THE OXFORD COMPANION TO

WINE

EDITED BY JANCIS ROBINSON

The Oxford Companion to

WINE

Edited by Jancis Robinson

Fourth Edition

Assistant Editor: Julia Harding

Advisory Editor, Viticulture: Richard E. Smart

Advisory Editors, Oenology:
Valérie Lavigne & Denis Dubourdieu

OXFORD
UNIVERSITY PRESS

OXFORD
UNIVERSITY PRESS

Great Clarendon Street, Oxford, OX2 6DP,
United Kingdom

Oxford University Press is a department of the University of Oxford.
It furthers the University's objective of excellence in research, scholarship,
and education by publishing worldwide. Oxford is a registered trade mark of
Oxford University Press in the UK and in certain other countries

First published 1994
Second edition 1999
Third edition 2006
Fourth edition 2015

Impression: 1

Published in the United States of America by Oxford University Press
198 Madison Avenue, New York, NY 10016, United States of America

British Library Cataloguing in Publication Data

Data available

Library of Congress Control Number: 2015941385

ISBN 978-0-19-870538-3

Printed in Slovakia by Neografia

Contents

Preface

This revision is by far the most thorough there has ever been to *The Oxford Companion to Wine*. Every single entry has been subjected to intense scrutiny.

It is quite a responsibility to be in charge of a work that I know from personal experience occupies a very special place in the lives of wine lovers and wine students all over the world. Interest in wine, both its consumption and its production, has never been greater, which means that the world of wine has never been as extensive, nor as fast-changing. All of this means that it is very, very different from the wine world described in the third edition of this *Companion*, published in 2006.

The great majority of existing articles needed considerable revision, some of them benefited from recasting and some needed a complete rewrite. In addition to this meticulous operation, we have added 300 new entries, from Accolade and additives to Zametovka and Zelen (see the List of new entries on p. xix). The fact that there was no entry in the third edition for terms such as minerality, Hong Kong, and CellarTracker demonstrates just how fast the wine world has been evolving. And of course it will continue to evolve. (Our references to the important wine-producing region Crimea had to be considerably revised in early 2014, for instance.) Frustratingly, the European wine authorities decided to change the entire structure of wine designations not long before we started work on our revisions, and many wine producers are still deciding how to react. For the moment two systems of nomenclature, both described in the *Companion*, can

be found on the labels of wines produced in Europe, still by far the world's most important wine-growing continent. The word 'growing' is significant. Throughout the wine world, the emphasis continues to shift from 'making' to 'growing' wine, just as we are seeing a step change in the style of wine to which thoughtful producers aspire. In terms of wine structure and alcohol levels, big is no longer as beautiful as it was at the end of the last century. And the range of grape varieties harnessed for serious commercial wine production is wider than it has been for decades. The scope of this *Companion* fully acknowledges all these trends.

Because the *Companion* was already very long and heavy (a common complaint which has inspired the publication of a digital version of this fourth edition), our esteemed publishers Oxford University Press were extremely strict with us about the total length of this new edition, which is less than 4% longer than the third edition in terms of the total number of words. This necessitated the deletion of a few of the more outdated entries but, more importantly, encouraged us to take a much more disciplined approach to existing entries than for any previous edition. Our intention has been to excise material that might be deemed incidental, marginal, or arguably otiose. Even so this fourth edition has a total of 4,104 entries, of which 315 are cross-references (there were 3,930 entries, of which 263 were cross-references, in the third edition). We are confident that this is the best edition of this work so far, although since there are far more and better-informed wine students around the world than ever before, we expect and welcome any suggested corrections and improvements via editorial@jancisrobinson.com.

I could not have even contemplated the necessary tasks without the exceptional vigilance and diligence of the *Companion*'s assistant editor Julia Harding MW. We have had to devote the best part of two years to revising the text and have as usual depended heavily on our advisory editors and an army of generous, knowledgeable contributors—all 187 of them, more than 50 new—and contacts (see our List of contributors and Acknowledgements). All of this has been helped considerably by the OUP team. Rebecca Lane got the ball rolling. Our editor

Cornelia Haase has offered us a delightful combination of charm and efficiency, and we are grateful to designer Elisabeth Heissler, production editor Bethan Lee, copy editor Marilyn Inglis, and proofreaders Bernadette Mohan and Michael Munro.

But I could not possibly have completed this edition had my husband Nicholas Lander not been such a patient, talented cook and tea-maker who has been remarkably tolerant of seeing his wife mainly in profile. I have not been much of a companion myself.

JANCIS ROBINSON

Contributors

Advisory Viticulture Editor:
Dr Richard E. Smart

Advisory Oenology Editors:
Dr Valérie Lavigne and Professor Denis Dubourdieu

Previous Oenology Editors:
Professor A. Dinsmoor Webb and Dr Patrick J. Williams

Contributors are listed in alphabetical order, first by surname, then by first name. MW stands for Master of Wine, MS for Master Sommelier, CM is Order of Canada, CBE is Commander of the British Empire, and OBE is Order of the British Empire. Unsigned entries are written by the Editor or Assistant Editor.

S.A. Sarah Ahmed publishes thewinedetective.co.uk and is a recognized authority on the wines of Portugal. She writes for *Decanter* and *The World of Fine Wine* magazines as well as contributing to *Hugh Johnson's Pocket Wine Book* and *The World Atlas of Wine*.

H.H.A. The late Hamish Aird, classicist and Sub-Warden of Radley College, Oxfordshire, in England.

J.A. Dr Jean Aitchison is Emeritus Rupert Murdoch Professor of Language and Communication at the University of Oxford. She gave the Reith Lectures in 1996.

M.A. Mail Amanov is Director of the Azerbaijan Institute of Viniculture and Winemaking.

K.A. Kym Anderson is the George Gollin Professor of Economics and foundation Executive Director of the Wine Economics Research Centre at the University of Adelaide, and Professor of Economics at the Australian National University's Crawford School of Public Policy. His unrivalled global statistical compendia of regional winegrape plantings by variety and of national wine markets are freely available at www.adelaide.edu.au/wine-econ.

A.A. Alberto Antonini studied in Bordeaux and at Davis in California. A roving consultant winemaker, he has made wine in California, Argentina, Chile, Spain, South Africa, Canada, Romania, Armenia, Uruguay, Australia, and his native Italy.

T.A. Tony Aspler CM, Canada's most widely published wine writer and educator.

S.E.A. Susy Atkins is a television presenter and wine writer who is based in Britain but travels widely.

H.G.B. The late Bill Baker, wine merchant and wine judge whose distinctive Reid Wines list was famously decorated with unusual vinous quotations and his wit.

J.B. Dr John Barker is a wine law specialist and the principal of John Barker Law. He is widely experienced in the field of wine regulation as a lecturer, author, and lawyer. He is a former General Counsel for New Zealand Winegrowers, President of the OIV's Law and Economy Commission, and Industry Chair of the World Wine Trade Group.

E.J.B. Dr Eveline Bartowsky is Senior Research Microbiologist at the Australian Wine Research Institute (see entry) in Adelaide, Australia. A specialist in malolactic conversion and wine bacteria research, she is also Manager of the AWRI Wine Microorganism Culture Collection.

N.J.B. Nicolas Belfrage MW is the author of four books and countless articles on Italian wine, the region in which he has specialized as merchant, importer and agent, and writer, since the 1980s.

H.B. Dr Helen Bettinson, Development Director of Fitzwilliam College, Cambridge, whose speciality is historical research.

D.B. David Bird MW is a Chartered Chemist and a Member of the Institute of Quality Assurance. He audits wineries throughout Europe and lectures on winemaking techniques. His publications include *Understanding Wine Technology*.

L.F.B. Dr LINDA BISSON is a microbiologist trained in genetics and currently specializing in yeast biology. She is a Professor of Enology and a geneticist in the Agricultural Experiment Station at the University of California at Davis (see entry).

J.A.B. The late Dr JEREMY BLACK was Director of the British School of Archaeology in Iraq and later a Fellow of Wolfson College, Oxford, and university lecturer in Akkadian. He wrote several studies on Sumerian and Babylonian literature and ancient philology.

B.B. BEVERLEY BLANNING MW is an independent UK-based wine writer who travels and tastes widely. She passed the Master of Wine exams at her first attempt in 2001, specializing for her dissertation in the subject of wine and health.

W.B. WILLIAM BOLTER, Bordeaux-based wine merchant, author, and winemaker who worked for Alexis Lichine (see entry) from 1958 to 1964.

R.G.V.B. Dr ROB BRAMLEY is a Principal Research Scientist with CSIRO in Adelaide, South Australia. Since 1998, he has been at the forefront of research aimed at understanding vineyard variability and the associated development of precision viticulture.

J.M.B. MICHAEL BROADBENT MW, founder of Christie's Wine Department and author (see entry).

R.B. Dr ROGER BROCK is a Senior Lecturer in Classics at the University of Leeds and specialist in Greek history and historiography.

S.B. STEPHEN BROOK, journalist and author whose works include *The Complete Bordeaux* and *The Wines of California*.

L.B. LARRY BROOKS studied plant pathology at the University of California at Davis (see entry) and has been a winemaker or winemaking consultant in California ever since.

N.B. NICK BULLEID MW is a freelance winemaking consultant in Australia and New Zealand and was for 13 years a visiting professor at Charles Sturt University (see entry). He is also a wine writer, wine judge, and wine producer in New South Wales.

R.N.H.B. ROBIN BUTLER is an antiques dealer with a particular interest in wine. He co-wrote *The Book of Wine Antiques* in 1986 and in 2009 wrote *Great British Wine Accessories 1550–1900*.

R.F.C. BOB CAMPBELL MW, New Zealand's best-known wine writer and founder of an exceptional wine school in Auckland.

D.L.C. Dr DIMITRA CAPONE, Research Scientist—Chemistry, at the Australian Wine Research Institute, has studied many aspects of wine flavour chemistry and recently received the 2013 Early Career (Life and Environmental Sciences) SA Science Excellence Award.

A.C. ALAIN CARBONNEAU, Professor of Viticulture at Montpellier SupAgro, President of the Group of International Experts in Vitivinicultural Systems for CoOpération (GiESCO), Director of *Publications et Actualités Vitivinicoles* (*PAV*), specialist in vine physiology, and inventor of the lyre training system.

T.R.C. TOM CARSON, youngest chairman of Australia's National Wine Show and chief winemaker and general manager of Yabby Lake Vineyard, Mornington Peninsula, Victoria.

B.C.C. BRUCE CASS is a California-based wine writer, educator, and editor of the *Oxford Companion to the Wines of North America*.

U.C. UMAY ÇEVIKER is a Turkish architect and WSET-educated wine enthusiast who has travelled and tasted widely. He has a particular affection for 'the unappreciated' in the wine world.

S.J.C. Dr STEVE CHARTERS MW, Director of Research, School of Wine and Spirits Business, Burgundy Business School, France, with research interests in the consumer's engagement with wine.

V.C. Dr VÉRONIQUE CHEYNIER, Director of Research at INRA (see entry), has been managing INRA Montpellier's internationally acclaimed research on grape and wine polyphenols for 20 years. In 2012 she was elected President of Groupe Polyphénols, the international society dedicated to the promotion of research on plant polyphenols.

N.C. NODAR CHKHARTISHVILI works as a consultant for the Georgian Scientific Research Centre for Agriculture.

M.C. PROFESSOR DR MONIKA CHRISTMANN is head of the oenology department at Geisenheim University with research and teaching responsibilities. She currently serves as Vice President of the OIV (see entry).

E.C.B. ELAINE CHUKAN BROWN was a commercial salmon fisherman in Alaska, then an academic philosopher, and is now a wine writer, not least at WakawakaWineReviews.com.

T.C. Dr TYLER COLMAN teaches wine classes at New York University. He blogs at DrVino.com and is the author of two wine books, *A Year of Wine* and *Wine Politics*.

M.J.C. Dr MICHAEL CONSIDINE is employed by both the University of Western Australia and the state's Department of Agriculture & Food. His primary expertise is in oxygen/redox metabolism. In his research in sulfur and redox metabolism he collaborates with Professor Christine Foyer of the University of Leeds, who co-authored his addition to the entry on sulfur dioxide.

B.G.C. The late Dr BRYAN COOMBE was an author, lecturer, and researcher who specialized in grapevine physiology at Waite Agricultural Research Institute, Adelaide. The American Society of Enology and Viticulture awarded him Best Viticulture Paper of the Year 1987 and Enology in 1991.

P.C. Dr PETER COUSINS is a grape breeder at E & J Gallo Winery, Modesto, California. He has bred and introduced several grape varieties to cultivation, including rootstocks, genetics research varieties, and improved clones. He has collected and studied grape germplasm in nature across North America.

G.L.C. Dr GLEN CREASY is a Senior Lecturer in Viticulture at Lincoln University's Centre for Viticulture and Oenology in New Zealand. His research specializes in cool-climate viticulture and grape and wine phenolics.

B.C. PROFESSOR BARRY CUNLIFFE CBE is Emeritus Professor of European Archaeology at the Institute of Archaeology, University of Oxford.

T.D.C. TAMLYN CURRIN is a wine writer who was born and brought up in Zimbabwe, but now lives in the UK and works for JancisRobinson.com.

R.D. Dr BOB DAMBERGS was Senior Research Scientist with the Australian Wine Research Institute (see entry). His primary research focus has been on developing objective measures of grape and wine quality. He has been a pioneer in the development of rapid analytical methods such as infrared spectroscopy that are now routinely used within the global wine industry.

D.Ds. Dr DANIEL DECKERS holds a PhD in Catholic theology, is a senior political editor of the *Frankfurter Allgemeine Zeitung*, and is devoted to the cultural history of German wine.

L.D. LI DEMEI is Associate Professor at Beijing Agriculture College with research interests in wine consumer behaviour. He consults for several wineries and was listed in the *Drinks Business* top 10 influential wine consultants in the world. He also writes regularly for decanterchina.com, for several Chinese wine magazines and for *La Revue du Vin de France*.

D.A.D. DR DONALD DIBBERN is a physician specializing in the diagnosis and treatment of allergic diseases, and a Fellow of the American Academy of Allergy Asthma and Immunology.

B.D. BARRY DICK MW has studied at Queens University, Belfast, and the University of Adelaide in Australia. He has made wine in Spain, California, Australia, Languedoc, and at Château Mouton Rothschild (see entry) and now acts as a consultant for producers, importers, and major retailers.

J. & M.D. The late PROFESSOR JAMES DOUGLAS was Visiting Professor of Political Science in various American universities while the late PROFESSOR DAME MARY DOUGLAS was Emeritus Professor of Social Anthropology at the University of London and was the leading British anthropologist of the second half of the 20th century.

P.R.D. DR PETER DRY, Adjunct Associate Professor, School of Agriculture, Food and Wine, University of Adelaide, and former consultant to the Australian Wine Research Institute (see entry).

D.D. DR DENIS DUBOURDIEU, Advisory Oenology Co-editor of this book, well-travelled winemaker, owner of six Bordeaux wine estates, and renowned Professor of Oenology and research scientist at the University of Bordeaux (see entry) who has had a particularly significant influence on white winemaking throughout France and abroad.

A.J.D. ANNE DUGGAN is Emeritus Professor of Medieval History at King's College, University of London.

A.D. ABI DUHR studied oenology at Geisenheim and Bordeaux. He lives and works in Luxembourg, where he is winemaker for his family's wine company and is in charge of Introduction to Oenology courses at the Lycée Technique Alexis Heck.

M.J.E. MARGARET EMERY was the librarian at Roseworthy Agricultural College from 1975 until 1995 and holds a Graduate Diploma in Wine.

M.E. MARCEL ESSLING is a Senior Viticulturist with the Australian Wine Research Institute (see entry) and belongs to the Technical Working Group on Maximum Residue Limits for the World Wine Trade Group. He advises the Australian wine sector on regulatory and technical aspects of agrochemical use in grape production.

N.F. NICHOLAS FAITH is a financial journalist whose numerous specialities include champagne, cognac, and railways.

C.C.F. CHRISTOPHER FIELDEN is a retired British wine merchant and collector of wine books.

M.F. MICHAEL FRIDJHON is South Africa's leading wine writer, Visiting Professor of Wine Business at the University of Cape Town's Graduate School of Business, Wine Wizard™, and liquor industry specialist.

D.F. DOUG FROST MW MS is a Kansas City author who is one of only four people in the world to be both a Master Sommelier and Master of Wine. He specializes in wines from America's less famous wine-producing states.

D.G. DENIS GASTIN is a widely published Australian-based wine writer, wine judge, and wine educator, specializing in Asia.

R.G. RICHARD GAWEL is a Research Scientist with the Australian Wine Research Institute (see entry) who established ways of describing red wines' mouthfeel (see entry). He specializes in the chemistry of polysaccharides and phenolics and their effect on white wine texture.

R.E.G. ROSEMARY GEORGE MW, wine writer, one of the first women to become a Master of Wine, whose books include the award-winning *Chablis* and, 25 years later, *The Wines of Chablis and the Grand Auxerrois*.

C.G. DR CAROLINE GILBY MW is a wine lecturer and writer specializing in Central and Eastern Europe. She has a PhD in plant sciences but left science to buy wine for a major UK retail chain, taking on responsibility for Eastern European wine, before going freelance.

J.G. DR JOHN GLADSTONES, author of *Viticulture and Environment* (1992) and *Terroir and Climate Change* (2011), is former Senior Lecturer in the University of Western Australia Department of Agriculture.

S.J.G. SAM GLAETZER, member of a well-known South Australian winemaking family, has a degree in civil and environmental engineering and a graduate diploma in

oenology. He started his career as an environmental engineer and winemaker at Treasury Wine Estates (see entry) before becoming managing director of Constellation Brands (see entry) in New Zealand.

D.C.G. DAVID GLEAVE MW is managing director of Liberty Wines, a London-based wine importer and distributor. He has been extensively involved with Italian wines since 1983, spending three months of every year in Italy. He has written widely on the subject, including the 1989 book *The Wines of Italy*.

W.G. WOJCIECH GOGOLIŃSKI is one of Poland's leading wine writers, founder of the Polish Sommeliers' Association, and a wine lecturer. He has written several books on wines and spirits.

H.G. HOWARD G. GOLDBERG writes for *The New York Times* and lives in New York City.

J.A.G. DR JAMIE GOODE has a PhD in plant biology and for many years worked as a scientific editor. He publishes wineanorak.com and is wine writer for Britain's *Sunday Express*. His first book, *Wine Science*, was published in 2005 and revised in 2014.

R.F.G. ROBERT GORJAK was raised in a wine-growing family close to Jeruzalem, Slovenia. He has written five guides to Slovenian wines and created Slovenia's first wine school. He divides his time between writing, teaching, and an active role in the Slovenian wine trade.

N.G. NAYAN GOWDA is a wine consultant and itinerant winemaker who has made wine from more than 50 different varieties in eight countries, including Kazakhstan, where he has overseen production at the country's only organic winery.

P.G. PAUL GREGUTT is a wine writer who has specialized in the Pacific Northwest since the early 1990s. He is the author of both editions of *Washington Wines & Wineries—The Essential Guide*.

R.d.G. RONALD DE GROOT is a wine writer and wine consultant who owns and edits the leading Dutch wine magazine *Perswijn* and the restaurant guide *Grootspraak*.

L.S.H. LISA SHARA HALL is a wine columnist and author who is based in Oregon and specializes in the wines of the Pacific Northwest.

Contributors

J.H. James Halliday, Australia's most prolific and most respected wine writer, an ex-lawyer who also found time to establish Coldstream Hills winery in the Yarra Valley.

J.M.H. The late Jake Hancock was Professor of Geology at Imperial College, University of London, and a member of the editorial board of the *Journal of Wine Research*.

R.H. Rosi Hanson, journalist, regular contributor to *Decanter* magazine, and author of a book on the recipes and traditions of the French wine harvest.

J.E.H. Julia Harding MW, assistant editor of *The Oxford Companion to Wine*, studied modern languages at Cambridge before becoming a freelance book editor. She qualified as a Master of Wine in 2004, winning the Robert Mondavi award for best theory papers and the Tim Derouet Memorial Prize for excellence in all parts of the exam and dissertation. She has been part of the JancisRobinson.com team since 2005 and co-wrote *Wine Grapes* in 2012. She is responsible for all entries on oenology and viticulture in this fourth edition of *The Oxford Companion to Wine*, as well as those on Bolivia, Georgia, and Uruguay.

S.H. Sam Harrop MW studied at both Auckland and Lincoln Universities before starting a career in winemaking in 1994 at Villa Maria. He moved to the UK in 1997 and worked for seven years as a winemaker for UK retailer Marks & Spencer before becoming an international wine consultant. He is also co-chair of the International Wine Challenge.

D.A.H. David A. Harvey works in the UK wine trade and writes about wine. He has been a sommelier and at one time worked for Frank Cornelissen on Etna, Sicily.

J.H.H. Dr Judith Harvey became a medical practitioner after a distinguished career as a research scientist and now writes on health-related matters.

M.v.H. Maarten van Helden is an associate professor and researcher of Dutch nationality. He graduated from Wageningen agricultural university and has been working since 1997 at Bordeaux Sciences Agro as an Associate Professor. He teaches plant protection and agro-ecology there, and conducts research on landscape ecology, ecosystem services, and pest management in viticulture.

P.A.H. Professor Paul A. Henschke is Emeritus Fellow, formerly Principal Research Microbiologist, at the Australian Wine Research Institute (see entry) in Adelaide, South Australia, and is Affiliate Professor at the University of Adelaide. He has more than 40 years' experience in yeast research.

M.H. Dr Markus Herderich is a food chemist and Group Manager—Research, at the Australian Wine Research Institute (see entry) and leads a research group of more than 30 professional scientists. His research interests include oenology, aroma chemistry, analytical chemistry, and metabolomics. He is also an Affiliate Associate Professor at the University of Adelaide and an expert at the OIV (see entry).

Hg.H. Dr Hildegarde Heymann is an author and Distinguished Professor of Sensory Science in the Department of Viticulture and Enology at the University of California at Davis (see entry). She has worked in all areas of sensory science and has evaluated numerous food and non-food products. Her main areas of expertise are descriptive analysis methodology and multivariate data analyses.

H.-P.H. Hans-Peter Hoehnen qualified at Geisenheim and worked in Australia, New Zealand, and his native Germany until 1997, when he moved to Thailand for three years. He is now a consultant in tropical viticulture and winemaking throughout South East Asia.

L.H.-S. Dr Leofranc Holford-Strevens is a classical scholar and author of *Aulus Gellius*. He works for Oxford University Press.

H.H. Huon Hooke is one of Australia's most respected wine writers. Based in Sydney, he makes his living entirely from writing, judging, and educating about wine. A journalist first and wine professional second, he has tertiary qualifications in both fields and has been writing on wine since 1983.

A.H. Alex Hunt MW is a London-based wine merchant with a particular interest in the philosophy and language of tasting, on which he has been extensively published.

D.J. Dr Dan Johnson is Managing Director of the Australian Wine Research Institute (see entry). He is Chairman of the Australian Wine Industry Technical Conference, and a member of many other wine sector boards and committees.

H.J. Hugh Johnson OBE is the world's most successful wine author and was introduced to specialist wine writing by the late André Simon (see entries on both).

R.J. Russell Johnstone was viticulture manager for Pernod Ricard Australia and now co-directs a consultancy business called Winecycle.

G.V.J. Dr Gregory V. Jones is an Associate Professor at Southern Oregon University, specializing in the study of how climate variability and change affect natural ecosystems and agriculture. He conducts applied research for the grape and wine industry in Oregon and has written widely on wine economics, grapevine phenology, climatological assessments of viticulture, and climate change.

T.J. Dr Tony Jordan started his career as research scientist and lecturer in oenology. He established the Chandon Australia Yarra Valley winery and vineyard for Moët Hennessy and later became CEO of the Moët Hennessy Wine Estates Group of Australian and New Zealand wineries. He now runs his own wine consultancy.

R.H.N.J. Rupert Joy is a wine writer and consultant with a particular interest in Moroccan wine, on which he wrote his thesis at ESC Dijon.

M.R.K. Michael Karam is a leading writer and author who specializes in Lebanese wine.

P.K. Dr Philip Kennedy completed a doctorate in classical Arabic poetry at the Oriental Institute of Oxford University and is now Associate Professor of Middle Eastern and Islamic Studies and Comparative Literature at New York University.

J.D.K. John Kesby, social anthropologist with a particular interest in metaphysical systems and myths, who taught at the University of Kent.

M.K. Mel Knox is based in California, where he has sold wine since 1972, taught wine appreciation classes at the University of California from 1974 to 1990, and sold French barrels since 1980. He is involved in wine production and was awarded the Mérite Agricole by the French government in 2010.

M.P.K. Dr Mark Krstic is Senior Research Scientist—Viticulture, at the Australian Wine Research Institute (see entry). He worked with CSIRO Plant Industries, the Victorian Department of Primary Industries, and the Grape and Wine Research and Development Corporation (GWRDC).

M.P.L. MARTIN LAM, food and wine consultant, was the owner, chef, and celebrated wine buyer of Ransome's Dock restaurant in London.

M.L.-G. MILES LAMBERT-GOCS researches the wine history and traditions of Eastern Europe, from Slovakia south through Greece.

E.L. ERICA LANDIN is a Swedish-American wine writer and journalist for a number of leading trade and consumer magazines, both in Sweden and internationally. She has an M.Sc. in medical biology and worked as an equities analyst in the biotech industry.

V.L. DR VALÉRIE LAVIGNE, Advisory Oenology Co-editor of this book, has a PhD in oenology from the University of Bordeaux. She is a research associate on secondment from cooper Seguin Moreau to the Institut des Sciences de la Vigne et du Vin (ISVV, see entry) in Bordeaux. Her research focuses on premature ageing of white and red wines and the aromas of Chardonnay wines. She is an oenology and viticulture consultant with Professor Denis Dubourdieu (see above) and Christophe Olivier in all of France's main wine regions as well as in Italy, Portugal, Spain, South Africa, Greece, and Egypt.

K.L. KONSTANTINOS LAZARAKIS MW was the first Greek Master of Wine and is a wine educator, judge and consultant. He is the author of *The Wines of Greece* (2005).

T.H.L. PROFESSOR TERRY LEE was Director of the Australian Wine Research Institute (see entry) in Adelaide, then worked for E & J Gallo (see entry) in California.

C.v.L. CORNELIS (KEES) VAN LEEUWEN is Professor of Viticulture at the Institut des Sciences de la Vigne et du Vin (ISVV, see entry) in Bordeaux. He is also the viticulturist at Château Cheval Blanc (see entry) in St-Émilion, and has written extensively on various aspects of terroir, soil, and wine quality.

H.L. HARRIET LEMBECK, noted wine educator and writer based in New York and a Charter Director of the Society of Wine Educators.

P.L. PETER LESKE, formerly Technical Services Manager at the Australian Wine Research Institute (see entry), is now a winemaker in the Adelaide Hills and a partner in Tempranillo specialist La Linea.

S.P.D.L. SIMON LOFTUS, retired renowned English wine merchant and award-winning author.

W.L. WINK LORCH, wine educator, writer, and editor, specializes in the wines of the Jura and French Alps. A founder of the Association of Wine Educators, she wrote *Jura Wine* in 2014.

P.E.M. PATRICK E. MCGOVERN is the Scientific Director of the Biomolecular Archaeology Project for Cuisine, Fermented Beverages, and Health at the University of Pennsylvania Museum in Philadelphia, where he is also an Adjunct Professor of Anthropology. He has published three books on ancient wine, including *Ancient Wine: The Search for the Origins of Viniculture* and *Uncorking the Past: The Quest for Wine, Beer, and Other Alcoholic Beverages*, together with numerous articles (see www.penn.museum/sites/biomoleculararchaeology).

E.M. DR EDI MALETIĆ is a Professor at the University of Zagreb, where he is head of the Department of Viticulture and Enology. A specialist in grapevine genetics, he was one of the scientists who discovered the Croatian roots of Zinfandel/Tribidrag.

A.J.M. ALEX MALTMAN is Professor of Earth Sciences at Aberystwyth University, Wales. For nearly forty years he has grown vines and made wine as a hobby, and travelled the world's vineyards. He has contributed articles on vineyard geology to both popular magazines and scientific journals.

J.E.M. JANE MASTERS MW (née Kay) originally trained as an oenologist at the Institut d'Oenologie in Bordeaux. After working for some years in France and Corsica, she ran the wine and drinks business of UK retailer Marks & Spencer. Since 2005 she has had her own international wine consultancy business, Mastering Wine.

R.J.M. RICHARD MAYSON, a leading authority on port, madeira and Portuguese wines in the English language. After working for The Wine Society in the UK, he wrote *Portugal's Wines and Winemakers*, *Port and the Douro* and the award-winning *The Wine and Vineyards of Portugal*. He owns a vineyard and produces wine in the Alto Alentejo, Portugal.

G.M. DR GABRIELLA MÉSZÁROS trained as a lawyer and now teaches and writes regularly about wine in Hungary. She is the owner, editor, and publisher of AKÓ Gastronomic Consulting and Editing Ltd. Her books include *Terra Benedicta – Tokaj and beyond* (2003), *Magyar Borok Könyve* (2001), the biannual Hungarian *Wineguide*, and *Bortankönyv 1* and *2* (2011, 2012).

S.M. SVEN MOESGAARD is one of the founders of commercial viticulture in Denmark. He is the owner of Skærsøgaard Wine and is his country's most awarded winemaker. He is an active member of the Danish Association of Winegrowers and has helped to shape Danish wine legislation and provisions for regional wine.

A.S.M. ADAM SEBAG MONTEFIORE went to live in Israel after working in the English wine trade. There he worked first for the Golan Heights Winery and then for Carmel Winery, and helped spearhead the development of Israeli wines. He is the wine writer for the *Jerusalem Post* and co-author of *The Wine Route of Israel* and *Wines of Israel*.

J.T.C.M. JASPER MORRIS MW is a Burgundy resident, burgundy specialist for three decades, burgundy director of Berry Bros & Rudd, and author of *Inside Burgundy*. A pattern seems to be emerging.

L.T.M. LUCIE MORTON is an independent viticulturist in the US. She writes, lectures, and consults on ampelography, rootstocks, and vineyard development, and is a founding member of the International Council on Grapevine Diseases. She translated *A Practical Ampelography* from Galet's original, and wrote *Winegrowing in Eastern America*.

L.M. LINDA MURPHY is co-author, with Jancis Robinson MW, of *American Wine: The Ultimate Companion to the Wines and Wineries of the United States*, managing editor of *Sonoma* magazine, former wine editor of the *San Francisco Chronicle*, and contributor to a wide range of wine publications.

P.A.N. DR PHILIP NORRIE is a medical practitioner and wine producer in New South Wales, Australia, with a particular interest in wine history.

I.N. IGOR NYKOLYN is general manager of the Ukraine Bureau of Vine and Wine (UBVW), a non-governmental national association founded in 2013 which brings together leading Ukrainian wine companies to support domestic enterprises, implement progressive legislation, promote wine on the alcohol market, save national traditions in wine regions, and develop international relations and exports.

K.O. KEN OHASHI is a leading Japanese wine and sake consultant and an international judge of wines and sake, running his own Red Bridge Consultancy in Tokyo. He is a Master of Sake.

J.J.P. JEREMY PATERSON, Senior Lecturer in Ancient History at the University of Newcastle-upon-Tyne, is a specialist in Roman economic and social history with a particular interest in the Roman wine trade, on which he has published.

W.H.P. WYATT H. PEABODY has been writing about wine and spirits since 1998, when he and his partners purchased and revitalized the two-decades-old *Underground Wine Journal*, launching it internationally. He later co-founded undergroundwineletter.com. He takes a special interest in Mexican wine.

E.P.-R. The late EDMUND PENNING-ROWSELL was one of the world's most respected wine writers, and author of *The Wines of Bordeaux* (see his entry).

G.P. PROFESSOR GARY PICKERING received his doctorate in Wine Science from Lincoln University in New Zealand (see entry), and is currently Professor of Biological Sciences and Psychology at Brock University in Niagara, Canada (see entry), as well as Adjunct Professor at Charles Sturt University in Australia (see entry). His researches include wine flavour (sensory and chemistry), taste genetics, and climate change adaptation. He is also an international wine judge.

T.P. PROFESSOR THOMAS PINNEY, retired Professor of English at Pomona College in Claremont, California, and author of the two-volume *History of Wine in America*.

J.P. JOHN PLATTER became a South African wine farmer and wine writer after a career as a foreign correspondent for United Press International. *Platter's South African Wine Guide* has become the country's best-selling wine book.

J.V.P. DR JOHN POSSINGHAM has degrees from the universities of Adelaide and Oxford and was foundation Chief of CSIRO's Division of Horticulture in Australia.

V.P. DR VLADIMIR PUKISH has a PhD in linguistics and is the PR director of Fanagoria winery in southern Russia. He is also a historian and ethnologist and has written a number of essays on ancient and modern Russian history, and on Ukrainian winemaking. He has translated a series of books on the history of winemaking.

A.H.P. ALEXANDER PURCELL is Professor of Entomology at the University of California at Berkeley. His research has focused on Pierce's disease and other bacterial diseases of plants spread by insect vectors.

J.M.R. DR JANE RENFREW (Lady Renfrew of Kaimsthorn) is a prehistorian and palaeoethnobotanist and is an Emeritus Fellow of Lucy Cavendish College, University of Cambridge, and a retired Affiliated Lecturer in the Department of Archaeology, University of Cambridge.

P.R.-G. PROFESSOR PASCAL RIBÉREAU-GAYON was head of the Faculty of Oenology at the University of Bordeaux and is recognized as one of the most renowned French authorities on making and tasting wine. His father, Jean Ribéreau-Gayon, was also Director of Bordeaux's Institute of Oenology and a descendant of Professor Ulysse Gayon, who worked with Louis Pasteur.

J.R. JANCIS ROBINSON OBE MW, editor of *The Oxford Companion to Wine*, is one of the world's leading authorities on wine. The first person outside the wine trade to have passed the notoriously tough Master of Wine exams, she now writes weekly for the *Financial Times* and daily for JancisRobinson.com, which has members in 150 countries. Voted the first ever International Wine Communicator of the Year in 1996, she has won multiple awards and written many books. Most recently she co-wrote both *The World Atlas of Wine* (7th edn, 2013) and *Wine Grapes* (2012).

G.R. DR GÁBOR ROHÁLY is a physician, a founding member of the Hungarian Wine Academy, and a wine writer who is widely credited with developing Hungary's wine vocabulary.

A.R. ANDRÉS ROSBERG is a member of the Argentine, Pan-American and International Sommelier Associations. He is a leading wine writer, educator and judge in his native Argentina.

A.H.L.R. ANTHONY ROSE, British lawyer-turned-wine writer for *The Independent* and *i* newspapers who has written regularly on auctions and investment in wine for a wide range of publications. He is a founder member of thewinegang.com.

B.T.A.R. BJØRN TORE AASTORP RUUD, Norwegian chef turned wine writer, has benefited from wine and spirit training in Norway, England and Mexico, where he is currently President of the Sociedad Mexicana de Vinos & Licores de Guadalajara.

V.R. VIACHESLAV RYBINSTEV was appointed Deputy Director of Research at the Magaratch (see entry) Wine Research Institute in Yalta in 1986 and has studied viticulture in Ukraine, Russia, Moldova, Kazakhstan, Uzbekistan,

Georgia, Armenia, Azerbaijan, Turkmenistan, Germany, and the south of France.

D.S. DAVID SCHILDKNECHT trained in philosophy but has over nearly four decades worked as restaurateur, retailer, importer, and wine writer. From 2005 to 2014 he wrote full-time for Robert Parker's *Wine Advocate*, covering Austria, Germany, much of France, and selected regions of North America.

J.S. JOHN SCHREINER is a Vancouver-based writer who has been commenting on the wines of British Columbia since 1975. He has written 15 books about Canadian wine.

H.S. PROFESSOR HANS SCHULTZ is President of Geisenheim University (see entry). He was formerly the Director of the Geisenheim Research Institute and Professor of Viticulture. He has also worked and studied at Charles Sturt University in Australia, at ENSA/INRA Montpellier, and at the University of California at Davis (see their entries). Professor Schultz grew up in the Mosel Valley, where his parents have a small vineyard and winery.

M.W.E.S. MICHAEL SCHUSTER, writer who runs his own wine school in London and has translated the work of Professor Émile Peynaud.

T.S. DR TOM SCOTT, part-time wine merchant and Honorary Professor in the Institute of Reformation Studies at the University of St Andrews, specializing in the economic and social history of Germany, 1300–1600.

M.A.S. DR MARK SEFTON was formerly a Principal Research Chemist at the Australian Wine Research Institute (see entry), where he led the Institute's research programme on the chemistry of volatile grape and wine aroma and flavour compounds, and is now an Adjunct Associate Professor of the University of Adelaide.

V. DE LA S. VICTOR DE LA SERNA, Madrid-based journalist for *El Mundo*, wine writer, and wine producer.

Y.S. YOUNG SHI divides her time between Shanghai, London, and the world's wine regions. She is co-founder of TasteSpirit.com and TS Wine Academy Director in Shanghai. As well as being a wine writer and educator, she represents Jancis Robinson in China.

C.A.S. CON SIMOS is Group Manager—Industry Development and Support, Australian Wine Research Institute (see entry). With extensive international winemaking experience, he now leads the group responsible for the transfer of knowledge and skills programmes to the Australian grape and wine sector.

R.K.S. REVA K. SINGH, a veteran of the Indian magazine industry, is the founder of *Sommelier India Wine Magazine*, India's first print and online publication on wine. In 2009 she founded and was co-chair of the Sommelier India Wine Competition (SIWC).

S.S. STEPHEN SKELTON MW established the vineyards at Tenterden in Kent (today's Chapel Down) in 1977 and made wine there until 2001. Today he is a viticultural consultant, setting up and advising vineyards in the UK, as well as an author and lecturer. He self-published *Wine Growing in Great Britain* in 2014.

R.E.S. DR RICHARD SMART, Viticulture Editor of this book and a substantial contributor to it. World-famous viticultural scientist and author, now a consultant known particularly for his studies and applications of canopy management, he has advised on viticulture in over forty countries.

B.C.S. PROFESSOR BARRY C. SMITH is the Director of the Institute of Philosophy at the School of Advanced Study, University of London, and founding director of The Centre for the Study of the Senses. He has published articles on the multisensory perception of flavour in *Nature, Food Quality and Preference, Flavour*, and *The World of Fine Wine*. He is editor of *Questions of Taste: The Philosophy of Wine* (2007) and has held visiting positions at the University of California at Berkeley, and the École Normale Supérieure in Paris.

W.S. WALTER SPELLER is the Italian correspondent for JancisRobinson.com and a wine writer specializing in Italy. He has contributed to the 7th edition of the *World Atlas of Wine* and *Decanter* magazine. He spends his time between Padova and his base in London.

R.J.S. RICHARD STÁVEK is an award-winning winemaker and wine consultant specializing in organic and biodynamic viticulture in the Czech Republic. He is also a wine judge and prolific wine writer.

P.K.C.S. PATRICIA STEFANOWICZ MW is a wine consultant and educator as well as a qualified architect and structural engineer. She is based in the UK and divides her working life between wine and construction project management.

T.M.S. TYSON STELZER, wine writer and scientist, is the world's most prolific writer on the topic of screwcaps. His books include *Taming the Screw: A Manual for Winemaking with Screw Caps*. His other speciality is champagne.

A.C.S. DR AMANDA STEWART is Assistant Professor of Enology and Fermentation at Virginia Tech (see entry), where her research investigates the impact of nitrogen in wine grapes on fermentation, aroma, and flavour. She has worked in the wine industry in Oregon and New Zealand.

C.S.S. DR CREINA STOCKLEY is Health and Regulatory Information Manager at The Australian Wine Research Institute (see entry). A clinical pharmacologist, she has been actively involved in research into the health effects of wine and wine-derived phenolic compounds, as well as in the preparation of alcohol policy and regulation. She was elected President of the OIV's (see entry) Commission IV Safety and Health in 2012.

L. & E.S. LUKAS SUSAJ lectures in ampelography at the University of Tirana, where he is a Professor. He has published widely in both Albania and abroad, as has DR ELISABETA SUSAJ, who is a lecturer on genetics and plant breeding at the Agricultural University of Tirana.

K.S. KEITH SUTTON is Honorary Research Fellow in Geography at the University of Manchester and spent 20 years researching Algeria's socio-economic development.

M.T. MICHAEL TABONE is a wine lecturer and writer. He is the main wine correspondent for the *Sunday Times of Malta* and a consultant for a number of importers, restaurants, and hotels. In 2001 he established Malta's first wine school.

P.T. PATRICIO TAPIA has a degree in journalism from the Universidad de Chile in Santiago and studied wine at Bordeaux University (see entry). He has written several books about South American wine and writes regularly for both *Wine & Spirits* magazine in New York and *Decanter* magazine in London.

G.T. GEOFF TAYLOR has worked in the UK wine trade since 1976, always in the technical/analytical area. He founded the leading UK wine analysis and consultancy laboratories, now part of Campden BRI, the world's largest independent technical/laboratory-based organization for the food and drink industry.

R.T. DU C. RÉMI TEISSIER DU CROS is a forest and wood engineer currently working at Tonnellerie Taransaud, France. He started his career at the French National Forest Inventory. Now he shares his time between research and development as an oak and wood specialist and quality management.

J.T. JOELLE THOMSON is a New Zealand-based journalist, editor and author of 14 books about wine and those who make it. She also has a weekly wine column, writes for joellethomson.com, and teaches at the NZ School of Food & Wine.

R.T. DR ROY THORNTON has a PhD in Applied Microbiology from Strathclyde University, Scotland. He developed new strains of wine yeasts at Massey University, New Zealand, and has written extensively on wine microbiology. He was a Senior Research Microbiologist at E & J Gallo (see entry) for five years before joining CSU Fresno (see entry).

S.T. DR STEVE TYERMAN is the Wine Industry Professor of Viticulture at Adelaide University. He was President of the Australian Society of Plant Scientists (2004–05) and is a member of the Australian Society of Viticulture and Oenology. In 2003, he was elected as a fellow of the Australian Academy of Science.

P.T.H.U. TIM UNWIN is Emeritus Professor of Geography at Royal Holloway, University of London. He is author of *Wine and the Vine* and was one of the founding editors of the *Journal of Wine Research*. He is currently Secretary General of the Commonwealth Telecommunications Organisation and Chair of the Commonwealth Scholarship Commission but retains a strong interest in wine and viticulture, serving on the wine committee of the Athenaeum Club in London.

J.R.U.-T. DR JOSÉ RAMÓN ÚRBEZ-TORRES is a plant pathologist currently working as a Research Scientist for Agriculture and Agri-Food Canada in the Pacific Agriculture Research Centre (PARC) at Summerland, British Columbia. His primary research focus is the etiology, biology, epidemiology, and control of fungal diseases of grapevines and fruit trees, with a special emphasis on grapevine trunk diseases.

T. V. TIM VANDERGRIFT is Technical Services Manager for Global Vintners International, the world's largest manufacturer of home-winemaking equipment and supplies. He has been active in the home beer and wine industry for two and a half decades. In addition to experience as a sommelier, he is also a BJCP certified beer judge and an all-grain brewer. He is a feature writer and columnist for *WineMaker* magazine and writes at timswineblog.com.

P.V.P. The late PAMELA VANDYKE PRICE was wine correspondent of *The Times* of London and a prolific author.

G.V.I. GIDO VAN IMSCHOOT MS is President of the Flemish Sommelier Association and was European Ambassador of Champagne in 2012. He lectures and has written six books on wine.

O.V. DR OLIVIER VIRET is head of the research division of plant protection in grape and field crops, viticulture, and oenology at Agroscope, the Swiss centre for agricultural research in Changins, with national responsibility for grapevine and wine research.

J.V. DR JOSÉ VOUILLAMOZ, Swiss grape geneticist, trained at the University of California at Davis, specializing in the study of the origin and parentage of grape varieties through DNA profiling. Co-author with Jancis Robinson and Julia Harding of *Wine Grapes* (2012), he has also authored and co-authored several scientific papers and other books about grapes. He is a member of the Académie Internationale du Vin.

M.W. MONTY WALDIN is a wine writer based in the UK. He has written several respected books on both organic and biodynamic vines and wines. His television series *Chateau Monty* (2008) was the first to document biodynamic wine production from pruning to bottling.

B.M.W. The late DR BERNARD WATNEY was initially a physician but his many interests included wine, wine labels, and corkscrews. He co-wrote *Corkscrews for Collectors*, which has since been translated into French and German.

A.D.W. The late A. DINSMOOR WEBB, Oenology Editor of the first edition of this book, retired in 1982 as Professor Emeritus from the University of California at Davis and then continued to write and to act as consultant oenologist worldwide.

R.E.W. ROBERT E. WHITE is Emeritus Professor of Soil Science at the University of Melbourne, Australia. He consults to the wine industry and provides technical advice on soil matters to the Australian Wine Research Institute (see entry) and is author of *Principles and Practice of Soil Science*, *Soils for Fine Wines*, and *Understanding Vineyard Soils*. He also co-edited the four volumes of Earthscan's *Soil Science*.

P.J.W. DR PATRICK WILLIAMS, Oenology Editor of the second edition of this book, was until his recent retirement the Deputy Director of, and a researcher for 24 years in, the Australian Wine Research Institute (see entry). The American Society of Enology and Viticulture awarded him Best Enology Paper of the Year in 1991 and 1993.

H.M.W. DR HANNEKE WILSON is the author of *Wine and Words in Classical Antiquity and the Middle Ages* and writes on wine for *Oxford Today*. She is the wine steward of Exeter College, Oxford, and does a little work for wine merchant Haynes Hanson & Clark. She is also the coach and senior member of the Oxford University Blind-Tasting Society.

N.G.W. NIGEL WILSON, Emeritus Fellow and Tutor in Classics at Lincoln College, Oxford, where he continues to look after the college cellar. His main work as a classical scholar is as an expert in Greek palaeography and the history of the classical tradition.

T.K.W. DR TONY WOLF is Professor of Viticulture and has served as viticulturist with Virginia Tech (see entry) since 1986. His education includes an MS from Pennsylvania State University and a PhD from Cornell, both in viticulture research. Dr Wolf has been widely published in scientific journals and was also editor and principal author of the 2008 *Wine Grape Production Guide for Eastern North America*.

S.D.W. STEVE WRATTEN is Professor of Ecology at Lincoln University in New Zealand as well as being on the staff of the Bio-Protection Research Centre. He has studied and worked in the Universities of Reading, Glasgow, London, Cambridge, and Southampton in the UK. He is the world leader in biological control of pests and is currently working on using ecological techniques to reduce the decline in populations of pollinators.

B.W.Z. BRUCE ZOECKLEIN is Professor Emeritus and former head of the Enology-Grape Chemistry Group at Virginia Tech (see entry). Before that he worked in the California wine industry and at the Viticulture and Enology Research Center, Fresno State (see entry). Dr Zoecklein has co-authored several books on wine chemistry and analysis. His research interests include secondary grape metabolites.

Acknowledgements

As for the three previous editions, this *Companion* owes most to a host of people around the world who have been extraordinarily generous with their time and knowledge, perhaps because wine is a subject which naturally inspires generosity and enthusiasm.

Dr Richard Smart, viticulturist extraordinaire, went to exceptional lengths to ensure that all the entries on viticulture were brought fully up to date and was always on hand to answer queries. He is Australian and a veteran contributor to the *Oxford Companion to Wine*, complemented in previous editions by the late A. Dinsmoor Webb of California and Dr Patrick Williams of Australia as Oenology Editors. In this edition we were particularly keen to increase the influence of the Old World on our scientific entries, so capably marshalled by Julia Harding MW. We were delighted therefore when renowned oenologist Professor Denis Dubourdieu of Bordeaux University's oenology department and his associate, the appropriately named Dr Valérie Lavigne, agreed to review the entries on winemaking. Nevertheless, when it came to final detailed updates to specific entries, it is remarkable how many specialists came to our aid from the Australian Wine Research Institute in Adelaide. We are hugely grateful to all those who shared their highly specialized knowledge with us.

A highly valued addition to the team for this edition was Dr John Barker, who, despite being based in New Zealand, has one of the clearest-eyed views of the latest contortions of EU wine regulation. The International Organisation of Vine and Wine (OIV) supplied data on international production and consumption of wine, notably that presented in Appendix 2. Global grape variety statistics were provided by Professor Kym Anderson of the University of Adelaide. And our co-author of *Wine Grapes* Dr José Vouillamoz was always there for us when we had a grape-related query, as well as considerably revising the entry on his native Switzerland.

We are particularly delighted to have a major new contribution on the origins of what he calls viniculture from the world's foremost authority on the subject, Patrick McGovern of the University of Pennsylvania Museum. All other historical entries have been reviewed by their authors to ensure that necessary updates have been made, and we are grateful that our many celebrated academics, especially Dr Jane Renfrew, have taken such trouble to incorporate new discoveries, often archaeological, in the relevant entries.

We owe an enormous debt to all our regional specialists, many of whom were far more helpful than they need have been. Walter Speller worked particularly hard to update all the Italian entries, adding new ones, too—as did David Schildknecht on Germany and, for the first time, Austria as well. Umay Çeviker first of all wrote about wine in his native Turkey at such length that his contribution would have made an exceptionally fine book in its own right, and then undertook the thankless task of condensing it into the harsh word count we allowed him. Huon Hooke was at first unwilling to undertake the considerable task of updating James Halliday's previous contributions on Australian wine because he felt he could not do it justice in the time suggested; I am particularly grateful to him for responding positively to an extended deadline. Caroline Gilby MW has given us the benefit of her unrivalled knowledge of wine production in Eastern Europe, while Denis Gastin has done the same for his rapidly expanding area of expertise, Asia—although by now Japan, India, and in particular China have become so important that for the first time in this edition they have warranted their own local specialist commentators.

Tamlyn Currin nobly wrestled with assorted and much-amended wine regulations to produce our unique lists of appellations and permitted grape varieties in Appendix 1. But there were also many individuals whose initials do not appear at the bottom of any entry but without whose advice or contacts our work would have been very much more difficult. We apologize to anyone whose name we have failed to record—all too easy, alas, when dealing with literally thousands of people during the preparation of this work. Those who made notable contributions to this fourth edition in particular, other than those recorded in the List of contributors, include:

Jonas Andersen
Foulques Aulagnon
Brigitte Batonnet
Melina Bertocchi
Gilles Besse
Bill Blatch
Fabiana Bracco
Miguel Cabral
Pascal Chatonnet
Alfredo Coelho
Jean-Michel Comme
Andrian Coulter
Veronika Crecelius
Helmut Dietrich
James Farquharson
Chris Foss
Tanya Garnham
Aziz Gasimov

Jacques Gautier
Philippe Gayral
Zorik Gharibian
Peter Godden
Mat Goodard
Hervé Hannin
Richard Hemming
Luiz Horta
Ben Howkins
Lynnette Hudson
Barbara Iasiello
Tim James
Andrew Jefford
Yann Juban
Eva Kaluzynska
Judy Kendrick
Tina Kezeli
Jan R. C. Lensing

Alan N. Lakso
Gelasio Lovatelli
Jacqui McRea
David Maghradze
Olga Markovets
Alessandro Masnaghetti
David Molyneux-Berry
Jacques Nadolski
Natalia Neronova
Ryan Opaz
Wendy Parr
Sofia Perpera
Daniel Pisano
Gill Pitts
Bruce Reisch
Marcelo Retamal
Francisco Roig
Denis Roudenko

Andrea Russo
Steffen Schindler
Joachim Schmid
Michael Schmidt
Camilla Sellars
Pavel Shvets
Clark Smith
Rory Stewart
Liz Thach MW
Gabriel Tinguely
Michel Valade
Andy Walker
Rob Walker
Tommy Wide
Eric Wilkes
David Wollan
Alder Yarrow

List of new entries

Below is an alphabetical list of all the terms given their own new entry in this fourth edition of *The Oxford Companion to Wine.*

access system, wine
Accolade Wines
Aconcagua
additives
Alaska
alternative packaging
alternative varieties
ambient yeast
Anatolia
antioxidants
Apera
apical dominance
Areni
argilo-calcaire
Arlanza
aromatics
Arvine
Atlas Peak
authentication
Baltic states
barrel alternatives

basalt
bead
Bikavér
Bío-Bío
biochar
Blauer Wildbacher
blogs, wine
Botryosphaeria dieback
Bourguignons, Coteaux
British Columbia
Cabernet Gernischt
Cachapoal
Cadillac Côtes de
    Bordeaux
calcareous
Calistoga
Cambodia
carbon
Carnuntum
Carricante
Casablanca
Casella Family Brands
cellar door
cellar rat
CellarTracker
Changyu

CMO
Côdega de Larinho
Colchagua
colluvium
complexity
Concha y Toro
concrete
Conegliano-Valdobbiadene
Costa Rica
counterfeit wine
Cserszegi Fűszeres
Curicó
Derenoncourt, Stéphane
Diamond Mountain
Distell
Divico
Dona Branca
DOP
earthworms
ecosystem, vineyard
Elim
Elqui
en rama
Erste Lage
eucalyptus character
films about wine

flotation
Franschhoek
frost protection
funds, wine
galet
geosmin
Glera
gneiss
Gomera, La
grafted vine
Granada, Vinos de
Gran Canaria
Gran Selezione
gravity-fed
Greco
Gredos
greywacke
Grignan-les-Adhémar
Grosse Lage
grubbing up
GSM
harmony
heritage clones
Historic Vineyard Society
Hong Kong
horses

hot-water treatment
IGP
indigenous varieties
infrared spectroscopy
ingredient labelling
Institut des Sciences de la Vigne et du Vin de Bordeaux (ISVV)
Integrated Production of Wine
IPT
Itata
Jacquez
Jakot
Jewish heritage in German wine culture
Judgment of Paris
Julius-Kühn-Institut
Justino's Madeira Wines SA
Kalecik Karasi
Kamptal
kegs
Kisi
Klassik
Koshu
Kremstal
La Crosse
ladybug taint
Laithwaite's
late harvest
Leithaberg DAC
Léon Millot
Lesotho
Leyda
lightstrike
lignification
Lima
Limarí
lime, active
liqueur wine
Longyan
Maillard reaction
Maipo
Malibu Coast
Malleco
Malvasija Istarska
malvidin
Mara
Marquette
Marufo
Maturana Blanca
Maule
Mavrotragano
Mediterranean fruit fly

microbial terroir
minerality
Minutolo
Mittelburgenland
molybdenum
Monção e Melgaço
Montecucco
moût de raisins partiellement fermenté issu de vendanges passerillées
Mtsvane
Muschelkalk
mycorrhiza
Nascetta
natamycin
natural alcohol
natural wine
Nero di Troia
Neusiedlersee-Hügelland
Norway
Nova Scotia
olfactory bulb
Ontario
optical sorting
orange wine
Ornellaia
oxygen transmission rate (OTR)
Pallagrello Nero
Pannobile
Pardillo
Paulée, La
PDO
Península de Setúbal
pétillant naturel
pet-nat
Pézenas
PGI
phylogeny
Picapoll Blanco
pie franco
Pinot Noir Précoce
Pirque
planting rights
plastic bottles
Plumpton
Pošip
pouches
premature oxidation
Prié
processing aids
prodelphinidin
provenance

proximal sensing
Puente Alto
quartzite
Quebec
qvevri
Rabigato
Rapel
red blotch virus
reducing sugars
reductive winemaking
Reggiano
Ridge Vineyards
Riesling Taste Profile
Rivairenc
Rollo
Romagna Trebbiano
Rotling
rotundone
San Antonio
San Diego County
San Francisco Bay
San Juan
Sauvignon Gris
Savagnin Blanc
Savagnin Rose
Schilfwein
selective harvesting
Selektion
sensitivity
Sideways
Sierra de Salamanca
single-vineyard wines
skin-fermented
smoke taint
social media
soil biota
soil compaction
soil health
soil potential
soil profile
Southern Wine & Spirits
spontaneous fermentation
Strevi
structure
submerged cap
Südburgenland
Süd-Oststeiermark
Südsteiermark
Suntory
sustainability
Swartland
Sweden

sweetness codes
Syrah decline
Szepsy, István
Tahiti
Tai Bianco
taint
Tai Rosso
Tejo
Thermenregion
Thrapsathiri
three-tier system
Tierra de León
Tintilla de Rota
Tokay
Topaque and Muscat
total package oxygen (TPO)
traditional terms
Traditionsweingüter Österreich
Traisental
Traminette
Transmontano
Treasury Wine Estates
TrentoDOC
Tribidrag
trunk diseases
Tsimlyansky Cherny
tuff
Tulbagh
ungrafted vine
urban wineries
vandalism
Verduzzo
Verduzzo Trevigiano
Vernaccia di Oristano
Vin de France
vine architecture
Vinea Wachau
viniculture
Vino de Calidad
VSIG
Wachau
Wagram
Wellington
Western Cape
Weststeiermark
Wine Group, The
wine-growing
wine without geographical indication
WSET
Žametovka
Zelen

Maps of the wine regions

Note to the reader

Entries are arranged in letter-by-letter alphabetical order up to the first punctuation in the headword, except that names beginning with Mc are ordered as if they were spelt Mac, and St and Ste (French) are arranged as if they were spelt Saint and Sainte. Château and châteaux appear in full as headwords, but are abbreviated to Ch and Chx elsewhere. Entries appear under the name of the château, and not under C.

Cross-references are denoted by red small capitals and indicate the entry to which attention is being directed. We have attempted to limit cross-references to other entries likely to amplify or increase understanding of the entry being read. They are not given in all instances where the name of an entry appears in the text.

All wine-producing countries have an entry. The most significant ones also have individual entries for regions within them. Some countries or regions have individual entries for specific appellations, depending on what's on the label and which wines are widely available or especially famous. We have tried to give all the most significant appellations their own entry, as we have the individual people, wine producers, and properties which have played or are playing an important part in the history of wine.

Measurements are given in metric accompanied by the United States equivalent. (See right for abbreviations.)

The format of this fourth edition is very similar to the third, including a Complete list of entries by topic to provide a specific guide to the scope of this book, and to suggest another way of navigating your way through it. A revealing List of new entries is included on pp xix–xx; all new entries are of course included in the thematic listings too (see pp xxv–xliii).

The appendices include a completely updated list of all significant wine appellations (very rarely found in printed form) together with details of those grape varieties currently specified by them, including many recent changes (an even rarer listing), as well as tables of total vineyard area by country, total wine production, and per capita wine consumption. All have been thoroughly updated to include the most recent OIV statistics available.

Abbreviations

ch, chx	château, châteaux
ft	feet
gal	US gallon
g/l	grams per litre
ha	hectare
hl	hectolitre
in	inches
l	litre
m	metre

Complete list of entries by subject

Regions

France
Abymes
Aix-en-Provence, Coteaux d'
Allier
Aloxe-Corton
Alsace
Ancenis, Coteaux d'
Anjou
AOC
Appellation Contrôlée
Apremont
Arbin

Arbois
Ardèche
Aubance, Coteaux de l'
Ausone, Château
Auvergne, Côtes d'
Auxerre
Auxey-Duresses
AXA
Ayse
Bandol
Banyuls
barrique

Barsac
Bartons
Basque
Bâtard-Montrachet
Baux de Provence, Les
Béarn
Beaujolais
Beaumes-de-Venise
Beaune
Beaune, Côte de
Bellet
Bergerac

Bienvenues-Bâtard-Montrachet
Blagny
blanc
blanc de blancs
blanc de noirs
Blanc Fumé
Blaye
Boisset
Bollinger
bonbonne
Bonnes Mares
Bonnezeaux

Italy cont.

spumante
Strevi
Südtirol
Superiore
Supertuscan
Taurasi
tenuta
Terlano
Tignanello
Tocai
Torgiano
Toscana
Trentino
Trentino-Alto Adige
TrentoDOC
Tuscany
Tyrol
Umbria
Valdadige
Valle Isarco
Valpolicella
Valtellina
vendemmia
Veneto
Venice
Verdicchio
Verduzzo
vermouth
Vernaccia di Oristano
Vernaccia di San Gimignano
Veronelli, Luigi
Vien de Nus
vigna
Vin Santo
vino
vino da meditazione
vino da tavola
Vino Nobile di Montepulciano

Spain

Abona
albariza
Alella
Alicante
almacenista
Almansa
amontillado
Andalucía
año
Aragón

Arlanza
Arribes
arrope
barrica
Basque
Bierzo
Binissalem
blanco
bodega
Bullas
butt
Calatayud
Campo de Borja
Canary Islands
Cariñena
Castilla
Castilla-La Mancha
Castilla y León
Cataluña
Catalunya
Cava
Cebreros
Chacolí
Cigales
clarete
Codorníu
Conca de Barberá
Condado de Huelva
Consejo Regulador
cosecha
Costers del Segre
Cream
crianza
Denominación de Origen
Denominación de Origen Calificada
DO
doble pasta
DOCa
DOP
DOQ
El Hierro
embotellado
Empordà
en rama
espumoso
Extremadura
film-forming yeasts
finca
fino
flor
Fondillón

Freixenet
Galicia
Garrido
girasol
Gomera, La
González Byass
Granada, Vinos de
Gran Canaria
Gran Reserva
granvas
Gredos
Jerez
joven
Jumilla
Lanzarote
La Palma
Madrid, Vinos de
Málaga
Mallorca
Mancha, La
Manchuela
manzanilla
Méntrida
Mondéjar
Monterrei
Montilla-Moriles
Montsant
Navarra
oloroso
pago
Palo Cortado
Penedès
Pla de Bages
Pla i Llevant
Priorat
Puerto de Santa María
PX
raya
Reserva
Rías Baixas
Ribeira Sacra
Ribeiro
Ribera del Duero
Ribera del Guadiana
Ribera del Júcar
Rioja
Rueda
sangría
Sanlúcar de Barrameda
sherry
Sierra de Salamanca

Sierras de Málaga
solera
Somontano
Spain
Tacoronte-Acentejo
Tarragona
Terra Alta
Tierra de Barros
Tierra de León
Tierra del Vino de Zamora
tinaja
tinta
tinto
Toro
Torres SA, Miguel
Txakoli
Uclés
Utiel-Requena
Valdeorras
Valdepeñas
Valencia
Valle de Güimar
Valle de la Orotava
Vega Sicilia
viña
Vino de Calidad
vino de la tierra
vino de mesa
vino de pago
VORS and VOS
Xérès
Ycoden-Daute-Isora
Yecla

Portugal

adega
Alenquer
Alentejo
Algarve
Almeirim
armazém
Arruda
Azores
Bairrada
Beira Interior
Beiras
Biscoitos
Borba
branco
Bucelas
Câmara de Lobos

Complete list of entries by subject

Vine-growing/Viticulture cont.

degree days
dehydration
desert
destalking
desuckering
dew
direct producer
disease-resistant varieties
diseases, vine
diurnal temperature variation
divided canopy
DNA profiling
dormancy
double pruning
downy mildew
drainage
drip irrigation
drosophila
drought
dry-farmed
drying grapes
dryland viticulture
dusting
earthworms
eating grapes
éclaircissage
ecological viticulture
ecosystem, vineyard
effeuillage
égrappage
Eiswein
El Niño
elevation
ELISA
encépagement
épamprage
erinose mite
erosion
esca
espalier
eucalyptus
eudemis
European vines
Eutypa dieback
Euvitis
evaporation
evapotranspiration
excoriose
fanleaf degeneration
fasciation

fertigation
fertility
fertilizers
field blend
field budding and grafting
flavescence dorée
flavonoids
flavonols
flavour compounds
flavour precursors
flétri
fleuraison
flooding
flood irrigation
flower cap
flowering
flowers in vineyards
flowers, vine
Foundation Plant Services
freeze
French hybrids
fresh grapes
frost
frost damage
frost protection
fructose
fruit
fruit fly
fruitfulness
fruit set
fumigation
fungal diseases
fungi
fungicide
galet
gallic acid
GDC
genetic modification
Geneva double curtain
geographical information system
geology
German crosses
gibberellins
girdling
GIS
glassy winged sharpshooter
global positioning system
global warming
glucose
gneiss
gobelet

GPS
grafted vine
grafting
grafting machine
granite
grape
grape quality assessment
grape varieties
grapevine
grapevine yellows
grasshoppers
gravel
green grafting
green harvest
greenhouse effect
grey rot
greywacke
grower
growth cycle
growth regulators
grubbing up
guttation
Guyot, Jules
hail
hail disease
hang time
harvest
harvest traditions
head
head training
heat stress
heat summation
heat-treated vines
hectare
hedging
helicopters
herbicides
heritage clones
hillside vineyards
Historic Vineyard Society
homoclimes
horizontal trellis
hormones
hot-water treatment
humidity
hybrids
IFOAM
incrocio
indexing
indicator
indigenous varieties

inflorescence
initiation
insecticides
insect pests
integrated pest management
integrated production
International Grape Genome
    Program
international varieties
internode
interspecific hybrid
invertase
iron
irrigation
isobutyl-methoxypyrazine
isopropyl-methoxypyrazine
KMW
labour
labrusca
ladybirds
ladybug taint
lake effect
late harvest
lateral shoot
latitude
layering
lead
leaf
leaf aldehydes
leaf fall
leafhoppers
leaf removal
leaf rollers
leafroll virus
leaf to fruit ratio
legno riccio
Lenz Moser
lightning
lignification
lime
lime, active
limestone
little leaf
loam
locusts
loess
low-input viticulture
lutte raisonnée
lyre
macroclimate
magnesium

a

abboccato, Italian for medium sweet (less sweet than AMABILE) or, literally, 'palatable' from *bocca* or 'mouth'. See also SWEETNESS.

ABC, acronym for the weary sentiment 'Anything But Chardonnay (or Cabernet)' which encouraged interest in grapes other than the (two most famous) INTERNATIONAL VARIETIES on the part of both producers and consumers. Rhône varieties were the earliest beneficiaries in the 1980s, but by the 2010s INDIGENOUS VARIETIES and ALTERNATIVE VARIETIES, the more obscure the better, were all the rage.

abocado, Spanish for medium sweet. According to European Union labelling regulations, *semiseco* is the official Spanish term.

Abona, small denominated Spanish wine region covering the semi-desert south of Tenerife in the vinously revitalized CANARY ISLANDS. Inland, at Vilaflor, it boasts Europe's highest vineyard, reaching 1,600 m/5,200 ft above sea level. It produces an increasing number of ORGANIC wines as well as whites of little distinction from the LISTÁN Blanco grape.   V. de la S.

Abouriou, early-ripening minor south western dark-berried vine variety that was still grown on 309 ha/763 acres of France in 2012. It is still theoretically allowed into Côtes du MARMANDAIS where Elian Da Ros makes a varietal version. Its wine is relatively high in tannin and low in acidity. French AMPELOGRAPHER Paul Truel identified the vine once grown in California as Early Burgundy as Abouriou.

Robinson, J., Harding, J., and Vouillamoz, J., *Wine Grapes: A Complete Guide to 1,368 Vine Varieties Including their Origins and Flavours* (London, 2012).

Abruzzo, mountainous region in central Italy with a significant coastline on the Adriatic sea to the south of MARCHE and an important producer of wine (see map under ITALY). Abruzzo is seventh among Italy's regions in terms of production, with a total output of just over 2 million hl (nearly 53 million gal) in 2011. Despite the presence of one of Italy's better red grape varieties MONTEPULCIANO d'Abruzzo, the warm climate, and favourable vineyard sites where the hills descend towards the Adriatic and enjoy the benefits of summer heat and solar radiation from the sea, most of the region's production is still undistinguished.

Abruzzo is particularly known for two varieties, the red Montepulciano and the white TREBBIANO D'ABRUZZO. Both varieties have been underachievers, mainly because of ignorance of site specifics and because YIELDS of more than 100hl/ha are allowed by law. This is not helped by the facts that until recently the entire region was covered by a single DOC, Abruzzo, and only 80% of each principal variety is required.

But the region has made convincing attempts at improving quality over quantity, doubtless helped by falling BULK WINE prices and the VINE PULL SCHEME of the EU which has seen total vineyard area decline from 36,000 ha (89,000 acres) to 30,000 ha in the first decade of this century, with half of that dedicated to DOC production. Montepulciano d'Abruzzo is generally produced in two styles: a young, quaffing style, robustly fruity and best drunk in its first two years, and a more serious, almost Syrah-like style, where the wildness of the fruit is often tempered by a bit of OAK.

The huge Abruzzo DOC has been divided into five subzones (Alto Tirino, Casauria, Teate, Terre dei Peligni, and Terre dei Vestini), areas that have traditionally been associated with a finer quality of Montepulciano, plus the tiny DOC Controguerra. Subject to stricter production rules, the subzones' VINE DENSITY must be at least 4,000 vines/ha compared with DOC Abruzzo's 2,500. The subzone system may well be the first step towards an increasing focus on TERROIR. With a minimum of 95% Montepulciano, three tiny, and potentially exciting, DOCs—Villamagna, Terre Tollesi, and Ortona—share the same tighter rules. The region currently has only one DOCG, Montepulciano d'Abruzzo Colline Teramare, which has still to prove its worth, but an important side effect is the concomitant reduction in permitted yields.

Montepulciano d'Abruzzo was once prized as a blending wine in Italy's north, Germany, and France, but an increasing amount of more serious examples from single producers, rather than from the omnipresent CO-OPERATIVES, is bottled than ever before. Once Montepulciano is given full attention in vineyard as well as cellar, some seriously fine and age-worthy wines should result, evidenced by the Montepulciano of Emilio Pepe and Valentini, the latter better known for his fabled long-lived Trebbiano d'Abruzzo. Most of Abruzzo's insipid whites labelled Trebbiano are not made of Trebbiano d'Abruzzo grapes at all, but the bland Trebbiano Toscano. Only if the first law of wine quality, lower yields, is respected, can a realistic assessment of Trebbiano d'Abruzzo's quality be made.   W.S.

Belfrage, N., *From Brunello to Zibibbo—The Wines of Tuscany, Central and Southern Italy* (2nd edn, London, 2003).

www.consorzio-viniabruzzo.it

abscisic acid, or **ABA**, HORMONE that occurs naturally in vines and regulates growth and physiology. It has been shown to be involved in the control of gene expression, thereby influencing certain characteristics of the vine such as the biosynthesis of ANTHOCYANINS. Its synthesis is encouraged by physiological stresses including short days and WATER STRESS. In the vine, abscisic acid is involved in LEAF FALL, shoot and root growth, bud dormancy, opening of STOMATA, and regulation of grape ripening. The irrigation technique PARTIAL ROOT-ZONE DRYING works by manipulating ABA levels.

R.E.S. & P.R.D.

Böttcher, C., and Davies, C., 'Hormonal control of grape berry development and ripening', in H. Gerós, M. Chaves, and S. Delrot (eds.), *The Biochemistry of the Grape Berry* (Bentham, 2012). doi: 10.2174/97816080536051120101.

Keller, M., 'Botany and anatomy', in *The Science of Grapevines: Anatomy and Physiology* (Elsevier, 2010).

Abu Nuwas (d. AD 814), half Arab/half Persian, was court poet and close friend of the Abbasid Caliph al-Amīn (reigned AD 809–813). He was one of the greatest ARAB POETS of classical Arabic/Islamic culture and, despite his eloquence in all the poetic genres, is remembered principally in the Arabic tradition for his wine poems (the *Khamriyyāt*). P.K.

Kennedy, P., *Abu Nuwas: A Genius of Poetry* (Oxford, 2005).

Abymes, named CRU just south of CHAMBÉRY whose name may be added to the eastern French appellation Vin de SAVOIE. The vineyards border those of APREMONT and the wines are similar: typically light, dry whites made from the local JACQUÈRE grape.

academe, originally a Greek word for a site of scholastic endeavour, and today a term embracing all that is achieved there. It impinges considerably on the world of wine.

Winemaking was already a sophisticated practical art by the beginning of the 19th century, and Europe's first formal viticultural training school was established in SACHSEN in what is now eastern Germany in 1811–12. In the second half of the century, however, the seminal work of Louis PASTEUR heralded its transition to an applied science worthy of academic study. Vine-growing and winemaking were soon recognized as academic disciplines and in 1880, coincidentally, both the University of California (now established at DAVIS) and the Institut d'Oenologie at the University of BORDEAUX began teaching and researching VITICULTURE and OENOLOGY. The devastation caused in the mid to late 19th century by FUNGAL DISEASES and the PHYLLOXERA pest may help to explain the coincidence.

During the 20th and early 21st centuries, academic institutions throughout the world have worked in tandem with their local wine industries both to teach the scientific principles of vine-growing and winemaking (increasingly regarded as the single discipline of wine-growing) and to research refinements and solutions. Other academic institutions of importance to wine include ADELAIDE, AUSTRALIAN WINE RESEARCH INSTITUTE, BROCK, CHANGINS, CHARLES STURT UNIVERSITY, CONEGLIANO, CORNELL UNIVERSITY, DIJON, FRESNO, GEISENHEIM, INSTITUT DES SCIENCES DE LA VIGNE ET DU VIN DE BORDEAUX, JULIUS-KÜHN-INSTITUT, KLOSTERNEUBURG, LINCOLN, MAGARACH, MONTPELLIER, PLUMPTON, SAN MICHELE ALL'ADIGE, STELLENBOSCH, VIRGINIA TECH, and WÄDENSWIL. Some of these are government funded, although grants for specific research projects are increasingly sought from industry.

In traditional wine regions, wine-growing was taught by apprenticeship, and apprentices were taught to respect TRADITION above SCIENCE. Formal academic training has long been the norm in the NEW WORLD, on the other hand. By the late 20th century, however, it was customary for even a seventh-generation Old World wine producer to have received some sort of formal academic training, certainly in his or her own region and very possibly abroad. This not only reflected a fundamental change of attitude towards the science of wine production on the part of Old World producers, but also played a crucial role in the widespread improvement in wine quality during the 1980s and 1990s. Academe, with its annual crop of graduates, could be said to have spawned FLYING WINEMAKERS. Wine courses today need not be focused on production or tasting, however, with such tertiary qualifications as the wine MBAs available in Bordeaux, Davis, and Sonoma.

Acadie. See L'ACADIE BLANC.

access system, wine. Technology allowing wine to be withdrawn from a bottle, INERT GAS being substituted for its volume, without pulling the cork and creating LEFTOVER WINE. Potentially of use to those serving fine wine by the glass professionally, or at home to very few people at a time. Coravin was the prototype.

Accolade Wines. In 2011 and 2012 the US company CONSTELLATION BRANDS sold its Australian, South African, and European wine interests to Australian Champ Private Equity, who renamed them Accolade Wines. In 2014 Accolade produced more wine than any other Australian company although TREASURY WINE ESTATES had higher revenues. Accolade's Australian BRANDS include Amberley, Banrock Station, Bay of Fires, Berri, Brookland Valley, Goundrey, HARDYS, Houghton, the leading Australian sparkling wine brand House of Arras, Leasingham, Moondah Brook, Omni, Renmano, Reynella, Stanley, and Yarra Burn. They also acquired Geyser Peak, Atlas Peak, and XYZ alongside Mud House and Waipara Hills of New Zealand. Kumala, South Africa's biggest-selling branded wine, is another important product, while the company also owns several mass-market California wine brands such as Echo Falls. Much of Accolade's wine is shipped around the world in BULK. At a facility outside Bristol, Accolade is the UK's major wine bottler and packager of wine in BOXES.

acetaldehyde, the most common member of the group of chemical compounds known as ALDEHYDES, a natural constituent of nearly all plant material, including grapes. Acetaldehyde is the next to last substance involved in the FERMENTATION pathway (and is therefore a minor constituent of all fermented products). Post-fermentation traces of acetaldehyde remain in all wines.

In pure liquid form, acetaldehyde has a particularly penetrating and unpleasant aroma. Above a certain level it can make the wine smell 'flat', vapid, and oxidized. At slightly higher concentrations, it contributes to the distinctive and characteristic smell of FINO sherry and other FLOR wines. Acetaldehyde binds with SULFUR DIOXIDE. It also adds to ANTHOCYANIN pigments, CATECHINS, and PROANTHOCYANIDINS (condensed TANNINS) and it is thus involved in the formation of PIGMENTED TANNINS and other derived pigments in wines.

Because it is the first compound formed when OXYGEN reacts with the ETHANOL in wine, winemakers are careful to minimize delicate white wines' exposure to air. (This is not so critical with heavier red wines, possibly because acetaldehyde reacts with tannins and anthocyanins.) Special care must be taken while BOTTLING white wines as this is when the introduction of oxygen can most easily damage the delicate aromas. When a bottle of white wine is only partially emptied, the freshness of its aroma is rapidly lost and replaced by a vapid OXIDIZED smell that is due to, among other reactions, the conversion of ethanol to acetaldehyde. The formation of perceptible acetaldehyde, accompanied by a browning of colour, is a typical sign of OXIDATION.

A.D.W., P.J.W., & V.C.

acetic acid, a simple two-carbon fatty acid which is the main flavour constituent responsible for the aroma and sour taste of VINEGAR. In wine it is the main component of what is called VOLATILE ACIDITY (VA).

Acetic acid is produced by a range of microbial activity including primary FERMENTATION, MALOLACTIC CONVERSION, and other fermentations carried out by spoilage organisms (LACTIC ACID BACTERIA, acetic acid bacteria, and spoilage yeasts including BRETTANOMYCES). If wine is exposed to OXYGEN after fermentation, ACETOBACTER can produce high levels of acetic acid from ETHANOL.

The sensory threshold for acetic acid is about 0.7 g/l. Levels above 1.1 to 1.2 g/l become unpleasant (sharp, vinegary) and are regarded as a wine fault in most wine styles. However, in some red-wine styles and botrytis-affected white wines, higher levels of VA can be perceived as giving the wine a more complex and desirable flavour.   T.J.

acetic acid bacteria, a family of genera which includes ACETOBACTER and GLUCONOBACTER.

acetobacter, genus within the family of ACETIC ACID BACTERIA (AAB) capable of spoiling wine by converting it ultimately into VINEGAR. They are found on all grapes but especially rot-affected grapes. Acetobacter can survive only in OXYGEN and are also one of the very few groups of bacteria which can live in the high-acid (low PH) environment of wine (although see also LACTIC ACID BACTERIA).

Ideal conditions for the growth of acetobacter are temperatures between 30° and 40 °C (86° and 104 °F), relatively high pH values of between 3.5 and 4.0, low alcohol concentrations, absence of SULFUR DIOXIDE, and generous supplies of oxygen. For these reasons, safe winemaking favours low storage temperatures, good levels of ACIDITY and alcohol, use of appropriate levels of sulfur dioxide as a disinfectant and, to minimize oxygen contact, barrels, vats, and tanks kept full at all times, that is with minimum ULLAGE. If this last cannot be avoided, the stored wine is blanketed with CARBON DIOXIDE, NITROGEN, or an INERT GAS MIXTURE.

                                                          A.D.W. & P.J.W.

acid, when used as an adjectival tasting term rather than a chemical noun (see ACIDS), is usually pejorative, a bit like 'tart' or 'sour', and means that the wine has too much ACIDITY.

acid adjustment, euphemism for DEACIDIFICATION or more usually ACIDIFICATION.

acidification is the winemaking process of increasing the ACIDITY in a grape must or wine. This is a common practice in warm wine regions (as common as ENRICHMENT, or CHAPTALIZATION, in cool wine regions), and is often the only course open to a winemaker wanting to make a balanced wine from grapes which have been allowed a growing season long enough to develop flavour by reaching full physiological RIPENESS. This is because in warm conditions a large amount of the grape's natural malic acid is degraded during the ripening process. A good level of ACIDS (and therefore low PH) not only increases the apparent freshness and fruitiness of many wines, it also protects the wine against attack from BACTERIA and spoilage yeasts such as BRETTANOMYCES, enhances the effectiveness of SULFUR DIOXIDE, and can improve COLOUR (as explained under acidity).

Acidification is usually sanctioned by local wine regulations within carefully delineated limits in order to prevent stretching of wine by adding sugar and water along with the permitted acid. In temperate zones such as Bordeaux and Burgundy, acidification is allowed, but with the understandable proviso that no wine may be both acidified and enriched.

The timing of the acid addition varies, but adding acid usually lowers pH so that an addition before or during FERMENTATION results in better microbiological control of subsequent processes and favours the formation of desirable aromas. Fine tuning of acid levels may take place at the final BLENDING stage but acid added at this stage can be too obvious.

Regulations vary from country to country but the most common permitted additives for acidification are, in descending order, TARTARIC ACID, CITRIC ACID, and MALIC ACID. Tartaric is the acid of choice for adding to grape juice before fermentation for several reasons: it is the natural acid of ripe grapes, it is the most effective option, and, unlike both citric and malic acid, which can be attacked by LACTIC ACID BACTERIA, tartaric acid is rarely degraded. Tartaric acid has the disadvantages, however, that it is the most expensive of the three and that significant amounts of the acid may be precipitated as TARTRATES and lost from the wine. If grapes are harvested with high levels of malic acid, tartaric acid may be added so that the wine retains sufficient acidity after MALOLACTIC CONVERSION. Malic acid is used infrequently because of its microbiological instability and its cost. Citric acid, while also being susceptible to microbiological attack, has the merit of being the least expensive and is used widely for inexpensive wines. It is often chosen for late acid additions because, unlike tartaric acid, it does not affect cold STABILIZATION. However, the use of citric acid for acidification is not permitted in wines made or sold in the EU. In many instances and where regulations permit (in the United States, for example), a blend of acids is often used.

One of the problems with acidification is that it is difficult to calculate how much acid to add to reach a desired final pH, in part because each wine or must has its own BUFFERING CAPACITY.

See also DEACIDIFICATION, a less common winemaking measure used in cool climates.

                                                          A.D.W. & J.A.G.

acidity is a general term for the fresh, tart, or sour taste produced by the natural organic ACIDS present in a liquid and one of the primary tastes sensed by tastebuds on the tongue (see TASTING). Wines, together with most other refreshing or appetizing drinks, owe their attractive qualities to a proper balance between this acidic character and the sweet and bitter sensations of other components. All refreshing drinks contain some acidity, which is typically sensed on the human palate by a prickling sensation on the sides of the tongue.

The acidity of the original grape juice has an important influence on wine quality because of its direct influence on COLOUR (see below), its effect on the growth of YEASTS and BACTERIA (harmful and beneficial), and its inherent effects on flavour qualities. It also plays a part in wine AGEING.

Grape juice acidity is highest just at the beginning of RIPENING, at which stage grapes have half as much concentration of acidity as lemons. See also VERJUS.

Acidity is one of the most important components in both grape juice and wine, and is also easily quantifiable. What is measured, although in different ways in different countries, is usually the TOTAL ACIDITY, which is the sum of the FIXED ACIDS and the VOLATILE ACIDS. To a scientist, acidity is the extent to which a solution is acid, caused by protons (hydrogen ions or H+), which may be present in either free or bound forms. Another way of measuring acidity is to measure the concentration of hydrogen ions (H+) free in solution, using the logarithmic PH scale. Generally the higher the total acidity of a wine, the lower is its pH.

Acidity helps to preserve the colour of red wines because the pH affects the ionization of ANTHOCYANINS, which in turn affects their colour. The lower the pH, the redder (less blue) the colour is and the greater the colour stability. As pH values rise (in less acid wines), pigments become increasingly blue and the colour becomes less stable with pigments eventually assuming muddy grey forms. Red wines from warmer regions and made without ACIDIFICATION can have colours that are less red (and often with a brownish tinge) than those from colder regions which produce wines with higher acidity.

Excessive acidity—resulting either from excessive concentrations of natural plant acids in less-than-ripe grapes or, more rarely, from over-enthusiastic acidification in the winery—makes wines sharp, tart, and sometimes unpleasant to drink. Too little acidity, on the other hand—the consequence of picking too late, or such heat during ripening that the natural plant acids are largely decomposed—results in wines that are flat, uninteresting, and described typically by wine tasters as 'flabby'.

See TOTAL ACIDITY for more details.

                                                          A.D.W., B.G.C., & P.J.W.

acids, members of a group of chemical compounds which are responsible for the sharp or sour taste of all drinks and foods, including wine. The most important acids contained in grapes are TARTARIC ACID and, in slightly lower concentrations, MALIC ACID. Malic acid occurs in many different plants and fruits, but vines are among the very few plants with large concentrations of tartaric acid in their fruit. The principal acid component in most plants is CITRIC ACID but VINIFERA vines are also unusual among plants in accumulating only very small amounts of citric acid.

Grapes contain a large number of acids other than their major constituents, tartaric and malic acids. Present in low concentrations are several of the fatty acids, of which the most common is ACETIC ACID, arising from the metabolic processes of fruit RIPENING.

Some other acids involved in the growth of vines accumulate in the berry in very small amounts and some of these persist into the wine. Other acids found in wines, while possibly present in traces in grapes, are formed mainly during FERMENTATION. Among those present in the largest concentrations are LACTIC ACID, SUCCINIC ACID, and CARBONIC ACID.

Various acids are also occasionally added during winemaking. (See ASCORBIC ACID, SORBIC ACID, and sulfurous acid, which is SULFUR DIOXIDE.)

Acids are important in wine not just because, in moderation, they make it taste refreshing, but also because they prevent the growth of harmful BACTERIA and spoilage yeasts such as BRETTANOMYCES and can keep it microbiologically stable. Most bacteria, and all of those of greatest danger to man, are incapable of living in distinctly acid solutions such as wines. Two groups of bacteria are major exceptions to this rule, however, the ACETOBACTER and the various LACTIC ACID BACTERIA.

A wine's concentration of acids is called its ACIDITY, which can be measured in various ways. Acidity is closely, if inversely, related to PH.   A.D.W. & P.J.W.

acidulation, winemaking process more commonly known as ACIDIFICATION.

Acolon, GERMAN CROSS of LEMBERGER and DORNFELDER that is increasingly popular, especially in Württemberg and the Pfalz, and plantings totalled 482 ha/1,190 acres in 2012.

Aconcagua, burgeoning wine region of CHILE including the subregions Aconcagua, Casablanca, and San Antonio.

active. See LIME, ACTIVE and CARBON, ACTIVE.

additives, as controversial in wine as in any other foodstuff, are mostly hidden from wine drinkers since wine is exempt from INGREDIENT-LABELLING regulations, although producers must state on the label if their wines contain SULFUR DIOXIDE. Other widely used and perfectly legal additives include YEAST to carry out FERMENTATION, lactic acid bacteria for MALOLACTIC CONVERSION, sugar to increase ALCOHOLIC STRENGTH (see CHAPTALIZATION), acid for ACIDIFICATION, OENOLOGICAL TANNINS for TEXTURE and COLOUR

stability, SÜSSRESERVE for sweetness, alcohol for FORTIFICATION, ASCORBIC ACID as an ANTIOXIDANT, DIAMMONIUM PHOSPHATE as a yeast nutrient, ENZYMES to improve juice extraction, and SORBIC ACID as a preservative. Additions may be allowed only in certain regions or within specific limits but these vary despite the OIV's attempts at standardization set out in their *International Code of Oenological Practices*. Instances of the use of illegal additives such as FLAVOURINGS and OAK essence may be more common than we think and prosecutions for ADULTERATION are seemingly rare. Additives should not be confused with PROCESSING AIDS.

See also HUMIDIFICATION, DOSAGE, MICRO-OXYGENATION, and ADULTERATION AND FRAUD.

OIV, *International Code of Oenological Practices* (2014), www.oiv.int/oiv/info/enplubicationoiv.

adega, Portuguese word for cellar or winery.

Adelaide, usual abbreviation in the wine world for the **University of Adelaide**, in South Australia, with which ROSEWORTHY Agricultural College was merged in 1991 to form what is now known as the School of Agriculture, Food, and Wine, Australia's principal and influential centre of wine education and research (see ACADEME and AUSTRALIAN INFLUENCE).

Most of the teaching in OENOLOGY, VITICULTURE, and wine business studies takes place in the South Australian capital city of Adelaide at the Waite and North Terrace campuses. At the Waite Campus, students undertake their winemaking in the multi-million-dollar Hickinbotham Roseworthy Wine Science Laboratory owned by the University of Adelaide. They also have access to collaborating partners in the Wine Innovation Cluster located on the Waite Campus that includes the Commonwealth Scientific and Industrial Research Organization (CSIRO) Plant Industry, the AUSTRALIAN WINE RESEARCH INSTITUTE (AWRI), and the South Australian Research and Development Institute (SARDI), all of them having established a considerable international reputation for research in viticulture and oenology.   S.T.

www.wineinnovationcluster.com

Adelaide Hills, fashionable, relatively high (450–550 m/1,480–1,800 ft), cool wine region in SOUTH AUSTRALIA and one of Australia's best for growing fine Sauvignon Blanc, part of the MOUNT LOFTY RANGES ZONE with CLARE VALLEY. Lenswood and Piccadilly Valley are officially recognized subregions. The 90 producers are also notable for sparkling wine made from Pinot Noir and Chardonnay. In the north of the region, lower-elevation west-facing slopes produce fuller-bodied wines from Shiraz. To complicate the picture, Shiraz (sometimes married with Viognier) also flourishes in the cooler parts to produce northern Rhône Valley

lookalikes. ALTERNATIVE VARIETIES are increasingly grown, the main successes being Tempranillo, Nebbiolo, Pinot Gris, and Fiano.

Adelaide Plains, a flat, warm to hot region immediately north of Adelaide with one notable winery, Primo Estate (which sources much of its fruit from outside the region).

Adelaide Zone, Australian super zone encompassing the MOUNT LOFTY RANGES ZONE, FLEURIEU ZONE, and BAROSSA ZONE, stretching from CLARE VALLEY in the north to the foot of the Fleurieu Peninsula, plus the gaps in between; hence Penfolds Magill Estate is a notable resident. Infrequently used as a GEOGRAPHICAL INDICATION on wine labels.

adulteration and fraud have dogged the wine trade throughout its history. The variability and value of wine have traditionally made it a target for unscrupulous operators, as catalogued in the LITERATURE OF WINE. The long human chain stretching from grower to consumer affords many opportunities for illegal practices. It is important to remember, however, that at various times the law has viewed the same practices differently, sometimes condoning, sometimes condemning them. What we know as adulteration, our ancestors may have classed as a legitimate part of the winemaking process. See also MANIPULATION.

The simplest and most obvious form of adulterating wine is to add WATER. This is not necessarily fraudulent. In Ancient GREECE, for example, no civilized man would dream of drinking undiluted wine, and even today wine made from extremely ripe grapes may achieve better BALANCE if slightly diluted. The practice becomes illegal when done surreptitiously to cheat the consumer or defraud the taxman.

Another means of stretching wine is to 'cut', or blend, it with spirits or other (usually poorer-quality) wines. BORDEAUX merchants in the 18th century cut fine clarets with rough, stronger wine imported from Spain, the Rhône, or the Midi to increase profits, but also because it was genuinely believed that the resulting fuller bodied concoction was more to the English taste. JULLIEN describes this common practice as *travail à l'anglaise*. Similarly, merchants in 18th-century OPORTO began to adulterate port with brandy. The systematization of this process by the Portuguese government eventually led to an accepted method of 'adulteration', entirely lawful, to produce PORT as we know it today.

Other ways of altering the nature of a wine were perfectly legal. In the past, wines turned sour after a year or two and techniques used to cure or disguise 'sick' wines were commonplace. Classical and medieval recipes suggested adding various substances ranging from milk (perhaps a precursor of FINING with CASEIN) and mustard to ashes, nettles, and LEAD.

Although home doctoring was routine, when these techniques were employed by merchants or taverners deliberately to mislead the customer, the practice was as illegal as it was ubiquitous. In the first century AD, PLINY the Elder bemoaned the fact that 'not even our nobility ever enjoys wines that are genuine'.

It is assumed today that, unless explicitly stated otherwise, wine is the product of naturally fermented grape juice. However, the practice of fabricating wine, as opposed to simply doctoring it, has a long and chequered history, often most prolific and ingenious at times when true grape wine has been difficult to obtain. In 1709 Joseph Addison wrote in the *Tatler* of the 'fraternity of chymical operators . . . who squeeze Bourdeaux out of a sloe and draw Champagne from an apple', apparently a profession of long standing. Even today in CHINA's relatively uncontrolled wine market, it is not uncommon to encounter chemical concoctions sold as wine.

Wines were also fabricated from raisins. In the 1880s and 1890s during the scourge of PHYLLOXERA, a thriving industry manufacturing wine from imported raisins sprang up on the Mediterranean coast. During American PROHIBITION in the 1920s, various methods were contrived to circumvent the law by producing wines at home from raisins, dried grape 'bricks', and tinned GRAPE CONCENTRATE (using techniques common to HOME WINEMAKING today).

One of the most common forms of fraud does not involve any doctoring or fabricating of the wine, but merely renaming it. Once a region made a name for its wines, others tried to steal it. In Roman times, ordinary wines were passed off as valuable FALERNIAN. From the 19th century, vine-growers have fought for the legal apparatus to protect their names (see APPELLATION CONTRÔLÉE) and today producers of some of the most expensive wines go to great lengths to design labels which cannot be counterfeited (see INVESTMENT).

The adulteration or fraudulent sale of wine can be dangerous. The consumer may even be put medically at risk, by the use of lead in ancient times and by METHANOL contamination in the 20th century.

Consumers, growers, and merchants are not alone in trying to prevent adulteration and fraud. Local authorities and (from the last century) governments have fought it. Regulations and legislation have been passed for many reasons: to protect the consumer; to preserve the good name of the local wine; or to facilitate TAXATION.

In medieval London it was illegal for taverners to keep French or Spanish wines in the same cellar as those from Germany to prevent mixing or substitution. A vintner found selling corrupt wine was forced to drink it, then banned from the trade. German punishments of the time were more severe, ranging from beatings and branding to hanging.

The legal apparatus existing to combat fraud and adulteration today is the culmination of many battles waged by both consumers and trade. In 1820 Frederick Accum published his *Treatise* stating that wine was the commodity most at risk. Thirteen years later Cyrus Redding reported no improvement and it was not until 1860 that the first British Food and Drug Act was passed.

As for wine-producing countries, the economic distress caused by phylloxera was the main stimulus to legislation. The French government produced a legal definition of wine in 1889, the Germans framed the first GERMAN WINE LAW in 1892 (superseded by the more thorough 1909 version), and the Italians in 1904. The French Appellation Contrôlée system, defining wines by geography rather than simply composition, did not become nationally viable until the 1930s.

Although once rife, adulteration and fraud have been considerably rarer in the wine trade since the adoption of CONTROLLED APPELLATION systems and methods by which to enforce them such as France's Service de la Répression des Fraudes. There have been examples of CONTAMINANTS in wine, both deliberate and accidental, but passing off has become increasingly difficult and, just possibly, less rewarding as wine consumers become ever more sophisticated and more concerned with inherent wine quality than the hierarchy of famous names. Consumers may with justification feel that the wine trade has attracted more than its fair share of charlatans because fraud in any field in which expertise is difficult to acquire and viewed with suspicion (such as wine and fine art) attracts more media attention than most other types of commercial fraud.

For details of modern fine wines encountered in fake form, see COUNTERFEIT WINE.   H.B. & J.R.

Accum, F., *Treatise on Adulteration of Food and Culinary Poisons* (London, 1820).

Barr, A., *Wine Snobbery: An Insider's Guide to the Booze Business* (London, 1988).

Johnson, H., *The Story of Wine* (London and New York, 1989).

Jullien, A., *Topographie de tous les vignobles connus* (Paris, 1816).

Loubère, L. A., *The Red and the White: A History of Wine in France and Italy in the Nineteenth Century* (Albany, NY, 1978).

Redding, C., *The History and Description of Modern Wines* (London, 1833).

Aegean Islands, islands in the Aegean Sea between modern GREECE and TURKEY. From 1050 BC onwards most of these islands were populated by Greeks. Some of the best Greek wine came from these islands, with CHIAN wine, from the island of Chios, ranked highly in both Ancient Greece and Ancient ROME. Wines from Lesbos, Thasos, and Cos also featured strongly. Chian wine was still highly valued in the Middle Ages and traded in quantity by the Genoans, for example. Today the islands, led by SANTORINI, are home to several important wines and appellations. In addition, a number of grape varieties such as ASSYRTIKO, MANDILARIA, and LIMNIO are considered quintessentially Aegean.

aeration, the deliberate and controlled exposure of a substance to air, and particularly to its reactive component OXYGEN.

The aeration of wine during WINEMAKING must be carefully controlled, since excessive exposure to oxygen can result in OXIDATION and the possible formation of excess ACETIC ACID. At the beginning of FERMENTATION some aeration is necessary since YEAST needs oxygen for growth. The cellar operation of TOPPING UP can expose the wine to an amount of oxygen that contributes to the BARREL MATURATION process. The amount of aeration involved in the cellar techniques of RACKING wine from one container (usually a BARREL) to another, DÉLESTAGE, and PUMPING OVER can also be positively beneficial to a wine's development. Specifically, aeration can often cure wines suffering from REDUCTION and can usually remove malodorous and volatile HYDROGEN SULFIDE and MERCAPTANS.

Often for the same reasons, some aeration before SERVING by pouring the contents of a bottle from a great height or from one container into another can also benefit some wines after BOTTLE AGEING, as can simply swirling the wine in the glass. See also DECANTING and BREATHING.

aerial imagery. See REMOTE SENSING.

Afghanistan, Middle Eastern country in which 62,000 ha/153,000 acres of vines were officially cultivated for TABLE GRAPES and DRYING GRAPES in 2011, according to OIV figures. At one time wine may have been made here and shipped along the old Silk Road to India, and there are reports of current winemaking on the Shamali Plains north of Kabul.

Africa. See ALGERIA, EGYPT, ETHIOPIA, KENYA, LESOTHO, MADAGASCAR, MOROCCO, NAMIBIA, SOUTH AFRICA, TANZANIA, TUNISIA, and ZIMBABWE.

age in a wine is not necessarily a virtue. See AGEING. See also VINE AGE.

ageing of wine, an important aspect of wine CONNOISSEURSHIP, and one which distinguishes wine from almost every other drink (see BACTERIA).

History

When a fine wine is allowed to age, spectacular changes can occur which increase both its complexity and monetary value. Ageing is dependent on several factors: the wine must be intrinsically capable of it; it must be correctly STORED (in a cool place and out of contact with air); and some form of capital INVESTMENT is usually necessary.

Although the BIBLE suggests that Luke understood that old wine was finer than new wine, the Romans (see Ancient ROME and, specifically, HORACE) were the first connoisseurs systematically to appreciate fine wines which had been allowed to age, although there is some evidence of wine ageing in Ancient GREECE. Certain wines (DRIED-GRAPE WINES, for example) were suitable for ageing because of their high sugar content and were stored in sealed earthenware jars or AMPHORAE. The best, FALERNIAN and SURRENTINE wines, required 15 to 20 years before they were considered at their best and were sometimes kept for decades.

The Greek physician GALEN (b. AD 130) noted that an 'aged' wine need not necessarily be old, but might simply have the characteristics of age. In other words it was possible, indeed very common, to age wines prematurely by means of heating or smoking them (see Ancient Rome). At one time the smoky taste of 'aged' wines became a vogue in itself, though Galen warned that they were not as wholesome as naturally old wines.

After the collapse of the Roman Empire, the appreciation of aged wines disappeared for a millennium. The thin, low-alcohol wines of northern Europe were good for only a few months, after which they turned sour and were sold cheaply. The only wines that could be enjoyed a little longer were the sweeter and more alcoholic wines of the Mediterranean such as MALMSEY and SACK.

By the 16th century, exceptions to this rule could be found in the huge casks of top-quality wine made from RIESLING wine kept beneath German palaces (see GERMAN HISTORY). These wines were preserved through a combination of sweetness and ACIDITY, the coldness of the cellar, and the cellarmaster's habit of constantly TOPPING UP the cask to avoid OXIDATION.

The real breakthrough came with the introduction in the 17th century of CORKS and glass BOTTLES. The ageing of wine in bottle was pioneered in England by connoisseurs of fine CLARET and port. English wine drinkers rediscovered pleasures largely unknown since Roman times.

Other methods of preserving wine were developed or rediscovered: the addition of spirits to a partially fermented wine to produce fortified wines (see FORTIFICATION); the systematic topping up of a SOLERA system to produce wines like sherry; and the heating of MADEIRA.

Demand for mature wines transformed the wine trade. Aside from a few wealthy owners, most vine-growers could not afford to keep stocks of past vintages. Only MERCHANTS could do that, and their economic power and hold over the producers increased during the 18th and 19th centuries. This was most demonstrably the case in BORDEAUX, BEAUNE, and OPORTO, where merchants amassed huge stocks, vast fortunes, and powerful reputations.   H.B.

Johnson, H., *The Story of Wine* (London, 1989).
Younger, W., *Gods, Men and Wine* (London, 1966).

Which wines to age

The ageing of wine is an important element in getting the most from it but, contrary to popular opinion, only a small subgroup of wines benefit from extended BOTTLE AGEING. The great bulk of wine sold today, red as well as white and pink, is designed to be drunk within a year, or at most two, of BOTTLING.

Wines which generally do not improve with time spent in bottle, and which are usually best consumed as soon as possible after bottling (although after a few weeks in bottle has eliminated any BOTTLE SICKNESS) include the following—although the following is only the most approximate generalization: wines packaged in any containers other than bottles—BOXES, for example; most basic WINE WITHOUT GEOGRAPHICAL INDICATION in the EU, JUG WINE in the US, and their everyday, commercial equivalents elsewhere; almost all BRANDED wines, with the possible exception of some red bordeaux; most wine coloured pink; all wines released within less than six months of the vintage such as those labelled NOUVEAU and the like.

Even among finer wines, different wines mature at different rates, according to individual VINTAGE characteristics, their exact provenance, and how they were made. Such factors as BARREL FERMENTATION for whites and BARREL MATURATION for wines of any colour play a part in the likely life cycle of the wine. In general, the lower a wine's PH, the longer it is capable of evolving. Among reds, generally speaking the higher the level of FLAVOUR COMPOUNDS and PHENOLICS, particularly TANNINS, the longer it is capable of being aged. Wines made from Cabernet Sauvignon and Nebbiolo grapes, for example, and many of those made from Syrah/Shiraz, should be aged longer than those based on Merlot or Pinot Noir—and certainly much longer than the average wine made from Gamay or Grenache. Among white wines, partly because of their higher acidity and FLAVOUR PRECURSORS, the finest Riesling and Loire Chenin Blanc evolve more slowly than wines based on Chardonnay.

In general terms, better-quality wines from the following regions or made from the following grape varieties should benefit from some bottle age, with a *very* approximate number of years in bottle in brackets (of course, it all depends on vintage, winemaker, storage conditions, and many other factors):

WHITES

Almost all wine retailing at under £10/$20: 1–2
Chablis: 3–15
Côte d'Or white burgundy: 3–10
Other wines based on Chardonnay: 2–6
Wines based on Riesling: 3–20
Wines based on Sauvignon Blanc: 1–5
Wines based on Viognier: 1–3
Wines based on Chenin Blanc: 3–15
Botrytized sweet wines: 5–35

REDS

Almost all wine retailing at under £10/$20: 1–3 (although some particularly good red Côtes du Rhône and old-vine Spaniards can provide exceptions)

Bordeaux, Madiran: 5–25
Burgundy: 4–20
Northern Rhône: 4–15 (Hermitage longer)
Southern Rhône: 3–10
Languedoc-Roussillon: 3–8
Barolo, Barbaresco: 6–25
Brunello di Montalcino: 5–13
Chianti: 4–10
Rioja: 5–20
Ribera del Duero: 3–15
Douro table wines: 4–12
Vintage port: 12–50
Other wines based on Cabernet Sauvignon: 7–17
Other wines based on Pinot Noir: 4–10
Other wines based on Syrah/Shiraz: 4–12
Other wines based on Grenache: 3–8

ICEWINE and all but the finest EISWEIN matures quite rapidly. Most fortified wines and their like, such as VINS DOUX NATURELS and VINS DE LIQUEUR, are bottled when their producers think they are ready to drink. Exceptions to this are the extremely rare bottle-aged sherries, vintage PORT (which is expressly designed for decades of bottle ageing), single quinta ports, and crusted port.

Producers of most SPARKLING WINES usually claim that their wines are ready to drink on release, but this may not be true when demand exceeds supply. Even if yeast AUTOLYSIS ceases when the wine is disgorged, better-quality young sparkling wines with their high levels of acidity can often improve considerably with an additional year or so in bottle.

Factors affecting ageing

STORING WINE in particular conditions can affect the rate at which wine ages; the lower the TEMPERATURE, the slower the maturation. Conversely, ageing can be hastened by stripping a young wine of its solids (by very heavy FILTRATION or FINING, for example), and by storing wine in warmer conditions. Thus, a wine stored in a centrally heated Manhattan apartment will mature very much faster than one stored in an unheated warehouse in Scandinavia. In general, the more slowly a wine matures, the greater the complexity of the flavour compounds that go to make up its BOUQUET (see below).

It is also popularly believed that in general, the smaller the BOTTLE SIZE, the faster its contents mature, presumably because of the greater proportion of OXYGEN in the bottle, both as a consequence of the bottling process and any possible oxygen ingress via the cork seal during ageing. This is part of the reason LARGE FORMATS carry a premium.

Wines under SCREWCAP tend to age very differently from the same wine under CORK, although it is too early for long-term scientific studies of this phenomenon.

For more details, see STORING WINE and CLOSURES.

How wine ages

The descriptions below concern only those wines designed specifically to be aged. The great majority of wines in commercial circulation are ready to drink when released.

Red wines To the untutored taster, older red wines seem to be softer and gentler than harsh, inky young ones. Those who notice such things will also observe a change in colour, typically from deep purple to light brick red. There should also be more SEDIMENT in an old wine than a young one. All these phenomena are related, and are related in particular to the behaviour of phenolics, the compounds of the grape, particularly the skins, including the blue/red ANTHOCYANINS which together with the astringent but colourless flavonoids form the PIGMENTED TANNINS (tannin-anthocyanin complexes) that are responsible for a red wine's COLOUR and TEXTURE.

Most phenolics are leached out of the grape skins and seeds during RED WINEMAKING. They react with each other, especially under the influence of the small amounts of oxygen dissolved in the wine during such processes as RACKING, topping up, and, later, bottling, to generate various derivatives including pigmented tannins. There is some evidence that these reactions start during the primary FERMENTATION process, and by about 18 months later the anthocyanins have mostly been converted to derived pigments responsible for the colour of older red wines. A fine red wine ready for bottling, therefore, may contain colourless tannins, a low concentration of anthocyanins, as well as pigmented tannins, and more complex COLLOIDS such as tannin-POLYSACCHARIDES, and tannin-PROTEINS. Reactions and aggregation continue in bottle. When the resulting polymers and particles reach a certain size, they precipitate as dark reddish-brown sediment, leaving wine that is progressively less astringent, some of the red/blue pigments and tannins having been precipitated. Thus, to a certain extent, holding a bottle of wine up to the light to determine how much sediment it has precipitated can give some indication of its maturity (although the amount of sediment deposited is a function not just of time, but of storage conditions and the initial composition of the wine, phenolic and protein content for example).

At the same time as these visible changes occur, the impact of the wine on the nose and palate also evolves. A wide range of FLAVOUR PRECURSORS that were attached to glucose detach themselves (through a natural, and time-dependent, process of HYDROLYSIS) and contribute their individual flavour characteristics to the older wine.

Other flavour compounds responsible for the initial primary AROMAS of the grape and those of fermentation (sometimes called secondary aroma, or secondary bouquet) are also interacting, with each other and with other phenolics, so that gradually the smell of the wine is said to be transformed, by a pathway as yet not understood, into a bouquet, of tertiary aromas, a very much more subtle array and arrangement of flavours which can be sensed by the nose (see TASTING).

ESTERS are formed from combinations of the increasingly complex array of wine ACIDS with ALCOHOLS. Continued esterification in bottle produces another range of possible aromas, all the more unpredictable since the esters are formed at very different rates.

The rate at which all these things happen is influenced by a host of factors: storage conditions (particularly temperature), the state of the cork or other stopper, the ULLAGE when the wine was bottled, its pH level, and SULFUR DIOXIDE concentration, both of which can inhibit or slow the all-important influence of oxygen.

OENOLOGISTS understand this much about the maturation of age-worthy red wine, but are unable to predict with any degree of certainty when such a wine is likely to reach that complex stage called full MATURITY, when it has dispensed with its uncomfortably harsh tannins and acquired maximum complexity of flavour without starting to decay. Part of the joy of wine has long been said to be the monitoring of the progress of a case of wine, bottle by bottle, but this is strictly a rich person's sport.

White wines If our understanding of red wine maturation is incomplete, even less is known about the ageing process in white wines. Nevertheless, research has shown the importance of certain grape GLYCOSIDES (and the hydrolysis of these constituents) during white wine ageing to the development of varietal aroma in the wine. White wines begin life in bottle with a much lower tally of phenolics, although those they have strongly influence colour and apparent astringency. White wines become browner with age, presumably because of the slow oxidation of their phenolic content.

Ageing potential is indirectly proportional to a white wine's concentration of phenolics. For example, fine Rieslings, which are relatively low in phenolics, can in general age much longer than comparable Chardonnays, which contain more phenolics.

Experienced tasters, however, often note that wines affected by NOBLE ROT have a much greater ability to last than their non-botrytized counterparts. Experience also seems to suggest that white wines which undergo barrel fermentation also seem capable of lasting longer than those fermented in inert containers and then transferred to barrel for barrel maturation. Nevertheless, some unwooded white wines also have a great ageing ability.

Most white wines which can mature over several decades rather than years are notably high in acidity, and few of them undergo MALO-LACTIC CONVERSION. Many of the venerable sweet wines which demonstrate exceptional ageing ability today may well have been bottled with higher levels of sulfur dioxide than are acceptable to the modern consumer. See also ATYPICAL AGEING.

Stages of ageing

Maturing fine wines go through a number of perceptibly different stages. Very young wines are usually delicious, full of fruit and vivacity, but slightly simple. At some (unpredictable) time after bottling, anything between a few months and a few years, many fine wines seem to close up, to become surly, to lose their aroma without having gained a bouquet. Their dimensions can be sensed but little else (see TASTING). A variable number of years afterwards, they begin to smell like wine again and to have considerably more palate LENGTH. After this they enter into their most satisfying stage at which the bouquet seems fully developed and astringency has receded, making the mouthfeel attractive, so that the wine is delightful in terms of flavour, texture, length, and all-important BALANCE. (Many serious white Rhône wines are particularly prone to this sort of mid-life crisis.) If, however, wine is aged for too long (and no one, alas, can predict when this will be), it enters a stage of decrepitude during which the acidity starts to dominate (see above). This unpredictable journey may help to explain apparently contradictory judgements of the same wine, from WINE WRITERS, wine professionals, and wine consumers alike.

Artificial ageing

This winemaking technique has been practised with varying degrees of enthusiasm according to the demands of the market. Current FASHION dictates that wine should be as 'natural' as possible (and, increasingly, that it should be youthful rather than mature), and so very few table wines are ever subjected to artificial ageing (even if many modern WINEMAKING techniques such as MICRO-OXYGENATION are in fact designed to hasten some natural processes). Wine can be artificially aged by exposing it to oxygen or extremes of temperature, by shaking it to encourage effects of dissolved oxygen, or by exposing it to radiation or ultra-sonic or magnetic waves. The making of MADEIRA and some other RANCIO wines deliberately incorporates exposure to high temperatures, while storing wine in some modern domestic conditions can expose wine to high temperatures rather less deliberately.

This century is seeing considerable experimentation with unusual storage conditions for ageing. Those deliberately storing bottles of wine under water have been encouraged by the condition of even century-old champagne dredged up from the Baltic (see record prices in AUCTIONS) while others are seeing what happened when wine is stored at especially high ELEVATIONS or at a variety of TEMPERATURES and HUMIDITIES.

See ANTHOCYANINS, ESTER, PH, PHENOLICS, TANNINS; also MATURITY and STORING WINE.

J.R., P.J.W., & V.C.

Ribéreau-Gayon, P., et al., *Traité d'Œnologie 2: Chimie du vin: Stabilisation et traitements* (Paris, 1998), translated by Aquitrad Traduction as *Handbook of Enology 2: The Chemistry of Wine Stabilization and Treatments* (Chichester, 2000).

Robinson, J., *Vintage Timecharts* (London, 1989).

Agiorgitiko, also known as **Aghiorgitiko** and St George, most planted and admirably versatile Greek red grape variety native to Neméa in the Peloponnese, whose wines may be made from no other variety. It blends well with other varieties (notably with Cabernet Sauvignon grown many miles north in Metsovo) and can also produce good-quality rosé. The wine produced by Agiorgitiko is fruity but can lack acidity. Grapes grown on the higher vineyards of Neméa can yield long-lived reds. Virus-free clones are being developed.

Aglianico, a dark-skinned top-quality southern Italian grape variety for long thought to be of Greek origin (the name itself was said to be a corruption of the word *Ellenico*, the Italian word for Hellenic) although DNA PROFILING has failed to find a relationship with any known Greek variety. It retained the name Ellenico or Ellenica until the end of the 15th century, when it took its current name of Aglianico. First planted around the Greek colony of Cumae, close to present day Avellino (home of TAURASI), it is today cultivated in the mountainous centre of Italy's south, in particular in the provinces of Avellino and Benevento in CAMPANIA, and in the provinces of Potenza and Matera in BASILICATA. Scattered traces of this early-budding vine variety can also be found in CALABRIA, in PUGLIA, MOLISE, and on the island of Procida near Naples. Italy's total plantings were 9,910 ha/24,488 acres in 2010. The vine can ripen so late even

this far south that grapes may be picked in November. Attempts to pick it earlier, or to increase yields, invariably lead to a failure to tame its rather ferocious tannins. The grape's best wines are deep in colour with full chocolate and plum aromas, fine-grained tannins, and marked acidity on the palate. Aglianico seems to prefer soils of volcanic origin and achieves its finest results in the two DOCs of Taurasi in Campania and AGLIANICO DEL VULTURE in Basilicata where elevations are lower and the wines rather softer and earlier-maturing. Its nobility is so obvious that it is now grown in both Australia and California.

Robinson, J., Harding, J., and Vouillamoz, J., *Wine Grapes: A Complete Guide to 1,368 Vine Varieties, Including their Origins and Flavours* (London, 2012).

Aglianico del Vulture, potentially superior wine, one of only a handful in BASILICATA, based on the tannic and ageworthy AGLIANICO grape planted on the slopes of Mount Vulture, an extinct volcano, between 200 and 700 m ELEVATION. The DOC zone consists of close to 400 ha/1,000 acres, all on soils of VOLCANIC origin in the north west of the zone and benefiting from cool nights at an elevation of 450 to 600 m (1,970 ft). The area was given its own DOC as early as 1971, while the Superiore and Riserva versions of the wines were elevated to DOCG in 2010. Minimum VINE DENSITY for both DOC and DOCG is a low 3,350 plants/ha, while the high permitted YIELDS of 10 tons/ha for the DOC is lowered to 8 tonnes/ha for the DOCG. Quality-focused producers, however, demand much lower yields from their vines to produce the sturdy, classic red wine with a real propensity for extended cellaring.

Legal ageing requirements differ too: the DOC version may not be released on to the market prior to the September following the year of harvest, while the DOCG requires 24 months of ageing, of which 12 must be in oak. Styles can differ wildly, with an emphasis on winemaking (French BARRIQUES still feature heavily) rather than on the vineyard. However, the best wines tend to be aged in large oak casks, as many a fine older vintage of D'Angelo demonstrates. Single vineyard or vineyard districts, some 70 in total, may feature on labels, but the zone would benefit from more refined GEOGRAPHICAL delimitation, specifically a much smaller CLASSICO zone to distinguish the HILLSIDES from the many vineyards on the plain.

W.S.

www.aglianicodelvulture.net

agricultural treatises are the source of much of our evidence for wine in Ancient GREECE and Ancient ROME. HESIOD was the first Greek to write on agriculture, in the 8th century

BC. CATO, VARRO, COLUMELLA, PLINY, and VIRGIL were all important Roman writers.

agriturismo, important late-20th-century phenomenon in rural Italy whereby unused or under-used farm buildings, a significant proportion of them on wine farms, are converted, typically with state aid, for TOURIST accommodation, thereby exposing many thousands of visitors each year to the practicalities of wine production. Spain has seen a similar **enoturismo** initiative.

agrochemicals, the materials used in agriculture to control pests and diseases. They include FUNGICIDES, insecticides, HERBICIDES, bird repellents, plant GROWTH REGULATORS, rodenticides, and soil fumigants. A broader definition might also include FERTILIZERS.

Viticulture requires fewer agrochemicals than many other field crops, partly because such a high proportion of vines are grown in warm, dry summer environments in which FUNGAL DISEASES are relatively rare, and also because vines require fewer fertilizers than most other crops (see VINE NUTRITION). Vines grown in humid, warm summers may require as many as ten or more SPRAYINGS, however. Vinegrowers, like other farmers, are in general becoming less reliant on agrochemicals as a result of increased environmental concerns (see SUSTAINABILITY), and as alternative approaches become available. Some diseases, notably BOTRYTIS BUNCH ROT, develop tolerance to the repeated use of some chemicals, and so their continued use is now subject to resistance-management strategies. Alternative approaches may take the form of INTEGRATED PEST MANAGEMENT (IPM) programmes, which aim to apply chemicals more rationally, or the adoption of some form of SUSTAINABLE, ORGANIC or BIODYNAMIC VITICULTURE, which aim to minimize the use of agrochemicals.

The use of agrochemicals in viticulture is strictly regulated by governments. The process of registering a new agrochemical with a government is lengthy, exacting, and costly. Such registrations specify, for example, withholding periods that must elapse between the last application and when the crop is harvested to allow residues of the agrochemical to diminish to suitably low concentrations. To save money, some manufacturers do not register chemicals with all governments, with the result that small and emerging wine industries, like that of the UK, are disadvantaged by having access to only a limited range of products.

In the case of wine, the effect the agrochemical may have on FERMENTATION is also assessed. For example, the fungicide folpet, which is used in some countries to protect vines against DOWNY MILDEW, may delay, or even prevent, fermentation by some wine YEASTS if present at certain concentrations.

Because an official maximum residue limit (MRL) may not exist for an agrochemical in all countries, world trade may be adversely affected. For example, the fungicide procymidone, which has been used in parts of Europe, is not registered in the US for use on any crop. When the American authorities detected residues of procymidone in some European wines in early 1990, they banned the importation of any European wine containing residues of procymidone until a permissible residue level was established. This had a serious effect on many sectors of the European wine trade.

The *Codex Alimentarius* ('food code' in Latin) was established by the Food and Agricultural Organization (FAO) and the World Health Organization (WHO) to upgrade and simplify international food regulations and to avoid such incidents. *Codex* MRLs have been set for some agrochemicals in a range of crops, and several countries accept *Codex* MRLs in the absence of their own. The US does not recognize *Codex* MRLs, however.

Although an agrochemical may be present in formulations bearing different proprietary names, it usually has a single common name that is recommended by standards organizations. For example, the fungicide Rovral® (from manufacturers Rhône Poulenc) contains the agrochemical iprodione that is also the active constituent of several other fungicides.

See also RESIDUES.   R.J., R.E.S., & M.E.

Mollah, M., and MacGregor, A., 'Review of the potential for agrochemicals used in viticulture to impact on the environment' (Mildura, 2002). www.gwrdc.com.au/wp-content/uploads/2012/09/CRV-01-04-Final-version.pdf.

Ahr, diminutive German wine region of 563 ha/1,391 acres in 2013 specializing in red wine and named after the river which flows east from the hills of the Eifel to join the Rhine near Remagen (see map under GERMANY). The most westerly vineyards are in dramatic, rocky, wooded scenery near Altenahr, where the steep slopes on either side of the river reach up to 300 m/980 ft above sea level, and sometimes narrow to the dimensions of a gorge. Many are covered in SLATE as well as BASALT and clay-rich GREYWACKE clay, well suited to SPÄTBURGUNDER (PINOT NOIR). The region lies between 50 and 51 degrees of LATITUDE, so that a good MESOCLIMATE is needed to ripen the grapes. Most of the best sites face south east to south west (see TOPOGRAPHY). The dark soil (see SOIL COLOUR), the reflected heat from the curious rock formations, and the protection from north winds that blow above the valley intensify summer warmth. Spätburgunder has gained ground steadily and for most of this century has been planted on more than 60% of the vineyard area. PORTUGIESER, FRÜHBURGUNDER, and RIESLING each represent 6–8% of plantings, the last favouring slate soils and evincing tropical fruit character similar to that encountered in the MITTELRHEIN. The Ahr used to be known for soft, late-picked, medium-sweet Spätburgunder but today's typical Ahr wine is a fully fermented, dry, OAK aged, tannic Spätburgunder of good colour from low-yielding vineyards. Almost 80% of the region's grape harvest is processed by four CO-OPERATIVE cellars, and the state of Rheinland-Pfalz owns the largest estate, 18.5 ha/46 acres based on the 13th-century Kloster Marienthal. A small collection of privately owned estates has enjoyed increasing demand and prestige in the wake of Germany's 1995–2005 red-wine boom.   D.S.

Aïdani, floral-scented variety grown on SANTORINI and other Greek islands for blending with mainly ASSYRTIKO. Aïdani Mavro is a dark-skinned mutation.

air drainage, important topographical and hence climatological consideration in VINEYARD SITE SELECTION. Cold air flows, or 'drains', downhill and so a continuous slope or HILLSIDE is much less prone to FROST and WINTER FREEZE than a hollow. In regions at risk from these phenomena, zones which accumulate cold air should be avoided as vineyard sites. In general, a vineyard site near the top of a free-standing hill is ideal since no cold air is imported from above.   R.E.S.

air dried. See BARREL MAKING.

Airén, is planted at such a low VINE DENSITY in its central Spanish homeland that it is planted on almost a quarter of all Spanish vineyard and covers more area than any other white wine variety in the world. Its 2011 total of 218,439 ha/539,544 acres is dramatically reduced from its 2004 total of 305,000 ha/753,350 acres, however, thanks to vigorous VINE PULL SCHEMES, particularly in La MANCHA and VALDEPEÑAS where it has traditionally been blended with dark-skinned Cencibel (TEMPRANILLO) grapes, which are steadily replacing Airén, to produce light red wines. It is increasingly vinified as an inexpensive white wine, however, to yield crisp, neutral dry white wines for early consumption. In several ways, therefore, Airén is the Spanish equivalent of France's UGNI BLANC. Airén vines are trained into low bushes and have remarkable resistance to the DROUGHTS which plague central Spanish viticulture. The variety is also grown around MADRID.

Aix-en-Provence, Coteaux d'. Mainly dry rosé and some red wines are made, in very varied but often spectacularly situated vineyards among the lavender and garrigue of PROVENCE. The arguably too-extensive area entitled to this appellation stretches from the frontier with Les BAUX DE PROVENCE subappellation created in 1995 in the west as far as the COTEAUX VAROIS, and includes ELEVATIONS varying from nearly sea level to over 400 m with considerable TEMPERATURE VARIABILITY. A growing total of nearly 4,000 ha/10,000 acres of vineyards produce serviceable if generally unsophisticated reds and pale pink wines for early, often local, consumption. CO-OPERATIVES are relatively important here, but a number of individual estates such as Chx Calissanne, Revelette, and a revitalized Vignelaure are trying to establish a distinctive style from Grenache with Cinsaut, Mourvèdre, the local Counoise, Syrah, Carignan, and Cabernet Sauvignon grapes. Neither of the last two may make up more than 30% of a blend. A little white is made from a wide range of southern, and SOUTH WEST FRANCE, grape varieties.

ORGANIC VITICULTURE has established a significant hold in this arid, MEDITERRANEAN climate.

Ajaccio. See CORSICA.

Alarije, white grape grown in the EXTREMADURA region of Spain. Called Malvasia Riojana in Rioja and Subirat Parent in Catalunya.

Alaska, far north-western state of the UNITED STATES where several wineries have been established to ferment grape juice imported from warmer states and to process other FRUIT WINES.

Alba, culinary capital of the LANGHE, famous for its red wines and white truffles, and where in the past, before estate bottling became the norm, producers would sell their grapes to bottlers and négociants on the Piazza Savona immediately after the harvest. Since 2010 it also is the name of a rather irrelevant DOC for Nebbiolo-Barbera blends covering all of Roero, Barolo, Barbaresco, and Dogliani. See also ROERO and NEBBIOLO D'ALBA.   W.S.

Albalonga is a 1951 Rieslaner × Silvaner vine cross grown to a very limited extent in Germany, notably Rheinhessen and the Pfalz. It inherits from Rieslaner both a firm core of acidity and good rot resistance while dehydrating to MUST WEIGHTS above SPÄTLESE. The wine can smell more like a red, with black fruits and floral aromas, and Wittmann in Westhoven has high prices and complex old bottles to testify to the potential of this exotic but rare variety.   D.S.

Albana, Italian vine made famous by the over-promoted ALBANA DI ROMAGNA. Now widely planted in the EMILIA-ROMAGNA region, its chief claim to fame is being mentioned in the 13th century by medieval agricultural writer PETRUS DI CRESCENTIIS. Most Albana is late ripening, thin-skinned, and prone to rot but the **Albana Gentile di Bertinoro** clone has thicker skins than most and results in relatively deep-coloured white wines with marked acidity, which is useful in the best, long-lived sweet versions. Total area planted had declined to 1,523 ha/3762 acres by 2010.

Albana di Romagna, white wine made in central Italy from Albana grapes, much-maligned in spite of its long historic presence in the region (see ALBANA). Unreasonably high yields of 100 hl/ha and careless winemaking by large CO-OPERATIVES led to Albana's mediocre reputation, which is why its elevation to DOCG in 1986 spurred criticism that the DOC system was flawed.

Only a handful of producers, aware of its intrinsic quality, started to give Albana their full attention, planting it on suitable sites (rather than simply where Sangiovese, Romagna's most important red wine grape, wouldn't ripen) and drastically reducing YIELDS to overcome Albana's supposed neutral and tart character.

Autumn rains, as well as vineyard sites without sufficient ventilation, regularly force growers to harvest before the grapes have reached full ripeness and aromatic development. However, with the right site, late-harvest dry Albana and impressive BOTRYTIZED sweet wines can be made.

Local research into the different CLONES of Albana has helped to save the rarest ones from extinction while a greater focus on the selection of suitable sites has led to the production of several single-vineyard wines, showing that the variety adapts equally well to the CALCAREOUS soils of the township of Bertinoro and the reddish CLAY soils of Faenza.

While frequently labelled as *secco* (dry), *amabile* (medium dry), *dolce* (sweet), and PASSITO, Albana's future undoubtedly lies in the late-harvest, dry version as well as the botrytized dessert wines, such as those of Fattoria Zerbina, while radical examples, such as Francesconi's Arcaia, are SKIN-FERMENTED—a reference to the variety's ancient past.   W.S.

Albani, Colli, white wine DOC from the hills south east of Rome based on MALVASIA CANDIA. For more information, see CASTELLI ROMANI.

Albania, Mediterranean country situated on the Adriatic coast between MONTENEGRO and GREECE with a history closely linked to agriculture, particularly viticulture. Albania claims one of Europe's longest histories of vine-growing. French historian Henri Enjalbert considered Albania, the Ionian Islands of Greece, and southern Dalmatia in what is now BOSNIA AND HERZEGOVINA may well have been the last European refuge of the vine after the Ice Age. Wine production is believed to have been practised by the inhabitants of Albania in the Bronze Age, and there are written accounts of vines being cultivated in Illyria (as Albania was known in

Classical times) as early as the 8th century BC. Until the Ottoman invasion in the late 15th century, vines were grown in every region, and every parish church had its vineyard. The Ottoman occupation of Albania (1479–1913), followed by a period of uncertainty between the two World Wars, and the isolationist communist regime suppressed the development of the Albanian wine industry, but there is a very considerable level of viticultural potential in this small country, particularly due to the presence of its distinctive INDIGENOUS vine varieties.

Albania is now a parliamentary republic with a population of 3.5 million inhabitants, and a total land area a little smaller than Belgium. Its climate is typically MEDITERRANEAN: cool and wet in winter and hot and dry in summer. It is a mountainous country, with only a quarter of its land suitable for agriculture, but over half its population lives off the land, on farms with an average size of 1.14 ha/2.8 acres. Viticulture is an important, and growing, sector in Albanian agriculture. About half of all vines are trained on PERGOLAS, as opposed to conventional vineyards. By 2013 there were 10,185 ha/25,157 acres of vineyard, of which 9,587 ha (23,689 acres) were in production, yielding 118,500 tonnes of grapes. This, together with around 83,000 tonnes of grapes grown on pergolas, generated approximately 122,500 hl/3,234,000 gal of wine, demonstrating steady growth in the Albanian wine industry.

Vines are grown throughout Albania, but the principal vine-growing regions are Fier in the north (1,665 ha/4,144 acres when last reported), Vlorë in the south (1,258 ha/3,108 acres), and Elbasan (1,003 ha/2,478 acres) in the centre. The total amount of wine produced in Albania in 2008 was 570,700 hl (equivalent to 16 litres per head of population) vinified in 72 commercial wineries. About 48% of the total vineyard area in Albania is planted with red wine grapes, 34% white wine grapes, and 18% TABLE GRAPES. The principal red wine varieties are Merlot (15%), Shesh i Zi (13%), Cabernet Sauvignon (11%), and Kallmet (10% and known as KADARKA in Hungary). The principal white wine varieties are Shesh i Bardhë (18%), Chardonnay (16%), Muskat i Bardhë (14% and made up of Muscat Blanc à Petits Grains, Muscat of Alexandria, and Muscat of Hamburg), and Trebbiano (11%).

However, there are many very interesting, minor indigenous varieties, the likes of Cëruja, Pulës i Zi, Vlosh, Serina e Zezë, and Debine e Bardhë. Their cultivation greatly declined during the Ottoman occupation, but many can still be found growing wild near pre-Ottoman archaeological sites such as those at Rozafa Castle, Berati town, and Byllis. Viticultural research in Albania is focused on the collection, characterization, and preservation of these varieties, and of the WILD VINES found in different areas of

Albania. Through CLONAL SELECTION, focusing particularly on the Kallmet and Vlosh cultivars, researchers are producing, characterizing, and evaluating certified virus- and disease-free plant material. They will then assess the suitability of these varieties for specific regions of the country.   L. & E.S.

Enjalbert, H., *Histoire de la vigne et du vin* (Paris, 1975).

Albariño, Spanish name of the distinctive, aromatic, high-quality vine grown in Galicia (and as ALVARINHO in the north of Portugal's Vinho Verde region). The grapes' thick skins help them withstand the particularly damp climate, and can result in white wines notably high in alcohol, acidity, and flavour. Albariño was one of the first Spanish white grape varieties produced as a varietal and encountered on labels. Most common in Spain in the RÍAS BAIXAS zone, it has become so popular (and expensive) that it represents about half of all white wine grapes. Sometimes oak-matured, and increasingly aged for several years in stainless steel tanks before release, it can age better than most light-skinned Spanish grapes however it is made. Occasionally blended with Loureiro, Treixadura, Caiño. Spanish plantings had grown to about 5,555 ha (13,721 acres) by 2012. Its wines are so widely exported that it is now also grown in California, Oregon, Washington, Australia, New Zealand, and Uruguay, and has been allowed in France since 2010.

Robinson, J., Harding, J., and Vouillamoz, J., *Wine Grapes: A Complete Guide to 1,368 Vine Varieties Including their Origins and Flavours* (London, 2012).

albariza, a local, Andalusian term for the white, chalky-looking soil typical of parts of the JEREZ region in southern Spain. Grapes grown on this soil type produce some of the finest FINO and MANZANILLA sherries. The soil has a high LIMESTONE content, about 40%, the remainder being CLAY and SAND. It appears dazzling white in summer, and has the characteristic of drying without caking, slowly releasing moisture to the vines during the growing season. This soil type is also present in the PENEDÈS region of north east Spain, where some of the best Spanish sparkling wine is produced (see CAVA).   M.J.E.

Albarola, neutral white grape disappearing from the Cinqueterre zone of LIGURIA in northwest Italy.

alberello, Italian term to describe free-standing BUSH VINES trained according to the GOBELET system.

Albillo, name of several different pale-skinned grape varieties grown and sometimes confused in various parts of Spain, most notably

Albillo Mayor in Ribera del Duero and other parts of CASTILLA Y LEÓN, and Albillo Real in CASTILLA-LA MANCHA and around MADRID where some old vines yield honeyed dry wines of real substance. However, considerable confusion is caused by the use of plain Albillo in Spanish statistics and wine regulations. Both Albillos produce wines that are generally low in acidity, full bodied, and aromatic.

Robinson, J., Harding, J., and Vouillamoz, J., *Wine Grapes: A Complete Guide to 1,368 Vine Varieties, Including their Origins and Flavours* (London, 2012).

alcohol, the common name for ETHANOL. The term alcohol, which can be applied to any of the ALCOHOLS, derives from the Arabic *al-kuhl*, meaning 'the fine powder used to stain eyelids' (today's kohl), and thus by extension any kind of fine impalpable powder that represents the concentration, or quintessence, of the raw material involved. It was then more widely applied to fluids that represented the essence, or spirit, of something, and thus to any product of distillation.

alcoholic, usually pejorative tasting term for a wine which tastes 'hot' and seems to contain excess ethyl alcohol, or ETHANOL.

alcoholic strength, an important measurement of any wine, is its concentration of the intoxicant ethyl alcohol, or ETHANOL. It can be measured in several different ways, the most common being the DEGREE first defined in France by Gay-Lussac in 1884. This was the number of litres of pure ethanol in 100 litres of wine, both measured at 15 °C/59 °F. Later a more precise definition, using 20 °C/68 °F as the reference temperature and some other minor refinements, was adopted in France and by most international organizations. The degree of alcohol is equivalent to its percentage by volume and is sometimes referred to as 'abv', alcohol by volume. In most countries it is mandatory to specify the alcoholic strength of all wines on the label, although it may be written either % or occasionally ° (see also LABELLING INFORMATION).

The alcoholic strength of wine that has not had alcohol added by FORTIFICATION is usually between nine and 16%, with the great majority of wines being between 12.5 and 14.5% alcohol—considerably higher than as recently as the 1980s thanks to CLIMATE CHANGE, current FASHION, a desire for riper PHENOLICS, and the resulting tendency to later picking after extended HANG TIME. A significant proportion of high-quality wine made today in warmer climates is deliberately subjected to some form of ALCOHOL REDUCTION to make it more palatable or to satisfy some legal requirement.

In Europe, fermented grape juice should usually reach at least 8.5% alcohol (9% in specified warmer zones) before it legally constitutes wine, although exceptions are made for PDO or PGI wines that have traditionally been low in alcohol such as German PRÄDIKATSWEIN and Italian MOSCATO. The technical European legal maximum alcoholic strength for wines that have had no alcohol added is 15%, but derogations are frequently made at this upper limit too (as long as they have not been ENRICHED), not least for Italy's strongest wines such as AMARONE. In the United States, grape-based 'table wine' must legally be between seven and 14%, while those between 14 and 24% technically qualify as 'DESSERT WINES'.

Since alcohol is the product by FERMENTATION of grape sugar, itself the product of PHOTOSYNTHESIS driven by sunlight, the alcoholic strength of a wine is, very generally, proportional to the proximity of its provenance to the equator and to the precosity of the variety, although many other factors play a part, especially the intentions of the winemaker. High vineyard ELEVATION, poor WEATHER in a particular year, high YIELD, and any RESIDUAL SUGAR, are just some of the factors which may decrease alcoholic strength. Severe PRUNING in the vineyard, and cellar techniques such as ENRICHMENT, CONCENTRATION, and fortification allow winemakers to manipulate alcoholic strength upwards. Some OLOROSO sherries, for example, can reach alcoholic strengths approaching 24% after EVAPORATION. (See also DRIED-GRAPE WINES.)

There is an important distinction between **actual alcoholic strength**, as defined above, and **potential alcoholic strength**, which refers to what the concentration of alcohol in a wine would be if all the sugars were converted to alcohol. **Total alcoholic strength** is the sum, post fermentation, of the actual alcoholic strength and the potential alcohol of any remaining fermentable sugars. **Natural alcoholic strength** refers to the alcoholic strength of a wine prior to any form of enrichment.

Regulation (EU) No 1308/2013 of The European Parliament and of the Council of 17 December 2013, *Official Journal of the European Union*, 347/2013.spc

alcohol reduction in wine can be achieved by a range of physicochemical methods permitted in some countries but not in others. These include the use of a low-temperature DISTILLATION technique such as the SPINNING CONE COLUMN, membrane separation techniques such as REVERSE OSMOSIS, ELECTRODIALYSIS, EVAPORATIVE PERSTRACTION, ULTRAFILTRATION, and NANOFILTRATION, as well as the more 'traditional' method of HUMIDIFICATION. A continuing quest in some quarters for extended HANG TIME and resultant increased ALCOHOLIC STRENGTH promoted the rapid development of such technologies. Research into the influences on alcohol levels of YEAST selection has so far had only limited success.

Contreras, A., et al., 'Evaluation of non-Saccharomyces yeast for the reduction of alcohol content in wine', *Applied and Environmental Microbiology*, 80/5 (2014), 1670–8.

Tilloy, V., Ortiz-Julien, A., and Dequin, S., 'Reduction of ethanol yield and improvement of glycerol formation by adaptive evolution of the wine yeast Saccharomyces cerevisiae under hyperosmotic conditions', *Applied and Environmental Microbiology*, 80/8 (2014). doi: 10.1128/AEM.03710-13.

alcohols, those organic chemicals, the simplest members of which consist of carbon, hydrogen, and oxygen atoms arranged so that there is an –OH group present. Many different alcohols are used in commerce and industry but the most common is ethyl alcohol, or ETHANOL, the alcohol that is the important, and intoxicating, ingredient in wines and spirits. The presence of ethanol in foods and beverages, commonly referred to simply as 'alcohol', is the product of yeast FERMENTATION of natural sugars.

Other alcohols with more than two carbon atoms of ethanol are also the product of fermentation and these are sometimes called higher alcohols, or FUSEL OILS. The higher alcohols separated from ethanol by DISTILLATION are normally used as solvents in industrial processes. The major constituent of higher alcohols or fusel oils is the five-carbon isoamyl alcohol.

A.D.W. & P.J.W.

aldehydes, a class of chemical compounds midway between the ALCOHOLS and the organic acids in their state of OXIDATION. They are formed during any phase of processing in which an alcoholic beverage is exposed to air. ACETALDEHYDE is the aldehyde of most interest to wine producers. Some aldehydes have quite potent odours, even if they are usually present in only trace concentrations in wines and spirits. As such, aldehydes contribute harmoniously to the overall character.

Those aldehydes containing more than the two carbon atoms of acetaldehyde are in general much more palatable. Vanillin, for example, is a complex aromatic aldehyde present in the vanilla bean and in many other plants, including some grapes where it is present as a GLYCOSIDE and is a FLAVOUR PRECURSOR. Vanillin also occurs as a component of the lignin structure of OAK wood. If new oak casks are used for wine maturation, some of this vanillin is extracted from the wood into the wine, where it may add complexity to the flavour. (See also OAK FLAVOUR.)

See also HERBACEOUS for the part played by **leaf aldehydes**.   A.D.W. & P.J.W.

Aleatico, Italian red grape variety with a strong MUSCAT aroma. DNA PROFILING at SAN

MICHELE ALL'ADIGE strongly supports a parent–offspring relationship with the classic MUSCAT BLANC À PETITS GRAINS, hence the Muscat flavour. Aleatico certainly has the potential to produce fine, if somewhat esoteric, fragrant, usually pale red from the Italian 2010 total of a few hundred ha. Two DOCs enshrine the word Aleatico in the wine lexicon of LAZIO and PUGLIA, but the variety is becoming increasingly rare, although successful attempts such as Avignonesi's to revive the wine in the Tuscan MAREMMA are under way. Sweet red Aleatico is one of the few wines to be exported from the island of ELBA, and the variety is grown on the island of Corsica, although it is not authorized for any APPELLATION CONTRÔLÉE wine. Aleatico is also surprisingly popular in the central Asian republics, notably KAZAKHSTAN and UZBEKISTAN.   J.R. & J.V.

Alella, town near Barcelona in CATALUÑA (see map under SPAIN) which gives its name to a small Spanish denominated wine zone making mainly white wines in increasingly urbanized countryside. To compensate for the loss of agricultural land, this tiny DO was extended northwards in 1989 but by 2012 there were only 315 ha/750 acres of vineyard left, a fraction of the area planted in 1956 when Alella was first awarded DO status. The zone used to be known for its old-fashioned, cask-aged, medium-sweet white wines. The chief grape variety is Pansa Blanca, the local name for XAREL-LO, which is now grown along with some CHENIN BLANC and CHARDONNAY to make both CAVA sparkling wines and dry, still white wine. The reputation of Alella was salvaged by Parxet/Marqués de Alella, which pioneered these new styles of wine. Alta Alella is an important new 21st-century producer.   V. de la S.

Alenquer, small DOP in a sheltered valley in LISBOA is most successful for fuller-bodied red wines.

Alentejo, DOP and VINHO REGIONAL (known as Vinho Regional Alentejano) in southern PORTUGAL corresponding to the province of the same name.

DOP wines must come from one (or more) of eight subregions: PORTALEGRE, BORBA, REDONDO, REGUENGOS de Monsaraz, GRANJA-AMARELEJA, VIDIGUEIRA, EVORA, and MOURA, which may appear on labels. Many good DOP producers prefer to label wines VR Alentejano, however, while some outside its DOP regions (notably in Beja) must be labelled VR Alentejano, despite their wines' evident high quality.

The sparsely populated Alentejo represents one-third of mainland Portugal and, in contrast to the north, cereal farms and cork plantations (*latifúndios*) stretch as far as the eye can see. For centuries, the Alentejo's main link with wine was CORK. Around half the world's cork supply is grown in Portugal, nearly all stripped from Alentejo's cork oaks. Southern Portugal bore the brunt of the military-led revolution that rocked the Lisbon establishment in 1974 and 1975 and the economy of the Alentejo was still in disarray in the early 1980s. However, as a result of financial assistance from the EU it has enjoyed a reversal of fortune. The injection of funds allowed the CO-OPERATIVE wineries in the towns of Portalegre, Borba, Redondo, Reguengos de Monsaraz, Granja-Amareleja, and Vidigueira (each built with government support in the pre-revolutionary 1960s and early 1970s) to improve wine quality and develop exports. Moreover, it resulted in an increase in the number of ambitious, privately owned estates from 45 to 260 between 1995 and 2010. By 2010 Alentejo not only commanded the biggest share of the domestic market in quality wines (in volume and value), but had also charmed export markets with its generous, fruit-led wines. By 2014 vines were planted on more than 20,000 ha/49,400 acres. Large farms offer considerable economies of scale compared with the smallholdings (*minifúndios*) of northern Portugal.

Summer temperatures frequently exceed 35 °C or even 40 °C (104 °F) and the climate in much of the Alentejo is not naturally conducive to the production of fine wine. However, cooler locations such as the higher Portalegre and Borba and Alentejo's water-retentive bands of SCHIST help, as does modern technology. TEMPERATURE CONTROL and IRRIGATION, which supplements an annual rainfall total that rarely reaches 600 mm/23 in, is essential. The production of red wine—principally blends from ARAGONEZ, TRINCADEIRA, ALICANTE BOUSCHET (which flourishes in the Alentejo), and CASTELÃO grapes—exceeds white, although a number of producers make surprisingly good blends of ANTÃO VAZ, ROUPEIRO and ARINTO. VERDELHO, ALVARINHO, and VIOGNIER also look promising.
                                                    S.A.

Metcalfe, C., and McWhirter, K., *The Wine and Food Lover's Guide to Portugal* (Haywards Heath, 2007). www.vinhosdoalentejo.pt

Alexander Valley, California wine region and AVA in northern Sonoma County north east of Healdsburg and south of Cloverdale. See SONOMA.

Alfrocheiro, one of the most promising, if not particularly widely planted (a national total of 1,492 ha/3,687 acres), red grapes in the DÃO region of PORTUGAL. Alfrocheiro's well constructed blackberry- and strawberry-flavoured wines have such appeal that it can also be found in the vineyards of ALENTEJO, TEJO, and BAIRRADA now. It is very susceptible to OÏDIUM and GREY ROT and is not therefore as popular with growers as with winemakers. However, it yields reasonably well, ripens early, and produces deep-coloured wines with good alcohol and acid balance. It is often referred to as **Alfrocheiro Preto** ('black Alfrocheiro'). In the Douro it may sometimes be called Tinta Bastardinha.   R.J.M.

Algarve, the southernmost province of Portugal, now better known for TOURISM than for wine (see map under PORTUGAL). There is, however, evidence of a long winemaking tradition in the Algarve, principally fortified wines. The entire province is designated as a VINHO REGIONAL and its four DOPs were centred on local CO-OPERATIVES at Lagos, Portimão, LAGOA, and Tavira (only one of which now remains). The climate and soils of the Algarve are generally thought to be better for citrus fruit and CORK trees than vines but private investment in a small but growing number of boutique wineries has proved that the Algarve can produce medal-winners. Still, attaining PHENOLIC ripeness can be challenging. The popular British singer Sir Cliff Richard has helped put the Algarve on the wine map by planting a vineyard and building a winery near the resort of Albufeira.   S.A.

Algeria was one of the world's leading wine producers in the 1930s when annual production of wine and wine-related products averaged 22 million hl/550 million gal, much of it exported to France, of which it was then a colony. Despite its turbulent recent history and strong ISLAMIC influence, it is now increasing wine production by about 10% a year once more. According to OIV figures for 2011, Algeria made just 627,000 hl/16.5 million gal of wine, from 77,000 ha/190,000 acres of vineyard. New initiatives, including a 10,000 ha/24,700 acre replanting programme, were begun in 1994.

History

In the late 1950s, France depended heavily on Algerian wine to provide its everyday blended red (and some smarter wines) with strength, colour, and concentration—all of them attributes entirely lacking in the ARAMON then grown so prolifically in the LANGUEDOC. Together with neighbouring MOROCCO and TUNISIA, Algeria accounted for two-thirds of international wine trade in the 1950s.

Although vine-growing was practised in pre-colonial Algeria, and indeed flourished in classical times, it was the French PHYLLOXERA crisis of the 1870s that was to convert the agriculture of this North African colony to vineyards (although there had been a certain influx of wine-growers from Baden in the mid 19th century—see GERMAN HISTORY). In the late 19th century, Algeria was so successfully developed as the prime alternative source for France's voracious wine drinkers that Algeria's total viticultural area grew from 16,688 ha/41,240 acres in 1872 to 110,042 ha/271,910 acres in 1890, largely thanks to settlers whose own European vineyards had been devastated by phylloxera, which eventually reached Algeria.

Vineyards reached their maximum extent of 400,000 ha/988,400 acres in 1938. By then viticulture had shaped Algerian colonial society and by the year of independence, 1962, a dozen crus were accorded the honour of official VDQS recognition by the French. To the European vineyard owners living in Algeria, the so-called *pieds noirs*, or 'black feet', it gave economic and political power; for non-Europeans it provided valuable employment, but also dependence as the wine trade more than anything else integrated the colony with metropolitan France.

By the start of Algeria's war of independence in the mid 1950s, viticulture was still the leading sector of the colonial economy, accounting for half of Algeria's exports by value, and in some regions had acquired monocultural status.

At Algerian independence in 1962 nearly a million French settlers left, as well as a sizeable army of occupation. Algeria's domestic wine market promptly collapsed and the inappropriateness of an Islamic country's heavy economic reliance on wine production became an immediate problem. The mass exodus of European technical skills adversely affected both quality and productivity. Most vineyards passed into a form of collective agriculture as total vineyard and, especially, total wine production began to decline. This posed economic problems as by the mid 1960s wine was still Algeria's second export commodity, after the country's burgeoning oil industry, and viticulture still provided half the man-days worked in the modern, commercialized sector of agriculture.

Marketing problems soon emerged after independence. France immediately reduced its imports of Algerian wine from 14.6 million hl/ 385 million gal in 1962 (about a fifth of France's own total production) to only 6.8 million hl/179 million gal in 1963. The USSR's agreement to buy 5 million hl/132 million gal a year between 1969 and 1975 eased these marketing difficulties somewhat but the agreed (barter) price represented less than half the prevailing world market rate. Negotiations with the EU resulted in reduced quantities of Algerian wine allowed into Europe.

These problems prompted various schemes in the late 1960s for the reconversion and reconstitution of Algeria's uneconomically ageing vineyards. The essential problem was, however, that few replacement crops such as cereals could match viticulture's employment opportunities.

By the early 21st century total vineyard area had shrunk to 65,000 ha/160,000 acres, about an eighth of the 1930s *vignoble*, with a growing proportion used for TABLE GRAPES rather than wine, about 60% in 2002, so that wine production levels have fallen even more drastically

than vineyard area. The OIV estimates that the vineyard total is rising once more although abandoned vineyards and wineries, lower yields, and lower prices have combined to make the relict Algerian wine industry a shadow of its former self.

Geography

Western Algeria accounts for over 65% of the area under vines, notably the districts of Aïn Temouchent, Mascara, Mostaganem, Sidi Bel Abbès, and Tlemcen. Médéa, Aïn Defla, and western Mitidja grow vines in the centre of the country, while El Tarf is on the border with TUNISIA in the east. Winters are mild, summers are hot, dry, and sunny. Climatically this is similar to much of southern and eastern Spain.

Wine industry structure

In its heyday Algerian vineyards were planted substantially with Carignan, Alicante Bouschet, Cinsault, and Grenache and, although the vines have not been well maintained, VINE AGE in Algeria is notably high. A replanting programme that began in the late 1990s has encouraged the planting of INTERNATIONAL VARIETIES, including Tempranillo, for red wines.

Most wine was vinified on a semi-industrial scale in wineries that favoured fast fermentations and early bottling, although its mechanization and hot-country technology at one time provided inspiration for many. The AUTOVINIFICATION tanks once common in the DOURO, for example, were developed in Algeria, where they were known as the Ducellier system.

The centralized ONCV long exercised a near monopoly on both the production and sale of wine, but in 2014 made only about 65% of the wine sold in Algeria in its 132 fermentation centres and 11 wineries. ONCV exported about 20% of its production but a private sector has been growing in importance.

Algeria is also a substantial producer of CORKS, which are mainly processed in Portugal and Spain.   K.S. & J.R.

Isnard, H., 'Vigne et décolonisation en Algérie', in A. Huetz de Lemps (ed.), *Géographie historique des vignobles: actes du colloque de Bordeaux: octobre 1977* (Paris, 1978), vol. i.

Sutton, K., 'Algeria's vineyards: an Islamic dilemma and a problem of decolonisation', *Journal of Wine Research* (1990), 101–20.

www.oncv-groupe.com

Alicante, city on Spain's Mediterranean coast long associated with strong, rustic wines which now gives its name to a denominated but shrinking wine zone of 9,100 ha/21,800 acres. This DO in the LEVANTE extends from the city towards YECLA on the foothills of Spain's central plateau (see map under SPAIN) and allows eight different styles of wine including DOBLE PASTA, fortified wines, and a SOLERA-aged wine called

FONDILLÓN, a speciality of the region made from very sweet, deliberately overripened grapes. A coastal subzone, the Marina Alta, produces mostly white MUSCAT-based wines. The climate becomes progressively hotter and the landscape more arid away from the coast and YIELDS rarely exceed 20 hl/ha (1.1 ton/acre). The principal grape variety is the red MONASTRELL (Mourvèdre). Other red varieties well suited to the MEDITERRANEAN climate include GARNACHA and BOBAL. Ninety per cent of the region's wine is produced in CO-OPERATIVES. The Bocopa co-op at Petrer and such private firms as Gutiérrez de la Vega, Bernabé Navarro, Salvador Poveda, Enrique Mendoza, Sierra Salinas, El Sequé, Celler de la Muntanya, Volver, and Bruno Prats Ibérica have made noticeable strides in quality.

Alicante is also a synonym for Garnacha Tintorera, or ALICANTE BOUSCHET, in Spain and is even sometimes used as a synonym for GRENACHE.   R.J.M. & V. de la S.

Alicante Bouschet, often known simply as **Alicante** and sometimes as **Alicante Henri Bouschet**, is the most widely planted of France's red-fleshed TEINTURIER grape varieties. It was widely planted for much of the 20th century but total French plantings had declined to 3,699 ha/9,136 acres by 2011, mainly in the Languedoc-Roussillon.

It was bred between 1865 and 1885 by Henri BOUSCHET from his father's crossing of Petit Bouschet with the popular Grenache, then often known as Alicante, and was an immediate success. Thanks to its deep red flesh, the wine it produced was about 15 times as red as that of the productive and rapidly spreading ARAMON.

Alicante Bouschet also played a major role in late-19th and early-20th-century viticulture as parent of a host of other Teinturiers, the products almost exclusively of crossings with non-VINIFERA varieties. In the second half of the 20th century it profited from its status as the sole Teinturier to be a *Vitis vinifera*, and is therefore officially sanctioned by the French authorities.

Outside France it is most widely cultivated in Spain, where it is also known as Garnacha Tintorera and where plantings totalled 18,950 ha/ 46,806 acres in 2011. It is particularly common in Galicia and Castilla-La Mancha. The total area planted in Portugal is much smaller but it can make wines as celebrated as Mouchão in the Alentejo.

Alicante is widely grown around the world but nowhere else in any great quantity.

Robinson, J., Harding, J., and Vouillamoz, J., *Wine Grapes: A Complete Guide to 1,368 Vine Varieties, Including their Origins and Flavours* (London, 2012).

Aligoté, Burgundy's 'other' white grape variety, may be very much Chardonnay's underdog but in a fine year, when ripeness can compensate for its characteristic ACIDITY, Aligoté is not short of champions and is arguably a beneficiary of CLIMATE CHANGE. It is a member of the PINOT (and GOUAIS BLANC) family, is therefore a sibling of Chardonnay, and was recorded in Burgundy at the end of the 18th century.

The vine is vigorous and its yield varies enormously according to the vineyard site. If grown on Burgundy's best slopes on the poorest soils in warmer years, Aligoté could produce fine dry whites with more nerve than most Chardonnays, but it would not be nearly as profitable.

In the Côte d'Or it is far less important than the two obviously nobler grape varieties Chardonnay and Pinot Noir, but there was still a total of 1,914 ha/4,727 acres in greater Burgundy in 2012, including 663 ha/1,638 acres in the Côte d'Or. It is now largely relegated to the highest and lowest vineyards, where it produces light, early-maturing wines allowed only the Bourgogne Aligoté appellation. Traditionally it was mixed with blackcurrant liqueur as a KIR. Only the village of Bouzeron in the CÔTE CHALONNAISE, where some of the finest examples are produced, has its own appellation for Aligoté, Bouzeron, in which the maximum yield is only 45 hl/ha (2.5 ton/acre) as opposed to the 60 hl/ha allowed for Bourgogne Aligoté. A little is grown by burgundy enthusiasts in the New World but it is extraordinarily popular (and rarely tart) in Eastern Europe where Moldova, Romania, Ukraine, and Bulgaria grow thousands of hectares of it and it is also a common feature in Russian vineyards.

allergies and intolerances. A key difference between allergy and intolerance is that allergic reactions have an immunological basis, while those with other causes are classed as intolerances. Intolerance of wine is far more common than true allergy to wine or grapes. The most common **allergens**, chemicals capable of causing an allergic reaction in humans, are proteinaceous compounds. Among possible allergens in wines are traces of the natural PROTEINS not precipitated and removed with the dead yeast cells after FERMENTATION, and traces of proteins from FINING agents used to clarify and stabilize the wine. Pollen-food allergy syndrome affects those severely sensitized to pollens which cross-react with similar proteins in fruit skins, causing oral itching. Grape allergy appears to be largely found around the Mediterranean, and chitinases may be the major allergen. Even traces of wasp venom found in wine have been reported to cause reactions. The biogenic amines HISTAMINE and tyramine produced by LACTIC ACID BACTERIA during MALOLACTIC CONVERSION and present at higher levels in red wines, have been implicated in triggering headaches and red-wine intolerance.

SULFUR DIOXIDE may be a cause of so-called 'white-wine allergy' (strictly speaking an intolerance) and some asthmatics may be particularly sensitive to SULFITES. Although used in both red and white wines, whites typically have both higher sulfur levels and more acidity (which increases its release from solution), resulting in airway irritation and wheezing for those sensitive to this.

Some people, particularly members of certain ethnic groups, experience symptoms such as face flushing and high pulse rate after consuming even quite moderate amounts of ETHANOL in any form. This alcohol intolerance is due to genetic variations in two enzymes involved in the metabolism of alcohol, alcohol dehydrogenase and acetaldehyde dehydrogenase, which are less efficient and result in higher levels of toxic metabolites after drinking.

See also HEALTH and LABELLING INFORMATION.

D.A.D

Armentia A., 'Adverse reactions to wine: think outside the bottle,' *Current Opinion in Allergy and Clinical Immunology*, 8 (2008), 266–9

Vally, H., and Thompson, P. J., 'Allergic and asthmatic reactions to alcoholic drinks', *Addiction Biology*, 8 (2003), 3–11.

Allier is the name of a *département* in central France best known in the world of wine for its OAK, although it is also home to the wines of ST-POURÇAIN.

alluvium, type of sediment which can be described as **alluvial**, giving rise to soils which are often fine grained and typically fertile consisting of mud, SILT, SAND, and sometimes GRAVEL or stones deposited by flowing water on flood plains, in river beds, in deltas, and in estuaries, often from many different and distant sources. Alluvial soils are variable in texture, DRAINAGE, and age, and often such changes can be seen over a few metres. Where these soils are stony and sandy, they are highly valued for viticulture, as in the MÉDOC region of France and Marlborough in NEW ZEALAND. See entries prefixed SOIL.

R.E.S.

almacenista. From the Spanish word *almacén* meaning 'store', an almacenista is the term for a SHERRY stockholder who sells wine to shippers. It has been used as a marketing term by the sherry firm of Lustau, who buy in and bottle wines from almacenistas.

Almansa, denominated wine zone in the eastern corner of CASTILE-LA MANCHA in central Spain (see map under SPAIN) with 7,100 ha/ 17,050 acres under vine. The Almansa DO borders the LEVANTE regions JUMILLA and YECLA, which produce similarly strong, sturdy red wines, traditionally used for blending but increasingly sold in bottle, principally from MONASTRELL and GARNACHA TINTORERA grapes, although SYRAH is increasingly planted. The climate is extreme. Temperatures rise to 40 °C

(104 °F) in summer but can dip below 0 °C (32 °F) in winter. Bodegas Almanseñas, Hacienda El Espino, and the Tintoralba co-op are the leading producers.

V. de la S.

Almeirim, DOP subregion of TEJO in central, southern Portugal dominated by a huge CO-OPERATIVE winery.

Aloxe-Corton, a small village of charm at the northern end of the Côte de Beaune in Burgundy. First references to vineyards in Aloxe date back to 696, while in 775 CHARLEMAGNE ceded vines to the Abbey of St-Andoche at Saulieu. Aloxe is dominated by the hill of Corton, planted on three sides with vineyards including the GRANDS CRUS Corton (almost all red) and Corton-Charlemagne (white).

Corton is the sole grand cru appellation for red wine in the CÔTE DE BEAUNE and covers several vineyards which may be described simply as Corton or as Corton hyphenated with their names. While all Corton tends to be a dense, closed wine when young, Bressandes is noted for its comparative suppleness and charm; Renardes for its rustic, gamey character; Perrières for extra finesse; and Clos du Roi for the optimum balance between weight and elegance. It is often regarded as the finest of the Corton vineyards. Other Corton vineyards are Le Charlemagne, Les Pougets, and Les Languettes, all of which more often produce white Corton-Charlemagne, and Les Chaumes, Les Grèves, Les Fiètres, Les Meix, Clos de la Vigne au Saint, and part of Les Paulands and Les Maréchaudes. Further Corton vineyards extend into LADOIX-Serrigny. Although Corton is planted almost entirely with Pinot Noir vines, a tiny amount of white Corton is made, including the HOSPICES DE BEAUNE cuvée Paul Chanson from Chardonnay.

The great white wines, however, are those made within the **Corton-Charlemagne** appellation, which stretches in a narrow band around the top of the hill from Ladoix-Serrigny, through Aloxe-Corton to PERNAND-VERGELESSES, where it descends down the western edge of the hillside. The MESOCLIMATE governing Corton-Charlemagne is fractionally cooler than that of Corton and the soils are different. Whereas red Corton is mainly produced on reddish chalky clay which is rich in marl, the soil at the top of the hill and on the western edge is lighter and whiter, its stoniness believed locally to impart a gunflint edge to the wines of Corton-Charlemagne.

There remains some Pinot Blanc in the otherwise Chardonnay-dominated Corton-Charlemagne vineyards, which formerly were widely planted with Pinot Beurot (see PINOT GRIS) and Aligoté.

A great Corton may seem ungainly in its sturdiness when young but should have the power to develop into a rich wine with complex, gamey flavours at eight to ten years old. Cortons should, with POMMARD, be the most intense and longest-lived wines of the Côte de Beaune. Corton-Charlemagne also needs time to develop its exceptional character of breed, backbone, and racy power. Needing a minimum of five years, a good example will be better for a full decade in bottle.

Although more than half the vineyard area is given over to the grands crus, Aloxe-Corton also has its share of PREMIER CRU and village vineyards producing mainly red wines which can be supple and well coloured but mostly do not justify their significant premium over the wines of SAVIGNY-LÈS-BEAUNE. Apart from Les Guérets and Les Vercots, which are adjacent to Les Fichots in the commune of Pernand-Vergelesses, the premiers crus of Aloxe-Corton form a band just below the swathe of grand cru vineyards, extending into Ladoix-Serrigny.

See CÔTE D'OR and map under BURGUNDY.

J.T.C.M.

Chapuis, C., *Aloxe-Corton* (Dijon, 1988), in French.

Alpine Valleys in NORTH EAST VICTORIA ZONE in Australia encompasses inter alia the Ovens, Buffalo, Kiewa, and Buckland Valleys, and an important producer of a range of mainstream and ultra-eclectic varieties (Arneis, Petit Manseng, Saperavi, etc.).

Alsace, historically much-disputed region now on the eastern border of France, producing a unique style of largely VARIETAL wine, about 90% of which is white. For much of its existence it has been the western German region Elsass. Because of its location it has been the subject of many a territorial dispute between France and Germany. Now separated from Germany by the river RHINE, and from the rest of France by the Vosges mountains, the language and culture of Alsace owe much to both origins, but are at the same time unique. Many families speak Alsacien, a dialect peculiar to the region, quite different from either French or German.

Of all the regions of France, this is the one in which it is still easiest to find villages outwardly much as they were in the Middle Ages, with traditional half-timbered houses and extant fortifications. The hilltops of the lower Vosges are dotted with ruined castles and fortresses, witnesses to past invasions.

Of more than 4,000 grape growers, about 950 bottle wine but more than 60% of total production is sold by one of the 20 biggest NÉGOCIANTS and CO-OPERATIVES. Even the large companies are usually family owned, however. One of the unique aspects of Alsace is that even the smallest producers regularly bottle at least six to eight different wines each year, while the larger producers may extend to a range of 20 to 30 different bottlings.

All Alsace wines are, by law, bottled in the region of production in tall bottles called *flutes* (which some think may hinder sales because they are hardly the height of FASHION).

History

For details of the earlier history of the region, see GERMAN HISTORY. Annexed by France in the 17th century, Alsace was reclaimed, with part of Lorraine, by the new German empire in 1871. The vineyards were used to produce cheap blending wines. After the twin crises of oïdium (POWDERY MILDEW) and PHYLLOXERA, HYBRIDS to give large, trouble-free crops were planted on the flat, easily accessible land on the plains. The finer, steeper, HILLSIDE sites, formerly revered, were largely abandoned.

Following the First World War, when Alsace returned to French rule, up to a third of these better sites were replanted with the VINIFERA varieties. A setback occurred with the Second World War, when export was impossible, and the area was once again overrun by Germany. Replanting of the better sites gathered momentum in the 1960s and 1970s, when Alsace once again started to build up export markets.

Geography and climate

Alsace lies between LATITUDES 47.5 degrees and 49 degrees north of the equator, giving a long, cool growing season. It is important for the vineyards to make the most of the sun's rays, and so most of the best vineyards are on south, south west, or south east facing slopes, sheltered from the wind by the Vosges. Average annual RAINFALL is one of the lowest in France, due to the influence of the Vosges mountains: 500 mm/19 in in Colmar, varying considerably according to site. Most vineyards are at an ELEVATION of between 175 m and 550 m (1,804 ft) in the Munster Valley, above which level much of the mountainside is covered with pine forests. Autumn humidity allows for the production of late-picked VENDANGE TARDIVE—and SÉLECTION DE GRAINS NOBLES—wines (see below) in good vintages.

The narrow vineyard strip runs from north to south, along the lower contours of the Vosges Mountains (see map under GERMANY), and spans the two French *départements* of Haut-Rhin and Bas-Rhin. The majority of large producers are based in the more southerly Haut-Rhin *département*, which is generally associated with better quality, especially for Alsace's characteristic Gewurztraminer (spelt Gewürztraminer in Germany) and Pinot Gris, producing fatter, more powerful wines towards the south of the region. In the Bas-Rhin, individual vineyard sites become even more important to ensure full RIPENESS.

There are at least 20 major soil formations within the Alsace wine region, covering several eras. Higher, steeper slopes of the Vosges have thin topsoil, with subsoils of weathered GNEISS,

GRANITE, SANDSTONE, SCHIST, and VOLCANIC sediments. The gentler lower slopes, derived from the Rhine delta bed, have deeper topsoils, over subsoils of CLAY, MARL, LIMESTONE, and sandstone. One of the most important subsoils is the pink *grès de Vosges*, Vosges sandstone, which was used extensively in the construction of churches and cathedrals, and which is much in evidence in Strasbourg. The plains at the foot of the Vosges are of ALLUVIAL soils, eroded from the Vosges, and are rich and fertile, generally more suited to the production of crops other than vines.

Winters can be very cold, spring is generally mild, and the summer is warm and sometimes very dry, with heavy HAIL and thunderstorms possible in summer and autumn. In some vintages summer DROUGHT can be a problem, and younger vines planted in the drier, sandy soils can suffer, whereas vineyards on the water-retentive clay soils have an advantage.

As a general rule, the heavier clay and marl soils give a wine with broader flavours, more body and weight, while a lighter limestone or sandy soil gives more elegance and finesse. Flint, schist, shale, and slate soils tend to give wines with a characteristic oily, minerally aroma reminiscent of petrol and sometimes described as 'gunflint', especially those made from the Riesling grape.

Viticulture

The varied styles of training in use depend partly on the steepness of the vineyard. Either single GUYOT, with up to 15 buds left on the cane, or double Guyot, with up to eight buds on each cane, may be found, with a VINE DENSITY of between 4,400 and 4,800 vines per ha (1,940 per acre). There are also some CORDON-trained vines, with SPUR PRUNING, generally on older vines. The range of maximum permitted yields is given below, although each year the permitted yield can be altered upwards or downwards by decree.

Vines are generally trained at a height of between 60 and 90 cm (35 in) above ground, depending on the site. Vines on the plain are generally trained high to avoid FROSTS, while sloping vineyards can be trained closer to the ground, benefiting to the maximum from the available SUNLIGHT.

The steepest vineyard slopes may be TERRACED, as for example the GRAND CRU sites of Rangen and Kastelberg, or vines may be planted in rows either following the contours of the slope, or vertically from top to bottom, depending on the risk of SOIL EROSION. COVER CROPS may be planted to prevent erosion and to give more of a grip to tractors on moderate slopes.

Although MECHANICAL HARVESTING is common on the plains, many vineyards are too steep for machines, and many grapes are still hand picked. The vintage is always protracted, with varieties ripening at different times. Generally, harvesting starts in mid September, and often continues well into November.

A few growers have experimented with late-picked, BOTRYTIZED wines, not merely for the four varieties permitted for the late-harvest wines described below, but also with such diverse varieties as Auxerrois and Sylvaner, which can make outstanding wines. One or two growers produce a small quantity of VIN DE PAILLE, from healthy, ripe grapes picked in October, and dried on straw over the winter months. There have also been experiments with EISWEIN, from healthy grapes picked in December, and even in early January.

Vine varieties

At the beginning of the 20th century, the many varieties planted in Alsace were divided into 'noble' and others. The number has been rationalized over the years, and now the region produces eight major varietal wines: RIESLING, Gewurztraminer (GEWÜRZTRAMINER), PINOT GRIS, PINOT NOIR, PINOT BLANC, MUSCAT, CHASSELAS, and SYLVANER. Chasselas is generally used for blending, and only a handful of producers still bottle it as a varietal. AUXERROIS is also planted, and is usually blended with and labelled as Pinot Blanc, although it does sometimes feature on a label. There has also been some interest in planting the ubiquitous CHARDONNAY, forbidden by law, but tolerated when labelled as Pinot Blanc, or used in the sparkling wine CRÉMANT d'Alsace.

Most growers, wherever in the region they are based, plant all of the above varieties. As some varieties fetch higher prices, and some are much more fussy about vineyard site, each grower must make an economic as well as a practical decision when deciding what to plant where. Pinot Blanc and Auxerrois are among the first to ripen, and are viticulturally easy to please. The later ripening Riesling and Sylvaner need to be planted on a sheltered site, and are much more demanding. Muscat and Gewurztraminer are the most unreliable producers; unsettled weather at FLOWERING time can seriously shrink the crop, so the site should be sheltered.

Riesling was (just) the most widely planted variety in 2012, accounting for nearly 22% of the area under vine. Plantations are steadily increasing, mainly in place of Sylvaner, which has been losing ground, and by 2012 accounted for only 7.5% of the area planted, with higher proportions in the Bas-Rhin than the Haut-Rhin. Pinot Blanc and the more common Auxerrois have also been on the increase, accounting for another 21% between them. Gewurztraminer is grown on almost as much land but usually represents a smaller percentage of the production, which can fluctuate alarmingly. Its average yield is the smallest of all the varieties. The largest plantations of Gewurztraminer are in the Haut-Rhin. Pinot Gris has become increasingly popular and accounted for more than 15% of plantings by 2012. Pinot Noir has also increased its share as the only red varietal of Alsace (though Pinot Gris and Gewurztraminer are definitely pink-skinned varieties). It represented almost 10% of the total vineyard area in 2012. The area planted with MUSCAT D'ALSACE and MUSCAT OTTONEL together represented barely 2% of vineyard area. The total area devoted to Chasselas and Chardonnay, together with the small amounts of other old varieties had fallen to 2.4% by 2012.

Riesling Considered by growers to be the finest variety, Alsace Riesling is almost invariably bone dry. Young Riesling can display floral aromas, although it is sometimes fairly neutral. With age it takes on complex, gunflint, mineral aromas, with crisp steely acidity and very pure fruit flavours. It is one of the most difficult varieties for beginners, but one of the most rewarding wines for connoisseurs.

Gewurztraminer Usually dry to off-dry, but its low ACIDITY, combined with high alcohol and GLYCEROL, often give an impression of sweetness. Gewurztraminer has a distinctive aroma and flavour, with hints of lychees and grapefruit. The naturally high sugar levels of Gewurztraminer make it ideal for late-harvest sweet wines, and this is the most frequent varietal found as Vendange Tardive. Poorly made examples can be blowsy, flat, over-alcoholic, sometimes oily. Gewurztraminer from the southern end of Alsace, around Eguisheim southwards, tends to have quite a different character, and is generally more aromatic as well as richer in weight.

Pinot Gris Once known as Tokay-Pinot Gris or Tokay d'Alsace, Pinot Gris has been the only permitted name on labels since 2007 according to an agreement between Hungary and the EU. Pinot Gris was for long underrated in Alsace. It combines some of the spicy flavours of Gewurztraminer with the firm backbone of acidity found in Riesling, giving a wine that ages particularly well. Young Pinot Gris is reminiscent of peaches and apricot, with a hint of smoke, developing biscuity, buttery flavours with age. It can be particularly successful in a Vendange Tardive style.

Muscat Two varieties of Muscat are found in Alsace: MUSCAT BLANC À PETITS GRAINS, known as Muscat d'Alsace, and Muscat Ottonel. Most wines are a blend of the two. Alsace Muscat is always dry, and has a fresh grapey aroma and flavour. The taste should be reminiscent of biting into a fresh grape, with young, crisp fruitiness. Muscat is low in alcohol, and quite low in acidity. Because of its sensitivity to poor weather at flowering, yields can vary considerably from year to year.

Sylvaner Sylvaner is difficult to grow, needs a good site and a warm vintage, yet fetches comparatively little money. Good Sylvaner has a slightly bitter, slightly perfumed aroma and flavour, with very firm acidity. It has moderate alcohol, and is at its best when it is young and fresh.

Pinot Blanc Also labelled Clevner or Klevner, Pinot Blanc is the workhorse of Alsace. As well as forming the base wine for Crémant d'Alsace, Pinot Blanc can produce very good, clean, dry white that is not particularly aromatic but has good acidity, with moderate alcohol.

Auxerrois This variety is rarely mentioned on the label, although it may form the total or the majority of many wines labelled as Pinot Blanc, Klevner, or Clevner. A wine from pure Auxerrois is spicy, soft, and quite broad, with low acidity and good alcohol. It is occasionally vinified successfully in oak.

Chasselas This variety's name is also seldom seen on the label. It is usually used for Edelzwicker, although the few growers who bottle Chasselas as a varietal can produce a very pretty, quite lightweight wine, dry with soft grapey fruit, low acidity, and light alcohol.

Edelzwicker Literally, this is German for 'noble mixture'. A blend of more than one variety can be labelled as Edelzwicker or, more occasionally, as Gentil. It can also be given a general name, such as 'Fruits de Mer'. Edelzwicker is generally one of the cheapest wines in the range. Chasselas, Pinot Blanc, and Auxerrois are common ingredients.

Pinot Noir The only red varietal of Alsace has been deepening in flavour and colour thanks to CLIMATE change. Good OAK-matured wines have increasingly resulted from warmer vintages.

See also KLEVENER DE HEILIGENSTEIN.

Winemaking

As in Germany, winemakers measure the sugar content of the grapes, or MUST WEIGHT, in degrees OECHSLE. CHAPTALIZATION, always outlawed for late-harvest wines (see below) and, since 2011, for AOC Alsace Grand Cru, is now relatively rare, even for AOC Alsace, thanks to climate change. Indigenous YEASTS are generally sufficient, and few winemakers add yeast cultures, except in an abnormally wet vintage. ACIDIFICATION is not practised.

The number of different varieties, all to be vinified separately, can present a logistical problem. Small operations with one PRESS (usually a bladder press, which gives cleaner juice) will organize picking to allow each variety sufficient time in the press before the next variety is picked.

Most winemakers deliberately prevent MALOLACTIC FERMENTATION in white wines by keeping them cool and lightly sulfured, preferring to keep the fresh grape aromas—although some CUVÉES manage to complete malolactic fermentation, often by accident. Although initially making such wines softer, more vinous, and less floral, it does not seem to have altered the quality or keeping ability of the wines, so an increasing number of reputable cellars are allowing malolactic fermentation to take place. Pinot Noir needs to go through malolactic to soften and STABILIZE the wine, and is therefore often kept in an isolated part of the cellar to prevent cross-contamination from LACTIC ACID BACTERIA.

Because over 90% of the wine is white, and because winemakers are emphasizing the primary grape flavours, most wine is vinified and stored in inert containers, and new wood is seldom used. Traditional cellars have large oval wood casks, many over 100 years of age, literally built into the cellar. Traditionally the same cask will be used each year for the same varietal. The build-up of TARTRATES forms a glass-like lining to the cask, and there is no likelihood of oak flavours masking the wine's character. If a cask has to be replaced, the new cask will be well washed out to remove as much as possible of the OAK FLAVOUR, and will be used for Edelzwicker until all oak flavours have disappeared. A few growers are experimenting with BARREL MATURATION, most widely for Pinot Noir, but also occasionally with Pinot Blanc, Pinot Gris, Auxerrois, and even Sylvaner.

The cellars are generally quite cold by the time FERMENTATION is taking place, so many cellars have no cooling system.

Growers have found that the BOUQUET and AGEING potential can be enhanced by fermenting Riesling, Sylvaner, and Muscat at between 14 and 16 °C (61 °F), while Gewurztraminer will take a warmer temperature, of up to 21 °C (70 °F). Most wines are bottled within a year of the vintage to retain freshness.

Alsace wines are in principle fermented dry. Around the turn of the century some of these supposedly dry wines had perceptible RESIDUAL SUGAR that was difficult to predict from the label, but wines have in general become drier—and some producers have introduced SWEETNESS codes on labels. Supposedly the only Alsace wines with significant residual sugar are the late-harvest wines described below.

The late-harvest wines

Regulations for Vendange Tardive and Sélection de Grains Nobles wines were drawn up in 1983.

Vendange Tardive, or Vendanges Tardives

Late-picked wines have always been produced in Alsace in small quantities in outstanding vintages. To be labelled as Vendange Tardive, a term to which Alsace producers claim exclusive rights in France, a wine must come from a single vintage, from one of the four permitted varieties Riesling, Muscat, Gewurztraminer, or Pinot Gris. The wine must not be ENRICHED in any way, and the minimum sugar concentration at harvest must be 220 g/l (95 °Oechsle) for Riesling or Muscat, and 243 g/l (105 °Oechsle) for Gewurztraminer or Pinot Gris. Picking must take place after a certain date, determined annually by the authorities, who must be informed beforehand of the grower's intention to pick a Vendange Tardive wine, and may inspect the vineyard at the time of picking to check the sugar concentration and quantity produced. The wine must also undergo an analysis and tasting after bottling, before the label is granted. Vendange Tardive wines do not have to be BOTRYTIS-affected. The most common varietal for Vendange Tardive wines is Gewurztraminer, which can easily attain very high sugar levels. Muscat is the rarest of all, and is only possible in occasional vintages. Vendange Tardive wine is not necessarily sweet, and may vary from bone dry to medium sweet. Quality varies as widely as sweetness levels.

Sélection de Grains Nobles

SGN is a further refinement of Vendange Tardive, where the grapes have reached even higher sugar levels. Wines labelled as Sélection de Grains Nobles, however, nearly always contain a proportion of grapes affected by botrytis, or NOBLE ROT, picked by hand, generally involving several passages through the vineyard. The same four varieties are permitted, with minimum sugar levels of 256 g/l (110 °Oechsle) for Riesling and Muscat, and 279 g/l (120 °Oechsle) for Gewurztraminer and Pinot Gris. The same legislation as for Vendange Tardive governs production (see above). Sélection de Grains Nobles wine is always sweet, although there is a variation in richness and quality, depending on the grape and the grower.

The appellations Alsace was awarded AOC status in 1962, with the one regional appellation Alsace, or Vin d'Alsace. In 2011 a further two appellations were introduced which may complement the general AOC Alsace:

AOC Alsace communales

This denomination is stricter than the regional appellation, and specifies grape variety, VINE DENSITY, PRUNING, VINE TRAINING, ripeness levels (MUST WEIGHTS), and YIELDS. The following 11 communes, or inter-communal entities, may be mentioned on the label, alongside 'AOC Alsace': Blienschwiller, Saint-Hippolyte, Côtes de Barr, Scherwiller, Côte de Rouffach, Vallée Noble, KLEVENER DE HEILIGENSTEIN, Val Saint-Grégoire, Ottrott, Wolxheim, and Rodern.

AOC Alsace lieux-dits

These are wines which express combinations of varietal and certain terroirs and have stricter requirements than the AOC communales. Wines from these lieux-dits express a number of nuances: primary fruit characters of individual grape varieties are blended with terroir-derived minerality.

Alsace Grand Cru

The appellation Alsace Grand Cru was first defined as a single, if sometimes controversial, appellation in 1975 when Schlossberg was the prototype. The wine had to come from a single named vineyard site, or lieu-dit, a single vintage, and (initially) be made from just one of four permitted varieties, Riesling, Muscat, Gewurztraminer, or Pinot Gris. By 1983 there were 26 lieux-dits, then 50 by 1992. Varietal exceptions have been allowed such as the blend allowed, under pressure from Deiss, in Altenberg de Bergheim, and the estimable Sylvaner of Zotzenberg. In 2007 Kaefferkopf became the 51st lieu-dit to be awarded AOC Alsace Grand Cru status and blends based on a majority of Gewurztraminer were permitted in addition to the four varietals. Four years later the umbrella Alsace Grand Cru AOC was divided into 51 individual AOC Alsace Grands Crus appellations, which affords each lieu-dit AOP-level guarantees of quality.

The wines from these vineyard sites make up only 4% of Alsace's total production but the precise boundary of each grand cru is the subject of much debate, and some of the négociants in particular have eschewed the appellation in favour of their superior brands. Beyer's Riesling Cuvée Particulière is from the Grand Cru Pfersigberg while Trimbach's Clos Ste-Hune, grown in a parcel within the Rosacker Grand Cru but without the words grand cru on the label, is a prime and hugely respected example. But some of the nominated grand cru sites are of only moderate quality. Some named vineyards cover an unreasonably large area, often extending over a number of hillsides, including a number of soils and aspects, some greatly superior to others.

While single-vineyard wines are an excellent way forward for quality wine production, much depends on the attitude of the grower, as well as on the quality of the vineyard site. The best sites and growers have undoubtedly benefited from the grand cru appellation, but many growers and co-operatives are producing

Grand Cru	Type of Soil	Commune	Area	Elevation	Exposition	Date
Altenberg de Bergbieten	Marl-limestone-gypsum	67 Bergbieten	29.07 ha	210 to265 m	south-east	23.11.1983
Altenberg de Bergheim	Marl-limestone	68 Bergheim	35.06 ha	220 to 320 m	south/south-east	23.11.1983
Altenberg de Wolxheim	Marl-limestone	67 Wolxheim	31.20 ha	200 to 250 m	south/south-west	17.12.1992
Brand	Granite	68 Turckheim	57.95 ha	250 to 380 m	south/south-east	23.11.1983
Bruderthal	Marl-limestone	67 Molsheim	18.40 ha	225 to 300 m	south-east	17.12.1992
Eichberg	Marl-limestone	68 Eguisheim	57.62 ha	220 to 340 m	south-east	23.11.1983
Engelberg	Marl-limestone	67 Dahlenheim and Scharrachbergheim	14.80 ha	250 to 300 m	south	17.12.1992
Florimont	Marl-limestone	68 Ingersheim and Katzenthal	21 ha	250 to 280 m	east	17.12.1992
Frankstein	Granite	67 Dambach-La-Ville	56.20 ha	220 to 230 m	east/south-east	17.12.1992
Froehn	Clay-marl	68 Zellenberg	14.60 ha	270 to 300 m	south/south-east	17.12.1992
Furstentum	Limestone	68 Kientzheim and Sigolsheim	30.50 ha	300 to 400 m	south/south-west	17.12.1992
Geisberg	Marl-limestone-sandstone	68 Ribeauvillé	8.53 ha	250 to 320 m	south	23.11.1983
Gloeckelberg	Granite clay	68 Rodern and Saint-Hippolyte	23.40 ha	250 to360 m	south/south-east	23.11.1983
Goldert	Marl-limestone	68 Gueberschwihr	45.35 ha	230 to 330 m	east	23.11.1983
Hatschbourg	Marl-limestone and loess	68 Hattstatt and Voegtlinshoffen	47.36 ha	210 to 330 m	south/south-east	23.11.1983
Hengst	Marl-limestone-sandstone	68 Wintzenheim	75.78 ha	270 to 360 m	south/south-east	23.11.1983
Kaefferkopf	Granite-limestone and sandstone	68 Ammerschwihr	71.65 ha	240 to 350 m	south/west	14.01.2007
Kanzlerberg	Clay-marl-gypsum	67 Andlau	3.23 ha	250 m	south/south-west	23.11.1983
Kastelberg	Schist	67 Andlau	5.82 ha	240 to 300 m	south-east	23.11.1983
Kessler	Sandy-clay	68 Guebwiller	28.53 ha	300 to 390 m	south-east	23.11.1983
Kirchberg de Barr	Marl-limestone	67 Barr	40.63 ha	210 to 330 m	south-east	23.11.1983
Kirchberg de Ribeauvillé	Marl-limestone-sandstone	68 Ribeauvillé	11.40 ha	270 to 350 m	south/south-west	23.11.1983
Kitterlé	Sandstone-volcanic	68 Guebwiller	25.79 ha	270 to 360 m	south/south-east/ south-west	23.11.1983
Mambourg	Marl-limestone	68 Sigolsheim	61.85 ha	210 to 360 m	south	17.12.1992
Mandelberg	Marl-limestone	68 Mittelwihr and Beblenheim	22 ha	210 to 250 m	south/south-west	17.12.1992
Marckrain	Marl-limestone	68 Bennwihr and Sigolsheim	53.35 ha	200 to 300 m	east/south-east	17.12.1992
Moenchberg	Marl-limestone and colluvial deposits	67 Andlau and Eichoffen	11.83 ha	230 à 260 m	south	23.11.1983
Muenchberg	Sandstone-volcanic-pebbles	67 Nothalten	17.70 ha	250 to 310 m	south	17.12.1992
Ollwiller	Sandy-clay	67 Wuenheim	35.86 ha	260 to 330 m	south-east	23.11.1983
Osterberg	Marl	68 Ribeauvillé	24.60 ha	250 to 320 m	east-south-east	17.12.1992
Pfersigberg	Limestone-sandstone	68 Eguisheim and Wettolsheim	74.55 ha	220 to 330 m	east/south-east	17.12.1992
Pfingstberg	Marl-limestone-sandstone	68 Orschwihr	28.15 ha	270 to 370 m	south-east	17.12.1992
Praelatenberg	Granite-gneiss	67 Kintzheim	18.70 ha	250 to 350 m	east-south-east	17.12.1992
Rangen	Volcanic	68 Thann and Vieux-Thann	22.13 ha	320 to 450 m	south	23.11.1983
Rosacker	Dolomitic limestone	68 Hunawihr	26.18 ha	260 to 330 m	east-south-east	23.11.1983
Saering	Marl-limestone-sandstone	68 Guebwiller	26.75 ha	260 to 300 m	east/south-east	23.11.1983
Schlossberg	Granitic	68 Schlossberg	80.28 ha	230 to 350 m	south	20.11.1975
Schoenenbourg	Marl-sand-gypsum	68 Riquewihr and Zellenberg	53.40 ha	265 to 380 m	south/south-east	17.12.1992
Sommerberg	Granitic	68 Niedermorschwihr and Katzenthal	28.36 ha	260 to 400 m	south	23.11.1983
Sonnenglanz	Marl-limestone	68 Beblenheim	32.80 ha	220 to 270 m	south-east	23.11.1983
Spiegel	Marl-sandstone	68 Bergholtz and Guebwiller	18.26 ha	260 to 315 m	east	23.11.1983
Sporen	Clay-marl-pebbles	68 Riquewihr	23.70 ha	265 to 310 m	south-east	17.12.1992
Steinert	Limestone	68 Pfaffenheim and Westhalten	38,90 ha	250 to 350 m	east	17.12.1992
Steingrubler	Marl-limestone-sandstone	68 Wettolsheim	22.95 ha	280 to 350 m	south-east	17.12.1992
Steinklotz	Limestone	67 Marlenheim	40.60 ha	200 to 300 m	south-south-east	17.12.1992
Vorbourg	Limestone-sandstone	68 Rouffach and Westhalten	73.61 ha	210 to 300 m	south/south-east	17.12.1992
Wiebelsberg	Sand-sandstone	67 Andlau	12.52 ha	200 to 300 m	south/south-east	23.11.1983
Wineck-Schlossberg	Granitic	68 Katzenthal and Ammerschwihr	27.40 ha	280 to 400 m	south/south-east	17.12.1992
Winzenberg	Granitic	67 Blienschwiller	19.20 ha	240 to 320 m	south-south-east	17.12.1992
Zinnkoepflé	Limestone-sandstone	67 Soultzmatt and Westhalten	71.03 ha	250 to 420 m	south/south-east	17.12.1992
Zotzenberg	Marl-limestone	67 Mittelbergheim	36.45 ha	215 to 320 m	east/south	17.12.1992

wines of average quality, cashing in on the grand cru name.

Crémant d'Alsace The appellation Crémant d'Alsace was created in 1976 and amended in 2011, formalizing the sparkling wines that had long been made in the region. By 2013 Crémant d'Alsace represented 24% of all AOC wines made in Alsace. Pinot Blanc is by the far the most significant ingredient, although some Riesling and Chardonnay is also used, and Pinot Noir is the only variety allowed for Crémant d'Alsace rosé. As with the late-harvest wines, growers have to identify before the start of harvest which parcels of vines are destined for Crémant d'Alsace production. See also CRÉMANT.

www.vinsalsace.com

	AOC	Maximum yields
Alsace	White	80 hl/ha
	Pinot Noir (rosé)	75 hl/ha
	Pinot Noir (red)	60 hl/ha
Alsace	White	72 hl/ha
communales	Red	60 hl/ha
Alsace	White	68 hl/ha
Lieu-Dit	Red	60 hl/ha
Alsace Grand Cru		55 hl/ha
Crémant d'Alsace		80 hl/ha

Maximum permitted yields for each Alsace AOC

Alta Langa. See LANGHE.

Alternaria, vine disease. See BUNCH ROTS.

alternative packaging for wine is slowly becoming more common, for reasons of convenience, economy, and/or SUSTAINABILITY. BOTTLES are still by far the most common, but see also BOXES, CANS, CARTONS, KEGS, PLASTIC BOTTLES, and POUCHES.

alternative varieties, Australian name for VINE VARIETIES other than the best-known INTERNATIONAL VARIETIES. They even have their own wine SHOW in Australia.

alternative viticulture, forms of viticultural practice such as ORGANIC and BIODYNAMIC, which usually aim to minimize environmental degradation. See also SUSTAINABLE VITICULTURE.

Altesse, SAVOIE's finest white grape variety, once known as ROUSSETTE, the name of several associated wines.

The variety is a shy, late producer but it resists rot well and the wine produced is relatively exotically perfumed, has good acidity, and is well worth ageing. Total plantings had grown to 369 ha/911 acres by 2012.

Robinson, J., Harding, J., and Vouillamoz, J., *Wine Grapes: A Complete Guide to 1,368 Vine Varieties, Including their Origins and Flavours* (London, 2012).

altitude, a term commonly used to describe the ELEVATION of a vineyard. While the terms are used interchangeably, altitude—used typically by pilots—actually refers to height above the Earth's surface whereas elevation refers to the height above sea level.

Alto Adige, the alpine and most northerly part of Italy which shares with its neighbour TRENTINO a preponderance of INTERNATIONAL VARIETIES and the absence of a detailed DOC system. With the Austrian Tyrol to the immediate north, its culture is firmly Germanic and its first language is German. Officially known as Südtirol—Alto Adige, and part of Austria until it was annexed by Italy after the Second World War, the region owes the Italian part of its name to the River Adige (Etsch), flowing south-east to the Adriatic. At the capital Bolzano the Adige is joined by the Isarco (Eisach) River from the north east, forming a y-shaped valley on whose slopes viticulture has been practised for millennia. Vineyards are planted from 300 m up to 1,000 m (3,280 ft), while the valley floor is reserved for other fruits, plus the occasional large-scale vineyard which can be worked mechanically and is therefore more lucrative than apple orchards.

Viticulture at often dizzying heights is a serious option since the Alps protect Alto Adige from cold winds from the north, while the steepness of the slopes creates excellent expositions for long, slow grape ripening. Marked TEMPERATURE variation helps to retain acidity in the grapes, resulting in the fresh, appetizing whites for which the region is especially known. Some districts, notably around the towns of Merano and Bolzano where the dark-skinned LAGREIN is cultivated, even enjoy a sub-MEDITERRANEAN climate.

International grape varieties, introduced in the 19th century under Hapsburg rule, are the norm here, with Pinot Bianco (475 ha/1,174 acres), Pinot Grigio (585 ha/1,446 acres), Chardonnay (494 ha/1,174 acres), and Merlot the most important, although they are dwarfed by plantings of the local SCHIAVA (1,157 ha/2,857 acres). Its pale, often dilute, early-maturing red wine was once enormously popular in Germany, Switzerland, and Austria, markets that are now looking for fuller-bodied reds which, increasingly, they can produce themselves. The annual Alto Adige Schiava Trophy is awarded by a group of quality-conscious producers in an attempt to reverse the varietal's fortunes.

Nearly two-thirds of Alto Adige production is controlled by CO-OPERATIVES, which process the harvest of hundreds, sometimes thousands, of grape farmers. The power of the co-ops is such that they can dictate the cultivation of certain grape varieties considered marketable. This is the main reason why, except for Schiava, Alto Adige's INDIGENOUS VARIETIES have received scant attention in the past, while Pinot Grigio became enormously popular among most growers. The regulations permit YIELDS up to 108 hl/ha and although high yields were still the norm in the early 2010s, improvements in the vineyard, notably the change from PERGOLA to lower-yielding GUYOT training systems, has led to increased wine quality. However, many of the old local varieties that survive are trained on pergolas. A new generation of producers taking over from parents who sold all their grapes to the co-op are reappraising these indigenous varieties and traditional training systems.

An extremely simple DOC system, and the absence of a DOCG, sustains the impression that Alto Adige is all about quantity and easily marketable varieties rather than attention to terroir. There are only three denominations: Lago di Caldaro DOC for the production of Schiava; Valdadige DOC including the whole of Alto Adige and neighbouring Trentino; and Alto Adige DOC with seven subregions—Colli di Bolzano, Meranese, Santa Maddalena, Terlano, Valle Isarco, Valle Venosta, and Lago di Caldaro. In such a crude DOC system, subregions seem only marginally important although Terlano and Valle Isarco have deservedly risen to prominence: the first because of its long-lived Pinot Bianco, notably from Cantina Terlano, which pays scrupulous attention to quality, the latter because of a handful of small estates producing crystalline wines from vineyards up to 1,000 m. Other Cantine Sociale notable for their high quality output include Colterenzio and San Michele Appiano. Matching suitable varieties to subzones has become much more precise, confirming the historic tradition of growing certain grapes on certain terroirs: Magré (Margreid) and Cortaccia (Kurtatsch) in the south west and Settequerce (Siebeneich) to the west of Bolzano for Cabernet and Merlot; Mazzon and Montagna (Montan) in the south east, and Cornaiano (Girlan) to the south west of Bolzano for Pinot Noir (unlike in BURGUNDY, Pinot Noir prefers a south-western ASPECT in this hotter region); Terlano (Terlan) for Sauvignon Blanc; Appiano (Eppan) and Monte (Berg) for Pinot Bianco; Ora (Auer) and the sandy and gravelly soils adjacent to Bolzano for Lagrein, with an intricate system of single vineyards called *Leiten* followed by their individual names; Termeno (Tramin) for TRAMINER; Caldaro (Kaltern), and Cortaccia in addition to Santa Maddalena for Schiava; Cortaccia, Magré, and Salorno for Pinot Grigio.

While most of Alto Adige's produce is enthusiastically consumed by the region itself, the Italian as well as the international markets have begun to take notice of Alto Adige as a source of highly original, fresh wines. Now that Pinot Grigio is produced throughout the entire peninsula, including Puglia in the far south, Alto Adige is no longer the cheapest source of this wine. By turning its attention to its very diverse terroirs and marketing them accordingly, it may well manage to shake off its undeserved reputation as a producer of commodity wines.

See also SANTA MADDALENA.   W.S.

www.altoadigewines.com

Alvarelhão, dark-berried vine planted all over northern Portugal, especially in Dão, Douro, Beiras, and to a limited extent in

Vinho Verde country. In GALICIA it is also known as BRANCELLAO and makes pale aromatic reds for early drinking.

Alvarinho, the Portuguese name of a distinctive white grape variety grown around the town of Monção in the extreme north west of Portugal's VINHO VERDE country (and, as ALBARIÑO, in neighbouring GALICIA). The grapes' thick skins help them withstand the particularly damp climate, and can result in wines relatively high in alcohol (12 to 13%), acidity, and flavour. Alvarinho was one of the first Portuguese varieties to appear on the labels of VARIETAL whites and is therefore one of the best known. Portuguese plantings had reached 2,340 ha/5,782 acres by 2010.

Robinson, J., Harding, J., and Vouillamoz, J., *Wine Grapes: A Complete Guide to 1,368 Vine Varieties, Including their Origins and Flavours* (London, 2012).

amabile, Italian for sweet (sweeter than ABBOCATO) or, literally, 'lovable'. See also SWEETNESS.

Amador, California county. See SIERRA FOOTHILLS.

Amarone, powerful, red DRIED-GRAPE WINE in the DOC VALPOLICELLA in Italy's north east. The wine, made of the same grape varieties as Valpolicella, consists of 45–95% CORVINA, 5–50% RONDINELLA, and up to 50% CORVINONE in the place of Corvina. It may also contain up to 15% of any red variety that is authorized in the province of Verona.

Strictly speaking, Amarone is a *recioto scapata*, literally a RECIOTO that has escaped and fermented to full dryness when the intention was to produce a sweet wine. The yeast, already struggling with the high sugar content in the must, would normally stop working because of rising alcohol levels, and before all the sugar had been converted. Stylistically, Recioto della Valpolicella and Amarone are similar, but the latter must be dry with no more than 12 g/l RESIDUAL SUGAR and at least 14% alcohol (but often more). The pleasant, bitter (*amaro*) aftertaste explains its name. Amarone is a style and its name must be followed by 'della Valpolicella' on the label.

Amarone has been produced in commercial quantities only since the 1950s. From the 1980s it has been a roaring success, especially in Scandinavia, Germany, and the United States, and production soared from 8.5 to 14 million bottles between 2005 and 2013. During the same period the total Valpolicella vineyard area increased from 5,719 ha/14,125 acres in 2000 to 7,288 ha/18,000 acres in 2013. Producers are allowed to transform up to 70% of their total grape production into Amarone, regardless of the quality or provenance of the grapes within the dramatically extended Valpolicella zone,

which has resulted in wide quality variation. Much more important for quality than the drying process is the provenance of the grapes. But proposals to restrict Amarone's production to HILLSIDE sites, and/or reducing production on the plains, have not come to fruition. By law the grapes for Amarone must be dried at least until the beginning of the December after the vintage. The drying process results in a metabolization of the acids in the grape and a polymerization of tannins in the skins, which explains the richness of good Amarone. The wine should be made from selected superior whole bunches, which are dried or raisined in special drying lodges. Traditionally, the drying of grapes was restricted to the Valpolicella hills, above the autumn fog line, where thermal fluctuation warded off the development of BOTRYTIS. Grapes were spread out on mats or wickerwork shelving, or strung up from the ceiling or rafters. Today, however, most producers pick the grapes directly into plastic crates and dry them in a temperature- and humidity-controlled warehouse. This technical approach, which ensures minimal handling of the grapes, minimizing the risk of damage and consequent development of rot or mould, has resulted in cleaner, more balanced, but also rather formulaic wines, while encouraging the current industrial-scale production of Amarone. Traditionally, the wines were aged in large BOTTI, although today barrique ageing is the norm, resulting in wines with a distinctly international style, but at the cost of originality. In the 2010s the pendulum started to swing back, away from heavy OAK influence, and towards lower alcohol, and little or no residual sweetness. Good producers include Bertani, Quintarelli, Le Salette, Monte dei Ragni, Corte Sant'Alda, Ca la Bionda, Monte dall'Ora, and the idiosyncratic Dal Forno.   W.S.

Morganti, P., and Sangiorgio, S., *L'Amarone della Valpolicella* (2nd edn, Verona, 2004).

Masnaghetti, A., *Valpolicella—Crus and Valleys* (Monza, 2014) e-book.

www.consorziovalpolicella.it

amateur winemaking. See HOME WINEMAKING.

ambient yeast, are those that are present in the vineyard and winery, as opposed to inoculated, cultured YEAST.

amelioration, which strictly means improvement, is a euphemism for chemical intervention in winemaking with the express purpose of compensating for nature's deficiencies. Thus in cooler wine regions the term is commonly used interchangeably with ENRICHMENT or CHAPTALIZATION. Amelioration is sometimes used more widely to include both ACIDIFICATION and DEACIDIFICATION, and sometimes for any chemical adjustment to the

constituents naturally present in grape juice or wine. Ameliorating operations condoned by each region's authorities tend to be those required, and vice versa, but limits are set. See also MANIPULATION.

American hybrids, group of vine HYBRIDS developed in the eastern United States, mainly in the early and mid 19th century and in some cases earlier but also much more recently with cold-hardiness in mind. Brianna, for example, was developed in 1983 by Elmer Swenson and involved no fewer than 93 distinct parents from eight different species. The term includes hybrids between native AMERICAN VINE SPECIES of the genus VITIS and a variety of the European vine species VINIFERA, resulting in such varieties as Black Spanish, NORTON, CONCORD, NIAGARA, HERBEMONT, DELAWARE, and Othello. The hybrids' most common parents are the American species *V. labrusca* and *V. aestivalis*, along with *V. vinifera*.

These varieties are used for wine production, for unfermented GRAPE JUICE and jelly, and for TABLE GRAPES. The fruit is typically highly flavoured, and palates accustomed to the taste of *V. vinifera* varieties find the FOXY character of many American vines strong and objectionable.

See UNITED STATES, history, for more background. Following the devastation wreaked by the pest PHYLLOXERA in Europe at the end of the 19th century, the French began experimental hybridizing of *V. vinifera* with American species, producing the so-called FRENCH HYBRIDS or 'direct producers'.   T.P., R.E.S., & P.C.

Morton, L. T., *Winegrowing in Eastern America* (Ithaca, 1985).

Reisch, B. I., et al., 'Grape', in M. L. Badenes and D. H. Byrne (eds.), *Fruit Breeding* (New York, 2012).

Sabbatini, P., and Howell, S. G., 'Vitis hybrids: history and current status', *Wines & Vines* (January 2014), 135–42.

American vines, loose term for both AMERICAN VINE SPECIES and also AMERICAN HYBRIDS.

American vine species, those members of the grapevine genus VITIS which originate in North and South America, including Mexico and the Caribbean. About half the vine species of the world are native to America, but they are poorly suited to WINEMAKING. However, when all efforts to grow European vine species VINIFERA in North America failed through pest, disease, or climatic extreme (see UNITED STATES, history), wine was made in North America of necessity from these species, detailed below.

After the development of AMERICAN HYBRIDS and the successful cultivation of *V. vinifera* vines in CALIFORNIA and elsewhere in the Americas, native vines were rarely used for wine. A notable exception is *V. rotundifolia*, particularly the SCUPPERNONG and related bronze- and

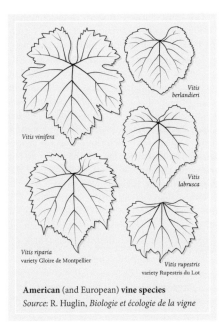

American (and European) **vine species**
Source: R. Huglin, *Biologie et écologie de la vigne*

Vitis vinifera has varied leaf forms among its many varieties, not always with five distinct lobes as shown here.

black-fruited varieties used for a sweet, musky wine popular in the southern United States, where they are both grown and cultivated.

The most important role for the American species has been to provide the genetic basis for ROOTSTOCKS on to which *V. vinifera* vines may be grafted (see MUNSON). This became a necessity in most of the world's wine regions by the end of the 19th century to counter the predations of the PHYLLOXERA louse, native to America and to which most American vine species developed resistance or tolerance. The species *V. berlandieri*, *V. riparia*, and *V. rupestris* are particularly important as sources of protection against phylloxera, and the great majority of the world's vineyards now grow on rootstocks derived from them.

These are some of the more important American vine species (although others are listed under VITIS):

Vitis labrusca Vine species found in the northeastern United States producing highly aromatic and strongly flavoured berries sometimes described as FOXY. The berries fall easily from the cluster when mature and are called 'slip-skin', in that a berry squeezed between fingers will eject the flesh as a complete ball (non slip-skin varieties, which are more usual, are squashed when squeezed in this way). Most of the fruit of this species is black, and the leaves are large, thick, and covered on the lower surface with dense white or brown hairs. *V. labrusca* is a common parent in American hybrids, including CONCORD and CATAWBA.

Vitis aestivalis Vine species found in the southern and eastern United States which, like *Vitis labrusca*, is a common parent in American

hybrids. The fruit, typically black, is not strongly aromatic and the berries adhere to the cluster when mature. This species shows good resistance to DOWNY MILDEW and POWDERY MILDEW and is therefore a common parent in VINE BREEDING programmes. Norton, which has a reputation for high-quality wine and is enjoying a revival in VIRGINIA, is a hybrid derived from *V. aestivalis*. Early Spanish settlers of north eastern MEXICO made wine from WILD VINES of this species as early as 1597.

Vitis riparia This vine species is widely distributed in eastern North America, from Canada to the Gulf of Mexico. The grapes are not strongly aromatic, with black skin and highly acidic juice. *V. riparia* is used directly as a rootstock and as a parent of many commercially important rootstocks; the species typically imparts low to moderate vine size to SCIONS and provides protection against phylloxera.

Vitis rupestris Unusual vine species that grows as a small shrub, found typically on gravelly banks of streams or in watercourses in Texas, Oklahoma, Arkansas, and Missouri. The leaves are small and kidney-shaped and roots tend to grow vertically downwards rather than spread horizontally. A common parent of many commercially important rootstocks because of its phylloxera tolerance or resistance and deep-rooting habit, which can provide protection against drought.

Vitis berlandieri Vine species found on the limestone soils of Texas and Mexico. The grape is black and its juice is high in sugar and acid without strong flavours. This species is known for being difficult to root from cuttings, but because of its high phylloxera and lime tolerance or resistance, it is a common parent of many commercially important rootstocks.

Other American species include *V. cinerea*, *V. vulpina* (*cordifolia*), *V. mustangensis*, *V. shuttleworthii*, *V. acerifolia*, *V. californica*, *V. arizonica*, *V. monticola*, *V. palmata*, *V. biformis*, and *V. tiliifolia*. See VITIS.   P.C.

Moore, M. O., 'Vitaceae', in Flora of North America Editorial Committee (eds.), *Flora of North America North of Mexico*, 12 (New York and Oxford, 2015).

Morton, L. T., *Winegrowing in Eastern America* (Ithaca, 1985).

Reisch, B. I., et al., 'Grape', in M. L. Badenes and E. H. Byrne (eds.), *Fruit Breeding* (New York, 2012).

American Viticultural Area. See AVA.

Amerine, Maynard (1911–98), preeminent American OENOLOGIST, teacher, and writer, was trained as a plant physiologist at Berkeley in California before joining the revived Department of Viticulture and Enology at DAVIS in 1935. There he participated in some of the most important branches of its work, including the assessment of VINE VARIETIES for the different

regions of California and the re-education of the wine industry to restore and advance the technical knowledge lost during PROHIBITION.

With A. J. WINKLER, Amerine developed the system of classifying wine regions by measuring heat summation. The list of his publications extends to nearly 400 items making substantial contributions to the literature of such subjects as wine JUDGING methods, wine and must ANALYSIS, COLOUR in wines, the AGEING of wine, the control of FERMENTATION, and the LITERATURE OF WINE.

Amerine served as chairman of his department from 1957 until 1962 and retired from the University in 1974, although he remained active as a writer and a recognized general expert on wine throughout his retirement.

T.P. & B.C.C.

Amigne, rare Swiss white grape variety and a speciality of Vétroz in the Valais used for dry, semi-dried on the vine, and sweet wines. DNA PROFILING has established that Amigne is a likely grandchild of PETIT MESLIER, an almost extinct variety of Champagne. The wine produced is either a powerful dry white with distinctive linden aromas or a sweet (see FLÉTRI) wine with flavours of citrus fruits and bitter almonds.   J.V.

amines. See HISTAMINE.

amino acids, the basic building blocks of PROTEINS, chemicals essential to all living systems. There are 20 amino acids involved in constructing thousands of proteins of living materials. When these proteins act as catalysts for specific biochemical reactions, they are called ENZYMES.

In ripe grapes, NITROGEN-containing compounds constitute about 1 g/l of juice, of which amino acids make up about half. The most common are proline, arginine, and glutamic acid (see UMAMI). During grape RIPENING, the concentrations of amino acids increase, arginine and proline especially; proline increases more than arginine if the fruit is exposed to light. High concentrations of arginine, resulting from soils with a high nitrogen content, present the danger of production of the carcinogen urethane (ethyl CARBAMATE) in wine.

YEASTS are able to make all the amino acids they require, but they will also use intact amino acids from the medium in which they find themselves if they are available. Thus FUSEL OILS are formed in wine as by-products of the nitrogen metabolism of the yeast cells living in grape juice. After fermentation has finished, yeast proteins break down, secreting smaller peptide units and amino acids into the wine if it is left in the presence of the LEES or dead yeast cells.

Bottle-fermented SPARKLING WINES owe some of their special flavour to the presence of substances associated with yeast breakdown, peptides, and amino acids (see AUTOLYSIS).

A.D.W. & B.G.C.

Rantz, J. A., 'Nitrogen in Grapes and Wine', Proceedings of the International Symposium, Seattle, June 1991, *American Society of Enology and Viticulture* (Davis, Calif., 1991).

amontillado, Spanish word which originally described sherry in the style of MONTILLA. Today it has two related meanings in the sherry-making process. The basic FINO wines become amontillado (Spanish for 'like Montilla') when the FLOR yeast dies and the wine is exposed to oxygen. This happens automatically if a fino type of sherry is fortified to 16% since the flor yeast cannot work in such an alcoholic environment. The wine turns amber and tastes richer and nuttier. A true Amontillado-style sherry is therefore an aged Fino. Cheaper Amontillados, the most common Amontillado encountered commercially, are created artificially by blending and are usually sweetened. They tend to be quintessentially medium. For more details, see SHERRY.

ampelography, the science of description and identification of the vine genus VITIS and its cultivated VINE VARIETIES. A volume of vine descriptions is also called an ampelography, the word coming from the Greek *ampelos*, meaning vine and *graphos*, meaning 'description'. Some system of distinguishing between grapevine varieties is clearly necessary since the early French **ampelographers** Viala and Vermorel (see below) were able to list about 24,000 names of varieties and their synonyms in their seven volume *Ampélographie* published between 1901 and 1910. Some system of vine identification is particularly necessary in the modern era of VARIETAL wines (see below for examples of mistaken identification, especially in the NEW WORLD).

There has long been an awareness of differences between vine varieties, and PLINY the Elder could already produce vine descriptions and state that synonyms were creating confusion in Ancient ROME. While regional ampelographies emphasizing the aptitudes of various cultivated varieties already existed in medieval Europe, it was not until the second half of the 19th century that a need for more systematic study developed. When serious vine diseases and pests were introduced to Europe from America (POWDERY MILDEW in 1845, PHYLLOXERA in 1863, DOWNY MILDEW in 1878, and BLACK ROT in 1885), it became essential to identify those species and varieties which showed most resistance to these hazards. Such species were soon used for VINE BREEDING and as ROOTSTOCKS.

Early ampelographic works emphasized fruit characters, and did not provide a key for classification, so that it was impossible to determine the name of a variety in a systematic fashion.

Further, the distinguishing features of the vine varieties themselves were not emphasized. The vegetative parts of the vine were not used for identification since they were thought too variable and not stable. The Austrian ampelographer Hermann Goethe proposed measuring the angle between leaf veins as an identifying character in 1876, and this concept was developed by the French ampelographer Louis Ravaz when in 1902 he published his, presumably much-needed, book *Les Vignes américaines*. Several large regional ampelographies were published near the turn of the century, including Pulliat (1888) and also Viala and Vermorel (1901–10) in France; Goethe (1878) in Austria; Rovasenda (1877) and Molon (1906) in Italy; and Hedrick (1908) and MUNSON (1909) in the US.

The most famous modern ampelographer, Dr Pierre GALET of MONTPELLIER, began his studies in 1944 by inspecting rootstock plantings, and this led to the publication of a distinguishing key in 1946. These studies were extended to include wine and table grape varieties and in 1952 his *Précis d'ampélographie pratique* was published, followed by, among other works, *Cépages et vignobles de France*. Galet's comprehensive quantitative description of leaf shape, attained by measuring the lengths and angles of the veins, the ratio of length to width, and the depth of sinuses, is highly objective.

Other characteristics have been considered for identification, including the timing of phenological or development stages such as BUDBREAK, fruit maturation, or even LEAF FALL.

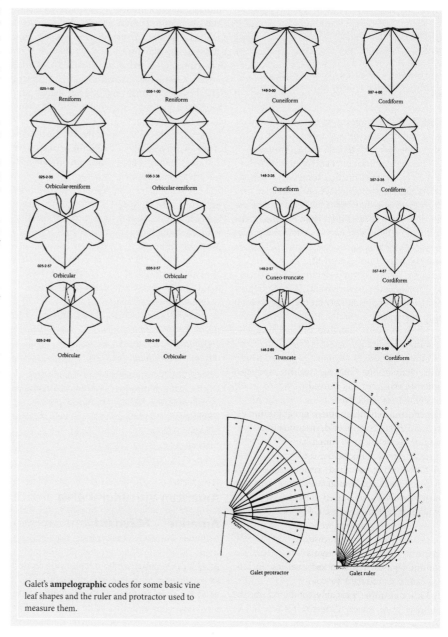

Galet's **ampelographic** codes for some basic vine leaf shapes and the ruler and protractor used to measure them.

Such features are known to be controlled by the environment, however, and can be used only in a relative sense for vine varieties in a single region.

The disadvantages of the technique are that, while some characteristics are quite stable, others, such as leaf shape, can vary markedly even on one vine. Major differences can be caused by environmental factors, but also and to a lesser degree by variation between different CLONES, plant age, and the influence of pests and vine DISEASES. There are, however, five characters which are quite stable: sex of the flower; grape skin colour; pulp colour; the taste of berries; and the presence of seeds.

Experience has shown that ampelography is a field of systematic botany requiring very specialized skills and interpretative ability, as well as an extraordinary memory. Very few people can walk into any vineyard and unequivocally identify varieties. Some modern acknowledged experts apart from Pierre Galet have included his colleague Paul Truel and successors Jean-Michel Boursiquot, Thierry Lacombe of Montpellier, and Anna Schneider of Italy, and the late Allan Antcliff of Australia.

A complex ampelographic procedure was proposed by the Office International de la Vigne et du Vin (OIV) in 1951, based on 65 morphological characters. The International Board of Plant Genetic Resources (IBPGR) and l'Union Internationale pour la Protection des Obtentions Végétales (UPOV) have also produced lists of descriptors and all three international systems have been harmonized by the introduction of numeric codes. Ampelographic studies have recently been facilitated by application of computers and electronic data storage and retrieval, (e.g. www.vivc.de), but final identification still relies heavily on the judgement of ampelographers.

Attempts were therefore made to develop objective, laboratory-based tests for vine identification, including isozyme analysis and gel electrophoresis of enzyme banding patterns but DNA PROFILING has proved by far the most successful and effective.

Unfortunately, misnomers are common, especially in the New World, in government collections as well as in commercial nurseries and thus vineyards. Some of the early introductions of vine cuttings to these regions were made before European vine-growers had correctly identified their own varieties. Sometimes name tags on bundles of vine cuttings, all of which look remarkably similar, were simply misplaced or transposed. In other cases, confusion was caused by different synonyms in different European regions. James BUSBY's celebrated vine collection introduced to colonial Australia in 1832, for example, probably contained CINSAUT cuttings under seven different regional synonyms, and CHENIN BLANC under three. Paul

Truel studied a large collection of French varieties at Domaine de Vassal on the Mediterranean coast (see INRA) in the 1960s and 1970s and found that as many as six distinct varieties grown in different parts of France were a single variety under different names, and there is even more variation in nomenclature between countries. The Graciano of Spain, for example, is the same as France's Morrastel, while the Ottavianello of Italy is the same as Cinsaut of France, but more complex examples abound.

Because its nursery has been able to provide virus-free, high-health vines, the FOUNDATION PLANT SERVICES at the University of California at DAVIS has been an important source of varieties for many establishing New World countries. Naming mistakes in this collection were legion, and caused inconvenience for both the California wine industry and importers of plant material from Davis. Some examples of such errors cited in California by French ampelographers Galet and Boursiquot, in Australia by Truel, and in New Zealand by Zuur include Abouriou (incorrectly called Early Burgundy), Petit Verdot (Gros Manseng), one clone of Pinot Noir (Gamay Beaujolais), Négrette (Pinot St George), Valdiguié (Napa Gamay), Melon (Pinot Blanc), Muscadelle (Sauvignon Vert), Tempranillo (Valdepeñas), a clone of Sauvignon Blanc (Savagnin Musqué), Trousseau Gris (Grey Riesling), and Touriga (Alvarelhão).

Generally rootstocks are more difficult to differentiate as they do not often fruit, so it is not surprising that problems have also occurred with their naming. In the 1990s, California growers were forced to replace the rootstock AXR1 as it succumbed to phylloxera. This replanting effort was thwarted by finding that the rootstock thought to be SO4 was in fact 5C Teleki, and Riparia Gloire was mixed with Couderc 1616.   R.E.S.

Galet, P., *Cépages et vignobles de France* (2nd edn, Montpellier, 1990).

Galet, P., *Dictionnaire encyclopédique des cépages* (Paris, 2000).

Galet, P., and Morton, L. T., *A Practical Ampelography* (Ithaca, NY, and London, 1979).

Robinson, J., Harding, J., and Vouillamoz, J., *Wine Grapes: A Complete Guide to 1,368 Vine Varieties, including their Origins and Flavours* (London and New York, 2012).

amphora, Latin word from the Greek for a vessel with two handles. Although the term may refer sometimes to fine wares, it is normally used to describe the large pottery containers which were used for the BULK TRANSPORT of many goods and liquids, including wine, in the Mediterranean world throughout classical antiquity (see Ancient EGYPT, for example). Despite the considerable variety of shape in amphorae, they mainly shared the characteristics of the two handles, a mouth narrow enough to

be stoppered, and a bottom which tapered to a point (only a few, notably those of southern France, had flat bottoms). When full, many amphorae were a considerable weight; so the spike on the bottom served as a third handle, an essential point of purchase, when lifting and pouring. To carry wine the inner surface of the porous amphora was sealed with a coating of pine resin (see RESINATED WINES). To stop the mouth, either CORK or a lid of fired clay was pushed down the neck and then secured with a sealing of mortar. Modern study of ancient amphorae began after the Second World War, when the use of the aqualung led to the discovery of many wrecks carrying cargoes of amphorae (see CELTS, for example). Later research has concentrated on the identification of kiln sites, where the vessels were produced. As a result, a much clearer picture of the pattern of trade in goods, such as wine, has emerged. The term amphora also became an expression of capacity, a cubic Roman foot, about 26 l/7 gal, although the actual vessels did not by any means conform to this. Indeed, it is likely that goods, such as wine, were frequently sold wholesale by weight and there were formulae for converting the weight of different goods into capacity.   J.J.P.

Peacock, D. P. S., and Williams, D. F., *Amphorae and the Roman Economy* (London, 1986).

Modern usage

Partly inspired by the likes of Gravner in FRIULI, and traditional winemaking techniques in Georgia (see QVEVRI), winemakers have been experimenting with FERMENTATION and AGEING in modern copies of amphorae, made from CLAY or, occasionally, CONCRETE. Concrete may provide a less oxidative environment and is easier to use and maintain but the level of oxygenation depends more on the size of the vessel and the width of the opening, and how it is sealed. Winemakers may design their own shapes. The more typical amphora shape, with a narrow base, allows less LEES CONTACT and better SETTLING and results typically in more vibrant wines than those whose shape is closer to that of CONCRETE EGGS, which tend to produce richer wines. Amphorae are generally freestanding in a cellar but some producers bury them, emulating Georgian traditions. Small amphorae with narrow necks are particularly difficult to clean. Ideally the pores of the clay should be very fine, giving a smooth surface that is easier to clean and does not need to be epoxy-lined. Some producers such as Ch Pontet-Canet in Pauillac, which ages its wine in a blend of amphorae, tronconic vats, and barriques, even mix fragments of gravel or crushed limestone from their vineyards into the concrete during the production process so as to maximize the possible local footprint on the resulting wine. Others use local clay. See also TINAJA.

Amtliche Prüfungsnummer. See AP NUMBER.

amurensis, an Asian vine species of the VITIS genus which takes its name from the Amur valley of northern China. The exceptionally cold climate in which it originates makes it useful to vine breeders seeking to introduce genes for cold hardiness. Professor Helmut BECKER in particular developed HYBRIDS which included both Riesling and *V. amurensis* in their complex pedigrees (e.g. Solaris). See also CABERNET SEVERNY.

amyl alcohols. See FUSEL OILS.

analysis of grapes, must, and wine is a regular and important part of the WINEMAKING process.

Grapes and must

Traditional analysis of grapes and must is chiefly concerned with just three components: sugar, acid, and PH. For TABLE WINE, for instance, the grapes should ideally contain SUGARS capable of producing wines with an ALCOHOLIC STRENGTH between about 10 and 14% by volume, which means that the grapes should have between 18 and 25% of fermentable sugar by weight (see MUST WEIGHT for the various ways in which this can be measured).

The ACIDITY of the grapes or must should also ideally be such that the TOTAL ACIDITY is in the general range of 7 to 10 g/l expressed as tartaric acid. Some acid is always lost during winemaking, primarily as the alcohol content of the wine increases and the solubility of wine acids decreases. Acidity may be further reduced by MALOLACTIC CONVERSION and cold STABILIZATION. It is therefore necessary to start with more acid in the grapes than is eventually wanted in the wine. However, it should be noted that the production of SUCCINIC ACID during fermentation may occasionally lead to a very slight increase in total acidity.

The chemistry of AGEING is strongly influenced by pH, and, although there is a relationship between pH and total acidity, it is important to measure pH separately. Two samples with the same acidity can have different pH readings because of the BUFFERING EFFECT of ions such as POTASSIUM and due to differing organic acid profiles.

Sugars are most simply measured by determining the DENSITY of a sample of CLARIFIED grape juice. Measurement of the juice's index of refraction (see REFRACTOMETER) can also provide a close estimate of its sugar content. In establishments with particularly well-equipped laboratories, modern chromatography can provide an extremely accurate sugar measurement. Sugar measurement is of primary concern in cool wine regions, as an indication of timing of HARVEST, the POTENTIAL ALCOHOL, and any

need for ENRICHMENT, but harvest decisions are often also governed by grape flavour profiles.

In warm wine regions, the accumulation of sugars poses a different problem; in hot, dry weather, sugar synthesis (see PHOTOSYNTHESIS) and acid loss occur so rapidly that picking decisions have to be taken fast, and frequent field analysis may be necessary, normally involving a hand refractometer for sugar.

On arrival at the winery, harvested grapes may also be tested with a probe linked to an autoanalyser. This will typically analyse for sugar content, total acidity, MALIC ACID, pH, and yeast-available NITROGEN.   B.G.C. & R.D.

Wine

Analysis of wine involves the measurement of various characteristics which relate to wine quality, stability, and legal requirements, ideally in a well-equipped laboratory. In most specialist wine laboratories, wine analysis also includes a critical tasting to ensure that the wine conforms to type and quality. Wine analysis is also used to help assess blends, shelf-life estimations, and to ensure that BLENDING and PACKAGING operations have been successfully performed.

Common measurements include those of alcoholic strength, total acidity, VOLATILE ACIDITY, pH, density, RESIDUAL SUGAR, microbiology, and SULFUR DIOXIDE. Laboratories in larger wineries may also be equipped to test for mineral elements such as IRON, COPPER, SODIUM, and potassium. All these parameters either play an important part in assessing quality and stability or are limited by law.

Not all wineries determine all these constituents, and many of the smaller ones have no laboratory at all and have to rely on samples sent to professional analysts.

Wine analysis advanced considerably in the early 21st century with the development of powerful specialist high-tech equipment such as Inductively Coupled Mass Spectrometry (ICPMS), Liquid Chromatography Mass Spectrometry Mass Spectrometry (LCMSMS), and Gas Chromatography Mass Spectrometry Mass Spectrometry (GCMSMS).

ICPMS is a powerful technique which enables the simultaneous measurement of 60 or more different elements (e.g. metals, trace metals) and can be used to check authenticity, for example, to make sure that wines or batches of allegedly the same wine are, in fact, identical.

Chromatography in very general terms is an analytical technique for separating, then identifying and quantifying the various components and chemicals within liquids such as wine. Of the various types of chromatography, the two most commonly used in wine analysis are complementary: liquid chromatography, generally used to separate non-volatile compounds, and gas chromatography, for separating volatile compounds. The techniques have evolved into

very sophisticated analytical tools and can now include a double mass spectrometer: the first confirms the mass of the compound separated, the second breaks down the compound into its components, enabling detection at lower levels, and more certain identification, than previously. Sub-nanogram per litre quantification is now possible. This is important because wine taints such as TCA can be detected by the human nose at nanogram per litre level.

LCMSMS is typically used for SUGARS, TANNINS, PHENOLICS, certain ACIDS, etc.

GCMSMS is typically used for anisoles (TCA, TBA, etc.), BRETTANOMYCES markers such as 4-ethyl phenol, pesticide RESIDUES, aroma profiling for varietals such as Sauvignon Blanc, etc. An additional adaptor, called an odour port or sniff port, can be used to enable simultaneous nosing (smelling) and identification. These are extremely powerful tools available to the modern wine analyst.

Stability prediction tests for TARTRATES, PROTEIN, COLOUR sedimentation, and microbiology are also crucial analyses to ensure a commercially sound and stable product.

Modern analytical methods based on INFRARED SPECTROSCOPY allow rapid analysis in the field and in the laboratory, allowing analysis of all components in the production chain, ranging from soil to finished wine.

See also NUCLEAR MAGNETIC RESONANCE, infrared spectroscopy; and SOIL TESTING for the analysis of soils.   R.D. & G.T.

Coulter, A., Cozzlino, D., and Dambergs, R. G., 'Instrumental analysis of grape, must and wine', in A. G. Reynolds (ed.), *Managing Wine Quality 1: Viticulture and Wine Quality* (Cambridge, 2010).

Anatolia, much of modern TURKEY, the land lying between the Black Sea and the Mediterranean. In Ancient Asia Minor, grapes were harvested in September and October. In business documents of the Old Assyrian trading colonies in Asia Minor (dating to approximately the 19th century BC), this season of the year was called *qitip karānim*, or 'grape picking'. The location of the ancient vine-growing areas is uncertain, but they were probably established in suitably warm, well-watered regions throughout the peninsula, as they are today along major river valleys and along the coasts.

Among the Hittites, the Anatolian civilization in central Turkey in the second millennium BC, a grape-harvesting festival took place every year. Viticulture was certainly important during the Hittite Old Kingdom (*c.*18th–15th centuries BC). The king's merit in the eyes of the storm god (who was regarded as the owner of the land) was reflected in the produce of the vineyards and in grain and livestock production. Wine was under the control of royal officials who distributed 'good wine' to certain pensioners (who complained when the quality was not satisfactory). Certain officials during the Old Kingdom bore a title which can be translated as 'wine chief', originally supervisor of the vineyards but later an exalted military rank comparable with general or field marshal.

In Hittite laws (also of the Old Kingdom), the price of grapes was regulated, together with the prices of barley and emmer (a species of wheat). One law makes provisions for damage caused to vines: the offender has to take the damaged vine himself and let the plaintiff take grapes from one of his own good vines at harvest time.

Another law prescribes penalties for the theft of a vine: six shekels of silver for a free man, three if the offender was a slave. Previously the fine was lower, but the offender had been obliged to undergo corporal punishment in addition. Six shekels was also the fine for a free man who damaged another's vine by fire. Viticultural images were used in ritual magic. In an archaic ritual performed during the foundation of a new palace, for example: 'They lay out a vine tendril and say, "Just as the vine puts down roots and sends up tendrils, so may the king and queen put down roots and send up tendrils!"'

Similarly in so-called 'vanishing god' texts we read: 'O Telepinu [a god of agriculture], hold goodness in your mind and heart, just as the grape holds wine in its heart!'

See also ORIGINS OF VINICULTURE and PALAEOETH-NOBOTANY AND THE ARCHAEOLOGY OF WINE. J.A.B.

Gorny, R. L., 'Viticulture and Ancient Anatolia', in Fleming, S. J., and Katz, S. H. (eds.), *The Origins and Ancient History of Wine* (New York, 1995).

Hoffner, H. A., Jr, *Alimenta Hethaeorum: Food Production in Hittite Asia Minor*, American Oriental Series 55 (New Haven, Conn., 1974).

Ancellotta, Italian red wine grape valued for its deep colour as a blending ingredient, up to 15% in LAMBRUSCO and up to 60% in REGGIANO. It is also widely used throughout central and northern Italy to add colour to wines deemed too pallid for today's market. Total Italian plantings were 4,342 ha/10,724 acres in 2010 with almost all of it in EMILIA-ROMAGNA. It is also grown in Brazil and the Valais in Switzerland.

Ancenis, Coteaux d', small AOC zone in the LOIRE around the historic town of Ancenis between Nantes and Angers for light whites from Pinot Gris (occasionally called Malvoisie) and reds and rosés from Gamay.

ancient vine varieties. THEOPHRASTUS (*c*.370–*c*.287 BC) remarked that there were as many kinds of grapes as there were kinds of soil (*Historia plantarum* 2. 5. 7; also *De causis plantarum* 4. 11. 6). He does not elaborate, but his remark shows how difficult it is to discuss VINE VARIETIES in the classical world. Are varieties that classical authors describe as different

really different varieties, or are they examples of the same variety behaving differently in different conditions? Soil is only one factor; climate and winemaking methods are others. We cannot resort to tasting samples or nursery specimens; all we possess are CLASSICAL TEXTS written by authors who were not modern, scientifically trained AMPELOGRAPHERS.

The Greeks did not write systematic treatises on wine so we must turn to the Latin writers on agriculture and natural history, particularly VIRGIL, PLINY, and COLUMELLA. Virgil's treatment, in *Georgics* 2. 98–108, is the briefest and least systematic of the three, and he does not distinguish different wines, such as Lesbos, from different grape varieties, such as Aminean and Bumastus (the latter primarily a TABLE GRAPE). There are so many varieties, he concludes, that no one knows the number.

Only Democritus knew how many grape varieties existed, Pliny says (14. 20), but his account does not survive. Pliny himself announces that he will give us only the most important vine varieties. Pride of place among the Italian grapes goes to the Aminean, which has five subvarieties, then to the Nomentan, and third comes the Apian, which has two subvarieties and is the preferred grape of Etruria. All other vine varieties, Pliny asserts confidently, are imports from GREECE. Of these, the Graecula, from Chios or Thasos, is as good as the Aminean. Eugenia is good but only when planted in the COLLI ALBANI. Elsewhere it does not produce good wine. The same goes for Rhaetic, which grows well in a cool climate, and the Allobrogian, which apparently ripens well in frost. These last three grape varieties produce wines which go lighter with age. The remaining varieties Pliny mentions are ones that he judges to be without distinction as wine grapes.

Columella agrees with Pliny for the most part but there are differences (3. 2. 7–31). He regards the Aminean as the best grape and puts the Nomentan second. He also recommends the Eugenian and Allobrogian wines, with the same reservation as Pliny, and the Apian. Then he mentions other varieties which are noted for their productivity rather than their flavour. He does not think highly of the Rhaetic, and he does not rank the Graecula with the Aminean. Vines were still being imported: Columella mentions three grapes which have only lately come to his notice so that he cannot give an opinion on their wines and also another grape which he says is a recent Greek import named Dracontion. Columella's aim is not to give a long and comprehensive list, for that would be impossible (he quotes Virgil's words, *Georgics* 2. 104–6). One should not quibble about names, he concludes, and, knowing that a variety can change out of all recognition if it is planted somewhere new, one should not approve a new grape until it has been tried and tested.

Columella's remarks indicate that farmers were prepared to experiment with new varieties, some of them imported from Greece. Some varieties were probably brought over with the Greek colonists from the 8th century BC onwards, others were growing in Italy long before they arrived. A Greek name is not a guarantee of Greek origin: some Greek names may be names given to Italian grapes which the Greeks of Sicily and southern Italy used when they started producing wine in their colonies. If so, these names reflect no more than the fact that the Greeks exploited the potential of these grapes commercially before the natives did.

H.M.W.

André, J., 'Contribution au vocabulaire de la viticulture: les noms des cépages', *Revue des études latines*, 30 (1952), 126–56.

McGovern, P. E., *Ancient Wine* (Princeton and Oxford, 2003).

McGovern, P. E., Fleming, S. J., and Kat, S. H. (eds.), *The Origins and Ancient History of Wine* (New York, 1995).

Tchernia, A., *Le Vin de l'Italie romaine* (Paris, 1986).

Ancient World. See Ancient ARMENIA, ASIA MINOR, CANAAN, CHINA, EGYPT, GREECE, INDIA, IRAN, MESOPOTAMIA, PHOENICIA, ROME, SUMER.

Andalucía, or **Andalusia**, the southernmost of Spain's autonomous regions, encompassing eight provinces and the DO regions of JEREZ, MÁLAGA, MONTILLA-MORILES, SIERRAS DE MÁLAGA, and CONDADO DE HUELVA (see map under SPAIN). Andalucía is the hottest part of Spain and has traditionally been associated with strong, alcoholic wines which have been exported from the Atlantic port of Cádiz since the PHOENICIANS first established their trading links around 1100 BC (see SPAIN, history). Wine continued to be produced during seven centuries of Moorish domination when Andalucía became one of the most prosperous parts of southern Europe. Since the 16th century, however, when cities such as Seville, Granada, and Córdoba were stepping-stones to the new colonies in SOUTH AMERICA, Andalucía has become one of the most impoverished regions of Spain.

Many wines of Andalucía bear a strong resemblance to each other, and particularly to SHERRY, which has fashioned the region's wine industry since the city of Jerez was won back from the Moors in 1264. Most are FORTIFIED, although grapes from the arid plateau around Córdoba and Jaén are often so rich in natural sugar that they do not require the addition of spirit to reach an ALCOHOLIC STRENGTH of between 14 and 18%. Until laws were tightened up following the foundation of the Jerez Consejo Regulador in 1934, wines from other parts of Andalucía would frequently find their way into sherry blends. Prince Alfonso de Hohenlohe's groundbreaking venture up in the Ronda hills, with an estate devoted to producing red and rosé table wines that first won acclaim in the late 1990s, opened up new perspectives for Andalusian wine which have been most convincingly confirmed in Granada province, where fine-wine estates have sprouted on the slopes of Sierra Nevada and around Ronda. R.J.M. & V. de la S.

Anderson Valley, cool California wine region and AVA on the western slope of the coastal mountain range 80 miles north of San Francisco. See MENDOCINO.

animals can cause serious damage in the vineyard, most obviously but not exclusively by eating grapes and foliage. Any reductions in foliage can prejudice fruit RIPENING and wine quality, and encourage sunburn.

Most mammals may be kept out by fencing, but fences have to be sunk into the soil for smaller, burrowing animals, and high and cantilevered for animals as large and mobile as kangaroos. Deer, rabbits, rodents, raccoons, and wild boar are some of the most common vineyard animal pests, but baboons can pose a threat in South Africa and ETHIOPIA, as can monkeys in JAPAN, hippos in Ethiopia, bears in Canada, kangaroos in Australia, and badgers in the UK, while rattlesnakes can present a danger to vineyard workers. Some vine-growers in New Zealand, on the other hand, deliberately use a combination of electric fencing and sheep to achieve judicious LEAF REMOVAL. Animals of relevance to wine production other than HORSES are referred to in VINE PESTS.

M.J.E. & R.E.S.

Bettiga, L. J., (ed.), *Grape Pest Management* (3rd edn, Oakland, Calif., 2013).

Anjou, important, revitalized, and varied wine region in the western Loire centred on the town of Angers, whose influence once extended all over north west France. Anjou was the birthplace of Henri II, and its wines were some of France's most highly regarded in the Middle Ages (see LOIRE, history). It was the DUTCH WINE TRADE, however, that developed the sweet white wine production of the region in the 16th and 17th centuries, and it would be some centuries before the citizens of Paris rather than Rotterdam had the pick of each Angevin vintage. White grapes predominated until the 19th century, when the Anjou vignoble reached its peak and PHYLLOXERA arrived. Subsequently a wide variety of less noble grape varieties were planted, including a number of HYBRIDS, although Chenin and Cabernet Franc with some Cabernet Sauvignon are now the lynchpins, with the total vineyard having shrunk by a half from its peak. Rosé is by far the most important of the wines with Anjou in their name, then red, with Anjou Blanc produced on a relatively small scale.

The region is relatively mild, being influenced by the Atlantic and protected by the woods of the Vendée to the south west. Rainfall is particularly low here, for the land between here and the ocean is unremitting flat, with annual totals of just 500 mm/19 in.

The GROLLEAU vine, and the sickly **Rosé d'Anjou** it all too often produced, are in retreat, although better vineyard management and an increase in the proportion of wine vinified by the négociants has resulted in an improvement in average quality. Much more refined, and incredibly long-lasting, is rosé **Cabernet d'Anjou**, made from Cabernet Sauvignon or, much more likely, Cabernet Franc. It can be quite sweet but usually has very high acidity which can preserve it for decades and makes it an interesting partner for a wide range of savoury dishes.

Cabernet Franc represents about one vine in three in Anjou and is increasingly favoured by growers there, encouraged by the creation in 1987 of the serious red wine appellation **Anjou-Villages**. The best area for such reds immediately south of Angers in the Coteaux de l'Aubance was given its own appellation **Anjou-Villages Brissac** in 1998. Lighter reds are produced as **Anjou Gamay**, from the Gamay grape of Beaujolais, with **Anjou Rouge** as the catch-all appellation for lighter, often quite crisp, red wines, although some excessively tannic wines result when growers draw off too much juice—and fruit—to make rosés.

Of dry white wines, **Anjou Blanc** is the most common, and is most successful when produced on the SCHIST and carboniferous rock close to the river. The wine must contain at least 80% Chenin Blanc, but Chardonnay, and Sauvignon, are allowed in the blend. Tiny amounts of sweet white **Anjou-Coteaux de la Loire**, made exclusively from Chenin Blanc, are also made. A significant and exciting development since the late 1990s has been the emergence of a new, high-quality style of dry Chenin Blanc in the Anjou, often using prime Layon sites to produce healthy, golden Chenin that is picked by hand in successive passages through the vineyard at full maturity before being fermented and then aged in 400 l double-barriques with a partial malolactic fermentation. Within the Anjou region are certain areas which have produced white wines of such quality that they have earned their own appellations—Coteaux de l'AUBANCE; BONNEZEAUX; Coteaux du LAYON; QUARTS DE CHAUME for sweet wines and SAVENNIÈRES for dry wines—many of them very fine indeed.

See also LOIRE, including map.

annual growth cycle of the vine. See VINE GROWTH CYCLE.

año, Spanish word for year. Some wines, particularly RIOJA, were once sold without a VINTAGE year but with the number of years' AGEING prior to bottling indicated on the label. **Ano** is the Portuguese word.

Ansonica, alternative name for Sicily's white INZOLIA grape used particularly in the Tuscan Maremma, where it can produce wines of real character.

Antão Vaz, white grape increasingly favoured by winemakers in the ALENTEJO, southern Portugal, where it is now producing sound, full-bodied VARIETAL wines and is used for blending with tarter varieties such as ARINTO. Total 2010 plantings were 1,209 ha/2,987 acres.

anther, the pollen-bearing part of the STAMEN of a flower such as that of the vine. Each of the five anthers of the grape has sacs in which a large number of pollen mother cells develop into pollen grains, about two to three weeks before FLOWERING. The small, dry grains of POLLEN are released, possibly before the CALYPTRA or flower caps have fallen (see POLLINATION). In deliberate VINE BREEDING stamens and caps are removed early, before caps would normally fall, to prevent self-pollination and permit deliberate cross-pollination. B.G.C.

anthesis, another word for FLOWERING.

anthocyanins, members of a complex group of natural phenolic GLYCOSIDES (see also PHENOLICS and FLAVONOIDS) responsible for the colour of black and red grapes. They are also responsible for the colour of red wines, both as wine components and as precursors of PIGMENTED TANNINS and other derived pigments which are formed through reactions of anthocyanins with other wine components. Anthocyanins are common in the plant world and are responsible for the red to blue colours of leaves, fruits, and flowers. The word comes from *anthos*, Greek for 'flower', together with the Greek-derived 'cyan' blue.

The particular anthocyanins found in grapes are limited in number, with mixtures of pigment molecules varying from species to species and from grape variety to grape variety. Indeed, chemical determination of the particular mixture of pigments present in an unidentified grape berry can aid vine identification. Pure VINIFERA varieties have mostly anthocyanin pigments with only one molecule of glucose (monoglucosides), while many of the AMERICAN VINES used in breeding ROOTSTOCKS and AMERICAN HYBRIDS also have significant amounts of anthocyanins with two molecules of glucose (diglucosides; a fact which greatly aided detection of non-*V. vinifera* wine in France in the mid 20th century; see University of BORDEAUX).

Anthocyanins have another important characteristic. They are capable of changing form, depending upon the PH, or degree of ACIDITY, of the medium in which they are dissolved, the different forms being red, blue, and colourless. In general, the more acid the grape juice or wine, the greater the degree of ionization of the anthocyanins (giving a higher proportion of the red flavylium cation), and the brighter red the colour; as the acidity decreases, the proportion of colourless and blue forms increases. In mildly acidic conditions, anthocyanins are also bleached by SULFUR DIOXIDE. At wine pH values, grape anthocyanins should be mostly in colourless forms unless the pigments are stabilized by CO-PIGMENTATION or through conversion to derived pigments including PIGMENTED TANNINS (see below).

The anthocyanin pigments are formed in the grapevine by a sequence of metabolic steps and are first visible when the berry begins to expand. The onset of this stage in the vine's metabolism is called VERAISON and is characterized by rapid growth and accumulation of sugar in the berry together with the first flush of colour in the berries.

The concentration of the pigments in the grape skin increases as the level of sugar increases in the grapes during ripening. The increase is intensified if sunlight falls on the berries, that is, if the berries are in an open CANOPY MICROCLIMATE. Anthocyanin production during ripening is very temperature-dependent and is also strongly influenced by the MACROCLIMATE. During veraison the anthocyanin pigments are formed and sequestered in the berry skins' outer cell layers in all but a few dark-berried grape varieties which have a portion of the pigment present in the pulp of the berry as well as in the skin (see TEINTURIERS).

One important operation during the FERMENTATION of most red wines, therefore, is to transfer the anthocyanin pigments from the skin cells to the wine. Colour transfer is achieved by keeping the skins adequately mixed with the fermenting wine (see MACERATION).

One might reasonably expect that the pigments in the new wine would be identical to those found in the grape skin. This may be the case for a few hours, but once the anthocyanins are mixed with the other phenolics as well as the many products of fermentation, they begin a series of reactions leading to a great diversity of derived pigments and colourless molecules. Derived pigments are classically assimilated to pigmented tannins arising from the addition of tannins to anthocyanins, either directly or through condensation reactions with ALDEHYDES. However, they also include rather small molecules formed by the reaction of anthocyanins with other wine constituents such as ACETALDEHYDE or PYRUVIC ACID, or hydroxycinnamic acid derivatives. Moreover, most of these reaction products are themselves unstable and the list of derived pigments found in wine keeps expanding, covering a wide range of colours. Within a few years, only traces of the relatively simple monomeric anthocyanins remain. With wine ageing, polymers containing anthocyanin molecules may become larger and form aggregates so that some of them exceed their solubility in the wine and are precipitated as SEDIMENT. See AGEING.   A.D.W., B.G.C., & V.C.

Cheynier, V., 'Flavonoids in wine', in O. M. Andersen and K. R. Markham (eds.), *Flavonoids: Chemistry, Biochemistry and Applications* (Boca Raton, Fla., 2006), 263–318.

de Freitas, V., and Mateus, N., 'Formation of pyranoanthocyanins in red wines: a new and diverse class of anthocyanin derivatives', *Analytical and Bioanalytical Chemistry*, 401/5 (2011), 1463–73. doi: 10.1007/s00216-010-4479-9.

Monagas, M., and Bartolome, B., 'Anthocyanins and anthocyanin-derived compounds', in M. V. Moreno-Arribas and C. Polo (eds.), *Wine Chemistry and Biochemistry* (New York, 2009).

anthracnose, one of the FUNGAL DISEASES of European origin which affects vines. It is also known as bird's eye rot or black spot. The disease is spread worldwide but is a particular problem in humid regions, as in the eastern UNITED STATES. Before the introduction of DOWNY MILDEW and POWDERY MILDEW, it was the most serious grape fungal disease in Europe, but since BORDEAUX MIXTURE was introduced in 1885 it has been controllable. The disease is caused by the fungus *Elsinoe ampelina*. Small black lesions are produced on the leaves and this area can die and drop out so that the leaves look as though peppered with gunshot. Small dark-coloured spots are also produced on young shoots, flower cluster stems, and berries. Anthracnose can reduce both the YIELD and quality of the fruit. The disease can be controlled by FUNGICIDES applied early in the growing season.   R.E.S.

Antinori, one of Italy's most important wine producers, based in TUSCANY. The modern wine firm was founded by brothers Lodovico and Piero Antinori in 1895, although the Antinori family can trace their history in the wine trade back to 1385, when Giovanni di Pietro Antinori enrolled in the Vintners Guild of Florence. Like the vast majority of the Florentine nobility, the Antinori were, for centuries, producers of wine on their substantial country properties.

The work of the 19th-century brothers was continued by Piero's son Niccolò, who extended the house's commercial network both in Italy and into foreign markets and purchased the Castello della Sala estate near ORVIETO in Umbria. The house developed a certain reputation for its white wines, sold under the Villa Antinori label, and for its Chianti, made in a soft and fruity style. Although the family fortunes flourished, Antinori was only a medium-sized operation in 1966 when Piero Antinori, the son of Niccolò Antinori, took over.

By the early 1990s, he had increased the annual production fifteen-fold, giving the house a commanding position in Tuscany, based on both the excellent quality of all the firm's wines at various price levels and, above all, on the innovative work of Antinori and its OENOLOGIST Giacomo Tachis in creating Tignanello, the prototype SUPERTUSCAN; Solaia, which, together with SASSICAIA (initially marketed by the Antinori and whose development was assisted by Tachis), showed the potential for outstanding Cabernet in Tuscany; and Cervaro, a white wine produced at the Castello della Sala based on Chardonnay grapes and, then unusual for Italy, BARREL FERMENTED.

Although it is firmly anchored in Central Italy, where its vineyard holdings were 1,475 ha/3,643 acres in 2014, Antinori has expanded steadily, securing holdings in every important or upcoming Italian wine region: Montenisa in FRANCIACORTA; the historic house of Prunotto in BAROLO; and Tormaresca, a large-scale operation in PUGLIA.

Internationally Antinori spread its wings quite early on, often through JOINT VENTURES, the most important of which is Antica in Napa Valley in 1993. (It was originally named Atlas Peak, now a BRAND acquired by ACCOLADE.) This was followed in 1995 by Col Solare in a joint venture with Ste. Michelle, in WASHINGTON state. In 2007, again in a joint venture with Ste. Michelle, the legendary Stag's Leap Winery of Napa Valley was acquired. Tuzko Bátaapáti in Hungary had been acquired in a joint venture with Fonterutoli's Lapo Mazzei in 1991. Meridiana in MALTA, producing INTERNATIONAL VARIETIES, was established in 1992, followed by Vitis Metamorfosis, a joint venture with Halewood in ROMANIA, and Haras de Pirque in CHILE's Maipo Valley.

Piero's brother Lodovico Antinori independently created the internationally famous Supertuscans ORNELLAIA and the all-Merlot Masseto at his own estate near BOLGHERI (now owned by the Antinoris' great rivals the FRESCOBALDI). With their sister Ilaria, the brothers have developed the Tenuta di Biserno project at Bibbona just north of Bolgheri. Lodovico, long a fan of Sauvignon Blanc, independently produces one in MARLBOROUGH, New Zealand, with Mount Nelson Estates.   W.S.

antioxidants. For their role in protecting must and wine against the effects of OXYGEN during winemaking and wine AGEING, see GLUTATHIONE, SULFUR DIOXIDE, ASCORBIC ACID, NITROGEN, and CARBON DIOXIDE. For their importance in the effects of wine consumption on HEALTH, see FLAVONOIDS and RESVERATROL.

AOC stands for APPELLATION D'ORIGINE CONTRÔLÉE, France's famous denomination for its best wines, sometimes known as Appellation Contrôlée (AC). In 2010, as a result of EU reforms introduced in 2008, this was superseded by Appellation d'Origine Protegée (AOP), France's PDO, but many continue to use the term AOC.

Aosta, or the **Valle d'Aosta** (**Vallée d'Aoste** to the region's many French speakers), is Italy's smallest region (see map under ITALY). The long, narrow valley formed by the River Dora Baltea as it courses through the mountains of Italy's extreme north west is Italy's connecting link to France and Switzerland and to the north of Europe beyond. As a consequence, wine labels may be written in either Italian or French.

In this rugged alpine landscape the vineyards, planted on HILLSIDES flanking the Dora Baltea, are frequently TERRACED on dizzyingly steep slopes. No more than 18,000 hl/475,000 gal of wine qualifying as DOC is produced from a total of 462 ha/1,140 acres of vines, with 300 ha qualified to produce DOC wines, in an average year. Despite such minuscule production levels, the region has no fewer than seven subzones suffixing a single overarching DOC, Valle d'Aosta, while a host of INTERNATIONAL and local varieties may appear on labels as single varietals.

At the crossroads between northern and southern Europe, the Valle d'Aosta has found itself with an extremely rich diversity of vine varieties. Native regional and other Italian varieties include NEBBIOLO, DOLCETTO, PETIT ROUGE, FUMIN, VIEN DE NUS, Prëmetta, Moscato di Chambave, and PRIÉ for Blanc de Morgex. French varieties include PINOT NOIR, GAMAY, SYRAH, GRENACHE, PINOT GRIS or Malvoisie, PINOT BLANC, and CHARDONNAY. There is also the ARVINE of Switzerland and the MÜLLER-THURGAU of Germany.

The three most important local varieties are Petit Rouge, which is the main ingredient in Chambave, Enfer d'Arvier, and Torrette; Prié Blanc in Blanc de Morgex; and Nebbiolo in Arnad-Montjovet and Donnas, which between them account for more than one third of the region's DOC production.

For such a small region, production has been in the hands of CO-OPERATIVES, which have a good reputation but have been joined by an association of small producers, Viticulteurs Encaveurs Vallée d'Aoste, aiming at reviving ancient local viticultural practices and favouring INDIGENOUS VARIETIES.

The most interesting wines are the Nebbiolo-based Donnas or Donnaz and the neighbouring Nebbiolo-based Arnad-Montjovet, as well as the family of fruity Petit Rouge reds such as Enfer d'Arvier, Torrette, and Chambave Rosso. But in the early 21st century its delicate alpine Chardonnay drew attention, as well as the minerally Blanc de Morgex et de La Salle

from some of the highest vineyards in Europe, up to 1,200 m/3,937 ft. The latter is made from ungrafted vines (PHYLLOXERA does not survive at such high ELEVATIONS) trained in a low PERGOLA. Thanks to the elevation, the grapes retain acidity well and fine TRADITIONAL METHOD sparkling wines are made. This acidity is also key to the region's relatively numerous sweet wines. The region's main challenge for the future is to retain its highest-quality steep vineyards when faced with an ageing population.   W.S.

Gallino, F., *Vino in Valle* (Torino, 2013).

aoûtement, French term for CANE RIPENING derived from *août*, French for August, the month in which it generally takes place in the northern hemisphere. The closest English term is periderm (shoot bark) formation. Careful observation shows that the first vineyards to start *aoûtement* and where it proceeds rapidly, are those which produce the finest wine. This is because early and rapid *aoûtement* indicates a modicum of WATER STRESS, as well as generous plant levels of CARBOHYDRATES, both of which contribute to rapid fruit RIPENING. *Aoûtement* has therefore been incorporated into vineyard SCORING systems used to predict wine quality.
                                                                    R.E.S.

Apera, registered in 2012 as the name to replace Sherry for Australian wines previously thus named. At the same time, Fino, Amontillado, and Oloroso were replaced by the more prosaic, but decidedly less Andalucian, Dry, Medium Dry, Medium Sweet, Semi-Sweet, and Sweet.

aperitifs, drinks served before a meal to 'open' (from the Latin *aperire*) the digestive system and stimulate the appetite, of which VERMOUTH and similar drinks are archetypal. Wines commonly served as aperitifs are dry, white, and not too alcoholic: CHAMPAGNE or any dry SPARKLING WINE; FINO and MANZANILLA sherry; MOSEL wines up to SPÄTLESE level of sweetness; less rich ALSACE whites; MUSCADET, CHABLIS, and virtually any light, dry, still white wine without too much oak or alcohol. Customs vary nationally, however, and the French have customarily served spirits, FORTIFIED WINES, VINS DOUX NATURELS, VINS DE LIQUEUR, and sweet wines such as SAUTERNES before meals. A common all-purpose aperitif, apparently acceptable to French and non-French alike, is the KIR, or *vin blanc cassis*, as well as a blend of white wine and sparkling water sometimes known as a spritzer. The port trade serves white port as an aperitif, sherry producers a dry oloroso or fino, too many amateurs a full-bodied Chardonnay.

aphids, small insects of the *Aphidiodae* family that feed by sucking the juices from plants. Several species of aphids attack grapes, but

apart from PHYLLOXERA, they seldom cause serious damage in vineyards.   M.J.E.

apical dominance describes plant growth which is greater at the apex of a stem or shoot, suppressing lateral growth further away from the apex, a physiological attribute which helped grapevines survive in forest habitats. In viticulture, the term describes preferential BUDBREAK for the buds nearest the cut end of the CANE, which grow earlier and more strongly than those below. To encourage fruitfulness along the entire cane and avoid staggered RIPENING, some viticulturists use an arched cane TRAINING system to promote mid-cane budbreak, bending the cane so that the middle section is higher than the base and the apex, but the benefits are not universally acknowledged. Movement of HORMONES in the cane prior to budbreak affects these growth responses.   R.E.S.

AP number, or **Amtliche Prüfungsnummer**, adorns the label of every bottle of German QUALITÄTSWEIN. This 10- to 12-digit number is an outward sign that the wine has passed GERMANY's much-vaunted official testing procedure, which involves submitting samples of the wine to ANALYSIS and a BLIND TASTING test in which the wine is checked for FAULTS by a changing panel of fellow winemakers and other tasters. The test is hardly the most stringent procedure; the pass rate is well above 90%. The first digit signifies which of the country's testing stations awarded the AP number (1 for Koblenz, 2 for Bernkastel, 3 for Trier—all three in the MOSEL-SAAR-RUWER—4 for Alzey in RHEINHESSEN, 5 for Neustadt in the PFALZ, 6 and 7 for Bad Kreuznach in the NAHE, where wines from SAALE-UNSTRUT and SACHSEN were also tested in the mid 1990s). The next code signifies the location of the vineyard. The penultimate pair of digits is the most significant, the bottler's own code, which supplies a unique identification of the particular lot. If a vintner has bottled two or more wines of otherwise identical labelling (same site, Prädikat, and degree of dryness) this number is often used to distinguish them. The final two digits signify the year in which the wine was tested.

apoplexy, vine disease. See ESCA.

appellation. See CONTROLLED APPELLATION.

Appellation Contrôlée, short for **Appellation d'Origine Contrôlée (AOC)**, is France's CONTROLLED APPELLATION, renamed Appellation d'Origine Protegée (AOP) in response to the EU reforms of 2008 (see PDO). This much-imitated, prototypical, and inherently protectionist system of designating and controlling her all-important geographically based names applies not just to wines but also to spirits such as cognac, armagnac, and calvados, as well as to many foods. It is administered by the INAO, a powerful Paris-based body which also controls the less restrictive denomination Indication Géographique Protégée or IGP (formerly VIN DE PAYS). AOP/AOC wines represent 46% of French wine production (ten-year average to 2013), IGP 28%.

History

France's role as a wine producer had been gravely affected by the viticultural devastation caused by POWDERY MILDEW, DOWNY MILDEW, and PHYLLOXERA in the second half of the 19th century (see FRANCE, history). Fine wines were available in much-reduced quantity, but the LANGUEDOC and ALGERIA had become vast factories for the production of very ordinary wine at very low prices. Laws passed in the first two decades of the 20th century were aimed at bringing an end to the ADULTERATION AND FRAUD that was by then widespread. These were based simply on the principle of geographical DELIMITATION, and specified particular areas within which certain wines had to be produced. Bordeaux, Banyuls, and Clairette de Die were among the first; disagreement about exactly which districts should be allowed to produce France's most famous sparkling wine led to riots (see CHAMPAGNE, history).

It rapidly became clear, however, that France's famous wines depended on more than geography. The wrong grape varieties and careless winemaking would not result in a suitable expression of these carefully delimited TERROIRS. By 1923, Baron le Roy, the most influential and well-connected producer of CHÂTEAU-NEUF-DU-PAPE, was implementing in his part of the southern Rhône a much more detailed set of rules including not just geographical delimitation but a specification of permitted VINE VARIETIES, PRUNING, and vine-TRAINING methods, and minimum ALCOHOLIC STRENGTH.

The French Appellation Contrôlée system evolved into a national reality in the 1930s when economic depression, widespread cultivation of HYBRIDS, and a serious wine surplus increased the incentive for wine merchants to indulge in nefarious blending. The producers of genuine Pommard, for example, had a very real interest in limiting the use of their name to themselves. In 1935 the INAO was created with the express mission of drawing up and enforcing specifications for individual AOCs, which broadly followed the Châteauneuf prototype, and in principle banned hybrids from AOC wine. The great majority of the appellation regulations for France's most famous wines and spirits are therefore dated 1936 or 1937, although they have been continuously revised since. The VDQS category, created in 1949 for wines deemed just below AOC status, was abolished after the 2010 vintage.

The legal powers of the INAO, both within France and in its dealings with the EU and beyond, were strengthened substantially in 1990, when it took the conscious decision to try to build the future of French wine on the concept of geographical appellations (eschewing even the mention of vine varieties on the main label) and adopted the specific aim of preserving agricultural activity in certain zones. But in 2004, when France's wine exports were clearly in significant decline and domestic sales stagnant, this policy was dramatically modified to make French wine labels easier to understand and the wines themselves more competitive in the global market. The aim was to raise the average quality of AOC wines and introduce some new regional Vin de Pays categories (most now rebadged as IGP). The INAO continues to wage war on all misused GENERIC wine and spirit names but, as an increasing number of French wine producers find the detailed AOP/AOC regulations too restrictive, the supremacy of the AOC system is no longer unchallenged orthodoxy.

The regulations' scope

The INAO's detailed regulations for its more than 300 AOP/AOCs are already voluminous and constantly revised, covering the following aspects for each appellation. The regulations for the IGP category (with 75 listed in 2014) are similar but generally less restrictive.

Production area All those communes allowed to produce the wine in question are listed, but within each of these communes only certain plots of land are deemed worthy, details of which are lodged with each commune's all-important *mairie* or administrative centre. Vines grown elsewhere within the commune are normally entitled only to be sold as a less specific appellation, an IGP, or VIN DE FRANCE.

Vine varieties The permitted grapes are specified in great detail, along with permitted maximum and minimum proportions. Vineyards will generally be inspected to ensure that the correct varieties are planted. Many appellation regulations include long lists of half-forgotten but once-significant local varieties. White grape varieties are permitted to a certain extent in a number of red wine appellations. See full details in Appendix 1.

Ripeness and alcoholic strength Specific MUST WEIGHTS are generally cited for freshly picked grapes before any CHAPTALIZATION, generally given in g/l of sugar. A maximum ALCOHOLIC STRENGTH after any chaptalization, if allowed, is also usually specified.

Yields Control of YIELDS is a fundamental tenet of the Appellation Contrôlée system, however sceptical some New World viticulturists are of the concept. The maximum yields cited in the regulations, the *rendement maximum autorisé* (RA), were almost routinely increased, however, by about 20% throughout the 1970s and 1980s thanks to a frequently used special derogation known as the *plafond limite de classement* or PLC. In 1993, the INAO announced its intention to curb yields (as the EU has done) but this has not been adopted with noticeable enthusiasm. The PLC has been abolished but it is still possible to request a derogation (up or down) if the application can be justified—by the VINTAGE weather conditions, for example.

This section usually includes information on a minimum VINE AGE allowed for AOP/AOC production.

Viticulture This usually specifies a minimum VINE DENSITY, the approved PRUNING regime down to the number of buds, and the permitted vine-TRAINING SYSTEM. In some southern appellations the (limited) extent to which IRRIGATION is allowed may be outlined.

Winemaking This long section may well specify such aspects as compulsory DESTEMMING, method of ROSÉ WINEMAKING (usually by SAIGNÉE), although there is generous use of the vague phrase *usages locaux*.

Pros and cons

France's Appellation d'Origine Contrôlée designation is in general a more reliable guide to the country's best wines than, for example, the QBA category of supposedly superior wines in Germany, the liberally applied DOC designation in Italy and Portugal, and its DO counterpart in Spain (all of the last three modelled on the AOC system). The French system is by no means perfect, however. Policing remains a problem, and the Service de la Répression des Fraudes is probably understaffed. Contraventions of the regulations, particularly over-chaptalization, or chaptalization and ACIDIFICATION of the same wine, are difficult to detect (although a complex bureaucracy controls overproduction). Misdemeanours are only very rarely publicized, and then usually only as a result of local politics.

A more serious disadvantage of the Appellation d'Origine Contrôlée system is the extent to which it stifles experimentation. In dramatic contrast to the New World, vinegrowers may plant only certain vine varieties. Those wishing to experiment are often restricted to selling the wine not merely as an IGP, but as Vin de France.

The Appellation Contrôlée regulations were drawn up not with a clean slate and a pencil devoted to the best possible options, but to legitimize the best current practices.

It is also fanciful to suggest that every wine produced within an appellation inevitably uniquely betrays its geographical provenance.

Few blind tasters would unhesitatingly identify a CÔTES DU MARMANDAIS, for example. And then there are the catch-all appellations such as BORDEAUX AOC, ALSACE, and CHAMPAGNE, whose quality variation is simply frustrating.

The full regulations for every appellation can be found online: www.inao.gouv.fr.

apps, wine. See INFORMATION TECHNOLOGY.

Apremont, named CRU just south of CHAMBÉRY whose name may be added to the eastern French appellation Vin de SAVOIE. This is the largest cru in Savoie and its wines are typically light, dry whites made from the local JACQUÈRE grape.

Apulia, Anglicized form of the Italian region PUGLIA.

Aquileia, or Friuli Aquileia, a lesser-known DOC from FRIULI comprising the entire province of Udine. The white must consist of at least 50% FRIULANO, while the Rosso must contain at least 50% REFOSCO dal Peduncolo Rosso. The balance in both can be any authorized variety, most of which are INTERNATIONAL VARIETIES, potentially compromising the wines' originality.

W.S.

Arab poets. The classical period of Arab civilization spawned a rich corpus of BACCHIC poetry which had its roots in pre-Islamic Arabia (AD 530 until the emergence of ISLAM). Wine was celebrated as one of a number of standard topics in the composite odes of pre-Islamic poetry. In its treatment, wine was underpinned by the rigid ethical code (*Muruwwa*, approximately *virtus*) that predicated the desert *Weltanschauung*, and thus gave voice to exaggerated notions of generosity. It was in this period, when wine was often compared to the saliva of women (to represent a kiss), that the seeds of the erotic register of later Arabic wine poetry were sown. Interestingly one such simile is even contained in the ode composed by Hassān Ibn Thābit, the Prophet's bard, to celebrate the conquest of Mecca shortly before Muhammad's death in AD 632. Traditional Muslim commentary, basing itself on the Islamic injunction against the consumption of wine, suggests that the simile is interpolated. But this argument is not entirely convincing; for Islam, while criticizing aspects of the culture of poetry, seems to have had little effect in censoring the poetic repertoire.

The essential model provided by this bedouin canon, which constituted the corner-stone of Arabian cultural and tribal identity, was absorbed virtually in its entirety into the nascent Islamic/Arab community; for this reason wine survived as a theme. Soon its treatment came to stand independently from the composite ode and, whilst the descriptive elements of Bacchic verse were based around a core of inherited imagery, a new defiant and anti-religious attitude was introduced that is reflected in a verse by the poet from al-Tā'if, Abū Mihjan al-Thaqafi: 'If I die bury me by the vine, so that its roots may satiate the thirst of my bones.' This solipsistic dirge, that shows the poet to have acquired notions of life after death, ignores the new imposing religious eschatology of the nascent Islamic community.

Islam did, of course, have a profound effect on the poets of Bacchism; for after a time, usually with the onset of old age, they would repent of their erring in pious Islamic terms. To replace them there was always a new generation of libertines, who were commonly men of high standing, such as governors and even, during the Umayyad period, caliphs. Al-Walīd ibn Yazīd, one of the last Umayyad caliphs (d. AD 744), was a notorious hedonist (although perhaps maligned by later Abbasid propaganda) whose attitude in some Bacchic fragments is aggressively atheistic: 'Give wine [to drink] . . . for I know there is no Hell-fire!' In this period Bacchism became an urban phenomenon, notably amongst the libertines of Kufa (modern Iraq), and was eventually to gain a high profile in the Abbasid court circle of Baghdad, particularly during the reign of al-Amīn (reigned AD 809–13). This son of Hārūn al-Rashīd is famous in literary history as patron and boon companion of the great ABU NUWAS (d. AD 814).

In his wine poetry, Abu Nuwas synthesized a variety of impulses to produce sometimes complex poems which articulated all the issues relevant to the social dialectic of wine culture in an Islamic society: he expanded both the fantastical and mimetic descriptive repertoire of the *khamriyya*; he fused the Bacchic and erotic registers of poetry to create well-wrought seduction poems that gave voice to a sceptical world-view; he structured his poems in such a way as to support the simple rhetoric in defence of wine; finally, with literary sleights of hand, he reconciled the hedonistic ethic with Islamic dogma. It has rightly been said about the finest of these poems that they parallel the impulses and complexity of some English Metaphysical poetry.

From the descriptions of Abu Nuwas and other poets we gain a detailed picture of Bacchic culture: we are familiarized with the wine itself (its provenance, preparation, colour, bouquet, taste, and age—although here a mythological dimension enters into the poet's expression); its effects (physical, psychic, and spiritual); the personages (the boon companion, the pourer, the singing girl, the taverner (Jewish, Christian, or Persian), and the servant girl); the decorum of drinking (generosity, aristocracy, the quest for freedom, the Satanic pact, and, ultimately, belief in divine mercy); the venues of drinking (the caliphal palace, the tavern, the monastery, gardens, and the vine itself); finally we learn about the variety of vessels (for drinking: glass, silver and gold cups or goblets, ewers; for storage: jars, tanks or casks, and leather bottles).

After Abu Nuwas, poets who treated wine (throughout the Islamic lands, including al-Andalus in southern Spain) had little new to say; they simply reworked the imagery he had established, whilst discarding the careful structure of his finest poems. It was only amongst Sufi mystics that a new, important dimension was added to Bacchic poetry. Foremost amongst these was Ibn al-Fārid (d. 1235). For these ascetics DRUNKENNESS represented divine intoxication; they simply borrowed the imagery of Bacchic culture to articulate the otherwise ineffable states of mystical experience. Although Abu Nuwas himself was a ribald, Sufi sensitivity is perhaps foreshadowed in some of his most ethereal descriptions of wine:

[Last night I could not sleep] so give me to drink of the maiden wine who has donned the grey locks of old age whilst still in the womb;
A wine which [when poured] is replenished with youth . . .
One preserved for a day when its [seal] is pierced, though it is the confidant of Time itself;
It has been aged, such that if it were possessed of an eloquent tongue,
It would sit proudly amongst people and tell a tale of an ancient time . . .

P.K.

'Khamriyya', The Encyclopaedia of Islam (new edn), vol. iv (Leiden, 1978), 998–1009.

Aragón, known as **Aragon** in English. Once a powerful kingdom whose sphere of influence stretched from the LEVANTE in the west as far as NAPLES and SICILY in the east, Aragón is now one of Spain's 17 autonomous regions. In the north east of the country, it spans the broad valley of the River Ebro which is flanked by mountains on either side (see map under SPAIN). The north is dominated by the Pyrenees, which feed water on to the arid Ebro plain. To the south and east the climate becomes progressively extreme as the land rises towards the central Spanish plateau.

The wines of Aragón used to be strapping potions with natural alcohol reaching levels as high as 17 or 18%. Red wines, made predominantly from the GARNACHA grape, were mostly sold in bulk for blending. However, four DO regions designated between 1980 and 1990 changed the profile of Aragón wines. SOMONTANO in the lush Pyrenean foothills east of the city of Huesca chose to almost entirely forgo INDIGENOUS grape varieties, a choice which has proven controversial and not always fruitful in terms of sales, but south of the Ebro wines from the DOs of CAMPO DE BORJA, CARIÑENA, and CALATAYUD have benefited from investment in modern winemaking technology, which has revolutionized the style of modern-day

Garnacha, sometimes blended with Tempranillo or Syrah. Throughout much of Aragón, large CO-OPERATIVES continue to dominate production, buying in grapes from smallholders.

R.J.M. & V. de la S.

Aragonez, once spelt **Aragónêz**, occasionally spelt **Aragones**, the traditional name for the Spanish red grape variety TEMPRANILLO in the ALENTEJO region, where it makes concentrated, deep-coloured reds. See under its northern Portuguese name TINTA RORIZ for more information.

Aramon is now, happily, a remnant of French viticultural history, a vine variety that burgeoned throughout the LANGUEDOC in the second half of the 19th century (the many who made their fortunes from wine around Béziers then were known by some as the **Aramonie**) and was displaced as France's most popular only in the 1960s by CARIGNAN. For decades, particularly after the development of railway links with the populous north of France, Aramon vines were encouraged to spew forth light, everyday wine-for-the-workers that was with good reason called *petit rouge*.

Aramon's great attribute, apart from its prodigious productivity of up to 400 hl/ha (22.8 tons/acre), was its resistance to POWDERY MILDEW, the scourge of what were France's established wine regions in the mid 19th century. The variety was taken up with great enthusiasm and rapidly spread over terrain previously considered too flat and fertile for viticulture. GALET notes that its effects were particularly noticeable in the Hérault, where, between 1849 and 1869, the land under vine more than doubled, to 214,000 ha/528,800 acres.

Unless planted on poor soils and pruned extremely severely, Aramon produces some of the lightest red wine that could be considered red, notably low in alcohol, extract, and character. To render the *rouge* sufficiently *rouge* for the French consumer, Aramon had invariably to be bolstered by such red-fleshed grapes as one of the TEINTURIERS, most often ALICANTE BOUSCHET. This gave Aramon a grave disadvantage compared with the deep, alcoholic reds of North Africa, and its popularity began to decline in the mid 20th century, a trend exacerbated by its toll from the 1956 and 1963 frosts. Aramon suffers from the twin disadvantages of budding early and ripening late and is therefore limited to hotter wine regions.

The total French area planted with Aramon shrank from 34,700 ha/85,700 acres in 1988 to 2,126 ha/5,251 acres in 2010.

Aramon Gris and **Aramon Blanc**, lighter-berried mutations, can still (just) be found, particularly in the Hérault.

Galet, P., *Dictionnaire encyclopédique des cépages* (Paris, 2000).

Robinson, J., Harding, J., and Vouillamoz, J., *Wine Grapes: A Complete Guide to 1,368 Vine Varieties Including their Origins and Flavours* (London, 2012).

Arany Sárfehér, white grape of HUNGARY traditionally grown on the sandy Great Plain for table grapes and sparkling wines. Its 2012 total of just over 1,000 ha/2,500 acres produced light, tart wine.

Arbin, CRU on the steep, warm, south-facing slopes east of CHAMBÉRY whose name can be added to the eastern French appellation Vin de SAVOIE. Use of the Arbin cru name is restricted to wines from the local MONDEUSE grape, some of the region's most concentrated reds.

Arbois, the most important appellation in the JURA region in eastern France and named after the region's main wine town. The scientist Louis PASTEUR was brought up in the town, and conducted observations here when invited to turn his attention to wine health. In the 20th century the town was made famous by wine producer Henri Maire, who did much for the revival of the Jura wine region after the Second World War and died in 2003. The wine company he founded still owns over 250 ha/618 acres of Jura's vineyards but since 2010 it has been owned by a Luxembourg-based financial institution and quality had not yet been demonstrably revived by late 2014. About half of Arbois is red, making it the most important Jura red wine appellation. The light-coloured POULSARD grape is a speciality of the subappellation of Arbois-Pupillin, where it is named Ploussard, and well-structured wines are made from TROUSSEAU in the warmer sites around the village of Montigny-les-Arsures. White wines are often VARIETAL Chardonnay made in unoxidized, Burgundian style, increasingly vineyard-designated. The old synonym *Naturé* is sometimes used for the local SAVAGNIN, especially to designate fresh, lemony, or so-called 'floral' white wines made from the variety, distinguishing them from the more usual oxidative styles. The oxidative styles may be a blend of Savagnin with Chardonnay, or Savagnin on its own, and they culminate in the nutty and long-lived VIN JAUNE. An Arbois 1774 was so much appreciated when tasted in 1994 that a second bottle was sold in 2011 for €57,000. VIN DE PAILLE is made under the Arbois appellation, whereas TRADITIONAL METHOD sparkling wine made is sold as CRÉMANT du Jura. See also MACVIN DU JURA.

Wines made from grapes grown within the commune of Pupillin have the right to the appellation **Arbois Pupillin**. Pupillin is home to one of the 'fathers' of the natural wine movement in France, retired wine producer Pierre Overnoy, whose estate is run today by Emmanuel Houillon.   W.L.

Arbois Blanc is also a synonym for the MENU PINEAU vine variety of the LOIRE.

arbour, an overhead trellis structure used for VINE TRAINING, particularly in southern Italy. See TENDONE.

archaeology has been of great importance in tracing the ORIGINS OF VINICULTURE and plays a part in the ancient history of most wine regions. For a discussion of the techniques available and some of the more significant finds, see PALAEOETHNOBOTANY. For some more specific aspects, see also AMPHORAE and the CELTS.

Ardèche, region of France on the right bank of the Rhône between the main concentrations of vineyards which constitute the northern and southern RHÔNE Valley in south-east France and now the name of an IGP for a wide range of generally VARIETAL wines. Reds are generally light. Chardonnay and to a lesser extent Viognier have been particularly successful here. Louis LATOUR of Burgundy was a pioneer, notably with Grand Ardèche Chardonnay, and the Vignerons Ardechois is a co-operative with high standards.

Areni, the characteristic red wine grape of ARMENIA, and also the name of a village on the border with Azerbaijan where the remains of a 4000 BC winery were identified in 2011. Wines are medium bodied with real zip.

Argaman, ISRAELI 1972 cross of CARIGNAN and the Portuguese SOUSÃO which produces dark, light-bodied red.

Argentina, the most important wine-producing country in South America, and, since the 1990s, one of the most dynamic wine producers in the world. Producing almost 15 million hl/396 million gal in 2013, Argentina is one of the world's six biggest wine producers. Almost a quarter of all Argentine wine is exported.

Of the country's 224,064 ha/553,674 acres of vineyard in 2013 (an increase of more than 10% on the 2000 total area), 92% grew grapes for wine. The shift from quantity towards quality has been particularly marked this century, with the proportion of dark-skinned grapes growing from 40 to nearly 50%. Argentina's famous pink-skinned varieties (mostly the CRIOLLAS and CEREZA) fell from 31 to less than 25%. By 2012, 66% of vineyards were planted with high-quality wine grapes, the rest being those deemed low quality or TABLE GRAPE varieties. (In 1990, only 37.5% of vineyards were planted with high-quality wine grapes.) Considerable investment in new vineyard areas, improved winemaking technology, and continued RESEARCH and innovation have all played a part in the transformation of Argentine wine from rustic ferment to world-class quality.

History

Unlike North America, where explorers and early settlers found VITIS *labrusca* growing in abundance, South America depended on the Spanish colonizers for imported European VINIFERA vines. The vine probably arrived in Argentina by four different routes. The first was directly from Spain in 1541 when vines are thought to have been cultivated, without great success, on the Atlantic coast around the river Plate. A year later, seeds of dried grapes were germinated as a result of an expedition from Peru to the current wine regions immediately east of the Andes. Another expedition from Peru in 1550 also imported vines to Argentina, while the fourth and most important vine importation came from Chile in 1556, just two years after the vine was introduced to Chile's Central Valley. (See SOUTH AMERICA, history, for more details.)

One of the most important grape varieties systematically cultivated for wine in South America was almost certainly the forerunner of Argentina's CRIOLLA CHICA, California's MISSION, and Chile's PAIS, which were to be the backbone of South American wine production for the next 300 years. Although Argentina was settled from both the east and the west, it was in the foothills of the Andes that the Jesuit MISSIONARIES found the best conditions for vine-growing. The first recorded vineyard was planted at Santiago del Estero in 1557. The city of Mendoza was founded in 1561 and vineyards in the province of San Juan to the north were established on a commercial scale between 1569 and 1589. Soon after that, in 1595, King Felipe II of Spain, who ruled over most of Central and South America, banned the production of wine, except by the Catholic Church. This was intended to protect Spanish wine producers and their exports to Mexico and was therefore not particularly enforced in South America, so secular producers remained, and the wine industry thrived. Contrary to popular belief, this heralded a period of almost 300 years (from the second half of the 16th century to the beginning of the 19th century) of sustained growth, innovation, and a search for wine quality, largely thanks to the powerful MONKS AND MONASTERIES.

Wine soon became the main economic activity, with the wealthiest families of Cuyo and the north west of Argentina—in what are today the provinces of Mendoza, San Juan, La Rioja, and Salta—engaged in wine production, either secularly, or through family members who were clergy, or both. Export routes to the cities of Buenos Aires, Córdoba, and Santa Fe to the east, to Bolivia to the north, and to Chile to the west were developed from the early 16th century, which created a dynamic proto-bourgeoisie, particularly in the Cuyo region. During this time, the most important grape variety cultivated was Uva Negra, later known as Criolla Chica, which was to be the backbone of South American wine production for the next 300 years. This and other old varieties, including various Muscats, were widely grown. Torrontés Riojano, the result of a natural crossing of Criolla Chica and Moscatel de Alejandría, dates from the 18th century.

By the skilful use of dams and IRRIGATION channels, originally established by the native population, the early settlers were able to produce sufficient wine to meet the needs of a growing population and they also learned how to produce wine that could stand up to a journey of perhaps 45 days by cart from Mendoza to Buenos Aires. The 18th century saw major changes. To ensure quality and ageing potential, particularly for wines that had to endure long journeys, wines were FORTIFIED or, sometimes, heated, a precursor of PASTEURIZATION. Some wines were even made, like SHERRY, under FILM-FORMING YEASTS. Wine PRESSES changed from being made of leather and/or oak to being built with bricks, lime, and slate. The first record of FERMENTATION vessels made from OAK instead of the old clay AMPHORAE, dates from 1740. The first AMPELOGRAPHIC studies were carried out during the second half of the century. The first winery census by the government took place in 1780. This was a period of dynamic growth, driven by solid institutions, commerce, peace, and the conjunction of a blooming bourgeoisie and the clergy's desire to make the most out of God's creation. By the end of the century, Cuyo was by far the most important wine region in Argentina, with about 8,000 people in the cities of Mendoza and San Juan, almost 300 vine growers, and a total annual production of 13 million litres of wine.

Then the wine scene went into a decline that lasted for almost 100 years. In 1767 the Jesuits were expelled from Spain and its colonies by royal decree and their estates were either abandoned or seized by the Spanish crown. A civil war lasted for much of the early 19th century. It was no longer safe to transport wine and wine was no longer the most important economic activity of the region.

Some good things happened, however, such as the introduction of glass BOTTLES, from 1820. The best example is the well-documented story of General San Martín, the son of a vine grower and probably Argentina's first wine CONNOISSEUR. After returning from leading a long campaign in Chile and Perú against the Spanish royalists, he went back to Mendoza and organized a dinner with some of the most important people of his time. At this meal, in 1823, he poured one of his favourite wines from Mendoza, and one from a renowned producer of Málaga—transposing the labels before doing so. By the end of the evening, when all attendees had proclaimed the virtues of the bottles with the Málaga label, he had demonstrated two things: that the wines from Mendoza compared well with those of Spain, and that they could age for eight years or more—which was the time his bottles had spent in his underground cellar during his crusade against the Spanish empire.

The second half of the 19th century saw Argentina enjoy a period of relative stability and prosperity built on exports of agricultural and cattle products. Many of those who had fled to Chile returned to Cuyo. Among them was Domingo Faustino Sarmiento, who subsequently became governor of San Juan, and then president of Argentina. He campaigned for the creation of an agronomy school, including viticultural research and a vine NURSERY used to gradually improve vineyards, under the direction of a Frenchman exiled in 1851. Under his direction top-quality French varieties, including Malbec, were imported—before the arrival of PHYLLOXERA in Europe, incorporating much of the genetic material that was later lost in Europe. Thus Torrontés, Malbec, and many high-quality varieties were already established in Argentina before a significant wave of European immigrants of the late 1800s and early 1900s further enriched Argentina's viticulture.

In 1885 the RAILWAY between Buenos Aires and Mendoza was completed, lending still greater importance to the vineyards in the foothills of the Andes. The immigrants, many from wine-producing areas of Italy, Spain, and France, brought with them many new vine varieties and their own regional vine-growing and winemaking skills. The foundations for Argentina's mammoth domestic wine industry were laid. This had interesting implications. Unlike many New World wine regions where winemaking was restricted to an elite, the origin of Argentina's modern era viticulture was popular. Even today there are over 25,000 vineyards, with an average size of less than 9 ha/23 acres. And the immigrants brought their wine-drinking culture with them, which turned Argentina into one of the largest domestic markets in the world, despite having a relatively low population. Today, Argentines drink about 75% of the national crop, a figure that has remained relatively stable.

By the early 20th century, Argentina was the seventh wealthiest developed nation in the world, but the subsequent economic depression and political crisis led to a disastrous drop in the export price of its primary products, and then a steep decline in foreign investment. The peso was often devalued almost routinely. While the landowning classes continued to

ARGENTINA

0   250   500 km

Wine-growing regions

PARAGUAY

Jujuy

Salta

Cafayete

Formosa

BRAZIL

Tucumán

Santiago del Estero

Catamarca

La Rioja

Santa Fe

San Juan

Córdoba

URUGUAY

Mt Aconcagua

Mendoza

Mendoza

San Luis

Buenos Aires

PACIFIC OCEAN

CHILE

Andes Mountains

Parana

Buenos Aires

La Pampa

Neuquén

Colorado

Río Negro

ATLANTIC OCEAN

Chubut

MENDOZA

North Oasis   Lavalle

La Consulta
Mendoza

Luján de Cuyo   San Martín

Las Compuertas   Maipú   Junín

Agrelo   Perdriel   Santa Rosa

Tupungato   Ugarteche   East Oasis

Gualtallary   Rivadavia

Vista Flores   Tunuyán

Altamira   San Carlos

Uco Valley

San Rafael

South Oasis

Andes Mountains

0   100 km

---

prosper for some time, or salted away their capital overseas, there was growing unrest among the largely disenfranchised, poorly paid urban masses. When General Juan Domingo Perón came to power in 1943 he appealed directly to the workers with promises of rapid industrialization, better working conditions, and organized, government-controlled unions.

For a while Argentina's fortunes revived, but in the mid 1950s Perón and his ambitious and charismatic wife Eva were deposed by the military. From then on a succession of opportunistic military governments led the country into spiralling decline. The urban masses created an unprecedented market for wine so that quantity not quality became the imperative.

Most producers were content to supply cheap, rustic VINO DE MESA to a domestic market that boasted the third-highest per capita consumption of wine in the world. In the late 1960s and early 1970s, at a time when the UK was drinking approximately 3 litres per capita per year and the Americans even less, the Argentines, despite all their troubles, were quaffing

90 litres of wine per head. By 1996 that figure had dropped dramatically to 41 litres per capita, and has finally stabilized at around 25 litres.

Throughout the 1960s, 1970s, and 1980s Argentina grew increasedly isolated, and suffered from social and political unrest, military governments, violence, stifling bureaucracy, corruption, war, and disastrous economic management. Accumulated inflation during the 1970s was over 1,400%, and over 8,000% during the 1980s. In 1983 Argentina returned to being a democratic country and has remained one ever since.

Faced with a dramatic drop in home consumption, added to the pressing need to earn foreign currency, the more enlightened producers decided to go upmarket and in the late 1980s, for the first time, gave serious consideration to the possibilities of exporting. A peak of hyper-inflation in 1989, however, prompted President Raúl Alfonsín out of office, who was replaced by Carlos Menem, inaugurating a period of political and economic stability not experienced for decades. Under his administration, business confidence in Argentina's future was revitalized at home and abroad, and encouraged investment in a wine industry where time had stood still (see also CHILE). Vineyards had been modernized during the 1980s, and technology and expertise were incorporated during the 1990s. Argentina's wine sector was ready to export but a law that artificially pegged the Argentine peso to the US dollar, resulted in, first, an overvalued peso at the end of the 1990s which made Argentine wines too expensive, followed by prolonged recession, and a 300% devaluation in 2001/02. While being traumatic for the people of Argentina, this presented a great opportunity for its wine industry since prices were then highly competitive, and both exports and foreign investment soared.

A 1980s VINE-PULL scheme had reduced the total vineyard area by a third, with Malbec a specific and dramatic casualty just before its potential was realized. Argentina's total vineyard fell from 314,000 ha/775,580 acres in the early 1980s to 205,000 ha/506,350 acres in 1993 before a new wave of high-quality varieties were planted.

Climate

Argentina's wine regions are widely dispersed, but are almost entirely confined to the western strip of the country bordering the foothills of the Andes, where the climate is CONTINENTAL, with the four seasons clearly defined. The vineyard area extends from the 23rd to the 42nd parallel in the south. Apart from the southern, largely fruit-growing areas of the Río Negro and Neuquén, the climate is semi-desert with annual rainfall rarely more than 250 mm/10 in.

Summer temperatures vary from 10 °C/50 °F at night to as much as 40 °C/104 °F during the day. Summers are hot in the regions of San Juan (except for the high elevation valleys of Pedernal and Calingasta), La Rioja, Catamarca, and the east of Mendoza (Santa Rosa, Rivadavia, San Martín, and Lavalle). In the Calchaquies Valley (Cafayate), upper Mendoza (Luján de Cuyo), Uco Valley (Tupungato, Tunuyán, and San Carlos), and Río Negro, summers are TEMPERATE to warm, making them Regions II and III in the Winkler system of CLIMATE CLASSIFICATION. In winter, temperatures can drop below 0 °C/ 32 °F with occasional light snowfalls. Heavy winter snow in the high Andes is important as this ensures plentiful supplies of particularly pure water for the irrigation systems on which the vines depend.

Total annual rainfall just east of the Andes is concentrated on the summer months, which encourages growth, but it seldom exceeds 300 mm/12 in a year with 200 mm/8 in being the average. Early summer HAIL, or *piedra*, is the main risk to the vines—as many as 6% of Argentine vineyards are netted against hail—together with FROST. It is customary in Mendoza to own vineyards in different parts of the province to minimize the risk of hail damage. As a result, and even though single-vineyard and TERROIR-DRIVEN wines are increasingly important, 100% varietal blends of wines from different parts of the province are also common.

The air is dry and particularly unpolluted. Vine FLOWERING may occasionally be adversely affected by a hot, dry, very strong wind called *zonda*, which blows down from the west mainly in late spring and early summer. Grapes almost invariably reach full maturity and the lack of humidity reduces the risk of FUNGAL DISEASES, resulting in very healthy vineyards and obviating the need for frequent and costly SPRAYING. Vineyards are typically sprayed much less often in Argentina than elsewhere, making ORGANIC VITICULTURE relatively easy. Full RIPENESS is easily achieved and CHAPTALIZATION is not allowed.

Regions

See map.

Mendoza In the far west of the country, only a (substantial) mountain range from Santiago in Chile, this is by far the biggest and most important wine-growing province in Argentina, accounting for more than 70% of all Argentina's wine production, although the area planted has declined from a peak of 255,000 ha/629,850 acres in 1980 to 159,137 ha/394,500 acres in 2013. The Andes dominate the western skyline, with Mount Aconcagua, at 6,960 m/22,837 ft, the highest mountain in the Americas. Vineyard elevations range between 600 to 1,600 m (1,970 to 5,249 ft) above sea level.

Provinces, such as Mendoza, are divided into departments, which in turn are subdivided into districts, and, in turn, into single vineyards. The most important wine-producing areas in and around Mendoza are:

The North Oasis and the East Oasis: Low elevation, warm weather areas, specializing in big volumes and entry-level wines—although some high-quality wines are also made here, mostly with Tempranillo and Bonarda. The area comprises the departments of Lavalle, Las Heras, Santa Rosa, La Paz, San Martin, and Rivadavia.

Luján de Cuyo: In the upper Mendoza Valley at elevations between 800 and 1,100 m (2,640 and 3,630 ft). Average rainfall is about 190 mm/ 7.2 in a year and the mean annual temperature is 15 °C/37.5 °F. Together with the department of Maipú, they form what the locals call *Primera Zona,* or 'first zone', Mendoza's most traditional high-quality region, just south of the city limits. It was here that Argentina's first CONTROLLED APPELLATION was created for Malbec in 1993, and this is where most of the traditional and renowned wineries of Mendoza are located—even if most of them also have vineyards in other parts of the province. The main districts in Luján de Cuyo are Las Compuertas, Vistalba (which are the two that reach the highest elevations),—Agrelo, Perdriel, Ugarteche, Chacras de Coria, and Mayor Drummond.

Maipú department: Just east of Luján and also south of the city, is slightly warmer because of its lower elevation. Cruz de Piedra, Barrancas, Russell, Coquimbito, Lunlunta, Fray Luis Beltrán, and Maipú districts (as in Luján, there is a department and a district within it with the same name).

San Rafael and General Alvear departments: The southernmost wine region of Mendoza, balances lower elevation with higher latitude, and focuses on classic varietals. This does not enjoy the reputation of some other areas, perhaps due to a higher incidence of hail and greater distance from the city, but it can still produce high-quality wines.

Valle de Uco (or Uco Valley): The rising star of Argentina, and arguably the most fashionable wine region in the country. It comprises the departments of Tupungato (with its districts El Peral, Anchoris, La Arboleda, Tupungato, and Gualtallary), Tunuyán (Vista Flores, Los Árboles, Los Sauces, Los Chacayes), and San Carlos (Altamira, La Consulta, Eugenio Bustos, El Cepillo), ranging between 1,000 and 1,600 m/ 3,280 and 5,250 ft. Its cooler weather, very poor SOILS, good DRAINAGE, and continuous breeze are responsible for particularly healthy vines which result in low YIELDS, and full-bodied wines with high natural acidity. Malbec, Chardonnay, and Cabernet Franc are reaching new heights here.

Pink-skinned grapes, notably CRIOLLA GRANDE and CEREZA, account for about a fifth of all Mendoza plantings and are used for inexpensive wine and GRAPE CONCENTRATE. Red wine grapes account for more than half of all plantings. Malbec predominates with a total of 31,169 ha/77,020 acres, almost double the area planted in 2003. The variety called Bonarda in Argentina (identical to CHARBONO) comes next with 15,803 ha/39,050 acres, and several producers have started to call it Bonarda Argentina to differentiate it from Italian wines and vines with the same name. Cabernet Sauvignon is also significant, and features with Malbec in many a top blend. Next most plamted red wine grapes are Syrah, Tempranillo, Merlot, Sangiovese, and Pinot Noir, demonstrating the mix of French, Italian, and Spanish cultural influences that characterize Argentina. PEDRO GIMÉNEZ is the most planted white wine grape, but attention is focused on Chardonnay, with 5,305 ha/ 13,108 acres planted particularly in the sophisticated, very high vineyards of the Uco Valley. Also important are the ubiquitous Torrontés Riojano, Chenin Blanc, and Sauvignon Blanc. Sémillon was traditionally Mendoza's white wine grape and is now making a comeback thanks to producers such as Mendel and Ricardo Santos. Over 150 different grape varieties are planted in Mendoza.

San Juan Argentina's second biggest wine-producing region had 47,741 ha/117,970 acres of vineyards in 2013. The capital of the province, San Juan, is 150 km/90 miles north of Mendoza. The climate at these lower elevations and latitudes is much hotter than that of Mendoza, with summer temperatures of 42 °C/107 °F not uncommon and with rainfall averaging only 150 mm/6 in per annum. TEMPERATURE variation is also much lower.

For long the home of high-yielding pink varieties, especially Cereza, whose high sugar content made them ideal for wine blending, concentrating, or for selling as fresh TABLE GRAPES or RAISINS, San Juan has been developed as a producer of better quality wine since the late 1990s. A rapid reduction in the volume of wine produced has already taken place and is likely to continue, especially for red-skinned grapes such as BONARDA and SYRAH, which has become the province's emblematic red, with 3,032 ha/7,492 acres planted (50% more than Malbec). Good-value basic reds are made with these two varieties. The region also produces smaller quantities of perfectly acceptable sherry-style wines, interesting Viognier, Chardonnay, and Pinot Gris in whites, and Petit Verdot and Tannat in reds. It also provides the base for most of Argentina's BRANDY and VERMOUTHS. The vast majority of San Juan's wine comes from Tulum Valley at an elevation of 650 m/ 2,132 ft just south of the capital city. Better quality wines can be found, as in Mendoza, further west at higher elevations, where the Ullum-Zonda Valley at 850 m/2,788 ft is producing good Reserva-level wines. Even higher, Pedernal (1,100 m/3608 ft) and Calingasta

(1,500 m/4,921 ft) valleys in the south west of the province are starting to produce world-class wines and have the potential to take San Juan to the next level.

La Rioja Historically the oldest of Argentina's wine-producing provinces, La Rioja had 7,287 ha/18,006 acres of vineyard in 2013, of which Torrontés Riojano was planted on a total of 2,145 ha/5,300 acres. La Rioja is little-known abroad, partly because almost the entire production of the province is crushed by the giant Co-operativa La Riojana in the town of Chilecito. They make Torrontés in several styles, including an aromatic dry one, a late harvest, and even a refreshing sparkling version. In recent years, a handful of new, small-scale producers have started to produce more interesting wines in higher elevation vineyards from lesser known areas such as Famatina and Chañar Muyo. This has increased interest in the region even if, as elsewhere, irrigation water can be scarce in parts.

Salta, Jujuy, Tucumán, and Catamarca The Calchaquí Valley crosses these far northwestern provinces. Catamarca used to have the biggest area under vine, but the province of Salta recently overtook it, and now boasts 2,932 ha/7,245 acres of vineyards, thus becoming the fourth most important wine-producing province after Mendoza, San Juan, and La Rioja. Viticulture in Catamarca is still rustic and lacking identity. Jujuy and Tucumán are starting to make quite interesting wines but on an extremely small scale. Salta is the most significant and widely recognized province for wine in this part of the country. It also has some of the world's highest vineyards (see ELEVATION) near the town of Payogasta. Donald Hess's Colomé Altura Máxima vineyard is planted at 3,111 m/ 10,206 ft.

Not just Salta but the entire Calchaquí Valley benefits from more than 300 days of sun per year, as well as considerable exposure to WIND and ULTRAVIOLET RADIATION. Even the lower vineyards in Salta are at 1,650 m/5,413 ft, and because of this elevation, the vine is forced to protect itself from extreme weather, resulting in lower YIELDS and thick skins, which produce concentrated, full-bodied wines that are also extremely fragrant. Promising varieties include Malbec, Cabernet Sauvignon, Bonarda, Syrah, and, particularly, Tannat, which expresses itself quite differently here compared with URUGUAY and MADIRAN. For white wines, Torrontés Riojano is very much at home and around Cafayate in the Calchaquies Valley it produces particularly aromatic, full-bodied, dryish whites. The vineyards lie between 24 and 26 degrees LATITUDE, with soils not dissimilar to those of Mendoza, but with a MESOCLIMATE that ensures a combination of good sugar levels at harvest

(from 21 to 25 °BRIX) and above-average TOTAL ACIDITY, thereby ensuring a wine of depth and balance. The main wine region in Salta is the lively tourist resort of Cafayate. Other small areas such as Tolombón, Colomé, Molinos, Yacochuya, and Tacuil also have excellent potential. With its stylish hotels and infrastructure, unspoilt colonial architecture, Andean food, impressive landscapes, and hearty wines, this area provides world-class TOURISM experiences.

Río Negro, Neuquén, and Chubut This southern area of Patagonia is much cooler than the higher-yielding areas to the north and, although there were some 3,398 ha/8,396 acres under vine in 2013 split roughly equally between Río Negro and Neuquén, they may not yet have reached their full potential. Neuquén is the result of 21st-century central planning while Río Negro has historically been Argentina's principal fruit-growing district, producing apples and pears in particular, as well as grapes. The cooler climate and heavier soils of the valley, combined with a long, warm ripening season under clear skies, make it ideal for the production of good-quality white wine (notably Torrontés Riojano, Sémillon and, in more recent times, a fairly decent Riesling), a fragrant, less concentrated version of Malbec, and great Pinot Noir, Merlot, and Cabernet Franc. Unlike most Argentine wine regions that are high and relatively close to the Andes, Río Negro province has a quite different topography. The valley is shaped by a river that runs from the west into the Atlantic, forming a green canyon surrounded by arid desert on both sides. Humidity and rainfall are markedly higher than further north. These growing conditions, together with some seriously old vineyards, attracted both Countess Noemi Marone Cinzano and Piero Incisa della Rochetta, from the family that owns SASSICAIA, who respectively established their Noemía and Bodega Chacra projects in the province some years ago. Both are now farmed biodynamically, with exciting results.

Unlike Río Negro, the province of Neuquén had no winemaking tradition whatsoever until very recently when the authorities realized that the province was going to run out of its non-renewable resources. They accordingly constructed an extensive channel that could irrigate about 3,000 ha/7,413 acres of land on which vegetables, orchards, and vineyards have been planted. Bodegas del Fin del Mundo led the project and now several producers make millions of bottles in state-of-the-art wineries, filling them mainly with Sauvignon Blanc, Chardonnay, Pinot Noir, and Malbec.

Last, but by no means least, the legendary Bernardo Weinert, from the eponymous Mendoza winery, has planted Pinot Noir, Chardonnay, Riesling, Gewürztraminer, and other early-ripening vines in the southernmost vineyard of the Americas, El Hoyo de Epuyén in Chubut, between the 42nd and 43rd parallels. This has inspired several others so that by 2014 vineyards totalled about 21 ha/51 acres and some were already producing rather Germanic high-acid, low-alcohol wines.

Buenos Aires, La Pampa, and Córdoba

The Argentine wine map is being redrawn virtually every day. Córdoba, which had 279 ha/690 acres of vines in 2014, had a long tradition of making artisanal wines and has now shifted its focus to high quality. La Pampa, a province known more for its cattle, has suitable vineyard land in the south for its 212 ha/524 acres of vines on the northern border of Patagonia, where Bodega del Desierto, under the supervision of Paul Hobbs of California, is showing the way. And even Buenos Aires province, by the Atlantic Ocean, now has 114 ha/280 acres of vineyards planted in deeper soils, on slopes rather than mountains, and in a MARITIME CLIMATE rather than a continental one. A handful of wineries are already in production, with the giant Trapiche already achieving great results with Pinot Noir and Sauvignon Blanc in its new vineyard close to Mar del Plata, the country's biggest beach resort a few hundred kilometres south of the city of Buenos Aires.

Vine varieties

Red Malbec, the dominant red wine grape that accounts for 16% of all plantings, seems more at home in Argentina than in its CAHORS homeland. From a total of 36,125 ha/89,266 acres of vines come deep-coloured, robust, fruity wines with enough alcohol, weight, and structure to benefit from OAK AGEING, with different expressions in each wine region. Cabernet Sauvignon is popular with Argentine growers, having increased enormously, from under 2,500 ha/6,200 acres in 1990 to 15,982 ha/39,492 acres by 2013. It is making better and better VARIETAL wines, and is typically blended with Malbec in the country's most celebrated bottlings. The second most planted red wine variety in Argentina, with 18,882 ha/46,658 ac, is the increasingly fashionable variety called Bonarda in Argentina (see CHARBONO). Total plantings of Syrah shot up from under 700 ha/1,730 acres in 1990 to 12,992 ha/32,103 acres by 2013, making it Argentina's fourth most planted European variety after Malbec, Bonarda, and Cabernet Sauvignon. It performs best in the hot San Juan province north of Mendoza. A wide range of Italian and Spanish varieties, including Tempranillo, Corvina, and Ancellota, were presumably brought to the country by the many European immigrants, but it is the French Cabernet Franc, Petit Verdot, and Tannat that are currently making waves. Other red wine varieties apart from Merlot, often blended with Cabernet,

include Pinot Noir, which seems to have found its home in Patagonia and the high-elevation vineyards of the Uco Valley.

White Although steadily losing ground, PEDRO GIMÉNEZ (distinct from Spain's PEDRO XIMÉNEZ) is still Argentina's most-planted light-skinned grape variety, with 11,773 ha/29,091 acres grown in 2013, particularly in Mendoza and the province of San Juan, where it is used mostly in basic blends. It is also used for making grape concentrate, which Argentina exports in vast quantities, particularly to JAPAN. The second most-planted light-skinned variety in 2013 was TORRONTÉS Riojano with almost 7,885 ha/19,500 acres, followed by Chardonnay with 6,394 ha/15,799 acres. Other white wine grapes, in order of importance, are Moscatel de Alejandría, Chenin Blanc, Sauvignon Blanc, Torrontés Sanjuanino, Ugni Blanc, Viognier, Sémillon, Sauvignonasse, Pinot Gris, Riesling, and others. The country's most distinctive white wine grape is Torrontés Riojano in its various forms, which can produce a (relatively) light wine with a strong, floral, MUSCAT aroma. Use of the right strains of yeast—a particularly effective local strain has been identified in La Rioja and is now being widely commercialized for this variety—and careful TEMPERATURE CONTROL during fermentation can result in a Torrontés of universal appeal. Originally it was planted almost exclusively in the northern province of Salta, particularly in the Calchaquies Valley and around Cafayate, but it can now be found in the province of Mendoza, where it is often used for blending, and increasingly in the Uco Valley, where it is producing steely, more structured, linear wines. Chardonnay is the wine that everyone wants to produce and the Argentines are no exception, particularly with an eye to the US and UK markets. Chardonnay has proved to be particularly well suited to parts of Argentina. Its own so-called Mendoza CLONE (see MILLERANDAGE) was developed at DAVIS in California and is widely planted in Australia and elsewhere.

Pinks These are the grapes which account for more than a quarter of all vines planted in Argentina whose skins at full ripeness are distinctly pink. CRIOLLA GRANDE, Criolla Chica, and CEREZA are some of Argentina's oldest varieties. Both Criollas and Cereza are extremely productive varieties of which one bunch on a well-irrigated vineyard can weigh as much as 4 kg/9 lb. They are typically planted in the hotter, flatter, most heavily irrigated vineyards. Moscatel Rosada is another important pink-skinned variety, of which there was a total of 7,084 ha/17,504 acres in 2013. The wine produced from these varieties is usually very deeply coloured white, occasionally pink, often quite sweet, and sold at the bottom end of the market, either in bulk or in litre bottles or cardboard cartons, as

everyday wine within Argentina, or blended with basic Malbec to produce a light red.

Alcalde, A. J., *Cultivares Viticolas Argentinas* (Mendoza, 1989).

Viticulture

Warm, dry summers; clear skies; poor, alluvial soils; and pure water for irrigation is a promising combination for viticulture. The drop in domestic sales in the 1970s and 1980s led to a search for new areas more suitable for the production of better-quality wine and since the 1990s Argentine viticulture has been transformed, with better IRRIGATION techniques, CANOPY MANAGEMENT, methods and timing of HARVEST, incorporation of technology, clonal and MASS SELECTIONS, and studies of the impact of MICROBIAL TERROIR and ULTRAVIOLET RADIATION, for example.

Most vines in Argentina are UNGRAFTED because the biotype of PHYLLOXERA present is a relatively mild one, perhaps because there is a relatively high proportion of SAND in vineyard soils. Some varieties that are vulnerable to NEMATODES, however, tend to be grafted. Rainfall is so low in most of the country that irrigation is a necessity. Traditionally, water was distributed by an intricate network of canals and ditches and then by FLOODING or furrows; Argentina's water distribution system is still one of the best in the world, despite having its origins in the 16th century. In more recent times, the channels of water that flow from the permanently snow-capped peaks of the high Andes have been augmented by deep boreholes. These take water from between 60 and 300 m (196 to 984 ft) below the surface and can produce as much as 250,000 l/66,000 gal per hour. They are used with the more efficient DRIP IRRIGATION systems that now operate on about 20% of Argentine vineyards. In this unique landscape the cultivated areas resemble green oases in the scorched desert surroundings (as in the irrigated vineyards of AUSTRALIA but with the majestic Andes as a backdrop). The vast majority of the soils are of alluvial origin, quite poor, and mostly made of sand and stones. Their structure varies from region to region but a loose greyish sandy texture predominates with substrates of GRAVEL, LIMESTONE, and CLAY. Areas with substrates of GRANITE, QUARTZ, and LIMESTONE are currently being researched. Different forms of CALCAREOUS soils are found in some of the finest terroirs of the Uco Valley, such as Altamira, Gualtallary, and Vista Flores, those that result in increasingly complex and individual wines.

Although the immigrants who arrived in the early 20th century brought with them the vertical *espaldera* TRAINING SYSTEM of low training of vines along three wires, the need for greater volume led most vineyard owners to adopt the productive *parral cuyano* trellis system in the

1950s and 1960s (see TENDONE). As in Chile, however, the classic method is increasingly favoured once more in order to facilitate both CANOPY MANAGEMENT and drip irrigation, although Cereza and Criolla Grande vines are still likely to be *parral* trained. By 2013 roughly half of all vines were *parral* trained, and most of the rest were trained with either high or low VSP *espaldera* systems. Only a very small proportion were either head trained or managed with other systems. Over 40% of vineyards were 25 years old or more, and in Salta there is even a vineyard planted in 1862. Only 20% of vines are under eight years old.

From BUDBREAK to HARVEST takes an average of five months and the long ripening season normally ensures full maturity. The national institute sets the date of the harvest, which usually begins in mid February and, depending on the variety and the region, extends until late April. Special permits have to be obtained to pick any later than the prescribed end date, mostly for late-harvest wines. Itinerant, low-paid grape pickers are no longer plentiful, thanks to the recent dramatic rise in the cost of living, so MECHANICAL HARVESTERS are slowly becoming more common.

Winemaking and labelling

The export-led drive towards improved quality has forced even the biggest producers of cheap wine into a reappraisal of their winemaking techniques in order to supply international demand for sound VARIETAL wines. This is even more noticeable in better-quality wines, which have benefited from new generations of technicians who have been trained abroad, and the input of foreign CONSULTANTS. Locals and foreigners co-operate at all levels. Furthermore, there has been an important cultural change. While old schoolers were secretive and competitive, winery owners and winemakers nowadays get together to taste each other's wines, share experiences and information, and are enthusiastic about wider issues in a sector that is now particularly dynamic.

In terms of labelling, a varietal wine must contain at least 85% of the variety cited, while any variety mentioned on the label must constitute at least 20% of the blend. Reserva wines have to be aged from six months (whites and rosés), to 12 months (reds), and Gran Reserva wines have to be kept twice as long. In European markets, however, as a result of negotiations that have been taking place since 2010, wines are classified either IP (Indicación de Procedencia) for table and regional wines, IG (Indicación Geográfica—see GEOGRAPHICAL INDICATION) for *V. vinifera* wines made from a specific region with certain minimum quality standards, and DOC (Denominación de Origen Controlado), for high-quality wines in which restrictions related to alcohol, winemaking

techniques, yields, ageing, and other criteria apply. Argentina has, so far, two DOCs—Luján de Cuyo and San Rafael—and roughly 90 IGs. So far, the DOCs are used by only a handful of producers. Plans are well advanced for the creation of IGs for areas producing truly distinctive wines, with two Uco Valley locations—Pajare Altamira in San Carlos in the south of the valley and Gualtallary in Tupungato in the west—the most advanced.

Wine trade organization

The majority of Argentina's vineyards are in the hands of specialist grape-growers. Wine producers exert increasing control on the grapes they buy, however, and almost all of them own at least some vineyards.

The big factors in the improvement of Argentina's wines have been the widespread use of foreign consultants, and FLYING WINEMAKERS. Several Argentine winemakers work in the northern hemisphere during harvest, therefore experiencing at least two vintages every year.

Collaboration between private and public sectors has been more successful in Argentina than anywhere else, and has resulted in a promotional plan for Argentine wine up to 2020, and the creation of the Argentine Viticultural Corporation (COVIAR) in which all interested parties are involved.

The great majority of Argentina's wineries, like the country's vineyards, are in Mendoza province, often on the outskirts of the city of Mendoza itself. Some of the most important wineries are still owned by Argentine families: Catena Zapata, López, Bianchi, Lagarde, Lávaque, Goyenechea, Roca, Domingo Hermanos, Toso, Zuccardi, La Rural, Weinert, Luigi Bosca, and even large groups such as Peñaflor or Nieto Senetiner. Others have been bought by large international groups: Navarro Correas (DIAGEO), Finca Flichman (SOGRAPE), Etchart, Graffigna, and Mumm (PERNOD RICARD), and Norton (the Austrian Swarovski family, who also have wine interests in CHINA). Some foreign investment has also gone into developing wineries from scratch. Examples include Chandon and Terrazas de los Andes owned by LVMH, Alta Vista, Monteviejo, Cuvelier Los Andes, Flecha de los Andes, Fabre Montmayou, LURTON, Atamisque, all French-owned; Alto Las Hormigas, AVE, Masi Tupungato, Chacra, Noémia, and Speri, all backed by Italian investors; the Chilean-owned Cruzat, Trivento, La Celia, Kaiken, Renacer, and Doña Paula; Spanish-owned Séptima de Codorniu, Freixenet, and O Fournier; Greek-owned Krontiras, Dutch-owned Salentein and Callia, American-owned Enrique Foster and Viña Cobos, and others. Foreigners have also had a big impact with JOINT VENTURES such as CaRo (Catena + Rothschild) and Cheval des Andes (Ch CHEVAL BLANC and Terrazas de

los Andes). And last, but not least, a largest number of wineries have been started from zero by Argentines—some completely new, some who sold their previous winery only to set up again. Examples include Benegas, La Amalia, Altocedro, Dominio del Plata, Patritti, Familia Schroeder, Huarpe, SinFin, Sophenia, Mendel, Tapiz, De Ángeles, Zorzal, Passionate Wines, and several others. All these producers, and many others, have played a vital part in promoting Argentina to the first world of wine.   A.R.

Anuario Internacional (Buenos Aires, annually).

Goldin, C., *The Secrets of Argentine Malbec* (Buenos Aires, 2004).

Goldstein, E., *Wines of South America* (Oakland, Calif., 2014).

Guía Austral Spectator (Buenos Aires, annually).

Lacoste, P., *Vinos de Capa y Espada* (Mendoza, 2013).

Rolland, M., and Chrabolowsky, E., *Wines of Argentina* (Mendoza, 2003).

www.winesofargentina.org

www.inv.gov.ar

argilo-calcaire, French term commonly used to describe soil that is a mixture of LIMESTONE and CLAY.

argols, another word for TARTRATES.

Arinarnoa, 1956 INRA cross of Merlot and Petit Verdot of which just over 100 ha/247 acres grew in the Languedoc in 2006. It is planted to a very limited extent in several more countries and can produce strong, dark red.

Robinson, J., Harding, J., and Vouillamoz, J., *Wine Grapes: A Complete Guide to 1,368 Vine Varieties, Including their Origins and Flavours* (London, 2012).

Arinto, more precisely **Arinto de Bucelas**, historic Portuguese white grape variety most commonly encountered in BUCELAS in which it must constitute at least 75% of the blend. It is also grown in many other parts of Portugal, notably Tejo and Lisboa. Arinto is respected for its high acidity and can yield wines which gain interest and, sometimes, a citrus quality with age. As an ingredient in VINHO VERDE it is known as Pedernã. Total plantings had fallen to 3,175 ha/7,846 acres by 2010.

Arinto do Dão is a synonym for MALVASIA Fina in DÃO.

Arinto Tinto, Portuguese synonym for Aragonez, or TEMPRANILLO.

Aristophanes, Greek writer of comedies at the end of the 5th century BC. In his plays he extols the hard-working peasant farmer in the fields around Athens. One of his characters is a vine-dresser, or early vineyard worker (Trygaios in *The Peace*), and the goddess of peace is called wine-loving and 'giver of grapes'. Aristophanes criticizes the young for idling and drinking too much. Women also come in for criticism as topers in several of his plays.

H.H.A.

Arlanza, DOP created in SPAIN in 2008 for land between RIOJA and RIBERA DEL DUERO along the Arlanza River, with 450 ha/1,080 acres under vine. Closer in climate to Rioja, it is the source of fresh, fragrant wines from old, often mixed vineyards (see FIELD BLEND) by producers Olivier Rivière and Sabiñares y Viñas.

V. de la S.

arm, viticultural term for that part of the vine's woody framework from which the CANES and SPURS arise. The location of arms depends on the VINE-TRAINING system used. They may be borne along CORDONS, positioned at intervals so that the buds, after PRUNING, are placed to space the bearing shoots desirably. Alternatively, the arms may be positioned on a short HEAD at the top of the trunk as happens with some CANE PRUNING systems. Arm is used interchangeably with cordon in some regions but if both are present, the arm is the shorter and the cordon is the longer.

B.G.C. & R.E.S.

armazém, Portuguese word literally meaning 'warehouse' or 'store'. In the towns of Vila Nova de Gaia (see OPORTO) and Funchal (see MADEIRA), *armazém* are the long, low LODGES where PORT and madeira are left to age.

Armenia, relatively small, mountainous, ex-Soviet republic in the south Transcaucasus. One of the oldest viticultural regions, its ELEVATION compensates for its LATITUDE, which is five to seven degrees more southerly than the famous vineyards of France. Only 10 to 15% of grapes are used for wine. In 2013 Armenia had 17,400 ha/43,000 acres of vineyard and produced 57,000 hl/1.5 million gal of wine (of which two-thirds are red), and 185,000 hl of brandy.

History

The Transcaucasian region, including Armenia, is one of the world's oldest centres of viticulture. Ancient Armenia was much bigger than modern Armenia and in classical times included much of eastern TURKEY, AZERBAIJAN, and GEORGIA in the area between the Black Sea and the Caspian Sea. The vine was an indigenous plant in the valleys of Armenia, where the climate was particularly suitable for it. The wild vine *Vitis vinifera silvestris* (ancestor of the cultivated VINIFERA vine species) was established there over a million years ago. Carbonized or petrified grape pips have been found at several neolithic sites in the Caucasus.

In 2011 it was announced that the earliest 'winery' in the world had been discovered at the cave of Areni I. Dating to *c*.3500–3000 BC, it comprised plaster floors which had been constructed as grape PRESSES to run the juice into underground jars (Armenian *karas*, Georgian QVEVRI) or *pithoi*. Grape remains in the vicinity pointed to the contents of the vessels as wine, and chemical analysis confirmed this. A contemporary cemetery within the cave suggests that the wine was used in burial services for the ancestors. See PALAEOETHNOBOTANY and ORIGINS OF VINICULTURE.

Archaeological evidence has also revealed irrigation canals, wine cellars with processing facilities, and large *karas* dating to the Iron Age. Raisins and grape seeds believed to be reminiscent of the varieties Voskeat, Makhali, and Garandmak cultivated today in the Ararat plain south west of Erevan were unearthed during excavations of the Teishebaini fortress from the 8th century BC. Wine cups and SULFUR sticks used in the 7th century BC were also found in the fortress.

Argishti I (785–753 BC), the king of Urartu (an ancient state which is regarded by modern Armenians as a predecessor of their homeland), made his capital Tushpa into a pleasant garden city planted with vineyards. An inscription of his descendant Rusa II (680–639 BC), who built Teishebaini (modern Karmir Blur), states: 'By command of the god Haldi I have planted these vineyards.' At Teishebaini wine cellars were excavated, with rows of *pithoi* buried up to mid body and stamped with the year of production and the quality of the wine. Herodotus (*Histories* 1. 194, see Ancient GREECE) described the river trade on the Tigris carried on by merchants operating from Armenia all the way downstream by the Assyrians. Transported on circular leather-covered rafts (like the modern *gufas* which could until recently still be seen on the river) was wine (*oinos* and therefore made from grapes; see WINE, etymology) in what he described as palm-wood casks.

But the Ancient Armenians fermented more than grapes. XENOPHON (*Anabasis* 4. 5. 26) describes how during his epic journey through the Near East he found in villages in eastern Turkey, 'also wheat, barley and beans; and barley-wine in *kraters* [see CRATER]. The actual grains of barley floated level with the brim, and reeds of various lengths but without nodes were in the bowls. When you were thirsty, you had to put one of these in your mouth and suck. It was a very strong wine, unless you mixed it with water. Once you got used to it, it was a very pleasant drink.'

In 301 AD Armenia became the first nation to adopt Christianity as the official religion of the state. The Christian faith shaped Armenian culture intimately and wine became not only an intrinsic part of religious rituals (see EUCHARIST) but was also used for medicinal purposes. Old manuscripts confirm Armenia's high level of viticultural development, yet this art often suffered periods of decline due to war and Arab, Turkish, and Persian invasions (see ISLAM).

J.A.B. & A.A.

By the end of the 19th century, Armenia's viticulture was on a small scale. In 1913 vineyards covered 9,200 ha/22,700 acres and after the First World War this was reduced to 5,100 ha. In that period the average area of a peasant farm was just 1 ha. In the 1920s, private wineries were nationalized and amalgamated into the large Ararat wine trust, which later established a network of wine-processing plants in RUSSIA and in UKRAINE.

In 1940, the vineyard area reached 16,300 ha/40,261 acres. In the post-war period grape culture was developed mainly on land that had not been cultivated before, and specialized state farms were established based on collective farms. In 1990, Armenia had 29,000 ha/71,630 acres of vineyards.

Modern viticulture

Bounded by the Small Caucasus in the north and east and by the narrow Ararat Plain in the south west, Armenia grows vines commercially at 400 to 1,700 m (1,300–5,580 ft), the elevation determining climate, which is dry and CONTINENTAL to dry subtropical, the annual rainfall being less than 500 mm/19 in. Summers are so dry that 85% of vineyards need IRRIGATION. Winters are sufficiently severe for 85% of vineyards to need WINTER PROTECTION, and there is a risk of FROST at both the beginning and end of the growing season. Only about 10% of vines are GRAFTED, and roughly three vines in four are grown on a four-wire VERTICAL TRELLIS.

Armenia has five viticultural zones: the Ararat Valley (65% of vineyards and most of the wineries), the foothills of the Ararat Valley (13%), the north east zone (10%), Vaiots Dzor region (10% of vines), and Zangezur region (2%). More than 400 different vine varieties are grown in Armenia, many of them for TABLE GRAPES, but notable wine varieties include the indigenous ARENI, Voskeat, Mskhali, Kakhet, RKATSITELI, Kangun, Akhtanak, Megrabuyr, and Karmrajut.

After a steady decline, wine production has started to recover slowly from a historic low in 2008, thanks in part to an influx of investment in vineyards and modern wine technology from the country's large diaspora. Since the late 1990s demand for Armenian wine has risen considerably, particularly in Russia, which is still Armenia's main export market. With the improvement in quality and the rise of more 'European'-style wines, Armenia is now slowly beginning to export its wines further afield to countries such as China, the US, and France. Areni grapes grown in the Vaiots Dzor region produce the most sought-after wine.

A.A.

armillaria root rot, worldwide FUNGAL DISEASE which lives in woody plant materials in the soil and attacks a wide range of plants including vines. It is sometimes called the mushroom, oak, or shoestring root rot. It is typically a problem on land where vines have replaced trees, and is frequently seen in new California vineyards where oak trees grew previously. Infected vines tend to occur in groups and slowly decline or sometimes die suddenly. The causal fungus, *Armillaria mellea*, produces white fungal mats with a distinct mushroom-like smell under the bark of the vine's lower trunk and roots. The land can be fumigated to ward off this fungus, for which there are no tolerant ROOTSTOCKS.   R.E.S.

Arnaldus de Villanova, sometimes called **Arnaud de Villeneuve**, was a Catalan who died in 1311. He taught MEDICINE at MONT-PELLIER, the most important medical school, with Salerno, in medieval Europe. He had an eventful life, attending the sickbeds of popes and kings and engaging in theological controversy. He was an influential physician, and his writings were still reprinted in the 16th century.

Arnaldus is not interested in wine for its own sake: his concern is with the medical proprieties of wine. One of his books, the *Liber de vinis* ('Book on Wines'), deals exclusively with wine as medicine, but references to wine appear throughout his works. The *Liber de vinis* is short: in the 16th-century editions of the complete works it occupies no more than ten folio pages. To a modern reader it is bound to appear a strange mixture: GALEN and the Arab philosopher Avicenna; alchemy and astrology; some first-hand observation. Arnaldus' medicine draws heavily on the voluminous writings of Galen (129–99 BC), physician to the Emperor Marcus Aurelius, but Galen was a far better scientist. Galen wrote in Greek, but knowledge of Greek was rare in the medieval west: some of his works were, however, translated into Arabic and thence into Latin. Through Moorish Spain, Arabic influence on European influence was strong: hence Arnaldus' references to Avicenna and other Arabic authors.

Arnaldus praises wine as a remedy against melancholy and says that it is good for the liver, the urinary tract, and the veins, because it purifies the blood. He recommends it to the old, especially in winter, because it warms the kidneys as well as the entire body, it reduces the swelling of haemorrhoids, it is beneficial to digestion, gives one a healthy complexion, comforts the mind, and, best of all, slows down the greying of one's hair. Most of his remedies, however, do not involve the drinking of neat or watered wine. He uses wines flavoured with rosemary or borage, recipes which go back to classical antiquity and which were supposed to cure a wide variety of ills; he exploits the antiseptic quality of wine for making poultices and, since the water was not usually reliable, to dissolve other medical substances.

One would not have been safe in Arnaldus' hands. An aside about making wine is spot on, however: the wooden casks in which wine was kept should be clean and free of odours, the grapes should mature properly, and any unripe grapes must be discarded.

He is popularly credited with introducing the first still to France, probably from Salerno, and George (1990) notes that he was granted a patent for his discovery of MUTAGE (which spawned wines such as those now known as VINS DOUX NATURELS) in 1299 from the powerful king of Majorca.   H.M.W.

Lucia, S. P., *A History of Wine as Therapy* (New York, 1963).

Sigerist, H. E., *The Earliest Printed Book on Wine* (New York, 1943).

Thorndike, L., *A History of Magic and Experiential Science*, 7 vols. (New York and London, 1923-57), ii. 841-61.

Arneis, white grape variety and dry, scented VARIETAL wine of PIEMONTE in north west Italy. Originally from ROERO, it was traditionally used to soften the red Nebbiolo grape. Perhaps because of this, it is also sometimes called BAROLO Bianco, or white Barolo, by some of its more fervent admirers. Although the wine has a certain history in Piemonte, it seemed on the verge of disappearing in the early 1970s when only two houses, Vietti and Bruno Giacosa, were bottling Arneis. In the 1980s, however, thanks to growing demand for white wine in Piemonte, particularly from houses more renowned for their Barolo and BARBARESCO, there was an explosion of interest in Arneis, and plantings totalled 969 ha/2,393 acres by 2010. This low-yielding variety ripens in the second half of September and gives wines with subtle if interesting perfumes. Modern winemaking has, in the best cases, dealt with the variety's inherently low acidity. The best examples tend to be unoaked and drunk young. It is not planted anywhere else in Italy, but is planted to a very limited extent in California, Oregon, Australia, and New Zealand. The best producers in Piemonte are Malvira, Deltetto, Cascina Chicco, and Bruno Giacosa.   D.C.G.

Arnsburger, white wine variety developed at GEISENHEIM for sparkling wine and exported to the island of MADEIRA due to an EU-funded project (with a German consultant). Planted on the north side of the island, the productive, disease-resistant variety is used to make rather tart, unfortified, dry white wine with limited local appeal.   R.J.M.

aroma, imprecise tasting term for a relatively simple smell such as that of a grape, fermenting MUST, or young wine. Originally from the Greek word meaning 'spice', it has evolved so that in generally current English it means 'pleasant smell' (as opposed to odours, which may be distinctly nasty). Wine-tasting professionals tend to use the word aroma to distinguish the smells associated with young wines from the more complex aromatic compounds which result from extended BOTTLE AGE, often referred to as BOUQUET. In Australia, the word aroma is often used to refer specifically to VARIETAL characteristics rather than those associated with winemaking or AGEING. Those who distinguish between aroma and bouquet differ as to the point in a wine's life cycle which divides the use of the two terms. For tasters schooled at the University of BORDEAUX, bouquet includes fermentation smells, for example, as well as all those associated with oak ageing and bottle ageing. Others, particularly Burgundians, may refer to grape aromas as primary aromas, fermentation and oak ageing aromas as secondary aromas, and bottle ageing aromas as either tertiary aromas or bouquet. See also FLAVOUR, AROMA WHEEL, FLAVOUR COMPOUNDS, and ESTER.
                    A.D.W.

aroma compounds. See FLAVOUR COMPOUNDS.

aromatics, informal category of white wines made from particularly aromatic grape varieties, a term commonly used in AUSTRALIA and NEW ZEALAND. Typical examples are VARIETAL Gewürztraminer, Pinot Gris, and Riesling. Other particularly aromatic grape varieties include Sauvignon Blanc and Viognier.

aromatized wines. See FLAVOURED WINES.

aroma wheel, graphical representation of TASTING TERMS used for AROMA, devised at the University of California at DAVIS by Ann C. Noble and others in the early 1980s. Her research into sensory evaluation of wine had indicated that there was no general agreement either on terminology or on its application. The aroma wheel was developed to provide a standardized lexicon which can be used widely to describe wine aroma in non-judgemental terms, grouping specific terms which can be defined to provide a basis for communication. In its attempt at clarification and categorization it is used by professionals and provides a good basis on which tasting terms for aroma can be taught to novices, even if with experience, most individuals tend to develop their own terms, which may be just as precise and descriptive. The aroma wheel does not include terms which describe the physical dimensions of a wine (such as 'full bodied' or 'tart').

The extensive use of the wine aroma wheel has led to the development of an analogous mouthfeel wheel to describe the TEXTURE and MOUTHFEEL sensations of red wines.

The **aroma wheel** was devised at the University of California at Davis by Professor Ann C. Noble in an attempt to instil some rigour into wine descriptions.

Source: American Journal of Enology & Viticulture, 38/2 (1987). Copyright © Dr Ann C. Noble and *American Journal of Enology & Viticulture*

Noble, A. C., et al., 'Modification of a standardized system of wine aroma terminology', *American Journal of Enology and Viticulture*, 38/2 (1987).

Arrábida, former IPR in southern Portugal named after the Serra da Arrábida and now part of the Palmela DOC. See TERRAS DO SADO.

arrachage, French term for GRUBBING UP vines. The *prime d'arrachage*, payment for participating in the European VINE PULL SCHEME, made its mark on the southern French landscape from the late 1980s.

Arribes. On Spain's border with Portugal, the Douro River flows through deep canyons and vineyards grow on the slopes and at the top of the steep hills. The indigenous dark-skinned JUAN GARCÍA dominated the 750 ha/1,852 acres of vineyards, with 14 wineries in operation in 2013.

arrope, a syrup used for sweetening wine in Spain, especially SHERRY, made by boiling down and thus concentrating unfermented grape juice. See GRAPE CONCENTRATE.

Arroyo Grande, California wine region and AVA. See SAN LUIS OBISPO.

Arroyo Seco, California wine region and AVA. See MONTEREY.

Arruda, DOP in western Portugal with a large CO-OPERATIVE. See LISBOA.

Arrufiac, also known as **Arrufiat**, is a light-skinned, quite tannic grape variety enjoying a modest renaissance in Gascony in SOUTH WEST FRANCE. An ingredient in PACHERENC DU VIC-BILH and Côtes de ST-MONT, it was rescued from obscurity in the 1980s by André Dubosc of the Plaimont CO-OPERATIVE. It is typically blended with the MANSENGS, COURBU BLANC, and PETIT COURBU.

artists' labels, wine LABELS illustrated by works of art, often a different one for each vintage. Baron Philippe de ROTHSCHILD commissioned the Cubist Jean Carlu to design a mould-breaking label for the 1924 vintage of Ch MOUTON-ROTHSCHILD, the first to be CHÂTEAU BOTTLED. He instituted this as an annual custom from the 1945 vintage, with the result that collectors may seek particular missing labels, thereby adding value to Mouton Rothschild even in lesser or earlier-maturing vintages (of which most bottles tend to have been opened). Since then, vintages of Mouton have enjoyed particular réclame in countries such as Japan, Denmark, Holland, and Spain associated with the artist responsible for that year's label. Wine producers all over the world have since emulated this practice, notably Leeuwin Estate of WESTERN AUSTRALIA, although none to such clever effect.

(Exhibition catalogue) *Mouton Rothschild—Paintings for the Labels* (Bordeaux, 1995).

Arvine, also known as **Petite Arvine**, the finest of the INDIGENOUS grape specialities of the Valais in SWITZERLAND. The wines tend to be nervy with considerable EXTRACT and, often, a vague suggestion of grapefruit and salt. Wines vary in sweetness between dry, mi-FLÉTRI, and downright sweet. Switzerland had 158 ha/390 acres of this grape by 2012.

ascorbic acid, vitamin C, one of the first VITAMINS to be discovered, and a winemaking additive used chiefly as an antioxidant. As well as being essential to mankind's diet, it is involved in plant metabolic processes. The green grape contains significant levels of vitamin C but much is lost during fruit ripening and winemaking. In a wine context, ascorbic acid (or its isomer erythorbic or iso-ascorbic acid) is of chief importance not to the wine drinker but to the winemaker as a permitted additive, within limits, for its ability to prevent OXIDATION by reacting directly with OXYGEN. The EU limit in a finished wine is 250 mg/l.

The chemistry of ascorbic acid in preventing oxidation in white juices and wines is complex and this has led to confusion about its effectiveness. When used alone as an antioxidant, ascorbic acid reacts very rapidly with oxygen and thus retards oxidation. However, the reaction of ascorbic acid with oxygen produces oxidative products that, in the absence of free SULFUR DIOXIDE, will in turn oxidize wine components. Thus ascorbic acid alone is not a suitable antioxidant in winemaking.

Free sulfur dioxide does not react rapidly with oxygen, thus it is not a good oxygen scavenger and does not fully control wine oxidation. However, the combination of ascorbic acid with free sulfur dioxide is a very effective antioxidant, even in the long term, provided that a level of free sulfur dioxide is maintained in the wine. The ascorbic acid reacts rapidly with any OXYGEN present and the oxidative products in turn react with the sulfur dioxide and are eliminated.

In combination, ascorbic acid and sulfur dioxide can be used throughout the white

winemaking process, from grape crushing and pressing to BOTTLING. In red winemaking, ascorbic acid is not used as some oxidative modification of PHENOLIC compounds, including TANNINS, is usually desirable. P.J.W.& T.J.

aseptic bottling. See STERILE BOTTLING.

Asia. Until the 1990s it was assumed—quite wrongly as it turned out—that this most populous of continents would never play an important role in the world of wine. There was something in the physical make-up of most Asians, it was thought by those in the continent which produces the lion's share of all wine, that made them prefer either non-alcoholic or grain-based drinks. This assumption was rapidly disproved in the mid to late 1990s when the world's AUCTION prices were inflated at an unprecedented rate thanks largely to sudden interest from buyers in Hong Kong, Singapore, and Taiwan. Thanks to a boom in the so-called tiger economies, and the much-vaunted HEALTH benefits claimed for red wine, wine-drinking changed from bizarre foreign practice to status symbol in a remarkably short time in countries as varied as Thailand, Taiwan, India, Korea, and—the country with the greatest potential as both consumer and producer—China. Wine-drinking had already infiltrated Japan, and several other Asian countries have embarked on their own domestic wine industries, often based on TABLE GRAPES initially, and sometimes bolstered by imported BULK WINE, since the early 1990s. For details of individual countries, see BHUTAN, Cambodia, CHINA, Hong Kong, INDIA, INDONESIA, JAPAN, Korea, MYANMAR, NEPAL, SRI LANKA, TAIWAN, THAILAND, and VIETNAM. See also the ex-Soviet Central Asian republics of AZERBAIJAN, KAZAKHSTAN, KYRGYZSTAN, TAJIKISTAN, TURKMENISTAN, and UZBEKISTAN. Countries such as AFGHANISTAN, IRAQ, IRAN, JORDAN, PAKISTAN, SYRIA, and Yemen devote most of their vineyards to the production of DRYING GRAPES but ISRAEL, LEBANON, and TURKEY all have flourishing wine industries.

Asia Minor. See ANATOLIA.

Asian lady beetle. See LADYBUG TAINT.

aspect, the direction in which a slope faces, an important characteristic of vineyard sites, especially in cool climates. For more details, see TOPOGRAPHY.

aspergillus, vine disease; see BUNCH ROTS.

aspersion, French for sprinkling and therefore a measure to reduce FROST DAMAGE to vines; see SPRINKLERS.

Aspiran, officially but not popularly known as **Rivairenc**, is a very old dark-skinned grape variety of the LANGUEDOC which once represented about a quarter of all vines in the Hérault

département, but was rarely replanted after PHYLLOXERA because it is not particularly productive. The odd hectare that remains yields limited quantities of light but perfumed red wine and it is a permitted grape variety in MINERVOIS. Its progeny **Aspiran Bouschet** is almost extinct in France but can be found in Mendoza and Chile.

Asprinio, light grape speciality of CAMPANIA in southern Italy, where it often makes slightly sparkling wines. DNA PROFILING at SAN MICHELE ALL'ADIGE showed that Asprinio and GRECO DI TUFO, each used to produce distinct varietal wines, are in reality identical. The 2010 vine census noted 158 ha/390 acres of Asprinio. J.V.

Assario, Dão synonym for MALVASIA Fina.

assemblage, French word for the important operation in the production of fine wines of deciding which lots will be assembled to make up the final blend. It plays a crucial role in SPARKLING WINEMAKING when some CUVÉES may be assembled from several hundred different components. Here the complementary nature of each component is of great importance, as is, for all NON-VINTAGE sparkling wines, adherence to a house style.

Assemblage is of almost ritual significance in BORDEAUX, where many CHÂTEAUX make their so-called GRAND VIN carrying the château name by selecting and BLENDING only the best lots. The rejected lots may either be blended together to make a SECOND WINE (and occasionally even a third wine) or be sold off in bulk to a NÉGOCIANT carrying only the local APPELLATION (Margaux or St-Julien, for example).

This selection process typically takes place between the third and sixth month after the HARVEST (much later in SAUTERNES) and involves the MAÎTRE DE CHAI (winemaker), any OENOLOGIST regularly working for the property, and the proprietor, who must bear the considerable financial sacrifice of exclusions from the *grand vin*, which may sell for three or more times the price of the associated second wine. It is at this stage that the decision is usually taken over whether to incorporate any PRESS WINE.

The normal procedure is to taste samples from each *cuve* or FERMENTATION VESSEL and then simply decide whether it is of sufficiently high quality for the *grand vin*. It has usually been assumed that any blend of wines from the same property is likely to be harmonious. In most other Old World wine regions, especially BURGUNDY, holdings are too small to allow this selectivity, although Chave of HERMITAGE in the Rhône, for example, is notable for keeping lots from different parcels of vineyard separate until a final assembly just before bottling.

Such a TERROIR-DRIVEN approach is slowly becoming more common in the New World, although it was more likely to involve the assembly of blends of various different quality levels and character. In this case there may be extensive experiments with small samples of each lot—known as bench blending—before final blends are decided upon. Here the wine-maker is concerned not just with each lot's inherent quality but also with its affinity with other components in the blend.

Assyrtiko, top-quality white grape variety grown increasingly widely in GREECE. Its origins lie on the island of SANTORINI but its ability to retain acidity in a hot climate has encouraged successful experimentation with it elsewhere, notably on the north-eastern mainland around Halkidiki. Its severe mineral profile has made it a successful blending partner for MALAGOU-SIA, Sauvignon Blanc, and Sémillon. Its wines can age relatively well. So obvious is its quality that by 2008 it was Greece's third most-planted white wine vine with 1,704 ha/4,211 acres, and it has even been imported into Australia.

Asti, town and province in PIEMONTE in north-west Italy whose name appears in local VARIETAL reds made from Dolcetto, Freisa, and Barbera d'Asti. Unlike its counterpart Barbera d'Alba, made from vines traditionally planted in lesser sites where Nebbiolo will not ripen, Barbera has always been given supreme vineyard sites in Asti. **Barbera d'Asti** was elevated to DOCG in 2010, with three superior subzones: Tinella, Colli Astiani or Astiano, and Nizza.

However Asti's name is most commonly associated with playful, aromatic, lightly sparkling wine with modest alcohol levels that is Italy's biggest-selling wine. In 1993, along with the superior MOSCATO D'ASTI, Asti Spumante was elevated to DOCG status and renamed **Asti**, largely in an effort to distinguish it from the host of FRIZZANTE or sparkling wines produced in Italy from a host of grape varieties of very varying quality.

Both Asti and Moscato d'Asti are produced from Moscato Bianco (MUSCAT BLANC À PETITS GRAINS) in the provinces of Asti, Cuneo, and Alessandria, where vineyards total 9,490 ha/23,440 acres shared by 4,000 growers spread over 152 communes. Production has increased from 40 million bottles in the 1970s to 107 million bottles (or 800,000 hl/17,597,539 gallons) in 2011, made possible by a VINE DENSITY of 4,000 vines/ha and a permitted yield of 100 tonnes/ha, although average vineyard size is just 2.45 ha/6 acres. Due to this fragmentation, large bottlers and NÉGOCIANT houses have traditionally dominated production. With the invention of the tank method (see SPARKLING WINEMAKING) at the end of the 19th century, industrial production of Asti became a reality. The combination of large-volume production and small-scale viticulture has necessarily made Asti a blended wine from many sources, masking geographical differences in sites and zones. However, more

and more producers are bottling their own produce, resulting in more artisanal wines, with SINGLE-VINEYARD bottlings becoming increasingly common.

Asti comes in several versions, each determined by its alcoholic content, RESIDUAL SUGAR, and intensity of sparkle. Asti differs significantly from Moscato d'Asti: it is more alcoholic (6 to 9.5% rather than Moscato d'Asti's maximum of 6.5%), and it is fizzier (at least 3 bar of pressure in the bottle rather than Moscato d'Asti's maximum of 2 bar). The best and ripest grapes are normally reserved for Moscato d'Asti.

Often scorned for the many mediocre wines released under the Asti name, the wine never lost its popularity. The image and sales of Moscato in general and Asti in particular received a huge boost in the 2000s when several rap artists who had formerly praised the virtues of Champagne switched to mentioning Moscato in their songs. The subsequent boom in the US led to increased demand, and a call from the larger producers to enlarge the vineyard area. The Asti Consorzio has expressed doubts, fearing that expansion may prejudice quality.   W.S.

www.astidocg.info

astringency is a complex of sensations resulting from the shrinking, drawing, or puckering of the tissues of the mouth. Earlier, astringency had been considered as one of the primary TASTE sensations, like sweetness, sourness, and particularly BITTERNESS, with which it has often been confused. It is now recognized as a tactile response not dependent on the taste receptors, however. The word is derived from the Latin *ad stringere*, meaning to bind, which presaged the finding that astringent materials could bind to, and precipitate, PROTEINS. The most important astringent materials are TANNINS, and it is these components of a wine that are responsible for the puckery, tactile sensation that is most noticeable in young red wines (but can be sensed in some white wines too, particularly those from hard-pressed or SKIN-FERMENTED grapes). However, an appropriate degree of astringency contributes very positively to the palatability of a red wine, and astringency is central to the TEXTURE and MOUTHFEEL of a wine. Some of the terms used by tasters to describe the astringency of a wine—hard, soft, green, resinous, leathery, gripping, aggressive, supple, for example—are the same as those used to describe the tannins of the wine. The astringent sensation may be modified by ACIDITY, SWEETNESS, PHENOLICS and particularly tannins and PIGMENTED TANNINS, and even serving TEMPERATURE. The effect of these components on apparent astringency has been an area of active research in contemporary OENOLOGY.

Kennedy et al. suggest that the 'stickiness' as well as the level of tannins is a factor in how astringent a wine tastes.   P.J.W.

Revelett, M. R., Barak, J. A., and Kennedy, J., 'Chromatography determination of red wine tannin stickiness', *Journal of Agricultural and Food Chemistry*, 62/28 (2014), 6626–31.

Vidal, S., et al., 'Taste and mouth-feel properties of different types of tannin-like polyphenolic compounds and anthocyanins in wine', *Analytica Chemica Acta*, 513 (2004), 57–65.

ATF, previously known as BATF. See TTB.

Athenaeus (flourished *c*.AD 200) was born in Naucratis, a Greek city in the Nile Delta in Egypt, and wrote in Greek. Nothing is known about his life, and his surviving work, the *Deipnosophistae*, meaning 'The masters of the art of dining', can be dated only from internal evidence. It describes at length how 23 men dine together in Ancient ROME and records their conversations; their two most frequent topics are HOMER and wine. Two of the participants are the physician GALEN and the lawyer Ulpian of Tyre; the others are not based on real persons. The work consists of 15 books, but the first two and part of the third survive only in excerpts.

Although wine is the second most frequent topic of the diners' conversation, Athenaeus shows little interest in CONNOISSEURSHIP and none at all in VITICULTURE. Rather than engaging in systematic discussion, Athenaeus assembles curious facts, makes lists, and proposes (often incorrect) etymologies: his enumeration of types of CONTAINERS for wine in Book 11 exemplifies all these tendencies. Most of the wines which he mentions do not belong to his own day, e.g. Coan, Chian, Mendaean, and Thasian. The famous passage attributed to Galen on the wines of Italy (26c–27d) promises to be a discussion of Italian wines in Galen's day, the second half of the second century, but it has none of the rigour and acumen of the great medical writer; in fact, it is almost certainly not by Galen at all. The passage is a series of bald statements, telling us mainly whether a wine is sweet or dry and whether or not it was strong; it does not offer any comparison with wines of earlier periods or different regions. It gives some optimum drinking dates: Alban is best at 15 years old; FALERNIAN needs a minimum of 10 years' ageing, is best after 15 to 20 and, if any older, gives headaches. Falernian can be sweet or dry: we know from other writings (mainly Galen's own) that dry wines were popular in the second century AD, whereas in PLINY's day good wines appear to have been sweet. Athenaeus himself gives us no such historical perspective, however: he is not a historian but a contented collector of snippets.   H.M.W.

Brock, R., and Wilson, H., 'Wine in Athenaeus', in D. Braund and J. Wilkins (eds.), *Athenaeus and his World* (Exeter, 2000).

Athiri, vine grown widely in southern Greece. Its soft, lemony produce is often used for blending, notably with the even higher quality ASSYRTIKO.

Atlas Peak, CALIFORNIA wine region and AVA in the mountains on the eastern side of NAPA Valley.

atypical ageing (ATA) or **untypical ageing** (UTA), known as *untypischer Alterungsnote* in Germany, where it was first documented in the late 1980s, is a term used to identify a phenomenon found in white wine-growing regions worldwide, although varieties such as MÜLLER-THURGAU, KERNER, and BACCHUS seem to be particularly susceptible. Heat and dry conditions immediately before and after VERAISON resulting in extreme WATER STRESS can lead to the development of this aroma/flavour defect. Wines from hot, dry growing seasons and sites are more prone to developing ATA. Vine NITROGEN deficiency may also be a contributing factor. Research suggests that the compound 2-aminoacetophenone (2-AAP) is primarily responsible and that indole-3-acetic acid (IAA) is its precursor. Affected wines lose VARIETAL character very early, develop atypical aromas and flavours described as naphthalene (moth balls), wet towel, or old furniture varnish, and may show an increase in bitterness. These characteristics are not the same as those typical of wines suffering from PREMATURE OXIDATION, where some varietal qualities may remain. Methods to minimize the development of ATA include avoiding extreme moisture stress around veraison, ensuring adequate plant nitrogen, and avoiding OVERCROPPING, which could delay maturity. ASCORBIC ACID additions (100–150 mg/l) in conjunction with proper SULFUR DIOXIDE levels in the wine may help to limit the extent of this phenomenon. J.E.H. & B.W.Z.

Henick-Kling, T., et al., 'Studies on the origin and sensory aspects of atypical aging in white wines', *Proceedings of 15th International Enology Symposium*, 2008, Trier, Germany.

Linsenmeier, A., et al., 'Ambivalence of the influence of nitrogen supply on o-aminoacetophenone in Riesling wine', *Vitis*, 46 (2007), 91–7.

Schwab, A., et al., 'Die "Untypische Alterungsnote" im Wein. Teil IV: Beeinflussung durch weinbauliche Maßnahmen', *Rebe & Wein*, 49 (1996), 181–7.

Zoecklein, B. W., 'Atypical ageing', Enology Notes, 77 (2003).

www.apps.fst.vt.edu/extension/enology/EN/77. html.

Aubance, Coteaux de l', small (barely 200 ha/500 acres) but sometimes excellent sweet white wine appellation in ANJOU on the left bank of the River Loire just south of the town of Angers and immediately north of Coteaux du LAYON. It takes its name from the Aubance, a tributary of the Loire. Total production is rather more than that of SAVENNIÈRES across the river to the west, but the best results come from Chenin planted on outcrops of heat-retaining SLATE. The standard of winemaking is high, and a high proportion of the racy, sweet white Chenin Blanc wines made here is snapped up locally or in Paris. Red and dry white Anjou make up the bulk of production in this zone, with some red Anjou Villages Brissac, but in exceptional years Coteaux de l'Aubance can be just as noble, if not always as long-lived, as the Loire's more famous sweet whites, and must owe their sweetness to a succession of TRIES through the vineyard, picking only the ripest grapes, a discipline, unusually, overseen by the INAO. According to the vintage, the wines may be BOTRYTIZED, and may carry the term Sélection de Grains Nobles on the label, or the grapes may be partly raisined on the vine. See also LOIRE, including map.

Aubun, rather ordinary black-berried vine variety of the southern Rhône. After a strange increase in popularity noted by the French agricultural census of 1979, its total area of French vineyard has declined to 464 ha/1,146 acres. It produces wine not unlike a softer version of CARIGNAN, and formed part of James BUSBY's original vine collection taken to Australia, where isolated plantings can still be found, as they can in California.

auctions of wine are the sale of wine by lots by an auctioneer acting as agent for the seller or, in certain instances, as the seller in his or her own right.

History

Auctions have long been an integral part of the wine TRADE. Wine was sold by auction in Ancient ROME and, in the Middle Ages, before it became commonplace for buyers to visit wine regions, wine shipped in barrel to its final destination (see CONTAINERS) was frequently sold by auction as well as by private contract. In Britain, wine auctions were common at trading ports such as Leith in Edinburgh, Scotland, where the auction room in The Vaults testifies to a once lively auction trade in casks of fine bordeaux. In Germany, the practice of selling wine by auction under the names of village and vintage became well established in the 18th century. The Nassauer'sche Domäne in the Rheingau was among the first to initiate the movement towards establishing conditions of sale by auction in the 1830s.

As wine trading became increasingly competitive with improved transportation and more sophisticated communications, the need for producers to sell their wine by auction diminished. Whereas historically wine auctions were used as a means of selling young or relatively young wine in barrel, today's commercial auction trade relies on bottled wines at all stages of maturity. Once wine was packaged in BOTTLES stoppered with CORKS from the end of the 17th century, it became capable of BOTTLE AGEING and full maturation. With, literally, a new lease of life for fine wine, exceeding decades and, in rare instances, even a century or more, fine wine transcended its previous status as a short-term commodity.

Once wine became capable of being traded across generations, it naturally attracted admirers, collectors, and investors (see INVESTMENT). It became something that, at its finest, could be regarded with the same admiration as a work of art or any other classic auction room collectible. Wine captured in bottle led to a market in older wines whose reputation, based on VINTAGE and name, created a comprehensible and measurable scale of values.

Sales of wine were generally held as part of house sales until wine departments were established in two of the world's leading auction houses, Christie's and Sotheby's. Christie's established its wine department in 1966, when Michael BROADBENT was recruited from the wine merchant HARVEYS OF BRISTOL to build up the department to meet the demands of an increasingly specialized and sophisticated international market. The first auction of the new era was held on 11 October 1966 and the first season achieved sales amounting to £220,634. Not to be outdone, Sotheby's entered the fray in 1970, holding the first auction of its newly formed wine department on 16 September 1970 in Glasgow.

While Christie's and Sotheby's dominated the wine auction scene for many decades, new auction systems and entrants have challenged the status quo. In the late 1970s, The Chicago Wine Company introduced and popularized the 'silent bid' wine auction system in the US. Archaic laws in New York state prevented the spread of wine auctions in one of the world's most lucrative markets until the late 1980s. Christie's and Sotheby's initially teamed up with local wine merchants until deregulation in the late 1990s. The French auction market was also deregulated in the late 1990s.

Inefficiencies in the auction wine market during the 1980s also led to increased competition from specialist FINE WINE traders, the great majority of them based in the UK. The dot.com boom in the late 1990s spawned electronic wine auction houses, and online selling in some form has been adopted by most wine auction companies, while online wine exchange businesses such as Liv-ex have brought further competition and depth to the secondary wine market.

Some notable annual auctions

Nevertheless, traditional auctions survive, most notably that of the HOSPICES DE BEAUNE. This former medieval hospice in Burgundy derives a substantial proportion of income for the modern hospital associated with it from the sale of wines produced from vineyards given as bequests over the centuries. Every third Sunday in November, the Hospices holds a charity auction accompanied by a long weekend of gargantuan feasting and decadent celebration (see TROIS GLORIEUSES). At the traditional candle auction, the lots are named after the Hospices' benefactors, each comprising a number of new 228-l/60-gal barrels. Since 2005 Christie's has partnered with the Hospices de Beaune, and together they organize the annual sale with tastings of the wines all over the world. In 2014, the 154th Hospices de Beaune auction, the sale achieved a record total of €8,887,888 million ($11.1 m). The success of the Hospices de Beaune auction in combining the sale of wines with the glare of publicity has been the role model for a number of latter-day imitators, from LIMOUX to the NAPA Valley.

A number of notable auctions in Germany, largely focused on Riesling, include those of the VDP's GROSSER RING in the Mosel, VDP Rheingau at KLOSTER EBERBACH, and VDP Nahe-Ahr in Bad Kreuznach. South Africa's Nederburg enhanced its reputation as a wine producer by establishing the Nederburg auction in 1975, at which lots of its top bottlings and those of other producers are offered for sale. The Nederburg sale in turn spawned the annual auction of the Cape Winemakers' Guild, a group of largely independent cellarmasters that started selling small lots of top wines at auction in 1985.

In the United States, distillers Heublein established the first New World wine auction in Chicago in 1969. Since then a combination of strict licensing laws and tax advantages to buyers led to a boom in charity wine auctions in the United States, led by the now famous annual Auction Napa Valley, which raised $18.7 million in 2014 for vineyard worker healthcare and children's education, and the Naples Winter Wine Festival in Florida. The prices paid at these charity events are often so inflated by goodwill and/or welcome exhibitionism, however, that they cannot be compared with the United States' thriving commercial auctions as reliable indicators of the market.

The professionals

Christie's is the oldest established wine auctioneer. Wine was a prominent feature in James Christie's first sale on 5 December 1766, which, along with household furniture, jewellery, and firearms, included the sale of 'a large quantity of Madeira and high Flavour'd Claret, late the Property of Noble Personage (Deceas'd)'. Three years later, on 7 and 8 September 1769, James Christie held his first sale entirely devoted to wine, a collection of 'Old Hock, Rich Burgundy, Calcavella [Portugal's CARCAVELOS], Malaga and TENT, the property of Captain Fletcher from the West Indies'.

Today's commercial auction scene is dominated by regular sales conducted by a number of professional auction houses, initially London-based. However in the late 1990s wine auctions elsewhere, particularly in the United States, started to present an increasingly serious challenge to London's hegemony as American cellars became an increasingly lucrative source of supply. In the early 1990s, wine auctions were at long last permitted in New York, but only in association with an established retailer. As a result, Sotheby's established a presence in association with Sherry-Lehmann, holding its first sale in New York on 8 October 1994 while Christie's teamed up with Zachy's. The total value of wine sales in the US overtook the UK total in the mid 1990s.

By 2015, the major companies holding significant live wine auctions around six main cities in the US were, in declining order of revenues achieved, Hart Davis Hart, Acker Merrall & Condit, Wally's, Zachy's, Sotheby's, Heritage, and Christie's. But the abolition of wine duties in HONG KONG in 2008 dramatically changed the geography of wine auctions, making Hong Kong another major wine auction hub. Acker Merrall & Condit, Sotheby's, Christie's, and Zachy's became major players in an Asian wine-auction scene centred on Hong Kong. With Singapore included, 2014 live-auction revenues for Asia, at $105.7 million, were second only to the US total of $160.1 million, and considerably ahead of Europe's total of $63.1 million.

In 2014, Sotheby's was the world's leading auctioneer with sales totalling $65.3 million, followed by Acker, Merrall & Condit with sales of $61.8 million, then Christie's at $54.7 million, Zachy's at $45.2 million, and Hart Davis Hart at $42.8 million. The other major players, in declining order of revenue, were Wally's, Bonhams, Heritage, Steinfels, Spectrum, and Artcurial. After the bumper years of 2011 and 2012, and the decline in global auction revenues by 16% in 2013, total revenues rose by 5.5% in 2014, possibly affected by increasing concern about PROVENANCE and adverse reaction to the exorbitant *en primeur* pricing of the 2010 Bordeaux vintage combined with economic uncertainty, particularly in the EU. $2,976 was the average lot price compared with $2,813 in 2013. Hart Davis Hart showed the best percentage of lots sold in 2014 with 99.7%, as against Sotheby's 91.1% and Christie's 86.8%.

Commercial auctions are also held in other countries, notably France, Holland, Switzerland, Italy, Singapore, and Australia.

The introduction of the silent-bid wine auction in the 1980s, followed by the deployment of internet auction technology in the late 1990s has changed the auction format irrevocably. The vibrant cut and thrust of the live auction room is to a certain extent dwindling as internet trading becomes part of our daily lives. The traditional live auction has been joined today not just by the addition of internet bidding, as well as by exclusive online and trading-exchange platforms such as those of Liv-Ex in the UK, and some fine-wine merchants accept online bids for customers' wines stored with them.

Trade structure

Wine auction customers are broadly split between private individuals and the wine trade. Private buyers may have any number of different reasons for buying wine. They may be consumers, collectors, and/or investors (see INVESTMENT). Trade buyers also buy for investment, to fill gaps in a restaurant or merchant's wine list, or as brokers for trade or private clients. Reasons for selling wine vary equally, the traditional three d's of death, debt, and divorce having turned into four, as doctors' orders have also become a factor. Private customers may want or need to sell in order to realize the value of their cellar, or part of it, or to finance further purchases, or as executors selling on behalf of an estate. The wine trade may sell to dispose of surplus or bankrupt stock.

Wines traded

Red bordeaux, or claret, remains the staple of the wine auction rooms. It is long lived, enjoys widespread appeal, and it is in relatively plentiful supply. And the relative value of a particular red bordeaux is more readily identifiable than that of any other wine style, the 1855 CLASSIFICATION providing some sort of easily comprehensible framework for evaluating the red bordeaux châteaux most widely traded in the saleroom.

The FIRST GROWTHS—Chx LAFITE, LATOUR, MARGAUX, MOUTON ROTHSCHILD in the Médoc, HAUTBRION and La MISSION HAUT-BRION in Pessac-Léognan, AUSONE and CHEVAL BLANC in St-Émilion, the unofficial first growths Ch PETRUS and Le PIN of Pomerol, and Ch d'Yquem in Sauternes—are undisputed members of today's élite. Owing to the classification's rigid composition, a second leading group of properties has emerged, commonly referred to as SUPER SECONDS. Qualification for this group requires not only the strictest commitment to quality, but a record of consistently high prices which reflects that policy. More recently, a third group of so-called GARAGE WINES emerged, inspired by the success of Le Pin. Despite a relative fall from grace after its Asian market peak in 2011, Lafite remains the unofficial leader of the five Médoc first growths.

Pre-PHYLLOXERA clarets are extremely rare and among the most highly prized items in any sale catalogue. Unique GRANDS FORMATS (large bottles) of old vintages, particularly of first growths, are much sought-after by collectors (see BOTTLE SIZE), although perhaps to a lesser degree than in the late 1980s. Specific VINTAGES play an important part, too, with the price of wines from consecutive years often fluctuating by a factor of three according to the reputation of the vintage. The most highly prized pre-war vintages of the 20th century are 1900, 1920, 1926, 1928, and 1929. In the immediate post-war period, the most sought-after trio are 1945, 1947, and 1949. In the latter half of the 20th century and early 21st century, 1953, 1959, 1961, 1982, 1990, 2000, 2005, 2009, and 2010 rank as the outstanding vintages.

A recent saleroom phenomenon is the way prices for relatively recent vintages have started to outstrip the prices of older vintages. Although the state of the global economy plays a part, much of this has to do with the taste, and ratings, of the influential American critic, Robert M. PARKER, who writes mainly about young wines. There are a number of additional reasons for the strength of young wine prices, among them the global trend towards drinking wines younger, the emergence of a new, determined group of collectors in Asia, and a relative shortage of great vintages tilting the balance of supply and demand even further towards demand.

Red bordeaux apart, burgundy is an increasingly significant player in the saleroom with Domaine de la ROMANÉE-CONTI, Henri Jayer, Leroy, Rousseau, Leflaive, Comte Georges de Vogüé, Coche-Dury, Domaine Dujac, Roumier, Jean-Frédéric Mugnier, and Méo-Camuzet among the most sought-after names. Champagne too has become an auction room collectible, notably KRUG, ROEDERER CRISTAL, DOM PÉRIGNON, and Salon. Vintage port is a saleroom regular, although demand for it has been relatively modest, with TAYLOR, FONSECA, GRAHAM, WARRE, DOW, and QUINTA DO NOVAL, the unofficial first growths, as it were, of a group of some 40 or more port houses. Rare madeira makes an occasional appearance at auction. Auction houses have played a key role in predicting and shaping the success of newer regions for collectible wines, such as Italy and Spain. Among Italy's blue chips, GAJA and certain wines from Giacomo Conterno, Bruno Giacosa, Rocche dei Manzoni, Luciano Sandrone, and Aldo Conterno represent solid collectibles along with SUPERTUSCANS Sassicaia, Solaia, TIGNA-NELLO, ORNELLAIA, and Masseto. From Spain older vintages of VEGA SICILIA, Marqués de Murrieta, Marqués de Riscal, CVNE, and Viña Tondonia from Lopez de Heredia are increasingly seen at auction. The finest wines of the Rhône, notably Hermitage, Côte Rôtie, and

Châteauneuf-du-Pape, often made an appearance in auction catalogues. Wines from Germany, Alsace, Loire, and TOKAJ make only an occasional appearance.

The wines of the New World, California and Australia in particular, are making an impact as their track record for ageing becomes more widely accepted and new wines appear on the secondary market. Demand for California wines is particularly strong in the US, less so elsewhere. While such older rarities as the 1941 Inglenook Cabernet can fetch very high prices, the focus today is on such CALIFORNIA CULT names as Araujo, Bryant Family, Colgin, Dominus, Harlan, Kistler, Opus One, Screaming Eagle, Shafer, and Sine Qua Non. It was a wine from Australia, PENFOLDS Grange, that was arguably the first New World wine to be recognized internationally as the equivalent of a Bordeaux FIRST GROWTH. Grange is already a saleroom classic, while Henschke's Hill of Grace is also regarded as an important single-vineyard Shiraz. Langton's Classification of Australian Wine, first published in 1991, recognizes the reputation and track record of Australian wine at auction, reflecting an increasingly diverse market largely underpinned by BAROSSA VALLEY Shiraz, and COONAWARRA and MARGARET RIVER Cabernet Sauvignon. The sixth edition, published in 2014, gives top 'Outstanding' billing to 21 wines including, PENFOLDS Grange and Hill of Grace apart, Bass Phillip Reserve Pinot Noir, Clonakilla Shiraz-Viognier, Grosset Polish Hill Riesling, Cullen Diana Madeline Cabernet-Merlot, Wendouree Shiraz, and Wynns John Riddoch Coonawarra Cabernet Sauvignon.

Record prices

Red bordeaux is the consistent pace-setter for wine auction PRICES, accounting for almost all red wine records. The record of £105,000 for a single bottle of 1787 Ch Lafitte (sic) paid by the late Malcolm Forbes at Christie's on 5 December 1985 survived much longer than the wine itself, which turned to vinegar when put on show upright under a bright light (see STORING WINE). It was Lafite again, on this occasion the 1869 vintage, which smashed through the barrier for a standard 75 cl. bottle when three bottles were sold at Sotheby's Hong Kong in October 2010 for HK$1.8 million ($230,000) each. In November 2010, a rare imperial (six-litre bottle) of Ch Cheval Blanc 1947 was sold for £192,000 at Christie's, Geneva, setting a world record for a single bottle, albeit an outsize one. The dizzying rise of the Domaine de la Romanée-Conti in the early 21st century has seen records consistently broken by the wines of this exceptional Burgundy producer. The most notable world record for a case of the GRAND CRU Romanée-Conti itself was the HK$3,675,000 (£295,838) paid at Christie's Hong Kong in

November 2013 for 12 bottles of the 1978 vintage.

Beyond Bordeaux and Burgundy, other rarities have achieved fabulous prices for varying reasons. Thus, individual bottles of the 1907 Heidsieck Champagne salvaged in 1998 from a ship torpedoed by a German submarine during the First World War made up to $275,000 at auctions around the world. The £25,000 paid for a bottle of the 1775 MASSANDRA 'Sherry de la Frontera' at Sotheby's in 2001 is the highest price ever paid for a bottle of FORTIFIED WINE. And in 2000 at Auction Napa Valley, the annual charity fundraiser, an imperial of 1992 Screaming Eagle Cabernet Sauvignon made $500,000 (£297,000).

How to buy and sell at auction

The public forum of the auction room and the intrinsically competitive aspect of bidding for lots often creates an atmosphere of tension and excitement in the saleroom in which it is easy for inexperienced participants to get carried away. The online-only format—which attempts to replicate the live auction environment—differs in that all lots are sold at exactly the same moment. The excitement of an online auction sale is greatest in the last 30 minutes before the auction closes. All the information required about a particular auction is published in the auction catalogue, including details of the lots, estimated prices, conditions of sale, and other general information on such matters as delivery charges, premiums, and other additions to the hammer price such as taxes and duties payable where applicable. Most auctioneers charge a buyer's premium at a house rate that is normally between 10 and 22.5% of the hammer price, and a seller's premium which can be negotiated with the auction house and varies according to the amount sold. The internet auction format has taken catalogues one step further, providing potential buyers with instant information regarding vintage conditions, regional information, and tasting notes.

The wines to be sold are in numbered lots. In addition to a number and an estimated price band from lowest to highest, the description of each lot identifies the wine by name, bottle size, and vintage where applicable. Increasing concern about COUNTERFEIT WINES has heightened awareness of the importance of PROVENANCE by both bidders and (most) auctioneers. Given the importance of the condition of the wine, especially older wines, and since wines are not generally available for inspection, the catalogue specifies exact FILL LEVEL, or ULLAGE levels ('mid shoulder' or 'bottom neck', for example, levels illustrated in the catalogue), the condition of the LABEL, whether the wine comes in its own wooden CASE (sometimes abbreviated to 'owc.'), and will generally mention if a cellar is of exceptional pedigree or in previously undisturbed condition. Auction house policy may vary on inspection and the condition of the wine to be sold. Some auctioneers offer pre-sale tastings of varying degrees of lavishness. Hong Kong has seen extravagant entertainment of potential bidders, usually including examples of the wines to be sold. New York sales often take place in smart restaurants with lunch laid on. Most London sales are arid, workmanlike affairs.

Lots which are of particular interest may be supplemented by the auctioneer's tasting notes.

Bidding may be by hand or, more often today, by waving a numbered paddle to attract the auctioneer's attention. Bidding is, unless otherwise stated, per dozen bottles.

Advance commission bids form a substantial proportion of bids received and more and more lots are being sold online. Commission, or absentee, bids are treated in exactly the same way as bids in the room. The successful bidders obtain their lot at one increment above the underbidder. In the event of two commission bids of the same amount, it is the one received first that takes precedence.

See COOPERAGE for details of French OAK auctions. A.H.L.R.

Ella Lister, 'Liquid assets', *The World of Fine Wine.*
www.winemarketjournal.com
www.wine-searcher.com
www.decanter.com

Aurore, otherwise known as Seibel 5279, a complex FRENCH HYBRID once widely planted in North America and still found occasionally in colder states. Adaptable and productive, it ripens early but is prone to ROT and its floral-scented wines are of no great distinction.

Ausbruch, German-language equivalent of the Hungarian Aszú, traditionally designating sweet wines made from BOTRYTIZED grapes which made the reputations of TOKAJ and of Rust on the shores of the NEUSIEDLERSEE. The methods involved historically in making Ruster Ausbruch are unknown but considerable circumstantial evidence suggests that FURMINT—still-dominant around Tokaj—long played a similar role in Rust, where that variety almost disappeared until a modest revival was mounted at the end of the 20th century. Ausbruch officially remains a trans-regional category of Austrian wine (stipulating botrytized grapes at a minimum MUST WEIGHT of 27 °KMW—equivalent to 139 °OECHSLE); in practice the term is widely used only in Rust, whose growers, as members of the Cercle Ruster Ausbruch, in 1991 set a lower limit of 30 °KMW. They further distinguished it from TROCKENBEER-ENAUSLESE as having finesse and effusive fruit rather than opulence and a target alcohol level of 12%. Ruster Ausbruch wines may be made from any of the many white grapes grown in

Rust, notably Chardonnay, Muskateller, Sauvignon Blanc, Pinot Blanc, and Welschriesling, as well as occasionally (and memorably) from Furmint, or even Pinot Noir. D.S.

Auslese, a PRÄDIKAT that means literally 'selected harvest' but is officially defined by the MUST WEIGHT at harvest. In Germany, specific minimum must weights are laid down for each combination of vine variety and region, and range from 83 to 105 °OECHSLE. In Austria, the minimum is 21 °KMW (approximately 105 °Oechsle). By the letter of the GERMAN WINE LAW, grapes for Auslese should have been picked at least one week after a preliminary picking of less ripe grapes but in practice an Auslese may well have been picked early in the harvest. At their finest, German Auslesen are long-lived, sweet, often BOTRYTIZED wines, and the finest botrytis frequently occurs early on. In Germany, high-alcohol, dry wines have occasionally been designated Auslese trocken, but with decreasing frequency. Many vintners long preferred to use the designation SPÄTLESE even if the must weight on which their dry wine was based far exceeded the minimum for Auslese; and the trend (now official policy within the VDP growers' association) is to dispense entirely with Prädikat designations for dry wines.

In Austria not only botrytized sweet wines but also most other wines that meet the minimum must weight for this Prädikat and harbour more than 9 g/l residual sugar (i.e. are not legally trocken) are labelled, if inconspicuously, as Auslese. D.S.

Ausone, Château, minuscule but exceptionally fine estate on the edge of the town of ST-ÉMILION. It was named in 1781 after the Roman poet Ausonius who certainly had a vineyard in the Gironde, but probably one facing the River GARONNE rather than in St-Émilion. Recorded in the 1868 Cocks et Féret's *Bordeaux et ses vins* (see LITERATURE OF WINE) as belonging to M. Cantenats, it then passed to a nephew, M. Lafargue, and then to his nephew, Edouard Dubois-Challon, who raised the reputation of the château to the leading position in St-Émilion up to the 1920s, when it was challenged by Ch CHEVAL-BLANC, the only other château to be ranked 'A' in the official CLASSIFICATION of St-Émilion in 1955. From 1939 to the mid 1970s, Ausone was not, with a few exceptional vintages, producing wines of the longevity of their 19th-century predecessors, although there was a marked improvement after the arrival of a new RÉGISSEUR, Pascal Delbeck, in 1976. Until the late 1990s, 50% was owned by Mme Dubois-Challon, widow of Edouard, and 50% by Alain Vauthier, who married Edouard's daughter Cécile, an unsatisfactory arrangement which ended with Vauthier taking control of, and

completely renovating, the extraordinary cellars in limestone caves originally excavated to provide stone for building the town. The wine itself has also been dramatically modernized, and the vineyard recuperated.

The estate consists of a mere 7 ha/18 acres—45% MERLOT vines and 55% CABERNET FRANC—on the steep slopes of the Côtes (see ST-ÉMILION) that run along the right bank of the DORDOGNE just below the town. Production of Ausone averages 1,500 cases.

Australia became the world's sixth biggest wine producer in 2005, producing 14.7 million hl/388 million gal of wine in 2004, but by 2013 production had fallen to 12.31 million hl/324 million gal and both Chile and China have been catching up. After a flurry of vineyard expansion in the 1990s, total vineyard area was almost 148,500 ha/367,000 acres in 2012, having declined slightly each year since 2007. The steady fall in vineyard area reflects the Australian wine industry's painful reorientation away from inexpensive, mass-market wine to more upmarket bottlings in keeping with Australia's relatively high production costs. Vines have been GRUBBED UP in all regions, but mostly in the hotter, drier, water-dependent regions such as RIVERLAND and RIVERINA. This was propelled by the DROUGHT that persisted for three seasons from 2007 when the cost of IRRIGATION water hit heights that made viticulture unsustainable.

Australia makes every one of the major wine styles from aromatic, dry white table wine through to wines fashioned in the image of vintage port. Some of its wines—the unwooded Semillons of the Hunter Valley, the fortified TOPAQUES AND MUSCATS of north east Victoria—have no direct equivalent elsewhere, but overall the wines manage to be at once distinctively Australian yet fit easily into the world scene.

Just over 2,500 wineries are spread through every state. Most of the wineries are small; 86% of them crushed 250 tonnes of grapes or less in 2014, and 87% of the annual CRUSH is accounted for by the 20 largest companies. The top five, TREASURY (Penfolds, Wolf Blass, Wynns, Rosemount, Yellowglen, Lindemans), ACCOLADE (Hardys, Houghton, Banrock Station, Bay of Fires), PERNOD RICARD (Jacob's Creek, Wyndham Estate, St Hugo), Australian Vintage (McGuigan, Nepenthe, Tempus Two), and Casella (YELLOW TAIL) account for more than half.

As in California, the overwhelming majority (over 2,300) of those small wineries have come into existence since 1970, offering weekend or retirement occupations for people from all walks of life. In typical Australian style, however, the owners have frequently appointed themselves as hands-on viticulturists and winemakers. Nevertheless, perhaps due to the trickle-down effect of the renowned AUSTRALIAN WINE RESEARCH INSTITUTE at Adelaide and the university wine schools (see ADELAIDE), standards are extremely high.

The Australian wine SHOW system has also played a major role in promoting technical excellence and in shaping style. The lessons of the show ring have been reinforced by the well-known penchant Australians have for travel. Indeed, Australia spawned the so-called FLYING WINEMAKERS, a group of oenological guns for hire who follow the vintage around the world. On a less formal basis, many Australian winemakers have made a point of travelling and working overseas, principally in Europe. See AUSTRALIAN INFLUENCE.

Add this experience to the technological base, take in the effect of the sunny Australian climate, and allow for the surge in plantings of such popular grape varieties as Chardonnay and Cabernet Sauvignon, and it is not hard to see why Australian exports increased out of all recognition between 1983–4 and 2003–4, from 8.9 million litres/2.35 million gal, worth AU$9.6 million, to 575 million litres/151 million gal worth AU$2.55 billion. This placed it behind only France, Italy, and Spain in value of wine exports, a position it continued to occupy in the early 2010s, despite producing only 4% of the world's wine.

It is not too fanciful to suggest that the wines have an openness, a confident, user-friendly style which reflects the national character (and climate). Australian winemakers have opted to preserve as much as possible of the flavour of the grape, yet to do so with a delicacy of touch, producing intensely fruity white wines and soft, mouth-filling red wines which appeal to the heart as much as to the mind. In so doing they (willingly) sacrificed structural complexity at the altar of simple fruit flavour, although by the end of the first decade of this century wine styles were changing, with levels of alcohol and obvious oak in decline.

Between 1975 and 1985, the Australian 'wine boom', sales of dry white wine quadrupled, while those of red wine were static, but since 1985 red wine sales have more than doubled. By 2014, white wine represented 39% of the local market; red and rosé together 32.5%, and sparkling was 6.7%. FORTIFIED WINES had declined steadily, from 70% in the 1950s to under 3%. Australia has the highest annual per capita wine consumption in the English-speaking world (see APPENDIX 2C), steadily rising to 23.3 l/6 gal in 2011, an increase of more than 10% since 2003. Wine 'casks' (see BOXES), usually containing 4 litres (1 gal), played a particularly important part in growing the Australian wine market, once accounting for more than half of all sales by volume, although by 2014 cask sales represented only 31% and were in steady decline as drinkers traded up and bottled wine became more affordable.

History

'On 24th January two bunches of grapes were cut in the Governor's garden from cuttings of vines brought three years before from the Cape of Good Hope.' The year was 1791, the chronicler Watkin Tench, and the site of the garden is now occupied by the Hotel Inter-Continental in Sydney's Macquarie Street.

Between 1820 and 1840 commercial viticulture was progressively established in New South Wales, Tasmania, Western Australia, Victoria, and finally South Australia. It was based upon comprehensive collections of VINIFERA vines imported from Europe: there are no native vines in Australia, and neither CROSSES nor HYBRIDS have ever taken root. Italian immigrants (in Riverland and Riverina), Silesians (in the Barossa and Clare Valleys), Dalmatians (in the Swan Valley of WESTERN AUSTRALIA), and Swiss (Yarra Valley and Geelong in Victoria) all played key roles in the establishment of viticulture.

By 1870, South Australia, Victoria, and New South Wales all had substantial industries: that year they produced 8.7 million l/2.3 million gal of wine. Twenty years later Victoria alone was making twice that amount, more than the other two states combined. But PHYLLOXERA (discovered near Geelong in 1877), changing land use, a swing from dry wine production to fortified wine, the establishment of irrigated vineyards along the Murray River, and the removal of state trade barriers after Federation in 1901 saw South Australia comprehensively usurp Victoria's dominant position.

By 1930, South Australia was producing over 75% of Australia's wine and the Barossa Valley had become the centre of production, processing not only its own grapes but much of those grown in RIVERLAND, then and now the engine-room of Australian bulk wine production in the same way as California's CENTRAL VALLEY. As the geographic base moved from the cooler parts of Victoria to the warmer regions of South Australia, and specifically as the Murray and then Murrumbidgee-based Riverina came into production, so the type of wine being produced changed.

Between 1927 and 1939 inclusive, Australia exported more wine to the United Kingdom than did France, mainly because of the Imperial Preference system which created trading advantages within the British Commonwealth. Most of this wine was fortified, the remainder being massively alcoholic and ferruginous red wine from north east Victoria, the Barossa Valley, and McLaren Vale, marketed (inter alia) under the Emu wine brand.

The industry of today started to take shape in the mid 1950s. Cold fermentation of white wine in STAINLESS STEEL was pioneered (see REFRIGERATION); the big wine companies moved into Coonawarra and (a decade later) nearby Padthaway; and the decline in fortified wine production and consumption contrasted with spectacular growth in the consumption of red table wine (up to 1970) and thereafter white table wine. The 1970s witnessed the arrival of the wine cask, of Cabernet Sauvignon and Chardonnay, the phenomenon of the boutique winery, and the re-establishment of viticulture across the cool corner of south eastern Australia, running east from Coonawarra and Padthaway right through Victoria.

Since the export boom started in the mid 1980s, the Australian industry has literally reinvented itself. Back in 1956, multi-purpose (eating, drying or winemaking) and non-premium varieties (Doradillo, Trebbiano, and such like) accounted for 85% of the crush, premium grapes for 15%. In 1986, the shares were 60% and 40% respectively; in 1994, 30% and 70%; and by 2004, 10 and 90%. There may be a change within the mix of premium varieties, but the percentage of multi-purpose grapes is unlikely to fall much further (if at all) because of the safety valve they represent.

Looked at another way, in 1994, the 'big three' varieties Chardonnay, Shiraz, and Cabernet Sauvignon provided 27% of production; in 2013 they provided just under 60%. The extent and speed of this vineyard reconstruction, achieved without subsidy or direct government support (although tax breaks were offered for vineyard investment for a time), is a prime reason why Australia has such a competitive edge over OLD WORLD producers.

The last two decades of the 20th century saw more of the same: it is obvious, then, that the FINE WINES of today bear no resemblance to all but a tiny handful of those of 60 years ago. The next 60 years will bring further refinement, a continuation of the trend towards quality, and a decrease in the use of chemicals in all aspects of grape-growing and, to a lesser degree, winemaking. It is certain that the industry will continue to grow, but only the bravest prophet would suggest a further degree of change equivalent to that of the second half of the 20th century.

Climate

With a land mass similar to that of the United States of America, winter snowfields larger than those of Switzerland, and with viticulture in every state, one-line descriptions of the Australian climate are hazardous. For all that, there are two basic weather patterns, one affecting Western Australia, South Australia, Victoria, and Tasmania (the southern states), the other governing Queensland and New South Wales.

The southern states experience a winter–spring rainfall pattern, with a dry summer and

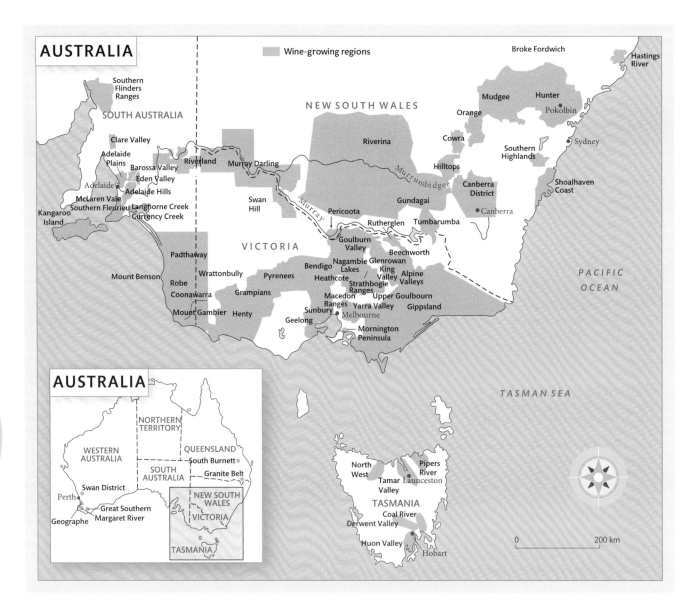

early autumn. Ridges of high pressure sweep across the southern half of the continent from Perth to Melbourne during the vines' growing season, uninterrupted by mountain ranges; daytime temperatures typically range between 25 °C/77 °F and 35 °C/95 °F.

There is a less profound MARITIME influence than in California; the sea temperature is warmer, and the diurnal temperature ranges are less (see TEMPERATURE VARIABILITY). The resultant even accumulation of heat in the premium wine regions is seen by Australian researchers to be a major factor in promoting wine quality (and, more controversially, style).

Using the California heat degree system developed by WINKLER, the climate varies between region I and mid region III, with a preponderance in region II. Because of the lack of summer rainfall, IRRIGATION is considered as important for quality as for quantity. In the

much hotter and drier Riverland of South Australia, Victoria, and New South Wales, it becomes as essential as it is in California's San Joaquin Valley, and is unashamedly used to boost production.

The other, more northerly, weather system derives from the tropics. It provides a more even rainfall pattern, higher temperatures, and higher humidity. This system defines the subtropical climate for much of the rapidly increasing Queensland wine industry, and the coastal regions of New South Wales. The Hunter Valley is prone to receive rather too much of its annual rainfall during HARVEST, only to suffer the subsequent dual burden of winter and spring DROUGHT. Its redeeming feature is the humidity and afternoon cloud cover which reduces stress on the vines and reduces the impact of its region IV heat load (see CLIMATE CLASSIFICATION for details).

Geography

Vine-growing in Australia is concentrated in the south eastern corner of this vast country. For more detail, see under the state or territory names which are, in declining order of importance as grape growers, SOUTH AUSTRALIA, NEW SOUTH WALES, VICTORIA, WESTERN AUSTRALIA, TASMANIA, QUEENSLAND, and CANBERRA. Considerable quantities of grapes and wine are trucked over state boundaries, however, for blending and bottling. EU laws demand that VARIETAL wines, labelled with a grape variety, be labelled with an officially recognized region. The **South Eastern Australia Zone** was created for this purpose and is a vast area encompassing all three of the most important wine states, including the important irrigated regions RIVERLAND and RIVERINA. This somewhat vague description is one of the most common on Australian lower-priced wine labels in export markets.

Viticulture

Equal pay for women, introduced in the latter part of the 1960s, had some unforeseen consequences. One was a major stimulus to the development of mechanized viticulture, initially MECHANICAL HARVESTING, which is responsible for about 80% of the nation's crop, but in due course extending to pruning and, in the latter part of the 1980s, to all aspects of CANOPY MANAGEMENT during the growing season. MECHANICAL PRUNING machines, which trim the canopy, lift and clip the foliage wires, pluck leaves in the fruiting zone, while simultaneously spraying herbicides were already common by the early 1990s. They have, however, fallen out of favour in some regions, and particularly in Coonawarra.

International cost comparisons carried out in the early 1990s for PENFOLDS established what common sense suggested: Australia is able to grow and harvest grapes more economically than California or France (although not necessarily more economically than Chile, Argentina, or South Africa). This big-company, broad-acre approach to viticulture was carried to its logical conclusion with the development of so-called MINIMAL PRUNING in the late 1970s. This involves no winter pruning at all; the vine is allowed to grow unchecked save for light trimming and skirting during the summer months, demonstrating a hitherto unsuspected capacity for self-regulation.

At the other end of the spectrum, Australasian viticulturists and researchers have been at the forefront in developing advanced TRELLIS SYSTEMS and canopy management systems. While these glory under such science fiction names as RT2T and TK2T, they can be seen as doing no more than recognizing what the French have practised for centuries: namely, that SUNLIGHT interception on buds and grape bunches is essential, as is a proper balance between CANOPY and crop level, or YIELD.

As in California, Oregon, and elsewhere, new vineyards in premium areas, particularly those in cooler regions, are being established with VINE DENSITIES two or three times greater than traditionally used, and with specifically adapted trellis systems. The aim is better-quality grapes at yields which may in fact be greater than those of traditional plantings.

The other major development is the move towards what is loosely called SUSTAINABLE VITICULTURE, with phrases such as INTEGRATED PEST MANAGEMENT coming into general (viticultural) usage. The Australian climate may prove less amenable than that of California (rather more growing season rainfall, higher humidity, and the scourge of DOWNY MILDEW), but there is an ineluctable move away from fungicides, PESTICIDES, and HERBICIDES towards more 'natural' grape growing (see ORGANIC VITICULTURE and BIODYNAMIC VITICULTURE).

While the Australian climate is less suited to sustainable viticulture than might appear at first sight, the overall health of the vineyards appears to be good. PHYLLOXERA has never entered the states of South Australia, Western Australia, Tasmania, nor most of New South Wales (including the Hunter Valley), and is not present in the bulk wine-producing Riverland. Small parts of Victoria remain affected, but very strict quarantine legislation, actively enforced and respected by viticulturists, prevented any spread from infested areas during the second half of the 20th century, with only one small exception.

Grafting, not as protection against phylloxera but for the entirely different purpose of changing vine variety, is practised (see TOP GRAFTING), and is playing a role in the shift towards premium grape varieties. However, the greater impetus comes from replanting and new plantings rather than from top grafting.

Winemaking

The typical medium-sized modern Australian winery is comprehensively equipped, especially in comparison with its counterpart in Europe. It has a laboratory capable of carrying out most basic ANALYSIS; a powerful REFRIGERATION system for cooling fermentation in insulated stainless steel fermenters, probably computer-controlled; and a must chiller to cool white grapes immediately after they have been crushed (unless they were machine harvested at night). The CRUSHER, PRESS, and FILTRATION equipment are usually of French, German, or Italian design and fabrication; and it is highly probable that there will be several large ROTOFERMENTERS supplementing the normal array of FERMENTATION VESSELS, including the Australian-designed Potter fermenters (see below).

The winery will routinely work 24 hours a day through the six to eight weeks of harvest using two shifts. The chief winemaker can work up to 18 hours a day. Scrupulous attention is paid to HYGIENE with caustic soda and citric acid solutions having replaced chlorine-based products.

Up to this point there is nothing particularly unusual in an international context, unless it be the extent of the refrigeration capacity and the rotofermenter capacity. It is the way Australian winemakers use the equipment, and the underlying technology, which differentiates them (and their wines) from winemakers (and wines) in most other parts of the world.

The basic aims—the maximum preservation of varietal fruit flavour, and an essentially soft and supple structure for both wood-matured white and wood-matured red wines—are achieved in a number of ways.

Primary FERMENTATION and the secondary MALOLACTIC FERMENTATION are initiated speedily by the use of cultured YEASTS, although ambient yeasts are used increasingly. White wine fermentations are carried out at relatively low temperatures (typically 12–14 °C/53–7 °F), usually with clear juice which has been cold-settled (see SETTLING), or filtered and protected against prefermentation OXIDATION (see PROTECTIVE WINEMAKING). The more complex, so-called 'dirty French' BARREL FERMENTATION of cloudy juice, LEES CONTACT, malolactic fermentation, and so forth is used for most of the best Chardonnay varietals and a handful of Sauvignon Blancs and Semillon/Sauvignon blends. The majority of AROMATICS and unwooded whites are made without malolactic fermentation, and are bottled within six to nine months after the harvest.

Because grapes grown in the warmer regions reach chemical RIPENESS and PHYSIOLOGICAL RIPENESS with relatively low levels of acidity, TARTARIC ACID is routinely added before or during the primary fermentation. In cooler areas, makers of white wines in particular endeavour to harvest the grapes with sufficient natural acidity to preclude, or at least minimize, acid additions. Nonetheless, Australian winemakers believe that if the ACIDIFICATION takes place at this stage, rather than later (and specifically rather than at BOTTLING), it cannot be distinguished from natural ACIDITY. CHAPTALIZATION, by contrast, is prohibited, even in the coolest regions, although certain forms of ENRICHMENT are permitted.

Red wines other than Pinot Noir are fermented at intermediate temperatures (22–8 °C) in a wide variety of fermentation vessels. The once-popular Potter fermenter (with a central vertical sieve cylinder for draining and PUMPING OVER) has been superseded by newer designs with single slope floors and sieves which hug either wall or floor, often with provision for wooden header boards for SUBMERGED CAP maceration. The handling of PINOT NOIR grapes is more complex: in this case, open-top fermenters are common, and an increasing number of wineries have the luxury of pneumatic devices for PUNCHING DOWN.

Extended MACERATION after fermentation is less commonly practised than in Europe or the United States, and is bypassed altogether with classic wines such as Penfolds Grange, which, like a significant proportion of fine Australian red wines, is pressed and put into barrel while still actively fermenting. The Australian belief is that post-fermentation maceration initially extracts more TANNINS, which entails extending the maceration to soften (by POLYMERIZATION) those tannins, and that this process dulls the fruit aroma and flavour, polymerization being an OXIDATIVE process (see OXIDATION). In the never-ending quest for complexity, it is common to put half the wine in new oak while still fermenting, the remaining half in old oak after extended post-fermentation maceration.

French OAK is preferred for top-quality white wines, for Pinot Noir, and much of the

Cabernet Sauvignon produced. American oak is widely used for SHIRAZ, Cabernet–Shiraz blends, and for some Cabernet Sauvignon. Overall, the trend is towards the use of French oak, perhaps in tandem with American oak. Better barrel-making of American oak is lessening the contrast with French oak, and giving less overt oak flavours. For lesser-quality wines, the use of OAK CHIPS or INNER STAVES (in conjunction with older barrels) is widespread.

After a false start due to an over-enthusiastic rate of use, 'micro-ox' has become standard procedure for lower-priced, big-volume red wines intended for immediate consumption. For the reasons given in MICRO-OXYGENATION, it may also be part of the production of premium wines in the larger, more sophisticated wineries.

Although in certain vintages many wine-makers wish it were otherwise, must CONCEN-TRATION equipment is not generally available. REVERSE OSMOSIS, as opposed to vacuum evapo-ration, is the preferred method, and some con-sultancy businesses bring the equipment on-site and carry out the procedure. The high cost limits its use.

Two issues have come to a head since 2000, seemingly unrelated, but both involving the use of SULFUR DIOXIDE. Up to that time, winemakers were following a politically correct path of re-ducing the total sulfur dioxide in their wines, and adding it in small, incremental doses. Laud-able though it may be from a perceived health point of view, the practice has been a root cause in the disconcertingly widespread appearance of BRETTANOMYCES, a problem which was rare as recently as the 1990s. The solution advocated by the AUSTRALIAN WINE RESEARCH INSTITUTE is to add sulfur dioxide in a dose of not less than 50 ppm if brett is detected. A back-up of sterile FILTRATION may be necessary in extreme circum-stances. In typical fashion, winemakers reacted swiftly, and the incidence of brett has rapidly retreated.

The other even more serious problem has been the increased incidence of RANDOM OXIDA-TION, particularly evident in cork-finished white wines, but also affecting red wines. The percent-age affected will grow with time, but once it first occurs, the percentage will be higher than that of CORK TAINT. Research into its causes has been underway for some time, but in the interim those who wish to continue to use corks are being advised to increase significantly the level of free sulfur dioxide at bottling.

In the early 21st century, wine styles changed to suit the public palate. While Australia still produces some rich, full-bodied red wines, there has been a move away from high alcohol so that 13.5 to 14.5% is a more likely range for South Australian Shiraz than the 14.5 to 15.5% norm at the turn of the century. Chardonnay alcohols also declined as winemakers realized that COOL-CLIMATE grapes could be harvested

earlier without any significant loss of flavour, so 12.5 to 13.5% is now very much more com-mon than 14%. Both Chardonnays and reds have also benefited from a reduction in the use of new, small oak BARRELS and the wines taste markedly less oaky. At the same time there was a move towards WHOLE-BUNCH FERMENTA-TION for at least a proportion of Shiraz lots. The result has been more complex, aromatic, softer wines with less assertive tannins and greater drinkability.

The Australian wine industry was built on FORTIFIED WINES but the most celebrated survi-vors of this category are the TOPAQUES AND MUS-CATS of Rutherglen and Glenrowan and a storehouse of ancient wines in wood at Sep-peltsfield in the BAROSSA VALLEY. The leading sparkling winemaker is Ed Carr, who is respon-sible for House of Arras, Australia's finest SPAR-KLING WINE brand based on Tasmanian grapes, as well as an array at various PRICE POINTS for HARDYS.

The twin problems of cork taint and random oxidation have led to the mass migration of winemakers from cork to SCREWCAP. In 2014, 85 to 90% of bottled wine was sealed with a screwcap.

Vine varieties

The following are the country's most widely planted varieties, red wine varieties first, in des-cending order of volume of wine produced.

Shiraz (432,340 tonnes in 2013) For long Aus-tralia's premier red wine grape in terms of area planted, Shiraz is also now securely planted on the throne. In 2013 it represented 46% of the red wine crush and nearly 24% of the all-grape total. It is grown in virtually every wine region, responding generously to the varying impera-tives of TERROIR and climate. The variety is iden-tical to the SYRAH of France and has a long Australian history. During the period in which Cabernet Sauvignon came into vogue, the fa-miliarity of Shiraz led to its being treated with a thoroughly undeserved degree of contempt. However, the old DRYLAND (non-irrigated) plantings of the Barossa Valley (producing vo-luptuously rich, potent wines) and the tradi-tional Hunter Valley wines (which become silky with age) initiated a surge of popularity in both domestic and export markets.

If Chardonnay was the ship which launched Australia's export armada, it is Shiraz which took command in the late 1990s, and continues to lead the fleet. It has led to the proliferation of Shiraz plantings in Old and New Worlds alike, as competitors have sought to match the Aus-tralian offering. But Australia has four advan-tages, three of which cannot be lessened. The first is the bank of old vines from 80 to 160 years old in New South Wales, Victoria, and South Australia, all UNGRAFTED and (usually)

dry-grown. The second is the equally long ex-perience vignerons have had in growing and making the wine. The third is an international icon, Grange, which only the northern Rhône can match. Fourth is the Joseph's Coat of styles from the huge range of terroir and climate, and the emergence of newer regions as promising as Heathcote. Here 500-million-year-old Cambri-an greenstone, an igneous rock, has weathered into a vivid red soil which, together with the climatic conditions, seems capable of becoming the greatest area for Shiraz in Australia.

Another new horizon for Shiraz is the loom-ing ability to differentiate CLONES (of this or any other variety). There appear to be a number of different clones, but we do not know whether Busby's cuttings taken from the Hermitage hill-side in 1832 were (as Busby's daily diary sug-gests) 'of three varieties of vines' (i.e. clones), or fewer, or more. Other importations may have added to clonal diversity, but there is also the belief that some apparently different clones may not be different at all, the difference in growth habit simply representing local terroir, climate, and several generations of viticultural techniques.

In the first decade and a half of the 21st century, Shiraz–Viognier blends from cooler-climate regions proliferated, as did Burgundian whole-bunch fermentation.

Cabernet Sauvignon looked likely to chal-lenge the supremacy of Shiraz as its production soared from 24,900 tonnes in 1989 to 317,472 tonnes in 2004, but then it dropped back to 249,689 tonnes by 2013. It barely existed in 1966 (100 ha/250 acres, 621 tonnes officially recorded). Its quality epicentre until the end of the 20th century was COONAWARRA, whence a disproportionate number of Australia's best Cabernet Sauvignons came initially, but MARGA-RET RIVER is now winning the race, eclipsing Coonawarra with its sheer number of outstand-ing wines. There is no question that the variety performs best in moderately cool regions with a climate similar to that of Bordeaux. Its thick skins and relatively loosely formed bunches provide a natural defence against DOWNY MIL-DEW and BOTRYTIS, which threaten so many re-gions during the growing season. Thus MARGARET RIVER, GREAT SOUTHERN, WRATTON-BULLY, CLARE VALLEY, and parts of central and southern VICTORIA produced most of the best Cabernets outside Coonawarra. That said, it is widely and successfully planted throughout Australia, except for the Riverland. While occa-sionally outstanding vintages such as 2002 manage to stand conventional wisdom on its head, the outlook is for the removal (or graft-ing) of Cabernet Sauvignon in the Riverina and Riverland regions.

Merlot The rate of growth of Merlot has out-paced all others since 1990 even though

Australia took an unusually long time to follow California's lead with the variety. In 1990, there were 509 ha/1,257 acres planted (almost 40% of which was not yet bearing) whereas in 2013, 131,575 tonnes were picked. As in California, there seems to be confusion over issues of flavour, structure, and style, well covered in the general discussion of the variety in this book. To the extent that there is consensus in Australia, it lies with structure and style: the wine should be medium-bodied, supple, and with soft, ripe tannins. As for flavour and style, some producers favour savoury, olive tones while others seek sweet, red berry fruit, just as some accept more new oak than others. The marketplace (both domestic and export) apparently regards these issues as irrelevant, and happily soaks up the wine in all of its manifestations.

Pinot Noir While Pinot Noir (of which 41,726 tonnes were picked in 2013) has not increased at the same death-defying rate as Merlot, its growth has surprised many. Calculating how much is used in sparkling wine production is not easy, but it is the major part. That said, when grown in the right regions, it can produce table wine of genuine, at times exhilarating, distinction. The most consistent regions are Geelong, Gippsland, Mornington Peninsula, Yarra Valley (all around Melbourne), and Tasmania. The Macedon Ranges and Adelaide Hills each have a handful of excellent producers, the remainder are inconsistent. Australia's very strict and cumbersome QUARANTINE provisions delayed the introduction of the newest Dijon clones of the now-retired Professor Raymond Bernard, giving New Zealand a distinct competitive advantage, but are now generally available.

Ruby Cabernet fell from 35,835 tonnes in 2004 to 13,206 tonnes in 2013. This strictly non-premium workhorse CROSS, used mainly for colour, is in retreat in the face of surplus Shiraz and Cabernet Sauvignon in Riverland and Riverina, where most Ruby Cabernet is planted. Most is used as a blend component in casks (see BOXES) and low-priced, generic, bottled wine.

Grenache fell from 25,935 tonnes in 2004 to 15,857 tonnes in 2013. Until the mid 1960s, 90% of Australia's red wine was fashioned from the three Rhône varieties: Shiraz, Grenache, and Mourvèdre. Then Cabernet Sauvignon and its Bordeaux handmaidens started to make inroads, followed in due course—though initially less convincingly—by Pinot Noir. Shiraz became less fashionable, Grenache and Mourvèdre even less so. Just when it seemed these varieties would cease to be at all significant, the worldwide interest in the Rhône varieties and wine styles reversed the trend. Century-old, dry-farmed, BUSH VINE Grenache in McLaren Vale (especially) and the Barossa Valley is once more in demand for TABLE WINE (previously most went into fortified wines)—see GSM. But, as ever, that portion of the crop produced from high-yielding, irrigated Riverland vineyards will make bland, lollyish wines. While total production has declined (and the drop is mostly in the irrigated regions), the best old-vine grapes from specialist regions such as McLaren Vale and the Barossa Valley are increasingly finding their way into super-premium bottlings, often at high prices.

Petit Verdot first hit the statistical radar in 1999, when 110 ha/272 acres were bearing (and well over twice that were still to come into bearing). In the face of overall red wine surplus, the meteoric rate of new plantings slowed with the planted area standing at 1,215 ha/3,000 acres in 2012. It has been planted in many places, in the cooler regions as a blend component with Cabernet Sauvignon, as in the MÉDOC, but its greatest success has come in the Riverland and Riverina. The warm climate guarantees its ripeness, and its strong colour, robust flavour, and substantial tannins result in wines with ample character, even when yields are high. Here it is typically presented as a single varietal wine, and enjoying much success. Riverland's Kingston Estate is its key champion.

Other red wine varieties Mourvèdre (often called Mataro) is used in precisely the same fashion as Grenache, and enjoyed the same recovery in the late 20th century, plantings increasing from 583 ha/1,440 acres in 1996 to 875 in 2006 but tapering off since, to 729 ha/1,800 acres in 2012. Other red varieties of importance: **Tempranillo** is the fastest-rising star, its plantings more than doubling between 2006 and 2012 to 712 ha/1,760 acres, and one wonders why it took so long for a variety which seems so well suited to Australian conditions to gain traction. **Sangiovese** leads the Italian band, with **Barbera, Dolcetto,** and **Nebbiolo** well behind and unlikely to close the gap. Enthusiasts have planted Sangiovese here, there, and everywhere, some with more success than others. A clear pattern is yet to emerge, but there seems to be greater potential than for Nebbiolo, although some superb Nebbiolos have been made, especially in the ADELAIDE HILLS and PYRENEES. Of the newer Italian varieties, **Montepulciano** and **Nero d'Avola** hold considerable promise. **Cabernet Franc** is becalmed; whether it is simply an issue of poor CLONES is not certain, but the wines generally lack focus except perhaps for some minor examples in MARGARET RIVER and GREAT SOUTHERN. **Malbec** has its moments of glory in both LANGHORNE CREEK and the CLARE VALLEY, where it has long formed a synergistic blend with Cabernet Sauvignon. **Durif** has been gaining ground for precisely the same reasons as Petit Verdot, providing wines with abundant colour and flavour from high yields in warm regions. Lesser varieties such as **Tannat, Saperavi**, **Sagrantino,** and **Lagrein** are now also in commercial production.

Chardonnay (397,239 tonnes in 2013, 22% of the nation's total crush). In Australia as elsewhere in the world, Chardonnay is seen as the grape of today and of tomorrow. In the first few years of this century, there were predictions of a glut which were not fulfilled. Plantings are still growing, albeit cautiously. In a climate of uncertainty about the desirability of new plantings, Chardonnay stands apart, with positive sentiment certain to see increased tonnages in the years ahead. It is grown in every wine region, bending as much to the wills of the viticulturists and winemakers as to the influence of climate and terroir. The style varies from simple to complex, quality from mediocre to excellent, factors increasingly recognized by a widening range of prices. Fluctuations in supply and demand have seen blends with Semillon, Colombard, Chenin Blanc, and so forth come and go; only Western Australia has persisted with an enduring market for Houghton HWB (previously White Burgundy) and Margaret River Classic.

Sauvignon Blanc The sustained increase in Sauvignon Blanc plantings and production (2,334 tonnes in 1995, 43,107 tonnes in 2004, and 98,212 tonnes in 2013) may come as a surprise to those who dislike the wine, mentally relegating it to second rank, but Sauvignon Blanc is now Australia's second most widely planted white variety. It will be no less surprising to viticultural economists who look at the price/quality competition from New Zealand and, in particular, Marlborough. One explanation is that Marlborough's success (supplying several of Australia's most popular wines) has engendered greater interest in and demand for the wine in both domestic and international markets. It also seems that the various interpretations of style (from cold-fermented in stainless steel and early bottled through to complex barrel-fermented wines with a splash of Semillon) all find their mark. The number of producers grows week by week, the apparently insatiable market demand pointing to increased plantings in the years ahead.

Semillon (rarely written Sémillon in the New World; 77,187 tonnes in 2013, a sharp fall from 103,171 tonnes in 2004) is in one sense Australia's traditional counterpart to Shiraz. Yet it is a conundrum. On the one hand, it has failed to make any substantial headway in export markets, arguably because it is not an internationally recognized single varietal: consumers buy white bordeaux, not Semillon/Sauvignon Blanc. In the domestic market, mature Hunter Valley Semillon (anywhere between five and 20-plus years old) has an ardent following in Sydney, but not elsewhere. Yet despite this, its production for high-quality dry wine continues to be strong: it is more than twice as important (in volume terms, at least) as Riesling. Historically in the Riverland and Riverina, where it produces large crops and wine superior to Trebbiano or Muscat Gordo Blanco, it was important, but most of the recent fall in plantings has been in these regions. At the other end of the scale, the best Semillons are 100% VARIETAL, including unoaked versions from the Hunter with an alcohol level of 10.5 to 11%, and those fermented in French oak, with or without a percentage of Sauvignon Blanc, from the Adelaide Hills and Margaret River at more conventional alcohol levels. The Semillon from the latter region, in particular, bears little or no resemblance to Hunter Valley Semillon, being much higher in alcohol (13 to 13.5%), richer, and more flavoursome in its youth.

Muscat Gordo Blanco Australia's MUSCAT OF ALEXANDRIA (70,564 tonnes in 2013) provides a more positively flavoured wine for cheap 'cask' blends than does SULTANA, but production is not likely to increase substantially (part is used for DRYING and part for grape juice). Muscat Gordo Blanco, in tandem with Gewurztraminer and Muscat Blanc à Petits Grains, has a new-found use with the FASHION for lightly sparkling, low-alcohol, slightly sweet wines labelled MOSCATO, which in Australia can be made from any of the Muscat-flavoured varieties.

Colombard (66,852 tonnes in 2013). The ability of this variety to retain ACIDITY has the same attractions in the warmer regions of Australia as in California, although its plantings are on nowhere near the same scale as those in California. The fifth most widely planted white variety in Australia, it shares its fortunes with those of Semillon, although it does not have any pretensions to the quality Semillon at its best can offer. Rather, it has a prodigious yield (routinely over 130 hl/ha) while retaining high levels of natural acidity, making it an ideal component in blended white wines sold in casks. Its strongholds are the Riverland and Riverina.

Pinot Gris/Pinot Grigio With 62,228 tonnes crushed in 2013 and growing steadily, Pinot Gris/Grigio has quickly risen to be Australia's sixth most widely planted white wine variety. Vinified either as an early-harvested, fairly neutral style loosely modelled on northern Italian Pinot Grigio, or picked riper to make a richer, more spicy, exotic and textural wine loosely

based on the Alsace Pinot Gris style, it has become a wine of such importance that it is no longer considered an ALTERNATIVE VARIETY. It is grown widely in the eastern states (but hardly at all in Western Australia, thanks to QUARANTINE laws) and performs especially well on the MORNINGTON PENINSULA.

Riesling (31,310 tonnes by 2013) will surely never regain the pre-eminent position it lost to Chardonnay in 1992 (and other white varieties since that time) but the long-heralded Riesling renaissance may just be at hand, even if the statistics need careful interpretation. In terms of tonnes crushed, the high point came in 1985, with 46,481, the low point in 2000 with 26,800. But during this time Riesling was being removed from regions to which it was not suited (notably the Riverland and Riverina). New plantings in appropriate regions were taking place, but there was a time lag as they came into bearing. The near-monopoly of the CLARE and EDEN VALLEYS for top-quality Riesling has been challenged by the GREAT SOUTHERN and, on a smaller scale, by TASMANIA, but there will be no seismic shift in the foreseeable future.

Verdelho (25,967 tonnes in 2004, down to 11,582 in 2013). Mid-19th-century writings were consistent in their view that this was Australia's most valuable white variety, the counterpart, as it were, of Shiraz. It was first imported in 1825 from Madeira by the Australian Agriculture Company, and on several other occasions thereafter. Quite why Australia should have embarked on an enthusiastic but solo (with the exception of Portugal) programme of making table wine with it is a mystery. It is a wine suited to everyday use from a vine that thrives in warm climates and yields well but not prodigiously, producing a popular, easy wine for relatively early drinking.

Other white varieties Marsanne has been grown at Tahbilk in the GOULBURN VALLEY for well over 100 years, having been taken there from Yeringberg in the YARRA VALLEY (in turn having come from Switzerland). Until relatively recently, Tahbilk's was the largest single-vineyard planting in the world, but the Rhône's sudden popularity in the US and elsewhere has seen it lose that title. Much smaller plantings of **Roussanne** are mainly used to blend with Marsanne. **Viognier** is exciting a great deal of interest, and in terms of area planted rivalled Verdelho by 2013. While most goes to make white wine, winemakers treasure it for the magic it works when CO-FERMENTED with Shiraz. **Gewurztraminer** has been around for a long time; blended with Riesling and made off-dry, it rightly inhabits Asian restaurant wine lists. Delicate—perhaps too delicate—dry, unblended versions are made on Tasmania and in the

cooler parts of Victoria. **Savagnin, Grüner Veltliner, Fiano, Vermentino, Arneis, Cortese, Garganega, Petit Manseng, Picolit, Schönburger**, and **Chenin Blanc** are but some of the more obscure white wine varieties also in commercial production.

Labelling laws
A common geographical designation found on lower-priced wines is the barely helpful SOUTH EASTERN AUSTRALIA, which takes in part of Queensland, all of New South Wales, all of Victoria, and that part of South Australia in which it is possible to grow grapes. In practice, it often signifies a wine made from fruit grown in areas as unglamorous as Riverland and/or Riverina.

Australia has had the major components of an APPELLATION system since 1963, initially through the framework of state legislation, but since 1987 effectively embodied in federal law, and since 1990 actively enforced by the official Australian Grape and Wine Authority (formerly the Australian Wine and Brandy Corporation) through the Label Integrity Programme (LIP). LIP annually carries out both general and specific audits, variously covering regions, varieties, and individual wineries, utilizing detailed production records which wineries must keep.

This is designed to ensure that where a variety or a region is specified, at least 85% of the wine is of that variety and/or from that region; that 85% is of the stated vintage; and, if more than one variety or region are specified, that they are listed in descending order. Thus Cabernet–Shiraz means the wine has more Cabernet Sauvignon grapes than Shiraz; Shiraz–Cabernet the reverse.

The missing link—a legislative definition of the boundaries of each region spurred on by the wine agreement signed between the EU and Australia in 1994—was completed in the late 1990s with the passing of regulations under the Federal Wine and Brandy Corporation Act. This has provided the framework for the methodical mapping of Australia into **zones, regions**, and **subregions**, all glorying under the ultimately bureaucratic and infinitely ugly term **Geographical Indications** (GI or GIs).

By 1996, each state had divided itself into **zones**: New South Wales has eight, Victoria six, South Australia eight, and Western Australia five. There was—and is—no requirement of geographic or climatic particularity, no rules for the drawing of the zone boundaries. Simple pragmatism ruled, although South Australia managed to complicate matters by introducing a **super zone**, and Western Australia came up with a series of utterly confusing and seemingly meaningless zone names. Compared with that which followed, it was a relatively simple and speedy process.

The legislation requires that a **region** is a single tract of land that is discrete and homogeneous in its grape growing attributes to a degree that is measurable; that it usually produces at least 500 tonnes of grapes a year; that it includes at least five differently owned vineyards each of at least 5 ha/12 acres; and that it may reasonably be regarded as a region.

A **subregion** must also be a single tract of land, comprising at least five independently owned wine grape vineyards of at least 5 ha each, and must usually produce 500 tonnes of wine grapes in a year. However, a subregion is required to be substantially discrete within the region and have substantial homogeneity in grape growing attributes over the area.

The ever-increasing spread of vineyards means new regions will continue to be created. The identifying of subregions is proceeding more slowly and thoughtfully; as of 2014, only 14 had been registered, notably in Western Australia's Great Southern region, the Hunter Valley, and Adelaide Hills. By 2014, 65 regions had been finally determined, and work continues on others.

The once widespread but now largely discredited use of GENERIC names such as claret, burgundy, champagne, port, and sherry has all but disappeared under the terms of the 1994 EU wine agreement. Such names were never permitted on export labels anyway. Australian Sherry and Port have almost vanished; what was once Sherry is now APERA and red FORTIFIED WINES will be sold as Tawny and Vintage. What was formerly Liqueur Tokay is now TOPAQUE or, more rarely, Dessert Muscadelle. For Dessert Muscat and Topaque, the voluntary categories of Classic, Grand, and Rare are now in common usage.

Wine trade organization

The structure of the wine sector, measured by the size of individual companies or groups, underwent profound changes in the first few years of the 21st century, and more are sure to come. The largest was the assimilation of Hardys by CONSTELLATION of the US to form the world's largest wine group. Soon afterwards, Constellation sold its Australian wine interests to local venture capitalists Champ Equity (see ACCOLADE). The most publicized change was the acquisition by Southcorp of Rosemount, and the financial haemorrhage which ensued. What seemed to be the most successful at the time was the 2000 acquisition of Beringer in California (by brewers Foster's who went on to swallow Southcorp/Rosemount) to form Beringer Blass, with the disappearance of the Mildara name. In 2011, Foster's separated its wine division from its brewing division and renamed it TREASURY WINE Estates. The 2002 merger of Simeon Wines and Brian McGuigan Wines, and the acquisition by that group of Miranda

Wines, Yaldara, and later Nepenthe, lifted McGuigan into the top four, where it remained in 2014—although in 2008 it was renamed, rather curiously, Australian Vintage Limited. Evans & Tate transformed itself from a small to medium winery based in the Margaret River to Australia's eighth-largest wine group by acquiring Cranswick Estate and was then taken over by McWilliam's in 2007. Arguably, the greatest success story was that of Riverina-based Casella Wines, nowhere in the top 20 companies in 2000, and by 2014 third-largest thanks to its enormous sales of YELLOW TAIL into the United States and elsewhere.

The sale of wine within Australia is relatively simple, and notably free of the restraints which apply in the United States, unless it be the all-up tax on retail wine sales of over 40%. Movement between the states is unhindered, and wine producers may sell to whomever they wish (distributors, retailers, or the public), wherever they wish. One of the particular freedoms of Australia is the BYO restaurant, 'BYO' standing for Bring Your Own. In Victoria, 'Licensed and BYO' restaurants which generously encourage patrons to bring their own wine are common. This ethic spreads across all restaurants in Australia. Most will permit patrons to bring their own wine upon payment of a CORKAGE fee, if the request is made in appropriate fashion.   J.H. & H.H.

Allen, M., *The Future Makers* (Melbourne, 2010).

Beeston, J., *A Concise History of Australian Wine* (3rd edn, Sydney, 2001).

Halliday, J., *Australia Wine Companion* (Sydney, annually).

Major, M. (ed.), *The Australian and New Zealand Wine Industry Directory* (Adelaide, annually).

www.wineaustralia.com

www.wineaustralia.net.au

www.winecompanion.com.au

www.csu.edu.au/nwgic

Australian influence on wine production, marketing, and even distribution is difficult to overestimate. When the chips are finally counted, Australia will be credited with having had an enormous influence on the wine world of the late 20th century. Its VITICULTURISTS (notably the viticulture editor of this book) pioneered sophisticated CANOPY MANAGEMENT techniques and all sorts of tricks such as niceties of irrigation (see PARTIAL ROOTZONE DRYING) and hi-tech SOIL MAPPING. Australia's winemakers travelled the world—especially the northern hemisphere where the HARVEST conveniently takes place during the southern hemisphere lull—quietly infiltrating all manner of wineries with Australian technology, obsession with HYGIENE, and record water usage (see FLYING WINEMAKERS). One of their distinguishing marks is their commitment to long hours, ignoring weekends and evenings, at the critical periods during and

immediately after harvest. Graduates of oenology and viticulture courses at Australian universities such as ADELAIDE and CHARLES STURT UNIVERSITY are now dispersed around the world, and the AUSTRALIAN WINE RESEARCH INSTITUTE (AWRI) is increasingly recognized as one of the most important, and practical, forces in ACADEME. It is significant that the world's largest and canniest wine company, E & J GALLO of California, deliberately recruited an Australian to lead its wine research department into the new millennium. Australia overtook France to be most important exporter of wine to the UK, one of the world's most significant wine importers, at the beginning of the century, and went on to perform the same trick in the US, but Australian wine was this popular only temporarily with Americans. The spectacular success of YELLOW TAIL tarnished its image so that it came to be dismissively associated with 'critter brands'. Such was Australia's late-20th-century success at developing and selling BRANDS to suit the modern international marketplace that for many years it was seen as a model even by such experienced wine exporters as the French. Alliances between Australian companies and global players in the drinks trade have been a notable feature of the GLOBALIZATION of the wine trade (see AUSTRALIA—Wine trade organization).

Australian Wine Research Institute

(**AWRI**) is a wine research, development, and extension organization owned and led by the Australian wine industry. Based in Adelaide, it also has offices in Victoria, New South Wales, and Tasmania. Formed in 1955, its governing board includes members elected by Australian winemakers and vine-growers who pay the Wine Grapes and Grape Research levy.

Research is designed to increase fundamental understanding, particularly of wine's composition, style, and sensory characteristics, but the AWRI has been famous among its peers for remaining responsive to the applied needs of producers and consumers. It has been particularly good at translating its research results into usable applications and fostering their adoption, and at spreading word of research and the development of practical solutions from around the world. In tough economic times the AWRI has been depending increasingly on income from commissions in ANALYSIS, benchmarking, and technical validation, as well as from providing export certificates and site audits.

The Institute conducts seminars and workshops and has published more than 1,540 papers and articles.

www.awri.com.au

Austria produces an average of 2.5 million hl/66 million gal wine a year but is more famous for the quality rather than the quantity of its wines, especially dry and sweet whites and also reds from the dark-skinned grapes grown on more than one-third of Austria's vineyard area. Average yields are relatively low, around 50 hl/ha (3 tons/acre).

History

Austria is among the many places into which CELTIC tribes are thought to have introduced grape growing, but historical records begin with the ROMANS. That Austria suffered under DOMITIAN's notorious AD 92 edict prohibiting viticultural expansion can only be assumed. But this much is documented: Emperor Probus, in rescinding that edict two centuries later, expressly encouraged new plantings both in Gaul and in Pannonia—the Great Plain that incorporates today's eastern Austria. From his 5th-century base in the Roman garrison town of Mautern, St Severin is believed to have planted the first WACHAU vineyards. Control of the subsequently burgeoning vineyards west of Vienna passed largely to a collection of Bavarian ecclesiastical institutions in the wake of Charlemagne's victories over the Avars in the late 8th century. Numerous important Austrian estates and vineyards are still owned and some operated by Roman Catholic institutions, which are by no means the exclusive bottlers of official Messwein, whose consumption transcends mass. The legacy of several Bavarian founders lives on in more than just the physical structures that they left behind, including the Wachau's towering stone terraces of Mediterranean inspiration, begun in the 11th century. Stift Göttweig, a huge wine-growing MONASTERY that dominates the landscape south of Krems, was founded by a bishop of Bavarian Passau in 1083; yet-larger KLOSTERNEUBURG dates from soon afterward; and the Salomon family of Krems-Stein's Undhof have for two centuries been renewing a land-for-wine rental contract with a charitable institution in Passau which first acquired those vineyards around 1200.

An Austrian tradition of small vineyard-holders dispensing their wine—institutionalized eventually as HEURIGER—is often said to have Carolingian origins; and by the Middle Ages, Vienna was notorious for copious consumption of wine, after which it was named. The evolution of viticulture in what was then westernmost Hungary led to several Neusiedlersee vineyard sites coming under direct royal control and by the mid-16th century, barrels of wine from Rust were branded 'R', leading to the town being declared a free city just over a century later. Successive waves of Ottoman invasions in the 17th century did not halt the expansion of vineyards. Moreover, many of the 'new settlers' for which the Neusiedlersee is named—waves of Croatians and southern Germans who arrived

to repopulate its shores—became wine growers, like their descendants.

The so-called Biedermeier era of Austrian stability that followed Napoleon saw the emergence not only of a prosperous, wine-drinking middle class, but also of vine science and vine nurseries, so that by the mid 19th century, the Hapsburg empire had become internationally renowned as a source for viticultural expertise and budwood. In 1860 a national school of viticulture and winemaking was established at Klosterneuburg. This was also a period of international success for Austrian wine, curtailed by PHYLLOXERA, identified relatively early by Klosterneuburg scientists. Meticulous wine historian Franz Schams identified many of the villages and vineyards that are still considered Austria's best as early as the 1830s, even if they often grew vine varieties different from those found there today. This was the case as recently as the mid 20th century, when plantings of GEMISCHTER SATZ (field blends) remained the norm. Silvaner (which was called Österreicher), flourished while Grüner Veltliner was encountered only in selected sectors, and Riesling was a real rarity.

The 20th century's world wars visited disaster on Austria, but each with distinctly different viticultural consequences. Following the collapse of the Austro-Hungarian empire in the wake of the First World War, vast wine regions were shed, including those of Moravia in what is now the CZECH REPUBLIC, FRIULI, CROATIA's Dalmatian Coast, SLOVENIA, SLOVAKIA, and much of today's ROMANIA. The Second World War brought physical devastation to Austrian vineyards on a significant scale and the plundering of virtually every wine cellar in the country by Soviet occupying troops. In rebuilding Austria's vineyards in the 1950s and 1960s, considerable attention was devoted to efficiency and where possible, MECHANIZATION (see, LENZ MOSER).

After four hard decades of vineyard revival, characterized by the remarkable ascendance of GRÜNER VELTLINER as Austria's national grape and by the international re-emergence of the Thermenregion and of the sweet-wine culture of the Neusiedlersee, Austria suffered yet another viticultural calamity of her own making. In mid 1985, dessert wines from the Burgenland region were found to have been laced with diethylene glycol, added by a handful of unscrupulous vintners or merchants to imitate the unctuous characteristics imparted by BOTRYTIS. While nobody is known to have been poisoned, the market for Austrian wine at home and abroad was devastated. Vinous integrity demanded a completely fresh start. Implementation of stringent quality standards, combined with consumer consciousness of estate bottling and wine purity, led to a rebuilding of Austrian wine culture in ways nobody could have

foreseen before the scandal. Through VINEA WACHAU, the Wachau's growers established quality benchmarks that went beyond Austria's new wine laws and set the stage for international prestige. Südsteiermark emerged from a century of obscurity to national stardom. And a young Viennese pharmacist named Alois Kracher returned home to transform his family's estate into a beacon of quality, rescuing the reputation of Burgenland, the very region from which had emerged the wines that poisoned an industry. By the late 1990s, Austrian wine was enjoying unprecedented export success and prestige that has continued to this day.

Geography, geology, and climate

NIEDERÖSTERREICH, STEIERMARK (Styria), and BURGENLAND are the three Austrian states that incorporate all but a tiny morsel of Austrian vineyard. Along a roughly 100 km/62 mile, almost continuously planted stretch of the Danube's left and occasionally right bank upstream of Vienna and north all the way to the Czech frontier, lie those regions of Niederösterreich known for their Grüner Veltliner and Riesling. And while the latter enjoys less than a 5% share of acreage, it not only makes up for this in notoriety and price, it also serves as a useful climatic touchstone. This part of Austria is where Riesling feels at home: cool enough, but dry—like the Vosges rainshadow of ALSACE. Another feature common to most of this sector—which incorporates the growing regions of Wachau, KAMPTAL, KREMSTAL, TRAISENTAL, WAGRAM, and WEINVIERTEL—is wide, regular diurnal temperature variation (see TEMPERATURE VARIABILITY). Austrian descriptions of some Niederösterreich vineyard soils may refer to Urgestein, usually translated as 'primary rock', a term and a concept long obsolete in GEOLOGY. It is used in Austria for relatively old, tough rocks such as GRANITE and GNEISS, which contrast with younger, softer materials such as LOESS (also common) and ALLUVIUM.

Vienna—an urban viticultural morsel that is itself officially a state—serves as a sort of fulcrum of Austrian wine growing. Its best-known vineyards, on the city's north-western edge, are dominated by Grüner Veltliner but were historically renowned for Riesling. Two smaller concentrations of vines on Vienna's southern fringe feature red grapes as well as white, and point towards the conditions that dominate in the adjacent Niederösterreich regions of THERMENREGION and CARNUNTUM, as well as the four growing regions of Burgenland that hug Austria's border with Hungary. Here, warm air from Hungary's Pannonian Plain dominates the grape-growing season, although winters are often bitterly cold, and precipitation is even lighter than in the wine regions dominated by Grüner Veltliner and Riesling to the west.

Most of Austria's red wine vines (about a third of the national total) are grown here, and Grüner Veltliner is less important than many other white grapes, whether for dry or the sweet wines responsible for the Neusiedlersee's centuries-old reputation.

The third viticultural part of Austria, the country's south east, corresponds to the three growing regions of Steiermark (Styria), overwhelmingly the most important of which is Südsteiermark, whose vineyards saturate a sector south of Graz and along a 40 km/25 mile stretch of the Slovenian frontier. Cool and well-watered, the steep hillsides here would no doubt support Riesling, but historical circumstance or caprice has dictated differently, and Sauvignon Blanc, Chardonnay, Pinot Blanc (Weissburgunder), Welschriesling, and Muskateller dominate along with Zweigelt for reds.

Vine varieties

Given the huge number of grape varieties grown in Austria and how many are INDIGENOUS or at least little-known elsewhere, an overview is in order. Among whites, Grüner Veltliner—with roughly a 30% share of plantings nationwide—has become known as Austria's national grape, even though its role in Burgenland is only modest and in Steiermark practically non-existent. Austrian wines from this grape—virtually always dry—capture an otherwise unprecedented range of flavours, including those of lentils, green beans, mange-tout, cress, rhubarb, beetroot, roasted red peppers, tobacco, white and black pepper, citrus zest, iris, and nutmeg. A tactile 'bite' or pleasantly sizzling peppery astringency—referred to by Austrians as *Pfefferl*—is often treated as a varietal signature. Arguably also without precedent is this grape's ability to achieve satisfying ripeness and completeness at levels of POTENTIAL ALCOHOL ranging from as little as 10.5% to as much as 15%. Grüner Veltliner wines can reflect vineyard identity as well as mature impressively in bottle for decades. There can be enormous variation in size and colour of berry; size and shape of cluster; vine VIGOUR; and wine flavour. The painstaking massal selection undertaken by the Wachau's Franz Pichler in the mid 20th century has made possible today's quality.

Riesling by no means takes a back seat to Grüner Veltliner in quality, although it occupies less than 5% of Austria's vineyards. As they do elsewhere, the wines vary considerably in strength and demonstrate an uncanny ability to reflect TERROIR. Most Austrian examples are dry and can tolerate alcohols over 13% rather better than their dry German counterparts, but after a brief flirtation with strengths of 14% or more, most growers actively seek, through viticultural adaptation and slightly earlier harvest, to keep levels below 13.5%.

Austrian Riesling is almost uniformly lower in acidity and tends towards less effusive aromas than its German counterparts, but at its best offers a crescendo of flavours on the finish. It tends to be leaner in texture than Alsace Riesling and to age a little faster than the best examples of Germany and Alsace, and Austria's best Grüner Veltliner.

Welschriesling, a traditional mainstay of Austrian viticulture, is planted on nearly twice as much land as true Riesling. It is prized commercially for light, bracing examples from Styria and considered a key player in Burgenland's botrytis belt. A few important growers also make dry or off-dry examples with considerable complexity, which suggests an increase in respect for the variety. Pinot Blanc—here generally called Weissburgunder—is arguably one of Austria's hidden strengths, capable of subtle and seductive complexity while uniting natural creaminess with refreshing animation; and having at least one or two eloquent champions in nearly every growing region. Chardonnay may be more common, but Austrian statistics have yet to thoroughly distinguish between the two, which collectively account for around 7% of the country's vineyard. Sauvignon Blanc is treated as the signature grape of Steiermark.

Gelber Muskateller—a variant of Muscat Blanc à Petit Grains—has a long tradition throughout Austria, even if the total planted is small. Light, bracing wines in Südsteiermark represent its one instance of commercial as opposed to merely aesthetic significance. Roter TRAMINER (here typically labelled simply Traminer, as it can be both its Gewürz-variant and a rare yellow Austrian strain) and Pinot Gris (here usually called Grauburgunder) are also grapes of long-standing if modest acreage in Austria. ROTER VELTLINER and NEUBURGER are two highly distinctive indigenous varieties whose wines tend towards high alcohol but are capable of remarkable longevity. Rotgipfler and Zierfandler are two more distinctive indigenous varieties associated with the THERMENREGION. BOUVIER and SCHEUREBE (here also called Sämling 88) deserve mention for their role in sweet wines from the Neusiedlersee; and FURMINT for its recent revival in Rust, in dry as well as AUSBRUCH wines.

Among red wine grapes, ZWEIGELT dominates Austria with a roughly 14% share of the national vineyard and (unlike Grüner Veltliner) has a significant presence in every wine region. Best known for the forward fruitiness of its solo expressions, it also figures in some more ambitious wines, especially when blended with other Austrian or Bordeaux varieties. Austrian red wine acreage grew rapidly at the beginning of this century. An exception appears to be Blaufränkisch, last pegged officially in 2013 at almost 7% of Austrian vine acreage, nearly all of

that in Burgenland. From the 1990s it was recognized that its wines can be profound and worth ageing if yields are modest and it is treated to long ÉLEVAGE. Black fruits, tobacco, resinous herbs, and black pepper are among the characteristics associated with Blaufränkisch wines, which demonstrate striking ability to reflect their soils and sites of origin. Selections whose grapes are smaller-berried and thicker-skinned than the late-20th-century norm are being actively sought.

St Laurent may or may not be an Austrian original, but it is today little known elsewhere, and given the fragility and finicky temperament it seems to have inherited from Pinot Noir, its under 2% share of acreage by no means secures its future. At their best, wines from St Laurent display rich fruit allied to even plusher texture than Pinot Noir (Blauburgunder) which represented 1.3% of Austria's vine surface in 2013. The Bordeaux red varieties are also grown to a limited extent and though uncommon, Syrah has some serious proponents in Burgenland and neighbouring Carnuntum. A picture of Austrian viticulture would be incomplete without mention of two traditionally widespread red wine varieties, BLAUBURGER and Blauer PORTUGIESER—at roughly 2% and 3% of acreage respectively. Like Müller-Thurgau among white grapes with its 4% share of Austrian acreage, these varieties are statistically significant if largely bereft of grower-champions and probably destined to decline.

Wine labelling

Austria shares much of its wine vocabulary with GERMANY, but a term can vary significantly in both the extent to and meaning with which it is employed in each country. Austrian wine law enshrines the term Kabinett for unchaptalized, dry Qualitätswein (Austria's equivalent of PDO) of up to 13% alcohol and from grapes of at least 17 °KMW (84 °OECHSLE). But in practice the term is seldom employed and where wines are so-labelled this is usually in small print. The term Spätlese imposes a higher minimum MUST weight and may be applied to wine with tasteable RESIDUAL sugar. But in practice that term is increasingly absent from Austrian wine labels. With the advent of DAC legislation, the term Reserve has effectively replaced Spätlese in those regions where that term was used for dry wines, while Klassik is used for wines formerly labelled Kabinett. There is, however, some use of the term Spätlese in Burgenland for lightly sweet wines from largely botrytis-free grapes. The official Austrian *Prädikats* of Auslese, Beerenauslese, and Trockenbeerenauslese apply to wines of incrementally higher minimum must weights and with noticeable residual sugar. They are used throughout the country but in practice are common only in those sectors of

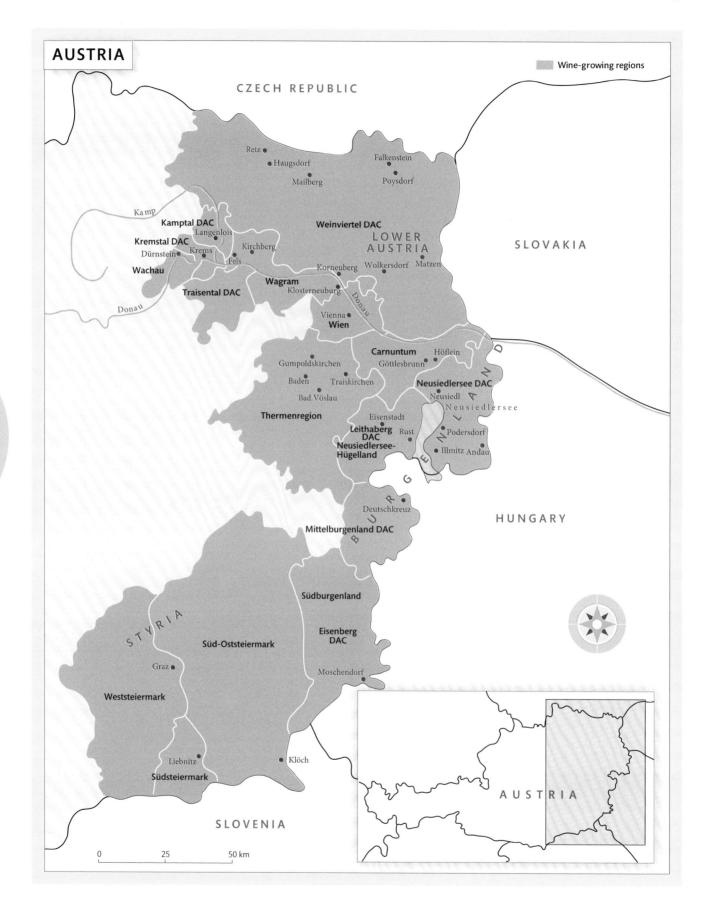

Burgenland that specialize in BOTRYTIZED sweet wine, which is also where the more specialized categories of Strohwein (STRAW WINE), EISWEIN, and AUSBRUCH are almost exclusively used. It can be safely assumed that an Austrian wine is dry-tasting unless it is labelled prominently with one of the so-called Prädikats. Growers therefore rarely use the word trocken (less than 9g/l residual sugar) prominently on their labels.

All Austrian wines meeting the standards set for Qualitätswein feature the so-called *Bande-role*, a neck band or capsule top featuring the red and white stripes of the national flag, which serves not only as a guarantee that the wine has met federal production limits and quality controls, including any implied by the terms on its label, but also acts (by means of a long string of tiny digits) to track the wine. The former Austrian legal category Tafelwein, now simply Wein (see WINE WITHOUT GEOGRAPHICAL INDICATION), refers to wines with must weights below those for Qualitätswein but a minimum of 8.5% alcohol. In practice, very little such wine is produced and virtually none is exported. Wines falling into the slightly more elevated official category Landwein, the equivalent of PGI, are almost as rare, although as elsewhere a few sometimes talented and visionary growers, frustrated by repeated failures to win Qualitätswein status, unapologetically or even proudly become refuseniks.   D.S.

Blom, P., *The Wines of Austria* (2nd edn London, 2006).

Moser, P., *Falstaff Ultimate Wine Guide Austria* (Vienna, annually).

Pigott, S., et al., *Wein Spricht Deutsch: Weine, Winzer, Weinlandschaften* (Frankfurt, 2007).

www.austrianwine.com

authentication

authentication. The gripping tale of skul-duggery arising from the Christie's 1985 AUCTION of the so-called 'Jefferson Lafite' was the first high-profile case in a subsequent litany of suspected COUNTERFEIT WINES, highlighting the growing need for the authentication of fine wine. Skyrocketing fine-wine PRICES, increased global demand, and the initial complacency of wine producers, auctioneers, and FINE WINE traders exacerbated the likely loss of revenues, BRAND VALUES, and consumer confidence still further.

With the emergence of new markets, ASIA in particular, the potential for irretrievable damage has led to a rise in the number of wine appraisal and authentication experts as well as the exploration by producers and collectors of methods of validating the authenticity of their wines. Such approaches are limited to a certain extent, however, by a lack of coordinated effort that would result in shared industry standards and solutions such as education, investigation, and law enforcement.

One of the most popular security measures aimed at reassuring customers has been the development of the Prooftag Bubble Tag. This device, used by, among others, Domaines Baron de Rothschild (Lafite) and Ch Palmer, consists of a translucent polymer with a randomly self-generated constellation of bubbles. The Bubble Tag authenticates a bottle's origins and allows access to information on the producer's website.

Another solution developed by eProvenance primarily to track and assure wine condition has been the use of RFID (Radio Frequency Identification) TEMPERATURE sensor technology along with a secure, online global database to monitor wine shipment temperatures across distribution channels. The RFID chip can be linked to a sequential serial number and randomly generated number for authentication purposes.

Other traceability and authentication measures in use or development include Argonne's anti-tampering cap that fits over a bottle's cork, proprietary paper with an ultra-violet signature, laser and other invisible product markings on bottles and/or labels, DNA codes, holograms, watermarks, NFC (near field communications) security tags, chips and electronic 'tongue' sensors whose tiny synthetic membranes built on a silicon chip can be developed to identify substances affecting quality or indicating wine fraud. No countermeasure though, however advanced, is yet known to be 100% proof against fraud or can be applied retrospectively to older vintages on the secondary market without the benefit of these technologies.   A.H.L.R

McCoy, E., www.wine-searcher.com/m/2014/07/five-ways-wineries-fight-counterfeits.

Wallace, B., *The Billionaire's Vinegar—The Mystery of the World's Most Expensive Bottle of Wine* (New York, 2008).

www.wineberserkers.com/forum

investdrinks-blog.blogspot.co.uk

autochthonous varieties

autochthonous varieties. See INDIGENOUS VARIETIES.

autolysis

autolysis, the destruction of the internal structures of cells by their own ENZYMES. In a winemaking context, the term most commonly applies to the action of dead YEAST cells, or LEES, after a second fermentation has taken place during SPARKLING WINEMAKING. Its effects are greatest if wine is left in contact with the lees of a second fermentation in bottle for at least five years, and minimal if LEES CONTACT lasts for less than 18 months. MOUTHFEEL is improved through the release of POLYSACCHARIDES and peptides; OXIDATION is inhibited through the release of GLUTATHIONE and reducing enzymes; and the production of certain MANNOPROTEINS reduces tartrate precipitation and improves protein stability. In addition, there is an increase in amino acids, which may be the precursors of those flavour characteristics typically associated with CHAMPAGNE such as acacia, biscuity or bready notes, and other complex aromas from BOTTLE AGEING.

Autolysis also occurs during ageing on lees of still white wines after fermentation. The changes in the chemical composition of such wines are highly desirable.

Charpentier, C., and Feuillat, M., 'Yeast autolysis', in G. H. Fleet (ed.), *Wine Microbiology and Biotechnology* (Switzerland, 1993).

autovinification

autovinification, method of vinification designed to extract maximum COLOUR from red grapes and used primarily in the production of red port. Autovinification, a process involving automatic PUMPING OVER, was developed in ALGERIA in the 1960s, where it was known as the Ducellier system. Faced with a shortage of LABOUR in the 1960s, port producers were forced to abandon the traditional practice of treading grapes by foot in LAGARES. Many isolated QUINTAS had no electricity and so shippers built central wineries. The power supply was erratic and too weak for sophisticated pumps or presses so the shippers installed autovinification tanks in order to extract sufficient colour and TANNINS in the short FERMENTATION period prior to FORTIFICATION. Autovinification is a self-perpetuating process induced by the build-up of pressure; no external power source is needed.

Crushed and partially destemmed grapes are pumped into specially constructed autovinification vats (see diagram overleaf) which are filled to within about 75 cm (29 in) of the top. The vat is closed and the autovinification unit (*a*) is screwed into place. As the fermentation begins, CARBON DIOXIDE is given off and pressure builds up inside the vat. This drives the fermenting must up an escape valve (*b*) which spills out into an open reservoir (1) on top of the vat. Eventually the pressure will also force the water out of a second valve (*c*) into a smaller, separate reservoir (2). When the water has been expelled, the carbon dioxide that has built up in the vat escapes with explosive force through valve (*c*). The fermenting must in reservoir (1) falls back into the vat down the central autovinification unit (*a*), spraying the floating CAP of grape skins, so extracting colour and tannin. At the same moment, the water in reservoir (2) returns to valve (*c*), again sealing in the carbon dioxide, and the process repeats itself. The cycle continues until the winemaker judges that sufficient grape sugar has been fermented to alcohol, and sufficient COLOUR has been extracted, at which time the wine is run off and fortified just as described in PORT, winemaking.

At the start of fermentation, when a small amount of carbon dioxide is given off, the autovinification cycle is slow. But when the fermentation is in full swing, the pressure build-up is such that the cycle takes only 10–15 minutes to complete.

a

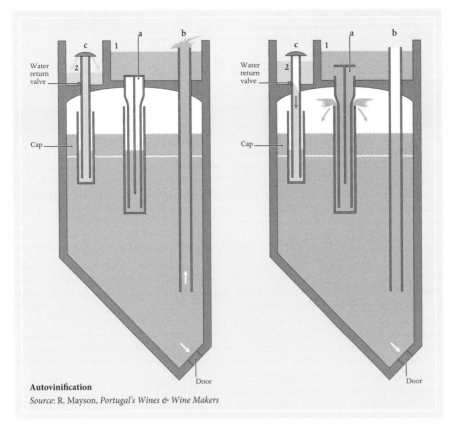

Autovinification

Source: R. Mayson, *Portugal's Wines & Wine Makers*

Originally autovinification vats were built from concrete and lined with resin-painted concrete. However, significant modifications have accompanied improvements in both wine-making technology and the power supply to the DOURO valley, where port is produced. Modern autovinification tanks are made from STAINLESS STEEL and are equipped with REFRIGERATION units to prevent the must from overheating. Some shippers have resorted to traditional pumping over, or *remontage*, although this generally provides insufficient EXTRACTION for better-quality port. Other shippers have successfully combined pumping over with autovinification, thereby giving the winemaker greater control over port fermentation than ever before, although lagares are preferred by many for top-quality ports.   R.J.M.

Auvergne, Côtes d', AOC which is administratively considered part of the greater LOIRE region, and basin, but these Massif Central vineyards, around Clermont-Ferrand, are in fact closer to the vineyards of the northern RHÔNE than they are to the river Loire itself. From fewer than 300 ha/750 acres of mainly Gamay, occasionally Pinot Noir, and some Chardonnay vines, light reds and some pinks and whites are made with considerable skill from some of the many small enterprises here. Gamay has long been grown here and this was one of the most important wine regions of France

in the 19th century, before which Pinot Noir was grown in preference to Gamay. The names of the communes Boudes, Chanturgue, Châteaugay, and Madargue may be appended to Côtes d'Auvergne for reds, Corent for rosés. Most wines are consumed locally; none is expensive.

Auxerre, once an important city in the Yonne *département* of north east France. Today CHABLIS is the Yonne's most famous and substantial wine appellation, but in the time of CHARLEMAGNE, the region centred on Auxerre 20 km/12 miles west had many more vineyards, being a larger centre of population and being conveniently situated on a river which leads directly into the Seine and thence to the PARIS basin. It is perhaps not surprising, given its historic importance, that so many vine varieties have the name or synonym AUXERROIS, meaning 'of Auxerre'.

Within the region, IRANCY has had its own appellation for Pinot Noir since 1999 and ST-BRIS for its Sauvignon Blanc. There are also regional appellations for light reds made mainly from Pinot Noir and whites from Chardonnay sold as BOURGOGNE with one of these suffixes: Chitry, Côte Saint-Jacques, Côtes d'Auxerre, Coulanges-la-Vineuse, Epineuil (reds only), and, for whites only, Vézelay and Tonnerre.

Auxerrois is both a synonym for the black-berried MALBEC in CAHORS, where it is the

dominant vine variety, and the name of a relatively important white-berried variety in Alsace. And as if that were not confusing enough, **Auxerrois Gris** is a synonym for PINOT GRIS in Alsace, while Chardonnay, before it became so famous, was once known as Auxerrois Blanc in the Moselle—as distinct from **Auxerrois de Laquenexy**, which is the variety today called Auxerrois in north east France (including Alsace) and LUXEMBOURG.

In 1999, DNA PROFILING at DAVIS showed that this Auxerrois is a progeny of Pinot and Gouais Blanc (see PINOT). There are still minuscule plantings of Auxerrois in the Loire but today it is most important in Alsace, the French Moselle (including CÔTES DE TOUL) and Luxembourg, where it is most valued, particularly for its low acidity. If yields are suppressed, which they rarely are, the variety can produce excitingly rich wines that are worth ageing until they achieve a bouquet with a honeyed note like that of mature Chablis, the wine which today could be described as 'from AUXERRE' or, in French, Auxerrois.

Virtually all of the French 2012 total of 2,419 ha/5,975 acres is in Alsace where it is much more popular than Pinot Blanc even though it is rarely seen on a label. Auxerrois produces slightly flabby, broad wines which are blended into, or may indeed constitute, many a wine labelled PINOT BLANC. Auxerrois is also a major ingredient in EDELZWICKER.

It is also planted to a limited extent in Germany, the Netherlands, and Canada.

Robinson, J., Harding, J., and Vouillamoz, J., *Wine Grapes: A Complete Guide to 1,368 Vine Varieties, Including their Origins and Flavours* (London, 2012).

Auxey-Duresses, a village in Burgundy producing medium-priced red and white wines not dissimilar to neighbouring VOLNAY and MEURSAULT respectively, although more austere in style. The vineyards, which include those of the hamlets of Petit Auxey and Melin, are located on either side of a valley subject to cooler winds than the main Côte de BEAUNE. PINOT NOIR vineyards, including such PREMIERS CRUS as Les Duresses and Le Climat de Val, are grown on the south east slope of the Montagne du Bourdon. White wines, made from CHARDONNAY, account for just above a quarter of the production, covering the slopes adjacent to Meursault. Some vines, atypically for Burgundy, are trained high.

In the past, wines from Auxey-Duresses were likely to have been sold under the names of grander neighbours. Some are now labelled as Côte de Beaune-Villages, although the village appellation is becoming more popular.

See CÔTE D'OR and map under BURGUNDY.

J.T.C.M.

auxins, one of a number of groups of natural HORMONES present in vines which regulate growth. They are produced in vine parts which are actively growing, such as shoot and root tips. Auxins favour cell growth over cell division, but are also involved in inhibiting the growth of LATERAL SHOOTS. Many chemicals have been synthesized which are chemically related and have a similar biological function. For example, the compounds 2,4-D and 2,4,5-T are auxin-like and form the basis of some HERBICIDES, which are used widely in cereal production. Vines, like tomatoes and cotton, are very sensitive to 2,4-D vapours such as can drift over vineyards when neighbouring farmers use aerial spraying, even from many miles away. Most vine-growing regions have now enacted laws to protect vineyards from the effects of such spraying.   R.E.S.

AVA, the acronym for **American Viticultural Area** and the UNITED STATES' relatively rudimentary answer to France's APPELLATION CONTRÔLÉE system of permitted geographical designations. The US federal government began developing this system in the early 1980s through its Bureau of Alcohol, Tobacco, and Firearms (BATF; see TTB). Under existing regulations, AVAs are theoretically defined by geographic and climatic boundaries and historic authenticity, rather than pre-existing political boundaries, although this is not invariably true and there is some overlap of borders. The system requires no limitations on varieties planted, YIELDS, or other specifics familiar to those who know France's AC or Italy's DOC laws. The only requirement for their use is that 85% of the grapes in a wine labelled with an AVA come from that region; if the wine is a VARIETAL, the legal minimum of 75% of the named variety must come from the named AVA. (Unlike the AC, or DOC system, however, neither the expression 'AVA' nor 'American Viticultural Area' appears on wine labels.)

Between 1983 and 1991, BATF approved more than 100 AVAs in the country at large, more than 60 of those in California, but applications slowed to a trickle in the 1990s as producers were discouraged by the bureaucracy involved without any obvious commercial gain. Yet the 2000s saw a new rush of AVA applications and approvals, as winery marketers realized that Americans were beginning to care about where the grapes were grown, and that labels from specific areas commanded more respect (and higher prices) than GENERIC blends. San Francisco Bay is an example of a relatively new AVA devised primarily for commercial rather than geographical reasons. But other AVAs make perfect sense, such as the 2011-approved Fort-Ross Seaview AVA, a cold, foggy, ocean-hugging region carved out of the impossibly large and nonspecific SONOMA COAST AVA.   L.M.

The TTB website has a complete list of AVAs: http://www.ttb.gov/appellation

Averys, historic wine merchant founded in the west of England port of Bristol in 1793 (three crucial years before the birth year of arch rivals HARVEYS of Bristol). The firm still operates from cellars in the city centre that were acquired in 1860 and where wine has been stored on-site since around 1746.

Ronald Avery (1899–1976) was the most significant of the wine merchant Averys. Born in the celebrated BORDEAUX vintage of 1899, he remained faithful to CLARET as his favourite red wine throughout his life. His time at Cambridge was cut short by the death of an uncle, who with his father ran the firm. To gain experience in the trade at a time when nearly all wine was imported in cask and bottled in Britain, he worked in cellars in London, Bordeaux, and Oporto before taking over the running of Averys in 1923.

In those days, wine merchants mostly bought from British agents or their principals, and visited the wine regions only for social purposes. But Avery had a keen, enquiring, even suspicious mind, became an excellent taster, and paid frequent visits abroad, particularly to Bordeaux. There he selected the casks he preferred, and when they arrived in Bristol docks was not averse to topping them up with another wine altogether. By the late 1930s Averys produced an exceptionally extensive list with a large range of German wines and 100 clarets extending back 20 years, including unusually good stocks of 1923 burgundy and 1929 bordeaux whose quality he was astute enough to discern. At one time the list included seven vintages, back to the famous 1921, of Ch CHEVAL BLANC, a wine then little known in Britain but of which he was very fond. After the Second World War, he and Harry WAUGH, a friend and rival then working for Harveys, were the first to import PETRUS into a distinctly unimpressed Britain. At this time he also became specially interested in authentic burgundy, much subject then to blending from sources in southern France and ALGERIA.

The British wine trade was then an occupation for gentlemen, and Ronald Avery was an eccentric example. Habitually unpunctual, he seldom arrived at his office before 1 p.m., but then stayed late, writing heavily annotated letters of recommendation that turned many customers into friends. At this period most amateurs of fine wine in Britain had an account with Averys.

An excellent navigator, Ronald Avery frequently crossed the English Channel to France in his large motor yacht, which he had to sell to reduce the borrowings entailed by his enthusiastic investment in the Bordeaux vintages of the late 1940s and 1950s. He died in 1976, after which time the firm was run by his son **John Avery** (1941–2012), a hugely enthusiastic MASTER OF WINE and wine collector who also travelled extensively and was an early champion

of NEW WORLD wines. The company lost its independence in 1987 and was acquired by LAITHWAITE's in 2006.   E.P.-R. & J.R.

Avesso, meaning 'contrary', a fitting description for this white grape planted in the VINHO VERDE region of northern PORTUGAL where, unlike the other principal grape varieties in the region, it ripens sufficiently to produce wines of 12–13% alcohol. Mostly planted close to the lower reaches of the River DOURO, it is now being produced as a VARIETAL wine. Plantings totalled 730 ha/1,804 acres in 2010.   R.J.M.

AWRI. See AUSTRALIAN WINE RESEARCH INSTITUTE.

AXA, vast insurance group based in France whose wine division **AXA-Millésimes** is very small in the context of the company and very big in the context of fine wine in general and Bordeaux in particular. Claude Bébéar, the company's president and founder, was led to buy the small St-Émilion property Ch Franc-Mayne in 1984 as an indirect result of his friendship with Jean-Michel Cazes of PAUILLAC. Seeing the investment potential of good Bordeaux properties, he founded AXA-Millésimes in 1987 and it was managed by Cazes alongside his own wine holdings including Ch Lynch Bages until 2000 when Cazes retired and Christian Seely took over. Initial acquisitions included Clos de l'Arlot in NUITS-ST-GEORGES, the CRU BOURGEOIS Ch Pibran and, also in Pauillac, the second growth Ch Pichon Baron, a fairy-tale chateau which has since been lavishly refurbished, re-equipped, and restored to its original name Ch Pichon-Longueville. In 1989 another landmark building Ch Cantenac Brown of MARGAUX was acquired, along with POMEROL's Ch Petit Village, sold by the Prats family of Cos in ST-ESTÈPHE. Three years later SAUTERNES first growth Ch Suduiraut and the Disznókő vineyard in TOKAJ were added, a sweet triumvirate being completed by the acquisition and subsequent restoration of the QUINTA DO NOVAL port business in 1993. AXA is by no means the only French insurance company to have invested in wine-related real estate but is the most wine-minded one. Ch Petit Village was almost sold to the owner of Ch Pavie in St-Émilion in 2001 and Ch Cantenac Brown was sold in 2005.

AXR1, variety of rootstock widely used in northern California until, in the late 1980s, it became fatally obvious that it was not resistant to PHYLLOXERA, something French vignerons had known for many decades. For more information, see ROOTSTOCK.

Ayse, sometime spelt **Ayze,** named, isolated CRU just outside Bonneville east of Geneva whose name may be added to the eastern French appellation Vin de SAVOIE. GRINGET is the principal grape variety used for the light white still and sparkling wines. Domaine

Belluard accounts for half of production and is highly regarded.

Azal, one of the less interesting white grapes grown to produce VINHO VERDE. Total plantings had fallen to 1,480 ha/3,657 acres by 2010. **Azal Tinto** is unrelated.

azeotrope, from the Greek 'to boil unchanged', a mixture of liquid chemicals which has a boiling point either higher or lower than any one of its components. The principal volatile components of wine tend to form azeotropes of two, three, or more components. Water, ETHANOL, volatile organic ACIDS, ALDEHYDES, ESTERS, acetals, and ketones, many of them powerfully aromatic, are among the azeotrope components in wines. The multiplicity of volatile compounds present in wine and our lack of detailed knowledge of all of the azeotropes possible makes it difficult to predict the composition of distillates (which depend on the varied boiling points of components).

Just as the formation of azeotropic mixtures in a liquid governs the boiling point and composition of the vapour during DISTILLATION, so it governs the composition of the vapours above a liquid in a glass at room temperature. When we smell a wine, our noses are recording the impression created by the azeotropic mixture rather than that of any single component.

A.D.W.

Azerbaijan, former Soviet Union state bordered by the Caspian Sea in the west and producing only a fraction of the wine it produced before the fall of communism. Divided into the mountain system of the large and small Caucasus and the Kura and Araka lowlands, it also includes the republic of Nakhichevan, an enclave surrounded by ARMENIA and TURKEY.

History

Grape-growing is likely to be one of the oldest branches of Azerbaijan's economy. Archaeology has revealed seeds of cultured grapes, stones for crushing grape berries, and stone fermentation and storage vessels dating back to the seventh millennium BC at Shomu-Tepe and second millennium BC in the settlements of Kültan, Galabaglar, and Galajig.

HERODOTUS, describing a campaign of the Scythian chief Madyas in ANATOLIA in the 7th century BC, mentioned that viticulture and winemaking were already developed in that region. The Greek geographer Strabo, in the 1st century BC, reported on grape culture in 'Albania', the old name of part of Azerbaijan.

The Arabian historians and geographers Abulfedy, Masudi, Khaukal, and El Mugaddasi recorded that vineyards existed near the towns of Gianji and Bardy during Arab domination. Viticulture of that region declined in the periods of war and revived in the time of peace. Viticulture was on a commercial scale after 1814, and developed especially fast at the end of the 19th century when two railways were built which provided access to the enormous wine market of RUSSIA.

By the beginning of the 20th century, small viticultural farms were established in the Ganja-Gazakh region as well as much larger enterprises in specialized zones of commercial grape and wine production. In 1940, the total vineyard area was 33,000 ha/81,500 acres, mostly planted by German colonists. The Second World War had reduced this total to 21,000 ha/51,900 acres by 1947. Revival came in 1954, when expansion in grape cultivation began once more and gross yields also increased.

See also ORIGINS OF VINICULTURE and PALAEOETHNOBOTANY AND THE ARCHAEOLOGY OF WINE.

Climate and geography

The climate and the soils of mountainous regions are determined to a considerable extent by latitude, elevation, relief, and exposition of slopes. The climate of Azerbaijan varies between moderately warm with dry winters, to cold with abundant rainfall.

The average annual temperature is 10.5 to 15.5 °C (51–60 °F). The active temperature summation (see CLIMATE CLASSIFICATION) is between 3,000 and 4,600 °C in its varied wine regions. Annual rainfall in the low and pre-mountainous parts of the country, where grapes are grown, is 250 and 600 mm (23 in) respectively.

Modern viticulture is concentrated east to west in the Shamakha, Ismaily, Gabala, Gandja, and Tovuz regions.

Viticulture

Only about 10% of the vineyards, mainly in Nakhichevan, need the WINTER PROTECTION that is so necessary in Russian vineyards. About half of all vineyards need IRRIGATION and only about 20% of them are grafted on to PHYLLOXERA-resistant ROOTSTOCKS. Irrigated vineyards are mainly in the Göy-Göl (formerly Helenendorf), Agdam, Mardakert, Tovuz, Gazakh, Fizuli, and Shamakha regions. The grapes of dry-farmed Gabala are particularly admired.

Vine varieties

The country has 17 vine varieties officially recognized for wine production—and 16 table grape varieties are planted, accounting for 15% of the total vineyard area. The most common varieties for red wine are the Azeri Madrasa, Saperavi, and Cabernet Sauvignon. Bayahshira is the main AUTOCHTHONOUS white wine grape and Rkatsiteli and Chardonnay are also planted. New vineyards are being planted with Pinot Blanc, Alicante, Mtsvane, Viognier, Syrah, Grenache, and Muscat.

Industry organization

In 1990, Azerbaijan reported 181,000 ha/447,000 acres of vineyard but by 2011, according to OIV statistics, total vineyard was just 16,000 ha/39,500 acres and total wine production 72,000 hl/1.9 million gal. Commerce in this oil-rich republic can best be described as entrepreneurial.

Ganja-Sharab, Qabala Sharab, Vinagro, ASPI, Fireland, Yarimada, and many other modern wineries were built in the early 21st century and the state is expected to continue to invest in the wine sector.

V.R. & M.A.

azienda, Italian for a business. An **azienda agricola** is a farm, the equivalent of a French DOMAINE, and the phrase should appear on a wine label only if the grapes were grown and the wine produced on that estate; an **azienda vinicola**, on the other hand, may buy in grapes from elsewhere, while an **azienda vitivinicola** combines both activities.

Azores, archipelago in the Atlantic and an autonomous region of PORTUGAL. Three of its nine islands grow vines and have their own DOP. See BISCOITOS, PICO, and GRACIOSA. In 2004, a VINHO REGIONAL category Açores was created for all red and white wines produced throughout the archipelago.

BA, common abbreviation, used particularly by English-speakers, for the sweet-wine designation BEERENAUSLESE.

Băbească Neagră, Romania's second most planted red wine vine variety, after Merlot, whose name, meaning 'grandmother's grape', compares directly with FETEASCĂ or 'young girl's grape'. It has long been grown in the east of the country but total plantings had fallen to 4,516 ha/11,159 acres by 2008, typically producing light, fruity reds that are considerably less 'serious' than Fetească Neagră.

Babo, alternative name for KMW, the Austrian unit of MUST WEIGHT. See KLOSTERNEUBURG.

Bacchus, common name in Ancient ROME for the classical god of wine whom the Greeks called Bacchos but, more usually, DIONYSUS. There was no official Roman festival of Bacchus: the Roman Senate suppressed the **Bacchanalia** in 186 BC because it saw them not only as a danger to the state, but also as a bacchanal in the modern sense, a scene of drunkenness and sexual licence. **Bacchic** poetry is verse with a vinous theme, a speciality of the ARAB POETS. Because the Romans concentrated on the vinous aspect of this much more complex god, and possibly because the word Bacchus is considerably easier to say and spell than Dionysus, the Roman name is much more commonly used in modern times, and is regarded as a word rich in wine connotations. The United States has its Society of Bacchus for committed wine enthusiasts, and the word is used emotively around the world to conjure up various conjunctions of wine and pleasure.

Dalby, A., *Bacchus. A Biography* (Los Angeles, 2003).

Bacchus is also the name of one of the most important GERMAN CROSSES. It was bred from a Silvaner × Riesling cross and the lacklustre MÜLLER-THURGAU and in good years can provide growers in Germany with musts notching up the all-important numbers on the OECHSLE scale as well as powerful flavours and character, and is therefore useful for blending with Müller-Thurgau. Unlike the more aristocratic and more popular cross KERNER, however, the wine produced lacks acidity and is not even useful for blending with high-acid musts in poor years since it too needs to be fully ripe before it can express its own exuberant flavours.

Bacchus's great allure for growers, however, is that it can be planted on sites on which Riesling is an unreliable ripener and will ripen as early and as productively as Müller-Thurgau. Total plantings in Germany reached a peak of around 3,500 ha/8,650 acres in 1990, about half in Rheinhessen, where its substance is valued as an ingredient in QBA blends. This total had fallen to 1,841 ha/4,547 acres by 2012 In the UK, Bacchus is valued for its must weights and is the second most planted white grape after Chardonnay. With the UK's generally lower yields and higher natural acid levels, it does not suffer from the flabbiness of warmer climate examples.

Baco, François, was, like BOUSCHET, a nurseryman who saw his name live on in the names of some of the most successful of the vine varieties he bred. Baco's specialities were FRENCH HYBRIDS and his most successful was **Baco Blanc**, sometimes called **Baco 22A**, which was hybridized in 1898 and was, for much of the 20th century until the late 1970s, the prime ingredient in armagnac—a role now occupied by UGNI BLANC but previously occupied by FOLLE BLANCHE, although the French vineyard census of 2011 still noted 661 ha/1,633 acres of the variety, mainly in armagnac country.

Baco Noir, or **Baco 1**, resulted from crossing Folle Blanche with a variety of *Vitis riparia* in 1902 and was at one time widely spread in France but today is best known for its light, fruity, non-FOXY reds in eastern Canada and, to a lesser extent, in upstate New York.

bacteria, very small micro-organisms which have serious implications in both viticulture and winemaking. Although not common pathogens of the grapevine, BACTERIAL DISEASES are potentially destructive and therefore very important.

In winemaking just two groups of bacteria are important, ACETOBACTER and LACTIC ACID BACTERIA. Since grape juice and wine are both high in ACIDITY, the great majority of bacteria, with the exception of these two groups, are incapable of living in them and, if introduced, do not survive. (Drinks such as cider, perry, orange juice, and beer are all much less acid than wine, are thereby subject to many forms of BACTERIAL SPOILAGE to which wine is immune, and therefore lack wine's AGEING potential.) No known human pathogenic bacteria can survive in wine, however, which is one of the reasons why it has been such a safe drink (safer than WATER at some times and in some places) through the ages.

Acetobacter (which do not harm humans) can turn wine, or any other dilute solution containing ETHANOL, into VINEGAR.

Acetobacter require OXYGEN for growth and survival and they die in the absence of oxygen (which is why care is taken to exclude oxygen from certain stages of winemaking and all stages of wine preservation—see LEFTOVER WINE).

Lactic acid bacteria produce LACTIC ACID and grow best in environments where there is a very small amount of oxygen. They are important as the agents of MALOLACTIC CONVERSION in wines, by which excess MALIC ACID is decomposed.

A.D.W., R.E.S., & P.J.W.

Kunkee, R., 'Bacteria in wine', in M. Amerine, *Technology of Wine Making* (4th edn, Westport, Conn., 1980).

bacterial blight

bacterial blight, vine BACTERIAL DISEASE caused by the bacterium *Xanthomonas ampelina*, so serious that it has led some Greek and French growers to abandon stricken vineyards. This disease shows its presence by retarding and killing young shoots. It is spread by rain and also by pruning tools. It can be controlled by removing and destroying infected plants and by disinfecting pruning tools between vines, as well as by COPPER sprays.   R.E.S.

bacterial diseases, group of grapevine diseases caused by BACTERIA, small organisms which do not commonly attack vines but which can be deadly and are difficult to control. Of the bacterial diseases, PIERCE'S DISEASE is the most important and QUARANTINE authorities around the world are anxious to stop it spreading from America. In parts of North and Central America (southern California, Florida, and eastern Texas, for instance), viticulture can be rendered commercially impossible by the natural presence of this disease. Other economically important bacterial diseases are BACTERIAL BLIGHT and CROWN GALL.   R.E.S.

Flaherty, D. L., et al. (eds.), *Grape Pest Management* (Berkeley, Calif., 1981).

Pearson, R. C., and Goheen, A. C. (eds.), *Compendium of Grape Diseases* (St Paul, Minn., 1988).

bacterial spoilage, range of wine maladies or FAULTS including gas, haze, cloud, and off-flavours generated by the activity of BACTERIA in wine. These bacteria are either ACETOBACTER or LACTIC ACID BACTERIA. Acetobacter's tendency to transform wine into vinegar can be checked by keeping air away from wine, on the part of both winemaker and wine drinker (see LEFTOVER WINE). Lactic acid bacteria are more varied in their effects, which include a wide range of unpleasant-smelling compounds, depending on the type of bacterium. These are relatively rarely seen today since great care is taken by winemakers (see STABILIZATION and HYGIENE) to guard against spoilage by lactic acid bacteria in the winery and to minimize the risk of a wine's being bottled with any spoilage bacteria (see FILTRATION, PASTEURIZATION, STERILE BOTTLING). If lactic acid bacteria do attack a wine in bottle, the results are usually detrimental to the taste and clarity of the wine, and gas is usually given off.   A.D.W.

Baden, GERMANY's longest wine region, stretching over 400 km/250 miles from the border with FRANKEN in the north across the Rhine from ALSACE to Lake Constance (the Bodensee) and German-speaking SWITZERLAND in the south (see map under GERMANY). The general and local climate, the varying soils, and the height above sea level have a marked effect on the wines of Baden's nine districts, or BEREICHE, which had a combined vineyard area of 15,822 ha/39,080 acres in 2013. In this southernmost growing region of Germany SPÄTBURGUNDER, GRAUBURGUNDER, and Weissburgunder (PINOT BLANC) account for 36, 11, and 8% respectively of the region's vineyard area, making it Germany's Pinot stronghold, and total red wine production surpassed 30% in 2011. Warm, dry conditions and frequently steep, terraced sites of volcanic origin typically combine to yield wines of naturally abundant alcohol, although, as in many other respects, this huge region harbours considerable diversity, and there are enough cooler sectors for growers so-inclined to bottle Pinots that are downright delicate, as well as to support a 7% vineyard share of RIESLING. Around 70% of Baden's vine acreage is farmed by growers who belong to one of the region's 80 CO-OPERATIVES (Winzergenossenschaften), a number approaching half of Germany's total.

The **Tauberfranken** district covers 680 ha/ 1,680 acres that intermittently follow the Tauber River until the confluence with the Main at Wertheim. Plantings in this frost-prone area, 70% of them for white wine, have for many years been declining, and hardy MÜLLER-THURGAU represents nearly half of all vines, with other crosses accounting for most of the rest. The wine is similar to that of FRANKEN and is also sold in its neighbour's flagon-shaped BOCKSBEUTEL.

East across the Odenwald, the vineyards of the Bereiche **Badische Bergstrasse** (400 ha/988 acres) and **Kraichgau** (1,250 ha/3,089 acres) run north and south of Heidelberg. The first district is simply a continuation of the HESSISCHE BERGSTRASSE. In both sectors, Müller-Thurgau and Riesling each hover around one-quarter of the acreage, the latter capable of yielding distinctive, delicate results in granite and sandstone sites along the Bergstrasse.

The extensive **Ortenau, Breisgau,** and **Kaiserstuhl** districts that parallel the Rhine east of the Black Forest between Baden-Baden and Freiburg are home to Baden's most prestigious estates although, as elsewhere in this region, grower co-operatives continue to account for a majority of total production. Thanks especially to the opportunities afforded by cool sites south of Baden-Baden, Riesling accounts for around one-quarter of Ortenau vines, with Pinot Noir planted on almost half. Steep porphyry and BASALT sites around Neuweier are especially known for their Riesling. Some 15 km/9 miles south at Waldum, that grape—on weathered GRANITE—vies with Pinot Noir for attention; while a few km closer to Offenburg, the village of Durbach, long a wine-trading centre, gives pride of place to Pinot, although Riesling (known here colloquially as Klingelberger) and Traminer (as Clevner) run close behind in importance and affection. Extending between Offenburg and Freiburg, parts of the Breisgau hug the Black Forest closely enough to benefit from more precipitation than neighbouring districts. Here CALCAREOUS soils promote firm fruity acidity resulting in Pinot Noir that marries richness with vivacity, and whose virtues have become increasingly evident over the past two decades, so that today many of the most intriguing red wines in Germany have Breisgau addresses. Among those villages to have demonstrated outstanding site potential are (from south to north) Mundingen, Köndringen, Malterdingen, Hecklingen, and (in a side valley well into the Black Forest) Münchweier. For all of the notoriety that is gradually coming to the Breisgau, the primarily VOLCANIC vineyards of the Kaiserstuhl to its immediate west, rearing steeply up from the Rhine, are Baden's most famous and coveted, in particular for their Pinots. Northwards from Breisach on the Rhine, Blankenhornsberg, Achkarren, Oberrotweil, and Bischoffingen harbour the most famous Kaiserstuhl vineyards. Largely on the basis of its LOESS and calcareous rather than volcanic soils, the diminutive (580 ha/1,430 acre) **Tuniberg** declared its independence from the Kaiserstuhl in 1991, though without having since then achieved special distinction with its Pinot Noir, most vinified by a single co-operative.

Hugging the Rhine in Germany's south-western corner from Freiburg to the Swiss frontier at Basel is the **Markgräflerland**, traditionally best known for its Gutedel (CHASSELAS), whose elegance and soil-sensitivity can challenge that of Switzerland's best examples. Like the Breisgau, the Markgräflerland is becoming increasingly recognized for innovative vintners and excellent Pinot Noirs, some from the calcareous soils of Istein and Efringen-Kirchen along the Rhine just north of Basel being especially impressive. The **Bodensee** district, most of whose vineyards stretch along the northern shore of the huge eponymous lake, is nearly 100 km/62 miles distant from the Markgräflerland and even further from any other districts of Baden. While known inside Germany more for its tourism than its wines, and hardly known at all outside Germany, this outpost of diverse German viticulture, like its immediate Swiss neighbours around Schaffhausen and Konstanz, can boast some distinctively delicious results.

D.S.

Baga, red grape found throughout central PORTUGAL but mostly in the BAIRRADA region, where, unusually for Portugal, it accounts for as much as 90% of dark-skinned varieties. It is a vigorous variety, resistant to POWDERY MILDEW but ripens late and has a tendency to rot in the damp Atlantic climate of Portugal's western seaboard, threatened by early autumn rains. This small, thin-skinned variety (*baga* means 'berry') produces dark, fairly acidic, tannic wines that can be undrinkably astringent if the grapes are under-ripe. Well-made wines such as those of Baga champion Luis Pato are full of fruit and capable of long ageing, however. A large amount of Baga ends up as rosé: Sogrape, producers of MATEUS rosé, have a large winery in the Bairrada region. Portuguese plantings totalled 9,885 ha/24,426 acres in 2010.

R.J.M. & J.R.

Baghdad, the capital of modern IRAQ, was founded by the first Abbasid caliph, al-Mansur, in AD 762. Early in its history the city became the focus of a Bacchic culture (see ARAB POETS), celebrated most eloquently by the poet ABU NUWAS. Although wine was imbibed in the Caliphal court and some outlying districts of the city (al-Karkh, for example), most wine was consumed where it was produced, in the small monasteries and towns that lay outside the city in various parts of Iraq. Their names are preserved in poetry and other sources ('Āna, Hīt, Qutrubbul in the vicinity of the city, for example, and Tīzanābādh further south near Kufa). P.K.

bag-in-box. See BOXES.

Bairrada, evolving DOP wine region in northern Portugal (see map under PORTUGAL). The coastal belt south of OPORTO has been producing wine since Portugal gained independence from the Moors in the 10th century. By the early 1700s, Bairrada's dark, tannic red wines were widely drunk in Britain, masquerading as or blended with PORT from the DOURO Valley to the north. Then in 1756, as part of his measures to protect the authenticity of port (see DELIMITATION), the Marquis of Pombal, Portugal's powerful prime minister, ordered that Bairrada's vineyards should be uprooted.

Despite the foundation in 1887 of the Escola Prática de Viticultura da Bairrada whose efforts to promote and develop the region included producing Portugal's first MÉTHODE CHAMPENOISE sparkling wine in 1890, it has taken Bairrada more than two centuries to recover.

For the best part of the 20th century, the merchant bottlers (see NÉGOCIANTS) and CO-OPERATIVES that still dominate production churned out cheap bulk wines for Portugal's African colonies. But this market collapsed in the wake of the 1974 revolution. Bairrada was awarded REGIÃO DEMARCADA (now DOP) status in 1979. Tapping new, more demanding export markets required the merchant bottlers to exert greater control over fruit sourcing and production through the acquisition of vineyards, buying grapes (instead of wine), and investing in winemaking facilities. Most

of Bairrada's 2,000 growers own a very small area of vines even today, so most send their grapes either to a merchant or to one of the region's three remaining co-operatives. Around 900 of them alone sell their fruit to SOGRAPE for MATEUS rosé. Bairrada's main quality impetus has come from the handful of dynamic individual winemaking estates that emerged in the 1980s and the successive wave that has reinforced its number. Stalwart supporters of traditional varieties, notably BAGA, have progressively tamed its worst excesses (fearsome tannins and acidity) by optimal VINEYARD SITE SELECTION (warmer, better-drained CALCAREOUS-clay soils are best), trimming this productive grape's yields, and gentler EXTRACTION. Others have taken advantage of DOP rule changes which, from 2003, permitted blending with more approachable, popular varieties such as Touriga Nacional, Cabernet Sauvignon, Merlot, and Pinot Noir. These incomers (sometimes with a dash of white grapes) have successfully fleshed out Baga and have even produced some very promising wines in their own right, especially the Bordeaux varieties, which are well-suited to Bairrada's MARITIME CLIMATE. Keen to reinforce the region's traditional varieties Baga, Maria Gomes, and Bical, from 2009 leading estate Luis Pato began once again to label its top wines Bairrada (as opposed to bottling all as Vinho Regional BEIRAS). By 2014 Baga represented only 40% of land under vine (down from 90%), but those who remain committed to producing single VARIETAL Baga are consistently making some of Portugal's leading reds. While they retain the capacity to age in bottle for two decades or more, with riper, finer tannins and better fruit expression, modern Baga is broachable earlier than in the past. Filipa Pato even makes an elegant FORTIFIED Baga using the region's and variety's hallmark freshness to good effect. White grapes, mostly Maria Gomes (or FERNÃO PIRES) and BICAL, once grown primarily by the merchants for TRADITIONAL METHOD sparkling wines, are increasingly valued by Bairrada's leading individual estates which make some remarkably TERROIR-focused, almost Burgundian whites and, more recently, artisanal traditional method sparkling wines based on Baga.

The Bussaco Palace Hotel owns a vineyard, Vinha da Mata, in Bairrada from which it has produced an impressively structured Baga-dominated red labelled VM since 2001. However, located on the cusp of Bairrada and Dão, it is best known for Buçaco red and white wines made from grapes sourced from both regions. Once regarded as some of the best table wines in Portugal, older vintages (dating back to the 1940s) are available only to guests dining at the hotel or one of its few associated establishments, apart from those few bottles that occasionally crop up at AUCTION. S.A.

Mayson, R., *The Wines and Vineyards of Portugal* (London, 2003).

Metcalfe, C., McWhirter, K., *The Wine and Food Lover's Guide to Portugal* (Haywards Heath, 2007).

Ahmed, S., 'Bairrada: the Baga beyond', *The World of Fine Wine*, 40 (2013) 92–99.

Baiyu, Chinese name for RKATSITELI.

balance is essential for quality in both vine and wine.

Vines

Vine balance is a viticultural concept little appreciated by wine consumers, yet one which is essential for producing grapes for premium winemaking. A vine is in balance when the LEAF TO FRUIT RATIO is in the correct range. The amount of early season shoot growth should also be in balance with the vine's reserves of CARBOHYDRATES. Vine balance concerns VIGOUR and it can be managed by the VITICULTURIST, with BALANCED PRUNING and WATER STRESS the principal tools. One of the best measures of vine balance is the ratio of fruit yield to pruning weight, now often called the Ravaz index, following its promotion by the French researcher of that name.

Balanced wine comes from balanced vines (a fact acknowledged even by such authors as Halliday and Johnson, who were previously critical of high YIELDS in any circumstances). A balanced vine has shoots of moderate vigour with no SHOOT TIP growth during fruit RIPENING. Leaves are of moderate size and number so excess SHADE is avoided, with both leaves and fruit well exposed to sunlight. Unbalanced vineyards are either too vigorous—in which case poor ripening results from shading and competition between the ripening grapes and shoot tips for carbohydrates—or not vigorous enough—in which case there is insufficient leaf area for proper ripening. Monitoring shoot tip growth is seen as an important management tool for vine balance. R.E.S.

Wines

Wine tasters say that a wine has balance, or is well **balanced**, if its ALCOHOLIC STRENGTH, ACIDITY, RESIDUAL SUGAR, TANNINS, and FRUIT, complement each other so that no single one of them is obtrusive on the PALATE. (Young wines are expected to exhibit more marked tannins than mature ones however.) This extremely important wine characteristic is unrelated to FLAVOUR, although see also HARMONY.

balanced pruning. The number of buds to be left on the vine at winter PRUNING should be judged relative to the vine's capacity early in the growing season to support the growth of shoots. In turn, a balanced pruned vine will have sufficient shoot growth to ripen the fruit it carries. The amount of late-season growth is

Balance

Vegetative cycle

Canopies tend to become more and more shaded and vegetative, leading to yield and quality reductions. Typical of vineyards on high potential soils with an inadequate trellis.

Shade
depresses budbreak, bunch initiation, fruit set, and berry growth

Canopy density
increases due to more leaf area

Fruit weight
per shoot is reduced

Shoot growth
is stimulated due to less fruit growth

Imbalance
between shoot and fruit growth

Balanced cycle

Light stimulates shoot fruitfulness leading to balance between shoot and fruit growth. Typical of vineyards trellised according to vigour.

Light
stimulates budbreak, bunch initiation, fruit set, and berry growth

Canopy density
decreases due to less leaf area

Fruit weight
per shoot is increased

Shoot growth
is depressed due to more fruit growth

Balance
between shoot and fruit growth

Source: R. Smart and M. Robinson, *Sunlight into Wine*

related to shoot growth early in the season. The amount of reserve, or stored, CARBOHYDRATES in the vine roots, trunk, and arms will determine how many developing shoots can be sustained. Of course, it is impossible to calculate the amount of stored reserves for each vine (which would involve excavation and chemical analysis), so dormant pruning weights are used as an indication. The underlying principle is that the more the amount of shoot growth in summer, the higher will be the pruning weight and also the stored carbohydrate reserves.

Pruning weights are simply measured by weighing the cane prunings removed at winter pruning and using this figure to judge the appropriate bud numbers to leave at winter pruning. For example, one formula is to keep around 30 buds for each kg/2 lb of pruning weight.

Experienced vine pruners can achieve a similar effect by looking at each vine, judging how it grew last growing season, and adjusting this year's number of buds accordingly.

If too few buds are left on the vine at winter pruning relative to the stored carbohydrates, then shoots in spring will grow quickly and have leaves which are too large and stems which are too thick. The vine will have a high LEAF TO FRUIT RATIO, which may result in poor fruit set (see COULURE). In any event, the leaf to fruit imbalance normally leads to a shaded CANOPY MICROCLIMATE and attendant problems of loss of YIELD and quality. Such a situation is common for vines planted close together on fertile soil.

On the other hand, if too many buds are left at pruning relative to stored carbohydrates, then the resulting large number of shoots will develop only slowly in spring. The leaves will be small and the stems spindly. The danger here is that the leaf area will be too low for the weight of grapes, which will ripen slowly and wine quality will suffer. This condition is often described as OVERCROPPING.

See also PRUNING.   R.E.S.

Smart, R. E., and Robinson, M., *Sunlight into Wine: A Handbook for Winegrape Canopy Management* (Adelaide, 1991).

Tassie, E., and Freeman, B. M., 'Pruning', in B. G. Coombe and P. R. Dry (eds.), *Viticulture*, ii: *Practices* (Adelaide, 1992).

Bali. See INDONESIA.

Balling, scale of measuring total dissolved compounds in grape juice, and therefore its approximate concentration of grape sugars. It is very similar to the BRIX scale used in the United States. For more details, see MUST WEIGHT.

Baltic states. Former SOVIET, now independent, states Estonia, Lithuania, and Latvia all produce wine, according to OIV statistics, but thanks to bulk imports as per the RUSSIAN (and Belorussian) model. Baltic OAK has been treasured for wine production.

Banat Riesling (**Banat Rizling**), white grape variety grown in SERBIA, and neighbouring parts of ROMANIA. Its produce tends to be somewhat heavy. Kreaca is a synonym.

Bandol, the most serious wine of PROVENCE, typically a deep-flavoured, lush red blend dominated by the MOURVÈDRE grape. Like CHÂTEAU-NEUF-DU-PAPE, Bandol produces quintessentially Mediterranean red wines which are easy to appreciate in youth despite their longevity.

The appellation is named after the port from which they were once shipped all over the world. Bandol is now a Mediterranean resort town with little to offer the wine tourist, and the vineyards are on south-facing terraces well inland called locally *restanques*. As in the smaller appellation of CASSIS just along the coast, the vines are protected from the cold north winds, but have to fight property developers for their right to continued existence. A total of about 1,400 ha were cultivated in the early 2000s but in 2011 fewer than 600 ha/1,482 acres were in production, perhaps partly because of property development.

This particularly well-favoured southern corner is one of the few parts of France in which Mourvèdre, the characteristic grape of Bandol, can be relied upon to ripen. Other dark-berried varieties grown include Grenache and Cinsaut, much used for the local herby rosés which can account for about three bottles of Bandol in every four some years, together with strictly limited additions of Syrah and Carignan. A small quantity of white Bandol is made from Bourboulenc, Clairette, and Ugni Blanc with a maximum of 40% Sauvignon Blanc, but little of it escapes the region's fish restaurants.

Winemaking techniques are traditional but evolving. All reds must have at least 18 months in cask and, thanks to the high proportion of Mourvèdre, at least 50%, REDUCTION is a constant threat. Mechanical harvesting is banned. Domaine Tempier is one of the few domaines to have a well-established market outside France but the likes of Domaines de la Bégude and de la Tour du Bon, and Chx La Rouvière, Pibarnon, Pradeaux, and Vannières have all made fine wines.

Lynch, K., *Adventures along the Wine Route* (2nd edn, New York, 2013).

Banyuls and **Banyuls Grand Cru** are the appellations for France's finest and certainly most complex VINS DOUX NATURELS, made from vertiginous terraced vineyards above the Mediterranean at the southern limit of ROUSSILLON, and indeed mainland France. The dry but powerful mostly red wine produced in the same vineyards is entitled to the appellation COLLIOURE, Banyuls-sur-Mer and Collioure being two of the four dramatic seaside communes included in these two appellations.

Grenache Noir must dominate the blend, constituting at least 50% of a Banyuls and 75% Banyuls Grand Cru (which latter appellation is ignored by individual producers of the calibre of Dr Parcé of Domaine du Mas Blanc, who could be said to have re-energized the appellation in the mid 20th century). The grapes yield poorly and are often part shrivelled before being picked in early October. Alcohol is added while the must is still on the skins so that a wide range of flavour compounds are absorbed into the young wine, which, after perhaps five weeks' further MACERATION, is then subjected to one of a wide range of ÉLEVAGE techniques. For much of the last century a portion of Banyuls would be kept in glass BONBONNES, sometimes outside, before being transferred to large old wood. This oxidative style gave way from the 1970s or so to a fruitier, earlier-maturing style. The occasional reminder of the very austere RANCIO style of Banyuls, sometimes matured in a SOLERA system that was made long ago can occasionally be found in the dustiest cellars. Some Banyuls is made to preserve the heady aromas of macerated red fruits while other Banyuls demonstrate the extraordinary levels of concentration that can be achieved by Grenache, heat, and time. Such wines are some of the few that go well with chocolate, although many a French chef has created savoury dishes, often with a hint of sweetness, to be served expressly with a particular Banyuls. This is the only French wine appellation, once routinely prescribed medicinally, able to offer 20- and 30-year-old wines as a serious proportion of its total production. See also RIVESALTES and MAURY.

Barbaresco, powerful red wine based on the NEBBIOLO grape grown around the village of Barbaresco in the PIEMONTE region in north west Italy. For long considered very much the junior of BAROLO in terms of its size and the power and prestige of its wines, Barbaresco emerged from Barolo's shadow in the 1960s to win recognition of its own striking qualities of elegance and aromatic intensity.

The wine is, in fact, a younger one than Barolo, its name appearing on labels only from 1894 when Domizio Cavazza, professor at the Oenological School of ALBA, founded the Barbaresco CO-OPERATIVE (now the much-admired Cantina di Produttori di Barbaresco) in that year. Before that the wines of Barbaresco were often blended with Barolo. Barbaresco did not enjoy Barolo's connection with the House of Savoy and the nobility of the royal court in Turin, and suffered relative commercial obscurity until the efforts of Giovanni GAJA and Bruno Giacosa in the 1960s demonstrated the full potential of the wine.

The production zone of Barbaresco is to the north east and east of the city of Alba and is only a third of that of Barolo (1,886 ha/4,660 acres) but, as in Barolo, the area under vine has increased dramatically in recent years, from 484 ha/1,200 acres in the early 1990s to 686 ha/1,695 acres in 2010. The wine is produced in the townships of Barbaresco, Treiso (formerly part of Barbaresco), Neive, and a fragment of Alba, although 95% of the cultivated vineyards lie in the first three. Neive calls itself 'the township of four wines' (the others being MOSCATO, BARBERA, DOLCETTO), and Nebbiolo only consolidated its position there after the Second World War. Even today Neive has fewer than 100 ha of Nebbiolo, less than that of Barbera or Dolcetto, and half the area planted with Moscato.

Although soil differences between Barolo and Barbaresco are regularly advanced as a major factor in the style difference, broadly speaking there are more similarities than differences. Barbaresco's soils can roughly be divided into two types. The CALCAREOUS clay of the Tortonion epoch is very similar to that in the Barolo communes of La Morra and Barolo, resulting in a perfumed, FRUIT-DRIVEN style. The second soil type, more compact and resembling somewhat the soils of the Barolo communes Monforte d'Alba and Serralunga d'Alba, is the so-called Sant'Agata fossil MARL, yielding more tannic wines.

Nebbiolo ripens earlier in Barbaresco than in Barolo, probably due to the vineyards' proximity to the River Tanaro, while the wines tend to be a bit lighter as the region is further east than Barolo. This lighter style of wine is reflected in the minimum ageing requirements, 26 months of which at least 9 months in oak, and 50 months for Barbaresco Riserva, compared with Barolo's 38 months of which 18 in oak, and 62 months for the Riserva counted from the year of harvest.

Winemaking techniques, which had previously favoured prolonged MACERATION and CASK AGEING, changed in the 1970s and 1980s, much as in Barolo, towards considerably shorter periods in French BARRIQUES in an effort to respond to modern tastes for rounder, fruitier wines. This was scorned by more traditional winemakers who argued that French oak suppressed Nebbiolo's gentle perfume. Today, a return to long skin maceration and ageing in large oak casks rather than barrique is favoured by an increasing number of Barbaresco producers. If Barbaresco is considered a lighter-bodied wine than Barolo (although these are wines which must have a minimum ALCOHOLIC STRENGTH of 12.5% and easily reach 13.5%), it is not lacking in the TANNINS and ACIDITY that mark the Nebbiolo grape; young Barbaresco is by no means an inevitably pleasurable glass of wine. It seems to mature slightly faster than Barolo, and is normally at its best between five and 15 years of age. The work done by the Produttori del Barbaresco, one of Italy's finest CO-OPERATIVES, and by individual producers such as Angelo GAJA and Bruno Giacosa, has helped to establish Barbaresco as a top-quality wine, while a number of smaller producers have begun tending their vineyards organically and biodynamically and are using traditional winemaking techniques, with long skin MACERATION, often up to 40 days, to produce highly original, long-lived wines with a muscular structure and perfumes of cherry, violets—and, with age, iron, tar and orange peel—which can easily be overwhelmed by new oak.

Single-vineyard bottlings are a relatively recent phenomenon, in Barbaresco as in the rest of Italy. The first efforts date from 1967, and there is a less firmly established written record of CRU designation here than in Barolo. Lorenzo Fantini's monograph on Piedmontese viticulture of the late 19th century indicates very few 'choice positions' in Barbaresco (and none whatsoever in Neive). The first attempts to list and rate the finest positions date from the 1960s (Luigi VERONELLI) and the 1970s (Renato Ratti).

NÉGOCIANTS' willingness to pay higher prices for grapes from certain vineyards, however, has established a certain consensus about which are the best: Asili, Montefico, Montestefano, and Rabajà in Barbaresco; Albesani and Gallina in Neive; and Pajorè in Treiso. A certain number of the most famous vineyards—San Lorenzo, Tildin, and Martinenga in Barbaresco, Santo Stefano in Neive—are, in effect, 'man-made' crus which have gained their current prestige from the dedicated work and exacting standards of producers such as Gaja, Giacosa, and Alberto di Gresy. An official list of single vineyards, the so-called Menzioni Geografiche Aggiuntive, was introduced in 2007, long before Barolo did the same in 2010. This list of single vineyards, also referred to as Crus, has sensibly retained all the historically known vineyards, without reducing their number by absorbing them in more famous vineyard names for commercial reasons, as has been the case with some communes in neighbouring Barolo.

D.C.G. & W.S.

Petrini, C. (ed.), *A Wine Atlas of the Langhe* (3rd edn, Bra, 2005).
www.langhevini.it

barbarians, uncivilized ancient European people who were introduced to wine, and therefore considered civilized, by CLASSICAL civilizations. See CELTS.

Barbarossa, name used for many, probably unrelated, Italian red grapes, one of which may be identical to the rare **Barbaroux** of Provence.

Robinson, J., Harding, J., and Vouillamoz, J., *Wine Grapes: A Complete Guide to 1,368 Vine Varieties, including their Origins and Flavours* (London & New York, 2012).

Barbera, productive and versatile red grape variety widely planted in northern Italy where total 2010 plantings were 20,523 ha/50,692 acres, a dramatic decrease since the nearly 50,000 ha/123,552 acres in the 1990s. No genetic link can be found with other Piemontese varieties, suggesting that it was imported into the region relatively recently.

Barbera ripens relatively late, as much as two weeks after the other 'lesser' black grape variety of Piemonte DOLCETTO, although in advance of the stately NEBBIOLO. Its chief characteristic is its high level of natural acidity even when fully ripe, which has helped its popularity in hot climates (it is also grown to quite an extent in Australia, Argentina, and, especially California).

Piemonte

Barbera was once known as 'the people's wine' of Piemonte for its versatility and its abundant production. During the 1980s and 1990s, however, a proportion of Barbera underwent a significant metamorphosis as producers, in a parallel development to the Sangiovese-based SUPERTUSCANS, experimented with BARREL MATURATION. The prototype was Giacomo Bologna's Bricco dell'Uccellone. New oak substantially modifies the character of Barbera, adding a real spiciness to its rather neutral aromas and a certain quantity of ligneous tannins which firm up its structure and soften the impact of its acidity. In addition, the extra oxygenation of the wine has helped to curb the variety's natural tendency to REDUCTION. Today Barbera comes in a bewildering range of styles, from the young, cheaplight, and spritzy to powerful, intense, highly priced wines that need extended cellaring, reflecting both variation of producer vision and the extreme heterogeneousness of the soils and MESOCLIMATES of the zones where it is planted.

Certain characteristics are constant none the less: a deep ruby colour (the wine was frequently used in the past to 'correct' the colour of Nebbiolo grapes grown in BAROLO and BARBARESCO); relatively low levels of TANNINS; pronounced ACIDITY which is aggravated by over-production, Barbera being a variety of exemplary VIGOUR and productivity. The DOC regulations, which regrettably permit generous yields (70 hl/ha in Alba, 63 hl/ha in Asti), relatively low ALCOHOLIC STRENGTH (12% in Alba and Asti, 11.5% in the Monferrato), and high minimum acidity in relation to the alcohol and body of the wines, do little to restrain yields or exalt quality.

ALBA, ASTI, and the MONFERRATO give their names to the three DOC zones of Piemonte, although the zones tend to sprawl across vast extensions of territory: there are 171 townships in the Asti DOC and 215 townships in the Monferrato DOC (with the two zones overlapping to a certain extent). The hills immediately to the north and south of Alba and Monforte d'Alba in the Alba DOC and, in the province of Asti, the area from Nizza Monferrato north west towards Vinchio, Castelnuovo Calcea, Agliano, Belveglio, and Rocchetta Tanaro are considered classic zones for Barbera. The finest wines tend to come from the DOCG **Barbera d'Asti**, where it is given serious attention while the DOC has been subdivided in three subzones of which Nizza is expeced to attain its own DOC. Historically, Nizza, because it is one of the warmest parts of the Asti zone, has produced the ripest and best Barbera. In Asti, Barbera is given the best vineyard sites, whereas in Alba these sites go to Nebbiolo.

An apparently unrelated **Barbera Bianca** was grown on 181 ha/447 acres, mainly in Acqui and Alessandria.

Elsewhere in Italy

Barbera dominates much of Lombardy, in particular the vineyards of Oltrepò Pavese, where it makes varietal wines of varying quality and degrees of fizziness, some fine and lively, as well as being blended with the softer local Croatina or BONARDA Piemontese grapes. It is a minor, and decreasing, ingredient in Terre di FRANCIACORTA and is found, as elsewhere in Italy, in oceans of basic VINO DA TAVOLA.

Barbera is also much planted immediately south east of Piemonte in the Colli Piacentini, the hills above Piacenza, of EMILIA-ROMAGNA. Here too it is often blended with Bonarda, particularly in the Val Tidone for the DOC red Gutturnio. It is also planted in the Bologna and Parma hills, the Colli Bolognesi and Colli di Parma, where it may also produce a VARIETAL wine which rarely has the concentration of Piemonte's best and is regularly fizzy.

The variety was planted in Argentina, many years ago, and in California and Australia more recently, thanks to a FASHION for Italian varieties. It can also be found in Slovenia.

Barbera del Sannio is known in Campania while **Barbera Sarda** is grown in Sardinia, but neither is related to the Barbera of Piemonte.

Bardolino, generally modest but attractive light red wine from the south eastern shores of Lake Garda in the VENETO region of north east Italy. As in the other two important Veneto DOCs SOAVE and VALPOLICELLA, the original production zone known as CLASSICO (Bardolino, Garda, Lazise, Affa, Costermano, and Cavaion) has been extended to a considerably larger zone whose wines are simply called Bardolino. The vineyard area of both zones combined is 3,000 ha/7,413 acres, producing some 240,000 hl/6.34 million gallons annually. Like Valpolicella the wine is made of Corvina, Rondinella, and Molinara grapes, with the possible addition of up to 20% of any authorized variety. Merlot is often used to bolster alcohol levels to the official minimum of 11.5% (10.5% for straight Bardolino DOC) so that after an additional year of ageing it can be labelled Bardolino Superiore, a category that has DOCG status. The rosé version, either still or sparkling, is called Chiaretto. TERROIR seems to have rather less effect on this relatively simple wine than it does on Soave and Valpolicella, because large parts of the Bardolino zone, whether Classico or not, lie on a plain. But the determining factor of the wine's general blandness are the high permitted yields of 11 tons/ha (or 80hl/ha). And yields even higher than this in vineyards trained on PERGOLA are encouraged by the region's many bottlers (some 100 in total) looking for BULK WINE at the lowest possible price. Between 2002 and 2007 the local CONSORZIO tried to improve quality by in-depth research into SOIL composition and CLONAL SELECTION. But the proposed system of subzones

had made little impact on the wines by the mid 2010s. Although Bardolino is undeniably light, Le Fraghe's Bardolino is proof that freshness and modest alcohol is not necessarily boring.

W.S.

www.ilbardolino.com

Barolo, the most powerful and dramatic expression of the NEBBIOLO grape, takes its name from the village of the same name 15 km/9 miles to the south of the town of Alba in the region of PIEMONTE in north west Italy.

Barolo as a name started to appear on labels only in the mid 19th century, coinciding with the introduction of glass BOTTLES in the region around 1844. Before that it had been sold in cask only. Camillo Benzo, Count of Cavour, the architect of Italian unity, played a decisive role in Barolo's fortunes by modernizing his family's estate in Grinzane, with the introduction of a monoculture of vines, an idea that may have been inspired by his frequent travels to France. He hired Frenchman Louis Oudart as his oenologist, and he is credited with creating the first modern Barolo by fermenting it fully to dryness, although 10 years before him, Cavour had begun working with Pier Francesco Staglieno who introduced fermentation in closed vats, which greatly reduced premature OXIDATION and levels of VOLATILE acidity in the wines.

Giulietta Falletti, Marquise of Barolo, also engaged Oudart for her vast estate extending to La Morra, Barolo, and Serralunga. Her wine, which attracted the attention of King Carlo Alberto di Savoia, allegedly inspired him to purchase and develop the estates of the castles of Verduno and Roddi for wine production, while Emanuele, Count of Mirafiori, Vittorio Emanuele II's son by the royal mistress Rosa Vercellana, developed the vineyards around the hunting lodge of Fontanafredda in Serralunga d'Alba. Due to this association with what was then Italy's reigning dynasty, Barolo earned the name 'the wine of kings, the king of wines'.

The core of Barolo has always been the townships of Barolo, La Morra, Castiglione Falletto, Serralunga d'Alba, and Monforte d'Alba, supplemented by outlying areas in a variety of other townships. The Agricultural Commission of Alba added Grinzano, part of Verduno, and a section of Novello in 1909, confirming the previous DELIMITATION work of the Ministry of Agriculture in 1896. This became the official definition of the zone in 1934, not without protests from Barolo and Castiglione Falletto, which considered themselves the true standard-bearers of authentic Barolo. Parts of Diano d'Alba, Roddi, and Cherasco were added in the DOC decree of 1966, an error at least on paper, although growers in the zone have generally been careful to plant Nebbiolo only where it can ripen properly, and the villages of Roddi and Cherasco have respectively a mere 22 and

2.34 ha (54.3 and 5.7 acres) planted to Nebbiolo for Barolo.

The majority of the Barolo zone falls within the five core townships mentioned above. This sensible demarcation of the zone, disciplined YIELDS (56 hl/ha (3.2 tons/acre) maximum), and reasonable requirements for AGEING (38 months in total with at least 18 months in oak) make this DOCG one of Italy's most intelligent).

Although Barolo is always powerful and concentrated, with pronounced TANNINS and ACIDITY, there are significant stylistic differences among the wines of the various zones which tend to reflect the two major soil types conveniently separated by the Alba–Barolo road which runs along the valley floor, dividing La Morra and Barolo to the west from Castiglione Falletto, Monforte d'Alba, and Serralunga d'Alba to the east. The first soil type, calcareous marls of the Tortonian epoch which are relatively compact, fresher, and more fertile, characterize the vineyards of the townships of La Morra and Barolo and, depending on the location of the vineyard, can produce softer, fruitier, aromatic wines which age relatively rapidly for a Barolo. The second soil type, from the Helvetian epoch, with a higher proportion of compressed sandstone, is less compact, poorer, and less fertile, with the result that the townships of Monforte d'Alba and Serralunga d'Alba yield more intense, structured wines that mature more slowly. The vineyards of Castiglione Falletto are on a spur that divides these two valleys, and produces wines that have some of the elegant and more forward character of the wines from Barolo combined with the structure and backbone of those from Serralunga.

All fine Barolo, however, shares certain common traits: colour that is never deep (for Nebbiolo, like Pinot Noir, never produces opaque wines), ruby tending relatively rapidly to garnet or brick; complex and expansive aromas of cherries and plums, evolving with time into dried cherries, rose petals, tar, liquorice, and—according to a few fortunate connoisseurs—the local white truffles. Full flavours are backed by substantial tannins, a dense texture, and lifted but never tart acidity. (Barolo from Helvetian soils may surpass 14% alcohol and 14.5% is by no means rare in hot vintages, although balance is the overriding aim.)

One development that has marked contemporary Barolo is ESTATE BOTTLING and the fact that virtually all producers offer at least one SINGLE-VINEYARD WINE. Until 1960 the marketing of the wine was dominated by NÉGOCIANT houses, unsurprisingly in a production zone where the average property is 1.9 ha (948 growers divided 1,886 ha/2,875 acres in 2010). Estate bottling represented both an attempt by peasant proprietors to reap greater economic benefits from their vineyards and a desire to put their name, as well as that of their holdings, before the public. Négociant houses, dealing in large quantities, necessarily blended the wines of different provenances into a house Barolo (just like their counterparts in BURGUNDY). When skilfully done, this did—and still does—accomplish the creation of balanced and harmonious wines which exemplify the general characteristics of Barolo. But certain privileged positions have long enjoyed greater prestige and given more distinctive wines in both the written tradition (from Lorenzo Fantini in the late 19th century to modern writers such as Luigi VERONELLI, Renato Ratti and, more recently, Alessandro Masnaghetti) and in the oral tradition of the zone, opinions made concretely significant by the higher prices paid by négociants for the grapes and wines of certain vineyards. While there is no absolute unanimity, most shortlists of the finest CRUS include Rocche dell'Annunziata and Cerequio in La Morra, spilling over into Barolo; Cannubi, Sarmazza, and Brunate in Barolo (the latter vineyard shared with La Morra); Rocche di Castiglione, Villero, and Monprivato in Castiglione Falletto; Bussia, Ginestra, and previously Santo Stefano di Perno (now included in the unreasonably enlarged Perno, see below) in Monforte d'Alba; Francia, Lazzarito and Vigna Rionda in Serralunga d'Alba.

The multiplicity of single-vineyard bottlings from the 1980s, in the absence of an official CLASSIFICATION, has had the paradoxical result of focusing attention on and reinforcing confidence in single producers. The situation has, at least partially, been addressed by the introduction of the Menzioni Geographiche Aggiuntive Ufficiali, an official list of registered single vineyards throughout the Barolo zone. They are not classified but they are identified as 'Crus', and Masnaghetti has attempted his own unofficial classification. Although most Barolo communes produced a historically faithful list, some, especially Monforte d'Alba, radically pruned the number of its vineyards by including swathes of them within more famous names. Bussia in particular has been unreasonably enlarged since the authorities failed to question this loss of historic vineyards and detail, important to consumers and professionals. This ruthless capitalization on famous vineyard names recalls the controversial creation of GROSSLAGE in Germany.

Like many of the world's powerful and age-worthy red wines, Barolo had to come to terms in the 1970s and 1980s with market demands for fruitier, less tannic wines that can more easily be drunk while young—not an easy transition for a zone which is devoted solely to Nebbiolo, a variety with high acidity and tannins, and where FERMENTATION and MACERATION have regularly lasted as long as two months. The leaders of the movement towards a softer style of Barolo were Renato Ratti, Paolo Cordero di Montezemolo, and the house of Ceretto, using ROTOFERMENTERS, allowing for speedy extraction of colour and a swift alcoholic fermentation (generally 7–14 days), and shorter ageing periods, resulting in less tannic, paler wines.

The proponents of this new approach were termed 'modernists', while those who retained faith in the old methods were called 'traditionalists'. This rather facile distinction fascinated the wine world in the 1970s and 1980s, but in retrospect it can be seen as nothing more than the continuing evolution of winemaking in this small zone. Traditional Barolo, a product of long maceration on the skins, from relatively high-yielding grapes in which the tannins had yet to polymerize fully, needed extended ageing in cask in order to soften the hard tannins the wine displayed in youth. In truth, this softening of the tannins was often brought about by oxidation, something that also oxidized the fruit. This resulted in wines that were garnet or brick in colour, with oxidation and the hard tannins still evident on the palate.

As the world of wine opened up in the 1960s, and as some of the producers in Barolo travelled further than Turin or Rome, they decided that their wines were badly in need of modernizing, triggering a move to TEMPERATURE CONTROL during fermentation, a reduction in the length of MACERATION, a move to PUMPING OVER rather than SUBMERGED CAP in the belief that a lower tannin level and shorter time in barrel were steps in this direction. Instead of a protracted length of time in large old oak, some producers started to introduce small oak BARRIQUES to the cellars in the late 1970s, in the belief that the sweeter oak tannins would help to moderate the aggressive grape tannins of the Nebbiolo. It was the same wish, to create more approachable if less typical wines, that favoured the plantings of INTERNATIONAL VARIETIES such as Merlot, Syrah, and Cabernet Sauvignon in the Barolo zone, not only to augment the colour but also to add impact and ripe berry notes to the more delicate character of Nebbiolo. Indeed, a proposal in the mid 1990s to reduce the minimum Nebbiolo content from 100 to 90% was defeated only after intense debate in the region.

At the beginning of the 21st century the differences between the modernists and traditionalists have come full circle. Some of the modernist versions aged in small French oak developed poorly in bottle, sometimes accompanied by PREMATURE OXIDATION, while the opulence of new oak aromas tended to obliterate Nebbiolo's fine perfume. The two camps have converged. Barriques are still in use, but a significant number of producers has returned to ageing in much larger casks, while increasing the total maceration on the skins to between 30 and even 60 days in some cases, crucially without resulting in harsh tannins or bitter wines.

No doubt, better clonal material, lower yields, and higher plant density, combined with increasingly sophisticated knowledge of viticulture on even the smallest estates has led to this increase of quality, and with that, an increase in the expression of variety and terroir.

An unparalleled series of exceptional vintages in the late 1990s and 2000s such as 1996, 1997, 1998, 1999, and 2001 saw demand in the US and German-speaking markets, and prices escalate. This led to an increase in plantings. In 2004, for example, there were 1,714 ha/4,285 acres under vine, almost half as much again as had been planted in 1990. This saw Nebbiolo planted in sites that were traditionally reserved for such lesser varieties as DOLCETTO and BARBERA. so there was grim pessimism among some producers that quality, just when it should be improving in order to justify the higher prices, would in fact decrease as these new plantings came to be used in the production of Barolo. CLIMATE CHANGE may have helped, but new plantings have slowed so that by 2010 the total Barolo vineyard was 1,886 ha/4,660 acres, and a string of excellent vintages such as 2006, 2008, and 2010 triggered demand for what, with just 13.2 million bottles produced in 2012, is increasingly recognized around the world as a fine wine in decidedly limited quantities.

See also BARBARESCO. **Barolo Bianco** is an occasional name for the ARNEIS grape.

D.C.G. & W.S.

Masnaghetti, A., *Barolo MGA: The Barolo Great Vineyards Encyclopedia* (Monza, 2015).

O'Keefe, K., *Barolo and Barbaresco* (Oakland, Calif., 2014).

Petrini, C. (ed.), *A Wine Atlas of the Langhe* (3rd edn, Bra, 2005).

Baroque, sometimes spelt **Barroque**, is the intensely local grape variety associated with white TURSAN. Although it is now grown almost exclusively in the Landes *département*, it was at one time known throughout SOUTH WEST FRANCE and was valued by growers in the early 20th century for its resistance to POWDERY MILDEW. More recently investment in the Tursan appellation by chef Michel Guérard of Eugénie-les-Bains has saved this characterful variety from extinction. His wine, Baron de Bachen, displays the unusual combination of high alcohol and fine aroma, something akin to ripe pears.

Barossa Valley, the heart of the Australian wine industry, the most famous wine region in AUSTRALIA, and the one in which most wine is produced, even if a high proportion of it is shipped in from vineyards outside the valley itself. There is an increasing trend towards planting off the valley floor and on higher ground on the hillsides. On the other side of the coin, the incalculable value of the viticultural bank of Shiraz, Grenache, and Mourvèdre vineyards, up to 170 years old, dry-grown (see DRYLAND VITICULTURE), and UNGRAFTED makes this a heritage area which can be neither duplicated nor replaced. According to Australia's official wine geography, the **Barossa Zone** includes the Barossa Valley and Eden Valley wine regions. For more detail, see SOUTH AUSTRALIA.

barrel, cylindrical container traditionally made from WOOD and historically used for the storage and transportation of a wide range of goods. Today, barrels are used almost exclusively in the production of fine wines and spirits, and are almost invariably made of wood, although some have experimented with various combinations of STAINLESS STEEL, clay, CONCRETE, etc. The bulge, or bilge, of barrels means that they can be rolled and spun easily, and that, when they are kept horizontal, any sediment naturally collects in one place, from which the wine can easily be separated by RACKING. The average worldwide production is one million barrels, with more than half made in France.

Barrels come in many sizes (see BARREL TYPES) and qualities (see BARREL MAKING). The word barrel is conventionally used for a wooden container small enough to be moved, while VATS are larger, permanent containers, sometimes with an open top. COOPERAGE is the collective noun for all wooden containers, whether barrels or vats (as well as the term for the cooper's business or premises), and the word CASK is used for wooden containers of all sizes.

BARREL MATURATION is the term used in this book for ageing a wine in a barrel, while CASK AGEING has been used as a general term for keeping a wine in a larger wooden container. BARREL FERMENTATION is the technique of fermenting wine in barrel.

A barrel is made up of STAVES shaped into a bulging cylinder, with hoops round it, a flat circular head at either end, and at least one hole for a BUNG. See BARREL MAKING for details.

History

Although HERODOTUS refers to palm-wood casks being used to carry Armenian wine to Babylon in Mesopotamia, it is generally accepted that it was the Iron Age communities of northern Europe, notably the CELTS, who developed the wooden barrel for the large-scale transport of goods. Its origins cannot now be recovered but Julius Caesar encountered barrels during his campaigns in France in the 50s BC. In the second half of the 1st century AD, PLINY described transport barrels in GAUL in a way that suggests they would have been unfamiliar to his Roman audience. The Latin term *cupa*, which later came to mean barrel, at this time normally referred to wood storage tanks, the remains of one of which have been found at POMPEII, near Naples. Barrels or barrel staves have been preserved in waterlogged conditions on sites in Britain (at Silchester), and along the RHINE and the Danube. The wood used was frequently silver fir.

Famous monuments such as that from Neumagen on the German River MOSEL testify to the use of barrels for the transport of goods. When the Roman army served in northern Europe, it used barrels regularly; they are frequently illustrated in scenes from the columns of Trajan and Marcus Aurelius which commemorated the campaigns of these emperors in the 2nd century AD. From the middle of the 3rd century references in literature and art to the use of barrels in Italy and, to a lesser extent, elsewhere in the Mediterranean are much more frequent. It is possible that the more widespread use of the barrel explains the disappearance of various types of AMPHORAE in this period. It also means that from this period on it is much more difficult to trace trade routes, since wood is much less likely to survive on archaeological sites. Barrels were certainly used for the transport of wine, but also for other liquids and goods such as salt.

See also BARREL MAINTENANCE, BARREL RENEWAL, BARREL STORAGE, GRAIN, INNER STAVES, OAK, OAK FLAVOUR, TOAST, WOOD INFLUENCE, WOOD TYPES.

J.J.P.

barrel alternatives, common term for a group of materials and techniques, including the use of OAK CHIPS, BARREL INSERTS, INNER STAVES, and sometimes MICRO-OXYGENATION, which are alternatives to BARRELS. They save both money and space and have become increasingly sophisticated, offering the winemaker a choice of different types of oak as well as different toast levels, but care is needed with the dosage and the length of time the products are in contact with the wine. Since 2006 certain barrel alternatives have been permitted in the EU, although their use is forbidden in some PDO wines.

barrel fermentation, winemaking technique of fermenting grape juice or must in small BARRELS rather than in a larger FERMENTATION VESSEL. The technique is used principally for white wines because of the difficulty of extracting through a barrel's small bung-hole the mass of skins and seeds which necessarily remains after red wine fermentation, although in the late 1990s, fermentation of red wine in barrel, said to improve oak integration and MOUTHFEEL, gained in popularity. In Burgundy, California, and especially Australia, however, some winemakers deliberately put pressed red wines which still retain some unfermented sugars into barrel, thus allowing completion of red wine FERMENTATION in barrel in an attempt to make softer, more approachable wines.

Encouraged by the success of this technique, a few winemakers are taking this further and fermenting small quantities of red grapes entirely in barrels, either by removing the barrel head for an open top fermentation, or by using a specially designed barrel in which the bung hole in the side of the barrel has been replaced by a porthole in the head, sometimes with a paddle inside to help break up the CAP. Proponents claim that putting the must into barrel immediately after crushing results in softer tannins, increased stability, and better colour concentration.

Barrel fermentation seems particularly well adapted to wine made from CHARDONNAY grapes and some of the finest SWEET WINES. Its advantages are that it offers the possibility of extracting a controlled amount of OAK FLAVOUR into the wine and, since barrels have a large surface to volume ratio, artificial mechanized TEMPERATURE CONTROL may not be needed. It also provides a natural prelude to BARREL MATURATION and LEES STIRRING since the lees and the wine are already in the same container.

White wine which is fermented and stored in oak with its yeast solids, or LEES, has a softened, less obvious, and more integrated oak flavour than wine that has been fermented in a larger container before being matured in barrels. This may be because the YEAST acts on the highly aromatic oak flavour molecules to transform them biochemically into much less aromatic substances. and because of the adsorption of aromatic compounds onto the yeast cell wall. (The secondary fermentation aromas, however, such as result from ESTERS, fatty acids, and higher alcohols, are substantially unaffected by barrel fermentation.) FINING also removes some oak compounds. Fermentation in barrel also gives large increases in POLYSACCHARIDES, or complex SUGARS, which add richness and apparent LENGTH of flavour on the palate. The amount of yeast mass in the barrel and the frequency of stirring have a direct and considerable effect on the quantity of polysaccharides formed. The yeast also make and release ENZYMES that could reduce the stability of aromatic compounds in the wine.

White wines matured for a few months on their lees in barrel usually have a much lighter colour than those put into barrel after fermentation to mature. Certain COLLOIDS are liberated during fermentation and LEES CONTACT; this stabilizes some of the PHENOLICS extracted from the oak, causing pigment to be precipitated.

Stirring up the lees in the barrel also affects oak flavour. If the lees are stirred, they act as an even more effective buffer between the wine and the wood, limiting the extent to which wood TANNINS, and colouring matter, are extracted into the wine. Wines subjected to lees stirring therefore tend to be much paler and less tannic than those whose lees are not stirred. Stirring also minimizes the effects of stratification in the barrel and is a more efficient way to bring wine components in contact with the lees, and thereby increase extraction of materials from them.

Fermentation in barrel can also have secondary flavour effects due to temperature, lot size, and precise level of TOAST. The often higher temperature of fermentation in barrel rather than vat causes a loss of floral flavours and a reduction of the most obvious white wine fermentation AROMAS reminiscent of tropical fruit. There are fewer fatty acid esters and fatty acids which are described as perfumed or soapy, and more higher alcohols, which makes the wine taste fuller bodied. And because each fermentation even of identical juice has a slightly different flavour outcome, the larger number of small volume lots that are common in barrel fermentation create more complexity. A 10,000-l/2,642-gal lot would create one fermentation flavour if it were fermented in one tank, for example, but the same lot volume fermented in 70 barrels would produce a much more complex array of flavours.

The disadvantages of barrel fermentation are the relatively small size of the barrel and the time and effort required to clean, fill, and empty it, although the extra degree of complexity gained by the wine is usually worth any extra production costs. The cost of new barrels themselves is such, however, that the technique is restricted to higher-priced wines. With so many fermentations in a non-sterile material, it is always possible that some barrels may be infected with BACTERIA or undesirable yeasts, so extra vigilance is required to eliminate any defective wines. Fermenting red wine in a barrel is more complicated because the CAP must be managed during fermentation and the skins and seeds have to be removed thereafter. Some barrels are specially designed with larger openings in the head to make this easier but some producers simply remove the head. If the barrels are stored on a racking system with rollers, barrels can easily be turned to keep the cap mixed with the fermenting must—rather like a mini wooden ROTOFERMENTER.

Fermentation produces a protective blanket of CARBON DIOXIDE on the surface of the wine in the barrel. As fermentation slows and stops, the CO_2 will be displaced by air, allowing uptake of some oxygen from the HEAD SPACE into the wine. The larger ratio of head space to wine volume in barrels, and the permeability of wood to oxygen, will allow more oxygen to enter the wine than would occur if the same volume were in a large tank. However, it is important to keep barrels full to limit the amount of oxygen exposure so that the wine does not become OXIDIZED or affected by BACTERIAL SPOILAGE. See TOPPING UP.

When barrels are expensive and wine is not, winemakers and winery owners seek ways of economizing on barrel purchases. For alternatives to barrels, see INNER STAVES and OAK CHIPS.   L.F.B., J.E.H., & D.D.

Dubourdieu, D., 'Vinification des vins blancs secs en barriques', in G. Guimberteau (ed.), *Le Bois et la qualité des vins et eaux-de-vie* (Bordeaux, 1992).

barrel inserts

barrel inserts, imprecise and expanding term for pieces of wood, usually OAK, added to a barrel too old to impart much OAK FLAVOUR. For the use of inserts in a tank, see INNER STAVES. See also BARREL RENEWAL and OAK CHIPS.

barrel maintenance

barrel maintenance. BARRELS are an important investment for a winery, in terms of both their cost and their precious contents. The contents of a barrel may well have a wholesale value of thousands of dollars, while new barrels cost £190 to £625 (US$300 to US$1,000) each, depending on quality and origin. The preparation of new barrels and the maintenance of used ones is therefore an important activity for winemakers, and can play a part in determining WOOD INFLUENCE.

Preparation for use

Barrels are treated prior to use both to check for leaks and to ensure that the barrel offers the right flavours to the wine. In Burgundy, where the barrels are filled with either white grape MUST in the case of white wines or just-pressed wine in the case of reds, treatment is minimal. Usually the barrel is merely rinsed or filled with cold water to check for leaks and so that the wood can expand properly, thus reducing initial leaks. In Bordeaux, barrels are traditionally filled with 15 to 20 l/4 to 5 gal of hot water. The barrel is spun and shaken so that, in theory, some of the rough TANNINS are washed out as the steam created during the spinning process exposes any leaks. (If a small leak is found, it can usually be plugged with a small piece of wood. A leak near the head may indicate that some adjustment is necessary. Occasionally a STAVE may have to be replaced.) In reality, it is the air-drying of the wood (see BARREL MAKING) that has more influence on the tannins than hot water.

New World wine regions used to be less systematic in their barrel preparation. In the late 1970s, it was still common to use soda ash, supposedly to remove unpleasant tannins, although it is now clear that soda ash prematurely ages the barrel and at the same time removes the barrel's TOAST and makes the wine taste more tannic. Most winemakers are wary of filling a barrel with lukewarm water as BACTERIA grow easily under such conditions. Nearly all winemakers will at least rinse the barrel prior to use and in parts of Europe ammonia is often used; although this is a harsh cleanser, it can provide nutrients for FERMENTATION. Ammonia may also be used deliberately to prepare barrels for a light vintage, supposedly to remove some of the wood tannins. although it more likely removes the toast. At some point prior to first use, the exterior of the barrel is often coated with linseed oil or a commercial product such as Mildecide to combat MOULDS, although this is done principally for aesthetic reasons and linseed is used mainly on larger vats. Several companies have developed high-pressure barrel washers that can be used in combination with hot water or steam to sanitize barrels with little impact on wood quality.

Identification

At many larger wineries a card is attached to the head of the barrel to enable the winemaker to follow the life of each individual barrel. In larger New World wineries, it is not uncommon to see the sort of bar code used by supermarkets, along with computerized tracking (see INFORMATION TECHNOLOGY). Some coopers now deliver barrels with bar codes, making it easier to identify them and improving their traceability. In smaller wineries, a few letters may suffice. In Burgundy, for example, the chalked letters 'CM/R' might serve to denote 'Chassagne Montrachet, Ruchottes'. And in very small cellars, the single individual in charge may know every barrel so intimately that formal markings are unnecessary. Some wineries are now experimenting with Radio Frequency Identification (RFID) systems.

Bungs

See BUNG.

Unused barrels and used empty barrels

Storage of empty barrels is always problematic, particularly because of the possible growth of harmful ACETOBACTER, and barrels may well be sheathed in plastic before being shipped long distances to minimize spoilage. Every month, empty barrels should be rinsed, carefully dried, and only then treated with SULFUR DIOXIDE, then bunged up. If they are not dried properly, there is a risk that sulfuric acid will be formed. Barrels so treated must be stored under the same conditions of low temperature and high, but not too high, humidity as full barrels.

Most winemakers prefer to avoid the cost and risks associated with the long-term storage of empty barrels by ordering very precise quantities and filling them as soon as possible. See also BARREL STORAGE.   L.B., J.E.H., & M.K.

Schahinger, G., and Rankine, B., *Cooperage for Winemakers* (rev. edn, Adelaide, 2005).

Taransaud, J., *Le Livre de la tonnellerie* (Paris, 1976).

barrel making involves far more than mere mechanics and the ability to fashion a watertight container out of nothing but bent wood. As outlined in detail in WOOD INFLUENCE, every stage of barrel manufacture has an impact on wine matured in that barrel. First, the tree is

cut down, usually during the autumn or winter when the sap is down. COOPERS usually buy long sections of trunk, from trees that are ideally over 100 years old, and then the process that turns logs into stave wood begins.

Cutting: sawing versus splitting

Logs of appropriate lengths are cut and then split into four lengthwise. The bark and sap wood are cut off so that STAVES may be cut from radial (rather than tangential) sections of wood.

Because American OAK is so much less porous than European, staves of American oak can simply be sawn from each quarter to maximize the yield of each log. This is traditional quarter sawing. The mill worker tosses a quartered bolt on to a conveyor belt. A band saw parallel to the conveyor belt lops off a stave, which is sent on its way, while the rest of the log comes back on the conveyor belt to be sawn again.

European oak could well leak if thus sawn, however, and staves have to be cut, or split, much more carefully, minimizing the risk of leakage by following the oak GRAIN. Traditionally therefore European oak was split by hand so that the axe blade could follow the grain. Nowadays mechanically operated axes are guided through the wood sections and the resulting staves trimmed, still following the grain.

Some coopers do saw European wood and may paint the end of the staves, the chime, to block end-grain leaks. Since twice as many staves are produced by sawing as by hand-splitting, the waste involved in traditional European COOPERAGE practices is considerable. French oak is so relatively expensive (the wood cost in a barrel was approximately €350 (£275/US$442) in 2013) that sawn French barrels seem an economically alluring proposition. Experiments so far, however, suggest that experienced tasters systematically prefer wines from French barrels made from traditionally hand-split staves—perhaps because sawing oak exposes more grains, and therefore more raw TANNINS, to the wine. Proponents of sawing maintain that the wood is worked so much during manufacture that it does not matter how the wood is cut, so long as the wood is sawed following the grain.

In France, wood split by hand from logs for use as staves is known as *merrain* and the men who do this work are known as *merrandiers*. Traditionally this work was done near the forest but nowadays many cooperages have their own stave-splitting facilities, either near the cooperage or in the forests.

Drying: air versus kiln

After the wood has been split or sawn, it must be dried. The drying process can be achieved either naturally in the open air or artificially using kilns. French oak has traditionally been

air dried one year for every 10 mm/0.4 in width so that it takes between 18 and 36 months to 'season' wood by drying it, in stacks of potential staves, in the open, preferably on a site far from any industrial activity or any other source of pollution. This ties up so much capital that many cooperages have been forced to substitute artificial drying techniques which generally take no more than 12 months.

Many quality-conscious winemakers will pay a premium for wood dried in the open air, however, and an increasing number of them actually select and buy their own wood in advance of seasoning. Natural drying tends to reduce and modify the structure of the extractable compounds of the wood while heightening its aromatic potential. It has for long been thought that, as wood is seasoned outdoors and turns grey, darkening the ground beneath it, harsh tannins are being leached out of the wood. Wine matured in air-dried wood certainly tends to taste less aggressively tannic than the same wine matured in kiln-dried wood. Australian research by Sefton and others, however, indicates that tannin levels in wood do not in fact change during seasoning, but that their sensory effect does, with French oak tannins becoming much less noticeable with seasoning and American oak tannins more so. In another Australian study, lots of the same wood were dried in Australia and in France. The Australian lot, dried under hot and dry conditions, was analysed and compared with the lot aged in France under cool and moist conditions. As the rate of chemical reactions increases dramatically with temperature rise, differences were to be expected. The concentration of certain lactones (see OAK FLAVOUR) was much higher in wood dried in Australia.

In the late 1980s, many American cooperages realized that the wine-barrel market called for an entirely different barrel from that traditionally supplied to bourbon producers and introduced air drying as well as offering barrels labelled with specific geographical origins, just like their French counterparts.

Studies by Nicolas Vivas of the University of BORDEAUX indicate that moulds and enzymes formed on and in the wood during air drying play crucial roles in the flavour of oak and any wine matured in it. Moulds formed on the surface of the wood liberate exocellular ENZYMES, principally heterosidases. They permit the transformation of certain bitter components into molecules which taste more neutral. At the same time, glucose and POLYSACCHARIDES are liberated from the structural elements of the wood. It has also been demonstrated that the moulds and enzymes help create micropores in the wood. Longer air-drying means more holes, giving additional life to the barrel.

Vivas has also shown that natural air drying lowers the level of dry EXTRACT, total PHENOLICS, and ellagitannins and raises the level of lactones, vanillins, and eugenols (see OAK FLAVOUR). He cautions that if oak is dried under warm and dry conditions such as those found in much of Australia and California, the results may be similar to those produced in artificial dryers.

Some cooperages maintain that it is not just the duration of the air-drying process that is important but the wood's exposure to rain and the temperature at which the wood is dried. Their wood may therefore be watered to simulate rain, but there has been little scientific analysis of results.

Assembling

Once the staves are dry enough, they can be assembled into barrels. Barrel making is made possible by the fact that wood can be bent when it has been heated. If the staves are shaped properly, the result will be a barrel. All edges will meet properly and the barrel will hold liquid without any agent other than the hoops which hold the staves together.

First, the staves are sized and trimmed into oblong lengths that might be called a double taper. Traditionally this work, known as 'dressing' the staves, was done by hand. The stave was 'listed', that is given the double taper shape, with a cooper's axe, known as a *doloire* in French. Then, the inside of the stave was 'scalloped' with a two-handled hollowing knife to allow for easier bending. Finally the staves were joined on a jointer, known as a *colombe*. Here the staves were given their final shape—rounded at the bilge (the middle) and narrowed at the heads (the ends). Nowadays most of this work is done by machines, saving much time and energy.

Finally, the cooper fits the staves into a frame so that each barrel will have the same circumference. An especially strong and wide stave is chosen for the stave into which the BUNG-hole will eventually be drilled (see below). Then these staves are arranged around an iron 'raising up' hoop, the result looking like a skirt or a teepee splayed out from the hoop at the top. This job calls for great manual dexterity, although in many American cooperages machines can do much of this work.

Shaping and toasting

Research has shown that the heating process is one of the most important in barrel manufacture, modifying the wood's physical and chemical composition and profoundly influencing any wine stored in the barrel. Heating allows the cooper to shape the barrel. Toasting degrades the wood structure and thereby produces aromatic compounds. There is controversy as to which type of toasting is best, with some suggesting that slower toasting is better for both the flavour and the structure of a wine matured

in that barrel. A deep medium toast produces the most desirable character for most woods, but there is variation in effect depending on geographic origin of the wood, the seasoning of the wood, and the wine style. Ellagitannins from the barrel, which combine with phenolics in the wine to form new and softer tannin compounds and improve colour stability, are reduced by toasting.

Various sources of heat can be used to shape the barrel: natural gas, steam and boiling water, or the fire of wood chips. Some cooperages combine techniques and shape the barrel with the aid of boiling water or steam, then finish the barrel with a fire toasting.

Coopers knocking down the hoops and bending the barrels over fire make an exciting spectacle for a high degree of co-ordination is required. The would-be barrel is rolled over a cylindrical, vented metal firepot, known as a *chaufferette*, in which small oak chips are burned. The coopers walk round the barrel knocking down the temporary iron hoops. They pound the hammer on a hoop driver—a short block of wood with a flat metal end—while watering the wood to keep it from getting too toasted too quickly. After the top of the barrel has been shaped, the coopers wrap cables around the base of the barrel and use a capstan to cinch up the base.

Coopers often categorize the toasting and bending of staves in three stages: the warm-up (*chauffage*); the shaping (*cintrage*); and the toasting afterwards (*bousinage*). It is the last stage which determines the level of TOAST inside the barrel, which depends crucially on the right combination of humidity and heat.

Natural gas, boiling water, and steam will heat the wood effectively and allow the cooper to bend the staves without the creation of blisters on the inside of the staves. Many winemakers prefer this technique as the barrel is easier to clean. Other winemakers prefer barrels shaped over a fire of wood chips, as the toast on the inside of the barrel provides an interesting 'toasty' flavour to the wine. These winemakers feel that any extra effort in BARREL MAINTENANCE is justified by the special flavour provided by this technique. The amount of time the barrel sits on the fire and the heat of the fire both have a dramatic impact on the appearance of the barrel's interior and on resultant wine flavour. Nowadays winemakers can order barrels 'toasted' to their specifications. Some cooperages use an electric ambient heater or a wood fire to toast the heads too, although these are usually left untoasted.

The heads

After the body of the barrel has been formed, then the heads, or barrel-ends, must be made and fitted. Five or six head staves are fitted together with wooden dowels or stainless steel

gudgeons (headless nails). Some cooperagess are now using a tongue and groove system. Then the head is cut to size, usually round but sometimes slightly oval in shape. Near each end of the body of the barrel, a groove, called the croze, is cut into the inside of the barrel. The head is cut at the edges so that it will fit into the croze.

Formerly all of this work was done by hand, but now virtually all of it is done on machines which have replaced an array of traditional cooper's tools with names (adze, chiv, etc.) to delight the dedicated Scrabble player. Finally the head is fitted into the barrel. To do this the hoops are loosened and the head is inserted into the croze.

Finishing

Before the barrel can be sold or shipped, its outside must be planed so that splinters will not dog cellar work. The barrel is tested for leaks, usually with steam or hot water injected through a small hole drilled in the bung stave. If the barrel passes the test, the small hole is drilled to bung-hole size and cauterized. The temporary iron hoops are removed and the final ones, usually made of metal and sometimes of chestnut, are fitted.

Developments

Several cooperages dry staves for up to four or five years. The fact that expensive barrels lose their value so quickly has initiated various schemes for BARREL RENEWAL. See also BARREL INSERTS, INNER STAVES, and OAK CHIPS for other ways of imbuing wine with OAK FLAVOUR without having to buy new barrels.

See also BARREL TYPES, OAK, and WOOD INFLUENCE.   M.K.

Chatonnet, P., 'Origin and processing of oak used in cooperage' and 'Aromatic compounds yielded by oak into wine', in *Le Bois et la qualité des vins et eaux-de-vie* (Bordeaux, 1992).

Schahinger, G., and Rankine, B., *Cooperage for Winemakers* (rev. edn, Adelaide, 2005).

Sefton, M. A., 'How does oak barrel maturation contribute to wine flavor?', *Australian and New Zealand Wine Industry Journal* (Feb 1991).

Sefton, M. A., et al., 'Influence of seasoning on the sensory characteristics and composition of oak extracts', in *International Oak Symposium* (San Francisco, 1993).

Taransaud, J., *Le Livre de la tonnellerie* (Paris, 1976).

Vivas, N., *Manuel de tonnellerie à l'usage des utilisateurs de futaille* (2nd edn, Bordeaux, 2002).

barrel maturation is the winemaking operation of storing a fermented wine in wooden BARRELS to create ideal conditions for the components of the wine to evolve and so that the wood imparts some OAK FLAVOUR. This is an increasingly common practice for superior-quality still wines of all colours and styles, providing them, as it does, with the ideal preparation for BOTTLE AGEING.

The most obvious advantage of barrel maturation is that it encourages CLARIFICATION and STABILIZATION of the wine in the most natural, if not necessarily the fastest, way. It also helps to deepen and stabilize the COLOUR, to soften the TANNINS, and to increase the complexity of the flavour compounds.

Although some oak flavour is extracted directly into the wine, one of the more obvious secondary flavour effects of maturing a wine in barrel results from the slow oxygenation of the wine. When barrels are filled, stoppered, and rolled, they receive a small but significant amount of OXYGEN. Leaving barrels upright and topping up the evaporated wine weekly can triple the amount of oxygen the wine receives. This uptake of oxygen, however slow or fast, tends to reduce fresh, grapey primary AROMAS and also causes small tannin molecules to agglomerate, which changes the colour towards gold in whites and softens the astringency in both reds and whites. In red wines, oxygen aids in the formation of PIGMENTED TANNINS with colours that are more permanent than those of monomeric ANTHOCYANINS. For more details, see AGEING. MICRO-OXYGENATION in barrel or tank is seen by an increasing number of winemakers (and accountants) as an attractive alternative to prolonged barrel ageing.

WOOD INFLUENCE outlines the factors that govern the process of barrel maturation: size, age, and wood type of the barrel, techniques used in BARREL MAKING, storage conditions, characteristics of the vintage, winemaking techniques, and time. See also TOAST for details of how this plays a part in providing a buffer between the alcohol and the wood's PHENOLICS.

The better properties in BORDEAUX provide the paradigm for the barrel maturation of wines based on CABERNET SAUVIGNON and MERLOT grapes. Here top-quality wines are put into barrels with a light to medium toast immediately after (occasionally before, see below) MALOLACTIC CONVERSION and left to mature for up to two years. RACKING every three or four months helps clarification, softens the oak flavour, and inevitably involves some oxygenation. Oxygenation is positively encouraged during the first six months by leaving the barrels with the BUNG up. Thereafter they are rotated so that oxygenation is reduced. FINING takes place at the beginning of the second year, further encouraging stabilization. The timing of BOTTLING is the final crucial human input of barrel maturation.

In the early 1980s, it was common for New World winemakers to practise these same techniques on wines made from the PINOT NOIR grape, but, because they lack the tannic structure of wines made from Cabernet Sauvignon or Merlot, such wines tasted bitter and excessively tannic. Heavier toast on the inside of the barrel can also act as a buffer between wood and wine. By racking Pinot Noir into barrel immediately after alcoholic fermentation and allowing malolactic conversion to take place in barrel, much better integration of wood and wine has been achieved, together with greater complexity of flavour.

As a result of this success, some California winemakers began to apply this Pinot Noir technique to varieties such as Cabernet Sauvignon, ZINFANDEL, and the RHÔNE varieties. Whereas in Bordeaux red wine has traditionally been racked into barrel only after malolactic conversion, a significant proportion of New World Cabernet, Syrah, Zinfandel, and Merlot is now racked straight into barrel after primary alcoholic fermentation with the result that wine and wood oak flavours are better integrated. Even in Bordeaux, particularly on smaller properties where the necessary barrel-by-barrel surveillance is easier, there is a FASHION for encouraging malolactic conversion in barrel in an attempt to make wines that are more flattering to taste young—particularly useful when selling EN PRIMEUR.

All over the world, many top-quality white wines are subjected to BARREL FERMENTATION prior to barrel maturation, another practice which tends to result in much better integration of wood and wine than putting white wine into barrel only after fermentation.

An alternative to barrel maturation for wines of all hues is CASK AGEING, whereby wine is stored in large, older wooden containers which impart very little wood oak flavour but exert some of the favourable aspects of wood influence, provided they are kept clean. Other alternatives, and possible supplements, to barrel maturation include ageing in inert CONTAINERS; ageing in clay vessels such as AMPHORAE, QVEVRI or TINAJAS; BOTTLE AGEING; and bottling almost immediately after fermentation as in NOUVEAU wines. See also INNER STAVES.

See BARREL MAINTENANCE and BARREL STORAGE for more details of some of the important practical aspects of barrel maturation. M.K. & L.B.

Naudin, R., *L'Élevage des vins de Bourgogne en fûts neufs* (Beaune, 1989).

Pontallier, P., 'Pratiques actuelles de l'élevage en barriques des grands vins rouges', in *Le Bois et la qualité des vins et eaux-de-vie* (Bordeaux, 1992).

Pracomtal, G. de, et al., 'Types of oak grain, wine élevage in barrel', *Practical Winery & Vineyard* (Jul 2014), 64–9.

Sefton, M. A., 'How does oak barrel maturation contribute to wine flavor?', *Australian and New Zealand Industry Journal* (Feb 1991).

barrel renewal is a way of saving money on expensive barrels that depreciate very quickly. One method popular in the New World involves shaving the interior of the barrel. A cooper removes the barrel head and shaves off all the pigmented wood from inside the barrel with a plane or grouter. In some cases, the barrel is allowed to dry out a bit, and then the cooper retoasts the inside in order to maintain the all-important buffer between the wine and the wood and seal the wood. This system is not perfect because it is difficult to toast wood that has been permeated by alcohol and is therefore not entirely dry. Retoasting seems most effective on relatively young (two- to three-year-old) barrels. Wine aged in shaved and retoasted older barrels rarely has the subtlety of wine matured in new barrels. Another technique involves removing the wine-soaked part of the barrel with dry ice.

An alternative approach is to insert pieces of OAK of various sizes and designs into the barrel. With larger pieces of wood, the barrel head has to be removed. A food-grade device reminiscent of the tray in an automatic dishwasher is inserted. This holds small oak planks which may be renewed every other year or so. Alternatively small planks are linked together and attached to the bottom of the bung so that they dangle in the wine. This technique can result in much better wines than those matured in shaved barrels. See also INNER STAVES and OAK CHIPS.

barrel storage has both aesthetic and practical ramifications. In most wineries there are visitors to impress, although they tend to find efficient modern reality less impressive than cobwebbed tradition. Some much-visited wineries fill their barrels in full view of the tourists before trucking the wine down the road to a clinical modern barrel warehouse, carefully regulated for both temperature and humidity. In Bordeaux particularly, it is traditional to anoint the band around the middle of the barrel with wine, giving it a neat pink stripe—indeed in some of today's most immaculate barrel cellars this is the only visible sign that a liquid called wine is involved at all.

Touristic considerations aside, most wineries usually employ one of the following techniques: (1) Barrels are placed on metal pallets and fork-lifted into place. This looks industrial but is easiest on the cellar staff. Barrels can be stored either rolled to the side or with the bung straight up. (2) Barrels are piled one, two, or even three high in neat rows. (3) Barrels are stacked in huge pyramids. These may look good but the barrels are hard to work and clean as disassembling the stack is a daunting task. (4) A single row of barrels is rolled on to fixed barrel racks. This looks good but is often inefficient in terms of LABOUR costs and use of space. (5) Barrels rest on rollers, supported by a steel framework, making access to each one easier and reducing the need to move the barrels, which can be rotated in situ so that LEES STIRRING becomes unnecessary and barrels may be emptied or drained without being removed from the stack.

Storage conditions of full barrels are important (see BARREL MAINTENANCE for unused barrels). If the cellar is too cold, the wine will not develop. If it is too warm, off-flavours and harmful bacteria may develop, and the wine may age too rapidly. If the cellars are too dry, too much wine can evaporate and the barrels themselves can dry out. The ideal temperature is usually around 10 to 18 °C/50 to 66 °F, with a relative HUMIDITY over 75%. Below 75%, water evaporates, but above that figure alcohol evaporates. In warm regions, winemakers like to keep the humidity high, but not so high that it becomes impossible to control the growth of moulds.

The winemaker must consider the dew point, that combination of temperature and humidity at which evaporation occurs. Storing empty barrels (and full ones too) at temperatures higher than 18 °C/65 °F invites problems, and storing barrels over 21 °C/70 °F for more than three weeks runs the risk of BACTERIAL BLIGHT and the formation of VOLATILE ACIDS. Constancy of temperature is not as important as it is in a cellar for full bottles, and a winter drop in temperature assists precipitation and therefore CLARIFICATION.

See also TOPPING UP.

barrel types

barrel types vary considerably and this list includes some terms used for COOPERAGE, or wooden containers, that are, strictly speaking, larger than BARRELS.

Before CONCRETE, STAINLESS STEEL, and other inert materials replaced WOOD as the most common material for wine FERMENTATION VESSELS and storage CONTAINERS in the 1960s, each wine region had its own legion of barrel types. Even today such terms as *feuillette*, TONNEAU, and FUDER may be used to measure volumes of wine long after the actual containers themselves have been abandoned. As recently as 1976, Jean Taransaud was able to list four pages of different barrel types used in various French wine regions (see below). By the second decade of this century there was a marked trend away from heavy oak influence and towards using barrels larger than the traditional sizes listed below, with capacities typically between 300 and 600 l (80 and 160 gal).

France

Barrel types, as most things French, are intensely regionalized. In many cases their capacity has changed over the years.

Bordeaux The **barrique bordelaise**, designated 225 l/59 gal for more than a century, is probably the most famous barrel of all and is used widely outside the region. It is about 95 cm/37 in high and the staves are only about 20 mm/0.8 in thick (although the export version may be a cm or two lower and have rather thicker staves). The traditional BARRIQUE, sometimes called the 'château' model, has a wooden crossbar at each head and both a top and a racking BUNG.

The TONNEAU, at 900 l/238 gal equivalent to four barriques, or 100 cases of wine, is still much used as a measurement by the Bordeaux trade, but this large cask no longer exists.

Burgundy Here the standard barrel is the 228-l (60-gal) **pièce**, which is relatively low (88 cm/37 in) and squat, supposedly for practicality given the narrow doorways and small scale of many Burgundian cellars, and to provide a deeper bilge for the LEES which accumulate in this region where RACKING is generally less frequent than in Bordeaux, for example. The staves are usually notably thicker than those of barriques, about 27 mm. Traditionally these barrels had chestnut hoops or iron hoops painted black, although some domaines have followed the American taste for more workmanlike galvanized hoops which need no repainting.

The traditional barrel in CHABLIS was the **feuillette**, at 132 l/35 gal about half the size of the *pièce*. This is still the unit in which prices are commonly given, even though the barrel itself is increasingly rare.

Some domaines on the CÔTE D'OR may still have their own size of *feuillette*, holding 114 l/30 gal, or even a **quartaut** holding 57 l/15 gal, used primarily for TOPPING UP or for the produce of a tiny holding in a GRAND CRU.

Cognac The standard cognac barrel now holds 350 l/92 gal, although in 1900 it held only about 275 l/73 gal, and only 200 l/53 gal before the French Revolution. Cognac coopers make a wide range of different barrels for various wine regions.

Champagne A 205-l/54-gal barrel is traditional here but those few houses which persist with BARREL FERMENTATION may also buy in Burgundy barrels.

Elsewhere in France A wide range of different barrel types is used in the Loire and the Rhône, from small new oak barrels to large wooden vats such as the 600-l/159-gal **demi-muid** used in Châteauneuf-du-Pape. In Alsace, large ovals, or **foudres** of varying capacities, are most common.

Germany

Although Germany formed its own group of daring iconoclasts, the Barrique Forum, in the early 1990s, most of the cooperage used until very recently has been large, old, and typically on the Mosel a **Fuder** holding 1,000 l/264 gal or on the Rhine a **Stück** of 1,200 l/317 gal. A **Halbfuder** and **Halbstück** are half these sizes respectively.

Spain

Spain's most characteristic barrel is the BUTT used for SHERRY. The American oak barrels used in RIOJA, and elsewhere, are 225-l/60 gal **barricas bordelesas** modelled on Bordeaux BARRIQUES. Spanish cooperage can vary considerably in size and shape, however, and new wood has only relatively recently been prized.

Portugal

The PIPE is Portugal's most famous wine measure. Portuguese cooperage, which can vary considerably in size and shape, may be made from French, American, or even Portuguese oak.

Italy

The large **botti**, or older wooden casks, traditionally used in Italy are typically made from Slavonian oak and have varying but substantial capacities. The barrique is increasingly common, however, sometimes called a **carato**, while the small barrels traditionally used for VIN SANTO are **caratelli** holding between 50 and 225 l/13-59 gal). Large wooden casks standing vertical rather than being laid horizontal may be called **tini**.

Hungary

Gönci holding 136 l/36 gal are traditional in the production of TOKAJI and are named after the village in which they were usually made.

United States

Before the US became the world's best customer for exported French oak barrels (see COOPERAGE), American winemakers bought 50-gal/190-l American oak barrels produced for the whiskey business. A decline in bourbon sales in the 1980s led to American cooperages tailoring an increasing proportion of their output to wineries' needs, although variations on the *barrique* and *pièce* imported from France are the most desired, and most common, barrels used by American winemakers. 70-gal/265-l barrels—Burgundy sized heads and Bordeaux length staves—have become popular for both aesthetic and practical reasons.

Australia and New Zealand

Barriques of 225 l/59 gal have become the most commonly used barrel, and if imported from France, are imported whole. **Hogsheads** of 300 l/79 gal and **puncheons** holding 450 or 500 l/118 or 132 gal may also be found in New World wineries and are regaining popularity. While the latter are too large to manœuvre with ease and do not impart OAK FLAVOUR as fast as many winemakers desire, they may prove more suitable than *barriques*, for example, for some lighter wines and for the 21st-century trend towards more restrained use of oak.

M.K. & J.R.

Taransaud, J., *Le Livre de la tonnellerie* (Paris, 1976).

barrica, Spanish term for a barrel or BARRIQUE. A *barrica bordelesa* is the specific term for a Bordeaux *barrique*, the most common BARREL TYPE used in Spain.

barrique, the most famous of the BARREL TYPES, Bordeaux's relatively tall 225-l/59-gal wooden cask with thinner STAVES than the Burgundian *pièce* and most other barrels.

In the Middle Ages, the commercially acute Bordelais virtually trade-marked their distinctive *barrique bordelaise,* carefully designating its dimensions and prohibiting its use outside the region. By the end of the 18th century, it had replaced the unwieldy TONNEAU four times the size for transportation as well as storage, and in 1866 it was officially decreed that it must hold 225 l/59 gal, rather than between 215 and 230 l/57 and 60 gal as previously. Even as recently as this, it was common for some of the most highly regarded wines of Bordeaux to be shipped in *barrique* for bottling, if not by the NÉGOCIANTS of Bordeaux, then by wine merchants outside France, particularly in northern Europe.

Today the word *barrique* is often used, particularly outside France, for all manner of wooden BARRELS. In Germany and Italy, for example, the word has been closely and emotively associated with those who employ BARREL MATURATION in small, new OAK rather than traditional CASK AGEING in *botti*, large, old, wooden casks.

Barsac, important sweet white wine appellation in BORDEAUX on the left bank of the River GARONNE just over the climatologically important cool river Ciron from the even bigger and more famous SAUTERNES appellation. All wines produced within Barsac are also entitled to use the appellation Sauternes (although the reverse is not the case). In 2013 just over 400 ha/2,000 acres of vineyard were declared as producing wine for the Barsac appellation, only a quarter the area declared for Sauternes. It is traditionally said that the wines of Barsac are slightly lighter than those of Sauternes, perhaps because the soils are more marked by SAND and LIMESTONE, and because the land is flatter, but much depends on individual properties and winemaking policies too. For more detail of viticultural and winemaking practices, see SAUTERNES. Some of the finest current achievers within the Barsac appellation are Chx Climens, Coutet, and Doisy-Daëne. See also the Barsac properties included in the Sauternes CLASSIFICATION.

Bartons, prominent family in BORDEAUX, originally from Lancashire in the north of England, which joined the Tudor Protestant Ascendancy in Ireland. Unlike most others who joined the BORDEAUX TRADE from abroad, the Bartons maintained their nationality, religion, and family connections with their country of origin. Thomas Barton arrived in Bordeaux in 1725, played a leading part in shipping fine CLARET back to Britain, and died in 1780 a very rich man. His son William (1723–99), with whom he bitterly quarrelled, formed his own company and was prominent in the trade on his own account. His son Hugh (1766–1854) married Anna, daughter of another prosperous merchant, Nathaniel Johnston. The association with Daniel Guestier of a Breton Huguenot family began in 1795 and Barton & Guestier was formed in 1802.

Highly successful, Hugh Barton bought Ch Langoa in ST-JULIEN in 1821, and acquired in 1826 part of the Léoville vineyard that was to become Ch Léoville-Barton, an even more prominent St-Julien. He died in England, having been succeeded by his son Nathaniel (1799–1867). The NÉGOCIANT Barton & Guestier continued to play a leading role in the Bordeaux trade, but PHYLLOXERA, the consequent shortage of authentic bordeaux, and the slump in English demand prior to the First World War led to unprecedented problems. Nathaniel's son Bertram Francis (1830–1904) worked first in the London office but came in 1873 to live in Bordeaux, rather than at Langoa. It was his third successor **Ronald Barton** (1902–86) who made Langoa his home. Business was difficult between the World Wars, and on the fall of France in 1940 Ronald had hurriedly to leave Langoa, which was soon occupied by the Germans. They did not pillage the cellars as Daniel Guestier told them that the estate belonged to a neutral Irishman, who, however, volunteered for the British army. Although the quality and reputation of SECOND GROWTH Ch Léoville-Barton and third growth Ch Langoa-Barton steadily improved, the profitability of Barton & Guestier gradually declined, and in 1954 the American firm of Seagram took half the shares of Barton & Guestier and later acquired complete control.

Ronald Barton's nephew **Anthony Barton** (1930–) joined Barton & Guestier in 1951, and subsequently left to form his own merchant business. In 1986 he moved into Langoa and took over complete control of the two classed growths, whose wines are both made at Langoa and have become models of sensibly priced, classic claret made for the long term. Today Anthony's daughter Lilian Barton Sartorius, who bought Ch Mauvesin Barton in Moulis in 2011 with her husband Michel, and grandchildren Damien and Mélanie are increasingly involved in these much-admired properties.

E.P.-R. & J.R.

Barton, A., and Petit-Castelli, C., *La Saga des Bartons* (Bordeaux, 1991).

Ray, C., *Fide et fortitudine: The Story of a Vineyard: Langoa-Léoville Barton 1821–1971* (Oxford, 1971).

basal buds, or **base buds**, the group of barely visible buds at the bottom of a shoot or cane. Normally they do not burst unless vines are severely pruned, and they are typically of low FRUITFULNESS.

R.E.S.

basalt, a dark-coloured, fine-grained igneous rock (see GEOLOGY) dominated by the two minerals feldspar and pyroxene, though they are usually too fine to be discernible. They weather to provide a good range of potential NUTRIENTS. Dark rocks such as basalt are often said to reradiate warmth at night, but Pogue's study in the Columbia Valley in WASHINGTON and OREGON states suggests that the thermal effects operate chiefly during the day.

Basalt is almost always found in association with VOLCANIC materials such as TUFF. In addition to the locations mentioned for them, basalt occurs in Victoria (e.g. King Valley and Macedon Ranges) and the HUNTER VALLEY in Australia, the Galilee region of ISRAEL (including the Golan Heights), and it dominates vineyards in parts of HUNGARY such as Tapolca near Lake Balaton, and Somlo Hill.

A.J.M.

Pogue, K., 'Influence of basalt on the terroir of the Columbia Valley American Viticultural area', www.whitman.edu, 2010, http://people.whitman.edu/~pogue/soave.pdf

Basilicata, mountainous, virtually landlocked area of southern Italy, is the country's third least populated region, with approximately 600,000 inhabitants. Its name has become synonymous with the extreme poverty in, and abandonment of, much of Italy's deep south. Little commercial or industrial activity exists, and the countryside has been drained by emigration since the end of the Second World War, while its unspoilt natural beauty still awaits any significant TOURISM boost to the regional economy. Little exists in the way of viticulture either; the region's total vineyard surface is 10,028 ha/24,769 acres, of which a third is classified as DOC. The Basilicata has only four DOC wines and one DOCG. AGLIANICO DEL VULTURE is qualitatively the most important with its vineyards situated on the slopes of an extinct volcano 56 km/35 miles to the north of Potenza. Confusingly, only the Superiore version of Aglianico del Vulture has been elevated to DOCG status.

Basilicata's other DOCs include Grottino di Roccanova (a 100% Malvasia Bianca di Basilicata, with a rather less exciting provision for a Sangiovese-based red), and Matera, a hastily and rather generously designated DOC based on Malvasia and the potentially interesting Greco Bianco for whites and Primitivo and Sangiovese for reds, while Matera Moro must contain at least 60% Cabernet Sauvignon. The Terre dell'Alta Val d'Agri DOC seems to have been designated to accommodate mainly INTERNATIONAL VARIETIES, for which demand is waning.

W.S.

Belfrage, N., *From Brunello to Zibibbo—The Wines of Tuscany, Central and Southern Italy* (2nd edn, London, 2003)
www.vinobasilicata.it

Basque country produces wines in Spain and France on either side of the western Pyrenees.

Spain

The Basque country (País Vasco in Castilian, Euskadi in Basque) is the most ferociously independent of all Spain's 17 autonomous regions. This densely populated, heavily industrialized strip of country facing the Bay of Biscay is not normally associated with wine, even though the important RIOJA region stretches north of the River Ebro into the Basque province of Alava where the Rioja Alavesa subregion is located—home to such important estates as Marqués de Riscal, Contino, Artadi, Martínez Bujanda, Remelluri, and Remírez de Ganuza. The three wholly Basque DOS are the tiny region of **Getariako** TXAKOLINA on the coast 25 km/15 miles west of San Sebastián, the smaller **Bizkaiko Txakolina** around Bilbao, and the newest one, **Arabako Txakolina**.

France

See BÉARN and IROULÉGUY.

Bastardo, Portuguese name for the Jura red wine grape TROUSSEAU. As Bastardo it is a minor variety in the Douro Valley, Dão, and Beiras with total plantings of 1,218 ha/3,101 acres in 2010. Over the Spanish border in Galicia it is known as Merenzao.

Bâtard-Montrachet, great white GRAND CRU in Burgundy's CÔTE D'OR. For more details, see MONTRACHET.

bâtonnage, French term for the winemaking operation of LEES STIRRING.

Baumé, scale of measuring total dissolved compounds in grape juice, and therefore its approximate concentration of grape sugars (see MUST WEIGHT). It is used in much of Europe, including France, and Australia and, like other scales used elsewhere (see BRIX and OECHSLE), it can be measured with either a REFRACTOMETER or a HYDROMETER. The Baumé scale is particularly useful in winemaking since the number of degrees Baumé indicates the POTENTIAL ALCOHOL in percentage by volume. (Grape juice of 12 °Baumé, for example, would produce a wine of about 12% alcohol if fermented out to dryness.) The rate of fall in Baumé is one method used to follow the course of an alcoholic FERMENTATION, but it should be noted that its product, ETHANOL, has a low DENSITY and progressively depresses hydrometer readings.

B.G.C.

Baux de Provence, Les. A spectacular and famous small hilltop settlement in the far west of PROVENCE dominated by Michelin-starred restaurants and their customers' cars gives its name to a local APPELLATION CONTRÔLÉE created in 1995 and substantially amended since. In the far north west, effectively on limestone rubble from the craggy Alpilles chain, Les Baux is slightly warmer and wetter than much of COTEAUX D'AIX-EN-PROVENCE from which it was ceded and the rules are stricter—possibly too strict. Red wines are made, from Grenache, Syrah, and Mourvèdre grapes, which must together make up at least 60% of the blend, together with Cinsaut, Counoise, Carignan, and Cabernet Sauvignon (which last must represent no more than 20% of the total, thus excluding the area's best estate, Domaine de Trévallon, from the appellation). Cinsaut takes the place of Mourvèdre in the rosés, which make up about a fifth of the appellation. Clairette, Grenache Blanc, and Vermentino are the principal grapes for the new white version, although some Marsanne and Roussanne may be included in the blend. Even more significant however is that the growers (unsuccessfully) asked that their appellation regulations should be the first in France to specify ORGANIC VITICULTURE. The Mistral helps to keep the vines healthy.

bead, the progress of bubbles in a SPARKLING WINE. A fine bead denotes a steady stream of small bubbles. See also FIZZINESS.

bearer, viticultural term used when pruning for what is effectively the fruiting unit of the vine, the selected long canes or shorter spurs bearing the buds that will produce the next season's shoots and crop. See also PRUNING.

Béarn, rarely exported wine made in SOUTH WEST FRANCE either in the MADIRAN or JURANÇON zones, or in a third zone around Salies-de-Béarn and Bellocq dedicated exclusively to the production of **Béarn-Bellocq**. Characterful reds (often very similar to Madiran) and firm rosés are made with up to 60% Tannat grapes blended mainly with Cabernet Franc and Cabernet Sauvignon, with Fer, Manseng Noir, and Courbu Noir, while the very rare, tangy white wines are made from such classic south west white grape varieties as Petit Manseng, Gros Manseng, and Raffiat de Moncade which are conserved in the letter of the appellation law if not in the reality of the vineyard. Total area of vineyards had fallen to below 200 ha/500 acres by 2011. Most Béarn wines are quite concentrated enough to go with a steak and Béarn's famous sauce, and most of them are made by the CO-OPERATIVE at Bellocq.

Beaujolais, quantitatively extremely important wine region in east central France producing a unique style of fruity wine which is often relatively, nay unfashionably, light but is increasingly being made in a more concentrated, 'Burgundian' style. For administrative purposes, Beaujolais is often included as part of greater BURGUNDY, but in terms of climate, topography, soil types, and even distribution of grape varieties, it is quite different. In some years, Beaujolais has produced more than the whole of the rest of greater Burgundy to the north put together, nearly a million hl of wine, almost all of which is produced from a single red grape variety, GAMAY Noir à Jus Blanc, and much of it by a single, distinctive winemaking method. Early-drinking Beaujolais at its best provides the yardstick for all the world's attempts to put red refreshment into a bottle, being a wine that is essentially flirtatious, with a juicy aroma which, combined with its promise of appetizing acidity, is sufficient to release the gastric juices before even a mouthful of the wine has been drunk. In the 1970s and 1980s the region became too dependent on selling embryonic PRIMEUR wine, so-called **Beaujolais Nouveau**. When demand for Beaujolais Nouveau reached its peak, in 1992, nearly half of all Beaujolais AC was sold in this youthful state, for immediate consumption and, from the point of view of the producer, as an immediate generator of cash flow. But producers paid the price of much-reduced demand for their wine in the late 1990s and early 2000s when they had to resort to compulsory DISTILLATION. In the French market place, Beaujolais had become almost a commodity, with attendant pressures on prices, so that generic blended Beaujolais was too often a thin, inky liquid that was in all senses lacklustre—or an ultra-commercial blend all too dependent on CHAPTALIZATION. But in the 21st century there have been distinct stirrings of a revival, not least because an increasing proportion of the wine is vinified traditionally rather than by CARBONIC MACERATION, from the 2003 vintage, which resulted in much denser wines than usual. As Harry WAUGH discovered so many years ago, a DOMAINE BOTTLED wine may well be the most direct route to quality.

To the Burgundian, Beaujolais wines are *les vins du Rhône*, not because they are from the RHÔNE Valley, but because the vineyards of the Beaujolais hills fall within the Rhône *département* that surrounds the city of Lyons.

History

The region is on the ancient Roman trade route up the Rhône and Saône valleys. It is hardly surprising, therefore, that there are records of Roman vineyards in the region, notably on Mont Brouilly (Brulliacus), just the sort of HILLSIDE VINEYARD site favoured by the Romans, and Morgon. Benedictine MONKS developed vineyards here as early as the 7th century and for much of the medieval period Beaujolais, in wine terms at least, was simply the southern neighbour of the great duchy of Burgundy.

Beaujolais is named after Beaujeu, the town in its western hills founded in the 10th century, and was ruled by the Dukes of Beaujeu before being ceded to the Bourbonnais for a time. The region achieved real viticultural identity when Philip the Bold issued his famous edict against the growing of Gamay in Burgundy proper. He was right in that Gamay performs so much better on the GRANITE hillsides of Beaujolais than on the LIMESTONE escarpment of the CÔTE D'OR.

The Gamay wines of Beaujolais continued to flow down the Saône to Lyons so that Beaujolais became known as the city's third river, after the Rhône and Saône. When communications with Paris by canal and then RAILWAY were developed, demand for Beaujolais the wine increased yet further, and the region expanded to include much less suitable, flatter, more fertile land in the south, the Bas Beaujolais. REDDING in the early 19th century does not mention the word and cites, of today's well-known names, only St-Amour, Moulin-à-Vent, and Chénas, noting that they sold for relatively low prices (the same is true today), and that they should be drunk young.

Geography and climate

The total vineyard area of the Beaujolais region is well over 15,000 ha/37,500 acres and includes nearly 100 communes with MÂCONNAIS on its northern boundary (indeed some vineyards may be classified as either Beaujolais Blanc or ST-VÉRAN). The climate is TEMPERATE and semi-CONTINENTAL; snow may fall in the foothills of the Massif Central to the immediate west by the time Beaujolais Nouveau is launched, but summers are sufficiently hot for the local houses to have the shutters and gentle, tiled roofs of the south of France.

In the northern, narrower part of the region, the TOPOGRAPHY is very varied, the landscape made up of gentle, rolling hills, based on GRANITE and SCHIST with some limestone, while the flatter, southern, more recently developed sector south of Villefranche has much richer soils, often with some clay, making much lighter wines, typically for earlier consumption, on the plains which stretch down towards Lyons. The result of the more favourable MESOCLIMATES on the granite hillsides is that ripening is always more advanced in the north so that, apparently paradoxically, picking begins with the better-quality wines.

The appellations

About half of all Beaujolais is sold under the basic appellation Beaujolais, which comes from the Bas Beaujolais and the flatter land to the immediate west of the main north–south autoroute around Belleville. The second most important Beaujolais appellation is Beaujolais-Villages, which must come from the hillier, northern part of the Beaujolais region, its vineyards pushing up into the foothills of the Massif Central. If a Beaujolais-Villages is the produce of just one village or commune, it can append the name of that commune. In the finest sectors of this superior, northern part are the so-called Beaujolais crus, ten named communes or CRUS whose wines are considered so distinctive, and so good, that they have earned their own appellations. Some of these have the most evocative names in the wine lexicon, but their existence as separate entities can be confusing for newcomers to wine since there is rarely mention of the word Beaujolais on their labels. For more details of individual cru, see, approximately from north to south, ST-AMOUR, JULIÉNAS, CHÉNAS, MOULIN-À-VENT, FLEURIE, CHIROUBLES, MORGON, REGNIÉ, BROUILLY, and Côte de Brouilly.

A small amount of **Beaujolais Blanc** and **Beaujolais-Villages Blanc** is made each year, mainly from Chardonnay grapes. White grapes do best on patches of limestone and are planted mainly on these outcrops in the north of the region so that they are effectively southern neighbours of MÂCON Blanc and taste exactly like it. Growers are supposed to devote no more than 10% of their vineyard to white grape varieties. Equally small amounts of refreshing Beaujolais Rosé are made.

Basic maximum permitted YIELDS for both Beaujolais and Beaujolais-Villages have been increased to 64 hl/ha, those for the Beaujolais crus to 58 hl/ha.

Viticulture

The GOBELET vine-training method is traditional in Beaujolais but in fact single GUYOT is much more likely in the southern Bas Beaujolais, with up to 12 buds. For Beaujolais-Villages as well as the crus, PRUNING methods must be much more restrained, either en gobelet or éventail (see TRAINING SYSTEMS). VINE DENSITY here has long been one of the highest in the world, between 9,000 and 13,000 vines per ha usually. All picking, typically in late September, has to be manual because whole bunches are needed for Beaujolais's winemaking technique.

Vine varieties

Gamay Noir à Jus Blanc (so called to distinguish it from the relatively widely planted red-fleshed Gamay TEINTURIERS) accounts for about 98% of the Beaujolais vineyard, which makes Beaujolais the most *monocépagiste* (single variety) region of any size in France. Virtually all the rest is Chardonnay, although Aligoté is also allowed until 2024 (so long as it was planted before 2004). According to the detail of the official regulations, up to 15% of white wine grapes may be included in most Beaujolais appellations.

Considerable research into CLONAL SELECTION has taken place since 1960 so that the modern grower can choose from six approved clones, the best quality coming from small, thick-skinned berries.

ROOTSTOCKS used are SO_4, 3309, or, the Beaujolais speciality for granitic soils, Vialla.

Winemaking

Beaujolais is distinguished not just by the Gamay grape, but by its characteristic wine-making method, CARBONIC MACERATION or, more likely, SEMI-CARBONIC MACERATION. Only in Beaujolais is this technique used so widely, and, in the Nouveau era, with such speed.

Another controversial issue in Beaujolais is chaptalization. In recent years the trend was to pick grapes at the legal minimum ripeness of 10% potential alcohol (10.5% for Beaujolais-Villages and crus), and then add sugar to bring the actual alcoholic strength dangerously close to the theoretical 12.5% maximum permitted final alcohol content.

Whole bunches arrive at the cellars and are emptied into cement or stainless steel FERMENTATION VESSELS generally of between 40 and 300 hl/1,056 and 7,920 gal capacity. The bottom 10 to 30% of grapes are crushed by the weight above them and ferment in the normal way. This proportion increases with time. CARBON DIOXIDE is given off by this fermentation, and leaves the upper grapes bathed in the gas so that they undergo intracellular fermentation and produce the sort of aromas reminiscent of pear drops and bananas so closely associated with Beaujolais.

This combination of two different sorts of fermentation, together with MACERATION of the lower grapes and must, continues for perhaps as little as four days for Beaujolais Nouveau and ten days, sometimes longer nowadays, for cru wines destined for the long term. The pomace is then pressed and, unlike other regions, the PRESS WINE is automatically included in the final blend. MALOLACTIC CONVERSION is then de rigueur. After some form of STABILIZATION, the wine is bottled either at under two months, in the case of Nouveaux, or perhaps not until the second Christmas after the vintage for the most concentrated, long-lived crus. Bottling often takes place in the cellars of the négociants who soak up the great majority of production (every BEAUNE merchant has to have its Beaujolais and Burgundians such as Louis JADOT, BOUCHARD PÈRE ET FILS, and grower Thibault Liger-Belair have invested directly in properties in Beaujolais), or possibly at one of the village CO-OPERATIVES, which produce about a third of all the region's wine, or in a grower's cellar, using a mobile BOTTLING line.

An increasing proportion of Beaujolais, particularly in the crus, is made like 'proper' red burgundy at a much more leisurely pace, given some CASK AGEING, and possibly even bottled by hand from individual barrels. North Beaujolais is a region where TRADITION and the best of peasant culture have survived, looking down, perhaps with wry amusement, at the decreasing but frenetic production of Nouveau in the Bas Beaujolais.

Serving Beaujolais

Beaujolais was traditionally served in a special 46-cl/1 pint bottle known as a *pot*. European standardization may not approve of this but the essential point is that most Beaujolais is designed to be *drunk* rather than discussed or collected. This is the archetypal lubrication wine, and can be particularly *gouleyant*, or gulpable, if served cellar cool. Most Beaujolais has been drunk within a year of harvest, most Beaujolais-Villages within two, most crus within three, although traditionally vinified wines, particularly Morgon, Moulin-à-Vent, Chénas, and Juliénas, from a good vintage can improve in bottle for up to ten and sometimes more years. The tendency with time, however, is for a serious old Beaujolais cru to taste increasingly like a red burgundy. The region was a cradle of the NATURAL WINE movement.

See also the individual Beaujolais cru appellations, listed in approximately ascending order of body CHIROUBLES, ST-AMOUR, FLEURIE, RÉGNIÉ, BROUILLY and Côte de Brouilly, JULIÉNAS, CHÉNAS, MORGON, and MOULIN-À-VENT.

www.discoverbeaujolais.com

Beaumes-de-Venise is a pretty village

in Vaucluse that produced such characterful southern red Côtes-du-Rhône-Villages that in 2005 it was awarded its own AOC for these spicy reds based substantially on Grenache and Syrah grown on over 600 ha/1,500 acres of vineyards. The village has some excellent high-ELEVATION terroirs but for decades it was most famous for its unusually fragrant, sweet, pale gold VIN DOUX NATUREL, Muscat de Beaumes-de-Venise, grown on less than 500 ha/ 1,235 acres.

Like the Muscats of the Languedoc (see FRONTIGNAN, LUNEL, MIREVAL, and, particularly, ST-JEAN-DE-MINERVOIS), this southern Rhône Muscat is made exclusively from the best Muscat variety, MUSCAT BLANC À PETITS GRAINS, and occasionally its darker-berried mutation. Fermentation is arrested by the addition of alcohol to produce a wine of just over 15% but Beaumes-de-Venise can be more delicate and refreshing than most Languedoc Muscats. Apart from the extremely rare and expensive VIN DE PAILLE, the Muscat is the Rhône's only sweet, still white (although see RASTEAU).

Beaune, vinous capital of BURGUNDY giving

its name to the Côte de Beaune section of the CÔTE D'OR vineyards. Beaune was founded as a Roman camp by Julius Caesar, became the seat of the dukes of Burgundy until the 13th century, and, although losing political supremacy to Dijon thereafter, has always been the centre of the Burgundian wine industry. In the 18th century, the first merchant houses such as Champy (1720) and Bouchard (1731) were established and Beaune remains home to such leading NÉGOCIANTS as Louis JADOT, Joseph DROUHIN, Louis LATOUR, and BOUCHARD PÈRE ET FILS.

Beaune wines are mostly red, made from Pinot Noir grapes, although plantings of Chardonnay have increased since the 1990s. There is more SAND in the soil here than in most Côte d'Or villages so the red wines tend to be no more than medium bodied, best drunk between five and ten years old. While neither as powerful as POMMARD nor as elegant as VOLNAY, Beaune wines are more supple than Corton (see ALOXE-CORTON) and can be a charming introduction to good burgundy.

Before the enforcement of APPELLATION CONTRÔLÉE regulations, many local wines were sold as Beaune as a readily marketable label of convenience. Now the town has a good rather than great reputation for its wines, perhaps because there are few outstanding DOMAINES in an appellation dominated by merchants. However, Beaune is blessed with an unusually high proportion, nearly three-quarters, of PREMIER CRU vineyards. Indeed those of village status are the exception, being limited to small parcels of land clinging to unsuitable upper slopes and some low-lying vineyards with richer soils. Otherwise the vineyards of Beaune form a broad swathe of premiers crus from the border with SAVIGNY-LÈS-BEAUNE to Pommard.

The finest vineyards are regarded as those situated almost directly between the town and the hill of Les Mondes Rondes: Les Grèves, Les Bressandes, Les Teurons, and Les Avaux. Beaune-Grèves includes Bouchard's noted Vigne de l'Enfant Jésus vineyard, while Beaune-Vignes Franches includes Louis Jadot's Clos des Ursules.

Other noted premier cru vineyards are Les Marconnets and Clos du Roi near the border with Savigny, and Clos des Mouches abutting Pommard. Although the red wines from this vineyard are not always memorable, Joseph Drouhin makes a rich, complex, and ageworthy white Clos des Mouches which is highly sought after.

Producers with a wide range of Beaune premiers crus (other than the négociants cited above) include Domaine des Croix and Albert Morot.

In 1443 Nicolas Rolin founded the Hôtel Dieu, Beaune's principal tourist attraction. For more details, especially of the famous annual auction, see HOSPICES DE BEAUNE.

See also CÔTE D'OR, and map under BURGUNDY.
J.T.C.M.

Beaune, Côte de. The Côte de Beaune is

the southern half of the escarpment of the CÔTE D'OR, named after the important town and wine centre of Beaune. The greatest white wines of Burgundy and some very fine reds are grown on this stretch. The principal appellations, from north to south, are Corton and Corton-Charlemagne (see ALOXE-CORTON), BEAUNE, POMMARD, VOLNAY, MEURSAULT, PULIGNY-MONTRACHET, and CHASSAGNE-MONTRACHET. See also the separate entry under MONTRACHET.

Red wines from the lesser villages of the Côte may be sold under their own names or as **Côte de Beaune-Villages**. This appellation is available for the wines of AUXEY-DURESSES, Chassagne-Montrachet, CHOREY-LÈS-BEAUNE, LADOIX-SERRIGNY, Meursault, MONTHÉLIE, PERNAND-VERGELESSES, Puligny-Montrachet, ST-AUBIN, ST-ROMAIN, SANTENAY, and SAVIGNY-LÈS-BEAUNE. See also MARANGES.

Whereas wines labelled Beaune come from the appellation adjoining the town, there is a small group of vineyards on the hill above whose wines are sold under the confusing appellation Côte de Beaune. Of these the best known are Clos des Monsnières and Les Topes Bizot. Both red and white wines are produced.

See also CÔTE DE NUITS and map under BURGUNDY.
J.T.C.M.

Becker, Helmut (1927–89), academic and

exceptionally cosmopolitan VITICULTURIST who was chief of the GEISENHEIM Grape Breeding Institute in Germany from 1964 until his death. VINE BREEDING dominated his work. He emphasized the need for deliberate cross-breeding for resistance to DOWNY MILDEW and POWDERY MILDEW. To achieve this end he used not only resistant genes from AMERICAN VINES, as many other vine breeders had, but also those from Asian species of VITIS, in particular *V. amurensis*. Under his leadership, the winemaking facilities of the institute were extended and became a model for small-scale winemaking in breeding stations around the world. The products of these micro-vinifications were filed like library books in the research institute's deep, cool cellar, in bottles closed with the CROWN CAPS of which Becker was a great proponent. Here Professor Becker would regale visitors with tastings of fine, Riesling-like wine made from NEW VARIETIES which were effectively HYBRIDS because of their non-VINIFERA genes, and therefore officially outlawed. (Some have since been officially embraced; see DISEASE-RESISTANT VARIETIES.)

He also intensified breeding of ROOTSTOCKS, aiming for complete PHYLLOXERA resistance rather than tolerance. This work yielded Börner, the first registered NEMATODE- and phylloxera-resistant rootstock (released after his death).

Apart from his research work, Helmut Becker was also a passionate teacher. He always saw viticulture from a global point of view and

b

collaborated with numerous scientists around the world, participating in and organizing conferences as a platform for scientific discussion. Thanks to his willingness to travel, his often iconoclastic views, and lively delivery in several languages (including some colourful English learned while a 17-year-old prisoner of war), he was arguably the most internationally famous viticultural authority in the 1970s and 1980s. He made a particular contribution to the New Zealand wine industry, emphasizing viticulture's role in achieving wine quality, and encouraging the importation of important clones and varieties. R.E.S.

Beechworth, small but fashionable region with just 17 producers in 2014 in the foothills of the Victorian Alps with several iconic producers, notably Giaconda, in the NORTH EAST VICTORIA ZONE.

beer. This alcoholic drink made, like wine, by FERMENTATION, but of cereals rather than grapes, has impinged on wine mainly as a commercial competitor, the rivalry having ancient roots. Both beverages were enjoyed in the civilizations of MESOPOTAMIA, Ancient IRAN, and Ancient EGYPT, where brewing was associated with bread-making. Although beer was occasionally used for religious purposes, it was generally the drink of the common people, whereas the aristocracy and priesthood drank wine.

See also COFFEE HOUSES for details of other drinks which were historically in commercial competition with wine. See SPARKLING WINES for one area in which the technical concerns of the beer industry parallel those of some winemakers. H.B.

Forbes, R. J., 'Food and drink', in C. Singer (ed.), *A History of Technology*, ii (Oxford, 1956).

Lutz, H. F., *Viticulture and Brewing in the Ancient Orient* (Leipzig and New York, 1922).

Beerenauslese, literally 'berry selection', refers to sweet Austrian or German wines, usually made from BOTRYTIZED grapes. By GERMAN WINE LAW, minimum MUST WEIGHTS are laid down for each combination of vine variety and region and vary from 110 to 128 °OECHSLE. The iconic examples, often prodigiously long-lived, are complex and rich yet exhilarating Rieslings. In Austria, a minimum of 25 KMW (approximately 105 °Oechsle) is stipulated, and wines bearing this PRÄDIKAT are commonly grown only around the NEUSIEDLERSEE in BURGENLAND (and then from diverse grapes), being rare elsewhere. D.S.

beetles, insects of the *Coleoptera* order, several of which attack grapevines as well as other horticultural crops and pastures. While particular species of beetles are often specific to a country or even region, beetles are a pest to grapevines worldwide. Black beetles (*Heteronychus arator*)

attack young vines in spring, and can cause ring barking. They are native to South Africa, and are also known as African black beetles, but cause damage in other countries such as Australia. Apple curculio beetle (*Otiorhyncus cribricollis*), thought to be a native of Europe, and vegetable weevil (*Listorderes costirostris*) also attack young vines in late spring and early summer, causing damage by eating vine leaves and/or young shoots. Beetles of importance in France are *Altica ampelophaga* and *Adoxus vitis*, which eat leaves, and *Otiorhyncus sulcatus*, which eats young shoots and buds. *Rhynchites betuleti* is called *cigarier* in French because it damages PETIOLES so the leaves roll up like cigars. Control of beetles, if necessary, is by application of the appropriate INSECTICIDE or an ORGANIC alternative. See also BORERS. M.J.E. & R.E.S.

Bettiga, L. J. (ed.), *Grape Pest Management* (3rd edn, Oakland, Calif., 2013).

Galet, P., *Précis de viticulture* (7th edn, Montpellier, 2000).

Beira Interior, large, diverse, but sparsely planted DOP in central Portugal, with three subregions. Both Castel Rodrigo and Pinhel have vineyards up to 700 m/2,296 ft elevation, shallow GRANITE-based soils, and a harsh CONTINENTAL climate. Old SÍRIA vines can make racy, mineral whites. Attaining PHENOLIC RIPENESS is challenging for reds, the best of which include Touriga Nacional and/or Alfrocheiro. In the warmer, lower south, Cova de Beira is in the lee of Portugal's highest mountain range, the Serra da Estrela. The best wines are reds, typically made from the varieties favoured in neighbouring Alentejo. Individual estates have started to exploit the potential of TERROIR here but in 2014 indifferent wines from local CO-OPERATIVES still predominated. S.A.

Beiras, once a VINHO REGIONAL covering most of central Portugal, embracing, from west to east, DOPs BAIRRADA on the Atlantic coast; the rugged, mountainous terrain of DÃO; and BEIRA INTERIOR, and including declassified wine from these areas. It was split into three separate regions in 2009: Beira Atlântico, Terras do Dão, and Terras da Beira.

Belgium, north European country which has traditionally been one of Bordeaux's best customers but is also evincing an increasing interest in NEW WORLD wines. It also produces an increasing amount of wine of its own: about 5,500 hl/145,000 gal in 2010, despite its LATITUDE.

About 80% of wines are white and 15 vine varieties are authorized, of which Pinot Blanc, Chardonnay, and Pinot Noir are most successful. As in ENGLAND, the proportion of SPARKLING WINE has grown considerably, to nearly 40% by 2010. GERMAN CROSSES such as Kerner and Regent are also common as well as Auxerrois and

Pinot Gris. Most vineyards are hardly more than 1 ha/2.5 acres and produce wine for local sale although quality has been increasing thanks partly to CLIMATE change. The wine industry of LUXEMBOURG to the south east is much bigger, more successful, and older, having been established in Roman times. Belgian viticulture has a long, if not continuous, history, however. In the era of CHARLEMAGNE, vines were grown extensively in southern Belgium to provide wine for MONKS and were not abandoned until the 15th century, when a combination of climate change, military ravages, and the increasing influence of BURGUNDY prejudiced the continuation of Belgian viticulture.

Belgian wine is made with varying degrees of competence but is, typically, light, dry, white similar to that made just over the border in the southern NETHERLANDS.

There are five PDOs in Belgium. The first was Hagelandse Wijn, created in 1997 in the Flemish Brabant region around Leuven. Its 30 ha/75 acres were farmed by 12 officially recognized producers in 2012. The second appellation was Haspengouwse Wijn, created in 2000 in eastern Limburg near the Dutch border covering 25 ha/62 acres. Côtes de Sambres et Meuse in the south of the country near Liège between these two rivers was created in 2004, the first appellation in the French-speaking part of the country with eight professional growers in Walloon sharing 35 ha/86 acres of vines. Heuvelland Vlaamse Mousserende Kwaliteitswijn was created in 2007. For growers eschewing the confines of a CONTROLLED APPELLATION, there are two Belgian PGIs—one for Flanders (Vlaamse Landwijn) and one for Wallonia (Vin de Pays de Jardins de Wallonie). Appellations are overseen by the Belgian Federation of Wine and Spirits. G.V.I.

beli, Eastern European term for white or light, as in the colour of grapeskins. Beli Pinot is PINOT BLANC, for instance.

Belina, strictly **Belina Drobna**, historic middle European name for GOUAIS BLANC.

Bellet, historic, distinctive, but minute appellation in the far south east of PROVENCE whose total vineyard area had by 2011 fallen to 50 ha/125 acres in the hills above Nice. It takes determination to find a bottle outside the Côte d'Azur, and even greater determination to find the vineyards themselves perched about 300 m/980 ft above the Mediterranean up the Var valley in the city's hinterland. Almost equal quantities of all three colours are produced. The scented, full-bodied whites made from the local Rolle (Vermentino) grapes with some Chardonnay and occasionally Bourboulenc are the appellation's most distinctive wines, and reflect well the MESOCLIMATE of these hillside vineyards, which is slightly cooler than in much of the rest of Provence. Rosés may be made from BRAQUET (while the intriguing Folle Noire (Fuella) is traditional for red wines, although it is often supplemented by Cinsaut and occasionally Grenache.

bench blending. See ASSEMBLAGE.

bench grafting, the viticultural operation of GRAFTING vines indoors rather than in the field. This procedure has allowed viticulturists around the world successfully to combat the ravages of PHYLLOXERA and to a lesser extent those of NEMATODES by economically grafting to resistant ROOTSTOCK. It permits mechanization and factory-style operations leading to mass production. The procedure is widely used in Europe, especially Italy and southern France, where it is an important industry. Dormant cuttings are saved for bench grafting, stored in the cold; after soaking in fungicide solution, rootstock cuttings are disbudded and SCION cuttings are cut into one-node pieces. Cuts of matching shape are made at the bottom of the scion and at the top of the rootstock, using cuttings of similar diameter. With a GRAFTING MACHINE, variously shaped cuts are used, such as 'omega' or 'saw-tooth'. After matching together, the newly grafted cuttings are packed with a moistened, coarse-grained medium in boxes and stacked in humid, warm rooms (28–9 °C/82–4 °F) until the union has CALLUSED (in about two weeks). Once they have hardened, grafts are waxed to reduce water loss, then planted out, usually in a field NURSERY. These plants are grown over the summer and then lifted from the nursery, the roots and shoots trimmed, before delivery to the client in winter, typically in bundles of 50.

Such was the demand for grafted plants in the 1990s that in many countries nurserymen have sold young grafted plants in the summer of grafting for immediate planting in the field. Such young plants are called 'green grafts' (although this is not the same as GREEN GRAFTING) and are about half the price of a dormant, grafted vine which the nurseryman would sell the following winter. Green graft vines are now commonly available in many countries, and although they are younger than dormant vines, with fewer reserves, they can grow almost as well as dormant vines. However, good care is essential following transplanting, especially with regard to water supply.

In recent years grapevine nurseries have struggled with problems of fungal pathogens in young grafted plants which can cause poor growth and even the death of the vine (see TRUNK DISEASES). B.G.C. & R.E.S.

Bendigo, historic (see GOLD RUSHES), temperate Australian region notable for full-bodied but smooth red wines. Lack of water for IRRIGATION (a potential problem with dry summers and periodic DROUGHT) limits expansion to fewer than 50 producers in an otherwise excellent region. See VICTORIA.

bentonite, FINING agent based on a montmorillonite clay found principally in the state of Wyoming in the western United States, and in many other areas of the world. Like most clays, bentonite is a hydrated compound of aluminium and silicon oxides, but it differs in ways that are useful to winemakers. When mixed with water, it swells and assumes a form that has significant powers of adsorption.

Bentonite, so called because it was first discovered in the Fort Benton rock series, is widely used in the NEW WORLD to ensure PROTEIN stability, particularly to remove heat-unstable proteins from white wines.

Bentonite fining is also used in making everyday white wines for the CLARIFICATION of MUST before or, for more commercial wines, during FERMENTATION to remove solids that would otherwise make the wine look darker, taste coarser, and possibly form clouds in bottle. It is not used at this stage for top-quality white grape must whose constituents should have a beneficial effect on flavour. Bentonite is frequently used for fining after fermentation, however, to hasten the settling of LEES and thereby reduce the time between rackings. Bentonite is not generally used for red wines because their higher concentration of TANNINS can remove proteins naturally (but see BOTTLE DEPOSIT).

Even the most unsophisticated wine drinker prefers a clear white to a hazy one, however strange the idea of a Wyoming clay treatment may seem. An unwanted outcome of fining with too high a dosage of bentonite is an inevitable loss of flavour resulting from adsorption of flavour molecules on the surface of the fining agent. A.D.W.

Béquignol, productive red wine vine virtually extinct in its Bordeaux homeland but still grown on nearly 700 ha/1,729 acres in Argentina, where it is mainly used to add colour.

Bereich, official term for a winegrowing district defined by the 1971 GERMAN WINE LAW. In some regions such as BADEN the Bereich names corresponded largely with already familiar designations for well-defined subregions. In other instances, they were (like the notorious GROSSLAGEN) simply invented for the occasion. Prominent labelling with Bereich names was common for cheaper German wines during the 1970s and 1980s but has largely disappeared.

Bergerac, extensive wine appellation in SOUTH WEST FRANCE producing mainly red, but also dry and sweet white, and rosé wines in the image of BORDEAUX to the immediate west of the region, often at more appealing prices. The greater Bergerac region, named after the principal town at its centre on the River DORDOGNE, is the principal appellation of the Dordogne *département*, and can boast more beautiful and varied countryside than that of its vinously more glamorous neighbour. Lacking distinctions other than touristic (and gastronomic; Périgord is the home of the truffle), it has long been difficult for the wines of Bergerac to escape from the shadow of Bordeaux's more serious wine reputation, but thanks to much more sophisticated use of OAK, pioneering producers such as Luc de Conti of Ch les Tour des Gendres and David Fourtout of Vignobles des Verdots as well as a handful of sweet winemakers, some truly fine wine is being made.

The climate here is somewhere between MARITIME and CONTINENTAL, but overripeness is a rare characteristic of Bergerac grapes and wines. Soils vary from alluvial silt to clay and, on the higher terraces, limestone. Within the region are smaller districts, generally on higher sites with more obvious potential, which have their own appellations for specific wine types. MONBAZILLAC on the left bank of the river is potentially the greatest of these, and is making more and more good-quality BOTRYTIZED wine. MONTRAVEL on the right bank makes lightish dry and sweet white wines in the west of the region. Both these appellations were created in the late 1930s just after the creation of the Bergerac appellation. PÉCHARMANT won its own red wine appellation in 1946, as did the almost extinct sweet wine appellation of ROSETTE, while the SAUSSIGNAC sweet white wine appellation was created in 1982. Partly because these names, with the exception of Monbazillac, are hardly the most famous in the wine world, many producers choose to sell their wines simply as Bergerac.

The vine was grown in the region in Roman times but the wines were most obviously exported and appreciated in the Middle Ages, when viticulture thrived under the influence of MONKS AND MONASTERIES. The history of BORDEAUX outlines why the English were so fond of them, and why, as wines of the HAUT PAYS, they were discriminated against by the Bordeaux merchants. After the HUNDRED YEARS WAR, the DUTCH WINE TRADE dominated exports of Bergerac, developing the production of SWEET WINES here, as elsewhere, from the 16th century and, especially, after Protestant refugees left Périgord for northern Europe after the Revocation of the Edict of Nantes in 1685.

Bergerac was slow to recover from PHYLLOXERA and 2011's shrinking total of 6,843 ha/16,100 acres is just a fraction of the area planted with vines in the early 1870s—and much less than the 12,000 ha/29,652 acres of total vineyard in the 1990s. Vines grown are the classic Bordeaux varieties: Cabernets and Merlot for red wines, and Sauvignon, Sémillon, and Muscadelle for whites. Sémillon is still the most planted light-skinned variety, Merlot the most popular grape for the red wines, which constitute the majority of production.

The most common form of Bergerac is as a still red wine generally very similar to red BORDEAUX AOC. An increasing proportion of red wine is sold as longer-lasting, more usually barrel-aged **Côtes de Bergerac**, however, for which yields are generally lower (a maximum of 50 hl/ha or 3 tons/acre) and ALCOHOLIC STRENGTH higher.

Some **Bergerac Rosé** is made, generally of Cabernet, but the second most common form of Bergerac is the dry white **Bergerac Sec**, increasingly well made thanks to the application of some of the techniques employed for better dry white bordeaux. About a quarter of all white wine is sweet, made mainly from Sémillon, and sold as **Côtes de Bergerac Mœlleux**.

Bergeron, local name for ROUSSANNE in the Savoie appellation of Chignin.

Bergwein, a seldom-encountered official category in AUSTRIA for wine made on slopes steeper than 26% regardless of their region of origin (thus most often applying to the otherwise disparate wines of STYRIA and the WACHAU).

Berlou. See ST-CHINIAN.

berry, botanical term for a class of fleshy fruit lacking a stony layer, so that all of the fruit wall is fleshy or pulpy. The grape berry, popularly known as the grape, is a prime example. It consists of two carpels, denoted by its two locules (internal spaces) in each of which are borne two ovules which may develop into SEEDS, giving in most cases a maximum of four seeds per berry. For more details, see GRAPE. B.G.C.

berry rots. See BUNCH ROTS.

berry size is considered by many to be a factor in wine quality. It is often said that smaller berries contribute to better wine quality, especially for red wines, since ANTHOCYANINS, PHENOLICS, and FLAVOUR COMPOUNDS are mostly contained in the skins. Smaller berries' higher surface-to-volume ratio results in a higher concentration of these skin compounds in the juice and hence in the wine. However, there are few scientific studies that confirm this and some consider a link between berry size and wine quality to be a myth.

Good-quality wine grape varieties typically have small berries, at least compared with both lower-quality varieties and TABLE GRAPES. The average weight of a premium wine grape at full ripeness is 1 to 2 g, whereas others weigh 3 to 10 g/0.35 oz. These values doubtless represent the selection of VINE VARIETIES for their end use, which has continued for centuries. This fact

in itself would seem to support the idea that small berries are a prerequisite for premium wine production.

It is not the case, however, that any vineyard management practice which leads to smaller berries will necessarily improve wine quality. Certainly, WATER STRESS causes small berries, although some of the effects on wine quality may be the result of water stress on VINE PHYSIOLOGY rather than the direct result of small berries. The other simple means of reducing berry size is PRUNING to many buds in winter, but this is contrary to the principles of BALANCED PRUNING. Such pruning is likely to reduce wine quality since the vine may struggle to ripen grapes with insufficient leaf area for efficient PHOTOSYNTHESIS.

Controlled studies in California (with Cabernet Sauvignon) and Australia (with Shiraz and Pinot Noir) have shown that smaller berries do not necessarily make better wine. These studies concluded that it is the vineyard factors which make berries small, water stress in particular, which contribute directly to wine quality, not the small berries in themselves. R.E.S.

Roby, G., et al., 'Berry size and vine water deficits as factors in winegrape composition: Anthocyanins and tannins', *Australian Journal of Grape and Wine Research*, 10 (2004), 100–7.

Walker, R., et al., 'Shiraz berry size in relation to seed number and implications for juice and wine composition', *Australian Journal of Grape and Wine Research*, 11 (2005), 2–8.

Bhutan, Himalayan micro-kingdom with a single wine grape vineyard established in the early 1990s with the technical assistance of Australian wine company Taltarni. The vineyard is at 2,300 m/7,500 ft at Paro, near the capital Thimphu, but it is not known whether any wine resulted. D.G.

Biancame, ancient vine planted on 2,599 ha/6,422 acres in 2010 along the east coast of northern Italy under several aliases, including **Bianchello**.

bianco means 'white' in Italian and the names of many Italian white wines therefore are Bianco d'/da/di/del Place-name. For more details, see under the place-name.

Note, however, that **Bianco** is also the name of a small town in CALABRIA where an ancient sweet white DRIED-GRAPE WINE, Greco di Bianco, is still produced today from grapes known locally as GRECO BIANCO. This variety is distinct from the GRECO of Campania and has been shown by DNA PROFILING to be identical to MALVASIA di Lipari.

Robinson, J., Harding, J., and Vouillamoz, J., *Wine Grapes: A Complete Guide to 1,368 Vine Varieties,*

Including their Origins and Flavours (London, 2012).

Bianco d'Alessano, Italian white wine grape of PUGLIA which has created a small-scale stir in Australia.

Biancolella, Ischian white wine grape which may be related to others in CAMPANIA.

Bible. The vine, including its chief product, wine, is mentioned more often in the Bible than any other plant. The Book of Genesis presents the invention of viticulture as a step in the development of civilization. 'And Noah began to be an husbandman, and he planted a vineyard. And he drank of the wine and was drunken' (Gen. 9. 20–1). The original Hebrew text and its translations state clearly that Noah was the first to make wine, just as Abel was the first shepherd, Cain the first city builder, Jabel the first dweller in tents and keeper of cattle, Jubal the first musician, and Tubal-cain the first smith (Gen. 4. 2–22). By becoming the first winemaker, Noah fulfils his father's prophecy: 'this same shall comfort us concerning our work and toil of our hands, because of the ground which the Lord hath cursed' (Gen. 5. 29). VITICULTURE is divinely ordained: the art of WINE-MAKING will soften the rigours of human existence in a fallen world.

But wine is intoxicating if taken in excess: the invention of wine is also the occasion of the first DRUNKENNESS. Noah 'was uncovered within his tent'. Yet Genesis does not condemn Noah for his drunkenness and indecent exposure: it is Ham, the son who draws attention to his father's nakedness instead of respectfully covering it as Japheth and Shem do, who gets the blame. The impropriety is Ham's, not Noah's, and Noah curses Ham's offspring.

Even if Genesis was not troubled by drunkenness, the early Christian commentators were. The Church Fathers found all manner of excuses for Noah's behaviour: that Noah did not know the possible effects of wine, for example; that he drank to blot out his sorrow at the death and devastation wrought by the Flood; or that he was not drunk in a literal sense. Allegorically, Noah's drunkenness signifies divine ecstasy, the joy experienced by the Christian at the EUCHARIST, when wine is drunk. This interpretation is first offered by St Cyprian (d. 258), and, once it had been adopted by St Ambrose in the 4th century, it became the standard gloss on this text. Going yet further, because events in the Old Testament are read as foreshadowing parts of the life of Christ, Noah prefigures Christ. The wine that Noah drinks is the cup that God the Father would not allow to pass from Christ in the Garden of Gethsemane (Matt. 26. 39; cf. Mark 14. 35, Luke 22. 41–2), as St Augustine stated in Book 16 of *The City of God* (written in 429). In the eyes of Augustine and those of medieval commentators after him, because Noah's drunkenness points forward to Christ's Passion, it is to be praised. Similarly, the speaker of Isaiah 63. 3, who has 'trodden the wine press alone', is interpreted as Christ, the man of sorrows (Isa. 53. 3).

In the Middle Ages, Christ in his Passion is often depicted as a man treading grapes or even—but not in English art—crushed in a wine press. These numerous mentions of grapes, wine, and the vintage in the Old Testament are allegorized as representing Christ's Passion: the bunch of grapes from the Promised Land (Num. 13. 24), for example; the vineyard in Isaiah 5. 1–7; and the wine in the Song of Songs.

Nowadays this method of biblical interpretation, known technically as typology, is used much less often: we may still hear Moses mentioned occasionally as a type of Christ but not Noah. Modern biblical scholars restrict themselves to pointing out that in a primitive society lack of respect for one's elders is a far more serious offence than drunkenness.

The Bible is not suitable reading for teetotallers. As the Psalmist says, 'wine maketh glad the heart of man' (Ps. 104. 15). Although we may not realize it, Psalm 23, 'The Lord is my Shepherd', sings the praises of wine. In the line which is familiar to most English speakers as 'My cup runneth over', the cup contains wine, and the original version, followed by the various Latin translations, speaks approvingly of its intoxicating properties. To be deprived of wine is a terrible thing. Whenever the Prophets threaten doom and destruction, they say that the Lord will withhold the benefits of the vintage from the Israelites, as in Micah 6. 15, Amos 4. 9, Isaiah 17. 6, and Joel 1. 10. In the New Testament, Timothy is advised to give up drinking water and instead to 'use a little wine for thy stomach's sake and thine often infirmities' (1 Tim. 5. 23, now no longer thought to be by St Paul).

A rare disapproving reference would seem to be Acts 2. 13, when sceptical observers dismiss the Pentecostal miracle of speaking in tongues as drunkenness: the apostles 'are full of new wine', but the disapproval is aimed at the unseemly babble, not at wine; in any case, Pentecost is not the time of the vintage so the insult is perhaps not to be taken literally. 'New wine' evokes images of joyful abandon and drunken revelry, as in Joel 1. 5, where the Israelites, Joel prophesies, will labour in vain: 'Awake, ye drunkards, and weep, and howl, all ye drinkers of wine, because of the new wine, for it is cut off from your mouth.' But as a sign of God's mercy 'the mountains shall drop down new wine' (Joel 3. 18).

Old wine is never mentioned in the Old Testament, but it is in the New. Where the Synoptic Gospels explain that new wine should not be put into old 'bottles', wineskins in fact, as a matter of HYGIENE (Luke 5. 37–9, Matt. 9. 16–17, Mark 2. 21–2), only Luke adds, 'No man also, having drunk old wine, straightway desireth new; for he saith, The old is better.' The old wine would not of course have been stored and aged in a wineskin but in a sealed non-permeable container such as an AMPHORA. In the hot climate of the Holy Land, old wine would have been better than new, especially if it was a heavy tannic red. Compare Greek and Latin authors, who always prefer old wine to new (see AGEING, Ancient GREECE, and CLASSICAL TEXTS).

On one occasion, Christ himself expresses a desire to drink new wine. At the Last Supper, as the Synoptic Gospels tell us (Matt. 26. 29, Mark 14. 25, Luke 22. 18), he will not drink the wine until he drinks it new in the kingdom of his Father (Luke omits 'new'). These passages describe how the Eucharist was instituted. The new wine which Christ will drink when God's everlasting kingdom has come carried with it all the associations of the joy of the vintage. And Christ was aware of the importance of wine. His first miracle was to turn water into wine at the marriage feast in Cana, when the wine had run out. The governor of the feast, who does not know where the wine has come from, says to the bridegroom, 'Every man at the beginning doth set forth good wine and, when men have well drunk, then that which is worse; but thou hast kept the good wine until now' (John 2. 10). One would dearly like to know what this wine was like. But how delightful that Christ should be portrayed as a man of taste and discernment and that this should be the first tangible proof of his glory and the miracle that convinced the disciples. 'This beginning of miracles did Jesus in Cana, of Galilee, and manifested forth his glory; and his disciples believed in him' (John 2. 11). H.M.W.

Daube, D., *Wine in the Bible*, St Paul's Lecture (London, 1974).

Zapletal, V., *Der Wein in der Bibel* (Freiburg im Breisgau, 1920).

Bical, Portuguese white grape variety grown mainly in BAIRRADA, and DÃO, where it is called Borrado das Moscas, or fly droppings. The wines have good acidity and can be persuaded to display some aroma in some still VARIETAL versions, although in Bairrada the grapes are often used in blends for sparkling wines. Some capacity for AGEING has been demonstrated, Bical developing an almost RIESLING-like bouquet after a decade in bottle. It was grown on 1,456 ha/3,620 acres in 2010.

Bienvenues-Bâtard-Montrachet, a great white GRAND CRU in Burgundy's CÔTE D'OR. For more details, see MONTRACHET.

Bierzo, increasingly fashionable small DO region in north west Spain (see map under SPAIN) which administratively forms part of CASTILLA Y LEÓN. However, the River Sil, which bisects it, is a tributary of the Miño (Minho in Portugal) and the wines have more in common with those of GALICIA than those of the DOURO 140 km/88 miles to the south. Sheltered from the climatic excesses of the Atlantic and the central plateau, Bierzo shows promise as a wine region. The MENCÍA grape is capable of producing balanced, fruity red wines in well-drained soils on the SLATE and GRANITE of this part of Spain.

In the late 1990s, a group of small, mostly young growers reproduced in Bierzo the same 'miracle' which had happened in Priorat one decade earlier—they resurrected a moribund wine region. One of the protagonists, Álvaro Palacios, was indeed one of the Priorat pioneers as well. With his nephew Ricardo Pérez Palacios, he reclaimed small, old vineyards on slate slopes and produced wines with no resemblance to the light quaffable reds traditionally produced from fertile valley vineyards. Other top names are Paixar, Pittacum, Dominio de Tares, Estefanía, Luna Beberide, Mengoba, Raúl Pérez, Peique, Gancedo, Losada, Casar de Burbia, and Castro Ventosa. V. de la S.

Barquín, J., Guitiérrez, L., and de la Serna, V., *The Finest Wines of Rioja and Northwest Spain* (London, 2011).

Biferno, one of only four DOCs in the Italian MOLISE region, and arguably its most important.

Big Rivers Zone in NEW SOUTH WALES, comprising the Murray Darling, Perricoota, Riverina, and Swan Hill regions.

Bikavér or, on export markets, **Bull's Blood**, is a HUNGARIAN red wine style that may be made in the EGER or SZEKSZÁRD regions. At one time the blend depended heavily on KADARKA, but this demanding local variety was replaced by KÉKFRANKOS, supplemented by Cabernet, Merlot, and Kékoporto (Portugieser). Both regions are now making serious efforts to produce elegant, fruity Bikavér wines worth ageing that are neither heavy nor aggressively tannic. Single-vineyard examples are increasingly found.

bin, traditional term for a collection of wine bottles, normally stacked horizontally on top of each other, or the process of so storing, or **binning**, them. Thus these bins needed BIN LABELS, and a **bin end** has come to signify a small quantity of wine bottles left over from a larger lot. Some Australian wine companies have a tradition of using the word bin in BRAND names.

bin labels were necessitated by the practice of binning unlabelled bottles.

The most common form of bin label was made of pottery and was approximately the shape of a coat hanger some 3–5 in/7–13 cm wide. At the apex there was an additional lug, pierced so that it formed a suspension ring. As many were nailed to the cellar masonry, they have often been broken or cracked during removal.

Early English bin labels (dating to the mid 18th century) are delftware (tin-glazed earthenware) with blue or deep magenta calligraphy (upper case) on a white to pale blue ground. Almost all later ones have black lettering on white pottery, although coloured lettering is very rarely seen. European labels came in a variety of forms and often with polychrome decoration; the language of the writing usually provides an obvious clue to the country of origin.

By the 19th century, labels developed rounded shoulders, the earlier ones being angled. Many had a portion of the face left unglazed where more precise details of the bin contents might be written. Home-made labels were sometimes fashioned from wood or slate and would likewise have written information.

In very large cellars and in commercial ones where the bin contents changed frequently, it was established practice to use circular bin labels with numbers that would cross-refer to the cellar records. Many of these, and the coat hanger variety, are marked with the manufacturer's name (Wedgwood, Copeland, etc.) or the vendor's name (e.g. Farrow & Jackson), almost invariably impressed during manufacture. Bin labels are not much collected in the world of wine antiques but the most sought-after are delftware examples, those with spelling mistakes, and rarities of name, colour, or form.

R.N.H.B.

Binissalem. Wines from Spain's first offshore DO on the Mediterranean island of MALLORCA are mostly destined for the Balearic holiday resorts. Binissalem's dominant grape, Manto Negro, is certainly capable of making well-balanced reds, although they can lack structure and character. The most common white variety is Moll, also called Prensal Blanc, which produces bland, neutral wines.

V. de la S.

Bío-Bío, cool, wet subregion of the Southern region of CHILE.

biochar is made by heating organic materials such as wood waste, crop residues, or animal manure to 350–500 ℃ in the absence of oxygen. It has been advocated as a soil amendment because of its long-term CARBON storage and because it has been shown to increase soil CATION EXCHANGE CAPACITY, water-holding capacity in sandy soils (see SOIL WATER), and biological activity (see SOIL BIOTA). In trials in several European vineyards, the biochar had to be activated by mixing it with COMPOST or manure. Despite early positive results, by the mid 2010s, no firm recommendations had been made for biochar use in viticulture, primarily because of the variation in commercially available products and their complex interaction with SOIL TYPE, CLIMATE, grape variety, COVER CROP, and microbial activity.   R.E.W.

Lehmann, J., et al., 'Biochar effects on soil biota—a review', *Soil Biology & Biochemistry*, 43 (2011), 1812-36.

Niggli, C., and Schmidt, H.-P., 'Biochar in vineyards', *Terroir, Ecology, Climate-farming*, 1 (2010), 318-22, www.ithaka-journal.net

biodiversity. See ECOSYSTEM.

biodynamic viticulture is, depending on your perspective, an enhanced or extreme form of ORGANIC VITICULTURE. This controversial practice has produced some impressive results but without the reassurance of conclusive scientific explanation.

Biodynamics is the oldest 'green' farming movement, pre-dating organics by 20 years. It is based on theories described in 1924 by the Austrian philosopher Rudolf Steiner (1861–1925) for agriculture in general. All biodynamic vineyards practise organic viticulture, but biodynamics differs from organics in three ways. The vineyard should become a self-sustaining individual or 'farm organism' (see SUSTAINABLE VITICULTURE and ECOSYSTEM): it should be treated regularly with nine herb- and mineral-based biodynamic 'preparations'; and key tasks such as planting, PRUNING, PLOUGHING, PICKING, and BOTTLING should be timed to harness beneficial 'formative forces' exerted by earthly and celestial—planetary, solar, stellar, and especially lunar—rhythms.

France's first biodynamic wine-grower, François Bouchet (1932–2005), began using the technique on his 6 ha/15 acre Domaine de Château Gaillard in Touraine in 1962. But France's biodynamic wine movement remained almost non-existent until the late 1980s, when Bouchet began helping leading names such as Domaine Leflaive of PULIGNY-MONTRACHET, Domaine LEROY in Vosne-Romanée, CHAPOUTIER in Hermitage, Huet in Vouvray, and Kreydenweiss in Alsace to convert to biodynamics.

These producers shared a belief that only a less technologically driven form of viticulture would allow wine QUALITY to keep improving, and were emboldened by former INRA soil microbiologist Claude Bourguignon's 1988 declaration that Burgundy's vineyards contained 'less life than Sahara desert sand'. Bourguignon made no claim to understanding how biodynamics works; but his research showed that levels of microbial life in vineyard topsoils (see SOIL BIOTA) were significantly greater on organic and biodynamic plots than on those of conventionally farmed ones. In addition, Bourguignon found significant increases of microbial life on biodynamic vine roots at depths of several metres compared with conventionally and even organically farmed vines, and that the roots were thickest, longest and most able to penetrate the soil, and to assimilate trace elements (see VINE NUTRITION, MICRONUTRIENTS, and MYCORRHIZA), when grown biodynamically.

The particularity of biodynamics is the use of animal sense organs such as cow horns as sheaths when making six of the nine biodynamic preparations. It is believed that animal organs enable the medicinal properties of the substances encased within—cow manure, ground quartz, oak bark, and the flowers of yarrow, chamomile, and dandelion—to become fully effective throughout the farm, keeping it within what Steiner called 'the realm of the living'. The animal organ sheaths disintegrate naturally or are discarded before the preparation material within is applied. Nevertheless, it is this aspect that convinces non-believers that biodynamics is an unscientific and disturbingly irrational cult.

The two main biodynamic field sprays are horn manure and horn silica. Only a handful of the former or a few grams of the latter are required per hectare. They are prepared by burying the cow manure or the ground quartz (silica) in a cow horn for six months over winter or summer respectively. Horn manure is sprayed on the soil in the afternoon, in autumn and early spring, to stimulate microbial life in the soil, helping maintain SOIL STRUCTURE and levels of ORGANIC MATTER, and encouraging deeper vine roots. Horn silica is sprayed over the vines, at sunrise, either side of FLOWERING to regulate plant metabolism and promote stronger, more upright vine growth, to LIGNIFY the wood, and to improve the nutritional and keeping qualities of the wine. One further field spray, the silica-rich common horsetail (*Equisetum arvense*), is sprayed as a fresh tea or fermented liquid manure to encourage fungal spores to remain in the soil rather than affecting the vine. It is a fundamental tenet that all three biodynamic spray preparations are 'dynamized' before application. This involves rhythmically stirring the material in water, first one way and then the other, to create a vortex. When the direction of stirring is changed the water is thought to undergo chaos, allowing beneficial 'formative forces' within the preparation to be transferred to the water and thence to the vineyard when it is sprayed. Organic fertilizer in the form of COMPOST is used to nourish the soil but biodynamic compost differs from other composts in that the remaining six biodynamic preparations made from yarrow, chamomile, stinging nettle, oak bark, dandelion, and valerian must be inserted into the compost pile, which should be manure-based. The compost preparations are said to infuse the manure with vitalizing living forces whose role is more important to vine growth and form than the actual composted manure. Where specific ingredients are not available, substitutes may be used. For example, *Casuarina stricta* is often substituted for common horsetail in Australia.

Late-20th-century MECHANIZATION saw the almost complete disappearance of livestock from vineyards. Biodynamic growers are at the forefront of reversing this trend by acquiring livestock for manure (cows), traction (horses, mules), weed control (sheep), or pest control (chickens to eat cutworms). In this way, vine monocultures begin changing towards the biodynamic ideal of self-sustaining farm organisms, creating a natural equilibrium in which pests and diseases become potentially far less potent.

Biodynamic growers see plants as comprising four 'organs': ROOT, LEAF/shoot, flower, and fruit, and these are respectively linked to the four elements of earth, water, air, and fire (solar heat). Each plant component is said to be favoured during particular points of the moon's sidereal cycle when the moon passes in front of one of the 12 constellations of the astronomical (rather than astrological) zodiac. Thus, for example, spraying horn manure on the soil for root growth is said to be most effective if the moon is in front of an earth/root constellation such as Bull, Virgin, or Goat. These windows occur every nine days or so but for two or three days only, so only the smallest vineyards, or those with abundant labour, can time all their agricultural work according to the biodynamic calendar. Biodynamicists claim that on conventional vineyards where neither biodynamic compost nor the field spray preparations are used, the effect of these earthly and celestial rhythms will not be felt as the soil and the vines will not have been sensitized to them.

Cellar work is also said to benefit from the biodynamic calendar, with, it is claimed, bottling best under Lion if the wine is designed to age (the heat/fruit 'force' will be most concentrated in the wine at this point, so bottling then will capture or seal it).

Where VINE PESTS need to be controlled in biodynamic farming, a number of the pests are collected, burnt, and their ashes scattered around the affected area to discourage future infestations.

Biodynamic viticulture alone will not a great wine make: good viticultural and winemaking practices such as CANOPY MANAGEMENT and cellar HYGIENE are also essential. Biodynamic winemaking standards are similar to those used for ORGANIC WINE, but impose stricter guidelines regarding ENRICHMENT, NUTRIENT additions, the use of energy-intensive practices (eg PASTEURIZATION), MICRO-OXYGENATION, and recyclable PACKAGING.

In 2013 over 700 vineyards worldwide comprising more than 10,000 ha/24,710 acres were certified biodynamic, either by the German-based Demeter International organization which *de facto* controls the Biodynamic (with a capital B) agricultural trademark, or by the wine-only and French-based Syndicat International des Vignerons en Culture Bio-dynamique (Biodyvin), or by Australia's government, which, uniquely, has its own biodynamic rulebook. Biodynamic vineyards range in size from a handful of hectares to several hundred.

Vineyards whose biodynamic conversion proved catalytic either locally or further afield, in addition to those mentioned above, include Nicolas Joly in Savennières (1985), Jean-Pierre Fleury in Champagne (1989), James Millton in New Zealand (1989), Ch Romanin in Provence (1990), Guy Bossard in Muscadet (1992), Michel Grisard in Savoie (1994), the Fetzer and Frey families in California (mid 1990s), Cazes in Roussillon (1998), Nikolaihof in Austria (1998), Álvaro Espinoza in Chile (1999), Cooper Mountain in Oregon (1999), Reyneke in South Africa (2000), Valgiano in Tuscany (2001), Comte Abbatucci in Corsica (2002), Stéphane Tissot in the Jura (2004), Domaine Vacheron in Sancerre (2004), Ch Pontet-Canet in Bordeaux (2005), Dr Bürklin-Wolf in Germany (2005), Cullen in Western Australia (2005), Noemía in Argentina (2006), and Southbrook in Canada (2008).

Despite scepticism in some quarters, biodynamic growers are becoming less reticent about their biodynamic practices, and increasing numbers of organic growers now claim to use some (usually the less esoteric) elements of biodynamics.

See also ORGANIC VITICULTURE, ORGANIC WINE, SUSTAINABLE VITICULTURE.   M.W.

Waldin, M., *Biodynamic Wine-Growing: Theory & Practice* (London, 2012).

biological viticulture

biological viticulture, a loose term since all viticulture involves biology, but for more details of the general philosophy implied, see ORGANIC VITICULTURE. In France, many ORGANIC WINES are sold as *vins biologiques*.

Biondi-Santi

Biondi-Santi, family synonymous with and, in 1865, responsible for the production of the first wine ever to be labelled BRUNELLO DI MONTALCINO. Before that time Montalcino's fame was based solely on a sweet, often sparkling white based on the MOSCADELLO grape, until Ferruccio Biondi-Santi isolated a particular type of Sangiovese on his Il Greppo estate using MASS SELECTION with better resistance to OIDIUM than Moscadello. It was subsequently called Sangiovese Grosso and officially registered as BBS 11. Ferruccio also increased vine density and lowered yields, while eliminating the white grapes that were routinely blended with Sangiovese then.

Tancredi, Ferruccio's son, is credited with founding the first Montalcino CO-OPERATIVE during the crisis years of the 1920s, while focusing on exporting the Bondi-Santi wines. He was soon joined by his son, Franco, who committed himself firmly to Il Greppo's traditional methods which, during the 1980s and 1990s, were challenged by a new generation of Brunello producers preferring to make a more concentrated, richer, and more internationally accessible style by harvesting ultra-ripe grapes, using shorter maceration time, and ageing the wines in French BARRIQUES. This modernist approach, which received glowing reviews from the-then all-powerful Italian wine guides, was especially successful in the US but made the Biondi-Santi style look outdated and light. However, in 2008 during the scandal described in BRUNELLO DI MONTALCINO, Biondi-Santi rose as the natural defender of Brunello, and was subsequently joined by a majority of the region's growers and wine producers who together prevented the proposed change in production rules to allow INTERNATIONAL VARIETIES into Brunello di Montalcino.

With the taste for rich, extracted wines on the wane, and a growing international appetite for more locally authentic, TERROIR-driven wines, Biondi-Santi's future looks promising, and is in the hands of Jacopo Biondi Santi who took over the reins of Il Greppo on the death of his father Franco in 2013.   W.S.

Boldrini, M., Bruchi, B., and Cappelli, A., *This is my land—Franco Biondi Santi, Montalcino and Brunello* (Siena, 2009).

O'Keefe, K., *Franco Biondi Santi: The Gentleman of Brunello* (Bergamo, 2005).

biotechnology

biotechnology. See GENETIC MODIFICATION for some examples of viticultural biotechnology.

birds

birds can be a more serious modern vine pest than PHYLLOXERA in some areas because they are so difficult to control, particularly during grape RIPENING when they feed on grapes. Birds have been feeding on grapes as they have evolved for about 60 million years, and in so doing have spread grape seeds in their excreta. This is one reason why grapes are thought to have developed small, black, sugary fruits which attract birds. (Subsequent selection of MUTATIONS has given us light-skinned grapes.)

For small vineyards in isolated regions, and particularly for early-ripening vine varieties, birds may destroy an entire crop. Unfortunately, the birds begin their destruction as soon as the grapes begin to ripen, so early harvest is not a solution. As well as the potential crop loss, bird pecks provide entry points for all sorts of BUNCH ROTS. Control measures are expensive and bird damage can make some vineyards uneconomic. Birds are often the greatest problem facing vineyards in new viticultural regions, especially if the vineyards are isolated (as in

ENGLAND and Long Island in NEW YORK, for example).

The species of birds which attack grapes vary from region to region. The ubiquitous starling is one of the most widespread problem species but blackbirds, partridges, robins, sparrows, thrushes, and finches are also common. Starlings, for example, can eat 60 to 80 g/2.8 oz of grapes a day. The planting of a vineyard and the consequent provision of an extra food source can actually lead to a population increase of birds. Many growers notice that bird damage depends on the availability of alternative food sources. In the MARGARET RIVER region of Western Australia, for example, silvereye birds do more damage to vineyards when nectar from local eucalyptus trees and saltbush berries are limited. Where vineyards are extensive, and the varieties ripen together, then damage to individual vineyards is minor.

Many bird protection devices are based on scaring birds by sight or sound. In time, birds become accustomed to new objects or noises in a vineyard so that, for example, the traditional immobile scarecrow can rapidly lose effectiveness. Other scaring devices include a wide range of auditory contraptions, guns, gas-powered cannon, tape across the vineyards, cats, etc.

NETTING of vineyards is becoming increasingly common. The nets are made of woven string or perforated plastic, can often be reused, and tractor-mounted rollers assist installation and removal. Since the nets provide for virtually 100% effective control yet do not harm birds, they are acceptable to growers and environmentalists alike.

Some local bird populations are affected by eating insects or grapes which contain pesticides used in vineyards, which bird lovers view as an argument against the use of AGROCHEMICALS. R.E.S.

Buchanan, G. A., and Amos, T. G., 'Grape pests', in B. G. Coombe and P. R. Dry (eds.), *Viticulture*, ii: *Practices* (Adelaide, 1992).

McKee, L. J., 'To net or not to net', *Wines & Vines* (March 2010).

bird's eye rot, vine disease. See ANTHRACNOSE.

Biscoitos, DOP on the Azorean island of Terceira making small quantities of fortified wine and, more recently, table wine from the VERDELHO grape. Biscoitos is so-called because volcanic stones in the soil resemble biscuits.

bitterness, one of the primary tastes (see TASTING) which can be detected via taste buds mainly on the tongue in many wines even if it is not as common as SWEETNESS and ACIDITY, and is often confused with the quite different tactile sensation of caused by ASTRINGENCY. Many Italian red wines are relatively bitter, as are some less successful examples of particularly aromatic grape varieties such as Gewürztraminer,

typically because of an excess of PHENOLICS. Poorly seasoned OAK can also make a wine taste bitter. Many flavoured VERMOUTHS, notably Punt e Mes, are deliberately very bitter. Sweetness can help to mask bitterness.

bitter rot, a FUNGAL DISEASE of ripe grapes that is active in warm, humid conditions. It is found only on damaged and almost senescent tissues, but the bitter fruit flavour can be detected in the finished wine. The cause is the fungus *Greeneria uvicola* and the disease is widespread in the eastern United States, Asia, Australia, and South Africa but not in France or Germany. The disease is easily controlled by most FUNGICIDES. R.E.S.

black dead arm. See BOTRYOSPHAERIA DIEBACK.

black foot, fungal disease found in young vines in both vineyards and NURSERIES which can lead to the decline and death of young vines. One of the so-called TRUNK DISEASES, its symptoms include poor growth, chlorotic leaves, brownish-black discoloration of rootstock trunks, roots, graft unions, and a reduction in root biomass. Affected young vines usually die during the growing season or in the following winter. Causal agents vary geographically but are soil-borne fungi in the genera *Campylocarpon*, *Cylindrocladiella*, and *Ilyonectria*. *Ilyonectria liriodendri* and *I. macrodidyma* are known to be the most prevalent and widespread. Control measures include field rotation, planting clean vines (see HOT-WATER TREATMENT), and avoiding planting in heavy, wet, and poorly drained soils. The most common phylloxera-resistant rootstocks used today are susceptible to black foot. L.T.M. & J.R.U.-T.

Agusti-Brisach, C., and Armengol, J., 'Black-foot disease of grapevine: an update on taxonomy, epidemiology and management strategies', *Phytopathologia Mediterranea*, 52 (2013), 245–61.

Gramaje, D., and Armengol, J., 'Fungal trunk pathogens in the grapevine propagation process: potential inoculum sources, detection, identification, and management strategies', *Plant Disease*, 95 (2011), 1040–55.

Gubler, W. D., and Petit, E., 'Black foot disease', in *Grape Pest Management no. 3343* (3rd edn, Oakland, Calif., 2013), 90–92.

black goo, name coined in 1995 by American viticulturist Lucie Morton to describe the symptoms of black spots and tarry ooze in XYLEM vessels produced by *Phaeomoniella chlamydospora* and *Phaeoacremonium* species, fungi that cause decline in young vines. It is now known as PETRI DISEASE. The same symptoms and fungi are found in older vines suffering from ESCA. See also BLACK XYLEM DECLINE. L.T.M.

black knot, vine disease. See CROWN GALL.

black measles, vine disease. See ESCA.

black rot, FUNGAL DISEASE which is one of the most economically important diseases of vines in the north-eastern United States, Canada, and parts of Europe and South America. The disease is native to North America and was probably introduced to other countries by contaminated cuttings. It was introduced to France, for example, on PHYLLOXERA-tolerant rootstocks as early as 1885. The disease is caused by the fungus *Guignardia bidwelli*, which attacks young shoots, leaves, stems, and berries. The disease spreads only in mild, wet weather. Crop losses can be high, up to 80%. Control of the disease is based on FUNGICIDES sprayed from spring up to fruit ripening and removing from the vineyard infected mummified berries. The disease is causing renewed concern because of its recent spread in Europe. As might be expected from the origin of the disease, some native American species are tolerant. R.E.S.

black spot, vine disease. See ANTHRACNOSE.

Blackwood Valley, relatively new, inland wine region with 16 producers on the same latitude as Margaret River in the South West Australia Zone of WESTERN AUSTRALIA.

black xylem decline, a more formal name for the condition BLACK GOO. Unhealthy young vineyards have been studied in South Africa for about 50 years, and more recently have been a cause for concern in California, where rapid expansion took place in the 1980s. Similar problems have been noted in Europe, Australia, and New Zealand.

The reason is not clear, but the majority of evidence implicates wood-rotting fungi, perhaps associated with infected planting material. The fungus *Phaeoacremonium* has been isolated from unhealthy vines; when combined with other fungi *Phellinus* and/or *Stereum* species, it appears to cause ESCA. There is some evidence that black xylem decline may be overcome by treating planting material with hot water, which is also useful against NEMATODES, PIERCE'S DISEASE, and PHYTOPLASMA disease. R.E.S.

Blagny, small village in Burgundy's CÔTE D'OR. For more details, see both MEURSAULT and PULIGNY-MONTRACHET.

blanc, **blanche**, masculine and feminine French adjectives meaning 'white' and therefore a common suffix for white wines and light-berried grape variety names.

blanc de blancs, French for 'white of whites', may justifiably be used to describe white wines made from pale-skinned grapes, as the great majority of them are. The term has real significance, however, only when used for white SPARKLING WINES, in the production of which dark-skinned grapes tend to predominate. A blanc de blancs CHAMPAGNE, for example, is, unusually, made exclusively from CHARDONNAY grapes.

Blanc de Morgex, alpine white wine made from the PRIÉ grape, a speciality of the Valle d'AOSTA.

blanc de noirs, French for 'white of blacks', describes a white wine made from dark-skinned grapes by pressing them very gently and running the pale juice off the skins as early as possible. Many such still wines have a slightly pink tinge (see WHITE ZINFANDEL, for example). The term has a specific meaning in the Champagne region, where it is used to describe a CHAMPAGNE made exclusively from PINOT NOIR and MEUNIER grapes, a speciality of the Aube district in Champagne. See also VIN GRIS and BLUSH.

Blanc Fumé is a French synonym for SAUVIGNON BLANC, notably in Pouilly-sur-Loire, centre of the POUILLY-FUMÉ, or **Blanc Fumé de Pouilly**, appellation, many of whose aromatic dry whites do indeed have a smoky, if not exactly smoked, perfume. Thanks to one imaginative American, FUMÉ BLANC is today a much more widely known term (see MONDAVI).

blanco, Spanish term for white as in *vino blanco*, or white wine.

Blandy, a name that is synonymous with MADEIRA, both the island and the wine. The Blandy family has extensive interests on Madeira, including hotels, travel, and media. John Blandy of Dorset came to live on the island in 1811, having been introduced to the island and its wines while serving in the navy. His son Charles was astute enough to buy up considerable stocks of mature wine during the outbreak of POWDERY MILDEW in 1852, which contributed to the success of the madeira wine firm Blandy Brothers & Co. in the second half of the 19th century. In 1874, Charles's daughter married a Cossart, of the other important madeira wine firm Cossart Gordon. The tourist showpiece of the madeira wine industry, the old São Francisco lodge in Funchal, was once the Blandy family home and offices.

The difficult years of the early 20th century saw the formation of the Madeira Wine Association, which Blandy's joined in the 1920s, eventually acquiring a controlling interest. The group is now known as the Madeira Wine Company, includes all the British madeira firms (Cossart Gordon, Leacock, Rutherford & Miles), and is one of the largest producers on the island. The SYMINGTON family, a major force in the port wine trade, acquired a controlling interest in the Madeira Wine Company in 1988 and and invested considerably in the company,

improving both winemaking and marketing. In 2011, marking the bicentennial of company, the Blandys reacquired a controlling interest from the Symingtons and are now actively engaged in reviving the madeira category.

Binney, M., *The Blandys of Madeira (1811-2011)*, (London, 2011).

blanketing, winemaking term for protecting grapes, juice, or wine, particularly from OXYGEN, by applying a gas, usually INERT GAS or sometimes CARBON DIOXIDE.

Blanquette de Limoux. See LIMOUX.

Blau or **Blauer** is the adjective meaning 'blue' in German, often used for darker-berried vine varieties. Blauburgunder and Blauer Burgunder are PINOT NOIR, for example, while Weissburgunder and Weisser Burgunder are PINOT BLANC.

Blauburger, Austrian red wine grape variety and, like the much more common ZWEIGELT, a cross made in the 1920s by Dr Zweigelt at KLOSTERNEUBURG, in this case of Portugieser and Blaufränkisch. Plantings had reached 1,000 ha/ 2,470 acres by 2009, the majority planted in Lower Austria, where it produces relatively undistinguished light reds although its deep colour makes it a useful ingredient in blends. There is also a little in Hungary and Germany.

Blauburgunder, sometimes **Blauer Burgunder**, common name for PINOT NOIR in Austria and Switzerland. In Germany, SPÄTBURGUNDER (occasionally **Blauer Spätburgunder**) is more common.

Blauer Wildbacher, ancient, dark-skinned, perfumed grape variety that is a speciality of western STYRIA where almost all of the 422 ha/1,042 acres grown in Austria are located. The variety has been increasingly popular with growers and almost all of it is made into the notably tart, local pink speciality, Schilcher. DNA parentage analysis suggests a parent–offspring relationship with GOUAIS BLANC.

Blaufränkisch is the Austrian name for the increasingly respected middle European black grape variety the Germans call LEMBERGER. From pre-medieval times it was common to divide grape varieties into the (superior) 'fränkisch', whose origins lay with the Franks, and the rest. It is today Austria's second most planted dark-berried variety after its progeny ZWEIGELT, producing wines of real character, if notably high acidity, when carefully grown. Its good colour, tannin, and raciness encourage the most ambitious Austrian producers, led by Moric, to lavish new oak on it and treat it like single vineyard burgundy. For many years it was thought to be the Beaujolais grape GAMAY. Bulgarians still call it Gamé, while Hungarians translate its Austrian name more directly as

KÉKFRANKOS. Austrian DNA PROFILING suggests a parent–offspring relationship with GOUAIS BLANC, known in Austria as Heunisch.

Its Austrian home is Burgenland, where most of its 3,225 ha/7,966 acres are situated. It is grown particularly on the warm shores of the Neusiedlersee, in Mittelburgenland, and at Eisenberg in South Burgenland. As Kékfrankos it grows even more prolifically on the Hungarian side of the lake, notably in Sopron, whose version has the distinction of having been singled out for mention by Napoleon. Today it is seen both at home and abroad as one of Austria's best local varieties. Blaufränkisch gives varied wine styles with red fruit flavours, firm acidity, and generally good weight, deep colour, and spicy character. The variety called Frankovka in the CZECH REPUBLIC and Serbia is one and the same and here can produce lively, fruity, vigorous wines for early consumption. In FRIULI in the far north eastern corner of Italy, the variety is called Franconia and can yield wines with zip and fruit.

The vine buds early and ripens late and can therefore thrive only in a relatively warm climate.

Blaye, fortified town across the Gironde estuary from Margaux in the BORDEAUX region which has been exporting wine much longer than the famous MÉDOC. It gives its name to a region of scattered vineyards with soils that vary considerably (much more than in neighbouring Côtes de BOURG) but are mainly clay and limestone. At the beginning of the 20th century it produced mainly white wine for distillation into cognac to the immediate north, and even today some of its white wine is distilled. Early 21st century tinkering with nomenclature resulted in most of the wines being sold as **Blaye Côtes de Bordeaux**, part of the Côtes de Bordeaux group. Mainly robust, early-maturing, red BORDEAUX BLENDS were produced from 5,218 ha/12,888 acres of vines in 2013 planted predominantly with Merlot. A much smaller number of growers produce reds according to the stricter rules of **Blaye** *tout court*. More than 300 ha/740 acres of Sauvignon Blanc and Sémillon vines are responsible for some particularly successful, lively dry white **Blaye Côtes de Bordeaux** while **Côtes de Blaye**, a dry white based on Colombard and Ugni Blanc, is a minority product nowadays.

bleeding. Vines are said to bleed when they lose fluid in spring from pruning cuts. This event can take place over several days, and is generally seen following the first few days of warm spring weather. Individual vines can lose up to 5 l/1.3 gal of water. The liquid which drips from the pruning cuts is mostly water, with low concentrations of MINERALS, SUGARS, organic acids, and HORMONES. This is the first visible sign of the start of the new VINE GROWTH CYCLE, and corresponds to renewed activity of the root system. Osmotic forces create root pressure, which forces water up through the plant. The term is also used occasionally in winemaking; see SAIGNÉE. R.E.S.

Galet, P., *Précis de viticulture* (7th edn, Montpellier, 2000).

blend, any product of BLENDING but specifically a wine deliberately made from more than one grape variety rather than a single VARIETAL (which may contain only a small proportion of other varieties).

blending different batches of wine, or *coupage* as it is known in French, is a practice that was once more distrusted than understood. In fact almost all of the world's finest wines are made by blending the contents of different vats and different barrels (see ASSEMBLAGE); CHAMPAGNE and SHERRY are examples of wines which are quintessentially blends. It is often the case, as has been proved by the most rigorous of experiments, that a wine blend is superior to any one of its component parts.

Blending earned its dubious reputation before the mid 20th century when wine laws were either non-existent or under-enforced, and 'stretching' a superior wine by blending it with inferior wines was commonplace (see ADULTERATION). Blending of different lots of the same wine as it is commonly practised today to ensure that quality is maximal and consistent was not possible before the days of large blending vats; before then wine was bottled from individual casks or vats, which is one explanation of the much higher degree of BOTTLE VARIATION in older vintages.

Modern blending, important in the production of both fine and everyday wines, may combine wines with different but complementary characteristics: heavily oak-influenced lots aged in new barrels may be muted by blending with less oaky lots of the same wine; wines that have undergone MALOLACTIC CONVERSION may be blended with crisper ones that have not. In the case of ordinary table wines, blending is an important ingredient in smoothing out the difference between one VINTAGE and its successor. Such practices are by no means unknown in the realm of fine-wine production, whether legally sanctioned or not. The wine regulations in many regions permit the addition of a certain proportion of another vintage to a vintage-dated wine, as they frequently do a certain proportion, generally less than 15%, of wine from a region or even grape variety other than that specified on the label.

In today's competitive and quality-conscious wine market, motivation for blending is more often improvement than deception.

Perhaps the most enthusiastic blenders are the Australians, who regularly blend the produce of two or more different wine regions, possibly many hundreds of miles apart. There are philosophical differences between them and the European authorities, but a compromise solution to allow the importation of such wines into the EU was reached in the mid 1990s.

For details of **fractional blending**, see SOLERA. For an alternative approach, in which grape varieties are mixed before fermentation, see CO-FERMENTATION.

blind tasting, form of wine TASTING in which the taster attempts to evaluate and/or identify wines without knowing their identity. Only by blind tasting can a true assessment of a wine's style and quality be made, so subjective is the wine-tasting process. Many professional tastings, those designed to make significant judgements about quality and possibly value, are therefore conducted blind. A comparative tasting, for example, comprises a group of wines of the same approximate age and provenance served blind together in order to evaluate them without prejudicial knowledge of their identity.

Blind tasting with the sole purpose of identification is a particularly masochistic but potentially rewarding exercise, conducted sometimes round the dining table, sometimes in the examination room (as part of a MASTER OF WINE exam, for example). The blind taster generally attempts to identify VINE VARIETY, geographical provenance, and VINTAGE. The first of these should be the easiest but, while wines from different varieties are generally considered to be distinctive, trained tasters have been found unable correctly to identify varieties in University of California blind-tasting tests. The percentage of correct identification was high for characteristic varieties such as Muscat at 59%; the success rate with Cabernet Sauvignon was 39%, while some minor varieties could not be identified at all.

In some cases, a wine's geographical provenance can be easier to detect than specific grape variety or blend of varieties. Red bordeaux and white Alsace, for example, tend to express place before grape.

In identifying vintage and general maturity, a wine's COLOUR can be particularly helpful, although, given the extent of vintage variation, a vintage several years from the actual one may well be a better guess than the vintage either side of it. Blind tasting does not usually involve blindfolding the taster (although if this is done, many tasters can even be confused as to whether a wine is red or white, particularly if the wines have similar weight and genetic antecedents as in red and white burgundy). Common practice is to disguise labels or even whole bottles by swathing them in foil, paper, or fabric and identifying them simply by number. A

tasting is said to be **single blind** if the tasters know what is being tasted but not which wine is which, whereas in a **double blind** tasting no clues are given.

The OPTIONS GAME was devised by Len EVANS as a way of combining the arcane process of blind tasting with general entertainment. Beginners often make the best blind tasters; experience can confuse.

blogs, wine. See INFORMATION TECHNOLOGY and SOCIAL MEDIA. For **wine bloggers**, see WINE WRITERS.

bloom on a grape's skin (*pruine* in French) is the whitish covering consisting of waxes and cutin which protects the berry against water loss and helps stop the penetration of spores. Blooming is another term for FLOWERING.

blue fining, largely outmoded though still used winemaking process whereby excess COPPER and IRON are removed from wine by FINING with potassium ferrocyanide. The process works because soluble copper and iron form insoluble compounds with the ferrocyanide ion. A century ago, before STAINLESS STEEL was widely available, winery equipment was often made of iron, copper, or bronze, an alloy of copper and tin. They would be attacked by the ACIDS in wine. Wines containing more than 10 mg/l of iron or 0.25 mg/l of copper could easily form a haze, so blue fining was needed to remove the excess copper and iron dissolved from the equipment after prolonged contact with the metals.

The process was developed by the German chemist Möslinger at the end of the 19th century and is still legally used, under strict controls, in many countries. In contemporary winemaking, iron may be introduced from metal grape bins and from BENTONITE fining; vineyard sprays such as BORDEAUX MIXTURE are still a common source of copper. Because of fears that hydrogen cyanide could be formed from potassium ferrocyanide, the use of blue fining is a major regulatory issue for wine treatments internationally and is illegal in many countries. A.D.W. & P.J.W.

Blue Nun, the most successful German wine BRAND, and for most of the 20th century a LIEBFRAUMILCH owned by H. SICHEL Söhne of Mainz. It was launched with the 1921 vintage in 1923 as a more accessible product than the host of German bottles adorned with Gothic script and long, complicated names. A label was developed for the easy, medium-dry style of young white wine sold in inns throughout Germany which initially showed several nuns in brown habits against a bright blue sky. The label, and subsequently the brand, became known as Blue Nun, featuring a single, alluring nun in a blue habit. Long before MATEUS Rosé, Blue Nun became a substantial commercial success as a result of heavy investment in advertising which preyed on the fears of what was then an unsophisticated wine drinking public. Blue Nun was advertised as the wine you could drink 'right through the meal', thereby solving the awkward problem of FOOD AND WINE MATCHING. It began to grow rapidly, mainly in Britain and America, in the 1950s when German wines enjoyed greater prestige than they do today and Blue Nun commanded about the same price as a SECOND GROWTH red bordeaux. At its zenith, in 1984/5, annual sales in the US alone were 1.25 million cases, with a further 750,000 cases sold elsewhere. Quality was reliably high, despite the quantities needed to satisfy world sales, and blending at the Mainz headquarters was conscientiously undertaken. A static wine market, economic recession, and increasing sophistication on the part of wine consumers saw worldwide sales fall to well under a million cases in the 1990s. H. Sichel Söhne and the Blue Nun brand were bought by F. W. Langguth Erben in 1995. The brand was relaunched and by 2014 its principal variants were Riesling (in bottle and BOX), 'Authentic White', and Sweet Red.

blush wine is a very pale pink popular American speciality made, rather like France's VIN GRIS, by using black-skinned grapes as if to make white wine. A marketing triumph emanating from California in the late 1980s (the name was originally coined by Mill Creek winery but the style was promulgated by Bob Trinchero of Sutter Home), it differs from ROSÉ mainly in ethos rather than substance, having become fashionable just when and where rosé was losing its market appeal (although a blush wine is likely to be perceptibly paler than a rosé). WHITE ZINFANDEL was initially the dominant type in this class, but it spawned many other pinks-from-reds such as VARIETALS labelled White Grenache, Cabernet Blanc, and Merlot Blanc, as well as GENERICS and wines made from HYBRID grapes such as MARÉCHAL FOCH and CHAMBOURCIN. Most are sweet, vaguely aromatic, and faintly fizzy. Blush wines' share of all wine consumed in the US was 22% in the late 1990s but by 2014 many consumers had graduated to drier, smarter rosés. See also SAIGNÉE.

B.C.C. & L.M.

Boal, often Anglicized to Bual, is the MADEIRA name for the MALVASIA Fina grape. Most of the Boal growing to a limited extent on Madeira today—though not nearly as limited as the island's other three 'noble' varieties—is **Boal Cachudo**. Portugal's Instituto da Vinha e do Vinho (IVV) lists four other subvarieties of Boal: **Boal Barreiro**, **Boal Branco**, **Boal Espinho**, and **Boal Ratinho.**

Bobal, a very important Spanish dark-skinned grape variety which produces deep-coloured red wines and even GRAPE CONCENTRATE in south east Spain, substantially but by no means exclusively for BULK WINE production. In 2011 its plantings still totalled 67,411 ha/ 166,505 acres, making it Spain's second most planted red wine grape after Tempranillo. Its reputation has been growing as producers such as Mustiguillo have managed to fashion velvety reds from high-ELEVATION vineyards in UTIEL-REQUENA. It retains its acidity better than MONASTRELL, which tends to be grown in slightly warmer, more southerly parts of Spain, and is notably lower in alcohol. It is allowed in four DO areas: Utiel-Requena, VALENCIA, MANCHUELA, and RIBERA DEL JÚCAR. Drought-resistant, and always grown as unirrigated bush vines, Bobal is extremely sensitive to springtime cold spells. Young vines may ripen unevenly. Although more rustic than the internationally famous Grenache and Monastrell, Bobal wines are fresher, with fine colour, a good dark berry component, and an ability to transmit terroir.

Bobal Blanco, also known as Tortosí, is still grown to a limited extent in Valencia but is Alcañón and not related to Bobal.

Boca, rare but historically important red wine DOC in the Novara Hills in the north of PIEMONTE, comprising 12 ha/30 acres divided among six producers. Nebbiolo grapes, called SPANNA here, should comprise 70 to 90% of these intriguing reds. Although marginal in size, Boca produces such good wines, notably Le Piane's, that they are attracting international attention.

Bocksbeutel, special bottle in the shape of a flattened flask used in the German wine region of FRANKEN and four communes in the northern Ortenau area of BADEN. The name probably derived from the Low German *Bocksbeutel*, a pouch to carry prayer-books and the like, rather than from any ostensible resemblance to a goat's scrotum (the literal translation). From the early 18th century onwards, the orginal purpose of the special bottle was to guarantee the authenticity of Würzburger Steinwein. Only after the First World War did it become common throughout Franken.

T.S. & D.Ds.

BOD, biological oxygen demand. See WINERY WASTE.

bodega, Spanish term for a wine CELLAR, a WINERY, or a tavern or grocery store selling wine.

body, tasting term for the perceived 'weight'—the sensation of fullness, resulting from DENSITY or VISCOSITY—of a wine on the palate. Wines at either end of the scale are described as **full bodied** and **light bodied.**

Next to water, ALCOHOL is the major constituent of wines. It has a much higher viscosity than water and is the major component responsible for the sensation of fullness, or body, as a wine is rinsed around the mouth. ALCOHOLIC STRENGTH is therefore clearly an important factor: the more potent a wine the more full bodied it is usually said to be.

Sweet wines are not necessarily full bodied (ASTI, for example, is sweet but very light bodied, thanks to its low alcohol content).

Contrary to popular conception, GLYCEROL makes only a very minor contribution to density, viscosity, and therefore to body (although it does have a slight effect on apparent sweetness).

Body is not related to wine quality, BALANCE and HARMONY being more important in a wine than whether it is full or light-bodied. One of the less desirable effects of the increase in comparative TASTING, however, is that full-bodied wines make a more obvious impression and have therefore tended to be glorified.

Amerine, M. A., and Roessler, E. B., *Wines: Their Sensory Evaluation* (2nd edn, New York, 1982).

Bohemia, western part of the CZECH REPUBLIC that is better known for the production of beer and GLASSES than for wine. There are some small vineyard areas around the towns of Mělník and Roudnice, and the Lobkowicz estates in particular have made some good-quality red wine. A substantial business making sparkling wines, generally from imported base wine, is based in the region.

bois noir. See GRAPEVINE YELLOWS.

Boisset, Burgundy's largest wine producer and one of the world's largest family-owned producers of good quality wine, with wineries in Burgundy, Beaujolais, the Rhône Valley, the south of France, and in California's Napa Valley, Russian River Valley, Sonoma Valley, and Monterey.

It was formed as recently as 1961 by Jean-Claude and Claudine Boisset when Jean-Claude was just 18. The early business was successful enough to acquire rival NÉGOCIANTS Charles Viénot and Thomas-Bassot in 1982. The company was floated on the stock market in 1985 and took over Pierre Ponnelle, Morin Père et Fils, Jaffelin, and Bouchard Aîné during the next six years. In 1994 the company then diversified into sparkling wine production via such acquisitions as Varichon et Clerc and Charles de Fère while consolidating its Côte de Beaune holdings by buying Ropiteau Frères, followed in the late 1990s by the Cellier de Samsons and Mommessin in Beaujolais, J. Moreau in Chablis, Domaine Bernard (now Louis Bernard) in the Rhône, and the fruit liqueur business L'Héritier-Guyot. Further acquisitions in Beaujolais and the Languedoc, including Caroline de

Beaulieu, followed. In 1998, Boisset formed its first overseas JOINT VENTURE to build Le Clos Jordanne winery with VINCOR of Canada, now part of CONSTELLATION. Others followed in 2003 with Pisano in Uruguay to form Progreso and Corpora in Chile to form Veranda. That same year the Boisset family regained full ownership of the company, now styled *négociant-éleveur* with a commitment to ORGANIC and BIODYNAMIC VITICULTURE in its flagship 40-ha/99-acre vineyard holding Domaine de la Vougeraie. The term '*viniculteur*' was coined to stress Boisset's degree of control of quality in vineyards both owned and bought from.

Having abandoned its joint ventures in Canada and South America, the company has determinedly expanded into California, building a Franco-American identity from 1992 with the acquisition of Lyeth Estate in the Alexander Valley. This was followed in 2003 by DeLoach in the Russian River Valley, Raymond in the Napa Valley in 2009, Sonoma's Buena Vista (California's first winery), and Monterey's Lockwood Vineyards in 2011. Also in 2011, Skalli, based in Sète in the LANGUEDOC, joined what has come to be known as the Boisset Collection. Jean-Charles Boisset is married to Gina GALLO.

Bolgheri

Bolgheri, small town in the Tuscan MAREMMA made famous by Marchese Mario Incisa della Rocchetta, who planted Cabernet Sauvignon vines for a house wine as early as the 1940s on his San Guido estate, labelling the resulting wine SASSICAIA. Bizarrely, the DOC created for Bolgheri in 1983 was only for whites and rosé, but it was amended in 1994 to include red wine and the subzone Sassicaia was created. Prior to this Sassicaia had to be labelled as VINO DA TAVOLA, but due to its high quality it became known as a SUPERTUSCAN, spawning many copies throughout Tuscany. The success of Sassicaia, Grattamacco (first vintage 1982), and ORNELLAIA (1985) triggered an investment frenzy in the region, which expanded from 250 ha/618 acres at the end of the 1990s to more than 1,000 ha/2,470 acres in 2010 when it was home to more than 50 wine estates. The proximity to the sea gives a more temperate climate than that found in the central Tuscan hills, resulting in grapes that ripen earlier, often before the autumn rains arrive.

The DOC's red wine production is based on Cabernet Sauvignon and Merlot, which are allowed as varietal wines or blends, while the indigenous Sangiovese may comprise no more than 50% of the wines. Unsurprisingly, most estates produce a classic BORDEAUX BLEND aged in BARRIQUES, a model which initially seemed to guarantee commercial success. The wines are generally of a high quality, but styles differ due to the diverse soil composition and location of the vineyards as well as differences in

winemaking. Although once hailed as one of Italy's future fine-wine regions, the lower elevations have proved too warm to produce wines of sufficient elegance to mimic Bordeaux, which seems to be the objective of most producers here.   W.S.

Masnaghetti, A., *Bolgheri—Cellars and Vineyards* (Monza, 2009) E-Book.

Bolivia

Bolivia in SOUTH AMERICA has a long history of vine-growing but its modern wine industry is very small. Viticulture was brought to Bolivia from neighbouring PERU in the 16th century by Spanish settlers and Catholic MISSIONARIES. Between 1550 and 1570 the first vineyards were established in the foothills of Sutó surrounding the recently founded Spanish city of Santa Cruz de la Sierra, and in the Luribay Canyon, south east of the city of La Paz. However, Bolivian viticulture really flourished two decades later, when the high valleys of the eastern slopes of the Andes were conquered. In 1595, there were vineyards in full production in the valley of the Mizque River, whence they expanded south to Tarija and east to Vallegrande by 1600, and thereafter to the districts of Tomina, Pilaya, Paspalla, Cinti, and Samaipata.

PHYLLOXERA and NEMATODES severely hampered Bolivian viticulture in much of the 20th century. Resistant ROOTSTOCKS and good-quality VINIFERA cuttings were imported in the 1980s in an effort to restore vineyard health and the proportion of grafted vines is increasing.

Bolivia produced only about 60,000 hl/1.6 million gal of wine in 2013. Of the 3,000 ha/7,400 acres under vine, 78% are in the Tarija region close to the Argentine border and 10% in Cinti slightly further north. The smaller vineyard area further north in the Valles Cruceños (8%), in the highlands south west of the city of Santa Cruz de la Sierra, is expected to expand in the near future.

The climate in Tarija is both CONTINENTAL and TROPICAL, modified by ELEVATION, so that the vines in the high Andean valleys are planted at 1,600 to 2,500 m/5,250 to 8,200 ft above sea level with very significant diurnal TEMPERATURE VARIABILITY and the risk of both FROST and HAIL. Tarija would be classified as Region III or IV according to the WINKLER system, and annual RAINFALL averages 300 to 500 mm/19 in. Conditions in Cinti are similar to those of Tarija except that it is even hotter with an average temperature of 23 °C (73 °F) rather than 18.2 °C (66.5 °F). Rain can be concentrated in the early months of the year, encouraging FUNGAL DISEASES. The traditional system of training vines up the indigenous pepper tree (*Schinus molle*) helped retard the development of such diseases, but ESPALIER vine-training systems, with a VINE DENSITY of 3,000 to 3,500 vines per ha, are more common. IRRIGATION is widely practised.

Kohlberg, Bolivia's largest winery, was instrumental in introducing modern winemaking equipment from Argentina in the late 1960s. La Concepción, one of Tarija's large producers, brought in virus-free CLONES from California in the late 1970s, and also buys CRIOLLA grapes from vines trained up trees at elevations up to 2,850 m/9,350 ft in Toropalca to the north. The quality gap between big and small producers is decreasing but the latter tend to sell most of their wine locally. Development funding from the Netherlands is helping Bolivian producers build an export programme and establish a generic organization to promote their wines.

MUSCAT OF ALEXANDRIA represents about 80% of all light-coloured VINIFERA grape varieties planted, and is widely used for distillation into the aromatic local brandy singani, which can be a fine counterpart to the PISCO of Peru and Chile. Table wines are also produced from Muscat, although plantings of a wide range of other varieties associated throughout the world with good-quality red and white wine are increasing. Some creditable Cabernet and Cabernet blends are produced, as well as examples of varietal Malbec, Tannat, Sauvignon Blanc, Riesling, and Torrontés.

The wine produced for domestic consumption by foot treading and vinification in clay jars is called *patero*.

Goldstein, E., *South American Wines* (Oakland, Calif., 2014).

Bollinger

Bollinger, family-owned Champagne house producing a range of top-quality wines based on Pinot Noir grapes. Bollinger was formed from the de Villermont family's holdings in the village of Aÿ near Epernay, where the company is still based. In 1829, Jacques Joseph Placide Bollinger formed a partnership with Amiral Comte Athanase Louis Emmanuel de Villermont and Paul-Joseph Renaudin to form the house of Champagne Renaudin, Bollinger & Cie. In 1837, Jacques Bollinger married de Villermont's daughter Louise Charlotte and became a French citizen. In 1865, the house started to ship low-DOSAGE champagne to Britain, which was unusual for a period in which most champagne reaching the country was sweet. Champagne Bollinger received the Royal Warrant as Official Purveyor of Champagne to Queen Victoria in 1884.

Control of the house eventually passed to Jacques's grandson (also named Jacques), who died young, leaving his widow Elizabeth 'Lily' Bollinger (1899–1977) in charge. Madame Bollinger oversaw the family vineyards on foot and bicycle for four decades, enduring the 1944 German bombardment of Aÿ while sleeping in the Bollinger cellars. After the Second World War, she increased the house's vineyard holdings, which in 2014 stood at 164 ha/405 acres, providing around 60% of its needs. By the time of her death in 1977, Madame Bollinger had seen sales double to 1 million bottles a year. She believed that nothing should change the traditional Bollinger style, and to this day the following five rules are obeyed: a majority of grapes from the house's own vineyards, 85% of which are Grand and Premier Cru; Pinot Noir dominance in the blend; BARREL FERMENTATION in over 3,000 old barrels to encourage MICRO-OXYGENATION; reserve wines aged in magnums; and bottle ageing for two to three times longer than required, even for the non-vintage Special Cuvée. Bollinger RD ('recently disgorged', with marked AUTOLYSIS as a result of being aged for a minimum of eight years) was introduced by Madame Bollinger with the 1952 vintage. Rarest of all Bollinger champagnes is the Vieilles Vignes Françaises, a BLANC DE NOIRS produced exclusively from ungrafted Pinot Noir vines that grow in two walled vineyards were never affected by PHYLLOXERA.

The Bollinger family company, Société Jacques Bollinger, acquired Burgundy producer Chanson in 1999. It also owns a majority stake in the SAUMUR house Langlois-Chateau, as well as a minority stake in the cognac house Delamain. In 2005 the company bought their neighbouring house in Aÿ, Champagne Ayala, one of the original GRANDES MARQUES.

See also CHAMPAGNE.

Ray, C., *Bollinger: Tradition of a Champagne Family* (3rd edn, London, 1988).

Bolognesi, Colli, small DOC zone in the hills of Bologna in north central Italy. See EMILIA-ROMAGNA for more details.

Bolzano, or Bozen in German, the main town of ALTO ADIGE in northern Italy. Local light red wines with a minimum of 85% SCHIAVA (Vernatch) may carry the name **Colli di Bolzano** or **Bozner Leiten**.

Bombino Bianco, was planted on 1,229 ha/3,036 acres of southern Italy, mainly in PUGLIA, in 2010. In ABRUZZO it is regularly confused with, and may even be identical to, TREBBIANO d'Abruzzo.

It ripens late and yields extremely high quantities of relatively neutral wine. Some of its synonyms, Pagedebit ('it pays the debts') and Straccia Cambiale ('tear up the invoices') in particular, allude to its profitability to the vine-grower. The dark-berried Puglian **Bombino Nero**, planted on almost as much vineyard, may well be related.

Bonarda, Italian red grape variety, or more accurately the name of three distinct Italian varieties: (1) the Bonarda of the OLTREPÒ PAVESE and COLLI PIACENTINI (also planted in southern PUGLIA), which is, in fact, not Bonarda at all but rather the CROATINA grape; (2) the **Bonarda Novarese**, used to soften SPANNA in its range of

DOC reds in the Novara and Vercelli hills, which again is not Bonarda, but UVA RARA, a variety more widely employed in the Oltrepò Pavese; and (3) the so-called **Bonarda Piemontese**, an aromatic variety which has been virtually abandoned because of its small bunches and low productivity, although it covered 30% of the region's vineyard before the advent of PHYLLOXERA. Scattered patches remain on the left bank of the Tanaro, particularly in the township of Govone, and the Italian vine census of 2010 found 749 ha/1,850 acres of 'Bonarda Nera', very much less than Croatina but more than Uva Rara. The only DOC wines in production which bear the name Bonarda are from the Oltrepò Pavese and are, confusingly, made from Croatina.

Bonarda is also the name of the second most widely grown red wine grape variety, after Malbec, in ARGENTINA, where total plantings had grown to 18,127 ha/44,774 acres by 2011, which means that Argentina has far more 'Bonarda' planted than Italy, although DNA PROFILING has shown that Argentine Bonarda is unrelated to any of the Italian Bonardas and is in fact identical to California's CHARBONO, which is the Douce Noire of Savoie. The variety makes particularly exuberant, fruity wines for relatively early consumption.

bonbonne, a large glass jar or carboy, also known as a demijohn, typically holding 25 l/6.6 gal, used as a neutral container to store wine, VIN DOUX NATUREL, or brandy, often after a period of wood ageing.

bonded warehouse, one in which no DUTY has been paid on the goods inside it. Prices for wines and, especially, spirits held **in bond** (IB) are therefore considerably lower than those quoted duty paid. It is sensible for any foreigner buying wine to store for possible shipment outside that country to buy it **in bond**.

Bondola, traditional *V. vinifera* grape of SWITZERLAND's Ticino, where it may be an ingredient in the local blend called Nostrano. Largely replaced by Merlot.

Bonnes Mares, great red GRAND CRU in Burgundy's CÔTE D'OR. For more details, see CHAMBOLLE-MUSIGNY and MOREY-ST-DENIS.

Bonnezeaux, particularly well-favoured enclave for sweet white wine production within the Coteaux du LAYON appellation in the ANJOU district of the Loire. In this respect Bonnezeaux resembles QUARTS DE CHAUME to the north west but, perhaps because of its greater extent (just under 100 ha/247 acres) spread across three south-facing *buttes* (small hills) of SCHIST and QUARTZ and much more exposed situation, it has not enjoyed such fame. A Bonnezeaux from a producer as reliable as Ch de Fesles can be a deep green-gold nectar at 10 to 20 years old. The wines are made exclusively

from Chenin Blanc grapes grown on steep slopes near Thouarcé. These grapes should ideally be attacked by NOBLE ROT, sometimes concentrated by shrivelling on the vine, and at the very least have been picked only after several TRIES through the vineyard. Yields average only about 22 hl/ha. See also LOIRE, including map.

books on wine. See the LITERATURE OF WINE and WINE WRITING. For references to wine in some more obviously literary works, see ENGLISH LITERATURE, WINE IN.

Borba, DOP subregion of ALENTEJO in southern Portugal.

Bordeaux, important French port on the GARONNE River leading to the GIRONDE Estuary on the west coast. Bordeaux gives its name to a wine region that includes the vineyards of the Gironde *département* and, as such, the wine region that produces more top-quality wine than any other, from a total vineyard area that ballooned in the mid 2000s to about 124,000 ha/276,760 acres but was down to about 112,000 ha/276,570 acres by 2014, divided among about 6,800 increasingly impoverished producers as the PRICE gap widened between the most famous wines and the rest. Bordeaux has a higher proportion of large estates than any other French wine region, and produces more of the world's FINE wine and TROPHY WINES than anywhere else. The most famous examples represent less than 5% of the region's total production, however, and Bordeaux's most pressing long-term problem has been selling the other 95% profitably. The best red bordeaux, known by the British as CLARET, are characterized by their subtlety and ability to evolve after years, sometimes decades, of BOTTLE AGEING. The worst can be thin and evanescent. The producers in between suffer because there are simply too many of them to make much impact.

The proportion of bordeaux that is white has fallen from about a quarter in the 1990s to just over 10%, just under a quarter of which is sweet, in the early 21st century. Small quantities of rosé, light red CLAIRET, and sparkling CRÉMANT are also made. The total quantity of wine produced each year varies considerably according to VINTAGE but currently averages about 5.5 million hl, which represents more than a quarter of France's total AOC wine production. See BORDEAUX AOC for bordeaux wine at its most basic, BORDEAUX, CÔTES DE for a group of right-bank appellations, BORDEAUX TRADE for an account of the workings of the wine trade in Bordeaux, and BORDEAUX, UNIVERSITY OF for details of its important contribution to wine ACADEME.

History to medieval times

The Latin poet Ausonius (*c*.AD 310–393/4) is not only the first author to mention that wine

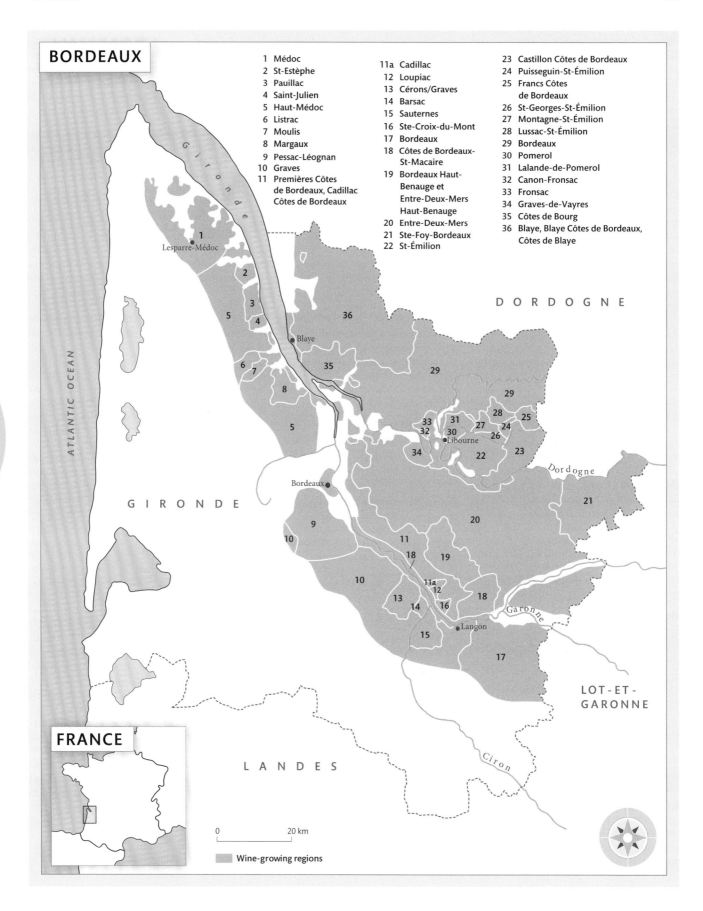

BORDEAUX

1 Médoc
2 St-Estèphe
3 Pauillac
4 Saint-Julien
5 Haut-Médoc
6 Listrac
7 Moulis
8 Margaux
9 Pessac-Léognan
10 Graves
11 Premières Côtes de Bordeaux, Cadillac Côtes de Bordeaux
11a Cadillac
12 Loupiac
13 Cérons/Graves
14 Barsac
15 Sauternes
16 Ste-Croix-du-Mont
17 Bordeaux
18 Côtes de Bordeaux-St-Macaire
19 Bordeaux Haut-Benauge et Entre-Deux-Mers Haut-Benauge
20 Entre-Deux-Mers
21 Ste-Foy-Bordeaux
22 St-Émilion
23 Castillon Côtes de Bordeaux
24 Puisseguin-St-Émilion
25 Francs Côtes de Bordeaux
26 St-Georges-St-Émilion
27 Montagne-St-Émilion
28 Lussac-St-Émilion
29 Bordeaux
30 Pomerol
31 Lalande-de-Pomerol
32 Canon-Fronsac
33 Fronsac
34 Graves-de-Vayres
35 Côtes de Bourg
36 Blaye, Blaye Côtes de Bordeaux, Côtes de Blaye

DORDOGNE

ATLANTIC OCEAN

GIRONDE

Lesparre-Médoc

Blaye

Libourne

Bordeaux

Langon

Dordogne

LOT-ET-GARONNE

LANDES

Ciron

FRANCE

0   20 km

Wine-growing regions

was grown in his native Bordeaux, he was also the region's first known wine-grower. In his poem 'De herediolo' ('On his small inheritance'), dated 379, he tells us that he grows 100 *iugera* (a *iugerum* is approximately two-thirds of an acre or 0.25 ha) of vines. His estate was probably at Bazas, near the river Garonne (although some have suggested St-Émilion). In two of his other poems, 'Mosella' ('On the Moselle'), and 'Ordo urbium nobilium' ('The list of distinguished cities'), he describes the banks of the Garonne overgrown with vines. Ch AUSONE is named after him.

Although Ausonius' descriptions indicate that viticulture was well established in Bordeaux in his lifetime, no definite earlier evidence exists. Given that the Allobroges tribe were growing wine around Vienne in the RHÔNE Valley in the 1st century AD, the Bituriges may have been doing the same in Bordeaux, but Strabo, author of the *Geography* (completed in 7 BC), merely says that Bordeaux ('Burdigala' in Latin and in Strabo's Greek) was a place of commerce, and PLINY, writing *c.*AD 77, does not tell us clearly that the Bituriges grew wine (although he does refer to a Biturica vine, which may have been associated with either the Bituriges tribe of Bordeaux or the other to the west of Bourges), so the likelihood is that viticulture spread to Bordeaux after it had come to the Rhône.

We know little about Bordeaux in the centuries following the fall of the Roman empire. The area was overrun by the Visigoths in the 5th century and when Clovis had defeated the Visigoths in 507 it became part of the Frankish kingdom. CHARLEMAGNE is said to have displayed a temporary interest in FRONSAC. With the economic expansion in Europe which started in the 11th century, demand for wine grew. Initially, the new port of LA ROCHELLE, on the Atlantic coast north of Bordeaux, brought wealth to the region in the 12th century; consequently, Bordeaux increased both its trade and its production. By 1200 wine was grown in BLAYE, BOURG, the lower DORDOGNE and the Garonne Valley, and in the GRAVES. The Graves was the largest producer, with Ch Pape-Clément its oldest named vineyard. In 1305 Archbishop Bertrand de Goth, who was to become Pope Clement V, presented it to the see of Bordeaux. Throughout the Bordeaux region more red wine was grown than white, but SAUTERNES and CÉRONS probably had white wine, although these white wines cannot have been like the botrytis-affected wines of today, for the deliberate commercial use of NOBLE ROT in Sauternes and Cérons dates from after the Middle Ages. Until the late 17th century the MÉDOC was too marshy to produce much wine and was known mainly for its corn: there were just a few vineyards in what is now called the Bas-Médoc, north of ST-ESTÈPHE. ST-ÉMILION was already a wine-growing district, however. Some of the wine of Bordeaux was neither white nor red but a mixture of white and red grapes fermented together called 'clairet' in Old French, which is the origin of the modern English word CLARET.

Bordeaux's pre-eminence began as a result of the English connection. In 1152, Eleanor of Aquitaine married Henry Plantagenet, who in 1154 became king of England (and duke of Normandy) as well as acquiring Eleanor's territories, GASCONY and most of western France. In order to win the favour of the citizens of Bordeaux, King John (1199–1216) granted them numerous privileges. The most important of these was exemption from the Grand Coutume, the export tax imposed on ships sailing from Bordeaux. Also, Gascon merchants were given favoured treatment in London. All this made Gascon wine cheaper for the English than any other imported wine. In the 14th century, most French wine consumed in England was from Gascony, and a quarter of Bordeaux's wine exports went to England. Against these protective measures La Rochelle could not compete, despite its superior position right on the coast, while Bordeaux was 60 miles/100 km up river. And when La Rochelle fell to the French in 1224, it ceased to be a commercial threat to Bordeaux.

Not all the wines sold by the Gascon merchants were from the immediate Bordeaux area. In the HAUT PAYS (Gaillac, Quercy, Nérac, and Bergerac) the climate was more reliable and these wines were stronger than those of Bordeaux. The Haut Pays wines were more expensive because they were taxed in Bordeaux; and those from the parts of the Haut Pays which had fallen to the French were not allowed into Bordeaux until St Martin's Day, 11 November, or even until Christmas, so that Bordeaux wines dominated the wines available for the fleet which arrived each autumn to deliver the year's new wine to England, Scotland, Ireland, the Low Countries, and the Hanseatic ports.

In 1453, at the end of the HUNDRED YEARS WAR, Gascony reverted to French rule; yet its trade with England soon picked up again, even though it never regained its 14th-century volume. Bordeaux had been a major port before it became a wine-producing area to feed its wine trade. Its winemakers were not patient monks, as they had often been in Burgundy, but opportunistic laymen, whose aim was to cash in on the huge demand for Bordeaux's chief export product, and so they switched from grain to wine. The thin wines of Bordeaux, which before the advent of glass BOTTLES and CORKS did not last from one vintage to the next, cannot have been anything like modern bordeaux.   H.M.W.

James, M. K., *Studies in the Medieval Wine Trade* (Oxford, 1971).

Penning-Rowsell, E., *The Wines of Bordeaux* (6th edn, London, 1989).

Simon, A. L., *The History of the Wine Trade in England*, 3 vols. (London, 1906–9).

Modern history

Trade with Britain continued after the English were expelled, but the DUTCH WINE TRADE gradually became dominant, not so much in wines for their own consumption but in inexpensive white wines for the rest of northern Europe and the Hanseatic states. The Bordeaux merchants had to fight hard to maintain their position in northern Europe, for the Dutch also bought from the Mediterranean countries.

It was the Dutch who drained the marshy MÉDOC in the mid 17th century, thereby creating the basis for the fine wines that made Bordeaux's reputation throughout the world. Before this the best wines were to be found in the well-drained GRAVES near the city, notably Ch HAUT-BRION. Today's leading Médocain estates—Chx LAFITE, LATOUR, and MARGAUX— were probably planted in the last third of the 17th century, and reached England, to be offered at auction in the COFFEE HOUSES of London, only after consignments had been captured at sea in the Anglo-French wars at the beginning of the 18th century.

The simultaneous trade war between Britain and France led to ever-increasing duties on French wines and the Anglo-Portuguese Methuen Treaty of 1703. In return for a Portuguese promise to admit British woollen goods in perpetuity, the British government agreed that duty on French wines should never be less than 50% higher than on the wines of Portugal (and, in fact, Spain). Officially, British wine imports from Bordeaux declined sharply but smuggling must have been rife, to judge from the prevalence of bordeaux in the household sales conducted by Christie's (see AUCTIONS) after their foundation in 1766. Conditions in both Bordeaux and Britain were ripe for the development of trade in fine CLARET: in the Gironde there was a new affluent bourgeoisie, members of the legal Bordeaux Parlement, with the means to plant and maintain expensive vineyards, while in Britain bordeaux's almost exclusive market was created by a wealthy, landowning aristocracy and, soon, the new industrial middle class.

The necessary link was a Bordeaux merchant class, sufficiently well established to be able to buy, cellar, and export these 'new French clarets'. These merchants came largely from the British Isles, and Germany, which had long been prominent in the inexpensive red bordeaux trade. BARTON & Guestier originally started in 1725; William, later Nathaniel, Johnston began in 1734; and BROKERS Tastet & Lawton in 1740. These are some of the longer survivors of many more. The German firms of standing appear to have arrived later: CRUSE from Danish Schleswig-Holstein, later incorporated into Germany, arrived in 1819; Eschenauer in 1821; and Kressmann in 1858. A substantial French merchant, with its roots in the RHÔNE Valley, was Calvet, which opened a Bordeaux office in 1870. It is also significant that the trade's 'bible' was the creation, in 1850, of an English teacher, Charles Cocks (see FÉRET).

Until well into the second half of the 20th century, most of these firms had their premises in the suburb of Les Chartrons, named after a medieval Carthusian monastery. The Quai des Chartrons, facing the River Garonne, and its side streets, was the headquarters of the so-called *aristocratie du bouchon* (aristocracy of the cork).

In 1852, Bordeaux was struck by oidium, or POWDERY MILDEW, the first of a series of vine plagues which were to devastate many other wine regions too. First noted in the sweet wine areas near the Garonne, it spread through the Graves and then into the Médoc. Between 1854 and 1856, all the properties which were rated CLASSED GROWTHS in the 1855 CLASSIFICATION produced a total of only 3,400 TONNEAUX of wine, not much more than half the crop in a prolific year. By 1858 this fungal disease was conquered by spraying with SULFUR, a practice which continues to this day (see below).

Trade with Britain increased as a result of the Anglo-French Treaty of 1860, for in the following year Gladstone, then Chancellor of the Exchequer, reduced duty on French wines to 2d. (less than 1p) a bottle. This was a particularly prosperous time for Bordeaux, which had also developed substantial markets in South America and Russia, and a small one in North America.

However, the severe onset of PHYLLOXERA in the late 1870s, followed by DOWNY MILDEW in the next decade, proved a serious setback to the trade in everyday GENERIC red and white bordeaux. For the first time ever an import BOND was established in Bordeaux, largely supplied with blending wine from the new vineyards of ALGERIA. On the other hand, excessive FERTILIZATION by important châteaux proprietors to compensate for losses by disease led to large crops of inferior quality and to a fall in reputation and price. In 1910, nevertheless, two out of every three bottles of French wine imported into Britain came from the Gironde. They totalled 110,000 hl/2.9 million gal, approximately the same as for BELGIUM, although Germany imported almost twice as much. In 1911, the Gironde *département* was delimited, leading eventually to the establishment of Bordeaux's APPELLATION CONTRÔLÉE system in 1936.

A serious slump followed soon after the First World War, with many châteaux changing hands, and this continued in the 1930s. After the First World War, the Russian market had disappeared, the South American one was much reduced, and the US market was closed

by PROHIBITION between 1919 and 1933, when it hardly had time to recover before the Second World War.

At this time the market for fine wines was largely confined to the Médoc and the châteaux in the Graves near to Bordeaux. It was not until after the Second World War—during which Bordeaux, and many large châteaux, were occupied by the German army—that any ST-ÉMILION property other than Ch CHEVAL BLANC was widely known outside France, and the same was true of POMEROL, even Ch PETRUS, although there was a good market for inexpensive St-Émilions in Belgium.

It was not until the end of the 1950s that those châteaux with an international reputation made sufficient profits to begin serious replanting and the installation of modern equipment, notably FERMENTATION VESSELS made of STAINLESS STEEL, although this was an option which many châteaux, including Lafite, Margaux, and MOUTON-ROTHSCHILD, did not take. From the mid 1960s, the United States market became increasingly important, especially for the classed growths. This was particularly marked with the successful 1970 vintage when large American purchases were made as futures, EN PRIMEUR, followed some years later in Britain. Previously, if a vintage was considered likely to be very fine, the BORDEAUX TRADE would sometimes buy SUR SOUCHE, but otherwise a vintage would not be marketed until shortly before or after BOTTLING, either by the château or by the Bordeaux merchants. In 1972, CHÂTEAU BOTTLING became compulsory for the classed growths, and was generally applied to the more important properties in the Graves, St-Émilion, and Pomerol. The leading red and white Graves had first been classified in 1953, and the St-Émilions in 1955 (see CLASSIFICATIONS). The Pomerols remain unclassified.

These en primeur campaigns reflected the changed financial situation in Bordeaux (although the generic wines, accounting for up to half the annual crop, continued, and continue, to be sold chiefly within 12 months of the harvest). No longer could most châteaux afford to hold several vintages in stock; nor could the Bordeaux merchants or their customers in France or abroad. For the most part in the 1970s and 1980s, consumers had to bear the financial responsibility of AGEING young red bordeaux, and some leading sweet wines.

The 'energy crisis' of 1973, in which Middle East oil producers greatly raised their prices, caused havoc in Bordeaux, where recent vintages had been sold en primeur at excessively high prices. This had applied at all quality levels, and one result was that in order to meet contracts for generic red bordeaux the distinguished house of CRUSE had bought wine from outside the region, involving altered Appellation Contrôlée documents. A sharp fall in prices occurred, as well as subsequent mass disposals

of stock by both merchants and leading châteaux. Some of the traditional firms were saved from bankruptcy only by foreign ownership, and the old world of the Chartronnais disappeared for ever. Later, classed growth châteaux passed into the financial control of such outsiders as insurance companies (see AXA for example) and multinational corporations.

The succession of fine vintages in the 1980s improved the situation of many châteaux, but competition was so keen on the Bordeaux market that the merchants were unable as in the past to build up the financial reserves to tide them over poor years. So when Bordeaux was hit by the heavily FROST-DAMAGED 1991 vintage and the record, diluted 1992, the en primeur trade virtually ceased internationally, and considerable financial problems arose—although the chiefly domestic trade in generic and humble appellation wines continued much as usual.

From the 18th century until 1939, the Bordeaux trade normally called the price tune, and with the exception of the *belle époque* from 1858 to 1878 the château owners had to fall into line. For the 30 years from 1961, the leading proprietors then held the whip hand in allocating their new wines to more than 100 Bordeaux merchants. In the early 1990s, when Bordeaux had no great vintages to sell, power was transferred to the consumer. The number of potential purchasers of fine bordeaux grew substantially, however, in the mid 1990s when the exciting 1995 and 1996 vintages were available, in the United States and for the first time in ASIA. This, coupled with widespread economic boom, helped create an unprecedented price spiral in Bordeaux in the 2000s. It faltered temporarily as a result of the invasion of Iraq and financial turmoil in Asia, only to accelerate when the undoubted quality of the 2009 and 2010 vintages coincided with unprecedented, and short-term, interest from investors, many of them without any wine-trade experience, notably but not exclusively from CHINA, a market that had been courted assiduously by the Bordelais. Prices of these vintages subsequently stagnated or fell and the Bordelais were faced with the combination of a succession of lacklustre vintages and a lack of interest in their wines by many consumers, particularly younger ones.

E.P.-R. & J.R.

Brook, S., *The Complete Bordeaux* (rev. edn, London, 2010).

Faith, N., *The Winemasters* (3rd edn, London, 2005).

Penning-Rowsell, E., *The Wines of Bordeaux* (6th edn, London, 1989).

Geography

The wine districts of Bordeaux hug the Gironde estuary and the Rivers DORDOGNE and GARONNE which flow into it (see map on p. 90). The largest and most important appellation is BORDEAUX AOC, but there are nearly 50 appellations in all even if many of them are rarely seen outside the region. The notably flat Bordeaux vineyards are rarely at elevations of more than a few metres above sea level.

Conventionally, in terms of the all-important fine red wines at least, the whole region is split into 'left bank' and 'right bank', or MÉDOC and GRAVES on the west side of the Gironde, and St-Émilion and POMEROL on the east side, leaving the vast ENTRE-DEUX-MERS ('between two seas') district in the middle. Within the Haut-Médoc, the superior, higher land closer to Bordeaux, are the world-famous communes, south to north, MARGAUX, ST-JULIEN, PAUILLAC, and ST-ESTÈPHE, together with the slightly less illustrious and, significantly, more inland appellations of LISTRAC and MOULIS. Most of the finest wines of the Graves, on the other hand, have come from an enclave awarded its own appellation in 1987, PESSAC-LÉOGNAN. Pomerol and St-Émilion have their 'satellite' appellations: LALANDE-DE-POMEROL; and Montagne-St-Émilion, Lussac-St-Émilion, St-Georges-St-Émilion, and Puisseguin-St-Émilion (for details of which see ST-ÉMILION). And just west of Pomerol are the historic appellations of FRONSAC and Canon-Fronsac. Other appellations on the right bank of the Garonne are BOURG, BLAYE, grouped as CÔTES de Bordeaux. The GRAVES DE VAYRES enclave near Libourne remains resolutely outside the fold. Although a certain amount of white wine is made between the two rivers, most of Bordeaux's best white wines are made south of the river Garonne: dry wines from Graves and Pessac-Léognan, and sweet white wines which include some of the finest in the world from SAUTERNES and BARSAC. (See Climate below for a more detailed explanation.) Other, lesser sweet white appellations in the south east of the region are CADILLAC, CÉRONS, LOUPIAC, PREMIÈRES CÔTES DE BORDEAUX, *Sainte-Croix du Mont, and Sainte-Foy Bordeaux which can also be red.

The most famous vineyards are on particularly well-drained soils, notably gravels in the Médoc and Graves, and more calcareous terrain in parts of St-Émilion and Ste-Croix-du-Mont. For more details of local soils and conditions, see under these appellation names.

Climate
The mild climate of Bordeaux is tailor-made to produce mild wines, wines that are marked more by subtlety than power. (It is the vine varieties, described below, which endow the wines with longevity.) Unlike the much more CONTINENTAL climate of inland France, or the more arid Mediterranean influence in the south of the country, the vineyards of Bordeaux are moderated and heavily influenced by their proximity to the Atlantic, here warmed by the Gulf Stream, and this gentle oceanic regulation of the climate extends well inland, thanks to the

wide Gironde Estuary. Most years the MARITIME CLIMATE protects the vines from WINTER FREEZE (although February 1956 was so cold that many vines were killed) and spring FROST (although April 1991 was so cold that much of that year's growth was frozen to extinction and the crop much reduced).

Spring is generally mild and damp, providing ample supplies of water for the growing season. Bordeaux's climate is hardly marginal, in that most grapes are usually ripened, but the late-ripening Cabernet Sauvignon may not reach full ripeness everywhere every year and the region's weather is sufficiently unpredictable that the period of the FLOWERING in June is critical, with unsettled weather, especially cold rain and strong winds, seriously prejudicing the quantity of the forthcoming crop. COULURE and MILLERANDAGE are perennial threats, especially to the Merlot crop, although average rainfall in June is markedly lower than in any other month.

Summers are usually hot, with occasional storms but rarely prolonged rainfall. The forests of the Landes to the south help to moderate temperatures (and to protect the wine districts from strong winds off the Atlantic), which reach an average maximum of 26 °C/79 °F in August, the hottest month. July is usually the driest and sunniest month. Annual average sunshine is well over 2,000 hours. Increasingly, however, during July and August it can be so hot and dry and the vines suffer such WATER STRESS that the ripening process stops altogether. HEAT STRESS may be such that vines have to be picked in August. But generally Bordeaux's grapes ripen steadily, swollen by occasional rainfall, until a harvest between mid September and mid October. Rainfall can vary considerably from vintage to vintage and within the Bordeaux region itself, with the Médoc being wetter overall, with an average annual rainfall of 950 mm/37 in, than more inland districts.

Excessive rain is the chief hazard at harvest, especially in a year during which full ripeness has yet to be achieved. In the sweet wine areas, on the other hand, humidity is sought in autumn, particularly morning mists which evaporate during the day to encourage the spread of NOBLE ROT. It is no coincidence that Bordeaux's sweet white wine districts are clustered together on either side of the Garonne, about 20 miles upstream of the city, where the river Ciron flows into the Garonne. The waters of the Ciron, shaded for most of its length by the forests of the Landes, are invariably cooler than those of the Garonne and encourage the autumn morning mists which promote the BOTRYTIS fungus. In years when these are followed by warm, dry afternoons, the benevolent form of botrytis, noble rot, forms and great sweet white wine may be made. In damp years the malevolent form, GREY ROT, simply rots the fruit.

Vine varieties
Bordeaux's most famous, and best travelled, grape variety is that on which the Médoc and Graves depend for their red wines, CABERNET SAUVIGNON. Bordeaux's most planted variety by far, however, is MERLOT, which in 2011 occupied 65% of all vineyard land, almost three times as much as the later-ripening Cabernet Sauvignon. Merlot predominates not just in the famous right-bank appellations of St-Émilion and Pomerol but more importantly in the Entre-Deux-Mers (BORDEAUX AOC country) and throughout the right bank, in whose damper, cooler soils Cabernet Sauvignon can be difficult to ripen. CABERNET FRANC, also important on the right bank, where it is often called Bouchet, is the third most planted grape variety. PETIT VERDOT is the only other red grape variety of any importance, playing a minor, but in ripe vintages useful, role in the Médoc. Cot, Pressac, or MALBEC is an ingredient in some right-bank wines on the other hand, and, perhaps thanks to some Argentine wines, is increasingly mentioned by producers, as is CARMENÈRE, a red grape variety of historical importance in Bordeaux (mentioned for reasons associated with CHILE).

In the early 1970s, Bordeaux's single most planted grape variety of either colour was SÉMILLON but it is now much less important except for sweet wine production. SAUVIGNON BLANC is Sémillon's traditional minor blending partner in sweet white bordeaux but is used increasingly for dry white wines, often unblended and by the 2010s is almost as widely planted as Sémillon. SAUVIGNON GRIS is now also allowed in many dry white bordeaux. The only other white grape variety fully sanctioned by the appellation laws is the Bordeaux and Bergerac speciality MUSCADELLE, but small quantities of UGNI BLANC, COLOMBARD, and Merlot Blanc are also planted and used in white BORDEAUX AOC. (The 2011 official national vine census rather remarkably records 6 ha/14.8 acres of Chardonnay in the Gironde département.)

In stark contrast to France's other famous fine wine, BURGUNDY, red bordeaux is quintessentially a wine made from a blend of different vine varieties. This is only partly because Merlot and Cabernet are complementary, the flesh of the former filling in the frame of the latter. It is also an insurance policy on the part of growers in an unpredictable climate. Merlot grapes bud, flower, and ripen earlier than Cabernet Sauvignon, and are much more susceptible to COULURE, which can seriously affect quantity. Cabernet Sauvignon, on the other hand, ripens so late that a cool, cloudy late summer can seriously affect its quality. Although the ENCÉPAGEMENT, the exact proportions of different vine varieties, varies from château to château, a typical Médoc recipe is 70% Cabernet Sauvignon, 10% Cabernet Franc, 20% Merlot, while a typical St-Émilion recipe might be closer to 70% Merlot and 30% Cabernet Franc.

Among dry white wines, the recipe is less predictable, although some all-Sauvignon wines are produced. The classic recipe for sweet white wines is 80% Sémillon to 20% Sauvignon Blanc. In the wake of the success of Pavillon Blanc de Ch Margaux an increasing number of white wines have emerged from the red wine country of the Médoc.

Viticulture

With their neat, low rows of densely planted, GUYOT-trained, low-vigour vines, Bordeaux's vineyards are some of the world's most recognizable. Vine TRIMMING is a perennial activity, and VINE DENSITY in less glorious vineyards averages between 5,000 and 6,000 vines per ha, although it is often as high as 10,000 vines per ha/4,000 per acre in the Médoc.

FUNGAL DISEASES thrive in Bordeaux's damp climate, and frequent SPRAYING is a fact of life here. (This may explain why Bordeaux has been slow to embrace ORGANIC VITICULTURE.) The incidence of EUTYPA DIEBACK became a serious preoccupation in the 1980s. BOTRYTIS BUNCH ROT is one of the most common hazards, although in sweet wine districts it is encouraged in its benevolent form as NOBLE ROT. Fertilizers (including manure from specially reared herds at some top properties) and pesticides have played their part in increasing YIELDS. CROP THINNING and selective LEAF PLUCKING during the growing season has been widely employed since the late 1980s—although vignerons are increasingly aware of the hazards of SUNBURN.

The flat, well-drained vineyards would submit easily to MECHANIZATION, although few have rows sufficiently widely spaced to permit MECHANICAL HARVESTING.

Traditionally the Bordeaux harvest would begin 100 days after the flowering, but the 1990s saw a tendency to leave the grapes on the vine longer to achieve fully ripe PHENOLICS. It has not been uncommon therefore to start picking 110 days or more after the flowering. Identifying the date of optimum maturity of each parcel of grapes, and managing to pick them as quickly as possible on and after that date, has become one of the chief preoccupations in Bordeaux. Grapes for dry white wines and Merlot are in general picked before Cabernet Sauvignon and, especially, grapes for sweet white wines, which may not be picked until November in SAUTERNES.

Bordeaux must be the only region able to command prices high enough to justify hiring HELICOPTERS in an attempt to agitate cold air during spring FROSTS, or to dry grapes during a wet vintage, as Chx MOUTON ROTHSCHILD and PÉTRUS have been known to do. Since the difficult vintages of the early 1990s, a high proportion of properties have invested in SORTING equipment in an attempt to maximize wine quality.

Winemaking

Winemaking techniques in Bordeaux's top estates are regarded as the paradigm by producers of Cabernet and Merlot wines, and fine sweet white wines, throughout the world. Under the guidance of the University of BORDEAUX, these techniques underwent considerable modernization in the 1970s and are continually being refined. Émile PEYNAUD in particular led the way towards much more approachable, more concentrated red wines, a trend intensified under the influence of consultant Michel ROLLAND. And the way in which dry white bordeaux is made was revolutionized in the 1980s, notably by Denis DUBOURDIEU.

Red wines Classic vinification of red bordeaux involves time and, because of the size of most top estates, considerable space in which to house the wine as it slowly makes itself (see RED WINEMAKING). The process begins in the vat hall or *cuvier*, then moves to a first-year CHAI in which a year's production is stored in barrel, continues in the second-year *chai*, and increasingly necessitates an area for bottle storage.

Grapes are almost invariably DESTEMMED before crushing, and fermented in large FERMENTATION VESSELS, known as CUVES in Bordeaux, which may be made of cement, stainless steel, or even wood, for between five and ten or more days. Some form of TEMPERATURE CONTROL was installed at most properties in the 1970s or early 1980s, but is needed for only the hotter vintages; indeed it is increasingly common practice to heat the *cuves* at the beginning of FERMENTATION. Fermentation TEMPERATURES are generally slightly higher in Bordeaux than in the NEW WORLD, with 30 °C/86 °F being a common maximum during fermentation. The concentration of PHENOLICS in ripe Bordeaux Cabernet Sauvignon grapes is such that the precise techniques of EXTRACTION are an extremely important aspect of vinification. Much modern research is concentrated on the relative merits of various PUMPING OVER regimes, usually several times a day. The post-fermentation MACERATION is therefore seen as crucial by most winemakers, who allow the newly made wine at least a week and sometimes much longer 'on the skins'.

Some degree of CHAPTALIZATION was for long commonplace, and generally well judged, in Bordeaux, although there has been some experimentation with CONCENTRATION techniques, including both osmosis and reverse osmosis, since the early 1990s. Ambient YEASTS are the norm and vines have been such an important crop in Bordeaux for so long that the indigenous yeast population is reliable and well adapted.

After fermentation and maceration, the FREE-RUN WINE is racked off the solids into another large vessel, either by PUMPING or, in the most meticulously or fortuitously designed properties, by gravity (see WINERY DESIGN). If the free-run wine is drained into a lower tank, the volume of harsher PRESS WINE can be reduced from more than 15 to about 10%, and the wine tastes softer and riper.

After, and increasingly before, MALOLACTIC CONVERSION, the wine is racked into BARRELS made of French OAK, often LIMOUSIN with the typical Bordeaux barrel being called a BARRIQUE. The luxury of new barrels was introduced only in the 1980s, and the proportion of new barrels used even at top estates tends to be lower than in the most lavish New World wineries: rarely more than 60%, and even lower in less ripe vintages. Traditionally, during the first year the wine is racked off its LEES into a fresh barrel every three months or so, as well as being clarified by egg-white FINING. Unless the property is unusually small, the wine is generally moved to a separate second-year *chai*, where it remains until the wine is blended immediately prior to BOTTLING, usually in early summer. The wine then undergoes the all-important period of BOTTLE AGEING, although this is likely, depending on the state of the market, to take place in the cellars of the BORDEAUX TRADE, the wine merchant, and, most typically, the consumer.

The ASSEMBLAGE is a crucial operation of selection, generally undertaken in the first few months after fermentation, during which it is decided which lots of wine will be blended together to form the principal GRAND VIN for that year, which lots will form the SECOND WINE, and which may be sold off at an even lower level, either in bulk or in bottle. In less successful years, less than half of the wine produced on an estate might be selected for the *grand vin*. The actual blending may take place at any time up to bottling, according to the producer's preference. MICRO-OXYGENATION became increasingly popular in the 21st century, being especially useful for preparing early SAMPLES for the all-important annual PRIMEURS tastings which determine the reputation of each vintage.

The procedure above is that followed by the CLASSED GROWTHS and those who aspire to that quality level. Most wine which qualifies merely as BORDEAUX AOC is more likely to be fairly ruthlessly filtered than fined, and is not given any BARREL MATURATION, but is bottled after a few months in tank. Some PETITS CHÂTEAUX may well treat their wines to a stint in barrique, but such barrels are likely to be hand-me-downs from properties whose wines sell at a higher price.

For Bordeaux's exclusively red wine appellations, see MÉDOC, HAUT-MÉDOC, ST-ESTÈPHE, PAUILLAC, ST-JULIEN, MARGAUX, LISTRAC, MOULIS,

ST-ÉMILION, POMEROL, FRONSAC, and some of the Côtes de Bordeaux (see BORDEAUX, CÔTES DE).

Dry whites WHITE WINEMAKING is relatively unremarkable in Bordeaux, except that the region was one of the last in France to cling to high doses of SULFUR in finished dry wines (perhaps because of its long history of turning its white grapes into sweet wines, which do need more sulfur), and in the upper echelons of white Graves and Pessac-Léognan BARREL MATURATION has one of the longest histories in the world. Bordeaux is also the home of cryomaceration, whereby additional flavour may be imbued by prefermentation SKIN CONTACT at low temperatures, known here as *macération pelliculaire*.

For Bordeaux's principal dry white wine appellations, see PESSAC-LÉOGNAN, GRAVES, ENTRE-DEUX-MERS, BLAYE, and of course BORDEAUX AOC.

Sweet whites Bordeaux's sweet white wine appellations are, in very approximate descending order of quality, SAUTERNES, BARSAC, SAINTE-CROIX-DU-MONT, LOUPIAC, CÉRONS, CADILLAC, PREMIÈRES CÔTES DE BORDEAUX, GRAVES Supérieures, STE-FOY-BORDEAUX, Côtes de Bordeaux-SAINT-MACAIRE, and Bordeaux Supérieur (for which see BORDEAUX AOC).

Basic sweet white bordeaux, often described as *moelleux*, is a simple, sugary wine for which demand is falling. It is typically made by stopping the alcoholic FERMENTATION once it has reached the level of sweetness required. (See RESIDUAL SUGAR.) This is generally achieved by a combition of techniques: chilling, SULFUR DIOXIDE addition, and sterile FILTRATION. Winemakers in Sauternes and Barsac, however, and their more ambitious counterparts elsewhere, aim to make very rich BOTRYTIZED wines from grapes at the full limit of ripeness, which may be described as LIQUOREUX. This involves a considerably more painstaking winemaking regime, even more dependent than any other on events in the vineyard, which is described in SAUTERNES. The wine's selling PRICE, which in the 20th century was depressed by the whims of FASHION, may also play a part in determining whether its maker is able or prepared to take the risks involved in trying to maximize ripeness of the grapes. In the late 1980s, some producers experimented with the supplementary and controversial technique CRYOEXTRACTION in order to concentrate sugars by freezing.

Brook, S., *The Complete Bordeaux* (rev. edn., London, 2010).

Parker, R., *Bordeaux* (4th edn, New York, 2003). www.bordeaux.com

Bordeaux AOC. The most important sort of wine produced in Bordeaux, quantitatively if not qualitatively, is that which qualifies for the simple appellation Bordeaux. About half of all the AOC wine produced in the region is on this lowest rung of the ladder of quality. Red

Bordeaux AOC was produced from 53,938 ha/ 133,226 acres of vineyard in 2013. Such wine is typically produced outside the more specific commune or regional appellations, although a great deal of red Bordeaux AOC comes from the ENTRE-DEUX-MERS region, whose eponymous appellation applies only to white wine. (A counterpoint to this is the fact that the appellations of the Médoc apply only to red wines, so that even the Médoc's smartest white wines, such as Pavillon Blanc du Ch MARGAUX, are not allowed any appellation grander than Bordeaux AOC. Similarly, dry white wines made from grapes usually grown for SAUTERNES qualify only for Bordeaux AOC.) The other area with the greatest concentration of vineyard dedicated to the production of Bordeaux and Bordeaux Supérieur is that north of Libourne, where Merlot grapes predominate.

The great majority of Bordeaux AOC produced is made, often by CO-OPERATIVES, to be sold for blending anonymously into humble GENERIC wines, of very varying quality, but there are also some individual properties, so called PETITS CHÂTEAUX, which lie outside any grander appellation but which express their own TERROIR and practise CHÂTEAU BOTTLING. Almost 90% of all Bordeaux AOC produced is red, and the white, if sweet, may be labelled **Bordeaux** Moelleux. Made from the same area, **Bordeaux Supérieur** is a generally more concentrated, ambitious wine than Bordeaux AOC with maximum yields 56 rather than 60 hl/ha that has been aged for at least 10 months. About four times as much Bordeaux AOC Rouge is made as Bordeaux Supérieur, or 'Bord Sup' as the BORDEAUX TRADE call it. Also included in the generic Bordeaux AOC appellation are the relatively rare **Bordeaux Rosé** and, slightly deeper-coloured **Bordeaux Clairet**, as well as the bottle-fermented sparkling wine CRÉMANT de Bordeaux. **Bordeaux Haut-Benauge** is the name given to the small amount of white wine, both dry and sweet, made in an enclave just across the Garonne from Langon (see also ENTRE-DEUX-MERS).

Most of these wines are designed to be drunk within a year of bottling if white, rosé, or clairet and within two or three years if red. The better examples are unmistakably lighter versions of Bordeaux's grander wines, while the worst can taste like homeless PLONK. With the exception of the best Bordeaux Supérieur reds, few producers can afford to age these wines in OAK, and even fewer of the wines have the concentration to benefit from it, especially since expensive viticultural techniques such as CROP THINNING are hard to justify at this price level, although exceptions are becoming numerous. Most of the Bordeaux BRANDS are Bordeaux AOC, most notably MOUTON CADET, which started off life with the much grander and more specific appellation of PAUILLAC.

Bordeaux blend, usually a red wine made up of some or all of CABERNET SAUVIGNON, CABERNET FRANC, MERLOT, PETIT VERDOT, and possibly MALBEC and CARMENÈRE. Its white wine counterpart is made from Sauvignon Blanc, Sémillon, and possibly Sauvignon Gris and Muscadelle. See also MERITAGE.

Bordeaux, Côtes de, group of appellation on the right bank of the Garonne that since 2009 has brought together the (mainly red) wines of four smaller regions. The details have been in flux but 2009 was the first Côtes de Bordeaux vintage and by 2013 the vineyards involved totalled 9,829 ha/24,278 acres. The group comprises **Cadillac Côtes de Bordeaux** (see CADILLAC), and **Castillon Côtes de Bordeaux** (see CASTILLON), which apply specifically to red wines; **Blaye Côtes de Bordeaux** (see BLAYE) for both red and dry white); and **Francs Côtes de Bordeaux** (see FRANCS), which can apply to reds and both dry and sweet whites). The appellation **Côtes de Bordeaux** *tout court* applies to any wine made from one or more of these geographically specific appellations, has slightly less strict requirements than them, and is generally used by merchants rather than individuals. These wines tend to have more personality than regular BORDEAUX AOC, the result perhaps of local pride, and can provide some of Bordeaux's better wine value.

Côtes de Bordeaux-ST-MACAIRE applies to white wines made in an enclave across the Garonne from the town of Langon. See also BOURG, GRAVES DE VAYRES, and STE-FOY DE BORDEAUX.

Bordeaux mixture, *bouillie bordelaise* in French, once much-used mixture of lime, copper sulfate, and water first recorded in 1885 by Alexis Millardet, Professor of Botany at BORDEAUX University, as an effective control of DOWNY MILDEW. Use of the mixture was a historic event since it was to become the most important chemical for the control of both FUNGAL DISEASES and BACTERIAL DISEASES for 50 years. It has subsequently been replaced by other FUNGICIDES, many of them containing copper. It is still used today by very traditional growers in some regions and it is one of the few preparations permitted in ORGANIC VITICULTURE and BIODYNAMIC VITICULTURE.

There is some debate as to how the treatment was discovered. It was common for Bordeaux vignerons to spray the outside vineyard rows with the blue-staining copper sulfate to deter thieves. No doubt it was noticed that this practice halted the devastation caused by downy mildew which had begun in 1883. Continued use of Bordeaux mixture can lead to accumulation of COPPER in the soil, which can reach toxic levels especially in acidic soils. Some vineyards affected by copper toxicity in the Bordeaux area are much reduced in vigour, but the problem can be overcome by adding LIME to the soil. Also, copper sprayed within 14 days of harvest can produce browning, turbidity, and SULFIDE characters in the wine and can result in incomplete FERMENTATIONS. R.E.S.

Figiel, R., 'Bouillie bordelaise: the other gift from Bordeaux vineyards', *Practical Winery & Vineyard*, 11/3 (1990), 27–9.

Bordeaux trade

Bordeaux trade. The sheer quantity of wine produced in Bordeaux, the fact that so much requires AGEING, and the historical importance of Bordeaux as a port (see BORDEAUX, history), mean that its wine trade is more stratified than most—even if wine is no longer the city's economically most important commodity.

Bordeaux wines have always been produced by one category of people and sold by another. The wine producers of the region range from world-famous estates with 200 ha/500 acres under vine, to owners of 2.5 ha or less, whose wines nowadays may also be world-famous (see GARAGE WINES) or whose grapes are delivered to one of the region's wine CO-OPERATIVES, or vinified in conditions of precarious HYGIENE for personal consumption.

The wine merchants, or NÉGOCIANTS, traditionally brought most of the wines they bought into their CHAIS in or around Bordeaux (notably its Quai des Chartrons) to be matured and shipped out to export customers, particularly in Britain and Scandinavia, either in barrels, or after bottling. They were joined in the early 20th century by merchants in LIBOURNE, who concentrated on markets in northern France and northern Europe (see POMEROL).

So great was the quantity of wine to be traded that numbers of middlemen were needed between producers and the merchants, of whom professional brokers, or *courtiers*, such as Tastet & Lawton have become an essential part of Bordeaux's vinous commercial structure. There were 89 of them in 2014. What the merchant supplied in addition to the mere buying and selling of wine was technical ability (his cellarmaster and team were likely to be considerably better technicians than the producers'), and financing for the grower.

This way of doing business changed considerably after 1945, when even some of the FIRST GROWTHS were still made available to the merchants in bulk, and most of the CLASSED GROWTHS have since 1959 been sold to the merchants on the condition that they are CHÂTEAU BOTTLED.

Since 1945, improvements in winemaking at all levels and, since the 1980s, PRICE increases and inflation levels which have made it impossible for even the biggest merchants to finance large quantities of wine, have tended to transform the role of the merchant from principal to broker. Some of the merchants have been more aggressive than most in adapting winemaking techniques at the bottom end of the market, particularly for BORDEAUX AOC, to international changes in taste. The mid 2000s saw a particular focus on the development of BRANDS in an effort to find a home for the increasing quantity of red wine produced in the region. The balance of financial power between the 300 merchants and 100 or so most signfiicant proprietors is a precarious one, ever-changing according to vintage quality and quantity and international demand. The Bordeaux trade is increasingly involved in STORING WINE and selling direct to the consumer, having constructed many substantial wine warehouses around the city's fringes. For examples of specific Bordeaux merchants, see BARTON, CRUSE, SICHEL, and MOUEIX. W.B. & J.R.

Brook, S., *The Complete Bordeaux* (rev. edn, London, 2010).

Faith, N., *The Winemasters* (3rd edn, London, 2005).

Loftus, S., *Anatomy of the Wine Trade* (London, 1985).

Penning-Rowsell, E., *The Wines of Bordeaux* (6th edn, London, 1989).

Bordeaux, University of

Bordeaux, University of, university complex whose Faculté (formerly Institut) d'Oenologie is a centre of oenological ACADEME of world renown. (Viticultural research is conducted under the auspices of INRA and Bordeaux Sciences Agro, the agricultural university of Bordeaux.)

The institute was founded in 1880 (the same year as the research institute that was to become the University of California at DAVIS) as a mere *station agronomique*, when Ulysse Gayon, the sole Professor of Chemistry at the associated University of Bordeaux, became its director.

Gayon had studied and worked with Louis PASTEUR, the founder of scientific OENOLOGY. He considered the *station*'s function was to promulgate sound methods of making and maturing wine. In addition to his contributions to the ANALYSIS of wines, he worked with Alexis Millardet on the development of the copper-based vine treatment designed to combat FUNGAL DISEASES which was to be known as BORDEAUX MIXTURE.

During the 40 years Gayon directed the *station*, its tradition of identifying the practical applications which could be made from research results was established, as was the importance of transmitting information to winemakers in unscientific language.

From 1927 the most significant research on wine and related subjects in the world was carried out at the University of Bordeaux through a collaboration between Jean RIBÉREAU-GAYON, the grandson of Ulysse Gayon, and Émile PEYNAUD, who did not officially join the University until 1949. From 1949, when Jean Ribéreau-Gayon became director of the *station*, the results of basic and extensive research became apparent to winemaker and consumer alike. Chromatography provided legally convincing evidence of the use of HYBRIDS in any wine sample, and encouraged their replacement by VINIFERA vine varieties in the vineyards of Bordeaux, and thereby a great improvement in the quality of the region's basic BORDEAUX AOC wines. At the same time, the understanding of the process of MALOLACTIC CONVERSION gave wine producers the knowledge they needed to control a fundamental step in winemaking and gave them much greater control over the style and quality of the wines they made. Research into the influence of TERROIR on wine style and quality has been conducted at Bordeaux since the early 1960s.

The importance of the education of OENOLOGISTS was officially recognized in 1956 with the creation of an École Supérieure d'Oenologie empowered to award a winemaker's diploma. This became the Institut d'Oenologie in 1963, which was transformed into the Faculté d'Oenologie in 1995. During this period, oenology achieved full recognition as a new science and in 1971 the institute formally became part of the university, its work and educational titles enjoying full academic status. The work of the institute has continued since 1976 under the direction of Pascal Ribéreau-Gayon, the son of the previous director.

The Faculté is currently engaged in research on subjects which vary from explorations of the nature and effects of different YEASTS to investigations into the characteristics of different TANNINS. The most significant result of research in the 1980s was arguably the dramatic improvement in aroma and subtlety of dry white bordeaux, in which field Denis DUBOURDIEU deserves much credit.

In addition to training oenologists who make wine throughout the world and belong to what is outside France referred to as the 'Bordeaux school' of winemaking, the Faculté supervises doctorates on vinous subjects and is one of only two French organizations to enjoy this privilege, along with SupAgro Montpellier (see INRA). A prominent feature of the professional training at the Faculté is the importance attached to tasting wines and analysing their characteristics. Since 1949 the Faculté has also given tastings and lectures for growers and cellar workers without scientific training, particularly through the Diplôme Universitaire d'Aptitude à la Dégustation (DUAD), which is one of the world's most in-depth courses in wine TASTING.

In 2009, the Faculté merged with Bordeaux Sciences Agro and part of the Institut National de la Recherche Agronomique to form the INSTITUT DES SCIENCES DE LA VIGNE ET DU VIN DE BORDEAUX (ISVV), which encompasses a high level of research and academic training in both oenology and viticulture. W.B. & C.v.v.L.

Bordo, occasional Romanian name for CABERNET FRANC and sometimes used in northeast Italy for CARMENÈRE.

bore, wine. For some reason, wine bores exist in public consciousness and, it has to be said, in reality in a more vividly pestilential way than art bores, music bores, or even sport bores. Perhaps this is because for most people wine is associated with sensual pleasure rather than analysis and verbal communication and so their wine-related boredom threshold is low. So far, wine bores are usually men, although women wine bores may be an eventual consequence of female financial emancipation. One woman's wine bore can be another person's wine expert, however.

borers, usually beetles or their larvae, which bore into the woody parts of plants, sometimes killing them. The branch and twig borer, *Melalqus confertus*, occurs throughout California and parts of Oregon and damages grape canes. Control is usually by cultural methods, by keeping vines healthy, pruning off all dying and dead parts and infested wood in winter. Beetle larvae causing problems to vineyards can be quite regionally specific. The fig longicorn (*Dihammus vastator*) beetle larvae causes vine damage only in the Hunter Valley region of Australia, for example. M.J.E.

boron, a MINERAL element required in minute quantities for healthy vine growth, and thus called a micronutrient. Boron deficiencies in vines are commonly found where SOIL ACIDITY and RAINFALL are high. Boron is required for the movement of SUGARS and the synthesis of AUXINS in the plant. A major effect of boron deficiency is poor FRUIT SET caused by the effect on POLLEN tube growth affecting germination, which can result in substantial reductions in YIELD. Bunches on boron-deficient vines often have many small berries. A quality gain from having more and smaller berries (see BERRY SIZE) is possible but this effect, while tantalizing, has not been proven.

Boron toxicity is also possible, sometimes due to over-application of fertilizer. Excess boron can, coincidentally, also come from bore water used for IRRIGATION. See also FERTILIZERS. R.E.S. & R.W.

Borraçal, synonym for Galicia's CAIÑO TINTO in Portugal's Vinho Verde region where it makes tart reds.

Borrado das Moscas, the DÃO region's name for the Portuguese variety BICAL.

Bosco, grown on just 82 ha/202 acres of LIGURIA, can make exciting sweet amber wine.

Bosnia and Herzegovina, an independent federal republic since 1992, previously part of YUGOSLAVIA. Located on the western Balkan peninsula with just 12 km/7.5 m of Adriatic coastline and high central mountains, it is divided into two entities: the Federation of Bosnia & Herzegovina, and Republika Srpska, plus the district of Brčko. Each has its own constitution and thus no single central body oversees the wine industry. The republic signed a Stabilization and Association Agreement with the EU in 2008 but by 2014 was yet to be accepted as a candidate for EU membership.

The vineyard area was estimated at 3,500 ha/8,645 acres in 2013 by the Federal Agro-Mediterranean Institute, with 46 commercial wineries owning 1,320 ha/3,261 acres. The remainder belong to around 11,000 small households and farms largely producing for the grey market or home consumption. The devastating war between 1992 and 1995 caused considerable damage to viticulture near the front line and production has not recovered to pre-war levels. More than 90% of the vineyards are in Herzegovina, across 10 municipalities. Mostar is the most important area with 1,074 ha/2,654 acres of vineyards. Plantings are 55% white, predominantly the local Žilavka, making high-quality white wine noted for an expressive aroma and generous body, balanced by good acidity. Records for this variety go back 600 years to the time of Bosnian King Tvrtko. Other local white wine grapes include Krkošija, Bena, and the Serbian Smederevka. Red wine varieties are dominated by local Blatina, a female variety that requires a cross-pollinator and is usually interplanted and blended, with Kambuša (Alicante Bouschet), Trnjak, or Merlot. Cabernet Sauvignon and Vranac are also found. A new wine law was enacted in 2014 and the problems of fragmentation of land and grey-market sales are expected to be addressed. C.G.

FAO Regional Office for Europe and Central Asia, 'The Wine Sector in Bosnia and Herzegovina', www.fao.org.
www.wineroute.ba

botanical classification, a system of classifying plants—including VINES, YEASTS, and the organisms responsible for FUNGAL DISEASES of the vine—which shows their relationship one to the other, and which also allows them to be uniquely described and identified. The basic unit of classification is the species; related species are sometimes grouped into genera (plural of genus); related genera into families; and related families into orders. In turn, species can be divided into subspecies, when different types have developed naturally, and into varieties, or occasionally cultivars (a contraction of cultivated variety), when different types have been selected by human hands. VINE VARIETIES can be further divided into three PROLES, according

to their geographical origins. Different CLONES of individual varieties have also been selected. To summarize:

Order	Variety
Family	Prole
Genus	Clone
Species	

Recent DNA analyses have considerably modified the earlier classifications created by botanists and although there are still some controversies, current consensus according to the Angiosperm Phylogeny Group of international systematic botanists is that GRAPEVINES belong to the order Vitales, comprising the Leeaceae family, which consists mostly of shrubs, and the Vitaceae family, which consists of approximately 14 genera and about 900 species primarily distributed in tropical regions in Asia, Africa, Australia, the neotropics, and the Pacific islands, with a few genera in temperate regions (*Vitis*, *Parthenocissus*, and *Ampelopsis*).

Most of the plants are climbers and have tendrils opposite leaves on the shoots, the grapevine being representative. Galet lists 13 genera other than *Vitis* in this family (excluding two extinct species) whereas Soejima and Wen, using more recent PHYLOGENETIC analyses, list 13 including *Vitis*; the largest genus is *Cissus* with about 350 species, from succulent species such as cacti to the lianas of tropical jungles. *Ampelopsis* and *Parthenocissus* are two more genera closely related to each other and are observably similar to grapevines. Ornamental plants related to the grapevine include the Virginia creeper in the US and Europe, the kangaroo vine in Australia, and Japanese ivy and Crimson Glory in Japan.

The family **Vitaceae** (according to Soejima and Wen):

Vitis	*Cyphostemma*
Acareosperma	*Nothocissus*
Ampelocissus	*Parthenocissus*
Ampelopsis	*Pterisanthes*
Cayratia	*Rhoicissus*
Cissus	*Tetrastigma*
Clematicissus	

There are also the fossil genera *Cissites* and *Paleovitis*.

The grapevine genus VITIS, created in 1700 by Tournefort, comprises about 60 species, including VINIFERA, first studied by Linnaeus in 1735. The full botanical binomial of the most common wine-producing vine species is therefore *Vitis vinifera* L., often abbreviated to *V. vinifera* or (botanically incorrectly) *vinifera* (the first person to describe the species often being listed, usually as initials, after the scientific name). Another convention is the use of Latin, often confected, and italics.

The genus *Vitis*

The *Vitis* genus has traditionally been divided into two distinct sections called *Vitis* (previously *Euvitis*) and MUSCADINIA and this has been confirmed by DNA classification. The two sections may be differentiated not only on the basis of appearance but also by chromosome number. *Muscadinia* has 40 chromosomes while *Vitis* has only 38. (This is a frustration to VINE BREEDERS, who would welcome ready access to the many pest and disease resistant genes of *Muscadinia*.)

Most *Vitis* species are native to North America (see AMERICAN VINE SPECIES) and Asia. The common wine grape species *Vitis vinifera* is native to Europe and the Near East and is commonly divided into two subspecies, the wild *Vitis vinifera* subsp. *silvestris* and the cultivated *Vitis vinifera* subsp. *sativa*. The latter shows great diversity as a result of selection and cultivation by man, and three basic eco-geographic groups of varieties, or proles, were created by Russian ampelographer Negrul in 1938 (*occidentalis*, *pontica*, and *orientalis*), reflecting differences between origin and end use. Each prole contains numerous grape varieties (or cultivars), for example 'Cabernet Sauvignon', which are themselves subdivided into numerous clones. (Botanists put the names of varieties in inverted commas.) See VITIS and VINIFERA for more details. The full botanical classification of Cabernet Sauvignon might therefore be: order Vitales, family Vitaceae, genus *Vitis*, section *Vitis*, species *vinifera*, proles *occidentalis*, variety 'Cabernet Sauvignon', clone INRA BX 5197.   R.E.S. & J.V.

Antcliff, A. J., 'Taxonomy: the grapevine as a member of the plant kingdom', in B. G. Coombe and P. R. Dry (eds.), *Viticulture, i: Resources*). (2nd edn, Adelaide, 2004).

Soejima, A., and Wen, J., 'Phylogenetic analysis of the grape family (Vitaceae) based on three chloroplast markers', *American Journal of Botany* 93/2 (2006), 278–87.

Zecca, G., et al., 'The timing and the mode of evolution of wild grapes (*Vitis*)', *Molecular Phylogenetics and Evolution* 62/2 (2012), 736–47.

Botryosphaeria dieback, FUNGAL DISEASE

affecting the TRUNK and ARMS of the vine caused by at least 22 species in the family Botryosphaeriaceae that occurs wherever grapes are grown, causing loss of production in both newly planted and mature vineyards. Botryosphaeriaceae fungi primarily infect vines through pruning wounds and although species differ in their impact on the vines, the most characteristic symptoms of the disease are perennial cankers in the wood (typically wedge-shaped) and lack of spring growth. Other symptoms include black or light-brown streaking of the XYLEM vessels, graft failure, cane bleaching, cane dieback, shoot NECROSIS, bud necrosis, and mortality. In some grape-growing regions, several Botryosphaeriaceae species are also thought to be involved in causing BUNCH ROTS. See also TRUNK DISEASES.   J.R.U.-T.

Úrbez-Torres, J. R., 'The status of Botryosphaeriaceae spp. infecting grapevines', *Phytopathologia Mediterranea*, 50 (2011), S5–S45.

botryticine. See NOBLE ROT.

botrytis, without the capital B it botanically deserves, is commonly used as an abbreviation for BOTRYTIS BUNCH ROT, for the fungus that causes it *Botrytis cinerea* Pers, for its benevolent form NOBLE ROT, and occasionally for its malevolent form GREY ROT. Grapes affected by noble rot and the wines produced from them are often called BOTRYTIZED, or **botrytis affected.**

Elad, Y., et al. (eds.), *Botrytis: Biology, Pathology and Control* (Dordrecht, 2004).

botrytis bunch rot, vine disease which, of all FUNGAL DISEASES, has the greatest potential effect on wine quality. The disease can have a disastrous effect on both yield and quality when the fungus affects almost ripe, or damaged grapes, typically in humid weather. This malevolent form is known as GREY ROT, the most common of the BUNCH ROTS. On the other hand, if it affects ripe, healthy, whole, light-skinned grapes, and the weather conditions are favourable, botrytis develops in a benevolent form called NOBLE ROT, which is responsible for some of the world's finest sweet wines. (If it affects red grapes, it always damages PIGMENTS, resulting in wines with a brownish tinge and, often, off-odours associated with rot.)

The causal fungus for both forms of botrytis bunch rot is *Botryotinia fuckeliana* of which only a certain form (the so-called conidial form), termed *Botrytis cinerea*, is found in vineyards. The disease is widespread as it attacks not only vines but also many cultivated and wild plants, and it survives as a saprophyte on dying and dead plant tissue.

Botrytis rot is a problem especially for vineyards in damp climates. In particular, rainfall near harvest causes severe infections, and thus can be a major climatic factor affecting the YIELD and quality of a particular vintage (as regularly happens in both BURGUNDY and BORDEAUX, for example). Botrytis spores germinate either on wet surfaces or where the ambient humidity is at least 90%. Optimal infection temperatures are 15 to 20 °C/59–68 °F.

Although the botrytis fungus most commonly affects bunches of ripe grapes, it can also affect other parts of the vine such as emerging shoots in spring and young bunches which fall off with obvious effects on yield. The more common problem, however, is when flower parts are infected and remain trapped in the developing bunches. Infections of the fungus can spread in the bunch as it approaches maturity, especially after VERAISON when the grape berries are infected directly through the intact berry skin, or through wounds. The fungi can penetrate even healthy berries, gaining access through minute breathing pores called STOMATA, but more commonly the entry is through the broken skin. Such injuries may be caused by bird pecks, insect damage (in New Zealand, THRIPS have been found to carry botrytis spores), mechanical abrasion, or by tightly compressed berries which burst when the vine takes up water after rainfall.

The mould spreads progressively through the whole bunch, especially when berries are in close contact, as with vine varieties with compact bunches. If the weather turns dry, infected berries tend to dry out, and major changes to the fruit's chemistry can result in grapes suitable for classic BOTRYTIZED wines influenced by noble rot. In continuing wet weather, however, the fungus rapidly spreads as grey rot, and the grape crop can literally rot before the owner's eyes. This explains the urgency of harvest when weather conditions are inclement. Early warning systems based on temperature or relative humidity have been developed to predict epidemics. Wines in such years are typically lower in alcohol as the fruit is harvested earlier. Research in Champagne has shown that botrytis can have a negative effect on the foaming properties of champagne.

Botrytis is a problem in other areas of viticulture. It is a common rot developing in stored TABLE GRAPES and also causes problems during GRAFTING operations in nurseries.

Vine varieties, and indeed various CLONES of vine varieties, differ in their susceptibility to botrytis depending on how tightly packed the berries are in the bunch, on the thickness of the skin, and to some extent also on the stage of ripeness. Varieties with compact bunches of high sugar content are the most susceptible. Sémillon, Sauvignon Blanc, Muscadelle, Carignan, Pinot Noir, and Merlot are particularly susceptible to botrytis bunch rot, with Chardonnay moderately susceptible and Cabernet Sauvignon quite tolerant. Interestingly, some varieties are made more resistant by producing PHYTOALEXINS which inhibit the fungus. Some varieties also have higher concentrations of preformed antifungal compounds.

Modern control measures take two forms. The first, the 'natural' approach, is to avoid excessive leafiness around the fruit, which means that bunches are better exposed to sun and wind which dry the fruit after rain or dew. Bunch thinning can also help. The removal of fallen leaves and prunings reduces the risk of overwintering spores and infection in spring due to rain splash. CANOPY MANAGEMENT practices such as leaf removal and improved trellis are most useful. Chemical control using a FUNGICIDE is the second route and still the most common method of control. The number of spray applications required depends on the climate. In wet regions, more than half a dozen sprayings may be needed, beginning at FLOWERING and ending before harvest. The last sprayings cannot be applied too close to harvest as yeast activity during fermentation may be inhibited, quite apart from any potentially harmful chemical RESIDUES.

While a relatively wide range of chemicals is now used for botrytis control, the fungus seems to be waging a war against the chemist. New chemicals seem to be used only for a few years before they become less effective, as the fungus develops resistance. Growers are now being forced to rely less on chemicals and to use more natural means of control. Newly bred varieties commonly have greater disease tolerance, and researchers are also attempting to control botrytis with two types of antagonistic fungus, *Trichoderma harzianum* and *Trichoderma atroviride*. This biological approach has led to the development of new products such as BOTRY-Zen® from New Zealand, using the competitive fungus *Ulocladium oudemansii*, which is claimed to be an effective control for botrytis. Modern researchers are investigating a number of new approaches to botrytis control using, for example, competitive bacillus bacteria, elicitors such as chitosan extracted from crustaceans, which stimulate the vines' defence mechanisms, and sanitizers such as hydrogen peroxide and peracetic acid which leave no residue. However, biological controls are variable in their efficacy.

See GREY ROT and NOBLE ROT for more details of the two different forms of botrytis. For details of how nobly rotten grapes are transformed into wine, and of the resulting wines, see BOTRYTIZED wines. R.E.S.

Bettiga, L. J., and Gubler, W. G., 'Bunch rots', in L. J. Bettiga (ed.), *Grape Pest Management* (3rd edn, Oakland, Calif., 2013), 93–103.

Galet, P., *Précis de viticulture* (7th edn, Montpellier, 2000).

Pearson, R. C., and Goheen, A. (eds.), *Compendium of Grape Diseases* (St Paul, Minn., 1988).

botrytized, or **botrytis-affected, wines** are those made from white grapes affected by the benevolent form of BOTRYTIS BUNCH ROT, known in English as NOBLE ROT. Distinctively scented in youth, and with considerably more EXTRACT than most wines, they are the most complex and longest lived of all the sweet, white table wines. The noble rot smell is often described as honeyed, but it can also have an (attractive) overtone of boiled cabbage.

History

There is no firm evidence that botrytized wines were recognized in antiquity, although Olney points out that a particularly fine Ancient Greek wine produced on Chios (see CHIAN) in the 5th century BC is described as *saprian* by ATHENAEUS, and that the literal translation of this may be 'rotten, putrid'. Noble rot is much more likely to occur in more humid climates than in the MEDITERRANEAN CLIMATE of the Aegean Islands, however, and the extremely unpleasant appearance of grapes infected by noble rot, and the difficulty with which they ferment, must have deterred many early winemakers.

Three important centres of botrytized wine production have their own accounts of the discovery that this particular sort of mouldy grape could be transformed into exceptional wine.

That of the TOKAJ region of north east Hungary is the oldest, dating from at least 1650 when the priest-cum-winemaker on a particular estate there delayed the HARVEST because of the threat of attack by the Turks. This allowed the development of noble rot and the grapes were duly vinified separately, as one would expect, and the resulting wine much admired. For diplomatic purposes it was introduced to the French court in the early 18th century, long before French vine-growers had recognized the existence of the noble fungus.

In Germany, the principle of picking selected bunches of grapes (AUSLESE) was understood in the 18th century, but that of the widespread picking of grapes affected by NOBLE ROT dates, in the Rheingau region which became most famous for botrytized wines, from about 1820. In spite of popular beliefs to the contrary, precisely when and where vine-growers first realized the value of noble rot is not certain, although the discovery in Germany is thought to have been in the particularly suitable climate of the Rheingau. SCHLOSS JOHANNISBERG has certainly promulgated its own claim that in 1775 the traditional harvest messenger, as usual licensed to deliver permission to pick from the owner, the distant prince-abbot of Fulda, was delayed, thereby supposedly allowing a noble rot infection to proceed, and resulting in Germany's first botrytized SPÄTLESE.

The sweet wines of Bordeaux and the Loire were much treasured in the Middle Ages, particularly by the DUTCH, but without any specific mention of a special fungus, or acknowledgement of any special attribute. The principal French legend concerning the 'discovery' of noble rot—and legend it is widely believed to be—dates from as recently as 1847, at Ch d'YQUEM (although the quality, style, and youthfulness of earlier vintages of Yquem, such as the 1811, suggest that noble rot must have played an important part in wine production there before that date).

The risks and costs involved in making naturally botrytized wine make it necessarily expensive. It has therefore been an economical proposition only when sweet wines are highly valued. Germany's botrytized wines have always been regarded as precious rarities for which a ready market can be found within Germany. France's output of botrytized wines is potentially much greater, but when sweet wines were out of FASHION in the 1960s and 1970s, enthusiasm for producing them inevitably waned, only to be rekindled in the 1980s.

Geography and climate

Many conditions have to be met before botrytized wines can be produced. Not only is a MESOCLIMATE which favours misty mornings and warm afternoons in autumn needed, but producers must have the knowledge and the will to sacrifice quantity for nothing more certain than possible quality. Botrytized wines are very much a product of psyche as well as nature.

The district with the potential to produce the greatest quantity of top-quality botrytized wine is SAUTERNES (although it all depends, as everywhere, on the precise WEATHER of the year). The confluence of the Rivers Ciron and GARONNE provide an ideal mesoclimate for the satisfactory development of noble rot. Nearby sweet white wine districts CÉRONS, LOUPIAC, CADILLAC, and STE-CROIX-DU-MONT may also produce small quantities of botrytized wines, although the price fetched by these appellations rarely justifies the additional production costs.

Botrytized wine is also made by the most meticulous producers in MONBAZILLAC and SAUSSIGNAC. With viticultural commitment and skilful vinification, these districts can make botrytized wines to rival all but the very best Sauternes made similarly from Sémillon, Sauvignon, and particularly Muscadelle grapes. One or two fine examples of this style have also emerged from Gaillac.

On the river Loire, appellations such as Coteaux de l'AUBANCE, Coteaux du LAYON, QUARTS DE CHAUME, BONNEZEAUX, MONTLOUIS, and VOUVRAY can produce botrytized wines in good years, and they are given even greater ageing potential for being made from the acidic Chenin Blanc grape.

Botrytized wines may also be made from such varied grapes as Mâconnais Chardonnays and Alsace Rieslings in exceptional years.

Germany is the other famous source of botrytized wines, usually labelled BEERENAUSLESE or TROCKENBEERENAUSLESE, although the quantities made vary enormously according to vintage. Riesling is the classic grape, although some of the GERMAN CROSSES can be persuaded to rot nobly in an exceptionally suitable year. Noble rot infections are much more reliable in the BURGENLAND district of Austria, where, thanks to the influence of the NEUSIEDLERSEE, considerable quantities of botrytized Beerenauslesen and Trockenbeerenauslesen are made most years. Over the border in Hungary, Tokaj is still closely associated with botrytized winemaking, as various parts of ROMANIA, notably COTNARI, once were.

Botrytized winemaking is an embryonic art in Italy, Spain, and most of Portugal, where producers and consumers tend to favour either DRIED-GRAPE WINES or FORTIFIED WINES.

In the New World, botrytized wines are made with increasing frequency. Nederburg Edelkeur was a South African prototype which enjoyed international acclaim in the 1970s. Griffith in NEW SOUTH WALES's Riverina was producing Australian botrytized Pedro Ximénez as early as the late 1950s, and is now a centre for the production of relatively early maturing botrytized whites, particularly Semillon. In Australia, New Zealand, South Africa, and in California particularly, a host of botrytized Rieslings has emerged.

California has also seen attempts to simulate noble rot, by growing spores of the botrytis fungus in a laboratory and spraying them on picked, healthy, ripe grapes before subjecting them to alternately humid and warm conditions for a couple of weeks. The first of these wines was made in the late 1950s by Myron Nightingale in the Livermore Valley. The result was called Premiere Semillon and has been followed by a series of similar wines made at Beringer in the Napa Valley.

As awareness of noble rot and botrytized wines grows, the number of winemakers anxious to experiment also increases, even if the market is not always rapturous, and they are usually at the mercy of the weather. Even ENGLAND has succeeded in producing botrytized wine.

Vine varieties

Any white grape variety may be infected benevolently by the botrytis fungus; red varieties simply lose their colour. and usually develop off-odours. Certain varieties seem particularly sensitive to the fungus and well adapted to the production of botrytized wines, however: Sémillon, Sauvignon Blanc, Chenin Blanc, Riesling, Gewürztraminer, and Furmint are traditional.

Viticulture

The chief viticultural aspect of making botrytized wines is the number of passages or TRIES through the vineyard which may have to be made in order to pick grapes only at the optimum point of botrytis infection, because noble rot is so crucial to quality. See SAUTERNES for a description of the likely routine there. In a year as difficult as 1974 at Ch d'YQUEM (admittedly the most conscientious Sauternes estate), 11 *tries* were made over a ten-week period. In 1990, on the other hand, noble rot spread rapidly and uniformly and the grapes were picked by early October. In some vintages the spread and quality of botrytis may be so patchy that some estates, for example Yquem, Rieussec, and Suduiraut in 2012, elect not make a GRAND VIN.

Hand picking of these varied but usually disgusting-looking grapes is essential, and the cost of LABOUR is one important element in the price of botrytized wines.

In wet vintages, some producers use modern freeze-concentration techniques, called CRYOEXTRACTION in French.

Winemaking

If picking botrytized grapes is painstaking, obtaining their juice and persuading it to ferment is at least as difficult because of its composition (see NOBLE ROT). PRESSING is a physically difficult operation, and, contrary to the usual practice, later pressings yield juice superior to the first pressing because it is richer in sugar and the chemical compounds produced by the botrytis fungus. The most dehydrated grapes in the press may not in any case yield juice until they have been pressed twice or three times.

A variety of winemaking methods are used, including the classic method described in SAUTERNES. Fermentation is necessarily extremely slow. The juice seems almost designed to inhibit YEASTS, being so high in sugar and antibiotics such as botryticine. Botrytized musts tend to lack nutrients such as thiamine and ammonia, which is another reason for stuck fermentations. Fermentation may be allowed to stop itself, or SULFUR DIOXIDE addition may be used. Care must be taken that these wines, which often have a RESIDUAL SUGAR level equivalent to about 6% alcoholic strength, do not suffer a SECOND FERMENTATION, and bottling, whether after two winters in new BARRIQUES as in the top Sauternes properties, or in the following spring as in the Loire and many German cellars, has to be undertaken with care. Higher levels of sulfur dioxide are needed during vinification and at bottling because the enzyme LACCASE produced by botrytis increases the risk of OXIDATION and is tolerant of high levels of sulfur dioxide. In addition, the chemical composition of botrytized wines means they have significant power to bind sulfur dioxide. This is why EU regulations permit a higher level of total sulfur dioxide for these wines than for all others. The development of *Botrytis cinerea* also results in the production of two POLYSACCHARIDES. One has antifungal properties and inhibits fermentation. The other, a β-glucan, can make FILTRATION much more difficult, especially if crushing, pumping, and pressing are carried out harshly.

Some wines, notably those made from aromatic varieties such as Muscat, are marked by a loss of varietal aroma. This is mainly because botrytis metabolizes the MONOTERPENES such as linalool and geraniol that are responsible for the distinctive aromas of such varieties.

Botrytized wines are capable of extremely long BOTTLE AGEING, for many decades in some cases.

Brook, S., *Liquid Gold: Dessert Wines of the World* (London, 1987).

Olney, R., *Yquem* (Paris, 1985, and London, 1986).

Ribéreau-Gayon, P., et al., *Traité d'Œnologie* 1: *Microbiologie du vin: Vinifications* (Paris, 1998), translated by J. M. Branco, as *Handbook of Enology* 1: *The Microbiology of Wine and Vinifications* (Chichester, 2000).

botte, Italian word for a large wooden cask, presumably from the same root as BUTT. The plural is **botti**.

bottle ageing, the process of deliberately maturing a wine after BOTTLING, whether for a few weeks as a conscious effort on the part of the bottler to allow the wine to recover from BOTTLE SICKNESS or, in the case of very fine wines, for many years in order to allow the wine to mature. Fine wines are usually vinified expressly so that they will benefit from ageing in bottle, with generous amounts of ACIDS, PHENOLICS, and FLAVOUR PRECURSORS extracted from the grape. These can often make them unattractive when consumed young, but provide them with all the necessary ingredients for bottle ageing. In some cases the high sugar, acid, and flavour compound levels, as in great Rieslings which may not contain much alcohol, can also benefit greatly from bottle ageing. However, some winemakers have adapted their winemaking techniques so that their wines have the capacity to age but are nevertheless approachable much earlier. See, for example, MICRO-OXYGENATION.

The exact identification of the compounds produced during bottle ageing and responsible for the complex BOUQUET of a mature wine is yet to be completely resolved.   A.D.W. & P.J.W.

bottle deposit in red wines is a lacquer-like pigmented deposit adhering to the inner bottle surface and is different from SEDIMENT. This deposition, which may begin in the first few months after bottling, may cover only a small area of the bottle shoulder or may eventually cover the entire glass surface with which the wine is in contact. Wine quality is not affected by bottle deposit and experience has shown that premium reds (particularly those made from RHÔNE varieties) tend to exhibit this deposit more than lower-quality wines. The deposit is an insoluble complex polymer of PIGMENTED TANNINS and PROTEIN.   P.J.W.

bottle fermented, description of some SPARKLING WINES made either by the traditional method, or by the transfer method. See SPARKLING WINEMAKING for full details.

bottles, still by far the most common CONTAINERS for finished wine. Being made of glass, bottles are inconveniently fragile and relatively heavy, but, importantly for long-term AGEING, they are inert. A standard bottle contains 75 cl/ 25 fl oz although see also BOTTLE SIZES.

History

Today it may be taken for granted that wine bottles of different colours and shapes will hold a precise capacity. Nor is it questioned that a paper LABEL will be firmly fixed to the bottle to give a plethora of information, much of it required by law. These are recent developments.

In classical antiquity wine was stored and transported in large, long jars called AMPHORAE. They varied considerably in size but it would certainly be difficult to pour a drinking quantity from such an awkward and big vessel, without using some sort of intermediate container. The Romans invented the technique of blowing glass bottles and some of these may well have been used to serve wine.

Pottery and stoneware jugs were used for centuries in Europe for serving wine, but glass took over as technology to make glass in commercial quantities spread in the 17th century, and by the end of it glass bottles were plentiful, although reserved for the upper classes.

Shape Early bottles have more or less globular bodies with long conical necks. The form developed (see illustration), becoming lower and wider in Britain, while on mainland Europe the flask-shape with an oval cross-section was popular. From c.1690 to 1720, the outline of a bottle resembled that of an onion—a wide compressed globular body with a short neck. Larger bottles were made too, whose shape resembled an inflated balloon or bladder. It is thought that all these forms were stored in beds of sand. By the 1720s the 'onion' became taller and the sides flatter—a form known by collectors as a 'mallet'. Naturally occurring impurities in the constituent ingredients gave glass an olive green hue which varied from pale to almost black and was beneficial to the bottled wine as it excluded light. Most bottles before 1700 had an applied ring of glass just below the neck which gave an anchorage to the string used to hold in a variety of stoppers. These bottles were of substantial weight and thickness too.

Wine drinkers made an important discovery in the 1730s. While it was known that some vintages of wine were better than others even in prehistory, their keeping and consequent maturing qualities were not realized until the introduction of BINNING, the storing of wine in bottles laid on their sides. The effectiveness of CORK as a CLOSURE was thereby enhanced because it was kept wet and expanded by the wine. All this was achieved by the abandoning of onion-, bladder-, and mallet-shaped bottles in favour of cylindrical ones which stack easily. Early cylindrical bottles have short wide bodies with tall necks, but as the century progressed the modern shape evolved. In 1821, Ricketts of Bristol patented a machine for moulding bottles of uniform size and shape, early examples of which are impressed 'patent' on the shoulder of the bottle and the legend 'H Ricketts & Co. Glassworks Bristol' on the base. Thus the modern wine bottle had evolved, all later shapes and colours being decided as a question of aesthetics rather than technical limitation.

Identification From 1636, at about the time of the first appearance of glass bottles in post-Roman Britain, it was illegal to sell wine by the bottle. This consumer protection measure was on account of vintners' willingness to take advantage of the varying capacity of blown bottles. From that time and for the next 230 years, wine was sold by the measure and then bottled. Customers who bought regularly had their own bottles and had them marked in order to distinguish them from any others that might be at the vintner's premises waiting to be filled. The usual marking was the attachment at the end of the production process of a disc seal of the same glass as the bottle, upon which was impressed the owner's initials, name, or heraldic device, often accompanied by the date. Innkeepers and taverners had appropriately marked, or 'sealed', bottles too. It may be noted here that these seals did not indicate the contents.

Sealed bottles are avidly collected today, the most prized being 17th-century ones, particularly those with dates incorporated in the seal. Named examples are preferred to ones with initials, and earlier ones to later.

Bottles with paper labels indicating the contents, first hand written and later printed, emerged during the opening years of the 19th century, but in Britain the law prohibiting wine from being sold by the bottle was not relaxed until 1860. Bottles with paper labels printed with pre-1860 vintages are probably relabelled or were intended for non-British markets.

Other materials Bottles in media other than glass are known, particularly in the 17th century, when glass was an expensive and scarce commodity. Leather bottles, jugs, and other vessels are sometimes associated with ale and beer but many will have been used in the service of wine. A large group of serving bottles is known, made in London, of white tin-glazed earthenware (termed delftware). They are onion shaped with handles and vary from about half to 1½-bottle capacity. Their most charming feature is the calligraphy, usually opposite the handle, for 'CLARET', 'Whit Wine' (sic), 'SACK', or, more rarely, 'PORT' or other wine. They are frequently dated (from c.1630 to 1660) and the legend is often embellished with a curlicue.

Size The size and shape of early bottles was, to an extent, a hit and miss affair. Perhaps the 'standard' size was the natural result of a lungful of air, but bottles were made in a variety of sizes from early times. The onion or bladder shape can sometimes be found in extremely large sizes holding up to 30 bottles. The general term for a large early bottle is a carboy but the word magnum was also used somewhat impressively for a bottle of about double normal capacity. For a long while a bottle was more or less 1¼ UK pints (70 cl or 25 fl oz) and a magnum was a quart (1.12 l or 40 fl oz). Until the 1970s, when EU and other legislation enforced standardization, bottles varied from about 65 to 85 cl, CHAMPAGNE and BURGUNDY tending to be larger than those for BORDEAUX, while SHERRY bottles were often smaller. R.N.H.B.

Butler, R., *Great British Wine Accessories 1550–1900* (Sudbury, Suffolk, 2009).

Van den Bossche, W., *Antique Glass Bottles: Their History & Evolution (1500–1850)* (Woodbridge, Suffolk, 2001).

Modern bottles

Choice of LABEL and FOIL are not the only ways in which a wine producer can make a visual statement to a potential customer. Wine bottles are now made in an almost bewildering array of shapes, weights, colours of glass, and design, quite apart from their capacity (see BOTTLE SIZES).

In some regions one specific bottle has been adopted by all but the most anarchic producers, and indeed adoption of a special local, regional, or appellational bottle became particularly fashionable in the 1980s. Examples of special bottles are the heavy, embossed CHÂTEAUNEUF-DU-PAPE bottle (which comes in several rival versions); the BOCKSBEUTEL of FRANKEN; the CHÂTEAU GRILLET bottle peculiar to a single property; and the long-necked green bottle particular to MUSCADET, although it can sometimes seem that every French appellation has developed its own exclusive bottle.

In general, Italians, with their firm belief in the importance of design, offer the most dazzling range of wine bottles. Some of the particularly artful shapes used for grappa have been adopted by wine producers in Austria and further afield, especially for halves of sweet wine. The problem with some special bottle shapes, however, is that they may well be difficult to store, both on the shelf (many a special bottle is simply too tall for the average supermarket display) and, particularly, in a wine rack designed for standard bottles.

Weight and darkness of glass seem to have been particularly highly valued by Argentines and Italians, although it has been a general rule throughout the wine world that the heavier a bottle, the greater the aspirations of the producer of the wine for its longevity, or at least its price. The weight of a 75 cl bottle can vary between about 350 g and, in extreme cases, almost a kilo. Bottling wine in the lightest, cheapest glass is one way of saving costs. Eschewing overweight bottles is one way of saving the planet. See SUSTAINABILITY.

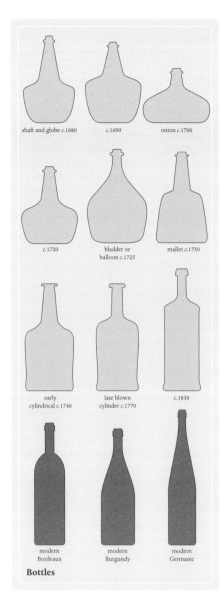

shaft and globe *c.*1680   *c.*1690   onion *c.*1700

*c.*1720   bladder or balloon *c.*1725   mallet *c.*1730

early cylindrical *c.*1740   late blown cylinder *c.*1770   *c.*1830

modern Bordeaux   modern Burgundy   modern Germanic

Bottles

Bottle shapes Special designs apart, there are certain standard bottle shapes associated most commonly with certain regions or, increasingly, the styles of wine associated with those regions. Ambitiously made Chardonnays the world over, for example, tend to be put into burgundy bottles. Since the geographical provenance of most wines should be clear from the label, understanding bottle shapes is most useful for the clues they provide as to the intended style of the wine inside them. Some RIOJA producers, for example, put their Garnacha-dominated, richer blends into burgundy bottles, while their Tempranillo wines designed for longer ageing are put into bordeaux bottles.

Most champagne and sparkling wines are sold in much the same shape of bottle, moulded to be thick and strong enough to withstand the pressure of up to six atmospheres inside each

bottle. Considerable energy and money is expended, however, on designing special bottles for PRESTIGE CUVÉES, Moët & Chandon's Dom PÉRIGNON bottle having set a formidable standard. The precise shape of the lip of a champagne bottle indicates whether the second fermentation took place under a crown cap, or under a cork as it does in some very rare cases.

Bottles vary in the extent to which they have a punt, or inverse indentation, in their base. Most champagne and sparkling wine bottles have a particularly deep indentation because it strengthens the glass, which is under considerable pressure, and, during disgorgement when bottles are inverted, makes it easy for bottles to be lifted by suction during SPARKLING WINEMAKING. Punts are less obviously useful for still wines—although they can make bottles look bigger and more impressive—and deep punts can provide useful purchase for the thumb when SERVING wine from a bottle.

The exact shape and design of the neck and lip of the bottle is determined by what is used to stopper it. Most CLOSURES other than cork need some sort of modification and the widespread adoption of SCREWCAPS has entailed considerable redesign of bottles. The 1990s saw a marked but mercifully brief FASHION for bottles with a flange but no CAPSULE around the top, which damaged many a CORKSCREW.

Bottle colour Wine keeps best in dark glass—as the Champenois, the most energetic researchers into the effects of bottle choice on wine, have found. ROEDERER Cristal, which has traditionally been sold in clear glass, is always swathed in an orange wrap designed to filter out ultraviolet light (see LIGHTSTRIKE for more on this phenomenon). On the other hand, dark glass prevents the consumer from being impressed by the colour of a wine. For this reason, most ROSÉS, not designed for BOTTLE AGEING in any case, are sold in clear glass. It is less clear why SAUTERNES and other sweet white bordeaux is sold in clear glass; TRADITION is presumably the explanation. Most wine bottles are, for reasons of both tradition and the orientation of glass furnaces, some shade of green, from pale blueish green to a colour that to all intents and purposes is black. For traditional reasons again, brown glass is used for some Italian wines, for many fortified wines, and was the traditional way of telling a HOCK or Rhine wine from a MOSEL in green glass. Some German producers use blue-green glass, however, a nod to Victorian times when blue glass was often used. One of the most distinctive glass colours for wine bottles is the yellow-green used for white burgundy, called *feuille morte* in France and therefore 'dead leaf' in much of the New World. Wines are occasionally marketed in bright blue and bright red bottles.

More clues from the bottle

Most wine bottles are moulded with the mark of their manufacturers, sometimes with their capacity, and all wine sold within Europe from the 1990s should have a LOT MARK, a small code stamped on the label, foil, or more usually bottle, so that each bottle can be traced back to its precise BOTTLING and dispatch.

bottle sickness, also known less politely as **bottle stink**, unpleasant and increasingly rare smell apparent in a wine immediately on opening which, unlike most FAULTS, usually dissipates after a few minutes. 'Bottling sickness' might be more a appropriate term to loosely describe two rather different phenomenon that occur in the early months after bottling, one caused by excess OXYGEN, the other by lack of oxygen.

Operations such as RACKING and FILTRATION used to STABILIZE a wine, together with the BOTTLING process itself, may involve aeration and agitation of the wine, resulting in high levels of dissolved oxygen (see TOTAL PACKAGE OXYGEN), which can make a wine taste closed and disappointing when the bottle is first opened. On the other hand, REDUCTION may lead to the production of volatile sulfur-related compounds, which can also lead to off odours. Except in extreme cases, DECANTING can alleviate such problems. The once-common phenomenon of high levels of SULFUR DIOXIDE at bottling may also make a wine smell unpleasant if opened soon thereafter.

bottle sizes are standardized in most countries. A bottle containing 75 cl (25 fl oz) is now accepted almost universally as the standard wine (but not spirits, which is more usually 70 cl) bottle, with the magnum being 1.5 l, exactly twice the capacity. The standard bottle is about the same size as the first bottles (see BOTTLES, history), whose size may have been determined by the size of container conveniently blown by a (glassblower's) lungful of air. The bottle has in its time been variously described as a suitable ration of wine for one person at a sitting, one person per day, and two people at a sitting (see CONSUMPTION).

Half-bottles usually contain 37.5 cl and are believed to hasten wine AGEING, partly because they contain more OXYGEN per centilitre of wine since the bottle neck and ULLAGE are the same as for a full bottle. Most wine bottlers have viewed halves and other bottles smaller than the standard bottle as an unwelcome inconvenience, and BOTTLING technology has been focused on standard bottles, but there continues to be strong demand for half-bottles, particularly in restaurants. There have been various attempts to launch a 50-cl bottle, particularly common for SWEET WINES, and some champagne producers have had notable success with single-serve quarter-bottles.

Capacity (l)	Bordeaux	Champagne/Burgundy
1.5 (2 bottles)	magnum	magnum
2.25 (3 bottles)	Marie-Jeanne	not found
3 (4 bottles)	double magnum	Jéroboam
4.5 (6 bottles)	Jéroboam*	Rehoboam
6 (8 bottles)	Impériale	Methuselah
9 (12 bottles)	not found	Salmanazar
12 (16 bottles)	not found	Balthazar
15 (20 bottles)	not found	Nebuchadnezzar

* 5 litres since 1978

With the exception of JURA's special 62 cl *clavelin*, the bottle capacities permitted within Europe for still wines are 10 cl, 25 cl, 37.5 cl, 50 cl, 75 cl, and 1, 1.5, 2, 3, 4, 5, 6, 8, 9, and 10 litres (and wine may be served in 18.7-cl bottles, sometimes referred to as 'splits', aboard trains, planes, and the like). Sparkling wine bottles come in 12.5-, 20-, 37.5- and 75-cl and 1.5-, 3-, 4.5-, 6- and 9-litre capacities. The larger-sized bottles, some of them no longer in production, have different names in different regions.

A 24-bottle sized Melchior and a 34-bottle sized Sovereign are also known, in theory. Bordeaux collectors particularly treasure larger bottles (often known as 'large formats' or *grands formats*) up to Impériale size, as they favour slow but subtle wine AGEING. Giant champagne bottles, on the other hand, tend to favour publicity rather than wine quality (sizes larger than a magnum tend to be filled with wine made in smaller bottles).

bottle variation is one of the more tantalizing aspects of wine appreciation. 'There are no great wines, just great bottles', is a popular saying among connoisseurs. It is only to be expected with a product as sensitive to STORAGE conditions as wine that bottles of the same wine will differ—perhaps because one has been exposed to higher temperatures or greater humidity. There can easily be a perceptible difference in quality and character between bottles from the very same CASE. SUBJECTIVITY may play a part, as well as a difference in FILL LEVELS, but it is also possible that the individual wines were subtly different before they went into bottle, or were bottled under different conditions. It was not until the 1970s, for example, that it became commonplace for Bordeaux châteaux to ensure that a uniform blend was made before bottling; some of the world's most artisanal producers still bottle by hand from cask to cask. Similarly, wines bottled on two different occasions may find themselves packed in the same case (although modern LOT NUMBER marking provides more clues in this respect). CORKS can also contribute to bottle variation with individual bottles exhibiting odours from TCA originating from the cork, and the ability of the cork seal to allow varying degrees of oxygen into bottles.

bottling, vital winemaking operation for all wines other than those packaged in containers other than bottles (see BOXES and CANS) and those few served straight from a cask or tank as BULK WINE.

Bottling techniques vary greatly according to the size, resources, technical ability, and modernity of the winery, although since the 1960s it has been customary almost everywhere to blend all casks or vats of a given lot of wine together before bottling, and to bottle it all at once. (Prior to this there could be considerable BOTTLE VARIATION between different bottlings of even FIRST GROWTHS. And see CHAPOUTIER for a report of this practice extending well into the 1990s.)

Until recently, bottling lines subjected the wine to considerable AERATION and agitation so that wines would not taste as they should for some weeks after bottling, when the dissolved OXYGEN had fully reacted with the wine components, including added SULFUR DIOXIDE (as explained in BOTTLE SICKNESS). At one time, wines containing RESIDUAL SUGAR might have been subjected to PASTEURIZATION and 'hot bottling' to ensure microbiological stability, but such methods have been largely replaced by membrane FILTRATION. High-quality, low-alcohol, slightly sweet young wines may well be treated to STERILE BOTTLING.

Today an increasing proportion of wine is bottled more carefully: improved technology, including the use of NITROGEN or CARBON DIOXIDE to eliminate exposure to oxygen, has significantly reduced the level of dissolved oxygen in the wine (see TOTAL PACKAGE OXYGEN). The expensive, high-volume, super-fast bottling lines used for everyday wines often provide the best results because problems with oxygen pick-up tend to be worse at slower speeds, at the start and end of the bottling run, or if there is a stoppage. Oxygen management is likely to be given higher priority in wines not intended for ageing. In this aspect of wine production, big may be beautiful.

Some smaller producers of high-quality wine have the funds to invest in their own hi-tech bottling line but many other small wineries, especially in France where *mis en bouteille au domaine* has considerable cachet, depend on the services of outside mobile bottling lines, bottling equipment mounted in a truck or lorry which can be brought to the winery for a day or more. Others still follow the ancient tradition of bottling wine from casks or even individual barrels in the cellar but in general this is a part of the production process that is most often outsourced to specialists.

The specific steps involved in bottling are the preparation of the wine itself (BLENDING, ANALYSIS, and possibly final FILTRATION) together with the preparation of the bottling line (sterilization and the preparation of the filler, corker or capper, labeller, capsuler, and casing machines, as appropriate). High-quality wines suitable for BOTTLE AGEING may not be labelled as soon as they are bottled, because they are stored for some time before being released and the labels may deteriorate in cellar conditions.

Bottling may take place either at any time from a few weeks after HARVEST (as with NOUVEAU wines) or when the wine is many years old (as in some of the most traditional Iberian BODEGAS). On smaller wine estates, bottling normally takes place at an otherwise quiet time for cellar staff such as in the spring or early summer.

Place of bottling may be many thousands of miles from where the grapes were originally grown, and even from where the wine was made, since BULK TRANSPORT is so very much cheaper than transporting wine in bottle and more environmentally friendly. A 20-foot container will hold approximately 1,100 9-litre cases of bottled wine but a disposable tank that fits into the same container will hold 24,000 litres of wine. The cost of bottling and bottles being so relatively high in California, Chile, and Australia, for example, some wines destined for sale in the US and Europe are bottled close to the market. According to the OIV, the total volume of wine shipped around the world in bulk rose 61% between 2005 and 2012 to represent more than 40% of all exported wine. In Eastern Europe and the former SOVIET UNION in particular, bottling has traditionally taken place much closer to centres of population than to the vineyard. Producers of hand-crafted, top-quality wines, however, usually prefer to conduct the bottling operation themselves since they have greater control over the process and are able to reduce to a minimum the amount of treatment the wine needs prior to shipping. However, for high-volume wines with a limited shelf life in bottle of around nine months, there is the advantage that the wine is likely to reach the retailers' shelves much sooner after bottling than wine bottled at source. See BOTTLING INFORMATION for the significance of various bottling claims on the label.

As with any mechanical process, many things can go wrong during the bottling operation. The bottled wine itself can develop problems which were not previously apparent. Most result from high levels of dissolved oxygen (see BOTTLE SICKNESS), incomplete STABILIZATION, or introducing yeast/bacteria during bottling and causing post-bottling fermentation, but other contaminants may also intervene, such as those associated with CORKS.

See also BOTTLES.   J.R., J.E.H., & B.D.

bottling information. Most wine labels should divulge where the wine was bottled. Common phrases for 'bottled' are *mis en bouteille* in French, *imbottigliato* in Italian, *embotellado* in Spanish, and *engarrafado* in Portuguese.

Wines bottled in the same place as they were vinified are described under CHÂTEAU BOTTLED, DOMAINE BOTTLED, ESTATE BOTTLED, ERZEUGERAB-FÜLLUNG, or GUTSABFÜLLUNG, but WINES WITHOUT GEOGRAPHICAL INDICATION may not be described as having been bottled at the domaine or château, for example, which last two terms are prohibited from their labels. If an address includes the name of a Protected Designation of Origin (see PDO), there are restrictions on the font size relative to that of any designation. Many of the wines bottled by an enterprise other than the one which made the wine are labelled relatively obliquely. Within the EU, the bottler's post code is usually employed instead of a full postal address. This is one of those well-intentioned rules designed to minimize the possibility of passing off, but it does make labels less informative to those not conversant with, for example, French *département* numbers or the two letters used for each Italian province.

Bouchalès is a dark-berried vine variety still grown to a limited extent in Bordeaux and in the Lot-et-Garonne *département*. It is not particularly easy to graft or grow and total French plantings fell from over 4,000 ha/9,900 acres in 1968 to less than 200 ha/500 acres by the 21st century.

Bouchard, Père et Fils, one of Beaune's large merchant houses (quite distinct from Bouchard Aîné), and the most important vineyard owner on Burgundy's Côte de BEAUNE. Based since 1731 in the 15th-century Château de Beaune, a landmark in this medieval wine town, the house was established by Michel Bouchard, a Dauphiné textile merchant, and taken over in 1995 by Joseph Henriot of the eponymous champagne house who once ran VEUVE CLICQUOT. By that stage the beleaguered ninth generation of Bouchards had vineyard land acquired over the centuries that totalled more than 90 ha/230 acres and Henriot has continued to add to this, with 86 of the firm's 130 ha/321 acres in GRANDS CRUS or PREMIERS CRUS. Bouchard have holdings in 22 different Beaune vineyards, including their exclusivity in Beaune-Grèves, Vigne de l'Enfant Jésus, and MONOPOLES Beaune, Clos de la Mousse, Beaune, Clos St Landry, and Volnay, Frémiets Clos de la Rougeotte. They are also particularly proud of their 0.89-ha/2.2-acre holding in Le MONTRA-CHET, and their particularly significant share of Chevalier-Montrachet with their holding of 2.33 ha/5.75 acres. In 1998, the Chablis firm William Fèvre was also acquired by the Henriot family and has been taken from strength to strength.

Wines from their own vineyards are undoubtedly Bouchard's best. For the much larger NÉGOCIANT business, the firm buys in considerable quantities of grapes and young wines for ÉLEVAGE in the firm's cellars in Savigny-lès-Beaune. Under Henriot, even relatively inexpensive red wines became noticeably deeper and more concentrated.

Bouchet, name for CABERNET FRANC commonly used in St-Émilion and elsewhere on the right bank of the GIRONDE, while Bouchy has been known in MADIRAN.

bouchon is French for CORK and **bouchonné** describes a faulty, CORKED wine.

bouillie bordelaise. See BORDEAUX MIXTURE.

bouquet, oft-ridiculed tasting term for the smell of a wine, particularly that of a mature or maturing wine. Although its original French meaning was 'small wood' (from the same root as the Italian *bosco* and the English *bosky*), bouquet is a French word for a bunch of flowers which has been used to describe the perfume of a wine since the first half of the 19th century. It is used loosely by many wine tasters to describe any pleasant wine smell or smells but, just as a bouquet (rather than a bunch) of flowers suggests a composition of several varied elements, many wine professionals distinguish between the simple AROMA of the grape and the bouquet of the more complex compounds which evolve as a result of FERMENTATION, ÉLEVAGE, and BOTTLE AGEING. There is little consistency in usage, however, and many authorities differ about the point in a wine's life cycle at which a wine's smell stops being an aroma and becomes a bouquet. See also AGEING, ESTER, FLAVOUR COMPOUNDS, and FLAVOUR PRECURSORS.

Bourboulenc is an ancient Provençal white grape variety. Ripening late but keeping its acidity well, it is allowed into a wide variety of Provençal and southern Rhône appellations (including Châteauneuf-du-Pape) but is rarely encountered as a dominant variety other than in the distinctively marine whites of La CLAPE and an increasing number of other Languedoc whites. France's total area of Bourboulenc was 566 ha/1,398 acres in 2011. Together with Maccabéo, it should constitute more than 50% of the blend for any white MINERVOIS, and the two, with Grenache Blanc, should dominate CORBIÈRES Blanc. Wine produced can be fine, crisp, and aromatic.

Bourg, small town in the BORDEAUX region on the right bank of the River DORDOGNE, just up river of its confluence with the Garonne, which is surrounded by the **Côtes de Bourg** appellation, also known as **Bourg** and **Bourgeais**. The 3,400 ha/8,398 acres of vineyard that produced Côtes de Bourg in 2013 have a characterful base of CLAY and LIMESTONE with sandy GRAVEL deposits and some MARLS. They are planted substantially with Merlot and the best reds can be more concentrated and ageworthy than those from the larger BLAYE area to the immediate north, and vineyards on the edge of the Gironde estuary are particularly well protected from FROST DAMAGE, thanks to the maritime influence. The star of the appellation is Ch Roc de Combes, related to St-Émilion's Ch Tertre-Roteboeuf, on a particularly well-favoured site on the Gironde itself. A little dry white wine is also made.

bourgeon is French for BUD, and **bourgeonnage** is the viticultural practice of thinning surplus developing buds before FLOWERING, a form of early CROP THINNING.

Bourgogne, the French name for both the region of BURGUNDY (La Bourgogne) and burgundy, the wines thereof (*le bourgogne*), which are red, white, and very occasionally rosé. In particular, Bourgogne refers to the most basic, generic category of APPELLATIONS in Burgundy.

For white wines the generic appellations are BOURGOGNE ALIGOTÉ, **Bourgogne Blanc** (made from Chardonnay grapes, although Pinot Blanc and Pinot Gris are tolerated), and Coteaux BOURGUIGNONS. For red wines the generic appellations are BOURGOGNE PASSETOUTGRAINS, **Coteaux Bourguignons**, and **Bourgogne Rouge**. The last is usually pure Pinot Noir, although it may technically include the César and Tressot once grown in the Yonne (Chablis country), and may be made from Gamay grapes if grown in one of the BEAUJOLAIS crus. A small amount of pink wine is sold as **Bourgogne Rosé**, or **Bourgogne Clairet**. In practice this may be the result of a SAIGNÉE of a red wine from a major vineyard in order to concentrate it—although by law this is not possible, since to declassify part of the crop into Bourgogne Rosé would necessitate declassifying the remainder into Bourgogne Rouge.

Bourgogne of whatever colour may be followed by a geographical suffix, either denoting a region (Hautes Côtes de Nuits, Hautes Côtes de Beaune, Côte Chalonnaise, Côtes d'AUXERRE, Côtes du COUCHOIS); a commune or group of communes (Chitry, Coulanges-la-Vineuse, Epineuil, Tonnerre, Vézelay); or in certain cases a vineyard (Côte St-Jacques at Joigny, and La Chapelle Notre-Dame, Le Chapitre, and Montrecul in the Côte d'Or).

Thus it is evident that the scope of 'Bourgogne', be it white, red, or pink, encompasses wide variations in provenance, quality, and style of wine, which may not be clear from the label. A Bourgogne Rouge or Bourgogne Blanc made by a grower in one of the major villages of the Côte d'Or (such as MEURSAULT for whites and VOLNAY or CHAMBOLLE-MUSIGNY for reds) is likely to be reliably fashioned in the image of classic CÔTE D'OR burgundy, however, and may well represent excellent value, being generally ready to drink sooner. There is every chance that the wine will be made from vines only just outside the village appellation yet will be sold at half the price.

CRÉMANT de Bourgogne is the generic appellation for sparkling Burgundy, either white or rosé, while the now rare red version is classified as **Bourgogne Mousseux**.

See also BOURGOGNE ALIGOTÉ, BOURGOGNE PASSETOUTGRAINS, and Coteaux BOURGUIGNONS.

J.T.C.M.

Bourgogne Aligoté

Bourgogne Aligoté, a generic appellation of around 1,600 ha/3, 950 acres in Burgundy for white wines made from the ALIGOTÉ grape. These wines vary between refreshingly crisp and disagreeably tart, although the latter characteristic suits their role as the basis for *vin blanc cassis*, or KIR. Aligoté is primarily for early consumption although wines from the best locations such as Chitry in the Yonne, Pernand-Vergelesses in the Côte de Beaune, and BOUZERON (which has its own appellation for Aligoté) can age well. The golden Aligoté d'Oré is a superior version of the grape, typically found in Bouzeron.

J.T.C.M.

Bourgogne Passetoutgrains

Bourgogne Passetoutgrains, red thirst-quencher from Burgundy made from Pinot Noir (which must be at least 30% of the blend) and Gamay grapes. Often deep in colour and rather savagely animal when young, Passetoutgrains with age can attain greater refinement as the Pinot Noir flavours start to dominate. The best examples come from vineyards in the CÔTE D'OR lying in the plain beyond the main D974 road which divides the finer vineyards from the generic. Almost two-thirds as much of this appellation is made each year as Bourgogne Rouge but relatively little leaves France.

J.T.C.M.

Bourgogne, Université de

Bourgogne, Université de. See DIJON.

Bourgueil

Bourgueil, potentially captivating red wines made on the north bank of the Loire in the west of the TOURAINE district. The climate here is particularly gentle and rainfall is low, as in much of ANJOU to the immediate west. Of the 1,300 ha/3,200 acres of vineyard well over half are on the south-facing slopes of limestone and gravel which lead west from St-Patrice almost on the river to St-Nicolas (see below), where fewer than a third of the vineyard is on the slopes

The CABERNET FRANC grape is mainly responsible for these medium-bodied wines, which are typically marked by a more powerful aroma (reminding some of raspberries, others of pencil shavings) and slightly more noticeable tannins than the wines of CHINON to the south. As in Chinon, the proportion of Cabernet Sauvignon allowed in the wine has been reduced from 25 to 10% of the blend. Bourgueil can be aged for

five or many more years in really successful, fully ripe VINTAGES while **St-Nicolas-de-Bourgueil**, produced on about 900 ha of often lighter soils in the west of the region, is generally a lighter, earlier maturing wine. These fragrant wines are extremely popular in Paris and northern France but have yet to be discovered by most non-French wine lovers.

A little dry rosé Bourgueil is also made, but the appellation does not, unlike Chinon, encompass white wines. See LOIRE, including map.

Friedrich, J., *A Wine and Food Guide to the Loire* (New York, 1996).

Bourguignons, Coteaux

Bourguignons, Coteaux. This 2013 appellation replaced Bourgogne Grande Ordinaire, applying to minor Burgundy vineyards, growing ALIGOTÉ, Chardonnay, MELON DE BOURGOGNE, Pinot Blanc, and/or Pinot Gris for whites, and Gamay, Pinot Noir, and CÉSAR (in the Yonne) for reds. The key to this is the inclusion of the Gamay grape because the rules for BEAUJOLAIS allow de- or re-classification as Coteaux Bourguignons.

J.T.C.M

Bouschet

Bouschet is, like Müller, Scheu, and Seibel, a vine-breeder's surname that lives on in the name of his creations, although in this case there were two Bouschets, a 19th-century father and son whose work, perhaps unfortunately, made the spread of ARAMON possible. In 1824 Louis Bouschet de Bernard combined the productivity of Aramon with the colour expected of a red wine by crossing Aramon with TEINTURIER du Cher and modestly calling the result Petit Bouschet. This expedient cross was popular in France throughout the second half of the 19th century and is still, just, to be found in Portugal. Louis's son Henri carried on where his father left off, producing more durably ALICANTE BOUSCHET and GRAND NOIR DE LA CALMETTE as well as a Carignan Bouschet.

Boutenac

Boutenac, subappellation in the north east of CORBIÈRES.

Bouvier

Bouvier, minor, low-acid white grape variety grown mainly in the Burgenland region of AUSTRIA, where it is particularly used for FEDERWEISSER, as well as for early-bottled wines. It can also be found in Slovenia, Slovakia, and Hungary.

Bouzeron

Bouzeron, village in the Côte CHALONNAISE famous for its BOURGOGNE ALIGOTÉ, which has had its own appellation, Bourgogne Aligoté de Bouzeron, since 1979, promoted to the simple appellation Bouzeron in 1997. Just 52 ha/128 acres produced wine in 2012.

Bovale

Bovale, dark-skinned grapes in SARDINIA distinguished as **Bovale Sardo**, a synonym for CARIGNAN, and the more common **Bovale Grande**, a synonym for GRACIANO. Both are used mainly for blending.

boxes, wine

boxes, wine. In the 1970s, an entirely new way of PACKAGING wine was developed, expressly to provide a significant volume of wine in a package that is not as breakable or heavy as a bottle, and is better able to preserve any wine left in the container. It comprises a collapsible laminated bag inside a strong cardboard carton, and wine is drawn out of a tap specially designed to minimize the ingress of potentially harmful OXYGEN. The difficulty of making the wine container completely airtight restricts the potential shelf life of **bag-in-box** wines. but there have been considerable improvements in this respect since the mid 1990s. There are two main types of bag: in the silver-coloured ones, the oxygen barrier is provided by a thin layer of aluminium, or aluminium-coated polyester, between layers of high-density polyethylene; in the clear bags, the oxygen barrier is made from polyvinyl alcohol. The main disadvantage of the former is 'flex cracking', which tends to occur during transportation and weakens the oxygen barrier. The oxygen barrier in the clear bag is less effective and becomes even less so as relative humidity increases.

The package, commonly holding four litres of wine, is particularly popular in Australia and New Zealand, where it is known flatteringly as the 'cask' or, more prosaically, 'bladder pack'. Wine boxes have also enjoyed success in northern Europe in the 3-l size. Boxes are generally filled with less expensive wines designed for early drinking and are bought either in bulk for parties or by those who want to enjoy a simple wine one glass at a time over several weeks. The wine inside a bag is best consumed within 4–6 weeks of opening, and has usually deteriorated quite markedly 9–12 months after filling, which is why some wine boxes are dated. (See LEFTOVER WINE for details of devices for preserving wine in partially empty bottles.) By 2014, almost 20% of all wine sold in the off trade (off-premise) in the US was packed in a box.

Brachetto

Brachetto, distinctively aromatic light red grape variety found principally round Asti, Roero, and Alessandria, where it is particularly successful, in the PIEMONTE region of Italy. It produces wines, notably **Brachetto d'Acqui** promoted to DOCG status in 1996, that are fizzy, light in alcohol (usually under 6%), and have both the colour and flavour of roses or strawberries—the light red equivalent of Moscato d'Asti. Occasional dry versions are made in Piemonte which has 1,459 ha/3,604 acres in total. Some is planted in Victoria, Australia.

Bragato, Romeo

Bragato, Romeo, Dalmatian-born graduate of Italian viticulture studies and employee of the Victorian government in Australia who was invited in 1895 to investigate the prospects for viticulture and winemaking in New Zealand. His report was very favourable, and became an important document encouraging the development of the industry. Bragato found many regions 'pre-eminently suited' to viticulture and a surge in plantings resulted.

Bragato identified PHYLLOXERA in New Zealand in 1895, and suggested the use of resistant ROOTSTOCKS, but his advice was initially ignored. Offered the position of government viticulturist in 1902, he immediately began importing and distributing these rootstocks (which were to be used again to fight phylloxera outbreaks of the 1980s). He established a research station at Te Kauwhata with experimental vineyards and a training winery, and also published a handbook *Viticulture in New Zealand*. Bragato and the fledgling wine industry were, however, not supported by his masters in the Department of Agriculture. In 1908 he lost control of the Te Kauwhata Research Station and in 1909 migrated to Canada in disgust.   R.E.S.

Bramaterra, tiny DOC in the Alto Piemonte of which unfortunately only 28ha remained in 2014. Wines should contain 50 to 80% Nebbiolo with CROATINA, UVA RARA, and VESPOLINA. The Bramaterra of Odilio Antoniotti aptly demonstrates the excellence of the terroir. See SPANNA for more detail.

Brancellao, Galician name for ALVARELHÃO of the Douro.

branco, Portuguese word meaning 'white'. *Vinho branco* is therefore white wine.

Brancott Estate, long known as Montana, once the dominant producer and exporter of NEW ZEALAND wine, responsible for about half the country's production. It was founded in 1934 when Ivan Yukich planted a vineyard in the Waitakere Ranges west of Auckland. His sons, Frank and Mate, adopted the vineyard's name, Montana, when they founded a wine company 30 years later. Montana helped drive, and greatly profited from, New Zealand's rapid rise in wine consumption from the early 1970s.

Increased wine production was originally achieved with the help of contracted grape growers, particularly in Gisborne and later in Hawke's Bay. In 1973, the North American wine and spirit giant Seagram bought 45% of Montana, the additional capital and expertise allowing the company to invest heavily in vineyards, specifically pioneering grape-growing in Marlborough. Seagram sold its share in the company in 1987.

In 2000, Montana acquired Corbans Wines, New Zealand's second largest wine producer. Between 2001 and 2005, the company, renamed Allied Domecq Wines (NZ), was the jewel in

the crown of the wine division of the eponymous British conglomerate before being acquired by PERNOD RICARD, which changed the New Zealand company's name to avoid confusion with the American state. In 2010 Pernod Ricard NZ sold five sparkling wine brands and seven still wine brands to Lion Nathan New Zealand. At the same time it also sold its Gisborne winery, all of its vineyards in the Gisborne region, and one Hawke's Bay winery to Lion Nathan and their JOINT VENTURE partner Indevin. By 'streamlining its production footprint' Pernod Ricard lost the company's dominant status and the New Zealand wine industry is no longer dominated by a single producer.
R.F.C.

brands, interpreted strictly as individual products marketed on the basis of their name and image rather than on their inherent qualities, have a much less dominant position in the market for wine than for drinks such as beer or cola, for instance, but thanks to GLOBALIZATION they are growing in importance. The leading industry resource IMPACT Databank calculated that the global market share of the top 25 wine brands in the world, while having grown significantly since the mid 1990s, was still less than 8% by 2004. It is perhaps significant that IMPACT is based in the UNITED STATES, where distribution is tightly controlled (see THREE-TIER SYSTEM, for example) and brands account for more than half of all wine sales. Most sectors of the wine market are relatively fragmented (although the FORTIFIED WINE business is not and has been built on brands), so that brand promotion is difficult to make cost-effective, and can leave **branded wines** looking poor value. By far the most common promotion in the 21st century has been based on PRICE and close relationships with the decreasing number of multiple retailers, many of which have been turning away from third party brands to their own exclusive labels.

Wine brands offer a familiar lifeline to new wine consumers baffled by a multiplicity of unfamiliar, often foreign, proper names. But as wine drinkers become more sophisticated, they learn to decode what initially seems the arcane language of wine names, usually by identifying the major VARIETALS, some of the more important place-names, and/or favourite producers. Thus, brands are most sought after in embryonic and fast-growing markets, such as northern Europe and the rest of the English-speaking world between the 1950s and the 1980s, and in Africa and some Asian countries today.

It may be difficult to market branded wines in a competitive market, but it can be even more difficult to maintain consistency of a product as variable as wine. Supplies are strictly limited to an annual batch production process. Wine cannot be manufactured to suit demand, and

different vintages impose their own characteristics on the product regardless of consumer taste. A high proportion of all wine drinkers were introduced to wine through brands, and it is to the credit of those brand owners most dedicated to maintaining quality standards whenever the introduction was a happy one.

Notably successful international individual wine brands are relatively few, and they have perforce to be based on wine of which there is no shortage of supply. BLUE NUN, LANCERS, MATEUS ROSÉ, and MOUTON CADET are all examples of brands which in the 20th century achieved annual sales measured in millions of cases. YELLOW TAIL was the miracle brand of the early 21st century.

There are those who argue that the grape varieties CHARDONNAY and PINOT GRIGIO, for example, have become brands in their own right, so strong is consumer recognition of the name. Others claim that in certain markets, buyers' own brands have become so important, and so cleverly marketed, that, for example, some retailers' names have established themselves as brands. The definition of a wine brand is certainly a loose one. In some respects, the New French CLARETS, named for the estate which produced them, were the first wine brands. Today, the French wine industry blames some of its difficulty in selling everything it produces on its failure to build brands, in conspicuous contrast to the bigger companies in Australia and the US. And any definition which incorporates the notion of relatively elastic supply and some studied promotion would allow that the most successful wine brands of all are the so-called *grande marque* (which translates directly as 'big brand') CHAMPAGNES.

Braquet, sometimes called **Brachet**, historic light red grape variety of PROVENCE which is still a valued, if minor, ingredient in the red and pink wines of BELLET near Nice. Yields are low and the vine is relatively delicate but the wine is truly distinctive. This variety is not related to the much more aromatic Italian BRACHETTO.

Brazil, **Brasil** in Portuguese, vast country and third most important wine producer in SOUTH AMERICA after Argentina and Chile with 82,507 ha/203,840 acres of vineyards in 2012 of which only a little over 10,000 ha were VINIFERA. Of the 3.88 million hl/102 million galls of wine produced in 2013, 43% was still red, 34% was still white, and a significant 22% was sparkling. Only about 9% of all wine made in Brazil is *vinho fino*, made from *V. vinifera* grapes. TABLE GRAPES are the main products of Brazilian vineyards.

The vine was introduced in São Paulo state by the Portuguese as early as 1532. Spanish vines were introduced by the Jesuits in Rio Grande do Sul in 1626, but viticulture was abandoned after the destruction of Jesuit missions in the south of the country. In the 18th century, settlers from the Azores tried for a third time to establish *V. vinifera* vine cuttings brought from Madeira and the Azores, but encountered severe problems in the hot, humid climate. The first vines to be successfully cultivated in Brazil were the American vine ISABELLA (more often called Isabel in Brazil) that was first planted on the south coast of Rio Grande in 1840, but it was not until the arrival of Italian immigrants in the high Serra Gaúcha region in the north east of Rio Grande do Sul that viticulture was definitively established in Brazil, and even then, in the late 1870s, it was mainly the AMERICAN VINES Isabel and CONCORD that were cultivated, subsequently supplemented by Italian varieties such as Barbera, Bonarda, Moscato, Peverella, and Trebbiano, and by Tannat as in Uruguay to the south.

Only in the early 20th century was any sort of national wine market established, with the development of communications between the centres of population such as Rio de Janeiro and the wine regions in the far south. The first CO-OPERATIVES were established in the late 1920s.

Wines with serious claims to quality were not developed until the 1970s, when several important multinational corporations, including MOËT & CHANDON, Seagram, Bacardi, Heublein, DOMECQ, and Martini & Rossi, established wine companies in Brazil and invested in modern winemaking equipment such as automatic TEMPERATURE CONTROL, STAINLESS STEEL, and imported BARRIQUES. Vine varieties such as Chardonnay, Welschriesling (Riesling Italico), Sémillon, Gewürztraminer, Cabernet Franc, Merlot, and Cabernet Sauvignon were also imported, and a programme of viticultural improvements embarked upon.

Modern Brazilian viticulture is concentrated in the extreme south of the country in the state of Rio Grande do Sul, principally in the high, hilly Serra Gaúcha region, north and inland of the state capital Porto Alegre, and also in the much smaller, newer Campanha, sometimes called Fronteira, wine region on the border with URUGUAY and Argentina.

Serra Gaúcha incorporates about 31,000 ha/ 76,000 acres of vines, all grafted, at an average ELEVATION of 700 m/2,300 ft, which is difficult to mechanize, and shared between so many small farmers that the average vineyard holding is just 2.5 ha. The relatively acid soils are shallow, not particularly fertile, and have a high proportion of water-retaining clay. Average RAINFALL here is very high for a wine region, about 1,800 mm/70 in, of which at least 700 mm falls during the growing season of September to February. The resulting effect on GRAPE RIPENING means that ENRICHMENT of some sort, usually CHAPTALIZATION, is almost always necessary. FUNGAL

DISEASES are a constant threat in this humid climate, and more than 80% of all vines are American vines or hybrids, still chiefly the usefully thick-skinned Isabel, grown to produce GRAPE JUICE, TABLE GRAPES, and wine of the most basic quality.

The most common vine-TRAINING SYSTEMS are TENDONE to minimize the ROT that is a perennial problem and ESPALIER to encourage ripening of red wine varieties. For the *V. vinifera* varieties, efforts are being made to reduce YIELDS, however, in attempts to maximize wine quality.

The grapes are often picked before full ripeness is reached and the white wines of Serra Gaúcha are usually high in MALIC ACID. Different wineries have different policies on the desirability of MALOLACTIC FERMENTATION for white wines. Red wines are, inevitably in this climate, relatively light (yields can easily be 14 tonnes per ha) and acid, although there has been some experimentation with new OAK.

Serra Gaúcha can produce good-quality grapes for red wine (and substantial quantities for local VERMOUTH), while Flores da Cunha in the east of the region is the source of much everyday wine. *V. vinifera* production is centred on Bento Gonçalves, a sort of tourist centre for the wine industry, immediately east of the Vale dos Vinhedos, Brazil's first DO. Created in 2009, it established Merlot and Chardonnay as the accepted grapes (with Cabernet Sauvignon, Cabernet Franc, and Tannat also allowed in red blends and Riesling Itálico (Welschriesling) for whites). Also within Serra Gaúcha, Garibaldi, where Moët-Hennessy Brasil is based, is the traditional area for SPARKLING WINE production, many of these wines being made in the image of SPUMANTE, for Italian influence is strong in the region. However, many producers such as Cave Geisse are establishing themselves outside these boundaries. Geisse, in Pinto Bandeira just east of Bento Gonçalves, have shown just how good Brazilian sparkling wine can be.

With the exception of the the Vale dos Vinhedos, all the major companies have moved their fine-wine focus to the Campanha region, which is notably less humid and produces deeper-coloured wines. There are around 1,400 ha/ 3,500 acres of vines, all *V. vinifera* varieties, planted in Campanha on the border with Uruguay, chiefly in the communes of Santana do Livramento and Pinheiro Machado. This is much flatter country, used substantially for pasture and cereal crops, with sandy soils and good DRAINAGE. Most vines are trained using some sort of espalier system, and the average annual rainfall is about 850 mm/33 in, considerably less than Serra Gaúcha but still high enough to prejudice ripening.

North of Serra Gaúcha, in the state of Santa Catarina, a Vinhos de Altura (High Altitude Wines) association has been formed, centred on the São Joaquim Plateau (above 900 m/

2,950 ft elevation), with promising results. Campos de Cima da Serra, a small new wine region between Serra Gaúcha and the Planalto Catarinense, has vineyards at about the same elevation.

Another, even more distinctive, relatively new wine region is in the São Francisco Valley in the arid north of the country just nine degrees of LATITUDE south of the equator on the border between the states of Bahia and Pernambuco. TROPICAL VITICULTURE here involves more than one harvest a year. Irrigation from vines dependent on water from the local river is the rule here for the 570 ha of *V. vinifera* vines among a total vineyard area of 12,500 ha/31,000 acres in the early 2010s. Production costs are usefully low but the wines produced are relatively basic. Despite these signs of viticultural life, local wine has yet to penetrate Brazilian culture very deeply, and average consumption is still extremely low, well below 2 l per head per year, except in the predominantly European communities of the south, although interest in Brazilian wine both domestically and on export markets is certainly growing.

Desimone, M., & Jenssen, J., *Wines of the Southern Hemisphere* (New York, 2012).

Goldstein, E., *Wines of South America* (Oakland, Calif., 2014).

www.winesofbrasil.com

breathing, an operation, believed beneficial by some consumers, involving pulling the cork and letting the open bottle stand for a few hours before it is poured. In fact, in such circumstances the wine can take only the most minimal of 'breaths', and any change is bound to be imperceptible (except possibly in the case of BOTTLE SICKNESS). The surface area of wine exposed to the air is so small that the effects of any AERATION as a result of this operation are negligible. See DECANTING for details of effective aeration.

Breede River Valley, important wine region in SOUTH AFRICA.

breeding. See VINE BREEDING.

Breganze, DOC in the VENETO region in north-east Italy, mainly for the INTERNATIONAL VARIETIES for which demand is waning, and increasingly in need of redefining itself in a more Italian, indigenous context. Wines of real interest are produced from Bordeaux varieties, but TAI BIANCO, the local VESPAIOLA for the BOTRYTIZED or DRIED-GRAPE sweet white speciality Torcolato, the red MARZEMINO, and the rare Gruaja, probably related to Valpolicella's NEGRARA Veronese, could add some distinction to the DOC. Maculan put Breganze on the map in the 1980s by focusing on quality instead of mere quantity by lowering yields, introducing modern winemaking equipment, and using BARRIQUES. Several estates followed his example, but the region as a whole receives little attention from the international market.

W.S.

Breton, name sometimes used in the middle Loire for the CABERNET FRANC grape. The reference is not to Brittany but to Abbot Breton, who is reputed to have disseminated the vine in the 17th century.

Brettanomyces, sometimes called **brett**, one of the YEAST genera found occasionally on grapes but more often in wines, especially those that have undergone BARREL MATURATION or CASK AGEING. *Brettanomyces* in its perfect or sporulating form is known as DEKKERA, but recent changes to the rules for naming fungi suggest precedence be given to the name *Brettanomyces*. While it is widely considered a spoilage yeast since it can produce off-flavours in wines, there are producers who suggest that at low levels some of the diverse flavours produced by *Brettanomyces* can improve red wine complexity. (In some beers, for example Belgium's spontaneously fermented lambic and gueuze beers, *Brettanomyces* and its effects are essential.)

The first isolation of *Brettanomyces*, originally designated *Mycotorula intermedia*, in wine was in the 1930s by Krumbholz and Tauschanoff. Although the number of *Brettanomyces/Dekkera* species has expanded and contracted due to changes in methods of identification, of the five species currently recognised, *Brettanomyces (Dekkera) bruxellensis* is the one most commonly found in wines worldwide. This species can grow in both red and white wine, although it is more often associated with red.

Brettanomyces is both an anaerobic and an aerobic organism. It is a resourceful microbe that can utilize a number of substrates at low levels and under restrictive conditions. The range and quantity of by-products produced by *Brettanomyces* depend on various factors, including levels of substrates, available precursors, and the size of the *Brettanomyces* population in the wine. The most important substrate is RESIDUAL SUGAR, although some OXYGEN is needed to maximize growth.

There are four key by-products of *Brettanomyces* growth which can affect the flavour and aroma of a wine: esterases, volatile fatty acids, tetrahydropyridines, and, arguably the most important, volatile phenols. Two critical volatile phenol compounds have been isolated from *Brettanomyces* activity: 4-ethylphenol (4-EP) and 4-ethylguaiacol (4-EG). 4-EP is often described as introducing an 'animal', 'medicinal', and 'sweaty saddle' flavour to wine. Its presence is an almost certain indicator of a *Brettanomyces* infection, and this is what most diagnostic laboratories test for to verify the presence of

Brettanomyces. 4-EG in wine has a more appealing smoky, spicy, clove-like aroma. Formation of tetrahydropyridines, which are responsible for MOUSY off-flavour, seems to result from a large population of *Brettanomyces* which is stimulated by exposure of wine to oxygen, for example when the wine is on ULLAGE.

Brettanomyces can create significant levels of volatile phenols in a short period of time and is difficult to manage in the cellar. However, the tools for monitoring *Brettanomyces* have never been more advanced, and winemakers can use microbiological techniques such as selective growth media containing cyclodeximide and odourless hydroxyphenolic acid precursor compound, or DNA-based identification methods, and analytical techniques such as gas chromatography/mass spectrometry to monitor high-risk wines.

Brettanomyces strains have variable sensitivity to SULFUR DIOXIDE. Recent research suggests that they might be adapting to it but that they can be controlled by maintaining at least 0.625 mg/l molecular sulfur dioxide. Wines are at greatest risk of spoilage if the onset of MALOLACTIC CONVERSION is delayed or if there is insufficient sulfur dioxidide during maturation. HYGIENE is an important factor in controlling the spread of *Brettanomyces* in the cellar. Areas that provide suitable niches for *Brettanomyces* are must lines, dirty crush equipment, barrels, or any tank or transfer line that is not cleaned effectively. There have also been suggestions that the fruit fly (see DROSOPHILA) can carry *Brettanomyces*. Once it is embedded in COOPERAGE, it can be difficult to eliminate from the cellar and barrels may need to be discarded to significantly reduce the populations. As with other microbes, the cleaner the winery, the more control one has over *Brettanomyces*. There are currently only two methods that virtually eliminate *Brettanomyces* at bottling: sterile FILTRATION and dimethyl dicarbonate (see DMDC).

S.H. & P.A.H.

Chatonnet, P., Dubourdieu, D., and Boidron, J. N., 'The influence of Brettanomyces/Dekkera sp. yeasts and lactic acid bacteria on the ethylphenol content of red wines', *American Journal of Enology and Viticulture*, 46/4 (1995), 463–8.

Conterno, L., et al., 'Genetic and physiological characterization of Brettanomyces bruxellensis strains isolated from wines', *American Journal of Enology and Viticulture*, 57 (2006), 139–47.

Curtin, C., Kennedy, E., and Henschke, P. A., 'Genotype-dependent sulphite tolerance of Australian Dekkera (Brettanomyces) bruxellensis wine isolates', *Letters in Applied Microbiology*, 55 (2012), 56–61.

Romano, A., et al., 'Sensory and analytical re-evaluation of "Brett character"', *Food Chemistry*, 114/1 (2009), 15–19.

Silva, P., Cardoso, H., and Gerós, H., 'Studies on the wine spoilage capacity of Brettanomyces/Dekkera spp.', *American Journal of Enology and Viticulture*, 55/1 (2004), 65–72.

Snowdon, E. M., et al., 'Mousy off-flavor: a review', *Journal of Agricultural and Food Chemistry*, 54/18 (2006), 6465–74.

bricco, or *bric* in the dialect of the north west Italian region of PIEMONTE, indicates the highest part of an elevation in the landscape or, in particular, a vineyard with a steep gradient at the top of a hill. The term was first used on a wine label by Luciano de Giacomi in 1969 for his Bricco del Drago, a blend of DOLCETTO and NEBBIOLO grapes from Alba, and has been extensively used for the other wines of Piemonte ever since.

Brindisi, Adriatic port and DOC for robust red wine made mainly from NEGROAMARO grapes, and Chardonnay-based whites shipped mainly in BULK. For more details see PUGLIA.

Britain, or **Great Britain**, has long been one of the most important markets for wine. It regularly imports more wine than any country other than Germany and has shown unusually healthy growth in wine CONSUMPTION since the late 20th century. Its long wine-MERCHANT tradition has made it one of the most discerning, yet open-minded, wine-consuming nations, and London has been an important centre for wine AUCTIONS and FINE WINE trading. Domestic vine-growing in England and Wales is still on too small a scale to affect consumers who expect to find the wines of the world on the shelves of their specialist merchants and, increasingly, supermarkets, although the British may now feel proud of the quality of English sparkling wine. A certain amount of wine is also made from imported GRAPE CONCENTRATE (see BRITISH MADE WINE). Historically, Britain's commercial influence helped shape the very existence of such wines as claret, madeira, marsala, port, and sherry (see BRITISH INFLUENCE ON THE WINE TRADE).

See also ENGLAND (especially for history and modern viticulture), SCOTLAND, and WALES.

British Columbia. With only 3,993 ha/9,866 acres by 2014 in CANADA's extreme Pacific west, about a third of the country's vineyards, British Columbia produces a significant share of the best Canadian wines. European vines thrive in a largely disease-free TERROIR once believed too cold for VINIFERA. The province is currently divided into five APPELLATIONS. The smallest (25.5 ha/63 acres) is the **Fraser Valley** near Vancouver. Most coastal wineries are in the bigger appellations, **Vancouver Island** (175 ha/432 acres) and **Gulf Islands** (46.5 ha/115 acres). Because of the cool maritime climate, early-ripening varieties (Ortega, Pinot Noir, Pinot Gris) predominate. Many wineries here buy additional grapes from the dominant appellation **Okanagan Valley** (3,262 ha/8,060 acres) and the nearby **Similkameen Valley** (280 ha/691 acres). These latter appellations, comprising 89% of British Columbia's vineyards, are 400 km east of Vancouver, protected from coastal rains by two moderate mountain ranges. The growing season is hot and arid. With the lowest precipitation in southern Canada, IRRIGATION is essential. The dominant varieties includethe major Bordeaux red varieties, notably Merlot, as well as Pinot Noir, Pinot Gris, Chardonnay, and Gewurztraminer.

The Okanagan Valley, one of the world's most northerly wine regions, is a superbly scenic glacial trench extending from the 49th parallel north for about 160 km. The defining feature is vast Okanagan Lake, the largest of the valley's chain of lakes which tempers baking summer heat (*see* LAKE EFFECT). The southern part of the Okanagan is the northern extension of the Sonoran desert. Vineyards, on sand or well-drained sandy clay loam, are mainly on slopes.

The first vines in the Okanagan were planted in 1859 by a French Oblate priest, Charles Pandosy. The first commercial vineyards were developed from 1928 by a horticulturist who planted VITIS LABRUSCA vines and sold grapes to the province's first two wineries.

Wineries in the 1960s began importing grapes from California but were also required to buy domestic grapes. Because local scientists opposed *V. vinifera*, new growers initially chose productive French and American HYBRIDS that were winter-hardy but yielded mediocre wine.

The quest for better wine led to *V. vinifera* trials. Inkameep Vineyards, established in the southern Okanagan by the Osoyoos Indian band, planted Riesling, Ehrenfelser, and Scheurebe in 1975.

The economic convulsion that swept away most second-rate wines was the free trade agreement concluded in 1988 between Canada and the United States. It stripped away the protections that domestic wines had enjoyed against competing imports. More than two-thirds of the Okanagan vineyards were pulled out after the 1988 harvest (which totalled 18,400 tons, a record not equalled until the 2005 vintage).

The industry regrouped in 1990, forming the British Columbia Wine Institute and adapting the ONTARIO-developed Vintners Quality Alliance (VQA) programme which imposed the first significant standards of wine quality and included mandatory tasting. Consumer confidence in the wines recovered, attracting new growers who, from 1993, bought fallow vineyards or converted orchards.

British Columbia's largest producers are independently-owned Mission Hill Family Estate and Jackson-Triggs Okanagan Estate owned by CONSTELLATION BRANDS. Groupe Taillan, owner

of Bordeaux's Ch Gruaud Larose and of the Okanagan's Osoyoos Larose, was the first European producer to invest in British Columbia.

As a wine region, British Columbia is still defining itself. More than 60 grape varieties are grown by more than 225 wineries. Almost every style of wine is produced, from sparkling wine to ICEWINE. The most successful are the BORDEAUX BLENDS, Chardonnay, and Pinot Gris, with credible Pinot Noir coming from selected sites.   J.S.

Danehower, C., *Essential Wines and Wineries of the Pacific Northwest: A Guide to the Wine Counties of Washingon, Oregon, British Columbia* (Portland, 2010).

Schreiner, J., *John Schreiner's Okanagan Wine Tour Guide* (5th edn, Vancouver, 2014).

www.winebc.com

www.winebc.org

British influence on the wine trade

For centuries, wine consumption in Britain has had significant ramifications in many of the world's most important wine regions. A cool, wet climate has limited the production of wine in ENGLAND, so that British wine drinkers historically had no choice but to look overseas for their supplies. Since they owe no permanent allegiance to any one wine region or wine-producing country, they have traditionally had a broad range from which to choose, although that choice has been dictated by convenience, FASHION, ECONOMICS, and POLITICS as often as by taste.

British influence on the wine trade resulted from more complex circumstances than a simple lack of native wines, however. (Otherwise, British influence on the wine trade would be no greater than, for example, Swedish or Danish—although see DUTCH WINE TRADE.) Britain enjoyed a unique combination of factors: relative prosperity and political power, a worldwide commercial empire supported by a strong navy, and a steadily increasing middle class. These circumstances not only helped to foster an interest in imported wines, but also provided the economic clout to acquire them. And at certain times in history, in specific wine regions, the British market was so influential that wine styles evolved, or completely new wines were invented, to satisfy its demands.

The first region fully to devote itself to British needs was SOUTH WEST FRANCE, when it belonged to the English crown. Indeed it could be argued that for 300 years, from 1152, Britain did have her own extensive vineyards. During this period BORDEAUX was transformed into the most important wine centre in France. Vineyards were planted or extended around the city and far up the rivers Garonne and Dordogne to quench the English thirst. The loss of Bordeaux to the French in 1453 saw a decline in exports to

England but this part of France was by now well established as a commercial wine region.

During the Middle Ages, wine was relatively cheap and plentiful in Britain. Wines from Germany, Portugal, Spain, Italy, Greece, the Mediterranean islands, and the Holy Land could all be found in London taverns, as well as those from France. It was not until the 16th century, however, that British merchants found, in southern Spain, a wine region to compensate for the loss of Bordeaux. Known collectively as SACK, the wines of Andalucía became immensely fashionable in Tudor times despite wars with Spain. Thousands of BUTTS of wine were sent back to England by British merchants settled in Sanlúcar and MÁLAGA. British taste and investment laid the foundations of what was to become the SHERRY industry.

The 17th century brought many problems for wine. The introduction of exotic new beverages such as coffee, chocolate, and teas (see COFFEE HOUSES), as well as the growing popularity of 'hopped' BEER, threatened the wine trade. The situation was not eased by the fact that the cost of wine had steadily grown to such a point that only the middle and upper classes could afford it. Crippling customs duties exacerbated the crisis. If the wine trade was to survive in Britain, some drastic changes were needed.

Medieval CLAIRET and Tudor sack had been staple beverages enjoyed by many Englishmen. British influence at the end of the 17th century was felt by a different sort of wine producer and encouraged the development of sophisticated superior-quality wines which only a limited clientele could afford. This select English market had particular influence in two areas of France: Bordeaux and CHAMPAGNE.

After the Restoration of Charles II in 1660, all things French were extremely fashionable in London. At this time individual producers in both Champagne and Bordeaux were making efforts to improve the quality of their wines. Champagne was promoted in London by French exiles (although it was English aristocrats who developed the taste for sparkling wine while French connoisseurs decried it as an aberration). Meanwhile a wealthy landowner from Bordeaux, Arnaud de Pontac, succeeded in creating a stir when he opened a restaurant in London, Pontack's Head in Abchurch Street, to sell the wines of his Graves estate of HAUT-BRION.

The English aristocracy were delighted by these new styles of French wines, CLARET, and paid through the nose for them. Thus London became the chief market for fine wine and in turn influenced the quality of the wines themselves, for in the wine trade it is export that makes reputations, raises standards, and, above all, provides the driving force for investment. New vineyards were planted in Champagne and in the MÉDOC to exploit these refined English palates and purses.

b

The next great instance of a British-inspired wine was PORT. The exorbitant cost of champagne and good-quality claret, combined with the supply difficulties that resulted from war with France, caused British merchants to look elsewhere. Political rapprochement with Portugal signalled the possibility of a new, and cheap, source of wine. The British moved into OPORTO, prospected the DOURO Valley for wine and vine-growing potential, and started a boom. Huge quantities of port were sent to Britain from the early 1700s, and as the century progressed the nature of the wine evolved to suit. Originally a rough red table wine, it was soon discovered to be improved by the addition of brandy, which made it even more palatable to the English, and considerably more stable for the sea voyage required. A whole new industry was created and the steep sides of the Douro Valley terraced and planted to victual the English shires.

Similarly, Sicily's MARSALA wine industry was developed by the British when, in the early years of the 19th century, Napoleon set up his Continental System hoping that, by depriving his enemies of French wine (among other things), he could cause British morale to collapse.

In 1860, William Gladstone stated that an Englishman's taste in wine 'is not an immutable, but a mutable thing'. He meant that British palates were capable of adapting to whatever was most available or pleasing at any particular period. A host of factors influenced taste and in turn demand influenced supply. Of all wine-drinking societies, Britain showed these developments most strikingly. Top-quality claret, sparkling champagne, and distinguished vintage port are today sought after all over the world. But ties of tradition and affection remain strong with the British market, a reminder of the fundamental part it played in the evolution of these and many other wines, and the wine trade in general.

Since the early 1980s, Great Britain has been targeted by many of the world's wine producers as one of the few substantial wine markets in which per capita wine consumption is growing. Only Germany imports more wine than Great Britain, but a substantial proportion of this is basic wine for processing into brandy, or tafelwein or SEKT, much of which is re-exported.

The presence of the principal AUCTION houses and the resultant BROKERS made London the focus of the fine-wine market, just as it is a production centre for the LITERATURE OF WINE and for wine EDUCATION.   H.B. & J.R.

Francis, A. D., *The Wine Trade* (London, 1972).

Johnson, H., *The Story of Wine* (London and New York, 1989).

Simon, A. L., *The History of the Wine Trade in England* (London, 1906-9).

British made wine, a curious alcoholic drink made in the image of WINE from ingredients, often GRAPE CONCENTRATE, imported into Great Britain. It is known as MADE WINE, and a decidedly manufactured product it is. Concentrated grape must, the consistency of thin honey, is imported in bulk throughout the year from wherever happens to be able to supply the best value (Spain was a notable source in the early 21st century). The must is reconstituted by adding water and is fermented using selected YEAST strains, under the most rigorous technical controls, according to the wine style required. Until the 1980s, almost all British wine produced was FORTIFIED, and made to resemble sherry or port, or flavoured with ginger or other spices or fruits. Since the early 1980s, British wines of normal TABLE WINE strength have also been made, much to the dismay of the producers of English wine (see ENGLAND), with whose products made from freshly picked grapes there is considerable confusion.

The British wine producers, few and relatively industrial, claim as initial historical precedent a Francis Chamberleyne, who was granted a charter by Charles I in 1635 to make wine from imported raisins. Wine continued to be made from imported raisins, but the real catalyst for the establishment of an economically viable British wine trade came when a technique for the CONCENTRATION of GRAPE JUICE was perfected by Emmanuel Roche of Toulouse, south-west France, who promptly shared it with two Greek brothers Mitzotakis, members of his wife's family, to help them sell a surplus stock of Greek grapes and grape juice in London in 1900. Their Crown Grape Wine Company (worryingly, on the site of a previous VINEGAR plant) eventually became Vine Products, whose premises outside the capital in Kingston-upon-Thames were described in the 1960s, in a reference to its production of sherry-style wines, as 'the biggest BODEGA in Europe'. This highly profitable concern was eventually taken over by Allied Breweries and, by the 1970s, was being run, somewhat incongruously, in tandem with HARVEYS OF BRISTOL, the principal producers of real SHERRY.

Abbott, J. H. C., *British Wines* (London, 1975).

Brix, scale of measuring total dissolved compounds in grape juice, and therefore its approximate concentration of grape sugars. It is used in the United States and, like other scales used elsewhere (see BAUMÉ and OECHSLE), it can be measured with either a REFRACTOMETER or HYDROMETER. Degrees Brix indicate the percentage of solutes (of which about 90% are sugars in ripe grapes) by weight in the liquid, at a temperature specified for the instrument used. One degree Brix corresponds approximately to 10 g/l sugar.

The **Balling** scale is similar although the specified temperature may differ.   B.G.C.

Broadbent, J. Michael (1927–), wine taster, writer, and auctioneer known particularly for his experience of fine, old wines. Broadbent trained initially as an architect in London but was not as enthused by its more prosaic aspects as by the fine wines to which a family friend had introduced him. He joined the late Tommy Layton as a wine trade trainee in 1952. Three years later he joined HARVEYS OF BRISTOL, then in its heyday, where he worked for Harry WAUGH and eventually became UK sales director. In 1966, partly as a result of his own personal enterprise in corresponding with the chairman, Broadbent was taken on by Christie's to revive their, and the London, wine AUCTION business. From then until 1992 he ran Christie's wine department and in that capacity traded in and tasted a greater number of fine and rare wines than anyone else in the world.

Naturally didactic, he lectured on wine since the late 1950s and conducted wine tastings all over the world, always emphatically insisting on correct tasting conditions. Never inhibited about airing his elegant wine vocabulary in public, he has painstakingly recorded his disciplined impressions of every wine tasted, nearly 120,000 of them in more than 150 notebooks.

It is these notebooks, retyped by his equally hard-working wife Daphne, which formed the basis for Broadbent's *Great Vintage Wine Book* and the more discursive *Vintage Wine*, unique records of wine-tasting history which stretch back to wines of the early 18th century. Unlike PARKER, his most obvious rival as publisher of personal TASTING NOTES, Broadbent eschewed scoring wines with numbers, preferring to award up to five stars to each wine.

Broadbent's life has been marked by competition, particularly with Sotheby's, and ambition. While at Christie's he not only wrote his own classic on the subject of *Wine Tasting*, first published in 1968 and much republished since, but instituted and directed Christie's Wine Publications, which issued many invaluable books—including the *Christie's Wine Review* anthologies—during the 1970s and 1980s. He also wrote a highly personal monthly column for the British magazine *Decanter* from its inception in 1977 until 2013.

Incurably active and apparently indefatigable, he became a MASTER OF WINE in 1960, a freeman of the City of London in 1964, chairman of the Institute of Masters of Wine in 1970, international president of the INTERNATIONAL WINE & FOOD SOCIETY in 1986, master of the City of London's Distillers' Company in 1990, council chairman of the Wine & Spirit Trades Benevolent Society in 1991, and even stood, unsuccessfully, for sheriff of the City of London in 1993. He was made a Chevalier de l'Ordre du Mérite National in 1979. His son Bartholomew could be said to have helped establish the United States as the prime market for vintage

PORT in the 1990s and continues as a wine importer there.

Broadbent, M., *Vintage Wine* (London, 2002).
Broadbent, M., *Wine Tasting* (London, various editions 1968–2003).

Brock, leading university in CANADA for wine-related ACADEME. It is home to the Cool Climate Oenology and Viticulture Institute (CCOVI) established in 1996. Graduates make wine all over the world with particularly large contingents in California and Ontario. CCOVI is also the home of North America's only undergraduate degree programme in the study of COOL CLIMATE grape growing and winemaking. Student exchange programmes include partnerships with Okanagan University College in British Columbia, the Nova Scotia Agricultural College, LINCOLN University in New Zealand, the University of Udine in Italy, and DIJON. In viticulture, studies include the effects on wine quality of different vine training systems, vine spacing, irrigation, and shoot thinning; Niagara TERROIR using GPS, control of disease (particularly POWDERY MILDEW) and pests (particularly Asian lady beetle—see LADYBUG TAINT), the elucidation of odour-active compounds in Canadian ICEWINES, and the effects of CANOPY MANAGEMENT and oenological treatments on red wine composition and taste. Studies in winemaking have focused, non-exclusively, on the production of Icewine. Niagara College offers a Winery & Viticulture course as well as a graduate course in Wine Business Management.   T.A.

brokers, important members of any trade, and increasingly important in the wine trade. Known charmingly as *courtiers* in French, brokers can play a vital role as middlemen between vine-growers and merchants, or NÉGOCIANTS, collecting and exhibiting hundreds of samples, or *échantillons*, taking a small percentage of any eventual sale. Another class of brokers, further along the distribution chain, guide those who sell wine through the maze of those who produce it, some of them nursing 'stables' of producers rather in the manner of a literary agent representing a rollcall of authors. And then, just one or two links away from those who actually pull the cork, there are the FINE WINE brokers, those who sell from a list of glamorous properties and vintages which may, but often do not, belong to them.

This last group, most of whom have been based in Britain clustered round the headquarters of the two London-based AUCTION houses like bees round a honeypot, represents one of the very few sectors of the wine trade that has been highly profitable. Several London firms did extremely well in the 1990s as the number of wine collectors and investors around the world increased exponentially and ASIA woke up to the delights of fine wine; Farr Vintners has

sold more wine than Sotheby's and Christie's combined for many years. The sort of wine of interest to this new breed of wine merchant typically sits in an unbroken CASE in a BONDED WAREHOUSE in Britain while being traded so profitably around the world. The profitability of this business was so obviously attractive to traditional MERCHANTS more used to trading and delivering individual bottles and cases of much less valuable wine that in the early and mid 1990s many of them set up their own broking divisions. Much of these brokers' trade is between their own established customers. By the turn of the century most of these fine-wine brokers had, often extremely profitable, outposts in HONG KONG.

Brouilly, largest of the Beaujolais crus, produces some of the most robust, most textured of these red wines. A steady 1,300 ha/3,200 acres of vineyards flank the volcanic Mont Brouilly. **Côte de Brouilly** is an entirely separate appellation including just 325 ha/acres of land higher up the hillside. The wine produced tends to be more concentrated and longer lived than that of Brouilly. Ch de Thivin is a landmark producer. For more details, see BEAUJOLAIS.

Brulhois, red wine AOC in SOUTH WEST FRANCE. About 118 ha/290 acres of Bordeaux varieties plus the Gascon TANNAT (which must constitute 15–40% of the blend) with a little FER remained in 2011 in the rolling farmland down river of Moissac on both sides of the River Garonne. From medieval times the Brulhois wines of the HAUT PAYS were blended with those of Bordeaux down river but the ravages of PHYLLOXERA in the late 19th century were followed by widespread planting of HYBRIDS. The district's wines made from recently replanted VINIFERA vines were given VIN DE PAYS status initially before an elevation to VDQS in 1984. The wines are usually well coloured and the best can offer a good meeting-point between Gascon and Bordelais influences. Most are made by one of the two CO-OPERATIVES and consumed locally.

Brunello, Montalcino name for the six to eight different clones of SANGIOVESE planted there.

Brunello di Montalcino, youngest of Italy's prestigious red wines, having been invented as a wine in its own right by Ferruccio BIONDI-SANTI, the first to bottle it and give it a distinctive name, in 1865. Conventional descriptions of the birth of the wine stress Biondi-Santi's successful isolation of a superior CLONE of SANGIOVESE, the Sangiovese Grosso or BRUNELLO. an investigation begun by his father Clemente Santi. The 1865 vintage of a wine Clemente had labelled 'brunello' had been a prize-winning entry in the agricultural fair of

Montepulciano in 1869, indicating that genetically superior material was available in the zone at an earlier date. (Some records show the wines of Montalcino referred to as Brunello as early as the 14th century; see TUSCANY, history.) Only four vintages—1888, 1891, 1925, 1945—were declared in the first 57 years of production, contributing an aura of rarity to the wine that translated into high prices and, in Italy at least, incomparable prestige. The Biondi-Santi were the only commercial producers until after the Second World War and a government report of 1932 named Brunello as an exclusive product of the family and estimated its total annual production at just 200 hl/5,280 gal.

Until the 1960s the region was almost exclusively known for sweet and often sparkling MOSCADELLO. With the arrival of the American company Banfi at the end of the 1970s Brunello's fortunes took a sharp turn. Banfi's owners, the Italo-American Mariani brothers who had had huge commercial success with LAMBRUSCO, bought up whole swathes of land in the hotter, southern part of the zone which until then had never been vineyards, planting them with Moscadello for the production of a fizzy sweet white. The plan failed spectacularly, after which the vines were grafted over to Sangiovese and INTERNATIONAL VARIETIES. Banfi started to produce Brunello in great quantity and had such commercial success with it that many outsiders were tempted to jump on the bandwagon. The region, which in the 1960s consisted of 11 producers on a mere 63.5 ha/157 acres swelled to almost 2,000 ha/4,940 acres shared by 258 producers in 2012. This dramatic increase was made possible by including land new to viticulture. in 1996 a new DOC, Sant'Antimo, was added to the production regulations to allow for the international varieties that inevitably turned up in the wake of the success of SUPERTUSCANS.

The question of Brunello's true identity culminated in a blending scandal in 2008 when Italy's financial police sequestered whole batches of wines from several producers after their investigations had shown that these wines were not the mandatory 100% Brunello, but illegal blends which contained international varieties. The scandal, known as Brunellogate (Brunellopoli in Italy), led to a controversial proposal, eventually rejected, to allow the addition of other varieties but actually highlighted the uncomfortable fact that the official Brunello zone may well include land unsuitable for Brunello vines.

Climate and elevation are perhaps more significant factors than specific clones in creating the characteristics of the wine: the town of Montalcino, 112 km/70 miles south of Florence, enjoys a warmer, drier climate than the various zones of CHIANTI. Indeed, it is the most arid of all Tuscan DOCG zones, with an annual rainfall of about 700 mm/28 in (compared with over 900 in central Chianti Classico). In addition, a cool maritime breeze from the south west ensures both excellent ventilation and cool evenings and nights. Sangiovese can reach its maximum ripeness here, giving fuller, more structured wines than anywhere else in Tuscany.

The zone can be split roughly in two. On the GALESTRO soils in the northern part of the zone, vineyards are at elevations up to 500 m, while in the south the soil has more clay, the average temperature is higher, and the wines tend to be fuller than the more aromatic wines from the north. Because of this some of the zone's producers have vineyards in both the north and south to give them the balance they seek in their wines. However, winemaking practices differ widely between estates, resulting in myriad styles of Brunello but the finest examples manage the tricky balancing act of combining layers of red fruit, bold structure, and elegance.

The DOC regulations of 1960, largely written by Biondi-Santi on the basis of the family's oenological practices, include five to six years' CASK AGEING for the RISERVA and established a model of Brunello as a full, intense, long-lasting wine, which was confirmed in 1980 by the DOCG rules. The minimum cask ageing period was lowered to 36 months in 1990 and then to two years in 1998. BARRIQUE ageing has become standard in Montalcino, however, as in much of Tuscany. Some producers balance the oak with the wine better than others, while many producers have returned to ageing in large oak casks (*botti*), which impart less or no oak flavour at all to the wine.

The financial burden imposed by the lengthy ageing period has led to a corresponding increase in the production of ROSSO DI Montalcino, the 100% Brunello DOC wine that can be marketed after one year. The existence of a second DOC into which lesser wines can be declassified has had a positive impact on the quality of Brunello di Montalcino, in addition to its obvious advantages for producers' cash flow.　　W.S.

O'Keefe, K., *Brunello di Montalcino—Understanding and Appreciating One of Italy's Greatest Wines* (Oakland, Calif., 2012).

www.consorziobrunellodimontalcino.it

Brun Fourca, ancient Provençal vine associated with but hardly grown in PALETTE.

brush, the flesh remaining attached to the end of the berry stalk, or stem, after a grape is pulled from the bunch, as occurs during MECHANICAL HARVESTING or DESTEMMING, for example. The brush's size varies between vine varieties, from a barely discernible bit of flesh to a 'tongue' up to 5 mm/0.2 in long. The brush is caused by strong adhesion between the berry and stem, causing tearing of the skin, combined with particular characteristics of the zone of the flesh at the top of the berry. The cells of the brush are rich in TANNINS. The French term is *pinceau*.

The word brush is also used in the US for the total cane growth evident after leaf fall.　　B.G.C.

brut, French word meaning 'crude' or 'raw', adapted by the CHAMPAGNE industry for wines made without (much) added sweetening or DOSAGE. It has come to be used widely for any SPARKLING WINE to indicate one that tastes bone dry. The upper limit for the RESIDUAL SUGAR of a brut champagne has been reduced from 15 to 12 g/l. A wine labelled **extra brut** should contain less than 6 g/l residual sugar. Particularly dry wines may be labelled **brut nature**, with less than 3 g/l residual sugar and are made without dosage. The word **bruto** may be used in Portugal.

Bual, Anglicized form of BOAL most often used for a style of MADEIRA, richer than SERCIAL and VERDELHO, yet not as sweet as that called MALMSEY.

Bucelas, tiny white wine DOP just north of Lisbon, Portugal's capital city (see map under PORTUGAL) and formerly spelt **Bucellas**. At one time it was fortified and it is thought to be Shakespeare's Charneco, mentioned in *2 Henry VI* and named after one of the local villages. The Duke of Wellington popularized the wine in Britain following the Peninsular Wars and for a time Bucelas was widely sold and appreciated in Victorian Britain as Portuguese Hock. ARINTO grapes can make acidic, dry white wine in this sub-Mediterranean climate. Although Bucelas had almost disappeared by the early 1980s, a number of new enterprises have revived its fortunes, making modern, zesty, fruity Arinto which, with ALVARINHO bottled solo in VINHO VERDE country, is a rare example of Portuguese varietal white. One producer even makes an oaked cuvée, TRADITIONAL METHOD sparkling wine, and late-harvest Bucelas.　　S.A.

bud, *bourgeon* in French, is the name given to a small part of the vine shoot which rests between the leaf stalk or PETIOLE and the shoot stem. In the summer it is covered by green scales, which turn brown in winter. The bud contains three miniature, compressed (primordial) shoots. Normally the best developed of these shoots (from the 'primary' bud) bursts at BUDBREAK. Grapevine buds are classified as compound and fruitful; their development is complex.　　B.G.C. & R.E.S.

Budai Zöld, Hungarian white grape grown around Lake Balaton making deep-coloured, full-bodied wine for local consumption.

budbreak, or **budburst**, a stage of annual vine development during which small shoots emerge from vine BUDS in the spring. This process begins the new growing season and signals the end of DORMANCY, their period of winter sleep. The first sign that budbreak is imminent is BLEEDING, when the vines begin to drip water from pruning cuts. The buds left at winter pruning begin to swell in the few weeks prior to budbreak, and budbreak itself is marked by the first signs of green in the vineyard, as the first young leaves unfold and push through the bud scales.

Budbreak takes place in early spring in cool climates, when the average air temperature is about 10 °C/50 °F. For many northern hemisphere regions, budbreak occurs in March, and for the southern hemisphere in September. Budbreak is more uniform when winters are cold but not subject to WINTER FREEZE. In warm to hot regions, budbreak is earlier, and in cooler regions it is delayed. In fact in TROPICAL VITICULTURE the vines never achieve proper dormancy, and budbreak can take place at any time of the year.

Not all varieties show budbreak at the same temperature. For example, French studies indicate that for the early TABLE GRAPE Pearl of Csaba budbreak occurs at 5.6 °C, MERLOT at 9.4 °C, and UGNI BLANC at 11.0 °C. Late pruning in winter delays budbreak, and this can be used to reduce the risk of winter FROST.

In temperate regions with warm winters, a few warm days, even in midwinter, can be enough to induce bud swelling, which can lead to budbreak if the warmth persists. One of the very few places around the world to show this problem is the MARGARET RIVER region in Western Australia. Because of the nearby moderating effects of the Indian Ocean, the midwinter (July) mean temperature is a warm 13 °C. CHARDONNAY vines are particularly prone to this premature budbreak, with only a few buds breaking on the vine in midwinter, and the rest somewhat erratically later in spring.

For vines which are properly pruned (see BALANCED PRUNING) most of the buds left at winter pruning will burst, and budbreak is near 100%. Budbreak is, however, normally lower for buds in the middle of long CANES. (When vines are left unpruned, as in MINIMAL PRUNING, it is the buds near the ends of canes which burst preferentially, as do higher buds (see APICAL DOMINANCE). The two buds on either side of the cane just below the pruning cut typically burst. This is because of the flow of HORMONES in the plant and is the reason for pruning to two bud spurs.

For the vine-grower, budbreak represents the beginning of about eight months' work before HARVEST, during which the vine must be protected from pests, VINE DISEASES, and trained as necessary. The biggest problem for many vineyards at this time of the year is spring frost, to which the young shoot growth is particularly sensitive.   R.E.S.

Huglin, P., *Biologie et écologie de la vigne* (Paris, 1986).

Iland, P., et al., 'Grapevine growth', in *The Grapevine: From the Science to the Practice of Growing Vines for Wine* (Adelaide, 2011).

budding, the viticultural operation of GRAFTING where only a single bud is inserted into the rootstock. The term is also used in the context of BUDBREAK.

budwood, name given to vine CUTTINGS when they are destined for GRAFTING. Depending on the cutting length and bud spacing, four to 12 buds may be taken from each cutting. The budwood is typically put into cold storage to await grafting in the spring.

buffering capacity, the measure of resistance to change in PH by the addition of either acids or bases.

Bugey, Vins du, collective name for the wines of the Ain *département* in the southern Jura Mountains just west of SAVOIE in eastern France, sometimes just called **Bugey**. Since the turn of this century total vineyard area has been a stable 500 ha/1,235 acres and after decades the wines were finally elevated to AOC from VDQS in 2009. From the three chief vineyard zones of Cerdon, Belley, and Montagnieu, the main ACs are Bugey, Bugey Mousseux or Pétillant, and ROUSSETTE de Bugey, with certain CRUS added as a suffix. Bugey was once part of Burgundy and under the medieval influence of MONKS AND MONASTERIES the area was an important wine producer. In recent times until the 21st century most of its varied wines were consumed locally, but international interest in them has grown alongside that for wines from Savoie and JURA. The delicate, medium-sweet, pink **Vin du Bugey Cerdon** at around 7 % alcohol is made by the MÉTHODE ANCESTRALE from the Gamay grape of nearby Beaujolais and some of Jura's POULSARD. It accounts for nearly half of the Bugey's annual four million bottle production. Also important are other white and pink TRADITIONAL METHOD sparkling wines. The still wines are mainly VARIETAL with more whites than rosé and reds. Chardonnay dominates whites, but there are small quantities of ALIGOTÉ and Pinot Gris as well as Savoie's ALTESSE, JACQUÈRE, MONDEUSE BLANCHE, and MOLETTE, with the Altesse performing well as Roussette du Bugey. Among reds, Gamay and Pinot Noir are joined by the interesting MONDEUSE NOIRE of Savoie. These were the wines with which the notable gastronome Anthelme Brillat-Savarin grew up.   W.L.

Bukettraube, white grape variety, a GERMAN CROSS of Silvaner and Trollinger. It is grown almost exclusively but to a limited extent in South Africa for sweet and occasionally BOTRYTIZED dessert wines, with a slightly grapey aroma.

Bulgaria, Eastern European wine-producing country whose western export success in the 1980s was built on inexpensive VARIETAL wines, especially Cabernet Sauvignon, now showing increasing potential as a producer of high-quality red. Viniculture has been practised in this part of the world for more than three millennia, even if it was interrupted by Ottoman domination for nearly 500 years from 1393 to 1878 (see ISLAM). The Turks retained substantial vineyards for TABLE GRAPE production, however, so that vine-growing has been consistently one of Bulgaria's principal agricultural activities.

Geography and climate

Bulgaria is a small country just 450 km/280 miles from the western border to the Black Sea and 300 km/200 miles from Romania to the north and Greece and Turkey to the south. With the exception of the Stara Planina (Balkan mountain range), which runs east to west, and the environs of the capital Sofia, vines are planted all over the country, although the modern wine industry has been based on rolling fertile flatlands. On the Danubian and upper Thracian plains, for example, the vineyards lie mainly between 100 and 300 m (330–990 ft) in ELEVATION, although some south-western vineyards are as high as 1,000 m/3,280 ft.

Summers tend to be hot, with temperatures up to 40 °C/104 °F, while the temperature can fall to −25 °C/−13 ºF in winter. Although the Black Sea has a moderating effect on the eastern side of the country, the climate tends to be dramatically CONTINENTAL.

The most common climatological hazards are FUNGAL DISEASES caused by humidity. In non-DROUGHT years rainfall and high temperatures combine to promote rot and both sorts of mildew. IRRIGATION and CHAPTALIZATION are not generally necessary.

History

The country has a long vinous heritage, dating back around 3,000 years. Numerous archaeological finds depict wine consumption, including discoveries at the Thracian temple complex near Starosel dated to the end of fifth century BC. PLINY the Elder stated that the first European wine grower was a Thracian named Evmolp. Grape growing developed under ROMAN occupation while the country's conversion to Christianity from 864 AD brought new impetus to wine consumption (see EUCHARIST). Ottoman rule from the 15th to the 19th century failed to destroy viticulture, and it has been suggested that as many as 50,000 ha/125,000 acres of vineyards remained when the country regained its independence in 1878.

At the beginning of the 20th century, the first Bulgarian wine CO-OPERATIVES were founded, based on the southern French model. The first of these was at Suhindol in 1909 and by 1939 there were 60, whose winemakers were often graduates of French universities. After the Second World War the new communist government, established in 1947, nationalized wine production and quickly set about collectivizing the vineyards. In 1949, the state wine and spirits monopoly Vinprom was set up to control all commercial production and trade. Typical holdings of barely half a hectare of vines gave way to much larger co-operative enterprises.

In 1952 a decree officially promoted viticulture and winegrowing in Bulgaria, followed by geographical DELIMITATION of wine regions in 1957. Until the early 1960s, INDIGENOUS VARIETIES dominated, especially DIMIAT, PAMID, and MAVRUD together with Georgia's RKATSITELI, often as unkempt BUSH VINES, but these were then supplemented by 80,000 ha/200,000 acres of vast, single-variety plantings of INTERNATIONAL VARIETIES, especially Cabernet Sauvignon, Merlot, Chardonnay, Sauvignon Blanc, and Muscat Ottonel on flatter sites and using higher TRAINING systems designed to increase YIELDS. Grape growing was often incorporated into agro-industrial complexes set up to grow a wide variety of crops on a huge scale. In the early 1960s Vinprom also established centralized processing and wine-bottling plants. By the 1970s Bulgaria had around 200,000 ha/500,000 acres of vines, of which 150,000 ha were designed to produce wine, chiefly for the SOVIET UNION and Comecon countries. During this period around 70% of all grapes were grown in these agro-industrial complexes, a further 20% in vineyards owned directly by Vinprom, and 10% by individual growers. Vinprom controlled 80% of winemaking facilities, with three smaller state-owned organizations producing the remainder. All exports went through the state monopoly Vinimpex, which set up wholly owned subsidiaries in key markets such as the UK. These decisions set the scene for Bulgarian wine in the 1980s. Initially the emphasis was on red wine production, so no great influx of new equipment was needed, although Soviet demand for sparkling and sweet wines was so great that investment in stainless-steel tanks, proper FILTRATION systems, and CONCRETE vats was initially financed by the Comecon Bank of the Eastern Bloc, the principal export market for Bulgarian wine. Subsequently, new technology was subsidized by cheap loans from the Bulgarian government and repaid from the income of the rapidly increasing exports to the west.

Western expertise came with the men from Pepsico, the giant American cola manufacturers. Eager to trade their soft-drink concentrate for a saleable product, they provided links with California's wine faculty at DAVIS, with Professor Maynard AMERINE, and with other western establishments and wineries.

Between the mid 1960s and mid 1980s, the Bulgarian wine industry made significant progress, in terms of both quality and exports of inexpensive but competently made varietals to the west, especially to Britain. Towards the end of this period Bulgaria was the fourth biggest exporter of bottled wines worldwide, but Gorbachev's arrival as Soviet premier had dire consequences for Bulgarian wine. His campaign to curb alcohol consumption in the Soviet Union involved uprooting huge tracts of Bulgarian vineyard, some but not all of inferior quality. Grape prices were then fixed every year, irrespective of quality, which encouraged the co-operatives to turn their attention away from vines to other crops. Dead, dying, or diseased vines were not replaced. Many vineyards were simply abandoned, and few were treated to any systematic training or pruning systems.

In 1985, when Gorbachev came to power, Bulgaria produced 4.5 million hl of wine, but by 1990 the total crop was just 1.8 million hl/40 million gal, and this at a time when exports to the west were at record levels.

Post communism

In 1990, the wine sector was suddenly liberalized and Vinprom disbanded in 1991 as part of the free-market reforms introduced in the wake of the fall of communism in 1989. Throughout the 1990s, the Bulgarian wine industry was in disarray as ineffectual attempts were made to return land to its pre-1944 owners, many of them absent. The inherited separation of grape-growing and wine production continued very largely unchanged until 1999, and even as recently as the mid 2000s very few wineries actually owned vineyards. Winemakers were rarely involved in managing viticultural issues. Grape growers tended to be focused on harvesting and being paid as quickly as possible—before being threatened by inclement weather or, a real threat, theft of grapes. At the same time, lack of professional viticulture and vineyard management meant that yields, already low, declined further. The position was not helped by a series of short crops, and by the end of the 1990s the Bulgarian wine industry was suffering from a serious shortage of fruit. This led to fierce competition for grapes, which encouraged early picking. This in turn led directly to much leaner, under-ripe wines at a time when western consumers expected ripe, fruity wine styles. Bulgaria rapidly lost market share.

In the 2000s, many wineries found themselves in trading difficulties, due to falling sales, reliance on bank loans, and lack of investment. Bulgaria joined the EU in 2007. Undoubtedly, pre-accession EU funding programmes such as SAPARD (Special Accession Program for Agricultural and Rural Development) and Phare were significant. Subsidies of up to 50% for both winery and vineyard investments brought in substantial foreign capital and also enabled some small, individual projects and wine estates—a novelty in Bulgaria at that time. The realization that wine quality could be regained only through control of fruit sourcing meant that many wineries took on the huge bureaucratic burden of consolidating landholdings. Today most wineries of any significance,

or with ambition, own vineyards, but since so many of them were planted or replanted relatively recently, VINE AGE is often low.

A number of smaller boutique wineries emerged in the early 21st century making premium wines and investing in vineyards. Maxxima's 1999 Reserve Cabernet and Merlot was one of the first seriously ambitious Bulgarian wines of the modern era. Damianitza winery followed suit not long after with Redark. New estates have been emerging every year so that there are currently around 260 wineries, of which around 70 are of commercial significance.

Vineyards

The landscape of the Bulgarian wine industry has changed dramatically since the fall of the Iron Curtain and even more so since the completion of privatization. As part of EU membership negotiations, Bulgaria confirmed a vineyard area of 153,000 ha/378,071 acres and indeed official data for 2006 showed an area under vine of 135,760 ha/335,470 acres, but this seems never to have been a realistic reflection of what was planted or likely to be planted. By the end of 2013, the country's Executive Agency for Vine and Wine recorded a potential vineyard total area of 81,000 ha/200,155 acres, of which only 68,840 ha/170,107 acres were already in full production. Even this may be an overestimate. Ministry of Agriculture surveys suggest that up to one-third of the vineyard area may have been abandoned. Nearly half of Bulgaria's vines are over 30 years old but since 2008 6,000 to 8,000 ha/14,800 to 19,800 acres have been renovated each year. This almost certainly reflects the purchase of vineyards by large wineries, as well as the emergence of small and medium-sized wineries with quality aspirations. The officially declared wine production in 2013 was 1.8 million hl/nearly 50 million gal, but there is also a significant black market for wine.

Markets

In 2013, 35% of Bulgarian wine was sold within Bulgaria, reflecting a considerable increase in domestic wine consumption, although this has been slowed by economic difficulties. Despite this, some sort of wine culture has been developing. Bulgaria also has a strong spirits culture, especially for the local *rakia*, whose consumption still exceeds that of wine. Russia is still the leading export market, followed by Poland, the Czech Republic, and Romania. In most markets Bulgarian producers are focusing on quality and at the expense of volume.

Winemaking

Foreign investment and SAPARD funds have been used to fund winery renovations and the installation of STAINLESS STEEL, TEMPERATURE CONTROL, and modern technology across much of the industry. OAK use is widespread, with leading producers usually opting for French oak, although some local oak is appearing now COOPERAGE standards are better. Use of OAK CHIPS in older barrels is still common. Most wineries now have locally trained winemakers who have frequently travelled and gained international experience, although Michel ROLLAND consults at Castra Rubra and Frenchman Marc Dworkin at Bessa Valley.

Grape varieties

Red varieties account for about 63% of plantings with whites dominating only in the eastern Black Sea region. Bulgaria may have been famous for its Cabernet Sauvignon, of which there were 8,437 ha/20,000 acres according to the most recent data, gathered in 2009, but Merlot has overtaken it to become the most planted variety with a total of 10,572 ha/26,125 acres. Local PAMID has fallen out of favour, dropping to 6,792 ha/16,783 acres, as its light body, low acidity and low EXTRACT means that it rarely produces anything better than light wines for early consumption. Shiroka Melnishka Loza or broad-leaved MELNIK is grown exclusively in the south west around the towns of Melnik, Sandinski, and Harsovo and its vines total 1,580 ha/3,904 acres. It is very late ripening and can require extensive ageing, though an earlier-ripening CROSS is also often labelled Melnik. Most interesting of the INDIGENOUS red grape varieties is MAVRUD, grown traditionally around Plovdiv but now planted more widely. It is increasingly appearing in flagship blends such as Santa Sarah's Privat and Rumelia's Erelia. Varietal Melnik is very popular on the home market and typically has powerful tannins that require careful management or lengthy oak ageing. Plantings of Gamza, the KADARKA of Hungary, comprise just 1.5% of vineyards now, most in the north of the country, where it can make interestingly spicy wines if yields are controlled, especially from boutique producer Borovitza winery. RUBIN looked set to become Bulgaria's signature grape but it has fallen from favour due to doubts over its wines' longevity, although some powerful, richly fruited versions are now being made, notably by Damianitza, Dragomir, and Santa Sarah.

Bulgarian researchers have been enthusiastic developers of crosses, including Buket (good versions from Borovitza and Miroglio) and Ruen, a Cabernet × Melnik cross registered for the south west. A number of lower quality varieties developed primarily for disease resistance such as dark-skinned Storgozia (a cross of the local Buket with VILLARD Blanc) and Shevka are locally important. The Georgian variety SAPERAVI has been imported. Recent plantings of Syrah and Pinot Noir have shown some successful results, while Cabernet Franc also shows promise.

Bulgaria grows a curious mix of white wine grapes, showing evidence of SERBIAN influence in its everyday DIMIAT (2,385 ha/5,893 acres) and Georgian influence in its plantings of RKATSITELI (3,121 ha/7,712 acres). Central European influence is evident in its MUSCAT OTTONEL (3,235 ha/7,994 acres). Most popular is a local pink-skinned variety called MISKET Cherven, or Red Misket (4,159 ha/10,277 acres), which is particularly noted for its FROST resistance, produces distinctly grapey white wines, and is grown mainly in the Valley of the Roses area (previously known as the Sub-Balkan region). Chardonnay (2,456 ha/6,069 acres) is the fifth most planted white variety followed by Traminer (746 ha/1,843 acres) and Ugni Blanc (723 ha/1,787 acres), while Riesling, Sauvignon Blanc, Aligoté, and more recently Viognier are also grown.

The regions and quality designations

Winemaking and oenological practices have been brought into line with EU requirements, along with CONTROLLED APPELLATIONS. There are just two PGI regions for Bulgaria—the Danubian Plain and Thracian Lowlands—arguably as a result of strong lobbying by large wineries used to sourcing grapes from all over the country. The border runs across the Stara Planina range from east to west. In addition, there are 52 PDOs and the previous distinction between Quality Wines with Declared Geographical Origin and Quality wines with Guaranteed and Controlled Appellation of Origin is no longer made.

The term 'Reserve' may also be used for wines in both quality categories that have been made from one variety that has been matured for at least one year before release. PDO wines account for only a small percentage of the Bulgarian market and only about 30% of the 52 PDOs are actually in use, whereas around 80% of wine is produced within the PGI category, with producers preferring to develop their own brands.

Danubian Plain Vidin, Pleven, Lovech, Rousse, Lyaskovets, Black Sea Region, Targovishte, Novo Selo, Lozitsa, Varbitsa, Svishtov, Suhindol, Pavlikeni, Novi Pazar, Veliki Preslav, Khan Krum, Evxinograd.

Thracian Lowlands Karnobat, Septemvri, Plovdiv, Yambol, Stara Zagora, Sliven, Shivachevo, Nova Zagora, Haskovo, Ivailovgrad, Lyubimets, Sandanski, South Black Sea, Struma Valley, Pomorie, Assenovgrad, Karlovo, Hissarya, Perushtitsa, Brestnik, Oriahovitsa, Stambolovo, Sakar, Melnik, Harsovo, Sungurlare, Slavyantsi.

Previously there were five regions—Danubian Plain, Rose Valley or Sub-Balkan region, Thracian Lowlands, Black Sea, and South West or Struma Valley—based on distinct climatic and soil differences. They are still widely used in literature and some in the industry are lobbying for these five, and more, to be reinstated. Some Bulgarian producers have started to accept the concepts of TERROIR and wines that reflect their geographical origin, in contrast to the historical approach of sourcing grapes all over the country. Traditionally the warmer south was more lauded for its rich reds, but the cooler north west overlooking the Danube is now producing some fine, elegant reds.   C.G.

National Vine and Wine Chamber, *Who is Who—Wines & Spirits in Bulgaria 2012* (Sofia, 2009).

Tanovska, T., and Iontcheva, K., *KATA Catalogue of Bulgarian Wine 2* (Sofia, 2014).

www.mzh.government.bg

www.divino.bg (Bulgarian only)

bulk method, alternative name for the Charmat or tank method of SPARKLING WINEMAKING.

bulk storage of wine is important in the production and BLENDING of everyday commercial wines. Large storage tanks are usually made of stainless steel and may hold as much as 800,000 l/176,000 gal. OXIDATION is always a risk and, if the tank is not completely filled with wine, the head space must be filled with an INERT GAS. Many commercial blends are bottled throughout the year from such tanks, which are kept at relatively low temperatures. The ideal storage temperature is 12–18 °C (54–64 °F). Extremes of heat or cold are likely to have a negative effect on quality. If consumers were to become more demanding of individuality in their wines, these large storage containers would become rarer and the wineries of the future might have only small and medium-sized storage containers.   A.D.W. & B.D.

bulk transport of wine is the movement of large quantities of wine within a single winery or from one place to another, typically from where it was held in BULK STORAGE to the BOTTLING location, which may not even be in the same hemisphere.

Bulk transport over long distances has increased considerably over the last 10 years in an effort to reduce both financial and environmental costs. Twice as much wine can be transported in the same space in bulk than in bottle, PACKAGING waste is reduced, and locally recycled glass may be used (although bottlers in the producing country suffer the consequences). According to the OIV, 40% of exported wine was moved in bulk in 2012, up more than 60% compared with 2005. In the same year, 80% of Australia's wine exports to the UK were in bulk, and in 2013, 65% of South African wine was exported in this way. Other benefits include the better thermal protection offered by a large volume of wine and longer shelf life for wine sold in BOXES.

Wine is most commonly transported in bulk from one installation to another by road tanker and/or ocean-going tank ships, although rail and barge are not unknown. The two main options are an ISO tank (a stainless-steel pill-shaped container within a standard ISO frame that can carry up to 26,000 litres) or a Flexitank (a hermetically sealed, collapsible, and flexible bag or bladder, which is fitted into a container and typically holds 24,000 litres). Pipelines are occasionally used to transport wine over short distances, for example between winery sites or to a neighbouring bottling facility.

Whenever wine is moved, it is important to guard against OXIDATION. The ability to control both the OXYGEN TRANSMISSION RATE of the containers and the temperatures to which the tanks are subjected—en route or at the dock—are critical to the quality of the wine. Flexitanks, because of their flexibility, offer more effective management of ULLAGE levels, a critical factor in controlling the level of dissolved oxygen, whereas the more solid construction of ISO tanks may offer better thermal protection from temperature variation. Wine being delivered to a receiving tank should be filled from the bottom of the tank and onto a blanket of INERT GAS such as carbon dioxide to prevent excessive aeration of the wine.   B.D.

bulk wine, or wine *en vrac*, as the French call it, is wine that is ready to drink, but has not been put into smaller CONTAINERS such as BOTTLES. This may be because it is about to be packaged, or because it will be sold to another producer. Most of the wine that is sold in bulk is marketed at less than 10 US dollars per bottle, and is not meant for long term ageing. BULK TRANSPORT is by far the cheapest way of moving wine and it is common for wine to move in bulk between producer and blender or bottler, possibly between continents and hemispheres.

In Europe, Germany has emerged as the major importer of bulk wine from the New World, buying mainly red wine from Chile, Argentina, California, Australia, and South Africa. Most of this is sold through importers/bottlers in Germany and then bottled for various discount chains. China has emerged as a significant buyer of bulk wine, sourced wherever it is cheapest. The UK remains a significant market for bulk wine, both for brands and for private labels, a continuation of the country's wine BOTTLING tradition.

When SURPLUS PRODUCTION became an increasingly geographically widespread phenomenon in the early 21st century, the bulk wine market became an important feature of international wine trade, helped considerably by online trading.

Brokers of bulk wine have become inceasingly important and their business is strongly influenced by factors such as the weather during FLOWERING where large quantities of wine are grown, currency movements, and FASHIONS in varietals (see SIDEWAYS, for example). They follow the bulk markets daily and provide information to their client base. The internet has been a significant tool in managing and communicating up-to-date market information but few of the companies formed in the internet boom days, in the hope of replacing more traditional BROKERS, survived because ebuyers need more information than simply price and location.

Bulk wine may even be sold in measured quantities drawn off from some form of BULK STORAGE. In southern Europe it is still commonplace to take a container, perhaps a BONBONNE or large plastic container, to be filled with bulk wine, which is charged by the litre.

Bullas, growing wine-producing zone in Spain's LEVANTE, now a DO. It shares many features with neighbouring JUMILLA and YECLA, including the predominance of the MONASTRELL grape.

Bull's Blood, once a wine BRAND named after a historic style of red wine made in HUNGARY, known as BIKAVÉR in Hungarian.

bunch, or cluster, the viticultural term for that part of the grapevine comprising BUNCHSTEM and BERRIES. *Grappe* is the French term. Before the berries SET, each berry position is occupied by a flower; a bunch develops from the INFLORESCENCE of the vine once the berries have set. In the grapevine the inflorescence grows at the node on the side of the stem opposite to a leaf, an unusual position within the plant kingdom. It is closely related to a TENDRIL, both deriving from the same embryonic organ, the anlage. Depending on the time of development, anlagen produce bunches, tendrils, or SECOND CROP.

Like a tendril, a grape bunch has two arms, called outer and inner. The inner arm develops the bulk of the bunch, while the outer arm may vary in form from a large, well-set 'wing' (as in UGNI BLANC) to a small tendril arm without berries, or it may even abort. Berries on wings sometimes ripen differently from those on the main crop.

Bunches vary hugely in size depending on that year's FRUIT SET and VINE VARIETY, from a few grams to many kilograms. They also vary in shape and tightness depending on the lengthening and flexibility of the BUNCHSTEM and branches and, of course, on setting and BERRY SIZE.   B.G.C.

bunch rots, or **berry rots**, occur in vines all over the world and can be caused by many species of fungi including YEASTS and BACTERIA. Yield losses can be as high as 80% and wine made from rotten fruit often smells and tastes tainted, typically mouldy, with a perceptible loss of fruit flavour. Vineyards badly infected with bunch rots themselves have a distinctive and unpleasant smell. Wet weather at HARVEST causes the worst cases of bunch rot, especially if grape skins are broken. The best known of the bunch rots is BOTRYTIS BUNCH ROT.

Some fungi, such as *Botrytis*, *Alternaria*, and *Cladosporium*, can infect healthy berries and these are called 'primary invaders'. 'Secondary invaders' such as *Aspergillus*, *Rhizopus*, and *Penicillium* gain access to berries split by rain, bird or insect attack, or diseases such as DOWNY MILDEW and POWDERY MILDEW, ESCA, or HAIL disease. So-called SOUR ROT is due to a mix of fungi, yeasts, acetic acid bacteria, and fruit fly larvae. Control measures can include SPRAYING, bunch thinning, increasing fruit exposure to wind and sun (see CANOPY MANAGEMENT), and avoiding other pests and diseases which can break berry skins. (See also FUNGAL DISEASES.) R.E.S.

Emmett, R. W., et al., 'Grape diseases and vineyard protection', in B. G. Coombe and P. R. Dry (eds.), *Viticulture*, ii: *Practices* (Adelaide, 1992).

Pearson, R. C., and Goheen, A. C., (eds.), *Compendium of Grape Diseases* (St Paul, Minn., 1988).

bunchstem, the stem of a grapevine inflorescence, or bunch of grapes, known by botanists as the peduncle and in French as a *rafle*. The form of the bunchstem, especially the position and length of lateral branches, determines the shape of the BUNCH and is one of many characters used to identify vine varieties in the science of AMPELOGRAPHY. Winemakers often refer to bunchstems as stems or stalks (see DESTEMMING, for instance). B.G.C.

bunchstem necrosis, or BSN, physiological condition which causes grape bunchstems to shrivel and die during RIPENING. This condition is also known as water berry in California, shanking in New Zealand, *Stiellähme* in Germany, and *dessèchement de la rafle* in French. Affected berries do not ripen properly and shrivel on the bunch, although it is rare for all berries to be affected. CABERNET SAUVIGNON vines are particularly prone to this disorder. Affected berries have lower SUGARS, ANTHOCYANINS, and fatty acids, but higher ACIDITY. The cause is unknown, but factors associated with the condition are vigorous shoot growth, the weather at FLOWERING, and levels of MAGNESIUM, CALCIUM, and ammonium in the plant tissue. Yield can be severely reduced, especially with MECHANICAL HARVESTING, as affected berries fall off. Wines can taste bitter and are poorly coloured. There is no widely accepted control, although magnesium sprays at VERAISON have sometimes reduced the problem. A similar disorder affects inflorescences at flowering and has been termed **early bunchstem necrosis,** or 'inflorescence necrosis'. R.E.S.

Bondada, B., and Keller, M., 'Not all shrivels are created equal–morpho-anatomical and compositional characteristics differ among different shrivel types that develop during ripening of grape (*Vitis vinifera* L.) berries', *American Journal of Plant Sciences*, 3/7 (2012), 879–98.

bung. A bung, made of glass, plastic, rubber, earthenware, silicone, or wood, is a barrel's stopper, analogous to the cork of a bottle. It is inserted in a **bung-hole**. If a barrel is stored so that the bung is at its highest point, this position is called **bung up** and the bung may be left so that gas can escape from the bung-hole. Some bungs even incorporate a device that encourages this. If a barrel is stored with the bung at either two or ten o'clock, the position is called **bung over**.

Since OXYGEN tends to enter a barrel around the bung-hole, silicone bungs are sometimes used to keep a particularly tight fit. These silicone bungs also have the advantage of being gentler on the **bung stave**, the stave in which the bung-hole is drilled, which is weakened and sometimes cracked by the constant hammering needed on wooden bungs.

Traditionally in Bordeaux and Burgundy barrels are filled and TOPPED UP through the top bung but racked via a RACKING bung on the head of the barrel. M.K.

Burgenland, home today to nearly one-third of Austria's vine acreage, divided between NEUSIEDLERSEE, NEUSIEDLERSEE-HÜGELLAND, MITTELBURGENLAND, and SÜDBURGENLAND. Although it produces important volumes of dry white wine, Burgenland is best known for red and BOTRYTIZED sweet wines. Wines grown and bottled within this state have long been allowed to indicate Burgenland on the label in preference to specifying one of its regions. Moreover, many wines are now required to stipulate Burgenland as their place of origin rather than citing a specific region on their labels, the designations Neusiedlersee and Mittelburgenland now being restricted to those meeting the requirements of their respective DACS. D.S.

Burger, white grape variety that was once very important in CALIFORNIA, where it was the state's most planted VINIFERA variety, having been promoted by one pioneer as greatly superior to the MISSION grape. The total had fallen to 1,165 acres/472 ha by 2012, mainly in the hot SAN JOAQUIN VALLEY, many of them planted in the early 1980s.

It is the almost extinct southern French variety Monbadon, probably a cross of Folle Blanche and Ugni Blanc that was cultivated to a limited extent in the Languedoc until the 1980s. It produces sizeable quantities of neutral wine.

Burgunder, common suffix in German, meaning literally 'of BURGUNDY', for such grape variety members of the PINOT family as Spätburgunder, Blauburgunder, Blauer Spätburgunder, or Blauer Burgunder (PINOT NOIR); Weissburgunder or Weisser Burgunder (PINOT BLANC); and Grauburgunder or Grauer Burgunder (drier styles of PINOT GRIS).

Burgund Mare means 'big Burgundian' in ROMANIA and is the local name for BLAUFRÄNKISCH.

Burgundy, known as BOURGOGNE in French, province of eastern France famous for its great red and white wines produced mostly from PINOT NOIR and CHARDONNAY grapes respectively. The province includes the viticultural regions of the Côte de Nuits and Côte de Beaune in the *département* of the CÔTE D'OR, the Côte CHALONNAISE and MÂCONNAIS in the Saône-et-Loire *département*, and CHABLIS and the wines of AUXERRE in the Yonne *département*. In 2011, the total area of Burgundy vineyard was 28,320 ha/ 69,950 acres. The total crop was 1,505,707hl of which 61% was white, 31% red, and 8% sparkling.

BEAUJOLAIS in the Rhône *département*, while sometimes being considered part of greater Burgundy, is a distinct region viticulturally, if not administratively, and is treated separately.

Ancient history

When the Romans (see Ancient ROME) conquered Gaul in 51 BC, they probably found the CELTS inhabiting what is now Burgundy already growing wine, if not yet in substantial quantities. In the early 21st century the remains of a small vineyard dating back to the 1st century AD, apparently for the use of those living in a Roman villa close to Gibriacum (GEVREY-CHAMBERTIN) has been unearthed. A tombstone in the village church of Corgoloin depicts what appears to be a Celtic god with a vine in his right hand; other gravestones have carvings of grapes. Also, archaeologists have found no Italian AMPHORAE of the mid 2nd century or later in Burgundy, which may indicate that from then on the region was producing enough wine of its own. From at least the 3rd century onwards, however, wine was transported from Italy in wooden BARRELS instead of amphorae, and wood is far more perishable than pottery.

The earliest literary evidence dates from AD 312. In a panegyric addressed to the Emperor Constantine the Great on the occasion of his visit to Autun (Augustodeunum), the citizens plead poverty. Part of the grim picture their orator paints is abandoned vineyards, the roots of the old vines so thickly intertwined that it would be impossible for a farmer to dig ditches. However old the vines were—and a mere human lifetime's worth of neglect would

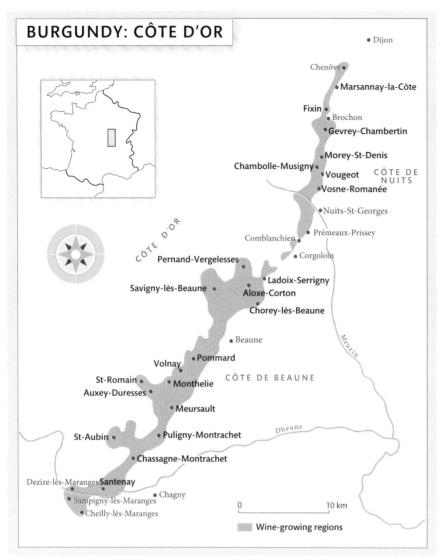

BURGUNDY: CÔTE D'OR

- Dijon
- Chenôve
- **Marsannay-la-Côte**
- **Fixin**
  - Brochon
- **Gevrey-Chambertin**
- **Morey-St-Denis**
- **Chambolle-Musigny**
- **Vougeot**
- **Vosne-Romanée**   CÔTE DE NUITS
- Nuits-St-Georges
- Prémeaux-Prissey
- Comblanchien
- Corgoloin
- CÔTE D'OR
- **Pernand-Vergelesses**
- **Ladoix-Serrigny**
- **Savigny-lès-Beaune**
- **Aloxe-Corton**
- **Chorey-lès-Beaune**
- Beaune
- **Pommard**
- **Volnay**   CÔTE DE BEAUNE
- **St-Romain**
- **Monthelie**
- **Auxey-Duresses**
- **Meursault**
- **St-Aubin**
- **Puligny-Montrachet**   Dheune
- **Chassagne-Montrachet**
- Dezize-lès-Maranges **Santenay**
- Chagny
- Sampigny-lès-Maranges
- Cheilly-lès-Maranges
- Meuzin

0 ——————— 10 km

■ Wine-growing regions

2011 harvest statistics	
Chablis and Auxerrois	329,586 hl (44 million bottles)
Côte de Nuits	104,795 hl (14 million bottles)
Côte de Beaune	209,243 hl (27 million bottles)
Côte Chalonnaise	100,880 hl (13 million bottles)
Mâconnais	354,267 hl (47 million bottles)
Regional appellations	406,936 hl (54 million bottles)

account for their tangled state—commercial viticulture had clearly been well established by the early 4th century.

As the Roman empire disintegrated, Burgundy came once more under barbarian rule, by the Franks, the Alamans, and the Vandals.

The Burgundians, Scandinavians by origin, founded a kingdom in the RHÔNE Valley, later including Lyons and Dijon, in 456; they were defeated by the Franks under Clovis's sons in 534. The first recorded words in praise of Burgundian wine date from the Merovingian period. Gregory of Tours, who finished his History of the Franks in 591, says that the hills to the west of Dijon produce a noble wine that is like FALERNIAN—the highest praise possible from a Dark Age Latinist. That wine, and the clear water flowing from the springs around the city, are sufficient reasons why in his opinion Dijon should become an episcopal see. In 587 King Guntramn, grandson of Clovis and son of Clotaire, gave a vineyard to the Abbey of St Benignus at Dijon, and in 630 the duke of Lower Burgundy donated vineyards at Gevrey, Vosne, and Beaune to the Abbey of Bèze, near Gevrey. The beginnings of monastic viticulture in Burgundy were in these Merovingian times.

Monastic influence

Nobles, peasants, and monks cultivated the vine under CHARLEMAGNE, when political stability brought prosperity. Medieval Burgundy owes its reputation as a producer of excellent wines largely to the MONKS AND MONASTERIES. The monks had several advantages over lay growers: they had cellars and store rooms in which to mature their wine; and, most importantly, they kept records and had the time and the degree of organization necessary to engage in systematic improvement. The first group of monks to acquire vineyards in Burgundy on a large scale were the Benedictines of Cluny. The foundation in 910 of the Abbey at Cluny in Mâconnais was the beginning of the Benedictine reform movement. Between 927 and 1157 Cluny became a vast organization with hundreds of dependent priories, not only in France but also in England, Germany, Spain, and Italy. Through benefactions from pious laymen, Cluny came to own all the vineyards around Gevrey by 1273, and in 1232 the duchess of Burgundy granted the Abbey of St-Vivant the vineyards now known as Romanée-Conti, La Romanée, La Tâche, Richebourg and Romanée-St-Vivant (see also DOMAINE DE LA ROMANÉE-CONTI). It also owned Pommard and vineyards at Auxey and Santenay.

The other group of monks to have a lasting effect on Burgundian viticulture were the Cistercians, an order founded in 1098 which took its name from the site of its first monastery, Cîteaux, east of modern Nuits-St-Georges. Although austerity and asceticism were the aims of the order, in contrast to the luxury and ostentation of the Benedictines, the Cistercians, often through donations, became rich and important landowners.

The Cistercians' first vineyard was given to them by the duke of Burgundy in 1098, not long after their foundation. Soon they were buying vineyards as well: in 1118 the Cistercians of Pontigny on the River Serein purchased, after much haggling, vineyards from the Benedictine monks of St-Martin at Tours from which they produced a white wine, the first CHABLIS. In 1110 the monks of Cîteaux were given land at Vougeot and went on to acquire more land there: it took them until 1336 to acquire enough to form one large vineyard, which they surrounded with a wall, the CLOS DE VOUGEOT. They bought or were given more vineyards all over the CÔTE D'OR and trained their lay brothers to work them: Beaune, Chambolle, Fixin, Pommard, and many more.

Aided by their skilled workforce, the monks had the time, the experience, and the learning necessary to experiment, record, and compare. By observing how different plots of vines produced different wines, the Cistercians discovered the importance of TERROIR and began to acknowledge different CRUS.

In the 12th and 13th centuries, white wine was preferred to red. In an age of murky drinking water, carefully made white wine was valued for its clarity. The wines that were most highly reputed, however, were not those of Burgundy but those of the Île-de-France centred on PARIS, which could easily be transported by RIVERS. Burgundy, on the other hand, was cut off, and its wines, which could only be transported north with much expense and difficulty along bumpy roads, were as yet little known. In medieval French texts, 'vin de Bourgogne' was from Auxerre, whose wines could easily reach Paris along the River Yonne: transport by boat was cheaper, easier, and less harmful to the wine than being carried by horse-drawn cart along bumpy roads. Until the 15th century what we call burgundy was known as 'Beaune'.

Upon his election in 1305 Clement V moved the papal court to Avignon. During this 'Babylonian captivity', which lasted until 1377, the court of the Avignonese popes was famous for its extravagance as well as its corruption, and demand for the wines of Burgundy to the north surged. The wines of 'Beaune' came generally to be regarded as second to none. Urban V (1362–70) went to Rome for three years in 1367 but, exasperated by the political infighting there, he returned to Avignon. In a letter, Petrarch made a vain attempt to persuade him to go back to Rome but had to admit that the best burgundy was not to be had south of the alps. The Babylonian captivity ended with Urban's successor Gregory XI, but the wines of Burgundy retained their high reputation.

The dukes of Burgundy

From a byword for largesse in Avignon, Burgundian wine became a status symbol with the Valois dukes, four generations of whom governed Burgundy from 1363 to 1477. The first duke, Philip the Bold (1363–1404), son of King John of France, took a keen interest in the wine of the region, its most important export. In 1395, he issued a decree declaring the GAMAY grape variety to be harmful to human beings and its planting contrary to Burgundian practice. The first mention of the PINOT NOIR grape, named Noirien, dates only from the 1370s, but in all probability the grape had been in use longer. Modern Gamay has a far higher yield than Pinot Noir, and documentary evidence suggests that the same was true in the 14th century. In the same decree, Philip inveighs against the use of organic FERTILIZERS, presumably because it also increased YIELDS. Philip was trying to maintain quality, while many growers thought that manure and Gamay would make for easy profits. Although Philip the Bold wanted every single Gamay plant uprooted by the next Easter, we find his grandson Philip the Good (1429–67) still thundering against the inferior vine, which he says is a threat to both

the wines and the dukes of Burgundy. Fearing for his immortal soul, Philip the Good's rapacious Chancellor Nicolas Rolin built the famous HOSPICES DE BEAUNE in 1443.

But what were these famous wines really like? The white wines of Burgundy were probably made from the grape that also produced the highly reputed white wines of north eastern France, the Fromenteau, which had pale red berries and white juice, and could well be the ancestor of our PINOT GRIS. (The CHARDONNAY of modern white burgundy did not appear in the region until after the Middle Ages.) Also, in the Middle Ages wines were drunk in the year following the vintage, so properly matured burgundy would then have been unknown.   H.M.W.

Derlow, R. K., 'The "disloyal grape": the agrarian crisis of late fourteenth century Burgundy', *Agricultural History*, 56 (1982), 426–38.

Dion, R., *Histoire de la vigne et du vin en France* (Paris, 1959).

Modern burgundy

The duchy of Burgundy was once so proud of having the finest wines and finest court in Christendom that it developed into a state, and very nearly a kingdom in its own right. The defeat and death of the over-ambitious Charles the Rash, however, led to its being reincorporated into the kingdom of France. As the monarchy became stronger, the power of the Church declined slowly, so that during the 17th century many of the famous vineyards donated to the Church during the Middle Ages were sold to the increasingly important bourgeoisie in Dijon.

Although transport difficulties (see RIVERS) still hindered burgundy's fame abroad, the famous giant Pierre Brosse managed to interest Louis XIV in his Mâcon and the Sun King's physician, Fagon, prescribed old burgundy instead of champagne as the most suitable wine for his monarch's health. Roads began to improve in the 18th century and the tolls and tribulations inherent in road travel diminished, encouraging the start of commercial traffic in Burgundy. The first NÉGOCIANT (merchant) houses were founded in the 1720s and 1730s, including Champy (1720) and BOUCHARD PÈRE ET FILS (1731), names which have survived to this day.

The earliest major work on the wines of Burgundy, Claude Arnoux's *Dissertation on the Situation of Burgundy*... was published in 1728. It demonstrates the fame of the red wines of the Côte de Nuits and the special reputation of the Œil-de-Perdrix (partridge-eye) pink wines of Volnay, while the existence of white wine in the Côte de Beaune earns only a brief mention.

Most vineyards remained in the hands of Church or nobility until the French Revolution.

From 1791, the vineyards were sold off, often split between several owners. Since then they have further fragmented as a result of the law of equal inheritance among children laid down in the Napoleonic Code. This process has caused much of the difficulty in understanding burgundy: the consumer must familiarize himself not only with a plethora of village and vineyard names but also with the relative merits of possibly dozens of producers of each one.

Burgundy prospered in the early 19th century, although wine PRICES were low even for the fine vineyards. In addition, there was widespread planting of the inferior GAMAY grape to provide wine that was plentiful and cheap, albeit mediocre. Transport conditions continued to improve with the opening of a canal system in Burgundy, and the Paris–Dijon railway in 1851.

Easy prosperity was first checked, however, by the spread of POWDERY MILDEW in the 1850s and then destroyed by the arrival of the PHYLLOXERA louse in the 1870s. This calamity was finally admitted in the Côte d'Or in 1878 when an infested vineyard in Meursault was surrounded by soldiers. The Burgundians did not find it easy to come to terms with the problem: there were riots in Bouze-lès-Beaune between factions in favour of treating vineyards and those against; a posse of growers in Chenôve actually attacked a team sent in to spray the vines; American ROOTSTOCKS, the eventual saviours of French vineyards, were banned from the region between 1874 and 1887. Eventually, however, common sense prevailed and by the 1890s post-phylloxera wines were again on the market. Only the best vineyards were worth replanting after the predations of phylloxera, a valuable side benefit of the disaster.

The Burgundians were well aware of the considerable variation in quality of the wines produced by different plots of land, or *climats*, as they are known in Burgundy. In 1855, Dr Lavalle published his influential *History and Statistics of the Côte d'Or*, which included an informal CLASSIFICATION of the best vineyards. This was formalized in 1861 by the Beaune Committee of Agriculture, which, with Lavalle's assistance, devised three classes. Most of the first class were in due course enfranchised as GRANDS CRUS when the APPELLATION CONTRÔLÉE system was introduced in the 1930s.

Most burgundy was sold through the flourishing NÉGOCIANT houses until the years of hardship after the First World War. The economic depression of the 1920s and early 1930s threatened to ruin many small growers. One solution was the CO-OPERATIVE, particularly useful in Mâconnais, where prices were lower. Another was for proprietors to bottle their own produce, a move which met with opposition from the merchants when growers such as the Marquis d'Angerville, Henri Gouges, and Armand

Rousseau pioneered the concept of DOMAINE BOTTLING in the 1930s. Whereas in 1962 wines produced and bottled by growers accounted for only 15% of production, by 1990 nearly half of all Côte d'Or wines were domaine bottled. In 2011 58% of all burgundy was sold by 250 négociants, 26% by the 3,800 domaines, and 16% by the 23 co-operatives.

Geography and climate

The vineyards of Burgundy are based on LIME-STONE originating in the Jurassic period. This takes the form of undulating CHALK hills in Chablis; a long narrow escarpment running south and a touch west from Dijon to Chagny, the CÔTE D'OR; more isolated limestone outcrops in the Côte Chalonnaise and Mâconnais; with the vineyards of POUILLY-FUISSÉ beneath the imposing crags of Solutré and Vergisson in the extreme south.

The climate in Burgundy is broadly CONTINENTAL. In contrast to BORDEAUX, Burgundy is noticeably colder in the winter months, similar in temperature in the spring, but a little cooler during the summer. Although usually dry in winter, Burgundy tends to suffer from particularly heavy rainfall in May and June and again in October, which may or may not fall after the HARVEST. Spring FROST can be a problem (especially in CHABLIS), while HAIL causes local damage almost every year. Indeed the incidence of hail seems to be on the increase, particularly in the Côte de Beaune, and is perhaps a by-product of CLIMATE CHANGE.

Overall, there is a shorter and more variable summer than in Bordeaux (which is why only early-ripening grape varieties can be grown there). And whereas the hardy CHARDONNAY vine can thrive under these conditions, producing what are widely considered the finest full-bodied dry white wines in the world, the temperamental PINOT NOIR vine is less regularly successful. For more details of Burgundy's special aptitude for top-quality wine production, see CLIMATE AND WINE QUALITY.

Burgundy used to be at the limit of successful RIPENING, the red wines of Auxerrois rarely achieving much depth or body, but they continue to improve—and ripeness is usually guaranteed throughout Burgundy. The region's greatest reds are produced on the escarpment of the Côte d'Or, especially in the Côte de Nuits sector. Among the white wines of Burgundy, the wines of Chablis, reflecting their northern origin, are green tinted in colour and comparatively austere to taste. The most revered white wines are those of the Côte de Beaune, there being very few in the Côte de Nuits, while the whites of the Côte Chalonnaise are lighter and

attractive to drink young. Further south, the white wines of Mâconnais enjoy enough sun to make fat and ripe wines, although they may lack finesse.

Viticulture

For details, see CÔTE D'OR; CHALONNAISE; and MÂCONNAIS.

Winemaking

For details, see CÔTE D'OR; CHALONNAISE; and MÂCONNAIS.

Vine varieties

Burgundy has one of the world's least varied ranges of vine varieties. Almost all of the region's best red and white wines are made from Pinot Noir and Chardonnay respectively. According to official 2012 statistics, Chardonnay is grown on 49% of the region's total vineyard area (a proportion swollen by the substantially white wine production of Chablis and the Mâconnais), followed by Pinot Noir (35%), Gamay (8%), Aligoté (6%), Sauvignon Blanc (1% for ST-BRIS), and others such as MELON, SACY, and CÉSAR combined comprising 1%.

Organization of Burgundian vineyards

The vineyards of Burgundy, especially those of the Côte d'Or, are the most minutely parcellated in the world. This is mainly because the land has been continuously managed and owned by individual smallholders—there was no influx of outside capital with which to establish great estates as in BORDEAUX. But the combination of the Napoleonic Code, with its insistence on equal inheritance for every family member, and the fact that the land has proved so valuable, has meant that small family holdings have been divided and subdivided over generations. One vineyard, or *climat*, as it is known in this, the cradle of TERROIR, may therefore be owned by scores of different individual owners, each of them cultivating sometimes just a row or two of vines (see CLOS DE VOUGEOT, for example).

Organization of trade

Unlike the BORDEAUX TRADE with its large volume of single appellations, and many stratifications of those who sell it, the Burgundian wine trade became polarized between growers and NÉGOCIANTS, or merchants. Because the laws of equal inheritance have been strictly applied in a region of such valuable vineyards, individual growers may for example produce just one barrel, enough to fill just 25 cases, of a particular appellation. The market for burgundy was originally built by the merchants, who would buy grapes and wine from many different

growers before blending and selling the results. Increasingly individual growers with leading vineyards have been bottling their own wines. Since the early 1990s, the distinctions between growers and merchants have become increasingly blurred, with many widely admired growers also producing another range of wines made from grapes they did not grow themselves, while most merchants have been increasing their vineyard holdings. For more details, see NÉGOCIANTS.

See also HOSPICES DE BEAUNE and see BOURGOGNE for details of Burgundy's generic appellations. For the names of individual appellations, see BEAUNE; NUITS; CHALONNAISE; and MÂCON.

J.T.C.M.

CHABLIS and BEAUJOLAIS are treated separately.

Burgundy Grands Crus (listed from north to south)	
Commune	**Grand Cru**
Côte de Nuits (all for red wine unless otherwise stated)	
Gevrey-Chambertin	Mazis-Chambertin
	Ruchottes-Chambertin
	Chambertin Clos-de-Bèze
	Griotte-Chambertin
	Charmes-Chambertin
	Le Chambertin
	Latricières-Chambertin
	Mazoyères-Chambertin
	Chapelle-Chambertin
Morey-St-Denis	Clos de la Roche
	Clos St-Denis
	Clos des Lambrays
	Clos de Tart
	Bonnes Mares (some)
Chambolle-Musigny	Bonnes Mares (most)
	Le Musigny (some white wine too)
Vougeot	Clos de Vougeot
Flagey-Échezeaux	Grands Échezeaux
	Échezeaux
Vosne-Romanée	Richebourg
	Romanée-St-Vivant
	Romanée-Conti
	La Romanée
	La Grande Rue
	La Tâche
Côte de Beaune (all for white wine unless otherwise stated)	
Ladoix-Serrigny	Corton (almost all red)
	Corton-Charlemagne
Aloxe-Corton	Corton (almost all red)
	Corton-Charlemagne
Pernand-Vergelesses	Corton-Charlemagne
	Charlemagne (no longer used)
Puligny-Montrachet	Chevalier-Montrachet
	Bienvenues-Bâtard-Montrachet
with Chassagne-Montrachet	Le Montrachet
	Bâtard-Montrachet
Chassagne-Montrachet	Criots-Bâtard-Montrachet

Coates, C., The Wines of Burgundy (Berkeley, 2008).

Hanson, A., Burgundy (2nd edn, London, 1995).

Morris, J., Inside Burgundy (London, 2010).

Norman, R. H., and Taylor, C., The Great Domaines of Burgundy (3rd edn, London, 2010).

Pitiot, S., and Servant, J.-C., The Wines of Burgundy (12th edn of P. Poupon's original, Paris, 2012).

www.bourgogne-wines.com

www.burgundy-report.com

Busby, James (1801–71), the so-called father of AUSTRALIAN viticulture, although more recently the term prophet has been considered more appropriate. James Busby was born in Edinburgh and became interested in agriculture in Ireland, where his father managed estates. Before leaving Scotland for Australia, Busby became convinced that wine could be made in the colony and so spent several months studying viticulture and winemaking in France. This allowed him to write his first book, *Treatise on the Culture of the Vine*, on the five-month voyage on the *Triton*. At 24, therefore, Busby was already an author of a viticultural textbook, although at the time it was considered too scientific and lacking in simple directions. A land grant of 800 ha/1,980 acres was made to Busby on the Hunter River in NEW SOUTH WALES in 1824, and the property was named Kirkton. Busby was initially employed to teach viticulture at the Male Orphan School near Liverpool, and to manage its 5,000-ha estate. Unfortunately the school was soon closed down, and in between several other posts Busby published in 1830 his second and much more successful book *A Manual of Plain Directions for Planting and Cultivating Vineyards and for Making Wine in New South Wales*. Busby, like others of his time, extolled the virtues of wine drinking compared with the then common excessive spirits consumption in the colony. His book contains the much quoted 'The man who could sit under the shade of his own vine, with his wife and children about him, and the ripe clusters hanging within their reach, in such a climate as this, and not feel the highest enjoyment, is incapable of happiness and does not know what the word means.'

Busby's greatest contribution to Australian viticulture was yet to be made. In 1831 he returned to England, and spent four months touring the Continent, primarily to make a collection of vine cuttings for Australia. His collection included cuttings for about 680 VINE VARIETIES (not necessarily all different) from the botanical gardens of MONTPELLIER, Luxembourg in Paris, and Kew in London, as well as from other parts of France and Spain. This collection was shipped to Sydney along with seeds of various vegetables, and by January 1833 was reported to be growing in the Sydney Botanic Gardens. In 1833 Busby published another book about his tour to Spain and France, and listed the varieties in his collection.

Busby's life entered a new dimension in 1833 with his appointment as the first British Resident at the Bay of Islands in New Zealand. The nearby town of Russell was a trading port for visiting whalers, and described as 'the hell hole of the Pacific'. Busby had neither the magisterial powers nor the constabulary to impose order but, through his and others' efforts, New Zealand became a British possession in February 1840 with the signing of the Treaty of Waitangi by some fifty Maori chiefs. Busby had little time for viticulture in New Zealand, although he did establish a vineyard at Waitangi which was destroyed in 1845 during clashes with the Maoris. He is credited with being the first person to make wine in New Zealand.

Unfortunately, the Sydney vine collection was not tended as well as it should have been. Some of the vines were distributed to Kirkton in the Hunter, and some to the Adelaide Botanic Gardens in South Australia. Many of Busby's imports were to become the basis of the Australian wine industry; indeed some CLONES of vine varieties such as Chardonnay and Shiraz still important today can be traced to Busby's imports. In later life Busby was aggrieved to discover that much of the credit for his vine introductions was erroneously given to William Macarthur, another pioneer of the Australian wine industry. Busby died in England in 1871. His great contribution to the Australian wine industry was his vine importations, his writings, and his enthusiasm for the notion that Australia should develop as John Bull's (England's) vineyard of the Antipodes.   R.E.S.

Evans, L., Australian Complete Book of Wine (Sydney, 1977).

Halliday, J., and Jarratt, R., The Wines & History of the Hunter Valley (Sydney, 1979).

bush vines, an alternative term to describe GOBELET-trained vines or HEAD TRAINING. The comparison with a bush is apt: the vines are trained to a short trunk, normally free standing (without a TRELLIS SYSTEM), and are pruned to a few spurs commonly arranged in a ring on short arms from the trunk. The term bush vines is used in Australia and South Africa, and there was a FASHION for using it on labels in the late 1990s, although many of these old, and typically low-vigour, vineyards have been replaced by vines with a trellis system.   R.E.S.

butt, BARREL TYPE associated particularly with SHERRY production in the Jerez region. It is usually made from American oak and has a capacity of between 600 and 650 l/172 gal. A *bota chica* or shipping butt holds 500 l and is sometimes used as a unit of measurement. New butts are an inconvenience in the sherry-making process and have to be seasoned by being used for the FERMENTATION of lower-quality wines.

Buzet, archetypically Gascon red wine appellation in SOUTH WEST FRANCE up the Garonne River from BORDEAUX energetically producing notably bordeaux-like wines. The recent history of the appellation, created in 1973, is inextricably intertwined with the dynamism of the local CO-OPERATIVE, Les Vignerons de Buzet, which makes all but a tiny proportion of Buzet. Notably ambitious, the co-operative laid the foundation stones of a barrel-ageing cellar in 1958, and has its own COOPER. Thus, the average Buzet is given much more sophisticated ÉLEVAGE than the average BORDEAUX AOC, without an enormous price differential.

The region, which extends along the left bank of the Garonne between Agen and Marmande, has known viticulture since Roman times but vine-growing was developed under monastic influence in the Middle Ages. The fortunes of the district's wines suffered during the HUNDRED YEARS WAR, when the district supported the English crown. The district was further hampered by the restrictions imposed by the Bordelais on all HAUT PAYS, or 'high country', wines, when the wines of the village of Nérac were particularly well known. PHYLLOXERA seriously affected viticulture in the late 19th century, and a ruling in the early 20th century that Bordeaux wines had to come from within the GIRONDE *département* was a further blow to a district which had habitually supplied BLENDING wines to the Bordeaux merchants.

By 2011 the total vineyard area was back to its late 1990s peak of more than 1,800 ha/4,450 acres. The gravels and clays of these inland hills are planted with classic red Bordeaux vine varieties Cabernet Sauvignon, Cabernet Franc, and, especially, Merlot. The co-operative has invested heavily in the most modern winemaking equipment, and its policy is to make strict selections according to TERROIR and quality each VINTAGE so that all red Buzet should receive at least a year's BARREL MATURATION. The co-operative also vinifies the produce of a number of individual parcels of land and bottles a plethora of them separately.

Byblos, ancient town in the LEBANON 40 km/ 25 miles north of modern Beirut. It had the reputation of being the oldest town in the world and was a PHOENICIAN centre of trading. Its wines were famous in classical times.

BYO stands for 'Bring Your Own' (Wine) and is a type of restaurant most common in Australia and New Zealand, where the term was coined. The term is associated with maximum wine-drinking pleasure at minimum cost to the restaurant-goer (in tandem with reduced profit to the restaurateur). New Zealanders claim that the BYO name and concept was born in 1976 when the New Zealand authorities, still notably cautious about the distribution of alcoholic drinks, devised the Bring Your Own licence for restaurants at which diners would be allowed to take their own wine. Australians in the state of Victoria, also famously restrictive in its legislative attitude to alcoholic drinks, maintain that Melbourne had BYO establishments in the 1960s. Wherever its origins, this arrangement has become common for a wide range of restaurants in Australia, New Zealand, and elsewhere, the wine often being bought in a nearby retail establishment. CORKAGE is sometimes but not always charged. The expression in the US is **BYOB** as in 'Bring Your Own Bottle', most commonly encouraged here and elsewhere either in restaurants too new to have a liquor licence and during quiet periods such as Mondays or when regular customers are on holiday.

C

Cabardès, LANGUEDOC appellation (since 1999) of 590 ha/1,457 acres to the north of Carcassonne which produces red and some rosé wines that testify to its location on the cusp of Atlantic and Mediterranean influences. The grape varieties planted also represent a Bordeaux/Languedoc cocktail of Cabernet Sauvignon, Cabernet Franc, Merlot, Cot (Malbec), and some Fer Servadou (of MARCILLAC fame), spiced and fleshed out with the more meridional Syrah, Grenache, and Cinsaut (mainly for rosé). The Bordelais varieties tend to prosper on the western, wetter, deeper soils, while wines produced from the hotter, shallower soils of the eastern Cabardès are more likely to have a high proportion of Mediterranean varieties. Winds almost constantly buffet the small hills punctuated by pines and garrigue, and minimize the local wine producers' dependence on AGROCHEMICALS. In contrast to the somewhat similar Côtes de la MALEPÈRE to the south of Carcassonne, production here is mainly in the hands of a small but committed band of individuals constrained by low financial returns. Winemaking equipment and methods are not always the most sophisticated, but the wines boast an originality and potential for longevity that is unusual for this part of France (which officials tend to classify as SOUTH WEST FRANCE rather than the LANGUEDOC to which its immediate eastern neighbour the Minervois belongs).

Cabernet is loosely used as an abbreviation for either or both of the black grape varieties CABERNET FRANC and CABERNET SAUVIGNON. In north-east Italy in particular there has been a certain lack of precision about the precise identity of the Cabernet grown and allowed into the many Cabernet DOCS, although Cabernet Franc has tended to predominate. Elsewhere, Cabernet is more likely to be an abbreviation for

Cabernet Sauvignon. Cabernet is also a popular prefix for recent German and Swiss hybrids such as **Cabernet Blanc, Cabernet Carbon, Cabernet Carol, Cabernet Colonjes, Cabernet Cortis, Cabernet Dorio, Cabernet Dorsa** (the most popular), **Cabernet Jura,** and **Cabernet Mitos.**

Cabernet Franc, fine French black grape variety, much blended with and overshadowed by its progeny the more widely planted CABERNET SAUVIGNON. Only in Anjou-Saumur and Touraine in the Loire Valley, on the right bank of the Gironde in Bordeaux, and in parts of north east Italy is it quantitatively more important than Cabernet Sauvignon, but Cabernet Franc is sufficiently widely grown to be one of the world's 20 most planted cultivars for wine.

In the vineyard it can be distinguished from Cabernet Sauvignon by its less dramatically indented leaves but the two share so many characteristics that they had for long been thought to be related. In 1997, thanks to DNA PROFILING, it was established that Cabernet Franc was, with the Bordeaux white vine variety SAUVIGNON BLANC, a parent of the noble Cabernet Sauvignon (see CABERNET SAUVIGNON for more details).

There is some evidence that the variety's origins lie in Spanish Basque country but by the end of the 18th century, Cabernet Franc was already documented as producing high-quality wine in the Libournais vineyards of St-Émilion, Pomerol, and Fronsac, where it is often called Bouchet today. Long before this, however, according to Odart, it had already been selected by Cardinal Richelieu, as a well-respected vine of south west France, to be planted at the Abbaye de St-Nicolas-de-Bourgueil in the Loire by an abbot called Breton, whose name persists as the Loire synonym for Cabernet Franc to this day.

Cabernet Franc is particularly well suited to cool, inland climates such as the middle Loire and the Libournais. It buds and matures more than a week earlier than Cabernet Sauvignon, which makes it more susceptible to COULURE, but it is easier to ripen fully and is much less susceptible to poor weather during harvest. In the Médoc and Graves districts of Bordeaux, where Cabernet Franc constitutes about 10% of a typical vineyard and is always blended with other varieties, it is regarded as a form of insurance against the weather's predations on Cabernet Sauvignon and Merlot grapes. Most Libournais bet on Cabernet Franc in preference to the later, and therefore more difficult to ripen, Cabernet Sauvignon to provide a framework for Merlot, Bordeaux's most planted variety.

In Bordeaux, plantings of Cabernet Franc and Cabernet Sauvignon were almost equal, at about 10,000 ha/25,000 acres, in the late 1960s but Cabernet Sauvignon was so often chosen in preference to Cabernet Franc by those replacing unprofitable white wine vineyards that by 2011 Cabernet Sauvignon covered more than twice Cabernet Franc's total area in the Gironde of 11,155 ha/27,553 acres.

As a wine, Cabernet Franc tends to be rather lighter in colour and tannins, and therefore earlier maturing, than Cabernet Sauvignon although CHEVAL BLANC, the world's grandest Cabernet Franc-dominated wine, proves that majestic durability is also possible. Cabernet Franc is, typically, light to medium bodied with more immediate fruit than Cabernet Sauvignon and marked fragrance, including sometimes some of the herbaceous aromas evident in unripe Cabernet Sauvignon.

Cabernet Franc is still planted all over south west France, although, in appellations such as Bergerac and Madiran (where Cabernet Franc is known as Bouchy), Cabernet Sauvignon has been gaining ground.

Cabernet Franc has been France's sixth most planted black grape variety throughout the twentieth century with about 40% of its 2011 total of 35,214 ha in the south west and just over a quarter in the greater Loire Valley. Steadily increasing appreciation (largely within France) of relatively light, early-maturing reds such as Saumur-Champigny, Bourgueil, Chinon, and Anjou-Villages fuelled demand for Cabernet Franc in the Loire at the expense of Rosé d'Anjou and Chenin Blanc whites. Here Cabernet Franc tends to be the dominant variety in perfumed, fresh red wines that can smell of raspberries and/or pencil shavings.

Cabernet Franc is also well established in Italy, particularly in the north east (see FRIULI and VENETO in particular), where it has sometimes been encouraged to yield such quantity that wines can be over-herbaceous and where some vines previously thought to be Cabernet Franc have been identified as Carmenère. Some Tuscan and central Italian producers of Cabernet Sauvignon grow the variety for blending purposes but in BOLGHERI and the rest of the Maremma it can yield wines of real interest and complexity, as it does at Tenuta di Trinoro in southern Tuscany. The 2010 Italian vineyard survey found a total of 6,313 ha of Cabernet Franc in Italy, less than half of the Cabernet Sauvignon total. Elsewhere in Europe, only HUNGARY takes Cabernet Franc particularly seriously—particularly in Villány.

Elsewhere, with a few notable exceptions such as Viader, Cabernet Franc has generally been grown for the express purpose of blending with Cabernet Sauvignon, following the Bordeaux recipe whether or not the climate suggests that such insurance would be wise. California's total plantings of the variety, 3,428 acres/1,388 ha in 2012 concentrated in Napa and Sonoma, have remained stable for years. The variety has been responsible for some well-balanced, fruity wines in WASHINGTON State where the winter-hardy Cabernet Franc is more resistant to WINTER FREEZE than Merlot, but it has been losing ground to the more fashionable Syrah and there were only 972 acres/303 ha by 2011.

In the cooler northern and eastern wine regions of North America (especially VIRGINIA, the Niagara Peninsula of CANADA, where ICEWINE has been made from it, Pennsylvania, and Long Island in NEW YORK State), Cabernet Franc has emerged as the red VINIFERA variety of choice, ripening much more reliably than Cabernet Sauvignon and providing much more EXTRACT than do most HYBRIDS.

ARGENTINA has barely 400 ha of Cabernet Franc, while Chile has 1,450 ha, some of the best being old vines in Maule.

In Australia Cabernet Franc plays a very minor, generally lacklustre part while most of the best of New Zealand's 166 ha/410 acres play a part in Hawke's Bay blends. Although the likes of Rijk's and Warwick make fine varietal versions, Cabernet Franc is planted on less than one per cent of South Africa's vineyards.

As the pendulum swings back from super-concentrated, high-alcohol reds, Cabernet Franc may well benefit.

Bowers, J. E., and Meredith, C. P., 'The parentage of a classic wine grape, Cabernet Sauvignon', *Nature Genetics*, 16/1 (1997), 84–7.

Enjalbert, H., *Les Grands Vins de Saint-Émilion, Pomerol et Fronsac* (Paris, 1983).

Galet, P., *Dictionnaire encyclopédique des cépages* (Paris, 2000).

Odart, A.-P., *Ampélographie universelle* (Paris, 1845).

Cabernet Frank, occasional north-east Italian name for CABERNET FRANC.

Cabernet Gernischt, Chinese name for CARMENÈRE, probably a misliteration of **Cabernet Gemischt** (mixed Cabernet).

Cabernet Sauvignon, the world's most renowned, but relatively recent, red wine grape, that is now the world's most-planted grape variety, total plantings having more than doubled beween 1990 (when it was the world's eighth most planted variety) and 2010 to nearly 300,000 ha. From its power base in Bordeaux, where it is almost invariably blended with other grapes, it was taken up in other French wine regions and in much of the Old and New Worlds, where it has been blended to create BORDEAUX blends and with INDIGENOUS VARIETIES and is often used to produce pure VARIETAL wine, especially in warmer climates.

Perhaps the most extraordinary aspect of Cabernet Sauvignon is its ability to produce a wine that is so recognizably Cabernet, even if remarkably few wine regions, considering its ubiquity, have so far proved reliable sources of seriously top-quality expressions of this potentially top-quality grape: MÉDOC, PESSAC-LÉOGNAN, NAPA, SONOMA, SANTA CRUZ MOUNTAINS, WASHINGTON State, BOLGHERI, COONAWARRA, MARGARET RIVER, and part of PENEDÈS spring most readily to mind. What makes Cabernet Sauvignon remarkable to taste is not primarily its exact fruit flavour—which is sometimes likened to blackcurrants or cigar boxes—but its structure and its ability to provide the perfect vehicle for individual vintage characteristics, winemaking and ÉLEVAGE techniques, and, especially, local physical attributes, or TERROIR. Unlike CHARDONNAY, which is as widely disseminated, late-ripening Cabernet Sauvignon must be grown in relatively warm climates, and can in some years fail to reach full RIPENESS even somewhere as mild as the Médoc.

It is Cabernet Sauvignon's remarkable concentration of PHENOLICS that really sets it apart from most other widely grown vine varieties. It is therefore capable of producing deeply coloured wines worthy of long MACERATION and long-term AGEING. Over the centuries, it has demonstrated a special but by no means exclusive affinity for densely textured French OAK. The particular appeal of Cabernet Sauvignon lies much less in primary fruit aromas (with which other varieties such as Gamay and Pinot Noir are more obviously associated) than in the much more subtle flavour compounds that evolve over years of BOTTLE AGEING from complex interaction between compounds derived from fruit, fermentation, alcohol, and oak. It is also true, however, that so distinctive is Cabernet Sauvignon's imprint on the palate memory that part of the reason why it is so widely planted is that even when irrigated to greedily high yields and hastily vinified without even a glimpse of wood, it can produce a wine with some recognizable relationship to the great Bordeaux growths of the Médoc and Graves on which its reputation has been built.

Cabernet Sauvignon's origins for long remained shrouded in mystery but all was revealed in 1997, thanks to DNA PROFILING. Bowers and Meredith of the University of California at DAVIS showed beyond all reasonable doubt that Cabernet Sauvignon's parents are none other than CABERNET FRANC and the Bordeaux white wine grape SAUVIGNON BLANC, a cross that is thought to have happened spontaneously in one of the many vineyards planted with a mixture of different vines in the old days. This neatly explains why Cabernet Sauvignon can smell like either or both of its parents, and why Cabernet Franc is mentioned in the literature long before Cabernet Sauvignon.

There are no early references to Cabernet Sauvignon in the LITERATURE OF WINE and the variety did not start to make any significant impact on the vineyards of Bordeaux until the end of the 18th century, when the great estates were built up and wine with real longevity emerged (see BORDEAUX, history). Baron Hector de Brane, once owner of Ch Mouton, together with his neighbour Armand d'Armailhacq, is credited with its promulgation, if not introduction, in the MÉDOC.

The distinguishing marks of the Cabernet Sauvignon berry are its small size, its high ratio of pip to pulp (one to 12, according to Peynaud, as opposed to one to 25 for Sémillon), and the thickness of its skins, so distinctively blue, as opposed to red or even purple, on the vine. The pips are a major factor in Cabernet Sauvignon's high TANNIN level while the thickness of its skins accounts for the depth of colour that is the tell-tale sign of a Cabernet Sauvignon in so many BLIND TASTINGS—as well as the variety's relatively good resistance to ROT.

The vine is susceptible however to POWDERY MILDEW, which can be treated quite easily, and the vine TRUNK DISEASES EUTYPA and EXCORIOSE, which cannot. It is extremely vigorous and should ideally be grafted on to a weak ROOTSTOCK to keep its VIGOUR in check. It both buds and ripens late, one to two weeks after Merlot and Cabernet Franc, the two varieties with which it is typically planted and blended in Bordeaux. Cabernet Sauvignon ripens slowly, which has the advantage that picking dates are less crucial than with other varieties (such as Syrah, for example); but this has the disadvantage that Cabernet Sauvignon simply cannot be relied upon to ripen in the coolest wine regions, especially when its energy can so easily be diverted into producing dangerously shady leaves, such as in Tasmania or New Zealand, unless CANOPY MANAGEMENT is employed. Cabernet Sauvignon that fails to reach full ripeness can taste eerily like Cabernet Franc (just as unripe Sémillon, co-incidentally, resembles Sauvignon Blanc).

Even in the temperate climate of Bordeaux, the flowering of the vine can be dogged by cold weather and the ripening by rain, so that Bordeaux's vine-growers have traditionally hedged their bets by planting a mix of early and late local varieties, typically in the Médoc and Graves districts 75% of Cabernet Sauvignon plus a mixture of Merlot, Cabernet Franc, and sometimes a little Petit Verdot. (See CABERNET FRANC for reasons why the Cabernet in St-Émilion and Pomerol is much less likely to be Cabernet Sauvignon.)

A practice that had its origins in judicious fruit farming has proved itself in the blending vat. The plump, fruity, earlier maturing Merlot is a natural blending partner for the more rigorous Cabernet Sauvignon, while Petit Verdot can add extra spice (if only in the sunniest years) and Cabernet Franc can perfume the blend to a certain extent. Except in warmer wine regions, wines made solely from Cabernet Sauvignon can lack charm and stuffing; the framework is sensational but tannin and colour alone make poor nourishment. As demonstrated by the increasing popularity of Merlot and Cabernet Franc and even Petit Verdot cuttings, some producers follow the Bordeaux example of blending their Cabernet Sauvignon with other varieties in newer wine regions, even those warm enough to ripen Cabernet fully, although the Médoc recipe is by no means the only one. In Tuscany it is sometimes blended with Sangiovese. In Australia and in Provence it is blended with SYRAH (SHIRAZ), with very different results.

Cabernet Sauvignon, with its sophisticated whiff of French glamour, was extraordinarily popular in the New World in the last two decades of the 20th century. Indeed, it could fairly be said that one of the first signs of 'modernization' of a wine region was its importation of and experimentation with Cabernet Sauvignon cuttings. Only those regions, such as England, Germany, and Luxembourg, disbarred for reasons of climate, have found it difficult to join this particular club.

French plantings of Cabernet Sauvignon increased enormously in the 1980s and 1990s but have fallen slightly this century so that in 2011 there were 51,769 ha/127,869 acres, of which just under half were in the Bordeaux *département* the Gironde (although within the Gironde the agriculturally more dependable Merlot is almost three times as popular). The vine's stronghold is the left bank of the River Gironde, most notably the famously well-drained gravels of the Médoc and Graves CRUS classés, whose selling price can well justify the efficacious luxury of ageing their wine in small, often new, oak barrels. Most of the FIRST GROWTHS are famous for their high proportion of Cabernet Sauvignon. Their wines, although differing in character, are known for their solidity and longevity.

The vine is also planted over much of SOUTH WEST FRANCE, often as an optional ingredient in its red, and occasionally rosé, wines, although only in BERGERAC and BUZET does it play a substantial part. In more internationally styled wines, however, it may add structure to the Négrette of GAILLAC and FRONTON, and the Tannat of BÉARN, IROULÉGUY, and MADIRAN. It is also increasingly used to add substance to the red Côtes de ST-MONT.

Plantings in the Languedoc-Roussillon have increased substantially since the 1980s so that the total was 16,967 ha by 2011, but Syrah and Merlot have proved much more successful, and Grenache and Carignan are also much more widely planted. The most obviously successful southern French Cabernet Sauvignons are those used as ingredients in low-yield blends with Syrah and other Rhône varieties, such as Mas de Daumas Gassac in the Hérault or, further east in Provence, Domaine de Trévallon and Ch Vignelaure. Provence had just over 3,000 ha of Cabernet Sauvignon in 2011.

Cabernet Sauvignon's only other French territory is the Loire, but Cabernet Franc is nine times as widely grown, not least because it is so much easier to ripen.

Outside France

Cabernet Sauvignon is by far the dominant variety for the world's fastest growing wine-producing county CHINA where total plantings were thought to have reached 20,000 ha by 2009, and this total may already have overtaken Bordeaux's. The variety, incidentally, was also very widely planted in the old Soviet Union where according to the most accurate estimates available, there were approximately 30,000 ha/75,000 acres of Cabernet Sauvignon before it was broken up. The variety is presumably still widely planted in RUSSIA, UKRAINE, and especially in MOLDOVA—although in the many wine regions susceptible to WINTER FREEZE, the cold-hardy hybrid CABERNET SEVERNY is popular. Cabernet Sauvignon is also grown in GEORGIA, AZERBAIJAN, KAZAKHSTAN, TAJIKISTAN, and KYRGYZSTAN.

Another country with an extremely important area planted with the world's noblest black grape variety is CHILE, whose grand total of (generally ungrafted) Cabernet Sauvignon grew from about 16,000 ha/39,500 acres to about 40,000 ha between 1997 and 2003, making it the country's most important vine variety even if the total has remained pretty stable while Chile experiments with new varieties. Here the fruit is exceptionally healthy and the wine almost rudely exuberant.

Not surprisingly, Cabernet Sauvignon also flourishes in the rest of South America's vineyards: in ARGENTINA, where in terms of quantity it is dwarfed by Malbec; in BRAZIL, URUGUAY, MEXICO, PERU, and BOLIVIA.

Cabernet Sauvignon, even less surprisingly, has been the bedrock of CALIFORNIA CULT wines. Such has been the quality of some of these wines that northern California could fairly be said to have proved itself Cabernet Sauvignon's second home, and in fact grows far more in total—almost 80,000 acres/32,400 ha. Although the dramatic growth in Cabernet plantings has stopped, it is California's most important variety by far apart from Chardonnay. In the better, and often extremely carefully tended, sites of northern California, Cabernet Sauvignon can ripen quite well enough to need no grower's insurance or winemaker's additional complexity in terms of other grape varieties and 100% Cabernet Sauvignon can be a hugely successful recipe. For more detail on the golden state's Cabernet achievements, see CALIFORNIA.

Cabernet Sauvignon is also one of WASHINGTON State's two major black grape varieties, and definitively overtook Merlot in 2006 so that plantings totalled 10,293 acres/4,167 ha by 2011. Cabernet Sauvignon's vigour and late ripening make it unattractive to growers in damp, cool Oregon but it has been most successful in other American states including Arizona and TEXAS. In CANADA, the warmer climate of Okanagan Valley in BRITISH COLUMBIA is much more suitable for Cabernet Sauvignon than ONTARIO. If Californians decided early on that the Napa Valley was their Cabernet Sauvignon hotspot, Australians did the same about Coonawarra and, subsequently, Margaret River. They, however, have for decades employed a much less reverential policy towards blending their Cabernet. Cabernet–Shiraz blends (a recipe recommended in Provence as long ago as 1865 by Dr GUYOT) have been popular items in the Australian market place since the 1960s. The richness and softness of Australian Shiraz is such that it fills in the gaps left by Cabernet Sauvignon even more effectively than can the French Syrah recommended by Dr Guyot.

Cabernet Sauvignon and Chardonnay vie for second most planted vine variety, but a long way behind Shiraz. In 2012 there were nearly 26,000 ha of Cabernet Sauvignon, mainly in South Australia, particularly Coonawarra. See AUSTRALIA for more detail on Australian Cabernet Sauvignon.

Cabernet Sauvignon was once important in NEW ZEALAND but by 2012 there were fewer than 300 ha, most of them in Hawke's Bay. It needs careful CANOPY MANAGEMENT to ripen fully, and Pinot Noir is now firmly the country's signature red.

Cabernet Sauvignon was equally revered in SOUTH AFRICA in the late 20th century but Shiraz had become almost as important by 2012 when total Cabernet Sauvignon vineyards had fallen to 11,800 ha/29,146 acres. Many vines are still plagued by LEAFROLL VIRUS which can prejudice full ripening.

Cabernet Sauvignon has been an increasingly popular choice for internationally minded wine producers in Spain, where it was planted by the Marqués de Riscal at his Rioja estate in the mid 19th century, and could also be found in the vineyards of VEGA SICILIA. It was otherwise virtually unknown on the Iberian peninsula until the 1960s, when it was imported into Penedès by both Miguel TORRES, Jr, and Jean León. It broadened its base in Spain, particularly Cataluña, in the late 20th century—not just for wines dominated by it but for blending, notably with Tempranillo. By 2011 there were 21,642 ha/53,455 acres of Cabernet Sauvignon in Spain, making it the fifth most planted red wine vine, yielding some successful reds, and some very boring basic varietals, from Penedès to Ronda. In Portugal, it is much rarer, planted on barely 2,000 ha of vineyard, mainly around Lisbon.

Italy, where Cabernet Sauvignon was introduced, via Piemonte, in the 1820s, now has a very substantial area of Cabernet Sauvignon, almost 14,000 ha by 2010, more than double the total recorded for Cabernet Franc. Tuscany and Sicily are the most important regions quantitively. Cabernet Sauvignon played a considerable role in the emergence of SUPERTUSCANS, and has been popular as a seasoning in an increasing proportion, not just of CHIANTI, but in a wide range of reds throughout the country. In the early 21st century there was a tendency, arguably regrettable, to amend DOC regulations to allow in a small proportion of INTERNATIONAL VARIETIES, notably Cabernet Sauvignon. Cabernet Sauvignon was for long a major ingredient in such Tuscan wines as Solaia, Sassicaia, Venegazzù, and Castello di Rampolla's Sammarco, and has even invaded the NEBBIOLO territory of Piemonte in such bottlings as Darmagi from GAJA and Alberto Bertelli's I Fossaretti.

East of Italy there are many thousands of hectares of Cabernet Sauvignon, which plays a particularly important part in the wine industries of BULGARIA where its 15,827 ha/39,109 acres in 2009 constituted 15% of the country's vines. Ukraine had the second biggest area of Cabernet Sauvignon with 8,468 ha/20,925 acres in 2009 but it is also very significant in Moldova where 7,590 ha were planted and the variety is by far the most important. Both Russia and Romania had a little over 3,000 ha. The variety can ripen reliably in the warm summers of eastern Europe and, as Bulgaria proved in the 1980s, can provide excellent value if grown and made carefully. Smaller amounts of Cabernet Sauvignon are grown in HUNGARY, AUSTRIA, and GREECE, where it was first planted, in modern times at least, at the Carras domaine.

Perhaps the most tenacious Cabernet Sauvignon grower has been Serge Hochar of Ch Musar in the LEBANON, where in the last 20 years it has become, along with Cinsaut, the country's most planted wine grape with more than 200 ha. It is also by far the most popular variety in ISRAEL's revitalized wine industry and can make fair, if often expensive, copies of California Cabernet there. There are other, rather less war-torn, pockets of Cabernet Sauvignon vines all over the eastern Mediterranean, notably in TURKEY and CYPRUS, as well as in North Africa. In ASIA, Cabernet Sauvignon is planted by virtually all nascent wine industries and is well established already in JAPAN, where its strong links with the famous châteaux of Bordeaux are particularly prized.

Wherever there are any vine-growers with any grounding in the wines of the world, and late-ripening grapes are economically viable, they are almost certain to try Cabernet Sauvignon—unless they inhabit one of Bordeaux's great rival regions Burgundy and the Rhône.

Bowers, J. E., and Meredith, C. P., 'The parentage of a classic wine grape, Cabernet Sauvignon', *Nature Genetics*, 16/1 (1997), 84–7.

Eyres, H., *Cabernet Sauvignon* (London, 1991).

Galet, P., *Dictionnaire encyclopédique des cépages* (Paris, 2000).

Lake, M., *Cabernet* (Sydney, 1977).

Peynaud, E., *Connaissance et travail du vin* (Paris, 1981).

Lewin, B., *Claret and Cabs—The Story of Cabernet Sauvignon* (Dover, 2013).

Cabernet Severny, red wine grape variety specially bred for cold climates at the All-Russia Potapenko Institute in the Rostov region of RUSSIA. It was created by pollination of a HYBRID of DIMIAT (known here as Galan) × *V. amurensis* with a pollen mixture of other hybrid forms involving both the European vine species *V. vinifera* and the famously cold-hardy Mongolian vine species *V. amurensis*. It is grown in Russia and colder parts of Canada.

Cabinet, term of approbation applied to German wines from the 18th century until 1971, when its use was outlawed by the new GERMAN WINE LAW. A wine labelled Auslese Cabinet, for instance, signified an AUSLESE especially prized by its producer. The term was also used for precious works of art and, implying a piece worthy of enshrining in the proprietor's cabinet, it was occasionally spelled with a K; *Kabinettstück* is still used in German in the sense of *pièce de résistance* and its cachet was borrowed by the 1971 Wine Law for the technically defined PRÄDIKAT known as KABINETT. D.S.

Cabrières, village and named TERROIR for reds and rosés within the LANGUEDOC AOC inside the CLAIRETTE DU LANGUEDOC zone. The CO-OPERATIVE dominates production, which has historically favoured rosé, which must contain at least 45% CINSAUT grapes.

Cachapoal, part of the Rapel subregion of the Central Valley in CHILE.

Cadillac, small sweet and medium-sweet white appellation of barely 130 ha/321 acres in 2013 just north of LOUPIAC in the BORDEAUX region, once particularly popular with the Dutch, named after the walled town built by the English in the 12th century. Its special combination of chalk and gravel theoretically justifies a distinction which is still too rarely found in the wines. Low selling prices make high-quality production methods such as those practised in SAUTERNES difficult to justify, and few producers are brave enough to try to make BOTRYTIZED WINES.

Cadillac Côtes de Bordeaux, part of the Côtes de BORDEAUX appellation, officially recognized in 2011, for the ambitious reds made on the south-facing slopes along the right bank of the Garonne between Bordeaux and Langon, once called PREMIÈRES CÔTES DE BORDEAUX. Merlot with Cabernet Sauvignon and Cabernet Franc are planted on about 1,000 ha/5,000 acres of vineyard dedicated to the production of these often good-value reds. The soils here are very varied, with the *coteaux* rising from the river bank offering the most valuably gravelly or CALCAREOUS terrain. Clay predominates on the plateau between the *coteaux* and the Entre-Deux-Mers boundary. The relatively small quantity of sweet white wines produced on this strip of land are called Premières Côtes de Bordeaux. There is a recognizable band of seriously ambitious producers here, especially of quite concentrated red wines which may lack the ageing potential of Bordeaux's more famous examples but can offer good value for drinking at three to five years old. Particularly successful properties include Chx Carignan, Carsin, Haut-Rian, Lezongars, Parenchère, and Reynon. See BORDEAUX for more detail.

Caecuban wine was ranked by the connoisseurs of Ancient ROME among the finest wines of Italy for the last century BC and the first half of the 1st century AD. Caecuban wine was produced on a small vineyard in the low-lying marshy region, south of Terracina, on the west coast of central Italy, between the sea and the Lago di Fondi. The vines were trained up poplars. Caecuban was a white wine, which following standard Roman practice was aged for a number of years, during which it deepened to a 'flame' colour. It was described as 'sinewy' and 'packing a punch' by the medical writer Galen. The vineyard was largely destroyed in the middle of the 1st century AD by the ambitious, though abortive, scheme of the Emperor Nero to dig a canal to link the bay of Naples with the Tiber. Caecuban never recovered and the name became simply a generic term for wine with the characteristic colour of the true wine. Small quantities of undistinguished red wine called Cécubo are produced in the district today.   J.J.P.

Cagnina, synonym for TERAN (or Terrano) in Italy's Romagna region.

Cahors, shrinking wine region in the Quercy district in SOUTH WEST FRANCE, producing exclusively red wine, uniquely in France dependent on the MALBEC or Cot grape. In the 1980s and 1990s, it benefited from considerable inward investment and since then has pinned hopes on Argentina's success with Malbec.

The wine producers of Cahors long suffered from the protectionist measures against such HAUT PAYS wines inflicted on Cahors by the merchants of Bordeaux. The River Lot provided an ideal trade route from the town of Cahors to the markets of northern Europe via the GARONNE and Bordeaux, and Cahors was making wines noted for their colour and BODY from at least the early Middle Ages. There are records of Cahors being sold in London in the early 13th century, but the HUNDRED YEARS WAR disrupted patterns of trade.

Cahors is influenced by the Mediterranean as well as by the Atlantic, and, although winters are rather colder than in Bordeaux, the wines tend to be more concentrated. They were appreciated as suitable blending material with the lighter wines of Bordeaux, and in the early 19th century were famed as the 'black wines of Cahors'. (Such was Cahors's international renown in the 19th century that imitation 'Cahors' was made by at least one of the Russian model wineries in the CRIMEA.) A method of making the wines even blacker had been adopted whereby a portion of the grape juice was boiled to concentrate its colour and fermentable sugars. The produce of this technique was designed specifically for blending rather than drinking. At this time there were almost 40,000 ha/100,000 acres of vineyards in the greater Cahors region, but PHYLLOXERA reduced it to less than a tenth of this, and resulted in considerable replanting with HYBRIDS. The

arrival of the RAILWAYS also gave the populous north ready access to the cheap and plentiful wines of the LANGUEDOC. Cahors fell into decline.

The establishment of the Caves d'Olt CO-OPERATIVE at Parnac in 1947 marked the modest beginning of a new era during which the proportion of noble grape varieties and the incidence of good winemaking equipment and technology have steadily increased so that by the late 1990s more than 4,000 ha of vines were producing Cahors, awarded full APPELLATION CONTRÔLÉE status in 1971—although this total had dropped to below 3,400 ha by 2011. Within south west France only BERGERAC makes more wine. Vines for Cahors may be planted either on the notably thin topsoil of the arid, limestone plateau, the *causses*, or on the sand and gravel terraces between the plateau and the river, the *coteaux*. The suitability of each is much debated (according to the location of the debater's own vines), although most agree that the *causses* tend to produce wine for long ageing, a more traditional style of Cahors, while the wine made on the *coteaux* can be drunk much younger.

The notorious WINTER FREEZE of 1956 had a marked effect on the Cahors *vignoble* and provided a clean slate at an appropriate moment in the appellation's evolution. By far the largest number of growers planted an overwhelming majority of Malbec, traditionally called here for obscure reasons Auxerrois, a traditional Cahors variety which is nowhere else associated with particularly long-living wines. The appellation rules stipulate at least 70% Malbec, supplemented by the tannic TANNAT and/or the supple MERLOT. Again, debate rages over the most suitable mix of grape varieties (although, like vineyard location, this is hardly a variable in practice, more a matter of long-term fact). Cahors is exceptional among the important south west French appellations in that neither Cabernet vine is allowed.

In the winery, MACERATION times are a genuine variable and can have a considerable effect on wine style, as of course does BARREL MATURATION. By the mid 2000s, the most prominent Cahors producers such as Ch du Cèdre, Ch Lagrezette, and Domaine Cosse Maisonneuve were making special cuvées so concentrated and velvety that they were difficult to distinguish from Argentina's most winning examples of the same grape—apart from their higher prices. The great majority of wine produced is much lighter however and can often betray a certain rustic or animal character.

Coteaux de Quercy stretches to the south.

Caíño Blanco is grown to a very limited extent in north-western Iberia while **Caíño Tinto** is the Galician name for the rather more common BORRAÇAL.

Cairanne, one of the highest and best of the Côtes du Rhône villages which may be appended to the appellation name. It is unusually well suited to Syrah. See RHÔNE.

Calabrese, meaning 'of Calabria', is a common synonym for NERO D'AVOLA while the rare, unrelated **Calabrese di Montenuovo** has been identified as a parent of SANGIOVESE.

Calabria, the rugged toe of the boot of Italy, is closer to SICILY than to Rome in every way. (In antiquity, Calabria was the name of the heel of Italy, part of modern PUGLIA.) It has lagged behind the rest of Italy in its agricultural and industrial development and it is probably not surprising that its wines have yet to make much impact on national and international markets.

Only 2% of Calabria's agricultural land, in 2011 a total of just 10,024 ha/24,769 acres, was planted with vineyards, most of them close to the northern Tyrrhenian coast or the southern Ionian coast. This represented an astonishing 30% decrease from the total at the turn of the century, thanks to the EU's 2008 VINE PULL SCHEME, an ageing workforce unable or unwilling to put in long hours on the mostly mountainous vineyards, and a general decline in demand for BULK WINE which took the brunt of the decline in wine production.

Of the region's nine DOCs, most are of strictly local interest. CIRÒ is the most important with 1,694 ha of a total of 1,985 ha DOC vineyards. This DOC produces a very modest 33 hl/ha from vineyards on gentle slopes on the coast of the Ionian Sea near the town of the same name. The other DOCs, such as Melissa Bianco, Donnici, Savuto, and Pollino, at one time seemed on the brink of extinction but almost all of them marginally increased their production in the early years of this century.

GAGLIOPPO, the principal red grape of the region, is the basis of Cirò, Savuto, and Pollino. The most emblematic and largest producer of Cirò is Librandi, which conquered the international market in the 1990s with a barrique-aged Gaglioppo–Cabernet Sauvignon blend called Gravello, nicknamed the SUPERTUSCAN of the south', while continuing to bottle their 100% Gaglioppo Cirò Classico. In 2010, arguably far too late, the Consorzio of Cirò changed the production rules to allow Cabernet Sauvignon and Merlot into the wine, in an effort to make this pale but highly original wine more internationally palatable. Lower yields, riper grapes, and BIODYNAMIC practices in the vineyard, followed by extended skin maceration time has yielded at least one more shining example of complex Cirò, produced by A'Vita.

In addition to the potentially great Gaglioppo, the still obscure but equally interesting MAGLIOCCO may ride the current wave of interest in INDIGENOUS VARIETIES. The white

Greco grape, partially dried, produces a strong, coppery dessert wine of real interest and personality in its DOC zone around the town of Bianco almost at the tip of the boot, making the confusingly named Greco di Bianco one of Calabria's most distinguished wines. On the whole, Calabria has considerable potential which may not be realized for many years yet.

W.S.

Belfrage, N., *From Brunello to Zibibbo: The Wines of Southern Italy* (London, 2003).

Caladoc, reliable dark-skinned cross of Grenache and Côt (Malbec) created in 1958 by French AMPELOGRAPHER Paul Truel to produce a Grenache-like variety less prone to COULURE. It is not allowed into any APPELLATION CONTRÔLÉE wine, although it is used to add TANNIN and aroma to some southern French reds. France grew a total of almost 3,000 ha/7,410 acres by 2012 and there were more than 1,000 ha in Portugal, mainly in Lisboa, by 2009. It is also grown in Spain, Lebanon, Morocco, and Argentina.

Calatayud, dynamic denominated wine zone with 5,000 ha/12,000 acres of vines in ARAGÓN in north-east Spain, in arid country on either side of the River Jalón, a tributary of the Ebro (see map under SPAIN). As in much of central Spain, YIELDS rarely rise above 20 hl/ha (1 ton/acre). Most grapes are sold to one of nine local CO-OPERATIVES. The GARNACHA grape, which accounts for around two-thirds of Calatayud's production, makes heady, potent red wine, although TEMPRANILLO and various INTERNATIONAL VARIETIES are now also planted. Investment in new technology, particularly STAINLESS STEEL and REFRIGERATION, is increasing the proportion of Garnacha-based rosés and crisp white wines made from VIURA. El Escocés Volante (Norrel Robertson MW), Bodegas y Viñedos del Jalón, and Ateca are the top producers. V. de la S.

calcareous is the technical adjective for geological materials that are 'limy', i.e. composed significantly of calcium carbonate. These include MARL, LIMESTONE (and its subvarieties CHALK and dolomite), and their associated soils (see GEOLOGY). **Calcaire** is the French for limestone.

In cool, non-arid vineyards, calcareous soils allow better water movement and access to nutrients than more acid soils. This is because calcium carbonate, unlike most geological minerals, can dissolve in the water in the soil and react with its natural carbon dioxide content to form soluble bicarbonate, which tends to buffer the pH (see SOIL ACIDITY and SOIL ALKALINITY) to around its optimum for nutrient availability. In addition, calcareous soils tend to flocculate clays, improving SOIL TEXTURE, microbial activity, and DRAINAGE. Limestone bedrock is normally highly fissured, and this also promotes water flow. Adding calcareous matter to overly acid soils (see LIME) helps achieve the same results, although it can be overdone, causing the problems associated with vines growing on highly calcareous rocks or pure limestone (CHLOROSIS, for example). These are vineyard effects; calcareous soils are unrelated to the ACIDITY of a finished wine. A.J.M.

calcium is a major nutrient required for vine growth and is rarely lacking in vineyards. It enhances cell wall structure and contributes to grape skin defence against microbial attack. Calcium is immobile in the plant. It is taken up by roots during the period of rapid growth up to VERAISON, after which point there is little increase in calcium concentration in the plant.

CALCAREOUS rocks come in many forms, including MARL, CHALK, LIMESTONE, marble, and dolomite. (see GEOLOGY). The presence of calcium MINERALS in soils increases friability and DRAINAGE, especially where such calcareous soils underlie CLAY. See SOIL TEXTURE and SOIL AND WINE QUALITY. In northerly European wine regions such as Burgundy and Champagne, the drainage encouraged by calcium in the soils accounts for some of their suitability for premium viticulture.

Calcium salts have important effects on soil pH and CATION EXCHANGE CAPACITY. The availability of elements as plant nutrients is broadly correlated with soil pH. Calcium in soils is usually accompanied by a pH of 6–7, at which point many plant nutrients and trace elements are at their most available (see SOIL ACIDITY, SOIL ALKALINITY). The presence of calcium in soils often correlates with the optimum pH for vine growth, which is why liming soils not only tends to improve soil texture but can also increase the availability of nutrients. However, above pH 7, many elements become unavailable, so soils extremely high in calcium carbonate are not ideal for viticulture and cause lime-induced CHLOROSIS. A.J.M.

Caldaro, or **Kaltern** in German, township in ALTO ADIGE, northern Italy. It gives its name to **Lago di Caldaro** or **Kalterersee**, a large DOC zone for lightish red wines which extends into neighbouring TRENTINO. Produced from SCHIAVA Grossa, Schiava Gentile, and/or Schiava Grigia, the wines' general lightness owes at least as much to the unreasonably high yields of 14 tons/ha allowed by law as to varietal characteristics.

California, highly successful 'wine state' of the UNITED STATES and the largest source of American wine by far, producing 90% of all US-grown wine, some years more than 660 million gal/25 million hl in total, and three out of every four bottles sold in the US, making the state effectively the world's fourth biggest producer of wine. California was also for many years the only source of VINIFERA wine in the US. California wine, like most things Californian, has arrived at its current position by a series of bold investments, natural disasters, scientific achievements, external pressures, and political calamities. That the US was not historically a nation of wine drinkers has tended to exaggerate the cycle of giant strides and general retreats, and even relatively recent events can fast become history (see below).

History

Franciscan MISSIONARIES planted the first *Vitis vinifera* vines in California around 1770 (the native *Vitis californica* and *Vitis girdiana* are unfit for wine). For the next eighty years the Franciscans' MISSION grape remained the basis of California wine-growing, which passed from the missions to small growers as the mission lands were secularized under the newly independent Mexican government beginning in 1822. After the US annexation of Alta California in 1847, and the discovery of gold in 1848, wine-growing spread throughout the state. California's fame as a new wine region spread even as far as North Caucasus (see RUSSIA).

Following the GOLD RUSH of 1849, both population and vineyards expanded rapidly in the districts around San Francisco Bay as frenzied commercialism gripped the region. Since almost all of the immigrants were male, there was enormous demand for domestic services such as laundries and restaurants as well as for less prosaic services and commodities, alcohol prominent among them. SONOMA Valley had been a centre of winemaking activity since the 1820s thanks to spirited competition between Mariano Vallejo, the Mexicans' military commandant for Alta California, and Agoston HARASZTHY. By 1891, Sonoma had 22,683 acres/9,180 ha under vine to the NAPA Valley's 18,000 acres. Driven in no small measure by the devastation of Europe's vineyards by PHYLLOXERA, the 1870s and 1880s saw an extraordinary burst of investment in vineyards and wineries, benefiting not just these NORTH COAST counties, but also LIVERMORE VALLEY, SANTA CLARA VALLEY, and LODI.

By the end of the century, nearly every region currently producing wine in California had been tried, and production was over 30 million gal/1.1 million hl, largely from the northern part of the state, especially Sonoma, Napa, and Santa Clara Counties. The vast central SAN JOAQUIN VALLEY began to develop for the large-scale production of inexpensive wines from the 1870s, especially in Fresno and Madera Counties. The state had officially encouraged wine-growing from the earliest years, recognizing it as one of California's most distinctive contributions to the US economy. A board of State Viticultural Commissioners did useful work from 1880 to 1895, and the wine research

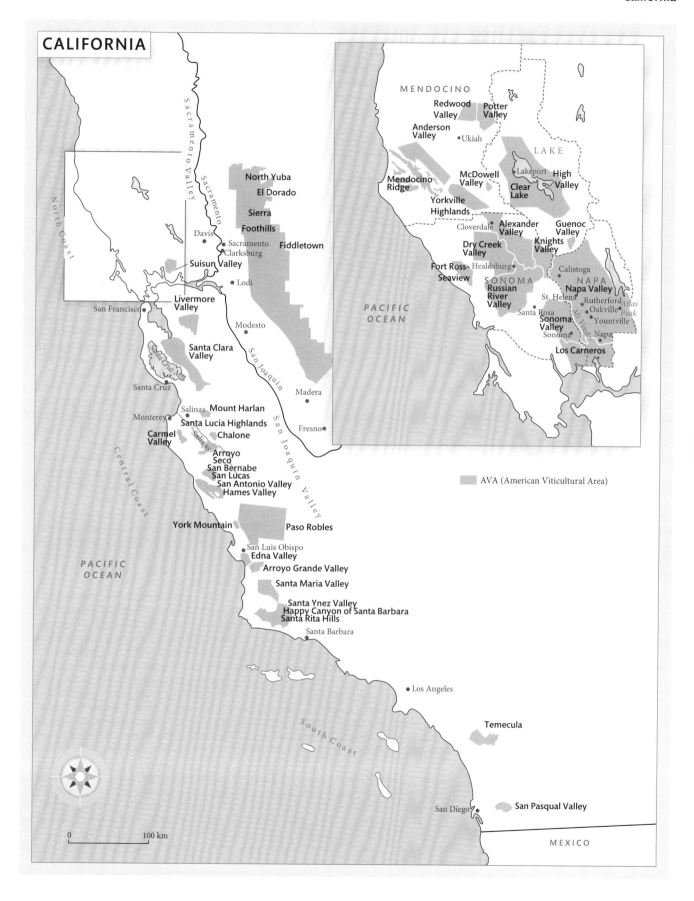

CALIFORNIA

MENDOCINO

Redwood Valley
Potter Valley
Anderson Valley
• Ukiah
LAKE
Mendocino Ridge
McDowell Valley
• Lakeport
High Valley
Yorkville Highlands
Clear Lake
Cloverdale
Alexander Valley
Guenoc Valley
Dry Creek Valley
Knights Valley
Fort Ross-Seaview
Healdsburg
• Calistoga
SONOMA
NAPA
Russian River Valley
Napa Valley
St. Helena
Rutherford
Atlas Peak
Santa Rosa
Oakville
Sonoma Valley
Yountville
Sonoma
Napa
Los Carneros

PACIFIC OCEAN

Sacramento Valley

Sacramento

North Coast

North Yuba
El Dorado
Sierra
Foothills
Fiddletown
• Davis
• Sacramento
• Clarksburg
Suisun Valley
• Lodi
Livermore Valley
• San Francisco
Santa Clara Valley
• Modesto
San Joaquin
Santa Cruz Mts.
• Santa Cruz
• Salinas
Mount Harlan
• Madera
• Monterey
Santa Lucia Highlands
• Fresno
Carmel Valley
Chalone
Salinas
Arroyo Seco
San Bernabe
San Lucas
San Antonio Valley
Hames Valley
San Joaquin Valley

Central Coast

York Mountain
Paso Robles
PACIFIC OCEAN
• San Luis Obispo
Edna Valley
Arroyo Grande Valley
Santa Maria Valley
Santa Ynez Valley
Happy Canyon of Santa Barbara
Santa Rita Hills
• Santa Barbara

AVA (American Viticultural Area)

• Los Angeles

South Coast

Temecula

San Pasqual Valley
• San Diego

MEXICO

0   100 km

◄ COVER CROP / ORGANIC VITICULTURE / CLARE VALLEY / AUSTRALIA Even companies as big as Penfolds have adopted organic viticulture, including its insistence on **cover crops**, as here in the Clare Valley, South Australia. © Andy Christodolo/Cephas Picture Library

and education of the University of California (first at Berkeley and subsequently in the warmer, more suitable location of DAVIS) began in 1880 and continues to the present.

California had neither viticultural traditions nor an entrenched peasantry in its early era, so aggressive research and education by E. W. Hilgard and Frederic T. Bioletti at the university produced immediate results. No later than 1881, scholars and growers alike saw clearly that the coastal counties were for finer table wines, the San Joaquin for everyday table wines and, perhaps, dessert wines of quality. Already California grew more than 300 *V. vinifera* varieties with CHASSELAS, ZINFANDEL, BURGER, and of course Mission, predominating, even if most of the nearly 800 wineries producing at California's 19th century peak (about the same number as a century later) sold their wines anonymously in bulk to a handful of blender/bottlers who offered broad ranges of wine types to the trade.

Over-planting, however, and attempts by a few powerful merchants to corner the wine market, caused the price of grapes and wine to crash in the 1890s. Prices dropped below production costs. This and the first signs of phylloxera in California were the twin blows which caused the first major setback for this burgeoning industry, devastating the state's wine production. PROHIBITION, legally in force between 1920 and 1933, destroyed its market. It was many decades before some areas recovered their pre-Prohibition status as wine regions, although Napa and Sonoma in the north and the Central Valley survived by producing and selling SACRAMENTAL and 'medicinal' wines, and shipping grapes and concentrate throughout the country for legal HOME WINEMAKING purposes.

Immediately after the Repeal of Prohibition, the market demanded mostly sweet wines. Relatively few, small producers attempted to make superior table wines from superior varieties, with little recognition. By the end of the Second World War, wineries that bottled their own production were the norm. By then overall numbers had dwindled to about 120 producing wineries. A trade far more familiar with whiskey than wine enouraged the survivors to produce 'full lines', echoing, not the old blender/bottlers, but importers who were now bringing in broad arrays of wines from Europe sold under GENERIC names. In the THREE-TIER SYSTEM of distribution it may have been the retailers who were most to blame for wanting to keep their domestic orders as simple as their import invoices, reinforced by the general ignorance of the American drinking public. California thus produced wines sold under such generic names as Burgundy and Chablis.

After a period of struggle that lingered beyond the Great Depression and the Second World War, a second grand burst of investment was evident between 1970 and 1985, most obviously in Napa but also in Sonoma. Although a new strain of phylloxera and another wave of prohibitionist sentiments in the late 1980s acted as a brake, growing populations around San Francisco pushed vineyard planting south into MONTEREY, SAN LUIS OBISPO, and SANTA BARBARA counties. Then in the late 1990s a third wave of expansion, in no small part fuelled by the overnight successes of internet and multi-media entrepreneurs in northern California, pushed experimental planting up into the SIERRA FOOTHILLS as land in the Central Coast, Napa, and Sonoma became increasingly expensive.

In the 1970s and early 1980s, America became interested in wine. New wineries proliferated, production rose, more suitable varieties were extensively planted, higher standards aimed at, and market demand swiftly answered. While California had fewer than 100 acres of Cabernet Sauvignon and practically no Chardonnay immediately after Prohibition in 1933, and only 600 and under 100 acres respectively of these two major INTERNATIONAL VARIETIES by 1960, California's total plantings of Cabernet and Chardonnay had reached 30,000 acres/12,000 ha and 50,000 acres/20,000 ha by 1991. In 2013, those totals were 80,000 acres/32,000 ha and 95,000 acres/380,000 ha (more Chardonnay than is grown in the whole of France) and the names Cabernet and Chardonnay had become respectively almost synonymous with red wine and white wine for many Americans.

By the turn of the century, the state had nearly 800,000 acres of vines of grape-bearing age. Only 500,000 acres of these produced specifically wine grapes, however, with a significant proportion of grapes being varieties such as THOMPSON SEEDLESS (Sultana) which has made California one of the world's most important producers of RAISINS.

As both consumers and trade matured in the 1970s, there was a proliferation of California wineries specializing in just two or three wines, most of them labelled as VARIETAL wines closely tied to their region of origin, a distinct step up from the generic wines that had dominated the state's production since Prohibition. By 2005 the number of wine companies in the state had shot past the late 1980s record of 800 to nearly 1,700, almost all of them this time selling their production under their own labels.

The market for wine in the United States has continued to grow in this century and California continues to supply two-thirds of all domestic requirements, shipping 215 million cases in 2013—3% more than in 2012. Meanwhile US wine exports, which were negligible after the Second World War, have grown steadily since the mid 1980s, with California supplying 95% of that volume. In 1986, the US exported only 7.3 million gallons/0.275 million hl with a value to the wineries of US$35 million. In 2013, those figures had risen to 435 million gallons/16.4 million hl with a value to the wineries of US $1.55 billion. The EU was the biggest importer, followed in order by Canada, Japan, Hong Kong, and China.

California's tradition has been to see grape variety as more important than place. In the 19th century, immigrant Germans and Frenchmen showed the way for a larger population of Anglo-Americans. A later wave of Italian immigrants kept things going during and after Prohibition. And in the second half of the 20th century, the wine industry has been populated by an eclectic gathering of engineers, painters, physicians, pilots, retired industrialists, reformed hippies, and other second careerists who somehow found a calling in wine, and who have driven themselves with the same energy that made them successes in other fields, sometimes in spite of location rather than because of it.

Vine varieties (see below) have sometimes been planted more in response to consumer demand than because they are known to be the most suitable for a particular site, but there is growing awareness of the importance of matching site and variety, certainly for higher-priced wines (see Geography below and AVA).   T.P., B.C.C., & L.M.

Adams, L., *The Wines of America* (4th edn, New York, 1990).

Carosso, V., *The California Wine Industry: A Study of the Formative Years* (Berkeley, Calif., 1951).

Pinney, T., *A History of Wine in America—From the Beginnings to Prohibition* (Berkeley, Calif., 1989).

Pinney, T., *A History of Wine in America—From Prohibition to the Present* (Berkeley, Calif., 2005).

Sullivan, C., *A Companion to California Wine* (Berkeley, Calif., 1998).

Climate

Those unfamiliar with California assign it a two-season MEDITERRANEAN CLIMATE. This is but a partial truth. Offshore ocean currents cause an intermittent fog-bank along California's coast, creating long stretches with insufficient sunshine to ripen most grapes. These fogs do not penetrate far inland, because of the 1,000-m/3,300-ft high coastal range, leaving the San Joaquin Valley too warm and sunny—too Mediterranean if you will—to grow fine table wines. However, in the sharply convoluted in-between of the Coast Ranges, jumbled terrain, variable fog and marine breezes produce more and less perfect growing season echoes of Castellina-in-CHIANTI, ST-ESTÈPHE, BEAUNE, and even Hattenheim in the RHEINGAU. There is no linear pattern. Napa, 20 miles north across the bay from San Francisco, is one of the warmer, drier regions on the coast. Westerly parts of Santa Barbara County, 300 miles/500 km to the south, are cooler and foggier than any part of Napa, while much of Mendocino, nearly

80 miles north of Napa, has hotter summers. Openings to the Pacific Ocean in the Coast ranges indicate the cool spots, while mountain barriers locate the warmer ones.

The rainy season follows a more orderly pattern. Total annual RAINFALL north of San Francisco is between 24 and 45 in (615–1,150 mm), while from San Francisco southwards totals range from 20 in to the low teens. DROUGHT occurs regularly, typically in 10- to 20-year cycles. The period 2010 to 2014 was the driest in memory, although a drought from 1987 to 1992 was also severe. Winters in California's grape-growing regions are mild to outright balmy. Damaging WINTER FREEZES are virtually unheard of.

Spring FROSTS vex growers more than any other fact of climate. Although late cold snaps occur infrequently, growers in the North Coast (north of San Francisco) are geared to mitigate the effects with overhead SPRINKLERS and WIND MACHINES, huge fans that keep cold air moving in the vineyards. Spring rains sometimes interfere with flowering and fruit set, but rarely disastrously.

Geography

California's wine regions extend over more than 600 miles/960 km of the state's 900-mile length from north to south. They also extend 135 miles west to east from the Pacific coast up into the Sierra Nevada Mountains. It is therefore difficult to typify soil types in California's vineyards because so much of the state's landforms have been emplaced on the North American tectonic plate, and then crumpled together by the action of the Pacific tectonic plate's sliding beneath it. Most vineyards have intrusions of several different soil types. Hence identification, and separate vinification, of different blocks within vineyards (see PRECISION VITICULTURE) became an increasingly valuable tool in the early 21st century for California's most quality-conscious winemakers. Until this century it was rare for wines from separately vinified vineyard blocks to appear as such in the market place; most were blended (for complexity) at the winery into a range of styles and price levels more easily understood by consumers. But by the second decade, single-vineyard, single-block, and/or single-clone bottlings proliferated, albeit produced in small amounts and typically restricted to Chardonnay, Pinot Noir, Cabernet Sauvignon, and Merlot.

The US federal government began holding hearings in 1983 to approve AVA (American Viticultural Area) names for use on labels. That process is ongoing, but it has been widely criticized for outcomes which often seem more marketing-driven or politically expedient than educational or terribly useful to consumers. Before 1983, California's geographical appellations, by and large, were its counties. Those county names, still much used in practice on wine labels, have been, in very approximate descending order of popularity, NAPA, SONOMA, SANTA BARBARA, MONTEREY, SAN LUIS OBISPO, MENDOCINO, AMADOR, EL DORADO, and LAKE. Up to 15% of a wine so-labelled may come from elsewhere.

AVAs are rudimentary, imposing no restrictions on varieties planted or vineyard practices. By 2014, California had more than 116 (out of a national total of 211), many such complete unknowns that county names remain more effective at communicating vineyard location.

Individual AVAs are detailed in this book under the name of the county or larger geographical unit in which they fall, except for CARNEROS, LIVERMORE VALLEY, SAN FRANCISCO BAY, SANTA CLARA VALLEY, SANTA CRUZ MOUNTAINS, and TEMECULA.

Kramer, M., *Making Sense of California Wine* (New York, 1992).

Robinson, J., and Murphy, L., *American Wine* (London/Berkeley, 2013).

See www.wineinstitute.org/ava/index.html for more information on AVAs.

Viticulture

In the years following Repeal of Prohibition, California viticultural practices were relatively uniform: head-trained, SPUR PRUNED vines spaced about 8 ft apart in rows about 10 ft/3 m apart. Dry farming was the rule in the North Coast, while flood IRRIGATION was the universal practice in the San Joaquin Valley.

During the 1960s, vine TRAINING began to move on to wires, with cane PRUNING for lighter-bearing vine varieties and CORDON for heavier yielders. Overhead sprinkler systems for irrigation became more common, especially in the emerging Central Coast. AXR1 became the ROOTSTOCK of choice because of its vigour and near universal adaptability, and heavy, dense canopies were the norm. Vine spacing remained at or near 8 × 10, or between 400 and 600 vines per acre (1,000 to 1,500 vines per ha).

Towards the mid 1980s, all of the old rules went by the way, impelled partly by a new mutation of phylloxera, the so-called biotype B, partly by a recurrence of PIERCE'S DISEASE, and, more significantly, by closer observation of the variables caused by California's turbulent geology. It was not uncommon in the early 1990s to see single properties on the North Coast with three or four different vine spacings, ranging between 800 and 2,000 vines per acre, and as many different systems of CANOPY MANAGEMENT. The aim was to take advantage of variations in soil structure and exposures as well as vine varieties. Since AXR1's resistance to phylloxera had proved disastrously low, rootstock selection was becoming a new art. The 1990s saw a major replanting programme, particularly in Napa and Sonoma, as a direct result of phylloxera and vine disease. The traditional alternative to AXR1 was Rupestris St George but around 30 different rootstocks were being trialled in the mid to late 1990s.

When the focus of winemakers' attention moved from flavour to TEXTURE in the 1990s, grapes tended to be picked at ever higher BRIX. Since 2000 it became common to see Cabernet Sauvignon destined for higher priced bottles left on the vine until 27 °Brix and pH levels above 3.7 were achieved. This technique was unpopular with growers since desiccation of the berries results in reduced tonnage, and less income. The technique also frequently requires an addition of WATER to mobilize YEAST and encourage FERMENTATION, and to reduce alcohol levels to below 16%. California wine legislation allows such 'watering back'. The result sought by these winemakers is mouth-filling EXTRACT, soft, luxurious texture from 'mature' tannins (see PHYSIOLOGICAL RIPENESS), and perhaps high scores from some American wine critics. These winemakers eschew herbal, green bean aromas in Cabernet in favour of berry and black stone-fruits' flavours, although enthusiasm for a more classic, herbal style has been growing. Cooler, wetter-than-usual growing seasons in 2010 and 2011 forced many to harvest Cabernet earlier than usual, and resulted in wines arguably closer to this style.

For much of its history California benefited from particularly adept Mexican LABOUR (cf. AUSTRALIA, for example), but ongoing 21st century federal crackdowns on illegal immigration, and restrictive work permit policies, have greatly reduced the Mexican labour force in California. MECHANICAL HARVESTING has long been common in the CENTRAL VALLEY and in much of MONTEREY, but NORTH COAST growers at even the highest levels of quality are looking into harvesting machines, and MECHANICAL PRUNING too. The phrase 'SUSTAINABILITY' rolls easily off the tongue of most of the state's professional grape growers today, although interestingly they were relatively slow to promote it to consumers. In the early 21st century however several regional marketing bodies such as the Napa Valley Vintners Association and Sonoma County Grapegrowers have pursued initiatives focused on sustainability, which encourage their members to adopt organic farming practices. ORGANIC VITICULTURE has grown from a cottage industry in the mid 1980s to a full-blown movement. Organic winemaking has been defined by the US government for labelling purposes since 2001. However, unlike European regulations, the US does not allow any addition of SULFITES which would raise the free sulfur dioxide level over 10 parts per million. The production of certified 'organic wine' in California is therefore limited to a small, and somewhat eccentric, segment of the industry. Many more wines go to market with a label claiming 'Certified Organic Grapes' but this number is far fewer than would be expected from the number of vineyards growing grapes without AGROCHEMICALS, in part due to a perceived lack of consumer confidence in wines labelled as organic. As in many other parts of the world, some growers choose not to seek organic certification merely because they see no financial advantage in the marketplace and wish to leave their options open. Although sceptics continue to exist, BIODYNAMIC VITICULTURE has an increasing number of proponents in California.

Winemaking

Without tradition as either guide or limitation, most California winemakers have consistently looked to achieve the kind of reproducible results their university training exalts. Understanding a process and then controlling it are, thus, the first two goals of the state's typical OENOLOGIST. Of all the steps in winemaking, FERMENTATION has received the most vigorous attention.

Temperature-controlled fermentation began in California in the 1940s. With the advent of STAINLESS STEEL tanks and more integral cooling systems in the 1960s, there came 'designed' fermentation curves for each major grape variety. Ultra-hygienic, infinitely controllable stainless steel tanks and sterile FILTRATION allowed MALOLACTIC CONVERSIONS to be brought under control at the same time. Today it is not at all unusual to have malolactic fermentation induced in one low PH batch of Chardonnay, deliberately inhibited in another (higher pH) batch, and then to blend these components for additional complexity in the resulting wine.

Throughout the modern era, ACIDIFICATION has been the norm across the state, but it is becoming slightly less commonplace as grapes are increasingly sourced from the more marginal climates of the coastal regions, where grapes often have higher natural ACIDITY than their counterparts in Bordeaux or Burgundy. DEACIDIFICATION is rarely practised or necessary. CHAPTALIZATION is not permitted, nor ever needed when wines and GRAPE CONCENTRATE from warm inland areas are consistently available for blending.

OAK barrels from French forests came into play as ageing vessels at the beginning of the 1960s; within a decade, BARREL FERMENTATION of white wines was the height of fashion. Chardonnay was and remains foremost among the varieties so fermented, but no white grape variety is immune. COOPERAGE activity in California surged in the 1990s after studies suggested that treatment and technique were more important than whether the oak was French or American. OAK CHIPS and INNER STAVES are commonly available in California but they, like MICRO-OXYGENATION, are used largely by producers of inexpensive, mass-market wines.

With the exception of some who use oak fermenters, red wines continue to be fermented in TANK, almost always in stainless steel, frequently in open topped vessels which allow manual or mechanical PUNCHING DOWN. After years of separating MUST from CAP just as the fermentation approached dryness, the vogue of the 1980s was extended MACERATION for as long as 25 days after the end of fermentation. Today a broad panoply of maceration techniques is employed in a quest called 'TANNIN management'. As outlined above, the goal is soft MOUTHFEEL achieved through a high degree of extract and ripe tannins.

YEASTS, the very engine of fermentation, are also much studied and carefully monitored. For years pure strains of specially cultured yeast ruled in California. Towards the end of the 1980s, however, winemakers began to use various combinations of these strains, and were increasingly prepared to experiment with AMBIENT YEASTS. The stated goal is greater aromatic complexity. California's naturally arid summer climate lends itself well to minimal use of FUNGICIDES. The cultivation of an ambient yeast population is therefore much easier than it would be in regions subject to frequent spraying. By the turn of the century even large commercial wineries were fermenting as much as a quarter of their production with naturally occurring ambient yeasts.

Wine types

The most important California wine type is the VARIETAL, the principal sorts of which are outlined below (see VINE VARIETIES).

The production of inexpensive wines, largely from the Central Valley, is in the hands of relatively few very large wineries. Most of the state's wineries concentrate on more expensive wines, many of limited production and available only in a few markets. Throughout the 1980s, production of red table wines, to which the state is well adapted, declined precipitously in response to the vagaries of the market. Only 14% of the table wines shipped from California in 1989 were red, the rest being white (53%), rosé (16%), and so-called BLUSH wines (17%). In 1991, this trend abruptly reversed itself thanks to the FRENCH PARADOX phenomenon. By 2013, Chardonnay still commanded 21% of the market, but the combined sales of Cabernet Sauvignon (12%) and Merlot (9%) equalled it. American wine diction tends to be based more on tax rates than wine characteristics. Table wine is anything with an ALCOHOLIC STRENGTH of 7 to 14%. Even the finest late-harvest imitations of TBAs (see TROCKENBEERENAUSLESE), the ones with 40% residual sugar, are table wines to the taxman. Dessert wine, meanwhile, is anything with more than 16% alcohol, even the driest of SHERRY types and dry but high-alcohol Zinfandels. Sparkling wine, sensibly, is the stuff with bubbles.

There is a long and complex history of producing sparkling wine in California, which, initially anyway, had few inhibitions about calling it champagne. HARASZTHY began attempts to make sparkling wines of quality in the 1870s, using the TRADITIONAL METHOD. F. Korbel & Bros. came right behind, with rather more success.

In the years since 1970, European- and especially French-owned firms have come to dominate production of California traditional method wines made by traditional techniques using traditional grape varieties. Domaine Chandon owned by LVMH was the forerunner. Piper-Sonoma, Mumm-Napa Valley, Roederer Estate, Maison Deutz, Domaine Carneros (Taittinger), and Scharffenberger (once Pommery, then Roederer) followed from France, Gloria Ferrer (Freixenet) and Codorníu Napa from Spain. There remains a strong domestic element led by Schramsberg, Iron Horse, and, more recently, J. Wine Co. During the 1990s, competition among foreign producers of sparkling wine in California produced a situation of immense benefit to consumers: quality rose dramatically while prices were ever more deeply discounted. In 1997, Deutz and Piper-Heidsieck sold their California properties and went back home to Champagne.

Producers of inexpensive mass-market bubblies make less complicated wines yet complicate the story. American law permits wines made from a wide range of non-traditional grape varieties, made sparkling either by the Charmat CUVE CLOSE process or the Carstens TRANSFER process (which has almost been abandoned since the adoption of GYROPALETTES for RIDDLING), to be called Champagne so long as that word is accompanied by a clear appellation of origin (almost always 'California') and indication of the method used. Such wines are the sparkling equivalents of generic table wines. The 2005 EU–US wine agreement permitted continued use of the term champagne for already established brands of such wines, although Schramsberg, most notably, dropped the word 'champagne' from its labels, confident in its 'sparkling wine'.

Vine varieties

California's mix of vine varieties is one of the world's most fluid, thanks to its high proportion of professional grape farmers selling their produce to wineries in free market conditions, to innate American flexibility, and to the technique of FIELD GRAFTING.

The most planted varieties in 2013, in declining order, were Chardonnay, whose total area had shrunk very slightly to 98,000 acres/39,000 ha, Cabernet Sauvignon, which passed the 86,000 acre mark, Zinfandel (a fairly steady 48,000 acres), Merlot (whose total plantings increased spectacularly from 11,000 to 52,000 acres between 1992 and 2003) at a steady 45,000 acres, Pinot Noir (whose total plantings had soared to 41,000 acres), French Colombard (22,000 acres), Syrah (19,000 acres), Sauvignon Blanc (a fairly steady 16,500 acres), and Pinot Gris (13,000 acres). Chardonnay, Cabernet Sauvignon, Merlot, and Zinfandel dominate labels, while French Colombard and Chenin Blanc are more often non-trumpeted ingredients in less expensive blends, the great majority of them either white or blush. Italian influence can be seen in limited plantings of Sangiovese, Dolcetto, Nebbiolo, Barbera, and Pinot Grigio (Gris). Other varieties gaining ground in the 2010s included Cabernet Franc and other Rhône varieties such as Grenache (red and white), Mourvedre, Petite Sirah, and Viognier.

AMPELOGRAPHY, the science of vine identification by human observation, has never been a popular sport with Californians. Nineteenth-century Californians were altogether casual about the identities of the vines they imported and grew. Modern researchers at Davis are using more sophisticated techniques of vine identification such as DNA PROFILING to try to sort out the ancestry of the varieties known in California as Petite Sirah, Valdepeñas (probably TEMPRANILLO), 'Pinot Blanc' (MELON, the Muscadet grape), Sauvignon Vert (MUSCADELLE), and Gray Riesling (TROUSSEAU Gris). Muscat Blanc should mean MUSCAT BLANC À PETITS GRAINS, although before a BATF (see TTB) ruling in the early 1990s it was also known as Muscat Frontignan and Muscat Canelli. Orange Muscat is a darker-berried mutation. Malvasia Bianca is a minor variety but has produced some impressive bottles of sweet and off-dry table wine.

The following are the most important varieties found on California wine labels, listed in declining order of acreage. For details of other California vine varieties, see under the variety name.

Cabernet Sauvignon Of all the transplants of European varieties to California, it is Cabernet Sauvignon that seems most at home, particularly in the Napa Valley. Cabernet had surfaced as a leading success in Napa by the 1880s according to producers and critics of the time. Its primacy there has been recognized by authorities ever since, although not always by the consuming public. Other parts of the state have been trying to catch Napa since the 1880s, and most convincingly since the 1970s. The result was a state total of 86,000 acres/35,000 ha by 2013, of which Napa's share, despite vigorous increases in Cabernet acreage, is less than a quarter.

The best ones offer rich textures and an entrancing tennis match of opposing flavours, berries on one side, herbs on the other. Whether by natural gift or historic dominance, Napa produces a majority of the memorably distinctive, age-worthy examples from California. Some show off particular subzones such as the Rutherford-Oakville west side (of which two of the first to establish their credentials were Beaulieu Vineyard's Georges de Latour bottling and Heitz Cellars' Martha's Vineyard), Howell Mountain, or the Stags Leap District (from which a Stag's Leap Wine Cellars offering famously 'beat' some of the great names of France at the JUDGMENT OF PARIS tasting in 1976). A long list of others come from less-defined regions or are blended from vineyards in differing parts of the valley.

Sonoma does not lag far behind with its finest examples, but they are fewer and more scattered in provenance. Its superior districts appear to be Alexander Valley and Sonoma Valley. The other coastal wine-growing northern county Mendocino shows a kinship in growing conditions, with a similar character if generally rather less winemaking finesse. The Central Coast is generally cooler, and not as widely known today for Cabernet, although notable success at everyday price levels has been achieved by some of the larger wineries in the warmer districts inland of the coastal mountains such as Paso Robles and the southernmost sections of the Salinas valley. The inland side of the Santa Cruz Mountains was historically a magnificent district for California Cabernet and several smaller vineyards (Ridge's Monte Bello would be a premier example) persist today. Meanwhile new plantings in the Sierra Foothills are beginning to show distinct promise for broadening the range of California Cab style with their lighter body, high-toned fruit, and the more aggressive tannins found at increased ELEVATION.

Zinfandel Conclusively shown in 2003 by Dr Carole Meredith of DAVIS to have originated in CROATIA (see ZINFANDEL), California's signature grape languished to the point of extinction in its native home. It is a thin-skinned variety with compact, often large, clusters which are prone to rot in wet conditions. But from the time it arrived in the 1850s, Zin flourished in the dry California climate. Virtually a California exclusive for more than a century, the variety for long suffered from an image problem. Apparently lacking any European forebear, let alone a famous one, it had to be taken on its own terms. Few critics had the independence of mind to do so, and so until the mid 1990s it was consigned to the category of a low-priced, honest, Italian-American working man's wine. All that has since changed. Well-made examples from 80-year-old and older vines (one of California's great viticultural treasures—see the HISTORIC VINEYARD SOCIETY) routinely command very respectable prices.

Although sometimes deliberately vinified to minimize this characteristic, Zinfandel can easily be chewier than a Cabernet. Beyond its robust textures, Zinfandel at the height of its powers tastes of the strain of raspberry Americans call boysenberry. Although it often has the structure and balance to age well, time does not replace its glorious flavours of berry with anything as pleasing. All the foregoing means that Zinfandel must come from a superior vineyard or be ordinary. Much inconclusive, artistic debate turns on VINE AGE, and on trellising versus the traditional BUSH VINES.

The variety finds its most congenial home on dry-farmed hillsides originally identified in parts of California at the turn of the last century by immigrant Italians. A centrepiece of this cultural community is Sonoma's Dry Creek Valley, the Russian River district, Mendocino County, Sonoma Valley and, though the fact is little recognized, Napa Valley. San Luis Obispo County's Paso Robles has a long, strong history with Zinfandel, as does Amador County in the Sierra Foothills and Lodi and the Delta region of the Central Valley. All of these tend to make headier, riper wines than Sonoma, and heady, port-style wines made from late-harvested old Zinfandel vines enjoyed a brief vogue in the early 1970s. See also WHITE ZINFANDEL.

Merlot The historical record suggests that Merlot succeeded rarely and excelled never on its own in California in the years before Prohibition, although as a blending component with Cabernet it did win some important international prizes in the foothill districts of Santa Clara county. When those practitioners disappeared, Merlot disappeared too. It was not apparently grown in the state between 1919 and 1969, when, at last, a few curious growers (notably Louis Martini, Gundlach-Bundschu, and, later, Duckhorn Vineyards) began experimenting with it as a possible blending grape to soften the tannins in Cabernet Sauvignon once more. In the mid 1990s, Merlot suddenly took off, becoming the faddish red varietal of choice, a less tannic alternative to Cabernet Sauvignon, particularly when offered in restaurants by the glass. Between 1995 and 2003, Merlot acreage doubled from 26,000 to 52,000. Thanks partly to being ridiculed in the film SIDEWAYS, this had dipped to 45,000 acres by 2013. There is much debate as to where in California is best suited to Merlot. Perception of the variety and its specific characteristics has in part been hampered by its mass-market success, which has yielded the bland sort of wines that may have caused it to disappear in the first place. However, more skilful growers and more determined winery owners have pushed several examples to heights heretofore not achieved, often with a stiffening soupçon of Cabernet Sauvignon. Of all the districts in which it has been tried to date, the most promising appear to be Napa's Stags Leap and Oak Knoll, the Santa Ynez Valley, and parts of

Napa Carneros. Many fine examples still go into blends with Cabernet Sauvignon, usually between 10 and 15%, or into MERITAGE-like blends in larger proportions.

Pinot Noir The secrets of Pinot Noir in California turned out to be two: marine-induced fog in the vineyards (or, increasingly, planting at elevations too high to be much influenced by fog) and less time in wood in the cellars than it was given in the early 1980s. Pinot Noir perplexed California winemakers for decades by producing truly outstanding wine once in a great while, but dull stuff most of the time. André TCHELISTCHEFF symbolizes the struggle, never having equalled by his own judgement the splendid pair he made for Beaulieu Vineyard in 1946 and 1947. The harder people tried to make something grand, the more often they fell short. In the 1970s, the search for more suitable vineyards began to move ever closer to the coast. By the end of the 1980s, three districts had emerged, if not triumphant then at least much closer to triumph. Unified only by their proximity to a saltwater shore, they are Carneros, the Russian River Valley of Sonoma, and Santa Barbara county, especially its Santa Maria Valley and Sta. Rita Hills. And by the late 1990s there was a great awakening of the virtues of growing Pinot Noir in the most marginal zones on the SONOMA Coast, in the areas of Cazadero, Fort Ross, Freestone, Occidental, and Annapolis, where scintillating acidity and fruit purity can be relied on.

More and more wineries were trimming the time they left their Pinot Noirs in French oak barrels from two years or more to one year or less. The shorter span confers complexity of bouquet, yet leaves the wines richer in texture and readier to age well in bottle. Pinot Noir enthusiasts tend to have their own favourites but Au Bon Climat, Davis Bynum, Gary Farrell, Rochioli, and Williams Selyem were some of the most consistently successful producers during the 1990s. Since then districts such as Anderson Valley, the new Fort Ross AVA in northern Sonoma, and the Santa Lucia Highlands on Salinas valley's western bench have created a considerable stir. Producers and growers such as Ted Lemon of Littorai, Gary Pisoni, Siduri, Flowers, and Merry Edwards represented the vanguard of an increasingly powerful new movement.

Syrah California's RHÔNE RANGERS have generated growing interest in this French variety. Fleshy, clean, and plum-scented, perhaps more reminiscent of Australian Shiraz than the more microbiologically-laden examples of the Rhône Valley. In fact California's surge in Syrah interest can trace its inception to a 1973 importation of cuttings from Australia. California Syrahs achieved remarkable success in only a few years with acreage growing from 2,200 in 1995 to 19,000 acres in 2013. The Sierra Foothills, the warmer canyons of eastern Santa Barbara County, the Hopland area of Mendocino, and Sonoma's Dry Creek Valley have particularly distinguished themselves. Some intrepid Californians are also growing Syrah and other Rhône varieties in exceedingly cool coastal regions such as the 'true' Sonoma Coast and the Sta. Rita Hills AVA of Santa Barbara County, with impressive results in a more focused, structured style than warm-region Syrahs.

Chardonnay The great white grape variety of Burgundy came late to California but, once arrived, it swiftly came to play vanilla to Cabernet Sauvignon's chocolate. It has become so ubiquitous that many consumers use the name almost synonymously with white wine. However, grown in appropriate vineyards and made with care, it can be glorious and is still the premier white varietal wine of the state.

Wente Bros resolutely grew and made Chardonnay in LIVERMORE VALLEY during the 1940s. They were almost alone until 1952, when Napa's Stony Hill winery brought new attention to the varietal wine. With its celebrated 1957, Hanzell added the effects of new oak barrels to those of the vineyard, inspiring first dozens then scores to clamber on to that bandwagon. After a 1973 from Ch Montelena came first against some respectable white burgundies in the Judgment of Paris in 1976, a whole new gold rush was on. Best estimates are that, by the early 21st century, California wineries were producing more than 1,500 different Chardonnays in each vintage.

During the 1970s, the majority of California Chardonnays were fermented in stainless steel, racked off their lees and presented untroubled by oak. As such, and given the warmer climate (Napa Valley is 37 rather than Burgundy's 47 degrees north of the equator), California did much to introduce the notion of FRUIT DRIVEN Chardonnays to the world. This approach was the technique advocated by UC DAVIS and was followed by most trained winemakers. Some more independent individuals began to experiment with what were then considered the much riskier techniques of BARREL FERMENTATION and LEES CONTACT.

Today, as in Burgundy, indeed because of Burgundy, California Chardonnay is often made as much or more in the cellar as in the vineyard. Barrel fermentation and OAK AGEING, MALOLACTIC CONVERSION, and all the other tricks in the winemaker's bag go into a wide range of styles from outright butterscotchy to straightforwardly fruity, with every stage in between and an increasing interest in an elusive characteristic described as MINERALITY. Most are dry, but a considerable number offer a softening dollop of sweetness (KENDALL-JACKSON's supposed 'recipe' was the subject of a famous 1992 court case). Partly thanks to more powerful YEASTS, Chardonnays with more than 14% alcohol are now common.

The grape variety has proven remarkably adaptable, growing well throughout the coastal counties, and not badly in the SIERRA FOOTHILLS. Chardonnay is most widely planted in Napa, Monterey, Santa Barbara, and Sonoma Counties, in almost equal measure, with the Santa Cruz Mountains home to some decidedly superior examples.

French Colombard The name of California's second most planted white wine grape is relatively rarely seen on wine labels but it is found in a wide variety of wines and not just the very cheapest—not least because up to 15% of varieties other than those specified on the label of a VARIETAL wine may be included, and French Colombard grapes are cheap—not least because most of it is planted in the Central Valley. As in south west France where it is known simply as COLOMBARD, the grape naturally, and usefully in California, retains a high level of acidity.

Sauvignon Blanc Dr Maynard A. AMERINE, long a voice of conscience for California winemakers when in post at the University of California at DAVIS, used to call Sauvignon Blanc California's greatest white grape. He would also confess that the variety's forceful flavours probably needed tempering to appeal to the American public. There, in a nutshell, is its career, whether under its own name or under the California-coined synonym FUMÉ BLANC. It makes outstanding wines that many find too specific to enjoy, especially against the milder charms of Chardonnay. Some age their Sauvignons in new oak, disguising it as a sort of poor man's Chardonnay. Others avoid oak and rely on the lees to imbue body and texture. Some blend in proportions of Semillon to temper the flavour and fill out a characteristically light body. A few do all of the above.

In 2013, it was grown on 16,500 acres, which meant it was by far the most widely planted premium variety after Chardonnay. Memorable Sauvignon Blanc examples have come from Livermore Valley, Sonoma Valley, Napa Valley, and Santa Barbara. Scores of producers compete well; nearly every region in the state produces at least agreeably balanced wines from the variety. Generally speaking, straightforwardly styled Central Coast Sauvignon Blancs (Santa Ynez Valley, Monterey) smack sharply of the herbaceous or grassy flavours for which Sauvignon is so widely noted. Their North Coast counterparts are more subtly herbaceous from the cooler zones (Russian River Valley, lower Napa Valley), almost melony from warmer areas (upper Napa Valley, upper Alexander Valley).

In recent years, an ever-increasing number of growers have been allowing grapes to become botrytis affected for sweet wines styled after SAUTERNES. Early results have charmed in youth, but tended to fade quickly.

Pinot Gris/Grigio The faddishness of the American market place has winemakers constantly on the look-out for a new trend (see ABC). By 1998, Pinot Gris had begun to be discussed as a potential candidate, and in 2004 Pinot Gris (often labelled Pinot Grigio) inched passed Sauvignon Blanc to become the second most widely sold white wine in America. No single style has emerged as dominant but California's generally warm climate and its experimentally inclined winemakers tend more toward Alsace richness than toward the crisper style found in Italy.

Riesling In the 1960s, Riesling was, with Cabernet Sauvignon, Chardonnay, and Pinot Noir, one of the Big Four in California. Beginning in the 1970s, its reputation began to decline, as an explosion in differing sweetness levels lacked a coherent set of semantic explanations. There may be a connection. During the 1980s, both sales and acreage tumbled, and scores of wineries abandoned Germany's noblest grape, leaving it in the hands of a few stubborn supporters. By the mid 2000s, barely 20 wineries produced a varietally labelled Riesling, none of them highly priced, but a flurry of interest in the variety generated from Washington State resulted in a doubling of acreage in California from just over 2,000 acres to more than 4,000 in the ten years from 2004.

California Riesling cannot be mistaken for its German counterparts, being riper in flavour and weightier with higher alcohol. Its finest homes, albeit vestigial, in California include Mendocino's Anderson Valley, the higher reaches of El Dorado County, Monterey's Arroyo Seco district, and Santa Barbara County.

Viognier The 1980s' explosion of interest in red Rhône varieties was echoed in the 1990s with their white counterparts. Although a handful of California producers dabbled initially with Marsanne and Roussanne, the majority of entrants cast their lot with Viognier. Indeed while in 1995 its cradle, the CONDRIEU appellation in France, boasted about 200 acres of the variety, California planted at least 600 acres in the 1990s alone, and boasted more than 3,000 acres by 2013. Pioneers included Joseph Phelps, Ritchie Creek, La Jota, and Calera but the first major commitment was made by John Alban, who planted 30 acres in San Luis Obispo's Edna Valley district in 1989. Quality and style have been about as variable as the prices, with many expensive offerings being mediocre at best, presenting an oaky, Chardonnay-like profile with little Viognier character. Many lesser priced wines with very little, if any, oak influence, can be charming. A more recent Rhône white grape to emerge has been Grenache Blanc. There isn't much of it, at under 300 acres in 2013, yet many a blend features it along with Viognier and Roussanne. These wines can be greater than the sum of their parts.   B.C.C. & L.M.

See also CARNEROS, CENTRAL COAST, CENTRAL VALLEY, LAKE COUNTY, LIVERMORE VALLEY, MENDOCINO, MONTEREY, NAPA, SAN LUIS OBISPO, SANTA BARBARA, SANTA CLARA VALLEY, SANTA CRUZ MOUNTAINS, SIERRA FOOTHILLS, SONOMA, and TEMECULA.

Bonné, J., *The New California Wine* (Berkeley, 2013).

Cass, B. (ed.), *Oxford Companion to the Wines of North America* (Oxford and New York, 2000).

Kramer, M., *Matt Kramer's New California Wine: Making Sense of Napa Valley, Sonoma, Central Coast, and Beyond* (New York, 2004).

Muscatine, D., Amerine, M. A., and Thompson, B. (eds.), *The University of California/Sotheby's Book of California Wine* (Berkeley, Calif., 1984).

Robinson, J., and Murphy, L., *American Wine* (London/Berkeley, 2013).

www.discovercaliforniawines.com

www.wineinstitute.org

www.cawg.org

California cult wines, a phrase coined in the 1990s to encompass wines made in the State of California, typically but not exclusively Napa Valley Cabernets, for which collectors, and possibly a few investors, would pay PRICES higher than those of Bordeaux's FIRST GROWTHS. They include such names as Araujo, Bryant Family, Colgin, Dalla Valle Maya, Grace Family, Harlan Estate, Moraga (bought by media mogul Rupert Murdoch in 2013), Screaming Eagle, Sine Qua Non, and Vineyard 29. What many of these names have in common is that they are made in extremely limited quantity, by talented winemaker consultant OENOLOGISTS (often female) currently favoured by FASHION.

California sprawl, term commonly used to describe the CANOPY of a vine trained on a simple TRELLIS SYSTEM although such systems are not restricted to California. It generally refers to a trellis with a single fruiting wire plus one foliage wire above this, though there are some variations. This results in a sprawling vine without rigorous SHOOT POSITIONING. This inexpensive form of training can lead to a shaded canopy with poor bud FRUITFULNESS and increased vegetative growth. Such vine forms are more typically seen in vineyards in hotter parts of California's CENTRAL VALLEY and are also common in the inland irrigation regions of Australia. See also CANOPY MANAGEMENT.

Calistoga, CALIFORNIA wine region and AVA in the northernmost part of NAPA Valley.

Callet, MALLORCAN grape of unclear origin often planted as a FIELD BLEND with Fogoneu Mallorqué or Fogoneu Francés, although Spanish statistics of 2008 recorded a total 134 ha/331 acres planted. Callet tends to produce small quantities of light-coloured wine with relatively little alcohol. Used mainly for rosés and in red blends.

callus, the white, formless tissue that grows from CAMBIUM tissue at cut and wounded surfaces of the grapevine on stems and roots. It is critical for vine GRAFTING since it signifies that the conditions for cell division are favourable and that the underlying graft or bud has united. High humidity, oxygen supply, and warm temperatures are the major requirements for rapid callus development. In the field, these conditions may be achieved by waxing or by wrapping the tissues tightly with plastic grafting tape. After BENCH GRAFTING, the cuttings are packed with moist material and held in a warm, humid room. (See also TISSUE CULTURE and illustration under GRAFTING.)   B.G.C.

Hartmann, H. T., et al., *Plant Propagation: Principles and Practices* (8th edn, Upper Saddle River, NJ, 2011).

Caluso, town in northern, pre-alpine PIEMONTE most famous for a DRIED-GRAPE WINE made of ERBALUCE grapes although dry versions, often from single vineyard sites, can be just as impressive.

calyptra, or flower cap, of the vine flower consists of the five petals joined together in the form of an inverted cup. The cap separates as a unit and falls from the grape flower at FLOWERING and exposes the STAMENS, which produce pollen, and the STIGMA, which receives pollen. The rate of capfall is slowed by cold and rain; the duration of capfall can stretch from a normal seven to ten days to as long as 15 to 20 days. FRUIT SET is impaired if the caps are retained and so this very small part of the grapevine can affect YIELD, especially for varieties such as MERLOT.   B.G.C.

Câmara de Lobos, or **Cama de Lobos**, occasionally found on bottles of ancient MADEIRA, is a wine district west of the capital Funchal on the south coast of the island associated with noble vine varieties and fine wine.

Camaralet, obscure vine allowed but hardly grown in BÉARN and JURANÇON in south-west France that can make strongly flavoured white wine.

Camarate, Portuguese wine grape making soft reds in BAIRRADA, where it is second most planted dark-skinned variety. It is known as MORTÁGUA in Arruda.

cambium, a zone of dividing cells in plants such as the grapevine; the inner cells develop into XYLEM and later differentiate into wood, while the outer cells develop into PHLOEM and, later, bark. The matching of cambial zones is important to the success of BUDDING and GRAFTING.

The cork cambium cuts off non-living suberized cells yielding bark, as during vine CANE RIPENING. Of course the cork most readily associated with wine is the CORK derived from the secondary cambium of QUERCUS *suber* and used as CLOSURES.   B.G.C.

Cambodia now has a single winery, Prasat Phnom Banan, just outside the city of Battambang, Cambodia's second largest city, with 2 ha/5 acres of Shiraz, Black Queen, and Kyoho vines imported from THAILAND. The first vintage was 2004.   D.G.

Campania, region of south-west Italy of which Naples is the capital. In the ancient world, Campania was the home of some of the most renowned wines of Italy, if not of the whole Mediterranean basin: SURRENTINE, MASSIC, and, most famous of all, FALERNIAN.

In spite of its southern location, Campania is known for its white wines, as daytime temperatures are largely mitigated by elevation in the mountainous inland (Campania boasts its own ski resorts) and its INDIGENOUS VARIETIES, showcased in Campania's many DOCs and DOCGs, are capable of retaining freshness and acidity in a warm climate. On the basis of its soil types the region can be broadly grouped into three parts. The volcanic, sandy soils of DOC Vesuvio and DOC Campi Flegrei (the 'fire fields' named by the Romans, who built thermal baths on the slopes of these extinct volcanoes) are almost in the suburbs of Naples, where the white FALANGHINA and red PIEDIROSSO are planted on their own rootstocks as PHYLLOXERA cannot survive there. Once considered workhorse varieties, Falanghina and Piedirosso now receive serious attention, including higher density vineyards and lower yields. The DOC Vesuvio is based predominantly on Caprettone, Falanghina, and Piedirosso, resulting in white and red LACRYMA CHRISTI.

The second soil type, alluvial sediments, prevails in the DOC Sannio on the Piana Campania Plain between Naples and Benevento. In the early 2010s, the much smaller DOCs Guardia Sanframondi, Sant'Agata dei Goti (with its own clone of the Falanghina as produced by Mustilli), Solopaca, and Taburno (its speciality being AGLIANICO) were all demoted to subzones of Sannio, while a new DOCG, Aglianico del Taburno, was created.

The third soil type is the porous LIMESTONE which typifies the hills of the DOC Irpinia. It was called tufo by the Romans (hence GRECO di Tufo)—incorrectly as it is not of volcanic origin. Within Irpinia lie the superior DOCGs TAURASI, FIANO di Avellino, and GRECO di Tufo, the latter two producing Campania's most famous and long-lived whites, typified by peaches and flint, and smoky notes in aged versions. Taurasi is arguably Aglianico's finest and longest lived expression.

A large part of Campania consists of hills and mountains with myriad expositions and elevations. The higher the ELEVATION, the cooler it is—so cool in fact that the grapes of Fiano di Avellino and Greco di Tufo are not picked before the beginning of October, and the late-ripening Aglianico may be picked even later in Taurasi. With the exception of MASTROBERARDINO, a general focus on quality has been recent (see TAURASI for more details).

The third large Campania DOC, Cilento, lies 50 km south of Naples, its coastline dominated by Paestum, site of the little-known Greek temple, while its rugged mountainous hinterland is planted with olive trees and vines. In spite of its extent, Cilento produces very much less wine than Sannio, producing small quantities of Fiano and Aglianico which can be worth seeking out, especially from such overachievers as Conciliis and Casebianche. North of Cilento the tiny DOC Costa d'Amalfi, grown in Campania's stunning answer to the French Côte d'Azur, has low-yielding vineyards clinging to any available ridge on this stony coast. Modern but very individual whites based on Falanghina and Biancolella, and reds based on Piedirosso and Sciasinoso, are produced by Marisa Cuomo and Tenuta San Francesco, while its subzone Tramonti is renowned for its many centenarian vineyards. Aglianico and Piedirosso also feature in the DOC Falerno del Massico to the north towards Lazio, its wines said to have already been appreciated by the Romans (see FALERNIAN). Curiously, a 100% Primitivo is also allowed here. While the demands of TOURISM have replaced the once-renowned viticulture of the island of Capri, ISCHIA has managed to retain 60 ha/150 acres of DOC vineyards on steep terraced slopes overlooking the Mediterranean, producing small quantities of complex whites based on the local Forastera and Biancolella, notably those of d'Ambra, and minuscule quantities of red wine based on Guarnaccia (MAGLIOCCO Dolce) and Piedirosso.   W.S.

Capalbo, C., *The Food and Wine Guide to Naples and Campania* (London, 2005).

Belfrage, N., From *Brunello to Zibibbo—The Wines of Tuscany, Central and Southern Italy* (2nd edn, London, 2003).

www.vinocampania.it

Campo de Borja, promising Spanish wine zone in the undulating plains around the town of Borja (after which the Borgia family was named) in the ARAGÓN region in the north east (see map under SPAIN), producing fairly alcoholic red wines. This is one of the most arid parts of the country and the 6,800 ha/16,300 acres of low-yielding vineyards, planted predominantly with GARNACHA vines, produce intensely sweet, dark grapes which are made into heady red wines. The Borsao Borja co-operative has revolutionized the region with its young, intensely fruity reds that have won a large following on export markets and shown the way to the future for the DO. The best wines, notably the result of an Australo-American JOINT VENTURE, can command prices that would not even have been dreamt of in the late 1990s.   V. de la S. & J.R.

Canaan, or the Levant, comprises the coastal and inland areas of the eastern Mediterranean which played an important part in spreading viniculture. The pharaohs of Ancient EGYPT were struggling to maintain their control of this area during the 14th century BC, as we can read in the Amarna letters, an extensive correspondence between the pharaohs and the local puppet rulers and officials of Canaan. 'See that much food and wine—everything in great quantities—is made available for the archers of the king,' writes one Egyptian monarch. In the Egyptian *Story of Sinuhe*, Canaan was described as having 'more wine than water'.

Records on cuneiform tablets from the kingdom centres on the city of Ugarit (c.1500–1200 BC; modern Ras Shamra near Latakia about 160 km/100 miles north of the vineyards of modern Lebanon) indicate extensive viticulture. A standard formulation in describing properties for real estate transactions at this date mentions 'a house, together with its [watch-]tower, its olive grove and its vineyard'. However, life was as difficult in this area then as it was in the 1980s, since a complaint addressed by the prefect of Ugarit to a local great king, who was acting as mediator, stated that the people of Siyannu, a neighbouring city, 'have cut down our vines'. The people of Ugarit were obliged to swear not to cut down the vines of Siyannu, and moreover to swear (somewhat ingenuously) that they knew nothing of the identity of the perpetrators of such acts in the past. A similar dispute was adjudicated on the same occasion, this time concerning an allegation that wine from Ugarit had been stolen and sold unofficially to dealers at Beirut, down the coast.

The southern Levantine wine industry, beginning c.4000 BC, had matured to such a degree that by the time of Scorpion I (c.3150 BC), one of the first rulers of a united Egypt, his tomb at Abydos was stocked with some 4,500 litres of wine imported from southern Canaan. From around 3000 BC, the Egyptian pharaohs financed the establishment of a royal wine industry in the Nile Delta under the tutelage of Canaanite viniculturalists. With the Egyptian winemaking success behind them, the

Canaanites on their sea-going 'Byblos ships' made of Cedar of Lebanon, ventured further and further out into the Mediterranean. They and their successors, the Phoenicians, applied a similar formula wherever they went: import wine and other luxury goods, entice the rulers with wine culture by presenting them with speciality wine sets, and then wait until they were asked to help in establishing native industries, including viniculture, by transplanting the domesticated Eurasian VINIFERA grapevine.

See also ORIGINS OF VINICULTURE and PALAEOETHNOBOTANY AND THE ARCHAEOLOGY OF WINE.

J.A.B. & P.E.M.

McGovern, P. E., *Ancient Wine* (Princeton and Oxford, 2003).

McGovern, P. E., *Uncorking the Past: The Quest for Wine, Beer, and Other Alcoholic Beverages* (Berkeley, 2009).

Canada

Canada, a prime beneficiary of CLIMATE CHANGE, has a thriving wine industry concentrated in four provinces, ONTARIO, BRITISH COLUMBIA, and to a lesser extent QUEBEC and NOVA SCOTIA, on vineyards that totalled 12,000 ha/ 30,000 acres in 2011 according to the OIV. Given the exigencies of the Canadian climate, grapes are invariably grown near large bodies of water that moderate the effects of Canada's severe winters and decrease the risk of damaging WINTER FREEZE and spring FROSTS (see LAKE EFFECT). Until the late 1970s, the majority of Canadian vines were the winter-hardy North American LABRUSCA varieties such as CONCORD and Niagara. Next to follow were early-ripening, winter-resistant FRENCH HYBRIDS such as VIDAL BLANC, SEYVAL BLANC, BACO NOIR, and MARÉCHAL FOCH, often called simply Foch in Canada. Since the late 1980s, however, growers have put greater emphasis on VINIFERA vine varieties, whose wines enjoy increasing success both at home and abroad.

The Canadian climate is particularly suitable for the production of SPARKLING WINES in all four of its wine-growing provinces but it first established a reputation for the consistently high quality and quantity of its ICEWINE. Canada is the world's largest producer, which is not surprising since sustained temperatures of −8 °C can be relied upon each winter. The APPELLATION system (VQA) of Ontario, for instance, sets the minimum sugar levels for Icewine at 35 °BRIX, substantially higher than those for Germany's EISWEIN.

History

The Canadian wine industry dates from the early 19th century (although see also VÍNLAND). In 1811, a retired German corporal, Johann Schiller, domesticated the *Vitis labrusca* vines he found growing along the Credit river west of Toronto and planted a 20-acre vineyard. In 1866, the country's first major winery Vin

Villa was established at Canada's most southerly point, on Pelee Island on Lake Erie, by three gentlemen farmers from Kentucky who planted 20 acres/8 ha of ISABELLA vines. By 1890, there were 41 commercial wineries across the country, 35 in Ontario. In the Okanagan Valley of British Columbia and along the St Lawrence river shoreline in Quebec, it was the Church rather than the regions' farmers which encouraged the planting of vineyards and fostered the art of winemaking.

PROHIBITION, which began in Canada in 1916, spurred the wine trade. Thanks to some fancy political lobbying by the grape-growers, wine was exempted from the general interdiction against alcohol. By the time the Great Experiment was brought to an end in 1927 (six years before Repeal in the United States), 57 winery licences had been granted in Ontario alone.

In that year, another experiment began, the creation of the provincial liquor board system, government MONOPOLIES which control the sale and distribution of all beverage alcohol sold in Canada and collect hundreds of millions of dollars in tax revenues. (By the mid 1990s, Alberta had privatized and British Columbia and Manitoba, Saskatchewan, and Prince Edward Island have some privately owned wine merchant stores competing with government monopolies.)

Until the mid 1970s, most Canadian wines were sweet, highly alcoholic products made from *V. labrusca* varieties and labelled Sherry or Port, depending on the colour. The advent of the 'boutique' (small, usually owner-managed) winery was signalled in 1974 when Inniskillin, near Niagara Falls, was granted the first commercial licence since Prohibition. This coincided with a shift in public taste towards drier, less alcoholic, TABLE WINE. The wineries that followed in Ontario and British Columbia were dedicated to the proposition that *V. vinifera* grapes could be grown on appropriate sites in spite of the harsh winters and unpredictable springs.

In 1988, an APPELLATION system called Vintners Quality Alliance (VQA) was introduced, first in Ontario and then, in 1990, in British Columbia. See Wine laws below.

The Canadian wine industry has spawned a considerable number of estate wineries in which grape-growers are developing agri-tourism by offering events, attractions, bed and breakfast accommodation, and winery restaurants as well as wine.

Climate

Geographically, the major concentration of Canadian vineyards is on the same latitude as the LANGUEDOC and CHIANTI, but lower winter temperatures, the freeze–thaw–freeze cycle of early spring, and unpredictable weather at HARVEST rank Canada as a cool climate wine region,

with all the vintage variation and winemaking challenges that entails.

While some of Canada's vineyards may enjoy hotter summers than either Bordeaux or Burgundy, the growing season tends to be shorter. According to one estimate, average sunshine hours during the growing season are 1,500 in the Niagara Peninsula, Ontario; 1,423 in British Columbia's Okanagan Valley; and 1,150 in Dunham, Quebec—compared with 1,315 in Burgundy. Grapes may require CHAPTALIZATION in some years. Drought can be a problem and some producers have installed irrigation systems. Many wineries have invested in wind machines to counter spring frosts.

Wine laws

Wine regulations vary from province to province. Most wine is retailed by provincial MONOPOLIES such as the Liquor Control Board of Ontario (LCBO).

The Vintners Quality Alliance Act in Ontario and similar legislation in BC establishes the legal framework for an appellation of origin system as well as minimum standards that must be met in order to obtain VQA approval. Compliance with the standards is legally enforced in Ontario and BC.

Minimum MUST WEIGHTS and limits to chaptalization are specified along with permitted grape varieties (not LABRUSCA).

Many Canadian wineries also bottle wines which contain imported produce and which are therefore entitled to neither a VQA appellation designation nor the more general Product of Canada label. Wines labelled International Canadian Blend, common in Canadian liquor stores, usually contain a majority of imported grape juice or wine.

See also BRITISH COLUMBIA, NOVA SCOTIA, ONTARIO, and QUEBEC.   T.A.

Aspler, T., and Bergeron, J.-F., *Canadian Wineries* (Toronto, 2012).

www.canadianvintners.com

Canaiolo

Canaiolo, or **Canaiolo Nero**, red grape variety grown all over central Italy and, perhaps most famously, a permitted ingredient in the controversial recipe for CHIANTI, in which it played a more important part than SANGIOVESE in the 18th century. It has declined considerably in popularity since it was relatively difficult to graft in the wake of PHYLLOXERA, and suffered from poor CLONAL SELECTION. Only just over 1,000/2,470 acres remained in total in 2010. The decline in popularity of the GOVERNO winemaking trick also hastened its decline since soft, full-bodied Canaiolo, without either the structure of Sangiovese or the scent of MAMMOLO, was most prized for its resistance to rot while being dried for *governo* use. Canaiolo of good quality does still exist in scattered spots in Chianti Classico, notably—and unsurprisingly—at the two RICASOLI properties of Castello di Brolio and Castello di Cacchiano in Gaiole in Chianti, in Barbarino Val d'Elsa (where the Castello della Paneretta and neighbour Isole e Olena both use Canaiolo in their Chianti Classico), and in the VINO NOBILE DI MONTEPULCIANO production zone. Efforts to salvage the variety by better clonal and MASS SELECTIONS are under way in Tuscany, but there are few illusions that this will be accomplished either easily or quickly. Canaiolo is also grown, to an even more limited extent, in LAZIO, SARDINIA, and the MARCHE.

A light-berried **Canaiolo Bianco** is also grown in Umbria, where, in ORVIETO, it is known as DRUPEGGIO, but has also been declining in popularity.

Canandaigua, based in Fairport in the Finger Lakes region of NEW YORK State, is a subsidiary of (and was the original name of) what is now CONSTELLATION BRANDS.

Canary Islands, Spanish islands in the Atlantic ocean off the coast of Morocco which were famous in Shakespearian England, as witness Sir Toby Belch's call for 'a cup of canary' in *Twelfth Night*. The mediocre wines for the tourist trade are being replaced by much more interesting products, much subsidized by the regional government, including young reds from NEGRAMOLL and the indigenous LISTÁN NEGRO grapes, and whites from Listán Blanco (Palomino), traditional and dry MALVASÍAS from La Palma and Lanzarote islands, and VIJARIEJO, MARMAJUELO, and Gual (which is the same as Madeira's Boal/BUAL). VINE AGE is high, soils often VOLCANIC. Although construction is encroaching on vineyards, the number of denominated zones has ballooned, and by the mid 2000s included one for each of the islands of LA PALMA, EL HIERRO, LANZAROTE, and GRAN CANARIA, and no fewer than five for the island of Tenerife (ABONA, TACORONTE-ACENTEJO, VALLE DE GÜÍMAR, VALLE DE LA OROTAVA, and YCODEN-DAUTE-ISORA). Suertes del Marqués of Valle de la Orotava is one of the most ambitious producers.   V. de la S.

Canberra, the capital of AUSTRALIA, is ringed by almost 40 wineries which together constitute a wine region called the Canberra District, even if, because freeholds are not granted in the Australian Capital Territory itself, they are all, bar one, over the border in the Southern New South Wales Zone. There is considerable site climate diversity due to variations in ELEVATION from 500 m to 800 m (1,640–2,625 ft). Thus Riesling, Viognier, Marsanne, Semillon/Sauvignon Blanc blends, Chardonnay, Pinot Noir, Shiraz/Viognier (Clonakilla the star performer), and Cabernet blends can and do prosper in the correct site. Overall wine quality has improved markedly since the early 1990s. See NEW SOUTH WALES.

cane, the stem of a mature grapevine shoot after the bark becomes woody (lignified) and tan-coloured at VERAISON and starts its overwintering form (see CANE RIPENING and CAMBIUM). After leaves have fallen, the canes of a vine display the total vegetative growth it made during the previous season (called the 'brush' in the US). The number of canes and their weight and average size are important guides to decisions about BALANCED PRUNING and CANOPY MANAGEMENT tactics. The canes are cut at winter PRUNING to reduce the number of buds and to select their position. The cutting may be to SPURS or canes.   B.G.C.

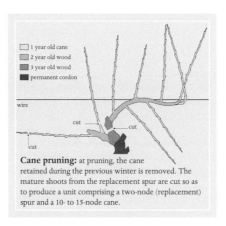

Cane pruning: at pruning, the cane retained during the previous winter is removed. The mature shoots from the replacement spur are cut so as to produce a unit comprising a two-node (replacement) spur and a 10- to 15-node cane.

cane pruning, a form of winter vine PRUNING in which the buds are retained on longer BEARERS called CANES, typically including six to 15 buds. This pruning system usually takes longer to perform by hand than the alternative SPUR PRUNING. Cane pruning is typically used for vines which have fewer FRUITFUL buds at the base of canes, which is the case especially in cool-climate wine regions. The tendency in warmer New World wine regions is to use spur pruning, which can be equally productive, requires less LABOUR, and can be MECHANIZED. For more details, see GUYOT pruning. See also MECHANICAL PRUNING.   R.E.S.

cane ripening, or lignification, *aoûtement* in French, is a viticultural term used to describe a stage in the development of the shoot when the stem matures, and changes colour from green to yellow and thence to brown. The change involves the formation of corky tissue known as periderm and cellular changes including the accumulation of CARBOHYDRATE reserves, which collectively prepare the stem to withstand the cold of winter. The process begins at the base of the shoot and progresses up towards the tip, as does the dormancy status of its buds. VERAISON, the change in colour of the grapes, usually occurs at about the same time.   B.G.C.

Cannonau, sometimes spelt **Cannonao**, the Sardinian name for the widely planted red

grape variety known in Spain as GARNACHA and in France as GRENACHE (see SARDINIA). A high proportion of the grapes are grown on the east of the island to produce a varietal **Cannonau di Sardegna**, which comes in several forms, but most commonly as a full-throttle dryish red. Although the variety has lost ground since the mid 1990s, partly because as a BUSH VINE it is low-yielding and expensive to cultivate, 5,422 ha/13,400 acres of Cannonau were recorded in the Italian vine census of 2010. The admirable Cannonau-based Turriga made by the Argiolas winery near Cagliari, whose development was greatly aided by the work of consultant Giacomo Tachis (see ANTINORI), showed what could be achieved from the island's old Cannonau vines.

Canon-Fronsac, underrated Bordeaux red wine appellation, the heartland of Fronsac. See FRONSAC for more details.

canopy, that part of the vine above the ground, formed by the leaf and shoot system. It includes the trunk, cordon or canes, shoots, leaves, and fruit. It is a term borrowed from forestry, and was first used for grapevines by Professor Nelson SHAULIS of CORNELL UNIVERSITY. See CANOPY MANAGEMENT.

canopy management, a portfolio of vineyard management techniques used to improve vineyard YIELD and wine QUALITY, and to control VINE DISEASES, especially where vines are of high VIGOUR. Canopy management techniques aim to produce a desirable CANOPY MICROCLIMATE essentially by improving the exposure of leaves and fruit to the sun. The phrase became popular in many parts of the New World in the 1980s and early 1990s as part of a growing awareness of the way in which canopy microclimate affects vineyards. This awareness was not restricted to the New World. Considerable experimental work was also conducted in Europe, and the effects of canopy microclimate are now recognized as partly responsible for the ability of distinguished vineyards to produce great wines (see TERROIR and VITICULTURE).

Some of the underlying principles of canopy management can be traced to early Roman writings. For example, 'BACCHUS loves hills' is partly explained by the fact that low-vigour vines growing on shallower soils on HILLSIDES have open canopies with good fruit and leaf exposure. In modern times, the principles were best formulated by the experimental work of Professor Nelson SHAULIS of Cornell University in New York state. During the 1960s, he showed that increased fruit and leaf exposure to sunlight improved both YIELD and GRAPE COMPOSITION AND WINE QUALITY. These early studies were also much involved with introducing MECHANICAL HARVESTERS and

MECHANICAL PRUNING. Shaulis influenced researchers from other countries, who extended this work to VINIFERA vine varieties and also considered effects on wine quality. Studies in Bordeaux by Dr Alain Carbonneau demonstrated wine quality benefits of canopy manipulation in the mid 1970s. Other notable early studies were by Intrieri in Italy, Kliewer in California, Reynolds in Canada, and Smart in Australia and New Zealand.

Canopy management techniques are essentially aimed at producing an 'open' canopy microclimate, which is characterized by good leaf and fruit exposure to the sun and other climate elements, and therefore not much shade. The benefits of such a microclimate include improvements to wine quality and yield, and a significant reduction in diseases such as POWDERY MILDEW and BOTRYTIS BUNCH ROT. The ULTRAVIOLET portion of the solar spectrum has been shown to increase PHENOLICS and colour in grapes and wine, and to suppress these diseases. Interest in overcoming the common problems of excessively vigorous vines caused canopy management techniques to become popular. This was particularly marked in the New World, where a lack of experience to guide site selection and management practices resulted in some vineyards whose vines were so leafy and the fruit so shaded that it affected ripeness and wine quality. These problems were exacerbated by the widespread adoption of AGROCHEMICALS developed after the Second World War to control pests, diseases, and weeds, which, along with practices such as FERTILIZATION and IRRIGATION, stimulated shoot growth, often excessively. Canopy management techniques, especially trellis change, can offset the negative effects of vines with excess VIGOUR, but are not always necessary for low-vigour vineyards such as those found in most of the classic fine wine regions of Europe; see TERROIR.

A common feature of vineyards with a reputation for producing high-quality wines is that they are of moderate to low vigour, and that the canopy microclimate is characterized by good exposure of leaves and fruit to the sun, and little shade. Canopy management techniques can emulate this microclimate. For example, by altering TRELLIS SYSTEMS, it is possible to remove the fruit from the deep shade of the depths of the canopy to the outside of the canopy in the sun. Canopy management can also increase yield, which is reduced by densely shaded conditions. In particular, BUDBREAK and FRUITFULNESS are reduced by shade, no doubt an example of adaptive physiology which allowed WILD VINES to fruit only when they had climbed to the top of forest canopies. With increasing global concern about the use of agricultural chemicals, there is a swing towards using canopy management to help control FUNGAL DISEASES and reduce reliance on sprays (see INTEGRATED PEST MANAGEMENT). Not only is it difficult and wasteful to force sprays to penetrate to the centre of dense canopies, but shaded conditions also encourage diseases such as botrytis bunch rot and powdery mildew.

There is a range of canopy management techniques, the applicability of which varies from vineyard to vineyard. The simplest of these are TRIMMING, which cuts off excessive shoot growth in the summer, SHOOT THINNING, which removes unwanted shoots early in the season, LEAF REMOVAL in the fruit zone, which allows more fruit exposure to sun and wind, and SHOOT POSITIONING, which makes trimming and leaf removal easy and effective. These more simple techniques of canopy management are quite traditional in many parts of the Old World and good examples may be seen in the neatly trimmed vineyards in many French regions. PRUNING also affects canopy density, as well as vine BALANCE. These practices may be termed 'Bandaid viticulture' in the sense that they overcome the problem only in the season during which they are applied, and need to be reapplied each year. More permanent solutions require changes to the trellis system, which affects the canopy shape, size, and density. The changes to the trellis usually involve increasing the canopy surface area and decreasing shading. For example, dense canopies in vineyards where rows are as much as 3.5 m/11.5 ft apart can be converted to a trellis system such as GENEVA DOUBLE CURTAIN, which effectively results in a canopy twice as long as the row. This is achieved by dividing the canopy into two curtains, thereby more or less doubling the canopy surface area. Other trellis systems such as the LYRE, SCOTT HENRY, and SMART-DYSON are also being widely used commercially, especially in New World vineyards.

There was resistance to the extension of the ideas of canopy management, however, even within the US, where the technique was effectively born. There was initially a marked reluctance for academic and commercial acceptance of these ideas in California, although they were eventually taken up 30 years behind other regions, and seen to be imported from France, Italy, Australia, or New Zealand. This resistance stemmed partly from the fact that Shaulis's initial studies were made with the American grape CONCORD—even though it was proven quickly enough that VINIFERA varieties responded in the same way.

There is less scope in the Old World for canopy management since ROW SPACING is traditionally narrower, and trimming and leaf removal are routine anyway. Centuries of trial and error have demonstrated the benefits of open canopies to improve wine quality and reduce vine diseases. However, in the Old World the benefits of canopy management are often not recognized as such by traditional viticulturists, many of whom ascribe the quality and disease effects solely to the associated lower yield or vigour, and more generally to the terroir. By the early 1990s, however, there were already examples in Old World commercial viticulture—in France, Italy, and Spain—where trellises had been altered for canopy management reasons. SPAIN's relaxation of laws prohibiting IRRIGATION, together with proven performance of canopy management techniques in La Mancha, meant that some Spanish vineyards have pointed the way to the use of New World viticultural technology in Europe.

Contemporary thinking about canopy management suggests the optimal degree of leaf and fruit exposure might vary according to variety and region. There have been instances where excessive fruit exposure has had negative effects on quality. For example, in association with high temperatures it can lead to loss of colour, an effect sometimes called 'berry pinking'; and berries may shrivel if they are exposed to too much heat.   R.E.S.

Iland, P., et al., 'Climate and the vine', in *The Grapevine: From the Science to the Practice of Growing Vines for Wine* (Adelaide, 2011).

Reynier, A., *Manuel de viticulture* (11th edn, Paris, 2011).

Reynolds, A. G., 'Viticultural and vineyard management practices and their effects on grape and wine quality', in A. G. Reynolds (ed.), *Managing Wine Quality 1: Viticulture and Wine Quality* (Cambridge, 2010), 365–444.

Smart, R. E., and Robinson, M., *Sunlight into Wine: A Handbook of Winegrape Canopy Management* (Adelaide, 1991).

canopy microclimate, the climate within and immediately around the grapevine CANOPY. This is the third level of climate definition (see also MACROCLIMATE, MESOCLIMATE) and in many ways the one of most relevance to contemporary viticulture because it can be so effectively manipulated, by CANOPY MANAGEMENT, to improve wine quality and yield and to reduce disease.

The canopy microclimate at the outside of the canopy is obviously affected by the macroclimate and mesoclimate, but that within the canopy depends on the way the canopy itself alters the climate. Bright SUNLIGHT falling on a dense canopy with few gaps in California's Napa Valley may be considered as an example. Suppose a leaf facing the sun at midday receives 100 relative units of sunlight. The second leaf in the canopy will receive less than ten units and the third will receive less than one. So the second leaf in the canopy has a light climate like that of a northern European vineyard on an overcast day. In other words, the number of layers of leaves in the canopy can have even more effect on canopy microclimate than can vineyard location. This drastic reduction in sunlight levels in the canopy is caused by the vine leaves absorbing and reflecting more than 90% of light falling on the upper surface; less than 10% penetrates through to the lower surface.

This simple example illustrates the importance of canopy microclimate, and indeed how its effects can override those of regional CLIMATE, CLONE, ROOTSTOCK, and so on. (See VITICULTURE.) A feature of reputable vineyards, be they in the Old World or the New, is that they are typically of low to moderate VIGOUR and as a result the canopies are not dense or shaded. Many vineyards with an extended VINE AGE are also like this. Leaves and fruit are well exposed to the sun, so the microclimate in the centre of the canopy is not too different from that of the canopy outside. For vigorous and high-yielding vineyards, on the other hand, the canopy interior is a dark, humid, and cool place by day. Not only are the processes of fruit RIPENING slowed, but FUNGAL DISEASES such as BOTRYTIS BUNCH ROT and POWDERY MILDEW are encouraged. Canopy management techniques can be used to provide high-vigour vineyards with the same canopy microclimate as that of low-vigour vineyards.

Of the various climatological elements such as sunlight, HUMIDITY, TEMPERATURE, RAINFALL, EVAPORATION, and WIND, the canopy has greatest effect on sunlight, wind, and evaporation. The values of these three elements in the centre of a dense canopy can be less than one-tenth of those above the canopy, while temperature and humidity values are more similar to those outside the canopy. It is the leaves of the vine canopy that are responsible for creating the distinctive canopy microclimate. They strongly absorb sunlight and the energy (strictly, momentum) of the wind so that values below just one leaf are very different from those above it. Since evaporation depends on sunlight and wind, it is easy to appreciate that these values will also be reduced below the first leaf layer.

It is obvious therefore that the amount of vine leaf area has a significant effect on canopy microclimate. If most leaves and fruit are exposed, then the canopy microclimate values will not be too different from those above the canopy. If, on the other hand, the canopy is dense and the majority of leaves and bunches are not visible (and so are shaded), then it is fair to conclude that WINE QUALITY and YIELD are both below the vineyard's potential. That a visual impression of the canopy can be so definitive in terms of the vineyard's ability to produce good-quality wines is the basis of a system of vineyard SCORING used to assess vineyard potential to produce quality wine.

It has often seemed paradoxical that exposed fruit would produce better wine quality, even in warm to hot climates where HEAT STRESS is anticipated. This is because grape bunches exposed to sunlight can reach temperatures 5 to 10 °C higher than what might already be higher than optimal air temperatures. Research in Washington state by Spayd and others has carefully separated light and temperature effects. They found a positive benefit of sunlight exposure on the fruit but this could be negated by high grape temperatures. Exposure to the ULTRAVIOLET part of sunlight also affected grape composition. They suggest exposing fruit to the morning rather than afternoon sun, to avoid the problems associated with high temperature such as depression of anthocyanins. This result reflects the practice common in Bordeaux, for example, of leaf removal on the eastern side of the canopy in the hottest part of the season and then on the western side only later in the season.   R.E.S.

Smart, R. E., and Robinson, M., *Sunlight into Wine: A Handbook of Winegrape Canopy Management* (Adelaide, 1991).

Spayd, S. E., et al., 'Separation of sunlight and temperature effects on the composition of *vitis vinifera* cv. Merlot berries', *American Journal of Enology and Viticulture*, 53 (2002), 171–82.

cans. Ordinary wine is occasionally packaged in cans (usually 25 cl), which have no harmful effect on wine destined for early consumption. The advantages are that cans are lighter and less fragile than BOTTLES, but the material from which they are made is not, unlike GLASS, inert. Cans are lacquered on the inside to give chemical resistance to the acid in the wine. However, if there is the slightest pinhole in the lacquer, the wine attacks the aluminium, producing foul-smelling HYDROGEN SULFIDE, and the wine may turn black.

cantina, Italian for a cellar, a wine shop (although the word ENOTECA is much more common), and a winery. A **cantina sociale** is a CO-OPERATIVE winery.

cap (*chapeau* in French), the layer of grape solids that floats on the liquid surface during red wine fermentation and requires careful management. The cap usefully limits the amount of OXYGEN available to the YEAST, thereby encouraging the formation of alcohol, but has to be broken up and SUBMERGED in order to encourage the extraction of the desirable PHENOLICS which add colour, flavour, and longevity to a wine. See MACERATION, PUMPING OVER, DÉLESTAGE, and PUNCHING DOWN.

CAP stands for Common Agricultural Policy, a plank of EU policy which has had long-term effects on world wine production.

Cape, a synecdoche used for SOUTH AFRICA, particularly during the apartheid era.

Cape Agulhas, district in SOUTH AFRICA close to the southernmost tip of the continent.

Cape blend, SOUTH AFRICAN term generally used to describe a red wine in which PINOTAGE is one of the blending components.

Cape Riesling, the old, misleading South African name for CROUCHEN Blanc. From 2010 wine produced from Crouchen Blanc must either be sold as such or as Cape Riesling, but may no longer be labelled Riesling alone.

Cape Verde Islands far into the Atlantic produce minuscule amounts of wine. There is virtually no rainfall, but condensation from the huge volcano permits some vine-growing on the island of Fogo.

capsule, French and occasional English name for the sheath over the top of a cork and bottle-neck, otherwise known as a FOIL, just as the **capsule cutter** is more widely known as a FOIL CUTTER. French wine released for sale within France must have its capsules embossed with a customs seal, known as a **capsule CRD** or **capsule congé**. The regulation requiring producers to use a different seal for exported wines was dropped in 2011.

Caramany, named GNEISS-dominated enclave in the extreme south west of the area designated for Côtes du ROUSSILLON-Villages. Syrah must constitute at least 40% of the blend, Carignan no more than 60%. The rest should be Grenache.

carbamates, or **urethanes**, relatively simple organic compounds found in very low concentrations in some foods and wines. Ethyl carbamate, or ethyl urethane, is a naturally occurring component of all fermented foods and beverages. In the case of the YEAST *Saccharomyces cerevisiae*, ethyl carbamate is formed by the reaction between ETHANOL and urea, which in turn is produced by the degradation of the amino acid arginine, one of the main NITROGEN sources in grape juice and musts. In the late 1980s, ethyl carbamate was added to the growing list of compounds suspected of human carcinogenicity on the basis of animal tests.

Most wine types contain ethyl carbamate concentrations well below the limit suggested by US authorities of 15 mg per litre. (60 in fortified wines). High-alcohol, particularly sweet wines which have been heated during production (such as MADEIRA), are likely to be the wines with the highest levels of ethyl carbamate, and higher than average levels may be produced from grapes grown in vineyards given excess nitrogen FERTILIZERS. The level may also be influenced by the yeast strain.   A.D.W. & J.E.H.

carbohydrates, organic compounds made up of CARBON, OXYGEN, and hydrogen and which include sugars, starch, and cellulose. Of particular interest to the wine consumer are the simple sugar molecules GLUCOSE and FRUCTOSE, which together make up the SUGARS in grape juice, and which are subsequently fermented into the alcohol which distinguishes wine from grape juice. Sucrose is the sugar molecule made up of glucose and fructose and is manufactured in the leaves of plants, including vines, by PHOTOSYNTHESIS. Sucrose can be converted to all other forms of carbohydrates, such as starch, as a storage compound in the roots and trunks, and cellulose, which is present in all cells. Sucrose is also the basic plant biochemical building block, and can be converted to proteins, fats, and organic acids.

A vine's reserves of carbohydrates are an important factor in its ANNUAL GROWTH CYCLE. STARCH is the principal form of carbohydrate reserve which is stored in the woody vine parts in the autumn. The starch is converted into sugars which, via RESPIRATION, provide the chemical energy for growing shoots early the following spring. The reason perennial plants, such as vines, can grow to such a large size is this ability to store surplus chemical energy each growing season, which is then available for shoot growth the following season. This allows more rapid growth than for a plant starting out from a seed, which has limited food reserves.

At about VERAISON, when the fruit starts to ripen, the vine begins to replace carbohydrate reserves used earlier that growing season. Sugars are moved into the trunk, arms, and roots, where they are converted to the insoluble storage material starch. As shoots accumulate starch they change colour, from green to brown; this is called CANE RIPENING. Ideally there should be a period of warm, sunny weather after HARVEST during which the leaves can manufacture the sugars to provide the final topping up of starch reserves. However, this ideal state of affairs can be disrupted, for example by large crops of grapes or late-season shoot growth which slows ripening and limits the amounts of starch formed. Similarly, an autumn FROST which destroys leaves can interrupt the orderly build-up of reserves in the vine. High levels of carbohydrate reserves of sugars and starches make vines better able to withstand WINTER FREEZE, providing them with a sort of biological antifreeze mechanism. Although starch is the main carbohydrate storage compound, there are some other minor compounds such as AMINO ACIDS and carboxylic acids which show the same pattern of autumn accumulation and spring depletion.

Early shoot growth in spring is entirely dependent on these stored reserves, which are mobilized in the woody parts and moved to the developing shoots. If there are too many new shoots growing for the reserves available, new growth will be checked. The concept of BALANCED PRUNING ensures that the number of buds retained is proportional to the reserves available. The new shoots become independent of these reserves when the leaves reach about half their final size, and photosynthesis is sufficient to support further growth.

See also WOOD, in which the carbohydrate cellulose plays an important part.   R.E.S.

Keller, M., 'Partitioning of assimilates', in *The Science of Grapevines: Anatomy and Physiology* (Elsevier, 2010).

carbon is an essential element that is distributed between the atmosphere (present as CARBON DIOXIDE), plants, animals, and the soil. When plant and animal residues and excreta are returned to the soil, they are colonized by a host of microorganisms, aided by larger soil organisms such as EARTHWORMS, which decompose these residues, releasing carbon dioxide and nutrients, and deriving energy for their growth. As the many different carbon compounds in the residues are decomposed, and organisms multiply and then die, the more resistant compounds and newly synthesized carbon compounds gradually accumulate to form a dark brown to black colloidal material called humus (see ORGANIC MATTER). This carbon cycle is important for the nutrition of vines and COVER CROPS, most especially in ORGANIC and BIODYNAMIC VITICULTURE.

See also BIOCHAR.   R.E.W.

carbon, active. See CHARCOAL.

carbonation, the cheapest and least effective method of SPARKLING WINEMAKING, involving the simple pumping of CARBON DIOXIDE into a tank of wine. In EU terminology, carbonated wines are aerated sparkling wines.

carbon dioxide, or CO_2, a naturally occurring atmospheric gas, commonly encountered as the sparkle in soft drinks, beers, and SPARKLING WINES. Its content in the atmosphere is only about 0.03%; yet upon that small amount depends the growth of all living systems, including man, vines, yeasts, bacteria, all plants, and the existence of all fauna depending on them for food. Not least, it is the ultimate raw material of wine and, via a series of biochemical reactions involving the grapevine, yeast cells, and the consumer, results in carbon dioxide's being both assimilated and produced.

The cycle begins with the combination of carbon dioxide and water into sugars in the vine leaves by PHOTOSYNTHESIS; conversion in the leaves and berries of some of that sugar into a variety of compounds, including those directly or indirectly responsible for ACIDS, COLOUR, and FLAVOUR in the grapes and wine; and, as the final step, transformation of the grape juice into wine by FERMENTATION. Carbon dioxide is released in substantial amounts during fermentation. It returns whence it came with the metabolism of the alcohol and other wine constituents back to carbon dioxide and water, primarily in the liver of the wine drinker.

Carbon dioxide passes into vine leaves through small pores, or STOMATA. The greater the atmospheric concentration, the more can pass in, and the greater the potential growth and YIELD of the vine (provided that other factors such as water, light, temperature, or nutrients are not more directly limiting).

Carbon dioxide concentrations in the Earth's atmosphere have increased by 25% since the beginning of the Industrial Revolution, largely through the burning of fossil fuels. By analogy, it seems certain that this has already helped to increase the yields of grapevines, and, very possibly, grape and wine quality. Theoretical arguments have been advanced that it may also have tended to raise the optimum ripening temperatures for grape and wine quality.

With increasing awareness of CLIMATE CHANGE and rising atmospheric carbon dioxide levels, it is worth considering the wine industry's role in what may be the Earth's greatest environmental problem. Dr Damien Martin of Plant and Food Research, New Zealand, has calculated that the activities of the world's wine producers typically lead to a net reduction in atmospheric carbon dioxide of 8 tonnes per ha of vineyard per year. The calculation estimates that for each ha almost ten tonnes are 'fixed' each year by photosynthesis, while each tonne of grapes produces 1.3 tonnes of carbon dioxide during fermentation and a further 0.6 tonnes treating WINERY WASTE.   J.G. & R.E.S.

In winemaking

Carbon dioxide is used throughout the winemaking process to displace OXYGEN from contact with crushed grapes or wine. At some wineries, carbon dioxide is deliberately pumped over white grapes as they are received at the winery and pass through the destemmer in order to minimize OXIDATION. Draining tanks, presses, storage and blending vats, filters, and bottling lines are all locations where carbon dioxide may be applied by fastidious winemakers.

Carbon dioxide also plays an important role in the fermentation of all wines. Like humans, YEAST metabolizes starches and sugars to produce water and carbon dioxide. In the human case, carbon dioxide from muscle or brain activity dissolves in the blood, is transferred to the lungs and then to the atmosphere as exhaled breath. In the case of yeast's metabolic activity in six-carbon sugar solutions such as grape juice, the three main by-products are water, ETHANOL, and carbon dioxide. If excess oxygen is available, the yeast obtains more cell-building energy from the sugar by converting it to carbon dioxide and water. With only a moderate oxygen supply, the yeast produces carbon dioxide and the ethanol that distinguishes wine from grape juice.

As winery visitors during vintage time may discover, while wine is fermenting, substantial quantities of carbon dioxide are given off; while not being inherently toxic to humans, carbon dioxide displaces oxygen so that, in a confined space such as a FERMENTATION VESSEL, suffocation is all too possible. Winery workers must exercise particular caution in this respect.

In most still wines, this carbon dioxide is encouraged to dissipate leaving only very small amounts in the finished wine—although the more protective the winemaking, the more substantial these traces may be, as in, for example, many German and other light, aromatic, white wines. (Winemakers may, however, choose to remove carbon dioxide from such wines by SPARGING them with NITROGEN just before bottling.)

In sparkling wines, however, substantial quantities of dissolved carbon dioxide, between two and six atmospheres, are encouraged to remain in the bottle by one of the methods outlined in SPARKLING WINEMAKING. Lesser quantities of carbon dioxide, between one and two atmospheres, may be encouraged in wines such as those labelled PERLANT, PÉTILLANT, or FRIZZANTE by inducing a second but less violent fermentation and preserving the carbon dioxide produced.

Since the 1960s, however, a number of winemakers in hotter, particularly New World, regions have pursued a deliberate policy of bottling wine, particularly white wine, with up to one atmosphere of carbon dioxide dissolved in it. This is because carbon dioxide, as it vaporizes from the wine, carries with it many ESTERS and thus tends to increase a wine's freshness and fruitiness, attributes which the winemaker may well wish to enhance. This is done by processing the wine at very low temperatures where carbon dioxide is much more soluble in wine, and bottling it early in order to preserve some of the gas given off during fermentation. The warmer the wine is served, the more obvious is the carbon dioxide to the taster.

While most tasters would be surprised and probably shocked to notice any carbon dioxide in a mature red bordeaux (in which case it could even be taken to be an unwelcome sign of FERMENTATION IN BOTTLE), it is not necessarily a fault in most types of white and rosé wines. Portugal's VINHO VERDE provides many examples of this deliberate wine style, as do many young whites from the MOSEL, and some Italian

red wines contain a perceptible level of carbon dioxide, sometimes as a result of the GOVERNO practice of adding dried grapes to provoke a second fermentation.

Carbon dioxide also plays an essential role in CARBONIC MACERATION. A.D.W.

Smart, R. E., 'A lump of coal, a bunch of grapes . . .', *Journal of Wine Research*, 21/2-3 (2010), 107–11. doi: 10.1080/09571264.2010.530092.

carbonic acid is the acid formed when CARBON DIOXIDE is dissolved in water, H_2CO_3.

carbonic maceration, red winemaking process which transforms a small amount of SUGAR IN GRAPES which are uncrushed to ETHANOL, without the intervention of yeasts. It is used typically to produce light-bodied, brightly coloured, fruity red wines for early consumption, most famously but by no means exclusively in the Beaujolais region of France.

Louis PASTEUR observed in 1872 that grape berries held in air differed in flavour from those held in a CARBON DIOXIDE atmosphere (although he, wrongly, suspected that grapes held in carbon dioxide would produce wines for long ageing).

Carbonic maceration is not normally used with white grapes, as undesirable flavours are formed. When used to make red wines, whole bunches of grapes are deliberately placed, with care to ensure that the berries are not broken, in an anaerobic atmosphere, generally obtained by using carbon dioxide to exclude OXYGEN. An intracellular fermentation takes place within the intact berry and a small amount of ethanol is formed, along with traces of many flavourful aromatic compounds. All of these contribute to the distinctive aroma and flavour of the resultant wines. The maceration period in this anaerobic environment and phase, where these aromatic compounds are produced, depends on temperature, and can be from one to three weeks.

It is likely that the same metabolic pathways are involved in carbonic maceration as in normal alcoholic fermentation but the flavour differences suggest that other processes are also concerned. Michel Flanzy, whose work dates from 1936, and other French researchers have observed that ordinary grapes held intact for several days under a carbon dioxide atmosphere, then crushed and allowed to ferment, produce a wine which is much brighter-coloured, less tannic, and more distinctively perfumed than one made normally. Some find this very particular aroma reminiscent of bananas, others of kirsch.

Detailed studies suggest that whole grapes held under carbon dioxide lose about a fifth of their sugar, gain about 2% in ALCOHOLIC STRENGTH, show a tenfold gain in GLYCEROL, lose about half of their harsh MALIC ACID, and

show an increase in PH of about 0.25 units, all within the intact berry. These measurements exclude any changes in FLAVOUR COMPOUNDS. It is thought that the distinguishing volatile compounds include the volatile PHENOLS, benzaldehyde, vinylbenzene, ethyl cinnamate, ethyl vanillate, and methyl vanillate.

Under commercial winemaking conditions, it is almost impossible to produce a wine that depends wholly on carbonic maceration. The two key elements are the retention of whole berries, and an anaerobic atmosphere. While carbon dioxide is readily available to exclude oxygen, when whole bunches are poured into a tank, in practice the weight of the grapes breaks open those at the bottom, which begin to ferment in the normal way due to the action of indigenous YEASTS, derived either from the grapes or from the winemaking equipment or environment. Immediately above this exist whole grapes surrounded by juice; above this, whole grapes in an atmosphere of carbon dioxide. This upper layer will undergo true carbonic maceration. The grapes in the middle layer will undergo similar intracellular transformations, but at a much slower rate, and with the presence of yeast in the surrounding juice.

Even when a CRUSHER is employed in traditional red winemaking, a proportion of whole berries is retained, depending on the size and condition of the berries and the operation of the crusher. These berries undergo carbonic maceration as the fermenting MUST at the bottom of the vessel gives off carbon dioxide which excludes all oxygen above it. Thus, alcoholic fermentation and carbonic maceration would proceed simultaneously.

This also applies to some red burgundy made today using WHOLE-GRAPE FERMENTATIONS. Winemakers in other regions around the world, working with varieties other than Burgundy's classic PINOT NOIR, carefully adjust their crushers, pumps, and CAP management regime to maximize such flavour modification techniques.

The technique is open to much regional and personal modification (see SEMI-CARBONIC MACERATION as an example). Some winemakers allow one or two days' maceration in carbon dioxide while others (or the same individuals in different vintages), may prefer to leave the grapes a week or two under the gas. It is generally considered that the necessary period of maceration is longer when the fruit is less ripe because carbonic maceration reduces the concentration of malic acid, which tends to be higher in greener grapes.

Although Beaujolais is the most famous wine region where carbonic maceration is the most common winemaking technique, it is also widely used for the Beaujolais grape Gamay in other parts of France. It has also been turned to positive use in the southern Rhône, and it assists in making commercial reds from the sometimes tough Carignan grape to yield red wines for early drinking in the Languedoc-Roussillon in southern France—although there is an increasing tendency to blend these with traditionally made wines.

Its use in the New World has been limited.   P.L.

Ribéreau-Gayon, P., et al., *Traité d'Œnologie 1: Microbiologie du vin: Vinifications* (Paris, 1998), translated by Branco, J. M., as *Handbook of Enology 1: The Microbiology of Wine and Vinifications* (Chichester, 2000), 348–58.

Sneyd, T. N., 'Carbonic maceration: an overview', *Australian and New Zealand Wine Industry Journal*, 4 (1989), 281–5.

Carcavelos, tiny DOP, renowned in its heyday for FORTIFIED WINES. However, its vineyards have almost been obliterated by the westward expansion of the capital city Lisbon along the Tagus Estuary (see map under PORTUGAL). A cynic's view of Carcavelos is that it was created by the Marquis of Pombal, Portugal's autocratic 18th century prime minister, because he had to do something with the grapes from his country residence at nearby Oeiras. He even flouted his own regulations and permitted Carcavelos to be blended with PORT. Thanks to Pombal, Carcavelos enjoyed a brief period of popularity in Britain in the early part of the 19th century (and see AUCTIONS for evidence of its renown even earlier). The wine may be made from a blend of up to nine different red and white grapes. It is usually fermented dry and fortified with GRAPE SPIRIT up to an ALCOHOLIC STRENGTH of 18 to 20%. A small amount of *vinho abafado* (fermenting grape must preserved by the addition of alcohol) is added after FERMENTATION to sweeten the wine. Between three and five years' CASK AGEING give the wine a nutty character akin to a tawny port. Although total vineyard area fell to less than 10 ha/25 acres, a 21st century municipal initiative spearheaded by the Mayor of Oeiras has resulted in the doubling of land under vine and a new fortified brand, Conde de Oeiras.   R.J.M. & S.A.

Cardinal, red TABLE GRAPE, a CROSS, grown for wine production in VIETNAM and THAILAND. *Cardinal* is also a (Burgundian) name for a red wine mixed with CASSIS.

Carema, almost alpine red wine zone of PIEMONTE in north-west Italy, bordering on the Valle d'AOSTA, is the northernmost zone of Piemonte in which the great NEBBIOLO is cultivated (although see also VALTELLINA). Viticulture is not an easy task in this mountainous region, and the TENDONE-trained vineyards have been wrested from steep gradients by means of TERRACES at 350 to 700 m (1,150 to 2,300 ft).

The wine itself has a recognizably Nebbiolo character, with higher ACIDITY and less body than the wines of the Langhe or than the group described in SPANNA. Although CHAPTALIZATION has often been allowed, interesting, perfumed, and surprisingly long-lived wines are regularly made in the warmer vintages, which are becoming more frequent thanks to CLIMATE CHANGE. Improved viticultural practices and lower yields have also helped to produce wines with more extract. Carema's total vineyard area was just 16 ha/40 acres in 2014, supplying a tiny handful of producers. Ferrando, founded in 1890, saved the DOC from obscurity thanks to its legendary Carema Etichetta Nera, a 100% Nebbiolo aged for three years in cask and produced in only the best vintages. The estate still possesses vintages going back to the 1950s as proof of Carema's longevity. Newcomer Dazero is one to watch. The minimum ageing period has been reduced from four to two years, oak or chestnut.   W.S.

www.caremavini.it

Carignan, known as **Carignane** in the US, **Carignano** in Italy (**Bovale Grande** in Sardinia), and **Mazuelo** and **Cariñena** in Spain, late-ripening black grape variety which was once so widely planted in LANGUEDOC-ROUSSILLON that it was France's most planted vine for much of the last century. Thanks to EU bribes it had fallen to fifth most planted red wine grape in France by 2011 when plantings totalled 41,718 ha/103,043 acres.

Nowadays Carignan seems a very odd choice indeed, although presumably it seemed obvious to many *pieds noirs* returning in the mid 20th century from ALGERIA, where the wine industry depended at one time on its 140,000 ha/350,000 acres of Carignan. In much of southern France its wine is high in everything—acidity, tannins, colour, bitterness—but finesse and charm. This gives it the double inconvenience of being unsuitable for early consumption yet unworthy of maturation. The astringency of basic red from the Languedoc has owed much to Carignan's ubiquity, although blending with Cinsaut or Grenache helped considerably, and CARBONIC MACERATION helped disguise, if not exactly compensate for, Carignan's lack of youthful charm. The vine is not even particularly easy to grow. It is extremely sensitive to POWDERY MILDEW, quite sensitive to DOWNY MILDEW, prone to rot, and prey to infestation by grape worms. Its diffusion was presumably beneficial to the AGROCHEMICAL industry. Its bunches keep such a tenacious hold on the vine that it does not adapt well to MECHANICAL HARVESTING and is mainly grown in BUSH VINES.

There must have been some attribute which led to the almost exclusive dissemination of Carignan throughout the Midi in the 1950s and 1960s, and there was: yield. The vine can quite easily be persuaded to produce almost 200 hl/ha (11 tons/acre), ideal for a thirsty but not discriminating post-Second World War market. It also buds late, which gave it extra allure as a substitute for the much lighter ARAMON, previously France's number one vine, which had been badly affected by the frosts of 1956 and 1963. It ripens late, too, however, limiting its cultivation to Mediterranean wine regions. The regulations for the Languedoc-Roussillon's appellations have been forced to embrace the ubiquitous Carignan, but it is hard to argue that, for example, Minervois or Corbières are improved by their (continually reduced) Carignan component. Those wines that depend most heavily on the 'improving' varieties such as Syrah, Grenache, and Mourvèdre and least on Carignan are almost invariably the most successful—with the exception of some wines made with care from well-sited old bush vines which can make concentrated marvels such as those of Domaine d'Aupilhac in Montpeyroux, Bertrand Bergé in Fitou, and Roc des Anges in Roussillon.

The fuller-bodied white mutation **Carignan Blanc** can still be found in some vineyards of the Languedoc and, in particular, Roussillon.

Although the vine (like Grenache) may have originated in Spain in the province of Aragón, it is not widely planted there today. Carignan is not even the principal grape variety in the wine that carries its most obvoius Spanish synonym CARIÑENA. It is grown chiefly in Cataluña today although it was historically, as Mazuela, a not particularly distinguished ingredient in Rioja. It also plays a major part in the wines of PRIORAT (where some of the finest Carignan-dominant wines in the world are to be found), COSTERS DEL SEGRE, PENEDÈS, TARRAGONA, and TERRA ALTA, so that Spain had total plantings of 5,863 ha/ 14,481 acres in 2011.

Because of its late-ripening habits, Carignan can thrive only in relatively hot climates. At one time it underpinned Israel's wine industry and there are still 1,645 ha/4,963 acres in Italy. As Carignano it is grown in Lazio and most commonly in Sardinia (perhaps as a result of that island's long dominance by Aragón), where it makes strong, rich, velvety reds and rosés, notably some seriously exciting Carignano del Sulcis. It is also grown in Cyprus, Turkey, and Croatia.

The vine, gaining a vowel as Carignane, has been important in the Americas. Although it is rarely seen as a varietal, there were still about 3,300 acres/1,336 ha in California's hotter regions in 2012 for the vine's productivity and vigour are valued by growers, if not consumers. It is also grown (to a much lesser extent) in Mexico, Argentina, Chile, and Uruguay. And occasional bottlings of savoury old-vine Carignan have surfaced in South Africa.

Let some interesting old Carignan vines be treasured but let it not be planted.

www.carignans.com

Cariñena, town in north-east Spain which lends its name to both a denominated wine zone and a vine variety, widely grown in southern France as CARIGNAN. Although it is thought to have originated in the area, the vine (officially known as Mazuelo in Spain) has been widely abandoned here in favour of GARNACHA, which seems better suited to the arid growing conditions in this, the largest of the four DO zones of the ARAGÓN region (see map under SPAIN). But Cariñena, like so many other regions of Spain, is trying to break with the the viticultural and winemaking flaws of the past. The minimum ALCOHOLIC STRENGTH permitted by DO regulations for red Cariñena was reduced from 14 to 12% in 1990. Tempranillo and Cabernet Sauvignon have also been planted, and the local red wine rarity Vidadillo rediscovered. Among the white vine varieties that cover a fifth of Cariñena's total vineyard area, Macabeo and Garnacha Blanca have been joined by Parellada from Penedès. The CO-OPERATIVES, led by San Valero, have been fully modernized, and some noteworthy private producers have joined them, notably Solar de Urbezo, Pablo, Bioenos, Añadas, and Grandes Vinos y Viñedos. V. de la S.

Carmel Valley, California wine region. See MONTEREY.

Carmenère is a very minor dark-skinned grape variety in Bordeaux today but was, according to Daurel, widely cultivated in the Médoc in the early 18th century and, with its parent CABERNET FRANC, established the reputations of its best properties. He reports that the vine is vigorous and used to produce exceptionally good wine but was abandoned because of its susceptibility to COULURE and resultant low yields. It yields small quantities of exceptionally deep-coloured, full-bodied wines that can taste decidedly herbaceous if the grapes are not completely ripe. Ch Clerc Milon, PAUILLAC classed growth, usually includes some in its ASSEMBLAGE and the odd VARIETAL emerged in Bordeaux in the early 2000s.

Its new power base is CHILE, where plantings had reached 10,000 ha/24,700 acres by 2012, particularly as a result of correct VINE IDENTIFICATION rather than new plantings. It was discovered in 1994 that a substantial proportion of the vines previously believed to be Merlot are in fact this historic variety, presumably imported directly from Bordeaux in the late 19th century. It ripens even later than Cabernet Sauvignon and if yields are limited, by grafting on to low-vigour ROOTSTOCKS, for example, has the potential to make very respectable wines, combining some of the charm of Merlot with the structure of Cabernet Sauvignon, although for many winemakers it is best as an ingredient in a BORDEAUX blend.

Correct identification also grew the official total of Carmenère plantings in Italy from 45 to 1,000 ha between the censuses of 2000 and 2010. Most of these were previously thought to be CABERNET FRANC in northern and north eastern Italy. Much is used for blending but the likes of San Leonardo in TRENTINO and Ca'del Bosco in LOMBARDY make a sturdy varietal Carmenero. Even more recently DNA PROFILING showed that the variety known as CABERNET GERNISCHT in CHINA is in fact Carmenère.

Daurel, J., *Les Raisins de cuve de la Gironde et du sud-ouest de la France* (Bordeaux, 1892).

Carmignano, historic central Italian red wine made 16 km/10 miles north west of Florence in a zone noted as one of TUSCANY's finest for red wine production since the Middle Ages. The vineyards are located on a series of low hills between 50 and 200 m (160–650 ft) above sea level, unusually low for the SANGIOVESE grape, which forms the base of the blend and gives wines with lower ACIDITY and softer TANNINS than the wines of CHIANTI CLASSICO.

The wines were first given legal status by Cosimo III de'Medici—himself a major proprietor in the Carmignano zone at the villa of Artimino—who included them in his selection of four areas of superior wine production in an edict of 1716 which prohibited other wines from using the names of the selected areas. The grand-ducal wines were sent regularly to Queen Anne of England, who apparently appreciated their quality. The wines were also praised by Giovanni Cosimo Villifranchi (1773) and Cosimo Ridolfi (1831).

The report of the Dalmasso Commission in 1932 (see ITALY and TUSCANY) assigned Carmignano to the nearby zone of Chianti Montalbano, where cooler temperatures and higher elevations result in Chianti wines of lighter body and higher acidity more suitable for early drinking. Independent status was restored in 1975, however, with the granting of a DOC for Carmignano, the only Tuscan DOC to require the inclusion of CABERNET SAUVIGNON (up to 20%) in a Sangiovese-based blend years before its use became common in the so-called SUPERTUSCANS and long before the production rules of Chianti and Chianti Classico were loosened to allow INTERNATIONAL VARIETIES in the blends. It was awarded DOCG status in 1990. Bizarrely, a provision for up to 10% white wine grapes remains, but is hardly used by any quality-conscious producers. The wine must be aged for at least 12 months in oak or chestnut casks.

The alleged tradition of Cabernet Sauvignon in the zone was of major assistance in detaching it from Chianti Montalbano. The vineyards of Ugo Contini-Bonacossi of Villa di Capezzana, who was instrumental in obtaining the DOC for the region, and the zone's major producer, were grafted with cuttings from Ch LAFITE in

the 1970s. He claimed to be reviving a local tradition begun by the Medici. This view is supported by the zone's Consorzio, which maintains that Cabernet Sauvignon vines were planted here as early as the 16th century at the request of Catherine de Medici, then Queen of France.

Although in the past many of the Carmignano wines were aged, at least partially, in French BARRIQUES, many producers have returned to ageing the wines in large oak casks, while Fattoria di Bacchereto uses clay AMPHORAE with impressive results.

The DOC for younger wines is Barco Reale (referring to the 'royal park', as distinguished in the Medici edict of 1716), the DOC which also applies to the zone's sweet VIN SANTO and its rosé often obtained by SAIGNÉE. The rosé has a long history here as Vin Ruspo, a reference to peasants' drawing off, or 'robbing', the pale juice from the cask at the beginning of fermentation. W.S.

Belfrage, N., *Brunello to Zibibbo—The Wines of Tuscany, Central and Southern Italy* (London, 2003).
www.consorziovinicarmignano.it

Carmine, California CROSS whose antecedents include Carignan, Cabernet Sauvignon, and Merlot. It has an intense Cabernet flavour and is planted to a limited extent in the US. Mainly blended.

Carnelian, like CARMINE, a black grape CROSS developed from Carignan, Cabernet Sauvignon, and Garnacha in and specifically for California by Dr H. P. Olmo of DAVIS. It was supposed to be a hot-climate Cabernet but too many of the Grenache characteristics predominate to make it easy to pick. Its California influence is limited, and restricted to the SAN JOAQUIN VALLEY, where total plantings fell to 782 acres/316 acres by 2011. It is also grown in Texas, Hawaii, and with surprising success in Western Australia where it was originally thought to be Sangiovese.

Carneros, also known as **Los Carneros**, a moderately cool, windy CALIFORNIA wine region, an AVA that spans the extreme south of both NAPA and SONOMA Counties. Carneros sprang to public notice in and outside California in the mid 1980s, partly on the strength of some impressive Pinot Noirs and as much or more because of traditionally made SPARKLING WINES blended from Chardonnay and Pinot Noir grown in Carneros. Acacia, Buena Vista, Carneros Creek, and Saintsbury were important producers of still wines throughout the 1980s; Gloria Ferrer, Domaine Carneros, and Codorníu Napa were the pioneer sparkling wine producers following the lead of Domaine Chandon of Yountville (see MOËT & CHANDON), which first sourced grapes here.

In fact this is one of the state's older wine districts. Agoston HARASZTHY planted grapes in it before 1870. A property originally called Stanly Ranch was famous as a vineyard by 1880. However, persistent fog and wind made vine-growing difficult and, when PHYLLOXERA struck hard in the 1880s, there began a swift slide into a long night. The Stanly Ranch was bought and replanted in 1942 by Louis M. Martini, but the push that brought Carneros both fame and more than 8,000 acres/3,200 ha of vineyard in 2013 did not begin until the 1970s.

Los Carneros ('the rams' in Spanish) sprawls across the last, low hills of the Mayacamas Range before it slips beneath San Francisco Bay. The larger part of the AVA lies within Sonoma County; grapes from that portion can also use the Sonoma Valley AVA. The smaller segment, in Napa County, is equally entitled to use Napa Valley as an AVA. In addition to Chardonnay and Pinot Noir, Carneros is gaining a reputation for Merlot and, to a limited extent, Syrah. Many wineries further north in Napa Valley either own vineyards or buy grapes, particularly Chardonnay, in the Carneros district in order to have a cooler climate blending component.

Growers and wineries within the AVA have banded together in a promotional body called the Carneros Quality Alliance (www.carneros.com).   B.C.C. & L.M.

Carnuntum, Austrian wine-growing region immediately east of Vienna, named after a Roman city whose ruins grace the Danube's shoreline. Its roughly 1,000-ha/2,500-acre vine surface features nearly every grape variety planted in Austria. Considering its GEOLOGICAL and MESOCLIMATIC diversity, it is likely that the region will continue to produce a wide variety of wine styles. But its most ambitious growers have discovered some highly distinctive combinations of variety and site, as witness the reputation of Gerhard Markowitsch (in Carnuntum's best-known wine village, Göttelsbrunn) as one of the top Pinot Noir producers; or the revival, spearheaded by Dorli Muhr and Dirk van der Niepoort, of Blaufränkisch on the once-renowned Spitzerberg, a LIMESTONE-rich remnant of the Carpathians that sits a mere 15 km/9 miles from SLOVAKIA's capital Bratislava and nearly touches the northern tip of BURGENLAND.   D.S.

carotenoids, important class of plant PIGMENTS whose red, orange, and yellow colours complement the green of chlorophyll and the blue and red of ANTHOCYANINS. They come from the chloroplasts in green grapes. Carotenoids are TERPENOIDS with 40 carbons and belong to the LIPID group of organic compounds. They include two main groups—xanthophylls and carotenes—which are prominent in grapes and provide the skin colour of so-called white grapes and are associated with vine leaf colours in autumn; carotenes also form a substrate for synthesis of many FLAVOUR COMPOUNDS and FLAVOUR PRECURSORS. Carotenoids serve as accessory pigments in the process of PHOTOSYNTHESIS.   B.G.C.

Carricante, white wine grape speciality of ETNA in Sicily and dominant grape in the blend for Etna Bianco. Wines are crisp with citrus notes and the best can age well. Plantings totalled just 200 ha/500 acres in 2010.

Carso, or **Carso-Kras**, small DOC consisting of just 53 ha of vineyards in FRIULI in north-east Italy, on a gravelly plateau between Gorizia and Trieste and bordering SLOVENIA. A smaller subzone, called Terrano Classico, is situated immediately around the city of Trieste. The DOC produces mainly dark, tannic reds high in acidity made from the Terrano grape (see TERAN), which responds well to BARREL MATURATION. Terrano is often confused with REFOSCO DAL PENDUCOLO ROSSO, which is also allowed in the Carso DOC, in addition to INTERNATIONAL VARIETIES such as Chardonnay, Sauvignon Blanc, GLERA, and Cabernet Sauvignon.   W.S.

Belfrage, N., *Barolo to Valpolicella—The Wines of Northern Italy* (2nd edn, London, 2003).
Robinson, J., Harding, J., and Vouillamoz, J., *Wine Grapes: A Complete Guide to 1,368 Vine Varieties Including their Origins and Flavours* (London, 2012).

Cartagène is the traditional, largely domestically produced, strong, sweet aperitif of the Languedoc, made, rather like a VIN DE LIQUEUR, by adding grape spirit to barely fermenting grape juice.

Cartaxo, DOP subregion of TEJO in central southern Portugal.

Carthage, ancient city on the north coast of Africa just east of modern Tunis which played a part in wine history as a result of the maritime expansion of the PHOENICIANS who settled there in the late 9th century BC. A famous passage of the historian Diodorus (20. 8) paints a vivid picture of the country estates of the Carthaginian elite of the late 4th century BC, flourishing on the fertile soils around Carthage with a mix of farming, which included viticulture. However, at no period did Carthaginian wine figure prominently in trade. It was eclipsed by North Africa's importance as a producer of corn and olive oil, most particularly in the period when it was part of the Roman empire. Still, there can be little doubt that Carthage's élite shared the same interest in viticulture as the rest of the Mediterranean world.

It was for them that a large work, written in Punic, of 28 books on agriculture was produced by a certain Mago. Little is known of the writer or of his date; but his work fits most easily into the great explosion of handbooks on agriculture written in the Hellenistic period, particularly in the 3rd and 2nd centuries BC. Like these other works, Mago's treatise is lost; our knowledge of its contents is entirely derived from references to it and quotations from it in the later writers. Of these the largest number are about vines, although it would be dangerous to infer from this very fragmentary selection that viticulture had particular prominence in his work. While Mago's work probably contained much that was taken from the earlier AGRICULTURAL TREATISES produced in the Greek world, it was not without information based on personal observation. As COLUMELLA (*De re rustica* 3. 12. 5–6) noted, Mago's advice to plant vines on north-facing slopes is particularly appropriate to Africa (see TOPOGRAPHY). Large extracts from Mago were translated into Greek and incorporated in a treatise on agriculture by Cassius Dionysius of Utica, near Carthage (VARRO, *De re rustica* 1. 1. 10). More surprisingly a decree of the senate ordered a translation of Mago into Latin (Columella, *De re rustica* 1. 1. 13). The most likely occasion for this must be in connection with one of the schemes for Roman settlement in North Africa in the period after Rome's destruction of Carthage in 146 BC. Columella was to call Mago 'the father of country matters', probably primarily because his work in its Latin version gave Romans convenient access to the vast literature on agriculture from the Hellenistic world.

The most famous Carthaginian of all is commemorated in the name of the co-operative and principal producer of CHÂTILLON-EN-DIOIS in the foothills of the French Alps, the Cellier Hannibal.   J.J.P.

Greene, J. A., 'Beginnings of Phoenician/Punic Wine Production', in Fleming, S. J., and Katz, S. H. (eds.), *The Origins and Ancient History of Wine* (New York, 1995).
Gsell, S., *Histoire ancienne de l'Afrique du nord* (Paris, 1951), iv. 1–169.

Cartizze. See PROSECCO.

cartons, method of packaging wine in what are effectively cardboard 'bricks', sometimes known as tetrapacks, that has been particularly popular for everyday wines in Latin American countries such as CHILE. They are starting to become more popular elsewhere in the light of concerns about SUSTAINABILITY. Cartons are light, made of renewable materials, exceedingly space-efficient, non-breakable, and easy to recycle. They also offer producers a much larger LABELLING area than BOTTLES. They are made mainly from paperboard, with polyethylene and aluminium, often with a resealable plastic closure, and can keep wine fresh for between 18 months and two years.

Casablanca, relatively cool wine valley in CHILE, part of the Aconcagua region.

casa vinicola, or AZIENDA vinicola, on the label of an Italian wine indicates a producer who buys in grapes or wine, like a French NÉGOCIANT.

case. BEER and milk may be sold in crates but, contrary to popular usage, wine is sold in cases. A case typically holds a dozen bottles, the basic trading unit in the fine-wine trade and much of the wholesale wine trade. It has been posited that the case contains 12 bottles because that is as many as a man can comfortably carry. Most cases are made of cardboard outers, with cardboard vertical or papier mâché horizontal dividers. Wine merchants truly dedicated to the mail-order business ensure that they use only particularly strong cases especially designed to minimize breakage.

Many FINE WINES designed for prolonged BOTTLE AGEING are dispatched from their producers in heavy wooden cases, however, usually made of rough pine, branded with the name, and often logo, of the producer on the **case ends** (which can be attractive enough for future use as decoration or table mats). These cases are usually nailed down and can be opened only with a chisel or screwdriver and hammer, often breaking the wooden lid. Wine sold in unopened cases is presumed, in the fine-wine market, to be worth sufficient premium that they are usually designated 'o.w.c.', or 'original wooden cases' in AUCTION catalogues. The German wine trade has long sold wine in six-bottle cartons and as wine PRICES rise, an increasing proportion of fine wine is offered in six-bottle cases.

A **split case** may be one that is torn, but may be one that contains six bottles of each of two different wines, or four bottles of each of three different wines. One bottle of each of 12 different wines becomes a **mixed case**.

casein, the principal milk PROTEIN, is used by winemakers as a FINING agent particularly useful for removing brown colours from white wines. It is also used to a lesser extent in the general CLARIFICATION of young wines. Precipitated from milk by the addition of ACIDS, casein is chiefly used in the form of sodium or potassium caseinate. When this salt is added to cloudy wine, it reacts with some of the wine acid forming a curd which adsorbs and precipitates most of the very small particles, including the PIGMENTS causing discoloration. In many countries, the use of casein must be declared on the label. See LABELLING INFORMATION.   A.D.W.

Casella Family Brands, Australian producer most famous for its YELLOW TAIL brand.

cask, wooden container for wine, often used interchangeably with BARREL, a cylindrical container small enough to be rolled. The term is also used less precisely, however, for any form of COOPERAGE, i.e. wooden containers of any size, whether larger, immobile storage containers such as the oval *Fuder* or *foudre* common in Germany and Alsace, or the *botte* of Italy, and also including quite large, immovable containers which may or may not be open topped.

In the 1970s, the Australian wine industry neatly, if misleadingly, coined the term **cask wine** for wine packaged in a bag packed inside a cardboard BOX, a wine type highly unlikely to have been either made or aged in wood of any sort (although OAK CHIPS may well have played a part in some).

cask ageing, winemaking practice of ageing a wine after fermentation (see ÉLEVAGE) in a large wooden container usually too old to impart any OAK FLAVOUR. It may well, however, exert some WOOD INFLUENCE and help considerably to achieve natural CLARIFICATION and STABILIZATION. White wines subjected to cask ageing for several months include some of the great white wines of the LOIRE, GERMANY, and ALSACE. Red wines subjected to cask ageing, sometimes for several years, include many of the traditional wines of the RHÔNE, ITALY, SPAIN, PORTUGAL, and GREECE.

The alternatives, and possible supplements, to cask ageing are BARREL MATURATION, AGEING in inert CONTAINERS such as stainless steel tanks, (with or without the use of INNER STAVES or OAK CHIPS), BOTTLE AGEING, and BOTTLING almost immediately after FERMENTATION as in NOUVEAU wines.

casse, historic wine FAULT involving spoilage either by an excess of IRON or COPPER or PROTEIN or TARTARIC ACID precipitation.

cassis is French for blackcurrant and is used often as a tasting note for red wines, particularly red wines based on Cabernet Sauvignon grapes. Dry white wine mixed with some blackcurrant liqueur is known as both a **vin blanc cassis** and KIR (while red wine mixed with blackcurrant liqueur is sometimes called a *cardinal*).

Cassis, small, mainly white wine appellation in PROVENCE. The encroachment of Greater Marseilles on this old fishing village keeps total plantings to just under 190 ha/470 acres in this sheltered amphitheatre, protected from the mistral by the Cap Canaille to the east, one of the highest cliffs in France.

Three-quarters of the wine is full, dry, herby white, made mainly from Clairette and Marsanne. A little rosé and even less red are also made, mainly from Mourvèdre (which ripens easily here—see nearby BANDOL), Grenache, and Cinsaut. Little Cassis is allowed to escape by the annual influx of summer visitors, however.

Castel, France's biggest wine company, was founded in Bordeaux by nine Castel brothers and sisters in 1949 and is still family-owned. As well as owning dozens of Bordeaux châteaux and selling prodigious quantities of wine, Castel is an important distributor of BEER and WATER in France and North Africa. Castel acquired BARTON & Guestier, the Bordeaux négociant, and bought the Nicolas retail chain in 1988, their chief rival Société des Vins de France in 1992, Domaines Virginie in the Languedoc in 1999, the British retail chain Oddbins in 2002 (which it subsequently sold off), and the Burgundy négociant Patriarche in 2011. It is also involved in a JOINT VENTURE for the production of Chinese wine and distribution ofFrench wines in CHINA with CHANGYU and, together with SUNTORY of Japan, owns a Bordeaux négociant and Chx Beaumont and Beychevelle.

Castelão, Portugal's usefully versatile, second most planted vine variety, having been definitively overtaken by Tinta Roriz (TEMPRANILLO) by 2012 when total Castelão plantings fell to 14,414 ha/35,602 acres. It makes varied but generally fruity, sometimes surprisingly long-lived reds all over southern Portugal. It is known variously as Periquita in Setúbal, João de Santarém in Oeste, and **Castelão Francês** in many regions.

Castel del Monte, DOC in PUGLIA in the far south east of Italy, associated with the NERO DI TROIA grape, although it may also be a 100% AGLIANICO or either of the two CABERNETS. The same flexible production rules are applied to the white, which was traditionally based on BOMBINO BIANCO, but varietal CHARDONNAY and SAUVIGNON BLANC are also allowed. Confusingly, no fewer than three parallel DOCGS were created in the early 2010s: Castel del Monte Bombino Nero DOCG, Castel del Monte Nero di Troia Riserva DOCG, and Castel del Monte Rosso Riserva DOCG (minimum 65% Nero di Troia), none with the track record for quality that this level implies. For more details, see PUGLIA.   W.S.

Castelli Romani, extensive DOC for the wines of the VOLCANIC hills south east of Rome in the region of LAZIO (see map under ITALY) which stretch from just outside the city gates (some of the vineyards are in fact within the administrative borders of the city) into the province of Latina, south of the township of Velletri. Nine different DOCS fall completely or partially within the zone, making Castelli Romani, once known for its MALVASIA-based whites, more akin to an IGT than a carefully delineated vineyard area. Except for the potentially interesting Cori DOC (based on the local BELLONE for whites and Nero Buono for reds), Colli Lanuvini (whites based on Malvasia and reds on Merlot and Sangiovese), and the recent, rather commercially opportunistic DOC Roma (a canvas for INTERNATIONAL VARIETIES blended with Malvasia in the case of whites and with Montepulciano for reds), the overwhelming majority of the DOCs are devoted to whites, of which the best known is the generally under-performing FRASCATI.

Malvasia is the traditional variety here and Malvasia di Candia is more widely grown than Malvasia di Lazio, principally for its high productivity, although better producers prefer the quality level of the latter. A wide variety of different strains of Trebbiano is also grown (Verde, Giallo, Toscano, Romagnolo, di Soave). High YIELDS—ranging from the 98 hl/ha (7 tons/acre) of the Colli Lanuvini to the more than 115 hl/ha of the Colli Albani and Marino—make many of the discussions of blends and subvarieties purely nugatory; interesting wines from Malvasia and Trebbiano cannot be made at these yields and there is little distinction between the wines of the different DOCs. Over three-quarters of the total production is in the hands of CO-OPERATIVES, the rest principally in the hands of large commercial wineries. Both have followed a marketing strategy based on high volume and low prices, counting on the advantages of the proximity of the millions of visitors who flock to Rome each year. If the Castelli Romani wines are principally intended for undiscriminating tourists, the character of the wines themselves has changed considerably. Once fermented on their skins, these wines were golden in colour, full in flavour and aroma. The colour deepened as the Malvasia, a variety whose wines oxidize quite rapidly, began to age, and the aromas and flavours followed suit. Modern Castelli Romani wines, from high-yielding vines, cold fermented off the skins, filtered, and stabilized, lack the defects of old but are essentially industrial. Several avant-garde estates in Marino and Frascati are producing good wines from Cabernet, Merlot, Syrah, Chardonnay, Sauvignon Blanc, and Viognier, while there is increasing interest in INDIGENOUS VARIETIES. The results have demonstrated that the soil and climate of the Castelli Romani can indeed produce good-quality wines, but few of these wines, self-consciously detached from the history and traditions of the zone, provide a key to resolving the area's viticultural problems, which, with a severe drop in demand for central Italy's standard Trebbiano–Malvasia wines, are becoming increasingly acute. This problem is exacerbated by high vineyard land PRICES, given that the hills are such an attractive place to live for Romans who want to distance themselves from the congestion of the city. For this reason, the total area of vineyard continues to shrink.

D.C.G. & W.S.

www.stradadeivinideicastelliromani.com

Castets, almost extinct vine, probably selected from an escaped seedling in a forest in the Aveyron, SOUTH WEST FRANCE. Unexpectedly, a parent of several NEW VARIETIES bred in SLOVAKIA in the 1970s.

Castilla, **Castile** in English, old central Spanish kingdom divided by mountains into CASTILLA Y LEÓN, or Old Castile, in the north and CASTILLA-LA MANCHA, or New Castile, in the south.

Castilla-La Mancha, known as Castile-La Mancha

in English (historically, Castilla la Nueva or New Castile), the lower, southern half of the plateau that makes up central Spain (see map under SPAIN). At elevations between 400 and 1,000 m (1,300–3,500 ft) above sea level, this is Spain at her most extreme. Winters are long and cold with temperatures often falling below 0 °C/32 °F for days on end. In summer the heat is gruelling. The thermometer regularly rises above 35 °C, even 40 °C (104 °F), and little if any rain falls between May and September. The vast expanse of country which is green in the spring quickly turns to a shade of burnt ochre in July and August as all but the deepest river beds dry up completely. The locals say that they suffer 'nine months of winter and three months of hell'. Despite these fierce conditions, Castilla-La Mancha produces half of all the wine made in Spain, with drip irrigation having amply compensated for the widespread vine pull since 2000. Around 465,000 ha/one million acres of vineyard yield an average of 20 million hl/530 million gal of wine (averaging much-increased yields of 43 hl/ha (2.6 tons/acre). One of Castilla-La Mancha's nine (plus eight PAGOS) DO regions, LA MANCHA itself, is planted mainly with the robust white wine vine AIRÉN.

Despite determined uprooting, there are still an estimated 180,000 ha of DROUGHT-resistant Airén in the zone of La Mancha alone (less than half of them producing DO wine), making it one of the world's most widely planted vine varieties—although Cencibel (alias TEMPRANILLO) has been catching up fast. By 2013 there were more than 73,000 ha in La Mancha alone and it dominates in the VALDEPEÑAS DO, while north west of Toledo, MÉNTRIDA produces sturdy reds from very ripe GARNACHA. Although the fourth DO, ALMANSA, belongs administratively to Castilla-La Mancha, the style of winemaking there is closer to that of the LEVANTE. MONASTRELL, Cencibel, and the red-fleshed Garnacha Tintorera are grown.

The mountainous DO of MONDÉJAR east of Madrid produces largely undistinguished reds, but the Ribera del Júcar and MANCHUELA DOs further east are producing much more interesting reds from Tempranillo, Syrah, and such INDIGENOUS VARIETIES as Bobal, Garnacha, and Monastrell, as well as possibly Spain's most fragrant renditions of Macabeo whites.

Attracted by the availability of grapes and low production costs, a number of large companies moved to the region bringing new winemaking technology with them. The large CO-OPERATIVES similarly modernized their production, although much of their bulk wine from Airén still goes into subsidized distillation (see WINE LAKE). So a new generation of cleanly made and often inexpensive red, rosé, and white wine from Castilla-La Mancha is finding favour with buyers both at home and abroad.

Another development that contrasts strongly with centuries of bulk wine production has been a blossoming of distinguished single-estate wines that have vastly outgrown clichés about La Mancha wines, all of them inspired by the pioneering efforts of the Marqués de Griñón at his Dominio de Valdepusa.   V. de la S.

www.lamanchawines.com

Castilla y León, Castile and León in

English, is the largest of the 17 autonomous regions of Spain. This northern part of Spain's central plateau, rising to between 880 and 1,000 m (2,900–3,300 ft) above sea level, takes up about a fifth of the entire country. Centred on its capital, the university city of Valladolid, most of Castilla y León is thinly populated table land almost encircled by mountains. It is separated from the hub of Spain (MADRID and CASTILLA-LA MANCHA or New Castile) by the central mountain range which rises to over 2,000 m near Avila and Segovia (see map under SPAIN). To the north, the Cordillera Cantabrica, which peaks at over 2,600 m, deflects the maritime influence of the Bay of Biscay.

The climate here is harsh. Short, hot summers are followed by long, cold winters when temperatures can drop to −10 °C/14 °F. Under often clear skies, temperatures drop quickly after sunset and, even in summer, nights are cool. FROST continues to be a threat until mid May. Rain falls mainly in winter and amounts to between 400 and 500 mm (15–19 in) a year. Much of the land is poor and unable to support anything other than nomadic flocks of sheep. However, the river Duero (known as DOURO in Portugal), which cuts a broad valley in the rather featureless plain, provides a natural water source. Grain, sugar beet, and vines are grown along its length.

A regional variant of the red TEMPRANILLO vine, variously called Tinta del País, Tinto Fino, Tinto Aragonés, and Tinta de Toro, is the chief good-quality grape variety in four of the nine DO wine regions in Castilla y León. The largest of these is RIBERA DEL DUERO, which extends for about 100 km/60 miles either side of the river and is internationally known for its red wines. Downstream of Ribera del Duero, since the 1990s RUEDA has established itself as Spain's leading white wine region while neighbouring TORO, straddling the Duero near the Portuguese border, gained worldwide recognition a decade later. CIGALES, north of Valladolid, specializes in rosé wine. BIERZO, abutting GALICIA in the north west, shows promise with its fragrant, characterful reds from the MENCÍA grape.   V. de la S.

Castillon. Named after the town of Castillon-la-Bataille, the battle being that which brought an end to the HUNDRED YEARS WAR, **Castillon Côtes de Bordeaux** is a dynamic, well-priced red wine appellation, part of the Côtes de BORDEAUX group, effectively an eastern extension of ST-ÉMILION in Bordeaux. With 1,850 ha/4,570 acres of vineyard in 2013 on mixed soils of clay, limestone, and some sandstone with silt, sand, and stones on the alluvial terrace above the River Dordogne, it is much bigger than its northern neighbour FRANCS but produces similarly sturdy red wines based on Merlot grapes with generally better structure than regular red BORDEAUX AOC. Vineyards closest to the river tend to produce more supple wine than those at higher elevations such as Ch de Belcier, one of the more important producers. The region, whose land is still relatively affordable, has benefited from the application of expertise from grander right-bank appellations.

Cataluña, **Catalonia** in English, a proud and industrious region on the Mediterranean coast which encompasses a part of southern France (see ROUSSILLON) and a part of north east Spain (see maps under FRANCE and SPAIN), some of whose inhabitants do not consider themselves French or Spanish, and even if they do, think of themselves as Catalan first. Cataluña is one of Spain's 17 autonomous regions with Barcelona its capital.

Barcelona and its densely populated hinterland is a hive of enterprise and industry and it is therefore no coincidence that Cataluña was at the vanguard of Spain's 20th-century winemaking revolution. The region began to stir in the early 1870s when José Raventos began making sparkling wine by the TRADITIONAL METHOD in the small town of Sant Sadurni d'Anoia. He founded the giant CODORNÍU firm, and his foresight generated the CAVA industry which earned its own Denominación de Origen (see DO) in 1986.

In addition to most of Spain's Cava, Cataluña produces an eclectic range of wines from traditional, powerful reds to cool-fermented dry whites.

Much of the credit for the transformation of Cataluña's wine industry in the late 20th century must go to the late Don Miguel Torres Carbó and his son Miguel A. TORRES, who imported INTERNATIONAL VINE VARIETIES to plant alongside INDIGENOUS VARIETIES such as GARNACHA, MONASTRELL, and TEMPRANILLO (called Ull de Llebre in

Catalan), and the Cava grapes, PARELLADA, MACABEO, and XARELLO.

The climate in Cataluña is strongly influenced by the Mediterranean. The coastal belt is warm and equable with moderate rainfall but conditions become progressively more arid and extreme further inland. There are ten DO regions: ALELLA, EMPORDÀ, CONCA DE BARBERÁ, COSTERS DEL SEGRE, MONTSANT, PENEDÈS, PLA DE BAGES, PRIORAT, TARRAGONA, and TERRA ALTA plus the new, controversial catch-all DO CATALUNYA. Of these, Penedès is the most important in terms of quantity, although the late-20th-century transformation of Priorat resulted in some of Spain's highest wine prices.

Cataluña has long been an important centre of CORK production and is a particularly important source of corks for sparkling wines.   V. de la S.

Catalunya, local Catalan name for the region of CATALUÑA and controversial DO created in the early 21st century for blends of wines made from anywhere in the region. The big bottlers such as TORRES were the chief proponents and are the chief beneficiaries.

Catarratto, Sicilian white grape variety that may well be the most widely planted grape variety in Italy. According to the 2010 Italian grape census, which distinguishes between **Catarratto Bianco Comune** and the less common but better quality **Catarratto Bianco Lucido**, probably two clones of the same variety, plantings still totalled 34,793 ha/ nearly 86,000 acres, despite EU efforts to diminish this total. The variety is planted almost exclusively in the far western province of Trapani and was in the past much used for the production of MARSALA. Today, it can be expected that much of the vine's produce is regarded as SURPLUS and is therefore either compulsorily distilled by the EU, or transformed into GRAPE CONCENTRATE. Despite its profusion, the variety is specified in the regulations of just three DOC zones; familiarity seems to have bred the usual contempt from locals. See SICILY for more details.

Catawba, deep pink-skinned American grape variety that was extremely popular in the 19th century and is still grown to a certain extent, particularly in NEW YORK State. Identified in North Carolina in 1802, even before CONCORD, it produces white and pink, still and sparkling rather FOXY wines from dry to very sweet.

catechin and its isomer **epicatechin** are PHENOLIC compounds (see also FLAVONOIDS) found mainly in grape seeds, but also in stems and berry skins and, in lower amounts, in flesh. They contribute to bitterness in wines and are the constitutive units of TANNINS (see also PROANTHOCYANIDINS), which are responsible for astringency and increasing the stability

of ANTHOCYANINS (see CO-PIGMENTATION and PIGMENTED TANNINS), leading to longer-lived COLOUR in wines. Because of the increased SKIN CONTACT involved during RED WINEMAKING, catechin concentrations are usually higher in red wines than in whites, but they are involved in browning reactions in both red and white wine. Catechin may play a role in protecting vine parts from microbial attack as a pre-existing chemical barrier, but it is also produced by vines in response to DOWNY MILDEW infection.

Catechin and epicatechin but also, by extension, other flavanol monomers such as gallocatechin and epigallocatechin, are often referred to as **catechins**. Like other flavonoids, catechins are antioxidant compounds that may contribute to the HEALTH benefits of moderate wine consumption. The study of catechins has been overshadowed by that of RESVERATROL and related stilbenes, which are present in wine in much lower concentrations. Perhaps this is because unlike resveratrol, these compounds are widely present in other fruits and vegetables and other beverages such as teas.

The concentrations of catechins vary with vine variety, with PINOT NOIR, then MERLOT, notably high among well-known red wine grapes, and SYRAH lowest. As with resveratrol, cool, damp climates seem to stimulate more catechin synthesis than do hot, dry ones.   G.L.C., R.E.S, & V.C.

Goldberg, D. M., et al., 'Catechin and Epicatechin. Concentrations of red wines: regional and cultivar-related differences', *American Journal of Enology and Viticulture*, 49 (1998), 23–34.

cation exchange is a process by which cations (positively charged ions) in solution in a soil exchange with other cations that are held on negatively charged CLAY and ORGANIC MATTER. These cations are called exchangeable cations and the amount held per kilogram of soil defines the CATION EXCHANGE CAPACITY. Cation exchange can result in potentially toxic concentrations of exchangeable ALUMINIUM in very acid soils (soil PH less than 5), whereas exchange of SODIUM for CALCIUM cations in soils with high concentrations of soluble salts can lead to very high pH soils (greater than pH 9) when the salts are leached out. See also ION EXCHANGE.   R.E.W.

White, R. E., *Understanding Vineyard Soils* (2nd edn, Oxford, 2015).

cation exchange capacity (CEC), the amount of positively charged ions a soil can hold, is a significant factor in the degree to which SOIL NUTRIENTS are available to the vine. CEC is determined by SOIL TEXTURE, the amount of ORGANIC MATTER in the soil, and the amount and type of CLAY. Sandy soil has a low CEC. Fine-textured soil such as clay, with a high level of organic matter, tends to have a high CEC.

Cato, Marcus (234–149 BC), Roman statesman advanced as a writer on agricultural and viticulture matters, known as 'Cato the Elder' or 'Cato the Censor' to distinguish him from his great-grandson. He grew up on his father's farm near Reate, north east of Rome, then fought against CARTHAGE in the Second Punic War and afterwards had a distinguished political career. He became known as a strict moralist, castigating the 'new' extravagance, ostentation, and luxury and advocating a return to the 'old' virtues of austerity, honesty, and hard work. He wrote books on many subjects and published his speeches. PLINY the Elder praises him for the breadth of his learning (*Natural History* 25. 4), and COLUMELLA (*De re rustica* 1. 1. 12) and Cicero (*Brutus* 16. 61) honour him as the father of Latin prose. His only surviving work, *De agri cultura* ('Concerning the cultivation of the land'), also known as *De re rustica* ('Concerning country matters'), is important not only because it is the first lengthy prose work in Latin. *De agri cultura* is not divided into books or arranged systematically in any other way: Cato's remarks on viticulture and winemaking are scattered throughout the treatise. The advice he gives is of a severely practical kind. His prime concern is making farming, including wine-growing, profitable through hard work and careful management. For instance, he stresses that the grapes should always be thoroughly ripe when harvested, or one's wine will lose its good reputation. And in the making and storing of wine he was aware of the importance of HYGIENE to prevent the wine turning to VINEGAR. After the vintage, the wine jars should be wiped twice a day, each with its own broom. After 30 days, when FERMENTATION is complete, the jars should be sealed or the wine can be drawn off its LEES if desired as an alternative to LEES CONTACT. The type of estate he has in mind produces chiefly wine and olive oil: hence his extensive section on the construction of presses.　　　H.M.W.

Astin, A. S., *Cato the Censor* (Oxford, 1978).
Thielschen, P., *Des Marcus Catos Belehrung über die Landwirtschaft* (Berlin, 1963).

caudalie, French term for a unit of sensory measurement equal to one second's LENGTH of a wine's impact on the palate after swallowing or spitting.

Cava, Spanish SPARKLING WINES made using the traditional method of SPARKLING WINEMAKING. The term Cava was adopted by the Spanish in 1970 when they agreed to abandon the use of the potentially misleading term Champaña. The word originates in CATALUÑA, which produces most but not all Cava, where it means 'cellar'. It was here in the town of Sant Sadurní d'Anoia that José Raventós, head of the family firm of CODORNÍU, made the first bottles of traditional method sparkling wine after a visit to France in 1872. Early growth in the industry coincided with the arrival of the PHYLLOXERA louse, which first appeared in Catalan vineyards in the 1880s. Vineyards that had once made sturdy red wines had to be uprooted and were replanted with MACABEO, PARELLADA, and XARELLO, the triad of grape varieties which is the mainstay of the Cava industry to this day. In 1889, the Raventos family were joined by Pedro Ferrer, who founded the firm of FREIXENET. Codorníu and Freixenet, both still family owned, are now two of the largest sparkling wine producers in the world, with their own winery outposts in CALIFORNIA.

Unlike any other Spanish DO, the Cava denominación is not restricted to a single delimited area. However, since Spain joined the EU in 1986, the EU authorities have insisted that Cava should be made from grapes grown in prescribed regions. As a result, the use of the term Cava is restricted to sparkling wines from a list of municipalities in Catalonia, VALENCIA, ARAGÓN, NAVARRA, RIOJA, and the BASQUE country. Ninety-five per cent of all Cava is made in Cataluña, however, mostly in and around the town of Sant Sadurní d'Anoia. Total production amounts to over 1.2 million hl/31 million gal a year (about a third that of Champagne).

The light, aromatic Macabeo (the Viura of Rioja) comprises about half of the blend for a typical Cava, its late BUDBREAK making it a popular choice for vineyards prone to spring frosts. The productive and indigenous Xarello vine which thrives at relatively low elevations is the second most important, and its earthy aroma has been one of Cava's distinguishing features. Parellada performs better above 300 m/900 ft, where it produces finer wines relatively low in BODY. Plantings of the French vine CHARDONNAY, officially authorized for Cava in 1986, seem to have peaked at 1,500 ha/3,700 acres, mostly around Sant Sadurní d'Anoia. The dark-skinned varieties GARNACHA, MONASTRELL, PINOT NOIR, and TREPAT are also permitted, Trepat only in rosé.

To qualify for the DO, Cava must be made according to the local, and in some respects less rigorous, adaptation of the champagne traditional method. The wine must spend at least nine months on its lees before DISGORGEMENT, achieve at least four atmospheres of pressure, and attain an ALCOHOLIC STRENGTH of 10.8–12.8% by volume. YIELDS, set at a maximum of 1 hl of must per 150 kg of grapes, are higher than those allowed in Champagne. Most REMUAGE is now carried out automatically in a *girasol* or GYROPALETTE, a Spanish invention which enables hundreds of bottles to be handled at a time.

The best Cavas have increasingly been produced by smaller, more artisanal firms such as Recaredo and Gramona. But the perceived mass-market image of the appellation has led to a growing disenchantment among better quality producers. By 2014 a number of them in Penedès—including Raventòs i Blanc, Albet i Noya, Mas Comptal, Loxarel, Colet, and Mas Bertran—had left the appellation altogether and joined the PENEDÈS DO. A new classification for single-vineyard Cava, Cava del Paraje Calificado, was introduced in 2014.　　V. de la S.

www.crcava.es

cave, French for a CELLAR or winemaking establishment and as close as the French language comes to an equivalent of a WINERY. A **caviste** is French for a specialist wine retailer, of which there are surprisingly few in France, presumably since so many consumers buy direct from the producer. See also CHAI.

cave co-opérative, French for one of France's nearly 700 wine CO-OPERATIVES. They vinify nearly 40% of all AOC wine and more than 70% of IGP.

http://www.coopdefrance.coop/

Cayetana, high-yielding Spanish white grape variety travelling under many aliases, including Pardina and Jaén Blanco in Spain and Mourisco Branco in Portugal where there were more than 1,000 ha in 2012. Official 2011 Spanish vine statistics still distinguished between the synonyms, but plantings totalled more than 39,000 ha/96,6000 acres. It produces low-acid, neutral-flavoured wines which oxidize easily. It is particularly popular, as Pardina, in the EXTREMADURA region, especially in Badajoz province on the border with Portugal, where much of its produce is distilled into Brandy de Jerez. In Rioja it may be known as Cazagal, and Baladí is another synonym. The variety is closely related to many other Iberian varieties.

Robinson, J., Harding, J., and Vouillamoz, J., *Wine Grapes: A Complete Guide to 1,368 Vine Varieties, Including their Origins and Flavours* (London, 2012).

Cayuga White, AMERICAN HYBRID with SEYVAL genes released in 1972 from Geneva in New York (see CORNELL). It is grown in the north east of the UNITED STATES and makes fruity white wines.

Cebreros, wine zone in CASTILLA Y LEÓN in west-central Spain, little known despite its outstanding feature, very old GARNACHA vineyards on steep SLATE slopes.

CEC. See CATION EXCHANGE CAPACITY.

cell, the structural unit of living organisms, the smallest unit capable of independent existence. YEAST and BACTERIA are examples of single cells while one grapevine has billions of cells. Each plant cell consists of a protoplast surrounded by a cell wall, but it can be differentiated into a host of forms. A cell in the flesh of a ripe grape berry, for example, can be 0.5 mm/0.02 in in length with a thin, wavy cell wall lined by an equally thin cytoplasm surrounding the vacuole, a 'sea' of water with dissolved sugars, acids, and hundreds of other solutes, otherwise known as grape juice. Other cells within the berry can be entirely different. A PHLOEM element aligns end to end with others to form a tube through which elaborated sap moves in a network throughout the plant. Adjacent fibre cells in the XYLEM are long and slim with thick walls hardened by the wood polymer, lignin. The complex functioning of the leaf provides other examples of cell forms: STOMATAL cells function to allow carbon dioxide in and oxygen and water vapour out; others function as the 'carbohydrate factory'; and cells in its dense network of veins are designed to move water and minerals up from the roots (in the xylem) and to move sugars and other elaborated organic nutrients out to the rest of the plant (in the phloem).

Despite this diversity, all cells of a plant have the same genetic information in their nuclei and, with some exceptions, may be separated and cultured as single protoplasts. By TISSUE CULTURE methods, these can then be used for the regeneration of another plant like the parent. The genetic material in each cell will therefore be 'tuned' for its differentiation and functioning by the dictate of its neighbours in that tissue and by its reaction to signals received from other tissues and organs.   B.G.C.

Taiz, L., and Zeiger, E., *Plant Physiology* (5th edn, Sunderland, Mass., 2010).

cellar, widely used word that is roughly the English counterpart to CAVE, CANTINA, and BODEGA in French, Italian, and Spanish respectively. It can therefore be applied to both wine shops and winemaking premises, but is here considered only in its domestic sense, as a collection of wine and the place in which it is stored.

Location

Traditional underground cellars have the great advantages of being secure, dark, at a constant low temperature without recourse to external energy sources, slightly damp, and rarely disturbed. As outlined in STORING WINE, these constitute ideal conditions. Few modern dwellings have anywhere that enjoys all these advantages, and to re-create them it may be necessary to spend lavishly on specialist help in constructing or adapting quarters with low lighting levels and specially controlled temperature and humidity (and as few visitors as the expender of all this money and effort can bear). It is also possible to buy special cabinets which look like refrigerators and can be programmed to maintain certain temperature and humidity levels,

but they are expensive and guzzle energy relative to their capacity. Less expensive options include insulating a small room or large cupboard, insulating a space under some stairs, using a dark corner of a distant spare room or a closet against an outside wall, or a secure outhouse (although care must be taken that the TEMPERATURE never falls so low as to freeze the wine and push the corks out). It is important that any makeshift cellar is far from any heat source, even a hot water pipe and, especially, a boiler, but a constant medium temperature is less harmful than violent temperature swings. Those living on ground level can even excavate, and depend on a trapdoor.

Accessibility is an advantage or disadvantage depending on the cellar owner's personality and attitude towards the cellar. Paying for professional storage may be the only realistic option for some, but in this case cellar records (see below) are essential.

Design

Wine can be stored in the unopened CASES in which it is bought, but this is practical only for wines years away from being ready to drink, and very steady and sturdy shelves are needed if more than one layer of cases is to be stacked. A system which incorporates cases without lids on individual runners is particularly space-efficient. Wine racks take up more room but allow bottles to be kept horizontal and corks damp (not strictly necessary for bottles with SCREWCAPS or SPARKLING WINE) and retrieved individually. Racks with slots for individual bottles offer the best access for very mixed cellars (metal and wood is the usual combination of materials used for these racks), but larger compartments, or BINS, can be used for larger quantities of bottles of the same wine.

It of course makes sense to keep the wines nearest MATURITY in the most accessible positions and vice versa (which dictates how wines may be kept in double-depth racks). There will be a slight temperature variation between the top and bottom of the cellar. Light levels are also likely to be higher at the top than the bottom, so there are at least two reasons why the fullest, least fragile, slowest maturing wines such as vintage port should be stored at the top and bottles as sensitive as, say, those containing sparkling wines should be stored close to floor level.

Contents

There is little point in devoting space and capital to storing wine unless it is difficult or expensive to replace (such as an EN PRIMEUR rarity), or will positively improve as a result of BOTTLE AGEING. It may therefore be worthwhile keeping the last bottle of nuptial champagne or holiday souvenir purely for sentimental reasons, but in general it is wise to be ruthless

about cellar space. Space in wine books and magazines is often devoted to a concept called the 'ideal cellar' and the recommendations usually make interesting reading, but in truth there is no such thing and an individual's ideal depends entirely on his or her tastes and consumption patterns. Even the advice that NON-VINTAGE champagne is always improved by a year or so in a personal cellar may be questionable in an era of champagne glut.

Records

Cellar records are not necessary but they can add to the pleasure of wine collectors with a love of order and memorabilia. (The other school enjoys the twin elements of chaos and serendipity in plundering their wine cellars.) Traditional cellar records have a good-sized page for each case of wine acquired, stating price, supplier, and date of purchase. Below this a dated tasting note for each bottle tasted can be inserted, together perhaps with details of the circumstances in which it was opened. The pages can be grouped by wine type (red bordeaux, for example) and individual bottles can be grouped appropriately together on pages. (Those using professional wine storage need, for obvious reasons, to keep full details of where and since when the wine has been stored.)

INFORMATION TECHNOLOGY can offer other, often much more sophisticated and flexible, possibilities for cellar record-keeping but it is worth remembering that individual wines are usually kept for many years longer than a home computer. CELLARTRACKER and its imitators store personal cellar records in cyberspace.

See also STORING WINE.

Gold, R., *How and Why to Build a Wine Cellar* (4th edn, San Francisco, 2007).
Sims, P., *Home Wine Cellar* (Toronto, 2004).

cellar door has a very specific meaning in Australia where it denotes the physical interface between a winery and its visiting customers. (It is also an expression famous for how beautiful it sounds to anglophones, regardless of its meaning.) See TOURISM.

cellar rat, colloquial term for a relatively junior WINERY worker, especially itinerant ones following in the footsteps of FLYING WINEMAKERS.

CellarTracker, WEBSITE that houses the world's largest collection of TASTING NOTES, more than 5 million by 2015. This fully searchable database is free to use (a donation is optional) and is made up of contributions from well over 300,000 mainly amateur users all over the globe. It was set up in 2003 by Eric LeVine, then employed by Microsoft, as a personal cellar-management tool but the SOCIAL MEDIA implications rapidly became apparent. Today wine lovers enjoy sharing impressions and keeping track of their own wine collections and those of others. The site is integrated with those of a host of WINE WRITERS.

www.cellartracker.com

cellar work, general term for all the processing steps requiring human intervention or monitoring in WINEMAKING. In its most general sense it encompasses all operations included in winemaking. In the narrower human sense of what cellar workers actually do, apart from overseeing grape reception, DESTEMMING, CRUSHING, FERMENTATION, CLARIFICATION, FILTRATION, BLENDING, STABILIZATION, and BOTTLING, it generally entails operating PUMPS, adding FINING agents and other additions or processing aids, and almost constant cleaning (see HYGIENE). Cellars in which small barrels are used for both fermentation and maturation involve the most physical work, including filling, RACKING and moving barrels, TOPPING UP, and possibly STIRRING. See also ÉLEVAGE.

Celts, peoples who inhabited western Europe before the rise of Ancient ROME. Many of them were introduced to wine by the Romans, when some were already skilled COOPERS.

The first clear evidence that wine drinking with its attendant rituals was penetrating the courts of the prehistoric barbarian élites in western central Europe (eastern France, southern Germany, and Switzerland) appears in the archaeological record in the 6th century BC.

Griffon-headed cauldrons, CRATERS, jugs and strainers, and fine painted Attic cups, all of which would have been used at a Greek SYMPOSIUM, were shipped to Mediterranean ports such as Massilia (Marseilles). From there they were transported along the navigable RIVERS into the hinterland to be used in the complex systems of gift exchange which bound these peoples to the Greek and Etruscan traders of the south. Along with these trappings of civilization came wine. How much of it, if any, was at this stage Greek or Italian is difficult to tell. What is certain is that the large ceramic AMPHORAE in which the wine was transported inland were manufactured along the coast of southern France in the vicinity of Marseilles, suggesting, but not proving, that most of the wine consumed was locally manufactured.

The courts of the élite, places such as Mont Lassois on the main south–north trade route between Burgundy and Paris (where the celebrated Vix crater, a bronze vase 1.64 m/5.4 ft high and clearly made in Ancient GREECE, was found), and Heuneburg in Germany, lasted for a comparatively short time. They were flourishing in the 530s and 520s BC but had ceased to exist by the end of the next century as the old social order collapsed in a turmoil of unrest caused by migrating bands of Celts who were to thrust deep into Italy, Greece, and Turkey.

By the end of the 3rd century BC, a new order was beginning to emerge in the western Mediterranean. Rome was growing rapidly in power and had won a decisive victory over the CARTHAGINIANS in Spain, but their military involvement was to last for almost two centuries before the peninsula could be regarded as fully conquered. This meant a continuous movement of military detachments, supplies, and officials using the ports and the roads in southern France linking Italy and Spain. Inevitably the cities and the native tribes of Provence and Languedoc got used to this traffic and no doubt profited from it. So too did Roman entrepreneurs keen to exploit the new markets being opened up. For them the love of wine which the Celtic tribes of the interior so evidently possessed was a heaven-sent opportunity to offload, with profit, the considerable wine surpluses being generated by the large estates of northern and western Italy. As one contemporary writer somewhat incredulously remarked of the Celts of GAUL, 'They will give you a slave for an amphora of wine thus exchanging the cupbearer for the cup.' While this does not necessarily imply the actual exchange rate it shows which surpluses the two societies were prepared to exchange with each other for mutual benefit.

In the Celtic world it was important for those aspiring to power to host elaborate feasts to entertain their followers and others. The more exotic the commodities offered, the greater the status of the host. Wine from the south was in considerable demand and was avidly consumed. The drunken Celt who took his wine undiluted—something no civilized man would have done—was several times remarked upon by contemporary writers.

Wine was usually transported by sea in large ceramic amphorae made in distinctive styles and fabrics which can be quite closely dated and assigned to specific localities of manufacture. This means that it is possible to study the developing wine trade in some detail, and, since several of the estates produced amphorae with their own identifying stamps, individual marketing strategies can be identified. By studying the relative proportions of Italic and local amphorae in the successive levels of settlement sites in southern France, it is possible to show that throughout the 2nd century BC, when Provence and Languedoc were finally annexed by Rome, there is little trace in the archaeological record that local wine was drunk at all. In parallel with this, the number of shipwrecks containing amphorae found off the southern French coast increases noticeably, presumably reflecting the corresponding increase in the volume of trade.

Once offloaded at ports such as Massilia and Narbo (Narbonne), the amphorae were transported inland by road or river. En route a *portorium* (or transport tax) was charged at each settlement through which the wine passed, trebling the price charged by the time it eventually reached the native consumers. From the borders of Provincia of Ancient Rome, modern Provence, the wine penetrated the territory of the neighbouring tribes. At two locations, one just outside Toulouse and the other at Chalon-sur-Saône, substantial quantities of discarded Italian amphorae have been found. No precise count can now be made but estimates in the tens of thousands are unlikely to be far from the truth. These must surely be major transshipment points where wine was decanted into skins or BARRELS (for which the Celts of the CAHORS region were particularly famed) for the more arduous journeys by cart into the wild interior. Not all wine was decanted, however. Considerable numbers of amphorae have been recovered from major native *oppida* (towns) at Montmerlhe, Essalois, Jœuvres, and Mont-Beuvray between 20 and 100 km (12–62 miles) beyond the frontier. From here much of it passed into the hands of the local nobility to be consumed with relish in their lavish feasts.

The volume of wine imported into Gaul at this time is difficult to estimate in detail but a conservative assessment suggests that it may have reached 100,000 hl/2.6 million gal a year. When it is remembered that the largest trading system operating in pre-industrial Europe—the Gascon wine trade to Britain and Flanders in the 14th century (see BORDEAUX)—was 750,000 hl/20 million gal a year, the intensity of the Roman operation can be appreciated.

By the end of the 2nd century BC Italian wine was reaching all parts of France mainly along the navigable rivers but some, still in its amphorae, was being reloaded on to ships in the GIRONDE estuary to be transported along the Atlantic coast of France to Brittany. There much of it was consumed, but a small quantity was carried by Breton sailors on the last leg of its journey via Guernsey to the British port on Hengistbury Head, overlooking Christchurch harbour, constituting the earliest attested importation of wine to ENGLAND, or Britain. One wonders whether after such a journey it was even barely drinkable. B.C.

Cunliffe, B., *Greeks, Romans & Barbarians: Spheres of Interaction* (London, 1988).

Tchernia, A., *Le Vin de l'Italie romaine* (Paris, 1986).

Tchernia, A., 'Italian Wine in Gaul at the end of the Republic', in P. Garnsey, K. Hopkins, and C. R. Whittaker (eds.), *Trade in the Ancient Economy* (London, 1983).

Cencibel, synonym for the Spanish black grape variety TEMPRANILLO, especially in central and southern Spain, notably in LA MANCHA and VALDEPEÑAS, where it is the principal dark-skinned variety.

Central Coast, one of CALIFORNIA's umbrella AVAS, this sprawling wine region technically encompasses all of the land from San Francisco to Los Angeles, and inland from the coast almost to the CENTRAL VALLEY. In practice, the important and unique viticultural areas referenced by the name are concentrated in a mid-section of this too-broad appellation, the counties of MONTEREY, SAN LUIS OBISPO, and SANTA BARBARA.

Central Ranges Zone, Australian zone in NEW SOUTH WALES comprising the Cowra, Mudgee, and Orange regions.

Central Valley. In CALIFORNIA, this great expanse is divided into the SACRAMENTO VALLEY in the north, which produces small quantities of wine, and the vast SAN JOAQUIN VALLEY in the south, which supplies the majority of the state's BULK WINE (and TABLE GRAPES and RAISINS). Plumbed by an extensive system of rivers out of the Sierra Nevada and IRRIGATION canals built since the 1920s, this large, fertile, sunny region is arguably the most productive farmland in the world with more agricultural output than the whole of China until 1990.

The Sacramento river from the north and the San Joaquin River from the south drain into the **Central Valley Delta**, which includes such AVAS as CLARKSBURG and, on slightly higher ground, LODI. One-third of America's produce comes from here.

CHILE also has a Central Valley, a large region comprising the subregions (from north to south) Maipo, Rapel, Maule, and Southern, and an appellation commonly found on many wine labels, especially those grown in more than one region.

Central Victoria, zone within the Australian state of VICTORIA comprising the Bendigo, Goulburn Valley, Heathcote, Strathbogie Ranges, and Upper Goulburn regions.

centrifugation, winemaking operation of CLARIFICATION using a **centrifuge**. In the past this has been used to clarify white grape juice before FERMENTATION, but the process is relatively expensive and slow. It is more effective when used to clarify new wines because of the greater difference in DENSITY between the yeast cells and the liquid than between the grape solids and the liquid.

While the force used in natural clarification is gravity, the centrifugal force used in centrifugation is 5,000 to 10,000 times greater and requires large amounts of electrical power and expensive specialist equipment to process only relatively small amounts of wine per hour. A.D.W. & P.J.W.

Centurian, CALIFORNIA vine cross with the same parentage as CARNELIAN but released three years later in 1975. The state's total acreage had fallen to less than 100 acres by 2011, all in the central SAN JOAQUIN VALLEY. It has viticultural advantages over Carnelian but no organoleptic distinction.

cépage, French for VINE VARIETY. A VARIETAL wine, one that is sold by the name of the principal grape variety from which it is made is known as a **vin de cépage** within France, a term which has had some pejorative sense in comparison with a geographically named wine which qualifies as APPELLATION CONTRÔLÉE. High-quality vine varieties such as Syrah (as opposed to such traditional varieties as Carignan and Alicante Bouschet) are described as **cépages améliorateurs**, or 'improving varieties', in the south of France.

Cerceal, or **Cerceal Branco**, white Portuguese grape variety with high acidity found mainly in the DOURO, DÃO, and BAIRRADA. Not the same as the SERCIAL of MADEIRA.

Cercial is the BAIRRADA synonym for Cerceal Branco, also known as Cercial do Douro.

Cerdon. See BUGEY.

Cereza, quantitively very significant pink-skinned grape variety in ARGENTINA where it is second only to Malbec in the total area planted: 28,189 ha/69,626 acres in 2011. A CROSS between CRIOLLA CHICA and MUSCAT OF ALEXANDRIA which takes its name from the Spanish for cherry, it produces mainly white and some rosé wine of extremely mediocre quality for early consumption within Argentina, typically sold in cardboard packs, as well as being used for GRAPE CONCENTRATE.

Cérons, historic (see BORDEAUX, history) but struggling sweet white wine appellation on the left bank of the River GARONNE. Just north of BARSAC and SAUTERNES, it produces wines which rarely demonstrate either the finesse of the first or the concentration of the second of these two more famous appellations, possibly partly because much more generous YIELDS are allowed, but also because selling prices make sacrifices for quality difficult. In effect, Cérons is a buffer zone between Barsac and the GRAVES, and its dry whites and reds are entitled to the Graves appellation. Clay is slightly more common here than in Barsac and Sauternes and the generally flatter land may also play a part in reducing the likelihood of BOTRYTIS. Less than 40 ha produced sweet whites in the early 2010s.

certified planting material, budwood, cuttings, or grafted plants which have normally been through a form of quality assurance to ensure trueness to type, freedom from known virus diseases and bacterial diseases, and typically designated clonal origin. Various bodies, often government controlled, offer such certification programmes around the world. See CLONE, CLONAL SELECTION, and VINE IMPROVEMENT.

Cesanese, the red grape variety of LAZIO. The superior **Cesanese d'Affile** clone (a minor ingredient in the cult wine Trinoro of southern Tuscany) is very slightly more common than **Cesanese Comune**, which has larger berries and is also known as Bonvino Nero. Total plantings of both were only 670 ha/1,656 acres in 2010.

César, minor vine speciality of the far north of Burgundy, where it can contribute backbone to such light, soft reds as IRANCY. DNA PROFILING at DAVIS suggested it is a progeny of PINOT and Argant.

Chablis is the uniquely steely, dry, age-worthy white wine of the most northern vineyards of BURGUNDY in north east France, made, like all fine white Burgundy, from Chardonnay grapes. Paradoxically, however, in the New World, particularly in North America in whose vineyards a wine as austere as Chablis is virtually impossible to produce, the name Chablis has been borrowed as a GENERIC name for the most basic white wine. The true Chablis appellation has increased considerably since the early 1990s and in 2012 included a total of 5,284 ha/just over 13,000 acres of Chardonnay vineyard around the small town of Chablis and 19 other villages and hamlets in the *département* of the Yonne, near the city of AUXERRE. Created in 1938, the Chablis appellation comprises four ranks, of which the top is grand cru Chablis, with seven named vineyards. Then come the premiers crus, including 40 vineyard names, then Chablis, by far the most common and infuriatingly variable appellation, and finally Petit Chablis, the lowliest. The best vineyard sites are on the south west facing slopes of the valley of the Serein, the small river that flows through Chablis to join the Yonne.

Chablis is quite separate from the rest of Burgundy, divided from the CÔTE D'OR by the hills of the Morvan, so that BEAUNE, for example, is over 100 km/62 miles to the south. In fact, the vineyards of Chablis are much closer to CHAMPAGNE and its southernmost vineyards in the Aube *département*, than to the rest of Burgundy, and until early in this century it was not unusual for wine from Chablis to find its way into the champagne makers' cellars in Rheims and Épernay.

History

Although it was the Romans who introduced vines to Chablis, as to so many other parts of FRANCE, it was the medieval church, notably the Cistercian MONKS of the nearby abbey of Pontigny, who firmly established viticulture as an essential part of the rural economy, possibly even introducing the Chardonnay vine. See BURGUNDY, history.

Towards the end of the 19th century, the Yonne as a whole was a flourishing wine region, with some 40,000 ha of vines. Vineyards lined the banks of the River Yonne, as far as Joigny and Sens. The best known of these Yonne wines was Chablis and the name was used to describe the ample quantities of dry white wine that was transported with great convenience along the Rivers Yonne and Seine to satisfy the vast and thirsty Parisian market.

Three factors were responsible for the sharp decline in the vineyard area at the end of the 19th century: first POWDERY MILDEW, which appeared in Chablis in 1886, for which a cure had already been found, as had one for PHYLLOXERA, which first reached Chablis in 1887. However, many growers were reluctant to replant their vineyards, for the opening of the Paris–Lyons–Marseilles RAILWAY in 1856 considerably reduced their share of the Paris market. Thanks to the railways, Chablis lost its advantage of proximity to the capital and was simply unable to compete with the cheap wines of the MIDI, which could now be transported easily to the capital. Consequently the vineyard area gradually declined until it reached a mere 500 ha in the mid 1950s, before the fortunes of the appellation revived.

Climate

Climate has always played an important role in determining the success and quality of Chablis. Essentially the climate is semi-CONTINENTAL, with no maritime influence, so that the winters are long and hard and the summers often, but not always, fairly hot. There is all the climatic uncertainty, and therefore vintage variation, both in quality and quantity, of a vineyard far from the equator.

One of the key factors in determining how much wine will be produced is the possibility of spring FROSTS, which can cause enormous damage to the young vine shoots. Depending on how advanced the vegetation is, the vineyards are vulnerable from the end of March until well into May. Since the end of the 1950s, after a decade of vintages particularly badly affected by frost, various methods of protection evolved. Heaters, or SMUDGE POTS, may be lit in the vineyards; they are expensive but efficient. The alternative technique of using SPRINKLERS, or aspersion, to spray the vines with water from the moment the temperature drops to freezing point has also been increasingly practised. Wind can seriously prejudice the effectiveness of aspersion, however. In the often parcellated vineyards of Chablis it can be all too easy to protect a neighbour's vines rather than one's own. Spraying must continue all the time the temperature is at 0 °C/32 °F or below. Electric cables, cleaner than smudge pots, may also be laid to raise ambient temperatures while taking advantage of France's reduced night tariffs. Such measures can be sufficiently effective to make the difference in some years between a

crop of reasonable quantity and virtually no crop at all. It is now perfectly possible to make a viable living from vines in Chablis, whereas in the 1950s, growers needed both eternal optimism and another crop, so that polyculture was common.

Vineyard expansion

It was the development of effective frost protection in the early 1960s that encouraged today's increase in the vineyard area of Chablis, which has not been without controversy. The seven CLIMATS of Chablis Grand Cru total 105 ha and are all on one slope facing south west just outside the town. They are Les Clos, Blanchots, Bougros, Vaudésir, Valmur, Preuses, and Grenouilles. There is also, in true Burgundian fashion, an anomaly. The tiny vineyard of La Moutonne is partly in Vaudésir and partly in Preuses, but for some illogical and doubtless bureaucratic reason, an official INAO decree confirming its status as a grand cru has never been issued, even though its wines certainly demonstrate that it qualifies.

Much of the dispute over the vineyard expansion has centred on the premiers crus. By the early 21st century there were 40 in all, totalling 784 ha. Some are often seen on labels, while others are more obscure, and some such as Vaudevey came into existence only with the expansion of the appellation. Their protagonists argue that they are on slopes that were planted before the phylloxera crisis and that their TERROIR closely resembles that of the long-established premiers crus. Some of the lesser-known vineyards may use a better-known umbrella name, so that for example L'Homme Mort may be sold as Fourchaume, as follows, with umbrella names followed by their associated premiers crus:

Mont de Milieu
Montée de Tonnerre: *Chapelot, Pied d'Aloue, Côte de Bréchain*
Fourchaume: *Vaupulent, Côte de Fontenay, L'Homme Mort, Vaulorent*
Vaillons: *Châtains, Séchet, Beugnons, Les Lys, Mélinots, Roncières, Les Epinottes*
Montmains: *Forêt, Butteaux*
Côte de Léchet
Beauroy: *Troesme, Côte de Savant*
Vauligneau
Vaudevey: *Vaux Ragons*
Vaucoupin
Vosgros: *Vaugiraut*
Les Fourneaux: *Morein, Côte de Prés Girots*
Côte de Vaubarousse
Berdiot
Chaume de Talvat
Côte de Jouan
Les Beauregards: *Côte de Cuissy*

By 2012 some 3,450 ha of vineyard was planted for AC Chablis, a fifth more than ten years previously and considerably more than was originally envisaged when the appellation was

granted, much of the arable land having been given over to vines. By 2012, 944 ha of a permitted 1,800 ha of Petit Chablis had been planted. Soil is another significant factor that should determine not only the unique flavour of Chablis, but also the vineyard area. Chablis lies on the edge of the Paris basin, where the rocks date back to the Upper Jurassic age, some 180 million years ago. On the other side of the basin is the Dorset village of Kimmeridge in southern England, which gives its name to the particular geological formation and period known as 'Kimmeridgean'. Basically the soil is what the French call ARGILO-CALCAIRE, containing a multitude of tiny fossilized oyster shells. The next geological layer is Portlandien, which is very similar in structure to Kimmeridge, but is generally deemed not to give as much finesse to the wine. The grand cru vineyards are all on Kimmeridge while Portlandien constitutes most of the outlying vineyards of Petit Chablis.

Viticultural practices in Chablis are very similar to those in the rest of Burgundy, apart from the overriding need to protect the vines from frost.

The use of oak

In the cellar, as elsewhere in France, winemaking techniques improved enormously in the late 20th century, so that there is a better understanding of such elements as MALOLACTIC CONVERSION and the need for TEMPERATURE CONTROL during fermentation. The most interesting and controversial aspect of vinification in Chablis is the use of OAK, Chablis being the one fine wine area where Chardonnay is not automatically oaked.

Those who favour stainless steel want the purest flavour of Chablis, with the firm streak of acidity and the mineral quality that the French describe as *goût de pierre à fusil*, or gunflint. Louis Michel's is generally considered to be the epitome of this style, although others who employ it successfully include Jean Durup, Jean-Marc Brocard, and A. Régnard.

Other producers, such as Vincent Dauvissat and Jean-Marie Raveneau, have never completely abandoned their barrels. They may ferment their wine in vats and then, once the alcoholic FERMENTATION is finished, the wine goes into oak for a few months' BARREL MATURATION. Those who favour the use of oak barrels believe that the gentle process of oxygenation adds an extra dimension of complexity to the flavour of their wine. The proportion of new barrels in a cellar in Chablis can vary. Some producers buy very few each year, wishing to avoid the marked vanilla flavours that new wood can impart, while William Fèvre, for example, depend on sister company BOUCHARD of Beaune for used barrels. Some, such as Gilles Collet, Jean-Paul Droin, and Domaine Laroche for some crus, ferment in barrel; others just age their wine in oak, with annual variations according to the quality of the wine. Generally only grand cru and premier cru Chablis is matured in wood. Paradoxically it is not unknown for a Chablis that has seen no wood, to take on, as it matures, a certain firm nuttiness that suggests some ageing in oak.

The Chablis market

Surprisingly perhaps until the early 1980s, Chablis was hardly appreciated in France itself as most of it was sold on the export market, usually through the large NÉGOCIANTS of Burgundy, based mainly in Beaune. Currently nearly a third of all Chablis is vinified by the local cooperative, La Chablisienne, which works well for its appellation. The trend, as elsewhere, has been for an increasing number of producers, who originally sold their wine in bulk to négociants, to bottle and sell their wine themselves. Some of them have even started their own NÉGOCIANT businesses.

Chablis has always been affected by significant variations in the size of the vintage and prices have fluctuated accordingly (much more dramatically, for example, than in the more regulated but climatically similar Champagne market). However, some of the commercial instability has disappeared with the growth in the vineyard area so that there is more Chablis available to satisfy world demand. Generally Chablis is a more prosperous appellation than it was in the 1970s, for with the possibility of frost protection the growers are much more certain of making a viable living from their vines than ever before.

Chablis remains one of the great white wines of the world. It is sometimes overshadowed by the greater opulence of a fine Meursault or Corton-Charlemagne, but it has an individuality of its own that sets it apart from the great white burgundies of the Côte d'Or. There is a unique streak of steely acidity, a firm flintiness, and a mineral quality that is not found elsewhere in Burgundy. Like all great white burgundy, it benefits from, but all too rarely receives, BOTTLE AGEING. A premier cru will be at its best at 10 years, while a grand cru could easily benefit from 15 or more years of maturation. A 1947 Côte de Léchet, not one of the best premiers crus, but from a great vintage, was still showing a remarkable depth of flavour with the characteristic *goût de pierre à fusil*, when it was 40 years old.   R.E.G.

Biss, A., and Smith, O., *The Wines of Chablis* (Bournemouth, 2000).

Bro, L., and Moreau, M., *Chablis, Porte d'Or de la Bourgogne* (Auxerre, 1998).

Cannard, H., *Les Vignobles de Chablis et de l'Yonne* (Dijon, 1999).

Fèvre, W., *Le Vrai Chablis et les autres* (Chablis, 1978).

George, R., *The Wines of Chablis and The Grand Auxerrois* (London, 2007).

Chacolí. Castilian spelling of the Basque wine TXAKOLI. Chacolí **de Guetaria** is Getariako Txakolina, Chacolí **de Vizcaya** is Bizkaiko Txakolina, while Chacolí **de Alava** is Arabako Txakolina.

chai, French, and particularly Bordelais, term for a place where wine and occasionally brandy is stored, typically in BARREL. Thus a smart Bordeaux CHÂTEAU will have (perhaps) the château building itself with no direct winemaking function, a CUVERIE in which fermentation takes place, a first-year *chai* in which the most recent vintage's crop undergoes ÉLEVAGE, and a second-year *chai* to which it is moved at some point before the year end in order to make way for the next year's crop. The New World counterpart to the *chai* is sometimes called the barrel hall. See also CAVE.

chalk, a soft and crumbly, highly porous (35 to 40%) type of pure white LIMESTONE and a word often used erroneously as synonymous with it. Chalk-derived SOILS are valued in viticulture for their excellent DRAINAGE, combined with a capacity of the SUBSOIL to store substantial amounts of water. Because vine ROOTS can usually penetrate to chalk bedrock, continuity of moisture supply is assured regardless of short-term fluctuations in RAINFALL. Pure chalk is of low fertility, resulting in a rather low vine VIGOUR and naturally good CANOPY MICROCLIMATE.

True chalk is much less common under vineyards than most wine books suggest, chiefly because calcarous (CALCAIRE in French) has been taken to mean chalky. Apart from some vineyards in southern ENGLAND, the principal wine region with chalk is CHAMPAGNE. Even here, the better vineyards are mostly on CLAYS, with only the longer roots reaching the underlying chalk. It is also widely believed that the SHERRY region around Jerez in south west Spain is on chalk, although the bedrock is not even pure limestone. The fact that Jerez, Cognac, and Champagne produce more or less exclusively white wines is one of the bases for the widely held misapprehension that there is a correlation between wine colour and SOIL COLOUR.

(See also DEACIDIFICATION for the use of chalk in winemaking.)   J.M.H. & J.G.

Hancock, J., and Price, M., 'Real chalk balances the water supply', *Journal of Wine Research*, 1/1 (1990), 45–60.

Chalk Hill, California wine region and AVA north of Santa Rosa and south east of Healdsburg. See SONOMA.

Chalone, small California wine region and AVA in the mountains east of the Salinas Valley. See MONTEREY.

Chalonnaise, Côte, red and white wine-producing region in the Saône-et-Loire *département* of BURGUNDY between the CÔTE D'OR and Mâconnais. The Côte Chalonnaise takes its name from the town of Chalon-sur-Saône, which had been an important CELTIC trading centre in Ancient GAUL. As well as generic BOURGOGNE Côte Chalonnaise, mostly red from the Pinot Noir grape, there are five village appellations: MERCUREY, which stands apart in both quality and price, produces mostly Pinot Noir with small quantities of white wine; GIVRY the same; MONTAGNY is exclusively a white wine appellation growing the Chardonnay grape; RULLY offers both red and white wines and is a centre for the sparkling wine industry in a small way; while BOUZERON uniquely has its own appellation exclusively for the Aligoté grape.

Although the soils in the Côte Chalonnaise are similar to those of the Côte d'Or, being based on limestone with a complex admixture of other elements, the vineyards are more scattered since there is no regular escarpment to provide continuity of suitable slopes.

Viticultural practices are broadly similar to those in the Côte d'Or. Vinification is sometimes carried out in barrels, although only the best producers use any new OAK. Bottling normally takes place in the summer before the new vintage.

Maximum yields for Mercurey are the same as those for VILLAGE WINES in the Côte d'Or, whereas the other appellations of the Côte Chalonnaise may produce a little more. Although cheerfully fruity while young, few wines from this region have enough body to age well. The Côte Chalonnaise is well served by CO-OPERATIVES such as the Cave de Buxy, such NÉGOCIANTS as Antonin Rodet and Faiveley, and growers such as Stéphane Aladame, Dureuil-Janthial, François Lumpp, Michel Juillot, and de Villaine.   J.T.C.M.

Chambertin, **Chambertin-Clos de Bèze**, **Chapelle-Chambertin**, **Charmes-Chambertin**, **Griotte(s)-Chambertin**, **Latricières-Chambertin**, **Mazis-Chambertin**, **Mazoyères-Chambertin,** and **Ruchottes-Chambertin**, great red GRANDS CRUS in Burgundy's CÔTE D'OR. For more details, see GEVREY-CHAMBERTIN.

Chambéry, not a wine at all but a delicate, aromatic VERMOUTH made in the French Alps. Of the huge volume of vermouth produced and assiduously marketed each year, the relatively rare Chambéry is one subtle enough to appeal to the wine drinker.

Chambolle-Musigny, village and appellation of particular charm in the Côte de Nuits district of Burgundy producing red wines from Pinot Noir grapes. A fine Chambolle-Musigny has a rich, velvety elegance which rivals the finesse of Vosne-Romanée or the power of Gevrey-Chambertin. There are two GRAND CRU vineyards, Le Musigny and Bonnes Mares (in part), and some exceptional PREMIERS CRUS worthy of promotion.

Le **Musigny** ranks with Romanée-Conti, La Tâche, Richebourg, Chambertin, and Chambertin-Clos de Bèze as one of the pinnacles of great burgundy (see DOMAINE DE LA ROMANÉE-CONTI, VOSNE-ROMANÉE, and GEVREY-CHAMBERTIN for details of these). The vineyard lies between the scrubland at the top of the slope and the upper part of CLOS DE VOUGEOT, on a slope of 8 to 10% which drains particularly well through the oolitic limestone. The soil is more chalk than clay, covered by a fine silt, a combination which leads to the exceptional grace and power of Le Musigny, an iron fist in a velvet glove.

Of the 10.7 ha/26 acres of Le Musigny which is split between Musigny, Petits Musigny, and La Combe d'Orveau, seven are owned by Domaine Comte de Vogüé. Other significant producers are Barthod, the Ch de Chambolle Musigny, Joseph Drouhin, Groffier, Mugnier, Jacques Prieur, and Roumier.

Adjacent to Le Musigny lies the premier cru Les Amoureuses, whose reputation and price suggest that this vineyard is worthy of elevation to grand cru. If a little less powerful than Le Musigny itself, the wines of Les Amoureuses demonstrate a very similar style. The next most sought-after premier cru, and the largest, is Les Charmes, although CLIMATE CHANGE has had the effect of shunting quality up the hillside to Les Cras and Les Fuées.

The other grand cru of Chambolle Musigny is **Bonnes Mares**, situated to the north of the village and overflowing into MOREY-ST-DENIS. The wines show more sturdiness than silkiness, are less graceful than Le Musigny but have evident power and structure. Bonnes Mares is noted for its ageing capacity. Ownership is spread over more than 30 proprietors, the largest being again Domaine Comte de Vogüé, a producer who also makes a very small quantity of white wine in Musigny labelled Bourgogne Blanc. Other notable producers based in Chambolle-Musigny include Barthod, Roumier, and Mugnier.

See also CÔTE D'OR, and map under BURGUNDY.

J.T.C.M.

Chambourcin is a dark-berried FRENCH HYBRID commercially available only since 1963 and popular in the 1970s, particularly around the mouth of the Loire. In 2011 France still grew a total of more than 600 ha/1,635 acres, all in the Loire Valley. This extremely vigorous, productive vine tolerates wet weather well and produces better-quality wine than most hybrids, being deep coloured and full of relatively aromatic flavour. Its winter-hardiness finds it well distributed, if not exactly common, in the US. It was successfully planted by Cassegrain in the warm, damp climate of Hastings Valley in NEW SOUTH WALES in Australia, a culture unfettered by anti-hybrid prejudice, and has since spread up and down Australia's east coast, including Queensland, with outbreaks elsewhere. It also looks promising in VIETNAM.

chambré, French word also used in English to describe a wine that has been deliberately warmed to room TEMPERATURE before serving (from *chambre*, 'room'). Most rooms nowadays are rather warmer than the ideal serving temperatures for most wines.

Champagne, name derived from the Latin term *campania*, originally used to describe the rolling open countryside just north of Rome (see CAMPANIA). In the early Middle Ages, it was applied to a province in north-east France (see map under FRANCE). It is now divided into the so-called 'Champagne pouilleuse', the once-barren but now cereal-growing CALCAREOUS plains east of Rheims, and the 'Champagne viticole' (capital letters indicate the geographical descriptions, lower case is used for the wine).

Champagne, with its three champagne towns Rheims (Reims in French), Épernay, and Aÿ, was the first region to make SPARKLING WINE in any quantity and historically the name champagne became synonymous with the finest, although Champagne is now responsible for less than one bottle in 12 of total world production of all sparkling wine. In common with other French regions making fine wines, notably Burgundy and Bordeaux, champagne formed the model for other aspiring winemakers, especially in Australia and the west coast of the United States, employing the same grapes, and the same SPARKLING WINEMAKING method, as the French originals (known now as the TRADITIONAL METHOD). This form of imitation, while flattering, became decidedly awkward for the Champenois in the late 1980s. Their response was to tighten up the regulations regarding their own wines, and thus substantially increase the average quality—although they are unable to increase the 35,000 ha/86,500 acres devoted to vines to any significant extent for fear of diluting the quality and character of the wine. See the detail of the expansion of the region proposed in 2007 in Geography below.

History

Champagne was at the crossroads of two major trade routes, north–south between Flanders and Switzerland and east–west from Paris to the Rhine. Its position made it prosperous, but also ensured that it has been fought over many times in the course of the past 1,500 years. One of the most important battles in history was fought at Châlons-sur-Marne (now Châlons-en-Champagne) in AD 455, when Attila the Hun was finally repulsed. Subsequent battles included a savage civil war, the Fronde in the middle of the 17th century. As late as 1914 the famous 'Taxis de la Marne' brought French reinforcements from Paris to repulse the German invaders, who had (briefly) occupied Épernay and reached the outskirts of Rheims. But successive conflicts merely interrupted the progress of the vineyard.

Although there are numerous legends concerning earlier vineyards, the first serious mention is at the time of St Rémi at the end of the 5th century AD. For nearly eight centuries after Clovis, first king of the Francs, was baptized in Rheims in 496, the city's position as the spiritual centre of France naturally boosted its fame.

Vines had already been planted around the city, mainly by the numerous local abbeys and by the local nobility. But until the 17th century there was no generic 'vin de Champagne'. Since the 9th century, wines from the MONTAGNE DE REIMS south of the city had been known as *vins de la montagne*, those from the Marne Valley as *vins de la rivière*, or river wines. A number of villages, notably Bouzy and Verzenay on the Montagne, and Aÿ and Épernay in the Marne Valley, were already being singled out for the quality of their wines. The wine trade was centred on Rheims and Châlons-sur-Marne, and the wines had the great advantage of immediate access to the Marne, which joined the Seine just east of PARIS (see RIVERS).

But the wines did not sparkle: they were light, pinkish still wines made from the Pinot Noir grape. In the last half of the 17th century, wine-making greatly improved, under the auspices of leading clerical winemakers, led by Dom PÉRIGNON, who transformed the Abbey of Hautvillers, above Épernay, into the region's leading centre of viticultural progress. The wines' fame grew greatly in the second half of the 17th century when they were introduced to the Court of Versailles, notably by the Marquis de Sillery, a large landowner in the region, and by the Marquis de St-Évremond, who introduced champagne to London society after he was banished to Britain in 1662.

In the cold winters normal in the region, the wines had a tendency to stop FERMENTATION and then to start refermenting in the spring. For a long time this was considered something of a nuisance, as the resulting release of CARBON DIOXIDE was often strong enough to break the flimsy bottles normal at the time. The development of stronger BOTTLES by British glassmakers permitted drinkers to enjoy the resulting sparkle. Indeed it was the café society of London, encouraged by St-Évremond, which probably first enjoyed true 'sparkling champagne' (see contemporary references in ENGLISH LITERATURE).

The habit was taken up by the licentious court round the duke of Orléans, who became regent of France after the death of Louis XIV in 1715, but serious winemakers (and their clients) continued to believe that sparkling champagne was inferior to the still wines of the region.

Moreover even the stronger bottles could not reliably withstand the pressure generated by the SECOND FERMENTATION. So, throughout the 18th century, only a few thousand bottles were produced every year, and up to half of them would break.

The champagne business we know today was born in the first 40 years of the 19th century. The first notable step was taken by Madame (VEUVE) CLICQUOT. One of her employees developed the system of PUPITRES to assist in the REMUAGE process. CORKS were improved, and a corking machine developed. Understanding, and then mastering, the second fermentation took longer. The scientist and minister CHAPTAL had understood that 'sparkling wines owe their tendency to sparkle only to the fact that they have been enclosed in a bottle before they have completed their fermentation'. But it took a young pharmacist from Châlons-sur-Marne, Jean-Baptiste François, to enable winemakers to measure the precise quantity of sugar required to induce a second fermentation in the bottle without inducing an explosive force.

François died in 1838, shortly after he had published his formulae. But within a generation Champagne had become the home of the world's first 'wine industry', one dominated by a number of internationally famous BRAND names. Most of these were those of young entrepreneurs from the Rhineland, such as Messrs KRUG, BOLLINGER, and ROEDERER, who showed greater commercial nous than the local merchants, only a few of whom, apart from Madame Clicquot and Monsieur MOËT, survived.

But for over half a century, until well into the 1950s, Champagne suffered from a number of problems which clouded its earlier successes. The important Russian market collapsed in 1917, and two World Wars, separated by the slump, closed the export markets on which the region depended so heavily. The arrival of the PHYLLOXERA louse in Champagne in 1890 intensified competition from other sparkling wines, from Germany as well as from other French winemakers, and intensified the fraudulent habits of some of the region's more unscrupulous merchants, who were wont to import juice and wine for bottling and sale as champagne.

The fraud compounded the misery caused by phylloxera to the region's growers and caused a near civil war in 1911. This was sparked by the first attempts to define the region entitled to produce champagne. An initial delimitation in January excluded Aube, a separate wine region 110 km/70 miles south east of Épernay, which provoked riots in the Aube. This led some members of the French government to suppress the delimitation entirely which provoked the infamous April 1911 riots in the Marne. In the end the delimitation was retained and eventually the Aube was included as a separate 'second zone', although it was included in the main

appellation when the boundaries were finally fixed in 1927.

The events of 1911 shook the whole winemaking community, and 25 years later the resulting desire for common action resulted in the combined group of growers and merchants known as the Commission de Châlons, set up in 1935 under the impetus of the remarkable Robert-Jean de Vogüé, head of Moët, and Maurice Doyard who was able to rally the growers. At a time when growers were virtually giving away their grapes, the Commission provided them with some stability. Six years later, the desire for joint action led to the formation of the CIVC, the Comité Interprofessionnel du Vin de Champagne, the pioneering attempt, much copied elsewhere, to provide winemaking regions with an organization which represented all the interests involved.

For 60 years from 1950, the region enjoyed unprecedented prosperity with sales peaking in 2007 at almost 340 million bottles. Traditional export markets, such as Britain, the United States, Belgium, Japan, and Switzerland, took increasing quantities. Nevertheless the French market has long consumed far more champagne than all export markets and accounts for two-thirds of sales. This emphasis had important structural implications, since the traditional BRANDS were less dominant in the domestic market than outside France, where they still account for over 90% of sales.

In the domestic market, nearly half total sales are made by individual GROWERS, CO-OPERATIVES, and co-operative unions. The first co-operatives in Champagne were founded just before the First World War. They grew rapidly in the early 1960s and by 1989 the region's 140 co-operatives represented over half the growers and a third of the area under vines. Some co-operatives merely press grapes, others make wine (much of which is returned to members for sale under their own label, a fact signified by the letters RC before the grower's code on the label; see LABELLING INFORMATION). Two or three co-operative unions, producing up to ten million bottles annually, became major forces, particularly in supplying buyers' own brands and subsequently uniting to promote their own brands.

The competition from the co-operatives added to the pressure on the, usually family-owned, MERCHANTS. In the 1960s and 1970s, MOËT & CHANDON absorbed Mercier and Ruinart, the latter the oldest firm in the region, and after further acquisitions, including VEUVE CLICQUOT and KRUG, today represents by far the dominant grouping in Champagne. The growers' increasing power was reflected in a rapid rise of grape prices during the 1980s and by the inflexibility with which grapes were allotted to the merchants. In 1990, under the impetus of Moët, the market was freed. During the 1990s the

price was indicative, not legally binding, and since 2000 there have been no controls on prices. A number of firms, especially those without their own vineyards, experienced difficulties and were sold and resold a number of times. So the trade has become increasingly concentrated, with the seven biggest houses accounting for 70% of the total.

Geography and climate

The region permitted to call its wines 'champagne' was strictly defined by law in 1927. It sprawls from Charly-sur-Marne a mere 50 km/30 miles east of Paris along the Vallée de la Marne subregion to the Montagne de Reims subregion and south from Épernay along the Côte des Blancs and its southern extension, the Côte de Sézanne. A separate subregion is the Côte des Bar in the Aube, 112 km south east of Épernay. Over the years, the acreage actually planted has varied widely, dropping to 11,000 ha/27,000 acres during the 1930s. In 2013, the appellation comprised 34,282 ha/84,676 acres of vines—up from the 1993 total of 27,500 ha: 66% in the Marne; 10% in the Aisne; and 23% in the Aube. Only a tenth of the vines are owned by merchants, who can now add to their holdings only under very strict conditions. The remainder is owned by about 15,000 growers (far fewer than there used to be), many of whom own less than a hectare of vines.

Much of the appellation (and Champagne is now the only major French region to have just one appellation), and all the better CRUS, are on the slopes of the hills typical of the region. The vines' roots dig deep into CALCAREOUS depths, providing ideal conditions of DRAINAGE and HUMIDITY. The Champagne vineyard's exposure to the cold northern winter inevitably makes grape-growing a precarious operation, with the quality of the wines varying from year to year. As a result, champagne is traditionally a wine blended, not only from a number of different villages and different grape varieties, but also from several vintages. The poverty of the soil requires constant addition of FERTILIZER, either the *cendres noirs*, the natural compost found on the region's hilltops, or, until the late 1990s, finely ground (and curiously multicoloured) household rubbish from Rheims, or even Paris.

The different qualities of grapes from the region's 320 widely spread CRUS led to the establishment of a scale of prices according to the status of each commune. In general grapes from the 17 'grand cru' communes fetch even higher prices than those from the 42 communes called premiers crus, although now that pricing has been freed, grape prices reflect the difference between individual vineyards rather than having one price for all vines in a given commune.

At a time when champagne sales were increasing apparently ceaselessly, a list of 45 new communes that could be allowed to produce champagne has been presented to the authorities, but a slowdown in sales, apparently inspired partly by wider economic concerns and partly by increasing consumer confidence in other sparkling wines, has made this revision of the delimitation a little less pressing.

Vine varieties

In the past, a number of grape varieties were planted in Champagne. But today almost the whole vineyard is planted with three:, Pinot Noir, Pinot Meunier, and Chardonnay. The Pinot Noir, which accounts for just over a third of the total acreage, is no longer as dominant as it was, but still accounts for 38% of all plantings and provides the basic structure and depth of fruit in the blend. In Champagne, the Chardonnay, planted on 30% of the total vineyard, was traditionally grown on the east-facing slopes of the Côte des Blancs but has proved suitable in many other subregions, especially the Côte de Sézanne. In Champagne it grows vigorously and buds early, thus making it susceptible to spring FROSTS. It imparts a certain austerity and elegance to young champagnes, but is long lived and matures to a fine fruitiness. The remaining 32% is planted with PINOT MEUNIER, a variety much more important in Champagne than anywhere else, particularly in the Valley of the Marne. It provides many champagnes with an early-maturing richness and fruitiness. There were 90 ha of Pinot Blanc planted together with tiny amounts of Pinot Gris, Arbane, and PETIT MESLIER from which at least one varietal champagne is made.

Thanks to new CLONES and viticultural methods, the YIELD of grapes has grown greatly: from an average of 3,670 kg/ha in the 1940s to 9,910 in the 1980s (or from 24 to 66 hl/ha (1.3–3.7 tons/acre)). The first limit was set in 1935. Nowadays, the Comité Champagne sets the yield each year, usually well below the maximum limit set by EU regulations which is 15,500 kg/ha. Since 1992, 160 (rather than the earlier limit of 150) kg of grapes are required to produce 102 l of juice, which means that the maximum permitted yield is 65 hl/ha.

VINE DENSITY is notably high, and vines are replanted after between 25 and 30 years. The grapes are usually picked in September, on dates now fixed per grape variety village by village but which are in general becoming earlier as a result of CLIMATE CHANGE. (ACID levels have also been falling.) They cannot be harvested unless they contain that year's fixed minimum level of POTENTIAL ALCOHOL. But since the level can be as low as 8%, sugar may be added (see CHAPTALIZATION) to boost the alcohol level to 11% after the alcoholic fermentation, and the second fermentation supplements the final ALCOHOLIC STRENGTH by up to another 1.5%. Most champagne is about 12.5% alcohol.

Winemaking

The pressing of the grapes is difficult, since the juice of what is to be a white wine must not be tainted by the skin of the mainly black grapes used. The traditional champagne PRESS was a vertical basket press, holding 4,000 kg/8,800 lb of grapes, a quantity known as a *marc* and a standard unit of measurement in the region. These presses are also called Coquard presses after the name of the manufacturer. A number of other types of press have since been introduced and the CIVC allows both hydraulic and pneumatic horizontal presses.

Since 1990, all pressing centres have had to comply with certain minimum standards. Traditionally, 2,666 l/704 gal were extracted from every *marc*: the first 2,050 l were the cuvée, the next 410 l the *premières tailles*, while the final 206 l were the *deuxièmes tailles*. The total yield has now been reduced by 115 l to 2,550 l per 4,000 kg (or 102 l per 160 kg, as the INAO regulations express it) and the *deuxièmes tailles* abolished.

The juice is allowed to settle for between 12 and 48 hours, at a low temperature. A small but increasing number of producers ferment the must in OAK, but the overwhelming majority of the grapes are fermented in STAINLESS STEEL vats holding between 50 and 1,200 hl (1,320–31,700 gal). The fermentation TEMPERATURE also varies, between 12 and 25 °C (54–77 °F). Most winemakers use a strain of YEAST specially developed by the CIVC.

Immediately after the first fermentation, most, but by no means all, champagnes now undergo MALOLACTIC CONVERSION. The result is called *vin clair*. Traditionally champagne has been made from wines from a number of different vineyards, and a major part of the work of a chef de cave in a champagne house is the art of blending, but many growers (and a few firms) make wines from a single commune or vineyard. Major firms use wines from between 50 and 200 communes for their blend. They also use between 10 and 50% of *vins de réserve* from earlier vintages, generally stored in stainless steel or cement vats. Before the wine is bottled, a measured dose of bottling liquor (*liqueur de tirage*), a mixture of wine, sugar, and specially developed yeasts, is added to the wine. The bottles are then capped, usually with a crown cap lined with plastic. Following TIRAGE, LEES CONTACT, RIDDLING, and DISGORGEMENT, a sweetening DOSAGE is usually added before final corking. A few champagnes are sold without any added sugar at all; most are BRUT.

For more information, see in SPARKLING WINEMAKING, traditional method.

Styles of champagne

In addition to their basic wine, their non-vintage brut, major firms also make single **vintage champagnes**, typically three or four in every decade. BLANC DE BLANCS is made exclusively from the Chardonnay grape while BLANC DE NOIRS is made exclusively from black grapes.

This century has seen a FASHION for pink or **rosé champagne** made either by adding a small proportion of red wine to the blend or, less usually, by letting the juice remain in contact with the skin of the grapes for a short time during fermentation. All the major firms have now followed the example of Roederer with their Cristal bottling and Moët & Chandon with Dom Pérignon and produce 'luxury', 'de luxe', or PRESTIGE CUVÉES to show their house styles at their best.

See DOSAGE for a list of the various different levels of RESIDUAL SUGAR in champagne. By far the most common style is Brut and, as average acidity levels in grapes have been declining, base wines taste softer, there is less need for compensatory sweetness, and the maximum permitted residual sugar in Brut wines has been reduced from 15 to 12 g/l. Age also reduces apparent acidity so that both riper grapes and more mature wines require less sweetness. An increase in both grape maturity and average age of reserve wines has encouraged a number of producers to launch wines with less or even no added dosage. Wines with residual sugar less than 6 g/l may be called Extra Brut, while those without any added dosage at all, and with residual sugar under 3 g/l, may be called Brut Nature, Pas Dosé, or Zéro Dosage. These bone-dry wines have become more common, but some champagne specialists believe some dosage is essential for a well-balanced champagne and are concerned that undosed champagnes cannot benefit from the effects of any MAILLARD REACTION.

The small proportion of still wines made in the region are sold under the appellations Coteaux CHAMPENOIS and the rare pink ROSÉ DES RICEYS. RATAFIA champenois is a local wine-based apéritif.   N.F. & J.R.

Bonal, F., *Le Livre d'or de Champagne* (Lausanne, 1984).

Faith, N., *The Story of Champagne* (London, 1988).

Juhlin, R., *4000 Champagnes* (Paris, 2005).

Stevenson, T., and Avellan, E., *Christie's Encyclopedia of Champagne & Sparkling Wine* (London, 2013).

Zarifian, E., et al., *Bulle de Champagne* (Paris, 2005).

www.champagne.fr

champagne method. See TRADITIONAL METHOD.

Champenois, Coteaux, appellation used for the relatively rare still wines of CHAMPAGNE in northern France. For every one bottle of still white Coteaux Champenois produced, perhaps 20 of still red Coteaux Champenois are produced (in a good vintage), and 16,000 bottles of sparkling champagne. The wines of this cool region with their naturally high acidity and light body are generally improved by dissolved CARBON DIOXIDE. It is difficult to justify the production of white Coteaux Champenois, from expensive Chardonnay grapes, but easier to understand why the Champenois like to be able to drink the odd bottle of local still red from time to time. The village of Bouzy on the MONTAGNE DE REIMS has a particular reputation for its red Coteaux Champenois, partly perhaps because of the appeal of the name Bouzy Rouge, as do Aÿ, Cumières, and Ambonnay. These red wines are of interest to outsiders only in the ripest vintages, while the whites and rosés tend to serve only to compliment the Champenois on their wise decision to concentrate on sparkling wines.

See also ROSÉ DES RICEYS.

Chamusca, DOP subregion of TEJO in central southern Portugal.

Chancellor, productive but minor red FRENCH HYBRID developed from two SEIBEL parents. For long it was known as Seibel 7053, but was named Chancellor in NEW YORK in 1970. Encountered occasionally in the UNITED STATES.

Changins, the federal viticultural research station in western SWITZERLAND near Nyon on Lake Geneva, is principally concerned with improving plant material, including CLONAL SELECTION; matching VINE VARIETY to specific TERROIR in both French-speaking Switzerland and Italian-speaking Switzerland; and developing viticultural techniques which reduce costs, improve wine quality, and minimize chemical inputs (see ORGANIC VITICULTURE). Areas of OENOLOGICAL research have included techniques for must SETTLING of white wines, red wine MACERATION, YEASTS, MALOLACTIC CONVERSION, FILTRATION, and ENRICHMENT. The station has developed a number of crosses such as GAMARET and GARANOIR, and more recently Divico, showing good resistance to both MILDEWS and to BOTRYTIS bunch rot.

The research station's counterpart in German-speaking Switzerland is WÄDENSWIL. The two stations combined under the administration of Agroscope (ACW) in early 2006.

Changyu. Changyu Pioneer Wine Co. is China's oldest and largest wine producer and, according to one independent analysis of 2010 turnover, was the world's fourth biggest wine company. It was founded in Yantai, Shandong province, in 1892 by Zhang Bishi, an officer in the Qing government. He introduced VINIFERA varieties from Europe in 1896. The winemaker then was Maximilian, son of Baron Auguste Wilhelm von Babo, founder of the pioneering viticultural college KLOSTERNEUBERG.

In the 1950s, Premier Zhou Enlai presented Changyu brandy as a diplomatic gift to the Geneva Conference delegates, recorded as 'diplomacy of Gold Medal brandy'. Chairman Mao instructed Changyu to develop its wine production 'so the people may enjoy a bit more wine'. Today it claims to have a total of 20,000 ha/49,400 acres of vineyard potential and an overall production capacity of 200,000 tonnes, much of it focused on basic and mid-market lines.

As for its premium production facilities, in 2002 the company formed a JOINT VENTURE with the French CASTEL group in Yantai to establish Chateau Changyu Castel winery, signalling a new era for Chinese wine in which the word CHATEAU takes on the special significance of a dedicated wine estate with TOURISM potential. The primary grape variety is CABERNET GERNISCHT. In 2006, Changyu and Aurora Icewine Co. of Canada built the Golden Icewine Valley in Liaoning Province, capable, it is claimed, of producing half of the world's ICEWINE. Its vineyard holdings of about 333 ha/820 acres are dominated by VIDAL. Thanks to the LAKE EFFECT, winters are cold, but not too dry. In 2007 the company used investments from the US, Italy, and Portugal, as well as China, to establish Chateau Changyu AFIP Global north east of Beijing, with 200 ha of vineyard dedicated principally to upmarket varietal Cabernet Sauvignon and Chardonnay. Chateau Changyu Baron Balboa was built in the extravagant image of a 19th-century French château in Xinjiang in the far west of China with 333 ha of vineyards and a NURSERY planned. Chateau Changyu Moser XV is a joint venture with LENZ MOSER of Austria in Ningxia while Chateau Changyu Rena in Shaanxi is Tuscan-inspired and has what is claimed to be the largest underground wine cellar in Asia.

In the mid 2010s, two more production facilities—Chateau Tinlot, named after former OIV chairman Robert Tinlot, and Chateau Keya-Brandy dedicated to spirits production—were being built in Yantai. Changyu acquired a cognac house in 2013, although presumably they were far from immune from the impact of Chinese austerity measures imposed then. By 2014 Changyu was already an established wine exporter and had bottling agreements in place in Bordeaux and New Zealand.   Y.S.

Chapoutier, family-owned merchant-grower based at Tain-l'Hermitage in France's northern RHÔNE. One of the Rhône Valley's great names established in 1808 and with 32 ha/80 acres of precious HERMITAGE vineyard, it languished somewhat in the late 20th century. During the 1980s, when Chapoutier's peers (GUIGAL and JABOULET, for example) and numerous small growers were catching the imagination of the wine world with the improving quality of their wines, Chapoutier wines stood out precisely because they seemed unexceptional by comparison. This situation changed dramatically in 1990 when Max Chapoutier's son Michel took over the running of the company, with outspoken passion and an early devotion to BIODYNAMIC VITICULTURE. In 1996, the firm became the first wine producer to have labels in Braille. But what really distinguishes the company is its combination of high quality, often vineyard designated, and almost restless vineyard acquisition. By 2014 Chapoutier had a total of 260 ha/642 acres of vineyard in France alone, plus 428 ha of land as yet unplanted. These included vineyards the length of the Rhône Valley, nearly 100 ha in Roussillon, and three characterful Riesling vineyards in Alsace. Chapoutier also control 15 ha of vines in the Douro Valley and a total of 58 ha in the Australian state of Victoria together with a much greater area of unplanted land, some of these ambitious projects being JOINT VENTURES. In 2014 further possibilities in the Gard *département* in the southern Rhône and in GEORGIA were under review.

Livingstone-Learmonth, J., *The Wines of the Northern Rhône* (Berkeley, 2005).

Chaptal, Jean-Antoine (1756–1832), French chemist, statesman, and polymath who rose from humble beginnings to become Minister of the Interior under Napoleon. He was the son of an apothecary, and studied chemistry at the University of MONTPELLIER, where a Chair of Chemistry was founded for him in 1781. In 1799, he wrote the article on wine for the monumental *Dictionnaire d'agriculture* of the Abbé Rozier, but is better known in wine circles for his *l'Art de faire le vin* (1807) and his support for the concept of increasing the ALCOHOLIC STRENGTH of wine by adding sugar to the must, the procedure now known as CHAPTALIZATION. Some winemakers throughout history sought to enhance either the quality or quantity of their product by adulterating the basic raw material, grapes, with other products. However, after the French Revolution of 1789, there was a considerable increase in the amount of poor-quality wine made in France. This provided the incentive for Chaptal to compile his famous *Traité théorique et pratique sur la culture de la vigne* (1801). Although he is best known for having introduced the metric system of weights and measures into France, as a practical scientist Chaptal was particularly concerned at the declining reputation of French wines, with increasing ADULTERATION AND FRAUD in the wine trade, and with the ignorance on the part of many French wine producers about the scientific advances that could help them. He was of the firm belief that it was perfectly natural, and desirable, to add sugar to wine in order to improve it. Although he encouraged farmers to use GRAPE CONCENTRATE, he recognized that sugar from cane or beet was also capable of having a similar effect. (Another of Chaptal's many achievements was his development of techniques for extracting sugar from sugar beet.) Chaptal's treatise synthesizing beneficial winemaking techniques current at the beginning of the 19th century marked a turning point in the history of wine technology. It was translated into Italian, Spanish, German, and Hungarian. Two American versions appeared and James BUSBY published a translation in Australia in 1825.   P.T.H.U.

Chaptal, J. A., *Traité théorique et pratique sur la culture de la vigne* (Paris, 1801).

Gough, J. B., 'Winecraft and chemistry in 18th century France: Chaptal and the invention of chaptalization', *Technology and Culture*, 39 (1998), 74–104.

Johnson, H., *The Story of Wine* (London, 1989).

Loubère, L. A., *The Red and the White: A History of Wine in France and Italy in the Nineteenth Century* (Albany, NY, 1978).

chaptalization, common winemaking practice, named after its French promulgator Jean-Antoine CHAPTAL, whereby the final ALCOHOLIC STRENGTH of a wine is increased by the addition of sugar to the grape juice or must, before and/or during FERMENTATION, although if it is added before, the higher sugar level will make it harder for the YEAST to multiply. Contrary to popular belief, Chaptal did not invent the process, which had been the subject of common experiment, not least by the innovative French chemist Pierre-Joseph Macquer.

Amelioration is a common English euphemism for chaptalization. The French sometimes call it *amélioration*; the Germans, who were introduced to the technique by the chemist Ludwig Gall in the mid 19th century, call it *Verbesserung*; while most southern Europeans consider it an appalling practice, chiefly because, thanks to their warmer climate, they have no need of it.

Although the practice is still commonplace, and is indeed the norm in northern Europe, potential alcoholic strength is increasingly raised by adding products other than beet or cane sugar (particularly grape products of which there has been a surplus in many wine regions). The addition of sugar, grape MUST, GRAPE CONCENTRATE, and rectified concentrated grape must (RCGM) in order to increase a wine's alcoholic strength are collectively known as enrichment, the general term for chaptalization and all related techniques and that officially sanctioned in EU parlance. Within the EU, permission to chaptalize depends on the EU climatic zone in which an area falls. For example, it is permitted in Zone A, which includes the UK and northern Germany, but it is not permitted in Zone C IIIb, which includes southern Italy. A country's own regulations may also forbid the practice, as throughout Italy.

In 1993, the EU, concerned about its wine SURPLUS, officially announced its disapproval of chaptalization and its intention to curb the practice because it tended to encourage higher YIELDS. Although this announcement made little difference to winemaking practices, chaptalization, once routine in northern Europe, is becoming less common, partly because grapes tend to be picked later and riper, perhaps partly because of CLIMATE CHANGE.

Producers of Pinot Noir, most notably in Burgundy but also in Oregon and elsewhere, often add sugar during alcoholic fermentation, particularly towards the end, even if some might not readily confess to it. The aim is not primarily to increase the final alcohol level but to extend the fermentation and thereby improve the flavour and texture of the wine. It is said that earlier picking followed by this fractional chaptalization (which is less disruptive to yeast metabolism) often produces better results than fruit picked later with higher sugar levels.

See ENRICHMENT for more details.

Gough, J. B., 'Winecraft and chemistry in 18th century France: Chaptal and the invention of chaptalization', *Technology and Culture*, 39 (1998), 74–104.

char, term sometimes used of barrels. See TOAST.

Charbono, the California name for the virtually extinct DOUCE NOIRE of the SAVOIE region in the French Alps, also known as Corbeau and Charbonneau. Charbono clings to existence on under 100 acres/40 ha on the North Coast, especially in the Napa Valley. As varietal wine it can be difficult to distinguish from Barbera grown under similar circumstances. DNA PROFILING has shown it is identical to the BONARDA of ARGENTINA.

Robinson, J., Harding, J., and Vouillamoz, J., *Wine Grapes: A Complete Guide to 1,368 Vine Varieties, Including their Origins and Flavours* (London, 2012).

charcoal, absorbent material occasionally used in wine processing to remove COLOUR and off flavours caused by BOTRYTIS or SOUR ROT. Charcoal is an impure amorphous CARBON obtained by the dry distillation of wood or some other material containing carbon (bones, peat, and plant debris have all been used). The sort of charcoal most frequently used in winemaking is generally known as **active carbon** and is much purer than the charcoal in common use as a fuel in 17th-century England.

Because of its very porous nature, charcoal has the particularly high ratio of surface area to weight required of an absorptive material. In winemaking it is used mainly to absorb the colloidal pigment polymers responsible for amber or brown colours in white wines, particularly in the manufacture of Pale Cream SHERRY. Off-flavours in wine are occasionally removed

using a grade of active charcoal with a smaller pore size, transforming an unsaleable wine into a neutral one for use in a basic blend. Charcoal is also used on juice to remove off flavours caused by botrytis or sour rot, for example (a process known as *Kohlschönung* in Germany, where the practice is relatively common). However, this may have a negative effect on the quality of the wine.   A.D.W.

Chardonel, cunningly named vine CROSS of Seyval Blanc and Chardonnay made at New York State's Geneva experimental station (see CORNELL) in 1953. Originally tested in eastern US under the name GW9, it was named and released only in 1990. The variety is more resistant to WINTER FREEZE, POWDERY MILDEW, and BOTRYTIS than Chardonnay, and is planted to a limited extent in cooler American states. Wines may resemble either Seyval Blanc or Chardonnay.

Smart, R, 'Chardonel, anyone?', *Practical Winery & Vineyard* (Jan/Feb 1998), 111–12.

Chardonnay, a name so familiar to wine lovers around the world that many do not realize that it is the name of a white grape variety. In its Burgundian homeland, Chardonnay has for long been the sole vine responsible for all of the finest white burgundy. As such, in a region devoted to geographical labelling, its name was known only to vine-growers. All this changed with the advent of VARIETAL labelling in the late 20th century, when Chardonnay virtually became a BRAND. It is perhaps fitting that a variety so governed by the whims of FASHION should have seen considerable stylistic changes in the sorts of wine sought by its legion of fans. Until the mid 1990s, rich, oaky varietals were the height of modishness but this has been followed by a trend towards leaner, more appetizing, and definitely less oak-dominated Chardonnays.

Chardonnay-mania reached a peak in the late 1980s and it was subsequently planted so widely that a glut was assured in the late 1990s, leading to a shortage of Chardonnay in the early 21st century in Australia, for example. There is hardly a country in which wine is produced that does not at least try to produce commercially acceptable Chardonnay in marketable quantities. During a single decade, the 1980s, the world's total area planted with Chardonnay vines quadrupled, to nearly 100,000 ha/ 247,000 acres—and by the mid 2000s had surpassed 174,000 ha/430,000 acres. By 2010, total global plantings were very nearly 200,000 ha, although the rate of increase had definitely slowed, thanks to what might be called 'the Bridget Jones effect'. Chardonnay came to be associated with mass market demand (see ABC). So popular is Chardonnay that synonyms are rarely used (although some Austrians in Styria persist with their name Morillon). The wine's relatively high level of alcohol, which can often taste slightly sweet, probably played a part in this popularity, as for a time did the obvious appeal of the OAK so often used in making Chardonnay. But it is not just wine drinkers who appreciate the broad, easy-to-appreciate if difficult-to-describe charms of golden Chardonnay. (The AUSTRALIAN WINE RESEARCH INSTITUTE's initiative, analysing the component parts of each major variety's flavour, found Chardonnay a particularly nebulous target, identifying flavour compounds also found in, among other things, raspberries, vanilla, tropical fruits, peaches, tomatoes, tobacco, tea, and rose petals.)

Vine-growers appreciate the ease with which, in a wide range of climates, they can coax relatively high yields from this vine (whose natural VIGOUR may need to be curbed by either dense planting, low-vigour ROOTSTOCKS or CANOPY MANAGEMENT). Wine quality is severely prejudiced, however, at yields above 80 hl/ha (4.5 tons/acre) and yields of 30 hl/ha or lower are usually needed for seriously fine wine. Growers' only major reservation is that it buds quite early, just after Pinot Noir, which regularly puts the coolest vineyards—those of Chablis, Champagne, and Chile's Casablanca Valley, for example—at risk from spring FROSTS. It can suffer from COULURE and occasionally MILLERANDAGE and the grapes' relatively thin skins can encourage rot if there is rain at harvest time, but it can thrive in climates as diverse as those of CHABLIS in northern France and Australia's hot RIVERLAND. Picking time is critical for, unlike Cabernet Sauvignon, Chardonnay can quickly lose its crucial acidity in the latter stages of ripening.

Winemakers love Chardonnay for its reliably high ripeness levels and its malleability. It will happily respond to a far wider range of winemaking techniques than most white varieties. The Mosel or Vouvray winemaking recipe of a long, cool fermentation followed by early bottling can be applied to Chardonnay. Or it can be treated to BARREL FERMENTATION and/or BARREL MATURATION, some of the highest-quality fruit being able to stand up to new oak. It accommodates each individual winemaker's policy on the second, softening MALOLACTIC CONVERSION and LEES STIRRING without demur. Chardonnay is also a vital ingredient in most of the world's best SPARKLING WINE, not just in Champagne, demonstrating its ability to age in bottle even when picked early. And, picked late, it has even been known to produce some creditable BOTRYTIZED wines, notably in the Mâconnais, Romania, and New Zealand. Chardonnay blends happily with other less fashionable, cheaper varieties such as Chenin Blanc, Sémillon, or Colombard to meet demand or PRICE POINTS at the lower end of the market. But perhaps this is because its own character is, unlike that of the other ultra-fashionable white, Sauvignon Blanc,

not too pronounced. Chardonnay from young or over-productive vines can taste almost aqueous. Basic Chardonnay may be vaguely fruity (apples or melons) but, at its best, Chardonnay, like Pinot Noir, is merely a vehicle for the character of the vineyard in which it is grown (see TERROIR). As in many other ambitious wines fashioned in the image of top white burgundy, its 'flavour' has sometimes been that of the oak in which it was matured, or the relics of the winemaking techniques used (see above). When the vineyard site is right, yields not too high, acid not too low, and winemaking skilled, Chardonnay can produce thrilling, savoury, dry, full-bodied wines that will continue to improve in bottle for one, two, or, exceptionally, more decades but—unlike RIESLING and the best, nobly rotten CHENIN BLANC and SÉMILLON—it is not a variety capable of making whites for the very long term, and white burgundies, in particular, have shown a tendency to PREMATURE OXIDATION.

Chardonnay's origins were long considered obscure, but DNA PROFILING finally provided the answer to this mystery. Along with a host of other varieties common in north eastern France, it is the progeny of Pinot Noir and GOUAIS BLANC (see PINOT).

There is a rare but distinct pink-berried mutation, **Chardonnay Rose**, as well as a headily perfumed **Chardonnay Blanc Musqué** version, sometimes used in blends. Some of the 34 official French CLONES of Chardonnay have a similarly grapey perfume, notably 77 and 809, which have been quite widely planted and can add a rather incongruously aromatic note to blends with other clones of the variety. The arguably overenthusiastic application of CLONAL SELECTION techniques in Burgundy means that growers can now choose from a wide range of Chardonnay clones specially selected for their productivity, particularly 75, 78, 121, 124, 125, and 277. Those seeking quality rather than quantity are more likely to choose 76, 95, and 96. Many New World wine regions began their love affair with Chardonnay on clones such as the Mendoza clone, only to find it rekindled by the introduction of better clones from Burgundy, sometimes known as Dijon clones. In California, the old Wente clone is held in high regard.

In France the total area planted with Chardonnay—47,487 ha/ 117,292 acres in 2111—has long been second only in rankings of paleskinned varieties to the Cognac and Armagnac grape Ugni Blanc. Chardonnay is significant in every single Fench wine region except for Alsace and Bordeaux and is particularly so in greater Burgundy, the Languedoc, and Champagne where Chardonnay, with more than 10,000 ha by 2013, was only just the least-planted of the three most important varieties there. France, once home to sizeable tracts of dozens of local grape varieties, has become increasingly dominated by this paradigm of an

INTERNATIONAL VARIETY. Chablis is quintessential Chardonnay country and plantings totalled very nearly 6,000 ha by 2011. In the Burgundian heartland, the CÔTE D'OR, Chardonnay plantings had increased to 2,230 ha by 2011 at the expense of ALIGOTÉ, but were outnumbered three to one by those of Pinot Noir. In the Côte CHALONNAISE and the MÂCONNAIS to the south, Chardonnay, with an overall total of 7,242 ha by 2011, was twice as common overall as Pinot Noir, Mâcon Blanc being by far the most common, and affordable, incarnation of white burgundy. Although the regulations allow Aligoté into Beaujolais Blanc and Pinot Blanc into white wines labelled Bourgogne and Mâcon, most of these less expensive white burgundies are in practice made predominantly from Chardonnay. To the initial horror of the INAO, there has been an increasing trend towards slipping the word Chardonnay on to white burgundy labels to increase their appeal to non-French consumers.

In the Languedoc, Chardonnay was first planted to add international appeal to the lemony wines of LIMOUX. By 2000 there were nearly 9,000 ha of Chardonnay in the Languedoc, a total that had grown to nearly 14,000 ha by 2011, nearly 6,000 of them in the hot Hérault département, although this is essentially red wine country.

Chardonnay is grown in virtually all European wine-producing countries, and makes copies of white burgundy of varying qualities, even if much of Spain south of Catalunya (where it plays a part in CAVA) is too hot, and Portugal wisely tends to concentrate on its INDIGENOUS VARIETIES. Even Germany, Rieslingland, now grows Chardonnay on 1,500 ha of vineyard, and it is an important ingredient in the sparkling wine production of England.

Italy has a long history of Chardonnay cultivation, especially on its subalpine slopes in the north, and the 2010 census identified nearly 20,000 ha/50,000 acres of Chardonnay throughout the country. For decades, Italians were casual about distinguishing between their Pinot Bianco (PINOT BLANC, also known as Weissburgunder in the Italian Tyrol) and their Chardonnay (traditionally called Gelber, or Golden, Weissburgunder in the Italian Tyrol). Alto Adige Chardonnay was the first Italian Chardonnay accorded DOC status, in 1984, although the vine has since been working its magic on producers all over Italy from Puglia to Piemonte and, of course, Aosta towards the French border. Nowadays much of Italy's Chardonnay is produced, often without much distinction, in Friuli, Trentino, and, to a more limited extent, Veneto, where much of it is used as ballast for GARGANEGA. Some fine examples are produced in favoured sites in both Friuli and Trentino but a considerable proportion is siphoned off to become SPUMANTE, as it is

HARVEST / CHILE Different vine **training systems** and **trellisses** are designed to encourage bunches to form at specific heights according to local conditions, for example to benefit from the warmth of the soil or to reduce frost risk. But waist-height is probably the most convenient for pickers such as these Chileans in the Polkura Hill vineyard in Colchagua. © Matt Wilson/Cephas Picture Library

in Lombardy, where it can add finesse to some fine fizz. Chardonnay gained ground rapidly in Italy in the 1990s, being planted in Tuscan spots where Sangiovese is difficult to ripen. Piemonte, cooler than Tuscany, has, not unsurprisingly, had more overall success with the variety. See under these geographical names for more details of Italian Chardonnays.

Much less dramatic Chardonnay is also produced in Switzerland, particularly in Geneva, the Valais, and Bündner Herrschaft (see map under SWITZERLAND). In Austria, a foreign vine known as Morillon in Styria and Feinburgunder in Vienna and Burgenland was not identified as the modish Chardonnay until the late 1980s. Austria's Chardonnays include relatively rich, oak-matured versions; lean, aromatic styles modelled on their finest Rieslings; and even sweet AUSBRUCH wines. See AUSTRIA. The variety is planted throughout Eastern Europe but, with the notable exception of some fine, artisanal Slovenian examples, yields and temperatures are often too high for real distinction.

Few would have believed in 1980, when California had just 18,000 acres/7,200 ha of Chardonnay, that by 1988 the state's total plantings would for a while overtake France's (rapidly increasing) total. In the 21st century France more than caught up, even though Chardonnay remains California's most planted variety with a 2012 total of 95,000 acres/38,461 ha. Thanks to the red wine boom, the rate of new plantings reached a peak in the mid 1990s. See under CALIFORNIA for more detail of the state's evolving but generally rich, heady style of Chardonnay.

Chardonnay, now North American for 'white wine', has been embraced with equal fervour throughout the rest of North America, from British Columbia in CANADA to Long Island in NEW YORK, although it is usually more restrained in character than in California. In 1990, Chardonnay overtook Riesling to become the most planted variety of any hue in WASHINGTON State but red wine is now far more important and the 2011 Chardonnay total of 7,652 acres makes it only the most planted white wine grape. Chardonnay is also increasingly well regarded in Oregon (where plantings totalled 950 acres in 2011 and the introduction of DIJON CLONES has had a profound effect on quality), Virginia, and Texas. The scale of America's romance with Chardonnay in general and oak-aged Chardonnay in particular was reflected in the international COOPERAGE business in the 1990s.

Various South American countries have been seeking out cooler spots to imbue their Chardonnay with real verve and concentration. Chile's Pacific-influenced regions including most notably Casablanca Valley and San Antonio/Leyda and the high-elevation vineyards of Argentina's Uco Valley are the most obvious examples and their best wines combine the New World virtues of accessibility and value.

In Argentina, where the variety has shown impressive finesse, Chardonnay overtook Ugni Blanc, Chenin Blanc, Semillon, and Sauvignonasse in the 1990s to become the country's second most planted white wine grape after Torrontés. Total Argentine plantings were more than 6,470 ha by 2011. Chile has even more, 10,970 ha, and Chardonnay was the country's most planted white wine grape (and third overall) for the first decade of this century but Sauvignon Blanc has once more taken the lead. The Australian wine industry's all-important export trade was for long centred on its particularly user-friendly and frequently adapted style of Chardonnay. Rich fruit flavours, often disciplined by added acid and flavoured by OAK CHIPS, have been available at carefully judged price points. Such was the strength of demand for Australian Chardonnay in the late 1980s that the area of Chardonnay vines increased more than fivefold during the decade so that in 1990, Chardonnay, with its 4,300 ha/10,600 acres, became Australia's most planted white wine grape variety (although 1,300 ha were too young to bear fruit). Plantings peaked in 2007 with more than 32,000 ha but reaction to a glut left total Chardonnay plantings at 25,491 ha in 2012, very slighty less than those of Cabernet Sauvignon, Australia's second most popular variety after Shiraz. The style of typical Australian Chardonnay changed more rapidly than any other nation's with steeliness, almost austerity, now seen as virtues. Nevertheless, the average life expectancy of typical Australian (and most other New World) Chardonnay is short, but glorious exceptions abound in cooler spots such as Adelaide Hills, Victoria, and Tasmania, and can give fine white burgundy a run for its money.

New Zealand's love affair with Chardonnay was relatively short. Only in the last decade of the 20th century did Chardonnay plantings outnumber those of the Sauvignon Blanc that has now been anointed queen of Kiwi vines. By 2012 total plantings of Chardonnay, just over 3,000 ha, had fallen to less than one-sixth those of Sauvignon Blanc, even though the naturally high acidity of New Zealand wines suits Chardonnay so well. Chardonnay has had a chequered history in South Africa. Planting material in the late 1970s and early 1980s was frequently smuggled rather than submitted for QUARANTINE, and at one time significant quantities of AUXERROIS contaminated the authenticity of 'Chardonnay' vineyards. For a while Chardonnay was the country's third most planted white wine grape, albeit a long way behind Chenin Blanc and Colombard, but in 2006 Sauvignon Blanc, as in New Zealand, overtook Chardonnay whose plantings in 2012 were under 8,000 ha.

Although Chardonnay can thrive in relatively hot climates (such as Australia's irrigation zones), it has to be picked before acids plummet (sometimes before the grapes have developed much real character, although this is usually caused by excessively high yields) and it does require relatively sophisticated techniques, including TEMPERATURE CONTROL, in the cellar. This is why it is not especially well suited to hot Mediterranean wine regions and well-balanced Chardonnays with real interest from the likes of Greece, Israel, and the Lebanon tend to be exceptions.

Charlemagne, king of the Franks 768–814, crowned Holy Roman Emperor in 800, the man who ushered in civilization, order, and prosperity after the long Dark Ages, ruling a Christian kingdom based at Aachen (Aix-la-Chapelle) which included virtually all of France, Belgium, Germany, and Switzerland.

Charlemagne's name is associated by modern wine drinkers with one of the greatest white burgundies, Corton-Charlemagne (whose vineyards include a plot known as Le Charlemagne), produced on land he gave to the Abbey of Saulieu in 775 (see ALOXE-CORTON for more detail). Charlemagne's secretary and biographer Einhard tells us, however, that Charlemagne was a moderate man: he never drank more than three cups of wine with dinner, and he hated to see people drunk (*Life of Charlemagne*, ch. 24). Only a temperate man is truly interested in wine: when he renamed the 12 months of the year in his native language, he called October 'windume-manoth', the month of the wine harvest (Einhard, ch. 28)—which was presumably true of the vineyards then established in parts of northern Europe considered too cool for viable wine production today.

This Old FRANKEN name reflects the growing importance of wine in the Carolingian era, for under Charlemagne and his heirs more and more vines began to be grown. Viticulture had of course been long established in a large part of Charlemagne's empire. The Greek colonists had introduced wine-growing to Massilia (now Marseilles) from 600 BC onwards. When the Romans, under Julius Caesar, conquered Gaul in 51 BC, they gradually expanded the small-scale viticulture of the Gauls, who had drunk mainly BEER. The Roman settlers planted their first vineyards in southern Gaul, and by the 2nd century wine was grown extensively in most of Gaul. The Romans also planted vines in the Moselle valley, on the left bank of the Rhine, and in the areas we now know as Alsace, the Pfalz, and Rheinhessen.

The spread of Christianity was one reason for the expansion of viticulture that took place during Charlemagne's reign and continued for another two centuries afterwards. The Church needed a daily supply of wine to celebrate the EUCHARIST. Also, monasteries, many of which were new foundations, needed wine for the monks and their guests (see MONKS AND MONAS-TERIES) and vineyards were planted all over northern France and even southern Belgium.

The Rule of St Benedict permitted a modest daily ration of wine, and more on holy days and feast days; important guests who stayed at the monastery had to be suitably entertained, for they might one day repay the monks generously for their hospitality. Monasteries usually had their own vineyards, and often these had been donated by local landowners who hoped for a place in heaven. Bishops also wanted wine, not just for the day-to-day running of their households but as a status symbol to put themselves on a par with the nobility of the district. Bishops, like monks, had their own vineyards, and some bishops may even have moved their sees to be nearer vineyards: at least, this may explain why the bishopric of Langres moved south to Dijon (at the north of the CÔTE D'OR), that of Tongres to Liège in modern Belgium, and that of St-Quentin to Noyon north of Paris. Thus Christianity fostered the production of two grades of wine, wine for daily consumption and a superior kind that was designed to impress prestigious guests.

In 816, the Council of Aachen added a third category of ecclesiastical viticulture. The Council prescribed that a college of canons, living under monastic rule, should be attached to every cathedral and that the canons should grow wine. Often they tended vineyards adjacent to those of their bishops; collegiate churches could be founded elsewhere in the diocese as well, and they also acquired their own vineyards.

Unlike education, viticulture was not the preserve of the Church, however: laymen also grew wine. The factor that decided where they established their new vineyards was not TERROIR but ease of transport. If the enterprise was to be commercially viable, the area had to be near a navigable RIVER or within easy reach, by road, of a major town or city. This is why so much wine was grown around PARIS, AUXERRE, and in CHAMPAGNE, despite the fact that it was too cold there for the vine to yield ripe and abundant fruit. If the summer had not been hot, there was nothing for it but to drink thin, acidic wine until the following autumn, unless one could afford to buy better wine from elsewhere. An interesting document from the last decade of the 8th century deals with the management of vineyards in secular ownership. It is known as the 'Capitulare de villis', or 'Concerning estates' (a capitulary being a collection of ordinances). Linguistic evidence and local references show that it was drawn up for Aquitaine, which was administered by Charlemagne's son Louis the Pious before he succeeded his father. The list of plants and herbs which it says must be grown in the estate's market garden owes more to the library than to real horticulture, but the advice it gives on wine-growing is sound and practical. Not only should the king's inspectors claim the portion of the vintage that is the royal household's due, they should also oversee hygienic procedures in the vineyard. Wine PRESSES should be clean, and grapes should not be trodden with the feet. Wine that is to be sent to the palace should be put into proper wooden BARRELS instead of leather wineskins. An inventory of the entire estate should be drawn up each Christmas, including the wine it has produced that autumn and any older wine left over.

The 'Capitulare de villis' has no connection with Charlemagne himself, and there is no solid evidence that he initiated the planting of any vineyard, although parts of France and the Rheingau were first planted in his day. Viticulture flourished, not because of a *dirigiste* policy but because political unity had brought prosperity. External threats, most importantly from the Moors and the Magyars, could not be prevented and had to be dealt with, but, within the frontiers of the Holy Roman Empire, peace reigned, and viticulture was so successful that there was a surplus of wine. Landowners had to resort to the right of 'banvin', by which none of their tenants was allowed to sell his wine until the lord had sold his own. In the south, wine was part of everyday life; in the north it was more of a luxury item but it could still be obtained readily.

How different things were in England! When the English scholar Alcuin, friend of Charlemagne and tutor to his court at Aachen, went back to his native country for a visit, he complained bitterly in a letter, dated 790, to a Frankish ex-pupil. The wine has run out, and his stomach aches with sour beer: please send wine. BEER has its uses, but it is not a civilized drink. In the 8th century, the Frankish kingdom was a better place for a wine drinker to be than Anglo-Saxon England.

See also GERMAN HISTORY.   H.M.W.

Bassermann-Jordan, F., *Geschichte des Weinbaus*, 3 vols., i (1907).

Dion, R., *Histoire de la vigne et du vin en France* (France, 1959; rpt 1977).

Duby, G., *Historie de la France rurale*, 4 vols., i (1975).

Einhard and Notker the Stammerer, *Two Lives of Charlemagne*, tr. Lewis Thorpe (London, 1969).

Latouche, R., *The Birth of Western Economy* (London, 1961).

Charles Sturt University

Charles Sturt University, one of Australia's foremost research and teaching institutions for grape-growers and winemakers. Courses started in 1976 within the Riverina College of Advanced Education, Wagga Wagga, New South Wales (NSW) to satisfy the need, within the rapidly growing wine industry, for a teaching institution in addition to ROSEWORTHY. In 1989, the College combined with other regional teaching institutions in NSW to form Charles Sturt University (CSU).

The School of Agricultural and Wine Sciences offers Bachelor of Wine Science and Bachelor of Viticulture degrees in either viticulture or wine science over three years full-time on campus or six years by distance education (DE). Initially a controversial option for the wine industry, DE is now the predominant means of learning, allowing students to continue in their current profession while studying. There is also a shorter Associate Degree in Wine Science (Winegrowing) as a four-year exit point from the longer Bachelor of Wine Business. The Master of Viticulture and Oenology has full-time and DE options and requires a research dissertation. CSU also offers its degrees through partner institutions in New Zealand and elsewhere in Australia.

In 1997, CSU joined the NSW Government's Department of Primary Industries and the NSW Wine Industry Association to form the National Wine and Grape Industry Centre, an alliance that conducts research and offers extension services to assist the wine industry in applying best practice.   N.B.

Charmat, the name of a bulk SPARKLING WINEMAKING process which involves provoking a second fermentation in a pressure tank. Also called *cuve close* or tank method.

Charneco, Portuguese white wine, probably fortified, popular in England in the 16th and 17th centuries and mentioned by Shakespeare in *2 Henry VI*. It is probably the forerunner of BUCELAS.   R.J.M.

Charta (pronounced 'karta'), an association of RHEINGAU wine producers founded in 1984 (although the first wines were vintage 1983), and the designation given to one or two special Riesling bottlings made annually by each member in accordance with the association's strict standard for YIELDS, MUST WEIGHTS, and permissible vineyards of origin. (Paradoxically, these may not be labelled with the names of specific vineyards, although if a grower offers both a QBA and KABINETT Charta bottling, they will typically originate from different single sites.) Charta Rieslings must be finished TROCKEN or HALB-TROCKEN—a stricture intended as homage to tradition—and pass three blind tasting tests, after which they are bottled in tall flute-shaped bottles embossed and labelled with a double Romanesque arch. (Some estates use this as an opportunity to commission Charta-dedicated ARTISTS' LABELS.) The qualitative impetus behind this association and its wines is often rightly associated with the subsequent emergence of ERSTES GEWÄCHS and GROSSES GEWÄCHS as quality wine categories, although the number of participating growers has fallen slightly in recent years from a high of nearly 50.   D.S.

Chasan, CROSS of Palomino (known in France as LISTÁN) and Chardonnay vines made under

INRA auspices by French AMPELOGRAPHER Paul Truel. The resulting wine bears a lightweight imprint of Chardonnay while the vine buds early. It is planted on a limited scale in the Midi, particularly in the Aude *département*, and France's total plantings were more than 660 ha/1,630 acres by 2011.

Chassagne-Montrachet

Chassagne-Montrachet, village in the Côte de Beaune district of Burgundy's Côte d'Or more famed for its white wines from the Chardonnay grape than for its equally plentiful red wines from Pinot Noir. Until the mid 1980s, the village produced more red wine than white, but the significant premium for white Chassagne led to considerable planting of Chardonnay, even on relatively unsuitable soils.

The better soil for Pinot Noir, limestone marl with a red gravel content, lies mainly on the south side of the village towards Santenay and incorporates most of the village appellation, although La Boudriotte and Morgeot, among the PREMIERS CRUS, make excellent red wines, as can Clos St-Jean closer to the village. Red Chassagne-Montrachet tends to be somewhat hard and earthy when young, mellowing with age but rarely achieving the delicacy of truly fine red burgundy.

The fame of Chassagne rests with the white wines at village, premier cru, and especially GRAND CRU level. Chassagne shares the Le Montrachet and Bâtard-Montrachet vineyards with neighbouring Puligny and enjoys sole possession of a third grand cru, Criots-Bâtard-Montrachet (see MONTRACHET for more details). Among the premiers crus, the best known are Les Chenevottes, Clos de la Maltroie, En Cailleret, and Les Ruchottes. Suitable white wine soil tends to have more oolitic limestone and less marl in its make-up.

The white wines of Chassagne are noted for their steely power, less rounded than MEURSAULT when young, sometimes similar to PULIGNY-MONTRACHET if less floral. Good vintages from good producers such as Ramonet and the extended Colin, Gagnard, and Morey clans should age from five to ten years. In 2011, some 3,935 hl of red wine and 10,805 hl of white were produced from 304 ha/750 acres of vineyards. This 75:25 ratio in favour of white wines is an inversion of the position 40 years earlier.

See also CÔTE D'OR, and map under BURGUNDY.

J.T.C.M.

Chasselas

Chasselas, even if by no means the most revered white grape variety, is widely planted under dozens of names around the world and has a particularly long, intriguing history. DNA PROFILING suggests its origins lie in French SWITZERLAND, where it certainly produces its finest wines today, often called Fendant, its common synonym in the Valais. Chasselas is still Switzerland's most planted white wine grape and is particularly common in the canton of Vaud, where over half of the total of more than 4,000 ha/10,000 acres are grown. Individual villages all over French Switzerland but particularly on the northern bank of Lac Léman have won acclaim for their TERROIR-specific interpretations of what can be a relatively neutral grape.

In France, it is rather despised, not least because, as Chasselas Doré or Golden Chasselas, it is France's most common TABLE GRAPE. Total French plantings had declined to just over 700 ha by 2011. It is rapidly disappearing from Alsace, where it is regarded as the lowest of the low and is generally sold as Edelzwicker or under some proprietary name that excludes mention of any grape variety. Planted in the area responsible for Pouilly-Fumé, it makes the distinctly inferior white labelled Pouilly-sur-Loire and, as might be expected, approaches respectability only as it nears Switzerland, in SAVOIE. Here it is the main grape grown in the *département* of Haute Savoie on the south side of Lake Geneva in the Vin de Savoie CRUS of CRÉPY, MARIGNAN, Marin, and Ripaille.

The variety's long history has enabled it to spread far and wide. In Germany, where it is known as Weisser GUTEDEL and is grown on more than 1,000 ha, mainly in BADEN, it has been known since the 16th century. It is no longer nearly as important in central Europe as it once was but can stil be found in Hungary, Romania, Russia, and Serbia. Outside Europe it is most important in Chile.

château

château may be French for 'castle' but in wine parlance it usually means a vine-growing, winemaking estate, to include the vineyards, the cellars, often the wine itself, and any building or buildings on the property, which can range from the non-existent (as in the case of Ch Léoville-BARTON, for example, which is made in the cellars of Ch Langoa-Barton), through the most rudimentary shack, to the sumptuous classical edifice called Ch MARGAUX. The term is most commonly used in BORDEAUX, where the 18th edition of the FÉRET guide lists more than 14,000 châteaux, although common use of the term developed only in the second half of the 19th century, when the owners of the great estates could afford to build grand lodgings to go with them. Only five of the original 79 properties in the Médoc, Graves, and Sauternes listed in the famous 1855 CLASSIFICATION, for example, were described as châteaux then. Bordeaux proprietors soon learnt the value of a Château prefix, and have long adopted the policy of renaming properties almost at will, in particular suffixing their own surname as, for example, Ch Prieuré-LICHINE and Chx Mouton- and Lafite-ROTHSCHILD. The word château is by no means uncommon outside Bordeaux, however, mainly within but sometimes outside FRANCE (where it tends to lose its circumflex). According to current French law, the word château may be used only of a specified plot, or collection of plots, of land, which means that it is perfectly possible for CO-OPERATIVES, for example, to produce a wine labelled as Château Quelquechose (see CHÂTEAU BOTTLING). Some producers make a range of wines carrying the name of the property, but reserve the word château for their top bottlings.

château bottling

château bottling, the relatively recent practice of BOTTLING the produce of a CHÂTEAU on that property. Such a wine is said to be **château bottled**, or *mis(e) en bouteille au château* in French, an expression used throughout France but particularly in BORDEAUX. (Its counterpart in BURGUNDY is DOMAINE BOTTLED, while in the NEW WORLD the term ESTATE BOTTLED is often used.)

Initially all wine was sold in bulk, and subsequently it was up to the MERCHANTS, whether in the region of consumption or production, to put the wine into bottle. Even as recently as the mid 20th century, the great majority of wine left the property on which it was produced in BARRELS. ADULTERATION AND FRAUD was therefore all too easy among less scrupulous merchants, and particularly tempting in the wake of the world wine shortages which followed POWDERY MILDEW and PHYLLOXERA at the end of the 19th century.

It was the young Baron Philippe de ROTHSCHILD who did most to promote château bottling when he took over Ch MOUTON ROTHSCHILD in the early 1920s. He succeeded in persuading all the first growths (and Ch Mouton Rothschild of course) of the wisdom of bottling all of their principal output, the so-called GRAND VIN, on their own territory. This involved a certain amount of investment, but the resulting reliability and cachet more than compensated.

Good bottling lines require a level of investment that is unrealistic for many a small wine property, however, so contract bottlers and mobile bottling lines are much in demand, and a producer may not be able to bottle at the precise time he or she would prefer. Others still bottle by hand, some with scant regard for HYGIENE and consistency. Such considerations mean that bottling at source is not necessarily superior to careful BULK TRANSPORT of the wine to a top-quality bottling plant.

Today, a producer of château bottled wine, described on the label as *mis(e) en bouteille au château*, is likely to care about quality. It is worth noting in addition that wines made from specific plots of land but vinified and bottled by CO-OPERATIVES may also be described as château bottled.

Château-Chalon

Château-Chalon, extraordinary wine made in the JURA region of eastern France with its own small appellation named after the hill-top village where it is produced. In the 17th century or even earlier the abbesses from the Abbey of Château-Chalon may have been the first in the region to make a VIN JAUNE style of wine, historically named 'Vin de Garde'. Unlike other Jura appellations, Château-Chalon must be a Vin Jaune and thus must be made exclusively from SAVAGNIN grapes grown on the local grey MARL. (Other wines produced by local growers are entitled to the Côtes du Jura appellation.) In 1952 the appellation was the first in France to instigate vineyard inspections pre-harvest before the vintage is approved. The noble decision was made not to bottle any wine under the appellation in 1974, 1980, 1984, and 2001. Like all Vin Jaune, the wine must be kept for at least six years and three months before bottling, most of this time spent in partially filled, untouched casks under the famous *voile*, or local benevolent FILM-FORM-ING YEAST. The resulting wine is exceptionally spicy and mineral-rich, pale to deep golden, and long lasting. It must be bottled in a special *clavelin* bottle containing 62 cl, supposedly the amount of wine that remains from a litre of wine kept in a cask in Ch-Chalon for six years. The result is a wine that shares some taste characteristics with SHERRY but has more finesse, working well as a gastronomic partner (especially with the local Comté cheese and poultry of Bresse, also APPELLATION CONTRÔLÉE products) and as a candidate for extended BOTTLE AGEING. It is said to develop 'curry' flavours in bottle, thanks to the compound SOTOLON. With only 50 ha/125 acres planted, production volumes vary wildly from zero to around 2,000 hl/52,835 gal in a good year.   W.L.

Château Grillet, one of France's smallest wine appellations and one of the few with a single owner (although see also DOMAINE DE LA ROMANÉE-CONTI). Ch Grillet's few hectares of vineyard represent an enclave within the CONDRIEU zone in the north of the northern Rhône (see map under RHÔNE). A virtual amphitheatre carved out of the granite shelters the narrow terraces of VIOGNIER vines from the north winds which can so seriously prejudice both quantity and quality in Condrieu. Already appreciated by Thomas JEFFERSON in the late 18th century, Ch Grillet has always been in single ownership. Until it was bought by François Pinault, owner of Ch LATOUR, in 2011 it belonged to the Neyret-Gachet family and descendants. Annual production was barely 2,000 cases of Ch Grillet's distinctive brown bottle, one of the last to grow from 70 to 75 cl. Since the 1970s, the wine maintained its high price more by its rarity than because it was obviously one of France's finest wines.

The new team in charge of the original 3.5 ha estate make a second wine, sold as Côtes du Rhône, and are refining rather than changing the style which is more austere and less headily perfumed than the best Condrieu. The result is a restrained, taut, longer-living wine which, unlike Condrieu, may improve in bottle for a decade or even two. The potential of the vineyard is undoubted, as earlier eulogies testify.

Châteaumeillant, small, isolated AOC in central France around the town of Château-meillant between ST POURÇAIN and TOURAINE (see map under FRANCE). Mainly Gamay with some Pinot Noir and a little Pinot Gris produce red and VIN GRIS from fewer than 100 ha/250 acres of VOLCANIC soils. One CO-OPERATIVE dominates production.

Châteauneuf-du-Pape, the most important, and variable, appellation in the southern RHÔNE in terms of quality, producing mainly rich, spicy, full-bodied red wines which can be some of the most alluring expressions of warm-climate viticulture, but can also be either impossibly tannic or disappointingly jammy. Only one in every 16 distinctively heavy and embossed Châteauneuf-du-Pape bottles contains full bodied white wine, which since the 1990s has been increasingly fresh and well made. Rosé is even rarer.

The wine takes its name, which means 'Pope's new castle', from the relocation of the papal court to Avignon in the 14th century, and in particular from the construction of summer quarters just north of the city in a village once known as Calcernier for its limestone quarry. It is now called Châteauneuf-du-Pape. The Gascon Pope Clément V (after whom Ch Pape-Clément in PESSAC-LÉOGNAN is named) arrived at Avignon in 1309 and is supposed to have ordered the planting of vines, but it was his successor John XXII who is credited with developing a papal vineyard in Châteauneuf-du-Pape.

The history of Châteauneuf-du-Pape the wine as such is relatively recent, however. As Livingstone-Learmonth points out, the region's wine was known simply as *vin d'Avignon* in the 18th century, when it was shipped northwards up river. In the early 19th century, a wine called Châteauneuf-du-Pape-Calcernier emerges, but from JULLIEN's description it sounds a much lighter wine than the Châteauneuf-du-Pape of today. Châteauneuf-du-Pape's reputation steadily grew within France until the arrival of the PHYLLOXERA louse began seriously to affect wine production, in the early 1870s, before most other French wine regions.

Reconstruction of the vineyards was financially devastating, and the Châteauneuf-du-Pape vignerons were just some of those affected by the ADULTERATION AND FRAUD that were rife in the early 20th century. By 1923, the most energetic and well connected of their number, Baron Le Roy of Ch Fortia, had successfully drawn up a set of rules for the production of Châteauneuf-du-Pape, with the co-operation of his peers, which was the prototype for the entire APPELLATION CONTRÔLÉE system. Among what have now become the usual regulations, it involved the first geographical DELIMITATION of the original production zone, land being defined as suitable if it were so infertile and arid that thyme and lavender would grow on it. Another notable feature was the minimum specified AL-COHOLIC STRENGTH, at 12.5% still the highest in France, and in the southern Rhône this must be achieved without the aid of external sugar addition, or CHAPTALIZATION. TRIAGE of picked grapes was mandatory and ROSÉ was outlawed (with a flick of the nose at the vignerons of TAVEL just across the river). When GIGONDAS drew up its own appellation rules, it incorporated many of these exigencies.

Perhaps it is because of the antiquity of Châteauneuf-du-Pape's wine regulations that quite so many VINE VARIETIES are theoretically permitted by the Châteauneuf-du-Pape appellation (because vines are such a long-term crop, appellation laws have to countenance the status quo to a certain extent). Three more varieties were added to the original ten in 1936. Today 18 varieties are authorized, without distinction between red and white wines. The Châteauneuf-du-Pape grape *par excellence* is GRENACHE and conversely Châteauneuf-du-Pape is its finest expression in France. Grenache dominates plantings in the Châteauneuf-du-Pape vineyards, and on their impoverished soils, with yields officially restricted to a base rate of just 35 hl/ha (2 tons/acre), it can produce wines which combine concentration with the usual sweet fruit of Grenache, although it is particularly prone to COULURE.

MOURVÈDRE is an increasingly popular ingredient, although it needs the warmest MESOCLI-MATES to ripen fully, while SYRAH from the northern Rhône has also been planted by producers who admire its TANNINS and structure, although, unlike Grenache and Mourvèdre, it needs care to avoid overripeness and is falling from favour in some quarters. CINSAUT is also grown, but to a declining extent. Of the other permitted dark-skinned varieties, MUSCARDIN, VACCARÈSE, PICQUEPOUL Noir, TERRET Noir, and COUNOISE, only the last is grown to any significant extent, and has its admirers, particularly at Ch de Beaucastel, one of the most rigorous producers of Châteauneuf-du-Pape, and one of the few to cultivate such a wide range of varieties. For white Châteauneuf-du-Pape, there is considerable variation in the proportions of Grenache Blanc, CLAIRETTE, BOURBOULENC, and ROUSSANNE planted, although Ch de Beaucastel have demonstrated that a VARIETAL Roussanne can be a worthy candidate for BARREL MATURATION.

PICARDAN, which is not widely planted, produces light, relatively neutral wine.

By 2013, the Châteauneuf-du-Pape appellation comprised 3,161 ha/7,808 acres of relatively flat vineyards at varying elevations and expositions above the river in Châteauneuf-du-Pape and the neighbouring communes of Bédarrides, Courthézon, Orange, and Sorgues. The terrain is traditionally characterized by the large pebbles, or *galets*, some of them several inches across, which cover many of the more photographed vineyards, supposedly retaining heat and speeding the ripening process of the traditionally low-trained GOBELET vines. Soils in Châteauneuf-du-Pape are more varied than this, however (see soil map in Johnson and Robinson, 2013), and those at the celebrated Ch Rayas, for example, are sandy CALCAREOUS without a *galet* in sight. On south-facing slopes, any reradiated night-time heat could well be too much, so, on very pebbly ground, the best vineyards may face at least partly north to moderate this. Most wines are blends from different subzones, but some of the many highly priced special cuvées in particular that have proliferated, sometimes to the detriment are the product of single vineyards.

The key with red Châteauneuf-du-Pape in general is to balance the accumulation of SUGAR IN GRAPES, and therefore alcohol content, with the PHENOLICS, and tannins in particular. Traditionally DESTEMMING has been avoided, and fairly hot fermentations have been accompanied by frequent PUNCHING DOWN or PUMPING OVER, so that some wines have been tannic, although it is also easy for others to be too alcoholic without the flavour and structure to support it. This is arguably France's appellation most evidently affected by CLIMATE CHANGE and musts can sometimes reach nearly 17% POTENTIAL ALCOHOL. Since the 1970s, a number of producers have used CARBONIC MACERATION or SEMI-CARBONIC MACERATION to produce lighter, fruitier wines which can be drunk from about three years rather than from five or six. This is by no means a high-tech wine region, however. Some notable wines include Ch de Beaucastel, Henri Bonneau (Réserve des Célestins), Chapoutier's Barbe Rac, Domaine de la Janasse, Domaine de Pegaü, Ch Rayas, and Domaine du Vieux Télégraphe but dozens more have left the CO-OPERATIVE system to make their own wine, some of which have established more recent reputations.

White Châteauneuf-du-Pape is a relative rarity, and may be made according to a wide range of formulae but overall quality has been steadily increasing. The wines are always full bodied and the less successful lack acidity and BOUQUET. They should usually be drunk young, although the all-Roussanne Vieilles Vignes bottling from Ch de Beaucastel can withstand several years in bottle. See also RHÔNE.

Johnson, H., and Robinson, J., *The World Atlas of Wine* (7th edn, London, 2013).

Parker, R. M., *The Wines of the Rhône Valley* (2nd edn, New York, 1997).

Châtillon-en-Diois, small appellation of about 60 ha/150 acres in area round DIE in the far east of the greater RHÔNE region in the cooler reaches of the Drôme Valley for still wines: light, Gamay-based reds and light whites made from Aligoté and Chardonnay. The local fizz, CLAIRETTE DE DIE, is more common.

Chaume, much-contested name for the sweet white wines of less than 80 ha/200 acres of Chenin Blanc. From 2014, they are to be known as Premier Cru Coteaux du LAYON Chaume.

Chautagne, named CRU in the upper Rhône Valley north of Chambéry whose name may be added to the French appellation Vin de SAVOIE. Production is dominated by the CO-OPERATIVE, and some fine red wines are made, from Gamay, Pinot Noir, and, especially, the local Mondeuse.

Chaves, DOP subregion of TRÁS-OS-MONTES in north-east Portugal.

Chelois, Seibel FRENCH HYBRID planted to a very limited extent in the north-eastern US.

Chelva, leading Spanish TABLE GRAPE also grown for RIBERA DEL GUADIANA in EXTREMADURA, western Spain. Also known as Montúa. Spain's plantings totalled more than 5,000 ha/12,500 acres in 2011.

Chenanson, productive CROSS of Grenache Noir and Jurançon Noir planted on about 450 ha/1,112 acres in southern France, presumably popular because it is more productive and deeper-coloured than Grenache.

Chénas, the smallest of the ten Beaujolais CRUS in the far north of the region in the shadow of MOULIN-À-VENT. By 2011 its total vineyard had shrunk to 243 ha/600 acres divided between the villages of Chénas and La Chapelle de Guinchay. Hubert Lapierre is one of the oldest domaines. For more details, see BEAUJOLAIS.

Chenin or **Chenin Blanc**, in its native region often called Pineau or Pineau de la Loire, is probably the world's most versatile grape variety, capable of producing some of the finest, longest-living sweet whites and a wide range of fine dry whites. It is also responsible for a considerable volume of sparkling wine and, in SOUTH AFRICA, where it is by far the most planted variety, it is even used as the base for a wide range of fortified wines and spirits. Although, in its most common high-yield, New World form, its distinctive flavour reminiscent of honey and damp straw is usually lost, it retains the naturally high acidity that dogs it in some of the Loire's less ripe vintages but can be so useful in hot climates.

South Africa, with a 2012 total of 18,200 ha, has almost twice as much Chenin planted as France's 2011 total of just under 10,000 ha/ 24,700 acres which remained unchanged for a decade. On the Cape, Chenin is prized for its acidity, productivity, and good resistance to disease and wind. The vine may have been one of the original collection imported in 1655 by Jan van Riebeeck. A dedicated band of Chenin Blanc specialists has emerged in South Africa, focusing on the best sites and on restoring to high-quality production old vineyard blocks.

In the 1980s, CALIFORNIA also had more Chenin planted than France, but total plantings had fallen to about 9,000 acres by 2012. In stark contrast to South Africa and the Loire, California has very few champions of the variety and most of it is used as the usually anonymous base for everyday commercial blends of reasonably crisp white of varying degrees of sweetness, often blended with the much more widely planted French COLOMBARD. Both of these workhorse varieties are planted primarily in the hot, dry Central Valley, a setting that might be described as the antithesis of Chenin's Loire homeland. (It also presumably helps extend quantities of, and add acidity to, cheaper wines labelled Chardonnay.) Chappellet's Chenin can be worth ageing and in Clarksburg at the north end of the Central Valley, it can take on a distinctive melony, musky flavour. In New Zealand it has almost disappeared, and Millton is virtually the only producer to understand the variety. Australia grew only about 500 ha in 2012 and treated it largely with disdain as low cost (high-yielding) blending material, usually extending Chardonnay, Semillon, and Sauvignon Blanc. Plantings had fallen to about 2,500 ha in Argentina by 2011, and to under 60 ha in Chile.

The variety was exported to Israel to establish vineyards there at the end of the 19th century.

If Chenin appears to lead a double life—biddable workhorse in the New World, superstar in Anjou-Saumur and Touraine—it is clear that the explanation lies in a combination of climate, soil, and yield. In California's Central Valley, the vine is often expected to yield 10 tons per acre (175 hl/ha), while even the most basic Anjou Blanc should not be produced from vines that yield more than 45 hl/ha. It is hardly surprising that Chenin's character seems diluted outside the Loire, where it has been known for centuries under various names such as Plant d'Anjou and Pineau de la Loire. DNA profiling suggests relationships with a wide range of varieties including SAVAGNIN, SAUVIGNON Blanc, TROUSSEAU, COLOMBARD, and even CABERNET SAUVIGNON.

The vine is vigorous and has a tendency to bud early and ripen late, both of which are highly inconvenient attributes in the cool Loire valley (though hardly noticeable characteristics in the hotter vineyards of the New World). CLONES that minimize these inconveniences have been selected and six had been officially sanctioned in France by the 1990s. It is prone to BOTRYTIS BUNCH ROT—usefully so for late-harvest styles.

About a third of all France's, which means the middle Loire's, Chenin was abandoned in the 1970s, often in favour of Cabernet Franc in Anjou-Saumur and Touraine and to make way for the temporarily more fashionable Gamay and Sauvignon de Touraine in the east of the middle Loire. It is today most planted in the heart of Anjou-Saumur and Touraine, as well it might be to judge from the superlative quality of the best wines of such appellations as ANJOU, BONNEZEAUX, Coteaux de l'AUBANCE, Coteaux du LAYON, JASNIÈRES, MONTLOUIS, QUARTS DE CHAUME, SAUMUR, SAVENNIÈRES (the grape's one definitively dry appellation), VOUVRAY, and CRÉMANT de Loire.

In most of the best Loire Chenins, and certainly all of the great sweet wines, Chenin is unblended, but up to 20% of Chardonnay or Sauvignon is allowed into an Anjou or a Saumur and even more catholic blends are allowed into whites labelled Touraine—although even here Chardonnay's pervasive influence is officially limited to 20% of the total blend. If middle Loire white has any character at all it is that of Chenin, increasingly valued as the region's signature grape, in contrast to the widely planted Sauvignon Blanc and Chardonnay. While basic Loire Chenin exhibits simply vaguely floral aromas and refreshingly high acidity (together with too much sulfur if made in one of the more old-fashioned cellars), the best have a physically thrilling concentration of honeyed flavour, whether the wine is made sweet (MOELLEUX), dry/sec (an inceasingly popular style, often incorporating some BARREL MATURATION), or demi-sec, together with Chenin's characteristically vibrant acidity level.

It is undoubtedly this acid, emphasized by a conscious distaste for MALOLACTIC FERMENTATION and concentrated in some years by BOTRYTIS, that helps preserve the finest Chenins for decades after their relatively early bottling. (In all of these respects, together with lateness of ripening and a wide range of sweetness levels that are customary, Chenin is France's answer to Germany's RIESLING.)

Chenin with its high acidity is a useful base for a wide range of sparkling wines, most importantly Saumur Mousseux but also Crémant de Loire and even some rich sparkling Vouvrays, which, like their still counterparts, can age beautifully. Treasured for its reliably high acidity, and useful perfume, it is also an ingredient, with Mauzac and Chardonnay, in the sparkling wines of LIMOUX.

Cheval Blanc, Château, very fine BORDEAUX property in ST-ÉMILION. In 1832, Henriette Ducasse married Libourne négociant Jean Laussac-Fourcaud, bringing with her 12 ha/30 acres of land including part of the narrow gravel ridge that runs through Figeac and neighbouring vineyards and reaches PETRUS just over the border in POMEROL. This became Ch Cheval Blanc, which, in the International London and Paris Exhibitions in 1862 and 1867, won the medals still prominent on its labels. In 1892, Albert reversed the order of his double surname, and it remained in the Fourcaud-Laussac family until 1998 when it was sold to Bernard Arnault, chairman of LVMH, and Belgian businessman Albert Frère. Pierre, one of the LURTONS, has been general manager since 1991.

The estate has 39 ha of vines: 51% Cabernet Franc, 47% Merlot, and 2% Cabernet Sauvignon. A total of 45 very different plots have been identified and, since an ultra-modern CHAI was built in 2011, have been picked and vinified separately. Average production is about 7,000 dozen bottles a year. Petit Cheval is the second wine. The high percentage of Cabernet Franc, a variety felicitously originally favoured by Jean Laussac-Fourcaud which has proved particularly well-suited to the often GRAVELLY soils of Cheval Blanc, gives the wines a deep colour and a rich, concentrated blackcurrant bouquet and flavour. Although excellent wines were made towards the end of the 19th century and before the First World War, the property's international reputation was made with the 1921, which had enormous concentration and sweetness. Other very successful wines were made in the 1920s, and even in 1934 and 1937, but its more modern fame was achieved with the rich, porty 1947.   E.P.-R. & J.R.

Chevalier-Montrachet, great white GRAND CRU in Burgundy's CÔTE D'OR. For more details, see MONTRACHET.

Cheverny in the middle LOIRE was promoted to full AOC status in 1993 and produces a wide range of wines in an enclave in the north east corner of TOURAINE near Blois (see LOIRE map) whose vineyards had grown to 632 ha/1,561 acres by 2012. Light reds and rosés may be made from Pinot Noir with some Gamay. But most Cheverny is based on Sauvignons Blanc and Gris, typically blended with a little Chardonnay and/or Chenin Blanc, which can offer a good-value northern riposte to Sancerre and Pouilly-Fumé. Wines made from the local ROMORANTIN grape have their own 53-ha appellation **Cour Cheverny**.

Chian wine, from the island of **Chios**, was highly prized in both ancient and medieval times. See AEGEAN ISLANDS and DRIED-GRAPE WINES for more details.

Chianti, the name of a specific geographical area between Florence and Siena in the central Italian region of TUSCANY, associated with tangy, dry red wines of very varied quality. The Chianti zone is first identified in documents of the second half of the 13th century which named the high hills between Baliaccia and Monte Luco 'the Chianti mountains' but without reference to the actual wine (although see TUSCANY, history). In the 18th century the name was applied to the townships of Castellina, Radda, and Gaiole that formed the nucleus of the medieval League of Chianti under Florentine jurisdiction. These townships became one of the very first wine regions anywhere to be officially DEMARCATED. In an edict drawn up in 1716 by Cosimo III, Grand Duke of Tuscany, the Chianti Classico borders were determined in order to protect authenticity and combat fraud. In the 1930s the Italian government's Dalmasso commission enlarged this historic zone to capitalize on the Chianti name (see CHIANTI CLASSICO). Thus it is that legally oenological Chianti extends over 15,500 ha/38,285 acres. Seven subzones can call their wines Chianti: Chianti Colli Fiorentini, CHIANTI RUFINA, Chianti Montalbano, Chianti Colli Senesi, Chianti Colline Pisane, Chianti Colli Aretini, and Chianti Montespertoli, while other parts of this extended region may produce a wine labelled simply Chianti. There are quality-oriented producers outside the Chianti Classico heartland, notably Chianti Rufina's Fattoria Selvapiana and Pacina in the Colli Senesi, whose wines are on a par with the best from Chianti Classico but much of the wine labelled simply Chianti lacks distinction.

Production regulations for Chianti and its seven subzones have always been more lenient (some would say lax) than for Chianti Classico. Although SANGIOVESE is the main variety in the wines, it may represent only 70% of the blend compared with the minimum 80% for Chianti Classico, and white wine grapes may still comprise up to 10% of the blend. Maximum permitted YIELDS at 9 ton/ha are higher than Chianti Classico's 7.5 ton/ha, while the minimum alcohol of 10.5% indicates a tolerance for less ripe fruit compared with Chianti Classico's minimum of 12.5%.

The very irregular quality of wine labelled simply Chianti has always had a detrimental effect on Chianti Classico's reputation, especially when the latter shifted its focus from quantity to quality from 1984 onwards when all of Chianti was elevated to DOCG status (in one of the worst vintages the area has known).

Large volumes of Chianti are bought by bottlers furnishing large retailers at the lowest possible price, which has done little to incentivize investments and increase overall quality.

However, some good-quality Chianti is produced, even if the wines are usually ready to drink earlier than those from Classico or Rufina. This is reflected in the law which states that Chianti may be released from 1 March following the vintage, while wines from individual subzones, and Chianti Superiore (with its minimum alcohol of 11.5%), must wait longer (1 October for Chianti Classico) before release.   W.S.

Belfrage, N., *Brunello to Zibibbo—The Wines of Tuscany, Central and Southern Italy* (London, 2003). www.consorziovinochianti.it

Chianti Classico, the heartland of the CHIANTI zone, was given its fundamental geographical DELIMITATION by the Medici Grand Duke Cosimo III in an edict of 1716, one of the first examples of such legislation, and was defined as the townships of Radda, Gaiole, and Castellina in addition to the township of Greve (including Panzano).

In 1924 the 'Consortium for the defence of Chianti wine and its symbol of origin' was founded to fight the cheap imitations seeking to take advantage of the growing international demand for Chianti Classico. At the request of the Consorzio in 1932 a government committee, known as the Commissione Dalmasso, was sent to the region to demarcate the original, CLASSICO zone but, much to the frustration of the Consorzio, the commission enlarged the zone with six additional subzones. The new enlarged region was what is now more or less Chianti proper, defended by the commission on the basis of presumed common oenological practices rather than suitability or historical evidence. To integrate such a large and diverse area, the production regulations set up by the Dalmasso commission were decidedly flexible, requiring only 50 to 80% of the region's most important red variety, SANGIOVESE. They also allowed white MALVASIA and TREBBIANO grapes in the blend, the latter two believed to have been traditionally interplanted with red wine varieties in the Chianti vineyards.

Little is known of the precise varietal composition of the wines before the 19th century, although the work of Cosimo Villifranchi (1773) suggests that the wine was a blend dominated by CANAIOLO with smaller amounts of Sangiovese, MAMMOLO, and MARZEMINO. Modern Chianti can be said to have been invented by Baron Bettino RICASOLI, who, in a letter in 1872, synthesized decades of experimentation and recommended that the wine be based on Sangiovese ('for bouquet and vigour') with the addition of CANAIOLO to soften the wine. Malvasia was suggested as appropriate for wines to be drunk young although its use was discouraged for wines intended for ageing.

By the 1960s the old sharecropping system was official abolished, leading to an exodus of workers looking for paid work in the growing industrial cities in the north. Mixed agricultural estates were transformed into a monoculture, without much attention paid to VINEYARD SITE SELECTION for the many newly planted vineyards. The government promoted high-yielding CLONES of Sangiovese as well as the white Trebbiano, believing that a focus on quantity rather than quality would help to improve the economic state of the region. The DOC regulations of 1967, guided by the 'Ricasoli formula', therefore required between 10 and 30% of the white grapes Trebbiano and Malvasia. They also allowed generous permitted YIELDS of 80 hl/ha (4.5 tons/acre), and put no limits on production per vine. Because of the resulting low quality and the fact that 100% Sangiovese wines were now outlawed, several quality-oriented producers decided they had no choice but to opt out of the DOC system and produce instead, often using new winemaking techniques such as BARREL MATURATION, wines labelled VINO DA TAVOLA which gained swift recognition (see SUPERTUSCANS). This presented the Consorzio with an embarrassing and absurd situation.

From the beginning of the 1980s the Consorzio finally understood that for Chianti Classico's quality—and price—to increase, it needed to focus on improving the output of the region's vineyards. This coincided with the fact that most vineyards, planted in the 1960s and exhausted from excessive yields, had to be replanted. Committing itself fully to quality, the Consorzio started an in-depth study, called Chianti Classico 2000, into different clones, ELEVATIONS, and soil compositions, the results of which were freely divulged to the producers. At the same time, many investors from outside the region, some foreign, were attracted by the low land prices. Many of these incomers had little prior knowledge of viticulture and winemaking, and relied heavily on consultant OENOLOGISTS. Overall wine quality then improved considerably. INTERNATIONAL VARIETIES were often added to make Sangiovese's initial high acidity and tannic structure more appealing to international palates.

At last, in 1996, Chianti Classico became autonomous, was granted its own DOCG, and was therefore no longer a subzone of Chianti. The suffix Classico was to be restricted to the original 7,000-ha/17,500-acres zone, with stricter regulations such as lower yields and a higher minimum of Sangiovese (80%). Many Chianti Classicos made today are 100% Sangiovese but an almost incredible 49 dark-skinned varieties are authorized to make up the additional 20%.

In spite of many a marketing campaign aimed at distancing itself from generic Chianti, the Consorzio of Chianti Classico has still to make the difference clear to the general public. The region is already subdivided into nine communes (Greve in Chianti, San Casciano in Val di Pesa, Tavarnelle Val di Pesa, Barberino Val d'Elsa, Castellina in Chianti, Poggibonsi, Radda in Chianti, Gaiole in Chianti, and Castelnuovo Berardenga), but by 2014 the Consorzio had not condoned subzone naming on labels (as, say, Côtes-du-Rhône Villages are clearly identified). Instead the Consorzio continues to argue that the region's elevation, exposition, and soil types (based on GALESTRO and Alberese) are too diverse to allow for a simple system, and prefers to cling to a single name to describe such a large viticultural area while ignoring the fact that the focus of many producers has noticeably shifted away from international varieties and BARRIQUE ageing. Today they are much more likely to age Sangiovese in traditional large oak casks in order to achieve more transparency and expression of the individual terroir, emphasizing the variety's characteristic tangy, dark-cherry flavours with a fine gravelly tannic structure in place of any vanilla from new oak. This trend has also led to a significant increase in single-vineyard Chianti Classicos.

Instead of identifying and promulgating subzones, in 2014 the Consorzio introduced a new 'top layer' known as GRAN SELEZIONE to the denomination pyramid, which consists of Chianti Classico as its base and Chianti Classico RISERVA (with a mandatory 24 months of oak and three months of bottle ageing) above it. This supposedly top selection, made on the basis of tastings, met with lukewarm enthusiasm, as the production regulations are only marginally stricter than those for the Riserva category with which it competes.   W.S.

Masnaghetti, A., *Chianti Classico—Vineyards and production zones* (Monza, 2014).

Belfrage, N., *Brunello to Zibibbo—The Wines of Tuscany, Central and Southern Italy* (2nd edn, London, 2003).

Consorzio Vino Chianti Classico, *Progetto di Ricerca e Sperimentazione. Chianti Classico 2000* (Florence 1996).

www.chianticlassico.com

Chianti Rufina, north-eastern and smallest of the seven subzones that form CHIANTI. Rufina was first identified as an area of superior production in Cosimo III de'Medici's grand-ducal edict of 1716, which names the zone Pomino, a village within Rufina, after the famous estate of the Albizi family. Pomino, now owned substantially by FRESCOBALDI, has its own DOC for blends of INTERNATIONAL VARIETIES, but the delimited zone of the DOC of 1967 followed to a substantial extent the territory first delimited by Cosimo III, with an extension of the zone to the west of the confluence of the Sieve and Arno rivers. This happens to be one case where the often contentious measure of enlarging the production zone was based on sound principles. (See CHIANTI CLASSICO.)

The vineyards of Rufina are south-west facing and have soils similar to those of Chianti Classico, consisting of GALESTRO, Alberese, and LIMESTONE at elevations from 200 to 700 m (655 to 2,300 ft). It is said that these higher elevations are responsible for the wines' trademark acidity and longevity, but relatively few of the Rufina wines currently on the market demonstrate these qualities. Only 22 producers bottle wine, while 120 growers sell their grapes to NÉGOCIANTS or bottlers, who often sell the result as Chianti rather than Chianti Rufina since it entails less bureaucracy.

All this obscures the fact that the best of Rufina can truly be outstanding (as evidenced by the wines of Selvapiana), if producers eschew high yields and the inclusion of 30% of international varieties (as well as up to 10% white varieties) in what is a historic Sangiovese-based wine. Specific characteristics of superior communes such as Pelago, Monsecco, Cafaggio, and Travignoli are inevitably lost in the usual big blends. Rufina's potential at least equals that of the much larger Chianti Classico, but the region has been slow to emulate the latter's continued efforts to improve overall quality.   W.S.

www.chiantirufina.com

Chiavennasca, synonym for the noble NEBBIOLO vine and grape in VALTELLINA.

Chignin, named CRU near Chambéry whose name can be added to the eastern French appellation Vin de SAVOIE. Most Chignin is a scented dry white made from the local JACQUÈRE grape variety. Technically a separate CRU, the rich, but dry **Chignin Bergeron** is made from the superior white ROUSSANNE grape, Bergeron being a local name for it.

Chile. With a particularly varied climate and topography, this long, narrow SOUTH AMERICAN country on the Pacific Ocean was long associated with reliable, inexpensive wines, but a new generation is beginning to show that it can produce more than bargains. The Spanish may have introduced viticulture, but since the 19th century, France has had the greatest influence on the Chilean wine industry, primarily with Bordeaux varieties such as Cabernet Sauvignon, Merlot, and Carmenère.

Chile is famously PHYLLOXERA-free, which means that GRAFTING is not necessary. Since the 1990s, new zones such as San Antonio and Limarí have supplemented the traditional valleys such as Maipo, Aconcagua, and Colchagua, and southern regions such as Itata and parts of Maule that were semi-abandoned have been rediscovered as sources of new flavours and styles. Chile is one of the world's most energetic wine exporters. Thanks to a flurry of planting, vineyards totalled 205,000 ha/506,000 acres by 2012 according to the OIV, and total wine production in 2013 was 12 million hl/317 million

gal, nearly three-quarters of which was destined for export.

History

The VINIFERA vine, and deliberate cultivation of it for wine, was brought to the Americas by the Spanish (see SOUTH AMERICA, history). Cortés imported vine cuttings, or more probably seeds, directly from Spain to Mexico where the first successful American vintage was produced, but it is not clear whether the vines first cultivated in the mid 16th century at Cuzco in PERU, the progenitors of the Chilean wine industry, came from Mexico or directly from Spain or Portugal. It is generally agreed, however, that Spanish settlers brought the vine to Chile some time in the 1550s, the vine probably arriving in the Central Valley with Juan Jufre and Diego Garcia de Cáceres in 1554. This was partly so that the early Spanish settlers could celebrate the EUCHARIST with its produce. Specific grape varieties mentioned by the Jesuit priest Alonso Ovalle include Moscatel, Torontel, Albilho, Mollar, and 'the common black grape' (presumably related to the PAIS).

Some early vineyards were ransacked by native Indians, notably in the far south of the country, but the capital Santiago has been associated with continuous wine production for more than four centuries. In the 17th century, Spain attempted to protect its export trade of wine to South America by banning new plantings of vineyards there, but with little success. Indeed in 1678, the Chilean governor recommended that not only should this ban be lifted but vineyards should be actively encouraged so that more farms, or haciendas, would be established. In the 18th century, Chile was known for the quantity and cheapness of wine it produced, much to the dismay of some Spanish wine producers.

The vine varieties grown and winemaking techniques of the early 19th century were well documented and fairly primitive by modern standards, the wines commonly being sweetened with boiled, concentrated must, for example. It was Chile's great good fortune that an energetic Frenchman, Claudio Gay, persuaded the Chilean government to set up the Quinta Normal, an experimental nursery for all manner of exotic botanical specimens, including European vines, as early as 1830. This meant that Chile had its own collection of *V. vinifera* cuttings safely banked in viticultural isolation before the onset of the world's late-19th-century vineyard scourges of POWDERY MILDEW and phylloxera, although it was private enterprise which, as so often, provided the spur to the nation's wine industry.

Now independent of Spanish domination, rich Chileans began to travel and experience a wider world, which included the fine wines of Europe, markedly different from the rustic

produce of Pais and Moscatel grapes. One of these was Silvestre Ochagavía Echazarreta, who in 1851 personally imported, along with a French winemaker, a range of those vine varieties regarded today as the most classic and internationally respected. These cuttings were to form the basis of Chile's modern wine industry. A class of gentlemen farmers was emerging in Chile, some of whom had made their fortunes as a result of Chile's rich mineral deposits. Owning a vine-growing country estate on the fertile land outside Santiago, preferably run by one of the many French refugees from phylloxera, was a sign of success in 19th century Chile.

It was not long before Chile could boast the world's only healthy wine industry, both viticulturally and financially, run effectively by ten rich families (several of them of Basque origin) and their descendants. As almost every other wine-producing country succumbed to the successive ravages of mildew and phylloxera, the Chilean wine industry enjoyed the rudest of health. The industry, still (as today) substantially in private hands, was so profitable, and per capita wine consumption so high, that it was increasingly energetically taxed and constricted as the 20th century wore on.

Domestic demand for Chile's basic wines declined, and wine prices plummeted in the 1970s and early 1980s. About half of Chile's vineyards were pulled up, some of them in quite suitable locations. The unsettled nature of Chile's politics and economics provided a natural brake on the progress of this unique industry, until the successful establishment of free market policies and the return of democracy in the 1980s stimulated growth in this potentially important aspect of the Chilean economy. Between 1987 and 1993, more than 10,000 ha/25,000 acres of vineyard were planted with INTERNATIONAL VARIETIES, significant investments were made in new winemaking technology, and the focus of the wine industry switched completely from quantity for the domestic market to quality for export markets.

Although Chile's wine-related activity continues to be concentrated among just four companies—CONCHA Y TORO, Santa Rita, Santa Carolina, and San Pedro—that account for approximately 80% of the country's total production, investors from other fields of commerce have more recently entered the fray via the likes of Loma Larga, Matetic, and Casas del Bosque. And from the mid 1990s a number of smaller producers has at last been emerging. The creation of MOVI, the Movement of Independent Vintners, and Chanchos Deslenguados, a group of independent producers allied to the NATURAL WINE movement, have broken Chile's historic wine oligopoly and have injected greater diversity into the Chilean wine scene.

The same applies to the discovery of new zones. Until the 1980s, Chile's finest wines

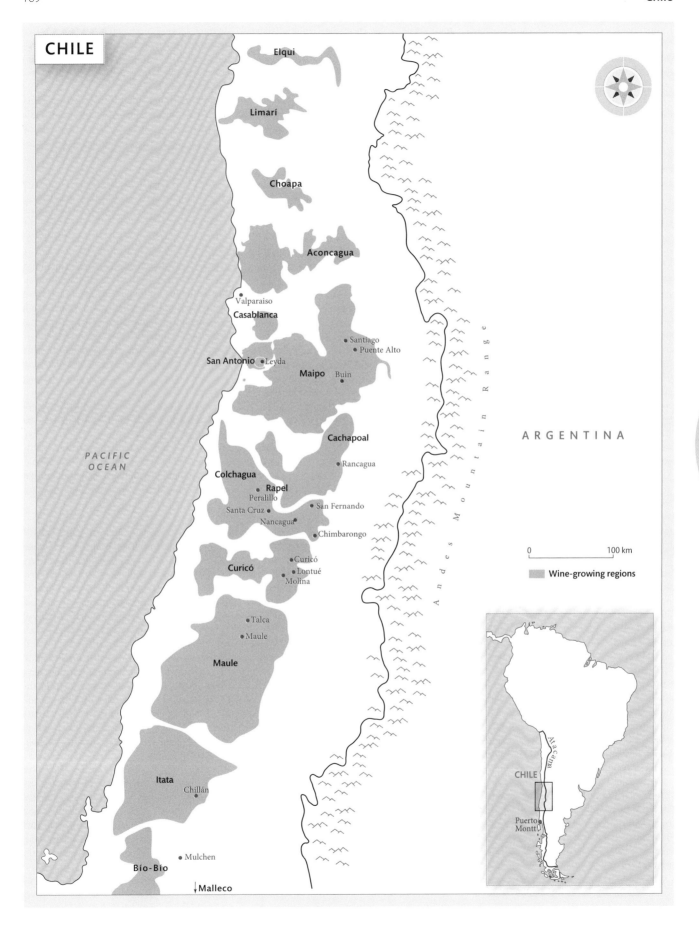

CHILE

Elqui

Limarí

Choapa

Aconcagua

• Valparaiso

Casablanca

• Santiago
• Puente Alto

San Antonio • Leyda

Maipo • Buin

Cachapoal

• Rancagua

Colchagua

Rapel

Peralillo

Santa Cruz • • San Fernando

Nancagua

• Chimbarongo

• Curicó

Curicó • Lontué

Molina

• Talca

• Maule

Maule

Itata

• Chillán

• Mulchen

Bío-Bío

↓ **Malleco**

PACIFIC OCEAN

A R G E N T I N A

Andes Mountain Range

0   100 km

Wine-growing regions

CHILE

Atacama

Puerto Montt

C

(primarily Cabernet Sauvignon) came from sectors close to the Andean Piedmont in the Maipo Valley, while the simple, keenly priced VARIETAL wines for which Chile was best known abroad were grown on the fertile, well-irrigated lands of Chile's Central Valley between the Andes and the Coastal Range.

The coastal Casablanca Valley established in 1982 has been followed by a series of newer, generally cooler wine zones. The San Antonio and Limarí Valleys in the latter half of the 1990s are the most obvious examples of more daring viticulture in less reliable climates and more extreme conditions. Projects that bear particular mention include the Flaño family's Alcohuaz winery at 2,000 m/6,652 feet ELEVATION in the Elqui Valley, guided by consulting winemaker Marcelo Retamal of De Martino. For white wines Casa Marín were trailblazers in Lo Abarca, just 4 km/2.5 miles from the cold Pacific Ocean in the San Antonio Valley. These projects would have been unthinkable in Chile even quite recently.

Geography and climate

Chile extends nearly 4,300 km/2,670 miles north-south. It is also very narrow (at its narrowest it is barely 15 km/49 miles wide). Squeezed between the Pacific Ocean and the Andes (80% of Chile is mountainous), land suitable for viticulture is limited, although quite varied. In 2012, a total of 128,637 ha/317,800 acres were planted with grapevines, nearly 74% dedicated to red wine grapes. The most widely planted variety was Cabernet Sauvignon with a total of 41,500 ha/102,500 acres, followed by Sauvignon Blanc planted on 14,131 ha/34,920 acres.

The two northernmost regions, Atacama and, especially, Coquimbo, specialize in the production of Chile's own controlled appellation grape spirit pisco, to which nearly 7,700 ha of vineyards were dedicated in the early 2010s. But early examples of wines grown well north of the capital Santiago, especially from Limarí and Elqui, swelled the total area of northern vineyards devoted to wine production to 3,600 ha.

Although there are experimental vineyards throughout the country (from latitude 23 °S in the north to 46 °S in the extreme south), the great majority of Chilean wine is produced between the latitudes of 32 and 38 degrees. A northern hemisphere counterpart of these latitudes would be North Africa and southern Spain, but in Chile temperatures are considerably mitigated by the influence of the Pacific and its cold Humboldt current. Chilean wine producers describe their climate as somewhere between that of California's NAPA Valley and that of Bordeaux.

Although the coastal areas are being energetically developed, most of Chile's wine has traditionally come from the Central Valley, a 1,000-km-long plateau which reaches as far south as Puerto Montt. The Central Valley is separated from the Pacific to the west by a relatively low coastal range whose peaks reach 300 to 800 m (1,000–2,600 ft) and is separated from Argentina's Mendoza wine region to the east by the Andes, which can reach elevations of 6,000 m here. Vines will grow up to an elevation of 600 m on the western slopes of the Central Valley, and 1,000 m on the sunnier eastern slopes of the valley on the foothills of the Andes. The Central Valley is dissected by rivers which, during the growing season, carry torrents of melted snow from the Andes to the Pacific: IRRIGATION made easy.

Although there are distinct variations between individual regions and even subregions (see below), the climate in the Central Valley is generally MEDITERRANEAN, with warm, dry summers, and rainfall, averaging between 300 and 800 mm (12–31 in) a year, restricted to the winter, thanks to the effect of the Pacific high-pressure area. Rainfall in the Central Valley tends to increase both in the south and east, on the slopes of the Andes. On the western edge of the valley, summer temperatures average 15 to 18 °C (59–64 °F) and may rise to 30 °C/86 °F, with clear skies, strong sunlight, and relatively low humidity of just 55 to 60%. On the eastern edge of the valley, however, under the influence of cold air drainage from the Andes at night, there is much greater TEMPERATURE VARIABILITY resulting in particularly good levels of ACIDITY and COLOUR in grapes.

Southern regions such as Bío-Bío and Malleco are also being developed for serious wine production. In carefully selected sites in places such as Mulchén and Traiguén, vines can yield good white wines, although FROST and excessive rain may prejudice quality south of Temuco. Meanwhile traditional and historic zones such as Itata have recently been rediscovered by wineries from the central zone such as De Martino and Miguel Torres. Old Cinsault and Moscatel de Alejandría vines planted there are paying dividends.

Regions and soils

Traditionally, Chile's wine regions were divided from north to south following administrative and provincial divisions rather than according to likely TERROIR effects. This system, common in many young wine regions, is slowly being modified. A first and very preliminary step was the 2013 geographical divisions of the wine valleys into Andes, Entre Cordilleras (between mountain ranges), and Costa (coastal). This transversal division from east to west aims to reflect the impact of the effects of the Andes as well as the Pacific—both cooling influences—in contrast to the valleys, where the climate tends to be warmer. This is a very general division. Dozens of exceptions are already evident, but this is at least a first step towards recognizing the influence of Chile's mountainous topography and the Pacific Ocean on the character of its wines.

From north to south the main wine regions, with their most significant subregions, are (see map):

Coquimbo: Elqui, Limarí
Aconcagua: Aconcagua, Casablanca, San Antonio (including Leyda)
Central Valley: Maipo (including Santiago, Talagante, Pirque, Puente Alto, Isla de Maipo, Buin), Rapel (including Cachapoal, Colchagua), Curicó (including Teno, Lontué), Maule (including Talca, San Clemente, San Javier, Parral, Linares, Cauquenes)
Southern region: Itata, Bío-Bío, Malleco

In general, Chile's vineyards are planted on flat, fertile land where water is readily available either naturally or through irrigation, so that vine root systems are relatively shallow. Alluvial soils predominate in Aconcagua and are also present to the south in Maipo, although here there are loams and occasionally clay soils too. In both the Maipo region and the Cachapoal district of northern Rapel, there are mixtures of loam, clay, and sand, some of which may be subject to EROSION on slopes. Soils are similar in southern Rapel and Maule while VOLCANIC soils extend from south of Curicó to the Bío-Bío region, interrupted only by sand and sandy loam around Linares. Some parts of Cachapoal, Colchagua, and the Southern region suffer from relatively poor drainage, can be quite swampy, and may need no irrigation.

Coquimbo Coquimbo, 500 km north of the capital Santiago primarily comprises the Limarí and Elqui Valleys (as well as the little-developed Choapa Valley) and was historically focused on TABLE GRAPES and pisco. There is intense SUNLIGHT throughout the year and less than 100 mm of annual rainfall. Although some fine wines have emerged, water shortages are threatening the region's survival. It was as recently as the mid 1990s that Viña Francisco de Aguirre started to produce exciting table wines in the Limarí Valley, 20 km from the Pacific coast where the likes of Tamaya and Tabalí had established themselves by the early 2000s. The cooling ocean influence plays an important part in delaying ripening in both Limarí and Elqui Valleys. The soils are rocky and clay, with a strong presence of alluvial stones near the rivers. The combination of clay and limestone, however, along with the proximity of the ocean, has yielded the best results in this northern zone. Tabalí and Tamaya Chardonnays and some Tamaya Pinot Noirs have been particularly impressive, while Falernia's Sauvignon Blanc from Elqui and some cool climate reds such as Syrah and Carmenère are also promising.

Aconcagua Named after the river which bisects it, Aconcagua is made up of three very distinct zones. The interior of Aconcagua is one of Chile's hottest, driest wine regions. In the summer, clouds are rarely seen, and temperatures are often above 30 °C/86 °F. Soils are mainly alluvial and the region produces some good red wines. Errázuriz and von Siebenthal are two of the few important wine exporters to have their base here, at Panquehue in the much gentler intermediate region, cooled by coastal breezes. This is home to the traditional Aconcagua vineyards responsible for such Chilean classics as Don Maximiano from Viña Errázuriz and their Seña grown closer to the coast.

A third area—also the responsibility of Errázuriz—is on the hillsides of the coastal range in Manzanar, strongly influenced by cold breezes off the Pacific Ocean. With clay and stony soils and gently rolling hills, this new area is part of the logical westward expansion taking place in several Chilean valleys. The climate and soils in the Aconcagua Costa zone are similar to those in Leyda and initial results with Sauvignon Blanc, Chardonnay, and Pinot Noir showed similar exciting potential.

Casablanca and San Antonio Although both zones are coastal and, politically speaking, belong to the Aconcagua Valley, Casablanca and San Antonio—the two largest sources of cold-climate whites in Chile—are different in various aspects. Casablanca's vineyards are cooled to WINKLER Region I by cool morning fogs, the result of the Pacific's icy Humboldt current (which has a similar effect thousands of miles up the coast in California). Frequent cloud slows ripening and reduces the average number of clear days per year to 180, as opposed to between 240 and 300 in the interior. Spring FROSTS are a real hazard here but specialist grape growers and most of the big companies have planted varieties such as Sauvignon Blanc, Chardonnay, and Pinot Noir extensively since the region's beginnings in the early 1980s. Casablanca runs from east to west, which means it is a transversal valley in which the easternmost zones—those furthest from oceanic influence—are warmer. There can be more than a month's difference in harvest dates between eastern Casablanca (also known as Upper or Alto Casablanca) and the western zone (Lower or Bajo Casablanca). Soils vary enormously although they generally tend to be sandy in Alto Casablanca and are increasingly granitic with a higher clay content with proximity to the coast.

Planting began in San Antonio in the late 1990s. Climate, soils, and topography are quite similar to Bajo Casablanca. The landscape typically features rolling hills, clay and granitic soils and, like nearly all of Chile's coastline, is cooled by coastal breezes. San Antonio Valley runs north to south, parallel to the coast, and has zones that are just a few km from the ocean, although the average direct distance between San Antonio's vineyards and the ocean is 15 km. Sauvignon Blanc is the valley's flagship variety, but some promising Pinot Noir, Chardonnay, and sparkling wine is also made.

Maipo The most famous wine region in Chile just south of the capital Santiago is not one of the largest. In 2012, some 12,971 ha/32,052 acres of vines were recorded, with a clear predominance of red over white grapes. Cabernet Sauvignon and Chardonnay were the most widely planted, although Merlot, Carmenère, and Sauvignon Blanc are also important. Annual rainfall averages just 300 mm/12 in a year, most of it falling in the winter. IRRIGATION is common, although the water can be quite high in salt around the Maipo river from which the region takes its name. POTASSIUM levels tend to be low throughout the region. Maipo is famous for producing Chile's most lauded Cabernet Sauvignon and some producers such as William Fèvre have begun planting up in the Andes as high as 1,000 m elevation with encouraging preliminary results.

Rapel About 150 km south of Santiago, Rapel had more than 42,000 ha/103,000 acres of vineyards in 2012 and is divided into two subzones—Cachapoal to the north and Colchagua to the south. Both are transversal valleys and run from the Andes to the Pacific Ocean. This results in pronounced differences in the wines (primarily reds) produced in the two subvalleys, depending on their proximity to the cooling influence of the Andes (Alto Cachapoal and Alto Colchagua). Some of Chile's finest Cabernet Sauvignons come from the Andean piedmont in Rapel. Significant individual zones have already been identified within them. Apalta within Colchagua, for example, has a reputation for fine Merlot, Carmenère, and Syrah won, to a large extent by the French-owned winery Casa Lapostolle and by Viña Montes. Cabernet Sauvignon, Carmenère, and Merlot are the most planted grape varieties, and the region has a particularly good reputation for full-flavoured red wines. Los Vascos winery, in which Ch LAFITE-Rothschild has an important stake, is at Peralillo. Large wineries such as Santa Emiliana, Santa Rita, Undurraga, and the smaller Viña Montes operation all made considerable vineyard investments in Colchagua in the 1990s. The latest trend in Rapel, specifically in Colchagua, has been to take maximum advantage of its transversal characteristics by exploiting coastal zones such as Lolol and especially Paredones (just 15 km/ 9.3 miles from the Pacific) whose Pinot Noir and Sauvignon Blanc rival those of Casablanca and San Antonio for quality and freshness.

Curicó Formed by the subregions Lontué and Teno, Curicó Valley was put on the international map when Miguel TORRES arrived there in 1979. According to 2013 statistics, the valley has 24,000 ha/59,000 acres planted. Curicó has basically two different mesoclimates. Towards the east, around Molina and north of the Claro river, the climate is cooler thanks to the breezes from the Andes. To the west, the coastal range minimizes the ocean influence and the climate is warmer, sometimes notably hot and dry. Even though the valley does not have any particular speciality such as Cabernet Sauvignon in Maipo or Sauvignon Blanc in Casablanca, the wide range of varieties planted reach a good general level of quality. The most recognized Curicó wineries, apart from Torres, are San Pedro, Valdivieso, Aresti, and Los Robles cooperative.

Maule Important wine region in Chile which includes the subregions of Talca, San Clemente, San Javier, Parral, Linares, and Cauquenes. According to official records, Maule's total area of wine grapevines has remained static at 30,250 ha/74,7200 acres for years (although there are some doubts about the efficiency of filing vineyard statistics in this region of smallholders). Well to the south of Santiago, this is one of Chile's cooler and cloudier regions, thanks to the Pacific influence, although it is hotter and drier than Bío-Bío to the south. The rustic PAIS vine variety used to dominate plantings, especially in the rain-fed areas, but Cabernet Sauvignon has been gaining ground. Vineyards in the rain-fed western areas often suffer from serious deficiencies of nutrients, especially NITROGEN and to a lesser extent POTASSIUM. Thanks to new investment and viticultural practices, Maule is no longer seen solely as a source of BULK WINE. Maule also has more CARIGNAN planted than any other valley, and the variety is now undergoing a revival among Chilean producers. The grapes from old vines in DRY-FARMED coastal zones provide the raw material for the VIGNO (Vignadores del Carignan/Carignan Vintners) group, an association that aims to promote this long-forgotten variety. The results have been spectacular.

Southern region The vineyards of southern Chile had fallen to 8,800 ha/21,750 acres by 2013, split quite evenly between red and white grapes. Formed by Itata, Bío-Bío, and the new Malleco subregion, this region is more open than Maipo and Rapel, lacking the protection of a high coastal range, so that rainfall is higher and average temperature and sunshine hours are lower. By far the most common vine variety is the humble PAIS, planted on a total of 2,464 ha/6,088 acres and now the object of a strong revival among small producers such as the French winemaker Louis Antoine Luyt (a pioneer in this endeavour), but also by large wineries such as Concha y Toro and VIA Wines. With more than 400 ha/988 acres planted, Cinsault is the region's latest rising star, especially in the DRY-FARMED zones of Itata, where it now produces simple, refreshing reds. The most widely planted white wine grape is Moscatel de Alejandría on about 3,000 ha/7,413 acres. Little by little, it is being taken more seriously by wineries such as De Martino who vinify it carefully with fine results. Research in the early 1990s in the Chillán area, however, suggested that, with DRIP IRRIGATION and appropriate training systems such as the LYRE, some good-quality wine from the best-known INTERNATIONAL VARIETIES could be made here. The proof of that lies in the Mulchén and Negrete areas where wineries such as Cono Sur and Gracia are producing crisp Riesling and ripe Pinot Noir. The embryonic Malleco area showed its mettle with excellent Chardonnay and Pinot Noir made by producers such as Aquitania, William Fèvre, and Alto Las Gredas.

Viticulture

IRRIGATION is essential in nearly half of all Chilean vineyards and, as in Argentina, is made possible by the melting snows of the Andes, diverted along a series of canals and channels as well as through the use of deep wells that exploit groundwater. This method is particularly important in coastal zones far from the Andes such as Casablanca. DRIP IRRIGATION was introduced only in the early 1990s. As a result of this ready and plentiful water supply, most vineyards have good access to water during the growing season. The irrigated vineyards are mainly in the north of the Central Valley, in the interior of the Aconcagua, Maipo, Rapel, Maule, and Curicó regions. On the slopes of the coastal range in the west of southern regions, rainfall is often sufficient, as it is in most of the Southern region. FERTILIZERS are widely employed, but their use is regulated to avoid an excess of VIGOUR. Drip irrigation allows FERTIGATION in some of the more viticulturally developed areas.

Average YIELDS in Chile are about 70 hl/ha (4 tons/acre). Over-irrigated, high-yielding vines can experience difficulties in RIPENING. This is particularly true of varieties which ripen relatively late, such as Cabernet Sauvignon and Chile's speciality CARMENÈRE, or of high TRAINING SYSTEMS. There is a predictably rich cultural diversity of training and trellis systems in Chile. Some vines, particularly those dedicated to TABLE GRAPES, are trained in variations on the TENDONE system in the high, arbour-like *parrón* trellis which encourages shade (like the *parral* of ARGENTINA). The standard Spanish practice of growing unstaked vines as free-standing bushes, trained into a GOBELET shape, has been common since the Spanish conquest but is today usually restricted to the País vine, notably in the south. The Bordeaux post-PHYLLOXERA immigrants introduced row trellising to Chile at the end of the 19th century and this has evolved in two distinct ways. Low, narrow rows of vines that are traditional in Europe tend to be double GUYOT pruned or spur cordons, depending on variety, and used mainly to produce better-quality wines. More common for basic wine production are more widely spaced vines (sometimes with cross-pieces, described as Californian), which permit the increasingly common phenomenon of vineyard MECHANIZATION. In the 1990s, most new plantings were in long narrow rows between 2 and 2.5 m (6.5–8 ft) apart, with vines planted 1.2 to 1.5 m apart. Australian CANOPY MANAGEMENT techniques were introduced in some vineyards in the early 1990s.

HARVEST of wine grapes begins at the end of February for such early-maturing varieties as Chardonnay, continues through to the end of April for Cabernet Sauvignon, and can last well into May for Carmenère.

No Chilean vine-grower feels he needs to study ROOTSTOCKS since the country is free of phylloxera and the consequent need for grafting. Some FIELD GRAFTING has been undertaken, however, in the rush to increase the proportion of fashionable grape varieties planted. And such is the prevalence of NEMATODES in Chilean vineyards, because of V. vinifera's low resistance to them relative to American vine species, that some authorities suggest using American rootstocks to combat this problem. Chile's vines are by no means free of VIRUS DISEASES.

Chile may be famously free of phylloxera, but POWDERY MILDEW and BOTRYTIS BUNCH ROT are annual and potentially extremely costly vine diseases, with VERTICILLIUM WILT another serious vine health hazard. DOWNY MILDEW infections occurred in some areas for the first time during the heavily EL NIÑO-influenced 1997–8 growing season. The absence of summer rains means that SPRAYING is generally much less frequent than in many other wine regions, however. ORGANIC VITICULTURE has been becoming more prevalent.

Vine varieties

VINE IDENTIFICATION arrived relatively late in Chile. Conscious of its unique status as a wine-producing country as yet unravaged by phylloxera, Chile imposes a particularly strict QUARANTINE on imported plant material, which has helped to maintain certain aspects of its viticultural isolation. The quality and identity of the vines grown was the most dramatic example of this. The majority of the vines called Sauvignon by the Chileans, for example, were almost certainly Sauvignon Vert, SAUVIGNONASSE (or Friulano) and occasionally Sauvignon Gris, rather than the more familiar Sauvignon Blanc.

Only a small but increasing proportion of Sauvignon Blanc, almost exclusively based on CLONES developed in California, had been planted by the early 1990s and even by the mid 2000s official statistics claiming 7,400 ha/18,300 acres of Sauvignon Blanc and just 200 ha of Sauvignon Vert probably did not reflect the true proportions of these two varieties. Thanks to the new plantations and more fastidious differentiation between Sauvignons Blanc and Vert, official statistics for 2012 suggest there are 14,131 ha/34,918 acres of Sauvignon Blanc versus just 792 ha/1,957 acres of Sauvignon Vert.

Similarly, vines called Merlot are usually in fact a mixture, and sometimes a FIELD BLEND, of Merlot and the old Bordeaux variety CARMENÈRE, first identified as such in Chile in 1994. The vine identification required to distinguish Merlot from Carmenère is continuing and since the mid 1990s the word Carmenère has increasingly appeared on wine labels both as a varietal and, perhaps more suitably, an ingredient in a blend. Although Chile is indubitably the Bordeaux of the southern hemisphere, for long it lacked a wine style to call its own but has dragooned Carmenère to be its answer to Argentina's Malbec, or Uruguay's Tannat.

Until the 1990s, the most commonly planted grape variety was the dark-skinned PAIS, identical to the CRIOLLA CHICA of Argentina and the MISSION of California, a direct descendant of vine cuttings imported by the Spanish colonists. Official statistics recorded just under 15,000 ha/37,050 acres of Pais in 2003, more or less the same as in 1997 but half the area planted with the variety in the 1980s. Although the variety is currently undergoing a revival, the area planted has continued to decline. By 2012 there were just 7,247 ha/17,907 acres planted, and the great majority are planted in the southern Maule and Bío-Bío regions.

The same survey of 2012 found nearly 41,000 ha/101,270 acres of Cabernet Sauvignon, the most important variety in Chile by quite a margin (almost three times as much as seven years previously), 14,131 ha/34,904 acres of Sauvignon Blanc, 11,649 ha/28,773 acres of 'Merlot' (all of 10,418 ha/25,732 acres of which had already been identified as Carmenère), more than 10,570 ha of Chardonnay, and just over 3,320 ha of MUSCAT OF ALEXANDRIA, about half of the total ten years before. The early years of this century saw a dramatic increase in plantings of Syrah, which totalled 7,744 by 2012, and Pinot Noir with a total of 4,012 ha (60% as much as is planted on the CÔTE D'OR).

Such new plant material as is allowed in has come mainly from DAVIS, but European investors such as Miguel Torres, a couple from Chablis, and Ch Lafite-Rothschild import their own cuttings directly from Europe, under strict quarantine regulations.

Winemaking

Chile has undergone possibly the most dramatic technological revolution in the wine world. Wineries were for decades underfunded as the domestic market could be satisfied with often oxidized white wines and faded reds made with the most traditional of equipment. All wines were made from grapes trucked, often in very high temperatures with scant regard for OXIDATION, to wineries equipped with little in the way of TEMPERATURE CONTROL, and made exclusively in vats made either of cement or the coarse local *raulí*, or evergreen beech, WOOD, usually coopered many decades previously. In the late 1980s, however, the wine industry made a commitment to the long-term future of Chile as a wine exporter and began to invest in the equipment necessary for that goal. Outside investors assisted the influx of both equipment and expertise, and since then the wineries of Chile were invaded, at a pace usually determined by the enterprise's size and cash flow, by pneumatic PRESSES, oak BARRELS, STAINLESS STEEL, and modern filters. Often one of the most necessary improvements was one of the technically least complicated: the provision of cool storage facilities. Today Chile's OENOLOGISTS are some of the world's finest.

Industry organization

Most of the big wine-exporting companies, many of them run by descendants of the wine dynasties of the mid 19th century, have their headquarters in Santiago or nearby in the Maipo region. The likes of CONCHA Y TORO, Santa Rita, Santa Carolina, and San Pedro own several wineries and many different vineyards, although it is also the norm to buy grapes from a wide range of growers. Estate wineries such as the historic Cousiño Macul, Los Vascos, Montes, or Portal del Alto, for which practically all grapes used are grown by the owner/winemakers, are increasing in number. Foreign investment has come from KENDALL JACKSON (MONDAVI), France (Chx MOUTON ROTHSCHILD and Lafite-ROTHSCHILD and many others), Spain (TORRES), presumably attracted by the relatively low cost of land, vineyard establishment, and running costs in Chile, although this is offset by the need to import all sophisticated equipment and cooperage. In the mid 1990s, however, some of the larger Chilean wine companies invested in Argentina, tempted by lower land costs across the Andes. Kaiken (Viña Montes) and Trivento (Concha y Toro) are two obvious examples.

Although the Chilean wine scene continues to be dominated by large corporations that have ready access to enormous expanses of vineyards and that produce millions of bottles, producers' groups such as MOVI (*Movimiento de Viñateros Independientes*) and *Chanchos Deslenguados* have shown that there is room for much more artisanal projects with their own styles and philosophies. Some of Chile's most exciting wines today come from members of these organizations.

Wine styles

Wines exported from Chile are, typically, extremely fruity and clean but did not until the early 1990s display the structure which can be imposed only by low yields and/or BARREL MATURATION. Yields are still relatively high, although there are some plots of very old vines which produce concentrated wine. Cabernet Sauvignon, Merlot–Carmenère, and Cabernet blends dominate Chile's red wine exports and can provide extremely good-value wines for drinking within two or three years, although an increasing proportion of wine capable of BOTTLE AGEING has been produced.

The new generation of white wines has been clean and well made and it is now possible to find well-defined, increasingly complex Chardonnay and Sauvignon Blanc from cooler areas such as Casablanca and San Antonio. Pink and sweet wines are certainly made and Valdivieso was the first to make sparkling wines using TRADITIONAL METHOD techniques, as early as 1879.

Table grapes may be vinified and sold as wine in Chile and the grape varieties Sultana and Ribier, or Alphonse Lavallé, are most commonly used for this purpose. Most of this wine is sold locally, or is exported in bulk. Wine made from a table grape variety sold locally should be labelled as such.

Chile overtook Australia as the world's fourth most important wine exporter in 2013, with prices if not the populace benefiting from very much lower LABOUR costs. J.R. & P.T.

Goldstein, E., *Wines of South America* (Oakland, 2014).

Richards, P., *The Wines of Chile* (London, 2006).

Tapia, P., *Descorchados, The South American Wine Guide* (Santiago, 2014).

Waldin, M., *Wines of South America* (London, 2003).

www.winesofchile.org

China

China, vast Asian country with its own indigenous vine species (see VITIS) but a relatively short modern tradition of growing VINIFERA grapes to make wine. In a remarkably short time, however, it has emerged as a major global wine force, with the world's fourth largest vineyard area and fifth largest wine production level in 2012 according to OIV statistics. Consumption doubled between 2006 and 2012, and is overwhelmingly (more than 80%) satisfied by domestic production.

Ancient China

Vines have long been grown in China. Geological fossils show that the *V. romanetii* Roman du Caill. ex Planch. existed in Linqu County, Shandong Province, 26 million years ago. As outlined in ORIGINS OF VINICULTURE, to date the earliest chemically attested instance of grapes being used in a fermented beverage, probably mixed with other fermentable ingredients, is at the Neolithic site of Jiahu in the Yellow River during the 7th millennium BC. The earliest written record of grapes in China is seen in *Qi Yue* in the *Odes of Bin* in the *Classic of Poetry*:

> In the sixth month they eat the sparrow-plums and grapes; in the seventh, they cook the kui and pulse; in the eighth, they knock down the dates; in the tenth, they reap the rice and make the spirits for the spring, for the benefit of the bushy eyebrows. (Translated by James Legge)

This indicates that people were already known to collect and eat various kinds of wild grapes in the Shang Dynasty (c.1600 BC–c.1000 BC).

The introduction of *V. vinifera* to China can be dated back to the 4th century BC. In the book *On Ancient Central Asian Tracks: Brief Narrative of Three Expeditions in Innermost Asia and Northwestern China*, Marc Aurel Stein describes the tidy plots of vineyard sites outside the courtyard of houses in the ancient city of Niya (first to third century AD) 150 km/93 miles north of the modern Minfeng county, Shan Shan prefecture in Xinjiang. A 1959 archaeological investigation of Niya by a team from Xinjiang Uygur Automonous Region Museum and a later Sino-Japanese 1988-96 operation excavated relics from an ancient tomb decorated with patterns of grape clusters, as well as dried grapes in containers. Carbon-14 dating indicates that the tomb is 2,295±75 years old. It would seem therefore that there was viticulture on a considerable scale in Niya from the third to first centuries BC. Archaeological expeditions in southern TURKMENISTAN and UZBEKISTAN, which unearthed grapes and both text descriptions and patterns of grapes from a fourth-century residential site also suggest that *V. vinifera* may well have been introduced to China from Central Asia along the Silk Route.

Two notable old varieties of *V. vinifera*, both TABLE GRAPES, are the dark-skinned Dragon's Eye (Longyan, or Longan, in Chinese) and pale Mare's Teat (Maru), the former long grown along the path of the Great Wall and, even longer, in the far west. Their import and successful cultivation in China shows us that viticulture prospered in Xinjiang, Gansu, Shanxi, and Hebei provinces. Shanxi wine continued to be popular after the decline of trade along the Silk Route following a break in relations with central Asia. It was not long before wine was also being made from the small native grapes of the *V. thunbergii* species, which grows wild in Shandong and Jiangxi provinces, and from the *Vitis heyneana* of Guangxi province,

V. davidii of Jiangxi and Hunan province, and *V.* AMURENSIS of north-eastern China.

See also ORIGINS OF VINICULTURE and PALAEOETH-NOBOTANY AND THE ARCHAEOLOGY OF WINE.

McGovern, P. E., 'Fermented beverages of pre- and proto-historic China', *The Proceedings of the National Academy of Sciences USA*, 101/51 (2004), 17593–8.

Modern history

Viticulture continued in China (JULLIEN classified the wines of what he called Chinese Tartary). In 1892, Zhang Bishi, who was born in Guangdong in China, moved to Indonesia as a successful businessman, and was then consul in southern Asian countries for the Qing government, returned to China and established the Changyu winery in Yantai. He introduced 120 *V. vinifera* varieties from Europe, including Welschriesling, and apparently employed the then Austrian consul as his winemaker. Qingdao (formerly rendered as Tsingtao), the other winery established by Germans in 1930, was first known as the Melco winery. Shang Yi winery (today's Beijing winery) was set up by French Catholics in 1910; Yi Hua winery was set up in Shanxi by Chinese in 1921, and Chang Bai Shan and Tung Hua (Tonghua) wineries at Jilin were set up and managed by the Japanese in 1936 and 1937 respectively. The wines produced by them were made mainly to cater for foreign communities in China.

In 1949, the wineries were expanded by the government and, for reasons of economy, they generally blended grape wine with other juices, water, colouring, and fermented cereals. Because of this, the term 'wine' was until recently widely misunderstood in China. The relevant Chinese character 'jiu' literally means alcohol in any form, so it was difficult to distinguish wine from beer or spirits. From June 2004, national wine production regulations were changed so that only alcoholic drinks based entirely on fresh grapes or grape juice may be called 'wine'.

Geography and climate

Most of China's 665,610 ha/1.7 million acres of vineyards (in 2012) are spread across provinces north of the Yangtze River, from the Xinjiang Uygur autonomous region in the extreme north west (where 21.5% of vines are planted) to the coastal regions of Hebei (11.4%) and Shandong (5.6%). Shanxi and Liaoning grow 5.3% of China's vines each, Henan grows 4.5%, Ningxia 4.4%, and Yunnan in south western China 4.1%. Owing to the general lack of exposure to Western wine culture and extreme CONTINENTAL conditions inland, production in all regions has been concentrated on TABLE GRAPES and DRYING GRAPES. China's 980 'alcohol manufacturing factories' (the literal translation of the word for winery) vinify only about one-sixth of the total

grape harvest (an estimated 10,543,154 tons of grapes for wine in 2012).

Temperatures in the coastal provinces of **Shandong**, **Hebei**, and **Tianjin**, which lie on the latitudes 36 to 40 °N, are generally suitable for wine production. Cool Pacific breezes moderate humidity levels and temperatures range from -5 °C/23 °F in the north in winter to 26 °C/79 °F in the south in summer. Monsoons and typhoons which sweep in from the South China Sea can prove hazardous, although monsoon winds rapidly aerate vines. Springs are generally dry, but summers and autumns can be muggy and wet, promoting FUNGAL DISEASES and ROT. Chinese peasants learnt, probably from the Soviet Union in the early 1950s, to establish their vineyards on flat land with fertile soil and to encourage high yields. Over-cropping, poor drainage and vineyards vulnerable to typhoons resulted in poor-quality fruit and therefore poor-quality wines in these coastal provinces.

Since the late 1990s the most spectacular vineyard expansion has been in **Xinjiang** on tableland north of the provincial capital Urumqi, the new industrial centre of the Manasi Basin near the city of Shiheze, and the Yanqi Basin in the south of Xinjiang. Natural rainfall is low but vineyards tap the huge alpine water resource of the perennially snow-capped Tian Shan (Heavenly Mountains) range through natural river systems and man-made canals. The soils are sandy LOAM over GRANITE. The region is relatively disease free and requires only minimal SPRAYING. Xinjiang may produce the biggest volume of wine in China, but most of it is sold in bulk to wineries in eastern regions.

Ningxia, an arid and semi-arid zone in the centre of China, has high sunshine hours and moderate temperatures compared with eastern and far western regions. The Yellow River provides irrigation water and, since the turn of the century, the local government has been providing financial incentives for investors in vineyards and wineries.

The neighbouring **Gansu** province has a similar climate but is a little cooler with a slightly shorter frost-free growing season. Gansu has long history of winemaking, and more and more vines have been planted there this century. But, like most wine regions in China's interior—whether Xinjiang, Ningxia, or Gansu—vines need WINTER PROTECTION. This practice swallows one third of a year's entire vineyard management costs and is already the biggest challenge for Chinese growers, let alone when China's likely increasing urbanization causes a shortage of LABOUR.

The Shangri-la area is a particularly interesting new wine region in an area close to Tibet within both **Yunnan** province (Deqin County) and **Sichuan** province (Danba and Xiaojin Counties). Vines are planted on steep valley

sides at ELEVATIONS between 1,600 and 2,900 m. This combination of low latitudes with high elevations confers moderate temperatures and a notably long frost-free season meaning that winter protection is unnecessary, rainfall is sufficient and generally well timed, and the dry air reduces the risk of vine disease. On the other hand, viticulture is not traditional in Shangri-La so training costs are high, and transport can be a challenge in these mountains where, in places, there are as many as 20 parcels of vines per hectare.

Wineries

Jesuit MISSIONARIES are believed to have been the first to encourage the planting of vineyards specifically to make wine here, in the mid 19th century. During the German and Japanese occupation of northern China at the turn of the 20th century, the first two wineries were established at Yantai and Qingdao. However, still and sparkling wine production in the five largest state wineries—Qingdao, Yantai Changyu, Henan Min Chuan, Beijing Eastern Rural, and Jilin Tung Hua—remained very unsophisticated until 1978 when China opened again to the outside world.

After 1979, several moves were made to allow foreign investors to install a modern wine industry in north-east China. In 1980, Cognac giant Rémy Martin set up the first JOINT VENTURE winery, Sino-French Joint Venture Winery (Dynasty), with the Tianjin Agriculture Bureau. The Henan Minquan winery first used the BRAND Great Wall for wine but the trademark was subsequently registered by the monopolistic China National Cereals, Oils, Foodstuffs Import & Export Corporation (COFCO), which established the business at Shacheng in Hebei Province in 1988. Both Dynasty and Great Wall applied modern winemaking techniques but produced relatively simple white table wines from the local Dragon's Eye (Longyan), MUSCAT OF HAMBURG, and other local TABLE GRAPES. The Huadong (East China) winery, China's first 'château-style' wine estate to plant and produce VARIETAL and vintage-dated superior white wines with an APPELLATION, Tsingtao, on the label, was established at Qingdao in 1985 and run by a British wine merchant from Hong Kong until 1990 when it was acquired and run by the multinational Allied Domecq, who abandoned it in 1999, since which time it has turned to mass production of inexpensive red wine. Another multinational, PERNOD RICARD, set up the Beijing Friendship (Dragon Seal) winery in 1987. All ventures relied on imported advanced vinification equipment, European VINIFERA vine cuttings, and foreign OENOLOGISTS to produce the first 'western-style' grape wines in China. State wineries followed their lead, among them, CHANGYU and Qingdao in Shandong.

In the mid and late 1990s, the Chinese government repeatedly encouraged the replacement of cereal-based spirits with fruit-based wines, motivated both by HEALTH concerns and by an acute grain shortage. Official recommendation of red wine as reducing the risk of cardiovascular disease sparked a wine boom throughout China. In 1996/97, Chinese wine consumers switched from favouring white to red wine. Thousands of cases of red wine were shipped in from Europe and rushed on to the market. Millions of litres of wine were shipped in BULK for local bottling. Distillers of traditional *baijiu* (white spirits) adapted their plants to make or bottle wines. Small wineries and bottling plants mushroomed all over China: more than 100 new wineries opened between 1996 and 2004.

By the beginning of the new century, a number of large wine companies had established wineries surrounded by vines and offering some TOURISM facilities. Examples included the high quality Grace Vineyard of Shanxi province; Changyu Castel in Yantai, Shandong; Chateau Bolongbao in Beijing; and in Hebei province Bodega Langes (a boutique winery and COOPERAGE owned by the Austrian owner of Norton in Mendoza); Rongchen winery, the first (of many) 'French chateau-style' wineries, the Sino-French Demonstration Vineyard, and Great Wall's Chateau Sungod.

The traditional vineyard area of the burgeoning north west once centred on the Turpan Depression oases, which can be 155 m/500 ft below sea level. Production had been almost entirely devoted to DRYING GRAPES and table grapes with only a small proportion of Sultanine being made into sweet, simple, often OXIDIZED dessert wines by Xinjiang's state wineries, without any means of TEMPERATURE CONTROL. Xingjiang's first western-style winery, Lou Lan, was established there in the 1970s, initially state-owned and then in private hands. Its French winemaker made some promising Cabernet Sauvignon. The big move forward, however, came with the launch of the huge ViniSuntime wine venture in 1998. It was sold to the Guoan subsidiary of CITIC (China International Trust and Investment Corporation) in 2008 and is now known as CITIC Guoan winery. In terms of grape throughput it rivals the traditional industry leaders in China—Changyu (its Chinese holding much diluted in the early 2000s), COFCO Great Wall, and Dynasty—with its 10,000 ha/24,700 acres of vines and several wineries.

This century saw other new ventures in Xinjiang such as the Yanqi Xiangdu winery, a Sino-French JOINT VENTURE that launched its first wines in 2004 under the Champs d'Or label, and Tiansai vineyard and Zhongfei winery that were set up in the same region in 2010 and 2012 respectively.

Other notable new wine ventures include in Ningxia province the sizeable Xi Xia King, PERNOD RICARD's Helan Mountain, Imperial Horse, LVMH's Domaine Chandon, COFCO's Château Yunmo, and Changyu's Chateau Moser XV, as well as the much smaller Helan Qingxue and Silver Heights. Mogao is another notable new winery in Gansu province.

In the far south west of China LVMH have set up another joint-venture winery in Deqin County, Yunnan province, with the Shangrila Wine Group. In Huanren county in Liaoning province in north east China, several wineries are now specializing in ICE WINE.

Grape varieties

Selecting and breeding TABLE GRAPES and wine grapes started in China in the 1950s. Before that, all vine varieties were the result of long-term natural selection and manual breeding. The aim of wine VINE BREEDING in China was to breed red wine varieties with cold resistance. Even nowadays, the European species (VINIFERA) in northern China (including Xinjiang and Ningxia) would be frozen to death without WINTER PROTECTION. The highly cold-resistant Mongolian species *Vitis* AMURENSIS has been widely used, not least for Gongniang No 1 and Gongniang No 2, which were bred in Jilin in 1952 and 1961 respectively. Gongniang No 1 can survive winter temperatures as low as −22 °C. The cold-resistant Beichun, Beihong, and Beimei varieties were bred in Beijing in 1954 by crossing MUSCAT OF HAMBURG with *V. amurensis*.

Later on, many institutes, such as the Shandong Grape Experiment Station, Yantai Winery (now Changyu), Zhengzhou Fruit Research Institute of Chinese Academy of Agriculture Sciences, and so on, successively bred such grape varieties as Meichun, Meiyu, Meinong, Hongzhilu (all of these four being Merlot × Petit Verdot crosses), Quanbai (Riesling × Petit Verdot), Quanyu (Riesling × Muscat of Hamburg), Yan 73, and Yan 74 (Alicante Bouchet × Muscat of Hamburg).

Most commercially cultivated wine grapes today are imported varieties. Since Changyu introduced 120 wine grape varieties from Germany, Austria, Spain, and Italy in 1892, this process has continued uninterrupted. During the 1950s and 1960s, the communist regime ensured that most imported varieties were from the Soviet bloc in Eastern Europe. Varieties such as RKATSITELI and SAPERAVI are still found in vineyards today. The introduction of varieties from the US, Italy, and France began as recently as the 1970s. The 1980s saw massive imports from Europe by Great Wall Wine Company, China National Research Institute of Food and Fermentation Industries, Xinjiang Shanshan Wine Company, Tianjin Agricultural Reclamation Group, Qingdao Huadong Winery

Co, Beijing Dragon Seal Winery Co, and so on. The huge wave of wine-industry development at the end of the 1990s encouraged imports of vine CUTTINGS on an even bigger scale. However, the fanleaf viruses that came with them led the central government to impose tighter controls of imported vine cuttings, which this century are mainly GRAFTED. Principal importers have been Domaine Franco-Chinois and Jianan Winery in Huailai, Hebei province; COFCO's Chateau Junding in Penglai, Shandong province; and Ningxia Daylong Wine Company and Ningxia Development Bureau for Grape and Flower Industry in Ningxia province.

Red varieties dominate, representing 80% of the total. Of this 80%, Cabernet Sauvignon accounts for about 60% with Merlot and Cabernet Gernischt (CARMENÈRE) about 10% each. Other red wine grapes include Syrah/Shiraz, Cabernet Franc, Pinot Noir, Saperavi, Petit Verdot, Carignan, and a small percentage of the Chinese varieties mentioned above. There is interest in planting more MARSELAN for its useful combination of YIELD and concentration of sugar and PHENOLICS. Of white wine varieties, Chardonnay accounts for at least 70% of the total, followed by Riesling (principally WELSCHRIESLING but also some true RIESLING), which represents about 10% plus Muscat Blanc à Petits Grains, Sauvignon Blanc, Rkatsiteli, Chenin Blanc, and Gewürztraminer. The old favourites Longyan and Muscat of Hamburg now account for less than 5% of all white wine made in China. There is interest in PETIT MANSENG for its sugar accumulation, high ACIDITY and good resistance to major VINE DISEASES. China's first vine NURSERY was established in the north of the Shandong Peninsula in the early 2000s as a joint venture between COFCO and the French nursery Arrive. In 2011, Guillaume set up a nursery in Gansu, and in 2013 Mercier set up another in Ningxia.

Viticulture

In long-standing wine regions vineyard development and grape supply were major problems for the wine industry. Traditionally grapes were supplied on contract through collective agencies and grown on intensively subdivided lands. Individual farmers may work less than an acre each and are entitled to choose their own crop, often preferring the less viticulturally risky TABLE GRAPES. China's parallel systems of planned and market-driven economy and deep-rooted peasant traditions clearly hindered modernization. The traditional fan trellis system, dense foliage, excessive YIELDS, heavy summer IRRIGATION, peanut COVER CROPS, early picking to avoid ROT, and grape prices determined by weight alone are typical. Many vineyards planted in low-lying valleys alongside rice fields have high water-tables and a high risk of FLOODING.

The majority of the traditional vines are ungrafted, with no widespread PHYLLOXERA problem encountered to date. The strong summer rains, humidity levels over 85%, and typically dense CANOPY encourage many vine diseases. ANTHRACNOSE, POWDERY MILDEW, DOWNY MILDEW, DEAD ARM, and WHITE ROT are commonplace, controlled by modern FUNGICIDES when available. BITTER ROT (*Greeneria uvicola*) is also a major problem, as a low level of infection affects the wine. Viticulturists still find it difficult to impose a proper SPRAYING programme on farmers, and winemakers find it difficult to impose the right dates for HARVEST. With more and more wineries competing for grapes, and generally insufficient rewards to growers for waiting until full RIPENESS, grapes tend to arrive early and all at the same time, necessitating investment in extra PRESS capacity at some wineries. With cheap and plentiful labour so far, all work is done manually with very limited MECHANIZATION. The low water-holding capacity and dry spring weather necessitate irrigation, controlled manually with pump and hose.

The most eye-catching development in recent years has been in China's north west; particularly in the Xinjiang Uygur Autonomous Region (which already had the largest vineyard area in China) and in the neighbouring provinces of Ningxia and Gansu. In these regions, most new wineries, founded after 2005, planted their own vineyards instead of buying grapes by contract.   D.G. & L.D.

www.grapewallofchina.com

Chinon, significant red wine appellation in the TOURAINE district of the LOIRE (see map) in which a small amount of rosé, and satisfying dry white from Chenin Blanc grapes, is also produced. The total vineyard area was about 2,300 ha/5,683 acres in 2014. The vineyards extend south of the Loire on the banks of the Vienne, not far east of the fashionable red SAUMUR-CHAMPIGNY, another product of mainly CABERNET FRANC grapes, here often called Breton. No more than 10% of Cabernet Sauvignon is allowed. The region's most famous son, the early-16th-century writer Rabelais, promulgated the wines of Chinon. In modern times, it is the gastronomic writers of Paris who have done much to increase demand for Chinon, and increase the extent of the vineyards that produce it (which had fallen to a few hundred hectares in the 1950s).

Two distinct styles of Chinon are made. A fuller, long-term BOURGUEIL-like wine comes from sites on the clay and TUFFEAU limestone slopes and plateaux, most notably the south-facing slopes of Cravant-les-Coteaux, and the plateau above Beaumont. Lighter wines are made from sand and gravel vineyards near the river (in effect the old flood plains of the Loire and Vienne), with the most elegant examples coming from the gravel beds around Panzoult. These wines are closer to St Nicolas-de-Bourgueil in style.

Chinon is quintessentially a wine of refreshment, being light to medium bodied, often extravagantly scented (lead pencils is one common tasting note), and with an appetizing combination of fruit and acidity. The wines have become markedly richer and more satisfying as growers grass over their vineyards and use higher trellises, de-budding, and deleafing to ripen grapes more successfully. The best wines can benefit from BOTTLE AGEING, but that is not the point of the wine, which keeps the Chinon market free of foreign speculation on the part of collectors. Chinon is essentially a Frenchman's wine, and it takes some local knowledge to seek out the best, often artisanal, bottlings. A high proportion of the wine is sold to merchants, whose blends vary considerably in quality.

chip budding, a popular method for the BUDDING of vines, with a long history. It is known as the yema bud in Europe and California. During the first growing season of the ROOTSTOCK, a piece is cut from its original wood and a matching chip piece with a bud is cut from a scion cutting. The chip is inserted in the stock with CAMBIUM zones matching, then wrapped tightly with budding tape (see illustration). Chip budding, which may take place at any time of year, may also be used for TOP GRAFTING.

See also FIELD BUDDING.   B.G.C.

Chiroubles, highest of the Beaujolais crus, producing some of the lightest but most

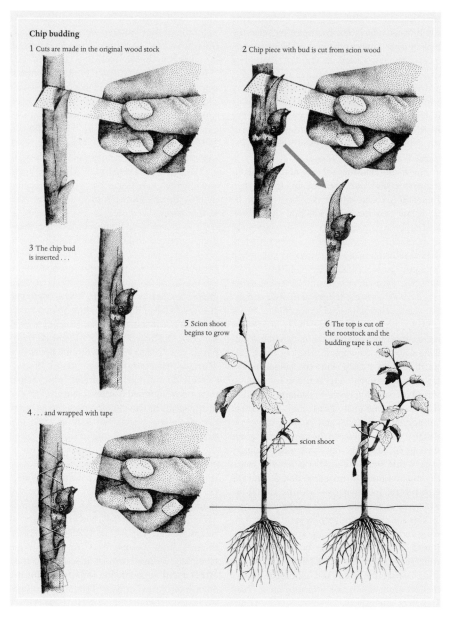

Chip budding

1 Cuts are made in the original wood stock

2 Chip piece with bud is cut from scion wood

3 The chip bud is inserted . . .

4 . . . and wrapped with tape

5 Scion shoot begins to grow

6 The top is cut off the rootstock and the budding tape is cut

scion shoot

genuinely refreshing wines. The soils are very similar to the sandiest parts of neighbouring FLEURIE and wines can be a little tart in poor vintages. Perhaps the most archetypically Beaujolais of all the crus, Chiroubles is best drunk relatively young. Total vineyard area had shrunk to 324 ha/800 acres by 2012. For more details, see BEAUJOLAIS.

Chitry, commune near AUXERRE whose name may be appended to that of BOURGOGNE.

chloroanisoles, group of compounds responsible, in most instances, for the musty odour of CORKED wine and one of which, TCA, was the first identified as contributing to the problem. The formation of chloroanisoles in cork bark comes about in a stepwise process involving as the final step the methylation of chlorophenols by microorganisms. It is the earlier steps, i.e. those leading to the formation of the chlorophenols, which continue to elude understanding. It appears that the chlorophenolic precursors have multiple origins, including, among other possibilities, formation during chlorine bleaching of cork bark, the use of organochlorine biocides on cork trees in the forests, and perhaps even direct biosynthesis in cork tissue. Even though chlorophenol fungicides have been banned in Europe since 1995, chlorophenols are very stable and still present in groundwater. Until the diverse origins of chlorophenols in cork bark are fully understood, the elimination of chloroanisoles, and hence their contribution to CORK TAINT, will remain a significant problem in cork production.   P.J.W.

chlorosis, vine disorder in which parts or all of the foliage turn yellow due to lack of chlorophyll. The most common and extreme chlorosis is that which is visible in spring and early summer and is caused by IRON deficiency, which is common on soils high in LIMESTONE. Lime-induced chlorosis became a problem in parts of France as a consequence of PHYLLOXERA invasion at the end of the 19th century, since AMERICAN VINE SPECIES sourced initially in the eastern US and used as phylloxera-resistant ROOTSTOCKS were more prone to iron deficiency than were the original VINIFERA root systems. This problem, known in French as **chlorose calcaire**, has been largely overcome now by the selection of lime-tolerant rootstocks suitable for calcareous soils, such as 41 B or the newer Fercal. In Burgundy and Champagne, where soils tend to be high in limestone, it has been difficult to find rootstocks with sufficient lime tolerance for healthy vine growth. This sensitivity of early post-phylloxera rootstocks to lime-induced chlorosis may provide part of the explanation for an apparent drop in quality in post-phylloxera wines, according to some historical authorities.

Chlorosis is a common symptom of deficiencies of other nutrients such as NITROGEN, SULFUR, and MAGNESIUM. It can also be caused by some VINE DISEASES. The effect may be general, as for FANLEAF DEGENERATION virus, or more localized, as in, for example, the so-called oil spot on leaves due to DOWNY MILDEW infection.   R.E.S.

Chorey-lès-Beaune, village near (lès in old French) Beaune in Burgundy producing red wines from Pinot Noir grapes. Chorey lies in the plain below the main RN74 road, as do most of the appellation's vineyards. There are no vineyards of PREMIER CRU status, and much of the wine is sold as Côte de BEAUNE-Villages. Exceptional producers based here are Domaines Tollot-Beaut and Jacques Germain, which make some of the finest wines of the Beaune appellation. A good Chorey is similar to a village SAVIGNY-LÈS-BEAUNE or a lesser ALOXE-CORTON. A tiny quantity of white Chorey-lès-Beaune is made from Chardonnay.

See also CÔTE D'OR and map under BURGUNDY.   J.T.C.M.

Christianity and wine. See EUCHARIST, RELIGION, BIBLE, MONKS AND MONASTERIES, and MISSIONARIES.

Chusclan, the most famous of the Côtes du RHÔNE villages on the right bank of the river making fruity reds for relatively early consumption. As in nearby TAVEL, its rosé is particularly appreciated.

Cienna, NEW VARIETY bred in Australia from the Spanish SUMOLL and Cabernet Sauvignon and released, with its sister variety Tyrian, in 2000. Both varieties have good sugar to acid ratios, low PH, good colour and flavour, and adequate yields. Cienna is very tannic.

Cigales, small wine zone in northern Spain, north of Valladolid in CASTILLA Y LEÓN (see map under SPAIN), higher and cooler than TORO, with impressive average VINE AGE. This DO has traditionally produced dry rosé wines made from Tinto del Pais (TEMPRANILLO) and some GARNACHA grapes, but an increasing number of dry reds show real potential and, so far, value.

Ciliegiolo, widely dispersed Italian red grape variety of Tuscan origin named after its supposed cherry-like flavour and colour. It has been declining in extent, although it can make some excellent VARIETAL wines, particularly Sassotondo's Maremma examples, and can be a usefully soft blending partner for SANGIOVESE, particularly in CHIANTI. Unexpectedly, DNA PROFILING revealed that Ciliegiolo is one of the parents of Sangiovese. Plantings totalled 1,829 ha/4,520 acres in 2010.

cincturing, viticultural practice involving removing, with a knife or special tool, a ring (3 to 8 mm (0.1–0.3 in) wide) of conducting tissue (PHLOEM) around a trunk, cane, or shoot, normally to improve FRUIT SET. Also called girdling or ringing in English and incision annulaire in French, the technique is more widely used for TABLE GRAPES than for wine production, which can rarely justify the necessary LABOUR cost. Cincturing stops both the upwards and downwards flow of nutrients and plant hormones, until the wound heals over.   R.E.S.

cineole. See EUCALYPTUS CHARACTER.

Cinsaut, sometimes written **Cinsault**, is a red grape variety known for centuries in the Languedoc region of southern France that has much in common with GRENACHE. Although it has good drought resistance and its best wines by far come from vines that yield less than 40 hl/ha (2.3 tons/acre), it can all too easily be persuaded to yield generously and unremarkably. The wines it produces tend to be lighter, softer, and, in extreme youth, more aromatic and charmingly cherry-fruited than most of its peers. Although prone to ROT, it is particularly well adapted for rosé production and is widely planted throughout southern France, especially in the Hérault and Var départements in Languedoc and Provence respectively. It differs from Grenache by virtue of its long history, its shorter growing season, and its easier adaptation to mechanical harvesting.

There was a threefold increase in French plantings in the 1970s, when Cinsaut was officially sanctioned as an 'improving' grape variety with which to replace ARAMON and ALICANTE BOUSCHET, mainly in the Aude and Hérault départements. Since then, the economic realities of quality's supremacy over quantity have slowed Cinsaut's fortunes and Languedoc producers have been much more likely to plant a variety with as much character and cachet as Syrah, Merlot, Mourvèdre, or Cabernet Sauvignon. Cinsaut is used almost exclusively to add suppleness, perfume, and immediate fruit to blends (typically compensating for the ubiquitous but curmudgeonly Carignan), although all-Cinsaut rosés are increasingly common.

It is an approved but hardly venerated ingredient in the CHÂTEAUNEUF-DU-PAPE cocktail and is often found further east in Provence, as well as in the north of CORSICA, where it has been widely pulled up in favour of more profitable crops.

Total French plantings of Cinsaut fell throughout the 1980s to less than 50,000 ha/123,500 acres (still more vineyard than Cabernet Sauvignon) and by 2011 were less than 19,000 ha. The variety was most important in the 1950s and early 1960s when ALGERIA, then constitutionally part of France, was an important wine producer and depended particularly heavily on its healthily productive 60,000 ha of Cinsaut. Since Algerian wine was then used primarily for blending in France, notoriously for adding body to less reputable burgundies, some of this North African Cinsaut may still be found in a few older bottles of 'burgundy'. It is still common in MOROCCO and has long played an important part in the wine industry of the LEBANON, where it formed the backbone of the wine industry for 150 years and is now experiencing a resurgence in popularity.

Cinsaut has in its time played a major part in South as well as North Africa (which makes it all the stranger that South Africa has had little ROSÉ culture). Having been imported from southern France in the mid 19th century, it was South Africa's most important red wine vine until the mid 1960s and was overtaken by Cabernet Sauvignon as the Cape's most planted red grape variety only in 1993. In 2012, it was South Africa's sixth most planted red wine grape with a little under 2,000 ha in total. Cinsaut was once known carelessly as Hermitage in South Africa (although there is no Cinsaut in the northern Rhône). Thus South Africa's own grape variety speciality, a cross of Pinot Noir with Cinsaut, was named PINOTAGE, now much more respected in South Africa than Cinsaut.

In both France and Australia (where its fortunes waned rapidly in the 1970s and 1980s), Cinsaut has occasionally been sold as a table grape under the name Œillade. In southern Italy, it is known as Ottavianello and is planted around Brindisi, producing light, unremarkable red wines. Cinsaut can also be found in Turkey.

Cirò, currently the only DOC of any quantitative significance in the southern Italian region of CALABRIA.

citric acid, a common plant acid, abundant in some fleshy fruits such as lemons, but rare in grapes. The grape is unusual among fruits in that its major acid is TARTARIC ACID (and MALIC ACID), rather than citric acid, whose concentration in the juice of most grape varieties is only about one-twentieth that of tartaric acid.

Citric acid is also one of the ACIDS used in winemaking for the purposes of ACIDIFICATION. It is inexpensive but unsubtle and is used almost exclusively for inexpensive wines. It is always added after rather than before fermentation since it can be converted to ACETIC ACID by the yeast. It is produced commercially by fermenting SUCROSE solutions; very small amounts are recovered from processing citrus fruits. It is also used for cleaning. In the EU it is not permitted for acidification but it can be used to prevent iron casse if BLUE FINING is not possible. See also DIACETYL.   B.G.C. & A.D.W.

CIVC. Thanks to the **Comité Interprofessionnel du Vin de Champagne**, CHAMPAGNE is one of the most thoroughly organized wine regions in the world. The CIVC was established in 1941 as a co-operative organization grouping champagne GROWERS, CO-OPERATIVES, shippers, and houses under the auspices of the government. Growers/co-operatives on the one hand and merchants/champagne houses on the other each have a president to represent them. The CIVC is charged with organizing and controlling the production, distribution, and promotion of the wines of Champagne, as well as undertaking fundamental research for the region. Until 1990 it set a price for the grapes and still intervenes to regulate the size of the harvest and decide whether any of it should be 'blocked', or retained as juice rather than vinified and sold. The CIVC is financed by a levy on production and a tax on champagne sales.

But most importantly the CIVC is responsible for defending the Champenois's exclusive right to use the word 'champagne'. A notable victory was won in the English courts in 1959 and since then the name has achieved legal protection in most major markets, although not in the United States for established brands. The CIVC has fought a number of battles to ensure that the name Champagne is not used for other products, including a cigarette and a brand of perfume.   N.F. & J.R.

Clairet, dark pink wine style that is a speciality of the BORDEAUX region, recalling the sort of red wines that were shipped in such quantity in the Middle Ages from Bordeaux to ENGLAND, and which originally inspired the English word CLARET. Dark-skinned grapes are fermented in contact with the skins for about 24 hours before fermentation of this lightly coloured wine continues to dryness. Bordeaux Clairet should be drunk as young as possible.

Clairette is a much-used name for southern French white grape varieties. **Clairette Ronde**, for example, is the Languedoc name for the ubiquitous UGNI BLANC, and various Clairettes serve as synonyms for the much finer BOURBOULENC.

True **Clairette Blanche**, however, is very old Languedoc variety grown on a total of 2,274 ha/ 5,617 acres of French vineyard in 2011, being allowed into a wide range of southern Rhône, Provençal, and Languedoc appellations, even lending its name to three (see below). Clairette is a traditional variety well suited to poor, dry soils, for long grown in what Galet calls 'the land of the olive tree'. Its small, thick-skinned grapes ripen relatively late, but can ripen dangerously fast at the end of the growing season. In the southern Rhône, it is particularly popular for adding aroma and acidity to a blend, not least with the fatter GRENACHE BLANC. Clairette is widely distributed throughout the eastern Midi, especially in the Gard, where it produces CLAIRETTE DE BELLEGARDE and in the Hérault for CLAIRETTE DU LANGUEDOC, two of the Languedoc's earliest controlled appellations, presumably because these white wines were so unlike the typical produce of the Midi. Its other stronghold is the Drôme *département* since Clairette is the main ingredient in CLAIRETTE DE DIE and CRÉMANT DE DIE.

Partly because it was an ingredient in PICARDAN, the variety spread far and wide, including to southern RUSSIA, in the 19th and early 20th centuries. At one time there were sizeable plantings in Algeria. It is known as Clairette Blanche in South Africa, where it was once as widely planted as in France. Some old plantings can still be found.

Clairette de Bellegarde is a tiny 16-ha/ 40-acre appellation for white wine in the south of the COSTIÈRES DE NÎMES appellation in the southern Rhône on the edge of the Camargue. Like CLAIRETTE DU LANGUEDOC, it is made entirely of the CLAIRETTE grape and needs all the streamlining that modern vinification can impart. Production is dominated by the Bellegarde co-operative. Drink this wine young.

Clairette de Die, pair of appellations for sparkling white wines centred on the town of DIE on the Drôme tributary east of the Rhône between Valence and Montélimar. According to PLINY, wine has been made here since Roman times. Die's gently fizzing wines may pre-date those of Champagne. Two very different sorts of sparkling Clairette de Die are made. The dry version, **Clairette de Die Brut**, is made from CLAIRETTE grapes by the transfer method (see SPARKLING WINEMAKING) and has an alcoholic strength of between 11 and 12%. It differs from CRÉMANT de Die in that the latter must be made from whole grapes and made sparkling by the TRADITIONAL method whereas Clairette de Die Brut may be separated from the lees of the second fermentation by filtration rather than DISGORGEMENT.

Clairette de Die Tradition is more distinctive. It is refreshingly grapey and gently fizzy, made from at least 75% MUSCAT BLANC À PETITS GRAINS, the rest Clairette, by the *méthode dioise ancestrale* (see SPARKLING WINEMAKING). The local co-operative, geographically and historically justified in calling itself the Cellier Hannibal, has been responsible for dynamizing the appellation and makes three in every four bottles carrying it.

Local still reds and whites may qualify as CHÂTILLON-EN-DIOIS.

Clairette du Languedoc is a slightly more important (73-ha/180-acre in 2012) appellation than CLAIRETTE DE BELLEGARDE, again exclusively from the Clairette grape. It is one of the named subappellations of the southern French LANGUEDOC AOC. Clairette du Languedoc has suffered an extremely confused image as, despite its relatively small production, a wide array of different wine styles has been produced, and is officially sanctioned, within the appellation. The wine can be anything from an ultra-modern, early-picked, yellowish green, dry wine for drinking almost before the end of the year in which it was harvested, to a deep brown RANCIO sweet, alcoholic VIN DE LIQUEUR fortified just as fermentation has started. The area qualifying for this confused appellation lies to the north east of Pézenas. The Adissan and Cabrières CO-OPERATIVES are the specialist producers.

Clape, La, named TERROIR within the LANGUEDOC AOC in southern France which can be unfairly penalized for its name in Anglophone markets. La Clape was once an island off the busy Roman port of Narbo (Narbonne). Today it is a quintessentially Mediterranean coastal mountain just south of Narbonne which has one of France's highest average annual totals of sunshine. On the clay-limestone southern slopes of the rocky massif, the climate is heavily influenced by the sea. Elevations of vineyards can vary by as much as 200 m/980 ft. La Clape is particularly well suited to growing BOURBOULENC, which must represent at least 40% of the grapes used in the production of La Clape's iodine-scented white wines in which Grenache Blanc and a little Viognier is also allowed. Most of the wine produced from about 1,000 ha/2,500 acres of vineyard within the appellation is full-blooded red, however, virtually indistinguishable from maritime CORBIÈRES, with Ch de la Négly a notable producer. The extensive l'Hospitalet domaine is headquarters of the dynamic Languedoc NÉGOCIANT Gérard Bertrand.

Clare Riesling. See CROUCHEN.

claret, English (not American) term generally used to describe red wines from the BORDEAUX region, or red bordeaux. Claret has also been used as a GENERIC term for a vaguely identified class of red table wines supposedly drier, and possibly higher in TANNINS, than those wines sold as generic burgundy (although, in the history of Australian wine SHOWS, it has been known for the same wine to win both claret and burgundy classes).

History
In medieval France, most red wine was the result of a short FERMENTATION, usually of no more than one or two days. The short period of contact with the grape skins meant that the resultant wines were pale in colour, and were probably very similar to the rosés of today. Such wines exported from Bordeaux were known as *vinum clarum, vin clar*, or CLAIRET, and it is from the last of these that the English term claret is derived. Other much darker wines were also made by pressing the remaining skins, effectively the same as modern PRESS WINE, and these

were known as *vinum rubeum purum, bin vermelh*, or *pinpin*.

Although the term *clairet* was widely used during the medieval period in France, the word claret does not appear to have been used at all extensively in England until the 16th century. In the second half of the 17th century, a new type of wine, of much higher quality and deeper colour, began to be produced in the GRAVES and on the sands and gravels of the MÉDOC to the north west of Bordeaux. These wines, the provenance of specific properties, where close attention was paid to grape selection, improved methods of vinification, and the use of new oak BARRELS, became known by the beginning of the 18th century as New French Clarets, and the earliest and most famous of them were HAUT-BRION, LAFITE, LATOUR, and MARGAUX (see BORDEAUX, history).   P.T.H.U.

Marquette, J., 'La Vinification dans les domaines de l'archevêque de Bordeaux à la fin du Moyen Âge', in A. Huetz de Lemps (ed.), *Géographie historique des vignobles*, i (Bordeaux, 1978).

Pijassou, R., *Un grand vignoble de qualité: le Médoc* (Paris, 1980).

clarete is a historic Spanish term for a wine somewhere between a rosé (which the Spaniards would call *rosado*) and a light red. It is etymologically, though not oenologically, related to CLARET.

claret jugs. See DECANTERS.

Clare Valley, fine wine region in SOUTH AUSTRALIA with a strongly CONTINENTAL climate: warm summer days and cool nights. This combined with differences in soil, elevation, degree of slope and aspect, enables the region to produce some of Australia's finest Riesling as well as excellent Shiraz, Cabernet Sauvignon, and Malbec. While wines are sturdy and powerful, alcohol levels are generally lower than those of the Barossa Valley or McLaren Vale. There are 40 producers, of which 15 sell but do not make wine there.   J.H. & H.H.

clarification, progressive winemaking operation which removes suspended and insoluble material from grape juice, or new wine, in which these solids are known as LEES.

Clarification proper may be the removal only of insoluble solids such as the dead yeast cells and fragments of grape skins, stems, seeds, and pulp, but is frequently understood to encompass also the removal of dispersed COLLOIDS and other materials which exist in supersaturated concentration in the must or new wine, and in older wine that has not been stabilized. These latter substances include excess TARTRATES, pectins and gums, some PROTEINS, and small numbers of micro-organisms such as YEAST and BACTERIA. Removal of all these substances, which are not visible to the unaided eye, is

frequently called STABILIZATION, since no subsequent clarification is needed. Clarification has become more critical now that most consumers have come to expect wines to be bright and clear.

Clarification can usually be accomplished naturally by simply holding the liquid in a storage tank until the larger particles settle (see SETTLING, or *débourbage*) and then siphoning, or RACKING, the clear upper layer from the compact layer of solids at the bottom of the tank. This takes time, however, especially if the wine is stored in small barrels where full clarification may take a year or two and several rackings.

Most winemakers, therefore, and certainly all concerned with high-volume production, may start with settling to remove the gross matter, then choose to accelerate the process by intervening with one or more of FILTRATION, CENTRIFUGATION, FLOTATION, and the much cheaper process of FINING, the addition of agents which aid agglomeration and settling of colloids in the must or new wine.

One important white winemaking decision is the extent to which grape solids should be removed from the must before FERMENTATION. With Chardonnays, for example, it may be desirable to have a relatively high proportion of grape solids which produce various characters during fermentation. Winemakers may wish to eliminate most grape solids from the juice of more aromatic varieties in order to accentuate varietal fruit flavours. Juice for everyday white wines may be clarified before fermentation simply to speed and ease processing afterwards. This clarification can be done by simply holding the cooled and SULFUR DIOXIDE-treated juice in a tank for 24 hours or so. Sometimes, pectin-splitting ENZYMES will be added along with the sulfur dioxide in order to aid the clarification. In the past, some winemakers added BENTONITE before fermentation in order to precipitate unstable proteins.

For a long time neither centrifugation nor filtration was practical for removing solids from must. Centrifugation, which depends upon differing densities between the solids and the liquid, is impractically inefficient because of the high density of the sugar-laden juice. Before the development of ROTARY DRUM VACUUM FILTERS, the finely divided grape solids would quickly plug the small holes of a filter, making the process prohibitively expensive. Today, however, rotary filters, press filters, and tangential filters may be used on lees which contain up to 15% solids.

Red wines are not commonly clarified before fermentation because the skins are fermented with the juice in order to provide colour and flavour. In some cases, however, pectin-splitting enzymes are added to red must before fermentation to aid subsequent clarification and increase the eventual yield of FREE-RUN wine. Many everyday new red wines are processed in order to prevent the subsequent precipitation of tartrates and some will have the malic acid removed or reduced by a MALOLACTIC CONVERSION to assure reasonable stability in bottle.

See also the similar but distinct processes associated with STABILIZATION. A.D.W. & D.B.

Clarksburg, California wine region and AVA. Much of the AVA is composed of deep-soiled islands in the CENTRAL VALLEY delta from a point near Sacramento west beyond the town of Clarksburg. Though its position in the river channel leaves its vineyards open to the strongest summer sea fogs, the vast proportion of surrounding water retards overnight cooling when fogs are not afoot, so Clarksburg is far from being California's coolest vineyard district. Although a spectrum of varieties grows within the zone, only CHENIN BLANC truly distinguishes itself. Indeed, only here in all of California does Chenin Blanc become regionally identifiable. For all practical purposes it has swallowed up the Merritt Island AVA, which lies within its western end.

classed growth is a vineyard, estate, or château included in a wine CLASSIFICATION. The term is used almost exclusively in BORDEAUX for those châteaux included in the 1855 classification of the Médoc and Sauternes, the 1955 classification of Graves, and sometimes for those properties included in the regularly revised St-Émilion classification. The term is a direct translation of the French term CRU classé.

Classic, official German wine designation introduced in 2000, though little used outside Germany, for dry-tasting wines (maximum 15 g/l RESIDUAL SUGAR) vinified from traditional grape varieties, harvested at at least 12% potential alcohol (11.5% in the Mosel). See also GERMAN WINE LAW. Not to be confused with the term KLASSIK as used (principally) in AUSTRIA.

classical art, wine in. Wine was so deeply embedded in the culture of the classical world that it is inevitable that it would figure prominently in the art of that world. The vessels used for mixing and drinking wine (see CRATER, for example) were frequently decorated with scenes which played on the association with wine. So, most notably, the fine Attic Black and Red Figure pottery of the 6th and 5th centuries BC sometimes contains rural scenes of men harvesting grapes and treading them, as well as scenes from the *komos* (revels) and the SYMPOSIUM, in which the craters and cups are depicted in use. Sometimes it is possible to suspect an ironic commentary taking place. A famous Red Figure cup by the so-called Dokimasia painter has scenes of revelry around the outside with the awkward spaces under the handles filled by men crouched or crawling, the worse for drink, while inside the cup an old man is depicted being sick.

Another playful irony is that nearly all these scenes can be found translated to another world, in which men are replaced by satyrs, uninhibited by the conventions of human society and presided over by the god DIONYSUS. Not surprisingly, Dionysus achieves a greater prominence in the art of the world of drinking than his place in the pantheon would suggest as his due. Feasting and banquets with wine also form the subject of some of the most memorable frescos from the tombs of the ETRUSCANS, where, for example, the Tomb of the Leopards at Tarquinia beautifully illustrates the funeral meal held near the tomb in honour of the dead.

Scenes of the vintage and the pressing of the grapes, with the role of humans frequently played by *amorini*, cupids, are found in great numbers at all periods throughout the Roman world, in paintings, sculptured reliefs, sarcophagi, decorated glass, and ivory plaques. Part of the explanation for the popularity of the themes, particularly on sarcophagi, is the obvious mystical symbolism of the vine and wine. Scenes of country life, including vines and the vintage, play a significant part in Roman painting from the 1st century BC onwards, and are most elaborately and impressively illustrated in mosaic. The vintage and tasks connected with viticulture, such as pruning and the cleaning and pitching of DOLIA, are often found in mosaics which illustrate the seasons or the tasks of the rural calendar. As a genre, these had a long history, which went back to the Hellenistic period in mosaic and may be connected with illustrated manuscript calendars. Fine examples in mosaic come from GAUL (St-Romain-en-Gal) and North Africa (the Maison des Mois at El Djem). From the 3rd century AD the élite of North Africa adorned their houses with mosaics which reflected the work of their estates. One of the most remarkable examples of realism in classical art must be the mosaic of the Labours of the Fields from Cherchel in Algeria, with men hoeing between TRELLISED vines.

The potential of the vine and wine as mystical symbols also explains why this was one of the themes of classical art which was most easily taken over by Christianity. A key monument is the church of Santa Costanza on the Via Nomentana in the north of Rome, a work of such rare beauty as to justify on its own a visit to that city. Santa Costanza was the mausoleum of Constantina, the daughter of Constantine, the first Christian emperor. Her huge porphyry sarcophagus has cherubs engaged in the vintage, a theme which is taken up by the remarkable mosaics which run round the ceiling of the ambulatory. The themes are traditional. Nothing is specifically Christian in these mosaics, but they are given a Christian connotation by the other, more overtly Christian, mosaics which would have adorned the dome. J.J.P.

Berard, C., et al., *A City of Images* (Princeton, NJ, 1989).

Dunbabin, K. M. D., *The Mosaics of Roman North Africa* (Oxford, 1978).

classical texts. The vine and the olive are the plants that characterize Mediterranean civilization. To grow them is the sign of a settled, not a nomadic, existence. Their products can be used as part of the daily routine, olive oil for cooking and washing, wine for drinking, or to mark a special occasion in the life of a community, when people would anoint their heads with fragrant oil and drink the best wine. In wine-producing countries wine can be an ordinary drink or a luxury item: classical literature reflects both.

This starts with HOMER (the end of the 8th century BC) and HESIOD (c. 700 BC), the earliest Greek authors. Wine is mentioned frequently in the grander context. In Hesiod's *Works and Days* the cultivation of the vine is part of the order of nature as laid down by the gods: the secular and the religious were not distinct spheres. HERODOTUS' *Histories* (5th century BC) have many observations on wine and its uses among foreign nations. The Greeks had no books on agriculture, but THEOPHRASTUS (c.370–c.287 BC) could be called the first systematic botanist. A very late Greek author, ATHENAEUS (fl. AD 200), is a good source of information on the wines of his day.

Among the Romans, VIRGIL (70–19 BC), HORACE (65–8 BC), and MARTIAL (c.AD 30–103/4) are the poets who display a particular interest in wine: Virgil chiefly in the *Georgics*, Horace throughout his poems, and Martial in many of his epigrams on the mores of his time. PLINY the Elder (AD 23/4–79) devoted an entire book of his *Natural History* to all aspects of wine. Other prose writers wrote treatises on agriculture: CATO (234–149 BC), VARRO (116–27 BC), COLUMELLA (1st century AD), and the derivative PALLADIUS (4th century AD). H.M.W.

classical vine varieties. See ANCIENT VINE VARIETIES.

classical wines. See GREECE and ROME for general comments, as well as CAECUBAN, FALERNIAN, MASSIC, OPIMIAN, and SURRENTINE wines specifically.

classical world. See Ancient GREECE and Ancient ROME.

Classico, Italian term appended to the names of various DOC or DOCG wines to indicate that they have been produced in the historic zone, the zone which, at least in theory, offers the ideal conditions of soil and climate and which gave the wine its name.

The name of the wine *without* the adjective Classico is usually applied to a significant expansion of the original production zone into areas which generally, but not always, cultivate the same grape varieties but in different, and usually less satisfactory, conditions, frequently with more lenient production requirements. The origins of this practice, which occurred well before the establishment of the DOC system in the 1960s, and has often been driven by economic motives, lie in the regulation of the use of the name CHIANTI established by the Dalmasso Commission in the 1930s (see CHIANTI CLASSICO). This precedent was widely followed as the various DOCs came into being between 1963, when the law regulating the demarcation of Italy's wine regions was passed, and 1975, since when a significant number of Italy's historically important wines are now produced in both a Classico and a regular version. These include BARDOLINO, CALDARO, CHIANTI, CIRÒ, Colli BOLOGNESI, Pignoletto, Garda, ORVIETO, SANTA MADDALENA, SOAVE, TERLANO, VALPOLICELLA, and VERDICCHIO.

The practice, not dissimilar to the creation of Germany's notorious GROSSLAGEN, reflects a permanent tension in Italy's DOC system itself. Often the most quality-conscious producers keen for promotion to DOCG status lobby for it to be restricted to the original Classico zone, but find themselves opposed by big companies with holdings throughout the enlarged zone.

classification

classification of various wine estates and vineyards is in general a relatively recent phenomenon, dictated by the increasingly sophisticated wine market of the last 150 years or so. It has to a certain extent been superseded by the even more recent phenomenon of SCORING individual wines.

There were earlier instances of classifying individual vineyards, however. The vineyards of JURANÇON in south-west France were officially evaluated as early as the 14th century. Tax collectors in GATTINARA did the same in the 16th century. In 1644, the council of Würzburg in FRANKEN rigorously ranked the city's vineyards according to the quality of wine they produced (see GERMAN HISTORY). The first mention of a classification of TOKAJ vineyards dates from 1700, although the classes were not ratified until 1737 (and the vineyards probably not officially mapped until 1786 under Emperor Joseph II).

Bordeaux

BORDEAUX, with its plethora of fine, long-lasting wine from well-established estates and its well-organized market, is the wine region which has been most subject to classification of individual châteaux. The most famous wine classification in the world is that drawn up in 1855 of what became known as the CLASSED GROWTHS of the MÉDOC, and one GRAVES (see following pages). In response to a request from Napoleon III's 1855 Exposition Universelle in Paris (possibly so that dignitaries there should effectively know what to be impressed by), the Bordeaux BROKERS

formalized their own and the market's ranking with a five-class classification of 60 of the leading Médoc châteaux plus the particularly famous and historic Graves, HAUT-BRION; and a two-class classification of SAUTERNES and BARSAC. This classification merely codified the market's view of relative quality as expressed by the prices fetched by individual estates' wines. (It also formalized previous informal lists of those wines widely regarded as the best by the likes of Thomas JEFFERSON, Wilhelm Franck, Alexander HENDERSON, and Cyrus REDDING.) The brokers issued the 1855 classification through the Bordeaux Chamber of Commerce, and were careful to explain that it was based on a century's experience. Within each of their classes, from FIRST GROWTHS, or PREMIERS CRUS, down to fifth growths, or cinquièmes CRUS, the brokers listed châteaux in descending order of average price fetched. Thus, it is widely believed, LAFITE, the 'premier des premiers', headed the list because it commanded prices in excess even of LATOUR, MARGAUX, and Haut-Brion (although others have argued that the first growths were simply listed in alphabetical order). In the original classification, the term CHÂTEAU was rarely used.

The 1855 classification has endured remarkably well considering the many and various changes to the management and precise extent of individual properties since it was compiled, with only Chx MOUTON ROTHSCHILD and Léoville-BARTON in the same hands. Ch Dubignon-Talbot has not produced wine since the arrival of PHYLLOXERA in the late 19th century. Edmund PENNING-ROWSELL notes that Palmer's low ranking may have been influenced by the fact that the property was in receivership in 1855, and that Cantemerle, a property relatively new to the Bordeaux market, was added to the bottom of the list in a different hand. The only official revision of this much-discussed list took place in 1973, when, after much lobbying on the part of Baron Philippe de ROTHSCHILD, Ch Mouton-Rothschild made the all-important leap from top of the second growths to become a first growth (although see also SUPER SECOND). It could be argued that such a classification contains an element of self-preservation in that highly classified properties are thereby able to command prices which sustain the investment needed to maintain their status, although the history of Ch Margaux in the 1960s and 1970s demonstrates that other factors may affect this hypothesis, and in the 1980s and 1990s many Bordeaux proprietors were driven by competition and ambition to invest, and in some cases price, at a level above that suggested by their official ranking. See Ch LÉOVILLE LAS CASES in particular.

The 1855 classification of Sauternes and Barsac is also printed on p. 183. Reflecting price and the *réclame* then attached to sweet wines, it elevated Ch d'YQUEM to premier cru supérieur, a

rank higher even than any of the red wine first growths, and listed 11 châteaux as first growths and 14 as seconds.

Other than Haut-Brion's inclusion in the 1855 Médoc classification, the wines of the Graves district were not officially classified until 1953. This one-class list, slightly augmented in 1959, appears on p 182. It avoided some possible controversy by employing a democratically alphabetical order (Ch Haut-Brion Blanc was added in 1960). It should be said, however, that there is a wide differential between the prices commanded by Ch Haut-Brion and its close rival Ch La Mission-Haut-Brion, and those fetched by Chx Bouscaut and de Fieuzal, for example. The Graves district was subsequently divided into Graves and PESSAC-LÉOGNAN.

The classification of ST-ÉMILION, formally drawn up in 1955, is most frequently amended, and therefore most controversial. Modifications were published in 1969, 1985, 1996, 2006, and 2012 and these are likely to continue on the basis of monitoring of wine quality, vineyard boundaries, prices, and the like (vineyards cannot be extended between reclassifications). The 2006 classification was disputed and suspended in the spring of 2007, and then reinstated six months later. The 2012 classification, reproduced on pp. 182–3, has met with slightly less opposition. St-Émilion classification's laudable topicality is mitigated by over-generosity in nomenclature, however. The top four properties Chx CHEVAL BLANC, AUSONE, Angélus, and Pavie are ranked, somewhat inelegantly, premiers grands crus classés A, while 14 properties qualify as premiers grands crus classés B. Below this are 64 grands crus classés, whose quality can vary considerably, and then in each vintage, on the basis of tastings, the deceptively grandiose rank of GRAND CRU (minus the classé) is awarded to scores of individual wines from properties below grand cru classé status.

POMEROL is the only important fine wine district of Bordeaux never to have been classified, although its star PETRUS is conventionally included with Chx Lafite, Latour, Margaux, Haut-Brion, Mouton-Rothschild, Cheval Blanc, and Ausone as an honorary first growth.

There have been regular attempts to revise and assimilate the various classifications of Bordeaux, most notably that drawn up by Alexis LICHINE in 1959. Most serious writers on bordeaux make their own revisions, more or less confirmed by the market.

See also CRU BOURGEOIS for those MÉDOC properties classified as just below the status of a fifth growth.

Burgundy

Burgundians were also well aware of the considerable variation in quality of the wines produced by different plots of land, or *climats*, as they are known in Burgundy. In 1855, Dr

Bordeaux

The Official Classification of Médoc and Graves of 1855

First Growths (Premiers Crus)

	Commune	Appellation		Commune	Appellation
Ch Lafite-Rothschild	Pauillac	Pauillac	Ch Haut-Brion*	Pessac	Graves, now Pessac-Léognan
Ch Margaux	Margaux	Margaux			
Ch Latour	Pauillac	Pauillac	Ch Mouton Rothschild**	Pauillac	Pauillac

Second Growths (Deuxièmes Crus)

	Commune	Appellation		Commune	Appellation
Ch Rauzan-Ségla	Margaux	Margaux	Ch Brane-Cantenac	Cantenac	Margaux
Ch Rauzan-Gassies	Margaux	Margaux	Ch Pichon Baron	Pauillac	Pauillac
Ch Léoville Las Cases	St-Julien	St-Julien			
Ch Léoville-Poyferré	St-Julien	St-Julien	Ch Pichon-Longueville,	Pauillac	Pauillac
Ch Léoville-Barton	St-Julien	St-Julien	Comtesse de Lalande		
Ch Durfort-Vivens	Margaux	Margaux	Ch Ducru-Beaucaillou	St-Julien	St-Julien
Ch Gruaud-Larose	St-Julien	St-Julien	Ch Cos d'Estournel	St-Estèphe	St-Estèphe
Ch Lascombes	Margaux	Margaux	Ch Montrose	St-Estèphe	St-Estèphe

Third Growths (Troisièmes Crus)

	Commune	Appellation		Commune	Appellation
Ch Kirwan	Cantenac	Margaux	Ch Cantenac-Brown	Cantenac	Margaux
Ch d'Issan	Cantenac	Margaux	Ch Palmer	Cantenac	Margaux
Ch Lagrange	St-Julien	St-Julien	Ch La Lagune	Ludon	Haut-Médoc
Ch Langoa-Barton	St-Julien	St-Julien	Ch Desmirail	Margaux	Margaux
Ch Giscours	Labarde	Margaux	Ch Calon-Ségur	St-Estèphe	St-Estèphe
Ch Malescot St-Exupéry	Margaux	Margaux	Ch Ferrière	Margaux	Margaux
Ch Boyd-Cantenac	Cantenac	Margaux	Ch Marquis d'Alesme Becker	Margaux	Margaux

Fourth Growths (Quatrièmes Crus)

	Commune	Appellation		Commune	Appellation
Ch St-Pierre	St-Julien	St-Julien	Ch La Tour-Carnet	St-Laurent	Haut-Médoc
Ch Talbot	St-Julien	St-Julien	Ch Lafon-Rochet	St-Estèphe	St-Estèphe
Ch Branaire-Ducru	St-Julien	St-Julien	Ch Beychevelle	St-Julien	St-Julien
Ch Duhart-Milon	Pauillac	Pauillac	Ch Prieuré-Lichine	Cantenac	Margaux
Ch Pouget	Cantenac	Margaux	Ch Marquis-de-Terme	Margaux	Margaux

Fifth Growths (Cinquièmes Crus)

	Commune	Appellation		Commune	Appellation
Ch Pontet-Canet	Pauillac	Pauillac	Ch du Tertre	Arsac	Margaux
Ch Batailley	Pauillac	Pauillac	Ch Haut-Bages-Liberal	Pauillac	Pauillac
Ch Haut-Batailley	Pauillac	Pauillac	Ch Pédesclaux	Pauillac	Pauillac
Ch Grand-Puy-Lacoste	Pauillac	Pauillac	Ch Belgrave	St-Laurent	Haut-Médoc
Ch Grand-Puy-Ducasse	Pauillac	Pauillac	Ch de Camensac	St-Laurent	Haut-Médoc
Ch Lynch-Bages	Pauillac	Pauillac	Ch Cos-Labory	St-Estèphe	St-Estèphe
Ch Lynch-Moussas	Pauillac	Pauillac	Ch Clerc-Milon	Pauillac	Pauillac
Ch Dauzac	Labarde	Margaux	Ch Croizet-Bages	Pauillac	Pauillac
Ch d'Armailhac***	Pauillac	Pauillac	Ch Cantemerle	Macau	Haut-Médoc

* This wine, although a Graves, was universally recognized and classified as one of the original four first growths.
** This wine was decreed a first growth in 1973.
*** Previously Ch d'Armailhaq, Ch Mouton-Baron-Philippe, and Ch Mouton-Baronne-Philippe.

The Official Classification of St-Émilion of 1955 (Reclassified 2012)

Premiers Grands Crus Classés

A. Ch Angélus   Ch Ausone   Ch Cheval Blanc   Ch Pavie

B. Ch Beau-Séjour Bécot   Ch Beauséjour (héritiers Duffau-Lagarrosse)   Ch Bélair-Monange   Ch Canon   Ch Canon La Gaffelière
Clos Fourtet   Ch Figeac   Ch La Gaffelière   Ch Larcisse-Ducasse   La Mondotte   Ch Pavie Macquin   Ch Troplong Mondot
Ch Trottevieille   Ch Valandraud

Grands Crus Classés

Ch L'Arrosée	Ch Clos de Sarpe	Ch La Fleur	Ch Haute-Sarpe	Ch Quinault L'Enclos
Ch Balestard La Tonnelle	Ch La Clotte	Morange	Ch Jean Faure	Ch Ripeau
Ch Barde-Haut	Ch La Commanderie	Ch Fombrauge	Ch Laniote	Ch Rochebelle
Ch Bellefont-Belcier	Ch Corbin	Ch Fonplégade	Ch Larmande	Ch St-Georges-Côte-
Ch Bellevue	Ch Côte de Baleau	Ch Fonroque	Ch Laroque	Pavie
Ch Berliquet	Ch La Couspaude	Ch Franc Mayne	Ch Laroze	Ch Sansonnet
Ch Cadet-Bon	Couvent des Jacobins	Ch Grand Corbin	Ch La Marzelle	Ch La Serre
Ch Cap de Mourlin	Ch Dassault	Ch Grand Corbin-	Ch Monbousquet	Ch Soutard
Ch Le Chatelet	Ch Destieux	Despagne	Ch Moulin du Cadet	Ch Quintus (formerly Ch Tertre-Daugay)
Ch Chauvin	Ch La Dominique	Ch Grand Mayne	Ch Pavie-Decesse	Ch La Tour Figeac
Clos des Jacobins	Ch Faugères	Ch Les Grandes	Ch Péby Faugères	Ch Villemaurine
Clos La Madeleine	Ch Faurie de Souchard	Murailles	Ch Petit Faurie de Soutard	Ch Yon-Figeac
Clos de l'Oratoire	Ch de Ferrand	Ch Grand-Pontet	Ch de Pressac	
Clos St-Martin	Ch Fleur Cardinale	Ch Gaudet	Ch Le Prieuré	

The Official Classification of Sauternes-Barsac of 1855

Superior First Growth (Premier Cru Supérieur)

Ch d'Yquem	Sauternes

First Growths (Premiers Crus)

	Commune		Commune
Ch La Tour-Blanche	Bommes	Ch Climens	Barsac
Ch Lafaurie-Peyraguey	Bommes	Ch Guiraud	Sauternes
Ch Clos Haut-Peyraguey	Bommes	Ch Rieussec	Fargues
Ch de Rayne-Vigneau	Bommes	Ch Rabaud-Promis	Bommes
Ch Suduiraut	Preignac	Ch Sigalas-Rabaud	Bommes
Ch Coutet	Barsac		

Second Growths (Deuxièmes Crus)

	Commune		Commune
Ch de Myrat	Barsac	Ch Naïrac	Barsac
Ch Doisy-Daene	Barsac	Ch Caillou	Barsac
Ch Doisy-Dubroca	Barsac	Ch Suau	Barsac
Ch Dolsy-Vedrines	Barsac	Ch de Malle	Preignac
Ch d'Arche	Sauternes	Ch Romer-du-Hayot	Fargues
Ch Filhot	Sauternes	Ch Lamothe-Despujois	Sauternes
Ch Broustet	Barsac	Ch Lamothe-Guignard	Sauternes

The Official Classification of Graves of 1959

Classified Red Wines of Graves

	Commune		Commune
Ch Bouscaut	Cadaujac	Ch La Tour-Martillac	Martillac
Ch Haut-Bailly	Léognan	Ch Smith-Haut-Lafitte	Martillac
Ch Carbonnieux	Léognan	Ch Haut-Brion	Pessac
Domaine de Chevalier	Léognan	Ch La Mission-Haut-Brion	Talence
Ch de Fieuzal	Léognan	Ch Pape-Clément	Pessac
Ch Olivier	Léognan	Ch La Tour-Haut-Brion	Talence
Ch Malartic-Lagravière	Léognan		

Classified White Wines of Graves

	Commune		Commune
Ch Bouscaut	Cadaujac	Ch La Tour-Martillac	Martillac
Ch Carbonnieux	Léognan	Ch Laville Haut-Brion	Talence
Domaine de Chevalier	Léognan	Ch Couhins	Villenave d'Ornon
Ch d'Olivier	Léognan	Ch Haut-Brion*	Pessac
Ch Malartic-Lagravière	Léognan		

* Added to the list in 1960

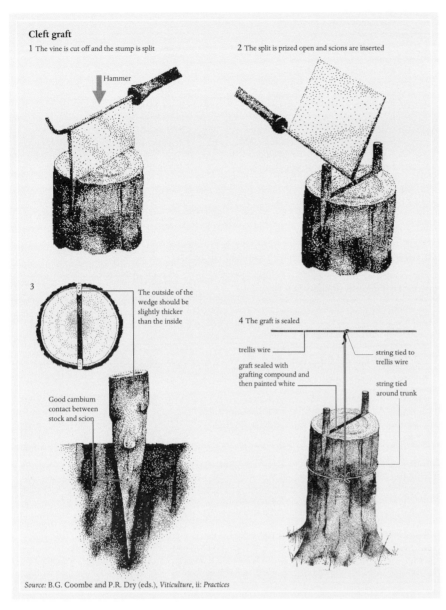

Cleft graft

1 The vine is cut off and the stump is split

Hammer

2 The split is prized open and scions are inserted

3

The outside of the wedge should be slightly thicker than the inside

Good cambium contact between stock and scion

4 The graft is sealed

trellis wire

graft sealed with grafting compound and then painted white

string tied to trellis wire

string tied around trunk

Source: B.G. Coombe and P.R. Dry (eds.), *Viticulture*, ii: *Practices*

medals and trophies in their famous SHOWS. Langton's Classification of Australian Wine, produced periodically, distinguishes wines on the basis of track record and reputation at AUCTION. In North America, on the other hand, it seems that classification may never appeal to the democratic California wine industry. See also CLIMATE CLASSIFICATION.

Caillard, A., and Langton, S., *Langton's Australian Fine Wine: Buying and Investment Guide* (4th edn, Sydney, 2005).

Markham, D., *1855: A History of the Bordeaux Classification* (New York, 1998).

Penning-Rowsell, E., *The Wines of Bordeaux* (6th edn, London, 1989).

Pitiot, S., and Servant, J.-C., *Les Vins de Bourgogne* (15th edn, Paris, 2014).

clay, refers to a particular type of MINERAL found in some rock types and in soil, and also a description of sediment or soil which is made up of particularly small particles. See SOIL TEXTURE and GEOLOGY. Soils described as 'clays' have a high content of clay minerals, but may also contain fine particles of calcium carbonate (in soils formed on LIMESTONE) and QUARTZ (in soils that have been weathering over a long period of time). Clay-sized particles interact with soil ORGANIC MATTER to form SOIL STRUCTURE. Different clay minerals predispose to variations in the stability of a soil's structure. For example, kaolinite clays tend to support stable structures whereas montmorillonite clays, which show marked swelling when wet and shrinkage on drying, may cause structural instability. Mica-type clay minerals can hold significant amounts of POTASSIUM cations within their structures, which can be slowly released on exchange with other cations in the soil water. Clay can be important in vineyard subsoils because of its water-holding capacity, as in parts of POMEROL, for example.   R.E.W.

For clay FERMENTATION VESSELS, see AMPHORA, QVEVRI, and TINAJAS.

Lavalle published his influential *History and Statistics of the Côte d'Or*, which included an informal classification of the best vineyards. This was formalized in 1861 by the Beaune Committee of Agriculture, which, with Lavalle's assistance, devised three classes. Most *climats* included in the first class eventually became grands crus when the APPELLATION CONTRÔLÉE system was introduced in the 1930s. See under BURGUNDY for a full list of Burgundian grands crus, and see under individual village names for details of their premiers crus.

Elsewhere

Few other regions of France have anything approaching an official classification, although see ALSACE for a list of those vineyards accorded grand cru status, CHABLIS for details of crus in this northern outpost of Burgundy, and CHAMPAGNE for some details of the classification of individual villages there.

There have been attempts, typically by WINE WRITERS, wine waiters, or producers' associations to produce classifications of the best vineyards, or best wines, of many countries, notably Germany (see GROSSE LAGE) and Italy (see VERONELLI), but these have generally been too controversial to be widely adopted. With the exception of the DOURO, where individual vineyards have been classified for the quality of port they produce, the wine regions of Portugal and Spain are in too great a state of flux to submit satisfactorily to classification, like those of eastern Europe and the rest of the Mediterranean.

In the New World, Australia prefers to classify not vineyards but individual wines, often much blended between areas, by awarding them

cleanliness, an important quality in wine (a wine should not have any off-odours) and in wineries, for which see HYGIENE.

Clear Lake, California AVA. See LAKE COUNTY.

cleft grafting, a popular method for changing VINE VARIETY in the vineyard (see TOP GRAFTING). The severing of the trunk may be at ground level or just below the head; the latter is preferred because DESUCKERING is simpler, less vine training is required, and the extra wood of the trunk aids the rapid establishment of the new vine. The trunk is cut horizontally in early spring and the stump split across the middle to about 5 cm/2 in depth. SCION pieces of one or two nodes are prepared from dormant canes with a long-tapered wedge. After the trunk is split and spread, the pieces are inserted one on each side so that

CAMBIUMS of ROOTSTOCK and scion are matched to facilitate their bonding. The wounds are sealed with grafting mastic, then with paint. NOTCH GRAFTING is an alternative. See diagram.   B.G.C.

Clevner, grape variety, usually part of the PINOT family. In SWITZERLAND, the name is often applied to PINOT NOIR or Blauburgunder grown in the canton of Zurich. In ALSACE, Clevner or Klevner are usually synonyms for PINOT BLANC but see also KLEVENER DE HEILIGENSTEIN.

climat, French, particularly Burgundian, term for a specific vineyard site defined by, as the name suggests, all of its climatological as well as geographical characteristics, otherwise known as TERROIR. Thus the Burgundian grower uses the word *climat* interchangeably with 'vineyard'. A *climat* is generally but not always smaller than a specific appellation. The term *climat* may for example be used to refer to a grand cru such as Richebourg. To further complicate matters, most appellations have over the centuries been subdivided into small parcels, each with its own traditional name, known by local geographers as a LIEU-DIT.

climate, long-term WEATHER pattern of an area, and an extremely important variable in the winemaking equation. For more details, see MACROCLIMATE in particular, but also CLIMATE CLASSIFICATION, CLIMATE CHANGE, CONTINENTALITY, COOL-CLIMATE VITICULTURE, LATITUDE, MEDITERRANEAN CLIMATE, RAINFALL, SUNLIGHT, TEMPERATE, TEMPERATURE, TEMPERATURE VARIABILITY, and, importantly, CLIMATE AND WINE QUALITY. For details of climate on a smaller scale, see MESOCLIMATE and MICROCLIMATE.

climate and wine quality. Climate of course influences both the QUALITY and styles of wine that an area can produce best. At the extremes, a climate can be so unsuitable for grape-growing that to produce good wines regularly is impossible or, at best, uneconomic. Cooler climates are best suited to producing light, delicate wines, while hotter climates are most suitable for FORTIFIED WINE production.

Temperature
Average mean TEMPERATURE during RIPENING strongly influences potential wine style. Defining grape maturity as that appropriate to making dry TABLE WINES, mean temperatures averaging above about 21 °C/70 °F in the final month to maturity lead to a rapid loss of MALIC ACID from the grapes, and to lower TOTAL ACIDITY and generally higher PH in the juice. Conversely, an average mean temperature below about 15 °C/59 °F in the final month minimizes acid loss to the point that acid levels may be too high. There is also often a risk that the grapes will not ripen fully at all.

Average conditions during ripening cannot be estimated directly from raw climatic statistics, because they depend in part on when ripening occurs. That, in turn, depends on the heat requirements of individual VINE VARIETIES to reach maturity. Some are early maturing and have a relatively low total heat requirement. These will ripen successfully in cool climates, and in hot climates ripen very early. Late-maturing varieties need a long, warm growing season and a high heat total to ripen at all. Jones classifies the main wine grape varieties into eight maturing groups.

Beyond that, individual grape varieties differ in their optimum ripening temperatures for quality. Many of the early-maturing varieties are best when ripened under relatively cool conditions. The berries of some of them are very sensitive to heat, particularly red wine varieties such as Pinot Noir. Such varieties nevertheless need warmth during ripening to give enough colour and body for red wines, a contradiction which explains their limited and specialized climatic adaptations. Other equally early-maturing varieties, usually for white wine, can tolerate considerable heat during ripening and can give good quality across a wide range of climates. Chardonnay, Verdelho, and to a lesser extent Sauvignon Blanc are good examples. Late-maturing varieties such as Grenache, Mourvèdre, Carignan, and Muscat of Alexandria need not only high heat totals to reach maturity, but also moderately high temperatures during ripening for maximum wine quality.

Temperature variability
Whereas potential wine style depends broadly on average mean temperature during ripening, quality appears to be related at least as much to short-term temperature variability from day to day. It has yet to be established whether less variable (or more equable) ripening temperatures are likely to result in better wine quality but highly variable temperatures risk greater damage, both by frosts after budburst and by extremes of heat in summer. See TEMPERATURE VARIABILITY.

Sunlight
Contrary to common perception, cool viticultural climates are probably more limited by their low temperatures than by lack of SUNLIGHT. Heat as summed over the season determines which grape varieties, if any, reach a satisfactory degree of RIPENESS. Sunlight duration acts mainly by controlling sugar in grapes and therefore potential wine alcohol content at a given stage of physiological ripening. In practice, however, the relative contributions of sunlight and temperature are hard to distinguish because low temperatures and low sunlight hours tend to go together. Poor seasons in cool climates are usually both sunless and cold.

Paradoxically, sunlight duration appears to limit wine style and (sometimes) quality fully as much in warm as in cool climates, even though their sunlight hours over the season are usually greater. The explanation lies in rates of RESPIRATION. Vines respire more sugar at high temperatures for their normal metabolism, but do not photosynthesize any faster; they therefore need more sunlight hours to generate a sugar surplus for ripening the fruit. It is why, for instance, Australia's often cloudy Hunter Valley produces only table wines despite being very warm; and why mild to warm, but cloudy, regions of northern New Zealand such as Auckland produce predominantly light table wines. Similar factors appear to apply through much of central and northern Italy.

Regions with unlimited sunlight hours and high sunlight intensity are nevertheless not necessarily at an advantage because they commonly suffer from excessive temperature variability (see above) and low relative humidities and WATER STRESS (see below). But in the absence of these adverse factors, ample sunlight does appear to be universally beneficial. A strong and constant sugar flow to the ripening berries assures not only their sweetness and sufficient alcohol in the wine, but also that colour, flavour, and aroma compounds are not limited by a lack of sugar substrate for their formation.

Timing of the sunlight is important. Studies such as that of Gadille in Burgundy show that the most critical period for quality is around the start of ripening (August in most European viticultural regions). Good conditions then assure an ample reserve of sugar in the vine, both for early conversion in the leaves and berries into flavour and aroma compounds, or their precursors, and so that sugar and flavour ripening of the berries can continue unabated under the cooler and less sunny conditions normally encountered later.

Rainfall
The general implications of rain for viticulture are discussed under RAINFALL.

Opinions differ as to optimum rainfall amounts during ripening. Most agree that any severe water stress at that stage is deleterious. On the other hand, heavy rain can lead to temporary juice dilution and sometimes to incomplete ripening, especially if accompanied by lack of sunshine. Wet ripening periods commonly signal poor vintages. Heavy rain close to maturity is especially damaging, because it can cause berry splitting and subsequent fungal infection of the bunches (see BOTRYTIS BUNCH ROT). This occurs most typically in certain varieties with tight bunches, such as Chenin Blanc and Zinfandel, and where the vines were under drought stress prior to the rain. HAIL at this time can be devastating.

Relative humidity and evaporation

Strong evaporative demands place the vines under water stress, which, in extreme cases, can cause leaf loss and substantial collapse of vine metabolism. Obvious fruit damage often follows through excessive exposure to the overhead sun. Milder water stress can still reduce PHOTOSYNTHESIS and sugar production in the leaves, and hence reduce both quantity and fruit quality. Mechanisms are discussed more fully under EVAPORATION and HUMIDITY.

Virtually all of the world's acknowledged great table wines have so far come from regions with moderately high relative humidities and low evaporation. This is partly because of their lack of stress (see above) and perhaps through their usually restricted temperature variability.

Wind

The effects of WIND STRESS are largely on vine health and yield, via reduced disease incidence on the one hand, and closure of the leaf STOMATA and especially direct physical damage on the other. Dry winds may also reduce wine quality through increased evaporation, as explained above.

On the other hand, the daily alternating land and sea breezes of the summer months that occur with some regularity in coastal regions of the dry continents markedly benefit both vine physiological functioning and wine quality. They are especially important in Australia and on the west coast of the United States, and are doubly advantageous. Dry land winds at night and in the early morning reduce the risk of FUNGAL DISEASES. Then mild, humid afternoon sea breezes reduce stresses on the vines and greatly improve day conditions for photosynthesis and ripening. The same applies on a reduced scale around inland lakes and rivers. See TOPOGRAPHY and TERROIR.

Summary

Two climatic types appear to offer the best compromises for both viticulture and wine quality. The first is that with cool to mild growing season temperatures and uniform to predominantly summer rainfall, such as is found in western and central Europe. Within that context, the best vineyard sites have specialized MESOCLIMATES with more than usual sunshine, warmth, and length of frost-free period.

The second broad climatic type, extending more or less contiguously from the first, comprises the cooler and more humid of the summer-dry MEDITERRANEAN CLIMATES, whenever summer heat is regularly moderated by afternoon sea breezes, and irrigation can be supplied in late summer if needed and permitted. Advantages over the uniform and summer-rainfall climates include more reliable summer sunshine and less risk of excessive rain and humidity during the ripening period.

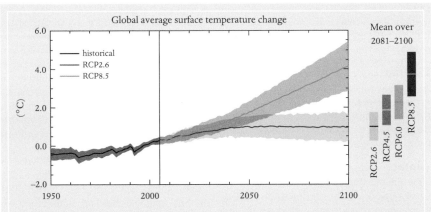

Climate-model output for two models from the 2013 Intergovernmental Panel on Climate Change Report. Solid lines represent annual mean surface temperatures for 1986–2005 and shading represents the uncertainties associated with the models. An RCP (Representative Concentration Pathway) is a greenhouse-gas concentration trajectory that is used for climate modelling (see www.ipcc.ch for more information).

The world's greatest table wines have traditionally come from the cool to mild temperate climates with uniform to summer-dominant rainfall. Partly this was because the limitations of frost and lack of warmth automatically confined viticulture there to the most equable mesoclimates, which happened also to have the best temperature regimes for wine quality.

For more detail, see TEMPERATURE, TEMPERATURE VARIABILITY, SUNLIGHT, RAINFALL, HUMIDITY, and WIND. See also COOL-CLIMATE VITICULTURE and CLIMATE CHANGE.   J.G. & R.E.S.

Becker, N., 'Site climate effects on development, fruit maturation and harvest quality', in R. E. Smart et al. (eds.), *Proceedings of the Second International Symposium for Cool Climate Viticulture and Oenology: 11–15 January 1988, Auckland, New Zealand* (Auckland, 1988).

Gadille, R., *Le Vignoble de la Côte Bourguignonne* (Paris, 1967).

Gladstones, J., *Viticulture and Environment* (Adelaide, 1992).

Huglin, P., and Schneider, C., 1998. *Biologie et écologie de la vigne* (2nd edn, Paris, 1998).

Jones, G. V., Reid, R., and Vilks, A., 'Climate, grapes, and wine: structure and suitability in a variable and changing climate', in P. Dougherty (ed.), *The Geography of Wine: Regions, Terroir, and Techniques* (Springer, 2012), 109–33.

climate change. Growing grapes for wine is a climatically sensitive endeavour, with narrow geographical zones providing the best production and quality characteristics. Therefore, the inherent uniqueness that wine region climates provide places the industry at greater risk from climate change than more broadly grown agricultural crops.

WEATHER and climate present three distinct spatial/temporal scales of risks and challenges to viticulture and wine production: first, individual weather events, which are mostly short term and localized (e.g. HAIL, WINTER FREEZES, FROST, and heavy rain); second, climate variability, which is measured on seasonal to decadal timescales and typically regionalized (e.g. DROUGHT or wet periods, warm or cold periods); third, climate change, which is recognized as long term and regional to global in scale (e.g. warming, cooling, changes in moisture regimes). In addition, one factor often influences and/or changes another—climate variability can change the frequency of individual weather events, or climate change can alter the nature of climate variability.

Historically climate change has been brought about by both internal and external natural processes such as volcanic events, ocean/snow/ice dynamics, solar variation, and meteoroid impacts. However, it is becoming increasingly evident that contemporary and future climate changes have become greatly influenced by human behaviour, through changes in atmospheric composition, deforestation, desertification, and urbanization. Probably the greatest concern for future climate change comes from increasing fossil fuel consumption and rising CARBON DIOXIDE (CO_2) levels in the atmosphere. While the magnitude of human influences on global climates is currently debated, the unabated use of fossil fuels and a growing population will continue to alter the Earth's surface and atmosphere and the way they hold and distribute heat. To study climate change, scientists use empirical methods (based on observations and/or proxy data, such as tree rings), dynamic methods (based on complex three-dimensional, mathematical models of our Earth–atmosphere system), or a combination of the two. Although climate models are far from perfect representations of climate reality and are constantly scrutinized, they continue to improve as technology and knowledge increase; combined with observations, they provide the best tools for climate change studies.

Historical and contemporary climate changes

The grapevine is one of the oldest cultivated plants and, along with the process of making wine, has resulted in a rich geographical and cultural history (see ORIGINS OF VINICULTURE). History has shown that wine-grape growing regions developed when the climate was most conducive. In addition, records of dates of harvest and yield for European viticulture have been kept for nearly a thousand years, revealing large swings in growing season temperatures and productivity. For example, Pfister's historical research describes how during the medieval 'Little Optimum', roughly AD 900–1300, average temperatures were up to 1 °C/1.8 °F warmer with vineyards planted as far north as the coastal zones of the Baltic sea and southern England. Recorded harvest dates for northern Europe from the High Middle Ages (12th and 13th centuries) show that fruit was ripening in early September as compared with late September to mid October during the late 20th century, and that growing season temperatures were roughly 1.7 °C/3 °F warmer. However, during the 'Little Ice Age' (14th to late 19th centuries), temperature declines were dramatic, resulting in northern vineyards being abandoned and growing seasons so short that harvesting ripe grapes even in southern Europe was difficult. Recent research by Chuine and colleagues used contemporary grape harvest dates from Burgundy to reconstruct spring-summer temperatures from 1370 to 2003. While the results indicate that temperatures as high as those reached in the warm 1990s have occurred several times in the region since 1370, the extremely warm summer of 2003 appears to have been hotter than any other year since 1370.

Today our understanding of climate change and the potential effects on VITICULTURE and wine production has become increasingly important as changing levels of greenhouse gases and alterations in Earth surface characteristics bring about changes in the Earth's radiation balance, atmospheric circulation, and hydrologic cycle. In its latest report, the Intergovernmental Panel on Climate Change (IPCC) has stated that warming of the climate system is unequivocal, and that since the middle of the 20th century, many of the observed changes are unprecedented over decades to millennia. Observed climate change in the period 1880 to 2012 shows that globally averaged combined land and ocean surface temperatures have increased 0.65–1.06 °C/ 1.17–1.91 °F (see figure). However, temperature changes have not been globally uniform, with a few regions experiencing decreases, some not changing at all, and many increasing more

dramatically. In addition, the warming trends have been found to be asymmetric with respect to seasonal and diurnal cycles, with greatest warming occurring during the winter and spring and at night (resulting in a smaller diurnal temperature range; see TEMPERATURE VARIABILITY).

Averaged globally, all 13 years in the 21st century rank among the 14 warmest on record and only one year during the 20th century (1998) was warmer than 2013. Other average climate-related observations include: over the last few decades the Greenland and Antarctic ice sheets have been losing mass; on average glaciers have continued to shrink worldwide; there have been decreases in snow-cover extent in the northern hemisphere and floating ice in the Arctic Ocean; global mean sea level has risen on average 19 cm over the past century; and worldwide precipitation over land has increased by 5–10%. Furthermore, changes in many extreme weather and climate events have been observed since the middle of the 20th century, including: the number of cold days and nights has decreased and the number of warm days and nights has increased on the global scale; the frequency of heatwaves has increased in large parts of North America, Europe, Asia, and Australia; some locations are showing a greater frequency of drought while other regions have seen the frequency of extreme rainfall events increase.

While contemporary research shows that the impact of climate change on viticulture and wine has been less than on other crops, numerous effects associated with plant growth, fruit characteristics, and pest and disease issues (see below) have been seen in wine regions and are likely to continue in the future. Recent analyses in many wine regions worldwide have documented changes in average climate conditions that have produced warmer and longer growing and DORMANT periods. Growing-season temperatures in many of the best wine-producing regions in the world increased 1.3 °C/2.34 °F during the last half of the 20th century. However, the warming was not uniform across all regions, with greater magnitudes in the western US and Europe and less warming in Chile, South Africa, and Australia. Also trends between day and night temperatures vary by region, with some seeing much more significant warming at night and others seeing more heat stress events through higher daytime temperatures. In addition to warmer growing seasons with greater heat accumulation, many of the world's wine regions have experienced a decline in FROST frequency and shifts in the timing of frosts. However, cold extremes still occur and there is some evidence that acclimation to more benign conditions can reduce growers' readiness to protect their vineyards from such events and make the plant system more susceptible to their effects. Furthermore, warmer winters in wine

regions could influence hardening potential for latent buds, ultimately affecting vine growth and productivity the next year.

Grapevine PHENOLOGICAL timing has shown strong relationships with the observed warming in wine regions, with trends ranging from 5 to 30 days earlier over numerous CULTIVARS and locations. Changes are greatest for the timing of VERAISON and harvest, and interval lengths between the main phenological events have also shortened with the length of time from budbreak to bloom, bloom to veraison, or veraison to harvest dates shortening by two weeks or more. An analysis over all locations and cultivars shows that grapevine phenology has been responding by roughly 5–10 days per 1°C/1.8 °F of warming over the last 30–50 years. With this earlier and more rapid plant growth, the potential for changes to ripening profiles and wine styles is evident. Many regions have seen trends to higher sugar and lower acidity levels that are significantly correlated with increases in temperatures. As a result of these changes in GRAPE COMPOSITION, combined with other complex consumer and economic issues (see HANG TIME, for example), higher alcohol levels have been observed in many regions. Furthermore, research in some regions shows that harvests that occur earlier in the summer, in a warmer part of the growing season, will result in hotter fruit being harvested, leading typically to loss of flavour and aroma compounds, as well as the potential for greater fruit desiccation unless irrigation is increased.

Research on climate change effects on pest and disease pressure indicates that we are likely to see increases in populations and severity, but also shifts to new areas further towards the poles with warmer winters and warmer night temperatures. See below for further examples.

Soil interactions with climate, pests and disease also strongly influence YIELD and QUALITY in wine. Numerous studies have shown that SOIL EROSION, degradation, and SALINITY are likely to be major indirect effects of climate change on viticulture and wine production. Climate change is expected to lead to a more vigorous hydrological cycle, including more total rainfall and more frequent high-intensity rainfall events. Furthermore, a changing climate and other demands on water will increase the pressure to restrict irrigation, ultimately increasing rootzone salinity with a greater impact on wine quality over time.

In addition, researchers have found that increases in carbon dioxide will cause more vegetative growth (see VIGOUR) in grapevines and increased water use efficiency, although the increased growth is likely to come at the expense of grape quality. However, while we understand some of the issues surrounding the impact of CO_2 on growing grapes, there has not been enough research to understand fully how increasing CO_2 concentrations along with warmer temperatures and changes in available water relate to vine growth, phenological timing and phase lengths, yield formation, fruit ripening and composition, and, most importantly, wine quality. Finally, an important indirect effect of increased CO_2 for the wine industry has also been identified: changes in the texture of OAK wood may alter its suitability for wine barrel production.

Future predicted climate changes

Current climate modelling work, using a range of predictions with regard to CO_2 emissions, indicates which are the largest contributors to total increases in temperatures, projects that the globally averaged surface temperature will increase 1.3–4.8 °C/2.34–8.65 °F by the 2081–2100 period relative to what was seen globally during the 1986–2005 period (see figure). This level of change is between two and ten times greater than that which was observed during the 20th century. The projected warming will continue to exhibit interannual-to-decadal variability and will not be regionally uniform, with variation in the rate of warming and whether the warming comes from greater increases in daytime or night-time temperatures. Research suggests that growing-season temperatures will increase by 2.0 °C/3.6 °F by 2050, with increased seasonal TEMPERATURE VARIABILITY. However, the warming rates in wine regions are likely to vary: locations in the northern hemisphere are expected to warm more than those in the southern hemisphere. In addition, regions at higher latitudes or inland are expected to warm more than those in coastal zones. Both observations and models also suggest that in Australia and California this projected warming is likely to lead to a decrease in rainfall in most viticultural locations, leading to greater water stress and reductions in WATER resources in the future.

Global studies have shown broad shifts to higher LATITUDES, with cool-climate zones being further north in Europe and North America. Similar poleward shifts are projected in the southern hemisphere, although this is likely to affect only small areas of New Zealand, Tasmania, and the southern regions of Argentina and Chile. Regional research on spatial modelling of suitable zones for viticulture in Europe show latitudinal, coastal, and elevation shifts from historic wine regions. Similar results have been found elsewhere with estimations that potential viticultural area could expand in some regions, while contracting in others.

Future climate change of the magnitudes predicted will have numerous effects on society and natural ECOSYSTEMS. Likewise, it presents numerous potential influences on, and challenges to, the wine industry, including additional changes in the timing of grapevine phenology, which is likely to result in a disruption of balanced composition and flavour in grapes and wine. In addition, the changes are not likely to be uniform across all regions and varieties, but are likely to be related to climatic thresholds for optimum growth and quality. Furthermore, the warming will clearly force decisions on the mix of varieties grown and the wine styles produced in particular regions: those that currently have a cool climate will have a greater choice of viable varieties, while in many of today's warmer regions, the future climates will be challenging for optimum grape growth and wine production. Current and future adaptations to changes in climate are many; they include better understanding of the cultivar limits to climate conditions, changes in vineyard management strategies (see PRECISION VITICULTURE), winemaking refinements, developments in soil-rootstock compatibility, and continued plant breeding and genetic research.

While the Earth's climate is always changing, strong regional identities have developed in terms of cultivars and wine styles. Therefore, any future climate change has the potential to influence cultural change. To prepare for the future, the wine industry will most certainly need to integrate planning and adaptation strategies to adjust to changes in climate.

H.S. & G.V.J.

Chuine, I. E, et al., 'Grape ripening as a past climate indicator', *Nature*, 432 (2004).

Fraga, H., et al., 'An overview of climate change impacts on European viticulture', *Food and Energy Security*, 1/2 (2012), 94–110.

IPCC, *Climate Change 2013–The Physical Science Basis. Working Group I Contribution to the Fifth Assessment Report of the Intergovernmental Panel on Climate Change* (Cambridge and New York, 2013).

Jones, G. V., et al., 'Climate change and global wine quality', *Climatic Change*, 73 (2005), 319–43.

Jones, G. V., Reid, R., and Vilks, A., 'Climate, grapes, and wine: structure and suitability in a variable and changing climate', in P. Dougherty (ed.), *The Geography of Wine: Regions, Terroir, and Techniques* (Springer, 2012), 109–33.

Moriondo, M., et al., 'Projected shifts of wine regions in response to climate change', *Climatic Change*, 119/3-4 (2013), 825–39.

Pfister, C., 'Variations in the spring-summer climate of central Europe from the High Middle Ages to 1850', in Schultz, H. R., and Jones, G. V., 'Climate induced historic and future changes in viticulture', *Journal of Wine Research*, 21/2 (2010) 137–45.

Wanner, H., and Siegenthaler, U. (eds.), *Long and Short Term Variability of Climate* (Berlin, 1988), 57–82.

Webb, L. B., Whetton, P. H., and Barlow, E. W. R., 'Observed trends in winegrape maturity in Australia', *Global Change Biology*, 17/8 (2011), 2707–19.

The effect of climate change on vineyard pests and diseases

Over the last few decades, climate change, and especially global warming, has correlated with the migration of some vineyard pests and diseases. For example, in France, the FLAVESCENCE DORÉE phytoplasma and the associated LEAFHOPPER vector *Scaphoideus titanus* were first described in Armagnac in 1956. The disease has been found in Bordeaux (1994) and has been increasing in the area ever since. The vector still seems to be moving further north, to Saumur-Champigny (2006), and then Burgundy and Champagne in 2012. The related phytoplasma disease *bois noir* (see GRAPEVINE YELLOWS) now occurs in southern Germany. The European grapevine MOTH (*Lobesia botrana*), originating from the warmer Mediterranean areas, also seems to be travelling northwards, replacing the cool-climate vine moth (*Eupoecilia ambiguella*) in some areas of the Loire Valley. This northwards insect migration is generally considered to be due to the impact of warming on insect distribution, which is known to be one of the first biological indicators of climate change.

Some vineyards in the southern hemisphere are facing warmer and drier weather conditions, which should not in theory favour disease development. In both hemispheres, however, trends towards higher temperatures are combined with more irregular and more intense rainfall. Generally, warmer and wetter conditions increase fungal disease pressure by encouraging more infection cycles. In European vineyards, DOWNY and POWDERY MILDEWS and BOTRYTIS BUNCH ROT are now considered more aggressive. By the mid 2010s powdery mildew was a more common phenomenon in Champagne than ever before, perhaps because of warmer temperatures. BLACK ROT, even though it was introduced more than a century ago from the US, has been spreading in many European countries, from Germany to Hungary, and even to places with warm, dry climates such as Portugal and central Italy. More generations of grapevine moths, mites, and leafhoppers are generally observed with higher temperatures, and additional late-season flights of insects such as European grapevine moths have been regularly observed in PHEROMONE traps in warm years in the Bordeaux region, even if without an increase in actual damage by the mid 2010s.

It is too early to be sure that extraordinary weather conditions such as hurricanes, floods, and droughts are the result of climate change because much longer-term data are required. Pathologists studying grapevine pests and diseases face a similar dilemma. Are recent changes in the distribution or impact truly part of longer-term effects brought about by climate change, or are they due to changes in, for example, vineyard management, PESTICIDE use, global transport, or a genuine movement into a new ecological niche for a species?

This is not to say that climate-change effects on diseases cannot be predicted. For example, Salinari et al. simulated likely future downy-mildew attacks in Acqui Terme in north-west

Italy, for the decades around 2030, 2050, and 2080. General Circulation Models predicted an increase in temperature and a decrease in precipitation; the former outweighed the latter in terms of influence and was sufficient to predict increased disease pressure and more severe epidemics. Two more sprayings would be required early in the season. However, pests and diseases may also change over the longer term. Fungi, for example, are able to adapt themselves not only to climate change but also to the sprayed AGROCHEMICALS used for their control. This is another challenge in situations with higher disease pressure, where more sprays are required to ensure sufficient control. Unfortunately, more reliance on sprayed chemicals can favour development of resistant fungal strains. The grapevine as host plant has also to be considered in terms of its sensitivity to pests and diseases in a changing climate. Crossing resistant cultivars (see DISEASE-RESISTANT VARIETIES) with sensitive *Vitis vinifera* varieties that have high qualitative traits could be a key factor in successfully adapting to changing vineyard climate. O.V. & M.v.H.

Salinari F., et al., 'Downy mildew (*Plasmopara viticola*) epidemics on grapevine under climate change', *Global Change Biology*, 12/7 (2006), 1299–307. doi: 10.1111/j.1365-2486.2006.01175.x.

climate classification, the description and grouping of climates for viticultural purposes.

History

Climate classification, particularly that of Köppen, has been commonly used in disciplines such as geography and ecology. However, specialized systems have been developed for viticulture. The first scientific study of viticultural climates was that of the French researcher A. P. de Candolle in the mid 19th century, a time when reliable climatic data were just starting to become available. De Candolle observed that BUDBREAK in European vineyards corresponded closely with the dates on which average mean temperature reached 10 °C/50 °F. He proposed that useful heat for vine growth and RIPENING could be measured by the amount that actual mean temperatures exceed 10 °C. Therefore, a summation of the excesses for all growing-season days would give a measure of the total usable heat for the year.

There is a need, however, for improved understanding of annual variations in climate. A Burgundy study has shown a correlation between early harvest dates for Pinot Noir grapes with dry winters and warm springs. An interesting classification involving many climate elements is proposed by Tonietto and Carbonneau. Some ideas on the role of day length at high latitudes were discussed by J. Branas and P. Huglin. Huglin compared climate conditions with the amount of heat

varieties need to ripen (the Huglin Index, HI), concluding that great wines can only be made when grapes are just able to achieve ripeness, slowly and late in the season, in the local climate. See also TERROIR.

California heat summation

The first extensive practical use of de Candolle's method was in California, where AMERINE and WINKLER, in 1944, delineated five viticultural regions on the basis of their Fahrenheit temperature summations over 50 °F/10 °C. One advance over de Candolle was to confine the summations to a fixed vine growth and ripening season extending from 1 April to 31 October.

The California summations (like most others) are in practice calculated from monthly averages of maxima and minima, each month's total being its average excess of the mean over 50 °F, multiplied by the number of days in the month. Amerine and Winkler proposed five regions for California based on heat degree days (HDD) but more recent studies of temperature conditions in western US vineyards by Jones et al. (2010) and in New Zealand by Anderson et al. have identified the need to update this classification by creating additional classes at both the lower and upper ends, as shown in the table below, since the original classification did not encompass present cool and hot limits.

Class/Region	C° units	F° units
Too cool	<850	<1500
(Region Ia)	850–1111	1500–2000
(Region Ib)	1111–1389	2000–2500
(Region II)	1389–1667	2500–3000
(Region III)	1667–1944	3000–3500
(Region IV)	1944–2222	3500–4000
(Region V)	2222–2700	4000–4900
Too hot	>2700	4900

Although successful in California, Amerine and Winkler's heat-summation system, also known as the Winkler Index (WI), is not fully accepted elsewhere. It works well in California partly because temperatures there are quite closely correlated with other climatic factors possibly related to viticulture and wine quality: directly with total SUNLIGHT, and inversely with HUMIDITY (see also CLIMATE AND WINE QUALITY). Temperature alone thus gives a reasonably adequate index of all the relevant climatic variables but, more importantly, it is the prime driver of vine PHENOLOGY.

Some other systems based on temperature have been simpler. Prescott in Australia found that the average mean temperature of the warmest month gave essentially as good a climatic indication as the seasonal temperature summation. Average growing-season temperature (GST) for the whole seven months

(see COOL-CLIMATE VITICULTURE), as used by Jones, likewise gives a reasonable measure of growing-season temperature regimes and is very strongly correlated with HDD. The GST index is being increasingly recognized and used.

Australian alternatives

The classification that Smart and Dry developed in Australia involves five separate climate elements of temperature, sunlight, rainfall, evaporation, and humidity, but is still tolerably simple and workable. Smart and Dry preferred to use the simple statistic of average mean temperature for January (MJT; July in the northern hemisphere) as a usable index of summer heat. It is complemented by an index of CONTINENTALITY (the difference between mean summer and winter temperatures) to show the amplitude of swings in temperatures through the 12 months, together with indices of sunlight, humidity, and water relations. The resulting five-way classification gives a reasonable overview of viticultural climates, and has been widely used for VINEYARD SITE SELECTION and regional comparison.

Gladstones' proposal for Biologically Effective Degree Days (BEDD) is too complex to cover in full here but in essence is a method predicting an average ripening date for any defined grape maturity type in any environment. It employs growing-season temperature summations over a 10 °C/50 °F base, but with refinements that entail:

- imposing an upper limit (19 °C) on the monthly average mean temperatures, beyond which no further increases are credited (this feature has been criticized by some for failing to emphasize the negative benefits of a very hot climate on wine quality);
- a correction factor proportional to the average day length of each month (long days giving greater biological effectiveness for a given greater mean temperature; see LATITUDE);
- a correction for each month's average daily temperature range (a narrow range resulting in greater effectiveness, for a given mean).

These considerations provide a predicted ripening date that forms the basis for evaluating or comparing environments as to their likely grape variety adaptations, potential for wine quality, and most natural wine styles. J.G. & R.E.S.

Amerine, M. A., and Winkler, A. J., 'Composition and quality of musts and wines of California grapes', *Hilgardia*, 15 (1944), 493–575.

Anderson, J. D., et al., 'Analysis of viticulture region climate and structure and suitability in New Zealand', *Journal International des Sciences de la Vigne et du Vin*, 46/3 (2012), 149–65.

Gladstones, J., *Viticulture and Environment* (Adelaide, 1992).

Jones, G. V., et al., 'Spatial analysis of climate in winegrape growing regions in the western United

States, *American Journal of Enology and Viticulture*, 61/3 (2010), 313–26.

Huglin, P., 'Nouveau mode d'évaluation des possibilités héliothermiques d'un milieu viticole', *Comptes Rendus de l'Académie d'Agriculture de France* (1978), 1117–26.

Prescott, J. A., 'The climatology of the vine (*Vitis vinifera*). 3. A comparison of France and Australia on the basis of the warmest month', *Transactions of the Royal Society of South Australia*, 93 (1969), 7–15.

Smart, R. E., and Dry, P. R., 'A climatic classification for Australian viticultural regions', *Australian Grapegrower and Winemaker*, 196 (1980), 8, 10, 16.

Tonietto, J., and Carbonneau, A., 'Système de classification climatique multicritères (C.C.M.) géoviticole', in *3rd International Symposium Zonification Vitivinicola* (Tenerife, May 2000).

climate effects on vine diseases. The climate has a major effect on VINE DISEASES, and indeed is a major factor determining where grapes are grown worldwide. The most commercially important vine diseases are due to fungi, and these are normally encouraged by warm, humid, and rainy conditions. Such regions as a consequence produce wines of higher RESVERATROL content, with purported HEALTH benefits. Most of the world's viticulture is therefore carried out in regions with dry summers and less attendant risk of disease, the Mediterranean area being a classic example. However, as the risk of fungal disease decreases, the likelihood of DROUGHT increases and, in those parts of Europe where irrigation is prohibited (such as southern France), the effects of drought can be substantial. Some regions such as California, Chile, and Western Australia can be so dry during summer that DOWNY MILDEW, one of the worst vine fungal diseases, is generally not present.

Sometimes climate effects on vine disease are subtle and difficult to discern. A good example is the phytoplasma disease FLAVESCENCE DORÉE, which is known to occur in epidemics, with severity varying markedly from year to year. This is thought to result from climate-induced natural variations in population levels of the insect vector. While the insect population swings are dramatic, the weather perturbations responsible may indeed be so slight as to be barely distinguishable from the average. RAINFALL (and sometimes dew) has a major effect on diseases. Water is important for spore germination and dispersal by splashing, as for downy mildew and DEAD ARM, and so a rainy spring can cause epidemics of both these diseases. Rain near the time of harvest causes grape berries to split, and so many BUNCH ROT fungi and bacteria can gain entry and ruin the fruit. Many fungi spores such as those of BOTRYTIS BUNCH ROT and downy mildew germinate in high humidity. The fungal disease POWDERY MILDEW develops in the shade of dense vine canopies, and is also encouraged by overcast weather. Years of low rainfall mean that the effect of pests which damage roots such as PHYLLOXERA and NEMATODES are more evident.

TEMPERATURE is a major factor in disease development and spread, with temperatures of 20 to 27 °C favouring the germination of powdery mildew spores. Freezing winter temperatures can cause vine trunks to split, allowing the entry of the CROWN GALL bacterium.

WIND is important in spreading diseases: for example BACTERIAL BLIGHT is spread in wet, windy weather. Otherwise wind helps reduce disease by drying leaves and fruit after rain and dew.

Climate has a significant effect on wine quality because of disease, and there is no more important example than that of botrytis bunch rot. Intermittent rainy, humid, and warm weather near the time of harvest causes anguish to grape-grower and winemaker alike, because of the risk of losing both yield and quality. Yet, following infection, a change to dry weather can encourage the formation of NOBLE ROT. Furthermore, costs of grape production are higher when the weather induces disease.   R.E.S.

Pearson, R. C., and Goheen, A. C., (eds.), *Compendium of Grape Diseases* (St Paul, Minn., 1988).

Clinton, dark-skinned *Vitis riparia* x Vitis labrusca AMERICAN HYBRID. It is planted in Brazil and its wine has a pronounced FOXY flavour. It has also been known in Italian SWITZERLAND.

clonal selection, one of the two principal means of improving a vine variety (the other being the elimination of VIRUS DISEASES). Clonal selection is the practice of selecting a single superior plant in the vineyard and then taking cuttings from this vine for PROPAGATION. The selection is generally made with a particular attribute such as YIELD or fruit RIPENESS in mind. Clonal selection contrasts with MASS SELECTION, where a group of superior vines is selected.

New grapevines, in common with many other perennial crops, are produced by vegetative propagation, that is by using cuttings which are genetically identical. (This contrasts with agricultural field crops, which are multiplied by seeds that are different one from another—although sexual reproduction leading to the production of seedlings is the means by which NEW VARIETIES are created.) In vegetative propagation, each bud from a so-called 'mother vine' essentially gives rise to a plant of the same CLONE (except for those very rare cases in which a bud mutation has taken place).

Clonal selection for vines was first demonstrated in 1926 in Germany, where it has been most widely practised. Other European countries have also developed clonal selection initiatives, but the practice is less well developed in some countries of the New World.

Clonal selection depends on the fact that adjacent vines in a vineyard may be different, sometimes discernibly different. More often the differences can be established only after some years of careful measurement. Differences on this scale would not normally be expected from soil variation. There are two possible explanations: the first being a difference in genetic make-up between the vines due to mutations; the second being a difference in the incidence of diseases in the vines.

Sometimes the disease is 'graft transmissible' and is carried from one vine generation to the next in CUTTINGS. The most common and commercially important transmissible disease agents are VIRUSES. Such disease agents are transmitted by careless selection of the BUDWOOD or ROOTSTOCK material used at GRAFTING (and thus a human influence), but it may also reflect the effect of viruses, VIROIDS, FUNGI or PHYTOPLASMA sometimes transmitted by NEMATODES or INSECTS. In any event, infection, especially due to a virus, can have a major impact on yield, fruit ripening, and wine quality.

There has been disagreement between viticultural scientists working in this area as to the relative importance of genetic difference *vis-à-vis* virus diseases. Professor Helmut BECKER, an acknowledged authority on clonal selection based at GEISENHEIM in Germany, argued for the genetic difference principle, while the virologists led by Austin Goheen of the University of California at DAVIS believed that virus infection was the more important. (More recently the possibility has been raised that differing viroid incidence may be responsible for clonal variation.) Most workers in the field would now agree that both influences are important, but these views have had significant consequences. Some European centres had been slow to test for and eliminate virus diseases, whereas in California the emphasis had traditionally been on virus elimination, typically by THERMOTHERAPY, rather than on clonal selection and evaluation in the field. During the 1980s and 1990s this situation changed, although not necessarily in time for California's replanting programme necessitated in the 1990s by PHYLLOXERA. In countries such as Australia, New Zealand, and South Africa, efforts to improve vines acknowledge both viewpoints.

Importantly, whether the vine to vine difference in the field is due to mutation or a graft-transmissible disease, the effects can be passed on from generation to generation by the cuttings. This is the basis of the viticultural technique of clonal selection.

The process of clonal selection is necessarily long and requires considerable investment of resources. To make reliable field selections requires several years of records (up to nine are used in Germany) followed by comparative trials of many different clones of the one variety for evaluation. After waiting three years for the first harvest, five to ten more years are necessary to monitor yields and fruit ripeness. These trials are often conducted in several locations and with several rootstocks. Clonal selection should also involve making trial wine to assure trueness to VARIETAL type. Selected clones may not therefore be released until 15 or more years after the initial selection in the field. And, given the possibilities of both mutation and the spread of viruses by natural means, clonal selection should be an ongoing process. There has already been a release of second generation clones in Germany; fields originally planted to one clone have been selected again for 'clones of clones'.

There is no doubt that clonal selection has played an important part in improving both yield and wine quality from modern vineyards. When grafting became popular in the 1880s to overcome phylloxera, virus diseases were inadvertently spread. Many vineyards of both the Old World and the New World planted as late as the 1960s contained off-types, rogue vines (i.e. not the intended variety), and virus diseases. As more healthy and true-to-type planting material becomes available as a result of clonal selection, then these problems disappear. Many reputable nurserymen worldwide will provide only plants propagated from clonally selected rootstocks and scions.

Mechanisms for clonal selection and propagation vary from country to country. Generally the studies are conducted by government-funded scientists (although it is not unusual for a leading Bordeaux château, for example, to be doing its own clonal selection from vines naturally adapted to that property). In France the extent to which planting material was infected by viruses up to the mid 1940s led to the formation of the Institut des Vins de Consommation Courante (IVCC). This organization and its affiliates tested selected clones and supplied CERTIFIED PLANTING MATERIAL. France AgriMer now oversees the certification process, although the research is generally carried out by the Institut Français de la Vigne et du Vin (IFV). In Germany, certification was introduced voluntarily after the First World War, and the scheme later became law. The EU adopted guidelines for propagation material through the EU in the early 1990s. In Australia, South Africa, and New Zealand there are well-established VINE IMPROVEMENT programmes utilizing clonal selection as well as virus elimination. In California, the programme is conducted by the FOUNDATION PLANT SERVICES at the University of California at Davis. In South Africa, there is a Vine Improvement Association and a number of organizations specialize in heat treatment to eliminate viruses (see THERMOTHERAPY).

For many vine varieties, the differences in appearance and performance between clones with the same virus status is small. This suggests that genetic differences are generally minor and that the mutation rate is low. Some varieties, such as Pinot Noir, show extreme variation between clones, which indicates that it is a very old variety that has had time to accumulate many mutations.

It is difficult to understand the effect of clonal selection on commercial wine quality since so many vineyards are planted with mixed clones. While most Old World countries have a wide range of clones available, sometimes, because of limited importations, a New World country might have only a few for any one variety. An extreme example is Sauvignon Blanc in New Zealand, where all commercial plantings up until the early 1990s can be traced to a single clone imported from the United States. Some producers and researchers are critical of the limited availability of only improved clones from nurserymen. They argue that either MASS SELECTION or a range of clones produces better, more characterful wine than a single virus-free, high-yielding clone. Unfortunately, some clones were released on the basis of purely viticultural evaluation, which has fuelled suspicion about their effect on wine quality. R.E.S.

clone in a viticultural context is a single vine or a population of vines all derived by vegetative PROPAGATION from cuttings or buds from a single 'mother vine' by deliberate CLONAL SELECTION.

Vine nurseries may sell a range of different clones of each vine variety, each with different attributes and characteristics and individually identified by numbers and/or names. In Germany, for example, there is a formal process of clonal evaluation and a systematic numbering system. Normally government agencies are involved in selection, evaluation, and distribution to nurserymen, and often the availability of clones and their acceptance varies regionally. Some clones are so outstanding that they become internationally distributed. Clones of Riesling from GEISENHEIM in Germany are examples of this. In the 1990s, there was considerable interest in Burgundian (sometimes called Dijon) clones; see particularly CHARDONNAY and PINOT NOIR.

By the late 1980s, many quality-conscious wine producers were wary of being dependent on a single clone of a particular variety—particularly Pinot Noir—deliberately seeking instead a mixture of clones or, less likely, vines from MASS SELECTION, for both viticultural and wine quality reasons. R.E.S. & B.G.C.

Galet, P., *Dictionnaire encyclopédique des cépages* (Paris, 2000).

Marsh, S. A., 'The contribution of Pinot Noir clones to the vineyards of the Côte d'Or. An evaluation focusing on clones 114, 115, 667, 777' (MW dissertation, London, 2004).

Mullins, M. G., Bouquet, A., and Williams, L., *Biology of the Grapevine* (Cambridge, 1992).

clos is French for 'enclosure', and any vineyard described as a Clos should be enclosed, generally by a wall. This is a particularly common term in Burgundy, but is also used elsewhere. Similarly, the term *cuve close* refers to the sealed tank which gives its name to a bulk method of SPARKLING WINEMAKING. The first new wave producers of PRIORAT adopted this term for their single-vineyard wines.

Clos de la Roche, leading red GRAND CRU in Burgundy's CÔTE D'OR. For more details, see MOREY-ST-DENIS.

Clos de Tart, Clos des Lambrays, and **Clos St-Denis**, red GRANDS CRUS in Burgundy's CÔTE D'OR. For more details, see MOREY-ST-DENIS.

Clos de Vougeot, also frequently known as **Clos Vougeot**, famous walled vineyard in BURGUNDY created originally by the monks (see MONKS AND MONASTERIES) of Cîteaux. Between the 12th and early 14th centuries the Cistercians purchased or received as donations the land, much of which needed clearing and planting, which subsequently became known as the Clos de Vougeot. By 1336, the 50-ha/120-acre plot was complete and enclosed by stone walls on all sides.

The Cistercians maintained ownership until the French Revolution, when all clerical estates were dispossessed, although Dom Goblet, the monk responsible for the vineyards and the wine, had a sufficiently fine reputation to retain his job in the short term. In due course, Clos de Vougeot was sold on to Julien-Jules Ouvrard in 1818, the year before he bought ROMANÉE-Conti, and remained in single ownership until 1889. Since then ownership has fragmented so that today there are over 80 proprietors.

A small chapel and rudimentary buildings, damaged during the religious wars, were rebuilt and enlarged in 1551, becoming the current Ch du Clos de Vougeot, a major tourist attraction. It is also home to the CONFRÉRIE des Chevaliers du Tastevin, a brotherhood which organizes copious feasts and the tastings for the Tastevinage. For this, producers submit wines to a jury; those selected are entitled to use the 'tastevíné' label, which should enable the wine to be sold more easily or at a higher price.

For more historical detail, see BURGUNDY, history. The vineyard and wines of Clos de Vougeot are described under VOUGEOT. J.T.C.M.

closures for wine containers are necessary to avoid harmful contact with OXYGEN and changed remarkably little until recent times. CORKS are still the principal closures used for wine BOTTLES, just as they were more than two centuries ago and probably long before that, although alternative stoppers have become increasingly common since the mid 1980s, thanks primarily to a rise in the incidence of CORK TAINT.

History

Cork was certainly known in Ancient GREECE, where, as in Ancient EGYPT, great care was taken to provide AMPHORAE with a wide variety of airtight stoppers. Roman authors such as CATO, writing in the 2nd century BC, refer to the need to seal jars with cork and pitch when the fermentation was complete. However, this use of cork does not appear to have continued into the early medieval period, possibly because the main potential supply of European cork was in southern Iberia, which had been conquered by the Moors in the 8th century. Medieval illuminations illustrate barrels generally sealed by wooden stoppers, with cloth frequently placed between the barrel and the stopper to provide a more airtight seal. Pitch and wax were also sometimes used to provide additional protection. In the long period during which wine was mainly stored in and served from the BARREL, the most common stopper was some form of BUNG.

With the development of glass bottles during the 17th century, it was necessary to devise new methods of stoppering. Glass stoppers, ground to fit individual bottles and tied to them with thread, were therefore introduced, and survived well into the 19th century. Indeed, as they are found in DECANTERS, they remain in use to this day, and are now also being introduced for bottled wine (see below). However, such stoppers were expensive, and gradually from the beginning of the 17th century cork became the most frequent substance used to seal bottles. The use of corks also required the invention of another piece of equipment, the CORKSCREW or, as it was first called, the bottlescrew. The earliest corks were not pressed completely into the bottles, and so could be pulled out without excessive difficulty. However, by the end of the 17th century the introduction of corkscrews enabled corks to be fully inserted into the necks of bottles.   P.T.H.U.

Johnson, H., *The Story of Wine* (London, 1989).
Simon, A. L., *Bottlescrew Days: Wine Drinking in England during the 18th Century* (London, 1926).

Modern closures

Modern technology, prompted by an increasing awareness of the extent of CORK TAINT and bottle-to-bottle variability, offers a range of alternatives to the traditional cork. To present a viable alternative to this natural substance they have to offer a reliable seal, present an inert substance to the wine, be easy to remove and reinsert, and be capable of being produced at a relatively low cost. Few have proved as successful as cork for long-term BOTTLE AGEING, however, and there is still considerable attachment on the part of many wine drinkers to the ritual

of pulling a cork. For more details, see CROWN CAPS, SCREWCAPS, and other alternatives below.

Synthetic closures

Popularly known as 'plastic corks', these have proved popular with both consumers and producers. They satisfy the wine drinker's need to wrestle with a CORKSCREW while alleviating the risk of CORK TAINT, but they have the disadvantage of not being biodegradable (although manufacturers are attempting to produce more SUSTAINABLE VERSIONS). It has proven surprisingly difficult to find synthetic materials that replicate the natural properties of cork in order to provide a tight seal while remaining easy enough to extract from, and reinsert into, the neck of the bottle. The first brands to establish a market presence, most notably Supremecorq and Integra, were based on a one-piece injection-moulded design. These early examples were hard to extract and almost impossible to reinsert. They also allowed too much oxygen ingress (see OXYGEN TRANSMISSION RATES), making them suitable only for wines intended for early consumption. The better-performing synthetic closures now available are made by an extrusion process with a separate smooth plastic sleeve. After a period of consolidation in the market, Nomacorc is now the dominant manufacturer of synthetic corks, and has released a 'Select' series of closures offering different oxygen transmission levels to suit different wine styles. There are indications that these improved synthetic closures may also be suitable for wines intended for ageing. Another concern surrounds the capacity of synthetic closures to 'scalp' flavour by absorbing volatile components from the wine (see FLAVOUR SCALPING). Natural corks also do this but to a lesser extent. Synthetic closures are cheaper than all but the poorest quality natural corks and have the advantage that, unlike screwcaps, they do not require producers to adopt new bottles and BOTTLING LINES.

Recent years have seen the development and marketing of a range of novel closures, such as Australia's Zork (which offers the convenience of a screwcap but pops like a cork), ProCork (a natural cork sealed at both ends with a barrier membrane to protect the wine from oxygen and taint), and glass stoppers such as Vinolok—although these last have proved inconveniently fragile. These alternatives are likely to capitalize on the growing frustration with the variable performance of natural cork, but the field is still wide open to more acceptable, and more aesthetically pleasing, alternatives to a piece of bark.

See also CAPSULES.   J.A.G.

Goode, J. A., *Wine Science: The Application of Science in Winemaking* (2nd edn, London, 2014).

cloudy wine. See FAULTS and STABILIZATION.

Cloudy Bay, seminal winery in the Marlborough region of NEW ZEALAND, the brainchild of David Hohnen of Cape Mentelle in WESTERN AUSTRALIA. Its debut release of a moodily labelled varietal Sauvignon Blanc in 1985 on export markets created a reputation for Marlborough Sauvignon and a cult following for Cloudy Bay almost overnight, even though initially the grapes were bought in and the wine made under contract at another winery. The enterprise, based in its own premises, became a distant offshoot of the VEUVE CLICQUOT, and hence LVMH, empire in 1990. It also produces Chardonnay, Pinot Noir, and a sparkling wine Pelorus.

cluster, alternative, viticultural term for a BUNCH of grapes.

CMO, abbreviation for the EU's common market organization, its regulatory framework for wine.

Coal River, wine region in TASMANIA.

Coastal, misleading, unregulated, and much-used term on California wine labels meant to, sometimes falsely, imply provenance cooler than the CENTRAL VALLEY.

Coastal Region, a conveniently extensive wine region in SOUTH AFRICA, home to several of the country's most important wine districts and wards, including CONSTANTIA, DARLING, FRANSCHHOEK (or Franschhoek Valley), PAARL, STELLENBOSCH, SWARTLAND, TULBAGH, and WELLINGTON. The name appears on labels of a substantial proportion of South African wines.

cochylis, a flying insect which can damage vines. See MOTHS.

Cockburn, PORT house which, in the second half of the 20th century, became the brand leader in the important British market with its Special Reserve ruby. The house was founded in 1815 by Robert Cockburn and George Wauchope, who were joined in 1828 by Captain William Greig and a year later by Robert Cockburn's sons Archibald and Alexander, who opened an office in London. In 1845, the brothers Henry and John Smithes joined the company, which became Cockburn Smithes and Co. John Smithes initiated an organized system of records for blending. He married Eleanor Cobb and both Smithes and Cobb families remained in the firm for many generations. The last family member Peter Cobb joined Cockburn's in 1960, became a director of the company in Oporto in 1980, and retired in 1999. In 1962, Cockburn's became an associate company of HARVEYS OF BRISTOL and, subsequently, part of the Allied-Domecq conglomerate (until 2005). It is now part of a new American company, Beam Wine Estates of the

US 2005. In 1961 Harveys had bought Martinez Gassiot, transforming the two houses from fierce competitors to partners. Cockburn had a fine reputation, commanding high prices, for their vintage ports in the mid 20th century, but had some unconventional views on vintage port declarations: it released the lighter 1967 rather than 1966 against the popular vote (Martinez joined it) but decided against declaring 1977 and 1980 before releasing a 1983. Cockburn's have long sourced wines in the higher reaches of the DOURO and reinforced this tradition with the purchase, in 1978, of 169 ha/418 acres of land (126 ha planted) at Vilariça, where important viticultural experiments were carried out, in particular trial of various clones of TOURIGA NACIONAL. This work was particularly useful when in 1989 the company acquired Quinta dos Canais, a 261-ha property on the north bank of the Douro, which has long provided the backbone of Cockburn's vintage port but which needed extensive renovation and replanting. In 2006 the SYMINGTONS bought the Cockburn vineyards and took over the entire company from Beam Global in 2010. Vilariça is now used for the production of unfortified Douro wine and the Symingtons are working to rebuild Cockburn's reputation as a producer of vintage port.   R.J.M.

Cocks et Féret. See FÉRET.

Cococciola, white wine variety of PUGLIA and ABRUZZO where it is blended with TREBBIANO. There were nearly 1,000 ha/2,470 acres in 2010.

Coda di Volpe Bianca, ancient, full-bodied white grape grown near Naples in CAMPANIA. Plantings had fallen to 555 ha/1,370 acres by 2010.

Códega, Douro synonym for SÍRIA, Portugal's widely planted white wine grape.

Côdega de Larinho, particularly soft, fruity white wine grape most common in the DOURO and TRÁS-OS-MONTES regions of northern Portugal. There were 793 ha/1,958 acres in 2013.

Codorníu, one of the world's largest producers of SPARKLING WINES made by the TRADITIONAL METHOD. The Codorníu group incorporates the Spanish CAVA brand Codorníu, and Masia Bach and Raimat (see COSTERS DEL SEGRE) which make both Cava and still wine. Cava is responsible for more than half of the company's turnover and Codorníu is particularly strong on the Spanish market. The history of Codorníu dates back to 1551, when the Codorníu family established their first winery in Sant Sadurní d'Anoia in PENEDÈS in Cataluña. In 1659, the heiress to the Codorníu winery, Anna Codorníu, married a member of the Raventós family. A direct descendant, Josep Raventós, decided to produce sparkling wine, uncorking the first

bottle of Spanish wine made in the image of CHAMPAGNE in 1872. Within ten years, the style was popular across Spain, and Codorníu claims as a result to have founded the Cava industry. Codorníu was the first to use Chardonnay and Pinot Noir as well as the traditional Catalan grapes Parellada, Macabeo, and Xarel-lo in its Cavas. The company's first Chardonnay-based Cava, named Anna de Codorníu, was launched in 1984 and Chardonnay has since become a common ingredient in many Codorníu Cavas. Raimat, in Costers del Segre, is the viticultural and research and development centre for the group. In 1991, the group opened Codorníu Napa, a new winery in the CARNEROS district of California, since renamed Artesa. In 1997, Codorníu acquired the traditional Bodegas Bilbaínas winery and 200 surrounding hectares in RIOJA Alta, then in 2000 it acquired a controlling stake in Cellers de Scala Dei, the oldest winery in PRIORAT. In 1999, the company built the Septima winery in Mendoza, Argentina and in 2000 built the Legaris winery from scratch in RIBERA DEL DUERO. Other wineries in Spain include Abadia de Poblet in CONCA DE BARBERÁ and Nuviana in Valle del Cinca in Aragón.

co-fermentation, the simultaneous fermentation of two or more varieties in the same vessel, is said to lift a wine's floral aromas, enhance its TEXTURE, and improve the brilliance and intensity of the colour.

The technique has its origins in the Old World, most notably in the CÔTE RÔTIE appellation in the northern Rhône. Here, the red variety SYRAH is co-fermented with the white variety VIOGNIER. Up to 20% Viognier is permitted, but 5–10% is more usual. This practice found increased favour in Australia and other parts of the New World from the 2000s. Co-fermentation does not have to be a combination of red and white grapes—in the United States, for example, co-fermentation may originally have been a natural consequence of FIELD BLENDS such as ZINFANDEL and PETITE SIRAH. Another notable historical example is found in the CHIANTI region of Italy, where the primary red grape, Sangiovese, was traditionally fermented with small amounts of the red variety Canaiolo Nero and the white varieties Trebbiano and Malvasia, although this practice has become uncommon.

Research by Dr Roger Boulton, Professor of Enology and Chemical Engineering at DAVIS, indicates that red varieties may contain low levels of co-factors (sometimes known confusingly as co-pigments), which are said to aid CO-PIGMENTATION and thus the formation of deeper and more stable colour in red wines. The addition of a variety with higher levels of co-factors may aid co-pigmentation, and co-fermentation may originally have been adopted because it was seen to increase colour stability and intensity.

When Syrah, or Shiraz, and Viognier are co-fermented, there are many different techniques used to add the Viognier: whole fruit at the crusher; whole grapes, or pressed skins and grapes or just juice added to the crushed Shiraz must.

Differing harvest dates may put constraints on co-fermentation but these can be overcome by modern REFRIGERATION techniques. Further research is needed to ascertain the best combinations of varieties and the best proportions. Too many white grapes might simply dilute the colour of a red wine.   T.R.C. & J.E.H.

Boulton, R., 'The copigmentation of anthocyanins and its role in the color of red wine: a critical review', *American Journal of Enology and Viticulture*, 52/2 (2001), 67–87.

coffee houses. The traditional drink of Arabs, coffee was introduced to western Europe in the mid 17th century. Like tea and chocolate, it was soon to pose a serious threat to the popularity of wine.

The first English coffee house was reputedly opened in a room in the Angel Inn in Oxford's High Street in 1650 and within a couple of years the trend had taken hold in London. By the 1660s, coffee houses were challenging the traditional English tavern, and not only because they served this novel beverage which was very cheap and had the added advantage of not making you drunk. Samuel Pepys, among others, frequented these 'penny universities' in order to catch up on the city's gossip or join a political debate.

Some of the more popular ones survive as gentlemen's clubs, whilst coffee houses in Europe evolved into that ubiquitous institution, the café.   H.B.

Aubertin-Potter, N., and Bennett, A., *Oxford Coffee Houses 1651–1800* (Oxford, 1987).

Ellis, A., *The Penny Universities: A History of the Coffee Houses* (London, 1956).

Lillywhite, B., *London Coffee Houses* (London, 1963).

co-inoculation. See MALOLACTIC CONVERSION.

Colares, exceptional but now minuscule DOP wine region on the west coast of Portugal just north of the capital Lisbon (see map under PORTUGAL). These vineyards were spared from the PHYLLOXERA pest in the 19th century thanks to their sandy composition but have struggled to survive today's commercial pressures. Located on a narrow strip of sand dunes on the cliff-tops above the Atlantic, with roots anchored in the clay below, 80% of the UNGRAFTED are RAMISCO. Made principally from MALVASIA de Colares, which is genetically distinct from other known Malvasia grapes, white Colares is distinctly salty and mineral, sometimes like a FINO sherry, while Ramisco can be reminiscent of a particularly austere PINOT NOIR.

The region was badly hit by the collapse of the Brazilian market in 1930 and a year later the Lisbon government created the Adega Regional, a CO-OPERATIVE winery, which all growers were eventually obliged to join for their wine to be entitled to the Colares denomination. In 1990, the EU forced the government to abolish the Adega Regional's monopoly (soon after a similar move in DÃO), but this was probably too late to save the wine from virtual extinction and by 2014 just 12 ha/30 acres of vineyard remained (compared with over 1,800 ha in the 1930s). In 1999, the local municipality intervened and 8.5 hectares of traditional vineyard were placed in the hands of a charitable foundation. Wines grown on the firmer calcareous-clay soils away from the coast have nothing like the same finesse and must be labelled either Vinho Regional Lisboa or just Vinho. R.J.M. & S.A.

Colchagua, part of the Rapel subregion of the Central Valley of CHILE.

cold soak, MACERATION technique particularly popular for Pinot Noir.

colheita, Portuguese word meaning 'crop' or 'HARVEST' and, by extension, 'VINTAGE'. It is also the name of a style of PORT or MADEIRA from a single year aged in wood for at least seven or five years respectively before bottling. R.J.M.

collage, French term for FINING.

collar rot, one of the FUNGAL DISEASES of the vine which particularly attacks young vines growing in cool, moist soil, via the *Pythium* fungus. The vines are weakened and may die. Vines grafted on to Rupestris St George ROOTSTOCKS are most susceptible. Control is achieved by removing soil from the base of the trunk and reducing soil moisture. R.E.S.

collecting wine became a popular hobby in the 1980s. Americans in particular have tended to call anyone who buys fine wine a **collector** rather than a wine enthusiast, connoisseur, or *amateur* (the French term), suggesting that the thrill lies in acquisition and possession rather than in consumption. Ever since the development of cylindrical BOTTLES in the 1730s, when it first became possible to maintain a personal CELLAR, there have been individuals whose purchasing patterns amounted to building up a specific **collection** of certain wines. The rapid economic growth of the late 1970s and 1980s, however, together with a succession of good vintages to be bought EN PRIMEUR and the emergence of a truly international consumer wine press (see Robert PARKER, for example), resulted in the emergence of a significant group of serious wine collectors around the globe (notably in the United States, Germany, and ASIA). They communicate and trade with each other through the AUCTION houses and the specialist BROKERS, and for some of them the purpose of collecting is to enable occasional but usually sumptuous marathon TASTINGS.

colli, plural **colline**, is the Italian word for hills, and its use in a wine name indicates that the wine is produced on slopes of a certain ELEVATION (it is an almost direct equivalent of France's CÔTE, Côtes, and Coteaux). Accordingly, articles about Colli Somewhere are listed not under Colli, but under S for Somewhere.

Elevation is obviously in the eye of the beholder, however, and the word *colli* is used to describe both mere knolls and near-mountainous viticulture at elevations of over 500 m/1,600 ft. *Colli* and its variations can be found not only as the title of various DOCs but also as a part of their descriptive apparatus: CHIANTI, for example, is produced in the Colli Senesi and the Colline Pisane (Chianti dei Colli Senesi, Chianti delle Colline Pisane). The absence of the word does not imply that a given wine is produced in the flatlands; much of Italy's finest wine—BARBARESCO, BAROLO, BRUNELLO DI MONTALCINO, VINO NOBILE DI MONTEPULCIANO—is produced from HILLSIDE VINEYARDS without that fact being indicated in the wine's name.

Collio, or **Collio Goriziano**, is a qualitatively important, predominantly white wine, DOC zone on the north eastern border of Italy with Slovenia. Collio did much in the early 1970s to increase Italians' confidence in their ability to make fine white wine.

Collio, a corruption of the Italian word for hills (see COLLI), is in the province of Gorizia (hence Colli Goriziano). Half of what was once a single wine zone was annexed in 1918 by Italy, with the border running straight through vineyards. The other half is now known as Goriška Brda (see SLOVENIA).

Within the region of FRIULI, it is the fourth biggest DOC in terms of area planted and volume of production after GRAVE DEL FRIULI, ISONZO, and COLLI ORIENTALI del Friuli, but its fragrant and lively whites, which account for 85% of total production, have created an image of quality for Friuli throughout the world. Collio's red wines, overwhelmingly from MERLOT and CABERNETS SAUVIGNON and FRANC, tend to resemble LOIRE reds, at times with an identical vegetal quality underlined by a certain lightness of body and texture.

The territory itself extends across the hills from the Judrio River in the west—the former boundary between Austria and Italy and now Collio's boundary with the climatologically similar Colli Orientali—to the Slovenian border in the east. Vines are planted on a calcareous marl alternating with layers of sandstone called 'flysch of Cormons' after an important township in the heart of the zone.

After two World Wars had ravaged the zone, it rebuilt itself based on viticulture, which became even more important at the beginning of the 1960s when the share-cropping system was abolished and many growers seized the chance to buy vineyards and impose a vine monoculture. Pinot Grigio became the inevitable cash cow and was planted widely. Other international, mainly white, varieties, notably Sauvignon Blanc and Chardonnay, as well the red Bordeaux varieties, followed suit and the early adoption of modern vinification techniques, particularly TEMPERATURE-CONTROLLED fermentation, resulted in what were then Italy's cleanest, most modern wines which found a ready international market.

However, in the past Collio was a white wine made from local varieties RIBOLLA Gialla, FRIULANO, and MALVASIA Istriana, labelled Collio without the suffix BIANCO. Today nine different varieties are allowed in the blend, while an additional 12 white and four red varieties can be a suffix to VARIETALLY labelled Collio. Competition from other regions which eventually began to produce similar wines forced producers to reconsider their history. Several producers, particularly Edi Keber, began producing a trdaitional white Collio blend. Today, Collio's vineyards are still dominated by Pinot Grigio, Sauvignon Blanc, and Chardonnay, but renewed interest in local varieties is unstoppable, while interest in Collio's subzones has been triggered by the rediscovery of a 1767 document which includes a CLASSIFICATION of Collio's vineyards into nine different categories, showing that a sophisticated system of CRUS was in place in the 18th century.

There are plans to introduce a new DOC category, Collio Classico, for the classic blend of Ribolla Gialla, Friulano, and Malvasia Istriana. A special bottle and capsule has also been introduced. See also SLOVENIA, which is capable of producing some extremely similar wines. Before the Second World War, Collio extended much further eastward, and many knowledgeable producers—some of whom have continued to own and farm vineyards across the border in Slovenia—claim that some of these sites are among the very finest of the entire zone. W.S.

Capalbo, C., *Collio—Fine Wine and Foods from Italy's North-East* (London, 2009).

Cosma, S., 'Dotato d'eccellentissimi vini, è il contado di Goritia . . .'. *Viticoltura nel Goriziano* (Monfalcone, 1992).

Brozzoni, G. (ed.), *Ribolla Gialla Oslavia. The Book* (Bergamo, 2011).

www.consorziocolliocarso.it

Colli Orientali del Friuli, literally the eastern hills of the FRIULI region in north-east Italy, comprise about 2,000 ha/4,942 acres of vineyard.

The territory of the DOC begins, as its name implies, to the east of the city of Udine near the SLOVENIAN border and continues to the border of the province of Udine. The dividing line between the Colli Orientali and Collio is neither geological nor climatic, but simply historical: Udine and its province became part of Italy in 1866 while the neighbouring area of Collio, in the province of Gorizia, was not reunified with the rest of Italy until the end of the First World War. The contiguous zones in fact have the same sort of soil: the so-called 'flysch of Cormons', with alternating strata of calcareous marls and sandstone.

Wine has a documented history here, as in most parts of Italy, since the days of the Roman empire, but the zone first began to attract significant attention in the 1970s, when cold fermentation techniques began to produce here, and in the Collio DOC, significant quantities of fresh, fruity, and aromatic white wines, predominantly based on INTERNATIONAL VARIETIES, especially Pinot Grigio, Chardonnay, and Sauvignon Blanc, pioneering efforts for Italy. Significant development of red wines came in the 1980s as producers began to move away from lighter, fruitier styles, while planting Merlot, Cabernet Sauvignon, Cabernet Franc, and Pinot Noir, producing a fuller, more structured style, frequently aged in small oak barrels for the then prevalent international taste for such wine.

A certain number of these reds were released as an ambitiously priced VINO DA TAVOLA, because individual producers wanted to either distance the wines from their allegedly more facile antecedents, or to make an unorthodox blend of varieties, or, more often than not, to copy the international success of the highly priced SUPERTUSCANS. White versions, particularly from Chardonnay or Pinot Bianco, were also either fermented or aged in BARRIQUES and these wines were also marketed as *vini da tavola* to distinguish them from the fresher style of whites, which remained the backbone of production.

This century, increased international competition has kindled renewed interest in Colli Orientali's unique INDIGENOUS VARIETIES, linked to five subzones where historically these local varieties were cultivated: Cialla for RIBOLLA GIALLA, VERDUZZO, REFOSCO DAL PENDUNCOLO ROSSO, and SCHIOPPETTINO; Rosazzo for Ribolla Gialla and PIGNOLO; Prepotto for Schioppettino; and Faedis for a scented local grape known as Refosco Nostrano.

Although international varietal wines, especially whites, still prevail, producers have begun to focus on the specifics of local TERROIRS instead of producing a certain wine style to order. The red Schioppettino, saved from extinction in the 1970s, is now cultivated by 22 producers who have founded an association

dedicated to its promotion. Colli Orientali del Friuli has not one but two historic sweet wines, based on the local white Verduzzo and PICOLIT grapes, either LATE HARVEST or DRIED-GRAPE WINES which can be complex and long-lived, their greatness recognized by their elevation to DOCG. DOCG Colli Orientali del Friuli Picolit includes the subzone Cialla, while DOCG Ramandolo applies to sweet Verduzzo and more or less covers the same area as DOC Colli Orientali Friuli. Although Verduzzo is planted throughout Friuli and in parts of neighbouring VENETO, nowhere else produces wines as great as Ramandolo.   W.S.

www.colliorientali.com

Collioure to tourists is one of the prettiest seaside villages on the Mediterranean coast just north of the Franco-Spanish border. To wine lovers it is a rare, particularly heady, deep, usually red table wine whose aromas of overripe fruits and spice reflect the fact that Collioure comes from exactly the same area as BANYULS. There is a pink version and a scented, particularly full, low-acid white wine. The characteristics of the vintage determine what proportion of grapes become Collioure rather than Banyuls, but the grapes for Collioure are certainly picked before those destined to become VIN DOUX NATUREL. This is the only wine zone untouched by MECHANICAL harvesting, so steep are the terraces. The region's MOURVÈDRE is grown expressly for Collioure, however, as it, Syrah, Grenache Noir, and Carignan are the red and rosé ingredients. As in Banyuls, yields from these BUSH VINES are some of the lowest in France, although 40 hl/ha (2.3 tons/acre) is decreed the official maximum.

colloid, substance consisting of ultramicroscopic particles suspended in another substance. Wine colloids are very finely divided solids in particles with diameters ranging from about five nanometres to one micrometre. These are principally large organic molecules, most of which are polymers made of POLYSACCHARIDES including PECTINS, and of smaller molecules such as PHENOLICS, PIGMENTED TANNINS, and TANNINS (see POLYMERIZATION). They do not contribute to a wine's VISCOSITY. When FINING and FILTRATION are successfully accomplished, less than 20% of colloids are removed so that wine quality is not affected.   D.D. & V. L.

colluvium is sediment that has moved downslope under the influence of gravity, whereas ALLUVIUM is transported by RIVERS. The difference is significant for viticulture given that HILLSIDE VINEYARDS—usually characterized by a thin veneer of fragments of the material higher up the same slope, commonly the bedrock that caps the hill—are generally considered superior to those on plains and valley floors, where alluvium dominates. The grand cru vineyards of CHABLIS, for example,

are sited mid-slope on the famous marly Kimmeridgian bedrock but a substantial proportion of the colluvium that coats the slopes consists of fragments of the younger Portlandian hilltop limestone (see GEOLOGY).

Studies by Wittendal have suggested that the majority of the grand cru vineyards in Burgundy's CÔTE D'OR are on colluvium. Colluvial sediment can comprise any geological material: for example, VOLCANIC bedrock in Coombsville, NAPA Valley; SCHIST and GNEISS in Central Otago, NEW ZEALAND; GRANITE on the slopes flanking the Curicó Valley in central Chile.   A.J.M.

Wittendal, F., 'Great Burgundy wines: a principal components analysis of "La Côte" vineyards', paper prepared for the 11th Œnometrics Conference 2004, Dijon, France, http://www.wittendal.com/w/gwpc/Great%20Burgundy%20Wines.pdf

Colombard is a natural cross of CHENIN BLANC × GOUAIS BLANC. This widely planted Charentais white grape variety was traditionally blended with Ugni Blanc (TREBBIANO) and FOLLE BLANCHE, but considered inferior to both, as an ingredient in cognac. As Colombard's star waned in France, almost half of total plantings being pulled up in the 1970s, it waxed quite spectacularly in California, where, as FRENCH COLOMBARD, it became the state's most planted variety of all, providing generous quantities of reasonably neutral but reliably crisp base wine for commercial, often quite sweet, white blends to service the prevailing FASHION for white wine.

Its disadvantages of being quite prone to rot and POWDERY MILDEW are much lesser inconveniences in the hot, dry Central Valley, where almost all of California's Colombard is planted. And Colombard's disadvantages for the distillers of Charentes, that its wine is more alcoholic and less acid than that of the other cognac varieties, are positive advantages for consumers of the wine in its undistilled state.

The annual rate of planting of French Colombard in California slowed to a standstill towards the end of the 1980s and then picked up briefly in the early 2000s but by 2012 total plantings were only about 22,500 acres/9,100 ha (whereas Chardonnay's total was almost 100,000 acres). Colombard is found in other American states, notably Texas.

It would take some sorcery to transform Colombard into an exciting wine, but pleasantly lively innocuousness is well within reach for those equipped with STAINLESS STEEL and TEMPERATURE CONTROL. In a nice example of transatlantic switchback, the producers of the Armagnac region set about duplicating California's modern winemaking transformation of the dull Colombard grape on their own varieties surplus to brandy production, thus creating the hugely successful Vin de Pays des Côtes de Gascogne. Colombard plantings have been steadily growing in France. It is the most planted variety in the Gers *département* where about two-thirds of France's 2011 total of about 9,000 ha/22,230 acres was concentrated, although it is grown all over SOUTH WEST FRANCE.

It is even more widely planted, as Colombar, in SOUTH AFRICA, where it was once important to the local brandy industry, and is now also popular for cheap, commercial off-dry white. Total Cape plantings have remained steady at just over 11,000 ha, making it the country's third most important wine grape, just behind Cabernet Sauvignon in 2012. As in Australia, it provides usefully crisp blending material with Chenin Blanc and the much more fashionable Sauvignon Blanc. Australia's total plantings had fallen to just over 2,000 ha in 2012, mainly in the irrigated inland regions.

Colombia, South American country with a tropical climate and a relatively short history of viticulture. For long Colombia depended on imported wines and spirits from Spain and developed a taste for sweet fortified wines such as MÁLAGA. The initial output of the first vines planted here in the 1920s and 1930s was therefore directed towards aping this style of wine, as well as to the production of TABLE GRAPES. When wine imports from non-South American countries were punitively taxed in the mid 1980s, however, consumers became accustomed to the dry table wines of Chile and Argentina and Colombia began to produce small quantities of dry wines from VINIFERA vines. The main grape-growing zone is in Boyacá department north east of the capital Bogotá. The country was thought to have 2,591 ha/6,400 acres of vines in 2013. Vines have to be defoliated by hand in order to provide a short period of DORMANCY (see TROPICAL VITICULTURE). Annual rainfall is 1,000 mm/39 in, although there are dry periods between December and March and between June and September. DOWNY MILDEW is the principal hazard. ISABELLA and Italia table grapes were grown in quantity but INTERNATIONAL VARIETIES are now grown by the likes of Marqués de Puntalarga and Marqués de Villa de Leyva.

Goldstein, E., *Wines of South America* (Oakland, Calif., 2014).

Colorino, rare, deep-coloured dark grape variety used traditionally to add colour to blends of CHIANTI and VINO NOBILE DI MONTELPULCIANO. Four different varieties of Colorino can be distinguished, with 2010 plantings totalling 421 ha/1,039 acres. The late 1980s and early 1990s saw an upsurge in interest in Colorino as an ingredient capable of adding TANNINS and colour to firm up the structure of Sangiovese without the aromatic impact of the Cabernet Sauvignon.
D.C.G.

colour of wines. Wines are classified as red, white, or rosé but can vary widely in colour within these broad categories, sometimes with little obvious distinction between a light red and a dark rosé.

Red wines
Red wines derive their colour from the natural organic red/blue ANTHOCYANIN pigments, of which there are varying concentrations in the skins of darker-skinned grapes (only TEINTURIER grape varieties have red pulp). These concentrations depend on the VINE VARIETY, the RIPENESS of the grape, viticultural practices, and the environmental conditions such as soil and weather, all of which may affect YIELD. The amount of anthocyanins leached into the resulting wine depends on many factors including BERRY SIZE, homogeneity of berry ripeness, length and temperature of the MACERATION of skins and new wine, together with the extent to which techniques to encourage EXTRACTION such as PUMPING OVER and PUNCHING DOWN are used. All these factors influence the intensity of colour in a young red wine.

The actual hue of a young red wine is influenced partly by the grape variety (Cabernet Sauvignon grape skins, for example, are blue-black, while those of Grenache are much more crimson), although much less than one might expect (see ANTHOCYANINS). A more important influence is the acidity of the grape juice. In low PH solutions, anthocyanins exist in bright red coloured forms, while as pH rises they change to a more colourless form. In general, therefore, the more acid the grape juice, the brighter the colour—although very high acid grapes may be unripe and deficient in available anthocyanins.

The anthocyanins as they occur in the grape are responsible for the colour of a red wine only in its very early life. In a red wine more than a few weeks old, the colour is due increasingly to products formed from anthocyanins, including PIGMENTED TANNINS, which are polymeric species resulting from reactions of anthocyanins with tannins. Pigmented tannins and other derived pigments have a wide range of colours, from orange to purple, but the purple species tend to be less stable so that brick-red pigments gradually become predominant.

Red wines which undergo BARREL MATURATION also tend to have more stable colour than those which do not, because small amounts of OXYGEN promote the formation of the wine's pigmented tannins. During AGEING, reactions of the phenolics and anthocyanins continue, forming an ever increasing diversity of larger pigmented tannins. The larger ones aggregate and precipitate as SEDIMENT, depleting the wine of pigment.

The bleaching effect of SULFUR DIOXIDE on grape anthocyanins also means that red wines with a high level of free sulfur dioxide tend to be paler than they would be with a lower level. However, most of the red pigments generated in wine by anthocyanin reactions are resistant to sulfite bleaching so that this effect decreases as the wine ages. Also, if red wines are bottled with high sulfur-dioxide levels, the normal chemical interactions among the phenolics and other wine constituents to generate BOUQUET are disrupted.

The colour of a young red wine can vary from blackish purple (as in a vintage PORT, for example) through many hues of crimson to ruby. With age, red wines take on brick and then amber hues, lightening with time. The colour at the rim of a glassful of wine can give the most telling indication of the hue and therefore age of a wine, while looking straight down through a glassful of wine from above can clearly indicate the intensity of colour (see TASTING).

During the 1990s, winemakers tended to make ever-deeper coloured red wines. This trend was encouraged by the increasing importance of large comparative tastings in JUDGING WINE. Because many (though by no means all) of the world's best red wines are deeply coloured (particularly those based on Cabernet Sauvignon and Syrah grapes, for example), and because EXTRACTION may be associated with depth of FLAVOUR, there was a tendency among wine judges to favour deeply coloured wines. This led to a considerable increase in the number of red wines which owe their deep colour to over-extraction and/or colour added in the form of OENOCYANIN or some Teinturier wine but which are often otherwise undistinguished. See, for example, the increase in plantings of the red-fleshed RUBIRED in California, home of proprietary colouring agents such as Mega Purple, which offer concentrated anthocyanins without tannins.

See also RED WINEMAKING and RED WINES for more information, including names for red wines in languages other than English.

White wines
Although red wines are red, white wines are not white. Very occasionally they are colourless, but they usually range from pale green, through straw, pale copper, and deep gold to amber.

The stems, skins, and pulp of the light-skinned grapes used for making white wines contain a large and complex mixture of phenolics similar to those found in dark-skinned grapes but not the red/blue-coloured anthocyanins. The absorption of light by these white-wine phenolics occurs mainly in the ultraviolet range, but extends into the visible range sufficiently to cause a light yellow colour in the wines we call 'white'. After CRUSHING of the grapes, these phenolics are exposed to oxygen and to the acids and other constituents of the grape juice, which causes a number of enzymatic and chemical reactions (including OXIDATION and polymerization) which result in changes of colour from light yellow to amber and eventually to brown. To minimize extraction of phenolic compounds into the must and subsequent oxidative browning, white wines are usually made with minimum SKIN CONTACT. Although most white wines are made from light-skinned grapes, white wines may be made from dark-skinned grape varieties (see BLANC DE NOIRS) using minimum skin contact and/or CHARCOAL treatments.

Different 'white' grape varieties contain a slightly different array of phenolics, which results in differently coloured wines. Palomino and Pinot Blanc, for example, are particularly prone to oxidation and browning, while Riesling has traces of non-phenolic compounds which can cause a greenish tinge to the basic yellow.

Must browning is due to enzymatic oxidation and is highly dependent on the phenolic content (especially hydroxycinnamic acids) of the juice. During fermentation, yeast cells can absorb some of the brown polymerized materials which are then removed with the LEES. (Much the same phenomenon allows the use of quite distinctly pale pink base wines from Pinots Noir and Meunier in the blend for BOTTLE FERMENTED sparkling wines which, after DISGORGEMENT, are white.) Some varieties used for white wines such as Gewürztraminer and Pinot Gris have greyish pink to purple skins and tend to result in deeply coloured wines with a strong pinkish yellow hue.

Careful protection from oxidation in prefermentation stages (for instance by addition of SULFUR DIOXIDE or ASCORBIC ACID) reduces must browning but maintains a rather high level of phenolics in the wine, especially if some skin contact has led to extraction of CATECHINS or PROANTHOCYANIDINS. This may result in increased browning susceptibility of the wine and, under some circumstances, may produce a pink tinge to the basic yellow.

The names of the fundamental phenolics on which each group of complex compounds is built are the benzoic acid group, the cinnamic acid group, the flavan-3-ols, and the flavan-3, 4-diols (these last two are important to tannins).

With age, small amounts of oxygen act on phenolic compounds to brown them and apparently deepen a white wine's colour. With extreme BOTTLE AGEING of many decades, a very old white wine can be the same medium intensity amber colour as a red wine of the same age.

White wine colour is also affected by the wine's levels of pH and sulfur dioxide; low pH and high sulfur dioxide concentration has a bleaching effect—as has hydrogen peroxide, which is occasionally used to make wine look paler.

Wines made from grapes affected by NOBLE ROT tend to have a particularly deep golden colour. Those which have been given extended skin contact tend to brown relatively early, while young white wines subjected to BARREL FERMENTATION and LEES CONTACT tend to be markedly paler than those fermented in STAINLESS STEEL and then transferred to cask for barrel maturation because darker pigments are absorbed by the lees.

During the 1990s, white wines have in general become paler, as unintended oxidation becomes rarer, barrel fermentation has become more common, and barrel maturation has become more skilfully handled. See also WHITE WINEMAKING and WHITE WINES.

Rosé wines

These wines, which vary enormously in hue and intensity, owe their combination of pink colour and white wine characteristics either to a very short SKIN CONTACT with dark-skinned grapes, or, for some everyday wines and pink sparkling wines, to the BLENDING of red and white wines. The proportions of anthocyanins, hydroxycinnamic acids, and tannins in the wine, depending on the grape variety and winemaking process, influence the pigment composition and thus the colour. In addition, wines that are pale bluish pink are likely to be the results of PROTECTIVE techniques, while those with an orange tinge may well have been exposed to some, possibly deliberate, oxidation. While a blindfolded taster can in some circumstances find it difficult to distinguish between low-tannin red wines and fuller-bodied white wines, it can be almost impossible on the basis of taste alone to distinguish a rosé wine from a white one.

See also ROSÉ WINEMAKING, ROSÉ WINES, and AGEING.   J.R. & V.C.

Columella, Lucius Junius Moderatus,

important but, for long, uncredited source of information on wine production in Ancient ROME. Little is known about his life except that he was born in Gades (Cádiz near JEREZ) and that he was an officer in the Roman army in Syria. He composed his treatise on farming, *De re rustica*, in AD 60–5. It is divided into 12 books, all in prose except the tenth, on gardens. This book was written in hexameter verse as an addition to VIRGIL's *Georgics*, which Columella admired. Columella's work shows by far the best grasp of technical detail of all the surviving Roman treatises on farming, and this is particularly clear in his treatment of VITICULTURE. Books 3 and 4, the most important of the treatise, deal with vine-growing, but much practical advice on winemaking is also contained in Book 12, which outlines the duties of the bailiff's wife. He discusses what grape variety to use in which type of soil; yield in relation to labour and capital outlay (he assumes that a well-managed vineyard will yield at least 20 AMPHORAE *per iugerum*, approximately 20 hl/ha (1.1 tons/ acre), and possibly 30); planting; propagating; pruning; training and dressing; grafting (Books 3–4); the vintage, and winemaking (Book 12). Half of an earlier, shorter, work called *De arboribus* ('On trees') also survives: it has a section on vines which is much briefer than the corresponding sections of *De re rustica*.   H.M.W.

Martin, R., *Recherches sur les agronomes latins* (Paris, 1971).

White, K. D., *Roman Farming* (London, 1970).

Comité Interprofessionnel, body representing all interests concerned with the production of a certain wine and the French counterpart to the CONSORZIO of Italy and Spain's CONSEJO REGULADOR. The model for all such organizations was the CIVC of Champagne.

Commandaria, a dark sweet-wine speciality of the island of Cyprus with a honeyed, raisiny flavour and alcohol content usually around 15%, produced from partially dried grapes.

Evidence suggests that Commandaria is the oldest named wine in the world still being made today, with records of its production methods dating back to 800 BC. It was praised by the Greek poet HESIOD, who described a sweet Cypriot wine, produced from sun-dried grapes, and is arguably the pioneer of the concept of CONTROLLED APPELLATION. Cyprus Nama, the forerunner of Commandaria, was famed throughout the classical world (*see* DRIED-GRAPE WINES). See the history of CYPRUS for how Commandaria got its name.

In 1993, Commandaria became the first Cypriot wine to be granted full, legal protection covering both its geographical origin and production techniques and was further regulated by government decree in 2005, while today it has PDO status. Commandaria must be produced within a strictly defined region comprising 14 wine-producing villages on the Troodos foothills about 30 km/20 miles north of Limassol, from the MAVRO (red) and XYNISTERI (white) grape varieties, grown as BUSH VINES, and planted at a low VINE DENSITY of 2,000 to 2,750 vines per hectare. Either grape variety may be used and both are usually, but the most subtle versions of Commandaria are made from white grapes only.

The wine must be vinified within the region and may be moved (for example to be aged elsewhere) only after fermentation is complete. Minimum MUST WEIGHTS are 13 °Baumé for Xynisteri and 14 ° for Mavro. Grapes are then sun-dried to a concentration of at least 21 or 23 °Baumé respectively. After fermentation, the wine must have an alcoholic strength of at least 10% without FORTIFICATION, and no more than 1.5 g/l VOLATILE ACIDITY. The wine may (but doesn't have to be) fortified by the addition of grape spirit at 95% to 96% or with grape distillate at around 70% alcohol to a maximum of

20% actual alcohol while its total POTENTIAL ALCOHOL must be at least 22.5%.

The wine must be aged for at least two years in wood although in practice ageing is typically much longer. Traditionally, producers use a blending SOLERA-like system called *mana* in which selected older barrels are topped up with younger wines, although recently successful single-vintage Commandarias have appeared as part of the revival of the island's long wine heritage.

Although even within Cyprus it is of very limited commercial importance (total production of the island's PDO wines was only 2,000 hl/ 52,830 gal in 2012, of which the majority would be Commandaria), Commandaria is one of the world's classic sweet wines.   C.G.

http://www.academia.edu/1037309/The_ Renaissance_of_Commandaria_A_Strategic_ Branding_Prescriptive_Analysis

Commanderie, common French term for a CONFRÉRIE.

commune, French for village or parish. The Italian counterpart is a **comune.**

competitions, wine. Well-run reputable wine competitions can be extremely lucrative for the organizers, and can play an important part in marketing, which is why some wine labels are adorned with MEDALS and the like, and some wine merchants' lists are dotted with lists of awards. Care should be taken when studying these claims that the competition was a recent and respected one, and that the successful wine was exactly the same bottling as the one on offer. Two of the most ambitious and successful international wine competitions are the International Wine Challenge held every year in London and the newer rival event organised in London by *Decanter* magazine. They attract thousands of entries from around the world and most of their garlanded wines are of genuinely superior quality. The International Wine and Spirit Competition is an older British rival. Most wine competitions in wine-producing countries are national rather than international. Some of France's most important are associated with agricultural shows, especially those of Paris and Mâcon; Germany has its DLG. Some of the more respected of the many wine competitions held regularly in the US are the Critics Challenge International Wine Competition, Dallas Morning News Wine Competition, the Indy International in Indiana, Long Beach Grand Cru, Los Angeles County Fair's International Wine & Spirits Competition, Pacific Rim International, Riverside International, San Diego International, San Francisco International Wine Competition, San Francisco Chronicle Wine Competition, Sunset International Wine Competition, and the New York Wine and Food Classic for NEW

YORK wines only. The explosion of interest in wine in CHINA has been accompanied by a rash of wine competitions there. It should be remembered, however, that few of the world's most revered producers enter such competitions, and certainly none of those who produce very limited quantities. It is difficult to imagine there will ever be a wine competition which will identify the best, rather than the best of those who have something to gain by entering. In Australia they are known as wine SHOWS.

For more details of how competitions and wine shows work, see JUDGING WINE.

Completer, ancient white grape variety grown in Graubünden in eastern SWITZERLAND. The wine produced—distinctive, pungent, acidic, and full bodied—is a speciality of Bündner Herrschaft. DNA PROFILING at DAVIS showed in 2004 that Completer is one of the parents of LAFNETSCHA. Subsequently, a few vines of Completer discovered among Lafnetscha vines supported this parentage and the unanticipated presence of Completer in the Valais.   J.V.

Complexa, Portuguese red wine variety bred from Castelão, Tintinha, and Muscat Hamburg in the 1960s and introduced to MADEIRA as an experimental, deeper-coloured, softer alternative to NEGRAMOLL.   R.J.M.

complexity, a TASTING TERM of approval when applied to FLAVOUR in wine, and commonly viewed as a central component of wine QUALITY. Complex wines possess multiple flavours as well as flavour diversity. The term implies coherence: chaotic or jarring flavours are not considered complex. It can also be used, typically when describing older wines, to suggest intricate subtlety, requiring sustained mental effort to grasp, as with a complex puzzle.   A.H.

compost, the name given to the product of microbial action on organic wastes under controlled conditions in piles or windrows. Compost can be created from WINERY WASTE, typically POMACE, and it may be mixed for example with animal manures and sometimes with municipal garden waste, which encourages microbial action and resultant high temperatures. The compost must be turned regularly to maintain aerobic conditions and be kept at a temperature of 55 °C/131 ° F for at least three days to destroy pathogens and weed seeds. Compost is applied to vineyard soils and, being rich in ORGANIC MATTER and NUTRIENTS, improves vine growth. However, compost making and distribution requires handling large quantities of material, and for this reason most vine-growers around the world use manufactured FERTILIZERS. The use of compost and other organic soil amendments is, however,

an integral part of ORGANIC and BIODYNAMIC VITICULTURE.   R.E.S. & R.E.W.

computers. See INFORMATION TECHNOLOGY.

Conca de Barberá, small but promising wine zone in Spanish CATALUÑA, sandwiched in between PENEDÈS, COSTERS DEL SEGRE, and TARRAGONA (see map under SPAIN). At around 500 m/ 1,600 ft above sea level, this DO experiences cold winters, and hot summer days are tempered by cool winds from the sea. Miguel TORRES of Penedès recognized the grape-growing potential of the LIMESTONE country around the Castillo de Milmanda and makes two of his most ambitious single-vineyard wines there: the white Milmanda and the red Grans Muralles. Some interesting rosé, and now red wines are also made from the local TREPAT vine. Most of Conca de Barberá's grapes are used to produce CAVA, however, and consequently few wines carry the name of the DO on the label.   V. de la S.

concentrated grape must. See GRAPE CONCENTRATE.

concentration, umbrella term for any winemaking operation which serves to remove volatile substances, mainly water, from grape juice or wine. Its most common application has been in the production of GRAPE CONCENTRATE But a range of more sophisticated concentration techniques is increasingly used on grapes and musts, often only on a certain portion of the total must, in order to produce more concentrated wines, notably in some of BORDEAUX's grandest cellars.

One component in a mixture can be concentrated using differences in boiling points, in freezing points, or in molecular size. The usual technique for making grape concentrate is to use differences in boiling points in a low-pressure, low-temperature evaporator. While very effective in concentrating sugar, this technique has the disadvantage of also removing volatile FLAVOUR COMPOUNDS.

A more recent and more sophisticated technique, used since 1989 in some parts of France as an alternative to ENRICHMENT, involves evaporating grape must under vacuum. Under vacuum, the water in the must evaporates at temperatures of about 20 °C/68 °F, no hotter than fermentation temperatures and therefore involving no dangerous loss of flavour. In practice, to achieve an acceptable rate of evaporation, temperatures rather higher have to be used, which can have a negative effect on the flavour of the final wine. The equipment needed (known in French as a *concentrateur sous vide*) is relatively expensive, but has the advantage of being able to handle unclarified grape must. Increasingly, though, vacuum concentrators are being superseded by REVERSE OSMOSIS machines.

Differences in molecular size have long been used to purify substances other than wine. The development of strong plastic membrane filters with very small pores of nearly uniform size means that the technique can be applied to purifying drinking water, and concentrating wine. However, filters with very small pores become easily clogged with grape must or wine. Reverse osmosis is an increasingly popular manipulation that makes use of a technique called tangential or cross-flow filtration to concentrate wine without clogging the filter because the flow of liquid is tangential to the membrane and at pressure.

Freeze concentration, using differences in freezing points, is used to make a range of sweet wines of varying qualities. The EISWEIN of Germany and Austria and the ICE WINE of Canada and elsewhere is made by picking frozen grapes from the vine, crushing them, and filtering the juice without allowing the mixture to thaw so that water is removed in the form of ice. Ice crystals are collected on the filter along with the more usual grape solids (skins, etc.) and the result is grape juice with a lower concentration of water, but a higher concentration of sugars, acids, and other soluble solids.

Natural freezing on the vine is replicated by producers in such different regions as SAUTERNES (where it is called CRYOEXTRACTION) and NEW ZEALAND. Freshly picked grapes may be frozen in special chillers prior to crushing and filtering. This technique is often practised selectively, not just for sweet white wines, but also on grapes destined to make dry white wines, not all of which are fully ripe. Since just-ripe grapes freeze at 0 °C/32 °F but fully ripe grapes freeze only at −6 °C or below, the mixture of grapes is chilled before crushing to an intermediate temperature so that it yields only the ripest juice (although it will yield nothing if there are no ripe grapes in the first place). The technique can only be practised on individual batches of grapes, however, so is relatively labour intensive.

One final method of concentrating grape must is also the oldest: desiccation. See DRIED-GRAPE WINES.

Because in general these methods remove only water from the grapes or must, all other components are concentrated. An increased concentration of fermentable SUGARS results in a wine with a higher ALCOHOLIC STRENGTH. Increased concentrations of PHENOLICS in many cases result in red wines with more BODY, potential for AGEING, and possibly more flavour. Increased ACIDITY, however, can result in wines that are aggressively tart, especially in less ripe years or in cooler wine regions. In some cases, particularly in cooler areas, musts which have been concentrated may have to be further subjected to DEACIDIFICATION, although in temperate climates TOTAL ACIDITY is usually only very slightly raised once TARTRATES have been precipitated.

Concentration is also used as a TASTING TERM.

J.R. & J.A.G.

Goode, J., *Wine Science: The Application of Science in Winemaking* (2nd edn., London, 2014).

Concha y Toro. The dominant wine producer in Latin America was founded in Pirque, CHILE, in 1883 by Don Melchor Concha y Toro, a prominent businessman and politician. Its 2014 total of 10,750 ha/26,564 acres made it one of the world's leading vineyard owners. Since the mid 20th century efforts have been focused on modernization and developing export markets.

The Casillero del Diablo ('the Devil's Cellar') BRAND is one of the world's most successful with global sales of over 3.8 million cases annually (1.3 million of which are in the UK).

In 1993 the company founded Cono Sur winery to provide more innovative styles of wine, specializing in Pinot Noir, and an early espouser of SUSTAINABILITY, a policy now applied throughout the group. Other significant winery projects followed, including Bodega Trivento in Mendoza in 1996 (now the fourth largest winery in Argentina) and Maycas de Limari in the new, cool Limari Valley in northern Chile. In 2011 Concha y Toro acquired Fetzer and Bonterra in Mendocino, California, thereby extending its vineyard holdings outside South America for the first time.

Concha y Toro is distinguished by the quality of its winemakers, wines, and management at virtually all price levels. Its top wines include Don Melchor Cabernet Sauvignon, Carmin de Peumo Carmenère, and the Terrunyo wine range. Since 1997, Concha y Toro has had a JOINT VENTURE, Almaviva in Puente Alto, with the Rothschilds of Ch MOUTON ROTHSCHILD.

Since the 1980s the company has been led by Eduardo Guilisasti, whose family have a majority shareholding (27.8%) of Viña Concha y Toro. His siblings Rafael, José, Pablo, and Isabel are also closely involved in the running of the business.

Concord, the most widely planted vine variety grown in the eastern United States, notably in NEW YORK State where there were more than 20,000 acres/8,000 ha in 2006. It started life as a chance seedling and the majority of its genes clearly belong to the American vine species *Vitis labrusca*. The pronounced FOXY flavour of its juice—synonymous with 'grape' flavour in the US—makes its wine an acquired taste for those raised on the produce of VINIFERA vines. It was named after Concord, Massachusetts, by Ephraim W. Bull, who introduced it, having planted the seeds of a WILD VINE there in 1843. It is particularly important for the production of GRAPE JUICE and grape jelly, but between 5 and 10% of it is used to produce a wide range of wines, some KOSHER, often with some considerable RESIDUAL SUGAR. Viticulturally, the vine is extremely well adapted to the low temperatures of New York and is both productive and vigorous. It is planted in many eastern states of the US and widely in Washington state where most grapes go into juice and GRAPE CONCENTRATE. There are also about 2,500 ha/6,177 acres of Concord in Brazil.

Robinson, J., Harding, J., and Vouillamoz, J., *Wine Grapes: A Complete Guide to 1,368 Vine Varieties, Including their Origins and Flavours* (London, 2012).

concrete, popular since the 19th century for the construction of large FERMENTATION VESSELS and tanks for storage and AGEING, it was upstaged by the introduction of shiny STAINLESS-STEEL vats from the 1970s onwards. Nevertheless, concrete's greater thermal inertia, longevity, cost-effectiveness, and overall influence on wine QUALITY are still appreciated by many top producers, including Bordeaux's PETRUS, and the material is experiencing a renaissance. Traditionally lined with epoxy resin to prevent direct contact between the concrete and the wine and to make cleaning easier, especially the removal of TARTRATE crystals, concrete tanks do have the potential disadvantage of allowing very little OXYGEN exchange, which is important in the evolution of TANNINS. Some producers therefore prefer unlined concrete for its greater oxygen ingress. Since the early 2000s, so-called **concrete eggs** have been gaining in popularity among a small group of producers around the world because the shape not only offers a high level of contact between the wine and the LEES but also appears to encourage convection currents that improve fermentation kinetics and reduce the need for BÂTONNAGE. They range in size from around 500 to 1,500 litres (130–400 gal) and are usually unlined but treated with tartaric acid solution before use. Early adopters include Michel CHAPOUTIER, South Africa's Eben Sadie, and Alfred Tesseron at Ch Pontet-Canet.

Condado de Huelva, Spanish denominated wine zone in ANDALUCÍA, close to the city of Huelva between the JEREZ region and the Portuguese border (see map under SPAIN). Nowadays few of its wines, which have typically been FORTIFIED and made in the image of its neighbour SHERRY, are exported but the region has a long history (see SPAIN, history). In 'The Pardoner's Tale', Chaucer refers to the wines of Lepe, a small town just outside the modern Condado de Huelva DO and a notorious source of blending wine, and by the early 16th century the wines of Huelva were being exported to northern Europe and the emerging colonies in South America. But from the 17th century, much of Huelva's production was sold to

Jerez, where it was blended anonymously into sherry SOLERAS. Huelva became a DO in its own right in 1964. The principal grape is the rather neutral ZALEMA along with a little PALOMINO (15% of the vineyard area).

Four styles of wine are made. Condado Pálido is a pale, dry, fortified wine matured in a solera under a blanket of FLOR so that it resembles a coarse FINO sherry. Condado Viejo is a RANCIO style of wine aged in a solera and resembling a somewhat rustic Jerez OLOROSO. Vino Naranja, literally 'orange wine', is Spain's only aromatized wine (through maceration with orange peel) with an appellation of origin (and bears no relation, therefore, to ORANGE WINE). Vino Joven, finally, is an unfortified dry table wine that now accounts for about half the regional production, and which can be a little fruitier than similar white wines produced in the Jerez area.   V. de la S.

Condrieu, distinctive and fashionable white wine made in minuscule quantities in the northern RHÔNE. It is made exclusively from the VIOGNIER grape, whose successful wines manage the unusual combination of a pronounced yet elusive perfume with substantial BODY. The recent wave of Viognier planting all over the world was originally inspired by enthusiasm for Condrieu.

This small appellation encompasses seven right-bank communes (which happen to span three *départements*, the Rhône, Loire, and Ardèche) just south of the red wine appellation CÔTE RÔTIE where the river turns a bend and the best vineyards are exposed to the south (see map under RHÔNE). The vine has probably been cultivated here for two millennia, since nearby Vienne was an important Roman city, although the total Condrieu *vignoble* fell to fewer than 10 ha/25 acres in the 1960s, when the wine was virtually unknown outside local restaurants, and when other fruit crops were much more profitable.

Since the 1970s, however, Condrieu's fame and price have risen steadily, and an increasing number of growers have been prepared to reconstruct small patches of vineyard on the steep slopes, often granitic in the south around the village of Chavanay, the best of which are traditionally said to have a topsoil of *arzelle*, or decomposed mica. The best sites should also be sheltered from the north wind, which can decimate the potential crop at FLOWERING, but little can be done to combat the inevitable SOIL EROSION. Average yields here are notoriously low (and very much lower than for Viognier planted further south), which is one reason why Condrieu is relatively expensive for a wine that is best drunk young, at between two and four years in general.

At one time, Condrieu was a sweet or medium-sweet wine but almost all is made dry today.

Vinification standards are extremely variable, particularly since some vignerons are relative newcomers (even if their grandfathers were experienced in making Condrieu). Two of the most experienced producers are Georges Vernay and GUIGAL, the appellation's dominant force whose top bottling is La Doriane. Policies on such fundamentals as the desirability of MALOLACTIC CONVERSION and use of OAK vary considerably in Condrieu.

In 1990, there were 40 ha/100 acres of vineyard old enough to produce AOC wine, but the total area under vine grew rapidly in the early 1990s so that by 2013 168 ha/415 acres were in production, but further expansion is difficult on these steep, indented slopes and many growers have had to content themselves with extending into a Viognier-based local Vin de Pays. CHÂTEAU GRILLET, France's other all-Viognier appellation, is an enclave within the Condrieu zone.

Conegliano, town that is home to the main experimental viticultural station in the VENETO region of north-east Italy. The Istituto Sperimentale per la Viticoltura, now called CRA-Vit (Consiglio per la Ricerca e la sperimentazione in Agricoltura—Centro di Ricerca per la Viticoltura), was established in 1923. One of its first directors was Professor Dalmasso, whose Dalmasso Commission made a significant report on the state of the Italian wine industry (see ITALY). His successor Professor Manzoni produced many crosses (see INCROCIO Manzoni) still cultivated today. In 1933, Conegliano became involved in combating ADULTERATION AND FRAUD in an area which was expanded in 1965 to include not just Veneto but also FRIULI. From 1986, the adulteration and fraud service became independent. At the same time, an experimental winery was established at Conegliano.

A 9-ha nursery for an ampelographical collection of vine varieties had been established in 1951, and another estate of 20 ha/50 acres was acquired nearby in 1963. From 1967, the institute's work was focused on viticulture, with four central units concerned with AMPELOGRAPHY and VINE IMPROVEMENT, biology and protection, PROPAGATION, and cultivation techniques. There are further units located around Italy and the institute is responsible for CLONAL SELECTION, research into ROOTSTOCKS, and an ampelographic collection of more than 2,000 VINE VARIETIES. Conegliano is home of the Italian national register for grape cultivars. Since 1999 it has been integrated in the national Agricultural Research Council (CRA) and is its centre of viticultural research.

Conegliano's influence extends all over Italy, not least because the oenological school, Italy's first, founded in 1876, is there and trained many of the country's producers and consultant OENOLOGISTS. In 2001 its name was changed to Istituto Statale di Istruzione Secondaria Superiore

G. B. Cerletti. Nowadays the Institute teaches oenology as well as viticulture in conjunction with the University of Padova.   W.S.

Conegliano-Valdobbiadene, DOCG for PROSECCO from the original production zone on the hills between these two towns.

confréries, French 'brotherhoods' or associations, dedicated in particular to advancing the cause of various foods and drinks throughout France. More than 150 of them, most of them founded in the second half of the 20th century, are devoted to such various products as macaroons, jams, olives, and local shellfish. A high proportion of them, almost half, are based on specific wines and other alcoholic drinks. One of the most famous is the Confrérie des Chevaliers de Tastevin in Burgundy (see CLOS DE VOUGEOT). The Commanderie du Bontemps du MÉDOC et des Graves, founded in Bordeaux in 1949 by the energetic Henri Martin, is also well known and is the LEFT BANK answer to the oldest of these *confréries*, the Jurade de ST-ÉMILION. The latter dates from the late 12th century, when the town councillors of this ancient town were given particular powers and responsibilities by the English crown, which then governed it (see BORDEAUX, history); it was reconstituted in 1947. These *confréries* are devoted to an annual programme of pageantry, feasting, robe-wearing, and the *intronisation* (enthronement) of honorary converts to the cause.

connoisseurship of wine is a (disappearing) art in search of a less emotive name. The word **connoisseur** in English, and its counterpart *connaisseur* in French, conjures up a frightening vision of an elderly male so steeped in wine, wine knowledge, and wine prejudices as to be completely unapproachable. Much more attractive and widely acceptable terms are those which convey not just knowledge but an element of relish such as wine lover, wine enthusiast, or the common and attractive French term *amateur du vin*. None of these terms, incidentally, has any connotation of gender.

Whatever the drawbacks of the term, connoisseurship or wine expertise is an art that can give pleasure, and involves less an arid grasp of the precise ENCÉPAGEMENT of each vineyard and fermentation regimes for each vintage than an intelligent appreciation of how wines are likely to taste in a given environment, at a certain stage in their evolution, before or after other wines, and, importantly, with different foods. This is what consumers rather than producers are for. Experience can contribute to connoisseurship, but only if the consumer tastes with humility, attention, and an open mind. Mentors are useful but some newcomers to wine have an instinctive grasp of connoisseurship. A true connoisseur meets each wine halfway and tries to show it in the best possible light, in stark contrast to professional wine JUDGING. Too many wine drinkers seem determined to judge rather than enjoy wine. See wine TASTING, AGE-ING, SERVING, and FOOD AND WINE MATCHING. A connoisseur is not necessarily a wine BORE and while deep pockets help, they are not a prerequisite.

Consejo Regulador, Spanish term meaning 'regulating council' (see COMITÉ INTERPROFES-SIONNEL). Spanish wine law is administered through a network of Consejos Reguladores representing each and every DO. They comprise vine-growers, wine producers, and merchants who between them decide on the ground rules for their region.

Consorzio, Italian word for a consortium or association, of wine-growers, NÉGOCIANTS, and CO-OPERATIVES representing the interests of a single wine region or DOC/DOCG. However, since the 2008 reforms of the EU wine market, the Consorzio role has changed drastically. QUALITY CONTROL, which used to be the Consor-zio's concern, is now in the hands of a neutral third party and Consorzios are now concerned more with promotion and marketing, while several have added to this the ambitious task of routing COUNTERFEIT wines in the international market. If at least 60% of production is controlled by Consorzio members, a mandatory levy can be imposed on any producer wishing to use the relevant DOC or DOCG name on labels, regardless of whether they are a member or not. Its counterpart in France is the COMITÉ INTERPROFESSIONNEL; in Spain the CONSEJO REGULADOR.   W.S.

Constantia, legendary, 18th- and 19th-century dessert wines from the Cape, SOUTH AFRICA, then a Dutch colony. Their fame was never matched by any other New World wines and at their height they commanded more prestige, more fabulous prices, and enjoyed more crowned patronage than the most celebrated wines of Europe (with the possible exception of Hungarian TOKAJI). Constantia was even ordered by Napoleon from his exile on St Helena.

The Cape wines were grown on a subdivision of the 750-ha/1,850-acre Constantia Estate just outside Cape Town, founded in 1685 by an early Dutch governor Simon van der Stel. However, it was Constantia's subsequent owners who achieved acclaim and prosperity, principally Hendrik Cloete, who purchased and restored one of the subdivisions in 1778. Quality and fame gradually declined in the late 19th century, partly as a result of the Cape's declining importance to the British wine market, and partly because Constantia's higher labour costs, especially after the abolition of slavery in 1834, and the lower yields associated with its cool climate, made wine production economically marginal. By 1885 Cloete's estate was bankrupt

and under the name of Groot Constantia has been state-owned ever since. In 1975, management of its activities passed into the hands of a control board and in 1993 into a trust. In recent times Groot Constantia has made sound, increasingly impressive, conventional wines. A neighbouring privately owned estate, Klein (Little) Constantia, an 1823 deduction from Groot Constantia, was the first to take up the challenge of recreating the legend. It replanted vineyards with Muscat of Frontignan (MUSCAT BLANC À PETITS GRAINS) in the early 1980s and now produces a white dessert wine known as Vin de Constance (without BOTRYTIS in the manner of the old Constantia) to local and international acclaim.

The sweet wines of Constantia, both red and white, the latter the more expensive, were made principally from this small-berried Muscat and its dark-berried mutation, probably including the lesser MUSCAT OF ALEXANDRIA together with the dark red PONTAC and CHENIN BLANC. Records show that slightly under 50% of Constantia wine in the early 19th century was sold either as red or white Constantia without any varietal claim. Analyses of recently opened bottles (still perfumed with a tang of citrus and smoky richness) reveal they were unfortified although high in alcohol, apparently confirming records that the grapes were left on the vines long after ripeness to achieve shrivelled, but not BOTRY-TIZED, concentration (see DRIED-GRAPE WINES for more details of the technique). Other stories suggest the wines may have been fortified by shippers for protection on the long, rough, and hot journey across the equator to Europe.

Today Constantia is a demarcated wine ward in Cape Town's southern suburbs, on the slim peninsula pointing into the south Atlantic, cooled by the sea for relatively slow summer ripening with average daily temperatures of 18–19 °C/64–66 °F, and very wet but moderate winters (average annual rainfall over 1,000 mm/ 39 in). Rich, loamy Table Mountain sandstone and decomposed granite soils nurture vigorous growth and even shy-bearing classic vines require ruthless TRIMMING and CROP THINNING. Here a handful of vineyards have, since the mid 1980s, once again been producing classic wines from land that once formed part of the historic 750-ha estate developed by Governor van der Stel.

See also SOUTH AFRICA, history.   J.P. & M.F.

Burman, J., *Wine of Constantia* (Cape Town, 1979).
James, T., *Wines of the New South Africa: Tradition and Revolution* (Berkeley, 2013).
Johnson, H., 'Groot Constantia', in *The Story of Wine* (London, 1989).

Constellation Brands, holding company of Constellation Wines, previously known as Canandaigua (still the name of its NEW YORK wine subsidiary). Based in Fairport, New York, Constellation Brands is a leading international

producer and marketer of virtually all forms of alcoholic beverage. Thanks to consistent acquisition, it became the world's largest wine business in 2004. In 2006 it acquired Canada's biggest wine company Vincor and remains the dominant player there. But in 2011 it refocused on its American roots and sold off all of the Australian, South African, and UK interests it had so recently acquired, including HARDYS, to what would become ACCOLADE. Constellation claims carefully to be 'the world's leader in premium wine' whose 100 BRANDS, in 2014, included Robert MONDAVI, Clos du Bois, Rex Goliath, Ravenswood, Black Box, Simi, Wild Horse, Mark West, Franciscan Estate, Toasted Head, and Mount Veeder in California; Manischewitz (America's best-selling KOSHER wine) in New York; Jackson-Triggs and Inniskillin in Canada; Kim Crawford and Nobilo in New Zealand; and Ruffino in central Italy.

consultants are used with increasing frequency in wine production, selling, and occasionally consumption. Consultant VITICULTURISTS are particularly useful since those who operate on an international scale can impart knowledge gleaned from a wide variety of different vine-growing environments, although strictly local specialists such as David Abreu in northern California can forge an international reputation. Like viticulturists, the more energetic consultant OENOLOGISTS can use their expertise in both hemispheres, although their work is necessarily limited by the timing of HARVEST. One of the first internationally famous consultant oenologists was Professor Émile PEYNAUD. Today his best-known successor from Bordeaux is Michel ROLLAND, although dozens of other highly respected consultants operate in Bordeaux alone and there are now hundreds of winemakers who travel the globe and offer, if not consultancy, then hard graft (see FLYING WINEMAKERS). Consultants play an increasingly important role in wine production everywhere but have long been particularly important in Bordeaux, California, and Italy, where the likes of Riccardo COTARELLA are liberally used for marketing purposes.

Many restaurateurs and hoteliers, most airlines, and even some wine retailers employ consultants in their wine selection. Some well-heeled collectors also take INVESTMENT advice from consultants.

consumption of wine throughout the world fell from a peak of around 285 million hl/7,500 million gal a year in the years 1976–80 to about 225 million hl in the early 2000s, a slight increase on the late-1990s level, and then peaked at about 255 million hl in 2007, only to fall in the wake of the global financial crisis to about 240 million hl by 2013. Total world PRO-DUCTION continues to be considerably more than this, resulting in a serious global wine SURPLUS that is most acute in Europe, the most important producer and consumer of wine if regarded as a continent. But on a national level, by 2014 the US had pulled ahead of France to become the world's biggest consumer of wine. The main reason for the drop in global consumption has been sharp falls in average wine consumption by France and Italy, traditionally the world's two most important producers and consumers of wine. The generation of Frenchmen and Italians who routinely consumed a litre of wine a day is with us no more, and wine consumption has been falling even faster in Spain. These plummeting consumption levels in Europe's most important wine-producing countries have been offset not just by steady growth in the US but by a dramatic increase in wine consumption in China, which was the world's fifth most important market for wine after the US, France, Italy, and Germany, by 2012. Sixth biggest market, according to OIV figures, was the UK which imports more wine than any country other than Germany.

The countries with the highest per capita wine consumption in the early 21st century were still mainly the most important wine producers: in declining order of consumption, Luxembourg, France, Portugal, Italy, Switzerland, Denmark, Croatia, Greece, Austria, Slovenia, Argentina, Belgium, Georgia, Serbia, Germany, Australia, Sweden, New Zealand, Netherlands, and only then Spain.

National annual per capita wine consumption figures in litres according to the OIV are to be found in Appendix 2.

See SURPLUS for statistics on global consumption since 1976 and see HEALTH for official medical advice on safe personal consumption levels of alcoholic drinks.

containers

containers for wine are used at four main stages in a wine's life: during the FERMENTATION that creates it, during its MATURATION, for its TRANSPORT, and for SERVING it. Moreover, while wine containers have changed throughout history, they have also varied through space, with each winemaking region becoming characterized by vessels of different dimensions.

History

A wide variety of materials were used for drinking and serving wine in the Ancient World, particularly CHINA. In prehistoric times in the eastern Mediterranean, wine was generally put in earthenware jars, or sometimes into wooden containers, soon after the grapes had been trodden or pressed, and this basic fermentation technology remained the norm until the 20th century, when VATS or tanks of concrete and STAINLESS STEEL were introduced. The basic receptacles used for storing and transporting wine in classical antiquity were pottery AMPHORAE,

which varied greatly in size and shape but which could be sealed, thus preventing the potentially harmful access of OXYGEN. Larger pottery vessels for storing wine in the Roman world were known as DOLIA. During the 1st century BC, experiments were also undertaken in transporting wine in these *dolia*, anchored amidships, but their use did not persist. By the end of the 2nd century AD, amphorae production declined in Italy, although it continued in other parts of the eastern and southern Mediterranean, and most wine was transported long distance in wooden BARRELS. For short distances, numerous other vessels, in particular animal skins, were also used, especially in Iberia.

Throughout the medieval period, wooden barrels served as almost the only vessels used for maturing and transporting wine, and their sizes came to reflect local custom and requirements. The standard barrel size in England, for example, the BUTT or PIPE, was fixed by statute in the 15th century at 126 imperial gallons (572.8 l). However, in southern Italy at the same time, their wooden *botti* held about 454 l, while in Bruges the butt had a capacity of about 910 l; in Spain it varied from 454 to 477 litres. Meanwhile, it had been discovered in Germany that wines from good vintages with a high sugar content kept in larger barrels, providing they were not subjected to RACKING, lasted longer. This led to the construction of huge wooden tuns, containing thousands of litres, among the most famous of which were the Strasbourg Tun of 1472, and the Heidelberg Tuns of 1591 and 1663.

For serving wine, small jugs made of pottery were generally used during the medieval period. However, from the 16th century, glass BOTTLES became more frequently used, and by the second half of the 17th century, these bottles began to be used to store and mature wines. Bottle shapes evolved so as to allow extended BOTTLE AGEING and thus were born VINTAGE wines, and CONNOISSEURSHIP. Moreover, the use of bottles also enabled completely new types of wine, such as CHAMPAGNE and vintage PORT, to be produced from the 17th century onwards.   P.T.H.U.

Allen, H. W., *A History of Wine: Great Vintage Wines from the Homeric Age to the Present Day* (London, 1961).

Peacock, D. P. S., and Williams, D. F., *Amphorae and the Roman Economy: An Introductory Guide* (London, 1986).

Unwin, P. T. H., *Wine and the Vine: An Historical Geography of Viticulture and the Wine Trade* (London, 1992).

Modern times

For details of containers used for fermentation, see FERMENTATION VESSELS, which may be either open topped or closed, and may have a capacity as big as 300 hl/7,925 gal. Wines are matured prior to bottling in closed containers (to avoid

OXIDATION), either in tanks made from materials such as STAINLESS STEEL or CONCRETE, or in some form of COOPERAGE, from small, new barrels to large, old casks, or in AMPHORAE, QVEVRI, CONCRETE eggs, or clay TINAJAS, or even glass BONBONNES. Wine may be blended in even larger tanks holding up to 15,000 hl. Wine is transported either in BULK, usually in food-grade 250-hl stainless steel tankers or disposable 'flexitanks', or in bottle. When transport containers are used for shipping wine in bottle, care is taken by some fine wine merchants and some fine wine producers that the wine is shipped only in reefers, or temperature-controlled containers, and sometimes only during cooler times of year. This is particularly important for wines which have undergone a minimum of FILTRATION and vital for NATURAL WINES. For more details, see TRANSPORT.

The most common container for wine on its final journey to the GLASS, occasionally via a DECANTER, is the bottle, but see PACKAGING for the increasing number of alternatives.

contaminants, potentially harmful substances found in wine, either as a result of air or water pollution, (see SMOKE TAINT, for example), vineyard treatment RESIDUES, poor winery HYGIENE, contaminated pallets, packaging materials, or transport containers, ignorance, or ADULTERATION AND FRAUD. They are often difficult to identify and very potent, with extremely low perception threshholds, although the ability to detect them is not universal, even among professional tasters. A contaminant becomes a TAINT only once it can be smelt or tasted.

Ignorance is possibly the most forgivable reason for contamination since the scope of what is regarded as, and can be measured as, a contaminant grows wider with the rapid progress of science and measuring techniques. LEAD, for example, which was deliberately added to wines by the Romans, is now known to be a serious neural toxin. CARBAMATES, on the other hand, have been regarded as contaminants only since the late 1980s. And it was only in the 1990s that the contaminating effect of some apparently innocuous treatments of wooden beams in some winemaking establishments became apparent (see TRIBROMOANISOLE).

Nowadays, contamination as a result of poor winery hygiene is extremely rare, although may be caused by products such as chlorine sanitizers that are designed to clean the winery but which form chlorophenols when they come into contact with phenols in rubber, resin, or plastic fittings, resulting in plastic or medicinal off-flavours in contaminated wine. A leak of brine from a refrigerant unit is another possible hazard. Research by Chatonnet et al. detected levels of phthalate contamination that exceeded the EU's specific migration limits for alcoholic drinks in 11% of the French wines tested, thought to be due mainly to the epoxy-resin coatings inside older vats.

Pollution is difficult to guard against. Wine producers are increasingly wary of some AGROCHEMICALS, however. Orthene, a fungicide used widely in the early 1980s, with no ill effects apparent during winemaking, produced a range of wines with an extremely unpleasant smell after several years' BOTTLE AGE. Many German wines made in the early to mid 1980s, particularly the 1983s, exhibited this particular contamination. The ST-ESTÈPHE property Ch Phélan-Ségur destroyed its entire 1984 and 1985 production because of Orthene contamination. Even after a particular product has been banned, it may still contaminate the environment. Chlorophenols, for example, are active ingredients in wood preservatives, fungicides, and biocides that have been used over many years and form CHLOROANISOLES. American authorities, in particular, have regularly applied stringent tests for traces of recently suspected contaminants, such as procymidone from agrochemical RESIDUES, to imported wines. Other potential contaminants from the vineyard include hydraulic oil leaked from mechanical harvesters or spray drift from PESTICIDES.

The wine trade, like every other commercial activity, has its villains, but they are increasingly rare. Fortunately, very few of the substances which the least scrupulous producers are tempted to add illegally to wine (SORBITOL, for example) are harmful—with the notable and horrifying exception of lethal doses of METHANOL added to one Italian producer's wines in 1987.

See also ADULTERATION, which sometimes involves the deliberate addition of contaminants.
J.R. & J.E.H.

Chatonnet, P., Boutou, S., and Plana, A., 'Contamination of wines and spirits by phthalates: types of contaminants present, contamination sources and means of prevention', *Food Additives & Contaminants: Part A*, 31/9 (2014), 1605–15. doi: 10.1080/19440049.2014.941947.

continental climate is one with a high degree of **continentality**, defined for any place as the difference between the average mean temperature of its hottest month and that of its coldest month. Climates with a wide annual range are called continental; those with a narrow range, MARITIME. The former tend to be in the interiors of the larger continents; the latter, near oceans or other large water bodies.

The most continental viticultural climates are those of central and eastern Europe, together with inland northern America (see RUSSIA and CANADA, for example). The European west coastal and most Mediterranean viticultural regions rank as intermediate, while the most maritime viticultural climate of all is that of MADEIRA. All viticultural regions of the southern

hemisphere, even those well inland, are classed (in this sense) as maritime. That is because the total land mass of the southern hemisphere is small relative to that of the oceans, which thus dominate temperatures.

The rapid autumn temperature drop in continental climates means that RIPENING can be precarious. VINTAGE variation therefore tends to be marked, and the effects of high YIELDS on ripening and wine quality are probably more evident than in maritime climates when autumn temperatures drop slowly, and ripening is relatively assured. Cool maritime climates such as those of ENGLAND and WALES, on the other hand, can result in viticultural problems due to insufficient warmth during FLOWERING and FRUIT SET.

European experience shows that ideal continental seasons can lead to superb wines when combined with appropriate cropping levels. Against that, maritime climates that are warm and sunny enough during flowering and setting can probably produce good quality more reliably, and thus have practical advantages for commercial viticulture.

See also CLIMATE AND WINE QUALITY and MEDITERRANEAN CLIMATE.   J.G. & R.E.S.

continuous method, SPARKLING WINEMAKING process developed in the USSR for SOVIET SPARKLING WINE and now used in Germany and Portugal.

contract winemaking. See CUSTOM CRUSH FACILITY.

controlled appellations, a method of LABELLING wine and regulating quality that is modelled on France's APPELLATION CONTRÔLÉE system. Controlled appellations such as the EU's PDO or protected designations of origin are distinguished within the broader category of GEOGRAPHICAL INDICATIONS by the inclusion of strict rules governing viticultural and winemaking practices that reinforce a close link between the inherent characteristics of the wine and its place of origin. Typical controls will include restrictions on yield, grape varieties, and vine management techniques. The restrictions of the controlled appellation model make them less common outside Europe, and even within Europe, controlled appellations are criticized on the grounds that they limit innovation and tend unquestioningly to maintain traditional practices and TRADITION. (See Appendix 1 for a complete list of controlled appellations for which particular grape varieties are specified, with their permitted grapes.)

Somewhat confusingly, in the United States, all geographical DELIMITATIONS (including AVAs) are legally known as 'appellations of origin', although they do not include rules on viticultural and winemaking practices.   J.B.

cooking with wine. Good wine used in the kitchen adds depth and dimension to a dish that no other ingredient can. The recipes of Apicius, the most famous Roman chef, show that wine was commonly used in his sauces and it has found a place in the kitchen ever since.

Wine is an essential ingredient in many dishes and can be used in every stage of cooking from the preparation and tenderizing of meat to providing the final, often sweet, finish to a dessert. It is all the more curious, therefore, that so little research has been done into exactly what happens to wine during cooking, particularly as a result of the application of heat. Since the boiling point of ETHANOL is 78 °C/172 °F, considerably lower than that of water, however, it is reasonable to suppose that any wine used in cooking becomes progressively less alcoholic if heated to above 78 °C for any length of time. As a sauce is 'reduced' with wine, the other components in the wine such as any RESIDUAL SUGAR and, especially, its ACIDITY become even more marked. This is presumably why over-reduced sauces can taste so acid, and why they can have an almost caramelized appearance and taste. Other uses for wine in cooking do not involve changing the wine's composition by heating.

There is much debate about the necessary quality of **cooking wine**, some regarding the saucepan or stockpot as the ideal repository for any wine considered too nasty to drink, others insisting that only the finest wine will do. Wine with an unpleasant flavour will not lose that flavour in the kitchen, and CORKED wine is not advisable. On the other hand, the complex BALANCE and full range of volatile FLAVOUR COMPOUNDS of a great wine will not survive the application of any fierce heat. The most important group of flavours the cook may want to extract from a wine are those of the fruit, which are then used to build sauces and slow-cooked dishes such as daubes; for this the wine must be well-made, and not too acidic, whether red or white.

The following are some of the most common ways in which wine is used in the kitchen.

Deglazing: pouring wine (or another liquid such as stock) into a pan in which something has been roasted or sautéed in order to dissolve the remnants of that operation in the liquid to make a sauce. Wine adds body and depth to the sauce. White VERMOUTH is often used as it brings complexity from the added herbal element of its composition. This might be in a sauce with cream, or in an emulsion such as beurre blanc.

Marinade: a method of imparting extra flavour, principally to meat and game, via a mixture based on carrots, shallots, onions, pepper, salt, vinegar, garlic, and red or white wine which takes the form of cooked and uncooked marinades. Instant marinades, using brandy, port, or madeira, are used for the ingredients of pâtés and terrines. After the meat has been removed, the marinade may be used for deglazing or for a more complicated sauce.

Stocks: wine is often used instead of, or as well as, water, to provide the essential base for soups and sauces. Red wine is used in game stock, white wine in chicken and fish stocks. (Wine, mainly white but sometimes red, features in many risotto recipes.)

Court-bouillon: a method of cooking fish, shellfish, or white meat in which herbs and spices are infused in white wine and water in which the food is subsequently poached.

Sauces: of the many which form the basis of classic French cuisine, *bordelaise* comprises red wine and shallots; *périgueux* uses madeira, veal stock, and truffles; *sauce Robert* is white wine, onion, and mustard; and *ravigote* is made with white wine and vinegar.

Stews and casseroles: wine, preferably from the same area as the dish, is an integral part of *coq au vin*, daube of beef, fish stew, *boeuf bourguignonne*, and many more classics of *la cuisine bourgeoise*. Acidic wine will detract rather than enhance.

Jellies: poached foie gras set in a Gewurztraminer jelly is an Alsace speciality. Sweet jellies can be made from Sauternes or any other sweet wine.

Desserts: wine has a surprisingly wide range of applications for sweet foods and patisserie. Red wine is used for poaching pears and macerating strawberries (a speciality of Bordeaux) while dessert wines such as MARSALA and SHERRY are used in, respectively, zabaglione and English trifle. In Italy, strong, usually sweet wines, typically VIN SANTO, are served with dry biscuits which are moistened in them.   J.R. & M.P.L.

Percival, F., 'Coq au what? Cooking with wine', *The World of Fine Wine*, 30 (2010).

Poussier, L., and Poussier, O., *Desserts and Wines* (London, 2004).

McGee, H., *On Food and Cooking* (New York, 1984).

cool-climate viticulture, and warm-climate viticulture,

are indefinite terms, depending on the speaker's or writer's viewpoint, but are probably applied most usefully to the coolest and warmest thirds of the climatic or geographic range used successfully for growing wine grapes. Intermediate climate viticulture (see below) lies between, while true hot-climate viticulture produces mainly TABLE GRAPES and DRYING GRAPES, and cannot, in general, produce high-quality wine grapes of any kind. The term cold-climate viticulture is sometimes used to refer to those wine regions that experience WINTER FREEZE and where winter injury of vines can dominate viticultural practices.

Major areas of cool-climate viticulture would certainly include the northern half of France (the LOIRE, CHAMPAGNE, CHABLIS, BURGUNDY, and BEAUJOLAIS,); ENGLAND, LUXEMBOURG, GERMANY, SWITZERLAND, DENMARK, and AUSTRIA; in the US, the Lower Columbia Valley of WASHINGTON and OREGON, and the coolest coastal strip of northern California (CARNEROS, ANDERSON VALLEY); the most southern vineyards of CHILE and some elevated vineyards of SOUTH AFRICA; the South Island and southern North Island of NEW ZEALAND; and in Australia, the whole of TASMANIA, small areas of the higher Adelaide hills in SOUTH AUSTRALIA, and southern VICTORIA, and elevated land associated with the Great Dividing Range in the south east. Gladstones's data (table 183) show all these to have regional average mean temperatures for the growing season (April to October inclusive in the northern hemisphere, October to April in the southern hemisphere) of below 16.0 °C/60.8 °F. Jackson and Schuster (1987) and Casteel (1992) deal specifically with this type of viticulture.

The distinguishing characteristic of cool viticultural climates is that they will regularly ripen only early-maturing grape varieties such as CHASSELAS, MÜLLER-THURGAU, GEWÜRZTRAMINER, CHARDONNAY, PINOT NOIR, and GAMAY; and only in especially warm MESOCLIMATES can varieties such as RIESLING, which ripens early to mid season, be ripened. RIPENING also tends to take place under cool to mild conditions. The combination leads to wines which, at their best, are fresh, delicate, and aromatic. Most are white or only pale red, because full development of ANTHOCYANIN pigments and TANNINS in the grape skins needs greater warmth. Other, warmer viticultural climates will be examined here for the sake of comparison.

Intermediate climate viticulture is that with growing seasons long and warm enough for regular ripening of mid-season grape varieties such as CABERNET FRANC, MERLOT, SYRAH (or Shiraz), and SANGIOVESE, and late-mid-season varieties such as CABERNET SAUVIGNON and NEBBIOLO, to make mainly medium- to full-bodied red table wines. Typical regions are BORDEAUX and the northern RHÔNE Valley in France; the RIOJA Alta in Spain; much of northern ITALY and TUSCANY; the intermediate and warmer coastal valleys of California, such as NAPA and SONOMA; the north and east coasts of the North Island of New Zealand; Margaret River and the south coast of WESTERN AUSTRALIA; the Barossa Valley and hills, Padthaway, and Coonawarra in SOUTH AUSTRALIA; and much of central and southern VICTORIA. Average mean growing season temperatures are in the range 16.0 to 18.5 °C (60.8 to 65.2 °F).

Warm viticultural climates, if sunny enough, will ripen early and mid-season grape varieties to high sugar contents and make the best sweet, fortified wines. They will also ripen late-maturing grape varieties such as MOURVÈDRE (Mataro), CARIGNAN, GRENACHE, TREBBIANO, and CLAIRETTE for making table wines. Examples are the south of France; the DOURO Valley of Portugal and the island of Madeira; the Adelaide district and McLaren Vale in SOUTH AUSTRALIA, the MURRAY DARLING regions of South Australia and Victoria, and the Hunter Valley and Mudgee in NEW SOUTH WALES in Australia. Corresponding average mean growing season temperatures are in the range 18.5 to 21 °C.

Typical hot-climate viticultural regions are those producing table and drying grapes in GREECE and TURKEY, and the San Joaquin Valley of California. Growing season average mean temperatures are mostly 22 °C or higher. Subtropical and TROPICAL VITICULTURE for table grapes and wine, using mainly non-VINIFERA grape varieties, also falls into this temperature category.

Relationships of temperature, particularly during ripening, to wine qualities are discussed under CLIMATE AND WINE QUALITY.   J.G. & R.E.S.

Casteel, E. (ed.), *Oregon Winegrapes Growers' Guide* (4th edn., Portland, Ore., 1992).

Gladstones, J., *Viticulture and Environment* (Adelaide, 1992).

Jackson, D., and Schuster, D., *The Production of Grapes and Wine in Cool Climates* (Nelson and Melbourne, 1987).

Coonawarra, important wine region with 43 producers in 2014 in South Australia's Limestone Coast Zone and traditionally the most popularly revered area of AUSTRALIA for Cabernet Sauvignon, grown on its famous strip of TERRA ROSSA soil. Its cool, MEDITERRANEAN climate is very similar to that of Bordeaux; it is slightly warmer and has less growing season rainfall, but Cabernet Sauvignon is normally picked in the second half of April (or, in Bordeaux terms, the second half of October). For more detail, see SOUTH AUSTRALIA.

cooperage is a collective noun for wooden containers (as in 'small OAK cooperage') but has been more traditionally used for both the activities and workplace of **coopers**, those who make and repair small BARRELS and larger wooden VATS. At one time all wine or spirit producers of any size would have their own small cooperage, but today the craft is perpetuated mainly by specialist cooperage businesses. The French term is *tonnellerie*.

History

Until relatively recently, coopers played an important role not only in the wine business but in myriad aspects of daily life. Almost all containers—buckets, barrels, tanks—were made by coopers from various woods (see BARRELS, history). Barrels were made to hold salted fish, flour, gunpowder, oil, turpentine, salt, sugar, butter, and many other household commodities since they retain liquids safely, keep the elements out, and are easy to manœuvre.

Coopers' guilds were already established by the end of the 9th century and, during the Middle Ages, laws relating to apprenticeships, master–apprentice relations, and guild memberships were codified throughout Europe (with nepotism already playing its part). At the end of the 18th century, there were approximately 8,000 coopers in Paris alone. It is still possible to meet coopers who are the last in a line of craftsmen dating back to the 17th century. Such men, who can probably make barrels with handtools alone, may well have served traditional apprenticeships that often involve extensive work in different regions of their own countries as well as abroad.

As Europeans colonized the New World, they inevitably took their coopering skills with them. John Alden, one of the more famous early North American colonists of Plymouth, Massachusetts, was a master cooper and by 1648 there were enough coopers to form a guild in this New England colony. America's important export trade of staves and logs to Europe began slightly later in the 17th century, when the Spanish controlled large parts of what is now the United States.

During the 19th century, coopering remained an important craft, but the advent of metal (and later plastic) containers ultimately reduced coopering to an adjunct of the drinks business. More than 1 million barrels were made for salted herring in Britain in 1913, for example, but by 1953 the number had dropped to around one-tenth of this figure and now this business is virtually extinct.

American PROHIBITION had a dramatic impact on the sale of fine wines and spirits, and in turn on the cooperage business—particularly in the United States but also in the British Isles, where only those coopers working on beer barrels were unaffected. Before the Second World War, most beer barrels were made of wood and many breweries had their own cooperages, but by the early 1960s wooden barrels had been replaced by metal ones. In much of the wine industry, too, wood was replaced by concrete, stainless steel, and other neutral materials, particularly for larger tanks (see CONTAINERS).

Cooperage today

As wooden barrels are expensive to buy, use, and maintain, they tend to be used only for products whose sale price can justify such a major investment or, in the case of older containers, by those who have inherited them.

Cooperages are found wherever there is a wine or spirits business that needs barrels, notably in America, Scotland, and France but also in Italy, Spain, Portugal, Ireland, eastern Europe, Germany, Australia, and South Africa. They make new vats and barrels (see BARREL MAKING) and/or repair or maintain older barrels and vats (see BARREL MAINTENANCE and BARREL RENEWAL).

There are no serious industry analysts of the contemporary cooperage business, such as there are in the automotive or electronics industry, since it is effectively just a small part of the timber industry. Nor is there any official regulatory or inspection body as there is in the wine trade. Consequently, statistics related to the cooperage industry are little more than educated guesses. Naturally all coopers maintain that their oak is the best wood, entirely hand split and seasoned in the open air but that their competitors cut corners. In the absence of facts, winemakers have to rely on results rather than rhetoric.

United States The great majority of wooden barrels traded today are made in the American Midwest for the ageing of bourbon whiskey. It is estimated that in 2013 about 2 million barrels were made there, primarily by two cooperages. No one really knows how many American oak barrels are used in winemaking but it is likely that 80,000–100,000 go directly to wineries in the United States alone.

Nearly all American logs come from privately held forests in the eastern half of the United States, notably in Minnesota, Wisconsin, Kentucky, Arkansas, Tennessee, the Virginias, the Carolinas, and Missouri. These logs are purchased by stave mill operators, some of whom also run cooperages. Cooperage use accounts for about 3% of all American white oak harvested every year. Most American oak is used for furniture, construction, veneer, and pulp.

The logs are cut into appropriate lengths, quarter sawn, planed, and then sold to cooperages. Customers for American oak staves are found not only in bourbon country, but in cooperages in California, Australia—and Spain, where American oak has until recently been used almost exclusively for wine maturation, most notably in RIOJA and JEREZ, for the historical reasons outlined.

For whiskey to be called bourbon, it must, according to American government regulations that are a blessing to the cooperage business, be aged in a 'new, charred white oak barrel', so large quantities of used whiskey barrels are commercially available, many of them relatively new. Over 2 million used bourbon barrels are sold each year to Spain, Scotland, Ireland, Japan, Thailand, India, Puerto Rico, Canada, and Taiwan, as well as to producers of other North American spirits. Most of them are used to mature spirits: various brandies, rums, and whiskies. The Scotch whisky industry is a particularly important consumer of American oak, at any one time using approximately 13 million casks in total. In some cases American oak barrels are sent to Jerez en route to Scotland, where some distillers still prefer to use casks infused with sherry flavours as was the norm in the 19th century, when sherry was shipped in

cask to British wine merchants, who would then pass on these casks to the Scotch whisky industry. Now that sherry is no longer shipped in cask, some Scotch whisky distillers in Scotland have their barrels 'broken in' in Jerez with sherry.

France The French cooperage business is much smaller than its American counterpart but is much more important to the wine business. According to the Fédération Française de la Tonnellerie, around 525,000 French oak barrels were produced in 2012, two-thirds of which were exported. The domestic market for these barrels is primarily in BORDEAUX, BURGUNDY, and Cognac, where most French cooperages are located. Probably half of the exported barrels go to the United States. The balance is shipped to 30 other countries, most notably Italy, Australia, New Zealand, South Africa, Chile, Argentina, and Germany. As well as selling to Bordeaux, Burgundy, Cognac, and Armagnac, French cooperages are also developing new 'export' markets selling to ambitious winemakers in French regions that had abandoned new barrels. The RHÔNE, LANGUEDOC, ROUSSILLON, and SOUTH WEST FRANCE, as well as the LOIRE and to a much lesser extent ALSACE, have all become important purchasers.

In France about one-third of all forests are owned by local or national government. However, the sale of over 80% of all lots, carefully delineated groups of trees, is administered by the Office National des Forêts (ONF). In September and October, wood auctions are held all over France but for the buyer of oak destined to be turned into barrels and vats the most important auctions are held in Nevers, Châteauroux, and Moulins.

A potential buyer bids on the trees in a delineated section, which should be at least 100 and preferably well over 120, sometimes 160, years old before providing suitable wood for casks. Buyers have the right to go into the forest, measure the trees, even to bore into them 30 cm/12 in to see how straight is the GRAIN. They must decide how much of each type of wood there is, how it can be used, and, of course, how much they should bid.

As not every tree in an auction lot can be used for STAVES, French cooperages usually work with wood brokers who have other customers. The most valuable part of a tree is that with the tightest and straightest grains which can be used for panelling. The furniture and construction industries are important customers.

French barrels cost at least double those made of American oak. French logs are much more expensive because they must be hand split rather than machine sawn and demand more expensive drying methods. (see BARREL MAKING). French cooperages also tend to be smaller and less automated than their American counterpars. But the special qualities of French oak ensure that it is the most sought after by modern winemakers and able to command a considerable premium.

As the use of French oak has become more widespread, staves are now shipped all over the world, notably to Australia, Italy, South America, South Africa, America, Spain, and Portugal, where they may be made up into barrels in local cooperages.

No system of APPELLATION CONTRÔLÉE limits the period of time French oak barrels may be used for any wine or spirit. Consequently the sale of used French oak barrels is not as organized as that for American barrels. In Burgundy, producers often use most of their new barrels for their grandest appellations and lesser appellations get proportionately fewer new barrels. In Bordeaux, one proprietor will often own several châteaux and will treat his or her most prestigious property to the luxury of new oak before passing the barrels down the chain to a lowlier property. Alternatively, used barrels are sold to wineries unable to command the sort of price that can support expensive new barrels, or where winemakers do not want the taste of new oak. In the New World, used barrels are often traded between wineries. Relatively young ones, especially those used for white wine, are highly valued, but barrels more than ten years old are usually sold to be cut in half for flower planters.

Hungary There are two major cooperages in Hungary, both affiliated to French cooperages, and many smaller ones.

Italy In Italy, a relatively small but lively cooperage industry makes barrels and vats primarily with oak imported from France and Slavonia (eastern Croatia).

Spain Barrels have been important to the Spanish wine and sherry industries for centuries and the cooper's craft is sustained there. In Jerez, new barrels are spurned for the maturation of fine SHERRY and will probably be used at least three times for FERMENTATION before being used to mature a top-quality OLOROSO. The older a cask, the more expensive it is, and some bodegas boast casks (or butts as they are usually called here) that are more than 200 years old.

Portugal The demands of the port industry, and a ready supply of Portuguese oak, have kept the cooper's craft alive in northern Portugal so that French coopers have even imported Portuguese craftsmen.

Australia Distance from most of the world's established coopers has inspired the establishment of several cooperages in South Australia, the wine state.   M.K.

Kilby, K., *The Cooper and his Trade* (London, 1971).

Taransaud, J., *Le Livre de la tonnellerie* (Paris, 1976).

co-operatives, ventures owned jointly by a number of different members, are extremely important as wine producers and have the advantage for their members of pooling winemaking and marketing resources and costs. Collectively, they usually have access to a broad range of financial advantages over individual producers, particularly subsidies in the EU, although these have been declining. In most countries they also enjoy the commercial advantage of being able to describe their wines as bottled by the producer, using such reassuring phrases as MIS(E) EN BOUTEILLE *à la propriété* and ERZEUGERABFÜLLUNG more usually associated with much smaller, individually managed wine enterprises. The better co-operatives are becoming increasingly skilled not just at winemaking but also at marketing specific bottlings designed to look and taste every bit as distinctive as the individually produced competition. The worst co-operatives play almost exclusively with subsidies and politics. Co-operatives are at their strongest in areas where wine's selling price is relatively low and where the average size of individual holdings is small, although co-operatives are also quite significant in CHAMPAGNE and there are several in the MÉDOC, for example. The majority of wine co-operatives were formed in the early 1930s in the immediate aftermath of the Depression.

France

France's *caves coopératives* (often referred to locally simply as *la cave*) are declining in number and influence, but in 2013 the national total of 690 were still responsible for half of all wine produced in France. The average number of members, or *adhérents*, of each co-operative is also declining (down from 240 in the 1960s to 122 in 2013) as holdings are amalgamated and members have been encouraged to grub up less suitable vineyards by the EU VINE PULL SCHEME. Co-operatives are a particularly strong force in the LANGUEDOC and ROUSSILLON, the greater RHÔNE Valley, PROVENCE, and CORSICA, where *la cave* can dominate local economic life. As subsidies and compulsory DISTILLATION have declined, co-operatives are being restructured and amalgamated into much bigger groupings. Co-ops' speciality is IGP wine—they produce more than 70% of the French total—but those which have established a reputation for particularly sound AOC wines sold outside their own region include Union CHAMPAGNE, La Chablisienne of CHABLIS, the co-operative at Tain l'HERMITAGE, the Plaimont co-operative organization in GASCONY, and a number of ALSACE co-operatives, notably that of Turckheim. The average quality of wine made in French co-ops has improved since the early 1990s but their sales

and marketing expertise has not in general, a major factor in France's CRISE VITICOLE.

www.coopdefrance.coop/fr/39/vin/

Germany

In GERMANY, co-operatives (known as *Winzergenossenschaft*, *Winzerverein*, *Winzervereinigung*, *Weingärtnergenossenschaft*, or *Weinbauernverband*) have played an increasingly significant role since 1868, when the first German wine co-operative was formally established in the AHR. As outlined in GERMAN HISTORY, co-operatives offered smallholders the chance to compete in the newly quality-conscious German wine market of the late 19th and early 20th centuries.

Nearly two in every three German vine-growers today belong to the local co-operative, although their vineyards are often a small, part-time activity which therefore, cumulatively, represent almost a third of the total German area under vine. Many of the 13 wine regions of Germany have a central co-operative cellar, or ZENTRALKELLEREI, which is fed grapes, wine, or must by more localized co-operatives. By 2014, the number of co-operatives in Germany had fallen to 179, of which 114 made wine on the premises.

The co-operative movement is particularly strong, and particularly successful, in the most southerly region of BADEN, where about 85% of all wine produced from over 50 individual co-operatives is sold under the auspices of the giant central Badischer Winzerkeller at Breisach. This vast enterprise is larger than any winery in France. The Baden co-operatives have been particularly active in transcending the co-operative image of quantity over quality by developing superior, small volume bottlings of distinctive wines. Co-operatives are also extremely important in the WÜRTTEMBERG region, where there are 41 co-operatives whose central cellar is at Möglingen. They are also important in Germany's four smallest regions, SAALE-UNSTRUT, AHR, HESSISCHE BERGSTRASSE, and SACHSEN. In the MOSEL region, the central co-operative cellar, Moselland of Bernkastel, not only processes about 20% of the region's output, but also handles winemaking and marketing for three central co-operatives in the Pfalz, Rheinhessen, and Nahe. In the other classic wine region, the RHEINGAU, the role of co-operative cellars is very much less significant.

Italy

In Italy, the *cantina sociale* is no less important, accounting for about 50% of the country's production. EU policies have favoured co-operatives in the past, often as a result of wily or politically well-connected operators of them. As EU subsidies dwindle, however, the quality of the wine, and the ability to run the co-operative on a commercial basis, becomes increasingly important. One of the most respected Italian co-operatives, in the far north west, is the Produttori del BARBARESCO, whose origins are 19th century. The influence of the *cantina sociale*, or *Kellereigenossenschaft* in German, is particularly strong in TRENTINO-ALTO ADIGE, where Cavit, incorporating eleven wineries and 4,500 members, is the region's biggest producer. In VENETO, co-operatives have traditionally been responsible for the bulk of production, particularly in Verona, where a large number of producers of Soave and Valpolicella either buy, or supplement their production through purchases, from the local co-op.

The co-operative Riunite of EMILIA-ROMAGNA was famous in the early 1980s for engulfing the United States, and other markets, in a tidal wave of LAMBRUSCO. Cantine Leonardo da Vinci, the Cantine di Montalcino, and the Cantina di Scansano are some of TUSCANY's better co-operatives. Further south, quantity, and not always quality, is the chief characteristic of the co-operatives that proliferate practically wherever the vine is grown, although Cantina di Taburno with Luigi Moio as CONSULTANT is a leading light. The Copertino co-operative in PUGLIA makes a good job of its eponymous red. The islands SARDINIA and SICILY are dominated by co-operatives, of which Settesoli in Sicily and Santadi in Sardinia are models of quality. Settesoli has cooperated in the local research institute in CLONAL SELECTION, variety and soil matching, and the conservation of almost extinct INDIGENOUS VARIETIES—all of which have helped to improve and increase wine quality in Sicily.

Spain and Portugal

As in Italy, co-operatives are extremely important in Iberia, where grapes are so often grown alongside other crops. More than 60% of each vintage was delivered to one of Spain's 1,000 wine co-operatives or Portugal's 300 (see PORTUGAL, history) in the late 1980s, although the proportion had dropped to 55% by 2014 in Spain, and after Portugal's entry into the EU in 1986 the private sector has grown significantly as regulations which favoured production by the co-operatives were relaxed and EU funds resulted in substantial investment in the wine industry. In consequence, by 2011, Portugal had 90 active co-operatives accounting for 43% of the country's production.

Although the movement began in the early years of the 20th century, it substantially increased in importance in the 1950s, when the wine market was relatively depressed. One of the earliest wine co-operatives was in Olite in NAVARRA, where the movement is particularly powerful and where it can absorb as much as 90% of grape production, although here, as elsewhere, links are being forged with individual producers to increase overall quality and technical expertise. It was only in the 1980s that many Iberian co-operatives even began to

consider bottling wine, so much of their produce was sold off either for DISTILLATION or as BULK WINE and even today they bottle only about 10% of their production. Co-ops are present in most Spanish wine regions but only a handful of small or mid-sized operations such as Martín Códax in RÍAS BAIXAS or the Capçanes, Masroig, and Falset co-ops in MONTSANT make wines of serious quality. In the vineyard vastness of La MANCHA, there are about 100 co-operatives of very varied quality, while YECLA and JUMILLA have export-minded co-operatives whose level of modern equipment and expertise is considerably above average. In the fortified wine regions of JEREZ, much of the rest of ANDALUCÍA, and the DOURO, co-operatives are less important than the long-standing links between vinegrowers and individual wine producers. The 20th-century Portuguese table wine industry was revolutionized by the government's formation of co-operatives, however not always for the better (see DÃO), although fortunately the 21st century has seen a greater focus on quality over quantity and a more vibrant private sector.

Rest of the world

Practically wherever wine is made, co-operatives thrive, although the movement is not particularly strong in the UNITED STATES and has had its own variants in eastern Europe. Co-operatives have played a particularly important role in the development of the wine industry in SOUTH AFRICA and ARGENTINA.

Copertino, DOC for robust red wine made mainly from NEGROAMARO grapes on relatively flat terrain in south east Italy. For more details, see PUGLIA. The co-operative winery of Copertino has begun identifying superior vineyard sites within the DOC.

co-pigmentation, a mechanism of colour stabilization, involving the interaction of ANTHOCYANIN pigments with another molecule (co-pigment).

In aqueous media, anthocyanins are present under different forms in equilibrium, including red and violet pigment species and colourless hydrated forms. The latter predominate at mildly acidic PH values such as encountered in plant cell VACUOLES and in wine. However, the anthocyanin pigmented forms stack vertically with other species present in the solution (co-pigments) to form complexes from which water is excluded. This results in enhanced colour intensity due to a shift of the balance from the colourless hydrated forms towards the dehydrated pigment forms involved in these stable complexes. The role of co-pigmentation in wine colour can be estimated by comparing red colour intensity before and after disruption of co-pigmentation complexes by dilution in a wine-like buffer. Co-pigmentation has been reported

to account for 30 to 50% of the colour of young red wines, on the basis of such measurements.

V.C.

Boulton, R., 'The copigmentation of anthocyanins and its role in the color of red wine: a critical review', *American Journal of Enology and Viticulture*, 52/2 (2001), 67–87.

Escribano-Bailon, M. T., and Santos-Buelga, C., 'Anthocyanin copigmentation—evaluation, mechanisms and implications for the colour of red wines', *Current Organic Chemistry*, 16/6 (2012), 715–23. doi: 10.2174/138527212799957977.

copita, special tulip-shaped glass in which SHERRY is customarily served in Spain. It is designed to maximize the AROMA, and larger sizes can be used as a glass for general wine TASTING. See GLASSES.

copper, a micronutrient required in very small concentrations for healthy vine growth. Copper is toxic to plants except in very dilute concentrations. Reports of copper deficiencies in vineyards are rare, probably because of the very small requirements by the vines, but also because of the widespread use of FUNGICIDES containing copper. In acid soils, the copper from fungicide sprays can actually reach toxic levels and some parts of the MÉDOC have been affected by copper toxicity. After the annual application of several kg of copper per ha, as in BORDEAUX MIXTURE, for about a century, the level of copper in the soil can be toxic and the vine growth became severely stunted. Generous applications of ORGANIC MATTER make the copper make less available to the vines. Additions of lime will help to neutralize the toxic effect of copper by raising the SOIL pH. See also CASSE.

R.E.S. & R.E.W.

Delas, J., 'Copper toxicity in viticultural soils', in P. L'Hermite and J. Dehandtschutter (eds.), *Copper in animal wastes and sewage sludge* (Springer, 1981).

Corbeau. See CHARBONO.

Corbières, quantitatively significant appellation in the Languedoc region of southern France producing some excitingly dense, herby red wines, a small amount of rosé, and a little increasingly well-made white wine from just over 10,000 ha/25,000 acres of vineyard in 2012. The terrain here in the Pyrenean foothills (see map under LANGUEDOC) is extremely varied, and so hilly that it is difficult to generalize about soil types and TOPOGRAPHY. In recognition of this, the appellation was in the 1990s subdivided into 11 so-called TERROIRS, although not without a certain amount of local dissent. The basic distinctions in this southernmost corner of the Aude *département* are between coastal zones influenced by the Mediterranean, the northern strip on the Montagne d'Alaric (some of which has more in common with MINERVOIS), the westernmost vineyards, which are cooled both by Atlantic influence and by their ELEVA-TION, and the rugged, mountainous terrain in the south and centre in which the FITOU appellation forms two enclaves.

Vineyards in the south west of the appellation are as high as 300 to 450 m (980–1,500 ft) above sea level, and HARVEST may not take place until well into October, while those in the Sigean area are right on the coast and can vary enormously in elevation but the high average temperatures and very low annual rainfall are partly compensated for by the marine influence. One of the most admired terroirs is that of Boutenac in the hills south of Lézignan, which has particularly poor soils on a LIMESTONE base in what is known locally as Corbières' 'golden triangle'. In 2005, **Corbières Boutenac** was granted its own 150-ha subappellation for wines that, unusually, must contain between 30 and 50% Carignan and satisfy certain minimum ageing periods.

With terrain this extensive and this varied, it is perhaps hardly surprising that progress within the appellation can become enmired in local politics.

In AOC Corbières, Syrah, Mourvèdre, Grenache Noir, and Lladoner Pelut must represent at least half the blend in all red wines, and the once-dominant Carignan may not make up more than half. Some producers particularly value the spice and concentration of wine from old vines, which in Corbières effectively means old Carignan. Warmer parts of Corbières can ripen Mourvèdre on a regular basis. Plantings of Cinsaut, useful along with Syrah for rosé, are more limited here than in neighbouring Minervois. Picquepoul Noir, Terret, and Grenache Gris are also allowed in red and rosé Corbières with some of the white wine grapes allowed in the rosé. White Corbières, a rare but often refreshing dry wine, is made principally from Bourboulenc, Maccabéo/Macabeu, Grenache Blanc, Marsanne, Roussanne, and Vermentino, providing an interesting aromatic palette for the increasing number of producers prepared to experiment with superior white winemaking. CO-OPERATIVES, Embrès-et-Castelmaure and Tuchan/Mont Tauch being particularly quality conscious, dominate the region, but there are many seriously ambitious individual estates offering keenly priced wines with considerable individuality.

Simms, P. and S., *The Wines of Corbières & Fitou* (Toulouse, 1991).

cordon, part of the vine's woody framework, arising from the top of the trunk and on which arms are borne (see diagram under PRUNING). Cordons can be at any angle but are generally trained along horizontal WIRES, or shallowly sloped wires as in some TENDONE trellises. The most common arrangement is a bilateral cordon in which two horizontal cordons are arranged in opposite directions from the top of the trunk, but any number of arrangements are possible. The unilateral cordon is common in some parts of Europe. Because of ease of management and MECHANIZATION, SPUR PRUNING using horizontal cordons is being increasingly adopted in the New World. Usually the cordon is trained to its permanent position and remains there. See vine-TRAINING SYSTEMS.   B.G.C. & R.E.S.

cordon de Royat, an old form of CORDON TRAINING used in France for wine grapes since the end of the 19th century (see illustration below). The system was proposed by Lefebvre, director of the French agricultural school of Royat. The classic form is a unilateral CORDON on a short trunk (about 30 to 50 cm (12–20 in)), the term unilateral meaning that the cordon is trained only to one side of the trunk. The cordon extends mostly from one vine to another. The vines are normally SPUR PRUNED to two-bud spurs. The number of spurs is limited for each variety under APPELLATION laws: in Burgundy, for example, to four spurs each for Pinot Noir and Chardonnay vines, and to eight for Gamay.   R.E.S.

cordon training, a form of VINE TRAINING in which the trunk terminates in a CORDON, and the vine is then typically subjected to SPUR PRUNING. The alternative is HEAD TRAINING, where the vines are usually subjected to CANE PRUNING. The cordon is normally horizontal and can be unilateral (trained only to one side of the trunk) or bilateral (to both sides). See also CORDON DE ROYAT and PRUNING.   R.E.S.

corkage, charge customarily levied in a restaurant for each bottle of wine brought in and consumed on the premises rather than bought from the restaurant's own selection (although see also BYO). The term is derived from the fact that the number of corks pulled represents the number of bottles consumed. There is considerable variation in the amount charged, and the grace with which the practice is accepted.

corked, pejorative tasting term for a wine spoiled by a cork stopper contaminated with CORK TAINT. A wine spoiled by cork taint may also be described as **corky** and the condition is known as **corkiness**. This is one of the most serious wine FAULTS as in most cases it irrevocably imbues the wine with such a powerfully off-putting smell that it cannot be drunk with any enjoyment. The unpleasantly, almost mould-like, chemical smell of TCA is occasionally present in smaller doses that may initially be noticed only by noses particularly sensitive to it or particularly familiar with the wine, but the odour usually intensifies with aeration and it is difficult for tasters to enjoy a wine once their attention has been drawn to its existence. Even a low level of taint often results in a slight dulling effect on the bouquet and palate, and levels well below the threshold of most drinkers have been shown to suppress fruit characters significantly.

The problem of corkiness was perceived by the wine industry to have increased from the 1980s which soured relations between the wine and the cork industries and led to a marked increase in the use of alternative CLOSURES, particularly including SCREWCAPS and SYNTHETIC CLOSURES. In the second decade of the 21st century, the greatest competitor to cork in terms of performance appears to be the screwcap.

It is commonly, but erroneously, believed that a wine with small fragments of cork floating in it is 'corked'. This may be a SERVING fault but is certainly not a wine fault.

Chastaingt, M., 'Trop de vins sont bouchonnés, la grogne s'amplifie', *La Vigne*, 140 (Feb 2003), 28-33.

Taber, G., *To Cork or Not to Cork* (New York, 2007).

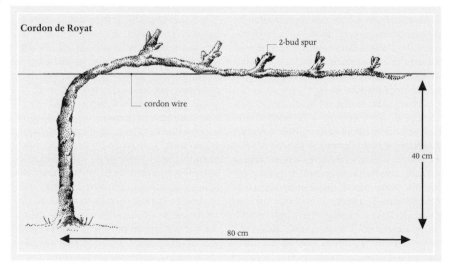

Cordon de Royat

2-bud spur

cordon wire

40 cm

80 cm

corks, wine bottle stoppers, without which the appreciation of fine wine, and in particular BOTTLE AGEING, might never have evolved. Cork's unique combination of qualities have made it by far the most popular stopper for wine, but in the late 20th century the science of wine production bounded ahead of the science of cork production, to the detriment of relations between the two industries (see CORKED wine).

History
See CLOSURES.

The cork tree
The cork tree, *Quercus suber*, is a relatively young species of OAK and is unusual in that its bark is so thick and resistant that it can be stripped from the trunk and large branches without hurting the tree.

It grows in sandy soils free of chalk and prefers annual rainfalls between 400 and 800 mm (15–30 in), temperatures which never fall below −5 °C/23 °F, and an elevation between 100 and 300 m (330–1,000 ft). This effectively restricts cork oaks to the coast of the western Mediterranean, particularly Spain, North Africa, and much of Portugal, where cork plays a significant role in the economy. The cork industry was born in Cataluña but was disrupted by the Spanish Civil War. The commercial stability of Algeria, which still grows more than 10% of the world's cork (though much less than Morocco), was called into question in the 1960s, so that, in the early 21st century, Portugal is the centre of the world's cork business and cork is an important contributor to the Portuguese economy. Portugal's cork forests, centred on the Alentejo, are today the most extensive, their 716,000 ha/ 1.77 million acres representing about 34% of the world's cork trees, significantly assisted in the late 1980s by EU grants.

Spain has the next largest total area planted with cork oaks, about 574,000 ha, most of them now in the south and west of the country, from which a high proportion of the cork is shipped across the border for processing in Portugal's more temperate climate (although, in the north east, Cataluña is still an important supplier of corks, especially to France and particularly to Champagne). So entrenched is the modern cork industry in Portugal—many of the processing centres are located just south of Oporto and therefore close to the PORT trade—that it produces more than half of the world's total output of cork, helped by imports not just from Spain but also from North Africa. Each cork region produces cork with slightly different characteristics. Portugal's most prized cork region is Evora. Although forestry management is important, the most significant determinants of quality occur at the processing stage, however.

Cork trees, if not a cork industry, also flourish along the west coast of Italy, on Sicily, Sardinia,

and Corsica, and along the Mediterranean coast of France, particularly in Provence, but little is made of these plantations commercially. There have also been trial plantings of cork trees in countries such as the United States and Japan.

The bark of the cork tree is sufficiently thick to yield commercially useful cork in its 25th year, and cork trees are regularly stripped during the summer months, no more than every nine years by Portuguese law. On average, modern husbandry means that each hectare of cork forest yields 230 kg/500 lbs of cork; the older the tree the more cork it will yield. Although the average life expectancy of a cork tree is about 170 years, there is one 200-year-old tree in the Montijo region south east of Portugal's capital Lisbon which has yielded 1,200 kg of cork from a single stripping. Cork farming, an activity often administered by the state, is an even longer-term undertaking than growing vines, which have an active wine-producing life of around 30 years.

The bark micro-structure is unique in that it consists of very small, closely packed, usually 14-sided cells which have undergone a process known as suberinization. This renders it light, elastic, inert, and relatively impermeable to gases and most liquids except particularly strong acids or bases. These qualities and its low conductivity make cork a useful and versatile commodity as an insulator, particularly for the automotive and construction industries, but the principal use for cork is still cork stoppers and, in particular, wine corks.

Cork processing
Modern cork processing follows traditional methods, albeit helped by increasingly sophisticated technology nowadays. The strips of cork bark yielded by the annual stripping are stacked and left outside for seasoning (just as other woods are in BARREL MAKING) for at least six months. Good drainage and airflow are important at this stage to minimize the risk of TCA development. Still in large strips, the cork is then boiled for about 90 minutes, both to make it more flexible and in an effort to kill off any moulds and other contaminants. The planks are then left to rest in the warehouse of the cork processing plant for three weeks before being sorted by hand and cut into strips as wide as the length of the final cork stopper. Corks are then punched out of these strips, usually by hand-operated punches but using an increasing degree of mechanization (machines are more efficient, but are so far unable to scrutinize each strip for impurities). Maximizing yield is a significant factor since only about 40% of all the commercially viable cork harvested is suitable for stoppers.

Corks are deliberately punched at right angles to the growth of the cork tree, so that any lenticels, occasional knots in the wood, remain

transverse and the risk of possible leakage due to lenticels is minimized. The ends of the cork stoppers are then polished to present a smooth surface to the wine.

Various treatments then follow, with the twin aims of cosmetic appeal and hygiene. Bleaching was done by immersing the corks in a bath of chlorine solution, but after it was discovered that chlorine increases the likelihood of TCA formation, and therefore the incidence of CORK TAINT, it has largely been superseded by hydrogen peroxide. Alternatives include moisture-saturated heat treatments to destroy moulds and BACTERIA but not cork's natural flexibility. After complaints from the wine industry in the late 20th century, the major cork producers invested substantially in quality control and continue to refine their armoury in the battle against TCA incidence

Corks are then graded on visual quality (the fewer markings the higher the grade), branded (most corks today are marked not only with the branding specified by the wine bottler, but also with an indication of the cork supplier), and often coated with some paraffin or silicon-based product that increases their extractability and, in many cases, eases their passage through high-speed BOTTLING lines.

Finally, corks are sealed into large plastic bags, typically with SULFUR DIOXIDE as a disinfectant, although irradiation and simple holes for aeration are used as respectively more and less sophisticated alternatives. Subsequent storage conditions are important to minimize possible contamination. Corks should ideally be stored in a ventilated, odour-free environment at a temperature between 15 and 20 °C (59–68 °F) in a humidity of 50 to 70%. Poor cork storage conditions can dramatically increase TCA incidence.

The range available
Although the first cork stoppers were tapered, the development of CORKSCREWS made tightly fitting cylindrical corks the norm. Modern corks are available in varying lengths, from 25 to as much as 60 mm (1–2.3 in), according to the BOTTLE AGEING aspirations, or extravagant exhibitionism, of the wine producer. (GAJA of Barbaresco, for example, perhaps the most ambitious cork buyer, personally selects his 60 mm corks from a supplier in Sardinia.) The longer the cork, the longer it is likely to remain an intact and viable stopper (see RECORKING), although some oenologists argue that longer corks result in lower FILL LEVELS, which may prejudice AGEING. There is a limit to the length at which cork effectiveness can continue to increase, since most bottle necks allow only 50–55 mm of cork length to make contact with the glass. There is much less variation in diameter, however, with 24 mm being the norm, although corks 21 and 26 mm wide are

not unknown, depending on the inside width of the necks of BOTTLES used.

The quality of the cork material itself also determines the price and potential life of the stopper, and corks may be graded into eight different quality levels. The cheapest form of cork, developed in 1891 by an American businessman, John Smith, is cork agglomerate, occasionally called 'agglo', reassembled crumbs of cork which can offer some of the benefits of intact cork itself. A more recent development is the 'technical' cork, such as the Altec and Diam closures made from cork flour mixed with a synthetic component (the Diam version has been treated with supercritical CO_2, see CORK TAINT). Agglomerate corks with discs of natural cork at each end, such as Twin Top® from the world's biggest cork supplier Amorim, are also very popular. In 2013 Amorim launched Helix (see CLOSURES), made from cork but with some SCREWCAP-like features. The best-quality cork is that with the least markings. The longest, finest cork can cost five times as much as the cheapest, shortest agglomerate cork. However, since corks are graded on visual quality, this has no bearing on the likelihood of TCA or other taints.

Stopper corks with plastic tops are used for some wines, particularly FORTIFIED WINES and some SWEET WINES, a single bottle of which may be consumed over an extended period.

Corks for SPARKLING WINES, commonly known, with scant regard for appellation laws, as champagne corks, have to be made to very particular specifications. Initially cylindrical, they are much wider than normal corks, about 30 mm, and have to be (half) driven into the bottle-neck, forcing them into a mushroom shape. Champagne corks are held in place, against the force of the pressure of undissolved gas inside the bottle, by a wire muzzle. Because such corks are too wide to be punched whole from the bark of most cork oaks, and to moderate the cost of such a large cork, champagne corks are usually made from cork agglomerate with one, two, or occasionally three discs of natural cork stuck on to the end which goes into the bottle-neck and is in contact with the wine.

Clues from the cork

In general, the narrower and more misshapen a cork extracted from a bottle, the longer it has been there. This is a particularly useful clue to the likely age of a non-vintage sparkling wine, or at least to the time that has elapsed since DISGORGEMENT. It can also provide a clue to the likely age of any other non-vintage wine, or fine wine which has lost its label or, perhaps in the case of vintage PORT, never had one (although see also RECORKING).

Most fine wine corks are emblazoned with the name of the wine producer (if not the wine itself) and, often, the vintage. Different countries adopt different conventions. Italian corks, which fit particularly tightly into their narrow bottle-necks, are often marked with a two-letter regional code (UD for Udine on many FRIULI wine corks, for example). Most British wine bottlers brand their corks with a W followed by their own numerical code. The regular French message is simply MIS EN BOUTEILLE *à la propriété*.

A short agglomerate cork suggests that the bottler had little regard for the ageing ability of this wine, while a particularly long cork is indicative at least of ambition or optimism.

If a cork has crystals on the end that has been in contact with the wine (white in the case of a white wine and dyed dark red by a red wine), these are harmless TARTRATES. If a cork seems damp or mouldy at either end, this is not necessarily a sign of any wine fault. Some wine waiters are taught to smell the cork and present it to the customer as an essential part of wine SERVICE, but the state of a cork is no sure guide to the state of the wine it stoppered.

For alternatives to corks, including so-called 'plastic corks', see CLOSURES, CROWN CAPS, SCREWCAPS, and SYNTHETIC CLOSURES. See also OXYGEN TRANSMISSION RATE.

Taber, G., *To Cork or Not to Cork*, (New York, 2007).

corkscrews, wide range of devices for extracting CORKS from the necks of wine BOTTLES.

It might be thought that cork extraction would prove an easy matter with any simple screw device, given the relatively soft, resilient nature of the stopper. However, there have been many hundreds of inventions since the middle of the 18th century with the aim of producing a better, more efficient corkscrew, and as yet none has been accepted as the perfect instrument. In particular, no corkscrew has yet been shown to be infallible with old PORT corks so PORT TONGS are sometimes employed instead. The extraction operation can vary considerably. Corks vary in length and, as they accommodate to the shape of the bottle-neck, they can also vary in shape. Furthermore, cork undergoes ageing in old bottles and may partially disintegrate on extraction. The necks of old port bottles, for example, usually have a slightly bulbous form, so that the lower part of the cylindrical cork is weakened where it ballooned out and became cone shaped. Italian wine bottles tend to be narrow at the neck, tightly compressing corks and making them relatively difficult to penetrate.

History

The free-blown, onion-shaped wine bottles (see BOTTLES, history) of the 17th century did not have a standard size of neck. Under these circumstances, tapered corks made a satisfactory stopper, especially as a portion remained proud of the bottle top, facilitating manual removal. The mould-made cylindrical glass bottle which evolved from about 1740 could be BINNED horizontally to keep the cork moist and at the same time to save space. This necessitated a driven cylindrical cork of standard diameter and the removal of such a cork required a special tool.

Simple corkscrews leave the operator to do the work of screwing in the worm and pulling out the cork unassisted. Various modifications of handle, shaft, and worm can increase the efficiency of these manœuvres: the handle should be formed to give a good pulling grip; the shaft can be fitted with a metal disc, or button, to obtain more complete contact with the cork; and the worm should be a steel helix 5.7 cm/ 2.2 in long, of good open pitch, and have an outer diameter of between 0.8 and 1 cm.

Although it is possible that simple corkscrews were in use by the mid 17th century in England, the earliest extant examples date from the 1690s.

Mechanical corkscrews are designed to reduce the amount of physical effort required during the three manœuvres of piercing, pulling, and disposing of the cork. Mechanical hand-held corkscrews can never be used with the rapidity of an efficient wall- or bar-mounted mechanical instrument, although the modern hand-held **Lever Pull**, really a miniature bar-screw in concept, can be used at remarkable speed.

National characteristics

Until fairly recently, the best corkscrews from the points of view of function, design, and quality of workmanship were made in wine-neutral Britain. The two-lever Italian corkscrew with a gimlet-like worm overcame the erstwhile problem of their short, tight corks.

The Germans rarely used other than the centre worm and often combined this with an inventive use of springs and ball bearings. In 1882, Karl Wienke of Rostock, Mecklenburg, conceived of using a knife-like handle as a lever. Known affectionately as the **waiter's friend**, it is still the essential tool of a SOMMELIER worldwide. The development of an articulated lever makes this model even easier to use as the cork is extracted in two stages, keeping it more upright and less likely to break.

The French were keen on nickel plating, contrasting with the bronzed finish of English pieces; well demonstrated by the lazy tongs models of both countries.

Americans printed the wooden handles with advertisements and became largely preoccupied with self-pullers and other models which used the frame of the corkscrew as a fulcrum and derived from the French *à cage* principle. **Screwpull**, invented in the 1970s by Herbert Allen, is the culmination of applying this principle using strong modern plastics and a teflon-coated helix. Many other manufacturers today use teflon-coated worms, copying the Screwpull principles.

A two-pronged extractor became jokingly known as the **butler's friend**, as it enabled the cork to be extracted and replaced without evident damage and, possibly, the wine to be replaced with one less fine.   B.M.W. & R.N.H.B.

Bibliographical note: Literally dozens of books about corkscrews have been published, with Donald Bull, Ron Maclean, and Ferd Peters particularly prolific authors of them.

cork taint

. Although research results vary, between 3 and 5% of all wines sealed under cork display a musty taint. This is caused by a number of potent organic compounds, the most significant of which is 2,4,6-trichloroanisole or TCA. These taint compounds are metabolic products of fungi naturally present in cork, or which have grown in the cork at various processing stages. Initially, the occurrence of this taint was ascribed to the washing of cork planks by chlorine-containing bleaches; these have since been replaced by peroxide, but cork taint has remained a problem. It seems that the structure of cork, which is permeated by fine pores (lenticels) to facilitate gas exchange, will always harbour fungi with the potential to produce taint compounds. A study by Duncan, Gibson, and Obradovic has demonstrated the presence of TCA in the bark of cork trees in a Portuguese cork forest. See CHLOROANISOLES. The effect of cork taint on the wine is often characterized as an off-putting, mouldy, wet cardboard or wet dog character. It suppresses fruit and shortens the length of finish of the wine. In its most subtle form, cork taint has a slight dulling effect on the bouquet and palate. At its extreme, high levels of cork taint render a wine quite unapproachable.

Only tiny amounts of TCA are needed to cause a taint problem since its aroma detection threshold in wine is about 3–4 ng/l. The cork industry has searched in earnest for methods to eradicate TCA from corks, and two new directions show promise. Oeneo's Diamant procedure, using supercritical carbon dioxide, has proved successful in stripping TCA from the cork flour used to make its popular DIAM closure; however, it is unsuitable for treating whole natural corks. Amorim's steam-based ROSA cleaning process removes most, but not all, of the TCA. OZONE is sometimes used as a preventive measure but its effectiveness is uncertain. The adoption by many cork producers of gas chromatography–mass spectrometry as a TCA detection tool has improved cork-quality control measures but it seems unlikely that it will ever prove possible to completely eradicate taint compounds from cork. However, an AUSTRALIAN WINE RESEARCH INSTITUTE study has

shown that cork may sometimes actually absorb TCA and other chloroanisoles from contaminated wine.

Research has identified the potential contribution of chemicals other than TCA to taint in wine. These include other chloroanisoles such as TeCA and PCA (see TETRACHLOROANISOLE), as well as alternatives to chloroanisoles. MDMP (see METHOXY-DIMETHYLPYRAZINE) has been identified as a key compound responsible for a 'fungal must' taint in wines that is possibly second only to TCA. TBA (see TRIBROMOANISOLE) also creates musty aromas in wine but is caused by contamination from the winery environment. This tallies with the observation that 'cork taint' can come from sources other than the cork: most notably from wooden structures in wineries that have been chemically treated, though the taint may still be transferred to the wine via the secondary contamination of the cork. But despite a few fairly high-profile instances of winery contamination, it seems that the cork is the culprit in the vast majority of cases.   P.J.W., T.M.S., & J.A.G.

Capone, D., et al., 'Flavour "scalping" by wine bottle closures', *Australian and New Zealand Wine Industry Journal*, 18/5 (2003), 16–20.

Chatonnet, P., et al., 'Identification and responsibility of 2,4,6-tribromoanisole in musty, corked odors in wine', *Journal of Agricultural and Food Chemistry*, 52 (2004), 1255–62.

Duncan, B. C., Gibson, R. L., and Obradovic, D., '2,4,6-trichloroanisole and cork production', *Australian and New Zealand Wine Industry Journal*, 12/2 (1997), 180–4.

Prak, S., et al., 'Fungal strains isolated from cork stoppers and the formation of 2,4,6-trichloroanisole involved in the cork taint of wine', *Food Microbiology*, 24 (2007), 271–80.

Simpson, R. F., Capone D. L., and Sefton, M. A., 'Isolation and identification of 2-methoxy-3,5-dimethylpyrazine, a potent musty compound isolated from wine corks', *Journal of Agricultural and Food Chemistry*, 25 (2004), 5245–430.

Stelzer, T., *Taming the Screw: A Manual for Winemaking with Screw Caps* (Brisbane, 2005).

corky bark, virus-like disease and one of the few which can kill vines. It is one of a complex of diseases known as RUGOSE WOOD. Symptoms of the disease resemble another one of the VIRUS DISEASES, LEAFROLL VIRUS, in that, during autumn, leaves turn red or yellow and roll downwards. Vines infected with corky bark retain their leaves after they would naturally have fallen. It can be transmitted to healthy grapevines by the longtailed mealybug *Pseudococcus longispinus*. There is no control for infected vineyards, and vine removal is the only solution if many vines are infected.   R.E.S.

Cornalin, ancient and almost extinct variety from AOSTA that was shown to be identical to

HUMAGNE ROUGE in the Swiss Valais by DNA PROFILING. It is therefore an offspring of ROUGE DU PAYS, confusingly renamed Cornalin in Valais in 1972.   J.V.

Cornas, red wine appellation in the northern RHÔNE (see map) with the potential to provide serious if rather earlier-maturing challengers to HERMITAGE on the opposite bank to the north. Cornas was renowned in the era of CHARLEMAGNE, and in the 18th century, but many of the terraced vineyards on its steep south-facing granite slopes fell into decline in the early 20th century. The appellation experienced a revival of interest in the late 1980s with the arrival of ambitious newcomers prepared to re-establish the TERRACES needed for high-quality vineyards, so that by 2013 there were 131 ha/324 acres of vineyards in production. Consultant OENOLOGIST Jean-Luc Colombo established a base here in the 1990s began making ultra-modern wine very unlike that of Auguste Clape, the standard-bearer during the lean years of the 1970s. Perhaps because Clape's very traditional wines demand considerable BOTTLE AGE, Cornas gained a reputation as a long-living wine, but the likes of Thierry Allemand, Domaine Courbis, Eric et Joël Durand, Mark Haisma, Vincent Paris, and Domaine du Tunnel are making a much more luscious style of Cornas.

Many of the best slopes such as Les Renards in the south are well sheltered from the cold north winds and enjoy some of the best positions in the northern Rhône. Cornas can provide some of the most satisfying red wine drinking, and offers a much more uniform and dependable quality level than the extensive ST-JOSEPH appellation to the immediate north.

Livingstone-Learmonth, J., *The Wines of the Northern Rhône* (Berkeley, 2005).

Cornell University has conducted viticultural research at its New York State Agricultural Experiment Station (NYSAES) in Geneva, NY, since the 1880s. VINE breeders have released 57 varieties of juice, table, and wine grapes since 1906. As part of the breeding programme, DISEASE-RESISTANT and winter-hardy AMERICAN VINE SPECIES are crossed with VINIFERA as well as with Asian species of the VITIS genus. The USDA-ARS Plant Genetic Resources Unit at Geneva makes over 1, 300 genotypes of cold-hardy *Vitis* germplasm available for grape breeders around the world.

The principles of sunlight utilization in grape canopies were elucidated by Dr Nelson SHAULIS leading to modern CANOPY MANAGEMENT such as shoot positioning and the GENEVA DOUBLE CURTAIN training system. The modern mechanical grape harvester was also developed by Shaulis, E. S. Shepardson, and grower Roy Orton.

Oenology studies at Cornell began in the 1960s. CAYUGA WHITE, Cornell's first wine grape variety, was released in 1972. More recent releases include CHARDONEL (1990), TRAMINETTE (1996), Valvin Muscat (2006), and Arandell (2013). Studies in microbiology, fermentation, flavour chemistry, and wine production are ongoing. Cornell's plant pathologists, grape physiologists, entomologists, extension specialists, and others develop technologies to enhance the quality and TERROIR of New York's grapes and wines and to sustainably control diseases and pests.

Cornell recently instituted new undergraduate degrees in OENOLOGY and VITICULTURE, with teaching at Geneva and on the main campus in Ithaca.

Cornifesto, minor dark grape in the DOURO, making light reds and ports.

Corse is the French, and therefore Corsican, name for CORSICA.

Corsica, mountainous Mediterranean island under French jurisdiction whose wines continue to improve. Situated on the 42nd parallel, Corsica is actually much closer to Italy (83 km/ 50 miles) than to France (170 km/100 miles). The island, about 180 km long and 80 km wide, comprises a series of mountains around which runs a perimeter of capes, gulfs, and sandy beaches. The average elevation is 586 m/1,900 ft. Corsica produces many different types and styles of wine. Average annual production is 350,000 hl/9.2 million gal with two-thirds of production now leaving the island. About 160,000 hl is sold in mainland France while 60,000 hl exported, particularly to the US, Germany, and Belgium.

History

The history of Corsica is closely related to that of Italy and this is reflected in the viticulture. Evidence suggests that vines were indigenous to the island and that their cultivation is one of the oldest in Europe, dating back to PHOENICIAN times and the settlement in 570 BC at Aleria on the east coast. Under Genoese rule in the 16th century, laws were enacted to control the harvest and tasting of wines; export of Corsican wines to destinations other than the republic of GENOA was banned. The English diarist James Boswell wrote in 1769, only a year after the Genoese ceded the island to France, of the excellence and diversity of Corsican wines. Napoleon was born in Ajaccio and Napoleonic laws still entitle the island to sell duty-free wines and tobacco.

The wine industry was revolutionized in the 1960s with the repatriation of many French *pieds noirs* from ALGERIA. Between 1960 and 1976 they imported and planted their own productive and often undistinguished vine varieties (see below) with such determination that the total vineyard area increased fourfold to over 30,000 ha producing 2 million hl of wine.

In 1980, however, as EU subsidies favoured uprooting vines rather than producing yet more liquid to be poured into the European WINE LAKE, Corsican vineyards began to be restructured, with a more determined emphasis on quality. The total area under vine was barely 6,000 ha/14,826 acres in 2013. The old highly productive varieties have been replaced by nobler vines, both imported and Corsican.

Geography and climate

With more than 20 peaks over 2,000 m/6,560 ft in elevation, over 55% of the surface area of the island lies above 400 m elevation, creating an array of valleys and hillsides with different elevations, expositions to wind and maritime influence, and MESOCLIMATES.

A variety of soils exists with four main soil types: granite on the west side; schist in the north and the Cap Corse, the mountainous finger of land pointing Francewards in the far north; chalk and clay in Patrimonio immediately south of it; and marly sand and alluvial soils from Solenzara to Bastia on the east coast.

Corsica is sunnier than anywhere in mainland France with an annual average of 2,885 hours, and, although total rainfall is higher than on the mainland, very little rain falls in the months of August and September. Due to the mountainous nature of Corsica, a jigsaw of MESOCLIMATES exists. The average temperature is higher in the north of the island than in the south. The sea, by absorbing heat during the day and radiating it at night, plays a major role in diminishing the day–night TEMPERATURE VARIABILITY. WIND is extremely influential, with Cap Corse, Bonifacio, and Calvi often experiencing winds of over 150 km/hour. Important winds include the mistral from Provence; libeccio from Gibraltar bringing rain; the dry, cold tramontane from the Alps; the damper gregale from the Appenines; and the warm sirocco blowing in from the Sahara.

Viticulture

Vines are cultivated up to 300 m/1,000 ft in elevation. Traditionally vines were pruned in GOBELET form but pruning and training methods such as CORDON DE ROYAT and single GUYOT became more widespread with mechanization. The most common ROOTSTOCK is 110 R. The strong winds help to keep the vines free of disease, the main viticultural concerns being DOWNY MILDEW, POWDERY MILDEW, and FLAVESCENCE DORÉE provoked by cicadelle attack. Irrigation is prohibited (often resulting in particularly intense flavours), and VINE DENSITY is an average 2,500 vines per ha (1,000 per acre).

Vine varieties

Niellucciu (SANGIOVESE), Sciacarellu (MAMMOLO), and VERMENTINO (Favorita) are the important Corsican varieties, representing more than two-thirds of all AOC wines, while INTERNATIONAL VARIETIES comprise about a quarter of vines planted on the island, having displaced the traditional varieties Cinsaut, Carignan, Grenache, and Alicante Bouschet.

A host of more traditional Corsican varieties exist but few are planted in any significant quantity. CRVI (Centre de Recherche Viticole Insulaire) is charged with researching and selecting 'new-old' Corsican varieties such as Bianco Gentile, Carcajolo, Codivarta, Morastellu, Genovese, Riminese, and Barbarossa.

Niellucciu, probably introduced by the Genoese before the 18th century, was the most planted variety, accounting for 35% of vineyard area or 2,380 ha/3,955 acres in 2013, many of them in the north of the island, where it thrives on the CALCAREOUS-clay soils of Patrimonio. Nielluccio may be vinified as either a rosé or, if well vinified, an intensely coloured red with good, structured tannins and a balanced acidity. Plantings of Sciacarellu had grown to 1,020 ha/ 2,520 acres ha by 2013. It is most successful on the granitic south west coast between Ajaccio and Sartène, producing relatively crisp, peppery reds and rosés, light in colour but high in alcohol. It is often blended with Nielluccio or Grenache.

The only significant white native grape variety is also the best travelled. Vermentino (1,156 ha/2,856 acres in 2013) is grown all over the island but performs best in the far north. It produces wines ranging from a pale, crisp version to a full-bodied golden wine with a ripe fruit flavour, depending on when it is picked. Although many of the wines are dry, sweet Vermentino wines are also produced. Codivarta, a white grape grown on the Cap Corse, is the only other local speciality cultivated to any appreciable extent.

Vinification

Almost 70% of all Corsican wine is made by CO-OPERATIVES, which, like some of the smaller wineries, took advantage of EU grants available for the installation of modern STAINLESS STEEL vats and REFRIGERATION equipment. White wines are usually therefore fermented at between 18 and 20 °C (64–8 °F), and clean-tasting rosés are made by SAIGNÉE and cool fermentation. MALOLACTIC CONVERSION is usually suppressed for whites and rosés. Red winemaking is relatively traditional with fermentation temperatures regularly rising to 30 °C, followed by malolactic conversion. The use of OAK was still relatively limited but increasing in the early 21st century, although Vermentino subjected to BARREL FERMENTATION and LEES STIRRING can yield good results, and wines such as the Cuvée des Gouverneurs from Orenga de Gaffory and Clos du Cardinal from Domaine Peraldi showed respectively that Niellucciu and Sciacarellu respond well to ageing in oak.

The wines produced

Rosé has become extremely important in Corsica, representing 67% of all production in 2013 (30% in 2003). In the same period white wine's share increased from 10 to 20%.

In 2013 total production was 368,000 hl (over 9.7 million gal), a substantial decrease on the 1988 figure of just under 600,000 hl. In 2013 AOC wines represented just over 30% of total production, while the proportion of wine which qualifies as IGP de l'Île de Beauté was nearly 64% with the remaining 6% being table wine.

Nine different appellations exist: Patrimonio, Ajaccio, Muscat de Cap Corse, Vin de Corse (Corsican wine), and Vin de Corse followed by Calvi, Coteaux du Cap Corse, Figari, Porto-Vecchio, or Sartène, all of them in the process of establishing their own viticultural identity.

Patrimonio Patrimonio on the north coast was the first region in Corsica to gain AC status, in 1968. About 410 ha of vines were shared between 33 domaines and YIELDS are restricted to 50 hl/ha (2.8 tons/acre). In the past, the wines of Patrimonio often included a mix of different imported grape varieties, notably Grenache, but from 2000, Niellucciu must account for 90% of the blend in red wines and Vermentino for 100% in the white. This has caused considerable controversy amongst the growers. Clos de Bernardi, one of the oldest estates reputed for its red, is situated in Patrimonio. Other growers such as Orenga de Gaffory, Gentile, Yves Leccia, and Arena have also invested much time and money to make dramatic improvements in quality.

Ajaccio Some of Corsica's highest vineyards are in this extensive zone on the west coast which produces mainly red and rosé wines from 14 producers with a total of 260 ha. Sciacarellu is the grape variety typical of the appellation and yields are set at 45 hl/ha. Domaine Peraldi, which overlooks the Bay of Ajaccio, is one of the best producers.

(Vin de) Corse This generic AC is the dominant one on the island comprising the wines grown on the eastern plain where the largest estates were established in the 1960s. These tend to be Corsica's least distinguished AC wines, although Niellucciu, Sciacarellu, and Grenache must represent at least 50% of any red or rosé, while whites must be at least 75% Vermentino. The 1,603 ha are shared between 17 individual producers and four co-ops.

(Vin de) Corse-Coteaux du Cap Corse The most northerly tip of the island, the Cap Corse, is renowned for its sweet Muscat and Rappu (a sweet MUSCAT-style red wine made from the ALEATICO vine variety). Some of Corsica's best dry white wines, such as Clos Nicrosi, are produced here on only 30 ha shared by five domaines.

(Vin de) Corse-Calvi Lower yields are required of this appellation which encompasses 227 ha and 12 producers in the north west of the island.

(Vin de) Corse-Figari comes from 130 ha of vines and six producers in the south west of the island where Clos Canarelli is the leading producer.

(Vin de) Corse-Porto Vecchio is made in the far south east on 88 ha of vines by four producers.

(Vin de) Corse-Sartène just north west of Figari has 226 ha of vineyard and ten producers.

Muscat du Cap Corse A full 37 producers make this distinctive VIN DOUX NATUREL from just 74 ha of MUSCAT BLANC À PETITS GRAINS on the northern tip of the island. Grapes are picked at between 14 and 15% POTENTIAL ALCOHOL and made, by the addition of alcohol at an early stage of fermentation, into a relatively elegant sweet wine. J.E.M.

www.vinsdecorse.com

Cortese, Italian white grape variety most closely associated with south east PIEMONTE, in the province of Alessandria where it was first recorded in the early 17th century. No relatives have so far been identified. Total plantings had reached almost 3,000 ha/7,000 acres by 2010 and it is the basis of no fewer than nine DOCs. Its most highly regarded wine is GAVI, produced initially to serve the fish restaurants of Genoa and the Ligurian coast not far to the south. The Cortese dell'Alto Monferrato a few miles west, like the Cortese grown on the Colli Tortonese, rarely achieves the ripeness, or winemaking proficiency, of Gavi. At its best, the wine is clean and fresh. The use of oak is usually misguided.

Corton and **Corton-Charlemagne**, respectively the great red and white GRANDS CRUS in ALOXE-CORTON in Burgundy's CÔTE D'OR.

Coruche, subregion of TEJO in central, southern Portugal.

Corvina, or **Corvina Veronese**, the dominant and best grape variety of VALPOLICELLA and BARDOLINO in north east Italy, producing fruity, red wines with a characteristic sour cherry twist on the finish. Wines from the better Valpolicella producers who reduced yields in the 1980s and 1990s demonstrated that lack of BODY was not an inherent characteristic of Corvina. Since then, it has enjoyed great success as the best variety for AMARONE. Producers such as Allegrini have also illustrated that wines made solely or predominantly from Corvina such as La Poja can be serious, barrel-aged reds. Corvina, sometimes called Cruina, has traditionally been confused with CORVINONE. DNA PROFILING at SAN MICHELE ALL'ADIGE in 2005 supported a parent–offspring relationship with RONDINELLA. Presumably fuelled by the popularity of Amarone, Italy's total plantings of Corvina Veronese increased substantially in the early 21st century to reach nearly 7,500 ha/18,525 acres by 2010.

Corvinone, red grape variety grown mainly in the VALPOLICELLA zone. It is so similar to CORVINA that it was long mistaken as merely a different CLONE of it although DNA profiling has established that it is a distinct variety. It is now highly regarded as a grape of specific use for such DRIED-GRAPE WINES as AMARONE and RECIOTO as its loose bunches and large berries make it particularly suited to DRYING. The Italian 2010 vine census noted that total plantings had grown to nearly 1,000 ha.

cosecha is Spanish for VINTAGE year.

Costa Rica in Central America saw its first commercial winery and limited plantings of Sauvignon Blanc, Pinot Noir, Syrah, and Grenache in late 2011 above the small city of Copey at an ELEVATION of 2,000 m/6,560 ft. Expertise was imported from Napa Valley.

Costers del Segre, small wine zone in north east Spain in semi-DESERT near the Catalan city of Lerida (see map under SPAIN) and in the lusher mountains bordering the Priorat DO to the east. The climate is severe. The thermometer often dips below freezing point in winter and exceeds 35 °C/95 °F in high summer. RAINFALL barely reaches 400 mm/15 in in a year. The River Segre, a tributary of the Ebro after which this fragmented DO is named, is little more than a seasonal stream.

The history of Costers del Segre was initially the history of one estate: Raimat, which covers 3,200 ha/7,900 acres of arid country 15 km/9 miles north west of Lerida. When Manuel Raventós, owner of CAVA producer CODORNÍU, first visited the property in 1914, he found infertile salt plains abandoned by farmers. An IRRIGATION artery, the Canal de Aragón y Cataluña, since transformed the estate into an oasis but it took over 50 years of planting cattle fodder, pine trees, and cereals before the soil was fit for vines. Today the Raimat vineyard covers 1,250 ha, which amounts to a third of the Costers del Segre DO. A labyrinthine irrigation system starts automatically whenever the temperature rises above 35 °C, and provides FROST protection when the thermometer falls below 1 °C. As a result, imported vine varieties such as Cabernet Sauvignon, Merlot, Pinot

Noir, and Chardonnay flourish alongside INDIGENOUS VARIETIES such as Tempranillo, Parellada, and Macabeo.

Elsewhere in the region, which splits into four separate subzones—Raimat, Artesa, Vall de Riu Corb, and Les Garrigues—other quality-conscious producers include Castell del Remei, Celler de Cantonella, Tomàs Cusiné, and L'Olivera. V. de la S.

Costières de Nîmes, the generally reliable and well-priced southernmost appellation of the RHÔNE. In French wine politics, it used to be considered part of the eastern LANGUEDOC but the climate, soil, topography—and wines—are closer to those just over the river in the southern Côtes du Rhône vineyards.

The relatively uniform soils are marked by large pebbles on gentle, typically south-facing slopes. A total of 25,000 ha/62,000 acres of land on the edge of the Camargue could qualify to produce wine for this appellation, and by 2013 4,193 ha/10,357 acres were dedicated to the production of appellation wine, about half of it red, and most of the rest rosé. This is an important zone for the production of IGP WINE. As in the nearby southern Rhône, Grenache is an important vine variety here and, with Mourvèdre and Syrah, must represent at least 60% of any red, with the last two constituting at least 20%. Carignan is in retreat, and Marselan may not represent more than 10%. This is an appellation in transition, not just geographically between the Languedoc and the Rhône, but temporally between being a BULK wine producer and a source of genuinely characterful, well-made wines. CO-OPERATIVES are less important here than in most of the Languedoc and most of the development and experimentation is taking place on dynamic, smaller estates.

Côt, or **Cot** is an important French synonym for the black grape variety of French origin also known as MALBEC and, in Cahors, Auxerrois.

Cotarella, Riccardo (1948–), one of Italy's most famous CONSULTANT oenologists, based in Umbria. Born in Orvieto, he graduated from the winemaking school in Conegliano in 1968 and started working for the Vaselli winery in Orvieto. Together with his brother Renzo (who is general manager for ANTINORI), he founded the Falesco winery at Montefiascone in 1979 with the aim of producing modern white wines to sell to the large bottlers. As the market for Italian wines began to change, Cotarella began to bottle his own wines. He leapt to prominence, however, with red wines from Umbria and Lazio based primarily on Merlot. Falesco's Montiano, first produced in 1993, became one of Italy's best known examples of this variety. His fame as a consultant was cemented when the 1993 Montevetrano, a red

wine from Salerno in Campania, was released. He now consults to wineries as diverse as Morgante in Sicily, Paola di Mauro in Lazio, Nottola and Castello di Volpaia in Tuscany, Terra di Lavoro in Campania, and La Carraia, Lamborghini, and Sportoletti in Umbria. In 1999 Cotarella and his brother acquired the Marciliano estate in Umbria. His wines are characterized by deep colour, richness, ripe fruit, low acid, and immense appeal. While his critics claim that he has been responsible for producing a more international style of wine, he and his brother can lay claim to having saved the indigenous white Roscetto or Rossetto vine from extinction, of which a complex barrel-aged version is produced, while also turning their attention to ALEATICO, of which they produce a sweet version. There is no doubt that he has improved quality in and focused a great deal of attention on previously little-known areas (not unlike Michel ROLLAND). In 2013 he was elected the president of Assoenologi, the Italian association of oenologists. D.C.G. & W.S.

Côte means literally 'slope' or 'hill' in French, **Côtes** is the plural, while **Coteau** (of which **Coteaux** is the plural) means much the same thing but possibly on a smaller scale. Since French vine-growers are great believers in the viticultural merits of hillsides, all of these make suitable wine names. Thus, any index of French wine names contains long lists of Côte, Côtes, and Coteaux de, du, de la, and des various place-names, suggesting, often with reason, that the wine comes from the slopes above these places. Some of these prefixes are eventually dropped, however. Côtes de Buzet, for example, was renamed plain BUZET in the late 1980s, and Côtes du Ventoux has become VENTOUX.

For this reason, and to save readers having to remember whether a wine is, for example, a Coteaux de or a Coteaux du Somewhere, such an entry would be listed under S for Somewhere, rather than under Coteaux. Their Côte and Côtes counterparts are listed similarly. The only exceptions to this are names in which the Côte, Côtes, or Coteaux are integral. They follow this entry.

Côte des Blancs, area of CHAMPAGNE on east-facing slopes south of Épernay noted for the quality of its Chardonnay grapes.

Côte d'Or, the heart of the BURGUNDY wine region in eastern France in the form of an escarpment supporting a narrow band of vineyards for nearly 50 km/30 miles southwards (and a touch west) from Dijon, capital of the *département* of the same name (see map under BURGUNDY). The name Côte d'Or apparently translates directly as 'golden slope', evoking its autumnal aspect, but some think it may be an abbreviation of Côte d'Orient, a reference to the fact that the escarpment on which the vines

flourish faces east. Viticulturally it is divided into two sectors, the Côte de NUITS, in which great red wines are made from the Pinot Noir vine, and the Côte de BEAUNE, where the reds are joined by the finest white wines made from Chardonnay.

The Côte d'Or represents the fault line separating the hills of the Morvan from the plain of the Saône, which, in the Jurassic period 195 to 135 million years BC, was an inland sea. The predominant rock is Jurassic LIMESTONE, which favours both Chardonnay and Pinot Noir vine varieties. However, the escarpment features many differing forms of limestone and other rocks. Oolitic limestone, which originated as a precipitation around marine debris of carbonate of lime from the seawater, is usefully porous, and provides good DRAINAGE compared with marlstone, which is made up of clay, sand, gravel, and marl, the result of decomposition of older mountains such as the Ardennes.

The escarpment is also broken up by streams—the Vouge in Vougeot, the Meuzin in Nuits-St-Georges, the Rhoin in Savigny, the Dheune and Avant-Dheune further south—running down from the hills eventually to join the Saône, and by dry valleys (*combes*) such as the Combe de Lavaux in Gevrey-Chambertin. These breaks vary the orientation of the vineyards: thus Clos-St-Jacques and Corton are both exposed more to the south than east while much of Corton-Charlemagne actually faces south west. The streams also affect the composition of the soil by bringing down alluvial deposits.

A cross-section of the Côte reveals topsoil too sparse on the hilltop and too fertile in the plain to produce wine of any quality. The vineyard area begins to the west of the Dijon–Lyons railway line but only the most basic wines made from Aligoté and Gamay are produced here. Approaching the main Dijon–Chagny road, the D974, the vineyards are still on flat, fertile land but Pinot Noir and Chardonnay are planted to produce BOURGOGNE Rouge and Bourgogne Blanc. These in turn give way to village APPELLATION vineyards; as the ground starts to slope upwards, drainage improves, and the soil is less fertile.

Where the slope becomes more pronounced and clay gives way to stonier topsoil, the vineyards are designated PREMIERS CRUS, reflecting the potential quality of the wines from land which drains well and enjoys greater exposure to the sun. The finest of these vineyards, in certain villages only, are classified as GRANDS CRUS (listed under BURGUNDY). The premier and grand cru vineyards are mainly at elevations between 250 and 300 m (800–1,000 ft) above sea level. Near the top of the slope, where the soil is almost too poor, there is usually a narrow band of village appellation vineyards providing fine but light wines.

Viticultural practices are relatively constant for both major grape varieties throughout the Côte d'Or. VINE DENSITY is notably high—about 10,000 vines per ha (4,000 per acre)—and vines are trained and pruned chiefly according to the single GUYOT system (although CORDON DE ROYAT is increasingly employed to restrict vigour in younger vines and those on over-productive rootstocks). Harvesting is still mostly manual, especially for Pinot Noir. Yields are usually restricted to 50 hl/ha (3 tons/acre) for red wines and 57 hl/ha (3.5 tons/acre) at village level, reduced by 2 hl/ha for premiers crus.

There are no set rules for the production of great red burgundy, and every domaine or NÉGOCIANT house revels in its own idiosyncrasies. Principal options include DESTEMMING of the grapes (wholly, partly, or not at all); MACERATION period; fermentation TEMPERATURE; length of BARREL MATURATION; type of OAK barrels; FINING regime; and the extent to which FILTRATION is practised. The better wines of the Côte d'Or are all matured for at least a year, more often 18 months, in 228-l (59-gal) oak BARRELS, a proportion of which are usually new. Before bottling, some producers fine and filter the wine; others prefer one treatment to the other; a few use neither in the belief that the wine thereby has more depth of flavour and capacity to evolve, even though it may throw a deposit.

The qualities of great red burgundy are not easy to judge young, especially since the wine tends to be less deeply coloured than equivalent wines from Bordeaux or the Rhône. When young, a fine burgundy should show a bouquet of soft red fruit, ranging from cherries to plums depending on the vineyard and vigneron; complexity comes with maturity, the fresh fruit components giving way to more evolved aromas, often redolent of truffles or undergrowth (sous-bois, according to French palates).

Some wines are weighty, others intensely elegant, but all should have concentration. Style depends in part on the character of the village: GEVREY-CHAMBERTIN, VOUGEOT, NUITS-ST-GEORGES, CORTON, and POMMARD tend to produce robust, long-lived wines; CHAMBOLLE-MUSIGNY, VOSNE-ROMANÉE, and VOLNAY epitomize finesse and elegance. Within each village, different vineyards display their individual characteristics according to the exact SOIL STRUCTURE, ELEVATION, and TOPOGRAPHY.

Differences in annual WEATHER patterns are crucial in determining quality in the region. Burgundy is at a climatic crossroads, experiencing Atlantic, Mediterranean, and Baltic weather systems. A cool breeze from the north (la bise) is ideal to temper anticyclonic conditions in the summer; a southern wind brings heat but also danger; HAIL and thunder often result when the warm wind swings round to the west, the wettest direction. This has become an increasing problem in recent

years with Volnay badly hailed in 2004, 2008, 2012, 2013, and 2014.

There is probably greater vintage variation in Burgundy than in any other wine region. In some VINTAGES–2004, 2008, and 2011 for instance–Pinot Noir grapes struggled to ripen fully, although growers who conscientiously restrict yields often produce excellent wines. The 1996 vintage, which produced fine wines for ageing, was unusual in that September sunshine ripened the grapes fully, judging by the sugar levels, yet cool nights maintained the acidity at levels normally associated with an unripe year. In other years, excessive rainfall can either swell the crop to produce dilute wines (as in 1982, 1992, and 2000) or encourage ROT (as in 1986 and 1994). Most difficult to judge are the hot vintages in which the fruit in the wine is either supported, or sometimes overwhelmed, by TANNINS (as in 1976 and 1983) or appears ultra-ripe (2003, 2009). Balance may be best achieved in those vintages where ripeness is only just attained, as in 2002 and 2010. However the greatest vintages of the past 40 years have been 1978, 1990, 1999, and, probably the finest of all, 2005. Certain vintages, such as 1985, 1989, 1997, and 2003 produce fully ripe grapes and many wines which are attractive to taste throughout their lives.

Great white burgundy is produced in the Côte de Beaune, notably in the villages of MEURSAULT, PULIGNY-MONTRACHET, and CHASSAGNE-MONTRACHET, along with a small enclave further north yielding the grand cru Corton-Charlemagne (see ALOXE-CORTON). The soils suited to Chardonnay production tend to be paler in colour than the iron-rich, redder soils on which the Pinot Noir thrives (see SOIL COLOUR). The Chardonnay vine is hardier than the Pinot, the grapes ripen more easily, and the wines require less delicate handling. It is easier to make good white burgundy than red but very little great white burgundy is made.

The grapes are pressed, usually without SKIN CONTACT, left to settle, then fermented in oak casks for up to a year (see BARREL FERMENTATION), although those with suitable cellars prefer to keep the wine for a second winter in wood. After the alcoholic FERMENTATION, the wines are racked into another set of barrels to remove the major deposits, the 'gross lees', but left on their fine LEES, which may be stirred up to nourish the wine (see LEES STIRRING), although this practice has been declining.

Fine white burgundy, when young, is more likely to show the character of the oak in which it has been vinified than the grapes from which it came. Hallmarks of quality are fullness of BODY, balance of ACIDITY, and persistence of flavour. Only after two or more years of bottle age will a fine Meursault or Puligny-Montrachet start to show the quality of the fruit. This will deepen with age and, although vegetal tones

may appear, they should not overwhelm the natural elegance of the wine. A village appellation wine should be at its best from between three and five years old, a premier cru from five to ten years, while a grand cru worthy of its status needs a full decade of BOTTLE AGEING but see also PREMATURE oxidation.

For more detail, see under names of individual villages or appellations. See BEAUNE, CÔTE DE and NUITS, CÔTE DE for a full list of the villages in each. To most of the villages and towns in the Côte d'Or was appended the name of their most famous vineyard, typically in the late 19th century. Thus, for example, Vosne became Vosne-Romanée and Puligny became Puligny-Montrachet.   J.T.C.M.

Coates, C., *The Wines of Burgundy* (Berkeley, 2008).

Morris, J., *Inside Burgundy* (London, 2010).

Norman, R., and Taylor C., *The Great Domaines of Burgundy* (3rd edn, London, 2010).

Pitiot, S., and Landrieu-Lussigny, M., *Climats et lieux-dits des Grands Vignobles de Bourgogne* (Paris, 2012).

Côte Rôtie

Côte Rôtie, one of the most exciting, if geographically extremely limited, red wine appellations in France, in the far north of the northern Rhône (see map under RHÔNE). In the 1970s, the area and its wines were somewhat moribund, a rather isolated outpost well north of Tain, where the major NÉGOCIANTS and the famous HERMITAGE vineyard are situated. One man, Marcel GUIGAL, is chiefly responsible for the renaissance of this zone (helped by the adulation of another, the American wine critic Robert PARKER).

Côte Rôtie may be the site where the vine was first cultivated in GAUL, and vineyards have been sculpted from these, some of the steepest slopes of viticultural France, since at least the time when nearby Vienne was an important Roman settlement. The vines then grown were identified with the local tribe, the Allobroges (see RHÔNE, history).

Vine-growing brought so little reward in the 1960s and 1970s that total plantings were only about 70 ha/175 acres in the early 1970s; by the mid 1990s, however, plantings had reached 150 ha (rather less than the extent of the single biggest wine château in the MÉDOC) and by 2013 276 ha of vineyards qualified for the appellation. Guigal's single-vineyard bottlings of La Mouline, La Landonne, and, later, La Turque reminded the wine-buying world of the potential majesty of wines hewn from the Côte Rôtie, or 'roasted slope', even if their concentration is not typical of the appellation.

Because of the turn of the river here, the vineyards banked up the SCHIST behind the unremarkable town of Ampuis face directly south east, and are angled so as to maximize the ripening effect of any SUNLIGHT, while being sheltered from the cold winds. The slopes have traditionally been distinguished, with associated legend, either as Côte Blonde, supposedly producing alluring wines for relatively early consumption (often as a result of blending up to the permitted maximum of 20% scented white VIOGNIER in with the mandatory SYRAH grape—see CO-FERMENTATION), or Côte Brune, associated with firmer, more durable, all-Syrah wines. The finest Côte Rôtie, local lore had it, was a blend of the two. More recently, the fame, and record prices, of wines flaunting specific vineyard sites has rather put paid to this theory, and the appellation is a hotbed of activity and ambition.

Syrah is trained particularly distinctively on these slopes (so steep in parts that winches have to be used), single GUYOT on single or double stakes. TERRACES are essential here, where they are known as *cheys* and have been in place for centuries. The theoretical minimum potential alcohol of these wines is 10%, but most growers manage to achieve considerably more ripeness than this, and wines are made, with more or less new OAK (more *chez* Guigal). More typical examples of Côte Rôtie can be relatively light and fresh with a particularly haunting savoury perfume. Côte Rôtie should always be more 'feminine' than Hermitage. Clusel-Roch, Jean-Michel Gerin, Jamet, René Rostaing, and Vidal Fleury also produce very fine Côte Rôtie.

Livingstone-Learmonth, J., *The Wines of the Northern Rhône* (Berkeley, 2005).

Cotnari

Cotnari, once-famous sweet white wine produced in wild, hilly countryside in the north Romanian Moldova Hills (see ROMANIA for geographical details). At one time it rivalled Hungarian TOKAJI as an elixir of FASHION sought after in the courts of northern Europe. It was still fashionable in Paris at the end of the 19th century, and it is clear that NOBLE ROT has played an important role here for several centuries, and continues to do so every three or four years today. It is still very popular in Romania.

The DOC allows wine to be made from any of the four local white grape varieties grown in the region, although Sauvignon Blanc, Chardonnay, Pinot Gris, Fetească Neagră, and Busuioacă de Bohotin are also permitted. The wines are often vinified from dry to semi-sweet, as single varieties, or as a traditional blend containing a minimum of 30% GRASĂ (which provides the body and sugar). TĂMÂIOASĂ Românească provides its 'frankincense' aromas (and sugar without losing acidity in the Cotnari MESOCLIMATE), Frâncușă gives the acidity (it must make up at least 30% in a blend, although it can suffer from poor FRUIT SET), and Fetească Albă the aroma. Occasionally, Grasă ripens to very high sugar levels and may be affected by noble rot. Such wines can be long-lived and impressive—and are released occasionally as 'collection' wines. Oak ageing is usually for only six months to one year, unlike TOKAJI AZSU, and Cotnari has a typically greenish tinge when young. C.G.

Couchois, Bourgogne, Côtes du, appellation created in 2001 for red wines made from Pinot Noir grown around the town of Couches north west of the Côte Chalonnaise. See BOURGOGNE.

Couderc Noir, a HYBRID of a dark-berried RUPESTRIS-*lincecumii* and VINIFERA, is one of several productive but undistinguished hybrids that proliferated in the MIDI in the early 20th century (see also BACO, CHAMBOURCIN, PLANTET, SEIBEL, SEYVE-VILLARD, VILLARD). Although not as popular as Villard once was, Couderc Noir was so widely planted that France's total area of Cabernet Sauvignon did not overtake that of Couderc Noir until well into the 1970s. By 2011 total plantings were less than 200 ha. The wine produced can be aggressively non-*V. vinifera* in taste.

Coulanges-la-Vineuse, commune near AUXERRE whose name may be appended to that of red, white, and rosé BOURGOGNE.

coulure, French term, commonly used by English speakers too, for one form of poor FRUIT SET in the grapevine. Excessive shedding of OVARIES and young berries results in relatively few berries per bunch, either during or soon after FLOWERING. To a great extent, coulure is a natural and necessary phenomenon, since the vine cannot possibly ripen the crop if all the flowers remained as berries. However, for some varieties in some years, coulure can be excessive and YIELD drastically reduced. Excessive coulure can have a disastrous effect on grape-growers' incomes, and can also affect grape supply and wine prices in certain years. GRENACHE vines are particularly susceptible to coulure, as are MALBEC, CABERNET SAUVIGNON, and MERLOT.

Coulure is caused by an imbalance in the levels of CARBOHYDRATES in vine tissue. Weather conditions around flowering which reduce PHOTOSYNTHESIS, such as periods of cloudy, cold, and wet weather, will cause coulure, and can have devastating effects on yield for some varieties. Coulure also happens where the total leaf area, and thus photosynthesis, is limited. Low carbohydrate levels can also be due to excessively vigorous shoot growth, combined with warm temperatures, which favour RESPIRATION. Very fertile soils, excessive application of FERTILIZERS, especially those high in NITROGEN, vigorous ROOTSTOCKS, and PRUNING too severely (see BALANCED PRUNING) can also cause coulure.

There is little growers can do to prevent coulure. It is not always possible to grow varieties which are not susceptible, as particular varieties may be required for a certain style or blend. CLONAL SELECTION can be effective in reducing susceptibility for some varieties, as for example with Merlot and Malbec. TOPPING shoots during flowering can reduce coulure by temporarily stopping competition for carbohydrates between actively growing SHOOT TIPS and INFLORESCENCES. Later pruning may also help because a delayed BUDBREAK will increase the possibility of warmer weather at flowering. Some chemical GROWTH REGULATORS can reduce coulure by inhibiting shoot growth. A Coulure Index (CI) was defined for the first time in 2009—the higher the numerical value, the greater the expression of the condition. R.E.S. & P.R.D.

Collins, C., and Dry, P. R., 'Response of fruitset and other yield components to shoot topping and CCC application', *Australian Journal of Grape and Wine Research*, 15 (2009), 256–67.

Iland, P., et al., 'Flowering and fruitset', in *The Grapevine: From the Science to the Practice of Growing Vines for Wine* (Adelaide, 2011).

Counoise is one of the more rarefied varietal ingredients in red CHÂTEAUNEUF-DU-PAPE, easily confused in the vineyard with the much lesser southern Rhône variety AUBUN, with which it may sometimes be mingled in older vineyards. It is authorized as a supplementary ingredient for most red wine appellations around the southern Rhône, including LANGUEDOC AOC (which allows Aubin as a synonym) but, although VARIETAL southern French versions are made, it is not widely grown outside Châteauneuf-du-Pape. Total French plantings increased in the 1980s to around 900 ha/2,200 acres but were only 369 ha in 2011.

As a vine, it leafs and ripens late and yields conservatively. As a wine, it is not particularly deeply coloured or alcoholic but adds lift, a peppery note, and lively acidity to a blend. Enthusiasts such as the Perrin family of Ch de Beaucastel typically use about 5% of Counoise in their red Châteauneuf-du-Pape and have disseminated it around California's Central Coast and beyond via their Tablas Creek vine NURSERY there.

counterfeit wine has, alas, become more common as fine wine has become more valuable. Wine of all sorts has been subject to ADULTERATION AND FRAUD for centuries but the escalation in prices of the most sought-after names, the rapid increase in the number of (often inexperienced) collectors, and the fact that a fine wine may be consumed many years after it was bought combined to provide irresistible opportunities for fraudsters in general and counterfeiters in particular in the late 20th and early 21st centuries.

In less developed markets poor-quality wine may be packaged in a poor copy of a famous wine's BOTTLE, LABEL, and CAPSULE but more sophisticated methods are generally called for, leading to a new breed of wine CONSULTANT who is expert in, inter alia, precise label design and typeface evolution for the most valuable wines. Wines that have been particularly popular with counterfeiters are, of course, the rarest which means that the likes of PETRUS, DRC, and Henri Jayer burgundies have appeared at auction unfeasibly often, just as vintages 1961 and 1945 of fine bordeaux have. A favourite recipe for fake top vintage Petrus, for example, has been a mixture of off-vintage Petrus with particularly ripe California red. Printers are necessary accomplices for counterfeiters.

The most common counterfeits include Chx Cheval Blanc 1921 and 1947, Lafite 1787 and 1870, Lafleur 1947 and 1950, Latour à Pomerol 1961, Margaux 1900, and Pétrus 1921 and 1947. Among other counterfeits, there have been discoveries of fake 1990 Penfolds Grange and of 1994 and 1995 Sassicaia, but even mid-range priced wines such as Rioja and MOUTON CADET have been victims.

Wine AUCTIONS provide the perfect arena for such frauds but counterfeit wines have also been sold by retailers and privately. This has led to an increase in interest in each bottle's precise PROVENANCE and calls for some sort of system akin to motor vehicles' logbooks (see AUTHENTICATION).

Producers of most wines targeted by fraudsters have been taking anti-counterfeit measures such as special invisible marks on varius aspects of packaging for ten or more vintages now, but mature fine wine should be bought only from the most impeccable of sources. Premiums for wines direct from château, domaine, or estate have risen.

Wallace, B., *The Billionaire's Vinegar* (New York, 2008).

Steinberger, M., 'A Vintage Crime', *Vanity Fair* (July 2012).

www.vanityfair.com/culture/2012/07/wine-fraud-rudy-kurniawan-vintage-burgundies

coupage, French and EU term for BLENDING. It means literally 'cutting' and retains a slightly pejorative overtone, tending to be reserved for wine blending at its least glamorous while the word ASSEMBLAGE is more commonly used for blending different lots of a fine wine. EU regulations prohibit the coupage of all sorts of different wines, including EU with non-EU wines, WINE WITHOUT GEOGRAPHICAL INDICATION with PDO and PGI wines, and different members of these inelegantly named categories of wine.

Courbu Blanc, Basque speciality often blended with PETIT MANSENG and GROS MANSENG, distinct from PETIT COURBU. See also HONDARRIBI ZURI. **Courbu Noir** is an almost extinct speciality of BÉARN.

courses, wine. See EDUCATION.

court-noué, common French term for FANLEAF DEGENERATION, a virus disease of the vine.

Cova de Beira, large subregion within BEIRA INTERIOR in central Portugal. Wines bearing the name are rarely seen on export markets.

cover crop, a crop of plants other than vines established in the vineyard, typically between the rows, generally for biodiversity (see ECOSYSTEM) and the benefit of the vineyard soil. Also known as a sward, or sod culture, and *couvert végétal* in French, it is an alternative to bare soil created by CULTIVATION or HERBICIDES. Sometimes cover crops are not deliberately sown but volunteer plants or WEEDS are allowed to grow instead. Cover crops are normally mown during the vine-growing season, and may be removed by cultivation or herbicide spray (but see ORGANIC VITICULTURE). Typical sown cover crops are grasses and legumes. The grasses used may be native to the area or specially introduced species such as perennial rye grass, fescue, or bent grasses, although often cereals such as barley or oats are used. Legumes sown as cover crops include clovers, medics, peas, vetches, and beans. Occasionally, deep-rooted cover crops such as chicory (*Chicorium intybus*) are sown to compete for soil water with over-vigorous vines. Cover crop management is more difficult in high-density, narrow-spaced vineyards, such as Bordeaux's left bank and Champagne (see VINE DENSITY).

A common reason for sowing cover crops is to increase the ORGANIC MATTER in the soil and hence improve its structure and capacity to hold water. When this is the aim, the species sown should, like cereals and grasses, grow quickly and produce plenty of bulk which can then be incorporated into the soil by shallow ploughing. Cover crops with a deep tap root such as radish and chicory, or hollow-stemmed such as oats, maintain soil structure by facilitating water infiltration. When a cover crop is slashed, the residues left on the soil surface reduce the amount of EVAPORATION from the topsoil. Vine roots will not develop as much near the soil surface in the presence of cover crops.

Cover crops are also commonly sown to stop SOIL EROSION in areas with storms and are especially useful in sloping vineyards. The roots of the cover crop bind the soil and resist the flowing water. Tall cover crops are also used in newly established vineyards to combat high winds, which can cause damage to young plants. Cover crops also help reduce SOIL COMPACTION.

Another important use of cover crops is to compete with the vines, especially when they are too vigorous, and to encourage earlier RIPENING and improve wine quality. Slight WATER STRESS hastens the ripening process, so cover crops, which compete with the vines for water and nutrients, especially NITROGEN, can help to generate this stress in areas of high summer rainfall. However, when winter legumes such as lupins, vetch, or beans are ploughed in during spring, they allow fixed atmospheric nitrogen to be released into the soil. In conditions of high soil moisture, this can lead to excessive vine VIGOUR. Some mowers throw the cover crop clippings under the vines, thus forming a MULCH.

Apparently weedy vineyards should not necessarily be dismissed as untidy; they may represent a deliberate ploy to improve wine quality. Deep-rooting crops such as mustard, lucerne (alfalfa), and chicory can be particularly useful to use up subsoil water which more shallow-rooted grasses cannot reach.

Cover crops should be grown with caution. In spring, they make the vineyard more prone to FROST than if the soil is bare. The cover crop may play host to insects which spread diseases such as FLAVESCENCE DORÉE. If the cover crop is not mown or cultivated in summer, it can use too much water or nutrients and the vines can suffer as a result. Because of competition with vines for nitrogen, the use of cover crops can also cause STUCK FERMENTATIONS (although ORGANIC growers claim the reverse is the case). These effects can be offset by close mowing or by killing the cover crop by ploughing or herbicides. Cover crops reduce the problems caused by dust from traffic on bare soil alleyways in the vineyard; dust can encourage MITES.

R.E.S., M.W., & R.E.W.

Ingels, C. A., *Cover cropping in vineyards: a grower's handbook* (Oakland, Calif., 1998).

Wheeler, S. J., Black, A. S., and Pickering, G. J., 'Vineyard floor management improves wine quality in highly vigorous *Vitis vinifera* "Cabernet Sauvignon" in New Zealand', *New Zealand Journal of Crop and Horticultural Science* 33 (2005), 317–328.

Cowra, well-established warm Australian wine region, best suited to Chardonnays, in NEW SOUTH WALES. The accent is more on yield than on quality, and most of the production goes to large wineries as a blend component in lower-priced VARIETAL or GENERIC wine styles.   J.H.

crater, big, deep bowl with a wide mouth used in Ancient GREECE for mixing wine, most often with water. The crater was characteristically 12 to 18 in (30–45 cm) high and could be either painted pottery or made of bronze. The most remarkable example is the huge bronze crater, over 5 ft/1.5 m high, probably of Spartan manufacture, which was found at Vix in France (see CELTS).   J.J.P.

Crato Branco, Algarve synonym for Portugal's SÍRIA grape.

Cream, the sweetest, darkest style of SHERRY (with the exception of PX, which is even sweeter and darker) created expressly for the sweet-toothed British market by HARVEYS OF BRISTOL. Bristol Milk was a style of sweet sherry sold successfully in the early 19th century by both AVERYS and Harveys. The story goes that a lady visitor to the cellars in 1882, on tasting Harveys' new, as yet unnamed, BRAND of sweet sherry observed, 'If that is Milk, then this is Cream.' Harveys Bristol Cream was thus named, and has become the most successful branded sherry in the world. This sweet style of sherry is eschewed by the Spaniards, for it is essentially the product of BLENDING not necessarily very distinguished sherries with sweetening and colouring wines. **Pale Cream** was another highly successful sherry style launched, with huge initial success, by Croft in the 1970s. Most Pale Cream is essentially the same as Cream but with the colour removed, by CHARCOAL or other treatments, although it may also be sweetened FINO. Cream sherries generally have a RESIDUAL SUGAR content that is the equivalent of 4.5 to 6.5 °BAUMÉ.

Crémant, term used as France's shorthand for the country's finest dry sparkling wines made outside Champagne using the traditional method of SPARKLING WINEMAKING. The term was adopted in the late 1980s, when the expression *méthode champenoise* was outlawed by the EU (and replaced by MÉTHODE TRADITIONNELLE). The principal provenances of modern Crémants are Alsace, Bourgogne (Burgundy), Loire, and Limoux. The best sparkling wines of LUXEMBOURG are also called Crémant. Crémant de Saumur and Crémant de Vouvray were the first non-champagne sparkling wines to use the term, and in the mid 1970s the Crémant de Loire appellation was born, soon followed by Alsace and Bourgogne. Bordeaux and Limoux joined the official Crémant appellations, created under INAO authority, in 1990, and were followed by Die in 1993, Jura in 1995, and Savoie in 2014.

Although grape varieties and TERROIRS vary from region to region, certain strict sparkling winemaking rules are imposed, including WHOLE-BUNCH PRESSING; a maximum yield of 100 l per 150 kg of grapes (the same as CHAMPAGNE prior to 1993); a maximum SULFUR DIOXIDE content of 150 mg/l; a minimum of 12 months between initial bottling and release.

Crémant d'Alsace

Sparkling winemaking using the TRADITIONAL METHOD in Alsace dates from the late 19th century and in the 1980s became an important commercial activity, representing almost a quarter of the region's output. Only the grape varieties Pinots Blanc, Noir, and Gris, together with the related Auxerrois, and Riesling and such Chardonnay as is planted in Alsace, may be used (i.e. no Gewurztraminer or Chasselas), and any rosé must be made entirely of Pinot Noir. Maximum yields are 80 hl/ha (4.5 tons/acre). The wines are well made, tend to have a

particularly fine mousse, high acidity, and to be relatively light in BODY. Only if substantial proportions of Riesling are used do they acquire strong flavour. Production is in the hands of nearly 500 different small-scale producers whose blending capability is usually limited. A total of 3,523 ha/8,705 acres were devoted to the wine in 2012.

Crémant de Bordeaux

A small and declining amount of sparkling wine has been made in the BORDEAUX region since the end of the 19th century. Today production is controlled by a handful of companies which have not established a clear style or identity for the white and pink wines.

Crémant de Bourgogne

This appellation, created in 1975, replaced that of Bourgogne Mousseux (now used exclusively for sparkling red burgundy), under which name sparkling burgundy of all colours enjoyed considerable commercial success in the 1950s and 1960s. All grape varieties grown in BURGUNDY are allowed into Crémant, although Gamay may not constitute more than a fifth of the blend. Yields are limited to about 65 hl/ha. RULLY in the Côte Chalonnaise and AUXERRE in the far north of Burgundy are the principal sources of Crémant de Bourgogne (CÔTE D'OR grapes being in general worth considerably more when sold as still wine), and there can be considerable stylistic differences between their produce. Crémant from southern Burgundy can be full and soft, a good-value alternative to bigger styles of champagne, while Crémant made in the north is usually much lighter and crisper. A total of 2,370 ha/5,860 acres were devoted to the wine in 2012.

Crémant de Die

Crémant de Die is a dry wine made by the traditional method from at least 55% CLAIRETTE grapes with no more than 10% of the Muscat Blanc that is grown for another of the region's three sparkling wines (see CLAIRETTE DE DIE for more details), and the balance Aligoté.

Crémant du Jura

The appellation was created in 1995 and by 2013 it represented more than 25% of Jura wine production. The wines may be white or rosé from any of the authorized JURA grape varieties, although the white must be at least half Chardonnay, and the rosé at least half Poulsard or Pinot Noir. In practice, few Crémants du Jura are made from anything other than these grapes, although some interesting white blends with Savagnin are available. All but the largest producers have their base wine made sparkling by one of two specialist companies who then return the finished wines to individual producers to market. The best

wines offer excellent value for money. As Chardonnay is Jura's most planted variety, the Crémant appellation is particularly useful for underripe grapes in this relatively wet region and has a beneficial effect on the quality of still Chardonnay wines.

Crémant de Limoux

This appellation represents the increasing champenization of the ancient sparkling wines of LIMOUX in a particularly cool, high corner of the southern Languedoc. In 1990, Blanquette de Limoux became an appellation reserved for sparkling wines made principally from the MAUZAC grape grown traditionally in the region, while Crémant de Limoux contains at least 50% Chardonnay plus Chenin Blanc (20 to 40%). The other two varieties allowed are Pinot Noir and Mauzac. A very high proportion is made by the CO-OPERATIVE, although the produce of nearly 300 growers is used to make this most southerly Crémant. A total of 846 ha/2,090 acres were devoted to the wine in 2012.

Crémant de Loire

Crémant de Loire was created in 1975 and encompasses the Anjou-Saumur and Touraine regions. Most of the middle Loire's wide palette of grape varieties may be used to produce Crémant, with the notable and sensible exception of Sauvignon Blanc, whose aroma has yet to prove itself an attractive sparkling wine ingredient. GROLLEAU grapes may not represent much of any blend, and in practice Chenin Blanc is the most common dominant component, clearly distinguishing the flavour of most Crémant de Loire from Crémants made from Pinots and Chardonnay to the east. Yields are limited to 50 hl/ha. Levels of winemaking are generally high among the nearly 200 producers (including four co-operatives and several important NÉGOCIANTS) and an increasing level of complexity in the bottle is evident. Some producers have been Loire offshoots of Champagne houses, notably Langlois Chateau of BOLLINGER, Gratien & Meyer of Alfred Gratien, and the ambitious Bouvet-Ladubay of Taittinger.

Crémant de Luxembourg

Luxembourg has a long tradition of sparkling winemaking, and its particularly acid wines were at one time valued as base wines for SEKT. The Crémant de Luxembourg appellation was created in 1991, following the INAO rules laid down for French wines. Permitted grape varieties are Elbling, Pinot Blanc, Rivaner (Müller Thurgau), Auxerrois, Chardonnay, and Riesling for white wines, Pinot Noir for rosé.

Crémant de Savoie

Blends should be composed of at least 60% JACQUÈRE and the local ALTESSE, with a minimum of 40% Jacquère, supplemented by the likes of local Chasselas, Aligoté, and Chardonnay. In 2014 when the appellation was introduced, sparkling wines comprised just 6% of SAVOIE wine production. SEYSSEL and AYSE have their own appellations for sparkling wines.

Crépy, cru (formerly a small appellation in its own right) within the eastern French region of SAVOIE on the south-eastern shore of Lake Geneva producing light, dry white wines from the CHASSELAS grape. They differ from their Swiss counterparts in being crisper as most are made without MALOLACTIC CONVERSION.

Crete, large island to the south east of GREECE famous for the Minoan civilization (*c.*2000–1400 BC). Its wines were most famous in the Middle Ages when the island was known as Candia. Today the most important viticultural centre is the area south of Heraklion, although ambitious producers are also to be found around Chania in the west and Sitia in the east. See also MALVASIA, MALMSEY, NAPLES, and VENICE.

crianza, Spanish term used both to describe the process of AGEING a wine and also for the youngest officially recognized category of a wood-matured wine. A crianza red wine may not be sold until its third (second for whites and rosés) year, and must have spent a minimum of six months in cask. Crianza white and rosé must be aged for at least 18 months, including six months in wood. In RIOJA and other regions such as RIBERA DEL DUERO, where the term is most commonly used, the wine must have spent at least 12 months in oak BARRICAS. An increasingly frequent, albeit unofficial, category now is **semi-crianza**, or **roble** (meaning OAK), for wine aged in cask for less time than the crianza minimum. With the term JOVEN fully accepted for fruity young wines without cask ageing, the slightly derogatory description *sin crianza* had all but disappeared by the late 1990s.

Crimea, important wine-producing peninsula off southern UKRAINE surrounded by the Black Sea. After decades of being controlled by and selling most of its wines in UKRAINE, it and its 25,000 ha/61,780 acres of vineyards were annexed by RUSSIA in 2014.

Grapes were grown here from at least the 4th century BC. Archaeological evidence includes stone fences, remnants of viticultural plots and wineries, and wine AMPHORAE in the Tauric settlement of Uch-Bash near Inkerman (which is as old as the 10th to 7th centuries BC). There have also been wine-related finds in the ancient town of Mirmecium in the east of the Kerch Peninsula. The unearthed tomb of a Scythian chief dated 500 BC was arranged with an amphora of CHIAN wine at its head.

Crimea's south coast became an important holiday region for Russian aristocrats in the 19th century and centre for sanatoriums in the 20th century. Cyrus REDDING noted in 1833 that 'the Crimea wines are thought the best in the empire'. The wine-loving Count Mikhail Vorontsov, governor-general of that part of Russia which then included the Tauric province (Crimea), began to build the Alupka Palace and associated winery in the 1820s which still produces FORTIFIED WINES in quantity, and also laid the foundations for the MAGARACH Institute for research into winemaking and viticulture. Vorontsov imported a wide range of grape varieties from Europe, but suffered many early winemaking failures, as did his successor as principal Crimean wine innovator, Prince Leo Golitzin. In 1882 he established the Novy Svet (New World) winery, which, inter alia, produced pre-revolutionary Russia's 'Shampanskoe' that even won a gold medal in Paris in 1900 and continues to produce sparkling wine to this day.

The Crimea has very favourable soil and climatic conditions for viticulture. Average July temperatures of 24 °C/75 °F and annual sunshine of 2,250 hours at Yalta result in extremely ripe grapes best suited to the production of strong, sweet wines, most of them made like VINS DOUX NATURELS.

Of the three main winemaking regions—South Coast, West Coast, and Steep Crimea—the South Coast continues to specialize in strong, sweet wines, with MASSANDRA the dominant winery producing about 70,000 hl/1.85 million gal a year on the outskirts of Yalta, mainly PORT-style wines and Kagor (its name inspired by Cahors), a deep-coloured wine made from MUST heated before fermentation. The West Coast is more readily associated with dry varietals produced by small, new-wave operations such as those of Pavel Shvets and Oleg Repin. Inkerman is also based here and produces vast quantities of wine, some based on imported BULK wine.

Other producers include Solnechnaya Dolina (Sun Valley), which makes mainly fortified wines, and sparkling-wine producer Zolotaya Balka (Golden Creek).

Criolla Chica is the Argentine name for the Listán Prieto of Spain, the PAIS of Chile, the MISSION of California, and the Negra Corriente of PERU. It is thought to be descended from the seeds of grapes, presumably well raisined after their voyage under sail across the Atlantic, imported by the Spanish conquistadores, possibly as early as the 16th century (see SOUTH AMERICA). Criolla Chica was planted on just 423 ha/1,045 acres in 2011 and is therefore much less common in Argentina than the other pink-skinned grape varieties CRIOLLA GRANDE and CEREZA. Its wine is generally paler but slightly better quality.

Criolla Grande, the fourth most planted vine variety in ARGENTINA after MALBEC, CEREZA, and BONARDA. Although the area planted with this coarse, pink-skinned grape has declined substantially, there were still 17,000 ha/42,000 acres in 2011. Almost all Criolla Grande is in Mendoza province. Criolla Grande is a low-quality CRIOLLA, and is much deeper skinned than CRIOLLA CHICA. The two Criollas, along with Cereza and Moscatel Rosada, form the basis of Argentina's declining trade in basic deep-coloured white or pale pink wine sold very cheaply in litre bottles or cardboard cartons.

Criollas, generic name for vine varieties that have been common in SOUTH AMERICA, particularly ARGENTINA, since the arrival of the conquistadores. They include CEREZA, CRIOLLA CHICA, CRIOLLA GRANDE, various local Moscatels, PEDRO GIMÉNEZ, and various TORRONTÉS.

Criots-Bâtard-Montrachet, great white GRAND CRU in Burgundy's CÔTE D'OR. For more details, see MONTRACHET.

crise viticole, la, widely used phrase for France's wine crisis of 1907 (see LANGUEDOC) and also that of the early 21st century resulting from plummeting wine sales both at home and abroad. Sales stagnation affected not just the Languedoc with its huge volumes of surplus VIN DE TABLE and VIN DE PAYS and its notoriously militant vignerons, but also APPELLATION D'ORIGINE CONTRÔLÉE wines, notably MUSCADET and to a lesser extent BEAUJOLAIS and the less favoured parts of BORDEAUX. CHAMPAGNE seemed relatively unscathed, leading to increased attempts to develop BRANDS of French still wines.

critter labels, informal category of mass-market wines with animals on their labels, mainly Australian, with YELLOW TAIL the prototype.

Crljenak Kaštelanski, 'the red wine grape of Kaštela', an island off CROATIA. It has turned out to be ZINFANDEL and is being planted once more by Croatians. See also TRIBIDRAG.

Croatia, or Hrvatska, is one of the most successful wine producers of the former YUGOSLAVIA on the Balkan peninsula. The Adriatic coastline of the mainland stretches 1,880 km/1,170 miles while its 1,244 islands add a further 4,398 km. In recent years Croatia has become hugely popular as a tourist destination with 10.4 million foreign visitors in 2012, vastly outnumbering its resident population of 4.3 million, and creating a ready-made market for its wines.

History

Viticulture in this region certainly dates back to the ancient Greeks and possibly earlier with the Illyrians. It is claimed that the UNESCO-listed

Stari Grad plain on the island of Hvar is the oldest continuously cultivated viticultural site in the world, dating back to the fourth century BC, with its original layout of geometric parcels, or *chora*, divided by stone walls. Grape growing increased in importance and became more organized under ROMAN occupation. The land was part of the Ottoman empire from the 15th century and was subsequently part of the Habsburg empire when grape growing flourished until the arrival of PHYLLOXERA. Under 20th-century communist rule, wine production became centred on large collectivized state wineries.

The break-up of Yugoslavia and the brutal wars of independence that followed in the early 1990s undoubtedly had a significant effect on viticulture. Even in 2013, more than 630 square kilometres (240 square miles) of agricultural land were classified as minefields. After a late start as an independent nation (compared with neighbours such as SLOVENIA and HUNGARY), Croatia has accelerated the development of a fascinating wine industry based on private wine producers, although it suffers from the common Balkan problem of fragmentation of land holdings. Croatia's vineyard survey ahead of EU accession in 2013 recorded nearly 60,000 growers/producers but only 39 with more than 39 ha, although the largest, the Agrokor Group, produces over 30% of all Croatian wine.

Geography

Croatia is a very diverse country between the latitudes of 46 ° and 42 °N with an unusually wide range of climatic influences. The biggest divide in terms of climate is between the two inland CONTINENTAL areas of Istočna kontinentalna Hrvatska, the eastern zone, and the western zone Zapadna kontinentalna Hrvatska, and the coastal zone Primorska Hrvatska. In 2012 according to the Croatian Bureau of Statistics there were 29,237 ha/72,246 acres of vineyard producing 1.29 million hl/34 million gal, of which 59% is produced in inland Croatia and 41% is grown in the coastal zone. More recently the country has been divided into four large (and more understandable) wine regions: the inland areas of Croatian Uplands and Slavonia and Croatian Danube, along with two coastal areas of Istria and Kvarner and Dalmatia. These are divided into 12 subregions and 61 wine districts. Wine categories include premium quality wines called Vrhunsko Vino, quality wines or Kvalitetno Vino, and table wines known as Stolno Vino. The first two categories are classified as PDO in EU terminology. Croatia claims to grow around 200 different grape varieties with around 40 of these identified as indigenous.

Istria and Kvarner has a mild climate with MEDITERRANEAN influences meeting the cold air flowing down from the Alps, and shares both climate and cultural influences with both north east Italy and Slovenia. Iron-rich red soils are widespread. White wines, particularly those made from the characterful local MALVAZIJA ISTARSKA, Croatia's third most planted variety (1,858 ha/4,590 acres in 2011), dominate. Most often vinified without oak in a fresh, fruity style with apple and white peach flavours, it also responds well to being picked later and vinified, often with extended SKIN CONTACT, in barrels that may be made of acacia rather than oak. Reds are less important in this region with the most characteristic a tart, firm varietal speciality called Teran (made from the local variety also known as Terrano, and Refošk in Slovenia, distinct from REFOSCO DAL PEDUNCOLO ROSSO). The name is the subject of dispute with Slovenia, which has registered Teran as a protected term. Merlot produces some fine elegant wines, and is sometimes blended with local Teran. Some Muskat Momjanski is also made, usually as semisweet or sweet whites. The island of Krk's speciality is the delicate white Žlahtina grape.

Dalmatia stretches south from Zadar to the country's southern border with MONTENEGRO and includes the important wine-growing islands of Korčula, Hvar, Vis, and Brač. Its often steep and rocky vineyards enjoy sunny summers and are noted for their treasure trove of INDIGENOUS VARIETIES. They produce some of the country's most powerful, full-bodied reds, frequently over 15% alcohol. This is the only Croatian region where reds predominate, especially PLAVAC MALI (Croatia's second most planted grape with 2,019 ha/5,000 acres in 2012). This is the grape responsible for Dingač and Postup from the seaside terraces of the Pelješac Peninsula and the Ivan Dolac cru of Hvar. CRLJENAK KAŠTELANSKI, rescued from just nine vines at Kaštela near Split in 2002, was shown by DNA PROFILING to be none other than ZINFANDEL (aka Tribidrag) and also a parent of Plavac Mali. Since this important discovery it has been planted much more widely. Babić is another good-quality red wine grape grown on famously stony coastal vineyards near Šibenik and the UNESCO-listed hillsides of Primošten. It is also being planted more widely now that its potential has been recognized. Pošip is the most important white wine grape and is producing increasingly exciting wines, especially from Korčula, Hvar, and Brač. Other interesting pale-skinned Dalmatian varieties include Grk, Debit, Vugava, Bogdanuša, Gegic, and Maraština. A wine traditionally called Prosek is made on islands such as Hvar and Brač but mainly for home or local consumption. Italy's PROSECCO producers have objected to the name.

The inland zone of **Slavonia and Croatian Danube** is the home of Croatia's most important white wine grape Graševina (WELSCHRIESLING, planted on 5,582 ha/13,787 acres). This relatively flat region of plains with a few low hills reaches as far north east as the foothills of the Fruška Gora Range. Pale-skinned grapes predominate and the long, notably warm autumns encourage the production of some impressive sweet, late-harvest whites. Graševina is often a workhorse grape but arguably reaches its peak around the historic town of Kutjevo, while Traminac (GEWÜRZTRAMINER) can also be notable, especially around Ilok. More recent arrivals of INTERNATIONAL VARIETIES such as Chardonnay and Sauvignon Blanc are proving successful. Reds are led by Frankovka (BLAUFRÄNKISCH) but some promising wines have now been made from Pinot Crni (Pinot Noir), Merlot, and Cabernet Sauvignon. Slavonia is also famous for its OAK, particularly beloved of Italian producers for their large oak casks (*botti*).

The **Croatian Upland** region surrounding the capital Zagreb is the coolest zone, with small family vineyards dotted across green hillsides. International white grapes predominate and some fresh, zesty Sauvignons, crisp Rieslings, and more recently some decent Pinot Gris and Pinot Noir, especially in Plešivica and even Zagorje in the north, have been produced. Some impressive ICEWINE has also been made. FURMINT under its local name of Moslavac is also grown, while the native variety Škrlet is found in the Moslavina district and makes fresh, fruity but quite simple wines.   E.M. & C.G.

www.hcphs.hr Institute of Viticulture and Enology
www.hgk.hr/wp-content/files_mf/winesofcroatie nsadrzajmail.pdf
www.tasteofcroatia.org
www.winesofcroatia.wordpress.com

Croatina, red grape variety from the borders of the PIEMONTE and LOMBARDY regions of northern Italy. The vine buds and ripens late but yields good quantities of fruity wine with a certain bite, designed to be drunk relatively young. Its common synonym is Bonarda, under which name it has an appetizing red VARIETAL DOC in the OLTREPÒ PAVESE zone of south west Lombardia. The variety is quite distinct from BONARDA Piemontese. Total plantings of Croatina were 5,684 ha/14,045 acres in 2010.

Croft, port shipper with a particularly long history. Its precursor Phayre and Bradley was established in 1678. The first Croft, from York, became a partner in 1736 and the company was known as Croft and Co from 1769. In 1911 the firm was taken over by Gilbey's, and the majority shareholding eventually passed into the hands of the multinational corporation Grand Metropolitan, subsequently an integral part of DIAGEO. Port shipper Morgan Brothers was acquired in 1952.

Croft expanded into the SHERRY business in the difficult era of the early 1970s. Croft invaded Jerez with energy and one novel idea: they launched an entirely new style of sherry, Pale

CREAM, which could offer the beguiling combination of a pale, sophisticated appearance with the reassuring sweetness of a cream. It was an enormous and much-imitated success, necessitating almost immediate expansion for Croft Jerez, in the form a series of ultra-modern bodegas known as Rancho Croft. Croft's Jerez adventure ended in 2001, when DIAGEO sold the bodegas to GONZÁLEZ BYASS for 54 million euros. Some of its best old soleras were acquired by a new, quality-minded company, Tradición.

The port business is now owned by the FLADGATE PARTNERSHIP.

crop thinning, viticultural practice which, it is claimed, improves wine quality by encouraging fruit RIPENING. It is known as *éclaircissage* or *vendange verte* (green harvest) in French. Some bunches are removed from the vine and those remaining should in theory ripen more quickly with the benefit of improved LEAF TO FRUIT RATIO. Crop thinning is usually carried out by hand, and is therefore expensive. MECHANICAL HARVESTERS are occasionally used to thin crops, removing individual berries or parts of bunches.

The YIELD is reduced more or less proportionately to the bunches removed (although the remaining berries may be slightly enlarged), which means that only those growers able to guarantee top prices for their produce can afford the operation. The technique became common in the early 1990s among the better wine producers in Bordeaux, where it had been practised at PETRUS since 1973.

Crop thinning is normally carried out at VERAISON, when it is obvious which bunches are slow to ripen. This is also referred to as colour thinning. It is cheaper if done earlier but there is a risk that the remaining bunches will become tight due to larger berries and so be prone to BOTRYTIS BUNCH ROT. Later bunch removal has more impact on yield, and earlier removal on fruit ripening. Crop thinning is common for varieties with large bunches such as Merlot, and for Pinot Noir, again especially for CLONES with large bunches.

Thinning is also appropriate when it is obvious that the vintage will be late, decreasing the chance of ripening a large crop, and when yield estimates suggest there is going to be more crop than can probably be ripened, especially in cool climates.

The theory of crop thinning is that the remaining fruit ripens earlier, and so has better levels of SUGARS and ANTHOCYANINS for red varieties. However, many studies have shown that these benefits are small in magnitude, and that crop levels need to be greatly reduced for a small change in GRAPE COMPOSITION. For many vineyards where the yield is in BALANCE with shoot growth, and the leaves and fruit are well exposed, then there will be little benefit from crop thinning. Some viticulturists, this author

included, believe that thinning may bring more pyschological than physiological benefit and that thinning is best done on the day of harvest.   R.E.S.

Reynier, A., *Manuel de viticulture* (11th edn, Paris, 2010).

cross, the result of breeding a new variety by **crossing** two VINE VARIETIES. If the varieties are of the same species, usually the European VINIFERA species, then the result may also be known as an **intraspecific cross**—MÜLLER-THURGAU would be one example. Crosses of the same species are different from HYBRIDS, sometimes called **interspecific crosses**, which contain the genes of more than one species of the VITIS genus.

Crouchen, or **Cruchen**, white grape variety producing neutral wines in both South Africa and Australia. It originated in the western Pyrenees of France but is no longer grown there in any quantity, thanks to its sensitivity to FUNGAL DISEASES. There are records of its shipment to Clare Valley in SOUTH AUSTRALIA in 1850 and for long it was confused with Semillon, which Australians were wont to call Riesling. It was therefore known principally as Clare Riesling in Australia until 1976, when AMPELOGRAPHER Paul Truel identified it as this relatively obscure French variety. Just over 100 ha/250 acres remained in 2012. The South Africans finally started to name their Crouchen correctly rather than calling it Cape Riesling just as it virtually disappeared from their vineyard statistics.

crown caps, small metal caps used on beer and soda bottles, have proved to be a very reliable closure for long-term wine bottle storage (see Helmut BECKER) and provide an extremely cheap and efficient closure for any sort of wine. Many wine drinkers find their association with what they regard as less sophisticated drinks unacceptable, particularly when it comes to wine service in a restaurant, but they have been enjoying a modest renaissance with the PET-NAT category. The crown cap is also used nearly universally for closing SPARKLING WINE bottles during the TIRAGE process; DISGORGING is much more difficult if a cork has to be extracted. Some sparkling wines have been released under crown seal in Australia, to avoid the possibility of CORK TAINT.

crown gall, BACTERIAL DISEASE which occurs on over 600 plant species, including vines, particularly when grown where winters are so cold that vines can be damaged (see WINTER FREEZE). High incidence of the disease can make vineyards uneconomic. All VINIFERA varieties are susceptible, but some *V. labrusca* varieties are more tolerant, one reason why such species tend to be grown in very cold climates.

The disease, also known as black knot, is caused by *Agrobacterium tumefaciens*. The

major symptom is the growth of fleshy galls (tumours) on the lower trunk which can girdle the trunk and portions of the vine above may die. At one time it was believed that the bacterium lived in the soil like its relative that causes galls on other plants. However, crown gall of vines lives inside the vine itself and so is spread at planting. Control of crown gall is difficult. Research in the early 1990s suggested that hot water treatment of dormant cuttings (50 °C/122 °F for 30 minutes) reduces the bacterium, and TISSUE CULTURE offers total elimination by producing nursery stock free of crown gall. Avoiding the disease in new plants can also help to reduce winter freeze injury to trunks. In the north eastern UNITED STATES, the growers train the vines with up to five trunks so that there is always a young healthy trunk to replace dead or dying ones. See TRAINING SYSTEMS.

In recent years, the crown gall bacterium has been the focus of intense research due to its application in GENETIC MODIFICATION in a wide range of plants other than vines. *Agrobacterium* has the ability to incorporate its own DNA (the genetic code) into the plant where it is combined with that of the host, and can thus be used to transfer new genes into the plant.   R.E.S.

Pearson, R. C., and Goheen, A. C., (eds.), *Compendium of Grape Diseases* (St Paul, Minn., 1988).

Crozes-Hermitage, the northern RHÔNE'S biggest appellation, regularly producing more than eleven times as much wine as the much more distinguished vineyards of HERMITAGE which it surrounds, and still considerably more than the similarly priced, and similarly extended, appellation of ST-JOSEPH across the river. Like both these appellations, Crozes-Hermitage is usually red and made exclusively of the SYRAH grape, although a certain proportion, just over a tenth, of full-bodied dry white wine is made from the MARSANNE grape supplemented by ROUSSANNE. Up to 15% of white grapes may theoretically be added to red Crozes at the time of FERMENTATION. Although some bottlers have treated the appellation with little respect for quality, a nucleus of excitingly ambitious producers such as Belle, Colombier, Graillot, Pochon, and Tardieu-Laurent emerged from the late 1980s to provide thoughtfully made Crozes-Hermitage of real distinction and mass. The best reds are softer and fruitier than Hermitage because the soils are richer (and because it is more difficult to justify BARREL MATURATION at Crozes prices), but they tend to share more of Hermitage's solidity than average St-Joseph. A more typical red Crozes, however, exhibits the burnt rubber smell and sinewy build of overstretched Syrah, although the COOPERATIVE in the town of Tain l'Hermitage, two-thirds of whose production is Crozes-Hermitage, should not be underestimated. Les

Chassis, between the *autoroute* south of Tain and the river, provides some of the finest red Crozes, including JABOULET's Domaine de Thalabert, which was for long the appellation's principal standard-bearer. Parts of Gervan just north of Tain enjoy a MESOCLIMATE very much closer to that of Hermitage than the flatter vineyards to the east, which are some of the few in the northern Rhône which can be harvested by machine. The clay-limestone alluvial soils of Crozes-Hermitage seem generally less well suited to white wine production, although there are some successful vineyards around Mercurol. The appellation, which dates from 1937, takes its name from a small village just north of Tain without any particular vinous claim. Total vineyard area in production expanded by about a quarter between 1990 and 2005 and by the early 2010s was more than 1,500 ha/3,700 acres. The best reds can be kept for five years or more (and in good years can happily survive for ten) but the average Crozes, red or white, is probably at its best drunk young.

Livingstone-Learmonth, J., *The Wines of the Northern Rhône* (Berkeley, 2005).

cru, French specialist term for a vineyard, usually reserved for those officially recognized as of superior quality. Such recognition was already known in Ancient ROME. In English the word is often translated as 'growth'. PREMIERS CRUS, for example, are called FIRST GROWTHS in BORDEAUX, according to one of their official CLASSIFICATIONS. A cru that has been 'classified' is a **cru classé**, or CLASSED GROWTH. GRANDS CRUS can also have a very specific meaning, notably in BURGUNDY and ALSACE.

The top-ranked communes in BEAUJOLAIS are called crus, and their produce is Cru Beaujolais.

In SWITZERLAND, the first two vineyards to be officially awarded cru status were the neighbouring Dézaley and Calamin in Vaud.

The term has been enthusiastically adopted in Italy, where there have been some attempts to define various superior vineyards as crus. The local dialect for such a site in PIEMONTE is SORÌ.

cru artisan was recognized by the EU in 2002 as a 'traditional expression' reserved for AOC wines from a particular category of wine estates in the Médoc, the Haut-Médoc, Margaux, Moulis, Listrac, St-Julien, Pauillac, and St-Estèphe. A cru artisan is more humble, and generally much smaller, than a CRU BOURGEOIS.

cru bourgeois, a category of red wine properties, or CRUS, designated bourgeois, or a social stratum below the supposedly aristocratic crus classés. While the crus classés represent about 25% of the Médoc's total wine production from 60 estates, the crus bourgeois, from a possible total of more than 250 generally

much smaller estates, represent a further 40% or so. The properties can vary, however, from simple smallholdings to others such as Ch Larose-Trintaudon, the largest estate in the Médoc with its own vast château buildings, or Ch Clarke of Listrac, on which Baron Edmond de ROTHSCHILD lavished a large fortune.

The description 'cru bourgeois' has been used orally for several centuries and appeared in an early edition of COCKS ET FÉRET in the mid 19th century, but the First World War and then the dire state of the international wine market at the end of the 1920s called for a new impetus. A first CLASSIFICATION of the crus bourgeois of the Médoc was drawn up in 1932, and one can only imagine the difficulties of bestowing this supposed commercial advantage, ranked into three different classes, on a few hundred Médoc wine farmers. Thirty years later, when the Syndicate of Crus Bourgeois set about revitalizing itself, it was discovered that, of the 444 members registered in 1932, more than 300 had been absorbed into other estates, or converted their land from viticulture to another crop such as pines instead. The lack of official recognition by the Minister of Agriculture when the list was first drawn up in 1932 was a constant source of difficulty and potential abuse of the title, but the designation Cru Bourgeois was officially recognized in the EU labelling laws of 1979 on condition that its use be codified by the French government.

In 2003 there was an ill-fated attempt to draw up a permanent classification of crus bourgeois properties but from 2008, cru bourgeois has been not an official designation of estates but a self-regulated accolade awarded annually to particular wines, on the basis of blind tasting by a professional panel and announced each September two years after the harvest. Thus the number of crus bourgeois varies from year to year but the proportion of crus bourgeois is usually particularly high in the HAUT-MÉDOC and MÉDOC appellations, and also in MOULIS and LISTRAC. In general this category can offer some of Bordeaux's best-value and most accessible wines. They are made mainly from Cabernet Sauvignon grapes but often contain quite a high proportion of Merlot, usually supplemented by some Cabernet Franc. Some BARREL MATURATION is usually involved in the making of the most highly priced crus bourgeois, even if only a small proportion of new OAK is lavished on this wine category. However, viticulture and winemaking at the best crus bourgeois can be very similar to that practised by the crus classés (even if the selling prices are much lower). The wines are generally ready to drink at between four and eight years old but the best may be aged up to 15 years.

Cruess, William Vere (1886–1968), biochemist, teacher, and author, was the link

between work in wine research and teaching of the pre-PROHIBITION and post-Repeal eras in CALIFORNIA and thus had a central role in the restoration of the California wine industry. Professor of Food Technology at the University of California at Berkeley, Cruess had researched FERMENTATION before Prohibition. In the 'dry years' he studied such things as the production of grape syrup and other VINE PRODUCTS. Immediately upon Repeal he undertook to re-establish viticultural and oenological research at the University of California and did so with remarkable speed and efficiency. His *Principles and Practices of Wine Making* (1934) was the first work for the guidance of commercial winemaking published after Repeal.

Cruet, named CRU east of the vermouth town of CHAMBÉRY whose name may be added to the eastern French appellation Vin de SAVOIE. Cruet is dominated by its CO-OPERATIVE, which makes a range of wines from all the principal Savoie varieties.

Cruse, the most patrician and numerous of the merchant families who occupied the Quai des Chartrons, playing an important part in the BORDEAUX TRADE in wine. Hermann Cruse came to Bordeaux in 1819 from Schleswig-Holstein and opened his office in the Chartrons. The family's fortune was made in 1848 and 1849, when Cruse made a vast speculation on the 1847 vintage, described by the BROKERS Tastet & Lawton as 'very abundant, exquisite but not big'. Since 1848 was the year of revolution in France when Louis-Philippe fled to England, and revolutions broke out in Germany, wine prices slumped. Cruse bought no fewer than 13,650 TONNEAUX from 130 CRUS, nearly all MÉDOC and particularly CRUS BOURGEOIS for the German market.

In 1852, Hermann Cruse bought Ch Laujac in the Bas-Médoc, still owned by the family. In 1865, he bought his biggest property, the first in a series of CLASSED GROWTH acquisitions, Ch Pontet-Canet in PAUILLAC. In the same year Edouard Cruse acquired Ch Giscours in MARGAUX, which they resold in 1913. In 1903, Frédéric Cruse inherited Ch Rauzan-Ségla in Margaux from his clergyman father-in-law, and this was sold in 1956. In 1945, Emmanuel Cruse purchased Ch d'Issan in a semi-derelict condition. It took many years to restore this fine, moated 17th century château and its cellars.

After the beginning of the 1970s, wine prices in Bordeaux rose sharply and by 1973 had reached a point for generic red BORDEAUX AOC that made it impossible for merchants to fulfil their contracts without substantial loss. A disreputable broker persuaded the Cruse company, then chiefly run by the younger generation headed by Lionel, son of Emmanuel, to buy

TABLE WINE for resale as APPELLATION CONTRÔLÉE Bordeaux. No doubt other firms were involved, but Cruse was the most prominent merchant of Bordeaux at this time and a much-publicized trial took place in 1974. The broker was sent to prison, and the Cruses received a suspended sentence together with a huge fine, substantially reduced on appeal. The firm never recovered from this and in 1979 was sold. In 1975 Ch Pontet-Canet was bought by Guy Tesseron, Emmanuel Cruse's son-in-law and a Cognac merchant who already owned Ch Lafon-Rochet. Ch d'Issan is still owned by the Cruse family and run by today's Emmanuel Cruse. The affair broadly coincided with the decline and sale, mostly to foreign concerns, of those houses that had formed the core of the Bordeaux trade, among whom the Cruses were for long the leaders.   E.P.-R.

Brook, S., *The Complete Bordeaux* (rev. edn, London, 2010).

Faith, N., *The Winemasters* (3rd edn, London, 2005).

crush, mainly American term for the whole HARVEST season, named after one of the first processes in the winery (CRUSHING) rather than what happens in the vineyard.

crusher-destemmer, common combination of winemaking equipment which carries out the operations of both CRUSHING and DESTEMMING.

crushing (*foulage* in French), winemaking operation of breaking open the grape berry so that the juice is more readily available to the YEAST for FERMENTATION and to increase the pulp and SKIN CONTACT. Modern winery equipment that permits sufficiently thorough crushing has effectively speeded up the onset and completion of fermentation. The additional advantages of this are that the rapid accumulation of alcohol discourages any activity on the part of wild yeast and BACTERIA. The principal result is that an overwhelming proportion of grapes finish as attractive and balanced wines rather than as VINEGAR or unacceptably faulty wines.

Crushing was traditionally done by foot, by treading grapes thinly spread on a crushing floor slanted towards a drain and bounded by low walls to prevent the loss of juice. Foot treading is a relatively inefficient method of crushing, however, and extremely expensive in areas where LABOUR costs are more than minimal—which is why it persisted in the production of PORT in the DOURO, although even there ROBOTIC alternatives have become more attractive.

Modern **crushers** operate on one of two general principles. One type uses intermeshed counter-rotating corrugated rollers spaced far enough apart to pass grape seeds (which exude bitter TANNINS and rancid oils if smashed) but smash anything larger. Such machines generally

incorporate a stem-separating unit (see DESTEMMING) and are therefore known as **crusher-destemmers**, **crusher-stemmers** in the United States, *fouloir-égrappoirs* in France. The other general type also incorporates a destemmer but crushes the clusters by impacting them with paddles on a more rapidly rotating concentric shaft. Some machines are roller destemmers, while others are destemmer rollers, and many modern machines are sufficiently flexible for either the rollers or the destemmers to be left out.

It is to minimize the period over which grapes are crushed that the grapes are increasingly transported from vineyard to winery in shallow containers, ideally no more than 20 to 60 cm (8–23 in) deep, and why pressing stations are increasingly located close to the vineyard.   A.D.W.

crust, name for the SEDIMENT that forms in bottle-aged PORT, consisting of molecules that have become too heavy to stay in solution. **Crusted port** is a style of port created by British shippers in order to provide some of the qualities of vintage port in a shorter time, and therefore at a lower price.

cryoextraction (**cryo** referring to very low temperatures), French term, now used more widely, for freeze CONCENTRATION, the controversial winemaking practice of artificially replicating the natural conditions necessary to produce sweet white ICE WINE. Freshly picked grapes are held overnight in a special cold room at sub-zero temperatures, −5 or −6 °C (21 °F) for example, and then pressed immediately. The freezing point of grape must depends on its concentration of sugars, so only the less ripe grapes freeze. PRESSING the grapes straight out of the cold room therefore yields only the juice of the non-frozen, ripest grapes, whose chemical composition remains unchanged. The colder the grapes are kept, the less but richer juice is obtained, and vice versa. The wine producer can therefore manipulate how much wine of what quality is made (unlike ice wine, which is entirely dictated by natural conditions). The technique is particularly useful in wet vintages in which the health and ripeness of individual berries may vary. In the late 1980s some Sauternes properties, including Ch d'YQUEM, experimented with the technique.

crystals in a bottle of white wine, on the underside of a cork, or on the inside of a vat, are harmless deposits. See TARTRATES for a full explanation.

Cserszegi Fűszeres, IRSAI OLIVER × TRAMINER cross developed in HUNGARY in 1960 and widely planted there for basic grapey wines. Plantings totalled 3,608 ha/8,900 acres in 2011, mainly in Kunság.

CSIRO (**Commonwealth Scientific and Industrial Research Organization**), founded in 1926, is one of the world's largest and most diverse research institutions. Its charter covers research into areas of economic, environmental, and social benefit to AUSTRALIA. Early research focused on solving immediate problems relating to the adaptation of northern hemisphere practices, irrigation, and pest and disease control to the new Australian viticultural frontiers.

After the Second World War, CSIRO's viticultural research broadened to include nematology (see NEMATODES), IRRIGATION, hydrology, and basic VINE PHYSIOLOGY. In the 1960s, there was an even greater shift in emphasis to viticultural research. A new laboratory was opened in Adelaide to accommodate a group of plant (largely vine) physiologists. An early result of research was the introduction of the complementary management techniques of MINIMAL PRUNING and MECHANICAL HARVESTING.

Around this time, the grapevine germplasm collection was established at Mildura and now contains around 680 varieties of many species. VINE BREEDING and selection has yielded a number of new varieties such as TARRANGO, TAMINGA, TYRIAN, and CIENNA as well as successful table and drying grapes.

In the 1990s, CSIRO extended its research to encompass computer modelling of vine growth, water and nutrient application, YIELD estimation, and PRECISION VITICULTURE. GENETIC MODIFICATION is an increasingly important avenue of research in viticulture worldwide, and CSIRO achieved the transformation of Sultana and a range of wine grape varieties in the late 1990s. The genes controlling colour were also identified.

New CSIRO wine-grape research initiatives include a focus on disease resistance, RIPENING, and flavour and aroma development in berries, this last aimed at understanding the management and genetics of grape flavour and aroma and links to final wine quality.

Results of CSIRO research have given Australian viticulturists access to improved varieties, ROOTSTOCKS resistant to salt and nematodes, and water and nutrient management strategies suited to different environments.   R.E.S.

Cuba. The ubiquitous Chardonnay is said to be grown on this Caribbean island in the tobacco-growing region of Pinar del Rio but most 'Cuban wine' is imported in bulk.

cultivar, term developed by professional botanists to mean a group of plants sharing common characteristics persisting under cultivation that have either been selected or otherwise genetically manipulated by humans. According to the rules of plant taxonomy, cultivar would be a more appropriate term than VARIETY but the term does not have a wide following outside professional botanists and horticulturists, except in South Africa, where it is widely and generally used. It has a major deficiency in that it has no adjectival form, and therefore no counterpart to VARIETAL.

cultivation, the vineyard process of ploughing the soil, normally to kill weeds. The type of cultivation and its frequency vary from region to region around the world. Initially cultivation was by hand-held hoes. Animals were subsequently used to pull ploughs. For modern vineyards, tractor-mounted discs or tines disturb the topsoil and kill weeds. Cultivation within the vine row requires a special plough that will avoid trunks. Initially these were manually operated to dodge in and out; later, touch or electronic sensors were used to activate a hydraulic mechanism. Because of root and trunk damage, this practice was replaced in many vineyards by the use of undervine HERBICIDES. However, since the last two decades of the 20th century, growers in both the Old and New Worlds wishing to avoid the use of AGROCHEMICALS have returned to undervine cultivation. This has been assisted by the development of hoes which are more efficient and have more sensitive and accurate 'tripping' mechanisms, thus reducing damage to the vines. Some producers, including those as notable as Ch LATOUR and Leflaive of Puligny-Montrachet, have even gone back to using HORSES.

Cultivation of the soil to control weed growth is particularly common in regions with irrigation or summer rainfall. A fastidiously cultivated vineyard is still regarded as a sign of good husbandry in some regions, but there is a growing recognition for many vineyards that cultivation damages SOIL STRUCTURE and can lead, for example, to problems of water infiltration. and SOIL COMPACTION. The planting of COVER CROPS or allowing volunteer plants to grow is becoming more common.   R.E.S.

Curicó, distinctive wine zone in the Central Valley of CHILE formed by subzones Lontué and Teno, officially part of the Maule region.

currants, small, dark DRYING GRAPES made from the vine variety called **Zante Currant** (in Australia) or Black Corinth (in California). As Korinthiaki, this dark-skinned variety originated in Greece, which is where most of the world's currants are produced, and takes its name from a corruption of the word Corinth. It has very occasionally been used for winemaking in California and Australia.

Currency Creek, a cool, maritime region with eight producers by 2014 in the Fleurieu Zone of SOUTH AUSTRALIA producing BORDEAUX BLENDS (white and red), plus Shiraz. All are elegant.

Curtefranca. See FRANCIACORTA.

custom crush facility, American term for a winery specializing in vinifying grapes on behalf of many different vine-growers, typically those without their own winemaking equipment. The various wines are kept separate and marketed by the growers under their own labels. Such operations have played an important part in establishing ambitious new wine producers, as in CALIFORNIA and Long Island in NEW YORK, and indeed whole new wine regions such as Marlborough and Central Otago in NEW ZEALAND, where new or small-scale growers can ill afford to build their own wineries.

Custoza, Bianco di, or **Custoza**, a straightforward dry white wine produced in the VENETO region of north-east Italy in a wide stretch of territory extending south westward from the city of Verona partially overlapping the BARDOLINO DOC zone on the shores of Lake Garda and immediately south of the lake. The total vineyard area had fallen to just over 1,200 ha/2,964 acres by 2011. The substantial presence of TREBBIANO Toscano grapes (constituting 10 to 45% of the blend), blended with GARGANEGA (20 to 40%), a local strain of FRIULIANO known as Trebianello (5 to 30%), and a variety of other grapes (Riesling Italico, Pinot Bianco, Chardonnnay, Malvasia Toscana), tends to yield a rather colourless, neutral wine on the fertile soils of this zone. While substantial research in SOIL composition and MESOCLIMATES was executed in 2010, resulting in the identification of ten subzones, this has yet to result in either innovation or an increase in quality.   W.S.

cut cane, viticultural technique designed to increase the sugar concentration in almost-ripe grapes. The term originated in Australia, where this technique is typically used to produce sweet wines, but it is apparently also used occasionally for dry red wines, for example, by Bertani in the Veneto, and even for Spätburgunder in Germany, even though it is illegal there. By cutting the canes almost at the time of HARVEST, water supply to the fruit is halted, and so the berries start to shrivel (as in the production of DRIED-GRAPE WINES). Sugar concentration is elevated as water is lost through the berry skin and ACIDITY may also be increased. The technique, resulting in grapes known as PASSERILLÉS in French, was developed to avert rain spoilage of DRYING GRAPES.
R.E.S. & D.S.

cuttings, cut lengths of canes used for vine PROPAGATION. Cuttings are the basis of propagation for commercial grape production, whether as own-rooted plants (see ROOTLINGS), or as scion varieties for GRAFTING on to ROOTSTOCK. Both methods are representative of asexual or vegetative propagation and the progeny are considered as CLONES of the source vines. In commerce, cuttings are cut from dormant vines in lengths of 30 to 45 cm (12–18 in).

Once made, the cuttings are kept cool and moist and planted in a nursery in spring for roots to form at the base, and a shoot to grow from the top bud. The plant is now called a rootling. It is lifted from the nursery in autumn and planted in its vineyard position the following spring.   B.G.C.

cutworms, the larvae of several species of moths, are one of the most serious pests of all sorts of crops worldwide. They hide in the soil or under the vine's bark during the day and emerge to feed and cause damage at night. Young vines are particularly prone to damage. When cultural practices, natural enemies, and climatic factors do not keep cutworms to tolerable levels, there are highly effective chemical agents which can prevent major losses. DDT was once used, but there are now effective contact insecticides.   M.J.E.

cuve is French for a vat or tank. Thus, a **cuverie** is the vat hall, typically where fermentation takes place. *Cuves* may be made of any material:—wood, concrete, or, most likely, stainless steel, and come in many different shapes and sizes. See FERMENTATION VESSEL.

cuve close, French for sealed tank, and a name for a bulk sparkling winemaking process (sometimes called Charmat) which involves provoking a second fermentation in wine stored in a pressure tank. For more details, see SPARKLING WINEMAKING.

cuvée, French wine term derived from CUVE, with many different meanings in different contexts. In general terms it can be used to mean any containerful, or even any lot, of wine and therefore wine labels often carry relatively meaningless descriptions incorporating the word *cuvée*. **Tête de cuvée**, on the other hand, is occasionally used for the top bottling of a French wine producer, particularly in Sauternes.

In CHAMPAGNE and other environments in which traditional method sparkling wines are made, *cuvée* is a name for the first and best juice to flow from the press (see SPARKLING WINEMAKING). The blend of base wines assembled for second fermentation in bottle is also known as the *cuvée*. Thus the term is often used in many champagne and sparkling wine names.

Elsewhere, particularly in German-speaking wine regions oddly enough, *cuvée* may be used to describe any ambitious blend, particularly of different vine varieties.

Cyprus, eastern Mediterranean island less than 100 km/60 miles from Syria to the east and Turkey to the north. The majority of wine production is concentrated in the southern Greek part of the island. The few wineries that do exist in the northern Turkish-controlled zone are of little commercial significance. The medieval Cyprus wine industry was commercially the most important in the Middle East, but for most of the 20th century, Cyprus wine languished in terms of quality. Investment from the 1990s led to an improvement in production techniques and resulting wines, with EU membership in 2004 stimulating even greater changes and restructuring of the industry. The Greek financial crisis hit this small island particularly hard and in spring 2013 it became the fifth EU country to require a bail-out from European funds. The total vineyard area had dropped to about 9,000 ha/22,200 acres by 2013 but still represented about 8% of the island's cultivated agricultural land.

History

Because of its position in the eastern Mediterranean, closer to the Middle East than to GREECE, Cyprus has changed hands many times. In antiquity, domination by various foreign powers alternated with brief periods of independence, and in 58 BC Cyprus became part of the Roman province of Cilicia in Asia Minor. Strabo (*Geography*, 7 BC) and PLINY mention the wine of Cyprus approvingly but it was not particularly famous. In AD 668 Cyprus was occupied by Arabs; when they were finally expelled in 965 Cyprus became an advance base of the Greek navy. In 1191, in the course of the Third CRUSADE, Richard I, king of England, conquered Cyprus and sold it to the Templars, who soon gave it back to him, whereupon he presented it to the rejected king of Jerusalem, Guy de Lusignan. Guy de Lusignan imposed a feudal system on Cyprus and governed the island as a separate kingdom, which it remained until it became a colony of the then powerful VENICE in 1489.

The Crusaders and Venetian expansionism made the island part of the Latin west, which soon became fond of its wines. The earliest record of Cyprus wine being drunk in the west is dated 1178 when Count Baldwin of Guines offered it to the archbishop of Rheims. The wine is clearly a rare luxury, designed to impress an ecclesiastical magnate. In the next century it became more widely available. The Old French poem *La Bataille des vins* (see MEDIEVAL LITERATURE) awards the palm to *chypre*, Cyprus wine, because it is stronger and sweeter than any wine that is to be had in western Europe (FORTIFICATION and MUTAGE were as yet unknown). We do not know when the wines of Cyprus first reached the English market, but in the 13th and 14th centuries they, along with other sweet wines from the east and from Italy (see ENGLAND), fetched higher prices than the wines of GASCONY and LA ROCHELLE. The Venetians shipped them from Cyprus to Venice in their galleys, and from Venice they distributed them all over Europe.

The distinctive sweet wine COMMANDARIA preserves in its name a piece of crusading history.

When the fall of Acre, in 1281, ended the Latin Christian presence in Palestine and Syria, the Knights Hospitallers moved their headquarters from Acre to Cyprus and thence to Rhodes. Like all religious orders, the Knights Hospitallers (or Knights of St John) acquired land on a large scale and grew wine. Their organization was strictly hierarchical, into priorates, then bailiwicks, and lastly commanderies. A commandery was a manor or group of manors under the authority of a commendator. Each commandery had its vineyard or vineyards: hence the name.   H.M.W.

Dion, R., *Histoire de la vigne et du vin en France* (Paris, 1959).

Simon, A. L., *The History of the Wine Trade in England*, 3 vols. (London, 1906–9).

Modern history

Ottoman rule (1571–1878) brought a steep decline in wine production, and in the importance of the wine industry, which remained in an underdeveloped state until the middle of the 19th century, the first of the modern wineries, Haggipavlu, not being founded until 1844. British administration of the island (1878–1960) saw a further revitalization of the industry, with Cyprus 'sherry', as this fortified wine was then allowed to call itself, becoming an important product for the first time. The invasion of northern Cyprus by Turkey in 1974, and subsequent political problems, hardly affected the wine industry, concentrated in the southern part of the island. Today, wine continues to play an important role in the agricultural economy of the Greek Cypriot, southern Republic of Cyprus.

After the Second World War, the majority of the island's wine exports fell into four categories, tellingly reflecting the needs of different countries: large volumes of very basic wine for eastern-bloc countries; wine intended for industrial uses such as VERMOUTH, SANGRÍA, or, in German-speaking countries, commercially prepared GLÜHWEIN; GRAPE CONCENTRATE sent chiefly in the early 1990s to Japan, Central and Eastern Europe, and the United Kingdom, where it was reconstituted and made into BRITISH WINE; and Cyprus fortified wine.

Climate and geography

Most vineyards are on the south-facing side of the Troodos Mountains, where a combination of ELEVATION and rain make viticulture possible on what would otherwise be too hot and dry an island. The best vineyards lie where the rains fall, in valleys at 600 m/1,980 ft up to nearly 1,500 m/4,950 ft. To bring the industry in line with the EU, a CONTROLLED APPELLATION scheme has been developed for Commandaria, Laona Akama, Pitsilia, Vouni Panayia-Ambelitis, Krasochoria Lemesou, Krasochoria Lemesou-Afames, and Krasochoria

Lemesou-Laona, all PDOs, although the scheme has so far been little used. There are also four regions for PGI wines: Pafos, Lemesos, Larnaca, and Lefkosia, accounting for nearly half of production.

Pitsilia and the northern (higher elevation) half of Commandaria have igneous soil and subsoil. Elsewhere soils are of sedimentary LIMESTONE with a particularly high active LIME content.

The climate is typically MEDITERRANEAN: mild winters and hot summers with precipitation confined to the winter months. Rainfall is low: 500 mm/19 in per annum is the mean for the lower-elevation vineyards and 900 mm/35 in for the higher. DRIP IRRIGATION is permitted, although limited water availability and very fragmented, small vineyard holdings make it rare in practice.

The great variation in temperatures between low- and high-elevation vineyards (resulting in mean minimum summer temperatures varying from 9 to 20 °C/48 to 68 °F) results in one of the most extended vintage periods in the world. Picking usually starts in mid July and continues until early November. Climatic hazards are restricted to HAIL and, in higher-elevation vineyards, spring and autumn FROST. The lack of humidity means that DOWNY MILDEW is unknown but growers regularly spray against POWDERY MILDEW. BOTRYTIS is found only in grape bunches that have previously been attacked by eudemis MOTHS or other INSECTS. Almost all vines are BUSH trained, the exceptions being non-indigenous varieties supported by TRELLISING systems.

Vine varieties

Cyprus has never been invaded by PHYLLOXERA, and its ungrafted vines are still protected by strict QUARANTINE—slowing the introduction of INTERNATIONAL VARIETIES. By 2012, even after considerable restructuring, 3,973 ha/9,815 acres of the island's 9,000 ha of wine-grape vineyards were still planted with the indigenous and rather unexciting grape MAVRO, so common that its name simply means 'black', while the local XYNISTERI accounts for another 2,064 ha. Xynisteri can make appealing, delicate dry whites if grown at high elevations, and occasionally more serious styles. Shiraz/Syrah (286 ha) has overtaken Cabernet Sauvignon (229 ha), Cabernet Franc (187 ha), and Carignan (226 ha) as the most significant incomer, having proved well suited to the island's hot, dry soils. indigenous Maratheftiko (known as Vamvakada around Pitsilia) (165 ha) is making increasingly interesting and impressive reds where efforts have been put into vineyard management, while tannic Lefkada can add some local spice to blends. Ophthalmo is another local red grown on 102 ha and, while better than Mavro, it does not produce wines of great interest. Other white wine varieties include Sultanina (507 ha), often vinified for wine though unexciting, followed by

Chardonnay (114 ha), and Muscat of Alexandria (100 ha), with limited plantings of Palomino, Sémillon, Sauvignon Blanc, and Riesling.

Maratheftiko has perhaps the greatest potential for quality. It is often found in mixed plantings due to its need for a cross pollinator. It ripens later than the Mavro that it is often planted with and is therefore difficult and expensive to pick at optimum ripeness in these older vineyards. Recent single-vineyard plantings are more promising. Lefkada, with small bunches and producing deeply coloured, very well-structured reds, has considerable potential as a blending grape but is generally too tannic as a VARIETAL wine. Typically, the land is worked by the older generation, and most vineyard work is done by hand. The increasing urbanization of younger Cypriots suggests a likely vineyard LABOUR shortage in future.

Modern-day industry structure

Until the late 1980s, almost all Cypriot wine was made in large wineries near the docks of Limassol or Paphos, at a considerable distance from the vineyards. Equipment was basic with little TEMPERATURE CONTROL or HYGIENE. At this time production was dominated by four large firms—SODAP, Keo, ETKO, and Loel. From the 1990s there was a marked change in the island's wine industry. The large companies invested in much-improved equipment, and wineries were built in the mountains nearer to the grape-growing areas, well away from the

heat of the coast. Smaller satellite wineries have also been built to allow producers to comply with regulations for production of PGI, and occasionally PDO, wines, and alongside this a number of small, quality-focused estates have been developed. Some foreign CONSULTANT winemakers were employed in the early part of this development, but less so in the 21st century as local winemakers have trained abroad.

When Cyprus joined the EU in 2004, its wine industry underwent further revolution. Where in the past subsidies were paid for exporting vast quantities of nondescript wine in bulk to manufacturers of cheap drinks (the Soviets were big customers), more recently they have resulted in removal of the worst vineyards and planting in the mountainous interior as well as relocating and equipping wineries. By 2014, 52 wine producers were registered (including multiple wineries owned by larger companies). The only grower-owned CO-OPERATIVE SODAP (which is now a reliable producer of good-value wine) crushed 24% of the island's crop in 2013 but the other registered wineries, 35 crush less than 100,000 kg of grapes a year, and only eight crush over 200 tonnes. The industry has largely changed focus from bulk towards quality and today the best producers are making genuinely exciting wines from their own vineyards and using modern equipment.

See also COMMANDARIA.   C.G.

www.cypruswinemuseum.com
www.winesofcyprus.co.uk

cytokinins, natural HORMONES in vines produced in the root tips and affecting the growth of other parts of the plant. Cytokinins favour cell multiplication and affect growth and development of shoots and INFLORESCENCES. Fewer cytokinins are produced in dry soils, and also in cold and wet soils, and this appears to be critical for BUDBREAK and early shoot growth.

Czech Republic, better known for its BEER, officially split from SLOVAKIA, the eastern part of what was Czechoslovakia, in 1993. It took less than a third of the productive vineyard area, just over 40% of wine production, and around two-thirds of the wine consumption of the original Czechoslovakia. The republic grew about 18,000 ha/44,480 acres of vines in 2014. In preparation for EU membership, in 1995 the Czech Republic passed wine laws modelled on the GERMAN WINE LAW, amending them in 2000 and 2004. In response to the EU reforms of 2008, the new terms CHZO (PGI) and CHOP (PDO) have been introduced.

The republic and its vineyards divide into two distinct regions: the tiny, touristy vineyards of BOHEMIA in towns such as Roudnice, Mělník, and Litoměřice on the banks of the River Labe (Germany's Elbe) in the north; and, quantitatively much more important, MORAVIA to the south along the Austrian and Slovakian borders.

About two-fifths of the vineyards lie on gentle slopes, usually topped by woodland, while the rest are on undulating plains which fall

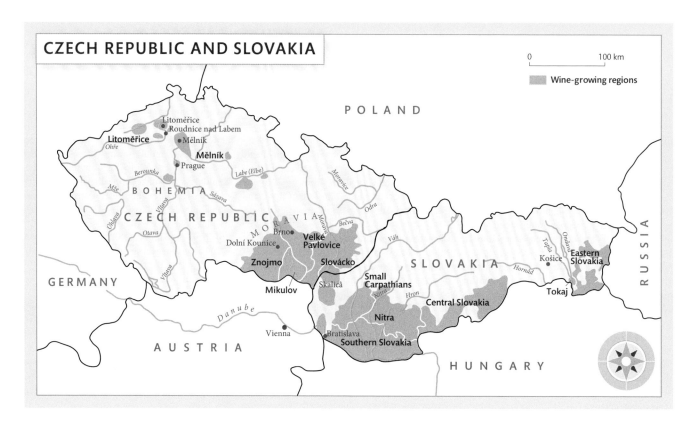

CZECH REPUBLIC AND SLOVAKIA

Wine-growing regions

away to the flatter Danube Basin. In terms of GEOLOGY, Bohemia and Moravia are very different, with the most notable phenomena being the GRANITE of Brno pluton in Dolní Kounice and the Jurassic LIMESTONE of the Palava Hills. The lower reaches where most vineyards are tend towards CLAY and SAND, but the major influences are the relatively low ELEVATION (between 100 and 250 m (330–820 ft) above sea level) and the CONTINENTAL CLIMATE. Rainfall in Moravia is relatively low, on average between a half and two-thirds of the annual rainfall in Burgundy and Alsace on the same latitude, which has encouraged the adoption of ORGANIC VITICULTURE. Because of their position north of the Danube, most of the slopes face south and are protected by higher land in the north. The vines are trained like those of Germany and Austria. Ryzlink Rýnský (RIESLING), Rulandské Bílé (PINOT BLANC), Ryzlink Vlašský (WELSCH-RIESLING), MÜLLER-THURGAU, Veltlínské Zelené (GRÜNER VELTLINER), and Sylvánské Zelené (SIL-VANER) are the major white wine varieties, together with the Muscat-scented IRSAY OLIVER and Chardonnay, whose international name survives intact. The country has the world's largest area of Svatovavřinecké (ST-LAURENT). Frankovka (BLAUFRÄNKISCH), Modrý Portugal (PORTUGIESER), and ZWEIGELTREBE are other significant red wine varieties. Pinot Noir has a long and successful history in Bohemia and has been enthusiastically planted in newer vineyards in Moravia too. Other popular varieties among whites include Frühroter Veltliner, Neuburger, Moravian Muscat (a cross between Muscat Ottonel and Prachttraube), and the dark-skinned varieties André, Alibernet, Cabernet Moravia, Neronet, and a host of newly developed, mainly local, CROSSES resistant to frost and fungal diseases, such as Cerason, Erilon, Laurot, Malverina, and SOLARIS, and those developed by the venerable Professor Vilém Kraus (1924–2013) and his disciples, such as Kofranka, Merlan, and Rubinet.

Grape RIPENESS is generally at a premium and is measured in °NM (normalized must weight measurement) similar to the KMW scale of Austria although 1 °CNM denotes 1 kg of sugar per 100 l of grape must while 1 °KMW denotes 1 kg of sugar in 100 kg of must.

Recently the OIV has had difficulty collecting statistics on total vineyard area since 2008 when it was put at about 18,000 ha/44,480 acres. CHAPTALIZATION is allowed and sometimes practised. Winemaking techniques have fully recovered from the communist era even if many of the mass-market wines are bolstered by wine imported in BULK. Bohemia Sekt is the dominant wine group. Nevertheless a handful of small and medium-sized producers such as Valihrach Dva Duby, Volarik, Madl, and Michlovsky make consistently good wines that justify a premium as well as standing up to increasingly competitively priced imports. Kočařík, Koráb, Stawek, Ševčík, and Vykoukal are members of a group of small, independent producers luxuriating in the name Authentists. Other producers make excellent SPARKLING WINE, ICE WINE and STRAW WINE.   R.J.S.

DAC, Districtus Austria Controllatus, denotes AUSTRIAN appellations of origin established and regulated by grower-dominated regional wine committees and intended to define and promote a typical style and flavour profile (including specified grape varieties) for each of Austria's growing regions. By 2014 there were nine of these. The first, WEINVIERTEL, was established in 2002 while the ninth, Wiener GEMISCHTER SATZ, applies to Viennese wines made from FIELD BLENDS or adjacent parcels of at least three varieties and was created in 2013. Kamptal, Kremstal, and Traisental DACs may be applied to both varietally labelled Riesling and Grüner Veltliner and for most there is both the basic KLASSIK and **DAC Reserve** with higher minimum alcohol and, sometimes, later release. LEITHABERG is subdivided into red and white blends. Six DACs share the name of an official growing region while EISENBERG is named for a village and vineyard site but effectively covers an entire region. DAC is one of the Austrian denominations that is classified as a PDO in EU terminology.

The capital letters DAC appear on labels in immediate conjunction with its name. It is theoretically possible for growers and their committees to decide to be covered by more than one DAC. In 2014 it also remained to be seen how the wine regions to which no DAC has yet applied would elect to define themselves; the three regions are within STEIERMARK, WACHAU, WAGRAM, THERMENREGION, and CARNUNTUM.

See also under the name of specific DACs.   D.S.

Dão, REGIÃO DEMARCADA since 1908, this DOP in north central Portugal produces some of the country's most elegant, mineral red wines (see map under PORTUGAL). Locked in on three sides by granite mountains and sheltered from the Atlantic, Dão benefits from long, warm summers and abundant winter rainfall. (which supports the pine forests whose resin notes can be detected in mature Dão wines, especially reds, but also those made from ENCRUZADO). Granitic sandy soils are well drained (sometimes too well drained—WATER STRESS can prejudice ripening in the lead-up to harvest). Vineyards are stocked with a wealth of indigenous grape varieties, including Portugal's flagship red grape TOURIGA NACIONAL which is thought to have originated here. For much of the second half of the 20th century however, the wines rarely lived up to expectations, a consequence of heavy-handed government intervention since the 1940s.

In a laudable attempt to impose some form of organization on the highly fragmented, largely subsistence economy in the north of Portugal, the Salazar government introduced a programme of co-operativization. Ten CO-OPERATIVES were built in Dão between 1954 and 1971 to much the same design. To make the programme work, the authorities passed legislation giving co-operatives the exclusive right to buy grapes. Private firms were effectively restricted to purchasing ready-made wine. The system served Dão badly. Wines became ever more standardized and, as co-operatives were poorly equipped and paid scant attention to HYGIENE, standards fell. This monopolistic legislation was felt to be incompatible with Portugal's membership of the EU and the law institutionalizing Dão's co-operatives was overturned in 1989. Some enterprising initiatives followed, led by SOGRAPE, which built a modern winery in the heart of the region and an influential band of single estates whose rising numbers has helped consolidate Dão's revival of fortunes.

Although about 80% of Dão wines are still red, thanks to the modern era's introduction of planting varietally blocked vineyards (traditional vineyards comprised FIELD BLENDS) high-quality Touriga Nacional, Tinta Roriz (TEMPRANILLO), Jaen (MENCÍA), and ALFROCHEIRO PRETO have become the mainstay of the region's leading wines. Efforts are also underway to revive some of the region's more obscure varieties. Although tannins are accentuated by the high acidity in the region's wines, modern reds are fruitier—much less austere and tannic—than in the past when many wines suffered from excessively prolonged MACERATION with stalks and protracted ageing in old casks or cement tanks. New French OAK and overripeness can mar TERROIR expression but the

DAC	Region	State
Eisenberg	Südburgenland	Burgenland
Kamptal	Kamptal	Niederösterreich
Kremstal	Kremstal	Niederösterreich
Leithaberg	Neusiedlersee-Hügelland	Burgenland
Mittelburgenland	Mittelburgenland	Burgenland
Neusiedlersee	Neusiedlersee	Burgenland
Traisental	Traisental	Niederösterreich
Weinviertel	Weinviertel	Niederösterreich
Wiener Gemischter Satz	Wien	Wien

pendulum (in some quarters at least) is swinging back in favour of greater restraint.

As for white wines, in line with national trends, they improved markedly in the early 21st century, becoming fruitier without sacrificing varietal complexity or the region's hallmark freshness. Encruzado is without doubt the jewel in the crown, making ageworthy VARIETAL wines that may be crisp and fragrant wines or more Burgundian if BARREL FERMENTATION is employed. Encruzado may also be blended with less structured varieties such as Malvasia Fina and Bical, known here as Borrado das Moscas ('fly droppings').   S.A.

Mayson. R., *The Wines and Vineyards of Portugal* (London, 2003).

Metcalfe, C., McWhirter, K., *The Wine and Food Lover's Guide to Portugal* (Haywards Heath, 2007). www.cvrdao.pt

DAP. See DIAMMONIUM PHOSPHATE.

Davis, the usual abbreviation in the wine world for the influential wine-related faculties of the University of California at Davis, a small city 70 miles north east of San Francisco in California's Central Valley. The city came to be known throughout the world as a centre for research and instruction in all aspects of agriculture because it was the home of the University Farm established in 1906.

Until the late 19th century, grape-growing and winemaking in California had been relatively haphazard, with numerous problems generally unrecognized. An act of state legislature in 1880 directed the nascent University of California to start research and instruction in VITICULTURE and OENOLOGY. The fact that Berkeley, the original site of the university, was too cold and foggy for grape-growing encouraged the establishment of the farm in the warm, inland climate of Davis.

The then Professor of Agriculture, Eugene Hilgard, soon recognized that grafting VINIFERA scions on to hybrid ROOTSTOCKS was the only practical solution to the world's PHYLLOXERA epidemic. He also recognized the importance of matching vine variety to soil and climate for fine wine production. Hilgard established early co-operation between ACADEME and practitioners.

PROHIBITION brought a temporary hiatus in Davis's wine-related activities. In 1959 UC Davis was declared an independent general campus, ending a half-century as a branch of UC Berkeley. The university hired a powerful group of academics including: the late Albert J. WINKLER, famous for his DEGREE DAY/heat summation method of CLIMATE CLASSIFICATION; Harold P. Olmo, breeder of NEW VARIETIES; and well known oenologist Maynard A. AMERINE. The department was also responsible for the development of assays now routinely employed in wineries internationally. This work continues today.

Current research efforts are dedicated to understanding the impact of viticultural practices such as REGULATED DEFICIT IRRIGATION, YIELD, clonal variation, and SITE SELECTION on wine composition and perceived quality. In addition, novel molecular and genetic technologies are being developed and applied to the improvement of both scion and rootstock varieties with the aim of producing vines less susceptible to pests and diseases and increasing understanding of grape berry maturation and flavour and aroma development. Genomics technologies are being used to further understanding of the yeast and bacterial fermentations of wine, to profile the presence and persistence of both wild and spoilage flora, and to map the winery and vineyard microbes (see SOIL BIOTA) and their impact on grape and wine quality. The department is similarly engaged in defining and profiling the key chemical components responsible for wine aroma and flavour, and linking the development and evolution of these components to vineyard practices, using consumers and professionals for sensory evaluation. The department is also playing an important role in defining the bioactive compounds of wines responsible for the health benefits of moderate consumption (see HEALTH). Sophisticated tools for the analysis of wine aroma, flavour, and ageability are also being pioneered and applied to the investigation of wine composition. Consumer preference profiling is being exploited to better understand the phenomenon of preference. Work continues on vine variety identification using DNA PROFILING. The Davis campus also houses the FOUNDATION PLANT SERVICES. The department's new facilities, opened in 2008, have ushered in a new era of SUSTAINABILITY.

Davis continues to be the principal centre for teaching viticulture and oenology in the Americas, and has trained numerous winemakers from around the world. It has become synonymous with a scientific approach to wine production and the understanding of wine quality as opposed to one informed solely by TRADITION and observation.   L.F.B.

day–night temperature difference. See TEMPERATURE VARIABILITY.

deacidification, winemaking process of decreasing the excessive ACIDITY of grape juice or wine made in cold wine regions or, in particularly cool years, in temperate wine regions. A number of techniques for making excessively acid wines more palatable have been developed and are usually strictly governed by local regulations.

MALOLACTIC CONVERSION is a way of lowering acidity biologically, but it is difficult to persuade LACTIC ACID BACTERIA to work in very acid conditions.

Winemakers generally prefer to rely on biological methods for reducing acidity but there are other forms of deacidification which rely on chemical processes, notably adding compounds to MUST or wine that will precipitate significant amounts of acidity as insoluble solids that can be filtered or settle out. Calcium carbonate, or chalk, is the most satisfactory of these, since its addition results in insoluble calcium TARTRATES and the liberation of harmless CARBON DIOXIDE. In some very cool regions, where grapes have higher malic acid levels, the addition of calcium carbonate can lead to an imbalance in the proportion of malic to tartaric acid. Double salt deacidification resolves this by reducing the acidity in the juice and yet maintaining similar proportions of tartaric to malic acid. Other methods include REVERSE OSMOSIS and ELECTRODIALYSIS.

Deacidifications are most effective after fermentation, partly because alcohol decreases the solubility of cream of tartar, thereby reducing some of the must acidity, and fermentation itself produces a better mix of flavour by-products in the more acid solution.

Deacidification is not the commonplace procedure that ACIDIFICATION is in warmer regions. It is practised in northern Germany, Luxembourg, Burgundy, the United Kingdom, Canada, New York State, Tasmania, and New Zealand's South Island in certain years.   A.D.W. & B.W.Z.

dead arm or **dying arm**, common names for several fungal diseases in vine wood that cause cankers and dieback. See TRUNK DISEASES, EUTYPA DIEBACK, PHOMOPSIS, and BLACK DEAD ARM.

dead fruit. See SURMATURITÉ.

dealcoholized wine is produced in an attempt to provide a drink that tastes like wine but has none of the negative implications for HEALTH or subsequent activity such as driving. Such wines also have fewer calories than regular wine, fewer than 150 calories per bottle in many cases. They may broadly be divided into dealcoholized wine, with an ALCOHOLIC STRENGTH of less than 0.5%, and partially dealcoholized wines in which the alcohol may be reduced to as little as 0.5%.

Wine may be dealcoholized in several ways, all of which involve removing ALCOHOL from normally fermented wine, using either thermal or membrane techniques, yet retaining all other components. (See also REDUCED-ALCOHOL WINES, which are low-alcohol wines made by either dilution or partial fermentation.)

One method, particularly common in Germany, is a process of vacuum distillation, whereby wine, at extremely low pressures at normal room temperatures, is separated into various fractions in a tall column. Under

d

vacuum conditions the boiling point of alcohol is reduced and it literally 'boils' away at room temperature. The non-volatile wine compounds such as MINERALS, ACIDS, PHENOLICS, SUGARS, and VITAMINS are fully preserved. By avoiding high temperatures, there is no risk of 'cooked' flavours.

Another similar method, pioneered in France by UCCOAR, the large wine group based in the LANGUEDOC, working in conjunction with researchers at the local INRA station, and launched in 1988, involves evaporation under vacuum at low temperatures and under INERT GAS. The resulting wine has the colour and most of the taste characteristics of the original wine, but an alcoholic strength of less than 0.5%.

REVERSE OSMOSIS can also be used, using osmotic pressure to separate, through an impermeable membrane, a solution of low concentration from one of higher concentration.

INRA at Narbonne have also developed another method of dealcoholizing wine called pervaporation. It depends on dense silicone membranes which at about 30 °C are particularly efficient at separating alcohol from water.

The SPINNING CONE COLUMN is being used increasingly, particularly in New World winemaking countries, as an alternative to vacuum distillation for the production of dealcoholized wines.

Taking the alcohol out of wine leaves it much less stable, so even higher standards of HYGIENE and STERILE BOTTLING conditions are necessary.

All of these methods of removing alcohol to produce no-alcohol or low-alcohol wines are expensive, however, relative to the methods of simply reducing alcohol.

Escudier, J.-L., 'Les Nouveaux Produits de la Vigne', *Bulletin de l'OIV*, May–June (1993).

Debina, the sprightly white grape variety that is solely responsible for the lightly sparkling white wines of Zítsa in Epirus high in north west GREECE near the Albanian border. At these elevations (600–700 m) acidity levels remain high.

débourbage, French term for SETTLING out solids from must or wine.

decanters, vessels, usually glass and stoppered, into which wine is poured during DECANTING.

The decanter as we know it today has changed form very little in the last 250 years, in that it is a handleless clear glass bottle with a capacity of about 1 l and, normally, a stopper. Stopperless decanters are known as carafes. The shape and the decoration have changed in line with fashion and as technology has allowed. Since the capacity is noticeably more than that of a standard 75-cl/27-fl oz bottle, it allows the wine to 'breathe' and develop (see AERATION).

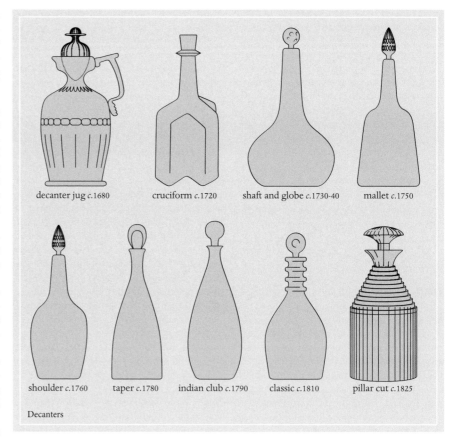

decanter jug *c*.1680   cruciform *c*.1720   shaft and globe *c*.1730-40   mallet *c*.1750

shoulder *c*.1760   taper *c*.1780   indian club *c*.1790   classic *c*.1810   pillar cut *c*.1825

Decanters

History

The decanter's origins lie with the Roman serving bottle, which was typically square. Some Roman glass bottles may have been used for serving wine, but the Romans also used silver. After the collapse of the Roman empire, glass production went into a sharp decline until the revival of the glass trade in Renaissance Italy. By the 16th century, Venice had emerged as the principal centre of glass-making.

While the glass trade was expanding, other developments were afoot. Popular throughout northern Europe during the 16th and early 17th centuries were bulbous earthenware jugs with flat, small handles and short, narrow necks.

A more sophisticated finish, sometimes employed, was a saltglaze which produced a textured surface not unlike an orange peel. In addition, Chinese porcelain jugs were being imported for the most sophisticated of tastes, while some preferred their wine served in carved rock crystal. Whether the jug was saltglaze, tigerware, porcelain, or crystal, all the better-quality pieces were given silver or silver-gilt mounts. For the grandest, gold was used.

Throughout the medieval period and well beyond, pouring vessels were also made in bronze and silver, but these media often gave way to glass once a centre of production became established in a country. The new glass serving

vessels represented the latest in fashion and technology and were quickly adopted by society. For almost a century, England, which was an important wine market, relied on imports until George Ravenscroft and others started producing glass using lead oxide as a flux in the 1670s. This, together with his flint glass, allowed the production of usable jugs and glasses. His developments gave Britain a lead that lasted for about 100 years.

Contemporary with the jug, decanters were also made which took the same form as bottles but with a much greater sophistication of material, decoration, and workmanship.

With the exception of very early decanter jugs, decanters first acquired stoppers in the 1730s.

In the early 19th century, the introduction of steam-driven cutting tools and better lighting from oil lamps produced a fashion for profusely cut decanters although plain ones continued to be made too. From the 1820s a wide variety of shapes and patterns gained favour at the expense of a well-defined progression of design.

The 1840s saw the return of the 'shaft and globe' shape that had been popular a century before. This form continued in fashion until the 20th century, gradually changing in proportion and weight of cutting. The 1870s saw acid-etched decoration of machine precision and other applications of mechanical and chemical technology which enabled decanters to be made in a variety of complex patterns. Some decanters from this time were raised on a foot, a new idea that remained popular for the remainder of the century.

Decanters were not the only vessels from which wine was served. Jugs were made in silver throughout the 18th century. Glass claret jugs were made during the 19th century and followed the pattern of decanters, the only difference being the addition of a handle and a modified rim to form a pouring lip.

Claret jugs of glass mounted with silver, silver plate, or gilt became popular from about 1835. One favoured design, incorporating a globular body with a wide neck, closely imitated the jugs of the late 16th century.

The Arts and Crafts movement influenced some designs for claret jugs, as did art nouveau and late-19th-century interest in Japanese forms. Novelty jugs would also be made in the form of a duck, walrus, seal, or some other animal, with the body in glass and the head in silver or silver plate. All these forms were prevalent in the closing 30 years of the 19th century.

While it is not possible to describe every sort of decanter, there is one type which should not pass unmentioned. It has a conical body giving it a very wide base and it usually has neck rings. Many are plain but some have cut decoration. Plain or decorated with cutting, all are considerably heavier than their standard counterparts. Originally called 'rodneys', today they are known as ship's decanters.   R.N.H.B.

Butler, R., *Great British Wine Accessories 1550–1900* (Sudbury, Suffolk, 2009).

McConnell, A., *The Decanter: An Illustrated History of Glass from 1650* (Woodbridge, Suffolk, 2004).

Modern decanters

Any container, a simple jug for example, can be used as a vessel for wine, so long as it is made of an inert material and can hold at least the contents of a bottle while, ideally, leaving a considerable surface area in contact with air. Some decanters, notably one designed in the late 1980s by the Ch LATOUR management, are shaped so that a bottle exactly fills them to their maximum width, thereby maximizing the potential for AERATION. Some decanters are designed specifically for magnums, or double-sized bottles. Others have handles, all manner of different shapes, engravings, shadings, and designs, including one to ensure circulation with a semi-spherical base that cannot be laid to rest other than in a special cradle by the host's elbow (see PASSING THE PORT). Wine need not be served from clear glass, or even glass at all, but most wine's COLOUR (whites as much as reds) can give great aesthetic and anticipatory pleasure.

See LEAD for details of the limited extent to which this toxic element may be leached from different sorts of decanters.

decanting, optional and controversial step in SERVING wine, involving pouring wine out of its bottle into another container called a DECANTER.

Reasons for decanting

The most obvious reason for decanting a wine is to separate it from any SEDIMENT that has formed in the bottle which not only looks unappetizing in the glass, but usually tastes bitter and/or astringent. Before winemakers mastered the art of CLARIFICATION, this was necessary for all wines. Today such a justification of the decanting process effectively limits it to those wines outlined in AGEING as capable of development in bottle, in most of which some solids are precipitated as part of the maturation process. Vintage and crusted PORTS in particular always throw a heavy deposit (since they are bottled so early in their evolution), as do red wines made with no or minimal FILTRATION. It is rare for inexpensive, everyday TABLE WINES to throw a deposit, and most large retailers insist on such heavy filtration that a deposit is unlikely (although not unknown in older, higher-quality reds). To check whether a wine bottle contains any sediment, stand it upright for an hour or more and then carefully hold it up to the light for inspection at the base (although some BOTTLES are too dark for this exercise to be effective).

Another, traditional but disputed, reason for decanting is to promote AERATION and therefore encourage the development of the wine's BOUQUET. Authorities as scientifically respectable as the late Professor Émile PEYNAUD argued that this is oenologically indefensible: that the action of OXYGEN dissolved in a sound wine when ready to serve is usually detrimental and that the longer it is prolonged—i.e. the longer before serving a wine is decanted—the more diffuse its aroma and the less marked its sensory attributes. His advice is to decant only wines with a sediment, and then only just before serving. If they need aeration because of some wine FAULT such as REDUCTION or MERCAPTANS, then the taster can simply aerate the wine by agitating it in the glass. His argument is that from the moment the wine is fully exposed to air (which happens when it is poured, but not to any significant extent during so-called 'BREATHING') some of its sensory impressions may be lost, and that decanting immediately before serving gives the taster maximum control.

It is certainly wise advice to decant fully mature wines only just before serving, since some are so fragile that they can withstand oxygen for only a few minutes before succumbing to OXIDATION. And it is also true that the aeration process of an individual glass of wine

can be controlled by the person drinking out of it. However, there are certain types of wines, ultra-traditional BAROLO most obviously, which may not have been included in Professor Peynaud's experiments with decanting regimes, which can be so concentrated and tannic in youth that to lose some of their initial sensory impressions is a positive benefit.

There is also the very practical fact that many hosts find it more convenient to decant before a meal is served rather than in the middle of it. There are also people who enjoy the sight of (perhaps both red and white) wine in a decanter so much that they are prepared to sacrifice the potential reduction in gustatory impact.

How to decant

Some authorities argue that bottles that have been stored horizontally should be disturbed as little as possible before being decanted, so transfer them to either a DECANTING CRADLE or a (much more expensive) decanting machine. The alternative and more common method involves much more contact between the deposit and the clear wine, standing the bottle upright for as long as possible before opening, certainly a few hours for wines which have a great deal of sediment, to allow the sediment to fall through the wine to the base of the bottle. Whichever method is used, ensure that the decanter looks and smells absolutely clean, and find a strong light source against which the bottle can be held (a candle, flashlight, desk light, or unshaded table lamp will do). After opening the bottle, as gently as possible, and wiping the lip of the bottle clean to avoid any possible contamination, particularly if the capsule is old enough to contain LEAD, steadily pour the contents of the bottle into the decanter watching the lower shoulder of the bottle with the light source behind it. The sediment should eventually collect in the shoulder and the pouring action can be halted as soon as any sediment starts to spill into the bottleneck.

To extract maximum volume of liquid from a bottle with sediment, or if there is no time to let all the sediment fall to the bottom of the bottle, or if a cork collapses into fragments in the bottle during extraction, the wine can be filtered into the decanter through clean fabric such as muslin, a paper coffee filter, or a special inert wine filter.

Peynaud, É., *The Taste of Wine* (London, 1987).

decanting cradles, bottle carriers, usually made of wicker or metal, which keep the bottle at a perpetually inclined angle with the bottleneck only slightly higher than the base of the bottle, so that the SEDIMENT does not have to fall through the wine to the base of the bottle between STORING horizontally and pouring.

Special **decanting machines** have also been constructed, designed to pour wine gently out of a bottle held horizontally so that the deposit hardly moves at all.

De Chaunac (Seibel 9549), early-ripening, productive, disease-resistant, dark-skinned FRENCH HYBRID grown for a wide range of wine styles in NEW YORK's Finger Lakes region and in Ontario in CANADA.

defoliation, loss of leaves, of a vine can be caused by various agents. If extensive and badly timed, it inevitably adversely affects fruit RIPENING and wine quality, although the precise effects depend on the time of the year. Defoliation is, of course, a natural process and happens at the end of each growing season in the autumn. Normally it is caused by the first frost, but it may also be through mechanical damage or merely senescence. By this time the vines have lost most of the green colour from their leaves anyway and they are no longer effective at PHOTOSYNTHESIS. Providing the vine's reserves of CARBOHYDRATES are topped up by late-season photosynthesis, there is no negative effect of defoliation.

However, defoliation can occur at any time of the growing season due to climate, disease, or pests. FROSTS at any time in the growing season can partially or totally defoliate vines. HAIL can also defoliate vines. A mild hailstorm may simply tear some leaves, but a severe hailstorm will rip off all the leaves, and cut shoots back to their thick stubs. FUNGAL DISEASES such as DOWNY MILDEW can also cause defoliation if left unchecked. Similarly, insect pests such as the western grapeleaf skeletonizer and GRASSHOPPERS, as well as grazing ANIMALS, can defoliate entire vines unless checked.

The vine responds to defoliation by producing new leaves on lateral shoots. However, this new growth will depend on stored carbohydrate reserves of the vine for a month or so, and so will weaken the vine until the new leaves are able to produce carbohydrates by photosynthesis and build up reserves again. While vigorous vines may be able to recover from a single defoliation, repeated defoliation can weaken the vine to the point of death.

Obviously, defoliation will have an impact on fruit growth and ripening. A low LEAF TO FRUIT RATIO causes a reduction in levels of fruit sugars (see SUGAR IN GRAPES), as well as in PHENOLICS, with an adverse effect on colour and flavour of the resultant wine. Note, however, that the vine can compensate for a lower than ideal leaf area by automatically increasing the rate of photosynthesis, so that practices such as LEAF REMOVAL and TRIMMING do not normally cause negative effects, as might be imagined. Good-quality wine can be made only from vines with a sufficient area of healthy leaves exposed to sunlight.   R.E.S.

dégorgement, French term for the DISGORGEMENT operations at the end of the traditional method of SPARKLING WINEMAKING.

degree, or *degré* in French, the ALCOHOLIC STRENGTH of a wine, and identical to the wine's percentage of ETHANOL by volume. This was traditionally regarded as the most vital statistic of all for everyday French VIN DE TABLE, whose price was generally quoted per *degré/hecto*, as though its only important characteristics were its potency and volume (although, at this quality level, wines with low alcohol levels tended to have been over-produced and to be low in fruit and concentration).

degree days, unit devised to measure the TEMPERATURE component of climate. See CLIMATE CLASSIFICATION for more details.

dehydration, winemaking process used in the production of DRIED-GRAPE WINES—and a frequent consequence of extended HANG TIME. The dehydration process transforms grapes into RAISINS and has to be arrested before completion if appetizing wines are to be made from the results.

Dekkera, the sporulating form of the yeast genus BRETTANOMYCES which can cause two distinct off-flavours in wines, often described as 'mousy', and 'animal' or 'medicinal'. Like *Brettanomyces*, Dekkera has variable sensitivity to SULFUR DIOXIDE. In practice, Dekkera is used as a European, particularly French, synonym for *Brettanomyces*, but recent changes to the rules for naming fungi suggest precedence be given to *Brettanomyces*.

Delaware, dark pink-skinned VITIS *labrusca* vine variety that is quite popular in NEW YORK and, for reasons that are now obscure, is also planted in JAPAN and KOREA. Its early ripening is presumably an advantage in Japan's damp autumns. The wine is not as markedly FOXY as that of its great New York rival CONCORD. It was first propagated in Delaware, Ohio, in 1849.

délestage, or rack and return, is a CAP management procedure which optimizes contact between must and solids during fermentation. When the cap has risen to the top of the tank, fermenting wine is taken from a bottom valve to a separate receiving vessel. The remaining POMACE is allowed to free drain for two or more hours. The wine is then gently pumped back over the top of the cap, using a low pressure pump or sprinkler system. This procedure, usually conducted once or twice during fermentation, is designed to ensure optimum diffusion of tannins and pigments from the fruit into the wine. It may also used to remove a proportion of the seeds and can thus reduce the extraction of bitter tannins from unripe seeds. When the tank is wide rather than tall, maceration is more

efficient so that délestage is not as useful. See also MACERATION.   B.W.Z. & D.D.

delimitation, geographical. The central purpose of geographical delimitation of a wine area, typically into a CONTROLLED APPELLATION, is to establish a distinctive identity for the wines produced within it, and provide a means whereby the provenance of those wines can be guaranteed. It is based primarily upon the assumption that different environments give rise to wines of different character (see TERROIR).

Since classical antiquity, wines from certain regions tended to be called after the area of their production, with many gaining particularly high reputations (FALERNIAN, for example), but the first legal vineyard delimitation may well have been that of CHIANTI, Pomino, and CARMIGNANO in 1716 by Cosimo III de' Medici, Grand Duke of Tuscany, in a document which further states that penalties will be incurred if any wine makes a false claim to be from those demarcated regions. The DOURO Valley of northern Portugal was famously first delimited in 1756, associated with the establishment of the Companhia Geral da Agricultura das Vinhas do Alto Douro. During the 18th century, there had been many disputes over the sources and qualities of wines exported from Oporto (see PORT), as well as conflicts between foreign wine shippers and the Portuguese growers, and the formation of the Companhia Geral with strictly defined areas of operation was designed to remedy the situation. At the heart of this legislation was the establishment of a specific area in the upper Douro Valley from which farmers were able to obtain higher prices for their wines compared with those produced elsewhere.

During the 18th century in other parts of Europe, CLASSIFICATIONS of the different qualities of wine were becoming increasingly common, with Thomas JEFFERSON, for example, commenting on the various categories of wines from Bordeaux and Burgundy in 1787. In the 19th century, more formal classifications emerged, with the most famous of these being the classification of the wines of the Médoc, and Lavalle's classification of the wines of the Côte d'Or, both of which date from 1855. By the early 20th century, in the wake of the devastation caused by POWDERY MILDEW and PHYLLOXERA, there were two fundamental problems facing the wine industry: ADULTERATION AND FRAUD. Many wines contained a range of additives designed to mask their flavour; and wine purporting to come from a respected source frequently contained wines from elsewhere. In order to overcome these problems, some groups of growers, such as those in Chablis and Bordeaux, decided to form their own associations designed to guarantee the origin of their wines. National governments then began to concern themselves more formally with the geographical delimitation of areas of wine production, with the French taking a first step in 1905 towards the creation of a national system of wine control based on the delimitation of areas of origin. Through further laws, most notably those of 1919 and 1927, this eventually culminated in 1935 in the law creating the APPELLATIONS D'ORIGINE CONTRÔLÉES.

Numerous systems were also developed in Germany, notably the GERMAN WINE LAW of 1930, but although this included the use of vineyard names, the perceived quality of Germany's wines was for long based not primarily on geography but on MUST WEIGHTS (see GERMAN HISTORY).

Italian wine laws also include an element of geographical delimitation, as represented in the creation of the Denominazione di Origine Controllata (DOC) system in 1963 and more recently in the 1992 legislation with its specific reference to Indicazione Geografica Tipica (IGT).

The precise practical methods of geographical demarcation vary from country to country, but are usually based on the compilation of a detailed vineyard register and include varying degrees of political intrigue (see, for example, ALBANA DI ROMAGNA). Producers wishing to gain a certain status must satisfy regional and national committees of both the quality, origin, and distinction of their wines. One of the most rigorous systems of geographical delimitation is that adopted in France under INAO auspices. This requires that commissions of inquiry examine the relationships between such factors as GEOLOGY, SOILS, TOPOGRAPHY, DRAINAGE, slope, exposure, and wine quality. In BURGUNDY, for example, the geological origin of the soils is a determining factor in differentiating the GRAND CRU vineyards.

The central feature of geographical delimitation as it applies to wine is not just that it is intended to lead to improvements in wine quality, thus enabling the wines to be sold at a higher price, but also that it is a legislative procedure whereby a privileged monopolistic position is created for producers within a demarcated area. Whether a given vineyard falls within or outside the legal boundary of a delimited wine region can have important commercial consequences, which is why the much more recent demarcation of America's AVAs, South Africa's WINE OF ORIGIN, and some of AUSTRALIA's even newer GIs (see GEOGRAPHICAL INDICATION), many of them based more on political than geographical boundaries, can be such a contentious process.

The creation of geographically delimited areas remains highly controversial.   P.T.H.U. & J.R.

Pomerol, C. (ed.), *The Wines and Winelands of France: Geological Journeys* (London, 1989).

Unwin, T., *Wine and the Vine: An Historical Geography of Viticulture and the Wine Trade* (London, 1991).

demi-sec, French term meaning 'medium dry' (see SWEETNESS). In practice, the term is used particularly for Chenin Blanc wines in ANJOU-Saumur and TOURAINE. See DOSAGE for official EU sugar levels in SPARKLING WINES.

Denmark. Despite its far northern LATITUDE, vines have been grown here since the Middle Ages. Denmark was acknowledged as a wine-producing country in EU regulations only in 2000, however, and the first commercial vintage was 2001, when there were only two wine producers. By 2014 there were 90, although many are very small-scale. Modern Danish viticulture is helped by CLIMATE change and depends on NEW VARIETIES (HYBRIDS or DISEASE RESISTANT) such as Rondo and Regent for reds and Solaris and Orion for whites. Most wines are relatively light. Most Danish wines have PGI status and a full dozen had been registered by 2007: Drenthe, Flevoland, Friesland, Gelderland, Groningen, Limburg, Noord-Brabant, Noord-Holland, Overijssel, Utrecht, Zeeland, and Zuid-Holland. A Protected Designation of Origin (PDO) for a sparkling wine, one of Denmark's specialities, was in the pipeline in 2014.   S.M.

Génsboel, B., and Gundersen, J. M., *Vinavl i Danmark (Winegrowing in Denmark)*, (Copenhagen, 2002).

Klitgaard J., *Danske Vingaarde (Danish Vineyards)*, (Fredericia 2009).

Denominação de Origem Controlada, the name of a controlled appellation in PORTUGAL, which replaced the earlier Região Demarcarda when Portuguese wine laws were revised for EU entry. For more details, see DOC.

Denominación de Origen, Spanish controlled appellation. See DO.

Denominación de Origen Calificada, Spain's superior CONTROLLED APPELLATION. RIOJA was the first, PRIORAT the second DO to be promoted to this status. See DOCA.

Denominazione di Origine Controllata. See DOC.

Denominazione di Origine Controllata e Garantita. See DOCG.

density, a measurement of the concentration of matter in units of mass per unit volume. In wine it is usually expressed as g/cc, and occasionally as g/ml, at 20 °C/68 °F (which must be specified since wine's mass per unit volume decreases as its temperature increases). Wine is an interesting mixture because it contains dissolved solids (SUGARS, ACIDS, PHENOLICS, and MINERAL salts) which increase its density above that of pure water, but it also contains ALCOHOL, which is less dense than water. The result is that very dry wines can have densities near 0.9 g/cc while very sweet wines that are low in alcohol

(such as some Italian MOSCATO, for example) can have densities around 1.03 g/cc.

A term closely related to density, and used in technical wine analysis, is **specific gravity**. The specific gravity is the ratio of the weight or mass of a volume of a liquid to the weight of an equal volume of water. It is thus a pure or unitless number which differs only slightly from density, according to temperature (since the density of water is only exactly 1 g/cc at a temperature of 3.98 °C).

Wine densities are also frequently reported in terms of one of the traditional scales used for measuring the sugar solution concentrations (see BALLING, BAUMÉ, BRIX, OECHSLE), which also measure wine density but in units other than g/cc. These scales all use different units (see MUST WEIGHT for equivalencies) from each other, with Oechsle bearing the most obvious relationship to specific gravity: a must with the specific gravity of 1.070, for example, is said to measure 70 °Oechsle. Density is usually measured with a HYDROMETER or mustimeter and while a range of alternative electronic density meters are available, hydrometers are the instrumental standard for this measurement.   A.D.W.

deposit. See BOTTLE DEPOSIT and SEDIMENT.

Derenoncourt, Stéphane (1963–), influential, self-taught, now international wine-making CONSULTANT based on Bordeaux's right bank. Originally from the far north of France, he first picked grapes in Fronsac in 1982 and continued as a lowly vineyard worker. He did not make wine until 1990, at Ch Pavie Macquin, and claims that his winemaking philosophy is informed by his experiences in the vineyard and by Burgundian sensibilities. A great believer in the virtues of tasting, he states perhaps even more explicitly than Bordeaux's other famous international consultant OENOLOGIST Michel ROLLAND, the importance of expressing TERROIR.

In 1999 with his wife Christine he acquired Domaine de l'A, an estate in CASTILLON and from this base was working on about 100 estates around the world by 2014, with a team of six young qualified oenologists and two technical consultants who are expected to have a practical grasp of viticulture too. About 50 of these estates were on Bordeaux's RIGHT BANK (including the stable of wines at Ch Canon-La-Gaffelière) but he now also has about 20 clients on the left bank (including Domaine de Chevalier), about a dozen elsewhere in France, and others in Spain, Portugal, Italy, Austria, Greece, Turkey, Ukraine, Morocco, Lebanon, Syria, India, Virginia, and California (Inglenook).

http://www.jancisrobinson.com/articles/winenews0508.html *Derenoncourt—the new Michel Rolland?* May 2004.

derived pigments. See ANTHOCYANINS.

desert, an arid, treeless region. True deserts are not conducive to growing grapes for wine, even where IRRIGATION water is available. Low HUMIDITY and extreme temperature ranges place stresses on the vine which usually preclude good grape quality. With irrigation they can still be very suitable for TABLE GRAPES, especially early-maturing varieties, and for DRYING GRAPES, but wine grapes seldom rise above mediocre quality. See CLIMATE AND WINE QUALITY.

Some near-desert regions used extensively for viticulture include the SAN JOAQUIN VALLEY of California; the southern reaches of the Okanagan Valley in BRITISH COLUMBIA; ARGENTINA's Mendoza Region; the Bekaa Valley of LEBANON; parts of ISRAEL; AZERBAIJAN on the west coast of the Caspian sea; parts of northern CHINA; the lower Murray Valley of SOUTH AUSTRALIA and VICTORIA; and the Little Karoo of SOUTH AFRICA.   J.G.

designations. Within the EU, there are now two broad categories for wine—with or without GEOGRAPHICAL INDICATION. Within these broad categories there are more precise designations. The former includes both Protected Designation of Origin (PDO) and Protected Geographical Indication (PGI), while the latter includes what used to be referred to as 'table wine'. Within the US, wines between 7 and 14% alcohol are designated table wine while those over 14%, whether sweet or dry, fortified or not, are officially designated DESSERT WINE.   J.B.

dessert wines usually mean SWEET WINES but according to American regulations, any wine between 14 and 24% alcohol is designated a dessert wine, even if dry and unfortified, and attracts a higher tax rate. The proportion of California wine that qualifies as dessert wine has been about 10% since 2005.

destalking. See DESTEMMING.

destemming, the winemaking process of removing the STEMS, or stalks, from clusters of grape berries. Known as *égrappage* or *éraflage* in French, it usually takes place immediately after and combined with the CRUSHING operation. Grape stems, and the attached BRUSH of pulp, contain TANNINS. If they are crushed or broken, these can be leached into the wine during FERMENTATION, making the wine taste bitter and astringent. Destemming also very slightly increases the resultant COLOUR and ALCOHOLIC STRENGTH because stems, if included, have a dilution effect. Fermentation is also likely to be slightly slower and cooler since including stems increases the interfaces between the fermenting must and air, or OXYGEN.

Although historically all wines were made without either crushing or stem removal, most white and the majority of black grapes are destemmed today. The exceptions are those white grapes subjected to WHOLE-BUNCH PRESSING and black grapes used for CARBONIC MACERATION and the increasing proportion employed in WHOLE-BUNCH FERMENTATION. Some producers, notably in BURGUNDY and parts of the RHÔNE, believe in retaining a certain proportion of the stems to add structure, colour, and mid-palate weight, to improve TEXTURE, to ease the drainage of the juice through the CAP during MACERATION of red wines and during PRESSING of white wines.

Modern destemming machines, or **destemmers**, are usually based on the principle of straining or sieving larger stems from the crushed grape mixture which is fed into a horizontal rotating perforated cylinder. As the mass is tumbled, the juice, skins, and seeds pass through the perforations into a collector. The stems, which are long enough to bridge across the perforations, are carried to the open exit end where they are collected in a separate receiver. Stem fragments small enough to fall through the perforations in the cylinder go into the juice, which means that they remain in contact with the juice until after fermentation in the case of red wines but are removed along with the skins and seeds before fermentation in the case of white wines (see WINEMAKING). A very few producers destem by hand, thereby keeping the berries whole. The gentler handling is very time-consuming but proponents believe it results in improved wine quality.

Goode, J., 'Stemming the tide', *World of Fine Wine*, 37 (2012), 90–7.

desuckering, the viticultural practice of removing unwanted young shoots. Known in most parts of France as *épamprage*, the practice is common to most vineyards of the world. Typically, the shoots removed are either on the TRUNK or in the HEAD of the vine, and grow in spring from buds surviving in the old wood. These shoots are termed WATER SHOOTS and for the majority of vine varieties have no bunches of grapes. Varieties differ in their production of water shoots; GEWÜRZTRAMINER, for example, produces many. The operation is carried out in spring, several weeks after BUDBREAK, when the water shoots are 10 to 15 cm (4 to 6 in) long. The work is relatively tiresome, as for many vineyards the shoots can be near the ground, although shoots can be removed from trunks mechanically by mounting a rotating cylinder with rubber straps attached on the front of a tractor.

In California, desuckering is also carried out on CORDON-trained vines and so can alternatively be termed SHOOT THINNING.   R.E.S.

Deutsche means literally 'German', thus **Deutscher** Wein is what appears on the labels of Germany's WINE WITHOUT GEOGRAPHICAL INDICATION (once called Tafelwein); **Deutscher Sekt** is that relative rarity, a SEKT or sparkling wine made in Germany that is actually made of German wine; and the **Deutsche Weinstrasse** is a particularly famous route through the vineyards of the PFALZ region in Germany.

The **Deutsches Weinsiegel**, or German Wine Seal, is a significant award made to superior bottlings assessed by BLIND TASTING panels, but only after the wine has been awarded an official AP NUMBER. Award-winning bottles can be identified by a large, round paper seal on the bottle-neck: a yellow seal for dry wines, green for medium dry, and red for other styles. These awards, and a national competition, are held under the auspices of the **Deutsche Land-wirtschafts-Gesellschaft**, or DLG, an agricultural society formed in the late 19th century to encourage quality and agricultural expertise. Prize-winning bottles carry gold, silver, or bronze strips across the neck.

dew, water which condenses on objects, such as leaves, when the air in immediate contact with them is cooled below dew point, the temperature at which the air becomes fully saturated by its current content of water vapour (see HUMIDITY). Dew contributes little directly to the water supply of the vine. However, the latent heat of vaporization that is released during condensation plays a positive role by slowing nighttime temperature drop. The risk of FROST is appreciably reduced when the air contains enough water vapour to result in dew.

Dew has a major (mostly unfavourable) impact on the incidence of VINE DISEASES. It provides the necessary conditions for spore germination and the establishment of several fungal disease organisms, most notably those for DOWNY MILDEW (*Plasmopara viticola*), BLACK ROT (*Guignardia bidwellii*), and the malevolent form of botrytis bunch rot, GREY ROT (*Botrytis cinerea*), even in the absence of wetting rain.

Spreading bunch infection by the last of these after (but only after) normal maturity has been reached constitutes the benevolent form, NOBLE ROT, which is responsible for most of the world's greatest SWEET WINES. See CLIMATE AND WINE QUALITY and TOPOGRAPHY.   J.G.

diacetyl, a product of MALOLACTIC CONVERSION with a powerful butterscotch or butter aroma. The ability to detect diacetyl depends on its concentration and the wine type and style. The perception threshold varies from 0.2 mg/l for Chardonnay, 0.9 mg/l for Pinot Noir to 2.8 mg/l for Cabernet Sauvignon. At low concentrations, it may be perceived as nutty or toasty and add desirable complexity. In excess, as was once common in NEW WORLD Chardonnays, it is perceived as distractingly obvious butteriness. The amount of diacetyl produced depends on the bacterial strain and the rate of progress of the malolactic conversion as well as temperature, oxygen availability, the wine's pH, SULFUR DIOXIDE content, and, importantly, CITRIC ACID concentrations.   P.J.W.

Bartowsky, E. J., and Henschke, P. A., 'The "buttery" attribute of wine—diacetyl—desirability, spoilage and beyond', *International Journal of Food Microbiology* 96 (2004), 235–52.

Diageo, the world's largest drinks company, is very much more interested in spirits than wine, and BRANDS above all else. It owns Piat d'Or, Blossom Hill, Beaulieu Vineyard (now singular), and Sterling in California. It acquired the premium California-based Chalone Wine Group from Ch LAFITE-Rothschild in 2004 but has no obvious wine strategy. Its London fine wine merchant Justerini & Brooks is somewhat anomalous but earns a Royal Warrant.

diammonium phosphate, or **DAP**, common YEAST nutrient added during FERMENTATION. Research has shown that it not only encourages fermentation but appropriate addition may also result in the production of complex compounds and ESTERS that make wines taste more fruity and floral. The current EU limit is 1 g/l and 0.3 g/l for the second fermentation of SPARKLING WINE.

Torrea, D., et al., 'Comparison of inorganic and organic nitrogen supplementation of grape juice—effect on volatile composition and aroma profile of a Chardonnay wine fermented with *Saccharomyces cerevisiae* yeast', *Food Chemistry*, 127 (2011), 1072–83.

Diamond Mountain, CALIFORNIA region and AVA on the north-western edge of NAPA VALLEY.

diatomaceous earth (**DE**), widely used in FILTRATION, is a naturally occurring, highly porous, chalk-like sedimentary rock mineral made mainly of silica and consisting of fossilized remains of diatoms, a type of hard-shelled algae. It is also known as Kieselguhr. There are, however, increasing concerns about potential health hazards and safe disposal of used DE.

Die, town between the RHÔNE Valley and the alps (see map under FRANCE) whose name features in the **Clairette de Die** and **Crémant de Die** sparkling wine appellations and **Coteaux de Die**, a light, still, dry white wine made from Clairette grapes. According to PLINY, the local tribe in Roman times, the Voconces, made a sparkling sweet wine, and practised an early form of TEMPERATURE CONTROL by plunging barrels full of fermenting must in the river. Most wines are sparkling and many of them are sweet and grapey. For more information, see CLAIRETTE DE DIE, CRÉMANT, and CHÂTILLON-EN-DIOIS.

diet, wine as part of. Some medical research suggests that wine may be drunk for dietary reasons. Wine contains various VITAMINS and MINERALS but in such small concentrations that, for them to make any sufficient contribution to the human diet, excessive amounts of ALCOHOL would also have to be ingested. 'Moderate' wine consumption has been shown to have a beneficial effect for several medical conditions, however, and wine consumption clearly plays a part in the much-vaunted **Mediterranean diet** (see HEALTH).

No wine is 'slimming', but dry **dealcoholized wine** is usually lower in calories than most.

In Mediterranean countries it has always been natural to drink wine because it is abundant and relatively cheap. But wine forms part of our diet for reasons beyond necessity or ease of access.

Traditionally societies have wanted to drink wine because it tastes good. It was popular not least because of the dangers associated with drinking unclean WATER.

The concept of maintaining good health through diet can be traced back to Ancient GREECE and the Greek Hippocrates, in particular, although wine was included in the dietary laws of Moses 1,000 years earlier.

As late as the 1860s, doctors were still matching wines to lifestyles, as they would be termed today. For example, Dr Robert Druitt suggested CLARET 'for children, for literary persons, and for all those whose occupations are chiefly carried on indoors'. The fuller-bodied wines of BURGUNDY, the MIDI, and GREECE he considered better suited to manual workers.   H.B. & J.R.

Corder, R., *The Red Wine Diet* (London, 2007).

Johnson, H., *The Story of Wine* (London and New York, 1989).

Newman, C., *The White Wine Diet* (London, 2004).

Dijon, town in northern BURGUNDY and the focus of the region's vinous ACADEME, the Institut Universitaire de la Vigne et du Vin Jules Guyot in the Université de Bourgogne (formerly the **Université de Dijon**). For some time OENOLOGY was taught by the charismatic vigneron René Engel, who was also a leading light in the Chevaliers de Tastevin, but Dijon was able to offer graduate diplomas in oenology from 1947. The course was further refined in 1955 when a viticultural research station and experimental winery (2.4 ha/10 acres) were established in nearby MARSANNAY.

Dijon offers the fifth-year Diplôme National d'Oenologue; two Masters: Vine, Wine, Terroir, and Fermentation Processes for the Food Industry; two Bachelors: Vine Science, and Marketing of Wine and Oenotourism. Four diplomas in continuing education also exist: Practical Oenology, Vine Science and Environment, Wine, Culture and Oenotourism, and Strategic Vineyard and Winery Management. Research concentrates on five main areas: mechanisms and factors of induced resistance in grapevines, the impact of CLIMATE CHANGE, microbiology, physical chemistry, and sensory analysis. The UNESCO chair of Culture and Traditions of Wine' and the Scientific Committee for Vine and Wine in Burgundy are hosted at the IUVV Jules Guyot.

Certain CLONES of Chardonnay, and PINOT NOIR clones such as 115 and 777, imported from Burgundy, are sometimes known as **Dijon clones**.

www.u-bourgogne.fr/IUVV

Dimyat, sometimes spelt **Dimiat**, BULGARIA's widely planted indigenous white grape variety whose total area had declined to 6,000 ha/15,000 acres by 2009. It is grown mainly in the east and south of Bulgaria, where it is regarded as a producer of perfumed everyday whites of varying levels of sweetness but usefully dependable quality. The vines yield copper-coloured grapes in great quantity. The wines should be consumed young and cool. Dimyat is probably related to GOUAIS BLANC and is a parent of CABERNET SEVERNY and others.

dining clubs, private societies of like-minded individuals who meet over meals. A high proportion of what are called dining clubs are in fact wining clubs devoted to the consumption and discussion of fine wines. See also SAINTSBURY.

Dinka, very ordinary but widely planted white grape variety in CROATIA. It is known as Kövidinka and Kevedinka in HUNGARY and SERBIA respectively.

Dionysus, the classical god of wine, for whom Bacchus was the more common name among the Romans. However, grapes and vines are not his only attributes, and neither is wine the only aspect of his cult.

Although some scholars have argued that wine is a secondary element in his cult and the god Dionysus was a late importation from the east, he is a wine god, an Olympian, and an important influence on Ancient GREECE. The earliest festival known to be devoted to Dionysus, the three-day feast of the Anthesteria, is a wine festival. It gives its name to the spring month of Anthesterion and celebrates the broaching of the new wine (the wine of the most recent vintage, which was always kept until the next spring). Clay tablets dating from the late Bronze Age (*c.*1200 BC), connect Dionysus with wine, and thus provide further evidence for the early cult of Dionysus as a wine god.

Dionysus has been taken to be a non-Greek because he is a god of epiphanies. He appears suddenly, from outside, to strike people with madness, most famously represented in Euripides' tragedy *The Bacchae* (probably written shortly after 408 BC).

The Bacchae is about Dionysiac frenzy and, although the play praises Dionysus for his gift of wine which lessens the cares of mortals, the

d

madness that he brings is not the result of excessive consumption of wine.

The essence of the cult of Dionysus is the surrender of personal identity. Hence one of Dionysus' symbols is the mask, and he is often depicted in VASE PAINTINGS of drinking ceremonies as a mask set up on a column draped in cloth. His other attributes are the thyrsus, a tall stick with a bunch of ivy leaves on top—ivy because it is evergreen and it produces its berries in the winter when the mountain ritual takes place and the vine is bare. He is also depicted with grapes or a wine cup, and often has an effeminate appearance with long flowing locks. He is frequently equated (especially by HERODOTUS in the 5th century BC) with the Egyptian god Osiris.

One well-known myth about Dionysus concerns the invention of wine. Dionysus discloses the secret of winemaking to the peasant Icarius and his daughter Erigone, with whom he had lodged as a guest, in return for their hospitality. Obedient to the god's command to teach the art to other people, Icarius shares his wine with a group of shepherds. At first they enjoy this delicious new drink, but as the unaccustomed wine overwhelms them they begin to suspect Icarius of having poisoned them. So they turn on him and batter him to death with their clubs. For a time his body cannot be found, but eventually Icarius' faithful dog Moera leads Erigone to the spot where he lies buried. Erigone hangs herself in despair. However, in death they receive their due rewards: Icarius becomes the star Boötes, his daughter the constellation Virgo, and Moera becomes Canis, or Sirius, the dog star. Boötes, also known in Greek as 'the grape-gatherer', rises in the autumn, at the time of the vintage, and in the warm climate of Greece the vintage may well have taken place some time before the autumnal equinox, still under the constellation of Virgo. It is also interesting to note that PLINY the Elder recommends the rising of the dog star, 2 August, as the day when wine jars should receive their inside coating of RESIN to make them airtight in readiness for the vintage.

Dionysus is a god who strives against reason, calm and order. As such he is a god of the people, dangerous and subversive to those in authority. His cult attracts further suspicion because it is surrounded by secrecy.

Gradually Dionysiac orgies appear to have become orgies in the modern sense, and among the Romans the cult of Dionysus was a disreputable affair. Livy gives a lurid account of the banning of the Bacchanalia, but it should not be forgotten that Livy was a historian of conservative tendencies, an admirer of Augustus, who lamented what he considered to be the recent slide into luxury and immorality. Bacchus certainly played little part in the official religion of Ancient ROME; he was too dangerous

a god. Among the Romans he survives in a sanitized version, jolly Bacchus the wine god, giver of wine and bringer of joy, who makes sorrow bearable. Satyrs and nymphs gambol about him harmlessly, and Silenus is a cheerful old soak. This is the Bacchus that survived into the Renaissance, familiar from the pictures of Titian and his contemporaries. The Romans reduced the complex god of the Greeks to little more than wine personified.   H.M.W.

Burkert, W., *Greek Religion*, trans. by John Raffan (Oxford, 1985).

Carpenter, T. H., *Dionysian Imagery in Archaic Greek Art* (Oxford, 1986).

Dalby, A., *Bacchus. A Biography* (Los Angeles, 2003).

R. Seaford, *Dionysus*, (London, 2006).

Wilson, H., *Wine and Words in Classical Antiquity and the Middle Ages* (London, 2003).

direct producer, term used for a group of vines, also known as FRENCH HYBRIDS, bred from the late 19th century onwards in an effort to combine the pest and disease resistance of AMERICAN VINE SPECIES with the desirable fruit characters of the European VINIFERA species. They are called direct producers, and sometimes hybrid direct producers, or HDPs, because, unlike *V. vinifera* VINE VARIETIES, they do not need GRAFTING on to PHYLLOXERA-tolerant ROOTSTOCKS. They are not all sufficiently phylloxera-tolerant, however, and added soil stresses such as DROUGHT or WEEDS can see them weakened by phylloxera.   R.E.S.

direct shipping, cause célèbre in the US which banned shipping of wine direct from winery to consumer, until a seminal Supreme Court decision in 2005 liberalized direct shipments into some states, yet allowed others to keep their borders closed to wine shipments from out of state. See UNITED STATES, regulations for more detail of this bypassing of the notorious THREE-TIER SYSTEM.

disease-resistant varieties, semantically expedient term for grapevines introduced by the German Bundessortenamt (Plant Variety Rights Office) in 1995 that were bred specifically to produce wines that taste like VINIFERA yet meet consumer demands for reductions in AGROCHEMICAL use by incorporating some non-*V. vinifera* genes for resistance to various common VINE DISEASES. The term replaces the previously pejorative terms HYBRIDS or INTERSPECIFIC HYBRIDS for some of their most promising results of VINE BREEDING. The German term is *Pilzwiderstandsfähige Rebsorten*.

There had been substantial bias against such new varieties, especially those including genes from AMERICAN VINE SPECIES, because of historical associations with poor wine quality and FOXY flavours. The bureaucratic hurdle of the EU's ban on non-*V. vinifera* vines for QUALITY WINE (designed initially to exclude the old AMERICAN

HYBRIDS and French hybrids) was bypassed by classifying these new disease-resistant varieties as *V. vinifera* subspecies *sativa*.

Merzling, the product of Seyve-Villard 5–276 and a Riesling × Ruländer cross, was the first variety so registered, and other German-bred varieties such as PHOENIX, RONDO, ORION, REGENT, Bronner, Johanniter, Saphira, Prinzipal, Hibernal, and Bolero have followed, all registered as *Vitis vinifera*. Thanks to this creative taxonomy, these disease-resistant varieties can be grown for quality wine production, though they still have to be registered for quality wine production in any given EU region. The Swiss are very proud of their new variety Divico, a GAMARET × BRONNER cross said to be resistant to DOWNY and POWDERY MILDEWS and to grey rot.   R.E.S., J.R., & J.E.H.

Basler, P., and Scherz, R., *PIWI-Rebsorten—Pilzwiderstandsfähige Rebsorten* (Wädenswil, 2011).

diseases, vine. See VINE DISEASES and individual diseases.

disgorgement, or *dégorgement* in French, an integral stage in the traditional method of sparkling winemaking entailing the removal of a pellet of frozen sediment from the neck of each bottle. For more detail and modern alternative techniques, see SPARKLING WINEMAKING.

Distell, dominant wine and spirits producer in the SOUTH AFRICAN market and the eleventh-largest wine company in the world. Formed in 2000 from the merger of Stellenbosch Farmers Winery and Distillers Corporation, it owns 1,500 ha/3,705 acres of planted vineyard and enjoys 40% by value of the country's domestic wine business, between 25 and 30% of the packaged wine exports, and over 70% of the domestic brandy trade. Its major premium wine labels include Nederburg and Fleur du Cap, while its popular and long-established brands include Chateau Libertas, Grand Mousseux, and Tassenberg.   M.F.

distillation, the separation of the constituents of a liquid mixture by partial vaporization of the mixture and the separate recovery of the vapour and the residue. When applied to wine, or any other fermented liquid, the result is a considerably stronger alcoholic liquid: brandy in the case of wine and other fermented fruit juices, calvados in the case of certain apples from northern France, whisky in the case of fermented barley.

distillation, compulsory. In an effort to curb, and dispose of, SURPLUS wine production, the EU authorities instituted a system in 1982 whereby any wine produced over a certain limit should theoretically be compulsorily bought, at a standard and not too attractive price, and distilled into industrial ALCOHOL (which policy resulted, perhaps inevitably, in an alcohol surplus). Average annual quantities distilled under this scheme in the 1980s were well over 30 million hl/790 million gal, or about a fifth of total European production. In 1993 the European Commission admitted that the scheme had done little to curb over-production, and announced stricter measures designed to offer less financial support to over-producers, and to curb abuse of the system more effectively. Between 1993 and 1996, the amount distilled was reduced to about 10% of production, but the Commission decided to crack down and, in 1998, proposed introducing just one 'crisis distillation' measure instead of a multi-tiered system. The proposed new measure was intended to deal only with exceptional cases of market disturbance and serious quality problems, but continued to play an important part in the European wine market. Following further reforms of the common market organisation (CMO) for Wine in 1999, distillation was 'no longer an obligatory measure in the event of serious wine market crises' and it could be applied to QUALITY WINE. An EU report published in 2002 concluded that distillation was not an efficient way of eliminating structural surpluses and suggested alternative measures such as paying growers a premium for GREEN HARVESTING. Compulsory distillation was finally phased out altogether in 2012 as a result of the wide-ranging 2008 reforms to the CMO. However, in 2014 Spain decided to distil 4 million hl (106 million gallons) to try to balance its own surplus.   J.R., E.K., & J.E.H.

European Court of Auditors, *The Reform of the Common Organisation of the Market in Wine: Progress to Date* (Brussels, 2012).

diurnal temperature variation. See TEMPERATURE VARIABILITY.

Divico, red grapevine CROSS created at CHANGINS by Jean-Laurent Spring from GAMARET and Bronner and released in 2013. Highly resistant to the major FUNGAL DISEASES. The first wines, tannic and fruity, are expected in 2018.   J.V.

divided canopy, group of vine-TRAINING SYSTEMS which involve separation of a leaf CANOPY into two or more subcanopies, sometimes called curtains. The expression was popularized by Professor Nelson SHAULIS in the 1960s and 1970s as part of his pioneering promotion of CANOPY MANAGEMENT. One of the most important divided canopy training systems is the GENEVA DOUBLE CURTAIN developed by Shaulis. The LYRE, SCOTT HENRY, and SMART-DYSON are more recent developments. The advantage of canopy division is that it increases the surface area of the canopy that is exposed to sunlight, while reducing canopy SHADE. Both yield and wine quality can increase as a result.   R.E.S.

DLG, source of German wine awards. See DEUTSCHE.

DMDC (**dimethyl dicarbonate**), a sterilant used by a number of producers of high-quality red wine outside Europe to eliminate the risk of BRETTANOMYCES growth in bottle. DMDC works by deactivating enzymes in the spoilage yeast. Any remaining DMDC reacts principally with the water in the beverage. It is currently approved in the United States, South Africa, Australia, and New Zealand for use in the production of dry wines. In the EU, it is authorized up to a maximum of 200 mg/l. While it was originally developed for commercial wines, it has been accepted more widely for higher quality wines.   S.H.

DNA profiling, also known as **DNA typing**, **DNA fingerprinting**, or **DNA testing**, allows the unequivocal identification of any living individual. This technique was developed in 1985 in forensic science to confound criminals, and was first applied to grape CULTIVARS in 1993 by Australian researchers. Since a grape variety is made of CLONES reproduced asexually by VEGETATIVE PROPAGATION, it is genetically comparable to a human individual. The identification technique is based on small pieces of variable DNA called molecular markers, the most successful using repetitive pieces of DNA called **microsatellites**. They exist in any living organism and their length varies from one individual to another. Analysis of 8 to 12 microsatellites is enough to obtain a unique 'genetic identity card', looking like a supermarket bar code, for every variety. This technique, for which data exchanges between laboratories is relatively easy, allowed, for example, identification of the enigmatic PETITE SIRAH in California and solved the long-standing mystery of ZINFANDEL's identity.

DNA profiling technique complements classical AMPELOGRAPHY and offers the advantage of unambiguously identifying grape varieties (as well as ROOTSTOCKS) from any part of the plant, (except pips, which are already progenies), independently of the factors potentially influencing the vine's morphology that can mislead ampelographers such as environmental conditions (e.g. drought), the development stage (e.g. woody canes used for trading, often impossible to identify visually), or sanitary state (e.g. viruses). There are between 5,000 and 10,000 grape cultivars in the world, for which about 24,000 names have been recorded, thus the same grape often has several names (synonyms) in different regions. Inversely, the same name can be used for several distinct varieties (homonyms). DNA profiling can be very helpful in correcting misnomers and detecting synonyms (e.g. Zinfandel and Primitivo) and homonyms (e.g. the REFOSCO group), and is thus useful in managing

important ampelographic collections. Although in 2002 DAVIS and Australia's CSIRO scientists independently found some microsatellite variations within a high number of Pinot, Chardonnay, and Primitivo clones, so far neither DNA profiling nor any other molecular method has managed unambiguously to identify different clones of a grape variety.

Microsatellites follow the laws of heredity: half of them come from the mother and half of them come from the father. Much like paternity testing in humans, by looking at a high number of microsatellites (30 to 50), it is possible with DNA profiling to reconstruct the parentage of a variety when both parents are still available. Researchers Carole Meredith and John Bowers at Davis were the first to uncover an unexpected parentage in 1997 when they surprised the whole wine world by announcing that CABERNET SAUVIGNON is the result of a (probably spontaneous) CROSS between Cabernet Franc and Sauvignon Blanc. Later on, in collaboration with Jean-Michel Boursiquot at MONTPELLIER, they revealed additional unexpected parentages such as those of CHARDONNAY and GAMAY (in 1999), and SYRAH (in 2000). Many additional parentages have since been discovered by these and other scientists around the world, including those of SANGIOVESE, MERLOT, and TEMPRANILLO.

DNA profiling has also been used to correctly ascertain the varietal identity of fresh and dried grapes as well as the varietal origin of free-run juice.

Through DNA profiling, parent–offspring pairs can also be determined when one parent is missing, though it is impossible to infer the direction of the relationship. Pedigree reconstruction makes available unprecedented information about history and migrations of grape cultivars, and provides a better understanding of the genetic events that led to today's range of cultivars. The largest pedigree that appears in Robinson, Harding, and Vouillamoz's *Wine Grapes* groups no fewer than 156 European wine grape varieties that are linked by parent–offspring relationships.

However, the 'holy grail' of reconstructing the exhaustive genealogical tree of all existing cultivars will almost certainly never be attained since many parents have disappeared because of frost, pests (e.g. PHYLLOXERA), or lack of interest.   J.V.

Bowers, J. E., and Meredith, C. P., 'The parentage of a classic wine grape, Cabernet Sauvignon', *Nature Genetics*, 16/1 (1997), 84–7.

Robinson, J., Harding, J., and Vouillamoz, J., *Wine Grapes: A Complete Guide to 1,368 Vine Varieties, Including their Origins and Flavours* (London, 2012).

Thomas, M. R., et al., 'Repetitive DNA of grapevine: classes present and sequences suitable for cultivar identification', *Theoretical and Applied Genetics*, 86 (1993) 173–80.

d

Sefc, K. M., et al., 'Microsatellite markers for grapevine: tools for cultivar identification and pedigree reconstruction', in K. A. Roubelakis-Angelakis (ed.), *Grapevine Molecular Physiology and Biotechnology* (2nd edn, New York, 2009), 565–96.

DO stands for Denominación de Origen, the name of Spain's PDO denomination, which is now widely called DOP, Denominación de Origen Protegida.

doble pasta, dark, full-bodied Spanish wine produced by running off a proportion of fermenting must after two days and adding more crushed grapes to refill the vat. The ratio of skin to pulp is effectively doubled, producing wines with a deep, black colour and very high levels of TANNIN. Doble pasta wines have traditionally been made in JUMILLA, YECLA, UTIEL-REQUENA, MANCHUELA, and ALICANTE, where they are used for blending but they are being superseded by GRAPE CONCENTRATE.   R.J.M.

DOC, initials which stand for Denominação de Origem Controlada in PORTUGAL and Denominazione di Origine Controllata in ITALY, those countries' PDO denomination for superior wines.

A DOC system has also been in operation in ROMANIA since 1975.

Denominação de Origem Controlada (Portugal)

In Portugal, DOC stands for Denominação de Origem Controlada. An alternative term, Denominação de Origem Protegida (DOP), introduced after the EU wine market reforms of 2008, is also available but by 2014 had not been widely adopted. On joining the EU in 1986, Portugal undertook revision of its wine laws to bring them into line with other European countries, most notably those of France. Each of the regions which had already been designated a REGIÃO DEMARCADA (RD) in earlier legislation (BUCELAS, CARCAVELOS, COLARES, DÃO, MADEIRA, SETÚBAL, VINHO VERDE, BAIRRADA, and DOURO) were subsequently designated as DOCs. The system equates roughly with the French AOC and sets out permitted grape varieties, maximum yields, periods of ageing in bulk and bottle, and analytical standards for specified types of wine. Samples must be submitted to the local body controlling that region's wine industry, who grant numbered seals of origin to producers whose wines have satisfied the regulations.

See VINHO REGIONAL (VR) for the denomination below DOC/DOP.   S.A.

Denominazione di Origine Controllata (Italy)

Italy's PDO denomination has had a chequered history. Italian wine was first regulated systematically in 1963 in an effort to bring Italy's wine laws into line with fellow EU founding nation France. A few of Italy's most famous wines had already been given legal recognition and protection in the 1930s but this new system was designed to be much more comprehensive and modelled on France's APPELLATION CONTRÔLÉE. This meant that individual production zones were DELIMITED; permitted VINE VARIETIES specified, often with specific percentages; levels of ALCOHOL, TOTAL ACIDITY, and EXTRACT were established; and limits, often very generously, placed on YIELDS. Viticultural and winemaking practices were regulated, albeit often in the haziest of terms: 'in conformity with existing practices' or 'so as to not change the nature of the wine' are frequent phrases in the rules of individual DOCs. As in the case of the French archetype, this new system was set up to protect wine regions against COUNTERFEIT products and imitations, but has often seemed more concerned with enshrining in law existing practice than in optimizing QUALITY IN WINE.

Towards the end of the 1970s, ambitious producers, particularly those in the CHIANTI CLASSICO zone, became disillusioned with DOC rules which required them to include white wine grapes in their red wines and began to label their best wines with the lowest category VINO DA TAVOLA (see SUPERTUSCANS). See also DOCG, a category designed to be superior to DOC.

In an attempt to correct this confusing situation, the DOC system was overhauled in 1992. Its main innovation was to introduce the principle of territorial subdivision by allowing larger DOC zones to be broken down into subzones, townships, hamlets, microzones, individual estates, and vineyards, and to give the entire structure a vertical and hierarchical basis; the smaller the geographical unit, the stricter the production limits and criteria. Producers wishing to use a single-vineyard name for their DOC and DOCG wines had to register their vineyard and define its extent with the authorities, a reform aimed at curbing the multiplication of invented single-vineyard names (following the Italian FASHION for individual CRUS) with no real territorial basis. (See BAROLO for consideration of this phenomenon.) While many of these reforms were sensible and well-intentioned, the excessively generous yields of most DOCs were rarely curbed.

Recently the old lack of flexibility in permitted grape varieties has been reversed so that many DOC regulations have been opened up to allow a broad range of grape varieties, almost always including INTERNATIONAL VARIETIES. Perversely, this has altered some of Italy's most distinctive wines beyond recognition (see the very different cases of CIRÒ and BRUNELLO DI MONTALCINO, for example). This liberalization and GLOBALIZATION comes at a time when interest in INDIGENOUS VARIETIES and authentic, TERROIR-driven Italian wine has never been greater.

In the past the failure of the DOC system was evidenced by the fact that by the 1990s DOC wine represented only a third of the potential production of vineyards designated DOC. In 2011, while Italian wine production as a whole had declined thanks to falling BULK WINE prices, a continuous decrease in wine consumption in Italy, and the EU's abolition of compulsory DISTILLATION, 35% of all Italian wine was DOC, even if a mere ten names accounted for more than half of it. PROSECCO (1.3 million hl), ASTI (790,000 hl), and MONTEPULCIANO D'ABRUZZO (959,000 hl) contributed the lion's share. Veneto, Tuscany, Emilia-Romagna, Abruzzo, and Trentino-Alto Adige produced 75% of Italy's total DOC production.

In 2014 there were 330 DOCs, 118 IGTs, and 73 DOCG wines. The introduction of the EU reforms to the common market organisation (CMO) for wine, which came into force in 2008, required all EU member states to register all of their denominations in an official list by the end of 2011, with any elevations or additions of wine regions after that date to be approved by the EU rather than just by individual member states. This prompted Italy to rush to create and elevate DOCs by the dozen and resulted in some that exist on paper only, or have been created purely out of commercial opportunism, such as DOCs VENEZIA and ROMA.   W.S.

Belfrage, N. 'The Law', *Life Beyond Lambrusco—Understanding Italian Fine Wine*, (London, 1985), pp 44–51.

DOCa, Denominación de Origen Calificada, is the highest Spanish wine quality denomination, the elite of DO/DOP, reserved for regions complying with certain conditions including above-average grape prices, and particularly stringent quality controls. RIOJA was the first Spanish region to be awarded DOCa status, in 1991, followed by PRIORAT in 2002.

doce, Portuguese for sweet. See SWEETNESS, and DOSAGE for official EU sugar levels.

DOCG, stands for **Denominazione di Origine Controllata e Garantita**, a legal category established in ITALY in 1963 for its highest-quality wines, at the same time as its DOC was created as an Italian version of the French APPELLATION CONTRÔLÉE system. The express purpose of this category was to identify and reward the finest Italian wines, which were to be 'guaranteed' (the G), and not merely 'controlled'. The 'guarantee' consists of a laboratory ANALYSIS of, among other aspects, the wine's minimum EXTRACT, and a panel tasting.

If the DOC system did not enjoy general credibility because it was eventually applied liberally and with little rigour, the DOCG title, in contrast, was conferred with admirable parsimony in its first years of existence. It was not even used until 1980, and by 1992, when the

DOC system was overhauled by law 164, only 11 wines had been deemed worthy of receiving the honour. The first five DOCGs to be conferred were BAROLO, BARBARESCO, CHIANTI, BRUNELLO DI MONTALCINO, and VINO NOBILE DI MONTEPULCIANO, the last of which was the first to be elevated, after having applied as early as 1969. The awarding of DOCG status to ALBANA DI ROMAGNA in 1986, however, was widely regarded as political in inspiration and a violation of both the letter and spirit of law 930 and, as such, a threat to the viability of the DOCG category itself. It met with such criticism that it was hoped it would have prevented repetition of such an episode.

The authorities nevertheless found themselves in a similar situation with the approval of DOCG for SOAVE, which, while merited in part of the zone, turned into a series of political compromises rather than a coherent attempt to define that which represents the best of Soave. By 2014, there were 73 DOCG wines, many created since the EU reforms of 2008 announcing that from 2011 all promotions would be approved by Brussels. Several of the new DOCGs make sense, such as AMARONE della Valpolicella, but many are likely to create confusion or trigger incredulity, notably elevations of SUPERIORE or RISERVA versions within an existing DOC, such as Bardolino Superiore and Verdicchio dei Castelli di Jesi Riserva, since these suffixes have so far proved unable to guarantee superior quality. In the past, the greatest successes of DOCG have been to decrease YIELDS and promote an image of quality in virtually every zone to which it has been introduced, but the latest flurry of additions has diluted their significance, especially in the all-too-frequent cases in which the elevation has not involved stricter production rules.   W.S.

doctors of medicine through the ages have displayed an uncommon affection for wine, and not just because of wine's uses as a MEDICINE and beneficial effects on HEALTH. Doctors have long been enthusiastic wine consumers (see Alexander HENDERSON, for example), collectors, and, more recently, producers. There are numerous examples of vineyard owners who combine viticulture with practising medicine. Docteur Peste's slice of the CORTON vineyard is sold each year in the HOSPICES DE BEAUNE auction, itself a medical charity, for example. The MOSEL in Germany has an example of what might be called double-doctoring, in that the producer Dr Thanisch owns a portion of the world-famous Doctor, or Doktor, vineyard of Bernkastel.

Particularly strong medical connections can be traced in the history of AUSTRALIAN wine. During the transport of convicts and subsequent migrant trade of the 19th century, doctors became accustomed to using wine as

medicine and many established their own vineyards on settling in Australia. More than 160 such cases can be cited, including the founders of what were for long Australia's three largest wine companies HARDYS, Lindemans, and PENFOLDS, as well as those of labels such as Angove, Houghton, Stanley, and Minchinbury. Australia was founded in the rum age, developed in the beer age, and is now maturing in the wine age.

See also LITERATURE OF WINE.   J.R. & P.A.N.

Norrie, P. A., 'Australia's three leading wine doctors', *Journal of Medical Biography*, 3 (1995), 218–24.

dolce, Italian for sweet. See SWEETNESS, and DOSAGE for official EU sugar levels.

Dolceacqua, or **Rossese di Dolceacqua**, wine from the north western coast of Italy. For more details, see ROSSESE and LIGURIA.

Dolcetto, an early-ripening, deep-coloured, low-acid red grape variety cultivated almost exclusively in the provinces of Cuneo and Alessandria in the north west Italian region of PIEMONTE. The wines produced are soft, round, fruity, and fragrant with flavours of liquorice and almonds. Most are designed to be drunk in their first two or three years, although well-made bottles of Dolcetto d'Alba and Dolcetto d'Ovada can easily last at least five years. Dolcetto therefore plays an important role in the economy of various estates, providing a product which can be marketed early while the wines based on BARBERA or, particularly, NEBBIOLO grapes demand extended ageing in cask and bottle. Unlike Barbera, it is rarely blended with other varieties, chiefly because it is so rarely planted outside VARIETALLY-minded Piemonte.

As a precocious ripener, ripening up to four weeks before the majestic Nebbiolo, Dolcetto also permits growers to exploit either higher or less favourably exposed vineyard sites and thus maximize the return on their holdings. In the precious BAROLO and BARBARESCO zones, for example, Dolcetto is rarely planted on a south-facing site unless the vineyard is too high to ripen Nebbiolo reliably. And in the zones of Dogliani, Diano d'Alba, and Ovada, Dolcetto is planted where other varieties may not ripen at all. There is a consensus amongst growers in the Dolcetto d'Alba DOC, source of much of the finest Dolcetto, that the variety prefers the characteristic white marls of the right bank of the Tanaro and cannot give maximum results in heavier soils.

If the grape is relatively easy to cultivate, apart from its susceptibility to FUNGAL DISEASES and a tendency to drop its bunches in the cold mornings of late September, it is far from easy to vinify. While low in ACIDITY, relative to Barbera at least, and therefore *dolce* (sweet) to the Piedmontese palate, Dolcetto ('little sweet one') does have significant TANNINS, which producers

have learned to soften with shorter fermentations. So rich are the skins of Dolcetto in ANTHOCYANINS that even the shortest fermentation rarely compromises the deep ruby and purple tones of the wine. Like Barbera, it is prone to REDUCTION. Because it is generally vinified early and fast (to make way for Barbera and Nebbiolo in the winery), most Dolcetto is made to be drunk early without ceremony. But a drop in sales in 2008 caused a Dolcetto crisis in Piemonte which unfortunately sullied the reputation of the now relatively obscure Dolcetto d'Ovada DOCG, which has been associated with fine, elegant Dolcettos that are worth ageing, while Dogliani or Dolcetto di Dogliani DOCG produces truly exceptional, ageworthy, and complex wines radically different from the many uninspiring but cheaper Dolcettos.

There are seven Dolcetto DOCs in Piemonte: Acqui, ALBA, ASTI (where little is planted, GRIGNOLINO being the young wine of choice), Diano d'Alba, Dogliani, Langhe Monregalesi, and Ovada. Alba, Ovada, and Dogliani are quantitatively the most significant, while the Langhe Monregalesi is a barely extant curiosity.

Ormeasco is LIGURIA's version of Dolcetto and is therefore the southernmost extent of Dolcetto territory in Italy. It grows just on the Ligurian side of the mountains that separate Piemonte from Liguria. In total, there were 6,128 ha/15,136 acres of Dolcetto planted in Italy in 2010.

A FASHION for Italian wine and food has spread Dolcetto to the US, Australia, and New Zealand.

Robinson, J., Harding, J., and Vouillamoz, J., *Wine Grapes: A Complete Guide to 1,368 Vine Varieties, Including their Origins and Flavours* (London, 2012).

Dôle. See SWITZERLAND.

dolium, a large earthenware vessel used in the Ancient Roman period. Sometimes with a capacity of several thousand litres, they were often partly buried in the floor of a barn to act as a FERMENTATION VESSEL and provide storage for wine until it was transferred to AMPHORAE. In the late 20th and early 21st centuries, a number of Roman wrecks were discovered off the south coast of France in which the cargo space was largely taken up by up to 14 *dolia*, thus creating the ancient equivalent of a tanker for the transport of wine in bulk.   J.J.P.

domaine, French word for an estate, typically a vine-growing and winemaking estate in BURGUNDY.

domaine bottling, the relatively recent practice of BOTTLING the produce of a DOMAINE on the property which produced it (although bottling at least in the region of production was advocated as early as 1728; see LITERATURE OF

WINE). Such wines are described as **domaine bottled**, or *mis(e) en bouteille au domaine* in French. The term is the BURGUNDY equivalent of Bordeaux's CHÂTEAU BOTTLING, whose history is mirrored by the practice of domaine bottling. Domaine bottling began in the economic crisis years of the early 1930s but it was not until energetic foreign wine merchants such as Frank SCHOONMAKER and Alexis LICHINE visited Burgundy in the second half of the 20th century that the better individual producers were encouraged, and in many cases subsidized, to bottle their own production, typically with the help of mobile BOTTLING lines. The movement gathered pace in the 1980s and 1990s and is now seen as standard. However, many domaines also now produce some merchant bottlings, and most of the classic NÉGOCIANTS are concentrating more on wines from their own vineyards. In either case the small print of bottling information may provide the only clue to the original provenance of the grapes: if the label states *mis en bouteille au domaine*, then the wine is made from fruit grown in their own vineyards. Otherwise the label is more likely to note: *mis en bouteille par . . .* followed by the producer's name.

See also ESTATE BOTTLED.

Domaine de la Romanée-Conti

Domaine de la Romanée-Conti, the most prestigious wine estate in Burgundy, based in Vosne-Romanée. 'The Domaine', as it is frequently called, is co-owned by the de Villaine and LEROY families and produces only GRAND CRU wines: one white, Le MONTRACHET, and six reds: Romanée-Conti and La Tâche (both MONOPOLES of the domaine), Richebourg, Romanée-St-Vivant, Échezeaux, and Grands Échezeaux. For more details of individual wines, see VOSNE-ROMANÉE and ÉCHEZEAUX. The Domaine is the exception to the law according to which no estate in Burgundy may be named after a specific vineyard. Its wines are notable for their richness and longevity.

History

What is now Romanée-Conti was identified by the monks of St-Vivant as Le Cloux des Cinq Journaux in 1512 and sold off, as Le Cros de Cloux, in 1584 to Claude Cousin. His nephew and heir Germain Danton sold again to Jacques Vénot in 1621. Vénot's daughter married a Croonembourg, which family retained the vineyard, now known as La Romanée (first mentioned in 1651), for four generations until it was sold to the Prince de Conti in 1760. The title Romanée-Conti was not used, however, until after dispossession by the revolutionaries and its sale by auction in 1794.

Romanée-Conti was bought by Julien Ouvard in 1819 and sold by his heirs to Jacques-Marie Duvault-Blochet 50 years later. Duvault-Blochet's eventual heirs were the de Villaine family. In 1911, Edmond Guidon de Villaine became director of what was now known as the Domaine de la Romanée-Conti, selling a half-share in 1942 to his friend Henri Leroy.

Over the years, Duvault-Blochet built up major vineyard ownership including part of Échezeaux, Grands Échezeaux, Richebourg, and the section of La Tâche known as Les Gaudichots. In 1933, the rest of La Tâche was bought from the Liger-Belair family, making a monopoly, and a small holding of Le Montrachet (0.67 ha/1.6 acres) was added in three slices between 1963 and 1980. The Domaine entered into a long-term contract to farm and produce the wines of Domaine Marey-Monge's holding of Romanée-St-Vivant before eventually buying the land in 1988. This necessitated selling part of their Échezeaux vineyards and a slice of Grands Échezeaux, although they continue to farm the land and bottle the wines. From 2009 the Domaine has also made a Corton, having leased three vineyards there from the estate of Prince Florent de Mérode. The produce of further vineyards owned by the Domaine in Vosne-Romanée and Bâtard-Montrachet is sold in bulk or kept for domestic consumption. Today the Domaine continues to be owned jointly by the de Villaine and Leroy/Roch families, with Aubert de Villaine and Henri-Frédéric Roch in place as co-directors.   J.T.C.M.

Meadows, A., *The Pearl of the Côte* (2010).
Olney, R., *Romanée-Conti* (Paris, 1991).

domestic wine production. See HOME WINEMAKING.

Domina, modern red CROSS of Portugieser × Spätburgunder (Pinot Noir) that combines combines the productivity of the first with the ripeness, tannins, and colour of the second, if not its finesse and fruit. The total vineyard area in Germany, mainly Franken, had reached 388 ha/958 acres by 2012.

Domitian, Roman emperor (AD 81–96) who, in the words of the eulogy by the contemporary poet Statius (*Silvae* 4. 3. 11–12), restored 'to chaste Ceres the acres which had so long been denied her and lands made sober'. By a famous edict, possibly from AD 92, Domitian banned the planting of new vineyards in Italy and ordered the destruction of at least half of the vineyards in the provinces (Suetonius, *Domitian* 7). He may also have sought to ban the planting within cities of small vineyards, of the sort which have been found at POMPEII. His purpose was not, as some have supposed, an attempt to protect the price of Italian wine at a time of general over-production, but a heavy-handed attempt to divert investment into the production of cereals, the supply of which was a perennial problem for the large cities of the Roman empire. There was no way that Domitian could enforce such a ban and, following the protests which we know came from Asia, he did not persist with the measure. Hence the much later efforts of the Emperor Probus (AD 276–82) to encourage the planting of vineyards should not be taken as a sign that the ban lasted for centuries, as has often been thought.   J.J.P.

Dom Pérignon. See PÉRIGNON, DOM.

Doña Blanca, also known as **Valenciana**, and Moza Fresca, variety grown in north west Spain, particularly in Monterrei, Bierzo, and to a much lesser extent Valdeorras, where it is known as Valenciana. DNA PROFILING has shown that it is identical to the Portuguese variety SÍRIA. In 2011 there were 579 ha/1,430 acres left in Spain.

Dona Branca, soft, northern Portuguese white wine grape planted on 390 ha/963 acres in 2012.

Donnaz, or **Donnas**, red wine based on NEBBIOLO grapes made in Italy's Valle d'AOSTA.

DOP, or Denominación de Origen Protegida, previously known as DO (which was still widely used in 2014), the mainstay of Spain's wine quality control system and equivalent to PDO. The EU's denomination reforms implemented in Spain in 2010 are followed by some of the more recent Spanish appellations, but both DO and DOP are permitted on labels.

Each region awarded DO/DOP status is governed by a CONSEJO REGULADOR made up of representatives of the regional government (or the Ministry of Agriculture in the three multiregional appellations Rioja, Jumilla, and Cava), vinegrowers, winemakers, and merchants who earn their livelihoods in the region. These regional governments decide on the boundaries of the region, permitted VINE VARIETIES, maximum YIELDS, limits of ALCOHOLIC STRENGTH, and any other limitations pertaining to the zone. Back labels or neck seals are granted by the Consejo to certify that a wine meets the standards laid out in the DOP regulations. A superior category, Denominación de Origen Calificada (see DOCA), was created in 1991.

Rioja (promoted to DOCa status in 1991) became Spain's first DO in 1926 when its own Consejo Regulador was established. Jerez and Málaga had joined the ranks by the end of the 1930s, and they were joined by several other regions immediately after the Civil War.

Spanish wine law has been subject to some criticism as the list of regions promoted to DOP status continues to lengthen (see also PORTUGAL). By 2014 there were 84 DOPs, including the 15 VINOS DE PAGO (no fewer than nine DOPs in the CANARY ISLANDS alone). The system has most often helped the newer, lesser-known DOPs improve quality levels to no small degree, but some older, well-known Consejos Reguladores continue to uphold certain local quirks, which may sometimes stifle enterprise and initiative among growers and winemakers, as INAO has been known to do in France.

See also the additional Spanish denomination VINO DE CALIDAD. V. de la S.

In PORTUGAL DOP stands for Denominação de Origem Protegida, a denomination which may eventually replace the country's DOC.

DOQ, or Denominaciò d'Origen Qualificada, the Catalan equivalent of DOCA.

Doradillo, Australian name for the bland CAYETANA Blanca, once grown in the hot, irrigated RIVERLAND of South Australia.

Dordogne, river in SOUTH WEST FRANCE which rises on the Massif Central south west of Clermont-Ferrand, flows through the Corrèze *département* (whence the merchants of LIBOURNE came), flows through BERGERAC and related appellations, and into the GIRONDE to form the more northerly of the two 'seas' referred to in the name of ENTRE-DEUX-MERS, with ST-ÉMILION, POMEROL, FRONSAC, and finally BOURG on its right bank.

dormancy, sleep, the normal state of vines in winter. This period nominally starts with autumn LEAF FALL, although buds are in a state of so-called organic dormancy from VERAISON onwards. The period of dormancy ends with BUDBREAK in the spring. PRUNING is carried out when the vines are dormant, and buds and CUTTINGS taken from the vines at this time are used in PROPAGATION. Tests on vines in winter show they are literally asleep or dormant, with minimal metabolic activity. R.E.S.

Lavee, S., and May, P., 'Dormancy of grapevine buds—facts and speculation', *Australian Journal of Grape and Wine Research*, 3 (1997), 31–46.

Dornfelder, the most popular German CROSS, bred in 1956 by August Herold, who had unwisely already assigned his name to one of its parents, the lesser HEROLDREBE, and so Dornfelder owes its name to the 19th-century founder of the Württemberg viticultural school. A HELFENSTEINER × Heroldrebe cross, Dornfelder incorporates every important red wine vine grown in Germany somewhere in its genealogy and happily seems to have inherited many more of their good points than their bad.

The wine is notable for its depth of colour (useful in a country where pigments are at a premium), its good acidity, and, in some cases, its ability to benefit from BARRIQUE ageing and even to develop in bottle. Producing wines that are velvety textured, slightly floral, and sometimes with just a hint of sweetness, Dornfelder is easier to grow than Spätburgunder, has much better resistance to rot than Portugieser,

stronger stalks than Trollinger, better ripeness levels than either, earlier ripening than Lemberger (Blaufränkisch), and a yield that can easily reach 120 hl/ha (6.8 tons/acre) (although quality-conscious producers are careful to restrict productivity). It is hardly surprising that it continues to gain ground in most German wine regions, especially Rheinhessen and the Pfalz, where results are particularly appetizing. Germany's total plantings have been rising steadily to reach a national total of 8,197 ha/20,246 acres by 2012.

dosage, the final addition to a SPARKLING WINE which may top up a bottle in the case of TRADITIONAL METHOD wines, and also determines the sweetness, or RESIDUAL SUGAR, of the finished wine. In French this addition is called the *liqueur d'expédition* and, in traditional method wines, usually comprises a mixture of wine and sugar syrup. Champagne is naturally so high in ACIDITY that even wines with relatively high residual sugar can taste bone dry. BOTTLE AGE or extended AUTOLYSIS are excellent substitutes for dosage, however, and, in general, the older the wine, the lower the necessary dosage to produce a BALANCED wine, and vice versa. The early 21st century saw a FASHION for champagnes made with no, or zero, dosage. The table below gives the legal classification of sweetness levels for sparkling wine and champagne within the EU. This information must be included on the label.

EU classification of sweetness levels for champagne and sparking wine	
RS g/l	**Example descriptions**
< 3 with no sugar added after the second fermentation	brut nature/natur herb/ bruto natural/pas dosé/zéro dosage
0–6	extra brut/extra herb/ extra bruto
< 15	brut/herb/bruto
12–20	extra dry/extra trocken/ extra seco /extra sec
17–35	sec/trocken/secco or asciutto/dry/seco
33–50	demi-sec/halbtrocken/ abboccato/medium dry/semiseco
> 50	doux/mild/dolce/sweet/ dulce

double pruning, a time-consuming viticultural technique in which the vines are pruned twice, which alters the timing of vine development (see PHENOLOGY). Double pruning may be carried out for one of two reasons: to delay BUDBREAK and hence reduce FROST hazard in cool climates; or to delay harvest and hence potentially increase wine quality in hot regions.

Since early winter pruning encourages earlier budbreak, frost injury risks are increased. Pruning lightly in the beginning of the winter delays budbreak of basal buds; a second or double pruning can be done after the danger of frost is passed.

The related technique of double pruning in hot climates was developed by R. E. Smart and P. R. Dry at ROSEWORTHY in South Australia in the 1970s to delay fruit ripening from the heat of midsummer to cooler conditions of autumn. The vines are pruned normally in winter and then again in early summer just after flowering. Yields are reduced by this process but wine quality is much improved. R.E.S.

Douce Noire, what CHARBONO is called in its SAVOIE home.

douelle or **douve**, French for a STAVE.

Douro, Portuguese DOP named after the river which rises as the Duero in Spain (see RIBERA DEL DUERO) before turning south to form the frontier with PORTUGAL, then weaving west where it cleaves through the hard, granite mountains of northern Portugal before finally slipping past OPORTO into the Atlantic swell (see maps under PORTUGAL and SPAIN). Most famous as the source of the FORTIFIED wine PORT, the Douro Valley is also well known for the production of (unfortified) table wine labelled Douro DOP. First demarcated in 1756, making it one of the world's oldest delimited wine regions (see DELIMITATION and PORTUGAL, history), the Douro Valley's since-modified irregular outline corresponds closely with an outcrop of pre-Cambrian SCHIST, which is hemmed in by GRANITE. For over two centuries, the demarcation applied only to port, but in 1979 it was extended to include table wine. Although (poorly made) 'blackstrap' table wines dominated Douro production until usurped by port in the latter part of the 18th century, the first glimmer of the region's true potential for table wines appeared when port shippers FERREIRA launched Barca Velha 1952, a red wine from the Douro Superior, upstream of the port heartland. Making TABLE WINES did not take hold, however, until the 1990s, following Portugal's accession to the EU. This provided invaluable funds for research and new equipment. It also led to the demise of the port shippers' de facto monopoly over exports, enabling estates to make and sell their own wine. In the spirit of Barca Velha, early efforts focused on ambitious, upmarket reds. But this century has seen the emergence of many a mid-priced and even entry-level Douro table wine as the number of port shippers and independent wine farms (quintas) making table wine has mushroomed. While quality is correspondingly more variable, the Douro still produces some of Portugal's most consistent red wines.

DOP wines are made from a single variety or, more typically, a blend of as many as 30 of the region's 100-plus approved INDIGENOUS varieties, which are similar to those used for port. Should winemakers stray from the approved list, wines are labelled Vinho Regional DURIENSE. The region's varietal versatility reflects the sheer diversity of the world's largest mountain vineyard (about 250,000 ha/617,763 acres, of which 45,203 ha/111,197 acres are under vine), whose TERROIR has been more artfully exploited as a result of the increased focus on Douro DOP wine. Divided into three subregions (the easternmost Baixo or Lower Corgo, Cima or Upper Corgo, and the Douro Superior/Upper Douro which reaches the Spanish border), in general terms it is progressively warmer and drier towards the east. However, since the steep slopes extend from around 150 m to a substantially cooler 900 m ELEVATION and face every which way (the Douro DOP not only tracks a 100 km stretch of the River Douro, but also the valleys of its tributaries), there is many an exception. The first decade of this century saw a sharper focus on fresh white wines sourced from higher sites often located on granite soils. Earlier picking and especially the use of older and larger OAK barrels is also resulting in greater freshness and restraint among the better reds. The quest for individuation led some to question 1970s viticultural studies whose outcome was a shift away from the tradition of FIELD blends towards varietally homogenous plantings of the supposedly superior red grape varieties, TOURIGA NACIONAL, TINTA RORIZ, TOURIGA FRANCA, TINTA BARROCA, and TINTO CÃO—five were even mandatory for new vineyards planted under the 1982 TRÁS-OS-MONTES Integrated Rural Development Project (which encouraged the restructuring of over 3,700 ha of abandoned vineyards). Traditional varieties that have been planted once more include TINTA FRANCISCA, Donzelinho Tinto, Touriga Brasileira, Folgasão, and also SOUSÃO (which is prized for its high acidity). For whites (mostly from old field blends), key varieties include RABIGATO, CÔDEGA DO LARINHO, VIOSINHO, GOUVEIO, MALVASIA Fina, and ARINTO.   S.A.

Mayson, R. J., *Port and the Douro* (3rd edn, Oxford, 2013).

de Almeida, J. N., 'Vine, wine and life – a portrait of the Douro Region in recent times', in Fundação Francisco Girão, *Francisco Girão An innovator in viticulture in the north of Portugal* (Volume II, 2011, Porto).

www.ivdp.pt

Douro bake, traditional expression for the character imparted to wines, especially PORT, matured in the hot, dry climate of the DOURO Valley (rather than the much cooler, damper atmosphere of VILA NOVA DE GAIA, where port has traditionally been matured by the shippers).

Some wines matured in the Douro seem to develop faster, losing colour, browning, and sometimes acquiring a slightly sweet, caramelized flavour—although poor and sometimes unhygienic storage conditions often have a greater impact on wine quality than the climate, and many reputable shippers successfully age large stocks of port in the Douro.   R.J.M.

doux, French for sweet. See SWEETNESS, and DOSAGE for official EU sugar levels.

Dow, important port shipper. See SYMINGTONS.

downy mildew, one of the most economically significant FUNGAL DISEASES affecting vines, often called peronospora in parts of Europe. It is a particular problem in regions with warm, humid springs and summers such as many wine regions in northern Europe. The disease is caused by the organism *Plasmopara viticola*. This fungus is indigenous to eastern North America, and so some species of native AMERICAN VINES such as *Vitis cordifolia*, *Vitis rupestris*, and *Vitis rotundifolia* are relatively resistant. Commercially important varieties of VINIFERA, however, are highly susceptible.

The fungus caused havoc in the vineyards of Europe when it was accidentally introduced before 1878, probably on American vines imported as grafting stock to combat PHYLLOXERA. By 1882, the disease had spread to all of France. The famous BORDEAUX MIXTURE was first used as a preventive spray to control this disease.

The disease is now widespread around the world, but a few areas with low spring and summer rainfall are essentially free of it. These include Afghanistan, northern Chile, Egypt, and Western Australia. It has occurred spasmodically in California and southern Chile.

Downy mildew attacks all green parts of the vine and young leaves are particularly susceptible. When severely affected, leaves will drop off. The loss of leaves reduces PHOTOSYNTHESIS and thus causes delays in fruit ripening and, typically, levels of fruit SUGARS, vine reserves of CARBOHYDRATES, and ANTHOCYANINS are depressed. BUDBREAK and early shoot growth can be delayed the following spring. Severe infections result in pale, puny reds and weak whites.

The symptoms of the disease are described quite aptly by the name. Leaves show patches of dense, white cottony growth on the undersurface. The earliest stage of the fungus is the so-called 'oil spot', easily seen on the upper leaf surface when it is held up against the light. PETIOLES, TENDRILS, young INFLORESCENCES, and developing berries are also affected. The fungus spends the winter in fallen leaves and can sometimes survive in the buds. Spores germinate in the spring when temperatures reach 11 °C/52 °F

and they are spread to the vine by rainsplash from the soil. Spores are further spread and germinated with high humidity (95 to 100% relative humidity), warm temperatures (18 to 22 °C), and moisture. The most severe epidemics of the disease occur with frequent rainstorms and warm weather. The low yields of the French vintages of 1886, 1910, 1915, 1930, 1932, 1948, 1957, and 1969, all of them produced after wet growing seasons, were probably due to downy mildew.

There are two principal protection approaches. The first and most common is to use protective sprays which are often based on COPPER. However, the protection lasts for only ten days or so, especially when the shoots are growing rapidly in early spring. Curative FUNGICIDES which act against established infections became available in the early 1990s, but these are more expensive. A modern approach is to install a VINEYARD WEATHER STATION which can predict outbreaks by measuring the weather.

An alternative but less popular approach to the control of this disease is to plant DISEASE-RESISTANT VARIETIES. European vine breeders, especially at GEISENHEIM and GEILWEILERHOF in Germany, have been particularly successful in developing varieties which require no, or less, spraying against downy mildew, with native American vines contributing the resistant genes. Increased environmental awareness may encourage their use, but there is substantial consumer resistance to new varieties.   R.E.S.

Emmett, R. W., et al., 'Grape diseases and vineyard protection', in B. G. Coombe and P. R. Dry (eds.), *Viticulture*, ii: *Practices* (Adelaide, 1992).

Galet, P., *Précis de viticulture* (7th edn, Montpellier, 2000).

Pearson, R. C., and Goheen, A. C. (eds.), *Compendium of Grape Diseases* (St Paul, Minn., 1988).

drainage, free movement of water through the SOIL PROFILE or across the land surface; or alternatively, the removal of surplus water by artificial means. The importance of good soil drainage for viticulture and wine quality cannot be overstated. For a detailed discussion, see Seguin. See also TERROIR and SOIL AND WINE QUALITY.

All good vineyard soils are well drained, whether naturally or by artificial drainage. Permanent waterlogging or prolonged waterlogging after the start of spring growth is lethal to vine roots. Even marginal waterlogging can be harmful, by causing restriction of root and soil microbial activity, and consequent starvation of the vine for nutrients and root-produced growth substances (see CYTOKININ). Soils that are cold and wet at the time of FLOWERING are a major factor in poor berry setting, or COULURE. However, if waterlogging is temporary and the soil dries out at or just after flowering, with mild water stress before veraison, it is still possible to produce fine wines, especially on alluvial soils when sand or gravel is layered over finer sediment. Such waterlogging may reduce root depth but will not necessarily affect eventual wine quality.

Waterlogging confined to the SUBSOIL can still be a serious disadvantage, through killing or inactivation of the deeper roots. This can result in a vine with only a shallow effective root system, readily subject both to later DROUGHT after the surface moisture has evaporated or been used, and to excessive water uptake following rains during ripening. Seguin argues that such irregularity in the supply of SOIL WATER can be seriously detrimental to wine quality. Subsoils that are regularly waterlogged can be identified by their bleached, blue-grey colour (see SOIL COLOUR) while well-drained subsoils are usually yellow to reddish, and mottled subsoils indicate intermittent waterlogging.

As a broad rule, light-textured and stony soils drain freely, while tight or heavy clay soils (see SOIL TEXTURE) restrict drainage. Subsoils composed of the latter type can result in water-tables 'perched' on top of them. These develop most commonly on gradients, where seepage of water down the slope through the surface soil is interrupted by barriers of rock, or of clay reaching or approaching the surface.

However, even heavy soils and subsoils can drain adequately if they have good crumb structure (see SOIL STRUCTURE). This depends on their chemical nature, including sufficient contents of CALCIUM and, in the upper layers, ORGANIC MATTER. Unstructured soils can easily pack down to form impermeable hardpans below the surface when subjected to trampling or wheeled traffic (see SOIL COMPACTION). Vineyards are commonly RIPPED before planting to facilitate drainage.

Several other management factors can influence soil drainage. Deeply tap-rooted green manuring or COVER CROPS, such as mustard or lupins, can help to create and maintain vertical channels which allow water to infiltrate freely into the deeper soil layers. The maintenance of an organic surface MULCH, whether applied or originating naturally from cover crops, attains the same effect through encouraging EARTHWORM activity. These useful creatures also help to distribute surface organic matter and nutrients through the SOIL PROFILE. Finally, the application of LIME or gypsum can help on some acid soils, by improving their crumb structure and permeability.

Artificial drainage, where required, can be of several types according to situation and need. Webber and Jones describe them in detail. All forms of artificial soil drainage are expensive, but, on otherwise valuable land for producing high-value grapes, they can be essential. Drainage did, after all, transform the Médoc from a marsh to one of the world's most admired wine regions (see BORDEAUX, history). J.G. & C.v.L.

Seguin, G., ' "Terroirs" and pedology of wine growing', *Experientia*, 42 (1986), 861–72.
Webber, R. T. J., and Jones, L. D., 'Drainage and soil salinity', in B. G. Coombe and P. R. Dry (eds.), *Viticulture*, ii: *Practices* (Adelaide, 1992).

draining, *égouttage* in French. In WHITE WINEMAKING the operation usually takes place just after CRUSHING, although some winemakers choose to move crushed fruit straight to the press. Any juice run off without pressing is called drainings. The FREE-RUN juice is drained off the grape skins in a **draining tank** or **draining vat**, many of which incorporate special design features to assist the separation of liquids from solids. Similarly, in red wine fermentation, the red wine run off the skins may also be called drainings.

DRC, famous initials in the world of fine wine, standing for the DOMAINE DE LA ROMANÉE-CONTI.

dried-grape wines, varied and growing category of generally intense, complex, often sweet wines made from partially raisined grapes. The production technique, involving either leaving the grapes to raisin on the vine or picking and then drying them by various methods, is associated with most of the celebrated wines of antiquity. This early CONCENTRATION technique continues one of the oldest traditions in the gastronomic world.

In the classical world this winemaking style may well have evolved because of problems of wine conservation, particularly for wines traded and consumed outside their area of origin, semi-dried grapes naturally resulting in sweeter, stronger and therefore more stable wines. (BOTRYTIZED wines and the technique of FORTIFICATION were developed many centuries later.) The dried grape tradition has proved particularly resilient close to its origins, notably in Italy.

Ancient history

The technique of twisting the stems of grape bunches to deprive them of sap, and leaving them to raisin on the vine, may have originated in CRETE, but vinification techniques for dried grapes were perfected in Ancient GREECE. The Ancient Greeks also learned from other inhabitants of the eastern Mediterranean, particularly the Hittites of ANATOLIA. The first description of how to make wine from dried grapes is provided by HESIOD, in the 8th century BC. His *Works and Days* describes how grapes should be dried in the sun 'for ten days and nights' and then in the shade for a further five, before fermenting the wine in jars.

Such methods were responsible for the famous wines of the islands (Chios, Lesbos, and Thasos) which were so highly prized by HOMER and succeeding writers. These wines were often noted as being at their best after many years' maturation, when they had 'lost their teeth': clear evidence of the longevity which only dried-grape wines could provide before the invention of stoppered bottles. Sealed AMPHORAE may have been relatively airtight containers but long journeys in Mediterranean heat demanded exceptionally robust wines.

Coincidental with the rise of the Greek city states was the emergence of the most adventurous traders of the Mediterranean, those of PHOENICIA. They exported the wines of Lebanon (and the winemaking practices of CANAAN) along the littorals of North Africa and to Spain, Sardinia, and Sicily. One of their colonies was CARTHAGE, founded in 814 BC, where in about 500 BC Mago wrote his seminal work on agriculture, now known only in the extensive quotations which survive in the works of succeeding classical authors, notably the Roman COLUMELLA. Redding quotes Mago in the following passage which summarizes the Graeco-Roman understanding of dried grape vinification:

Let the bunches of grapes quite ripe, and scorched or shrivelled in the sun, when the bad and faulty ones are picked out, be spread upon a frame resting on stakes or forks and covered with a layer of reeds. Place them in the sun but protect them from the dew at night. When they are dry (sufficiently shrivelled) pluck the grapes from the stalks, throw them into a cask and make the first must. If they have been well drained, put them, at the end of six days, into a vessel, and press them for the first wine. A second time let them be pounded (or trodden) and pressed, adding cold must to the pressing. This second wine is to be placed in a pitched vessel, lest it become sour. After it has remained twenty or thirty days, and fermented, rack it into another vessel and stopping it close immediately, cover it with a skin.

Other writers in Ancient ROME such as CATO, PLINY, HORACE, and VIRGIL add other details (such as storing these wines in the rafters, as with modern Tuscan VIN SANTO), but in general repeat the principles laid down by their Mediterranean forebears.

The Romans, like the Greeks, planted vineyards wherever they went—in Spain, France, Germany, and central Europe, perhaps even in England. Only in the last would the climate have been too austere for the production of *passum* (PASSITO) wines; elsewhere the practice became embedded in the complex strata of vinicultural history, a rich seam of vinous tradition to be mined in later centuries, after the long upheavals which followed the collapse of the Roman empire.

Evolution since the Middle Ages

Italy The *vinum reticum* of Verona praised by Pliny was presumably the ancestor of today's RECIOTO and AMARONE. It was relatively common for wines to be made from grapes dried on the vine cut off from the flow of sap by having their stems twisted, or *torcolato* (the name of a modern white Recioto made in Veneto's BREGANZE from partially dried, though not (today) twisted, VESPAIOLA grapes). The dried-grape tradition was presumably enhanced in 1204 when Venice conquered Crete, the stronghold of this classical heritage. The result seems to have been a revival of dried-grape winemaking throughout the growing Venetian empire, not just in Veneto but on the islands and coast of what is now SLOVENIA and CROATIA.

In early-14th-century PIEMONTE, such wines were in great demand and are mentioned again in the mid 17th century, but the tradition survives only as a curiosity today. In TUSCANY, however, VIN SANTO survives as an apparently unbroken tradition, practised by most of the best estates. Versions exist in other parts of Italy, notably in TRENTINO (see VINO SANTO). Other survivals include the VERDUZZO of Ramandolo, the generally overrated PICOLIT of FRIULI, the remarkable Rosenmuskateller of TRENTINO-ALTO ADIGE, SFORZATO or Sfursat of VALTELLINA, ALBANA *passito* from Romagna, and SAGRANTINO *passito* from Umbria. In the south and islands, examples of this renascent tradition are too numerous to mention in detail but include a range of wines based on raisined MOSCATO, ALEATICO, MALVASIA, and Nasco grapes, not to mention Vecchio Samperi, the rare unfortified wine in the style of MARSALA from de Bartoli. Perhaps the best-known example of *passito* wine in southern Italy today is Vallone's Amarone-like Graticciaia, dried not three months under the winery roof but about ten days under the Puglian sun, still hot immediately after the grape harvest. And the island of Pantelleria is famous for a wine made from dried MOSCATO grapes.

Elsewhere It is clear from REDDING that dried-grape wines were much more common in early-19th-century France than today. He mentions the VIN DE PAILLE of Alsace, two types from Argentat in the Corrèze (way upriver of modern BERGERAC), one of them slightly sparkling, and what sounds like a magnificent example from the Sciacarello grape made at Sartène in CORSICA. He also makes clear that Muscat de RIVESALTES was then a true raisin wine, often the result of twisting grape stems on the vine, and not, as now, a fortified blend. In contemporary France, the tradition survives only in the vins de paille of Hermitage and the Jura, made as curiosities by two or three producers in each region, in quantities so tiny that they rarely reach the market.

In Spain, the classical traditions continued in muted form through the Muslim occupation and were revived thereafter. The most notable surviving derivatives are the Andalusian specialities SHERRY, MONTILLA, and MÁLAGA, whose richer styles have always been made with semi-dried grapes, but these are not pure dried-grape wines because most (although not Telmo Rodriguez' Molino Réal Malaga) are now fortified. Elsewhere in Spain the tradition is almost extinct.

Surprisingly few dried-grape wines can be found in Greece today. The rich wines of Sámos date from the replanting of the island's vineyards in the 16th century but those of SANTORINI (Thíra of the ancients) are descendants of the classical prototypes, as is the now fortified COMMANDARIA of Cyprus.

There are records of straw wine (Strohwein) being made in FRANKEN in Germany; a rich red dried-grape wine just over the border in Switzerland from Italy's VALTELLINA; a 'green' wine of remarkable strength produced near Cotnar on the borders of Moldova and Romania (see COTNARI); and of course the rather special case of TOKAJI in Hungary. The last survives; most of the others have vanished. The only notable additions to the once splendid roll-call of wines from the old Austro-Hungarian empire are a few straw wines and reed wines from AUSTRIA.

Redding mentions Shahoni, the 'royal grape' of the province of Cashbin in Persia, claiming that 'the grapes are kept over the winter, and remain on the vine a good deal of the time in linen bags', and also lists from Argentina a 'sweet wine, resembling Malaga, made at Mendoza at the foot of the Andes, on their eastern side' and the famous CONSTANTIA from South Africa, now being revived. In modern times there have also been experiments with dried-grape wines in California and Australia (see CUT CANE).   S.P.D.L.

Modern production techniques

Grapes with maximum EXTRACT and SUGARS are required, which normally entails restricting YIELDS. Such grapes may be picked either before, at, or after full RIPENESS. Twisting the stalk was once practised in Veneto but most growers now prefer to dry their grapes off the vine.

Those who pick slightly before full maturation claim there is less risk of ROT, thicker skins, enhanced resistance during drying, and higher acidity, all of which favour aroma, freshness, balance, and longevity—and concentrate the grapes which remain on the vine.

Only the ripest, healthiest grapes are generally picked, which today means a pre-selection by experienced pickers (although see RECIOTO). Healthy grapes are vital since any incipient mould or rot soon spreads during the drying process. Skins must remain intact, to which end

the grapes may well be laid in small trays for transport to the winery. The bunches should be *spargolo*, loose rather than compact, so that air circulates around the individual berries during the all-important drying process.

Sun drying is still practised in places such as the Sicilian island of PANTELLERIA off Tunisia, in southern PUGLIA, and the Greek island of SANTORINI. The process can be many times faster than drying under cover, but this can result in excessive colour, caramelized flavours, and loss of aroma, bypassing some of the microbiological transformations which are the essence of fine dried-grape wine.

Most grape drying for commercial purposes happens in a winery loft, where windows may be opened to let in plenty of air (essential against the development of rot and mould). Bunches are hung up vertically (on hooks, or on long strings), or laid out horizontally on neutral, bone-dry materials. Straw is rarely used because of its attractions for mice. Wire mesh, nylon nets, and wooden or plastic fruit boxes were 20th-century developments; more traditional cane and rush mats and bamboo racks remain popular in much of Italy. Today, in zones where dried grapes constitute an important factor in the local wine economy, purpose-built grape-drying plants are being created complete with temperature control and wind machines.

The duration of the drying process is dictated by the grape variety, the type of wine required, and microclimatic conditions during drying. Sugar-rich Greek grape varieties such as Muscat, Aleatico, and Malvasia require less time than more northern varieties. Three weeks may suffice for a Muscat whereas a Veronese variety such as GARGANEGA for a white Recioto or CORVINA, CORVINONE or RONDINELLA for a red Recioto or Amarone will need three to four months, in some cases, for Recioto, even up to six months. Ideal conditions include considerable currents of dry air, and humidity is such a problem in some valley sites that drying facilities are being moved to higher elevations. Excessive heat is generally regarded as negative, as is excessive cold.

The main effect of drying grapes is loss of water and the consequent concentration of sugars. The relationship between water loss and sugar gain is relatively direct so that a water loss of a third from grapes picked at 12 °BAUMÉ would result in a wine of 16% alcohol (if all the sugar were fermented out). Depending on the wine style desired, the loss of grape weight by evaporation varies between 10 and 60%, with the norm for a PASSITO wine being somewhere in the region of 35 to 40%, so the potential alcohol is raised by just over a third.

Other components behave less predictably. The TOTAL ACIDITY in grapes undergoing a 40% dehydration rises not by 40% but by around 25%.

These and other organic substances undergo various transformations, and there may be development of certain aromas and loss of others in the process. The longer the drying period, the greater the biological change of organic substances and resultant wine quality.

NOBLE ROT may develop on the grapes during dehydration but it is not desired by most practitioners, particularly those making the drier styles of dried-grape wines such as Amarone. A further problem is insect infestation, particularly of bees, wasps, and hornets.

Crushing or pressing should ideally be as gentle as possible. Gravity, but certainly not CENTRIFUGATION, may be used to clarify white must, while in the case of red wines, stems may be totally or only partially removed.

The must of raisined grapes is so concentrated that it slows FERMENTATION, an effect accentuated in cooler climates, especially where the long drying period may mean that the grapes are crushed in midwinter and the ambient temperature is naturally low. In Italy, fermentation may therefore safely take place in wood, and may need to be started by heating or by adding specially cultured local YEAST. In traditional areas, the right yeasts have been in the atmosphere for centuries. *Saccharomyces uvarum* begins the job in Valpolicella, according to Masi, while *Saccharomyces bayanus* is able to work at higher temperatures and at the ALCOHOLIC STRENGTH of 16% or more that is necessary for many Amarones.

Some producers allow the fermentation to stop and start for months or even, as in the case of the late Giuseppe Quintarelli, two to three years, and allow Nature to decide how sweet the final wine will be. Most, however, use RACKING and, increasingly, REFRIGERATION to stop fermentation.

The wine is then generally racked off its LEES and the lees sometimes used to enrich normal VALPOLICELLA, the process called RIPASSO. In Tuscany, the so-called GOVERNO process is employed.

Dried grape wines tend to be particularly high in VOLATILE ACIDS, a direct result of high sugar levels (accentuated if any BOTRYTIZED grapes have been included). The ACETIC ACID of such a wine may well exceed legal levels, sometimes entailing unacceptably high SULFUR DIOXIDE additions. Many argue that high levels of volatile acidity are essential to the quality of such wines, and some maintain that false 'passito' wines can be exposed precisely by improbably low levels of acetic acid.

Dried grape wines may be divided into two categories: those in which the fresh primary AROMAS are retained and those in which primary aromas are sacrificed to the development of a more complex BOUQUET. The former include most wines based on aromatic varieties such as Muscat, Brachetto, Aleatico, and Riesling, as well as sweet whites where the emphasis is on fruit, such as Recioto di Soave. These are subjected as far as possible to PROTECTIVE winemaking techniques.

Vin de paille and Vin Santo, with their RANCIO character, are the most notable examples of the OXIDATIVE style. Amarone and Recioto della Valpolicella of the traditional type are also treated oxidatively, the aim being to incorporate in the final tasting experience an evolution of aromas due in some measure to exposure to oxygen. Traditional Amarone and Recioto are, typically, the result of prolonged maceration, deliberately frequent racking, and ageing for years in large, old barrels. Strong, dry Valpolicella Amarone is a notable example, as is Vin Santo with the rancio character encouraged by traditionalists. Since the 1980s, there has been a movement away from such classic styles, however, and modernist Amarone and Recioto producers are aiming for more FRUIT-DRIVEN wines.

Italy produces more dried-grape wine than anywhere else, not least because of the dramatic increase in AMARONE production, but experimentation with the technique has spread to Australia, South America, North America, and much of Europe.   N.J.B.

Loftus, S., Belfrage, N., *Dried Grapes* (Southwold, 1992).

Masi, Grupo Technico, *Amarone and Recioto; Historical and Technical Notes* (private communication, Verona, 1990).

Redding, C., *The History and Description of Modern Wines* (London, 1833).

Tachis, G., *Il Libro del Vin Santo* (Florence, 1988).

drinking, the activity for which wine was designed, now threatened by rising average ALCOHOLIC STRENGTH. TASTING is different.

drinking vessels. Before the development of glass-making enabled the production of GLASSES (the most common modern wine drinking vessels), a wide variety of drinking vessels were used for wine. Pottery cups were commonplace, and goblets made of a variety of metals, but even earlier than this wine was sucked through a reed, either from a bowl such as a CRATER, or possibly from a hollowed-out gourd or similar vessel provided by Nature. See Ancient EGYPT, INDIA, and ARMENIA.

Modern history

The majority of drinking vessels are glass but despite its use for thousands of years, glass has not always been available (see GLASS, HISTORY OF). In such times, the principal alternative was silver. There are other occasions when glass was too fragile for a particular environment. Clear drinking glasses were an expensive commodity beyond the means of most people in the 18th century, but then so was wine—at least in countries where wine was not produced.

Silver was most commonly used for wine drinking vessels until the Venetian glass industry burgeoned in the 16th century. Although glass became preferred, trade in it was limited and, but for exceptional grand occasions and settings, in each country wine was usually consumed from indigenous vessels.

The social history of drinking and eating habits and customs has inevitably played an important part in the history of drinking vessels. FASHIONS change and, for example, a plain tall narrow glass is now preferred for champagne over the cut saucer-bowl version that was in vogue in the mid 20th century. The first introduction of suites of glasses in limited sizes was in the late 18th century but the designated use for each size can only be conjectural.

It is often observed that many 18th-century drinking glasses are small, but they have to be considered in context. They were not placed on the table for the diner to quaff at will. Rather, they were brought by the footman to each diner when requested and were taken after each draught to await another request. It may be speculated that the larger goblets were used by gentlemen after the servants had been dismissed towards the end of the meal.

By the mid 19th century, service *à la russe* had become fashionable, with its place settings of cutlery and glasses with which a diner today would be familiar. The 'new' arrangement dispensed with the need for a footman for each diner and it was the cause of the widespread use of long sets of glasses with each diner having up to six glasses for different wines, not to mention tumblers and finger bowls.

Glass Drinking vessels in both silver and glass were made by the Romans. The glass-making craft went into decline after the collapse of the Roman empire and, although glass was made in small quantities, it was not until the Renaissance that glass-making gained a prominent place in the decorative arts in VENICE. By the 16th century, Venice was producing fine and elegant drinking glasses. The soda glass was almost colourless and very thin. The often-decorated baluster stems had elements of very narrow section.

Draconian attempts to prevent the secrets of glass-making from leaving Venice were put in place in order that the city should retain its supremacy. However, a few of those with the knowledge left and small factories sprang up all over Europe in consequence. To raise revenue, the English monarch granted glass-making monopolies on payment of a fee and in 1574 Elizabeth I let a lapsed monopoly fall to Giacomo Verzelini. A few of his glasses, closely following Venetian models, sometimes dated, and usually engraved, survive. England and subsequently Britain became the dominant production centre.

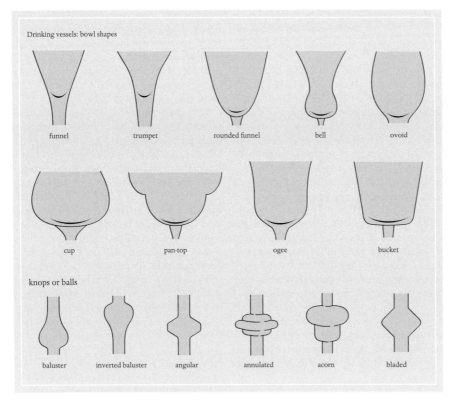

Drinking vessels: bowl shapes

funnel trumpet rounded funnel bell ovoid

cup pan-top ogee bucket

knops or balls

baluster inverted baluster angular annulated acorn bladed

d

In the early 17th century, wood-fired furnaces were outlawed in England, hence the setting up of glass houses in coal-producing areas—Newcastle, Stourbridge, and Bristol. As described in DECANTERS a major advance in glass technology was made in the 1670s by George Ravenscroft with the introduction of lead and flint glass and it was this which enabled British glass-makers to hold world supremacy for the ensuing hundred years. However, drinking glasses were still being made in Italy and in large numbers in what is now Germany and the Netherlands throughout the 17th century.

The earliest lead glass was frequently unstable and soon after manufacturers developed crizzling: a myriad of short cracks within the glass that gave it a milky effect. Ravenscroft and others in England soon improved the recipe and technique, enabling them to produce glasses of a rich weight and colour, quite unlike the light, pale products of Venice. The soda glass of Venice lent itself to thin and elegant shapes, often embellished with lattice designs in opaque white glass within the form or with coloured elements. The English lead glass, by contrast, was heavy and with a grey tint, capable of being drawn into bold plastic forms.

The drinking glass can be divided into three parts: the bowl, stem, and foot. Made separately, the parts were put together during the final stages of production. The bowl can take a variety of shapes, each with a name recognized in the large glass-collecting fraternity. Trumpet,

ovoid, bell, and bucket are obvious shapes, but rounded funnel, ogee, cup, and pan-top are also illustrated above.

The stem of a wine glass is perhaps the element offering most opportunity for decorative treatment. The stem may be straight or with swellings called knops. The early examples were generally heavily knopped, the main element of the stem often of baluster outline but with other swellings above, or below, or both. The knops, like the bowls, have names such as acorn, bladed, baluster, annulated, and ball, all of which are more or less self-descriptive (see diagram).

Beneath the stem is the foot. Most wine glasses have a foot of a flattish conical section, some raising the stem 5 mm (0.25 in) or more away from the table, others by three times as much. Most glasses before the mid 18th century have an additional feature called a folded foot. Long before English glass became pre-eminent it was realized that if, when the foot was made, the rim was folded underneath itself, a much sturdier glass was the result. Some glasses have a domed or tiered foot rather than a conical one.

During the 1670s and 1680s, wine glasses followed the Venetian forms, some of which had changed little over 100 years. By the 1690s, the particular qualities of lead-glass began to be appreciated and resulted in manufacture of glasses of substantial weight and a solid form quite distinct from the

Venetian tradition. Over the next 20 years, designs were refined to what many consider the zenith of glass-making, characterized by bold, pure, unadorned form. Many glasses were lightened by air bubbles or tears being blown within the stem and occasionally at the base of the bowl but the form remained substantial. These glasses are referred to as heavy balusters.

The heavy balusters became lighter as time progressed, partly perhaps because of taxation on the weight of glass. The bold designs became more fussy, with increased numbers of elements in the stem, and the stem itself became thinner. The heavy balusters had given way to light balusters and balustroids by the 1730s and 1740s. Some glasses had stems moulded of polygonal section; these are known as Silesian stems. During the 1740s and 1750s many glasses had stems that had inserted in them a series of small bubbles. When twisted and stretched these formed helices of air within the stem, or air twists. By this time, too, it was becoming fashionable for the stems to be straight sided and folded feet were at the end of their span.

A popular form in the 1760s was the result of twisting opaque white or coloured glass into the stem, instead of air bubbles.

The next phase of glass-making was the facet stem—quite simply the cutting of the stem with shield, diamond, or hexagonal facets. Traditionally air twists have been dated in the 1750s, opaque twists in the 1760s, and facet stems in the 1770s. It seems far more likely in view of the general shape and proportion of these styles that they were made more or less concurrently but, whatever the truth, it marked the end of the golden age for British glass collectors. Facet stems continued to be made to the end of the century, with the stems becoming shorter and the overall proportion degenerating.

During the 18th century, there were forms of embellishment other than pure shape. Wheel-engraving produced fine decoration in the 1730s and 1740s, sometimes being delicate bands of flowers and scrolls around the rim, while glasses engraved with Jacobite and Williamite symbolism had their enthusiastic followers. In the 1760s, the enamelled decoration of William and Mary Beilby of Newcastle enjoyed royal and other esteemed patronage while in the following decade the gilt decoration of James Giles drew its admirers, as did the stipple engraving of David Wolff.

The 19th century saw the fast decline of design, with many drinking glasses cut to match the cut decanters of the period. At this time, too, the idea of having glasses in different sizes and shapes for different drinks was becoming widespread, although this idea was not unknown in the 1780s. By the mid century, glasses could be ordered in large suites with sizes from goblet to liqueur matching the decanters, claret jugs, and finger bowls. Decoration was either cut or acid etched and in a variety of patterned styles.

The 20th century saw an interest in antiques and a large quantity of glass was made, much of it in the Georgian style. For the amateur it can be difficult to distinguish between a Georgian decanter of, say, 1815 and a copy made 100 years later. Wine glasses with green and cranberry-coloured bowls on clear stems also became popular at this time.

Silver During the 16th century and before, glass was a very highly prized commodity and wine would normally have been consumed from silver or silver gilt goblets. Early wine cups—often with a cover—were invariably heavily decorated and were considered status symbols. Many that remain are so large that their use must have been communal. Smaller cups for individual use date back to the Middle Ages but by the 1570s a standard pattern of a wide, shallow bowl on a baluster stem emerged. The making of silver drinking cups appears to have almost stopped by about the 1650s, probably due to the impact of Venetian glass and the subsequent burgeoning of glass-making in England.

There was a revival of silver drinking goblets in the 1780s which lasted for some 25 years. These were usually quite large, having ovoid bowls often made in prevailing styles during the 19th century in small numbers.

Other materials Drinking vessels were made in a variety of other media. Before long-distance maritime trade became frequent, ostrich eggs and coconuts were particularly prized for their exotic rarity and were mounted in silver as cups. At a more basic level, the horns of various animals were used for drinking, and wood was lathe-turned into cups and goblets. Antique cups of pottery and earthenware are also occasionally found.   R.N.H.B.

Bickerton, L.M., *18th Century Drinking Glasses, An Illustrated History* (Woodbridge, Suffolk, 1987).

Butler, R., *Great British Wine Accessories 1550–1900* (Sudbury, Suffolk, 2009).

Seddon, G. B., *The Jacobites and their Drinking Glasses* (Woodbridge, Suffolk, 1995).

drip irrigation, a form of IRRIGATION in which WATER is applied literally as drops to each vine from a pressure-reducing plastic device (the dripper) attached to a plastic pipe. The technique was developed in Israel and Australia in the 1960s, and has been widely adopted wherever irrigation is permitted. Drip irrigation has transformed viticulture since, unlike flood irrigation, it allows irrigation of vineyards on undulating land, and uses a limited water supply to maximum advantage. The technique requires extensive filtration of irrigation water and now soluble FERTILIZERS can be added

directly to it, a process known as FERTIGATION. Refinements include burying irrigation lines, which usefully reduces evaporation from the wet soil surface (and has obvious applications in regions where irrigation is prohibited).   R.E.S.

drone. *See* REMOTE SENSING.

drosophila, an insect pest of grapevines. Fruit fly, MEDITERRANEAN FRUIT FLY, vinegar fly, and pomace fly are all names applied to various species of *Drosophila*, in particular *Drosophila melanogaster*. *Drosophila* feed and reproduce in fermenting fruits of all kinds and can frequently be found in the domestic fruit bowl. The major damage they cause in grapes, with a drastic reduction in wine quality, is the spread of BUNCH ROTS. *Drosophila* multiply rapidly—with a period of only six to eight days for the egg-to-egg reproductive cycle in hot climates—which explains why this fly has been used so much for the study of genetics. They are also a common problem in wineries during vintage, when insects can contaminate wine by spreading harmful bacteria. Maggots may develop in overripe fruit. Control is difficult, and includes the destruction of breeding places, such as piles of rejected fruit and POMACE.

While *Drosophila melanogaster* is an inconvenience, the Spotted Wing Drosophila (*Drosophila suzukii*) is an acknowledged pest which is causing concern in many vineyard and fruit-growing regions. This small insect has been known in Japan as a pest of soft-skinned fruits such as strawberries, cherries, and grapes since the early 1900s. It was first noted in North America on California strawberries in 2008, and has now spread north to Oregon and British Columbia, south to Mexico, and had travelled as far east as Quebec by 2013. The insect was first reported in Spain in 2008, and by 2012 had been reported in nine countries. The main cause for concern is that the female has a strong ovipositor, enabling her to lay eggs in ripening fruit. Eggs hatch in a day and maggots feed inside the fruit, with no visible sign of their presence from the outside. There is as yet no evidence of wine taint but the damage to the fruit may encourage BOTRYTIS BUNCH ROT and SOUR ROT.   R.E.S.

Alessandro, C., Ioriatti, C., and Anfora, G., 'A review of the invasion of *Drosophila suzukii* in Europe and a draft research agenda for integrated pest management', *Bulletin of Insectology*, 65/1 (2012), 149–60.

drought, a severe and prolonged deficit of RAINFALL, compared with that normally received. Its implications for viticulture depend on the region and its normal climate. In cool and wet viticultural regions, drought years often produce the best vintages, especially of red wines. This is because excessive vegetative growth, or excess VIGOUR, is arrested; YIELDS are

limited; BERRY SIZE remains small with the purported benefits of a high ratio of the colour- and flavour-containing skin to juice; and sunshine and warmth are greater than average. Such effects are well known in Europe and New Zealand.

Such beneficial effects nevertheless depend on the drought's not being too extreme. Severe WATER STRESS reduces yield and is almost always detrimental to wine quality, especially if it occurs during RIPENING.

Most dry viticultural climates are regularly warm and sunny enough, and drought is nearly always detrimental: whether directly, in the case of DRYLAND VITICULTURE, or indirectly via a lack and/or reduced quality of IRRIGATION water. California suffered a periodic drought for three years 2012 to 2014, causing stresses on underground water reserves. Eastern Australia also suffered a severe drought in the first decade of the 21st century. Drought in such climates drastically reduces growth and yield, and if very severe can disrupt the ripening process more or less completely. In DESERT regions, drought is the norm, and commercial viticulture may only survive if sufficient irrigation is available.

See also CLIMATE AND WINE QUALITY.

J.G. & R.E.S.

Drouhin, Joseph, one of the most respected grower-merchants in Burgundy. Founded in 1880, the firm is based above historic cellars in the city of Beaune, dating from the 13th century. Joseph's son Maurice, who took over control of the firm in 1918, built up its reputation for quality and acquired a number of important vineyard holdings, starting with the Clos des Mouches (see BEAUNE). After the Second World War, exports of Joseph Drouhin wines increased considerably.

Robert Drouhin took over control of the house in 1957 and made many significant vineyard acquisitions, particularly on the CÔTE DE NUITS, including Musigny, Griotte-Chambertin, Bonnes Mares, and Grands Échezeaux. In 1968, an outpost in CHABLIS was established so that, of all Beaune merchants, Drouhin is the best placed in this northerly region with holdings in several grands crus and premiers crus. In 2014 the firm's (all organically cultivated) holdings totalled 78 ha/193 acres. The firm has also made and sold Marquis de Laguiche MONTRACHET since 1947.

The firm has its own NURSERY. At 12,500 plants per ha its VINE DENSITY is one of the highest in Burgundy (where the average is 10,000). Drouhin was one of the first firms to investigate and embrace the fundamentals of modern winemaking, although many traditional techniques are also used. The clean, rigorous wines are never among Burgundy's richest but are serious expressions of each appellation. Today the firm is run by Robert's children Philippe, Véronique, Laurent, and Frédéric, who is manager.

Somewhat ironically in view of Maurice's stated aim that Joseph Drouhin should concentrate on burgundy exclusively, Robert Drouhin was the first Burgundian to make a significant investment in a wine region outside France. **Domaine Drouhin Oregon**, established in 1987, owns 150 ha in OREGON and 1988 was its first commercial vintage of Pinot Noir, made from bought-in fruit. Domaine Drouhin Oregon is produced by Véronique. In 1994, the firm was acquired by its Japanese distributor Snobrand but the Drouhin family bought back the majority in 2003.

Drumborg. See HENTY.

drunkenness and its history is inextricably entwined with that of wine, since one of the chief reasons wine has been cherished, and prohibited, is its property to intoxicate. Excessive wine drinking has therefore always had moral or religious connotations, beginning with the 'shameful' intoxication of Noah after the Flood (see BIBLE).

Varying definitions of what constitutes excessive drinking have prevailed at different times and in different societies, with opinions sometimes diverging within that same society. It is also important to note that drinking has always accompanied festivity and ritual, and that societies have developed rules to contain it. The fear that these rules may be violated and society threatened is therefore apparent at almost every stage in the history of drunkenness.

Wine drinking is first documented in the ancient civilizations of the Middle East; the same is true of drunkenness (see SUMER and Ancient EGYPT). An early Mesopotamian tablet describes a man drunk from strong wine: 'he forgets his words and his speech becomes confused, his mind wanders and his eyes have a set expression.' The suggested HANGOVER cure includes liquorice, beans, and wine, to be administered before sunrise and before he has been kissed. The request of an Egyptian woman living in the 17th Dynasty may have been typical: 'Give me 18 cups of wine, behold I should love drunkenness.' Other races were quick to point the finger of over-indulgence at the Egyptians.

Sources show that drunkenness was both tolerated and at times denounced in these ancient civilizations. Although wine played a part in all their religions, the voice of disapproval most frequently heard was clerical. The Ancient Jews also displayed a somewhat equivocal attitude towards wine drinking. The Old Testament contains many warnings against drunkenness alongside the positive benefits of temperate wine drinking. Some Jewish religious sects, such as the Nazarenes, chose to abstain altogether.

Society in Ancient GREECE also showed a marked ambiguity in attitudes towards wine drinking. On the one hand strict guidelines were laid down to curb any excess. Plato advised no wine before the age of 18 and moderation until 30. The all-male drinking party known as the SYMPOSIUM was, when properly observed, a strictly controlled ritual of drinking combined with poetry, entertainment, and debate. The aim was pleasant intoxication without loss of reason. See HERODOTUS for some more details.

On the other hand, some Greek wine drinkers drank specifically to lose their reason. The worshippers of the wine god DIONYSUS deliberately became intoxicated and indeed this was, in their eyes, a fundamental point of their religion. The authorities took fright at their wild behaviour, identifying drunkenness with a breakdown in social order. Despite attempts to ban the cult its popularity continued into the Roman era but attitudes toward drunkenness shifted somewhat afterwards. The Christian Church, while hallowing wine as a sacrament (see EUCHARIST), sought to dissociate itself from the riotous habits and heavy drinking of earlier religions. Behaviour reminiscent of the Dionysiac cult was met with excommunication. When St Bernard developed the Cistercian order in Burgundy he originally intended abstinence for his brethren; this was soon dropped. Monks earned a reputation for excessive drinking in the Middle Ages but this reflected their dominance in wine-growing as much as in wine consumption (see MONKS and MONASTERIES).

There were periods in Ancient INDIA when drunkenness was considered a desirable state. Drunkards in the Middle East faced a formidable obstacle, however, in Muhammad's total prohibition on wine (see ISLAM). Wine drinking did not cease because of it, but had to be covert. Drinking among the upper classes of Persian society, for example, took place at secret parties reminiscent of Greek symposia with their strictly ritualized etiquette and emphasis on poetry and discussion (see ARAB POETS).

Meanwhile in Europe the scope for drunkenness was considerably increased with the discovery of DISTILLATION in the 12th century. Intoxication reached new heights as demand for this new liquor spread across the continent. The Dutch and Germans gained reputations throughout Europe for their drunkenness. In 17th-century Holland, drinking hours were applied to keep drinking in check. In Britain, too, drunkenness on the streets was increasingly blamed on spirits. By the 18th century wine was relatively expensive and only the middle and upper classes could afford this route to drunkenness.

The Victorians were not the first to confront the problem of drunkenness, but they put it on a new footing. Alcoholism was defined as a

disease in the mid 19th century and came to be identified with degeneracy of race. In Britain, wine was not seen as the main culprit—indeed it was seen by many, including Prime Minister Gladstone, as the remedy against drunkenness. The new catchword was 'temperance', and, whilst in the minds of some this meant the encouragement of moderate wine drinking to combat the medical and social ills of addiction to spirits, to a growing band of (often religiously inspired) campaigners it denoted complete abstinence. The governments of Britain and the United States adopted differing interpretations. Gladstone lowered the duty on light table wines to improve the health and morals of the British whilst American states gradually voted themselves 'dry', culminating in full-blown PROHIBITION, which came into force in 1920. See also HANGOVER.   H.B.

Lucia, S. P. (ed.), *Alcohol and Civilization* (New York, 1963).

Sournia, A., *Histoire de l'alcoolisme* (Paris, 1986), trans. by N. Hindley as *A History of Alcoholism* (Oxford, 1990).

Vickers, M., *Greek Symposia* (London, 1978).

Drupeggio, name for the high-acid CANAIOLO Bianco that adds interest, with Trebbiano grapes, to Grechetto, Malvasia, and Verdello, in the ORVIETO wine of central Italy. Total plantings had fallen to 286 ha by 2010.

dry, adjective often applied to wines, usually to describe those in which there is no perceptible SWEETNESS. Such wines may have as many as 10 g/l RESIDUAL SUGAR, or even more in wines with particularly high ACIDITY (which tends to counterbalance sweetness). In this sense, virtually all red wines are dry, while white, rosé, sparkling, and fortified wines can vary considerably between **bone dry**, **dry**, **medium dry**, medium sweet, and sweet.

Some wines, particularly reds, are said to have a 'dry finish' if they are especially astringent.

For the technical definition of 'dry' as laid down in recent EU labelling regulations, see SWEETNESS.

Dry Creek Valley, California wine region and AVA north west of Healdsburg. See SONOMA.

dry extract. See EXTRACT.

dry-farmed or **dry-grown**. See DRYLAND VITICULTURE.

drying grapes, which become **dried grapes**, second most common commercial use for viticulture, less important than wine but more important than TABLE GRAPES. Drying is a means of preserving grapes for eating (and precedes fermentation in the production of DRIED-GRAPE WINES). Dried grapes are an ancient food supply. The low moisture content of the dried grape (10 to 15%) and high sugar concentration

(70 to 80%) make the product relatively unsuitable for survival of food spoilage organisms.

Grapes have been dried since antiquity. Records of grape drying found in EGYPT date back to 3000 BC, and records of dried grapes are found in biblical times. Aristotle in 360 BC referred to the seedless character of the Black Corinth grape, today's CURRANT. Legend has it that Hannibal fed his troops with raisins during the crossing of the Alps in 218 BC.

The common English name RAISIN comes from the French *raisin sec*, or dry grape. Three varieties dominate world trade in drying grapes: SULTANA (also known as Thompson Seedless in America, and Kishmish or Sultanina in Asia and the Near East); Zante Currant or Black Corinth (California); and MUSCAT OF ALEXANDRIA (Gordo Blanco in Australia and White Hanepoot in South Africa). In Australia and California, grapes usually destined for the dried-grape industry have been diverted into wine at times of severe wine grape shortage.

In 2009, the biggest producer of dried grapes was Turkey, which had overtaken the US, followed at some distance by Iran, Chile, Greece, South Africa, and Uzbekistan. World production has remained steady at just over 1.2 million dried tonnes. Climate is a major factor determining where grapes are grown for drying. Temperatures should be high and there should be plenty of sunshine, while humidity and rainfall should be low. In such conditions, the evaporation rate is reliably high, but this usually means that the vineyards need IRRIGATION. Rainfall prior to harvest or during drying has catastrophic results, as the fruit can split and rot.

Harvested grapes are placed outside on wooden or paper trays, or concrete or clay slabs. After about 10 to 14 days, the bunches must be turned over to dry the other side. An alternative method widely used is to dip the grapes in solutions containing vegetable oils and potassium carbonate to speed their drying. In Australia and South Africa, special drying racks with roofs are used. These can help reduce rain damage, and allow drying solutions to be sprayed on the fruit.

Alternative methods of drying fruit on the vines have been developed in Australia and California. The canes supporting the bunches are cut at the base, but left on the trellis wires. (This is the derivation of the CUT CANE method of producing sweet wines in Australia.) The vines may be sprayed with the drying emulsion, and then mechanically harvested when dried. Dried grapes should not be packed with more than 13% moisture, and sometimes grapes dried in the field need to be dried further.

Quality factors in raisins are size, hue, and uniformity of colour, surface condition, texture of both skin and pulp, and lack of any contamination. The highest-quality raisins are produced from the ripest fruit. See also CURRANTS,

MUSCATELS, SULTANAS, and RAISINS for specific sorts of dried grape.   R.E.S.

Whiting, J. R., 'Harvesting and drying of grapes', in B. G. Coombe and P. R. Dry (eds.), *Viticulture*, ii: *Practices* (Adelaide, 1992).

dryland viticulture, viticulture relying entirely on natural RAINFALL, and a term used, sometimes as a sales pitch, only in regions where IRRIGATION is common.

There can be little doubt that some European areas with both moderate rainfall and Mediterranean climates, now practising fully dryland viticulture, could in some circumstances improve their wine quality if limited irrigation were allowed. Excessive WATER STRESS causes loss of PHOTOSYNTHESIS and eventually of the leaves themselves, and can seriously prejudice normal RIPENING.

On the other hand, even in New World regions where irrigation is widely practised, dryland vineyards are often prized for the quality of their fruit, for which some wineries will pay a premium, thereby allowing such vineyards to remain economical. As WATER shortages become more prevalent, dryland viticulture is likely to become more common., at least in regions of moderate rainfall.   J.G. & R.E.S.

Dubourdieu, a father and son of particular importance in the history of white winemaking in BORDEAUX. The father Pierre (1923–), owner—with son Denis—of Ch Doisy-Daëne in BARSAC, produced the first dry white wine in the SAUTERNES area and it is still made today. He was also instrumental in helping the Vaslin company improve the action of their grape PRESSES and he has clearly been an inspiration to his son Denis, co-oenology editor of this book, with whom he has worked on many experiments.

Denis Dubourdieu (1949–) is a research scientist at the University of BORDEAUX, and owner and winemaker at Ch Reynon in CADILLAC CÔTES DE BORDEAUX, Clos Floridène and Ch Haura in the Graves, and Ch Doisy-Daëne and Ch Cantegril in BARSAC. In 2014 he bought Ch Doisy-Dubroca, a small classified estate next to Doisy-Daëne. He is also, with his associates Dr Valérie Lavigne and Christophe Olivier, an international CONSULTANT in OENOLOGY.

He and his research team have been a significant influence on white winemaking, not just in Bordeaux but throughout France and abroad. His early areas of research were into the nature of *Botrytis cinerea*, and in particular NOBLE ROT; earlier picking dates to enhance the AROMA of wines made from aromatic white grape varieties; and the influence of fermentation TEMPERATURES and selected YEAST on white wines. More recently he investigated FLAVOUR COMPOUNDS in grape pulp and skins, identification of which

can assist in the matching of vine varieties to soils, and in aspects of vinification strategy such as picking dates, fermentation temperatures, and—a favourite research area of his—the extent of prefermentation maceration (see SKIN CONTACT). In particular, he elucidated the chemical nature of the varietal aromas of SAUVIGNON BLANC wines and their odourless precursors located in the grapes; he has also demonstrated for the first time that yeast metabolism is involved in the transformation of FLAVOUR PRECURSORS into wine aromas. He has also clarified the significant REDUCTIVE and FINING properties of yeast LEES during BARREL FERMENTATION and BARREL MATURATION, rationalizing the ancient practice of BÂTONNAGE and also explaining why white wines fermented and aged in barrel are less oaky, oxidized, and astringent than those put into barrel only after fermentation and without lees. Denis Dubourdieu and coresearchers also studied the aroma compounds associated with oak BARRELS; they identified furan-methanthiol as the molecule responsible for the 'toasty' flavour of wines aged in oak. They also extensively investigated various off-odours in wines: those associated with REDUCTION, OXIDATION (including PREMATURE OXIDATION); GRASSY aromas due to ISOBUTYL-METHOXYPYRAZINES; and the ethylphenols associated with BRETTANOMYCES contamination. Most importantly for wine enthusiasts, his explanations of many of the phenomena of vinification have helped winemakers exploit them on a practical level.

Dubourdieu, D., 'Vinification des vins blancs secs en barriques', *Le Bois et la qualité des vins et eaux-de-vie* (Bordeaux, 1992).

Ribéreau-Gayon, P., Dubourdieu, D., Donèche, B., and Lonvaud, D., *Traité d'Œnologie* 1: *Microbiologie du vin: Vinifications* (Paris, 1998), trans. by J. M. Branco, as *Handbook of Enology* 1: *The Microbiology of Wine and Vinifications* (Chichester, 2000).

Ribéreau-Gayon, P., Glories, Y., Maujean, A., and Dubourdieu, D., *Traité d'Œnologie* 2: *Chimie du vin: Stabilisation et traitements* (Paris, 1998), trans. by Aquitrad Traduction as *Handbook of Enology* 2: *The Chemistry of Wine Stabilization and Treatments* (Chichester, 2000).

Ducellier, name associated with a special fermentation vat designed to extract, without electricity, maximum colour and tannins even in short fermentation periods. The system was devised for winemaking in ALGERIA but is now most commonly used to make PORT. See AUTOVINIFICATION.

Duché d'Uzès, soft reds and rosés from Grenache and Syrah and some whites from Viognier and Grenache Blanc grown on fewer than 300 ha/750 acres in the Gard *département* in the far west of the southern RHÔNE. Promoted to AOC in 2012.

dulce, Spanish for sweet. See SWEETNESS and DOSAGE for official EU sugar levels.

Dunkelfelder, dark-skinned GERMAN CROSS notable mainly for the depth of its colour, a useful commodity in Germany's blending vats. It is increasingly popular with growers if not consumers. German plantings totalled 314 ha/776 acres in 2012, half in Pfalz. Also grown in Switzerland and England.

Duras is perhaps the oldest vine variety still used in the once-famous red wines of GAILLAC. Its presence distinguishes them from the complex mosaic of other blending permutations that comprise the reds of SOUTH WEST FRANCE. It is not grown in the Côtes de Duras, nor anywhere else in any significant amount outside the Tarn *département*, where Gaillac is the chief appellation. In the Tarn, however, like its blending partner FER, it has steadily gained ground, thanks to Gaillac's powerful internal lobby against incoming INTERNATIONAL VARIETIES. Total plantings were 861 ha/2,127 acres in 2011. The wine is deeply coloured, full bodied, and lively. Varietal Duras produced in Gaillac eloquently demonstrates a marriage of CÉPAGE to TERROIR well worth defending. The vine buds inconveniently early but gives wines of particularly good structure and acidity.

Duras, Côtes de, red and white wine appellation on the north eastern fringe of BORDEAUX which is regarded as one of the wine districts of SOUTH WEST FRANCE. It is bounded by Côtes du MARMANDAIS to the south, BERGERAC to the north, and ENTRE-DEUX-MERS and Ste-Foy-Bordeaux to the west. The town of Duras, with its impressive castle, marks the eastern extremity of the Entre-Deux-Mers plateau and the 1,545 ha/3,816 acres of vines still planted either on limestone hilltops, mainly for white wine grapes, or on slightly more sheltered limestone and clay slopes for red wine grapes. The vine varieties are essentially those of Bordeaux, and a specifically Duras character in the red wines is certainly difficult to discern (although more luxurious winemaking techniques such as BARREL MATURATION are increasingly employed). White Côtes de Duras can display originality, however, in fresh, dry Sauvignons and the sweet or MOELLEUX wines sometimes produced from the Bordeaux grape varieties Sémillon, Sauvignon Blanc, and Muscadelle together with the south western specialities ONDENC and MAUZAC. Some Chenin Blanc has also been imported from the Loire. Historically, the region was commercially penalized by the Bordelais as part of the HAUT PAYS, but the Huguenots who fled to the NETHERLANDS remained faithful to its wines.

Durbanville, an important ward in the Coastal Region in SOUTH AFRICA, part of the Tygerberg district.

Durella, tart, white grape of VENETO whose 469 ha in 2010 produce both sparkling and sweet wines.

Dureza, scarcely cultivated Ardèche darkberried vine variety famous chiefly as a parent of Syrah, with MONDEUSE BLANCHE.

Duriense, VINHO REGIONAL whose boundaries correspond to the DOURO region, but producers may use a much wider range of grape varieties. As a result, a handful of credible examples of Pinot Noir, Syrah, Alvarinho, Sauvignon Blanc, Riesling, and Chardonnay bear witness to the Duriense's great diversity of TERROIR. See DOURO for more details.   S.A.

Durif is a well-travelled black grape variety, revealed in 1999 as probably a cross of PELOURSIN with SYRAH, propagated eponymously by a Dr Durif in south eastern France in the 1880s.

Today it has almost disappeared from France but it is still cultivated in both North and South America as the dominant proportion of all vines called PETITE SIRAH.

As Durif, it was long grown in Australia's RUTHERGLEN making a prodigiously inky, alcoholic wine of surprising quality. In the late 1990s and early 2000s, it was enthusiastically planted by RIVERINA growers who value how it retains deep colour and strong flavour even when heavily cropped and are responsible for over half the national total of 500 ha/1,250 acres in 2012.

dusting, a vineyard practice designed to apply AGROCHEMICALS in dry powder form. Typical of such operations is the application of finely ground elemental SULFUR dust to control the fungal disease POWDERY MILDEW. Most vineyard agrochemicals are applied as a liquid formulation with water as the carrier, and applied by SPRAYING.   R.E.S.

Dutch East India Company, powerful trading organization which played a seminal part in the wine history of SOUTH AFRICA. Founded in March 1602 by the amalgamation of four Holland and two Zeeland companies which had been set up between 1596 and 1602 to conduct trade in East Asia, the General United Chartered East-India Company in the United Netherlands (Vereenigde Oost-Indische Compagnie: VOC) dominated European trade with the Orient for the rest of the 17th century, with counters and outposts strung out along the extended sea routes which linked the Netherlands with southern Africa, India, Ceylon, Sumatra, Java, Borneo, and Japan. Apart from its participation in the bulk transport of fortified wines such as MADEIRA and spirits to the ends of its seaborne empire, it played a vital part in the Dutch penetration of southern Africa and in the establishment of viticulture on the Cape of Good Hope. See SOUTH AFRICA, history.   A.J.D.

Dutchess, white AMERICAN HYBRID based on *V.* LABRUSCA, *V. aestivalis*, and *V. vinifera* grown with limited success in New York State. Created in 1868 by Andrew Jackson Caywood in Poughkeepsie, New York.

Dutch wine trade, a major influence on the history of international trade in wine. By the middle years of the 17th century, the Dutch republic had achieved a dominant position in the world trade in wines and spirits (and much else besides), greater, even, than that of ENGLAND, whose Navigation Acts in the 1650s were directed specifically at Dutch freight. John Locke recorded in 1678 that the Dutch conducted more trade through BORDEAUX than England. Amsterdam, Rotterdam, and Dordrecht were world emporia. Its geographical position, at the estuaries of three great RIVERS, Schelde (Scheldt), Maas (Meuse), and Rhine, made it a natural point of convergence for river-based traffic; its wealthy bourgeoisie created a consumer demand distributed throughout the region, in addition to that of the nobility; and, lastly, its relative proximity to long-established and highly productive wine-producing areas enabled it to become a major conduit for the highly prized wines of the Rhineland and Alsace (see GERMAN HISTORY).

The RHINE (and its distributaries Waal and Lek) was virtually a wine highway, linking Cologne with Dordrecht and Rotterdam. Moreover, Middelburg in Zeeland, on the island of Walcheren at the estuary of the Schelde, had been the principal port of call for a centuries-old and highly lucrative seaborne traffic which linked the Atlantic seaboard with Scandinavia and the lands of the Baltic; formerly the principal staple (official market) for the whole of the Netherlands and earlier still the out-port serving the Flemish and Brabançon cities of Bruges, Ghent, and Antwerp, it had been secured for the independent Netherlands after the rising against Spain in 1568.

Hanseatic League

Although merchants from the region had been handling wine from very early times, it was not until the late 13th century that the Dutch, principally Hollanders and Zeelanders, entered the thriving maritime commerce which linked the countries of the Atlantic seaboard with the Baltic, as associates of the German Hansa (the Hanseatic League). This powerful alliance of about 80 merchant towns had by that time established a virtual monopoly of Baltic and Scandinavian trade by organizing large fleets of merchant vessels to transport basic commodities in bulk. From 1237 they began to acquire rights in English markets; and from 1252 they acquired trading privileges in Flanders, with reduced customs in Bruges and its out-port Damme.

Thus they gained access to the Atlantic trade and the estuaries of the 'wine rivers' of Europe: Adour, Lot-Tarn-GARONNE, LOIRE, Seine, Schelde (Scheldt), Maas (Meuse), and Rhine-MOSEL, to which would later be added the Guadalquivir, for SHERRY, and the DOURO for PORT, or at least their prototypes. French wines, chiefly from Gascony and Poitou, French salt from the bay of Bourgneuf, English wool, and Flemish cloth constituted the major commodities traded for the produce of the northern lands. This was the commerce which enriched the cities of Ghent, Bruges, Ypres, Antwerp, and many others. Wine consumption was a mark of wealth in northern lands. At a time when a wage-earning man might have to spend a third of his income on bread, noble households devoted more than a third of their expenditure to wine, although cheap wine was readily available in taverns and inns, where it had to compete with locally brewed BEER and ale.

Zeelanders and Hollanders played an increasing role in the transportation of wines from Bordeaux and LA ROCHELLE to England, Flanders, and the Baltic from the last quarter of the 13th century onwards, gradually supplanting the Flemings and Brabançons, and they were joined in the course of the 14th century by mariners and traders from Dordrecht, Zierikzee, and Middelburg. In the first quarter of the 14th century, wine represented respectively 31% and 25% of imports into England and the Low Countries (Flanders, Zeeland), although this very high proportion was never equalled again. Much of this wine was re-exported: Gascon wine from England; Poitevin, Loire, and Rhine wines from Flanders and Zeeland.

The Dutch dominated the Bourgneuf salt trade during the 15th century, acquired a large share in the export of CLAIRET from Bordeaux and of the cheaper, white Poitevin wines from La Rochelle, and established a direct trade between Bourgneuf and the Baltic, carrying principally salt and wine, and returning to the Low Countries with fish, furs, and grain. The chief commercial centre was the thriving port of Middelburg, recognized by the Habsburg government in 1523 as the official French-wine staple for the whole of the Netherlands, where merchant ships of all countries transported their wares.

After England's loss of Gascony in 1453, before which wine was exported from Bordeaux to England and then re-exported by licence, the Dutch secured the lion's share of the direct trade out of Bordeaux so that Hanseatic and Dutch vessels shipped huge quantities of wine to Middelburg. The western French wines of Poitou, Saintonge, and Aunis were transported in Dutch and Breton ships. Expensive sweet Mediterranean wines (from the Peloponnese,

Crete, Cyprus, and Rhodes) were carried by ships from GENOA and VENICE. Some Rhine wines also found their way to Middelburg, but the bulk of these highly favoured wines travelled down the Rhine by barge to Dordrecht. From Middelburg and Dordrecht wines could radiate by sea or pass by river to Antwerp, and thence to the rest of the region and beyond. The Dutch employed fleets of full-rigged ships of relatively large tonnage (up to 200 tons), which enabled them to undercut the freight charges of their competitors by a significant margin.

Expansion outside Europe
During the 16th century, three major changes, economic, religious, and political, contributed to the further expansion of Dutch commerce. The first was the fragmentation of the Hanseatic League itself, of which the Dutch were major beneficiaries and agents, and which enabled them to establish a virtual monopoly of Scandinavian and Baltic trade. The second, and much more dramatic, event was the undermining of Antwerp's commercial dominance by Spanish attempts to retain control of the Netherlands during the last third of the 16th century. The third was the declaration of independence from Spain made in 1581 by the seven northern provinces (Holland, Zeeland, Utrecht, Gelderland, Groningen, Friesland, Overijssel). Although the United Provinces did not secure final international recognition until the treaty of Westphalia in 1648, they were from the 1580s a formidable maritime force, opposed to Spanish hegemony on religious and political grounds. After Antwerp's capture by Spanish forces in 1585, the United Provinces blocked the entry to the River Schelde and so cut the principal artery which linked Antwerp to Middelburg and the North Sea. The Dutch economy was thus for the first time decisively detached from the rest of the Netherlands in terms of capital, shipping, and the expertise of refugee Jews, who had earlier fled Spain and Portugal and migrated north with their commercial knowledge and connections to Amsterdam, which grew to become the major commercial, maritime, and banking centre of the western world for the next century or so. Amsterdam, in north Holland, became heir to the Hanseatic League's Baltic trade and to Antwerp's international banking and commerce.

By the end of the 16th century, the Dutch fleet equalled the combined commercial fleets of Spain and Portugal, and far outstripped those of France and England. It was thus able to take advantage of Iberian colonial expansion in the Americas and participate in South East Asian commercial colonialism. The DUTCH EAST INDIA COMPANY was founded in 1602; the West India Company in 1621. These major enterprises, which transformed the Netherlands into a colonial power and a major competitor of the

English, French, and Portuguese, were driven not by wine but by the desire to control as much as possible of the commerce of the New World and Asia: sugar, tobacco, calico, spices, and their manufactured products. But the handling of wine remained a significant part of the commercial interests of the independent Netherlands, whose fleets competed for markets around the globe. Wine, brandy, and vinegar constituted nearly 40% of Dutch imports from France in 1645; most of the 224 ships which loaded wine at Bordeaux in 1682 were Dutch; and wines, fortified wines, and spirits were carried to the furthest corners of their trading empire, to North America, Surinam, the Caribbean islands, South Africa, Ceylon, and the Malay archipelago (Sumatra, Java, Borneo).

Influence on wine styles
Dutch interest in the transport of and trade in wines helped shape the evolution of wine production according to the dictates of changing taste and the requirements of the long-distance transportation of a perishable product by sea. Until the end of the 17th century, most wines could not survive from one vintage to the next, and many were spoiled and undrinkable within six months of the vintage, partly because they were transported in large oak casks, 'tuns' of 900 l weighing 1,000 kg, inclusive of the wood, which constituted the units of freight. Even before the creation of overseas colonies, wine destined for the Baltic had to overwinter at some convenient point. The grape harvest occurred too late in the year to permit immediate transportation to the northern lands, since the Baltic and White Seas often became impassable from November onwards. To overcome these disadvantages the Dutch popularized *mistelles*, wines fortified by the addition of brandy to stop fermentation and prolong the life of the wine, and *vins pourris*, made from overripened grapes. They also introduced the French to the stabilizing effects of SULFUR candles (known in French as *allumettes hollandaises* for many years), and encouraged the production of distilled liquors, based on both grain and grape. Amsterdam and Rotterdam became the principal international markets for wines and brandy in the 17th century, sustained by regular and reliable supplies, bulk storage, and an international network of merchants. One effect was the increase in planting white grape varieties in western France, to satisfy the tastes of the Dutch market.

At the same time, they practised BLENDING wines from different areas to increase the bulk of more popular varieties, to improve the taste or increase the BODY of inferior wines, or simply to make them conform to the changing palates of consumers. From the 15th century, for example, the English came to prefer stronger and sweeter wines than formerly. Thus the weak *clairet* of Gascony was 'strengthened' by blending with CAHORS or Portuguese wines. When in the 16th century the English developed a liking for SACK, the white wines of southern Spain (exported through Seville and Cádiz), and when at about the same time the CANARY ISLANDS and MADEIRA began producing sweet wines (malmseys and madeiras) from the MALVASIA grape (introduced from Crete), the Dutch entered that trade too, and made significant inroads into the rapidly growing trade in Portuguese wines (via Lisbon, Lamego, and Oporto). And, of course, it was the Dutch who had the technical skills with which to drain the marshes of the MÉDOC in the mid 17th century, thereby enabling production of what were to be recognized as some of the finest red wines in the world.

Dutch prominence in the wine trade in the 16th and 17th centuries was merely one aspect of their general primacy in all aspects of international commerce during that period. They were principally merchants and shippers, controlling all aspects of trade, purchase, transport, storage, and sale to local merchants and retailers. Their purchasing power enabled them often to dictate advantageous terms to the producers and the large tonnage of their ships enabled them to transport their wares at relatively low cost. Such was their access to the wine-producing areas of Europe that they were able to circumvent the English embargo on all French wines during the Anglo-French war of 1690–6 by passing them off as Spanish, Portuguese, or even Rhenish, and transporting them in the appropriate casks.

By the 1690s, however, this dominance was being seriously undermined by an aggressive trade war with England, culminating in the Franco-Dutch war of 1692–4, in which Holland's commercial enemies conspired with France against her. A combination of protectionist legislation in England, widespread piracy, the successful French invasion of 1692, and the rapid rise of English seaborne trade (especially from Bristol and London) marked the end of the Dutch supremacy, though not of Dutch involvement in the world trade in wines and spirits.

The Dutch also played the crucial role in dictating the style of modern MUSCADET.   A.J.D.

Craeybeckx, J., *Un grand commerce d'importation: les vins de France aux anciens Pays-Bas (xiii–xvi siècle)*, École Pratique des Hautes Études, section VI, Centre des Recherches Historiques (Paris, 1958). Israel, J. I., *Dutch Primacy in World Trade 1585–1740* (Oxford, 1989).

James, M. K., *Studies in the Medieval Wine Trade* (London, 1971).

duty is levied on wine importation and movement into circulation from BOND in many countries at an extremely variable level. In general, countries in which viticulture is an economically (and therefore politically) important activity, such as France and Italy, tend to have extremely low duties on wine, while countries, such as the UK, which produce little or no wine, and/or those with restrictive policies on the sale of alcoholic drinks, such as Norway, tend to have high duties. Wine duty may be a flat rate per litre, as in the UK, or calculated ad valorem as in China and much of Asia. In Hong Kong customs officials used to be issued with a set of current prices for all commonly encountered wines.

Wine is not often a good buy in so-called **duty-free** shops, however, as profit margins are rarely low enough to warrant the weight and breakability of wine bottles. In 1993, the relaxation of duty-free allowances when crossing borders within the EU led to widespread loss of trade to British wine merchants as consumers crossed the English Channel to take advantage of bulk buying in France. In 2008 HONG KONG transformed itself as a wine market by becoming the only significant one with zero wine duty in Asia. For some historical background, see TAXATION.

Early Burgundy, California name for a grape once grown there in some quantity and eventually identified as the ABOURIOU of SOUTH WEST FRANCE.

Early Muscat, bred in California as a TABLE GRAPE but has been successful on a very small scale as a wine grape in Oregon.

earthworms, segmented ANIMALS which have an important role in improving soil conditions for plant growth. Their burrowing improves soil mixing and aeration, and their feeding breaks down and redistributes ORGANIC MATTER, facilitating NUTRIENT uptake by the vine. Because a high level of mixing of organic matter is associated with SOIL FERTILITY, an abundance of earthworms is generally considered beneficial by many growers, especially those involved in ORGANIC VITICULTURE. Earthworms are encouraged by MULCHES, which reduce soil surface temperature, provide organic matter, and help retain moisture. They are discouraged by bare, HERBICIDE-treated soils and their species diversity and biomass are reduced by CULTIVATION and by copper-containing FUNGICIDES. See also SOIL BIOTA.
R.E.S.

eating grapes. See TABLE GRAPES.

échantillon, French for sample. See SAMPLING.

Échezeaux, GRAND CRU of the village of Flagey-Échezeaux in Burgundy's Côte de Nuits, producing red wines from Pinot Noir grapes (see map under BURGUNDY). While wines of VILLAGE or PREMIER CRU status in Flagey-Échezeaux are sold under the name of neighbouring VOSNE-ROMANÉE, the majority of the commune's vineyard land is shared between the two grands crus Échezeaux and Grands Échezeaux.

Échezeaux is perhaps fortunate to be rated grand cru in its entirety (37.6 ha/92.9 acres), as many of its wines are relatively light. The vineyard is made up of 11 LIEUX-DITS ranging from Les Treux, which has a deep clay soil with indifferent drainage, to Les Échezeaux du Dessus, where the soil is shallower and chalkier and the wine correspondingly finer. It is not the equal, however, of neighbouring Grands Échezeaux (9 ha), which also abuts CLOS DE VOUGEOT.

There are 21 owners of Grands Échezeaux and over 80 of Échezeaux. Proprietors of both include DOMAINE DE LA ROMANÉE-CONTI, Domaine d'Eugénie, Domaine Lamarche, and Domaine Mongeard—Mugneret.

See also CÔTE D'OR.
J.T.C.M.

éclaircissage. See CROP THINNING.

ecological viticulture. See ORGANIC and BIODYNAMIC VITICULTURE, and SUSTAINABILITY.

economics of wine, is a field of study that aims to improve our understanding of what affects the demand for and supply of different types of wines and wine grapes, and thereby the prices, quantities, and qualities of wines sold in domestic markets and traded internationally. This area of study has grown considerably in recent years, for several reasons. One is the increasing GLOBALIZATION of wine. Another is that wine growers have shown, perhaps more clearly than any other farmers, the possibilities for adding value to their primary product, particularly by differentiating it according to its TERROIR or via marketing investments. Wine producers are increasingly investigating which specific attributes of wine appeal to consumers in order to better target their production and marketing efforts. Some producers also benefit from INVESTMENT IN WINE. The demand for the best vintages of iconic wines as a way of storing

wealth has grown along with affluence, including in newly wealthy countries such as China.

The basic point that excess supply can depress prices was well understood at the time of DOMITIAN's order in the first century AD to pull up half of the Roman Empire's vines planted outside Italy in the hope of holding back collapsing Italian wine and grape PRICES. More recently Jean Milhau argued in his 1935 book, *Etude économétrique du prix du vin en France*, that wide variations in producer prices and incomes were due to huge swings in harvest volumes while CONSUMPTION remained insensitive (inelastic) to price. He argued that prices could be stabilized within certain limits by regulating the volumes released from the wineries' stocks and by distilling SURPLUSES. That idea became the cornerstone of France's wine policy enacted in 1935, which also created a separate market organization for quality wines (see INAO). After the Second World War, integration of (initially six) European economies led to a single market by 1970 and a common wine policy (see EU). That policy soon involved compulsory DISTILLATION to support producer prices in an attempt to stem the flow of cheaper wines from Italy into France and appease social unrest in the LANGUEDOC—the so-called 'wine wars' of the 1970s. Its long-lasting effects included driving YIELDS up and quality down.

The study of wine demand initially focused on estimating the responsiveness of consumers to changes in price (relative to other beverages), taxes, and income. It then broadened to studying the many other aspects of wine that appeal to buyers such as the reputations of regions, varieties, brands, closures, production methods, and vintages. Economists, most notably Orley Ashenfelter of Princeton University, have contributed to the reputation of VINTAGES by using econometric analysis to forecast the future value of each vintage's iconic wines, based on RAINFALL and TEMPERATURE data during the growing season. When Ashenfelter forecast in 1991 that the 1989 and 1990 vintages were likely to be outstanding for red bordeaux, many professional wine writers and judges at the time disagreed, but now there is almost unanimous agreement that they were exceptionally good. More recently, economists have drawn on behavioural studies and neurosciences to explore, for example, the impact of price information on the perceived quality of wine. Some studies suggest that blind tasters often prefer cheaper wine if they are unaware of its price but, if told it is expensive, their perception of a wine's quality is raised, according to brainscans.

Even though international trade in wine has grown in significance only during the past quarter-century, economists have cited wine for nearly two centuries in their teaching of international trade theory. This is because wine was used by English economist David Ricardo when in 1817 he introduced the compelling notion of comparative advantage to explain the benefits of free trade between textile-exporting England and wine-exporting Portugal following the METHUEN TREATY.

There is now both an American and a European Association of Wine Economists (www. wine-economics.org and www.euawe.org respectively), each of which has an annual conference. The *Journal of Wine Economics* has been published commercially since 2006 and wine economics is recognized by ACADEME both at UC DAVIS and the University of ADELAIDE.   K.A.

Milhau, J., *Etude économétrique du prix du vin en France* (Montpellier, 1935).

Spanhi, P., *The Common Wine Policy and Price Stabilization* (Aldershot, 1988). *Journal of Wine Economics* (Cambridge, three issues annually from 2013).

ecosystem, vineyard, the collection of plant and animal communities which interact with each other and with their non-living environment in the vineyard such as WIND, RAINFALL, TEMPERATURE, and SOIL NUTRIENTS. It has only recently been adequately acknowledged that a vineyard is a living, functioning ecosystem. Such ecosystems deliver to mankind ecosystem services (ES) such as biological control of pests, diseases, and weeds, carbon capture from the atmosphere, nutrient provision to the vines, and some protection from FROST and wind. This 'commodification' of natural ecosystem functions began in the 1970s, with publications such as that of Westman.

The practices adopted in most vineyards worldwide usually severely reduce these free services, with the result that high levels of artificial inputs are needed (see AGROCHEMICALS).

This is often called 'substitution agriculture', in which products derived from fossil fuels are substituted for nature's services. For example, a typical vineyard may receive 15 FUNGICIDE applications in one season, which is costly to the business and to the environment (many of these compounds have detrimental effects on flora and fauna above and below ground). The same negative effects arise from PESTICIDE applications and even from FERTILIZER use. The latter can generate external costs arising from environmental damage beyond the vineyard—water pollution, for example.

Increasingly, individual wine companies and regional producer groups are developing schemes to reduce these inputs by identifying economic thresholds so that a problem is treated only when the economic damage would exceed the cost of the treatment, and by enhancing nature's services around and within the vineyard. However, few of the many so-called SUSTAINABLE VITICULTURE schemes around the world are based on a sound knowledge of agro-ecology. For example, some operate sophisticated recording systems to track inputs of water, energy, fertilizers, and pesticides, but that is not the same as a research-led attempt to improve ES to minimize such inputs and the impact that they have on the environment. A good example of a research- and community-led approach to functional vineyard biodiversity is the Greening Waipara project in New Zealand. At its peak this involved 50 vineyard companies and the planting of thousands of indigenous New Zealand plants under and between the vine rows and around the vineyard properties. These plants delivered a wide range of ES, including eco-TOURISM, education, and biological control of vine pests.

A well-researched approach to ES is summarized by the acronym SNAP—shelter, nectar, alternative food, and pollen. These are the four key requirements of beneficial insects, although they are usually absent—or present only at a low level—in vineyards because viticulture generally involves a monoculture. For example, parasitic wasps are a very important group of biological control agents, and having floral nectar available can increase these insects' longevity in a vineyard from three to 30 days because of the sugars and amino acids that nectars contain. Unfortunately inter-row grasses, often heavily used and promoted for vineyard COVER CROPS, do not offer much SNAP. These grasses are wind-pollinated, so even if they are left to flower, they produce no nectar. The 'trilogy' of the best-performing flowering plants for vineyards is (sweet) alyssum, buckwheat, and phacelia (tansey). In New Zealand, it has been established that one inter-row in 10 or 15 drilled with one or more of these plants is sufficient to enhance the biological control of key pests throughout the vineyard because of

the distance these wasps disperse from the flowering strips. Planting flowering buckwheat between vine rows to provide nectar for these harmless wasps is a protocol adopted in vineyards in Australasia, the US, and Europe. The pests targeted include the lightbrown apple MOTH, the European grapevine moth, and MEALY BUGS, among others. A further example of 'ecological engineering' is the use of MULCHES under vines to intervene in the life-cycle and spore production of BOTRYTIS BUNCH ROT. This simple practice has brought the incidence of this disease on grapes to below the economic spray threshold. These examples show the great potential for enhancing vineyard environmental health, whether the wine grower is 'conventional', ORGANIC, or BIODYNAMIC.   S.D.W.

Gurr, G. M., Wratten, S. D., and Snyder, W. E. (eds.), *Biodiversity and Insect Pests: Key Issues for Sustainable Management* (Wiley-Blackwell, 2012). http://bioprotection.org.nz/research/programme/greening-waipara.

Westman, W. E., 'How much are Nature's services worth?', *Science*, 197/4307 (1977), 960–4.

Wratten, S., et al. (eds.), *Ecosystem Services in Agricultural and Urban Landscapes* (Wiley-Blackwell, 2013).

Ecuador bottles a considerable quantity of wine (including a SCHEUREBE), but the extent of its vineyards is considerably more limited. TROPICAL VITICULTURE, enforced DORMANCY, and the considerable application of FUNGICIDES are essential here on the equator where it rains most days. The limited plantings of INTERNATIONAL VARIETIES that there are here are either at ELEVATIONS of over 2,500 m/8,000 ft near the capital Quito or on the coast in the hinterland of Guayaquil. In 2014 there were three wineries, all small.

Goldstein, E., *Wines of South America* (Oakland, 2014).

edel means 'noble' in German and thus **Edelfäule** is German for NOBLE ROT, and EDELZWICKER is the name chosen to add lustre to a not particularly noble blend in ALSACE. Similarly, Gutedel is the German synonym for the not particularly noble CHASSELAS grape.

Edelzwicker, Alsace term, originally German, for what is usually a relatively basic blend. See ALSACE.

Eden Valley, wine region (High Eden is a subregion) abutting SOUTH AUSTRALIA's Barossa Valley, with high ELEVATION, 43 producers, and a fine reputation for lime-juice-accented and long-lived RIESLING and elegant, medium-bodied Shiraz (Henschke's Hill of Grace, for example).

Edna Valley, California wine region and AVA on the ocean side of the coastal mountains. See SAN LUIS OBISPO.

education, wine. Education plays an important part in the production, sale, and enjoyment of a product as complex and, in many countries, as foreign as wine. Detailed knowledge of wine involves an appreciation of history, geography (inevitably including a host of foreign names), science, and technology, quite apart from the development of practical tasting skills.

Education for wine-producing professionals is discussed under ACADEME and is, naturally, concentrated in the world's wine regions. Some universities, such as BORDEAUX, offer courses, especially in tasting, that are open to wine merchants and the general public. There is even more overlap between wine trade education, courses designed specifically for the wholesale and retail trade, and consumer education; the most enthusiastic wine consumers may well want to know more about wine than the less academically inclined wine traders. The Institute of MASTERS OF WINE, for example, the leading international wine trade educational body which opened its notoriously stiff series of trade examinations to those unconnected with the wine trade in the early 1990s, admitted its first 'MW' without any connection with the wine trade, a Hollywood lawyer, in 1993.

While trade education is usually undertaken by this sort of professional body (the leading international organization is the London-based WSET), consumer education may be undertaken by professional lecturers and wine merchants. This can take the form of TASTINGS so informal as to constitute a party, tutored tastings, BLIND TASTINGS, or some form of wine TOURISM. This century has seen an explosion of interest in wine courses, especially in the US where many of those who run them belong to the Society of Wine Educators, in the UK with its Association of Wine Educators, and in Asia.

Other forms of wine education include both print and online articles (see WINE WRITERS), books (see the LITERATURE OF WINE), various forms of audio-visual instruction such as television and radio programmes, aspects of SOCIAL MEDIA, and software (see INFORMATION TECHNOLOGY). Interactive wine tasting is a way of combining the practical with the theoretical.

effeuillage. See LEAF REMOVAL.

Eger, much-disputed town in north-east HUNGARY whose wines have been exported with success since the 13th century, although various Turkish incursions interrupted this trade. Eger's most famous siege was during the Ottoman occupation of the 16th century when, according to legend, the defenders of Eger were so dramatically fortified by a red liquid which stained their beards and armour that the Turks retreated, believing their opponents to have drunk BIKAVÉR, or Bull's Blood.

The town gives its name to a PDO on the foothills of the volcanic Bükk Mountains where rainfall is low and spring tends to come late. This is one of Hungary's cooler wine-producing areas, and therefore the wines have good aromas and acidity. The geological makeup is diverse, with CALCAREOUS sections alternating with patches of LOESS, ALLUVIAL SOILS, and extensive VOLCANIC rocks, especially TUFF. The southern slope of the Nagy Eged Hill, reclaimed from woods and shrubs, is one of the three most valuable vineyard sites in Hungary. The topsoil here is not volcanic. Pajdos, Síkhegy, and Grőber are all very distinctive sites, too.

The renowned grape of Eger's halcyon days, KADARKA, is being rediscovered, and Pinot Noir and Shiraz are also being planted. Grown on over 200 ha/500 acres, KÉKFRANKOS (Blaufränkisch) continues to dominate and tends to have firmly etched acidity that demands MALOLACTIC CONVERSION. As for white wines, Eger, like Balatonfüred-Csopak and Somló, produces some of the finest Olaszrizlings (WELSCHRIESLING) in all Hungary. Other fine whites are made from Chardonnay, Leányka, Királyleányka, and Hárslevelű.   G.R & G.M.

egg whites play a surprisingly important part in the production of fine red wines. Their particular albumin content makes them highly desirable FINING agents for red wines because they act relatively gently, adsorbing harsh and bitter TANNINS in preference to the softer tannins. Five egg-whites are usually sufficient to fine excess COLLOIDS from a 225-l/59-gal barrel of young red wine. The separation of yolks from egg whites can form an important part of CELLAR WORK in some seasons (and egg yolks can be a significant waste product of winemaking).

Egiodola, tannic French 1954 vine CROSS of Fer Servadou with Abouriou whose total French plantings had fallen to 229 ha by 2011 but it is being trialled in Brazil.

égrappage, French term for DESTEMMING grapes meaning literally 'debunching'.

Egypt, North African country which makes small quantities of wine, about 43,000 hl/1.1 million gal a year from its 70,000 ha/173,000 acres of vineyard in 2011, which are mainly devoted to producing TABLE GRAPES. The Ancient Egyptians provide us with some of the oldest depictions of winemaking techniques, however.

Ancient Egypt

Remains of grapes have been found in late Predynastic sites (c.3300–3000 BC), but the vine is not part of the native flora of the country, and was probably introduced from CANAAN in Predynastic times, despite HERODOTUS' false claim (*Histories* 2. 77) that there were no vines in Egypt. The southern Levantine industry had

matured to such a degree that by the time of Scorpion I (c.3150 BC), one of the first rulers of a united Egypt, his tomb at Abydos was stocked with some 4,500 l/1,900 gal of imported wine from southern Canaan. The wine was laced with terebinth tree resin, to which fresh fruit (grapes and figs) and a variety of herbs (including thyme and savory) had been added. Beginning around 3000 BC, the Egyptian pharaohs financed the establishment of a royal wine industry in the Nile Delta.

The best grapes were considered to come from the Nile Delta; by the New Kingdom (c.1550–1050 BC), viniculture had been introduced to the oases of the western desert and the middle Nile. Vines, irrigated, and manured with bird droppings, were grown in walled gardens, sometimes among other fruits such as olives, and trained over pergolas (see TENDONE).

As in Ancient GREECE and Ancient ROME, there were two distinct winemaking operations: treading, or CRUSHING, to yield some FREE-RUN juice, and PRESSING the remainder with a sack-press. When harvested, grapes were trodden by foot by men who could hang on to overhead supports, or suspended ropes. The vat was deliberately shielded from the heat, and an offering of the must was made to the goddess Renenutet. Tomb paintings illustrate wine production amply, although the precise details are not always clear. After treading, the pressing was often carried out in a special sack-press with a pole fixed in a loop at either end of what was effectively a giant jelly bag. This was then twisted by several men in opposite directions and the liquid was collected in a vessel beneath. The liquid flowing out of the sack-press is always depicted as red. In Old Kingdom times (c.2686–2181 BC) the wine was transferred to large jars, later called AMPHORAE.

In scenes dating from the New Kingdom must flows from the trough along a small conduit into a receptacle. In the sack-press apparently only the skins would have been pressed. Probably the free-run juice and the PRESS WINE were fermented together. Depictions show only the transfer of the must from the press into amphorae. In one illustration the contents of the press are transferred to large fermentation vats, then pressed in the sack-press and transferred into amphorae.

The actual alcoholic fermentation took place in the amphorae, from which the Ancient Egyptians would then deliberately exclude air, just like many modern winemakers. The filled amphorae were covered with cloth or leather lids, smeared with Nile mud, and then sealed. Small holes to allow the continuing escape of CARBON DIOXIDE were later blocked up.

White wine is likely attested in the Scorpion I tomb, based on the yellowishness of the residue, and in some of the amphorae in the Tutankhamun tomb, based on chemical analyses.

Egyptian wines were generally RESINATED WINES from the beginning of the royal winemaking industry to the end of the Pharaonic period. Wine was also drunk for medicinal purposes, when it was sometimes flavoured with Levantine and Egyptian herbs, *kyphi*, a mixture of gums, resins, herbs, spices, and possibly other less pleasant ingredients such as the dungs of various animals and birds, and asses' hair.

Wine trade organization It is clear from the seals on amphorae and from the titles of certain officials that the manufacture and delivery of wine were already organized at royal level in the earliest periods. Wine is often shown in scenes on wall paintings. Lists from the Fifth Dynasty distinguish five types of wine according to its origin. 'Wine from Asia' and Canaan is also mentioned, and Canaanite wine amphorae are found in the New Kingdom. Inscriptions on amphorae of that period usually indicate year, vineyard site, owner, and chief winemaker (rather more information than is given on most modern wine labels). Most but not all centres of wine production lay on the western arm of the Nile Delta.

Wine drinking Wine was drunk by gods, kings, and nobles, especially at feasts, and was rated only slightly behind BEER, which was the most common beverage of ancient Egypt. Amphorae, often painted with vine leaves, are depicted on tables or resting on stands. The wine was sieved as it was poured out. Servants would fill small beakers for serving, sometimes carrying a second small jug (possibly containing water to dilute the wine, but more likely a herbal concoction). The wine was drunk from bowls or amphorae (which sometimes rested on stands). The king Akhenaten and his family are shown drinking at the royal capital Tell-el-Amarna (14th century BC). Priests received wine as part of their daily rations, likewise army officers and foreign mercenaries; but the workmen of Amarna received none, an indication of its value. By contrast, the workers who had built the pyramids received a daily allotment of two 'bottles' or about 4–5 l/1–1.3 gal of beer.

Religion and wine Wine is said to be the drink of gods, and also of the dead (along with beer and milk). Thus it was important in cult worship and is frequently mentioned in lists of offerings, sometimes several sorts together. It was frequently offered as nourishment to deities by the king or private persons, also symbolizing purification. LIBATIONS of wine and water were made at temples and tombs throughout the country.

The goddess Hathor, 'the mistress of DRUNKENNESS', was the Egyptian equivalent of the Sumerian beer goddess, Ninkasi. She was closely associated with a lesser goddess 'who makes beer', Menqet. One festival to honour Hathor, appropriately designated the 'the Drunkenness of Hathor', at her temple in Dendera, recalled the story of how the goddess had gone on a rampage to destroy a rebellious humanity in her form as the lioness goddess, Sekhmet. Just in time, Re diverted her from her mission by filling the inundated fields with 'red beer', which Hathor interpreted as a sign that she had accomplished her task. She then over-indulged, and forgot to carry out the devastation of mankind. The yearly celebration at Dendera coincided with the inundation of the Nile during the summer, when reddish iron-rich soils were washed down from the Atbara River in Sudan, giving the waters the appearance of 'red beer'. By drinking an alcoholic beverage at the festival—both wine and beer—and celebrating with music and dance, humanity shared in Hathor's transformation into her more benign form as the feline Bastet.

Classical authors identified Osiris as the benefactor who bestowed wine on mankind, comparing him in this respect to the Greek god DIONYSUS. The grape certainly became a symbol of the dying and rising god. Vines depicted in tomb paintings symbolized the deceased's hope for resurrection. Other texts refer to wine as the perspiration of Re or as the eyes of the god Horus. His pupils are said to be grapes through which wine flows. In the later periods the term 'Green Eye of Horus' was used to refer to wine.

See also ORIGINS OF VINICULTURE and PALAEOETHNOBOTANY AND THE ARCHAEOLOGY OF WINE. J.A.B. & P.E.M.

James, T. G. H., 'The Earliest History of Wine in Egypt', in Fleming, S. J. and Katz, S. H. (eds), *The Origins and Ancient History of Wine* (New York, 1995).

Lesko, L. H., 'Egyptian Wine Production during the New Kingdom', in Fleming, S. J. and Katz, S. H. (eds), *The Origins and Ancient History of Wine* (New York, 1995).

See articles 'Wein', 'Weinkrug', 'Weinopfer', and 'Weintrauben', in *Lexikon der Ägyptologie* (Wiesbaden, 1975–86), cols. 1169–92 (the standard scholarly reference work on the subject).

Modern wine production

Brewers Heineken own the leading and thoroughly modern Egyptian wine producer Gianaclis, about 75 km/47 miles from Alexandria, and in 2014 there were two others. SULTANA and a wide range of INTERNATIONAL VARIETIES are grown, on trellises, mainly in the north of the country, although VINE AGE is low and the growing season is too short for Riesling, Sauvignon Blanc, and members of the Pinot family. Satellite technology is harnessed to apply DRIP IRRIGATION with precision. Grapes are picked between late June and early August and are generally chilled before transport to sophisticated modern wineries equipped with STAINLESS STEEL. French oak BARRIQUES are used for some top wines but most are drunk young.

Ehrenfelser is one of the more frost-resistant better GERMAN CROSSES, developed at GEISENHEIM in 1929. Although it was said to be a RIESLING × SILVANER cross, DNA PROFILING has shown that the latter is not one of its parents. It is not nearly as versatile in terms of site as KERNER, which became a more obvious choice as a flexible Riesling substitute. Total German plantings of Ehrenfelser had fallen to 67 ha/165 acres by 2012, mainly in the Pfalz and Rheinhessen.

Einzellage, literally 'individual site' in the wine regions of GERMANY. Almost all of Germany's vineyards are officially registered as one of these approximately 2,600 **Einzellagen**, which can vary in size from a fraction of 1 ha to more than 200 ha/494 acres. The average size of an Einzellage is about 38 ha, about the same size as a typical BORDEAUX estate. As in BURGUNDY, for example, the vines may be divided among many different owners, who are allowed to put the name of the Einzellage only on QUALITÄTSWEIN. Such names must usually be preceded by the name of the village in which they were produced; thus a wine from the Mandelring vineyard in the village of Haardt is called Haardter Mandelring.

The same formula of town + vineyard name is also followed for so-called GROSSLAGEN, which are in reality collections of many individual sites in the vicinity of—but by no means always clustered around—the town in question. The result is one of the most misleading features of the German Wine Law, since unless the consumer knows that a designation such as Piesporter Michelsberg refers to a wide range of generally undistinguished sites, they will be deceived—by intention, sadly—into thinking that the wine in question was grown on the steep slate terroir immediately around Piesport. In a few instances such as SCHLOSS JOHANNISBERG and Schloss Vollrads in the RHEINGAU, the name of the property itself legally suffices as provenance, and the Scharzhofberg vineyard in the SAAR is considered so important that it dispenses with the prefix Wiltinger, but such official exceptions are rare. Recent practice, though, among VDP members (some would say affectation, but intended to ape Burgundian grand cru labelling conventions) is to dispense with the names of villages in front of any site deemed worthy of bottling as a GROSSES GEWÄCHS. J.R. & D.S.

Pigott, S., and Johnson, H., *The Wine Atlas of Germany* (London, 1995).

Eire. See IRELAND.

Eisacktaler, German for Valle Isarco, DOC in ALTO ADIGE producing pure, dry white wines.

Eisenberg, tiny wine village in Austria's BURGENLAND adjacent to and named for a high hill dominated by iron-rich SCHIST—its twin over the Hungarian border Vaskereztes sharing the same etymology. Since 2008 it has lent its name to an official DAC for BLAUFRÄNKISCH wines grown throughout SÜDBURGENLAND. The KLASSIK wines of Eisenberg DAC must reach 12% alcohol and may not be approved or sold until 1 June and 1 September respectively of the year after their vintage. Wines of this DAC labelled Reserve must be raised in cask or small barrels; reach 13% alcohol; and cannot be approved or marketed before 1 January and 1 March of the second calendar year following their harvest.   D.S.

Eisheiligen, Germany's Ice Saints, those whose commemoration days fall between 11 and 14 May, including St Pancras and St Boniface. After 15 May, *Kalte Sophie* or St Sophie's day, the risk of spring FROST in the vineyards is deemed past.

Eiswein designates German wines produced from grapes frozen on the vine, and pressed while still frozen. The deliberate picking of Eiswein with any significant frequency seems to have originated in the 1960s, and from the 1980s the practice became routine at the majority of top estates, excepting those that farm vineyards not prone to deep frost. Freezing concentrates not just the SUGAR in the grapes, but also ACIDITY and EXTRACT, and Riesling Eiswein is routinely the highest in acid (as well as some of the highest-priced) of any German wines. For best results, a frost of at least −8 °C/18 °F is required, for which grapes are generally harvested between five and eight in the morning of the first sufficiently cold November or December days. Eiswein picked in January or even February is not unknown, but is seldom of as high a quality. Such a wine is labelled for the calendar year of the growing season. Before 1971, Eisweine were frequently labelled for the date of picking or nearest Saint's Day (Nikolauswein, for example, designated a wine harvested December 6), but such information is currently not permitted on the label. Since 1982, Eiswein has been a separate PRÄDIKAT with the minimum MUST weight of a BEERENAUSLESE, namely 110–128 OECHSLE depending on the region and variety in question. In AUSTRIA too, the requisite must weight is the same as that of a Beerenauslese, 25 KMW (approximately 127 °Oechsle). The harvesting of Eiswein has become much more routine as a result of the widespread (if controversial) use of semi-permeable PLASTIC SHEETING that hugs the vines to protect grapes from birds and rain while waiting for a suitably deep frost. (Protection from wild boar is another matter, and more potential Eiswein is lost to these marauders

than to any other cause.) While the classic concept of Eiswein for most growers is a wine from BOTRYTIS-free grapes, this is not a legal requirement, and the use of film in fact often promotes humidity and thus a low level of botrytis in the shrouded grapes. If the harvest does not achieve the requisite ripeness or the character deemed appropriate to Eiswein by the individual vintner, the wine usually ends up being bottled as an AUSLESE or subsumed into another wine, even though this practice is technically legally questionable.

See also ICEWINE in Canada.   D.S.

Eiximenis, Francisc (*c.*1340–*c.*1409), Catalan Franciscan friar and author of *Lo Crestià* ('The Christian'), an encyclopedia of the Christian life. Thirteen books were planned but only four were finished. It is aimed at a popular, not a learned, audience, and hence it is written not in Latin but in the vernacular, Catalan. As a result it has had no influence on other European authors of the Middle Ages (see LITERATURE OF WINE).

Its third book, *Lo terç del Crestià*, dated 1384, is concerned with sin. The section on gluttony deals with DRUNKENNESS (chs. 350–9) and the etiquette of wine drinking (chs. 362–7, 393–5). Eiximenis is aware of the medical properties of wine, but his interest is in the moral aspects of drinking. Drunkenness, he says, leads to every conceivable vice, but, taken in moderation, wine is a good thing. All other nations, except perhaps the Italians, drink too much: only the Catalans have the art of sensible drinking. This means three cups at dinner, three at supper: one should never have more than four, and there is to be no drinking between meals. Although he disapproves of the fastidious habits of connoisseurs, he does tell where the best wines are to be found. They are the strong, sweet wines of the Mediterranean, particularly MALMSEY (Malvasia), the Cretan Candia, and Picapoll from Mallorca (Majorca). He ranks Italian wines above French wines, and insists that strong wines (these do not include the wines of France) should be mixed with water, the stronger the wine the more water.   H.M.W.

Gracia, Jorge J. E., 'Rules and regulations for drinking wine in Francisc Eiximenis' *Terç del Crestià* (1384)', *Traditio*, 32 (1976), 369–85.

Gracia, Jorge J. E., 'Francisc Eiximenis' *Terç del Crestià*: edition and study of sources, chs. 359–436' (Ph.D. thesis, University of Toronto, 1971).

Elba, Mediterranean island off TUSCANY. Viticulture played an important role in the economy of the island in the ancient world, and PLINY described Elba as '*insula vini ferax*' (an island with abundant production of wine). This continued until the late 19th and early 20th centuries, when a quarter of the cultivated surface was occupied by vines. Emigration from the

island and the increasing attractions of the booming tourist industry have drastically reduced the role of wine in the overall economic picture, however, to the point where hardly 100 ha/250 acres of the Elba DOC are in production, three-quarters of it white wine. The whole of Elba is covered by one DOC, called Elba, with whites based on TREBBIANO Toscano, VERMENTINO, and Ansonica (Sicily's INZOLIA), and reds on the ubiquitous SANGIOVESE. The one DOCG is a sweet DRIED-GRAPE WINE, the red ALEATICO PASSITO.   D.C.G. & W.S.

Elbling is an ancient, and some would say outdated, vine variety that has been cultivated in the Mosel Valley since Roman times. At one time it was effectively the only variety planted in LUXEMBOURG and dominated the extensive vineyards of medieval Germany (see GERMAN HISTORY). Today it is increasingly unpopular in Luxembourg and in Germany, where only 538 ha/1,329 acres remained in 2012, most of it in the upper reaches of the MOSEL above Trier where chalk dominates slate and Riesling has difficulty ripening. Much of the Elbling grown here is used for SEKT. While the vine is distinguished for its antiquity and productivity, its wines are distinguished by their often searing acidity and their relatively low alcohol. DNA PROFILING in Austria suggested a parent–offspring relationship with GOUAIS BLANC.

El Dorado, California county and AVA. See SIERRA FOOTHILLS.

electrical resistance tomography. See PROMIMAL SENSING

electrodialysis, a sophisticated, electrically driven membrane FILTRATION process which allows the removal of selected ions (electrically charged molecules), has been used since the 1960s to desalinate water and was adapted for use in the STABILIZATION of wine by INRA in the 1990s. In this context it is used to remove potassium, TARTRATES, and bitartrates. Despite the relatively high capital costs of the technology, it is gaining acceptance in the wine industry because it uses 80% less energy than cold stabilization, is much faster, and total running costs are up to 40% lower. The volume of water used to extract the tartrate salt has been significantly reduced by the use of REVERSE OSMOSIS and there are said to be no adverse effects on wine quality. No further filtration is required to remove the potassium bitartrate crystals before bottling, although the wine does have to be filtered prior to electrodialysis to avoid clogging the membranes. One of the greatest advantages of this process is that it allows great control over what and how much is removed from the wine.

Electrodialysis may also be used to remove calcium, another potential source of instability, reduce saltiness, and lower the PH of a wine without ACIDIFICATION.

Unlike ION EXCHANGE, which is far less selective, electrodialysis is permitted and widely used in the EU and most other wine-producing countries that regulate winemaking processes—but only for tartrate stabilization. There are a number of units in wineries in Italy, France, Germany, and Spain, and others in South Africa, and the US. Mobile units are in use in the EU, the US, Chile, Argentina, Australia, and New Zealand.

Wollan, D., 'Membrane and other techniques for the management of wine composition', in A. G. Reynolds (ed.), *Managing Wine Quality 2: Oenology and Wine Quality* (Cambridge, 2010), 133–63.

electromagnetic induction. See PROXIMAL SENSING.

élevage, French word that describes an important aspect of winemaking but has no direct equivalent in English (other than the Anglicization 'elevage'). *Élevage* means literally 'rearing', 'breeding', or 'raising' and is commonly applied to livestock, or humans as in *bien élevé* for 'well brought up'. When applied to wines, it means the series of cellar operations that take place between FERMENTATION and BOTTLING, suggesting that the winemaker's role is rather like that of a loving parent who guides, disciplines, and civilizes the raw young wine that emerges from the FERMENTATION VESSEL. The word *élevage* implies that all this effort is worth it, and is therefore normally applied only above a certain level of wine quality.

For details of the various stages of *élevage*, see RED WINEMAKING and WHITE WINEMAKING. A.D.W.

elevation, the height above mean sea level of a location such as a vineyard, often mistakenly referred to as altitude. Local elevation of vineyards above valley floors or flat land determines their air drainage and TEMPERATURE relations, including liability to FROST (see also TOPOGRAPHY; MESOCLIMATE; CLIMATE AND WINE QUALITY).

The elevation of a vineyard can have important effects on its climate and therefore on its viticultural potential. Other things being equal, temperature falls by about 0.6 °C (1.1 °F) per 100 m (330 ft) greater height. Planting vineyards at higher elevations is commonly considered a means of avoiding the impact of increasing temperatures related to CLIMATE CHANGE. For example, TORRES in Cataluña is developing vineyards in the nearby Pyrenees, while Prager has been planting much higher land than previous generations in the Wachau.

The lower temperatures at higher elevations retard both vine BUDBREAK and, in particular, RIPENING. Small differences in elevation can have surprisingly big effects on wine quality and, indeed, on the ability of individual grape varieties to ripen at all. Becker refers to a major Rhine Valley study illustrating this. Lower temperatures can be further compounded by the generally greater rainfall and cloudiness at higher elevations.

With the increased market emphasis on TABLE WINES since the 1960s, ever higher vineyard sites have been sought, especially in the world's warmer wine regions (see CLIMATE AND WINE QUALITY and TEMPERATURE). Examples include the Adelaide Hills in SOUTH AUSTRALIA, the Central Ranges of NEW SOUTH WALES, Tupungato and other high-elevation plantings in ARGENTINA, the foothills of the Andes in CHILE, as well as the newer HILLSIDE VINEYARDS of California, Sicily, and Greece. Some of these vineyards have been planted not just in search of cooler temperatures, but to escape the deeper, more fertile soils of the valley floors and to achieve vine BALANCE in shallower, hillside soils.

Elevated vineyards also experience more ULTRAVIOLET RADIATION, which is likely to increase quality because of stimulation of PHENOLIC synthesis.

Most of the world's highest established vineyards are in Latin America but they are being challenged by new plantings in the Himalayas. Three of the world's highest commercial vineyards are Swiss-born Donald Hess's plantings in the northern province of Salta, Argentina. Colomé, near Molinos, is at 2,200–2,300 m (7,218–7,546 ft); El Arenal, Payogasta, is at 2,400–2,500 m (7,874–8,200 ft); Altura Máxima, also near Payogasta, is at 3,111 m (10,207 ft). BOLIVIA has vines up to 2,850 m in the Cotagaita Valley. In the Himalayas in Asia, there are small commercial vineyards up to 2,900 m in the south west of CHINA. A small vineyard planted in 2012 at 2,089 m (6,855 ft) in Big Bear in southern California's ski country is claimed to be North America's highest. The highest European vineyards are probably those of ABONA in the Canary Islands, which are at elevations up to 1,600 m/5,280 ft, although there are vines up to 1,150 m/3,770 ft and 1,250 m/4,100 ft in SWITZERLAND and AOSTA respectively. J.G., J.R., & R.E.S.

Becker, H., 'Site climate effects on development, fruit maturation and harvest quality', in R. E. Smart et al. (eds.), *Proceedings of the Second International Symposium for Cool Climate Viticulture and Oenology: 11–15 January 1988, Auckland, New Zealand* (Auckland, 1988), 11–15.

Gladstones, J., *Viticulture and Environment* (Adelaide, 1992).

Iland, P., et al., 'Climate and the vine', in *The Grapevine: From the Science to the Practice of Growing Vines for Wine* (Adelaide, 2011).

Elgin, predominantly white wine district in the Cape South Coast region of SOUTH AFRICA. This relatively new district has cool, high vineyards in apple-orchard country east of Cape Town and is a source of fine Chardonnay and Sauvignon Blanc, as well as some successful Pinot Noirs.

El Hierro, Spanish DO covering the whole of the eponymous island in the CANARY ISLANDS, with just 190 ha/450 acres of vineyards. The dominant grape is the white Vijariego, but it's the red Baboso Negro (ALFROCHEIRO PRETO) which has won the Tanajara estate some international recognition. V. de la S.

Elim, very cool ward in SOUTH AFRICA's Cape Agulhas district on the southernmost tip of Africa within the Cape South Coast region. Baboons, lack of CRUSH facilities, and low temperatures have been threats to its survival.

ELISA, acronym for enzyme-linked immunosorbent assay, a serological test which can also be used to detect vine pathogens. First used in plant pathology in the mid 1970s, the technique is now used routinely to determine the presence of a wide range of vine pathogens, and test kits are available commercially. R.E.S.

Weber, E., Golino, D., and Rowhani, A., 'Laboratory testing for grapevine diseases', *Practical Winery & Vineyard* (Jan/Feb 2002), 13–27.

ellagitannins. See OAK FLAVOUR and PIGMENTED TANNINS.

El Niño, anomalous seasonal ocean current along the coast of Peru, and part of a much larger atmospheric phenomenon called the 'southern oscillation', which can have a substantial impact on vineyard production in several countries where climate is affected by the Pacific Ocean. The phenomenon recurs every two to ten years, and is associated with atmospheric pressure changes in the South Pacific; it can be predicted well in advance.

Typical but severe effects were felt in 1998, which started with serious FLOODING in California and continued there throughout spring and early summer to retard the likely harvest dates. The Australian 1997–8 growing season on the other hand was generally affected by DROUGHT, decreasing quantity but sometimes increasing quality. There was a similar weather pattern in New Zealand. Chile's wine regions experienced a generally cooler, wetter growing season with DOWNY MILDEW in some areas for the first time. In Argentina around Mendoza, summer storms before vintage created BUNCH ROT problems. Latest reports are that hopes are fading of a strong El Niño in 2014 to alleviate drought in California. R.E.S.

Elqui, valley in the northern Coquimbo region of CHILE increasingly known for its wine as well as its pisco.

embotellado is Spanish for bottled.

Emerald Riesling, one of the earliest of the vine varieties developed at the University of

California (see DAVIS) by Dr H. P. Olmo to emerge in VARIETAL (white) wine. It is a CROSS of a variety labelled Muscadelle (but not true MUSCADELLE) and Grenache and had its heyday in the late 1960s and early 1970s before slumping towards oblivion. Just 152 ha/375 acres remained in 2011, mainly in the very south of the SAN JOAQUIN VALLEY, and nearly all of the grapes disappear into generic blends. It has also been tried in SOUTH AFRICA and makes off-dry wine in ISRAEL.

Emilia, western part of EMILIA-ROMAGNA.

Emilia-Romagna, Italian wine region which stretches across north-central Italy from the eastern Adriatic coast to include vast tracts of inland Emilia in the west, which is quite distinct from coastal Romagna in the east (see map under ITALY).

There are four very individual areas, each producing distinct wines: the hills around Piacenza in the north east bordering LOMBARDY; the plain in central Emilia around Parma, Reggio nell'Emilia, and Modena; the hills around Bologna; and the hills in Romagna between Imola and Rimini bordering TUSCANY to the south east.

The Colli Piacentini, geologically and climatically similar to the contiguous OLTREPÒ PAVESE of Lombardy, is divided in three subregions, Monterosso Val d'Arda, Valnure, and Trebbianino Val Trebbia, which may appear on labels. Many of its FRIZZANTE or lightly sparkling whites from MALVASIA Candia, the rare ORTRUGO (recently elevated to DOC, without, confusingly any geographical DELIMITATION) and Trebbiano; and reds from BARBERA and CROATINA (incorrectly called BONARDA here), are made by the tank method (see SPARKLING WINEMAKING) in industrial volumes.

However, the traditional complex, bottle-fermented versions are slowly gaining ground again, notably those from Ermano Croce. The area's most interesting other developments come from the subzone of Rivergaro-Vigolzone, with complex varietal PINOT NOIR and BARBERA, CABERNET blends, and Malvasia di Candia for whites. La Stoppa and Denavolo achieve excellence here, both preferring to label their wines IGT rather than DOC. The DOC Gutturnio, once a suffix to Colli Piacentini and with a CLASSICO subzone as its heart, produces red wine based on Barbera and Croatina, has untapped potential, both for still as well as frizzante versions.

The flat Emilia plain is often associated with one wine only: LAMBRUSCO. Since the 1970s this light, frothy, and often slightly sweet red has been a huge export success, and industrial-sized production has completely dominated Lambrusco's image. There are no fewer than four different Lambrusco DOCs, representing distinct styles, which rarely surface in the glass of the industrial versions (see LAMBRUSCO for more detail).

The Colli Bolognesi, the hills immediately south west of Bologna, are dominated by international varieties Cabernet Sauvignon, Merlot, and Chardonnay. The good results achieved here can be traced back to the pioneering estate Terre Rosse, whose founder Enrico Vallania planted these varieties in the 1960s, aiming at making long-lived wine without any use of OAK. The local white Pignoletto, producing fresh, lively and often lightly sparkling whites, has been elevated to DOCG, but few producers aim for quality, as most Pignoletto ends up in the tanks of large bottlers and huge CO-OPERATIVES, an exception being Alberto Tedeschi.

The Romagna Hills, covered by the enormous DOC Romagna, are home to both some of the best and worst of the region's output. Total production is dominated by co-ops turning out industrial quantities of insipid SANGIOVESE and TREBBIANO. The image of ROMAGNA SANGIOVESE has suffered particularly from this indifference, much to the frustration of a group of quality-focused producers (see SANGIOVESE DI ROMAGNA for more details). The oft-scorned Romagna ALBANA (see DOCG), grown in the same extensive area as Romagna Sangiovese and elevated to DOGC in 1986 to considerable scepticism, is beginning to prove its worth with fine PASSITO and BOTRYTIZED versions as well as some serious barrel-fermented dry wines, often from single vineyards.   W.S.

www.consorziovinidiromagna.it
www.revinireggiani.it
www.enotecaemiliaromagna.it

Empordà, DO in the extreme north east corner of Spanish CATALUÑA separated from ROUSSILLON only by the French border (see maps under SPAIN and FRANCE). The zone has a long history of wine production, which was nearly extinguished when PHYLLOXERA swept through the vineyards in the 1900s. Many of the TERRACES that climb the low foothills of the Pyrenees were never replanted. The climate is MEDITERRANEAN, although strong year-round winds protect the vineyards from FROST and VINE DISEASES, but can subject vines without WINDBREAKS to severe stress. Empordà used to produce heavy RANCIOS, sometimes called Garnatxa, the Catalan name for the GRENACHE grape. This vine variety and Cariñena (CARIGNAN) still account for 80% of production, although for long they were mostly turned into bulk rosé for the local market. Inspired by the quality-conscious Castillo de Perelada estate however, smaller producers such as Mas Estela, Masia Serra, and Mas Oller have significantly changed the perception of a region that used to be known as Empordà-Costa Brava.   V. de la S.

Enantio, new 1980s name for vine grown in TRENTINO to produce deep red wine. Recent DNA PROFILING at SAN MICHELE ALL'ADIGE revealed a likely parent–offspring relationship with NEGRARA Trentina and it seems to be closely related to TEROLDEGO and LAGREIN too. The Italian 2010 vine census found 724 ha/1,788 acres of the variety it still called Lambrusco a Foglia Frastagliata, 'toothed leafed Lambrusco', which is unrelated to any other LAMBRUSCO.

encépagement, widely used French term for the mix of *cépages*, or VINE VARIETIES, planted on a particular property. These proportions (typically for a MÉDOC estate, for example, Cabernet Sauvignon 60%, Cabernet Franc 20%, and Merlot 20%) do not necessarily correspond to the proportions of each grape variety in a given wine, partly because different varieties vary generally in terms of productivity, but also because factors such as FLOWERING and FROST may dramatically influence the yield from each variety in a given growing season.

Encostas d'Aire, DOP on the slopes of the Serra d'Aire in western Portugal. See LISBOA.

Encruzado, fine Portuguese white grape variety most commonly planted in DÃO. It can yield well-balanced, full-bodied VARIETAL wines capable of ageing. Total 2012 plantings were 350 ha/865 acres.

engarrafado, Portuguese for bottled.

England, the largest and warmest country in Great BRITAIN and the only one which produces wine in any quantity, albeit on a small scale relative to most European wine-producing countries.

History

Perhaps the Romans introduced viticulture to England, but, whether they did or not, they cannot be held responsible for introducing the grapevine itself, because archaeologists have found prehistoric remains of the pollen of VINIFERA vines at Marks Tey in Essex, as well as seed at Hoxne in Suffolk (see PALAEOETHNOBOTANY).

Both these finds go back to the Hoxnian Interglacial, i.e. the period between the Second and Third Ice Ages, when summers were warmer than they are now. Grape seeds dating from the Hoxnian have also been found in the NETHERLANDS, north GERMANY, Denmark, and Poland. Since the British Isles were still part of continental Europe at the time (they did not become separated until after the Fourth Ice Age), this shows that *Vitis Vinifera* had spread to regions of northern Europe which are now too cold for grapes. The seeds and pollen found in East Anglia are not accompanied by remains of cereals or other signs of agriculture. A more recent find at a Roman site at Wollaston in the

Nene Valley near Wellingborough in the south Midlands is of what appear to be planting holes together with grape pollen, suggesting that this was the site of a vineyard.

Seeds have been found at Roman sites in London, Bermondsey, Silchester in Hampshire, and Gloucester, and stalks at a Roman villa near Boxmoor in Hertfordshire, but all without any evidence of cultivation, so these may be the remains of imported raisins. And even if grapes were grown in England, we cannot prove that they were made into wine. Wine was certainly imported from Italy, even before the Roman invasion of AD 43: remains of AMPHORAE testify to that. (See CELTS for evidence that a small quantity of wine was carried to Hampshire at the end of the 2nd century BC.) The earliest wine drinkers in Britain were the Belgae, a Celtic tribe that had invaded Britain in two waves, the first in 75 BC and the second in 20 BC, after the Romans had put down the Belgic rebellion in Gaul. The British Belgae kept in close contact with their kinsmen in Gaul, who were prodigious drinkers of Italian wine. In the reign of Cymbeline (Cunobelin), AD 10–40, galleys came up the River Colne to Camulodunum (one mile from Colchester in Essex).

Consumption of wine probably increased after the Roman invasion of Britain, for remains of amphorae and pottery drinking cups are common finds on the sites of Roman towns and country houses. Recent finds show that amphorae were manufactured at Brockley Hill, Middlesex, which appears to have been an important pottery centre, and also at other London sites. They are of a type that, according to archaeological evidence from southern France, were used as containers for locally produced wine; the London amphorae were probably the work of immigrant potters from France. The amphorae all date from AD 70–100: perhaps this short period could be explained by the edict issued by the Roman emperor DOMITIAN, which, by reducing the number of vineyards in the provinces, put a stop to the Romano-British wine industry. Remains of imported amphorae are rare after AD 300 but it seems unlikely that the Romano-British were now producing enough wine to meet their own needs. In any case, from the 3rd century onwards wine began increasingly to be transported not in amphorae but in wooden BARRELS, which are perishable, so one would not expect to find many amphorae dating from the 4th century AD and certainly no wooden casks.

Our earliest conclusive evidence for wine-growing in Britain, then, must be Bede's *Ecclesiastical History*, which he finished in 731. It opens with a general description of Britain and Ireland, including geography, climate, agriculture, animals, nations, and languages. 'Britain,' Bede says, 'is rich in grain and timber; it has good pasturage for cattle and draught animals, and wines are cultivated in various localities' (Book 1, ch. 1). Unfortunately, that is all he tells us about Anglo-Saxon viticulture–although in any case Bede has been shown to be a less than reliable source of information on viticulture in Ireland. As well as growing their own, the Anglo-Saxons certainly bought wine from the Franks. In the 8th and 9th centuries, Southampton was one of the largest ports of northern Europe and well placed for trade with northern France, especially Rouen (see PARIS). In return for animal hides, the merchants of Southampton obtained gold, silver, glassware, and wine. However, as Viking pirates began to capture more and more ships, overseas trade was disrupted, and if imported wine was available at all it must have been a rare luxury item.

The Anglo-Saxons' daily drink was BEER, but they needed wine for the EUCHARIST: supply being erratic, it made sense for monasteries to have their own vineyards, as some had probably been doing since Bede's day (see MONKS AND MONASTERIES). A charter, dated 955, of King Edwy, great-grandson of King Alfred, grants a vineyard at Pethanesburgh, Somerset, to the monks of Glastonbury Abbey. But not all vineyards were owned by monks. The Laws of King Alfred regard viticulture as important enough to make it an offence for anyone to destroy a vineyard; no mention is made of monasteries here. An 11th-century document lists looking after the vineyard as one of the duties of the manager of a secular estate and, out of the 38 vineyards named in Domesday Book, only 12 were monastic. More importantly, if the figure is accurate—and William the Conqueror's surveyors did their work thoroughly—38 vineyards cannot possibly have produced a plentiful supply of wine for the whole of England. (According to the Bayeux Tapestry's depiction of William's invasion of England in 1066, he judged it as important to take wine as arms with him.)

Wine continued to be grown in England during the 12th and 13th centuries. There were vineyards as far north as south Yorkshire, and the praise lavished on the wines of Gloucestershire by the 12th-century chronicler William of Malmesbury demonstrates that English wine was no thin, sour plonk. Worcestershire, too, was renowned for its wine. This golden age of English viticulture was the result of a long period of warm summer weather, which started in the mid 11th century (see CLIMATE CHANGE). It ended abruptly in the 14th century, when the ocean currents changed and summers became wet and cloudy. Moreover, when on his marriage to Eleanor of Aquitaine Henry II acquired Gascony, and when King John (1199–1216) granted the citizens of BORDEAUX numerous privileges in order to win their favour, Gascon wine became cheaper to buy for the English than any other wine, imported or home produced. Around 1,300 commercial vineyards were grubbed up all over England, and grapes made way for more profitable crops: this is how the Vale of Evesham, still famous for its plums and apples, came to be planted with fruit trees. Monastic viticulture continued for longer, but between 1348 and 1370 the Black Death carried off a third or more of the population, lay and ecclesiastic alike. Not only did many monks die, but the ensuing shortage of labour deprived the monasteries of their unsalaried workforce, the lay brothers. English viticulture did not cease altogether, but it was no longer commercially viable, even for the monks.

But with a wine-drinking Norman aristocracy, domestic production could never have satisfied demand. Via Rouen, then governed by the king of England, who was also duke of Normandy (until John lost Normandy), the English had ready access to the wines of the Île-de-France (see PARIS), which in 1200 were the most expensive on the English market, although people bought more of the wines of Poitou (see LA ROCHELLE) and Anjou (see LOIRE), and probably with reason, for they must have been less acidic. With the rise of Bordeaux, this changed, and until the end of the HUNDRED YEARS WAR the English bought more wine from Gascony than from anywhere else, with wine being second only to wool in importance for English trade at this time. Wine was shipped to England, principally to the port of Southampton, twice a year from Bordeaux, in the autumn and in the spring. Even if the vintage had been early, the new wine did not usually reach England before November; the wines that arrived in the spring were the wines 'of rack', so-called because they were not racked off their LEES until the spring. The wines, 'of rack', an early form of SUR LIE, fetched higher prices. Since there was nothing better in which to keep the wine than wooden casks, OXIDATION was the norm and wine did not keep from one year to the next. The wine of the previous year was therefore sold off cheaply at AUCTION as soon as the new vintage appeared on the market in England. White wine was more expensive than red.

French wines were not the only wines to be drunk in 14th-century London. From the 1350s onwards, sweet wines from southern Europe began to be introduced (see VENICE, NAPLES, and GENOA), and they became the most expensive available. The most highly prized of these was 'vernage', the Italian VERNACCIA. Another favourite was 'malvesye', or MALMSEY, supplied mainly by Cyprus and Crete. Because of their additional strength and sweetness, these wines lasted longer than the thinner, drier wines that the English had been used to and were greatly prized. The wines of Alsace and the Rhine were highly valued because they were so brilliantly clear. Spanish wine, which was higher in alcohol than other wines, was regarded mainly as cheaper heady plonk, and better, more expensive, wines were often cut with it (see SPAIN, history).

Attempts were made to protect the consumer from ADULTERATION AND FRAUD, but their frequency suggests that they were not always successful. In 1321, a proclamation was made that in London all wines should be graded 'good' or 'ordinary' and the casks marked; everyone would have the right to see his wine drawn and maximum prices were fixed. Merchants and innkeepers refused to cooperate and were promptly fined. The marking of casks was probably abandoned, but the right to see one's wine being drawn is reiterated from one writ and proclamation to the next, and one even says that taverners should keep red wines and white in different cellars: a note of desperation is clearly creeping in. A London proclamation of 1371 makes clear what the unfortunate drinker was subjected to: overcharging, adulteration, and wine that was off. It makes one grateful for clearly labelled, tamper-free modern packaging: the glass BOTTLE and modern CLOSURES have improved the wine drinker's life almost beyond imagination.   H.M.W.

Dion, R., *Histoire de la vigne et du vin en France* (Paris, 1959).

Dion, R., *Studies in the Medieval Wine Trade* (Oxford, 1971).

Simon, A. L., *The History of the Wine Trade in England*, 3 vols. (London, 1906–9).

Modern English wine

The revival of viticulture in the British Isles, mainly in England, but also Wales (and even Scotland), that began in the mid 20th century has matured into a small but significant industry with a planted area in 2013 of 1,884 ha/4,655 acres, of which 1,571 ha/3,882 acres were already producing wine. Average annual production was around 3 million bottles. While initially English wines were often thin and acidic, CLIMATE CHANGE has led to a revolution in the VINE varieties grown and in QUALITY IN WINE. This is especially true of the BOTTLE-FERMENTED sparkling wines which are increasingly being compared to champagne. English and Welsh wine is subject to EU winemaking regulations and is made strictly from freshly picked, UK-grown grapes (see BRITISH MADE WINE).

The revival of viticulture began in 1945 when Raymond Barrington Brock (Ray Brock) started what became the Oxted Viticultural Research Station, a privately funded experimental NURSERY where, over the next 25 years, Brock trialled 600 different vine varieties. Buoyed by the success of some of Brock's trials, the first commercial vineyard, all 0.4 ha/1 acre of it, was planted at Hambledon in Hampshire by Major-General Sir Guy Salisbury-Jones in March 1952.

More vineyards followed, slowly at first, but as wines were produced from these early vineyards, more pioneers took up the cause and by the mid-1960s there were over 40 vineyards spread across the south of England and Wales. The hot summer of 1976 provided the spur for many new growers to enter the industry and the area under vine rose to a high point of 1,065 ha (2,632 acres) in 1993, after which it declined as competition increased and consumer demand for the still wines then typically based on GERMAN CROSSES waned. This decline continued until 2003 heralded an era of much warmer summers, and considerable success in tastings and the marketplace of SPARKLING WINES made from the champagne varieties Chardonnay, Pinot Noir, and Pinot Meunier. Together they spurred a new wave of planting.

The biggest change in UK vineyards has been in the range of vine varieties grown. Varieties such as MÜLLER-THURGAU, REICHENSTEINER, MADELEINE × ANGEVINE 7672, HUXELREBE, SCHÖNBURGER, and BACCHUS, plus the French-American hybrid SEYVAL BLANC (which together accounted for 74% of the UK area under vine in 1980) have been widely replaced by Chardonnay and Pinot Noir, which were planted on about half of all English vineyard in 2014 and are almost exclusively used for sparkling wines. For still wines, Bacchus is by far the most widely grown variety. Red wine varieties, excluding Pinot Noir and Pinot Meunier, account for around 10% of plantings.

The majority of UK vineyards are situated in the warmer southern counties with almost 80% of the 537 officially recorded vineyards (of 0.10 ha or more) and the 131 wineries located in the south east, the south, and the south west. East Anglia accounts for a further 12% of vineyard. The best are in the traditional fruit-growing regions of the UK on sheltered sites below 100 m/330 ft above sea level. To many people's surprise, vineyards are planted in almost every county of England, and Yorkshire boasts around a dozen wine producers. However, the chances of achieving commercial viability lessen the further north a vineyard is situated, with YIELDS and quality in some of the more challenging regions considerably lower than in the prize-winning southern counties.

The main problems of growing grapes above LATITUDE 50° are those of achieving adequate yields and sufficient wine quality to generate the income required to finance the considerable investment needed to buy land and establish vineyards and wineries. Although much of the south of the UK and some of the western regions have a climate that is softened by the Gulf Stream, the MARITIME CLIMATE brings summer gales and high summer RAINFALL which can disrupt FLOWERING so that yields are dramatically reduced. In 2012, for example, spectacularly bad weather during pollination reduced

the total UK crop by about two-thirds, with some large producers picking not a single grape. Official average yields are very low, 20 hl/ha in the first decade of this century, but well-sited, well-managed vineyards can expect to average 50–60 hl/ha.

Harvesting usually takes place between the end of September and the end of October, depending on variety and region, but in 2013, the latest grape harvest ever recorded in the UK saw some growers still picking Chardonnay on 20 November. Natural MUST WEIGHTS tend to be low by global standards with most grapes achieving 7–9% POTENTIAL ALCOHOL, although with certain varieties and in warmer years, 11, 12, and even 13% have been recorded. Levels of natural acidity tend to be high, with PHS around 2.9 to 3.2 and TOTAL ACIDITY (as tartaric) between 8 and 15 g/l. Under EU winemaking regulations, CHAPTALIZATION is allowed by up to 3% every year, and 3.5% in 'abnormal' years. ACIDIFICATION is not permitted (nor often needed) except in sparkling wines post-DISGORGEMENT where 1 g/l may be added for STABILIZATION purposes (as in Champagne and other EU regions where sparkling wine is made).

The UK has its own APPELLATION system, set up under EU regulations with four distinct categories. Those qualifying as PDO are known as Quality Wines; PGI wines are called Regional Wines; Varietal Wines are WINES without geographical indication labelled varietally which have gone through a certification process; and the rest which carry neither grape variety not vintage and are labelled simply UK Wine.

England and Wales are increasingly recognized as legitimate wine-producing regions with wines regularly winning trophies and gold medals in UK and international wine COMPETITIONS. Where once the industry was populated by amateurs and retirees, today's modern vineyards are staffed by well-trained and experienced viticulturalists and winemakers, many trained at PLUMPTON. While many smaller vineyards rely on TOURISM and sales to local outlets, more and more UK wines are stocked by bigger retailers, and are to be found on quite smart wine lists. Some of the larger vineyards are even starting to export their wines. See also IRELAND.   S.S.

Skelton, S. P., *The UK Vineyards Guide 2010* (London, 2010).

Skelton, S. P., *Wine Growing in Great Britain* London, 2014).

www.englishwineproducers.co.uk

www.ukva.org.uk

English literature, wine in. References to specific wines in English literature are relatively common, and provide a useful record of FASHIONS in wine styles and the history of wine imports to the British Isles, from the time of Chaucer to the present day. Literary references to wine drinking are legion, presumably because it encouraged conversation, civilized, bawdy, or sometimes nonsensical. Generic 'wine' is mentioned too often to report, and more detailed and revealing references specifying wine type or provenance are scarce in English literature before the 17th century.

The first English writer to demonstrate a serious interest in wine was Geoffrey Chaucer (1345–1400), himself the son and grandson of a vintner. *The Canterbury Tales* are dotted with references to specific wines (see CONDADO DE HUELVA, for example). The Prologue details contemporary eating and drinking habits, while the 60-year-old knight in 'The Merchant's Tale' drank spiced wine in the form of 'ypocras, clarree, and vernage' (see VERNACCIA) for 'courage' in the bedchamber.

BORDEAUX was England's chief medieval wine supplier and it dominates wine references in the literature until long after Aquitaine was ceded to France. William Shakespeare's (1564–1616) 'good familiar creature' in *Othello* would undoubtedly have been bordeaux, although 'sherris SACK' was Falstaff's favoured drink in *1 Henry IV*, and Sir Toby Belch's call for 'a cup of CANARY' in *Twelfth Night* also demonstrates the increasing importance of Spanish wines. Shakespeare's contemporaries Robert Herrick, John Webster, and Burton certainly refer to wine, but only Robert Burton (1577–1640) mentions the evocative names of Alicant, Rumney, and Brown Bastard (respectively, wines from ALICANTE, sweet wines made in the Greek style, and a sweet blend from Portugal, presumably based on BASTARDO grapes).

Samuel Pepys's (1633–1703) life seems to have been a succession of drinks if his diary provides an accurate record, with references to TENT, Canary, Rhenish (wine from the RHINE), and English wine from vineyards around London (see ENGLAND). Pepys also famously provides the first reference to New French CLARETS, and in particular that of 'Ho Bryan' (HAUT-BRION). Pepys mentions champagne, as does the comic playwright Sir George Etherege (?1634–91), who qualifies the reference with 'sparkling'. These, together with a brief note from Dean Swift (1667–1745), are the earliest mentions of what must have been a very new product (see CHAMPAGNE, history). Edward Ravenscroft (*fl.* 1671–97), the relatively obscure author of a rollicking farce *The London Cuckolds* (1682), is very forthcoming, with sack and PORT mentioned almost as many times as pretty women. John Gay (1685–1732) even published in 1708 a rather indifferent poem entitled 'Wine' which mentions the mysterious drink 'Golorence'.

In the 18th century, the number of references to wine by English dramatists, novelists, and poets rises dramatically. R. B. Sheridan (1751–1816) insists about claret in *School for Scandal*

that 'women give headaches, this don't', and champagne appears more than once in his *Paris Sketchbook*. David Garrick (1716–79) provides one of the first mentions of burgundy in English: 'rich Burgundy with a ruby tint'. As today, however, opinions about the relative merits of various wine regions are divided. The observation of Tobias Smollett (1721–77) in his *Travels through France and Italy* that 'the Wine known as Burgundy is so weak and thin' is a useful indication of the general derision of any wine region other than Bordeaux.

Samuel Johnson (1709–84) and Parson Woodforde (1740–1803) both give disquieting insight into the prodigious quantity of food and drink which then customarily appeared at table. Boswell reports Johnson's observation that 'few people had intellectual resources sufficient to forgo the pleasures of wine. They could not otherwise contrive how to fill the interval between lunch and dinner.' And during travels in Germany, 'I drank too much Moselle, imagining it to be a mere diuretic.' The next day he 'was uneasy from the Moselle'. There is a disparaging reference to Florence wine which 'neither pleases the taste nor exhilarates the Spirits'.

Jane Austen (1775–1817) admits to some of her characters drinking wine, although only in appropriate quantities of course. Among very few references to specific wines, the treasured South African CONSTANTIA is considered a suitable restorative for a young lady in *Sense and Sensibility*. Keats refers to claret frequently in correspondence but his most famous vinous reference is in 'Ode to a Nightingale' ('O, for a draught of vintage!' etc.). George Crabbe (1754–1832), whose works illustrate his somewhat grim sense of humour, describes the sorts and conditions of men who drink various wines in 'Champagne the courtier drinks the spleen to chase, the Colonel Burgundy, Port His Grace . . .' Crabbe's approver Lord Byron (1788–1824) is entertaining on the subject of wine and DRUNKENNESS, and recommends 'hock and soda-water' as a hangover remedy. He also turned wines into verbs, as in 'We clareted and champagned till two' in a letter to Thomas Moore. In his *Don Juan* VI. 607–8, one of the most misquoted pieces of literature (often confused with Keats), Byron eventually declares, 'If Britain mourn her bleakness we can tell her, the very best of vineyards is the cellar', an admirable sentiment.

The 19th-century writers indicate the increasing range of wines imported to the British Isles, and the widening appreciation and understanding of them. In *Melincourt*, Thomas Love Peacock (1785–1866) describes wine as both 'a hierarchical and episcopal fluid' and 'the elixir of life', and further references appear in *Crotchet Castle*. Peacock was clearly a burgundy aficionado, daring to suggest that 'an aged

Burgundy runs an ageless Port'. George Meredith (1828–1909), who married the widowed daughter of Peacock, shares his interest in burgundy; precise references to Musigny and Romanée appear in *The Egoist* and *One of our Conquerors*. R. S. Surtees (1805–64), the master of comic fox-hunting novels, brings port, champagne, and 'tolerable St Julien doing duty for Ch Margaux' into such pieces as *Handley Cross* and *Mr Sponge's Sporting Tour*. He sagely advises against the excesses of the previous century, 'no side dishes, no liqueurs, only two or three wines'.

At a somewhat more elevated level, William Thackeray (1811–63) names Beaune and Chambertin and also refers to claret, sherry, and madeira, and comments, 'if there is to be Champagne have no stint of it . . . save on your hocks, sauternes, and moselles, which count for nothing'. This last quotation is from *Pendennis*, in which appears the character Captain Shandon, heavily based on William Maginn (1793–1842), who wrote under the pseudonym Sir Morgan O'Doherty, Bt. As a regular contributor to *Blackwoods Edinburgh Magazine* Maginn wrote many wonderful 'Maxims', many of which refer to or include wine and food: they are well worth searching out, as is the 'Spectator ab extra' of A. H. Clough (1819–61), an entire poem devoted to food and drink of which the first stanza has particular appeal for this writer:

> Pass the bottle and damn the expense
> I've heard it said by a man of sense
> That the labouring classes could scarce live a day
> If people like us didn't eat, drink and pay.

Henry James (1843–1916) is particularly descriptive about Burgundy and its vineyard in *A Little Tour of France*. Robert Louis Stevenson (1850–94) also enthuses over Burgundy in *Travels with a Donkey in the Cévennes*. His ill health led to frequent foreign journeys even as far afield as California: *The Silverado Squatters* is the first literary work to include reference to the vineyards there.

Other serious 19th century writers who regularly included comments on wine are Robert Browning (1812–89), who clearly enjoyed Chablis; Charles Dickens (1812–70), whose novels, as one might imagine, mention punch more often than wine; and, most amusingly, Saki, or H. H. Munro (1870–1916), who delights in his many comments on wines and the manners of those who serve it, such as 'the conscious air of defiance that a waiter adopts in announcing that the cheapest Claret on the list is no more'. Finally, Edward Fitzgerald (1809–83), the erudite translator of the 11th century ARAB POEM *The Rubáiyát of Omar Khayyám*, must be cited, as one particular passage has cut wine merchants to the quick ever since publication: 'I often wonder what the Vintners buy, one half so precious as the goods they sell.'

The 20th century sees further geographical extension of the wine regions mentioned in English literature, and a greater awareness of the variety and quality of the products available. Hilaire Belloc (1870–1953) wrote much in praise of all sorts of drink, notably 'Advice' full of vinous references, and his 'Heroic Poem in Praise of Wine', which expresses the sentiment, 'Dead Lucre: burnt Ambition: Wine is best'. The *Forsyte Saga* of John Galsworthy (1867–1933) abounds with references to hock, especially Steinberger. Aldous Huxley offers the somewhat jaded assessment that 'Champagne has the taste of an apple peeled with a steel knife', while Eric Newby in *Love and War in the Apennines* also paints a grim picture of the wine 'the Italians call *vini lavatori*'. But the balance is redressed by P. G. Wodehouse, whose characters' 'form' can often be restored by various vinous substances. Evelyn Waugh's diaries and letters inform us of his own serious wine-drinking habits, although only *Brideshead Revisited* among his works contains many specific wine references. He wrote a monograph *Wine in Peace and War* for wine merchants Saccone & Speed and was paid, according to his son Auberon, at the rate of a dozen bottles of champagne per thousand words. More recent novelists whose work displays a deep understanding of wine include Sybille Bedford, and Dick Francis, who in one of his novels treats good wine extensively. Wine is one of several alcoholic drinks to figure largely in Kingsley Amis's work.

Are spy stories literature? Ian Fleming's James Bond has rather common tastes in champagne, and more than once Fleming mentions a vintage of Taittinger or Dom Pérignon which was never made. This usefully illustrates the way in which wine, mentioned by authors throughout the history of literature, is used more for illustrative purposes than anything else. In ingested form, however, wine has probably offered writers more inspiration than opium, and their references to it have helped us better understand the chronology of importation and imbibing of wine through the ages. See also MEDIEVAL LITERATURE. H.G.B.

One wine-soaked novel I would like to have discussed with the late Bill Baker who wrote the article above is Paul Torday's successor to *Salmon Fishing in the Yemen*. The hero of *The Irresistible Inheritance of Wilberforce* drinks himself, knowledgeably, to death. J.R.

enologist is the American and South African spelling of OENOLOGIST, just as **enology** is the alternative spelling of OENOLOGY, the study of wine and, especially, winemaking.

enoteca, term used frequently in Italy for a wine shop with a significant range of high-quality wines, while quite a few still offer the local wine or wines as *vino sfuso*, or in BULK, which are poured straight from the cask into demijohns brought along by customers. It contrasts with a *bottiglieria*, a shop with a more pedestrian selection, and a *vineria*, run by a *vinaio*, more of a tavern, in which wine is sold by the glass as well as by the bottle. Various **enoteche** in Italy offer tasting facilities and some serve food to accompany the wines—from the mere appetite-stimulating to the most ambitious *haute cuisine*. The word comes from the same root as OENOTRIA, the Ancient Greeks' name for Italy, and *theke*, Greek for a case or receptacle.

Enotria, corruption of the Ancient Greek name for what is now Italy. See OENOTRIA.

enoturismo. See AGRITURISMO.

en primeur, wine trade term, French in origin, for wine sold as futures before being bottled. It comes from the word PRIMEUR. En primeur sales are a relatively recent speciality, but not exclusivity, of CLASSED GROWTHS by the BORDEAUX TRADE (see BORDEAUX, history). Cask SAMPLES of wines have customarily been shown in the spring following the vintage. Thousands of trade and media representatives descend on Bordeaux each spring for carefully organized programmes of tastings. Sales are solicited, through BROKERS and then NÉGOCIANTS, as soon as proprietors decide to announce their opening PRICE and market reaction is keenly monitored by interested parties. A particular property often releases only a certain proportion, or *tranche*, of its total production, depending on its need for cash and reading of the market.

This form of early sale has long been available to the wine trade, but was undertaken by wine consumers only from the late 20th century. It has been most popular in times of frenetic demand such as in the very early 1970s (when some wine was even sold *sur souche*, or on the vine before the grapes were picked) and since the 1980s, when a succession of good VINTAGES coincided with widespread economic prosperity and the accessibility of early VINTAGE ASSESSMENTS from the wine trade and press. The consumer pays the opening price as soon as the offer is made and then, up to two years later, having paid the additional shipping costs and DUTY, takes delivery of the wine after it has been bottled and shipped. The theory is that, by buying wine early, the consumer not only secures sought-after wines, he or she also pays less. This is by no means invariably the case, however, as outlined in INVESTMENT IN WINE.

En primeur purchases have many disadvantages in periods of economic recession. Not only may prices stagnate or even fall, but there is a much higher risk that one of the many commercial concerns in the chain between wine producer and wine consumer will fail, leaving the consumer with the possibility of having paid for the wine without any certainty of receiving it. There is also the important fact that en primeur purchases inevitably mean investing in an embryonic product. A third party's assessment of a single cask SAMPLE taken when it is just six months old is a poor justification for financial outlay on a liquid that is bottled only a year later (and is particularly hazardous for a wine as notoriously transient as red BURGUNDY), unless the wine market is extremely buoyant.

Buying en primeur may make financial sense only for the most unanimously lauded vintages and the most sought-after wines, and then only in a rising market, although it can of course give a great deal of pleasure to those with a strong wine-COLLECTING instinct.

en rama, literally 'raw', a condition of fino or manzanilla SHERRY whereby, unlike mass-market BRANDS, it is only very lightly clarified before being bottled and sold.

enrichment (*amélioration* in French, *Anreicherung* in German), winemaking operation whereby the fermentable sugars of grape juice or must are supplemented in order to increase the ALCOHOLIC STRENGTH of the resultant wine. This is traditionally and habitually done to compensate for natural underripeness in cool regions or after particularly cool summers in warmer regions. The original process, often generally called CHAPTALIZATION after its French promulgator CHAPTAL, involves adding sugar, whereas the wider term enrichment encompasses the addition of sugar, grape must, concentrated grape must, and rectified concentrated grape must, or RCGM, and is the term favoured in official EU terminology. According to a 2012 report, in Europe an average of 55 million hl (1,453 million gal) of wine are enriched every year, corresponding to 30% of total EU wine production; 27 million hl of wine are enriched using concentrated must or RCGM, and 28 million hl using sucrose, using 5 million hl of must and 90,000 tonnes of sucrose.

Enrichment is the winemaking counterpoint to ACIDIFICATION, which is the norm in hot wine regions. Most regions' wine regulations set limits for these processes and most of them, as in Bordeaux and Burgundy, for example, forbid the enrichment and acidification of the same batch of wine.

Geography

Enrichment is the norm in climates which cannot be relied upon to bring grapes to full ripeness every season: throughout northern Europe, for example, in the north-eastern wine regions of the UNITED STATES, throughout CANADA, BRAZIL, in JAPAN, and in much of NEW ZEALAND, especially for red wines.

At the coolest limits of vine cultivation it is a prerequisite of wine production. The poorest summers in ENGLAND, for example, yield grape sugar levels in some varieties that have difficulty reaching the legal minimum NATURAL ALCOHOL level of 5%. In regions as cool as England and Luxembourg, the so-called Zone A of the EU, musts may be enriched to a maximum increase in alcoholic strength of 3% (3.5% in particularly unripe years).

Winemakers in Europe's Zone C1, which includes Burgundy, for example, may enrich their musts by up to 1.5 %.

In Bordeaux, also in Zone C1, chaptalization has also been the norm historically but thanks to CLIMATE CHANGE, and the development of alternative techniques for juice CONCENTRATION, the practice of enrichment is becoming a choice rather than a necessity.

Enrichment is also much relied upon, especially for more commercial wines, in Eastern Europe, Switzerland, Austria, and Germany. Indeed the major distinction between Germany's better-quality wine classified as PRÄDIKATSWEIN and ordinary QBA wine was for long that Prädikatsweine could not be enriched by added sugar (although they could include SÜSSRESERVE of comparable ripeness added after fermentation for sweetening purposes). Similarly in AUSTRIA, sugar may not be added to wines of Kabinett quality or above. See PRÄDIKATSWEIN for the current situation.

In southern France, notably Languedoc-Roussillon, the southern Rhône, Provence, and Corsica, and throughout the rest of the south of the EU, chaptalization is expressly forbidden, but enrichment using concentrated must of various sorts is often permitted, and even encouraged, depending on the quality level of the wine and the characteristics of the VINTAGE. This sort of enrichment by adding concentrated must is commonplace in northern Italy, and has provided an end use for vast quantities of otherwise SURPLUS wine made in southern Italy (see Materials below).

Winemakers prohibited from practising enrichment tend to scorn the practice as artificial and manipulative (just as those in cooler regions, prohibited from adding acid, are wary of the practice of ACIDIFICATION).

There are wine regions, however, such as TASMANIA, the recently planted vineyards on the southern tip of SOUTH AFRICA, and even some of the higher vineyards of northern Italy, in which chaptalization is prohibited, to the detriment of wine quality in many seasons, simply because they belong to a political unit whose other wine regions are too hot to need it.

Materials

SUCROSE is the usual enrichment material used. In northern Europe this has normally been refined sugar beet, or occasionally cane sugar.

In an effort to help drain Europe's WINE LAKE, however, EU authorities tried to encourage the use of high-strength grape sugar syrups made from surplus wine, especially in Italy and southern France (see GRAPE CONCENTRATE and RECTIFIED GRAPE MUST for more details), but compulsory DISTILLATION and other market reforms have been more effective at reducing the SURPLUS. Enrichment using grape concentrate is also permitted in Australia, but sugar may be added only to induce the second fermentation for sparkling wines.

Adding grape concentrate rather than sugar, however, has the effect of diluting flavour, as those determined to make only the very best German wines are well aware.

Technique

The enrichment material may be added before and/or during FERMENTATION. Both sugar and acid tend to inhibit yeast growth, however. Adding the enriching sugar when fermentation is already fully under way avoids the delay which could ensue if it were added to the unfermented must. It is also favoured as a way of extending the fermentation by some winemakers, especially in Burgundy.

About 1.8 kg/4 lb of sugar is needed to raise the alcoholic strength of 1 hl of wine by 1% (slightly less for less dense white and rosé wine musts), which means that stacks of sugar sacks can be a regular sight in many large and not-so-large French wine cellars.

When conducted properly, enrichment increases the volume of the wine negligibly, has no tastable effect on the wine, and merely compensates for Nature's deficiencies in a particular growing season. Enriched wines certainly should not taste sweet, since all of the fermentable SUGARS should have been fermented into ALCOHOL; the wine should merely have more BODY and BALANCE than it would otherwise have done.

The non-winemaking observer may wonder, however, why in an age in which many consumers wish to curb their consumption of alcohol, and there is a global wine surplus, the wine industry systematically and deliberately increases the alcohol content of so many of its products, in many cases to compensate for overcropped vines (see YIELD).

In recent years, concentration techniques such as vacuum evaporation and REVERSE OSMOSIS have become popular ways to enrich musts by removing water. In many ways, these subtractive techniques may be less 'unnatural' and open to abuse than additive techniques such as chaptalization. See also MANIPULATION.

Entraygues–Le Fel, miniature AOC on the right bank of the upper Lot in SOUTH WEST FRANCE. Reds are based on FER grapes and the even rarer whites on Chenin Blanc, although many a local oddity is allowed in too.

Entre-Deux-Mers, large, pretty area of the BORDEAUX wine region between the Rivers DORDOGNE and GARONNE; hence a name which means 'between two seas'. A high proportion of the vineyard land in this pretty, green region (which has much in common with BERGERAC to its immediate east) produces light red, often slightly austere wine made from MERLOT and CABERNET grapes and sold as BORDEAUX AOC. Indeed, since vine-growers converted their white wine vineyards to red varieties in the 1960s and 1970s, the Entre-Deux-Mers district has become the chief source of red Bordeaux AC. The Entre-Deux-Mers region contains a number of other appellations, some of them enclaves such as GRAVES DE VAYRES, STE-FOY BORDEAUX, and Côtes de Bordeaux-St-Macaire. Haut-Benauge is another whose dry white wines have their own appellation, **Entre-Deux-Mers-Haut-Benauge**. The PREMIÈRES CÔTES DE BORDEAUX and its sweet white winemaking enclave lie between the Entre-Deux-Mers appellation and the river Garonne, in the same territory as produces red CADILLAC CÔTES DE BORDEAUX. Wines sold as Entre-Deux-Mers are dry whites made, with degrees of winemaking skill which vary from minimal to dazzling, mainly from SAUVIGNON BLANC together with SÉMILLON, MUSCADELLE, and SAUVIGNON GRIS grapes. After Bordeaux AC, this is the biggest dry white wine appellation in the Bordeaux region, on a vineyard area that had fallen to 1,325 ha/ 3,273 acres by 2012. Clay and sandy clay predominate although there are pockets of limestone, especially just across the Dordogne from St-Émilion. This is one of the few French wine districts to have adopted the LENZ MOSER system of high vine TRELLISING to any great extent. Most Entre-Deux-Mers should be drunk as young as possible. These dry whites are generally drunk young without great ceremony.

Matthews, T., *Village in the Vineyards* (New York, 1993).

enzymes, proteins present in all biological systems that act as catalysts by inducing or accelerating specific biochemical reactions. Enzymes, named using the suffix -'ase', are characterized by both the specificity of the chemical group or substrate they act on and the reaction which they catalyse. Endogenous enzymes are those that the organism itself produces whereas exogenous enzymes are those that are prepared commercially.

Endogenous enzyme activities of the vine are central to the biological processes by which grape berries develop and ripen. Wine is the enzymatic transformation or FERMENTATION of grape juice by thousands of endogenous enzymes originating from the grape juice, YEAST cells and other microbes.

Winemakers influence the outcome of these reactions (via PH, TEMPERATURE, SULFUR DIOXIDE levels, choice of yeast and bacteria) to produce specific wine styles.

As not all endogenous enzymes are efficient under winemaking conditions, since the 1970s winemakers have increasingly used exogenous enzymes to speed up or improve some processes. Enzyme research is active and the range of exogenous enzymes available is increasing. They are produced mainly from natural fungi, *Aspergillus niger* and Tricoderma species. Examples of these enzymes and their uses are described below.

Pectinases (polygalacturonase, pectin lyase, and pectin methyl esterase), also known as pectolitic enzymes, often in combination with cellulase and hemicellulase, are used to break down PECTINS in cell walls to enhance juice extraction in white wines (see PRESSING) and colour EXTRACTION in reds during fermentation. Pectinases also reduce juice viscosity and thereby accelerate CLARIFICATION by breaking down pectin molecules in the juice.

Glycosidases release AROMA compounds (especially in varieties high in TERPENES such as Muscat, Riesling, and Gewurztraminer) bound to sugars in an odourless GLYCOSIDE form thereby increasing the aromatic intensity of the wine. This process also occurs naturally but very slowly.

Glucanases are used to assist the development of TEXTURE in wines aged on yeast. The enzyme breaks down the cell walls releasing MANNOPROTEINS into the wine. Glucanases are also used in wines affected by BOTRYTIS BUNCH ROT, which can have high levels of glucans (polysaccharides of glucose) which make FILTRATION more difficult. Beta-glucanase breaks down these molecules, making the wine easier to filter.

Botrytis also produces the enzyme laccase, which promotes very rapid OXIDATION and browning of juice and young wine exposed to oxygen. At the end of fermentation, exposure to any oxygen has to be avoided until the combination of higher ALCOHOLIC STRENGTH, TANNINS, and added SULFUR DIOXIDE reduce the laccase activity, thereby making the wine stable to enzymatic oxidation. Alternatively, heat treatment of the wine can be used to inactivate (denature) the enzyme.

Lysozyme, an enzyme isolated from egg whites, attacks the cell walls of LACTIC ACID BACTERIA and is used to inhibit MALOLACTIC CONVERSION.   P.J.W. & T.J.

Lourens, K., and Pellerin, P., 'Enzymes in winemaking', www.wineland.co.za (Nov 2004).

épamprage, French term for DESUCKERING.

epicatechin. See CATECHIN.

Épineuil, red wine commune near AUXERRE whose name may be appended to that of BOURGOGNE.

éraflage, French term for DESTEMMING grapes.

Erbaluce, old but minor white wine grape speciality of Caluso in the north of the PIEMONTE region of north west Italy. Most dry Erbaluce is relatively light bodied and acidic. Erbaluce's most famous, if rare, manifestation is the golden sweet Caluso PASSITO. Total Italian plantings were 319 ha/788 acres in 2010.

erinose mite. The grapevine is the only known host in the plant kingdom to the grape erineum mite, *Colomerus vitis*, sometimes called grape leaf blister mite. The mite is widely distributed, but usually causes only minor damage in commercial vineyards. The damage first appears as pinkish or reddish swellings or galls on the upper surfaces of the leaves. Beneath the gall, the concave portion of the leaf is lined with a felty mass of plant hairs or 'erinea'. This is one of the most unsightly grape pest problems, yet it has negligible effects on vine performance. Control is usually by preventive applications of SULFUR dust, and, as this is often applied to control POWDERY MILDEW, these mites are often incidentally controlled.   M.J.E.

Ermitage, alternative and historic name for HERMITAGE in the northern Rhône. Occasional synonym for MARSANNE.

erosion. See SOIL EROSION.

Erste Lage, literally 'first [class] site', is an expression that has entered German and Austrian wine discourse in recent years with several distinctive meanings best explained in historical context. While Germany's VDP growers' association professed an ongoing interest in vineyard CLASSIFICATION from the 1980s, this was always in the context of delimiting a luxury or premium class of dry wines, for which the name ERSTES GEWÄCHS was long entertained. Following the RHEINGAU growers' 1999 success in gaining legal recognition by the state of Hessen for the designation Erstes Gewächs, the VDP nationally adopted the name GROSSES GEWÄCHS for an almost identically conceived category, applying it by implication to those vineyard sites classified as worthy of generating a wine so-designated. In 2003, the Mosel regional VDP, most of whose members placed emphasis on residually sweet Riesling, adopted 'Erste Lage' for wines from top-ranked sites that failed the test of legal dryness imposed on Grosse Gewächse. In 2006, the VDP adopted 'Erste Lage' as 'the unifying overarching concept in all regions for wines of the uppermost category', thus making Grosses Gewächs a name for legally dry (TROCKEN) wine from an Erste Lage. Inspired in part by the VDP's classification efforts, Austria's TRADITIONSWEINGÜTER ÖSTERREICH unveiled in 2010 their own classification in which the top vineyard category was also referred to as 'Erste Lage'

and signified on labels by a logo intentionally patterned after that utilized by the VDP, featuring a prominent Arabic number 1. (Neither 'Grosses Gewächs' nor 'Erste Lage' were or are recognized by German or Austrian wine law, and neither name is permitted on labels.)

In 2013, concerned that their use of Grosses and Erstes in reference to the same group of vineyards was confusing, and in an attempt to institute a category of what are in effect PREMIER CRU vineyards to accompany the grand cru Grosse Gewächse, the VDP revised its terminology. Henceforth, any vineyard deemed capable of supporting a Grosses Gewächs is officially known within the VDP as a GROSSE LAGE, whereas Erste Lage now refers to a new classificatory tier of vineyards that each regional VDP is at liberty to generate. By 2014 most regional branches had drawn up such a list of Erste Lagen or were in the process of doing so. Four regions—AHR, MOSEL, NAHE, and RHEINHESSEN—however, indicated their intention to eschew this additional classificatory level. Austria's Traditionsweingüter have signalled no interest in changing the name of their uppermost classification tier to reflect new VDP nomenclature.   D.S.

Erstes Gewächs, designates dry wines from a limited number of ostensibly top sites in the RHEINGAU and HESSISCHE BERGSTRASSE. Quality-conscious Rheingau growers introduced this term in the 1990s to refer to their top dry wines from classic grape varieties, which they then bottled with the same double Romanesque arch insignia as used for CHARTA bottlings. Their lobbying resulted in the 1999 recognition of this category by the German state of Hessen and in its being permitted on labels. Given this protection of 'Erstes Gewächs' under the laws of a single state, the VDP growers' association elected to promote the term GROSSES GEWÄCHS, utilizing it in a very similar way, albeit without any state or national legal recognition. In 2013 it was agreed within the VDP that, to avoid confusion about the association's prestige category of dry wine, its Rheingau members would henceforth replace the designation 'Erstes Gewächs' with 'Grosses Gewächs' (signified on bottles by a logo and the initials 'GG'), which also meant adopting the stricter limits on RESIDUAL SUGAR that defined the latter. Rheingau growers who are not members of the VDP continue to use the legally protected term Erstes Gewächs.   D.S.

erythorbic acid, alternative antioxidant to ASCORBIC ACID.

Erzeugerabfüllung, German word meaning 'producer bottling', applicable to all the finest wines of Germany. As in France (see MIS EN BOUTEILLE), the term may be used by CO-OPERATIVES to describe blends of wines from many different member-producers over whose viticultural techniques the bottler may or may not exercise significant control. The terms GUT-SABFÜLLUNG and Schlossabfüllung are officially defined in slightly more restrictive terms and are nowadays seldom used.　　　　　D.S.

esca, fungal disease believed to be as old as vine cultivation. Although it occurs in most of the world's wine regions, it is most severe in vineyards located in warmer and drier MEDITER-RANEAN CLIMATES, for example, in France, Italy, Portugal, Spain, and California. A disease affecting older vines (more than ten years old), it is characterized by white rot and apoplexy (sudden death) and is considered to be a complex of diseases that start with cuttings used in PROPA-GATION (see TRUNK DISEASES). The Greek word *yska* signified both rotten grape wood and the spongy Basidiomycete fungal bodies.

Shoot tip and tendril dieback is the earliest symptom, observed in mid spring, followed later in the season by tiger-striping of the leaves, which eventually turn reddish. A third symptom, grey- to dark-brown speckling on the berry skin (hence the name 'black measles') is economically worse for table-grape growers than for wine-growers. The last symptom, apoplexy, is characterized by a sudden wilting of the vine, including shrivelling of the fruit and fallen leaves. Vines affected by apoplexy may appear completely healthy the following season. Internal wood symptoms include light- to dark-brown and black streaking similar to that observed in vines with PETRI DISEASE. In older vines, a white rot characterized by a yellowish spongy mass of wood can be observed in the centre of the trunk and/or cordons.

The fungi *Phaeomoniella chlamydospora* and *Togninia minima* are known to be the main pathogens associated with esca. However, up to 24 other species of *Phaeoacremonium* and several *Cadophora* species have been reported to occur in vines showing symptoms of esca. Additionally, several species in the genera *Fomitiporia, Fomitioporella, Inonotus, Inocutis,* and *Phellinus* are regarded as the causal agents of the white rot.

Although there is currently no cure for the esca complex, research has shown that stress avoidance and the protection of pruning wounds using registered FUNGICIDES can significantly reduce the incidence and severity of the disease. ORGANIC and BIODYNAMIC growers are also trialling biological controls that incorporate various strains of the non-pathogenic Trichoderma fungus to combat esca and other fungal diseases including BOTRYTIS BUNCH ROT.　　　　　L.T.M. & J.R.U.-T.

Current research can be found at http://www.icgtd.org.

Gubler, W. D., et al., 'Esca (black measles) and Petri disease', in L. J. Bettiga (ed.), *Grape Pest Management* (3rd edn, Oakland, Calif., 2013), 120–5.

Mugnai, L., Graniti, A., and Surico, G., 'Esca (black measles) and brown wood-streaking: two old and elusive diseases of grapevines', *Plant Disease*, 83 (1999), 404–16.

Esgana Cão, synonyms for the Portuguese white grape variety known on the Island of Madeira as SERCIAL. Its full name on the mainland means 'dog strangler', presumably a reference to its notably high acidity. It can, occasionally, be found as an ingredient in VINHO VERDE and BUCELAS.

Espadeiro, minor grape variety producing mainly crisp pink wines on 333 ha/823 acres in Portugal's VINHO VERDE country. It can produce quite heavily and rarely reaches high sugar levels.

espalier, a relatively unusual TRAINING SYS-TEM, more desirable for aesthetic than commercial reasons, for vines or other fruit trees, by which the plant is trained to grow in a single plane to form a flat shape, for example against a wall (see diagram below). Espalier training leaves a trunk and one or two arms with several canes which are trained in the same plane with a trellis or wire for support. Different vines are trained to different heights in the French Espalier de Thoméry.　　　　　R.E.S.

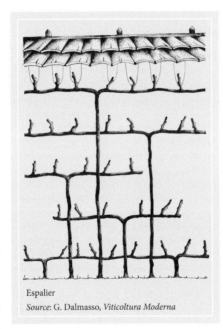

Espalier

Source: G. Dalmasso, *Viticoltura Moderna*

espumoso, Spanish for sparkling. TRADITIONAL METHOD Spanish sparkling wine that is exported is most often labelled CAVA.

Esquitxagos, misleadingly interesting synonym for VALENCIA's bland white wine grape MERSEGUERA.

Estaing, miniature AOC on the left bank of the Lot in the Aveyron *département* in SOUTH WEST FRANCE. Reds are based on FER and Gamay grapes and the even rarer whites on Chenin Blanc, although the Cabernets and many a local oddity are allowed in too. The climate here makes MARCILLAC downstream look positively balmy.

estate bottled, term used on labels which has a very specific meaning in the United States, where an estate-bottled wine must come from the winery's own vineyards or those on which the winery has a long lease; both vineyards and winery must be in the geographical area specified on the label. This is the American counterpart of CHÂTEAU BOTTLED or DOMAINE BOTTLED.

estate wine, term in common parlance, but not in federal law, in the US that suggests loosely that the wine came entirely from grapes farmed on the winery's own property. 'Estate wine' may be casually construed conversationally to be exactly synonymous with ESTATE BOTTLED, which has legal status, but technically it is not.

In South Africa 'estate wine' is a specific term for a wine that was grown, made, and bottled on a single geographical unit registered with the Wine and Spirit Board. Many German producers refer to their most basic bottling of Riesling as their Estate Riesling, Gutsriesling in German.

esters, compounds formed by reaction of ACIDS with ALCOHOLS. The two most common forms of esters in wine are FERMENTATION esters, commonly found in the aroma of young white wine, and esters that are chemically formed during AGEING.

The fresh, fruity aroma of young wines derives in large part from the presence of the mixture of esters produced during fermentation, which is why it is usually called fermentation AROMA. The precise nature of esters formed during fermentation is strongly influenced by the fermentation temperature, as well as the YEAST strain and other factors. For more details, see TEMPERATURE.

Since wines contain much more ETHANOL than any other alcohol, and since the most common ester-forming volatile organic acid is ACETIC ACID, it is not surprising that the most common ester in wine is ETHYL ACETATE, but many more combinations are possible from among the acids and alcohols present, and help to explain why wines differ so greatly in their aroma and, after years in bottle, BOUQUET. (See also ISOAMYL ACETATE.)

A number of esters that do not have a particularly marked odour are also present in wines. Among these are those resulting from reaction of the ethyl alcohol produced by fermentation with TARTARIC, MALIC, SUCCINIC, and other acids of the grape and wine, and such a process lowers the acidity and can mellow a wine.

When an acid reacts with an alcohol, water is produced in addition to the ester. This reaction is assisted or catalysed by the hydrogen ion, a substance plentiful in acid (low PH) solutions such as wines. Hydrogen ions not only catalyse the formation of esters from acids and alcohols, they also function as catalysts for the splitting of esters into their acid and alcohol segments. The result of these two tendencies, formation and splitting, is that wines contain mixtures of the four participants in the reactions: organic acids, alcohols, the several esters from the possible combinations, and water. The relative amounts of the four participants in the two reactions is governed by their concentrations and the reaction rates for formation and splitting. Given enough time, a state will be reached in which the net formation of esters just balances the splitting of them. This is known as the equilibrium state. In practice, the equilibrium state in wines is not reached but merely approached, because the formation rates for some esters are extremely slow under wine storage conditions.

The fact that esters are formed at different rates, some of them reaching equilibrium only after decades, helps to explain the changes in wine aroma and bouquet during ageing.   A.D.W. & P.J.W.

Margalit, Y., *Concepts in Wine Chemistry* (San Francisco, 3rd edn, 2012).

Estremadura, old name for the DOP known since 2009 as LISBOA.

estufa, Portuguese word meaning 'hothouse' or 'stove', also applied to the tanks used to heat wine on the Island of MADEIRA, thereby accelerating its development and maturation. The heating process Itself is called **estufagem**. *Estufas* simulate the effects of the long tropical sea voyages in the 18th and 19th centuries when madeira (and SETÚBAL) was, at first accidentally and then deliberately, stowed in the hold of a ship to age prematurely as a result of the temperature changes involved in a round trip, or *torna viagem*, across the tropics.   R.J.M.

ethanal, synonym for ACETALDEHYDE.

ethanol, common name for ethyl alcohol, the most potable of the ALCOHOLS and an important, intoxicating constituent of wine and all other alcoholic drinks. Ethanol, often called simply 'alcohol', is colourless and odourless but can have considerable impact on how a liquid tastes.

Ethanol is the most potent component of wine (and the most obvious of those that distinguish it from GRAPE JUICE), but it is probably the least discussed by wine consumers (unless in the context of HANGOVERS). For although ethanol does not have a taste, it has an effect, not just on the human nervous system, but on how a wine tastes. The ethanol content in a perfectly

BALANCED wine should be unfathomable, but wines that are slightly too high in alcohol can have a hot aftertaste.

Wines relatively high in ethanol—over 13.5%, for example (see ALCOHOLIC STRENGTH)—can taste sweet even if they contain practically no RESIDUAL SUGAR. Wines whose ethanol level robs them of their BALANCE may 'burn' or taste 'hot', especially in the aftertaste. Ethanol contributes to VISCOSITY and some argue that wines described as full bodied, or having considerable BODY, are high in ethanol while wines that are low in viscosity and body are low in ethanol. However, this is an oversimplification because many different compounds contribute to a wine's body and MOUTH-FEEL. Ethanol may also play a role in wine conservation since low-alcohol wines may be prey to BACTERIAL attack. See ALCOHOLIC STRENGTH for ways in which the ethanol level may be manipulated.

Ethanol is produced in two ways, the most traditional and natural of which is by the fermentation by YEAST of solutions that contain SUGARS, such as that involved in wine production. It is required in huge volumes by industry, however, as a solvent for perfumes and as a raw material for the synthesis of products such as drugs, plastics, lacquers, polishes, plasticizers, and cosmetics. Most of the ethanol used by industry, other than that produced by distilling the European wine SURPLUS, is produced in factories by hydrating ethylene, a component of petroleum.

See ALCOHOLIC STRENGTH for the varied concentrations of ethanol to be found in different wines, HEALTH for the effects of alcohol consumption in the form of wine, and REDUCED-ALCOHOL WINES.   A.D.W.

Ethiopia in north-east AFRICA can produce quite respectable red wine and some white from vines grown at relatively high ELEVATIONS. The Awash winery in Addis Ababa, based on vineyards established by the Italian troops who occupied part of the country from 1936 to 1941, has been joined by a CASTEL project with 162 ha/400 acres of vines planted between 2007 and 2009 near Ziway, 160 km/100 miles south of the capital. It sells INTERNATIONAL VARIETALS under the brand names Rift Valley and Acacia from vineyards surrounded by a wide trench designed to deter pythons, hippopotamuses, and hyenas.

www.theguardian.com/world/2014/jul/23/first-bottles-ethiopian-wine-castel

ethyl acetate, the most common ESTER in wine, and a natural organic compound present in most fruits, berries, other foods, and alcoholic drinks. Ethyl acetate is present in much higher concentrations than any other ester because it is formed by the reaction of the most common volatile organic acid in young wine, ACETIC ACID, with the most common alcohol produced by FERMENTATION, ETHANOL.

The perception threshold of ethyl acetate is generally about 120 mg/l, and a moderate concentration is unlikely to be perceived. At higher concentrations, however, it can become unacceptably dominant and increasingly impart the character described as VOLATILE and, eventually, vinegary.

Wines exposed to oxygen first lose their fresh fruitiness and become vapid in smell and taste because of the ACETALDEHYDE resulting from the oxidation of ethanol. The OXIDATION goes further to yield acetic acid from the acetaldehyde intermediate and then, when some of this acetic acid reacts with ethanol, ethyl acetate is produced. By the time this stage is reached, the wine is no longer wine but wine vinegar, which combines the sharp, acid taste of acetic acid with the odour of ethyl acetate.   A.D.W.

ethyl alcohol, scientific name for ETHANOL, the alcohol most commonly encountered in wine and other alcoholic drinks.

ethylphenol. See BRETTANOMYCES.

Étoile, L'. See L'ÉTOILE.

Étraire de l'Adui, or Étraire de la Duï, is a historic and increasingly rare vine grown before PHYLLOXERA on the fringes of the south east Rhône valley and Savoie. Related to PERSAN.

Etruscans. The origins of viticulture in TUSCANY are as problematic as the origins of the Etruscan peoples who flourished in central north Italy from the 8th century BC until being absorbed by the Romans from the 3rd century onwards. However, at its height, Etruscan society was heavily influenced by the culture of the Greek colonies of southern Italy. They imported fine Greek pottery for use in the SYMPOSIUM and made their own copies. The dinner and drinking party was a favourite theme in the lavish paintings which adorned their tombs. Indeed, the Etruscans became a byword among Greek and Roman moralists for luxurious living and eccentric customs, such as allowing wives to participate in banquets. There are literary references to Etruscan wine from the late 3rd century BC, but much earlier, from the late 7th century, the wine was exported in a distinctive type of AMPHORA well beyond Italy to southern France. Various wines are attested throughout the region in the classical period, although none was universally recognized as of the highest class. See ORIGINS OF VINICULTURE.   J.J.P.

Bouloumie, B., 'Le Vin etrusque', *Quaderni della scuola di specializzazione in viticoltura e enologia* (Turin), 7 (1983), 165–88.

Cerchiai, C., *L'alimentazione nel mondo antico: gli Etruschi* (Rome, 1987).

Heurgon, J., *Daily Life of the Etruscans* (London, 1964).

EU stands for European Union, previously known as the **European Community**, a group of 28 advanced Western industrialized countries co-operating on both economic and political fronts. Twenty-four of the 28 members produce wine (of which seven only in marginal quantities), making the Union the world's leading wine economy, producing around 175 million hl/4,623 million gal every year, and accounting for 45% of the world's wine-growing areas, 65% of production, 57% of global consumption, and 70% of exports.

The area under vine in the EU stood at 3.48 million ha/8.6 million acres in 2013, down from almost 4 million ha in 1987. This represents nearly 47% of the total global vineyard area (these OIV statistics include vines used to produce DRYING GRAPES and TABLE GRAPES, and these two categories represent a higher proportion of total vineyard area in Asia than in Europe). According to official EU data, of the 3.2 million ha of vines planted for wine production in the EU, over 2 million ha produce grapes for PDO wines, almost 0.7 million ha for PGI wines, and nearly 0.5 million ha for WINE WITHOUT GEOGRAPHICAL INDICATION. Spain has the most extensive area under vines in Europe (958,000 ha planted for wine), and indeed the world, although Italy produces more wine than Spain, which used to have the lowest-yielding vines in the EU (see SPAIN for how this has changed).

The EU wine-producing countries are, in descending order of average wine production: Italy, France, Spain, Germany, Portugal, Romania, Greece, Hungary, Austria, Croatia, Bulgaria, Slovenia, Czech Republic, Slovakia, Luxembourg, Cyprus, Malta, the United Kingdom, and Belgium. (DENMARK, the NETHERLANDS, POLAND, IRELAND, and SWEDEN also produce a small amount of wine.) In 2012–13, total EU production of wine was around 152 million hl/4,015 million gal (world production in 2012–13 was approximately 277 million hl, according to OIV statistics). Official figures for YIELDS in EU wine-producing countries averaged 47 hl/ha (2.69 tons/acre) in 2012–13. Germany, Italy, and Luxembourg reported the highest yields in 2012–13 (88 hl/ha, 71 hl/ha, and 66 hl/ha respectively), and Cyprus, Slovakia, and Romania the lowest (13 hl/ha, 17 hl/ha, and 20 hl/ha respectively, but as with all such collated data, national reporting is often inaccurate).

Although the EU includes some of the most industrialized nations of the world, it is in Europe that wine production is of greatest social and economic importance. Wine accounted for 3.9% of the EU's agricultural production by value in 2010–11. In France, the proportion was 13.4%, 8.8% in Austria, 3.9% in Italy, 2.6% in Spain, and 5.8% in Portugal.

The EU is an important net exporter of wine, and the trade was worth 8.1 billion euros in 2011, representing 22.8 million hl, over 14% of production. The EU's imports from outside the Union were 13.6 million hl in 2011, worth 2.4 billion euros. In 2011, the four top exporters to the EU were Australia, Chile, South Africa, and the United States, representing almost 85% of wine imports from outside the EU. Wine imported into the EU, known as 'third country wine', must conform to European wine law and may not be blended with wine made within the EU.

According to OIV figures, the EU's citizens drank an estimated 120 million hl of wine in 2010 (at that time only 16 member states), just over 23 l per inhabitant, considerably more than the world average for consumer countries. Between 1995 and 2010 consumption fell by about 8 million hl, most noticeably since 2008.

The EU wine sector is subject to an overarching regulatory framework called the 'common market organization' (CMO), which is part of Europe's common agricultural policy (CAP). The wine CMO includes rules on the free movement of wine between member states, winemaking practices, and labelling and trade with 'third countries' outside the common market. Its defining feature, until 2008, was the segregation of the wine sector into QUALITY WINE, which was regulated to manage 'quality', and TABLE WINE, which was granted subsidies to control production and the market. This essentially political and cultural divide was imported from France's wine law, reflecting that country's efforts to manage production in the poorer Midi while protecting the more privileged producers of well-known wine regions.

From the very first wine CMO in 1970, it was evident that accommodating the more liberal rules (and cheaper wines) that existed in Italy and the stricter regime prevailing in France within a single market would be a significant challenge. Blockades and violent protests through the 1970s and early 1980s, fuelled by rampant overproduction of table wine and nationalistic sentiment, testified to the difficulty of the task. The accession of Spain, Portugal, and Greece in the mid 1980s multiplied the complexity of the problems.

The wine CMO went through several iterations over the years, resulting in a proliferation of subsidies and controls, such as DISTILLATION, GRUBBING UP of vines, PLANTING RIGHTS, and price supports, ostensibly intended to bring supply and demand in the wine sector into balance. These largely failed because policymakers were torn between maintaining the incomes of the poorer table wine producers and realigning the wine sector with the demands of the modern wine market. Usually the political imperative to prop up the table wine producers won out, resulting in a ballooning budget.

By the mid 2000s, a rethink of the wine CMO had become essential and politically achievable. The sharp decline of traditional table wine, soaring production of wines with a geographical indication, the accession of new EU member states, budget constraints, and competition from the NEW WORLD were all factors.

The reform introduced in 2008 took the radical step of dissolving the quality wine and table wine categories. In their place a new hierarchy was created: protected denominations of origin (PDOs—covering AOC, DOC, DO, etc.); Protected Geographical Indications (or PGIs—covering VIN DE PAYS, IGT, Landwein, Vino de la Tierra, etc.); and WINES WITHOUT GEOGRAPHICAL INDICATION. The last were granted permission to use grape variety names on the label, thereby allowing the creation of a new class of VARIETAL wines. Each member state has its own precise terminology based on these overarching categories. The new hierarchy brought wine into alignment with the PDO/PGI system for other foods in the EU.

A revised set of support measures was made available to all categories of wine (not just wines without geographical indication), with a total budget of around 1.2 billion euros per year. In the first years of the reform, a key focus of support measures was, as before, to balance supply and demand, with grubbing up measures contributing to a reduction in the total EU vineyard of 370,000 ha (10%), an exercise considerably more successful in some countries than others. Winemaking rules were linked to OIV recommendations as a means of benchmarking them internationally. Labelling was also simplified and liberalized to some extent. Whether or not these changes will be sufficient to align EU wine production with the contemporary wine market remains to be seen.

Alongside the wine CMO, the EU has negotiated a series of agreements with several non-EU wine-producing countries, including Australia (1998, 2008), Canada (2003), Chile (2002), South Africa (2002), Switzerland (2002), and the USA (1984, 2005). These agreements cover concerns such as reciprocal arrangements regarding oenological practices, the reciprocal protection and control of wine denominations (which in some cases implies the phasing out of GENERICS), trade facilitation, dispute-resolution procedures, and in some cases tariff quotas. On the EU side, these agreements form a key part of a long-term strategy to secure protection for their GEOGRAPHICAL INDICATIONS, while for non-EU countries the incentive has been to improve their ability to compete in the EU market.

The thorny issue of planting rights was still unresolved in 2014.   J.B. & J.E.H.

Commission Regulation (EC) No. 606/2009, *Official Journal of the European Union*: this document outlines the EU regulations on oenological practices.
European Court of Auditors, *The Reform of the Common Organisation of the Market in Wine: Progress to Date* (Brussels, 2012).

European Union Directorate General for Agriculture and Rural Development, *Agriculture in the European Union: Statistical and Economic Information Report 2012* (Brussels, 2012). http://ec.europa.eu/agriculture/markets/wine/facts/index_en.htm.

eucalyptus character refers to an aroma and flavour found in red wine, most commonly but not exclusively in Australia and California and also in Chile, described variously as 'eucalypt', 'camphor', or 'minty'. For some winemakers this characteristic is a selling point whereas others prefer to avoid it, or at least to limit its presence as far as possible. In 2010 the AUSTRALIAN WINE RESEARCH INSTITUTE (AWRI) assessed consumer response to eucalypt flavour in red wines and found that even at very low levels, most consumers reacted to the flavour, and more consumers preferred wines with the 'minty' flavour than disliked it.

Most species of Eucalyptus, which are native to Australia but are now grown on every continent, contain essential oils in their leaves and, depending on the species, the main component of the oil is a volatile compound called 1,8-cineole, commonly known as eucalyptol. It is present in a wide range of foods, beverages, and therapeutic products. Research on California Merlot has determined that 1,8-cineole can be perceived even in very low concentrations such as 1.1 µg/l and can be recognized at 3.2 µg/l.

While the compound may be found in wines made from grapes grown with no Eucalyptus trees nearby, research has indicated that Eucalyptus trees growing close to vineyards are the primary source of the flavour in wine and that only negligible levels found in wine are from grape-derived FLAVOUR PRECURSORS.

In one study, grapes harvested from rows further than 25 m (80 ft) from Eucalyptus trees gave wines with very low levels of 1,8-cineole while those grown closer to the Eucalyptus trees contained significantly higher amounts. The compound is at its highest levels in the skin of the grape berry, and is extracted during fermentation on skins. While the absorption of the compound by grape berries is important, it is much less a factor than the presence of Eucalyptus leaves or bark in harvested grapes. Machine harvesting of rows close to Eucalyptus trees will, more than likely, produce bins of grapes containing numerous Eucalyptus leaves, and these have a very significant effect on eventual levels of 1,8-cineole in wine. Even during hand harvesting, Eucalyptus leaves can be trapped within the grape bunches. The key to managing 1,8-cineole levels in wine is therefore to control the amount of MOG (material other than grapes). M.P.K. & D.L.C.

Capone, D. L., Jeffery, D. W., and Sefton, M. A., 'Vineyard and fermentation studies to elucidate the origin of 1,8-cineole in Australian red wine', *Journal of Agricultural and Food Chemistry*, 60 (2012), 2281–7.

Capone, D. L., et al., 'Evolution and occurrence of 1,8-cineole (Eucalyptol) in Australian Wine', *Journal of Agricultural and Food Chemistry*, 59 (2011) 953–9.

Farina, L., et al., 'Terpene compounds as possible precursors of 1,8-cineole in red grapes and wines', *Journal of Agricultural and Food Chemistry*, 53 (2005) 1633–6.

Herve, E., Price, S., and Burns, G., 'Eucalyptol in wines showing a "eucalyptus" aroma', in A. Lonvaud, G. De Revel, and P. Darriet (eds.), *Actualités Oenologiques: VIIème Symposium International d'Oenologie, Bordeaux* (Paris, 2003) 598–600.

Eucharist, wine in the. The significance of wine in the Christian sacrament of Eucharist derives from the meanings of wine in the BIBLE and from the purposes of a variety of religious rituals. God's generous love of his people is symbolized by his gift of 'the fermented blood of the grape for drink' (Deut. 32. 14). The contrast of old wine and new wine is often used, new wine bursting its container, a proof of exuberance.

In Jewish sacrifices, wine to signify wellbeing and abundance, and animal blood to signify life itself, were both offered by being poured out as a libation, and so given back to God, in acts of thanksgiving, worship, and atonement for sin. Neither was consumed by the participants. In the celebration of the annual Passover supper, wine was drunk in joyful commemoration of the deliverance (redemption) by God of the whole people from enslavement to the Egyptians.

On the dark side, red wine is often compared with bloodshed. Contact with blood could be a defilement. Lapses into pagan ritual sacrifices involving human blood earned God's particular condemnation. Drinking from a cup and especially drinking it to the dregs was an expression indicating deep suffering rather than rejoicing, and the CRUSHING of grapes in the wine PRESS was a metaphor for the punishment of God. When Christ in spiritual agony in the garden of Gethsemane, anticipating his betrayal and death, prays for 'this cup' to be taken away from him (Matt. 26. 39–42), there is an echo of Isaiah's 'the stupefying cup', the cup of God's wrath (Isa. 51. 22), and Ezekiel's 'cup of affliction and devastation' that has to be drunk (Ezek. 23. 33).

In the light of this tradition, the words of Christ to his disciples would have been mysterious, even scandalous, yet evocative: 'If you do not eat the flesh of the Son of Man and drink his blood you have no life in you ... for my flesh is real food and my blood is real drink. Whoever eats my flesh and drinks my blood lives in me and I live in that person' (John 6. 53–6). At his last supper before his crucifixion, Christ takes the cup and says, 'Drink from this all of you, for this is my blood, the blood of the new covenant poured out for many for the forgiveness of sins' (Matt. 26. 28). It was wine, so it should have been for rejoicing, but drinking from a cup could have the connotations of the cup of suffering, and as for drinking blood, that would be an inconceivable abomination. Yet his next words, 'From now on ... I shall never again drink wine until the day I drink the new wine with you in the kingdom of my father' (Matt. 26. 29), suggest his joyful renewed presence with his followers at the messianic banquet that the Old Testament prophet Isaiah described when in the last times God would make for his people a feast of good things, including wine (Isa. 25. 6). Finally Christ commands his Church do this in memory of him.

So, the Eucharist of the risen Christ becomes the principal act of Christian faithfulness. In it the participants share in the redemptive death and resurrection of Christ through sacramental communion with his body and blood, signified by consuming consecrated bread and wine. By his blood shed on the cross the Eucharist has power to give peace and unity and continuously makes the Church into a unified, living body. It is called eucharist or thanksgiving since, at his last supper with his disciples, Christ pronounced over the wine (and bread) the traditional thanksgiving to God when he inaugurated a new covenant between God and his people in his own blood to be poured out in the sacrifice of the cross. Wine, in particular, would recall the blood shed by Christ whom some contemporaries greeted as the Lamb of God.

Controversy

Rites intended for unity tend paradoxically to be the focus of disunity, and the Eucharist is no exception. The eucharistic wine challenges the Old Testament tradition from which it originates. For the Jews, blood shed in animal sacrifice reconciled God and humans—it made atonement, literally, putting man and God 'at one'. Christ puts his own death in the place of that of the sacrificial animal. The Christian doctrine of drinking wine that has (sacramentally) become blood, even the blood of Christ the son of God, would be rejected as scandalous by Jews. Conversely, the Christian sacrifice of bread and wine in the Eucharist is a rejection of the shedding of blood in animal sacrifice.

After the Reformation, seemingly irreconcilable views about the Eucharist separated Protestants and Roman Catholics, notably about the exact meaning of the Eucharist as a 'memorial' of Christ's death and as a sacrifice, and about the sense in which the wine (and bread) become the body and blood of Christ. After the disputes of the Reformation there are now welcome signs of a reconvergence of views in which the emphasis is placed on the real presence of Christ in the Eucharist as a sacramental sign of his redemptive death.

A lesser controversy concerns receiving communion in the form of both bread and wine. In the course of centuries the Church had developed the practice of allowing the laity to take communion only under the form of bread, reserving communion under both species for the celebrant. The Church maintained that, since Christ is fully present under both species, this was only a matter of Church discipline and practical convenience—problems of hygiene with the cup and so on. All the great Reformers—Wyclif, John Huss, Luther, Calvin—campaigned for the restoration of communion wine for the laity, wishing to reduce the distinction between the celebrant and the congregation, and this has become universal in the Reformed tradition. In the 1960s, the Second Vatican Council allowed, subject to the local bishop's permission, communion under both kinds for the Catholic laity.

Sacramental signs are supposed to be 'natural', that is, unmistakable and able to be specified unambiguously. So the sacramental wine has to be fermented juice of the grape: it should not be turned to VINEGAR, nor heavily diluted with water; it must be real wine. But tradition fixes what the sacramental signs are and tradition varies. The fermented juice of the grape is what has always been meant by 'wine' in those parts of the world where Christianity arose. However, in spreading over the globe, Christianity encounters regions where the grapevine has never grown and where there never has been wine of the grape. The question arises in the world of MISSIONARIES whether the tradition could be modified to include rice 'wine', for example, or palm 'wine'.

There are other pastoral issues for sacramental wine. Christian missions among the urban poor in the 19th century were sensitive to the dangers of alcoholism. Was it right to put temptation in people's way? Was it even right to accord high ritual status to alcohol? John Wesley, the father of the Methodist tradition, took it for granted that the Eucharist should be celebrated with wine. In the second half of the 19th century, the alternative of celebrating with grape juice ('unfermented wine') gradually became common in the Methodist Church, under the influence of 'temperance' movements in both Britain and the United States.

A similar question was raised in relation to alcoholic priests in the Catholic Church. In 1974, bishops were authorized to grant to priests who had been treated for alcoholism permission to drink the unfermented juice of the grape instead of wine at the Eucharist. This authorization was revoked in 1983: in the Roman Catholic Church the symbolism of wine is recognized to be so central that even alcoholic priests are not now dispensed from taking at least a trace of wine when celebrating the Eucharist (by 'intinction', dipping the bread in the consecrated wine).

See also RELIGION and MONKS AND MONASTERIES.

J. & M.D.

Albert, J.-P., 'Le Vin sans ivresse: remarques sur la liturgie eucharistique', in D. Fournier and S. d'Onofrio (eds.), *Le Ferment divin* (Paris, 1992).

Jeremias, J., *Die Abendmahlsworte Jesu* (3rd edn, Göttingen, 1960), trans. as *The Eucharistic Words of Jesus* (London, 1966).

Tillard, J. M. R., *The Eucharist. Paths of God's People* (New York, 1967).

eudemis, a flying insect which can damage vines. See MOTHS.

eugenol. See OAK FLAVOUR.

European Union. See EU.

European vines, much-used description for varieties of the common vine species VINIFERA of the VITIS genus, as opposed to AMERICAN VINE SPECIES and Asian vine species.

Euskadi. See BASQUE.

eutypa dieback, one of the FUNGAL DISEASES included in the TRUNK DISEASE complex which, by rotting the wood, can be very destructive and cause whole vineyards to be replanted. Sometimes it is known as dying arm, and is called **eutypiose** in France. Distribution is worldwide, over a wide range of climates, but with the highest incidence in regions with more than 300 mm rainfall a year. Today it is the most common trunk disease in South Australia, where it was first discovered in 1957, south-west France, and in the North Coast and Sacramento regions of California. Studies conducted in the late 1990s estimated the loss of net income caused by eutypa dieback to grape-growers in California at $260 million a year and at $20 million a year in Australia for Shiraz alone.

Eutypa is caused primarily by the fungus *Eutypa lata*, which also attacks many other plants, especially apricots, although recent research has identified at least 11 other Diatrypaceae fungi associated with the disease. Symptoms rarely show in vineyards less than eight years old, but this can be several years after infection has occurred. Spores are released when it rains, can be spread up to 100 km by wind, and infection in grapevines occurs mainly via PRUNING wounds in mild temperatures.

Eutypa dieback can be easily diagnosed in the spring: young shoots are stunted and yellow with small, misshapen, cupped leaves caused by toxins in the infected trunks or arms and/ or secondary metabolites produced by the fungus. Symptoms in the wood include wedge-shaped cankers. No *Vitis vinifera* variety is immune, but some such as Cabernet Sauvignon, Sauvignon Blanc, Grenache, and Syrah are more susceptible. Removing infected arms and trunks, commonly known as vine surgery, may allow the vine to thrive. Painting or spraying the fresh pruning wound with approved FUNGICIDES is very effective in preventing infection. This disease does not affect wine quality, but it can have drastic effects on yield, as old vineyards degenerate long after the onset of the initial infection. Given the commercial interest in wine made from old vines (see VINE AGE), this disease is particularly regrettable.

R.E.S. & J.R.U.-T.

Gubler, W. D., Rolshausen, P., and Trouillas, F. P., 'Eutypa dieback' in L. J. Bettiga (ed.), *Grape Pest Management* (3rd edn, Oakland, Calif., 2013), 110–16.

Rolshausen, P. E., et al., 'Evaluation of pruning wound susceptibility and protection against fungi associated with grapevine trunk diseases in California', *American Journal of Enology and Viticulture*, 61 (2010), 113–19.

Sosnowski, M. R., et al., 'Evaluating treatments and spray application for the protection of grapevine pruning wounds from infection by *Eutypa lata*', *Plant Disease*, 97 (2013), 1599–604.

Sosnowski, M. R., Wicks, T. J., and Scott, E. S., 'Control of Eutypa dieback in grapevines using remedial surgery', *Phytopathologia Mediterranea*, 50 (2011), S227-84.

Euvitis, considered by many botanists to be one of two sections of the genus VITIS (see BOTANICAL CLASSIFICATION), the other being MUSCADINIA. These two are considered to be two separate genera by others, since *Euvitis* and *Muscadinia* vines differ in chromosome number and in appearance. All of the commercially important wine, table, and drying grapes belong to the genus *Euvitis*. R.E.S. & J.V.

Wan, Y., et al., 'A phylogenetic analysis of the grape genus (*Vitis* L.) reveals broad reticulation and concurrent diversification during neogene and quaternary climate change', *BMC Evolutionary Biology*, 13 (2013), 141. doi:10.1186/1471-2148-13-141.

EU wine is wine at its most basically European, a blend of WINES WITHOUT GEOGRAPHICAL INDICATION from more than one country in the EU. The constituents of an EU wine tend to vary with the vagaries of the bottom layer of the European wine market. One of the most common blends, however, has been cheap white vino from Italy, neutralized by extensive FILTRATION, CENTRIFUGATION, and, sometimes, CHARCOAL treatment, 'Germanized' by the addition of some German *Wein* made from a heavily aromatic variety such as MORIO-MUSKAT. In France, EU wine blends have included blends of French red *vin* and a much deeper coloured *vino* from southern Italy, and blends of French white *vin* with the much cheaper Spanish *viña*.

The market for such concoctions is, thankfully, shrinking.

Evans, Len (1930–2006), promoter, taster, judge, consumer, teacher, and maker of wine who did more to advance the cause of wine in AUSTRALIA than any other individual. Born in Felixstowe, England, he was an architect *manqué*, like his friend Michael BROADBENT, but in Evans's case the distraction was professional golf rather than wine. He emigrated to New Zealand in 1953 and arrived in Sydney, Australia, two years later, where his stepping stone into what was to become a lifetime's immersion in wine was working for the new Chevron Hilton Hotel. His energetic enthusiasm for wine was such that by 1965 he was the first National Promotions Executive for the Australian Wine Board. Evans was one of the few to see that the future lay in table wine rather than in the sweet fortified drinks in which Australia then specialized. A natural performer and publicist, Evans caused such a stir that Australians were apparently convinced that real men could indeed drink table wine, and since then table wine has become increasingly important to Australia's social life and economy.

By 1969 he was writing books and articles on wine, had left the Wine Board, and was starting up the Rothbury Estate in the HUNTER VALLEY and establishing his own restaurant-cum-dining club at Bulletin Place by Sydney Harbour. He collected people, preferably famous, with as much enthusiasm as seriously fine wine, but distinguished himself in his practical relish of both. He did not just transform BLIND TASTING into a competitive sport, but even oversaw the creation of a game predicated on it, the OPTIONS GAME, which was subsequently put to work raising substantial sums for charity under Evans's direction.

In the late 1970s, it seemed as though Evans, by now an intimate of the great and the good of the wine world, was about to take it over. Financed by a tax lawyer friend Peter Fox, he acquired properties in GRAVES, SAUTERNES, and the NAPA Valley, with plans to staff them using an early version of the FLYING WINEMAKER concept. His exceptional tasting skills had also been recognized by his numerous invitations to judge at Australia's important wine COMPETITIONS, and by his appointment as chairman of judges (the first of many) at the Royal Sydney Show.

In 1981, Peter Fox was killed in a crash and the Evans Wine Company was thrown into turmoil. From the remains, Rothbury survived, as did the Petaluma winery in the ADELAIDE HILLS, with which Evans was involved from the start. Evans attempted to rusticate himself at his much embellished mud hut 'Loggerheads' overlooking Rothbury.

From then he continued to write, broadcast, and keep tables or halls full of people entertained,

while reminding them that wine is for drinking. He was awarded an Order of the British Empire as well as numerous wine industry distinctions and was made a Chevalier de l'Ordre du Mérite Agricole in 1994.

In 1996, Rothbury, by now incorporating Saltram and St Huberts, was the subject of a hostile takeover bid from brewers Fosters, owners of Beringer Blass wines. Evans Family Wines and the establishment of Tower winery and luxurious lodge in the Hunter Valley became his chief commercial preoccupations although he continued to the end to play an important part in educating those with clear potential in the Australian wine industry. He is commemorated by the Len Evans Tutorial, an annual orgy of blind tasting.

Oliver, J., *Evans on Earth* (Melbourne, 1992).

evaporation, conversion of water (or other liquids) from the liquid to the gaseous or vapour state, brought about by the input and absorption of heat energy. It has important implications for both growing vines and maturing wines. High evaporation is favoured by high SUNLIGHT, high WIND speed, and low HUMIDITY.

Viticulture

There are three sorts of evaporation in the vineyard. First, there is evaporation from the soil, which is especially significant while the soil surface is wet. Then there is evaporation from the vine leaves, and lastly from other parts of the vine (bunches wet from rain, for example), which can have important disease implications.

The power of the atmosphere to evaporate water is related inversely to its humidity and directly to its temperature. Unfortunately the direct climatic records of evaporation, or potential evaporation, are sparse. The records are further confused by the fact that different countries use different instruments for measurement of evaporation. Nevertheless broad averages for regions can be estimated with fair accuracy, and these allow calculation of IRRIGATION requirements, for example.

Evaporation from the soil reduces the amount of water available to the vine and so can encourage WATER STRESS. It also creates humidity in the vineyard.

Evaporation out of grapevine leaves (a process known as TRANSPIRATION) takes place mainly through pores, or STOMATA, which form openings in the waxy leaf surface. It is regulated by opening and closing of the stomata, with partial closure taking place at night. Transpiration from individual leaves is increased by their direct exposure to sunlight, which provides the energy needed for evaporation. The combined water loss from a vineyard is the sum of the evaporation from the soil and transpiration from the vines (and possibly a COVER CROP or weeds), and is called evapotranspiration.

Inadequate evaporation from wet leaves and bunches is, of course, a factor in FUNGAL DISEASE infection. Vine-growers in many climates deliberately trim vines and remove leaves from the vicinity of the bunches, partly to allow in more light, but partly also to encourage evaporation, and thus avoid diseases such as BOTRYTIS BUNCH ROT (see CANOPY MANAGEMENT).   J.G. & R.E.S.

Wine maturation

Evaporation also causes a loss of liquid stored in tight wooden containers, such as wine undergoing BARREL MATURATION. WATER, the principal component in wines, diffuses through small pores of OAK, eventually reaching the outer surface of the stave, where it evaporates into the atmosphere. ALCOHOL also diffuses through the stave, but at a rate considerably slower than that of water.

The atmosphere in contact with the barrel STAVE contains many molecules of water vapour (more when humidity is high, fewer in dry conditions) but relatively few molecules of alcohol. This diffusion–evaporation process means there exists a concentration gradient of water across the barrel stave which is determined by the relative humidity. Accordingly, high humidity slows the net transfer of water from the barrel interior to the atmosphere. Whilst the rate of alcohol transfer is not affected by high humidity, alcohol loss is enhanced relative to the decreased water loss. To summarize, wine subjected to barrel maturation in a high-humidity storage cellar will decrease in ALCOHOLIC STRENGTH whereas that stored in a dry cellar will increase.

This is why, in the low-humidity SHERRY bodegas of JEREZ, it is common practice to sprinkle water on the earth floors to raise the relative humidity and therefore prevent the alcoholic strength of the wine under FLOR film yeast from increasing to the point at which the yeast would be killed.

Evaporation makes regular TOPPING UP of a barrel necessary. The space left by evaporation is called the ULLAGE.   A.D.W. & P.J.W.

evaporative perstraction is a membrane technique used as a means of ALCOHOL REDUCTION, as described in detail by Wollan.

Hogan, P. A., et al., 'A new option: osmotic distillation', *Chemical Engineering Progress*, 49 (July 1998).
Wollan, D., 'Membrane and other techniques for the management of wine composition', in A. G. Reynolds (ed.), *Managing Wine Quality 2: Oenology and Wine Quality* (Cambridge, 2010), 133–63.

evapotranspiration, total loss of water from a vineyard. See EVAPORATION and TRANSPIRATION.

Évora, UNESCO World Heritage Site, capital, and DOP subregion of the ALENTEJO in southern Portugal.

ex cellar(s), professional way of buying direct from wine producers and the price they quote, which excludes TRANSPORT and DUTY in the importing country and any retailer's margin. This price will invariably be less than one quoted to a tourist or consumer at the CELLAR DOOR.

excoriose, vine disease. See PHOMOPSIS.

extract, or **dry extract**, or **total dry extract (TDE)**, the sum of the non-volatile solids of a wine: the SUGARS, non-volatile ACIDS, MINERALS, PHENOLICS, GLYCEROL, glycols, nitrogenous compounds, and traces of other substances such as PROTEINS, PECTINS, and gums. Sometimes sugars are deliberately excluded to give sugar-free extract. Wines' extract, including sugars, usually starts at between 17 and 30 g/l but can vary considerably depending on the wine's SWEETNESS, COLOUR (red wines usually having a higher extract than whites, thanks to their greater phenolic content), and age, since some extract is precipitated as SEDIMENT over the years. Cooler and wetter years, with higher levels of acidity in the grapes, are likely to produce wines with higher levels of dry extract, and BOTRYTIS is also likely to increase its concentration.

Historically, extract was determined by the simple but time-consuming expedient of evaporating a measured quantity of wine and weighing the residue, but this method is imprecise and has generally been replaced by using what is known as the Tabarié formula, techniques involving the measurement of ALCOHOLIC STRENGTH, the DENSITY, and the RESIDUAL SUGAR (if sugar-free extract is required).

To be high in extract, a wine does not necessarily have to be high in alcohol or BODY. Many fine German wines are high in extract, and yet are low in alcohol and are light bodied, especially low-yield Rieslings. Dry extract helps a wine to age well but there is otherwise no correlation between high extract and high QUALITY IN WINE.

Ribéreau-Gayon, P., et al., *Traité d'Œnologie 2: Chimie du vin: Stabilisation et traitements* (Paris, 1998), translated by Aquitrad Traduction as *Handbook of Enology 2: The Chemistry of Wine Stabilization and Treatments* (Chichester, 2000), 81–98.

extraction in a wine context usually refers to the extraction of desirable PHENOLICS from grape solids before, during, and after FERMENTATION, although **over-extraction** is a common fault when colour is associated with quality so that phenolics dominate the wine, often making wines heavy and tannic. Such wines lack FRUIT and BALANCE. See MACERATION for more details.

Extremadura, one of the 17 autonomous regions in SPAIN and, perhaps surprisingly, the country's fourth most important wine region. Spain's wild west is hardly ideal for growing grapes. Sheep are reputed to outnumber people in this semi-arid upland area between CASTILLA-LA MANCHA and PORTUGAL (see map under SPAIN). Most of the wine is sold in bulk for DISTILLATION and ends up as brandy de Jerez. The Tierra de Barros ('land of mud') zone near the Portuguese border, which shares climate and soil features with neighbouring ALENTEJO, witnessed a certain rebirth after 1990.

The regional administration settled in the late 1990s for a single DO for most of the wine areas in Extremadura—RIBERA DEL GUADIANA. Cencibel, Garnacha, Graciano, and, increasingly, Cabernet Sauvignon and Syrah dominate amongst red grape varieties, and Pardina amongst white ones. But the region was still underperforming in 2014. CORK is an important crop here.   V. de la S.

Ezerjó, white grape variety still planted on about 1,000 ha of vineyard in HUNGARY but scarcely known outside it. Most of the wine produced is relatively anodyne, but Móri Ezerjó produced from the vineyards near the town of Mór enjoys a certain following as a light, crisp, refreshing drink. It also produces strong, sweet wines, BOTRYTIZED in good vintages. Ezerjó means 'a thousand boons'.

Faberrebe, or **Faber**, waning, early-ripening German vine cross bred by Dr Scheu at Alzey in Rheinhessen in the early 20th century. Most of its 435 ha in 2011 were in the Rheinhessen. A little is also grown in England.

Factory House, handsome Georgian monument in OPORTO, standing on land granted in 1806 in perpetuity 'from this day and forever to the consul of the British nation and his corporation and their successors', is a testament to the historic role of the British in the port wine trade. The only surviving example of any Factory House, it is possibly the only actual building constructed as a meeting place for a 'factory', a body of traders or 'factors' buying and selling any commodity in a foreign country. The Portuguese were probably the first to establish such a factory, which they called a *feitoria*, in one of their earliest West African settlements. The first British factory was established by the East India Company near Bombay in 1613. By the beginning of the 18th century, British factories had been established in all major Portuguese ports, including of course Oporto, from which wine was an important export (see PORTUGAL). The Factory House, probably the first and only permanent meeting place for the Oporto factory, was begun in 1786 and finished, under the supervision of the consul John Whitehead, four years later. The cost of the land and the building was paid by the 'Outward Fund', voluntarily levied by the British shippers on their own exports of port.

The British factory's enjoyment of their grand, and determinedly exclusive, new clubhouse was cut short by the French invasion of Portugal in 1807. The official reopening of the Factory House took place at a dinner based on the number 11 on 11 November 1811. In the previous year, George III and the Prince Regent

of Portugal had signed a commercial treaty that stipulated that there should be no more British factories in Portugal. The factory itself was therefore abolished and replaced by the British Association in Oporto as British port traders trickled back to enjoy a period of unparalleled prosperity.

The British Association is made up exclusively of members drawn from the British port shippers. By the early 21st century, the remaining British-owned port companies accounted for less than a third of all sales by volume but were still firmly entrenched in Oporto, as evinced by the city's Cricket and Lawn Tennis Club, the oldest British school in Europe, and an Anglican church.

The Factory House continues to be maintained for the exclusive use of the remaining British port shippers, although at such traditional Wednesday lunches as still take place, there are often more Portuguese (directors of the British companies and their friends) than British around the table.

Delaforce, J., *The Factory House at Oporto* (London, 1983).

fake wine. See COUNTERFEIT WINE and ADULTERATION AND FRAUD.

Falanghina, **Falanghina Beneventana** of Benevento province is the less common of Campania's two distinct Falaghinas while the leafy-smelling **Falanghina Flegrea** of Campi Flegrei is Campania's signature white wine grape which may have provided a basis for the classical FALERNIAN and is now the base for Falerno del Massico and Sannio DOCs. It produces attractive, unoaked, fragrant wines of real interest. Modern fermentation enabled producers to preserve its aromas, which gave it a new lease of life from the mid 1990s. The

Italian 2010 vine census did not distinguish between the two but found more than 3,000 ha/7,500 acres in total—nearly twice as much as in 2000.

Falernian or **Falernum** was the most famous and most highly prized wine of Italy in the Roman period. It was produced on the southern slopes of Monte Massico, the range of hills which runs down to the west coast of Italy in northern CAMPANIA. With a precision which was unusual for the Romans, three distinct zones, or CRUS, were distinguished: Caucinian on the hilltops, Faustian on the slopes (probably in the region of present-day Falciano), and Falernian proper at the edge of the plain. Recent archaeological survey has revealed numerous Roman farms in this region and part of a vineyard of Roman date has been excavated. The vines were trained up trees and also on trellises on poles of willow.

Falernian was a white wine of at least two types, one relatively dry, the other sweeter. As with other Roman fine wines such as CAECUBAN and MASSIC, it was normal to age it considerably. It was considered drinkable between 10 and 20 years. Its distinctive colour, deep amber, was probably the result of MADERIZATION, which may also explain the references to 'dark' Falernian in one source. The frequent descriptions of the wine's 'strength' and 'heat' suggest a high ALCOHOLIC STRENGTH. One curious claim was that it was the only wine which could be set alight! Despite the concern of PLINY in the second half of the 1st century AD that the reputation of Falernian was being endangered by a commitment to quantity rather than quality, the wine remained in the front rank until at least the 4th century AD.

The contemporary revival is Falerno del Massico, produced in white, blended red, and all-PRIMITIVO grape versions in modern CAMPANIA. See also ATHENAEUS.   J.J.P.

fanleaf degeneration, sometimes called
fanleaf virus, one of the oldest known VIRUS DISEASES affecting vines. Records of it date back some 200 years in Europe and there are indications that it may have existed in the Mediterranean and Near East since grape culture began. Rather than being a single disease, it is in fact a complex of related diseases which include forms known as yellow mosaic and veinbanding. Shoot growth is typically malformed, leaves are distorted and asymmetric, and teeth along the edge are elongated. Shoots show abnormal branching with double nodes (see FASCIATION), short internodes, and zigzag growth. Leaves on infected plants look fanlike—hence the name. Bunches are smaller than normal, with poor FRUIT SET and many SHOT BERRIES. Sensitive varieties such as Cabernet Sauvignon can lose up to 80% of potential yield and have a shortened productive life.

The disease can be detected by INDEXING using varieties of other species of VITIS such as Rupestris St George, or with other plants such as *Chenopodium*, or by serological tests using ELISA. The virus can be spread by infected planting material, and this reached widespread proportions in the late 1880s with the adoption of grafting vines on to ROOTSTOCKS resistant to PHYLLOXERA. A second means of spread was discovered in California in 1958. The NEMATODE *Xiphinema index* spreads the disease within a vineyard by feeding on the roots of infected plants and then healthy ones. Thus the symptoms of the disease spread slowly around an original infected plant.

There is no control for an infected vineyard and it must be removed. The virus particle can survive in root pieces for over six years. Nematode populations can be reduced by FUMIGATION. Current research aims to develop resistant rootstocks for planting in infested vineyards but has so far been only partly successful. The most successful method is to plant virus-free vines in a nematode-free soil. Fanleaf-free planting material is readily obtained by THERMOTHERAPY or TISSUE CULTURE. (See also NEPOVIRUSES.)   R.E.S.

Bovey, R., et al., *Virus and Virus-Like Diseases of Vines: Colour Atlas of Symptoms* (Lausanne, 1980). Pearson, R. C., and Goheen, A. C. (eds.), *Compendium of Grape Diseases* (St Paul, Minn., 1988).

Fara, tiny red wine DOC of 15 ha in the Novara
Hills of eastern PIEMONTE in north-west Italy. The wines are made from 50 to 70% NEBBIOLO, here called SPANNA.

Far North Zone in SOUTH AUSTRALIA has a
single region, Southern Flinders Ranges, and seven producers in 2014.

fasciation, a growth abnormality, of shoots
in particular, in which the stem is broadened and flattened as though there were several shoots fused side by side. It is relatively rare in grapevines, although some varieties seem to be prone. The cause is unknown but it is a common symptom of FANLEAF DEGENERATION infection.   B.G.C.

fashion has played a part in wine consump-
tion, and therefore eventually wine production, for at least two millennia. The wine drinkers of Ancient ROME favoured white wines, preferably old, sweet white wines (see FALERNIAN, for example). Indeed, throughout much of the modern age, sweet, heady wines have been prized above all others. In the early Middle Ages, the wine drinkers of northern Europe had to drink the thin, tart, sometimes spiced ferments of local vineyards because TRANSPORT was so rudimentary, and RHINE wines were considered the height of fashion. But when these consumers were introduced to such syrupy Mediterranean potions as the wines of CYPRUS and MALMSEY, wines traded energetically by the merchants of, for instance, VENICE, a fashion for this richer style of wine was established. By the 16th century, for example, light, white ALSACE wine was regarded as unfashionable by the German wine drinker (see GERMAN HISTORY), who was, as now, beginning to favour red wines. Many fashions were restricted to one particular district or region, particularly before the age of modern communications. It is clear that the wines favoured by the French court in the medieval period, for example, were considerably influenced by fashion and, possibly, more pragmatically political considerations (see MEDIEVAL LITERATURE and ST-POURÇAIN).

Towards the end of the Middle Ages, fashion seems to have begun to favour not just RESIDUAL SUGAR, but ALCOHOLIC STRENGTH too. Such wines as SACK and TENT from southern Spain were valued for their potency, although by the end of the 17th century, seafaring and exploration brought a new range of drinks to the trendsetters of northern Europe (see COFFEE HOUSES) which were very much more fashionable than any form of wine.

A new age demanded new products, and the most durable of these were the so-called New French Clarets (see CLARET and BORDEAUX, history), whose initial success was largely due to fashion. In the 18th century, however, no wines were more fashionable than a clutch of what a modern salesperson might call 'speciality items': Hungarian TOKAJI, South African CONSTANTIA, and Moldavian COTNARI. These were available in necessarily very limited quantities, but the wine styles created during or soon after this period illustrate the wine qualities regarded as fashionable then: PORT, MADEIRA, MÁLAGA, and MARSALA are all remarkable for their colour, alcohol, and often sweetness.

By the 19th century, much more detailed evidence of the wines then considered most fashionable is available, not just in the form of CLASSIFICATIONS and a number of books specifically comparing different wines (see LITERATURE OF WINE), but also in the form of price lists—for wine PRICES have reflected fashions in wine throughout history. It would surprise the modern wine drinker, for example, to see the high prices fetched by German wines compared with the classified growths of Bordeaux from the late 19th to the mid 20th centuries. The late 19th century was also a time when CHAMPAGNE was considered exceptionally modish in northern Europe, notably in St Petersburg.

In the 1920s and 1930s, wine in almost any form was extremely unfashionable. This was the age of the cocktail on one side of the Atlantic and of PROHIBITION on the other. These phenomena, together with the marked decline of traditional markets and a worldwide economic depression, threatened many small-scale vine-growers with penury (this was the era during which so many wine CO-OPERATIVES were established).

It was not until well after the Second World War, when some measure of real economic recovery and stability had returned, that wine slowly re-established itself as a fashionable drink (although it had long been a drink of necessity in wine-producing areas). As foreign travel became an economic possibility for the majority of northern Europeans, consumers in non-producing countries began to link wine with a way of life they associated with leisure, the exotic, and warmer, wine-producing countries.

By the late 1970s, wine CONNOISSEURSHIP itself was beginning to be fashionable, and the economic boom of the 1980s provided the means for a new generation of collectors. This led inevitably to a fashion for marathon 'horizontal' and 'vertical' TASTINGS of scores of bottles at a time. Buying wine EN PRIMEUR was particularly fashionable in this decade of superlative VINTAGES.

What has been most remarkable about fashions in wine consumption in the late 20th and early 21st centuries, however, has been how rapidly wine production has reacted to them, and in some cases created them (see MOSCATO, PINOT NOIR, MERLOT, wine BRANDS, ROSÉ WINES, pale cream SHERRY, LOW-ALCOHOL wine, and wine BOXES among others). The speed of producer reaction is doubtless related to the development of wine criticism, and its publication in the more immediate media of websites, newspapers, newsletters, magazines, radio, and television, rather than books (see WINE WRITING).

Perhaps the most significant fashion of the 1970s and 1980s was for VARIETAL wines, especially but by no means exclusively in the NEW WORLD. This led to a dramatic increase in the area planted with INTERNATIONAL VARIETIES—Chardonnay, Cabernet

Sauvignon, briefly Merlot, and then, thanks to a single film SIDEWAYS, Pinot Noir, in particular.

On a much more limited scale, the development of a cult following for the distinctive wines of CONDRIEU in the northern Rhône meant that VIOGNIER, the vine variety from which it is made, was introduced to wine regions as far afield as ROUSSILLON, South Australia, and California in the late 1980s and early 1990s. Viognier would feature again in the brief, early-21st-century fashion for CO-FERMENTATION. The 1990s saw an even more significant development, however, a dramatic shift in consumer taste away from white wines to red. Just when a high proportion of northern CALIFORNIA's post-PHYLLOXERA replantings and AUSTRALIA's ambitious new plantings were assigned to the then fashionable Chardonnay, it became clear that the wine drinker of the 1990s, particularly the new army of ASIAN WINE consumers, would in fact prefer red—partly for heavily touted, perceived HEALTH benefits.

In the vineyard, one notable recent fashion, partly fuelled by the perceived tastes of Robert M. PARKER Jr, was to seek not just RIPENESS, but PHYSIOLOGICAL RIPENESS, resulting in prolonged HANG TIME and a marked increase in average ALCOHOLIC STRENGTH. By the second decade of this century, however, there were signs of a retreat from this style, just as in the cellar late-20th-century winemakers reacted quickly to successive fashions for and then against obviously OAKY wines, both white and red. And as the fashions for co-fermentation and international varieties have waned, INDIGENOUS and alternative varieties have waxed markedly.

Of course, fashions change rapidly—and inconveniently for a plant that takes three years to produce a commercial crop (see TOP GRAFTING)—and can be at least national if not parochial. What is fashionable in southern England, for example, may not be fashionable in Sydney or San Francisco. But for certain periods there are wine types and whole wine regions which can be said to be generally out of fashion outside their region or country of production. Obvious recent examples have included lighter-bodied, higher-acid reds such as those of the Loire and Beaujolais, as well as sherry, which could hardly be accused of being light in body or high in acid. Such is the fickle nature of fashion.

fats. See LIPIDS.

fattoria, Italian for a farm, also used for a wine estate. A *fattoria* is generally bigger than a PODERE, which is often a small farm carved out of a larger property and designed to be just large enough to support a sharecropper/tenant and his family.

Faugères, reliable appellation in the LANGUEDOC region in southern France. A total of 1,890 ha/4,668 acres of vineyard, mainly at relatively high ELEVATIONS (often well above 250 m/820 ft) on schistous foothills of the Cévennes, look down on the plains around Béziers. The Faugères appellation vineyards are planted with quintessentially Mediterranean grape varieties to produce big, southern reds that taste like a cross between the spice of the southern RHÔNE and wild, rustic CORBIÈRES to the south west. The ubiquitous Carignan, which by 2014 was limited to 40% of any blend) is being replaced by Syrah, Grenache, or its relative Lladoner Pelut, and Mourvèdre, and Cinsaut is still grown for fruit and rosés. Roussanne is encouraged in white Faugères, which since 2004 has had its own appellation based on at least 30% of this variety with Grenache Blanc, Marsanne, and Vermentino. This is one of the Languedoc's distinctive and consistent appellations.

faults in wines

faults in wines vary, of course, according to the taste of the consumer. Some diners will quite wrongly 'send back' a wine (see SERVING WINE and SOMMELIER) simply because they find it is not to their taste. Taste varies not only according to individuals but also according to nationality. Italians are generally more tolerant of BITTERNESS, Americans of SWEETNESS, Germans of SULFUR DIOXIDE, the French of TANNINS, and the British of decrepitude (see MATURITY) in their wines, while Australians tend to be particularly sensitive to MERCAPTANS and most Americans view HERBACEOUSNESS as a fault rather than a characteristic. To winemakers, however, wine faults are specific departures from an acceptable norm, the least quantifiable of which may be a lack of TYPICALITY.

Visible faults

Faults in a wine's appearance are generally either hazes, clouds, or precipitates in the bottle. STABILIZATION is designed to avoid all these hazards. (In the past, BACTERIA sometimes affected a wine's VISCOSITY, but this problem is rare today.) Haze and cloud in bottled wines can have a variety of causes, of which the most common today is the growth of the micro-organisms YEAST or bacteria. Mycoderma is a yeast-related fault which forms a film on the wine's surface (and so may be visible to winemakers, if not to wine consumers). Clouds from heat-unstable PROTEINS and from heavy-metal contamination do occur but they are much less frequent than they were in the era of copper and brass pipes and taps.

Precipitates, especially crystalline ones, are found from time to time and are usually the harmless result of excess potassium or calcium TARTRATES finally coming out of solution. (Tartrate stabilization usually prevents this.) From white wines, these may form as needle-like colourless or white crystals on the end of the cork in contact with the wine or in the bottom of the bottle, where they look misleadingly like fragments of glass. From red wine, tartrate crystals are usually dyed red or brown from the adsorbed PHENOLICS. See SEDIMENT.

Visible bubbles in a supposedly still wine are frequently viewed as a fault. Some wines, particularly off-dry whites, are deliberately bottled with a trace of CARBON DIOXIDE gas to make them taste more refreshing. Bubbles in a bottle of older wine, particularly a red wine, usually indicate unintentional FERMENTATION IN BOTTLE, however, and are definitely a fault.

While most consumers would agree that cloudy wines are faulty (although see NATURAL WINE), there is much less agreement about COLOUR. Some wine judges in COMPETITIONS automatically disqualify rosé wines with a hint of amber, even though it is difficult to make a blueish-pink wine out of the GRENACHE grape variety, for example—and wines of all sorts and hues turn amber with age.

OXIDATION, which can brown wines prematurely, is a fault in young table wines but is best confirmed by the nose.

Smellable faults

Some wines smell so stale and unpleasant that the taster is unwilling even to taste them. The most likely explanation for this is a mouldy cork causing CORK TAINT. Such a wine is said to be CORKED, but a wine served with small pieces of cork floating in it indicates a fault in the SERVICE of the wine rather than a fault in the wine. Contact with fragments of sound cork does not harm wine.

Other off-odours can vary considerably. Oxidized wines (see above) smell flat and aldehydic. VINEGARY wines indicate the presence of ACETIC ACID due to microbiological activity by bacteria and yeast. ETHYL ACETATE, HYDROGEN SULFIDE, mercaptans, excess sulfur dioxide, and the smellable compounds generated by some bacteria can all be reasons for judging a wine faulty. (See also REDUCTION.) The picture is complicated, however, by the fact that we all vary in our sensitivities to most of these compounds (see TASTING and LADYBUG TAINT), and some of them may be more acceptable in some sorts of wine than others. Acetaldehyde, for example, is the principal odorant of FINO sherries, but definitely indicates over-oxidation in white wines, and makes red wines taste vapid and flat. Although the average palate should not detect acetic acid on a fault-free wine, there are some much-admired, full-bodied red wines (such as some PORT, PENFOLDS Grange, and VEGA SICILIA) whose VOLATILITY is much higher than the norm. Many fine German winemakers at one time deliberately used relatively high concentrations of sulfur dioxide to preserve some of their best wines for a long life in bottle.

A wine may not smell clean because of the influence of one or several CONTAMINANTS such as agrochemical RESIDUES. If it smells of geranium leaves, there has probably been some bacterial degradation of SORBIC ACID, although this can easily be controlled by adding sulfur dioxide at the same time.

A wine may smell MOULDY either because of BACTERIAL SPOILAGE, or because it has taken on the smell of a less-than-clean container.

Another much-discussed microbiological fault, which can cause a wine to smell mousy or animal/medicinal, has been attributed to the action of yeasts of the BRETTANOMYCES genus, closely related to DEKKERA. More detailed studies on the causes of mousy off-flavour in wine have indicated that LACTIC ACID BACTERIA, including particular strains of *Lactobacillus*, and to a lesser extent *Oenococcus* and *Pediococcus*, are capable of producing the off-flavour compounds responsible for this most unpleasant fault. It cannot normally be smelled in wine unless it is alkalinized or rubbed in the palm of the hand (an action which neutralizes wine acidity). This mousy flavour is volatile only at neutral or high PH, which explains why it is not immediately apparent but builds up in the back of the mouth once a wine has been swallowed or expectorated, as the palate slowly returns to neutral pH through the buffering action of saliva.

See also GEOSMIN, GERANIUM, MOULDY, TRIBROMOANISOLE, METHOXY-DIMETHYLPYRAZINE, and ISOBUTYL-METHOXYPYRAZINE.

Tastable faults

Most faults are already obvious to the nose and need only confirmation on the palate (which is why in a restaurant it is, strictly speaking, necessary only to smell a sample of wine offered by the waiter). Some contaminations, notably from metal, are easier to taste than smell, however, and a wine that is excessively tannic or bitter (see BALANCE) will not display this fault to the eye or nose. See also CONTAMINANTS.   A.D.W. & S.H.

Bird, D., *Understanding Wine Technology* (3rd edn, Newark, 2010).

Peynaud, É., *The Taste of Wine* (London, 2010).

Favorita, local synonym for the VERMENTINO cultivated near ALBA, both on the left bank of the Tanaro in the ROERO zone, and slightly less successfully on the right bank in the LANGHE Hills. Gagliardo has championed the variety in Roero. The 2010 vine census lists Favorita, Vermentino, and PIGATO separately, the first totalling 219 ha.

Federspiel, the middle of the three official categories of dry whites for which alcohol and minimum MUST WEIGHT are stipulated and that characterize Austria's WACHAU—specifically from unchaptalized grapes of minimum

83 °OECHSLE, or 17 °KMW, and harbouring between 11 and 12.5% finished alcohol by volume. The name originates from falconry. See also STEINFEDER and SMARAGD.   D.S.

Federweisser, German term for young wine popularly consumed before bottling—generally cloudy and often still fermenting—and typically referred to in Austria as Sturm or HEURIGER. Confusingly, the term Federweisser is used in German-speaking Switzerland to refer collectively to white wines made from black grapes.

feinherb, a traditional term of approbation permitted on German wine labels since 2000 that is neither amenable to intelligible literal translation nor legally defined. Many growers use it successfully as it was envisioned by most of those who lobbied for its instatement, as a substitute for HALBTROCKEN, a concept whose appeal to German consumers fell significantly towards the end of the last century. Others use it for wines of overt, albeit modest, sweetness.   D.S.

Fendant, Valais name for the most planted white wine in SWITZERLAND, the productive CHASSELAS.

Fer, alias **Fer Servadou** (and many other aliases), is a characterful, tannic black grape variety traditionally encouraged in a wide range of the sturdy red wines of SOUTH WEST FRANCE. In MADIRAN, where it is often called Pinenc, it is a distinctly minor ingredient, alongside Tannat and the two Cabernets. In GAILLAC, where it is known as Brocol or Braucol, it has overtaken DURAS to become the dominant variety. It is technically allowed into wines as far north as Bergerac, but today it is particularly important to the red wines of the Aveyron *département*, ENTRAYGUES, ESTAING, and the defiantly smoky, rustic MARCILLAC. The iron-hardness of the name refers to the vine's wood rather than the resulting wine, although it is well coloured, concentrated, and interestingly scented. Fer has also been invited to join the already crowded party of varieties permitted in CABARDÈS.

French plantings had grown to 1,569 ha/3,875 acres by 2011 and DNA PROFILING has shown it to be a progenitor of CARMENÈRE.

Féret, sometimes known as *Cocks et Féret*, important directory of Bordeaux châteaux which was first published in 1846 as *Bordeaux, its Wines and the Claret Country* by the Englishman Charles Cocks who died in 1854 (see LITERATURE OF WINE). A French version followed in 1850, with the emphasis on classifying wines in order of merit, also published in Bordeaux by Féret. It played a significant part in establishing the 1855 CLASSIFICATION and continues to be updated, expanded, and published by members of the Féret family to this day. It has always

provided a useful historical record of the evolution of different properties' and districts' reputations. (The 1868 edition, for example, ranked PETRUS as a mere CRU BOURGEOIS.) As a sign of the times, the 19th edition of what is now known simply as *Bordeaux et ses vins* was published in 2013, in e-book format, in French, English, and Mandarin.

Cocks, C. and Féret, C., *Bordeaux and its Wines* (19th edn, Bordeaux, 2013).

Mustacich, S., 'The Book that Defined Bordeaux', WineSpectator.com, 2013 http://www.winespectator.com/webfeature/show/id/48495

fermentation, as it applies to wine, is the process of converting SUGAR to ETHANOL (ethyl alcohol) and CARBON DIOXIDE effected by the anaerobic (oxygen-free) metabolism of YEAST. It comes from the Latin word *fervere*, to boil; any mass containing sugar that has been infused with yeast certainly looks as though it is boiling, as it exudes carbon dioxide bubbles.

History

Before yeast's metabolic processes were properly understood, the word fermentation was also used to describe a much wider range of chemical changes that resulted in the appearance of boiling and in some of which carbon dioxide evolved. These have included the leavening of bread, the production of cheese, and the tumultuous reactions of acids with alkalis. Today such changes involving the intervention of yeast or BACTERIA in aerobic processes are not usually considered true fermentations.

By the middle of the 19th century, our understanding of science was such that opinions were divided about the nature of 'organized ferments' as opposed to 'unorganized ferments' in fermentation. Thanks to Louis PASTEUR, we now know that it is the organized ferments and their agents yeasts and bacteria that are primarily responsible for alcoholic fermentation. They act through their internal ENZYMES (enzymes were responsible for Pasteur's unorganized ferments), which, functioning as catalysts, mediate the series of reactions involved in the conversion of sugar into alcohol and carbon dioxide.

The net change during fermentation of one glucose molecule giving two alcohol and two carbon dioxide molecules expressed as a chemical equation is:

$$C_6H_{12}O_6 \rightarrow 2C_2H_5OH + 2CO_2$$

Many years and the research talents of several scientists, notably Embden, Meyerhof, and Parnas, have elucidated the successive steps in the apparently simple conversion of sugars to the metabolic end products, alcohol and carbon dioxide.

The complex process

The first steps in the process attach phosphate groups to the sugars. Next comes a series of steps in which the six-carbon sugar is split into two three-carbon pieces, one of which is then rearranged into the structure of the other. After some further rearrangements, this three-carbon molecule loses its terminal carboxylic carbon atom in the form of carbon dioxide gas. The residual part is the two-carbon compound ACETALDEHYDE, which goes next to alcohol if oxygen is lacking, or into another multi-step series of reactions eventually yielding energy, water, and more carbon dioxide if generous amounts of oxygen are available.

The net change when oxygen is present in excess is one glucose plus six oxygen molecules giving six carbon dioxide and six water molecules, as shown by this chemical equation:

$$C_6H_{12}O_6 + 6O_2 \rightarrow 6CO_2 + 6H_2O$$

Ideally for the yeast, therefore, the process should be carried out with generous quantities of oxygen available, for then much more cell-building energy is produced. For winemaking man, however, it is important that this process can be modified by limitation of the oxygen supply because then alcohol, rather than water, is produced along with carbon dioxide. Without the alcohol there would be no wine.

(It is interesting that this same series of steps in decomposition of sugar is employed by man during muscular activity, another form of fermentation. In man, and other mammals, the three-carbon compound PYRUVATE is converted to LACTIC ACID and supplies energy for muscular action.)

A number of intermediate compounds are involved. The biochemical reactions converting one compound into its successor in this series are not 100% efficient, with the result that small amounts of certain of the intermediate compounds accumulate in the wine. These compounds and the products of their reaction with other substances in the mixture contribute to what is known as fermentation, or secondary, AROMAS. Included among these compounds are acetaldehyde, ETHYL ACETATE, and numerous other ESTERS and FUSEL OILS.

Physical chemistry tells us that the reaction of six-carbon sugar to ethanol and carbon dioxide yields generous amounts of energy. A significant portion of this energy is captured during the process and used by the yeast for its own purposes. Another major portion of the energy, however, is not captured but appears as waste heat. Unless this waste heat is removed from the fermenting mass, its temperature will rise, reaching levels which damage or kill the yeast cells and stop the reaction, resulting in a STUCK FERMENTATION which can be very difficult to restart. Heat removal is not a major problem when fermentations are conducted in a small FERMENTATION VESSEL because the greater ratio of surface to volume furnishes sufficient radiation and conduction surfaces from which the heat can be dissipated. In a large container, however, the amount of heat liberated may be so large that it cannot all be radiated or conducted away and in such cases some REFRIGERATION system is needed.

Monitoring fermentation

Progress of a fermentation can be monitored in several ways. The most obvious is by simply observing activity in the fermentation vessel. As long as carbon dioxide is vigorously given off, the yeast are still working. Laboratory fermentations are sometimes followed by weighing the fermentation vessel at frequent intervals, thus obtaining a record of the weight of carbon dioxide gas lost and therefore, by calculation, the amount of sugar remaining. Chemical analyses of the unfermented sugar remaining, or of the alcohol produced, are accurate measures of the course of fermentation but are seldom used as they are complex and time consuming. The technique most commonly used in the operating cellar is a measurement of the DENSITY of a sample of fermenting juice.

Density can be determined quickly and with reasonable accuracy by floating a calibrated HYDROMETER in the juice. Although most hydrometers are calibrated to read the remaining sugar's percentage in weight, it must be remembered that this calibration is for a sugar in water solution. When alcohol, less dense than water, is added to the solution during fermentation, the hydrometer reading no longer gives a true reading of the sugar remaining. Indeed, when all of the fermentable sugar has been converted into alcohol, these hydrometers will give the apparently ridiculous reading of less than no sugar. The problem of deciding when the fermentation is complete matters because the presence of small amounts of sugar renders the wine susceptible to bacterial attack and necessitates different treatment after fermentation. Today there are quick, simple paper strips or pills which can reliably detect the presence of even very small amounts of fermentable sugars. Hand-held density meters are becoming increasingly common; these are faster and data can be downloaded directly into a computer. Larger producers may have tanks that monitor fermentation using in-line densitometers or pressure sensors, with readings automatically fed into the computer system.

Factors affecting fermentation

The time required for complete fermentation of white grape juice or crushed red grapes varies greatly. The TEMPERATURE maintained in the fermenting mass is the principal factor affecting duration of fermentation (as well as resultant character of the wine), more even than the initial sugar concentration (see MUST WEIGHT), YEAST type, the aeration of the MUST, and the quantity of micronutrients in the juice, especially NITROGEN. In general, red wine fermentations are complete within four to seven days but white wines, which are frequently fermented at much lower temperatures, may sometimes require longer, possibly two to three weeks, occasionally months (see DRIED-GRAPE WINES, for instance).

Other factors which influence the course of a fermentation include agrochemical RESIDUES and various chemical additions such as too high a concentration of SULFUR DIOXIDE. In the most commercially minded wineries, fermentations may be deliberately hastened so that a single fermentation vessel may be used twice or even three or more times a season.

In the making of certain styles of wine, such as PORT, VIN DOUX NATUREL, and other VINS DE LIQUEUR, the fermentation may be arrested deliberately by the addition of alcohol, usually grape spirit.

The above is an outline of the most usual sorts of fermentation but there are many variants, including BARREL FERMENTATION, CARBONIC MACERATION, ROSÉ WINEMAKING, and, quite distinct from the primary or alcoholic fermentation, FERMENTATION IN BOTTLE, MALOLACTIC CONVERSION, and SECOND FERMENTATION.

See also MACERATION, the process that inevitably accompanies red wine fermentation, and also RED WINEMAKING, WHITE WINEMAKING, and SPARKLING WINEMAKING.   A.D.W.

Halliday, J., and Johnson, H., *The Art and Science of Wine* (London and New York, 1992).

Ribéreau-Gayon, P., et al., *Traité d'Œnologie* 1: *Microbiologie du vin: Vinifications* (Paris, 1998), translated by J. M. Branco, as *Handbook of Enology* 1: *The Microbiology of Wine and Vinifications* (Chichester, 2000).

fermentation in bottle plays an important part in SPARKLING WINEMAKING. In most still wines, however, it is one of the wine FAULTS most feared by winemakers. It usually results from the presence of some RESIDUAL SUGAR together with live cells of either YEAST or BACTERIA under conditions which favour their growth. (High ALCOHOLIC STRENGTH and high levels of SULFUR DIOXIDE inhibit the growth of such micro-organisms.) It is also possible that a completely dry wine will appear to start fermenting in bottle if it contains a high concentration of MALIC ACID since live LACTIC ACID BACTERIA may metabolize the malic acid causing a MALOLACTIC CONVERSION in bottle.

The implications of a fermentation in bottle for the wine consumer can range from an inconsequential level of carbon dioxide in the wine to the generation of such large quantities of the gas that it explodes. This latter, potentially dangerous, occurrence is most likely if the wine contains significant amounts of fermentable sugar and is kept at warm room temperatures. If the fermentation is bacterial rather than by yeast, gas is usually produced, together with off-flavours, cloud, or haze (see BACTERIAL SPOILAGE).

A low level of gas in a wine, particularly a young white wine, is by no means necessarily a sign of unwanted fermentation in bottle. Many winemakers deliberately retain (from fermentation) or incorporate a low level of CARBON DIOXIDE to enliven some wines.   A.D.W.

fermentation vessel.

The container in which FERMENTATION, and MACERATION in the case of red wines, take place can vary enormously in size, material, and design: from a small plastic bucket (in the case of some HOME WINEMAKING) to an oak BARREL (in the case of white wines and a very few red wines undergoing BARREL FERMENTATION) to a CONCRETE tank or egg to what is effectively a vast, computerized STAINLESS STEEL tower (for high-volume everyday wines). Stainless steel has the advantage that both cleaning and TEMPERATURE CONTROL are much easier than for wooden or concrete fermentation vessels and most modern white and rosé wines, and many reds, are fermented in stainless steel tanks.

Wooden fermentation vessels are still used by many winemakers, however. Traditional wine producers in Germany, Alsace, and the Loire may well use large, old, wooden CASKS which offer natural STABILIZATION and CLARIFICATION. Unless scrupulous attention is paid to cellar HYGIENE, however, harmful bacteria can linger in the staves of wooden casks.

Red wine may be fermented either in large wooden casks or open-topped wooden vats. An open top requires constant surveillance since BACTERIA can attack the floating CAP of skins, which will dry out and fail to achieve proper MACERATION without REMONTAGE or PIGEAGE. The cap may alternatively be kept SUBMERGED with a headboard or some other design feature.

Wooden fermentation vessels are particularly treasured by some traditionalists for red wine maceration, however, as they retain heat especially well, which favours the extraction process, and tend to have a much higher diameter to height ratio than some inappropriate stainless steel tanks, which favours the contact between wine and solids.

Modern stainless steel tanks, and design modifications of them such as various autovinifiers (see AUTOVINIFICATION), computer-controlled fermentation vessels, self-draining vessels, and Vinomatic automatic vinifiers, are closed at the top and automatically offer a high degree of hygiene.

Lined concrete vats are also widely used for fermentation, even at such highly respected properties as PETRUS in Pomerol, where stainless steel is regarded as more sensitive to temperature variation and offering less aeration.

fermented in bottle,

legitimate description of a SPARKLING WINE made by the traditional, transversage, or transfer methods described in SPARKLING WINEMAKING. Only traditional method wines could claim to be **fermented in this bottle**, however.

Fernão Pires,

Portugal's most planted white wine grape, grown throughout central, southern PORTUGAL. Adaptable, it is not only productive, it also manages to make distinctively scented, reasonably crisp wines. Known in BAIRRADA as Maria Gomes, Fernão Pires was still planted on a total of 13,409 ha/33,120 acres of Portugal in 2012 and to a very limited extent in South Africa, Australia, and California.

Ferreira,

one of the leading Portuguese port shippers, established in 1715. Dona Antónia Adelaide Ferreira, the *grande dame* of the DOURO Valley, was perhaps one of the most dedicated personalities in the PORT industry in the latter half of the 19th century. Born in 1811 in Régua, Dona Antónia devoted her life to the Douro, ruling her vast estates as a benevolent dictator. She invested much of her considerable fortune in planting and improving her properties throughout this harsh terrain. The father of her first husband, António Bernardo Ferreira, founded one of the largest and most stately quintas in the Douro, the Quinta do Vesúvio, which the family owned until its sale in 1989 to the SYMINGTONS. Today Ferreira own three properties in the Douro: Quinta do Porto, Quinta do Caêdo near Pinhão, and Quinta da Leda high up in the Douro, as well as buying in wine from other properties owned by the family. Quinta do Seixo, bought by Ferreira in 1979, has now been rebranded as a SANDEMAN property. In the 1980s, the properties were the subject of considerable research and investment, with the company pioneering the vertical system of planting whereby vine rows are aligned uphill rather than along contours. Until 1987, Ferreira was owned by descendants of Dona Antónia, but the company now belongs to SOGRAPE. Ferreira is the leading brand of port in Portugal and pioneered the production of high-quality dry red wines in the DOURO, of which their famous Barca Velha was the prototype in 1952.

fertigation,

the viticultural practice of mixing soluble FERTILIZERS with IRRIGATION water for direct application to vines. The technique is most often used with DRIP IRRIGATION systems, for which each vine has a water outlet. Fertilizers are placed in a tank through which the irrigation water passes, and so the vine is fed with appropriate amounts of water and nutrients as the growth proceeds. Some nutrients such as NITROGEN are readily available in a soluble form (urea); others such as PHOSPHORUS require a relatively expensive formulation to render them immediately soluble. Some vineyard additions such as gypsum and lime are quite insoluble and so require special formulations.   R.E.S.

fertility,

viticultural term for the FRUITFULNESS of buds or shoots, and also of vineyard soils, see SOIL FERTILITY.

fertilizers.

Vines, in common with other plants, may require additions of fertilizers to overcome the deficiency in the soil of a particular nutrient (see SOIL NUTRIENTS). However, grapevines do not require such fertile soils as many other crops. Indeed, the vineyards most highly regarded in terms of the quality of wine they produce are generally grown on relatively infertile soils. While a modicum of nutrient stress may enhance quality, this is not to suggest that the fewer the soil nutrients the greater the wine quality. For example, a severe NITROGEN deficiency will limit shoot, root, and leaf growth, and fruit yield, and also cause a STUCK FERMENTATION, potentially contributing to poor wine quality. Typically, a vineyard producing wine will receive less fertilizer than one producing table grapes.

Fertilizers are commercial formulations which are rich in plant nutrients. Typically they are manufactured (for example, superphosphate) but may be a mined natural product (for example, rock phosphate). COMPOST is not commonly used in large commercial vineyards because of its lack of cost-effectiveness. More commonly, compost made from a combination of plant materials and animal manures (mainly poultry, sheep, or pig) is used in smaller vineyards where its use is encouraged for ecological benefits (see ORGANIC VITICULTURE and BIODYNAMIC VITICULTURE). Animal manures are also used alone, but again, unless they are readily and cheaply available (as from the cattle deliberately kept at Ch MARGAUX, for example), then their use is restricted because of the relatively high cost of applying sufficient nutrients in this form.

The mineral elements most likely to be deficient in vineyards are nitrogen, POTASSIUM, PHOSPHORUS, ZINC, BORON, IRON, MANGANESE, and MAGNESIUM. The fertilizers commonly used to overcome some of these deficiencies are therefore urea, calcium or ammonium nitrate, potassium chloride or potassium sulfate, superphosphate, zinc sulfate, boric acid or borate, and magnesium sulfate. Fertilizers supplying the macronutrients (see SOIL NUTRIENTS) nitrogen, phosphorus, and potassium are normally applied in amounts giving up to 50, 15, and 25 kg of nitrogen, phosphorus, and potassium, respectively, per ha per year. They can be spread on the ground under vine or applied through an irrigation dripline by FERTIGATION. The micronutrients (see SOIL NUTRIENTS) are required in small amounts only, typically less than 5 kg per ha, applied every 4–5 years. Thus fertilizers compensating for deficiencies of the micronutrients zinc, manganese, boron, iron, and MOLYBDENUM can be applied either mixed with other fertilizers to the ground, or sprayed onto the leaves.

The efficiency of fertilization varies with the type of fertilizer and the soil. For example, phosphate fertilizers are not readily available to plants grown in acid soils high in iron and aluminium oxides, so LIMING might increase growth because it makes more phosphorus available to the vine. Similarly, with high rainfall or irrigation, the nitrate form of nitrogen is leached so easily that it is lost to the vine roots unless they are very deep. The nitrate may end up contaminating nearby streams and groundwater, as has been reported in many countries, making fertilizer use in viticulture (and other forms of agriculture) the subject of scrutiny by those concerned with SUSTAINABILITY.

Fertilizer use can affect wine quality. Too much nitrogen can stimulate vine growth to such an extent that RIPENING is prejudiced and the resultant wines are thin, pale, and HERBACEOUS. Excessive use of potassium may also detrimentally increase wine PH and affect the colour stability of red wines.   R.E.S. & R.E.W.

Coombe, B. G., and Dry, P. R. (eds.), *Viticulture*, ii: *Practices* (Adelaide, 1992).

White, R. E., *Understanding Vineyard Soils* (2nd edn, Oxford, 2015).

Fetească, **Fetiaska**, or **Feteaska**, means 'young girl' and is associated with three important eastern European vine varieties. The 'royal' **Fetească Regală** was (just) the most planted variety in 2013 in ROMANIA where it produced crisp, scented whites from nearly 13,000 ha/ 32,000 acres of vineyard. Total Romanian plantings of 'white' **Fetească Albă**, which almost certainly originated in MOLDOVA and is often used for sparkling wines, were said to have grown to 12,633 ha/31,203 acres. In neighbouring Moldova and UKRAINE, statistics do not distinguish between the two pale-skinned Feteascăs, which are typically blended and sold simply as **Fetească**. The dark-skinned **Fetească Neagră**, whose red wines show potential when well vinified and yields are severely restricted, was much less common and planted on just over 2,500 ha of Romania and is also grown in Ukraine. DNA PROFILING suggests that the dark-skinned Fetească is a particularly old variety and may not be related to either of the light-skinned ones. (In Romanian, Fetească, meaning young girl's grape, contrasts directly with BĂBEASCĂ, grandmother's grape.)

Fiano, strongly flavoured classical vine responsible for CAMPANIA's **Fiano di Avellino**

DOCG in southern Italy. Wines made from this variety are assertive but lack the aromatic lift of **Fiano Aromatico**, or MINUTOLO. It is also planted in Puglia, Molise, and increasingly in SICILY. The 2010 Italian vine census did not distinguish between the two Fianos but found a total of 1,376 ha/3,400 acres. Total Australian plantings had reached 1000 ha by 2012.

Fiddletown, California wine region and higher of the two AVAS in the SIERRA FOOTHILLS.

Fié, occasionally written **Fiét** or **Fiers**, old Loire synonym for SAUVIGNON GRIS. This CLONE has largely been abandoned because of its remarkably low yield, but producers such as Jacky Preys of Touraine pride themselves on their richer versions of Sauvignon made from particularly old Fié vines.

Fiefs Vendéens, small, oceanic AOC zone south of the Muscadet zone near the mouth of the Loire, qualified by one of the communes Brem, Chantonnay, Mareuil, Pissotte, or Vix, each with its own permitted ENCEPAGEMENT. Most wines are red, from Cabernet Franc, Négrette, and Pinot Noir but there are rosés, often with Gamay, and some whites based on Chenin Blanc.

field blend, a mixture of different vine varieties planted in the same vineyard, as was once common, particularly when VINE IDENTIFICATION was less reliable. It is rare today but some of the oldest vineyards in CALIFORNIA, the DOURO, and ROUSSILLON are thus planted. See also CO-FERMENTATION.

field budding and grafting, viticultural operation of planting ROOTSTOCK rootlings in their vineyard position and inserting SCION buds. Many types of insertion may be used but CHIP BUDDING is common. The success rate is highest in warm to hot climates but can be erratic, and careful attention is needed to watering, nutrition, and the tending of each vine. This method is therefore most suitable for small vineyards with good soils and a well-trained workforce.

(See TOP GRAFTING for details of the viticultural operation of changing VINE VARIETY in an established vineyard.)   B.G.C.

fifth growth. See the CLASSIFICATION of Bordeaux.

fill level, an aspect of individual bottles of wine which can be closely related to the condition of the wine. The lower the fill level when a wine is bottled, the more the space between the top of the wine and the bottom of the cork (the so-called HEAD SPACE or ULLAGE) in which OXYGEN may be trapped in the bottle and may hasten the AGEING process. Most bottlers try to ensure that there is minimal ullage space in the bottle immediately after BOTTLING, a depth of

5–10 mm/0.2–0.4 in to allow for expansion if ambient temperature ever exceeds the usual bottling temperature of 20 °C. On modern bottling lines, the bottle may be flushed with INERT GAS before and after filling in order to limit as far as possible the oxygen in the head space (see TOTAL PACKAGE OXYGEN). Subsequent reductions in temperature cause a reduction in the wine's volume, thereby apparently lowering the fill level.

For wines designed for early consumption, this is unlikely to make much difference, but fill levels are important indicators of the condition of a fine and, especially, mature wine, so that fill levels should always be specified by the AUCTION houses and other fine wine traders. The lower the fill level, the more likely a harmful level of OXIDATION and therefore the lower should be the selling price. Despite this perception, experience shows many wines which age in bottle with substantial ullage exhibit no signs of oxidation. Some sorts of wine seem more resilient to low fill levels than others—vintage port and Sauternes are examples—and a low fill level can apparently, sometimes usefully, hasten the ageing process of an extremely TANNIC wine.

During long-term BOTTLE AGEING, some wine is likely to be absorbed by the CORK, resulting in a drop in fill level of perhaps 7 mm after ten years. (To reduce this absorption effect, Ch MOUTON-ROTHSCHILD adopted a policy of using shorter corks from the 1991 vintage.) Some wine may also evaporate from the top of the bottle during this time, especially if some was trapped between the cork and the inside of the bottle-neck during bottling. Other reasons for a low fill level include poor control during bottling, wine being bottled at too high a temperature, and a faulty cork. In any event, it is always wise policy to pick bottles with the highest fill levels off the shelf, and to drink bottles of wine from the same case from lowest to highest fill level since the wine in bottles with the lowest fill level is likely to be the most evolved.

Note that the fill level in wine GLASSES should ideally be less than half the height of the glass and never more than two-thirds, in order to provide somewhere for the AROMA to collect.

film-forming yeasts, sometimes called **film yeasts**, flowers of yeast, or mycoderma, comprise a group of grape- and wine-associated species of wild YEASTS, all of which require OXYGEN for their characteristic growth and metabolism. For this reason they appear on the surface of wine in barrels or vats that are not kept completely filled. Some, such as FLOR, being strains of *Saccharomyces cerevisiae* and genetically closely related to wine fermentation strains, can add desirable aromas and flavours, whereas other species, often referred to as 'non-*Saccharomyces* yeasts', produce off-flavours, while others have a relatively neutral sensory impact.

The commonly encountered film-forming non-*Saccharomyces* species belong to the genera *Candida* (which contains only anamorphic species—those which cannot form sexual spores) and *Pichia* (teleomorphic species—spore formers). *Candida mycoderma*, previously called *Mycoderma vini*, is now classified as *Candida vini* and *Candida valida*. *Pichia membranifaciens* is the teleomorphic form of *Candida valida*, and *Pichia anomala*, formerly *Hansenula anomala*, is the anamorph of *Candida pelliculosa*. These yeasts are widely dispersed in vineyard regions and are among the types encountered in spontaneous or wild yeast fermentations. When sugar is present, they are producers of alcohol and carbon dioxide, but have low alcohol tolerance. Thus, while they are active in the early stages of spontaneous fermentations when traces of oxygen remain, they become dominated by the more alcohol-tolerant *Saccharomyces* species, which finish the sugar conversion. After fermentation, exposure of the wine to oxygen can stimulate film formation. These yeast species typically form more ESTERS, predominantly ETHYL ACETATE, and ALDEHYDES, and sometimes ACETIC ACID, than do *Saccharomyces*, consequently producing an undesirable, oxidized flavour profile.

Initially, small islands of a thin film form on the surface of wines in tanks or barrels that are not completely full, and, if left unchecked, can develop into a creamy to grey, dense biomass, referred to as 'velum' in flor wine production. These yeasts require oxygen for film formation and thus act as a signal to the winemaker that a more frequent TOPPING UP regime is required. If wine has to be kept under ULLAGE, then maintaining a headspace of inert gas and an adequate concentration of sulfur dioxide in the wine will usually prevent film formation. For white wines, the ACETALDEHYDE produced is a negative factor, but for red wines, short exposure to a film of *mycoderma* does little damage.

Film-forming strains of *Saccharomyces* yeasts perform a vital function in the production of wines such as flor sherry, VIN JAUNE, and TOKAJI.   A.D.W. & P.A.H.

Sponholz, W.-R., 'Wine spoilage by microorganisms', in G. H. Fleet (ed.), *Wine Microbiology and Biotechnology* (Chur, 1993), 395–420.

Fugelsang, K. C., and Edwards, C. G., *Wine Microbiology—Practical Applications and Procedures* (Springer, 2007).

films about wine

films about wine. As wine has become more deeply embedded in popular culture, not least in the US, so films about wine proliferated in the 21st century, but wine features strongly in at least three in the 20th century. Perhaps the earliest of the modern era was Hitchcock's *Notorious*, a 1946 spy thriller whose plot turns on the whereabouts of the key to a wine CELLAR. Food was perhaps more important than wine in the 1987 classic *Babette's Feast* but her one sumptuous blow-out meal served to her austere Danish employers included SHERRY, 1860 VEUVE CLICQUOT champagne, an 1846 CLOS DE VOUGEOT, and a cognac. There is no doubt about wine's role in the 1996 thriller *Blood and Wine* which stars Jack Nicholson as a Florida wine merchant who turns to crime. The 1998 remake of *The Parent Trap* set male parent Denis Quaid on a Napa Valley wine estate.

By far the most powerful mainstream film about wine ever was SIDEWAYS, the 2004 comedy set in CENTRAL COAST wine country. Its success spawned many other film treatments in which wine is more or less deeply embedded but the most high-profile was *Bottle Shock*, a 2008 comedy drama based extremely approximately on the JUDGMENT OF PARIS California vs France taste-off. The same year saw the release of the New Zealand film *Dean Spanley*, featuring Sam Neill, actor and wine producer, whose plot turns on the interaction between the clergyman played by Neill and TOKAJ.

At almost the same time as *Sideways* was released came the first of a series of documentary films about wine. Ex-sommelier Jonathan Nossiter's *Mondovino* was a passionate if somewhat tendentious complaint about growing GLOBALIZATION in wine. Four years later, in 2012, *Somm* documented four young Americans' real-life quest for the MASTER SOMMELIER qualification involving BLIND TASTING tests deliberately made gruelling. Soon afterwards came *Red Obsession*, a high-quality Australian documentary about the Chinese love affair with red wine, bordeaux in particular. Ex-California wine merchant Martine Saunier meanwhile starred in a series called 'A Year in . . .' shot mainly in her native France.

filtration, fundamental but controversial winemaking process, a means of CLARIFICATION involving the removal of solid particles from a wine. At the end of FERMENTATION, wine contains a vast amount of particulate matter, including yeast cells, bacteria, grape cellulose, proteins, and pectins. All of these have to be progressively removed in order to produce a clear wine.

There are two principal categories of filtration: depth filtration and surface or absolute filtration. **Depth filtration** involves the use of a relatively thick layer of a finely divided material such as DIATOMACEOUS EARTH, or pads made of cellulose fibres. As the cloudy wine passes through the layer, small particles are trapped in the tortuous channels and clear liquid passes through. This form of filtration is useful for removing large quantities of solid matter because the thickness of the filtration layer presents a large volume of medium in which the particles are trapped. The ROTARY DRUM VACUUM FILTER is the extreme example of depth filtration because it can be used to separate wine from the thick deposits at the bottom of a fermentation tank. A sheet filter fitted with thick pads of cellulose fibres is used for removing fine particles in preparation for the final filtration prior to bottling. The risk involved in using depth filtration is that by increasing the pressure or flow-rate beyond the specified maximum, particles can be forced through the filter to the clean side.

Surface filtration depends on a thin but strong film of plastic polymer material with uniform-sized holes which are smaller than the particles being removed from the solution. It is thus impossible for particles to cross the filter, hence the alternative term absolute filtration. The shortcoming here is that the filter can become blocked if it is presented with too much particulate matter. Tangential or cross-flow filtration is an ingenious development of surface filtration where the liquid flows parallel to the filter surface and keeps the filter membrane clear, avoiding clogging. The commonest form of surface filter, as used in many wineries, is the membrane filter, which consists of a set of membrane cartridges within a simple cylindrical housing. These are manufactured in a variety of pore sizes, the most common being 0.45μ.

Although the use of this pore size is often incorrectly called **sterile filtration**, the filtered wine is not totally sterile—as in the production of intravenous liquids—but merely devoid of yeasts and bacteria that could cause degradation of the bottled wine at some time in the future. A more accurate term would be aseptic filtration.

Filtration of wine is somewhat controversial in that it is recognized that minimum intervention is the best approach since every time wine is handled, processed, or even moved, there can be a slight loss of quality. The best approach is to let nature do the job by SETTLING, as it will, given time. However, this is a slow process which has to be accelerated for large-scale production. Correctly applied, filtration is perfectly satisfactory for the production of good-quality wine in large volumes.   D.B.

finca, Spanish for estate. **Finca Élez** is a Spanish DO created especially for the high-elevation estate of Manuel Manzaneque.

Findling, white wine grape grown to a limited extent in the MOSEL. Possibly related to MÜLLER-THURGAU.

fine wine is a nebulous term, used by the AUCTION houses to describe the sort of wines they sell, which roughly coincide with those described in INVESTMENT. For example, within

Bordeaux, a wine would have to be of CLASSED GROWTH level or equivalent to qualify as 'fine'.

The extent to which this category of wine coincides with the best wine the world produces has declined slowly but steadily since the 1970s. Buying from, selling to, and in many cases in direct competition with, the auction houses are the **fine wine traders**, a small group of wine merchants who specialize in servicing the needs of collectors and the like. See BROKERS for more details.

See also PHILOSOPHY AND WINE.

fining, winemaking process with the aim of CLARIFICATION and stabilization of a wine whereby a **fining agent**, one of a range of special materials, is added to coagulate or adsorb and precipitate quickly the COLLOIDS suspended in it. Fining (*collage*, or 'sticking', in French) is important because, by encouraging these microscopic particles to fall out of the wine, the wine is less likely to become hazy or cloudy after bottling.

Most young wines, if left long enough under good conditions, would eventually reach the same state of clarity as fining can achieve within months, but fining saves money for the producer and therefore eventually the consumer. Fining is most effective in removing molecules of colloidal size, which include polymerized TANNINS, PIGMENTED TANNINS, other PHENOLICS, and heat-unstable PROTEINS. (Other reasons for clouds, hazes, and deposits in bottled wines include TARTRATES and BACTERIA. See STABILIZATION for details of other methods of removing them.)

Over the centuries, a wide range of fining agents has doubtless been essayed, but scientific and technical advances have eliminated those (such as dried blood powder) that are dangerous to health and those (such as various gums) that are less than fully effective in improving the wine. Many fining agents, deriving variously from EGG WHITES, milk, fish bladders, and American BENTONITE clay deposits, may strike consumers as curious winemaking tools but it should be recognized that only insignificant traces, at most, of the fining agent remain in the treated wine. Nevertheless, in many countries, including the EU, Australia, New Zealand, and Canada, the use of any fining agent that is considered an 'allergenic substance' must be declared on the label if such a substance is above the detection limit in the finished wine (see LABELLING INFORMATION), and therefore many winemakers are dropping the use of animal-derived proteinaceous fining agents and using only bentonite. In 2012 the OIV halved the detection limit for potentially allergenic proteinaceous fining agents set out in its oenological code. It is, however, important to distinguish between ADDITIVES such as OENOLOGICAL TANNINS, which are intended to change the

flavour or structure of the wine, and PROCESSING AIDS such as bentonite, which are used to improve stability and/or clarity.

Today two general classes of fining agents are used: powdered mineral or plastic materials that are insoluble (including PVPP), and protein-based organic compounds in liquid form. Bentonite, an unusual form of clay, is particularly effective in adsorbing certain proteins and, to a limited extent, bacteria. SILICA functions similarly but somewhat less effectively. Kaolin, another type of clay, is even less effective than silica. Activated carbon (CHARCOAL) has been used to remove brown colours and is also effective in removing some off-odours. Potassium ferrocyanide may still be used as a fining agent for removing copper and iron (see BLUE FINING).

Organic compounds used as fining agents include proteins such as the CASEIN from milk, albumin from egg whites, ISINGLASS from the swim bladders of fish, and GELATIN from waste meat, which form insoluble complexes with the unstable pigments and tannins. There is a tendency to move away from animal-based products in the interests of VEGETARIANS AND VEGANS; it is possible to obtain vegetable gelatin, and proteinaceous fining agents derived from peas and potatoes have been developed.

Everyday wines, both white and red, are normally fined earlier and to a greater extent than fine wines. Given the extra time accorded the making of fine wines, many of the potentially unstable components polymerize earlier and deposit without human assistance from man. In general, white wines need fining to preserve their lighter colour and to prevent heat-unstable proteins forming a cloud, while red wines need it for a reduction of astringent and bitter tannins. The fining operation removes components that are soluble but potentially subject to polymerization and cloud, or may precipitate with time.

See also FILTRATION, which cannot remove these soluble substances and acts only on particulates.   A.D.W., J.E.H., & D.B.

fino, Spanish word with two related meanings in the SHERRY-making process. *Fino* is one of two types of wine made naturally in the sherry bodega (*oloroso* being the other). Fino is also a style of sherry, the commercial result of filtering and bottling a *fino*, the palest, lightest, and driest apart from MANZANILLA, and quintessentially the product of the *fino* type of sherry preserved and influenced by the film-forming yeast FLOR. It may be made in any of the three sherry towns, although Fino de Jerez is by far the most common, and that made in Puerto de Santa María is known as Puerto Fino. Most Fino sold in Spain has an alcoholic strength of about 15.5% and is bone dry, and this is now also the norm for export brands. A freshly opened bottle of true, dry, light Fino is one of

the most appetizing wines in the world. For more details, see SHERRY.   V. de la S.

first growth is a direct translation of the French PREMIER CRU but its meaning tends to be limited to those BORDEAUX wine properties judged in the top rank according to the various CLASSIFICATIONS: Chx LAFITE, LATOUR, MARGAUX, HAUT-BRION, MOUTON ROTHSCHILD, CHEVAL BLANC, AUSONE, d'YQUEM, together often with the unclassified but generally acknowledged star of POMEROL, PETRUS. Just below these red bordeaux in terms of status are the so-called SUPER SECONDS.

Fitou, red wine appellation on 2,204 ha/5,444 acres of LANGUEDOC vineyard in two enclaves within the CORBIÈRES zone where it meets ROUSSILLON (see map under LANGUEDOC). When the boundaries of this, the first dry red wine appellation of Languedoc, were drawn up in 1948, local politics prevailed and Fitou has remained with, apparently, a great tract of Corbières bisecting it. The clay-limestone soils of Fitou Maritime, i.e. coastal Fitou, are quite different from the arguably potentially more interesting schists of Fitou Montagneux, ie mountainous Fitou, 40 minutes' drive inland—the purity in the wines of Domaine Bertrand-Bergé argue convincingly for the virtues of a mountain climate. The low-yielding vines on the infertile soils of these Pyrenean foothills are capable of great expression, but the appellation underperformed in the 1970s and 1980s. The region is even more in the grip of CO-OPERATIVES than its northern neighbour, with the Mont Tauch co-operative in Tuchan, the oldest in the Languedoc, responsible for half of all production and, for a while, performing better than many individual producers. In 2014, however, Mont Tauch narrowly avoided brankruptcy and reverted to supplying BULK WINE rather than bottling and marketing their own wine.

The traditional varieties Carignan and Grenache must make up 60% of the final blend with a minimum of 20% of each (this is one of the few appellations that demands a minimum Carignan component). A minimum of 10% of Syrah (better suited to Fitou Montagneux) and/or Mourvèdre (which thrives in Fitou Maritime) must be also included in the blend.

The two territories demarcated for Fitou may also produce RIVESALTES and MUSCAT DE RIVESALTES.

fixed acids, those organic ACIDS of wines whose volatilities are so low that they cannot be separated from wine by DISTILLATION. The two main fixed acids of wine are TARTARIC ACID and MALIC ACID, but several other non-volatile acids are present in small amounts. Unfortunately, the distinction between fixed and volatile acids is not precise because there are some acids which have intermediate volatilities. Among these are LACTIC ACID and SUCCINIC

ACID, both found in wine. The fixed acids are important in wines because they are the acids that give wine its refreshing tartness, as well as its natural resistance to bacterial attack. VOLATILE ACIDS, on the other hand, are more obviously smelly than fixed acids and generally produce fruity or, when present in excess, vinegary aromas. TOTAL ACIDITY, a standard wine measurement, is the sum of the fixed acids and volatile acids.   A.D.W.

Fixin, appellation abutting Gevrey-Chambertin in the Côte de Nuits district of Burgundy, producing red wines of a similar style to its neighbour, though currently of lesser fame. Fixin wines have a similar sturdiness to Gevrey but have less powerful fruit and fragrance.

There are five PREMIER CRU vineyards: Les Arvelets and Les Hervelets (seemingly interchangeable; certainly wine grown in the former may be labelled the latter), Clos de la Perrière, Clos Napoléon, and Clos du Chapître. Dr Lavalle, writing in 1855, noted Le Chapître, Les Arvelets, and Clos Napoléon but he singled out Clos de la Perrière for special praise since at that time the Marquis de Montmort sold it at the same price as his Chambertin.

See also CÔTE D'OR and map under BURGUNDY.
                                                J.T.C.M.

fizziness is the bubbling that occurs in a SPARKLING WINE when the bottle is opened and the wine is poured into a glass. In a sealed bottle the cork maintains a pressure of up to 6 atmospheres and there is equilibrium between the dissolved CARBON DIOXIDE and the carbon dioxide in the HEAD SPACE. When the bottle is opened and the wine is poured into a glass, the pressure above the wine is reduced to ambient pressure of about 1 atmosphere and the wine is said to be supersaturated with carbon dioxide.

In this state, carbon dioxide does not suddenly rush from the wine as bubbles. Carbon dioxide is lost by individual molecules diffusing through the surface and by bubble formation at so-called nucleation sites, which are located on impurities (dirt) stuck to the glass or floating in the wine. Photographic research by Liger-Belair shows these sites are largely hollow cylindrical cellulose fibres from paper or cloth.

Carbon dioxide molecules diffuse into minute gas pockets in the nucleation sites, forming a bubble, and when the bubble grows big enough, buoyancy causes it to lift off and rise to the surface of the wine. This process is then repeated so a stream of bubbles is seen emerging from each site. As the bubbles rise, carbon dioxide from the supersaturated wine continues to diffuse into them and thus they get bigger.

Bubbles reaching the surface of the wine can clearly be seen to have different diameters. This is because different nucleation sites have different shapes and sizes and because the nucleation sites are at different distances from the surface, so the bubble diameters grow by different amounts as they rise. The loss of carbon dioxide is very slow: a bottle or glass of gently bubbling fizz takes many hours to go flat.

It is often observed that the bubbles in old cellared bottles of CHAMPAGNE are smaller and slower (lazier) moving to the surface. This is simply because the bottle has, over the years, slowly lost pressure and thus the degree of supersaturation with carbon dioxide is less, resulting in slower bubble growth, both at the nucleation sites and on the way to the surface.

Most fully sparkling wines such as champagne are sold with a pressure of between 5 and 6 atmospheres, about three times that inside a car tyre, which is the pressure which a normal champagne cork and bottle can withstand without undue risk. Such wines may be described as *mousseux* or CRÉMANT in French, *espumoso* in Spanish, SPUMANTE in Italian, and SEKT in German. Fizziness in champagne seems to be decreasing in the 21st century, perhaps due to the greater use of reserve wines.

Many wines are somewhere between still and this level of pressure, however. Wines with a gentle but definite sparkle may be described as PÉTILLANT in French, FRIZZANTE in Italian, and SPRITZIG in German, although many variations in nomenclature exist. European wine law defines a sparkling wine as any wine with an excess pressure of more than 3 atmospheres (for quality sparkling wine, for example, one with a PDO, it is 3.5), while a semi-sparkling wine has a pressure of between 1 and 2.5 atmospheres. The amount of pressure can be controlled by the winemaker by varying the amount of sugar added at the second fermentation or TIRAGE stage or, in the case of CARBONATION, simply by controlling the amount of gas dissolved in the wine.

Some wines sold as still wines may fizz very gently, however. This could be a sign of a FAULT but is more likely to be a deliberate winemaking feature. See CARBON DIOXIDE for more details.
                                                J.R. & T.J.

Jordan, A. D., and Napper, D. H., 'Some aspects of the physical chemistry of bubble and foam phenomena in sparkling wine', *Proceedings of the Sixth Australian Wine Industry Technical Conference* (1986).

Liger-Belair, G., *Uncorked: The Science of Champagne* (rev. edn, Princeton, 2013).

Fladgate Partnership. The Fladgate Partnership Vinhos S.A. was formed in 2001 when Taylor Fonseca Vinhos S.A. (see TAYLOR'S and FONSECA) purchased CROFT and Delaforce (subsequently sold) from DIAGEO. The group, whose name was inspired by Taylor's full name—Taylor, Fladgate, & Yeatman—remains family owned and is run by descendants of the Yeatman family. In 2014 it had 631 ha/1,558 acres of properties in the DOURO Valley with over 1.4 million vines.

Taylor's vintage PORT is consistently one of the most admired and longest lived, and its Quinta de Vargellas single-quinta bottling can often be almost as concentrated. Vargellas, Taylor's best-known property in the remote eastern reaches of the Douro, was acquired in 1893 when it was still suffering from the ravages of PHYLLOXERA. This acquisition marked the start of Taylor's now considerable landowning and farming activities. Quinta de Terra Feita in the Pinhão Valley, which had been supplying port to Taylor's since the 1890s, was bought in 1974. In 1990, Terra Feita de Cima was added, followed in 1993 by São Xisto next door to Vargellas, which was further extended in 1999. Quinta do Junco was acquired in 1998. In the late 20th century Taylor's popularized the filtered LBV (late bottled vintage) style of port. In the early 21st century it pioneered the release of special, small-volume releases of luxury ports.

In 1948, Taylor, Fladgate, & Yeatman acquired Fonseca and have continued to build on the firm's reputation for excellent, dramatic vintage ports. Quinta do Cruzeiro in the Pinhão Valley had been supplying wine for Fonseca since the 19th century and was acquired in 1973. Five years later the company bought Quinta do Panascal in the Távora Valley, which is a key ingredient in Fonseca vintage port as well as producing single quinta vintage ports. Quinta de Santo António was replanted in the 2000s and is entirely ORGANIC. Fonseca's best-known wine is probably the superior ruby reserve port Bin 27. Vintage ports from earlier-maturing years are sold under the name Guimaraens and are blended from the same properties as produce Fonseca vintage port.

In 2001 port shipper Croft was acquired from Diageo, including the 109-ha/269-acre Quinta da Roêda near Pinhão which has long provided the backbone for Croft's vintage blends. In 2008 the brand was used to launch rosé port, Croft Pink, on an unsuspecting world.

In 2013 The Fladgate Partnership purchased shipper Wiese & Krohn and its impressive stocks of mature tawnies. Eschewing Douro table wines, its focus is premium port, with a global market share of more than 33% of this category. The company has also ventured into wine-related hotels, first in the Douro and, since 2010, the Yeatman in Vila Nova da Gaia overlooking Oporto.

flash détente, also known as flash EXTRACTION, is a technique originally used to extract flavour from fruit such as bananas and mangoes on Réunion that was successfully applied to wine by researchers at INRA in the early 1990s, and patented in 1993. A certain proportion of fully ripe and fully DESTEMMED grapes is rapidly heated to up to 95 °C (200 °F) and then immediately put under vacuum. This very fast method of first heating then cooling has been shown to break up the structure of the skin cells, thereby increasing the extraction of colour, POLYSACCHARIDES, and PHENOLICS by between 30 and 50%. *Flash détente* (literal meaning 'instant relaxation') has so far been authorized for use in certain appellations in southern France such as the Côtes du Rhône and units have been installed there, in Bordeaux, and even in Japan. French and Italian versions have been exported to Australia, the US, and South America. See also THERMOVINIFICATION.

flavescence dorée, a PHYTOPLASMA disease (previously known as mycoplasma disease) of the vine which is spread by insects. It has the potential to threaten many of the world's vineyards and is becoming more widespread due to CLIMATE CHANGE. For more details, see GRAPEVINE YELLOWS.   R.E.S.

flavonoids, a large group of PHENOLIC compounds that includes ANTHOCYANINS, CATECHINS, and the FLAVONOLS. More than 45,000 flavonoids from a wide variety of plant sources have been described. In wine, they contribute to COLOUR, ASTRINGENCY, TEXTURE, and possibly BITTERNESS, although this last is less well documented. Up to 90% of the phenolic content in red wine is made up of flavonoids; in white wines the proportion may be lower because of less EXTRACTION from the skins, stems, and seeds. The antioxidant and cancer chemopreventive capacity of many flavonoids may contribute to the HEALTH benefits of moderate wine consumption.   G.L.C.

flavonols, a group of PHENOLIC yellow PIGMENTS belonging to the FLAVONOID family found mostly as GLYCOSIDES such as glucosides and glucuronides. QUERCETIN glycosides, the most common flavonols in grapes, are abundant in vine leaves and present in skins and stems. Their concentration can be enhanced in grapes (and therefore in wine too) by exposing the berry cluster to the sun (see CANOPY MANAGEMENT). Indeed, Price and colleagues argue that the quercetin level in grape berries can be used as an index of the sun exposure they have experienced. Like CATECHIN, quercetin may enhance PIGMENT stability in young wines through CO-PIGMENTATION and has anti-oxidant properties similar to those of RESVERATROL (see HEALTH). The release of flavonol aglycones from the corresponding glycosides may also result in a hazy wine as these molecules are poorly soluble in wine.

B.G.C., P.J.W., & V.C.

Price, S. F., et al., 'Cluster sun exposure and quercetin in Pinot Noir grapes and wine', *American Journal of Enology and Viticulture*, 46 (1995), 187–94.

flavour, arguably a wine's most important distinguishing mark. As outlined in TASTING, most of what is commonly described as wine's flavour is in fact its AROMA (or alternatively, in the case of older wines, its BOUQUET). This, the 'smell' of a wine, may be its greatest sensory characteristic, but is also the most difficult of its attributes to measure and describe. A wine's flavour could, in its widest sense, be said to be the overall sensory impression of both aroma (as sensed both by the nose and from the mouth), and the taste components, and may therefore incorporate the other, more measurable, aspects of ACIDITY, SWEETNESS, BITTERNESS, occasional saltiness, ALCOHOLIC STRENGTH, FIZZINESS, and ASTRINGENCY. It has, further, been proposed that the definition of flavour be enlarged to include not just how a wine smells, tastes, and feels (including, for example, the burning sensation associated with particularly alcoholic wines), but also individual tasters' psychological predetermination, the all-important factor of SUBJECTIVISM including personal preferences, expectations, and ALLERGIES AND INTOLERANCES determined by individuals' cultural, regional, psychological, and physical influences. (See PHILOSOPHY AND WINE.) In this book, however, the word flavour is used interchangeably with aroma. See also FLAVOUR COMPOUNDS and FLAVOUR PRECURSORS.

flavour compounds, imprecise and inclusive term for substances in wines that can be smelled or tasted (see TASTING), sometimes called aroma compounds. The term flavour compounds is used more particularly for the volatile compounds which are sensed olfactorily, by the nose, and which contribute to both AROMA and, later, BOUQUET, the flavour changing rapidly and markedly during the first few months of a wine's life and then more and more slowly as it matures. Certain compounds are associated with particular VINE VARIETIES although the exact chemical nature of compounds associated with varietal flavours is still the subject of study.

These volatile aroma compounds are in vastly smaller concentrations than those of the non-volatile taste compounds such as GLYCEROL or various ACIDS, some little more than one part per trillion. The flavour differences between varieties arises from differences in the types and amounts of volatile aroma compounds in their berries. It is commonly stated that these occur in the skins, but grape juice also contains significant amounts, and sometimes in different proportions from those found in the same grapes' skin.

Hardie and O'Brien propose that flavour compounds may be present in grapes because they fulfilled an evolutionary role in attracting insects to assist POLLINATION, defending the developing berry flesh against attack from insects and microbes, attracting birds and animals which would eat grapes and so disperse the seeds, and inhibiting germination of competitive plant species. In accordance with selection theory, the variation in flavour and aroma compounds between different VITIS groups of diverse origin is considered to reflect the range of ecological conditions existing during evolution.

The study of grape aroma has attracted scientific attention because of its importance in wine quality, long appreciated but methodologically difficult because of the abundance of candidate compounds, every one of which is potent but scarce. Research quickened in the 1980s as better measuring techniques emerged, notably gas chromatograph-mass spectrometers.

Some of the types of compounds so far identified among the aroma volatiles in the grape are as follows: *monoterpenes*, e.g. linalool, nerol, geraniol, found in floral grapes such as Muscat, Gewürztraminer, and Riesling; *norisoprenoids*, CAROTENOID-derived, e.g. damascenone (rose oil), megastigmatrienone (tobacco, spice), found in Chardonnay; *shikimate-derived*, e.g. raspberry ketone, vanillin, zingerone, found in Syrah/Shiraz; *nitrogen-containing*, e.g. methoxypyrazine (grassy), found in Cabernet Sauvignon and Sauvignon Blanc; *aliphatics*, some gamma LACTONES, an important component of OAK flavour. See METHOXYPYRAZINES and MONOTERPENES.

A large proportion of these compounds occur in grapes combined with SUGARS as GLYCOSIDES and as such are odourless FLAVOUR PRECURSORS. They revert to their aromatic form after hydrolysis of the glycoside by the action of ENZYMES or acids, a process that has been shown to be important in wine ageing.

Most recently, a series of volatile thiol compounds (see MERCAPTANS) has been found to be involved in the varietal aromas of Sauvignon Blanc, Scheurebe, Gewürztraminer, Pinot Gris, Riesling, Muscat, Sylvaner, Pinot Blanc, Petit Manseng, Sémillon, Cabernet Sauvignon, and Merlot. Importantly, these sulfur-containing compounds are present in grape juice and are released, in very low concentration, during fermentation by the action of yeast.

There is no doubt that increasing knowledge about flavour compounds, and their manipulation in the vineyard and winery (as, for example, by the addition of selected enzymes), represents the most important likely technological advances in the wine industry at the beginning of the 21st century. As emphasized above, our knowledge of this area is constantly expanding, especially as new measuring techniques are being developed (see INFRARED SPECTROSCOPY and GLYCOSYL-GLUCOSE ASSAY).

Although the chemical characterization of VARIETAL FLAVOURS is still in progress, it is instructive to consider the example of the methoxypyrazines studied by Allen et al. These remarkable compounds, associated with the 'green', herbaceous, or vegetative aromas in Cabernet Sauvignon and Sauvignon Blanc grapes, can be detected at one part per trillion in water (the equivalent of one grape berry in a million tons of grapes).

Contemporary studies of flavour compounds are beginning to provide important links between viticulture and wine quality such as the relationship between CANOPY MICROCLIMATE and the development of flavour compounds, which Allen et al. found can be increased tenfold using appropriate vineyard practices.

The above examples indicate the enormous effect that flavour chemistry is likely to have on our understanding and manipulation of wine quality, although it also raises the more sinister possibility of 'manufacturing' wines by the addition of traces of flavour compounds to neutral, low-quality wines. Concern about this issue has increased since the discovery in 2004 that illegal flavourings had been added to certain Sauvignon Blanc wines at a winery in South Africa to enhance the varietal character of the wine.

See PHENOLICS, AGEING, and BOTTLE AGEING.

R.E.S., B.G.C., & P.J.W.

Allen, M. S., et al., 'Contribution of methoxypyrazines to the flavour of Cabernet Sauvignon and Sauvignon Blanc', in P. J. Williams et al. (eds.), *Proceedings of the Seventh Australian Wine Industry Technical Conference* (Adelaide, 1990).

Dubourdieu, D., et al., 'The role of yeasts in flavor development during fermentation: the example of Sauvignon blanc', in J. M. Rantz (ed.), *Proceedings of the American Society of Enology and Viticulture 50th Anniversary Annual Meeting, 19–23 June 2000* (Davis, 2001), 196–203.

O'Brien, T. P., 'Some considerations of the biological significance of some volatile constituents of grape (*Vitis* spp)', *Australian Journal of Botany*, 36 (1988), 107–17.

Williams, P. J., and Francis, I. L., 'Wine flavour research—experiences from the past offer a guide to the future', in J. M. Rantz (ed.), *Proceedings of the American Society of Enology and Viticulture 50th Anniversary Annual Meeting, 19–23 June 2000* (Davis, 2001), 191–5.

flavoured wines, somewhat amorphous category of wines whose basic wine grape flavour is modified by the addition of other flavouring materials. VERMOUTH is a flavoured FORTIFIED wine, while the Greek RETSINA is perhaps the most strikingly flavoured unfortified wine.

History

Spices have traditionally been added to wine (as they have to food) to provide some variety in taste, or, more likely, to hide any imperfections of taste. A wine that tasted like VINEGAR would have been much improved by such additions.

The ancient cultures of the Mediterranean added spices, herbs, and honey (and also drugs or resins such as myrrh) to their grape and date wines. Descriptions and recipes abound in ancient texts from MESOPOTAMIA to Ancient ROME. (See also Ancient EGYPT and Ancient GREECE.) The Greeks were reputed by the Romans almost never to drink their wines straight, and PLINY lists virtually everything from pepper to absinthe as wine flavourings.

Flavourings such as herbs and honey would not only cover off-flavours but would give appeal to light-bodied wines (see GERMAN HISTORY). There have long been local specialities of wines flavoured with herbs, spices, flowers, or nuts.

In medieval times, wine usually needed some improvement within a few months when it began to turn sour. This was often done at home and the most popular recipe was for 'hippocras', made with red or white wine. Sugar, honey, cinnamon, ginger, and pepper were the usual ingredients, and the name came from Hippocrates' sleeve, a reference to the muslin bag through which the infused wine was strained. Hippocras remained popular in England well into the 17th century, when it was enjoyed by Pepys, undergoing various changes of name and composition to emerge as punch, so beloved by the Victorians.

Meanwhile in Europe, spiced wines, often fortified with alcohol, evolved into the vermouths we know today. H.B.

Pliny the Elder, *Natural History*, trans. by H. Rackham (London, 1938), Book 14.

Younger, W., *Gods, Men and Wine* (London, 1966).

Modern variations

The category has been much expanded in recent years, however, by the emergence of flavoured, often low-alcohol wines—an attempt to persuade those who do not see themselves as wine drinkers to buy wine diluted and disguised as something else. They come in all degrees of alcoholic strength, sweetness, and fizziness and are popularly flavoured with fruits, even nuts, and chocolate. Such products should be distinguished from FRUIT WINES, whose alcohol derives from the sugars of the (non-grape) fruit itself.

A.D.W.

flavourings are available to wine producers, and are used, illegally, to an unknown extent. Of the three sorts of flavourings available to the beverage industry—natural, nature-identical, and artificial—the last can be discounted because they are easily detectable, and natural and nature-identical flavourings are readily available, no more expensive, and still relatively difficult to detect. Natural and nature-identical flavourings which can impose the characteristics of a range of noble grape varieties such as CABERNET SAUVIGNON and SAUVIGNON BLANC are marketed. Modern analytical techniques

(see ANALYSIS) are able to detect additions at very low levels and there have been a number of successful prosecutions. Since these flavourings are so intense, they can be effective at concentrations as low as 0.001% and the addition of, for example, 100 ml/3.6 fl oz of essence to a 100-hl/2,640-gal vat is an operation which could be performed easily and discreetly. G.T.

flavour precursors include GLYCOSIDES, or sugar derivatives, of compounds that would otherwise be flavour-active. These flavourless compounds occur naturally in grapes (and many other fruits) as products of the normal metabolic activity of the fruit, and they are both numerous and more abundant than the free FLAVOUR COMPOUNDS. Their importance to wine comes from their ability to release and so augment the level of flavour compounds, some positive, some less so. In the case of glycosides, this release is by HYDROLYSIS. This may be a prolonged process during AGEING, for example, or one accelerated through the use of ENZYMES in the winemaking process. Both chemical and sensory studies at the AUSTRALIAN WINE RESEARCH INSTITUTE have demonstrated that flavour precursors are important in development of VARIETAL flavours and BOUQUET in wines. Because many flavour precursors are glycosides, quantification of this class of compound through measures of GLYCOSYL-GLUCOSE in grapes has been suggested as an indicator of grape quality although research is underway to find quicker analytical techniques.

A new category of grape flavour precursor, involving the coupling (or conjugation) of a volatile thiol compound to the AMINO ACID cysteine, was discovered by Professor Denis Dubourdieu's research group at BORDEAUX University in 1998. The action of yeasts during alcoholic fermentation serves to free some of the highly potent thiol compounds from their S-cysteine conjugated precursor form. P.J.W.

Francis, I. L., et al., 'The role of yeasts in flavor development during fermentation: the example of Sauvignon blanc', in R. J. Blair, et al. (eds.), *Proceedings of the Tenth Australian Wine Industry Technical Conference 1998* (Adelaide, 1999), 104–8.

Tominaga, T., Peyrot des Gachons, C., and Dubourdieu, D., 'A new type of flavour precursors in *Vitis vinifera* L. cv. Sauvignon blanc: S-cysteine conjugates', *Journal of Agricultural and Food Chemistry*, 46 (1998), 5215–19.

American Chemical Society, 'Hydrolytic flavor release in fruit and wines through hydrolysis of nonvolatile precursors', *Flavor Science: Sensible Principles and Techniques* (Washington, DC, 1993).

flavour scalping refers to the partial absorption from wine of some aroma and FLAVOUR COMPOUNDS by wine bottle CLOSURES and other types of packaging material (such as the bladders used in wine BOXES) during storage. This process mostly affects wine components that are the least soluble in water. Various flavour-scalping studies of sensorially relevant compounds in wine, some looking at changes in the same wines over several years, have shown that some compounds are not significantly scalped by any closures, while other compounds can be scalped by up to 98% depending on the closure type. The extent of absorption is a function of time in the bottle or other package and the sorptive capacity of the closure, with some SYNTHETIC CLOSURES having a much greater sorptive capacity than natural bark CORKS or technical closures made of processed cork bark. SCREWCAPS have little or no sorptive capacity. Bottles sealed with a particular closure will exhibit little bottle-to-bottle variation in this phenomenon. Flavour scalping does not necessarily diminish wine quality since some wine components can have an unfavourable impact on wine aroma; it does not affect all wines equally and, indeed, will not affect many wines at all.

M.A.S., D.J., & D.L.C.

Capone, D., et al., 'Flavour "scalping" by wine bottle closures', *Australian and New Zealand Wine Industry Journal*, 18/5 (2003), 16–20.

flétri, French term used to describe grapes which have been dried, or partially dried, before fermentation to increase the sugar content. It is used most commonly in SWITZERLAND and occasionally in the Valle d'AOSTA. See also DRIED-GRAPE WINES.

fleuraison or **floraison**, French terms for FLOWERING.

Fleurie, one of the ten BEAUJOLAIS CRUS, and surely the appellation with the prettiest name in France, comprised 822 ha/2,030 acres of vines in 2012. It has a particularly efficacious CO-OPERATIVE, and produces wines which, it is easy to believe, have a particularly floral perfume. Partly because of its name perhaps, Fleurie is one of the most expensive Beaujolais. Soils vary from sandy in the south west where the lightest wines are grown, to clay towards MOULIN-À-VENT in the west where wines can be quite meaty and full bodied.

Fleurieu Zone in SOUTH AUSTRALIA encompasses the regions of Currency Creek, Kangaroo Island, Langhorne Creek, McLaren Vale, and Southern Fleurieu, where Tapanappa's Foggy Hill vineyard is notable for Pinot Noir.

flight, name for a series of different but related servings of wine, served in a bar or restaurant by the GLASS or as part of a TASTING. Australians tend to call them brackets.

Floc de Gascogne is the Armagnac region's answer to the PINEAU DES CHARENTES of Cognac. This strong, sweet red and white VIN DE LIQUEUR, awarded AOC status in 1990, is made by arresting the fermentation of local grape juice at an early stage by adding young armagnac, which in this case must have been produced by the same enterprise. The resulting liquid, of which about 17% is alcohol, is aged for at least nine months (although not necessarily in wood, as for Pineau). It is usually drunk as an aperitif but is also much used by Gascony's famously resourceful chefs.

flooding of vineyards is normally a major inconvenience. Vines can be damaged if there is flooding while they are growing, but not if they are DORMANT. Floodwaters can also destroy TRELLIS SYSTEMS if debris catches in wires. EL NIÑO has made vineyard flooding in California commonplace but fortunately it is usually confined to the winter months.

Flooding (where feasible and controlled) was at one time a measure deliberately used in France, Argentina, and elsewhere to prevent or to minimize the effects of PHYLLOXERA, the root louse that devastated many of the world's vineyards in the late 19th century. Flooding when the vines are dormant can drown the lice but leave the vines unharmed, if not prolong their life expectancy. Unfortunately this treatment was also a factor in the abandonment of many of France's good HILLSIDE VINEYARDS, and replanting on flatland where the MESOCLIMATE and soils are inferior for wine quality (see LANGUEDOC in particular).

Natural winter flooding was used for vineyard IRRIGATION in antiquity, and is still so employed at Langhorne Creek in SOUTH AUSTRALIA, where the annual flood waters of the Bremer river are diverted across some of the vineyards each winter, bringing rich silt which tops up the soil fertility and water to recharge the reserve of moisture held throughout the deep, water-retentive SOIL PROFILE. This gives the vines enough moisture to carry them right through the summer and results in high YIELDS, despite a summer-dry climate with only 500 mm/20 in of annual RAINFALL. However, new vineyards in the region use DRIP IRRIGATION.

J.G. & R.E.S.

flood irrigation. See IRRIGATION.

flor, or **flor yeasts**, are benevolent FILM-FORMING YEASTS which are able to form a veil, velum, or film of yeast cells which floats on the surface of a wine. Flor yeasts are typified by those native to the JEREZ region of southern Spain which produce Fino and Manzanilla SHERRY. These yeasts have been assigned many names by different microbiologists over the years, including *Saccharomyces bayanus*, *S. beticus*, *S. capensis*, *S. cheriensis*, *S. fermentati*, *S. montuliensis*, and *S. rouxii*. However, they are now considered to be synonyms of *S. cerevisiae*.

Flor yeasts are all capable of fermenting sugar in an anaerobic phase of their metabolism. In Jerez they are the active sugar-fermenting yeast. When all fermentable sugar has been consumed, these yeasts have the capacity to switch to another metabolic phase in which they use alcohol and oxygen from the atmosphere to produce a waxy or fatty coating on the cells' exterior which permits them to float on the wine's surface. The flor yeasts begin to form as small white curds on the surface of the wine, typically in the spring after fermentation as the ambient temperature begins to rise. These increase in size until the surface is completely covered by a thin white film which gradually thickens and browns. They also produce ACETALDEHYDE and other products which characterize the aroma of film or flor sherries.

Many studies have shown that these desirable yeasts will form films only in the narrow ALCOHOLIC STRENGTH range of 14.5 to 16.0%. Below 14.5 the usual result is VINEGAR; above 16.0 the yeast struggles and dies, resulting in an *oloroso* style of sherry. Film sherry cannot be made in STAINLESS STEEL tanks because the yeast uses so much alcohol that the wine becomes watery and eventually acetifies. In wooden barrels such as the BUTTS of Jerez, in the area's low-humidity cellars, there is enough preferential EVAPORATION of water through the wood that the water loss just balances the alcohol used by the yeast, the end result being sherry.

Flor yeasts have been studied in detail by Fornachon in Australia, by Niehaus in South Africa, and by CRUESS in California, all regions hospitable to the flor yeast strains and the PALOMINO grape used for sherry, and where wines similar to sherry have been produced (although see also CYPRUS).

Flor or a similar film-forming yeast has been observed on wines in many and varied parts of the world, both ancient and modern.

Flor wines are made in MONTILLA, RUEDA, and Huelva (see CONDADO DE HUELVA) in Spain, and the ALGARVE in southern Portugal, where flor is also used to make a rather crude aperitif wine. See also JURA, whose VIN JAUNE is very similar to sherry, and TOKAJI in Hungary. Similar wines are also made in ROMANIA and, by Plageoles, in GAILLAC.

A.D.W. & P.A.H.

Flora, CALIFORNIA aromatic white vine cross. Perhaps the most delicately aromatic of Dr H. P. Olmo's DAVIS creations (see also CARNELIAN, EMERALD RIESLING, RUBY CABERNET, SYMPHONY), Flora is grown to a very limited extent in California, Australia, and New Zealand.

flotation is a technique of must CLARIFICATION borrowed from the ore refining and concentrating industry. It is based on the tendency of grape solids to adhere to rising bubbles. If very small bubbles of air are introduced at the

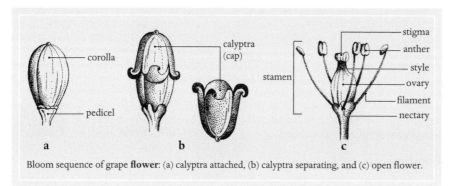

Bloom sequence of grape **flower**: (a) calyptra attached, (b) calyptra separating, and (c) open flower.

bottom of a vat of must, easily oxidized PHENOLICS in the juice will react and some will be removed along with the other suspended solids which are carried to the top of the tank by the finely divided air bubbles. Oxidized phenolics, which are brown, not removed by flotation will probably be adsorbed and removed with the LEES after fermentation. (It is also possible to use compressed nitrogen instead of air.) The advantage of this technique is that the resultant wine resists further oxidative browning. However, there must be no yeast or fermentation activity in the must as this prevents flocculation. Flotation is best suited to large wineries where the process can run continuously.

flower cap of the vine is known as the CALYPTRA.

flowering, important event in the annual growth cycle of vines, the process preceding the fertilization of vine flowers and their subsequent development into berries. The sequence of events includes the opening of individual flowers, with the CALYPTRA (fused cap of petals) being shed, POLLEN being liberated, and ovules becoming fertilized. Fertilization leads to BERRIES being set (see FRUIT SET), the stage following flowering.

Compared with many other plants, the vine has unattractive small green flowers, and the flowering process in the vineyard is so notably unspectacular that it is likely to be missed by the casual observer. The vine-grower, however, is aware that this process is particularly important in the chain of events that leads up to HARVEST, and, with some varieties and some weather conditions, a poor flowering can mean financial disaster for the vineyard owner.

Flowering, or bloom, takes place about six to 13 weeks after BUDBREAK, the period being shorter for warm climates and early varieties. The vine flower usually contains both male parts (STAMENS) and female parts (a pistil-containing OVARY). The flowering process begins as the cap falls away, exposing the stamens. POLLINATION is the process whereby pollen grains are shed and land on the moistened stigma surface where they germinate. They then penetrate the style and fertilize the ovary, leading to fruit set and the creation of a berry. The fertilized ovaries form SEEDS, with up to four per berry. The wall of the flower tissue enlarges to form the SKIN and PULP of the grape berry. See diagram.

Most wine grape varieties have perfect, or hermaphroditic, flowers, that is with well-developed and functional male and female parts. Some varieties such as CURRANT, SULTANA, and Perlette, more suitable for DRYING GRAPES and TABLE GRAPES, have non-functional or defective female parts. Berries from such varieties are typically seedless or have small, poorly developed seeds, and therefore tend to be small because of a lack of HORMONES produced by normal seeds.

Cold, wet, and windy weather at flowering has a bad effect on flowering and fruit set and, in countries such as ENGLAND where grapevines are grown at the cool limit of viticulture, is a major cause of poor YIELDS. Studies in Europe (in CHAMPAGNE, for example) have shown that regional vineyard yield can be correlated with the concentration of pollen in the lower atmosphere, which in turn can also be correlated with weather conditions. Many studies have shown that the vine flower is probably self-pollinated, with insects and wind making little contribution; even flowers surrounded by a bag tend to set perfectly (although cross-pollination between flowers is possible). However, grape flowers do release a pungent, reputedly aphrodisiac, odour, from odour glands at the base of the pistil, which is known to attract insects.   R.E.S.

Keller, M., 'Phenology and growth cycle', in *The Science of Grapevines: Anatomy and Physiology* (Elsevier, 2010).

flowers, vine. The grapevine flower is not showy, and has little attraction for birds, but it has the normal complement of sepals and petals surrounding the sexual parts: the male in the stamens and the female in the pistil. Flowers are grouped together on an inflorescence (see BUNCH). The five petals are locked together to form a cap or CALYPTRA and, at FLOWERING, they fall off, usually as a unit joined at the base; this is called 'capfall', an important PHENOLOGICAL stage. Once the caps are off, the STAMENS expand to their full length and the inflorescence begins to look fluffy. A wet, glistening coating covers the stigma at the top of the pistil when it is ready to receive large numbers of POLLEN grains lodged on this surface.

Different species and varieties of grapevine have one of three types of flower. The most common, and most FRUITFUL, are those with bisexual or hermaphrodite flowers, whose pistil and stamens are both functional. Some vine varieties (such as MADELEINE ANGEVINE and Maratheftiko) may have female or pistillate flowers, with a well-developed, functional pistil but with reflexed stamens which contain usually sterile pollen; with cross-pollination, using fertile pollen, these varieties become fruitful. And other varieties, particularly ROOTSTOCKS, may have male or staminate flowers (with functional stamens but no pistil) and therefore do not bear fruit. Most species of VITIS, in their native habitats, have male and female flowers on separate vines, which ensures cross-pollination and hence genetic diversity among the seedling progeny (see SEXUAL PROPAGATION). Commercial VINE VARIETIES are almost invariably bisexual and self-fruitful, and genetic diversity is avoided by VEGETATIVE PROPAGATION.

Flowering occurs in late spring when shoots have developed 17 to 20 visible internodes. This is a crucial stage in the reproductive development of the grape since a host of mishaps may lead to unsuccessful pollination or failure to develop into a berry (see FRUIT SET).   B.G.C.

Mullins, M. G., Bouquet, A., and Williams, L. E., *Biology of the Grapevine* (Cambridge, 1992).
Pratt, C., 'Reproductive anatomy in cultivated grapes: a review', *American Journal of Enology and Viticulture*, 22 (1971), 92–109.

flowers in vineyards may be deliberately planted at row ends or even between rows as COVER CROPS. Rose bushes at row ends are commonplace in the Médoc and, increasingly, elsewhere, either for aesthetic reasons or because they may act as early indicators of a POWDERY MILDEW attack. Flowers may also be planted between the rows as a pollen source to attract insects which are considered beneficial to vineyard ECOSYSTEMS.

Flurbereinigung, refers to wholesale restructuring to which most of Germany's vineyards have been subjected since the 1950s, involving improved accessibility, grading, consolidation of growers' highly fragmented holdings, and of course replanting. Without this restructuring, many vineyards would long since have been abandoned as not economically viable to till. But the process—which must be agreed to by a majority of landholders who share its costs with the state—is often contentious. Owners of vineyards marginally located or extremely difficult to access are offered the opportunity of opting out, and some entire vineyards have been deemed too onerously steep and rocky to be amenable to restructuring. It is largely as a result of these two situations that ancient terraces and vines, some UNGRAFTED, remain in certain sites, especially along the SAAR and MOSEL.   D.S.

flying winemakers, term coined by English wine merchant Tony LAITHWAITE for a team of young Australian winemakers he hired to work the 1987 vintage in French CO-OPERATIVE wineries. The idea was to apply Australian hard work and technological expertise to inexpensive grapes, thereby producing a unique range of wines for his mail-order wine business. The scheme originally depended on the fact that AUSTRALIA has a substantial number of highly trained winemakers (see ACADEME) who are relatively idle during HARVEST time in the northern hemisphere, where most of the world's wine is made. This sort of bought-in OENOLOGY initially worked best in areas with a considerable quantity of relatively inexpensive grapes but whose technical potential was yet to be realized. It thus excluded the classic wine regions and much of the NEW WORLD but decisively included southern France, much of Italy (especially Puglia and Sicily), and Iberia, eastern Europe, some of the more open-minded South African wineries, and South America. The concept was such a success that it was much imitated and developed into a phenomenon with a long-term impact on winemaking techniques and wine styles all over the world (see GLOBALIZATION) in the 1990s, although the marked increase in local oenological training and skills has made the phenomenon less common.

By the late 1990s, several teams of itinerant winemakers had developed from permanent bases in both France and Britain. But in general hundreds of career flying winemakers have been replaced by much smaller numbers of recent oenology graduates who combine travelling with work experience in cellars and vineyards around the world before finding their vocational location or returning home. INFORMATION TECHNOLOGY has enabled virtual winemaking from a distance of several time zones and many thousands of miles. By the 21st century, the winemaker who had only ever made wine in a single location was almost the exception.

Foch, common North American name for the MARÉCHAL FOCH vine.

Fogoneu, minor red wine grape of the Balearic island of Mallorca usually blended with CALLET and MANTO NEGRO.

foil, alternative name for the CAPSULE which covers the cork and neck of a wine bottle. The term is most commonly used for bottles of sparkling wine because in this case it is almost invariably made of metal foil, whereas the 'foil' covering tops of bottles of still wine may be made from a wide range of materials. Traditionally LEAD or lead alloys were used to manufacture foils, but in Europe these were found to be a major source of soil contamination in disposal sites, and lead contamination of wine was traced to this source, so the use of lead foils has been phased out, and was prohibited in the US and the EU in 1993. Older bottles with lead foils should be wiped carefully around the bottle-neck between pulling the cork and serving. Various plastics and tin are used, as is, increasingly, paper. Of the two most common types, one is made from polyvinyl chloride (PVC) with an aluminium top and is heat shrunk onto the bottle (alternatives made from more environmentally friendly polyethylene terephthalate (PET) are also available); the other is a polylaminate consisting of layers of polyethylene and aluminium which is spun into place. The foil is there largely for aesthetic reasons since the CLOSURE should provide an airtight seal and only a faulty one will allow any seepage of wine. Very occasionally, in the case of an oversight during bottling, a wine may be bottled with a foil but no cork; a tight foil has been observed to act as an effective bottle stopper in at least one case. The length and design of a foil is another purely aesthetic matter, although some clear identification on the top of the foil can be very useful in a CELLAR full of bottles on wine racks.

foil cutter, gadget for SERVING wine which helps cut the FOIL neatly just below the lip of the bottle with the advantages that this avoids unsightly and possibly dangerous torn metal edges, and that there is no likelihood of the wine's being poured over a foil which might taint it. Some foil cutters are blades incorporated into CORKSCREWS; others are separate prongs with small circular blades which cut the foil when rotated. Life without a foil cutter is quite feasible; living without one after being introduced to it is not.

Folgasão, mysterious vine producing promising whites from 258 ha, mainly in Trás-os-Montes in Portugal.

Folle Blanche, white grape variety, probably GOUAIS BLANC progeny, once grown in profusion along the Atlantic seaboard of western France, providing very acidic but otherwise neutral base wine for distillation by the largely DUTCH WINE TRADE. It never regained its position after PHYLLOXERA ravaged the vineyards of Europe in the late 19th century and France's total plantings of Folle Blanche continue to decline: from 12,000 ha/29,640 acres in 1968, to 1,366 ha/3,374 acres in 2011, mainly for GROS PLANT

production. It has also been grown to a very limited extent in California, and possibly northern Spain.

Folle Noire, occasional synonym for various French dark-berried grape varieties including JURANÇON and Fuella Nera. Unrelated to FOLLE BLANCHE. See BELLET.

Fondillón, strong RANCIO wine from ALICANTE made from the dark-skinned MONASTRELL grape and matured like an *oloroso* SHERRY.

Fonseca, common Portuguese surname associated with two important but unrelated wine producers in PORTUGAL.

Fonseca is a highly respected PORT shippers, now part of the FLADGATE PARTNERSHIP. It was founded by the Fonseca and Monteiro families and acquired by a Portuguese gentleman, Manoel Pedro Guimaraens, in 1822. With the exception of the 1955 produced by Dorothy Guimaraens, every single Fonseca vintage port between 1896 and 1991 was made either by Frank Guimaraens or his great-nephew Bruce. Bruce's son, Australian-trained fifth-generation David Guimaraens, continues the good work. Fonseca Guimaraens, as it was then known, was acquired by Taylor, Fladgate, and Yeatman in 1948 but the two houses maintain separate identities and styles of port within the group now known as the Fladgate Partnerhip under which more detail can be found.

José Maria da Fonseca is a family company based in the south of the country at Azeitão in ARRÁBIDA on the Setúbal peninsula. Originally a producer of rich, fortified SETÚBAL, it is now more important as a producer of a wide range of unfortified Portuguese wines, notably under the name Periquita designed for the international market. See TERRAS DO SADO.

In the mid 1990s, José Maria da Fonseca took over its sister company J. M. da Fonseca Internacional, which had been hived off as a separate business in the 1960s for the production of LANCERS.

food, wine as. See DIET.

food and wine matching is either an extremely complex, detailed subject, a set of rules embedded in one's national culture, or an activity only for gastro-bores, according to one's point of view.

To the French, not surprisingly, wine is simply part of *gastronomie* in general, and few French people would dream of describing a wine without suggesting which dish or dishes it should be served with. France has traditionally looked to its chefs for expertise in TASTING and selecting wine, and it was only in the late 1980s that wine began to be viewed as a distinct subject in its own right.

In the United States, food and wine matching, or pairing, became a subject of intense scrutiny in the 1980s as wine producers, under pressure from so-called neo-Prohibitionists, sought to distance wine from drinks consumed principally for their alcohol content by putting it firmly on the dining table.

For some of the most fanatical wine enthusiasts, food is an obstacle between palate and wine glass, whose flavours can get in the way of a decent wine-tasting session.

It is certainly true that it is perfectly physically possible to drink any sort of wine with any sort of food. It is also true that 'white wine with fish and red wine with meat' is an absurd generalization built on a couple of sound maxims. There are also certain foods which have very specific effects on wine, and others which distort the PALATE to such an extent that wine tastes very odd or downright nasty in their wake.

But, as Hanni points out, wine and food matching is an ongoing process of sensory adaptation. If a sensory message to the brain is constantly repeated (such as the taste of sourness in food), then it will suppress our sensitivity to the source of stimulation, making the wine that follows taste less sour.

The following should be read in conjunction with the article on TASTING.

Some specific reactions

The wine merchant's maxim 'buy on an apple and sell on cheese' has a sound basis in gustatory fact. Fresh, uncooked apples, like most fruits high in both SWEETNESS and ACIDITY, make many wines taste thin and metallic; any wine that impressed when tasted with an apple must have been seriously good. Hard cheese such as cheddar, on the other hand, tends to make wines taste softer and fuller. Strongly acidic foods such as dishes containing lemon juice and VINEGAR were for long cast as villains in terms of serving with wine, but thanks to sensory adaptation can make a slightly too acid wine taste fuller and more agreeable (while reacting badly with top-quality wines). Raw garlic can react with water to produce a burning sensation in many palates, while an acidic drink such as wine (Provençal rosé with *aïoli*) neutralizes the garlic and refreshes the palate. Hanni has demonstrated that, to the majority of palates, freshly ground pepper is a sensitizing element that may ruin the nuances of a fine, old wine, but can flatter a young, light-bodied wine by making it taste stronger, fuller, and more complex.

Some wine-unfriendly foods

Globe artichokes and asparagus: A significant proportion of the population are sensitive to a substance in artichokes which has been dubbed 'cynarin' and which has the effect on them of making water taste sweet, and making wine taste metallic. McGee reports the evidence for this. A similar effect has been observed with fresh asparagus.

Some forms of chocolate are not only so sweet that it is difficult to find a wine sweeter than they are, they also coat the inside of the mouth. In this case a very strong, very sweet wine will overcome these disadvantages; lively young port, PX, Australian TOPAQUE AND MUSCAT, and the sweetest VINS DOUX NATURELS, seem to manage.

Some general rules

White wines generally (although not universally) taste more acid than red wines, so it makes sense to serve them with simple fish dishes which would normally call for the sort of acidity in lemon juice or vinegar.

Sweetness in food (which can be from as unexpected a source as tomatoes or balsamic vinegar) increases the perception of sourness, BITTERNESS, and ASTRINGENCY in wine, while making the wine appear less sweet, stronger, and less fruity.

Very acid foods (such as those dressed with vinegar or citrus juice) decrease our perception of sourness in wine, making the wine taste richer and more mellow. If the wine is at all sweet, it will taste sweeter.

Foods dominated by bitterness, sweetness, and UMAMI accentuate any bitterness in a wine.

Red wines high in TANNINS taste less tannic if served with heavily textured foods containing uncoagulated proteins for the tannin molecules to combine with, so it can make sense to partner a rare steak with a young wine based on Cabernet Sauvignon, Syrah, Nebbiolo, or Sangiovese.

Bitterness and astringency in wines can be muted by judicious use of salt in the food served with them.

Astringency in wine is suppressed by foods that are acid, salty, or fatty and accentuated by food that is sweet or spicy.

Salty foods may make sweet wines taste sweeter.

Full-bodied, aromatic white wines such as Gewürztraminer have traditionally been recommended with spicy foods, but contemporary Asians suggest that particularly those containing chili may well go best with lightly chilled, assertively fruity, possibly even tannic, reds.

Many cheeses are too pungent or greasy textured for very fine or mature red wine. Sweet wines, whether fortified or not, can be more flattered by the savoury, salty nature of cheese, and are less overwhelmed by it than, say, a mature red bordeaux.

Most dry wines taste horrible with sweet foods, which seem to emphasize their acidity. Even quite sweet wines can taste very thin and nasty if served with dishes that are sweeter than they are. It is therefore advisable to choose only relatively sweet, full-bodied wines with the sweet course. Germany's delicious sweet AUSLESEN are usually best sipped without food.

Clever use of lemon juice, vinegar, fresh pepper, and chewy meats can compensate for the shortcomings of ordinary wines. With very fine wine, however, it is probably safest to serve relatively neutral foods. A general observation in matching food and wine is that there are nearly always at least two ways of doing it: in one the wine completely parallels the food profile, in the other opposes and contrasts with it. For example, smoked eel can successfully be paired with, respectively, a creamy Chardonnay with heavy lees influence or a steely Riesling with green apple and mineral notes.

Some particularly successful combinations

Riesling and smoked salmon or other smoked fish.

Riesling (even medium-sweet Riesling) with onion tart.

Chablis with oysters.

Cru Beaujolais with charcuterie, particularly *rosette de Lyon*.

Red bordeaux and lamb.

Red burgundy with feathered game.

Sauternes and Roquefort or other blue cheese.

See also ORDER OF WINES.

Goldstein, E. & J., *Perfect Pairings* (Berkeley, 2006).

Hanni, T., *The Cause and Effect of Wine and Food* (St Helena, 1991).

Goldstein, E. & J., *The Components of Taste* (St Helena, 1998).

Lee, J. C., 'Some Prefer Red With Chili', *Wall Street Journal* (Nov 2004).

Poussier, L., and Poussier, O., *Desserts and Wines* (London, 2004).

McGee, H., *On Food and Cooking* (New York, 1984).

www.matchingfoodandwine.com

foot treading, traditional method of CRUSHING only rarely found outside Portugal's DOURO Valley, where it is still used for the production of some of the finest ports. CHAPOUTIER of Hermitage and some BURGUNDY producers also use feet for breaking up the CAP of their top red table wines.

Forastera, simple white wine grape from the island of Ischia near Naples with total plantings of just 56 ha in 2010.

Forcallat Tinta, blending grape grown on 635 ha/1,568 acres of VALENCIA and Murcia, making curious-smelling, light-coloured red wine.

forests, by supplying wood of a certain sort, have an important impact on the character and flavour of wine made using COOPERAGE made from that wood. See WOOD TYPES and, particularly, OAK for details of individual forest locations.

Forez, Côtes du. A range of hills between the upper reaches of the Loire and Lyons in eastern France give their name to light, vigorous red and rosé wines made, like BEAUJOLAIS, from the GAMAY grape. The wines, designed for early drinking, may taste reminiscent of those of the Côte ROANNAISE to the north. Both regions, part-granitic, have known greater glory. Full AOC status was granted to Côtes du Forez in 2000. It is higher than the Côte Roannaise, has a slightly less dependable climate, and has taken an almost exclusively CO-OPERATIVE route. The Vignerons Foréziens co-operative is based in Boën-sur-Lignon and has won acclaim for its policy of developing quality through a series of different cuvées. Plantings had fallen to below 100 ha/250 acres by the early 2010s.

Fortana, tart red wine grape grown on 400 ha/1,000 acres in 2010 around Ravenna and Ferrara in EMILIA-ROMAGNA, also known as Uva d'Oro.

fortification, the practice of adding spirits, usually **grape spirit**, to wine to ensure microbiological stability, thereby adding ALCOHOLIC STRENGTH and precluding any further FERMENTATION.

The principle behind this addition of alcohol is that most BACTERIA and strains of YEAST are rendered impotent, unable to react with sugar or other wine constituents, in solutions containing more than 16–18% alcohol, depending on the strain of yeast.

The stage at which spirit is added has enormous implications for the style of fortified wine produced. The earlier it is added in the fermentation process, the sweeter the resulting wine will be. VINS DE LIQUEUR such as PINEAU DES CHARENTES, for example, are simply blends of sweet, unfermented, or hardly fermented grape juice with grape spirit, known as *mistelles* in France (see MISTELA). An even stronger charge of alcohol is added before fermentation to a significant proportion of the rich grape juice used in the production of Australia's TOPAQUE AND MUSCAT. For most port-style wines (including the sweeter styles of MADEIRA) and for all VINS DOUX NATURELS, fortification takes place during fermentation. Much of the natural grape sugar is retained by arresting fermentation before its completion, thereby boosting alcoholic strength to a pre-ordained level: usually 18–20% in PORT but 15–16% in most vins doux naturels. In the making of sherry, similar wines such as MONTILLA, and the drier styles of madeira, spirit is added to dry, fully fermented wine only at the end of fermentation. Any sweetness in such wines is usually due to a pre-bottling addition of sweetening agent, often itself a mixture of grape juice and spirit (see MISTELA, PX).

The spirit used for fortification comes from a variety of different sources and could be based on grapes, sugar beet, cane sugar, agricultural by-products, or even petroleum. Local regulations specify the types of spirit allowed for a given fortified wine and only grape spirit is allowed for fortified wines of any quality. Carbon dating usefully allows the immediate detection of petroleum-based spirit in any wine, however.

The method of DISTILLATION of the spirit plays a part possibly even more important than its source. The most neutral spirits are the products of a continuous still, which contain a minimum of flavour congeners (the impurities which contribute to the character of a spirit) and tend to be used in the fortification of wines that are designed for early consumption and deliberately exhibit the characteristics of the base wine (the MUSCATS of southern France, for example). Spirits produced by pot still distillation on the other hand are much more violently flavoured and are rarely added to fortified wines. A.D.W. & J.E.H.

fortified wines are those which have been subject to FORTIFICATION and therefore include SHERRY, PORT, MADEIRA, VERMOUTH, MÁLAGA, MONTILLA, MARSALA, TOPAQUE AND MUSCAT, VINS DOUX NATURELS, and several strictly local specialities. Liquids such as VINS DE LIQUEUR (see also MISTELA) made by adding spirit to grape juice rather than wine are not, strictly, fortified wines. Practically all warm wine regions (see AUSTRALIA, CALIFORNIA, CYPRUS, SOUTH AFRICA, for example) make some sort of fortified wine, often in the image of port and sherry even if they are not allowed to use those protected names, within Europe anyway. It is an almost invariable rule that anywhere hot enough to produce good fortified wine is too hot to provide the ideal climate for its consumption. See also LIQUEUR WINE.

Fort Ross-Seaview, relatively new California AVA. See SONOMA.

foulage, French for the winemaking operation of CRUSHING grapes.

Foundation Plant Services (FPS), a self-supporting service department of the University of California at DAVIS which produces, tests, maintains, and distributes disease-tested plant propagation material. It also provides plant importation, quarantine, and testing services.

fourth growth. See the CLASSIFICATION of Bordeaux.

foxy, usually deeply pejorative tasting term for the peculiar flavour of many wines, particularly red wines, made from AMERICAN VINES and AMERICAN HYBRIDS, vine varieties developed from both American and European species of the VITIS genus, particularly *Vitis labrusca*. (Wines made from many other hybrids—SEYVAL and NORTON, for example—are completely free of **foxiness**.) The CONCORD grape, widely planted in NEW YORK State, is one of the most heavily scented, reeking of something closer to animal fur than fruit, flowers, or any other aroma associated with fine wine, although the 'candy'-like aroma is, incidentally, quite close to that of the tiny wild strawberry or *fraise des bois*. Ortho-amino-acetophenone is the compound chiefly responsible for this aroma in NIAGARA grapes while methyl anthranilate does the job in Concords. Earlier harvesting or long CASK AGEING reduces some of Concord's foxy characteristics. H.L. & B.G.C.

fractional blending, prosaic English name for the labour-intensive SOLERA system of maintaining consistency of a blended wine, particularly SHERRY, over many years.

France, the country that produces more fine wine than any other, and in which wine is so firmly embedded in the culture that such French people as are interested in wine have a quasi-spiritual relationship with it. Per capita wine consumption in France has fallen dramatically, however, from over 100 l a year in 1977 to under 50 l by the early 21st century, thanks to social changes, increased restrictions on advertising alcohol, and on driving with it in the bloodstream. By the end of the 20th century, wine export markets were also being shrunk by competition from other wine-producing countries with their own wine SURPLUSES, a strong euro, and a distinct lack of marketing skills, particularly a lack of BRANDS, on the part of the French wine industry, although the rest of the wine-producing world increasingly envied France's primacy in wine TRADITIONS.

The total area planted with vines shrank considerably (see EU and its VINE PULL SCHEME) particularly in the 1990s and 2000s: down from 1.23 million ha/3.04 million acres in the late 1970s to under 800,000 ha by the early 2010s (including those vines dedicated to cognac, armagnac, and TABLE GRAPES), but France still has more land under vine than any country other than Spain. Average annual wine production fell from 65 million hl in the late 1980s to under 50 million hl in the early 2010s.

There are few wine producers anywhere who would not freely admit that they have been influenced by the great wines of BORDEAUX, BURGUNDY, CHAMPAGNE, or possibly the RHÔNE (see map). Other qualitatively significant wine regions, perhaps better appreciated within France than abroad, include ALSACE (for historical details of which see GERMAN HISTORY), BEAUJOLAIS, CHABLIS, JURA, LOIRE, PROVENCE, SAVOIE, and SOUTH WEST FRANCE. France's most important wine region by far in terms of quantity has long been the LANGUEDOC, and ROUSSILLON to the immediate south, but vine pull schemes have shrunk the regions' vineyard area and much improved the average quality of wine produced there.

FRANCE

BELGIUM

LUXEMBOURG

GERMANY

ENGLISH CHANNEL

Champagne

Moselle

Rheims
Bouzy
Château-Thierry
Épernay · Châlons sur Marne
Avize
Sézanne
Paris
Toul
Côtes
de Toul

Strasbourg

Alsace

Colmar

Bar sur Aube

Les Riceys

Chablis

Loire Valley Vendôme Orléans
Auxerre
Gien St Bris
Dijon
Angers
Tours
Blois
Saumur
Nantes
Chinon
Haut-Poitou

Sancerre
Nevers
Burgundy Côte
d'Or
Côte
Chalonnaise

Arbois
Jura

SWITZERLAND

Mâconnais
Mâcon

Châteaumeillant

Beaujolais

Geneva
Annecy

Fiefs
Vendéens

Poitiers

St-Pourçain-
sur-Sioule

Seyssel

Savoie
Chambéry

ATLANTIC
OCEAN

La Rochelle

Saintes

Angoulême

Roanne
Côte
Roannaise
Côtes
d'Auvergne

Côtes
du
Forez

Lyons

Northern
Rhône
Grenoble

ITALY

Valence
Die

Blaye

Bergerac

Dordogne

Massif
Central

Rhône

Bordeaux
Bordeaux Duras Monbazillac

Entraygues
Marcillac
Rodez

Estaing

Nyons
Southern
Rhône

Marmande
Buzet

Agen

Cahors

Nîmes

Avignon

Provence

Nice

Fronton Gaillac

Montpellier

Coteaux d'Aix
en Provence
Aix en Provence
Côtes de Provence
Marseilles
Cassis Bandol

South West
Tursan
Bayonne Béarn
Irouléguy Jurançon
Pau Madiran

Auch
Toulouse

Languedoc

Béziers

Carcassonne
Limoux

Perpignan

Roussillon

Pyrenees

SPAIN

MEDITERRANEAN
SEA

Calvi Patrimonio

Corsica Vin de
Corse
Ajaccio

Sartène Porto
Vecchio

0   200 km

■ Wine-growing regions

The Mediterranean island of CORSICA is also under French jurisdiction, although it shares many characteristics with the Italian island of SARDINIA.

Although the first instance of geographical DELIMITATION was in Portugal's DOURO Valley, France is the birthplace of the widespread application of the notion that geography, or TERROIR, is fundamental in shaping the character and quality of a wine. This resulted in the early 20th century in the much-copied APPELLATION CONTRÔLÉE system. Its governing body is INAO. Appellation contrôlée, or AOC, wines represent the wines of which France has traditionally been most proud, sold under the geographical name of the appellation rather than by vine variety, in contrast to the substantially VARIETAL wines of the NEW WORLD. AOC wines, prime candidates as the EU's new PDO category, represent an increasing proportion of all wine produced in France, about 46% in the 21st century. According to these new distinctions, those wines previously categorized as VDQS or VIN DE PAYS had either to be promoted to AOC status or recategorized as IGPs which represented about 28% of all French wine in the early 2010s. About 17% of all French wine goes to be distilled into cognac, armagnac, or other brandies, and the remaining just under 10% which does not satisfy the relatively stringent regulations for AOC and IGP wines is sold as mere VIN DE FRANCE. This category, created in 2010, includes very basic wines that would previously have sold as vin de table as well as an increasing number of much better-quality wines deliberately made outside the restrictions of AOC and IGP rules. This is also the fate of wines rejected by AOC tasting panels.

Curiously, and perhaps because wine is so deeply entrenched in French history and culture, wine CONNOISSEURSHIP and to a certain extent the wine TRADE are not as evolved in France as, for example, in Australia, Belgium, Great Britain, Switzerland, and the United States. Although things are slowly changing, the average French citizen has bought and drunk little other than the wine produced closest to him or her, whether geographically or by virtue of family or friendship. This has tended to stifle the development of wine retailing, although the number of specialist wine MERCHANTS, known here as *cavistes*, has increased significantly since the early 1980s. As might be expected in a country associated with so many forms of gastronomic excellence, wine appreciation in France is closely tethered to the table. Wine is rarely drunk without food, and France's chefs and SOMMELIERS have been regarded as the rightful repositories of wine knowledge.

Although France is by far the world's principal wine exporter, rivalled only by Italy, it is also a major wine importer, with the proportion of wine imported in BULK, about a third higher than any other country's. Wine has been imported ever since Massilia was settled by the Greeks (see below), but it was the development of the Languedoc as a virtual factory for particularly light red wines at the end of the 19th and the beginning of the 20th centuries that meant vast quantities of strong, deep-coloured red wines had to be imported for BLENDING (*coupage* in French), from North African colonies initially, and subsequently from southern Italy and, to an increasing extent, Spain.

France is so important as a role model to the world of wine that many terms used internationally are French in origin (BLANC DE BLANCS, PIGEAGE, and VERAISON are just three varied examples). France is recognized the world over as a centre of wine research and ACADEME and has benefited ever since the time of Colbert in the late 17th century from the country's ability to identify and solve potential problems on a national level (see OAK). The OENOLOGICAL and viticultural faculties of the universities of BORDEAUX and MONTPELLIER have long enjoyed international prestige, and considerable viticultural research emanates from INRA stations.

One of France's great commercial strengths in recent years has been that it is the world's prime source of oak for top-quality wine and brandy COOPERAGE. France is the world's leading exporter of barrels.

History

Around 600 BC, Greek immigrants arrived from Phocaea in ANATOLIA and founded Massalia (Marseilles) as a Greek city (see Ancient GREECE). One of the colonists' importations was viticulture, although in 2013 Patrick McGovern found evidence that they were probably preceded by Etruscans (see ORIGINS OF VINICULTURE). In the 2nd century BC, the settlement, now known as Massilia, had become vital to the Romans, now a major power (see Ancient ROME), if they were to safeguard their trading route with Saguntum (modern Sagunto, near Valencia in Spain). When Massilia was attacked first by the Ligurians and then by the Celtic tribes of the Allobroges and the Arverni (of modern AUVERGNE), self-interest made the Romans take on the defence of the city. As a result they gained a new province, named at first Provincia (modern PROVENCE) and later, with the foundation of the Roman city of Narbo (modern Narbonne) in 118 BC, Gallia Narbonensis. Massilia remained Greek until 49 BC.

In the eyes of the Greek colonists, vines grew where olives and figs grew: the commercial exploitation of the three together had long been characteristic of Mediterranean agriculture, so it did not occur to a Mediterranean people that the vine could be cultivated further north than the olive and the fig. The wines of Massilia were available in Rome, but they were cheap and nasty. Even before Caesar's conquest of Gaul in 51 BC, the Gauls had consumed Italian wine in prodigious quantities, as the evidence from AMPHORAE found in France shows. The Greek geographer Strabo, who finished his *Geography* in 7 BC, said that Massilia and Narbo produced the same fruits as Italy, but that the rest of Gaul was too far north for the olive, the fig, and the vine (4. 2. 1). His statement may have been too sweeping, however, and in the 1st century AD good wine certainly did come from Gaul. PLINY tells us in his *Natural History* that in Vienna (modern Vienne in the RHÔNE Valley) the Allobroges produced RESINATED WINES which were a source of national pride and for which they charged high prices (14. 57). For more details, see GAUL.

Thus the first French wine of note was a Rhône wine. Yet at the same time or earlier the inhabitants of Gallia Narbonensis may themselves have taken the vine beyond the familiar territory of the olive and the fig, to GAILLAC in modern SOUTH WEST FRANCE. Archaeological evidence shows that in the second half of the reign of the Emperor Augustus (he was Imperator from 27 BC to AD 14), amphorae were being made in large numbers in workshops near Gaillac, and near Béziers in the LANGUEDOC. This suggests that they were needed for wine that was grown there and not imported. The RIVERS Tarn and GARONNE would have provided convenient transport to the Atlantic coast, where BORDEAUX was already a trading post. Since these wines are not mentioned by any classical author, they probably did not reach Rome, unlike the wines of Vienne.

Gaillac and Vienne are beyond the northern limit for olive trees, but they do sustain another tree that is considered characteristic of Mediterranean vegetation, the evergreen oak, QUERCUS *ilex*. Where the evergreen oak grows, the climate is hot enough to produce a good grape harvest every year, without fail. Yet viticulture advanced further north, away from the evergreen oak, to where the success of the vintage is no longer guaranteed. Bordeaux and BURGUNDY were next in line; by the 3rd century AD, wine was grown in both regions, despite the possibility of cold, wet summers when the grapes might not ripen fully. Yet even if the harvest failed occasionally, the demand for wine was such that the expansion of viticulture made economic sense.

The Romans had regarded the CELTS as drunks, and hence a source of great profit, immoderate fools who drank wine unmixed with water until they fell into a stupor, but when the drunken Celts started growing their own wine, its reputation was soon to surpass that of the Italian wines that they had once imported. After Bordeaux and Burgundy came the LOIRE and the Île-de-France (the PARIS basin including CHAMPAGNE). By the 6th century AD, even the west of Brittany had vines, and wine was grown further north than it is now, well north of Paris.

As the Roman empire disintegrated, Gaul ceased to be a Roman province and was overrun by Germanic invaders. The Visigoths, the Burgundians, and the Franks established kingdoms in Gaul; eventually, Aquitaine and Burgundy were subjected to Frankish rule. Under the Romans, the Gauls had been governed from the south; the Franks had come from the north, and Clovis, the first of the Merovingian kings (481–511), established Paris as the capital city of a kingdom that hardly extended further than the Île-de-France. Under CHARLEMAGNE and his heirs, the royal court's principal seats were Aachen (Aix-la-Chapelle) and Paris. Hence political power, and the wealth that went with it, were concentrated in the north. In the Mediterranean, wine was part of everyday life, but in Paris and Aachen, on the northernmost limits of viticulture, wine was a luxury item, and from a luxury item it became a status symbol. Also, because Gaul was largely Christian by the 6th century, the Church's requirements added impetus to northern viticulture (see EUCHARIST). Monasteries and churches needed wine; local magnates, both lay and spiritual, wanted good wine.

McGovern, P. E., et al., 'The Beginning of Viniculture in France', *The Proceedings of the National Academy of Sciences USA* 110:25 (2013): 10147–10152.

Monastic influence

Monasteries had their own vineyards (see MONKS AND MONASTERIES and BURGUNDY), and so, often, did cathedrals. From the Carolingian era onwards, lay viticulture generally used the system of 'complant', which meant that a winegrower would approach an owner of uncultivated land with an offer to plant it for him. Since it takes about five years for new vines to start yielding a decent quantity of fruit, the grower would be given that length of time to work the vineyard; after that, half the land would revert to the owner, while the vines on the other half would become the possession of the grower, on condition that part of the harvest, or sometimes a monetary payment, be given every year in perpetuity. The Loire wine QUARTS DE CHAUME, for instance, owes its name to the complant mode of ownership and production: the *quart*, or fourth, being the share the vigneron owed the landowner (in 1440, the Abbey of Ronceray d'Angers); *chaume* meaning an uncultivated plot that is to be planted with vines. As labour grew more expensive, the conditions became more favourable to the grower: in the course of the 13th century, the owner would often no longer reclaim the half of his property, but the grower, and his children and his children's children after him, would continue to make their annual payments in wine or money. The system made it possible for wild country to be colonized and cultivated at no expense to the landowner: in this way, the new wine-growing region of Poitou (see LA ROCHELLE) was planted so efficiently in the 12th and 13th centuries. The advantage to the grower was that he was not a serf, tied to the land, but a free man, entitled to a large share of what he produced. It was therefore in his interest to make wine for which he could get a good price; nevertheless the owner exercised ultimate control, for the decision how and with what grapes to plant the vineyard was his, and he had the right to terminate the contract and evict the vigneron if the wine was not good enough.

In the Middle Ages, wine was France's chief export product, and the reasons why certain nations drink some wines in preference to others go back to this period. The English drink CLARET because BORDEAUX was at one time governed by the English crown and later remained the largest supplier of wine to England. The Scots drink claret because of the Auld Alliance with France against England. The Flemish and the Dutch have traditionally bought wines of Burgundy because Flanders and the southern part of the Netherlands were part of the dukedom of Burgundy and

Burgundy's trade routes were mostly overland to the north. But transporting wooden BARRELS of wine along bumpy roads was difficult and expensive: whether a region exported a large share of its wine or produced wine mainly for its own consumption depended on its proximity to navigable RIVERS rather than on the quality of its wines. Apart from its trade with the north, which did not develop until the 15th century, Burgundy did not export much wine, whereas regions accessible by water, such as the LOIRE, the Île-de-France around PARIS, and GASCONY, did. The chief ports were La Rochelle, Rouen, and Bordeaux respectively, with Bordeaux serving both the Bordeaux area and the HAUT PAYS.

The ships used to transport wine before the 12th century were longboats like the Viking ships. But in the 12th century, the new ports of La Rochelle and Gravelines (on the English Channel near St-Omer), as well as the new Flemish ports of Nieuwpoort (near Ypres) and Damme (near Bruges), adopted a new type of ship, the cog. The cog was a broadly built ship, with a roundish prow and stern, more manœuvrable than the old kind and specifically designed for carrying freight. Its capacity was far larger than that of the old longboat, and soon all other ports started using it as a more efficient way of transporting wine. The cog doubled up as a warship if need arose.

The unit in which wine was measured, the TONNEAU, derived from Bordeaux. A tonneau, or wooden barrel, could hold 252 old wine gallons, or 900 l/238 US gal. A Paris tonneau was 800 l, but, because of the prominence of Gascon merchants in London and English merchants in Bordeaux, the Bordeaux measure became the standard. Many cogs could hold as many as 200 tonneaux; in practice, a barrel containing 900 l was too heavy to handle, and casks half or a quarter the size were used. Such was the importance of the medieval wine trade that, from being the space occupied by a tun of wine, a tonneau, or ton in English, became the unit in measuring the carrying capacity of any ship, whatever its load. H.M.W.

Dion, R., *Histoire de la vigne et du vin en France* (Paris, 1959).

Duby, G. (ed.), *Histoire de la France rurale*, i (Paris, 1975).

Lachiver, M., *Vins, vignes, vignerons* (Paris, 1988).

Modern history

The social turmoil of the French Revolution at the end of the 18th century made few important changes to the patterns of wine production (although it did engender an entirely new class of consumers, and new styles of *restauration* for them). Until the middle of the 19th century, the vine was cultivated much more widely in France than it is today, and such now-abandoned areas as, for example, the Côtes d'AUVERGNE on the Massif Central, Paris, and the

MOSELLE were flourishing wine regions. As communications improved, the patterns of the wine trade changed, although Bordeaux continued to operate with a certain degree of autonomy, thanks to its geographical position and long-established trading links with northern Europe, first ENGLAND and then the DUTCH WINE TRADE. The 17th and 18th centuries saw an explosion of interest in wine production in the Gironde, and by the mid 19th century, when the world's most famous wine CLASSIFICATION was formalized at a magnificent exhibition in Paris, the great CHÂTEAUX of the MÉDOC were enjoying a period of prosperity that would not be rivalled until the 1980s. Wine continued to be important to the Burgundian economy, and French wine was recognized throughout the civilized world as one of the cornerstones of civilization itself. CHAPTAL had devised ways of improving overall wine quality (for ADULTERATION AND FRAUD was rife in the immediate aftermath of the Revolution), and France was beginning to produce its own wine experts such as the widely travelled and independently minded JULLIEN. A historian might say that a catastrophe to end this golden age was inevitable.

In fact there was a series of catastrophes, all viticultural, which had devastating effects on both the quantity and quality of wine produced. Oidium, or POWDERY MILDEW, was the first of a series of disastrous imports from North America, presumably the result of the 19th century passion for collecting botanical specimens. Unlike European vines, most American vines are resistant to this FUNGAL DISEASE and so it was not until it had been imported to Europe that its effects, of reducing quantity, quality, and colour, were noted, in 1852. The 1854 vintage in France was disastrous, the smallest for more than 60 years. French vineyards were just returning to health, thanks to the development of SULFUR dusting, when another curious vine condition was noted: inexplicable debilitation and, eventually, death. The cause was a tiny louse, PHYLLOXERA, which was to ravage the vineyards of the world, but affected southern France first, causing the greatest commercial havoc there while a remedy was sought. Since phylloxera affects only the roots of vines, the only effective solution was eventually found to be to graft European vines on to resistant American ROOTSTOCKS. But the renewed importation of North American plant material seems to have brought with it two more deadly American fungal diseases, DOWNY MILDEW, whose effects on wine quality and quantity were first noted in 1878 and lasted until well into the 20th century, and BLACK ROT, which was evident from the mid 1880s.

It is hardly surprising therefore that French vignerons saw their salvation in planting HYBRIDS, vines with at least some genes from AMERICAN VINE SPECIES to provide a defence against these completely new and unforeseen hazards to one of France's greatest glories. First, after considerable debate, American hybrids were planted and then, in the early 20th century, so-called FRENCH HYBRIDS were developed which tasted more like the European VINIFERA vines' produce.

There was such a crisis in wine quality in the late 19th century that the great scientist PASTEUR was asked to look into the matter, and the result was a giant step forward for the science of winemaking, in which France has long been at the forefront of research (see University of BORDEAUX in particular).

By the turn of the century, the plains of the LANGUEDOC had been transformed into a great factory producing light red for drinkers in northern France, now commercially accessible thanks to the development of the RAILWAYS. These light wines were given weight, alcohol, and colour by the produce of new vineyards in ALGERIA and the economy of this North African colony was transformed.

Two World Wars left France's wine business in serious need of reorganization, and since the mid 20th century it has certainly been the world's most thoroughly and harmoniously organized, with the development of the powers of the INAO and increasing emphasis on the importance of the APPELLATION CONTRÔLÉE system for which it is responsible. Vigorous, and successful, efforts have been made to uproot hybrids from France's vineyards, to ensure that a sound standard of scientific training is available to France's thousands of vine-growers and winemakers, and that a thorough programme of research is dedicated to the concept of wine quality.

Thanks to falling sales both at home and abroad towards the end of the 20th century, La CRISE VITICOLE dominated the French wine business in the early 21st century.

Geography and climate

France does not have the monopoly on fine wine production, but its geographical position is such that it can produce wine from an exceptionally wide range of grape varieties with a good balance of sugar and acidity, although CLIMATE change is evident throughout the country. With wine regions lying between LATITUDES 42 degrees and 49.5 degrees, France can provide the two most suitable environments identified in CLIMATE AND WINE QUALITY for growing grapes. In the south, the MEDITERRANEAN CLIMATE can be depended upon to ripen grapes fully, but not so fast that they do not have time to develop an interesting array of FLAVOUR COMPOUNDS and PHENOLICS. In the west, relatively high latitudes are tempered by the influence of the Atlantic's Gulf Stream. In the east, centuries of viticultural tradition have established what seem to be potentially perfect marriages between grape variety and particularly favoured terroir in the more

CONTINENTAL climate of Burgundy, Alsace, and Champagne, France's most northerly wine region where, over the centuries, the ideal wine style has evolved to take advantage of the area's climate and special geology.

France also has a wide variety of SOIL TYPES, much charted and revered (although see GEOLOGY and SOIL AND WINE QUALITY for a discussion of the limited extent to which they may affect wine quality).

Vine-growing in modern France is concentrated in the south but there are vineyards in all regions other than the most mountainous and the coolest, which excludes most of the Massif Central, the high-elevation mass in the middle of the country, much of the alpine region on the south east, and the flat north western sector closest to Great Britain. See map.

Vine varieties

France conducts a full agricultural census only every decade or so. The most recent was conducted in 2011 and published in 2012.

CARIGNAN was France's most planted vine variety for many decades, thanks to its ubiquity in France's largest wine region, the Languedoc-Roussillon, but by the turn of the century Merlot had assumed this role and its total plantings had grown to 114,306 ha/282,336 acres by 2011. GRENACHE was second most planted with 87,723 ha, while UGNI BLANC, grown chiefly for distillation into brandy, was still France's third most planted variety with 83,230 ha. Syrah overtook Cabernet Sauvignon to become the country's fifth most planted variety with a total of 66,859 ha to Cabernet's 51,769 ha. Carignan had been so thoroughly routed in the Languedoc Roussillon, and Chardonnay so widely planted, that the latter overtook the former to become France's seventh most planted variety with 47,487 ha. The only other varieties planted on more than 30,000 ha were Cabernet Franc and Pinot Noir, although Sauvignon Blanc was very nearly that widely grown. The picture overall is one of increasing domination of French vineyards by the INTERNATIONAL VARIETIES.

HYBRIDS, so widely planted in the mid 20th century, are all but a distant memory.

One of France's strengths is her increasingly appreciated and revived treasury of traditional INDIGENOUS VARIETIES, either imported as a result of shifting political power (many of France's most planted red varieties were originally Spanish), or the apparently autochthonous likes of those still to be found in limited quantity in SOUTH WEST FRANCE. They are less numerous than in ITALY, but that probably reflects France's national efficiency and centralism.

Viticulture

Most vineyards in France are immediately recognizably French. With its generally reliable

rainfall and supply of soil water, northern France has the highest VINE DENSITY in the world, with up to 13,000 plants per ha, and the vines are typically planted in neat, low-trained rows, often using GUYOT systems of pruning and training (typically dictated by the detail of APPELLATION CONTRÔLÉE regulations). LEAF TRIMMING during the growing season is common. French vignerons have in general had centuries to match cultural practices to local conditions, although in the early 20th century many less suitable terrains were planted in an extension of classic zones. IRRIGATION is usually unnecessary in northern and western France, and is strictly, if sometimes only theoretically, controlled in the south. The relatively humid climate of western France means, however, that frequent SPRAYING against FUNGAL DISEASES is often necessary. In the early 1990s, concern was increasingly expressed at the use of AGROCHEMICALS in many French wine regions, particularly Burgundy, where ORGANIC VITICULTURE and BIODYNAMIC VITICULTURE is increasingly common. Other common viticultural hazards are FROST in the north, HAIL in Burgundy, and DROUGHT in the south, both of the last two on the increase. Crop levels can vary considerably since the weather during FLOWERING is by no means predictably fine, WINTER FREEZE has been known to kill a substantial proportion of vines, as in 1956, and spring frosts can seriously affect total national production, as in 1991.

French viticultural research is of a high level, and co-ordinated nationally under the auspices of INRA, which has stations all over the country. Many of the world's vine-growers regard French NURSERIES as their prime source of planting material, and there has been considerable work on CLONAL SELECTION.

France's vine-growers are probably the most regulated and restricted in the world, however. For all wines other than the basic VSIG, dates of HARVEST are limited by regional annual decree, and YIELDS are minutely regulated. A low yield is generally regarded as the safest prerequisite for wine quality, but in the 1980s, the maximum basic yield allowed by Appellation Contrôlée regulations was routinely increased by a so-called *plafond limite de classement*, or PLC, supplement often as high as 20%. Yields are now set annually. Since the late 1980s, CROP THINNING has been the norm for many quality-conscious producers. The 1990s saw the introduction of SORTING tables to increase wine QUALITY. MECHANIZATION was introduced to lowlier appellations in the late 1980s and 1990s. PRECISION VITICULTURE techniques are currently being refined at the better, larger properties.

Winemaking

In many wine regions, TRADITION has long been as important as SCIENCE in determining winemaking techniques, although France's winemakers can and do draw on many centres of OENOLOGICAL academe for instruction and research (see ACADEME for a list of those described in further detail in this book).

Techniques vary enormously in France's hundreds of thousands of *caves* but in general, and in sharp contrast to the New World, PROTECTIVE JUICE HANDLING and an obsession with winery HYGIENE are relatively rare. Mastery of MALOLACTIC CONVERSION and OAK AGEING, on the other hand, have long been taken for granted.

Part of French winemakers' easy relationship with BARREL MATURATION comes from the fact that France is the centre of the world's COOPERAGE industry, or at least that part of it of interest to winemakers.

France is also the birthplace of CHAPTALIZATION, and a high proportion of her wines have depended on some degree of ENRICHMENT although CLIMATE CHANGE suggests that France may need to introduce more widespread ACIDIFICATION too, forbidden for wines that have been chaptalized. Another winemaking practice once regarded as quintessentially foreign in France, the use of OAK CHIPS, is now tolerated for IGP and VSIG wines. Further up the quality ladder there was some experimentation with CONCENTRATION techniques although this is on the wane.

Wine in France is red. Less than a quarter of all wine consumed in France is white, and in the hot summers of the south of France, rosé is more likely to be consumed than white, as a sort of red for high temperatures.

Wine quality categories

Of the average French harvest, wines from the most revered quality wine category AOC represent the most significant proportion, while the most basic wine for immediate consumption, that classified as Vin de France, or VSIG, is made in ever-decreasing quantity. In between these two categories lie the category of IGP wines introduced in 2010 which replaced wines previously sold as Vins de Pays, and those awaiting promotion to AOC status called VDQS. The remaining proportion of an average year's French wine production is designed for DISTILLATION into brandy. France dominates the production of fine brandy with its cognac and armagnac.

For details of the history, climate, geography, vine varieties planted, and wines produced, see under regional, or even more geographically specific, names, including PARIS. For individual regions, see also ALSACE, BEAUJOLAIS, BORDEAUX, BUGEY, BURGUNDY, CHABLIS, CHAMPAGNE, CORSICA, JURA, LANGUEDOC, ROUSSILLON, LOIRE, PROVENCE, SAVOIE, RÉUNION, RHÔNE, and SOUTH WEST FRANCE. See also VIN and immediately following entries, as well as CRÉMANT for some of France's better-quality sparkling wines.

Bettane, M., and Desseauve, T., *Le Classement* (Paris, annually).

Jefford, A., *The New France* (London, 2002).

Johnson, H., *The Story of Wine* (London and New York, 1989).

Johnson, H., and Robinson, J., *The World Atlas of Wine* (7th edn, London, 2013).

Le Guide Hachette des Vins (Paris, annually).

www.vins-france.com

www.inao.gouv.fr

Franciacorta, important wine region in the hills immediately east of Brescia, with a relatively short history of producing TRADITIONAL METHOD sparkling wine from Chardonnay and Pinot Noir with some Pinot Bianco. Its name is a corruption of the medieval Francae Curtes, Curtes meaning communes and Francae meaning 'exempt of taxes', referring to the region's privileged position at the time.

Spread over 19 villages, the area is also demarcated as DOC Curtefranca (formerly known as Terre di Franciacorta) for still white and red wines made from INTERNATIONAL VARIETIES. In the 1980s and 1990s these answers to Bordeaux and Burgundy, often treated to lavish amounts of new OAK, sold well but are now overshadowed by Franciacorta's sparkling success. Franciacorta's history begins in 1961 with the release of the first traditional method sparkling wine ever to be produced in the region by the house of Guido Berlucchi. The resulting demand for Berlucchi wines attracted a series of able entrepreneurs from Milan and Brescia to invest in Franciacorta.

Franciacorta modelled itself closely on Champagne, while the local CONSORZIO adopted an admirable code of self-regulation for the sparkling wines with production regulations at least as strict as those for the wine's French model: a minimum VINE DENSITY of 3,300 vines per ha; TENDONE and GENEVA DOUBLE CURTAIN training systems forbidden; a maximum yield of 65 hl/ha; and fractional PRESSING. The wines must undergo lees ageing for a minimum of 18 months for non-vintage wines, 30 months for vintage-dated wines, and 60 months for wines labelled Riserva. The Sáten designation refers to a BLANC DES BLANCS that has spent at least 24 months on the lees. The DOSAGE, and hence the wine pressure, is lower than for regular Franciacorta. One contrast to champagne is that Franciacorta with zero dosage works well every year, thanks to warm days and cool evenings in summer, assisted by the moderating influence of nearby Lake Iseo. Mineral-rich gravels and limestone soil predominate.

The success of the wines of Ca' del Bosco and Bellavista, with their scrupulous attention to detail, continues to attract newcomers to the region, to such an extent that the area under vine has grown from 800 ha/2,000 acres in the late 20th century to 2,800 ha in 2011, producing 21 million bottles of sparkling wine each year. Quality of the wines is generally high, showing a real capacity for ageing, while large players co-exist well with smaller, more artisanal producers, often focusing on organic and biodynamic viticulture. W.S.

www.franciacorta.net

Franconia, English name for the German wine region FRANKEN, and a local name for the BLAUFRÄNKISCH grape variety in FRIULI in northern Italy.

Francs, village which gives its name to the small Francs Côtes de Bordeaux appellation on the RIGHT BANK between ST-ÉMILION and BERGERAC, part of the Côtes de BORDEAUX group. The original settlement took its name from a detachment of Franks sent there by Clovis after defeating the Visigoths (see FRANCE, history). The wines have considerably more personality than regular BORDEAUX AOC and the area's revival in the 1980s owed much to the Belgian Thienpont family (also associated with Le PIN and Vieux-Château-Certan). In 2013, 361 ha/892 acres of vineyard were producing sturdy Merlot-based reds on high clay-limestone slopes, many of which enjoy a favourable west south west exposure. Tiny amounts of Sémillon-based white, both dry and sweet, were also made in memory of a style once traditional for this area. For more detail, see BORDEAUX.

Franken, known in English as **Franconia**, distinctive wine region in central GERMANY, with a total of 6,176 ha/15,255 acres of vineyard in 2013. Severe winters and autumns as well as spring frosts are among the challenges that result in some of Germany's most variable YIELDS, but this has not deterred a near tripling of total vineyard area since the 1960s. The features for which Franken wine is best known are arguably neither its grapes nor its distinctive soils and wines, but the fact that nearly all of it is marketed in squat, flattened BOCKSBEUTEL bottles at prices most German growers can only dream of, and most is consumed within the region itself.

While representing slightly less than one-quarter of planted surface (still significantly surpassed by MÜLLER-THURGAU), SILVANER is nonetheless rightly considered Franken's flagship grape, yielding robust, ageworthy, and minerally complex results. RIESLING and PINOT NOIR are also capable of excellence in selected sectors and sites. Several of the many vine crosses prominent in mid-20th-century Germany—notably BACCHUS, KERNER, SCHEUREBE, and RIESLANER—are, like Müller-Thurgau, more successful than usual in Franken, whose soils high in active lime seem to tame these grapes' less appetizing characteristics. Dry wines not only dominate in this region, but already did so during the 1970s and 1980s when Germany's Riesling-centric growing regions were only moving in that direction. Nobly sweet elixirs are relatively rare but can be stunningly complex and long-lived, like their Riesling relatives in other parts of Germany.

South of the city of Aschaffenburg along the right bank of the Main, Franken's westernmost vineyards Mainviereck and Miltenberg feature dramatically steep SANDSTONE terraces whose late-20th- and early-21st-century revival has resulted in some of Germany's most impressive Pinot Noirs (as well as distinctive Riesling), notably from the Schlossberg and Centgrafenberg vineyards of Klingenberg and Bürgstadt respectively. Some 25 km east but still along the Main, vineyards around Marktheidenfeld mark the transition from Triassic sandstone to fossiliferous MUSCHELKALK, Riesling sharing space with Silvaner. Vineyards dominate the eastern half of a huge northerly bow inscribed by the Main, as well as a plunge to the south that embraces the city of Würzburg, whose Stein, Innere Leiste, and Pfülben vineyards are among Franken's most celebrated sources of Silvaner and (in rather austere renditions) Riesling. Eastern viticultural Franconia includes numerous smaller outposts, but many vineyards are near the Main. Eschendorf, not far west of Würzburg is especially notable for its Lump vineyard, where Muschelkalk intersects with the distinctive Triassic MARL known as Keuper, a geological formation that dominates vineyards in the Steigerwald of Franken's southeast whose best-known wine village and site are, respectively, Iphofen with its Julius-Echter-Berg.   D.S.

Frankovka, Slovak synonym for the red BLAUFRÄNKISCH grape.

Franschhoek, or Franschhoek Valley, important wine district in the Coastal Region of SOUTH AFRICA and home to many historic cellars. Established in the late 17th century to accommodate the influx of French Huguenots (the name means 'French Corner'), it is an important TOURISM centre within easy driving distance of Cape Town.

Fransdruif, or just **Frans,** traditional Afrikaans name, meaning 'French grape', for the PALOMINO grape in South Africa.

Frappato, increasingly celebrated Sicilian red grape variety, which can add fruit and floral freshness to NERO D'AVOLA and NERELLO Mascalese in the south east of the island, notably Cerasuolo di Vittoria DOC. Probably a descendant of CILIEGIOLO, it wasgrown on a total of 752 ha/1,857 acres in 2010.

Frascati, LAZIO's most famous DOC, of which it has become regrettably difficult to find examples of ageworthy and complex white wine. Named after the town of Frascati immediately east from Rome, the wine was for centuries based on the local MALVASIA del Lazio (a cross between MUSCAT OF ALEXANDRIA and SCHIAVA

Grossa) which imparted a light Muscat note to the wine. Since the 1960s up to 30% of the high yielding TREBBIANO Toscana could be included, which has diluted its character to that of a rather neutral white for everyday drinking, of which most is absorbed by Rome and its many tourists.

The expanding suburbs of Rome have slowly crept up on Frascati's vineyards, but despite this continuing decline in producing area, to 839 ha/2,205 acres in 2012, they still managed to produce some 95,000 hl of wine. This exceptionally high average yield of 112 hl/ha has done little to achieve either more character in or higher prices for the wine.

In an effort to improve the situation, the entire zone was elevated to DOCG for Frascati Superiore, for which the production regulations demand lower YIELDS (11 tonnes/ha rather than the 14 tonnes/ha for plain Frascati), and with a higher mininum alcohol of 11.5% (rather than 11%), implying, at least in theory, a wine made from riper grapes with more extract. The traditional sweet version of Frascati, **Cannellino di Frascati**, was also elevated to DOCG level. Although in the past this was merely a medium-sweet wine, the 2011 regulations stipulate a higher alcohol level and that grapes must be at least late harvested. They may also undergo partial drying, while the minimum RESIDUAL SUGAR must be at least 35g/l. Oak ageing is explicitly allowed, if not mandatory, for this wine.

While Frascati's production is dominated by large operations, and relative industrial winemaking technology, even the largest of these regularly produce at least one superior bottling based on a higher percentage of Malvasia, often complemented by the local Bellone grape, especially suitable for sweet wines, and GRECO Bianco, and sometimes BARREL fermented. These examples express much more faithfully the original Frascati characteristics, but due to Frascati's generally modest reputation they have difficulty in finding a market willing to pay the premium. A classic example of true Frascati is the Superiore version of Casal Pilozzo.   W.S.

Belfrage, N., *Brunello to Zibibbo. The Wines of Tuscany, Central and Southern Italy* (London, 2003).

Canuto, F., and De Santis, L., *Frascati* (Rome, 2002).

www.consorziofrascati.it

fraud, wine. See ADULTERATION AND FRAUD.

free-run is the name used by winemakers for the juice or wine that will drain without PRESSING from a mass of freshly crushed grapes or from a FERMENTATION VESSEL. Depending on the type of vessel used for DRAINING and the winemaking process, it constitutes 60–85% of the total juice available and is generally superior to, and much lower in TANNINS than, juice or wine whose

extraction depends on pressing. Most modern white wine is made from grapes that pass through a CRUSHER-DESTEMMER before going into a draining tank with a perforated bottom through which the free-run juice passes to the fermentation vessel. In some wineries, free-run juice is collected by draining through specially designed, perforated-bottom screw or drag-link transfer conveyors which move the MUST directly from the crusher-destemmer to the PRESS, bypassing draining tanks completely. Many winemakers boast of using only free-run juice in the production of fine white wines, but PRESS WINE, the wine produced by pressing what is left, may be useful as a BLENDING element.

In RED WINEMAKING, the free-run wine is that which, after SETTLING, is drained or RACKED away from the LEES. In some wineries, free-run red wine is also recovered from specially designed transfer conveyors. Whatever remains goes into the press to yield press wine, which can be even more useful for its tannin concentration when making up blends of red wines.   A.D.W.

freeze. See WINTER FREEZE.

freeze concentration. See CONCENTRATION.

Freisa, or **Freisa Piccola,** is a distinctive, wild strawberry-flavoured red grape variety indigenous to the PIEMONTE region of north west Italy and, more specifically, to the provinces of Asti, Alessandria, and Cuneo in scattered vineyards which reach almost to the gates of the city of Turin.

The vine has been known in Piemonte for centuries. DNA PROFILING has shown that Freisa has a parent–offspring relationship with NEBBIOLO and may be closely related to VIOGNIER. Freisa musts can be quite high in both ACIDITY and TANNINS like Nebbiolo, although its wines are coarser in terms of the tannins and flavours.

The wine exists as a VARIETAL in a range of styles, but traditionally as a slightly frothy wine from a SECOND FERMENTATION, which retains some unfermented RESIDUAL SUGAR to balance the slight bitterness from the LEES. The frizzante or sparkling version of Freisa with its decisively purple colour and aromas of raspberries and violets is reminiscent of good LAMBRUSCO, if much more tannic and tart.

It is DOC in both dry and sweet (*amabile*) styles in the following areas: the larger Freisa d'ASTI and the minuscule Freisa di Chieri, the LANGHE, the MONFERRATO, and the rare Pinerolese. Its popularity has declined rapidly in recent years in its native Piemonte.

Modern technology, in the form of pressurized tanks, now permits producers better control of both the residual sugar level and the amount of CARBON DIOXIDE in the wine, and this type of Freisa, which does not undergo a second fermentation in the bottle, tends to be distinctively drier and almost imperceptibly fizzy. Today producers such as Aldo Vajra, Coppo, and Ascheri make a more ageworthy, completely dry, and completely still type of Freisa aged in BARRIQUE and a handful make a Freisa Nebbiolata, in which the wine is refermented on the skins of Nebbiolo used for BAROLO. Tannins abound in this style.

By 2010, total Italian plantings had fallen to just over 1,000 ha/2,500 acres. It is also known in California.

Freixenet, the largest producer of TRADITIONAL METHOD sparkling wine and most significant exporter of CAVA in the world. The brand was born at the beginning of the 20th century when Pedro Ferrer Bosch and his wife Dolores Sala Vivé decided to concentrate on sparkling wines. The company, still family-owned, was named after an estate in Mediona, PENEDÈS, which had been in Pedro Ferrer's family since the 13th century, known as La Freixeneda, meaning a plantation of ash trees. His wife's grandfather founded the former Sala company, which started exporting wines to the USA in the second half of the 19th century. The company was initially keen to establish export markets, a policy which has paid off in the latter half of the 20th century. It now has four production centres in San Sadurní d'Anoia: Freixenet SA, Segura Viudas SA, Castellblanch SA, and Torrelavit SA, as well as wineries in a number of DO regions around Spain: Solar Viejo in Rioja, Morlanda in Priorat, Garbó in Montsant, Valdubón in Ribera del Duero, and Vionta in Rías Baixas. The combined production of Cava alone is now more than 140 million bottles per year. Best-known brands are the medium-dry Carta Nevada, launched in 1951, and Cordon Negro, a brut Cava in a distinctive black bottle. Freixenet's overseas interests include the Bordeaux négociant Yvon Mau, Henri Abelé in Champagne, the Wingara Wine Group and Katnook Estate in Australia, Gloria Ferrer in the CARNEROS district of California, Finca Doña Dolores, a sparkling wine estate in MEXICO, and Finca Ferrer in the Uco Valley of Mendoza in Argentina.

S.E.A. & V. de la S.

French-American hybrids. See FRENCH HYBRIDS.

French Colombard, common California name for one of the state's most planted grape varieties, the French white COLOMBARD, now much more widely planted in California than in France. Originally brought from Cognac, Colombard was sold as a varietal wine in the 1970s and 1980s when there was a shortage of white wine grapes. Most of it is grown in the SAN JOAQUIN VALLEY for JUG whites and CHARMAT sparklers.

French hybrids, group of vine HYBRIDS bred in France in the late 19th and early 20th centuries, usually by crossing or hybridizing AMERICAN VINE SPECIES with a European VINIFERA variety (see VINE BREEDING). These are also known as direct producers, hybrid direct producers, HDPs, or, in French, *hybrides producteurs directs*. One early response to the invasion of the American PHYLLOXERA louse in Europe was to plant American varieties, since most had phylloxera tolerance. In Europe they proved to be both hardy and resistant to a wide range of FUNGAL DISEASES, but, because of the strange, often FOXY, flavour of the wine they produced, it has been illegal to plant the likes of ISABELLA, NOAH, Othello, Black Spanish (Jacquez), and Herbemont in France since 1934.

The aim of the early hybridizers was to combine the pest and disease resistance of the American species with the accepted wine quality of the European wine species V. vinifera. A group of French breeders such as François BACO, Castel, Georges COUDERC, Ferdinand Gaillard, Ganzin, Millardet, Oberlin, Albert SEIBEL, Bertille SEYVE, and Victor VILLARD, and, more recently, Joanny Burdin, Galibert, Eugene Kuhlmann, Pierre Landot, Ravat, Jean-François Seyve's sons Joannes and Bertille (who married Villard's daughter and developed the important SEYVE–VILLARD series of hybrids), and Jean-Louis VIDAL, produced thousands of new hybrid varieties with such aims in mind. They used AMERICAN HYBRIDS as parents as well as American vine species. *V. aestivalis, V. rupestris, V. riparia,* and *V. berlandieri* were common parents because of their excellent disease and pest resistance, and a reduction in the strong fruit flavour associated with *V. labrusca*. Some of the ROOTSTOCKS used today were bred by these hybridizers, particularly Castel, Couderc, Ganzin, and Millardet. Active hybridizers in other countries included the Italians Bruni, Paulsen, Pirovani, and Prosperi.

These hybrids were widely favoured because of disease resistance and high productivity, so by 1958 about 400,000 ha/988,000 acres of French hybrids were planted in France, or about one-third of the total vineyard area. Wine quality was, however, often inferior, especially from the earlier French hybrids. With continued crossing and back crossing, the objectionable features in the taste of the wine could be reduced (see diagram for NEW VARIETIES). French planting regulations since 1955 have deliberately discouraged vine varieties associated with poor wine quality, however, both hybrids and *V. vinifera*, and so by 2012 there were fewer than 205,000 ha of hybrids. With the exception of Baco 22A, which may be used for armagnac, hybrids are being systematically phased out of French wine and brandy production, even though there were still sizeable

plantings of Villard Noir, CHAMBOURCIN, and PLANTET for red wines and some Villard Blanc and SEYVAL BLANC for white wines, according to the FranceAgriMer statistics for 2012. Other hybrid varieties that are authorized, if not actually encouraged, in France include Baco 1, Chancellor, Couderc Noir, Garonnet, Oberlin Noir, various Seyve-Villard hybrids, and Varousset for red wine and Rayon d'Or for white wine.

The French hybrids have been planted outside France and have made significant contributions at some time or other to the wine industries of the eastern UNITED STATES (see NEW YORK in particular), CANADA, ENGLAND, and New Zealand, where French hybrids were planted in the majority of vineyards into the 1960s, and used for FORTIFIED WINES. From the 1960s onwards, in almost all of these regions, these hybrids have been systematically replaced by *V. vinifera* varieties for reasons of wine quality, although in some sites in Canada and New York subject to WINTER FREEZE, only a hybrid such as Vidal will survive (and has produced some fine ICE WINE), while Seyval Blanc is still grown to a limited extent in England.   R.E.S. & J.E.H.

Galet, P., *Précis de viticulture* (7th edn, Montpellier, 2000).

Galet, P., and Morton, L. T., *A Practical Ampelography: Grapevine Identification* (Ithaca, NY, and London, 1979).

Sabbatini, P., and Howell, S. G., 'Vitis hybrids: history and current status', *Wines & Vines* (January 2014), 135–42.

French paradox, term coined in the United States in 1991 to express the infuriating fact that the French seem to eat and drink themselves silly with no apparent ill effects on their coronary health. Immediately after this thesis was aired on prime-time television in the United States, and red wine consumption cited as a possible factor in reducing the risk of heart disease, US sales of red wine quadrupled and GALLO had to put their leading branded GENERIC Hearty Burgundy on allocation. For more details, see HEALTH. A similar association between red wine consumption and health benefits has played an important part in the wine boom in ASIA.

Frescobaldi, one of Florence's most prominent noble families since the 13th century, are among the largest landholders in TUSCANY with a wide range of agricultural activities. The Frescobaldi holdings can be divided into three distinct blocks: the first, Tenuta di Castiglioni to the south west of Florence, where the family started to produce wines as early as the 1300s; the second, to the east of Florence, produces classic CHIANTI RUFINA from the Nipozzano estate and the wines of Pomino; the third block is Castelgiocondo in MONTALCINO, whose acquisition in 1989 made Frescobaldi the largest potential producer of Brunello. In 2000, Frescobaldi ventured outside Tuscany when it acquired the Conti Attems estate in FRIULI. In 2004, they acquired control of the ORNELLAIA estate in BOLGHERI, their first foray into what had been an Antinori fief. Also in the Maremma Frescobaldi now produce INTERNATIONAL VARIETALS on their Tenuta dell'Amiraglia.   W.S.

The Frescobaldi were the first Italian producers of a BARRIQUE-aged white wine, beginning in the mid 1970s with the grapes from their Benefizio vineyard at Pomino. Their single-vineyard Chianti Rufina, Montesodi, was also among the first superior all-Sangiovese wines aged in small barrels.

fresh grapes. See TABLE GRAPES.

Fresno, abbreviation for California State University, Fresno, in the heart of the San Joaquin Valley, where over 65% of California wine grapes are grown. In 1997, it became home to the first licensed, bonded winery in a university in the US. The Department of Viticulture and Enology was formed in 2001. Students receive a very practical education, and expertise is required in both disciplines. The university has extensive vineyards for all aspects of grape production. Students make all wines produced from San Joaquin grapes, by Fresno State Winery, many of them award-winning.   R.T.

Friulano, name adopted for SAUVIGNONASSE in the early 21st century in FRIULI for the region's leading white wine variety once known, to the fury of Hungarians, as Tocai Friulano. Total plantings have been slowly declining but were 2,911 ha/7,193 acres according to the 2010 vine census, in all major DOC zones (COLLI ORIENTALI, COLLIO, GRAVE DEL FRIULI, and ISONZO). Buttrio, Manzano, and Rosazzo in the Colli Orientali, and the areas between Cormons and Brazzano, between Brazzano and Dolegna, and Capriva di Friuli in the Collio DOC are classic subzones. The wine itself is light in colour and body, floral in aroma, and has pronounced green almond notes. It is designed to be drunk young.

Friuli, or **Friuli-Venezia Giulia**, the northeasternmost region of ITALY, borders on Austria to the north and SLOVENIA to the east and has long been a confluence of three distinct peoples and cultures: Italian, Germanic, and Slavic. (See map under ITALY.) Despite endorsements of local wines by the usual succession of popes, emperors, princes, and princelings, Friuli's history of distinctive wines remained largely hidden until the late 1960s, when the introduction of both German winemaking philosophy and TEMPERATURE CONTROL—innovations usually credited to producer Mario Schiopetto—gave

Italy's first, fresh, fruity, internationally styled white wines. This created a FASHION which has waned as Friuli's international varietals became less distinctive, and as interest in INDIGENOUS VARIETIES waxes. This style of (predominantly white) WINEMAKING is one of the characteristic features of the region's production; the other is the large number of wines produced by each single estate.

Friuli's geographical position on land successively disputed by Romans, Byzantines, Venetians, and Habsburgs ensured that a large number of varieties would be available for planting. The white TOCAI Friulano, RIBOLLA, MALVASIA di Istria, VERDUZZO, PICOLIT and red REFOSCO, SCHIOPPETTINO, PIGNOLO, and the acidic Tazzelenghe are considered indigenous (although see ROBOLA, for example). RIESLING, WELSCHRIESLING (here called Riesling Italico), TRAMINER, MÜLLER-THURGAU, and BLAUFRÄNKISCH (locally called Franconia) are imports from Austria. The French varieties PINOT BIANCO, PINOT GRIGIO, CHARDONNAY, SAUVIGNON, CABERNET, MERLOT, PINOT NERO, and CARMENÈRE were introduced during the 19th century Habsburg domination (and greatly expanded during the replanting of Friuli's vineyards after the ravages of PHYLLOXERA), a domination which lasted until 1918 in the case of the province of Gorizia.

The result has been the multiplicity of single VARIETAL wines in each DOC: 18 for the 2,000 ha/ 4,942 acres of the COLLI ORIENTALI, 17 for the 1,500 ha of COLLIO. If the proliferation of DOC wines with varietal names attached to specific zones has created some confusion among consumers, the geography of Friuli's DOC structure is actually fairly easy to understand. Udine marks the northern border beyond which low temperatures make viticulture an impractical proposition in most cases: to the south of Udine exist two distinct bands of territory for the growing of grapes: the two hillside DOCs of Colli Orientali and Collio with calcareous MARL soils, and the ALLUVIAL plain with plentiful quantities of sand, pebbles, and rocks deposited by the various rivers—the Tagliamento, the Natisone, the Judrio, the Isonzo—which crisscross the plain. These flatlands are divided into five DOCs, moving from west to east: LISON-PRAMAGGIORE (shared with Veneto), LATISANA, GRAVE DEL FRIULI, AQUILEIA, and ISONZO. The HILLSIDE VINEYARDS give wines of greater personality. The white, and red, wines of this latter zone have shown a real suitability for small BARREL MATURATION. Isonzo, which borders on Collio, stands out among the DOCs of the plain and, in the 1990s, began to produce wines which, from the best producers, can challenge those of the hillsides.

The region's overall production was about 2.2 million hl in 2011, more than twice as much as its challenger as a source of crisp international varietals TRENTINO-ALTO ADIGE.

Plans exist to elevate the entire region of Friuli-Venezia-Giulia to DOC, although the advantages of doing so are unclear.

For more details of notable specific wines, see also AQUILEIA, CARSO, COLLI ORIENTALI, COLLIO, GRAVE DEL FRIULI, ISONZO, LATISANA, LISON-PRAMAGGIORE, and see specific grape varieties FRIULANO, PICOLIT, PIGNOLO, REFOSCO, RIBOLLA, SCHIOPPETTINO, and VERDUZZO.   W.S.

Zanfi, A., *Friuli—Terre, Uomini, Vino* (Poggibonsi, 2004).

www.winesfriuliveneziagiulia.it

frizzante, Italian wine term for semi-sparkling wine (as opposed to SPUMANTE, which is used for fully sparkling wines). *Frizzante* wines generally owe their bubbles to a partial second fermentation in tank, a sort of interrupted CHARMAT process (although see also Prosecco Col Fondo). A wine labelled frizzante must have between 1 and 2.5 bar pressure, and spumante at least 3 bar.

Fromenteau, name for several grape varieties, used as a synonym for both the ROUSSANNE of the Rhône and SAVAGNIN of the Jura. **Fromenteau Gris** is a synonym for PINOT GRIS.

Fronsac, small but once famed red wine appellation in the Bordeaux region just west of the town of Libourne on the RIGHT BANK of the River DORDOGNE (see map under BORDEAUX). The wooded low hills of Fronsac, and **Canon-Fronsac**, the even smaller and more famous appellation to the immediate south, constitute Bordeaux's prettiest countryside, and the region's elevation, unusual so close to the Gironde estuary, gave it great strategic importance. Fronsac was the site of a Roman temple, and then of a fortress built by CHARLEMAGNE, who is locally supposed to have taken a particular interest in this wine. The wine benefited further in the mid 17th century when the Duc de Richelieu, also Duc de Fronsac and a man of considerable influence, replaced the fortress with a villa in which he entertained frequently. According to Enjalbert, the first great right-bank wines were produced, around 1730, in Canon-Fronsac. Even well into the 19th century, the wines of Fronsac were much more famous than those of POMEROL on the other side of Libourne.

The low-lying land beside the river and any alluvial soils further inland from the Dordogne and its tributary the Isle are entitled to only the BORDEAUX AOC, while the Fronsac and Canon-Fronsac appellations are concentrated on the higher land where LIMESTONE predominates and SANDSTONE is also characteristic. Merlot and Cabernet Franc (Bouchet) are the dominant grape varieties, densely planted on the land entitled to the Fronsac appellation and the more restricted area, mainly around the villages of St-Michel-de-Fronsac and Fronsac itself, which are entitled to the supposedly superior Canon-Fronsac appellation. The region with its cool soils performs particularly well in hot vintages.

Wines made in the 1960s and 1970s were often both austere and slightly rustic. The 1980s saw considerable refinement of techniques, and investment in winemaking equipment, notably some new barrels, so that Fronsac added suppleness to its density. It does not have the lush character of Pomerol but can offer a keenly priced alternative to more famous red bordeaux, with the juicy fruit of a St-Émilion and the ageing potential of a Médoc. Even the commercial muscle of the MOUEIX family, who owned Chx Canon-Moueix, La Dauphine, and Canon de Brem, as well as distributing several others, from the 1980s until the early 21st century, failed to win the region the success it probably deserves. The largest and most picturesque property on the entire right bank is Ch de la Rivière. By 2013 Fronsac had only about 750 ha/1,852 acres planted, and Canon Fronsac about 250 ha, with red wine grapes only.

Enjalbert, H., *Great Bordeaux Wines: St Émilion, Pomerol, Fronsac* (Paris, 1983; Eng. trans. 1985).

Frontenac, relatively recent dark-skinned HYBRID grown for port-style wines, in the Upper Plains and American Midwest. It high acidity generally requires some RESIDUAL SUGAR. The mutation Frontenac Gris has produced some white wine but the more recent mutation **Frontenac Blanc** may well prove more popular.

Frontignac, name used occasionally for grapey, sweet wine, particularly in SOUTH AFRICA, providing it has been produced from MUSCAT DE FRONTIGNAN. Australian synonym for MUSCAT BLANC À PETITS GRAINS.

Frontignan is the name of the wine for long called Muscat de Frontignan, the most important of the Languedoc's four Muscats. Now a distinctly unglamorous town on the semi-industrial lagoon between Montpellier and Sète, Frontignan was famous for the quality of its MUSCAT for centuries. It was probably one of France's earliest vineyard sites, being close to the saltmarshes around Narbonne. PLINY the Younger singled out this particular 'bees' wine' for mention in his letters. ARNALDUS DE VILLANOVA, who is credited with the discovery of the process by which most Muscat de Frontignan is made today (see VIN DOUX NATUREL), claimed that his daily ration of the wine, as advised by the then all-powerful Aragón monarch, made him feel years younger. It was popular in both Paris and London in the 17th and 18th centuries, doubtless with wider appeal then than the dry reds of south west France that were also shipped north. 'Frontiniac' was specifically praised by the philosopher John Locke in

1676, while both Voltaire and, even further afield, Thomas JEFFERSON were well-documented and enthusiastic purchasers. In the 18th and 19th centuries, Frontignan clearly made red as well as white wines which were compared with those of that other favourite of our sweet-toothed ancestors, CONSTANTIA. See also LANGUEDOC, history, for details of a claimed link between Frontignan and Ch d'YQUEM.

Muscat de Frontignan, despite being one of the first appellations, and certainly the first vin doux naturel appellation, to be officially recognized, fell into decline for much of the 20th century. Only the rather lighter Muscat de BEAUMES-DE-VENISE somehow escaped the malaise that affected the market for France's sweeter wines, until the 1980s, when the winemakers of Frontignan awoke as if from a deep sleep and started to produce a much higher proportion of more delicate, more refreshing, yet more characterful golden Muscats (although some dark, turgid, raisiny Frontignan can still be found). As in all Languedoc Muscats (see LUNEL, MIREVAL, and ST-JEAN-DE-MINERVOIS), only the finest Muscat variety, MUSCAT BLANC À PETITS GRAINS, should be used and the final wine must be at least 15% alcohol with a sugar content of at least 110 g/l. Cheaper Muscats made well outside the region but marketed vigorously to tourists do nothing for the image of this once-great appellation. Co-operatives dominate output, but Ch de la Peyrade can take much of the credit for revitalizing winemaking in Frontignan, whose seaside vineyards may not be the Mediterranean's most picturesque but are at least reliably warm enough to maximize Muscat Blanc's potential.

A small proportion of Muscat de Frontignan is fortified so early it qualifies as a VIN DE LIQUEUR.

Fronton, red and rosé AOC of 1,353 ha/3,342 acres in 2012 of vineyards just north of Toulouse in SOUTH WEST FRANCE. It is distinguished by its local red grape variety the NÉGRETTE, which must constitute at least 50% with Syrah being the most important of the many other permitted south western varieties. The character of the wines can vary considerably according to the exact TERROIR and ENCÉPAGEMENT. Soils on the gravelly terraces of the Tarn are particularly poor. The CO-OPERATIVE is an important producer. Fronton has been producing wine since before the time of CHARLEMAGNE and in the 12th century the vineyard was already associated with 'négret'. Today the great majority of it is drunk in Toulouse.

frost, the ice crystals formed by freezing of water vapour on objects which have cooled below 0 °C/32 °F. Such frosts are known as white frosts, or hoar frosts. Black frosts cause freezing and extensive killing of plant tissue

itself, without any necessary hoar formation. Frost is a major viticultural problem as it can damage and kill shoots and fruit, in spring and autumn. FROST PROTECTION is expensive and not always effective; see also FROST DAMAGE.

Frost frequencies are, in many studies, imputed arbitrarily from weather records. Temperatures as recorded in the standard Stevenson screen used by meteorologists, at 1.25 m/4.1 ft above the ground, are always higher than at ground level. A screen temperature of 2.2 °C/36 °F is normally assumed to indicate a light ground frost, and one of 0 °C a heavy ground frost. Temperatures at vine height of −1 °C or lower after BUDBREAK in spring will usually cause serious injury to the young shoots. Even 'light' frosts can often cause damage somewhere in the vineyard, because their incidence tends to be patchy, depending on TOPOGRAPHY. Geiger covers this aspect in detail.

Two main types of frost are distinguished: radiation and advection. Radiation frost occurs typically on still, dry, cloudless nights. Without cloud, mist, or much water vapour to absorb and trap heat radiated from the ground and plant tissues, heat escapes freely to space and rapid surface cooling results. Air in immediate contact with these surfaces then becomes cooled. The coldest air, being densest, remains or collects close to the ground and in depressions. Lowest air temperatures in the early morning on flat land are at 5 to 15 cm/2–5 in above ground, rising with height to a relatively warm 'inversion' layer, commonly some 15 to 30 m/100 ft above, beyond which temperatures gradually fall again with elevation. This pool of cold, dense air close to the ground is stable unless dispersed by wind, or unless it can flow away by gravity to still lower regions (see TOPOGRAPHY).

Advective frosts result from such flows of already chilled air from elsewhere. They can originate locally, following valleys or other natural courses of AIR DRAINAGE, or arrive from up to several hundreds or perhaps thousands of kilometres away.   J.G.

Geiger, R., Aron, R. H., and Todhunter, P., *The Climate near the Ground* (Lanham, Md., 2009).

McCarthy, M. G., et al., 'Soil management and frost control', in B. G. Coombe and P. R. Dry (eds.), *Viticulture*, ii: *Practices* (Adelaide, 1992).

frost damage occurs in vineyards mostly in spring but also in autumn and occasionally summer, when the air temperature drops below freezing (see also FROST). Ice forms in the plant tissue of buds which have begun to break, young shoots, leaves, and inflorescences, which may subsequently turn brown and die. The vine can respond by growing more shoots from BASAL BUDS, but these are typically less fruitful and the crop is reduced and delayed. Frost in the autumn causes DEFOLIATION, which is a problem if the fruit is not ripe and the vine's reserves of CARBOHYDRATES have not been restored. Frost has much more impact on YIELD than on wine QUALITY, although if SPRINKLER irrigation is used before harvest to ward off autumn frost, it can have serious consequences for RIPENING.

FROST PROTECTION can be difficult and expensive but frost is so destructive that vineyard owners are forced to adopt extreme measures.

Typically cool-climate regions are more prone to spring frost. For example, in 1991 frost damage was so great in western France, particularly for the earlier budding white grape varieties, that total French wine production, which averaged nearly 55 million hl in 1991–2000, was less than 43 million hl/1,135 million gal.

However, spring frost damage to vines is by no means confined to cool viticultural climates. In fact it is not necessarily most characteristic of them. That is because the VINE GROWTH CYCLE is adapted to the general run of temperatures experienced, with spring budbreak delayed in cool climates until the average mean temperature reaches about 10 °C, as described under CLIMATE CLASSIFICATION. More damaging is short-term TEMPERATURE VARIABILITY, such that an early spring warm enough to induce budbreak may frequently be followed by a return to killing frosts after growth has started. Paradoxically, such events can occur in otherwise hot vineyard regions, such as the high plains of TEXAS. This is because their early spring is often hot, which encourages early budbreak, but this may be followed by cold of arctic origin which can severely damage vines.

Note the distinction between frost and WINTER FREEZE, a related but different vine injury.

R.E.S.

frost protection. The origins of FROST point to logical methods of avoiding it. The first is to plant on slopes from which surface-chilled air can drain away freely (see AIR DRAINAGE). Free-standing and projecting hills are best because they have no external sources of chilled air and what slips away must be replaced from the warmer atmosphere above (see TOPOGRAPHY). This is the most effective form of frost protection, but typically is generally an option only when developing vineyards in new regions that allow such VINEYARD SITE SELECTION.

Planting on frost-prone sites is normally confined to grape varieties with naturally late budbreak, such as (where the growing season is long enough) CABERNET SAUVIGNON, CARIGNAN, MOURVÈDRE, CLAIRETTE, and TREBBIANO. RIESLING, SYLVANER, MÜLLER-THURGAU, and SAUVIGNON BLANC are classed as having mid-season budbreak. Unfortunately some of the prime-quality varieties grown in COOL CLIMATES, such as PINOT NOIR and CHARDONNAY, burst early and are very vulnerable to spring frosts (see CHABLIS, for

instance). The selection of individual sites with minimal frost risk is crucial for such varieties. The risk in any situation can be reduced to a small extent by late PRUNING, but this can delay the effective time of budbreak by only up to about a week or, at the most, ten days.

Another method, employed on flat land subject to radiation frosts, is to use high TRELLIS SYSTEMS so that the main vine growth stands above the coldest air layer that settles close to the ground on still nights. In practice, however, there is little difference in frost sensitivity of commercial trellis systems, and this method offers limited benefit. Plant cover between the rows also needs to be cultivated or slashed by the time of budbreak, so as to lower the effective cooling surface. The soil should preferably be quite compacted so that it most readily absorbs day heat to depth and reradiates it continuously through the night. STONES AND ROCKS in the soil surface assist in this.

Stationary WIND MACHINES are often employed to break up the sedentary cold air layer and mix in warm upper air; these have become part of the vineyard landscape in NAPA and SONOMA Valleys and in Marlborough, for example. They are expensive to install and use a lot of fuel, but in the long run are less expensive than HELICOPTERS, which are widely used for the same purpose in NEW ZEALAND and can cover a much wider area but have to be hired by the hour. There's also a mobile fan machine that gathers cold air and blasts it vertically upwards, mixing it with the warmer air.

Fog-creating machines have also been used to mix the inversion layer and to minimize frost damage. SMUDGE POTS and other burners can also create limited local heating which may help to promote convectional mixing of upper and lower air, together with smoke (by-laws permitting), which reduces further radiative heat loss from the soil. A new development in the battle against frost is the Lazo machine, which is a liquid propane gas-powered burner towed behind a tractor on frosty nights. Hot air is blown by a fan out of the burner at 1000 °C but cools quickly so the vines are not burned.

In vineyards with sprinkler IRRIGATION, the SPRINKLERS can be turned on when temperatures fall to danger levels. This 'aspersion' technique both warms the vines and soil directly, and (if the soil was previously dry) improves its heat conductivity so that more warmth comes up from below. The release of latent heat as the water freezes on the vines protects the vine tissue from injury. However, the additional water in the vineyard may be unwelcome. More recent experiments, including the use of heated vineyard wires, blowing heated air through irrigation systems, and the gas-heated blower described above, have not so far been widely adopted.

R.E.S.

fructose is, with GLUCOSE, one of the two principal SUGARS of the grape and sweet wines. It is a six-carbon atom sugar, or a hexose. Common table sugar, SUCROSE, is made up of one molecule of fructose and one of glucose.

The grapevine leaf in the presence of sunlight, water, and carbon dioxide makes sucrose by a complicated series of steps called collectively PHOTOSYNTHESIS. The sucrose is transferred in the plant sap from the leaf to the grape berry. There the sucrose is split into fructose and glucose, the forms in which it is stored in the berry. The vine is unusual among fruiting plants in the extent to which it is capable of concentrating the two sugars fructose and glucose in its berries; sugars routinely represent 18–25% of grape juice weight, while 12% is the norm in apple and pear juice.

Fructose accumulates in the grape berry along with glucose but at lower concentrations during the early stages. However, at RIPENESS, and especially when grapes are overripe, fructose levels often exceed glucose. The glucose–fructose ratio is thus an indicator of grape ripening (roughly 1:5 at veraison but less than 1 at full ripeness). This is important because fructose is remarkable in that it has between 1.3 and 1.8 times the sweetening power of either glucose or sucrose (which has led to its manufacture in large quantities for use in so-called diet foods).

During FERMENTATION of grape juice, both fructose and glucose are consumed. Furthermore, in the acid and enzymic environment of grape juice, any sucrose present is split into its constituent parts, fructose and glucose, and will consequently be fermented. With selected strains of wine YEASTS, nearly all the fructose and glucose are converted to alcohol and carbon dioxide, leaving the wine with only traces of fermentable sugars.

A.D.W. & B.G.C.

früh is German for 'early'. Thus, for example, Früher Roter Malvasier is early red MALVASIA.

Frühburgunder, Blauer, increasingly highly regarded, small-berried mutation of Spätburgunder (Pinot Noir) which ripens a good two weeks before it. By 2012, total German plantings had grown to 262 ha/647 acres, in southern Germany, particularly on the red sandstone soils around Miltenberg and, historically, Bürgstadt in FRANKEN. Low-yielding examples can taste of black fruits.

Frühroter Veltliner, 'early-ripening, red-skinned VELTLINER', is a white wine grape variety most commonly encountered in Austria, where plantings, mainly in the Weinviertel district of Lower Austria, had fallen to about 400 ha/1,000 acres by 2012. The wine produced is often less distinguished than that made from Austria's most common grape variety GRÜNER VELTLINER, being notably lower in acidity in many cases. Yields are also generally lower. DNA PROFILING in Austria showed that Frühroter Veltliner is not related to Grüner Veltliner at all but is a spontaneous cross between ROTER VELTLINER and SILVANER. It makes rather neutral wine and is well suited to producing white wines in a NOUVEAU style.

In Germany, it has been known in Rheinhessen, as **Frühroter Malvasier** or occasionally Roter Malvasier. It is slightly less rare in north west Hungary, the Czech Republic, and Slovakia.

fruit. To a VITICULTURIST, fruit is a synonym for GRAPE, the former used more commonly than 'grapes' in English-speaking countries. To an OENOLOGIST or wine taster, fruit is a perceptible element essential to a young wine. Young wines should taste fruity, although not necessarily of grapes, or any particular grape variety. During BOTTLE AGEING, the fruity FLAVOUR COMPOUNDS in a good wine evolve into more complex elements which are described as BOUQUET; in a less good wine, the fruit simply dissipates to leave a non-fruity wine sometimes described as 'hollow'. The word **fruity** is sometimes used in wine descriptions concocted for marketing purposes as a euphemism for 'sweet'. Details of grape ripening are to be found under RIPENING.

fruit-driven, a TASTING TERM used to convey the fact that a wine has a dominance of grape-derived fruit flavour. For a wine to merit this description, the dominance of fruit overrides flavours in the wine that originate from other processes or treatments which the wine has undergone such as BARREL FERMENTATION, BARREL MATURATION, LEES CONTACT, MALOLACTIC CONVERSION, or, in the case of a sparkling wine, the influence of yeast AUTOLYSIS. Wines described as fruit-driven are, typically, NEW WORLD reds. Traditionally, classic European reds and whites were more likely to exhibit complex secondary flavours and aromas, often due to more OXIDATIVE winemaking. However, winemaking styles around the world have converged significantly since the late 20th century and by the mid 2010s, a significant and increasing proportion of European wines could be described as fruit-driven, while many New World winemakers were looking for more complex styles of wine in which fruit flavours play an important but secondary role.   P.J.W. & J.E.H.

fruit fly. See DROSOPHILA and MEDITERRANEAN FRUIT FLY.

fruitfulness, viticultural term describing the number of bunches of grapes on each shoot. It can also be used to describe the potential productivity of buds. A shoot of low fruitfulness will have zero or one bunch only, while a **fruitful** one may have two or three or, very rarely,

four. Some varieties are known to be very fruitful, an example being the so-called FRENCH HYBRIDS, no doubt due to their part-American parentage. At the other end of the fruitfulness spectrum is SULTANA, which has notoriously low fertility of buds at the base of canes. Most of the commercially important wine grape varieties fall between these two extremes and two bunches per shoot is most common. Where fruitfulness is low, the vine-grower must prune to CANES as opposed to SPURS, as shoots which arise from short spurs will typically be of lower fruitfulness, arising as they do from BASAL BUDS.

Interestingly, potential fruitfulness is determined at about the time the vines flower, as the buds are developing on the growing shoot. This process is known as INITIATION and is encouraged by warm, sunny weather and an open CANOPY that allows the sunlight to penetrate to the developing buds and adjacent leaves. By late summer it is usually possible to estimate the potential number of bunches which will be produced the following year by dissection and microscopic examination of the buds. The vine-grower anxiously assesses fruitfulness just as soon as the small bunches are evident on the developing shoots in spring. Normally, the higher the bunch number the higher is the potential yield of that season, although of course there are many other critical stages, especially FRUIT SET, before the harvest is brought in.   R.E.S.

Iland, P., et al., 'Development of inflorescence primordia', in *The Grapevine: From the Science to the Practice of Growing Vines for Wine* (Adelaide, 2011).

fruit set, known as *nouaison* in French, an important and delicate stage of the vine's development after FLOWERING which marks the transition from flower to grape berry. The setting period of about a week is a critical one for the vine-grower, since it is a major determinant of the size of the crop, yet the grower can do little to change the course of events. Only 'set' or fertilized flowers grow into the berries from which wine is made; the others fail to grow and eventually fall off. Fruit set occurs immediately after flowering, and is the result of successful POLLINATION achieving fertilization of the ovules and the development of seeds. The GRAPE SEED contains an embryo, formed by the union of the sperm cells from the POLLEN and the egg cell of the OVARY. Most wine grape varieties contain up to four seeds. The more seeds there are, the larger is the berry.

Not all flowers set, or form berries, and normally only about 30% of flowers become berries, although the range can be from almost zero to 60%. Those flowers that do not set fall from the bunch in a process called 'shatter' in English. It is not clear whether fruit set is more influenced by organic nutrition (CARBOHYDRATE

supply) or by HORMONES, but the crucial role played by the weather during this period is beyond dispute.

At one extreme, common in hot DRYLAND regions, high temperatures, low humidity, and attendant WATER STRESS can reduce fruit set, as can hot, dry winds. On the other hand, cold, cloudy, and rainy weather at flowering commonly reduces fruit set, and such conditions can cause widespread yield losses. Strategies to improve fruit set include using BALANCED PRUNING to avoid rapid shoot growth, ensuring balanced VINE NUTRITION (particularly NITROGEN, BORON, and ZINC) and water supply, TOPPING shoots during flowering, application of certain chemical GROWTH REGULATORS such as CCC (2-chloroethyltrimethyl-ammonium chloride) before flowering, or CINCTURING vine trunks at flowering.

Fruit set can be said to have been poor in specific situations when fruit yield is lower than normal as a consequence of either COULURE, which leaves few berries per bunch, or MILLERANDAGE, which leaves a high proportion of seedless berries and 'live green ovaries' (LGOs) per bunch, or both.   R.E.S., B.G.C., & P.R.D.

Iland, P., et al., 'Flowering and fruit set', in *The Grapevine: From the Science to the Practice of Growing Vines for Wine* (Adelaide, 2011).

fruit wines, made by the FERMENTATION of fruits other than grapes, include cider and perry, but not beer or sake, since they derive their fermentable sugars from hydrolized starch. They are particularly common in cool climates such as in North America and Scandinavia.

A wine-like beverage can be made from almost any fruit, berry, or other plant material containing sugar. Most of these sources contain so little fermentable sugar, however, that it is usually necessary to add sugar from another source (a form of ENRICHMENT) to obtain sufficient ALCOHOL for stability (see STABILIZATION). Table sugar, or SUCROSE, is usually used, and most fruits other than grapes have excessive concentrations of ACIDS that split the sucrose into fermentable GLUCOSE and FRUCTOSE. YEASTS also contain a natural ENZYME which will convert sucrose to its component glucose and fructose.

In most cases, acid levels are so high that it is necessary to dilute the crushed fruit to reduce tartness in the resulting wine. In most fruits other than grapes, much of the acid mixture is CITRIC ACID (which predominates in the citrus fruits), although in apples and a few others it is MALIC ACID. (Grapes are distinguished by their high levels of TARTARIC ACID, which is more resistant to attack by BACTERIA.)

Lack of yeast NUTRIENTS is a further problem in persuading fruits other than grapes to ferment. Commercial preparations made from autolysed yeast together with sufficient nitrogen, phosphorus, and potassium to make up the fruit's natural deficiency are commonly available to those who practise HOME WINEMAKING.

Very few fruit wines improve with BOTTLE AGE. Characteristic fruit flavours fade very rapidly and most are best consumed well within a year of bottling.   A.D.W.

Fuder, German for large wooden BARREL, typically one with a capacity of 1,000 l/264 gal used in the MOSEL region. (The STÜCK is more commonly used in RHINE regions.) A **Halbfuder** contains 500 l and was traditionally used for transporting wine from the Mosel.

full. A wine is described as full, or **full bodied**, if it is high, but not excessively high, in ALCOHOL and VISCOSITY. See BODY for more details.

Fumé Blanc is the curious descendant of the Loire synonym BLANC FUMÉ for the white grape variety SAUVIGNON BLANC. In the early 1970s, California's famous ideas man Robert MONDAVI had one of his most famous inspirations, that of renaming the then unfashionable Sauvignon Blanc, Fumé Blanc, thereby imbuing it with some of the glamour of imported French Pouilly-Fumé. He also gave it some OAK AGEING and a dark green bordeaux-shaped BOTTLE (both entirely alien to Pouilly-Fumé). This less-than-authentic formula proved a runaway success and Fumé Blanc became the highly successful name of a wine type in America, New Zealand, and elsewhere, even if there is little agreement about what exactly that wine type is.

fumigation, the viticultural practice of fumigating vineyard soils with the aim of killing soil-borne VINE PESTS or VINE DISEASES. It is usually carried out before planting. The earliest example of viticultural fumigation was the use of carbon bisulfide in France to combat PHYLLOXERA in the 1880s. Approximately 68,000 ha/ 167,960 acres were treated, requiring the painstaking insertion of about 30,000 holes per ha (12,000 per acre). Phylloxera is now controlled by GRAFTING, and today fumigation is used primarily to control the NEMATODE vector *Xiphenema index* of the virus disease FANLEAF DEGENERATION, but also for ARMILLARIA ROOT ROT, CROWN GALL, and occasionally squirrels and gophers.

Fumigation is difficult since it requires deep injection and a volatile chemical or gas which will permeate every pore to kill effectively. The exercise is most effective if the soil is porous and is not too wet. Newly fumigated vineyards in environmentally conscious areas such as California are covered with a large plastic sheet to prevent the fumigant being lost to the atmosphere. Some fumigants were banned in the early 1990s since they were found to contaminate groundwater. Methyl bromide, a very

volatile soil sterilant, is being phased out under international agreement and alternatives are being actively researched.   R.E.S.

Fumin, renascent dark-berried vine speciality of the Valle d'AOSTA whose firm produce, from more than 30 ha in 2010, is usually blended.

funds, wine. Wine funds aggregate investors' funds with a view to creating a professionally managed, balanced portfolio of FINE WINES. The first credible wine funds were the UK-based operations The Wine Investment Fund and the (now defunct) Vintage Wine Fund, which opened for business in January 2003.

Wine investment funds emerged as a result of the steady growth in the value of fine wine and with it the new respectability of fine wine as a part of SWAG, the tangible asset class that comprises silver, wine, art, and gold. The prestige conferred by fine-wine ownership and the thrill of the chase have contributed to the phenomenon of wine investment in general and the wine investment funds in particular.

Wine investment has become increasingly accepted as a means of diversifying an investment portfolio in times of economic uncertainty. In parallel with art funds, there has been a glut of wine funds in recent years with, in 2014, more than a dozen such operations across Europe, the US, and Asia with estimated investments under management of between £150 and £200 million.

Wine funds are aimed at professional investors and high net-worth individuals. While certain professional businesses have now been active for many years, other funds have been hampered by low liquidity, growing too fast in a relatively small market, questionable valuation standards, and poor portfolio selection. Among those that had run into difficulty by 2014 are the UK's Vintage Wine Fund and the Luxembourg fund Nobles Crus.

Wine funds necessarily rely on a continuing rise in overall fine-wine prices in order to provide returns to their investors. It was of considerable concern to wine funds and their investors that the first half of the 2010s saw a gradual decline in fine-wine prices. Fund managers taking a long-term view are presumably the ones most likely to succeed.   A.H.L.R.

Lister, E., 'Liquid Assets', *World of Fine Wine*, 32, 33, 34.

fungal diseases, very large group of vine diseases which are caused by small, mostly microscopic, and filament-shaped organisms. Since fungi lack chlorophyll they need to live on other organisms to obtain nourishment. Fungal diseases have been of major significance in affecting grape production over centuries, with important consequences for both quantity and quality. Today they receive little public

attention since they can successfully be controlled by a wide range of agricultural chemicals. In fact the famous fungicide BORDEAUX MIXTURE was used commercially to control DOWNY MILDEW in 1885 and for 50 years was the most important control of other fungal and bacterial plant diseases. Fungal disease epidemics are commonly related to weather conditions; examples are downy mildew and BOTRYTIS BUNCH ROT, both of which are favoured by warm, wet or humid weather, while POWDERY MILDEW is favoured by overcast weather.

Many of the economically important fungal diseases originated in America and therefore common varieties of the European VINIFERA species have no resistance. Thus, when powdery mildew was introduced in 1847, and then downy mildew in 1878, French *V. vinifera* vineyards were devastated. Fungal diseases can attack shoots and leaves but also developing bunches and ripe fruit. Some fungi such as *Armillaria* and *Verticillium* attack roots. Of more recent concern are a group of fungi which cause TRUNK DISEASES. They spread in vineyards and are also common contaminants of young vines propagated in grapevine NURSERIES.

Botrytis is the fungus with which wine consumers are probably most familiar. In its benevolent form (see NOBLE ROT), it contributes to a high proportion of the most famous SWEET WINES. The more common malevolent form (see GREY ROT) causes substantial yield and quality losses, on the other hand.

Common fungal diseases are ANTHRACNOSE, ARMILLARIA ROOT ROT, BLACK ROT, BOTRYTIS BUNCH ROT, BUNCH ROTS, COLLAR ROT, DEAD ARM, DOWNY MILDEW, ESCA, EUTYPA DIEBACK, POWDERY MILDEW, TEXAS ROOT ROT, VERTICILLIUM WILT, WHITE ROT. Other groups of vine diseases include BACTERIAL DISEASES, PHYTOPLASMA diseases, and VIRUS DISEASES.   R.E.S.

Emmett, R. W., et al., 'Grape diseases and vineyard protection', in B. G. Coombe and P. R. Dry (eds.), *Viticulture*, ii: *Practices* (Adelaide, 1992).

Pearson, R. C., and Goheen, A. C., (eds.), *Compendium of Grape Diseases* (St Paul, Minn., 1988).

fungi, a group of small and often microscopic multicellular or filamentous organisms which derive their energy living as saprophytes on dead plant or animal tissue, or as pathogens on living tissue. Fungi include YEASTS important in fermentation and many organisms causing vine FUNGAL DISEASES.

fungicide, type of PESTICIDE that is effective against FUNGAL DISEASES in vineyards. The first of the modern fungicides used for any crop was the BORDEAUX MIXTURE used on grapevines against DOWNY MILDEW in 1885. Fungicides are applied by SPRAYING at times which are deemed effective to prevent fungal development or control existing disease. Fungicides are thus classified as protectants or eradicants, depending on the timing of application. Protectant fungicides are applied before the fungus infects the vines and they prevent infection by inhibiting fungal development on the plant surface.

Eradicant fungicides are effective when applied after the infection has occurred. They can either inhibit or kill fungi present on or in the vine, thus preventing these fungi from further disease development. A typical characteristic of eradicants is their ability to penetrate plant tissues, most being systemic. Some eradicant fungicides can be applied one week or more after infection and still be effective.

Systemic fungicides have the ability to infiltrate and move within plants. Movement may be relatively localized, such as from one side of a leaf to the other (translaminar), or extensive, via the vine's vascular system. Contact fungicides are not absorbed by plant tissue. They act on the surface and good coverage of the target is critical. Examples include SULFUR and COPPER formulations. Copper ions are toxic to zoospores of downy mildew and prevent infection on the surface of plant tissue.

Mixtures of active ingredients may be used in formulations for different purposes, and may take advantage of synergistic effects: copper oxychloride and zineb mixtures, for example, or to create mixtures of protectant and eradicant fungicides, as for copper oxychloride and metalaxyl. Some fungicides may be used against more than one fungal pathogen: mancozeb is effective against both downy mildew and ANTHRACNOSE, for instance, whereas others have a narrow range of action.

It is important to keep levels of fungicide RESIDUES below limits specified for toxicological reasons. For wine grapes, there is an additional consideration: residues of some fungicides will inhibit yeast activity, thus affecting fermentation and resultant wine quality.

As with other pesticides, the potential for development of resistance to fungicides varies according to the type of fungicide. Fungicides can be grouped according to their mode of action as either multi-site or specific-site inhibitors. Multi-site inhibitors are toxic in more than one way and the chance of developing resistant strains by mutation is therefore low. This group includes protectant fungicides which have been widely used in viticulture for decades without any significant decrease in efficacy. Single-site inhibitors have more specific toxicity and, because they inhibit only one or a few steps in fungal metabolism, the chance of resistant strains arising is much greater. Many of the newer fungicides fall into this group. Strategies that delay or prevent the development of resistant strains include restrained use, the use of mixtures of multi- and single-site inhibitor fungicides, and alternation of single-site inhibitors during the season. Over time, resistance to fungicides used for POWDERY MILDEW and BOTRYTIS BUNCH ROT has developed.

Some 'natural' substances have been tested and proven to be effective against fungal pathogens. Activated potassium bicarbonate, paraffinic oil, and milk or whey have been researched for powdery mildew control. In some cases commercially available products have been developed. Species of *Trichoderma* have been found to compete with downy mildew and BOTRYTIS and reduce infection levels. Other compounds, it is suspected, elicit plant disease resistance mechanisms; and if applied ahead of infection can reduce damage by fungal disease. See also AGROCHEMICALS. P.R.D. & M.E.

American Phytopathological Society
www.apsnet.org/edcenter/intropp/topics/Pages/Fungicides.aspx
Fungicide Resistance Action Committee
www.frac.info

furfurals. See OAK FLAVOUR.

Furmint, fine, fiery white TOKAJ grape variety grown most widely in Hungary, just over the Slovakian border from Tokaj, and in 'Styrian' Slovenia and Croatia as Šipon. It is also being revived in Austria's Burgenland, particularly Rust where both Heidi Schröck and Triebaumer make fine dry and sweet versions. DNA PROFILING has shown that it has a parent–offspring relationship with GOUAIS BLANC and HARSLEVELŰ.

Helpfully for the great sweet wine that is Tokaji, the grapes are particularly sensitive to NOBLE ROT, yet the wine is characterized by very high acidity, which endows the wine with long ageing potential, high sugar levels, and rich, fiery flavours. In Tokaji it is usually blended with up to half as much of the more aromatic grape variety Hárslevelű, and some Sárga Muskotály (MUSCAT BLANC À PETITS GRAINS) is also sometimes included in the blend.

Furmint can easily produce wines with an ALCOHOLIC STRENGTH as high as 14%, and sturdy, characterful dry Furmint can age well and be a delicious wine, even when drunk very young. Although most of Hungary's just over 4,000 ha/10,000 acres of Furmint are in Tokaj, in Somló it can also make extremely concentrated dry wines. The vine buds early but ripening slows towards the end of the season and the BOTRYTIZED (*aszú*) grapes may not be picked until well into November in some years.

The vine has been known in Tokaj since at least the late 16th century, and it is still grown to a limited extent in South Africa, where it was imported in tandem with the other Tokaj grape Hárslevelű. Some think it may be identical to GRASĂ.

fusel oils, a general collective term for the complex, unpleasant-smelling, and varied mixtures of natural organic chemicals that are separable as wine is distilled into brandy in a continuous still. They are predominantly byproducts of the nitrogen metabolism of the YEAST during fermentation and of only minor importance to the wine drinker since they represent such a small proportion of wine.

futures in wine, wine bought before it is bottled and therefore long before it can be delivered. See EN PRIMEUR and INVESTMENT.

FYROM. See MACEDONIA.

Gaglioppo, predominant red grape variety in CALABRIA in the far south of Italy. whose mid ruby, quite tannic wines can be hauntingly scented, sometimes of roses. DNA PROFILING has shown it is a siblng of NERELLO Mascalese. It thrives in dry conditions and is occasionally found further north. Italy's total plantings of the variety had fallen to 4,213 ha/10,406 acres by 2010.

Gaillac, dynamic, variegated wine district in SOUTH WEST FRANCE that is also of considerable historic importance. As outlined in the history of FRANCE, archaeological evidence suggests that Gaillac may have been one of the first viticultural centres of ancient GAUL, with wine production well established in the early years of the 1st century AD.

Gaillac certainly seems to have been producing wine long before BORDEAUX, the port through which its wines would have been shipped after being transported down the Rivers Tarn and GARONNE. Barbarian invasions then curbed wine production until it was revived by MONKS at the Abbey of St-Michel-de-Gaillac in the 10th century and Gaillac wines were highly prized both locally and in northern Europe, especially ENGLAND, in the Middle Ages. Gaillac's export trade was thwarted, however, by the protectionist measures imposed by the merchants of Bordeaux on HAUT PAYS wines.

The wines may be called Gaillac after the small town at the centre of the production zone, but the most important settlement in the region by far is Albi just up river, with its extraordinary brick cathedral, a monument to the strength of religious belief. The Albigensian Crusade and the religious wars of the 12th and 13th centuries inevitably disrupted trade, although there is evidence that the English were

once more buying Gaillac with enthusiasm in the 16th century, and the region, along with 'Limouth' (LIMOUX), was already associated with SPARKLING WINE production in 1680.

The powerful, deeply coloured red wines of Gaillac continued to be prized by blenders in the early 19th century when ADULTERATION AND FRAUD were rife, but the arrival of the PHYLLOXERA louse towards the end of the century drove many local farmers to exploit crops other than the vine.

Today Gaillac's rolling fields are put to many uses, but the area devoted to AC wine production grew from about 1,600 ha/3,900 acres of vines in the early 1990s to of 2,961 ha/7,314 acres by 2012. (There has been a certain influx of aspirant wine producers from outside France, perhaps because land is relatively inexpensive.) The district is distinguished by its rich heritage of local VINE VARIETIES, and by its unusual diversity of wine styles.

The most distinctive local white grape variety is white- or pink-skinned MAUZAC (which is also characteristic of Limoux), whose wines have a strong apple peel aroma and sometimes a certain astringency. LEN DE L'EL is another strictly local variety whose wine can lack acidity and MUSCADELLE is the third principal variety which, together, must make up at least half of any white wine. The local ONDENC and Sauvignon Blanc are also allowed (although iconoclasts such as Robert Plageoles happily ignore these and produce a range of VARIETAL Gaillacs in an extraordinary range of styles, including sweet and sparkling wines and a vin de voile aged under a FILM-FORMING YEAST).

Some of Gaillac's finest wine is BARREL MATURED sweet white made from the same grape varieties and distinguished either as **Gaillac doux** or, if grown on certain demarcated

LIMESTONE slopes, as **Gaillac Premières Côtes** (which may also produce whites that are dry, or sec). Maximum yields for these last two appellations are lower than those for regular Gaillac. Some of these wines, such as Domaine Rotier's Cuvée Renaissance can be very luscious indeed, BOTRYTIZED in some years.

Gaillac also produces sparkling wines, with the most interesting and artisanal, the medium-sweet, lightly sparkling wines made by the *méthode gaillacoise*, a close relation of the *méthode ancestrale* (*see* SPARKLING WINEMAKING), sold by some with the sediment still in bottle.

Red wine, which can be an exciting south western ambassador, with the structure of a good bordeaux but more spicy flavours, is Gaillac's most common product, however, substantially based on the full-bodied DURAS and tannic FER (called Braucol locally), sometimes supplemented by Syrah as well as other local varieties. The relatively recent arrival GAMAY was imported to provide Gaillac vignerons with income from PRIMEUR wines. The APPELLATION CONTRÔLÉE regulations of Gaillac hint at thousands of man-hours of local political manœuvre.

Gaja, one of the most renowned producers of high-quality, estate-bottled wines in PIEMONTE, traces its origins to 1856 when the Gaja family opened a tavern in their home town of BARBARESCO and began serving their own wines to accompany the food. By the end of the 19th century, the wines were already being bottled and supplied to the Italian army in Abyssinia, a highly unusual development in their home district of the Langhe, where a tradition of bottled wine assumed real significance only from the 1960s. The firm became an important force after the Second World War under the direction of Giovanni Gaja, who began an important series of vineyard purchases in what is now the Barbaresco DOCG zone, a strategy that has given the house a total vineyard area in 2014 of 100 ha/247 acres, dwarfing all other family-owned Barbaresco houses, and an excellent selection of superior vineyard sites.

Gaja wines gained worldwide recognition under Giovanni's son Angelo Gaja, who took over the direction of activities in the late 1960s; trained at the oenological school of Alba and at MONTPELLIER, an indefatigable traveller in the world's major viticultural areas, and a tireless and charismatic champion of his native region and its wines, he gave a new international perspective to the wines, pioneering small BARREL MATURATION of both Barbaresco and BARBERA, and introducing international grape varieties—CABERNET SAUVIGNON, CHARDONNAY, and SAUVIGNON BLANC—to the vineyards of Piedmont (his Cabernet Sauvignon is called Darmagi, Piemontese for 'what a shame', supposedly his father's reaction). He also acquired land in nearby BAROLO, with the 1988 Barolo Sperss marking a return to the zone from which the Gaja family made a wine from purchased grapes until 1961.

In the 1990s, Gaja expanded his horizons even further, purchasing the Pieve di Santa Restituta estate in Montalcino, where the first BRUNELLO DI MONTALCINO produced under his supervision was made in 1993, and, more recently, the development of the Ca' Marcanda estate in BOLGHERI on the Tuscan coast.

In 1999, Gaja announced that he was renouncing the name he had made so famous and selling all the wine previously sold as Barbaresco DOCG, including his fabulously expensive single-vineyard Sorì San Lorenzo, Sorì Tildin, and Costa Russi bottlings, as DOC Langhe Nebbiolo, the catch-all appellation for declassified Barolo and Barbaresco and for wines containing up to 15% 'foreign' varieties such as Cabernet Sauvignon, Merlot, and Syrah. Gaja defended this controversial move by arguing that the estate's traditional Barbaresco, made by blending grapes from different vineyards (considered historical practice in the zone), had suffered in prestige being considered a 'basic' Barbaresco in comparison with single vineyard bottlings, a trend he was striving to counteract.   W.S.

Steinberg, E., *The Vines of San Lorenzo* (New York, 1992).

Galen, Greek physician whose work in the 2nd century AD was influential in Greece, Rome, and beyond. He identified the antiseptic properties of wine. See ATHENAEUS and MEDICINE.

Galen: *Selected Works*, trans. by P. N. Singer (Oxford, 1997).

galestro, the Italian name for the friable rock of the MARL-like soil that characterizes many of the best vineyard sites in CHIANTI CLASSICO, and also the name of a Tuscan white wine based on TREBBIANO created at the end of the 1970s to soak up the surplus of white grapes that developed when producers began to reduce the amount of Trebbiano used in their CHIANTI. It has largely faded although ANTINORI, under its Santa Cristina label, still produces a verson.

galet, or **galet roulé**, is a French term for a pebble, cobble, or even a boulder (see GEOLOGY) that is well rounded due to abrasion through continual rolling in fast-moving water.

The celebrated river-worn galets of CHÂTEAUNEUF-DU-PAPE and other parts of the southern RHÔNE are composed of strikingly pure white QUARTZITE. Although it is probably the underlying CLAYS and sands that are more significant for vine growth, these galets are so iconic that the name is now applied to rounded rock fragments in other vineyard regions, irrespective of their composition. In the Boutenac area of CORBIÈRES, for example, the galets are formed from a brown-stained quartzite; in California's ARROYO SECO, galets are a mixture of rock types; and Walla Walla, WASHINGTON, has old river channels filled with galets of dark BASALT.   A.J.M.

Galet, Pierre (1921–), father of modern AMPELOGRAPHY based in MONTPELLIER. Galet was born in Monaco and his upbringing in the Mediterranean climate of southern France undoubtedly helped to prepare him for a life spent outside surrounded by vines. Galet's working life was devoted to the science of describing and identifying VINE VARIETIES on the basis of minute botanical observation—an expertise he perfected while hiding from German occupation authorities in the international *Vitis* collection in the grounds of the Department of Viticulture at Montpellier. From 1946 to 1989, Galet was part of an elite teaching group that included Jean Branas, Denis Boubals, and François Champagnol at ENSA Montpellier, regarded as the national, if not international, centre of viticultural ACADEME. He taught thousands, including Paul Truel, whose own work based at Montpellier has been of worldwide significance, and Jean-Michel Boursiquot, who has succeeded him. Other acolytes include Lucie Morton, who translated some of his work into English for successful publication in the United States, Umberto Camargo in Brazil, Erika Maul Dettweiler in Germany, and Anna Schneider in Italy.

His most tangible achievements, however, have been as author (and publisher, he has consistently published and sold his own books). His four-volume *Cépages et vignobles de France* came out between 1956 and 1964, and battered copies are still circulated although he has since updated it to include handsome separate volumes with colour illustrations on American and French varieties, published in 1988 and 1991 respectively. His two-volume work on *Maladies et parasites de la vigne* came out in 1977 and 1982, while the fifth edition of his invaluable handbook *Précis de viticulture* appeared in 1988. In 2000, Hachette published his 936-page international dictionary of vine variety names and their synonyms; a new edition was anticipated in 2014.

Beyond teaching, much of his work involved vine identification for the practical purpose of, for example, settling a legal dispute, or advising a wine region on which varieties were actually growing in some of its old vineyards. This sort of work took him all over the Americas, North Africa, Cyprus, Afghanistan, Nepal, Thailand, and South Korea (Truel inspected the vineyards of Australia and Portugal). Able to identify hundreds of vine varieties at a glance, he was made an Officier de l'Ordre du Mérite Agricole and won many important awards, including a prize in 1983 from the OIV for the entirety of his published work. Few individuals embody such concentrated expertise. The reprint pamphlet cited below gives some of the flavour of this expert who had little patience with those not prepared to get their shoes dirty in the vineyard.
                                               J.R. & L.T.M.

Galet, P., 'La Culture de la vigne aux États-Unis et au Canada', *France viticole* (Sept–Oct 1980 and Jan–Feb 1981).

Galet, P., *Dictionnaire des cépages* (Paris, 2014).

Galicia, Spain's wet, Atlantic north west and one of the country's 17 autonomous regions encompassing the DO wine regions of RÍAS BAIXAS, RIBEIRO, RIBEIRA SACRA, MONTERREI, and VALDEORRAS. Separated by mountains from CASTILLA Y LEÓN, Galicia has developed in isolation from the rest of Spain, the region being geographically and culturally closer to northern Portugal than to Madrid (see map under SPAIN). The locals, many of whom are of Celtic descent, speak Gallego, a close relative of Portuguese. The wines also used to share an affinity with the light, acidic VINHO VERDE produced south of the Miño (Minho in Portuguese), the river that divides this part of Spain from Portugal, but they have become fuller and more substantial with the recovery of INDIGENOUS VARIETIES and the use of modern winemaking techniques.

Wines were exported from Galicia as early as the 14th century, but northern European merchants quickly moved on in search of fuller-bodied wines from the DOURO in northern Portugal. The progressive fragmentation of agricultural holdings left the region with a subsistence economy and in the 19th century the countryside suffered from depopulation as people moved away to find work. Many of the magnificent TERRACES in the PORT vineyards of the Douro were constructed by itinerant labour from Galicia. Since Spain joined the EU in 1986, however, Galicia has benefited from a massive injection of funds which has transformed its wine industry.

Galicia is one of the wettest parts of Iberia. On the coast, RAINFALL averaging more than 1,300 mm/50 in a year is compensated for by an annual average of over 2,000 hours of sunshine. Vines flourish in these humid conditions and YIELDS in excess of 100 hl/ha (5.7 tons/acre) are unequalled anywhere else in Spain. Most of the vineyards are to be found towards the south in the provinces of Orense, Pontevedra, and also in Lugo to the east. Rías Baixas, with its prized ALBARIÑO grape, was the engine of Galician rebirth and its vibrant, dense wines can command high prices. But success has also meant, in the case of some producers, excessive yields and an abusive reliance on such techniques as the use of selected yeasts. On the Miño River, wines are often blends of Albariño, Loureira, and Caiño. Inland, the Ribeiro DO is making impressive progress.

Local whites are based on complex blends, dominated by Treixadura and Torrontés, while reds from native varieties are making a timid comeback. In the inland Valdeorras and Ribeira Sacra DOs, light reds from the Mencía grape are prevalent, but the appley, white Godello grape is their main asset. The newest DO, Monterrei, has historic significance and it, too, has joined Galicia's dramaic improvement in wine quality.

V. de la S.

Barquín, J., Guitiérrez, L., and de la Serna, V., *The Finest Wines of Rioja and Northwest Spain* (London, 2011).

gallic acid, a measurement of TANNIN.

Gallo, based in Modesto, CALIFORNIA, the largest winemaking operation in the world. Gallo was developed by the brothers Ernest (1909–2007) and Julio (1910–93) from the vineyards of their father, who shipped grapes for HOME WINEMAKING during PROHIBITION. On the eve of Repeal in 1933, the brothers obtained a licence to manufacture and store wine, and on the demise of Prohibition at the end of that year began the rapid expansion of their business. The received story is that they had only a couple of pamphlets published before Prohibition to guide their first winemaking efforts, but their father and uncle had been associated with the wine business before Prohibition, and winemaking in some form went on in the CENTRAL VALLEY, where the Gallos lived and grew grapes, throughout Prohibition. They perhaps knew more than a good story later would allow for.

Nevertheless, Ernest Gallo's success in establishing a national distribution network, first, while still in his teens, as a grape broker, and then for wine, stands as an extraordinary feat, particularly in view of the business milieu of the era, still dominated by the thuggish outlaw element nurtured by Prohibition.

Julio's special charge was production. By 1935, just two years after Repeal, the winery was producing 350,000 gal/13,300 hl of wine, and in 1936 the brothers built a new facility with a capacity of 1.5 million gal. The new winery's design showed their concern for the highest level of technical efficiency, as its capacity showed their determination in pursuing new and larger markets. In common with most large California wineries, the Gallos at first sold largely in BULK to bottlers; in 1937 they began to promote their own label and to devise their own marketing methods. The development of the firm thereafter was as a completely self-contained enterprise: it either owned its own vineyards or signed growers to long-term contracts; it built its own glass factory, maintained its own sales force, acquired control over distributorships, operated its own research department, its own print shop, and its own transport company.

By 1950, Gallo had the largest wine-production capacity in the United States. By 1967, it held first position in sales, and has continued to do so. Storage capacity at its four wine-producing facilities by 1992 was 330 million gal/12.5 million hl, many times more than any of Europe's largest wineries. In the process of its growth, Gallo encouraged the planting of superior vine varieties, the use of modern crop management methods, and the best available winemaking technology.

Moreover, Gallo's sales and marketing operation was long considered the academy for such functions in America. At one time, almost all the top wine sales executives in the US had at least a short stint with Gallo on their resumés. In the 1950s and 1960s, Gallo so revolutionized concepts of wine retailing in America that it was said that Gallo salesmen knew more about a store's inventory than its owner. No wonder Gallo has been accused of having a domineering influence over the rest of the industry, particularly, through its sheer size, in the councils of the trade organization the (California) Wine Institute.

Known from the beginning for sound, inexpensive wines of every kind, including FLAVOURED WINES, wine coolers, and FRUIT WINES, brandy, and bulk process SPARKLING WINES, Gallo inevitably became synonymous with basic JUG WINE. From 1977, however, Gallo made a determined effort to associate its name with better quality wines, VARIETALS sold in bottles stoppered with a CORK. By the early 1980s, Gallo was already the largest purchaser of grapes in the Napa Valley. By the end of the 1980s, Gallo had become the largest vineyard owner in Sonoma County. In 2002, they purchased Louis Martini Winery, one of Napa's most venerable institutions. Two of Julio's grandchildren, Matt and Gina, run a winery in Dry Creek Valley estimated to have a capacity of 7 million gallons. It is also estimated that they own 5,000 acres of vineyard spread all over Sonoma County, although even at this size, Gallo-Sonoma accounts for only a small percentage of the company's total volume. The company's estate wines are sold under the name Gallo Estate, as well as third-generation winemaker Gina Gallo's Gallo Signature Series wines, while names such as MacMurray Estate Vineyards, Rancho Zabaco, and Frei Brothers Reserve are used for wines made from grapes purchased from Monterey, Sonoma, and Mendocino respectively. Less expensive wines sold under other Gallo brands such as Barefoot, Turning Leaf, Carlo Rossi, and Livingston Cellars are made in Livingston, south of Modesto. The firm, never particularly export-orientated, is wholly owned by the family and is notoriously secretive. Ernest Gallo's first on-the-record interview took place well after his eightieth birthday.

The Gallo brothers became as jealous of their own name as producers in the CHAMPAGNE region, prohibiting CHIANTI CLASSICO producers from using their traditional symbol of the black cockerel, or Gallo Nero, in the US and even preventing their own younger brother Joseph from using his own name on the cheese he produced.

Gallo, E. and J., *Our Story* (New York, 1994).
Hawkes, E., *Blood and Wine: The Unauthorized Story of the Gallo Wine Empire* (New York, 1993).

Gamaret, red grape CROSS bred in Switzerland by André Jaquinet at CHANGINS from Gamay and Reichensteiner. The variety, which has good rot resistance, makes quite powerful structured wines and total Swiss plantings had reached nearly 400 ha/988 acres by 2009. It is more popular than fellow cross GARANOIR, is authorized in Beaujolais, and occasionally found in Italy.

Gamay Noir, ancient Burgundian red grape variety solely responsible for the distinctive, evolving and unfairly unfashionable wines of BEAUJOLAIS. Galet cites 30 different Gamays, many quite unrelated to the Beaujolais archetype, many of them particular CLONAL SELECTIONS of it, and many more of them red-fleshed TEINTURIERS once widely used to add colour to vapid blends. Red-fleshed versions can still be found, particularly in Mâconnais and Touraine, and France grew almost 200 ha/500 acres of **Gamay Teinturier de Bouze** in 2011. The 'real' Gamay is officially known as **Gamay Noir à Jus Blanc** to draw attention to its noble pale flesh, and is a natural offspring of Pinot and Gouais Blanc (*see* PINOT).

The introduction of Gamay to the vineyards of the CÔTE D'OR in the late 14th century was viewed as scandalous by those whose livelihood did not personally depend on rearing productive vines, and great efforts were made to retain PINOT NOIR at the expense of the less noble newcomer.

The vine is a precocious one, budding, flowering, and ripening early, which makes it prone to spring FROSTS but means that it can flourish in regions as cool as much of the Loire. It can easily produce too generously and the traditional GOBELET method of training is designed to match this aptitude to the granitic soils of the better Beaujolais vineyards.

Although today an increasing proportion of Beaujolais, particularly from the CRUS, is vinified like red burgundy with full BARREL MATURATION and is expected to age for several years in bottle, Gamay juice for long tended to be vinified in a hurry, not least because of strong market pressure in the 1970s and 1980s for Beaujolais NOUVEAU. As a wine, Gamay tends to be paler and bluer than most other reds, with relatively high acidity and a simple but vivacious aroma of freshly picked red fruits, often overlaid by the less subtle smells associated with rapid, anaerated fermentation such as bananas, boiled sweets, and acetone in the Nouveau era. In Mâconnais and Switzerland, it is often blended with Pinot Noir, endowing the nobler grape with some precocity, but often blurring the very distinct attributes of each.

Gamay and Beaujolais are entirely interdependent. Few wine regions are so determinedly *monocépagiste* as Beaujolais; in 2011 all but 400 ha of the Rhône *département*'s nearly 17,548 ha/43,343 acres of vines were Gamay Noir. Vinification techniques vary but most common is a local variant on CARBONIC MACERATION. Similar, often lighter and arguably truer, wines are made from the Gamay grown in the small wine regions of central France, particularly those around Lyons and in the upper reaches of the Loire such as CHÂTEAUMEILLANT, Coteaux du LYONNAIS, Coteaux du GIENNOIS, Côtes d'AUVERGNE, Côtes du FOREZ, Côtes ROANNAISES, and ST-POURÇAIN.

Outside Beaujolais, and perhaps because its wines have been seen as too different from the intense, fashionable norm, the Gamay vine has been losing ground. In the Côte Chalonnaise and Mâconnais between Beaujolais and the Côte d'Or, the Gamay was displaced as principal grape variety by Chardonnay during the 1980s, and Pinot Noir plantings had surpassed those of Gamay by the 21st century. The unexcitingly muddy quality of Gamays made here is expected to continue this trend. Gamay took up just 168 ha of the Côte d'Or's valuable vineyard in 2011.

Gamay is widely planted in SAVOIE, grown especially in the cru of Chautagne. It is also grown all over the Loire, especially in the Loir-et-Cher *département* upstream of Tours, but is not glorified by any of the Loire's greatest appellations. Gamay de Touraine can provide a light, sometimes acid, but usually cheaper alternative to Beaujolais, but it is most widely grown west of Touraine, alongside Sauvignon, for such light, lesser-known names as CHEVERNY and Coteaux du VENDÔMOIS. Considerable plantings in the south west, greater Loire, and the Mâconnais brought France's total area of Gamay Noir up to 28,208 ha/69,673 acres.

Outside France there has been even less incentive to develop this under-appreciated variety. (One notable California grower who bothered in the early 1980s to import and vinify true Gamay was Charles F. Shaw, whose name acquired fame only when it had been acquired by Franzia and applied to a trend-setting wine retailed at $1.99 in the early 2000s, known colloquially as Two Buck Chuck.) Today just a few hundred acres remain of the less distinguished vine known in California **Napa Gamay** (*see* VALDIGUIÉ). Oregon, on the other hand, harbours one of two fine exponents of the variety.

Gamay is also grown in small quantities in Canada and Australia, and is confused on a grand scale with BLAUFRÄNKISCH (to which it may well be related) throughout eastern Europe. It is grown to a limited extent in Italy, and plays a relatively important role in the vineyards of TURKEY, SERBIA, KOSOVO, and, to least effect, in MACEDONIA.

It is chiefly valued, however, outside Beaujolais, by the Swiss, who grow it widely and, often blending with Pinot Noir, take it seriously—although, like Beaujolais's least conscientious producers, some of them chaptalize the life out of it (*see* SWITZERLAND).

Galet, P., *Dictionnaire encyclopédique des cépages* (Paris, 2000).

Robinson, J., Harding, J., and Vouillamoz, J., *Wine Grapes, a complete guide to 1,368 vine varieties, including their origins and flavours* (London, 2012).

Gambellara, dry white wine from the VENETO region of north east Italy. Based on GARGANEGA grapes (a minimum of 80%, with 20% of TREBBIANO di Soave or Trebbiano Toscano (VERDICCHIO)), it is produced in the townships of Gambellara, Montebello Vicentino, Montorso, and Zermeghedo, only a short distance from SOAVE but in the neighbouring province of Vicenza rather than that of Verona. Gambellara is tiny compared to its neighbour: based on about 600 ha compared with Soave's 5,645 ha/13,943 acres in 2012 but with generally more Garganega and lower yields. Since the enlargement of the PROSECCO zone, much of Garganega planted on the plains to the south of the town of Gambellara have been replaced with GLERA, to capitalize on Prosecco's ongoing success. So HILLSIDE VINEYARDS represent a healthy 60% of the Gambellara total. Although much Gambellara is as bland as the vast majority of Soave, several producers with vineyard holdings in the hills have turned to quality rather than quantity. The biodynamic La Biancara Estate, for example, which espouses fermentation on skins, has helped change the perception, even if it cites IGT rather than Gambellara on the labels of some of its wines, not least because of a quality control system unwilling to recognize the wines as typical. A good Gambellara is characterized by notes of camomile and yellow fruits, while taking on honeyed smoky notes after several years in the bottle.

The DOC Gambellara zone is elevated to DOCG for the sweet RECIOTO di Gambellara which has a long history in the region, while Gambellara CLASSICO is not a smaller, historic subzone, but a wine with higher alcohol and from (marginally) lower yields.   W.S.

www.consorziogambellara.com

Gamé, Bulgarian name for BLAUFRÄNKISCH.

Gamza, name for KADARKA in BULGARIA.

garage wines, unofficial, late-20th-century term for wines made with ambition in such small quantity that a garage would suffice as winery. Their makers have been known as **garagistes**. Although the term is now used globally, the phenomenon was first observed on Bordeaux's RIGHT BANK, with miniature wine estates producing ultra-modern, deep-coloured, early-maturing, often sweet, oaky, flattering reds typically produced in quantities of a few hundred cases from low YIELDS, careful SELECTION, MALOLACTIC CONVERSION in barrel, 15 to 18 months of 100% new BARREL MATURATION, minimal FILTRATION, and, often, Michel ROLLAND as consultant oenologist. Le PIN in Pomerol was the archetype, and is the only one to have experienced sustained demand. As Le Pin's PRICES soared in the 1990s, a host of garage wines appeared in St-Émilion (where there is more available land than in most smart Bordeaux appellations) in the late 1990s. Demand for such wines waned considerably in the 21st century and prices continued to slide in the mid 2000s.

Echikson, W., *Noble Rot* (New York, 2004).

Garanoir, red grapevine CROSS created at CHANGINS by André Jaquinet from Gamay and Reichensteiner. It makes less concentrated, softer, fruitier wines than its sister cross GAMARET and was planted on 214 ha/528 acres in Switzerland in 2012.

Garganega, vigorous, productive, often over-productive, late-ripening white grape variety of the VENETO region in north east Italy. Its most famous incarnation is SOAVE, in which it may constitute anything from 70 to 100% of the blend, often sharpened up by the addition of TREBBIANO di Soave (VERDICCHIO), but increasingly plumped up by CHARDONNAY and other imports. In the Soave CLASSICO zone, with yields kept well in check, and where it is allowed to ripen fully, it can produce the fine, delicate whites redolent of lemon and almonds which give Soave a good name. Naturally high in acid, it can give balanced yet steely wines that have an alluring, delicate spiciness. The vine is also responsible for GAMBELLARA—indeed Garganega di Gambellara is its most important subvariety—but Garganega has such a long history in Veneto that it has developed myriad, if rarely particularly interesting, strains, clones, and subvarieties. Other wines in which it plays a major part include Bianco di CUSTOZA, Colli Berici, Colli Euganei, and it is also grown to a more limited extent in both FRIULI and UMBRIA. The Italian vine census of 2010 lists total plantings of Garganega as a fairly steady; 11,291 ha/27,888 acres, but the surprising DNA PROFILING discovery in 2007 that it is identical to the GRECANICO DORATO of Sicily is not incorporated so that the over 4,000 ha of the latter are listed separately. Garganega also seems to be a parent of a wide range of Italian varieties. It is also grown in Australia.

Robinson, J., Harding, J., and Vouillamoz, J., *Wine Grapes, a complete guide to 1,368 vine varieties, including their origins and flavours* (London, 2012).

Garnacha is the Spanish, and therefore original, name for the increasingly fashionable grape known in France and elsewhere as GRENACHE. Its most common and noblest form is the dark-berried and light-fleshed **Garnacha Tinta** (**Garnaxa** in Catalan). As this variety, ubiquitous in much of Spain, is being re-evaluated from weed to asset (partly in response to the RHÔNE RANGER phenomenon but also spurred by PRIORAT's initial success), VARIETAL versions are becoming more common, as are blends with the firmer TEMPRANILLO, and the word Garnacha is increasingly seen on wine labels.

Even after extensive grubbing up in the 1980s and 1990s, when the variety was under-appreciated, a total of 82,300 ha/203,300 acres made Garnacha Tinta Spain's second most planted red wine grape after Tempranillo in 2004. By 2011, Spain's Garnacha Tinta total had fallen to 63,676 ha/15,728 acres, very slightly more than the BOBAL total and barely a third the Tempranillo total. It is grown particularly in north and east, being an important variety in such wine regions as Rioja, Navarra, Empordà-Costa-Brava, Campo de Borja, Cariñena, Costers del Segre, the Gredos Mountains, Madrid, La Mancha, Méntrida, Penedès, Priorat, Somontano, Tarragona, Terra Alta, Utiel-Requena, and Valdeorras. In Rioja it provides stuffing and immediate charm when blended with the more austere Tempranillo. The cooler, higher vineyards of Rioja Alta are reserved for

Tempranillo, while Garnacha is the most common grape variety of the warm eastern Rioja Baja region where the vines can enjoy a long ripening season. The juiciness apparent in these early maturing riojas can be tasted in a host of other Spanish reds and, especially, rosados. Garnacha has been adopted with particular enthusiasm in Navarra, where it has been the dominant grape variety and dictates a lighter, more obviously fruity style of red and rosado than in Rioja. In many other areas Garnacha is typically dry-farmed as an old bush vine (average vine age is high) so that the wines can be quite concentrated and tannic.

Perhaps the most distinctive, and certainly the most expensive, Spanish wine based on Garnacha Tinta (often incorporating some **Garnacha Peluda**, or 'downy Garnacha', more commonly known as LLADONER) is Priorat, the concentrated Cataluñan cult wine in which the produce of old Garnacha vines is often blended with Carignan grapes, and may be modernized by blending it with young Merlot, Cabernet, or even Syrah fruit.

Garnacha Blanca is the light-berried GRENACHE BLANC of which in 2011 there were about 2,200 ha/5,434 acres in Spain, where it plays a role in full-bodied, north eastern whites such as those of Alella, Priorato, Tarragona, Rioja, and Navarra. TERRA ALTA claims one-third of world production of the variety, from particularly old vines.

Garnacha Tintorera, Spanish synonym for the red-fleshed ALICANTE BOUSCHET, Tintorera being Spanish for 'dyer' or TEINTURIER. Spain grew 20,082 ha/29,602 acres acres of this variety in 2011, more than a third as much as GARNACHA Tinta.

Over half is in Castilla-La Mancha, south of Madrid where its deep colour is presumably much appreciated.

Garonne, river that rises south of Toulouse in SOUTH WEST FRANCE and flows north west towards the Atlantic and on which the city of BORDEAUX is situated. The confluence of the Garonne and the DORDOGNE, between MARGAUX and BOURG, marks the southern end of the GIRONDE estuary. The Garonne was an important trade route through south west GAUL in the era of Ancient ROME and continued to play a vital role in the medieval wine trade, where there was particular commercial rivalry between the wines produced up river in the HAUT PAYS, either on the Garonne or on its tributaries the Lot and the Tarn, and those produced in the immediate vicinity of Bordeaux.

Today the Garonne links, travelling north west down river, FRONTON, LAVILLEDIEU, BRULHOIS, BUZET, Côtes du MARMANDAIS, CADILLAC CÔTES DE BORDEAUX, GRAVES, and

Bordeaux's sweet white wine areas SAUTERNES and BARSAC.

garrafeira, word used by winemakers, wine bottlers, and wine collectors in PORTUGAL meaning a 'private wine cellar' or 'reserve'. The term was once widely used on wine labels to denote a red wine from an exceptional year that has been aged for at least 30 months before sale, including at least 12 months in bottle. White and rosé garrafeira wines, which are now fairly rare, must be aged for at least 12 months, including at least 6 months in bottle, to qualify. The law states that both red and white DOC wines must have an ALCOHOLIC STRENGTH at least 0.5 per cent above the legal minimum for the DOC region. Traditionally most garrafeiras were blends of wines from different parts of the country, labelled with the name of the merchant who bottled them. Under legislation introduced in the early 1990s, all garrafeiras must display their region of origin.   R.J.M.

Garrido, minor speciality of the CONDADO DE HUELVA region in southern Spain.

Garrut is a CATALAN synonym for Monastrell or MOURVÈDRE.

Gascony, proud region in SOUTH WEST FRANCE which today comprises armagnac country and such wines as MADIRAN and JURANÇON. Its name appears on labels of the highly successful IGP Côtes de Gascogne. In the Middle Ages it was incorporated into Aquitaine and was therefore, like BORDEAUX, under English rule for nearly 300 years from the middle of the 12th century.

Gattinara, small but historically important wine region in the hills between the towns of Vercelli and Novara, producing NEBBIOLO-based red wine in the north west of Piemonte (see SPANNA for more on its neighbours). It was important enough to have been CLASSIFIED in the 16th and 17th centuries but had only 95 ha/234 acres of vineyards in 2011. In the 19th century, these hills were far more widely planted with Nebbiolo than the LANGHE, and the wines were more highly prized than either Barolo or Barbaresco. The long decline of viticulture here was halted when Gattinara was awarded DOCG status in 1990. In 2004 an overarching DOC, Coste della Sesia, including the Lessona and Bramaterra zones, was created in an effort to safeguard its wine production. Although production regulations faithfully reflect the historical practice of blending in the local UVA RARA and/or VESPOLINA grapes, used in the past to compensate for unripe Nebbiolo grapes in cool vintages, practically all Gattinara is now made of 100% Nebbiolo, a sign of improved viticulture, lower yields, and, possibly, CLIMATE CHANGE. Gattinara is a seriously ageworthy wine with long mandatory ageing of 35 months (47 months for Riserva), and single-vineyard wines are the rule rather than the exception. The region as whole did not escape the fashion for BARRIQUE ageing entirely, although most wines today are aged in large oak casks. Gattinara tends to be lighter and a little more acid than Barolo, yet more perfumed with tangy acidity and a long ageing capacity while still representing excellent value.   W.S.

Gaul, part of western Europe closely approximating to modern France which existed before the rise of classical ROME. The élites of the CELTIC communities beyond the alps were large-scale consumers of wine, long before they were producers. The accoutrements of the Greek and Roman dinner party are frequently found amid the grave goods of Celtic chieftains. Their passion for wine was even claimed as the motive for the Gallic invasions of the Mediterranean world from the 4th century BC onwards (see e.g. Livy, 5. 33). The widespread ready market in Gaul for wine, as well as the slaves who were offered in exchange, was a major stimulus for exports from Italy, particularly in the last century BC (Diodorus, 5. 26). The cultivation of vines arrived with Greek settlers at Massilia (Marseilles) about 600 BC. From them the Gauls 'got used to living by the rule of law, and to pruning the vine, and planting the olive' (Justin, 43. 4. 1). But the real impetus came with the arrival of Roman settlers from the end of the 2nd century BC. By the end of the 1st century BC southern France and the RHÔNE valley (Gallia Narbonensis) were planted with all the fruit that Mediterranean visitors expected. But beyond the Cévennes was a world where 'no vine, olive, or fruit grew', as the great scholar VARRO (De re rustica, 1. 7. 8) noticed while on campaign there. The reasons for this were part sociological and part ecological. Some tribes banned the drinking of wine and even massacred traders, in the belief that it undermined their manliness and was the explanation of their defeats by Julius Caesar's armies. More significant was the need for vines which were resistant to FROST. The 1st century AD was a time of considerable development in the south, including wines from Baeterrae (Béziers) and around Vienne (see CÔTE RÔTIE), where the Allobrogica vine was noted for producing a wine with a natural resinated taste. Wines from this region competed in the markets of Italy and the western Mediterranean, as the finds of the distinctive local AMPHORAE confirm. Elsewhere in Gaul it is more difficult to trace the introduction of viticulture. The GARONNE was an important trade route from an early date; so it is highly likely that the BORDEAUX region was developed in the 1st century AD. On the other hand, the first references to vineyards in BURGUNDY, on the MOSELLE, and in the area of PARIS belong to the 4th century AD. However, recent archaeological finds suggest that

viticulture may have developed considerably earlier in many regions than the inadequate literary sources suggest. For example, the discovery of kilns producing amphorae for wine from the late 1st century AD onwards on the LOIRE and its tributaries is testimony to the presence of viticulture in an area for which there is no other evidence. The scale of production should not be exaggerated. The modern map of wine production in France owes less to the Romans than to the Christian Church in the post-Roman period (see CHARLEMAGNE and MONKS AND MONASTERIES).   J.J.P.

Dion, R., *Histoire de la vigne et du vin en France des origines au XIXe siècle* (Paris, 1959).

Ferdière, A., *Les Campagnes en Gaule romaine*, ii (Paris, 1988).

Gavi, or **Cortese di Gavi**, is a renowned Italian dry white DOCG zone of 1,455 ha/3,595 acres and the most interesting expression of the CORTESE grape in PIEMONTE. It is produced in 11 communes (Bosio, Carrosio, Capriata d'Orba, Francavilla Bisio, Gavi, Novi Ligure, Pasturana, San Cristoforo, Serravalle Scrivia and Tassarolo) in the south east of the province of Alessandria. Although the name of each commune (and even single vineyards) may appear on labels, stylistic differences are not (yet) evident, and most wines are blends of more than one commune. The red DOLCETTO grape was also important here until PHYLLOXERA devastated the vineyards. At its best, Gavi is fruity and aromatic, occasionally with mineral notes and a tangy, citric finish. In the past the wines tended to be rather neutral, caused by excessively high maximum yields, which have recently been reduced to 9.5 tonnes/ha or 60 hl/ha, and lower yet for single-vineyard wines. For a white wine best known in its still form, Gavi comes in a surprisingly wide range of styles: FRIZZANTE, SPUMANTE, and METODO CLASSICO (with a minimum required lees ageing of 18 months), and MÉTHODE ANCESTRALE all allowed. Although there are several BARRIQUE-aged examples, most producers stick to the conventional winemaking practice of temperature-controlled fermentation in stainless steel, leading to a certain sameness in the wines. More interesting Gavi tends to come from producers such as Castello di Tassarolo who focus on ORGANIC and BIODYNAMIC practices while fermenting the wine with ambient YEAST.

Thanks partly to the high quality achieved by the pioneering La Scolca estate in Rovereto di Gavi, the wine enjoyed great commercial success in the 1960s and the early 1970s, first in the Italian market and subsequently abroad, before the emergence of FRIULI as an important source of fresh white wine from international varieties. Increasing competition in its category from TRENTINO and ALTO ADIGE, as well as from Friuli, has subsequently put Gavi under a certain

commercial pressure, but the trend towards INDIGENOUS VARIETIES may well work in Gavi's favour.

www.consorziogavi.com   W.S.

GDC, vine-TRAINING SYSTEM. See GENEVA DOUBLE CURTAIN.

Geelong, cool wine region in the Port Phillip Zone of the Australian state of VICTORIA that is especially good for complex, intense Pinot Noir and Chardonnay. Shiraz also does well. Most of the 45 producers are small, family-owned and operated.

Geilweilerhof. See JULIUS-KÜHN-INSTITUT.

Geisenheim, former research institute for viticulture, horticulture, beverage technology, and landscape architecture and, since 2013, known properly as **Hochschule Geisenheim University**. Founded in 1872 by Eduard von Lade to improve the science of growing fruit, particularly apples, it has continued a tradition of combining education with applied research. In 1876 Professor Müller joined Geisenheim as a biologist and in 1882 developed the cross MÜLLER-THURGAU, which later became one of the most planted in Germany.

Today research in VITICULTURE and OENOLOGY focuses on environmental stress effects on grapevine physiology and fruit maturation, with particular emphasis on the possible effects of CLIMATE CHANGE on viticulture and on biotic stresses such as DISEASES; quantifying 'greenhouse gas' emissions from viticultural soils; studying the effects of elevated CARBON DIOXIDE on all aspects related to grapevine development and fruit quality; the development of new biological and technological strategies to minimize the use of PESTICIDES in both ORGANIC and conventional viticulture; molecular and physiological studies of PESTS and diseases; secondary metabolites formed during fruit development, focusing on AROMATIC precursors and PHENOLICS and their dynamics during fruit processing and winemaking; WATER STRESS and the use of new technologies to guide irrigation for grapes and horticultural crops; molecular and traditional genetics, including VINE BREEDING for DISEASE RESISTANCE, CLONAL SELECTION for improved quality and vine health, plant regeneration *in vitro*, research on the adaptation of ROOTSTOCKS to different soil and climate conditions; the genetics of PHYLLOXERA resistance and of YEAST and BACTERIA, and the detection of GENETICALLY MODIFIED organisms; all aspects of wine microbiology; steep-slope viticulture (see HILLSIDE VINEYARDS) and the development of new technologies for MECHANIZATION such as REMOTE SENSING, GLOBAL POSITIONING SYSTEMS in machine guidance, efficient SOIL WATER management, as well as an economic evaluation of vineyard management under these conditions; new technologies in juice and wine production and their effects on wine AGEING; the allergenic potential of wine ADDITIVES; and alcohol management in the vineyard and winery. Other areas of activity include identifying and describing objective parameters for wine quality as well as developing criteria for cork and alternative CLOSURES. Other studies focus on wine ECONOMICS and market research, including studies on consumer preferences, the dynamics of the global wine market, success factors in marketing, enterprise management, and economic analyses of different segments of the wine industry.   M.C.

www.hs-geisenheim.de

http://www.facebook.com/hsgeisenheim

gelatin, the gel familiar in jelly and jello, used by winemakers as a FINING agent. This animal product is particularly useful for precipitating excess TANNINS as large insoluble molecules which can be removed by FILTRATION. Gelatin is deliberately avoided by those making VEGETARIAN AND VEGAN WINES.

Gelber Muskateller, name for MUSCAT BLANC À PETITS GRAINS used in Austria which grew more than 700 ha of this and Roter Muskateller combined in 2013. The variety is popular in Styria for light, dry wines and makes some fine sweet wines in BURGENLAND. In Germany there were 245 ha of Gelber Muskateller, mainly in the south of the country, in 2012.

gemischter Satz, German term for an interplanting or FIELD BLEND of multiple grape varieties, and by implication for a wine made from the CO-FERMENTATION of fruit from such plantings. Once common, such plantings are now rare throughout the German-speaking world, with the exception of Vienna where, although a distinct minority, in 2013 they became the basis for that urban growing region's DAC known as WIENER GEMISCHTER SATZ.

generic wine, one named after a wine type (and usually borrowed European place-name) as opposed to a VARIETAL, named after the grape variety from which the wine was made. The term has been used particularly in AUSTRALIA and the UNITED STATES. Under American law, wines labelled as generics may be made from any grape variety or blend of varieties, and called either after their colour (red, white, rosé) or after places. With nothing else to call their results, early CALIFORNIA wineries borrowed European place-names shamelessly. Before PROHIBITION one could buy, not just St-Julien and Margaux made in the state, but wines named after particular châteaux. After Prohibition, stricter laws limited the borrowings to a handful of so-called **semi-generic** names, most commonly Burgundy, Chablis, Champagne, Chianti, Rhine, Sauterne (*sic*), Sherry, and Port, but did nothing to demand

even the faintest approximations of the original in terms of grape varieties or style. Chablis could and can be just as sickly sweet as Rhine, and both can be made from THOMPSON SEEDLESS or any other white grape. Burgundy, Chianti, and Claret could all come from the same tank, and probably have done. Towards the end of the 1980s, Red Table Wine, White Table Wine, and Rosé began to replace place-names on many of the more reputable labels. However, Chablis, Burgundy, and other borrowed names remain in widespread use by a number of large-volume producers, giants GALLO foremost among them. A wine agreement between the US and EU finally drafted in 2005 permitted the continued use of these semi-generic terms on established BRANDS for an unspecified period.

Generic names can still be found on many wine labels, particularly in non-exporting or developing wine regions. No third-country wine entering the EU may carry a geographical name recognized as a European wine name. Thus, for example, the Australian company PENFOLDS had to change the name of their most famous wine from Penfolds Grange Hermitage to Penfolds Grange and, more fatuously, EU officials have objected to established New World place-names incorporating the word Port.

Outside Europe, CHAMPAGNE is still widely used as a generic name for SPARKLING WINE, although not usually for the best-quality products.

generoso is a Spanish and Portuguese term for a FORTIFIED wine.

genetic modification, sometimes called **genetic manipulation** or **genetic engineering**, a modern approach to breeding which involves transfer of genes between organisms. This new technology has applications in both VITICULTURE and OENOLOGY, and the techniques used are extremely useful for the study of other aspects of vine biology and for more wide-ranging YEAST research.

A proposed benefit of genetic modification is the ability to insert foreign genes, responsible for a particular desirable characteristic, into the genetic material of traditional VINE VARIETIES such as Cabernet Sauvignon, without altering the genes concerned with their other characteristics. There are hopes of introducing resistance to FUNGAL DISEASES and VIRUS DISEASES as well as to INSECT PESTS by the use of this technique, as well as improving berry ripening and quality. Whether such genetically modified vines can retain the same variety name remains to be legally tested. Research groups around the world have produced genetically modified vines; since the late 1990s and early 2000s, field trials have been in progress in Germany, Italy, Australia, and the US with the aim of improving fruit quality and disease resistance.

Many governments have introduced strict testing procedures for genetically modified organisms and consumer resistance in parts of Europe has been considerable. It is expected that the commercial availability of genetically modified vines will depend on market acceptance of wines derived from these plants.

See also TISSUE CULTURE and INTERNATIONAL GRAPE GENOME PROJECT.

Biotechnology's powerful array of tools also allows modification of the DNA of YEAST. In essence, a gene which codes for a protein having a particular property can be added, replaced, or removed to change that property. In this way, a genetically modified (GM) yeast can acquire a new property, such as haze reduction, or show enhanced varietal flavour formation by introducing a gene that liberates a TERPENOID or thiol aroma compound (see MERCAPTANS), or can be freed of an undesirable property, such as the elimination of HYDROGEN SULFIDE production. In theory, any property for which a gene or a series of genes is/are known can be modified. Indeed, properties that do not exist in wine yeast, such as tannin biosynthesis, can in theory be introduced by taking genes from other organisms that have the required ability. Genetically complex properties, such as fermentation robustness or temperature profile, for which relevant genes have not yet been identified, cannot yet be modified at the gene level.

GM yeast tend to arouse the same concerns as do any other GM products. They have been approved for use in wine production in only a few countries, including the US and Canada, and to a very limited extent. For example, the GM wine yeast ML01, produced in Canada, has two new genes which enable it to consume malic acid, negating the need for the bacterial MALOLACTIC CONVERSION. This yeast is used to improve the taste and colour stability of wine as well as to avoid the production of undesirable compounds (HISTAMINES). This yeast is approved also in Moldova. If wine has been produced using a GM yeast, it does not have to say so on the label, provided that the yeast has been removed and is no longer detectable (see PROCESSING AIDS). That the use of GM wine yeast is limited may seem surprising since, for example, 'human-alike' insulin has been produced by GM yeast for use globally for a decade. Nonetheless, GM wine yeast have been under development by many institutions worldwide for more than two decades. Even if GM yeast is not more widely approved for use in winemaking, this technology facilitates an understanding and modification of the genetic basis for many important winemaking properties of yeast and can therefore greatly assist yeast modification by conventional breeding techniques. The recent development of non-GM yeast in which hydrogen sulfide production has been eliminated is a good example of the benefit of this GM technology. P.A.H.

Cebollero, E., et al., 'Transgenic wine yeast technology comes of age: is it time for transgenic wine?', *Biotechnology Letters*, 29/2 (2007), 191–200.

Perl, A., and Eshdat, Y., 'Grape', in E. C. Pua and R. R. Davey (eds.), *Biotechnology in Agriculture and Forestry 60: Transgenic Crops V* (Springer, 2007), 189–208.

Schuller, D., and Casal, M., 'The use of genetically modified *Saccharomyces cerevisiae* strains in the wine industry', *Applied Biochemistry and Biotechnology*, 68/3 (2005), 292–304.

Vivier, M. A., and Pretorius, I. S., 'Genetic improvement of grapevine: tailoring grape varieties for the third millennium–review', *Institute for Wine Biotechnology and Department of Viticulture & Oenology*, University of Stellenbosch (2000). www. sawislibrary.co.za/dbtextimages/17161.pdf.

Geneva double curtain

Geneva double curtain, often abbreviated to **GDC**, a vine-TRAINING SYSTEM whereby the CANOPY is divided into two pendent curtains, trained downwards from high CORDONS or CANES. The system was developed by Professor Nelson SHAULIS of Geneva Experiment Station in upstate New York in the early 1960s. The vines are planted in about 3-m/10-ft rows and the trunk divided at about 1.5 m height to form two parallel cordons about 1.3 m/4 ft apart. The foliage is trained downwards from these cordons, forming the so-called double curtains. This training system was one of the first examples of a DIVIDED CANOPY developed in the New World and, by reducing shade, it increases both yield and grape quality (see CANOPY MICROCLIMATE). While initially developed for the American variety CONCORD, the system has been applied to VINIFERA wine grapes, especially in Italy. It was one of a number of TRELLIS SYSTEMS advocated as part of CANOPY MANAGEMENT in the 1990s. The GDC system is particularly useful for wide row spacing vineyards of high VIGOUR.

While most wine grape varieties have more erect shoots than the American vines it was developed with, it has been found suitable for use in many vineyards, and some notable increases in yield and wine quality have resulted from use of the system. R.E.S.

Smart, R. E., and Robinson, M., *Sunlight into Wine: A Handbook for Winegrape Canopy Management* (Adelaide, 1991).

Genoa

Genoa, north-west Italian port and the principal city of the LIGURIA region. After the fall of Ancient ROME and the barbarian invasions, Genoa was occupied by the Lombards, a Germanic tribe, in 642. Under the Lombards, the region disintegrated economically, and the old Roman highways across the Apennines and along the coast were not maintained. It took Genoa until the early 11th century fully to recover from the effects of Lombard rule.

Genoa was therefore initially at a grave disadvantage compared with the city that was to become its deadly rival, VENICE. The Genoese navy had fought to protect its ships from Saracen sea power in the two centuries before the Crusades, together with Amalfi, Pisa, and Venice, and Genoa had established trading posts in the Byzantine empire, although it was nowhere near as successful in this as Venice. Nevertheless, Genoa's rise, like Venice's, was at first based on its eastern trade, and by the time of the Crusades it was battling with Venice, and occasionally Pisa, for economic control of the eastern Mediterranean. The Latin kings of Jerusalem were dependent on Venetian, Genoese, and Pisan naval power for their protection, and so they granted these cities trading areas in their ports. Whereas Venice continued to trade mostly with Constantinople and the Near East, Genoa's interests centred largely on Palestine and Syria. Along with sugar, glass, and textiles, it shipped wine from vineyards there, many of which had been planted by Christian settlers, to Italy, where these strong, sweet wines were accounted a luxury and bought by rich merchants for their own consumption.

Along with luxury goods acquired in the East, Genoa also began to export cheap bulky goods such as grain, salt, oil, alum (for dying woollen cloth), and wine to western and northern Europe. The overland route was prohibitively expensive, and so from the 13th century onwards Genoa organized regular sailings to Bruges and Southampton in galleys, which used their oars to get into and out of ports swiftly, regardless of the prevailing winds. The voyage still took several months, and only strong, sweet wines such as VERNACCIA ('vernage'), produced mainly in Liguria, and the MALMSEYS of the Aegean had any chance of arriving in drinkable condition. The Venetians did not follow the Genoese galleys until 40 years later. In the late 14th century, Genoa abandoned its galleys in favour of the much larger cogs, which had a capacity of 700 to 800 tons and could travel from Genoa to Southampton with only one stop on the way, at Cádiz (see SPAIN).

See also NAPLES and ITALY. H.M.W.

Lopez, R. S., 'The trade of mediaeval Europe: the South', *The Cambridge Economic History of Europe*, 7 vols. ii: *Trade and Industry in the Middle Ages* (Cambridge, 1987).

Melis, F., 'Produzione e commercio dei vini italiani nei secoli XIII–XVIII', *Annales cisalpines d'histoire sociale*, 1/3 (1972), 107–33.

Geographe

Geographe, moderately cool, gently hilly wine region in the South West Australia Zone of WESTERN AUSTRALIA. Most of the 40 producers are tiny.

geographical delimitation

geographical delimitation and **geographical designation**. See DELIMITATION, GEOGRAPHICAL.

geographical indication

geographical indication (**GI**) is a catch-all term that is intended to accommodate the various approaches to geographical DELIMITATION across the globe. It encompasses those straightforward systems typical of NEW WORLD countries that control only the origin of the grapes, as well as the European CONTROLLED APPELLATION model that also regulates conditions of production such as variety and yield.

GIs can vary greatly in size and consequently in the promise of specificity that they convey. South Eastern Australia and France's Pays d'Oc are immense, covering many thousands of hectares, whereas the smallest, such as the Burgundy grands crus, cover just a few hectares. But in every case, they should be more than a mere indication of source. They must signify a link between a place and the characteristics of the wines that are produced there.

Geographical indications were recognized as a special form of intellectual property in 1994

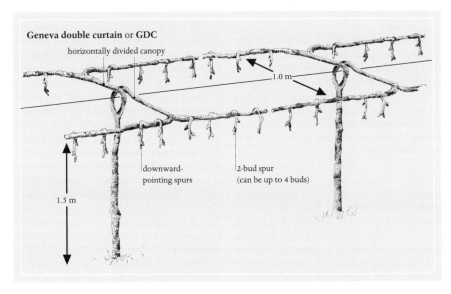

Geneva double curtain or GDC

horizontally divided canopy

1.0 m

downward-pointing spurs

2-bud spur (can be up to 4 buds)

1.5 m

through the WTO's Agreement on Trade Related Aspects of Intellectual Property. The agreement defines a GI as 'an indication that identifies a good as originating in the territory of a country, or a region or locality in that territory, where a given quality, or reputation, or other characteristic, of the good is essentially attributable to its geographical origin'. This definition applies not only to wine but to all products.

Every one of the 158 member countries of the WTO is required to provide a means for the legal protection of GIs against misuse. Wines and spirits have a higher level of protection than other products but it would be fair to say that each country interprets its obligations differently, resulting in a diverse range of approaches to GI protection as well as a reasonable amount of controversy.

Many countries have incorporated the term 'geographical indication' directly into their legislation, including Australia and China. The EU created the Protected Geographical Indication (PGI) category for wines in 2008 although this is seen as a lower guarantee of typicality than the more strictly controlled Protected Designation of Origin (PDO) category.   J.B.

Harvey, M., and Way, V., *Global Wine Regulation* (Melbourne, 2013).

geographical information system

(GIS), database which can store, analyse, and display in map form geographically related data such as soil type, climate, elevation, and crop history. GIS is an essential tool in PRECISION VITICULTURE.   R.G.V.B.

geology

is the scientific study of the solid Earth, although the term has also come to refer to the materials and processes involved with it. Vineyard geology, therefore, means the ground in which the vines are rooted. The loose earth on the surface is derived from bedrock and, if it can support plant life, is called SOIL. Because grapevines can thrive in strikingly stony soil and root into bedrock, the distinction in vineyards between rock and soil is unusually blurred.

Many of the world's vineyards are located on sediment that is now distant from its source, while in others the soil is derived from the local bedrock, which may be visible as outcrops protruding through the loose material. All exposed bedrock is under constant chemical and physical attack (weathering), breaking it down into the smaller fragments generally called stones (see STONES AND ROCKS). Smoothed pieces a few centimetres or so across are referred to as pebbles, or cobbles if larger. As the material is further fragmented, into SAND, SILT, and CLAY, it becomes soil. Loose material on hillsides tends to slip down the slope due to gravity (see COLLUVIUM). The world's largest vineyards

are on flat plains, carved by rivers over millennia and now covered by ALLUVIUM. All these fragmented products and the bedrock itself are composed of minerals.

Minerals

In geology, minerals are natural, inorganic solids in which the constituent atoms have an ordered, systematic structure. (In the nutrient sense, MINERALS are soluble single elements.) The two most abundant elements in the outer part of the Earth are oxygen (46%) and silicon (28%), consequently the most common minerals are various silicates, in which the two elements are rigidly bonded together, alone in the case of QUARTZ (silicon dioxide) but usually with a number of other elements.

Some minerals relevant to vineyard geology are not silicates but are composed of a single element, such as CARBON (the mineral graphite), largely responsible for the colour of rocks such as dark SHALES; and SULFUR, found in VOLCANIC areas. Non-silicate compounds include the oxides (e.g. hematite, the iron oxide giving the distinctive red colour of TERRA ROSSA) and sulfates such as gypsum. Especially important are the carbonates, particularly calcium carbonate (the mineral calcite). Materials dominated by calcite, such as LIMESTONE and MARL, are described as CALCAREOUS.

The silicate minerals are complex and numerous, including the family of mica minerals such as silvery muscovite and shiny black biotite; iron-calcium-magnesium minerals such as pyroxene and amphibole; serpentine, a magnesium silicate unusual in that it can be inimical to grapevines; feldspar, a large group of important rock-forming minerals; and quartz, often referred to as silica. This last can assume a wide variety of forms, including the grey, rather opaque form known as flint, *silex* in French. Although the term flint frequently appears in tasting notes, like all forms of silica (and virtually all minerals and rocks) the material is actually odourless and tasteless.

Clay is used to denote a particularly fine grain size in soils but it is also the name of a family of flaky silicate minerals that are especially varied and intricate. Because individual flakes of clay minerals are very tiny, they can choke the pores in the soil and curb drainage. Moreover, some clay minerals expand when wet, adding to the clogging effect but also offering water storage capabilities. Equally important, each tiny clay flake presents an enormous surface area for its size, and, because of clay chemistry, is commonly very reactive. Clays are therefore the basis of much of the CATION EXCHANGE CAPACITY (CEC) of soils. The fertility of vineyard soils that are stony and barren-looking, without much in the way of organic matter, comes largely from the CEC of the sparse clay minerals (see SOIL FERTILITY).

Rocks

Fundamental though minerals are, more noticeable in many vineyard soils are the larger stony pieces: the rigid, solid aggregates of minerals termed rock. Rocks are classified into three groups according to their origin.

Igneous rocks are solidified from a melt. Lava chills at the Earth's surface to form rocks such as BASALT, often with associated volcanic products such as TUFF. Molten material at depth tries to move upwards, progressively cooling until the mass finally solidifies while still deep underground, forming a plutonic igneous rock which may eventually be exposed at the surface by erosion of the overlying rocks. GRANITE is the most widespread plutonic igneous rock in vineyards.

Sedimentary rocks come about because of the weathering of outcrops into loose particles, in geology called sediment. Over time, it tends to be moved across the land surface and out to sea, but at any stage the sediment may be stationary long enough for the grains to become naturally bonded together into a coherent mass, a sedimentary rock. The particle sizes that constitute SANDSTONE, siltstone, and claystone correspond to the grain-size terms for soils described above. Conglomerates have reasonably smooth pebble-sized fragments; in breccia the fragments are angular. Claystone is often referred to as mudstone, especially if it incorporates silt-sized fragments. Shale is a variety of mudstone which tends to splinter along uneven weaknesses, giving a rock that is soft and easily eroded. From the Latin for clay (*argilla*) comes the adjective argillaceous, in French *argilo-*, added to rock names where there is a significant clay content. In warm, shallow seawater, accumulations of dead organisms made of calcite and chemical precipitates of calcium carbonate become hardened into limestone, including subvarieties CHALK and dolomite, the latter rich in magnesium. Some clay content gives an argillaceous limestone; even more, a marl or even a calcareous claystone. A certain cachet is often attached to calcareous materials in vineyards but largely for circumstantial rather than scientific reasons.

Metamorphic rocks are formed when rocks deeper underground experience greater pressure and are progressively warmed, slowly undergoing a variety of chemical and physical changes. At any stage, the changes may cease and a combination of uplift and erosion may lead to the material being excavated and visible at the surface. The metamorphic processes can imbue the rock with a planar aspect and a tendency to split. Where it is not possible to discern the individual minerals responsible for this, the rock is known as a SLATE. If the minerals are visible—though then the clean-splitting property is less marked—it is called a SCHIST. If the secondary planes consist of bands of different minerals, it is termed a GNEISS. Marble is the metamorphic equivalent of limestone; QUARTZITE is metamorphosed quartz-rich sandstone.

Geological time and fossils

Vineyard descriptions often mention periods of geological time. A famous example is the controversy over whether or not true CHABLIS can be produced from Portlandian as well as Kimmeridgian soils. These two terms refer to intervals of geological time rather than to the actual nature of the material, what geologists call its lithology. For viticulture, it is really the lithology and its properties that are relevant, not in which remote geological time the bedrock happened to form. However, the age of the overlying soil, typically hugely younger than its parent bedrock, is relevant in that it influences SOIL DEPTH and SOIL FERTILITY.

Fossilized seashells catch the eye in a number of the world's vineyards (see MUSCHELKALK, for example), but for the vines they are indistinguishable from any other piece of rock. Nearly all fossils are the result of durable geological minerals (most commonly calcite and quartz) replacing and replicating the shape of the original organism. Consequently, despite much mythology, fossils bring nothing different to the nutrition of the vines or the composition of the resulting wine.

Role of vineyard geology

Fundamentally, it is the interplay between erosion and variously arranged bedrock of differing toughness that governs the lie of the land and all that stems from that (see, for example, ELEVATION, HILLSIDE VINEYARD, and TOPOGRAPHY). More directly, the intensity and spatial orientation of planes of weakness in bedrock influence water and vine root penetration, and its propensity for weathering helps determine the SOIL DEPTH. SOIL COLOUR affects the thermal and ULTRAVIOLET RADIATION behaviour of soil and therefore vine performance.

However, much research indicates that the chief physical effect of geology is its influence on how easily water is stored and transmitted in soil (see DRAINAGE). Two properties are fundamental: porosity expresses what proportion of the substance is space, available for water storage; permeability represents how well water can flow through the material. A good vineyard soil balances the two (see SOIL WATER and SOIL STRUCTURE). In bedrock, water flows partly by using interconnected pores between the constituent mineral particles and partly along the cracks and fissures which exist to some extent in all solid rock.

The other dominant role of geology is its provision of SOIL NUTRIENTS essential for vine growth. Most are needed only in very small quantities, and the majority of rocks possess

ample supplies. However, their availability to vine roots is another matter, because the elements are tightly bonded in the physical soil framework and somehow have to become loosened, dissolved, and transported. In fact, it has been estimated that although a typical vineyard sited on GRANITE will contain abundant potassium, as little as 2% might actually be available to the vines. MYCORRHIZAL fungi and other microorganisms may be involved, but usually chemical weathering acts to generate clay minerals which, thanks to their CATION EXCHANGE CAPACITY, can release elements into water in the soil so that the roots can absorb them (see VINE NUTRITION and VINE PHYSIOLOGY). (It is at present unclear if fine variations within the optimal range of nutrient uptake affect subsequent metabolism and vinification processes.) Thus vines get little nutrition from intact rock, and stones and bedrock have relatively little direct role in nutrient supply. The vine roots do not distinguish the origin of their nutrients: a complex geology does not lead to complex wines.

Geology and wine flavour

Before modern science, winemakers thought, understandably, that vines and hence wine were made entirely of matter derived from the soil, and laid the basis for the European tradition of a special alliance between soil and wine that continues today (see TERROIR). Despite discoveries such as the pre-eminent roles of PHOTOSYNTHESIS and microbial FERMENTATION, it still seems *de rigueur* in winery descriptions to at least mention the vineyard geology, and often to extol some special virtue. For some enthusiasts, the Earth–wine relationship approaches the mystical, an intimacy unparalleled in any other agricultural product.

In practice, in much of the world the geological factors outlined above tend to be overridden by artificial manipulation: earth moving, RIPPING, DRAINAGE installation, COVER CROPS, and the rest. Two particularly conspicuous interventions are IRRIGATION and the application of FERTILIZERS: WATER STRESS is engineered; nutritional imbalances are routinely corrected.

The extent to which the natural vineyard geology affects wine flavour is unclear. Claims that wines made identically from adjacent sites taste different simply because the geology differs are hard to evaluate because other natural factors will vary along with the geology, particularly concerning MESOCLIMATE, CANOPY MICROCLIMATE, and soil microbiology. Similarly, because its properties interact with a whole matrix of other factors, a soil that is superb in one place may well perform differently elsewhere. Wines of comparable character can come from very different soils, and statements that certain types of geology are always best for a particular grape variety lack consistency, as do

assertions about which soils give what qualities to wine. Some wine attributes are given names that sound geological, such as 'mineral', 'earthy', or 'flinty', but they have no literal connection with the soils. Vineyard minerals and rocks are practically insoluble and do not volatilize—prerequisites for giving taste and odour.

Scientifically, geology is clearly important for vine performance and can therefore influence the character and flavour of the finished wine. But its role is indirect, subtle, and complex. Anecdotes notwithstanding, vineyard geology cannot—in any direct, literal way—be tasted in wine. A.J.M.

Maltman, A. J., 'The role of vineyard geology in wine typicity', *Journal of Wine Research* 19 (2008), 1–17.

Park, G., *Introducing Geology: A Guide to the World of Rocks* (2nd edn, Edinburgh, 2010).

van Leeuwen, C., et al., 'Influence of climate, soil, and cultivar on terroir', *American Journal of Enology and Viticulture*, 55/3 (2004), 207–17.

Geoponika, a compilation of advice on agriculture put together about AD 950 at the behest of the scholarly Byzantine Emperor Constantine VII Porphyrogenitus, as part of a grand scheme of digests of knowledge. It may have been based on a compilation of some three centuries earlier by Cassianus Bassus. Of the 20 books, the largest section, Books 4–8, consisted of a long list of precepts on viticulture and winemaking. It survives in part. The information is of variable quality. Much can be traced back to the Roman AGRICULTURAL TREATISES but it includes material from authors, particularly of the Hellenistic period, whose work is otherwise unknown to us. J.J.P.

Georgia, independent state between the Black Sea and the High Caucasus. One of the world's great and historic centres of both wild and cultivated vines, it contains the autonomous republics of Apkhazeti and Adjara, and the former autonomous district of South Ossetia.

History

Wine is integral to the culture of Georgia, a small country whose history is a succession of struggles for independence from such empires as the Assyrian, Roman, Persian, Byzantine, Arabian, Osmanli, Russian, and, latterly, the Soviet Union. Throughout all these struggles, Georgia retains a strong identity, including its own language, customs, Christian religion, and a national reverence for wine which persisted for more than 8,000 years and which is kept alive in Georgia's famous *supra*, a feast punctuated by traditional dancing, singing, and toasts, lubricated with jugfuls of wine and moderated by the *tamada* or toastmaster. Archaeology provides ample evidence that viticulture was long an important occupation of the Georgian people and wine drinking an integral part of their culture. Grape seeds, special knives for vine pruning, stone presses, pottery, silver and gold vessels for wine, and jewellery depicting grape bunches and leaves dating back to between 6000 and 5000 BC have all been unearthed in Shula-veris-Gora and nearby Neolithic sites in Lower Kartli. Rich ornaments of fruited vines are found on the walls of ancient temples in Samtavisi, Ikalto, Zarzma, Gelati, Nikortsminda, and Vardzia. According to Apollonius of Rhodes (3rd century BC), the Argonauts, having arrived in the capital of Kolkhida-Aia (nowadays Kutaisi) centuries earlier, saw twining vines and a fountain of wine in the shade of the trees.

Georgian legends and folklore bear witness to that people's love of the grapevine. Georgia adopted Christianity in the 4th century, and the first cross was made of vines to show that the Christian faith and the vine were the most sacred treasures of the nation.

The Middle Ages were Georgia's golden age of wine. For many centuries, viticulture was of great agricultural and economic importance to the country. In the second half of the 19th century, vineyards covered 71,200 ha/176,000 acres, but FUNGAL DISEASES and PHYLLOXERA had reduced the total vineyard area to 37,400 ha by the beginning of the 20th century. In order to restore vineyards destroyed by phylloxera, the country had to import phylloxera-resistant ROOTSTOCKS.

The 20th century was the era of Soviet wine-making; during this time, a number of Georgian terroirs were identified and developed but quality was routinely, and efficiently, sacrificed for the vast quantities required by the Russian market. GORBACHEV's anti-alcohol campaign of 1985–7 dramatically reduced the market for Georgian wine although it mainly affected the state vineyards since no Georgian farmer would be willing to pull out his own vines. In 1990, as the Soviet Union was disintegrating, the total area of the vineyards was 115,599 ha/285,500 acres, down from a peak of 134,300 ha in 1976. Viticultural investment was sorely needed. By 2004, the total was 37,419 ha, of which almost 10,000 were of very young vines.

See also ORIGINS OF VINICULTURE, PALAEO-ETHNOBOTANY AND THE ARCHAEOLOGY OF WINE.

P.T.H.U.

Viticulture and vine varieties

Vines in Georgia (unlike those in RUSSIA) do not need WINTER PROTECTION, and new vineyards are planted to grafted seedlings. Vineyards mostly use TRELLIS SYSTEMS and various TRAINING SYSTEMS such as CORDON, GUYOT, fan-shaped systems with numerous canes, Georgian systems with canes trained in one or two directions, and pergolas.

WILD VINES are widely distributed in Georgia, where *Vitis vinifera* subs. *silvestris* can still be seen. By both natural and artificial selection, they have given rise to more than 500

identifiable INDIGENOUS VARIETIES and clones. Of the 37 authorized varieties, the two most widely planted are the indigenous RKATSITELI and SAPERAVI. Although INTERNATIONAL VARIETIES such as Aligoté, Pinot Blanc, Chardonnay, Cabernet Sauvignon, and Merlot are permitted, around 95% of Georgian wine is made from indigenous varieties, including the light-skinned Chinuri, Goruli Mtsvane, Khikhvi, Kisi, Krakhuna, Mtsvane Kakhuri, Tsitska, and Tsolikouri; and the dark-skinned Aladasturi, Aleksandrouli, Ashughaji, Asureuli Shavi, Chkhaveri, Mujuretuli, Ojaleshi, Otskhanuri Sapere, Saperavi, Shavkapito, Tavkveri, and Usakhelouri. Many of these Georgian varieties were ignored during the Soviet era because of their low YIELDS but are now being more widely planted and appreciated for quality potential and for their distinctiveness in a world awash with international varieties. However, one of the difficulties Georgia currently faces in exporting wines is that foreign consumers are unfamiliar with the names and flavours of these traditional Georgian grape varieties. The ancient and uniquely Georgian tradition of fermenting, storing, and ageing wines in clay QVEVRI buried underground has never been lost. Even though qvevri makers are a dying breed, qvevri wines have begun to attract international attention, particularly among proponents of NATURAL WINE.

Climate and geography

Georgia's topography and geology are complex. Mountains of the High Caucasus in the north account for about 30% of its total area. The peculiarities of the relief determine a great diversity in the country's soil and climatic conditions, which, in turn, influence grape culture. The climate varies from moderate to subtropical. The annual rainfall is 300–800 mm (12–32 in) in the east and 1,000 to 2,800 mm (40–110 in) in the west. HAIL is a perennial threat.

Georgia, has ten viticultural regions: Kakheti and Kartli in south-eastern Georgia; Meskheti in the south; Imereti in the centre; Racha and Lechkhumi in the north; Adjara, Guria, Samegrelo, and Apkhazeti near the Black Sea. These encompass 18 CONTROLLED APPELLATIONS recognized by the EU.

Kakheti, which has always been the most important wine region in the country, is home to almost 70% of Georgia's vineyard, produces about 80% of its wine, and comprises the richest agricultural land in the south east of the country in the Alazani and Iori Valleys. The climate here is moderate, in parts subtropical, with an active temperature summation of 3,800 to 4,000 °C/6,800 to 7,200 °F and an annual rainfall of 400 to 800 mm (32 in). Cinnamonic forest soils (reddish with high mineral content and enriched with clay) and CALCAREOUS soils, some of them alluvial, are found in the region.

In terms of mesoclimatic conditions and types of wines produced, Kakheti can be subdivided into three main subregions and 14 appellations (e.g. Tsinandali, Mukuzani, Kvareli, Manavi, Napareuli, Kindzmarauli). The principal grape varieties in Kakheti are Saperavi for reds and Rkatsiteli, Mtsvane Kakhuri, Khikvi, and Kisi for whites. Alongside more modern technologies, these regions produce the distinctive traditional Kakhetian wines, made peculiarly tannic and flavourful by FERMENTATION in special clay qvevri followed by an extended MACERATION of up to six months, very much as wines were made thousands of years BC. Kindzmarauli's speciality is semi-sweet reds. It is in this region that Georgians and incomers have invested most of their hopes for the future of Georgian wine.

Kartli is the heart of Georgia, inspired the original name for the country Sakartvelo, and occupies a vast territory in the Mtkvari Valley, including the Mukhrani Lowlands and Gori. These wines are the most European and the region produces the fruit for 15% of Georgia's sparkling wines and brandy production. The zone is moderately warm, with hot and dry summers; vineyards have to be irrigated because of the low rainfall (350 to 500 mm (19 in) per year). Main grape varieties are Chinuri and Goruli Mtsvane for whites and Tavkveri for reds. The capital of Georgia, Tbilisi, where wineries making mainly sparkling wines and brandy are located, is in this zone. Tbilisi's oldest winery, founded in 1897, has a unique collection of ancient wines.

Imereti is the 'stomach' of Georgia, its gastronomic capital and keeper of national traditions. In the first half of the 19th century, Imereti's capital Kutaisi was the centre of Georgian winemaking and wine-trading. Imereti is in the eastern part of west Georgia, in the basins and in the gullies of Rioni, Kvirila, and other rivers. The most important grape varieties are Tsitska, Tsolikouri, and Krakhuna for whites and Aladasturi and Otskhanuri Sapere for reds. Nowadays the most important Imereti wine regions are Zestaphoni, Terjola, Vani, and Bagdati; the one appellation is Sviri. As well as modern European methods, Imereti also uses a very particular winemaking technique, similar to Kakheti's except that grape skins are added to the clay jars (here called *churi*) during fermentation, a little like Italy's GOVERNO, and this is followed by a maceration of six to eight weeks.

Racha and Lechkhumi comprise Georgia's smallest wine region but one of the country's most important winemaking centres. Vineyards are mainly in the Rioni and Tskhenistskali Valleys. Moderate rainfall (1,000 to 1,300 mm

(50 in) a year), southern exposed soils, and the assortment of local vine varieties such as Tsulukidzis Tetra and Tsolikouri for whites and Aleksandrouli, Mujuretuli, Usakhelouri, and Ojaleshi for reds encourage grapes with a sugar content as high as 30%. The region is famous for its natural semi-sweet wines such as the reds of the Khvanchkara appellation. Demand for these wines is so high that Aleksandrouli and Mujuretuli grapes fetch some of the highest prices in the country.

Meskheti, one of Georgia's most ancient winemaking regions, this is the origin of some of the oldest Georgian grape varieties and is in the very early stages of a challenging revival. Vineyards are traditionally terraced high on the slopes along Mtkvari River at 900–1,700 m (2,950–5,580 ft), where it is very dry and irrigation is needed.

Towards the Black Sea. The regions of Apkhazeti, Adjara, Guria, and Samegrelo are all known for both semi-sweet and dry wines. Guria, in the south west, is humid and subtropical. Vines are mainly in the Suspa and Gubazouli Valleys and mostly still trained using the tradional methods known as *maghlari* (up trees) or *olikhnari* (up low trees or tall poles) and the main varieties are Chkhaveri, Jani, Mtevandidi, and Skhilatubani. Samegrelo, the ancient region of Colchis, is also humid and subtropical with long summers and cold winters. Ojaleshi is the main variety, plus Chergvali, Cheshi, Chvitiluri, and others, all mostly *maghlari* trained. Apkhazeti is the historic winemaking region of north-western Georgia planted mainly with Avasirkhva, Amlakhu, and Kachichi. Adjara, which has many different climatic microzones, has seen a revival of viticulture and winemaking in recent years. The local varieties are Brola, Khopaturi, and Mekrenchkhi.

The future for Georgia

Georgia may be playing catch up with the modern technology of many countries but has an enviably strong wine and hospitality culture, national belief in its wines, a wide range of high-quality indigenous grape varieties, a unique tradition of fermenting a small percentage of its wines in qvevri, and no shortage of historically established TERROIRS. Georgia's wines, especially the semi-sweet reds, have always been in great demand in Russia and other states of the former Soviet Union, notwithstanding the politically motivated Russian ban on imports of Georgian wine between 2006 and 2013. The embargo forced exporters to improve quality and to look further afield to more demanding markets such as western Europe, the US, Japan, China, and Hong Kong. Although annual per capita consumption is around 15–20 l

(4–5 gal), exports are crucial since much of the domestic demand is satisfied by HOME WINEMAKING. According to a 2011 report by the Georgian Wine Association (GWA) and other stakeholders, half of the 150,000–200,000 tons of grapes harvested annually in Georgia are used for 'family wine'. Imported wines represent just 1% of the total domestic market.

Foreigners have invested in the Georgian wine industry since the mid 1990s, with support first from the European Bank for Reconstruction and Development (EBRD) and more recently from the World Bank. This has helped to build new wineries, train winemakers, and improve regulatory oversight, but progress is often hampered by the constant need to avoid trade impasses with near neighbours.

Georgia continues to pursue its course of moving closer to Europe and promoting its wines more effectively around the world through the Georgian Wine Association and the Georgian National Wine Agency, which has received increasing governmental support since 2013.   J.E.H

geosmin, a compound with a strong earthy or muddy aroma that is a by-product of soil bacteria and is usually associated with wine FAULTS. Found in red and white wines made with rotten grapes, it is also present in some wines with CORK TAINT. The same aroma arises when rain falls on dry earth. See also MICROBIAL TERROIR.

La Guerche. S., et al., 'Origin of (-)-geosmin on grapes: on the complementary action of two fungi, botrytis cinerea and penicillium expansum', *Antonie van Leeuwenhoek*, 88/2 (2005), 131–9. doi: 10.1007/s10482-005-3872-4.

geranium, pejorative TASTING TERM for the smell of crushed geranium leaves that is given off by wines in which LACTIC ACID BACTERIA have reacted with the fungistat (a chemical that prevents fungi from growing) SORBIC ACID. This geranium smell, which occurs in very varied concentrations and for which the compound 2-ethoxyhexa-3,5-diene is responsible, first appeared in wines during the 1970s, when sorbic acid use became common. Its formation can be prevented by adding SULFUR DIOXIDE at the same time as the sorbic acid to prevent the growth and activity of the lactic acid bacteria responsible.   A.D.W.

German crosses, an important group of VINE VARIETIES that are the result of VINE BREEDING, an activity that was particularly vigorous in the first half of the 20th century but which continues to this day, most notably at GEISENHEIM and GEILWEILERHOF.

The man who bred Germany's first commercially successful modern cross was in fact Swiss, Dr Hermann Müller (see MÜLLER-THURGAU),

whose eponymous vine variety was to become the most planted in Germany in the second half of the 20th century, almost 100 years after it was developed. A succession of new crosses followed in the 20th century, notably from research institutes at Geisenheim, Geilweilerhof, Alzey, Würzburg, and Freiburg, producing a large number of NEW VARIETIES usually designed to achieve the high MUST WEIGHTS encouraged by the GERMAN WINE LAW. The most successful white wine varieties, in descending order of area planted in Germany at the beginning of the 21st century, are KERNER, BACCHUS, SCHEUREBE, FABER(REBE), HUXELREBE, ORTEGA, MORIO-MUSKAT, REICHENSTEINER, EHRENFELSER, SIEGERREBE, OPTIMA, and REGNER. Others include PERLE, NOBLING, WÜRZER, KANZLER, SCHÖNBURGER, FREISAMER, FINDLING, RIESLANER, JUWEL, ALBALONGA, and, more popular in England than Germany, GUTENBORNER and PHOENIX. Few of these crosses make distinctive, attractive, and characterful wines, although Kerner, Ehrenfelser and, particularly, Scheurebe and Rieslaner can make fine wines if sufficiently ripe. More typically, the vines have been planted to yield good quantities of high must weight wines.

Successful German crosses for red wine include DORNFELDER, HEROLDREBE, and HELFENSTEINER, bred by Dr August Herold in the 1950s, as well as a host of others bred usually for their COLOUR, often using red-fleshed TEINTURIERS, including REGENT, DOMINA, Deckrot, DUNKELFELDER, Dacapo, Carmina, Sulmer, and Kolor. RONDO has proved very popular in England.

See also DISEASE-RESISTANT VARIETIES.

German history. This article encompasses the history of wine production not just in GERMANY but also in ALSACE.

The origins of viticulture to AD 800

Although the WILD VINE *Vitis vinifera silvestris* may be traced back to prehistoric times on the upper Rhine, the cultivated, wine-yielding vine species *Vitis* VINIFERA—and with it viticulture in Germany—almost certainly owe their origins to the Romans (see Ancient ROME).

Although archaeological discoveries have unearthed curved pruning knives near the sites of Roman garrisons on the left bank of the Rhine which can be dated to the 1st century AD, we cannot be sure they were used for vines. Emperor PROBUS (276–82) is traditionally regarded as the founder of viticulture in Germany but firm literary evidence only occurs with the tract *Mosella*, written around 370 by the Roman author Ausonius of Bordeaux, who lyrically describes the steep vineyards on the banks of the river.

Continuity of viticulture is suggested by the use of typically Roman forms of TRELLIS SYSTEMS on low and high frames (*Kammer(t)*-, and *Lauben-* or *Rahmenbau*), which survived in

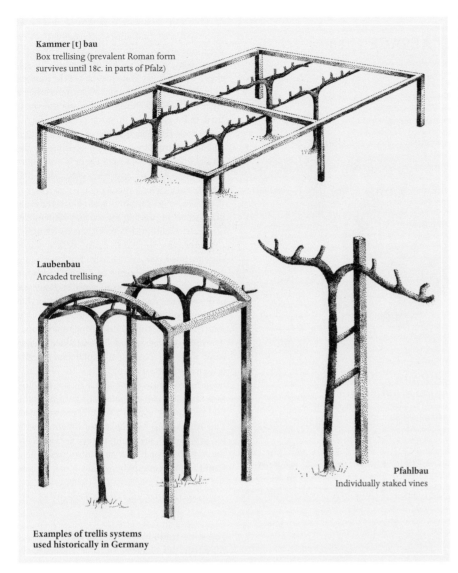

Kammer [t] bau
Box trellising (prevalent Roman form
survives until 18c. in parts of Pfalz)

Laubenbau
Arcaded trellising

Pfahlbau
Individually staked vines

**Examples of trellis systems
used historically in Germany**

Viticulture's importance in the Middle Ages

From the foundation of the Carolingian empire, the history of German wine can be traced with greater confidence. CHARLEMAGNE's numerous capitularies (law codes, relating particularly to landholding) contain instructions to his officials to plant vines. His true significance, however, lay in the support he gave to the spread of Christianity, for churches and convents were the principal cultivators and consumers of quality wine (see MONKS AND MONASTERIES).

Many vineyards still famous today originate in monastic settlements of the High Middle Ages. In the RHEINGAU, Archbishop Ruthard of Mainz (1088–1109) founded a Benedictine abbey on the slopes above Geisenheim, the Johannisberg, later known as SCHLOSS JOHANNISBERG. In 1135, his successor, Archbishop Adalbert, gave the Steinberg vineyard above Hattenheim to the Cistercians, whose KLOSTER EBERBACH remains the informal headquarters of the German wine trade to the present. On the River MOSEL, Archbishop Baldwin of Trier founded the Carthusian priory of St Alban in 1335, which was endowed with vineyards at Eitelsbach on the Ruwer, the Karthäuser Hofberg. In FRANKEN (Franconia), too, the bishops of Würzburg actively encouraged viticulture along the River Main.

Elsewhere, secular princes played a leading part, especially in the Palatinate, where the count-electors had promoted Bacharach on the Rhine as the entrepôt for wine from their many territories on both banks of the river.

Although viticulture was dominated by the Church and the aristocracy, bourgeois ownership of vineyards was common, too, either corporately by city councils or by individual merchants and investors.

The rapid expansion of viticulture after the millennium, which only came to a halt in the 16th century, can largely be attributed to the recovery in population and the rise of towns as centres of consumption and exchange: 'a wine landscape is an urban landscape' ran the medieval tag. But the spread of vineyards into the higher valleys, often far from urban centres, can only be explained by the foundation of the new ascetic religious orders, Cistercians and Carthusians, who established their houses from the 12th century at a deliberate distance from civilization. In Alsace, for example, vineyards followed convents into the remote valleys of the Vosges. Apart from the heartlands of medieval viticulture in Alsace, the Palatinate, and the Mosel Valley, all of which witnessed the further intake of land for vineyards up to 1500, wine-growing had spread by 1300 to the Rheingau, and throughout BADEN (with vineyards on Lake Constance from the 8th century), WÜRTTEMBERG, and Franken.

parts of the Palatinate as late as the 18th century. Evidence of wine-growing under the Merovingians can be seen in the pious donations of their kings: Dagobert I (622–88) gave vineyards at Ladenburg on the Neckar (in what is now the most northerly, Oberrhein district of BADEN) to the church of St Peter in Worms. This grant is especially significant, since it offers one of the earliest pointers to vines on the right bank of the Rhine.

Until the era of CHARLEMAGNE, nevertheless, wine-growing was concentrated west of the Rhine: from Alsace down river into the Palatinate (the modern German wine regions of PFALZ and RHEINHESSEN), and thence downstream along the middle Rhine as far as Koblenz. Wine-growing extended up three left bank tributaries: the NAHE Valley down to Bingen, where wine-growing is securely documented from 750; the Mosel (with its own tributaries, the SAAR and RUWER), where the tradition of

Roman viticulture was vigorously maintained by monastic foundations such as St Maximin and St Martin in Trier; and the most northerly European wine-growing district, the AHR Valley south of Bonn, where vines had been planted on sheltered slopes from at least the 3rd century AD.

East of the Rhine, in the districts beyond the frontier of Roman occupation, the spread of viticulture went hand in hand with the missions of Christian monks such as St Kilian in Franken and St Columban in Bavaria.

Apart from the existence of red wines, cited by the north Italian poet Venantius Fortunatus around 570, next to nothing is known about grape varieties and the quality of wine in this period.   T.S.

Scott, T., 'Medieval viticulture in the German-speaking lands', *German History*, 20 (2002), 95–115.

g

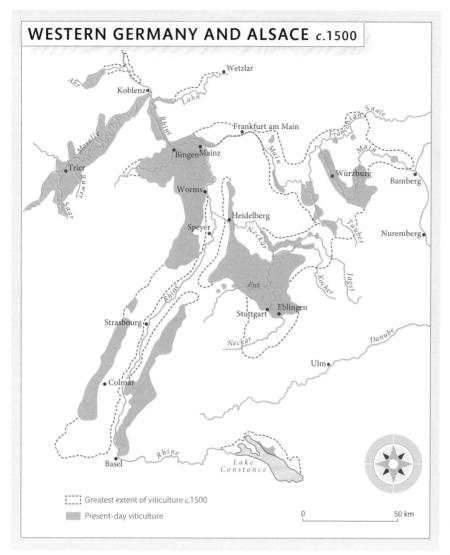

WESTERN GERMANY AND ALSACE *c.*1500

- Greatest extent of viticulture c.1500
- Present-day viticulture

0   50 km

Riesling (see GEMISCHTER SATZ). Of the better grapes, MUSCAT (red and white) was grown on the Rhine and in Alsace, TRAMINER chiefly in the latter. RIESLING is first documented at Rüsselsheim on the River Main just east of the modern Rheingau in 1435, though a century earlier a vineyard in Kinzheim in Alsace was known as 'zu dem Russelinge'. The variant orthography of these early references, however, makes it difficult to determine whether the Riesling or the Räuschling grape is meant. There is every likelihood that Riesling had been established and recognized as a high-quality grape much earlier than the sources suggest, for in 1477 Duke René of Lorraine, in praising the red and white wines of Alsace, mentioned in particular its Riesling.

In the Middle Ages, many Alsace wines were fortified (see FORTIFICATION) or spiced (see FLAVOURED WINES) in order to compete with the fuller bodied Mediterranean wines such as SACK and MALMSEY. Red wine was made from the Blauburgunder (PINOT NOIR) grape on the upper Rhine in Alsace and throughout Germany where it was spread by Cistercian MONKS from the 12th century (Affental had already acquired a reputation by 1330). In Württemberg, by contrast, where much of the production, then as now, consisted of light red wines, the TROLLINGER grape already predominated. The Ahr Valley may have been planted with red grapes, but they cannot have included the Pinot Noir, which was not introduced there until the 18th century.   T.S.

Scott, T., 'Medieval viticulture in the German-speaking lands', *German History*, 20 (2002), 95–115.

The wine trade in the Middle Ages

Although the quantity of wine harvested in medieval Germany never approached that of France, Italy, or the Iberian peninsula, production on the left bank of the Rhine always exceeded local consumption, so that commerce in wine became an economic necessity. Until the rise of towns, the wine trade was largely in the hands of the Church. Because the best vineyards lay along the Rhine and its tributaries, shipments of wine could pass easily down one of the great arteries of European trade to northern Germany, the Low Countries, Scandinavia, and England. Ease of transport, however, was offset by the numerous tolls which local lords levied on cargoes shipped down the Rhine.

Cologne and Frankfurt dominated Germany's medieval wine trade, a point tellingly illustrated by the decision of Kloster Eberbach, the important abbey in the rural depths of the Rheingau, to acquire its own cellars in Cologne in 1162 and in Frankfurt 50 years later. But their pattern of trade differed.

Throughout the Middle Ages, Cologne's trade with the Baltic, Scandinavia, and England was far more extensive than Frankfurt's. The

By 1500, even the rolling uplands of Swabia and the heavily afforested valleys of northern Franken had been cleared for vines. There viticulture reached its greatest extent in the 15th century, covering perhaps four times the area under vines today (see map of Western Germany and Alsace *c.*1500).

In eastern Germany, the Ottonian emperors promoted viticulture in their Saxon dynastic lands from the late 9th century. Vines were planted on the Elbe around Dresden and Meissen, and on the Saale and Unstrut, especially around Freyburg (see SAALE-UNSTRUT). Even in Brandenburg around Berlin and Jessen, east of Wittenberg up to Torgau, vines were grown on a commercial basis from the 14th to the 16th centuries. In the eastern part of the empire Kloster Pforte near Naumburg played a similar role to that of Kloster Eberbach in the Rheingau.

The sites chosen for planting were by no means those on which wines still thrive today.

Low-lying level sites were preferred; in Alsace, acknowledged as producing the best wines of medieval Germany, vineyards stretched across the plains from the Ried down to Mulhouse. From the 10th century, vines were at last being planted on slopes in TERRACES, with low walls to prevent SOIL EROSION. The famous slopes of the Rheingau were initially planted in the 11th century: first the Rüdesheimer Berg, then in the 12th century the Johannisberg and Steinberg, with the slopes of Rauenthal not planted until the 13th.

Vine varieties Workaday wine was made everywhere from the ELBLING grape, by far the commonest medieval variety, with RÄUSCHLING widely planted in Baden. SILVANER, which arrived in Franconia only in 1659, was extensively grown, but rarely as a high-quality grape in its own right; until the 20th century, it was generally planted together with Traminer and

city's wine trade reached its peak in the late 14th and early 15th centuries. Cologne continued to play a major role in the export of the best German wines, but its trading area was increasingly exposed to the rise of BEER as the everyday drink of northern Germany. It was Frankfurt's merchants who increasingly specialized in Alsace wines, although their popularity was challenged during the 15th century by wines from the Palatinate and the Rheingau.

Although German wines were firmly established in northern Europe during the Middle Ages, there were limits to their share of the market. In the southern Low Countries 'Rhine wine' was consumed, but it had to compete with the heavier wines of Burgundy, Auxerre, and also Bordeaux. In England, too, German wines faced a stiff challenge from France, as the trade with Gascony flourished from the 12th century. But German wine was not confined to northern markets. Alsace wines were extensively exported to southern Germany, Switzerland, and central Europe.   T.S.

Scott, T., 'Medieval viticulture in the German-speaking lands', *German History*, 20 (2002), 95–115.

Crisis and decline, 1500–1650

The Thirty Years War, which ravaged Germany in the early 17th century, left few viticultural regions unscathed, but the real problem arose from the loss of manpower through the casualties of war. The decline in exports of ALSACE wines is symptomatic of the difficulties. Wine consumption was dictated by FASHION, and by 1500 taste was moving away from the often spiced (see FLAVOURED WINES) white wines of Alsace towards those of the PALATINATE and the RHEINGAU, as well as to the lighter wines of FRANKEN. At the same time, demand for heavier red wines was increasing, so that Alsace found itself having to plant more PINOT NOIR vines together with 'Lampersch' (a red wine variety from Lombardia in Italy) to compete with imports from France and the Mediterranean.

The excessive expansion of vineyards up to 1500 brought about a slump in the land market by 1540, with a consequent collapse in the price of wine, much of it in any case of dismal quality, having been grown on sites quite unsuitable for viticulture.

It is no coincidence that the widespread agrarian rebellion of 1525 known as the German Peasants' War was concentrated in the wine-growing areas, where the peasantry had been exposed to the fluctuations of the market, demands by lords for higher taxes on its crop, and the need to subdivide holdings into unprofitably small parcels by the laws of partible inheritance (see BURGUNDY, history), and yet was compelled to cling to its foothold in commercialized viticulture for want of alternative employment.

Throughout the century, viticulture retreated from the cooler, more remote valleys; poor-quality vineyards in the plains were abandoned in favour of slopes with better exposure and drainage. As the century wore on, the demand for grain for bread and brewing swelled, so that corn prices outstripped wine prices, and much land reverted to tillage. Nevertheless, on the eve of the Thirty Years War around 350,000 ha/865,000 acres of land in Germany were still under vines, over four times the extent of viticulture today. The 16th century also saw greater emphasis on better-quality white varieties.

A first classification Although the use of individual site names to distinguish quality (as opposed merely to identifying different vineyards) was largely unknown before 1800, there is one striking instance of ranking by quality in this period. In 1644 the council of Würzburg in FRANKEN classified the city's vineyards into four groups.   T.S.

Bibliographical note: There is no reliable survey in English. Readers of German may consult Bassermann-Jordan, F. von, *Geschichte des Weinbaus*, 3 vols. in 2 (2nd edn, Frankfurt, 1923; repr. Landau 1991).

Weinhold, R., *Winzerarbeit an Elbe, Saale und Unstrut: eine historisch-ethnographische Untersuchung der Produktivkräfte des Weinbaus auf dem Gebiet der DDR* (Berlin, 1973).

Schröder, K. H., *Weinbau und Siedlung in Württemberg*, Forschungen zur deutschen Landeskunde, 73 (Remagen, 1953).

Militzer, K., 'Handel und Vertrieb rheinischer und elsässischer Weine über Köln im Spätmittelalter', in A. Gerlich (pub.), *Weinbau, Weinhandel und Weinkultur* (Stuttgart, 1994).

Recovery and improvement, 1650–1800

The recovery of German viticulture after the depredations of the Thirty Years War was slow and painful. Only FRANKEN (Franconia), which had been the scene of fierce fighting in the 1630s, experienced a swift recuperation in vineyards and wine prices in the 1650s. In the PALATINATE, viticulture was not fully restored until the 1710s. There many growers, despairing of making a decent living, emigrated to America in the early 18th century. The region was further afflicted by the wars of Louis XIV of France from 1674 to 1700, as indeed were districts on the left bank of the Rhine as a whole, including the MOSEL.

The vineyards of BADEN and WÜRTTEMBERG, which had suffered least the previous century, may have declined by as much as 80% by the end of the 18th century. In ALSACE, however, the loss of manpower was partly compensated for by policies to encourage immigration from France, Lorraine, and Switzerland.

Efforts to improve viticulture from the late 17th century onwards pursued a double strategy: to encourage the planting of better-quality grape varieties, often on selected new sites, while at the same time prohibiting the clearing of land for vines where only poor quality could be expected. In what is now the MOSEL, for instance, the Abbey of St Maximin had been replanting at Grünhaus on the RUWER since 1695; as many as 100,000 new cuttings, it has been reckoned, were put down. But at the other end of the scale, more land was constantly being taken in by small growers, so that the prince-archbishops of Trier issued an edict in 1720 banning the clearing of forest for new vineyards.

In 1750, another decree enjoined the production of natural, unsugared ('naturrein') wines, and in 1786 the last archbishop-elector, Clemens Wenceslas (r. 1768–1801), a keen champion of viticulture, ordered that inferior grapes be grubbed up and replaced with the RIESLING vine. At Bingen, the archbishop of Mainz decreed in 1697 that the famous Scharlachberg ('scarlet slope', perhaps because it once grew red wines) be planted exclusively with Riesling.

Likewise in the Rheingau, Constantine, prince-abbot of the ancient Benedictine abbey of Fulda, which had acquired the site and castle of Johannisberg (see SCHLOSS JOHANNISBERG), ordered the replanting of the vineyards with Riesling and 'Orléans' vines in the 1760s. In this period, the sources begin to distinguish the quality of Rhine wines according to village or, on occasion, site.

Vine varieties In Alsace, improvement owed nothing to the French crown, everything to local initiatives by institutions such as the Jesuit College at Sélestat, which began to plant Riesling in 1756 in place of lesser vines. Alsace saw the development of two new varieties in the 18th century. In 1756, Johann Michael Ortlieb of Riquewihr pioneered an early-ripening clone of RÄUSCHLING, the Kleiner (small) Räuschling (also known as Ortlieber or, in Alsace, as KNIPPERLÉ). In 1740, the mayor of Heiligenstein by Barr, Erhard Wantz, introduced a new variety under the name of KLEVENER.

In much of southern Germany, Silvaner was displacing ELBLING, but the real innovation was the development of PINOT GRIS by Johann Seger Ruland in Speyer around 1711. It has nothing to do with the Hungarian wine TOKAJI. Although it spread quickly, the Ruländer suffered a rapid decline because its early ripening meant that its harvest could not be held back until the later maturing Riesling, so that peasant growers preferred to let it rot rather than gather it early only to have to deliver up a fine wine as a tithe to their feudal lords. Not until tithing was abolished in the wake of the French Revolution did Ruländer establish its rightful place among German wines of distinction.

The 17th and 18th centuries also saw the first attempts to make specially selected or late-picked wines. The term CABINET to indicate a wine of reserve quality is first encountered at Schloss Vollrads in the Rheingau in 1716, then at Kloster Eberbach in the Rheingau in 1739. The picking of individual ripe berries off the stalks (*Abrappen*) was also deployed, particularly with Traminer grapes, to make what were in effect AUSLESEN, although the wines were relatively short lived. Nevertheless, the potential of picking grapes affected by NOBLE ROT was well recognized by the early 18th century.

Despite these advances, the period up to 1800 was a troubled one for German wine in export markets. Cologne and Frankfurt maintained their leading role in overseas trade, and the 18th century witnessed the first wine AUCTIONS of quality wines. Cologne's merchants were proud of their adherence to the oenological equivalent of the brewing purity laws (*Reinheitsgebot*), which forbade blending Rhine wines with those from the south, especially France and Italy. Yet their stranglehold on the market in Rhenish wines was challenged in the 1670s when English merchants began to buy at source. T.S.

Bibliographical note: There is no reliable survey in English. For readers of German, Bassermann-Jordan, cited above, remains an indispensable guide but some information may be gleaned from O. W. Loeb and T. Prittie, *Moselle* (London, 1972).

The rise of modern viticulture, 1800–1900

The French Revolution and its aftermath wrought profound changes in German viticulture. During the Revolution itself, the PALATINATE was invaded and occupied, although in the succeeding Napoleonic Wars it was barely affected. The whole of Germany on the left bank of the Rhine was ceded to France, which proceeded to reorganize the region's administration into four departments.

On the MOSEL, these political upheavals led to around one-fifth of the vineyards, many of them owned by the Church, changing hands, and once the estates of the empire had agreed upon the abolition of all ecclesiastical principalities at the diet of Regensburg in 1803, another 25% came under new ownership.

Although after the fall of Napoleon the Church regained some of its estates, a new and substantial class of peasant and bourgeois vineyard proprietors had been created. On the right bank of the Rhine in the RHEINGAU, Johannisberg (see SCHLOSS JOHANNISBERG) passed through several hands, including Napoleon's general Marshal Kellermann, before it fell to Austria at the Congress of Vienna in 1815 and was bestowed upon the then Foreign Minister Prince Metternich. On the Main, the estates of the prince-bishops of Würzburg in FRANKEN, or

Franconia, were acquired after a short interlude by the Bavarian crown in 1816.

In ALSACE, however, the repercussions of the Revolution were quite different. Once it had become part of the French customs area, growers hastened to increase production in order to capitalize upon a huge internal market. The result was the renewed planting of inferior vine varieties on low-lying sites. Moreover, the imposition by France of tolls on foreign wines hurt Alsace in particular, since it elicited reprisals from Baden, Württemberg, and Switzerland, all still important customers for Alsace wines.

At the Congress of Vienna, the political map of Germany was redrawn. The Mosel became part of the Prussian Rheinprovinz; RHEINHESSEN (west of the Rhine) was absorbed into the grand duchy of Hesse-Darmstadt together with the Bergstrasse; the Rheingau fell to the dukes of Nassau; and what remained of the Palatinate, the Pfalz proper, was reunited with Bavaria. From 1805/6 Saxony (see SACHSEN) and WÜRTTEMBERG had been elevated to kingdoms, BADEN to a grand duchy. The regulation of customs dues between these independent states became a matter of urgent necessity.

When Bavaria and Württemberg joined Prussia to create the general customs union (Zollverein) of 1834, followed by Baden and Hesse-Darmstadt the next year, all the major wine-growing districts were in open competition with each other. As a result, the better wines prevailed, and the market in lesser wines collapsed, although at least the Zollverein enabled German wines to compete on more favourable terms in the domestic market with French wines, especially those from BORDEAUX, which had begun to reach the north German cities in huge quantities in the 1820s. Baden and Württemberg were the worst hit by the new competition. In Baden the tithe was abolished in 1833, but the area under cultivation constantly receded, and many vintners emigrated to ALGERIA or VENEZUELA.

The development of the transport network, above all the RAILWAYS, allowed rapid and easy distribution of the better wines from the more favoured regions, so that Württemberg's production declined by 40% in the 19th century. Franken, too, suffered because of Bavaria's link with the Palatinate and the loss of manpower to the emerging industry; the area under vines shrank by 60% between 1850 and 1900.

Only the foundation of the German empire in 1871, however, put an end to all internal customs barriers. Yet the reabsorption of Alsace and Lorraine in that year brought little relief to wine-growers there. Alsace may have constituted 26% of German vineyards yielding 39% of production after 1871, but its wines were threatened by imports of cheap wines from France, sweetened wines from across the Rhine, and preferential trade treaties signed by

Germany with Austria and Italy in 1891 and with Spain in 1893.

Quality in the ascendant Quality of production became the central concern of German vine-growers and administrators after 1800. The beginnings of quality DELIMITATION can be traced to the 1830s. Wine ordinances in the German states began to prescribe that grapes of different levels of ripeness should be harvested separately. Their measurement was greatly facilitated by systems for weighing the must to achieve a specific MUST WEIGHT, refined in the 1830s by the Pforzheim physicist Ferdinand OECHSLE, whose system is still in use today.

Growers' associations for the improvement of wines and viticulture were founded in many German territories. The state authorities, moreover, played a vital role by establishing schools of viticultural research and teaching. Württemberg was the pioneer in 1860 with its academy at Weinsberg, followed by Prussia's establishment of the institute at GEISENHEIM in 1872, after it had annexed the Rheingau from Nassau in 1866. The Hessian wine academy at Oppenheim dates from 1885; in 1899 citizens of Neustadt an der Weinstrasse founded a wine school to serve the Palatinate; Mosel (Trier) and the Nahe (Kreuznach) acquired a Prussian academy in 1893. These endeavours were underpinned by the creation of state domaines. The earliest was set up by Baden at Meersburg on Lake Constance in 1802, followed shortly thereafter by the Bavarian state domaine in Würzburg and the Herzogl. Nassauische domaine at Kloster Eberbach from its abbatial estates throughout the Rheingau. After its acquisition of Nassau, the domaine was owned by Prussia. At the end of the century, Prussia established further state domaines: in 1896 on the Saar/Moselle with estates at Ockfen, then extended to Avelsbach and Serrig, and on the Nahe at Niederhausen in 1902.

The emphasis on quality, however, placed the smaller peasant growers in a quandary. Without the capital to invest in better vines and winemaking equipment, they were left with inferior grape varieties on poorer sites in a shrinking market. The only solution, albeit imperfect, was to seek safety in numbers by banding together in CO-OPERATIVES. The first such growers' union was formally established on the River AHR in 1869.

Towards the end of the century, viticulture fell victim to Germany's late industrialization, which sucked LABOUR into the cities. In terms of marketing, the German wine trade was torn between the lure of the controlled addition of sugar, pioneered by the chemist Ludwig Gall (the German counterpart to Jean CHAPTAL in France), which helped to make thin, sour wines from sun-starved soils saleable (see CHAPTALIZATION), and the reputation which attached to untreated, 'naturrein' wines. The first national Wine Laws of 1892 and 1901 had permitted controlled sugaring, but the Wine Law of 1909 restricted sugaring to 20% of the undiluted wine. In 1910, four groups of natural wine auctioneers formed the Verein Deutscher Naturweinversteiger (VDNV), today known as the VDP.

One answer was to turn the more acidic vintages into sparkling wine, known in German as SEKT. With some good vintages in the 1860s, Sekt had become a highly popular drink in Germany by the late 19th century.

The true threat to German viticulture, however, lay in VINE PESTS and VINE DISEASES—DOWNY MILDEW in particular and the PHYLLOXERA louse (*Reblaus* in German), which first appeared in Germany in 1874 in Bonn-Annaberg and Karlsruhe before being found in vineyards in the Ahr Valley in 1881.　　　　　　T.S.

The 20th century wine industry

The first half of the 20th century was a period of deep recession in the German wine industry. The area under vines shrank still further, from around 90,000 ha/220,000 acres in 1914 to less than 50,000 ha/123,000 acres in 1945. Both World Wars placed severe strains on Germany's domestic economy and caused considerable dislocation in its export markets. Exports had reached a peak of 190,000 hl/5 million gal by 1914, but in the aftermath of the First World War the situation was bleak.

The major growing regions on the left bank of the Rhine were occupied by France until 1930. In the PFALZ region, moreover, the activities of separatist groups severely disrupted civilian life up to 1924, which hit the wine industry in particular. A series of bad vintages from 1922 until 1932 in combination with the raging inflation and the economic hardship of the Weimar period ruined many wine merchants and growers, especially the smaller proprietors. A flood of imports from France and Luxembourg, as specified by the Versailles Treaty, undercut the prices which German producers could charge; many growers faced bankruptcy, and by 1928 exports had collapsed to no more than 39,000 hl/1 million gal per annum.

The Nazi era helped to revive domestic consumption of German wine, but the National Socialist policy of subordinating all private associations to state control (*Gleichschaltung*) meant, for the wine industry, that all independent professional bodies except the VDNV were abolished and replaced by a single Union of Viticulture under one president, thereby destroying the enterprise and initiative of individual growers and regional wine associations. The end of the Second World War heralded the return of some of the consequences of the First. German growers faced a shortage of labour but an abundance of cheap imports from France

and Algeria. In their zone of occupation in the Pfalz and Moselle, the French requisitioned wine and blocked its movement on a grand scale.

The parlous state of exports in the 1930s persuaded some merchants, principally those trading to the United Kingdom, to try to increase sales by marketing BRANDS, which could contain more than one grape variety, were sourced from more than one region of production, and were usually sweetened. This is the origin of LIEBFRAUMILCH.

Undoubtedly the most significant step forward for German viticulture in the first half of the century was the Wine Law of 1930, which went far towards rectifying the deficiencies of the 1909 law. It provided a clear definition of what constituted a natural, as opposed to a sweetened, wine, forbade the blending of red and white, and of German and foreign wines.

Viticulture Between 1950 and 1990 German viticulture underwent a dramatic transformation. The area under vine once again expanded steadily, and in the modern era is well over 100,000 ha/250,000 acres. But the most startling development was the increase in YIELDS. At the beginning of the century the average of 20 hl/ha (1.1 tons/acre) was no more than what might have been expected of an abundant vintage in any preceding century. By 1950 that had doubled to 40 hl/ha, and by the 1980s frequently exceeded 100 hl/ha (5.7 tons/acre), although today's more discriminating growers are cropping less heavily.

From the 1950s there was a radical restructuring of German vineyards, known as FLURBEREINIGUNG. The number of individual sites has been substantially pruned, and since the GERMAN WINE LAW of 1971 a new vineyard register has been compiled and average wine quality has improved immensely. Despite these advances, the outlook for German wines is still uncertain while they remain largely unfashionable.　T.S.

See also JEWISH HERITAGE IN GERMAN WINE CULTURE, and GERMANY for more on the modern wine scene.

Hallgarten, S. F., *German Wine* (London, 1976).

Langenbach, A., *German Wines and Vines* (London, 1962).

Loeb, O. W., and Prittie, T., *Moselle* (London, 1972).

Pigott, S., *The Mosel and Rheingau, including the Ahr, Nahe and Pfalz* (London, 1997).

German Wine Law

was once a source of pride for German wine producers but many now do their best to amend or ignore it. The German Wine Law of 1971 substantially revised the 1930 Wine Law (see GERMAN HISTORY), particularly in vineyard rationalization, and was precipitated by the demands of the EU wine regime. Compared with the anarchic chaos of Italy's wine-labelling habits, and the convoluted

geography of France's APPELLATION CONTRÔLÉE (AOC) system, the German Wine Law of 1971 was a marvel of precision. Each vineyard was delineated and registered (see EINZELLAGE), and collective sites, or GROSSLAGEN, were also delineated, in a manner that it is hard to deny was designed to deceive consumers. Their produce could be used to make wine at any quality level, depending not on YIELDS but exclusively on the ripeness, or MUST WEIGHT, of the grapes.

The least ripe grapes qualify for the bottom rung, once known as Deutscher Tafelwein, now simply as Deutscher Wein, which represents less than 5% of all wine produced in a typical German vintage. All the rest is graded as QUALITÄTSWEIN according to the generous terms of the German Wine Law. German officials make much of the fact that every quality wine is analysed and tasted and has to earn its AP NUMBER, but the failure rate is so low as to cast doubt on this highly bureaucratic 'control'.

The lower layer of Germany's quality wine is made from grapes whose ripeness qualifies for QBA status, a 'quality wine from a specified region'. This is the category which may be CHAPTALIZED and under which most German wine is usually sold. Wines made from riper grapes, however, are qualified as Prädikatswein, 'wine with distinction': the official PRÄDIKAT categories being KABINETT, SPÄTLESE, AUSLESE, BEERENAUSLESE, TROCKENBEERENAUSLESE, and EISWEIN. The volume produced in each of these categories varies tremendously according to the weather. In 2003, for example, more than half of all German wine produced had a Prädikat, while the cold, wet 1984 vintage yielded less than 6%. This emphasis on must weights was understandable in a country where the perennial challenge was, until the effects of CLIMATE CHANGE, to ripen grapes fully, but did little to encourage real quality and harmony in Germany's wines (see GERMANY and GERMAN HISTORY). Many quality-conscious producers themselves declassify wines from one Prädikat to a lower one, or from Prädikatswein to QbA, because the wine does not reach their own personal evaluation of what constitutes, say, an Auslese.

The German Wine Law has been substantially amended since 1971. In 1982 the little-used LANDWEIN category was introduced, and at about the same time Eiswein, with its entirely different production technique, was admitted as a Prädikat in its own right alongside Beerenauslese and Trockenbeerenauslese.

In 1989, the German parliament agreed to comply with EU regulations to limit yields, but a measure of how much progress was still to be made was that the maximum yield proposed for the noble RIESLING vine in the supposedly noble wine region MOSEL was 120 hl/ha (6.8 tons/acre) (more for other grape varieties).

During 1993, much more stringent amendments were proposed, for enactment in time for the 1994 vintage, with stricter controls on yields.

More significantly, the minimum MUST WEIGHTS required for various Prädikats in the Ahr, Mittelrhein, Mosel-Saar-Ruwer, Saale-Unstrut, and Sachsen were raised, and there were moves, albeit limited, to substitute a much clearer labelling system whereby the consumer could tell at a glance whether a wine comes from a single site or Einzellage, or from one of the collective GROSSLAGEN.

As if German wine categories were not numerous or confusing enough, several new ones have been added to the Wine Law—HOCHGEWÄCHS, CLASSIC, and SELECTION—but none has had a significant lasting impact in the marketplace. Two even more recent amendments to German Wine Law that represent signs of their times are permission to irrigate vines and to acidify musts or wine in years of drought and extreme heat.

The prestigious VDP growers' association has long imposed much more stringent requirements on its members than the German Wine Law, and continues to refine its requirements.   D.S.

Germany, the most distinctive major wine producer in Europe with both wines and problems quite unlike those of anywhere else. Grape growing in Germany is a small but culturally conspicuous part of the whole country's farming industry. Germany's annual wine production of between 7 and 10 million hl from about 100,000 ha/247,000 acres has made her Europe's fourth biggest wine producer for many years. Unlike France and Italy, however, Germany makes about as much wine as she consumes, while also being the largest importer of wine in the EU. Most unfortunately, undistinguished bulk wines have since the 1970s routinely been allowed to benefit from both the GERMAN WINE LAW and the reputations of top-flight vineyards, thus threatening to debase both. And the majority of German wine is still sold in bulk, often on price rather than quality. These unfortunate factors notwithstanding, the profile of German wine—in particular that of Riesling—has risen significantly in prestige at home and abroad since the late 20th century. What's more, while nearly all of Germany's growing regions can still be considered COOL-CLIMATE and capable of producing wines with incomparable finesse, the struggle to ripen grapes sufficiently that dominated viticulture and choice of sites here for centuries has eased dramatically thanks to CLIMATE CHANGE as well as viticultural and attitudinal changes.

History

See GERMAN HISTORY.

Geography and climate

Over the centuries, the German vineyard has expanded and contracted, often in response to the price and availability of grain. See GERMAN HISTORY and map there. Many of Germany's best vineyards are on the steepest slopes, quite unsuited to anything other than the vine. Overlooking the Rivers RHINE, Neckar, Main, Nahe, Ahr, MOSEL and its tributaries, their high cost of cultivation is justified only by the quality of the wine they can produce. In the steep vineyards, three times as many man-hours are spent tending the vine as is the case on flat or gently sloping terrain, where the natural position of the vine-grower is on the seat of a tractor.

Several other factors limit MECHANIZATION in the vineyards, amongst which are the smallness of the holdings and the tradition of selective harvest. Vine-growing in Germany was once the work of peasants, controlled by the Church and the nobility. Statistically, it is now a mainly female, mainly part-time occupation, based on an average holding of 1.3 ha/3.2 acres, although the average age of hobby and other part-time vine growers suggests that their numbers will decline, and by 2013 75% of total vine acreage was held by growers with more than 5 ha/12.5 acres. In the 21st century, picking is generally done by 'guest workers' from eastern and southern Europe, among whom Poles are pre-eminent. Most German growers do not make wine but supply grapes to merchants or, more likely, to the CO-OPERATIVE cellars which receive the crop from about 30% of the total German vineyard. For more geographical detail, see map of Germany and Alsace opposite; see also entries under the names of individual wine regions which are, in declining area of total vineyard, RHEINHESSEN, PFALZ, BADEN, MOSEL, WÜRTTEMBERG, FRANKEN, NAHE, RHEINGAU, MITTELRHEIN, SAALE-UNSTRUT, AHR, HESSISCHE BERGSTRASSE, and SACHSEN. Most German wine labels carry the name of the region in which the wine was produced.

Viticulture

The vine-growing regions of the EU are divided into climatically different zones. In Germany, Baden shares Zone B with a number of French regions including Alsace, Champagne, and the Loire Valley. Although the remaining German regions are all in Zone A, their MACROCLIMATES and MESOCLIMATES are perhaps the most varied of all the world's vineyards. Mesoclimatic variations within a single site or EINZELLAGE can result in simultaneous pickings of the same variety which exhibit significant differences in potential alcohol and flavour. According to research at GEISENHEIM, the average alcohol content of wine of the same vineyard can vary from one vintage to another by over 6%. The degree of LATITUDE, topographical features such as a favourable exposition to the sun, shelter from frequent cold winds or damaging FROSTS, and the ELEVATION are some of the factors which dramatically influence the quality of its viticulture.

Some 6 to 7% of Germany's vines are individually supported by POSTS, particularly in the Mosel where tight spacing between vines on steep slopes is the norm.

But this method is in decline as old vineyards continue to be subjected to FLÜRBEREINIGUNG and workers with the requisite skills disappear. (More than one prestigious Mosel estate reports all of their vines being tied by a single woman well past retirement age.) Elsewhere, vines are trained on WIRES in rows, often with wide spacing, although an international 21st century FASHION for tight spacing is influencing German replanting. Some 4 to 5 % of all vines—particularly in the Mosel, where some villages and vineyards never succumbed to PHYLLOXERA—are UNGRAFTED. But this proportion is also in decline, as is average VINE AGE due to ongoing Flürbereinigung. And incidences of phylloxera led to a 2013 ban on planting ungrafted vines even in those Mosel vineyards where this was previously permitted. Although German research stations, most notably Geisenheim, have for nearly a century been famous for their clonal selections, which dominate Germany's vineyards, many growers are increasingly enthusiastic about MASS SELECTIONS.

Among growers whose aim is to produce top-quality fruit, PRUNING is usually to six to eight buds per square metre, depending on the variety. To produce a more concentrated must, excess bunches of grapes are removed in the months following the FLOWERING in June (see CROP THINNING). The aim in VINE TRAINING in recent decades has been not just to harvest healthy grapes, but sometimes also to reduce costs by facilitating MECHANICAL PRUNING and MECHANICAL HARVESTING. Machines are increasingly used even at prestigious estates, sometimes employed for speed after human hands have cost-intensively performed a 'negative Auslese' to remove rotten or otherwise imperfect fruit. Among the many factors insufficiently emphasized in the current GERMAN WINE LAW is YIELD. The VDP growers' association and certain local organizations have attempted to impose voluntary production limits, even though quality and BALANCE in vine and wine are difficult to quantify in hl/ha. Germany's average yields have long been the highest of any significant wine-producing country, are generally well over 70 and sometimes over 100 hl/ha.

Ripeness can vary significantly from one bunch to another on the same vine as well as within the cluster, not to mention the presence or absence of BOTRYTIS. Riesling growers in some regions of Germany, notably the Rheingau, have for two centuries responded with selective picking of individual clusters or even berries, and in the course of the late 20th century, this

A ojo de buen cubero

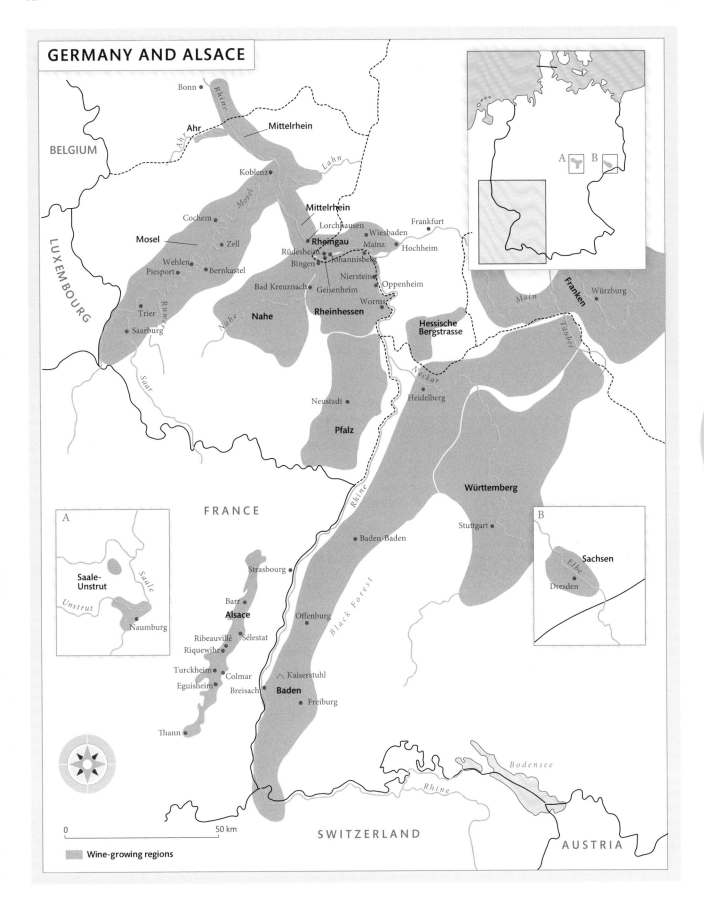

GERMANY AND ALSACE

Bonn

Rhine

Ahr

Mittelrhein

BELGIUM

Koblenz

Mosel

Cochem

Zell

Mittelrhein

Lahn

Lorchhausen

Frankfurt

Wiesbaden

Rheingau

Mainz

Hochheim

Rüdesheim

Johannisberg

Bingen

Nierstein

Oppenheim

LUXEMBOURG

Wehlen

Piesport

Bernkastel

Bad Kreuznach

Geisenheim

Worms

Trier

Nahe

Rheinhessen

Saarburg

Saar

Hessische
Bergstrasse

Neckar

Franken

Würzburg

Main

Tauber

Neustadt

Heidelberg

Pfalz

Rhine

Württemberg

Stuttgart

FRANCE

Baden-Baden

B

Sachsen

Elbe

Dresden

A

Saale-
Unstrut

Saale

Unstrut

Naumburg

Strasbourg

Barr

Alsace

Offenburg

Black Forest

Ribeauvillé

Sélestat

Riquewihr

Turckheim

Colmar

Kaiserstuhl

Eguisheim

Breisach

Baden

Freiburg

Thann

Bodensee

Rhine

SWITZERLAND

AUSTRIA

0   50 km

Wine-growing regions

became even more widespread among quality-conscious Riesling growers throughout Germany with at least a portion of most vintage's crop, resulting in sweet wines of PRÄDIKAT AUSLESE and above, but often also ensuring entirely healthy fruit for the dry (TROCKEN) or off-dry (HALBTROCKEN) wines that make up the majority of production. Such nobly sweet elixirs have high prices, thanks to the intensive LABOUR required, and they tend to predominate among bottlings sold at one of the VDP's several prestigious auctions, although by the second decade of this century there had been a noticeable (if perhaps temporary) decline in the frequency of such offerings due to combinations of weather, economic recession, and consumer preference. A minority of influential growers have begun to produce wines picked from entire blocks that vary considerably in their ripeness or botrytization, rather than selecting fruit in multiple passes through the vineyard for multiple bottlings. Prior to the late 20th century, block-picking of this sort characterized the vast majority of German wines, even those from Riesling.

While Germans exhibit a high level of support for SUSTAINABLE and ORGANIC agriculture, vines' disease sensitivity, difficulty of vineyard access, and the high RAINFALL that characterizes many of the best German vineyards have combined to slow the spread of organic viticulture compared with neighbouring Austria and France. In the Mosel, for example, pesticides or herbicides sprayed from helicopters are the only effective means of reaching vines on ultra-steep, rocky slopes. Such sprays easily drift into neighbouring vineyards, a deterrent to going organic. Under such circumstances, there is no point in a small landholder attempting to work organically, as the sprays will inevitably drift into his or her vineyards. Clemens Busch in the Mosel is an organic and BIODYNAMIC pioneer, but he has been able to acquire a contiguous block of prime vineyard in the Pündericher Marienburg that accounts for virtually his entire production.

Winemaking

While Germany has been a leader in winemaking technology as well as viticultural research, a movement towards minimal intervention and rediscovering traditional methods is a significant part of today's German wine scene. The resulting tension is reflected in the practices of most cellars. Sophisticated PRESSES, typically operating at two atmospheres or less, are sometimes essentially programmed to re-enact the regimen of ancient basket presses, and not a few strong young German growers have rehabilitated antique specimens of the latter. CENTRIFUGES, FILTERS, FINING agents, and ENZYMES are employed by many estates to ensure ultra-clean juices that are then fermented with carefully selected YEAST cultures. But the virtues of minimal gravity settling, retention of solid matter, and SPONTANEOUS FERMENTATION (which in the Mosel never went entirely out of fashion), are being affirmed by a growing share of vintners. Early racking, clarification, and bottling of young white wines is still the norm, but the role of LEES CONTACT as well as lighter fining and filtration, and later bottling in enhancing flavour and stability are taken increasingly seriously many wine growers. Charcoal-fining to remove off-aromas and flavours in vintages featuring GREY ROT and other fungal infections is still common but is increasingly seen as a last resort.

Extremely varied weather this century has forced German growers to practise, most unusually, ACIDIFICATION (initially in 2003) and, in 2010, 2012, and 2013, to rediscover DEACIDIFICATION techniques. Resort to CHAPTALIZATION is nowadays rare within the ranks of Germany's top growers—hard as that is for any grower born before 1960 to imagine. Many other techniques that have become prevalent elsewhere remain illegal in Germany, notably CRYOEXTRACTION (EISWEIN may not be made using a freezer), REVERSE OSMOSIS, and other post-harvest means of must CONCENTRATION.

Since the 1980s, dry wine has come to dominate the market in Germany itself, almost completely so in fine-dining establishments and among consumers of premium-priced bottlings, where TROCKEN is today viewed virtually as an imprimatur of drinkability, not to mention social respectability. But many German vintners remain committed to making wines with some sweetness, especially from Riesling, albeit very differently than of old. Addition of SÜSSRESERVE, the usual means of rendering or fine-tuning sweet wine during the 1970s and 1980s, has almost completely given way to practices such as arresting fermentation through a combination of low temperatures, adding SULFUR, and STERILE BOTTLING. The results of stopped-fermentation are chemically and organoleptically different from those of adding Süssreserve. Only the latter allowed growers to experiment in order to determine optimum BALANCE and achieve a desired RESIDUAL SUGAR level. At least as common today as taking measures to guarantee residual sugar, is supplemental yeasting, warming in tank or cask, and BLENDING to guarantee that the residual sugar of the finished wine is under the legal limit for a trocken (9 g/l in the case of Riesling of healthy acidity). Riesling especially, if left to its own fermentative devices, has a habit of coming to rest HALBTROCKEN, a state that most contemporary German growers seem somehow to find ideologically repugnant, and many German consumers seem to spurn.

BARREL MATURATION in casks of varying sizes is nowadays practised for only a minority of German white wines other than those made from Burgundian grapes. The use of small new barrels for maturing red wines or whites from Burgundian varieties is becoming increasingly fashionable in Germany, just as elsewhere. But the traditional 1,200-litre Stückfass and 600-litre Mosel Halbstück were never abandoned, and are today increasingly employed, especially by top estates. And as elsewhere, 300- and 600-litre and even larger casks as well as CONCRETE vessels are increasingly supplementing or replacing the classic 228-litre Burgundian PIÈCE for Pinots of both colours

Vine varieties

Before the concept of QUALITY IN WINE started to spread from the estates of the Church and the nobility in the 18th century, different vine varieties were grown as FIELD BLENDS as a hedge against crop failure. In these circumstances, the question of grape RIPENESS was less important and, until the early 19th century, many harvests were gathered before their time, to avoid the risk of uncontrollable ROT. The attraction of Riesling was probably its performance in the vineyard rather than because of its wine. Amid the chaos and competition of a mixed plantation, Riesling made a mark, sufficient for large estates to start growing it as a single vine. As the value of late and selective harvesting became understood, the reputation of Riesling wine rose above that of all other white grape varieties.

The 1971 GERMAN WINE LAW, however, significantly disadvantaged Riesling in the marketplace. Levels of wine quality were defined by MUST WEIGHT alone. Such a system may have some validity when applied to a single vine variety growing in a narrowly defined area but, given a broader application, it becomes increasingly unreliable, as the consumer eventually discovered. Achieving certain minimum must weights is scarcely a guarantee of quality, and a host of GERMAN CROSSES propagated simply to ripen fast virtually guaranteed the debasement of the 1971 Wine Law's purported distinctions of PRÄDIKAT, not to mention that of late-ripening Riesling. But, as was the case a century ago, Riesling is increasingly recognized as Germany's calling card, the pendulum has swung back even in areas of the Pfalz and Rheinhessen previously dominated by German crosses. Planted on 23% of German vineyards in 2013, Riesling has strengthened its lead over MÜLLER-THURGAU, still (just) Germany's second most planted vine variety in 2013 with less than 13%. Less welcome to many self-styled traditionalists has been the decline of what was once Germany's third white wine grape, SILVANER, to a mere 5%. It has been overtaken by GRAUBURGUNDER (Pinot Gris) with more than 5%, double its acreage of the mid-1990s, while Weissburgunder (PINOT BLANC, nearly 5%) is not far behind. Germany is becoming a hotspot for Burgundian varieties; even Chardonnay represented nearly 2% of all plantings. Like other once-important German crosses Kerner and Bacchus, Scheurebe has been declining in importance. Red wine grapes have become very much more important, thanks to CLIMATE CHANGE perhaps, and in 2013 represented 36% of all plantings. SPÄTBURGUNDER (Pinot Noir, with nearly 12% of total German vineyard area) was the third most planted variety overall. DORNFELDER represented 8% of all vineyard area while PORTUGIESER, TROLLINGER, REGENT (first planted in the mid-1990s), and Schwarzriesling/Müllerrebe (PINOT MEUNIER) were all planted on more than 2,000 ha/5,000 acres by 2013. Lemberger (better-known as BLAUFRÄNKISCH) was catching up fast. Chardonnay is by no means the only INTERNATIONAL VARIETY to have been embraced by German growers; Sauvignon Blanc, Merlot, and Cabernet Sauvignon were each grown on more than 350 ha of Germany in 2013 and a host of Cabernet crosses were also planted, especially in Pfalz and Rheinhessen.

Wine labelling

The overwhelming majority of German wine is officially QUALITÄTSWEIN. A portion of this, the amount varying according to quality of vintage and subject to long-term labelling trends, is bottled unchaptalized and bears a so-called Prädikat, of which there are six: KABINETT, SPÄT-LESE, AUSLESE, BEERENAUSLESE, TROCKENBEERENAUS-LESE, and EISWEIN. One such trend is toward omitting these designations of Prädikat for dry wines. Whereas a Beerenauslese, Trockenbeerenauslese, or Eiswein is almost inevitably bottled with a high level of residual sugar, designation of a wine as Kabinett, Spätlese, or Auslese bears no direct relation to the sweetness of the finished wine. Among wines not labelled as trocken (dry), FEINHERB, or halbtrocken (medium dry; see SWEETNESS for the official EU classification of such terms), an Auslese will generally, though not always, taste noticeably sweeter than a Spätlese, which will in turn taste sweeter than a Kabinett.

The tradition of picking parcel by parcel and even selectively within parcels, combined with what many Germans would claim is a national passion for minutiae, can make for dozens of different bottlings at a given wine estate. And German Riesling, in particular, is arguably capable of more stylistic diversity than any other combination of place and variety. The resulting multiplicity of bottlings, combined with the divided ownership of individual sites, has made it very difficult for vineyard names (other than those of a few hundred or so) to have any widely recognized associations of flavour, bouquet, or style. Reacting to this, some bottlers have abandoned the use of the names of individual sites or even of Prädikat in favour of

their own estate-internal categories, and the most prestigious growers' association, the VDP, advocates both simplification of labelling and the association of renowned vineyard names with a specific, recognizable style. The German Wine Law has in recent decades added new layers of terminology while adapting but not jettisoning the old. The results can be bewildering, and many growers and consumers would argue that the very foundation of the 1971 Wine Law, so single-mindedly rooted in ripeness as measured by sugar at harvest, is itself rotten.

A CLASSIFICATION of German estates similar to the 1855 one of the Médoc and Graves had prominent proponents among journalists and growers in the late 1980s. From the mid-1990s, momentum gathered for a system of classifying vineyards, with the sites at the apex of a qualitative pyramid being designated an ERSTES GEWÄCHS (first growth) or GROSSES GEWÄCHS (great growth). The VDP membership has voluntarily bound itself to such a system, but its category of Grosses Gewächs has no legal standing and those words may not appear on the relevant bottles. Since 2000, when strictures against including non-mandated information on the label were eased, a variety of estate-specific designations has proliferated including star-ratings, references to soil type, and (where the authorities choose not to raise a fuss) mention of plots other than official EINZELLAGEN (vineyard sites).

From the 2014 vintage, the designation of vineyard site in the state of Rheinland-Pfalz (i.e. in the AHR, MITTELRHEIN, MOSEL, NAHE, PFALZ, and RHEINHESSEN wine regions) became yet more specific but potentially more confusing for consumers. A grower may apply to have entered into the state's official list of vineyards any site name that is registered in the official cadastre map. Once a name has been entered, any grower may use it on the label of a wine originating in the delimited area, provided the name appears in conjunction with that of the relevant commune, and regardless of whether or not the grower chooses to indicate the relevant official EINZELLAGE. As a result, wines from all of Germany's predominant Riesling regions (except the RHEINGAU, which is in Hessen) may be labelled using the same formula—village + vineyard—but with three very different degrees of specificity for the vineyard: GROSSLAGE, Einzellage, or cadastre name. The first 20 such cadastre vineyard names to be registered, within weeks of the new legislation's enactment, included several (e.g. Im Kahlenberg and Auf dem Krötenpfuhl, both in Bad Kreuznach) virtually identical to those of the official Einzellagen (Kahlenberg and Krötenpfuhl respectively) in which the more narrowly delimited vineyards are located. While many will welcome the opportunity afforded to highlight potentially

outstanding sites, including the original core vineyards around which the 1971 Einzellagen were constructed (and whose names they generally, if often imprecisely, adopted), it is hard to argue that this new legislation makes an already complicated situation clearer or simpler.

Nor is it clear at what point either the vicious cycle of over-production and depressed prices from nugatory flatlands, or the attrition of excellent, steep vineyard land for lack of farmers, will see an end. But there are also propitious early-21st-century signs. The international reputation of Germany's revered Riesling is higher han at any time in almost a century. Unprecedented levels of technological sophistication are meeting their equal in quality aspirations, responsibility to the environment, and the rediscovery of ancient viticultural wisdom. And a reaction appears to have set in both against the stylistic straitjacket of German consumers' and opinion-makers' fanaticism for legally dry wine and against the threat of global gustatory uniformity, promising German wines and vintners an opportunity to flourish with that dazzling stylistic diversity of which they and especially the Riesling grape in their soils are uniquely capable.

See also AHR, BADEN, FRANKEN, HESSISCHE BERGSTRASSE, MITTELRHEIN, MOSEL, NAHE, PFALZ, RHEINGAU, RHEINHESSEN, SAALE-UNSTRUT, SACHSEN, and WÜRTTEMBERG.   D.S.

Braatz, D., Sautter, U., and Swoboda, I., *Wine Atlas of Germany* (Berkeley, 2014).

Pigott, S., *Wein Spricht Deutsch: Weine, Winzer, Weinlandschaften* (Frankfurt, 2007).

Reinhardt, S., *The Finest Wines of Germany* (London, 2012).

www.winesofgermany.co.uk

www.deutscheweine.de

Gevrey-Chambertin, small town in the Côte de Nuits producing some of Burgundy's most famous red wines from Pinot Noir grapes. The area allowed the appellation was sharply reduced in the late 1990s to exclude some less favoured land towards the plain, but with about 400 ha/1,000 acres under vine, including an overflow of vineyards into neighbouring Brochon, which does not have its own APPELLATION, as well as 87 ha/215 acres of grands crus, this is still the largest viticultural source in the Côte d'Or. In 1847, Gevrey annexed the name of its finest vineyard, Chambertin, somewhat tediously dubbed the king of wines and wine of kings (although it was in fact the Emperor Napoleon's favourite wine).

Gevrey-Chambertin wines are typically deeper in colour and firmer than their rivals from Vosne-Romanée and Chambolle-Musigny. Good examples may take time to develop into perhaps the richest and most complete wines of the Côte d'Or. Given the ease with which the village name sells, there used to be plenty of under-achievers in Gevrey-Chambertin, especially at grand cru level, but the quality of wines today from producers such as Denis Bachelet, Alain Burguet, Pierre Damoy, Claude Dugat, Dugat-Py, Duroché, Sylvie Esmonin, Fourrier, Géantet-Pansiot, Harmand-Geoffroy, Denis Mortet, Rossignol-Trapet, the exceptional Armand Rousseau, Sérafin, and Trapet is reassuring.

In all, Gevrey boasts nine grands crus, the pick of which are Chambertin and Chambertin-Clos de Bèze. The latter, comprising 15.4 ha/38 acres, may equally be sold as Le Chambertin. It is hard to differentiate between the two qualitatively although Clos de Bèze is slightly further up the hill than Chambertin, with a less deep soil, giving wines which are fractionally less powerful but full of sensual charm.

Le Chambertin, 12.9 ha (plus the 15.4 of Clos de Bèze), is the flagship: if not quite as sumptuous as Musigny or Richebourg, or as divinely elegant as La Tâche or Romanée-St-Vivant, Chambertin is matched only by Romanée-Conti (see VOSNE-ROMANÉE) for its completeness and its intensity.

Two other grand cru vineyards, Mazis-Chambertin and Latricières-Chambertin, lie on the same level as Chambertin and Clos de Bèze; one, Ruchottes-Chambertin, is to be found a little higher up the slope, while Charmes-Chambertin, Mazoyères-Chambertin, Griotte-Chambertin, and Chapelle-Chambertin are further downhill.

Mazis-Chambertin (12.59 ha), also written Mazy-, is usually regarded as being next in quality to Chambertin and Clos de Bèze, especially in the upper part, les Mazis Haut. The flavours are just as intense, the structure perhaps just a little less firm. Latricières (6.94 ha) is less powerful, although the wines are explosively fruity when young, with an entrancingly silky texture, especially when a sunny vintage warms up the cool clay soil. Ruchottes (3.50 ha), thanks to a particularly thin calcareous soil, is lighter in colour, angular in style, but again impressively intense in a fine, lacy style.

Griotte-Chambertin (5.48 ha), which possibly owes its name to the grill-pan shape of the vineyard rather than the griottes cherry aromas which the wine seems to have, and Chapelle-Chambertin (5.39 ha) are also a touch lighter in style. Charmes-Chambertin covers 31.6 ha if Mazoyères-Chambertin is included, which is usually the case. Together this constitutes the largest grand cru in the village and, as with Clos de Vougeot and Échezeaux, its size precludes homogeneous quality. Some of the vineyard, such as the part stretching down to the main road, the D974, should perhaps not be classified as grand cru, although a good Charmes is one of Gevrey-Chambertin's most seductive, fragrant wines when young.

Some of the grands crus are matched, if not surpassed, by the best of the premier cru vineyards, especially those with an ideal south eastern exposition such as Les Cazetiers and Clos St-Jacques. Indeed, Domaine Armand Rousseau, the most famous name in Gevrey thanks to the eponymous Armand's pioneering DOMAINE BOTTLING in the 1930s, charges significantly more for Clos St-Jacques than for several grands crus in an impressive range of wines.

See also CÔTE D'OR, and map under BURGUNDY.

J.T.C.M.

Gewürztraminer, often written **Gewurztraminer**, is the aromatic variant of the pink-skinned SAVAGNIN, shown by DNA PROFILING to be identical to TRAMINER, and is responsible for some of the most distinctively perfumed, full-bodied white wines of all. Gewürztraminer may not be easy to spell, even for wine merchants, but is blissfully easy to recognize—indeed many wine drinkers find it is the first, possibly only, grape variety they are able to recognize from the wine's heady aroma alone. Deeply coloured, opulently aromatic, and broader than almost any other white wine, Gewürztraminer's faults are only in having too much of everything. It is easy to tire of its weight and its exotic flavour of lychees and heavily scented roses, although ALSACE's finest Gewürztraminers are extremely serious wines, with an occasional savoury note reminiscent of bacon fat in some of the most complex examples, capable of at least medium-term ageing.

This by now internationally famous vine variety's genealogy is both ramified and fascinating. In our book *Wine Grapes* we cite no fewer than six groups of historical references for both Savagnin and Traminer, the variety that is like Gewürztraminer but with pale green berries and much less scent that was first noted in the village of Tramin or Termeno in what is now the Italian Tyrol (see ALTO ADIGE) in the 13th century. DNA profiling in Austria has furthermore demonstrated a parent–offspring relationship between Pinot and Traminer (hence Gewürztraminer), connecting two of the oldest grape varieties in Europe.

Traminer, like its parent PINOT, mutates easily, however, and Gewürztraminer is the name adopted in the late 19th century for the dark pink-berried MUSQUÉ mutation of Traminer (and adopted as its official name in Alsace in 1973). Although much has been read into the direct German translation of *gewurz* as 'spiced', in this context it simply means 'perfumed'. Traminer Musqué, Traminer Parfumé, and Traminer Aromatique were all at one time French synonyms for Gewürztraminer. As early as 1909, the AMPELOGRAPHER Viala acknowledged Gewürztraminer as an accepted synonym for Savagnin Rosé, and this aromatic, dark-berried version is known as Roter

Traminer in German and Traminer or Termeno Aromatico, Traminer Rosé, or Rosso in Italy. Its long history in Alsace means that it is occasionally known as some sort of KLEVNER, particularly in this case Rotclevner.

Gewürztraminer has become by far the most planted variant of Traminer. The grapes are certainly notable at harvest for their variegated but incontrovertibly pink colour, which is translated into very deep golden wines, sometimes with a slight coppery tinge. Winemakers unfamiliar with the variety have been known to be panicked into extracting colour and flavour. Gewürztraminers also attain higher alcohol levels than most white wines, with over 14% being by no means uncommon, and acidities can correspondingly be precariously low. MALOLACTIC CONVERSION is almost invariably suppressed for Gewürztraminer and steps must be taken to avoid OXIDATION.

If all goes well, the result is deep golden, full-bodied wines with a substantial spine and concentrated heady aromas whose acidity level will preserve them while those aromas unfurl. In a lesser year or too hot a climate the result is either an early-picked, neutral wine or an oppressively oily, flabby one that can easily taste bitter to boot.

Viticulturally, Gewürztraminer is not exactly a dream to grow. Relative to the varieties with which it is commonly planted, it has small bunches and is not particularly productive. Its early budding leaves it prey to spring frosts and it is particularly prone to VIRUS DISEASES, although the viticultural station at Colmar has developed such virus-free clones as those numbered 47, 48, and 643.

The finest examples still came almost exclusively from Alsace but the number of interesting examples made elsewhere has been growing.

Germany relegates its (Roter) Traminer to a very minor rank, well behind Riesling, with about 880 ha in total in 2012, including some plantings of the non-aromatic sort which is very occasionally bottled separately. The variety needs relatively warm sites to avoid spring frost damage and to assure good FRUIT SET so that in northern Germany Riesling is usually a more profitable choice for growers. Almost two thirds of Germany's Traminer is planted in Baden and the Pfalz, where it can produce wines of discernible character but they can tend to flab. At Rhodt in the Pfalz, a Traminer vineyard said to be nearly 400 years old styles itself the world's oldest.

There were about 300 ha of Traminer planted in AUSTRIA in 2013 but here too it has been consigned to the non-modish wilderness, even though some examples, particularly later-picked semi-sweet wines from Styria and botrytized sweet wines from Burgenland, can exhibit an exciting blend of race and aroma and can develop for many years in bottle.

The variety is grown, in no great quantity but usually distinctively, throughout eastern Europe: called Tramini in Hungary; Traminec in Slovenia; occasionally just Rusa in Romania; and Mala Dinka in Bulgaria. Most of the vines are the aromatic mutation and demonstrate some of Gewürztraminer's distinctive perfume but often in extremely dilute, and often sullied, form, typically overlaying a relatively sweet, lightish white. Hungarians are particularly proud of their Tramini grown on the rich shores of Lake Balaton. It is grown by the Romanians in Transylvania, by the Bulgarians in the south and east, and also, as Traminer, in Russia, Moldova, and Ukraine, where it is sometimes used to perfume Soviet sparkling wine.

It is grown in small quantities, sometimes called Haiden or HEIDA, in Switzerland and in ever smaller quantity in Luxembourg. In Iberia, Torres grow it in the High PENEDÈS for their Viña Esmeralda and it is essentially a mountain grape even in Italy, where about 200 ha of Traminer Aromatico are still grown in its seat, Alto Adige. The less scented and less interesting Traminer is also grown to a limited extent, and Italian winemaking together with vineyard elevation do nothing to emphasize Gewürztraminer characteristics in the resulting wines, although the international nature of the variety may encourage a small renaissance of popularity.

In the New World, Gewürztraminer presents a challenge. Many wine regions are simply too warm to produce wine with sufficient acidity, unless the grapes are picked so early (see HARVEST, timing), as in some of Australia's irrigated vineyards, that they have developed little Gewürztraminer character. Australia's 'Traminer' vine population of about 900 ha, concentrated in some of the less exciting corners of South Australia and New South Wales, has made a modest recovery in the early years of this century, its wine typically used to perfume and sweeten Riesling in commercial blends.

The variety has been more obviously successful in the cooler climate of NEW ZEALAND, although even here total plantings are not much more than 300 ha, despite some lively examples from Gisborne on the east coast of the North Island where it is taken particularly seriously by Vinoptima. This, incidentally, was one of the earliest identifications of varietal/geographical matching in the southern hemisphere.

Another happy home for Gewürztraminer is in the Pacific Northwest of America, particularly in Washington and Oregon, although the variety has lost ground to Riesling in Washington and to Pinot Gris in Oregon. Washington had almost 800 acres in 2011 and could demonstrate some appetizing life in several well-vinified examples, even if too many were too sweet. In Oregon, too, the smoky fume of

Alsace is apparent in some bottlings from its 200 acres in 2012, generally of late harvest or ICE WINES, although rot can be a problem in this wetter climate.

Gewürztraminer remains a relatively minor variety in California, however, whose 1,700 acres/688 ha, almost half of them in Monterey, too often bring forth oil rather than aroma (see CALIFORNIA for more on the wines). There are a few hectares of Traminer in Argentina, and some increasingly convincing bottlings from Chile, particularly from cooler, southern vineyards, but generally South America relies on TORRONTÉS and MOSCATEL to provide aromatic whites. Limited plantings in South Africa have so far yielded sweetish wines but some of the right aromas.

It seems likely that serious Gewürztraminer will remain an Alsace speciality for some years yet.

Galet, P., *Dictionnaire encyclopédique des cépages* (Paris, 2000).

Robinson, J., Harding, J., and Vouillamoz, J., *Wine Grapes, a complete guide to 1,368 vine varieties, including their origins and flavours* (London, 2012).

Ghemme, ancient, tiny red wine zone high up in the subalpine Novara Hills in the north of the PIEMONTE region of north-west Italy. Its promotion to DOCG in 1997 was intended to rescue its minuscule vineyard surface, less than 60 ha today. Like GATTINARA across the River Seisa in the Vercelli Hills with its satellites LESSONA and BRAMATERRA, Ghemme is made from the NEBBIOLO grape (with a mandatory minimum of 85%) while the addition of BONARDA, UVA RARA, and/or VESPOLINA. For more details, see SPANNA, the local name for Nebbiolo.

GI, abbreviation for GEOGRAPHICAL INDICATION.

gibberellins, naturally occurring plant HORMONES which regulate vine growth as for other plants. Isolated in 1941 from a rice fungus, they have been much studied since. In the vine they are formed in growing tissue in the leaves, roots, and berries. Many thousands of hectares of Thompson Seedless (SULTANA) vines are treated by spraying with gibberellins during FLOWERING and shortly afterwards, and this results in larger berries suitable as TABLE GRAPES. Other seedless varieties respond similarly to this treatment. Trials at GEISENHEIM and Oppenheim in Germany involving the application of gibberellic acid to seeded grapes during full bloom, causing berry shatter (see FRUIT SET), resulted in a substantial reduction in both BOTRYTIS infection and the development of SOUR ROT. The technique is already in commercial use in northern Italy and has proved to be an important way to reduce botrytis problems in Italy and Germany.   R.E.S. & H.S.

Giennois, Coteaux du, small AOC which extends on both banks of the Loire from just north of POUILLY-FUMÉ in the upper Loire to the town of Gien. Although the zone is quite extensive, and encompasses both calcareous and flint soils, it comprised only just over 200 ha/495 acres in 2012. Most of the wines are crisp, pale whites made exclusively from Sauvignon Blanc but some light red and rosé are also made from a blend of Gamay and Pinot Noir. Joseph Balland-Chapuis is one of the most dedicated producers in this region, where spring FROSTS are a perennial threat.

See also LOIRE, including map.

Gigondas, good-value red and rosé wine appellation in the southern RHÔNE. From just over a third of the total area, the best wines are remarkably similar to good red CHÂTEAUNEUF-DU-PAPE, with the benefit of higher elevations and more LIMESTONE. Overall wine standards are high, even if Gigondas winemaking can in some cases be more rustic than high-tech. Gigondas shares Châteauneuf's low maximum YIELD, 35 hl/ha (2 tons/acre); high minimum natural ALCOHOLIC STRENGTH, 12.5%; and a compulsory TRIAGE to eliminate imperfect grapes. Unlike Châteauneuf, however, it exists in rosé form.

In 2013 the total *vignoble* was 1,216 ha/3,003 acres of rugged, herb-scented vineyard just below the spectacularly jagged wall of rock, the Dentelles de Montmirail. Grenache grapes must constitute between 50 and 100% of the blend with Syrah and particularly Mourvèdre the most popular blending partners.

The district has been noted for its wine since Roman times. Later a significant proportion of the land under vine formed part of the estates of the princes of Orange. In the 20th century, however, lacking a Baron Le Roy of its own (see CHÂTEAUNEUF-DU-PAPE), it laboured under the commercial disadvantage of qualifying merely for the Côtes du Rhône appellation for several decades. In 1966, it was elevated to Côtes du Rhône-Villages, and in 1971, won its own appellation. The best wines can repay BOTTLE AGEING for a decade or more.

Gippsland Zone, vast, relatively cool zone east of Melbourne, VICTORIA, noted for Pinot Noir and Chardonnay. So far it has no regions simply because combined production from its 43 producers has not reached the critical 500-tonne mark. Depending on one's view, there are either three (east, west and south) distinct climates, or six (the latter view propounded by Phillip Jones, the elusive proprietor of Bass Phillip, regarded by many as source of Australia's best PINOT NOIR).

girasol. See GYROPALETTE.

girdling, making an incision round a vine trunk, cane, or shoot, usually to improve fruit set. For more details, see CINCTURING.

Girò, red grape used for dry, sweet, and fortified wines on SARDINIA. It is unrelated to the aromatic, pink-skinned **Giró Blanc** grown on Mallorca.

Gironde, the estuary which separates the MÉDOC from BLAYE and the south western extreme of cognac country gives its name to the *département* in which the city of Bordeaux and the Bordeaux wine region is to be found. The Rivers DORDOGNE and GARONNE flow into the Gironde (see map under BORDEAUX).

GIS. See GEOGRAPHICAL INFORMATION SYSTEM.

Givry, famous as the preferred wine of King Henri IV (perhaps because it was the birthplace of his mistress Gabrielle d'Estrées), produces mostly red wine in the Côte CHALONNAISE district of Burgundy. White wine constitutes only a seventh of total production, but is often particularly interesting with a soft bouquet reminiscent of liquorice. The reds have more structure and ability to age than those of neighbouring RULLY, but less depth than Mercurey. About half the vineyard area is designated PREMIER CRU, but the vineyards which most merit the higher rank are those on the hillside between Clos Salomon and the Cellier aux Moines.   J.T.C.M.

glass, history of. For more than 3,000 years, glass has played a unique role in the history of wine, in terms of both serving (GLASSES, DRINKING VESSELS, and DECANTERS) and storage (BOTTLES).

Glass vessels were known in the Ancient world (first appearing in EGYPT c.1500 BC) and became common during Roman times, when the techniques of glass-blowing spread throughout the Roman empire. Wine was sometimes drunk from glass tumblers and surviving examples show astonishingly intricate craftsmanship. Glass bottles were used as decanters for carrying wine to table, but not for storage because they were too fragile.

Glass-making continued after the collapse of Roman power. By the time of the Renaissance, VENICE had become the centre of luxury production. Venetian glassware was exported throughout the known world and Italian craftsmen settled across Europe setting up new workshops. In Tudor England, aristocrats preferred Venetian-style glasses to silver (which was considered too common) but glass was so expensive that several diners were expected to share each beaker.

Glass bottles at this time were used by apothecaries rather than wine merchants, although the wines produced around Florence were sometimes transported in *fiaschi* wrapped in straw. The problem with glass was that it was too light and therefore too fragile to withstand either transport or storage. The most common containers for wine were BARRELS for bulk, and leather, tin, or stoneware bottles.

A turning-point in the history of glass (and the history of wine) came early in the 17th century, when a timber shortage led to the introduction of coal-fired furnaces in England. Hotter furnaces made possible the production of bottles that were not only darker and heavier, but stronger. At first these dark, onion-shaped bottles were used mainly as decanters and for personal use, but by the beginning of the 18th century they were used for the long-distance transport of wine. Initially the French had to rely on English imports, but by 1790, there were five factories around Bordeaux (still an important centre of glass production) producing 400,000 English-style bottles.

This development was revolutionary because it made possible the ageing of wine. The necessary corollary was the CORK, whose use became common at this time. The advantages of BOTTLE AGEING were most noticeable in PORT, a staple drink in Georgian England. As the practice of BINNING wine became more common, the shape of wine bottles evolved towards the taller cylindrical shape (c.1760) we know today.

Meanwhile a revolution in drinking glasses had emanated from the two southern English workshops of George Ravenscroft, who in 1675 had discovered how to make LEAD crystal. This gave rise to a whole new style of English glassware quite distinct from intricate Venetian fashions. Increasingly, different glasses were designed and produced to be used specifically for certain wines, and by the end of the 18th century the concept of a uniformly decorated glass service was well established throughout Europe.   H.B.

Klein, D., and Lloyd, W., *The History of Glass* (London, 1984).

glass, wine by the. In an increasing proportion of the world's restaurants and bars, particularly in the United States, wine is served by the glass. This is especially useful for those who want to drink less than a half or full bottle, or want to taste as many different wines as possible in a FLIGHT of different small servings, or want to practise focused FOOD AND WINE MATCHING in a group that has ordered a wide range of different dishes. When carefully administered, with a high level of professional service and due attention to LEFTOVERS in opened bottles, possibly using special storage systems involving INERT GAS, this is an admirable service to the consumer. See also ACCESS SYSTEM, WINE.

glasses, not just the final CONTAINER for wine but an important instrument for communicating it to the human senses (see TASTING). Wine can be drunk from any DRINKING VESSEL but clean (and only clean) GLASS has the advantage of being completely inert and, if it is clear, of allowing the taster the pleasure (or in the case of BLIND TASTING the clues) afforded by the wine's appearance: colour, clarity, and so on.

For this reason, wine professionals and keen amateurs prefer completely plain, uncoloured, unengraved, uncut glass, preferably as thin as is practicable to allow the palate to commune as closely as possible with the liquid. Thin-rimmed glasses are particularly highly valued.

The ideal wine glass also has a stem—indeed Americans call wine glasses 'stemware'—so that the wine taster can hold the glass without necessarily affecting the wine's TEMPERATURE (a critical element in wine tasting). The stem also enables a glass to be rotated easily (although it takes a certain knack); rotation, as explained in TASTING, is essential for maximizing AROMA or BOUQUET. This rotation process also means that the ideal wine glass narrows towards the rim, to minimize the chance of spillage during rotation, and to encourage the volatile FLAVOUR COMPOUNDS to collect in the space between the surface of the wine and the rim of the glass.

Individuals have their own aesthetic preferences, but any glass which fits the above criteria will serve as a wine glass, including some relatively inexpensive examples. There is a sensual thrill to be had, however, in really thin crystal. This is usually expensive, although central Europe, and BOHEMIA in particular, has a long tradition of producing fine glasses at good prices.

For many households, a single wine glass shape and size will do, perhaps supplemented by smaller glasses for FORTIFIED wines and an elongated one for SPARKLING WINES. Purists, however, use slightly different glasses for different sorts of wine, conventionally (although not particularly logically) a smaller glass for white wines, and traditionally Germanic shapes for German and Alsace wines.

In this respect there is no greater purist than Georg Riedel, an Austrian glass-maker who is unusual for his wine CONNOISSEURSHIP. He has designed a series of different glasses not just for young red bordeaux and mature red bordeaux, but also, for example, different glasses for vintage port and tawny port, for Brunello di Montalcino and for Chianti. These designs are all based purely on analysing how different taste characteristics are optimized on the nose and palate by minute variations in glass design. Those determined to take full advantage of all Riedel permutations may need to give up a room or two to accommodate the necessary number of glasses, however, and in practice most people content themselves with just two or three possible glass types, often chosen as much on appearance as on efficacy.

Special glass types

Over the centuries, various specific glasses have come to be associated with different wine types.

CHAMPAGNE and other sparkling wines were for long drunk in a flat, saucer-like glass called a **coupe**, but this has been abandoned in favour of the tall **flute**, which preserves the wine's MOUSSE. This has evolved into a slightly more bulbous **tulipe**, which combines height with narrowing towards the rim.

In Spain, SHERRY has traditionally been served in the **copita**, and tastes infinitely better in a part-filled glass in this elongated tulip shape than it does brimming over a cut-glass thimble as it is so often served elsewhere.

The ideal PORT glass is not so very different from the copita, although it is usually rather bigger in order to allow maximum appreciation of the complex bouquet of a vintage port. Glasses like this are ideal for almost all fortified wines, which, for obvious reasons, are conventionally served in smaller quantities than table wines.

BURGUNDY, particularly red burgundy, has come to be served in glass balloons, sometimes so large they resemble fish-bowls. The idea, apart from lusty exhibitionism, is that a good burgundy can offer such a rich panoply of aromas that they should be given every chance to escape the wine and titillate the taster. Most wine connoisseurs use the shape on a reduced scale.

The wines of ALSACE and GERMANY are sometimes served in particular forms of glass such as the **Rohmer**, often with green or brown glass stems, mainly for traditional reasons. There are still those who teach wine serving who regard serving these wines in standard white wine glasses as an intolerable aberration.

See also SERVING WINE.

glassy winged sharpshooter, LEAF-
HOPPER insect (*Homalodisca vitripennis*) of great significance in some southern California wine regions since the 1990s as it is a vector of PIERCE'S DISEASE. It is able to fly longer distances than other leafhoppers, so the disease spreads more quickly. It has been detected in Australia but has not become established and poses no immediate threat to vineyards as the Pierce's disease bacterium is not present.   R.E.S.

Glenrowan, historic Australian wine region
in North East Victoria Zone (see VICTORIA), famous for Ned Kelly, FORTIFIED wines, and full-bodied reds. *See* TOPAQUE AND MUSCAT.

Glera. The PROSECCO grape was renamed Glera
in 2009 so that Prosecco could attain (greatly expanded) geographically protected status.

globalization of the world's wine markets
continues to accelerate. There was always some trade between Mediterranean countries, and a degree of trade expansion in the five decades to World War I, but until the late 20th century intercontinental interactions involved little

more than the exporting of CUTTINGS and traditional production expertise. Most wine was consumed in the country of production, and those countries were mostly in Europe. But since the 1980s, with the fall in TRANSPORT and communication costs, the wine industry has embraced new modes of internationalization. They include a greater export focus by the main producers, mergers and acquisitions of what are becoming multinational wine companies (see below), the not-unrelated growth of supermarket chains operating internationally as wine retailers, and the increase in OENOLOGISTS and VITICULTURISTS employed in multiple countries.

Globalization has brought changes in demand. Deregulation of wine retailing in Britain and elsewhere allowed rapidly expanding supermarket chains to compete with traditional sellers of wine and attract new consumers. Those chains responded to the new consumer preferences by sourcing robust, fruity wines that are more approachable and affordable than FINE WINE but better than traditional basic European wine. For national advertising to be profitable for those chains, and for wineries (and in some cases the supermarket chains themselves) seeking to build BRANDS, large quantities of homogenous wine are needed year after year. New World producers were initially more adept at responding to this new demand and one of the consequences was *la* CRISE VITICOLE.

The share of global wine production exported, which had previously been below 15% and mostly Mediterranean or intra-European, grew dramatically from the late 1980s and by 2012 exceeded 35%. Meanwhile the New World's share of global wine exports rose from 3% in the late 1980s to 25% (if sparkling wine is excluded) by 2004. Recognizing their poor performance, Europe's producers began belatedly in the mid 2000s to adapt their practices to compete. The world's three leading wine-exporting countries, Italy, Spain, and France, as a group now export almost half their production volume, up from just one-fifth a generation ago. Between 2002 and 2012 the share of wine that is exported from the New World in BULK rose from less than 15 to more than 35%. Bottling in the country of destination can reduce both costs and the carbon footprint. It also reflects the growth of supermarkets' own brands, and their demands for prompt delivery of other branded wines. The new bulk shipping technology offers greater opportunities to blend wines from any region of the world, and so may add to the commoditization of the popular wine category.

The dramatic expansion in international wine trade is part of a general tendency for global trade to grow faster than production, fuelled in part by the lowering of trade

restrictions and the freeing up of markets for foreign currency exchange. This greater openness means winemakers and hence grape growers are far more exposed now than pre-1990 to exchange rate volatility, and also to greater import competition in their domestic market as consumers seek an ever-broader range of wines. Wide fluctuations in exchange rates after the global financial crisis of 2008 substantially altered national shares in key markets.

Greater openness and international travel also alter tastes and preferences. Nowhere has this been more obvious than in China. Chinese wine imports grew more than 50% a year during 2006–12, fuelled largely by imports of low and medium-quality wine. Further large increases in wine consumption and probably imports are expected as China's middle class grows.

Mergers and acquisitions accelerated from the mid 1980s when Louis Vuitton bonded with Moët-Hennessy to form LVMH. At about the same time UK-based Grand Metropolitan (now Diageo) invested in California wineries, and Paris-based PERNOD RICARD added Jacob's Creek to its portfolio of brands via Orlando Wyndham in Australia. Global drinks company interest rests mainly with sparkling wines, brandies, and vermouths, however, which have lent themselves much more easily to global branding than still wines. Seagram and Pernod had both entered the mass market before, only to leave it to wine-focused operators such as CONSTELLATION BRANDS and CASTEL; DIAGEO did the same in the mid-1990s. Pernod Ricard signalled a return to the fray by acquiring Montana (renamed BRANCOTT Estate) and other significant wine brands when Allied Domecq broke up in 2005.

A second phase of international consolidation drew Australian producers closer to the American market with the merger of California's Beringer with the Mildara Blass subsubsidiary of Australian brewers Foster's in 2001, and the acquisition of Hardys of Australia by Constellation in 2003. Foster's subsequently separated its wine business from beer to form Treasury Wine Estates, and Constellation sold their Australian arm, now called Accolade, to a private equity firm in 2011. Companies such as ANTINORI, GALLO, and MONDAVI have also been involved in a changing roster of JOINT VENTURES which have helped to globalize wine. The latest development is the purchasing of vineyards and wineries, often for distribution reasons, by Chinese firms, particularly in France but also in some New World countries.

The emergence of large international wine companies and brands, built on economies of scale, and the ease with which technology and know-how can now be transferred, have led to significant shifts of wine grape production from western Europe to the globe's cheapest growing regions. But globalization is bound by TERROIR and the need for companies to offer differentiated wines of place—one of the main reasons why the largest wine companies control only a fraction of the world market. See also BRANDS.   K.A.

Anderson, K. (ed.), *The World's Wine Markets: Globalization at Work* (Cheltenham, 2004).

Anderson, K., and Nelgen, S., *Global Wine Markets, 1961 to 2009: A Statistical Compendium* (Adelaide, 2011, available as a free ebook at www.adelaide.edu.au/press/titles/global-wine).

Simpson, J., *Creating Wine: The Emergence of a World Industry, 1840-1914* (Princeton, 2011).

global positioning system (GPS), a satellite-based navigation system which allows detailed mapping of specific vineyard features to a positional accuracy of 1 m/3 ft through the use of differential corrections. Differential GPS (dGPS) is an essential component of PRECISION VITICULTURE.   R.G.V.B.

global warming. See CLIMATE CHANGE.

gluconobacter, a genus within the acetic acid bacteria family associated more with grapes than wine because of its high sugar tolerance. Like ACETOBACTER species, gluconobacter species are capable of spoiling wine by converting it into vinegar.

glucose is with fructose one of the two principal SUGARS of the grape and of sweet wines. Like fructose, it is a six-carbon-atom sugar, or a hexose.

The two major sugars that accumulate in grapes occur in about equal amounts; at the beginning of RIPENING, glucose exceeds fructose (up to fivefold), but in wines made with over-ripe grapes there is less glucose than fructose at the end of FERMENTATION. Glucose also serves a very important function as the major sugar used by the vine for forming GLYCOSIDES (see also FLAVOUR COMPOUNDS). Common table sugar, sucrose, is made up of one molecule of glucose and one of fructose. See FRUCTOSE for details of the unusual relationship between these sugars and the grape.   B.G.C. & A.D.W.

Glühwein, German for 'glow wine', seems a particularly apt name for the MULLED WINE that has cheered many an alpine skier. Pre-mixed wine, sugar, and spices are also available under this name.

glutathione, or **glutathion**, sulfur-containing compound (tripeptide) found in grape juice and an important antioxidant which has been shown to play a significant part in the ageing of wines, and in protecting them from PREMATURE OXIDATION. It also has an important role in the formation of the precursors of volatile sulfur compounds and in stabilizing the volatile sulfur

compounds which characterize the aroma of Sauvignon Blanc and possibly some other white grape varieties.

Pre-harvest, glutathione plays a major role in GRAPE COMPOSITION, for example, by increasing the stability within the cell of polyphenols, aldehydes, and other sensory precursors which conjugate with glutathione.

glycerol, or **glycerine**, member of the chemical class of polyols and a minor product of alcoholic fermentation. The name derives from the Greek word for sweet and glycerol does indeed taste slightly sweet, as well as oily and heavy. It is present in most wines in concentrations ranging from about 4 to 6 g/l, although BOTRYTIZED wines may have concentrations of around 10 g/l.

Glycerol does have a slight effect on the apparent sweetness of a wine but, contrary to popular conception, glycerol makes only a very minor contribution to the apparent VISCOSITY of a wine, and bears no relation to the TEARS observed on the inside of many a wine glass. Whereas sensory tests have demonstrated that glycerol imparts sweetness at a threshold of about 5.2 g/l in white wine, a level of more than 28 g/l would be needed before any difference in viscosity were noted.   A.D.W. & T.H.L.

glycolysis. See YEAST.

glycosidase. See ENZYMES and FLAVOUR PRECURSORS.

glycosides are naturally occurring molecules made up of two parts joined by a glycosidic linkage; one of the parts is a sugar, frequently GLUCOSE, and the other may be a non-sugar, called an aglycone. Common aglycones are phenolic compounds, for example ANTHOCYANINS, although TERPENOIDS and a number of other compound types are found **glycosylated** in many plant tissues, including fruits. Glycosides present in wines come from the grape and here the sugar is usually glucose, although it too may be connected to a second, non-glucose sugar residue. Formation of a glycoside changes the physical and chemical properties of molecules that are glycosylated. Glycosides are usually more water soluble, and invariably much less volatile than the aglycones from which they were derived. It is still not clear why they form in plants but glycosylation is presumed to aid detoxification and the transport of aglycones, or to make plant tissues rigid. Plants and fruits often have a higher concentration of glycosides than aglycones. The sensory properties of flavour-active aglycones are profoundly diminished by glycosylation and such glycosides, known as FLAVOUR PRECURSORS, are a reserve of FLAVOUR and contributors to VARIETAL flavour expression (as opposed to aspects of flavour that arise from vinification) and BOUQUET in wines. Following the recognition of

glycosides as flavour precursors, a development in the mid 1990s was the determination of this class of compound in grapes and wines through measures of glycosyl-glucose. See also INFRARED SPECTROSCOPY.   P.J.W.

glycosyl-glucose assay, or **G-G assay**, an experimental measure of grape and wine composition, developed in the mid 1990s, complementing, and additional to those already available (see GRAPE COMPOSITION AND WINE QUALITY and GRAPE QUALITY ASSESSMENT). The basis of the G-G assay is the recognition of the role of GLYCOSIDES as FLAVOUR PRECURSORS of varietal wine flavour. The assay as applied to a grape, juice, or wine sample involves (*a*) isolation of the glycosides, (*b*) their complete hydrolysis to yield glucose, and (*c*) quantification of the glucose. The results are expressed as the amount of glycosides in micromoles, either per litre or per berry as appropriate. The G-G assay has been applied to both light- and dark-skinned grape varieties, at early stages of berry development through to harvest, to musts and juices during fermentation, and to wines before, during and after AGEING. The assay is particularly important for white varieties, where there are few alternative ways of analysing secondary metabolites. Accordingly, the assay allows the viticulturist and oenologist to relate the glycoside component of grape composition, obtained before harvest, to the glycoside concentration of a wine, irrespective of its style, years after its vinification. It has revealed the decrease in G-G in wines with ageing as glycoside HYDROLYSIS progresses, the range in glycoside concentration in juices of the same varieties grown in different regions, and the different rates of increase in glycoside concentration in fruit grown under different conditions. In the late 1990s, the assay was advocated as a valuable new tool to viticulturists wishing to investigate the influence of vine-growing practices on grape composition. As such it holds promise of an objective measure of fruit composition pertinent to wine quality. However, the assay is relatively complex and time consuming, requiring specialized skill. For this reason there has been little uptake by commercial wineries, and new methods utilizing INFRARED SPECTROSCOPY that offer rapid analysis of G-G in grapes are more popular.   P.J.W.& R.D.

Whiton, R. S., and Zoecklein, B. W., 'Evaluation of glycosyl-glucose analytical methods for various glycosides', *American Journal of Enology and Viticulture*, 53 (2002), 315–17.

Williams, P. J., and Francis, I. L., 'Wine flavour research—experiences from the past offer a guide to the future', in J. M. Rantz (ed.), *Proceedings of the American Society of Enology and Viticulture 50th Anniversary Annual Meeting, 19–23 June 2000* (Davis, 2001), 191–5.

GM and **GMO**. See GENETIC MODIFICATION.

GM 6494–5. See RONDO.

gneiss, a dense, tough, coarse-grained rock (pronounced 'nice') in which distinct bands have developed, distinguishing it from other metamorphic rocks. These irregular bands, typically of paler feldspar and quartz alternating with darker biotite or amphibole, range in thickness over a few millimetres to centimetres with an irregularity that distinguishes the appearance of gneiss from the layers seen in some sedimentary rocks (see GEOLOGY). It is resistant to weathering and usually yields thin, rather acid soils but it is surprisingly common in vineyards, for example, in AUSTRIA's Kamptal and Wachau regions, in MUSCADET, ROUSSILLON, and CÔTE RÔTIE in France, in parts of the US state of VIRGINIA, and in CANADA's Okanagan Valley. A.J.M.

gobelet, or **goblet**, a form of vine-TRAINING SYSTEM, used since Roman times, whereby the spurs are arranged on short arms in an approximate circle at the top of a short trunk, making the vine look something like a goblet drinking vessel. The vines are free standing (apart from a small supporting stake when young) and the system is best suited to low-VIGOUR vineyards in drier climates. This is a form of HEAD TRAINING and is generally subject to SPUR PRUNING. The trunk is short, typically 30 to 50 cm (12–19 in), and the foliage is unsupported by WIRES.

The gobelet is widespread in France, from Beaujolais southwards, although it is now less common than it was because it is generally more economical to train vines on trellis systems rather than have them free standing. The traditional spacing was 1.5 by 1.5 m (5 ft), but the distance has been increased to allow tractor access and the vineyards are typically cultivated in both directions. Sometimes the vines are

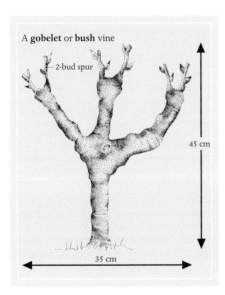

A **gobelet** or **bush** vine

2-bud spur

45 cm

35 cm

trained with several trunks. With low-vigour vineyards the foliage can be relatively erect, but shoots may trail on the ground in high-vigour vineyards, and there can be substantial SHADE. Grape yield and quality may suffer as a result. The system is used widely in many Mediterranean countries and is most suited to low-vigour vineyards. In Italy, the system is called *alberelli a vaso*, in Spain *en vaso*, and in Portugal *en taça*. In many New World countries such as Australia, South Africa, and California, the traditional and low-vigour gobelet-trained vineyards were often called bush vines; they have increasingly been replaced by vines with some form of trellising to accommodate the improved vigour of newer vineyards. R.E.S.

Galet, P., *Précis de viticulture* (7th edn, Montpellier, 2000).

goblets. See DRINKING VESSELS.

Godello, fine white grape variety native to north west Spain and northern Portugal rescued from near extinction in the 1980s and grown on more than 1,200 ha/2,964 acres of north west Spanish vineyard by 2011. As Godello it is responsible for well-structured, tense dry whites in VALDEORRAS, although DNA PROFILING suggested that it is identical to a Portuguese variety known as Verdelho do Dão in Dão and Gouveio in the Douro. Total plantings in Portugal were 675 ha in 2012, rather more than of the distinct GOUVEIO REAL.

Goldburger, bland Austrian gold-skinned cross of WELSCHRIESLING and Orangetraube. About 120 ha/300 acres of this vine remain, almost all of them in BURGENLAND, mainly used for sweet wines.

Goldkapsel, unregulated term of approbation referring to German Rieslings. Use of gold capsules to signify superior quality was a response, initially and still primarily in the MOSEL, to the 1971 GERMAN WINE LAW's prohibition on labels of traditional terms such as CABINET, feine, feinste, or hochfeinste. Because the band of permissible MUST WEIGHT for Auslese is especially broad and Auslesen are the products of selective picking, usually in very small volumes, there is ample room for gradations. Some growers even designated really fine examples **lange Goldkapsel** (long gold capsule) and the abbreviations GKA and LGKA became established. From the 1990s the designations spread to wines of all possible PRÄDIKATS including, at some estates, dry wines, the standards employed being entirely estate-specific. Wines referred to in this way on price lists sometimes lack a physical gold capsule, and in recent years some growers have snuck the tiny letters GKA or LGKA on to a label without the authorities finding grounds to object. D.S.

Goldmuskateller, German name for the golden-berried MOSCATO Giallo grape speciality in ALTO ADIGE.

gold rushes have played a significant role in the development of New World wine production through their influence both on demand for alcoholic beverages and also on LABOUR supply. In CALIFORNIA, commercial viticulture had emerged during the 1830s, and with the discovery of gold in 1848 there was a massive increase in demand for all types of alcohol in the gold-mining counties of Amador, Calaveras, El Dorado, Nevada, Placer, and Tuolumne. However, by the 1850s, once the first flush of gold fever was over, a number of the immigrants, seeking to profit from the rising price of wine, turned to grape-growing and winemaking as a more reliable source of income. By 1857 it is estimated that there were some 1.5 million vines in California, and only three years later, after the enactment of legislation in 1859 which exempted vineyards from taxation, this total had risen to some 6 million.

Viticulture had been introduced into AUSTRALIA on the establishment of the new colony in New South Wales in 1788. Its subsequent spread followed the increasing pace of colonization and settlement, with new vines being planted almost as soon as each new colony was founded. During the first half of the 19th century, however, despite the activities of proponents such as James BUSBY, winemaking remained a minority interest. The gold rush of 1851 changed this by attracting numerous immigrants to VICTORIA, with large numbers coming from France, Switzerland, Italy, and Germany, countries which had long traditions of viticulture and winemaking. Many, failing to make a success of prospecting, turned to farming, and in particular to viticulture, with the result that the pattern of vineyards in Victoria closely reflected the scattered distribution of the gold. In particular, during the 1870s and 1880s, the gold-mining areas of Ballarat, Bendigo, Great Western (now Grampians), and the Murray river all became important wine regions. P.T.H.U.

The Otago gold rush of the 1860s was responsible for the abandoned gold mines that are still a feature of wine country in this part of New Zealand.

Halliday, J., *The Australian Wine Compendium* (London, 1985).
Pinney, T., *A History of Wine in America: From the Beginnings to Prohibition* (Berkeley, Calif., 1989).

Gomera, La, rugged, mountainous CANARY Island with its own small DO and 120 ha/300 acres of terraced vines planted at elevations between 300 and 600 m.

González Byass, the largest producer of SHERRY, still run by the family that founded the house. In 1835, 23-year-old Manuel María

González Angel set up business as a shipper in JEREZ in southern Spain. Within months he had joined forces with D. Juan Dubosc to make their first large shipment to London: 48 hogsheads and a quarter cask, sent to Robert Blake Byass, who was to become their UK agent. In 1844, the company purchased its first vineyards, and in 1846 the first wines were bottled in Jerez. The FINO brand Tio Pepe was born by the mid-1800s, named after Manuel's uncle José Angel y Vargas (*tío* being Spanish for uncle), who helped his nephew establish the SOLERA. In 1855, Robert Blake Byass became a shareholder in the business, but it was not until 1870, when his sons and the sons of the founder entered the firm that it became González Byass & Co. The company remained in the hands of the two families until, in 1988, the González family financed the purchase of the 45% of shares held by the Byass family, later placing most of these with IDV, the British drinks subsidiary of the conglomerate Grand Metropolitan. The family bought the shares back from IDV in 1997, also the year in which Mauricio González Gordon, from the fourth generation of the family to work in the company, retired as chairman. His successors were Chon Gómez-Monche, another fourth-generation family member in the company and, from 2001, family friend Carlos Espinosa de los Monteros. In 2006, Mauricio González Gordon, fifth generation, became chairman.

By 2014 the company owned 1,372 ha/3,390 acres of vineyards throughout Spain, and controlled a further 1,893 ha owned by independent farmers. In the mid 1990s, the company began releasing expensive vintage-dated dry sherries, renewing a Jerez practice from the days before the solera system was adopted. The company also produces brandy, its most renowned brand being Lepanto.

In the early 1980s the González Byass began to expand and diversify, buying wineries Bodegas Beronia in Rioja, Cava producer Cavas Vilarnau, Viñas del Vero in Somontano, Finca Constancia in Castilla-La Mancha, and Finca Moncloa in Cádiz. In 2001, the company acquired the Spanish interests of CROFT.

González Gordon, M., *Sherry: The Noble Wine* (3rd edn, London, 1990).

Gorbachev, Mikhail (1931–), last President of the Soviet Union (1985–91) and significant in the history of wine because of his 1985–8 national campaign against alcohol abuse. Measures were energetically directed not just against vodka consumption but also against the production and importation of wine. The immediate domestic effect was that the total vineyard area in the Soviet Union (which until the fall of communism included such wine-producing republics as MOLDOVA, UKRAINE, the CRIMEA, UZBEKISTAN, RUSSIA, AZERBAIJAN, GEORGIA

and, producing very much less wine, ARMENIA, KYRGYZSTAN, TAJIKISTAN, KAZAKHSTAN, and TURKMENISTAN) fell by a third between 1980 and 1990 to the 1960 level of just over 1 million ha/ 2,471,000 acres. In 1990, the Soviet Union still accounted for 12% of the world's total area of vineyard and 5% of the wine produced. By 1996, according to OIV statistics, those same countries accounted for 11% of the world's vineyard but only 3% of the wine produced.

The effects of Gorbachev's anti-alcohol campaign were equally dramatic in countries from which the Soviet Union had been importing huge quantities of wine; see for example, BULGARIA, ROMANIA, HUNGARY, GEORGIA, and CYPRUS. These countries suddenly had to find new customers for an important proportion of their annual grape harvest—customers who would certainly be more demanding than their Soviet predecessors—or simply abandon vines and wine production to a significant degree.

Wine produced within the old Soviet Union, on the other hand, was viewed by some of the newly independent republics as a potential earner of hard currency, by others as useful barter. As individuals struggled for economic survival in the new free market economies, the markets were flooded with alcohol substitutes, cheap vodkas, brandies, and wines from central and western Europe. For more detail, see under the names of individual republics.

Gordo or **Gordo Blanco**, originally Spanish synonyms for MUSCAT OF ALEXANDRIA since adopted by Australia.

Gouais Blanc, genetically important, light-skinned grape variety commonly planted in central and north eastern France in the Middle Ages which produced rather ordinary, acid wine, while the more highly valued Pinots were planted on more favoured sites. DNA PROFILING has shown that Gouais Blanc and Pinot had a great number of important progeny in Northern France (see PINOT). Following that discovery, researchers became more interested in this ancient variety and realized that, besides its numerous synonyms in France, Gouais Blanc is also identical to Belina Drobna and Heunisch Weiss or Weisser Heunisch in Eastern Europe, and to Liseiret and Preveiral in Italy. Moreover, dozens of additional possible parent–offspring relationships have been suggested between Gouais Blanc and French or European varieties, including RIESLING, BLAUFRÄNKISCH, and FURMINT. Gouais Blanc has been called a 'key variety' for grape diversity in Europe by some researchers, and some others have even nicknamed it the 'Casanova of grapes'. Varietal Gouais Blanc is produced by Josef-Marie Chanton of Visp in Switzerland's Valais under the name Gwäss and some is also

grown in Australia where is has been known as Best's No 4.   J.V.

Goulburn Valley, long-established temperate wine region with 24 producers in all in Australia's Central VICTORIA Zone). Nagambie Lakes is a subregion with Tahbilk and Mitchelton its leading wineries.

goût, French noun for TASTE in all its senses. Some wines, particularly old CHAMPAGNES, are described as suiting the **goût anglais**, or English taste (supposedly for wine necrophilia). Sweet champagne was described as to the **goût russe** in the days of the imperial court. (The late-19th-century Champenois defined champagne sweetened to satisfy the *goût russe* as one with 273 to 330 g/l of RESIDUAL SUGAR, as opposed to the *goût anglais* of 22 to 66 g/l.)

A wine made from fruit adversely affected by HAIL, for example, might be described in French as having a **goût de grêle**. Another much discussed and loosely applied TASTING TERM is **goût de terroir**, sometimes used about those aspects of flavour deemed to derive from the TERROIR rather than the grape variety but sometimes erroneously used synonymously and pejoratively with the term 'earthy'.

Gouveio Real, minor pale-skinned vine variety of which 587 ha/1,449 acres remained in northern Portugal in 2012, mainly in the Douro where it makes full-bodied whites. It is distinct from **Gouveio**, a Portuguese synonym for the GODELLO of north west Spain.

governo, also known as *governo alla toscana*, since it is most closely associated with TUSCANY, is a winemaking technique once widely used in the various CHIANTI production zones, and occasionally in UMBRIA and the MARCHE. The technique consisted of setting aside and drying grapes from the September and October harvest, pressing them in mid to late November, and introducing the resulting unfermented grape juice into young wines which had just completed their alcoholic FERMENTATION, thereby restarting the fermentation. This practice led to a slight increase in the ALCOHOLIC STRENGTH of the wines, but its principal and most desirable effect was to encourage the MALOLACTIC CONVERSION, which was not always easy in the cold cellars of the past, with wines made from a grape as high in ACIDITY as SANGIOVESE. A side-effect was to increase the level of CARBON DIOXIDE in the wine, some of which inevitably remained in young Chianti, bottled and marketed in the spring after the harvest. One of the precise purposes of the *governo* was to make the wines marketable at an earlier date by accelerating the malolactic conversion. Occasionally a second addition (*rigoverno*) is made in spring, producing a deeply coloured, fragrant wine with low acidity.

Today *governo* is much less widely used as producers have striven to transform Chianti's image from quaffing wine to a serious candidate for BOTTLE AGEING. The technique was also used in the VERDICCHIO production zone in the Marche, to add fizz and a slight sweetness—from the high sugar content of the dried grapes—to counteract Verdicchio's occasionally bitter finish. It has virtually disappeared here now.

GPS. See GLOBAL POSITIONING SYSTEM.

Graciano, sometimes called **Graciana**, is a richly perfumed black grape variety once widely grown in Rioja in northern Spain. It had fallen from favour because of its inconveniently low yields, thereby depriving modern Rioja of an important flavour ingredient with considerable freshness, but by 2011 plantings had grown to almost 2,000 ha/5,000 acres, from which some increasingly interesting VARIETAL bottlings are made in Rioja and Navarra, and there were experimental plantings as far afield as Toledo. This is Portugal's TINTA MIÚDA, France's Morrastel, and it has also been certified through DNA PROFILING that the Tintilla de Rota grape of Jerez and BOVALE SARDO on Sardinia are both Graciano. The Parraleta of Somontano is also Graciano.

The vine buds very late and is prone to DOWNY MILDEW but can produce wine of great character and extract, albeit notably acidic in youth. As Morrastel, it was popular in Languedoc-Roussillon until the middle of the 19th century, when Henri BOUSCHET stepped in to provide growers with a more productive, more disease-resistant, but wildly inferior cross of Morrastel with Petit Bouschet, **Morrastel-Bouschet** which in time replaced virtually all of the original Morrastel in French vineyards. True Morrastel, or Graciano, is still grown in southern France in minute quantities and Languedoc's viticultural archivists have recently shown interest in it.

The variety known as Xeres in California, which has also been planted on a similarly limited scale in Australia, is probably Graciano, as is Graciana, the variety of which there are small plantings in Mendoza, Argentina.

Robinson, J., Harding, J., and Vouillamoz, J., *Wine Grapes, a complete guide to 1,368 vine varieties, including their origins and flavours* (London, 2012).

Graciosa, DOP on the Azorean island of the same name making small quantities of dry white wine.

grafted vine, a vine consisting of a SCION grafted to a ROOTSTOCK, typically produced by a grapevine NURSERY or a viticulturist. The vines may be sold by the nursery as a growing plant soon after GRAFTING, with limited root and shoot growth and ready for planting in early summer, or as a dormant vine. The latter are grown on in a field nursery after grafting for around six months, are then removed, trimmed of shoots and roots, and prepared for despatch for planting the following spring.

Most countries in the world have PHYLLOXERA infestation, and therefore grafted vines are common. Countries such as Chile, where phylloxera is not present, or Australia, where phylloxera is contained by QUARANTINE, may use UNGRAFTED vines, which are not resistant to phylloxera but grow satisfactorily in many situations and are cheaper.   R.E.S.

grafting, the connection of two pieces of living plant tissue so that they unite and grow as one plant, has been a particularly important element in growing vines since the end of the 19th century, when it was discovered that grafting on to resistant ROOTSTOCKS was the only effective weapon against the PHYLLOXERA louse.

History

The grafting of vines as a means of PROPAGATION was well known in Ancient ROME, and it is referred to as early as the 2nd century BC by CATO in his treatise *De agri cultura*. Knowledge of grafting survived through the medieval period, but it was in the 19th century that it came into particular prominence as the only method of satisfactorily ensuring the continued production of wine in the face of the threat posed by phylloxera. European varieties of VINIFERA had little resistance to phylloxera. It was only through the grafting of *V. vinifera* cuttings on to American species of *Vitis*, which had some phylloxera resistance, that traditional European grape varieties could continue to be cultivated, and thus wine with the commercially acceptable taste thereof could still be made. Early experiments to counter phylloxera had generally centred on chemical treatments or flooding, but during the 1870s, those, such as Laliman, who had been advocating the use of AMERICAN VINE SPECIES as rootstocks gained increasing support. Eventually, at the 1881 International Phylloxera Congress in Bordeaux, it became generally accepted that grafting of French scions on to American rootstock was the best solution, and this led to much experimentation to identify the best rootstocks for particular soil types. On a regional scale, however, widespread adoption of grafting awaited the efforts of people such as Gustave Foëx, director of the agricultural school at MONTPELLIER, who in 1882 produced a small booklet recommending the use of American vines, written in a clear style specifically designed for the small wine producers of the Languedoc. Traditionally grafting was done by hand, either in the field (FIELD BUDDING) or indoors (BENCH GRAFTING), using such techniques as the whip and tongue method. Today, however, most grafting in Europe is done by machines which join together scion and rootstock, usually in an omega-shaped cut. In California and to a lesser extent South Africa, field grafting is still common.   P.T.H.U. & R.E.S.

Foëx, G., *Instruction sur l'emploi des vignes américaines à la reconstruction du vignoble de l'Hérault* (Montpellier, 1882).

Gale, G., *Dying on the Vine: How Phylloxera Transformed Wine* (Berkeley, Calif., 2011).

Laliman, L., *Études sur les divers travaux phylloxériques et les vignes américaines* (Paris, 1879).

Ordish, G., *The Great Wine Blight* (London, 1972).

Paul, H. W., *Science, Vine and Wine in Modern France* (Cambridge, 1996).

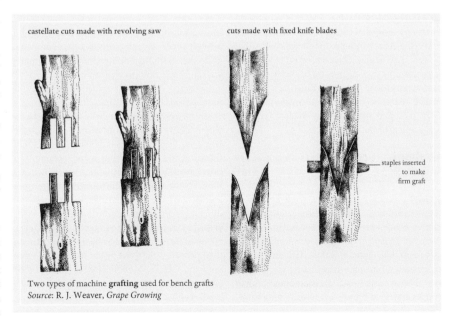

castellate cuts made with revolving saw   cuts made with fixed knife blades

staples inserted to make firm graft

Two types of machine **grafting** used for bench grafts
Source: R. J. Weaver, *Grape Growing*

Modern viticultural practices

Vines are grafted or budded to take advantage of the desirable properties of the rootstock variety. Foremost is resistance or tolerance to soil-borne pests and diseases, especially phylloxera and NEMATODES. Other properties are tolerance to soil SALINITY, to high LIME levels, to soil water-logging or DROUGHT, and an ability to modify VIGOUR or to hasten or delay RIPENING. If conducted in the vineyard, as FIELD BUDDING AND GRAFTING, the practice offers a method of changing a VINE VARIETY. If conducted indoors, before planting, it is called BENCH GRAFTING, which may in warm climates be complemented by NURSERY grafting.

The uniting of the SCION with the rootstock is achieved by a slow growth process: a mass of undifferentiated cells, the CALLUS, develops at each cut edge of the respective CAMBIUMS (zones of dividing cells), so it is important to position the two cambiums opposite each other and close together. Thereafter, the scion piece is part of the whole plant vascular system.

A number of factors determine success or failure in grafting, in addition to the skill involved in cutting and matching of cambiums. The first is that the graft needs specific environmental conditions such as warm temperatures (24–30 °C/75–86 °F) and high humidities (90–100%) around the union. The second is the compatibility of the scion/stock combination. The third, and probably the most serious, is that some rootstocks are difficult to root (see ROOTLING), which can affect the overall success of grafting. It has been shown that grafting success is reduced if the scion or rootstock is infected by the fungus *Botryosphaeria* (see TRUNK DISEASES).

Particular forms of graft include CLEFT GRAFTING, NOTCH GRAFTING, WHIP GRAFT. See also GRAFTED vine and GREEN GRAFTING.   B.G.C. & R.E.S.

grafting machine, a device used in GRAFTING by making cuts through the vine rootstock and scion pieces with mirror-image shapes that permit snug fitting. Shapes used include castellate and omega. Grafting machines are an essential part of the factory-like methods used for BENCH GRAFTING, but innovative growers have used modified machines for NURSERY grafting and FIELD BUDDING AND GRAFTING.   B.G.C.

Graham, important port shipper. See SYMINGTONS.

grain is visible on the end of a barrel STAVE at the bevelled edge, which is also known as the chime. Since staves are split along the radial plane, it can be seen across the width of the stave end. Each light and then dark alternation represents a one-year growth ring for the oak tree. The average width of each annual growth ring is called the grain by coopers and barrel users.

Every year, the tree forms a new growth ring in the cambium layer under the bark. Seen under a microscope, a ring can be broken down as a succession of spring wood (or early wood) and summer wood (late wood). Vessels in spring wood are more numerous and wider than in summer wood. Summer wood therefore has a higher density of fibres and parenchyma and fewer vessels.

Grain can be measured in two ways: either by the number of growth rings per centimetre (per inch) or by the average width of these rings. Grain is generally considered tight if there are 4 to 5 rings per cm or if the rings are narrower than 2 to 3 mm.

Many factors affect grain size. In addition to the work of the forester, who selects and raises the trees in each plot year after year, thereby regulating tree growth and therefore grain, different soil and climate conditions in oak forests produce different types of grain. Trees growing in dry areas, with a high population density and on poor soil, tend to have tight grains. But grain also varies through the life of the same tree. The older the tree, the more slowly its diameter grows and the tighter its grain. Similarly, the grain at the foot of a tree will be wider than at the top.

It is acknowledged that grain is wider for *Quercus robur* and therefore tighter for *Quercus petraea* (see OAK). This is due to the effect of differences in the ecological behaviour of each species. In general, *Quercus robur* requires more water and light, and hence exhibits faster growth and wider grains where it tends to be grown. *Quercus petraea*, which better withstands dry soils and a lack of light, tends to be located on the top of hills. But these species frequently co-exist in the same forest plots, in which case individuals of either species will rarely show significant differences in grain size. These species are sold together by forest managers. Sorting by grain, coopers tend to find a larger percentage of *Quercus robur* with wide grain than with tight grain although this empirical approach is in no way systematic.

Contrary to popular belief, tight grain is more porous than wide grain. Indeed, a slowing down in oak growth primarily affects summer wood, and the proportion of early wood in the ring (the large vessels) is greater. Tight grain therefore has more spring wood per cm and thus has more void than wide grain, which has more summer wood and therefore more fibre and parenchyma. This explains why there are differences in wines aged in barrels with wide grain compared with those aged in tight grain. However, it is important to distinguish between total porosity (the void in the wood) and open porosity, which is connected to the exterior environment and allows OXYGEN exchange. Studies show that open porosity varies significantly with no direct relationship to grain.

Barrel permeability is therefore more complex and less influenced by grain than by other anatomical factors of wood, particularly the number of tyloses, which block the vessels (see OAK).

Comparisons of barrels made from tight-grain versus wide-grain French oak showed that tight grain released more aromatic compounds (e.g. eugenol, whisky lactones) over time than wide grain, and wide grain released more wood TANNINS (ellagitannins). It was also observed that the release of various compounds from the wood was different from one grain type to another. Since porosity is higher for tight grain, it is easier for the wood to interact with wine, which releases the most accessible compounds in the wood more quickly.

See also WOOD INFLUENCE.

Pracomtal, G. de, et al., 'Types of oak grain, wine élevage in barrel', *Practical Winery & Vineyard* (Jul 2014), 64–9.   R.T. du C.

Graisse, also known as Plant de Graisse, minor white grape variety grown in the Armagnac region.

Grampians, temperate Australian wine region formerly known as Great Western in the Western Victoria Zone (see VICTORIA). Great Western is now a subregion of Grampians. Top-class Shiraz is produced here and senior wineries among the total of 19 are Bests and Seppelt, both established in the 1860s.

Granaccia, Sardinian synonym for VERNACCIA DI ORISTANO.

Granada, Vinos de. The Andalusian province of Granada between the high Sierra Nevada mountain range and the Mediterranean has an old viticultural tradition, 5,500 ha/13,585 acres, and just 20 wineries in 2012. Average vineyard ELEVATION of the DOP Vinos de Granada is above 1,000 m, including continental Europe's highest vineyard at 1,368 m. The elevation and humidity provide a much cooler growing environment than the latitude would suggest.   V. de la S.

Gran Canaria, CANARY Island with its own DO and 224 ha/553 acres of trellised vines planted up to 1,300 m.

grand cru means literally 'great growth' in French. In Burgundy's CÔTE D'OR a grand cru is one of 34 particularly favoured vineyards (see BURGUNDY for list), a decided notch above PREMIER CRU. In CHABLIS and ALSACE, grand cru is a separate, elevated AOC accorded to specific vineyards listed in the relevant entries. In Bordeaux, the words grand cru usually apply to a specific property or château and depend on the region in which it is located (see CLASSIFICATION). See also QUARTS DE CHAUME.

Grande Rue, La, red burgundy GRAND CRU vineyard in VOSNE-ROMANÉE.

grandes marques, obsolete, self-imposed term for some of the major houses or BRANDS of CHAMPAGNE. The original Syndicat des Grandes Marques was founded in 1882 but was disbanded in 1997. The term means literally 'big brand' in French and is still used informally.

grand format, BOTTLE SIZE larger than the standard 75 cl size and of particular interest to collectors and investors (provided it is filled with FINE WINE).

Grand Noir de la Calmette hardly deserves a name that suggests it is the great black grape variety of the BOUSCHET experimental vine-breeding station, Domaine de la Calmette. Bred from Petit Bouschet and the common ARAMON, it has a very high yield and, from its TEINTURIER parent, red flesh (although not as red as Alicante Bouschet's). Often known simply as **Grand Noir**, it was widely planted in France until the 1920s and is now almost extinct there. See also GRAN NEGRO.

Grand Roussillon, little-used VIN DOUX NATUREL appellation in ROUSSILLON used effectively for declassified RIVESALTES. It may be any of the three colours and also comes in RANCIO form.

Grands Échezeaux, red GRAND CRU in Burgundy's CÔTE D'OR. For more details, see ÉCHEZEAUX.

grand vin, name current in BORDEAUX for the main wine produced by a CHÂTEAU (as opposed to a SECOND WINE or *second vin*).

granite, a coarse-grained, pale-coloured igneous rock of plutonic origin (see GEOLOGY). Feldspars are the dominant constituent, with lesser amounts of quartz together with minerals such as mica and amphibole. The feldspars are rich in POTASSIUM, the chief mineral nutrient for vines and an indirect influence on wine flavour, although typically only a small proportion is actually available to the vine. Granitic soils tend to have low fertility, and because the quartz grains resist weathering, such soils are sandy and well-drained. They are widespread and are favoured for viticulture although they tend to be acid. Examples include DÃO and parts of SARDINIA, the northern RHÔNE, BEAUJOLAIS, as well as the Granite Belt of QUEENSLAND and parts of South Africa's Western Cape, coastal CHILE, and California's Sierra Foothills east of the CENTRAL VALLEY.   M.J.E. & A.J.M.

Granite Belt, the first established wine region in the extreme south of QUEENSLAND, Australia, cooled by its high ELEVATION. Of the 46 producers, Golden Grove Estate, Symphony Hill, Sirromet, Robert Channon, and the tiny Boireann can produce wines of international quality.

Granja-Amareleja, subregion of ALENTEJO adjacent to the Spanish border in one of the most arid parts of southern Portugal.

Gran Negro or **Grão Negro**, local name for GRAND NOIR DE LA CALMETTE in Galicia, in particularly Valdeorras, where there were still 568 ha/1,402 acres in 2011. It was introduced here after the PHYLLOXERA invasion. As **Grão Negro** it is also grown in southern Portugal.

Gran Reserva, Spanish term for a wine supposedly from an outstanding VINTAGE which has been subject to lengthy AGEING, the exact period varying from DO to DO, before release. Rioja produces the great majority of all Gran Reservas and here red wines must spend a minimum of two years in BARRELS of approximately 225 l. The wine may not leave the BODEGA until the sixth year after the vintage. White and rosé wines must spend a total of at least four years in cask and bottle, including at least six months AGEING in barrel, to qualify. For much of the 20th century, Gran Reservas represented Spain's finest and most expensive wines, but many of the country's most celebrated winemakers are nowadays concerned to preserve more FRUIT in their top bottlings and do not necessarily equate quality with time spent in wood.

See also RESERVA.

Gran Selezione, controversial category of supposedly superior CHIANTI CLASSICO DOCG introduced in 2014.

granvas, Spanish term for sparkling wine made by the tank or Charmat SPARKLING WINE-MAKING method.

grape, the berry or fruit of the grapevine, or VINE, whose juice is the essential ingredient for making WINE. A grape is *raisin* in French, *uva* in Italian and Spanish, and *Rebe* in German. The grapes produced by commercial viticulture are sold either as TABLE GRAPES or DRYING GRAPES, or crushed and processed into wine or GRAPE JUICE, GRAPE CONCENTRATE, or RECTIFIED GRAPE MUST. Wine production is, however, the most important use, accounting for some 80% of the world's grape production. The solids, including stems, skins, seeds, and pulp, left after these juicing processes are called grape POMACE. There are several hundred grapes to a BUNCH for wine grape varieties, and berries are individually relatively small.

The form and appearance of grape berries varies hugely between VINE VARIETIES. Their shape varies from flattened, through spherical and oval, to elongated and finger-like; colour from green to yellow, pink, crimson, dark blue, and black; and size from as small as a pea (as in CURRANT, for example) to the huge, egg-like berries of some recently bred table grape varieties which may weigh as much as 15 g/0.5 oz each. The majority of wine grapes, however, are spherical to short oval, 1–2 g in weight, and are coloured yellow (called 'white' by vine-growers) or very dark purple (called 'black' or 'red').

Grape berries are borne on the end of a stalk, the PEDICEL, which in turn is borne on the BUNCHSTEM, or peduncle. At the end opposite the pedicel is a small stub of dead tissue which is the remnant of the style and stigma (see FLOWER). Some varieties, for example Riesling, have corky lenticels scattered over the skin. When cut open (see diagram below), the grape is seen to have two units (carpels) side by side, each enclosing a space (a locule) in which are the seeds. When the berry enlarges, the space becomes compressed by encroaching flesh. The significant parts of a berry are the flesh, skin, and seeds.

Flesh or pulp

The flesh or pulp (*pulpe* in French) is the bulk of the berry or PERICARP. The pulp contains the juice in the VACUOLES of pericarp cells. A section across the flesh (see overleaf) shows that there are about 40 large parenchyma cells from beneath the skin to the single cell layer that is the inner lining. A central core of vascular strands connects to a mesh of veins that encircles the outer edge of the flesh like a chicken-wire cage and provides the vascular connection with the rest of the vine; the veins contain the XYLEM, which transports water and minerals from roots, and PHLOEM, which is the all-important pathway for sugar from the leaves. Another zone with a different texture is the so-called BRUSH, which is the lighter-coloured part of the flesh near the junction with the pedicel.

The pulp and the juice are the most important part of the grape to the winemaker, and the wine drinker, for they contain the main components of the finished wine. Because the juice of all grapes (apart from the specialist TEINTURIER varieties) is a pale grey, whatever the colour of the grape's skin, white wine can be made from grapes of all colours, so long as the juice is not left in contact with dark skins. Red wines can be made only by leaching colour from such skins, while pink wines can be made either from short contact with dark skins or more prolonged contact with pink or red skins.

Skin

The grape's skin (*pellicule* in French) is the tough, enveloping layer around the grape that holds it together. The outside layer, or bloom, consists of wax plates and cutin, both of which resist water diffusion and hence water loss from the berry. They also impede penetration of fungal spore growths and other biological infections. This waxy layer forms the grape's

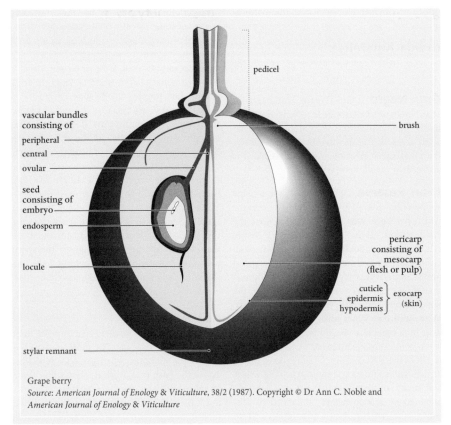

Grape berry

Source: American Journal of Enology & Viticulture, 38/2 (1987). Copyright © Dr Ann C. Noble and American Journal of Enology & Viticulture

g

See also GRAPE COMPOSITION AND WINE QUALITY, GRAPE QUALITY ASSESSMENT, and RIPENING. (For other parts of the vine plant, see VINE MORPHOLOGY.)   B.G.C. & A.D.W.

Coombe, B. G., 'Research on development and ripening of the grape berry', *American Journal of Enology & Viticulture*, 43 (1992), 101–10.

grape composition and wine quality.

Grape composition is the essential basis of wine quality, and knowledge of grape composition is critical for those winemakers interested in making the appropriate wine style. The concentrations of all component chemical groups play a part. Grape SUGARS, for example (see MUST WEIGHT), determine the possible potential ALCOHOLIC STRENGTH of the wine. ACIDS and nitrogenous compounds (see NITROGEN) affect the course of FERMENTATION and exert their own effects on flavour. POTASSIUM salts have effects on PH and thus on microbiological activity and oxidative STABILITY. PHENOLICS contribute to levels of COLOUR and TANNINS. A multitude of volatile compounds alter aroma (see ACIDITY, AMINO ACIDS, FLAVOUR COMPOUNDS, SUGARS).

Grape composition is constantly changing during RIPENING. A central factor in grape ripening is the steady increase in sugar concentration after sugar accumulation has been triggered at VERAISON. Another feature is that acidity declines, due mainly to the RESPIRATION of malate but also to dilution by berry growth and the formation of salts, especially with potassium, which increases concurrently with sugar. Colour and tannins increase in skins early during ripening. Less is known about the timing of the increase in aroma compounds because until recently they have been difficult to measure, but in some varieties intensity appears to develop late in the ripening process, after sugar concentration has levelled (see GRAPE QUALITY ASSESSMENT). Monitoring the GLYCOSIDE concentration in ripening grape berries is possible using the GLYCOSYL-GLUCOSE ASSAY, which measures the increase in these components, including the important FLAVOUR PRECURSORS of the fruit. More recent developments in INFRARED SPECTROSCOPY have made possible quicker analysis of these precursors as well as a wide range of components in both grapes and wine. Quality epitomizes the integration of these chemical groups in such a way that there is a balance between individual components, coupled with an intensity of VARIETAL character.

In recent years, well-funded producers such as E. & J. GALLO have determined fruit quality based on a range of measurements of grape composition, which are tracked over time during ripening, and which contribute both positive and negative quality attributes to wine. The score relates to VINTAGE and regional effects on wine as well as to winemakers' assessment of MOUTHFEEL, and variability within individual

typically whitish surface, called the BLOOM. The fatty acids and sterols from the bloom supply important nutrients for the growth of YEAST, either added or ambient yeast in the atmosphere, during FERMENTATION.

Below the wax and cutin are the cell layers that form the skin; the first is the true epidermis, below this are about seven cell layers forming the hypodermis in which are concentrated most of the berry PIGMENTS, yellow CAROTENOIDS, and xanthophylls, and the red and blue ANTHOCYANINS important in the making of red wine. As well as some TANNINS, a significant amount of a grape's FLAVOUR COMPOUNDS are also associated with the skin layers. There may well be differences in the precise locations of the PHENOLICS (pigments, tannins, and flavour compounds). Those compounds located closest to the pulp are presumably extracted first.

There are other differences in the chemical composition of skin compared with the underlying flesh: besides phenolics, they are rich in POTASSIUM. Skins constitute between 5 and 12% by weight of a mature grape berry, depending on the vine variety. The thickness of grape skin can vary from about 3 to 8 µm.

Seeds

Seeds, *pepins* in French, of grapes vary in size and shape between varieties; for example, those in MUSCAT BLANC À PETITS GRAINS are about 5 mm long while those in the table grape Waltham

Cross are nearly 10 mm. Their number per berry tends to be a characteristic for each variety with one or two predominating. Four is possible since each carpel bears two ovules; however, some freak Alphonse Lavallée (Ribier) berries with double the number of carpels may have eight seeds. Often, incompletely developed seed structures occur, called stenospermic (thin-seeded), alongside fully developed seeds. The greater the number and amount of seed development, the larger the berry; this relationship is largely a reflection of differences in amount of cell division in the pericarp. The plant hormone GIBBERELLIN may substitute for the berry-enlarging effect of seeds, as it is when Sultana is grown for the table, for example.

Seeds are only of minor importance in winemaking although if they are crushed, as those who eat seeded grapes know, the bitter tannins they contain are released. Unlike the stems, which are relatively easy to separate from the berries, seeds always accompany the juice and skins into the draining tanks or press for white wines, or into the fermentation vessel for red wines. In WHITE WINEMAKING, the contact time between juice and seeds and absorption of tannins from the seeds is minimal. In RED WINEMAKING, on the other hand, the prolonged contact between the seeds and an increasingly alcoholic solution means that tannins are very likely to be dissolved. Grape seeds have served as a source of edible or industrial oil.

vineyards (see SAMPLING and PRECISION VITICULTURE).   B.G.C., R.D., & R.E.S.

Boss, P. K., 'Towards the prediction [sic] wine outcomes from grape compositional measures', *Proceedings of the ASVO Workshop on Assessing Grape Quality* (Mildura, 2011).

Cleary, M. T., et al., 'A perspective on grape chemical quality assessment to support streaming and harvest decisions', *Proceedings of the ASVO Workshop on Assessing Grape Quality* (Mildura, 2011).

grape concentrate is what is left when the volatile elements are removed from fresh grape juice. Rarely used to produce really fine wine, it can provide a useful supply of grape SOLUBLE SOLIDS for use long after the HARVEST. Grape concentrate is the main ingredient, for example, in so-called MADE WINES produced without the benefit of freshly picked grapes (see BRITISH WINES and HOME WINEMAKING). Grape concentrate can also be used in BLENDING to soften and sweeten dry wines of everyday commercial standard made in cooler regions. It is widely used in Germany, for example, where it is called *Süssreserve*. For more details of grape concentrate used for sweetening purposes, see SWEET RESERVE. Grape concentrate is also in some circumstances used for ENRICHMENT, increasing the eventual alcohol content of a wine (it is a permitted prefermentation additive in Australia, for instance, although sugar is not). It is also used to sweeten some other fruit juices and foodstuffs, and is sometimes used as an alternative to honey. Concentrate is also used to produce a small category of high-intensity red and purple colourants, used to enhance colour and add body to wines.

Historically, winemakers made a form of grape concentrate by simply boiling grape juice until the volume was reduced by at least one-half. This resulted in a liquid with a strong cooked, caramel flavour, however, and such an additive is used exclusively for sweet, dark, strong wines such as rich SHERRY, MÁLAGA, and MARSALA. In Spain it is known as *arrope*.

Today, the caramelizing effect is avoided by CONCENTRATION of the grape juice under very low temperatures in vacuum evaporators. Modern low pressure concentrators represent a heavy investment for a winery selling anything other than the most expensive wine. They therefore tend to be operated by specialists who may use them to concentrate other fruit juices at other times of year. Most grape juice is subject to CLARIFICATION and is reduced in TARTRATES before concentration so that the solids precipitated are minimal when water is removed. See also RECTIFIED GRAPE MUST.

Red grape concentrate may be made by first heating the grapes to extract PIGMENTS into the juice before concentration.   A.D.W.

grape juice is a sweet, clear, non-alcoholic liquid. Winemakers generally use the term to refer to MUST that has undergone CLARIFICATION and STABILIZATION. Preserved by holding at temperatures so low that any YEAST or BACTERIA are inhibited, such juice was often used in commercial winemaking to soften or sweeten new, dry wines. Since the development of efficient juice concentrators, however, it has generally been supplanted in winemaking by GRAPE CONCENTRATE, which can be stored much more cheaply, is inherently stable against microbiological attack, and dilutes the wine much less.

A certain amount of grape juice is bottled and sold as a drink, however, although grape juice is a minor beverage compared with juices of other fruits such as citrus and apple. Since it so readily ferments, it needs to be protected from yeast contamination. This is usually done by PASTEURIZATION and/or ULTRAFILTRATION and heavy additions of SULFUR DIOXIDE. Many VINIFERA varieties lose their pleasant, fresh taste after pasteurization, and the American grape juice industry uses the non-*V. vinifera* CONCORD variety. The juice from grapes harvested at optimum ripeness for wine has a rather cloying sweetness which can overshadow the refreshing ACIDITY. Interestingly, it is very difficult to distinguish VARIETAL character in most grape juices, other than such conspicuous flavours as those associated with MUSCAT and Concord grapes. Wine drinkers generally find grape juice bears disappointingly little relation to wine.   A.D.W.

grape juice composition. The relative proportions of the compounds that make up grape juice are constantly changing as the berries ripen, so the time of HARVEST greatly affects composition. Most of the sugary solution that results when grapes are squeezed or crushed derives from the contents of the VACUOLES of the cells of the pulp or flesh, although heavy crushing and pressing adds further solution from vacuoles of the skin and vascular strands, thereby mixing many different compounds into the must. Thus the composition of the juice that issues when berries are crushed changes with the pressure and time of crushing; the first, FREE-RUN juice has fewest suspended solids and skin extracts; further pressing yields juice with more PHENOLICS and POTASSIUM salts, and hence lower TOTAL ACIDITY.

Fermentation of juice with skins present, as in red winemaking, yields still more FLAVOUR COMPOUNDS and PIGMENTS that are enriched in the cells of the skin. See GRAPE.

See also ACIDITY, AMINO ACIDS, ANTHOCYANINS, ASCORBIC ACID, CAROTENOIDS, CITRIC ACID, FRUCTOSE, GLUCOSE, GLYCOSIDES, LIPIDS, MALIC ACID, MINERALS, PECTINS, PROTEINS, SOLUBLE SOLIDS, STARCH, SUCROSE, TANNINS, TERPENOIDS, VARIETAL character, VITAMINS, and the all-important SUGAR IN GRAPES.   B.G.C.

grape quality assessment is needed by winemakers for long-term strategic planning and, in the short term, for the planning of each vintage, especially in fixing HARVEST dates. Assessment is often a matter of combined judgement by grape-growers and winemakers, using experience of the performance of previous vintages as the main guide, supplemented by tasting of berries and by measurements of GRAPE COMPOSITION (see SAMPLING and ANALYSIS). In some regions, sugar content (see MUST WEIGHT) is sufficient to indicate forthcoming wine quality, especially in cool regions (unless, of course, major catastrophes such as disease intervene). In warm to hot regions, sugar alone is an unreliable guide to quality and additional measurements are needed: TOTAL ACIDITY and PH of the juice are useful, as well as some measure of the colour of skins in some red grapes. The importance of aroma is increasingly recognized, but it is difficult to measure. Valuable information can be obtained by collecting and storing juice samples at intervals during grape development and running comparative 'sniffing tests', but these are costly and difficult because of their subjective nature. An experimental technique, GLYCOSYL-GLUCOSE ASSAY, was developed in the mid 1990s to supplement these methods. This gives a measure of the total GLYCOSIDE concentration in grapes, which include FLAVOUR PRECURSORS of some varietal FLAVOUR COMPOUNDS. A more recent development in grape quality assessment is the use of near INFRARED SPECTROSCOPY to measure rapidly many different grape constituents, including red grape colour, expressed as the concentration of total ANTHOCYANINS.

Many other characteristics of the harvest contribute to the assessment of its quality. Foremost is the amount and type of berry ROT which has been quantified in wineries in many countries. Other factors are the presence of broken skins due to heavy RAINFALL, HAIL, or physical damage. The extent of berry shrivel, evenness of ripening, contamination with leaves, clods, and other non-grape material, and BERRY SIZE are other important factors. Careful vine-growers will also take account of the appearance of the vineyard, the state of the CANOPY, condition of the leaves, and the general vineyard management.

See also ACIDITY, ANTHOCYANINS, FLAVOUR COMPOUNDS, GRAPE COMPOSITION AND WINE QUALITY, PHENOLICS, SUGARS.   B.G.C. & R.D.

grape sorting. See TRIAGE.

grape varieties. This term is often used interchangeably with vine varieties since different varieties of vine have predictably different grapes or berries. The effect of grape varieties on wine quality is discussed under VINE VARIETIES. Different varieties of vine produce grapes with very different and distinct characteristics (many of them outlined here under the names of individual varieties). Wines made predominantly from a single grape variety, usually specified on the label, are called VARIETAL wines.

See under the names of individual varieties. Specialized varieties are listed for both TABLE GRAPES and DRYING GRAPES.

grapevine, an alternative name for the plant on which most of the world's wine trade depends. It is known by most wine producers and consumers as the VINE, although botanically there are many other plant species which are vines.

grapevine yellows, generic term for a group of related PHYTOPLASMA diseases of grapevines which pose a serious threat to vineyards in many wine regions of the world because there is no known control. The best-known of these diseases, FLAVESCENCE DORÉE, can kill young vines and makes old vines uneconomical. It is spread by infected plants from the nursery and further spread by insects called LEAFHOPPERS, to which many common vineyard WEEDS are alternative host plants. The disease occurs sporadically in epidemics, and varieties vary in their sensitivity to it.

Flavescence dorée, the first recorded phytoplasma grapevine disease, appeared in the Armagnac region in south-west France on the vine variety BACO 22A in 1949. It spread rapidly throughout France towards the end of the 20th century. In 1982, only isolated vineyards in Armagnac were affected by flavescence dorée, as well as a very restricted area in the Languedoc. By 1987, this disease had spread to Cognac, throughout Languedoc and to the northern and southern Rhône, and by 1992 to the Loire Valley, Bordeaux, and the Côtes du Rhône, and by 2014 it was threatening the Côte d'Or from the Mâconnais. Several variants have also been noted, including bois noir in northeastern France, Bordeaux, and Switzerland, known as Vergilbungskrankeit in Germany, leaf curl and berry shrivel in New York state, and a form known as Australian grapevine yellows. A similar disease has been described in Romania, Israel, Chile, and Italy, and more recently in Slovenia, Croatia, Hungary, and Spain. That these diseases are more or less related has been shown by a form of DNA PROFILING called polymerase chain reaction. These diseases are related to phytoplasma diseases which attack many other crops and native plants such as, for example, some which affect pawpaw and tomato in Australia.

The first sign of grapevine yellows can be delayed BUDBREAK and very slow shoot growth until FLOWERING. Later, shoots on infected vines stop growing while leaves yellow and curl downwards. Later in the season, shoots droop as though made of rubber. When affected early in the season, bunches fall off. Otherwise, the berries shrivel and taste bitter. The disease can kill young vines, and old vines do not recover completely from infection. Symptoms seem to vary from year to year, and crop levels fluctuate. During epidemics, as for example in the PROSECCO region in northern Italy in 1995, yields of some vineyards dropped to one-tenth of a normal crop. The Australian experience is that vineyards with well-established infections yield at about half the rate of healthy vineyards.

Different species of leafhopper seem to be associated with the spread of different forms of grapevine yellows. Flavescence dorée is transmitted in the field by *Scaphoideus titanus*. Originally native to the eastern United States and Canada, this insect was apparently introduced to Europe after the Second World War. Vergilbungskrankheit and bois noir are spread by the leafhopper *Hyalesthes obsoletus*, and in Australia the vector is currently unknown.

Other plants can furthermore act as reservoirs of the disease in that insects spread the disease to and from them and grapevines. These so-called host plants include many broadleaf weeds and COVER CROPS such as nettles, mallow, chicory, dandelion, thistles, bindweed, deadly nightshade, and many clovers. The infection spreads rapidly when the appropriate insect vector and host plants are also present in or around the vineyards, which phenomenon is increasing as vineyard CULTIVATION is practised less frequently and cover crops and weeds are more common (see ORGANIC and BIODYNAMIC VITICULTURE). Disease epidemics in France and Italy have been associated with the natural fluctuations in leafhopper populations, and this is probably the case everywhere.

There is no effective control of grapevine yellows diseases. Insecticide sprays can reduce the leafhopper populations—especially of *Scaphoideus*—and reduce the spread of the disease. The removal of broad leaf cover crops and weeds reduces insect levels and opportunities for feeding on host plants. However, if the vineyards are small and are surrounded by native vegetation then this can be impractical. The disease can be spread by infected planting material. Young plants can be dipped in hot water before they leave the nursery (typically 50 °C/ 120 °F for 30 to 45 minutes when fully dormant), which will kill phytoplasma as well as some other diseases, but regrettably not all nurseries follow this practice.

Chardonnay and Riesling are among the most susceptible VINIFERA varieties, followed by Grenache, Tannat, Pinot Noir, and Pinot Gris. Some AMERICAN VINE SPECIES are tolerant. Grapevine yellows diseases may eventually be as destructive to the world's viticulture as was PHYLLOXERA, because they are widespread, are spreading even further due to CLIMATE change effects on insect distribution, and cannot be controlled with resistant ROOTSTOCKS. Wine quality does not appear to be affected, but the supply of grapes, especially of Chardonnay and other sensitive varieties, can be.   R.E.S.

Bovey, R., et al., *Virus and Virus-like Diseases of Vines: Colour Atlas of Symptoms* (Lausanne, 1980).

Pearson, R. C., and Goheen, A. C.. (eds.), *Compendium of Grape Diseases* (St Paul, Minn., 1988).

Grapput, or **Grappu**, synonym for the rapidly declining French grape variety BOUCHALÈS.

Grasă, the 'fat' white grape of COTNARI in ROMANIA, where it is grown exclusively. Total plantings had reached 566 ha/1,398 acres by 2013. It can reach extremely high MUST WEIGHTS but needs the balancing acidity of grapes such as Tămâioasă Românească in a blend. In 1958, Grasă grapes in Cotnari reached a sugar concentration of 520 g/l. The vine is usefully sensitive to NOBLE ROT and is thought to be the same as Hungary's Köverszolo but this had not been proved by DNA PROFILING in 2014.

Grașevina, Croatian name for the republic's most planted vine variety, WELSCHRIESLING, whose origins may well be Croatian.

grasshoppers, insects of the families *Acrididae* and *Tettigoniidae* which can feed on the vine. Reductions in vineyard leaf area impair grape RIPENING, with potentially severe effects on wine quality. In California, for example, the devastating grasshopper (*Melanoplus devastator Scudder*) is particularly harmful to vineyards, causing damage by defoliation, usually in mid to late summer. In eastern Australia, the Australian plague locust (*Chortoicetes terminifera*) can be a major pest. Dense swarms can build up in pasture areas, and descend very quickly on vineyard areas, especially when pastures dry out. Control where necessary is usually by insecticides.   M.J.E.

Buchanan, G. A., and Amos, T. G., 'Grape pests', in B. G. Coombe and P. R. Dry (eds.), *Viticulture*, ii: *Practices* (Adelaide, 1992).

grassy, TASTING TERM usually used synonymously with HERBACEOUS.

Grau, German for grey or *gris*.

Grauburgunder, German synonym for PINOT GRIS used for the increasingly popular dry wines made from this grape in Germany. (Sweeter wines are sometimes labelled RULÄNDER.) Its success in producing spicy, full-bodied dry wine accounts for the marked increase in total area planted with the variety in Germany: its 5,402 ha/13,343 acres by 2012, an increase of 90% since 2000 make it the country's fourth most planted white wine grape and far more popular than Weissburgunder (Pinot Blanc). Only Italy grows more of this grape variety (see PINOT GRIGIO) than Germany. It needs a good site with deep, heavy soils to maximize the impressive level of extract of which it is capable. It is a particularly popular speciality of the warm BADEN region, although there are more than a thousand hectares in both RHEIN-HESSEN and PFALZ, too.

Grave del Friuli, vast DOC zone in the FRIULI region of north-east Italy which sprawls across the southern portion of the provinces of Pordenone and Udine (with the largest portion in the former). This is flatland whose GRAVEL- and sand-based soil has been deposited over the millennia by the many rivers and streams that cross the territory before adding their waters to the Adriatic. It owes its name to the same etymological root as the gravelly GRAVES region of Bordeaux in France.

The DOC, with 4,300 ha/10,620 acres of vineyard, is responsible for more than 50% of Friuli's output, and is so large (it includes seven out of the ten Friuli DOCs) that it is more akin to an IGT than anything else. Exceptionally high permitted yields (13 tonnes/ha or 91 hl/ha) make it difficult to see how the DOC contributes to good-quality wine production here. And although it encapsulates other, smaller DOCs, their production rules are generally not much more restrictive so that Grave del Friuli cannot even be used by producers for declassified wines. Almost all INTERNATIONAL VARIETIES are grown here, with piercingly herbaceous Sauvignon Blanc once being the DOC's flagship but now encountering fierce international competition. That is not to say that the DOC is unsuitable for the production of high-quality wines, but its formidable size precludes generalizations.   W.S.

gravel, a soil or unconsolidated rock in which pebbles are the most obvious component, known in French as *graves*, from which the two appellations below, and the DOC above, take their names. Gravel is the most distinctive soil type of Bordeaux's so-called LEFT BANK wine regions. It is said that glaciers, slowly moving down to the Atlantic coast from the distant Pyrenees, followed the course of the nearby river, pushing back its high right bank. When glaciers melted, the pebbles remained near the surface. The vineyards of the GRAVES are, not surprisingly, characterized by their gravelly surface and gravel is nowhere so prevalent as at Ch HAUT-BRION, where in places it is 16–20 m/50–65 ft deep. Such soils offer excellent DRAINAGE, imposing on the vine the slight WATER STRESS favoured for wine quality. See VINE PHYSIOLOGY and SOIL AND WINE QUALITY.

Gravel soils are also highly prized for quality wine production on the plateau of ST-ÉMILION, in CHÂTEAUNEUF-DU-PAPE, GRAVE DEL FRIULI, and in the Gimblett Gravels region of Hawke's Bay and

Marlborough in NEW ZEALAND. Such soils are also widespread in the Ningxia region of CHINA. However, many gravel areas may well be used for viticulture simply because they are too difficult to work and too infertile for any other form of agriculture. It is notable that Chx Haut-Brion and La Mission-Haut-Brion are now viticultural oases in the southern suburbs of Bordeaux, indicating that the land is more valuable for housing than for vines.

See entries prefixed SOIL.

M.J.E., R.E.S., & J.M.H.

Enjalbert. H., *Great Bordeaux Wines: St Émilion, Pomerol, Fronsac* (Paris, 1983: Eng. trans. 1985).

Graves, French for gravelly terrain, and a term at one time used for many of Bordeaux's wine districts, but now the name of one particular large region extending 50 km/30 miles south east of the city along the left bank of the river GARONNE (see map under BORDEAUX). Graves is Bordeaux's only region famous for both its red and white wines, although its aristocratic, mineral-scented, Cabernet-dominated red wines are made in much greater quantity than its dry whites. In the early 1990s, about 1,800 ha/4,500 acres were planted with red wine grapes, while about 950 ha produced dry white Graves. By 2013 the areas were 2,520 and 752 ha respectively. **Graves Supérieures** is an AOC for sweet wines, to which 178 ha were dedicated in 2013, producing wines very similar to, but generally slightly drier and coarser than those from the enclave entitled to the CÉRONS appellation.

The Graves, and in particular the outskirts of Bordeaux, the Grabas de Burdeus, is the birthplace of CLARET. In the Middle Ages, much of the light CLAIRET dispatched in such quantity to England was grown in these vineyards within easy distance of the quayside; the Médoc was largely marshland (see BORDEAUX, history). Ch Pape-Clément is Bordeaux's first named château, while HAUT-BRION was the first New French Claret noted in London, by Samuel Pepys, in 1663. Thomas JEFFERSON noted that in late-18th-century 'Grave' wines were considered the finest Bordeaux had to offer. It was presumably this historic fame which had Ch Haut-Brion, Graves's most famous property, included with the finest Médoc châteaux in the famous CLASSIFICATION in 1855.

For centuries Graves encompassed all the vineyards south of the border with the MÉDOC in a great sweep around the city and upstream along the Garonne as far as Langon, with the exception of the enclaves for sweet white wine appellations BARSAC, CÉRONS, and SAUTERNES. In 1987, the separate appellation of PESSAC-LÉOGNAN was formed, a northern slice of the original Graves appellation which includes all of its most famous properties, and the southern suburbs of Bordeaux itself.

The creation of this new premium appellation had the effect of somewhat declassifying the historic name Graves, although some excellent wines are conscientiously made within the modern Graves appellation on the varied GRAVEL terraces which have been deposited there over alluvial deposits with the occasional sandy outcrop over the millennia. The reds, which can truly taste like country cousins of their more urbane neighbours in Pessac-Léognan, can often be good value, and mature earlier than their Médoc counterparts. It is in this area that some serious barrel-fermented, or at least oak-aged, dry whites are made, from Sauvignon and Sémillon grapes in varying proportions.

Graves de Vayres, a small BORDEAUX district, named after the historic town of Vayres, which has nothing to do with GRAVES but is just across the river DORDOGNE from the town of Libourne. From a total of 312 ha/770 acres in 2013 of, not surprisingly, gravelly soil, with patches of sand, the appellation produces light red wines made substantially from MERLOT grapes, although many of them are sold under the simple BORDEAUX AOC. White wines are now usually dry, often based on Sémillon, occasionally given BARREL MATURATION, and were produced from just 67 ha in 2013.

gravity-fed, describes a WINERY that is constructed on different levels, often into a hillside, or uses lifts, so that grapes, must, or wine are moved by gravity rather than by PUMPS in the belief that wine quality is improved by more gentle handling.

gré, French for SANDSTONE.

Great Southern, high-quality, cool climate wine region with 63 producers in 2014 in the extreme south west of WESTERN AUSTRALIA, including subregions Albany, Denmark, Frankland River, Mount Barker and Porongurup. Each has its own TERROIR and climate dictated in part by the distance from the south coast of Western Australia.

Great Western. See GRAMPIANS.

Grecanico Dorato, white grape variety grown on Sicily shown by DNA PROFILING in 2007 to be the GARGANEGA of the Veneto. The wines currently made may not be maximizing its full potential.

Grechetto, strictly **Grechetto di Orvieto**, sometimes **Greghetto**, characterful central Italian white grape variety most closely associated with UMBRIA. It is an ingredient in ORVIETO and in the whites of TORGIANO and the Colli Martini DOC, typically blended with Trebbiano Toscano and Verdello. The grapes' thick skins provide good resistance to DOWNY MILDEW. **Grechetto di Todi** is a synonym for PIGNOLETTO and DNA PROFILING suggests a parent–offspring relationship between the two Grechettos. Several DOC regulations specify simply 'Grechetto'. There were over 1,500 ha/3,750 acres of 'Grechetto Bianco' in the 2010 vine census (and 500 ha of Pignoletto).

Greco, or **Greco di Tufo** (which has its own DOCG for the zone around the village of Tufo), is a late-ripening Campanian white wine grape that has been shown by DNA PROFILING to be identical to ASPRINIO. The variety also grows in northern Puglia, Lazio, and Tuscany, and is genetically distinct from GRECO Bianco. Wines tend to be dry, assertive, and to have more body than aroma. The 2010 vine census notes a total area of 829 ha/2,048 acres and a smaller, separate total for Asprinio.

Greco Bianco, also known as **Greco Bianco di Gerace**, is the name of a CALABRIAN vine variety best known for its sweet whites made from semi-dried grapes grown around the town of Bianco on the south coast. The 2010 vine census notes a total of 774 ha/1,912 acres. It is unrelated to the Campanian GRECO (di Tufo) but has been shown by DNA PROFILING to be identical to MALVASIA di Lipari.

At least four other varieties have a synonym that begins Greco Bianco. The popularity of the name shows how widely Greek origins were assumed.

Greco Nero, name for at least five different dark-berried CALABRIAN vine varieties. The 2010 vine census does not distinguish between them and notes a declining total of 827 ha/2,043 acres.

Gredos, mountain range 80 km west of Madrid in SPAIN in which are parts of three appellations in three political regions, Vinos de MADRID, MÉNTRIDA in Castilla–La Mancha, and Vinos de la Tierra de Castilla y León (Cebreros sector) in Castilla y León. They form a specific viticultural area which one day may have its own appellation. Small vineyards in the mountains are planted with old Garnacha and ALBILLO Real vines with some Garnacha Blanca on granite and slate soils. A group of young growers began revitalizing the region in the early years of this century.   V. de la S.

Greece, renascent Mediterranean wine producer with a particularly rich history of wine made in classical times from the 7th century BC and on in the Roman era (see Ancient ROME). Early Greek colonization led to the vine being taken to all parts of the Mediterranean, thus laying the foundations for viticulture and the whole later development of wine in this area. In modern Greece, the total vineyard area had fallen to around 110,000 ha/275,000 acres by 2013, with only about half producing grapes for wine. DRYING GRAPES and TABLE GRAPES are important to the agricultural economy. About 70% of annual wine production of between 3.5 and 4 million hl (about 100 million gal) is of white wine.

Ancient Greece

Origins Wine was important in Greek society from the earliest times, forming part of the Greek cultural identity. The Ancient Greeks were aware that other societies, such as the Babylonians in MESOPOTAMIA and the inhabitants of Ancient EGYPT, made and drank wine, but for them it was a luxury, and they normally drank BEER (a drink disparaged by Greek writers as inferior and fit only for foreigners) or else 'wine' made from dates or lotus. Complete ignorance of viticulture was the mark of savages; so too was the drinking of undiluted wine, which was associated with northern barbarians such as the Scythians (in modern CRIMEA).

The vine was initially domesticated in Greece in the late neolithic, and widely cultivated by the early Bronze Age. Wine was clearly a significant element in the culture of Minoan CRETE before 2000 BC: remains of grapes and of installations for wine production (treading floors and spouted vats) have been found by archaeologists at palaces and villas, and some of the large storage jars found in the palace complexes probably contained wine rather than olive oil; an ideogram for 'wine' has been identified in the early script Linear A, and artistic evidence suggests the use of wine in ritual contexts. Given the links between Crete and Egypt in this period, the Minoans might be expected both to have learned viticulture from their neighbours and to have exported to supply the demand there and elsewhere in the Near East. In turn, Crete will have influenced contemporary Thíra (modern SANTORINI), where vines and grapes are depicted on painted pottery.

Mycenae There is no doubt of the importance of wine in Mycenaean culture (c.1600–1150 BC), which followed and developed on the mainland from Minoan culture: evidence from Mycenae, Tiryns, and Sparta includes grape pips and residues of wine, as well as the seal of a jar bearing the impression of vine leaves, while the palaces have revealed many storage jars, including a complete cellar at Pílos which contained at least 35 large jars, some labelled as containing wine. The evidence of the Linear B script, preserved on clay tablets fired hard in the destruction of the palaces, confirms that wine was important: the palace records contain many references to it, and include words for 'wine', 'vineyard', and, apparently, 'wine merchant', not to mention allusions to the god DIONYSUS. Finds of Mycenaean pottery abroad imply that they were exporting wine and oil to Syria, Palestine, Egypt, Cyprus, Sicily, and southern Italy, while the discovery of a few small CANAANITE jars (the earliest AMPHORAE) at Mycenae may suggest that connoisseurs were also importing foreign wines; certainly wine appears to have been a luxury item largely restricted to the élite.

Early Greek literature In the poetry of HOMER and HESIOD, the earliest Greek literature, wine is an essential part of life. It is naturally drunk by Greek and Trojan heroes at their feasts, but also used in the rituals of sacrifice, prayer, and burial, to solemnize agreements, and for therapeutic purposes; it is also the human drink, whereas gods drink nectar. A depiction of the vintage, in an enclosed vineyard, is part of the encapsulation of human life on the shield which Hephaestus makes for Achilles (*Iliad* 18. 561 ff.). Wine is the touchstone of civilization: even the Cyclopes in the *Odyssey* drink it, but without cultivating the vine, unlike the pleasure-loving Phaeacians, and, when offered the fine wine of Maron, Polyphemus swigs it neat until he falls into a stupor. Homer implies that the vine was widespread in Greece in his time, describing a number of places as 'rich in vines' (including Phrygia: in this as in other respects the Trojans are as civilized as the Greeks), and he gives us our earliest reference to specific wines, Pramnian and Ismarian, while Hesiod mentions Bibline. Advice on viticulture forms part of Hesiod's *Works and Days*: he mentions pruning and the harvest, including drying the grapes before vinification to make early forms of DRIED-GRAPE WINES.

The extent of viticulture In the classical period, vines were grown throughout Greece, and, through colonization, the Greeks carried viticulture to Sicily and southern Italy (which the Greeks called OENOTRIA, 'land of trained vines'), southern France, and the Black Sea. Some producers operated on a large scale, with extensive estates: we can infer the existence of vineyards of 8 to 10 ha and 30 ha/74 acres on the island of Thásos in the northern Aegean in the late 5th century BC and of one of about 12 ha in Attica in the middle of the 4th century, and Diodorus records a cellar at Acragas in Sicily with a storage capacity of 12,000 hl/317,000 gal and a vat holding 400 hl/10,500 gal (*Library of History* 13. 83). However, most viticulture was probably on a small scale, part of the normal peasant system of polyculture, which in Greece was founded on grain, vines, and olives; vines require more labour than cereals, but wine and grapes clearly played an important part in the Greek diet.

Trade Viticulture was also important to the economy of many cities, as is shown by the number of states whose coinage bears wine-related designs. Greek wine was traded within Greece, with Athens, the largest and richest city, offering the best market, and exported throughout the Mediterranean world, especially to Egypt, the Black Sea, Scythia, and Etruria (modern TUSCANY). Soon the colonial cities began to produce and export their own wine. (See CELTS for archaeological evidence of the geographical extent to which Greek wine and drinking rituals were adopted.) Amphorae from Marseilles are found along the southern coast of France and up the RHÔNE Valley, while in the CRIMEA archaeology has revealed extensive estates, their vineyards protected from the prevailing winds by low walls and planted with INDIGENOUS vines which were gradually domesticated, rather than with imported varieties.

The scale of the Greek wine trade can be inferred from the widespread finds of amphorae and the seals which indicate their origin. The richest evidence is from the island of Thásos, which took elaborate precautions to regulate its wine trade, both to maximize tax revenues and to prevent fraud which would damage its reputation; amphorae were required to be of standard sizes and were sealed with the name of an annual magistrate, which acted as a guarantee of authenticity; other states also used this system. Thásos also protected her commerce by forbidding her citizens to import foreign wine.

Viticultural practices No vine grown today can be confidently traced back to any Ancient Greek variety, although we know the names of 50 or more, some of which were cultivated in Italy in Roman times, and names such as GRECO, GRECHETTO, and AGLIANICO (i.e. Helleniko) reflect popular traditions of continuity (although DNA PROFILING suggests that these are more romance than reality). Roman writers noted that the YIELDS of Greek varieties were low, although their quality was good. In the 4th century BC, the botanically expert THEOPHRASTUS was aware of the need to match varieties to soil type and MESOCLIMATE, and recommended PROPAGATION by cuttings or suckering. A variety of VINE-TRAINING regimes was used: often vines were supported by forked props or trained up trees, but a few varieties naturally formed bushes, and sometimes plants were simply left to trail on the ground; training on trees meant climbing up, or using trestles, to pick the grapes. PRUNING was known to have an important effect on yields and quality, and land leases sometimes specify that the lessors be allowed to oversee it towards the end of a lease, as well as regulating the use of manure as fertilizer.

Vinification The HARVEST was, as in modern Greece, early by European standards: Hesiod recommends early September. Vase paintings suggest that, in many cases, PRESSING took place near the vineyard: the grapes were trodden inside a handled wicker basket which in turn stood in a wooden trough with low legs, from which the juice ran through a spout into an earthenware vat sunk in a hole in the ground; sometimes a sieve was placed over the mouth of the vat. As pickers brought grapes in,

they were added to the basket, while the treader held on to the basket handles or a ring or rope overhead (or a convenient vine) to keep his balance, and worked at CRUSHING in time to a flute. There are also scenes of treading in the vat itself, in which case the skins and pips will not have been strained out, and the wine will have taken colour from the skins, an early form of PIGEAGE. In either case, the vats will then have been covered and the juice taken for FERMENTATION in jars of larger capacity (*pithoi*); these could be 3 m/10 ft high, with a mouth a metre across. Larger and more specialized establishments had permanent stone treading floors rather than wooden ones, but otherwise the process was the same; although the beam PRESS was normally used for olives, there is little evidence for its use in wine production in classical Greece, and the screw press probably appeared only in Roman republican times. Small-scale producers may well have employed more primitive forms of pressing such as torsion in a fabric container, but no evidence for these survives.

References to the drying of grapes in Hesiod and the *Odyssey* (see DRIED-GRAPE WINES) suggest that this was the early norm, but in later times practices varied: a Lesbian wine, Protropon, was made from FREE-RUN juice, while in other cases grapes were deliberately harvested unripe to produce a wine with high ACIDITY (Omphakias); fresh MUST itself was sometimes drunk, as was boiled must. Finally, the solids left after treading could be moistened with water and trodden again to yield a low-quality PIQUETTE called Deuterias or Stemphulites.

Although wine was often transferred from the fermentation vessels once fermentation was over, it is clear that it had not been subjected to proper RACKING or FINING since a sieve or strainer through which to pour the wine is a standard feature of the SYMPOSIUM, and although Theophrastus may refer to the addition of gypsum, which was later used for the purposes of both CLARIFICATION and ACIDIFICATION, he describes this as an Italian practice. References to 'strained wine' suggest that it was unusual, and the straining may have been done at the point of sale, rather than during production.

Common additives The basic wine could be 'improved' by various additives: the use of a small percentage of seawater or brine seems to have begun in the 4th century BC, apparently as a flavouring, although it probably also had preservative qualities, and the technique was associated with particular areas of production, notably the island of Kós, and marked a shift in taste during antiquity. We also hear of the addition of aromatic herbs, to produce a sort of VERMOUTH, and of perfume being added both in production and by the consumer, as well as of the use of boiled must and, on Thásos, of the

addition of a mixture of dough and honey to produce a special CUVÉE for consumption on state occasions. BLENDING of different wines was also practised: Theophrastus gives one example, a mixture of hard but aromatic wine from Heraclea with soft Erythraean (a salted wine) which lacks BOUQUET, and says that there are many other blends known to experts (see TASTING, ancient history). There is some evidence, mainly in the Bronze Age, for the deliberate addition of pine or terebinth resin, but it is likely that storage (below) was normally a more significant cause of such flavours.

Containers for wine Finished wine was normally stored in AMPHORAE lined with resin or pitch (see RESINATED WINES) to limit porosity, which will have affected the taste to some extent, and pitch was also used to secure the stopper, which was usually of pottery, although the use of cork was known. Amphorae of the classical period held between 20 and 75 l (5–20 gal), depending on their origin, and added 5–15 kg (11–33 lbs) to the total load. These commercial amphorae are, of course, to be distinguished from the much smaller painted pots, also called amphorae, which were used to present the wine when it was drunk. In the *Odyssey* (2. 340 ff.), Telemachus had wine drawn off from the big *pithoi* in which it had been ageing into amphorae for his journey abroad. Homer also refers quite frequently to wine kept in wineskins, but in classical times skin bags were probably mainly filled for rapid consumption; despite being lighter and, perhaps, less fragile, they will have flavoured the wine, being usually made from the skin of a sheep or goat.

Selling wine In Athens, wine was bought mainly from wine sellers for immediate consumption: after the purchaser had sampled the wine, the required amount was ladled or siphoned from the amphora into a jug or small amphora which the purchaser usually provided: wealthier customers, however, and those holding parties, will have bought an amphora at a time. Evidence on price is scanty, but for imported wine of good quality, such as Chian or Mendean, in Athens in the 4th century BC a *chous* of about 3.25 l cost between a quarter of a drachma and 2 drachmas (a drachma being a day's wage for a craftsman). Of course, these were luxury wines, with prices to match: one Athenian, urged to improve his morals by the Areopagus, the Council of Elders, cited drinking Chian, along with keeping a mistress, as evidence of a life of blameless hedonism appropriate to a gentleman. See also MERCHANTS, ancient history.

Specific wines Some idea of the leading wines of classical Greece can be obtained from references in literature, particularly lyric poetry and

g

the Athenian comic poets; these make it clear that in Athens, at least, there was a degree of CONNOISSEURSHIP, different poets singing the praises of different wines while disparaging their rivals. The most frequently praised wines are those of Thásos, Lésvos, Mende, and Khíos (especially one called Ariousian), while those of Ismaros (in Thrace), Náxos, Peparethos (modern Skópelos), Acanthos and, from the 4th century, Kós were also admired.

This makes it clear that, although other areas had their admirers, the regions which produced the best wines were, by general consent, the AEGEAN ISLANDS, particularly to the east, and Chalkidike (modern Halkidiki near Ch Carras, see below) and Thrace on the northern mainland.

Two other much-praised wines, Pramnian and Bibline, are problematic. Pramnian, whose name goes back to Homer, is associated with a number of places—Lésvos, Smyrna, and the island of Ikaros (modern Ikaría, in the Dodecanese)—and indeed, according to ATHENAEUS, some considered it a generic name for dark wine, or long-lived wine; however, there was also a vine variety called Pramnian, and it seems most likely that Pramnian, which perhaps originated on Ikaría, came to be used as the name of wine of the style of the original, 'neither sweet nor rich, but dry, hard and unusually strong', whether or not made from the original vine.

In the case of Bibline, the problem is a confusion of names, since there was also Bybline wine, from Byblos in PHOENICIA, which is highly praised for fragrance by the 4th century BC gastronome Archestratus; Bibline, however, took its name from a region in Thrace where it originated, and came from a vine called Bibline, which was apparently subsequently introduced elsewhere. Since scribes were prone to confuse the two, allusions cannot always be reliably attributed to one or the other, but it is plain that both had excellent reputations. On these interpretations, both Pramnian and Bibline will also fall within the top zone outlined above. In all cases, wines are praised in terms of their origins; we never hear of particular estates or producers as being superior.

What was Greek wine like? First, it could be of three colours, white, black or red, and tawny, the last being less frequently mentioned; Homer's wine is always dark. Greeks were sensitive to aromas, and often speak of wines being fragrant; more specifically, they refer to wine as 'smelling of flowers', an expression often almost equivalent to our BOUQUET, although the way in which the comic poet Hermippus talks of a mature wine 'smelling of violets, roses and hyacinth' shows that it was not always metaphorical; the same passage attributes a scent of apples to Thasian wine. The sweetest wines were said to lack bouquet, which could,

according to Theophrastus, be supplied by blending, spicing, or perfuming.

In taste, wine is often praised as sweet, honeyed, ripe, and soft, and this must have appealed to the Greek palate, to judge from the production of PASSITO, or dried-grape wine, and even sweet wine further concentrated by boiling. Given the likely ripeness of the grapes, the limitations of natural YEASTS, and, perhaps, the risk of STUCK FERMENTATION without TEMPERATURE CONTROL, sweetness must have been the most frequent outcome, and is often assumed by Greek writers: Aristotle distinguishes among heavy drinkers between drunkards and the sweet-toothed. However, this was not always the case: as noted earlier, grapes were sometimes picked unripe, and some varieties, like Pramnian, were naturally more austere; one vine was allegedly called 'smoky' because the wine was so sharp as to bring tears to the eyes, like smoke. Medical writers discussing the qualities of wines class them as dry or sweet white; and dry, sweet, or medium red/black, so there was obviously a wide range of styles.

Wine ageing Given the vagaries of vinification, much Greek wine will not have lasted long, succumbing either to OXIDATION, which medical and scientific writers noticed and discussed as a form of decomposition, or to spoilage due to inadequate storage, the risk of which was noted by Aristotle. It is not surprising that the people of Thásos traded in VINEGAR as well as wine, and that sour wine was a regular cheap drink, especially since the risk of oxidation must have increased as a large jar was emptied.

Nevertheless, some wines clearly aged, since old wine was highly regarded by the Greeks: 'praise old wine, but the flowers of new songs,' said the poet Pindar, and comic poets noted that women preferred old wine but young men. The old wine praised by Hermippus (above) was described as *sapros*: literally, 'rotten' or 'decomposed', but obviously referring in the case of wine to the production of secondary flavours through AGEING; older wine was also described as having 'lost its bite'. We never find discussion of particular VINTAGES (unlike Roman wines and specific vintages such as OPIMIAN wine mentioned by Roman writers), and there is little reliable evidence as to how long good wine might keep: Theocritus speaks of drinking four-year-old wine, perhaps from Kós, in the early 3rd century BC, and in the same era Peparethian wine was regarded as a slow developer in requiring six years to reach maturity, while the elder PLINY (in the 1st century AD) considered all foreign wines middle-aged at seven years old; comparisons with the wines of Ancient ROME, which evidently matured more slowly, might allow one to guess that few Greek wines lasted more than ten years, a good age for a wine in the heroic age

(*Odyssey* 3. 390–2), but not a very long time by modern standards, especially when we remember that the CONTAINERS were very much larger than modern ones, so that the rate of development should have been proportionately reduced.

The uses of wine Wine had many uses for the Greeks. It was of course important as a food and drink (it was doubtless often safer than water), and the SYMPOSIUM, which centred around the drinking of wine, was one of the most important Greek social forms. Wine was almost always drunk diluted with water: the ratio varied, normally ranging between 2 : 3 and 1 : 3, which would give a range in ALCOHOLIC STRENGTH of about 3 to 6% and generally at the lower end of this range (roughly the same as British draught beer). Weaker mixtures are disparaged in comedy (and even 1 : 3 called for a good wine), but 1 : 1 was considered by some dangerous to the health, and the regular drinking of unmixed wine, a habit confined to barbarians, was believed by some Spartans to have caused the insanity and death of their King Cleomenes. The mixed wine was also normally cooled, sometimes in special pottery coolers; the very rich added snow.

The medical uses of wine were numerous, and much discussed by medical writers. Its advantages as a pick-me-up, tonic, and analgesic were obvious, and by experience it became clear that certain wines were nourishing, diuretic, good for the digestion, and so on, but the qualities of different types were also discussed in terms of the four essential qualities (hot, cold, wet, dry) in order to decide how they should be used to correct imbalances in the bodily humours.

There are occasional references to procedures for making wine-based medicines, either by adding drugs to the wine or by treating the vines with an appropriate agent, although these usually seem closer to folklore than science; certain wines also had the reputation of producing medical side-effects: those of Troizen (just across the Saronic Gulf from Athens), for example, were said to render the drinker sterile. The Greeks were also well aware of the hazards of consuming wine to excess, and Athenaeus mentions popular remedies for a HANGOVER.

After social aspects, however, the most important aspect of wine was its place in religion. A LIBATION (*sponde*) of wine was offered whenever wine was drunk as a sort of first fruit (at the symposium different gods were invoked for each bowlful) and drink offerings were part of the formula for prayers; hence treaties and truces were referred to as *spondai*, because they were sanctified by prayers and libations. Wine was used to quench the burning offerings on the altar at a sacrifice, and was one of the liquids poured on the ground as an offering to the dead.

More than this, however, wine was directly associated with a particular divinity: Dionysus was the patron god and the symbol of wine, as Demeter was of cereals, and one of the 12 major divinities (a further indication of the basic importance of wine to the Greeks).   R.B.

Wine festivals

For the Athenian of the 5th century BC, festival days in honour of the gods at set times of year gave the sort of relaxation now provided by weekends. Many of them were associated with wine drinking, vine-growing, and the HARVEST. The most important of these, the Anthesteria, in honour of Dionysus, celebrated the opening of wine jars in February to test the new wine. It included processions and ritual wine drinking contests and was probably closest to the modern idea of a wine festival. None the less, at the heart of the festival was the serious business of the dedication of the new wine to Dionysus.

Other festivals included the Oschophoria, a vintage celebration in September which seems to have been restricted to aristocratic families: two young men led a procession carrying vine branches with the grapes still on them (*oschoi*) in honour of Dionysus. The Apatouria in the same month was the festival when young males were registered in their *phratries*, or clans, and there was much associated pouring of wine. The last day of this festival was called Epibda and came to mean 'the morning after'. Strangely, there does not seem to have been a particularly important festival at the time of the grape harvest. At the country Dionysia celebrated in the country around Athens, a jar of wine and a vine headed the procession.

The great festivals of Athens, the Panathenaia and the City Dionysia, were less dominated by the vine (perhaps because they were held further from the vineyards) but there is no doubt that wine was enjoyed at them.   H.H.A.

Bibliographical note: There is no modern book specifically on Greek wine, works on ancient wine (cited under Ancient ROME) tend to pass rapidly on to Rome, where the evidence is much fuller; however, Roman sources are not necessarily reliable evidence for Greek practice 500 years earlier. Of the ancient sources, ATHENAEUS' *Deipnosophistae* collects much classical literary material (especially Books 1–2, 25e–40 ff.) and Theophrastus' *Enquiry into Plants and On the Causes of Plants* (especially 3. 11–16) contains a lot of botanical lore; all are accessible in translation in the Loeb Classical Library. On Athenaeus, see Brock, R. and Wirtjes, H., 'Athenaeus on Greek wine', in D. Braund and J. Wilkins (eds.), *Athenaeus and His World* (Exeter, 2000), 455–65, 587–8 with further general bibliography. The Minoan and Mycenaean periods are discussed in McGovern, P. E., Fleming, S. J., and Katz, S. H. (eds.), *The Origins and Ancient History of Wine* (Luxembourg, 1995), chs.

15–18. Grace, V., *Amphoras and the Ancient Wine Trade* (2nd edn, Princeton, NJ, 1979), is a good general introduction to AMPHORAE; see also Koehler, C., in McGovern, Fleming, & Katz, ch. 20. Sparkes, B. A., 'Treading the Grapes', *Bulletin Antieke Beschaving*, 51 (1976), 47–64, collects and discusses the pictorial evidence for the vintage. Wilson, H., *Wine and Words in Classical Antiquity and the Middle Ages* (London, 2003), is mainly concerned with the literary, social, and religious uses of wine but also deals with AGEING. On festivals, see Parke, H. *Festivals of the Athenians* (London, 1977).

Medieval history

In the medieval Greece that was part of the Byzantine empire, wine was grown by private individuals and by monasteries (see MONKS AND MONASTERIES). Monasteries were foremost among the great landowners because, as in western Europe, they received donations and bequests from the laity. In the 8th and 9th centuries, agriculture was exceptionally profitable; its chief products were wine and fruits and also cotton and medicinal herbs. As in antiquity, the best wines came from the AEGEAN ISLANDS, Khíos first of all, and Thásos and Crete. The wines of THRACE and ANATOLIA (Cappadocia in particular) were ranked second to these. Evidence from shipwrecks shows that wine was still transported in amphorae in the 7th century, whereas wooden BARRELS were commonly used in western Europe from the 3rd century AD. After the 7th century, the Greeks, too, started using wooden casks, which are lighter and easier to handle than amphorae.

In the 12th century, Constantinople (on the site of modern Istanbul) was the centre of the Byzantine empire's wine trade. Wines were shipped to Constantinople from the Aegean islands, from Thebes, and also from near Monemvasia, a port on the southern Peloponnese, which gave its name to MALVASIA and its English corruption MALMSEY. Monasteries were exempted from customs duties and were therefore at an advantage compared with private growers and traders: the monasteries of Patmos and Mount Áthos, for instance, made large profits from selling their wines in Constantinople.

But the private growers and wine merchants of Greece faced a much greater problem than unfair competition from monks. In 1082, the Emperor Alexius I Comnenus had granted VENICE trading facilities at Constantinople and in 32 towns without payment of taxes of any kind. As a result so much money disappeared to the west that Byzantium was economically ruined. Wine producers and wine merchants suffered badly. With no duties to pay, the Venetians were able to sell wine much more cheaply than any Greek could. Often this was imported Italian wine, but most of the wine came from Crete, known then as Candia, which was a colony of Venice (and

which was to remain one until the mid 17th century). Worse still, many taverns in Constantinople were owned by Venetians so, in Constantinople at least, they controlled the retail trade as well.

It took until the middle of the 14th century for the Byzantine government at least to try to protect the empire's own trade. After earlier failed attempts, the Venetians agreed in 1361 to accept a distinction between wholesale and retail trade and to impose a tax on their own, with the proceeds of course going to Venice, on taverns run by Venetians. In the 15th century, tax was finally levied on wine imported by Venetians, but by then it was too late, for Byzantium's wine trade was no longer viable. Crete and CYPRUS, under Venetian ownership, continued to produce the strong, sweet wines that were capable of surviving the long sea voyage to western Europe, but the harbour of Monemvasia, close to Byzantium's own supply of Malvasia wines, was now too small to take the larger ships that the west had increasingly come to adopt. Monemvasia had been an entrepôt for ships from Cyprus and Crete bound for the west; from the late 14th century onwards, it lost out to Cyprus and Crete as a port and the south west Peloponnese declined as a producer of export-quality wine. All trade in Greek wine ceased in the late 15th century, when, after the fall of Byzantium, the Ottoman Turks occupied the Peloponnesian shore and drove out its inhabitants.   H.M.W.

Kazhdan, A. P. (ed.), *The Oxford Dictionary of Byzantium*, 3 vols. (Oxford, 1988).
Lambert-Gócs, M., *The Wines of Greece* (London, 1990).
Nicol, D. M., *Byzantium and Venice* (Cambridge, 1988).

Modern history

The centuries of domination by the Ottoman Turks were to blight Greek viticulture and winemaking until well into the 20th century. Winemaking was not normally forbidden to the Christian population, but communication difficulties resulted in a localized peasant industry viewed by the Turkish rulers as a useful means of raising revenue through TAXATION. Thus, while FRANCE, for example, was developing fine-wine regions and their markets, Greece remained in what might be termed the vinous Dark Ages.

The battle for independence was prolonged and tortuous, and the exhausted and impoverished modern Greek state, founded in 1913, had preoccupations more important than the creation of a fine wine industry. It was not until well after the two World Wars and the subsequent bitter civil war that Greece began to modernize its fragmented wine industry, widely regarded as a source of cheap, often poorly made wines suitable only for the domestic market. You need two kinds of aristocracy to produce fine wine: one able to afford quality-oriented viticulture and production and another able to afford buying high-quality wine. Greece had neither.

The Vine Institute of Athens, which experiments with winemaking techniques and advises winemakers, was founded in 1937, and some of the major modern wine companies had been established in the late 19th century, but were then chiefly concerned with DISTILLATION, BULK wine sales being a subsequent addition. Only in the 1960s was any significant proportion of Greek wine sold in bottle rather than directly from the barrel.

From the 1960s, however, there was considerable investment in modern technology, and its results were evident from the 1970s with the emergence of Greece's first generation of trained OENOLOGISTS (it is to the Greek language that we owe the very term OENOLOGY). The 1980s signalled a new era for Greek wines. A number of oenologists decided to move out of the large companies and start their own smaller but high-profile projects, while several other Greeks established what might be called LIFE-STYLE wineries. By the early 21st century the mavericks of the 1980s had commercially successful mid-sized wineries; most, but not all, of the large producers of the past dominated in volume terms; while an increasing number of small ventures appeared in both traditional and entirely new areas. Greeks consume more than 95% of the wine produced in their country. However, several of the top wineries have been steadily investing in exports, encouraged by the financial turmoil experienced by Greeks in the early 2010s.

Geography and climate

At latitudes of between 34 and 42 degrees north, Greek vineyards are commonly but mistakenly thought to be some of the world's warmest. The diverse topography and the mountainous landscape create mild or even cool MESOCLIMATES, as largely unsuspected by summer tourists enjoying the Greek sun in a coastal resort.

The climate is generally predictably MEDITER-RANEAN, with short winters and very hot summers in which DROUGHT can be a serious threat in some years, particularly in the south. There can be considerable variation between the CON-TINENTAL-influenced cooler vineyards in the mountains, whether on the plateau of Mantinia in the Peloponnese or in Epirus and Macedonia, where grapes may not even reach full RIPENESS, and the intense heat of Pátras or islands such as Crete and Rhodes on which some grapes may be picked in July.

Most of the vineyards are sufficiently close to the sea for maritime breezes to moderate temperatures, but lack of water, particularly on the islands and in the south, is a major problem.

Although some rain does fall in the autumn, the first three months of the year are generally the wet months, and many wine areas have no rain at all for six months, which can make the establishment of young vines extremely difficult. IRRIGATION is recognized as an annual necessity in many areas.

Most of Greece is extremely mountainous. Vines can be found growing on flat land near sea level, such as at Ankhíalos; on foothills as at Rapsani on the lower slopes of Mount Olympus; and at elevations as high as 1,200 m/3,200 ft on the highest slopes in Neméa.

There are many soil types in Greece but the soils devoted to vines or olives are generally of low fertility. Subsoils on the mainland tend to be LIMESTONE, while on the islands they are mainly VOLCANIC. CLAY, LOAM, SCHIST, and MARL are all found, as well as sandy clay and CHALK.

Viticulture

The Greek land tenure system means that much of the vineyard area is in the hands of smallholders. Little by little, the large companies which buy in so many of their grapes have been working more closely with these vinegrowers and promulgating more modern viticultural techniques. Grape PRICES were for long determined by sugar levels, which too often resulted in dangerously low levels of ACIDITY, but these problems have been largely resolved by the big commercial concerns and the more modern CO-OPERATIVES. The more ambitious of the small estates now practise thoroughly modern viticultural techniques.

Traditionally most vines were left to grow as BUSH VINES, but almost all new vineyards have been designed with TRELLIS SYSTEMS on wires. However, in certain areas, unique trellis and pruning systems have been adapted, after centuries of trial and error, to local conditions. Pre-eminent examples are the basket-trained vines on the windy sites of SANTORINI, aplotaries in Paros, where vine canes are left to grow on the ground, or even the vines trained around olive trees in Messinia. CORDON systems of pruning and training are more common than GUYOT.

Viticultural CONSULTANTS, mainly university professors, have been instrumental in improving Greek vineyards. VIRUS DISEASES of the vine are common in some vineyards and certain grape varieties. The most common rootstocks are 110 R or 41 B.

Vine varieties

Greece is a still underdeveloped source of INDIG-ENOUS, ancient grape varieties of which more than 300 have been identified. Many of them are used solely for the important TABLE GRAPE or dried-fruit industries, however, and many others are used in tiny quantities on a purely local basis. There is still considerable work to be undertaken in VINE IDENTIFICATION, not just in

rediscovering classical varieties, but in discovering the relationships between Greek varieties and those grown elsewhere, in ITALY, CYPRUS, TURKEY, ALBANIA, MONTENEGRO, KOSOVO, CROATIA, and MACEDONIA in particular. The success of varieties such as MALAGOUSIA (virtually unheard of in 1993 but currently responsible for top-quality wines from no fewer than 30 producers), Vidiano, Limniona, Kydonitsa, and many more suggests it will take decades for Greek viticulture fully to capitalise on the full potential of its native grapes.

The specifically Greek wine grape varieties can offer unique characters and flavours. Although, for example, Debina remained a speciality of Epirus in the north west, and Xinomavro of Macedonia in the north east, Greek vine-growers are increasingly experimenting with varieties such as ASSYRTIKO and AGIORGITIKO in areas far from their traditional homes as their value in blends is being recognized.

The most important white wine grapes in Greece are Assyrtiko, RODITIS, ROBOLA, SAV-ATIANO, MOSCHOFILERO, VILANA, DEBINA, and both MUSCAT BLANC À PETITS GRAINS and MUSCAT OF ALEXANDRIA. The Greek port of Monemvasia also gave its name to the MALVASIA grape. Among Greek red grape varieties, the most important to the modern Greek wine industry have been Agiorgitiko, LIMNIO, MANDILARIA, and XINOMAVRO. See regional details below for more local grape varieties.

In addition to these native varieties, a number of INTERNATIONAL VARIETIES have been imported, particularly from France, which some estimates put at around 15% of total plantings. These include Chardonnay, Sauvignon Blanc, and Ugni Blanc among whites and both Cabernet Sauvignon and Cabernet Franc, Merlot, Grenache Noir, Cinsaut, and Syrah among red grape varieties. Some Greek wines may be VARIETAL versions of these, but it is far more usual to find these foreign varieties playing a minor role in blends with Greek varieties. Greek wine consumers, the Greek wine industry's best customers, enjoy the flavours of French varieties, but a strong lobby within Greece argues that Greek wine should not be made from international varieties, and any new wine applying for appellation status is likely to encounter difficulties if the principal grapes used are not Greek in origin. This creates a dissonance between what consumers and legislators regard as the top tier of Greek wine. Areas such as Drama and Kavala in northern Greece regularly produce wines of outstanding quality and undeniable commercial appeal but they are denied APPELLATION status since they focus on international varieties.

Winemaking

Since the mid 1980s, almost all Greek wineries have had some sort of REFRIGERATION and the

GREECE

REPUBLIC OF
MACEDONIA

BULGARIA

ALBANIA

Vardar

Drama

THRACE

Mt Ismaros ▲

Avdíra

Goumenissa

Amyndeo

Náoussa

MACEDONIA

Strimon

Thessalonika

Epanomi

LEMNOS

Mt Vermio ▲

Aliakron

Mt ▲
Olympus

Côtes de
Meliton

TURKEY

CORFU

Zitsa

Metsovo

Tyrnavos

Rapsani

Ioánnina

Meteora

Pinios

AEGEAN
ISLANDS

EPIRUS

THESSALY

Vólos

Akheloos

Ankhíalos

IONIAN
ISLANDS

AEGEAN
SEA

SÁMOS

Atalanti

EUBOEA

CEPHALONIA

Thebes

Andros

ATTICA

Pátras
Pátras

Gulf of Corinth

Corinth Canal

Tinos

ZAKYNTHOS

Corinth

Neméa

Athens

Mantinia

Alfios

CYCLADES

IONIAN
SEA

PELOPONNESE

PÁROS

Kalamata

Monemvasia-
Malvasia

SANTORINI

RHODES

Monemvasia

MEDITERRANEAN
SEA

CRETE

Chania

Archanes
Daphnes

Heraklion
Peza

0   100 km

Sitia

■ Wine-growing regions

sort of HYGIENE afforded by the use of STAINLESS STEEL vats. Even the oldest co-operatives have now made such investments.

As in other Mediterranean areas, the 1980s were characterized by early picking and cool fermentations enabled by temperature control that resulted in clean but characterless white wines of about 11.5% alcohol. Such techniques as SKIN CONTACT, slightly later picking, and deliberate OXIDATION of the must prior to fermentation were used by some of the more daring producers from the early 1990s to develop more interesting wines. In the 2010s, winemaking technology is as modern as anywhere, although

the trend is a return to TRADITIONAL METHODS such as fermentation using ambient yeasts and reduced SULFUR additions.

Better-quality red wines have traditionally been matured in large, old casks. After a couple of decades of over-using French, mainly new, BARRIQUES for the BARREL MATURATION of reds and even some whites, the pendulum is swinging back to more subtle oaking.

Wine laws
Greek wine laws were drawn up in the early 1970s and refined in the early 1980s as Greece prepared to join the EU. It is hardly surprising,

therefore, that the laws conform strictly to EU guidelines, in the past often employing the use on the label of the French terms APPELLATION d'Origine Contrôlée. In 2009, in line with general EU changes to GEOGRAPHICAL INDICATIONS, one quality category was designated PDO or Protected Designation of Origin. The words Réserve or Grande Réserve indicate superior wines with extended AGEING.

PGI, or Protected Geographical Indication wines, which constitute the next tier and of which there were 114 in 2014, may be made in a wide variety of specified areas, nearly always from a range of vine varieties that includes both

Greek and foreign grape varieties. Commercially the most important PGI areas are Attica, Drama, Peloponnese, Epanomi, and Thívai (or Thebes).

The large category of WINE WITHOUT GEOGRAPHICAL INDICATION, known now simply as Greek wine but formerly as table wine, includes wine BRANDS that were Greece's most successful wines, as well as some more interesting wines made outside the appellation regulations. The Greeks have also used the term Kava to indicate high-quality table wine which is made only in small quantities and which has been subject to prolonged ageing, a term akin to Réserve and Grande Réserve, but allowed only for PGI wines.

The first official list of Greek wine appellations was drawn up in the 1950s, although some more recent wine areas, such as the Monemvassia-Malvasia appellation near the fortified island and port of Monemvasia at the southernmost tip of the Peloponnese (see MALVASIA), were subsequently grafted on to the official list. Of the 33 PDOs in Greece's widely differing regions, some are produced only in tiny quantities. Some are in danger of extinction, many are rarely seen outside their area of origin, while some are well known and thriving.

Wine regions

Wine is made all over Greece, often on a very small, traditional scale. The following includes those quality wine regions which have established their own identity within Greece and sometimes abroad; see map.

Northern Greece The regions of Macedonia and Thrace are noted mainly for their red wines, although wines of all hues are made there today. Náoussa, home of red wine from Xinomavro grapes, is on the south-eastern slopes of Mount Vermio, at ELEVATIONS of between 200 and 500 m (660–1,650 ft), where there is usually no serious lack of rain and winters are cool enough for vine DORMANCY. Náoussa must be aged for at least a year in OAK, traditionally in old wooden casks, but there has been considerable experimentation with new, small barriques. A system of defining the better slopes has resulted in two categories of Náoussa: young wine from the lighter, sandy soil and more age-worthy wine from clay and limestone soils. Náoussa wines can be aged for several decades and maintain an ethereal, Barolo-like personality.

Xinomavro is also grown in this area to produce Goumenissa, where it is blended with Negoska grapes, and to make Amyndeo, which lies on the opposite, north-western slopes of Mount Vermio from Náoussa but at elevations as high as 650 m/2,100 ft. In this appellation, Greece's coolest, sparkling rosé is made as well as reds. Centenarian vines in sandy, PHYLLOXERA-free soils produce some Xinomavros with admirable COMPLEXITY.

Côtes de Meliton on the slopes of Mount Meliton in Sithoniá is the appellation specially created by Domaine Carras, a wine estate developed with the well-publicized assistance of Professor Émile PEYNAUD of Bordeaux. Here both white and red wines are made with a mixture of Greek and international vine varieties, notably Cabernet Sauvignon. The estate pioneered the rediscovered elegant indigenous white MALAGOUSIA.

Since at least 1990, the coastal area of Kavala and its landlocked neighbour Drama have been enormously influential in introducing a particularly modern style of Greek wine, with exceptional red BORDEAUX blends and Assyrtiko/Sauvignon Blanc white blends. Many wineries based here are considered the trendsetters by many young producers in other areas, as well as by Greek wine connoisseurs.

Thrace, an area famous for its wines in antiquity, is slowly reclaiming its past glory, mainly around Mount Ismaros and in Avdira, using the local Mavroudi red grape, as well as blends of Greek and international varieties.

Not far from the town of Ioánnina and near the border with ALBANIA lies Zitsa, which produces a dry or medium-dry, lightly sparkling white wine from the local DEBINA grape that is able to achieve full flavour ripeness at only 11% alcohol. To the immediate south west, in the mountains around Ioánnina, are Greece's highest vineyards at Metsovo (up to 1200 m/4,000 ft), which used to yield the popular Katogi brand from locally grown Cabernet Sauvignon grapes, although the brand is now made from Cabernet and Agiorgitiko grapes grown in the Peloponnese.

Central Greece On the east coast in Thessaly, Rapsani is produced on the foothills of Mount Olympus from Xinomavro (here grown at its most southerly point) blended with Krassato and Stavroto grapes and given CASK AGEING. This appellation is undergoing much-needed revival and old vintages suggest real potential for long-lived, concentrated reds. Most wines grown here are of strictly local interest but quality-minded producers are emerging from areas such as Tyrnavos, the island of Euboea, Atalanti, and Meteora and reviving indigenous varieties such as the red Limniona grape.

Peloponnese This dramatically formed, large southern peninsula has the greatest number of Greek wine appellations, as well as some interesting PGE wines. On the plateau of Mantinia in Arcadia, at elevations of about 600 m/2,000 ft, the pink-skinned Moschofilero grape produces a fresh, dry, aromatic, slightly spicy, sometimes lightly sparkling white, and, with extended SKIN CONTACT, can also yield an interesting rosé. At Neméa, not far from the Corinth canal which separates the Peloponnese from

mainland Greece, the Agiorgitiko grape is grown on marl and deep red soil. If yields are not too high, it can produce intense, fruity red wine from three different zones whose elevation varies between 250 and 900 m (800–3,000 ft). Grapes from the lowest vineyards frequently lack acidity and can be used to make a sweet wine. The finest, dry wine is said to come from vineyards between 450 and 700 m (1,500–2,350 ft) above sea level, but the potential of the highest, coolest parts of the appellation is now being explored. As in Náoussa, new French barriques were used extensively but gentler oaking is becoming the norm. SEMI-CARBONIC MACERATION has been used to make a sort of Neméa NOUVEAU. Since the late 1990s, Neméa has seen, more than any other Greek region, a flurry of investment in high-tech wineries, resulting in some outstanding bottlings. Leading vineyards have been replanted with a higher VINE DENSITY.

The vineyards around Pátras on the north coast are responsible for four different appellations. Pátras itself is a dry white wine made from Roditis grapes grown on the slopes around the town. Muscat of Pátras is a dessert wine made strong and sweet like a VIN DOUX NATUREL from Muscat Blanc à Petits Grains grapes, as is Rion of Pátras, which is almost extinct owing to the encroachment of buildings on the vineyard area. Mavrodaphne of Pátras is a very popular appellation, on the other hand, in which Mavrodaphne grapes may be supplemented by the locally grown Korinthiaki (Corinth or CURRANT) grape grown mainly for DRYING GRAPES. Fermentation is arrested when alcoholic strength has reached about 4% (as in making PORT) and the wine, like tawny port, is then aged in wood. Examples aged for 10–12 years in cask can be delicious.

The newest Peloponnese appellation is Monemvassia-Malvasia, a PDO oak-aged sweet white wine, made from sun-dried grapes from several varieties, including Assyrtiko, Monemvassia, and the rare Kydonitsa. Other significant viticultural areas include Ilía, where Refosco has been grown for more than a century, and Messinía, where some of the finest Greek Cabernet Sauvignon is grown.

The islands Among the Ionian islands off the west coast, Cephalonia is best known for its wine, particularly the powerful dry white Robola. Vines here were individually trained on high, stony land, and mainly UNGRAFTED, leading Venetians to call Robola a *vino di sasso*, or wine of stone. Some varietal dry, unfortified red table wines from Mavrodaphne are also made, possibly the finest examples of this genre. Mavrodaphne and Muscat dessert wines, similar to those of Pátras, are also produced on the island.

From the Cyclades come the wines of Páros, SANTORINI, and, more recently, Tinos. PDO

Páros red is a powerful, quite tannic wine made from a curious blend of grapes in which the deep colour of the Mandilaria is lightened by the addition of half as much of the white grape called Monemvassia (see MALVASIA). PDO Malvasia of Paros is a sweet white, from sun-dried Monemvassia and a small percentage of Assyrtiko. Rainfall is low but the maritime location helps raise humidity. Vines are trained along the ground as protection against the strong winds. Strong winds are also a characteristic of SANTORINI.

The island of Rhodes has been an important producer of wine since classical times. Today there are four appellations: one for a sweet Muscat made in very limited quantities; one for a dry white based on Athiri; and a red and a rosé, both based on Mandilaria, here known as Amorgiano. Only grapes grown on the higher reaches of the north or north eastern slopes qualify for appellation wines. The Rhodes co-operative, the CAIR, also makes a considerable quantity of sparkling wine.

Two of Greece's most famous wines are made on the AEGEAN ISLANDS. Lemnos was the original home of the Limnio grape, which is still grown there, producing the POP Lemnos red wine. But the most famous appellation wines of the islands are both Muscats. The dry version is becoming more important, but the VIN DE LIQUEUR Muscat of Lemnos made from Muscat of Alexandria grapes is widely admired, being surprisingly delicate.

Muscat of Sámos can claim to be Greece's most famous wine (after RETSINA). Muscat Blanc à Petits Grains is grown up to 800 m/2,600 ft above sea level, often on TERRACES on the island's steep hillsides, and the vintage can last a full two months, depending on vineyard ELEVATION. Muscat of Sámos comes in several forms: Sámos Doux is a MISTELA-type vin de liqueur, while Sámos Vin Doux Naturel is made by stopping the fermentation even earlier. Anthemis is an outstanding example of barrel-aged Samos VDN. Potentially finest of all, however, is Sámos Nectar, an unfortified dried-grape wine made from grapes dried in the sun so that they are capable of being fermented into a wine of 14% alcohol, which is then given three years in cask. France is the single largest market, importing in BULK more than half of the island's annual production.

The last of the appellation wines of any commercial importance comes from CRETE from a variety of grape varieties unique to the island, together with Mandilaria. The pale red Liatiko reaches high alcohol levels and ripens very early, sometimes as early as July, while the powerful, deep-coloured Mandilaria produces particularly robust red wines. The most important local white grape is Vilana. Local red wine appellations for dry and sometimes sweet wines are Archanes and Dafnés, while Sitia may be dry white or white or sweet red, and Peza, the

most common wine appellation on the island, may be either dry red or white. The latest appellation additions are Handakas-Candia for dry whites, plus Malvasia of Handakas-Candia and Malvasia of Sitia, both dedicated to sweet whites made from sun-dried grapes. Most vineyards are on the north of the island, protected from the hot winds from North Africa by the mountain range. Crete has a number of very rare vine varieties such as Vidiano, Dafni, Thrapsathiri, and even a single plant of Samos Muscat Noir that have been rescued from extinction by observant growers. See also AEGEAN ISLANDS, CRETE, RETSINA, and SANTORINI.   K.L.

Lazarakis, K., *The Wines of Greece* (London, 2005). Manessis, N., *The Illustrated Greek Wine Book* (Corfu, 2000).

www.newwinesofgreece.com

green, pejorative tasting term for a wine made from grapes that did not reach full RIPENESS.

green grafting, viticultural term for BUDDING and GRAFTING in the vineyard or nursery using green stem tissue. Green grafting offers less flexibility in timing than CHIP BUDDING and T-BUDDING because the ROOTSTOCK shoots must be green, and so it must take place in late spring or early summer. As with T-budding, the SCION pieces to be inserted may be from stored winter cuttings or the current season's green shoots.   B.G.C.

green harvest. See CROP THINNING.

greenhouse effect and viticulture. See CLIMATE CHANGE.

Grenache Blanc, the white-berried form of GRENACHE NOIR, was once important in France, where it was overtaken by Sauvignon Blanc as fourth most planted white grape variety (after Ugni Blanc, Chardonnay, and Sémillon) as recently as the late 1980s. Although in decline, the variety is still grown on a total of 5,541 ha/13,686 acres of France, throughout the Languedoc Roussillon, where it produces full-bodied whites that vary from fat and soft to nervy, floral, terroir-driven cellar candidates. In table wines it is typically blended with the likes of Grenache Gris, Clairette, Bourboulenc, Marsanne, Roussanne, Viognier, Macabeo, and Rolle, adding supple fruit if not necessarily longevity. It need not necessarily be consigned to the blending vat, however. If carefully pruned and vinified, it can produce richly flavoured, full-bodied varietals that share some characteristics with Marsanne and can be worthy of ageing in small oak barrels. It is also an ingredient in white Châteauneuf-du-Pape and is a significant ingredient in Roussillon's VINS doux naturels. The variety is also found in varietal

form in California and occasionally in South Africa.

See GARNACHA BLANCA for details of the variety in Spain.

Grenache Gris, the least important of the three Grenaches is a pink-skinned mutation of GRENACHE NOIR and is most imprtant in Roussillon where two-thirds of France's 1,565 ha/3,866 acres in 2011 were grown. It is more perfumed than GRENACHE BLANC and can add interest to table wines. A small amount of 'Garnacha Roja' is grown in northern Spain.

Grenache Noir, increasingly fashionable vine variety that in the late 20th century was the world's second most widely planted, sprawling, in several hues, all over Spain and southern France but by 2010 had slumped to seventh place, thanks largely to the EU vine pull scheme. It probably owes its early dispersal around the western Mediterranean to the strength and extent of the ARAGÓN kingdom. As GARNACHA, it probably originated in Spain in the northern province of Aragón before colonizing extensive vineyard land both north and south of the Pyrenees, notably in Roussillon, which was ruled by Spain, and more particularly by the kingdom of Aragón, for four centuries until 1659. From here Grenache presumably made its way east and was certainly well established in the southern Rhône by the 19th century. It is also known today that Grenache was not planted in Rioja before phylloxera struck in 1901. The productive, resistant Grenache then practically replaced native varieties in Rioja Baja and made significant inroads in Alta and Alavesa. Grenache is undoubtedly, however, the same grape variety as Sardinia's CANNONAU, which the Sardinians claim as their own, advancing the theory that the variety made its way from this island off Italy (where it is also known as Granaccia and Tocai Rosso) to Spain when Sardinia was under Aragón rule, from 1297 until 1713.

Whatever its origins, Grenache has been uprooted to such an extent in Spain (total area down from 170,000 ha/420,000 acres in the late 1980s to just over 63,000 ha in 2012) that France has the world's largest Grenache presence, 87,723 ha/216,676 acres in 2011—more than any variety other than Merlot. For a vine that covers so much terrain, it has until recently been a name rarely encountered by name by the wine drinker, much of it being blended with other varieties with more colour and backbone. Grenache produces essentially very fruity, rich, sweet-tasting wine, with varying degrees of tannin depending on the degree of WATER STRESS.

With its strong wood and upright growth, Grenache Noir is well suited to traditional BUSH VINE viticulture in hot, dry, windy vineyards. It buds early, can be prone to COULURE

g

and ripens relatively late (after Cabernet Sauvignon). In regions allowing a relatively long growing cycle it can achieve heady sugar levels, and indeed does not achieve full PHYSIOLOGICAL RIPENESS without them. The wine produced is, typically, paler than most reds (although low yields tend to concentrate the pigments, and tannins, in Spain and some Châteauneuf-du-Pape vineyards), with a tendency to oxidize early, a certain rusticity, and more than a hint of sweetness. If the vine is irrigated, as it has tended to be in the New World, it may lose even these taste characteristics. If, however, as by the most punctilious Châteauneuf-du-Pape producers, it is pruned severely on the poorest of soils and allowed to reach full maturity of both vine and grape, it can produce excitingly dense reds that demand several decades' cellaring. The rediscovery of Rhône reds in the late 1980s (see RHÔNE RANGERS, for example) encouraged some New World producers to invest more effort in their own Grenache, even though its sturdy trunk has made it less widely popular in the modern era of MECHANICAL HARVESTING.

See GARNACHA for details of the variety in Spain.

In France, the majority of Grenache is planted in the southern RHÔNE Valley. Here seas of Côtes du Rhône of varying degrees of distinction are produced alongside smaller quantities of CHÂTEAUNEUF-DU-PAPE, GIGONDAS, and the like. Although blending has been the watchword here, notably with the more structured Syrah, older vintages of such monoliths as the famously concentrated Châteauneuf-du-Pape Ch Rayas show what can be done by Grenache and determination alone. The variety's kingdom spreads north to the Drôme *département*, where it also dominates, on nearly 8,000 ha. Grenache is responsible for much of southern France's fruitiest, fullest rosé, most obviously and traditionally in Tavel and in neighbouring Lirac, but also much further eastwards into Provence proper where Grenache is strongly identified with its significant rosé production. In Languedoc-Roussillon, Grenache plays a generally unsung supporting role, together with its downy-leaved close relative LLADONER PELUT, which is also habitually cited in the APPELLATION CONTRÔLÉE regulations for red wines. In Roussillon, Grenaches of all three colours (see also GRENACHE BLANC and GRENACHE GRIS) are valued not only for their dry wines but are the vital ingredient in the region's distinctive VINS DOUX NATURELS.

Grenache Noir is being uprooted in Corsica but in Sardinia, as Cannonau, it still plays a dominant role in the island's and reds and dessert wines. The vine is also grown around the Mediterranean, notably in Croatia.

Grenache's ability to withstand drought and heat made it a popular choice with New World growers when FASHION had little effect on market forces. Extensive historic acreage in the central San Joaquin valley, and some in Mendocino, constituted the majority of the 6,000 acres/2,429 ha that remained in California in 2012. The wine typically made from these old vines—cheap, sweet, gimmicky Grenache Rosé or 'White Grenache'—had done little for Grenache's image in California but the state's RHÔNE RANGERS have rejuvenated the variety's image with new plant material imported straight from the Rhône Valley in their Central Coast vineyards. Grenache has benefited from Washington state's love affair with Rhône wines although fewer than 300 acres had been planted by 2011, less than a tenth as much as Syrah.

Grenache was Australia's most planted black grape variety until the mid 1960s. Shiraz (Syrah) overtook it in the late 1970s but it was not until the early 1990s that Australia's Cabernet Sauvignon output overtook that of Grenache. By 2013 the total area planted with Grenache in Australia had fallen to about 1,800 ha/4,446 acres, high-yielding vines in Riverland having been pulled out while more cosseted vines have been planted in McLaren vale and Barossa valley. Varietal Grenache has been less popular in Australia than GSM blends, and has not featured much in South America.

Robinson, J., Harding, J., and Vouillamoz, J., *Wine Grapes, a complete guide to 1,368 vine varieties, including their origins and flavours* (London, 2012).

Grés de Montpellier

Grés de Montpellier, named TERROIR within the LANGUEDOC AOC in southern France created in 2005 for red wines made mainly from Syrah and Mourvèdre with Grenache Noir in 46 communes in a broad sweep of hinterland of the city of Montpellier generally cooled by breezes from the nearby Mediterranean.

grey rot, sometimes known as **grey mould** and sometimes just **rot**, the malevolent form of BOTRYTIS BUNCH ROT and one of the most harmful of the FUNGAL DISEASES that attack vines. In this undesirable bunch rot form, the *Botrytis cinerea* fungus rapidly spreads throughout the berry flesh and the skin breaks down. Other fungi and bacteria then also invade the berry and the grapes become rotten. Badly infected fruit develops off-flavours, ACIDITY is significantly reduced, and PHENOLICS are OXIDIZED by LACCASE; badly infected vineyards themselves have a characteristic mouldy and often vinegary smell. Wines produced from such fruit smell mouldy and red wines look pale and grey-brown. When the *Botrytis cinerea* fungus attacks healthy, ripe, white wine grapes and the weather conditions are favourable, it results in so-called NOBLE ROT, which can produce some of the world's finest sweet wines. If the grapes are dark-skinned, unripe, or damaged, or the weather is unremittingly humid, the fungus wreaks so much damage that it is called grey rot.

greywacke, pronounced 'graywacky', from the German *Grauwacke*, is a tough, dark grey sandstone, with a high CLAY content. Most sedimentary rocks (see GEOLOGY) show a fairly uniform grain size, whereas greywacke, formed in turbid deep-sea water, shows characteristically jumbled grain sizes, with thick accumulations of coarse material (typically of QUARTZ, feldspar, and rock fragments) closely intermixed with fine clay. On land it weathers slowly, giving stony, free-draining soils.

Greywacke is found in South Africa's Western Cape; in California's RUSSIAN RIVER VALLEY; and in Germany's MOSEL, AHR, and MITTELRHEIN; but perhaps most famously in NEW ZEALAND, where the bedrock spine of both islands is composed largely of greywacke, and detritus derived from it dominates the gravels of regions such as Hawke's Bay, Marlborough, and Waipara.

A.J.M.

Grignan-les-Adhémar, name adopted in 2010 for an extensive (1,361 ha/3,362 acre) appellation on the eastern fringes of the southern RHÔNE for mainly red wines. (Its original name, Coteaux du Tricastin, was abandoned because it was too readily associated with a nearby nuclear power plant.) Although the climate here is definitively MEDITERRANEAN, the higher vineyards and more exposed terrain produce rather lighter wines than those of the Côtes-du-Rhône which they resemble. The best wine comes from sheltered, south-facing slopes, but acidity levels are usually noticeable beneath the superficial warmth of the southern vine variety perfume. The region was substantially redeveloped by *pieds noirs* returning from North Africa in the late 1960s. Large areas of scrub were cleared and planted with southern Rhône vine varieties. Grenache and Syrah are the principal vine varieties grown. Of the permitted white varieties, Grenache Blanc, Clairette, Bourboulenc, Marsanne, Roussanne, and Viognier may also be included. The wines are similar to those of the much larger VENTOUX appellation to the immediate south, which was also promoted to full APPELLATION CONTRÔLÉE status in 1973.

Grignolino, very localized, curiosity of a grape variety of the PIEMONTE region in northwest Italy sold almost invariably as a pale red VARIETAL wine with an almost alpine scent and a tangy ACIDITY. Grignolino is a native of the MONFERRATO hills between Asti and Casale and serves the same function as DOLCETTO in the province of Cuneo: that of providing a wine that can be drunk young with pleasure while the brawnier wines of the zone are shedding their youthful asperity—although Grignolino is more difficult to match with food than the fuller Dolcetto. The light colour and relatively low alcohol (11 to 12%) can be deceptive; the wine draws significant TANNINS from the abundant pips of the Grignolino grape and takes its name from *grignole*, the dialect name for pips in the province of Asti.

The wine remains an unquestionably local taste and, with its unusual combination of pale colour, perceptible acidity, and tannins, somewhat *sui generis*. In recent years, its popularity has declined rapidly, with a number of producers grubbing up vineyards as even local markets turn away from this variety. It has its own DOC areas, Grignolino Monferrato Casalese (195 ha) and Grignolino d'Asti (209 ha), the latter only minimally overlaps with DOCG ASTI. Total plantings in Italy in 2010 were 1,314 ha/3,246 acres, practically all in Piemonte. W.S.

Grillet, Château. See CHÂTEAU GRILLET.

Grillo, Sicilian white grape variety once used as the base for the best MARSALA. Grown on bush vines, it produced potent, full-bodied base wines that were supplemented by a proportion of the more aromatic INZOLIA. DNA PROFILING established that Grillo is a natural CROSS of Sicily's Catarratto with Muscat of Alexandria. At its best, it gives full-bodied wines of real interest, although they lack the aromatic intensity that has made Inzolia's transformation from fortified to dry white wine variety so much easier. Plantings have grown substantially. Virtually all of Italy's 6,294 ha/15,553 acres in 2010 were in Sicily, although the Rossese Bianco of Liguria has been shown to be identical to Grillo. See SICILY for more details.

Gringet, not, as was long thought, a synonym for SAVAGNIN but a distinct variety used mainly for light, floral, still and sparkling wines in AYSE, a SAVOIE cru.

Groenekloof, cool, predominantly white wine ward in the Darling district in SOUTH AFRICA.

Grolleau Noir, sometimes known as **Groslot**, is the everyday red grape variety of TOURAINE. It produces extremely high yields of relatively thin, acid wine and it is to the benefit of wine drinkers that it is so systematically being replaced with Gamay and, more recently, Cabernet Franc. It was once much more important but total French plantings have been steady this century at around 2,200 ha/5,500 acres in 2011. The status of the variety is such that it is allowed into the rosé but not red versions of APPELLATION CONTRÔLÉE wines such as ANJOU, SAUMUR, and Touraine. It has played a major part only in Rosé d'Anjou, in which it is commonly blended with Gamay, which ripens just before it. Plantings of **the** pink-skinned mutation **Grolleau Gris**, in much the same part of France, had fallen to 459 ha/1,138 acres by 2011.

Groppello Gentile, red grape variety grown to a limited extent on about 300 ha, mainly in the Italian wine region of LOMBARDY, it is the most important of the Groppellos.

Groslot is a common synonym for the Loire's rather commonplace red vine variety GROLLEAU.

Gros Manseng, assertive and increasingly popular Basque white grape grown on about 3,000 ha/7,500 acres of SOUTH WEST FRANCE in 2011 to produce drier versions of Jurançon and various Béarn wines, as well as being one of the more characterful ingredients in Gascon dry whites. The vine looks similar to but is distinct from the rarer, thinner-skinned PETIT MANSENG. It yields more generously and produces discernibly less elegant, less rich, but still powerful wine. Unlike the smaller-berried Petit Manseng, it is not sensitive to COULURE. Gros Manseng, unlike Petit Manseng, is rarely used for sweet wines.

Gros Plant, or, to give it a name that is more of a mouthful than the wine usually is, **Gros Plant du Pays Nantais**, is the country cousin of MUSCADET. Made from FOLLE BLANCHE vines, called Gros Plant here, with Colombard occasionally playing a minor part, it is grown in a wide arc east but mainly south of the city of Nantes on the Loire. Gros Plant is one of the most acidic-tasting wines made anywhere, and its aggressively dry style serves only to accentuate its inherent tartness—exacerbated by the grapes' tendency to rot here before they ripen. The Folle Blanche vine responsible was introduced to this region by the DUTCH WINE TRADE, and outnumbered the Muscadet vine until the ravages of PHYLLOXERA in the late 19th century. Gros Plant was promoted from VDQS to AOC in 2011. About a third as much Gros Plant is made as Muscadet, although a much smaller proportion ever leaves the region. As in Muscadet, it may be described as '*sur lie*' if aged with LEES CONTACT until at least March.

Gros Rhin, Swiss synonym for SILVANER, to distinguish it from Petit Rhin, or Riesling.

Grosse Lage, term adopted in 2013 by Germany's VDP association for those vineyards classified by its members as their best and hence capable of generating a GROSSES GEWÄCHS. Prior to that, the term ERSTE LAGE was used for such vineyards, but has been used from 2013 for a lesser tier of vineyards (effectively the premiers crus, with Grosse Lagen being the grands crus). D.S.

Grosser Ring, the Mosel branch of the VDP growers' association. Founded in 1908 in Trier, where its annual September auctions are still a prestigious feature of Germany's wine calendar as well as an indicator of vintage quality and market health, the group comprises 31 growers (as of 2014). D.S.

Grosses Gewächs (pronounced 'guh-*vex*') is a prestige wine category devised by Germany's VDP and in use (though no longer exclusively by its members) since 2002. Wines so designated (but not necessarily so labelled, as the terminology is not recognized by the GERMAN WINE LAW) are from traditional grapes and vineyard sites classified (by the VDP) as (superior) GROSSE LAGEN. The sites in question are typically EINZELLAGEN but occasionally subdivisions thereof (whose names are not technically allowed on labels). Grosses Gewächse (pl.) must be cropped at YIELDS of no more than 50 hl/ha, be hand harvested, at no less than the MUST WEIGHT required for SPÄTLESE (although Grosses Gewächs wines are nowadays labelled without PRÄDIKAT), and be subjected to sensory review. Besides attempting to classify, protect, and promote the best vineyard sites of Germany, the VDP regulations for Grosses Gewächs were also intended to stipulate a recognizable style of relatively full-bodied, legally TROCKEN wine (though that designation is also absent from their labels). Grosses Gewächs wines must be bottled in glass embossed with a logo featuring a grape cluster and the numeral 1 and (since vintage 2007) are labelled with the initials GG. In a departure from conventional German labelling practice, and to emphasize continuity with the Burgundian notion of a GRAND CRU, vineyard names on the labels of Grosse Gewächse are not preceded by the names of their respective villages, with the result that some names—Herrenberg and Schlossberg, for example—can be found on wines from several different sites. Within the VDP, Grosses Gewächs encompasses Rheingau wines formerly labelled ERSTES GEWÄCHS. D.S.

Grosslagen, are collective vineyard sites delimited by the 1971 GERMAN WINE LAW (and under no circumstances to be confused with the superior class of single vineyard sites defined by the VDP as grosse lagen). Sometimes co-opting a traditional place name but often made up for the occasion, a Grosslage designation is conjoined to the name of a particular wine village, but typically covers vineyards (each officially known as an EINZELLAGE) in far-flung and far less prestigious villages, the thinly disguised intent being, by means of the German labelling template village + vineyard, to trade on the prestige earned by sites outside the Grosslage. Thus, Niersteiner Gutes Domtal, in fact, refers to vast acreage spread across 15 disparate villages and 32 Einzellagen of which a mere one—tiny and obscure—happens to be within the communal limits of the Rheinhessen's justly famous wine village Nierstein. Another notorious example is Piesporter Michelsberg in the

Mosel. A Wiltinger Scharzberg Grosslage was even registered to trade deceptively on the prestige of the Saar's famed Scharzhofberg vineyard. Grosslage names are frequently applied to blends of lesser grapes in areas best-known for their fine Rieslings. Thankfully, the use of Grosslage designations has greatly diminished since the 1990s and is largely confined to inexpensive wines destined for sales in supermarkets. A very few Grosslage names—most notably Bernkasteler Badstube—are widely used even by the most quality-conscious among growers, because they incorporate solely high-quality sites, many of whose individual names have never been well-known.

Grosslage is still an officially recognized term in Austria but is not used on labels.   D.S.

Pigott, S., and Johnson, H., *The Wine Atlas of Germany* (London, 1995).

Gros Verdot, an unusual Bordeaux variety without the concentration or interest of PETIT VERDOT. May be grown in South America.

grower, the all-important producer of the raw material for winemaking. This individual may be called a grape-grower, more precisely a vine-grower, possibly even a wine-grower (or winegrower) if he or she also vinifies. Terms in other languages include *vigneron* and *viticulteur* in French, and *vignaiolo* in Italian. Wine producers who grow their own grapes and vinify them into wine but on a limited scale are often referred to somewhat carelessly and often inaccurately as **small growers**. A significant proportion of all vine-growers produce only grapes, however, which they sell to CO-OPERATIVES, merchant-bottlers (see NÉGOCIANT), or larger wine operations.

growth cycle of the vine. See VINE GROWTH CYCLE.

growth regulators, synthetic substances which act on vines like HORMONES to regulate their growth and development. A synthetic AUXIN, 4-CPA, has for example been used to improve FRUIT SET. Synthetic GIBBERELLINS have been used to increase berry size, especially for the seedless SULTANA, and a synthetic ethylene-releasing compound termed ethephon can be used to hasten grape maturity and enhance colouration in particularly cool climates. More recently applied to viticulture, hydrogen cyanamide encourages early and complete BUDBREAK, which can be useful for TROPICAL VITICULTURE. These chemicals are mostly used for TABLE GRAPES and their application to both table grapes and wine grapes is regulated by rules governing the use of AGROCHEMICALS. Some hormones effective on grapevines—ABSCISIC ACID and CYTOKININS, for example—have not been produced commercially for use in the vineyard.   R.E.S.

grubbing up vines is known as *arrachage* in France, where it became a common practice as part of the EU's various VINE PULL SCHEMES aimed at reducing the European WINE LAKE. In the NEW WORLD it is generally referred to as ripping out.

The more traditional reason for grubbing up a vineyard is that the VINE AGE is so high and the average YIELD so low that the vineyard is no longer economic (although the prestige associated with old vines, or VIEILLES VIGNES, may retard this process). Weak demand for wine grapes, signalled by wineries failing to renew contracts with growers and/or continued periods of low prices, sometimes below production costs, also leads to vineyard removal.

A vineyard may be grubbed up because its owner wishes to change VINE VARIETY or CLONE, although this may be achieved by TOP GRAFTING, or field grafting on to the existing trunks and root systems. Vineyards are normally grubbed up when invaded by a pest as deadly as PHYLLOXERA (as thousands of acres were in northern California in the late 1980s), and a disease such as LEAFROLL VIRUS, ESCA, or GRAPEVINE YELLOWS may damage production to such an extent that grubbing up is the only option. In the early 2010s, TRUNK DISEASE infection had become a major reason for vineyard removal in California and around the world, as the proportion of dead and missing vines increases with age.

If the vineyard is to be replanted, care must be taken that the soil is free of pests and diseases. FUMIGATION may be necessary; see also NEMATODES.

Grumello, subzone of VALTELLINA in the far north of Italy.

Grüner Veltliner. The most commonly planted vine variety in AUSTRIA is grown elsewhere in eastern Europe and is increasingly respected worldwide. This well-adapted variety is planted on 14,641 ha/36,163 acres of Austria, particularly in Lower Austria, where it represents more than half of total white grape production, and in the Vienna region, where it comprises about a third of all plantings. DNA PROFILING in Austria has shown that Grüner Veltliner is not genetically related to ROTER VELTLINER or FRÜHROTER VELTLINER.

The vine can be productive and is relatively hardy, but ripens too late for much of northern Europe. Yields of 100 hl/ha (5.7 tons/acre) are possible, invariably using the LENZ MOSER system of vine training, in the least distinguished vineyards of the Weinviertel in Lower Austria and the resulting wine is inoffensive if unexciting. However, at its best, arguably in the Wachau, Kamptal, Kremstal, Weinviertel, Wagram, and in the hands of some of the most ambitious growers in Vienna, Grüner Veltliner can produce wines which combine perfume and substance. The wine is typically dry, full-bodied, peppery, or spicy, and with time in bottle can start to taste positively Burgundian. Grüner Veltliner can produce a variety of wine styles from base wines for Austrian SEKT, simple wines served at HEURIGER, popular medium-bodied peppery wines to very opulent, concentrated wines. Grüner Veltliner may be regarded as Austria's biggest asset and adorns restaurant wine lists around the globe. It can be difficult for non-German speakers to pronounce so is often abbreviated to 'Gruner', 'GV', or even 'Gru-Ve'.

The variety has long been grown just over Lower Austria's northern border in the CZECH REPUBLIC, where it is known as Veltlin or Velt-línské Zelené and in the Sopron vineyards of HUNGARY as Zöldveltelini. It is also (just) known in Germany's Rheinhessen and is being assayed in Australia, New Zealand, and North America.

GSM on a wine label indicates the popular, southern-Rhône-inspired blend of Grenache, Syrah/Shiraz, and Mourvèdre. Particularly common in Australia but also made in California and Washington state.

GST. See CLIMATE CLASSIFICATION.

guaiacol. See BRETTANOMYCES, OAK FLAVOUR, and SMOKE TAINT.

Guarnaccia, Calabrian synonym used for CODA DI VOLPE BIANCA. Guarnaccia Nera is a Campanian synonym for MAGLIOCCO DOLCE.

Guenoc Valley, California AVA. See LAKE COUNTY.

Guigal, family-owned merchant-grower based at Ampuis, CÔTE RÔTIE, in the northern RHÔNE. Although established as recently as 1946 by Étienne Guigal, Établissements Guigal is the most famous of any of the Rhône valley's merchants or growers with collectors and investors. This is very largely due to the efforts of its manager since 1961, Étienne's only son Marcel, a man of exceptional modesty and a gifted, meticulous winemaker. Guigal owns slightly more than 30 ha/75 acres of prime vineyard in Côte Rôtie, and it was the wines made from three of its best parcels, extravagantly praised by influential American wine writer Robert PARKER in the early to mid 1980s, that first drew international attention to Marcel Guigal. It would be fair to say that the quality of Guigal's top wines, along with Parker's persistent enthusiasm for them among many other Rhône wines, spearheaded a resurgence of interest in the whole region.

Guigal's so-called CRU wines (La Mouline, La Landonne, and La Turque) are dark, dramatic, mouth-fillingly rich and oaky expressions of the SYRAH grape (supplemented by up to 11% of co-planted VIOGNIER in the case of La Mouline); made from low yields of very ripe, late-picked fruit aged for three and a half years in 100% new oak, and bottled without FINING or FILTRATION. They are particularly impressive when young and their quality is beyond question, but opinions are divided about their style; purists in particular feel that their character is masked by excessive oak. Reputation and rarity combined (only 400 to 700 cases of each are made each year) have also made them extremely expensive and therefore game for criticism, fair or not. More recent offerings include the more plentiful Côte Rôtie Ch d'Ampuis, La Doriane, a special CONDRIEU, and, from the 2001 vintage, Ermitage Ex Voto. Because of the ballyhoo over his top wines, it is easy to overlook the fact that Guigal's NÉGOCIANT wines, made substantially from bought-in grapes, are also very good and deservedly popular.

In 1984 Guigal bought and revitalized the firm of Vidal Fleury, the company where Étienne Guigal worked at 14 years old (from 1923 until 1940) before founding his own. Vidal Fleury is run quite independently of Guigal although Marcel, helped increasingly by his son Philippe, makes its Côte Rôtie wines.

M.W.E.S.

Gumpoldskirchen, wine centre in lower AUSTRIA famous for its fiery, full-bodied whites made from ZIERFANDLER (or Spätrot) and ROTGIPFLER grapes. Now part of the district known as THERMENREGION.

Gundagai, small wine region in Southern New South Wales Zone. Makes ripe, fleshy Shiraz and soft, peachy Chardonnay.

Gutedel, meaning 'good and noble' in German, is not the most obvious synonym for CHASSELAS but is still used in Germany, particularly in the Markgräflerland, southern Baden, which along with neighbouring areas of Alsace and Switzerland, is sometimes referred to as the Gutedel Triangle on account of this variety's ubiquity and continued popularity. The wines, generally juicy and straightforward, may have notes of almond and hay in the better examples, and particularly old vines in calcareous sites can evince both distinction and minerality. A dark-berried form, **Roter Gutedel**, is also known in Baden.

Gutenborner is a very minor white-berried GERMAN CROSS bred from Müller-Thurgau × Chasselas Napoleon which has had some success in sheltered sites of ENGLAND. Its main attribute is its ability to ripen in cool climates.

Gutsabfüllung. See ERZEUGERABFÜLLUNG.

guttation, botanical term applied to vines losing water through small pores at the leaf margin, due to root pressure. It can be seen early in the morning for vines in wet soil under cool conditions. See also BLEEDING.

Gutturnio, red wine from EMILIA-ROMAGNA in Italy.

Guyot, Jules, respected 19th century French scientist with a particular interest in viticulture and winemaking whose name lives on in the system of CANE PRUNING which he promulgated. His practical treatises on growing vines and making wine were translated into English in the second half of the 19th century and are enthusiastically followed by NEW WORLD vignerons.

Although cane pruning had been used in France for a very long period, it was promoted by Dr Guyot in 1860. The basic principle of Guyot pruning is to leave six- to ten-bud canes and for each a single two-bud spur at the base; shoots from this spur form the cane the following year (see PRUNING). The **Guyot simple** form, also known as single Guyot, has one cane and one spur. The length of the cane (in French *long bois* or *aste*), or at least the number of buds thereon, may be fixed by APPELLATION laws. **Guyot double**, or double Guyot, the most common vine-TRAINING SYSTEM in

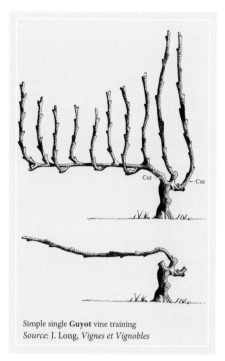

Simple single **Guyot** vine training
Source: J. Long, *Vignes et Vignobles*

Bordeaux, has two canes and two spurs, and the canes are trained to each side. Sometimes the canes are arched, as in the Jura. Galet lists regional variations of the Guyot. R.E.S.

Galet, P., *Précis de viticulture* (7th edn, Montpellier, 2000).

gyropalette or **girasol**, special metal crate holding many dozen inverted bottles of traditional method sparkling wine in a remote-controlled, movable frame. This is the mechanized form of RIDDLING and was developed in Cataluña in the 1970s. They are now widely used in CHAMPAGNE, ITALY, and elsewhere. *Girasol* is Spanish for sunflower, which also turns during a 24-hour period.

For more details, see SPARKLING WINEMAKING.

g

HACCP. See QUALITY ASSURANCE.

hail, frozen raindrops or ice bodies built up by accretion, typically falling in thunderstorms. To the normal ill effects of heavy summer RAINFALL is added direct physical damage to the vines and fruit. That to the vines ranges from ripping and stripping of the leaves to bruising and breaking of the young stems: effects which can carry over to the following season or even much longer. Damage to young bunches may destroy or at best reduce the crop, although compensatory growth of the remaining berries may minimize the effects on final YIELD. Hail damage while berries are ripening, on the other hand, is invariably a disaster. Smashed berries are prey to ROT and ferment on the vine, rendering even undamaged parts of the bunches unusable. BURGUNDY is particularly and apparently increasingly prone to hail damage, as is Mendoza in ARGENTINA. Hail is said to cost French agriculture more than half a billion euros a year.

Hailstorms characteristically follow irregular but well-defined pathways through an area, sometimes devastating parts of a vineyard but leaving other parts untouched. Local TOPOGRAPHY may result in a tendency for the storms to follow preferred pathways, but largely their incidence is unpredictable. Various prevention techniques have been tried, including seeding the clouds with silver iodide or dry ice, from planes or cannon, to reduce the size of the hailstones so that some melt before they reach the ground, and using hail cannon that generate shock waves intended to disrupt the formation of hail. Covering the vines with netting is another laborious and expensive option which reduces the impact of hailstones but also reduces the amount of SUNLIGHT reaching the vines—desirable only in the hottest wine regions. The technologies can hardly be described as proven, but

have found supporters among vine-growers understandably desperate to protect their hard-won crops. Insurance against hail is rarely cost-effective. J.G. & J.E.H.

hail disease. See WHITE ROT.

halbtrocken designates German wines that have between 5 and 18 g/l of RESIDUAL SUGAR depending on the TOTAL ACIDITY. Levels above 12 g/l are permitted governed by the formula: maximum residual sugar equals total g/l of acidity plus 10, up to an absolute limit of 18. Among Riesling wines, which are most often encountered in halbtrocken format, 8 g/l of acidity is routinely reached, so that effectively halbtrocken refers to wines with between 10 and 18 g/l residual sugar. Among the top German producers in this century there has been a tendency to bottle fewer wines that fit the criteria for halbtrocken, as well as labelling those that do as FEINHERB or without any reference to degree of SWEETNESS. In Austria, any wine is officially halbtrocken (and then labelled as such, albeit in tiny print) if it exceeds the maximum residual sugar set for TROCKEN (which varies with total acidity) but does not exceed 12 g/l. D.S.

Hammurabi (end of 18th century BC), king of BABYLONIA responsible for uniting MESOPOTAMIA with its capital Babylon. His law code survives on baked clay tablets and contains the earliest references to wine shops and wine sellers.

Hanepoot, traditional Afrikaans name for SOUTH AFRICA's most planted Muscat vine variety, MUSCAT OF ALEXANDRIA.

hangover, one of wine's least welcome effects, normally following some DRUNKENNESS or certainly excessive consumption. Drinking wine

with or after food and drinking at least as much WATER as wine can lessen the likelihood of a hangover. Homeopathic prophylactics include milk thistle extract (silymarin) and nux vomica. There is no evidence that wine hangovers are different from those caused by any other form of ALCOHOL, although inexpensive wine, non-organic wine, wine consumed with grain-based alcholic drinks, and bottle-aged PORT have all been accused of increasing the risk of hangover. The only indisputably effective control is moderation.

hang time, American expression that has come to be associated with the controversial practice of postponing the harvest beyond traditional ripeness. This can result in partly shrivelled and dehydrated berries that yield overripe flavours and such high alcoholic strength that MUSTS often need dilution with water. Proponents of long hang time argue that wines made from such grapes have better aroma and flavour and softer tannins. The practice appears to be less popular in the second decade of this century than it was in the last decade of the 20th. Very ripe, dehydrated grapes weigh less than those picked at conventional ripeness, generally resulting in lower payments for growers paid by weight. R.E.S.

Haraszthy, Agoston (1812–69), early CALIFORNIA wine-grower and promoter, frequently but wrongly identified as the 'father of California wine'. Born in Austro-Hungary, he went to the United States in 1842 and to California in 1849, where he engaged in multifarious activities, including politics, horticulture, and gold-refining. In 1856, he bought a SONOMA county vineyard and established the Buena Vista winery, still extant today. In 1861, as a member of the state commission on viticulture, he travelled to Europe and sent back many thousands of vine cuttings to California. His account of this trip and of his work as a wine-grower in California, *Grape Culture, Wines, and Wine-Making* (1862), first brought California as a wine state to the attention of the nation and is Haraszthy's main claim to importance in the history of wine in America.

After losing control of the Buena Vista winery he migrated to Nicaragua, where he died in mysterious circumstances. In the years after his death it came to be believed that Haraszthy was the first to show the possibilities of wine-growing in the state, the first to introduce superior grape varieties into California, and in particular the first to introduce the ZINFANDEL vine. None of this is true, but the story has become legendary and difficult to dislodge.   T.P.

McGinty, B., *Strong Wine: the Life and Legend of Agoston Haraszthy* (Stanford, 1998).

Pinney, T., *A History of Wine in America* (Berkeley, Calif., 1989).

hard, TASTING TERM applied to wine that is high in astringent TANNINS and apparently lacking in FRUIT. See TEXTURE.

Hardys, one of Australia's best-known wine brands, with a long and distinguished history. Founder Thomas Hardy was just 20 when he sailed from Devon, England to the new colony of South Australia in 1850. Three years later he founded his winery at Bankside on the River Torrens in Adelaide. Within a few decades he brought his sons into the business creating Thomas Hardy & Sons, exported South Australia's first wine to the UK, and stimulated the McLaren Vale region's development. When he died in 1912, he was regarded as one of the fathers of the Australian wine industry and Hardys was cemented in wine history. In 1976 Thomas Hardy & Sons purchased the Emu Wine Company, thereby acquiring Western Australia's Houghton Wines. In 1982 Hardys completed a neat circle, buying Chateau Reynella in McLaren Vale, whose founder John Reynell had introduced the young Thomas Hardy to winemaking. In 1992 the family business became a public company, merging with Berri Renmano—a RIVERLAND wine CO-OPERATIVE—to create BRL Hardy. Hardys is now the flagship brand of ACCOLADE WINES and comprises a full range of wines capped by the Thomas Hardy and Eileen Hardy labels commemorating respectively the founder and Eileen, the wife of one of his grandsons, Thomas Mayfield Hardy. Eileen was a courageous matriarch who continued the business when it might otherwise have faltered following the untimely death of her husband in a plane crash. Subbrands include Sir James, Tintara, Oomoo, and William Hardy. Banrock Station and Stamp of Australia are important export labels.   H.H.

harmony, TASTING TERM for a component of wine QUALITY related to BALANCE, but encompassing FLAVOUR as well as structure. A wine is harmonious if all its aromatic and structural elements are in proportion, with no individual element being too prominent, and if they complement each other to form a coherent whole. For example, a wine with herbaceous, barely ripe aromas but, in contrast, full BODY and low ACID on the palate might be said to lack harmony.   A.H.

Harriague, name for TANNAT in Uruguay. Inspired by a Basque viticultural pioneer there.

Hárslevelű, white grape variety, whose name means 'linden leaf', which is most widely grown in HUNGARY, where it produces characteristically spicy, aromatic white wines. This is the variety which brings perfume to FURMINT, the variety that has been shown to be its parent by DNA PROFILING whose grapes make up the majority of the blend for the famous dessert wine TOKAJI. Hárslevelű is widely planted elsewhere in Hungary, to a national total of 1,659 ha/4,098 acres in 2011, and produces a range of VARIETAL wines which vary considerably in quality and provenance. Good Hárslevelű is typically deep green-gold, very viscous, full, with the powerful flavour of linden honey. In Somló, it produces a less aromatic wine with some minerality while in Villány-Siklós it gives a softer, more perfumed wine.

The variety is popularly associated with the village of Debrö in the Mátra foothills (although much of the wine sold as Debröi Hárslevelű has been a much less specific and less distinguished off-dry blend).

The variety is also grown over the border from Hungary's Tokaj region in SLOVAKIA Austria's Burgenland, Romania, and in South Africa.

harvest, both the process of picking ripe grapes from the vine and transferring them to the winery (or field pressing station), and its occasionally festive, if frenetic, duration.

This transition period in the winemaking cycle from vineyard to cellar is also known as VINTAGE (crush in much of the New World), and RÉCOLTE or *vendange* in France, *vendemmia* in Italy, *Ernte* in Germany, COSECHA in Spain, *vindima* in the DOURO and *colheita* in the rest of Portugal.

Timing

A critical aspect of harvest is its timing, choosing a point during the grape RIPENING process when the balance between its natural accumulation of SUGARS and its decreasing tally of natural plant ACIDS is optimal (see SAMPLING, grapes).

Typically this is a frenzied period, especially in hotter climates where warm, dry weather can rapidly accelerate ripening, causing different varieties to ripen at the same time, and sometimes putting pressure on available FERMENTATION VESSEL space. In cooler climates, the threat of humid weather and possible ROT, heavy RAINFALL making vineyard access difficult, HAIL damage, or even FROST can also put unwelcome pressure on picking schedules. ACIDIFICATION and ENRICHMENT are respectively the most common rescue operations in the case of grapes picked slightly after or before ideal maturity. MICRO-OXYGENATION may also help reduce the HERBACEOUSNESS resulting from slightly unripe fruit.

Timing of the harvest is additionally complicated by the fact that the fruit in different parts of a single vineyard may vary in ripeness, and the picking of a single plot may take several days.

Although the timing of harvest depends on fruit RIPENESS, it also depends on the region, the grape variety, and the type of wine required (Pinot Noir grapes destined for sparkling white wine are invariably picked much earlier than they would be for a still, red wine, for example). Harvest typically takes place in autumn (see VINE GROWTH CYCLE): September and October in the northern hemisphere and March and April in the southern hemisphere. In very hot climates harvest may start in midsummer, however, while at the coolest limits of vine cultivation grapes may be picked when all the leaves have fallen from the vine and there is snow on the ground.

Harvest can, at least theoretically, take place somewhere in the world in every month of the year. Some German EISWEIN is not picked until the January following the official year of harvest (which it must by law carry on the label, no matter when it was picked). The common vintage period for most southern-hemisphere wine is March and April. In very cool southern-hemisphere vineyards such as Central Otago in NEW ZEALAND, grapes may remain on the vine until early June.

By July the harvest has usually begun in the earliest regions of the northern hemisphere, the warmest vineyards of CYPRUS and the vineyards of the south-eastern states of the UNITED STATES, for example. In August, grapes for the production of California sparkling wine are usually picked. For the majority of wine regions in the northern hemisphere, September and October are the harvest months, with the cooler and later regions and varieties extending into November. Northern-hemisphere fruit may still be on the vine in December, particularly for Eiswein in Germany or ICEWINE in Canada. In very hot southern-hemisphere vineyards, picking particularly precocious grapes before the end of December is not unheard of.

Manual harvesting

The traditional method of harvesting, by hand, consists of cutting the stem of individual bunches (peduncle) and putting the bunches into a suitable container. This method, as opposed to MECHANICAL HARVESTING, can be employed regardless of terrain, row spacing (see VINE DENSITY), and precise vine-TRAINING SYSTEM. It also allows pickers to select individual bunches according to their ripeness and to eliminate unhealthy fruit affected by ROT or DISEASE. Very occasionally pickers may be instructed to leave unripe fruit on the vine although this is not always easy to determine by the time of harvest and vines are usually stripped clean.

Occasionally individual berries are harvested, in the case of bunches affected by BOTRYTIS, an operation that is possible only with a high LABOUR input. This is most famously practised at Ch d'YQUEM in Sauternes and in other vineyards specializing in botrytized sweet wines in SOUTH WEST FRANCE, Austria, and Germany (see AUSLESE, BEERENAUSLESE, and TROCKENBEERENAUSLESE) but the technique may also be employed in the production of (necessarily expensive) dry wines when the vineyard has been attacked by less noble rot.

The cost of manual harvesting increases dramatically when yields are low, for particularly widely spaced vines, or on particularly steep vineyards as in the MOSEL.

The efficiency of hand picking, as opposed to MECHANICAL HARVESTING, depends on vineyard conditions. If the fruit is at a convenient height and the crop heavy, an experienced picker can harvest up to 2 tonnes /4,400 lbs a day. Output is reduced by worker fatigue, or in regions where the fruit is at a less convenient height: close to the ground as in traditional Bordeaux vineyards, for example; or grapes trained on the overhead TRELLIS SYSTEMS of southern Italy, northern Portugal, Argentina, and Chile. Light crops are also particularly expensive to pick by hand, where bunches are small because of the grape variety (GEWÜRZTRAMINER, for example) or because of poor fruit set (see COULURE). In such circumstances, even an experienced picker may have less than 500 kg/1,100 lb to show for a day's work.

Manual harvesting requires little equipment. The stems are cut by small secateurs or hooked-tip knives. The fruit is put into a small container holding perhaps 5 or 10 kg of fruit. This was traditionally, and still is in parts of Europe, a wooden trug, cane basket, or leather hod strapped on to the pickers' backs, but nowadays it is most likely to be an unromantic but lighter and easier-to-clean plastic container which may be emptied at intervals into a larger container for transport to the winery, or field pressing station, typically by tractor. These larger containers, often called 'gondolas' in the New World, holding between 500 kg and 2 tonnes, are passed down the row before being towed to the winery. In many vineyards, the fruit is simply emptied into the back of a trailer, although the shallower the depth of fruit, the less damage it will suffer, and so containers full of grapes are increasingly stacked on trailers for transport to the grape reception area.

The harvest workforce varies from region to region. In much of Europe, picking teams include both experienced locals and casual workers, often students and itinerant workers. Iberia traditionally supplied picking teams that would systematically work their way northwards through Europe from region to region as they successively reached ripeness. Similarly, Australian vineyards of the 1950s and 1960s were traditionally picked by the large numbers of itinerants who moved between the sugar-cane fields of northern Australia and the vineyards of the south. But increased mechanization in the sugar-cane industry has necessitated increased mechanization of the Australian wine industry. In the western United States, the typical grape-picker is Mexican. Wine farms in South Africa enjoy access to relatively inexpensive labour although since 1994 regulatory protection for rural employees has been strengthened. When in the late 1980s the Iron Curtain was torn down and EU membership raised wages in Spain and Portugal, eastern Europe became an important source of itinerant labour for vineyard owners in northern Europe.

Providing this annual influx with accommodation, sustenance and, often, transport is an increasingly onerous task each harvest. It is said that in many wine regions mechanical harvesting is the direct result of protest by the spouses of vineyard owners, to whom much of this annual workload has traditionally fallen.

See also MECHANICAL HARVESTING.

R.E.S. & A.D.W.

Coombe, B. G., and Dry, P. R. (eds.), *Viticulture*, ii: *Practices* (Adelaide, 1992).

Loftus, S., *Puligny-Montrachet: Journal of a Village in Burgundy* (London, 1992).

harvest traditions celebrate the culmination of a year's hard work in the vineyard and, in areas which have not yet succumbed to MECHANIZATION, encourage the pickers in their backbreaking task.

France

Harvest traditions are at their strongest in France. The church plays a role in many European villages, where a symbolic bunch of grapes is blessed before the harvest and a thanksgiving service held at the end (see also RELIGION). (New World producers such as Robert MONDAVI of California have emulated this tradition.)

Vineyard owners and other members of their families try to be present for the harvest even if they usually work in a distant city. At the end of the harvest a certain amount of horseplay almost inevitably accompanies the picking of the last rows, and one or two pickers end up being thrown into the sticky mass of grapes (a tradition endangered by the increasing use of shallow plastic containers to transport grapes to the cellar).

Traditionally, the tractor pulling the final load is decorated with flowers before it drives, horn blaring, to the cellar. On some estates the pickers still offer a bouquet of flowers to the owner and speeches are made. Large or small, almost all estates celebrate the end of harvest with a party and some regions have their own name for this: *la paulée* in BURGUNDY, *la gerbebaude* in BORDEAUX, and *le cochelet* in CHAMPAGNE.

Most harvest traditions are gastronomic, however, and the major events in a picker's day are the three meals which punctuate it (or four if the *casse-croute*, a second breakfast normally taken in the vines, is counted). In France, the women who run the kitchens during the harvest are usually part of a family team, helped by local women who may work in the vines during the rest of the year. For 11 months these women cook only for their families and friends, but for one month they must turn themselves into restaurateurs of a special kind. Working in often rudimentary kitchens, they must feed demanding pickers both well and economically. Soups, rabbit dishes, and dishes such as *pot-au-feu, coq au vin*, and *blanquettes* are often requested by pickers nostalgic for an era when long, slow cooking was the norm. A harvest would not be a harvest in Burgundy without a *bœuf bourguignon*, for example, and in Bordeaux the bonfires of *sarments*, or vine shoots, on which are grilled steaks and sausages, may be kept blazing to form the focus of informal dancing and singing after dinner.

The harvest cook's work is regularly interrupted to administer first aid, and when the cook's long day ends, she (and it is still usually she) is likely to be kept awake by pickers at play. Small wonder that there is something of a revolt among the younger generation of vine-growers' spouses, who may anyway have full-time jobs elsewhere. Caterers are increasingly used, and high unemployment has in some cases substituted for students in search of a good time local people who would rather increase their earnings by forgoing lunch. Bureaucratic regulations are creating increasingly onerous paperwork; stricter standards may soon be enforced in respect of the lodgings provided for pickers. These developments are contributing substantially to the substitution of MECHANICAL HARVESTERS for human pickers, and therefore to the death of harvest traditions.

The menus for each day, handwritten in notebooks every year, enlivened by anecdotal remarks, together with the photograph albums kept on many estates, may eventually be the only record of harvest traditions. R.H.

Rest of Europe

Harvest traditions are most likely to survive where vineyards are picked by approximately the same people each year, which is why few survive in Italy and Germany, where grapes are increasingly picked by immigrants with no tradition of grape-picking in their families. As mechanization invades a wine region, so harvest traditions retreat, presumably until revived as a public relations exercise. This means that harvest traditions are more likely to survive where LABOUR costs are relatively low.

A prime example of this has been the DOURO Valley, where PORT is made, although even here rural labour shortages are having an effect. Even in the early 21st century, however, it was still just possible to associate a genuine sense of folk tradition and celebration with the harvest, as some local pickers invade the QUINTAS at which they and their families have traditionally worked every autumn for decades. The increasingly depopulated TRÁS-OS-MONTES region has supplied many of the teams, or *rogas*, of pickers who brought noise, chatter, and traffic to a region marked by its silence the rest of the year.

At a few properties in the Douro, pickers' feet were still expected to provide a more bucolic, gentler, and more effective alternative to the mechanical CRUSHER, or robotic lagar (see FOOT TREADING). The *roga*, or sometimes only its male members, is expected not only to pick the grapes, but to make the wine as well. Donning shorts, and with their arms around each others' shoulders, they march methodically backwards and forwards across the granite LAGARES, often thigh-high in sticky purple grapes, to a chant or beat of a drum. Once a floating CAP of skins has visibly been separated from the juice beneath, *liberdade* (liberty) is declared and the march evolves into dancing, traditionally to the sound of an accordion but nowadays, more often than not, to recorded music from a stereo system. Traditionally the leader of the *roga* would present the owner of the farm or winery, the *patrão*, with a decorated vine branch at a final celebratory vintage feast.

New World

Such traditions as have evolved around the harvest, or crush, in the New World tend to be the direct result of having large numbers of people, often from very different backgrounds, doing work unfamiliar to many of them, in the open air. The weather conditions, especially the temperature and sunshine, have greatest effect on worker comfort, and indirectly on the development of traditions. In many parts of the New World, harvest can be a time of heavy physical work for moderately low pay under trying conditions. Where the weather is hot, the harvest can start very early in the morning, and meal breaks are short as there is often little opportunity to relax in a hot, dusty, vineyard with little available shade.

Many of the social aspects of harvest are changing with use of the mechanical harvester. One harvester and operator can pick as much in three shifts during the 24 hours as could hundreds of human pickers during the day.

Hanson, R., *Recipes from the French Wine Harvest* (London, 1995).

Harveys of Bristol, once-powerful force

in JEREZ and the British wine trade in the mid 20th century and owners of the world's most significant brand of sherry, Harveys Bristol Cream, and thereby creators of an entire style of sherry (see CREAM).

In 1946, the firm had taken on Harry WAUGH, a talented wine buyer, salesman, and teacher, to vitalize Harveys' fine wine business, and to rival that of their neighbours AVERYS. During the 20 years that Waugh and chairman George McWatters, a member of the Harvey family, were there, Harveys was to take the wine trade lead in training, in sponsorship of the arts and other activities, and in presentation of its wares to an increasingly discerning public.

In 1962, Harveys acquired the port shippers COCKBURN, and its ports became as internationally successful as Harveys' sherries; so successful in fact that, after a fierce take-over battle, the firm was acquired by the Showerings group, famous for cider, perry, and BRITISH WINE, in 1966. Two years later, Showerings merged with the giant Allied Breweries Group (later to become Allied-Lyons). A decline in the sherry market forced substantial rationalization so that by the early 1990s, Harveys were concentrating on their fortified wine BRANDS Harveys Bristol Cream and Cockburn's Special Reserve.

These activities were run in parallel with, but at an increasing distance from, Harveys' fine wine business, which declined considerably in prestige after the Showerings takeover, even though in 1963 the firm had acquired a quarter share in the Bordeaux first growth Ch LATOUR. The parent company Allied-Lyons acquired a majority holding in the château before selling it in 1993, taking over the sherry firm DOMECQ the following year. Both Harveys and Cockburn were sold to the American company Beam Wine Estates in 2005 after the break-up of Allied Domecq.

Hastings River, warm and humid wine

region on the north coast of NEW SOUTH WALES. Mildew-resistant hybrid CHAMBOURCIN is an important red variety. Many other grapes are sourced from more reliable regions. TOURISM is the principal rationale for the wineries' existence.

Haut, French for 'high'. See the rest of the name if there is no relevant entry under H.

Haut-Brion, Château, the most famous

property in the GRAVES district in BORDEAUX producing both red and white wines, today, after years of fierce competition, run in tandem with Ch La MISSION HAUT-BRION. Manuscripts from the beginning of the 15th century mention extensive vineyards around the LIEU-DIT Aubrion. But the real founder of the estate was Jean de PONTAC who, as early as 1525, defined the vineyard as it is today and built the château in 1549. His great-nephew Arnaud III de Pontac, Président of the Bordeaux Parliament, invented the 'New French Claret Haut-Brion', a new type of red wine benefiting from ageing, which laid the foundations of great bordeaux. In 1660, the cellar records of the British King Charles II mention that no fewer than 169 bottles of the 'wine of Hobriono' (sic) were served at the royal table. The wine was praised by Samuel Pepys, the London diarist, who recorded on 10 April 1663 that he 'drank a sort of French wine called Ho Bryan that hath a good and most particular taste I never met with.' In 1666, the son of Arnaud III de Pontac, François-Auguste, opened a tavern in London called Pontack's Head which soon became '...the most fashionable place in all of London...' where luminaries such as Locke, Swift, Defoe, Dryden, and the members of the Royal Society came to dine or buy Haut-Brion.

Thomas JEFFERSON also praised it on his visit to Bordeaux in 1787 as American minister in France. In 1801, Charles-Maurice de Talleyrand Périgord, Minister of Foreign Affairs to Emperor Napoleon I, bought Ch Haut-Brion and used its wines and the talent of the famous chef Antonin Carême, 'king of chefs and chef of kings', to diplomatic ends. In 1855, on the occasion of the Exposition Universelle held in Paris, Ch Haut-Brion was listed as one of four first growths in the famous CLASSIFICATION of Bordeaux wines.

After a further series of not very successful owners in a very difficult time, the château was bought in 1935 by Mr Clarence Dillon, an American banker. Today the property is run by his grandson Prince Robert of Luxembourg with his mother, the Duchess de Mouchy. In 2004, Jean-Philippe Delmas became estate manager when his innovative father, Jean-Bernard, retired.

The 50.5 ha/124 acres of vineyard are planted with just 40% Cabernet Sauvignon, 49% Merlot, and 11% Cabernet Franc. Average production is 9,000 cases. The SECOND WINE was renamed Le Clarence de Haut-Brion (from Ch Bahans-Haut-Brion) in 2007 in honour of Clarence Dillon. About 500 cases of the property's rare dry white Ch Haut-Brion Blanc are produced from a 2.9 ha vineyard planted with 52% Semillon and 48% Sauvignon Blanc. About 1,000 cases of a second white wine, La Clarté de Haut-Brion, common to both Chx

Haut-Brion and La Mission Haut-Brion are also produced.

In early summer 2011 family-owned Domaine Clarence Dillon purchased Ch Tertre Daugay in St-Émilion and renamed it Ch Quintus. Two years later the neighbouring property, Ch L'Arrosée, was also acquired with the intention of restoring the united properties to their former glory. The second wine is Le Dragon de Quintus.

Hautes Côtes de Beaune and Hautes Côtes de Nuits, sometimes known collectively

as the **Hautes Côtes**, vineyards dispersed in the hills above the escarpment of the Côte d'Or in Burgundy. Most of the production is red wine from Pinot Noir, with some white wine made from Chardonnay or occasionally Pinot Blanc or Pinot Gris, but at ELEVATIONS reaching 500 m/ 1,640 ft the grapes do not ripen easily. This is also suitable ground for BOURGOGNE ALIGOTÉ, especially as the blackcurrant bushes needed for the production of CASSIS can often be seen growing alongside.

Forty-seven communes are included in the Hautes Côtes appellations. The most prolific villages include Meloisey, Nantoux, and Échevronne above the Côte de Beaune and Villars-Fontaine, Magny-lès-Villars, and Marey-lès-Fussey above the Côte de Nuits. There is a good CO-OPERATIVE for the Hautes Côtes wines located just outside Beaune. Many leading growers in the Côte de Nuits such as the Gros family now also offer affordable wines from the Hautes Côtes.

See also CÔTE D'OR, and map under BURGUNDY.

J.T.C.M.

Haut-Médoc, the higher, southern part of

the Médoc district of Bordeaux which includes the world-famous communes of MARGAUX, PAUILLAC, ST-ESTÈPHE, and ST-JULIEN, as well as the less glamorous ones of LISTRAC and MOULIS. Red wines made here outside one of these appellations, many of them CRUS bourgeois, usually qualify for the appellation of Haut-Médoc. For more details, see MÉDOC.

Haut Pays, French term meaning 'high

country' which was used in the Middle Ages to describe the area upstream of BORDEAUX which produced wines (and had done for longer than Bordeaux since at the beginning of the Christian era winemaking spread north west from Narbonne towards the Atlantic). This included GAILLAC, BERGERAC, Quercy (modern CAHORS), and Nérac (BUZET). The more dependable climate here often produced wines stronger than the light, thin wines then made in the Bordeaux region itself and were seen as a serious commercial threat. The port of Bordeaux penalized them by taxing them heavily and barring them from the port until the region

had exported its own wines. See also HUNDRED YEARS WAR.

Haut-Poitou, AOC zone almost due south of

SAUMUR in which a few hundred hectares of vines on limestone and marl produce crisp, well-made red, white, and rosé wines. Whites are mainly Sauvignon Blanc although up to 40% Sauvignon Gris is permitted. Reds are mainly Cabernet Franc with various Gamays, Merlot, and Pinot Noir allowed to make up the rest. The CO-OPERATIVE at Neuville dominates production.

Hawaii, chain of islands in the Pacific and

one of the 50 UNITED STATES. It produces mainly FRUIT WINES, notably a sparkling pineapple wine, as well as some grape wines from varieties such as SYMPHONY, CARNELIAN, and a little Syrah grown at high ELEVATIONS on the islands of Big Island and Maui respectively. The humid climate encourages FUNGAL DISEASES.

HDD. See CLIMATE CLASSIFICATION.

head, or crown, of a vine is the top of the

TRUNK where CORDONS branch, or where some SPURS are retained to produce new CANES in cane pruning.

head space, that space in a container hold-

ing a liquid that is not taken up by that liquid. In wine containers it is often called the ULLAGE, or ullage space. In large, modern wineries, the head space of stainless-steel tanks is often deliberately filled by an INERT GAS as a preservative measure. Similarly, many modern BOTTLING lines use inert gas to exclude oxygen from the head space.

head training, a form of VINE TRAINING

whereby the trunk has a definite head, or knob, consisting of old wood rather than arms of a CORDON. Head-trained vines are normally subject to CANE PRUNING, but may, after SPUR PRUNING, be described as GOBELET. The head may be anywhere between 40 cm/1.25 ft and 1 m/3.3 ft from the ground. The GUYOT system is a common cane-pruned form of head training.   R.E.S.

health, effects of wine consumption on. Until the 18th century, wine played

a central role in medical practice, not least because it was safer to drink than most available water, as outlined in MEDICINE. But wine of course contains ALCOHOL, and it and its primary breakdown product ACETALDEHYDE are toxic to the body's tissues. Its contribution to damage to the liver, pancreas, and brain, and to accidents, is well known. Less well known is that the incidence of certain cancers, wasting of nerves and muscles, blood disorders, infections, psoriasis, raised blood pressure, strokes, and infertility increases with heavy consumption. Alcohol consumption during pregnancy can affect the

developing foetus, stunting its growth, and causing birth defects, and behavioural and intellectual problems (termed 'foetal alcohol spectrum disorder'). This has resulted in a proliferation of health warning labels on wine bottles in many countries (see LABELLING).

Since the early 1990s, however, a substantial and increasing body of research has shown that modest consumers have lower mortality than heavy consumers or non-drinkers, suggesting that alcohol consumption (and perhaps especially wine consumption) can have a net beneficial effect on health. The evidence to date is so convincing that the link between moderate consumption and reduced risk of heart disease is acknowledged by the World Health Organization in its commentaries on alcohol. Moderate consumption is very generally considered to be 20–30 g alcohol per day for men and 10–20 g alcohol per day for women.

Coronary heart disease

The most beneficial effect of wine is its contribution to reduced mortality from coronary heart disease, the western world's major killer. This develops when plaques of cholesterol build up in the arteries supplying the heart muscle. These furred-up arteries cannot supply the heart muscle with enough oxygen, resulting in the pain of angina. Heart attacks happen when blood clots block these narrowed arteries completely, cutting off the oxygen supply. Heavy drinkers develop increased cholesterol levels as well as raised blood pressure, weakened heart muscle, and a susceptibility to potentially fatal abnormal heart rhythms. Given this record, it was not just the temperance movement which believed that moderate consumption must surely be doing some harm. Yet there is now a mass of evidence that those who drink moderately are less likely to develop coronary heart disease and to die from it than either those who drink heavily or those who have never drunk alcohol. Furthermore, it is the alcohol in alcoholic drinks which has been identified as the single most important ingredient in prevention of coronary heart disease.

Alcohol, it seems, moderates the level of inflammatory blood chemicals called cytokines which adversely affect blood cholesterol and blood-clotting proteins. Blood carries LDL (low-density lipoprotein) cholesterol, which forms the plaques which block arteries, and HDL (high-density lipoprotein) cholesterol, which mops them up. Moderate alcohol consumption improves the balance between the harmful and beneficial forms of cholesterol. Blood clots are formed by platelets—small shards of old cells which float harmlessly in the blood until they are chemically triggered to stick together in a tangle of threads of fibrin protein. Alcohol has two anticoagulant effects which make blood less likely to clot in the wrong place. It makes the platelets slightly less sticky, and it reduces the level of fibrin available to form a clot. An added benefit for moderate consumers, and particularly moderate wine consumers, is increased vascular elasticity, enabling a more rapid flow of blood through the arteries and lowering risk of heart and blood pressure problems.

The anticoagulant effect of alcohol lasts less than 24 hours. This may explain why the risk of a heart attack is reduced during the day following a couple of drinks. The traditional wine drinker's glass or two with the evening meal provides a steady, safe level of alcohol. In contrast, the beer or spirit drinker's Saturday night binge leaves him or her temporarily over-anti-coagulated (and at increased risk of a stroke due to bleeding) until he or she has metabolized the alcohol, then at increased risk of heart attack until the next night out. Binge drinking of wine carries the same health risk as any other alcoholic drink taken to excess.

Alcohol is not the only compound of cardiovascular significance in wine. Red wine, much more than white, is rich in PHENOLICS, which have antioxidant, anti-blood clotting, and anti-inflammatory properties. There are hundreds of phenolic compounds in wine, but attention has focused on RESVERATROL. Like alcohol, resveratrol modulates the breakdown of LDL cholesterol in the laboratory, and so may help to reduce the formation of plaques in the body. Heart attacks are not the only problem caused by furred-up arteries. They cause peripheral vascular disease, which leads to angina-type pain in the leg muscles when their activity exceeds the ability of the arteries to the legs to provide oxygen. Most strokes are caused by blockages of blood vessels, so it is not surprising that moderate alcohol consumption reduces the risk of strokes. However, the anticoagulant effects of alcohol, which are beneficial if the stroke is caused by a blood clot, are likely to make the stroke worse if it is due to bleeding into the brain.

A growing number of studies conclude that the way alcohol is consumed—the pattern of drinking—is key to potential health benefits. Studies show that regular moderate consumption, predominantly with meals, significantly reduces the risk of a heart attack.

It is therefore likely that it is the combination of alcohol, its phenolic compounds, and the usual consumption pattern of wine (versus that of other alcoholic drinks), that makes wine the most beneficial alcoholic beverage for cardiovascular health. These factors may explain the FRENCH PARADOX. See also FLAVONOLS.

Cancers

Awareness of the influence of lifestyle on cancer risks has stimulated research into the relationship between drinking and cancers. Alcohol consumption increases the risk of cancers of all parts of the digestive tract except the stomach. The link becomes progressively weaker from mouth to rectum. The risk is tripled for cancer of the mouth and throat, and doubled for cancer of the oesophagus. The mucosal surfaces of these organs come into direct contact with imbibed alcohol, and it has been suggested that the risk of developing these cancers is less if the alcohol is consumed with food.

Food and drink passes from the oesophagus to the stomach, and there is good news about alcohol and stomach cancer. Ulcer sufferers were traditionally advised to avoid alcohol lest it irritate the lining of the stomach. However, gastritis, peptic ulcers, and stomach cancer are now known to be strongly associated with infection by the bacterium *Helicobacter pylori* and a short course of treatment designed to eradicate *H. pylori* is saving many former sufferers a lifetime of treatment and abstinence. Furthermore, studies have shown that moderate wine and beer drinkers are significantly less likely to be infected with *H. pylori* than non-drinkers, possibly due to the anti-microbial effects of alcohol. If moderate consumers are less likely to have *H. pylori* infection, they should have fewer ulcers, a deduction supported by evidence from the US. Recent studies suggest that regular moderate consumption may reduce the chances of infection with *H. pylori* more than occasional consumption of heavier amounts of alcohol. St Paul's advice to 'use a little wine for thy stomach's sake' proves to have been wise.

Drinking alcohol is associated with a modest increase of the risk of cancer of the bowel (colon and rectum). As with cancers of the upper digestive tract, the risk is greater with high consumption of alcohol.

Studies of the incidence of breast cancer show that even the moderate consumption of alcohol is associated with an increase in risk. Four to five drinks per day increase the risk by 50% compared with only one drink per day.

Preliminary studies suggest that moderate alcohol consumption may offer some protection from cancer of the prostate and the kidney and non-Hodgkin's lymphoma, but more evidence is needed to confirm this.

Respiratory problems

SULPHITES are produced naturally by FERMENTATION and so occur at low levels (10–50 mg/l) in all wines. Small amounts are also routinely added to most wines as a preservative. Asthmatics who are sensitive to sulphites may experience respiratory problems after drinking wine with concentrations of sulphur dioxide above 45 mg/l. So in many countries, wines containing more than 10 mg/l are labelled accordingly. Biogenic amines such as HISTAMINE are generally present in low concentrations in wine, but they can contribute to respiratory problems in histamine-allergic or sensitive individuals (see ALLERGIES AND INTOLERANCES), especially if they consume wine together with foods high in histamine such as some cheeses. Wine also contains salicylates that can trigger respiratory problems in salicylate-allergic individuals.

Headaches

Biogenic amines in wine, such as HISTAMINE and tyramine, can trigger migraines for some migraine sufferers. Red wine generally contains more biogenic amines that white. It has also been suggested that PHENOLIC compounds could be a trigger. In the test tube phenolics liberate serotonin (5-hydroxytryptamine) from cells; this is the chemical messenger that plays a part in the initiation of migraine.

Additionally, the alcohol in wine and its breakdown product, ACETALDEHYDE, act on the brain. The pain of headaches is referred via pain receptors to the surface of the head from deep structures such as the brain and its related tissues. The headache experienced after consuming alcohol is generally related to blood alcohol concentration (BAC). Alcohol and acetaldehyde readily diffuse from the blood into the fluids of the brain and spinal cord where they directly irritate the brain's cells and tissues, causing pain at the front surface of the head. The more wine consumed, the higher the BAC, the more the brain will be irritated, and the more severe the headache.

Dementia

The intoxified brain does not function well (whatever its owner may temporarily believe), and the deleterious effect on intellectual function of long-term assault with heavy alcohol is well known. It comes as a pleasant relief to find that moderate wine consumers have improved cognitive function compared with both heavy wine consumers and non-drinkers, and are less likely to develop dementias such as Alzheimer's disease. Studies suggest that RESVERATROL may additionally be 'dementia-protective' by increasing the brain's blood flow as well as directly benefiting the cells and tissues of the brain.

Musculo-skeletal problems

Excessively heavy drinkers are prone to fracture their bones such as the hips and vertebrae; a consequence of the effects of too much alcohol on their bone density and structure in addition to an increased rate of falls. Alcohol has been shown to have directly damaging effects on cellular bone formation as well as indirectly affecting the pancreas and cytokine and endocrine systems which also influence cellular bone formation. However, studies show an association between moderate alcohol, and in particular wine, consumption and improvement in bone density. Men and post-menopausal women at risk of osteoporosis may find one or two glasses of wine a day beneficial rather than harmful.

Rheumatoid arthritis has been shown to be less common in those who take moderate alcohol in any form, potentially from alcohol's anti-inflammatory actions, although any improvement in sufferers' symptoms may be due to the pleasure of a glass of wine rather than its physiological effects.

Diabetes mellitus

Although diabetics are obliged to watch carefully what they eat and drink, alcohol taken with a meal does not substantially alter their blood sugar level and is therefore an appropriate element in a diabetic's diet. As the World Health Organization acknowledges, moderate consumers of alcohol, and particularly wine drinkers, have a significantly lower risk of developing Type-2 diabetes mellitus than heavy drinkers and non-drinkers. Type-2 diabetes is the form of diabetes which typically develops in middle age and is usually treatable with diet and tablets. Type-2 diabetes is due not so much to lack of insulin but to decreased response to it. Research shows that moderate drinkers are more sensitive to insulin than non-drinkers, probably because alcohol moderates the effect of the cytokines, which appear to contribute to the development of Type-2 diabetes.

Gastrointestinal problems

As already described, alcohol is associated with an increase in the incidence of all gastrointestinal cancers except those of the stomach. But wine is more active against the bacteria that cause travellers' diarrhoea than bismuth, another traditional and distinctly less palatable remedy. More encouraging news: moderate drinkers are at reduced risk of developing gallstones.

Sensible drinking

Health authorities in many countries have disseminated 'low risk' or 'sensible drinking levels', suggested maxima for personal consumption of alcohol usually expressed in 'units', or STANDARD DRINKS, of alcohol, though there is wide variation between what constitutes a unit and how many of them may safely be consumed.

These limits are at best only a rough guide as individuals' reactions to alcohol must always be taken into consideration when assessing recommended consumption levels. Sex, age, build, genetic make-up, state of health, drinking with or without food, and drug intake all affect the way alcohol is metabolized. For instance, glass for glass, women, regardless of their weight or size, absorb relatively more alcohol than men because of differences in levels of stomach enzymes, their lower body water content meaning that alcohol is more concentrated in their tissues and, if they are also taking the

contraceptive pill, more slowly eliminated. This may explain why women who drink in excess of the recommended daily units experience significantly greater risks of poor health outcomes than men who do likewise. Additionally, women's tissues are more susceptible to the damaging effects of alcohol. Conversely, it appears that the relationship between moderate consumption and better general health is stronger for women.

Aside from any specific health benefits, it emerges that self-reported health—a good predictor of all-cause mortality—is best for moderate consumers, and especially for moderate wine consumers. Indeed, in 2011 the US Center for Disease Control and Prevention proposed that moderate alcohol consumption was one of four healthy lifestyle behaviours related to a lower mortality risk, along with not smoking, eating a healthy diet, and physical activity. The mortality risk for those who also consumed alcohol was significantly lower than for those exhibiting only the three other behaviours. And there is a benefit that the studies of mortality cannot identify. A final word, which won't appear in studies of mortality. The healthy can enjoy a drink, but for those whose lives are restricted by chronic disease a glass of wine may be one of the few pleasures left. That is a substantial health benefit.   J.H.H. & C.S.S.

Baglietto, L., et al., 'Average volume of alcohol consumed, type of beverage, drinking pattern and the risk of death from all causes', *Alcohol and Alcoholism*, 41/6 (2006), 664–1.

Chiva-Blanch, G., et al., 'Effects of wine, alcohol and polyphenols on cardiovascular disease risk factors: evidence from human studies', *Alcohol and Alcoholism*, 48/3 (2013), 270–7.

Ford, E. S., et al., 'Low-risk lifestyle behaviors and all-cause mortality: Findings from the National Health and Nutrition Examination Survey III Mortality Study', *American Journal of Public Health*, 101 (2011), 1922–9.

Simons, L. A., et al., 'Lifestyle factors and risk of dementia: Dubbo Study of the elderly', *Medical Journal of Australia*, 184/2 (2006), 68–70.

Stockley, C. S., 'Is it merely a myth that alcoholic beverages such as red wine can be cardioprotective?', *Journal of Science of Food and Agriculture*, 92/9 (2012), 1815–21.

Heathcote, exciting (Shiraz) Australian wine region, once part of Bendigo, VICTORIA. Jasper Hill is the leading winery; from the northern Rhône, Alain Graillot and CHAPOUTIER were among the growing roster of producers, some 55-strong by 2014.

heat stress affects vines when air temperatures are high. Very high daytime temperatures, of more than 40 °C/104 °F, cause the vine to 'shut down', or virtually cease PHOTOSYNTHESIS, as the ENZYMES responsible can no longer work.

High temperatures also lead to WATER STRESS, especially when accompanied by bright sunshine, low humidity, and strong, dry winds. High temperatures cause fast RESPIRATION in vines and this leads to, for example, low levels of MALIC ACID in mature fruit in hot regions. VARIETAL character and red COLOUR in grapes are also depressed by high temperatures. Australian research into the physiological impact of CLIMATE CHANGE has shown that, in a biochemical sense, sugar and ANTHOCYANIN accumulation in ripening berries is 'decoupled' by elevated temperatures. Some researchers claim that more moderate daytime temperatures, in excess of only 25 °C, can depress colour formation and varietal flavour expression.

R.E.S.

Sadras, V. O., and Maran, M. A., 'Elevated temperature decouples anthocyanins and sugars in berries of Shiraz and Cabernet Franc', *Australian Journal of Grape and Wine Research*, 18 (2012), 115–22.

Spayd, S. E., et al., 'Separation of sunlight and temperature effects on the composition of *vitis vinifera* cv. Merlot berries', *American Journal of Enology and Viticulture*, 53 (2002), 171–82.

heat summation, a computation involving addition of mean temperatures over the growing season that forms part of many systems of CLIMATE CLASSIFICATION.

heat-treated vines, vines which have undergone **heat treatment**, or THERMOTHERAPY, to eliminate virus disease. But see also HOT-WATER TREATMENT.

hectare, common agricultural measurement of area equivalent to 100 ares, 10,000 sq m, or 2.47 acres.

hedging. See TRIMMING.

Heida, Swiss-German synonym for SAVAGNIN BLANC and a speciality of Visperterminen.

Helfensteiner is famous principally as a parent of DORNFELDER, the more successful German red wine cross. The cross of FRÜHBURGUNDER × TROLLINGER has all but disappeared, even from Württemberg.

helicopters are more expensive than fixed-wing aircraft, which limits their application to viticulture. Their manoeuvrability is a bonus, however. They are particularly useful for crop SPRAYING, and the turbulence created by the rotors helps the spray to penetrate (although there are the usual problems where individual landholdings are small). They are commonly used as airborne WIND MACHINES in New Zealand and very occasionally in Europe to stir up cold, dense air just above the vineyard surface with warmer air above to prevent spring FROST DAMAGE. It is not uncommon, for instance, to have helicopters on standby when the risk of frost is high. On occasion they have been used in an attempt to dry excess moisture off vine leaves and bunches immediately after heavy RAINFALL at HARVEST.

Hemel-en-Aarde. See WALKER BAY.

Henderson, Dr Alexander (1780–1863), Scotsman who qualified as a doctor and then moved to London and contributed to a wide range of publications, including the *Encyclopaedia Britannica*. After visiting the wine regions of France, Germany, and Italy, he wrote *The History of Ancient and Modern Wines*, which was published in 1824 (eight years after JULLIEN but nine years before REDDING). Some of the most useful aspects of his book perhaps reflect some aspects of his medical training: his observations on the art of wine TASTING.

Henriques, Justino. See JUSTINO'S MADEIRA WINES SA.

Henty (including Drumborg), particularly cool Australian wine region in the Western Victoria Zone (see VICTORIA) used as a source of grapes for sparkling wines; also fine table wines, especially Riesling (Crawford River, Seppelt). It has just ten producers.

herbaceous, TASTING TERM for the leafy or grassy aroma of crushed green leaves or freshly cut grass. **Herbaceousness** is generally considered a defect only when present in excess (although American tasters are much less tolerant of it than, for example, the British). Wines made from the produce of SAUVIGNON BLANC, SÉMILLON, CABERNET SAUVIGNON, CABERNET FRANC, or MERLOT vines which failed to ripen fully are often excessively herbaceous. In general, the younger the vines, the greater their VIGOUR, and the earlier the grapes are picked, the more pronounced the herbaceousness. One cause of vegetative herbaceous aromas, particularly in wines of Sauvignon Blanc and Cabernet Sauvignon, is the presence of METHOXYPYRAZINES originating from the grape; see also FLAVOUR COMPOUNDS. Another source of herbaceousness is six-carbon atom LEAF ALDEHYDES.

Numerous investigations have shown that they, and the corresponding six-carbon atom ALCOHOLS, derive from linoleic and linolenic, which are both fatty acids found in plant leaves and in the fruit. These decompose rapidly once the grape berry is crushed to yield hexanal, hexenal, and the related unsaturated alcohols, all six-carbon atom compounds which can react further during FERMENTATION to produce a wide range of flavour compounds which are responsible for the aroma called herbaceous. Another reason why a wine may taste herbaceous is from vine leaves inadvertently crushed with the grapes (see MOG). Early MECHANICAL HARVESTERS

were particularly prone to do this, and the grapes were often so mangled that it was impossible to separate the wet leaves from them. Wines made from such a blend would also not surprisingly be high in leaf aldehydes and taste distinctly leafy or herbaceous, a problem accentuated when such mechanical harvesters are used on relatively young vineyards. More sophisticated machine harvesters have reduced leaf contamination considerably.

A.D.W. & P.J.W.

Herbemont, dark-skinned *V. aestivalis x V. vinifera* HYBRID grown in Brazil because of its resistance to FUNGAL DISEASES.

herbicides, chemicals applied to vineyards to control the growth of WEEDS. They may be either pre-emergent (or residual) or post-emergent (knockdown). The latter group comprises two types, contact and systemic herbicides. Residual herbicides act against germinating seedlings of the weeds, while post-emergent herbicides damage growing weeds. Typically, herbicides are applied only to the strip of ground directly under the vine, and weeds growing between the rows are controlled by cultivation or mowing. Herbicides are used even between rows in some vineyard regions, though there can be risks of soil erosion or loss of water infiltration without the organic matter produced by COVER CROPS in this zone.

In areas of winter rainfall, a contact or systemic spray is typically applied in late autumn to early winter, followed by a pre-emergent herbicide in the early spring. In regions with summer rainfall, or irrigated areas, further contact or systemic sprays may be needed to control weeds that grow during the growing season. Most herbicides used in vineyards are low-hazard chemicals which present no danger to the operator (see AGROCHEMICALS). Many of the knockdown chemicals are inactivated by soil, and so leave no soil RESIDUES.

Continued use of some herbicides leads to the increased presence of so-called 'escape' weeds, however, which were previously suppressed by competition from other weeds. Herbicides can encourage high soil surface temperatures, and loss of ORGANIC MATTER, so that there may be fewer EARTHWORMS where herbicides are used continually. Some herbicides can even damage vines, either by wetting vine leaves inadvertently, or when herbicides are leached into the root zone, as can happen with young vines, sandy soils, and irrigation.

Concern about environmental pollution as a result of herbicide use has been growing (see ORGANIC and BIODYNAMIC VITICULTURE), and more and more vine-growers are substituting under-vine ploughing for herbicide use—helped by the increasing sophistication of machinery for this type of cultivation. See WEED CONTROL. Although

the use of herbicides is relatively inexpensive, it does encourage the vine roots to go to the more fertile soils nearer the surface. R.E.S.

heritage clones, term used particularly in parts of the New World with a relatively long history of vine growing, such as California and Australia, for CUTTINGS from particularly historic vines. Examples in Australia are those from century-old ungrafted vines which may be traced back to early imports into the colony from pre-PHYLLOXERA Europe. They are typically virus-free, having been exported from Europe before the introduction of the GRAFTING that is known to spread virus disease. In California such selections as Calera, Mt. Eden, Swan Pinot Noir, and Rudd and Wente Chardonnay CLONES are regarded as part of the state's viticultural heritage.

heritage varieties. See INDIGENOUS VARIETIES.

Hermitage, the most famous northern RHÔNE appellation of all, producing extremely limited quantities of seriously long-lived reds and about a third as much full-bodied dry white wine which some believe is even more distinguished. Although the appellation is only the size of a large Bordeaux estate, Hermitage was one of France's most famous wines in the 18th and 19th centuries when the name alone was sufficient to justify prices higher than any wine other than a FIRST GROWTH bordeaux (which were sometimes strengthened by the addition of some Hermitage until the mid 19th century). The origin of the name Hermitage is not so much shrouded in mystery as obscured by many conflicting legends, most of them concerning a hermit, *ermite* in French. Not least of the puzzles is how and when Ermitage acquired its H (dropped for some modern bottlings, notably by CHAPOUTIER), although there was no shortage of English-speaking enthusiasts of the wine in the 18th century (including Thomas JEFFERSON). The first recorded mention of Hermitage in English was in Thomas Shadwell's 1680 play *The Woman-Captain*, 'Vin de Bon, Vin Celestine, and Hermitage, and all the Wines upon the fruitful Rhône'. These 'manly' wines were also a great favourite with the Russian imperial court, but the economic upheavals of the first half of the 20th century affected Hermitage as much as any Rhône appellation. While the surrounding appellation CROZES-HERMITAGE has, like most of the Rhône valley, seen considerable changes and extension over the last 20 years, Hermitage is a constant, give or take a winemaking tweak or two.

The wine comes from an almost unenlargeable 136 ha/336 acres of particularly well-favoured vines on the extraordinary hill of Hermitage, a south-facing bank of granite, thinly covered with extremely varied and well-charted soil types, which almost pushes the town of Tain l'Hermitage into the river Rhône just as it turns sharp left (see map under RHÔNE). Wines produced here in the Roman town of Tegna were already known to writers such as PLINY and MARTIAL.

The combination of heat-retaining granite and a reasonably steep southern exposition does much to encourage grape RIPENING here. It is not surprising that such a celebrated vineyard has been for long divided into various CLIMATS, all with their own soil types and reputations for wine types. Professor Pierre Mandier, a geologist at Lyons, has charted the hillside in considerable detail. The most famous *climats* are at the western end of the hill, which benefits from the highest temperatures. Les Bessards has a topsoil of sandy gravel on granite and produces some of the sturdiest wines. Le Méal produces more aromatic wines from a soil with more limestone, and bigger stones towards the top of the slope, where l'Hermite is crowned with a small stone chapel owned by Paul JABOULET Aîné and has more sand and fine LOESS. Clay predominates in the lower *climats* of Les Gréffieux and Les Diognières. Other famous *climats* include Beaume(s), Maison Blanche, Péléat, Les Murets, Rocoule, La Croix, and Les Signeaux in the extreme east. Although white and red grapes are planted all over the hill, some of the finest white Hermitage comes from the higher vineyards, and clay-limestone soils are considered the best suited.

Producers such as Jean-Louis Chave, the modest master of Hermitage, delight in blending the produce of holdings all over the hill to produce a complex, well-balanced expression of each vintage. Producers with less diversified holdings may produce less complex wines, some of them labelled with a single *climat*.

Unlike CÔTE RÔTIE upriver, red Hermitage is in practice made from the SYRAH vine alone (although the AC regulations permit the addition of up to 15% white grapes); indeed Hermitage has laid claim to be the cradle of Syrah, while white Hermitage may be made from the robust MARSANNE or the nervier, and less common, ROUSSANNE.

SOIL EROSION is a frequent problem here, the result as much of exposure as of gradient, although the hill is steep enough in parts for TERRACES to be necessary, and some retaining walls are used as advertising sites for the local merchants.

The appellation regulations limit yields to a basic 40 hl/ha (2.3 tons/acre) and 45 hl/ha for whites, but ENRICHMENT may be allowed in some vintages, so long as the ALCOHOLIC STRENGTH of the resultant wine is no more than 13.5% for reds and 14% for whites.

Wine making philosophies vary here, but are essentially traditional. Red wines are the result of relatively hot FERMENTATIONS matured in often quite old COOPERAGE of varied capacity, according to vintage characteristics. Red Hermitage should be very deeply coloured and headily perfumed. They can evolve for two or three decades after which they may be mistaken for great red bordeaux. Some of the finest red wines of Hermitage come from Chave, Le Pavillon from Chapoutier, La Chapelle from Jaboulet, and Le Gréal from Sorrel.

White wines are possibly even more varied, according to the blend of grape varieties used, RIPENESS, whether MALOLACTIC CONVERSION has taken place, and whether WOOD is used for fermentation and/or AGEING. Almost all white Hermitage is notably full in BODY, and some of the more serious examples such as Chave's and Chapoutier's Chante Alouette are among the longest-living dry white wines of France.

In very ripe years, some of Hermitage's white grapes may be transformed into VIN DE PAILLE so long as the must is not enriched and the yield is no more than 15 hl/ha. This sweet white Hermitage is delicious but all too rare.

Hermitage has also been used as a synonym for SHIRAZ in Australia, where, for example, PENFOLDS Grange was originally called Penfolds Grange Hermitage. Hermitage was also the historic South African synonym for CINSAUT and is sometimes used in Switzerland for Marsanne.

Livingstone-Learmonth, J., *The Wines of the Northern Rhône* (Berkeley, 2005).

Norman, R., *Rhône Renaissance* (London, 1995).

Parker, R. M., *Wines of the Rhône Valley* (2nd edn, New York, 1997).

Herodotus, prolific Ancient Greek writer. The *Histories* of Herodotus (490/480–425 BC), a native of Halicarnassus in Asia Minor, are not a history in the modern sense: the Greek word *historia* means 'an investigation'. Herodotus' main subject is the conflict between the Greeks and the Persians, and as such his book is history; but it is also an investigation into the geography and anthropology of the east in Herodotus' own day, for as a young man he had travelled widely in the Greek-speaking world and in Egypt and Africa.

Forming part of Herodotus' descriptions of the customs of foreign nations are some intriguing observations about wine and DRUNKENNESS. He says that the Assyrians use palm-wood casks to transport wine, in boats built in Armenia, down the Euphrates (1. 194). In fact, Herodotus' curiosity concerns the construction of the boats: their cargo is mentioned in an aside and he expresses no surprise at the Assyrians' use of palm-wood BARRELS instead of AMPHORAE. He has just told us that the date palm supplies the people with food, honey, and wine and that Assyria is the world's largest producer of grain. The country does not grow vines (1. 193) but, as we know from other sources, Babylon imported wine from ARMENIA. This is probably what the casks contained: with date palms growing all around, transporting fermented date juice would not have made sense. See also MESOPOTAMIA.

All of Book 2 and the beginning of Book 3 are taken up with Herodotus' description of Egypt before he goes on to relate the Persian conquest of that country. He states that the Egyptians have no wine but drink a wine made from barley (2. 81). This cannot be true, for we know that the vine was grown there in the 5th century BC. Egyptian wine may have been too scarce, however, for Herodotus to have come across it on his travels. Egypt certainly imported wine from Greece and PHOENICIA, as Herodotus mentions (3. 8). He says that it came in earthenware jars, and that when the wine had been finished the mayor of the town had to collect the empty jars and send them to Memphis, where they would be filled with water and sent to the Syrian desert. This system was devised by the Persians immediately after they had conquered Egypt so that they could reach Egypt through the Syrian desert without risking death through thirst.

When the Persians have subjugated the Egyptians, the king, the megalomaniac Cambyses, marches against the Ethiopians. The expedition is a disaster, and the Ethiopians recognize the Persians' superiority in one respect only: they have wine, and that is the reason for their longevity (3. 23). But Cambyses is too fond of it, and when he is told so by a court official he wrongly deduces that the Persians regard this as the cause of his madness (3. 35). His madness and cruelty seem to have been congenital (3. 38). Wine can cause madness, though: Cleomenes, king of Sparta, went mad and died as a result of drinking wine unmixed with WATER, a nasty habit he had picked up from those notorious drunkards the Scythians (6. 85). Only a barbarian would drink unmixed wine. The Persians are all great drinkers of wine, and their frequent drunkenness explains one of the strangest of their customs. The sensible part is that any decision they take when they are drunk they reconsider when they are sober. But the opposite also holds: any decision taken when they are sober has to be reconsidered when they are drunk (1. 135). Far from regarding drunkenness as undesirable and immoderate behaviour, the Persians, if Herodotus is to be trusted, view it as an altered state of consciousness that is as valuable as sobriety.   H.M.W.

Herodotus, *The Histories*, trans. Aubrey de Sélincourt, rev. A. R. Burn (Harmondsworth, 1972).

Heroldrebe is the marginal dark-berried GERMAN CROSS to which the prolific breeder August Herold of the Weinsberg in Württemberg put his name. This PORTUGIESER × LEMBERGER cross yields regularly and prolifically, about 140 hl/ha (8 tons/acre), but ripens so late that it is suitable only for Germany's warmer regions, particularly the Pfalz. Total plantings had fallen to 133 ha by 2012. It spawned DORNFELDER.

Herzegovina. See BOSNIA AND HERZEGOVINA.

Hesiod (*c.*700 BC), the earliest agricultural writer of Ancient GREECE, wrote *Works and Days*. Most of this is homely advice for the farmer: 'Be sparing of the middle of the cask, but when you open it, and at the end drink all you want; it's not worth saving dregs.' He is the first writer to tell of simple rustic pleasures: 'I love a shady rock and Bibline wine [from BYBLOS], a cake of cheese, and goat's milk, and some meat of heifers pastured in the woods, uncalved, of first-born kids. Then I may sit in the shade and drink the shining wine, and eat my fill, and turn my face to meet the fresh west wind, and pour three times an offering from the spring which always flows, unmuddied, streaming down, and make my fourth LIBATION one of wine.' Hesiod gives the time for the grape HARVEST as 'when Orion and the dog star [Sirius] move into the mid sky'.   H.H.A.

Hessische Bergstrasse. The northern vineyards on the western slopes of Germany's Odenwald have formed one of Germany's smallest wine regions since 1971. They comprised just 450 ha/1,111 acres in 2013, geologically diverse although dominated by LOESS, of which close to half in 2012 was planted with RIESLING, some capable of making distinguished dry wine, notably in Hambach's Centgericht and Steinbach vineyards. The largest and most prestigious estate is the Hessische Staatsweingüter (known nowadays for their fabled headquarters as KLOSTER EBERBACH) while a majority of the region's growers deliver their crops to the co-op in Heppenheim known as Bergsträsser Winzer.   D.S.

Heuriger, derived from the word for 'today' but signifying by implication 'this season', or 'the latest', is an AUSTRIAN institution whose social dimensions extend far beyond the only weeks-old wine so-described. Emperor Josef II in 1784 formally established the right of Austrian wine growers to dispense their young wines by the glass (along with a rudimentary repast) at establishments whose function was signified by the hanging of bush-like bundles of evergreens over the door, for which reason such establishments are still referred to within Austria as a *Buschenschank*. The still-cloudy, often only partially fermented young wine is variously known as Staubiger ('dusty one'), FEDERWEISSER, or Sturm ('storm'). Groups of Heurigen with their rows of tiny press houses at the edge of a village or its vineyards are prevalent throughout the former Hapsburg Empire, but within Austria many of these still double as

dispensaries. The institution of Austrian wine taverns transcends those temporarily opened each season to serve the latest vintage by the glass or pitcher. Many of Austria's top wine estates still run a year-round Heuriger at least on weekends out of economic necessity, sometimes less on account of the direct income than because this is a traditional means of establishing one's brand and local market niche. The Heurigen of Austria's thirsty capital Vienna and of the adjacent THERMENREGION are especially numerous and seasonally frenetic.   D.S.

higher alcohols. See FUSEL OILS.

hillside vineyards. Even in Ancient ROME it was said *Bacchus amat colles*, or BACCHUS loves the hills, suggesting that hillside vineyards have long been regarded as a source of high-quality wine.

This is partly because hillside soils are typically shallow, so that vineyard VIGOUR is relatively low, a factor commonly associated with high wine quality. Over millions of years soil tends to be washed down the hillsides and accumulates on the valley floors. Vines planted there will typically be more vigorous as the soils are deeper and the roots will be able to reach more water and nutrients.

Vines may also be planted on hillsides for reasons of MESOCLIMATE, as hillsides are less prone to FROST because cold air can drain freely away at night (see AIR DRAINAGE and TOPOGRAPHY). If the slopes face the equator, they receive more sunshine during the day and are warmer. In hotter regions, vineyards may be planted on hillsides to take advantage of cooler temperatures at higher ELEVATIONS. Since the early 1980s, there has been an increasing tendency to plant elevated sites in Australia, Argentina, South Africa, and California, for example, in order to produce a more COOL CLIMATE style of table wine.

Hillside vineyards: the warmth received by direct radiation on the vineyard depends on the elevation of the sun combined with the inclination of the vineyard towards the sun. The elevation of the sun controls the thickness of the atmosphere (an absorbing medium) through which the radiation passes. The inclination of the vineyard is independent of this variation.

$I = k \sin \alpha + q \sin \beta$
Where I = Intensity of radiation received in vineyard
         k and q = constants
         α = angular elevation of sun
         β = angle of inclination of the vineyard to the horizontal along a meridian

Hillside vineyard sites have their drawbacks. SOIL EROSION is an obvious example, and in California's NAPA Valley there are strict regulations to avoid erosion. Working on steep slopes is particularly tiring, productivity is affected, and the costs are higher. In most vineyards of the world, rows run up and down the slopes. Where the slopes are too steep for tractors, as in the CÔTE RÔTIE, parts of the MOSEL Valley, and SWITZERLAND, everything must be done by hand, or by machines winched down into the vineyards. Where rows run across the slopes, the vineyard is normally laid out in TERRACES, as in Portugal's DOURO Valley or France's hill of HERMITAGE.   R.E.S.

Hilltops, moderately cool, high-ELEVATION wine region in NEW SOUTH WALES, Australia. Provides elegant, medium-bodied Shiraz, Cabernet Sauvignon, Tempranillo, Nebbiolo, and Australia's only Rondinella/Corvina blend from moderately low-yielding vineyards.

hippocras, popular medieval FLAVOURED WINE.

histamine, the amine involved in a range of ALLERGIC and allergy-like reactions in humans, was once thought the primary cause of some people's reactions to red wine. Improved methods of wine ANALYSIS have demonstrated that the amounts of histamine in wine, typically <10 mg/l in whites and <30 mg/l in reds, are well below that required to cause a reaction in the great majority of people. However, low levels of diamine oxidase, the enzyme which breaks down histamine, in certain people may result in intolerance of wine containing even low levels of histamine. Other biogenic amines, including tyramine, as well as the unfortunately named putrescine and cadaverine, may also be present in tiny amounts and potentially be involved in wine intolerance. These are formed during fermentation and can be minimized with certain winemaking practices. See also LACTIC ACID BACTERIA.   J.H.H. & D.A.D.

Maintz, L., and Novak, N., 'Histamine and histamine intolerance', *American Journal of Clinical Nutrition*, 85/5 (2007), 1185–96.

Historic Vineyard Society was formed in northern California in 2010 to preserve the state's rich heritage of old vines by carefully assembling a registry of those planted before 1960 (although some date from the 19th century). The society was inspired by the speed with which historic vineyards were GRUBBED UP to make way particularly for fashionable Pinot Noir in Sonoma in the wake of the film SIDEWAYS.

Hochgewächs, like CABINET, an ancient approbation co-opted by GERMAN WINE LAW, in 1987 (but little-used today), for wines meeting higher standards than the minima set for QBA but not qualifying for a PRÄDIKAT.

Hochschule Geisenheim University. See GEISENHEIM.

hock, traditional generic English term for (white) Rhenish wines, from the RHINE regions of GERMANY, sometimes for the wines of Germany in general. It is a contraction of hockamore, an English rendering of the adjective Hochheimer, denoting wines from the important wine centre of Hochheim on the river Main just west of Frankfurt (see RHEINGAU).

The earliest firm reference in English occurs in Thomas D'Urfey's play *Madam Fickle; or, The Witty False One* in 1676: 'Here's a glass of excellent old Hock.' The *Oxford English Dictionary* gives a first reference in 1625 in John Fletcher's play *The Chances*, but this depends on a corrupt reading of hock for hollock, a light red wine. However, it is likely that the term was already current in England by the 17th century, for its use is closely linked to the growth in popularity of Rhenish and Main wines, which began to supplant the wines of ALSACE in export markets after 1500 (see GERMAN HISTORY).

At the outset, hock appears to have described only wines from the middle Rhine: in an address to the Royal Society in 1680, Anthony van Leeuwenhoeck, the inventor of the microscope, spoke of 'vinum Mosellanicum, vinum Rijncoviense and vinum Rhenanum, quod vulgo hogmer dicitur' (called 'hogmer' in the vernacular). In 1703, Johann Valentin Kauppers in his *De natura . . . vini Rhenani* could still distinguish between 'Rhine wines' and wines from the Rheingau, but in the course of the 18th century hock became the general designation of German wines sold in Britain.   T.S.

Term used particularly in Britain in the 20th century for a German Rhine wine, typically a simple QBA wine. It was by no means uncommon for the same wine to be offered as Hock to a gentlemen's club and LIEBFRAUMILCH to a supermarket buyer. Hock has also occasionally been used for non-German wines as a GENERIC term.

Holland. See NETHERLANDS.

Homer, writer(s) in Ancient GREECE of the two epic poems: the *Iliad* (telling the story of Achilles and the Trojan wars) and the *Odyssey* (the return of Odysseus from Troy to his home, Ithaca, and his adventures on the way). Homeric poems are usually dated to the 8th century BC and wine features regularly in both books. See also CLASSICAL TEXTS.

home winemaking, small-scale domestic activity indulged in either for fun, to save money, or both. Because such wine attracts no DUTY, it is especially popular in countries with high excise duties. Some countries with no or minimal viticulture such as Britain have a long tradition of making FRUIT WINES and wines based on plants, flowers, or even root vegetables.

Home winemaking became popular in the United States during PROHIBITION, when making an annual allowance of 200 gal/7.5 hl of fruit juice per household (a limit that still applies in the US) was the only legal way the average American household could procure alcoholic drink. Technology was primitive, and tales of exploding bottles were common, but the pursuit was so popular that vineyard acreage in California doubled between 1919 and 1926.

After Repeal, home winemaking continued, mostly in the hands of European immigrants with strong winemaking traditions. However, by the early 1990s, the growth in home winemaking had slowed, with fewer than half a million Americans making roughly 2.5 million cases of wine a year, mainly from grapes grown in California and shipped by rail to the rest of the country, but also from juice or GRAPE CONCENTRATE. In Great Britain, the hobby peaked in the late 1980s, with grape concentrate the usual raw material, producing MADE WINE, which lacks the fresh fruitiness of wine made from the juice of freshly picked grapes.

It was Canada that revolutionized home winemaking. Kits based on canned grape juice concentrate had been introduced in the 1950s but a new type of kit made by Canada's Brew King, using a combination of concentrates and flash-PASTEURIZED fresh grape juice and including much of the necessary equipment, encouraged many new recruits.

In addition, the introduction in the Canadian provinces of Ontario and British Columbia of 'Wine On Premise' shops, where customers could vinify an unlimited amount of wine for personal use, free of any tax, led to kits capturing more than 20% of the total wine market in Canada within 10 years, worth more than one-third of a billion Canadian dollars.

Today the world's major wine kit manufacturers are all based in Canada but distribute throughout Canada, the US, Europe, Iceland, and South East Asia. Together, they sell enough wine kits to produce more than 10 million cases of wine per year, using grape material sourced throughout the world.   J.R. & T.V.

homoclimes, geographical term meaning 'similar climate'. It has been a popular approach to VINEYARD SITE SELECTION in the New World to search for homoclimes of classical French regions. Homoclimes can be found efficiently and accurately with digitized maps and GEOGRAPHICAL INFORMATION SYSTEMS. Homoclimes are typically sought using temperature and rainfall data. For example, Tamar Ridge Vineyards has used this approach to identify new vineyard regions in Tasmania with the same climate as distinguished the MARLBOROUGH region of New Zealand.   R.E.S.

Hondarrabi Beltza, rare Spanish BASQUE red wine grape related to Cabernet Franc and grown to produce red and rosé TXAKOLI. The pale-skinned grapes making white Txakoli are called **Hondarribi Zuri**, of which Spain's total plantings had grown to 665 ha/1,642 acres by 2011. But these vines are probably a mix of COURBU BLANC, CROUCHEN, and, according to one reference sample for DNA PROFILING, the American hybrid NOAH. Hondarrabi is also known as Hondarribi.

Hong Kong has become the hub of ASIAN wine markets since 2008 when duty on wine was slashed to zero, with this very intention. Duties on wine imported to the rest of CHINA are substantial and therefore many of the army of new Chinese wine collectors buy and keep their FINE WINES in this southern enclave. The number of wine STORAGE FACILITIES, wine MERCHANTS, wine AUCTIONS, and wine trade fairs in Hong Kong has soared accordingly. By the second decade of this century, auction totals in Hong Kong had overtaken those in all of Europe, and virtually every fine wine trader had a Hong Kong outpost. Reliable statistics are not available but a very considerable quantity of fine wine is thought to cross the border into China from Hong Kong, some of it hand-carried. Hong Kong's first URBAN WINERY, The 8th Estate, has been making wine from imported grapes since 2007 and was joined by Portrait Winery in 2010.

Horace (Quintus Horatius Flaccus) (65–8 BC), the Latin poet, did not write a systematic guide to viticulture but wine does figure prominently in his work, and reflects his Epicurean philosophy of enjoying its pleasures in moderation. He tells us that at the Sabine farm which his patron Maecenas gave him he does not grow wine (*Epistles* 1. 14), but as a token of his gratitude he serves Maecenas the local wine, laid down by the poet himself in the year that his patron had recovered from a serious illness (*Odes* 1. 20). This matching of the wine to the guest and the occasion is a constant feature of Horace's invitation poems, and other poems about drinking: see also *Odes* 1. 9 and 4. 2 (simple wines for intimate occasions), 3. 21 (a wine from the year of the poet's birth for an honoured guest), 1. 37 (a grand old CAECUBAN to celebrate the defeat of the monstrous Cleopatra), 3. 14 (a wine that goes back to the Social War, 91–88 BC, to celebrate Augustus' return), 3. 28 (Caecuban of Bibulus' consular year, 59 BC, in honour of Neptune).

Horace cannot afford the very best wine, old FALERNIAN: to spend a feast day drinking that would be the greatest happiness (*Odes* 2. 3). Note that to Horace good wine is always old wine: the Romans (and the Greeks) preferred old wine to the wine of the current vintage.

Epistles 1. 19 is Horace's contribution to the debate about poetic inspiration. Callimachus (*c*.310/05–*c*.240 BC) first raised the question of whether water, symbol of the purity of poetic labour, or wine, which brings poetic frenzy, is the better drink for a poet. On the authority of Cratinus (*c*.520–*c*.423 BC), Horace sides with the wine drinkers, for were not Homer and Ennius (see Ancient GREECE), the fathers of Greek and Latin epic respectively, wine bibbers? 'Laudibus arguitur vini vinosus Homerus', Horace asserts: 'in his praises of wine, wine-bibbing Homer betrays himself.' To the modern reader, Horace seems to have more in common with today's civilized wine enthusiast than any other classical writer. H.M.W.

Commager, S., 'The function of wine in Horace's Odes', *Transactions of the American Philological Association*, 88 (1957), 68–80.

Eyres, H., *Horace and me* (London, 2013).

Griffin, J., *Latin Literature and Roman Life* (London, 1985).

Wilson, H., *Wine and Words in Classical Antiquity and the Middle Ages* (London, 2003).

horizontal trellis. See TENDONE and TRAINING SYSTEM.

hormones, natural substances present in trace concentrations in vines and other plants which move from one organ or part of the plant to another to regulate growth and development. Synthetic GROWTH REGULATORS may have similar chemical structures, and a similar mode of action. There are three groups of hormones which promote growth, these being AUXINS, GIBBERELLINS, and CYTOKININS, and two groups which inhibit growth, ABSCISIC ACID and ethylene. R.E.S.

horses are making a return to vineyards as an alternative to TRACTORS in response to concerns about SOIL COMPACTION. See also BIODYNAMIC VITICULTURE, CULTIVATION, LABOUR, and SUSTAINABLE VITICULTURE.

Hospices de Beaune, charity auction which has taken place in BEAUNE annually since 1851 on the third Sunday in November, a key feature of the Burgundian calendar. The beneficiaries are the combined charitable organizations of the Hôtel Dieu, founded in 1443 by Nicolas Rolin, chancellor of the duchy of Burgundy, and the Hôpital de la Charité.

The produce of vineyard holdings donated by benefactors over the centuries is auctioned at prices usually well in excess of current commercial values. Nevertheless, the results serve as some indication of the trend in bulk wine prices for the new vintage.

The cuvées sold are named to commemorate original benefactors such as Nicolas Rolin and his wife Guigone de Salins or more recent ones such as de Bahèzre de Lanlay, an inspector of aerial telegraphs. The Hospices de Beaune also provides the occasion for 'Les Trois Glorieuses', the three great feasts held over the weekend at CLOS DE VOUGEOT on Saturday night, in Beaune on Sunday night, and in MEURSAULT for the extended lunchtime bottle party that is the Paulée de Meursault on Monday.

The Hospices de Nuits also holds a charity wine auction; see NUITS-ST-GEORGES.

See also AUCTIONS. J.T.C.M.

hot bottling. See PASTEURIZATION.

hot pressing. See THERMOVINIFICATION.

hot-water treatment is used by QUARANTINE authorities and vine NURSERIES to sterilize dormant grapevine CUTTINGS or nursery plants. These are immersed in hot water at around 50 °C/122 °F, or slightly warmer, for a few minutes to destroy surface contaminants and for up to 30 minutes for internal diseases such as FUNGI and PHYTOPLASMA. Hot-water treatment is also used to control CROWN GALL bacteria, NEMATODES, and PHYLLOXERA and other insects. The process is currently receiving much attention because it may be a way to control TRUNK DISEASES. There should be no damage to the plants if the temperature is accurately regulated and storage protocols followed. See also THERMOTHERAPY. R.E.S.

Howell Mountain, California wine region and AVA east of St Helena, defined by elevation of about 1,400 ft/425 m. See NAPA Valley.

Hrvatska. See CROATIA.

Hugel, one of the best-known and oldest wine producers in Alsace, having been established in 1639. The family business is run today by the 12th and 13th generations. The Hugels, based in Riquewihr, make fine wines from their own 30 ha/74 acres of vineyard around the village planted mainly with Riesling and Gewurztraminer, together with a little Pinot Gris and Pinot Noir. Their Tradition range can be excitingly full and the Jubilee range masterful. The Hugel family also pioneered the resurrection of Alsace's late-harvest wines and were instrumental in drawing up the rigorous requirements for these VENDANGE TARDIVE and SÉLECTION DE GRAINS NOBLES wines. They are arch exponents of these styles themselves, and produce them, and the Jubilee range, exclusively from their own ALSACE GRAND CRU vineyards. The Hugel family, of which six family members worked in the Riquewihr wine business in the mid 2000s, have long been champions of maximizing quality in Alsace's finest wines, and are vociferous opponents of the Alsace Grand Cru appellation, which they feel is no guarantee of quality. The Hugels buy in grapes, never wine, for their basic generic range of wines from about 100 ha/250 120 ha/300 acres of vineyard under contract from more than 300 growers. Marc Hugel is in charge of winemaking.

Humagne Blanche, Swiss Valais white grape which, unexpectedly, is not related to HUMAGNE ROUGE. The wine produced is elegant, though less expressive than PETITE ARVINE. DNA PROFILING has shown that Humagne Blanche is the parent of LAFNETSCHA, and that it is also found in south-west France as MIOUSAT. J.V.

Humagne Rouge, relatively rare red wine grape of the Swiss Valais region whose wines are wild, rustic, and relatively high in TANNINS. They are particularly recommended with venison. DNA PROFILING at CHANGINS and Aosta showed that this variety is identical to CORNALIN of the Valle d'AOSTA and confirmed that it is not related to HUMAGNE BLANCHE. J.V.

humidification, euphemism for the (sometimes illegal but increasingly common) winemaking operation of adding water to reduce ALCOHOLIC STRENGTH.

humidity, or moisture content, of the atmosphere has considerable implications both for vine growth and for STORING barrels and wine, whether in bulk or bottle. Humidity is normally measured as per cent relative humidity (% RH): the amount of water vapour a given volume of air holds, as a percentage of the maximum it could hold at the same temperature. The latter amount increases with temperature, so the RH of air containing a constant amount of water vapour falls as temperature rises, and vice versa. Humidity can also be expressed as saturation deficit, which is a direct measure of the evaporative power of the atmosphere. Actual EVAPORATION is further influenced by WIND and SUNLIGHT.

Relative humidity follows a regular daily cycle, normally being highest in the early morning, when temperature is lowest, and lowest in the early to mid afternoon, when temperature is highest. Broadly speaking, high humidity is conducive to the spread of FUNGAL DISEASES, especially when combined with high temperatures. High morning humidity creates DEW, which is also important for some diseases. The afternoon humidity, together with sunshine, temperature, and wind, dominate in determining evaporation, and therefore the likelihood of WATER STRESS. The contrast between morning and afternoon relative humidities tends to be greatest inland, and least near coasts.

Gladstones argues that high humidity levels, critically those in the afternoon, are conducive to high wine quality. Where the vines suffer little water stress, PHOTOSYNTHESIS is relatively continuous and there is maximum production of SUGAR IN GRAPES and its derivatives in the form of berry colour, flavour, and aroma. Higher humidity will limit TRANSPIRATION so there will be less uptake of certain minerals into the vines and fruit, including POTASSIUM. Must and natural wine PH should therefore be lower, with benefits for brightness of wine COLOUR, freshness of wine flavour and aroma, and greater resistance to OXIDATION and BACTERIAL SPOILAGE.

Viticultural regions of the world with high afternoon relative humidities during the fruiting period include all those of Germany, Switzerland, Austria, and HUNGARY; Burgundy, Alsace, Champagne, the Loire Valley, Bordeaux, and the Mediterranean coastal strip of France; marginally central and northern Italy, and the upper Rioja region of Spain; Madeira and some exposed coastal areas of Portugal; most of the coolest parts (Region I: see CLIMATE CLASSIFICATION) of the coastal valleys of California, Oregon, and Washington; the Cape Town/Constantia area in South Africa; Margaret River and the south coast of Western Australia; coastal Victoria; and all of Tasmania and New Zealand. Many of these regions have experienced marked increases in humidity recently because of CLIMATE CHANGE; warmer air can hold more moisture.

Typical areas of intermediate humidity include the southern Rhône Valley of France; most inland table wine-producing areas of Portugal, such as Dão, and of Spain; Bulgaria; intermediate and warmer parts of the coastal valleys of California, such as the Napa and Santa Clara Valleys; Stellenbosch and Paarl in South Africa; the Western Australian west coast and hills; Barossa, Adelaide Hills, Langhorne Creek, and Coonawarra in South Australia; Grampians and other parts of the Great Dividing Range in Victoria; and the Hunter Valley and marginally Mudgee in New South Wales.

Viticultural regions with low afternoon relative humidities are nearly all hot as well, and tend to have high TEMPERATURE VARIABILITY. Such regions include the middle and upper Douro Valley of Portugal (to a moderate degree); the Central Valley of California; the Little Karoo in South Africa; and the Murray and Murrumbidgee Valley areas of South Australia, northern Victoria, and southern New South Wales.

The tendency for more humid wine regions to have higher quality reputations is evident from the above list, but compelling evidence for this based on VINE PHYSIOLOGY is yet to be developed.

For details of humidity and barrels, see EVAPORATION. For details of humidity and wine storage, see STORING WINE.   J.G. & R.E.S.

humus. See ORGANIC MATTER.

Hundred Years War. The sporadic fighting between the kings of England and France known as the Hundred Years War (1337–1453) changed both the political map of Europe and the nature and volume of the medieval wine trade. Both crowns claimed ownership of the wine regions of western France, which, through the wealthy port of BORDEAUX, supplied England with almost all her wine.

The hostilities had a marked effect on the wine trade. First the large and commercially successful vineyards of the HAUT PAYS, or 'high country', upstream from Bordeaux (GAILLAC, BERGERAC, BUZET, CAHORS) were for the most part under French control. This increased English reliance on the lesser vineyards of Bordeaux and its environs, encouraging their expansion.

Secondly, the ships carrying wine back to England faced the risk of greater piracy. Convoys organized for their protection proved expensive. Reduced supplies and greater freight costs led to a dramatic rise in the price of wine in England.

After Bordeaux's surrender at CASTILLON in 1453, England remained a major market for her wines, although the overall volume of this trade was not to reach the pre-war peak for many centuries. English merchants became more willing to look beyond western France for their wine imports while Bordeaux attracted a wider clientele of merchants from northern Europe.

See also BORDEAUX, history.   H.B.

Dion, R., *Histoire de la vigne et du vin en France* (Paris, 1959).

James, M. K., *Studies in the Medieval Wine Trade* (Oxford, 1971).

Renouard, Y., *Études d'histoire médiévale* (Paris, 1968).

Hungary, important central European wine-producing country with its own particularly distinctive range of vine varieties and wines. Hungary usually produces less wine than its eastern neighbour ROMANIA, but considerably more than, for example, AUSTRIA and BULGARIA. Just over 65,000 ha/160,000 acres were devoted to vines in 2011, and almost 70% of them produced white wines. Total Hungarian wine production has been decreasing and is now usually below 4 million hl/105 million gal a year, of which about a fifth is exported.

History

Vine-growing and winemaking have been practised in what is modern Hungary since at least Roman times, when it was part of the Roman province of Pannonia. The Magyar tribes who arrived here at the end of the 9th century found flourishing vineyards and familiarity with winemaking techniques. Under Bela IV (1235–70), the king who rebuilt Hungary after the Mongol invasion of 1241, wine production was given such priority that immigrants from areas with particular expertise in vine-growing and winemaking were deliberately invited to rebuild the devastated areas, and by the end of his reign wines from the two towns of SOPRON and EGER were being exported in relatively large quantities. Hungary's most famous wine, TOKAJI, is first mentioned in records in the late 15th century, although it was almost certainly dry at this time.

Following the defeat and death of Louis II at the battle of Mohács in 1529, much of the country was under Muslim rule for a century and a half, during which wine production survived, but did not thrive (see ISLAM).

The most important development in the 17th century was the emergence of especially rich Tokaj Aszú. As early as 1641, a Vine Law for the entire Tokaj-Hegyalja district was drawn up which regulated VINEYARD SITE SELECTION, the construction of TERRACES, IRRIGATION, manuring, and hoeing (which had to be done for the last time on 20 August before the official harvest date of 28 October). By 1570, NOBLE ROT was recognized, and the laws for Aszú formulated. For more details, see TOKAJI.

In 1686, the city of Buda was liberated from the Turks, followed within the next few years by all of the rest of Hungary, which then became part of the vast Habsburg empire. A bid for independence led by Ferenc Rákóczi failed in 1711, but had the effect of spreading the fame of Tokaj wines to the court of the French king, Louis XIV, to whom Rákóczi had wisely sent sample bottles as gifts. This was the beginning of Tokaj's formidable international reputation.

The vineyards of Tokaj were some of the first to be submitted to CLASSIFICATION, in 1700, and the first national vineyard classification anywhere, a five-level rating, was undertaken in Hungary in 1707–8 as part of general appraisal of the country's resources.

PHYLLOXERA struck Hungary in the 1870s, devastating the southern vineyards at Pancsova initially but eventually spreading to the Northern Massif and Tokaj-Hegyalja. Replanting on phylloxera-resistant ROOTSTOCKS began in 1881, but scientific proof that the phylloxera louse could not thrive in sandy soils had just been published, encouraging the planting of new vineyards in the Great Plain, between the Danube and Tisza Rivers, where vines were also discovered to be particularly suitable plants for stabilizing the shifting sands.

Zsigmond Teleki (1854–1910) bred the famous 5 BB Teleki rootstock which proved perfectly suited to producing high-quality grapes even when planted in the desolate, intensely CALCAREOUS hillsides of Villány. When Teleki died in 1910, his sons Andor and Sándor continued the NURSERY business with great success until the Second World War, maintaining subsidiaries in six countries. Ironically, Franz Kober in Oppenheim eventually collected most of the recognition by subjecting Teleki's CLONES to further selection and indeed the rootstock is more

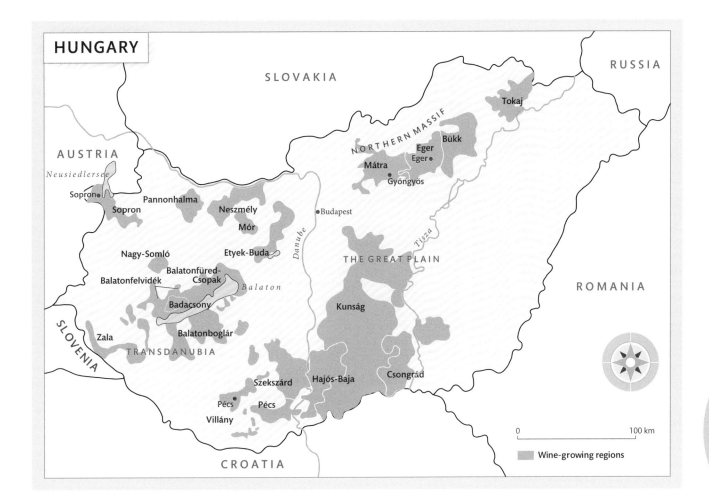

commonly known today as 5 BB Kober. Móricz Preysz (1829–77) was the pioneer of PASTEURIZATION, publishing his work on the technique, needed then to stabilize Tokaji, in 1861, two years before Louis PASTEUR developed pasteurization.

In 1947, the National Association of Hungarian Vine-Growers, Wine Trades and Wine-Growing Communities, which had originally been founded in 1830 to promote co-operation and study for the benefit of all in the wine industry, was forced to suspend its activities when the communist state monopoly took control. An era of state farms and state wineries followed, during which all wine exports were funnelled through the state-controlled trading company Monimpex (and half of all production at one point handled by just two state wineries designed to export huge quantities of very ordinary wine to the SOVIET UNION). Unlike the similarly organized BULGARIAN wine industry, that of Hungary suffered a period of stagnation and generally low technology during this era, which stultified the development of Hungarian wine until the somewhat complicated return of a free-market economy and private enterprise in the late 1980s. A considerable proportion of all Hungarian vines had remained in private

hands in the communist era, and this has enabled Hungary to adapt production to the more stringent requirements of western importers more quickly than other ex-Comecon countries.

In the post-communist division of vinicultural spoils (see below), there was no shortage of western interest in the unique Tokaji wines, and technology in other areas benefited from temporary invasion by foreign—typically antipodean (see AUSTRALIAN INFLUENCE)—winemakers. The early 21st century has seen a marked increase in the number of ambitious, quality-focused wineries with improved VINEYARD site selection, selection of suitable plant material, respect for TERROIR, and improved winemaking.

Geography

Hungary, which lies between the latitudes 45 and 50 degrees north, is land-locked but includes Central Europe's largest lake, Balaton. The River Danube (called Duna in Hungary) flows through the country from north to south, dividing it in almost equal halves. To the west lies Transdanubia, while to the immediate east of the river is the Great Plain. North east of the capital Budapest are the volcanic hills which

constitute the Northern Massif, whose south-facing slopes are particularly well suited to vine-growing. In the extreme north east of the country is the Tokaj (formerly Tokaj-Hegyalja) region, which borders SLOVAKIA. See TOKAJI for more details.

Soils are very varied. The Great Plain is mainly SAND and LOESS, while the area around Lake Balaton is of complex BASALT volcanic rock with CLAY and sandstone. Other soils include LIMESTONE and SLATE, particularly around Balatonfüred. In Tokaj, the soils are VOLCANIC with a topsoil of decayed lava. The best wines often come from volcanic soils, producing full, well-structured wines rich in MINERALITY.

See below and separate entries for EGER, SZEKSZÁRD, TOKAJ, and VILLÁNY for details of individual wine regions.

Climate

Hungary's climate is essentially CONTINENTAL and Central European, involving fairly predictably cold winters and hot summers. The relatively northerly latitude (on a par with Burgundy) makes it ideally situated to produce aromatic and semi-aromatic varieties such as Sauvignon Blanc and Gewurztraminer, while its continentality allows full ripening of such red varieties as Cabernet Sauvignon, especially in the south. The sun shines for a high average of about 2,000 hours a year, and the total heat summation (see CLIMATE CLASSIFICATION) during the vegetative ripening period is approximately 2,500 °C. Prolonged, sunny autumns which favour the development of NOBLE ROT are by no means rare, however. The largely volcanic hills are particularly well adapted to white-wine production.

Vine varieties

Wine labelling is mostly VARIETAL. Hungary had a particularly rich selection of INDIGENOUS VINE VARIETIES, many of which were largely abandoned when PHYLLOXERA invaded the country's vineyards in the late 19th century. A potentially exciting selection of localized white grape varieties can still be found, although some such as KÉKNYELŰ, found almost exclusively in Badacsony on the north shore of Lake Balaton, and JUHFARK, known mainly in Somló, are dangerously close to extinction.

Indigenous varieties which are relatively widely planted include EZERJÓ, a light speciality of the Mór region west of Budapest; FURMINT is the most characteristic ingredient of Tokaji; HÁRSLEVELŰ, which is usually a lesser Tokaji ingredient and is also widely grown throughout Hungary. The indigenous Leányka and Királyleányka are used for light-bodied aromatic wines. Newer crosses such as the Muscat-like IRSAI OLIVÉR and the grapey cross CSERSZEGI FŰSZERES are now being more widely planted for their own intrinsic character and quality. Other light-berried crosses include ZÉTA, ZENGŐ, ZEFIR, and ZENIT. Hungary's most characteristic red grape variety is KADARKA, although PORTUGIESER (once known as Kékoportó) can also make some appetizing wines here.

The usual range of central European vine varieties is grown: Olaszrizling (the Hungarian name for WELSCHRIESLING), Zöldveltelini (Austria's GRÜNER VELTLINER), Cirfandli (Austria's ZIERFANDLER, a speciality of Pécs); and, for red wine production, KÉKFRANKOS (along with Nagyburgundi, the Hungarian name for BLAUFRÄNKISCH), and Austria's ZWEIGELT.

A wide range of vine varieties have been imported into Hungary from western Europe, however, including Chardonnay, Sauvignon Blanc, Sémillon, Riesling (sometimes called Rajnai Rizling or Rheinriesling), Gewürztraminer (Tramini), Muscat Ottonel and Yellow Muscat, the deeper-hued Muscat Blanc à Petits Grains (both of which are sometimes called Muskotály), and Pinot Gris, whose distinctively Hungarian synonym is Szürkebarát. Red wine varieties imported from the west include Merlot and, to a much lesser extent, Cabernet Sauvignon and Cabernet Franc, and a small amount of Pinot Noir and Syrah.

Wine regions

Hungarian law in this century established 22 wine regions. In 2009, in keeping with the EU reforms of CONTROLLED APPELLATION terminology, these were replaced by 36 PDOS (Oltalom alatt álló eredet megjelöléssel or OEM in Hungarian) and six PGIS (Oltalom alatt álló földrajzi jelzéssel or OFJ): Zempléni, Zemplén/Felső-Magyarországi, Felső-magyarország, Duna, Dunántúl, and Balaton. The following PDOS may be considered pre-eminent: Badacsony, Balatonboglár, EGER, Etyek-Buda, Somló, SOPRON, SZEKSZÁRD, TOKAJ, and VILLÁNY. Names such as Mátra, Neszmély, and Pannonhalma may also be familiar from export labels. The wine regions fall into three major geographical groups, as outlined below.

Transdanubia The wine regions in this western part of Hungary, between the Austrian border and the Danube, are increasingly bringing their own marked characteristics to the wines. The area is heavily influenced by the waters of Lake Balaton, the NEUSIEDLERSEE in Austria, and the Danube itself. Wines from this area may be labelled PGI Dunántúl.

Traditionally the northern side of Lake Balaton was the vine-growing area, with the famous Badacsony Hill on the volcanic slopes at the south-west end. The surface area of water in the lake has a considerable ameliorating effect on the MESOCLIMATE (see TOPOGRAPHY) and the wines tend to be full and powerful. This is home to the ancient Kéknyelű, but also makes fine Pinot Gris (Szürkebarát), as well as Olaszrizling. Balatonfüred-Csopak also lies on the northern shore, on sandstone, slate, and marl, and produces a range of western varieties and Olaszrizling. Balatonfüred-Csopak is known for its Olaszrizling and the Csopak Kódex association has been formed to regulate and recognize the quality of the best examples.

On the slopes of an extinct volcano north west of Lake Balaton is the historic, now small, wine region of Somló, whose wood-aged, blended wines once enjoyed a similar reputation to those of Tokaj. Juhfark was once prized here, along with Furmint, but Olaszrizling, Hárslevelű, and Traminer have been in the ascendant. Somló has been attracting increasing investment as its potential for elegant, age-worthy wines with a distinctive MINERAL character becomes evident, and some promising Juhfark is being made once more.

On the south shore of the lake is a relatively new area, Balatonboglár, where the fertile soils include SAND and LOESS. Important grapes grown here are Olaszrizling, Királyleányka, Zöldveltelini, Irsai Olivér, Chardonnay, Muscat, Merlot, and Pinot Noir. Base wines for excellent sparkling wines such as Garamvári's Chateau Vincent are also produced here.

Sopron, the most westerly wine region of northern Transdanubia and effectively a continuation of NEUSIEDLERSEE-HÜGELLAND, Austria's most revered source of sweet white wine, is dominated by ambitious growers of Austro-German extraction. Sopron is mainly a red wine region and the principal vine varieties are Kékfrankos, Cabernet Sauvignon, Cabernet Franc, Merlot, Pinot Noir, and Syrah, which can be particularly elegant when grown on the SCHIST soils here.

In the north are two increasingly important white wine areas: Neszmély and Mór, between Sopron and Budapest, which are best known for crisp but well-balanced Olaszrizling and Sauvignon Blanc, tart Ezerjó, Leányka, and aromatic Gewurztraminer.

Southern Transdanubia has three important wine regions close together in the far south of the country just west of the Danube. Villány is most famous for the saddle of land in the Villány Hills which manages to produce highly prized reds even in difficult years. Several producers are exploiting these natural advantages. Cabernet Franc is most successful here, although Kékfrankos, Merlot, and Zweigelt are also good. More and more good Syrah is also produced.

Szekszárd has traditionally been associated with Kadarka, which it has managed to ripen more healthily than most regions, owing to its long, warm summers but plantings total barely 100 ha/250 acres. This native red variety has been supplanted by vigorous Kékfrankos, Merlot, and Cabernet but Szekszárd producers tend to achieve a higher average quality with their Kadarka, Kékfrankos, and BIKAVÉR wines. The area around Bátaszék, 15 km/9 miles to the south, is a cooler subregion that can produce some particularly good Sauvignon Blanc and Grüner Veltliner. ANTINORI owns a winery here.

Pécs, Hungary's warmest wine region, is at constant risk of DROUGHT. A wide range of vine varieties is cultivated here, often on very small estates. They include Olaszrizling, Chardonnay, Kadarka, Cabernet, Merlot, and Pinot Noir.

The Northern Massif This range of hills running north east from Budapest along the border with Slovakia contains four wine regions, Mátra, EGER, Bükk, and TOKAJ.

In the foothills of the Mátra Mountains, the soils are mainly VOLCANIC and most of the wine produced is white. Muscat, Olaszrizling, and Királyleányka predominate, alongside some elegant, fruity reds. In western Europe at least, the area is well known for the German-owned Danubiana Estate on which modern Chardonnay, Sauvignon Blanc, and Sémillon have been made for export.

Just to the east of the Mátra foothills, in the foothills of the Bükk Mountains, is the wine region named after the historic town of EGER. Spring often comes late here and the rainfall is low. Some white wines are made, principally from Olaszrizling, Leányka, and Chardonnay but the region is best known for ageworthy red wine, notably Egri Bikavér, once known on export markets as Bull's Blood. Once one of the most famous wine BRANDS, this blend represented a triumph of marketing although quality varied considerably towards the end of the communist era. Eger is once again making fine wine. At one time the blend depended heavily on Kadarka, but as elsewhere this troublesome native variety was replaced by Kékfrankos, supplemented by Cabernet, Merlot, and Portugieser (Kékoportó). The Bükk region generally favours white wines.

In the past, only Tokaji, made even further east, has rivalled Bull's Blood for recognition outside Hungary, although the situation has been changing rapidly as winemaking and exporting skills have passed into private, and often non-Hungarian, hands.

The Great Plain This vast, flat expanse (known as Alföld in Hungary) south of Budapest and between the Danube and Hungary's second river, the Tisza, accounts for nearly half the country's vineyards. The plain was heavily planted after the PHYLLOXERA invasion because of phylloxera's intolerance of sandy soils, and because vines were better at stabilizing the soil than the fruit trees planted earlier.

MECHANIZATION is easy on this flat land, but the DROUGHT in summer and FROST in both late spring and autumn are a perennial threat, and the combination of sandy soil and high summer temperatures means that soil temperatures can be very high indeed.

INTERNATIONAL VARIETIES or Olaszrizling, Rajnai Rizling (RIESLING), Kékfrankos, Kadarka, Cserszegi Fűszeres, and Ezerjó are planted here. The Great Plain encompasses the PGI Duna-Tisza közi and the PDOS Csongrád, Hajós-Baja, and Kunság but wine quality is generally indifferent. The more recent PDO Duna may be used for wines from those three more specific and well-established regions.

Structure of the trade

Prior to the reintroduction of a capitalist system in the early 1990s, the Hungarian wine industry was under the control of the state.

In the early 1980s, Hungary was a significant wine exporter, each year shipping out more than 3 million hl/79 million gal, or 60% of production, notably very ordinary quality wine in bulk to the SOVIET UNION and East Germany. These markets shrank abruptly at the end of the

1980s (see GORBACHEV), leading to sudden oversupply and extreme uncertainty among vinegrowers and winemakers.

The state of flux of the early 1990s, caused partly by uncertainty over property rights and exact boundaries, was followed by a far more stable economic and political environment. The influx of western European capital and EU finance enabled much-needed investment in modern winery equipment, resulting in a marked improvement in quality for all wines but particularly for flavoursome dry whites.

See also EGER, SZEKSZÁRD, TOKAJ, and VILLÁNY.

G.R. & G.M.

Liddell, A., *The Wines of Hungary* (London, 2003).

Rohály, G., *Rohály's Wine Guide: Hungary* (Budapest, annually).

Rohály, G., et al., *Terra Benedicta* (Budapest, 2003).

Hunter Valley Zone, historic NEW SOUTH WALES wine zone within striking distance of Sydney in which **Hunter** is a region and Broke Fordwich, Pokolbin, and Upper Hunter are subregions, with other subregions pending. There were 135 producers in 2014.

Huxelrebe is an early-21st-century German vine CROSS that enjoys some popularity both in Germany and, on a much smaller scale, in ENGLAND. Although like SCHEUREBE and FABERREBE it was actually bred by Dr Georg Scheu at Alzey, this cross takes its name from its chief propagator, nurseryman Fritz Huxel. It was bred in 1927 from GUTEDEL (Chasselas) and Courtillier Musqué (which is also an antecedent of the popular hybrid MARÉCHAL FOCH). The cross is capable of producing enormous quantities of rather ordinary wine—so enormous in fact that the vines can collapse under the strain. If pruned carefully, however, and planted on an average to good site, it can easily reach Auslese MUST WEIGHTS even in an ordinary year and produce a fulsome if not exactly subtle wine redolent of honey, musk, and raisins for reasonably early consumption. In England, its ripeness is a useful counterbalance to naturally high acidity. In Germany, it is grown almost exclusively in the Pfalz and Rheinhessen and, although it continues to lose ground, there were still 548 ha/1,354 acres in 2012. Günter and Wittmann manage to spin gold from it.

hybrids, in common viticultural terms, the offspring of two varieties of different species, as distinct from a CROSS between two varieties of the same species, which is also known as an intraspecific cross. (See VITIS for details of the various species of the vine genus.) EU authorities prefer the somewhat cumbersome term 'interspecific cross' to the word hybrid, which has pejorative connotations within Europe.

Hybrids can occur naturally by cross-pollination, as happened, for example, in early American viticulture (see AMERICAN HYBRIDS). More commonly, however, hybrids have been deliberately produced by man (see NEW VARIETIES and VINE BREEDING) to combine in the progeny some of the desirable characteristics of the parents. This viticultural activity was particularly important in the late 19th century, when European, and especially French, breeders tried to combine the desirable wine quality of European VINIFERA varieties with AMERICAN VINE SPECIES' resistance to introduced American pests and diseases, especially the PHYLLOXERA louse, which was devastating European vineyards (see FRENCH HYBRIDS).

Grafting European vines on to American ROOTSTOCKS proved the eventual solution to phylloxera, and many of today's commercially important rootstocks are hybrids. Early rootstocks were often pure varieties of a single American vine species chosen for their resistance to phylloxera. It was subsequently found, however, that hybrid rootstocks with combinations of genes from several American vine species allowing tolerance of various soil conditions and diseases, were more successful in the nursery.

Different species of *Vitis* contain genes with natural tolerance or resistance to winter cold, lime-induced CHLOROSIS, SALINITY, DOWNY MILDEW, POWDERY MILDEW, BOTRYTIS BUNCH ROT, CROWN GALL, PIERCE'S DISEASE, NEMATODES, WINTER FREEZE injury, and phylloxera. It is logical, therefore, to explore the possibilities of new hybrid varieties for wine production in an age of increasing concern about the AGROCHEMICALS which are used to control some of these. Vine breeders such as those at GEILWEILERHOF have proved that new hybrids, now called DISEASE-RESISTANT VARIETIES, may, without recourse to agrochemicals, produce useful quantities of wine which, in controlled tests, cannot be distinguished from that of their pure *V. vinifera* counterparts. As a result, EU authorities now allow such varieties as RONDO, REGENT, PHOENIX, and ORION (all relatively recent hybrids) into wines with GEOGRAPHICAL INDICATION.

Hybrids can yield good wine with no recognizably non-*V. vinifera* characteristics; see SEYVAL BLANC in England's cool climate, CHAMBOURCIN in summer rainfall areas such as parts of NEW SOUTH WALES, and some AMERICAN HYBRIDS.

The pedigree of many modern hybrids can involve seven or eight generations of crosses so that their ancestry is typically complex and includes *V. vinifera*, American varieties, possibly Asian varieties, and also early released French hybrids.

R.E.S.

Mullins, M. G., Bouquet, A., and Williams, L., *Biology of the Grapevine* (Cambridge, 1992).

hydrogen sulfide, or H₂S, is the foul-smelling gas, reminiscent of rotten eggs, which even at very low concentrations (parts per billion) is easily recognized in wine because it is highly volatile and has a very low sensory detection threshold. Although it can form at any stage of wine production, hydrogen sulfide is produced most commonly during alcoholic FERMENTATION, either in the early to middle, vigorous, phase or towards the end. Hydrogen sulfide production during the vigorous phase, which coincides with rapid yeast growth, is associated with a deficiency in the amount of NITROGEN (often referred to as yeast-assimilable/available nitrogen or YAN) in the grape must or juice. The nitrogen content of grapes is highly variable and depends on many factors, including grape variety, soil type and NUTRIENT status, climate, and vineyard management practices, such as type and amount of nutrient application, IRRIGATION, and use of COVER CROPS. Nitrogen-deficient grape musts are often supplemented with nitrogen, typically in the form of DIAMMONIUM PHOSPHATE (DAP), which usually suppresses the appearance of hydrogen sulfide. Addition of SULFUR DIOXIDE, often made to the must shortly before inoculating with YEAST, as an antioxidant and to inhibit AMBIENT YEAST and BACTERIA, can also increase the amount of hydrogen sulfide produced by some yeast strains.

Because grape must does not contain sufficient sulfur-containing AMINO ACIDS, which are essential for yeast protein synthesis and cell growth, yeast use inorganic sulfur sources—sulfate, and, when added, sulfite—present in the must. The inorganic sulfur is metabolically reduced to hydrogen sulfide, which is immediately incorporated into a nitrogen precursor molecule (*o*-acetylhomoserine) to synthesize the sulfur amino acids cysteine and methionine. However, if a deficiency of nitrogen occurs, the cell is unable to synthesize the nitrogen precursor molecule and, consequently, hydrogen sulfide escapes into the wine. The addition of nitrogen (i.e. DAP) reduces the accumulation of hydrogen sulfide in the wine, not by stopping its formation in the yeast cell but by allowing the yeast to make the amino acid precursor. In contrast, recent research suggests that hydrogen sulfide which forms during the late stages of fermentation or immediately after PRESSING results from the metabolic breakdown of yeast cell reserves of GLUTATHIONE, which contains sulfur in addition to nitrogen; the sulfur is surplus to needs and is released as hydrogen sulfide, whereas the nitrogen is used, for example, to repair damaged proteins. Adding nitrogen does not prevent the production of this form of hydrogen sulfide but the choice of yeast strain can help. Novel strains of wine yeast that are not capable of producing significant amounts of hydrogen sulfide have recently been developed at both the AUSTRALIAN

WINE RESEARCH INSTITUTE and at DAVIS using convential breeding and selection techniques. Other practical strategies—AERATION of the ferment, for example—are still being assessed.

Small amounts of sulfur used as vineyard fungicide can easily be reduced to hydrogen sulfide by the highly REDUCTIVE conditions generated by fermenting yeast. Reducing or eliminating sulfur residues by ceasing sulfur applications several weeks before HARVEST can help. Research suggests that the role of sulfur residues as a source of sulfide in wine is overstated. In rare instances, a VITAMIN deficiency caused by the growth of non-*Saccharomyces* yeasts before fermentation can also cause hydrogen sulfide formation. Hydrogen sulfide can also form through direct contact of wine with certain metals such as ZINC and even with the layer of manganese sulfide which can form on the surface of stainless steel. Iron and aluminium also serve as catalysts for the formation of sulfides. Residues of copper, which is commonly added to wine to remove the odour of hydrogen sulfide, can, under highly reductive conditions, for example during prolonged storage in tank or after packaging, catalyse the formation of hydrogen sulfide. The benefits and disadvantages of copper usage in winemaking are currently being reassessed.

Even traces of hydrogen sulfide can spoil the aroma of some wines. Fortunately, however, hydrogen sulfide is very volatile and can usually be removed by the stripping action of CARBON DIOXIDE produced during fermentation. However, hydrogen sulfide formed towards the end of fermentation or, worse still, after fermentation is completed is of greater concern to the winemaker. If allowed to remain in the wine, it can react with other wine components to form MERCAPTANS (i.e. thiols), and disulfides (see SULFIDE), which have pungent garlic, onion, or rubber aromas. The origin of mercaptans and other stinky sulfur compounds during fermentation is unclear, although recent research suggests that chemical formation as well as yeast are involved. The smell of rotten eggs is always a FAULT in a finished wine but acceptance of the presence of trace amounts of mercaptans and disulfide is more controversial. This can usually be removed from the new wine by a small addition of copper sulfate, whereas hydrogen sulfide, having a very low boiling point, is effectively eliminated during RACKING, where it is carried along with released carbon dioxide. Unfortunately, copper sulfate may react not only with off-flavours but also with varietal aromas. In the case of robust wines (especially reds), sulfur compounds can also be removed by AERATION, traditionally achieved by stirring, SPARGING, or by racking. A process of racking in association with temporary removal of yeast lees has been shown to be particularly effective in the removal of hydrogen sulfide. Finally, the

type of CLOSURE, which affects the ingress of oxygen, can also influence the development of sulfidic odours in packaged wine.   P.A.H.

Feuillat, M., 'Les capsules à vis pour le bouchage des vins: des essais faits en Bourgogne il y a 40 ans', *Revue des Oenologues*, 114 (Jan 2005).

Mestres, M., Busto, O., and Guasch, J., 'Analysis of organic sulfur compounds in wine aroma', *Journal of Chromatography A*, 881 (2000), 569–81. doi: 10.1016/S0021-9673(00)00220-X.

Rauhut, D., 'Usage and formation of sulphur compounds', in H. König, G. Unden, and J. Fröhlich (eds.), *Biology of Microorganisms on Grapes, in Musts and in Wine* (Springer, 2009).

Ugliano, M., 'Oxygen contribution to wine aroma evolution during bottle aging', *Journal of Agricultural and Food Chemistry*, 61/26 (2013), 6125–36. doi: 10.1021/jf400810v.

Ugliano, M., et al., 'Effect of nitrogen supplementation and *Saccharomyces* species on hydrogen sulfide and other volatile sulfur compounds in shiraz fermentation and wine', *Journal of Agricultural and Food Chemistry*, 57/11 (2009), 4948–55. doi: 10.1021/jf8037693.

Viviers, M. Z., et al., 'Effects of five metals on the evolution of hydrogen sulfide, methanethiol, and dimethyl sulfide during anaerobic storage of Chardonnay and Shiraz wines', *Journal of Agricultural and Food Chemistry*, 61/50 (2013), 12385–96. doi: 10.1021/jf403422x.

hydrolysis, a chemical reaction with, or involving, water and often catalysed by the hydrogen ions of acids. Hydrolysis is the reaction whereby an ESTER is split into its acid and alcohol components and GLYCOSIDES into their sugar and aglycone parts. The reaction is of great importance to the AGEING of wine when slow hydrolysis affects the FLAVOUR PRECURSORS releasing aroma-active aglycones from their flavourless glycosides.   P.J.W.

hydrometer, an instrument used for measuring the soluble solids, sugar content, or MUST WEIGHT of juice and wine before and/or during fermentation, consisting of a closed glass tube with a bulbous base, weighted so that it floats upright. The floating depth is inversely proportional to the DENSITY of the solution and is read by matching the bottom of the meniscus against a scale within the stem. This scale may be calibrated as for BAUMÉ, BRIX/Balling, OECHSLE, or % alcohol by volume (see ALCOHOLIC STRENGTH). As with all such density measurements, correction for the TEMPERATURE of the solution is necessary.   B.G.C.

hygiene, an essential discipline in modern cellar management, involving cleanliness of winemaking premises and equipment, and a great deal of WATER.

History

Winery hygiene was clearly already regarded as important in Ancient ROME, as suggested by writers such as CATO and references in classical literature to SULFUR.

At the heart of the transformation from traditional mouldy cellars to their spotlessly clean modern counterparts has been a desire by winemakers to obtain much greater control over the processes of vinification and the maturation of wine, primarily through an emphasis on hygiene. While the pace of scientific research on the microbiology and biochemistry of winemaking has quickened appreciably since 1945, its origins lie in the middle of the 19th century with the experimental work of Louis PASTEUR. Until then, the precise reasons why pressed grapes would ferment into wine, and would then become unpalatable if left open to the air for any length of time, were unknown. Practical experience had convinced Roman winemakers of the need to use chemicals such as sulfur to help prevent spoilage, and by the late 15th century in Germany it was recognized that wine kept in large barrels that were subjected to regular TOPPING UP would last longer than wine kept in small barrels which were left on ULLAGE. However, it was Pasteur who first reported in western Europe that wine deteriorated mainly as a result of the actions of micro-organisms, and that these could be killed by heating the wine in the absence of oxygen (although see HUNGARY history).

Much of the impetus for the changes in winery hygiene in the late 20th century came from the New World, and in particular from institutions such as the Department of Viticulture and Enology at the University of California, DAVIS, where the driving mentality during the 1950s and 1960s was towards the eradication of poor-quality wine. This, it was argued, could best be achieved through tight control of the FERMENTATION process, excluding the chance interference of a range of micro-organisms. More recently, innovative research at the AUSTRALIAN WINE RESEARCH INSTITUTE has also played a significant part in advancing the importance of winery hygiene. Above all, greater hygiene has enabled the adverse effects of ACETOBACTER and other spoilage micro-organisms such as BRETTANOMYCES to be avoided.   P.T.H.U.

Current practice

Hygiene is regarded as vital by modern winemakers (although it is still ignored by some traditional or peasant winemakers, several of whom somehow manage to produce top-quality wine). Old cellars, while usually more picturesque, are almost impossible to keep clean and free of BACTERIA and wild YEASTS.

Most modern wineries, on the other hand, are designed with sanitation and hygiene in mind. STAINLESS STEEL tanks can be easily cleaned and sanitized; hard floors are designed to drain dry; and all equipment is sited and mounted so that it can be cleaned thoroughly around, above, and below the unit. Vast quantities of water are used, together with non-foaming detergents and sterilizing agents, by carefully trained staff. In many wineries, all places where finished wine is exposed to the atmosphere are in separate, essentially sterile rooms, and care is taken particularly during BOTTLING, to its limit in STERILE BOTTLING. See also WINERY WASTE.

Some local winemaking traditions supposedly rely on cellar moulds (see TOKAJI in Hungary, for example).

Hygiene, or sanitation, is also important where the grapes are received, as overripe and damaged fruit can easily attract insects, particularly DROSOPHILA and other fruit flies. Piles of POMACE and stems should also be distanced from the winery as these can also become a breeding ground for insects.   A.D.W.

Mitham, P., 'Clean wineries for quality wines', *Wines & Vines* (Nov 2013), 34–9.

Paul, H. W., *Science, Vine and Wine in Modern France* (Cambridge, 1996).

Winkler, A. J., *Viticultural Research at University of California, Davis, 1921–1971* (Davis, Calif., 1973).

hyperoxidation. See WHITE WINEMAKING.

IBMP, or **2-isobutyl-3-methoxypyrazine**. See ISOBUTYL-METHOXYPYRAZINE.

ice wine, direct Anglicization of the German EISWEIN, sweet wine made from ripe grapes picked when frozen on the vine and pressed so that water crystals remain in the press and the sugar content of the resulting wine is increased. This sort of true ice wine is a speciality of CANADA, where it is written ICEWINE (see below). It is also increasingly made elsewhere including AUSTRIA, LUXEM-BOURG, OREGON, and Michigan in the UNITED STATES. The term has also been used in other English-speaking, wine-producing countries for wines made by artificial freeze CONCENTRATION, or CRYOEXTRACTION.

Icewine, made in BRITISH COLUMBIA, QUÉBEC, NOVA SCOTIA, and particularly ONTARIO, is CANADA's version of EISWEIN and the crown jewel of its wine industry. Average annual production in Ontario alone is 900,000 litres and routinely retails at more than C$50 per half-litre. The word Icewine has been trademarked by VQA Canada which imposes the world's most stringent standards on the production of ICE WINE. In Ontario, grapes for Icewine must have reached temperatures as low as −8 °C/18 °F before being harvested (as for Germany's Eiswein) but sugar levels must reach at least 35 °Brix, considerably higher than the minimum requirements in Germany and Austria. From the 1997 vintage, all grapes used for VQA Icewine had to be processed by VQA member wineries or Ontario grape growers who have registered as VQA processors, and strict monitoring systems are in place. All Icewine must be VARIETAL and made from VINIFERA grapes or the French hybrid VIDAL. Grapes must be grown and pressed within a recognized Viticultural Area. Residual sugar at bottling must be at least 125 g/l. No SWEET RESERVE may be added. Canadian wineries were the first to make sparkling Icewine and to make Icewine from red wine grapes. T.A.

Schreiner, J., *Icewine—The Complete Story* (Toronto, 2002).

icon wine, an expression favoured by marketing people for highly priced wine. Icons are generally regarded as ultra-premium wines, which cost more than super-premium wines, which are in turn more expensive than premium wines. The rest is all but undrinkable.

Idaho, state in the NORTHWEST region of the UNITED STATES which, as a wine region, has much in common with its neighbour eastern WASHINGTON. With vineyards at an elevation of around 2,500 ft/762 m, however, it is close to if not beyond the normal viticultural fringe. Its diurnal temperature variation (see TEMPERATURE VARIABILITY) is even greater than that of eastern Washington, with the effect of a paradoxical combination in grapes of high acid and high sugar. This posed interesting challenges for both grape-grower and winemaker in the past. In recent years, however, major developments in the vineyard—lower yields, drip irrigation, open canopies and, above all, planting in warmer localities—have had a dramatic influence on wine quality. In few places has GLOBAL WARMING been more of a blessing. Winters can still be severe but rarely as devastating as they were in the 1970s and 1980s. Regarded then as a marginal climate, primarily noted for wines from hardier white varieties such as Riesling, Gewurztraminer, Chenin Blanc, and Chardonnay, Idaho now grows notable wines from Merlot, Cabernet Sauvignon, and Syrah. It is no surprise to find successful Rieslings, from off dry to ICE WINES.

The industry has been dominated by Ste Chapelle Winery, one of the Northwest's largest (fifth in size in the Pacific Northwest) and more successful wineries, situated in the Snake River valley to the west of Boise, in an area renowned for its cherries, apples, and peaches, always an indication of wine grape potential. Ste Chapelle was Idaho's first winery and its largest. It is likely to continue to grow after its 2012 purchase by Precept Wines which owned 470 of the state's 1,600 acres/500 ha of vines in 2013 and aims to produce a total of 1 million cases of wine a year from Ste Chapelle and sister operation Sawtooth Estate, up from the 170,000 cases made in 2013. Ste Chapelle has played a leading role in improving Idaho viticulture along with the University of Idaho via their experimental vineyard at the research station in Parma. There is substantial cross-border traffic in wine and grapes between Idaho and Washington. L.S.H. & L.M.

Perdue, A., *Northwest Wine Guide* (Seattle, 2003).
Robinson, J., and Murphy, L., *American Wine* (London/Berkeley, 2013).

IFOAM, International Federation of Organic Agriculture Movements. See ORGANIC VITICULTURE.

IGP, short for Indication Géographique Protegée, France's PGI category which has been taking over from the old VIN DE PAYS. To qualify as an IGP, a wine must not be blended across zones, must be produced in limited quantities, must be made of certain specified grape varieties, must reach a certain minimum ALCO-HOLIC STRENGTH, and must be submitted to a tasting panel, as well as coming from a specified area. By 1993, more than one-fifth of all wine produced in France was sold as a Vin de Pays of some sort. The proportion rose to more than 30% by the turn of the century and remains relatively constant (just under 30% in 2012).

French wine producers have a clear choice between making an AOC/AOP (PDO) wine or an IGP wine, or a wine without geographical indication (VSIG) that will be labelled VIN DE FRANCE, either because yields are too high to qualify for an AOC, or because the mix of grape varieties is not permitted by the (usually very detailed) AOC regulations. In general, IGP wines may be produced from grapes which yield up to 90 hl/ha (5 tons/acre) while 50 hl/ha or so is a more likely maximum YIELD permitted by AOC regulations.

There are three levels of IGP wines and they are much less numerous than the old Vins de Pays, which included many a complicated name with no resonance outside their (often small) production zone. Six are at regional level: Pays d'Oc from the LANGUEDOC and ROUSSILLON; Val de LOIRE; Atlantique, part of SOUTH WEST FRANCE around BORDEAUX and north of the Gironde; Comté Tolosan, the rest of South West France; Comtés Rhodaniens, incorporating ARDÈCHE, BEAUJOLAIS, JURA, SAVOIE, and the northern RHÔNE; and Méditerranée from the south east of France and Corsica. Almost 30 are departmental, named after one of France's *département*, such as Aude, Gard, or Gers. Even more are locally specific. These may be named after some historical or geographical phenomenon such as Cité de Carcassonne and Alpilles. Some of these IGP names represent strokes of genius. The image of Corsica is transformed in the name l'Île de Beauté. Le Pays Cathare recalls the colourful history of this part of the western Languedoc, while one of Roussillon's most popular IGPs rightly emphasizes the region's ethnic origins in Côtes Catalanes. The most important single IGP by far is Pays d'Oc, France's prime source of VARIETAL wine. About 85% of all IGPs are grown in Languedoc-Roussillon, Provence, or the southern Rhône. A further 6% come from the Loire. This category has also provided a useful way of selling the surplus produce of vines grown in regions specializing in brandy production. Crisp, dry white Vin de Pays, now IGP, Côtes de Gascogne has been the commercial saviour of vignerons in Armagnac country since the early 1980s, while the Cognac counterpart is now named Charentais.

The following were the IGPs agreed as of 2014:

Agenais	Franche-Comté
Alpes-de-Haute-Provence	Gard
Alpes-Maritimes	Gers
Alpilles	Haute Vallée de
Ardèche	l'Aude
Ariège	Haute Vallée de
Atlantique	l'Orb
Aude	Haute-Marne
Aveyron	Haute-Vienne
Bouches-du-Rhône	Hautes-Alpes
Calvados	Île de Beauté
Cévennes	Isère
Charentais	Landes
Cité de Carcassonne	Lavilledieu
Collines Rhodaniennes	Le Pays Cathare
Comté Tolosan	Maures
Comtés Rhodaniens	Méditerranée
Côte Vermeille	Mont Caume
Coteaux d'Enserune	Pays d'Hérault
Coteaux de Coiffy	Pays d'Oc
Coteaux de Glanes	Périgord
Coteaux de l'Ain	Puy-de-Dôme
Coteaux de l'Auxois	Pyrénées-Orientales
Coteaux de Narbonne	Sable de Camargue
Coteaux de Peyriac	Saint-Guilhem-
Coteaux de Tannay	le-Désert
Coteaux des Baronnies	Sainte-Marie-
Coteaux du Cher et de	la-Blanche
l'Arnon	Saône-et-Loire
Coteaux du Libron	Saône-et-Loire
Coteaux du Pont du Gard	Thézac-Perricard
Côtes Catalanes	Urfé
Côtes de Gascogne	Val de Loire
Côtes de la Charité	Vallée du Paradis
Côtes de Meuse	Vallée du Torgan
Côtes de Thau	Var
Côtes de Thongue	Vaucluse
Côtes du Brian	Vicomté d'Aumelas
Côtes du Lot	Vin des Allobroges
Côtes du Tarn	Vins de la Corrèze
Drôme	Yonne
Duché d'Uzès	

IGT stands for **Indicazione Geografica Tipica**, corresponding to the EU denomination PGI. Either IGT or IGP (the Italian version of PGI) may appear on labels. This category of wines was created in ITALY by law 164 in 1992 as an approximate equivalent of the French VIN DE PAYS. It officially enabled producers to give more information on the labels of their myriad esteemed, and often extremely expensive, wines then selling as a VINO DA TAVOLA. IGT was created as the basis of a quality pyramid with DOC in the middle and DOCG at the top. Many producers are unable or unwilling to opt for any denomination higher than IGT, either because they produce wines from vine varieties and/or use winemaking techniques not permitted by the local DOC regulations, or because the quality control system, which must establish a wine's TYPICAL-ITY, is unable or unwilling to adapt to changes in viticulture and winemaking. Wines produced and bottled without SULFUR DIOXIDE, unfiltered wines, and SKIN-FERMENTED white

wines fall victim to this. Particularly popular IGTs include delle Venezie, Puglia, Terre Siciliane, Toscana, and Veneto.   W.S.

Île de Beauté is IGP language for CORSICA and, along with the Loire's similar denomination as 'Jardin de la France', one of the most alluring French names in the category.

imbottigliato is Italian for bottled.

impériale. See BOTTLE SIZES.

Imperial Tokay, historical name used for wine produced on the vineyard properties of the Austrian Habsburg emperors in the TOKAJ-Hegyalja region of Hungary, especially during the 19th century. The Habsburg holdings were concentrated in the village of Tarcal, particularly the highly respected Szarvas vineyard that had been confiscated from the rebellious Prince Ferenc Rákóczi II in 1711. The term became widely known in western Europe following the creation of the Austro-Hungarian Monarchy in 1867. However, Imperial Tokay was usually misunderstood either as being necessarily far superior to all other Tokaji wines, or as being an alternative term for Eszencia.   M.L.-G.

INAO, the **Institut National de l'Origine et de la Qualité** (formerly the Institut National des Appellations d'Origine), is the organization in charge of recognizing, granting, administering, regulating, and protecting the French APPELLATIONS CONTRÔLÉES, or AOC, now known as *appellation d'origine protégée* or AOP (see PDO) and the other official *signes* (signs) such as IGP that identify quality and origin for agricultural products, including not just wines and spirits but also other alcoholic drinks, dairy products, olive oil, meat, honey, fruit and vegetables, etc. In 2014 there were more than 300 AOC/AOPs for wine (more than 350 if you count every ALSACE grand cru separately), 75 IGPs/VINS DE PAYS, as well as 50 AOPs for dairy products, and 45 for meat, poultry, olive oil, etc.

Since IGP wines came under the INAO umbrella in 2009, it has controlled a massive proportion of all French wine, more than 90% of volume in 2012. Nearly 75,000 vine-growers therefore depend on its rules, its undoubted restrictions, its protection, and its efforts to continue France's reliance on geographically based wine names. The organization is based in Paris but run by regional committees and administrative offices.

INAO was founded in 1935 and, since for much of the 20th century France's leading role in the world of wine was undisputed, it provided a role model for the administration of more embryonic GEOGRAPHICAL

INDICATION schemes in other countries. During the 1980s, however, commercial competition from non-French wines, and even from some French vin de pays on export markets, encouraged a re-examination of the role of INAO. The result was an even stronger INAO, given additional powers in 1990, fiercely dedicated to the notion of controlled, geographically determined appellations for products that owe their characteristics to their region of origin and a prescribed mode of production, empowered to protect them against imitation both in France and abroad, and determined that France's viticultural future in particular depended on her ability to trade on her uniquely well-established wine names.

Falling sales called into question INAO's policy of prohibiting all VINE VARIETY names on wine labels, on the premise that French wines express TERROIR rather than mere fruit flavour. Certain producers positively relish their freedom to sell VARIETAL wines, or vins de cépages as they are known, and often despised, within France. Thanks to changes in EU rules, WINES WITHOUT GEOGRAPHICAL INDICATION may now also state the variety and vintage on the label.

Any group of wine producers can apply to INAO to establish an AOP or an IGP. They have to prepare a dossier by giving reasons for the request, proof of the traditional use of the name of the proposed appellation, full details of the terroir and how it affects production, and economic details concerning markets, sales, prices, and comparative prices of similar products. Once it has been agreed by INAO, it has to be approved by the EU and published in the *Journal Officiel de l'Union Européenne*.

incrocio, Italian for vine CROSS. A wine made from **Incrocio Manzoni** grapes, for example, is made from one of Signor Manzoni's many crosses of one VINIFERA variety with another. His Incrocio Manzoni 6.0.13, Riesling × Pinot Blanc, often known simply as Manzoni Bianco, is the most widely planted with 382 ha/943 acres in 2010, throughout Italy but especially in the south. Incrocio Manzoni 2.15 is Prosecco × Cabernet Sauvignon. Incrocio Terzi No 1 is a Barbera × Cabernet Franc cross grown in Lombardy.

indexing, method of testing vines for VIRUS DISEASES and PHYTOPLASMA diseases and their like. Sap from the plant to be tested is exposed to so-called indicator plants which show typical symptoms if the disease is present. Sap from the two plants can be mixed by abrading leaves or by grafting. Cabernet Franc, for example, is used as an indicator vine variety to test for LEAFROLL VIRUS. Indexing tests

are now being replaced by serological methods; see ELISA. R.E.S.

Weber, E., Golino, D., and Rowhani, A., 'Laboratory testing for grapevine diseases', *Practical Winery & Vineyard* (Jan/Feb 2002), 13–27.

India, large Asian country where wine consumption, production, and quality are increasing steadily. A growing middle class (likely to number 250 million by 2015) should maintain this trend, despite high taxes, licensing fees, discriminatory inter-state policies, and a number of dry states.

History

The vine was probably introduced into northwest India from Persia during the Indus civilization in the 4th millennium BC, but wine may not have been made from its fruit for many centuries. The gradual invasion of Aryan tribes from central Asia during the 2nd millennium BC produced the Vedic period (c.2000–800 BC), a blossoming of culture in north west India. The Aryans enjoyed gambling, music, and intoxicating drink, and in the four Vedas, the world's oldest religious texts, two drinks are mentioned: *soma*, a milky drink ceremoniously prepared immediately before a sacrifice and probably containing hallucinatory hemp; and *sura*, a potent secular drink made from either barley or paddy (rice) fermented with honey.

While praising the rowdy and hard-drinking Aryan warrior god Indra, the Vedas clearly condemn the effects of drinking. Later, Hindu, Buddhist, and Jain texts reveal similar dichotomies. Kautilya, chief minister under the Mauryan King Chandragupta (ruled c.324–300 BC), was the author of the Arthasastra, a remarkable text on statecraft in which he condemns alcohol and yet chronicles the king's drinking bouts and mentions *madhu* (wine) of various varieties and qualities. This is the first documentation of wine made from grapes in India.

Down the centuries, wine has maintained its status in India as a drink of the Kshatriya caste of aristocrats and warriors rather than of the masses, who have preferred more potent alcohol prepared from the staple local agricultural cereal crops.

The contradictory attitudes towards intoxicating drinks continue into modern times. The Muslim (see ISLAM) Mughal emperors' royal vineyards were in the Deccan; the alcoholic emperor Jehangir (who ruled 1605–27) would drink himself insensible on double- and triple-distilled wine (brandy), violating the Qurʾān's command not to lose one's sensibilities through intoxication.

Secular independent India's Constitution, adopted on 26 January 1950, states total

PROHIBITION of alcohol among its aims (in deference to Mahatma Gandhi, the father of the nation). However, only a few states such as Gujarat, Tamil Nadu, Andhra Pradesh, and Haryana ever enforced, variously, limited or total prohibition. Today Gujarat (Mahatma Gandhi's home state) is the only major state that still has prohibition.

Although the orthodox of all faiths may abstain, Indians everywhere (except Gujarat) are free to consume wine and other alcohol if they choose.

Indian viticulture was encouraged in the 19th century as the Victorian British upper classes enjoyed drinking wine. Vineyards were established in Kashmīr, Bārāmati, Surat, and Goalkonda. A number of Indian wines were exhibited at the Great Calcutta Exhibition of 1884 and elicited favourable comment. But in the 1890s, Indian vineyards, like their European counterparts, succumbed to PHYLLOXERA.

Since Independence in 1947, wine production has increased very slowly as it requires long-term investment and, ideally, a strong local market. Goa continued to produce low-quality fortified wines made in the image of port, an industry initiated by Portuguese colonists in the 16th century.

Until the 1990s, the small Indian wine industry went virtually unnoticed outside the country, partly because of the quality of the wine, made by rudimentary village operations, with the exception of a large winery and distillery established in Hyderābād and Bangalore in 1966 by the Shaw Wallace group, producing Golconda and Bosca wines.

Viticulture

India's 111,000 ha/274,287 acres of vineyards produce more than 1.2 million tons of grapes a year, of which less than 10% are used for wine while the bulk is used as TABLE GRAPES and RAISINS. Established vineyards of mainly table grapes are found in the temperate north west of the country and as far south as the state of Tamil Nadu. Two-thirds of the country's area under vine, however, is in the south-central states of Mahārāshtra (86,000 ha/212,510 acres), Karnataka (18,100 ha/44,726 acres), and Tamil Nadu (2,700 ha/6,672 acres). In Mahārāshtra, cultivation is concentrated around Pune, Nāsik, Baramati, Sangali, and Sholhāpur on the west of the Deccan Plateau, about 300 km/180 miles in length and 60 km in width, 135 km inland from Mumbai. The remainder of southern India's plantings are near Bangalore and around Hyderābād.

Plantings range from elevations of 300 m/984 ft on the Deccan in Mahārāshtra and 200 m/660 ft in Karnataka and a few at

800 m/2,600 ft on the slopes of Sahyadri. With India's hot summer and heavy monsoon, temperatures in growing areas range from 8 °C/46 °F in winter to 45 °C in summer, 625–1,500 mm (25–60 in) of rain falling between June and August depending on the region. There is little unseasonal rain. Humidity levels are high particularly during the monsoon, moderated only by afternoon winds. Eastern regions suffer most from humidity and extreme heat.

THOMPSON SEEDLESS (Sultana) is by far the most widely planted variety, accounting for over half the total vineyard area, although INTERNATIONAL VARIETIES are increasingly planted by the leading wine companies. Indigenous TABLE GRAPES such as Anab-e-shahi are grown along with Bangalore Blue (ISABELLA) and Bangalore Purple, which are the major varieties in Tamil Nadu, Andhra Pradesh, and Karnataka along with some Gulabi (MUSCAT OF HAMBURG), and small amounts of Perlette. These varieties account for less than 10% of Indian grapes, however, with a small proportion used for low-quality sweet wines in Goa and south India..

Vines are trained high on wire and bamboo with wide ROW SPACING to retain SOIL WATER, prevent SUNBURN, and maximize aeration of the vines, minimizing the risk of FUNGAL DISEASES. Since the early 1980s, DRIP IRRIGATION has been used throughout the growing season and YIELDS are high, up to 700 or 900 hl/ha (40 or 50 tons/ha). Pruning takes place in April and September with harvest (always manual in India) in February and March. In warmer regions, particularly Andhra, Karnataka, and Tamil Nadu two harvests a year are possible. See TROPICAL VITICULTURE.

The contemporary wine industry

The current renaissance of Indian viticulture began with pioneers Chateau Indage (known later as Indage Vintners) in 1984 near Pune in Mahārāshtra and Grover Vineyards in 1988 north of Bangalore in Karnataka, both of which set themselves the goal of exporting. Indage produced a surprisingly elegant sparkling wine for the international market. A short-sighted and aggressive overseas expansion programme and diversification in 2007/08 resulted in its collapse soon afterwards. Grover Vineyards trialled 33 vine varieties initially and settled principally on Cabernet Sauvignon and Clairette, which grow on PERGOLAS. Its first wine was released in 1992. With French oenologist Michel ROLLAND as its wine CONSULTANT, Grover's quality and reputation grew steadily, especially for its flagship La Reserve, a Cabernet-Shiraz blend. In 2012 Grover Vineyards merged with Nashik-based Vallée de Vin (whose main brand is Zampa) to form Grover

Zampa Vineyards with the aim of growing considerably.

Sula Vineyards, founded by former Silicon Valley engineer Ranjeev Samant, set up its winery in Nashik in Mahārāshtra in 1999 with the help of Californian Kerry Damskey. Sula produced India's first varietal Chenin Blanc, Sauvignon Blanc, Riesling, and Zinfandel. In 2005 Sula overtook Grover to become India's largest wine producer following the demise of Indage Vintners. Today Sula's market share is around 70%, with sales of over seven million bottles in 2013. Sula wines are exported to 20 countries around the world. Under Sula Selections, the company also imports and distributes wine and has spearheaded wine TOURISM in India.

Other prominent wineries with national distribution are Four Seasons owned by United Spirits (with Diageo as a major shareholder), Nine Hills of Pernod Ricard India, and Fratelli Wines, India's first Indo-Italian collaboration based in Akluj, near Pune. Superior Nashik-based wineries with national distribution include Vintage Wines, whose Reveilo brand specialises in the Italian varieties Sangiovese, Nero d'Avola, and Grillo, and Vallonnée, a small producer of French-inspired wines.

Promising wine producers include York Winery near Sula Vineyards, where Moët & Chandon produced their first vintage of Chandon sparkling wine in October 2013; Charosa Wineries set up in 2008 by industrialist Ajit Gulabchand in Nashik; KRSMA Estates, a boutique winery near the UNESCO heritage site of Hampi in Karnataka; and Alpine Wineries near Mysore (also in Karnataka) which has 240 ha/1,200 acres planted with Stéphane DERENONCOURT as consultant. Smaller producers such as Big Banyan (John Distilleries), Kinvah (Nandi Hills Winery), and Luca (Nirvana Biosys in Haryana) sell their wines only in a few states.　　　　　　　　　　　　R.K.S.

Chandra, A., 'Indian wine journey 2012–2013', *Sommelier India Wine Magazine* (April–May 2013), 22–3.

Gill, B., 'The trials and travails of the Indian wine industry', *Sommelier India Wine Magazine* (Aug–Sept 2013), 20–25.

Gill, B., 'The Nandi Hills meets Nashik', *Sommelier India Wine Magazine* (April–May 2013), 16–22.

Singh, R., 'A vinous getaway', *Sommelier India Wine Magazine* (June-July 2013), 30–2.

www.igpb.in

www.karnatakawineboard.com

indicator. See INDEXING.

indigenous varieties, VINE VARIETIES that are intensely local to a particular area and have a relatively long tradition of being grown there.

Researchers in SWITZERLAND and GASCONY were some of the first to rescue near-extinct local varieties in the 1980s but they have been followed by a host of others in the early 21st century, particularly but not exclusively in Italy. A discernible FASHION for indigenous varieties emerged as a reaction to an earlier one for INTERNATIONAL VARIETIES.

Indonesia had six wineries by 2014, all on the resort island of Bali. The industry pioneer, Hatten Wines, is still by far the largest winemaking enterprise, now turning out 1 million bottles a year. It began making wines from locally grown grapes in 1994, operating from an old rice wine factory at Sanur Beach in the south east of the island, but most of its grapes are grown near the city of Singaraja at the northern extreme of the island (8 °latitude). Here, the ELEVATION provides some modest respite from the relentless TROPICAL heat and humidity but climatic conditions are such that the vines crop almost continuously. These vineyards were planted originally for TABLE GRAPES with the French VINIFERA table grape Alphonse Lavallée (Ribier) growing on overhead PERGOLAS. MUSCAT varieties were planted more recently and Shiraz and CHAMBOURCIN have been trialled for more robust reds. Indico Wines, now called Singaraja Hills, was the second winery on Bali, established in 1998. Sababay Wines is the third winery working principally with domestically grown grapes. The others produce wine from imported grapes or MUST, to avoid the onerous taxes on imported alcohol. Hatten's range of wines made from Australian must is sold under the Two Islands label.　　　D.G.

inert gas, a gas used to protect wine from OXIDATION by the air, such as NITROGEN, CARBON DIOXIDE, or argon.

inert gas mixture, mixture of gases that does not include OXYGEN. Traditionally, such mixtures have been composed of NITROGEN and CARBON DIOXIDE but more recently argon is being included in these mixes, either in place of, or along with, nitrogen. Such mixtures are used in wine storage processes in lieu of nitrogen because the greater density of carbon dioxide and argon causes them to layer and so more efficiently exclude oxygen. Inert gas mixtures may not have been used in winemaking as often as nitrogen because the carbon dioxide fraction dissolves in wine, possibly leaving a higher-than-desirable residual concentration of this gas. Argon, like nitrogen, has a very low solubility in wine and inert gas mixtures of either or both of these two with carbon dioxide can, with modern metering equipment, be selected to leave a residual level of dissolved carbon dioxide that is optimal for the style of wine under storage. Inert gases are also used to flush the oxygen from hoses and pumps, and during BOTTLING. A.D.W. & P.J.W.

Inferno, subzone of VALTELLINA in the far north of Italy.

inflorescence, the structure that bears the flowers (see BUNCH for more details). At FLOWERING, the grape flower becomes a BERRY and the inflorescence a bunch.

information technology (IT) has revolutionized the world of wine as much as any other. Computers are now used throughout the production process. In the vineyard they can schedule and control IRRIGATION, for example, or measure weather and predict and even control SPRAYING regimes. They can assist VINEYARD SITE SELECTION by analysing and mapping data on CLIMATE, SOIL, VIGOUR, and TOPOGRAPHY. By monitoring, for example, WATER STRESS or FERTILIZATION needs in different parts of a vineyard, IT can help control WINE QUALITY and BERRY SIZE, and in the long term can contribute towards SUSTAINABILITY. In the winery, IT can weigh and sample GRAPES, SORT them, control CRUSHING and PRESSING operations, ensure the most vigilant TEMPERATURE CONTROL, and eventually oversee BOTTLING.

Thanks to information technology, wine ANALYSIS is today much more sophisticated than could have been imagined even a decade ago, and there have even been attempts to mechanize the process of TASTING. During fermentation, IT-integrated tanks provide temperature and wine composition data for each tank, not just in the winery but for a CONSULTANT who may be thousands of miles away. During ELEVAGE, the content and history of individual tanks, barrels, and pallets, can also be tracked.

Information technology has greatly assisted such techniques as DNA PROFILING in vine variety identification, and the possible new technique of 'fingerprinting' a vineyard by analysis of its MINERALS.

Those who sell wine, whether to consumers or in BULK to the trade, can use information technology to administer all aspects of TRANSPORT, STORAGE, stock control, and retailing, as well as being able to present their wares directly to potential customers via the Internet—which can be an advantage when selling a commodity as tightly regulated, heavy, and fragile as bottles of wine. The Internet has spawned a new generation of independent, often very small, online wine merchants, and has greatly widened the appeal of wine AUCTIONS.

As well as offering wine consumers a new market place, for both buying and selling, and a new medium for wine information, opinion, and EDUCATION via myriad websites and blogs, the Internet has provided them with an unprecedented forum for discussion, not just about the wines themselves but also about WINE WRITERS, a

new sort of consumer power, even if one that tends to attract wine BORES. See SOCIAL MEDIA. Websites such as Twitter, Facebook, and Instagram are spreading the diversity of wine to a much less specialized, more democratic readership, encouraging the discovery of wines from a broader range of countries and sources. These tools have helped wine producers, retailers, and regions to find new routes to the consumer.

Those who keep and wish to share detailed cellar records and TASTING NOTES have reason to be grateful for the flexibility and sorting ability of IT (see CELLARTRACKER). And price comparison websites such as wine-searcher.com have revolutionized wine retailing and encouraged fair PRICING on a global scale.

As Internet technologies develop, the international wine market is being revolutionized. For example, our mobile phones can now provide us with more information than we could have dreamt of simply by being pointed at a wine label or QR code. Microchips inserted in cases of wine have already provided fine-wine lovers with myriad data on shipping TEMPERATURES. They are expected to play an increasing part in fighting COUNTERFEIT WINE and much else besides.

infrared spectroscopy is fast becoming a routine ANALYSIS method in wine laboratories. This ground-breaking technique relies on the fact that all organic compounds have a unique spectral fingerprint in the Near Infrared (NIR) and Mid Infrared (MIR) regions of the electromagnetic spectrum. In the past it has been difficult to interpret these fingerprints on grape or wine samples but by the 2010s, the availability of cheap instrumentation, computing power, and software development meant that it had become a standard method of analysis in food and agriculture, including the wine industry.

The critical advantages of IR spectroscopy are that very little sample preparation is required, no dangerous laboratory chemicals are needed, multiple analyses can be tested simultaneously, and, once the methods have been developed and programmed into the instrument, very little user training is required. NIR is less sensitive than MIR but the lower absorbance makes it more penetrating, capable of analysis of grape must, whole grapes, grapevine tissue, and soil. The penetrating power of NIR can also be utilized to analyse packaged wine non-destructively, by scanning through the bottle. MIR is more sensitive and is better suited to the analysis of clarified grape juice and wine.

IR spectroscopy may be used to analyse, for example, SUGAR, PH, ACIDITY, moisture content, TANNIN, ANTHOCYANINS, and GLYCOSYL-GLUCOSE. Grapes can also be analysed for negative quality indicators, such as fungal spoilage by BOTRYTIS and POWDERY MILDEW. Water potential of

grapevine leaves is used as an indicator of WATER STRESS, and can be analysed non-destructively by IR spectroscopy to aid IRRIGATION scheduling. Grapevine wood (see CANE and TRUNK) can be analysed for starch and sugar, to determine over-wintering vine storage reserves. Wines can be analysed for most routine measures such as DENSITY, ALCOHOL, pH, total acidity, sugar, VOLATILE ACIDITY, anthocyanins, tannin, and organic ACIDS. In addition to quantitative methods, with appropriate software, qualitative methods such as classification of growing region and grape variety can be performed with the IR fingerprint, allowing the possibility of rapid wine AUTHENTICATION. R.D.

Gishen, M., Cozzolino, D., and Dambergs, R. G., 'The analysis of grapes, wine, and other alcoholic beverages by infrared spectroscopy', in E. C. Y. Li-Chan, P. R. Griffiths, and J. M. Chalmers (eds.), *Applications of Vibrational Spectroscopy in Food Science* (New York, 2010), 539–56.

ingredient labelling. Since detailed specification on labels of ingredients in foodstuffs is mandatory in most major markets, it has been proposed that wine should also be subject to this requirement. Few wine producers are in favour since it would be complicated and could well dispel what is seen as the simple romance of wine—although presumably producers of NATURAL WINE may welcome any public airing of the wide array of ADDITIVES and PROCESSING AIDS used by their more industrial rivals. Even some of the most lauded wines in the world may have to cite YEAST (unless AMBIENT), sugar (if CHAPTALIZED), TARTARIC ACID (if acidified), together with BACTERIA, NUTRIENTS, and VITAMINS, and all producers are already obliged to mention SULFITES. One large UK retailer, the Co-op, has provided ingredient labelling on its wines since 1999. See also LABELLING INFORMATION.

initiation, botanical term for the start of the vine's fruiting when the first signs of bunches are evident as small pieces of tissue in the developing bud. These buds are themselves developing beside the leaf stalk on the shoots as they grow in spring. Initiation starts simultaneously with the FLOWERING stage of the growing season. Warm, sunny weather conditions at this time favour initiation, with one, two, occasionally three, or very rarely four bunches per shoot initiated. When this shoot bursts the following year, it will be termed FRUITFUL. Cold, cloudy weather depresses fruit bud initiation.

Part of the annual variation in vineyard YIELD is thus due to weather conditions affecting initiation during the year previous to the crop being harvested. The time when the vines are flowering is the most critical period for bunch initiation. To most vine-growers, a 'light crop year' often refers in an oblique way to weather conditions which affected initiation a little over 12 months previously, although other factors such as FRUIT SET can also affect yield.   R.E.S.

Huglin, P., *Biologie et écologie de la vigne* (Paris, 1986).

injection, alternative name for CARBONATION, the cheapest and least effective method of SPARKLING WINEMAKING involving the simple pumping of CARBON DIOXIDE into a tank of wine.

inner staves, or **inserts**, planks of wood, usually oak, placed in a stainless steel tank and held in position by a metal framework, are a way of imparting oak flavour to wine more cheaply than by fermenting or ageing in BARRELS since the staves are easily replaced. Inner staves are sometimes used in conjunction with MICRO-OXYGENATION to mimic the use of barrels for fermentation or maturation without the cost of barrels, a barrel cellar, and barrel cellar workers. A more recent development is the use of oak staves in oxygen-permeable tanks made of food-grade polyethylene. See also BARREL INSERTS.

INRA (**l'Institut National de la Recherche Agronomique**). Founded just after the Second World War in 1946, the French specialist organization for agronomic research is under the control of both the Ministry for Scientific Research as well as the Ministry of Agriculture.

There are 18 separate research centres in France; the one in Montpellier has specialist units in OENOLOGY and VITICULTURE which actively cooperate with Montpellier SupAgro, with which it shares a campus. INRA Bordeaux specializes in viticulture.

Advances in viticulture since INRA's creation have been enormous. The Institute's most significant contribution has been the introduction of CLONAL SELECTION in France to help combat VIRUS DISEASES and thus improve quality and YIELDS. INRA's current viticultural and oenological research priorities focus on vine–environment interaction, vine resources (at the Domaine de Vassal, see below), quality control, and technological innovation.

INRA's work helped establish the best use of FERTILILZERS on high-quality vineyards, and current research aims to reduce the use of FUNGICIDES, whose extravagant use in the 1970s and 1980s led to an urgent need for more sophisticated control regimes. This development, known as *la lutte raisonnée* ('the rational struggle') in France, aims to use these products minimally and only when necessary rather than according to a predetermined programme of regular applications. As the ill effects of the last generation of AGROCHEMICALS become clearer, particularly in respect of COPPER toxicity, this is expected to become the area of greatest viticultural change.

The importance for eventual wine quality of the grapes' condition at HARVEST has long been recognized by both viticulturists and oenologists, and INRA is also studying the effects on wine quality of various vine-TRAINING SYSTEMS. More basic research is concentrated on the exact nature of grape RIPENING, which is still not fully understood. Research priorities include: organoleptic properties of PHENOLIC compounds, wine STABILITY, biology of wine YEASTS, and control of FERMENTATIONS.

INRA's collection of 7,000 VINIFERA varieties and HYBRIDS, held at the Domaine de Vassal on the Mediterranean coast, has been a centre for the analysis, preservation, and management of biodiversity, especially with regard to pest and disease resistance and wine quality. The sandy soils are free of both PHYLLOXERA and the nematode *Xiphinema index*. Some NEW VARIETIES, CHASAN, for example, have also been developed here and, thanks to the work of AMPELOGRAPHERS such as Paul Truel, Domaine de Vassal became a worldwide focus for vine identification. But in 2014, as the vineyard lease was about to expire and there were concerns about SALINITY and the health of the vines there, plans were formed to move the collection to INRA's experimental unit Pech Rouge on La Clape near Narbonne. Pech Rouge is largely dedicated to the development of experimental ideas and the transfer of technology in partnership with the Institut Français de la Vigne et du Vin (IFVV) and other professional bodies.

The Montpellier Pôle Vigne-Vin brings together the various research and technology departments involved in the vine and wine industry in Montpellier and the Institut des Hautes Études de la Vigne et du Vin at Montpellier SupAgro to help them disseminate technological innovation, and to deliver high-level training programmes for agronomists and oenologists.

In 1991, the Institut d'Oenologie de Bordeaux (see University of BORDEAUX) and INRA Bordeaux formed a Pôle de Recherche Scientifique sur la Vigne et le Vin with a view to working more closely together in the two areas in which scientific research can improve the quality of wine.   W.B. & J.E.H.

insecticides. See PESTICIDES.

insect pests. A wide variety of insects attack grapevines. Injury may occur as a result of direct feeding action, where reductions in leaf amount or leaf health can delay RIPENING with serious implications for wine quality, or by carrying (vectoring) a particular VIRUS DISEASE or PHYTOPLASMA disease.

Alternatively the vine root system can be attacked, which leads to development of WATER STRESS and restricted VINE NUTRITION. While minor stress may enhance wine quality (see VINE PHYSIOLOGY), the more likely outcome of root damage by insects such as PHYLLOXERA (the most destructive of all insect pests) is severe stress or vine death. Some insect pests, such as phylloxera, attack only grapevines, while many attack a range of different plants.

Different insect pests attack grapes and vines in different parts of the world, and in different districts, and what may be an important pest in one area may be unimportant or non-existent in another. The most important insect pests in European vineyards are the BEETLES *écrivain* and *cigarier* and the MOTHS cochylis, eudemis, and eulia, and MITES. MEDITERRANEAN FRUIT FLY can be a pest in some areas of Australia, but is not present in the United States, while LEAFHOPPERS are serious pests in California but not Australia. Other insects, such as CUTWORM and GRASSHOPPERS, are general agricultural pests worldwide.

Insect pests which affect only the appearance of grapes concern growers of TABLE GRAPES but not growers of wine grapes, who are more likely to be concerned with effects on YIELD or wine quality. Grape RIPENING can be seriously delayed, for example, when the WESTERN GRAPELEAF SKELETONIZER reduces leaf area and thus reduces PHOTOSYNTHESIS; vineyards can be destroyed as young plantings by cutworms, or when mature by MARGARODES and phylloxera. Perhaps more insidiously, insects such as fruit fly (see DROSOPHILA) can carry spores associated with BUNCH ROTS, and MEALY BUG can transmit LEAFROLL virus. LADYBIRDS are also thought to cause wine taint if harvested with the fruit. Leafhoppers spread the serious GRAPEVINE YELLOWS and PIERCE'S DISEASE and make such disease notoriously difficult to control. The larvae of some insect BORERS, such as the fig longicorn borer (*Acalolepta vastator*) in the Hunter Valley, can live inside grapevines and cause damage to the trunk.

In general, insect pests are relatively easy to control in vineyards, although insecticides (see PESTICIDES) are among the more dangerous AGROCHEMICALS for operators to apply. Modern approaches to viticulture are more environmentally aware than previously, and so persistent chemicals such as DDT are no longer used and INTEGRATED PEST MANAGEMENT, designed to reduce insecticide use, is becoming increasingly common (see also ORGANIC and BIODYNAMIC VITICULTURE). For example, predatory mites are encouraged, to control levels of damaging mites.

See also entries for the specific pests APHIDS, BEETLES, BORERS, CUTWORMS, DROSOPHILA, ERINOSE MITE, GRASSHOPPERS, LEAFHOPPERS, LEAF ROLLERS, LOCUSTS, MARGARODES, MEALY BUGS, MITES, MOTHS, PHYLLOXERA, SCALE, THRIPS, WESTERN GRAPELEAF SKELETONIZER.   M.J.E. & R.E.S.

Bettiga, L. J., (ed.), *Grape Pest Management* (3rd edn, Oakland, Calif., 2013).

Buchanan, G. A., and Amos, T. G., 'Grape pests', in B. G. Coombe and P. R. Dry (eds.), *Viticulture*, ii: *Practices* (Adelaide, 1992).

Institut des Sciences de la Vigne et du Vin de Bordeaux (ISVV) brings together under one roof in Villenave d'Ornon, a southern suburb of Bordeaux, the grape and wine research teams and students of several different academic institutions, including BORDEAUX University's faculty of oenology, Bordeaux Sciences Agro, and INRA Bordeaux. The current director general is Denis DUBOURDIEU.

integrated pest management, or IPM, a term which dates back to the mid 1970s in Europe. Initially developed for insect pests, IPM now encompasses the control of diseases, weeds, and physiological vine disorders and has the potential to increase economic returns for the grower and improve environmental and human safety by reducing, limiting or even eliminating the use of AGROCHEMICALS.

IPM is considered by conventional growers as a form of SUSTAINABLE VITICULTURE but most IPM management systems differ from ORGANIC VITICULTURE because they tolerate the use of industrially synthesized products such as HERBICIDES, PESTICIDES, and FERTILIZERS. However, IPM aims to stop the regular, calendar-based spraying of chemicals in a potentially wasteful manner and instead to apply such treatments in a more accurately timed way and targeted to specific threats. IPM is often seen as a first step towards organic or even BIODYNAMIC VITICULTURE.

Thus IPM takes account of the environment, particularly weather phenomena, the occurrence and life cycles of pests, and the incidence of natural enemies and alternative host plants. It requires a knowledge of the biology of the pest, monitoring the occurrences of the pest and any natural predators, recording environmental conditions, and then integrating all this information into a decision-making process.

A number of VINE PESTS and diseases have been studied under the aegis of IPM philosophy. For example, the European grapevine MOTHS *Lobesia botrana* and *Eupoecilia ambiguella* can cause extensive damage, and studies have shown that their population levels can be limited naturally by VIRUS DISEASES and protozoan diseases. Similarly, MITES which damage vines can be controlled by other species of predatory mites, but sometimes the latter's beneficial effect can actually be limited by the application of pesticides, in particular some FUNGICIDES. Indeed, the increased use of some agrochemicals has altered the balance of predator to pest mites.   R.E.S. & M.W.

Cavalloro, R., *Integrated Pest Control in Viticulture* (Rotterdam, 1987).

integrated production, or IP, European system of viticulture aimed at reducing environmental degradation in vineyards while at the same time maintaining economic viability of viticulture. It is similar in philosophy to SUSTAINABLE VITICULTURE. As the name suggests, it has its roots in INTEGRATED PEST MANAGEMENT, or IPM.

IP was developed as a concept in 1974, and major development has come from France, Germany, and, especially, Switzerland. Integrated production emphasizes a holistic approach to viticulture, by considering the vineyard as an 'agro-ecosystem'. The reduction of chemical inputs, especially nitrogen FERTILIZER and broad spectrum INSECTICIDES, is a first step. Where rainfall is sufficient, COVER CROPS are established, ideally to include legumes. CANOPY MANAGEMENT is also important to reduce SPRAYING against BOTRYTIS and POWDERY MILDEW. Some spraying is permitted, with restrictions more on frequency than on type of spray material.

South Africa's INTEGRATED PRODUCTION OF WINE (IPW) is a voluntary scheme established in 1998 and emphasizes the importance of balancing the needs of the natural habitat with those of wine-growers. See also ORGANIC and BIODYNAMIC VITICULTURE.   R.E.S. & M.W.

Malavolta, C., and Boller, E. F., 'Guidelines for integrated production of grapes', IOBC Technical Guidelines (3rd edn, 2007), www.iobc-wprs.org/ip_ipm/IOBC_Guideline_Grapes_2007_ENGLISH.pdf.

Integrated Production of Wine (IPW) in SOUTH AFRICA is a voluntary environmental SUSTAINABILITY scheme established in 1998. The scheme's criteria are based on international standards and were drafted taking account of International Federation of Wines and Spirits (FIVS) and the OIV's guidelines for sustainable viti-viniculture. For grape production these include SOIL PREPARATION, VINE NUTRITION, IRRIGATION, CANOPY MANAGEMENT, GROWTH REGULATORS, INTEGRATED PEST MANAGEMENT, and handling of AGROCHEMICALS. Only grapes that qualify for IPW may be used for IPW wines. The cellar and wine-production guidelines cover issues such as SULFUR DIOXIDE levels as well as WINERY WASTE management. The production practices of members and aspirant members of the scheme are evaluated and audited by the Wine and Spirit Board. Wines which are not required to have passed through the WINE OF ORIGIN certification and which have achieved an appropriate level of IPW compliance are marketed with an IPW certification seal. The World Wildlife Fund (WWF) Biodiversity & Wine Initiative operates with the IPW certification scheme and aims to minimize the loss of natural habitat by working with producers who commit to set aside protected areas for long-term conservation.   M.F.

International Grape Genome Program (IGGP), a framework for multinational collaborative grapevine research, with an emphasis on grapevine genomics. This project fosters efforts to characterize grape genes responsible for resistance to pests and diseases, vine growth, and fruit quality. These efforts result in the identification of genetic markers capable of expediting and optimizing classical VINE BREEDING. They also lead to the identification of grape genes that could be used to genetically modify and improve grapevines while having limited impact on variety integrity, a process known as cisgenics. See GENETIC MODIFICATION and PIERCE'S DISEASE.

www.vitaceae.org.

international varieties, loose term for those VINE VARIETIES with an international reputation for their VARIETAL wines. They are planted in almost every major wine region in which they stand a chance of ripening. Foremost among them are the red wine variety CABERNET SAUVIGNON and the white wine variety CHARDONNAY (which many consumers take to be either a place or, more usually, a BRAND). Other strong candidates as international varieties are MERLOT, PINOT NOIR, and, especially, SYRAH/SHIRAZ among reds and SAUVIGNON BLANC, RIESLING, MUSCAT, GEWÜRZTRAMINER, VIOGNIER, PINOT BLANC, and PINOT GRIS among whites. As winemakers and wine consumers constantly search for new excitement, the list of possibilities grows longer. MOURVÈDRE, TEMPRANILLO, SANGIOVESE, and NEBBIOLO could already be said to have joined this elite with all manner of others in the wings. But the second decade of this century, as part of a backlash against GLOBALIZATION, saw a certain backlash against international varieties in favour of INDIGENOUS VARIETIES and ALTERNATIVE VARIETIES.

International Wine & Food Society (IWFS), the oldest and most cosmopolitan of the gastronomic societies for consumers rather than professionals. Initially simply the Wine & Food Society, it was founded in London in 1933 by André SIMON and like-minded friends. Its aim, other than providing a readership for a journal *Wine and Food* which Simon planned to edit, was to promote the highest quality of raw materials and an appreciation of how they could best be served and consumed. An early motto was 'Not much, but the best'. Launched in full economic depression (partly as a reaction to the culinary decline which resulted from it), the society attracted its fair share of criticism initially, and might well have withered had not the Repeal of PROHIBITION opened up North America to the proselytizing of M. Simon. Soon there were branches all over the United States where it is most important today, although the IWFS remains based in London.

Total numbers have declined but in 2013 there were still 6,000 members in 130 branches in 30 countries. The Society, now much imitated, is a non-profit-making concern and has always taken a particular interest in wine. André Simon and his early colleague A. J. A. Symons launched the first pocket VINTAGE CHART in 1935 and it is annually revised by a special committee of the IWFS to this day, providing useful income through sales to publishers of diaries and the like. The journal was published regularly between 1934 and 2000 and was at one stage edited by Hugh JOHNSON.

Internet. See INFORMATION TECHNOLOGY.

internode, the part of the stem between NODES. The internode length varies between different VINE VARIETIES and with growing conditions. It is shorter with weak shoots, low temperatures, WATER STRESS, mineral deficiencies (especially of NITROGEN), and the position along the shoot (with the nodes closest together at the base and the tip). Shoots on vigorous vines have long internodes, and are large in diameter. Measured lengths vary from about 1 mm to 350 mm/13.6 in but commercially used cuttings usually have internode lengths between 50 and 150 mm. B.G.C.

interspecific hybrid denotes the result of sexually crossing more than one grapevine species, while a CROSS of varieties of the same species is **intraspecific**. See HYBRID and VITIS for some background.

intolerance of wine. See ALLERGIES AND INTOLERANCES.

invecchiato, Italian for aged.

invertase, a very important ENZYME in the grape berry for converting the larger molecule SUCROSE to its constituent molecules of GLUCOSE and FRUCTOSE in the ripening fruit so that sugar develops (see SUGAR IN GRAPES). The name invertase comes from the so-called 'invert' sugars of glucose and fructose. The reaction of this enzyme differs from that of other enzymes in that it is not reversible. This is one of the most widespread enzymes in the plant kingdom, and indeed one of the most efficient. It can metabolize 1 million times its own weight of sucrose with no loss of activity. The enzyme is located in the vacuole of berry cells, where it functions readily in the acidic environment. R.E.S.

investment in wine is the acquisition of wine for gain, whether as a means of making money or financing consumption or a combination of the two.

'This crisis is perfectly rational. It was even foreseeable. The day I saw in *Time* magazine a photograph of a bank vault with a bottle of Lafite in it, I assembled my staff and told them: "the crisis has started". Indeed from the

moment when you start to think of wine as an investment and not as something to be drunk, that's the end' (Baron Elie de ROTHSCHILD of Ch LAFITE-Rothschild, quoted in *The Winemasters* by Nicholas Faith).

The principal object of wine investment is to make a profit on wine which has increased in value as it matures. The essential premise on which wine investment is based is that demand for the wine in question exceeds supply, a premise that is often hard to gauge with accuracy. Such investment may be made purely for financial gain or to purchase wines with a view to financing consumption. The investor's prime objective is to secure wines of limited availability or high FASHION that may not appear again on the market.

Wine investment is not an activity confined to private individuals or investment companies outside the wine trade. Buying 'earliest, cheapest, lowest' is usually available to those in the know or with solid contacts. Indeed, historically, the wine trade itself, with its inside knowledge, has been known to 'take a position' on a vintage, buying grapes on a speculative hunch. This practice, known as buying *sur souches*, i.e. while the grapes are still on the vine, was referred to in Roman times by Pliny the Younger (8. 2) and became part of the folklore of the BORDEAUX TRADE, as discussed below.

Speculation and buying for consumption need not be mutually exclusive. Indeed, spreading the risk by buying mixed portfolios of wine with both disposal and consumption in mind makes sound sense and is normally advised by companies dealing in wine investment. In times of economic uncertainty, a tangible asset such as wine can bring with it comfort and prestige, and with a life expectancy for tax purposes of less than 50 years, it does not generally attract capital gains tax in the UK, unlike the US where the higher, collectible capital gains tax is charged when collectors sell wine. There may, however, be circumstances in which even UK tax officials would regard wine investment as a business and tax it accordingly. Vintage PORT, in particular, with a life expectancy of 50 years or more, is liable not to be regarded as a wasting asset for tax purposes. The popularity of wine as an investment has led to the creation of a number of investment schemes, or wine FUNDS, based in the UK, some of which are regulated by the Financial Services Authority (FSA), unlike those of wine merchants whose main aim is to move stock. Since 2012, the FSA has attempted to tighten the rules to prevent consumers from being sold risky investments.

But wine investment is inevitably a gamble, especially for anyone under the mistaken impression that making money from it is simply a question of holding on long enough to one's stock. Speculation in wine tends to be especially risky because wine is subject to the

unpredictable fluctuations of market forces. Buyers' and sellers' markets come and go and wine PRICES are as liable to go down as up. BORDEAUX, for reasons discussed below, is the principal medium of wine investment. The name Bordeaux is virtually synonymous with wine investment and its turbulent past bears witness to fortunes made and unmade in the name of wine.

In more recent years, the wine investment scene has embraced a wider portfolio of wine regions, notably Burgundy, Italy, Spain, California, and Australia. It has also attracted unscrupulous wine brokers who have manipulated secondary wine market data and extrapolated media reports to build a case for wine investment. Promises of high returns have often not been fulfilled because of fat broker margins, high storage costs, weakening currency exchange markets, company failure, and shady dealings. COUNTERFEIT WINE accounts for a small proportion of the fine and rare wine market, but in periods of high speculation and expectations, some fraudsters have attempted to circulate wines of questionable provenance, especially in emerging and particularly buoyant markets and notably DOMAINE DE LA ROMANÉE-CONTI, SASSICAIA, PETRUS, Ch MOUTON ROTHSCHILD, and PENFOLDS Grange.

Bordeaux: cyclical history

The first great boom in Bordeaux resulted from a period of prosperity which coincided with shortages caused by POWDERY MILDEW, or oidium, in the 1850s. The canny merchant Hermann CRUSE had struck the first speculative blow already, when, in 1848, he had bought up vast quantities of the 1847 vintage, only to release his hoard at undisclosed prices following Napoleon III's imperial accession. British Chancellor of the Exchequer (later to be Prime Minister) Gladstone's reduction of duty on French wine following the 1860 Anglo-French Commercial Treaty and the Single Bottle Act of 1861 (which paved the way for the off-licence, and thus a retail trade in alcoholic drinks) further fuelled demand for red bordeaux.

Following the fine vintages of 1864 and 1865, prices doubled. Two successive lean years then led to speculative buying of the hard and slow-maturing 1868 vintage, *sur souches*. Chx Lafite and Margaux offered their 1868 to the Bordeaux market, achieving record prices which were not to be surpassed for another 58 years. But this was already the beginning of the end of the first golden era of wine. The Bordeaux merchant Edouard Kressmann mirrored Hermann Cruse's earlier coup with his successful speculative purchase of the fine 1870 vintage harvested during the Franco-Prussian War. The 1875 vintage marked the end of this flamboyant period, however, as the imminent plagues of DOWNY MILDEW and PHYLLOXERA cast a blight over the vineyards of Bordeaux (see BORDEAUX, history).

History was to repeat itself nearly a century later. During the post-war period of economic regeneration, the turning-point came in 1959 when, following two devaluations of the French franc, the Americans first decisively entered the market for fine Bordeaux wines. The 1959 vintage was hailed as the vintage of the century, a term which has subsequently come to be applied ad nauseam to almost any vintage of note (usually revealing more about the ability of the Bordelais to feed speculation than about the quality of the vintage at issue). The clamour increased for the small but spectacular vintage of 1961. Between 1958 and 1961, the prices of the FIRST GROWTHS, on which most of the speculative activity was focused, more than quadrupled. By 1961, they had widened the gap between themselves and the other CLASSED GROWTHS to such an extent that their reputation as blue chip investment wines became even more firmly established.

Towards the end of the decade, the devaluation of the French franc in 1969 and the rivalry between Chx LAFITE and MOUTON ROTHSCHILD contributed to a fresh climate of speculation that was to grip Bordeaux in the early 1970s. An opening price battle between the first growths heralded the start of a boom, underpinned by a widespread feeling that demand would outstrip supply for the foreseeable future. A flood of foreign investment capital washed into Bordeaux to lap up the 1970 and 1971 vintages. Extortionate prices were asked—and paid—for the 1972 vintage, even though it turned out to be lean and mean.

A market develops

As inflation soared, red bordeaux became a wine investor's primary haven. The AUCTION houses Christie's and Sotheby's, whose new wine departments were established in, respectively, 1966 and 1970, provided the ideal forum for acquisitions and disposals. During the same period, numerous investment schemes were established to attract corporate finance, while wine merchants such as Justerini & Brooks set up their own schemes to cater for the speculative appetites of consumers. (Such schemes were to be the precursors of the government-backed Business Expansion Schemes set up in the British economic boom of the mid 1980s in the wake of a fresh outbreak of speculation fever.)

Rising oil prices and the collapse of American financial hegemony already signalled impending disaster by the spring of 1973. Tastings of the 1972 vintage coincided with the prospect of a large 1973 vintage, which turned out to be unexceptional in quality. An East Anglian wine merchant, writer Simon Loftus of Adnams, was offered—and refused—£1 million by a respectable City finance house to buy 1972 vintage

wines. Circumstances were aggravated by a scandal in which the Bordeaux house of CRUSE was charged with—and subsequently convicted of—fraud. By 1975, Chx Lafite and Mouton-Rothschild had buried the hatchet and offered surplus stocks through Christie's.

Speculation fever was rekindled by the annus mirabilis of 1982, when an exceptional red Bordeaux vintage coincided with a relatively weak French franc and a strong American dollar. Opening prices of the first growths, FF170, were more than double those of the 1980s. The fashion for buying EN PRIMEUR, boosted by the superb 1982 vintage, created a new wave of populist investment fervour. The momentum for this new form of speculative buying was buoyed by a succession of fine vintages during the 1980s, and by, for the first time, accessible press comment on the relative merits of individual, if embryonic, wine samples (see WINE WRITING). The 100-point SCORING system, introduced by the American critic Robert PARKER, brought fresh impetus to invest and an independent basis for assessing fine wine.

In the early to mid 1990s, despite particularly fine crops in 1985, 1986, 1989, and 1990, the market took a downward turn. The unfulfilled promise of increasing consumption was further aggravated by an embarrassing surplus of fine bordeaux. Following two successive great vintages in 2009 and 2010, with exorbitant prices to match, three consecutive vintages of average quality called into question the entire future of the en primeur market and the Place de Bordeaux as the principal incubators of the secondary market. Meanwhile, volatile market forces, notably the Asian market crash of 1997/8, followed by 9/11 in 2001, and more recently the 2008 credit crunch and global debt crisis of 2011, all contributed to a series of price drops by undermining stability and confidence. Confidence was also dented by the proliferation of unscrupulous peddlars of wine investment schemes (some of whom owned very little wine and knew even less about it, but were adept at cold calling) and some widely publicized counterfeit wines.

The electronic trading platform Liv-ex doubles as an independent monitor of market activity and prices. By 2014 its expanded indices showed a growing spread of investment-grade wines from outside Bordeaux, in particular from Burgundy, Champagne, the Rhône, Italy, and the New World. While Bordeaux remained the staple wine of the secondary market with an estimated 70 to 80% of the overall secondary market, the first decade and a half of this century saw a rapid rise in the fortunes of Burgundy, in particular the DOMAINE DE LA ROMANÉE-CONTI, as an investment vehicle. New cuvées were added to the Liv-ex Burgundy and Italy subindices, while the launch of a new Liv-ex 1000 list in 2014 reflected the changing shape

of a fine wine market estimated at around £3 billion.

How to minimize the risks

The lessons of the recent past are that, in order to fulfil the promise of any investment, timing, knowledge, and skill (not to mention a measure of luck) are all essential preconditions for would-be investors, whether individuals or companies. Timing requires knowledge both of market conditions and of the potential of a wine for maturing. The finer the wine, generally speaking, the longer it takes to reach its peak, and the longer it remains on a plateau of maturity. It takes knowledge and skill to be aware of and interpret the likely future trends of individual properties and vintages, taking into account their real and perceived qualities. (One of the best ways to acquire such knowledge is to keep abreast of the pronouncements of the most influential wine critics such as Robert Parker on Bordeaux and California, but anyone buying for investment would be well-advised to read a range of expert opinions on any particular wine or vintage and keep track of price indices such as those published by winemarketjournal.com.)

At the same time, investors need to be aware of less immediately obvious features of wine investment such as the importance of optimum storage conditions (see STORING WINE), the costs of storage, insurance and on-selling involved, disposal options, length of holding time, and ownership issues such as obtaining evidence, insofar as possible, to one's title to the goods. The better the guarantee of storage in ideal conditions, the higher the likely provenance premium. At the commercial auction houses, the vendor can expect to receive the current auction market price on disposal. At the same time, vendors should be aware of the requirement to pay a vendor's premium, or, if a disposal is effected through a specialist wine BROKER or FINE WINE trader, of commission on the disposal.

Investors need also to take full account of the buying options. If the conditions are right, the simplest and most attractive method of purchasing has been buying en primeur, or futures, but this is no longer offering the returns it once did. Indeed, it may well have run its course.

Wine may also be bought at AUCTION, in which case issues of PROVENANCE and storage conditions are paramount. For both reasons, any such purchase should be made at a commercial auction house holding regular, professionally run sales. And wine should ideally be bought in complete, original CASES offered in BOND, to avoid the additional expenses of paying duty and tax. As demand has increased since the 1990s, with rising incomes, and prices have risen to encourage investors other than the traditional wine lover, investment wine today is increasingly formalized through brokers and wine FUNDS.

Suitable wines for investment

The factors that make wine a worthwhile investment are numerous and complex. For one thing, political and economic auguries, specific market conditions, and likely future trends need all to be taken into account. Purchasing is usually best done in a buyer's market when conditions allow investors to take advantage of low prices such as occurred in the mid 1970s following the Bordeaux crisis, or during a glut as occurred at the end of the 1980s. A period of relatively high inflation, too, in contributing towards the creation of demand and putting pressure on supplies, such as occurred at the end of the 1960s and early 1980s, may also help bring about the desired preconditions for investing in wine. The emergence of new secondary fine wine markets such as the 21st century phenomenon of the Asian fine wine market can also promote capital growth in wine.

Wine purchased for investment must be available at a price attractive enough to give the purchaser, after a reasonable period of holding on to stock, a return on his or her initial outlay that is at least comparable with other forms of investment. It follows that the type and format of wine chosen must be intrinsically capable of increasing sufficiently in value over a period of time. Generally speaking, investment wines should be capable of ageing for a good 20 years or longer so that investors are able to hold on to the wines and sell when the market is right (although the fine wine market today seems to prefer young wines to old). Investment wines must either have an established reputation or, where the investor is in a position to evaluate likely trends, be lesser-known wines with the potential to gain in value. Investment-grade wines should come from a good, preferably great, vintage and should be capable of being easily traded. Account should be taken of the fact that magnums and LARGE FORMAT bottles may attract a premium on disposal.

Only a handful of wines fulfil these limited but strict criteria. Beyond wines with established reputations, the market for investment becomes too highly specialized for any but the best-informed insiders to dabble in with any degree of confidence or measure of success. When in doubt, *caveat emptor*, buyer beware, is always the best maxim.

'At one moment the example of a fashionable person will make a wine held in very little estimation before and perhaps worthless in reality the prime wine of a table for a season. In England it is the fashion, or accident, which frequently makes the demand considerable for a particular species' (Cyrus Redding).

See also AUCTIONS, EN PRIMEUR, and PRICE.

A.H.L.R.

Faith, N., *The Winemasters* (2nd edn, London, 1999).

Penning-Rowsell, E., *The Wines of Bordeaux* (6th edn, London, 1989).

Redding, C., *A History and Description of Modern Wines* (3rd edn, London, 1851).

Lewin, B., *What Price Bordeaux?* (US, 2009).

Wine Price Risk Management: *International Diversification and Derivative Instruments*: Apostolos Kourtis, Raphael N. Markellos and Dimitris Psychoyios.

Barclays Wealth Insight Report Profit or Pleasure? *Exploring the Motivations Behind Treasure Trends* www.ledburyresearch.com/media/document/barclays-wealth-insight-volume-15.pdf.

The World of Fine Wine, www.worldoffinewine.com.

Liv-ex, www.liv-ex.com

Inzolia, sometimes spelt **Insolia**, white grape variety grown mainly in Sicily and to a much more limited extent in Tuscany, where it is known as Ansonica Bianca, under which name the 2010 vine census lists an Italian total of 6,132 ha/15,050 acres. Its genetic roots seem to be in western Sicily where it was valued as a relatively aromatic ingredient, with Grillo, in top-quality MARSALA. Today it is more often encountered as a VARIETAL, or blended with the much more common CATARRATTO, in dry white table wines. The best examples show a certain nuttiness, the worst could do with more acid and more flavour.

ion exchange, chemical process used in, for example, water softening which has useful applications in winemaking, particularly for TARTRATE stabilization, but it has the serious disadvantage of increasing the sodium content of wine and may also alter the taste and aroma of wines. Its use is permitted in most winemaking countries but is strictly regulated.

Bird, D., *Understanding Wine Technology* (3rd edn, Newark, 2010).

Rankine, B., *Making Good Wine* (rev. edn, Sydney, 2004).

IPT, or **indice de polyphénols totaux**, common French measurement of total PHENOLICS, including TANNINS and ANTHOCYANINS.

IPW. See INTEGRATED PRODUCTION OF WINE.

Iran, large country in the Near East once known as PERSIA, under which heading details of Iran's important vinous history are to be found. Alcoholic drinks of all sorts are officially prohibited in modern Iran (see ISLAM) but HOME WINEMAKING is not unknown. According to OIV statistics, total vineyard area was still 238,000 ha/588,000 acres in 2011. The country is an important producer of DRYING GRAPES.

Irancy, small Burgundy AOC near AUXERRE created in 1999 for light reds from Pinot Noir with up to 10% of the local CÉSAR or Pinot Gris grapes.

Iraq, Middle Eastern country in which only 12,000 ha/29,600 acres of vines remained in 2011, grown chiefly for DRYING GRAPES and TABLE GRAPES, according to OIV statistics. In ancient times it was part of MESOPOTAMIA, where there was a thriving trade in wine. See also BAGHDAD for evidence of early medieval viticulture, and ISLAM for an explanation of Iraq's modern relationship with wine.

Ireland may well have been a more faithful customer of GASCON wines than was England. Several Irishmen have played a part in the history of Bordeaux wine: the BARTONS provide one example, and the Lynch of PAUILLAC's Ch Lynch-Bages was also Irish.

Despite several attempts at commercial viticulture, in conditions not dissimilar to those of ENGLAND, very few Irish vineyards have outlasted their original creators. By 2014 only two were making wine commercially: Lusca in Lusk just outside Dublin and Amurensis Walk vineyard at Kinsale.

iron, a mineral element essential for healthy vine growth in small amounts. Normally enough iron is taken up from the soil to meet the plant's needs, but iron deficiency in leaves is not uncommon. So-called lime-induced CHLOROSIS is a well-known disorder of the vine when it is grown on alkaline or CALCAREOUS soils. Leaves turn yellow, particularly between the veins, because iron is unavailable for the manufacture of chlorophyll. In alkaline and calcareous soils, iron is in an insoluble form which makes it unavailable to the vine roots. Soils can be measured for their ability to provide sufficient iron to the vine (see SOIL ALKALINITY).

The problem cannot be solved simply by adding to the soil a fertilizer such as iron sulfate because the iron will be made unavailable by the soil alkalinity. The answer is to add iron in a protected form, such as a chelate, where iron is bound in an organic complex preventing it from being precipitated in an insoluble form. Most commonly, however, lime-induced chlorosis is overcome by using a suitable ROOTSTOCK.

R.E.S. & R.E.W.

Champagnol, F., *Éléments de physiologie de la vigne et de viticulture générale* (St-Gely-du-Fesc, 1984).

Irouléguy, unique and isolated French wine appellation in BASQUE country in the extreme south west of the country fuelled almost entirely by national pride. The language and lettering used on labels here are distinctively Basque, with a heavy sprinkling of Xs. These vineyards of lower NAVARRA and the Spanish TXAKOLI are the last officially recognized vestiges of what was once a thriving wine industry (which can now be traced as far as URUGUAY). Although there were 470 ha/1,160 acres of vines in 1906, vines were almost abandoned until the late 20th century. An APPELLATION CONTRÔLÉE was granted in 1970, and by the early 1990s, the vineyard area was once again expanding. About 232 ha of scattered vineyards on soils including limestone, schist, red clay, and gravel were cultivated by 2012 by about 60 vignerons (one of them the ex-winemaker at PETRUS, no less) in rolling pastoral countryside in the far western Pyrenees, up to more than 400 m/1,300 ft above sea level, under heavy Atlantic climatic influence in the west. The vines are protected from north winds and enjoy more sunshine than most French wine regions. The local Tannat grape and/or Cabernet Franc must constitute between 50 and 90% of the light, crisp reds with the rest made up of Cabernet Sauvignon. A little distinctively fragrant white wine is also made from the indigenous varieties COURBU, PETIT COURBU, GROS MANSENG, and PETIT MANSENG. The fragrant, relatively substantial rosé is mostly Tannat with the two Cabernets but up to 10% of the white grapes may also be included.

irrigation, the application of water to growing plants such as vines, effectively a man-made simulation of RAINFALL, which can be useful, even essential, in drier regions. Few vineyard practices are more maligned, or misunderstood, than irrigation.

In its commonly visualized form, irrigation is carried out in hot, arid regions, and employs furrow or sprinkler distribution to maximize yield for TABLE GRAPES, DRYING GRAPES, and BULK wines. That is the background for the widely held view, especially in France, that only DRYLAND VITICULTURE can produce outstanding wines, and that irrigation inevitably reduces quality.

Widespread adoption of DRIP (or trickle) IRRIGATION since the 1960s has now greatly blurred the distinction. Although originally developed for and used in true arid climates, such as in ISRAEL, the technique has found its major viticultural use for supplementary watering in regions which are not so arid. That is, the vineyards rely mainly on natural rainfall, and irrigation is used to make up deficits. It is extensively used in MEDITERRANEAN CLIMATES which are regularly dry during the critical growth and ripening periods; or else in climates with more uniform rainfall but which might periodically suffer from dry periods. In both of these situations, the capacity to avoid severe WATER STRESS potentially improves grape and wine quality, provided that irrigation does not excessively stimulate vine growth and yield. See also SOIL AND WINE QUALITY; SOIL WATER.

Irrigation is one of the oldest agricultural and viticultural techniques and was clearly practised, for example, in Ancient EGYPT, and in Ancient ARMENIA too. The need for irrigation depends entirely on CLIMATE. Where EVAPORATION is high and rainfall low, vines suffer water stress. Many of the world's vineyards are in Mediterranean climates where the rain falls mostly over the winter, and the summers are dry and hot. Water stress in the vineyard during the summer depends on how much of the winter rain can be stored in the soil. Soils such as sand and gravel can hold only limited amounts of water, silts and clays much more. Vines with only shallow roots because of restricting soil conditions also experience water stress. On the other hand, some soils are able to store so much water from winter rainfall that vines can grow through the summer without significant water stress. Typically these are deep loamy or silt soils, and are commonly found on valley floors. Some of the deeper soils of California's Napa Valley are representative, and these may be found side by side with shallower soils where there is a need to irrigate.

While a modicum of WATER STRESS is desirable to encourage fruit RIPENING and enhance wine quality, excessive water stress has serious implications. In these circumstances, irrigation applied in a restricted fashion can actually improve quality (see PARTIAL ROOTZONE DRYING and REGULATED DEFICIT IRRIGATION).

It is easy to understand irrigation's notoriety, however. When vines have access to generous supplies of water, whether from irrigation or soil-stored water, they grow rapidly, producing long shoots, big leaves, big berries, and where YIELD is increased, then ripening is delayed, especially in shaded canopies. All of these are features of vineyards which produce poor-quality wine grapes. Yield is also greatly increased; depending on the severity of the water stress, irrigation may improve yield by 300% or more. In SPAIN, for example, increased use of irrigation, often in association with the planting of higher-yielding CLONES, has led to a marked increase in production despite significant EU-subsidized GRUBBING UP.

Irrigation is widely practised in the New World but less frequently in the Old (although irrigation is commonplace in some of the oldest vineyards in the world in the Near East and central Asia). At one time it was in principle banned in much of the EU other than for young vines, but it is now much more widely permitted, sometimes, as in Austria, with the proviso that it is used to improve quality rather than to increase yields, although how or whether this is actually controlled is another matter. Restrictions do still apply in much of France in the period just prior to harvest, with special derogations in times of DROUGHT. While some still believe that irrigation is intrinsically inimical to wine quality, and there are many examples of deliberate over-irrigation, some of those who deliberately install irrigation systems in southern Europe are motivated by the desire to make better wine. The modern view is that excessive water stress can be as damaging to quality as can excessive irrigation and that in drier regions carefully controlled irrigation can be a useful technique for maximizing yield and/or quality.

The mechanics

Soils vary in their ability to store water. The 'field capacity' is the maximum amount of water a thoroughly wetted soil will retain after normal drainage. The driest moisture content at which vines can extract water from the soil is called the 'permanent wilting point'. Between these two limits is the amount of available water in a soil. The ability to store water is highest for silt soils and lowest for coarse sands and gravels. The latter soils are preferred for fine wine production as there is less likelihood of excessive water supplies to the vine following rainfall.

The irrigation strategy employed by a vine-grower depends on his or her ambitions for quality and yield. For maximum yields the vines are not allowed to experience water stress at any stage of the growth cycle, and vines are irrigated to maintain moisture levels near field capacity. Such strategies are common for bulk wine production, which is often undertaken in hot, dry climates. Irrigation amount is measured as a depth of water applied: for unrestricted irrigation in a hot climate, up to 800 mm/31 in of water can be applied during the growing season. Smaller quantities of water are applied to vines producing better-quality wine. The regions in which they are grown are typically cooler and more humid, so the EVAPORATION is less, and also the rainfall is often higher. Further, it is desirable to have the vines experience a little water stress, so application amounts can be as low as 100 mm/4 in, or in some years even zero, depending on the weather.

There are several ways of deciding when to irrigate. In desert regions where the climate is relatively constant, such as much of Argentina, California, and inland Australia, irrigation is generally done by the calendar. The interval between irrigations can be longer in the early spring and late autumn, but the vineyards are irrigated most frequently in midsummer, when evaporation is highest. Weather stations, either communal or located in the vineyards, are used to measure EVAPOTRANSPIRATION. In areas with more rainfall, and especially where it is irregular, irrigation has to be much more carefully timed according to measurements of either the soil moisture or, less frequently, the plant water stress.

Soil moisture can be measured in several ways. The appearance and feel of the soil can be a useful guide, but while the surface is dry the subsoil can be still wet. Instruments used include tensiometers, gypsum blocks, neutron moisture meters, and, more recently, capacitance probes and time domain reflectometry (TDR). Data may be recorded in the field or transmitted by telemetry to the viticulturist's computer.

Plant stress can be assessed by the experienced viticulturist observing stress symptoms such as drooping shoot tips, tendrils, and leaves. Leaf temperature can also be measured, as can plant water potential, by using a so-called PRESSURE BOMB, which is common in California.

The amount of water applied depends on many factors. Water supplies are limited in many vineyard areas, so water is used sparingly and only to avoid the worst effects of severe water stress. More difficult than unlimited irrigation for high yields is to apply a limited amount of water so that a desired level of vine water stress is maintained to promote ripening and improve quality.

Methods of irrigation vary considerably. The ancient method, still used in some desert areas for bulk wine production, is **flood irrigation**. Water fed from a supply canal is run down the rows and is soaked up by the dry ground. For this to work, the vineyard floor must be flat and the rows not too long. Furrow irrigation (see ARGENTINA) is similar but allows greater control. More recent developments have been **sprinkler** and DRIP IRRIGATION (also known as trickle irrigation). Sprinklers are typically about 20 m/65 ft apart and span several rows. Dripper supply lines, usually long plastic tubes, are placed down each row, usually with one dripper at each vine.   R.E.S.

McCarthy, M. G., et al., 'Regulated deficit irrigation and partial rootzone drying as irrigation management techniques for grapevines', in *Deficit Irrigation Practices*, FAO Water Reports 22 (Rome, 2002), www.fao.org/docrep/004/y3655e/y3655e11.htm#k.

Nicholas. P. (ed.), *Soil, Irrigation and Nutrition* (Adelaide, 2004).

van Leeuwen, C., et al., 'The use of physiological indicators to assess vine water uptake and to manage vineyard irrigation', *The Australian Grapegrower & Winemaker*, 449 (June 2001), 18–24.

Irsay Oliver, aromatic, relatively recent white vine CROSS grown in SLOVAKIA and the CZECH REPUBLIC, and in HUNGARY, where there were 1,090 ha/2,692 acres in 2011, as **Irsai Olivér**. This eastern European cross of Pozsony Fehér × Pearl of Csaba was originally developed in the 1930s as a table grape. It ripens extremely early and reliably (although it is prone to POWDERY MILDEW) and produces relatively heavy, but intensely aromatic, wines strongly reminiscent of MUSCAT.

Isabella, sometimes **Isabel** and **Isabelle**, widely distributed VITIS *labrusca* AMERICAN HYBRID of unknown origin. It is said to have been named after a southern belle, Mrs Isabella Gibbs, and to have been developed in South Carolina in 1816. It can withstand tropical and semi-tropical conditions and has been planted widely, notably in MOLDOVA, BRAZIL, where it is by a substantial margin the most common vine variety, and INDIA where it is known as Bangalore Blue. In New York state, it was one of the first hybrids to be planted after PHYLLOXERA's late-19th-century devastation but it has largely been replaced by CONCORD. New plantings were banned in France in 1934. The vine is high yielding but the wines are very obviously FOXY.

Ischia, island and tourist destination in the Bay of Naples in the Italian region of CAMPANIA (see map under ITALY) which has managed to preserve a small part of the vineyards which once covered a significant part of the island. The DOC Ischia wine, produced from 60 ha/148 acres of vineyards, is most commonly a white blend based on 45 to 70% FORASTERA grapes with BIANCOLELLA. Reds are typically a blend of GUARNACCIA and PIEDIROSSO (locally known as Per'e Palummo), the latter of which, on its own, may be either a dry red or a sweet DRIED-GRAPE WINE. While these red wine grapes are widespread in Campania, Forastera and Biancolella are almost exclusively grown on Ischia on steep, terraced vineyards, often accessible only by monorail. Only few producers persevere but Casa d'Ambra is notable.   W.S.

isinglass, a particularly pure PROTEIN obtained from the bladders of sturgeon and other freshwater fish that has been used for FINING wine for centuries. As early as 1660, King Charles II of England regulated the use of isinglass by merchant VINTNERS.

Like GELATIN, isinglass reacts with the excess TANNINS in harsh young red wines. Although expensive, and difficult to prepare, isinglass is also occasionally used in the CLARIFICATION of white wines to be bottled without a final polish FILTRATION, as it has about the same clarifying property. However, there is a noticeable trend away from the use of animal-derived products for fining, mainly in the interests of VEGETARIANS AND VEGANS.   A.D.W.

Islam, the Muslim religion founded by the Prophet Muhammad (spelt variously Mohammed, Mohamet, etc.) in the 7th century AD, has had, and continues to have, the most profound effect on the history of wine. The consumption of any alcoholic drink was prohibited by Muhammad so that wine is neither officially consumed nor enthusiastically produced in most of the Near and Middle East, some of North Africa, and parts of Asia. Wine is therefore no longer produced in much of the land most closely associated with the ORIGINS OF VINICULTURE, and the rise of Islamic fundamentalism in the late 20th century represents a considerable constraint on the world's wine consumption.

Muhammad's prohibition

Wine (in Arabic *khamr*) was not prohibited from the outset of the Prophet Muhammad's preaching (between 610 and 632). Islam, both dogma and practice, emerged initially as the product of continuous revelation (the Qur'ān, often spelt Koran) during the Prophet's lifetime and his responses to the vicissitudes of the early Islamic community (these are recorded in the *hadīth* literature and constitute the second most substantive source of Islamic law). There are four verses in the Qur'ān which refer to wine; the first is quite positive (*Sūra* 16, verse 69): 'We give you the fruit of the palm and the vine from which you derive intoxicants and wholesome food.' The following two verses are cautionary but are not considered by Muslim jurists to enjoin abstinence from alcohol (Sura 2, verse 216, and Sura 4, verse 46): 'They will ask you concerning wine and gambling. Answer, in both there is great sin and also some things of use unto men, but their sinfulness is greater than their use.' 'Believers do not approach your prayers when you are drunk, but wait till you can grasp the meaning of your words; nor when you are polluted—unless you are travelling the road—until you have washed yourself.'

There is consensus amongst medieval Muslim jurists, however, that the fourth verse, which came in response to disturbances in the community, was tantamount to an injunction (although it is not couched in the same language as the prohibition on other dietary items, such as pork) (Sura 5, verse 92) 'Believers, wine and games of chance, idols and divining arrows are abominations devised by Satan. Avoid them so that you may prosper. Satan seeks to stir up enmity and hatred among you by means of wine and gambling and to keep you from the Remembrance of Allah and from your prayers.'

Although this verse was understood universally to articulate prohibition, there was dissension when it came to establishing the precise nature of forbidden wine. *Khamr*, the word used in the Qur'ānic verses, is the Arabic generic term for wine. There were, however, many types of fermented beverages known to pre-Islamic and later Arabs. The second caliph, 'Umar ibn al-Khattāb, is reported in the *hadīth* literature to have settled the question: 'Wine has been prohibited by the Qur'ān; it comes from five kinds of fruits: from grapes, from dates, from honey, from wheat and from barley; wine is what obscures the intellect.' The issue remained whether beverages prepared in a way different from wine were prohibited. For example *tilā'* appears to have been allowed by 'Umar; this was a kind of syrup made from grape juice which was cooked until two-thirds of it evaporated. However, the same source relates that 'Umar punished a man who became drunk on this concoction.

Another tradition quotes the Prophet stipulating the kinds of vessels in which fruit juice beverages could be made or stored: '. . . I forbid four things: *dubbā'* (a gourd), *hantam* (glazed wine jars), *muzaffat* (a vessel smeared with pitch) and *naqīr*.' When asked about the nature of *naqīr* he answered: 'It is a palmtrunk which you hollow out; then you pour small dates into it and upon them water. When the process of fermentation has finished, you drink it with the effect that a man hits his cousin with the sword.' The community was, therefore, enjoined to store fruit beverages in leather skins that prevented fermentation.

Nabīdh, date wine, is the drink about which there has been the most controversy. Several traditions state that this beverage was amongst the drinks prepared by Muhammad's wives and drunk by him: 'Aisha said: 'We used to prepare *nabīdh* . . . in a skin; we took a handful of dates or a handful of raisins, cast it into the skin and poured water upon it. The *nabīdh* we prepared in this way in the morning was drunk by him in the evening; and when we prepared it in the evening he drank it the next morning.' Despite this, three of the four Sunni schools of law as well as the Shiah prohibit *nabīdh*. The Hanafi school allows it when used in moderation, although intoxication is still prohibited.

Most jurists now consider discussions about types of wine to be secondary casuistry. What is deemed crucial, on the basis of *hadīth*, is that any beverage which intoxicates should not be consumed.

Despite the Qur'ānic injunction, even those types of wine recognized to be *harām* continued to be imbibed in many periods of Islamic history; this is best reflected in the rich tradition of Bacchic poetry which had its roots in pre-Islamic Arabia but flowered as a poetic genre in the early Abbasid period (see ARAB POETS). This canon of literature is largely mimetic and most certainly reflects the drinking habits of a significant sector of the Islamic community, notably—in some cases—the caliph and his entourage.

The wines consumed
Both Arabic poetry and other sources such as agricultural works tell us much about wine as a product. Although wine was produced in al-Tā'if in the Hijaz (156 km/97 miles south east of Mecca) from pre-Islamic times, it was imported mainly by Jewish and Christian merchants from SYRIA and MESOPOTAMIA. With the expansion of Islam, Arabs were introduced to finer wines grown mostly in the Christian monasteries of Iraq. 'Ana in upper Mesopotamia is only one of many areas that were known for viticulture. It was in the taverns around monasteries and in the monasteries themselves that most wine was consumed, as well as some of the outlying towns of Baghdad, districts of Baghdad

itself (especially al-Karkh), and not infrequently in the caliphal court at the very heart of the Islamic community.

The most lauded of beverages were four types of wine—white, yellow, red, and black—made from both red and white grapes, from a variety of vine varieties whose names are preserved in medieval agricultural books (Heine gives details of 21 of them, including KIŠMIŠ). In poetry, the date wine *nabīdh* was despised (cf. above). Grape wine was always mixed with water before drinking (one-third wine to two-thirds water, about the same dilution as in Ancient GREECE). The poets were fascinated by the bubbles which this mixing produced; although wine was celebrated as an ancient product ('It has aged since the time of Adam'), it may be that it was often very young and thus still fermenting when consumed. There were three classes of age: young wine, which was less than a year old, low in alcohol, and had little bouquet; middle-aged, which was a year old; and old wine, which one source claims was usually sour.   P.K.

Heine, P., *Weinstudien, Untersuchungen zu Anbau, Produktion und Konsum des Weins im arabisch-islamischen Mittelalter* (Wiesbaden, 1982).

'Khamr', *The Encyclopaedia of Islam*, vol. iv (new edn, Leiden, 1978).

Kueny, K., *The Rhetoric of Sobriety: Wine in Early Islam* (Albany, NY, 2001).

Effect of Islam on wine history
In the Middle Ages, Muslim conquest by no means outlawed wine production, however. Muhammad's caliph successors were based in Damascus and, subsequently, in BAGHDAD, which had its own local wine industry. Wine production continued in Moorish Spain (the Alhambra built by the Moors in 14th century Granada has its Puerta del Vino), Portugal, North Africa, Sicily, Sardinia, Corsica, Greece, Crete, and other eastern Mediterranean islands, usually under the heavily taxed auspices of Jews or Christians, even though they were ruled by Muslims. The Ottoman Turks made repeated raids on various eastern European wine regions in the Middle Ages, and, if the TOKAJI legend is based on fact, could therefore be said to have been indirectly responsible for the discovery of BOTRYTIZED WINES. For some more details, see SPAIN, GREECE, and CYPRUS.

It is because of the dissemination of Muslim techniques associated with alchemy that the art of DISTILLATION is said to have spread through western Europe. Indeed the word ALCOHOL is of Arab origin.

isoamyl acetate is an ESTER present in all fermented beverages. At higher concentrations, it is sometimes associated with banana-like aromas, and is often found in cool-fermented white wines and red wines that have undergone CARBONIC MACERATION. Research suggests that

this ester may have an influence on the varietal aroma of certain wines such as PINOTAGE and on the aftertaste of certain young Alsace wines.

Francis, I. L., and Newton, J. L., 'Determining wine aroma from compositional data', *Australian Journal of Grape and Wine Research*, 11 (2005), 114–26.

isoamyl alcohol. See FUSEL OILS.

isobutyl-methoxypyrazine, more properly, **2-isobutyl-3-methoxypyrazine**, or **IBMP**, smells of green or bell peppers and grass and is found in all green matter. The perception threshold in red and white wines is 615 ng/l and the concentration is higher in unripe grapes and in fruit with low sun exposure because it is very sensitive to UV light. This is why it is more often found in late-ripening varieties such as Cabernets Sauvignon and Franc and Carmenère. IBMP is very common in Sauvignon Blanc, where it is not generally considered a fault.

Isonzo del Friuli, or **Friuli Isonzo**, small DOC in the extreme north east of Italy in the FRIULI region overlapping with the COLLIO zone. The plain to the south of the Collio hills formed by the Isonzo River on its way to the Adriatic is, from a geological point of view, split in two. The left bank of the Isonzo River, the part closest to the sea, is like GRAVE DEL FRIULI a mixture of gravel and soil formed by fluvial and glacial deposits. The subzone on the right bank, inland towards COLLI ORIENTALI, is a less fertile red gravel, and produces Isonzo's finest wines. This distinction has been recognized in the DOC regulations since 2003, with wines from the right bank being entitled to put Rive Alte on the label, while those from the left bank can use the subzone Rive di Giare. Wines labelled with the Rive Alte subzone must be made from Pinot Grigio, Chardonnay, Sauvignon Blanc, Friulano, and/or Merlot. Rive di Giare must be made from Pinot Grigio, Sauvignon Blanc, Malvasia Istriana, Refosco dal Penduncolo Rosso, and/or Merlot.

The zone included just over 900 ha/2,223 acres of DOC vineyard in the early 2010s. As in the rest of Friuli, the wines tend to be produced as VARIETALS. The whites are generally fresh, simple and fruity, while the reds are soft and forward, both colours often determined by the still very high yields of between 12 and 13 tonnes/ha allowed here Practically all white wine grapes may also be used to produce a late-harvest or a sweet DRIED-GRAPE WINE, while rosés may either be varietal or a blend of white and red wine.

The flat plains of Isonzo, encircled by mountains to the north and east and running into the sea in the south, have long persuaded outsiders that the zone is little different from its southern neighbour, Grave del Friuli. However, the good DRAINAGE provided by the gravel soils, and a gap in the mountains to the north east, through which flows a cool moderating breeze, sets it apart from Grave. In the past, some of Friuli's top producers bought grapes in Isonzo. The high prices paid for the grapes held back the emergence of the zone's producers, but today the likes of Vie di Romans, Lis Neris, Pierpaolo Pecorari, Ronco del Gelso, Mauro Drius, Borgo San Daniele, and I Feudi di Romans are producing wines that rival the best from the rest of Friuli.   D.C.G. & W.S.

isopropyl-methoxypyrazine (IPMP).

See METHOXYPYRAZINES.

Israel, the biblical land of milk and honey (see CANAAN), lays claim to being the cradle of the world's wine industry. In 2013 locals estimated that about 5,500 ha/13,585 acres of vineyards were producing about 260,000 hl/6.86 million gal of wine a year. (OIV figures for total vineyard area in 2011 were 9,000 ha.)

History

The fruit of the vine was economically important in the Holy Land and was designated one of the seven blessed species of fruit specified in the book of Deuteronomy (see BIBLE). The dangers of immoderate wine consumption were fully recognized, and excess strictly forbidden. Vine-growing continued under Christian rule, even after the destruction of the Second Temple in Jerusalem, until AD 636, when the spread of ISLAM brought about destruction of the vineyards. The Crusaders temporarily restored wine production between AD 1100 and 1300, but with the exile of the Jews, vine-growing ceased.

At the end of the 19th century, Jews returned to the Holy Land from the Diaspora, and 1882 saw the beginning of the modern era with the support of Baron Edmond de ROTHSCHILD. His massive benefaction made viticulture an important part of the agricultural resettlement programmes. French experts provided expertise. Two wineries with deep underground cellars were built, Rishon Le Zion in 1890 and Zichron Ya'acov in 1892, which remain the largest wineries in Israel. The Société Co-operative Vigneronne des Grandes Caves was founded in 1906, trading under the name Carmel. The Rothschilds owned the wineries until 1957, when they were donated to the co-operative. The industry grew and thrived, exporting KOSHER wine to Jewish communities throughout the world for over 100 years.

The quality revolution began in the 1980s: planting vineyards with INTERNATIONAL VARIETIES in cooler, higher-elevation areas, combined with internationally trained winemakers and expertise, originally from California, had dramatic effects. Yarden wines from the Golan Heights Winery first won international acclaim in the 1980s.

Geography

Israel is a sliver of a country, stretching a mere 424 km/263 miles in length. The north and centre of the country may be divided into the fertile coastal plain and the mountainous region that runs down the spine of the country, which falls away to the Jordan Rift Valley in the east. The Negev Desert, combining arid and semi-arid areas, makes up over half the country.

The climate is MEDITERRANEAN with long, hot, dry summers and short, cool, rainy winters, with occasional snow at higher elevations in winter.

Viticulture

Israeli viticulture tends to be an ongoing battle with the elements. There is a chronic lack of water and the coastal area can be hot and humid. The wine industry has gradually moved northwards to Galilee and eastwards towards Jerusalem in search of higher elevations. Most vines are cordon spur pruned in a VSP. MECHANICAL HARVESTING is usually preferred although older vines are planted as BUSH VINES and are hand picked. CANOPY MANAGEMENT is crucial to reduce VIGOUR and protect the grapes from SUNBURN. DRIP IRRIGATION, pioneered by the Israelis in the 1960s and developed worldwide, is the norm. Harvesting starts mid July and may last until the first week of November, but most grapes are picked from August to mid October.

Wine regions

There are five registered regions. Galilee in the north includes the Upper Galilee, Lower Galilee, and Golan Heights.

Shomron includes Mount Carmel, with the majority of the region's vineyards, the Sharon Plain and the Shomron Hills.

Samson covers the central coastal plain south east of Tel Aviv, the Judean Lowlands, and Judean Foothills.

The Judean Hills, which rise from the foothills west of Jerusalem, run from north of Jerusalem down to the beginning of the desert area.

Finally, the Negev region covers the south of the country.

Soils vary from sandy and TERRA ROSSA on the coast, LIMESTONE and CHALK on the hills, VOLCANIC in the north, and LOESS in the south.

Grape varieties

Most of the best red wines are made from Cabernet Sauvignon, Merlot, and Shiraz/ Syrah. There are some interesting varietal Cabernet Francs and characterful old-vine Carignans and Petite Sirahs. Carignan is the variety that has spanned the modern wine history of Israel, having been planted even before Rothschild involvement. Unique to Israel is ARGAMAN, a local cross designed for inexpensive blends.

Among the whites, Chardonnay and Sauvignon Blanc are supplemented by Gewurztraminer, Riesling, and Viognier. The DAVIS creation EMERALD RIESLING has enjoyed more commercial success in Israel than elsewhere. The only winery still using local varieties such as Hamdani, Jandali, and Dabouki is that in the Cremisan Monastery between the West Bank and Jerusalem, and researchers are busy comparing their DNA with that of better-known INTERNATIONAL VARIETIES, and with ancient grape seeds found by archaeologists (see PALAEOETHNOBOTANY).

Modern wine production

Small wineries continue to proliferate. The 21st century brought new investors: Carmel was bought by an international consortium; Barkan was purchased by Israel's largest brewery; and Tabor by Israel's largest beverage company. By 2013 the 40 commercial wineries harvesting more than 50 metric tons a year were complemented by hundreds of small wineries and GARAGISTES. The three largest wineries were Carmel, Barkan, and the Golan Heights, which together controlled 65% of the Israeli market, followed by Teperberg, Binyamina, Tabor, Tishbi, Galil Mountain, Dalton, and Recanati. These ten wineries have well over 90% of the market and most of the exports. Reputable small wineries include Clos de Gat, Domaine du Castel, Flam, Margalit, Tzora, and Yatir. Most wineries are modern, the technology is advanced, and internationally trained winemakers predominate.

See also KOSHER (although by no means all Israel's wine is kosher).   A.S.M.

Heskett, R. and Butler, J., *Divine Vintage: Following the Wine Trail from Genesis to the Modern Age* (New York, 2012).

Rogov, D., *The Ultimate Rogov's Guide To Israeli Wines* (Jerusalem, 2012).

Sacks, E., and Montefiore, A., *The Wine Route of Israel* (3rd edn, Tel Aviv, 2012).

www.wines-israel.com

Istria. See CROATIA.

www.vinistra.com

Italian Riesling, or **Italian Rizling**; sometimes **Italianski Rizling**, occasional synonym for RIESLING ITALICO. See WELSCHRIESLING.

Italy, with FRANCE one of the world's two mammoth wine producers, sometimes producing as much as 50 million hl/1,320 million gal a year. Italy has more land under vine than any other country other than France and SPAIN, although thanks to the European VINE PULL SCHEME, the total has been reduced from close to 1.4 million ha/3.4 million acres in the early 1990s to barely half that, a forecast 750,000 ha/ 1.85 million, acres by 2015. Italy and France are routinely the world's biggest wine exporters. A significant but declining proportion of the wine exported from Italy has been inexpensive wine for BLENDING in and possible re-export from

ITALY

SWITZERLAND

AUSTRIA

HUNGARY

Alps

Alps

TRENTINO-
ALTO ADIGE
Bolzano

FRIULI
Udine
Gorizia

SLOVENIA

VALLE
D'AOSTA

Alps

LOMBARDIA

Trento

VENETO

Trieste

CROATIA

FRANCE

Novara
Vercelli

Milan
Pavia

Verona
Venice

Turin

Asti

Po

Alba

Piacenza

PIEMONTE

EMILIA-
ROMAGNA

BOSNIA AND
HERZEGOVINA

LIGURIA

Bologna

Genoa

SAN
MARINO

LIGURIAN

Florence

A p e n n i n e s

SEA

Bolgheri

TOSCANA

MARCHE

Ancona

Siena

ADRIATIC SEA

Montalcino

Perugia

Elba

UMBRIA
Orvieto

CORSICA

LAZIO

ABRUZZO

Rome
Frascati

MOLISE

Bari

SARDEGNA

Naples
Ischia

PUGLIA

CAMPANIA

Oristano

Capri

BASILICATA

Taranto

TYRRHENIAN
SEA

Cagliari

CALABRIA

Lipari

MEDITERRANEAN SEA

Palermo

Marsala

TUNISIA

SICILIA

Pantelleria

0   200 km

France and Germany, but a good 60% of exports are now in bottle and Italy's top wines are sought after around the world, especially in the US and German-speaking markets.

Unlike either France or Spain, Italy cultivates the vine virtually everywhere in the peninsula, from the Alps in the north to islands that are closer to the coast of North Africa than to the Italian mainland (see map). Viticulture traditionally impinged on the national consciousness, on the national imagination, and on daily life in a way that is hardly conceivable to those not accustomed to the Mediterranean way of life and its dietary trinity of bread, olive oil, and wine. It was unthinkable for Italians to sit down and eat without wine on the table until about the late 1980s since when per capita wine consumption, as in France and Spain, has been plummeting.

To consider the history of wine in Italy is to consider the history of Italy itself, however; wine and Italian civilization are virtually synonymous. The Ancient Greek name for much of Italy already acknowledged the importance of viticulture to the peninsula: OENOTRIA, or 'land of trained vines'.

Italy, Magna Graecia, and Roman Italy

The pastoral past of the tribes of Italy may be reflected in the use of milk in LIBATIONS rather than wine (see PLINY, *Natural History*, 14. 88), but viticulture and wine will have made an early impact as part of GREEK and ETRUSCAN culture (see ORIGINS OF VINICULTURE for more details). SICILY may have played a key role in the development of viticulture on the mainland. The Sicilian Murgentina grape, which flourished in volcanic soils, was successfully transplanted near POMPEII on the slopes of Vesuvius, where it was called locally the Pompeian grape. This in turn was introduced further north around Clusium (Chiusi) in Etruria, where it proved particularly prolific. Again, the Eugenia, the high-quality grape from Tauromenium (Taormina in Sicily), successfully found a home in the Colli ALBANI south of Rome, but was a failure elsewhere.

Incidental mentions by the historians suggest that by the time that Hannibal invaded Italy in the late 3rd century BC, vines could be found throughout the peninsula, from beyond the Po valley, down the Adriatic coast, and in CAMPANIA; but little wine was of particular note before the middle of the 2nd century BC according to Pliny (*Natural History*, 14. 87). It was Pliny, too, who in a key passage (*Natural History*, 14. 94 ff.) made a particularly acute observation. He noted that OPIMIAN wine of the year when Opimius was consul (121 BC) was accepted as one of the greatest VINTAGES, but that this applied generally to wine in that year, not to any particular CRUS. An edict of the censors of 89 BC imposing a price limit on costly wines refers only to wine made from the Aminnean grape (see ANCIENT VINE VARIETIES), not to any estates.

The creation of the grands crus of Roman Italy belongs to the 1st centuries BC and AD. This fact is more or less confirmed by ARCHAEOLOGY. The expansion of villas connected with wine production and overseas trade, as evidenced by their AMPHORAE, may have begun in the late 3rd or 2nd centuries, but the real growth is later. Three factors were involved in this development. First there was the exceptional growth of the city of ROME, which created a huge market for wine. Secondly, there was the opening up of trade routes to GAUL and SPAIN, which stimulated the growth of vineyards in the areas immediately behind ports; and finally there was the interest of the Roman aristocracy with an ever-increasing level of wealth to invest. So it is no accident that the areas in which the great wines of Roman Italy developed were LAZIO and Campania, regions within easy reach of the Roman market and where the Roman élites had their country homes. In the Colli Albani, the mainly sweet wines of Alba itself were highly prized, as were those of Velletri. The Emperor Augustus gave a boost to the wines of Setia (Sezze) by favouring them above all others. Beyond Terracina, CAECUBAN, produced in the marshes around the Lago di Fondi, was in the very front rank of wines. The wines from the slopes of Monte Massico, particularly the various types of FALERNIAN, long remained the most favoured. In northern and central Campania, the wines of Cales, along with Gauranum (from Monte Barbaro, overlooking the northern end of the bay of Naples) had reputations which were close to that of Falernian. Then on the bay of Naples itself were the noted vineyards of Pompeii and the Sorrento peninsula. The very light, white wine of this region, SURRENTINUM, made from the Aminnean Germana Minor grape, enjoyed very high status in the 1st century AD, although it did not win universal approval ('high-quality vinegar' was the view of the Emperor Tiberius).

Few wines outside Lazio and Campania ever approached the status of these wines and none exceeded it. To the north and west, Etruria (TUSCANY) had a great variety of wines, but only those of Luni and Genoa in Liguria made much impact. In Magna Graecia (southern Italy), a number of areas produced wines of some note, including Tarentine (from Taranto). The Adriatic coast of Italy presents an interesting test case. It would be difficult to guess at the importance of the wines of this area simply from the rather limited literary evidence. But the evidence of amphorae shows that PUGLIA and Ancient Calabria and, perhaps, areas further up the east coast exported wine to all the countries round the Adriatic and to the Greek world from the 2nd century. Brindisi certainly was the focus for a flourishing export trade. Further north, Hadrianum, the wine of Atri, and the adjoining Praetuttian vineyards (roughly the northern area of Montepulciano d'ABRUZZO) achieved a high reputation in the 1st century AD. A significant development is to be associated with the time of the first Roman emperor, Augustus (31 BC–AD 14); this was the increasing prominence of northern wines from the Po valley and beyond. The distinctive type of amphora which carried the wines of this region was sometimes stamped with the names of men who rose to prominence in the entourage of Augustus and had estates in the region. These amphorae doubtless carried Praetuttian, the wines of Ancona, of Ravenna, and of the towns along the Via Aemilia. VIRGIL, Augustus' court poet, reflected the emperor's liking for the wines of Verona (see VENETO), made from the Rhaetic grape (although, because of its distance from the sea, it is unlikely this area's wines achieved more than a passing prominence). Augustus' wife Livia did her bit to promote the wines of the FRIULI region, by publicly ascribing her longevity to an exclusive diet of the wine of Pucinum, beyond Aquileia.

Archaeology has combined with history to give us this picture of viticulture in Roman Italy, which differed in significant ways from the current scene. It should always be remembered that, as now, there would be an enormous consumption of undistinguished, local wines, which never travelled, and are rarely to be identified in the historical record.   J.J.P.

Pliny, *Natural History*, trans. by H Rackham (Loeb Classical Library, 1945), Book 14.

Tchernia, A., *Le Vin de l'Italie romaine* (Rome, 1986).

Medieval history

The fall of the Roman empire did not put an end to viticulture in Italy, but barbarization and economic collapse meant the disappearance of the market for fine wines. With Goths, then Lombards, in Rome and most of the north, and the remains of the empire administered precariously from Ravenna, Falernian, and Caecuban had become distant memories. Yet the Italian diet remained based on bread, olives, and wine, and so wine continued to be grown as one of the necessities of Mediterranean life.

The Dark Ages were a period of economic stagnation; except for the importation of luxury goods from the Near East, trade was local. We know little about the wine that was grown until the 11th century, when population, production, and exchange increased, and Italy, particularly northern Italy, became politically and economically the most important part of Europe (see GENOA and VENICE). Between the 11th and the 14th centuries, the population of Italy doubled to between 7 and 9 million inhabitants. People of all social classes migrated to the towns, including members of the nobility. As a result, urban communes came to govern the countryside. South of Tuscany, however, the aristocracy lived near the land and the feudal system, with its lack of distinction between trade and agriculture persisted.

One of the reasons for the strength of the Italian economy was that it had monopolized the trade in luxury items and their distribution throughout Europe. These included the strong, sweet wines of Crete, Cyprus, and other parts of the Aegean (see MALMSEY), but also goods produced in Italy itself, such as high-quality wool and silk (from Lucca and Florence). When it became possible to transfer credit throughout the Mediterranean and western Europe (instead of having to carry and exchange actual coins), Florence became the banking capital of Europe. The Florentine house of ANTINORI is a good example of several of these developments. The Antinoris were, and still are, a noble Tuscan family that moved from the country to the city; having made their money in banking, they diversified into selling wine and also used their capital to buy up land to grow their own wine.

The rich merchants of the cities became a new market for fine wines. Good wine became a sign of affluence and a source of profit: it is no coincidence that the merchant dynasties of Bardi and FRESCOBALDI should have gone into wine-growing, buying up land for the purpose. All over Italy, the usual way to improve land was to deforest it and plant it with vines. When there was enough moisture, the vines were raised on trees, stakes, or trellises (see TENDONE), in the Roman way, to increase yields by exposing the grapes to the sun. Thus sown and planted crops could be raised in the same fields. In the drier regions, particularly in the south (with the exception of CAMPANIA), the vines were left to grow unsupported, as BUSH VINES, or left to trail on the ground in vineyards or at least in separate plots.

Vine-growing as well as winemaking in medieval Italy were much as they had been in the days of the classical AGRICULTURAL TREATISES, and in one crucial respect things were worse: since AMPHORAE and other impermeable earthenware vessels were no longer available, wine was kept in wooden BARRELS, which were hard to clean and were not airtight. Unless a wine contained high proportions of two natural preservatives, sugar and alcohol, it would not last out the year.

The Roman VINE VARIETIES seem to have disappeared. In his treatise on agriculture (c 1304) PETRUS DE CRESCENTIIS, who had read the classical authorities and often repeats their advice, does not mention any of the famous Roman CÉPAGES. He lists some 37 contemporary Italian varieties, but he makes no attempt to relate those to the grapes encountered by his classical predecessors. The list he gives is mostly concerned

with the northern half of Italy, and especially his own city of Bologna. The list is not a great help to the modern scholar, because his descriptions are too brief for identification and many of the names are unrecognizable (although see below). None of Petrus' 17 red wine varieties has a familiar name, and Petrus does not devote much space to them. Like most medieval drinkers, he preferred white wines to red.

From the 13th century onwards, wine was medieval Italy's most profitable cash crop. Share-cropping was traditional throughout the country, with the landowner taking half the wine or more if production was high. Sometimes a contract was drawn up for a longer period at a fixed rent. Smallholders survived in the highlands, but in Tuscany and the northern plain they could not afford to stay on the better land. Peasants occasionally retailed their wine, but usually the landowners regulated sales to the towns. Consumption was high (the figure for Florence, c.1338, is a gallon a week for every man, woman, and child, but estimates for Milan and Venice are very much higher), yet production more than met demand, particularly in Campania.

Italy is mountainous and has few navigable RIVERS, which made internal transport costly and difficult before the coming of the RAILWAYS. Also, because Italy was not a political unity, there were obstacles in the form of tolls, duties, and differences in coinage, weights, and measures. Transport by sea was cheap and export to other countries no more laborious than much internal trade, so merchants in northern Italy or near the sea readily turned to foreign markets. The northern districts sold wine in Switzerland and Germany, the Marche exported to the Levant via Venice, which enjoyed tax privileges in Constantinople, and Genoese ships took the wines of Liguria to Spain, Flanders, and England. Nevertheless, the volume of Italy's international wine trade was merely the surplus production of a fertile vine-growing country. The Italians could afford not to deprive themselves of any of the wine they wanted to drink and still make money out of what remained.

See also GENOA, NAPLES, VENICE, and TUSCANY.

H.M.W.

Jones, P., 'Italy', in *The Cambridge Economic History of Europe*, 7 vols., i: *The Agrarian Life of the Middle Ages* (Cambridge, 1966).

Marescalchi, A., and Dalmasso, G. (eds.), *Storia della vite e del vino in Italia*, 3 vols. (Milan, 1993).

Modern history

That the revival of Europe's trade in the early Middle Ages began in the Mediterranean is by now universally accepted. It is therefore no surprise that specific references to what were

to become some of Italy's most important grapes and wines can be found as early as the late 13th and early 14th centuries. Barbera was already mentioned during this period, and Nebbiolo, Trebbiano, and Garganega were specifically named by Petrus de Crescentiis in his *Liber ruralium commodorum* of c.1304. The country's chronicles, both civic and monastic, of the 14th and 15th centuries abound with descriptions of the leading wines of their day—at times identified by grape variety, at times identified by their production zone. Many of them coincide, at least nominally, with the current wines of these same zones.

English records seem to indicate that wines such as Vernaccia, Trebbiano, and Greco were all known as such at this time. Sante Lancerio, cellarmaster to Pope Paul III, recounted the wines of his day in an account of papal travels in 1536, describing, criticizing, and praising the prominent products of his epoch, amongst which we find Aglianico, Aleatico, and Greco from the south, Vino Nobile di Montepulciano, Trebbiano di Romagna, Sangiovese di Romagna from the centre, and Cinqueterre from the north. And in Andrea Bacci's work we find a full-fledged treatise on Italy's wines, an attempt to deal with and describe the country's viticultural production on a national basis and in a national context, a surprising phenomenon inasmuch as Italy was far from being a nation in the modern sense in the late 16th century.

But it was precisely at this time—in the 17th, and then in the 18th, centuries—that the development of Italian viticulture and wines began to diverge from those of her neighbours. This critical period, which saw the rise of modern wine in BOTTLES stoppered with CORK and from specific producers, left Italy virtually untouched. Old bottles from this period are non-existent, nor is there any evidence of a long history of bottled wine from individual properties. Although some of Tuscany's leading NÉGOCIANT houses trace their history back to the Middle Ages (see ANTINORI and FRESCOBALDI), they, and the few Piedmontese houses which can trace their history to the late 18th century, sold bulk rather than either bottled wine or estate wines until relatively recently.

Any overall evaluation of the quality of Italian wine in the 18th century is impossible, but signs of deterioration do exist. The 'Florence' wines so greatly appreciated in the late 17th and early 18th centuries by Lady Sandwich, by Swift, and by Bolingbroke are described as 'disagreeably rough' by Sir Edward Barry in 1775, and there is good reason not to dismiss his words as a mere subjective reaction. Pietro Leopoldo, grand duke of Tuscany, during an inspection tour of his realm in 1773, reported a significant loss of viticultural commerce with England due to the lessened quality of the wines of Chianti. More importantly, Italy's wines, including many of its most famous ones, did not assume their current form until quite recently: Barolo and Barbaresco were allegedly sweet wines until the middle and end of the 19th century, respectively (although this may well have been simply because the wines did not routinely ferment to complete dryness); Chianti did not become a predominantly Sangiovese wine until the late 19th century; Brunello di Montalcino did not even exist as a wine until the end of the 19th century (see BIONDI SANTI who, like MASTROBER-ARDINO, was bottling wine by then); Orvieto and Cinqueterre were predominantly sweet wines until the modern epoch; the best-known wines of central Italy such as Orvieto, Verdicchio, Frascati, and the other white wines of the Castelli Romani were regularly fermented on their skins until the 1970s. The INTERNATIONAL VARIETIES which today play so important a role in the viticulture of Italy's north east—Trentino-Alto Adige, Veneto, and Friuli—began to assume a significant role only after the replanting of the country's vineyards in the wake of the ravages of PHYLLOXERA in the early 20th century. The crisp and refreshing white wines of Friuli are entirely a post-Second World War phenomenon; Sicily's first dry table wines, in contrast to the better-known sweet wines or blending wines of the island, were created only in 1824, by Duke Edoardo di Salaparuta.

Cyrus REDDING's observation that 'Italian wines have stood still and remained without improvement, while those of France and Spain...have kept pace to a certain extent with agricultural improvement and the increasing foreign demand' testifies to two and half centuries of marking time, of neglect, and probably of deterioration of quality.

The reasons for this period of stagnation, which in Italian historical literature is often called the period of Italy's *decadenza*, are not difficult to determine. The country experienced an extended domination by foreign powers, first by the Spanish Habsburgs both in the north and the south, then by Spanish Bourbons in the south and Austrian Habsburgs in the north. Meanwhile the increased influence—both temporal and spiritual—of Counter-Reformation Catholicism effectively removed the country's destiny from its own hands. Even more significant was the general shift of trade and commerce from south to north, from the Mediterranean to the Atlantic, which transformed Italy's geographical position for the first time in two millennia from that of a central to that of a peripheral power. Italy was on the fringes of a Europe in which the most prosperous and progressive areas, the northern

markets, were virtually inaccessible to her, and were increasingly dominated by the fine wines of France and Germany.

The unification of Italy in 1861, and a slow but steady period of economic growth, did much to reverse the decline of the previous two and a half centuries, although economic growth and modernization were neither unfaltering nor swift. It was only the economic boom after the Second World War which allowed the Italians to attain a truly European standard of living. It also created a class of consumers with both an interest in wine and the means to purchase it, which gave Italian wine producers the essential confidence in their own capacities and their own products which are the only real basis for making good-quality wine. Although a keen importer of champagne, the Italian wine market has been understandably preoccupied by Italian wine, and in the late 20th century came to be shaped by a handful of annual wine guides. Most of them encouraged INTERNATIONAL VARIETIES at the expense of Italy's rich heritage of INDIGENOUS VARIETIES, and for many years encouraged the use, sometimes overuse, of French BARRIQUES—not to mention favouring particular consultant OENOLOGISTS. This century has so far seen a decline in all these fads, however.

Major developments in the recent history of Italian wine are described under DOC, DOCG, and IGT.

Geography and climate

Generalizations about a peninsula 1,200 km/ 750 miles long extending through about 10 degrees of LATITUDE are not easy. The dominant geographical feature of the 'boot' is the Apennines, which begin close to the border with France and then form the central ridge, the national spinal column, down the peninsula to the 'toe' in Calabria. In the far north are the alps; in Sicily, the Madonie form yet another chain of central mountains, while Etna rises up to 3,350 m/10,990 ft. Good-quality viticulture is almost entirely a HILLSIDE phenomenon in Italy; there are no Italian equivalents of the *vignoble* of Bordeaux, and the Grave del Friuli and other flat viticultural areas of Friuli do not produce wine at the same quality level as the higher nearby districts of Collio and Colli Orientali. Unlike that of France, Italian agriculture has traditionally been organized vertically instead of horizontally: instead of growing grapes in certain given areas and other crops in different areas, Italians have used the richer soils of the valley floors for the cultivation of grain and vegetables and for the grazing of cattle, reserving the hills of the same areas for the cultivation of the vine and the olive.

A significant number of the country's most admired wines come from CALCAREOUS soils. Piemonte, Tuscany, the hillside zones of Friuli, and the Salento in Puglia all provide examples of this. The other dominant soil type is VOLCANIC, present in such zones as Soave, the Castelli Romani to the south west of Rome, the interior of Campania and Basilicata, and Sicily.

Climate is inevitably affected by ELEVATION. Latitude is not a sure guide to temperature and further south is not always synonymous with hotter temperatures. Elevation, exposure, wind currents, TOPOGRAPHY, SOIL COMPOSITION, and proximity to the sea are other relevant factors. If Cabernet Sauvignon can be grown at 46 degrees 30 minutes of latitude (north of Bordeaux), it is due to the narrow, heat-trapping alpine valleys of Alto Adige. Umbria is generally cooler than Tuscany albeit further to the south; a wide span of central Italy—Umbria, the Marche, Lazio—is more renowned for its white wines than for its reds, while Piemonte, in the far north on the French and Swiss border, is principally a producer of powerful red wines. Even Sicily confirms the rule that, in the case of Italy, geography is not destiny: the island as a whole produces considerably more white wine than red, and the western part of the island, in particular the province of Trapani in the extreme south west of the island, produces almost exclusively white wine (see MARSALA).

While the climate of the far north of Italy may be CONTINENTAL, that of central and southern Italy is MEDITERRANEAN. Italy's indigenous red grape varieties—with the exception of Dolcetto—are almost invariably later ripeners. Nebbiolo, Barbera, Refosco, Corvina, Sangiovese, Sagrantino, Aglianico, Negroamaro, Nerello Mascalese, and Nero d'Avola all require sustained heat throughout the summer and early autumn to ripen properly and lose their tannic and acidic asperity, and successful ripening is therefore far from automatic. Poor VINTAGES are by no means a strange or inexplicable phenomenon in Italy, although increased viticultural knowledge, strict grape selection, and CLIMATE change resulting in warmer growing seasons and notably earlier harvests, has made completely disastrous vintages a thing of the past, as in other wine producing countries.

Viticulture

Two distinguishing features mark Italian viticulture: first, the late development of vineyards as such and a significant presence until relatively recently of polyculture in grape-growing areas; second, the long-standing dominance of vine-TRAINING SYSTEMS created expressly for high YIELDS and easy MECHANIZATION. Polyculture was a common phenomenon throughout Europe at one time. What is distinctive about Italy is the extent to which this practice lasted into the modern epoch. Grain and vegetables such as potatoes were planted between rows of vines even in Barolo and Barbaresco until the 1950s, and central Italy was dominated by an almost standard type of mixed culture in which vines, planted amidst olive groves and rows of grains, were trained up trees to prevent the grapes from being eaten by the animals allowed to roam freely in the fields. Some modern vineyards, planted exclusively with vines in regular rows, did exist, particularly in Italy's north west, but viticulture in general was merely part of a general system of agriculture, one cash crop among many. It is no surprise, therefore, that when Italy's vineyards were replanted in the 1960s and 1970s, frequently with the assistance of EU funds, vineyards were generally adapted to the new exigencies of mechanization and productivity. Whereas in France the practicalities of mechanization were adapted to the existing low trained-trained vines and high VINE DENSITY with their proven ability to give high-quality grapes, Italian vineyards were redesigned when they were replanted, in a way that would make them compatible with the new large TRACTORS and other machines which were then becoming generally available. The result was spacings of up to 3 m/10 ft between the rows and high training systems. This low-density viticulture, with an average of between 2,500 and 3,300 vines per ha, coupled with the generous YIELDS that were common in the initial period of Italy's DOC epoch (roughly 1965–80), had as their inevitable result the very high yields per vine, often as much as 5 kg/11 lb of grapes, and a reduction in vine longevity.

The higher training systems, especially PERGOLA, while offering improved protection against HAIL and FUNGAL DISEASES, reduced the amounts of reradiated heat and often resulted in less ripe grapes with higher acidity, rougher tannins, and lower levels of EXTRACT. In the 1980s, there was renewed interest in higher vine density and lower yields per vine. Initial experiments with planting densities in central Italy have shown greatly improved results from densities of 7,500 to 10,000 per ha and little if any improvement with yet higher densities. Expansive vine-training systems such as TEN-DONE or even more extreme horizontal systems such as Sylvoz, Casarsa, and other accentuatedly productive CORDON systems are no longer as popular, and there was a visible return to more quality-orientated systems, GUYOT or COR-DON DE ROYAT in particular, the latter being popular for the ease with which it adapts to mechanization.

CLONAL SELECTION aimed at identifying and reproducing qualitatively superior clones of native vine varieties and the most appropriate ROOTSTOCKS to graft them on to has been a relatively recent activity, although important research programmes were conducted specifically for Sangiovese, Nebbiolo, and some other indigenous varieties in the 1990s. The popularity of Kober 5 BB and other over-productive rootstocks, a feature of the planting period from 1965 to 1980, is unlikely to be repeated.

With the general BULK WINE market in decline and increased demand for higher quality wines, Italy has gradually embraced viticultural methods much more focused on quality, while its total vineyard surface has steadily declined. At the same time a new generation has begun to reassess its ancient training and cultivation systems. In some cases Guyot has been abandoned in favour of a reappraisal of pergola systems which in cooler, higher, marginal regions—provided yields are kept low—may be the only training system that achieves full ripeness. And the ALBERELLO (bush vine) system once standard in the south may be LABOUR-INTENSIVE but tends to result in high-quality wine.

Winemaking

If Italian viticulture has tended to follow its own course, with little attention paid to the practices of other countries, the same cannot be said of its OENOLOGY and winemaking practices. Indeed, substantial investments in cellar equipment have made Italian winemaking facilities some of the most modern in Europe, and Italians make equipment such as BOTTLING lines that is some of the best, and most exported, in the world.

Chaptalization is forbidden but ENRICHMENT with concentrated grape must is permitted in some areas and within certain limits.

Wooden FERMENTATION VESSELS, once abandoned with vigour in favour of STAINLESS STEEL, have been gradually making a comeback, while CONCRETE vats and tanks are still widely used for both FERMENTATION and storage. TEMPERATURE CONTROL is widely accepted for the production of both red and white wines, and the PUNCHING DOWN of the cap of red wines has been generally replaced by regular PUMPING OVER during fermentation, although there is noticeable trend towards using the traditional SUBMERGED CAP technique, especially in Barolo and Barbaresco. The lengthy fermentations and MACERATIONS of the past, sometimes up to six weeks, were shortened, substantially so by most producers and slightly less so by avant-garde producers seeking the highest quality. This resulted in perhaps less distinctive wines but ones that were faster maturing and easier to sell. A new generation,

however, combines both ancient and modern techniques in an ongoing investigation into what leads to original wines.

WHITE WINEMAKING techniques changed drastically in the 1970s and 1980s, with the introduction of cool fermentations, FILTRATION, and CENTRIFUGES. The most fundamental change of all was to end the practice of fermenting white wines on their skins, which was once widely practised in Friuli and throughout central Italy. Gains in lightness and freshness were obvious, but were achieved at the price of a certain standardization. Producing white wines of more character without sacrificing the newly achieved crispness and cleanliness is the current challenge for Italian white winemaking and there has been a return in some quarters to fermenting white wines on the skins. Winemakers are increasingly conscious of traditional practices, inspired by Mario Soldati's account of them.

Fermentation may have evolved considerably in the second half of the 20th century, but ÉLEVAGE underwent more profound modifications during the same period. Large casks, usually oval rather than upright, were long the preferred containers for AGEING red wine in Italian cellars; long ageing periods, particularly for what were considered the grandest wines, were an almost unvarying rule; wood of a certain age was generally preferred to new wood (although this may often have been for financial rather than qualitative reasons). Many of Italy's most renowned red wines have tannins which need a considerable time in cask to soften and round, and periods of two years in cask (for Chianti Classico Riserva, and Vino Nobile di Montepulciano), or even three years in cask (for Brunello di Montalcino and Barolo), are by no means uncommon.

OAK has generally been the preferred wood for casks, much of it from Slavonia or elsewhere in central Europe. In the south of Italy, in areas such as Basilicata and Sicily, where chestnut forests abound and there are no local sources of oak, the traditional chestnut cooperage has been gradually replaced by oak casks to achieve a more international style and to avoid the bitterness which old chestnut casks can impart, although several producers, notably Tasca d'Almerita of Sicily, are gradually returning to chestnut.

The 1980s and 1990s saw Italian cellars invaded en masse by new French BARRIQUES, perhaps an inevitable development in convincing the world of Italy's potential. Sangiovese and Barbera were the first varieties to be widely aged in new small oak barrels, and the generally positive results led to widespread use of BARREL MATURATION, yielding both excellent results and some heavily over-oaked wines. This century there is a marked return to larger, older casks (with considerations of HYGIENE paramount) in order to avoid dominating the flavours of Italy's indigenous grape varieties with those of oak.

General inexperience in modern winemaking techniques was a chronic problem in Italy, and for Italian wine to be considered 'fine' it was felt, rightly or wrongly, that it had to emulate red bordeaux. This led to a major boom, particularly in the 1980s and 1990s, in the employment of consulting OENOLOGISTS. Media coverage of the exploits of individual consultants threatened to overshadow the significance both of specific estates and of individual TERROIRS.

Vine varieties

No country has more INDIGENOUS VARIETIES—many hundreds—than Italy and this is increasingly celebrated by a new wave of growers keen to rediscover local specialities. Virtually every article about individual wines reveals the country's wealth of vine varieties. Italy conducts a viticultural census every ten years. According to the 2010 report, the most planted variety was Sardinia's TORBATO Bianco, with a total of 32,000 ha/79,000 acres, closely followed by the much more widespread SANGIOVESE with 29,200 ha, down from 86,000 ha in 1990. Third most planted was Sicily's white wine grape CATARRATTO with 25,900 ha. The only other varieties planted on more than 20,000 ha were the PRIMITIVO of Puglia with 23,000 ha and the BARBERA of north western Italy with 20,000 ha. Perhaps surprising was that the next most planted variety, with 19,700 ha, was Chardonnay, its total presumably boosted by its popularity with producers of sparkling wines. Varieties planted on a total of between 10,000 and 20,000 ha, in declining order, are Nero d'Avola, Montepulciano, Merlot (down from 48,000 ha in 1990), Trebbiano Toscano, Cabernet Sauvignon, Pinot Bianco, Pinot Grigio, and the Soave grape Garganega. The relatively modest total area planted with Pinot Grigio, 10,000 ha, may surprise those aware of the oceans of neutral white wine exported from Italy labelled with that varietal name.

Large-scale plantings of INTERNATIONAL VARIETIES—principally French, although there is also some Riesling and Gewurztraminer—were initially confined to the country's north east (which, in many cases, was under either direct Austrian rule or strong Austrian influence until 1919). They are planted in an arc stretching from Franciacorta, in the eastern part of Lombardia, through Trentino-Alto Adige, the northern part of Veneto (the provinces of Vicenza and Treviso), and Friuli. Subsequent plantings of international varieties tended to follow international FASHION: various

members of the Pinot family in the 1970s; Chardonnay, Sauvignon Blanc, and Cabernet in the 1980s; Syrah and Viognier in the 1990s. Central Italy, with only the late-ripening Sangiovese an important red grape and with the relatively uninteresting Trebbiano Toscano as its major white grape, has seen considerable plantings of Cabernet, Merlot, and Syrah, especially on the Tuscan coast. But overall the fashion for international varieties is waning, even if some producers and producer associations still seem to view the inclusion of some of them in official regulations as a passport to commercial success.

Organization of trade

Italy's wine trade resembles those of its European neighbours in terms of a division of labour between individual properties, commercial and NÉGOCIANT houses, and CO-OPERATIVE wineries. What distinguishes Italy is the overwhelming importance of the latter two categories, a dominance which is the direct result of the extreme fractioning of vineyard property with individual holdings averaging just 1.8 ha/4.45 acres. Middlemen for the marketing of the wines, be they négociants or co-operatives, are thus indispensable links in the distribution chain which connects growers to consumers. Private estates of a certain size are an important reality in Tuscany, Puglia, and Sicily, and, to a lesser extent, in Friuli, while the development of a significant number of prestigious small 'domaines' in the finest zones of Piemonte might be considered a riposte to BURGUNDY.

Large commercial houses were a relatively late development in Italy, virtually all of them having been founded after the unification of the country in 1861 and thus being a century younger than comparable houses in France, Spain, and Portugal. The reasons for their late foundation and slow growth are far from mysterious: Italy was not a country prior to her unification and the movement of merchandise across the borders of the many small states which existed in the peninsula was a costly and cumbersome procedure. REDDING cites 'a vexatious system of imposts' as a major cause of Italian viticultural backwardness in the 19th century, a backwardness which was a hindrance commercially, as well as technically. There was very little in the way of a national market, and little knowledge of even the finest products outside their specific production zones. Even today, négociant houses are a major presence only in Tuscany, Veneto, and Sicily, while co-operative wineries play a significant role in virtually all Italian regions.

Co-operatives became the dominant force in the production and distribution of Italian

wine in the late 20th century, a logical development considering the political dominance of the Christian Democratic party in the country's various governments and the favour shown to co-operative movements in the social doctrine of the Roman Catholic church. Income maintenance has been as significant a concern as the products themselves; this objective has entailed large volumes, which, thanks to ample subsidies, could be marketed at low prices. Quality has not always been the strong point of the resulting wines, although individual co-operatives, particularly in the north, have always been responsive to the market and conscious of the need to create products that would please consumer palates. Italy enjoyed particular success in the 1970s and 1980s with its exports of the Riunite co-ops' LAMBRUSCO. Pinot Grigio could be said to have replaced this sweet, foaming red as the commercial ballast of Italy's wine exports.

As EU and national subsidies are reduced, Italian wines will have to respond more readily to free market economics. While the total volume of wine produced has declined considerably, consumption within Italy has declined even faster, and Italy now exports around 70% of its wine, making full use of EU marketing incentives to help sell its wines in third markets.

There can be few doubts that Italy's new prosperity and the worldwide popularity of Italian food have changed prospects and possibilities for Italian wine and created a new viewpoint amongst the country's producers. And there can be even fewer doubts that admirers and enthusiasts of Italian wine have never had such an embarrassment of riches as at the beginning of the third millennium AD.

For details of individual regions, see ABRUZZO, ALTO ADIGE, PUGLIA, BASILICATA, CALABRIA, CAMPANIA, EMILIA-ROMAGNA, FRIULI, LAZIO, LIGURIA, LOMBARDIA, MARCHE, MOLISE, PIEMONTE, SARDINIA, SICILY, TRENTINO, TUSCANY, UMBRIA, Valle d'AOSTA, and VENETO.

For details of terms to be found on Italian wine labels, see CLASSICO, DOC, DOCG, IGT, and RISERVA. According to the reorganized EU wine categories, a wine that fails to qualify as any of these is a WINE WITHOUT GEOGRAPHICAL INDICATION and is labelled simply VINO.   W.S.

Anderson, B., *Wine Atlas of Italy* (London, 1990).

Belfrage, N., *From Barolo to Valpolicella: The Wines of Northern Italy* (2nd edn, London, 2003).

Belfrage, N., *From Brunello to Zibibbo: The Wines of Southern Italy* (2nd edn, London, 2003).

Fabrizio, G., Guerini, E., and Sabellico, M., *Gambero Rosso Vini d'Italia* (Roma, 2014).

Gariglio, G., and Giavedoni, F. (eds.), *Slow Wine* (Bra, 2014).

Giavedoni, F., and Gily, M. (eds.), *Guida ai Vitigni d'Italia. Storia e Charatteristiche di 600 Varietà Autoctone* (Bra, 2011).

Johnson, H., and Robinson, J., *The World Atlas of Wine* (7th edn, London, 2013).

Robinson, J., Harding, J., and Vouillamoz, J., *Wine Grapes—a complete guide to 1,368 vine varieties, including their origins and flavours* (London, 2012).

Soldati, M., *Vino al Vino* (7th edn, Milan, 2010).

Masnaghetti, A. (ed.), *Enogea—Newsletter Bimestrale Indipendente (bi-monthly newsletter about Italian wine)*, (Faenza).

http://dati-censimentoagricoltura.istat.it

www.federdoc.com/pdf/VQPRD-2013.pdf

Itata, subregion of the Southern region of CHILE.

IVDP, Instituto do Vinho do Douro e do Porto, which governs the production of both PORT and DOURO wine.

Jaboulet Aîné, Paul, important RHÔNE Valley merchant and wine producer, whose most famous wine is Hermitage la Chapelle. The house was founded in the early 19th century by Antoine Jaboulet and takes its name from the older of his twin sons. Jaboulet's own vineyard holdings in production, which provide between a quarter and a third of the firm's needs, totalled more than 115 ha/2,85 acres in 2014, in every northern Rhône appellation. Recent acquisitions included additional holdings in Hermitage and Crozes-Hermitage, a stake in Condrieu (first vintage 1996), Domaine St-Pierre in Cornas (1994), most of Domaine Raymond Roure in Crozes-Hermitage (1996), Domaine des Pierrelles in Côte Rôtie (2006), and Domaine de Terre Ferme in Châteauneuf-du-Pape (2007). Of the raw materials bought in, from 150 growers the length of the Rhône valley, two-thirds is wine rather than grapes, and in the late 1990s quality was notably variable. The firm was based in its old cellars in Tain l'Hermitage from 1834 until 1984 when a modern winery and warehouse was built in La Roche de Glun just south of the town. Jaboulet sell a range of more than 20 different wines, most of them in the firm's own deep-PUNTED bottle, and the best are their own special cuvées. Their CROZES-HERMITAGE, Domaine de Thalabert, was some of the earliest proof offered to wine drinkers outside France that this appellation could produce serious, age-worthy wine. The firm's La Chapelle 1961 is an acknowledged classic. The white Hermitage, Chevalier de Stérimberg, demonstrates the late Gérard Jaboulet's admiration for the ROUSSANNE grape. In 2005, after years of under-performance, the company was sold to the Frey family, owners of Ch La Lagune in Bordeaux and investors in Champagne Billecart Salmon.

Livingstone-Learmonth, J., *The Wines of the Northern Rhône* (Berkeley, Calif. 2005).

Norman, R., *Rhône Renaissance* (London, 1995).

Jackson Family Wines. See KENDALL-JACKSON.

Jacob's Creek, leading wine BRAND of PERNOD RICARD, France's share of the Australian wine boom. Some bottlings in the Reserve range, especially Steingarten Riesling, can be impressive.

Jacquère is the most planted white grape variety in SAVOIE, where it produces high yields of lightly scented, essentially alpine dry white. Plantings were a steady 983 ha/2,428 acres in 2011.

Late ripening and relatively hardy, it has also been successfully grown for IGP blends in some CONDRIEU and other northern Rhône vineyards, and is found further south.

Jacquez, dark-skinned American hybrid grown in TEXAS thanks to its resistance to PIERCE'S DISEASE, and in Brazil for everyday wines and juice

Jadot, Louis, merchant-grower based in BEAUNE, dealing exclusively in Burgundy and owners of 68 ha/168 acres of vineyards in the CÔTE D'OR, 87 ha/214 acres in BEAUJOLAIS, and 18 ha/44 acres in Fuissé in the MÂCONNAIS. The company has been owned by the Kopf family since 1985. Founded in 1859 by the eponymous Louis Jadot, the company was run from 1962 to 1992 by André Gagey, who joined the firm as an assistant in 1954. When Louis-Alain Jadot, last of the family line, died prematurely in 1968, Gagey was asked by the family to become general manager, and he has now been succeeded by his son Pierre-Henry. Jadot's success has been very much due to the combined talents of André Gagey and winemaker Jacques Lardière. who retired in 2013 to be succeeded by François Barnier. Both red and white NÉGOCIANT wines, made from bought-in fruit, are thoroughly reliable, but the firm's reputation is based on the high quality of its domaine wines. Jadot's holdings have continued to increase, not least in Beaujolais, notably Ch des Jacques in the 1990s and Domaine Ferret in 2008. The company also manages and vinifies the Côte d'Or vineyards of Domaine Gagey and Domaine Duc de Magenta A large, beautiful, and flexible new winery was built on the Jadot premises in 1997 and another one in Givry in the Côte Chalonnaise in 2008 exclusively dedicated to the BOURGOGNE appellation. Among the reds, the Côte de Beaune wines stand out, with the MONOPOLE Beaune, Clos des Ursules, being especially fine. The domaine whites are wines of concentration, class, and distinction. Never over-oaked, they are a clear expression of their TERROIR and wines such as their Puligny-Montrachet Les Folatières, Corton-Charlemagne, and Chevalier-Montrachet Les Demoiselles, are regularly among the best bottles of white burgundy to be had.   M.W.E.S.

Jaen, **Jaen Tinto**, and **Jaen du Dão**, synonym for the MENCÍA red wine grape in Portugal's DÃO region, where it ripens early to produce deep-coloured wines that are notable for their lack of acidity. Occasionally seen as a VARIETAL, it is normally stiffened with Touriga Nacional and Alfrocheiro. The vine, planted on a total of 2,747 ha/6,785 acres in northern Portugal in 2013, is identical to Galicia's Mencía. **Jaén Blanco** is a synonym for CAYETANA Blanca.

Jahrgang, German for VINTAGE (as in the year rather than the HARVEST process, for which the word is *Ernte*).

Jakot, Slovenian name for the FRIULANO vine variety, the old name Tokaj spelt backwards.

Japan. Grape-growing and, to a lesser extent, wine production have a long history in this Far Eastern country, even though wine drinking on any appreciable scale is a relatively recent phenomenon. Between 1990 and 2012 wine consumption more than doubled but is still only 2.6 l per capita—low by European standards, but by far the highest in Asia. There are now more than 200 domestic wineries in all 47 prefectures and sales under domestic labels accounted for 32% of total wine sales in Japan in 2010.

History

Legend has it that grape-growing began at Katsunuma, in Yamanashi prefecture of central Honshu. As the story goes, in the year 718 the Buddha Nyorai passed vines to a holy man by the name of Gyoki, who planted the vines at Katsunuma, where he built the Daizenji Temple.

It was the grape itself, rather than wine, in which the Japanese were initially interested. The monks taught that grapes had medicinal value. The statue of Nyorai, which Gyoki had carved in his honour and which is still housed in the temple today, was named Budo Yakushi (*budo* meaning grape; and *yakushi* meaning teacher of medicine) by pilgrims to the temple.

Wine may, perhaps, have been made from local grapes in Katsunuma in earlier times but wine consumption in Japan had not been documented until the arrival of Portuguese MISSIONARIES in the 16th century. The Jesuit missionary St Francis Xavier carried wine as gifts for the feudal lords of Kyushu in southern Japan whom he visited in 1545. Others who followed him continued the practice so that the locals acquired a taste for wine and began to import it regularly.

They called the wine *tintashu*, combining the Japanese word for sake (*shu*) with a derivative of the Portuguese word for red (TINTO).

During the Tokugawa shogunate of the 17th century, the missionaries were expelled, Christians persecuted, and practices associated with Christianity, such as drinking wine, condemned. Ironically, however, the choice of Edo as the Tokugawa capital (on the site of modern Tokyo) was a boost for the farmers of nearby Yamanashi: their grapes quickly came to be prized for the tables of the shogun's court.

Eventually, in 1874, the first attempts at commercial winemaking were undertaken in Yamanashi, where grape-growing had begun over a millennium before. Three years later, in 1877, two disciples of the founder of one of the earliest commercial wineries visited France to study European viticulture and oenology. The early product was not good, but the effort was enough to convince local authorities to permit the import of European VINIFERA and AMERICAN VINES as the basis for a new industry.

Today, the viticultural industry is modest, but entrenched—and still focused mostly on producing TABLE GRAPES, rather than on providing top-quality raw material for WINEMAKING.

Geography and climate

Three prefectures (Yamanashi, Nagano, and Yamagata) on the main island Honshu account for almost 40% of the 17,600 ha/43,564 acres (a little less than in the early years of the century) under vine throughout Japan.

Production is in the order of 198,300 tonnes of grapes per year, although only one-tenth of these grapes is used for winemaking. The bulk of the production is for the table, and the grape varieties under cultivation and viticultural practices reflect this.

Japan's climate is not naturally suited to viticulture and successful grape-growing has always been a struggle.

In **Yamanashi** prefecture, where a quarter of Japan's grapes are grown and where 58 wineries are located, a monsoonal climate presents a serious problem of excess water and HUMIDITY. Here, and in most of the prefectures of Honshu, vines traditionally have been trained on to overhead wires or platforms (*budodana*) so that the bunches will hang lower than the foliage and be more freely exposed to circulating air. This PERGOLA method of cultivation, known in Japan as Tana-Shitate, was developed as a defence against FUNGAL DISEASES and has been reasonably effective. VINE DENSITY is notoriously low. There may be only 50–100 vines per hectare but other growers use training systems such as CORDON DE ROYAT for European varieties, entailing much higher vine density.

Grapes from the district of Katsunuma, with about 15% of the prefecture's vines, are those generally preferred by winemakers. Katsunuma

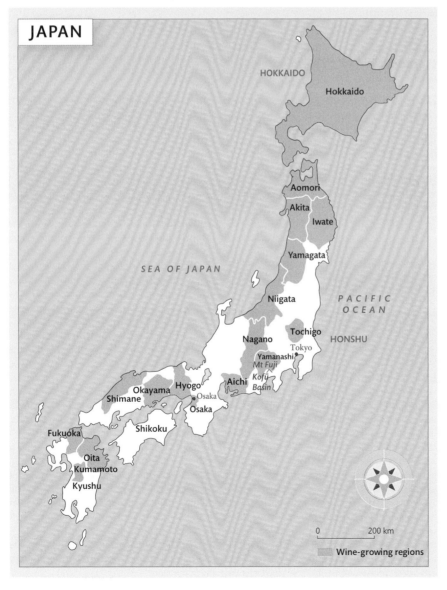

JAPAN

HOKKAIDO

Hokkaido

Aomori

Akita

Iwate

Yamagata

SEA OF JAPAN

Niigata

PACIFIC OCEAN

Nagano

Tochigo

HONSHU

Tokyo

Yamanashi

Mt Fuji

Aichi

Kofu Basin

Hyogo

Okayama

Osaka

Shimane

Osaka

Fukuoka

Shikoku

Oita

Kumamoto

Kyushu

0   200 km

Wine-growing regions

fares considerably better climatically than districts lower down in the Kofu Basin. Rainfall is lower, it has better DRAINAGE because of its higher ELEVATION, gets a refreshing breeze, which helps control rot and mildew, has a wider diurnal temperature variation (see TEMPERATURE VARIABILITY) and better ripening conditions for wine grapes generally.

Nagano and **Yamagata**, the prefectures where most of the recent growth in the industry has been concentrated, do better again but conditions are still far from ideal. Nagano had 26 wineries and Yamagata 11 in the mid 2010s.

In the 1960s, a second frontier of the modern Japanese industry was opened up in an even more unlikely location, in central **Hokkaido**, Japan's northernmost island. This is an extremely cold environment for grape-growing. Average temperatures rise to only about 23 °C/73 °F in July, August, and the early part of September. By the end of September, average temperatures are about 15 °C and, by October, below 10 °C. Vineyards are covered in deep snow for most of the winter and vines are given WINTER PROTECTION by being buried in heaped soil to avoid damage. In Hokkaido, canes are trained low along horizontal wires, in contrast to the Tana-Shitate technique. This region is characterized by much lower summer rainfall than on Honshu with some new boutique wineries specializing in ORGANIC VITICULTURE emerging in and around the developing area of Iwamizara.

Japanese vineyard soils are in general very acid see PH, SOILS.

Vine varieties

History, the dominant demand for TABLE GRAPES, and the climatic vagaries with which growers have had to contend over the years, have combined to result in the rather exotic range of grape varieties which form the basis of viticulture in Japan.

The most significant Japanese variety, and the undoubted sentimental favourite of the Japanese, is KOSHU. This is the descendant of the vines carried along the Silk Road to Japan 800 to 1,200 years ago and, in the public eye at least, is virtually synonymous with the industry of Katsunuma, which has over 90% of the total Koshu vineyard area.

Koshu has survived as an important variety because it has adapted to the difficult growing conditions in Yamanashi prefecture and because it is supported by long tradition.

A Koshu cousin, Ryugan (also known as Zenkoji, and probably distinct from the Longyan of CHINA), is grown only in tiny quantities, chiefly in Nagano prefecture in central Honshu. As with Koshu, Neo-Muscat and Ryugan produce grapes which are best suited to the table, but which are also made into light and generally sweetish wine.

However, the vines which are by far the most widely planted throughout Japan, accounting for almost 90% of the total area under vine, are HYBRIDS based on *Vitis* LABRUSCA, most of which were introduced directly from the US.

They have generally performed well in the difficult local growing conditions and, most importantly, have provided the best commercial results for growers attuned primarily to the table-grape market. In particular, as the highest prices are attracted by the first fruit onto the market each season, the fact that many of them are early-ripening varieties has been very attractive to growers.

Kyoho, a local hybrid of the American variety CONCORD, is now the most widely grown in Japan, comprising 35% of the vineyard area. DELAWARE follows with 20%. Campbell Early was once a clear second, but is now fourth. Kyoho has been further bred to produce a rash of minor varieties aimed at achieving better-quality table grapes, including Pione (possibly identical to Thailand's POKDUM), which is now the third ranked variety and produces quite creditable VARIETAL rosé. Another popular hybrid is Muscat Bailey A, planted on more than 450 ha/1,110 acres and gaining in popularity as a wine grape. It makes fresh, fruity, light-bodied wine although oaked versions are not unknown.

All of these varieties actually find their way into wine, even though the vines were not bred originally, nor are grown specifically in modern Japan, for this purpose. Grapes which for some reason fail to satisfy requirements as table grapes, or those which ripen late in the season, often end up at the wineries, providing the domestic component of many of the lower priced local labels.

Industry organization

Japan's first (and much-vaunted in Europe) 'wine boom' saw per capita consumption double during the 1980s, albeit from a low base. Consumption levelled off towards the end of the decade but a second wine boom quickly gathered momentum around 1993, when a strong yen encouraged a surge in imports.

Initially they had focused on investment in modern winemaking equipment and on training their winemakers in the methods used in the major wine-producing nations (Suntory even went so far as to buy the ST-JULIEN classed growth Ch Lagrange, and the 1980s saw several substantial Japanese investments in the German, California, and Australian wine industries). They had hoped that this, along with various practices in the winery aimed at extracting more flavour and body from the flimsy local fruit base, would be sufficient to match the competition from the foreign producers whose attention to the Japanese market had been attracted by its rapid growth, by the potential

associated with 128 million affluent people, by favourable exchange rates, and by the relaxation of import barriers.

The domestic industry has also tried to hold its ground by using imported BULK WINE, GRAPE CONCENTRATE, MUST, and even imported grapes to extend the quantity and improve the quality of its own base material. Labelling laws have allowed considerable leeway for producers in this regard and some wines sold under domestic BRANDS are known to contain the barest minimum of genuine domestic material. Although the market share of domestic labels has fallen from 75% in 1982 to 35% in 2010, four in every five of these domestic bottlings contain wine made by using imported bulk wine and/or grape concentrate. Some leading winemaking prefectures impose their own labelling regulations to satisfy customers' demands for authenticity of domestic wine, however. Since the National Tax Agency designated Yamanashi as a GEOGRAPHICAL INDICATION, all wines so labelled must be made from 100% Yamanashi grapes. Wine must be made from 100% Koshu to be labelled Koshu. Nagano prefecture east of Yamanashi established their own strict NAC regulations (Nagano Appellation Controlee) in 2003, before Yamanashi.

But the structure of the industry militates against rapid progress. The average vineyard size is less than 0.5 ha/1.2 acres.

Price maximization is essential to maintain a viable income for small grape-growers and when table grapes can command a price four or five times the price winemakers are prepared to pay, it is hard to imagine that the bulk of the existing growers will change their ways. Vineyards dedicated solely to producing wine grapes are the answer but there are still too few of them.

The large domestic wine producers rely overwhelmingly on bought-in grapes. Most of them also have vineyards, but these are small and primarily for experimental purposes. Some of the giants also focus on quality and play a leading role in CLONAL SELECTION and research into other techniques best suited to the climate, soil type, and ELEVATION in Japan.

Cabernet Sauvignon and Cabernet Franc have been planted in the west of Yamanashi prefecture with some reasonable results; Chardonnay, Petit Verdot, and Merlot look fairly well suited to Nagano; and northern European varieties such as Müller-Thurgau, Zweigelt, and particularly Kerner, have done well in Hokkaido. Yet European varieties comprised little more than 1% of the total area under vine in the mid 2000s and, with the exception of a few hectares of Cabernet Sauvignon, almost all have been planted since the 1970s.

In contrast to the fragmentation of the grape-growing industry, winemaking is extraordinarily concentrated.

Five giant, diversified beverage conglomerates—Mercian, Suntory, Asahi (Ste Neige), Sapporo (Polaire), and Kikkoman soy sauce maker subsidiary Manns Wine (Solaris, Manns)—account for more than 80% of the total sales of domestic wine (including locally bottled imported bulk wines and blends). But some of the best wines in Japan are made by much smaller family-owned or city-owned wineries. In Hokkaido, new wineries such as Taru and Domaine Takahiko have emerged following the success of Tokachi winery. In Yamanashi, benchmark Koshu is produced by Marufuji (Rubaiyat label), Katsunuma (Aruga Branca), and Grace wineries. Other small wineries with a reputation for quality include L'Atelier de Beau Paysage, Kanai Jozojo, Kizan Yoshu-Kogyo (in Yamanashi prefecture) and Hayashi Noen, Izutsu, Obuse Domaine Sogga, and Kido (all in Nagano prefecture), Takeda (Yamagata), Okuizumo (Shimane), Coco Farm (Tochigi), Kuzumaki specializing in *yamabudo* varieties and hybrids (Iwate), Kumamoto specializing in Chardonnay and Tsuno (the southernmost winery in Japan, in Miyazaki prefecture).　K.O.

Jasnières, white wine appellation of just 50 ha/124 acres in an enclave within the less favourably exposed Coteaux du LOIR district in the northern Loire. The appellation all but expired in the 1950s but Joël Gigou at Domaine de la Charrière and others such as Domaine Renard-Potaire have injected new passion into the making of these traditionally dry wines from the Chenin Blanc grape. Locals see Jasnières as 'the SAVENNIÈRES of Touraine', so dry and steely are these traditional wines in their youth, and so well do they respond to BOTTLE AGEING. In particularly ripe vintages since the late 1980s, however, extraordinarily rich, appley, BOTRYTIZED wines have been fashioned, either dry or sweet according to the extent of NOBLE ROT infection. The soils are characterized by their high flint content, on the south-east-facing slopes on the north bank of the Loir. Annual production of Jasnières is about double that of white Coteaux du Loir. See also LOIRE, including map.

Jefferson, Thomas (1743–1826), third president of the United States, a wine lover whose interest in wine and hopes for American wine-growing typified the early Republic. As a VIRGINIA farmer, Jefferson grew grapes from all sources, native (see VITIS, AMERICAN VINE SPECIES) and VINIFERA, at his estate Monticello for 50 years with uniform lack of success: no Monticello wine ever materialized, but the hope never died. His vineyard at Monticello has been restored to the form it had in 1807.

As ambassador to France (1784–9), Jefferson made himself expert in wine, travelling to all the major French wine regions as well as to those of Germany and Italy. He tasted, discussed, and

bought largely, and acted also as agent and adviser for his friends in the selection and purchase of wines. The record of this activity contained in his papers is a small encyclopedia of pre-Revolutionary wine and wine production. As president (1801–9), Jefferson was celebrated for the variety and excellence of his cellar at the White House in Washington, which abounded in CHAMBERTIN, MARGAUX, HERMITAGE, YQUEM, and TOKAY.

After his retirement from public life, living on a much-reduced scale, Jefferson turned to the wines of the south: the reds of BELLET and MONTEPULCIANO, for example, and the Muscat of RIVESALTES. He spared no effort to ensure a good supply from good sources. At all times, Jefferson was eager to assist the many efforts to solve the riddle of successful wine-growing in America: he gave land next to his Virginia estate to support Philip Mazzei's Italian Vineyard Society, an ambitious effort to grow wine by importing Italian vines and vineyard workers; he encouraged such neighbours as James Madison and James Monroe in their viticultural experiments; it was during his administration that land on the river Ohio in Indiana was granted to Swiss-born J. J. Dufour for the enterprise that resulted in the first successful commercial wine production in the UNITED STATES.

By such assistance, and by minimizing wine TAXATION, Jefferson hoped to make the US a wine-drinking country. He could be extravagant in his optimism: a wine from the native Alexander grape he called equal to Chambertin; a sweet SCUPPERNONG from North Carolina he thought would be 'distinguished on the best tables of Europe'. The US, he affirmed, could 'make as great a variety of wines as are made in Europe, not exactly of the same kind, but doubtless as good', even though his own experience contradicted the proposition.

Jefferson's personal pleasure in wine was clear: 'Good wine is a daily necessity for me,' he wrote. He also saw wine as an element in his vision of a nation of independent yeomen: 'no nation is drunken where wine is cheap,' hence wine should be the nation's drink. Despite his failures in practical vine-growing, Jefferson is the great patron of the idea that the US should be a wine-growing nation.　T.P.

Bottles of late-18th-century wines such as Ch LAFITE, supposedly ordered and even initialled by Jefferson, fetched record-breaking prices at AUCTION in the late 20th century but were subsequently shown to be COUNTERFEIT.

de Treville Lawrence, R. (ed.), *Jefferson and Wine* (2nd edn, The Plains, Va., 1989).

Gabler, J. M., *Passions: The Wines and Travels of Thomas Jefferson* (Baltimore, 1995).

jerepigo or **jerepiko**, unfermented dessert 'wines' in South Africa, the Cape's version of MISTELLE produced by adding alcohol before

fermentation to grape juice, generally from inland regions. Many are made from MUSCADEL, which name on the label may legally serve to indicate style as well as variety. Initially about 17% alcohol, many are now closer to a more recent lower limit of 15%, often with intense ripe fig and MUSCAT flavours. These traditional, warming wines, both red and white, once popular in South African winters but now sold in ever-declining volumes, probably derive their name from JEROPIGA.

Jerez, or **Jerez de la Frontera**, city in ANDALUCÍA, south west Spain, that is the centre of the sherry industry. Jerez is also the name of the DO which produces sherry. In Spain the wine is known as *vino de Jerez* (or simply *Jerez*), and sherry is an English corruption of the Spanish word (while in France the town and drink are known respectively as *Xérès* and *xérès*). The town owes its full name to the fact that in the Middle Ages it was on the frontier between Christian and Moorish Spain. For more details of Jerez's history and organization, see SHERRY.

jeroboam. See BOTTLE SIZES.

jeropiga, Portuguese term for grape must prevented from fermenting by the addition of grape spirit. *Jeropiga* is often used to sweeten FORTIFIED WINES. (*Vinho abafado*, on the other hand, is partially fermented before spirit is added; see CARCAVELOS.)

jetting. See SPARKLING WINEMAKING.

Jewish heritage in German wine culture. By their Christian names, they could not be distinguished from their colleagues in Prussia or elsewhere in Germany. But by their family names, many of the late-19th-century champions of the wine trade in Germany could be easily identified as Jewish: the sons of Hermann SICHEL, who spread from the old Rhenish wine capital Mainz throughout Europe and conquered the New World; Leo Levitta, who was raised in Rüdesheim on the Rhine; Julius Langenbach, a citizen of Worms, the town that centuries ago hosted one of the largest Jewish communities north of the Alps; and Sigmund Loeb, who had deserted the windy Hunsrück only to become one of the most renowned wine merchants of Trier and president of the Moselle Trade Association. In the last quarter of the 19th century, some excellent vintages, peace in notoriously war-torn Europe, and the free-trade spirit during the first wave of GLOBALIZATION helped propel Jews to the forefront of the German wine trade. Their centuries-old mercantile skills helped, as did the European aristocracy and nouveau-riche bourgeoisie's desire to acquire what were then regarded as the world's finest wines, as well as a thirst among emigrant communities throughout the Americas for wine from their German homeland.

Although Jews formed a significant part of the national and international German wine trade, there is no evidence that they endured particular scrutiny during the anti-semitic stirrings at the end of the 19th century. There was certainly some unease when Jewish brokers and merchants formed quasi-monopolistic structures, such as those in Franken and the southern Pfalz. But according to the few sources available, there was neither stigma nor bias toward Jews by government officials in the prosecution of wine ADULTERATION AND FRAUD. And during the First World War, German Jews turned out to be as patriotic as everybody else. Sigmund Loeb's only son Otto was not the only one to fight in France.

When the war was over, the main export markets for German wine were off limits. The victorious UK despised the symbols of German prepotency, PROHIBITION had closed the US market, and Russia was torn apart by the Bolshevist revolution. In the 1920s, most parts of Western Europe stumbled from one political and economical crisis into another. The German wine market was close to collapsing and, as a result, so was the business of brokers and merchants. Once again, the Jews drew on their skills and their international networks. Alfred Fromm moved from Franken to Bingen across the Rhine from the Rheingau where he set up a new export business; the Sichels created the famous BLUE NUN—one of the first BRANDS in wine history. When Hitler was elected in 1933, some 60% of German wine was traded by Jewish agents and merchants, which was the main reason the Nazis held back from cracking down immediately on the Jewish wine community. The other reason: by exporting high-value wine, Jewish merchants delivered the precious foreign currency that the Nazis needed for the German war machine.

Only after the Olympic games in 1936 in Berlin, by which time non-Jewish wine marketing had consolidated, did the Nazis crack down on Jewish brokers, merchants, and retailers. Families such as the Levittas split up with some members heading into exile; Sigmund Loeb's son, Otto Wolfgang, had already founded a subsidiary in London, O. W. Loeb, and managed to introduce opera lovers at the Glyndebourne Festival to Moselle wines; the Sichels eventually escaped to London and the US.

The 'Reichskristallnacht' in November 1938 marked the beginning of the final extinction of Jewish entrepreneurship in Germany. Those who had not left Germany were forced to sell their businesses or lost permission to do so. Although there are no detailed records, it seems that quite a number of merchants survived the Holocaust, thanks to their international contacts. However, the brokers whose work was based on their local networks were murdered or gassed. Ludwig Levitta, one of the finest palates of his time, was deported with his wife and son to Theresienstadt and perished at Auschwitz in 1943.

In spite of the Holocaust, most of the exiled Jews did not hesitate to engage in the German wine trade again and to restore the reputation of German wine in the UK and the US. Alfred Langenbach (d. 1964) published *The Wines of Germany*, the first comprehensive survey of German wines ever published in the English language (London 1951). Fritz Hallgarten (d. 1991) documented his experiences in his memoir *Rhineland-Wineland* (London 1951), and Otto W. Loeb (d. 1974) drew on his and his father's unique knowledge for his book, *Moselle* (1971).

By that time, Otto W. Loeb's efforts to initiate hundreds of members of Cambridge University Wine & Food Society into the mysteries of German Riesling and the wines of California had borne plenty of fruit—Hugh JOHNSON was one of the best and brightest of his adepts. Alfred Fromm (d. 1998) had joined Franz W. Sichel in influencing the reorientation of the California wine industry towards quality wine. Today, with Peter Max F. Sichel (b. 1923) still active in the wine world from his base in New York and O. W. Loeb of London still selling fine German wine, the Jewish heritage of German wine cultural is still alive and, one hopes, will never be forgotten.   D.Ds.

João de Santarém, name used for the widely planted CASTELÃO red wine grape in parts of the TEJO region of Portugal.

Johannisberg, Valais name for fuller-than-average dry white wine made from SILVANER grapes in SWITZERLAND.

Johnson, Hugh (1939–), world's bestselling wine author. Johnson's passion for wine began when he was at Cambridge University, where he read English. One of the great stylists of the LITERATURE OF WINE, he was immediately taken on as a feature writer for Condé Nast magazines on graduation. As a result of his close friendship with André SIMON, the founder of the International Wine & Food Society, he became General Secretary of the society and succeeded the legendary gastronome as editor of its magazine. At the same time he became wine correspondent of the *Sunday Times* and embarked on his first book *Wine*, whose publication in 1966 established him as one of the foremost English gastronomic writers of the time. More than 750,000 copies have been printed, in seven languages. He revised it in 1974.

His next book was even more successful, even though it allowed only limited scope for Johnson's matchless prose. *The World Atlas of Wine* represented the first serious attempt to map the world's wine regions, and first appeared in 1971. More than 4.5 million copies in a total of 20 languages have been sold of this and subsequent editions in 1977, 1985, 1994 the fully updated 2001 edition, 2007, and 2013 editions, co-written with J. R.

Pausing only to write a best-selling book on trees, *The International Book of Trees*, inspired by his acquisition of an Elizabethan house in 12 acres of Essex countryside, he went on to devise and write a best-selling annual wine guide, *The Pocket Wine Book*, which has sold more than 12 million copies in a dozen languages, since its first edition in 1977.

The more expansive *Hugh Johnson's Wine Companion* followed in 1983 and was revised in 1987, 1991, 1997, and 2003. It sold widely in the US as *Hugh Johnson's Modern Encyclopedia of Wine*, and in France as *Le Guide mondial du connaisseur de vin*, and in Germany as *Der Grosse Johnson*. This prolific output, encouraged by Johnson's publishers Mitchell Beazley, was supplemented by *The Principles of Gardening*, another bestseller, and a succession of co-authored and less serious wine books (including even a 'pop-up' version).

Johnson's most distinctive work, however, did not appear until 1989. *The Story of Wine* is a *tour de force*, a single-volume sweep through the history of wine in which Johnson's literary skills and breadth of vision are headily combined. The book was written to coincide with an ambitiously international 13-part television series, *Vintage: A History of Wine*, written and presented by Johnson. In 1992, he co-authored *The Art and Science of Wine* with Australian James Halliday. *A Life Uncorked* (2005) is his most reflective and autobiographical work.

Between 1986 and 2000 Johnson sold the Hugh Johnson Collection, glassware and other wine-related artefacts, with notable success in Japan, where he was a consultant to Jardines Wines and Spirits. He also served (1986–2001) on the administrative council of first growth Ch LATOUR, as a consultant to British Airways, and has been president of the Sunday Times Wine Club run by LAITHWAITE's since its inception in 1973. In 1990, Johnson co-founded The Royal TOKAJI Wine Company, a reflection of his interest in wine history. Other activities include regular journalism on and enthusiastic gardening. For 25 years from 1975 he was editorial director of the *Journal of the Royal Horticultural Society*. In 2005, none too hastily one might argue, the French made him a Chevalier de l'Ordre National du Mérite.

Johnson is one of the most vocal opponents of SCORING wine, and his writing has been characterized more by a sensual enthusiasm for wine in all its variety than by the critical analysis of individual wines which characterizes writers such as the American Robert PARKER.

His daughter Kitty followed him into wine writing.

Johnson, H., *Wine: A Life Uncorked* (London, 2005).

joint venture, common phenomenon in the late 20th century whereby two enterprises with very different strengths combine to produce a wine or wines. The modern prototype was that announced in 1979 between Baron Philippe de ROTHSCHILD of Bordeaux and Robert MONDAVI of California to produce Opus One, the luxuriously priced Napa Valley Cabernet Sauvignon, combining Mondavi's knowledge of and holdings in the Napa Valley with the prestige and winemaking expertise associated with Baron Philippe's first growth Pauillac Ch MOUTON-ROTHSCHILD. Most joint ventures are designed to justify a premium over the other wines made *in situ* by virtue of a much-heralded connection with a glamorous outsider. Both Mondavi and the Mouton team embarked on subsequent joint ventures but they have been joined by dozens of other companies attracted by the global nature of today's wine business (see GLOBALIZATION). Joint ventures are particularly well suited to new wine regions such as those in CHINA and INDIA, for example, where the winemaking expertise of an established wine producer blends well with an enterprise which can offer local knowledge and contacts.

Jongieux, named CRU in the upper Rhône valley just north of Chambéry whose name may be added to the French appellation Vin de SAVOIE. Vineyards allowed this special appellation produce a range of still wines from such varieties as Mondeuse, Pinot Noir, Gamay, Jacquère, Altesse, and Chardonnay. Within Jongieux is the separate Marestel cru, which may append its name to ROUSSETTE de Savoie.

Jordan, Middle Eastern country which produces a small amount of wine each year from a total wine grape area of about 400 ha/1,000 acres, of which Zumot, an organic producer of the Saint George label founded in 2000 at Sama Al Sarhan in northern Jordan, the main region of production, own nearly 300 ha/741 acres. Cabernet Sauvignon, Shiraz (sic), Merlot, Chardonnay, Sauvignon Blanc, and Pinot Grigio were the most popular varieties. Most of the country's 4,000 ha/9,884 acres of vines are dedicated to TABLE GRAPES. M.R.K.

Heskett, R., and Butler, J., *Divine Vintage: Following the Wine Trail from Genesis to the Modern Age* (New York, 2012).

joven, Spanish for young. Some wines destined for early consumption are sometimes sold as a Vino Joven.

Juan García, crisp, lively, local dark-skinned vine speciality of the ARRIBES zone in north west central Spain, where it is usually mixed in the vineyard with other, lesser vines. A total of 1,345 ha/3,322 acres are planted and, on rocky hillside sites, it can produce highly perfumed if relatively light reds. It is also known as Mouraton and is a natural cross of CAYETANA Blanca and ALFROCHEIRO.

Juan Ibáñez, synonym for the MORISTEL red wine grape in northern Spain.

judging wine, an activity that most wine drinkers undertake every time they open a new bottle, but also a serious business on which the commercial future of some wine producers may to a certain extent depend. For details of domestic, amateur wine judging, see TASTING.

The judging process at a more professional level can vary from a gathering of a few friends, a few bottles, and much hot air, to a COMPETITION in which wines have been carefully categorized by wine type, style, and possibly price and are tasted BLIND, in ideal conditions, without any consultation until a possible final discussion of controversial wines. Back-up bottles are always needed in case of CORKED bottles, and to verify whether any other FAULT is confined to a single bottle. SCORING systems vary but typically involve awarding a specific allocation of points for various different aspects such as appearance, NOSE, PALATE, perhaps TYPICALITY, and overall quality. MEDALS and trophies are often awarded as a result. Wine SHOWS, often part of much broader annual agricultural shows, are particularly important in Australia, where to be invited to act as a judge, or even associate judge, is a great honour. Wine judges usually wear white coats, work in silence, and may be expected to evaluate as many as 200 wines a day.

For the results of professional wine judging on an individual or small group basis, see WINE WRITING.

Judgment of Paris, famous blind tasting comparing hand-picked California and French wines organized in Paris in 1976 by British wine writer, then Parisian caviste, Steven Spurrier. Much to the fury and embarrassment of the renowned French tasters, California surprised everyone by winning hands down. The French claimed that this was simply because NEW WORLD wines mature faster, but a repeat tasting held 30 years later simultaneously in London and Napa had much the same result. The tasting made the reputations of producers such as Stag's Leap Wine Cellars and Mayacamas.

Taber, G., *Judgment of Paris—California vs. France and the Historic 1976 Paris Tasting that Revolutionized Wine* (New York, 2005).

jug wine, term used in CALIFORNIA for the most basic sort of wine, an American counterpart to VIN ordinaire or PLONK. After PROHIBITION was repealed in 1933, most inexpensive California GENERIC table wine was bottled in half-gallon and gallon (1.9- and 3.9-l) glass jugs or flagons with SCREWCAPS to satisfy a demand largely made up of thirsty immigrant labourers from the Mediterranean and eastern Europe. As this market segment has aged and died without direct replacement, jug wines have waned.

Juhfark, distinctive white grape variety once widely grown in HUNGARY. whose total plantings had fallen to 186 ha/acres by 2011. After the PHYLLOXERA invasion it never regained its importance and is today found almost exclusively in the Somló region, where it produces tart wine which ages well. The vine, whose name means 'ewe's tail', is inconveniently sensitive to both frost and downy mildew.

Juliénas, one of the ten BEAUJOLAIS crus in the far north of the region. In 2012 568 ha/1,403 acres of Gamay vines produced wines with real backbone. Les Mouilles and Les Capitans LIEUX-DITS tend to make relatively sophisticated wines.

Julius-Kühn-Institut, viticultural research station at Siebeldingen in the Pfalz region of GERMANY known to insiders by its previous name of Geilweilerhof and specializing in breeding vine varieties which combine resistance to FUNGAL DISEASES with superior wine quality. As early as 1926, Peter Morio and later Professor Husfeld were working on combining the desirable characteristics found in AMERICAN VINE SPECIES with the wine quality produced by VINIFERA varieties. Today some Asian species of the genus VITIS are also explored. Much of the focus of research is on improving VINE-BREEDING efficiency, with particular reference to pest and disease resistance, frost and drought resistance, as well as important wine constituents (particularly aroma and PHENOLIC compounds), the genetic resources of *Vitis*, grape genomic research, and biotechnology. Some of the most famous varieties from Geilweilerhof are MORIO-MUSKAT, BACCHUS, OPTIMA, and DOMINA. In the early 1990s, the successful breeding work of Professor Alleweldt led to the release of the first fungus-resistant varieties such as PHOENIX (1992), and a host of other new DISEASE-RESISTANT VARIETIES such as Sirius, Orion, and REGENT (1994). By 2004, Regent was planted on more than 2000 ha/5,000 acres in Germany, representing a breakthrough in the acceptance of NEW VARIETIES. Other new cultivars were released in 2004: Villaris and Felicia (white), and Calandro and Reberger (black). Geilweilerhof provides three grapevine databases on its website. The journal *Vitis* has been published by the Geilweilerhof Institute of Grape Breeding since 1957. See also GEISENHEIM. M.C.

www.jki.bund.de/en/startseite/institute/rebenzuechtung.html

Jullien, André (1766–1832), seminal wine writer, Parisian wine merchant, and one of the first explorers of the *world* of wine, venturing even as far as 'Chinese Tartary' in order to discover and assess all international wine regions and their produce. His was an extraordinary outlook, and it must have been a demanding journey, in an era when his peers barely ventured beyond the threshold of their wine shops. He had clearly read the contemporary LITERATURE OF WINE, which, until that point, concerned itself almost entirely with the details of how to grow vines and how to make wine (see CHAPTAL, for example). His aim was to discover and categorize the characteristics of as many different CRUS as he could find, travelling throughout eastern Europe, along the Silk Road to Asia, as well as discovering the vineyards of Africa. There can be few contemporary wine writers today who are as well travelled. The result was the publication in Paris in 1816 of *Topographie de tous les vignobles connus*, a substantial volume full of useful detail which includes the most comprehensive wine CLASSIFICATION (into five classes according to quality) ever undertaken. Much of it was translated into English and published, in abridged form, as 'a manual and guide to all importers and purchasers in the choice of wines' in London in 1824. In effect, Jullien's work set the style for a high proportion of modern wine writing.

For more details of Jullien's classification, see the LITERATURE OF WINE.

Jumilla, denominated wine region in the LEVANTE north of Murcia in central, southern Spain (see map under SPAIN) producing mainly strong red wines. The climate is arid, with RAINFALL amounting to just 300 mm/11.7 in a year. The principal grape variety in this DO is the red Monastrell (MOURVÈDRE), which ripens in the summer temperatures of around 40 °C/104 °F to produce wines that can reach a natural ALCOHOLIC STRENGTH of 18%. Average YIELDS of 12 to 15 hl/ha (0.7–0.8 tons/acre) have been uneconomically low, but more recent planting of GRAFTED vines has improved prospects.

About half of the region's much-reduced total area of 27,000 ha/64,800 acres lies in Castilla-La Mancha and the rest in the region of Murcia. For this reason, Jumilla is one of the three DOs in Spain regulated by the Agriculture Ministry and not by regional authorities.

Much of the wine from Jumilla was traditionally produced by the DOBLE PASTA method and used for blending with lighter wines from other parts of Spain. The vast San Isidro CO-OPERATIVE dominates the region's production, although since the mid 1980s a number of smaller, private producers such as Carchelo, Casa Castillo, Finca Luzón, El Nido, and Hijos de Juan Gil have been striving, with some success, to tame Monastrell, often by blending it with Tempranillo or Merlot.

Jumilla's recognition on international markets, notably thanks to the wines of Casa Castillo and El Nido, is not matched in Spain so that most of the best wines are exported.

V. de la S.

Jura, small eastern French wine region between Burgundy and Switzerland that produces an extremely wide range of wines relative to its extent, made from five main grape varieties, some unique, and including such unusual wine types as VIN JAUNE, VIN DE PAILLE, and MACVIN DU JURA, as well as a certain amount of MARC du Jura. Since the late 2000s the region has caught the imagination of sommeliers and wine amateurs worldwide.

Although this was once an important wine region, with nearly 20,000 ha/49,400 acres of vines in the early 19th century, there were only about 1,900 ha of vineyards planted in 2014 out of a possible 11,000 ha for the appellation. Most vineyards are on west-facing slopes at ELEVATIONS of between 250 and 450 m/820 and 1,476 ft on the foothills of the Jura mountains east of the Bresse plain. The chief town is Lons-le-Saunier, although ARBOIS is deemed to be the wine region's capital. Although it has a certain symmetry with the CÔTE D'OR on the other side of the Saône, the GEOLOGY is quite different with various colours of CLAY-rich MARL from the Triassic and Early Jurassic geological epochs. To limit SOIL EROSION especially on steeper slopes, today many vineyards are partially grassed down. Vines were often traditionally trained with bended canes, but most today are in double GUYOT, relatively high off the ground. The climate here is even more CONTINENTAL than in Burgundy and winters can be very cold. There is significantly higher rainfall too.

Five grape varieties are of importance in modern Jura (although more than 40 played a role at the end of the 19th century). Pinot Noir and Chardonnay have been borrowed from Burgundy, although they have been grown in the Jura vineyards since the Middle Ages. In 2012 Chardonnay accounted for 42% of total plantings. Its consistent ripening and YIELD make it popular with growers who use it to make dry white wines of several styles as well as for both CRÉMANT du Jura and Macvin. Since better terroir selections and different winemaking techniques have been adopted, some Chardonnays now rival those from the Côte d'Or. More unusual are those made in an oxidative style with or without the influence of FLOR-like yeast called the *voile*, or veil. Pinot Noir is increasingly valued either as a VARIETAL wine, in a red blend, or as part of the blend for both white and rosé Crémant. The most extensively planted red grape POULSARD, often called Ploussard, grown particularly in Arbois-Pupillin, makes light reds or deep-coloured rosés, sometimes with an orange tint. It is also used for vin de paille. Another local red wine grape variety, TROUSSEAU, needs the additional warmth of gravelly soils to ripen and is grown chiefly near Arbois, where some producers are capable of fashioning it into deep-flavoured varietals.

Jura's really distinctive grape variety, however, is the white SAVAGNIN, also called Naturé, very closely related to TRAMINER and hence GEWÜRZTRAMINER. Grown to a limited extent all over the region, it is especially known as the sole permitted variety for the extraordinary, nutty, long-lived vin jaune, sold in the distinctive 62 cl *clavelin* squat bottle. (Most other Jura wines are sold in another specially shaped bottle with the word Jura stamped on the shoulder.) See VIN JAUNE and CHÂTEAU-CHALON, which specializes in this unusual drink.

See also the more varied appellation Arbois which, like Côtes du Jura, makes red, pink, and white still wine along with vin jaune and vin de paille. The appellation L'ÉTOILE is reserved for white wines only, including vin jaune and vin de paille, while Château-Chalon is reserved for vin jaune only. Crémant du Jura, sparkling wines which are generally white and occasionally rosé, and white, rosé or red Macvin may be produced anywhere in the region.

Winemaking techniques are generally traditional, with almost no use of new oak barrels, but much use of older barrels, small and large, although many reds are matured only in tank. White wines may be made conventionally, in which case they may be described as OUILLÉ (topped up), or OXIDATIVELY, or as in the case of vin jaune, under film-forming yeasts. The ORGANIC and the NATURAL WINE movements are relatively important in Jura.

The wines are distinctive, particularly those which contain the local grape varieties, and whereas they were for many years drunk almost entirely within the greater Franche-Comté region which encompasses Jura, by 2012 around 7% of production was exported. With marked acidity and mineral characteristics, they make particularly good candidates for FOOD AND WINE MATCHING. **Côtes du Jura**, the region's second most important appellation after Arbois, includes an extended but scattered vineyard area stretching around 80 km/50 miles from north to south, and wines may be red, white, or dark pink; still or sparkling; vinified normally or matured slowly into vin jaune. About a third of the wine produced is still red or pink.

W.L.

Lorch, W., *Jura Wine* (London, 2014).

Jurançon is a name closely associated with SOUTH WEST FRANCE, of a distinguished white wine both dry (Jurançon Sec) and sweet (labelled simply Jurançon), of a relatively important, if undistinguished, dark-berried vine variety, and of an entirely unimportant light-berried vine.

The wine

This fashionable, tangy, distinctive white wine has been celebrated and fiercely protected since the Middle Ages, and Jurançon was one of France's earliest APPELLATIONS CONTRÔLÉES. In the 14th century, the princes of BÉARN and the parliament of NAVARRA introduced the concept of a CRU by identifying and valuing specific favoured vineyard sites. Locals claim this as France's first attempt at vineyard CLASSIFICATION, just as they claim the drop of Jurançon with which the infant Henri IV's lips were rubbed at his baptism in 1553 was responsible for most of his subsequent achievements. The Dutch were great enthusiasts for this wine and there was also a flourishing export trade across the Atlantic until PHYLLOXERA almost destroyed the wine. Jurançon's reputation was further advanced in the early 20th century by the enthusiasm of the French writer Colette. The principal varieties are the INDIGENOUS PETIT MANSENG and GROS MANSENG, but the dry version may include up to 50% made up of other local varieties PETIT COURBU, COURBU, Camaralet de Lasseube, and Lauzet. In the early 21st century vines were grown on about 800 ha/2,000 acres of vineyards in this hilly, relatively cool corner of southern France near Pau at the relatively high average ELEVATION of 300 m/984 ft. Spring FROSTS are such a threat that many vines are ESPALIER trained, but the Atlantic influence ensures sufficient RAINFALL. Vineyards on a mixture of limestone, sand, clay, and stones are protected by the Midi d'Ossau mountain. While the wines from Monein tend to be particularly rich in traditional style, those from the Coteaux (Chapelle-de-Rousse) tend to be crisper and more mineral.

Gros Manseng is chiefly responsible for Jurançon Sec, the more common dry but strongly flavoured version of this wine, for which yields of 60 hl/ha (3.4 tons/acre) are allowed. Petit Manseng, with its small, thick-skinned berries, is ideal for the production of Jurançon's real speciality, long-living, relatively inexpensive sweet Jurançon made from grapes partially dried on the vine (see PASSERILLÉ) which in some years may not be harvested until December, at a maximum yield of 40 hl/ha but often much less. If several TRIES are made through the vineyard (two are mandatory), the results may be bottled separately. OAK is used to increasing effect. These MOELLEUX wines, whose green tinge seems to deepen with age, serve well as aperitifs and with a wide range of foods.

The vine varieties

Vines called Jurançon have in their time been cultivated in practically every region of south west France, other than Jurançon itself. The dark-berried version **Jurançon Noir** was once the high-yielding ARAMON-like workhorse of this part of France and 567 ha/1,400 acres were still in production in 2011, mainly in Gers and Tarn. **Jurançon Blanc** was once quite widely planted for armagnac prduction but is nearly extinct.

Justino's Madeira Wines SA, the largest single shipper of MADEIRA, bottling under a variety of names including Cruz, the largest single BRAND of Madeira (and PORT) in France. Established in Funchal in 1870, Justino's operates from modern industrial premises outside the city. The company was formerly known as Justino Henriques but was renamed to avoid confusion with Henriques & Henriques, which is also now controlled by the French import and distribution group La Martiniquaise.

Juwel, white grape variety and one of the GERMAN CROSSES. A few vines linger, mainly in RHEINHESSEN.

Kabinett, one of six so-called PRÄDIKATS applying to German wine that has not been chaptalized, and designating—depending on growing region and grape variety—must weights between 67 and 82 °OECHSLE. As such, Kabinett designates the lightest end of the German wine spectrum, and Mosel Kabinetts that have RESIDUAL SUGAR are often as low as 7 or 8% alcohol. The term Kabinett, like the pegging of quality designations to minimum must weights itself, is entirely a product of the 1971 GERMAN WINE LAW. The name was chosen for its association with the English word CABINET, widely used in Germany prior to 1971 as a general term of approbation for wines in all styles. It still has resonance in the German marketplace even for wines from regions such as BADEN and the PFALZ where dry Kabinetts may significantly exceed 13% alcohol, and where among reputed producers most vintages since 1987 have involved no CHAPTALIZATION. In the early 2010s many of the regional VDPS elected to eliminate the use of the term, while others have decided to limit its use to non-dry Rieslings.

Austrian wine law enshrines the term 'Kabinett' for unchaptalized, dry Qualitätswein of up to 13% alcohol and from grapes of at least 17 KMW (84 °Oechsle), but the term is little used, particularly since the advent of DAC status for much of LOWER AUSTRIA, whereby 'Reserve' on labels of Riesling or Grüner Veltliner effectively replaces 'Spätlese trocken' and non-Reserve DAC bottlings are those that would formerly have been labelled 'Kabinett.'   D.S.

Kadarka, eastern European late ripening red wine grape of uncertain origin. As Gamza, it is most widely planted in Bulgaria where it is considered indigenous. Some Albanians stake a claim to it, called Kallmet there. And it is also said to be native to western Romania where it is known as Cadarča. BULGARIA's 3,000 ha/7,500 acres of Gamza are planted mainly in the north, where it can produce wines of interest from long growing seasons if yields are restricted. In Hungary the variety grew on a total of only just over 500 ha/1,250 acres and has been substantially replaced by the viticulturally sturdier KÉKFRANKOS, and by PORTUGIESER in Villány. It is still cultivated on the Great Plain and in the Szekszárd wine region just across the Danube to the west but its tendency to GREY ROT and its habit of ripening riskily late limit it to certain favoured sites. The vine is also naturally highly productive and needs careful control in order to produce truly concentrated wines, ideally trained as BUSH VINES. Fully ripened Szekszárdi Kadarka can be a fine, soft, full-bodied wine worthy of ageing but is produced in minuscule quantities. Kadarka is too often overproduced and picked when still low in colour and flavour.

Because of its—largely historic—fame, this is a variety which is often included in any large NURSERY collection of vine varieties.

Kalecik Karasi, vine variety that makes particularly fruity reds north east of Ankara in TURKEY where there are about 3,500 ha/8,645 acres.

Kalterer or **Kalterersee**, German for the TRENTINO and ALTO ADIGE DOC known as Caldaro or Lago di Caldaro in Italian based on SCHIAVA grapes.

Kamptal, named for the Kamp river that traverses it, is an AUSTRIAN wine-growing region immediately north east of KREMSTAL. Centred on the town of Langenlois and incorporating the nearby villages of Gobelsburg, Kammern, Legenfeld, and Zöbing, its diminutive perimeter is deceptive since an extremely high density of vineyards comprising 4,000 ha/9,800 acres represent more than 8% of Austrian vine acreage, third in regional size after the WEINVIERTEL and NEUSIEDLERSEE. In common with the nearby WACHAU (of which it was once loosely considered part), the Kamptal shares that region's wide diurnal temperature variation (see TEMPERATURE VARIABILITY) but with slightly less rain and greater vulnerability to frost—as well as its dominance of LOESS and old rocky soils occasionally intermingled with sand and gravel. But the Kamptal can boast even greater geological diversity, as witness the Permian sandstone that defines its best-known vineyard landmark, the massive, terraced Heiligenstein, arguably among the top 20 sites for Riesling the world. The nearby Gaisberg is this region's other renowned vineyard for Riesling, which makes up 9% of Kamptal acreage, while in between those two, the gently sloping, loess-dominated Lamm is the region's most famous site for Grüner Veltliner, which is planted on half of all Kamptal vineyard. Successful flirtations with other varieties are numerous, especially Chardonnay, Pinot Blanc (Weisser Burgunder), Sauvignon Blanc, Pinot Noir, St Laurent, and Zweigelt (on 14% of surface area). Known also for its density of ambitious, environmentally conscious growers, Kamptal has benefited from vintner Willi Bründlmayer's status as a longstanding unofficial ambassador for Austrian wine as well as from the chairmanship of Austria's TRADITIONSWEINGÜTER by Michael Moosbrugger, a Bründlmayer protegé who has had responsibility for the monastic estate of Schloss Gobelsburg since 1996.

Kamptal DAC is the official Austrian DAC appellation for Kamptal Grüner Veltiner and Riesling varietal wines launched in 2008. Those referred to as Klassik must be at least 12% alcohol and free of BOTRYTIS and wood notes. They can be released from 1 January following their harvest. DAC Reserve wines must be at least 13%, may taste 'subtly' of botrytis or wood, and may not be sold before 15 March. Wines that do not qualify as Kamptal DAC must be labelled with their state of origin NIEDERÖSTERREICH. This applies in particular to the 40% of Kamptal wines made from grapes other than Grüner Veltliner or Riesling.   D.S.

Kangaroo Island, unique, cool, maritime region (fauna, flora, etc.) south of Adelaide in SOUTH AUSTRALIA. Bordeaux-based FLYING WINE-MAKER Jacques Lurton has established a vineyard and winery (The Islander), the leading product an eclectic blend of Sangiovese, Cabernet Franc, and Malbec.

Kanzler, Müller-Thurgau × Silvaner cross bred at Alzey in 1927 of which only 31 ha/77 acres remained in 2012 because it does not yield well.

Kazakhstan, independent central Asian, former Soviet republic. Rich in natural resources and enjoying a certain prosperity, Kazakhstan is the largest land-locked country in the world, south of Russia and bordering China. It has an extreme CONTINENTAL climate, with summer temperatures exceeding 30 °C/86 °F, and winter temperatures averaging –20 °C/ –4 °F. Its capital is Astana in the north. Less than 4% of Kazakhstan offers favourable soil and climatic conditions for commercial grape culture. According to OIV estimates, total vineyard area was 13,000 ha/32,100 acres producing 189,000 hl/5 million gal of wine in 2011.

History

Evidence of grape culture in Kazakhstan dates back to the 7th century AD. The Turkestan area of the Shymkent region (where the grapevine was imported from the Samarkand and the Fergana regions of UZBEKISTAN) and the Panfilov area of the Taldy-Kurgan region (where grapevines are popularly believed to have come from CHINA's western Xinjiang province) are the country's most ancient viticultural areas.

At the end of the 19th century, grapes were grown on a small scale by private farms. The development of commercial grape culture began in the 1930s, when the first fruit- and wine-growing state farms such as Issyk in the Alamty region, Uch-Bulak in the Zhambyl region, and Juvaly and Kaplanbek in the Shymkent region were established. Viticulture developed rapidly after 1957. Vineyards occupied 4,997 ha in 1958, and 22,311 ha/55,130 acres in 1976. Twenty-six specialized fruit- and wine-growing state farms in the south and south east of the country owned 85% of the total vineyard area with the rest divided between collective farms and individuals.

Modern viticulture

According to OIV figures Kazakhstan's total vineyard area was 6,938 ha/17,144 acres in 2010 producing 172,00 hl/over 3.7 million gallons of wine (compared with 13,000 ha/32,120 acres producing 236,000 hl/over 6.2 million gal of wine in 2002). The active temperature summation varies from 1,800 °C in the north east to 4,500 °C in the south, and winters can be very cold. The annual rainfall is 700 to 1,000 mm/ 27–39 in in the Zaili and Talas Alatau but is as little as 100 to 150 mm (4–6 in) in some areas of the Aktobe region.

Commercial vine culture is principally located in the Almaty, Zhambyl, South Kazakhstan, and Kyzlorda regions. IRRIGATION is the norm, and most vineyards also need WINTER PROTECTION.

The 21st century has seen an increased investment from foreign and domestic sources in both vineyards and wineries. There has been a small but steady influx of viticultural and winemaking CONSULTANTS from the UK, Australia, France, and Italy who have worked with local producers to improve QUALITY. As with other parts of the former Soviet Union, there has been a move to produce fresher, more international styles, and a move away from the sweet, heavy wines of the past.

More than 40 grape varieties are allowed for commercial culture, of which 24 are for TABLE GRAPES, an important crop here. Wine varieties include RKATSITELI, RIESLING, PINOT NOIR, SAPERAVI, ALIGOTÉ, ALEATICO, Bayanshira, Kuljinski, Maiski Cherny, CABERNET FRANC, CABERNET SAUVIGNON, Rubinovy Magaracha, Hungarian Muscat (probably MUSCAT OTTONEL), and Muscat Rosé.   V.R. & N.G.

kegs, increasingly popular form of wine PACKAGING. The combination of recyclable stainless-steel kegs with plastic tubing and INERT GAS keeps large volumes of wine fresh. Kegs have been adopted with enthusiasm in many American bars and restaurants as a much more effective deliverer of fresh wine by the glass than BOTTLES. Large bag-in-BOX packages fitted with pumps are sometimes called kegs. Some retailers particularly concerned with SUSTAINABILITY encourage their customers to fill their own containers from kegs.

kék means 'blue' in Hungarian and, as such, can be a direct equivalent of BLAU in German or even NOIR in French.

Kékfrankos, Hungarian name for the increasingly fashionable red grape variety known in Austria as BLAUFRÄNKISCH (of which it is a direct translation) and grown on 8,000 ha/ 20,000 acres of Hungary, mainly on the Great Plain, in Eger, and, most successfully, in Sopron near the Austrian border where it is responsible for some of Hungary's finest reds.

Kéknyelű, revered but very rare white grape variety grown in HUNGARY, notably in Badacsony on the north shore of Lake Balaton, and named after its 'blue' stalk. Yields are very low; wines are crisp and perfumed.

Kékoportó, name for the PORTUGIESER grape in HUNGARY. The greatest concentration of the 1,216 ha/3,003 acres planted in 2012 were in Villány.

Keller is German for a cellar, even a small domestic cellar, while **Kellerei** is used in much the same way as the word CAVE in French, for any sort of wine-producing premises whether above or below ground. A German wine specifying a Keller rather than a WEINGUT on the label is usually the produce of a merchant rather than an estate. In ALTO ADIGE, the Italian Tyrol, **Kellereigenossenschaft** is a common name for one of the many wine CO-OPERATIVES. **Kellermeister** is German for cellarmaster, a position very similar to MAÎTRE DE CHAI in France.

Kendall-Jackson, original brand name of the winery and vineyard empire begun by Jess Jackson (Kendall was his former wife's maiden name) in Lake county, California, during the mid 1970s. By the early 1990s, expansion and acquisition had resulted in such a proliferation of brand names that the Artisans & Estates division was created to differentiate other labels, many of them of the highest quality, from the Kendall-Jackson labels. Now all the brands are under the Jackson Family Wines banner, but in US trade jargon 'K-J' is still used for the whole collection, as well as for the Kendall-Jackson labels specifically.

In many ways, Jess Jackson exemplifies the entrepreneurial nature of the CALIFORNIA wine industry as well as the go-go climate of the 1980s.

Most prominent players in the world of wine started with a significant viticultural or financial inheritance. Jackson did not, which adds grist to popular conjecture about his personality. Born in 1930, Jackson grew up poor and put himself through college and law school at UC Berkeley working as a police officer and a longshoreman. He made his own financial stake over thirty years as an attorney in San Francisco.

He entered the wine industry almost accidentally in 1974 when he purchased a small pear and walnut ranch on the western side of Clear Lake as a weekend retreat. He planted grapes, but had trouble selling them for a decent return, so he began to investigate converting them to wine. By 2009, estimates had his family-owned wine venture selling 3.5 million cases a year. In 2013, Jackson Family Wines owned 11,000 acres/4,450 ha of vineyards in California alone, in Santa Barbara, Monterey, Sonoma, Napa, Mendocino, and Lake counties. There are three dozen brands in the stable (and several thoroughbred racehorses, too), with a particular proclivity for mountain-grown Cabernet Sauvignon and coastal Pinot Noir. Villa Arceno wine estate in Tuscany, Viña Calina in Chile, and a cooperage in France are also among the holdings, along with a project in South Africa. In 2013, Jackson Family Wines made a major play in Oregon's Willamette Valley, purchasing two planted vineyards, a parcel of land suitable for Pinot Noir, and Solena Estate Winery, totalling nearly 1,000 acres/404 ha.

Yet back in the 1980s, Kendall-Jackson happily disregarded the California industry's movement toward vineyard designations, concentrating instead on blending from various regions to achieve certain taste characteristics. To say this strategy worked would be a grave understatement. Jackson's first wines were put together under the auspices of CONSULTANT Ric Forman in 1982, then continually improved under the hand of winemaker Jed Steele, who arrived in 1983. The hallmarks of K-J's blended Chardonnays were refreshingly strong ACIDITY, creamy oak vanillins (see OAK FLAVOUR), exotic pineapple fruit flavour, and softness and immediate drinkability from just-perceptible RESIDUAL SUGAR. Classically inclined show judges put up token resistance to the residual sugar, but consumers had no such reservations.

Speculation is that a dollop of Muscat-based SWEET RESERVE is the mystery ingredient driving this successful recipe. Verification is not available because Jackson went to court in 1992 to prevent Jed Steele from revealing what he claimed were 'trade secrets', on his departure from K-J. Despite a noteworthy historical precedent in the California wine industry of shared information, Jackson prevailed.

In 1987, Jackson and his second wife, Barbara Banke acquired 1,000 acres in Santa Barbara county and Cambria Winery and Vineyard, with Banke the listed owner. Since that time, acquisitions have been so frequent that any book is obsolete on the subject long before publication. Particularly notable was the Napa Valley 1995 purchase of the 1,800-acre Gauer Estate vineyard in Alexander Valley which supplies Stonestreet Wines. Matanzas Creek was added later along with Arrowood. The flagships, in addition to Stonestreet (Jess Jackson's middle name), include Hartford Court (Russian River Pinot Noir and Zinfandel), La Crema (Pinot Noir from California and Oregon), Cabernet-centric Lokoya and La Jota in Napa Valley, and Cardinale, a proprietary red blend from Napa.

Jess Jackson died in 2011 after a long bout with cancer, at age 81. Barbara Banke is now at the controls, and this land-use lawyer has made many moves since his death, including a march into Oregon.   B.C.C. & L.M.

Kenya, African country virtually on the equator, with a very limited production of wines, and some packaging of imports from South Africa. Since the mid 1980s, VINIFERA vines have been cultivated and have been harvested every eight months, providing three vintages every two years, chiefly from vineyards around Lake Naivasha (see TROPICAL VITICULTURE). Rainy seasons are March to May and October to December and some producers may revert to one growing season from June to September. The only commercial wine producer in 2014 was Rift Valley Winery, whose 20 ha/50 acres of vineyards are at ELEVATIONS over 1900 m/6,235 ft. A locally grown Sauvignon Blanc/Chenin Blanc blend and rosé are sold under the Leleshwa brand. A refugee from the Médoc has planted a small vineyard in Laikipia.

Platter, J. & E., *Africa Uncorked* (London, 2002).

Kerner, the most successful GERMAN CROSS which, because of its Riesling-like wines, is still planted on 3,030 ha/7,484 acres of Germany, mainly in Pfalz and Rheinhessen. It is also relatively popular in Württemberg, where it was bred from a red parent TROLLINGER (Schiava Grossa) × Riesling. The large white berries produce wines commendably close to Riesling in flavour except for their own leafy, sometimes candied and mawkish, aroma and slightly coarser texture. It is a cross which does not need to be subsumed in the blending vat but can produce respectable VARIETAL wines, up to quite high PRÄDIKAT levels, on its own account. Kerner is popular with growers as well as wine drinkers because of its late budding and therefore good FROST resistance. The mere 82 ha/202 acres of Kerner noted in Italy's 2010 vine census produce some widely admired wines in Alto Adige. It is also planted in Switzerland, England, Canada, quite successfully in JAPAN, and to a very limited extent in South Africa.

Kevedinka, ordinary white grape variety in Serbia. See DINKA.

kir, alternative name for a *vin blanc cassis*, dry white wine and blackcurrant liqueur, named after a hero of the Burgundian resistance movement during the Second World War, Canon Kir, who was also mayor of Dijon. Blackcurrants are probably a more important crop on the HAUTES CÔTES than grapes and most of the best-quality blackcurrant liqueurs, or *eaux-de-vie de cassis*, are made here. The typical base wine is the relatively acid Bourgogne ALIGOTÉ and to most palates a dash of full-strength liqueur is all that is needed. A **kir royal** is made with sparkling rather than still white wine.

Királyleányka, meaning 'princess', central European vine making lightly perfumed, crisp whites. Much of Hungary's 855 ha/2,111 acres

total is grown in Balatonboglár but there are also fine examples from Eger and Mátra.

Kisi, GEORGIAN vine variety making headily perfumed, well structured whites.

Kişmiş, Kismis, Kishmish, Middle Eastern synonyms for the common SULTANA.

K-J. See KENDALL-JACKSON.

Klassik, when noted with an uppercase 'K' on an AUSTRIAN label (or price list) refers to unoaked, fruit-forward wines. The most established such category is Steierische Klassik, used for wines grown in the state of STEIERMARK and associated especially with the crisp, dry wines of SÜDSTEIERMARK that are intended for early drinking. The term Klassik is also used—though generally without appearing on the relevant labels—for the lighter of two categories of wine within many of Austria's DACS. Klassik is also sometimes colloquially employed in Germany for the least expensive or simplest bottlings, as some French growers use the term *Tradition* to denote the basic bottling even though the word rarely appears on labels. Klassik is not to be confused with the specific category of German wine known as CLASSIC.   D.S.

Klein Karoo, inland semi-desert ostrich- and sheep-farming region that is also an official wine region in SOUTH AFRICA also known as Little Karoo. The town of Calitzdorp is widely regarded as the port-style wine capital of South Africa.

Klevener de Heiligenstein is an ALSACE oddity, a vine speciality of the village of Heiligenstein in the Bas-Rhin introduced in 1740 by its mayor Erhard Wantz, possibly from Chiavenna in the Italian alps. It is a locally adapted SAVAGNIN ROSE, occasionally known as Clevner de Heiligenstein, grown within five neighbouring communes of Heiligenstein to produce a dry wine, less scented than Gewurztraminer, with less alcohol and a little more acidity. In good vintages it can age well. In 2011 it was recognized as an appellation communale of Alsace. See also GERMAN HISTORY.

Klevner, like CLEVNER, is, and more particularly was, used fairly indiscriminately in Alsace and other German-speaking wine regions for various vine varieties, notably but not exclusively for various members of the PINOT family. References to Klevner in Alsace in the mid 16th century are common.

Kloster Eberbach, monastery in the RHEINGAU region of Germany with a tradition of viticulture; now seen as the cultural wine centre of the Rheingau. Kloster Eberbach was founded in 1135 by Bernard of Clairvaux. Throughout the Middle Ages, Cistercian monks produced wine at the monastery, and

k

made its name as one of the most important wine estates of its time. Through viticultural enterprise, the monastery became extremely powerful, owning a fleet of ships which sailed the Rhine. Kloster Eberbach nowadays lends its name to the vast Hessian State Domaine or Hessische Staatsweingüter, whose incomparable Cabinetkeller boasts abundant stocks of wines from the 19th century. Close to the adjacent MONOPOLE Steinberg vineyard is a 21st century, lavishly appointed production facility.

See also MONKS AND MONASTERIES.

S.E.A. & D.S.

Klosterneuburg, small city on the right bank of the Danube west of Vienna in AUSTRIA whose Augustinian monastery (*Stift*) has been a major vineyard owner since the Middle Ages. Since 1860 it has housed Austria's centre for viticultural and oenological research (see ACADEME), also giving its name to Austria's standard measurement of MUST WEIGHT, commonly referred to by its abbreviation KMW. While the vineyard holdings of Stift Klosterneuburg include substantial tracts in the nearby growing regions of WIEN, THERMENREGION, and CARNUNTUM, its home vineyards immediately upstream from Vienna have the official status of a GROSSLAGE within NIEDERÖSTERREICH.   D.S.

KMW, or Klosterneuburger Mostwage, named for its origins at KLOSTERNEUBURG, is AUSTRIA's traditional unit of measurement for MUST WEIGHT, equivalent to approximately 5 °OECHSLE.

Knights Valley, inland California wine region and AVA between the northern end of Napa Valley and the southern end of Alexander Valley. See SONOMA.

Korea, rugged, mountainous peninsula on the Asian mainland, between China and Japan, for long a producer of TABLE GRAPES and of commercial wine since 1977 when the large beverages group, DooSan Baekwha, launched its Majuang label, which still accounts for the majority of domestic wine produced. The first wine was a substitute for imported SACRAMENTAL WINE for the Korean Catholic Church but its ultimate goal was to reach local consumers with an affordable alternative to costly imported table wines. Wine consumption in Korea has soared this century but the market is still almost entirely reliant on imports. DooSan's early local rivals have mostly abandoned their wine ventures but recent entrants, notably Chateau Mani and Kenneth Kim Vineyards, have mounted a limited challenge. The tiny East of Eden Winery has attracted attention with its sweetish red wine made from the exotic wild *Vitis* AMURENSIS mountain grape (literally *sanmeoru*). An increasing number of wineries are working principally with this variety because the extremely cold winters and rainy, humid summers are far

from ideal for *Vitis vinifera* vines. Vineyards are scattered throughout the country and totalled 19,000 ha/47,000 acres in 2011 according to OIV figures. The limited proportion attached to commercial winemaking operations are either in the south east of the peninsula in the provinces of North and South Gyeongsang on sandy or stony sedimentary soils, and favoured by a milder MARITIME CLIMATE, or in the provinces of Gyeonggi and Chungcheong in the north west. The main varieties grown for the table are the hybrid Campbell Early, comprising two thirds of the total vineyard area, and Kyoho. Varieties grown specifically for wine are Riesling, Seibel, White Muscat (MUSCAT BLANC À PETIT GRAINS), MUSCAT BAILEY A, although Campbell Early is also used for wine. Some local labels, including Marjuang, rely on locally bottled imported BULK WINE. To the credit of the producers and the regulatory authorities, this information is declared on the label—all in Korean, of course.

D.G.

kosher (meaning pure). To the Jewish people, there is no communal, religious, or family event without wine. The vine was one of the seven fruits blessed in the Bible and there is even a special blessing devoted to wine: 'Blessed are You, Lord our God . . . who creates the fruit of the vine.'

Adhering to the Jewish dietary laws (*kashrut*) is essential for all Orthodox Jews. Kosher wine laws were established in ancient times, so an observant Jew could avoid drinking *Yayin Nesech*, a wine used for idol worship and *Stam Yayin*, wine made by non-Jews.

With kosher food the focus is on the source of the food, whereas with kosher wine, the emphasis is on the handler. At the winery, for a wine to be considered kosher, only religious Jews may handle the product and touch the winemaking equipment from the time the grapes arrive at the winery.

Only kosher items or substances may be used in the process. The kosher certification provides a similar quality assurance to the ISO systems. All raw materials such as added YEASTS, BARRELS, and FINING agents have to be prepared under the strictest quality and hygiene standards. Origin and traceability are key. Examples of fining agents not permitted include (animal-derived) gelatine, (dairy-derived) casein, and isinglass (because it comes from a non-kosher fish). Kosher wine is suitable for VEGETARIANS, and if egg whites are not used for fining, also for vegans.

In Israel, there are additional agricultural laws which date back to the agrarian society in Biblical times:

1. *Orlah*. For the first three years, fruit from the vine may not be used for winemaking.
2. *Kilai Ha'Kerem*. Cross-breeding. Growing other fruits between the vines is prohibited.

3. *Shmittah*. Every seventh year, the fields should be left fallow. However, because of economic realities, the land is symbolically sold to a non-Jew for the duration of this sabbatical year.
4. *Trumot and Ma'aserot*. Just over 1% of the production is poured away in remembrance of a tithe once paid in the time of the Holy Temple in Jerusalem.

The idea of giving the land and its workers a seventh-year sabbatical and reserving part of the harvest for the poor was socially progressive in biblical times. Today, *Shmittah* and *Trumot and Ma'asarot* remain mainly symbolic.

'Kosher for Passover' means the wine and barrels have not come into contact with bread, grain, or products made with leavened dough. Most kosher wines are also 'Kosher for Passover'.

The rules are full of ritual and tradition. It is notable, however, that there are no regulations affecting the quality of the wine, and standard winemaking procedures are followed in the HARVESTING, FERMENTATION, MATURATION, BLENDING, and BOTTLING.

The issue of *Yayin Mevushal* is more controversial. *Mevushal* wines must be flash PASTEURIZED to 175 °F/80 °C. The requirement relates to wine handling and to service to those more strictly religious, especially with regard to kosher catering. If *mevushal*, the wine remains kosher even if served by a non-observant waiter. Most of the finest kosher wines are not *mevushal*.

The Jewish SACRAMENTAL WINE category has done untold damage to the image of kosher wines. These wines are usually made from a mixture of grape MUST and wine, and often from LABRUSCA varieties such as CONCORD. They are used by Jewish communities or families to make kiddush—the blessing over wine for festivals and the Sabbath. Manischevitz and Palwin are well-known examples of kiddush wines.

Most wine enthusiasts prefer to use kosher table wines, which are of increasingly good quality. Some of the best are produced by Capçanes in Catalunya and Covenant in California. Leading Israeli producers of kosher wine include Castel, Carmel, Yarden, and Yatir. Even non-kosher wineries, such as Chx Léoville-Poyferré and Valandraud have been known occasionally to make a kosher cuvée.

The largest producers of kosher wine are Israel, the US, and France, but almost all wine-producing countries produce some kosher bottlings today.   A.S.M.

Koshu, best-known INDIGENOUS grape variety in JAPAN. The pink-skinned TABLE GRAPE has thick skins and withstands Japan's humid summers relatively well. Most Koshu is PERGOLA-trained but most ambitious growers are reducing YIELDS via Ichimonji-Tansho, a high culture system with spur pruning, while the likes of

Grace have started to train it low on CORDON DE ROYAT, reducing yields further and producing some of the most concentrated examples of Koshu. Koshu wine can rarely be accused of an excess of flavour but it can be a fine accompaniment to sashimi. Still, sparkling, sweet, and oaked versions are made. DNA PROFILING by Nami Goto in 2014 suggested that Koshu is a natural hybrid between an as-yet-unidentified variety of *Vitis vinifera* and an unknown variety, which is itself a hybrid between an individual of *Vitis davidii* and another unidentified variety of *Vitis vinifera*.

www.koshuofjapan.com

Kosovo, territory south of SERBIA that unilaterally declared its independence in 2008, but whose status is still in dispute, especially with its northern neighbour. Recently recognized by the EU as a potential candidate country for membership, it has a predominantly ethnic ALBANIAN population. Conditions for grape growing are good thanks to more than 200 sunny days each year, adequate summer rainfall, and vineyards at ELEVATIONS of 300 to 400 metres (985–1,310 ft) surrounded by spectacular mountains.

Wine has been produced in this region for around 2,000 years. In the 1950s, the YUGOSLAV regime recognized the potential for high-volume wine production in the region and developed four large-scale state wineries. Much of the wine went to the Serbian capital Belgrade for blending, with the notable exception of Amselfelder, a light, medium-sweet red marketed in Germany by Racke (and now Grands Chais de France). Shipments of Amselfelder reached 32 million litres/8.5 million gal in 1980s and Kosovan vineyards then totalled about 9,000 ha/22,200 acres.

The collapse of Yugoslavia in the 1990s and then the 1998–9 war meant that the vineyard area fell to under 4,000 ha/9,884 acres. A Serbian-imposed trade embargo also hindered the wine industry's attempts at recovery. Most of the land has now been privatized, with just 20% still in social ownership in 2014. Only one of the large state wineries has been sold successfully. Rahovec was bought in 2006 by two Albanian brothers living in the US and has been extensively modernized. It has been renamed Stone Castle, has 650 ha/1,606 acres of vineyards, and is the major exporter of Kosovan wine, mainly INTERNATIONAL VARIETALS and VRANAC. Small private producers are also emerging. Today 90% of all cultivated vineyards lie in southern Kosovo in the zones of Rahovec/Orahovac and Suhareka/Suva Reka.   C.G.

www.wineroutes-ks.com

Kotsifali. Generous, spicy, if soft wines are produced from this red grape speciality of the Greek island of CRETE where it is the second most common variety after Liatiko. They are best blended with something more tannic such as MANDILARIA.

Kövérszőlő, one of the oldest and rarest grape varieties in TOKAJ, and possibly the same as GRASĂ in Cotnari, Romania.

Kövidinka, Hungarian name for the ordinary white eastern European grape variety DINKA.

krater. See CRATER.

Kratošija, relatively important grape in Montenegro that is the same as ZINFANDEL.

Kremstal, wine region whose 2,250 ha/5,600 acres of vines represent roughly 5% of AUSTRIA's vineyards and characterized by considerable geological and microclimatic diversity. Long considered part of the WACHAU, the towering rocky terraced vineyards on the region's western edge—in particular those of the Krems-Stein suburb—segue seamlessly into those of today's official Wachau. These include two of Austria's greatest Riesling vineyards, the (Steiner) Hund and Pfaffenberg as well as the estimable Kögl and Wachtberg that are closer to the city of Krems proper. The valley of the diminutive River Krems incorporates only 7 km/4.3 miles of vineyards that are dominated by LOESS close to Krems city limits, rising to magnificent steepness upstream around Senftenberg, whose Ehrenfels, Hochäcker, and Pellingen vineyards are home to Riesling (10% of total Kremstal vineyard) and Grüner Veltliner. The eastern and north-eastern fringes of Krems are dominated by mounds of loess, anticipating the soil character and exposures of the WAGRAM region that runs along the Danube's left bank towards Vienna. Grüner Veltliner overwhelmingly dominates in this sector, which helps explain why it amounts to over half of the entire Kremstal vineyard area. Gneixendorf and Stratzing north of Krems (and bordering KAMPTAL) as well as Rohrendorf and Gedersdorf to the city's east are important wine villages in this sector. Kremstal also incorporates extensive vineyards on the Danube's right bank, where sand and gravel from the Danube, that meandered around numerous islands until late 20th century dredging, vie with loess for vine roots' attention. An especially diverse admixture of other varieties—including even Cabernet and Merlot from Bordeaux—colour growers' price lists. Heading east from Mautern (in the Wachau), the villages of Furth, Palt, Oberfucha, and Tiefenfucha are dominated by the massive mountaintop Göttweig monastery—itself an important vineyard owner—while further downstream Hollenburg hugs the Danube's shoreline and abuts TRAISENTAL, to which, however, it is not assigned.

Kremstal DAC is the official 2007 Austrian DAC appellation for Kremstal varietals Grüner

Veltliner and Riesling, which together account for about two-thirds of all Kremstal vines.

D.S.

Krug, small but important Champagne house founded in Rheims in 1843 by Johann Krug, who was born in Mainz, Germany, in 1800 and had come to work in Champagne, seeking French citizenship. From 1824 he was known as Joseph. By 1866 the firm occupied its current modest cellars, around whose courtyard the Krug family lived until 2014. Krug does not make an ordinary NON-VINTAGE champagne but specializes exclusively in PRESTIGE CUVÉES, of which the multi-vintage Grande Cuvée is the flagship, having replaced the rather fuller-bodied Private Cuvée in 1979. Grande Cuvée was first made with a blend of 60 to 70 wines from five to six different years, in addition to the current harvest, but a total of 148 wines from more than ten years went into the blend in 2014. Consistently producing champagne that is among the most admired in its region of origin, Krug is the only house to persist in BARREL FERMENTATION of its entire production of base wine, in old 205-l/54-gal casks. In 1971, Krug acquired and replanted the Clos du Mesnil, a walled vineyard of less than 2 ha/5 acres. Its Chardonnay grapes provide one of Champagne's very few single-vineyard, or CRU, wines of which the 1979 vintage was the first. The 0.68 ha/1.7 acres of Clos d'Ambonnay planted exclusively with Pinot Noir is responsible for an ever more expensive wine launched with the 1995 vintage. Small quantities of the finest vintage Krug, released at very similar prices to Grande Cuvée, are released, as Krug Collection, about ten years after their initial release. In 2012, acknowledging the considerable variation between the Grande Cuvées produced each year, Krug introduced back label codes identifying when each cuvée was disgorged. Krug has been owned by LVMH since 1999 although sixth-generation Olivier Krug is part of the tasting committee and represents the house in Champagne and abroad.

Arlott, J., *Krug: House of Champagne* (London, 1976).

Fountain, N., *Krug—A Journey through history* (Reims, 2011).

Krug, Charles (1825–92), German-born American wine producer, came to San Francisco in 1852 as a newspaper editor. After vineyard ventures in San Mateo and SONOMA, perhaps at the urging of HARASZTHY, Krug settled in the NAPA Valley in 1860, founding a winery near St Helena in 1861. Krug was not the first Napa Valley winemaker but he soon became the most eminent of his day and inevitably came to be called the 'father of Napa wine'. His success came in part because he understood public relations and because he developed his own sales organization. The winery he founded was acquired by the MONDAVI family in 1943 and is still notable among Napa Valley establishments, although Robert Mondavi left to set up on his own in 1965 after an acrimonious dispute with his brother Peter whose family still run the enterprise.

Although Charles Krug did not come from a German wine region (he was born near Kassel), he exemplifies the important contribution to pioneer wine-growing made by Germans in all parts of the US where the vine was successfully cultivated.   T.P.

Kuč. See TRBLJAN.

kvevri. See QVEVRI.

KWV, the South African Co-operative Wine Growers' Association, or Ko-operatiewe Wijn-bowers Vereniging van Zuid Afrika, was a statutory body established in 1918 after years of glut and grower bankruptcy, to fix production quotas and to minimize extreme swings between surplus and shortage. Over time, and as a result of the close ties between successive white governments and the influential grape-farming lobby, it became the dominant force in the South African wine industry. In 1998 it was relieved of its statutory authority and converted from CO-OPERATIVE to a company. It is now a moderately sized player in the domestic and export market, producing increasingly impressive wines in its premium ranges, as well as aged brandies which enjoy international renown.   M.F.

Fridjhon, M., and Murray, A., *Conspiracy of Giants* (Johannesburg, 1986).

James, T., *Wines of the New South Africa: Tradition and Revolution* (Berkeley, 2013).

South African Wine Industry Directory (Paarl, annually).

Kyrgyzstan, mountainous central Asian republic on the border between KAZAKHSTAN and China of only minor wine-producing importance. Kyrgyzstan, whose capital is Bishkek, has a CONTINENTAL climate and three zones favourable for viticulture: the Chuia and the Talas valleys, the south of the country, and the Issyk-Kul depression. Commercial viticulture is developed in the first two zones. The country's grape and wine industry specializes in the production of TABLE GRAPES and DRYING GRAPES although about 14,000 hl/369,840 gal of wine, mostly strong and sweet, was produced from the country's 6,000 ha/14,820 acres of vineyard in 2011, according to OIV statistics.

The Issyk-Kul depression is at an elevation of 1,600 to 1,800 m (5,250 to 5,900 ft) around Lake Issyk-Kul. This viticultural region does not experience large temperature fluctuations. Because the July average daily temperature is 18 °C/64 °F and that of January is 3 °C/37.5 °F, no WINTER PROTECTION is needed. The central part of this region, on the south and north banks of Lake Issyk-Kul, is particularly favourable for viticulture and the production of dessert wines and base materials for sparkling wines. Practically all vineyards in Kyrgyzstan have some form of IRRIGATION.

Grape varieties used for wine include RKATSITELI, PINOT NOIR, Bayan Shirey, Kuljinski, CABERNET SAUVIGNON, RIESLING, SAPERAVI, Budeshuri Tetri, Mairam, Mourvèdre Kirghizski, Hungarian Muscat, and Black Muscat.   V.R.

In 1999, the ANTINORI family of Italy undertook a small vineyard development north of Lake Issyk-Kul, together with an experimental winery, with the aim of demonstrating to an essentially nomadic population the virtues of stable, long-term agriculture. Eight hectares of spur-pruned, cordon-trained Chardonnay, Riesling, and Pinot Noir yielded their first crop in 2002. The growing season is relatively short but serviceable wines have been made for Russian and Chinese markets.

labelling information. The amount of information required on wine LABELS seems to increase dramatically each year. In the past, approaches to wine labelling differed significantly between countries but the demands of international trade have led to a gradual convergence in the types of information required on a label (if not necessarily the underlying philosophies). The following basic items of information are now mandatory in virtually every country in some form or another.

Wine designation: usually this will be a self-explanatory term such as 'wine' or 'sparkling wine'. Wines made within the EU must, where applicable, indicate their status as a PDO or PGI and/or the name of the relevant PDO or PGI. In the US, the 'class and type' designation may be a generic term such as 'table wine' (for wines between 7% and 14% alcohol) or a grape variety name.

Country of origin: most wine-producing countries take this to refer to the origin of the grapes, although in some countries it can refer to the place where the wine was blended (see CANADA, for example).

Name and address of importer, producer, or bottler: this is usually provided in a fairly straightforward fashion, although, within Europe, there are controls on the size of an address which happens to incorporate the name of a CONTROLLED APPELLATION on the label of a WINE WITHOUT GEOGRAPHICAL INDICATION, or even a PGI wine, so some sort of postal code is sometimes substituted.

Volume of wine: usually expressed in millilitres (ml or mL) or, in Europe, centilitres (cl or cL). See BOTTLE SIZES and BOXES.

Alcoholic strength: stated as a percentage of alcohol by volume (often abbreviated to 'alc. x% vol' or 'x% vol'). Earlier terms such as degrees (°) or, in Italy in particular, *gradi* have been

phased out. Tolerances can differ considerably, from the +/− 0.5% alcohol variance permitted in the EU and China to +/− 1.5% in the US, Australia, and New Zealand. However, for wines that are made to be exported to a range of countries, winemakers tend to stay within the strictest tolerances. See ALCOHOLIC STRENGTH.

Lot marking: packaged wine must be marked with a lot number unique to an individual batch or bottling so that it can be traced in the event of any complaint or recall. In Europe, the mark is usually an L followed by a coded date of packaging.

Health-related information: this is increasingly required on wine labels. In order to comply with international rules, in most countries it is now obligatory to state on the label that a wine contains SULFITES if it contains more than 10 mg/l of SULFUR DIOXIDE. Sulfur dioxide is used to a certain extent in the making of virtually all wine and is a by-product of FERMENTATION, therefore virtually all wine contains this level of sulfites.

Several jurisdictions, including the EU, Australia, New Zealand, and Canada, also require a reference to the presence of egg or milk residues if the wine has been FINED with EGG WHITES, milk, or CASEIN and if these are present above detection limits in the finished wine, even though there is scant evidence of any health issues associated with the tiny concentrations found in wine as a result of such processing. See also VEGETARIAN AND VEGAN WINES.

Health 'warnings' of various sorts are increasingly found on wine labels. In some cases they are required by law (such as the US Surgeon General's warning), while in others they are voluntary initiatives (as in the UK). The pregnancy advisory pictogram that originated in France now appears on labels all over the world.

The following items of information are generally optional but, if used, are subject to certain

rules. Note that exporting producers must comply not only with the rules in their own country but also with those in the market to which they are exporting.

Geographical reference: typically, all but the most basic wines, or the most experimental, are distinguished by some form of geographical label reference that is more specific than the country of origin. In most cases this will be a GEOGRAPHICAL INDICATION of some sort, possibly accompanied by the name of a smaller area such as a vineyard name. The minimum permitted proportion of the blend that must be sourced from the named area ranges from 75% (USA, Chile), to 80% (China), to 85% (NZ, Australia, AVAs, European PGIs) to 100% (Argentina, South Africa, European PDOs). In some jurisdictions, it is not permitted to have more than one geographical indication on the label, which is one of the reasons for the creation of mega-GIs such as SOUTH EASTERN AUSTRALIA that facilitate blends drawn from a wide area.

Vintage year: the year in which the grapes were harvested, although in rare cases (e.g. Canadian ICEWINE harvested in the new year) the vintage may in fact be the year in which the most of the growing took place. The minimum content of wine sourced from the vintage ranges from 75% (Chile), to 80% (China), to 85% (Australia, NZ, South Africa, US, European PGIs) to 95% (AVAs, Argentina, South Africa, European PDOs). See VINTAGE YEAR and NON-VINTAGE.

Varietal information: in most European countries, if a single variety is specified on a label of wine, then it must comprise at least 85% of the wine. In the US, it must comprise at least 75% (or 51% in the case of some particularly FOXY native varieties). If more than one variety is mentioned on the label, in many countries, e.g. the US, Europe, South Africa, and Chile, together they must comprise 100%.

Bottling information: the relationship between the source of the grapes and the producer or bottler is indicated by exactly how this is expressed. See BOTTLING INFORMATION for more details.

On a CHAMPAGNE label, the following codes printed next to the registered number of the bottler are useful:

NM: *négociant-manipulant*, one of the big houses/firms/négociants;

RM: *récoltant-manipulant*, a grower who makes his or her own wine;

CM: *coopérative de manipulation*, one of the co-operatives;

RC: *récoltant-coopérateur*, grower selling wine made by a co-op;

MA: *marque d'acheteur*, buyer's own brand;

SR: *société de récoltant*, a small family company (rare);

R: *récoltant*, very small-scale growers (very rare).

Environmental labelling: labels indicating the status of a wine as ORGANIC, BIODYNAMIC, SUSTAINABLE, or similar are now common. Such claims are usually validated by accreditation to a particular programme or standard, some national, some international.

Sweetness: see SWEETNESS.

Fizziness: see FIZZINESS. J.B.

labels, the principal means by which a wine producer or bottler can communicate with a potential customer and consumer (although see also BOTTLES, CASE, FOIL).

Wine labels are a relatively recent development, which awaited the widespread sale of bottled wine, and use of glues strong enough to stick to glass in about 1860. Before then wines were sold unlabelled and stacked in BINS, and served in decanters, so BIN LABELS and DECANTER LABELS are the precursors of today's wine-bottle label. For many years, wines were identified by branded CORKS rather than by paper labels, a habit that persisted longest for vintage PORT.

Every wine in commercial circulation has to have a main label, as its passport quite apart from its function as a sales aid. Many wines also have a **neck label**, typically carrying the VINTAGE year, so that the producer need not have new main labels printed for each new vintage (although labelling requirements can change so rapidly that in practice this sometimes seems necessary). See LABELLING INFORMATION for details of the information available on a main label. As wine consumers have become ever more sophisticated and curious, however, an increasing proportion of bottles carry a **back label** giving additional background information. This can vary from a genuinely useful outline of grape varieties used, vintage conditions, approximate SWEETNESS level, and serving

advice, to a collection of fine-sounding words involving the 'finest' grape varieties picked at 'perfect ripeness' in 'optimum conditions' and vinified according to the 'highest standards', but which contain no genuine information whatsoever. Now that the amount of mandatory information required on wine labels is so considerable, some design-conscious bottlers try to beat the system by conveying all of this detail on what is obviously meant to be the back label, while applying to a second label (which the retailer, but not the labelling inspector, is meant to treat as the main label) a dramatic design statement without all the clutter of the mandatory information.

Labels matter to lawyers and officials, and they matter enormously to the retail wine trade, in which they communicate far more effectively with many consumers than any recommendation or award, but they are relatively unimportant to wine sales from a website or catalogue or in the hotel and restaurant industry. The efforts of some new wine producers to design a really distinctive label may thus be partly wasted, although they may be appreciated. The Italians have been as innovative in label design as in that of bottles, and some NEW WORLD designs can be arresting, effective, innovative, and sometimes all three. ARTISTS' LABELS have a certain following. Producers of established wines have usually inherited a label and rarely do anything more than slightly modify it. The fact that the label of PETRUS would win no design award seems to do little to hinder sales. The label design of wine BRANDS, however, is an extremely important factor in their success.

Labels are usually, but not always, applied straight after BOTTLING as part of the same mechanized process. Some very small-scale producers still apply their labels by hand with pots of glue. Producers of champagne and other sparkling wines take particular care to use strong, water-resistant adhesive in applying their labels since their bottles are likely to spend their last hours in public circulation immersed in a bucket of water.

Wine labels have such a fascination of their own, and can help recollection of the circumstances of their consumption, that wine **label collecting** is a recognized activity. Some of those who practise it call themselves vintitulists.

labour. Viticulture, unlike winemaking, has long required a substantial input of labour. The Romans used slaves while MONKS AND MONASTERIES played an important part in medieval vine-growing. A peasant class was long necessary to maintain viticulture in Europe, and increasingly vineyard labour was paid for by leasing part of the vineyard to the labourer, share-cropping or, in French, MÉTAYAGE. The close association

between vine-growing and humans began to alter towards the end of the 20th century, however, mainly because of changes in technology.

There have traditionally been three levels of labour input to viticulture: man alone, man plus draught animal, and man plus machines. In the future, robots may do some vineyard tasks. In ancient vineyards, all work was done by man, which consisted of WEED CONTROL, PRUNING, TRIMMING, DESUCKERING, LAYERING, and HARVESTING. The labour input was high, and vineyards on the plains required between 70 and 80 man-days per hectare per year. This means that any one person might tend about 3 ha/7 acres, with due allowance for using other labour at times of peak demand such as harvesting and pruning. The YIELD from such vineyards was not high compared with modern standards. A generous 33.5 hl/ha (2 tons/acre) meant that one man's labour might produce a maximum of about 15 tonnes of grapes. For HILLSIDE VINEYARDS, one man might tend only about 100 sq m of vineyard, although this was not necessarily full-time work, with a likely output of tens of kilograms of grapes per person per year. Such vineyards relying totally on manual labour are increasingly rare, as the price of labour has increased much more than the price of wine, but some may be found all around the Mediterranean.

Intensive labour input continued for many vineyards up until the mid to late 19th century, when the invasion of POWDERY MILDEW, DOWNY MILDEW, and PHYLLOXERA led to the need for SPRAYING, and ROOTSTOCKS. Previously many vineyards had been planted haphazardly without rows, and with high density, almost like a field of wheat. As need be, unhealthy vines were replaced by layering from adjacent vines. With the need to spray, and also for ploughing, draught animals became more common, not only horses but also mules and oxen. Indeed, milk cows were also used; in France's Auvergne, for example, cows provided meat, milk, and labour. Vines then needed to be planted in rows to make easy the passage of the animal, and there were typically many fewer plants per hectare because of the cost of GRAFTING plants on rootstocks. One horse was able to work 7 ha, and one man was needed for every 3 ha. A typical family farm consisted of about 7 ha of vines, one horse with two drivers, and one labourer.

After the Second World War, the pattern of viticulture changed in France and elsewhere with the widespread introduction of MECHANIZATION. This was no simple matter, as there were conflicts between generations of farmers about replacing horses with TRACTORS, and substantial changes in the support services in rural villages. Mechanics and fuel salesmen replaced blacksmiths and fodder merchants. In the end, economic necessity determined the future; one man and a tractor was now able to tend 30 ha of vineyards, although with manual labour including pruning, trimming, and harvesting, 1 ha still required 43 days' work throughout the year.

In the 1960s, the mechanization revolution intensified. Under-vine ploughing had been largely replaced by HERBICIDES, and then there was the introduction of MECHANICAL HARVESTING followed by that of MECHANICAL PRUNING. Some sprays were even applied from the air, using aeroplanes or HELICOPTERS. There are some vineyards in south-eastern Australia where the total annual labour input is less than 50 man-hours per hectare: all operations are carried out mechanically including harvesting and pruning; spray units treat multiple rows at once; and weed control is by herbicides. On large estates, one worker is required for each 30 ha with this degree of mechanization, and the output can be more than 500 tonnes of wine grapes. This figure, compared with less than 15 tonnes per person about a century earlier, demonstrates how labour productivity has increased through mechanization. A counter-trend, albeit generally on a smaller scale, is the move towards ORGANIC and BIODYNAMIC grape growing, the latter in particular requiring considerable human input.

Australian examples are relevant because of the acute rural labour shortage here and in New Zealand, although Asian and Pacific island immigrants, as well as working students, were providing some solutions in the first decades of the 21st century. The wine industries of South America and, especially, South Africa have never known a labour shortage while in California and elsewhere on the West Coast of the US, Mexico has provided an exceptionally skilled viticultural labour force.

Future developments are not obvious. With improved computer technology there is renewed interest in developing robots for grapevine pruning, as at Canterbury in New Zealand and Purdue in Michigan in the US but the variability of vineyards, of terrain, and of the weather make the task of robot development and use more difficult than for the factory floor.

It seems likely, however, that an increasing proportion of vineyard tasks will be mechanized, even in countries where labour resources are not necessarily limiting or expensive. Mechanization is seen to offer benefits of timeliness as well as of economics, which encourage its further adoption. However, on a few estates where the slopes are too steep for mechanized ploughing, or where there is a wish to avoid SOIL COMPACTION, notably in ALSACE and BURGUNDY, and increasingly in Bordeaux's upper echelons, producers have returned to using ploughs pulled by draught animals such as horses.

Once the grapes have been delivered to the winery, winemaking requires relatively little labour. A WINEMAKER is required to make decisions and, increasingly, program a computer which may control such operations as TEMPERATURE CONTROL and RACKING wine from one container to another (see INFORMATION TECHNOLOGY).

Only BARREL MATURATION and, particularly, LEES STIRRING require much manual labour (see CELLAR WORK). Otherwise, cleaning is the chief manual operation.   R.E.S. & J.R.

Coombe, B. G., and Dry, P. R. (eds.), *Viticulture*, ii: *Practices* (Adelaide, 1992).

Galet, P., *Précis de viticulture* (7th edn, Montpellier, 2000).

labrusca, species of the *Vitis* genus native to North America. The juice of its grapes, and wine made from them, usually have a pronounced flavour described as FOXY. See VITIS.

L'Acadie Blanc, winter-hardy grape variety speciality of Nova Scotia and Quebec in CANADA. Named after the French term for Nova Scotia, it is a cross of Cascade (a complex HYBRID created by SEIBEL) and SEYVE-VILLARD 14–287 made in 1953 at Vineland Research, Ontario (now part of Guelph University). It ripens early, has good disease resistance, and is particularly suitable for regions with very short growing seasons.

laccase, a powerful oxidative ENZYME particularly associated with BOTRYTIS BUNCH ROT which turns grape must brown.

La Clape. See CLAPE.

Lacrima di Morro d'Alba, fast maturing, wild strawberry-scented red grape speciality of Morro d'Alba in the MARCHE. The 2010 Italian vine census noted 420 ha/1,037 acres.

La Crosse, promising, cold-hardy, complex American hybrid widely dispersed in the Midwest.

lactic acid, one of the milder ACIDS in wine, present in much lower concentrations than either MALIC ACID or TARTARIC ACID. Lactic acid, named after *lactis*, Latin for milk, is most frequently encountered as the principal acid in yoghurt, sour milk, pickled cucumbers, and sauerkraut. Lactic acid is a common participant in both plant and animal metabolic processes. It is the end-product of intense muscular activity in animals (see ACIDS); a by-product of the alcoholic FERMENTATION process in wines and beers; and the end-product of the metabolic action of the many LACTIC ACID BACTERIA.

In wine, lactic acid can be produced by bacteria both from traces of sugar and from malic acid. The function of the second MALOLACTIC CONVERSION, which a high proportion of red wines and some white wines undergo, is to transform harsh malic acid into the much milder lactic acid.   A.D.W.

lactic acid bacteria, or **LAB**, an abbreviation of **lactic acid producing bacteria**, known by some winemakers simply as **lactics**, are some of the few BACTERIA that can survive in such an acidic solution as wine. They all produce LACTIC ACID. Those of importance to winemaking can be subdivided into the three genera: *Oenococcus* (of which the best known species is *Oenococcus oeni*, formally called *Leuconostoc oenos*), *Lactobacillus*, and *Pediococcus*. They are the agents of MALOLACTIC CONVERSION in wines, by which the harsh MALIC ACID is effectively decomposed into the milder lactic acid. *Lactobacillus* and *Pediococcus* are also involved in the production of pickles, sauerkraut, and yoghurt.

Oenococcus species function best in environments that contain very small amounts of OXYGEN, which is why their growth on grapes is limited., whereas *Lactobacillus* and *Pediococcus* also grow well in aerobic environments. Lactic acid bacteria can inhabit wooden vats and barrels in traditional wineries and can be so deeply embedded in the wood fibres that even the highest standards of HYGIENE are unable to remove them. They can have the positive effect of conducting malolactic conversion in wines with an excess of malic acid. In newer wineries, lactic acid bacteria may need to be deliberately introduced to achieve this effect. Unfortunately, however, many strains of lactic acid bacteria can generate off-flavours and turbidity in wines., making *Oenococcus oeni* the preferred species for malolactic conversion. This is most likely to happen when traces of sugar remain as nutrients in the wine. Some species of LAB can also produce biogenic amines, notably HISTAMINE, tyramine, and putrescine. A recent Spanish study found ranges of 1–13 mg/l and showed differences between grape varieties and LAB species. Low PH prevented biogenic amine formation. Malolactic conversion and short storage periods in bottle (3–6 months) showed increases in histamine concentration, whereas longer periods of storage led to a general decrease in histamine. Many countries have informal legal limits on histamine but legal limits are still a matter of debate. See also ALLERGIES.

Fortunately, however, lactic acid bacteria are very sensitive to SULFUR DIOXIDE and are much easier to control than ACETOBACTER, the other group of bacteria of winemaking importance. Lactic acid bacteria grow best in very weakly acidic solutions and in the presence of ETHANOL in a temperature range of 15–30 °C (59–86 ºF). Bacteriologists regard them as 'fastidious' in that they require a wide range of micronutrients. They are also intolerant of high concentrations of ETHANOL.

Their effect on new or young wine can therefore be limited by sulfur dioxide, low temperatures, and frequent RACKING so as to eliminate the possibility of providing micronutrients from the YEAST decomposition products in the LEES.   A.D.W. & E.J.B.

Landete, J. M., et al., 'Biogenic amines in wines from three Spanish regions', *Journal of Agricultural and Food Chemistry*, 53 (2005), 1119–24.

Moreno-Arribas, M. V., Smit, A. Y., and du Toit, M., 'Biogenic amines and the winemaking process', in A. Reynolds (ed.), *Managing Wine Quality 2: Oenology and Wine Quality* (Cambridge, 2010), 494–522.

lactones. See OAK FLAVOUR.

Ladoix, the appellation from the village of **Ladoix-Serrigny** in the Côte de Beaune district of Burgundy's Côte d'Or, producing about 70% red wines from Pinot Noir grapes, sometimes sold as Côte de Beaune-Villages (see BEAUNE, CÔTE DE). White wines are growing in popularity, especially those grown towards the top of the slope. Unusually in Burgundy, some of the premiers crus are designated for red wine only (e.g. Les Joyeuses) or white wines only (e.g. Les Gréchons) while bizarrely a small number of premier cru vineyards located in Ladoix such as Les Moutottes are sold under the name Aloxe-Corton. Furthermore, 6 ha of Corton-Charlemagne and 22 ha (out of 160) of Le Corton, including part of Le Rognet and Les Vergennes, are actually sited in Ladoix (see ALOXE-CORTON for more details).

See also CÔTE D'OR, and map under BURGUNDY.   J.T.C.M.

ladybirds. See LADYBUG TAINT.

ladybug taint, also known as **lady beetle** or **ladybird taint**, is an off-flavour found in both grape juice and wine that contributes undesirable peanut- and/or green-like aromas and flavours, and possibly excessive bitterness. Two lady beetle species that migrate to vineyards during autumn—the seven-spot ladybird/ladybug (*Coccinella septempunctata*) from Europe, and particularly the multicoloured Asian lady beetle (or harlequin ladybird, *Harmonia axyridis*)—are known to cause the taint in the US and Canada. Both were originally introduced to North America to control aphids. It is unlikely that the beetles directly harm the grapes. Instead, they cause contamination after they are inadvertently harvested with the fruit and are incorporated in the MUST. The compounds responsible are alkyl-methoxypyazines—components of the insects' haemolymph—and are difficult to remove from affected juice and wine, although juice settling and must-heating prior to fermentation can help. While not always openly acknowledged, ladybug taint is a problem in some wines and vintages across many of the world's wine regions, including the US, France, Germany, and Canada. The first major incidence in northern North

America was in 2001, while the 2004 and 2011 vintages in Burgundy were probably the first two to be widely discussed in this context. In Europe, however, the culprit seems to be the common seven-spot ladybird.   G.P.

Botezatu, A., and Pickering, G. J., 'Ladybug (*Coccinellidae*) taint in wine', in A. G. Reynolds (ed.), *Managing Wine Quality 2: Oenology and Wine Quality* (Cambridge, 2010), 418–29.

Pickering, G. J., et al., 'Influence of *Harmonia axyridis* on the sensory properties of white and red wine', *American Journal of Enology and Viticulture*, 55/2 (2004), 153–9.

Vincent, C., and Pickering, G., '*Harmonia axyridis* (Pallas), Multicolored Asian Ladybeetle (Coleoptera: Coccinellidae)', in P. Mason and D. Gillespie (eds.), *Biological Control Program in Canada (2001–2010)*. (Canada, 2013), 192–8.

Lafite, Château, subsequently **Ch Lafite-Rothschild**, FIRST GROWTH in the MÉDOC region of BORDEAUX. The vineyard, to the north of the small town of PAUILLAC and adjoining Ch MOUTON ROTHSCHILD, was probably planted in the first third of the 17th century. Inherited in 1716 by the SÉGURS, who also owned Ch LATOUR, it was sold in 1784 to Pierre de Pichard, an extremely rich president of the Bordeaux Parlement who perished on the scaffold. The estate was confiscated and sold as public property in 1797 to a Dutch consortium which in 1803 resold it to a Dutch grain merchant and supplier to Napoleon's armies, Ignace-Joseph Vanlerberghe. When he fell on hard times, he resold it to his former wife in order to avoid its falling into a creditor's hands. Perhaps for the same reason, or to avoid splitting it up under French inheritance laws, in 1821 she apparently sold it to a London banker, Sir Samuel Scott, for 1 million francs. He and then his son were the nominal owners for over 40 years. But when the real proprietor Aimé Vanlerberghe died without issue in 1866, the family decided to sell it and pay the fines owed because of the concealment. In 1868, after a stiff contest with a Bordeaux syndicate, it was knocked down to Baron James de ROTHSCHILD of the Paris bank, for 4.4 million francs, including part of the Carruades vineyard. Baron James died in the same year and the château has remained in the family ever since. Baron Eric de Rothschild took over direction of the property from his uncle Baron Élie in 1974. In the famous 1855 CLASSIFICATION, Lafite was placed first of the premiers crus, although there is controversy as to whether the order was alphabetical or by rank. Yet, as Christie's AUCTIONS in the 1960s and 1970s of 19th century British country mansion cellars showed, in Britain Lafite was nearly always the favoured first growth.

The château itself is a 16th century manor. The vineyard, one of the largest in the Haut-Médoc, had grown to 112 ha/276 acres by 2014:

72% Cabernet Sauvignon, 25% Merlot, 2% Cabernet Franc, and 1% Petit Verdot. Annual production has been reduced to about 36,000 cases, of which up to 60% may be the SECOND WINE, called Carruades de Lafite but not restricted to wine produced on the plateau in the vineyard known as Les Carruades. See ROTHS-CHILDS AND WINE for other wine investments made by the owners of Ch Lafite.

E.P.-R. & J.R.

Penning-Rowsell, E., *The Wines of Bordeaux* (6th edn, London, 1979).

Lafnetscha, rare Swiss Valais white grape often mistaken for COMPLETER. In fact, DNA PROFILING at DAVIS showed in 2004 that Lafnetscha is an offspring of HUMAGNE BLANCHE of the Valais and Completer of Graubünden in Switzerland.   J.V.

Lafões, DOP with considerable unrealized potential in central northern Portugal making light, dry white wines similar to those of neighbouring Vinho Verde, sometimes referred to as *verdascos*. Red wines are more similar to those of nearby DÃO.   R.J.M.

lagar, term used in PORTUGAL for a low-sided stone trough where grapes are trodden and fermented. Most have now been replaced by conventional fermentation vats except in the DOURO Valley, where some of the best ports continue to be foot-trodden in *lagares*. In the late 1990s, ROBOTIC *lagares* were introduced in the Douro by the SYMINGTON family and have become an important factor in the making of premium quality port. See PORT for more detail.

Lagoa, DOP centred on the sole remaining CO-OPERATIVE winery (Única–Adega Cooperativa do Algarve) DOC in the ALGARVE, southern Portugal.

Lagorthi, name for VERDEA in Greece where it is admired for its aromatic whites but is all too rare.

Lagos, fishing port, holiday resort, and DOP in southern Portugal. See ALGARVE.

Lagrein, increasingly popular and well-connected INDIGENOUS red grape variety grown in 2010 on 653 ha/1,613 acres in ALTO ADIGE and TRENTINO. Although often over-produced, it can produce **Lagrein Scuro** or **Lagrein Dunkel**, somewhat tannic reds of real character, as well as fragrant yet sturdy rosé called **Lagrein Rosato** or **Lagrein Kretzer**. Lagrein can be slightly bitter on the finish and its presence, valued for both TANNINS and colour, can at times be detected in blends. DNA PROFILING has established that Lagrein is, inter alia, a progeny of Teroldego, a grandchild of Pinot, and a cousin of Syrah.

Robinson, J., Harding, J., and Vouillamoz, J., *Wine Grapes, a complete guide to 1,368 vine varieties, including their origins and flavours* (London, 2012).

Lairén, very old minor southern Spanish white grape variety also known as Malvar and often mistaken for AIRÉN.

Laithwaite's, the world's biggest family-owned wine retailer and Britain's biggest wine company. It was founded as Direct Wines in 1969 by Tony Laithwaite, a geography student who worked on a modest wine farm in CASTILLON, fell in love with wine, and began driving it back to the UK to sell from a railway arch in Windsor. His wife Barbara came on board the next year and steered the company with awesome efficiency until 1991. A key milestone was launching the Direct *Sunday Times* Wine Club in 1973, with HUGH JOHNSON as president. This feet-first introduction to the logistics of selling wine by mail order was enabled by Laithwaite's whimsical charm and lateral thinking; he has always prided himself on operating outside the wine trade mainstream.

Never to be seen at the usual round of trade tastings, Laithwaite travelled the world instead and claims responsibility for introducing the British to the wines of Bulgaria, Romania, Moldova, Czechoslovakia, Australia, New Zealand, Languedoc, Chile, Portugal ('the post-MATEUS new era'), and even England. Laithwaite's, Barbara Laithwaite, and one of their three sons now have, separately, their own English vineyards.

It was Tony Laithwaite who coined the expression FLYING WINEMAKER and in the 1980s made full use of putting southern hemisphere winemakers to work in some of Europe's more primitive CO-OPERATIVE cellars. This fitted perfectly with the Laithwaite *modus operandi* of selling exclusive labels at high margins to customers who delighted in apparently buying them from their personal, compulsively literate friend Tony Laithwaite, a relationship which seems to have survived his transfer to the *Sunday Times* Rich List. By the 1990s the great majority of British direct wine sales, via whichever society or special offer, were fulfilled from Laithwaite's state-of-the art warehouse in the Berkshire countryside. They at last gained a major toehold in the traditional wine trade by acquiring the historic AVERYS of Bristol between 2002 and 2006, and sell and store considerable quantities of FINE WINE as well as their trademark quirkier offerings.

The Laithwaites had long before acquired and replanted the Castillon vineyard on which Tony Laithwaite did his apprenticeship, and in 2007 opened their own substantial winery, the Chai au Quai, nearby. In 2003, to capitalize on the number of highly-trained, under-funded and, often, under-employed oenology graduates in South Australia, Laithwaite's opened the RedHeads Studio in McLaren Vale, a CELLAR RATS' playpen from which the company was able to buy the cream of the crop.

But the real game changer came in 2006 when Laithwaite's acquired two businesses in the US, one in Connecticut and one in Illinois, which gave the firm a base from which to invade the growing American wine market. Today they operate the *Wall Street Journal*'s wine club as well as Laithwaite's Wine and Virgin Wines in the US.

The next year they expanded into direct wine sales in Australia, and also operate the wine club of *The Australian* newspaper and Virgin Wines there. By 2014 they had franchised wine merchants in Taiwan and Hong Kong together with supply agreements in Switzerland, Germany, Sweden, Denmark, and Poland. By 2014 revenues were £318 million.

www.jancisrobinson.com/articles/a200906165.html 'Britain's biggest wine company' (June 2009).

Lake County, smallest viticultural district among CALIFORNIA's NORTH COAST counties and among the least understood. In this warm inland district east of Mendocino county and north of Napa County, a vigorous but short-lived 19th century industry died out with PROHIBITION, leaving scant historic guidance to the growers who restored vineyards to the region during the 1970s. The county's 9,000 acres/3,642 ha of vines and its small population of 30 wineries is concentrated in the Clear Lake AVA.

Clear Lake AVA

Nearly all of the AVA's vineyards nestle between steep hills west of the lake, the largest entirely within California. By the early 1990s, the district, north of NAPA and east of MENDOCINO, had grown some excellent Sauvignon Blanc and pleasant, early-maturing Cabernet Sauvignon. Zinfandel is well adapted, although few producers take advantage. The Red Hills AVA, within the greater Clear Lake appellation, has proved to be adept at Cabernet Sauvignon, with its volcanic and sometimes obsidian-laced soils providing tannic structure and minerality. Although several wineries (especially the original KENDALL-JACKSON facility) are located near the town of Lakeport, a considerable proportion of the region's grapes go to wineries in Napa, Mendocino, and SONOMA Counties.

Guenoc Valley AVA

Inland wine region and AVA promoted by Orville Magoon's Guenoc winery, now owned by William Foley. Slightly north of Napa Valley, it's more famous for the fact that it was once the estate of British actress Lily Langtry than it is for its wines.

High Valley AVA

North east of Clear Lake, this relatively new AVA has myriad soil types, volcanic and alluvial, and has the potential to grow many varieties. Sauvignon Blanc and Tempranillo appear to be the early favourites.

lake effect, the year-round influence on vineyards from nearby large lakes which permits vine-growing in areas such as the north east UNITED STATES and Ontario in CANADA despite their high LATITUDE. In winter, the large lakes provide moisture to the prevailing westerly winds, which creates a deep snow cover, protecting vines from WINTER FREEZE even in very low temperatures. The lake may eventually freeze, depending on the size. In spring, the westerly winds blow across the frozen lake and become cooler. These cooler breezes blowing on the vines retard BUDBREAK until the danger of FROST has passed. In summer the lake warms up. By autumn/fall, the westerly winds are warmed as they blow across the lake. The warm breezes on the vines lengthen the growing season (balancing the late start to the growing season) by delaying the first frost. In other parts of the world, lakes and large inland seas also moderate climate through temperature effects alone. See MARITIME CLIMATE.   H.L.

Lalande-de-Pomerol, appellation to the immediate north of POMEROL that is very much in the shadow of this great red wine district of Bordeaux. It includes the communes of Lalande-de-Pomerol and Néac and produces lush, Merlot-dominated wines which can offer a suggestion, sometimes a decidedly rustic suggestion, of the concentration available in a bottle of fine Pomerol but at a fraction of the price. Including about 1,100 ha/2,700 acres of vineyards, the Lalande-de-Pomerol appellation is much bigger than that of Pomerol, and its soils are composed of clay, sand, and some well-drained gravels in the south where it is divided from the Pomerol appellation only by the Barbanne river. At one time, the Barbanne separated that part of France which said *oc* for yes (see LANGUEDOC) from that part which said *oïl* and spoke the *langue d'oïl*. Because land here is so much cheaper than in Pomerol, recent years have seen investment from those who already own properties in St-Emilion and, particularly, Pomerol. Obvious examples include La Fleur de Boüard, co-owned with Ch Angelus, and La Chenade and Les Cruzelles, co-owned with Ch l'Eglise Clinet.

La Mancha. See MANCHA.

Lambrusco, central Italian VARIETAL wine based on the eponymous red grape variety, or rather varieties, that was enormously popular with the mass market in the US and northern Europe in the 1980s. So successful was it that special white, pink, and 'light' versions were somewhat perversely created, the colour and alcohol often being deliberately removed. In spite of, or perhaps because of, this enormous commercial success, Lambrusco is the most scorned and least understood of all Italian wine styles.

The many different vines called Lambrusco are grown principally in the three central provinces of EMILIA—Modena, Parma, and Reggio nell'Emilia—although significant plantings can be found across the River Po in the province of Mantova, and occasional plantings can be found as far afield as PIEMONTE, TRENTINO, and even BASILICATA.

The wine varies considerably, and so do the vines. The 2010 Italian vine variety census distinguished between one Lambrusca and no fewer than ten different forms of Lambrusco of which the most planted were **Lambrusco Salamino** (a national total of 5,003 ha/12,357 acres), **Lambrusco Grasparossa** (2,726 ha/6,736 acres), **Lambrusco Maestri** (2,223 ha/5,493 acres), **Lambrusco di Sorbara** (1,606 ha/3,968 acres), and **Lambrusco Marani** (1,394 ha/3,444 acres). (See also ENANTIO.) Others identified by the 2010 Italian vine census are, in declining order of area planted, from 240 ha down to 18 ha, **Lambrusco Viadanese, Lambrusca di Alessandria, Lambrusco Oliva, Lambrusco Montericco**, and **Lambrusco Barghi**.

The total production of Lambrusco in 2013 was a staggering 165 million bottles, with less than 40 million produced under DOC rules, the majority being labelled IGT Emilia. Efforts to increase the quality of Lambrusco have led to a change in production rules so that for IGT Emilia, the SECOND FERMENTATION for Lambrusco must be within Emilia. While most Lambrusco found on export markets is medium sweet or sweet, the traditional wine is dry, and much favoured by Italians themselves, the pronounced ACIDITY and FIZZINESS being thought to help digest Emilia's hearty cuisine.

Most Lambrusco made today is a fairly anonymous, standardized product made in industrial quantities by CO-OPERATIVES or large commercial wineries using the Charmat or bulk method (see SPARKLING WINEMAKING) together with heavy FILTRATION, STABILIZATION, and, frequently, PASTEURIZATION. 'Proper', dry Lambrusco seemed in danger of disappearing at one stage, but an increasing number of artisan producers can be found in the various DOC zones, and even the large producers are starting to make dry styles.

The distinctive qualities of the different vine varieties and different zones have tended to disappear with large volumes, inter-regional blending, and industrial techniques. However, five Lambrusco DOCs were created on the basis of distinct terroir and varietal differences. The first four are exclusive to the small province of Modena.

DOC Modena encompasses the whole of Modena province, with some 9,000 ha/22,240 acres planted to any Lambrusco, and 5,000 ha/12,355 acres registered as DOC. The two largest producers, Chiarlo and Cavicchioli, produce 40 million bottles between them annually.

DOC Lambrusco Salamino di Santa Croce is the northern-most DOC on an extensive plain of alluvial sediment, sand, and silt. The vines are high-yielding resulting in simple, violet-scented, fruity wines with medium tannins. Luciano Saetti's exceptional single-vineyard Lambrusco proves that quality can be obtained here, if not without the sacrifice of lower yields.

DOC Lambrusco di Sorbara on an alluvial plain, produces pale, rosé-like wines which tend to be dry and lively. Elegant wines come from potassium-rich sandy soils, while further on to the plain where clay soils dominate, the wines are heavier. Francesco Bellei makes a complex Lambrusco Rifermentazione Ancestrale (see MÉTHODE ANCESTRALE).

DOC Lambrusco Grasparossa di Castelvetro is the furthest south. This early budding, early ripening, and least vigorous Lambrusco is planted on undulating foothills around Castelvetro on sandy soils containing silt and marl. Considered the finest DOC of Lambrusco, its wines are rich in aroma, colour, extract, and tannin so that they may contain a little RESIDUAL SUGAR in compensation.

DOC Lambrusco Mantovano is a tiny DOC in Lombardia producing dry red sparkling wines mainly for local consumption.

Lambrusco is one of the suffices of the DOC REGGIANO in EMILIA-ROMAGNA, although Reggiano Lambrusco may include up to 60% of the deep-coloured ANCELLOTTA grape. Within this large area lies the superior Colli di Scandiano e Canossa, where Lambrusco Grasparossa is planted on HILLSIDES only, and whose yields are a fraction of those allowed in DOC Reggiano.

W.S. & T.D.C.

Francesco F., 'Lambrusco—Da Modena a Mantova Passando per Reggio' (*Enogea* Agosto/Settembre 2009).

Robinson, J., Harding, J., and Vouillamoz, J., *Wine Grapes, a complete guide to 1,368 vine varieties, including their origins and flavours* (London, 2012).

Lancers, BRAND of medium-sweet, lightly sparkling wine made by the firm of J. M. da FONSECA at Azeitão, near SETÚBAL in PORTUGAL. The brand was created in 1944, when Vintage Wines of New York saw that American veterans of the Second World War were returning home from Europe with a taste for wine. Lancers, initially sold in a stone crock, continues to be moderately successful in the United States, whereas MATEUS Rosé, created two years earlier, tends to be better known in Europe. A fully sparkling Lancers, made by the CONTINUOUS METHOD, was introduced in the late 1980s. R.J.M.

Landot, or **Landot 4511**, cold-hardy FRENCH HYBRID making soft red wine in the northeastern United States.

Landwein, rarely seen PGI category of dry Austrian or German wine. In GERMANY, Landwein must have an ALCOHOLIC STRENGTH of at least half a per cent more than the minimum level for German WINE WITHOUT GEOGRAPHICAL INDICATION. Austria's much higher minimum is 14 °KMW (68 °OECHSLE), reflecting the warmer climate.

Langenlois, dominant village of Austria's compact but bountiful KAMPTAL growing region.

Langhe, plural of **Langa**, name given to the hills to the north and south of the city of Alba in the province of Cuneo in PIEMONTE on the right bank of the River Tanaro. The soils, composed of clay marls, are the classic ones for the NEBBIOLO grape, and produce the Langhe's most famous wines BAROLO and BARBARESCO, although they can also yield BARBERA, DOLCETTO, and MOSCATO of excellent quality. The hills gradually rise to the south of Monforte d'Alba, creating a climatic limit to the cultivation of Nebbiolo, and to the south of Dogliani up to 600 m/1,970 ft. The area is increasingly important for the production of TRADITIONAL METHOD sparkling wines based on Chardonnay and Pinot Noir under the DOCG Alta Langa.

Langhe is also the name of a regional DOC, overlapping with the DOCG ROERO on the left bank of the Tanaro (and therefore not part of the Langhe geographically). The Langhe DOC is used for non-traditional grape varieties such as Chardonnay, Sauvignon Blanc, Riesling, Arneis, and Nas'cetta, and as a DOC category into which more geographically limited DOC wines can be declassified: Dolcetto d'Alba can become Langhe Dolcetto, for example, or Barbera d'Alba may become Langhe Rosso. Most Barolo and Barbaresco producers who bottle a cheaper Nebbiolo for relatively early drinking label it Langhe Nebbiolo as, perversely, the DOC Nebbiolo d'Alba is almost entirely confined to the left bank of the Tanaro, coinciding with Roero, and includes only tiny parts of the classic Barolo communes. W.S.

Arnulfo, C., *Langhe e Roero. From the Soil to the Glass* (Cuneo, 2012).
www.langhevini.it

Langhorne Creek, productive wine region with 26 producers in SOUTH AUSTRALIA cooled by Lake Alexandrina and the nearby Southern Ocean. It has an unusual ability to produce large yields of medium-bodied red wines which achieve sensory ripeness (an important ingredient in Orlando Wyndham's red JACOB'S CREEK) in its temperate climate. Smaller wineries which limit yields on estate vineyards are producing high-quality Shiraz, Cabernet Sauvignon, and blends thereof. Verdelho and Malbec are local specialities.

language of wine. Wine-talk is a problem: 'When trying to talk about wine in depth, one rapidly comes up against the limitations of our means of expression … We need to be able to describe the indescribable. We tasters feel to some extent betrayed by language,' comments Émile PEYNAUD.

Wine-talk is triply disadvantaged: first, people TASTE and smell wine differently from each other; second, a partially obscure conventional vocabulary has arisen: the wine flavour described as gooseberry, for example, does not taste very much like gooseberries (quite apart from the difficulties caused by the fact that gooseberries are known only in a limited number of cultures); third, the need to impress customers in a cut-throat market has led to ear-catching and sometimes bizarre descriptions: 'a fascinating old, old smell of unswept floorboards', 'old tarpaulin fringed with lace', 'Wham bam thankyou mam red, all rich, gooey, almost treacly fruit-dark plums and prunes awash with liquorice and chocolate and cream'.

In many ways, wine descriptions are in their linguistic infancy, parallel to the days when linguistic sounds could be described only by comparison to other sounds: in the 16th century, English *a* was described as like 'the balling of the sheepe when she feedeth', for example. Phonetics now has an International Phonetic Alphabet, with agreed parameters, but this is still far from true of wine terminology.

Descriptive terms should be distinguished from expressive or evaluative ones, it is sometimes argued. Yet even this proves to be difficult for wine: even the most straightforward descriptions are bizarre by the standards of 'normal' usage. An English speaker asked to describe the colours red and white is likely to mention blood versus snow, yet a red wine is typically reddish-purple and a white one pale straw, each with a range that goes beyond the usual boundaries for red and white. Other wine colour terms are equally odd: black, as in Greek MAVRODAPHNE 'black-daphne' or the old 'black wine' of CAHORS, refers simply to a hue darker than is usual for wines.

Yet colours illustrate one useful way in which wine terms can be partially analysed, by looking at the internal structure of the wine vocabulary. Red and white are opposites on a scale with rosé in the middle. Such antonyms are an anchor-point in descriptions. Possibly for this reason, the terms sweet versus dry are the first technical terms to be widely understood, and are now regularly found in supermarket classifications, even though, outside a wine context, the average person would oppose sweet to sour, and dry to wet.

Technically, antonyms such as sweet versus dry are gradable, in that sweet means 'sweet in relation to a norm', even though the norm is far from clear. Further opposites/scales have not generally caught on, though some recur in descriptions, as young vs. mature, light vs. heavy, crisp (nicely acidic) vs. flabby—though a basic problem is that a word such as flabby tends to be used as a general derogatory term, so is also found in opposition to terms such as hearty, sturdy, meaty, which indicate a wine with BODY.

Synonyms are also useful in understanding vocabulary structure, and words for wines with 'body' abound: beefy, big, broad, chunky, powerful, robust—though none has yet won out over others.

As the above examples show, most wine descriptions involve adjectives, though ones with a somewhat specialized interpretation. Adjectives depend for their meaning on the words to which they are attached: an old wine will be younger than an old house, but possibly older than an old friend, who may well not be aged. Many wine adjectives consist of a noun plus ending -y, as buttery, chalky, chocolatey, earthy, flinty, flowery, fruity, grapey, herby, meaty, nutty, oaky, peppery, silky, spicy, sugary, velvety.

Readers of wine columns sometimes get the misleading impression that 'anything goes'. Yet the majority of wine flavour descriptions cover a fairly narrow range, mostly of other food words, as appley, gamey, grapefruity, minty, peachy, plummy, raspberry—though these are often 'code' terms, in that a wine described as grapefruity or minty does not (to the uninitiated) taste very much like either. Terms that move outside these food flavours relate easily only to a small portion of wine qualities, as with the power terms listed above for wines with body. A further set relate perceived smoothness to fabrics, so wines may be velvety, silky, satiny—though even here, the range of fabrics is limited: a wine may be soft, though is not normally woolly. Shape and TEXTURE terms tend to be applied to wines with a high degree of ACIDITY, as angular, austere, flinty, steely. The AROMA (nose) is perhaps the aspect of wine that has caused the greatest controversy in recent years, and seems to be hardest to convey: cat's pee, pencil shavings, sweaty saddles, tobacco had relatively little attention paid to them, yet fury erupted when a serious critic referred to a wine as smelling of hamster cages. Any successful metaphor must achieve cultural resonance, and avoid cognitive dissonance: it must fit in with existing traditions and preconceptions or risk being rejected.

Yet in many cases, wine descriptions are unclear only out of context or when single words are used. Humans often think about word meanings in terms of 'prototypes' or typical examples. Prototypes are bundles of characteristics: so a robin, a prototypical bird, has a red breast, is fairly small, has wings, slender legs, and so on. Similarly, a bunch of features characterize particular wines, some of them accurate, some evocative: a Sauvignon Blanc, for example, popularly referred to as 'cat's pee on a gooseberry bush' is spoken of as acidic, clean, refreshing. However, increasingly, wines are acquiring shorthand labels for these bundles of characteristics: some Chardonnays, such as those produced in MEURSAULT, were traditionally labelled buttery for a fairly rich white wine—a description accepted even by those that love Meursault wines, but dislike butter. A Rioja is recognized and labelled oaky, even by those who have no idea why this tag is used.

All of this suggests that wine knowledge is becoming increasingly sophisticated. A future hope is that a more sophisticated classification system of the vocabulary of wine can match the knowledge of its drinkers.

See AROMA WHEEL, TASTING, TASTING NOTES, TASTING TERMS, TASTING NOTES LANGUAGE, and PHILOSOPHY OF WINE.   J.A.

Ayto, J., *The Diner's Dictionary: Word origins of food and drink* (2nd edn, Oxford, 2012).

Gluck, M., 'Wine language: useful idiom or idiot speak?', in Aitchison, J., and Lewis, D. M. (eds.), *New Media Language* (London, 2003).

Lehrer, A., *Wine and Conversation* (2nd edn, Oxford, 2009).

Peynaud, E., *The Taste of Wine* (Paris, 1983; London, 1987).

Languedoc, France's best-value, most fluid wine region and certainly its most important in terms of volume of wine produced, and in terms of the importance of viticulture to the region's economy. The Languedoc takes its name from a time when its inhabitants spoke Occitan, the language in which *oc* (rather than *oïl*) is the word for 'yes', hence *langue d'oc*. It comprises the three central southern *départements* of the Aude, Hérault, and Gard, a sea of little other than vines just inland from the beaches of the Mediterranean (see map opposite and FRANCE).

For administrative purposes, the Languedoc is often bracketed with the region to its immediate south, as in **Languedoc-Roussillon**, although the ROUSSILLON has a perceptibly different character, and is better equipped to replace vines with the other fruit crops it has for long cultivated.

Between them at the turn of the century a total of 31,541 vignerons cultivated 241,537 ha/596,596 acres of vineyard, a quarter of all French vines. (It had represented a third a decade earlier.) But strenuous EU-inspired VINE PULL SCHEMES aimed at reducing Europe's wine SURPLUS were specifically targeted at France's deep south with considerable success. By 2010 just 19,752 vignerons grew 192,286 ha/474,946 acres of vines, still more than a quarter of all French vines but the plains of the Languedoc have been transformed, with other crops widely replacing vines.

Despite its quantitative importance, Languedoc-Roussillon produces only about an eighth of France's AOC wines. For many years, the Languedoc's only appellation was Fitou, but in 1985 Corbières, Minervois, and the catch-all appellation Coteaux du Languedoc were elevated from VDQS to AC status and others have followed. Indeed the taxonomy of Languedoc wines has been revised several times in recent years, and the Coteaux du Languedoc AOC replaced by LANGUEDOC AOC.

A high proportion of the vast area technically included in these AC zones is dedicated to non-appellation wine, however, either because the ENCÉPAGEMENT is outside the appellation specifications, or because the vigneron continues to be more interested in quantity than quality. The Languedoc is still by far the principal producer of VSIG, as well as producing nearly 60% of France's intermediate IGP, much of it labelled regionally and, typically, VARIETALLY, as Pays d'Oc. In a very real sense the Languedoc is France's most anarchic wine region. Not only is it the only one in which vignerons still take direct and often violent action in protest at the organization of their sector of the wine business, a phenomenon all too visible in the 2000s, it is also the one in which wine producers are most obviously dissatisfied with the detail of the, admittedly relatively recent, appellation laws. Some important producers routinely ignored

the AOC system completely and put most of their effort into making high-quality IGP wines.

Not much more than 10% of the Languedoc's wine output was white in the early 2010s. The best Languedoc whites, after a decidedly OAKY phase, have become increasingly fine and interesting. The small proportion of dry rosé is mainly for local consumption. A substantial quantity of VIN DOUX NATUREL is made (see MUSCAT), and LIMOUX is the Languedoc's centre of SPARKLING WINEMAKING. The Languedoc is still principally a source of red wine, however, a typical representative being no longer a thin, pale remnant of the region's past as a BULK WINE supplier but a dense, exciting, increasingly supple ambassador of some of France's wildest countryside.

History

Vines were planted as early as 125 BC on the hills near the Roman colony of Narbo, modern Narbonne, which today produce Corbières, Minervois, and Languedoc AOC. Narbonne was then an important Roman port, protected by what was then the island of La CLAPE. Cargoes would be taken up river as far as Carcassonne and then transported overland to join the GARONNE and thence to the Roman legions in Aquitaine. The hinterland of Narbonne and Béziers came to produce so much wine that it was exported to Ancient ROME, although the

edict of DOMITIAN was designed to put a stop to this.

It was not until the Middle Ages, under the auspices of the Languedoc's MONKS AND MONASTERIES, that viticulture once again thrived (although today only the Abbaye de Valmagne retains its wine-producing role). Already the University of MONTPELLIER was established and ARNALDUS DE VILLANOVA oversaw several important developments for wine and spirit production there. The development of greatest potential significance for the Languedoc and its wines was the late-17th-century construction of the Canal du Midi, which connected the Mediterranean with the Atlantic. The Bordelais were by now so experienced at protectionism, however (see HAUT PAYS, for example), that the wine producers of the Languedoc failed to benefit substantially from this new distribution network until the end of the 18th century.

Much more profitable were the efforts of the DUTCH WINE TRADE in the late 17th century to develop northern European markets for *picardan*, a sweet white wine made from Clairette and Picquepoul grapes that was well known in Holland by 1680, and subsequently for eaux-de-vie. The port of Sète was established in 1666 and became particularly important for exports to ENGLAND and the NETHERLANDS, Narbonne having long since silted up. Sweet wines were also produced, notably a DRIED-GRAPE WINE made

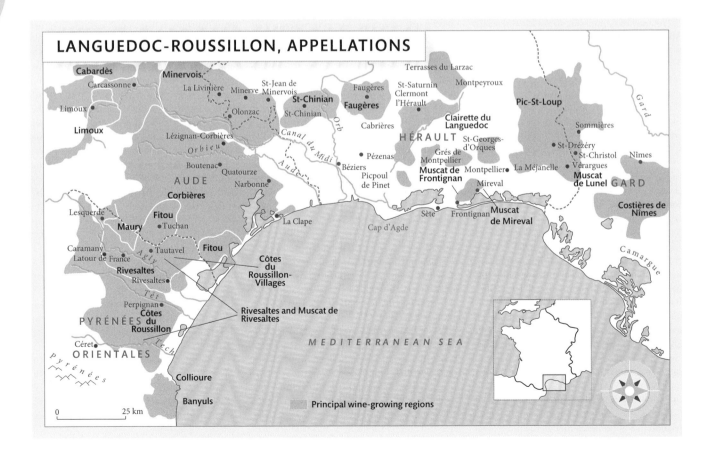

LANGUEDOC-ROUSSILLON, APPELLATIONS

from Muscat grown at FRONTIGNAN, whose inhabitants insist that it was as a result of a visit by a Marquis de Lur-Saluces to Frontignan after the great frost of 1709 that Ch d'YQUEM became a sweet wine property, and that their straight-sided bottle was adopted for bordeaux.

By the mid 19th century the vineyards of the Languedoc could be divided into the HILLSIDE VINEYARDS, vines planted on gravelly terraces at mid elevation (roughly approximating to the majority of modern Languedoc appellations), and vines, mainly ARAMON and TERRET grapes, planted on the plains for distillation into brandy.

In 1855, the Languedoc's fortunes were to change for ever, as a result of its first RAILWAY connection, via Lyons, with the important centres of population in the north. A link via Bordeaux was opened the next year. Between 1850 and 1869, average annual wine production nearly quadrupled in the Hérault département. The arrival of PHYLLOXERA could hardly have been worse timed, but, thanks to feverish experimentation and the eventual adoption of GRAFTING, as well as HYBRIDS and some of the new BOUSCHET crosses, the Languedoc vineyard was the first to be reconstituted after the devastations of this American louse. By the end of the 19th century, the Languedoc became France's principal wine supplier, producing 44% of France's entire wine production, from 23% of the country's total *vignoble*.

This superficial success was at some cost, however. Dr GUYOT had in 1867 warned against the increasing influence of VINE VARIETIES and practices designed to produce quantity rather than quality, and against the over-industrialization of the Languedoc wine trade. By the turn of the century, the plains of the Languedoc, the Hérault particularly, were being milked of thin, light, pale red that needed blending with the much more robust produce of new colonial vineyards in ALGERIA to yield a commercially acceptable drink. France had sown the seeds of her (continued) dependence on wine imports. Such was the extent of commercial interference in the French table wine market, including widespread ADULTERATION AND FRAUD, that prices plummeted and France's social crisis of 1907 provoked what were merely the first in a long series of wine-related riots.

Since then the vignerons of the Languedoc, typically but by no means always members of one of the region's hundreds of CO-OPERATIVES, many of them formed in the 1930s and most now part of a larger group, have been some of the world's most politicized. Their sheer number has given them political power, but the fall in demand for basic *vin de table* and difficulty in selling even the keenly priced VIN DE PAYS, which took its place as the Languedoc's principal product, led to increasing frustration among growers.

Land here is relatively inexpensive, which has drawn a wide range of new investors, both producers with an established record in a more famous wine region and complete outsiders keen to set up LIFESTYLE WINERIES.

Geography and climate

The great majority of the Languedoc's vines (and virtually all of those which have been RIPPED out recently) are or were planted on the flat, low-lying alluvial plain, particularly in the southern Hérault and Gard. In the northern Hérault and western Aude, however, vines may be planted several hundred metres above sea level, in the foothills of the Cévennes and the Corbières Pyrenean foothills, sometimes at quite an angle and on very varied soils which can include gravels and limestone.

The climate in all but the far western limits of the Languedoc (where Atlantic influence is apparent) is definitively MEDITERRANEAN and one of the major viticultural hazards is DROUGHT. Annual rainfall is often as little as 400 mm/15.6 in by the coast. July and August temperatures often exceed 30 °C/86 °F; such rain as does fall tends to fall in the form of localized deluges. WIND is common throughout the growing season, with the *tramontane* bringing cool air from the mountains.

Viticulture

The Languedoc is the land of the proud peasant farmer. The size of the average holding is small, and usually much divided between parcels inherited from various different branches of the family. Basic, straggling BUSH VINES still predominate, although an increasing proportion of vines, especially the newer INTERNATIONAL VARIETIES, are being trained on WIRES. IRRIGATION is theoretically permitted only within strictly specified limits, and in practice only the best and the worst producers tend to have any form of available irrigation system. The flatter, larger vineyards lend themselves to MECHANICAL HARVESTING but their parcellation, and ripping out, has slowed the inevitable invasion. The region is by no means free of FUNGAL DISEASES and some sprayings are usually necessary.

Vine varieties

The dominant late-20th-century vine variety CARIGNAN has been definitively routed by the VINE PULL SCHEME of the EU, and by 2011 was only the third most planted variety in the Languedoc after Syrah and then Grenache Noir. Merlot, grown mainly for IGP wines, covered almost as much ground as Carignan, with Cabernet Sauvignon, not nearly as much at home here as Merlot, some way behind. The ever-changing regulations of most red wine appellations in the Languedoc specify various combinations of Syrah, Grenache, and Mourvèdre with declining proportions of Carignan,

and most often, usually as minor blending ingredients, Cinsaut (especially good for rosés and fruity reds) and the Grenache relative LLADONER, or Lledoner, Pelut.

By far the most planted white wine grape, though even less common than Cabernet Sauvignon, is Chardonnay, used for both varietal IGP wines and the still and sparkling wines of Limoux. Sauvignon Blanc is the next most planted and Viognier fourth most popular white wine grape—further signs of how important INTERNATIONAL VARIETIES are to white wine production here. Each white wine appellation has a different cocktail of preferred ingredients from a palette of traditional pale-skinned Languedoc varieties which include Bourboulenc, Clairette, Grenache Blanc, Maccabéo, Picquepoul Blanc, and Vermentino, although Roussanne, and Marsanne are also specified occasionally.

Winemaking

With some high-profile exceptions, winery equipment and techniques are still relatively unsophisticated in the Languedoc, where selling prices have rarely been high enough to justify major investment. DESTEMMING equipment, for example, was widely regarded as a luxury until this century, and new oak BARRELS beyond the means of most producers. (In any case, the fruit is so intense in many red wines that, like the same varieties in the southern Rhône, they do not necessarily benefit from new, small oak.) The great majority of Languedoc wine is made in one of the co-operative cellars that still dominate production and whose will to make good-quality wine varies considerably. Fermentation and ÉLEVAGE typically take place in large concrete *cuves*, although stainless steel is slowly invading the region. Partly in an effort to tame the natural astringency of Carignan, full or partial CARBONIC MACERATION was for long the most common red winemaking technique. BOTTLING often takes place at a merchant's cellar rather than on the premises where the wine was made. The wine container most frequently seen by the consumer in the region is probably the road tanker (a high proportion of the locals buy their wine in bulk rather than bottle).

For more specific information, see the individual appellations CABARDÈS, CLAIRETTE DU LANGUEDOC, CORBIÈRES, FAUGÈRES, FITOU, LANGUEDOC AOC, LIMOUX, MALEPÈRE, MINERVOIS, Picpoul de Pinet, and ST-CHINIAN, and also the vin de liqueur CARTAGÈNE, and various MUSCAT vins doux naturels.

Clavel, J., and Baillaud, R., *Histoire et avenir des vins en Languedoc* (Toulouse, 1985).

www.languedoc-wines.com

Languedoc AOC, previously known as Coteaux du Languedoc, varied and probably too extensive appellation whose zone includes some of France's best-value vineyards and most of the land suitable for growing vines above the coastal plain in a swathe through the Hérault *département* from Narbonne towards Nîmes. This territory was once known as Septimanie and is in effect a giant south-facing amphitheatre, although of course there are many local variations in TOPOGRAPHY. As elsewhere in the Languedoc, much of the land technically included within the appellation is used for other purposes (other crops, IGP, or VSIG wine, for example). The total vineyard area dedicated to producing Coteaux du Languedoc by 2000 was about 10,000 ha/24,799 acres, a considerable increase on the 6,500 ha declared in the early 1990s, and remained pretty constant for the first decade of this century, despite the region's enthusiastic vine pull scheme.

Although much of the zone qualifies for the basic Languedoc appellation, a number of sub-appellations, CRUS, or specific TERROIRS have been identified and are allowed to append their own name to that of the appellation on labels. PICPOUL DE PINET established its own appellation and identity in 2013 and TERRASSES DU LARZAC followed in 2014. Other subappellations waiting with particular impatience for independent existence are CABRIÈRES, La CLAPE, GRÉS DE MONTPELLIER, LA MÉJANELLE, MONTPEYROUX, PÉZENAS, PIC-ST-LOUP, QUATOURZE, ST-CHRISTOL, ST-DRÉZÉRY, ST-GEORGES-D'ORQUES, ST-SATURNIN, and SOMMIÈRES.

For more information, see under the increasing number of individual subappellation names.

www.languedoc-wines.com

Lanzarote, Spanish DO including the whole of this relatively flat island in the CANARY ISLANDS. There are still 1,950 ha/4,680 acres of vineyards, with a clear domination by the white Malvasía grape, as on LA PALMA. Lanzarote's vines are often planted in individual shallow indentations in the black volcanic soil. The technically up-to-date El Grifo winery has been a pioneer in the development of modern dry Malvasía of some originality, and the overall quality of the other producers, led by Los Bermejos, Stratvs, Mozaga, and La Geria, has advanced significantly. V. de la S.

La Palma, Spanish DO including the entire eponymous island in the CANARY ISLANDS. Current vineyard surface has dropped to 800 ha/1,920 acres, planted at varying heights (200 to 1,400 m/656 to 4,600 ft above sea level) on the volcanic island. A large range of grape varieties are cultivated, but La Palma's most distinguished wine is traditional sweet Malvasías, almost forgotten in recent years but whose reputation, as Canary SACK, goes back to Elizabethan England. V. de la S.

large format, BOTTLE SIZE larger than the standard 75 cl size and of particular interest to collectors and investors (provided it is filled with FINE WINE).

La Rochelle, port on the Atlantic coast about 160 km/100 miles north of BORDEAUX in the *département* of Charente-Maritime. In the Middle Ages, La Rochelle was a New Town, having been founded in 1130, in an age of economic expansion. The climate at La Rochelle is hot and dry enough for the winning of sea salt, and salt was initially the basis of La Rochelle's economy. Merchants came from the north to buy salt, but they also wanted wine, and it was in response to that demand that the people of La Rochelle turned to viticulture. Because of its favourable climate, Poitou was a more reliable producer than the Seine basin (see PARIS), Rheims (see CHAMPAGNE), BURGUNDY, or the RHINE. Hence the English and the Flemish turned more readily to the wines of Poitou, all the more so because these wines were less acidic than those of Rheims and Paris. La Rochelle also exported its wines to Normandy, Scotland, Ireland, and even Denmark and Norway. In 1199, Poitou was the wine the royal household bought most of, with the wines of ANJOU and the Île-de-France coming second and third. But in 1224, when La Rochelle fell to the French, it had to cede its position as leading wine supplier to Bordeaux, although the wines of La Rochelle remained popular with the English in the 14th and 15th centuries.

The grape varieties were probably those of Burgundy and the Paris region: MORILLON, which was an early form of PINOT NOIR, and Fromenteau, thought to be the ancestor of PINOT GRIS. In documents of the 13th and 14th centuries, a third cépage appears: it is called Chemère, Chemière, Chenère, or Chenère Blanche, and it is likely to have been the parent of CHENIN BLANC. In accordance with medieval preference, most of the wines that Poitou made were white.

See also DUTCH WINE TRADE and HAUT-POITOU.

H.M.W.

Dion, R., *Histoire de la vigne et du vin en France* (Paris, 1959).

Laški Rizling, the name current in SLOVENIA, SERBIA, and some other parts of the former Yugoslavia for the white grape variety known in Austria as WELSCHRIESLING (under which name more details and more of its many synonyms appear). The vine is cultivated most successfully in the higher vineyards of Slovenia (just over the border from the spirited Welschrieslings of STYRIA), and Fruška Gora in Serbia, where it can produce equally crisp and delicately aromatic wines. Few of these superior examples have been exported, however, whereas for decades in the second half of the 20th century a Slovenian BRAND, Lutomer Riesling (eventually renamed Lutomer Laški Rizling after German lobbying), was the best-selling white wine in the UK, its heavily sweetened style conveying little of the intrinsic character of the variety. The Rizling Vlassky is the variant known in the CZECH REPUBLIC.

late harvest, a general term used to describe grapes that have been harvested later than is normal for dry wines in order to make a SWEET WINE, generally without the aid of NOBLE ROT. They are generally left on the vine so that the berries are rich in sugar (see MUST WEIGHT), or even longer so that the fruit starts to desiccate, resulting in DRIED-GRAPE WINES. See VENDANGE TARDIVE for a highly regulated French example of a late-harvest wine.

lateral shoot, sometimes called simply a **lateral**, secondary shoot that grows from the axil of a leaf on the main shoot. Its origin on grapevines is linked with the complex development of the BUD. At most nodes, especially on weak vines, the lateral shoot is short (less than 20 mm/0.8 in), fails to become woody, and drops off in autumn leaving a prominent scar at the side of the bud. But on more vigorous shoots, especially at the middle nodes or at the end where vigorous shoots have been topped or trimmed, the lateral shoot grows in the same way as a primary shoot producing hardened permanent wood. Sometimes, lateral shoots are fruitful (see SECOND CROP). Laterals that develop on secondary shoots are called tertiaries; quaternaries have even been seen on extremely vigorous vines. B.G.C.

Latin America. See SOUTH AMERICA and MEXICO.

latitude, angular distance north or south of the equator, measured in degrees and minutes. The main northern hemisphere viticultural regions extend between 32 and 51 degrees north, and most of those in the southern hemisphere between 28 and 42 degrees south. Viticulture is spreading polewards and is likely to continue to do so due to CLIMATE CHANGE. Whereas ten years ago 52 degrees north in ENGLAND (and Ireland) was around the northern limit, vines are now planted in NORWAY and SWEDEN, up to 59 degrees north. The southern extension is just over 46 degrees south in Central Otago, NEW ZEALAND and it seems highly unlikely that the vine could thrive further south than this in South America. Some vines are also cultivated for wine production in tropical highlands or irrigated desert conditions as close to the equator as eight or nine degrees. See TROPICAL VITICULTURE.

Comparisons between hemispheres based purely on latitude are misleading. Northern hemisphere vineyards are on average warmer during the growing season at given latitudes, a fact partly related to their greater CONTINENTALITY. But even over the whole year, the northern hemisphere is on average warmer than the southern hemisphere at similar latitudes, partly because of the greater land mass and its disposition around the North Pole, and partly (in the case of western Europe) because of warming by the Gulf Stream.

Similarly, comparisons between vineyard regions based on latitude can be misleading since TEMPERATURE, which is influenced more by distance from the sea and ELEVATION than by latitude, has a greater impact on VINE PHYSIOLOGY, PHENOLOGY, and wine style.

When wine regions with equal average mean temperatures during the growing season, or equal temperature summations (see CLIMATE CLASSIFICATION), are compared, grapes tend to ripen more fully when grown at high latitudes, i.e. further from the equator. Alternatively, later maturing grape varieties can be ripened. The reasons for this phenomenon of great significance for wine quality remain unproven, but two main mechanisms have been proposed.

There is speculation that because summers at higher latitudes have longer days, this may be an advantage for grape production and even wine style, but arguments for this are conjectural. It can be noted that high-latitude viticultural climates tend to have higher relative HUMIDITIES and less day-to-day TEMPERATURE VARIABILITY during the growing season than those at low latitudes (apart from where the latter are coastal). Both factors have likely implications for ripening and for grape and wine quality. See CLIMATE AND WINE QUALITY, HUMIDITY, TEMPERATURE VARIABILITY, and map under WORLD PRODUCTION.   J.G. & R.E.S.

Gladstones, J., *Viticulture and Environment* (Adelaide, 1992).

Latium, Anglicized version of the Italian wine region LAZIO.

Latour, Château, famously long-lived FIRST GROWTH in the MÉDOC region of BORDEAUX. The originally square tower from which the château takes its name was one of a defensive line against ocean-going pirates. Vines were already planted here in the late 14th century and at least a quarter of the land was vineyard by 1600. At the end of the 17th century, a number of smallholdings were accumulated into one ownership under the de Mullet family. The New French Clarets they produced made their first publicized appearances in AUCTIONS in London COFFEE HOUSES early in the 18th century. Owned from 1677 by the Clauzel family, it passed by marriage to the powerful SÉGURS, who also owned LAFITE, MOUTON, and Calon-Ségur. On the death in 1755 of the Marquis Nicolas-Alexandre de Ségur, 'Le Prince des Vignes', his properties passed to his four daughters, three of whom in 1760 acquired Latour. Their male descendants owned the château, which in 1842 became a private company, until its

purchase by the British Pearson family in 1963, with 25% acquired by HARVEYS OF BRISTOL, and a diminishing minority remaining in the hands of the French families. The property was greatly improved, with STAINLESS STEEL tanks controversially installed as FERMENTATION VESSELS in time for the 1964 vintage, partly on the advice of director Harry WAUGH. In 1989, the estate was sold to multinational corporation Allied-Lyons, already owners of Harveys, for the equivalent of £110 million. In 1993, Allied-Lyons sold their 94% share of the property to French businessman François Pinault (who acquired the London AUCTION house of Christie's in 1998), when Latour was valued at £86 million.

Thanks to 21st century expansion, the estate comprised 90 ha/222 acres of vineyard by 2014 with 75% Cabernet Sauvignon vines, 24% Merlot (increased from 15% in the 1980s), and a very small amount of Cabernet Franc and Petit Verdot, with an average annual production of a total of 30,000 cases of the three wines made there. In 1966 a SECOND WINE, Les Forts de Latour, made from the produce of young vines and from three plots on the other side of the St-Julien–Pauillac road was introduced as a permanent fixture. A third wine is also bottled and sold as Pauillac. Latour's wines generally require much longer to develop than those of the other first growths, and they often have greater longevity. Latour is also known for its ability to produce good wines in lesser vintages.

It also possesses better archives, back to the 14th century, than any other wine estate in Bordeaux and so has spawned an unusual and useful array of monographs.

In 2012 Latour's director Frédéric Engerer decided to withdraw from the annual Bordeaux PRIMEUR market, the first major Bordeaux château to do so, with a view to releasing wines only as they are ready to drink.

Other wine estates owned by François Pinault and under the same management are Domaine d'Eugénie in VOSNE-ROMANÉE acquired in 2006, CHÂTEAU-GRILLET in the northern Rhône Valley (2011), and Araujo Estate in NAPA Valley (2013).

Faith, N., *Latour* (London, 1991).

Higounet, C. (ed.), *La Seigneurie et le vignoble de Château Latour* (Bordeaux, 1974).

Penning-Rowsell, E., *Château Latour: A History of a Great Vineyard 1331–1992* (London, 1993).

Latour-de-France, small village on brown schist that once guarded the border between France and Spain, and whose name may be a suffix to the appellation Côtes du ROUSSILLON-Villages. It may have been accorded this distinction less because of the superior quality of the wine than because the name had been successfully promoted to the French wine consumer by wine merchants Nicolas, who once bought the majority of production. Grape varieties

allowed are Carignan, Grenache, Mourvèdre, Syrah, and Lladoner Pelut. For more details, see ROUSSILLON.

Latour, Louis, one of Burgundy's most commercially astute, and oldest, merchants. Jean Latour first planted vines in Aloxe-Corton, then called simply Aloxe, in 1768; his family had grown vines on the plain to the east of Beaune since the 16th century. Jean's son was the first in a long line of Louis Latours and enlarged the domaine considerably and it was not until the late 19th century that the family added wine brokering to their vine-growing activities.

With an eye to the developing export markets, the third Louis Latour bought the Lamarosse family's NÉGOCIANT business in Beaune's historic Rue des Tonneliers in 1867, and was so successful that in 1891 he was able to buy Ch Corton-Grancey in Aloxe-Corton, one of the earliest purpose-built, GRAVITY-FED wineries in the world. With this acquisition came one of the most handsome, and most photographed, houses in the Côte d'Or, together with extensive winemaking premises, and some notable vineyards around the hill of Corton to add to the Latour family holdings, which already included some Chambertin; Romanée-St-Vivant, Les Quatre Journaux; and Chevalier-Montrachet, Les Demoiselles. (Today Domaine Louis Latour represents the largest single holding of Grand Cru vineyards on the CÔTE D'OR.) It was the third Louis Latour who is reputed to have realized the hill of Corton's potential for great white wine when he replanted some of the hill now designated Corton-Charlemagne with Chardonnay vines after PHYLLOXERA had laid waste vineyards originally planted with Pinot Noir and Aligoté.

Innovations of succeeding Louis Latours include a succession of 'new' and increasingly daring white wines. What was then known as Grand Pouilly, and subsequently became known as Pouilly-Fuissé, was introduced to the United States in the 1930s, immediately after the Repeal of PROHIBITION. A wine known as MÂCON-Lugny was introduced as a respectable alternative to Côte d'Or white wines in close co-operation with the Lugny CO-OPERATIVE. Louis Latour also pioneered the planting of Chardonnay vines in the relatively unknown ARDÈCHE in the early 1980s. The firm has 350 ha of vines under contract to local growers, whose produce is vinified at Latour's winery in Alba. In the late 1980s, Louis Latour bought land in the Var *département* in PROVENCE, planting the Beurot selection of Pinot Noir to produce gentle red wines sold as Pinot Noir, Domaine de Valmoissine. Louis Latour acquired Chablis producer Simonnet-Febvre in 2003 and Beaujolais producer Henry Fessy in 2008. Continuing their development of Pinot Noir and Chardonnay grown in fringe areas, they more recently acquired land in the Terres Dorées in BEAUJOLAIS and in Auxois midway between Chablis and Dijon.

The house enjoys a solid reputation for its white wines, but has incited controversy over its continued endorsement of PASTEURIZATION of even its finest red wines. In 1997, they celebrated the bicentenary of the négociant business and the firm is currently run by the eleventh generation Louis-Fabrice Latour.

Lauzet, almost extinct and not especially exciting vine allowed into JURANÇON.

Lavilledieu, Vins de, almost extinct IGP in SOUTH WEST FRANCE on terraces between the GARONNE and Tarn rivers north of FRONTON. Lavilledieu has a long history, dating back to the pre-Christian era and revived by monks (see MONKS AND MONASTERIES) who cleared the forest of Agre and replaced trees with vines in the 12th century, but its wine production today is minuscule. A wide variety of south western vine varieties are allowed (notably the NÉGRETTE of Fronton).

law impinges on wine principally in the areas of penalizing ADULTERATION AND FRAUD of all sorts; regulating wine DESIGNATIONS, CONTROLLED APPELLATIONS, and LABELLING INFORMATION; and controlling the sale and service of any alcoholic drink as, for example, in state liquor laws or licensing laws. In the UNITED STATES, the consumption of any alcoholic drink is restricted to those over 21, for example, and DIRECT SHIPPING of wine to consumers in many states is forbidden.

layering, known as *marcottage* in French, is an ancient method of vine PROPAGATION which involves taking a long cane from one vine and training it down to the soil, then burying a section to normal planting depth but with the end bent up and emerging in a desired position. This is a useful method of filling empty spaces in established vineyards but only if resistant ROOTSTOCKS are not required. Thus layering may be used only in areas without PHYLLOXERA, NEMATODES, and other soil-borne pathogens (such as BOLLINGER's Vieilles Vignes vineyard, the Nacional vineyard at QUINTA DO NOVAL or COLARES in Portugal, and much of Australia and Chile). The foster vine may be left connected to the parent or may be separated after it has reached normal size.   B.G.C.

laying down wine is an English expression for holding wine as it undergoes BOTTLE AGEING. Thus most people lay down wine in their (however notional) CELLARS. Considerable quantities of red bordeaux are **laid down** by collectors all over the globe, for example.

Layon, Coteaux du, large appellation with more than 1,000 ha/2,500 acres of Chenin Blanc made generally medium-sweet white (much richer from the best independent vignerons) in the ANJOU district of the LOIRE. The communes of Beaulieu (-sur-Layon), Faye (d'Anjou), CHAUME, Rablay (-sur-Layon), Rochefort (-sur-Loire), St-Aubin (de Luigné), and St-Lambert (du Lattay) may append their names to the appellation if yields are restricted to 30 hl/ha (as opposed to 35 hl/ha for Coteaux du Layon). Two small areas within the area produce wines of such quality that they have earned their own appellations, BONNEZEAUX and QUARTS DE CHAUME. They, and most of the best vineyards of the Coteaux du Layon, are on the steep slopes on the right bank of the Layon tributary of the Loire. TERROIR is all here, for Coteaux du Layon should be an intense wine made ideally from several TRIES through the vineyard, selecting BOTRYTIZED grapes, or those that have begun to raisin on the vine. Producers such as Claude Papin of Ch Pierre Bise vinify grapes picked on slate, schist, clay, and sandstone separately to demonstrate the variation in style and potential longevity. Yields vary enormously according to the conditions of the vintage, but are officially limited to 35 hl/ha and 30 hl/ha for wines labelled Coteaux du Layon plus the name of one of the villages Beaulieu (-sur-Layon), CHAUME, Faye (d'Anjou), Rablay (-sur-Layon), Rochefort (-sur-Loire), St-Aubin (de Luigné), and St-Lambert (du Lattay). The appellation that includes the seven village crus is spread along about 20 km/12 miles of south-west facing slopes, in an extremely narrow strip of vines, above the Layon tributary of the Loire, together with a few slopes around St-Lambert, on buttes that catch drying winds straight off the Atlantic.

After a period in the late 1990s when maximum possible sugar levels were sought at all costs, growers today tend to pick between 18 and 23% potential alcohol, producing wines with RESIDUAL SUGAR of around 100 g/l, perhaps up to 200 g/l from the finest *tries*, which are sweet but not too rich to drink with gusto. In favourable vintages, some great wine is produced in this appellation, but producers are dogged by the depressing effect on selling prices of a substantial quantity of extremely ordinary just-sweet wine sold under the name Coteaux du Layon. Botrytized, particularly sweet wines may be labelled Sélection de Grains Nobles.

Wines may be sold as DEMI-SEC, MOELLEUX, and, sweetest of all, LIQUOREUX.

See also LOIRE, including map.

Lazio, the region known as Latium in English, the ancient homeland of the Latins (see ITALY, history), the seat of Italy's government and administration in the capital, Rome (see map under ITALY), and the large IGT Lazio covering the entire region. The region's total area of vineyard has declined considerably, to not much more than 17,000 ha/42,000 acres by the early 2010s.

More than a third of the total Lazio vineyard is now dedicated to making DOC wine. White wines, almost exclusively from MALVASIA and TREBBIANO Toscano grapes, represent the majority of Lazio's total vinous output, with the wines of the CASTELLI ROMANI representing by far the majority, although this DOC, like most of Lazio's 27 DOCs, has a provision for the production of red wines based on Sangiovese and Montepulciano as well as Cabernet Sauvignon and Merlot. Malvasia and Trebbiano blends are also produced in quantity in the DOC zones of Cerveteri and Est!Est!!Est!!!, as well as in Lazio's most famous DOC, FRASCATI.

Lazio has no significant red DOCs although an occasional good-quality red is made, usually in the image of red bordeaux, by some of the region's best estates. Examples include Falesco, where Riccardo COTARELLA makes the widely admired Montiano; the legendary Boncompagni Ludovisi estate near Rome that belongs to Piero ANTINORI's wife; the Di Mauro estate in Marino; and the newer Castel De Paolis estate in Grottaferrata. Most of these reds from INTERNATIONAL VARIETIES are labelled IGT Lazio, while the DOC Cori, based on the local Nero Buono di Cori grape, and the DOC Cesanese di Affile and the DOCG Cesanese del Piglio based on CESANESE grapes, are the only truly local reds. While high-quality Cori and Cesanese wines are still in the minority, Cesanese in particular has shown promise.   W.S.

www.vininelazio.com

Le. For anything prefixed Le, see under the next letter of the name.

lead, one of the familiar and widely dispersed heavy metals, which occurs naturally in trace amounts in all plants, therefore in grapes, and therefore, usually in microgram per litre quantities only, in wines. This ubiquitous element, which has no known biological function in plants or animals, is now known to be a neural toxin of particular danger to children. This has resulted in the reformulation of many products, particularly petroleum products, so as to exclude lead.

History

Lead has been associated with wine since the time of Ancient ROME. The Romans recognized that lead not only prevented wines from turning sour (and rescued those that already had) but also made them taste sweeter (see PLINY). What they did not know, however, is that, even when taken in only very small quantities over a long period, lead is a poison.

Its dangers were understood from the end of the 17th century when a German doctor, Eberhard Gockel of Ulm in Württemberg, noticed that the symptoms suffered by some of his wine-drinking patients matched those observed in lead miners. Gradually legislation was passed in Europe banning the use of lead in wine but the practice continued. At last, in 1820, the campaigner Frederick Accum complained that 'the merchant or dealer who practises this dangerous sophistication, adds the crime of murder to that of fraud'.

Poisoning could result not only from the wilful addition of lead to wine. The Romans heated grape juice in lead vessels in order to produce *sapa*, a sweet concentrate used as a wine additive and in cooking, and even in the 19th century wine BOTTLES were cleaned with lead shot, thereby contaminating the wine.   H.B.

Viticultural aspects

Grapes containing lead may produce wine containing lead. Recent health concerns about lead in wine have led to studies of lead in grapes. There are two principal sources of lead. One is from lead-rich automobile exhaust particles settling on both grapes and soil. This is a problem for roadside vineyards in particular, but one which is declining as the use of unleaded fuels increases. The other source is from prior use of the now-banned chemical insecticide lead arsenate, which has contaminated many vineyard soils, especially where SOIL ACIDITY is high.
                                                                                    R.E.S.

Lead in modern wine

Most of the traces of lead from grapes are precipitated out with the LEES during winemaking. However, as analytical methods continue to improve, microgram quantities per litre are likely to be found in most wines.

The equipment used in modern wineries should not result in any lead contamination. The few wines which contain lead in milligram per litre concentrations derive it principally from capsules or FOILS which contain lead, or from lead-crystal DECANTERS. (Modern bottles are made of lead-free glass.) Seepage of wine around the cork can corrode the foil and, if the lip of the bottle is not thoroughly cleaned before pouring, the wine may be contaminated by some of the lead salt. To protect those who do not clean obvious lead salts from a bottle lip before pouring, however, the use of lead capsules or foils is now declining or prohibited in many regions.

Lengthy storage of wines in lead-crystal decanters provides time for the wine acids to leach some lead from the glass, but keeping a wine in a lead-crystal glass or decanter for the usual period of no more than a few hours is too short for dangerous amounts of lead contamination. One study found a lead concentration of around 5 mg/l in port left in a lead-crystal decanter for four months, so that 10 l of it would have to be consumed in a short time

for a potentially toxic human intake of lead! The amount of lead leached from glassware is determined by the raw materials used to make it and research reported in the *Lancet* suggests that lead concentrations in wine increased by 50% after one hour in a low-quality Yugoslavian decanter, but by only 15% after three hours in better-quality decanters.

Analyses of thousands of representative samples of wine suggest that the lead content of wines is decreasing in general but in the early 1990s ranged from 0 to 1.26 mg/l, with the average lead content being 0.13 mg/l, values well below any legal maximum.

An Australian study found that there was minimal uptake of lead from wine when it was consumed with food.   A.D.W. & J.R.

Accum, F., *Treatise on Adulteration of Food, and Culinary Poisons* (London, 1820).

Eisinger, J., 'Early consumer protection legislation: a 17th century law prohibiting lead adulteration of wines', *Interdisciplinary Science Reviews*, 16/1 (1991), 61–8.

Gulson, B. L., et al., 'Contribution of lead in wine to the total dietary intake of lead in humans with and without a meal: a pilot study', *Journal of Wine Research*, 9/1 (1998), 5–14.

Pliny the Elder, *Natural History*, trans. H. Rackham (London, 1938), book 14.

leaf (*feuille* in French). Vine leaves range in size up to that of a dinner plate but are normally the area of a human hand (100 to 200 cm^2). Their individual area correlates with shoot VIGOUR and also varies with vine variety (Merlot has large leaves, for example, while Gewürztraminer has small leaves). The vine is a leafy plant with sometimes many hectares of total leaf area per hectare of vineyard. A proportion of these leaves will be shaded and therefore not PHOTOSYNTHETIC. The total leaf and shoot system of a vine is known as the CANOPY.

The green, flat zone of the leaf connected to the stem by the PETIOLE is known as the leaf blade, or lamina. The lamina of a grape leaf expands to nearly its full area in six or more weeks, growing to a shape and form characteristic for each VINE VARIETY. The arrangement of the five lobes, the shape of the 'teeth' at the edge of the leaf, the size and shape of the sinuses, and especially the angle and lengths of the main veins are features that are measured (ampelometry) for vine variety identification by AMPELOGRAPHERS.

Leaf colour is responsive to VINE NUTRITION, becoming yellow all over with deficiencies of nitrogen and sulfur, or patterned with yellow or red and/or dead zones with most other deficiencies. Similarly, yellow and dead areas on leaves occur with some virus infections and as a result of herbicide contamination, although usually in different patterns. With the onset of autumn, leaf colour changes naturally from

green to yellow or red, depending on the vine species and the presence of certain VIRUS DISEASES. See LEAFROLL VIRUS.   B.G.C.

leaf aldehydes make wines taste HERBACEOUS.

leaf fall, the process which occurs naturally in autumn, often after the first frost, which marks the end of the VINE GROWTH CYCLE. Ideally this is some time after HARVEST, so that the vine has been able to build up its reserves of the CARBOHYDRATES important for growth the following spring. See also DEFOLIATION.   R.E.S.

leafhoppers, members of the insect family Cicadellidae which can cause both direct and sometimes serious indirect damage to vineyards. In California, both the grape leafhopper, *Erythroneura elegantula*, and the closely related and biologically similar variegated grape leafhopper, *Erythroneura variabilis*, cause damage to grapes. They begin to feed on grapevine foliage as soon as it appears in spring, and do so by sucking out the contents of leaf cells. As injury progresses, heavily damaged leaves lose their green colour and PHOTOSYNTHESIS is much reduced. TABLE GRAPES are spoilt by spots of leafhopper excrement. The damage caused is in direct proportion to the numbers. When there are 20 or fewer leafhopper nymphs per leaf, no control is required.

There are, however, a number of natural enemies of leafhoppers, the most important being a tiny wasp, *Anagrus epos*.

Some other leafhopper pests do not cause direct damage but spread important grape diseases. PIERCE'S DISEASE of the Americas is spread by so-called sharpshooter leafhoppers (subfamily Cicadellinae). The bacteria that cause Pierce's disease inhabit the XYLEM of the plants, and xylem sap-feeders can transmit the bacteria from plant to plant. FLAVESCENCE DORÉE is caused by a PHYTOPLASMA that inhabits the PHLOEM and appears to be transmitted exclusively by the leafhopper *Scaphoideus littoralis*.

M.J.E., R.E.S., & A.H.P.

Bettiga, L. J. (ed.), *Grape Pest Management* (3rd edn, Oakland, Calif., 2013).

Pearson, R. C., and Goheen, A. C. (eds.), *Compendium of Grape Diseases* (St Paul, Minn., 1988).

leaf removal, vineyard practice aimed at helping to control BOTRYTIS BUNCH ROT and other BUNCH ROTS, and at improving GRAPE COMPOSITION and therefore wine quality. Typically the leaves are removed around the bunches to increase exposure to the sun and wind. The bunches dry out more quickly after dew and rain so that moulds are less likely to develop. Increased exposure to sunlight, especially to ULTRAVIOLET RADIATION, helps the berries produce more of the PHENOLICS important in wine quality. Grape SUGARS are also increased and

MALIC ACID and METHOXYPYRAZINES are reduced, all of which contribute to improved wine quality. Leaf removal is also used to improve the colour of black and red TABLE GRAPES.

For optimal effects on wine quality, leaves should be removed after FRUIT SET and before VERAISON, although it is more usual to remove them at the onset of veraison. In Europe it is common to remove leaves nearer to the time of harvest, primarily to reduce the risk of BOTRYTIS BUNCH ROT. Recent studies by Poni in Italy have shown that removal of lower, mature leaves on the shoot by the time of flowering reduces fruit set or berries per bunch. As a result, the bunches are looser with less berry-to-berry contact, and so less prone to botrytis bunch rot. Sugar and anthocyanin levels were also found to be higher. Early leaf removal can be considered a means of yield control. Traditionally leaf removal has been done by hand, requiring about 50 hours of labour per hectare (2.5 acres), but machines which take less than five hours per hectare to remove leaves by suction and/or cutting have been developed.

Recent studies around the world have questioned excessive leaf removal in warm to hot climates, because there can be negative effects on fruit composition and wine quality (see SUNBURN, increasingly seen in some regions). This is due to the bunches being heated by the sun, leading to undesirably high temperatures within the grape berries in the afternoon when air temperature is also higher. The alternative is to do less removal on the western side of the canopy.

Decreasing dependence on AGROCHEMICALS in the vineyard has led to renewed interest in leaf removal in both Old and New Worlds. As well as making the fruit less prone to FUNGAL DISEASES by improving aeration, leaf removal can also increase the effectiveness of such chemicals as may be applied to protect the fruit.   R.E.S.

Poni, S. L., et al., 'Effects of early defoliation on shoot photosynthesis, yield components, and grape composition', *American Journal of Enology and Viticulture*, 57/4 (2006), 397–407.

Smart, R. E., and Robinson, M., *Sunlight into Wine* (Adelaide, 1991).

leaf rollers

leaf rollers, also called **leaf folders** (see MOTHS), insects which cause damage to vines at the caterpillar stage (and nothing whatever to do with LEAFROLL VIRUS disease). As the name suggests, they form the leaf into a roll, and feed on the edge of the leaf inside the roll. The roll restricts the exposed leaf surface, and the feeding reduces the leaf area. In California, both the grape leaf roller (*Desmia funeralis*) and the omnivorous leaf roller (*Platynota stultana*) are serious vineyard pests. In Australia, a native leaf roller, the light brown apple MOTH (*Epiphyas postvittana*), is the country's most serious insect pest, feeding on a wide range of native and imported plants, including grapevines. As well as feeding on young shoots, the larvae cause damage by feeding on berries, resulting in yield reductions of up to 10%, and allowing the entry of BOTRYTIS and other BUNCH ROTS. The light brown apple moth was found in California in 2007 and aerial spraying of PHEROMONES caused some public outrage.

See also BEETLES for a European insect which causes leaf rolling.   M.J.E.

Bettiga, L. J. (ed.), *Grape Pest Management* (3rd edn, Oakland, Calif., 2013).

Buchanan, G. A., and Amos, T. G., 'Grape pests', in B. G. Coombe and P. R. Dry (eds.), *Viticulture*, ii: *Practices* (Adelaide, 1992).

leafroll virus

leafroll virus, virus disease that is widespread in all countries where grapes are grown. The disease is now thought to be due to a complex of ten different filamentous viruses referred to as grapevine leafroll associated viruses (GLRaVs). Of all the VIRUS DISEASES of vines, it can have the most serious effects on wine quality. These dramatic effects are not understood by the many appreciative TOURISTS in wine regions who marvel at the attractive autumnal red colours of vineyards. Few realize that these colours often indicate the presence of a serious disease, although other factors may contribute to autumnal colours. Leafroll virus causes yield to be reduced by as much as 50%. Wine quality is also affected because of delayed RIPENING. Thus wines from infected vines are lower in alcohol, colour, flavour, and body. The disease does not kill vines, so they are infrequently removed. Yet removal is the only known treatment to overcome the effects of the virus.

Characteristic symptoms are downwards and backwards rolling of the leaf blade in autumn. The area between the leaf veins turns red for black-fruited varieties, and, less obviously, yellow for white-fruited varieties. Some varieties such as Cabernet Franc and Chardonnay show the classic symptoms; others such as Riesling and most ROOTSTOCKS show no symptoms at all. Infected vines may be stunted but this is hardly sufficient for diagnosis.

Leafroll probably originated in the Near East along with VINIFERA and was carried along with grape cuttings. The disease is spread chiefly by humans, using cuttings or buds from infected vines. Cuttings for budwood are taken when the vines are dormant and no leaves are present to show symptoms, making it impossible to distinguish healthy from infected plants. Once infected planting material is used, then the new vineyard is immediately infected, and will perform at below its potential for its lifetime.

This virus disease, like many others, has become more widespread as GRAFTING on to PHYLLOXERA-resistant rootstocks has become more commonplace because grafting increases the chances of using infected material. Thus, many Old World vineyards planted early in the 1900s show the virus. Some tasters believed that grafting to phylloxera-resistant rootstocks from the 1880s onwards led directly to a decline in wine quality. In fact this supposed drop in quality may have been an effect of increased spread of leafroll virus due to grafting.

Of recent concern are reports of the natural spread of GLRaV, especially strain 3, beginning in South Africa in 1985, and subsequently to Spain, Italy, Australia, California, and New Zealand. This strain can have significant effects on YIELD and GRAPE COMPOSITION. MEALY BUGS and soft scale have been shown to be vectors. Successful management programmes have been introduced in South Africa, New Zealand, and California, involving removing affected vines, control of vectors, and replanting with disease-free vines. Since disease symptoms are harder to detect on white wine grape varieties, CHIP BUDDING a dark-skinned grape variety on the trunk of the white vine can reveal the virus.

Because there is no control for this disease, growers should ensure that they plant only material that is tested free of the virus. The University of California at DAVIS led the world in developing a 'clean stock' programme, now known as FOUNDATION PLANT SERVICES, with the result that vineyards planted in California since the early 1960s are generally virus free. In addition, this virus-tested planting stock has been exported and, for example, many of the vineyards of Australia and New Zealand are planted with such material. The virus is detected by INDEXING, or by using immunoassays such as ELISA, or by electron microscope searches for the virus particles. Healthy planting material is produced by eliminating viruses using THERMOTHERAPY or heat treatment or, more reliably, by TISSUE CULTURE. Propagation is recommended from these 'clean' mother plants.   R.E.S.

Almeida, R. P. P., et al., 'Ecology and management of grapevine leafroll disease', *Frontiers in Microbiology*, 4 (2013). doi: 10.3389/fmicb.2013.00094.

Baker, A., 'Grafting technique takes aim at blight of the wine industry', Idealog (Oct 2012), www.idealog.co.nz/blog/2012/10/grafting-technique-takes-aim-blight-wine-industry.

Fuchs, M. F., 'Grape leafroll disease', Cornell University IPM factsheet, www.nysipm.cornell.edu/factsheets/grapes/diseases/grape_leafroll.pdf.

leaf to fruit ratio

leaf to fruit ratio, viticultural measurement which indicates the capacity of a vine to ripen grapes. The ratio of vine leaf area to fruit (grape) weight determines just how well a vine can mature grapes and how suitable they will be for winemaking. Although it is less understood and discussed, it can have an even more important effect on wine quality than YIELD, although it is the latter that is highly regulated in most

European CONTROLLED APPELLATIONS and frequently discussed by OENOLOGISTS.

This ratio indicates the vine's ability to manufacture compounds important for grape RIPENING. If most leaves are exposed to the sun, then the leaf area is proportional to the ability of the vine to make SUGARS by PHOTOSYNTHESIS. Against this should be set the weight of grapes to be ripened. Some studies, however, show that photosynthetic rate can somewhat adjust to a low leaf to fruit ratio, and so the effect of over-severe LEAF REMOVAL in the fruit zone, for instance, may not be as detrimental to ripening as anticipated.

A low value of leaf to fruit ratio, for example 5 sq cm per g grape weight, indicates that the fruit will ripen sluggishly, and so levels of SUGAR IN GRAPES will increase slowly along with PHENOLICS and FLAVOUR, but PH will be relatively high for the corresponding sugar level. The other extreme of, say, 30 sq cm per g grape weight suggests a very leafy vine with a small crop of grapes, but one which will ripen quickly and completely, and so produce better wine quality than for the low leaf to fruit ratio. Such low yields, however, may be uneconomic, and so most vine-growers would aim to manage their vineyards with a sufficient but not excessive leaf to fruit ratio (see vine BALANCE). A value of between 10 and 15 sq cm per g grape weight is considered adequate for ripening of most vine varieties, although higher values are considered necessary by some for PINOT NOIR and perhaps MERLOT. Also, high leaf to fruit ratios must be carefully managed in the vineyard, so as to avoid any negative effects on wine quality due to canopy SHADE.   R.E.S.

Kliewer, W. M., and Dokoozlian, N. K., 'Leaf area/crop weight ratios of grapevines: influence on fruit composition and wine quality', *American Journal of Enology and Viticulture*, 56/2 (2005), 170–81.

Martínez de Toda, F., and Balda, P., 'Delaying berry ripening through manipulating leaf area to fruit ratio', *Vitis* 52/4 (2013), 171–6.

leafy, tasting term usually used synonymously with HERBACEOUS.

Leányka, meaning 'maiden', widely planted HUNGARIAN white wine grape, sometimes confused with the FETEASCĂ ALBĂ of Romania. Varietal Leányka has long been produced in EGER and neighbouring Bükk and Mátra. Total plantings were 837 ha/2,067 acres in 2011. It may be a parent of KIRÁLELEÁNYKA. For more details, see HUNGARY.

Leatico, synonym for ALEATICO.

Lebanon, one of the oldest sites of wine production, incorporating some of the ancient eastern Mediterranean land of CANAAN and, subsequently, most of PHOENICIA, whose people were arguably the first to treat wine as a tradable commodity (see ORIGINS OF VINICULTURE). In Baalbek, the ancient Greek city in the Bekaa Valley which is the vine-growing centre of Lebanon, is the temple of BACCHUS, built in the middle of the 2nd century AD and excavated, displaying much of its former glory, in the early 20th century.

In the Middle Ages, the rich wines of Tyre and Sidon were particularly treasured in Europe, and were traded by the merchants of VENICE, to whom these ports belonged for much of the 13th century. In 1517, what is now Lebanon was absorbed into the Ottoman Empire and winemaking was forbidden, except for religious purposes. This allowed Lebanon's Christians, mainly Maronites and Greek and Armenian Orthodox, to produce wine and in 1857 the Jesuit missionaries of Ksara introduced new vine varieties and production methods from French-governed Algeria, laying the foundations of the modern Lebanese wine industry.

The French administration that governed Lebanon between the wars created unprecedented demand for wine, while Lebanon's post-independence role as a cosmopolitan, financial hub allowed the new wine culture to take hold. It lasted until 1975 when the country descended into a 15-year civil war that stunted the development of the sector. Although only two harvests were lost to the fighting, only Chateau Musar, which recognized the need to penetrate new markets if it was to survive, genuinely thrived during this turbulent period. With peace came new opportunities and growth. The success of Chateau Kefraya, which began producing wine in 1979 after decades of supplying grapes to others, and the popularity of New World wines, galvanized Lebanon's few established wineries and inspired a new generation, many of whom were producers of arak, the aniseed-flavoured eau-de-vie that is the country's national drink, to exploit the potential of the Bekaa Valley's formidable terroir. In the 20 years since the mid 1990s the number of wineries increased from five to over 40. Around 90% of Lebanon's production may still come from ten producers, but they have proved they can produce world-class wine and stepped out of the shadow of the celebrated but quirky Chateau Musar. In 2013, total production was estimated to be 9 million bottles from 2,000 ha/5,000 acres of grapevines dedicated to wine production (OIV reckoned the total vineyard area was 14,000 ha/34,595 acres in 2011). In the same year, a National Wine Institute was formed with a view, inter alia, to creating a system inspired by France's APPELLATION d'origine contrôlée.

The Bekaa Valley (more a plateau than a valley, and sitting at an ELEVATION of around 1,000 m/3,280 ft between the Lebanon and Anti-Lebanon mountain ranges) is still the epicentre of the wine industry. The majority of the vineyards are in the Western Bekaa, Zahlé, and more recently in the drier regions of Baalbek and Hermel. The Bekaa enjoys dry summers, cool nights, and consistent rainfall so that the grapes rarely ripen before the middle of September (considerably later than some southern French vineyards, for example). Minimal vineyard treatments are needed today and almost half of all vines for wine production are trained on WIRES rather than sprawling in vigorous BUSH form. Average yields are around 5 tonnes/ha.

Other regions are emerging. The northern district of Batroun is home to eight producers, while there are also serious wineries in Mount Lebanon, the Chouf, and the south. All have different TERROIRS and have, albeit modestly, contributed to expanding Lebanon's variety of styles.

French influence on the country is still apparent in the grape varieties most commonly planted. For nearly 150 years, Cinsaut, Carignan and to a lesser extent Mourvèdre, Grenache, and Ugni Blanc were the dominant varieties but the post-war resurgence saw major plantings of fashionable INTERNATIONAL VARIETIES such as Cabernet Sauvignon, Merlot, Syrah, and Chardonnay in the mid 1990s. These were soon followed by Tempranillo, Cabernet Franc, Sauvignon Blanc, Viognier, Muscat, Sémillon, and Clairette. In total, around 30 varieties are grown, including a parcel of the little-known French variety ARINARNOA.

With red wines Lebanese producers fell heavily for Bordeaux and Rhône blends but Cinsault, Carignan, Grenache, and Mourvèdre (and to a lesser extent Tempranillo) are proving increasingly popular. Chardonnay and Sauvignon Blanc, and to a lesser extent Viognier, make up a diverse cast of pale-skinned varieties, and Lebanese whites, once an afterthought, are now being taken seriously. The increasingly popular Obaideh, and Merweh (or Merwah), were long considered indigenous but they may be genetically identical to Chardonnay and Sémillon respectively.

The Hochar family's distinctively Levantine red Chateau Musar is still Lebanon's most celebrated wine, a gamey blend of 50 to 80% Cabernet Sauvignon fleshed out with Cinsaut and Carignan. It has been both fêted as a work of genius and dismissed as an anachronism, flawed with excessive VOLATILE ACIDITY and hype, but its fans around the globe are legion. Influenced by a close relationship with the BARTONS of Bordeaux in the early 1960s, the Hochars introduced DESTEMMING and MATURATION in new French OAK BARRELS. Musar also produces small quantities of an equally full-bodied, oak-aged white, primarily from the two local varieties, and even smaller quantities of rosé.

Lebanon's biggest producer is Chateau Ksara, sold to a consortium of Lebanese businessmen in 1973 and now responsible for more than a third of all the wine sold in Lebanon, including most notably its top Bordeaux blend Cuvée du Troisième Millénaire, and Le Souverain, a Cabernet Sauvignon/Arinarnoa blend.

Chateau Kefraya, Lebanon's second biggest winery, was founded in 1979 and claims to use grapes only from its own 300 ha vineyards in the village of Kefraya. Its Cabernet/Syrah blend Comte de M 1996 convinced the outside world that there was more to Lebanese wine than Chateau Musar. The majority shareholder is the colourful Druze politician Walid Jumblatt.

Of the new generation, Massaya, a Franco-Lebanese alliance formed in 1997 between the Lebanese Ghosn brothers and heavyweight French investors from Bordeaux and Châteauneuf-du-Pape, set the early pace, followed closely by Château St Thomas and Domaine Wardy. All producing respected wines by what is a growing number of French-trained Lebanese winemakers, they have been joined by a resurgent Domaine des Tourelles (Lebanon's oldest commercial winery), Ixsir, an ambitious $12 million winery in Batroun, Château Marsyas, Château Ka, Domaine de Baal, Château Khoury, and Château Belle-Vue, all of which make wine well up to international standards.

M.R.K.

Heskett, R., and Butler, J., *Divine Vintage: Following the Wine Trail from Genesis to the Modern Age* (New York, 2012).

Karam, M., *Wines of Lebanon* (London, 2005).

www.lebanonwines.com

www.winesoflebanon.co.uk

lees, old English word for the dregs or sediment that settles at the bottom of a container such as a FERMENTATION VESSEL. Wine lees are made up of dead YEAST cells, the cell membranes of pulp, stem and skin fragments, and insoluble salts and macromolecules that are deposited during the making and ageing of wine.

In the production of everyday wines, clear wine is separated from the lees as soon as possible after FERMENTATION, to ensure that yeast AUTOLYSIS is avoided and clarification and stabilization can be begun. Some wines, both red and, especially, white, may be deliberately left on some or all of of their **fine lees** (as opposed to the coarser **gross lees**, from the French *grosses lies*, off which most wines are racked early in their life if greater complexity and reduction of MALIC ACID are desired), for some months in order to gain greater complexity of flavour. This is called LEES CONTACT.

Fine wines left on lees for a considerable time usually require much less drastic processing than more ordinary wines that were separated early from the lees, because the semi-stable colloidal PHENOLICS and tartrates gradually precipitate during this AGEING period.

Deposits of FINING agents used in CLARIFICATION such as bentonite, silicic acid, and casein are also referred to as lees. They are usually simply settled to permit the recovery of as much wine as possible, but in some large wineries are processed by ROTARY DRUM VACUUM filtration to salvage a bit more wine with a strong lees flavour.

Once the maximum amount of good wine has been recovered, usually by RACKING after prolonged SETTLING, or by the harsher process of FILTRATION, the lees are valuable only for their potassium acid tartrate (cream of tartar) and small amounts of alcohol. After the recovery of tartrates and alcohol, lees can be returned to the vineyard, where they can serve to add some NITROGEN to the soil. Other methods of lees disposal need to ensure they minimize the environmental impact of waste ORGANIC MATTER.

A.D.W.

lees contact, increasingly popular and currently fashionable winemaking practice known to the Ancient Romans (see CATO) whereby newly fermented wine is deliberately left in contact with the LEES. This period of lees contact may take place in any container, from a bottle (as in the making of any BOTTLE-FERMENTED sparkling wine where yeast AUTOLYSIS produces desirable flavour compounds) to a large tank or vat—although a small oak BARREL is the most common location for lees contact. It may take place for anything between a few weeks and, in the special case of some sparkling wines, several years (see SPARKLING WINEMAKING). Most commonly, however, lees contact is prolonged for less than a year after the completion of FERMENTATION.

Lees contact encourages the second, softening MALOLACTIC CONVERSION because the LACTIC ACID BACTERIA necessary for malolactic conversion feed on micronutrients in the lees. This has the effect of adding complexity to the resultant wine's flavour. Many producers, particularly those of white BURGUNDY and other wines based on CHARDONNAY grapes, try to increase the influence of the lees on flavour by LEES STIRRING, or *bâtonnage*, as this practice is known in French. Both lees contact and lees stirring also enhance the structure and MOUTHFEEL of a wine since some molecules released from the dead yeast cells by autolysis can significantly reduce astringency and increase body.

The results of lees ageing on Chardonnay in barrel have been summarized by Gambetta et al.: yeast lees contribute to floral and fruity aromas but overall they reduce the ESTER content of the wine and release polysaccharides (mainly MANNOPROTEINS) into the wine; the lees adsorb both positive ester-derived aromas but also negative off-odours; they attenuate the impact of wood from the barrel; and create an overall REDUCTIVE environment that protects the wine from OXIDATION but also increases the risk of unpleasant-smelling sulfur-related compounds.

White wines made with deliberate lees contact are sometimes described as SUR LIE, a description commonly used to differentiate one type of MUSCADET from another, although in this case small barrels rarely play a part in the process. Lees contact even in BULK STORAGE is increasingly used as a way of increasing flavour in everyday white wines.

Red wines, with their more robust flavours, gain less obvious benefit from lees contact but there is a growing trend to leave red wine on the lees even though it increases the risk of BRETTANOMYCES. Ageing red wines on lees has been shown to reduce BITTERNESS and ASTRINGENCY and give roundness and more BODY to red wines (Del Barrio-Galán et al., 2011)—more so than ageing in barrel alone (Fernández et al., 2011). This is due at least in part to the adsorption of condensed TANNINS to yeast lees (Mazauric and Salmon, 2005, 2006) or to yeast POLYSACCHARIDES. Ageing on lees has also been shown to improve the colour stability of red wines (Escot et al., 2001).

Wines left in contact with lees in large stainless steel tanks after fermentation are very likely to develop HYDROGEN SULFIDE, disulfide, or MERCAPTAN odours. This is why it is important to rack new wine from its gross lees (see LEES) so that the lees level does not become too thick, or to keep the wine separate from the lees for a month, during which time they lose their ability to generate sulfur compounds.

Del Barrio-Galán, R., Pérez-Magariño, S., and Ortega-Heras, M., 'Techniques for improving or replacing aging on lees of oak aged red wines: the effects on polysaccharides and the phenolic composition', *Food Chemistry*, 127/2 (2011), 528–40.

Escot, S., et al., 'Release of polysaccharides by yeast and the influence of released polysaccharides on color stability and wine astringency', *Australian Journal of Grape and Wine Research*, 7/3 (2001), 153–9.

Fernández, O., et al., 'Effect of the presence of lysated lees on polysaccharides, color and main phenolic compounds of red wine during barrel ageing', *Food Research International*, 44/1 (2011), 84–91.

Gambetta, J. M., et al., 'Factors influencing the aroma composition of Chardonnay wines', *Journal of Agricultural Food Chemistry*, 62 (2014), 6512–34. doi: 10.1021/jf501945s.

Mazauric, J. P., and Salmon, J. M., 'Interactions between yeast lees and wine polyphenols during simulation of wine aging: I. Analysis of remnant polyphenolic compounds in the resulting wines', *Journal of Agricultural and Food Chemistry*, 53/14 (2005), 5647–53.

Mazauric, J. P., and Salmon, J. M., 'Interactions between yeast lees and wine polyphenols during simulation of wine aging: II. Analysis of desorbed polyphenol compounds from yeast lees', *Journal of Agricultural and Food Chemistry* 54/11 (2006), 3876–81.

lees stirring, or *bâtonnage*, as it is called in French, is the once fashionable winemaking operation of mixing up the LEES in a barrel, cask, tank, or vat with the wine resting on them. It is an optional addition to the process of LEES CONTACT and is often employed, particularly for whites which have undergone BARREL FERMENTATION. As the French name suggests, such stirring is usually done with a stick, although some racking systems allow the barrel itself to be rotated in situ.

Lees stirring is done partly to avoid the development of malodorous HYDROGEN SULFIDE. Unless a thick layer of lees is stirred, oxygen does not reach the bottom layer and strong enough REDUCING conditions develop to change any small amounts of SULFUR into hydrogen sulfide (see LEES CONTACT).

Stirring up the lees in the barrel also affects OAK FLAVOUR, however. If the lees are stirred, they act as an even more effective buffer between the wine and the wood, limiting the extent to which wood TANNINS and PIGMENTS are extracted into the wine. Wines subjected to lees stirring therefore tend to be much paler and less tannic than those whose lees are not stirred.

Regular lees stirring also stimulates the release of MANNOPROTEINS, thereby improving the stability of the wine. Some producers have become more circumspect in their use of this technique in the belief that it makes the wine heavier, and that over-zealous stirring may increase the risk of PREMATURE OXIDATION.

left bank, an expression for that part of the BORDEAUX wine region that is on the left bank of the river GARONNE. It includes, travelling down river, GRAVES, SAUTERNES, BARSAC, PESSAC-LÉOGNAN, MÉDOC, and all the appellations of the Médoc. The most obvious characteristic shared by the red wines of these appellations, as distinct from RIGHT BANK appellations, is that the dominant red wine grape variety is Cabernet Sauvignon rather than Merlot and Cabernet Franc, although there are many other distinctions.

leftover wine in an opened container such as a half-empty bottle is prey to OXIDATION and steps must be taken in order to prevent it turning to VINEGAR—which could happen within hours or even minutes for a very old wine, within two or three days for most young table wines, and FINO and MANZANILLA sherry, and most bottle-matured PORT, within a few weeks for a robust wood-matured port such as common or garden Ruby or Tawny or OLOROSO

sherry, or within months, possibly years, for most MADEIRA.

Because OXYGEN is the villain in this piece, the easiest way to avoid spoilage of leftover wine is to decant it into a smaller container, perhaps a half-bottle, which approximates as closely as possible to the volume of wine left. There are also patent devices for filling the ULLAGE in a bottle or decanter with INERT GAS, by pumping or spraying, or an attempt can be made to create a vacuum with a pump device. Some drop small, inert objects such as GLASS MARBLES into an opened bottle to restore the fill level to the bottle neck. Leftover wine, no matter what the container or colour, is best stored cool to slow the reactions involved in its deterioration.

The most satisfactory way of disposing of wine leftovers is surely to drink them, and the leftovers of some wines, particularly concentrated young red wines, can taste better, and certainly softer, after a day or even two on ullage (see AERATION and DECANTING).

Leftover wine can also be used quite satisfactorily as COOKING wine or to make vinegar. See also RECORKING.

legno riccio, Italian name for the RUGOSE WOOD complex of vine VIRUS DISEASES.

legs, outmoded tasting term and alternative name for the TEARS left on the inside of a glass by some wines.

Leithaberg DAC, official Austrian DAC appellation named for the predominantly LIMESTONE and SCHIST Leitha Hills (the Leithagebirge) that, prior to the creation of BURGENLAND, formed the Austro-Hungarian border, and extend to the western and northern fringes of the NEUSIEDLERSEE. The Leithaberg DAC applies to wines grown in much, but not all, of the NEUS-IEDLERSEE-HÜGELLAND growing region (the commune of RUST and its immediate environs representing the most important exception) provided these meet the following criteria. Reds must be at least 85% BLAUFRÄNKISCH—a grape variety that represents somewhat more than a quarter of this region's vineyard surface area—together with any combination of Pinot Noir, ST-LAURENT, and/or ZWEIGELT. They must be oak-aged and cannot be sold before 1 September of the second year following harvest. Whites may be made from any combination of Pinot Blanc, Chardonnay, Grüner Veltliner, and/or NEUBURGER. All wines must be at least 12.5% alcohol. Since its inception for vintage 2008 (2009 for whites), wines that do not attain Leithaberg DAC status must be labelled Burgenland for their state or origin—although this was already common practice, since the term Neusiedlersee-Hügelland never really caught on for labelling purposes. With the advent of a Leithaberg DAC, reference to the Leitha Hills

in names and on labels has been outlawed for all but Leithaberg DAC wines.   D.S.

Lemberger, also known as **Blauer Lemberger** and occasionally **Limberger**, is the German name for the black grape variety much more widely grown in Austria as BLAUFRÄNKISCH and in Hungary as KÉKFRANKOS. Germany has very much less of the variety planted, but like all red varieties it has steadily become more popular so that by 2012 there were 1,786 ha/4,411 acres in all.

Lemberger once had a limited following in WASHINGTON state but plantings had fallen to 73 acres/30 ha in 2012.

Len de l'El, also spelled **Len de l'Elh**, was once a major and is now a compulsory minor ingredient in the white wines, especially the sweet ones, of GAILLAC. Its name is local dialect for *loin de l'œil*, or 'far from sight'. This vigorous vine needs a well-ventilated, well-drained site if it is to escape rot in lesser years. All but one of France's 630 ha/1,556 acres in 2011 were in Gaillac country.

length or persistence of flavour is an important indicator of wine quality. See the tasting term LONG.

Lenz Moser, a TRAINING SYSTEM developed in Austria in the 1920s by Dr Lenz Moser III. It employs wider rows (about 3.5 m/11.5 ft) and higher trunks (1.3 m) than had previously been the norm, thereby reducing VINE DENSITY. Lenz Moser's ideas influenced Professor Nelson SHAULIS, who developed the GENEVA DOUBLE CURTAIN.

The Lenz Moser system found favour in parts of Europe in the mid 20th century because it decreases LABOUR and therefore production costs, without any need for special machinery. French and German studies found reductions in fruit quality, however, probably because of SHADE in the fruit zone and it is now much less common even in Austria. It is also known as high culture, or *Hochkultur* in German. The name is probably more familiar as the biggest wine producer in Austria, with operations as far afield as China.   R.E.S.

Léon Millot, minor French hybrid producing small quantities of dark red wine in northern Europe and North America where its early ripening is valued.

Léoville Las Cases, Château, the flagship wine of ST-JULIEN and one run as though it were a FIRST GROWTH (down to the pricing policy) by Jean-Hubert Delon. It was perhaps the most obvious candidate as a SUPER SECOND but challengers proliferate.

The biggest of the three parts into which the extensive original Léoville estate was divided after the French Revolution was awarded to the original owners, the Abbadie-Léoville family, represented by the Marquis de Las Cases. From 1900 it was run by Théophile Swawinski, a distinguished Médoc viticulturist who also administered Ch Pontet-Canet for the CRUSE family. From him it passed to his son-in-law André Delon, grandfather of Michel Delon, Jean-Hubert's late father, who with his father Paul acquired majority ownership of the property in 1930. In 1994 the Delons succeeded in buying out the remaining minority shareholders, descendants of the Las Cases family. Unlike the BARTON family, who acquired the pretty Ch Langoa at the same time as the Léoville-Barton vineyards, the Delons have no magnificent château building, but, perhaps more importantly for them and for the world's wine drinkers, the Las Cases vineyard is made up substantially of one, well-placed contiguous plot rather than the more intertwined parcels of **Léoville-Barton** and **Léoville-Poyferré** (also second growths).

The Delon policy is admirably strict in terms of viticulture, wine quality, and longevity. These firm, deep-coloured, Cabernet-based wines are supported by a strict selection process which can make Clos du Marquis one of Bordeaux's finest SECOND WINES, similar to Les Forts de LATOUR in that a particular 40 ha of land, outside the original Léoville estate, are always designated for this fine wine; definitely not a dump bin for less satisfactory *cuves*.

A further 60 ha are devoted to Ch Léoville Las Cases, comprising 60% of the original estate. The Delons' policy is to release EN PRIMEUR prices very late, typically after the first growths and at a level far closer to them than those of their fellow second growths. In the early 1990s, the Delons, already owners of Ch Potensac in the MÉDOC, also acquired the POMEROL property Ch Nénin.

Leroy, famous name in French wine, not just because **Baron le Roy** of CHÂTEAUNEUF-DU-PAPE was instrumental in the development of the APPELLATION CONTRÔLÉE system, but also in the CÔTE D'OR. The NÉGOCIANT house **Maison Leroy** was founded in the small village of Auxey-Duresses in 1868 and its extensive warehouses there still house substantial stocks of fine, mature burgundy. Henri Leroy joined the family firm in 1919 and made his fortune exporting fortified wine from the Charentes to Germany between the two World Wars. This enabled him to buy a half share in the world-famous DOMAINE DE LA ROMANÉE-CONTI (DRC), a share inherited equally by his two daughters Pauline Roch-Leroy and **Lalou Bize-Leroy** on his death in 1980.

Lalou, a prodigious taster, rock climber, and glamorous dresser, had been co-director of the Domaine since 1974 and contributed considerably to its winemaking policy of quality above

all. She also ran Maison Leroy, but Burgundy's steady move towards DOMAINE BOTTLING made her job of buying the finest raw materials for her négociant skills of ÉLEVAGE increasingly difficult. In 1988, helped by an £8 million investment from her Japanese importers Takashimaya, she succeeded in buying the Domaine Noëllat of VOSNE-ROMANÉE, an already fine canvas on which to paint her vision of the perfect domaine, soon renamed **Domaine Leroy**. This domaine now comprises more than 22 ha/54 acres of some of the Côte d'Or's finest vineyards, including a total of nearly 7 ha in nine different GRANDS CRUS.

This effectively entailed setting up in competition with DRC, since the Domaine Leroy is based in the same village and, like DRC, has holdings in the grand crus ROMANÉE-ST-VIVANT and RICHEBOURG. Unfettered by the commercial considerations of the dozen or so shareholders in DRC, Lalou was able to institute fully BIODYNAMIC VITICULTURE, almost uneconomically low YIELDS, and to invest in every possible winemaking luxury. The wines, which come from a much broader range of (mainly red wine) appellations than those of DRC, are extremely concentrated, expressing as definitively as possible their exact geographical provenance, as well as considerable oak sometimes.

Independently of her sister Pauline, Lalou owns the Domaine d'Auvenay, another biodynamically farmed enterprise founded in 1988, with total holdings of around 4 ha in 80 parcels, including small plots in five different grands crus.

A sales company, **Société Leroy**, enjoyed the exclusive distribution rights to DRC wines, some of the most highly priced in the world, in all markets except the US and UK until a bitter dispute in 1992 which ousted Lalou from co-directorship of DRC. Today, only Domaine Leroy prices rival those of DRC.

Lalou's daughter Perrine Fenal is increasingly involved in the Domaine de la Romanée-Conti.

Les Baux. See BAUX.

Lesotho. One hectare (2.5 acres) of mainly Chenin Blanc with some Pinotage was planted in 2008 in this land-locked country surrounded by South Africa at an ELEVATION of 1,850 m/ 6,070 ft some 25 km/15.5 miles east of Maseru, with guidance from the South African winery Groot Parys 1,100 km/685 miles to the south. Challenges include spring hail, summer rain, and lack of local viticultural experience, but in 2013 the Thamea family was in discussions with local chiefs with a view to planting a further 5 ha/12 acres. The growing season is four weeks longer than in most of SOUTH AFRICA.

Lesquerde, far western subappellation of Côtes du ROUSSILLON-Villages in a mountain enclave dominated by granite. Carignan,

Grenache, and Syrah provide the backbone of these concentrated reds.

Lessona, tiny but historically important red wine district in the Vercelli Hills in the subalpine north of the PIEMONTE region of north-west Italy. On just 6.45 ha/16 acres three producers produce a wine from Nebbiolo grapes, optionally softened with some Bonarda or Vespolina. Sella and Massimo Clerico were joined in 1999 by Paolo De Marchi of Isole e Olena in Chianti Classico, who has revitalized his family estate, Villa Sperino, attracting international attention, and undoubtedly helped to save Lessona from extinction.

For more details, see SPANNA.

L'Étoile, small appellation in the JURA region of eastern France which specializes in traditional, OXIDATIVE white wines aged in non topped-up barrels. These are often pure Chardonnay but may be Chardonnay blended with the local SAVAGNIN grape. It also produces VIN DE PAILLE, CRÉMANT DU JURA, and the extraordinarily nutty VIN JAUNE. Historically l'Étoile was known for sparkling wines, which today are sold as CRÉMANT du Jura.   W.L.

Leyda, occasional name for SAN ANTONIO Valley in CHILE.

Liatiko, ancient Cretan vine that is still this Greek island's most planted, producing relatively soft, light red, usually blended with the stronger MANDILARIA and KOTSIFALI to make sweet reds, exported in great quantity by Venetian merchants in medieval times.

libation, the pouring out of wine (and occasionally other liquids: water, oil, honey) as a religious act. The practice of offering a libation to a god was universal in the Greek and Roman world. Whenever wine was drunk in formal gatherings, such as symposia, a libation was poured while a prayer was said to invoke a chosen god. Libations also regularly accompanied prayers and sacrifices on all sorts of occasions. The origins of the practice are to be found in the offering of the first fruits to gods; but libation should also be seen in the context of the way in which social intercourse between humans (and by analogy between humans and gods) was maintained by the mutual exchange of gifts. Libations poured on the ground were also specifically seen as a gift for the dead. 'The souls are nourished by libations', as Lucian says.   J.J.P.

Burkert, W., *Greek Religion* (Oxford, 1985).

Libourne, small port on the RIGHT BANK of the Dordogne in the Bordeaux region. It is now the commercial centre for the right-bank appellations, although it was established in the 13th century, much later than ST-ÉMILION's port Pierrefitte, and was at the time considered a parvenu in comparison with FRONSAC. In modern history, its wine trade is much more recent than the Chartronnais of the BORDEAUX TRADE in the great city across the Garonne, and its more modest traders concentrated initially on selling in northern mainland Europe rather than in the British Isles. Of merchants based here on the banks of the river Dordogne, J. P. MOUEIX is the most important. For more details, see POMEROL, the wine region on the eastern outskirts of the town.

The wines St-Émilion, Pomerol, and especially Fronsac are sometimes referred to collectively as **Libournais**.

Lichine, Alexis (1913–89), was born in Russia but, unlike André TCHELISTCHEFF, another Russian who was to shape the American wine industry, he and his family left before the Revolution, and he was educated in France.

After the Repeal of PROHIBITION, Lichine sold wines, first in a shop in New York and subsequently for the gifted American wine importer Frank SCHOONMAKER. After the Second World War, in which he served with distinction, he returned to finding French and German wines from individual estates and selling them in an America where wine was all but unknown.

His success in doing this was considerable and came from a flair for seeing and recounting the romantic side of wine and winemaking, as well as appreciating the pleasures wine can bring.

During the 1950s, he became a major figure in the French wine world, setting up his own company, Alexis Lichine & Co., to sell only CHÂTEAU BOTTLED and DOMAINE BOTTLED wines, for the most part from major properties. He sold this company to British brewers Bass-Charrington in 1964, and gradually left the commercial world to make wine and write books. For more detail, see the LITERATURE OF WINE.

Lichine assembled a group of investors to buy and renovate the MARGAUX second growth Ch Lascombes in 1952, and ran the property with great success before selling it, again to Bass-Charrington, in 1971.

He also bought in 1951 the fourth growth Ch Prieuré at Cantenac just outside Margaux. He officially renamed this property, based on an old Benedictine priory, Ch Prieuré-Lichine in 1953 and it was at this property, typically one of the first to welcome passing visitors, that he died in 1989. His son Sacha ran the property until its sale in 1999 and now makes acclaimed rosé on a Provençal estate Ch d'Esclans.   W.B.

licoroso, Portuguese sweet FORTIFIED WINE (as opposed to a GENEROSO, which may be dry or sweet).

lie or **lies**, French for LEES.

Liebfraumilch, quintessentially mild, slightly sweet white wine from GERMANY'S RHEIN-HESSEN, PFALZ, NAHE, or (rarely) RHEINGAU regions known almost exclusively in export markets where it weaned many a potential wine drinker off soft drinks but is now in steep decline. In its heyday in the 1980s, it accounted for an extraordinary, some would say horrifying, 60% of all German wine exported. These wines were generally dominated by SILVANER, MÜLLER-THURGAU, or KERNER grapes, but the **Liebfrauenstift-Kirchstück** (Our Lady's Cloister) in Worms from which the name Liebfraumilch was derived continues to be a source of good Riesling.

lieblich, appears (albeit usually in small print) on labels of AUSTRIAN wines whose RESIDUAL SUGAR is between 19 and 45 g/l. The term is not seen on German labels but it often used informally to describe German wines sweeter than those labelled TROCKEN, HALBTROCKEN, or FEINHERB.

Liechtenstein. The principality's vineyards extend from Balzers in the south to Eschen in the north but are concentrated on the capital Vaduz, above and at some distance from the river RHINE, where the climate is strongly influenced by the warming föhn effect of the wind from the south. There are about a hundred vine growers and just four commercial wine producers, of which the biggest is Hofkellerei des Fürsten von Liechtenstein, run in tandem with a much larger operation in Austria's WEINVIERTEL. Most of Liechtenstein's wine is sold directly to local consumers.

Ospelt, M. and Müller, W., *Weintradition Liechtenstein* (Triesen, 2004).

lieu-dit, French term used quite generally to refer to the local, traditional name of a small area of land, usually defined by topography or history. Such locally given names are also used more specifically, especially in Burgundy, to refer to a plot of land or vineyard within a larger appellation. In practice these names are used on labels for vineyards below PREMIER CRU in rank, for example Les Tillets in the commune of Meursault.

lifestyle winery, term coined in NEW ZEALAND for a small winery established and run, typically by an educated young to middle-aged couple who have access to funds generated by another career, more for its bucolic appeal than as a strictly commercial proposition.

lifted, tasting term for a wine with a high but not excessive level of VOLATILE ACIDITY. Such a wine may also be said have **lift** conferred on it.

light. A wine is described by wine tasters as light, or **light bodied**, if it is low in ALCOHOL and VISCOSITY. See BODY for more details. Wines are sometimes also described as light as opposed to FORTIFIED.

light brown apple moth. See LEAF ROLLERS and MOTHS.

lightning, a climatic phenomenon, an electric discharge from the atmosphere under storm conditions, which may strike a vineyard and, by travelling along a wire, damage vines around the point of contact. Most vines recover after a lightning strike, however.

lightstrike, known as *goût de lumière* in French, is the damaging effect that light at short wavelengths in the ultraviolet and blue end of the spectrum can have on wine, as well as products such as beer and milk. The light provokes a chemical reaction with riboflavin and AMINO ACIDS in the wine, resulting in malodorous sulfur-related compounds such as dimethyl disulfide (DMDS) and methanethiol, which smell variously of cardboard, garlic, and cooked cabbage. White wines in clear bottles exposed to artificial light, particularly fluorescent light, even for a relatively short period of time, are the most likely to be affected, although bright daylight is equally damaging. Sodium lighting is often used in cellars in Champagne for this reason. Green glass is better than clear but not as good as amber, and red wines are less likely to be affected because PHENOLICS, especially TANNINS, help to protect the wine. Coating or sleeving the bottle is another solution but again adds to the production costs. Some champagne producers such as Roederer protect their best bottles by wrapping them in amber-coloured cellophane. Reducing the intensity and changing the direction of shop lighting would be a much cheaper solution but harder to control. Research by the CIVC is trying to identify an LED light that excludes those wavelengths that cause lightstrike.

Descoins, C., Meurens, M., and Mathlouthi, M., 'Influence de la translucidité de la bouteille sur l'apparition du goût de lumière dans le Champagne', *Revue des Oenologues*, 120 (2006), 1–4.
Hartley, A., *The Effect of Ultraviolet Light on Wine Quality*, WRAP report (London 2008).

lignification, botanical term for the process in which SHOOTS or STEMS become woody. See also CANE RIPENING.

Liguria. The crescent-shaped strip that runs along Italy's Mediterranean coast from the French border to the edge of Tuscany is Italy's third smallest wine-producing region after the Valle d'Aosta and Molise. See map under ITALY, and see GENOA, VERNACCIA, and ITALY for some historical detail. The extremely rugged terrain—the Apennines descend virtually all the way to the sea—combined with the minute size of individual properties make agriculture in general and viticulture in particular a marginal activity, and the greater economic possibilities offered by the thriving tourist industry, commercial flower-, vegetable-, and olive-growing have steadily drained manpower from the region's vineyards ever since the Second World War. However, Liguria's total vineyard area, 1,568 ha/3,873 acres, has been stable in recent years, with more than half of it dedicated to the production of DOC wine.

A crossroads of trade and traffic between Italy, France, and Spain, Liguria has long cultivated myriad vine varieties, and a census of the province of Imperia in 1970 revealed no fewer than 123. Many of these have since been abandoned, although renewed interest in INDIGENOUS VARIETIES has saved several from extinction, notably the white Scimiscià, which in 2003 was officially included in the national register. The region is concentrating its efforts on the white wine grapes VERMENTINO (PIGATO) and the less characterful Bosco, and the red varieties ROSSESE, SANGIOVESE, and DOLCETTO (the last of these called Ormeasco in Liguria). Ormeasco, Pigato (now proved identical to Vermentino), Rossese, and Vermentino each have their own overarching DOC within the Riviera Ligure di Ponente zone, a wide stretch of territory between Genoa and the French border, which has been divided in five smaller subzones: Albenga, Finale, Quiliano, Riviera dei Fiori, and Taggia.

Liguria's most renowned wine, the white Cinqueterre, is perhaps most famous for its vertigo-inducing vineyards perched on TERRACES sculpted into cliffsides high above the Ligurian Sea. The wine itself, made from Vermentino plus Albarola and/or Bosco, occasionally rises above thirst-quenching level. The rare Sciacchetrà, a sweet Cinqueterre made from PASSITO grapes, is enjoying a modest comeback.

Production of Vermentino is concentrated in Castelnuovo Magra, to the south of La Spezia in the Colli di Luni DOC zone, and in Diano Castello and Imperia in the province of Imperia. The name Pigato is traditional in Ranzo and Pieve di Teco, to the north of the city of Imperia. Ormeasco (Dolcetto) is produced almost exclusively in Pornassio and Pieve di Teco. The ROSSESE grape, sometimes called 'Italy's Pinot Noir', has its own DOC near Ventimiglia, Rossese di Dolceacqua or simply Dolceacqua. The wine, combining aromas of blackcurrants and roses with power and delicacy, is produced on steep vineyards clinging to the coast, fighting a losing battle against greenhouses for vegetables. This admired but tiny DOC is divided among 14 villages, each with their own CRU vineyards at 400 m/1,312 ft ELEVATION, sometimes higher. A new generation, determined to save the steep vineyards from being abandoned, is focusing on the production of high-quality wines which seem ripe for elevation to DOCG status.   W.S.

Lima, inland DOP subregion of VINHO VERDE in north-west Portugal on the Lima River, best known for particularly floral VARIETAL wines made from the LOUREIRO grape. Single-estate examples are among Vinho Verde's fresh, aromatic, mineral best.

Limarí, valley in the northern region of Coquimbo in CHILE increasingly known for its wine.

lime, in the forms of slaked lime (calcium hydroxide) or ground limestone (calcium carbonate), may be added to soils to neutralize SOIL ACIDITY. Ground limestone is immobile in the soil, except in light sands, and must therefore be thoroughly incorporated to be fully effective. **Liming** is therefore most appropriately used, if needed, before vine PLANTING. It is easy to achieve in the topsoil but very difficult in the subsoil (below 50cm/20 in). The CALCIUM in lime or limestone also helps to give the soil greater crumb structure and friability (see SOIL STRUCTURE). Gypsum (calcium sulfate) can be used for the latter purpose on soils where acidity is at an appropriate level. One common problem of over-liming is lime-induced CHLOROSIS (iron is involved in photosynthesis and deficiency results in yellowing of leaves). See also LIME, ACTIVE.   J.G. & R.E.W.

lime, active, refers to calcium carbonate that is available to the vine because it is finely divided and therefore more soluble than LIMESTONE rock. Its presence in the soil is not necessarily due to underlying limestone, which is generally hard and insoluble, and may be the result of weathering and soil-forming processes. There is no direct relationship between the amount of active lime in the soil and wine quality. However, active lime raises a soil's PH above 7 and may enhance the vine's root development. Too much may lead to lime-induced CHLOROSIS. See also LIME and SOIL ALKALINITY.
                              J.E.H. & R.E.W.

limestone, a rock made of the mineral calcite (calcium carbonate); dolomitic limestone or dolomite is a mixture of calcium-magnesium carbonate. Limestone is *calcaire* in French.

Common limestones differ from CHALK (a soft form of limestone) in being hard and not readily penetrated by plant roots, except through cracks. Unless mineral material is brought in by wind or water, the depth of soil formed on limestone depends on the impurities (CLAY, SILT, and SAND) in the limestone because the dissolution of calcite produces only calcium and bicarbonate ions. Some limestone soils, such as the Mediterranean TERRA ROSSA, are red-brown in colour; these are moderately alkaline and have a good clay-loam texture and structure.

Some limestone soils overlie substantial reservoirs of SOIL WATER, of high quality for

IRRIGATION. The longer roots of well-established vines may reach these reservoirs, if they are not too deep. Deep RIPPING to shatter the hard limestone may be carried out before planting, typically to 1 m (3 ft) depth, but any slabs of limestone brought to the surface may need to be removed. Limestone-derived soils are in general valued most highly in cool viticultural regions. The great wines of BURGUNDY come from vines grown on the slopes of the CÔTE D'OR escarpment, where Jurassic limestone is the predominant rock but not the only type of limestone found there.

The red limestone-derived terra rossa of Coonawarra in SOUTH AUSTRALIA similarly produces some of Australia's best red wines from Cabernet Sauvignon and Shiraz, both vine varieties being close to the cool limit for their reliable ripening.

In warm climates, however, such as in the south of France, and the Riverland of South Australia, limestone soils are not regarded as superior, or even necessarily as suitable for viticulture (see SOIL AND WINE QUALITY).
                              R.E.S. & R.E.W.

Limestone Coast Zone, moderately cool, high-quality wine area in SOUTH AUSTRALIA encompassing Coonawarra, Mount Benson, Mount Gambier, Padthaway, Robe, and Wrattonbully regions. The zone is much greater in extent, with the districts of Bordertown and Penola candidates for official recognition as regions. Bordertown, the furthest north, is the warmest area (robust Shiraz, Cabernet Sauvignon, etc.). Mount Gambier, to the extreme south, is the coolest, best suited to Pinot Noir and Chardonnay.

Limnio, dark grape variety native to the island of Límnos in GREECE, where it can still be found. It has also transferred successfully to Khalkhidhikhi in north east Greece, however, where, sometimes blended with Cabernet, it produces a full-bodied wine with a good level of acidity and some herbal aromas. **Limniona** resurrected from mainland Greece is unrelated according to DNA PROFILING.

Limousin, old French province centred on the town of Limoges, and a term encountered most frequently in the wine world as a term for the region's OAK.

Limoux, small town and appellation in the eastern Pyrenean foothills in southern France. For centuries it has been devoted to the production of white wines that would sparkle naturally after a second fermentation during the spring. They became known as **Blanquette de Limoux**, Blanquette meaning simply 'white' in Occitan. Locals claim that fermentation in bottle was developed here long before it was consciously practised in CHAMPAGNE, dating the production of cork-stoppered sparkling wines at the Abbey of St-Hilaire from 1531 (Limoux is just north of CATALUÑA, a natural home of the CORK oak) although Stevenson casts doubt on both the date and claims that the wine was sparkling.

The region's vineyards are so much higher, cooler, and further from Mediterranean influence than any other Languedoc appellation (even Côtes de la MALEPÈRE to its immediate north) that many are Atlantic-influenced even though they are just inland from the CORBIÈRES hills. Within the region there are distinctly different zones, according to factors such as ELEVATION, soil types, and the influence of the Atlantic or Mediterranean.

The grape used traditionally was the MAUZAC, called locally Blanquette, but increasing amounts of Chardonnay and, to a lesser extent, CHENIN BLANC have been planted so that in the 1980s the Limoux vineyards were much valued as one of southern France's very few sources of CHARDONNAY grapes from mature vines. Still wines made from them were then in great demand, especially for export markets. This international success was cleverly capitalized upon by Toques et Clochers, an annual charity AUCTION of different Chardonnay barrel samples, inspired by the famous HOSPICES DE BEAUNE auction but embellished by the involvement of some of France's most famous chefs. These often lean, oak-aged Chardonnays regularly fetched prices far in excess of their then classification as VINS DE PAYS so the Limoux appellation was thoroughly overhauled in 1993. It now encompasses still whites made mainly from Chardonnay (although Chenin Blanc may be included and at least 15% Mauzac must be included), with, unusually, compulsory BARREL FERMENTATION.

In 2005, a red wine Limoux appellation was added, with Merlot compulsorily making up at least 50% of the blend, and Côt (Malbec), Syrah, and Grenache constituting at least 30%. Cabernet Sauvignon and Cabernet Franc may play a part—truly an Atlantic and Mediterranean blend. Such (relatively light) wines used to be sold as IGP de la Haute Vallée de l'Aude, a name now more commonly encountered on the region's most promising red wine grape, Pinot Noir.

But Limoux is essentially a sparkling wine town. Blanquette de Limoux is the region's most famous product, grown on 635 ha/1,568 acres of vineyard in 2012, sparkling wine made up of at least 90% Mauzac, although Chardonnay and/or Chenin Blanc may play a minor part. The **Crémant de Limoux** appellation was devised in 1990 for less rustic, more internationally designed sparkling wines. In 2012, some 846 ha/2,090 acres were devoted to the production of Crémant de Limoux. See CRÉMANT for more details.

Limoux's distinctly marginal speciality is Blanquette Méthode Ancestrale (see SPARKLING WINEMAKING), a sweeter, often slightly cloudy, less fizzy sparkling wine made exclusively from Mauzac grown on 65 ha/160 acres in 2012 and left to ferment a second time in bottle without subsequent disgorgement of the resultant sediment. Like the GAILLAC Mousseux made from Mauzac by the *méthode gaillacoise* with similar regard for tradition and disdain for technology, these hand-crafted wines are low in alcohol, high in Mauzac's old apple-peel flavours, and can taste remarkably like a superior sweet cider.

Limoux's sparkling wine business is dominated by the dynamic local CO-OPERATIVE, which sells a range of bottlings under such names as Aimery and Sieur d'Arques, but there are also some fine individual estates in the pretty hills here.

Stevenson, T., *How The English Invented Champagne*, (Kindle Book, 2014).

Lincoln University Centre for Viticulture and Oenology, research and teaching institution at Lincoln, Canterbury, in the South Island of NEW ZEALAND. Research focuses specifically on the growth and production of Pinot Noir and Sauvignon Blanc, in particular how cool-climate growing conditions, such as those in New Zealand, affect the flavours, aromas, MOUTHFEEL, PHENOLICS, and TANNINS of these grape varieties. Lincoln is a specialist land-based university with a traditional agricultural science background, from which the VITICULTURE and OENOLOGY programme grew in 1989. Lincoln is the largest wine training facility in New Zealand with study options up to PhD level. All programmes emphasize the integration of grape growing and winemaking from vine to glass. The focus is on such aspects of wine production as VINEYARD SITE SELECTION, planting material, vine management, harvest parameters, grape handling, fermentation control, and wine finishing as well as vine physiology and FERMENTATION chemistry.   J.T.

www.lincoln.ac.nz

linguistics. See LANGUAGE OF WINE.

lipids, a group of chemicals that includes oils, fats, and waxes. Lipids are distinctive in plants because, despite the plant's watery environment, they are not soluble in water, which is also the basis of their important roles. They make up the membranes of plant CELLS which keep apart entirely different zones of metabolic activity, often with large differences in ACIDITY on either side of the membrane. They make energy-rich reserves of food as in seeds, grapeseed oil being a good example. Also they coat the surface of the plant with a water-impermeable layer of waxy cutin which stops desiccation.

A host of other compounds have lipid-like structures, including important plant pigments such as chlorophyll and CAROTENOIDS. The sediment in MUST contains a significant amount of lipids that play an important role in FERMENTATION. If CLARIFICATION of the must is too severe (so that the turbidity is less than 150 NTU), the risk of sluggish fermentation is higher than in more turbid juices with higher levels of solids.   B.G.C. & D.D.

Liqueur Muscat, old name for the very special sort of STICKIE made in AUSTRALIA from Brown MUSCAT grapes. For more, see TOPAQUE.

liqueur wine is the official EU term for FORTIFIED WINES that have an ALCOHOLIC STRENGTH of not less than 15% and not more than 22%. See also VIN DE LIQUEUR.

liquoreux, French term meaning 'syrupy sweet', used for very rich, often BOTRYTIZED, wines that are markedly sweeter than MOELLEUX wines.

liquoroso, Italian for a strong, usually sweet, FORTIFIED, wine.

Lirac, large and growing (782 ha/1,932 acres by 2013) appellation on the right bank of the southern RHÔNE producing mainly full-bodied reds, and a small amount of rosé and full bodied white wine. The rosés can offer good-value alternatives to nearby TAVEL, made in very similar conditions and from the same sort of grape varieties, while the reds generally resemble a particularly soft, earlier maturing Côte du Rhône-Villages, although there are one or two notably more ambitious exceptions such as Domaines du Joncier and de la Mordorée and some of the better producers in CHÂTEAUNEUF-DU-PAPE across the river who also make a Lirac. The appellation includes three communes other than Lirac, of which Roquemaure was an important port in the 16th century from which wines would be shipped as far north as England and Holland (see RIVERS). In the 18th century, Roquemaure was a much more important wine centre than Châteauneuf-du-Pape.

Modern red and rosé Lirac must contain at least 40% Grenache with Mourvèdre and/or Syrah making up at least 25%, while in 2014 Carignan was limited to 10%. Many of the minor Châteauneuf varieties may make up the rest, while Bourboulenc, Clairette, Grenache Blanc, and Roussanne are the main white wine grapes. Quality has increased considerably.

See map under RHÔNE.

Lisboa, VINHO REGIONAL in western Portugal sometimes known colloquially as Oeste (West) and known until 2009 as Estremadura. Although it incorporates no fewer than nine DOPs—ALENQUER, Arruda, BUCELAS, CARCAVELOS, COLARES, Encostas d'Aire, Lourinhã, Óbidos, and Torres Vedras—as at 2010 all but 6% of wine from this sizeable coastal strip qualified as VINHO REGIONAL (VR) or VINHO. Much is produced by the 15 large CO-OPERATIVES who dominate the region, selling it in returnable 5 l/1.3 gal flagons known as *garrafoes* that are to be found in taverns and restaurants all over the Portuguese-speaking world. Some wine also goes to make Portugal's national brands of VERMOUTH. Focused principally on quantity not quality, Lisboa is Portugal's most productive region for table wines. Unfortunately Bucelas, Carcavelos, and Colareas, historically the most distinguished wine regions, are now too small to be qualitatively significant. The latter two have particularly struggled to sustain their culture of winemaking where so much land was sold to property developers in the 1960s and 1970s, catapulting land costs beyond the reach of most prospective vineyard investors. However, hitherto uncelebrated pockets of excellence are slowly but surely emerging elsewhere, typically defined by Lisboa's propitious clay and limestone soils and planted to recently introduced promising varieties, notably TOURIGA NACIONAL, Tinta Roriz (Tempranillo), and ARINTO, together with such INTERNATIONAL VARIETIES as Syrah, Cabernet Sauvignon, Grenache, Pinot Noir, Sauvignon Blanc, Riesling, and Viognier. (Although, keeping the faith, newcomers Biomanz and Casal Figueira produce some exciting wines from esoteric local grapes.) More often than not these wines are labelled VR (even though relaxed DOP regulations permit new grapes), and count among their number the best and most promising wines from the area as a whole (DOP or VR). More elevated areas (up to 500 m/1,640 ft ELEVATION) and those close to the coast are at last starting to reveal their potential for fresh, mineral-scented whites, also Pinot Noir. S.A.

Lison-Pramaggiore, DOC mainly in the VENETO region of north-east Italy created in 1986 by the fusion of two previous DOCs, the CABERNET di Pramaggiore and TOCAI di Lison. The DOC Lison was created in 1971 for the production of Tocai Bianco and Tocai Rosso, now officially known as Tai Bianco (identical to FRIULANO) and Tai Rosso (the same as GRENACHE) after Hungary successfully claimed ownership of the Tocai name. It was joined in 1972 by Pramaggiore to accommodate Merlot. With the unification of the two DOCs in 1985 a raft of new varieties such as Pinot Bianco, Chardonnay, Pinot Grigio, Sauvignon Blanc, and Friuli's Refosco was allowed, with Malbec added in 2000. As a result of the EU viticultural reforms of the late 2000s the entire Lison part of the DOC was, questionably, elevated to DOCG status. The subzone Lison Classico DOCG is reserved for wines coming from the original heartland of the zone.

The vineyards themselves are in the wide plain created by the Piave River as it descends from the hills of Conegliano and Montello towards the Adriatic and, as such, can be considered an eastward continuation of the PIAVE DOC zone, extending into the Pordenone province of FRIULI. The wines are fresh and pleasurable, if not memorable, with Cabernet (predominantly Franc rather than Sauvignon) regularly giving the most interesting results. Cooler vintages, together with the high percentage of Cabernet Franc and high yields in the vineyards (90 hl/ha), tend to bring out a HERBACEOUSNESS which may be more appealing to local markets than to international ones. W.S.

www.lison-pramaggiore.it

Listán, synonym for PALOMINO FINO, the white grape variety that can produce superb sherry around JEREZ. As Listán, or Listán Blanco, some of its most interesting wines are those grown on the CANARY ISLANDS' volcanic soils, where it can produce table wines of much greater tension, individuality, and distinction than most of those on the Spanish mainland. The rebirth of Canary wines in the 1990s thus gave this much-maligned variety a new lease on life. The Spanish vine census of 2011 cites the total area of 'Listán Blanco de Canarias' as 9,000 ha/(a suspiciously round number that is the equivalent of 22,240 acres). **Listán de Huelva** is a distinct but minor Andalucian pale-skinned variety while the dark-skinned, well-travelled PAIS of Chile is known in Spain as **Listán Prieto**.

Listán Negro, recently appreciated INDIGENOUS grape which dominates wine production on the island of Tenerife in the CANARY ISLANDS, planted on 4,519 ha/11,161 acres in 2011. CARBONIC MACERATION has managed to coax exceptional aromas out of this medium-bodied wine. The grape may also be called Almuñeco.

Listrac, or **Listrac-Médoc**, one of the six communal appellations of the Haut-Médoc district of Bordeaux. In relation to the other five (MARGAUX, ST-JULIEN, PAUILLAC, ST-ESTÈPHE, and even MOULIS, with which it is often compared), Listrac seems the least well favoured. It is, just, the furthest of them all from the Gironde estuary and the vineyards are planted on 540 ha/ 1,334 acres in 2013 of mainly clay-limestone on a gentle rise which, at an ELEVATION of about 40 m/131 ft, constitutes some of the highest land in the Médoc. Although the Merlot grape is increasingly planted, the wines can be relatively austere in youth. The most cosseted property is probably the late Baron Edmond de ROTHSCHILD's Ch Clarke, given extra ballast by oenologist Michel ROLLAND, although Ch Fonréaud is generally reliable. Yields of 45 hl/ha (2.6 tons/ acre) are officially tolerated here, whereas the limit is 40 hl/ha in Moulis and other Haut-Médoc village appellations.

For more information, see MÉDOC and BORDEAUX.

Parker, R., *Bordeaux* (4th edn, New York, 2003).
Penning-Rowsell, E., *The Wines of Bordeaux* (6th edn, London, 1989).

literature of wine. The literature that concerns wine specifically, as opposed to references to wine in more general writing (for which see ENGLISH LITERATURE), is a complicated tapestry of texts and books that has been woven from a broad variety of strands from classical times to the present day. Most writers concern themselves with how and where grapes are grown, how and where wine is made, and how individual wines taste, but their methods vary considerably and there are works on wine which are also works on travel, on history, on medicine, on agricultural matters, and on gastronomy.

Early works and agriculture

Many early works are richer in references to the effects of drinking wine (see DRUNKENNESS) than to the wine itself. CLASSICAL TEXTS constitute the earliest known literature of wine (although see also Ancient MESOPOTAMIA). While Mago of CARTHAGE clearly inspired many subsequent writers, his text does not survive and the first known classical writers to concentrate on wine and winemaking were probably CATO (234–149 BC) and VARRO (116–27 BC). Cato, particularly, was keen on the profit motive in winemaking and his instructions appear mainly to have been aimed at quantity rather than quality, even suggesting, at one point, how Coan wine (from Kós, one of the AEGEAN ISLANDS) could be faked from Italian grapes.

Much more modern in his outlook towards the production of wine was COLUMELLA (2 BC–AD 65), whose family, based near Cádiz in southern Spain, may well have owned vineyards. His *De re rustica* gives detailed advice on such matters as CLONAL SELECTION, the planting of vineyards, and the need for wines to be as natural as possible. 'The wine is clearly the best which can solely give pleasure by its own nature.' PLINY the Elder (AD 23–79) was the last great classical writer on wine and winemaking, although he was clearly influenced by Varro. The works of all these three, and the more derivative PALLADIUS in particular, were translated and used as textbooks throughout Europe until the end of the 16th century.

In these books, viticulture was treated merely as a part, albeit a major part, of the broader subject of agriculture. This tradition was continued by such writers as PETRUS DE CRESCENTIIS (1230–1310), an Italian lawyer who was forced to leave his own country and spent 30 years in exile in Spain and France. One volume of his monumental *Liber ruralium commodorum* dealt specifically with wine-growing and making. The work was translated into French on the instructions of Charles V.

The first French writer to attempt to classify wines in any way was Charles Étienne (1504–64). His *Vinetum . . .* first appeared in Lyons in 1536. This was subsequently translated into French and incorporated in *L'Agriculture et maison rustique des maistres Charles Étienne et Jean Liebault*, 1564 (Liebault was Étienne's son-in-law). This was a best seller and was translated into English by Richard Surflet in 1606. It was followed in due course by the *Nouvelle Maison rustique* by Louis Liger of AUX-ERRE, which appeared in many editions throughout the 18th and early 19th centuries. While this book deals with a broad selection of rural topics, the section on wine is particularly fascinating with its details of the then popular wines of Orléans, Burgundy, and Champagne. The characteristics are also given of 50 different VINE VARIETIES grown in France both as table grapes and for winemaking, of which 'morillon noir' is today's PINOT NOIR and 'gamet' is today's GAMAY. More than 15 varieties of MUSCAT are mentioned, but CABERNET SAUVIGNON is notably absent (in the late 1990s DNA PROFILING explained why).

In some ways, an English equivalent was Philip Miller's *Gardeners' Dictionary*, which first appeared in 1731. Here, under the headings Vitis and Wine, are detailed articles on such subjects as grape varieties, Burgundy, Champagne, and English vineyards, although he says of these last, 'There have of late years been but very few vineyards in England, tho' they were formerly very common.'

As wine was the everyday drink throughout much of Europe, in parallel with the books on the agricultural aspects of wine there were others devoted, perhaps only in part, to its keeping and serving. In England the anonymously written *Mystery of Vintners* appeared in 1692 and *L'Art d'améliorer et de conserver les vins* (1781) was first published in Paris, under the title *Dissertation sur les vins*, in 1772. Further editions came out in Liège and Turin soon afterwards. The information they gave was often plagiarized and adapted to appear in such general books as *The Laboratory, or School of Arts* (1799).

Wine as medicine

The role of wine in the world of MEDICINE had been important from the earliest of times. It was used widely as a medium for the infusion of medicinal herbs and many wine-based remedies were given in such books as *The Secrets of Alexis of Piedmont*, which appeared in a number of languages from 1555 onwards.

Indeed the first book specifically on wines in English, *A New Book of Wines* (1568), was written by William Turner, who studied medicine at Cambridge. He warned of the danger of

drinking the sweet, heavy wines of the Mediterranean as opposed to the healthy, light wines of the Rhine.

This medicinal tradition was adapted by the wine merchant Duncan M'Bride in his *Choice of Wines . . .* (1793) which included general discussion about the wines that were available at the time and their potential application for various medical conditions. Particularly recommended was Toc-kay de Espagne (*sic*), of which only M'Bride knew the source.

A much later sequel is *Wine is the Best Medicine* (1974, updated 1992) by the Frenchman Dr E. A. Maury. This had a more rational approach to the subject, with a variety of individual French wines being recommended for everything from flatulence to cystitis.

DOCTORS have always had a major role to play in English wine literature. Sir Edward Barry was a Bath physician whose *History of Classical Wines* appeared in 1775. He has been criticized for relying too closely on the work of the 16th century papal medical adviser Barrius, but he also includes an appendix on modern wines and viticulture in England.

Doctors were also responsible for the first two 'modern' books to deal with wine in depth. Whilst the title of *A Practical Treatise on Brewing, Distilling and Rectification*, by R. Shannon, MD (1805), might put off the oenophile there is 'A Copious Appendix on . . . Foreign Wines, Brandies and Vinegars'. This work is particularly strong on the wines of Portugal and Spain, but does not hesitate to lift, unattributed, from Miller on the wines of Burgundy.

Dr Alexander HENDERSON's *The History of Ancient and Modern Wines* (1824) is perhaps the first book in English to attempt to give descriptions of a broad range of wines, based upon his own travels to France, Germany, and Italy. It is also the first book to try to analyse the science of TASTING.

The golden age

In the number of wines it talks about, Henderson's book is overwhelmed by what must be the most remarkable book on wine ever published, the *Topographie de tous les vignobles connus* (1816) by André JULLIEN, a Parisian wine merchant who was born in Burgundy. In this are rated all the wines, not just of France, but of all known wine regions of the time including California, South America, South Africa's Cape, and 'Chinese Tartary'! He forecasts (or perhaps helps to shape) the 1855 CLASSIFICATION in Bordeaux by rating as first-class wines Lafitte (*sic*), Latour, Ch-Margaux, and Haut-Brion.

Outside Europe, his favourites all seem to be dessert wines, including TOKAJI, CONSTANTIA, COMMANDARIA, and COTNARI. Both his firsthand experience and his reading must have been gargantuan for him to compile such a work of reference. He followed this up with

another classic *Manuel du Sommelier* (1822). Cavoleau's *Oenologie française* was a similar work to the *Topographie*, but limited to French wines, which came from the same publisher 11 years later.

The 19th century was a golden age for wine writing in Britain. Shannon and Henderson were followed by Cyrus REDDING (1785–1870), a journalist whose interest in wine was stimulated during five years based in Paris. An avid traveller, he wrote *A History and Description of Modern Wines* (1833) as a result of first-hand observation of the ADULTERATION AND FRAUD which were then prevalent in the wine trade.

Many of the books were written by wine merchants, often criticizing the practices of their colleagues, or vaunting their own specialities. Perhaps the most enjoyable to read is Thomas Shaw, whose *Wine, the Vine and the Cellar* (1863) is an agreeable blend of reminiscences, knowledge, and simple advice. He was convinced even then that 'in wine tasting and wine talk there is an enormous amount of humbug'. Another of his campaigns was against excessive DUTIES on wine and this led to the famous Gladstone budget in 1862 in which they were considerably reduced.

Charles Tovey was a wine merchant in Bristol in south west England and in the introduction to *Wine and Wine Countries* (1862) he says that 'there can be no question that the Wine Trade is losing its position by the introduction into it of unscrupulous traders'. He drew heavily upon his 50 years' experience in denouncing and describing their deceits.

This same theme was continued by his London colleague James L. Denman, who wrote copiously on wine adulteration. His more particular interest, however, both commercial and literary, was the wines of Greece.

Another doctor to write on wines was John Thudichum, who had come to London from Germany, where his father had written technical books on wine. One of his particular hobbyhorses was the adding of gypsum to SHERRY, but his credibility within the trade was compromised by extensive research that he had carried out in Jerez, trying to produce AMONTILLADO by purely chemical means. His *Treatise on Wines* (1872), written with another doctor, A. Dupré, does, however, give a clear picture of viticulture and vinification at that time.

Specialist books

While all these books give a general idea of the wines of Europe and, in some cases, the world, some specialist books on individual regions had also begun to appear. One of the first of these was published in London as early as 1728. This was the *Dissertation sur la situation de Bourgogne* by the French tutor to the son of a Mr Freeman. Arnoux, in this brief book, describes the various wines of Burgundy and how they are made. He also makes a plea for them to be imported into England in bottle rather than in cask. This book must have met with some success, for it was soon translated into English and was subsequently used by Philip Miller in his *Gardeners' Dictionary* and by Robert Shannon.

It was more than a century until the next two classic books on the vineyards of Burgundy appeared and coincidentally it was in the same year, 1831. Morelot's *Statistique de la vigne dans le département de la Côte d'Or* is largely what its title suggests, although the second half of the book deals with both viticulture and vinification in the region. The *Histoire et statistique de la vigne et des grands vins de la Côte d'Or* by Lavalle is a more readable book, for it gives many historical details concerning Burgundy and its wines, as well as more details of the characteristics of the wines from the various villages and ownership of the vineyards. Later editions have etchings of vineyard scenes.

In Bordeaux, the first book of significance was the *Variétés bordelaises of* Abbé Beaurein (1784–5), which noted that the English were at last showing interest in the wines of the Médoc. The first major book dealing solely with the wines of Bordeaux, however, was the *Traité sur les vins du Médoc* of William Franck (1824), which ran into several editions. In many ways this was the forerunner of Charles Cocks's book *Bordeaux, its Wines and the Claret Country* (1846), which was translated into French four years later and became the classic reference work on Bordeaux wines, known after its original authors as COCKS ET FÉRET. An interesting independent view of the region is also given by the Paris merchant Charles Pierre de Saint in *Le Vin de Bordeaux* (1855).

Writing on Portuguese wines was dominated by the English. In 1787, John CROFT wrote *A Treatise of the Wines of Portugal* and this was followed by the many works of James Forrester (1809–61), who, from his position in the trade, took a strong position against the many adulterations that were taking place.

The 19th century saw the rapid expansion of vineyards in the New World and guidance was sought in Europe as to how to make the finest wines. From this came two interesting works. The first was the *Journal of a Tour through some of the Vineyards of Spain and France* by James BUSBY, which was published in Sydney in 1833. This is a fascinating account of a three-month trip, mainly by stagecoach, to find the right vine varieties for planting in Australia. The interpretation of what he learned appeared in two further books. The journey, almost 30 years later, by Agoston HARASZTHY, one of the pioneers of California viticulture, was largely by train. Perhaps because of his origins, he spent more of his time in the various states of Germany and none at all in France. His *Grape Culture, Wines and Wine-Making*, a journal of this tour, appeared in New York in 1862 and did much to establish the reputations of both Haraszthy and California wine.

A third, and earlier, New World traveller to have left his memories of vineyard visiting is Thomas JEFFERSON, later to become president of the United States. During his five years as minister to France (1784–9) he took advantage of his situation to visit many of the vineyards of Europe, and his diaries leave a fascinating picture of a layman's perception of the world of wine as it then was.

One final wine writer of Victorian times was the journalist and publisher Henry VIZETELLY. His books on champagne, port, and sherry are notable for their many illustrations. These works, with their beautiful engravings, many used by modern publishers, are the forebears of the lavishly illustrated wine books published today.

Technical literature

Parallel with this growth in books on the vineyard regions and their wines, there was a considerable body of work on VITICULTURE and WINEMAKING. In France at the end of the 18th century the Burgundian Béguillet and Maupin, from Paris, both wrote detailed works which were widely read.

In England, William Speechly, gardener to the Duke of Portland, wrote a *Treatise on the Culture of the Vine* (1790) which went into three editions. This dealt with both hothouse and open-air vines in ENGLAND and discusses some of the vineyards which were then planted there and the wines they produced.

Three French writers of the 19th century whose names live on in the world of wine are Jean-Antoine CHAPTAL (1756–1832), Dr Jules GUYOT, and Louis PASTEUR (1822–95). Chaptal was the essential polymath, rising from humble beginnings to become Minister of the Interior under Napoleon. In 1799, he wrote the article on wine for the monumental *Dictionnaire d'agriculture* of the Abbé Rozier, but is better known for his *L'Art de faire le vin* (1807) and his support for the concept of increasing the alcohol strength of wine by adding sugar to the must, the procedure now known as CHAPTALIZATION.

Jules Guyot was instructed under the Second Empire to carry out a survey of the vineyards of France and to make recommendations as to how viticulture might be improved. His three works on viticulture in north and central France (1860), the east (1863), and the west (1866) give a vital picture of France before the arrival of PHYLLOXERA. His name lives on as a method of vine TRAINING. It is largely to him that we owe the parade-ground look of today's vineyards in place of the rabble-like appearance of vines subjected to the traditional practice of LAYERING.

Louis Pasteur's *Études sur le vin* (1866) deal with the question of vinification and particularly the advantages of the heat treatment, or PASTEURIZATION, of wine. His is also the first detailed work on the role that YEASTS have to play in FERMENTATION. Another important work on the techniques of vinification was *Le Vin* (1867), by the Burgundian Comte de Vergnette-Lamotte. Over ten years from 1901, Montpellier professor of viticulture Pierre Viala, backed by industrialist Victor Vermorel, produced his unsurpassed seven-volume *Ampélographie*, a guide to 5,200 grape varieties with the 627 most important considered in detail and 500 of them beautifully illustrated in colour by Jules Troncy and Alexis Kreÿder.

Modern wine writing

The 20th century saw a great resurgence in wine writing, particularly in Britain. Much of the credit has been laid at the door of Professor George SAINTSBURY, whose vinous reminiscences, *Notes on a Cellar-Book* (1920), were written when he was 75 years old. While this erudite miscellany of thoughts is an enjoyable read, there are many who consider it overrated despite its commercial success. (It was reprinted twice within four months and has run through many editions since.)

What it did prove, however, was that there was a demand for books on wine and authors soon appeared to satisfy that demand. In the main, they fall into two fields, the reminiscent and the relevant. One of the finest of the former is H. Warner Allen, a journalist with a deep love for wine and its history. Much of his work is memories of bottles of vintages long past. His *A History of Wine* (1961) is, however, necessary reading for any wine enthusiast. Others who might be said to be in this group were Maurice Healy and Stephen Gwynn. All of them were highly educated men, for whom drinking fine wines was a part of everyday life.

The relevant school was nobly fronted by André SIMON (1877–1970), even if much of his work is also reminiscent. His early writings were largely on the history of the wine trade and he was, all his life, passionately interested in wine books, compiling a number of bibliographies on food and drink (see below). As a member of the wine trade, he introduced a degree of accuracy to his work that is missing from some of the 'gentlemen' wine writers cited above. In all he wrote more than 100 works in which his knowledge is matched by his readability.

Contemporary wine writing in Britain continues this parallel, with works coming from writers who have taken to wine and wine professionals who have taken to writing. While the choice might seem to be between elegance and erudition, the distinction is not always so straightforward. (See JEWISH HERITAGE IN GERMAN WINE CULTURE for an outline of the contribution of Jewish wine importers to English literature on German wine.)

From the British wine trade have come such as Tommy Layton, a prolific writer on the wines of Loire, Alsace, Spain, and Italy; his one-time office boy Michael BROADBENT, whose *Great Vintage Wine Book* and *Vintage Wine* are unrivalled collections of tasting notes on thousands of wines going back to the 17th century; Clive Coates on the wines of Burgundy and Bordeaux; both Anthony Hanson MW and Jasper Morris MW on Burgundy; the late John Radford on Spanish wines; Gerald Asher, now based in the United States; Steven Spurrier; and many others. Kermit Lynch and Terry Theise are perhaps the most accomplished writers to have emerged from the US wine trade.

Representing the world of the professional writer were the biographer and founder of the Good Food Club, Raymond Postgate, whose *The Plain Man's Guide to Wine* proved so successful that it went through 16 editions in 26 years; Edmund PENNING-ROWSELL, whose frequently revised book on the wines of Bordeaux was a masterpiece of research; the polished journalist Cyril RAY; and John Arlott, another journalist (and cricket commentator) whose enjoyment of wine and the pleasure it brings shone through his writing.

The late 20th century saw something new in the world of wine books: writers deliberately writing for their customer, the reader, rather than for their own pleasure, their work often embellished with ambitious illustration. Oz Clarke and Tom Stevenson have been particularly prolific, Andrew Jefford regrettably less so. But the most successful and innovative of these have undoubtedly been Hugh JOHNSON and Jancis Robinson. Even more successful than the former's *Wine* and *The Story of Wine*, is his *World Atlas of Wine*, which first appeared in 1971 and has sold more than four million copies. From the 5th edition, this has been co-authored by Jancis Robinson. She has written widely herself, notably producing *Wine Grapes*, with Julia Harding and José Vouillamoz, and editing *The Oxford Companion to Wine*.

In the rest of Europe, much of the wine literature was originally written in English, although the Dutch writer Hubrecht Duijker, with a series of heavily illustrated and highly instructive works on Bordeaux, Burgundy, Rioja, and other wine regions, achieved a broad international readership. Few French writers are read outside France, although each region has had its specialized writers such as Pierre Poupon, Pierre Forgeot, and Jean-François Bazin in Burgundy, René Pijassou and Bernard Ginestet in Bordeaux. An exception, for the technically minded, is Pierre GALET's work on AMPELOGRAPHY, a worthy successor to Pierre Viala's earlier volumes. The works of Émile PEYNAUD on winemaking and wine TASTING

have also been widely read outside France. In Spain, José Peñín leads the growing number of writers on wine, as VERONELLI did in Italy.

In the United States, wine writing became a boom industry in the late 20th century. This was led by Alexis LICHINE, who before the Second World War joined the wine trade with Frank SCHOONMAKER, himself a successful writer on wine. During the war he served as social aide-de-camp to General Eisenhower and afterwards bought vineyards in Bordeaux and Burgundy, eventually writing two highly successful and informative books, *Wines of France* and *Alexis Lichine's Encyclopedia of Wines and Spirits*.

Other effective American wine authors include the late Alexis Bespaloff, who worked for the Alexis Lichine wine company, Joe Bastianich, Matt Kramer, Karen MacNeil, Ed McCarthy, and Mary Ewing Mulligan MW (whose book in the 'for Dummies' series has been particularly successful), Kevin Zraly and, the most powerful wine writer of all, Robert PARKER, who has written several books and wine guides, most notably on Bordeaux and the Rhône.

Wine writing in Australia was led by Len EVANS followed by the even more prolific James Halliday. These vineyard owners have been followed by a host of career wine writers such as Max Allen and Peter Forrestal. In New Zealand the field has been led by Bob Campbell MW and Michael Cooper.

It is easy to chart through wine literature the change in public perception of wine, from élitist to populist, a move encouraged by wider travel and higher disposable incomes. Pocket books, often published annually, were particularly popular at the turn of the century as have been specialist buyer's guides such as Bettane & Desseauve's on French wines, Peñín's on Spain, Platter's on South Africa, Gambero Rosso on Italy, and many, many more.

The dramatic increase in interest in wine seen from the late 20th century has led to a corresponding increase in the range of wine books available but, perhaps more significantly, in the media by which wine writing is disseminated. Publications on wine are less often now literary works than a manual, a newsletter, an app, a blog, or a website. Books themselves are no longer the exclusive domain of print publishers. They may be self-published, like the works of Ben Lewin MW and Allen Meadows (aka Burghound) and they are increasingly available in digital form.

The literature of wine is infinite and, as appreciation of wine spreads around the world, so will the demand for words on wine. From Cato the Censor to Robert Parker is a long road, but the road is far from being at its end. See also LANGUAGE OF WINE, MEDIEVAL LITERATURE, WINE WRITING, and INFORMATION TECHNOLOGY.   C.C.F.

Useful bibliographies:

Amerine, M. A., and Borg, A. E., *A Bibliography on Grapes, Wines, Other Alcoholic Beverages and Temperance: Works Published in the United States before 1901* (Berkeley, Calif., 1996).

Gabler, J. M., *Wine into Words: A History and Bibliography of Wine Books in the English Language* (2nd edn, Baltimore, 2004).

Simon, A., *Bibliotheca vinaria* (London, 1913, and facsimile: London, 1979).

Vicaire, G., *Bibliographie gastronomique* (Paris, 1890, and facsimile: London, 1978).

little leaf, a symptom of ZINC deficiency of vines. An associated symptom is a PETIOLAR sinus that is wider than normal.

Livermore Valley, California wine region and AVA in Alameda County east of San Francisco Bay. Livermore hides behind hills high enough to screen out nearly all of the sea fogs common on the bay itself. It is therefore warm and—a passage between the cool, marine air of the bay and the hot, rising air of the CENTRAL VALLEY—windy, as evinced by thousands of turbines blanketing the hills of Altamont Pass at the eastern edge of the valley.

If the gods had got it all right, Sauvignon Blanc and Semillon would dominate the 1,400 acres/566 ha planted to vines in Livermore Valley in the early 1990s. Those two grape varieties, linked by their history in Bordeaux, first came with French emigrants during Livermore's first great blossoming in the 1870s and 1880s (see CALIFORNIA, history). These original growers believed in the virtues of its stonier-than-GRAVES soils. Today the difficulty of selling Semillon to Chardonnay-besotted Americans has begot changes. Zinfandels and Petite Sirahs have emerged as the best quality wines; Chardonnay is widely planted and promoted. Steven Kent Winery has had particular success with both Cabernets.

For 40 years, vine acreage has been under severe pressure from urbanization but scions of pioneer Wente Vineyards have crafted a land-use compromise with the political authorities which is an important example for California: 10 acres of land are set aside for open space or agricultural uses whenever permits are issued for an acre of home or business development. An immediate result has been two prime golf courses surrounded by vineyards and homes.

B.C.C. & L.M.

Livinière, La. Commune in the hilly far north of MINERVOIS in the LANGUEDOC which successfully campaigned hard and justifiably for a special subappellation for its 244 ha/603 acres of red wine grapes in which Syrah and/or Mourvèdre must constitute at least 40% of the blend, as opposed the 20% required by the Minervois appellation. Its ELEVATION and rockier soils seem to imbue quality.

Lladoner Pelut or **Lledoner Pelut**, the downy-leaved variant of GRENACHE also known as GRENACHE Poilu or Velu in the south of France and GARNACHA Peluda or Lledoner Pelut in Spain. Both vine and wine closely resemble Grenache Noir except that it is less susceptible to COULURE and therefore yields more consistently and, usefully, reaches PHYSIO-LOGICAL RIPENESS at lower sugar levels. It is officially and widely sanctioned in Languedoc-Roussillon, often being specified in appellation regulations alongside Grenache. But by 2011 France's total had fallen to 366 ha/904 acres, largely in Roussillon while Spain grew 574 ha/1,418 acres, mainly in Castilla-La Mancha and it is also grown in Spanish Cataluña. VARIETAL versions are rare.

Robinson, J., Harding, J., and Vouillamoz, J., *Wine Grapes, a complete guide to 1,368 vine varieties, including their origins and flavours* (London, 2012).

loam, the ideal soil for the growth of most plants, consisting of a balanced mixture of clay, silt, and sand (see SOIL TEXTURE). With enough ORGANIC MATTER, loams have a friable, crumby structure (see SOIL STRUCTURE). These desirable characteristics are enhanced where CALCIUM is prominent among the ions bonded to the clay particles and organic matter. A good loam has a high capacity to store water and plant nutrients but, unlike stiff clay, is not close textured enough to impede the free DRAINAGE of water. Rich, loamy soils can encourage excessive VIG-OUR in vines, however, particularly in cool to mild climates with ample RAINFALL, so loams (which exist in almost all regions) are not always ideal for viticulture.   J.G.

locusts can damage vines. See GRASSHOPPERS for more detail.

lodge, term used by British shippers of PORT and MADEIRA for a building where wine is stored and matured, especially in Vila Nova de Gaia in OPORTO and Funchal in Madeira respectively. It is derived from the Portuguese word *loja* meaning 'shop' or 'warehouse'. The Portuguese themselves tend to use the term ARMAZÉM.
                                                                R.J.M.

Lodi, town in the CENTRAL VALLEY of California that also gives its name to an AVA. Cooler than either the northern or southern halves of the valley, this prolific farming region was populated from the late 19th century by largely German smallholders who formed large CO-OPERATIVES to sell their grapes to large marketing companies such as CONSTELLATION BRANDS, Sebastiani, and JFJ Bronco in the late 1970s and early 1980s. The deep, rich-soiled valley floor was built up by alluvial deposits from rivers running out of the Sierra Nevada then pooling before running out to the Pacific through the Central Valley delta and San Francisco Bay. Lodi is inland from, less watery, and thus warmer than the CLARKSBURG AVA to the north west, but much less warm than Madera, Fresno, and other districts further south in the San Joaquin Valley.

Zinfandel has shown the greatest adaptability to Lodi's growing conditions, and is planted on nearly 12,000 acres/5,000 ha. Zinfandels from here tend to cluster at the fleshy, plummy, ripe end of the spectrum but represent good value in today's market place. Since the mid 1980s, Chardonnay and Merlot plantings have increased substantially but high YIELDS tend to reduce their distinctiveness beyond recognition. Viognier produces nicely fragrant examples from Lodi, inexpensively priced, and there is

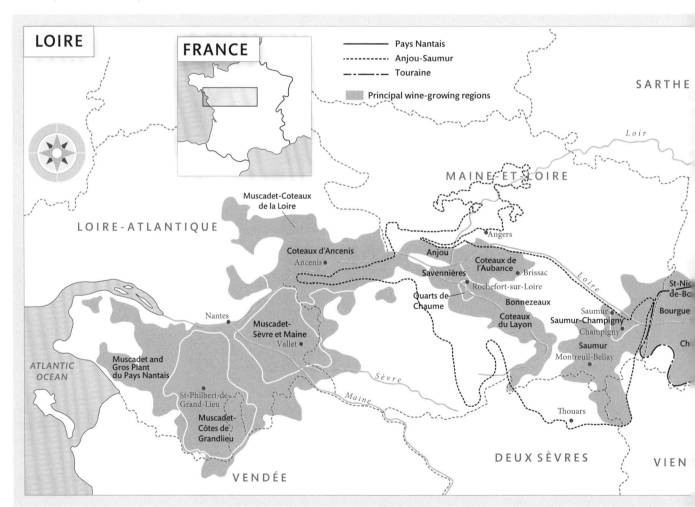

great recent excitement in Albariño and Grenache/Garnacha, particularly from Bokisch Vineyards.

In 2006, the Lodi AVA was dissected into seven sub-AVAs: Alta Mesa, Borden Ranch, Clements Hills, Cosumnes River, Jahant, Mokelumne River, and Sloughhouse. Wine distinctiveness has yet to be demonstrated.

B.C.C. & L.M.

loess, an accumulation of CLAY and SILT particles that have been deposited by the wind. Loess is typically pale-coloured, unstratified, and loosely cemented by calcium carbonate. Favoured for viticulture because it is porous, permeable, readily warmed, and easily penetrated by roots, it is common in WASHINGTON state and TOKAJ, and is found in some vineyards in AUSTRIA, GERMANY, and CHINA. A.J.M.

Loir, Coteaux du, northerly wine outpost of the greater LOIRE region on the confusingly named Loir tributary about 40 km/25 miles north of Tours in the Sarthe *département*. Viticulture seriously declined here, but enthusiasts such as Joël Gigou at Domaine de la Charrière

have invested in a bright future for the varied wines of this small, 70-ha/173-acre area, of which JASNIÈRES is the most famous appellation. All three colours of wine are made, with PINEAU d'Aunis the principal dark-skinned grape, even though acidity can be very high in less ripe years. Cabernet Franc may stiffen reds and Grolleau is allowed into its light, dry rosés. Gamay and Cot (Malbec) are allowed in both. Dry white wines are made from Chenin Blanc but tend to lack the concentration of Jasnières.

See also LOIRE, including map.

Loire, France's most famous river and name of one of its most varied wine regions which produces France's third biggest volume of wine after BORDEAUX and the RHÔNE. Loire wines are greatly appreciated locally and in Paris, but—with the famous exceptions of Sancerre and Pouilly-Fumé—are still widely underrated outside France. This may be partly because the Loire's best red wines are often distinguished by their freshness and delicacy rather than by their weight and longevity, and because so many of its finest white wines are made solely from Chenin Blanc, a grape variety associated

with some rather ordinary wine outside the middle Loire: Anjou-Saumur and Touraine.

History

We know little about the early history of viticulture in the Loire valley, but recent archaeological discoveries suggest that it was extant at least in the upper Loire in the 1st century AD (see GAUL), and it was certainly well established by the 5th century. In a letter to a friend, probably prepared for publication c.469, Sidonius Apollinaris (c.430–c.480), who was born in Lyons but spent a large part of his life in the Auvergne, praises the country of the Arverni (the Auvergne) for its landscape, its fertile fields, and its vineyards. In 475, ROME was forced to cede the Auvergne to the Visigoths, but the depredations of the barbarians left vine-growing safe.

In the next century, Gregory of Tours (c.539–94) makes frequent mention, in his *History of the Franks*, of viticulture in the Loire region. As bishop of Tours, he took a great interest in the wine of his diocese (modern TOURAINE). He tells us that, in 591, drought was followed by rain so that the grain harvest was ruined but the

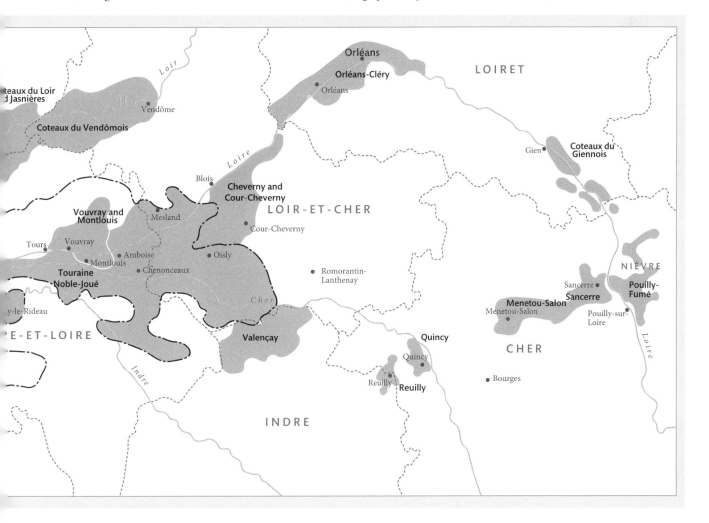

vines yielded abundantly. He also tells in detail of the Bretons' often successful attempts to seize the vineyards and/or grapes of the Nantes region (modern MUSCADET) in the 6th century.

The wines of the Loire continued to be held in high regard, and not only by the Bretons, who gave up plundering and bought the wines they wanted. The inhabitants of west Brittany had grown some wine themselves, but in the 13th century they gave up viticulture in favour of growing grain and instead purchased their wines from Nantes. Like Nantes, Touraine produced wine of export quality, and by the end of the 11th century the wine of SANCERRE was already well reputed. In the 12th century it was exported to Flanders and sold via Orléans.

From the late 11th century onwards, the aspiring bourgeoisie of the newly rich Flemish cities wanted more and more of its chief status symbol, which was wine (see DUTCH WINE TRADE). With its excellent river connections, the Loire region was especially well placed to meet this growing demand. Some of its wine was shipped to Flanders, or further north, or to England: some of it was carried to PARIS by river to be consumed there or sold on. Angers in particular grew rich on the Flemish guildsmen's desire for social advancement, and vines were planted even just outside its city walls. The count of ANJOU granted Angers the monopoly of carrying wine on the rivers Maine and Loire as far as the Breton port of Ingrandes; in addition, merchants could not buy their wines direct from the vineyards but had to buy them at Angers. These two privileges put the producers of SAUMUR at a disadvantage. The wines of Saumur were not fashionable in France, and Saumur was badly placed for overseas trade. In England in the late 12th century, before the rise of BORDEAUX, Anjou was the only wine to rival Poitou, shipped from LA ROCHELLE, in popularity. Anjou remained highly esteemed in England throughout the Middle Ages.

In France itself, the Loire wine that was most prized was one that has now all but disappeared from public regard: ST-POURÇAIN, made on the river Sioule in the Loire basin. King Louis IX served it at a banquet in Saumur to celebrate his brother Alphonse's 21st birthday. St-Pourçain fetched high prices during the 14th century and was a favourite with the papal court at Avignon. The wines of the Coteaux de LAYON did not become famous until the 15th century.

For more historical detail, see entries under individual wine names.   H.M.W.

Dion, R., *Histoire de la vigne et du vin en France* (Paris, 1959).

Geography and climate

So long is the extent of the viticultural Loire that generalizations are impossible. The Loire's vineyards vary from the CONTINENTAL climate which produces Sancerre and Pouilly-Fumé, to the Muscadet region warmed by the Gulf Stream. Loire wine regions represent today, however, the north western limit of vine cultivation in Europe (with the exception of ENGLAND's vineyards). Spring FROST can be a serious problem, as it was in 1991, when it destroyed up to 90% of the crop in some of the Loire's wine regions. The character of Loire wines can vary considerably from VINTAGE to vintage, since in a cool summer the grapes may struggle to reach full RIPENESS, while a particularly hot year such as 1989, 1990, 1997, 2003, 2005, 2009, and 2011 may result in some exceptional sweet white wines, some of them BOTRYTIZED in the middle Loire, but can rob the Loire's dry white Sauvignons of their nerve, and leave some Muscadet dangerously limp.

The region is sufficiently far from the equator, however, that few of its red wines can be accused of being tannic, and the naturally high acidity associated with these latitudes, and some of its grape varieties, make much of the Loire's produce ideal base wine for SPARKLING WINES.

Viticulture

The Loire is essentially a region of increasingly consolidated family holdings; the average holding has increased from 10 to 25 ha in recent years and many farmers have abandoned their other crops to concentrate on viticulture. In the middle Loire, rainfall is relatively low, but SPRAYING against FUNGAL DISEASES is still frequent elsewhere. VINE DENSITY is relatively high, between 4,000 and 5,000 plants per ha (1,600–2,000 per acre) on average, and up to 10,000 plants per ha in some Sancerre vineyards. Excess VIGOUR was a problem in the late 1980s and early 1990s, and resulted in HERBACEOUS flavours in many of the red wines, although CANOPY MANAGEMENT has generally resolved this. COVER CROPS have long been the norm, and CROP THINNING was introduced in the early 1990s. MECHANICAL HARVESTING is relatively common, but cannot be used for the sweet white wines of the middle Loire, where successive TRIES through the vineyards are needed to select only the ripest grapes.

Winemaking

White winemakers of the Loire traditionally followed very similar principles to their counterparts in Germany, assiduously avoiding MALOLACTIC CONVERSION and any new OAK influence, preferring instead to ferment and store wines in inert containers, and to bottle wines early, possibly after some LEES CONTACT in the case of Muscadet. For years, Loire reds suffered from a lack of EXTRACTION.

The result of the particularly competitive wine market of the 1980s and a drop in demand for sweet wines in the late 1990s, however, was to stimulate a rash of experimentation in cellars along the length of the Loire. BARREL MATURATION and in some cases BARREL FERMENTATION were introduced for both reds and whites (see ANJOU, specifically). Some producers encouraged their white wines to go through malolactic conversion, while red winemakers worked hard to extract greater colour and TANNINS from their red wine musts, by the use of prolonged SKIN CONTACT, TEMPERATURE CONTROL, and PUMPING OVER regimes. (It should be said that, in many a Loire autumn and winter, temperature control is just as likely to include heating the must as cooling it.) Skin contact prior to fermentation was also introduced for some white wines, especially Sauvignons.

CHAPTALIZATION has been the norm in the Loire, for both reds and whites, except in exceptionally hot vintages.

Vine varieties

At the mouth of the Loire, MELON de Bourgogne and FOLLE BLANCHE predominate. The upper Loire is, in the early 21st century anyway, the terrain of Sauvignon Blanc for white wines and Pinot Noir for reds and rosés. The majority of the most successful sites in the middle Loire have proved themselves suitable for either CABERNET FRANC or CHENIN BLANC, but in the thousands of hectares of vineyard planted around them, there is a greater diversity of vine varieties than anywhere else in France, including a mix of CABERNET SAUVIGNON, MALBEC, GAMAY, MEUNIER, PINOT GRIS, CHARDONNAY, and of course seas of Sauvignon and Pinot Noir. This is usually explained in terms of spheres of Bordeaux and Burgundy influence, but it indicates that, outside its most famous appellations, the regions of the Loire have been searching for their own wine identities. The vineyards of the Loire were particularly badly hit by PHYLLOXERA. The heavily calcareous soils in many regions meant that CHLOROSIS was a common problem when vines were replanted grafted on to resistant ROOTSTOCKS. The Loire, with its relatively cool climate, persisted with a higher proportion of HYBRIDS longer than any other French wine region. The limits on the role of Chardonnay and Cabernet Sauvignon included in the rules of so many Loire appellations show that the authorities at least are aware of the danger of the Loire losing its own identity and there are signs of a revival of some varieties that are exclusive to the Loire such as PINEAU D'AUNIS, MENU PINEAU, ROMORANTIN, and Meslier-St-François although the distinctly ordinary GROLLEAU is in retreat.

Wines produced

Of all French wine regions, the Loire produces the greatest diversity of wine styles: from still through all types of sparkling wine, including the generic CRÉMANT de Loire; from bone dry and searingly tart to unctuous LIQUOREUX (although still with a high degree of acidity); and all hues from water white to (quite) deep purple. Rosés are a speciality of the Loire, whether the various VINS GRIS made well upstream, the famous Rosé d'Anjou, various pink Cabernets, or the generic ROSÉ DE LOIRE. The most common IGP wine produced in the Loire is known as **Val de Loire**.

Travelling upstream, the major districts, with each appellation for which there is a separate entry, are (see map):

Pays Nantais: MUSCADET; GROS PLANT du Pays Nantais; Coteaux d'ANCENIS; FIEFS VENDÉENS.

Anjou-Saumur: ANJOU; SAVENNIÈRES; Coteaux du LAYON; QUARTS DE CHAUME; BONNEZEAUX; Coteaux de l'AUBANCE.

SAUMUR.

Touraine: TOURAINE; CHINON; BOURGUEIL; VOUVRAY; MONTLOUIS; CHEVERNY; VALENÇAY.

Upper Loire: REUILLY; QUINCY; MENETOU-SALON; SANCERRE; POUILLY-FUMÉ.

Northern outposts: Coteaux du LOIR; JASNIÈRES; Coteaux du VENDÔMOIS.

On the bend: ORLÉANS; Coteaux du GIENNOIS.

Southern outposts: HAUT-POITOU; CHÂTEAUMEILLANT; ST-POURÇAIN; Côtes d'AUVERGNE; Côte ROANNAISE; Côtes du FOREZ (although some of these are very far from the Loire and its climatic influence).

Friedrich, J., *A Wine and Food Guide to the Loire* (New York, 1996).
www.loirevalleywine.com
www.richardkelley.co.uk
jimsloire.blogspot.co.uk

Lombardy, known as **Lombardia** in Italian, is the largest and most populous region of ITALY and the driving force behind the country's post-Second World War economic boom, the dynamo which has given Milan and its hinterland one of Europe's highest standards of living.

Lombardy's principal centres of viticulture are in the hills, divided among no fewer than 22 DOCS and five DOCGS which cater mainly for the many local palates, and are rarely seen on export markets. Currently the five most important areas, each producing very distinct styles of wine, if of various quality, are FRANCIACORTA, LUGANA, OLTREPÒ PAVESE, VALTELLINA, and LAMBRUSCO Mantovano around the city of Mantua. These 1,000 ha/2,475 acres of vineyards are a continuation of the Lambrusco cultivation area in Emilia-Romagna. Most of its produce is on an industrial scale but more artisanal dry wines are appearing on the domestic market.

One of Lombardy's truly indigenous varieties, GROPELLO, cultivated immediately south west of Lake Garda, was awarded its own Valtènesi DOC in 2011, but up to 50% of authorized, mostly INTERNATIONAL VARIETIES are also allowed into the blend. This seems highly questionable since the vast Garda DOC introduced in the late 1990s includes all of the Valtènesi

zone and already allows a wide range of VARIETAL whites (including Pinot Grigio, Chardonnay, and Garganega) and reds (Merlot, Cabernet Sauvignon, Corvina, Marzemino, and others).

For more detail on specific notable wines see BONARDA and CROATINA. W.S.

long, much-derided tasting term for wines whose impact on the PALATE is particularly persistent. A wine that is long is usually of high quality. On the basis of studies in other food systems, it is assumed that wine COLLOIDS have a role to play in lengthening the palate of a wine. This occurs through interaction of various FLAVOUR COMPOUNDS with particular colloids resulting in some or all of the wine's flavour compounds being retained in the mouth, along with the associated polymers, after the wine has been swallowed. Delayed release of the flavour compounds then accounts for the persistent or long palate of the wine. See also TASTING and CAUDALIE. P.J.W.

Longyan, red-skinned grape grown in CHINA whose name means 'dragon's eyes'.

Los Carneros. See CARNEROS, wine region and AVA of California.

lot marking. See LABELLING INFORMATION.

Loupiac, sweet white wine appellation on the right bank of the GARONNE in the BORDEAUX region sandwiched between CADILLAC and STE-CROIX-DU-MONT with 344 ha/850 acres of Sémillon and Sauvignon vines in production on clay limestone soils in 2012. The wines of Loupiac were first cited in the 13th century (the Loupiac region was once much bigger), although in much of the 20th century the wines failed to fetch the prices necessary to justify truly meticulous winemaking. The best vineyards are on clay-limestone slopes overlooking the river and are well situated to benefit from NOBLE ROT, provided producers are prepared to take the necessary risks. Good Loupiac such as that produced at Domaine du Noble and Chx du Cros and Loupiac-Gaudiet is generally deeply coloured, early maturing, and noticeably full bodied; the use of new OAK became gradually more common from the late 1980s (see SAUTERNES for more details).

Loureiro, occasionally **Loureira**, fine, 'laurel-scented', ancient MINHO white grape variety that is the most planted in this VINHO VERDE country in northern Portugal and also grown in RÍAS BAIXAS in north-west Spain. Plantings totalled a substantial 5,162 ha/ 12,750 acres in Portugal, including some much further south, but less than a tenth as much in Spain, where ALBARIÑO is much more important. It has often been blended with TRAJADURA (Treixadura in Spain) but can also be found as a particularly aromatic VARIETAL wine. It can yield quite productively in

the north of the Vinho Verde region and produces its best quality, usually quite low in alcohol, around Braga, Ponte de Lima, and the coast.

low-alcohol wine is usually REDUCED-ALCOHOL WINE but may also be, like DEALCOHOLIZED WINE, regular wine from which alcohol has been deliberately removed, usually but not necessarily with harmful effects on flavour and quality. Such wines are usually reduced to an ALCOHOLIC STRENGTH which excludes them from DUTY, reducing their price. See also COOLERS.

Low Countries, historical region of northwest Europe including the NETHERLANDS, BELGIUM, and LUXEMBOURG, which once played an important part in the wine and spirit trade. See DUTCH WINE TRADE.

Lower Austria. See NIEDERÖSTERREICH.

Lower Murray Zone, in SOUTH AUSTRALIA, has a single but very important region, the RIVERLAND.

low-input viticulture, an alternative to conventional viticulture which aims to minimize all inputs to the vineyard. This may be of AGROCHEMICALS, with the aim of improving the environment (see ORGANIC and BIODYNAMIC VITICULTURE), or of inputs such as LABOUR, with the aim of improving the vineyard's profitability. This approach was popular in Australia and the phrase became a catchword in the 1990s. However, the philosophy is more appropriate to the production of BULK rather than FINE WINE.

Luberon, wines made on the fashionable slopes of the Luberon, where vineyards add colour and bucolic allure to one of the more sought-after corners of Provence. The appellation, which comprised 3,317 ha/8,193 acres of vineyard in 2013, is a sort of buffer state between the RHÔNE and PROVENCE, or more precisely between the VENTOUX appellation and that of Coteaux d'AIX-EN-PROVENCE (although French officialdom places it firmly in the Rhône).

The appellation was created only in 1988 and produces significant quantities of wine, mainly medium-bodied rosés with lightish reds based on Grenache and Syrah which must constitute 60% of the blend, although Mourvèdre is another approved principal ingredient in both reds and rosés. Those who try hard can produce herb-scented reds with some concentration and ageing potential. Whites are made in almost the same quantity as reds, from Grenache Blanc, Clairette, Bourboulenc, Vermentino, and possibly some Marsanne and Roussanne, with the proportion of Ugni Blanc limited to 50%. The region's rather cooler nights (and winters) than in most Côtes du Rhône vineyards help to produce some of the crisper, more interesting white wines of the southern Rhône. Rosés may incorporate up to 20% of white grapes, and have particular allure when drunk locally to the sound of cicadas.

Lugana, dry white Italian wine based on the eponymous grape previously known as Treb-biano di Lugana, the same as TREBBIANO DI SOAVE, so akin to VERDICCHIO produced to the south and south west of Lake Garda in the province of Brescia, straddling the provinces of Lombardy and Veneto.

The region, comprising some 1,000 ha/2,470 acres of vineyard, turns out a sizeable 127,000 hl of wine, made possible by yields of more than 120 hl/ha. The resulting insipid wines, often bottled outside the production area, obscure the fact that genuine Lugana comes from a narrow band of strikingly white, clay-limestone soils on the south shore of Lake Garda known locally known as *menadel*.

The DOC can be divided in two parts, of which the first is this narrow strip and the second, south of the Strada Provinciale 11, in the hills near San Martino della Battaglia, with sandier soils and less expressive wines. However, any differences of TERROIR are obliterated by high yields, and in the blending tanks in which most of the wine ends up. However, ageworthy versions of Lugana were not uncommon in the past. Proof is available in the form of Ca' Lojera estate's version which is aged for five years and has inspired the official creation of a Riserva category.   W.S.

www.consorziolugana.it

Lunel is the centre of the **Muscat de Lunel** appellation for sweet golden VIN DOUX NATUREL made from MUSCAT BLANC À PETITS GRAINS grapes grown on potentially interesting infertile inland soils between Montpellier and Nîmes. Yields are low and vinification techniques improving although many local vine-growers have been more interested in developing lower alcohol, dry Muscats or wines that qualify as LANGUEDOC AOC. A single CO-OPERATIVE is responsible for almost all the wine produced, which, as any geographer might suspect, tastes like a cross between the Muscats of FRONTIGNAN and ST-JEAN-DE-MINERVOIS. Lunel's historical claim to fame is less convincing than Frontignan's: its Muscat was dispatched to console Napoléon on the island of St Helena. The town does call itself the Cité du Muscat, however.

Lunel is also the occasional Hungarian name for a yellow-berried form of Muscat Blanc à Petits Grains grown in the TOKAJI region.

Lurtons, ramified family of property owners and winemakers in BORDEAUX, owning more wine estates in the Bordeaux region than any other single family. In 2014 no fewer than twelve Lurtons were working in wine, surely making this the largest wine family in the world. The original Lurton property is the modest Ch Bonnet in the ENTRE-DEUX-MERS, which belonged to Léonce Recapet, François Lurton's father-in-law. Although he and Fran-çois acquired Ch Brane-Cantenac in MARGAUX in 1925, the current extent of the Lurton empire is largely due to the efforts of the brothers André and Lucien, both of whom bought numerous properties during the 1960s, 1970s, and 1980s. The elder brother André, who now owns Ch Bonnet and whose estates are mainly in the GRAVES (Chx La Louvière, Couhins, Rochem-orin, Cruzeau), was a particularly potent force in the renaissance of the Graves region during the 1980s. A man of vision, energy, and a flair for promotion, he led the campaign for the new appellation of PESSAC-LÉOGNAN and became the first president of its Syndicat Viticole.

André's younger brother Lucien may have been less promient but built up an impressive empire of CLASSIFIED growths (among them Chx Brane-Cantenac, Durfort-Vivens, and Desmi-rail in Margaux, Bouscaut in Pessac-Léognan, and Doisy-Dubroca and Climens in Barsac) before passing them on in 1992 to his ten children. After establishing an international wine consultancy business in 1988, André's sons Jac-ques and François gradually acquired land, planted vines, and built wineries. By 2014 François owned wineries in Spain, Languedoc, Chile, and Argentina, as well as a bottling operation in Bordeaux for his branded Sauvignon Fumées Blanches. Jacques continues as a CONSULTANT and owns a vineyard on Kangaroo Island, SOUTH AUSTRALIA. Their sister Christine moved from managing Ch Dauzac in MARGAUX to overseeing communications for her father.

Lucien's sons have been busy in Margaux. Denis runs Ch Desmirail, Henri Ch Brane Cantenac, and Gonzague Ch Durfort Vivens. Gonzague and his wife Claire Villar, who owns several estates in the Médoc, created Trinité vineyard in SONOMA. Lucien's daughter Marie-Laure has a clutch of CRUS BOURGEOIS while her sister Sophie has Ch Bouscaut in Pessac-Léognan. Thierry has the BORDEAUX Supérieur Ch Camarsac while Bérénice is in charge of the Barsac star Ch Climens. Brigitte founded Belon-drade y Lurton in RUEDA but this ground-breaking estate is now run by her ex-husband and their son Jean.

In 1991 Pierre Lurton (son of Dominique, André and Lucien's younger brother) became the estate manager at Ch CHEVAL BLANC, the St-Émilion first growth and, later, Ch d'YQUEM for LVMH. He has his own 90-ha/222-acre estate, Ch Marjosse, making Bordeaux Supérieur and Entre-Deux-Mers. His brother Marc took over the family estate Ch Reynier in Entre-Deux-Mers to which he added Ch de Bouchet.

www.lurton.com

Lussac-St-Émilion, large satellite appellation of ST-ÉMILION in Bordeaux with 1,447 ha/ 3,574 acres making robust reds in 2013 on a gravel plateau in the west and cooler clay soils in the north.

Lutomer, known as **Ljutomer** in SLOVENIA, small town in the far east of the country which lent its name to a UK-bottled BRAND, popular in the mid 20th century, most famously of LAŠKI RIZLING.

lutte raisonnée, literally 'reasoned strug-gle', is an approach to viticulture which tries to minimize the application of AGROCHEMICALS so that they are used only when absolutely necessary and not as a matter of routine. See also INTEGRATED PEST MANAGEMENT and SUSTAINABLE VITICULTURE.

Luxembourg, or **Luxemburg**, was for long the EU's smallest and coolest wine producer before being rivalled in both respects by ENGLAND, BELGIUM, the NETHERLANDS, and DENMARK. The rarely exported wines produced are relatively dry and, depending on grape variety, reminiscent of those of Alsace or England in style. With the exception of an increasing number of light reds and rosés made from Pinot Noir and ST LAURENT vines, the wines made on the western, Luxembourg bank of the river MOSELLE are white. In 2014, there were 1,295 ha/3,213 acres of exceptionally productive vineyard. Average YIELDS have been decreasing but the official limits in 2014 were still as high as 115 hl/ha for Elbling and Rivaner and 100 hl/ha for other vine varieties. Except in very ripe years such as 2003, 2005, 2009, 2010, and 2011, CHAPTALIZATION is a necessity here and the wines can be marked by relatively high acidity (although DEACIDIFICATION may be practised by some producers). A national law passed in 1996 was designed to encourage higher-alcohol wines, a tendency encouraged by global warming (see CLIMATE CHANGE).

History

The German MOSEL, below Trier, and the Luxembourg Moselle above it, had to surmount the same problems—cool climate and political change—for centuries but since the First World War the two regions have adopted different solutions. After the war, during which the Grand Duchy remained neutral, Luxembourg was required to break the free-tariff agreement that had been made with Prussia in 1842. Thus a ready market for Luxembourg's sharp whites made from the Elbling grape evaporated and Germany looked elsewhere for base wines for SEKT and suitable blending material for the Rheinpfalz's flabbiest wines. The Champagne house Mercier opened up an offshoot in Luxembourg in the late 19th century. A new economic agreement with Belgium signed in 1921 did little to soak up the surplus; Belgian taste is for the richness of Pomerol, the vinous antithesis of Elbling. Thus Elbling has been replaced by nobler, or at least softer, varieties.

Geography and climate

Luxembourg's vineyards are in two of the Grand Duchy's eastern cantons, Remich and Grevenmacher. On the ALLUVIAL plain of Remich, the heavier soils tend to produce less aromatic, heavier, earlier-maturing wines from such villages as Remich, Wintrange, and Schengen. Parts of the narrower valley of Grevenmacher to the north have been reshaped by terracing, as in the Mosel across the German border, but yields are lower, CALCAREOUS soils predominate, and wines such as the village of Ahn's fine Rieslings are particularly slow maturing. Luxembourg suffers a wide range of cool-climate-related problems such as spring FROSTS, HAIL, and COULURE, so that yields can vary substantially.

Vine varieties

Most Luxembourg still wines are VARIETAL wines and are almost invariably labelled as such. Rivaner is the name used here for the MÜLLER-THURGAU that so effectively replaced Elbling in the 20th century that by the early 1980s it was planted on half of the Grand Duchy's total vineyard, being relatively easy to ripen whatever the local conditions. Its ability to yield obligingly high quantities was so abused by many growers, however, that it became synonymous with mediocrity and declined considerably to 330 ha/815 acres by 2013, about a quarter of the country's vineyard. Much of it was replaced by Pinot Gris (193 ha/477 acres), highly regarded for its low acidity and its ripening potential. Pinot Blanc (158 ha/390 acres) and Pinot Noir (116 ha/286 acres) have also been enthusiastically planted, chiefly for CRÉMANT sparkling wine. Pinot Blanc's close relative AUXERROIS enjoys higher status in Luxembourg than anywhere else in the world (and certainly higher than in Alsace, where ten times as much is planted). Its low acidity is a positive attribute this far from the equator and when yields are curbed, barrel-aged Luxembourg Auxerrois can produce smoky, full-bodied wines worth ageing. Total plantings in 2013 were 188 ha/465 acres. Although some Chardonnay and Gewürztraminer are planted, the only other significant variety is Riesling (158 ha/390 acres), whose stately ageing curve put many Luxembourg wine drinkers off for years, but a new generation of producers seems to have understood the need to pick Riesling later and achieve more consumer-friendly flavours.

Appellations

Appellation Protégé (AOP), Luxembourg's answer to the APPELLATION CONTRÔLÉE system of France, is highly individual and would be difficult to apply to a bigger wine industry. There is just one appellation, Moselle Luxembourgeoise, which is allowed to practically all wines, both still and sparkling, although they are all submitted to analysis and a tasting. Since vintage 2014, superior wines may be ranked as Vin de Charte (which includes the old Domaine & Tradition, Charte de Schengen, Charte des Vignerons Indépendants), Grands Premiers Crus, and Premiers Crus. For these different quality levels, maximum permitted yields are 60 hl/ha for Vins de Charte, 75 hl/ha for Grand Premier Cru, and 85 hl/ha for Premier Cru. (The maximum yield allowed on the French MOSELLE is 60 hl/ha.)

Since 1993, there has been some limited experimentation with ICE WINES and other sweet wines, with official regulation in 2001. Pinots Blanc and Gris and Riesling picked at −7 °C/19 °F with a MUST WEIGHT of at least 120 °Oechsle may be labelled **Icewine** (sic). The same regulations allow Auxerrois, Pinot Blanc, Pinot Gris, and Gewürztraminer with 105 °Oechsle and Riesling with 95 °Oechsle to be sold as **Vendange Tardive**, while the appellation **Vin de Paille** may be used for Auxerrois, Pinot Blanc, Pinot Gris, and Gewürztraminer with at least 130 °Oechsle.

For details of Luxembourg's appellation for traditional method sparkling wines, see CRÉMANT de Luxembourg.

Industry organization

As in the German Mosel, the average vine-holding is extremely small—3.62 ha/9 acres in 2013—although it is gradually increasing as more and more of the smallest holdings are sold to larger landowners. The number of growers more than halved during the 20 years up to 2013, to 357. Almost 30% of vines are grown by independent domaines which make wine themselves. Several wine CO-OPERATIVES together function as Vinsmoselle and represent 59% of the Grand Duchy's wine production.

A.D.

LVMH, scrupulously even-handed acronym for Moët Hennessy-Louis Vuitton, the French luxury goods conglomerate which has a dominant interest in the CHAMPAGNE industry, not least through its subsidiaries, which include MOËT & CHANDON, KRUG, VEUVE CLICQUOT, and Ruinart, and a leading position in Cognac through Hennessy. In 2004 the group acquired Glenmorangie and Ardbeg malt whiskies and other spirit brands including Belvedere vodka. LVMH's still wine assets include CLOUDY BAY, Cape Mentelle in WESTERN AUSTRALIA, Terrazas de los Andes in MENDOZA, Numanthia in TORO, and in 2014 it acquired Clos des Lambrays in MOREY-ST-DENIS. Since the late 1950s the company has developed a substantial position in the premium SPARKLING WINE market through the creation and development of the Chandon brand. It now produces Chandon in Argentina, Brazil, the US, Australia, China, and India. In 1998, LVMH acquired a substantial stake in Ch d'YQUEM, while its chief executive Bernard Arnault became co-owner of Ch CHEVAL BLANC. For more details of LVMH's champagne interests, see MOËT & CHANDON.

www.lvmh.com

Lyonnais, Coteaux du, light white, pink, but mainly red wines made chiefly from about 280 ha/692 acres of vines in the hills both north and south west of the city of Lyons, considered part of greater Burgundy by French wine authorities, and drunk mainly by its inhabitants. The red wines, all Gamay, can be every bit as good as nearby BEAUJOLAIS, although the appellation was granted only in 1984. A small amount of white wine is also made, from Chardonnay and Aligoté. The CO-OPERATIVE at Sain-Bel vinifies three-quarters of production.

lyre, a vine-TRAINING SYSTEM whereby the CANOPY is divided horizontally into two curtains of upward-pointing shoots and which resembles a lyre in shape (see illustration). The system was developed in Bordeaux in the early 1980s by Dr Alain Carbonneau, now Professor of Viticulture at MONTPELLIER. Carbonneau was much influenced by the pioneering studies of Nelson SHAULIS in CANOPY MANAGEMENT. The lyre system improves the CANOPY MICROCLIMATE and leads to improvement in

Cross-section of **lyre**-trained vines during the growing season.

Vine training to the **lyre** system showing spur pruning (cane pruning can also be used).

Source: R. Smart and M. Robinson, *Sunlight into Wine*

yield and wine quality because of better leaf and fruit exposure to sunlight. Either SPUR PRUNING or CANE PRUNING can be used. Further use of this system has been delayed by the unavailability of suitable MECHANICAL HARVESTERS. The system is being adopted in New World vineyards in particular, especially in California, and to a lesser extent in Australia, New Zealand, Chile, and Uruguay, but it has also been trialled in Beaujolais.

The lyre system is essentially an inverted GENEVA DOUBLE CURTAIN, with the two adjacent curtains of foliage trained upwards rather than downwards. Both systems are used to reduce the shading of dense canopies. The lyre system is typically recommended for medium-vigour vines, whereas the GDC can harness higher vine vigour. The lyre system has shown substantial improvements in wine quality where it has been evaluated. R.E.S.

Coombe, B. G., and Dry, P. R. (eds.), *Viticulture*, ii: *Practices* (Adelaide, 1992).

Smart, R. E., and Robinson, M., *Sunlight into Wine: A Handbook for Winegrape Canopy Management* (Adelaide, 1991).

lyric poetry. There are many references to wine in the lyric poets of Ancient GREECE. Archilochos, writing in the middle of the 7th century BC, describes the comfort brought by wine on a long sea journey:

Along the rowers' benches bring your cup
And lift the lids of the big wine jars up
And drain the good red wine: we can't, 'tis clear
Be sober all the time we're watching here.

Fifty years later, Alkaios of Lesbos (who knew and admired the poetess Sappho) has many references to wine, often in vigorous verse: 'Wet your lungs with wine; for the dog star is coming round, and everything is thirsty with heat.' In an early variant of not waiting for the sun to be over the yard-arm, he writes: 'Drink! Why wait for the lamps? The day is almost done!'

The curmudgeonly Theognis, writing at the same time, probably from Megara on the isthmus of Corinth, extols the value of wine and the dangers of DRUNKENNESS. 'Stand by ready to pour for those who want to drink. We cannot have a party every night. Still because I am moderate in my use of honeyed wine, I reach my house before I think of soothing sleep, and I make clear how divine a beverage for man is wine.' H.H.A.

Macabeo is northern Spain's second most planted white grape variety (considerably after AIRÉN), whose total had grown to 37,514 ha/ 49,400 acres by 2011, and, as **Maccabéo** or **Macabeu**, was still planted on 2,172 ha/5,367 acres of French vineyard, mainly in ROUSSILLON. It buds and ripens too late to be grown much further north but is quite productive.

It is grown in most Spanish regions apart from Galicia and the far south with the greatest areas in CASTILLA-LA MANCHA where it makes relatively bland dry whites, and in CATALUNYA where it is an ingredient in CAVA, generally blended with Xarello and Parellada. More than 2,000 ha/4,942 acres remain in each of ARAGÓN and RIOJA where, as Viura, it replaced Malvasia Fina and Garnacha Blanca after PHYLLOXERA. Average VINE AGE is high in Rioja and can be matched by wine QUALITY if yields are restricted. In early-picked form, in Roussillon it is either a fairly characterless white, a useful ingredient in rosé, or, as in Spain, a common lightener of potent reds in which it is officially sanctioned up to 10% of the total blend (up to 30% in rosé). In the LANGUEDOC, in the white wines of Minervois and Corbières, it may be blended with BOURBOULENC, GRENACHE BLANC, and a host of other southern white varieties.

Macabeo spread to southern France from Spain and was well established at one time in North Africa, where the vine can tolerate hot, dry conditions.

Robinson, J., Harding, J., and Vouillamoz, J., *Wine Grapes, a complete guide to 1,368 vine varieties, including their origins and flavours* (London, 2012).

Macedonia, country in the central Balkans, bordered by BULGARIA, SERBIA, KOSOVO, ALBANIA, GREECE, officially the Republic of Macedonia but still described by the UN as FYROM (Former Yugoslav Republic of Macedonia) due to an ongoing dispute over the name Macedonia, which Greece has registered as a PGI. The geographical and historical region of Macedonia covers a much larger area, including parts of Greece and south-western Bulgaria. At one time, under the rule of Philip II (359 BC) and then his son Alexander the Great (until his early death in 323 BC), it was the most powerful state in the world. By 146 BC it had been defeated and became a Roman province. Like the rest of the Balkans, Macedonia came under Ottoman rule for five centuries until 1913. The region of Macedonia was then partitioned between Bulgaria, Greece, and Serbia (this last part went on to become today's republic). After the Second World War, Macedonia became part of the kingdom of Serbs, Croats, and Slovenes, later to become part of YUGOSLAVIA. Secession from Yugoslavia was recognized in 1992, and Macedonia largely avoided the intra-ethnic bloodshed that afflicted so many of its neighbours. A rebel uprising in 2001 was brought to a relatively peaceful conclusion, with increased recognition for the ethnic ALBANIANS, who make up about a quarter of the population. The Republic of Macedonia became an EU candidate country in 2005 although progress towards membership is hampered by the dispute with Greece over names.

The Republic of Macedonia lies between the latitudes of 40 to 43 degrees north. It is landlocked and geographically defined by a central valley formed by the Vardar River, while mountains border the country, with 16 peaks over 2,000 m (6,562 ft). To the south lie three lakes including the UNESCO-listed Lake Ohrid, believed to be one of the oldest lakes in the world. The country is seismically active and the climate is transitional from MEDITERRANEAN to CONTINENTAL. Hot, dry summers with 270 sunny days are typical and annual rainfall ranges from 500 mm/20 in in the centre to 1,700 mm/70 in in the mountains, making it the driest region in the Balkans. The grape-growing regions are sufficiently hot that ACIDIFICATION but not ENRICHMENT is allowed.

Wine is a significant crop in Macedonia, and is the second most important agricultural export after tobacco. In the 1980s Macedonia accounted for as much as two-thirds of YUGOSLAVIA's wine production, reaching a peak of 1.8 million hl/47.5 million gal in the early 1990s. Production has fallen since but by 2013 had recovered to around 1.2 million hl. Two-thirds of this was exported, mainly as cheap BULK WINE and chiefly to Germany.

Accurate information about vineyard area and varieties is elusive but the best estimate in 2013 was about 23,500 ha/58,070 acres planted to wine grapes. In 2013, there were 81 registered wineries of which 90% had a capacity of under 50,000 hl/1.3 million gal, but there were four very large wineries producing 150,000 to 500,000 hl of wine a year. There are 16 wine districts within three wine regions: **Pcinya-Osogovo** in the east, the western region of **Pelagoniya-Polog**, and the most important central region of Vardar River Valley (also known as **Povardarie**), which accounts for more than 85% of vineyard area, particularly the Tikveš district, location of 41% of the country's vineyards.

Recent investment in large, modern wineries and new vineyards has been substantial and some foreign CONSULTANTS have been drafted in to modernize winemaking. A number of smaller estates and premium boutique wineries have also appeared, and there is increasing interest in vineyards at higher elevations in the steep hills close to the border with Greece, for example—all indications of the growing emphasis on quality over quantity. Red wine varieties predominate, particularly Vranec (the usual spelling of VRANAC here). Stanušina, also known as Ohridsko Crno, is the only genuinely INDIGENOUS VARIETY so far identified. Other red varieties include Kratošija (Tribidrag or ZINFANDEL), Cabernet Sauvignon, Merlot, Syrah, and even some promising Petit Verdot. Overripeness and high alcohol levels are becoming much less common than in the past, although producers suggest that Vranec has to reach 14% to reveal its rich fruit flavours. White wine grapes are generally destined for brandy or rakija production although dry whites are starting to show promise thanks to more sophisticated winemaking. They include Žilavka, Župljanka, Temjanika (MUSCAT BLANC À PETIT GRAINS), Smederevka, Rkatsiteli, Graševina (WELSCHRIESLING), Chardonnay, and Sauvignon Blanc. C.G.

www.balkanwineroute.com
www.winesofmacedonia.org

Macedon Ranges, very cool, sparkling and fine table wine region in the Port Phillip Zone in the Australian state of VICTORIA with 49 producers, including Bindi and Curly Flat.

Maceratino, increasingly rare white grape grown on 176 ha/435 acres of the MARCHE in 2010. Possibly related to the local VERDICCHIO.

maceration, ancient word for steeping a material in liquid with or without a kneading action to separate the softened parts of the material from the harder ones. This important process in RED WINEMAKING involves extraction of the PHENOLICS (TANNINS, colouring materials, or ANTHOCYANINS, other GLYCOSIDES, including FLAVOUR PRECURSORS, and non-glycosylated FLAVOUR COMPOUNDS) from the grape skins, seeds, and stem fragments into the juice or new wine. Some maceration inevitably takes place in the FERMENTATION VESSEL. It is governed by TEMPERATURE, contact between the solids and liquid and the degree of agitation, time, and by the composition of the extracting liquid, in this case the grape juice as it becomes wine. Although everyday red wines are made simply by a rapid fermentation lasting just two or three days, many winemakers encourage an additional maceration period after fermentation has been completed, particularly for long-lived wines such as red BORDEAUX. If fermentation is slow to start, possibly due to the low temperature of the grapes and/or the use of ambient yeast, the winemaker may take advantage of the 'accidental maceration' that results.

The maceration process can never extract all of the phenolics from red grapes, however, because the enclosed membranes of individual CELLS within the skin layer containing the phenolics are not broken by the CRUSHING operation that breaks open the berry. The diffusion of anthocyanins through these membranes is slow, and the maceration process is further complicated by the fact that reactions progressively occur among the compounds newly released from their confining cells leading to the formation of PIGMENTED TANNINS. Winemakers must use trial and error, often over many years, to decide which are the optimum maceration conditions for each grape variety and season. Rapid laboratory analyses can help to estimate colour and tannins (and Ferré has shown in his *Traité d'œnologie bourguignonne* that extraction reaches a maximum of 80% of the grapes' available colouring matter on the sixth day of maceration), but the winemaker's eye and palate often prove surer guides.

Both heat and alcohol encourage the extraction of desirable compounds, which is fortunate since both are produced by fermentation. As fermentation continues, heat is produced and the increasingly alcoholic liquid becomes a better and better solvent for the organic compounds to be extracted.

But the grape solids (mainly skins) have to be encouraged to make sufficient contact with the liquid for optimal extraction. The bubbles of CARBON DIOXIDE gas generated by the fermentation process tend to make the grape skins and seeds float to the surface in the fermentation vessel to form a layer known as a CAP. Without human intervention, a thick and drying layer of grape skins will be buoyed up by this stream of carbon dioxide and the extraction of desirable skin components will cease.

For generations, winemaking ingenuity has been harnessed to devising methods of breaking up and submerging the cap and keeping the skins mixed with the fermenting liquid. Keeping skins and liquid in contact is relatively simple with small batches of fermenting grapes (see PUNCHING DOWN). With larger batches, a system of either grids or coarse mesh screens must be devised to keep the cap SUBMERGED, or liquid from the bottom of the tank must be pumped to the top and sprayed over the skins (see PUMPING OVER and DÉLESTAGE).

Several proprietary systems have been devised to extract the desirable organic compounds from the grape skins into the fermenting wine. Some of these use a quick high-temperature phase to disrupt the cells containing anthocyanins and liberate the desirable organic compounds (see THERMOVINIFICATION and FLASH DÉTENTE); others use mechanical stirrers or rotating tanks (see ROTOFERMENTERS) which keep the skins and liquid in contact; or some form of AUTOVINIFICATION. In general, heat and mechanical agitation systems are used for ordinary wines, while the more sensitive techniques of punching down or pumping over are preferred for finer wines, although care must be taken that any pumps used are relatively gentle. The shape of the vat also influences the behaviour of the cap.

Along with temperature, liquid composition, and intimacy of contact, the fourth factor influencing colour, tannin, and flavour extraction is time of contact, a factor, albeit less than perfectly understood, over which winemakers can have total control (provided they have access to sufficient vat space). In general the longer the solids and liquids are in contact, the greater the degree of extraction, but it depends on the frequency of pumping over or punching down. It has been shown, however, that the extraction of the desirable compounds slows down considerably after the new wine approaches 10% alcohol and is at its height during the earlier phases of fermentation. The total maceration time varies according to the phenolic content of the skins (itself a function of grape variety and weather) and according to the desired style of wine. Within certain limits, the greater the degree of extraction, the longer the life expectancy of a wine—although care must be taken to avoid extracting the harshest phenolics. In red winemaking, maceration usually lasts at least as long as fermentation does, but may be prolonged for a further week to three or even four weeks afterwards. Care must be taken to avoid the increased risk of high levels of VOLATILE ACIDITY. Some musts, naturally low in tannins, may be heated after the completion of fermentation to encourage the extraction of phenolics.

Some wine producers favour a prefermentation **cold maceration** of red grapes rather than maceration of skins in an alcoholic liquid. This optional winemaking operation involves the maceration of grape skins with juice while the mass is held at a low temperature. In theory each of the extractable compounds in the skins has its own temperature coefficient governing the extraction rate, and the theory of cold maceration is that a more favourable combination of phenolics is extracted by water and added SULFUR DIOXIDE than is obtained with an alcoholic solution. A quite different red winemaking technique is CARBONIC MACERATION, practised particularly in Beaujolais and for other red wines designed for early consumption.

See also BARREL FERMENTATION for an outline of a red winemaking option which dispenses with post-fermentation maceration altogether.

In WHITE WINEMAKING, maceration is usually actively discouraged by separating the juice from the skins as soon as possible in order to avoid extraction of tannins, since no colouring matter is required and the resultant astringency is generally viewed as a fault in white wines. Some winemakers deliberately allow a certain period of SKIN CONTACT for white grapes before they are crushed, however, and in the late 1980s this technique (known as **macération pelliculaire** in French) was encouraged by Denis DUBOURDIEU among others in order to produce more flavourful dry white bordeaux. Sauvignon and, particularly, Sémillon grapes are held for between four and eight hours at about 18 °C/64 °F, resulting in juice higher in flavour compounds, tannins, POTASSIUM salts, and POLYSACCHARIDES, and wines with more BODY and a slightly higher PH. At the opposite end of the spectrum, fermenting white wine on the skins is regaining popularity, particularly but not exclusively in tandem with the use of clay fermentation vessels such as AMPHORAE, TINAJAS, and QVEVRI. See SKIN-FERMENTED and ORANGE WINE.

Maceration is also important in the production of fruit-flavoured spirits such as the *crème de cassis* used in making a *vin blanc cassis* or KIR which is the aromatic and deeply coloured product of blackcurrants macerated in alcohol.
A.D.W. & P.J.W.

macération carbonique, French term for CARBONIC MACERATION.

macération pelliculaire, French term for the prefermentation maceration of white grapes described in MACERATION and known elsewhere as SKIN CONTACT.

macération préfermentaire, French term for prefermentation MACERATION.

Mâcon, important commercial centre on the River Saône and capital of the **Mâconnais** dynamic district of BURGUNDY which produces considerable quantities of white wine and some red. Unlike in the Côte d'Or to the north (see map under FRANCE), vineyards on the rolling limestone hills of the Mâconnais are interspersed with land dedicated to livestock and arable farming. Côte d'Or producers as renowned as Leflaive and Lafon are investing in this southerly region.

The climate and ambience of the region differ from the Côte d'Or however: southern tiles are used for roofs, cicadas can be heard in summer, and the vineyards benefit from more sun, less rain, and little risk of frost. BEAUJOLAIS is to the immediate south of the Mâconnais.

Viticultural practices are broadly similar to those in the CÔTE D'OR, except for the widespread use of LYRE training systems, although yields may be a little higher, up to a permitted 55 hl/ha (3 tons/acre). Vinification is sometimes carried out in barrels, although only the best producers use new OAK. Bottling normally takes place in the summer before the next vintage.

The appellations of Mâconnais, in approximately ascending order of quality are, for white wines made from Chardonnay: **Mâcon**; **Mâcon-Villages** or **Mâcon** followed by a particular village name (for more details of which, see MÂCON-VILLAGES); ST-VÉRAN; Pouilly-Vinzelles, Pouilly-Loché, and Pouilly-Fuissé (for more details of which, see POUILLY-FUISSÉ). Red wine appellations are **Mâcon** and **Mâcon** followed by a particular village name. Almost all these red wines are made from the Gamay grape

since, although Pinot Noir is permitted, such wines may be sold as BOURGOGNE Rouge at a higher price than Mâcon fetches.

In 1998, the village of Viré and the adjacent hamlet of Clessé were given their own single appellation VIRÉ-CLESSÉ.

Leading producers include the Bret Brothers, Guffens-Heynen and his négociant company Verget, Merlin, Vincent, and Thévenet.
J.T.C.M.

Mâcon-Villages, appellation covering the great majority of the white wines of MÂCON. The wines may be sold either as Mâcon-Villages or as Mâcon followed by the name of the particular village. Viré and Lugny have been the best known by virtue of their CO-OPERATIVES. The full list of 27 villages or groups of villages with the right to the appellation is: Azé, Bray, Burgy, Bussières, Chaintré, Chardonnay (whence the grape may have taken its name), Charnay-lès-Mâcon, Cruzille, Davayé, Fuissé, Igé, Loché, Lugny, Mancey, Milly-Lamartine, Montbellet, Péronne, Pierreclos, Prissé, La Roche-Vineuse, St-Gengoux Serrières (reds only), Solutré-Pouilly, Uchizy (whites only), VERGISSON, Verzé, and Vinzelles.

Most Mâconnais wines are vinified in stainless steel or glass-lined concrete vats for early bottling and consumption within a year or two of the vintage. A handful of growers are producing significantly finer wines through low yields followed by BARREL FERMENTATION and BARREL MATURATION. J.T.C.M.

macroclimate, also called regional climate, means a climate broadly representing an area or region on a scale of tens to hundreds of kilometres (Dry and Smart). Unlike the more precise terms MICROCLIMATE and MESOCLIMATE, macroclimate approximates to what is normally meant by the word 'climate'. It is usually taken from a long-established recording station within the region. However, some such stations may not be representative of the local vineyards, especially if they are sited in or near an urban environment or on flat land or in a valley (see TOPOGRAPHY).

Macroclimatic data have to be used with caution when applied to viticulture. Informed adjustments are nearly always needed for differences in ELEVATION, slope, aspect, and perhaps even SOIL type, before reasonable estimates can be made for the mesoclimates of actual vineyards. This is especially so in cool regions, where small differences in effective temperature can make big differences in time and completeness of RIPENING. J.G. & R.E.S.

Dry, P. R., and Smart, R. E., 'Vineyard site selection', in B. G. Coombe and P. R. Dry (eds.), *Viticulture*, i: *Resources* (2nd edn, Adelaide, 2004).

macro-oxygenation, an umbrella term for the deliberate exposure of wine to OXYGEN

that contrasts with the very specific technique of MICRO-OXYGENATION. See AERATION, PUMPING OVER, DÉLESTAGE, RACKING, BARREL FERMENTATION, and BARREL MATURATION. See also MICRO-OXYGENATION and TOTAL PACKAGE OXYGEN.

Macvin du Jura, powerful VIN DE LIQUEUR made in the JURA in eastern France by blending hardly fermented grape juice with MARC du Jura. This somewhat sweet but curiously earthy drink should be served cool as an APERITIF or with ice cream dishes. A version involving spices and heated must was made as early as the 14th century. Macvin was awarded its own APPELLATION CONTRÔLÉE, the 400th created by INAO, in 1991.

Madagascar, large tropical island off the east African coast which was a French colony between 1896 and 1960 and has a wine industry that has since been run largely by Chinese immigrants. The island had about 3,000 ha/7,410 acres of vines in 2009 according to OIV figures. Mainly HYBRID vines are grown in the central *hauts plateaux* area at elevations of between 750 and 1,350 m. Swiss settlers encouraged the Betsileo farmers to apply their expertise growing rice on high terraces to viticulture in the 1960s. The hundreds of vine-growers, with just a few hectares of vineyard each, are centred on Fianarantsoa and Ambalavo. See TROPICAL VITICULTURE.

Platter, J. & E., *Africa Uncorked* (London, 2002).

Madeira, Atlantic island belonging to Portugal, nearly 1,000 km/625 miles from the Portuguese mainland and 750 km/466 miles off the coast of North Africa, now a DOP for fortified wines and an IGP (Indicação Geográfica Protegida) (see TERRAS MADEIRENSES) for unfortified wines. Of these, the FORTIFIED madeira, probably the world's most resilient and longest living wine, is much the most famous. This volcanic island rising steeply from the ocean is an unlikely place to find such an exciting and individual wine. But Madeira flies in the face of generally accepted winemaking norms.

History

Like PORT, madeira seems to have begun as an unfortified wine. There are few early records but Madeira's strategic position in the middle of the Atlantic put the island at an advantage and the island's capital Funchal became a natural port of call for ships en route to Africa, Asia, and South America. By the end of the 16th century (less than 200 years after the discovery of the island), there is firm evidence that Madeira's wine industry was well established. However, the early madeira wines were unstable and many deteriorated long before they reached their destination. Alcohol (probably distilled from cane sugar) was therefore added to some wines in order to help them survive a long sea voyage, although FORTIFICATION did not become general practice until the middle of the 18th century.

In the second half of the 17th century, ships en route to India (including many of the DUTCH EAST INDIA COMPANY fleet) called regularly at Funchal to pick up casks of wine termed pipas or PIPES. It was soon found that madeira somehow tasted better after pitching and rolling across the tropics in the hull of a ship. With this came a fashion for *vinho da roda*, wines that had benefited from a round trip, as opposed to *vinho canteiro*, wine which matured on the island, called after the trestles (*canteiros*) on which the pipes rested in the madeira LODGES. Wines continued to undergo long, tropical sea journeys to induce this special flavour until the 1900s, when the practice became impractical. Over the preceding century most shippers turned to using ESTUFAS, rooms or tanks in which the wine could be artificially heated to simulate the rapid maturation brought about by a long sea journey—although the finest madeiras continue to be aged naturally on *canteiros* (see Winemaking below).

With the colonization of North America in the 17th century, Madeira established an important export market on the east coast. By the end of the 18th century, the new North American colonies were buying a quarter of all the wine produced on the island. Madeira was held in such high esteem that it was used to toast the Declaration of Independence in 1776. Colonial troops returning to Britain opened up a new market for madeira there, but high-quality madeira is still much appreciated in the United States. The Madeira Club of Savannah survived PROHIBITION and continues to meet regularly over a quarter of a millennium after the first pipes of madeira were landed on the coast of Georgia.

As well as being extremely fashionable in Britain and the United States, the drink was also popular with Portuguese settlers in Africa, and in Brazil, and demand began to outstrip supply.

In 1851, however, the first of a series of crises struck the island's wine industry. Oidium or POWDERY MILDEW reached the island (in the same year as it was first identified in BORDEAUX) and quickly spread through the dense vineyards, almost wiping out production in just three years.

The industry revived after it was found that oidium could be controlled by dusting the vine leaves with SULFUR but shortly afterwards the PHYLLOXERA louse struck, leaving the island's wine-based economy in ruins. From the mid 1870s, vines all over the island were uprooted and replaced by sugar cane. Wine shippers abandoned Madeira and many vineyards were never replanted.

Phylloxera-resistant AMERICAN VINE SPECIES were introduced a decade or so later but many farmers, seeking a rapid return to prosperity, cultivated VITIS *labrusca, riparia, rupestris,* and hybrid vines rather than using them merely as ROOTSTOCKS onto which Madeira's traditional VINIFERA varieties could be grafted.

Madeira's wine industry returned to normal levels of production at the beginning of the 20th century and shipments to traditional markets were restored. But the island's economy was dealt another blow, first by the Russian Revolution in 1917, and immediately thereafter by the introduction of Prohibition, in the United States. Many firms were forced to close, but a number chose to amalgamate to form the Madeira Wine Association, renamed as the Madeira Wine Company in 1981.

Although at the end of the 17th century there were about 30 wine shippers operating on Madeira, by the mid 2010s there were just six exporters of madeira, of which Justino's (Justino Henriques) is now much the largest wine producer on the island, although the best known is probably the Madeira Wine Company comprising BLANDY, Cossart Gordon, Leacock, and Rutherford & Miles among more than 20 brand names. In 1988, the SYMINGTON family of OPORTO took control of the company and thoroughly overhauled the winemaking practices and equipment. In 2011 they sold their stake back to the Blandy family.

France, Germany, and the Benelux countries are the largest markets for modern madeira, although most of the wine destined for these countries is of very basic quality and bought for cooking rather than drinking. The United States, Japan, and the United Kingdom are the main markets for better-quality madeira.

Viticulture

Madeira is a difficult place to grow grapes. Nearly all the island's vineyards are planted on tiny step-like terraces called *poios*, carved from the red or grey BASALT bedrock. Although most of the newer vineyards are CORDON-trained, most vineyards are planted on low trellises (known as *latada*) similar to those of the VINHO VERDE region on the Portuguese mainland. These serve to raise the CANOPY above the ground, making the grapes less vulnerable to FUNGAL DISEASES that thrive in this damp, subtropical climate. With a mean annual temperature of 19 °C/66 °F and high rainfall, powdery mildew and BOTRYTIS BUNCH ROT are constant threats.

Viticulture at this latitude is only made possible by elevation. Madeira rises to over 1,800 m/5,900 ft and the mountains are almost perpetually covered in cloud as moisture in the warm oceanic air is forced to condense. Annual rainfall on the island's summit reaches nearly 3,000 mm/117 in, over three times the total in the island's capital Funchal on the south coast, where EVAPORATION is high. The network of IRRIGATION channels called *levadas* now extends to over 2,000 km/1,200 miles, supplying the 1,600 growers farming just under 500 ha/1,250 acres of piecemeal VINIFERA vineyard authorized to produce madeira. MECHANIZATION is rendered impossible by both the terracing and the small size of the vineyard plots. As a result, cultivation costs are rising and many vineyards on the south of the island have fallen prey to property speculation while others on the north side, mostly planted with American HYBRIDS, have been abandoned.

Vine varieties

The most planted variety by far is the red-skinned NEGRAMOLL (often referred to as Tinta Negra or Tinta Negra Mole) which has been the principal *V. vinifera* variety on the island since phylloxera arrived at the end of the 19th century. It was for long denigrated, somewhat unfairly in view of its versatility. Along with the recently introduced COMPLEXA grape, it can make good madeira, but wines based on Negramoll rarely have the keeping qualities of those based on the so-called 'noble' varieties. Plantings of the traditional varieties SERCIAL, VERDELHO, BUAL, MALVASIA, and the almost extinct Terrantez, are slowly increasing once again since their rout as a result of phylloxera. Other varieties planted are principally disease-resistant AMERICAN HYBRIDS such as Cunningham and Jacquet, although they are no longer permitted as ingredients in madeira and should be used exclusively in the production of the island's rustic table wine. Small quantities of ARNSBURGER and Cabernet Sauvignon are planted on the north side of the island for the production of unfortified wine. Listrão (Palomino) is planted on the nearby island of Porto Santo where they make a small quantity of their own fortified wine for the local market.

Winemaking

Madeira is made in a number of different ways and methods of production vary enormously according to the market and the price that the wine commands. Production revolves around the use of the ESTUFA system and its natural alternatives.

The *estufagem* process has been much improved in recent years with concrete tanks having been largely replaced by stainless steel (*cubas de calor*) ranging in size between 20,000 and 50,000 l/13,200 gal and most widely used for large-volume production. Hot water circulates either through a stainless steel coil in the middle of the tank or a jacket, heating the wine to a maximum temperature of 55 °C/130 °F for at least 90 days. The process is carefully monitored by the wine industry's controlling body IVBAM (Instituto do Vinho, do Bordado e do Artesanato da Madeira) which also, rather quaintly, represents Madeira's other traditional industries, embroidery and handicrafts.

A second type of *estufagem* (used exclusively by the Madeira Wine Company) takes place in 600-l/158-gal wooden casks or lodge pipes which are stored in warm rooms (*armazens de calor*) heated by the nearby tanks or by steam-filled hot water pipes. Temperatures usually range between 30 °C and 40 °C and the wines develop over a longer period, usually six months to a year. This is a gentler process than the bulk method generally used, and is used for higher-quality (see below).

The very finest madeiras are produced without any artificial heating at all. Some of the smaller shippers and stockholders (*armazenistas*) refuse to resort to the *estufa* to age their wines. These madeiras are left to age naturally in 600-l pipes stowed under the eaves of lodges in Funchal, heated only by the sun. These *vinhos de canteiro* mature in cask for at least 20 years, although some may remain in this state for a century or more before bottling, and are usually destined for vintage lots.

One of Madeira's most pressing problems was a lack of good-quality base wine caused by a shortage of grapes from *V. vinifera* vine varieties. The white Sercial, Verdelho, Malvasia, and Terrantez varieties, which used to be classified as 'noble' by the ruling Madeira Wine Institute, are challenging to grow and still in relatively short supply (see below). Most madeira is therefore made from the versatile and more productive Tinta Negra.

Traditionally, shippers bought unfermented MUST direct from the growers, who trod the grapes by foot in LAGARES. Today few winemakers use *lagares* and the main shippers buy grapes rather than must, from farmers all over the island. Most firms ferment in 25,000-l/ 6,600-gal vats made from stainless steel but a few still use lined cement or even ferment small quantities of wine in cask. The noble varieties are usually pressed and fermented separately from Negramoll. Malvasia and Bual are traditionally fermented on their skins while Sercial and Verdelho musts are separated from the grape skins before fermentation.

Higher-quality wines (usually those made with a high percentage of the more expensive noble grapes) are made by arresting the fermentation with 95% strength grape spirit to produce a wine with an ALCOHOLIC STRENGTH of between 17 and 18%. Wines made from Malvasia and Bual are fortified early in the FERMENTATION process, leaving up to 7 °Baumé (see MUST WEIGHT for conversions into other scales of measurement) of RESIDUAL SUGAR in the wine. Verdelho and Sercial are fermented until they are practically dry, although they may be sweetened at a later stage with either *vinho surdo* or *abafado*. *Surdo* is an intensely sweet MISTELA fortified to an alcoholic strength of 20%, often

before fermentation has begun, while *abafado* is a drier wine arrested at a later stage.

Producers of cheaper wines prefer to ferment all wines dry, leaving the fortification until after the wines have passed through the *estufa*. This saves on the cost of valuable alcohol, a few degrees of which are lost through evaporation during *estufagem*. The wines are sweetened after fortification according to style and are often adjusted with caramel.

The wines' age is counted from the point at which *estufagem* has been completed. Until 2002 the most basic wines were generally shipped in bulk (*granel*) but this practice has now been suspended.

Styles of madeira

The quality of even the most basic madeira improved greatly in the late 1990s and early 2000s. Inexpensive wines which used to smell cooked and taste coarse and stewed are now much fresher and cleaner, even if they are not as fine and incisive as cask-aged examples. Finer wines are distinguished by their high-toned RANCIO aromas and searing ACIDITY. Madeira varies in colour from pale gold to orange-amber to deep mahogany brown with a yellow-green tinge appearing on the rim of well-aged examples.

Standard blends Madeira's wines were traditionally named after the principal noble grape varieties grown on the island: Sercial, Verdelho, Bual (or Boal), and Malvasia (or MALMSEY), these names denoting increasingly sweet styles of madeira. But since phylloxera destroyed many of Madeira's best vineyards at the end of the 19th century, much of the island's wine has in reality been made from either AMERICAN HYBRIDS or the local *V. vinifera* variety Negramoll. The use of American hybrids has technically been illegal since 1979. From the beginning of 1993, Madeira has been made to conform to the EU requirement that a VARIETALLY named wine must contain at least 85% of wine made from the specified grape variety. Insufficient quantities of the noble varieties resulted in renaming most standard blends simply 'Dry', 'Medium Dry', 'Medium Sweet', 'Medium Rich', and 'Rich' or 'Sweet'.

Sercial Among the noble grapes, Sercial is usually grown in the coolest vineyards, at heights of up to 800 m/2,640 ft or on the north side of the island. Many growers erroneously believe that the variety is related to Germany's RIESLING grape but it is in fact the same as the ESGANA CÃO (meaning dog strangler) which grows on the Portuguese mainland, the grapes exhibiting the same ferocious levels of ACIDITY. At high ELEVATIONS, Sercial ripens with difficulty to make a 10% base wine which is dry, tart, and astringent when young. With fortification and

ten or more years' ageing in cask, a good Sercial wine develops high-toned, almond-like aromas with a nervy character and a searing dry finish. The Sercial wines range in residual sugar from 0.5 ° to 1.5 °Baumé.

Verdelho Verdelho, which also tends to be planted on the cooler north side of the island, ripens more easily than Sercial and therefore lends itself to producing a medium-dry wine with Baumé readings of between 1.5° and 2.5° after fortification. With age, the wines develop an extraordinary smoky complexity while retaining their characteristic tang of acidity.

Bual Bual, or Boal in Portuguese, is grown in warmer locations on the south side of Madeira. It ripens to achieve higher sugar levels than either Sercial or Verdelho and, after fortification to arrest the fermentation, Bual wines range from 2.5 to 3.5 °Baumé. These dark, medium-rich, raisiny wines retain their acidic verve with age. Confusingly, Bual is known by the name MALVASIA Fina in mainland Portugal and this is now its official name.

Malmsey The MALVASIA grapes which produce malmsey are usually grown in the warmest locations at low elevations on the south coast, especially around Câmara de Lobos. Subvarieties include Malvasia Candida and Malvasia Babosa, which ripen to produce the very sweetest madeira wines, gaining richness and concentration with time in cask. A productive sub-variety known as Malvasia de São Jorge is grown on the north of the island and is officially 'authorized' rather than 'recommended', pending investigation into its true identity. Sugar readings in a malmsey range between 3.5 and 6.5 °Baumé, but the wines are rarely cloying as the sweetness is balanced by characteristically high levels of acidity. Like all high-quality madeira made from noble varieties, malmseys are some of the most resilient in the world and will keep in cask and bottle for a century or more.

Historic styles Madeira's unparalleled ability to age means that styles of wine long abandoned by the island's wine shippers may still be found, and enjoyed. Rainwater is a light, off-dry or medium-dry style of madeira bottled before it is five years old and named after wine which was supposedly diluted by rain during shipment to the United States. Rainwater madeira is still made in small quantities, although the law is vague on what exactly constitutes the style. Two other styles of madeira based on the noble TERRANTEZ and BASTARDO grapes are rarely made since both varieties are almost extinct on the island, although Terrantez is making a modest comeback. Intensely sweet wines made from three types of Moscatel (MUSCAT) grape, usually produced for blending, are occasionally bottled on their own.

Qualities of madeira

A generally accepted hierarchy (from the youngest and most basic to the oldest and most distinguished) parallels the different styles of madeira as follows. Age designations do not refer to an exact, minimum, or average age but are effectively an indication of style.

Bulk wine (*granel*) accounted for between 30 and 40% of the island's production until shipments were suspended in 2002. Only denatured wines (usually spiced with salt and pepper for culinary use) may now be exported in bulk.

Three Year Old, sometimes designated 'Finest' or *corrente*, blended wines, bottled after *estufagem* and ageing in tank, rarely in wood. All are based on the Negramoll and Complexa grapes.

Five Year Old Reserve madeira is a blended five-year-old wine, some or all of which will have undergone *estufagem* in tank. A proportion of the blend is likely to have been aged in cask. Most are made from the Negramoll and Complexa grapes but some are made from the so-called noble varieties (see above). The use of the term 'Reserve' was complicated by the fact that one shipper, Pereira d'Oliveira, bottled *frasqueira* (vintage) wines as 'Reservas'.

Ten Year Old Special Reserve is a wine in which the youngest component in the blend will be around ten years old, having aged in cask, usually without recourse to *estufa* tanks. These wines are mostly made from the noble grape varieties and labelled accordingly.

Extra Reserve is a category which is rarely seen but the term is used to denote a blended, 15-year-old wine.

Twenty Year Old, Thirty Year Old, and Over Forty Years Old Although officially permitted, these designations are rarely used as a wine from a single year with 20 years of age qualifies as a vintage or *frasqueira* madeira.

Solera wines were made using the SOLERA system more commonly associated with SHERRY. This blended style began in the 19th century but, having been much abused, was temporarily prohibited for madeira by EU law—although some very good old bottlings of 19th-century soleras can still be found. Under the new definition a solera must be based on a wine from a single year, of which not more than 10% can be withdrawn in any one year. This must be replenished with a wine of similar quality, the maximum number of additions being ten, after which all the wine in the solera must be bottled at the same time.

Colheita or 'Harvest' wines are from a single year, or harvest, bottled after spending at least five years in ageing in cask. These are effectively early bottled *frasqueira* or 'vintage' wines which share the individuality if not the concentration or the complexity of a wine aged for a minimum of twenty years (see below).

Frasqueira (Vintage) is the official term which denotes 'vintage' madeira: wine from a single year which, unlike vintage PORT, must age in cask for a minimum of 20 years. Many wines spend considerably more time in wood than this and often spend their later years in 20-l/5-gal glass carboys, or *garrafões*, before bottling. The wines are extremely resistant to OXIDATION and may be kept in bottle for many years. Vintage madeira, especially Sercial, is capable of many decades' BOTTLE AGEING. Shippers carrying stocks of old vintages are so confident of madeira's ability to withstand oxidation that they keep the bottles standing upright so that there is no risk of a poor or tainted cork spoiling the wine.

Serving madeira

Madeira is probably the most robust wine in the world. Little can harm the wine after it has gone through the *estufa*, or been aged for twenty or more years in cask. Most shippers storing bottles upright RECORK their most venerable vintages, say, once every 20 years. All wines tend to throw a deposit with age, but madeira throws less than most. Decanting is therefore recommended for older, vintage wines but is not always necessary. Such wines should be left to breathe for a short time, even a few days, before serving simply to allow any BOTTLE SICKNESS to dissipate. Drier Sercial and Verdelho styles benefit from being served 'cellar cool' rather than iced. Sweeter Buals and Malmseys should be served at room temperature. Once opened, a bottle of madeira has the advantage of lasting for many months, even years.   R.J.M.

Cossart, N., and Berk, E., *Madeira, The Island Vineyard* (Sonoma, 2011).

Huetz de Lemps, A., *Le Vin de Madère* (Grenoble, 1989).

Liddell, A., *Madeira: The Mid-Atlantic Wine* (London, 2014).

Mayson, R., *The Wines and Vineyards of Portugal* (London, 2003).

www.vinhomadeira.pt

Madeira Wine Company. See BLANDY.

Madeleine Angevine, early-ripening

cross most common as a TABLE GRAPE but the parent of several wine grapes, including the confusingly named **Madeleine × Angevine 7672**, first sent to the UK from Alzey Research Institute in Germany in 1957. It makes some light, grapey wines in England and has been planted in SWEDEN and DENMARK.

maderization, occasionally **maderization**,

is the process by which a wine is made to taste like MADEIRA, involving mild OXIDATION over a long period and, usually, heat. Such a wine is said to be **maderized**. Although this tasting term is occasionally applied pejoratively to mean that a wine is OXIDIZED, it should properly be applied only to wines with a high enough ALCOHOLIC STRENGTH to inhibit the action of ACETOBACTER, which would otherwise transform the wine into VINEGAR. Very few maderized wines are made today by simply ageing the wine at cellar temperature; the oxidation process is instead hastened by heating or 'baking' the wine as on the island of Madeira. Oxidation reactions, like most organic chemical reactions, can be roughly doubled in speed by a temperature rise of 10 °C/18 °F. For example, a wine requiring ten years at a cellar temperature of 20 °C to develop a maderized character could manifest approximately, although not exactly, the same character after about two and a half years at 40 °C or 15 months at 50 °C. Maderized wines are normally amber to brown in colour and have a distinctive cooked or mildly caramelized flavour. Wines processed at excessively high temperatures may taste burnt and harsh. Most such wines and especially those made from AMERICAN VINES or AMERICAN HYBRIDS are fortified and sweetened before being marketed. Madeira and similar wines such as early sherry-style wines made in California were particularly popular in the 18th and early 19th centuries but have since fallen out of FASHION. See also RANCIO wines.   A.D.W.

made wine, somewhat inelegant name for wine made not from freshly picked grapes but from reconstituted GRAPE CONCENTRATE. The advantages for producers are that it can be made throughout the year, and that grapes can be sourced wherever they happen to be cheapest. CYPRUS has been an important source, as has Spain more recently. BRITISH MADE WINE is one of the most commercially successful made wines, but made wines have also been produced in notable quantity in JAPAN and eastern Europe. The produce of many HOME-WINEMAKERS is made wine.

Madiran, dynamic distinctive red wine appellation in SOUTH WEST FRANCE which has gently remodelled its concentrated, traditionally tannic wines, GASCONY's signature red.

There are said to have been vineyards here in Gallo-Roman times, and certainly the wines of Madiran were appreciated in the Middle Ages by pilgrims en route for Santiago de Compostela. About 1,200 ha/3,000 acres south of the greater armagnac region produce Madiran. Soils are mainly clay and limestone with so-called *grebb*, or *grip*, granules and pebbles strengthened with iron and manganese oxide from Pyrenean glacial alluvial deposits. The climate in Madiran is softened, and often moistened, by the Atlantic to the west, but autumn is usually dry.

The traditional grape variety is TANNAT, its very name hinting at the naturally astringent character of its high TANNIN level. The AOC regulations have increased the minimum permitted stiffening dose of Tannat to between 60 and 80%, with many top cuvées depending heavily on Tannat. The balance should be Cabernet Sauvignon, Cabernet Franc, and/or Fer. The wine traditionally needed long BOTTLE AGEING but some of Madiran's most dynamic winemakers have been experimenting with ways of softening the impact of Tannat (DESTEMMING is mandatory), including hand-picking only the ripest grapes, gentle handling, new oak, and MICRO-OXYGENATION to produce wines which have density, potential for ageing, but considerable charm in youth. Madiran can taste like a classed growth claret given the sort of Gascon twist needed to cope with *magret de canard*. The leader of the appellation has been Alain Brumont, who produces both Montus and Bouscassé. Other reliable producers include Ch d'Aydie, Domaine Berthoumieu, Domaine Capmartin, Ch Laffitte-Teston, and Patrick Ducournau, who pioneered micro-oxygenation.

From the same area comes white PACHERENC DU VIC-BILH. Some producers make a sticky, near-black VIN DE LIQUEUR from Tannat.

Perry, D. M., *Madiran and Pacherenc du Vic-Bilh* (Accrington, Lancs, 2014).

Madrid, Vinos de. The Spanish capital Madrid is much less well known as the name of a wine denomination. The DO Vinos de Madrid forms a semicircle around the southern suburbs. Of the three officially recognized subzones, the most important is round the town of Arganda del Rey to the east of Madrid. White wines are made from the Malvar and AIRÉN. Reds are produced from Tinto Fino (TEMPRANILLO), also known (in east central Spain, but not in Madrid) as Tinta Madrid, Garnacha (GRENACHE) and, increasingly, Cabernet Sauvignon, Syrah, and Merlot. A handful of producers have shown real potential, particularly those in the western part of the region (see GREDOS).   V. de la S.

Magarach, wine research institute at Yalta in the CRIMEA, founded in 1828, more than 50 years before DAVIS or the Institute of Oenology at the University of BORDEAUX. Although its activities have been unusually wide ranging (including some innovative by-product recycling such as alcohol-free bioactive additives from Cabernet Sauvignon), the Institute Magarach has been particularly distinguished in developing HYBRID varieties and special vinification techniques.

The extent of its three experimental vineyards has been reduced from nearly 2,000 ha/5,000 acres to around 600 ha/1,482 acres and they include a collection of vines with more

than 3,500 varieties from 41 countries. Some of the most successful of 30 vine varieties designed to combine quantity with quality are **Magarach Ruby** or Roubinovyi Magaracha (CABERNET SAUVIGNON × SAPERAVI), **Magarach Bastardo** or Bastardo Magarachski (BASTARDO × Saperavi), and Magarach Early or Ranni Magaracha. A newer generation of DISEASE-RESISTANT VARIETIES has since been developed with specific resistances to various PESTS and DISEASES. Since 1893 the institute has collected 1,080 genera of microorganisms for winemaking.

At one time much of Magarach's effort was directed towards producing convincing copies of various classic wine styles (Magarach Malmsey, for example). The institute's own cellar harbours nearly 220,000 sample bottles, some of them containing wine from the mid 19th century.

Specific research avenues tend to have a particularly practical aspect, involving hundreds of patents. New vine varieties created by the institute grow in RUSSIA, MOLDOVA, KAZAKHSTAN, AZERBAIJAN, and elsewhere.   I.N.

Magliocco. CALABRIA in southern Italy was home to a total of 538 ha/1,330 acres of dark-berried Magliocco vines in 2010, made up of **Magliocco Canino**, a late-ripening likely relative of Sangiovese, and the probably more common and more tannic, **Magliocco Dolce**. Librandi have made efforts to revive it as a varietal but it is also often blended with GAGLIOPPO.

magnesium, mineral element essential for healthy vine growth. It is an essential component of chlorophyll, and so CHLOROSIS is a common symptom of magnesium deficiency. The most conspicuous symptom is discoloration between the main veins of the leaf, which becomes particularly noticeable around VERAISON. This zone is yellow for white varieties, and red for dark fruit varieties. This deficiency can be severe in some situations, reducing YIELDS, and slowing fruit RIPENING. Magnesium deficiency may be associated with BUNCHSTEM NECROSIS, in which the bunch stems and berries shrivel before ripening. Maturity is affected and wine quality suffers.

Soils high in POTASSIUM encourage magnesium deficiency. Similarly, some ROOTSTOCKS such as SO4 and Fercal are incapable of taking up sufficient magnesium and tend to show deficiency symptoms. Magnesium deficiency is overcome by applying fertilizers to the soil or by spraying leaves.   R.E.S. & R.E.W.

White, R. E., *Understanding Vineyard Soils* (2nd edn, Oxford, 2015).

magnum, large BOTTLE SIZE containing 1.5 l/54 fl oz, or the equivalent of two bottles. It is widely regarded as being the ideal size for BOTTLE AGEING fine wine, being large enough to

slow the AGEING process, but not so big as to be unwieldy, or unthinkably expensive (unlike some other LARGE FORMATS). Magnums generally command a premium.

Mago, influential classical writer on agricultural, including viticultural, matters. See CARTHAGE and PHOENICIA for more details.

Maillard reaction. Named after French chemist Louis-Camille Maillard, this chemical reaction between REDUCING SUGARS and AMINO ACIDS or PROTEINS is commonly seen in the browning of untreated foods and in the taste of toast and seared meat. In wine, Maillard-reaction products are important in complex aromas of bottle-aged CHAMPAGNE and in the nutty, port-like, and bacon flavours of wine made from raisined grapes. See also RANCIO.

Maipo, important subregion in the north of the Central Valley in CHILE where Santiago, Talagante, Pirque, Puente Alto, Isla de Maipo, and Buin are located.

maître de chai, term often used in France, particularly in Bordeaux, for the cellarmaster, as opposed to the RÉGISSEUR, who might manage the whole estate, or certainly the vineyards. It means literally 'master of the CHAI'. As SCIENCE and ACADEME invade winemaking, the winemaking decisions are increasingly made by an OENOLOGIST.

Málaga, city and Mediterranean port in ANDALUCÍA, southern Spain (see map under SPAIN), which lends its name to a denominated wine zone producing rich, raisiny FORTIFIED WINES. Since the 1960s, Málaga has become more famous as the tourist gateway to the Costa del Sol, but its wine industry has a long and distinguished history dating back to around 600 BC, when the Greeks first planted vines in the area. The Moors continued to make wine, calling it *xarab al Malaqui*, or Málaga syrup, probably to remove any reference to alcohol but also evoking the extraordinary sweetness of the grapes growing in the hills above the city. In the 17th and 18th centuries, Málaga, often spelt **Malaga**, was exported worldwide and by the mid 19th century there were over 100,000 ha/247,000 acres of vineyard, making Málaga Spain's second largest wine region. (See, for example, the part it played in the history of ARGENTINE wine.) Exports of Mountain, as the wine became known in Great Britain and North America, totalled between 30,000 and 40,000 BUTTS (as much as 220,000 hl/5.8 million gal) a year.

In the mid 19th century, Málaga was dealt a double blow, first by POWDERY MILDEW, then, in 1876, by the arrival of PHYLLOXERA. Málaga was the first wine region in Spain to be affected by the louse and its effect on the local economy was devastating. The terraced vineyards, then covered with Muscat grapes, to the north and east of the city were abandoned and many families emigrated to South America. Málaga never really recovered until the 1960s, when tourism became Málaga's major industry. From a peak immediately prior to the arrival of phylloxera of 113,000 ha/279,000 acres, the region's vineyard area was only 1,200 ha in the early 21st century, making Málaga one of Spain's smallest DOs. Where there were once over 100 BODEGAS near the port in the centre of the city, the number of producers had risen from two in the late 1990s to 14 by 2003.

Málaga's vineyards are still split into four zones, the most important of which is the Antequera plateau 50 km/30 miles north of the city of Málaga itself. The principal grape variety nowadays is PEDRO XIMÉNEZ, which gives high sugar levels in the hot, dry climate (although considerable amounts of the more productive AIRÉN vine were also planted in the 1980s). In the cooler mountain zone immediately north of the city, Moscatel de Alejandría (MUSCAT OF AL-EXANDRIA) is the dominant vine, and is grown mainly for the production of RAISINS in the two coastal zones to the east and west of Málaga. In order to compensate for the lack of grapes in the region, Pedro Ximénez may also be imported from MONTILLA-MORILES, which abuts Málaga to the north, although according to regulations it may not exceed 10% of the volume.

Traditionally, Málaga was a DRIED-GRAPE WINE made by leaving the grapes in the sun on grass mats for between seven and 20 days to concentrate the natural sugars. Today the wines are made using a number of different methods. The sweetness is normally obtained by arresting the fermentation with grape spirit (as for MISTELA), although some grapes are still dried and can be fermented to 18% alcohol leaving considerable RESIDUAL SUGAR. A third way of adjusting the sweetness is with *arrope*, unfermented grape must that has been boiled down to 30% of its normal volume. This may be added either before or after fermentation.

The wines mature in different sizes of oak COOPERAGE arranged into SOLERAS. The Consejo Regulador recognizes 16 different types of wine ranging from sweet to dry with an ALCOHOLIC STRENGTH between 15 and 23%. Most wines are deep brown, intensely sweet, and raisiny, some tasting slightly burnt through the addition of too much *arrope*. Dry wines are paler with a rather undistinguished nutty character. The most common styles are as follows:

Lágrima: intensely sweet wine made from FREE-RUN juice without any mechanical pressing.
Moscatel: sweet, aromatic wine made exclusively from Moscatel de Alejandría grapes.
Pedro Ximénez (occasionally labelled Pedro Ximen): sweet wine made exclusively from Pedro Ximénez grapes.
Solera: sweet wine from a dated solera.

See also SIERRAS DE MÁLAGA.

R.J.M. & V. de la S.

Malaga Blanc, dominant grape variety in THAILAND, where it is used mainly as a TABLE GRAPE but also produces relatively soft white wine. Originally from the south of France, where it is named Panse de Provence, it is believed that this grape was introduced to Thailand in 1685 by the first Embassy of the King Louis XIV of France to King Narai the Great of Siam. The grapes' thick skins make them usefully resistant to heavy rain.

Malagousia or sometimes **Malagoussia**, elegant white western Greek grape variety rediscovered by Evangelos Gerovassiliou. It yields full-bodied, perfumed wines in many Greek regions.

Malbec, black grape variety once popular in Bordeaux, still the backbone of CAHORS, but given a new lease of life by its obvious success in ARGENTINA. It has many synonyms, of which Galet cites as the true name Côt, or Cot as it is known in much of western France, including the Loire, where it was once quite widely grown. In the Libournais it is known as Pressac, and in Cahors, suggesting origins in northern Burgundy, it was called Auxerrois until Argentine success encouraged adoption of the name Malbec. It also encouraged enthusiasm for the variety in France where total plantings have increased slightly this century, to 6,208 ha/15,334 acres in 2011, some 3,560 ha/8,797 acres in Cahors country. In cooler climates Malbec has some of the disadvantages of Merlot (sensitivity to COULURE, and spring frost) without as much obvious fruit quality. Indeed it can taste like a rather rustic, even shorter-lived version of Merlot, although when grown on the least fertile, high, rugged, limestone vineyards of Cahors it can occasionally remind us why the English used to refer to Cahors as 'the black wine'. Cahors APPELLATION CONTRÔLÉE regulations stipulate that 'Cot' must constitute at least 70% of the wine. Other appellations of SOUTH WEST FRANCE in which Malbec may play a (smaller) part are Bergerac, Buzet, Côtes de Duras, Fronton, Côtes du Marmandais, Pécharmant, and Côtes du Brulhois. It is also theoretically allowed into the Midi threshold appellations of Cabardès and Côtes de la Malepère but is rarely found this far from Atlantic influence.

At one time, especially before the predations of the 1956 frosts, Malbec was quite popular in Bordeaux and is still permitted by all major red bordeaux appellations, but total Bordeaux plantings fell from 4,900 ha/12,100 acres in 1968 to just over 1,000 ha/2,471 acres in 2011, most obviously in Bourg, Blaye, and the Entre-Deux-Mers region. Blended with Cabernet and Gamay, it is also theoretically allowed in a wide range of mid Loire appellations—Anjou, Coteaux du Loir, Touraines of various sorts, and even sparkling Saumur—but has largely been replaced by Cabernets Franc and Sauvignon.

It is in Argentina that Malbec really holds sway, and is now planted on more than 31,000 ha/76,500 acres all over Argentina, making it the country's most planted variety by far. Varietal Argentine Malbecs have some perceptibly Bordelais characteristics, of flavour rather than structure. The wines are generally much more ripe and velvety than their French counterparts, although they are similarly capable of extended AGEING and there is now a will to make rather more delicate, fragrant Malbecs. For more detail, see ARGENTINA.

The commercial success and clear appeal to modern wine drinkers of Argentine Malbec has spawned a new fashion for the variety elsewhere, not least in Chile, where varietal bottlings increased considerably in the early 21st century although total plantings are little more than 1,000 ha/2,471 acres. Chile's version tends to be more tannic than Argentina's and may be blended with the other Bordeaux grapes which Chile grows in such profusion. Viu, Chile's Malbec specialist, and others blend it with Cabernet Sauvignon.

Australians have so far shown no great respect for their Malbec and had been uprooting it systematically until the early 1990s, although poor clonal material was probably partly to blame. Plantings totalled just over 450 ha/1,112 acres in 2012 and some Clare Valley producers have made fine wine from it. In New Zealand producers such as Villa Maria value it as an ingredient in BORDEAUX BLENDS, which is also its usual fate in California (see MERITAGE). Malbec was quite significant in California before PROHIBITION) and plantings have steadily increased this century, to just over 2,600 acres/1,050 ha by 2012.

Many of the small amounts of Malbec, Malbech, or Malbeck planted elsewhere around the world doubtless owe their continued existence to Argentina's success with the variety.

Goldin, C., *The Secrets of Argentine Malbec* (Buenos Aires, 2004).
Robinson, J., Harding, J., and Vouillamoz, J., *Wine Grapes, a complete guide to 1,368 vine varieties, including their origins and flavours* (London, 2012).

Malepère shares many of the wine characteristics of CABARDÈS, another small AOC where the Midi and Aquitaine meet near Carcassonne in the far west of the LANGUEDOC. Climatically, it belongs even more definitively to south west France than to the Languedoc, from which it is geographically protected by the Hautes Corbières peaks. The vineyards, mainly clay and limestone, are immediately north of LIMOUX. The wines, mainly red and some rosé, are made up of a blend of Bordeaux and Languedoc varieties but in the case of Malepère, with its wetter, more Atlantic climate, it is the Bordeaux varieties that predominate. Merlot must make up at least half the blend of reds, with Cabernet Franc and Cot (Malbec) constituting at least 20%, but Cinsaut, Grenache, Lladoner Pelut, and Cabernet Sauvignon are also allowed as minor ingredients. Rosés are based on Cabernet Franc. Wine production is dominated by several large CO-OPERATIVES, of which the determinedly *océanique* Cave du Razès is responsible for almost two-thirds of the region's production.

Malibu Coast, AVA in southern CALIFORNIA approved in 2014 for a 50-mile/80 km stretch of coast north of Santa Monica encompassing the previously established Malibu-Newton Canyon and Saddle Rock-Malibu AVAS in Los Angeles county. About 50 growers share barely 200 acres/81 ha of predominantly Cabernet vines.

malic acid, one of the two principal organic acids of grapes and wines (see also TARTARIC ACID). Its name comes from *malum*, Latin for apple, the fruit in which it was first identified by early scientists. Present in nearly all fruits and berries, malic acid is now known to be one of the compounds involved in the complicated cycles of reactions by which plants and animals obtain the energy necessary for life. One of these cycles of reactions is known as the citric acid, Krebs, or tricarboxylic acid cycle and its elucidation was one of the outstanding triumphs of biochemistry.

Another, which comes into play during the final stages of RIPENING in many fruits, including grapes, causes the decomposition of malic acid. When all of the malic acid has been used up in this latter series of reactions, the fruit becomes overripe, or senescent. The malic acid decomposing reaction is much more rapid in hot summer temperatures, probably because of the more rapid RESPIRATION of malate in the berry. This is, at least in part, one reason for the lower TOTAL ACID concentrations in grapes grown in warmer regions. It accumulates in young grape berries reaching high levels at about VERAISON— sometimes as high as 20 g/l—but, as ripening progresses, the level of malate declines to concentrations of between 1 and 9 g/l when the grapes are ripe. This large range in ripe grapes is an important source of variation in quality and style.

Tartaric acid, the other main grape acid, does not participate in several of the reaction pathways in which malic acid is an essential component, which is why the hotter the summer, the lower the likely proportion of malic acid in the grapes. Malic acid's different chemical structure allows it to participate in many more of the enzymatic reactions involved in living systems than tartaric acid because it can be pumped across plant membranes serving as a transportable energy source. Because the

concentrations of tartaric acid are relatively and desirably stable, attention is given to the tartrate/malate (T/M) ratio, which varies from about 1 to 6 and is characteristic for each grape variety. High malate varieties, with a low ratio, are desirable for hot districts and examples are SYLVANER, COLOMBARD, BARBERA, and CARIGNAN.

Malic acid is lost not just through the citric acid cycle, and through other reaction cycles during grape ripening, but also in many cases as a result of MALOLACTIC CONVERSION. Temperatures of 18–22 °C/64–72 °F encourage the LACTIC ACID BACTERIA involved in malolactic conversion. The winemaker can exercise some control over this loss of malic acid if necessary, however, since the growth and activity of these organisms can be slowed or inhibited by moderate concentrations of SULFUR DIOXIDE. In addition, since the lactic acid bacteria responsible for malolactic conversion require many micronutrients (vitamins, growth factors, nitrogenous compounds), early and thorough separation of the new wine from its LEES can inhibit bacterial activity and preserve malic acid.

Malic acid is available commercially for use in acidifying foods and beverages and in numerous industrial processes. At one time it was isolated from fruits and other plant tissues but is more usually synthesized from another organic acid today.   A.D.W. & B.G.C.

Malleco, cool, wet subregion of the Southern region of CHILE.

Mallorca, Spanish Balearic island in the north-west Mediterranean which was once the seat of the kings of ARAGÓN. In the 19th century, the island was famous for its sweet MALVASIA wines, which all but disappeared when the vineyards fell victim to PHYLLOXERA. Of the 2,500 ha/ 6,175 acres of vines currently in production on the island, 400 belong to the BINISSALEM, Spain's first offshore DO wine region on the island's central plateau, with good, original reds from the local MANTO NEGRO grape. A second DO in the south-eastern part of the island, PLA I LLEVANT, was added in the late 1990s. See also the CALLET grape.

Malmesbury, ward in the SWARTLAND district of SOUTH AFRICA, and an increasingly important source of good-quality wines from often innovative wine producers, many smallscale.

malmsey, English corruption of the word MALVASIA, derived from the port of Monemvasia which was important in Ancient GREECE. The word was first used for (probably a wide range of) the unusually sweet, rich wines of Greece and the islands of the eastern Mediterranean, particularly Crete, then called Candia (see GREECE, medieval history). Sweet white wines

were prized in the Middle Ages, particularly but not exclusively by northern Europeans, who regarded their own wines as thin, and admired the longevity of these liquids, very possibly DRIED-GRAPE WINES, so sturdily high in sugar and alcohol. The acute merchants of GENOA, NAPLES, and VENICE were able profitably to capitalize on this stability in their trading links between east and west.

As European temperatures fell as a result of CLIMATE CHANGE, these richer wines held even more allure. Venetians in particular created a demand for malmsey in 15th-century England. George, duke of Clarence and younger brother of England's King Edward IV, was popularly believed to have been drowned in a BUTT of malmsey in the Tower of London in 1478.

Malvasia vines came to be planted all round the western Mediterranean (even today, Malvasia and MALVOISIE are two of the most commonly used synonyms for various, often quite unrelated, VINE VARIETIES). Malmsey, which originally denoted any strong, sweet wine, was eventually used specifically for the sweetest style of MADEIRA, particularly that made from Malvasia grapes.

Between 2010 and 2012, a number of new PDOS were introduced in GREECE for barrel-aged, sweet white wines made from sun-dried grapes, mainly from a mix of varieties, referred to under the group name of Malvasia. Malvasia of Monemvasia in the Peloponnese, Malvasia of Handakas-Candia, and Malvasia of Sitia in Crete, and Malvasia of Paros are in essence Greece's modern claim to the legendary style of the Middle Ages.

malolactic conversion, widely known as **malolactic fermentation**, and often abbreviated to **MLF** or **malo**, is the conversion of stronger MALIC ACID naturally present in new wine into LACTIC ACID (which has lower ACIDITY) and CARBON DIOXIDE. The term conversion is more accurate because it is not literally a fermentation process, although the release of carbon dioxide may initially give that impression. It is accomplished by LACTIC ACID BACTERIA, which are naturally present in most established wineries but may have to be cultured and carefully introduced in newer establishments where malolactic conversion is desired. This process is unrelated to and almost never precedes the main, alcoholic FERMENTATION, for which reason it is sometimes called a secondary fermentation. Nevertheless, it is not uncommon for malolactic conversion to be complete by the end of the alcoholic fermentation.

It is written chemically thus:

$$COOH-CHOH-CH_2-COOH \rightarrow COOH-CHOH-CH_3 + CO_2$$

malic acid→lactic acid + carbon dioxide

Malolactic conversion is conducted for three reasons: decrease in wine ACIDITY, wine stability (see STABILIZATION), and sensory (aroma and flavour) changes. It is desirable in wines which have excessive acidity, particularly red wines produced in cooler climates. It can also add flavour and complexity to both red and white wines, as well as rendering the wine impervious to the danger of malolactic conversion in bottle. Recognition and mastery of malolactic conversion (which would traditionally happen as if by accident when temperatures rose in the spring) was one of the key developments in winemaking in France and elsewhere in the mid 20th century. By the early 1990s, most fine red wines, many sparkling wines, and a small but increasing proportion of the world's white wine involved full or partial malolactic conversion, thanks either to the lactic acid bacteria present in the winery or to cultured LAB added to the wine. In hotter climates or warmer years in cooler areas, some winemakers deliberately suppress malolactic conversion in some or all batches of a wine in order to maintain the wine's acidity. Some grape varieties seem to have a greater affinity with malolactic conversion than others. Among white grapes, Chardonnay is a generally successful candidate for the process, while most producers of Riesling and Chenin Blanc deliberately avoid it, despite the high natural acidity in these latter two. Malolactic conversion may reduce unduly the acidity of a wine made from very ripe grapes and already low in acidity, and production of the buttery-smelling DIACETYL during malolactic conversion needs to be managed since excess diacetyl can be unpleasant, as was often observed in early trials with malolactic conversion in some white wines. Malolactic conversion's effect on decreasing TOTAL ACIDITY is often most marked on those wines which were highest in malic acid before it took place, i.e. the products of particularly cool growing seasons. In some cases, the winemaker may even have to ACIDIFY after malolactic conversion.

Like most BACTERIA, lactic acid bacteria grow best in very weakly acidic solutions and at temperatures above 20 °C/68 °F. Malolactic conversion is strongly influenced not only by temperature but also by the wine's PH: if it is less than 3.1, it is very difficult, but commonly practised under such conditions in Champagne and Burgundy. Lactic acid bacteria are intolerant of even moderate concentrations of SULFUR DIOXIDE and high concentrations of ETHANOL. Malolactic conversion can therefore be encouraged by adding lactic acid bacteria to the wine soon after alcoholic fermentation has finished. Alternatively, they can be added to the MUST at, or soon after, the start of alcoholic fermentation; this is often referred to as co-inoculation or simultaneous inoculation. At this point

conditions are ideal for the lactic acid bacteria—the fermenting wine is warm, its alcohol content is low, the sulfur dioxide added before fermentation has already been volatilized, and the dying yeast cells, or LEES, provide the necessary micronutrients. Co-inoculation is becoming increasingly popular but some oenologists believe it to be detrimental to wine quality because it happens very quickly and at higher temperatures. If malolactic conversion has not been initiated during the alcoholic fermentation (or during post-fermentation MACERATION of reds), the new wine may be transferred to barrels or stainless steel tanks where the malolactic conversion will take place. Barrels in which malolactic conversion has taken place in a previous vintage may encourage the onset of this process but it is very important to know what was in the container before so that no form of spoilage is encouraged. Putting fine red wine in barrel prior to the onset of malolactic conversion became fashionable in the early 21st century because it was believed to improve the oak integration and make the wines more approachable when young (particularly useful for EN PRIMEUR tastings), although some winemakers would take the opposite view.

Malolactic conversion may well be regarded as undesirable in some wines, particularly in certain styles of white and sparkling wine. In this case, sulfur dioxide additions and cool temperatures can prevent the activity of lactic acid bacteria. Sterile FILTRATION can insure against the commercial embarrassment of malolactic conversion's taking place in bottle. If a bottled still wine starts to fizz, this is the most likely cause and is most commonly encouraged by the combination of heat and residual lactic acid bacteria. See FAULTS IN WINE for more.

A.D.W. & E.J.B.

Abrahamase, C., and Bartowsky, E., 'Inoculation for MLF reduces overall vinification time: new research based on laboratory and winery trials in Shiraz delivers potential time and cost benefits', *The Australian & New Zealand Grapegrower & Winemaker*, 578 (2012), 41–6.

Bartowsky, E. J., 'Malolactic fermentation', in V. K. Joshi (ed.), *Handbook of Enology: Principles, Practices and Recent Innovations* (New York, 2011), 526–63.

Lonvaud-Funel, A., 'Understanding wine lactic acid bacteria. Progress and prospects in controlling wine quality', paper presented at the ASEV 50th anniversary annual meeting, Seattle (Washington, 2000).

Malta, the central Mediterranean island, has a small wine industry that can trace its history back to Phoenician times, but it was the arrival of the Knights of St John in 1530 that laid the foundations of today's wine industry. Viticulture in Malta flourished until the arrival of the British in 1800, when many vineyards (and

olive groves) were uprooted in favour of cotton. By the end of the 19th century, when demand for Maltese cotton had diminished, a replanting programme of sorts was started and in spite of the outbreak of PHYLLOXERA in 1919, viticulture flourished once again. By the 1950s 1,000 ha/ 2,470 acres were under vine.

The majority of vines planted were TABLE GRAPE varieties which produced wines so low in sugar and acid that considerable adjustments were needed in wineries rarely equipped for high-quality wine production. The most popular were Ġellewża, which makes soft, fleshy reds and aromatic, fruity dry rosés, while Gennarua and the superior Girgentina make weighty white wines. Most of these indigenous vines are grown as BUSH VINES without IRRIGATION and harvested at the end of August. By the mid 1980s, area under vine was just 320 ha/ 790 acres.

Some 1950s experiments with Muscat and Trebbiano were relatively successful but it was not until the 1970s that another serious attempt was made with wine grape varieties, this time Cabernet Sauvignon planted by Marsovin at Wardija in the north of the island. TOURISM boomed in the 1980s and demand for wine grew. The principal wineries were allowed to produce 'Maltese' wine from imported grapes or MUST. During the 1990s, many new vineyards were planted and with the help of DRIP IRRIGATION and French and Italian expertise, various other VINIFERA varieties were planted.

Only when Malta joined the EU in 2004 were labels required to distinguish between wines made from domestic and imported grapes. The EU also funded 1,000 ha/2,471 acres of new vineyards which made the island self-sufficient. In 2007 Malta introduced its DOK (equivalent to the EU's PDO) and IGT (PGI) production protocols very similar to Italy's system. Of dozens of different varieties so far planted on the island, Syrah, Sirkuzan (NERO D'AVOLA), and more recently, Mourvèdre so far show most promise.

Land holdings vary from 0.1 to 20 ha. Most small farmers sell their grapes under contract to either Delicata, Marsovin, or Camilleri. The last two wineries merged in 2013. A group of farmers formed a CO-OPERATIVE based in the ancient gardens of Buskett in the middle of the island. Meridiana is another important winery now wholly owned by ANTINORI. Ta Mena is a relative newcomer with mainly Sirkuzan vineyards on the sister island of Gozo. Best known of the smaller producers is San Niklaw in the village of Zejtun where Mourvèdre does well.

Vineyards typically have relatively shallow, poor, LOAMY topsoil on SAND, LIMESTONE, and CLAY with richer and more fertile clayey soils in the north. Some ALLUVIAL soils can be found in the valleys. The climate is MEDITERRANEAN with hot, dry summers and cool, rainy winters.

The average mean temperatures vary from 12.8 °C/55 °F in January to 25.6 °C/78 °F in July. Average rainfall is 575 mm/27 in but is so concentrated in the winter months that IRRIGATION is needed.   M.T.

Malvar. See LAIRÉN.

Malvasia, name used widely, especially in Iberia and Italy, for at least 20 different grape varieties. Wines produced from them are, typically, deeply coloured whites but some are, usually light, reds.

The word Malvasia itself is thought to be the Italian corruption of Monemvasia, the southern Greek port which, in the Middle Ages, was a busy and natural entrepôt for the rich and highly prized dessert wines of the eastern Mediterranean, notably those of Crete, or Candia (see GREECE, history)—although it is not known which grape varieties were responsible for these wines. They may not even have included any of the varieties known today as Malvasia of some sort. But so important was wine from Monemvasia during the time of the Venetian republic that wine shops in VENICE were called *malvasie*.

The French corruption of Malvasia has been used particularly loosely (see MALVOISIE). The word was also corrupted into MALMSEY in English, which was for long an important style of MADEIRA, traditionally based on the Malvasia di Lipari grape. The Germans call their various though rare forms of Malvasia **Malvasier**.

Italy grows more wine called Malvasia of some form than any other country, with 15 different varieties distinguished in its 2010 vine census. Most planted, with 4,876 ha/ 12,049 acres, was **Malvasia Bianca di Candia**, which produces relatively neutral wine in Lazio and throughout Central Italy. The variety known as **Malvasia di Candia Aromatico**, quite widely planted in Italy and Greece, is apparently different and closer to **Malvasia di Casorzo**, a red-berried, relatively rare speciality of Piemonte. Italy's second most planted Malvasia is simply called Malvasia Bianca in the 2010 census, which noted total plantings of 4,354 ha/10,759 acres. Third most common was **Malvasia Bianca Lunga** was counted as 2,259 ha/5,582 acres in 2010 (although that called simply Malvasia Bianca may well be Malvasia Bianca Lunga too). This is the variety, once called Malvasia del Chianti, most common in Tuscany for both dry wines and VIN SANTO and is also grown, as Marăstina, in Croatia (which is probably close to the Croatian variety called MALVAZIJA ISTARSKA, known as Malvasia Istriana when grown in north east Italy where it can produce some fine VARIETAL examples).

Total plantings of **Malvasia del Lazio**, a cross of MUSCAT of Alexandria and SCHIAVA GROSSA, had fallen to below 600 ha/1,482 acres. The

speciality of Basilicata, **Malvasia Bianca di Basilicata**, may be related to Malvasia Bianco di Candia. Plantings had fallen to 210 ha/519 acres by 2010. Other, less quantitatively significant pale-skinned grapes called Malvasia noted in the Italian vine census of 2010 included the widespread **Malvasia di Lipari**, which is grown on the Italian island of the same name for sweet PASSITO WINES; also known as Malvasia di Sardinia (and differentiated on the Italian census) for that island's Malvasias of various sweetnesses; as Greco Bianco di Gerace for the sweet wines of the Calabrian port of Bianco; as Malvasia Cândida to produce malmsey on the island of MADEIRA where only tiny plantings remain); and as various Malvasias in Catalunya and the Canary islands.

The Italian vine census also distinguishes between a further dark- or pink-berried Malvasias of which **Malvasia Nera di Brindisi** (identical to Malvasia Nera di Lecce and a cross of Malvasia Bianca Lunga and the Puglian red wine grape Negroamaro) is the most planted with 879 ha/2,172 acres, making it more common than southern Italy's other red wine Malvasia, **Malvasia Nera di Basilicata**. (At the time of writing DNA profiling had not yet established whether these two southern Italian dark-skinned Malvasias were distinct but they are both used to produce with robust pink wines characteristic of southern Italy.) **Malvasia Nera Lunga** was less quantitatively important than either and is a speciality of Asti in Piemonte. The census also notes a further hectare of a variety called simply Malvasia Nera, as well as **Malvasia di Schierano** that makes light, fragrant reds in Piemonte.

The variety more commonly planted to produce malmsey on Madeira today is a much newer variety called **Malvasia Branca de São Jorge** whose wines are usefully high in both sugar and acidity. Portugal grows several other Malvasias of note. The most important true Malvasia is **Malvasia Fina**, which goes under many aliases, including the slightly confusing one of BOAL, of which there were more than 3,000 ha/7,413 acres in 2012. It is most important in the dry whites of Dão although it is widely grown in other northern Portuguese regions such as Douro. Dark-berried **Malvasia Preta**, also known as Moreto and Mureto, is grown on 1,540 ha/3,805 acres of vineyard mainly in the Douro for port and red table wines. Pale-skinned **Malvasia de Colares**, the dominant grape of the shrinking COLARES region where 1,010 ha/2,496 acres, mainly ungrafted, remained in 2012. Malvasia Rei is the Portuguese synonym for PALOMINO FINO, while Malvasia Castellana is another name for SÍRIA.

In Spain, Malvasía di Sitges is Malvasia di Lipari but **Malvasía di Lanzarote** is an historic speciality of that particular Canary island and can make full-bodied, aromatic whites of real

interest. It may be a cross of Malvasia di Lipari and the local MARMAJUELO. About half of all 4,000 ha/9,884 acres Malvasía growing in Spain in 2012 was in the Canary islands while most of the rest was Malvasia Castellana, a synonum for the Síria of Portugal, called Sigüente in EXTREMADURA, in Castilla–León. None was noted in Rioja even though it was traditionally responsible for white rioja.

The aromatic, thick-skinned variety known simply as Malvasia Bianca in California and grown on about 1,300 acres/526 ha of mainly Central Valley vineyard was brought there from Piemonte and is known strictly as **Malvasia Bianca di Piemonte**. It makes full bodied, tangy, flirtatious whites there.

So common is Malvasia as part of a grape name or synonym that no fewer than 70 are listed in the index of the book *Wine Grapes*.

Robinson, J., Harding, J., and Vouillamoz, J., *Wine Grapes, a complete guide to 1,368 vine varieties, including their origins and flavours* (London, 2012).

Malvazija Istarska, characteristic and characterful white wine grape of the Istrian peninsula in northern CROATIA. Known as Malvasia Istriana in north-east Italy. It is genetically close to MALVASIA di Lipari, Malvasia Bianca Lunga, and Malvasia Nera di Brindisi.

malvidin is the PHENOLIC pigment primarily responsible for the colour of red wine. It is found in wine as malvidin 3-glucoside and various acylated derivatives.

Malvoisie is one of France's most confusing vine names, perhaps because, like PINEAU, the term was once used widely as a general term for superior wines, notably those whose origins were supposed to be Greek. There is no single variety whose principal name is Malvoisie, but it has been used as a synonym for a wide range of, usually white-berried, grape varieties producing full-bodied, aromatic whites. Despite the etymological similarity, Malvoisie has only rarely been a synonym for MALVASIA. Malvoisie is today found on the labels of some Loire, Savoie, and Aosta wines made from such plantings of PINOT GRIS as remain, as Malvoisie du Valais is a common synonym for, usually sweet, Pinot Gris in Switzerland. It is also sometimes used for BOURBOULENC in the Languedoc, for CLAIRETTE in Bordeaux, and for SAVAGNIN in the Austrian Tyrol. VERMENTINO is sometimes called Malvoisie in Roussillon and Corsica.

Malvoisie Rouge d'Italie is an occasional synonym for FRÜHROTER VELTLINER in Savoie and northern Italy.

Robinson, J., Harding, J., and Vouillamoz, J., *Wine Grapes, a complete guide to 1,368 vine varieties, including their origins and flavours* (London, 2012).

Mammolo, heavily perfumed, historic red grape variety producing wines which supposedly smell of violets, or *mammole*, in central Italy. It seems to have played a significant genetic role in several Tuscan vine varieties. A permitted ingredient in CHIANTI, and VINO NOBILE DI MONTEPULCIANO, it was planted on 50 ha/123 acres in 2010. Today it is quantitatively much more important as Corsica's SCIACARELLO.

Mancha, La, Europe's largest single demarcated wine region in the heart of Spain (see map under SPAIN). By 2012 the vineyards of the DO La Mancha had shrunk to 160,000 ha/385,000 acres of arid table land from the satellite towns south of Madrid to the hills beyond VALDEPEÑAS nearly 200 km/125 miles to the south. The Moors christened it Manxa, meaning 'parched earth', and that is an apt description of the growing conditions in southern Castile, CASTILLA-LA MANCHA. RAINFALL is unreliable, with annual totals averaging between 300 and 400 mm/12 to 16 in. Summers are hot with temperatures rising to over 40 °C/104 °F, while winters are bitterly cold with prolonged FROSTS.

The doughty AIRÉN vine seems to be well suited to these extreme conditions and is therefore popular among La Mancha's 18,000 smallholders. It was planted on a grand total of about 180,000 ha of La Mancha, and about 65% of all land dedicated to the DO. It is planted at the remarkably low VINE DENSITY of between 1,200 and 1,600 vines per hectare (485–650 per acre) because of the very dry climate. FUNGAL DISEASES are almost unknown in La Mancha's dry growing season and cultivation is therefore relatively easy. Average YIELDS of between 40 and 45 hl/ha (1.9 tons/acre) have increased significantly with the increase in TRELLIS systems and DRIP IRRIGATION which extended to more than 40% of vineyards by 2014.

Technological development has given La Mancha a new lease of life and opened new and more discerning markets for the region's fresh, inexpensive, if rather neutral dry white wines. Red wines, made increasingly from Cencibel (TEMPRANILLO) grapes, have also improved enormously and a number of enterprising growers are experimenting with other grape varieties, including CABERNET SAUVIGNON, SYRAH, PETIT VERDOT, GRACIANO, VERDEJO, SAUVIGNON BLANC, and CHARDONNAY, now admitted and even encouraged by DO regulations. Despite the reduction in total vineyard area, annual production has risen from 2 to 7 million hl/185 million gal produced annually, a large part is still distilled into industrial alcohol or sent to JEREZ to make brandy de Jerez.   V. de la S.

www.lamanchawines.com

Manchuela, one of Spain's newest wine regions, granted a DO in 2000, with vineyards totalling more than 55,000 ha/130,000 acres (although only 3,700 ha of these were registered for DO wines in 2014) on the eastern border of CASTILLA-LA MANCHA, straddling Cuenca and Albacete provinces. This is the home of the Bobal grape, which is mainly used for rosés and unoaked young reds, with Tempranillo growing in importance for oak-aged reds. At least one private estate was making a name for itself by adapting Syrah to the local clay-limestone TERROIR and making blends with the best local varieties Monastrell, Garnacha, Garnacha Tintorera (ALICANTE BOUSCHET), and Bobal. The white Macabeo also produces very drinkable fragrant whites in northern Albacete, while the local Albilla de Manchuela has been rediscovered as a good quality grape. Overall, this high plateau, which reaches an elevation of more than 1,000 m/3,280 ft in western Cuenca shows great potential but has mostly lacked the investment required to develop it.

V. de la S.

Mandilaria, distinctive speciality of various Greek islands, including Crete, where it is often blended with the much softer KOTSIFALI. The grapes have thick skins and therefore the wine produced is deep coloured and notably high in TANNINS. It can produce harmonious dry reds such as Peza, or even sweet reds. Known as Amorghiano on Rhodes. Total plantings in 2012 were just under 1,000 ha/2,500 acres.

manganese, a soil nutrient essential for vine growth but in very low quantities. Manganese deficiency causes leaf yellowing, and is found most commonly on soils high in LIMESTONE and other alkaline soils. Acid soils (see SOIL ACIDITY) which are poorly drained and high in manganese can cause toxicity, reducing both vine growth and YIELD.   R.E.S. & R.E.W.

manipulation, a slightly pejorative term referring to a range of interventions made by winemakers. Wine is unusual among alcoholic drinks in that once the grapes have been picked and put into a container, it can more or less make itself. However, winemakers almost always intervene in a variety of ways in order to achieve particular quality or stylistic goals. These range from traditional techniques such as DESTEMMING, CRUSHING, SAIGNÉE, CHAPTALIZATION, BARREL FERMENTATION, LEES STIRRING, AGEING in barrel, RACKING, CLARIFICATION, and FILTRATION to more modern steps such as the use of ENZYMES, cold MACERATION, CRYOEXTRACTION, cultured YEASTS, REVERSE OSMOSIS, MICRO-OXYGENATION, SPINNING CONE COLUMNS and OAK CHIPS—or, more likely, a combination of these methods. Many of these practices are controlled by regulations in most wine-producing countries. In general, those that have been practised for many years (such as chaptalization) are less controversial, even though they may be more interventionist and open to abuse than modern equivalents (such as reverse osmosis).   J.A.G. & J.E.H.

Goode, J., *Wine Science : The Application of Science in Winemaking* (2nd edn, London, 2014).

mannoproteins are POLYSACCHARIDES released from YEAST cells during FERMENTATION and by AUTOLYSIS during LEES ageing. Their release is generally considered beneficial and is encouraged by slightly higher fermentation temperatures and the length of time the wine is in contact with the yeast lees. Mannoproteins have the potential to protect white and rosé wine from PROTEIN HAZE and can inhibit TARTRATE crystal formation. They may also reduce the perception of ASTRINGENCY by disrupting the binding of salivary proteins with TANNINS. Finally, mannoproteins released during yeast autolysis have been demonstrated to improve the foaming properties of SPARKLING WINE.   R.G.

Moine-Ledoux, V., and Dubourdieu, D., 'Role of yeast mannoproteins with regard to tartaric stabilisation of wines', *Le Bulletin de l'OIV*, 75/857–8 (2002), 471–82.

Núñez, Y. P., et al., 'Isolation and characterization of a thermally extracted yeast cell wall fraction potentially useful for improving the foaming properties of sparkling wines', *Journal of Agricultural and Food Chemistry*, 54/20 (2006), 7898–903.

Quijada-Morín, N., et al., 'Polyphenolic, polysaccharide and oligosaccharide composition of Tempranillo red wines and their relationship with the perceived astringency', *Food Chemistry*, 154 (2014), 44–51. doi: 10.1016/j.foodchem.2013.12.101.

Waters, E. J., et al., 'Preventing protein haze in bottled wine', *Australian Journal of Grape and Wine Research*, 11 (2005), 215–25.

Manseng Noir, Basque vine variety that DNA PROFILING suggests is identical to the Ferrón of RIBEIRO. See also the white wine grapes GROS MANSENG and PETIT MANSENG.

Manseng, usually Petit Manseng, can also be found in Uruguay, where it, like TANNAT, was taken by Basque settlers in the 19th century.

Manto Negro, most common grape on MALLORCA, producing scented but light reds which tend to age and even OXIDIZE early. It may be best blended with a more structured grape such as CALLET.

manzanilla, a specially refreshing style of SHERRY that is made quite naturally in the seaside sherry town of SANLÚCAR DE BARRAMEDA. Like FINO, it is a very pale, light, dry style of wine that is heavily influenced by FLOR yeast, but manzanilla is made in the particularly humid, maritime air of Sanlúcar, which tends to result in a thicker layer of flor, a slower maturation process, lower alcohol content, and slightly higher acidity—especially since grapes are often picked slightly less ripe than for *fino*. As the wine matures, and the flor dies, a manzanilla may develop into a **Manzanilla Olorosa** and then a **Manzanilla Pasada**, which is a

Sanlúcar equivalent of a fino amontillado. Most manzanilla is now lightly fortified to 15% alcohol. For more details, see SHERRY.

Manzoni. See INCROCIO.

Mara, red grapevine CROSS created at CHANGINS from Gamay and Reichensteiner and released in 2009, 19 years later than its sister crosses GAMARET and GARANOIR. The wines are fruity, spicy, and rich in colour. It was planted on about 6 ha/14 acres in Switzerland in 2012.   J.V.

Maranges, the southernmost VILLAGE WINE appellation in the Côte de Beaune district of Burgundy, produces medium-bodied red wines of some charm when young. The vineyard stretches across the three villages of Cheilly, Dezize, and Sampigny, each of which takes Les Maranges as a suffix. Formerly the wines were sold either under the village name or, much more frequently, as Côte de Beaune-Villages. Since 1988, such wines may be called Maranges or **Maranges Côte de Beaune**. White wines counted for only 10% of production in 2012 but are becoming more common.

See also CÔTE D'OR, and map under BURGUNDY.
J.T.C.M.

marc, the general French term both for grape POMACE and, more widely, for pomace brandy. It is used to distinguish the product from a *fine*, which may be made by distilling local wine. Most traditional wine regions make marc from the pomace, grape skins, and pips left after pressing. This was rarely for financial gain but often because peasant wine-growers hate to see anything they have grown go to waste.

Marche (**Marches** in English), the easternmost region in the central belt of Italy stretching from TUSCANY through UMBRIA to the Adriatic coast (see map under ITALY). It shares a variety of characteristics with these neighbours to the west: a TOPOGRAPHY shaped by land rising from the coastal plains to rolling hills and, westward, to the central spine of the Apennines; and a TEMPERATE climate that, though it is marked by hot, dry summers, is not as uniform as its western neighbours. In the northern part of the region around Ancona, the climate is CONTINENTAL, while in the south near Ascoli Piceno it is MEDITERRANEAN. This has an impact on the grape varieties that perform best in the north and south of the Marche. Some viticultural characteristics are shared with Tuscany and Umbria: CALCAREOUS soils from the sea which once covered an important part of central Italy; HILLSIDE VINEYARDS; and large-scale plantings of SANGIOVESE, MONTEPULCIANO and VERDICCHIO vines. The Marche has been the last of the three central Italian regions to realize its potential for good-quality wines, however, partly because the region is off Italy's

main commercial axis of Milan–Bologna–Florence–Rome–Naples, and partly because of the lack of any urban centre more important than Ancona. However, the local white VERDICCHIO, produced in large volumes by co-ops and large bottlers, is a continuous export success, although it has obscured the fact that high-quality wines, provided yields are kept in check, can and are being made.

The Marche has several authentic wine styles that are now of serious interest with more vineyards (10,376 ha/25,629 acres) dedicated to DOC wines (10,376 ha) than ever. Of its 15 DOCs and three DOCGs, Verdicchio di Castelli di Jesi with 2,762 ha of vineyards is Marche's largest.

For red wines, Montepulciano, with 4,289 ha/10,598 acres, is the second most planted variety after Sangiovese (6,215 ha/15,357 acres) and produces its finest expression in Conero DOCG. Rosso Conero DOC is very similar except that notably higher yields are allowed: 13 rather than 9 tonnes/ha. The best producers stick to much lower yields.

The ubiquitous Sangiovese features in no fewer than six of the Marche's 15 DOCs. Traditionally it was blended with Montepulciano in the Rosso Piceno DOC, but the once-obligatory minimum 50% has been reduced to 15%, while VARIETAL Sangioveses are also now allowed within this DOC. Rosso Piceno Superiore indicates a smaller historic zone with marginally lower yields. The quality of both DOCs can be irregular, from fine oak-aged wines to modest stainless steel-fermented, early-drinking versions. Sangiovese from the Colli Pesaresi near the coast in the north of the region, can be particularly elegant, notably that of Fattoria Mancini. A local speciality are the medium-bodied, fresh, perfumed reds of the growing Lacrima di Moro d'Alba zone near the town of Moro d'Alba in the north eastern corner of the Verdicchio di Castelli di Jesi zone. Offida white wines, promoted in the early 2010s from DOC to DOCG, can be produced either from the Pecorino or Passerina grapes, while red Offida must be at least 85% Montepulciano. Offida Pecorino, in particular, has benefited from the ambitions of a new generation of wine producers determined to unleash its potential by lowering yields. Curiously the parallel DOC Terre di Offida is reserved for white wines only.

See also VERDICCHIO.   W.S.

Merlini, P., and Silvestri, M., *Un Altroviaggio nelle Marche* (Rome, 2012).
www.imtdoc.it

Marcillac, isolated, small, but growing AOC in SOUTH WEST FRANCE whose vigorous red wines can have real character. This is the liveliest wine district of the Aveyron *département* (although see also the ENTRAYGUES–LE FEL and ESTAING), but it can be hard to preserve the viticultural tradition here in the harsh climate of the Massif

Central at elevations up to 600 m/2,000 ft. Although there were several thousand hectares of vines here in the late 19th century, by 2012 there were 188 ha/464 acres of VINIFERA vines dedicated to the appellation (many growers responded to the PHYLLOXERA crisis by planting HYBRIDS). Marcillac, usually red and sometimes rosé, must be made of at least 90% FER, here often called Mansois, a hard-wooded vine capable of making peppery, aromatic mountain wines with excellent structure. BARREL MATURATION has been introduced to temper the high acidity of wines which, unlike many of the Bordeaux duplicates produced in the south west, are highly distinctive. The local CO-OPERATIVE at Valady is an important producer, as is Le Vieux Porche.

marcottage, French term for the LAYERING method of vine propagation in the vineyard.

Maréchal Foch, red wine grape variety named after a famous French First World War general. This FRENCH HYBRID was bred by Eugène Kuhlmann of Alsace, who cited the VINIFERA variety Goldriesling as one parent. It has good winter hardiness and ripens very early. It was once widely cultivated in the Loire and is still popular in CANADA and NEW YORK, where it is spelt **Marechal Foch**, is sometimes called simply Foch, and may be vinified using CARBONIC MACERATION. It produces fruity, non-FOXY wines which can stand on their own two feet.

Maremma, long, loosely defined strip of TUSCAN coastline south of Livorno (Leghorn) extending southward through the province of Grosseto. (Lazio also has its part of the Maremma, between Civitavecchia and the border with Tuscany, but this is not a viticultural zone.) Since 1995 it has also been the name of an IGT which was elevated to DOC in 2011 but, perversely, without more rigorous production rules. Within its borders lie no fewer than eight DOCs and four DOCGs, but although the area is extremely extensive, in 2012 only 1,665 ha/4,113 acres were declared DOC Maremma—modest in comparison with CHIANTI CLASSICO's 6,818 ha/16,847 acres. It cannot be used for declassifying wines from the many DOCs within the region, therefore it is potentially attractive only to producers in obscure DOCs whose names do not resonate with wine lovers. The Alta Maremma (Upper Maremma) is the highest part of the region in the north between Massa Marittima and Roccastrada where vineyards are situated at ELEVATIONS between 150 and 500 m (490–1,640 ft), providing a cooler MESOCLIMATE than the warm Maremma plain, and resulting in more elegant wines.

In etymological terms, the word Maremma derives from the Latin *mare*, or sea, and is related to the French *marais*. Like the MÉDOC in Bordeaux, the low-lying parts of the

Maremma were swampy or marshy for much of their history with chronic problems of malaria.

Production of bottled wine is consequently a recent phenomenon and quality wine can be said to date from the first bottles of SASSICAIA in the 1970s, although the zone of Morellino di Scansano, high and relatively malaria free, enjoyed a certain reputation in the past. Thanks to the success of Sassicaia and, later, ORNELLAIA, the mid 1990s saw an investment boom in the Maremma, its apparent potential for large-scale vineyards on relatively inexpensive land attracting many prestigious producers. Because the much warmer climate here results in riper grapes, it quickly became a source of blending wine for beefing up other Tuscan DOCs. The history of the region is so recent that eight of its 12 DOCs and DOCGs did not exist prior to 1989 (Bolgheri itself having been elevated only in 1983), while several small DOCs owe their status to the success of remarkably few producers, Suvereto being an example.

Sassicaia laid the foundation stone for successful Cabernet-based wines, and many estates tried to copy the style while often supplementing their vineyards with plantings of Merlot and Syrah, but the results often lack the elegance and age-worthiness of the prototype. BARRIQUE ageing is still the standard, although large oak casks are increasingly used instead. Even if almost every DOC within the Maremma has a provision for the production of INTERNATIONAL VARIETIES, be it as an added percentage or as varietally labelled wines, Sangiovese is still the most common and mandatory ingredient in most of the wines here.

In the Maremma there are three important areas, all promoted to DOCG in 2009. Morellino di Scansano DOCG is Maremma's classic zone for Sangiovese near Grosseto around the town of Scansano. Vineyards rise up to 450 m while Sangiovese (here called Morellino) tends to be fuller bodied on lower-lying vineyards. Like Chianti Classico, the wines must contain a minimum of 85% of Sangiovese. Montecucco Sangiovese DOCG, north east of Grosseto and further inland than Morellino di Scansano, shares its provision of a minimum of 85% Sangiovese. Unremarkable in the past, it has attracted newcomers unable to afford vineyards in Chianti Classico and Montalcino who have begun to produce high-quality Sangiovese wines. Montecucco DOC is for whites based on Vermentino and reds with up to 60% Sangiovese. Val di Cornia Rosso DOCG on the Tuscan coast south east of Suvereto, on a spit of land jutting out into the Mediterranean, is for blends of Sangiovese, Merlot, and Cabernet while the Val di Cornia Bianco DOC is for whites made from Vermentino and Ansonica (the DOC Ansonica Costa dell'Argentario on the coast near the rocky promontory of Argentario is reserved for whites with a minimum of 85% Ansonica, the same variety as Sicily's INZOLIA).

The DOC Monteregio di Massa Marittima, extending over a large area between the coast and the town of Roccastrada, features Sangiovese for reds and Vermentino for whites, complemented by international varieties. Rising up to 500 m, the hills here are virgin vineyard land but the few wines produced here are generally elegant and fresh, suggesting that it has an interesting future.

Bolgheri apart, the Maremma has not turned out to be the promised land it appeared to be in the mid 1990s, although it may eventually produce some excellent wines from vineyards planted with the right varieties and clones, and, crucially, in the best sites.   W.S.

Margaret River, most important wine region in WESTERN AUSTRALIA, air conditioned by the warm Indian Ocean. First-class Chardonnay (Leeuwin Estate) and Cabernet/Merlot (Cullen et al.) from a total of nearly 150 producers.

margarodes, otherwise known as ground pearls, are a serious insect pest in some vineyards, although they are, fortunately, found only in certain restricted regions. Margarodes weaken and kill vines with a similar action to PHYLLOXERA, and afflicted vines normally die about four years after a decline in VIGOUR is noted.

While many species of margarodes occur on a wide range of host plants worldwide, the most damaging to vines is the *Margarodes vitis* of South America. There are ten species of margarodes in South Africa, five of which infest vine roots, with *Margarodes prieskaensis* being one of the most damaging. The pre-adult insect is a round cyst which attaches itself to the roots, and is covered by a hard, waxy covering. The insects are conspicuous by their foul odour.

The mature cysts can remain inactive in the soil for many years. Winged male and female forms mate above the soil surface and eggs are laid in the vicinity of vine roots in early summer. There are no sources of resistance to ground pearls within the VITIS genus which includes vines, so control by grafting on to resistant ROOTSTOCKS seems unlikely.   R.E.S.

Margaux, potentially the most seductive appellation of the Haut-MÉDOC district of Bordeaux. At their stereotypical best, the wines of Margaux combine the deep ruby colour, structure, and concentration of any top-quality Médoc with a haunting perfume and a silkier texture than is found to the north in ST-JULIEN, PAUILLAC, and ST-ESTÈPHE. Mid-20th-century vintages from its two finest properties Ch Margaux (see below) and Ch Palmer certainly demonstrated this and helped to develop this conception of Margaux. Margaux is the most southerly, most isolated, and most extensive of the Médoc's communal appellations (see map under BORDEAUX). Although it is made of several non-contiguous parcels of the best portions of vineyard land, inferior parcels qualifying merely as Haut-Médoc, the appellation takes in not just the substantial village of Margaux, but also the neighbouring communities of Cantenac, Soussans, Labarde, and Arsac.

In total almost 1,500 ha/3,750 acres qualified for the Margaux appellation in the mid 2010s, and within its boundaries there are inevitably considerable variations in both topography and soil type. Within the apellation is limestone, chalk, clay, and sand, but most of the finest wines should come from gentle outcrops, or *croupes*, where gravel predominates and DRAINAGE is good—although properties here are particularly parcellated and intermingled with one estate often comprising very different, and often distant, plots of land. Ch Margaux, for example, has vineyards in both Cantenac and Soussans.

Margaux has in the past enjoyed enormous *réclame*, and more Margaux properties were included in the 1855 CLASSIFICATION of the Médoc and Graves (more than 20) than from any other appellation. The appellation clearly still has great potential, but in the 1970s, 1980s, and even 1990s a curious number of châteaux failed to keep pace with the substantial improvements in wine quality achieved in the other three major appellations of the Médoc.

Ch Margaux itself, the FIRST GROWTH standard-bearer as well as name-bearer for the appellation, was revived only in 1978 after more than a decade of disappointing vintages (see below for more details). Of the five second growths within the appellation, Chx Rauzan-Ségla, Rauzan-Gassies, Durfort-Vivens, Lascombes, and Brane-Cantenac, the first was seriously revived only when the owners of the couture house Chanel bought it in 1994 (restoring the 'z' in its name), and the second has been one of the most notable under-performers in the whole Médoc. Among the original ten third growths, Desmirail, Ferrière, and Dubignon-Talbot were practically abandoned for years, the last apparently for ever. Only Ch Palmer, officially a third growth, could be said to have represented the appellation with any glory and consistency in the second half of the 20th century. Ch Palmer, part owned and managed by the Bordeaux branch of the SICHEL family, produced a wine that could without hyperbole be described as legendary in 1961.

Rauzan-Ségla and Rauzan-Gassies were originally one estate and, according to Penning-Rowsell, probably the first other than the first growths to establish a reputation abroad. Rausan-Ségla (as it was then spelt), the larger part, or rather many different parts, was for long owned by the CRUSES and since then passed through several corporate hands, the last of which installed effective new winemaking equipment in the mid 1980s before the sale to the Wertheimer family of the fashion house Chanel.

Ch Lascombes passed from Alexis LICHINE to a British brewer in 1971 and is now run, with considerable RIGHT BANK influence, by an American-led consortium. The large Ch Brane-Cantenac estate, like Durfort-Vivens owned by a LURTON, has been producing lighter wines than its status in the 1855 classification suggests.

Of Margaux's many third growths other than Palmer, Kirwan has yo-yoed rather; Issan was for long more famous for its romantic moated château than for its wines (see CRUSE); Giscours has experienced a renaissance under new ownership; Cantenac-Brown was only temporarily owned by AXA; Malescot St-Exupéry, originally called St-Exupéry, is slowly taking on more flesh; Boyd-Cantenac is too often dull; while Marquis d'Alesme-Becker, originally called Becker, can be uncomfortably lean.

More care has recently been lavished on Ch Prieuré-Lichine than on Margaux's other fourth growths Chx Pouget and Marquis de Terme, although the latter is much improved since the mid 1980s. Chx Dauzac and du Tertre, Margaux's fifth growths, have seen considerable recent investment.

One of the Médoc's most famous white wines is made here, even though it qualifies only as BORDEAUX AOC (see below).

Brook, S., *The Complete Bordeaux* (rev. edn, London, 2010).

Ginestet, B., *Margaux* (Paris, 1984).

Penning-Rowsell, E., *The Wines of Bordeaux* (6th edn, London, 1989).

Margaux, Château, exceptional building and the most important wine estate in the village of MARGAUX in the Bordeaux wine region, and a FIRST GROWTH in the 1855 CLASSIFICATION. There is much potential for confusion since both Ch Margaux and GENERIC wine from the commune of Margaux are colloquially referred to as 'Margaux', but the former is likely to cost many times more than the latter.

With vineyards dating back to the 16th century, Ch Margaux was one of the four New French Clarets captured in the Anglo-French wars at the beginning of the 18th century, and sold in the COFFEE HOUSES of the City of London (see BORDEAUX, history). Thomas JEFFERSON on his visit to Bordeaux in 1787 picked it out as one of the 'four vineyards of first quality'. Sequestered in the French Revolution after the owner's flight to England, it was bought by the Marquis de la Colonilla in 1804 and rebuilt in the First Empire style, by L. Combes, as we know it today—the grandest CHÂTEAU of the Haut-MÉDOC. After passing through several hands, shares were bought by a Bordeaux wine

merchant, Fernand Ginestet, in 1925, and the family share was slowly increased to give his son Pierre Ginestet complete ownership in 1949. Also a merchant, he was badly hit by the 'energy crisis' in the early 1970s and had to seek a buyer. The French government refused to allow the American conglomerate National Distillers to buy it, but in 1977, the château was acquired by the French grocery and finance group Félix Potin, headed by the Greek André Mentzelopoulos, domiciled in France. A great deal of money was spent on restoring the neglected vineyard, *chais*, and mansion and Émile PEYNAUD was taken on as consultant. André Mentzelopoulos died suddenly in December 1980, and first his wife Laura and then his daughter Corinne took over control, assisted by Paul Pontallier, the young director who joined the estate in 1983 (coincidentally one of the property's most successful vintages). Between 1992 and 2003 the Italian Agnelli family of Fiat motor cars became involved in ownership of the estate, but Corinne Mentzelopoulos remained in charge and is now the sole owner with her children. A brand-new winery designed by British architect Sir Norman Foster has been in place since 2014 with a research lab, a particular interest of Pontallier's, given pride of place.

The 80 ha/197 acres of red wine grapes are planted with roughly 75% CABERNET SAUVIGNON grapes, 20% MERLOT, and 5% comprising CABERNET FRANC and PETIT VERDOT. Average total red wine output has been reduced to just over 20,000 from 30,000 cases, of which the resurrected Pavillon Rouge de Ch Margaux is the excellent SECOND WINE. A third wine has been made since 1997 and offered for sale from the 2009 vintage. A hitherto somewhat uninspiring white wine Pavillon Blanc was transformed into an ambitious dry wine. It is made in a new and separate temperature-controlled cellar, with BARREL FERMENTATION, exclusively from SAUVIGNON BLANC grapes planted on 12 ha of separate vineyard.   E.P.-R. & J.R.

Faith, N., *Château Margaux* (London, 1980).

Maria Gomes, Bairrada and Vinho Verde synonym for the Portuguese white grape variety FERNÃO PIRES.

Maria Ordoña, Galician synonym for TROUSSEAU.

Marignan and **Marin** are both named CRUS on the south eastern shore of Lake Geneva whose name may be added to the French appellation Vin de SAVOIE. The wine is typically a light, dry white made from the Chasselas grape.

Marino. See CASTELLI ROMANI.

maritime climate, the opposite of a CONTINENTAL climate, has a relatively narrow annual

range of temperatures. Places with a maritime climate tend to be near oceans or other large bodies of water (see LAKE EFFECT, for example). Compared with nearby inland regions, spring temperatures tend to be lower, autumn temperatures higher, because effectively water masses gain and lose heat more slowly than land masses. There is also less difference between daily maximum and minimum in summer. For the effects on wine quality and style, see CLIMATE.

marl, the crumbly combination of LIMESTONE and CLAY which is often added to soils lacking limestone (see LIME). Many of the finest wines of the CÔTE D'OR are from grapes grown on predominantly CALCAREOUS marl with some limestone. Whitish marl is found naturally to some extent in the vineyards of BEAUNE and POMMARD. It assumes more importance in MEURSAULT, where it forms the best soil for grapes grown for white wines. There is pebbly marl in the JURA region of France, and TAVEL in the southern RHÔNE has soils which are predominantly Cretaceous marl. In the German region of RHEINHESSEN, the soil is partly derived from marl. See entries prefixed SOIL.   M.J.E.

Marmajuelo (also known as **Bermejuela**), rare but outstanding white grape variety grown on the CANARY ISLANDS.

Marmandais, Côtes du, Bordeaux satellite AOC in SOUTH WEST FRANCE on either side of the river GARONNE. The town of Marmande, on the Garonne, gave it its name and provided a ready means of transporting the wines to Bordeaux and then to northern Europe, especially the NETHERLANDS, from the Middle Ages until the early 19th century. The arrival of the PHYLLOXERA louse caused many farmers to abandon viticulture, however, and vines are just one of many crops in these gentle Marmandais hills. Geographically the region is simply an extension of eastern GRAVES in the south and ENTRE-DEUX-MERS in the north. Bordeaux grape varieties CABERNET SAUVIGNON, CABERNET FRANC, and MERLOT predominate, and the cooler climate here tends to result in light versions of red, and some rosé, bordeaux. But these varieties may not exceed 85% of a blend, and Côtes du Marmandais's distinction is in the local variety ABOURIOU, which, with FER, Cot (Malbec), Gamay, and Syrah, must make up the rest. Total vineyard area increased sharply in the 1990s but declined again so that by 2012 it was only 787 ha/1,944 acres. A very small amount of white wine is made, mainly from Sauvignons Blanc and Gris.

Much of the increasingly sophisticated wine production is in the hands of CO-OPERATIVES but Elian Da Ros has provided much-needed glamour as an ambitious individual producer.

marque, French for BRAND.

Marqués, occasional name for LOUREIRO.

Marquette, increasingly popular cold-hardy American hybrid bred in Minnesota and grown in Canada and various chilly American states. Makes quite assertive red wine.

Marsala, town in western SICILY and the FORTIFIED WINE produced around it. For over 200 years one of Sicily, and Italy's, most famous products, Marsala has fallen on hard times as declining quality, evaporating markets, and plunging production levels have called into question the very survival of the wine, or at least of its better types, although there are modest signs of revival.

History

Although the province of Trapani, where the wine is produced, has always been a centre of Sicilian viticulture, Marsala can said to have been born with the arrival in Marsala in 1770 of John Woodhouse, an English merchant and connoisseur of PORT, SHERRY, and MADEIRA, who noted a striking similarity between the wines of the subzone of Birgi and the fortified wines of Spain and Portugal. Woodhouse 'invented' Marsala in 1773 by adding 8 1/2 gal of grape spirit to each of the 400-l/105-gal barrels which he shipped to England, and proceeded to open a warehouse and cellars in the township of Marsala in 1796. The victualling of Nelson's fleet in 1798 doubtlessly assisted in spreading the name of the wine, and Woodhouse was followed by another Englishman, Benjamin Ingham, who founded a Marsala firm in 1812 and contributed greatly to improving the area's viticulture. The largest Marsala house, Florio, whose premises once occupied a full km of seafront, was founded by Vincenzo Florio from CALABRIA in 1832. Marsala's production and marketing has always been dominated by large commercial houses, although there has been little continuity over time. These three pioneering houses failed to survive the 1920s and were absorbed by the vermouth house of Cinzano in 1929, and of the various Italian houses founded in the 19th century only Rallo, Pellegrino, and Vito Curatolo Arini remain today, with the last being the only producer still run by descendants of the founding family.

Winemaking and viticulture

Marsala has always been a fortified wine, but production techniques have changed over the decades and modern Marsala, as codified in the DOC regulations of 1969, can be fortified only by adding grape spirit. Alcohol levels will also be slightly increased by MUTAGE, creating a sweet so-called *sifone* by adding 20 to 25% of pure alcohol to a must of late-picked, overripe grapes. The viticulture of the zone has been considerably modified. Vines are trained on either WIRES or TENDONE systems rather than the traditional GOBELET, and the traditional superior grapes of the region, GRILLO and INZOLIA, have been partially supplanted by the higher-yielding CATARRATTO. This and enthusiastic IRRIGATION has led to significant increases in yield (the DOC rules allow an excessively generous 10 tons/ha) and a corresponding drop in the grapes' sugar levels. All these factors have led to poorer base wines, which has led to more routine sweetening and a loss of the intrinsic character of the wine itself, at its best when a dry Marsala Vergine.

In the past the ageing of the better categories of Marsala (Superiore and Vergine) in ancient and poorly maintained casks did little for the quality of these wines, which, in theory, should be the standard-bearers of the zone. What has been most damaging to Marsala, however, has been the proliferation of so-called 'Marsala Speciale', cloying wines flavoured with coffee, chocolate, strawberries, almonds, or eggs, all of which enjoyed a DOC status equal to the real wine from 1969 to 1984, helping to create the impression that Marsala is best kept in the kitchen. The revision of the DOC in 1984 banned the use of the name Marsala for these *speciale* forms, although the misconception these cooking wines created persists, while obscuring the fact that Marsala Superiore and Marsala Vergine (made by SOLERA) are the only true descendants of the historic tradition of Marsala.

Modern Marsala now comes in three different colours—Oro (golden), Ambra (amber: the colour coming from *mosto cotto*, which also serves as a rather poor-quality sweetener of other wines), and Rubino (ruby, made from NERO D'AVOLA, PERRICONE, and/or NERELLO MASCALESE grapes)—and each colour comes in a Secco (a maximum of 40 g/l of RESIDUAL SUGAR), a Semisecco (40 to 100 g/l), and a sweet (over 100 g/l) version. There are, in addition, five further types, depending on the CASK AGEING that the wines receive: a subsequent one year for Fine, two years for Superiore, four years for Superiore Riserva, five years for Vergine, ten years for the Stravecchio version of Vergine. The 1984 revision of the DOC also banned the use of *mosto cotto* in Marsala Oro and Marsala Rubino. *Mosto cotto* is still required for Marsala Ambra, and represents a foolish attempt to create the impression of a cask-aged wine by deepening its colour with concentrate, although since 1984 it has been greatly reduced to a minimum of 1%. The almost extinct Vergine version, however, the purest and most interesting type of all, cannot be made with *mosto cotto*.

Although some 1,672 ha/4,130 acres of vineyards were registered as DOC in 2012, producing 135,612 hl of Marsala (the equivalent of 18 million bottles), truly fine wines that are the result of long cask ageing are rare, if not completely extinct. Marco de Bartoli, the most innovative producer of the zone, may not state the Marsala name on the labels of his Vecchio Samperi, a prototype high-quality Marsala Vergine, as it is made without the required addition of alcohol, although it has the mandatory 18% alcohol by volume. W.S.

Belfrage, N., *Brunello to Zibibbo—The Wines of Tuscany, Central and Southern Italy* (2nd edn, London, 2003).

Nesto, B., and Di Savino, F., *The World of Sicilian Wine* (Berkeley, 2013).

www.consorziovinomarsala.it

Marsannay, northernmost appellation of the Côte de Nuits district of the CÔTE D'OR (see map under BURGUNDY). It is unique in Burgundy for having APPELLATION CONTRÔLÉE status for red, white, and pink wines. The vineyards of Couchey and Chenove are included with those of Marsannay. Prior to 1987, the wines were sold as generic BOURGOGNE followed by the specification Marsannay or Rosé de Marsannay. The latter style of wine is a speciality of the village pioneered in 1919 by Joseph Clair and taken up by the local CO-OPERATIVE. Leading producers are Audoin, Bouvier, Bruno Clair, Fournier, and Sylvain Pataille.

The small white wine production has yet to show particular character. The red wines are attractive and fruity, if lighter than those of neighbouring FIXIN. There were no PREMIER CRU vineyards in 2014 but vineyards such as Clos du Roy and Les Longeroies may yet be elevated.

J.T.C.M.

Marsanne, widely dispersed pale-skinned vine variety, making full-bodied, scented white wines. Probably originating in the northern RHÔNE, it has all but taken over here from its traditional blending partner and probable close relative ROUSSANNE in such appellations as ST-JOSEPH, ST-PÉRAY (where it is sometimes known as Roussette), CROZES-HERMITAGE, and, to a slightly lesser extent, HERMITAGE itself, where wines such as CHAPOUTIER's Chante Alouette show that the variety can make exceptionally good wines for ageing. The vine's relative productivity has doubtless been a factor in its popularity, and modern winemaking techniques have helped mitigate Marsanne's tendency to flab. It is increasingly planted in the south of France, where, as well as being embraced as an ingredient in most appellations, it is earning itself a reputation as a full-bodied, characterful VARIETAL, or a blending partner for more aromatic, acid varieties such as Roussanne, VIOGNIER, and ROLLE. The wine is particularly deep coloured, full bodied with a heady, if often heavy, aroma of glue, sometimes honeysuckle, verging occasionally on almonds, sometimes bitter in youth. It is not one of the chosen varieties for Châteauneuf-du-Pape, in which GRENACHE BLANC supplies many of Marsanne's characteristics, but France's total plantings had grown to 1,515 ha/3,742 acres by 2011—mainly in the Rhône valley but supplemented by plantings in Languedoc-Roussillon. A little is planted in Italy and Switzerland, where as Ermitage it produces both light, dry and complex sweet wines in the Valais, but even more interest has been generated in California as part of the RHÔNE RANGERS movement, although total acreage was only just over 100 acres/40 ha in 2012. Australia has some of the world's oldest Marsanne vineyards, notably in the state of Victoria, and a fine tradition of valuing this Rhône import and the hefty wines it produces, which have sometimes developed relatively fast in bottle. Total plantings had fallen to under 200 ha/500 acres by 2012, however.

Marselan, particulary successful CROSS of Cabernet Sauvignon and Grenache Noir made by INRA in 1961. The variety was developed specifically for the LANGUEDOC, where it copes with both wet and dry growing seasons, is resistant to FUNGAL DISEASES and COULURE, and is small-berried. It can offer respectable levels of both colour and flavour. By 2011 total French plantings had reached a very respectable 3,423 ha/8,455 acres of which almost 1,000 ha were on the cusp of the Languedoc and southern Rhône in the Gard département. It has also spread successfully to Spain, California, Argentina, Brazil, and China.

Martial (Marcus Valerius Martialis) (c.AD 40–103/4), born in Bilbilis, in Spain; he was poor and wrote Latin poetry for a living. In his *Epigrams*, in 15 books, more than 1,500 short poems in all, he writes about the vices he sees around him in Ancient ROME but he prudently uses pseudonyms to disguise the names of those he satirizes: e.g. 'Hesterno fetere mero qui credit Acerram, fallitur in lucem semper Acerra bibit' (1. 28). ('He who thinks that Acerra reeks of yesterday's wine is wrong. Acerra always drinks until daybreak.') Since snobbery and pretentiousness are two of his main targets, he often mentions wine. Misers and the *nouveaux riches* drink OPIMIAN wine (1. 26, 3. 82, 9. 87, 10. 49), and when Martial satirizes the classical cult of old wine (old wine was always preferred to new and was known by its consular year), he invents a wine that has not even got a consular year, because it was laid down before the Republic (13. 111). He generally presumes detailed knowledge about wine on the reader's part, as for instance in 2. 53, 4. 49, 3. 49. The reader needs to know which wines were good and which were not in order to get the point of the epigram. At the end of Book 13 (106–25) is a series of epigrams listing 21 types of wine.

Martial expresses his opinions of certain wines tersely, as in the following (13. 122), 'Acetum' (Vinegar):

Amphora Nilliaci non sit tibi vilis aceti
esset cum vinum, vilior illa fuit.

(Don't think an amphora of Egyptian vinegar is mean stuff. When it was wine, it was meaner still.)   H.M.W.

Griffin, J., *Latin Literature and Roman Life* (London, 1985).

Marufo, lesser PORT grape variety, also known as Mourisco Tinto, which produces red wines relatively light in colour in northern Portugal. Favoured by a few for light tawny ports, it was grown on 3,344 ha/8,260 acres in 2012.

Marzemino, interesting, late-ripening red grape variety grown in northern Italy, from Lombardia to Friuli but mainly in TRENTINO. DNA PROFILING at SAN MICHELE ALL'ADIGE revealed parent–offspring relationships with both TEROLDEGO and REFOSCO DAL PEDUNCULO ROSSO, thus anchoring the genetic roots of this variety in northern Italy. Once much more famous than now, it does not have particularly good resistance to FUNGAL DISEASES, and is often allowed to over-produce, but it can yield lively wines, some of them lightly sparkling. A big-berried clone dominated plantings with just over 1,000 ha/2,500 acres in Italy in 2010.   J.R. & J.V.

mas, southern French term for a domaine.

The most famous wine-producing *mas* is **Mas de Daumas Gassac**, established by outsiders to the world of wine just south east of MONTPEYROUX in the Languedoc in the 1970s. Aimé Guibert was the first to prove that a French non-appellation wine, labelled merely VIN DE PAYS de l'Hérault, can be an extremely serious, long-living red which can fetch the same sort of prices as a Bordeaux CLASSED GROWTH. Mas de Daumas Gassac also makes some rosé and some ambitious white, from a blend of unusual but trend-setting grape varieties including VIOGNIER, PETIT MANSENG, PETIT COURBU, PETITE ARVINE, AMIGNE, and NEHELESCHOL.

Mackenzie, A., *Daumas Gassac: The Birth of a Grand Cru* (London, 1995).

Masdeu, strong red wine made on and named after an exceptionally well-maintained estate near Perpignan in ROUSSILLON which found a market via London wine merchants and salerooms in the middle of the 19th century as a cheaper alternative to port.

Shaw, T. G., *Wine, the Vine and the Cellar* (London, 1864).

Massandra, winery built to extremely high specifications on the outskirts of Yalta in the CRIMEA in the 1890s to supply Livadia, the tsars' summer palace. Miners were imported from GEORGIA to tunnel into the rock to excavate three layers of cool, damp cellars. Prince Golitzin (see CRIMEA) was the first winemaker and was succeeded by the first of the Yegorov family, members of which made wine at Massandra for almost a century from 1898. The most successful wines are strong and sweet, many of them VINS DOUX NATURELS as well as FORTIFIED. The modern installation at Massandra is used not for winemaking, but for AGEING and BOTTLING. Massandra staff oversee production in a number of satellite wineries from the 2,500 ha/6,175 acres of vines under Massandra control; today the produce of nine different wineries is sold under the Massandra name but the comments below apply solely to the original operation. Grapes grown on the southern hillsides and in mountain valleys are responsible for such unique dessert wines as White Muscat of the Red Stone (sometimes translated as White Muscat from Red Rock), White Muscat Livadia, Rosé Muscat Yuzhnoberezhny (South Coast), Black Muscat Massandra, Tocay Yuzhnoberezhny, Pinot Gris Ai-Danil, and Kokur Surozh.

The **Massandra Collection** was begun by Prince Golitzin, its oldest member being an 18th-century wine made in the image of SHERRY known as Jerez de la Frontera 1773, but it is today made up substantially of the best Crimean wines. Approximately 10,000 bottles have been added each year and some wines in the collection are decades old. After considerable quantities were poured into the sea before the Nazi invasion, the Collection was evacuated during the German occupation of Yalta 1941–4, some as far as to Georgia, but was back in place in time for the historic Yalta peace conference in 1945. In the early 1990s Sotheby's offered two consignments of strong, very sweet, durable wines from the Massandra Collection at AUCTION in London as part of the auctioneer's trading arrangements with the disintegrating Soviet Union. A further sale was held in 2004.

Massic, a white wine which was among the most famous wines of Roman Italy and was much praised by the Roman poets. The type of grape is unknown. The wine was produced on Monte Massico, the line of hills which runs down to the sea on the west coast of Italy between the rivers Garigliano and Volturno. This zone is adjacent to the territory which produced FALERNIAN and some writers treat Massic as a subtype of that famous wine. The wine was transported to Sinuessa on the coast, where there were numerous kilns producing the AMPHORAE in which the wine was exported.   J.J.P.

mass selection, *sélection massale* in French, viticultural technique used to provide buds for the PROPAGATION of vines. Field vine selection can be either by mass selection, when many vines are selected to provide budwood, or by CLONAL SELECTION, in which a single mother vine is selected to provide CLONES. In mass selection, the identity of individual vines is not maintained, which is the principal difference between the two approaches.

Mass selection can be either negative or positive. If negative, then undesirable vines in a vineyard are marked so that cuttings are not taken from them. These vines might include those with low yield, poor fruit maturity, virus disease symptoms, higher than average incidence of fungal diseases, or off-types (MUTATIONS). Negative mass selection is also a good opportunity to mark 'rogue vines' (those of another variety) to ensure that mixed plantings do not occur in the future. Positive selection identifies the best vines, for example those with good fruit set, larger and looser bunches and good fruit maturity.

Usually the vineyard assessment is made several times over the season. For example, rogue vines and NEPOVIRUS symptoms are easier to pick out in the spring, whereas differences in grape ripening are obviously best determined just before harvest. Vines are commonly marked by paint on the trunk.

Since there is not the same detailed recording and selection of individual vines, the gains in yield or quality from mass selection are typically less than for clonal selection, but the resultant wine, made from vines with a mixture of different characteristics, may be more interesting than one made from a single clone. The benefits to be had from mass selection will depend on how heterogeneous was the field from which the selection is made. Obviously there will be little benefit of mass selection if the vineyard is quite uniform, but if there is a high proportion of rogue vines, off-types, or virus diseases, then the nurseryman might expect substantial benefits.

Unfortunately, in many viticultural regions of the world, cuttings are taken in winter from vineyards which have not benefited from even the most cursory inspection in the preceding summer. In the winter all vines appear similar, and so mistakes of mixed plantings, off-types, and virus diseases are spread unwittingly from one vineyard to the next generation by propagation. R.E.S.

Coombe, B. G., and Dry, P. R., *Viticulture*, i: *Resources in Australia* (2nd edn, Adelaide, 2004).

Galet, P., *Précis de viticulture* (7th edn, Montpellier, 2000).

Masters of Wine, those who have passed

the examinations held every year by the **Institute of Masters of Wine** (**IMW**), the wine trade's most famous and most demanding professional qualification. The Institute had its origins in the British wine trade in the early 1950s, when a counterpart to the qualifying examinations for other professions was devised by a group of wine merchants in conjunction with the VINTNERS' COMPANY. The first examination was held in London in 1953 and six of the 21 candidates were deemed to have qualified as Masters of Wine. The Institute of Masters of Wine was formed in 1955. The examinations consist of five written papers and three 'practical' (i.e. wine tasting) papers and since 1999 those who pass all of them must write an approved research paper to qualify as an MW. The examinations are distinguished by the breadth and depth of their scope. University courses (see ACADEME) offer more detailed instruction in the OENOLOGY or VITICULTURE of a particular country or region, while the MW examinations test knowledge of both subjects on a worldwide basis, as well as of such varied subjects as ÉLEVAGE, BOTTLING, transport, QUALITY CONTROL, marketing, commercial aspects of the wine trade, the effects of wine consumption on HEALTH, and general wine knowledge. Each tasting paper requires candidates to describe, assess, and, often, identify up to 12 wines served BLIND. These wines, including SPARKLING and FORTIFIED WINES, may come from anywhere in the world.

Despite a notoriously low pass rate (although it has risen markedly in recent years and candidates have always been allowed to pass practical and theoretical parts in separate years), by 1978 the number of Masters of Wine had reached 100, including two women. In 1982 the Institute held its first, relatively academic, symposium, at Oxford, but also lost four of its members and realized that some expansion would be necessary for its survival (it had no executives and no premises until 1987). In 1983 it relaxed its entry requirements and allowed candidates from the fringes of the wine trade, such as WINE WRITERS, to take the examinations. In 1987 the examinations were opened up to those outside the United Kingdom and the next year the first overseas candidate, an Australian, passed the examinations, at this stage still held in London. Since 1991 examinations have been held, on the same dates, in London, Australia, and North America. By 2014 there were 319 Masters of Wine (including 96 women) based in 24 countries, and several MWs with no professional connection with wine at all; 123 members live and work outside the UK.

Numbers of candidates have increased even more rapidly than numbers of Masters of Wine. The examinations are increasingly demanding as the wine world expands, and the standard of preparation offered by the Institute was raised considerably in the mid 1990s and early 2000s. If the aims of the Institute have at times been less clear than the status of its members, and for many years it offered examinations but remarkably little education, this is changing, thanks to annual residential courses, regular seminars, tastings, and a mentoring scheme.

Mastroberardino, historically the most important producer of TAURASI in the southern Italian region of CAMPANIA. Staunch defenders of the AGLIANICO grape, which was widely replaced after the Second World War by the higher-yielding Trebbiano and Sangiovese, they convinced their grape suppliers to continue growing it by paying higher PRICES for it. Mastroberardino was the first, and for a long period the sole producer to bottle TAURASI rather than selling it off in BULK. The family split in 1994, with one branch retaining the vineyards but setting up under the Vignadora label, and the other branch retaining the name but seeking grapes elsewhere.

Mataro is one of the many synonyms of MOURVÈDRE used primarily in Australia, and by those who do not realize how fashionable Mourvèdre has become.

Mateus. The Palace of Mateus near Vila Real just north of the DOURO Valley in northern Portugal lent its name to **Mateus Rosé**. Bottled in a flask not unlike the BOCKSBEUTEL, this medium-sweet, sparkling rosé blend became one of the world's most famous wine BRANDS. Created in 1942 by Fernando van Zeller Guedes, it was inspired by his family's VINHO VERDE, naturally pétillant red and white wines. The sparkling rosé was sweetened to make it more appealing to export markets. Production began at the end of the Second World War (at very much the same time as that of its rival LANCERS). It was originally successful in Brazil and, while that market collapsed after the war, the brand proved hugely popular in post-war Britain and then the US. At its peak in 1978, Mateus, by then supplemented by a white version, accounted for over 40% of Portugal's total table wine exports with worldwide sales amounting to 3.5 million cases. A small quantity of Mateus Rosé is still made at Vila Real but most of the wine is now produced at Anadia in BAIRRADA. Faced with falling sales of Mateus in the early 1990s, SOGRAPE, the Guedes family firm which owns the Mateus brand, has diversified into other areas, including PORT. Surfing the wave of popularity enjoyed by ROSÉS this century by launching a Mateus Rosé Tempranillo made in VALENCIA, a pink Shiraz (sic) from France, and, in a break with tradition, two still varietally blended rosés bottled in Bordeaux bottles. The original Mateus blend is now labelled 'The Original'. S.A.

Matrasa, or **Madrasa**, dominant, dark-berried vine of AZERBAIJAN. It is found in other central ASIAN republics and may also be called Kara Shirei and Kara Shirai. Also spelt Matrassa.

Maturana Blanca, recently revived INDIGENOUS white wine grape in RIOJA. **Maturana Tinta** is a Rioja synonym for TROUSSEAU.

maturation of wine. See AGEING.

mature, tasting term for a fine wine that seems to have enjoyed sufficient AGEING for it to have reached the peak of its potential. In practice, it is also used by the most polite, or determinedly optimistic, tasters to describe wines that are past that point. Any hint of orange at the rim of a red wine suggests MATURITY.

maturity, desirable state in a wine when it is consumed. In a sense, the most basic wine designed for early drinking is mature almost as soon as it is bottled, but mature when applied to a wine carries with it the implication that the maturity is the result of a certain amount of BOTTLE AGEING. Such a (red) wine is deemed fully mature when it has dispensed with its uncomfortably harsh TANNINS and acquired maximum complexity of flavour (sometimes described as BOUQUET) without starting to decay. The period of maturity varies considerably with wine type, but is probably longer than most wine consumers believe. A wine that has been followed since its youth and begins to taste mature may continue to delight, and possibly evolve for the better, for a decade or more. For more details of the process, and of the difference between individual wine types, see AGEING. For maturity in grapes, see RIPENING.

Robinson, J., *Vintage Timecharts* (London and New York, 1989).

Maule, increasingly valued southern subregion of the Central Valley of CHILE.

Maury, centred on the village in the Agly Valley of the same name, was one of ROUSSILLON's famous VINS DOUX NATURELS, a cousin from the hilly hinterland of seaside BANYULS, and produced in greater quantity. But in 2012 an appellation for its red wines was authorized, in recognition of the increasing importance of these less alcoholic, TERROIR-DRIVEN, dry wines in the region, previously sold as VIN DE PAYS des Côtes Catalanes (its whites are IGP Côtes Catalanes), at the expense of strong, sweet wines. Maury is on high inland SCHIST at the northern limit of the Côtes du Roussillon-Villages area in the Agly valley. The ruins of the Cathar castle of Quéribus, a constant reminder of the area's harsh natural environment, dominate the village of Maury. Summers are hot and dry, though slightly cooler in the higher west of the appellation. Both dry reds and red *vins doux naturels* are based substantially on Grenache Noir, with Carignan, Mourvèdre, and Syrah playing a subsidiary role in the dry reds and Grenache of other hues doing the same for the fast-declining production of *vins doux naturels*. The latter are invariably strong and sweet, those described as *grenat* or *tuilé* being based on Grenache Noir, although Grenache Blanc and Grenache Gris may be used for the occasional

vin doux naturel described as *ambré* or *blanc*. The CO-OPERATIVE, Les Vignerons du Maury, dominates production but since the 1990s the region has attracted an exceptional number of incomers too.

Mauzac, or more properly **Mauzac Blanc**, is a declining white grape in SOUTH WEST FRANCE, especially in its birthplace GAILLAC and LIMOUX, where it is the traditional and still principal vine variety. It produces relatively aromatic wines which are usually blended, with Len de l'El around Gaillac and with Chenin and Chardonnay in Limoux. France's total area of Mauzac had fallen to 1,806 ha/4,461 acres by 2011. Thanks to energetic winemakers such as Robert Plageoles, since the late 1980s there has been a revival of interest in Gaillac's Mauzac, which comes in several different hues, sweetness levels, and degrees of fizziness. During the 1970s and 1980s in Limoux, total plantings of Mauzac rose but have declined as the appellation, for both still and fizzy wines, has been invaded by Chardonnay.

The vine, whose yields can vary enormously according to site, buds and ripens late and grapes were traditionally picked well into autumn so that musts fermented slowly and gently in the cool Limoux winters, ready to referment in bottle in the spring. Today Mauzac tends to be picked much earlier, preserving its naturally high acidity but sacrificing much of its particular flavour reminiscent of the skin of shrivelled apples, before being subjected to the usual SPARKLING WINEMAKING techniques. Some gently sparkling Gaillacs are still made by the traditional *méthode gaillacoise*, however, just as a small portion of Limoux's Blanquette is made by the *méthode ancestrale*. Mauzac Noir is much rarer and unrelated.

Mavro means 'black' in Greek and is the common name of the dominant but undistinguished grape on the island of CYPRUS.

Mavrodaphne, dark-skinned grape variety grown particularly round Pátras in the Peloponnese in GREECE, where it is the foundation of a port-like dessert wine, **Mavrodaphne of Pátras**, which responds well to extended CASK AGEING. This aromatic, powerful variety, also grown to a much more limited extent on the island of Cephalonia, is occasionally vinified dry but only for use in blends.

Mavrotragano, increasingly appreciated, distinctive red wine grape INDIGENOUS to the Greek island of SANTORINI.

Mavroudi, generic name for several Greek red wine grapes.

Mavrud, indigenous Balkan grape variety most closely associated with BULGARIA, capable of producing intense, tannic wine if allowed to

ripen fully. Grown on about 1,700 ha/4,220 acres in central southern Bulgaria in 2009 and a speciality of Assenovgrad near Plovdiv, it is small berried, low yielding and has a long vegetative period. The robust wine produced responds well to oak ageing, although it tends to age rather faster than Bulgaria's other noble indigenous vine MELNIK.

Mazuelo, official Spanish name for CARIGNAN. Also known as **Mazuela** in RIOJA.

McDowell Valley, California AVA. See MENDOCINO.

McLaren Vale, intensively planted, historic SOUTH AUSTRALIAN wine region especially noted for rich reds, from 126 producers in 2014. These have a distinctive and often useful dash of dark chocolate in their makeup. More controversial is their level of alcohol: seldom less than 14.5% and sometimes in excess of 15.5%. The winemakers' response is that they are not seeking high alcohol, simply waiting for the right flavour development.

MDMP. See METHOXY-DIMETHYLPYRAZINE.

mead, a fermented alcoholic drink, called *hydromel* in France and *Honigwein* or *Met* in Germany, made from honey, which, it is claimed, pre-dates either wine or beer. Monks kept bees for candlewax and any surplus honey was fermented into mead. The dissolution of the monasteries meant the virtual demise of mead-making in Britain. Since the Second World War, some larger companies have marketed a mixture of wine and honey as mead, but the tradition of genuine mead-making persists. Grape mead is grape juice mixed with honey before fermentation.

mealy bugs, small, white insects of the family Cicadellidae which suck vine sap. Young mealy bugs infect new growth in the spring, typically the undersurface of leaves at the base of the shoot. They also can feed on the fruit, canes, and trunk, and one species, the vine mealy bug *Planococcus ficus*, can feed on roots. Mealy bugs become mature and reproduce in early summer, and there can be three or more generations a year. Mealy bugs prefer a humid environment, and so are mostly found in a dense vine CANOPY.

The vine mealy bug, first identified in California's Coachella valley in the early 1990s, is now widespread in the San Joaquin valley and the Central Coast, where it is regarded as a serious problem. It is spread by infected new plantings and can be controlled by briefly dipping the dormant plants in hot water.

Mealy bugs do not cause significant commercial damage by their sap-sucking action alone, but there can be two indirect effects. First, they produce copious quantities of a sugary, sticky liquid called honeydew, which collects over the bunches and foliage, and on which fungus grows, often giving it a sooty appearance. Grapes affected by this impart a distinctive and undesirable taste to wine, and the fruit may be fit only for DISTILLATION. Mealy bugs of the genera *Planococcus* and *Pseudococcus* have been implicated in the spread of LEAFROLL VIRUS, which has serious implications for the loss of vineyard yield and grape quality. Mealy bugs have been confirmed as spreading leafroll virus in South Africa, Israel, the US, Australia, and New Zealand.

Where mealy bug infestations are serious, a schedule of preventive sprays is necessary, but the waxy covering of the insect and the sheltered locations make control difficult.

M.J.E. & R.E.S.

Buchanan, G. A., and Amos, T. G., 'Grape pests', in B. G. Coombe and P. R. Dry (eds.), *Viticulture*, ii: *Practices* (Adelaide, 1992).

Golino, D. A., et al., 'California mealybugs can spread grapevine leafroll disease', *California Agriculture* 56 (2002), 196–201.

measles, as it affects vines, see ESCA.

mechanical harvesting, harvesting by machine in place of the traditional manual HARVEST. Undoubtedly one of the greatest changes from ancient to modern vineyards has been the adoption of machine harvesting, which was first introduced commercially in the 1960s. Whereas manual grape harvesting required literally hordes of pickers to descend on vineyards and complete the harvest, now the vintage may be completed by just one harvester driver, perhaps with a supporting driver and vehicle to receive the harvested grapes. Depending on the YIELD and vineyard TOPOGRAPHY, to harvest a vineyard by hand requires between one and ten man-days per hectare, as opposed to less than five man-hours per hectare by machine.

Mechanical harvesting has been adopted for different reasons in different parts of the world. In some of the earliest developments instigated by Nelson SHAULIS and E. S. Shepardson at the Agricultural Experiment Station in Geneva, in upstate New York, a major consideration was potential cost savings. In Australia, of the first countries to embrace the new technology, the scarcity of LABOUR was important, and welfare payments were another factor. In France, the increasing bureaucracy and costs involved in employing people even temporarily added allure to machine harvesting in the 1980s and 1990s. The net effect was that seasonal workers were more difficult to find, they demanded higher wages, and were also perhaps less reliable, all of these factors promoting machines over man at vintage time. Machine harvesting may have been developed in the United States, but the technology was rapidly refined in France.

History

Mechanical harvesting can either increase the efficiency of manual labour, or virtually replace it. Very early attempts at mechanization emphasized the first approach, but it has been the second approach which has been the more successful, by developing machines which essentially replace most of the manual operations.

Many forms of integrated machine harvesters have been developed and evaluated, although by the early 21st century, most machines worked by striking the CANOPY to remove fruit and catching it with horizontal conveyor belts. The early New York development was the 'vertical impactor', which used a metal finger to strike the vine cordon; the shock dislodged the berries. However, the most common form of harvesting now is the 'horizontal slapper' which uses fibreglass rods to strike the foliage and dislodge the fruit, sometimes as single berries, sometimes as bunches.

Effect on wine quality

The effect of machine harvesting on wine quality has been the subject of much scientific study, commercial experience, and popular conjecture. The majority of studies have shown that sophisticated mechanical harvesting has no negative effect on wine quality, and some have even argued that there is a positive effect. Certainly most forms of machine harvesting damage some grapes so that parts of berries and bunches are mixed with the juice of broken berries. However, the juice can be protected from OXIDATION by SULFUR DIOXIDE addition, especially if moved quickly in a closed container to the winery. This problem can be minimized by harvesting at night, a practice widely adopted in hotter wine regions where grapes harvested by day can arrive at the winery at over 40 °C/104 °F. Indeed, in these circumstances, machine picking at night is a bonus for wine quality in comparison with hand harvesting by day.

Another disadvantage of machine harvesting is that there can be excessive SKIN CONTACT, which, depending on its duration, usually dictated by transport times, can lead to white wines becoming too high in PHENOLICS. The skin contact involved in transporting mechanically harvested white grapes to a winery can also cause a significant increase in the concentration of PROTEINS in the wine, necessitating higher rates of BENTONITE fining. Long distances between the winery and vineyard may make a mechanical harvest for delicate white wines an impossibility. Machine-harvested grapes can also contain leaves and petioles (see MOG), which may cause taints. Despite much evidence in favour of machine harvesting, some producers will remain with hand harvesting. The gentler nature of hand harvesting (which can also involve some degree of selection, e.g. avoiding unripe

bunches or those affected by BUNCH ROT) is preferable for many top-quality wines, especially sparkling wines, for which WHOLE BUNCHES may be pressed without first crushing. However, in Australia, for example, machine harvesting of grapes for sparkling wine is being evaluated.

R.E.S.

Coombe, B. G., and Dry, P. R. (eds.), *Viticulture*, ii: *Practices* (Adelaide, 1992).

Galet, P., *Précis de viticulture* (7th edn, Montpellier, 2000).

Morris, J. R., and Brady, P., *Vineyard Mechanization: Development and Status in the United States and Major Grape Producing Regions of the World* (ASHS, 2011).

mechanical pruning involves using machines for PRUNING vines in winter. (For what is sometimes referred to as summer pruning, see TRIMMING.) Viticulture is a very traditional form of agriculture and many who tend the vines regard the annual winter pruning as their prime opportunity to interact physically with each vine. Because of this, and because they feel that mechanical pruning cannot offer the precision of manual pruning, many vinegrowers oppose mechanical pruning, even at the expense of hours of back-breaking labour in cold and sometimes wet weather.

Early experiments in mechanical pruning were carried out in Australia and New York state in the mid 1970s. The machinery was not as elaborate as that for MECHANICAL HARVESTING, which was undergoing simultaneous development. The pruning machines were simply reciprocating cutters or flails mounted on a tractor. In Australia circular saws were widely used, and sometimes these were mounted on a machine harvester with the picking head removed.

Machine pruning is simple in the extreme, as the vine canes (generally around a metre in length, and with, say, 15 buds) are cut back to their base leaving typically a SPUR with two or more buds. (CANE PRUNING cannot, of course, be mechanized but surplus cane removal after hand cutting can be, and in New Zealand machines have been developed to strip last season's growth off the trellis wires, offering partial mechanization.) Early commercial experiments followed mechanical pruning with hand pruning to tidy the vines' appearance, by thinning out spur numbers and cutting them to a uniform two-bud length, hence the term mechanical pre-pruning. This cuts pruning time in half. Encouraged by early experiments in Australia, however, most vines have since been left untended after machine pruning. Although they look ugly in late winter, soon after BUDBREAK they cannot be distinguished from handpruned vines. Because more buds are left on the vine (up to fivefold)), the YIELD usually increases for the first year or so, but many studies show no significant effect on wine quality. However, because of an increase in pruning wounds, some affecting thicker, older wood, such vines may be more prone to TRUNK DISEASE.

Mechanical pruning is now widespread in Australia, especially in the hotter wine regions, mostly using tractor-mounted circular saws, with a single pass cutting through wood of various ages across the top of the vine. Robots developed for cane pruning, using 3D vision, were field tested in New Zealand in 2014 following two years' research at the University of Canterbury. Other parts of the world have been much slower to embrace mechanical pruning, however, especially those where LABOUR is plentiful and relatively inexpensive. Mechanical pre-pruning is becoming more widespread for the extensive vineyards of southern France. In cooler regions such as northern Europe, mechanical pruning is less useful because machine pruning leaves too many buds, tending to increase yield and slow RIPENING.

The 100 to 150 hours per hectare required for hand pruning can be reduced to less than ten hours per hectare with mechanical pruning. Some of the substantial cost savings associated with this reduction may be lost if too extensive hand pruning follows. The logical extension of mechanical pruning is not to prune at all, so-called MINIMAL PRUNING.   R.E.S.

Morris, J. R., and Brady, P., *Vineyard Mechanization: Development and Status in the United States and Major Grape Producing Regions of the World* (ASHS, 2011).

Smart, R. E., 'Mechanical pruning—it seemed a good idea at the time', *Australian Journal of Grape and Wine Research*, 29/5 (2014), 38-44.

mechanization. Most WINEMAKING operations other than TASTING and overseeing individual barrels can be fully mechanized, but mechanization has been much slower to invade the vineyard. Robotic technology is used, for example, in the production of PORT, in the movement of pallets around the winery, and in the preparation of grape samples. For more details of viticultural mechanization, see MECHANICAL HARVESTING, MECHANICAL PRUNING, TRIAGE, and, most importantly, LABOUR.

medals from wine COMPETITIONS and other JUDGINGS are coveted by many wine producers. There is a certain hierarchy of medals, however. State and national wine shows are important to the wine trade in AUSTRALIA, but a Hobart gold medal may be reckoned less glamorous than a Canberra silver. In France, medals awarded by the fairs in Paris and Mâcon are usually indications of real quality, as are those awarded in Germany by the Deutscher Landwirtschaft Gesellschaft, or DLG.

medical aspects of wine consumption. See HEALTH.

medical profession. See DOCTORS.

medicine, wine in. From ancient times to the 18th century, wine enjoyed a central role in medicine (see LITERATURE OF WINE). The earliest practitioners of medicine were magicians and priests who used wine for healing as well as religious purposes (see RELIGION). Receipts for wine-based medicines appear in papyri of Ancient EGYPT and the tablets of SUMER in about 2200 BC, making wine man's oldest documented medicine.

The beginnings of systematized medicine are commonly attributed to the Greek Hippocrates (c.450 BC), who recommended the use of wine as a disinfectant, a medicine, a vehicle for other drugs, and as part of a healthy DIET. He experimented with different wines in order to discover how each might be most appropriately used—whether diluted or not, for example—to cure a specific ailment, from lethargy or diarrhoea to easing difficult childbirth.

The most famous physician of Ancient ROME was GALEN (2nd century AD), whose medical experience was shaped by treating injured gladiators in Asia Minor, although Aurelius Cornelius Celsus (25 BC–AD 37) had already written extensively about the medical uses of various wines from different regions of Greece and Italy. Galen learned (like the Good Samaritan of the BIBLE) that wine was the most effective means of disinfecting wounds, even soaking exposed abdominal contents in wine before returning them to the abdominal cavity in the case of severe stomach wounds. His post as imperial physician involved tasting the emperor's wines in order to select the best and most healthy.

Ancient Jewish civilization prized wine for its medicinal properties. In the Talmud it is stated that: 'Wine is the foremost of all medicines: wherever wine is lacking, medicines become necessary.'

The Koran presented Arab doctors with a dilemma. The likes of Avicenna (11th century AD) recognized the importance of wine in healing, but since its consumption was forbidden throughout the world of ISLAM he had to be careful to prescribe it as a dressing only (although he noted boldly that 'wine is also very efficient in causing the products of digestion to become disseminated through the body'). Arabs studied medicine from Greek sources then transmitted it back, slightly amended, to the west. The works of Galen, for example, reached medieval Europe partly via the great medical school of Salerno in Italy, where they were translated from Arabic to Latin, and partly through direct translation from Greek. It was then that the notion of wine as an essential element in a healthy diet gained ground.

The medicinal use of wine continued throughout the Middle Ages, in MONASTERIES,

hospitals, and universities. The earliest printed book on wine is by a doctor, one ARNALDUS DE VILLANOVA of the University of MONTPELLIER, who had written at the beginning of the 14th century. Building on the observations of his classical forebears, he offers not only remedies for curing human ailments with appropriate wines, but also recipes for curing 'sick' or bad wines too.

A new dimension was added to the role of wine in medicine with the introduction of DISTILLATION in the western world in the 12th century. Hieronymus Brunschwig, the German pharmacologist, wrote in the 15th century that '*Aqua vitae* [the water of life, or ALCOHOL] is commonly called the mistress of all medicines', but warned, 'it is to be drunk by reason and measure'.

Medicinal attitudes towards wine began to change in the latter half of the 19th century—although wine was still being added to sterilize water as late as the 1892 cholera epidemic of Hamburg (vindicated by modern research indicating that wine contains substances which make it a more effective anti-bacterial agent than pure alcohol), and strong, sweet wines such as PORT and BANYULS were still being prescribed as aids to recuperation in the early 20th century. Alcoholism was defined as a disease and the injurious side-effects of excessive drinking studied. The appearance of temperance societies, sometimes supported by the medical establishment, caused many to re-evaluate the role of wine in DIET and medicine.

One further aspect of the conjunction of wine and medicine is the great influence that DOCTORS have had since ancient times, not just as wine consumers (and producers) but also in promoting or damaging the commercial potential of certain wines. Undoubtedly Roman connoisseurs took note of the recommendations of Galen and others, while in 17th-century France the commercial battle between wine regions reached new heights when Louis XIV's physician prescribed burgundy in preference to champagne. Other examples of vinous prescriptions abound.

For a modern view of the medical effects of wine consumption, see HEALTH.   H.B. & P.A.N.

Darby, W. J., 'Wine and medical wisdom through the ages', in *Wine, Health and Society* (San Francisco, 1982).

Lucia, S. P., *A History of Wine as Therapy* (New York, 1963).

Sigerist, H. E., *The Earliest Printed Book on Wine* (New York, 1943) (contains Villanova's *Tractatus de vinis*).

medieval literature. The only medieval successor to the Roman AGRICULTURAL TREATISES is PETRUS DE CRESCENTIIS' *Liber ruralium commodorum* of c.1304; otherwise there are few medieval authors who wrote specifically on wine.

One of these is Henri d'Andely, whose *Bataille des vins* dates from just after 1223 and it belongs to the genre of the medieval debate poem. The king of France, Philip Augustus, wants to know which is the best wine: his preference is for whites. Some 70 wines are tasted and the crown of victory passes all the French wines by, for it goes to the wine of CYPRUS.

Another Old French poem about wine is *La Disputoison de vin et de l'iaue* ('The Debate between Wine and Water'), written some time between 1305 and 1377, when the papal court was at Avignon. The debate reflects the changing FASHIONS of the time, including those for the wines of BEAUNE, GASCONY, LA ROCHELLE, ST-POURÇAIN-sur-Sioule, and PARIS.

Of the Middle English poets, Chaucer is the one who displays most knowledge of wine, although he tends to mention different wines only briefly. Chaucer's father and grandfather were among the most important VINTNERS in London and held the office of deputy to the king's butler, who was the person responsible for the collection of taxes on imported wines. Jugs of MALMSEY ('malvasye') and VERNACCIA ('vernage') are, for example, the extravagant presents that the monk in 'The Shipman's Tale' gives his friend the merchant, whom he is about to cuckold.

Wine is just wine in the medieval drinking songs, too. Most of them are in Latin, and they are not so much in praise of drinking as of DRUNKENNESS. The 9th-century poem about Adam, abbot of Angers, for example, has an address to BACCHUS as its refrain. One of the *Carmina Burana*, 'Potatores exquisiti' (*CB* 179), asks all serious topers to banish moderate drinkers from parties and to drink until speech becomes impaired and walking impossible. Even when one is on one's own, the object of drinking should be inebriation.   H.M.W.

Hanford, J. H., 'The mediaeval debate between wine and water', *Publications of the Modern Language Academy of America*, 28 (1913), 315–67.

Raby, F. J. E., *The Oxford Book of Medieval Latin Verse* (Oxford, 1959).

Waddell, H., *Medieval Latin Lyrics* (London, 1933).

Wilson, H., *Wine and Words in Classical Antiquity and the Middle Ages* (London, 2003).

Mediterranean, famous sea, wine-producing climate, diet, and many other things besides. By classical times, vines were grown for wine in almost all the countries bordering the Mediterranean sea and on many of the islands; from Spain in the west to Byblos in the east, from northern Italy to Egypt, the vine made inexorable progress, with AMPHORAE of wine traversing the sea regularly. Historically, the Mediterranean was the focus of viticulture, and most wine was produced in MEDITERRANEAN CLIMATES. In the Middle Ages, particularly when temperatures rose overall (see CLIMATE CHANGE) and when consumers were accustomed to very light, acid wines, viticulture spread much further north than the shores of the Mediterranean (see PARIS, ENGLAND, and GERMAN HISTORY, for example).

Mediterranean climate, a climate type characterized by warm, dry, sunny summers and mostly mild, wet winters. It occurs throughout the Mediterranean basin, on the west coast of the United States, in Chile, southern and south western Australia, and the Cape Province of South Africa. The autumn and spring seasons range from mostly dry on the hot, equatorial fringes bordering deserts, to wet at the poleward fringes, where Mediterranean climates merge into those with a more or less uniform rainfall distribution as in central and western Europe.

Mediterranean climates have some distinct advantages for viticulture over uniform or summer-rainfall climates, provided that supplementary IRRIGATION can be given as needed. Sunshine is mostly more reliable and generous. There is less risk of rainfall in the growing season and of excessive rainfall during ripening and harvest. As a result of these rainfall patterns, the risk of FUNGAL DISEASES is generally lower. And to the extent that many Mediterranean climates have the disadvantages of low HUMIDITY and high TEMPERATURES during the ripening period, precise VINEYARD SITE SELECTION can help to minimize these disadvantages, by seeking out cooler coastal or high-elevation sites, for example.

Further favouring Mediterranean climates is the fact that some of the main advances in both vineyard management and winemaking technology have particular application there. DRIP IRRIGATION in a summer-dry climate allows a degree of control over SOIL WATER availability and vine VIGOUR, and permits the use of MESO-CLIMATES and soils (see SOIL AND WINE QUALITY) that were too dry for viticulture before. Improved CANOPY MANAGEMENT has at least as great an application as in other climates.

                                                    J.G. & R.E.S.

Mediterranean fruit fly, *Caratitis capitata*, can be a grape pest in some areas such as parts of Australia and South Africa. Infestations of grapes are often due to a build-up in other soft fruits such as figs, apricots, peaches, nectarines, or citrus. Despite being a major destructive pest for many fruit crops, it is not regarded as serious for vineyards. See also DROSOPHILA.

                                                          R.E.S.

Médoc, the most famous red wine district in Bordeaux, and possibly the world. The Médoc stretches north west from the city of Bordeaux along the left bank of the Gironde estuary, a virtually monocultural strip of flat, unremarkable land sandwiched between the *palus*, or coastal marshes, and the pine forests which extend for miles south into the Landes. The vineyard strip is about 5 to 12 km/3 to 8 miles wide, and runs northwards, with various intermissions for scrub, pasture, polder, and river bank, more than 70 km/50 miles from the northern suburbs of Bordeaux to the marshes of the lower, more northerly part of the Médoc, the so-called Bas-Médoc (see map under BORDEAUX). Wines produced in the Bas-Médoc use the **Médoc** appellation, while those on the higher ground in the south eastern section are entitled to the **Haut-Médoc** appellation, although many of them qualify for the smarter individual village, or communal, appellations. From south to north, these are MARGAUX, MOULIS, LISTRAC, ST-JULIEN, PAUILLAC, and ST-ESTÈPHE.

As outlined in BORDEAUX, history, the Médoc is a relatively recent wine region. Before the Dutch diligently applied their drainage technology to the polders of the Médoc in the mid 17th century, the region was salt-marsh, of interest for grazing rather than vine-growing. The ditches were so effective, and Bordeaux merchants so keen to supply vinous rivals to GRAVES and the powerful Portuguese wines that had been shipped in great quantity to the important British market, that New French Clarets were born, and great estates established in the Médoc on the back of their commercial success. In the mid 19th century, the Médoc enjoyed a period of prosperity unparalleled until the 1980s.

The climate on this peninsula is Bordeaux's mildest, moderated both by the estuary and by the Atlantic ocean just over the pines. These forests protect the vineyard strip from strong winds off the ocean, and help to moderate summer temperatures, but it is only in the Médoc and the Graves district further south that Bordeaux vignerons are confident of ripening Cabernet Sauvignon grapes with any frequency. The Médoc is also Bordeaux's wettest region, which makes ROT a constant threat and SPRAYING a habit.

A typical estate, or CHÂTEAU, in the greater Médoc district hedges its viticultural bets and grows at least three different grape varieties: a majority of Cabernet Sauvignon, supplemented principally by Merlot, together with some Cabernet Franc with, perhaps, a little late late-ripening Petit Verdot and occasionally some Malbec. However, Merlot often predominates in the damper, cooler soils of the Bas-Médoc as it is easier to ripen in lesser vintages, and Cabernet Sauvignon comprises only about half of all the vines planted in the district.

While the Médoc possesses few distinctive geographical features, many man-hours have been spent charting the subterranean Médoc. It has long been argued that its great distinction is its soil, in particular its GRAVEL. Many a geological theory has been employed to explain exactly how, and whence, these gravel deposits arrived in the Médoc, and efforts have been made to correlate exact soil and rock types with the quality of wine produced from vines grown on them. Dr Gérard Seguin of the University of BORDEAUX was one of the first to show that the soil's physical attributes are very much more important than its mineral composition, and that one of the most important soil attributes is good DRAINAGE (see SOIL AND WINE QUALITY). The gravels of the Médoc are ideal in this respect, and are particularly important in such a damp climate—although in hotter vintages mature vines can benefit from the extensive root systems encouraged by the gravel. The gravels of the Médoc are also good at storing valuable heat, thereby promoting RIPENING.

It is traditionally said that the best vines of the Médoc are those which grow within sight of the Gironde, and certainly this is true of all the district's FIRST GROWTHS. Some argue that this is because the gravels deposited here are younger and more effective for vine maturation, others that the MESOCLIMATES of coastal vineyards tend to be slightly warmer, others that vines on higher ground have to establish more complex root systems.

A total of about 1,500 vine-growers farm this land, about a quarter of which forms part of one of the classed growths ranked in the famous 1855 CLASSIFICATION of the Médoc (and Graves).

The Haut-Médoc appellation

The landscape of the Haut-Médoc may not be remarkable but it is peppered with grandiose château buildings erected and embellished with the money to be made from selling CLASSED GROWTH red bordeaux. Certainly the Haut-Médoc today is nothing if not stratified, thanks largely to the effects of the 1855 classification of its most famous estates, which recognized 60 of them as first, second, third, fourth, and fifth growths, commercial and social positions from which none but Ch MOUTON ROTHSCHILD has so far been able to escape.

Most of these classed growths are entitled to a village appellation such as Pauillac or Margaux (see map under BORDEAUX), but five of them are in communes without their own appellations and qualify merely as Haut-Médoc. The most highly ranked of these is the third growth Ch La Lagune in Ludon just outside the city, a property which has retained its reputation for robust, concentrated wines. Just north of this well-run property is the fifth growth Ch Cantemerle. The commune of St-Laurent, inland from ST-JULIEN on the main road through the forests of the Médoc, boasts the improving fourth growth Ch La Tour-Carnet and two improving fifth growths, Chx Belgrave and Camensac.

The area classified as Haut-Médoc as opposed to any more specific commune grew

very slightly to 4,600 ha/11,360 acres by 2004 at which level it has remained. Many of these vineyards are CRUS BOURGEOIS offering some of the best value to be found in Bordeaux. The best wines share the deep colour, concentration, tannins, and some of the ageing potential of the classed growths, and are made in a very similar fashion, with the maximum permitted YIELD usually 55 hl/ha (as opposed to the 57 hl/ha permitted for the Médoc's four important village or communal appellations), and a leap of faith and selling price is needed to justify the use of new BARRELS. Some other particularly ambitious properties include Chx Beaumont, Belgrave, Belle-Vue, Bernadotte, Cambon La Pelouse, Citran, Coufran, Labat, Lamothe-Bergeron, Lanessan, Sénéjac, Sociando-Mallet, and Tour du Haut-Moulin.

The appellation Médoc

The total area qualifying for the basic Médoc appellation increased dangerously fast in the 1990s and early 2000s and reached nearly 5,700 ha/14,000 acres by 2004, 1,000 ha more than in 1996 and considerably more than that of the generally finer Haut-Médoc. It was still 5,531 ha/13,667 acres in 2013. Growers were encouraged by what they thought would be a steady increase in worldwide demand for red bordeaux. They were wrong and many found themselves in severe financial difficulties by the mid 2000s. Permitted yields are generally the same as for Haut-Médoc, and a high proportion of the wines are dominated by Merlot. Much of the wine produced on these lower, less well-drained, heavier soils is solid if uninspiring claret sold in bulk to CO-OPERATIVES or to the BORDEAUX TRADE for blending into GENERIC Médoc, if the growers are lucky. Estates on which an effort is made to produce something more distinctive than this, usually by restricting yields and refining winemaking, include Chx Les Grands Chênes, Les Ormes Sorbet, Potensac (run particularly fastidiously by the owners of Ch LÉOVILLE LAS CASES of St-Julien), Preuillac, La Tour de By, Tour Haut-Caussan (one of Bordeaux's rare ORGANIC WINES), and Vieux Robin. Goulée is a particularly concentrated blended Médoc made by the owners of Ch Cos d'Estournel.

For more details, see BORDEAUX.

Brook, S., *The Complete Bordeaux* (rev. edn, London, 2010).

Penning-Rowsell, E., *The Wines of Bordeaux* (6th edn, London, 1989).

Seguin, G., ' "Terroirs" and pedology of wine growing', *Experientia*, 42 (1986), 861–72.

Méjanelle, La, small named TERROIR within the LANGUEDOC AOC in southern France, just east of MONTPELLIER. Unlike the rest of the Coteaux du Languedoc, this is a historic zone of individual estates, most notably Ch de Flaugergues.

Syrah, Grenache, and Mourvèdre dominate in these particularly Mediterranean vineyards, at a much lower elevation than much of the rest of the Languedoc AOC.

Melnik, powerful ancient late-ripening BULGARIAN red grape variety that is grown on 1,580 ha/3,902 acres in 2013 exclusively in the Struma Valley around the historic town of Mělnik close to the Greek border in what was Thrace. It may therefore have been cultivated here for many centuries (see GREECE, Ancient) and its wines certainly taste more Greek in their extract, tannin, and alcohol than typical of modern Bulgaria. Its full name is **Shiroka Melnishka Losa**, or 'broad-leaved vine of Melnik', and its berries are notably small with thick, blue skins. Some wines have the aroma of tobacco leaves, another local crop. Oak ageing and several years bring out a warmth and style not unlike a NEBBIOLO. This is probably the Bulgarian wine with the greatest longevity, but see also MAVRUD. An early ripening clone, Ranna Melnishka Losa, yields wines with rounder fruit and softer tannins.

Melon, or **Melon de Bourgogne**, the most planted grape variety in the Loire valley, planted on 10,798 ha/26,671 acres in 2011 and famous in only one respect and one region, MUSCADET. As its full name suggests, its origins are Burgundian, and this is one of the many progeny of Pinot and Gouais Blanc (see PINOT). Melon was outlawed from Burgundy just like Gamay at various times during the 16th and 17th centuries. Unlike its fellow white Burgundian and sibling Chardonnay, several of whose synonyms include the word Melon, it is not a noble grape variety but it does resist cold well and produces quite regularly and generously. It had spread as far as Anjou in the Middle Ages according to Bouchard and so it was natural that the vine-growers of the Muscadet region to the west might try it. It became the dominant vine variety of the Loire-Atlantique in the 17th century, when DUTCH traders encouraged production of high volumes of relatively neutral white wine, in place of the thin reds for which the region had previously been known, as base wines for Holland's enthusiastic distillers.

Melon's increasing importance today rests solely on MUSCADET, although it is also grown to a limited extent in Vézelay in northern Burgundy.

Many of the older cuttings of the variety called PINOT BLANC in California were in fact Melon.

Bouchard, A., 'Notes ampelographiques rétrospectives sur les cépages de la généralité de Dijon', *Bulletin de la Société des Viticulteurs de France* (1899).

Galet, P., *Dictionnaire encyclopédique des cépages* (Paris, 2000).

Mencía, increasingly valued red grape variety grown so widely in north-west Spain that plantings totalled 8,601 ha/21,244, notably in BIERZO, RIBEIRA SACRA, and VALDEORRAS (see map under SPAIN). DNA PROFILING laid to rest the once-popular theory that Mencía and Cabernet Franc were related, but more recently showed that the variety called JAEN, or Jaen du Dão, is Mencía. In addition, the rediscovery by young wine-makers of old, low-yielding hillside plots of Mencía has dispelled the notion that this variety necessarily produces light reds since wines of great concentration and complexity have emerged from these forgotten vineyards on deep schists and produced a PRIORAT-like revolution in the region. It was the fertile plains on which Mencía was replanted after PHYLLOXERA, with resulting high yields, that gave the variety its reputation for dilution.

Mendocino, one of CALIFORNIA's largest and climatically most diverse counties. All of its 17,000 acres/6,900 ha of vineyards are in the southern half. Even there, the meteorological range between the coastal Anderson Valley AVA and the interior McDowell Valley AVA (barely used) is extraordinary.

Isolation from San Francisco kept its 19th-century vineyards small, and delayed their impact outside the county. The same isolation kept wine for surreptitious resale there throughout PROHIBITION. Most of the plantings flank the town of Ukiah, near the headwaters of the Russian River. Redwood Valley was the first to have its own AVA, later joined by tiny Cole Ranch, Mendocino Ridge, Covelo, Dos Rios, McDowell Valley, Potter Valley, Yorkville Highlands, and Anderson Valley.

Mendocino AVA

The coverall AVA in Mendocino county includes the more specific Anderson Valley, Yorkville Highlands, Mendocino Ridge, McDowell Valley, and Potter Valley AVAs, as well as the county's most substantial vineyard plantings along the Russian River course from Redwood valley southward through Ukiah to Hopland and on south into Sonoma county's Alexander Valley. Cabernet Sauvignon and Sauvignon Blanc have been reliable in the large zone along the Russian River. Zinfandel and Petite Sirah from third-generation Italian–American growers on the benchlands can reach great heights in the hands of an artisan wine maker. Fetzer and its sibling Bonterra, whose grapes are grown organically, are the dominant wineries by size; Frey is notable as a producer of ORGANIC WINE, from grape to bottle.

Anderson Valley AVA

Scouts for Louis ROEDERER of Champagne say they hunted in California until they found somewhere with weather as bleak as Roederer's home in north-eastern France, and that Mendocino county's coast-hugging Anderson Valley fitted their requirement perfectly. Visually, scores of scenes sluiced out by a short, swift river, the Navarro, make landscape painters lunge for canvas and brushes. Close framed by steep hills, the valley has only a couple of patches that might pass for floor and, unusually for California's valley vineyards, only one or two of the 20 or so are flat. Anderson Valley is hardly 10 miles end to end, but a steady rise in elevation from 800 to 1,300 feet combines with a rising wall of hills to make the inland end at Boonville warmer and sunnier than the oft-befogged area between Philo and Navarro, where most of the vines grow.

Redwood logging, sheep and apples reigned here until grapes came, a little wave of them in the 1970s, a bigger one in the 1980s, and then a spate of celebrity weekend homes in the 1990s. A couple of extraordinary Gewürztraminers have come from Anderson Valley AVA. Some of its Rieslings and Chardonnays have been memorable. Ridgetops to the west have yielded a succession of wonderfully oak-ribbed Zinfandels from a scattering of tiny patches. Greenwood Ridge, Handley, and Navarro vineyards are the mainstay wineries for table wine production, with Roederer Estate and its sister winery, Scharffenberger, producing admirable TRADITIONAL METHOD sparkling wines.

Pinot Noir now looms large in Anderson Valley, with Duckhorn's Goldeneye operation leading the way. The chilly Pacific breezes that channel through the valley are conducive to the growing of crisp, aromatic, elegant Pinot Noirs, and respected producers from outside the region such as Littorai, Williams Selyem, and Siduri have long sought grapes from the valley. Local producers are finally realizing what they have, and retaining more and more of their grapes.   B.C.C. & L.M.

Mendoza, the most important wine-producing province in ARGENTINA.

Menetou-Salon is just west of, and very much smaller than, the much more famous SANCERRE, near the city of Bourges, producing a not dissimilar range of red, white, and rosé wines which can often offer better value—from 535 ha/1,321 acres of vines in 2012. Sauvignon Blanc grown here is capable of making wines every bit as refreshingly aromatic as Sancerre. Soils in the appellation are mainly LIMESTONE and can be very similar to those in the more famous zone to the east, although Menetou's vineyards are flatter and less compact, resulting in a less favourable mesoclimate. The best zone is around the village of Morogues, a name used on the labels of producers such as Henry Pellé. The village of Parassy also has a high concentration of vineyards. Sauvignon Blanc represents about 60% of the appellation's total production, while Pinot Noir grapes are responsible for scented, light reds and pinks for early consumption, this lightness owing much to relatively high permitted yields—yet more evidence of the similarity between Sancerre and Menetou-Salon.

See also LOIRE, including map.

Méntrida, Spanish town and wine zone south west of Madrid in CASTILLA-LA MANCHA (see map under SPAIN) traditionally producing robust red wines from GARNACHA grapes. The one producer who is making high-quality wine in this part of Spain, Marqués de Griñon, grows CABERNET SAUVIGNON, CHARDONNAY, SYRAH, and PETIT VERDOT in his vineyard at Malpica de Tajo, which used to be just outside the denomination but has now been incorporated within it. He spurned the opportunity to jump rank from what was then the lowest to the local DO and was rewarded in 2002 with his own single-estate DO (see VINO DE PAGO), Dominio de Valdepusa. Meanwhile, a small number of producers in Méntrida proper and in its mountainous northern area, part of the GREDOS region, began making significant progress with local Garnacha and Albillo Real grapes as well as with Syrah and Cabernet Sauvignon.

R.J.M. & V. de la S.

Menu Pineau, old LOIRE WHITE WINE grape sometimes called Arbois Blanc or Orbois and a progeny of the prolific GOUAIS BLANC. A few hundred hectares remain, producing such wines as VALENÇAY, CHEVERNY, occasionally one labelled TOURAINE, and the odd NATURAL WINE. It is a vigorous vine whose wines are softer than those of CHENIN BLANC.

Meranese, or **Meraner** in German, red wines based on SCHIAVA grapes, from around the town of Merano in ALTO ADIGE.

mercaptans, or thiol compounds, are a group of usually potent and often foul-smelling chemical compounds formed by YEAST metabolism during alcoholic FERMENTATION or by yeast reacting with SULFUR in the LEES after fermentation. If not removed from the new wine (which can usually be achieved by simple AERATION, by prompt RACKING, for example) less volatile and even more unpleasant compounds tend to be formed.

At extremely low concentration, some mercaptans can have less undesirable and even pleasant odours. An example of this phenomenon is to be found in the mercaptans recently discovered as important contributors to the varietal aroma of Sauvignon Blanc and other wines, see FLAVOUR COMPOUNDS and FLAVOUR PRECURSORS. Professor Denis DUBOURDIEU and his group at the University of BORDEAUX, who have extensively investigated the role of mercaptans in wine aroma, have also found that benzyl mercaptan contributes to the empyreumatic aroma, i.e. reminiscent of smoke or 'gun flint', of Chardonnay, as well as some Sauvignon Blanc and Sémillon wines. Even OAK FLAVOUR is affected by mercaptans, and furfuryl mercaptan, a compound with a powerful coffee aroma, can be released into wines during maturation in barrels with toasted STAVES. While the detailed chemical and biological mechanisms responsible for the formation of mercaptans in wines are not known in every case, Professor Alain Maujean has reviewed and discussed the known chemistry of sulfur in winemaking.

P.J.W.

Blanchard, L., Tominaga, T., and Dubourdieu, D., 'Formation of furfurylthiol exhibiting a strong coffee aroma during oak barrel fermentation from furfural released by toasted staves', *Journal of Agricultural and Food Chemistry*, 49 (2001), 4833–5.

Maujean, A., 'The chemistry of sulfur in musts and wines', *Journal International des Sciences de la Vigne et du Vin*, 35 (2001), 171–94.

Tominaga, T., Guimbertau, G., and Dubourdieu, D., 'Contribution of benzenemethanethiol to smoky aroma of certain *Vitis vinifera* L. wines', *Journal of Agricultural and Food Chemistry* 51, (2003), 1373–6.

merchants are almost as important to the wine world as producers and consumers, and may have been for at least four millennia. Four very different types of wine merchant are considered below, but they share a dependence on the vine and the attractions its produce has for the consumer.

Ancient Greece

As outlined in the ancient history of TASTING, specialized wine merchants already existed as a class in Ancient GREECE. They developed the art of wine tasting which, with cunning, could be applied to the art of selling wine, as recorded in detail by the 3rd century AD writer Florentinus (preserved in the *Geoponica* 7. 7):

Purchasers of wine should be offered a taste when the north wind blows [when, as he has already explained, wines taste at their best]. Some people try to trick their customers by using an empty cup which they have dipped in very good wine with a great aroma. The quality of the wine leaves its trace for some time, so that the bouquet seems to belong to the wine now poured in the cup, and in this way they deceive the customer. More unscrupulous dealers put out cheese and nuts in the shop, so as to tempt the customers who come in to eat something; the aim is to prevent them from tasting accurately. I record this not as a suggestion for us to follow, but so that we shall not suffer from these practices. The farmer will often need to taste the wine, both new and old, to detect wine which is about to deteriorate.

N.G.W.

Modern Britain

The British wine merchant is, almost necessarily, an importer, or a customer of one. Wine merchants were important in medieval England and Gascony, when they were known as VINTNERS in English. Even today, a wine merchant in Britain enjoys a social standing perceptibly higher than that of, for example, a grocer. This is somewhat ironic since the majority of the wine sold in Britain has been sold by grocers, as opposed to specialists, since at least 1987. This was largely due to the efforts of the licensed supermarkets to improve the range and quality of wines they sell, although it is also simply a function of the fact that so many Britons pass through a supermarket at some point every week. The independent specialist wine merchant has to struggle to compete with the low margins funded by the sheer quantity of wine a chain of supermarkets can sell. They do so by offering personal service, advice, sale or return facilities, credit, mail order, glass loan, and so on, with the supermarkets and such specialist chains as have survived the onslaught of competition from supermarkets hot on their heels.

France

The French term most often translated as merchant is *négociant*, most often a producer/bottler rather than a specialist retailer (known as a *caviste* in French and still a relatively rare phenomenon), since so many wine purchases in France have been made direct from the producer (*vente directe*) or, increasingly, at the supermarket (*grande surface*). See NÉGOCIANT and BORDEAUX TRADE for more details.

US

As American wine enthusiasts proliferate, so do wine retailers in the US, even though they have to deal with the constraints of the THREE-TIER SYSTEM and, in many states, compete with large supermarkets groups. Unlike their British counterparts, the best routinely sell mature FINE WINE by the single bottle rather than by the CASE.

See also wine TRADE.

Mercurey, most important village in the Côte CHALONNAISE district of Burgundy. While most of the production is in red wines made from Pinot Noir, a small quantity of unusually scented white wine from Chardonnay is also made. With 650 ha/1,600 acres under vine, Mercurey produces almost as much wine as the other principal Côte Chalonnaise appellations Givry, Rully, and Montagny combined. The appellation, including the commune of St-Martin-sous-Montaigu, includes 32 PREMIER CRU vineyards making up over 20% of the total.

The red wines tend to be deeper in colour, fuller in body, more capable of ageing, and half as expensive again as those of the neighbouring villages. Maximum yields for Mercurey are the same as those for VILLAGE WINES in the CÔTE D'OR, unlike the other appellations of the Côte Chalonnaise.

Mercurey is said to have been the favourite wine of Gabrielle d'Estrées, although her lover Henry IV preferred neighbouring Givry. The leading producers are Ch de Chamirey, Faiveley, Michel Juillot, Lorenzon, Raquillet, and de Villaine.

J.T.C.M.

Merenzao, relatively rare red grape in VALDEORRAS in north-west Spain, sometimes known as María Ordoña. See also TROUSSEAU.

Mérille, basic red wine grape once widely planted in SOUTH WEST FRANCE, and still very occasionally found in FRONTON blends.

meristem culture. See TISSUE CULTURE.

Meritage (rhymes with heritage), name coined in 1981, by the winner of a competition in the *Los Angeles Times*, for American wines made in the image of a BORDEAUX BLEND, devised to distinguish these wines from VARIETAL Cabernet Sauvignon, Merlot, etc., most usefully on wine lists. This trade-marked name is legally available on labels only to American wineries that agree to join the Meritage Alliance (previously Association) and for wines that are made exclusively from two or more of the varieties Cabernet Sauvignon, Cabernet Franc, Merlot, Malbec, Petit Verdot grapes for red wines (the less widely planted St-Macaire, Gros Verdot, and Carmenère are also allowed), and Sauvignon Blanc, Sémillon, and Muscadelle for whites. Nearly but not all of the members are in CALIFORNIA. The term is now relatively rarely used in California but is common in other US states such as VIRGINIA.

B.C.C.

www.meritagealliance.com

Merlot or **Merlot Noir**, black grape variety originally associated with the great wines of St-Émilion and Pomerol but it has become so popular worldwide that by 2010 it was the second most-planted variety overall, not far behind CABERNET SAUVIGNON. Its late 20th-century increase in popularity may be most readily associated with a short-lived FASHION for it in the United States, but in reality total American Merlot plantings lag behind those of Cabernet Sauvignon by quite a margin and it is in Bordeaux, and in France overall, that earlier-ripening Merlot is so decisively the most planted red wine grape with a total that had reached 114,306 ha/282,336 acres by 2012 (when Cabernet Sauvignon's total had fallen to 51,769 ha/127,923 acres).

It was already documented as a good-quality vine variety in the Libournais in 1784 according to the historian Enjalbert, and in 1868 was noted by A. Petit-Laffitte as the Médoc's premier variety for blending with the much younger grape variety Cabernet Sauvignon. DNA PROFILING has shown it is the progeny of CABERNET FRANC and an obscure western French variety recently named Magdeleine Noire des Charentes. In consequence, Merlot turns out to be the probable half-brother of Cabernet Sauvignon, which helps to explain why Merlot-dominant red bordeaux can taste so like Cabernet-dominant red bordeaux. Merlot the wine is generally plumper, fruitier, and softer than Cabernet but its flavour is arguably much less emphatic.

If any single wine promoted TEXTURE rather than flavour to the front rank of concerns for American winemakers it was Merlot, 'Cabernet without the pain' (cf. ASTRINGENCY). Indeed one of its flavour characteristics in France, a fragrance bordering on HERBACEOUSNESS, is seen as a positive drawback by many American tasters.

Throughout Bordeaux and SOUTH WEST FRANCE and, increasingly, much of the rest of the world, Merlot plays the role of constant companion to the more austere, aristocratic, long-living Cabernet Sauvignon. Its early-maturing, plump, lush fruitiness provides a more obvious complement to Cabernet Sauvignon's attributes than the CABERNET FRANC that often makes up the third ingredient in the common BORDEAUX BLEND. It also provides good viticultural insurance in more marginal climates as it buds, flowers, and ripens at least a week before Cabernet Sauvignon (although this makes Merlot more sensitive to frost, as was shown dramatically in 1991 when some RIGHT BANK properties hardly produced any wine at all). Its early flowering makes it particularly sensitive to COULURE, which weaker ROOTSTOCKS can help to prevent. Merlot is not quite so vigorous as Cabernet Sauvignon but its looser bunches of larger, notably thinner-skinned grapes are much more prone to ROT. It is also more sensitive to DOWNY MILDEW. (Spraying can be a particularly frequent phenomenon in the vineyards of Bordeaux.) Merlot responds much better than the late-ripening Cabernet Sauvignon to damp, cool soils, such as those of St-Émilion and Pomerol, that retain their moisture well and allow the grapes to reach full size. In very well-drained soils, dry summers can leave the grapes undeveloped. Unlike Cabernet Sauvignon, Merlot is extremely sensitive to the timing of HARVEST, and acid levels can be dangerously low if picking is delayed too long. Merlot arguably reaches its apogee in the finest wines of Pomerol such as PETRUS and Le PIN.

For the vine-grower in anything cooler than a warm or hot climate, Merlot is much easier to ripen than Cabernet Sauvignon, and has the further advantage of yielding a little higher to boot. It is not surprising therefore that, in France and northern Italy, total Merlot plantings have for long been greatly superior to those of Cabernet Sauvignon.

This is particularly marked in Bordeaux, where Cabernet Sauvignon dominates Merlot only in the famously well-drained soils of the Médoc and Graves—and even here Merlot plantings increased considerably in the late 1990s, typically at the expense of Cabernet Franc. Elsewhere, not just in St-Émilion and Pomerol but also in Bourg, Blaye, Fronsac, and, importantly, those areas qualifying for basic Bordeaux or the rest of the so-called BORDEAUX CÔTES appellation, Merlot predominates.

Merlot is also more widely planted than either sort of Cabernet in the rest of SOUTH WEST FRANCE. Wherever in this quarter of France the APPELLATION CONTRÔLÉE regulations sanction Cabernet Sauvignon (see CABERNET SAUVIGNON for details), they also sanction Merlot, although the latter is favoured in the Dordogne while the Cabernets are preferred in Gascony.

With Syrah, Merlot has been a major beneficiary of the Languedoc's replanting with 'improving' grape varieties. Total plantings in the Languedoc more than doubled between 1988 and 1998 and had reached 28,251 ha/69,780 acres by 2011. Most of this is destined for fruity, easy, early-drinking Pays d'Oc wines for the only Languedoc appellations to sanction Merlot within their regulations are CABARDÈS and MALEPÈRE.

Merlot has long been grown in Italy and the country's national total had reached 28,042 ha/69,293 acres by 2010. It is planted particularly in the north east, often alongside Cabernet Franc, where vast quantities of the wine called there 'Merlott' are grown on the plains of both GRAVE DEL FRIULI and PIAVE, even if better, more concentrated wines come in smaller quantities from higher vineyards. In FRIULI indeed, where Merlot performs perceptibly better than most CABERNET, there is even a Strada del Merlot, a tourist route along the Isonzo river. Individual denominations for Merlot abound in FRIULI, VENETO, and TRENTINO-ALTO ADIGE. Merlot is also planted on the Colli BOLOGNESI in Emilia-Romagna. The variety is planted in 14 of Italy's 20 regions. In general, little has been expected from or delivered by the sea of light, vaguely fruity Merlot from northern Italy, which makes it all the more remarkable that the variety is being taken seriously by a handful of producers in Tuscany and Umbria and, more recently, in Friuli itself. ORNELLAIA in BOLGHERI and the Fattoria di Ama in CHIANTI CLASSICO were some of the first to show that Italy could provide something more in the mould of serious Pomerol, with Masseto and L'Apparita respectively. Many Italian producers still in thrall to INTERNATIONAL VARIETIES prefer Merlot to Cabernet Sauvignon, both for ripening more easily and for being a less dominant blending component with native Italian varieties. In the south of Italy it can be a challenge to give Merlot definition.

Merlot is vital to the wine industry of Italian SWITZERLAND and is made at a wide range of quality levels, including some very fine wines indeed.

In eastern and central Europe Merlot plays a very important role. It has also been popular over Italy's north eastern border in western SLOVENIA and all down the Dalmatian coast in CROATIA, where it can be attractively plummy when yields are restricted. It is also known in HUNGARY, notably around Eger in the north east and Villány in the south but, as in AUSTRIA, Cabernet Franc is much more highly regarded. It is also the most widely planted red wine variety in ROMANIA, where total plantings had grown to 11,625 ha/28,714 acres by 2012, and it occupies a similar position over the border in MOLDOVA. Merlot is almost as widely planted in BULGARIA, particularly the south of the country, as Cabernet Sauvignon, with which it is often blended.

The fact that it is slightly lower in acidity as well as international *réclame* may have hindered its progress in some warmer climates such as Iberia and most of the eastern Mediterranean, where it is not generally as common as the more structured Cabernet Sauvignon. For example, in 2012, Spain grew more than 21,000 ha of the latter and less than 13,500 ha of Merlot, most successfully in Penedès.

In the 1990s, and until SIDEWAYS punctured its reputation, Merlot was suddenly regarded as 'the hot varietal' in the Cabernet-soaked state of California, and demonstrated decisively that it had a particular affinity with the conditions of Washington state and those of Long Island in NEW YORK state.

In 1985, California had a total of hardly 2,000 acres/800 ha of Merlot. This had already risen to about 8,000 acres by 1992 when the faddish American mass market discovered the variety as softer and milder than the state's Cabernet Sauvignons, and demand soared. By 2003, there were 52,000 acres in the ground in California, although the intensity of the FASHION for Merlot led to stretching and over-enthusiastic IRRIGATION for a while. Plantings, in all but the coolest regions of the state, seem to have settled down at around 45,000 acres. See CALIFORNIA for more detail of the wine style.

Merlot has had little success in Oregon's vineyards, where the much cooler climate makes coulure too grave a problem, but in Washington's sunny inland Columbia basin, Merlot has produced consistently fine, fruity, well-structured reds about which there are more details under WASHINGTON. Merlot is the state's second most popular black grape variety with 8,235 acres/3,334 ha in 2012, although

Merlot's susceptibility to WINTER FREEZE can occasionally prove disastrous in this desert climate. Merlot is also grown increasingly in other North American states, notably in NEW YORK's Long Island.

In South America, Merlot has become extremely important to Chile's prolific wine exports. Vines called Merlot have done particularly well in the damper soils of the more southerly wine regions in Chile's Central Valley, although it took some time to distinguish satisfactorily between true Merlot Noir and CARMENÈRE (which almost equalled Merlot's total Chilean plantings of 11,432 ha/28,237 acres by 2012. See CHILE for more detail. It is also planted to a more limited extent in ARGENTINA, URUGUAY (where it can blend well with the local TANNAT), BRAZIL, and BOLIVIA.

Merlot has never really taken off in AUSTRALIA, where plantings in the irrigated interior proliferated in the 1990s to satisfy US demand but have remained steady at around 10,000 ha this century, just over a third as extensive as those of Cabernet Sauvignon.

Merlot clearly has potential in New Zealand, too, particularly Hawke's Bay, and plantings were about 1,200 ha in 2012, making it the country's second most planted red wine grape after Pinot Noir and far more popular than the late-ripening Cabernet Sauvignon. South Africa has produced some interesting varietal Merlots as well as using it to good effect in various BORDEAUX BLENDS, but it is only the fourth most popular red wine variety after Cabernet Sauvignon, Shiraz, and even Pinotage.

Enjalbert, H., *Les Grands Vins de St-Émilion, Pomerol et Fronsac* (Paris, 1983).

Robinson, J., Harding, J., and Vouillamoz, J., *Wine Grapes, a complete guide to 1,368 vine varieties, including their origins and flavours* (London, 2012).

Merseguera, lacklustre Spanish white grape variety (Esquitxagos in Penedès) widely grown in ALICANTE, JUMILLA, and VALENCIA. The vine is vigorous and fertile and has compact bunches of large grapes.

Meslier St-François is, like MENU PINEAU a white grape variety that is a local speciality of the Loir-et-Cher *département* in the westward bend of the Loire but has been disappearing at an even faster rate. DNA PROFILING revealed it as a natural cross of GOUAIS BLANC and CHENIN BLANC.

mesoclimate, a term of climatic scale, intermediate between regional climate or MACROCLIMATE, and the very small scale MICROCLIMATE. It encompasses the more specific terms TOPOCLIMATE and SITE CLIMATE, and has largely replaced both in specialist usage (although the word microclimate is widely and incorrectly used by non-specialists for mesoclimate). The usual scale of a mesoclimate is in tens or hundreds of metres, so one speaks correctly of the mesoclimate of a particular vineyard or potential vineyard site.

The full definition of a mesoclimate (or site climate) requires detailed on-the-spot records, but these are seldom available over the long periods (conventionally 30 years or more) needed to iron out short-term climatic fluctuations, and thus to be fully representative. The process can be considerably shortened if site records can be calibrated continuously against those of a nearby and reasonably comparable older climate-recording station. The differences, once established as consistent over a number of seasons, can be applied to the longer-term records of the latter.

In the absence of any local temperature measurements it is still possible to make fair estimates by interpolating within known regional trends, and then allowing for differences in elevation at the rate of 0.6 °C/1.1 °F per 100 m/330 ft. Following that, individual mesoclimates can be approximated more closely still by allowing for features of TOPOGRAPHY such as slope and aspect, and even soil type, as discussed in general terms by Geiger. J.G.

Geiger, R., *Das Klima der bodennahen Luftschicht* (4th edn, Brunswick, 1961), trans. by Scripta Technica, Inc., as *Climate near the Ground* (Cambridge, Mass., 1966).

Gladstones, J., *Viticulture and Environment* (Adelaide, 1992).

Iland, P., et al., 'Climate and the vine', in *The Grapevine: From the Science to the Practice of Growing Vines for Wine* (Adelaide, 2011).

Mesopotamia. In ancient Mesopotamia, which lay in the fertile land between the rivers Tigris and Euphrates and is often thought of as the cradle of civilization, the most widely consumed alcoholic drink at all periods was probably BEER. However, grape wine is already mentioned in cuneiform texts preserved on clay tablets from Ur dating to approximately 2750 BC. Vines do not grow so well in the low-lying and humid south of Mesopotamia, and wine seems to have been imported from the more mountainous north. This is probably the origin of the poetic Mesopotamian name for wine, 'beer of the mountains'.

By the first millennium BC, wine was as widely used as beer, at least in privileged circles. Unfortunately, little information is available about the methods of production. Some wines, such as the so-called 'bitter wine' of Tupliash, an area lying to the east of the river Tigris, seem to have been drunk FLAVOURED with herbs.

But from the beginning of the first millennium BC, it appears that wines were more commonly identified by their place of origin than by their type. These are mostly regions in the north or north west of Mesopotamia (in modern northern Iraq and northern Syria), but also including Suhu (a region in modern Iraq on the middle course of the river Euphrates, downstream from the modern Syrian border). In an inscription detailing offerings made to the god Marduk in his temple at Babylon, King Nebuchadnezzar II (r. 604–563 BC) mentions 'beer of the mountains', 'clear wine', and the wines of eight different named regions.

A few documents (in the form of clay tablets) survive from the early 8th century BC from the Assyrian capital Kalhu (modern Nimrud). These are the remnants of a once vast archive detailing the administration of wine rations to the 6,000-strong palace household, from the king and queen down to assistant cooks and shepherd boys. It has been estimated that the *pithoi* in the Fort Shalmaneser magazine could have held as much as 15,000 litres. The storeroom of the North West Palace was on the same scale, and combined with other cellars that remain to be discovered, the wine supplies must have been adequate to meet the needs of the palace. The king's wives received the largest daily allotments, perhaps as much as a litre a day. By comparison, six skilled workers or ten ordinary workers had to share the same amount. A harem of women from Arpad, a city of the realm, were given a *sappu* of wine each day, but the number of women and size of the jar are unknown.

Wine and beer were frequently offered, among many other foods and drinks, to deities as part of the cult, and the practice of LIBATION was widespread in temple ritual.

Among the Babylonians and Assyrians, wine was widely used, as was beer, for medicinal purposes (see MEDICINE), especially as a vehicle for various concoctions often of rather dubious, if not frankly revolting, ingredients.

See also Ancient SUMER, and see HERODOTUS for details of the earliest recorded mention of the use of BARRELS for transporting wine, down the Euphrates. See also ORIGINS OF VINICULTURE and PALAEOETHNOBOTANY AND THE ARCHAEOLOGY OF WINE. J.A.B.

Bottéro, J., 'Getränke' ('Drinks'), *Reallexikon der Assyriologie und vorderasiatischen Archäologie* (the standard reference work on the subject, 1st pub. in Berlin, 1928, and still being completed).

Kinnier Wilson, J. V., *The Nimrud Wine Lists* (London, 1972).

Powell, M. A., 'Wine and the vine in Ancient Mesopotamia', in Fleming, S. J., and Katz, S. H. (eds.), *The Origins and Ancient History of Wine* (New York, 1995).

metabisulfite, often added to freshly picked grapes to prevent OXIDATION of the must. See SULFUR DIOXIDE.

metals. See MINERALS.

metatartaric acid. See TARTRATES.

métayage, French word for a system of sharecropping particularly common in the CÔTE D'OR whereby a vine-grower, or *métayer*, rents a vineyard or, more likely in Burgundy, part of a vineyard, and pays rent in the form of wine or grapes.

methanol, another name for **methyl alcohol**, also known as wood alcohol, is the member of the chemical series of common ALCOHOLS with the lowest molecular weight. Methanol is highly toxic. The immediate risk of ingesting any quantity of methanol is blindness, but consumption of between 25 and 100 ml (4 fl oz) can be fatal. As recently as the mid 1980s, some Italian wines were found to have been contaminated with methanol (see ADULTERATION).

Wines naturally contain very small quantities of methanol: about 0.1 g/l, or less than one-hundredth of the normal concentration of ethanol. Some methanol is naturally present in grapes and further traces are formed during FERMENTATION but most is formed by demethylating the pectin materials that are naturally present in the grape (see COLLOID and ENZYMES). Red wines, and particularly those subjected to prolonged MACERATION, are likely to have higher methanol concentrations than average. Brandy in general has rather higher levels of methanol than wine because the DISTILLATION process concentrates it. And wines and brandies made from fruits other than grapes tend to have higher methanol concentrations because grapes have fewer pectins than most other fruits. It would be impossible to ingest a dangerous level of methanol from such drinks, however, without ingesting a fatal amount of ethanol long beforehand.

Methanol is often encountered in everyday life because it is a common solvent for household products as well as being used as fuel for chafing dishes. A.D.W.

méthode ancestrale, sometimes called **méthode artisanale** or **méthode rurale**, very traditional and newly FASHIONABLE way of making a lightly sparkling, wine, usually with some RESIDUAL SUGAR and, often, some sediment. For more details, see SPARKLING WINEMAKING.

méthode champenoise, French term for the intricate traditional method described in detail in SPARKLING WINEMAKING. From 1994 the term was outlawed by EU authorities in favour of one of the following: 'méthode traditionnelle'; 'méthode classique'; 'méthode traditionnelle classique'. English-language equivalents are 'fermented in this bottle' and TRADITIONAL METHOD.

méthode classique, term for the traditional method of SPARKLING WINEMAKING approved by the EU.

méthode dioise ancestrale, SPARKLING WINEMAKING process used for CLAIRETTE DE DIE.

méthode gaillacoise, GAILLAC's version of the MÉTHODE ANCESTRALE. See SPARKLING WINEMAKING.

méthode traditionnelle and **méthode traditionnelle classique**, alternative terms for the traditional method of SPARKLING WINEMAKING that are approved by the EU.

methoxy-dimethylpyrazine, more properly **2-methoxy-3, 5-dimethylpyrazine**, or MDMP, exists in cork and becomes a taint in wine at concentrations above the perception threshold of approximately 2–4 ng/l in red and white wines. This compound is identified by aromas of fresh cork, woody, and dusty smells.

An AUSTRALIAN WINE RESEARCH INSTITUTE study in 2004 isolated this compound and confirmed that it is responsible for a taint described in Australia as 'fungal must'. It has been suggested that this may prove to be second only to TCA as a cause of CORK TAINT in Australian wine.

Simpson, R. F., et al., 'Incidence and nature of "fungal must" taint in wine corks', *Australia and New Zealand Wine Industry Journal*, 20/2 (Jan/Feb 2005), 26–31.

methoxypyrazines, FLAVOUR COMPOUNDS which result in HERBACEOUSNESS. They contain nitrogen and are secondary products of AMINO ACID metabolism. Three methoxypyrazines have been identified for Cabernet Sauvignon and Sauvignon Blanc grapes: ISOBUTYL-METHOXYPYRAZINE (IBMP), secbutyl-methoxypyrazine (SBMP), and isopropyl-methoxypyrazine (IPMP). Sensory evaluation has confirmed the contribution of IBMP, which has a very low threshold of 215 ng/l in white wine, to the aroma described as characteristic of capsicum or bell pepper and green gooseberries. It is generally the most dominant of the three. IPMP, the most abundant of the three, has a more earthy aroma, characteristic of cooked or canned asparagus (found in some New Zealand Sauvignon Blanc).

Related studies have demonstrated that the levels of IBMP and IPMP compounds in grape berries matches what is known commercially about the herbaceous wine character. First, the berry concentrations of IBMP drop markedly during ripening, as does the herbaceous character, and more so with increased sun exposure. Secondly, concentrations of IBMP are higher for grapes grown in cooler climates; Australian samples have been found to have much lower levels of IBMP than French or New Zealand samples, for example. In wine, methoxypyrazines are particularly stable against OXIDATION. Their sensory impact may be influenced through binding with other wine components. R.E.S. & D.D.

Allen, M. S., et al., 'Contribution of methoxypyrazines to the flavour of Cabernet Sauvignon and Sauvignon Blanc', in P. J. Williams et al. (eds.), *Proceedings of the Seventh Australian Wine Industry Technical Conference* (Adelaide, 1990).

Goode, J., *The Science of Sauvignon Blanc* (London, 2012).

Lacey, M. J., et al., 'Methoxypyrazines in Sauvignon blanc grapes and wines', *American Journal of Enology and Viticulture*, 42/2 (1991), 103–8.

Marais, J., 'Effect of grape temperature, oxidation and skin contact on Sauvignon Blanc juice and wine composition and wine quality', *South African Journal of Enology and Viticulture*, 19/1 (1998), 10–16.

Roujou de Boubée, D., et al., 'Location of 2-methoxy-3-isobutylpyrazine in Cabernet Sauvignon grape bunches and its extractability during vinification', *American Journal of Enology and Viticulture*, 53/1 (2002), 1–5.

Methuen Treaty, accord signed between Britain and Portugal in 1703 which gave Portuguese goods preferential treatment in Britain and encouraged the imports of Portuguese wine, at the expense of wine from the rest of Europe, notably France, at a time when PORT was evolving into the strong, sweet drink we know today.

metodo classico and **metodo tradizionale**, Italian terms for SPARKLING WINES made by the traditional method.

Meunier, how PINOT MEUNIER is known in CHAMPAGNE.

Meursault, large and prosperous village in the Côte de Beaune district of Burgundy's CÔTE D'OR producing mostly white wines from the Chardonnay grape (see map under BURGUNDY). Although Meursault contains no GRAND CRU vineyards, the quality of white burgundy from Meursault's best PREMIERS CRUS is rarely surpassed.

The finest vineyards are Les Perrières, Les Genevrières, and Les Charmes. Between them and the village of Meursault are three more premiers crus, Le Poruzot, Les Bouchères, and Les Gouttes d'Or. Another group by the hamlet of BLAGNY are sold as Meursault-Blagny if white or Blagny premier cru if red. while, at the other end of the village, Les Santenots is sold as Meursault Santenots if white and Volnay Santenots if red, as it usually is. Apart from Les Santenots, and the lean but fine red wines of Blagny, the other red wines of Meursault tend to be grown low on the slope and do not feature among the best of the Côte de Beaune.

Les Perrières was cited as a 'tête de cuvée' vineyard in the original CLASSIFICATION of 1861 and might well have been classified as a grand cru. Its character derives from the quantity of stones, which reflect the sun back onto the vines. If Les Perrières is regularly the richest wine in Meursault, Les Genevrières comes close, producing particularly elegant wines. Les Charmes is the biggest of the three major vineyards and produces the most forward wines, seductive even in their youth.

Meursault also enjoys a wealth of good wines from other named vineyards such as Chevalières, Tessons, Clos de la Barre, Luchets, Narvaux, and Tillets. These are frequently more interesting than the village wines of PULIGNY-MONTRACHET, where the water table is higher. Furthermore, it is possible to dig cellars significantly deeper in Meursault, which enables many growers to prolong BARREL MATURATION through a second winter, which improves the depth, stability, and ageing potential of the wines. Meursault comprises 316 ha/780 acres of village appellation and 132 ha of PREMIER CRU. A tiny fraction of both is red.

Meursault also hosts one of the three glorious feasts of Burgundy during the third weekend in November (see TROIS GLORIEUSES). On the Monday after the HOSPICES DE BEAUNE sale, some 600 local growers and guests gather at noon for the Paulée de Meursault, an end-of-harvest feast revived in the 1920s by Comte Jules Lafon. Everybody brings their own bottles to share with other tables. The occasion slightly belies the local proverb that he who drinks only Meursault will never be a drunkard. Comte Lafon remains one of the finest producers of Meursault, alongside Boisson-Vadot, Bouzereau, Coche-Dury, Ente, Fichet, Javillier, both Jobards, Mikulski, Prieur, Roulot, and others in a village rich with individual domaines.

J.T.C.M.

Mexico is at long last developing a wine culture. The total vineyard area in the Americas' oldest wine-producing country, may have fallen to 29,000 ha/72,000 acres by 2011 but only just over 10% of this land is devoted to wine production. Most of it was planted in the 1960s in response to huge domestic demand for brandy. This demand was fuelled by protectionist import taxes on both wines and spirits, which also encouraged foreign investment from the likes of Martell and DOMECQ, brandy producers who built on the efforts of long-standing indigenous wine producers such as Casa Madero, L. A. Cetto, and Santo Tomás. According to SAGARPA, the Mexican Secretary of Agriculture, 160,440 hl/4,238,376 gallons of wine were made in 2011, while OIV estimates were 393,000 hl.

Mexico's history of wine production dates from 1521, just a year after the arrival of the Spanish conquistadores, who had no intention of forswearing wine in this new continent (see SOUTH AMERICA, history). Cortés issued an edict three years later ordering all new Spanish settlers to plant 1,000 vines for every 100 natives on the land they had been granted. In 1531, King Carlos V commanded that every vessel headed for the New World should carry vines for cultivation, which made the country self-sufficient in wine (and curbed exports from Andalucía) by the end of the 16th century. The first commercially produced wine in the oldest winery in the Americas was made in 1597 at the Mission of Santa Maria de las Parras in what is now the Casa Madero winery. Father Juan Ugarte is credited with spreading viticulture northwards from mission to mission into what is now the state of CALIFORNIA. The notable growth of Mexican viticulture and winemaking came to an abrupt end in 1699 when King Charles II of Spain's protectionist edict prohibiting wine production in Spain's new colonies was applied with particular vigour in Mexico. Only SACRAMENTAL WINE was allowed.

Thanks to PHYLLOXERA, Mexico's vineyard was but a few hundred hectares at the beginning of the 20th century but in 1948 the National Association of Winemaking was established by 15 producers, and a fragile domestic market for wine began to develop in the 1960s. The country's total vineyard area doubled in the 1970s, although there is enormous variation in characteristics between the various vineyard regions. Average annual wine production was about 2 million cases in the 1980s but, thanks to a 1989 free trade agreement with the EU and a flood of cheap imports from Europe, it shrank in the 1990s.

The seven Mexican states producing wine are Querétaro, Aguascalientes, Zacatecas, Coahuila, Chihuahua, Sonora, and, by far the most important and promising, Baja California in the north west of the country. Baja California's principal wine regions are Valle de Guadalupe, Valle de Grulla, Valle de Santo Tomás, Valle de Ojos Negros, and Tecate. Annual rainfall here is only about 12 in/300 mm but vines can thrive in the MEDITERRANEAN climate, not unlike California's with its Pacific influence, wherever IRRIGATION water can be found, although YIELDS are relatively low. Generally SANDY SOILS in Baja California mean that PHYLLOXERA is unknown, most vines are ungrafted, and VINE AGE is high. Vine varieties are Cabernet Sauvignon, Merlot, Grenache, and Syrah together with PETITE SIRAH, ZINFANDEL, COLOMBARD, and CHENIN BLANC from California, plus NEBBIOLO, BARBERA, and TEMPRANILLO.

The most important wineries are: Casa de Piedra, Paralelo, Monte Xanic, Cavas Valmar, and Viñas Liceaga, all established in the 1980s and 1990s; the much older L.A. Cetto, Casa Pedro Domecq, and Santo Tomás; and the much smaller Adobe Guadalupe, Mogor-Badan, Sinergi, and Montefiori. FREIXENET of Spain also established Finca Doña Dolores in 1983 near Cadereyta to produce Sala Vivé sparkling wine. There has been a dramatic increase in quality and ambition among the best Mexican wine producers in the early 21st century as well as a surge in international investment.

Mexico's own influence on New World wine has also been considerable, if indirect. Without Mexicans as the prime LABOUR source for vineyard work, California's late-20th-century wine industry might have developed quite differently.

B.T.A.R. & W.H.P.

www.uvayvino.org

Michigan, Midwestern state in the UNITED STATES whose vineyards between the Great Lakes of Superior, Michigan, Huron, and Erie enjoy a slightly less harsh climate than the rest of the state. The cooling effects of the lakes in summer, and their warming capabilities in the cold, snowy winter (see lake effect), make viticulture viable. The industry is well developed with over 90 wineries, several doing robust business. Wineries such as Bel Lago, Black Star Farms, Chateau Grand Traverse, Fenn Valley, Good Harbor, Left Foot Charley, Old Mission Cellars, Peninsula Cellars, St Julian (delicious sherry styles), 2 Lads, Tabor Hill, and L. Mawby (with its excellent sparkling wines) hit the high notes. Aromatic white varieties are best here—especially Riesling—with Pinot Blanc, Pinot Gris, and Gewurztraminer not far behind. Pinot Noir has so far been best used for sparkling wine, yet Cabernet Franc has shown glimmers of excellence in warmer vintages.   L.M.

Robinson, J., and Murphy, L., *American Wine* (London/Berkeley, 2013).

microbes, or **micro-organisms**, extremely small living beings, a few of which are capable of causing VINE DISEASES and FERMENTATION. Those affecting wines and vines are usually referred to as YEASTS and BACTERIA. **Microbiology** is the study of such micro-organisms, which need **micronutrients** as well as nutrients for growth. See also MICROBIAL TERROIR.

microbial terroir. While there is now greater understanding of the roles played by SOIL, GEOLOGY, climate, and viticulture in TERROIR and its expression in wine, the study of vineyard microbiology, in the soil and on the berries, and its influence on wine QUALITY and FLAVOUR is just beginning.

Recent research suggests that fungi and bacteria found on grape skins, including the YEASTS that play a part in spontaneous fermentation, may also contribute to terroir. In California, Bokulich et al. demonstrated that region and site—notably climate—as well as grape variety play a role in determining the fungal and bacterial populations found in MUST. Research by Gayevskiy and Goddard and by Taylor et al. in New Zealand revealed regional differences both in fungal communities on ripe Chardonnay and in indigenous *Saccharomyces cerevisiae* populations found in spontaneous ferments. Subsequent and related research has suggested a link between these regionally distinct yeasts and wine composition.

ORGANIC MATTER may also play an important intermediary role between vineyard geology and what we smell and taste in a wine. Given the at-best indirect relationship between geology and wine flavour, notwithstanding the common use of tasting terms such as MINERAL or stony, bacteria and fungi in vineyard soils may bridge the gap between odourless, flavourless ROCKS and the organoleptic distinctiveness of wines from specific origins. For example, as Maltman explains, the smell of wet or warm earth and stones known as petrichor and the earthy odour called GEOSMIN are derived not from the stones themselves but from the release by wetting or warming of volatile organic compounds that form a film on soil and rock surfaces. See also SOIL AND WINE QUALITY and SOIL BIOTA.

Bokulich, N. A., et al., 'Microbial biogeography of wine grapes is conditioned by cultivar, vintage, and climate', *Proceedings of the National Academy of Science*, 111/1 (2014), E139-48. doi: 10.1073/pnas.1317377110.

Gayevskiy, R., and Goddard, M. R., 'Geographic delineations of yeast communities and populations associated with vines and wines in New Zealand', *ISME Journal*, 6 (2012), 1281-90. doi: 10.1038/ismej.2011.195.

Maltman, A., 'Minerality in wine: a geological perspective', *Journal of Wine Research*, 24/3 (2013), 169-81. doi: 10.1080/09571264.2013.793176.

Taylor, M. W., et al., 'Pyrosequencing reveals regional differences in fruit-associated fungal communities', *Environmental Microbiology*. doi: 10.1111/1462-2920.12456.

microbullage, French term for MICRO-OXYGENATION.

microchâteau, a Bordeaux GARAGE WINE.

microclimate, widely misused term meaning strictly the climate within a defined and usually very restricted space or position. In viticulture, it might be at specified positions between rows of vines, or distances above the ground.

Common use of the term microclimate to describe the climate of a vineyard site, hillside, or valley is clearly wrong. The correct term for these is usually MESOCLIMATE, or possibly site climate or topoclimate.

CANOPY MICROCLIMATE is that within and immediately surrounding the vine canopy, or green parts of the vine. There are microclimates on or close to the surfaces of individual leaves, grape bunches, or even berries. Microclimates exist at various positions or depths within the soil. All these distinctions are important in understanding vine responses to environment.

Microclimate is potentially influenced by management practices, such as vine TRELLISING, vine TRAINING, and TRIMMING; vine VIGOUR and the factors affecting it; and SOIL MANAGEMENT and mulching. In this respect it differs in important ways from climatic definitions of greater dimension, such as MACROCLIMATE and MESOCLIMATE, which are wholly or largely uninfluenced by management.

Microclimate distances are normally measured in millimetres to a maximum of a few metres; those of mesoclimate, in tens or hundreds of metres.   J.G. & R.E.S.

micro-oxygenation, also known by the French term *microbullage*, and colloquially as 'microx' or 'mox', is a vinification technique initiated in 1990 by winemaker Patrick Ducournau in MADIRAN to control the AERATION of wines in tank. The method was authorized by the European Commission in 1996 and is used mainly but not exclusively on red wines. Its guiding principle is that all wines require OXYGEN to a greater or lesser extent, its aim being to enable the winemaker to deliver precise and controlled levels at various stages in the WINEMAKING process. It also addresses the issue of wine storage, effectively transforming large inert storage vessels into selectively permeable containers of infinitely variable dimensions.

Micro-oxygenation can be used during the early stages of alcoholic FERMENTATION to build a healthy YEAST population and help avoid a STUCK FERMENTATION. It also helps to maintain yeast viability, thus minimizing the production of sulfides, which may later cause REDUCTION problems. Injections of oxygen during ÉLEVAGE can also help counter the problem of reduction. But, proponents believe, its chief attribute is that it mirrors the effects of oxygen on wines treated to BARREL MATURATION: wines in barrel are exposed to oxygen passively and continually, whereas wines stored in tank are exposed to significant amounts of oxygen only during RACKING and somewhat violently. Used in conjunction with OAK CHIPS or INNER STAVES, the technique can provide an efficient, cost-effective alternative to oak barrels. Micro-oxygenation seems to favour POLYMERIZATION of tannins and the retention of PIGMENTED TANNINS resulting respectively in a softer taste and more stable colour. Some Bordeaux producers use micro-oxygenation on new wine during maceration before PRESSING as a way to begin this process while the must has all its constituents available. Proponents claim that it is also an effective remedy for GREEN or vegetal characters that are the result of slightly underripe fruit but there is no evidence of this. It has been suggested that the introduction of oxygen in this way appears to accelerate the ageing process but this is contested by those who make the equipment and promote its use. In fact, the effect of micro-oxygenation depends very much on the amount of oxygen and the period of time over which it is added.

The micro-oxygenation apparatus consists of a system of two chambers and valves connected to a cylinder of oxygen. The gas is moved into a first chamber that is calibrated to the volume of wine. It then moves into a second chamber and is delivered into the wine, a timer controlling the periodic injection of a predetermined dose. The gas passes through a small polyamide tube into the tank and diffuses through a porous ceramic stone hung near the bottom of the vessel. A typical dosage rate is between 0.75 and 3 cc of oxygen per litre of wine per month and the treatment might take four to eight months. In the absence of good scientific studies on the effects of this technique, micro-oxygenation is still largely an art. There are no firm guidelines for how much micro-oxygenation a wine can take; winemakers have to guess this and monitor the process carefully by regular tasting.

The technique was first developed as a response to the fierce TANNINS of Madiran's TANNAT grape and seems particularly well suited to tannic grape varieties. It has also been used on wines high in tannin but relatively low in ANTHOCYANINS, some SANGIOVESE, for example.

Micro-oxygenation does not necessarily preclude barrel maturation. A variation on this technique is used in barrel as a gentler alternative to racking, and one which binds less SULFUR DIOXIDE, for example. A measured amount of oxygen is injected into the wine in barrel, again with a small ceramic stone. This 'punctual' micro-oxygenation has been dubbed *cliquage*. The wine is otherwise aged conventionally in barrels, which allow continuous micro-oxygenation due to the structure of the wood and produce big, rich red wines that remain relatively supple.

By the beginning of the 21st century, approximately 2500 micro-oxygenation units were in use throughout France, particularly in BORDEAUX, where it is used on a property as grand as Ch Canon La Gaffelière, the St-Émilion grand cru classé (see CLASSIFICATION), and in at least 11 countries on five continents. Perhaps its largest take-up, however, was in Chile, where it is particularly appreciated for its ability to moderate the greenness and vegetal character found in some Chilean red wines. Results so far suggest the technique is particularly suitable for fashioning wines for short- to medium-term consumption from tannic or potentially reductive grape varieties.

Lemaire, T., 'La micro-oxygénation des vins', École Nationale Supérieure Agronomique (Montpellier, 1995).

Parpinello, G. P., et al., 'Effect of micro-oxygenation on sensory characteristics and consumer preference of Cabernet Sauvignon wine', *Journal of the Science of Food and Agriculture*, 92/6 (2012), 1238–44. doi: 10.1002/jsfa.4688.

Midi, common name for the south of France. Like 'Mezzogiorno' in Italy, it means literally 'midday' and refers to regions where midday is a time of extreme heat and inactivity, at least in summer. Midi is often used synonymously with LANGUEDOC and ROUSSILLON, although strictly speaking the Midi encompasses PROVENCE as well.

mildew. See DOWNY MILDEW and POWDERY MILDEW.

Milgranet, rare, recuperated vine speciality of French vineyards north and west of Toulouse producing particularly firm red wine.

Millau, Côtes de, small AOC with 50 ha/ 125 acres of vines in the Gorges du Tarn in the far east of SOUTH WEST FRANCE making reds and some rosés mainly from Gamay and Syrah, and the odd Chenin-based white. The Aguessac CO-OPERATIVE dominates production.

millerandage, a condition of the grape bunch in which there is an excessively high proportion of seedless berries and 'live green ovaries' (LGOs) relative to seeded berries. Poor FRUIT SET in the vine is a consequence of either COULURE or millerandage. Seedless berries are sometimes known as chicken berries (normal seeded berries are the hens). Whereas seedless berries will mature normally, LGOs do not and remain firm and green. They have been known as shot berries in the past, but this nomenclature is inappropriate because they do not fit the definition of a berry. The condition is due either to inclement weather at FLOWERING, which affects some varieties, MERLOT, for example, more than others, or alternatively to BORON deficiency, or FANLEAF DEGENERATION.

Millerandage can cause a major loss of YIELD. Some winemakers believe that millerandage is good for wine quality because of the widely held view that small BERRY SIZE makes better-quality wine. This is based in part on experience with certain CLONES, for example, the so-called Mendoza clone of Chardonnay in Australia and New Zealand that typically displays a high proportion of seedless berries. A **Millerandage Index** (MI) was defined for the first time in 2009—the higher the numerical value, the greater the expression of the condition.

P.R.D.

Iland, P., et al., 'Flowering and fruit set', in *The Grapevine: From the Science to the Practice of Growing Vines for Wine* (Adelaide, 2011).

millésime is French for VINTAGE. A vintage-dated wine is therefore said to be **millésimé**.

minerality, imprecise tasting term and elusive wine characteristic that, along with the descriptor **mineral**, became common currency in the early years of this century. Although descriptors such as flinty/gunflint (*pierre à fusil*), stony, and chalky have been in circulation for many years, particularly with reference to white wines such as those from SANCERRE and CHABLIS, the term 'minerality' has been adopted much more recently by winemakers, marketers, and WINE WRITERS. If there is little agreement as to its exact meaning, there is even less as to its causes, but it is particularly useful for describing not only an aroma and flavour, but sometimes also a TEXTURE that is undeniably present in some wines from a wide range of regions and varieties, especially, but not exclusively in COOL-CLIMATE whites. It is easier to say what it is not—fruity, vegetal, or animal—than what it is. Other descriptors that are often associated with minerality include wet stones, smoky, oyster shell, struck match, salty, iodine. As Parr et al. (2013) point out, the term has also become, for many, an indicator of quality.

Although many TASTING TERMS are metaphorical (there are no blackcurrants in wine made from Cabernet Sauvignon and no oatmeal in barrel-aged Chardonnay), there is a strong temptation to interpret 'mineral' rather more literally, suggesting or presuming that aromas and flavours thus described are derived from the vineyard site and that they are therefore a demonstration of the concept of TERROIR.

However, geologists and soil scientists are clear that there can be no direct connection between the flavour of a wine and the GEOLOGICAL minerals in the rocks that underlie a vineyard or the MINERAL elements in the soil that are nutrients for the vine. In any case, the minerals found in wine are below the threshold of sensory perception. This has not deterred researchers such as Ballester, Parr, and Heymann from trying to elucidate the meaning, reference, and underlying causes of what Ballester describes as 'an ill-defined sensory concept' although there has so far been little progress in identifying compounds in wine that are associated with the perception of minerality.

It has been suggested by both sensory and chemical analysis that the wine components giving rise to the term 'minerality' include high ACIDITY and low PH (possibly due to an alkaline soil such as LIMESTONE or chalk), and sulfur-related compounds such as MERCAPTANS, the latter also commonly described as reductive aromas and flavours (see REDUCTION), and usually attributed to reductive winemaking practices and/or the use of a CLOSURE that has a very low OXYGEN TRANSMISSION RATE, including the majority of SCREWCAPS. As Heymann et al. point out, the exception to this lack of precision is the identification by Tominaga et al. of the aroma compound benzene methane thiol (benzyl mercaptan), which is said to give Sauvignon Blanc wines, in particular, a flinty or smoky aroma.

Given these suggested connections, it is not possible to determine whether minerality is a TERROIR or a WINEMAKING effect. In any one wine it could easily be either or both. Whereas once New Zealand Sauvignon Blanc wines were typically described and appreciated as FRUIT-DRIVEN and Loire Sauvignons as flinty, the former, almost exclusively sealed under screwcap, are now sometimes considered more sophisticated and complex than they were due to the perception that they are more 'mineral'.

While research has found some common ground among tasters who use this term, there may never be an agreed, precise definition, and further research into the chemical composition of wines perceived as mineral is in progress. Perhaps once we are able to describe and explain the mechanisms that translate vineyard site and viticultural practices into wine characteristics (see, for example, SOIL BIOTA, SOIL AND WINE QUALITY, YEAST), we will also be able to use the word minerality with greater precision.

See also LANGUAGE OF WINE and TASTING NOTES LANGUAGE.

Ballester, J., et al., 'Exploring minerality of Burgundy Chardonnay wines: a sensory approach with wine experts and trained panellists', *Australian Journal of Grape and Wine Research*, 19 (2013) 140–52.

Green, J., et al., 'Sensory and chemical characterisation of Sauvignon blanc wine: Influence of source of origin', *Food Research International*, 44 (2011) 2788–97.

Heymann, H., Hopper, H., and Bershaw, D., 'An exploration of the perception of minerality in white wines by projective mapping and descriptive analysis', *Journal of Sensory Studies*, 29/1 (2013), 1–13. doi: 10.1111/joss.12076.

Maltman, A., 'Minerality in wine: a geological perspective', *Journal of Wine Research*, 24/3 (2013), 169–81. doi: 10.1080/09571264.2013.793176.

Tominaga, T., Guimbertau, G., and Dubourdieu, D., 'Contribution of benzenemethanethiol to smoky aroma of certain Vitis vinifera L. wines', *Journal of Agricultural and Food Chemistry* 51, (2003), 1373–6.

Parr, W. V., et al., 'The nature of perceived minerality in white wine: preliminary sensory data', *New Zealand Winegrower* (Feb/March 2013), 71–5.

Parr, W. V., et al., 'The evocative notion of minerality in wine: sensorial reality or smart marketing', *Proceedings of the Third Edition of the International Conference Series on Wine Active Compounds* (2014).

minerals are the dissolved inorganic constituents of vines, grapes, and wine, often called nutrients, and primarily obtained from geological minerals in the ground. Minerals in the geological sense are typically complex, crystalline compounds, and mostly insoluble (see GEOLOGY). In the nutrient sense, the term 'mineral' usually refers to individual elements, especially those that are essential (along with carbon, OXYGEN, and hydrogen) for vine growth, such as POTASSIUM, CALCIUM, and MAGNESIUM, although the term can also encompass nitrates, phosphates, sulfates, and the like.

The processes in vineyard soils whereby nutrients are derived from the geological minerals, for example weathering and cation exchange (see ION EXCHANGE), are very variable, and vine roots are able, up to a point, to select and balance their nutrient uptake. If you take into account differing viticulture and winemaking practices, not to mention possible CONTAMINATION in the vineyard or winery, and different analytical methods, then it is clear that the mineral content of a finished wine has no obvious relationship with its vineyard geology. (See also MINERALITY, NUTRITION, and SOIL AND WINE QUALITY.)

Unsurprisingly, analyses of the mineral content of wine are highly varied, though concentrations are always small. Potassium is the exception, with reported values generally between 500 and 1,500 mg/l. The other main minerals present in wine, but at lower concentrations, are calcium and magnesium. SODIUM, and elements such as IRON, MANGANESE, and COPPER, are reported in the range 0.1–100 mg/l. Values for the forty or so remaining minerals that have been detected in wine are in fractions of a mg/l. (Notable is wine's high ratio of potassium to sodium, the ratio advocated for cardiac patients' diets, and the relatively low concentration of iron, despite the traditional view that wine is an important source of this particular mineral.)   A.J.M.

mineral vine nutrition. See VINE NUTRITION.

Minervois, improving western LANGUEDOC appellation for characterful reds, generally suppler than those from CORBIÈRES to the south, together with some rosé and a little white, whose total vineyard area had fallen to 3,245 ha/8,015 acres produced on varied inland terrain in the Aude and eastern Hérault *départements* (see map under LANGUEDOC). The appellation takes its name from the village of Minerve, scene of one of the bloodiest sieges of the Cathar sect in the 13th century. There is considerable archaeological evidence that the Romans practised viticulture here. Cicero records the dispatch of wine to Rome from the *pagus minerbensis*, and La Livinière, the first Minervois village to be accorded its own appellation, **Minervois-La Livinière**, is said to take its name from *cella vinaria*, Latin for 'wine cellar'. More recently, the vineyards of Minervois were invaded first by PHYLLOXERA and then by the CARIGNAN vine, which is no longer permitted in AOC wines.

Since 1985, when Minervois was granted APPELLATION CONTRÔLÉE status, strenuous efforts have been made to upgrade overall quality, and a number of both CO-OPERATIVES and individual wine producers have made considerable investments both in winery equipment and in planting better vine varieties. Mourvèdre and Syrah must account for at least 20% of the blend, with Grenache also Lladoner Pelut allowed to make up a 60% minimum. Various combinations of Bourboulenc, Rolle (Vermentino), Maccabéo, Roussanne, Marsanne, and Grenache Blanc are responsible for the varied quality and character of white Minervois, the first two being best suited to the south eastern part of the appellation closest to the Mediterranean, while the last two perform best in western, Atlantic-influenced sites. White Minervois is increasingly aromatic and sophisticated.

The appellation can be divided into five climatic zones: Les Côtes Noires in the far north west on the coolest, most Atlantic-influenced foothills of the Montagne Noire; La Clamoux on alluvial terraces and flatter land in the south west towards Carcassonne; La Zone Centrale in the middle of the appellation at an elevation of around 400 m; La Causse on high land and poor, dry soils in the north east where yields are lowest; and Les Serres in the warmest, most MEDITERRANEAN south east.

In the extreme north east of the region, some of France's rarest and most delicate VIN DOUX NATUREL is produced: MUSCAT DE ST-JEAN-DE-MINERVOIS.

Minho, VINHO REGIONAL in north-west Portugal named after the Minho province, itself named after the river (called Miño in Spain with which it forms the boundary—see map under PORTUGAL).

Its boundaries are identical to those of VINHO VERDE DOP but producers may use different grape varieties and make wines with higher levels of alcohol than the usual Vinho Verde maximum of 11.5%. If produced other than in the MONÇÃO AND MELGAÇO subregion, the popular variety ALVARINHO must be labelled Minho. Some producers prefer Minho to Vinho Verde because of the latter's historic reputation for low-quality wines.   S.A.

minimal pruning, a viticultural technique developed by the CSIRO in Australia whereby the vines are essentially left without any form of PRUNING from one year to the next. The technique has particular application to higher-yielding, low-cost vineyards in warmer areas but was also used in some cooler regions producing high-quality wines, especially Australia's COONAWARRA region where there is a shortage of LABOUR.

The technique was developed and popularized in the late 1970s and 1980s but its scientific interest can be traced back to a difference of opinion between two eminent viticultural scientists in the late 1960s. When Professor Nelson SHAULIS of CORNELL UNIVERSITY in New York state was visiting the CSIRO at Merbein in Victoria, Australia, he debated with Dr Peter May and Allan Antcliff whether an unpruned vine might die. To settle the question a SULTANA (Thompson Seedless) vine was left unpruned; to general surprise, it produced a large crop that ripened satisfactorily. At this time there was interest in MECHANICAL PRUNING, and in many ways minimal pruning is a natural extension of that method. The technique has now been extensively evaluated for vine varieties for both wine production and DRYING GRAPES and in both hot and cooler climates.

One might imagine that an unpruned plant would exhaust itself and die if its growth and cropping were not controlled by pruning. Interestingly, the opposite is true. The production of Sultana vines, which have now not been pruned for almost forty years, has continued to be satisfactory. Although vines are not killed by pruning, it has been shown to have a weakening effect on them. Furthermore, minimal or zero winter pruning is what vines experience in their natural state, and primitive vines survived in the wild for millions of years before they were first cultivated by man and pruned. A feature of unpruned, or minimally pruned, vines is that there are many short shoots, whereas a pruned vine has fewer shoots which in turn grow more vigorously. A minimally pruned vine typically produces more fruit than one conventionally pruned, especially in the first year or so of minimal pruning. In addition, a minimally pruned vine establishes a large leaf area earlier in the growing season, which is advantageous for PHOTOSYNTHESIS.

Ripening of this increased crop can be delayed, and if RIPENING is inadequate, due to cool weather for example, then wine quality can be reduced. In hot regions a harvest delay of a week or so is of little consequence, but in cooler climates the delay may be disastrous. Research by Rousseau et al. over a seven-year period in the Languedoc found that minimally pruned vines had higher yields and ripened 7–25 days later or, for later-ripening varieties such as Mourvèdre, not at all.

Minimally pruned vines look extremely wild and untidy compared with vines pruned by hand. After several years, old wood builds up in the centre of the thicket that is an unpruned vine, and this can exacerbate the threat of pests such as MEALY BUG. During the growing season, however, the vine's appearance may not be too different from that of normally pruned vines. Where minimal pruning is practised in hotter, dry climates, shoots stop growing quite early in the summer, and so the CANOPY can be relatively open with good fruit exposure, a requirement of a good CANOPY MICROCLIMATE. Where the climate is cooler and more humid and the vines are growing in fertile, moist soil, however, shoots may continue to grow, and the bunches of grapes may effectively be buried under several layers of leaves. This shaded canopy may then result in reduced colour and flavour in the grapes and eventual wine. R.E.S.

Coombe, B. G., and Dry, P. R. (eds.), *Viticulture, ii: Practices* (Adelaide, 1992).

Rousseau, J., et al., 'Incidence of minimal pruning on wine quality', *Acta Horticulturae* (ISHS), 978 (2013), 309–16. www.actahort.org/books/978/978_36.htm.

minimum intervention. See NATURAL WINE.

Minutolo, very aromatic Puglian white wine grape once known as Fiano Aromatico but unrelated to both FIANO and any Muscat, even though it can taste quite like MUSCAT OF ALEXANDRIA. It was rescued from extinction in the early 21st century.

Miousat, light-berried vine rarity of GASCONY which has been rescued from oblivion there but is still grown in very limited quantities. According to DNA PROFILING it is HUMAGNE BLANCHE.

Mireval is the large village that gives its name to Muscat de Mireval, the sweet golden VIN DOUX NATUREL appellation that adjoins and is somewhat overshadowed by FRONTIGNAN to the west of it. Production, from about 260 ha/640 acres of Muscat Blanc à Petits Grains, has been almost exclusively in the hands of the CO-OPERATIVE, called La Cave de Rabelais in honour of the only well-known writer to have mentioned it. The wine is virtually indistinguishable from Frontignan and to those who live outside Mireval there seems little justification for Muscat de Mireval's independent existence, although soils here may be a little more CALCAREOUS than those of Frontignan.

mis(e) en bouteille is French for bottled. A wine that is **mis(e) en bouteille au château** is CHÂTEAU BOTTLED, while **mis(e) en bouteille au domaine** is DOMAINE BOTTLED. **Mis(e) en bouteille du château/domaine** is a term used by CO-OPERATIVES for their bottlings of wines they vinified from the grapes of individual properties. In French the BOTTLING operation is often referred to as **la mise**.

Misket, name for at least three different perfumed whie wine grapes in BULGARIA. By far the most important is the old, pink-skinned **Misket Cherven** which makes soft, grapey, dry wines in the south of the country. **Misket Varnenski** is a Dimiat x Riesling cross developed for the eastern Varna province, while **Misket Vrachanski** is a more aromatic but even rarer cross.

Mission, California and Mexican name for the PAÍS of Chile and CRIOLLA CHICA of Argentina, both synonyms for Listán Prieto. Historically very important as a survivor from the earliest VINIFERA vine varieties to be cultivated in the Americas, this was the original black grape variety planted for sacramental purposes by Franciscan MISSIONARIES in MEXICO, the south west of the UNITED STATES, and CALIFORNIA in the 17th and 18th centuries. Mission was an important variety in California until the spread of PHYLLOXERA in the 1880s and about 600 acres/240 ha persist, mainly in the south of the Central Valley.

Pinney, T., *A History of Wine in America* (Berkeley, Calif., 1989).

missionaries have doubtless played a role in the establishment of viticulture all over the world and, particularly, in documenting these achievements. Missions and missionaries had a particularly profound effect, however, on the history of wine production in much of Latin America, in California, in New Zealand, and, to a certain extent, in Japan.

Soon after European colonization of South and Central America, missionaries, particularly Jesuit missionaries, established missions alongside more commercial ventures and, whatever the commercial interest in establishing viticulture, the missionaries grew vines to provide some wine for the EUCHARIST (although see SOUTH AMERICA, history). Both Argentina and Chile date their wine industries from the first successful attempts to cultivate the vine at missions in the foothills on either side of the Andes in the late 16th century, and by the 17th century, Peru's viticulture, which probably predated that of both Chile and Argentina, was concentrated around Jesuit missions in coastal valleys. Mexico, however, is the Americas' oldest wine-producing country, and grape seeds were planted almost as soon as Cortés had landed there. Jesuit missionaries are believed to have been the first to cultivate vines for the specific purpose of winemaking in Baja California (northern Mexico) in the 1670s. It was not until the late 18th century that they established their series of missions up the west coast of what is now the American state of CALIFORNIA, and brought with them the so-called MISSION grape from Mexico.

Two centuries earlier, in 1545, Portuguese Jesuit missionaries had introduced wine to the feudal lords of southern JAPAN, who developed a taste for wine and continued to import it. Much more recently, it was Jesuit missionaries who sowed the seeds of the modern wine industry in CHINA.

At much the same time or even earlier, in the early 19th century, French Marist missionaries played a significant role in New Zealand's wine history by introducing vine cuttings from Europe, brought expressly to provide sacramental wine. The first Catholic bishop of the South Pacific, from Lyons, arrived with cuttings in 1838 and by 1842 they were reported to be performing well. The Mission winery in Hawke's Bay, founded by Catholic priests in 1851, is still in production and run as an adjunct to a Marist seminary.

See also RELIGION and MONKS AND MONASTERIES.

Cooper, M., *The Wine and Vineyards of New Zealand* (Auckland, 1984).

Seward, D., *Monks and Wine* (London, 1979).

Mission Haut-Brion, Château La, important GRAVES wine estate now under the same ownership as its long-standing rival Ch HAUT-BRION.

Four wines are now produced here: Ch La Mission Haut-Brion red and white (the latter known as Ch Laville Haut-Brion until 2009), the red SECOND WINE La Chapelle de La Mission Haut-Brion, and a second white produced in common with Ch HAUT-BRION over the road, under the same ownership.

La Mission's winemaking history is as old as its neighbour's. In the 16th century, Arnaud de Lestonnac, brother-in-law of Jean de Pontac (founding father of Ch Haut-Brion) was already producing wine at la Mission. Then, all through the 18th century, the Pères Lazaristes worked to restore the property to its rightful worth. The property became well known in part thanks to the patronage of the Maréchal de Richelieu. The property was revitalized by the Woltner family, who acquired it in 1919 and in many subsequent vintages managed to make even more concentrated, long-lived wines than their FIRST GROWTH neighbour, typically fermented at much lower temperatures than Ch Haut-Brion. In 1983, however, La Mission was sold to the Dillons, so that both these famous estates, the flagships of the newer PESSAC-LÉOGNAN appellation (although much of La Mission is in fact in the Bordeaux suburb of Talence rather than Pessac), are run, retaining their quite distinct premises and characters, by the same team. La Mission's red wine vines are planted on 26 ha/64 acres of vineyard and produce about 5,500 cases of the red grand vin. White wine grapes are planted on 3.6 ha/8 acres, planted with slightly more Sémillon grapes than Sauvignon to produce approximately 600 cases.

Missouri, Midwestern state in the UNITED STATES which has played an important part in the country's wine history. In the 1860s, Missouri made more wine than CALIFORNIA and NEW YORK combined. Wine production blossomed under a heavy influx of Germans in the Missouri river valley, west of St Louis, and today this area is billed to its many wine TOURISTS as 'the Rhineland of Missouri'.

When the AVA system was initiated in the 1980s, Missouri's Mount Pleasant rushed its application through the process, and America's first AVA was therefore Augusta, the site of many of Missouri's best vineyards today. It remains one of America's top ten wine-producing states and enjoys robust support from the state government, with agricultural stations, experimental wineries and talented researchers, marketers, and consultants. Many of Missouri's 114 wineries (such as Adam Puchta, Augusta, Crown Valley, Montelle, Mount Pleasant, St James, Amigoni, and especially Stone Hill) are remarkably successful in national wine COMPETITIONS. HYBRIDS and AMERICAN VINE varieties comprise a significant amount of plantings and VARIETAL Seyval Blanc, Vidal Blanc, Chambourcin, Vignoles, and Norton have set a standard for these varieties in other states.

D.F. & L.M.

Robinson, J., and Murphy, L., *American Wine* (London/Berkeley, 2013).

mistela is the Spanish term, **mistelle** the French, and **mistella** (or *sifone*) the Italian for a mixture of grape juice and alcohol. The FERMENTATION process is arrested by the addition of alcohol, leaving a sweet, stable, alcoholic liquid arguably less complex than an equivalent wine that owes its alcohol content to fermentation. It was the commercially vigorous and adaptable Dutch who developed this sort of drink, so much more stable over long journeys than wine (see DUTCH WINE TRADE). In Spain, such usefully stable sweetening agents are used in blending wines such as SHERRY and MÁLAGA, but are also sometimes sold, like France's PINEAU DES CHARENTES, for drinking as an aperitif. Other examples of wines that either comprise or may include *mistelle* are some VIN DE LIQUEUR, some VIN DOUX NATUREL, and Australia's TOPAQUE AND MUSCATS.

mites, minute insects which feed on leaf surface cells and which can be an important grapevine pest worldwide. Those that feed on the leaves include grape (or grapeleaf) rust mite (*Calepitrimerus vitis*); Pacific spider mite (*Tetranychus pacificus*), which is the most destructive; two-spotted spider mite, which is only occasionally found on grapes; and Willamette mite (*Eotetranychus willametti*). Mite feeding slows PHOTOSYNTHESIS and can reduce grape RIPENING.

In Europe, red mite (*Panonychus ulmi*) and two types of yellow mite (*Eotetranychus carpini* and *Tetranychus urticae*) cause the most damage. They feed on green parts of the vine and can affect FRUIT SET and CANE RIPENING, as well as reducing leaf health.

Predatory mites often keep these mites sufficiently under control, although it is important not to destroy them with other sprays. Sulfur sprays applied for erinose or POWDERY MILDEW are effective on some types of mite. White oil applied before BUDBREAK or miticides during summer can control mites. See also ERINOSE MITE.

M.J.E.

Mittelburgenland, wine region whose roughly 2,200 ha/5,400 acres of vines make up nearly 5% of AUSTRIA's total. It runs from just south of the city of Sopron to just north of Koszeg, both in HUNGARY but long pre-eminent urban centres of this primarily German- and to a lesser extent Croatian-speaking area that until the creation of Austrian BURGENLAND through a 1921 plebiscite was known as German West Hungary. Mittelburgenland began styling itself Blaufränkischland even before the potential for this age-worthy red wine grape here and elsewhere in Burgenland emerged in the late 1980s and 1990s. BLAUFRANKISCH represents significantly more than half of Mittelburgenland vines today. The varied geological underpinnings of Mittelburgenland's hillsides and plateaus—featuring SCHIST and occasional BASALT, LOESS as well as CLAY-LIMESTONE—play a role in the diversity and complexity of its Blaufränkisch wines. Especially important wine communes include—in a band along the region's northern edge—Neckenmarkt, Horitschon (with contiguous Raiding), and Deutschkreuz; and in its extreme south, Lutzmannsburg. Blaufränkisch is most often supplemented in this region by Zweigelt, Merlot, or Cabernet Sauvignon—with all of which it is frequently blended—although there are also plantings of Pinot Noir (Blauburgunder) as well as St. Laurent. Plantings of Syrah increased in the early 21st century. Such Blaufränkisch pioneers as Albert Gesellmann and Franz Weninger focused on showcasing top individual vineyards, beginning with Horitschon's Hochäcker. Early in the new millennium, Roland Velich—from a family of growers of sweet and dry white wines in NEUSIEDLERSEE—staked Blaufränkisch claims of avowedly Burgundian stylistic inspiration but combined with multisite blending modelled on J. L. CHAVE. His Moric wines showcasing old vines in Neckenmarkt and Lutzmannsburg soon achieved internationally coveted status.

Mittelburgenland DAC is the official Austrian DAC appellation for Mittelburgenland varietal Blaufränkisch, which constituted 55% of all Mittelburgenland vines in 2009. The KLASSIK versions of Mittelburgenland DAC wines must be 12.5–13% alcohol (13–13.5% if sitedesignated), and those labelled Reserve should have at least 13% alcohol. They should not be released before respectively 1 May and 1 August of the year following their vintage, and those of Reserve class not before 1 January and 1 March respectively of the second calendar year following their vintage. Ageing in new wood is in principle restricted to Reserve bottlings. Since its vintage 2005 inception, wines that do not qualify for the Mittelburgenland DAC or are not successfully submitted by their growers for inclusion may not be labelled Mittelburgenland but must instead be labelled Burgenland for their state of origin, which is how many growers chose to label their wines beforehand anyway.

D.S.

Mittelrhein, one of the smallest wine regions in GERMANY better known to the outside world for its cliffs and castles than its Rieslings, which however can be outstanding. Most of the 469 ha/1,158 acres of vines planted in 2013, 67% of them Riesling, grow within sight of the river RHINE, often looking down upon it from a considerable height (see map under GERMANY). The first commercial vineyards start just south of Bonn and none is found on the west bank of the river until Koblenz is reached, 58 km/36 miles upstream. Thereafter, they climb both sides of the Rhine gorge, wherever site, the MESOCLIMATE, and much hard work make vinegrowing a more or less viable exercise. The temperature is raised by the large volume of water in the Rhine (see TOPOGRAPHY), and in summer there is usually enough rain to maintain the health and strength of the vines on their porous, steep, heat-trapping slate and quartzite slopes.

Most of the good wine comes from about 12 km south of Koblenz, around Boppard (the Hamm vineyard), and from the far south near the RHEINGAU at Bacharach and adjacent Steeg, whose most notable vineyards are Hahn, Posten, Wolfshöhle, and St Jost. Because of CLIMATE CHANGE, top growers have been relying on vineyards in nearby Oberdiebach to produce Rieslings of 12% alcohol or less, thus saving some of the region's dwindling treasure of old vines. Just upstream from Bacharach, Oberwesel also harbours some well-sited Riesling. At their best, Mittelrhein Rieslings combine the minerality and tension of the Mosel-Saar-Ruwer and Nahe Rieslings with tropical fruit flavors. SPÄTBURGUNDER—which accounts for just 9% of Mittelrhein's vineyards—can also yield serious quality around both Boppard and Bacharach. While the top growers of this region make up in quality for what they lack in numbers, it is only TOURISM that sustains the Mittelrhein's part-time or hobby vine growers in a wine region that has been shrinking for a century.

D.S.

MJT, mean January/July TEMPERATURE.

moelleux, French term meaning literally 'like (bone) marrow', or 'mellow'. Wines described as *moelleux* are usually medium sweet, while very rich BOTRYTIZED wines may be described as LIQUOREUX.

Moët & Chandon, Champagne house producing the single most important champagne BRAND in the world, and part of the vast LVMH group. The Champagne house was founded by Claude Moët, born in 1683 to a family which had settled in the Champagne district during the 14th century. He inherited vineyards and became a wine merchant, establishing his own firm in 1743. He was succeeded by his son Claude-Louis Nicolas and his grandson Jean-Rémy Moët, who used his impressive connections to open up international markets for his wine. Jean-Rémy was a close personal friend of Napoleon Bonaparte, and was awarded the cross of the Légion d'Honneur in the final years of the emperor's rule. In 1832, Jean-Rémy handed over the firm to his son Victor and his son-in-law Pierre-Gabriel Chandon. At the same time, the company acquired the Abbey of Hautvillers and its vineyards (see PÉRIGNON, DOM). In 1962, Moët & Chandon's shares were quoted for the first time on the Paris Stock Exchange, leading to a period of considerable expansion. First, Moët bought shares in Ruinart Père et Fils, the oldest Champagne house, in 1963. Five years later, it acquired a 34% stake in Parfums Christian Dior, increasing this to a 50% stake shortly afterwards. In 1970, Moët took control of Champagne Mercier, a popular brand in France, and capped it all by buying out Dior and merging with the cognac house of Hennessy in 1971 to form the holding company Moët Hennessy. The acquisitions continued unabated, including, in 1981, a stake in the American importers Schieffelin. At one stage the company's American investment also involved the Simi winery in Sonoma, Moët having established Domaine Chandon, a seminal sparkling California winemaking establishment in the Napa Valley, in 1973.

This was by no means the company's first venture into the New World. Bodegas Chandon was established in Argentina in 1960, and Provifin, now Chandon do Brasil, followed in 1974, both companies making considerable amounts of wine for the domestic market, much of it sparkling. In Germany, too, a SEKT business had been established in the form of Chandon GmbH in 1968. In 1985, the group founded Domaine Chandon, Australia, to make a premium sparkling wine sold as Domaine Chandon in Australia and Green Point in the UK, and in 1987 established a company in Spain for the production of a CAVA although the winery and vineyard associated with Masía Chandon were subsequently sold to FREIXENET.

In 1987, Moët Hennessy merged with the Louis Vuitton Group, makers of luxury leather goods and then owners of Champagne houses VEUVE CLICQUOT, Canard-Duchêne, and Henriot, and Givenchy perfumes. The LVMH group's composition continues to evolve but in 2005 it owned five Champagne houses: Moët & Chandon, Mercier, Ruinart, Veuve Clicquot, and KRUG (having once also owned Pommery, and

Lanson briefly while stripping it of its extensive vineyard holdings before selling it on). Of these, Moët & Chandon and Mercier are run most closely in tandem.

Moët, the brand, continues to sell at over twice the rate of its nearest competitors and claims that one in four bottles of Champagne exported comes from the house. It is the leading brand of champagne in most world markets with a share of the champagne market in the United States that can be as high as 50%.

The house prestige cuvée is named after Dom PÉRIGNON, the legendary figure of the Abbey of Hautvillers, and broke new ground in terms of packaging, pricing, and qualitative ambitions when it was launched in 1936.   S.E.A.

MOG, or material other than grapes, refers to leaves, canes, vines, and other debris picked inadvertently with the grapes at harvest. The amount of MOG is increased by MECHANICAL HARVESTING.

Moldavia. See MOLDOVA.

Moldova, one of Europe's poorest countries, may have been one of the geographically smallest states of the former Soviet Union but it had more vineyard than any other apart from UKRAINE and the TABLE GRAPE producer UZBEKISTAN. According to industry reports, there were still 142,000 ha/350,090 acres of vineyard in 2011, including 112,000 ha planted with VINIFERA wine grapes. It has real potential for wine quality and range, thanks to its extensive vineyards, temperate CONTINENTAL CLIMATE, and gently undulating landscape sandwiched between eastern ROMANIA and UKRAINE. It declared its independence from the Soviet Union in 1991 as the **Republic of Moldova** with the same boundaries as the previous Moldavian Soviet Socialist Republic. The eastern part of the country is the breakaway zone of Transnistria (not currently recognized by any UN member state), described by the Republic of Moldova as the 'Transnistria autonomous territorial unit with special legal status'. Moldavian is the main official language, which is very similar to Romanian and spoken by around two-thirds of the population.

History

Archaeological evidence—of leaves of *Vitis teutonica*—confirms that the vine was widely grown in this area, Bessarabia, millions of years ago. Grape seeds dating back to 2800 BC have been found, as well as AMPHORAE, and the well-documented voyages to this region by the Greeks and then Romans can only have encouraged this particular branch of agriculture. HERODOTUS visited the colonies of Ancient GREECE at the mouth of the rivers Dnepr and Dnestr in the middle of the 5th century BC and reported that wine drinking was already common there.

After the feudal state of Moldova was formed in the second half of the 14th century AD, trade was established with RUSSIA, UKRAINE, and Poland, and Moldovan viticulture developed rapidly, reaching a high point in the 15th century during the era of Stephan the Great.

The Turkish occupation of Bessarabia (or Bogdan as it was known in the Ottoman empire) was a severe blow to Moldovan wine production (see ISLAM), and it was only after the country was annexed to Russia in 1812 that the industry was revived. By 1837, vineyards totalled 14,500 ha/35,750 acres and total wine production was more than 100,000 hl/2.6 million gal. Moldova, with neighbouring Wallachia, formed the basis for independent Romania in the middle of the 19th century. In 1891, Moldova's vineyard totalled 107,000 ha, much of it planted with vine varieties imported from France, but was severely ravaged by PHYLLOXERA and POWDERY MILDEW until GRAFTING was adopted in 1906. The tsars provided incentives to grow European vine varieties, which still predominate. By 1914, the province of Bessarabia (the part of Moldova between the rivers Prut and Dnestr) was Russia's most important source of wine. In 1940, the country was annexed by Russia and the vineyards were once again devastated, by the effects of the Second World War. The post-war period revival period saw energetic reconstruction and the spread of INTERNATIONAL VARIETIES so that by 1984 Moldova's vineyard area reached a peak of 258,000 ha/637,530 acres.

Since then, GORBACHEV's anti-alcoholism campaign, followed by the economically devastating effect of the Russian bans on imported Moldovan wine in 2006 and 2009, shrank the vineyard area to its current total, although a 2013 industry analysis suggested that only around 60,000 ha/148,263 acres have commercial production potential because of the advanced VINE AGE and poor quality of many vines. As yet no official vineyard register is in place.

Climate and geography

Much of Moldova is low and hilly, rarely rising above 350 m/1,150 ft above sea level and with a gradual descent towards the Black Sea in the south. The climate is ideal for viticulture, with average summer temperatures of around 20 °C/68 °F. Spring (and occasionally winter) FROST can be a problem but the active temperature summation is between 2,700 °C in the north and 3,400 °C in the south. (see CLIMATE CLASSIFICATION). The main rivers are the Dniester and the Prut. The country's four historical wine production zones are: Bălți (most northerly), Codru (central), Ștefan Vodă (south east), and Valul lui Trajan (south west). The last three of these have been established as PGIS while the remaining region of Bălți grows only 3% of the country's vines, mainly for distillation.

Codru in the centre of Moldova has a CONTINENTAL climate with mild winters thanks to the protective, forested hills to the north. Annual rainfall is 550 mm to 680 mm (22–27 in) and 2,135 sunshine hours. It is noted for fresh, floral whites and structured, COOL-CLIMATE reds that can age well. **Valul lui Trajan** is the most important region for *Vitis vinifera* and it has a more MEDITERRANEAN CLIMATE with low annual rainfall (350 mm to 500 mm) and an elevation of 280 to 300 m, while average annual sunshine is approximately 2,500 hours. Warm, dry summers, mild winters, and well-drained soils make this region best regarded for its rich reds. **Ştefan Vodă** in the south east has a TEMPERATE continental climate, with influence from the Black Sea. Rainfall is 450 mm to 550 mm a year but elevations are very low at just 60 to 70 m while annual sunshine hours are 2,200. Its most famous district is Purcari (and the renovated historic winery of the same name), noted for long-lived reds, especially Negru de Purcari. This blend of Cabernet Sauvignon, Saperavi, and Rara Neagră was famously the only wine exported from Moldova in Soviet times.

Although at the end of the 20th century much of the vineyard was controlled by state farms, by the second decade of this century around 75% of vines were in private ownership with the remainder owned by wineries. Wineries are all fully privatized with the exception of state-owned enterprises Cricova and Mileştii Mici (famous for the largest collection of bottled wine in the world and for the largest network, 200 km, of underground cellars).

Viticulture

Unlike Russia to the north east, Moldova is able to grow the great majority of its vines without WINTER PROTECTION. Most vines are CORDON-trained on medium-height trellises. Very little IRRIGATION is in place and 90% of vineyard work is done by hand due to low wages and reasonable availability of LABOUR. Average VINE AGE is notably high but some 30,000 ha/74,131 acres of vineyard were replanted between 2006 and 2013, with substantial holdings now owned and managed directly by private wineries. Several aid organizations have been working in Moldova to support the wine industry given the economic significance of wine.

Vine varieties

Moldova has a more European range of grape varieties than any other state of the former Soviet Union, with about 70% light-skinned grapes. According to official figures, 73% of varieties are European (including Aligoté 23%, Sauvignon Blanc 9%, Chardonnay 4%, Riesling 3%, Traminer 2%, and for reds Merlot 9%, Cabernet Sauvignon 8%, Pinot Noir 7%). A further 17% are described as Caucasian, including Rkatsiteli (15%) and Saperavi, while just 10% are local varieties including FETEASCĂ ALBA, FETEASCĂ REGALĂ, FETEASCĂ NEAGRĂ, and Rara Neagră (aka BĂBEASCĂ NEAGRĂ). Recent industry emphasis has been directed towards developing these INDIGENOUS VARIETIES both as varietal wines and in blends.

Wines produced

Prior to the first Russian ban in 2006, wine quality was distinctly poor as old Soviet winemaking technology was commonplace, and little attention was paid to HYGIENE or controlling OXIDATION. This was driven by the reliance on Russia (which had 80% of the export market), where demand was for semi-dry or semi-sweet wines, based on price and packaging with little attention paid to wine quality. The bans, believed to have been politically motivated, provided Moldova with the motivation to improve. Modern equipment is now widespread among key players whose vineyard ownership allows them to control grape quality, and winemakers often have foreign training or experience. Heavy bureaucracy has been abandoned and this has encouraged the establishment of small boutique wineries and an association of small wineries. Modern wine styles usually show good natural acidity and relatively moderate alcohol levels with good varietal expression. Reds can be long-lived, but are still sometimes too GREEN and made from under-ripe grapes. Moldova continues to make some FORTIFIED WINES, accounting for around 4% of production in 2012, notably Cagor, a 16%, partially fermented red, often based on Cabernet. Sparkling wines, both tank- and bottle-fermented, accounted for 6.2% of production in 2012, with state-owned Cricova the most notable producer. Famous reds made in the early 1960s such as Negru de Purcari and Rosu de Purcari have been revived since 2003.

Modern industry structure

The wine industry is a strategic and economically important sector for Moldova, accounting in 2012 for 3.2% of GDP, 7.5% of Moldova's exports by value, and 14.4% of agricultural output, while 7% of the country's arable land is vineyard. There were 140 wine companies in 2014 although only 34 produced quality wines. Production in 2012 was approximately 1.36 million hl/nearly 36 million gal (although average production has typically been closer to 1.5 million hl, compared with around 4 million hl before the first Russian ban in 2006). The vast majority is exported (40% as bottled wine, the rest as BULK). By volume, leading export destinations are the former Soviet states, which take 68% (compared with 90% in 2004). Of these, Russia remains most important (at 38%), followed by KAZAKHSTAN (15%), Ukraine (11%), and Belarus (6%). Domestic consumption of commercial wine is slowly increasing but is dwarfed by consumption of homemade wines (often from HYBRIDS such as Lidia and Isabella) estimated at 37.8 l/10 gal per capita. A Wine of Moldova brand was launched in 2014 to encourage exports outside the old Soviet bloc.

C.G.

Association of Small Producers: www.winemoldova.com

Molette is a common white grape variety, yet another progeny of GOUAIS BLANC, used particularly for the sparkling wines of SEYSSEL in SAVOIE. The base wine produced is neutral and much improved by the addition of some ALTESSE.

Molinara, red grape variety grown in 2010 on 595 ha/1,470 acres, mainly in the Veneto region of north east Italy, particularly for VALPOLICELLA. Its wines tend to be high in acidity, light in colour, and prone to OXIDATION, so the variety is losing ground to CORVINA, RONDINELLA, and INTERNATIONAL VARIETIES in the zone.

Molise, after the Valle d'AOSTA, Italy's smallest and least populated region, is a mountainous area situated south of ABRUZZO in the south east of Italy just north of PUGLIA. Impoverished by a continuous emigration of manpower for almost a century, the region has only 5,152 ha/12,730 acres of vineyards of which a mere tenth is devoted to DOC wine production. Production is almost entirely in the hands of CO-OPERATIVE wineries, which sell much of the wine in BULK.

The proximity of Abruzzo—to which the Molise was joined administratively until the 1960s—has left its mark on Molise's viticulture: the two predominant vine varieties are MONTEPULCIANO d'Abruzzo and TREBBIANO d'Abruzzo. There have been attempts to diversify, however, with the planting of grape varieties from southern Italy, especially neighbouring Campania, such as FIANO, GRECO DI TUFO, and AGLIANICO. INTERNATIONAL VARIETIES have also been planted. The region has one overarching DOC, Molise, and three other DOCs within it: Biferno, Pentro d'Isernia, and Tintilla del Molise. While this last is based on one of the very few INDIGENOUS VARIETIES of any commercial significance in Molise (and which may only be planted in vineyards of at least 200 m ELEVATION), all other DOCs are catch-all denominations based on Trebbiano Toscano and Montepulciano d'Abruzzo and including VARIETAL bottlings, notably of Cabernet Sauvignon and Aglianico.

In the past, the best wines of the region, produced by the Di Majo Norante winery, chose the IGT route in response to the world's lack of interest in Molise's DOCs although today many of their wines, made exclusively from southern Italian varieties, are now bottled as DOC wines, evidence that, however slowly, things are moving forwards for Molise.   W.S.

Belfrage, N., *Brunello to Zibibbo—The Wines of Tuscany, Central and Southern Italy* (2nd edn, London, 2003).

Moll, robust but potentially interesting white grape grown on the Spanish island of MALLORCA, also known as Prensal.

molybdenum, trace element important for plant growth but not previously considered necessary for grapevines, although a deficiency may contribute to poor FRUIT SET. Recent research in Australia suggests that foliar molybdenum sprays can overcome a vegetative growth disorder and berry development disorders of Merlot. More research is required.

CRCV, 'Grapevine nutrition 8: molybdenum', www.gwrdc.com.au/wp-content/uploads/2012/09/2006-FS-Molybdenum.pdf.

monasteries. See MONKS AND MONASTERIES.

Monastrell, Spain's third most important black grape variety, known in France as MOURVÈDRE, grown on 48,116 ha/118,847 acres, mainly in Murcia and Castilla-La Mancha.

The origins of the variety are almost certainly Spanish. Murviedro is a town near Valencia (Mataro, another name for the variety, is another near Barcelona). It is certainly easier to grow in Spain than in the cooler reaches of southern France for it buds and ripens extremely late, later even than CARIGNAN. Provided the climate is warm, the upright, vigorous Monastrell adapts well to a wide range of soils and recovers well from spring frost. (It is sensitive to low winter temperatures, however.)

The wine produced from Monastrell's small, sweet, thick-skinned berries tends to be heady stuff, high in alcohol, tannins, with a somewhat gamey, almost animal, flavour when young, and well capable of ageing provided both OXIDATION and REDUCTION, to which it is particularly prone, is carefully avoided in the winery. It is the principal black grape variety in such DOS as ALICANTE, ALMANSA, JUMILLA, VALENCIA, and YECLA.

See MOURVÈDRE, its more usual name outside Spain, for more details of where else it is grown.

Monbazillac, increasingly serious sweet white wine appellation within the BERGERAC district in south-west France immediately south of the town of Bergerac on the left bank of the DORDOGNE. Monbazillac has a long history of sweet wine production, which here seems to pre-date the influence of the DUTCH WINE TRADE (one property's label still boasts 'Réputé en Hollande depuis 1513').

Like SAUTERNES, it is made from Sémillon, Sauvignons Blanc and Gris, and, particularly successful here, Muscadelle grapes and the vineyards lie on the left bank of an important river close to its confluence with a small tributary, in this case the Gardonette. This environment favours autumn morning mists and the development of NOBLE ROT, particularly on north-facing slopes, and an increasing number of producers are willing to take the risks involved in trying to produce fully BOTRYTIZED wines. In a determined quest for quality, MECHANICAL HARVESTING was banned from 1993 and successive TRIES through the vineyard insisted upon. The top-quality botrytized, often orange-tinged wines offer exceptional value. Basic maximum permitted yields here are 40 hl/ha (2.3 tons/acre), as opposed to the 25 hl/ha in Sauternes, but in a good vintage such as 1996, the average yield in Monbazillac was 26 hl/ha (as opposed to Sauternes' 22.5 hl/ha). By 2012 the area of vineyard dedicated to Monbazillac had grown to 2,122 ha/5,241 acres, considerably more than Sauternes, where picking generally takes place earlier so vintage characteristics can be very different.

In the past, too much Monbazillac was simply a sweetened, heavy wine, sometimes redolent of SULFUR DIOXIDE, blended and bottled by a NÉGOCIANT with little passion for the possibilities that exist within this region. Since 1993, there has been a clear distinction between serious sweet Monbazillac and early-picked dry white wine which is sold as Bergerac Sec. The leading property by far is Ch Tirecul La Gravière, which makes extremely intense, rich nectar.

Monção e Melgaço, inland DOP subregion of VINHO VERDE in north west Portugal on the left bank of the River MINHO best known for single VARIETAL wines made from the ALVARINHO grape which flourishes in its relatively warm, dry, sheltered location. Substantial investment at Monção's large CO-OPERATIVE and, since the late 1990s, a proliferation of quality-focused individual estates and privately owned brands have reinforced Monção e Melgaço's reputation for making some of Portugal's best white wines. While retaining the region's freshness and distinction, Alvarinho wines here tend to be more muscular and fruity than Albariño from Rías Baixas across the river. Some wines can respond well to OAK.

Mondavi, important family in the recent history of CALIFORNIA wine, with **Robert Mondavi** (1913–2008) in particular doing more than anyone to raise awareness of the civilizing influence of wine in general and of California as a source of top-quality wine in particular.

Robert's father Cesare came to the US in 1906 from the MARCHE on Italy's east coast. He and his Italian wife Rosa ran a boarding house for miners in Minnesota before moving to LODI in California's San Joaquin valley in 1921, whence, throughout PROHIBITION, they shipped grapes back east to America's temporarily swollen band of HOME WINEMAKERS. Immediately after Repeal, Cesare turned to winemaking and was joined in the late 1930s by his sons Robert and Peter.

As early as 1936, the Mondavis made their crucial move out of the hot Central Valley (leaving GALLO to build up the world's largest winery there) into the cooler NAPA Valley where they were determined to make table wines, rather than the then much more popular dessert wines. Robert's first job in the wine industry was at the Sunny St Helena winery, then called Sunnyhill, part-owned by Jack Riordan, a friend of his father. The Mondavis acquired the nearby Charles KRUG winery in 1943. Robert Mondavi's obsession with constant fine tuning of wine quality grew here, inspired by old bottles from the Inglenook winery, and guided by oenologist André TCHELISTCHEFF. During the 1950s, he became increasingly fascinated by the CABERNET SAUVIGNON grape and in 1962 visited BORDEAUX for the first time, a seminal visit which was to convince him of the necessary conjunction between fine wine and gracious living.

This led to disputes with his younger brother Peter which were exacerbated by Cesare's death in 1959 so that by 1965 Robert was excluded from the Charles Krug winery, where Peter and his descendants remain, and won compensation only after a long and bitter lawsuit. The opening of the Robert Mondavi winery on the Oakville highway in 1966, strikingly Californian, in the mission style, thanks to architect Cliff May, marked the beginning of a new chapter not just for the Mondavis but for California wine. Just as Baron Philippe de ROTHSCHILD had signalled a new era for Bordeaux when he took over at Ch MOUTON ROTHSCHILD in the 1920s, so the Robert Mondavi winery was at the forefront of developing VARIETAL wines based on Europe's most famous vine varieties (each, innovatively, made differently); continual experimentation with different BARRELS, TOAST, FINING, and FILTRATION regimes; special Reserve bottlings; comparative tastings with France's most famous wines; wine TOURISM; and cultural events associated with the winery and its wines. It was therefore no surprise when in 1979 a JOINT VENTURE was announced between Robert Mondavi and Baron Philippe: Opus One, with its own lavish winery since 1992, was a Napa Valley Cabernet-based wine made jointly by Tim Mondavi and Mouton's winemaker. Also in 1979 the company bought a co-operative in Lodi which, producing the high-volume, lower-priced range of Woodbridge wines then known as 'fighting varietals', has been its single most profitable venture by far.

During the 1990s, Robert Mondavi extricated himself from day-to-day operations, which then also included joint ventures in Chile and Tuscany, a controlling interest in ORNELLAIA, an ambitious venture in the Languedoc, and the Byron winery in the Santa Maria Valley.

Although the Robert Mondavi winery had considerable assets in the form of 1,500 acres/ 607 ha of prime Napa Valley vineyard, and annual production of Napa Valley wine peaked in the early 1990s at about 500,000 cases (more than any other producer), borrowings and the prospect of significant inheritance taxes forced this family-owned winery to make a public share issue in 1993. In 2004, the board voted to sell the company and it was purchased by CONSTELLATION BRANDS, which disposed of many of the joint ventures, although not Opus One.

Mondavi, R., *Harvests of Joy* (New York, 1998).

Mondéjar, denominated wine zone in northern Castilla-La Mancha, Spain, near Guadalajara, created in 1996 and producing table wines of modest distinction. Tempranillo is the main variety in the 2,100 ha/5,000 acres of vineyards.

Mondeuse Blanche is a light-berried vine found in SAVOIE, producing a dry, relatively soft white wine. DNA PROFILING has shown that it is not a white MUTATION of MONDEUSE NOIRE, but a parent, with DUREZA from Ardèche, of the famous SYRAH.

Mondeuse Noire, one of the oldest and most distinctive red grape varieties of SAVOIE, bringing an Italianate depth of colour and bite to the region in contrast to the softer reds produced by the Gamay imported only after PHYLLOXERA. The juicy, peppery wines are powerfully flavoured and are some of Savoie's few to respond well to careful oak ageing (although when grown prolifically on Savoie's more fertile, lower sites Mondeuse can easily be a dull wine too, which may explain why the variety has been underrated).

Total French plantings of Mondeuse Noire fell sharply in the 1970s and were barely 200 ha/ 500 acres in 2000 but they were nearly 300 ha by 2011 when a renaissance was very much underway. Most Mondeuse is sold as a varietal Vin de Savoie, sometimes with a CRU name added. It is also grown in the Vin du BUGEY region, and from the 2010s it underwent a small revival in Switzerland where it was once well respected. It is grown on Etna in Sicily and in California. It was long confused with REFOSCO DAL PEDUNCULO ROSSO in California where it is a relative rarity, as it is in Australia.

Monferrato, extensive DOC in the hills to the east of Turin in the provinces of Asti and Alesssandria in Piemonte. Traditionally known for light and often sparkling Barbera del Monferrato, lately the region's wines have gained in quality resulting in the elevation of Barbera del Monferrato Superiore to DOCG, entailing 14 months of ageing as well as a higher alcoholic content compared with that of the normal DOC. While Monferrato serves as an overarching DOC, allowing also for the production of INTERNATIONAL VARIETIES, which, however, cannot be mentioned on labels, the region boasts a handful of interesting smaller denominations dedicated to local varieties. Grignolino del Monferrato Casalese DOC is a pale and tannic red regularly offering more interest than most italian rosés; Ruchè di Castagnole Monferrato DOCG, a rare, aromatic red wine with classic Piemontese tannic structure; and Strevi, a sweet wine made from dried Moscato grapes, while Monferrato Casalese is a dry white made from Cortese and not unlike Gavi. Although Monferrato is overshadowed by its more illustrious neighbours, notably the Langhe, its highly original wine styles deserve more attention.   W.S.

Monica, basic red grape variety grown in 2010 on 1,400 ha/3,459 acres of Sardinia, where some varietal Monica di Sardinia is thus labelled. It is thought to have originated in Spain (although it is not known in modern Spain). Its wines are generally undistinguished and should be drunk young, although more recent wines from the Santadi co-operative suggest that with YIELDS lower than the current 15 tonnes/ha, Monica could be a pleasurable, if not always memorable, wine.

monks and monasteries. Wine has always had spiritual and religious significance (see RELIGION AND WINE), and monks and monasteries have long been regarded as playing a crucial part in wine history.

While wine and the vine played a prominent role in most religions of the eastern Mediterranean during antiquity, it was in Christian religious symbolism and practice that it achieved particular significance, as an essential element of the EUCHARIST. Such Christian symbolism built on earlier Jewish beliefs in which the vine or vineyard was used as one of the favourite symbols for the nation of ISRAEL in the Old Testament. The adoption of Christianity as the state religion of the Roman empire during the 4th century AD (see Ancient ROME) meant that wine was to attain a position of the utmost ideological prominence in European society. While monasteries in the eastern Mediterranean and northern Africa continued to make wine in late antiquity, as evidenced in particular by their wine PRESSES, the religious significance of wine is widely regarded as of particular importance at two main periods in its history: first, in ensuring the survival of viticulture following the collapse of the western Roman empire; and secondly in the introduction of viticulture and winemaking to the Americas.

It has generally been argued that Christian communities' need for grape-based wine with which to celebrate the Eucharist was one of the main factors enabling viticulture and winemaking to survive in western Europe following the fall of Rome in AD 476. It is assumed that when transport was difficult, it was easier for isolated Christian communities in northern Europe to cultivate their own vines rather than import wine. Moreover, monks are widely regarded as the only individuals capable of nurturing viticultural and winemaking traditions.

There is, however, little firm evidence for this hypothesis. The Germanic tribes which overran the western Roman empire were known to be fond of wine, and there is little reason to suppose that they consciously destroyed vast expanses of European vineyards. This is supported by the evidence of surviving elements of the Gallo-Roman aristocracy, who recorded the continued cultivation of vines during the second half of the 5th century in areas of GAUL such as Clermont-Ferrand. Bishops and monks certainly did own vineyards and organized the production of wine throughout the period from the 6th to the 10th century, but it is significant that in most instances they appear to have gained their vineyards mainly as grants from royalty or the secular nobility. This implies that substantial non-monastic vineyards survived and were developed in the aftermath of the Germanic invasions of the 5th century. The real role of monasteries therefore seems not so much to have been in the preservation of a tradition of viticulture following the collapse of Rome, but rather in building up substantial holdings of vineyards, and thus in being among the most important winemakers of medieval Europe (see also CHARLEMAGNE).

During the Middle Ages, monastic houses came to possess some of the most renowned vineyards of Europe. The Benedictines (who, like the Carthusians, are now popularly associated with a high-quality liqueur based on distilled wine) thus owned extensive vineyards. In BURGUNDY the monks of Cluny owned most of the vines in what is now GEVREY-CHAMBERTIN, while the abbey of St-Vivant owned vineyards in what is now called VOSNE-ROMANÉE. Along the Loire, the Benedictine abbey of St-Nicolas held vineyards in what is now ANJOU, and Benedictine monasteries at BOURGUEIL and La Charité also produced quantities of wine. Further south, the Benedictine abbey at ST-POURÇAIN produced what was one of the most renowned wines in medieval France. In CHAMPAGNE, the Benedictines held six monasteries in the diocese of Rheims, while in the RHÔNE they held vineyards at both CORNAS and ST-PÉRAY. In BORDEAUX, they owned such properties as Ch Prieuré in Cantenac (now carrying the suffix of a more recent owner, Alexis LICHINE) and Ch Carbonnieux in GRAVES. In Germany, the abbey at St Maximin in the RUWER was producing about 9,000 l/2,370 gal of wine a year towards the end of the 8th century. Although they also owned many German vineyards, especially in RHEINHESSEN and

FRANKEN, the Benedictines' best known German wine estate was SCHLOSS JOHANNISBERG in the RHEINGAU (see GERMAN HISTORY).

The more ascetic Cistercians, likewise, owned numerous important vineyards throughout Europe. The Clairvaux Abbey had extensive vineyards in CHAMPAGNE, and the Cistercians of Pontigny are reputed to have been the first to plant the CHARDONNAY vine in CHABLIS. Their most famous vineyard, however, was the extensive, walled CLOS DE VOUGEOT, and their other holdings in Burgundy included vineyards in MEURSAULT, BEAUNE, and POMMARD. Cistercians also produced fine wines in SANCERRE and PROVENCE. Their most important wine-producing abbey in Germany was KLOSTER EBERBACH in the RHEINGAU, but there were many others, notably at Himmerod and Machern in the MOSEL and Maulbronn in WÜRTTEMBERG. As major landowners throughout Europe, other monastic orders also owned extensive vineyards; the Carthusians, for example, had particular interests in CAHORS, SWITZERLAND, and Trier in the Upper Mosel. (See also PRIORAT.)

The second main viticultural role widely attributed to the monks was their influence on the development of vineyards in the Americas. In the 17th century, the Jesuits were major wine producers on the coastal plain of PERU, and in the 18th century, with the expansion of Spanish interests in CALIFORNIA, the Franciscans, particularly under the leadership of Júnipero Serra, played an important part in introducing viticulture and winemaking to Alta California. Most of the missions established in California during the 1770s and 1780s thus cultivated vines and made wine, with the Mission of San Gabriel becoming particularly famous for its wines, although the majority of mission vineyards nevertheless remained very small.

In the 21st century, monastic winemaking continues, despite the earlier effects of the Reformation in northern Europe. Abbeys and monasteries still producing wine include Göttweig, Heiligenkreuz, and KLOSTERNEUBURG in Austria and Muri-Gries near Bolzano in ALTO ADIGE while at St Hildegard above Rüdesheim in the German Rheingau almost all the work is actually done by the sisters. Perhaps the most unexpected wine-producing monastery is Cremisan, sandwiched between Israel and Palestine.

Quite apart from the general role played by monastic orders in the history of wine, certain individual monks and monasteries enjoy vinous fame on their own account. The classic example of this is the work of Dom PÉRIGNON in improving the quality of the wines of Hautvillers in CHAMPAGNE at the end of the 17th century.

See also MISSIONARIES.   J.R. and P.T.H.U.

Cushner, N. P., *Lords of the Land: Sugar, Wine and Jesuit Estates of Colonial Peru, 1600–1767* (Albany, 1980).

Goodenough, E. R., *Jewish Symbols in the Greco-Roman Period*, vols. v and vi (New York, 1956).

Seward, D., *Monks and Wine* (London, 1979).

Unwin, T., *Wine and the Vine: An Historical Geography of Viticulture and the Wine Trade* (London, 1991).

monopole, Burgundian term for wholly owned vineyard or CLIMAT.

monopolies. State, province, or national exclusive controls over the sale, and occasionally production, of all alcoholic drinks have a long history. In INDIA, the manufacture of the sort of wine drunk in the immediately pre-Christian era was a state monopoly. In countries such as ALGERIA and, to a lessening extent, EGYPT, the state has controlled wine production as well as distribution. The administrators of many ancient civilizations saw the economic and social advantages of exercising a monopoly over the distribution of wine and beer (the only alcoholic drinks known in antiquity). State monopolies on selling alcoholic drinks have been features in many Scandinavian countries, Pennsylvania in the UNITED STATES, and much of CANADA, although some of these monopolies were broken in the 1990s. The disadvantage for consumers can be a restriction of choice, and in many cases severe restrictions on where and how wine is sold, sometimes with all the safeguards and ignominy associated with the distribution of dangerous drugs. The advantage for producers can be that a sale to a monopoly represents a relatively high-volume order. The two biggest monopolies in terms of volume of wine sold are the Liquor Control Board of Ontario (LCBO) in Canada, which sold about 135 million litres of wine in the 12 months to 31 March 2013, and Systembolaget in Sweden, which sold nearly 200 million litres in 2012.

monoterpenes have ten carbon atoms and are members of the group of natural products called TERPENOIDS. Monoterpenes are major contributors to the characteristic flavour properties of MUSCAT grapes and wines, and contribute to the floral aromas of many non-Muscat wines such as RIESLING. Individual monoterpenes that are found in grapes and contribute to the attractive flavour properties of wines include the ALCOHOLS geraniol, nerol, linalool, and citronellol, although more than 40 have now been reported. Monoterpenes were among the first grape and wine FLAVOUR COMPOUNDS to be elucidated, and the first to be discovered in glycosylated form (see GLYCO-SIDES) as FLAVOUR PRECURSORS.   P.J.W.

Strauss, C. R., et al., 'Role of monoterpenes in grape and wine flavor', in *Biogeneration of Aromas*, American Chemical Society (Washington, DC, 1986).

Montagne de Reims, the 'mountain of Rheims', or the forested high ground between the CHAMPAGNE towns of Rheims and Épernay.

Its lower slopes are famed for the quality of PINOT NOIR base wine they produce.

Montagne-St-Émilion, the largest satellite appellation of ST-ÉMILION in Bordeaux with 1,591 ha/3,930 acres in production in 2013. Most soils are some mixture of clay and limestone with gravel and sand.

Montagny, the appellation for white burgundy produced in the communes of Montagny-lès-Buxy, Jully-lès-Buxy, Buxy, and St-Vallerin in the Côte CHALONNAISE. The wines have a little more body and more acidity than other whites from this region. Previously, all vineyards could be designated PREMIER CRU on condition that the wine had an ALCOHOLIC STRENGTH of 11.5%. Now Montagny has been brought into line with other appellations, though a high proportion of vineyards have been classified as premier cru. Much of the production passes through the excellent CO-OPERATIVE founded in 1929 at Buxy, which boasts the motto 'with the good wines of Buxy everyone sings and everyone laughs'.   J.T.C.M.

Montalcino, town in TUSCANY in central Italy famous for its long-lived red BRUNELLO DI MONTALCINO. Rosso di Montalcino is also made of 100% Brunello grapes but needs be aged for only one, rather than four, years.

Montana. See BRANCOTT ESTATE.

Montecucco, source of promising Sangiovese in the MAREMMA.

Montefalco. See SAGRANTINO.

Montenegro, or **Crna Gora**, meaning 'black mountain', is a small country on the Adriatic coast to the east of Croatia, also bordered by BOSNIA & HERZEGOVINA, SERBIA, KOSOVO, and ALBANIA. It was formerly part of YUGOSLAVIA, and finally became independent in 2006. Today it is an official candidate country for EU membership and an increasingly popular tourist destination. Its wine regions lie between 41.5° (and 42.5° N, with ELEVATIONS reaching 600 m/1,970 ft and a MEDITERRANEAN CLIMATE. Montenegro had 4,512 ha/11,150 acres of vineyards in 2012 divided into the Coastal zone and Lake Skadar basin (including the better known subregions of Podgorica and Crmnica). The national register records 380 grape growers. The country's dominant producer is 13 Jul-Plantaže (still with majority ownership by various state institutions), which owns 2,310 ha/5,708 acres in one of Europe's largest single vineyards, the Cemovsko Polje in the Crmnica region. Red wine grapes account for 80% of plantings. Local varieties VRANAC and Kratošija (ZINFANDEL) account for 70% of red wine grapes, along with INTERNATIONAL VARIETIES such as Cabernet Sauvignon, Merlot, Grenache, Syrah, and Marselan. INDIGENOUS VARIETIES Krstač and Žižak are the most important whites, supplemented with Chardonnay, Rkatsiteli, Sauvignon Blanc, and Pinot Blanc. 13 Jul Plantaže's DNA PROFILING of local varieties suggests that Vranac, Krstač, and Žižak are indigenous to Montenegro, and hints, given the genetic variability, that Kratošija (Zinfandel) may have originated here before it reached Croatia. Extensive work on CLONAL SELECTION has also been carried out, aimed at raising the quality of Vranac, Montenegro's deep-coloured and richly flavoured flagship grape. Most white wine is consumed locally while, by contrast, 13 Jul-Plantaže exports two-thirds of its production to 35 countries and is Montenegro's largest exporter.   C.G.

Montepulciano, name of a vigorous red grape variety planted on much of central Italy, and the name of a Tuscan town at the centre of the zone producing the highly ranked red wine VINO NOBILE DI MONTEPULCIANO (which is not made from this grape variety).

On a 2010 total of 34,824 ha/86,052 acres of vineyard, the grape variety is recommended for 20 of Italy's 95 provinces but is most widely planted in ABRUZZO, where it is responsible for the often excellent-value **Montepulciano d'Abruzzo**, and in the MARCHE, where it is a principal ingredient in such reds as Rosso Conero and Rosso Piceno. It is also grown in MOLISE and PUGLIA. At its best, it produces wines that are deep in colour with ripe, robust tannins. Both the colour and the tannins make it a favoured blending ingredient with producers looking to boost their more feeble efforts. Unfortunately, high yields, often abetted by official advice in the 1970s and 1980s that producers should train their vines high, and a tendency to REDUCTION in the wines, have ensured that general quality is not as high as it should be. DOCG for Montepulciano d'Abruzzo Colline Teramane, for Montepulciano grown in the hills in the area around Teramo in the northern part of Abruzzo, came into effect with the 2003 vintage, perhaps an attempt to promote future, rather than to recognize current, quality.

The variety ripens too late to be planted much further north, although Montepulciano has recently shown it can yield dependable quantities of deep-coloured, well-ripened grapes with good levels of alcohol and extract in UMBRIA and the Tuscan MAREMMA. It is sometimes called Cordisco, Morellone, and Uva Abruzzese. A tiny amount is grown in California, Australia, and New Zealand.

Monterey, one of the major agricultural counties south of San Francisco in CALIFORNIA, with a reputation as 'America's salad bowl'. The coast may be exceptionally picturesque while the county's inland Salinas Valley is planted with vast stretches of lettuces, broccoli, artichokes, carrots, tomatoes, capsicum, and strawberries which have their own kind of beauty, as described in John Steinbeck's novels, notably *The Grapes of Wrath*. Chardonnay, Pinot Noir, and some Riesling were the varieties in FASHION in the second decade of the century, plus a shrinking acreage of the Cabernet Sauvignon and Merlot that were once dominant despite the chilly conditions.

As a wine region, Monterey is not cut from the normal cloth. Rainfall is so low that grapes cannot be grown there without IRRIGATION. Water supply is ample, however, from the underground Salinas river, which defines the large valley so open to the Pacific Ocean that sea fogs and bracing winds cool and darken its northern end so that few or no grape varieties will ripen there. Into this contradictory situation came an army of would-be growers who, between 1968 and 1975, took Monterey from one isolated vineyard to the most heavily planted county on the American west coast, with a peak of 37,000 acres/14,980 ha. Nearly every year from 1975 to 1995 saw a steady reduction in vine acreage with vines increasingly concentrated in the southerly warmest and sunniest parts of the Salinas valley. That trend has since reversed, with acreage increased from 20,000 to nearly 70,000 between 1995 and 2010. The first Monterey wine successes came from near the towns of Soledad and Greenfield and that area, now the Arroyo Seco AVA, remains near the forefront, although it has since been eclipsed by the Santa Lucia Highlands, a more recent AVA that flanks Arroyo Seco and reaches further north along the western foothills.

Monterey AVA

The blanket AVA for Monterey county encompasses Arroyo Seco AVA, Carmel Valley AVA, San Lucas AVA, Hames Valley AVA, San Antonio Valley, Chalone AVA, Santa Lucia Highlands AVA, San Bernabe AVA and all other vineyards not included in these more specific regions. The San Lucas AVA was sponsored by the vast Almaden Vineyards when it owned large acreages in them; it has not been actively used on labels since Almaden left the region although it contains a hefty percentage of Monterey's total acreage in vines. The borders of the AVA are overlapped by the largest contiguous vineyard in the world, San Bernabe's 13,000 acres owned by Delicato, which also has bases in the Central Valley and Napa Valley, and pushed through AVA status for San Bernabe in 2004. Both Hames Valley and San Lucas would be considered hot by the overall standards of Monterey county.

Arroyo Seco AVA

A fairly coherent district within the vastness of Monterey county's Salinas valley has its anchor point at the scruffy farm town of Greenfield. Most of its vineyards lie to the west of that town, on either bank of the dry wash for which it is named in Spanish, but some range east and north to the even scruffier precincts of Soledad. Chardonnay is the mainstay for most of the wineries who draw upon it, but some cleave resolutely, and less successfully, to Cabernet Sauvignon. Rieslings from the area, with their reliable aroma of nectarines, can be of great interest, typically made in an off-dry to medium-sweet style. The earliest plantings here came in the early 1960s.

Carmel Valley AVA

The only seaward-facing wine district in Monterey county, with a much more affluent, less agricultural population than Salinas valley. It has a handful of small wineries and vineyards draped across steep slopes in the drainage area of the Carmel river, 10 to 12 miles/19 km inland from Carmel bay. Bernardus leads in terms of quality; Talbott Vineyards in Santa Lucia Highlands owns the Diamond T vineyard here.

Chalone AVA

Chalone's reputation was made by the winery of the same name set high in the Gavilan mountains, on the east side of Monterey's Salinas valley, notably with Chardonnay, Pinot Blanc, and Pinot Noir. Although Chalone looks directly down to the Arroyo Seco AVA, it remains worlds apart in climate (being above the fog) and soils, which for Chalone are crystal laden and CALCAREOUS.

Santa Lucia Highlands AVA

On the western side of the Salinas Valley, Santa Lucia Highlands' Chardonnay, Pinot Noir, and Syrah vines grow on terraces at up to 1,200 feet/365 m elevation, looming over the row crops on the valley floor. The AVA is arguably Monterey's most celebrated, with commensurate bottle prices, its grapes prized and purchased by wineries throughout California. Paraiso Vineyards, Hahn Estates, and the McFarlands of Sleepy Hollow Vineyard are among the pioneers who realized that the moderate ELEVATION and protection provided by the Santa Lucia coastal range mitigated the marine gusts that can turn grape leaves inside-out. The Garys, Morgan Double L, Pisoni, Rosella's, and Tondre Grapefields vineyards have the most cachet with producers and consumers.   B.C.C. & L.M.

www.montereywines.org

Robinson, J., and Murphy, L., *American Wine* (London and Berkeley, 2013).

Monterrei, relatively new DO in southern Galicia, on Spain's border with Portugal. Most of the wine is still sold in bulk, and the recovery of local grape varieties is less developed than elsewhere in Galicia. This is still more a project based on distant glories, than a current reality. But one vigneron, José Luis Mateo of Quinta da

Muradella, whose vineyards straddle the Portuguese border, has attracted international attention to this fledgling region with TERROIR-rich wines made with a bevy of red and white INDIGENOUS VARIETIES, including the aptly named Monstruosa, with its huge berries.   V. de la S.

Monthelie, a village producing red and occasionally white wine in the Côte de Beaune district of Burgundy's CÔTE D'OR (see map under BURGUNDY). It is so dominated by wine production that local saying has it that a chicken in Monthelie is likely to die of hunger at harvest time.

The wines resemble those of VOLNAY but are neither quite as rich nor as elegant, although they age well and are more powerful than those of AUXEY-DURESSES, the neighbouring appellation to the south with which the PREMIER CRU vineyard Les Duresses is shared. The other premier cru vineyards of Monthelie (which were expanded considerably in 2006) such as Meix Bataille and Champs Fulliot lie adjacent to Volnay. Some Chardonnay was planted in the 1980s, for Monthelie also borders the white wine village of MEURSAULT.   J.T.C.M.

Montilla-Moriles, southern Spanish denominated wine zone in ANDALUCÍA, 40 km/25 miles south of Cordoba (see map under SPAIN), producing both FORTIFIED and unfortified wines in the style of SHERRY, usually known simply as **Montilla**. For many years wine from the country around the towns of Montilla and Moriles found its way into sherry SOLERAS. The practice largely ceased in 1945 when the area was awarded a separate DO, although wines made from the PEDRO XIMÉNEZ grape, some of them very fine, are still legally exported to JEREZ and neighbouring MÁLAGA for blending. Since it became a region in its own right, Montilla has had to contend with a popular image as an inferior, cheap alternative to sherry.

The soils in the centre of the region associated with lower YIELDS and better wines resemble the chalky ALBARIZA of Jerez, although most of Montilla-Moriles is SANDY and parched. The climate is relatively harsh with summer temperatures rising to 45 °C/113 °F and short, cold winters. The Pedro Ximénez vine, which accounts for over 70% of production, seems to thrive in the hot conditions, yielding extremely sweet grapes. The wines therefore achieve ALCOHOLIC STRENGTHS between 14 and 16% without FORTIFICATION. Other grape varieties include the Lairén (AIRÉN) and MUSCAT OF ALEXANDRIA, which tend to produce lighter wines for blending. The PALOMINO vine, which is the basis for most sherry, has not been successful in Montilla.

Wine making practices in Montilla parallel those for sherry. Pale, dry FINO and AMONTILLADO style wines are made from FREE-RUN juice, while heavier styles similar to OLOROSO are made from the subsequent pressings.

Pale Dry Montilla matures under a film of FLOR, initially in cement or earthenware TINAJAS, then in a solera similar to those in Jerez. However, in the hot climate of Montilla-Moriles, far removed from the cooling winds of the Atlantic, the flor is usually less thick than in Jerez and the wines tend to have less finesse as a result (see SHERRY). Heavier oloroso styles are fortified and aged for longer in soleras, where they become dark and pungent. Around half the region's wines are not fortified, which puts them at an advantage in certain markets where duties are levied on alcoholic strength. The region is now most celebrated for its very sweet but not that strong PX wines, of which some producers are now making young, vintage-dated examples.

V. de la S.

Liem, P., and Barquín, J., *Sherry, Manzanilla & Montilla—A Guide to the Traditional Wines of Andalucía* (New York, 2012).

Montlouis, or **Mountlouis-sur-Loire**, overshadowed white wine appellation in the TOURAINE district of the Loire that exists across the river from the much larger and more famous VOUVRAY, although it has its own characteristics. As in Vouvray, the CHENIN BLANC grape is grown exclusively for Montlouis, which is made in all degrees of sweetness and FIZZINESS, according to each VINTAGE's peculiarities. An increasing proportion of still wine is bone dry and aged in OAK.

Although TUFFEAU also forms a base from which many a house and cellar is hewn, topsoils here on the south bank just downstream of Touraine-Amboise are lighter and sandier than in Vouvray, and the wines are less sharply defined, tending to mature considerably earlier (which can be a great advantage). About a third of the wine produced from Montlouis's 400 ha/1,000 acres of Chenin Blanc is the usefully sturdy and characterful **Montlouis Mousseux**, or **Montlouis Pétillant Naturel**, the first AOC for a gently sparkling, fruity PÉTILLANT NATUREL wine made by the MÉTHODE ANCESTRALE.

Montonico Bianco, ancient light-berried vine, probably of Greek origin, grown on 200 ha/495 acres in CALABRIA. **Montonico Nero** is a synonym for GAGLIOPPO.

Montpellier, University of. The agricultural component of this community of universities is known today as Montpellier SupAgro (Centre International d'Études Supérieures en Sciences Agronomiques). The École d'Agriculture de Montpellier was created in 1872 in response to the viticultural crises caused by PHYLLOXERA, POWDERY MILDEW, and DOWNY MILDEW in France. The first Professor of Viticulture, of a succession who built Montpellier's international reputation, was Gustave Foëx, who established the first important collection of European (*Vitis* VINIFERA) and AMERICAN VINE species (*V. riparia*, *V. labrusca* in particular) and

varieties. It remains the world's most comprehensive, with more than 7,500 genotypes in total nowadays. He experimented with phylloxera-resistant ROOTSTOCKS and published a guide to American vines which went into six editions. Ever since the Foëx era, AMPELOGRAPHY has been a speciality of Montpellier. Pierre Viala was Professor of Viticulture at the end of the 1880s, when he went to the US expressly to collect phylloxera-tolerant vine species suitable for CALCAREOUS soils. Thanks to his effort, *Vitis berlandieri* was used to obtain rootstocks such as 41 B, which allowed the replanting of the Cognac and the Champagne regions. From 1890, Viala worked at the Institut National Agronomique in Paris, where he published a treatise on vine diseases and then, with Jean Vermorel, the classic seven-volume *Ampélographie* between 1902 and 1910. Viala's successor was Louis Ravaz, who had created Cognac's viticultural research station and specialized in research on BLACK ROT and downy mildew. He also published an important work on American vines, extended Montpellier's vine collection, founded several publications, and was to become the first vine physiologist. From 1930, Jean Branas occupied the Chair of Viticulture of the renamed École Nationale Supérieure Agronomique de Montpellier (ENSA.M), and was particularly interested in vine biology, VINE NUTRITION, and VIRUS DISEASES. He published several important books on viticulture and took control of French vine nurseries. He began a CLONAL selection programme in the sandy, NEMATODE-free soils of La Petite Camargue in the western Rhône delta following the experience of the world vine repository at the Domaine de Vassal west of Sète (see INRA).

Denis Boubals succeeded Branas in 1975. His work focused on the causes and heredity of resistance to powdery and downy mildews, to phylloxera, and to nematodes. He has published numerous works on viticulture with a special interest in VINE VARIETIES suited to the south of France. His two main collaborators were Pierre GALET—whom Jean-Michel Boursiquot has succeeded—and the physiologist François Champagnol.

Alain Carbonneau is the current Professor of Viticulture of Montpellier SupAgro, which was created in 2003 as an integration of ENSA.M and similar organizations specialized in tropical agriculture. At INRA, first in Bordeaux and then in Montpellier, he deepened fundamental studies on VINE ARCHITECTURE, MICROCLIMATE, the VINE and its environment, and GRAPE QUALITY. He also concentrated on applied technologies taking into account wine QUALITY, ECONOMICS, and TERROIR sustainability. He designed and experimented with new TRAINING SYSTEMS such as the LYRE.

Today's very varied integrated research and development projects are undertaken at the Pech Rouge experimental unit just south of

Narbonne, where the main activities are applied oenology, berry and wine quality, SUSTAINABLE VINICULTURE, the effects of stress and CLIMATE CHANGE, and genetic resistance to parasites. The famous collection of vines is currently being transferred from the Domaine de Vassal to Pech Rouge. A.C.

Montpeyroux, the highest named CRU within the LANGUEDOC AOC and one of the most exciting. It produces mainly but not exclusively red wine. Although Syrah, Grenache, and Mourvèdre are the principal varieties and, between them, must constitute 60% of any blend, Carignan was long the dominant vine variety and Domaine d'Aupilhac has shown from the early 1990s that fine wine can be made of old-vine Carignan, and Cinsaut. DROUGHT is a common summer problem and yields on these rocky slopes are notably low.

Montrachet, or **Le Montrachet**, the most famous GRAND CRU white burgundy, the apogee of the Chardonnay grape produced from a single vineyard in the Côte de Beaune district of the CÔTE D'OR. Claude Arnoux, writing in 1728, could find no words in either French or Latin to describe its qualities, though he noted that it was very expensive and that you needed to reserve the wine a year in advance. Dr Lavalle's view (see BURGUNDY, history), expressed in 1855 and not necessarily valid today, was that whatever the price for a good vintage of Le Montrachet, you would not have paid too much.

Le Montrachet covers a whisker under 8 ha/20 acres straddling the borders of Puligny and Chassagne, two communes which have annexed the famous name to their own (see PULIGNY-MONTRACHET and CHASSAGNE-MONTRACHET). Part of the secret lies in the LIMESTONE, part in its perfect south east exposition, which keeps the sun from dawn till dusk. Curiously, the vines in the Puligny half of the vineyard run in east–west rows, those in Chassagne north–south, reflecting the contours of the land.

The principal owners and producers of Le Montrachet are the Marquis de Laguiche, Baron Thénard, DOMAINE DE LA ROMANÉE-CONTI, BOUCHARD Père et Fils, Domaines Lafon and Prieur in Meursault, and Domaines Ramonet, Colin, and Amiot-Bonfils in Chassagne. In 1991, Domaine Leflaive of Puligny purchased a smallholding. The largest slices belong to the Marquis de Laguiche, whose wine is made by Joseph DROUHIN and Baron Thénard, some of whose wine is distributed by NÉGOCIANTS.

Four more grands crus are associated with Le Montrachet: Chevalier-Montrachet, Bâtard-Montrachet, Bienvenues-Bâtard-Montrachet, and Criots-Bâtard-Montrachet.

Chevalier-Montrachet (7.36 ha) is situated directly above the Puligny section of Le Montrachet, on thin, stony soil giving wines which are not quite as rich as the latter. Particularly sought after are the Chevalier-Montrachet, Les Demoiselles, from Louis LATOUR and Louis JADOT, and Chevalier-Montrachet, La Cabotte from Bouchard Père et Fils.

Bâtard-Montrachet (11.86 ha), on the slope beneath Le Montrachet, also spans the two communes, producing rich and heady wines not quite as elegant as a Chevalier-Montrachet. In the Puligny section of Bâtard is a separate enclave, **Bienvenues-Bâtard-Montrachet** (3.68 ha), while an extension of the Chassagne section is the rarely seen **Criots-Bâtard-Montrachet** (1.57 ha).

See CÔTE D'OR for details of viticulture and winemaking. J.T.C.M.

Arnoux, C., *Dissertation sur la situation de Bourgogne* (Dijon, 1728).

Ginestet, B., *Montrachet* (Paris, 1988).

Loftus, S., *Puligny-Montrachet* (London, 1992).

Norman, R., *Grand Cru* (London 2010).

Montravel, dry white and some red wine appellation of 144 ha/356 acres of vineyard in 2012 in the extreme west of the BERGERAC district in SOUTH WEST FRANCE just over the boundary of the GIRONDE *département* with the DORDOGNE, and thus close to Bordeaux's Côtes de FRANCS, which also has a tradition of sweet white winemaking. Each of Sémillon and the two Sauvignons must make up at least a quarter of the blend. Muscadelle is also approved. The overall quality of these dry wines increased considerably in the late 1980s, with a certain amount of BARREL MATURATION having been introduced, but they are chiefly a local phenomenon.

The appellations **Côtes de Montravel** and **Haut-Montravel** are used for small quantities of sweet wines (from 36 and 8 ha respectively in 2012), with the former generally denoting a MOELLEUX and the latter, a description rarely used, for an even sweeter version. The appellation was extended in 2001 to red wines made from Bordeaux grape varieties, mainly Merlot.

Montsant, DO created in CATALUÑA in 2001 which used to be known as the Falset subregion of the TARRAGONA DO. Its 1,900 ha/4,700 acres of vineyards were given their own identity in order to highlight its superior quality. It has less of the schist soils of its neighbour PRIORAT but otherwise its old Garnacha and Cariñena vineyards on steep slopes enable it to produce wines of very similar style and quality at much lower prices.

Montù, also known as **Montuni**, late-ripening black grape indigenous to the plains of EMILIA in Italy.

Moravia, eastern, wine-producing part of the CZECH REPUBLIC whose wine region lies just north of the Weinviertel of Austria.

Moravia Agria is the name of a grape making refreshing reds in MANCHUELA, while Moravia Dulce is MARUFO.

Morellino di Scansano, particularly successful Sangiovese in the MAREMMA.

Moreto do Alentejo, undistinguished red grape variety that is widely planted in Portugal, notably but not exclusively in the ALENTEJO, where there were 1,127 ha/2,784 acres in 2012.

Morey-St-Denis, important village in the Côte de Nuits district of Burgundy producing red wines from Pinot Noir grapes (see map under BURGUNDY). Morey suffers, perhaps unfairly, in comparison with its neighbours CHAMBOLLE-MUSIGNY and GEVREY-CHAMBERTIN because its wines are usually described as being lighter versions of Gevrey or firmer than Chambolle, according to which side of the village they are located. Indeed, in the past, the wines were often sold under those names. Geologically there is no need for Morey-St-Denis to feel inferior as the same stratum of LIMESTONE runs from the Combe de Lavaux in Gevrey through Morey to the Combe d'Antin in Chambolle.

There are four GRAND CRU vineyards, moving southwards from the border with Gevrey-Chambertin: Clos de la Roche (16.9 ha/42 acres), Clos St-Denis (6.6 ha), Clos des Lambrays (8.8 ha), Clos de Tart (7.5 ha), plus a small segment of Bonnes Mares overlapping from Chambolle.

Although Morey chose to append St-Denis to its name in 1927, Clos de la Roche is probably the finest vineyard. The soil is rich in MARL, giving greater depth, body, and ageing ability than most other vineyards.

Clos St-Denis, sandwiched between Clos de la Roche and the village itself, may be the quintessential wine of Morey-St-Denis—a touch lighter than Clos de la Roche, supple and succulent, the more charming of the two early in life, with a trace of austerity, but the pinnacle of finesse.

Excellent examples of both Clos de la Roche and Clos St-Denis have been made by Domaine Ponsot, Domaine Dujac, and various Ligniers. While Domaine Ponsot was one of the first to bottle their own wines in Burgundy, Domaine Dujac is the comparatively recent creation (in 1968) of Jacques Seysses, an inspirational grower whose example significantly influenced the generation taking over their family domaines in the 1980s.

Clos des Lambrays, all but a monopoly, was promoted from PREMIER CRU to GRAND CRU. Clos de Tart, singled out by Dr Lavalle in 1855 as the only tête de cuvée vineyard in Morey, has always been a MONOPOLE: founded by the Cistercian sisters of Notre Dame de Genlis in 1250, it remained in their hands until the French

Revolution, when it was auctioned in one piece. In 1932, one of the Marey-Monge family sold it to the current owner, Mommessin.

Successful premier cru vineyards in Morey-St-Denis include Les Ruchots, Clos de la Bussière (*monopole* of Domaine Georges Roumier), Les Millandes, Clos des Ormes, and Les Monts Luisants. Domaine Ponsot also produces a rare and curious white wine from the last, based on a plot of Aligoté planted in 1911.

See also CÔTE D'OR.   J.T.C.M.

Morgon, important BEAUJOLAIS cru which encompasses about 1,100 ha/2,717 acres of vines around the commune of Villié-Morgon. The wines produced are considered notably denser and longer lived than most Cru Beaujolais and the appellation has even been used as a verb, as in describing the process by which a young Beaujolais becomes more like a Pinot Noir-dominated red burgundy with time in bottle: *il morgonne*. Soils here are more weathered and the total ripeness is likely to be greater than in most crus, although some consider that only the wines made on the ex-volcanic cone known as Côte de Py just south of Villié-Morgon have the real depth traditionally associated with Morgon.

Morillon is an old north eastern French name for PINOT NOIR and is still a common name for the powerfully aromatic CHARDONNAY of STYRIA in southern Austria. It was a widely used Burgundian vine variety name in the Middle Ages and was, for example, an old name for Chardonnay in Chablis country.

Morio-Muskat is Germany's most popular MUSCAT-like vine variety by far, although it is almost certainly unrelated to any Muscat. The precise identity of Peter Morio's GERMAN cross remains a mystery but its obvious grapiness is not. It was particularly popular with the eager blenders of the PFALZ and RHEINHESSEN in the late 1970s, when its total German area reached 3,000 ha/7,410 acres, and demand for LIEBFRAU-MILCH was high: a drop of Morio-Muskat in a neutral blend of Müller-Thurgau and Silvaner was the cheapest way of Germanizing it. Total plantings are falling fast, however, and Germany had only 488 ha by 2012 as this aggressively blowsy cross has undoubtedly had its day. The grapes can rot easily and ripen a week after Müller-Thurgau, which means that BACCHUS can be a better alternative for Germany's cooler northern wine regions.

Moristel, light, loganberry-flavoured speciality of SOMONTANO in northern Spain, also known as Juan Ibáñez. The light red wine produced oxidizes easily. It may be better in a blend than as a VARIETAL.

Mornington Peninsula, maritime, cool-climate wine region south east of Melbourne in the Australian state of VICTORIA and a summer playground for rich and poor alike. Site climate and soil type vary widely across this long east–west peninsula, and the differences are apparent in the wine styles from a total of 76 producers.

Morocco, with its high mountains and cooling Atlantic influence, has arguably the greatest potential for producing good-quality wine in North Africa. Viticulture, which existed in the Roman era, was probably introduced by Phoenician settlers. But it was the French colonists who brought large-scale wine production so that Morocco played a significant part in the world's wine trade in the 1950s and 1960s, although it never produced as much sheer quantity as neighbouring ALGERIA. At independence in 1956, Morocco had 55,000 ha/135,850 acres of carefully husbanded vineyard. With the departing French colonists went winemaking expertise, capital, and a large proportion of domestic consumption. This was compounded in 1967 by new EEC (now EU) quotas which literally decimated Morocco's exports. Frozen out of European markets and faced with stiff competition from other over-producing Mediterranean countries, most producers GRUBBED UP their vineyards and replaced them with cereal crops. Between 1973 and 1984, the great majority of vineyards were taken over by the state, which by 1984 had also established a firm grip on the sale of wine, including grape price-fixing regardless of quality.

By the early 1990s, only about 13,000 ha of the nation's 40,000 ha of vines were planted with wine vines, over half of them, many virused, were 30 years old or more and therefore economically unproductive. Average yields were well under 30 hl/ha (1.7 tons/acre). The state had a virtual monopoly of the domestic market. The only independent producer to prosper in this post-colonial climate was Brahim Zniber, head of North African wine giant Les Celliers de Meknès and also owner of its main domestic competitor, Thalvin-Ebertec (since 2001), as well as of Sincobar, so that by the mid 2000s the Sniber group had a 90% share of the domestic market. Zniber, who bought his first vineyards from departing French producers in the 1950s and started bottling wines in 1976, encouraged the introduction of a CONTROLLED APPELLATION system and pioneered VARIETAL wines.

In a bid to revive Morocco's rural economy, the late King Hassan II successfully attracted foreign investment in viticulture during the 1990s. Several large Bordeaux groups, including CASTEL, William Pitters, and Taillan, took up the offer of long leases on prime vineyard land from the state holding company SODEA. This policy of seeking inward investment, continued by King Mohammed VI, had a galvanizing effect on the industry from the mid 1990s. Thousands of hectares have been replanted with better quality grape varieties by foreign investors, Celliers de Meknès, and a few smaller entrepreneurs so that vineyards totalled 48,000 ha and there were eight significant wine producers by 2011. State-of-the-art bottling and vinification plants have been built by Celliers de Meknès and Castel, with the refrigeration necessary for TEMPERATURE CONTROL and oak barrels for maturation of the likes of lauded red Château Roslane. Well over 75% of Moroccan wine is red. Historically the uninspiring Carignan dominated the Moroccan *vignoble* although there was a later wave of planting Cinsaut (still the country's most planted variety), which can produce agreeable VIN GRIS. With rosé, this pale orangey-pink wine accounts for almost 20% of total wine production. Alicante and Grenache were once important but Castel have energetically replanted their vineyards with INTERNATIONAL VARIETIES. Whites, which represent a very small proportion of total production, are made from the likes of Clairette and Muscat. They have tended to produce heavy, often musty, non-aromatic white wines although the Roussanne of Domaine Val d'Argan in splendid isolation on the southern coast near Essouira is a laudable exception.

Morocco's appellation system, closely modelled on the French APPELLATION CONTRÔLÉE, is called Appellation d'Origine Garantie. AOG rules delimit the geographical area of production and set maximum yields but do not dictate grape varieties. The system has yet to achieve any real significance in terms of guaranteeing quality—Thalavin-Evertec make some of the country's best wines and do not even use it—but the following are AOG zones, mostly in the cooler, fertile regions of the north. Negotiations with the EU were ongoing in 2014.

The East: Beni Sadden, Berkane, Angad
Meknès/Fès region: Guerrouane, Beni M'tir, Saiss, Zerhoune
The Northern Plain: Gharb
Rabat/Casablanca region: Chellah, Zemmour, Zaër, Zenatta, Sahel
El-Jadida region: Doukkala

The Meknès region of the Middle Atlas, where vines are planted at an elevation of around 600 m/1,968 ft, and Berkane (once famous for its Muscat VIN DOUX NATUREL) have traditionally enjoyed the finest reputation but there are vast new plantings around Benslimane and Beni Mellal. Some of the best modern wines come from grapes grown in the Zaër highlands, closer to the capital Rabat. Thanks to the Atlantic influence, good wines are also produced further south along the coast: in the Doukkala, for instance, where Castel's Boulaouane domaine produces the wine for France's leading foreign wine brand. Castel concentrate on the French market and own the Sidi Brahim red-wine brand.

Although Morocco is often described as having a semi-arid MEDITERRANEAN CLIMATE, the Atlas Mountains and Atlantic Ocean combine to create cool MESOCLIMATES in the north. Nevertheless, summer temperatures can reach 35–38 °C/95-100 °F; rainfall between May and October is very low; and drought cycles and SUNBURN are worsening. Another problem can be the strength of the prevailing WINDS from the Atlantic of up to 65 km/40 miles per hour. Vine TRELLISING and careful row orientation have become more common, and all main producers now practice DRIP IRRIGATION.

With a current annual output of just 333,000 hl/8.8 million gal, Morocco's wine production remains modest. Although huge quantities of very poor wine are still produced, the wine industry is now dominated by private companies, all of which make consistently palatable—if, as yet, unexceptional—wines. The local market is buoyed by strong demand from the tourist industry and the country's affluent urban elite, as well as by the high duties on imported wines. Moroccan law prohibits the sale of alcohol to Muslims, but in practice the law is seldom if ever applied. Alcohol is freely available in all the main cities outside the holy month of Ramadan. Not everyone approves of this permissive approach—least of all Morocco's growing ISLAMIST movement, which seeks to ban or limit alcohol consumption.

See also CORKS, of which Morocco is a relatively important producer.   R.H.N.J. & J.R.

Joy, R., *A Survey of Moroccan Wine* (ESC Dijon, 2003).

Platter, J. & E., *Africa Uncorked* (London, 2002).

www.vindumaroc.com/

morphology. See VINE MORPHOLOGY.

Morrastel is the main French synonym for Rioja's GRACIANO. **Morrastel-Bouschet**, is a much lesser CROSS that produced substantial quantities of notably deep red wine in the Languedoc in the mid 20th century.

Mortágua, confusing western Portuguese red wine grape synonym with multiple meanings: for CAMARATE in Arruda, for TRINCADEIRA in Torres Vedras, and, occasionally in Dão and Setúbal, for TOURIGA NACIONAL.

Moscadello, sometimes **Moscadelleto**, name for the MUSCAT BLANC À PETITS GRAINS grown in and around MONTALCINO in central Italy. Moscadello was the major wine of Montalcino for centuries, being cited by English travellers in the 17th and 18th centuries, long before anyone even noted the presence of important reds. The firm Villa Banfi made an important investment in selling this sweet grapey, fizzy white wine in the 1980s, hoping to repeat the commercial success of LAMBRUSCO but to little avail.

Moscatel, Spanish and Portuguese for MUSCAT. The term may be applied to both grape varieties and wines. Thus **Moscatel de Grano Menudo** is none other than MUSCAT BLANC À PETITS GRAINS, while **Moscatel de Alejandría**, **Moscatel de Málaga**, and **Moscatel Romano** are MUSCAT OF ALEXANDRIA. **Moscatel Rosado**, on the other hand, may be a South American speciality (see below). Most of the vines known simply as Moscatel in Spanish- and Portuguese-speaking countries are Muscat of Alexandria, although northern Spain has some of the superior small-seeded variety.

Inexpensive wines called simply Moscatel abound in Iberia and are in general simply sweet and grapey.

See also Moscatel de SETÚBAL.

Moscatel de Alejandría, Spanish name for MUSCAT OF ALEXANDRIA.

Moscatel de Austria, grape variety grown on just over 50 ha of Chile and used in the production of the national aromatic brandy pisco. Identical to Argentina's TORRONTÉS SANJUANINO.

Moscato, Italian for MUSCAT and the name of a sweetish VARIETAL wine style for which there was a FASHION in certain quarters towards the end of the first decade of this century (see ASTI for details), which resulted in an increase in plantings of Muscat even in California. The Italian vine census of 2010 identifies seven different Moscatos. **Moscato Bianco**, sometimes called **Moscato di Canelli**, is the finest Muscat grape variety MUSCAT BLANC À PETITS GRAINS and is that most commonly encountered in Italy, with total plantings of 11,500 ha/28,471 acres, making it one of the country's most planted white wine grapes, cited in almost 20 DOCS. This is the Moscato responsible for all the light usually sweet and sparkling wines of Asti and MOSCATO D'ASTI. **Moscato Rosa del Trentino** (found in TRENTINO and ALTO ADIGE, often called Rosenmuskateller) is a very much rarer red-skinned grape which seems to exist in three different incarnations, of which a mutation of Moscato Bianco is only one. The golden-berried **Moscato Giallo** (Goldmuskateller) is more widely planted, on 1,127 ha/2,785 acres, and has a parent-offspring relationship with Moscato Bianco. **Moscato di Terracina** is a recently revived aromatic white grown on 125 ha/309 acres of Lazio. **Moscato di Scanzo** is a dark-berried speciality of Bergamo which makes small quantities of decadently aromatic, sweet passito reds. Moscato Nero di Acqui is a synonym for MUSCAT OF HAMBURG, as is MUSCAT OTTONEL, though neither is much grown in Italy.

Wines called Moscato are produced all over the country and are usually made from Moscato Bianco grapes. In the south and, especially, the islands, they are typically golden and sweet.

Few of Italy's regions do not have their own Moscato-based wines. The majority of these are low in alcohol and at least lightly sweet, ideal accompaniments to fruit and fruit-based desserts.

Italy's south, in particular SICILY, was once renowned for its Moscato wines, many of them made from MUSCAT OF ALEXANDRIA, more commonly known as ZIBIBBO in Italy. The revived popularity of Moscato di Pantelleria (see SICILY) in the 1980s coincided with, and perhaps influenced, new attempts to achieve a more luscious style of Moscato in Piemonte, and a new category of passito wines, far sweeter than Moscato d'Asti and frequently given BARREL MATURATION, began to emerge in the late 1980s. Small quantities of Moscato passito have long been made in the Valle d'AOSTA, principally near the township of Chambave.

Moscato d'Asti, fragrant and lightly sweet, gently fizzy, dessert wine made in the PIEMONTE region of north-west Italy now of DOCG status. It is produced from MOSCATO BIANCO, Italy's name for the aristocratic MUSCAT BLANC À PETITS GRAINS, whose production in and around the town of ASTI increased enormously in the 20th and early 21st centuries. Santo Stefano Belbo is considered the cradle of Moscato in Piemonte, and at the end of the 19th century almost 80% of all Moscato was grown in the CALCAREOUS soils of Canelli, Santo Stefano Belbo, Calosso, Castiglione Tinella, and Cassinasco. Strevi, Riccaldone, and Acqui Terme in the province of Alessandria, then and now a source of excellent Moscato, produced another 5% of the total. These are still considered the classic zones for fine Moscato, although expansion of the zone has revealed a real vocation for Moscato on the slopes of Cossano Belbo, Mango, Neviglie, and Trezzo Tinella. Moscato d'Asti is therefore something of a misnomer, since much of the production is not in the province of Asti at all but in the province of Cuneo (stretching as far as Serralunga Alba in the eastern part of the BAROLO zone), and a significant proportion is in the province of Alessandria. Renewed commercial success, especially in the US, has put pressure on the CONSORZIO to enlarge the production zone further, but by 2014 this had so far been resisted.

As a wine, Moscato d'Asti is often lumped together with ASTI, although the two wines are discernibly different. With a maximum of 2 atmospheres of pressure in the bottle, less than a third that of Asti, Moscato d'Asti is only slightly frothy while Asti is fully sparkling. Its ALCOHOLIC STRENGTH is considerably lower (maximum 6.5% as opposed to Asti's 6.5 to 9.5%), and Asti often tastes sweeter than the more flavourful Moscato d'Asti, even if its RESIDUAL SUGAR is usually slightly lower.

The ripest, and best, MOSCATO grapes are used to produce Moscato d'Asti. By law, the minimum potential alcohol of grapes selected for Moscato d'Asti must be 10%, while for Asti the minimum is 9%. The 'wine' is classed as 'partially fermented grape must', for the juice is chilled and filtered immediately after pressing and fermented only when required in order to ensure that the beguiling aromas of the Moscato grape are not lost. Fermentation is stopped when the wine reaches 5.5% alcohol; the unfermented sugar lends a hedonistic grapey character to the wine, and helps to exalt the Moscato's heady perfumes.

Moscato d'Asti is not a classic dessert wine, its chief virtues being its delicacy, its intense aromas, and a sweetness that is as much suggested as forthrightly declared. While Moscato d'Asti's reputation as 'the perfect breakfast wine' contains a nugget of truth, Moscato d'Asti Vendemmia Tardiva is a full-blown, still, sweet wine made from late-harvested or DRIED GRAPES.

Moscato d'Asti production may have grown enormously but is still only a fraction of Asti's (25 million bottles compared with the 75 million bottles of Asti) but it is now fully accepted as a classic and unusually refreshing expression of one of the world's most important and popular grape varieties.   W.S.

www.astidocg.info

Moscato di Sardegna, relatively new and as yet relatively unrealized DOC for sweet, still or sparkling white wines made in SARDINIA in the image of MOSCATI D'ASTI.

Moscato di Strevi. See STREVI.

Moscato Spumante, often the most basic form of light, fizzy, Italian white wine made in the style of ASTI but usually with the most basic, industrial ingredients. Not to be confused with the infinitely superior MOSCATO D'ASTI, nor with METODO CLASSICO versions.

Moschofilero, vine variety with deep pink-skinned grapes used to make strongly perfumed, delicate white wine in GREECE, particularly on the high plateau of Mantinia in the Peloponnese, where conditions are sufficiently cool that harvest is often delayed until well into October. Its name, like that of Italy's VESPAIOLO, indicates the extent to which insects are drawn to these ripe grapes. There are strong flavour similarities with fine MUSCAT but the origins of this distinct vine variety are as yet obscure. Small quantities of fruity light pink wine are also made from this spicy variety, which is also increasingly used for sparkling wines. So popular has it become that Greece had more than 1,000 ha/2,500 acres planted by 2013 (as opposed to 1,800 ha of Muscat).

Mosel, major German growing region with 8,776 ha/21,676 acres of vineyard in 2013, formerly known as Mosel-Saar-Ruwer. It is associated with long-lived wines of delicacy and dynamic complexity, including some of the world's finest sweet wines. The total area planted has been declining slowly and, except in the best-known vineyards, Riesling grapes command a price that only just covers the costs of farming the generally steep, stony, sheer slopes with their densely planted and often archaically trained vines. (See GERMANY, Viticulture.) As the River Mosel twists from Trier to Koblenz, the vineyards are at their steepest on the outer edge of the curve. Those on the flatter inner edge are frequently planted with varieties other than Riesling on land more suited to agriculture than to viticulture. TOPOGRAPHY is all important here, but SOIL, too, is critical. Virtually every top Mosel, Saar, or Ruwer site is dominated by Devonian SLATE, which has been used in the region for hundreds of years as a building material. Even vineyards naturally short of slate have had it added to help retain warmth. Some of the vineyards between the almost vertical spurs of rock were created in the 16th century with the aid of explosives, a dangerous operation when there was a wine village below. Vineyards have been subjected to the wholesale renovation known as FLURBEREINIGUNG) later and to a lesser extent than those of most other German regions, the principle obstacle being sheer steepness and difficulty of access to the slopes for earth-moving equipment, whose production costs remain among the highest in Germany. Vineyards associated with some of the Mosel's most important villages also proved resistant to the late-19th- and early-20th-century ravages of PHYLLOXERA, and in those places many vines are UNGRAFTED (and could until very recently be replanted without grafting), a dwindling but arguably precious legacy.

The Mosel normally has a warm summer with an average temperature in the hottest month of July of 18 °C (64 °F). The MESOCLIMATE is of rather more significance and varies considerably. In some Saar and Upper Mosel vineyards, there is a risk of FROST DAMAGE particularly in spring, but also in late autumn and winter. Even in relatively gentle winters, some nights are usually cold enough for EISWEIN production in most vineyard sites, although marauding wild boar have a well-justified reputation for Christmas or New Year's feasting on any grapes left hanging.

Vine varieties

In the 18th century, many villages produced red wine (see GERMAN HISTORY). By the early 19th century, white wine dominated and the ELBLING vine was planted on nearly two-thirds of the vineyard area. It still predominates in the largely CALCAREOUS slopes of the Upper Mosel. But overall Riesling, grown in over 90% of all Mosel vineyards in 1954, dominates with a 60% share. Where there is less steepness or slate, MÜLLER-THURGAU and other GERMAN CROSSES dominate. There was a temporary surge in plantings of the more profitable Dornfelder in the late 1990s in response to increased domestic demand for red wine. None of these non-Rieslings, except for tiny pockets of SPÄTBURGUNDER (PINOT NOIR) and PINOT BLANC, excel. The key to a fine Mosel Riesling is its backbone of fruity-tasting TARTARIC ACID, which balances any RESIDUAL SUGAR present, along with a frequent if vague impression of wet stone. A low-alcohol Mosel Riesling often tastes merely off-dry even when it has more than 30 g/l residual sugar. TROCKEN wine is increasingly common, representing a return to dryness such as characterized Mosel Riesling when it achieved international acclaim in the late 19th century, albeit in an era with later growing seasons and lower MUST weights than today's. As a result some dry Mosel Rieslings may be 13% or more natural alcohol, but the quintessential Mosel remains for many non-Germans a delicate (7–9% alcohol) Riesling that is fresh and subtly sweet yet invigorating. Only a minority of Mosel growers (notably along the Saar) seriously pursue the goal of non-trocken but far-from-sweet Riesling. (Throughout Germany, most prominent growers have given up on HALBTROCKEN as a concept.) Yet, at levels of residual sugar hardly detectable as such, ravishing dry-tasting Mosel Riesling of 10–12% alcohol is possible.

Processing close to one-fifth of its region's fruit and half of that Riesling makes Moselland CO-OPERATIVE in Bernkastel the world's largest producer of Riesling. Much of the rest—especially from grapes other than Riesling—is bottled by merchant houses. But although the standing of Mosel wine in Germany has been debased by over-production and price warfare, not to mention by the legal adoption of names of famous villages and vineyards to designate GROSSLAGEN, the small, upper tier of excellent estate-bottled wine has guaranteed Mosel Riesling a high profile and devoted following abroad, which has affected the German market as well. There may be more talent concentrated among the vintners of the Mosel than anywhere else in Germany today. The tendency since the 1990s has been for the best vineyards to be consolidated in ever-fewer but more adept winemaking hands.

Geography

The **Lower Mosel** boasts the highest percentage of Riesling vines on the River Mosel, if only a minority of its top sites. Curving downstream from Zell to the confluence of the Rhine and Mosel at Koblenz, this subregion incorporates many small, steep vineyards which can be maintained only by hand, and the lowest percentage of flat or gently sloping sites workable by tractor. The individual holdings are not as large as those of the Middle Mosel and their sheer incline and rockiness as well as their relative isolation in a narrow, steeply walled valley have traditionally put them at a commercial disadvantage relative to their neighbours upstream. During the 1980s and 1990s, the Deutsches Eck growers' association had some success in raising commercial consciousness as well as wine quality for these villages jointly with those of the neighbouring MITTELRHEIN region, a close cultural and geological cousin. More recently, the name Terrassenmosel is being used as a way of distinguishing, and of creating a quality image for these steepest of Mosel vineyards, nearly all planted on terraces dating back many centuries. The stony, relatively dry MESOCLIMATE here, as well as the frequent convergence of blue Devonian slate, red slate, and quartzite, can result in fascinating and distinctive wines, as a few of the top growers—some beginning to enjoy international attention—are proving. The precipitous walls of slate outside Koblenz at Winningen—most notably the Uhlen vineyard—are regaining a reputation for high ripeness and excellence that was essentially forgotten for nearly a century. Upriver from Winningen, in Kobern, Gondorf, and Hatzenport, several estates are demonstrating Riesling's delicious potential. Numerous villages above and below Cochem still harbour significant Riesling plantings although their wines are scarcely recognized by name even inside Germany. At Bremm, the terraced Calmont rises 200 m/656 ft from the river. With a 65% incline, it is one of the world's steepest vineyards and, like sites immediately upstream in Neef, St Aldegrund, and Alf, its potential is being demonstrated and its vine presence hanging on for dear life thanks to a few intrepid growers able to access their vineyards using hair-raising monorails.

Of perhaps 100 EINZELLAGEN with outstanding potential in the Mosel, over half are in the **Middle Mosel**, which extends upstream from Pünderich with its complex, slatey, crenulated Marienburg, a long, steep wall accessed by boat from the village. A roster of towns and their top sites begins with the blue and red slate sites of Enkirch (Batterieberg, Ellergrub, Steffensberg), Wolf (Goldgrube), Kröw (a different Steffensberg), and Kinheim (Rosenberg). Along the bow of the Mosel between Enkrich and Wolf is the traditionally important merchant base as well as wine-growing centre of Traben-Trarbach, some of whose once-renowned sites (notably Traben's Gaisberg and Würzgarten) cling to the Mosel's right bank beneath the hamlet of Starkenberg. Others (Hühnerberg, Ungsberg, Schlossberg, Taubenhaus)—outstanding for Pinot Noir as well as Riesling

and happily subject to some ambitious recent reclamation—hug the steep, narrow valley of the Kautenbach as it rushes down to meet the Mosel at Trarbach. The red slate of Erden (Treppchen and Prälat) generates some of the Mosel's most celebrated Rieslings, with a prominent and luscious citric undertow. Neighbouring Ürzig, virtually all of whose top vineyards are united under the name Würzgarten, gives the best Erdeners a run for their money with frequently spicy and strawberry- or kiwi-scented Rieslings from iron-rich, finely eroded Permian soil unique in the Mosel.

Below Ürzig the Mosel inscribes one of its periodic tight turns and then enters a straight stretch whose south-facing slopes enjoy international fame: Zeltingen (Himmelreich, Schlossberg, Sonnenuhr), Wehlen (Sonnenuhr), Graach (Himmelreich, Domprobst), and Bernkastel. Flavours of orchard fruits, vanilla, and nut oils typify many of the wines from these sites, and in the case of Bernkastel, a characteristic note of black cherry. In a departure from usual German practice, the names of the best individual sites at Bernkastel, with the exception of the famous Doctor, are—partly on account of their diminutive size—less prestigious and well known than is their collective identity as the unusually distinguished GROSSLAGE Badstube. After another twist, the river flows past Lieser (Niederberg Helden) and a side valley at Mülheim (Sonnenlay) and Veldenz (Elisenberg, Grafschafter Sonnenberg), all three towns getting well-deserved recent exposure in the hands of talented vintners. Next comes Brauneberg (Juffer, Juffer-Sonnenuhr), whose unusually well-watered walls of southeast-facing slate enjoyed a pre-eminent position in the Mosel pecking order throughout the 19th century, and earn high praise today for stunningly rich yet refined Rieslings. Nor do Kesten (Paulinsberg) or Wintrich (Geierslay, Ohligsberg) any longer want for conscientious vintners to prove that their Rieslings have more than historical interest.

Astride a tight loop in the Mosel hangs the amphitheatrical slopes of Piesport, whose Goldtröpfchen site is among the region's best and internationally best-known (although the adjacent Domherr, Kreuzwingert, and Schubertslay have first-rate potential as well). Honeyed richness and tropical and black fruit flavours characterize the best of these wines, but too many growers trade too easily on the site's name. Use of the Grosslage name Piesporter Michelsberg for wine from uninspiring surrounding vineyards brings the name of this historic wine village into disrepute. The clay- and iron-rich slate of Dhron, deployed along a tiny, eponymous tributary of the Mosel, is re-establishing the expectations for longevity and distinctive complexity that Riesling labelled Dhroner Hofberger commanded through the mid-20th

century. One of the Mosel's narrowest switchbacks and most vertiginous walls of blue slate occurs upstream from Piesport at Trittenheim (Altärchen, Apotheke) and neighbouring Leiwen (Laurentiuslay), wines from the former being characteristically richer and from the latter sleeker and more distinctly mineral. Thanks to a bevy of wine-growing talents, the reputation of these sites is itself now steeply ascendant. Upstream, Thörnich (Ritsch), Detzem (Maximiner Klosterlay), and Pölich (Held) offer glimpses of their potential greatness. The same is true of vineyards just below Trier at Longuich (Maximiner Herrenberg), where the abbey of St Maximin, arguably the pre-eminent medieval viticultural institution of the Mosel, established its main press house, and planted a forest that has served successfully as a hail shield for five centuries. Some sites just below Longuich at Mehring (Blattenberg, Zellerberg) have potential although their high clay component tends to result in a broader, less dynamic style of Riesling.

The Mosel tributaries **Saar** and **Ruwer** make up a mere 11% of the official Mosel growing region, but their reputation is out of proportion to their surface area. As every additional 100 m/ 328 ft above sea level results in a drop in average temperature of over 0.5 °C/0.9 °F, the extra ELEVATION of the Saar, Ruwer, and the upper reaches of the Mosel means they are generally cooler than the Middle Mosel. Saar and Ruwer Riesling achieved its renown for the brightness, animation, and clarity it preserved even in rich and selectively picked, sweet wines and today it manages to ripen fully in most vintages.

The main Ruwer vineyards begin near the village of the same name, and end some 10 km/6 miles upstream. A long legacy of high quality combined with MONOPOLE vineyard status has made Eitelsbach's Karthäuserhofberg and Mertesdorf's Maximin Grünhaus (with its famed Abtsberg and Herrenberg vineyards) the Ruwer's best-known estates outside Germany, but Kasel, immediately upstream, boasts excellence (from Nies'chen and Kehrnagel) including holdings by the vast, internationally prominent Reichsgraf von Kesselstatt estate, whose principle cellars are located further upstream. The predominantly red slate Ruwer vineyards often favour flavours of red fruits, pungent green herbs, and brown spices, and they can excel with both TROCKEN (the dominant taste today) or with sweetness ranging from hidden to overt and BOTRYTIZED.

Travelling upstream from the Saar's confluence with the Mosel near Trier, comes a hairpin turn with outstanding vineyards along its right bank at Filzen and Kanzen, the latter's Altenberg among the entire Mosel's handful of finest vineyards. Across the river at Wawern, the Herrenberg and Goldberg—perpendicular to the river—are being revived. The Saar straightens to north-south orientation just upstream from Kanzem at Wiltingen, whose Braune Kupp, Gottesfuss, Kupp, and Hölle are all first-rate. The fame of Wiltingen's towering Scharzhofberg is nowadays rightly associated with the superb custodianship of successive Egon Müllers. Although it was for centuries cited as one of the Mosel's greatest vineyards, it does not lie along the Saar. Rather, with the neighbouring Braunfels, it faces south overlooking an ancient bed of that river, which inscribes a roughly 10-km eastward crescent of important vineyards—some revived since the late 20th century, some still neglected—at Oberemmel (Agritiusberg, Hütte, Raul), Krettnach (Altenberg, Euchariusberg), Niedermennig (Herrenberg, Sonnenberg), and Falkenstein (Hofberg). Upstream from Wiltingen come Schoden (Herrenberg), Ayl (Kupp) and Ockfen (Bockstein). This sector engenders confusion in vineyard nomenclature. The best part of Kupp (like that of its right-bank counterpart Bockstein) is contiguous and lies perpendicular to the river, but the official EINZELLAGE incorporates disparate sites, including the recently revived but not legally recognized Schonfels perched over the Saar. And steep, elongated, uniquely cobbled, riverside Saarfeilser Marienberg straddles both Schoden and Wiltingen such that one of its three owners is not permitted the use of its name. Saarburg's dominant Rausch vineyard is another geological anomaly, for incorporating diabase. Furthest upstream of the Saar's vineyards are those of Serrig (Herrenberg, Schloss Saarsteiner, Würtzberg), overlooking across the River Kastel's tiny Maximiner Prälat, once among the gems of the medieval St Maximin abbey's necklace of vineyards, condemned by its steepness and poor access to return from 2012 to scrub, a reminder of how precarious are the Saar's vineyard treasures, numerous recent revivals notwithstanding.

Parallel to the vineyards along the Saar are those of the **Upper Mosel**, which hug that river's right bank above Trier. Here the Elbling grape still dominates (with about 500 ha); Riesling is rare; and the soils are calcareous like those in the adjacent left bank Moselle vineyards of LUXEMBOURG, whose dominant AUXERROIS is also planted on these German shores. Some recent projects suggest outstanding and as yet largely untapped potential with Burgundian grape varieties here. D.S.

Carlberg, L., *Mosel Wine*. www.larscarlberg.com

Pigott, S., *Wein Spricht Deutsch: Weine, Winzer, Weinlandschaften* (Frankfurt, 2007).

Reinhardt, S., *The Finest Wines of Germany* (London, 2012).

Steinberg, E., *Understanding Mosel Wines* (2012 e-book).

Moselle, French name for the river known in German as MOSEL which rises in the Vosges Mountains of France, forms the border between LUXEMBOURG (in which it plays a key part in wine production) and Germany, and joins the River Rhine at Koblenz in Germany, 545 km/340 miles later.

France

In the far north east of the country, Moselle is a small AOC which, with Côtes de TOUL, constitutes what the French call their *vins de l'est* or 'wines of the east', the last remnants of what was once an important and flourishing Lorraine wine industry. Extensive vineyards around Metz supplied PINOT NOIR grapes to Champagne in the 19th century and subsequently provided base wine for SEKT when the region became German after the Franco-Prussian war of 1870. PHYLLOXERA arrived late here and the region was relatively unaffected until 1910. The poor-quality HYBRIDS chosen for replanting, together with increasing industrialization (see RAILWAYS) and the proximity of the First World War battlefields, hastened the decline of this wine region. White Auxerrois and Müller-Thurgau are the two most common vine varieties for these delicate, crisp, still wines, and varietal Pinot Gris and Müller-Thurgau are both permitted. Light reds and rosés are based on Pinot Noir with Gamay.

As a result of the success of some German wines in the English-speaking world, Moselle became a GENERIC name for any light, medium-dry, faintly aromatic wine. In the middle of the 19th century, Sparkling Moselle was a popular partner to Sparkling HOCK.

Mosel-Saar-Ruwer, from 1971 until 2007 the official name, incorporating the names of two major tributaries, that appeared on all labels of wine from the German growing region now known simply as MOSEL.

Moster, occasional Austrian synonym for CHASSELAS.

mother vine, an identified, preferred individual vine from which CUTTINGS or other vegetative propagation materials are taken. They are the consequence of CLONAL SELECTION and VINE improvement programmes. Such vines are certified only if they have been tested for virus diseases. However, the widespread use of nursery clones over the last few decades, especially for ROOTSTOCKS, has inadvertently created another problem since mother vines infected with TRUNK DISEASES, which are FUNGAL rather than viral, have led to the spread of these diseases. B.G.C. & R.E.S.

moths, the larval stages of one or more small leafroller (tortricid) moth species damage grapes in almost all wine-growing regions of the world. Despite the name, most of these species do not 'roll leaves' but mainly feed on flowers and fruit. In Europe the main species are the **European grapevine moth** (*Lobesia botrana*) and the **vine moth** (*Eupoecilia ambiguella*), with occasional outbreaks of the **grape tortrix** (*Argyrotaenia ljungiana*), and the **long palped tortrix** (*Sparganothis pilleriana*); in North America the **grape berry moth** (*Paralobesia viteana*) and the **orange tortrix moth** (*Argyrotaenia citrana*); in Australia the **light brown apple moth** (*Epiphyas postvittana*) and in New Zealand the **grapevine moth** (*Phalaenoides glycine*). Most of these species can also develop on other (wild) host plants around the vineyard and transfer to the vines.

These species generally have several generations per season, the first generation attacking flowering stages or leaves, and later generations the fruit stage. The larval feeding causes little direct damage but feeding punctures in berries can increase the risk of BOTRYTIS BUNCH ROT or other infections, including several fungi of the genus *Aspergillus* that can produce a mycotoxin (OCHRATOXIN A). Accidental introductions of several of these species have occurred worldwide, even in the recent past: European grapevine moth to Japan, Chile, Argentina, and California (2009, Napa Valley); light brown apple moth to North America (2007), Hawaii, and New Zealand.

A few other species of moths (Tortricidae but also from the Sphingidae, Pyralidae, Zygaenidae, and Noctuidae families) that mainly feed on the leaves or buds can be found in vineyards but these are generally considered of minor importance.

Leafroller damage is very variable depending on the climate, seasonal weather, surrounding landscape (other vineyards and vegetation), and control by different natural enemies such as parasitic wasps and flies and predatory lacewings, BEETLES, true bugs (hemiptera), etc. Therefore monitoring of these pests is a key factor for successful INTEGRATED PEST MANAGEMENT. Adults are generally monitored using PHEROMONE or food traps, eggs and larvae can be counted. Intervention thresholds are very difficult to establish because of the risk of secondary infection (Botrytis) and the influence of climatic conditions on all insect stages and the secondary fungal infections

When population levels are high enough to require control, the measures are mainly based on mating disruption or INSECTICIDES. In ORGANIC VITICULTURE, disrupting mating as well as organic pesticides such as BT (*Bacillus thuringiensis*) allow sufficient control if applied at the right developmental stage, between egg-hatching and the caterpillars entering the berries. Attempts at biological control using natural enemies such as egg parasitoids have been largely unsuccessful. M.v.H.

Bettiga, L. J., (ed.), *Grape Pest Management* (3rd edn, Oakland, Calif., 2013).

Gilligan, T. M., et al., 'Discovery of *Lobesia botrana* ([Denis & Schiffermüller]) in California: an invasive species new to North America (Lepidoptera: Tortricidae)', *Proceedings of the Entomological Society of Washington*, 113/1 (2011), 14–30. doi: 10.4289/0013-8797.113.1.14.

Moueix, important family in the BORDEAUX TRADE, notably, but by no means exclusively, in ST-ÉMILION and POMEROL. The Moueix family came from the Corrèze, a severe district in central France, noted for its hard-headed men. Jean Moueix (1882–1957) bought Ch Fonroque in St-Émilion in 1930, and his son Jean-Pierre (1913–2003) joined him that year, with the purpose of selling only the hitherto somewhat neglected wines, nearly all red, produced on the RIGHT BANK of the Dordogne, from the Côtes de CASTILLON downstream to BLAYE. In 1937, Jean-Pierre formed Établissements Jean-Pierre Moueix on the quay in LIBOURNE. Increasingly successful in the postwar period, it became from 1970 the major NÉGOCIANT there selling the finer châteaux wines, at a time when the traditional merchants were failing.

In 1956, the 70-year-old firm of Duclot in the city of Bordeaux was acquired to deal mainly with the 'left bank' districts (MÉDOC, GRAVES, etc.), as well as selling direct to private customers in France. As Duclot Export it is prominent in the export trade. From 1968 Duclot has been headed by Jean-Pierre's elder son Jean-François (b. 1945). Fonroque was inherited by Jean-Antoine Moueix (1908–57), and then by his son Jean-Jacques (1935–2013), a director of the Libourne firm, now retired.

In 1970, the younger son, Christian (b. 1946), became a director of J. P. Moueix, with special responsibilities, along with the firm's OENOLOGIST Jean-Claude Berrouet, for the 17 estates owned or farmed by the firm. In 1982, Christian started a JOINT VENTURE in Yountville, NAPA Valley, with two daughters of John Daniel, former owner of Inglenook, before buying them out in 1994. From a 50-ha/124-acre vineyard and an architectural landmark winery opened in 1998, a Bordeaux-style wine named Dominus is produced. He now runs the Libourne négociant with his son Edouard who lives in what was Ch Belair in St-Émilion and is now Belair Monange, incorporating the vines of Magdelaine next door.

In the 1950s, Jean-Pierre Moueix began to acquire châteaux on the right bank: Trotanoy (1953), La Fleur-Pétrus (1950), Lagrange (1959), La Grave (Trigant de Boisset) (1971), and Certan-Giraud, renamed Hosanna (1999), in Pomerol; and Magdelaine (1952) in St-Émilion.

In the 1970s and 1980s, the firm expanded into FRONSAC, acquiring Canon, Canon de Brem, La Croix-Canon, and Canon-Moueix in the superior Canon-Fronsac appellation and La Dauphine in Fronsac. These properties were sold en masse in 2000.

A number of other properties are farmed on behalf of their owners, including Chx Lafleur-Gazin and Latour-Pomerol in Pomerol. However, much the most important acquisition was a half-share of PETRUS in 1964. Moueix had had the exclusive selling rights since 1945, and when the owner, Mme Loubat, died in 1961 she left it to her nephew and niece and the former sold his share to M. Moueix. Jean-François Moueix and his children now own it all.

Jean-Pierre Moueix, a man of great probity and courtesy, was a notable collector of art and books, and the château in which he lived beside the river Dordogne on the edge of Libourne was once full of the works of such leading modern artists as Picasso and Francis Bacon, some of them fetching record prices at auction after his demise.   E.P.-R. & J.R.

mouldy, pejorative tasting term used for wine spoiled by the growth of minute fungi on grapes or winery equipment. Many different types of mould grow on grapes in the vineyard, depending on region and vintage conditions but ROT is the most common. For more details, see FUNGAL DISEASES.

Mouldy COOPERAGE can also cause this sort of aroma. Empty barrels are difficult to keep clean and free of mould because the humid conditions inside them are ideal for the growth of these organisms. Once spores of mould become embedded in the pores of a wooden vessel, it is almost impossible to remove them completely. See BARREL MAINTENANCE.

The word mouldy, along with musty, is also used to describe a wine that is affected by CORK TAINT.   A.D.W.

Moulin-à-Vent means 'windmill' in French and is the name of one of the most famous of the BEAUJOLAIS crus, named after a local windmill. The area includes delimited vineyards within Chénas and Romanèche-Thorins. Of all the wine produced in the Beaujolais region, Moulin-à-Vent, or at least the wines grown on the slopes closest to the windmill itself, is expected to last the longest, taste most concentrated, and therefore, in a way, to be the least typical. With time, the wines begin to taste more like old Pinot Noir than Gamay, and some 50-year-old Moulin-à-Vent can be quite a satisfying drink, even if an atypical Beaujolais. It has also generally been the most expensive. The area planted increased in the 1980s and was about 610 ha/1,507 acres in the early 2010s. Ch des Jacques, bought by Louis JADOT, is a notable name.

Moulis, or **Moulis-en-Médoc**, smallest of the six communal appellations of the Haut-Médoc district of Bordeaux (the others being MARGAUX, ST-JULIEN, PAUILLAC, ST-ESTÈPHE, and neighbouring LISTRAC). Although it includes only about 600 ha/1,500 acres of vineyards, there is considerable diversity of TERROIR in Moulis, in terms of both topography and soil composition. Countryside that is positively rolling by Médoc standards, and soils that include various gravels, clays, and limestone, result in wines as varied as the occasionally brilliant Ch Chasse-Spleen, the good-value Ch Maucaillou, and a host of properties whose names include the word Poujeaux. The finest of these is usually long-lived Ch Poujeaux itself. Like Listrac, Moulis is not CLASSED GROWTH country. Perhaps because of this, the best wines can offer good value, being as well structured as any Haut-Médoc, often with some of the perfume of Margaux to the east.

For more information see MÉDOC and BORDEAUX.

Brook, S., *The Complete Bordeaux* (rev. edn, London, 2012).

Mountain, 19th-century English term for MÁLAGA, which is indeed flanked by mountains. The name is no longer used (excepy by Spain's roving winemaker Telmo Rodriguez for his sweet golden Málaga) but is commonly found on DECANTER labels produced before PHYLLOXERA devastated the Málaga region in 1876.

Mount Barker, cool subregion of the Great Southern region, Western Australia, with 14 producers and a strongly CONTINENTAL climate especially suited to Riesling, Shiraz, and Cabernet Sauvignon. (Also a town in the ADELAIDE HILLS.)

Mount Benson, relatively new seaside wine region in the Limestone Coast Zone of SOUTH AUSTRALIA with nine producers. Two distinguished residents are CHAPOUTIER of the Rhône Valley and (via a large modern winery) G&C Kreglinger, relatives of the Thienponts who own Vieux Château Certan and Le PIN in POMEROL. The region makes elegant, light to medium-bodied wines.

Mount Lofty Ranges Zone encompasses the Adelaide Hills, Adelaide Plains, and Clare Valley wine regions in SOUTH AUSTRALIA.

Mount Veeder, California wine region and AVA in the mountains between Napa and Sonoma. See NAPA Valley.

Moura, DOP subregion of the ALENTEJO in southern Portugal.

Mourisco. **Mourisco Branco** is CAYETANA BLANCA. **Mourisco Tinto** is MARUFO.

Mourvèdre, warm climate red grape variety whose considerable fortunes in Spain have been declining (see MONASTRELL) while it has become markedly more fashionable elsewhere. Plantings in France, where it is enjoying a resurgence of popularity in the south, had grown to 9,375 ha/23,156 acres by 2011, the second biggest national total after Spain's. It cannot be grown successfully much further north than the southern Rhône, however, since it is so late ripening. It is the characteristic grape variety of BANDOL and is increasingly popular with producers of CHÂTEAUNEUF-DU-PAPE because it ripens at lower sugar levels than GRENACHE. In California and Australia it was often called Mataro but has been enjoying a new lease of life as either varietal Mourvèdre or in a blend with Grenache and Syrah/Shiraz, sometimes called GSM.

Mourvèdre dominated Provence until the arrival of PHYLLOXERA and the search for productive vines to supply the burgeoning market for cheap table wine. For many decades it marked time in its French enclave Bandol (in 1968 total French plantings were as little as 900 ha) but is now regarded as an extremely modish and desirable 'improving variety' throughout the Languedoc and Roussillon, especially now that clones have been selected that no longer display the inconveniently variable yields that once resulted from degenerated vine stock.

In southern France, Mourvèdre produces wines considered useful for their structure, intense fruit, and, in good years, perfume often redolent of blackberries. The structure in particular can be a useful foil for Grenache in Provence and Cinsaut further west. In Bandol, it is typically blended with both of these, and the statutory minimum for Mourvèdre is now 50%. Mourvèdre is condoned in a host of APPELLATION CONTRÔLÉE regulations all over the south of France from Grignan les Adhémar to Collioure, including Châteauneuf-du-Pape and environs. It usually plays a useful supporting role, being fleshier than Syrah, tauter than Grenache and Cinsaut, and more charming than Carignan. Somewhat belatedly, Australia realized it had all the wherewithal to produce authentic Rhône blends, despite the loss of precious old-vine Grenache and Mourvèdre in South Australia in the late 1980s (due to an ill-advised VINE PULL SCHEME). Old-vine Grenache–Shiraz–Mourvèdre (or any combinations thereof) have proliferated since the 1990s as resources have been moved from fortified to table wine production, athough plantings of Mourvèdre, still called Mataro in official statistics, had fallen to 729 ha by 2012.

Although grown at least since the 1870s, California's unfashionable Mataro was fast disappearing until the RHÔNE RANGERS made the connection with Mourvèdre and pushed up demand for wine from these historic stumps, notably in Contra Costa county between San Francisco and the Central Valley, where there were considerable new plantings in the early 1990s thanks to demand from the likes of Bonny Doon and Cline Cellars. By 2012, the state's total plantings had risen to about 950 acres/385 ha. Rhône mania recently spread north to Washington where there were 165 acres by 2011. South Africa had 359 ha/887 acres which mainly disappeared into blends in 2008. It is also grown on Cyprus.

mousse, French term for FIZZINESS.

mousseux, French for sparkling. Some *mousseux* wines are made by the traditional method (see SPARKLING WINEMAKING) while others may be made by the much less painstaking CHARMAT process.

mousy, TASTING TERM commonly associated with the wine FAULT caused by BRETTANOMYCES yeasts and some bacteria, including some, but not all, LACTIC ACID BACTERIA. Although the exact mechanism of mousy taint formation is not totally clear, for example why some wines are spoiled and others are not despite the presence of microorganisms capable of producing the fault, it is evident that low levels of SULFUR DIOXIDE, high PH, and exposure to OXYGEN render a wine vulnerable to this spoilage. Mousiness is usually apparent only after a wine has been swallowed or expectorated. Once detected, the taint renders the wine undrinkable and worsens in the glass, but as many as 30% of winemakers are unable to detect it. Three different compounds (2-acetyltetrahydropiridine, 2-ethyltetrahydropiridine, and 2-acetylpyrroline) are responsible. P.J.W.

Grbin, P. R., et al., 'Developments in the sensory, chemical and microbiological basis of mousy taint in wine', in C. S. Stockley, et al. (eds.), *Proceedings of the Ninth Australian Wine Industry Technical Conference: 16–19 July 1995* (Adelaide, 1996).

moût de raisins partiellement fermenté issu de vendanges passerillées is the cumbersome French name for partially fermented grape must extracted from raisined grapes and is a term used on labels of some French SWEET WINES since Alsace has sole rights to VENDANGE TARDIVE. According to EU regulations, the must has to have a total sugar content of at least 272 g/l and the finished wine at least 8% alcohol.

mouthfeel, non-specific tasting term, used particularly for red wines, to indicate those

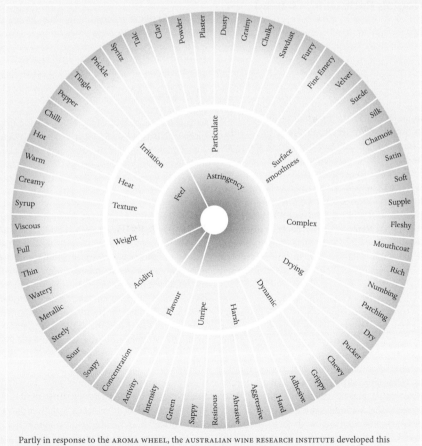

Partly in response to the AROMA WHEEL, the AUSTRALIAN WINE RESEARCH INSTITUTE developed this **mouthfeel** and astringency wheel in 1998.

textural attributes, such as smoothness, that produce tactile sensations on the surface of the oral cavity (see diagram). For more detail, see TEXTURE.

Gawel, R., Oberholster, A., Francis, I. L., 'A mouth-feel wheel: terminology for communicating the mouth-feel characteristics of red wine', *Australian Journal of Grape and Wine Research*, 6 (2000), 203–7.

Mouton Cadet, the most successful Bordeaux BRAND, began life in 1927, a poor vintage in which Baron Philippe de ROTHSCHILD created what was effectively a SECOND WINE called Carruades de Mouton for Ch MOUTON ROTHSCHILD. Penning-Rowsell notes that it was not a success, and its successor in 1930 was named Mouton-Cadet, since Philippe was the *cadet*, the youngest, of the family. Eventually, as Mouton Cadet, it developed a prosperous life of its own, and demand was so great that the flexibility of the BORDEAUX AOC appellation was needed.

Today Mouton Cadet is available in red, white, and rosé versions, having been repackaged and reblended in 2004 to rely predominantly on FRUIT-DRIVEN Merlot and Sauvignon Blanc, with tighter control over its many suppliers all over the Bordeaux region.

Mouton Rothschild, Château, important wine estate in PAUILLAC in the BORDEAUX wine region and the only one ever to have been promoted within the 1855 CLASSIFICATION, to FIRST GROWTH.

Originally part of the LAFITE estate with which it is intermingled, it became in the middle of the 18th century a separate entity, owned by the de Brane family. In the first half of the following century, Baron Hector de Brane (or Branne) became known as 'the Napoleon of the vines' for his work in developing the Médoc vineyards, and, in company with his neighbour Armand d'Armailhacq, in supposedly introducing the CABERNET SAUVIGNON vine. In 1830, he sold Mouton to a M. Thuret and retired to his Ch Brane-Cantenac in the commune of MARGAUX. At this time, Mouton had little international repute, and the first entry in a Christie's AUCTION catalogue was in 1834. In 1853, Thuret sold it to Baron Nathaniel de ROTHSCHILD, of the English branch of the family, two years before the 1855 classification which placed Mouton Rothschild at the top of the second growths, a position unsatisfactory to the family, but not seriously contested until Baron Philippe de Rothschild took over the running of it from his father in 1922. He startled Bordeaux by employing a poster artist, Carlu, to design an art deco label, including the Rothschild arrows, for the 1924 vintage, and then proposing CHÂTEAU BOTTLING of all the first growths (and Mouton Rothschild). He also instigated what was initially a SECOND WINE, called MOUTON CADET.

On his return in 1945 after the Second World War, Baron Philippe initiated the series of ARTIST'S LABELS, each year designed by a well-known artist, including Cocteau, Braque, Dali, Bacon, and Henry Moore. He also began a campaign to elevate Mouton to first growth status, which he achieved in 1973. He and his American wife Pauline created a magnificent Musée du Vin, or wine museum, filled with *objets d'art* and open to the public since 1962 on application. In 2013 a new vat room was inaugurated as well as an exhibition space for the artworks which have illustrated the Mouton labels so famously, and which have been exhibited around the world.

The 80-ha/200-acre vineyard is planted with 80% CABERNET SAUVIGNON grapes, 16% MERLOT (much increased in the late 1990s), 3% CABERNET FRANC, and 1% PETIT VERDOT. Average production is between 13,000 and 16,000 cases. A second wine, Petit Mouton, was introduced in 1994 and a dry white AC Bordeaux Aile d'Argent in 1991. The wine is famously concentrated and intensely aromatic in good vintages. See ROTHSCHILDS for details of other wine investments and JOINT VENTURES.   E.P.-R. & J.R.

Herman, S., and Pascal, J., *Mouton Rothschild, The Museum of Wine in Art* (Paris, 2003).
Ray, C., *Mouton Rothschild* (London, 1974).

Moza Fresca, GALICIAN name for the grape known as SÍRIA in Portugal.

Mtsvane, name of two distinct varieties grown in GEORGIA.

Mudgee, relatively isolated and well-defined wine region in NEW SOUTH WALES, associated with generous, smooth reds based on the ubiquitous Cabernet Sauvignon and Shiraz. Mudgee was a pioneer of Italian varieties in Australia and they are increasingly grown. There are still almost 40 producers but the total area under vine is shrinking.

mulch, materials put on the vineyard soil surface to assist vine growth. Mulch is useful because it keeps soil damp, stops it getting too hot, and hinders the growth of weeds. They are generally composed of ORGANIC MATTER, providing NUTRIENTS for the vine's growth as the mulch decomposes. Organic mulches have a desirable effect on SOIL HEALTH, by increasing microbial populations and diversity. A common indicator of this is more EARTHWORM activity, related to improved SOIL STRUCTURE and better water infiltration.

Animal manure and straw were common mulches of the past but in some modern vineyards these have been replaced with thin plastic film. Young vines are planted through holes in the plastic. The response of young vine growth to plastic is often remarkable, especially for vineyards which rely on rainfall rather than

IRRIGATION for their water. The film controls weed growth, stops water evaporating from the soil surface, and in spring it warms the soil, promoting root growth. The appearance of a vineyard with plastic film under the vines does not please all wine TOURISTS, nor those who favour more 'natural' means of vine establishment, and after a few years the plastic film rips and is blown around the vineyard.

A major disadvantage to straw mulch has been the cost of placing a sufficiently deep mat below each vine. This cost can be reduced by modern techniques of mechanically unrolling bales of hay, or alternatively by throwing the straw under the vine as the COVER CROP is mown.

So-called organic vineyards use mulches of living plants as well as dead material. The main disadvantage of living mulches for the young vines is that there may be too much competition for water and nutrients, and so the living mulch may need to be killed off. However, when a thick plant mulch breaks down, then nutrients are released and the soil is improved. Either living or dead organic mulches can cause problems because of INSECTS and FUNGI which can be harboured in the litter around the vine trunk. Generally speaking, however, mulch has more positive than negative effects in the vineyard.   R.E.S.

mulled wine is wine that has been heated with sugar and spices and also, sometimes, slices of fruit and even brandy. This was a particularly common way of serving wine in the Middle Ages, since honey and spices helped to compensate for any shortcomings in wine QUALITY (which were likely to be considerable as the months since the HARVEST wore on in this age when wine was served directly from the barrel). The verb 'mull' was current at least from the beginning of the 17th century. Recipes vary but red wine is almost invariably used, and cinnamon and cloves are common. It is far less difficult to make good mulled wine than to find DRINKING VESSELS that retain the heat but are not uncomfortably hot to hold. See also GLÜHWEIN.

Müllerrebe, which translates from German as 'miller's grape', is the common, and logical, name for Germany's selection of PINOT MEUNIER, grown on more than 2,000 ha of mainly Württemberg and Baden in southern Germany.

Müller-Thurgau, waning white grape variety which could fairly be said to have been the bane of German wine production but which is at long last on the wane there. This cross was developed in 1882 for entirely expedient reasons by a Dr Hermann Müller, born in the Swiss canton of Thurgau but then working at the German viticultural station at GEISENHEIM. His understandable aim was to combine the quality of the great RIESLING grape with the viticultural reliability, particularly the early ripening, of the SILVANER. Most of the variety's synonyms (Rivaner in Luxembourg and Slovenia, Riesling-Sylvaner in New Zealand and Switzerland, Rizlingszilvani in Hungary) reflect this combination. Late-20th-century DNA PROFILING by researchers at GEILWEILERHOF established that the variety is actually Riesling × Madeleine Royale, a now extinct TABLE GRAPE of unknown parentage obtained from a cross made in 1845. The variety is all too short on Riesling characteristics, typically smelling vaguely peachy with a fat, flaccid mid-palate, too often with a slight suspicion of rot, to which its rather large, thin-skinned berries are prone.

The vine certainly ripens early, even earlier than Silvaner. Unlike Riesling, it can be grown anywhere, producing prodigious quantities (sometimes double Riesling's common yield range of 80 to 110 hl/ha (4.6–6.3 tons/acre)) of extremely dull, flabby wine.

Müller-Thurgau was not embraced by Germany's growers until after the Second World War, when the need to rebuild the industry fast presumably gave this productive, easily grown vine allure. In the early 1970s, it even overtook the great Riesling in total area planted (having for some time produced far more wine in total) and remained in that position throughout the 1980s. Typically blended with a little of a more aromatic variety such as MORIO-MUSKAT and with a great deal of SÜSSRESERVE, Müller-Thurgau was transformed into oceans of QBA sugarwater labelled either LIEBFRAUMILCH or one of the internationally recognized names such as Niersteiner, Bernkasteler, or Piesporter (see GROSSLAGEN). But by the late 1990s, Riesling was once again Germany's most planted grape variety although at more than 13,000 ha in 2012, total plantings of Müller-Thurgau in Germany are arguably still (too?) significant.

The wood is much softer than Riesling's and can easily be damaged by hard winters. The grapes rot easily (as can be tasted in a number of examples from less successful years), and the vine is susceptible to DOWNY MILDEW, BLACK ROT, and, its own bane, ROTBRENNER, but it will presumably continue to flourish while there is a market for cheap German wine.

Outside Germany it can be much more exciting. In northern Italy's ALTO ADIGE, where extensive acreage of ancient vines testifies to the promotional success by early proponents of Dr Müller's cross, bottlings from easily a score of today's best domaines and grower co-operatives testify to the refinement, minerality, complexity and sheer refreshment value that is possible with Müller-Thurgau—just not, it seems, in Germany. Most of the best Alto Adige wines are grown on very steep, stony, high-ELEVATION sites of which Tiefenbrünner's Feldmarschall is an extreme example. Italy's total area planted in 2010 was 1,312 ha/3,242 acres.

The variety thrives all over central and eastern Europe. It is planted, appropriately enough, in SWITZERLAND, playing an increasingly important role in the vineyards of the German-speaking area in the north and east. In AUSTRIA (sometimes called Rivaner) total area planted had fallen to 1,972 ha by 2012, mainly in Weinviertel where it makes generally light, inconsequential wines. Across Austria's southern border, it is also grown as Rizvanec, in eastern SLOVENIA and is even more important to the east and north of Austria in the CZECH REPUBLIC and HUNGARY. As Rizlingszilvani, it covers thousands of hectares of vineyard around Lake Balaton and produces lakesful of flabby Badacsonyi Rizlingszilvani. In the 1970s Müller-Thurgau was planted enthusiastically by New Zealand grape growers on the recommendation of visiting German experts as a preferable substitute for the HYBRIDS that were all too prevalent in the country's nascent wine industry but 'Riesling-Sylvaner' has now virtually disappeared.

Elsewhere in the New World, most growers are not driven by the need for early-ripening varieties (and would find the flab in the resultant wine a distinct disadvantage), although some Oregon growers have experimented successfully with it, and credible examples have been produced in the Puget sound vineyards of western Washington state.

Northern Europe's two smallest and coolest wine producers, ENGLAND and LUXEMBOURG, have in their time depended heavily on Müller-Thurgau, called Rivaner in Luxembourg.

Munson, T. V. (1843–1913), Texan credited with putting PHYLLOXERA-resistant roots on French vines, and saving Europe's vineyards from devastation. Thomas Volney Munson was a lifelong student of viticulture, especially AMERICAN VINE SPECIES. At Kentucky University he became interested in TEXAS and its grapes and travelled tens of thousands of miles in 40 states gathering WILD VINE specimens, and studying soils and climates. He travelled by horseback and train, hunting from rail cars and jumping off to collect specimens whenever the train stopped. In 1876, Munson settled on the Red River near Denison in Texas, which he described as a 'grape paradise' because of the six or eight species of wild vines there. He developed a vineyard and nursery business as well as becoming the authority on the wild grape species of North America. Munson's passion was for VINE BREEDING, and he produced about 300 varieties using local VITIS species *lincecumii, champini,* and *candicans*. None however became commercially important.

Being aware of phylloxera's predations in Europe, Munson began GRAFTING European vines to American species as ROOTSTOCKS to grant resistance. He passed on the results of his research to Viala, Planchon, and other French experts. In the 1880s and 1890s, French growers accordingly imported huge quantities of American species for use as rootstocks, especially from Texas and Missouri. The French government made Munson a Chevalier du Mérite in 1888, only the second American to have achieved this honour (Thomas Edison having been the first). R.E.S.

Murray Darling, large Australian wine region straddling the Darling River and both sides of the Murray River in VICTORIA and NEW SOUTH WALES. While totally dependent on IRRIGATION (the soils have little water-holding capacity and there is negligible growing season rainfall) and high yields of low-cost grapes, international competition is leading to higher standards of fruit quality being demanded by the big companies which purchase the massive annual grape production.

Muscadel or **Muskadel**, South African name for MUSCAT BLANC À PETITS GRAINS, the term being generally used only for very sweet, but not very modish JEREPIGO. The total area planted in South Africa was 729 ha/1,800 acres in 2012, mainly in inland Robertson. This was the Muscat chiefly responsible for the famous 18th-century CONSTANTIA dessert wine.

Muscadelle is the famous also-ran third grape variety responsible, with SÉMILLON and SAUVIGNON BLANC, for the sweet white (and duller dry white) wines of Bordeaux. By 2011 France's total plantings had fallen to 1,554 ha/3,838 acres, 857 ha of them in the Gironde, where the majority of Muscadelle vines are not in the great sweet white wine areas of SAUTERNES, but in the unfashionable and vast ENTRE-DEUX-MERS, including the fringe sweet white appellations as PREMIÈRES CÔTES DE BORDEAUX, CADILLAC, LOUPIAC, and STE-CROIX-DU-MONT. Muscadelle is relatively more important to BERGERAC than to Bordeaux and it is valued as the finest ingredient in some of the best MONBAZILLAC.

The variety, unrelated to any member of the MUSCAT family, shares a vaguely grapey aroma with them but has its relatively ancient origins in SOUTH WEST FRANCE. DNA PROFILING has shown a parent-offspring relationship with the prolific GOUAIS BLANC. The usefully productive Muscadelle leafs late and ripens early and has rarely demonstrated great subtlety in the wines it produces. The occasional VARIETAL French Muscadelle can demonstrate a certain 'green' tang but its use is almost exclusively in blends, adding the same sort of youthful fruitiness to south western sweet whites as MEUNIER does to the north east sparkling whites called champagne.

The variety known as Sauvignon Vert in California is Muscadelle. In only one corner of the wine world does Muscadelle produce sensational varietal wine, however, that now known as TOPAQUE in Australia. For years

Australians thought the grape they called Tokay, which produced these dark, syrupy, wood-matured concentrates for after-dinner drinking, was Hungarian, but the French AMPELOGRAPHER Paul Truel identified it as Muscadelle in 1976. Total national plantings had fallen to 82 ha by 2012, just 33 of them in RUTHERGLEN.

Muscadet, one of France's dry white commodity wines currently undergoing revolution while trying to survive. The Muscadet region extends mainly south east of Nantes near the mouth of the Loire on a shrinking total vineyard area of about 12,000 ha/29,600 acres of gently rolling, Atlantic-dominated countryside where hundreds of wine farmers maintain family vine holdings, increasingly consolidated and devoted to one grape variety. The white MELON de Bourgogne, a reliable but relatively neutral variety, was introduced to the region in the 17th century by the DUTCH WINE TRADE, who were in need of distilling material for their brandewijn and had the means to transport it. The terrible winter of 1709 killed a high proportion of the red wine grapes previously grown here and transformed it into a predominantly white wine region.

The most significant, and varied, appellation by far, representing more than two-thirds of production, is **Muscadet-Sèvre et Maine**, named after two small rivers which flow through this, the most monocultural part of the Pays Nantais south and east of Nantes. Indeed, more Muscadet-Sèvre et Maine is produced every year than in any other Loire appellation. Particularly ambitious wines are made on the clay soils of Vallet, while those from the schist and granite slopes around St-Fiacre are also much admired. The appellation known as **Muscadet-Coteaux de la Loire** is in the north and **Muscadet-Côtes de Grandlieu** is in the south west of the region. **Muscadet** is the basic appellation, not made in great quantity and usually less exciting.

According to stricter regulations drawn up in the late 1990s, basic Muscadet is excluded from that substantial proportion of the wines that are matured SUR LIE, their flavour at least theoretically enriched by LEES CONTACT which must be bottled between March and November in the year following the harvest. So neutral is the Melon grape that Muscadet producers have long been able to store their wines over the winter without RACKING them off the lees, and without the risk of picking up off-flavours. This leaves the wines with rather more flavour and a small amount of CARBON DIOXIDE before bottling, which must be done where the wine was made and either during the spring or autumn following the harvest.

At its worst, Muscadet is an anodyne, watery, dry white with or without a little sparkle, but at its best it captures the essence of France's north Atlantic coast and provides an authentic, light, tangy, almost salty foil for its seafood. Since the mid 1980s, producers have been experimenting with such techniques as BARREL FERMENTATION and LEES STIRRING and since the late 1990s those producers seeking maximum ripeness levels have also employed pre-fermentation SKIN CONTACT. In 2011, the first crus communaux within the Muscadet de Sèvre et Maine were announced; these are designed to be superior, terroir-driven Muscadets with stricter yields (45 hl/ha maximum) worth ageing in bottle, and worth being aged on lees for so long that they miss the deadline to qualify for the 'sur lie' description outlined above. Clisson is an area of very well-drained pebble and gravel mix whose wines are particularly long-lived. Gorges on the River Sèvre has soils that range from gabbros to clay and quartz. Its wines develop a certain smokiness in bottle. Le Pallet is an especially warm pocket of vines on the right bank of the Sèvre, and further crus such as Mouzillon-Tillières, Château Thébaud, Monnières Saint-Fiacre, and Goulaine are expected to follow. A little PRIMEUR is also made. Muscadet can no longer be dismissed as a simple, homogeneous wine.

Other wines produced in the Pays Nantais are GROS PLANT, Coteaux d'ANCENIS, and FIEFS VENDÉENS. See also LOIRE, including map.

Friedrich, J., *A Wine and Food Guide to the Loire* (New York, 1996)

Muscadinia, a section of the botanical genus VITIS, although some botanists have suggested that it should be considered a separate genus rather than a section of *Vitis*. *Muscadinia* includes the two species, *V. rotundifolia* (including *V. rotundifolia* var. *munsonia*) and *V. popenoei*, according to recent PHYLOGENIES. *Vitis* contains the true grapevine, as outlined in BOTANICAL CLASSIFICATION. *Muscadinia* and *Vitis* differ in chromosome number and morphology.

Members of the *Muscadiniae* occur only in the south-eastern UNITED STATES, MEXICO, and (according to the Institute MAGARACH) in UKRAINE, but seem related to *Vitis ludwigii* found as fossil seeds in Tertiary sediments of northern Europe. There is speculation that *Muscadinia* can be regarded as transitional between the temperate genus *Vitis* and *Ampelocissus*, which is adapted to tropical climates. Species of the three genera have similar characteristics.

The **Muscadines**, as they are called, typically have small bunches of large, thick-skinned berries. The two species included in *Muscadinia* are found in America and Mexico. The best known is *Vitis rotundifolia*, of which only SCUPPERNONG is grown commercially for wine-making. The very thick skins and musky flavour of Muscadines produce fruit and wine quite different from that of European VINIFERA vines. Scuppernong's cluster has only a few berries which ripen unevenly and drop off when ripe. The large berries have a thick, slippery pulp that is difficult to press and excessive pressure brings bitterness from the skins. Muscadines are typically low in sugar concentration, and usually require CHAPTALIZATION.

A few thousand hectares of Muscadine grapes are grown in the cotton belt in the south-eastern United States.

The Muscadines have natural resistance to PIERCE'S DISEASE and can therefore be planted in some areas unsuitable for VITIS species and HYBRIDS of them. They are also usefully resistant to PHYLLOXERA, NEMATODES, DOWNY MILDEW, and POWDERY MILDEW, which makes Muscadine germplasm valuable in VINE BREEDING. For long the different chromosome numbers of *Vitis* (2n = 38) and Muscadines (2n = 40) proved a barrier to breeding, since progeny were typically infertile. However, recent advances have allowed Muscadine germplasm to be incorporated into VINE IMPROVEMENT programmes.

R.E.S. & J.V.

Aradhya, M., et al., 'Genetic structure, differentiation, and phylogeny of the genus *Vitis*: implications for genetic conservation', *Acta Horticulturae* 799 (2008), 43–9.

Lu, J., Schell, L., and Ramming, D. W., 'Interspecific hybridization between Vitis rotundifolia and Vitis vinifera and evaluation of the hybrids', *Acta Horticulturae*, 528 (2000), 479–86.

Pinney, T., *A History of Wine in America from the Beginnings to Prohibition* (Berkeley, Calif., 1989).

Wan, Y., et al., 'A phylogenetic analysis of the grape genus (*Vitis* L.) reveals broad reticulation and concurrent diversification during neogene and quaternary climate change', *BMC Evolutionary Biology*, 13 (2013), 141. doi:10.1186/1471-2148-13-141.

Muscardin, red grape variety occasionally making a light, crisp, floral contribution to CHÂTEAUNEUF-DU-PAPE blends.

Muscat, one of the world's great and historic names, of both grapes and wines, that has been benefiting from a FASHION for wines labelled MOSCATO. Muscat grapes—and many different Muscat varieties, several closely related, in several hues of berry—are some of the very few which produce wines that actually taste of grapes. MUSCAT OF HAMBURG and MUSCAT OF ALEXANDRIA are grown as both wine grapes and TABLE GRAPES (although it has to be said that Hamburg is much better in the second role). MUSCAT BLANC À PETITS GRAINS is the oldest and finest, producing wines of the greatest intensity, while MUSCAT OTTONEL, paler in every way, is a relative parvenu. See also various MOSCATELS and MOSCATOS.

Muscat grapes were probably the first to be distinguished and identified and have grown around the Mediterranean for many, many centuries. With such strongly perfumed grapes (thanks to a particularly high concentration of MONOTERPENES), described in French as MUSQUÉ as though they were actually impregnated with musk, Muscat grapes have always been attractive to bees and it was almost certainly Muscat grapes that the Greeks described as *anathelicon moschaton*, and PLINY the Elder as *uva apiana*, 'grape of the bees'. Some even theorize that Muscat derives its name from *musca*, the Latin for flies, also attracted to these scented grapes.

Muscat wines, carrying many different labels including Moscato (in Italy) and Moscatel (in Iberia), can vary from the refreshingly low-alcohol, sweet and frothy ASTI SPUMANTE, through Muscat d'ALSACE and other bone-dry Muscats made for example in Roussillon, to sweet wines with alcohol levels between 15 and 20%, usually by MUTAGE (as in the VINS DOUX NATURELS of southern France and Greece). Since a high proportion of the world's Muscat is dark-berried, and since a wide variety of wood-ageing techniques are used, such wines can vary in colour from palest gold (as in some of the more determinedly modern Muscats de FRONTIGNAN) to deepest brown (as in some of Australia's sweet, fortified Muscats (see TOPAQUE AND MUSCAT).

Most Muscat vines need relatively hot climates (although see MUSCAT OTTONEL and GERMAN HISTORY in which the medieval cultivation of both light- and dark-berried Muscat vines is documented). There either are or have been many famous Muscats around the Mediterranean. See MOROCCO, GREECE, SICILY, and SARDINIA.

Robinson, J., Harding, J., and Vouillamoz, J., *Wine Grapes, a complete guide to 1,368 vine varieties, including their origins and flavours* (London, 2012).

Muscat Bailey A, a HYBRID (Bailey x MUSCAT OF HAMBURG) grape that is becoming a major variety for wine in JAPAN producing a broad range of wines from rosé to full-bodied reds. Takeda Winery in Yamagata Prefecture has the oldest wine-producing vines, planted in the 1940s.

Muscat Blanc à Petits Grains is the cumbersome but descriptive full name of the oldest and noblest variety of Muscat with the greatest concentration of fine grape flavour, hinting at orange-flowers and spice. Its berries and seeds are, as its name suggests, particularly small, and they are round as opposed to the larger, oval berries of MUSCAT OF ALEXANDRIA—in fact another synonym for this superior variety is Muscat à Petits Grains Ronds. But its berries are not, as its principal AMPELOGRAPHICAL name suggests, invariably white. In fact there are pink-, red-, and black-berried versions (although the dark berries are not so deeply pigmented that they can produce a proper red wine) and some vines produce berries whose colour varies considerably from vintage to

vintage. Many synonyms for the variety include reference to the yellow or golden (*gallego, giallo, gelber*) colour of its berries. And Brown Muscat is one of Australia's names for a Muscat population that is more dark than light, and resembles South Africa's Muskadel in that respect (thereby providing more evidence of early viticultural links between these two southern hemisphere producers). *Wine Grapes* lists no fewer than 60 synonyms of this ancient variety, including Muscat of Frontignan, Frontignac, Muscat Blanc, Muscat d'Alsace, Muskateller, Moscato Bianco, Moscato d'Asti, Moscato di Canelli, Moscatel de Grano Menudo, Moscatel de Frontignan, Muscatel Branco, White Muscat, Muscat Canelli, and Muskadel (in South Africa). Any Muscat with the words Alexandria, Gordo, Romain, Hamburg, or Ottonel in its name is *not* this superior variety.

This particular Muscat may very well be the oldest known wine grape variety, and the oldest cultivated in France, having been established in Gaul around Narbonne, notably at FRONTIGNAN, by the Romans—and possibly even before then brought to the Marseilles region by the Greeks. DNA PROFILING has found close genetic relationships between this Muscat and several modern Greek and Italian varieties such as Moschofilero and Malvasia respectively. Muscat Blanc also seems to be a parent of several other varieties with Muscat in their name, including Muscat of Alexandria. Muscat Blanc has clearly been established for many centuries round the Mediterranean, where its early budding poses few problems. It was certainly already widely esteemed in the vineyards of Roussillon by the 14th century. It is Piemonte's oldest documented variety. That it is recorded as growing in Germany, as MUSKATELLER, as early as the 12th century, and is the first documented variety grown in Alsace, in the 16th century, suggesting that spring frosts may have been less common then, for the variety has now been replaced by the more accommodating Muscat Ottonel in Alsace.

Muscat Blanc also yields more conservatively than other Muscats and is sensitive to a wide range of diseases, which has naturally limited its cultivation—although it has travelled for so long and so widely that it is particularly widely distributed.

This is the Muscat that predominates in Italy, which has the single biggest area planted with it (see MOSCATO). In France, contrary to almost all other white grape varieties, this Muscat has recently been gaining ground and was planted on almost 8,000 ha/20,000 acres, plus 286 ha of the red-berried mutation, by 2011 mainly in the LANGUEDOC-ROUSSILLON, partly because of the development of dry Muscat unfortified wine there. It has overtaken Muscat of Alexandria to become the most common white wine grape in Roussillon, and is also important in

the Hérault *département*. This is the Muscat solely responsible for France's golden sweet Muscats of BEAUMES-DE-VENISE, FRONTIGNAN, LUNEL, MIREVAL, and ST-JEAN-DE-MINERVOIS. Muscat has also benefited from the development of a virtually CLAIRETTE-free grapey (Tradition) version of the Rhône's fizzy CLAIRETTE DE DIE. This is the predominant Muscat of CORSICA.

As Moscatel de Grano Menudo it is still grown in Spain but to a limited extent; most Spanish wines labelled Moscatel are made from Muscat of Alexandria. In eastern Europe MUSCAT OTTONEL with its shorter growing season is generally more popular but Muscat Blanc is grown in Slovenia as Rumeni Muščat, in Hungary as Sárga Muskotály, the third ingredient in TOKAJ, and in Romania where it is known as TĂMAÎIOĂSA Alba, and Bulgaria and Russia where it is called Tamyanka. It was almost certainly this Muscat that was responsible for the famous, long-lived Muscats of CRIMEA.

Germany has apparently been in thrall to the flashily ersatz MORIO-MUSKAT cross, but total plantings of Muscat Blanc, as Gelber Muskateller, had grown to just under 200 ha/500 acres, mainly in Pfalz, by 2012. This small comeback may be at least partly due to the influence of Müller-Catoir, whose distinctively pungent dry wines from this variety earned a keen following. Dry, racy Muskatellers from Styria and occasionally the Wachau have been particularly popular in Austria.

If anywhere could be said to be Muscat's homeland it is GREECE and its total area of Muscat Blanc à Petits Grains, at more than 1,800 ha in 2012, is more than twice as common as Muscat of Alexandria (the prime Cypriot Muscat). The small-berried Muscat is accorded the honour of being the only variety allowed in Greece's most rigidly controlled Muscats such as those of Sámos, Pátrai, and Kefallinía. For the moment, Greek Muscat, like its many variations on the MALVASIA theme, is almost invariably sweet, alcoholic, and redolent of history, but drier versions more suited to drinking with food are on the increase. See GREECE for more details.

In the New World, the variety reaches its apogee in Australia where it has been known as Brown Muscat and Frontignac with all manner of colour of grape skins and its most glorious incarnation is RUTHERGLEN Muscat. Official Australian 2012 grape variety statistics distinguished between a stable total of about 300 ha of dark-skinned, small-berried Muscat and a total of light-skinned, small-berried Muscat that had increased to over 800 ha, thanks to plantings in RIVERLAND and RIVERINA, presumably in response to the FASHION for MOSCATO. For South Africa, see MUSCADEL. Muscat of Alexandria has been very much more important than this finer Muscat in California with most Muscat Blanc in the central SAN JOAQUIN VALLEY.

But the FASHION for MOSCATO has encouraged new plantings, in San Luis Obispo as well, so that the state total was 2,000 acres/800 ha by 2012.

Robinson, J., Harding, J., and Vouillamoz, J., *Wine Grapes, a complete guide to 1,368 vine varieties, including their origins and flavours* (London, 2012).

Muscat d'Alsace

is an Alsace synonym for the vine variety MUSCAT BLANC À PETITS GRAINS. For more details of what to expect of a wine labelled Muscat d'Alsace, see ALSACE.

Muscat de Beaumes-de-Venise

is the often delicate VIN DOUX NATUREL from the southern Rhône village of BEAUMES-DE-VENISE under whose name there are more details.

Muscat de Frontignan

is the old name for the once internationally famous wine of FRONTIGNAN. It is also a synonym for the grape variety solely responsible for it, MUSCAT BLANC À PETITS GRAINS.

Muscat de Lunel

. See LUNEL for details of this southern Languedoc VIN DOUX NATUREL. It is yet another synonym for the grape variety solely responsible for it, MUSCAT BLANC À PETITS GRAINS.

Muscat de Mireval

. See MIREVAL for details of this relatively unimportant southern Languedoc VIN DOUX NATUREL.

Muscat de Rivesaltes

has become the most important appellation of the Rivesaltes region in ROUSSILLON grown on 4,856 ha/11,994 acres of VINEYARD and is by far the biggest Muscat appellation in France. Unlike the four Muscat VINS DOUX NATURELS listed above, and the one listed below, it is currently made mainly from MUSCAT OF ALEXANDRIA with some MUSCAT BLANC À PETITS GRAINS, although the latter is encouraged in new plantings. Much of it is of decidedly ordinary quality, based on planting of the lesser Muscat of Alexandria on the plain, although Domaine Cazes and Domaine de Chênes produce some superior bottlings. For more details, see RIVESALTES.

Muscat de St-Jean-de-Minervois

is the golden VIN DOUX NATUREL speciality of ST-JEAN-DE-MINERVOIS in the northern Languedoc and is produced in very limited quantities from MUSCAT BLANC À PETITS GRAINS.

Muscat du Cap Corse

, Corsican VIN DOUX NATUREL. See CORSICA.

Muscat of Alexandria

is a Muscat almost as ancient as MUSCAT BLANC À PETITS GRAINS, and also has dozens of synonyms, but its wine is usually distinctly inferior. In hot climates it can thrive and produce a good yield of extremely ripe grapes but their chief attribute is sweetness. (In cooler climates, its output can be seriously affected by COULURE, MILLERANDAGE, and a range of FUNGAL DISEASES.) Wines made from this sort of Muscat tend to be strong, sweet, and unsubtle. The aroma is vaguely grapey but can have slightly feline overtones of geranium rather than the more lingering bouquet of Muscat Blanc.

Some indication of its lack of finesse as a wine producer is the fact that a considerable proportion of the Muscat of Alexandria grown today is destined for uses other than wine: California for example uses most of its 3,800 acres/1,538 ha for RAISINS; Chile distils most of its thousands of hectares of Muscat of Alexandria to make pisco; it is even grown under glass in Britain and the Netherlands to provide grapes for the fruit bowl.

Its name suggests origins in Egypt but genetics suggest Greek origins, and that it is a progeny of Muscat Blanc à Petits Grains. It was disseminated around the Mediterranean by the Romans, hence its common synonym Muscat Romain. Its southern Italian synonym is ZIBIBBO under which details of its Italian incarnations can be found.

Today it is most important to wine industries in that old arc of maritime history Iberia, South Africa, and Australia, where it may be known respectively as Moscatel, Hanepoot, and Muscat Gordo Blanco or Lexia, a particularly Australian contraction of the word Alexandria. Spain's total plantings had grown to 10,234 ha/25,278 acres by 2011, eight times as much as of the other major Muscat, called Moscatel Grano Menudo here. It is not known, however, exactly how much of this serves the wine industry, typically with sweet MOSCATELS of various sticky sorts. Muscat of Alexandria's various Spanish synonyms include Moscatel de Alejandría, Moscatel de España, Moscatel Gordo (Blanco), Moscatel Blanco, and Moscatel de Chipiona.

In Portugal, its most famous incarnation is Moscatel de SETÚBAL but Portugal's under 1,000 ha of Muscat of Alexandria grapes, often called Moscatel Graúdo, have also been harnessed to produce aromatic, dry, much lower alcohol Muscats. This is also the fate of the majority of Australia's static total of 2,400 ha of 'Gordo Blanco', the country's dominant Muscat, once used mainly for fortified wines, although from cooler vineyards it can produce sound, unfortified wines that are sweet because late picked. Dry wine produced from the Gordo Blanco grown in Australia's irrigated Riverland is typically used for blending with, and often softening, more glamorous grape varieties.

Muscat of Alexandria is the dominant Muscat in South Africa—HANEPOOT is its traditional Afrikaans name—and was the country's fourth most planted white wine variety in the late 1990s, but it is in marked decline and by 2012 less than 2,000 ha remained, mainly in hotter inland regions. For years it provided sticky, raisiny wines for FORTIFICATION, as well as everything from GRAPE CONCENTRATE to RAISINS. Today some drier, lighter wines are also made from it. It is still grown to a relatively limited extent in Argentina, Peru, Colombia, Ecuador, and even Japan. Although Muscat Blanc is more important in GREECE, Muscat of Alexandria is grown widely there and is the Muscat that predominates in Turkey, Israel, and Tunisia, although in much of the Near East nowadays these grapes are eaten rather than drunk. In France, total plantings of Muscat d'Alexandrie, or Muscat Romain, have decreased slightly to about 2,700 ha, almost exclusively in Roussillon where it was introduced for Muscat de Rivesaltes.

Muscat of Frontignan

is a common synonym for MUSCAT BLANC À PETITS GRAINS and this is the Muscat variety that is solely responsible for the VIN DOUX NATUREL of the same name. See also FRONTIGNAN for details of the wine that justifies this synonym.

Muscat of Hamburg

is the lowest quality of the wine-producing MUSCATS. DNA PROFILING at CONEGLIANO showed that it is a natural cross of MUSCAT OF ALEXANDRIA and TROLLINGER (also called SCHIAVA Grossa). It comes exclusively in black-berried form and is far more common as a TABLE GRAPE than a wine grape. Its chief attribute is the consistency of its plump and shiny dark blue grapes, which can well withstand long journeys to reach consumers who like black-skinned Muscat-flavoured grapes. In France it was grown on 3,376 ha/8,339 acres in 2011 and was the most important table grape. It is also relatively important as a table grape in Greece, in eastern Europe, and Australia. It was extremely popular as a greenhouse grape in Victorian England, where it occasionally took the name of Snow or Venn, two of its more successful propagators.

In the world of wine production, its importance is limited but it does produce a fair quantity of light, grapey red throughout eastern Europe, some 'Black Muscat' in California, and in CHINA, crossed with the indigenous VITIS *amurensis*, it has spawned a generation of varieties adapted for wine production.

Muscat Ottonel

is the palest of all the Muscats, both in terms of the colour of wine produced and in terms of its character. Its aroma is altogether more vapid than the powerful grapey perfumes associated with MUSCAT BLANC À PETITS GRAINS and MUSCAT OF ALEXANDRIA. It was bred in 1839 and released in 1852 in the Loire, probably as a TABLE GRAPE from CHASSELAS and another minor variety.

Its tendency to ripen earlier than these other two Muscats has made it much easier to cultivate in cooler climates and nowadays Muscat Ottonel is the dominant Muscat cultivated, on a few hundred hectares, in ALSACE. This low-vigour vine, which does best in deep, damp soils, is also grown throughout eastern Europe, notably in AUSTRIA, where it is planted in Burgenland. It may well be that it is at its best as a late-harvest wine, for there are some fine, apparently long-living examples from both HUNGARY and ROMANIA (where the variety is often known, respectively, as Muskotály and TĂMAÎIOĂSA Ottonel). Romania and Bulgaria, where it is often labelled MISKET, probably have the biggest areas of the variety: more than 2,500 ha and 5,000 ha respectively.

Muscat Romain, or Roman Muscat, is a common name for MUSCAT OF ALEXANDRIA in Roussillon.

Muschelkalk, literally 'shell limestone' in German, is the time-honoured name used in Germany and neighbouring countries for a particular group of CALCAREOUS rocks deposited during a precise geological interval in northern mainland Europe. Muschelkalk consists mainly of limestones, various argillaceous and dolomitic limestones, and marls, each with distinctive fossils. Parts of southern PFALZ, RHEINHESSEN, and central FRANKEN in Germany, and NEUSIEDLERSEE-HÜGELLAND in Austria's Burgenland, are sited on Muschelkalk, as are a number of grand cru vineyards in ALSACE.

Classically and internationally, Muschelkalk is the name for the middle division of the three that originally defined the Triassic period of geological time. However, rocks formed at this time away from northern Europe are quite different from those lauded by German producers. See GEOLOGY for more. A.J.M.

mushroom root rot, vine disease. See ARMILLARIA ROOT ROT.

Musigny, Le, great red GRAND CRU in Burgundy's CÔTE D'OR. For more details, see CHAMBOLLE-MUSIGNY.

Muskateller, German for MUSCAT, almost invariably the superior MUSCAT BLANC, or some mutation of it. **Gelber Muskateller**, for example, is the gold-skinned version which is increasingly recognized as superior to MUSCAT OTTONEL in Austria, where it is particularly popular in STYRIA. In Germany, homeland of MORIO-MUSKAT, Gelber Muskateller is a distinctly minority interest, and there is even less of the red-skinned **Roter Muskateller**.

Muskat-Ottonel is what Germans call their minuscule plantings of MUSCAT OTTONEL.

Muskat-Silvaner, or **Muskat-Sylvaner**, was once, tellingly, the common German-language synonym for SAUVIGNON BLANC used in Germany and Austria.

Muskotály, name used in HUNGARY for Muscat, usually MUSCAT OTTONEL but also occasionally a yellow-berried form of MUSCAT BLANC À PETITS GRAINS, here called Muscat Lunel or Sárga Muskotály.

musqué is a French term meaning both 'perfumed', as in musky, and 'muscat-like'. Many vine varieties, including CHARDONNAY, have a Musqué mutation which is particularly aromatic and may add to the variety's own characteristics a grapey scent reminiscent of MUSCAT.

must is the name used by winemakers for a thick liquid that is neither GRAPE JUICE nor WINE but the intermediate, a mixture of grape juice, stem fragments, grape skins, seeds, and pulp that comes from the CRUSHER-DESTEMMER that smashes grapes at the start of the winemaking process. The French equivalent is *moût*, the Italian and Spanish is *mosto*, and the German is *Most*, but the word 'must' has been used in English for at least a thousand years with several small nuances of specific meaning. All refer to the mixture of crushed, chopped, or smashed fruit being prepared for, or undergoing, FERMENTATION. A.D.W.

must chilling, important white winemaking operation, particularly in the NEW WORLD, which delays the onset of fermentation until after pressing, and helps prevent OXIDATION. See REFRIGERATION and TEMPERATURE. France's first must chiller was installed, by Australians, in the Languedoc, in the early 1990s.

must weight, important measure of grape RIPENESS, indicated by the concentration of dissolved compounds in grape juice or must. Since about 90% of all the dissolved solids in grape juice are the fermentable SUGARS (the rest being acids, ions, and a host of other solutes), any measurement of these solids gives a reliable indication of the grapes' ripeness, and therefore the POTENTIAL ALCOHOL of wine made from them (see FERMENTATION).

Must weight may be measured approximately in the vineyard before harvest using a REFRACTOMETER, or in the winery, using a refractometer or a HYDROMETER, calibrated according to one of several different scales used in different parts of the world for measuring the concentration of dissolved solids. This variation is not so surprising when one considers how crucial this statistic is to the winemaking process and therefore how early in the evolution of each country's wine industry a scale will have been adopted. Each scale merely requires a different calibration of the hydrometer, usually with a reading of zero indicating that the DENSITY of a solution is exactly one, as in pure water.

BAUMÉ is the scale most commonly used in much of Europe, including France, and in

Baumé (degrees)	Brix/ Balling (degrees)	Oechsle (degrees)	Potential alcohol (% vol)
10	18.0	75	10
11	19.8	84	11
12	21.7	93	12
13	23.5	101	13
14	25.3	110	14
15	27.1	119	15

Australia. The number of degrees Baumé indicates the concentration of dissolved compounds in a solution calibrated so that it indicates fairly well the potential ALCOHOLIC STRENGTH of a wine made by fermenting the must to dryness, although the figures in the table above are approximate.

In the United States, and increasingly in Australia, ripeness is most commonly measured in degrees BRIX, also sometimes called Balling, both terms borrowed from the sugar-refining industry. The Brix reading simply indicates the percentage of solids (of which about 90% are sugars) by weight.

Winemakers in Germany most commonly use the OECHSLE scale, which simply indicates the density of the juice: a grape juice with a specific gravity of 1.085 is said to be 85 °Oechsle. This scale is much discussed since the GERMAN WINE LAW has tended to equate quality with degrees Oechsle. Austria has its own, similar scale, devised at KLOSTERNEUBURG, which measures ripeness in degrees KMW (or Babo).

Since it takes about 16.5 g/l (0.6 oz/1.76 pt) of sugar to produce 1% alcohol by fermentation (in white wines, closer to 18 g/l in reds, depending on the efficiency of the YEAST strain), it is possible to calculate approximately the potential alcohol using any of these scales. All of these must weight measurements can be roughly converted among themselves, with Baumé values about five-ninths of Brix/Balling values, and 14.7 °Brix/Balling = 60 °Oechsle. Some equivalences are outlined in the table above, although, according to published scales, the relationship between the different measurements is not a strict one. See nomograms in Hamilton and Coombe.

A typical dry wine is made from grapes which measure between 12 and 14 °Baumé, between 22 and 25 °Brix or Balling, and between 93 and 110 °Oechsle. Grapes grown in ENGLAND in particularly cool years, however, may reach a natural must weight of around 50 °Oechsle, while some grape varieties in the SAN JOAQUIN VALLEY of California can easily reach 30 °Brix, as they gradually dehydrate under the intense heat. One German wine harvested at Nussdorf in the PFALZ in 1971 was picked at 326 °Oechsle and was still fermenting 22 years later, having reached just 4.5% alcohol; another picked in 2011 in Rheinhessen came in at 338 °Oechsle but the volume was too small and the sugar too high to ferment.   B.G.C. & A.D.W.

Hamilton, R. P., and Coombe, B. G., 'Harvesting of winegrapes', in B. G. Coombe and P. R. Dry (eds.), *Viticulture*, ii: *Practices* (Adelaide, 1992).

mutage is the process of stopping a MUST from fermenting, sometimes by adding SULFUR DIOXIDE but usually by adding alcohol, thereby creating an environment in which YEASTS can no longer work. Mutage transforms fermenting must into a **vin muté** such as a VIN DE LIQUEUR or a VIN DOUX NATUREL. The alcohol may be added before or after the grape juice has been separated from the skins. Mutage plays a crucial part in making PORT, although the term is not used.

mutation, spontaneous change to genetic material occurring during cell division in organisms such as grapevines. Since so many VINE VARIETIES are of ancient origin, they have accumulated a substantial load of mutations. ANCIENT VINE VARIETIES were invariably dark-skinned; light-skinned varieties are the result of mutation. Generally mutations are deleterious, but man has had many centuries in which deliberately to select those vines which perform best (a process now formalized as CLONAL SELECTION), so beneficial mutations have been maintained.

Mutation is particularly common among vine varieties with a long history such as PINOT NOIR, CARIGNAN, SAVAGNIN, GRENACHE, and TERRET. Although mutation is not always as spectacular as a change in berry colour, most of these varieties have forms called variously Noir (black), Gris (grey), Blanc (white), Rose (pink), Vert (green), Rouge (red), and sometimes more.

Mutations commonly seen in grapevines include leaf, berry, and pulp colour, berry size, seedlessness, compactness of bunches, productivity, flavours, date of ripening, deeply lobed leaves, very large inflorescences, and absence of inflorescences. Mutation can also cause polyploidy (multiple sets of chromosomes), which leads to 'giant' plants and berries. The two Gamay TEINTURIERS, Gamay Teinturier de Fréaux and Gamay Teinturier de Chaudenay, are thought to be mutations of Gamay de Bouze. A mixture of normal and mutant tissue is known as a chimera, and the varieties Pinot Noir and (Pinot) Meunier are partners in a so-called periclinal chimera. Such plants are essentially composed of a mutant 'skin' enclosing a 'normal' interior. Pinot Meunier is essentially similar to Pinot Noir, with the exception of white hairs on the shoot tip and young leaves.

Mutation can be induced by chemicals such as colchicine and by ionizing radiation. A form of genetic variation known as somaclonal mutation is induced during TISSUE CULTURE, and it is thought that this will be a useful means of increasing clonal variation among existing varieties.   R.E.S., J.R., & J.V.

Pelsy, F., 'Molecular and cellular mechanisms of diversity within grapevine varieties', *Heredity*, 104 (2010), 331–40. doi:10.1038/hdy.2009.161.

Reisch, B. I., Owens, C. L., and Cousins, P. S., 'Grape', in M. L. Badenes and D. H. Byrne (eds.), *Fruit Breeding* (New York, 2012).

This, P., Lacombe, T., and Thomas, M. R., 'Historical origins and genetic diversity of wine grapes', *TRENDS in Genetics*, 22/9 (2006). doi:10.1016/j.tig.2006.07.008

muzzle, the wire which holds a SPARKLING WINE cork in place. Known in French as a **muselet**.

MW, abbreviation for MASTER OF WINE.

Myanmar (formerly Burma), tropical South East Asian nation, bordered by THAILAND, Laos, CHINA, INDIA, and Bangladesh, has two wineries, both focused on classic VINIFERA wine styles. Myanmar Vineyard Estate, with elevated vineyards (1,200 m/3,937 ft) on LIMESTONE slopes on the southern extension of the Himalayan ranges, west of the Shan state capital Taunggyi, first produced wine commercially in 2004. Sauvignon Blanc, Shiraz, and Cabernet Sauvignon are produced under the Aythaya label. Red Mountain Estate is located a bit further south, on the shores of Inle Lake, a popular tourist resort. Its first commercial vintage was 2008.   D.G.

mycoderma. See FILM-FORMING YEASTS.

mycoplasma. See PHYTOPLASMA.

mycorrhiza, the symbiotic relationship between vine ROOTS and arbuscular mycorrhizal fungi in the soil that increases the surface area of the roots and allows the vine to access and utilize NUTRIENTS in the soil more effectively. The fungi have been shown not only to improve the uptake of nutrients but also to increase resistance to plant pathogens and to improve SOIL STRUCTURE.

Baumgartner, K., 'Encouraging beneficial AM fungi in vineyard soil', *Practical Winery & Vineyard* (Jan/Feb 2003), 57–60.

n

Nagyburgundi, occasional Hungarian synonym for BLAUFRÄNKISCH although Kékfrankos is more common.

Nahe, wine region in GERMANY whose total vineyard area had decreased to 4,187 ha/ 10,342 acres by 2013 scattered over a wide area on either side of the river Nahe (see map under GERMANY). Vineyards begin upstream at Martinstein, with Monzingen being the first famous and ancient wine village, mentioned as early as 778. The region was defined in anything like its current form only as part of the GERMAN WINE LAW of 1971, bringing together several geologically and climatically distinct areas.

First there is the by turns bucolic and geologically dramatic stretch of the river between Monzingen and Bad Münster am Stein. Here many of the vineyards have been modernized and reconstructed where necessary and practical (see FLURBEREINIGUNG), and steep, often terraced slopes produce world-class RIESLING on a geologically complex mix including SANDSTONE, porphyry, melaphyr, and SLATE. A single vineyard, such as the tiny Oberhäuser Brücke (a MONOPOLE of the Nahe's foremost vintner, Helmut Dönnhoff), can incorporate four fundamentally different soil types, and it does not seem to be mere imagination that such geological complexity is mirrored in the taste of the wines. The general climatic tendency is to warm as the Nahe meanders downstream. Excellent ventilation, low precipitation, and balmy autumnal temperatures, in addition to the steep, southward inclination of vineyard slopes, offer ideal circumstances for late-ripening Riesling.

The foremost wine villages (with their most notable vineyards) along this stretch of the Nahe, travelling downstream are Monzingen (Frühlingsplätzchen, Halenberg), Meddersheim (Rheingrafenberg), Schlossböckelheim (Felsenberg, Kupfergrube), Oberhausen (Brücke), Niederhausen (Hermannshöhle, Kerz), Norheim (Dellchen, Kirschheck), and Traisen (Bastei, Rotenfels). Wines of pronounced, often pungent spice and mineral inflection with frequent red fruit notes are characteristic for many of the best vineyards in this area. The state domaine of Niederhausen-Schlossböckelheim founded by the state of Rheinland-Pfalz in 1902 (and privatized in 1998) greatly helped to establish any international reputation that Nahe Riesling had managed to enjoy prior to the 1980s.

The second outstanding area, also famous for its Rieslings, lies on the northern outskirts of Bad Kreuznach, immediately adjacent to the city. Here the vineyards are substantially LOESS and CLAY, heavier and on gentler slopes than those elsewhere along the Nahe, producing relatively substantial wines. But in certain sites, gravel offers excellent drainage and greater vinous finesse. Viticulture around Bad Kreuznach was traditionally dominated by large landholders who also had important holdings in the Middle Nahe. Foremost among these were two branches of the Anheuser family and the Reichsgraf von Plettenberg, each of which made contributions from the 1930s—but particularly after the Second World War—to the gradual recognition of what is today known collectively as Nahe wine. Best-known among Bad Kreuznach's vineyards are the Brücke, Kahlenberg, and Krötenpfuhl.

The third area of particular distinction is the Lower Nahe near the confluence with the Rhine at Bingen, 116 km/72 miles from the source of the Nahe. Here, steeply terraced vineyards on a slate and quartzite base resemble those of the nearby MITTELRHEIN. Flavours of citrus, stone fruits, and salty or wet stone mineral notes typify the Rieslings of this subregion where Scheurebe, Weissburgunder, and traditional Silvaner can also succeed. Top sites include a trio along the Troll-Bach at Dorsheim just west of the Nahe: Burgberg, Goldloch, and Pittermännchen; as well as two sites along similar tributary streams at Münster-Sarmsheim: Dautenflänzer and Pittersberg.

The three aforementioned areas by no means exhaust the historic or current sources of excellent Nahe wine. These include the Alsenz near its confluence with the Nahe at Bad Münster (notably the Altenbamberger Rotenberg and Ebernburger Schlossberg), as well as a number of villages located several miles north and west of the Nahe, notably Roxheim (Berg, Höllenberg), Sommerloch, Wallhausen (Johannisberg), and Bockenau, whose towering Felseneck has this century produced quite outstanding, and diverse, wines. Sporadic vineyards occur along the Nahe's tributary Glan from Oberhausen's Leistenberg south to Meisenheim more than 12 km away. Among these, the recently revived and dramatically terraced Kloster Distibodenberg in Odernheim harbours not only outstanding wine potential but also Germany's oldest known vine vestiges, dating back nearly to the eponymous cloister's most famous resident, Hildegard of Bingen.

Vine varieties

RIESLING, while steadily increasing its share, still represents just under 28% of Nahe vineyard, but overwhelmingly dominates all of the best addresses.

MÜLLER-THURGAU was the most widely grown vine variety for a time, but its area has declined dramatically in recent decades to 13% of vineyard by 2011. SILVANER has fallen to less than half that much, whereas PINOT BLANC and PINOT

GRIS—while small in total surface area—are responsible for some distinctive successes at many of the Nahe's front-running estates. In response to a German red wine boom from the late 1990s, SPÄTBURGUNDER (PINOT NOIR) reached 6% and DORNFELDER a remarkable 11%, although it remains to be seen whether it will establish permanent importance.

Until the mid 20th century, the Nahe enjoyed scant national let alone international reputation, in large part due to its wine being subsumed anonymously into RHINE blends. Even today, when nearly half of all Nahe wine is sold in bottle directly to the consumer, much inexpensive Nahe wine is blended to suit the needs of German supermarkets and grocery chains. CO-OPERATIVES have never had the importance here that they enjoy in other German growing regions. For wines of finesse one must turn to the private estates, nine of which are members of the prestigious VDP association. Among them, in keeping with current German fashion, the proportion of dry wines has increased since 1980 but residually sweet Rieslings with mouth-watering fruit-mineral interaction are still important for the region's reputation.

Good Nahe wine at all quality levels had for long been underpriced in Germany but by the late 1990s the leading estates could command prices on a par with the RHEINGAU. In the mid 2000s, there are also some worrying signs. Significant tracts of potentially top-flight vineyard land have been abandoned due to lack of vintners ambitious—or perhaps foolhardy—enough to try to make a living from the steepest slopes, and entire subregions such as the Alsenztal, a sea of vines less than a century ago, are threatened with extinction.   D.S.

Pigott, S., et al., *Wein Spricht Deutsch: Weine, Winzer, Weinlandschaften* (Frankfurt, 2007).

Reinhardt, S., *The Finest Wines of Germany* (London, 2012).

Namibia in southern AFRICA had three very small wine estates in 2014: Neuras in the south, Thonningii in the north, and Kristal Kellerei in the central area close to Omaruru.

nanofiltration, a membrane separation technique which is looser than REVERSE OSMOSIS and tighter than ULTRAFILTRATION but is not legally permitted for use with wine.

See ALCOHOL REDUCTION.

Wollan, D., 'Membrane and other techniques for the management of wine composition', in A. G. Reynolds (ed.), *Managing Wine Quality 2: Oenology and Wine Quality* (Cambridge, 2010), 133–63.

Napa, small city north of San Francisco in CALIFORNIA that gives its name to **Napa county** and, California's most famous wine region and an AVA, the **Napa Valley**. Although Napa was one of the last of California's coastal counties to receive the vine, the Napa Valley has earned the state's wine most of its fame both inside and outside the UNITED STATES in the 20th and 21st centuries. In America if not the wine world, 'the Valley' is Napa Valley. Natural beauty and proximity to San Francisco have attracted, not just willing investors, but owners and winemakers with aggressive desires to make names for themselves in this cultured pursuit. The first generation of them began the climb to prominence between 1880 and 1919. The third spurred Napa out in front of the pack during the boom times between 1966 and the early 1990s. The fourth has at times threatened to turn Napa into a parody of conspicuous consumption. But it was an undervalued interim group that kept the flame alive through the lean years between 1933 and 1966, when California wine was at its ebb. Six companies, Beaulieu Vineyard, Beringer Vineyards, the Christian Brothers, Inglenook Vineyards, Charles KRUG, and Louis M. Martini, pursued fine wine under their own labels when most districts sold commodity products in bulk (see CALIFORNIA, history). Their vineyards provided half the model that attracted the dizzying investments of the 1970s and 1980s, when vineyard acreage tripled and the number of Napa wineries shot from fewer than 20 to more than 200. The other half of the attraction model was provided by the original 'boutique wineries' Mayacamas and Stony Hill, which had sprung up from this fertile ground in the late 1950s. The oldtimers inspired such prominent wineries as the Robert MONDAVI winery, Trefethen, Freemark Abbey, Chateau Montelena, and Sterling Vineyards, while the small artisan model begat smaller operations such as Heitz, Stag's Leap Wine Cellars, Diamond Creek, Caymus, and Schramsberg.

The Napa Valley proper is a long, lazy arc with its foot in San Francisco Bay and its head on the western shoulder of Mount St Helena, the highest point in Napa county. Like most of the north south valleys around San Francisco Bay, it has a cool end at the bay (in the south) and a warm one away from it (in the north), although it is barely more than 40 miles/64 km end to end, and sometimes less than a mile wide. With more than 46,000 acres/18,200 ha of vineyard in the Napa Valley AVA, the main valley has little more land to plant, although a succession of smaller valleys in hills to the east such as Chiles and Pope valleys offer some room for expansion.

Napa's magic is derived in no small part from a magnificent diversity of exposure, climate, and soil, which has led to several sub-AVAs within the generously drawn main AVA. In the early 1990s, growers proposed dividing the Napa Valley into communes much as the Haut-MÉDOC is divided. The scheme has more or less succeeded with sub-AVAs in the middle of the valley from south to north being Oak Knoll, Yountville, Oakville, Rutherford, St Helena, and Calistoga, and those on hills and mountains being Atlas Peak, Diamond Mountain, Howell Mountain, Mount Veeder, and Spring Mountain. Growers in outlying areas who had historically sold their grapes to wineries in the centre of Napa Valley demanded inclusion in the Napa Valley AVA and gained federal approval over time for sub-AVA status, despite early resistance from some who believed the great Napa franchise would be diluted by such segmentation. Their fears have proved unfounded, but to protect the Napa Valley name, by regulation, both the name Napa Valley and the subappellation names appear on labels.

Distinctions among the wines makes even greater refinement of internal boundaries seem inevitable. With or without diversity, Napa has been such a congenial home to Cabernet Sauvignon that one could argue a case for Napa's having caused its popularity, not the other way around. Versatile growing conditions give Napa growers the options of Chardonnay, Sauvignon Blanc, Merlot, Zinfandel, Syrah, Malbec, Cabernet Franc, and Petit Verdot, with replantings in the wake of PHYLLOXERA broadening the menu.

The following are the most significant subappellations.

Atlas Peak AVA

If it weren't for the efforts of Italy's Marchese Piero Antinori to grow Sangiovese in Napa Valley, Atlas Peak might not exist as an AVA. While Sangiovese proved to be not only difficult to grow in this rocky region in eastern hills, California Sangiovese was difficult to sell, no matter who made it. Antinori sold the Atlas Peak brand and later relaunched it as Antica (a conjunction of Antinori and California). The results have been stellar, Chardonnays and Cabernet Sauvignons focused and ageworthy. Stagecoach Vineyards, whose plantings cross into the non-AVA Pritchard Hill region, is a source of grapes for numerous producers.

Calistoga AVA

One of Napa Valley's oldest winegrowing regions finally earned AVA status in 2009, after years of debate over two wineries' use of the word Calistoga when their grapes did not come from that region. Home to historic Chateau Montelena, Araujo Estate (now owned by François PINAULT), and visitor magnet Sterling Vineyards, the AVA can be very warm (35 °C) during the summer, with cooling breezes from Knights Valley to the west dropping temperatures to 12 °C overnight, making quality grapegrowing possible. Cabernet Sauvignon is the region's strong suit, and Zinfandel is very happy here (Storybook Mountain Vineyards is proof), yet the cost of land and greater profitability of Cabernet has largely restricted Zin plantings.

Diamond Mountain District AVA

This AVA is defined by its elevation (400 to 2,200 feet) and ability to capture plenty of sunshine in the daytime and cooling breezes from the Pacific Ocean in early morning and late afternoon. Weathered red sedimentary soils contribute graphite notes to the tannic Cabernet Sauvignons, which benefit from extensive BOTTLE AGEING. Von Strasser sets the pace.

Howell Mountain AVA

Howell Mountain won its pre-PROHIBITION fame for Zinfandel, but the current generation of growers and winemakers, led by Dunn Vineyards, La Jota, O'Shaughnessy, and Robert Craig has turned sharply towards Cabernet Sauvignon as the variety of choice. The district ranges upward from 1,400 ft/430 m elevation in Napa's rugged east hills, and has as its anchor the Seventh Day Adventist community of Angwin.

Mount Veeder AVA

Mount Veeder stretches out along ridgetops that separate the Napa and SONOMA valleys immediately west of the town of Napa, and is centred on the peak from which its name comes. Its oldest extant winery is Mayacamas, its largest the Hess Collection. Most of the plantings in it are Cabernet Sauvignon and Chardonnay, although Hess has made an investment in Malbec. Jackson Family Wines' Lokoya has emerged as a mini-cult brand.

Oakville AVA

This is one of the most prestigious winegrowing districts in America. Stretching across the valley floor and piedmont areas just north of the Yountville hills, it encompasses famous historic vineyards such as ToKalon and Martha's, cult Cabernets such as Harlan (on the western hills) and Screaming Eagle (on the eastern side), as well as a long list of highly successful wineries such as Far Niente, Groth and Opus One. As with most districts in Napa, there is a range of soils, drainage characteristics, and exposures. In general the weather is somewhat warmer than Yountville or Stags Leap because of the way the hills baffle winds off the bay. But most commentators would consider Oakville a bit cooler than Rutherford, thus lending an elegant nuance to Cabernets by comparison. Oakville's famous To Kalon vineyard, planted by Hamilton Crabb in 1868, is now shared by Robert Mondavi winery and grower Andy Beckstoffer. Each owns a portion of this historic site, and wines made from Beckstoffer's blocks are labelled as Beckstoffer To Kalon, to distinguish them from Mondavi's To Kalon wines.

Rutherford AVA

With Oakville, the name of Rutherford was put before BATF (see TTB) during 1991 as part of the grower plan to divide all of the Napa Valley into community-based sub-AVAs. The original petition would have further divided Rutherford into Rutherford and Rutherford bench, but that refinement was dropped before hearings began. Before AVAs, Rutherford bench was an innocently coined name meant to distinguish the long, snaky alluvial band stretching along the Napa Valley's west side, from St Helena down to Yountville, from the more westerly valley floor closer to the Napa River. At the time, Rutherford bench was a source of equal parts mirth and ire in Napa: it's not a bench and it extends through Oakville. Today folks are comfortable with Rutherford as the AVA, although the west side of this middle stretch of valley, the so-called 'bench', is home to many of California's premier patches of Cabernet Sauvignon, including Beaulieu Vineyard Nos. 1 and 2, Staglin, Inglenook (previously Niebaum-Coppola Rubicon), Bella Oaks, Bosche, Sycamore, and more.

Stags Leap District AVA

Well south and on the eastern side of the valley, Stags Leap District (shunning the apostrophe) celebrates Cabernet Sauvignon and Merlot, and virtually nothing else, with the exception of Shafer Vineyards' Relentless Syrah. Other varieties grow well, but not with enough regional distinctiveness to call attention to themselves, nor to command the prices paid for the AVA's Cabernets and Merlots. The hallmarks of its Cabernets are a greater emphasis on sour cherry and blackberry flavours than in counterparts from other parts of Napa, and suppler TANNINS. Eroded volcanic and old river sedimentary soils, reflective heat from the Palisades rock formations on the AVA's eastern edge, and refreshing breezes from San Pablo Bay to the south make Stags Leap District a nearly perfect growing environment for red wine grapes. Curiously, it was little planted to Cabernet before 1970. It takes its name from a BASALT palisade north east of Napa city, under the towering wall of which its vineyards lie, and from which deer are reputedly driven by indigenous hunters. Clos du Val and Stag's Leap Wine Cellars were the pioneers, since joined by Cliff Lede, Chimney Rock, Pine Ridge, Shafer, Silverado Vineyards, Sinskey, and others.

Oak Knoll District of Napa Valley AVA

This relatively cool AVA created in 2004 is mostly on the valley floor, south of Yountville and Stags Leap but north of the city of Napa. As in Carneros, San Pablo Bay breezes cool the area at morning and night, yet daytime warmth is plentiful. Trefethen is one of its oldest wineries; Robert Biale, Lewis Cellars and Monticello Vineyards are also notable. Merlot grown here is promising, and Biale's Zinfandels are legendary.

Yountville AVA

This is the region in which Bordeaux's Christian MOUEIX staked his Napa claim, and where MOËT & CHANDON entered the California winemaking business in 1973. Chandon established Domaine Chandon for the production of TRADITIONAL METHOD sparkling wines and found success from the start, with California ripe fruit marrying with champagne production methods. Moueix entered the picture in 1981, first partnering with John Lail's Napanook vineyard decendant daughers Robin and Marky, then taking over for his Dominus brand of ageworthy Cabernet Sauvignons. The small town of the same name has one of the Valley's highest concentrations of restaurants.

See also CALIFORNIA, including map.

B.C.C. & L.M.

Lapsley, J. T., *Bottled Poetry: Napa Winemaking from Prohibition to the Modern Era* (Berkeley, Calif., 1996).

Sullivan, C., *Napa Wine: A History from Mission Days to Present* (San Francisco, 1994).

www.napavintners.com

Naples

Naples, large south Italian port and capital of the CAMPANIA region. The area around Naples had once produced all the greatest wines of Ancient ROME, not only FALERNIAN, but also CAECUBAN, MASSIC, and SURRENTINE, but in viticultural terms it was never to be that famous again. With the fall of the Roman empire and the economic decline of Italy, the market for fine wines collapsed.

Its oriental trade, which dates from Naples's medieval period under Byzantine rule, included the strong sweet MALMSEY of Crete, but PUGLIA produced similar wines itself, mostly for consumption in southern Italy. Naples also traded in the VERNACCIA of Liguria, which it sold to Sicily, Majorca, and PARIS. These wines were known collectively as *vini grechi*, because like the wines imported from the Aegean they were high-quality sweet wines, capable of surviving a long sea voyage. The wines of Campania, which were not in the Greek style but dry, were called *vini latini*. They were considered inferior and were not long lived enough to be sent overseas to northern Europe. The highest regarded of the *vini latini* were those of Mount Vesuvius, which were sold to other parts of Italy by the merchants of Naples and Salerno. In addition, Naples sold CALABRIAN wines to Aragón and the Balearic islands.

All this made Naples the most important Mediterranean wine-trading port in the 14th century, yet, because of its many changes of regime and its severance from Sicily in 1282, Naples never became a political or economic power to match the northern city states. Geographically it was far better placed than VENICE and GENOA to conduct the lucrative trade in Aegean wines and other luxury goods with

n

northern Europe, but by the late 13th century, when Genoa began to send its galleys to Southampton and Bruges, Naples was no longer in a position to compete.

(Today the name Naples is more readily associated by American wine lovers with an important charity AUCTION held in the city of the same name in Florida.) H.M.W.

Lopez, R. S., 'The trade of mediaeval Europe: the South', in *The Cambridge Economic History of Europe*, 7 vols., ii: *Trade and Industry in the Middle Ages* (Cambridge, 1987).

Melis, F., 'Produzione e commercio dei vini italiani nei secoli XIII–XVIII', *Annales cisalpines d'histoire sociale*, 1/3 (1972), 107–33.

Nascetta, floral white wine grape recently revived in the LANGHE where there were just over 20 ha/49 acres by 2010.

Nasco, ancient light-berried vine making soft white wines from about 140 ha/346 acres around Cagliari on SARDINIA.

natamycin, an antiobiotic used to control the growth of yeasts and moulds in the food industry but not generally permitted as a wine ADDITIVE except in SOUTH AFRICA. Residues higher than the permitted level (0.005 mg/l) were found in wines from Argentina around the end of the first decade of the 21st century due to the contamination with antibiotics of certain oenological products but strict controls on exports have reduced this to a very local issue.

natural alcohol, defined in EU regulations as the total alcoholic strength of a wine before any ENRICHMENT.

natural wine, relative rather than absolute term for wine produced by small-scale, independent growers from hand-picked grapes grown using SUSTAINABLE, ORGANIC, or BIODYNAMIC VITICULTURE—increasingly but by no means exclusively certified as such. Natural wine enthusiasts favour physical rather than chemical interventions during winemaking, and thus no ADDITIVES and minimal additions of SULFUR DIOXIDE, and preferably none at all.

The contemporary natural wine movement's amorphous, countercultural ethos is both a reaction to the over-oaked, over-extracted, over-technologically manipulated 'blockbuster' wines in FASHION around the turn of the 20th century, and an implicit challenge to a contemporary wine industry it sees as increasingly additive-prone yet lazily content with a legislative status quo imposing less-than-rigorous LABELLING requirements for the several hundred potential PROCESSING AIDS, agents, and additives available to winemakers (see INGREDIENT LABELLING). Europe's pioneers of natural wine found it incongruous that sulfur dioxide be permitted in wine made from organically grown grapes, for example (although see ORGANIC WINE).

The natural wine movement originated in France: first in Beaujolais in the 1960s, where the pioneers' desire was to make pure wines with no added sulfur dioxide in the image of their grandparents' wines, and more recently in the Loire, where 'naturalistas' felt generous norms on additions of sulfur dioxide and sugar for CHAPTALISATION during winemaking were perversions of the AOC/AOP concept that wine should express a unique sense of place.

Critics argue natural wine's fondness for minimal levels of sulfur and CLARIFICATION create turbid wines prone to instability and spoilage by rogue bacteria and yeast; and that, if containing such potential instability in natural wines means shipping and storing them using energy-intensive TEMPERATURE CONTROL, then this constitutes rather un-'natural' constraints.

Nevertheless the sudden popularity of such wines with sensitive Japanese wine drinkers and with younger customers in Parisian wine bars gave the movement first commercial, then international legitimacy, a rare example of agenda-setting by drinkers rather than the mainstream wine intelligentsia. Some drinkers undoubtedly gravitated towards natural wine to reduce or eliminate their exposure to sulfur dioxide, believing the latter exacerbated HANGOVERS and affected ALLERGIES AND INTOLERANCES, but many cite both purity of taste and 'warts and all' individuality as key attributes of the natural wine style.

Signature natural wine styles include PÉTILLANT NATUREL sparkling wines made using the MÉTHODE ANCESTRALE (see SPARKLING WINEMAKING); red wines fermented using WHOLE-BUNCH FERMENTS whose lightish colours and ephemeral tannins are designed to be easy to drink rather than to score many PARKER POINTS; and so-called ORANGE WINE, robust, dry, SKIN-FERMENTED whites made like red wine. M.W.

nature when applied to a French wine usually means 'still'. Nature, with a capital N, is viewed by wine producers as friend or enemy and everything in between depending on whether they are, respectively, TRADITIONALISTS or technocrats. See NATURAL WINE.

Naturwein, German term for wine that has not been CHAPTALIZED, widely used before it was abolished by the 1971 GERMAN wine law, which replaced it with the notion of wine with PRÄDIKAT. See GERMAN HISTORY.

Navarra, known in English as **Navarre**, autonomous region in north east SPAIN which also lends its name to a denominated wine zone with 11,500 ha/27,500 acres of vineyard in 2012. The kingdom of Navarra once stretched from BORDEAUX to Barcelona but today this extensive denomination is overshadowed by the neighbouring DO zone RIOJA, a small part of which extends into the province of Navarra (see map under SPAIN). The wines share a common history.

Pilgrims en route to Santiago de Compostela fuelled the demand for wine in the Middle Ages. Later, in the mid 19th century, both Rioja and Navarra benefited greatly from their proximity to France after it was invaded by the PHYLLOXERA louse. Because northern Spain was affected considerably later than south west France, vineyards here were expanded and large quantities of Navarran wine were sold to producers in France until phylloxera arrived in Navarra itself in 1892. The region recovered fairly quickly but the area under vine in 1990 was less than a third of that a century before.

The region splits into five subzones according to climate, from the cooler slopes of the Baja Montaña close to the Pyrenean foothills and the slightly warmer Valdizarbe and Tierra Estella districts in the north of Navarra, to Ribera Alta in the centre of the region, and Ribera Baja round the city of Tudela in the south. Rainfall totals range between 600 mm (23 in) in the north and 400 mm in the south and east, while summer temperatures become correspondingly warmer. With over 30% of Navarra's vineyards, Ribera Baja has traditionally been the most important of the five subzones, although most of the new planting in the late 1980s and early 1990s took place in the cooler north.

The Garnacha grape (see GRENACHE) has dominated Navarra's vineyards but plantings of TEMPRANILLO increased considerably in the 1990s. Garnacha lends itself to good, dry rosé, which Navarra continues to make in large quantities. Some distinctive sweet whites are made from Moscatel de Grano Menudo (Muscat Blanc à Petits Grains) grown in the south. This century the region's wines have suffered on both domestic and foreign markets, being penalized for the widespread planting of imported varieties, which include Tempranillo in these parts, plus a reliance on high-yielding young vineyards. The new varieties and technical improvements have been largely promoted by the oenological research station, EVENA, set up at Olite by the CONSEJO REGULADOR and the regional government. V. de la S.

Barquín, J., Guitiérrez, L., and de la Serna, V., *The Finest Wines of Rioja and Northwest Spain* (London, 2011).

www.navarrawines.com

NDVI. See NORMALIZED DIFFERENCE VEGETATION INDEX.

Néac, small red BORDEAUX appellation to the immediate north east of POMEROL.

Nebbiolo, great black grape variety responsible for some of the finest and longest-lived wines in the world. It has been known in the

PIEMONTE region in the north west since at least the 13th century, and is its most distinctive and distinguished vine. The quality of wines such as BAROLO and BARBARESCO inspires hopeful planting of the variety all over the world.

Nebbiolo in Italy

Documents from the castle of Rivoli dating from 1266 when Conto Umberto de Balma is recorded as obtaining a wine named 'Nibiol' provide early evidence of Nebbiolo's existence. PETRUS DE CRESCENTIIS' *Liber ruralium commodorum* in 1304 made an unambiguous link between the 'Nubiola' grape, which he termed 'delightful', and 'excellent wine'. Some have postulated that the name derives from *nobile*, or noble, but a more likely derivation is from *nebbia*, or fog, a frequent phenomenon in Piemonte in October when the grape is harvested. and also possibly a reference to the thick bloom on ripe Nebbiolo berries.

Modern Piemonte has shown its respect for Nebbiolo in a more concrete, if less poetic way by restricting its planting to a few selected areas: of the 2012 total of 4,476 ha/11,056 acres, 80% were planted in the province of Cuneo, predominantly in Barolo, Barbaresco, and Roero.

Nebbiolo is always the first variety to bud and the last to ripen, with harvests that regularly last well past the middle of October, and the variety is accordingly granted the most favourable HILLSIDE exposures, generally south to south west. Perhaps as important as the vineyard site, however, are the soils: Nebbiolo has shown itself to be extremely fussy and has in the past century given best results only in the calcareous marls to the north and south of Alba on the right bank of the Tanaro in the DOCG zones of BARBARESCO and BAROLO respectively. Here Nebbiolo-based wines reach their maximum aromatic complexity, and express a fullness of flavour which balances the relatively high ACIDITY and substantial TANNINS which are invariably present. Historically, much more Nebbiolo was planted in the Novara and Vercelli hills. Total vineyard area declined rapidly during Italy's industrial revolution in the 1950s but there are signs of a resurgence; see SPANNA, the local name for Nebbiolo here.

NEBBIOLO D'ALBA, a tamer, less savage version of the grape, only suggests the heights which the variety can gain in more choice positions. The ROERO district on the left bank of the Tanaro has predominantly sandy soils which produced better and better wine throughout the 1990s. Roero wines are notably lighter in style and generally age faster than Barbaresco and Barolo.

Nebbiolo, often called Picutener, also plays the leading role in the postage stamp-size DOC of CAREMA on the border of the Valle d'Aosta, in the neighbouring and equally Lilliputian DOCs of Donnaz and Arnad-Montjovet in the Valle d'AOSTA itself. In Lombardia in VALTELLINA NEBBIOLO is known as Chiavennasca, with more than 800 ha, the only sizeable zone where Nebbiolo is cultivated outside Piemonte. These four areas, subalpine in latitude and definitely cool during the growing season, produce a medium-bodied style of Nebbiolo in which the fruit must frequently struggle against the grape's tannic asperity and acidic sharpness; the added ripeness of warmer vintages is even more valuable here. Sometimes the ripeness is achieved by drying the grapes, for example Valtellina's full-bodied, luscious but dry red wine speciality SFORZATO, or Sfurzat.

These zones apart, Nebbiolo is rarely cultivated elsewhere in Italy, although it is an ingredient in the FRANCIACORTA cocktail and, curiously, some 81 ha of the variety can be found on the island of Sardinia.

Three principal CLONES of Nebbiolo are conventionally identified: Lampia (the most common), Michet, and Bolla. The last of these is declining because of the pale colour of its wines, while Michet is Lampia afflicted with a virus which causes the vine's canes to fork. More importantly, however, this clone, while producing smaller bunches and YIELDS and particularly intense aromas and flavours, does not adapt itself to all soils, and is slowly being replaced by superior clonal material, which can achieve Lampia's intensity, but without its viral defects. Most producers, mindful of the relatively embryonic state of clonal research, prefer to rely on a careful MASS SELECTION in their vineyards rather than staking their future on a single clone. More systematic clonal research in the 1990s has only confirmed that Nebbiolo has serious problems with VIRUSES, perhaps the result of excessive inbreeding in an ancient variety so concentrated on a relatively small area, a fact which is hampering the multiplication of the better clones which have thus far been identified.

The total area planted with Nebbiolo declined towards the turn of the century but seems to be increasing once more in the Langhe. The 2010 vine census notes over 5,500 ha/12,700 .

D.G. & W.S.

Genetic relationships

Through DNA PROFILING, researchers in Anna Schneider's laboratory at Torino and José Vouillamoz at DAVIS found that **Nebbiolo Rosé** is not a clone of Nebbiolo but is a distinct variety. Furthermore, Nebbiolo Rosé turned out to have a parent–offspring relationship with Nebbiolo. Several additional parent–offspring relationships were discovered between Nebbiolo and traditional varieties from Piedmont (FREISA, VESPOLINA, and Bubbierasco) and Valtellina (Negrera and Rossola). While the complete pedigree of Nebbiolo is still unknown, these relationships indicate that Nebbiolo probably has its roots in Piedmont and/or Lombardy. In addition, a possible parent– offspring relationship was suggested between Freisa and VIOGNIER, so that Nebbiolo and Viognier are likely to be cousins.   J.V.

Robinson, J., Harding, J., and Vouillamoz, J., *Wine Grapes, a complete guide to 1,368 vine varieties, including their origins and flavours* (London, 2012).

Outside Italy

Vine-growers all over the world are experimenting with Nebbiolo. The results often lack the haunting aromas that characterize the variety but isolated examples in regions as far apart as Oregon, Washington state, and Australia's King Valley in Victoria suggest the quest may not be fruitless. Nebbiolo has so far somewhat reluctantly accompanied Barbera to both North and South America (including Mexico). In California, Sangiovese has proved generally more successful but there were 165 acres/67 ha of Nebbiolo in the ground in 2012. High yields have tended to subsume the variety's quality in South America. The few hundred hectares planted in Argentina are mainly in San Juan province. But as the special charms of Barolo and Barbaresco are inceasingly appreciated around the world, it is unlikely that growers will give up hope of making great Nebbiolo outside Italy.

Nebbiolo d'Alba is an Italian DOC red produced from NEBBIOLO grapes grown in 2012 on a growing total of 649 ha/1,603 acres of vineyard in 34 communes surrounding the city of ALBA in PIEMONTE. Seven of the communes are partially inside the Barolo DOCG zone, although the areas which can produce Nebbiolo d'Alba—the southern sections of Monforte d'Alba and Novello, the north eastern tip of La Morra, all but a western slice of Diano d'Alba, the northern parts of Verduno, Grinzano Cavour, and Roddi—have been excluded from the Barolo zone. Most of the vineyard land is on the northern bank of the river Tanaro in the Roero hills (which, absurdly, does not belong under the administration of Alba as it lies outside the LANGHE), on sandier soils that yield wines that are softer, less intense, and faster maturing than a Barolo or a Barbaresco, more generically 'Nebbiolo' and less pointedly characterful. The demarcation of the DOC Nebbiolo d'Alba comprises the whole of the DOCG ROERO, and therefore can be used by Roero producers for declassification of their wines, but as such is infrequently used. This may change, as the Roero DOCG is much less famous than Nebbiolo d'Alba.   D.C.G. & W.S.

Nebbiolo delle Langhe, or **Langhe Nebbiolo**, formerly a VINO DA TAVOLA of the PIEMONTE region in north west Italy. In the 1980s a few leading Barolo producers—Aldo Conterno and Elio Altare in particular—pioneered special CUVÉES based on Nebbiolo but including INTERNATIONAL VARIETIES given small oak BARREL MATURATION. These wines commanded a much higher price and enjoyed an entirely different prestige from the average Nebbiolo delle Langhe. The approval of an overall regional DOC for Piemonte in 1995 remedied this situation by creating a new DOC called Langhe Nebbiolo into which producers in Barolo, Barbaresco, and Roero may declassify their wines, while the much more appropriate NEBBIOLO D'ALBA is unavailable to most of Barolo and Barbaresco producers, as in a bizarre quirk of legislation, most of this DOC is reserved exclusively for Roero, although Roero is geographically, politically, and historically separated from the Langhe. W.S.

necrosis, a term used to describe death of tissue. For example, necrotic spots of leaf tissue caused by DOWNY MILDEW appear blackish brown. For many vine foliar diseases and disorders, the yellowing of leaf sections, or CHLOROSIS, precedes necrosis.

négociant, French term for a MERCHANT and one used particularly of wine merchants who buy in grapes, must, or wine, blend different lots of wine within an APPELLATION, and bottle the result under their own label. Making a perfectly balanced blend from a number of imperfect parts is a potentially noble calling, but one that once provided so many opportunities for ADULTERATION AND FRAUD that it brought the entire profession into question, if not ill repute, at least until the late 1980s. Nowadays, with the bureaucracy involved in the AOC system, cheating requires real ingenuity.

The role of the négociant is particularly worthwhile in BURGUNDY, where the oldest négociants, traditionally concentrated in Beaune, have been joined since the later 20th century by a new breed of smaller operators, often run alongside a grower's own DOMAINE. So many individual growers produce tiny quantities from each of a number of different appellations that it can make sense to make up commercially more significant quantities and bottle them together. Many of the larger Burgundy négociants have significant vineyard holdings of their own. BOUCHARD PÈRE ET FILS and BOISSET, for example, are two of the CÔTE D'OR's most subtantial vineyard owners. Louis LATOUR, Louis JADOT, and Joseph DROUHIN are other important Burgundian négociants. The term **négociant-éleveur** implies that the négociant oversees the ÉLEVAGE of the wine it sells (not always the case).

Like all important French wine regions, Bordeaux also has a great concentration of négociants, many of which own CHÂTEAUX (while some of the CLASSED GROWTHS are run alongside a négociant business). For more details, see BORDEAUX TRADE.

Negramoll and **Negra Mole**, Iberian dark-skinned grape variety and by far the most commonly planted vine variety on the island of MADEIRA where it is often called Tinta Negra or Tinta Negra Mole. As Negramoll it is also grown in the CANARY ISLANDS. DNA PROFILING recently showed it is identical to the Andalucian variety Mollar currently grown on more than 400 ha of EXTREMADURA. It is therefore indubitably a VINIFERA variety (unlike many of the vines that replaced the so-called noble varieties SERCIAL, VERDELHO, BUAL, and MALVASIA on Madeira after the ravages of POWDERY MILDEW and PHYLLOXERA in the 19th century). On Madeira it yields relatively high quantities of sweet, pale red wine which turns amber with the madeira production process and then yellow-green with age. A variety called **Negra Mole** but considered distinct is grown in Portugal's the Alentejo.

Negrara, name related to the colour of the berries (*negra* meaning 'black'), and corresponding to a group of several distinct CULTIVARS in northern Italy. **Negrara Trentina** is the most common variety, and recent DNA PROFILING revealed a parent–offspring relationship with ENANTIO. J.V.

Négrette, black grape variety special to the vineyards north of Toulouse in SOUTH WEST FRANCE. In FRONTON, it must dominate the blend and in Vins de LAVILLEDIEU it must constitute at least 30%. Wine made from Négrette is more supple, perfumed, and flirtatious than that produced from the more famous south western black grape variety TANNAT, and is best drunk young, with its fruit, sometimes described as having a slightly animal, or violet, flavour, unsuppressed by heavy oak ageing. The variety is inconveniently prone to POWDERY MILDEW and BOTRYTIS BUNCH ROT and is therefore better suited to the hot, dry climate of Toulouse than to many other wine regions. Total French plantings had fallen slightly to 1,160 ha/2,865 acres by 2011. A little is also planted in California where it was once known as Pinot St George.

Negroamaro, sometimes written **Negro Amaro**, dark-skinned southern Italian grape variety that fell victim to the EU VINE PULL SCHEMES with the total area planted falling from 31,000 ha/76,500 acres in 1990 to just 11,460 ha/28,318 acres by 2010. It is particularly associated with the eastern half of the Salento peninsula, in the provinces of Lecce and Brindisi, where it forms the base, blended with small proportions of Malvasia Nera and (not necessarily legally) the more structured Primitivo, for DOCs such as Salice Salentino, Copertino, Brindisi, Leverano, and Squinzano. It is later ripening than Primitivo, with chunkier tannins. It is also used to produce some lively rosé. For more details, see PUGLIA. The name means 'dark, bitter' but the wines are sometimes a bit soft.

Neheleschol, extremely ancient Middle Eastern light-berried vine with enormous bunches, planted experimentally at MAS de Daumas Gassac in the Languedoc.

nematodes, microscopic roundworms generally found in soil which can seriously harm vines and other plants. Some feed on bacteria or fungi and are part of the normal vineyard ECOSYSTEM. Others, however, feed on grapevine roots and thus reduce both the size and efficiency of the root system. Although the vines do not necessarily die, they suffer WATER STRESS and deficiencies in VINE NUTRITION and grow weakly. Some species of nematodes are important because they transmit VIRUS DISEASES. The viruses spread by nematodes are called NEPOVIRUSES. They can be spread throughout the vineyard from just one infected plant by nematode feeding. Often they show up as a few yellow vines in the vineyard.

The fact that nematodes damage vines was first established in about 1930, in California. Because of characteristic and visually striking root damage, the root knot nematode, *Meloidogyne* species, was considered most important. However, in 1958 it was discovered that FANLEAF DEGENERATION was spread by nematodes of the species *Xiphenema index*, the so-called dagger nematode. This milestone discovery in plant pathology was made by Hewitt and colleagues of the University of California at DAVIS. It had been reported in France as long ago as 1883 that fanleaf degeneration spread through the soil, and some French authorities believed until the 1950s that the PHYLLOXERA louse was responsible for the spread.

Root knot nematodes occur mainly in sandy soil. Their presence is visible to the naked eye since the knots (swollen tissue or galls) on the roots formed in response to their feeding resemble a string of beads. One female can lay up to 1,000 eggs, and with up to ten generations a year in warm climates they can spread rapidly. The root lesion nematode *Pratylenchus* also damages vines by feeding on their roots. Virus particles can survive for many years in root fragments after an infected vineyard is removed. Replanting a new, 'virus-free' vineyard can lead to disappointment, as reinfection with nematode feeding can follow.

At one time vineyards in which nematodes were previously present were subjected to FUMIGATION with injected chemicals before planting, but the nematicide DBCP, which was considered capable of controlling all nematodes, is now banned. Methyl bromide was highly effective but was banned in 2005 because of environmental considerations. In California, where methyl bromide was widely used for vineyard replanting, INTEGRATED PEST MANAGEMENT is suggested as an important alternative.

Nematode diseases are often spread on infected planting material or by the movement of infected soil on cultivation implements or by irrigation water. Infected nursery plants can be freed of nematodes by HOT-WATER treatment. Biological control using ROOTSTOCKS is possible and generally preferred. Some VITIS species (*V. solonis*, *V. champini*, and *V. doaniana*) show resistance to nematodes. Among the most nematode-resistant rootstocks are Couderc 1613, Ramsey, Schwarzmann, Harmony, and Dog Ridge.   R.E.S.

Hardie, W. J., and Cirami, R. M., 'Grapevine rootstocks', in B. G. Coombe and P. R. Dry (eds.), *Viticulture*, i: *Resources* (Adelaide, 1988).

Zyl, S., van Vivier, M. A., and Walker, M. A., 'Xiphinema index and its relationship to grapevines: a review', *South African Journal of Enology & Viticulture*, 33/1 (2012).

www.sawislibrary.co.za/dbtextimages/74400.pdf.

Nepal, apparently home to one of the highest vineyards in the world (2,750 m/9,000 ft). Two hectares of VINIFERA vines were planted in 1992 at Jomsom in the Annapurna region by a local politician keen to foster a new industry in this remote corner of the world, but it is not known if wine resulted.   D.G.

nepoviruses, group of 13 VIRUS DISEASES which are spread from plant to plant by the feeding of NEMATODES (microscopic worms) on roots. They also have in common a polyhedral structure, hence the name 'nepovirus': 'ne' for nematode and 'po' for polyhedral. Such diseases can be very destructive and almost impossible to control. This is because the virus can survive for years in nematodes and root fragments even after all infected vines have been removed. So, even if a new, supposedly virus-free, vineyard is planted, it will quickly become infected by the nematode feeding. Among the important virus diseases in this group are FANLEAF DEGENERATION, tomato ringspot, and tobacco ringspot.   R.E.S.

Pearson, R. C., and Goheen, A. C., (eds.), *Compendium of Grape Diseases* (St Paul, Minn., 1988).

Nerello. The most important and increasingly respected red grape on Etna, **Nerello Mascalese**, also known as **Nerello Calabrese**, makes fine, firm, pale but long-lived wines; DNA PROFILING suggests it may be a cross of Sangiovese and Mantonico Bianco. Total plantings in 2010 were nearly 3,000 ha/7,413 acres, many of the vines being extremely old. There were 508 ha/1,255 acres of **Nerello Cappuccio** whose wines are rather softer and earlier-maturing. See SICILY.

Nero d'Avola, the characteristic red grape variety of southern Siciliy, also known as Calabrese, suggesting origins in Calabria on the mainland. The 2010 Italian vine census cited 16,595 ha/40,990 acres of 'Calabrese', still the island's most planted red wine grape. Producers on the island value the body, deep colour, and sweet-cherry fruit which Nero d'Avola can bring to a blend. VARIETAL Nero d'Avola responds well to BARREL MATURATION. Like Syrah, Nero d'Avola requires a good site, warmth, and low VINE TRAINING to succeed. Avola itself is in the southern part of the province of Siracusa, and nearby Pachino, on the extreme south eastern tip of the island, is particularly reputed for the quality of its Nero d'Avola grapes. For more information, see SICILY.

Nero di Troia, fine red wine grape speciality named after a village near Foggia making firm, savoury wines in Castel del Monte in PUGLIA that was recently renamed from Uva di Troia by locals mindful of the success of NERO D'AVOLA. The 2010 vine census found a total of 1,126 ha/2,781 acres.

Netherlands, north European country more often referred to as Holland, whose inhabitants are known as the Dutch. In the 17th century particularly, they played a dominant role in the world's wine and spirit trade (see DUTCH WINE TRADE), and played a key role in draining the MÉDOC lowlands bordering the Gironde. For a long time, Holland was the world's largest importer of SHERRY—until 1997, when it was surpassed by the British Isles.

The country also has its own small, indigenous wine industry with an impressive history, despite the coolness of the climate. There are records of wine-producing vines growing in Limburg in southern Holland in 1324 and vine-growing around Maastricht ceased only in the early years of the 19th century, discouraged by a series of cold summers and the economic turbulence of the Napoleonic era. It was not until 1967 that the Netherlands became a wine producer once more when Frits Bosch created his Slavante vineyard of just 800 sq m. In 2014 there were about 180 active vine-growers, with an estimated total of 240 ha/590 acres of vines planted. The largest producers in the southern part of the country, around Maastricht, are medal winners Apostelhoeve, Hoeve Neekum, and Wijngoed Fromberg in Ubachsberg. The small village of Vijlen houses the biggest vineyard so far, St. Martinus, with 11 ha. Zeeland, in the sunny south west, is home to one of the best Dutch producers: Kleine Schorre. In the southern part of the country mainly VINIFERA varieties such as Riesling, Müller-Thurgau, Auxerrois, Chardonnay, Pinot Blanc, and Pinot Gris are grown for white wines while Pinot Noir produces light reds. Wine-growing in more northerly and eastern parts of the country has grown considerably since the introduction of new DISEASE-RESISTANT VARIETIES such as Regent and Rondo for reds and Johanniter, Merzling, and Solaris for white wines. Notable producers here are Betuws Wijndomein at Erichem, Wijnhoeve De Colonjes at Groesbeek, and Wijngaard Hof van Twente, Bentelo. One of the most dynamic producers in the east is the Achterhoekse Wijnbouwers CO-OPERATIVE, whose wines have achieved some international recognition. Further growth is expected because wine is a more profitable crop than most, and offers TOURISM possibilities.   R.d.G.

nets can literally save a grape crop. See BIRDS and HAIL.

Neuburger, sometimes distinguished white grape variety grown almost exclusively on almost 600 ha in AUSTRIA. DNA PROFILING in Austria showed it is a cross, possibly accidental, of ROTER VELTLINER × SYLVANER, which makes nutty wine that tastes like an even fuller-bodied Weissburgunder. It is also encountered in the Czech Republic, Slovakia, and Transylvania in ROMANIA.

Neusiedlersee refers to both the l33 km-long, notably shallow lake of mysterious origin that plays a critical role in the wine-growing MESOCLIMATES of the northern half of Austrian BURGENLAND, and to an official wine region along that lake's northern and eastern shores, with roughly 9,100 ha/22,500 acres of vines making up 8% of Austria's total.

A quick tour of this region beginning on the border with the NEUSIEDLERSEE-HÜGELLAND wine region and just to the west of the lake's northernmost extension highlights its geological, MESOCLIMATIC, and vinous diversity. The villages of Winden and Jois alternately feature slopes of mica SCHIST and LIMESTONE, and sites such as the Alter Berg and Junger Berg are gradually re-establishing reputations with BLAUFRÄNKISCH and Pinot Noir (Blauburgunder). Among white wines, the Pinot Blanc (Weissburgunder) in this sector—while not widely planted—also distinguishes itself. At the northern tip of the lake, the low range of hills between the Parndorfer Platte and the lakeshore at Weiden and Gols features combinations of gravel, sand, and clay that support all the local red grape varieties—notably Blaufränkisch, St. Laurent, Pinot Noir, and ZWIEGELT—as well as Merlot, Cabernet, and even some Syrah. The wealth of white grapes in this sector includes Chardonnay, NEUBURGER, Pinot Blanc, and Sauvignon Blanc. Few villages in Austria are more singularly devoted to viticulture nor so crowded with family wineries than Gols, among which estate-bottlers Hans 'John' Nittnaus was the pioneer in the 1980s, champion of unblended Blaufränkisch. Josef 'Pepi' Umathum is notable for his rigorous Blaufränkisch vine selection, part of a multifaceted local cultural preservation project. Wide diversity of vine varieties is perpetuated around Mönchhof, Halbturn, and Frauen-kirchen further south and east—the so-called Haideboden sector—more dominated by the warmth of the Great Pannonian Plain and less by the lake, a dominance that reaches its Austrian apex at Andau on the Hungarian frontier, known for its rich reds and in particular for the most powerful Zweigelt of all.

Along the alternately sandy and gravelly eastern shore of the Neusiedlersee as it descends toward the Hungarian border and an expanse of reedy swampland east of SOPRON, the villages of Podersdorf, Illmitz, and Apetlon are home—like Rust on the opposite shore—to Austria's most renowned BOTRYTIZED sweet wines, along with occasionally remarkable dry whites. Fog and humidity from the Neusiedlersee and a mosaic of small lakes engender frequent BOTRYTIS, while sunshine reflected off their surfaces and the bright white expanses of sand and dried mineral salts, serves to project light into the grape clusters; conjoined with this sector's generally low rainfall, ensures that the rot remains NOBLE. In this so-called Seewinkel sector of the Neusiedlersee grape varieties include Chardonnay, MUSKATELLER, Sauvignon Blanc, Traminer, Pinot Blanc, and WELSCHRIESLING plus significant amounts of BOUVIER, Muscat Ottonel, ZWEIGELT, and SCHEUREBE (known locally as SÄMLING 88). Strohwein—STRAW WINE known locally as *Schilfwein*—benefits from the local reeds and prevalent sunshine and contrasts with the region's far more prevalent botrytized AUSLESE, BEERENAUSLESE, and TROCKENBEERENAUSLESE wines, while EISWEIN is also made with relative regularity.

Somewhat confusingly, in 2011 **Neusiedlersee** became one of Austria's DAC appellations of origin, associated exclusively with ZWEIGELT-dominated red wine blends produced in the eponymous region, as a result of which only wines meeting the requirements for that DAC may cite Neusiedlersee as their place of origin, while others—including the sweet wines for which this region has long been best-known—must now state Burgenland as their place of origin. Wines of Neusiedlersee DAC are referred to as KLASSIK if overwhelmingly from Zweigelt, raised in tank or large cask, and with at least 12% alcohol. Wines from this DAC labelled Reserve must comprise at least 60% Zweigelt with the rest from other indigenous grapes, be at least 13% alcohol, and aged in large casks or small barrels.   D.S.

Neusiedlersee-Hügelland, official wine region in AUSTRIA with 4,150 ha/10,250 acres of vineyard (nearly 8% of the national total) along the western edge of the NEUSIEDLERSEE and adjacent slopes and foothills of the Leitha Hills. It incorporates RUST, one of Austria's historically most prestigious wine communities, and produces excellent dry red and both dry and sweet white made from a wide range of grape varieties. Neusiedlersee-Hügelland is rarely seen on wine labels, however, since the local growers seem to find it cumbersomely long, and confusing because it incorporates the name of another region NEUSIEDLERSEE across the eponymous lake. Wines grown in Neusiedlersee-Hügelland are more likely to be labelled with the name of the state, Burgenland. Eisenstadt and two of its village suburbs—Grosshöflein and St Georgen—are home to potentially outstanding Blaufränkisch as well as impressive Pinot Blanc, Neuburger, and under-appreciated Grüner Veltliner that tends to be overshadowed by examples grown in NIEDERÖSTERREICH, all of which benefit from the CALCAREOUS soils and the breeze that blows here. A mere kilometre or so east, Schützen-am-Gebirge reflects a transition to soils based on weathered GNEISS and mica SCHIST, outstanding for Blaufränkisch but also supportive of white varieties, which dominate the next village north, Donnerskirchen, where even Riesling flourishes thanks to the cooling effect of forests and breezes on an especially high stretch of hills. Closer to the lake, and running north-south, Breitenbrunn, Purbach, and Oggau also make good whites and reds. Although Rust is famous for BOTRYTIZED sweet white (see AUSBRUCH), it is also where modern appreciation of varietal Blaufränkisch arguably began, with Ernst 'ET' Triebaumer's 1986 Mariental bottling. (At the time Anton Kollwentz of nearby Grosshöflein had only recently bottled Austria's first Cabernet Sauvignon and would, like Engelbert Prieler of Schützen, become another early champion of Blaufränkisch.) Möbisch, on Lake Neusiedl immediately south of Rust, as well as St Margarethen, Siegendorf, and Zagersdorf—more or less midway between the lake and the Leitha range—are among other red wine villages worth noting, producing distinguished BLAUFRÄNKISCH and some of Austria's finest St. Laurent.   D.S.

Nevers is the town that gives its name to the central French *département* of Nièvre, most famous in the wine world for the wines of POUILLY-FUMÉ and for its OAK.

New Latitude Wines, term coined by Thai wine writer Frank Norel in 2003 for wines made in the TROPICAL fringes of the global wine map, although it could equally well apply to those from high latitudes where viticulture has recently been encouraged by CLIMATE CHANGE. See LATITUDE.

New South Wales, AUSTRALIA's most populous state, consumes far more wine than it produces, but its wine geography is developing rapidly.

The **Hunter Valley** (now an official wine zone), 130 km/80 miles north of Sydney, has always had a special hold on the affections (and wallets) of Sydneysiders. It is also one of the internationally known regions, notwithstanding its relatively small contribution (less than 3%) to the country's total crush, and its perverse climate. That climate is abnormally hot for a fine wine district, although the heat is partially offset by high HUMIDITY, by afternoon cloud cover, and by substantial rainfall during the growing season—less beneficially in the years in which most of the rain falls during harvest.

Out of this climatic witches' brew comes exceptionally long-lived dry SEMILLON, the best peaking somewhere between ten and 20 years of age and assuming a honeyed, buttery, nutty flavour, and texture which suggests it has been fermented or matured in oak, when (traditionally) none was used. Most remarkable is the ALCOHOLIC STRENGTH, often as low as 10%. Since 1970, CHARDONNAY also has proved its worth: Australia's first Chardonnays of note were made in the Hunter Valley by Tyrrell's. Here the lifespan is usually shorter, but there are exceptions. Whether young or old, Hunter Chardonnays are generous and soft, with peachy fruit and considerable VISCOSITY.

SHIRAZ was the traditional red counterpart to Semillon in the Hunter, making extremely distinctive, moderately tannic, and long-lived wines with earth and tar overtones, sometimes described as having the aroma of a sweaty saddle after a hard day's ride. At 20 to 30 years of age, the best acquire a silky sheen to their texture and move eerily close to wines of similar age from the RHÔNE Valley in south east France.

CABERNET SAUVIGNON is another relatively new arrival, planted for the first time since the 19th century at Lake's Folly winery in 1963. By and large, Hunter Valley wines tend to be more regional than varietal in their statement, a tendency which becomes more marked with age.

Riesling, Sauvignon Blanc, and Pinot Noir are among prominent varieties which have been tried and found unsuited to the climate and TERROIR. VERDELHO has made a remarkable comeback (highly regarded in the 19th century, then all but forgotten) as a soft, flavoursome wine requiring neither oak nor patience to show its wares.

Overall, the Hunter Valley produces better white wines than it does red, with Semillon its one unique contribution. If one is to differentiate the Upper Hunter, a separate viticultural subregion well to the north, from the Lower Hunter, the bias towards white wine becomes more acute in the former. Rosemount once enjoyed acclaim for its Upper Hunter Chardonnay, although the company all but abandoned the district in the 21st century.

Nowhere in Australia is the rate of change and the pace of growth more apparent than it is in New South Wales. The development of viticulture along the entire length of the western (or inland) side of the Great Dividing Range could not have been foreseen at the start of the 1990s, but from the end of the 20th century it has been making a significant contribution to the national crush.

The principal zones are the Central Ranges Zone and the Southern New South Wales Zone, providing two and a half times as much wine as the Hunter Valley. The former takes in the regions of Mudgee, Orange, and Cowra; the latter takes in the regions of Hilltops, Canberra District, Gundagai, and Tumbarumba.

Of these, **Mudgee** is by far the oldest, with an unbroken history of viticulture and winemaking stretching back to 1858. It is first and foremost red wine country, however well the ubiquitous Chardonnay does here. Indeed, Mudgee was the source of a precious VIRUS-free clone of Chardonnay almost certainly brought to Australia in the early 19th century. As with the Hunter Valley, Mudgee has never been attacked by PHYLLOXERA.

The climate is as hot as that of the Hunter Valley, but the summer rainfall is significantly lower, and it is rare for harvest rain seriously to interrupt proceedings. The red wines—Shiraz and Cabernet Sauvignon—are deeply coloured and intensely flavoured, and are ideal blend components for the products of the Hunter Valley's frequent wet vintages. Both PERNOD RICARD and TREASURY WINE ESTATES have largely abandoned Mudgee, and the region's biggest winery, Robert Oatley Vineyards, has also scaled back its Mudgee brands. As a result of all this, the vineyard area has declined.

ELEVATION is as important as LATITUDE in shaping the climate (and the ensuing wine style) of the regions south down the Great Dividing range to **Orange**. With most of its vineyards established on hillsides forming part of the extinct volcano Mount Canobolas at elevations of between 600 and 1,000 m, Orange is the coolest of these regions (apart from the southern outpost of Tumbarumba in the Australian Alps). Zesty, lively Chardonnay, some of Australia's best Sauvignon Blanc, and midweight Cabernet Sauvignon, Merlot, and Shiraz with clearly articulated varietal character are the order of the day. Here, as in the **Hilltops** region (which produces wines of slightly fuller style and weight), warm but not excessively hot summer days and cold nights are followed by a cool, dry autumn which assists in the slow ripening and relatively late harvest dates.

McWilliam's has thrown its lot in with the Hilltops region for reds and Tumbarumba for whites; indeed, many small producers in other New South Wales regions are either growing or sourcing white grapes from Tumbarumba.

Canberra District wineries are mostly small, clustered just outside the border of the Australian Capital Territory, but rely heavily on tourist (and local resident) trade to promote CELLAR-DOOR sales. The climate is not dissimilar to that of Orange and Hilltops: strongly CONTINENTAL with warm to hot days, cold nights, and a dry summer. Riesling, Chardonnay, Pinot Noir, Shiraz, and Viognier need VINEYARD SITE SELECTION, but with appropriate matching can be truly excellent.

Cowra (and nearby Canowindra) is significantly warmer, basically because the vineyards are at a lower elevation. Here broad acre farming is made easy by the flat plains, and yields (with the aid of IRRIGATION, of course) are substantial. Softly fleshy Chardonnay is the mainstay, with soft Cabernet Sauvignon, Shiraz, and Merlot seldom achieving enough concentration and structure to match the quality of Chardonnay.

The Big Rivers Zone, encompassing Riverina, Perricoota, and the New South Wales side of the Murray Darling and Swan Hill regions, which it shares with Victoria (they fall on both sides of the Murray River, the border between the two states), produces 75% of the state's grape crush.

Riverina (sometimes called the Murrumbidgee Irrigation Area, or MIA) is centred around Griffith 450 km/275 miles south west of Sydney. With the notable exception of BOTRYTIZED Semillon (made in a SAUTERNES style), the wines are on a par with those produced in the Perricoota, Murray Darling, and Lower Murray regions. Replanting in the late 1990s and early 2000s put increasing focus on Chardonnay, Shiraz, Merlot, and Cabernet Sauvignon, while Tempranillo and Italian varieties such as Pinot Grigio, Vermentino, Fiano, Sangiovese, and Barbera are the newest arrivals. Substantial quantities of MUSCAT GORDO BLANCO and the multipurpose SULTANA are still harvested. High yields are sought, and under normal conditions Chardonnay is the best variety. It takes a cool year for the red varieties to rise above pedestrian quality.

Overall the wines reflect the very warm climate and the quasi-hydroponic growing regimes. The technical excellence of the wineries assures clean, fault-free, mildly fruity wines well suited to the drinker of cask wine (in BOXES), and to the requirements of overseas BULK markets such as the own brands of the British supermarket chains.   J.H. & H.H.

www.nswwine.com.au

new varieties, somewhat loose and relative term used to describe VINE VARIETIES specifically and deliberately developed by man, which effectively means developed since the late 19th century (although it is sometimes used parochially to describe varieties new to a region).

There is interest in breeding new varieties which are resistant, for example, to environmental stresses, fungal and bacterial diseases, and nematodes and insects (see VINE BREEDING).

Of these, the major goals are varieties tolerant of the fungal diseases DOWNY MILDEW, POWDERY MILDEW, and BOTRYTIS BUNCH ROT or resistant to PIERCE'S DISEASE. Unfortunately, new varieties, especially HYBRIDS but even some CROSSES, suffer from the stigma of the poor wine quality of the early French hybrids. The uptake of newly developed grape varieties has been further hindered by consumer preference for traditional varieties, particularly the INTERNATIONAL VARIETIES, a consequence in part of VARIETAL labelling.

The early French hybridizers mentioned in FRENCH HYBRIDS were not the only French vine breeders to have developed new varieties. Louis BOUSCHET and his son Henri used controlled pollination from 1824 to create a range of seedlings which after selection became known as the Bouschet crosses. Of these the TEINTURIER variety ALICANTE BOUSCHET is the most important and indeed is the only one to be officially recommended for planting in France. Another early and successful VINIFERA vine breeder was Hermann Müller, whose variety MÜLLER-THURGAU was once the most planted in Germany. A succession of new crosses followed, notably from research institutes at GEISENHEIM, GEILWEILERHOF, Alzey, Würzburg, and Freiburg. For details of these, see GERMAN CROSSES.

Other new varieties such as Zweigelt, Blauburger, and Neuburger were bred in Austria, the first two at KLOSTERNEUBURG. The emphasis in RUSSIA has been on breeding varieties with cold tolerance as well as disease tolerance, and there are substantial areas, not just in Russia but in other ex-Soviet republics, planted with varieties such as Saperavi Severny, Stepniak, Fioletovy Ranni, and Cabernet Severny. In NEW YORK state and CANADA, the emphasis also has been on developing varieties with cold and disease tolerance, often relying on the French hybrids for resistant genes. Recent releases such as CAYUGA WHITE, Melody, CHARDONEL, and TRAMINETTE, all bred at CORNELL, are being more widely planted. The names of the last two varieties, incorporating those of their respective *V. vinifera* parents, may make them more acceptable to consumers. There is particular enthusiasm for grapevine breeding in the American Midwest, where new varieties seem to be valued as much by consumers for their local origins as by growers for their cold-hardiness and disease-resistance (see, for example, LA CROSSE, MARQUETTE, and TRAMINETTE).

New varieties in France, most of them developed in association with the University of MONTPELLIER, have been *V. vinifera* crosses such as PORTAN, CALADOC, Chenanson, Ganson, Gramon, Monerac, CHASAN, Arriloba, Odola, and Perdea, as well as EGIODOLA and ARINARNOA developed by INRA at Bordeaux. In France, new varieties must first be registered with the Comité Technique Permanent de la Sélection des Plantes Cultivées (CTPS) as a prelude to

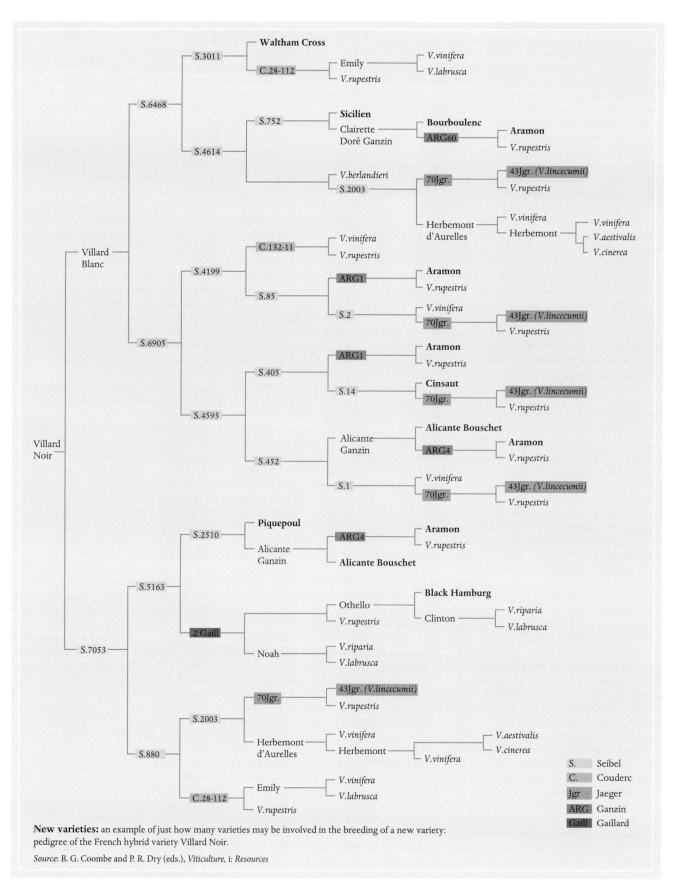

New varieties: an example of just how many varieties may be involved in the breeding of a new variety: pedigree of the French hybrid variety Villard Noir.

Source: B. G. Coombe and P. R. Dry (eds.), *Viticulture*, i: *Resources*

their recognition in the EU. Active breeding programmes are underway in many parts of Europe, notably in the CZECH REPUBLIC and in SLOVAKIA.

Australia has a vine-breeding programme designed to produce varieties suitable for hot climates, and Goyura, TARRANGO, Tullilah, TAMINGA, TYRIAN, and CIENNA have all been released. In California such new varieties as CARNELIAN, RUBY CABERNET, EMERALD RIESLING, SYMPHONY, and FLORA have all enjoyed popularity at some point while RUBIRED, unlike similarly red-fleshed ROYALTY, is widely planted to add colour to blends.

New varieties of particular interest today are interspecific hybrids because of the opportunities they offer for natural disease resistance with much reduced use of AGROCHEMICALS. These DISEASE-RESISTANT VARIETIES have complex genealogies which may include, not just *V. vinifera* genes, but also those of various AMERICAN VINE SPECIES, French hybrids, and even Asian vine species.

A full account of vine breeding and the inheritance of characteristics is given by Huglin.

See also VINE BREEDING. R.E.S.

Covert, C., 'Cold climate grape varieties from eastern U.S. breeding programs', *FPS Grape Program Newsletter* (Oct 2008), iv.ucdavis.edu/files/24502.pdf.

Huglin, P., *Biologie et écologie de la vigne* (Paris, 1986).

Mullins, M. G., Bouquet, A., and Williams, L., *Biology of the Grapevine* (Cambridge, 1992).

New World

New World, term much used in the wine world, initially somewhat patronizingly but with increasing admiration in the last quarter of the 20th century as the New World's share of global exports rose from 3 to 23%, to distinguish the colonies established as a result of European exploration, beginning with some of the longer voyages in the 15th century. As such it contrasts with the OLD WORLD of Europe and the other Mediterranean countries where the vine was widely established by the 4th century. The differences between the Old and New Worlds of wine have been steadily eroded as those in the Old World have increasingly adopted technical innovation and those in the New World are increasingly exposed to the better aspects of TRADITION and further develop the notion of REGIONALITY.

History

The new colonists needed wine for religious reasons (see EUCHARIST), and the planting of the vine was a matter of high priority when the conquistadores invaded SOUTH AMERICA. Cortés was already arranging to plant vines in MEXICO by 1522. By 1530, vines were cultivated in both Mexico and JAPAN, and by the 1550s in PERU, followed soon after by CHILE. The New World's oldest winery in continuous use is Casa Madero at San Lorenzo in north-eastern Mexico, where the first vintage in the Americas was made, from VITIS *aestivalis*, in 1597.

The European settlement of SOUTH AFRICA followed a decision by the DUTCH EAST INDIA COMPANY soon after 1640 to establish a victualling post at the Cape of Good Hope, to serve the growing Batavia trade. Dutch settlement began in 1652 and the first vines were planted in 1655.

British settlers planted the first vines in the UNITED STATES of America in Virginia in 1619; thus began a series of unsuccessful attempts to establish European or VINIFERA vine varieties on the east coast of America. Settlers there were dismayed that they could not cultivate this sort of vine when local wild vines, AMERICAN VINES, grew in profusion in the forests. At that time they were not to know the nature of the pest and disease scourges which were attacking their plantations, and were subsequently to invade Europe (see DOWNY MILDEW, POWDERY MILDEW, and PHYLLOXERA). PIERCE'S DISEASE presumably also played a role in the devastation of these European vines on some sites. Added to these problems in many areas were those of much colder winters than *V. vinifera* varieties can withstand.

There were not the same problems in Baja California, where Spanish-Mexican Jesuit MISSIONARIES established vineyards in the 1670s. Although prone to summer DROUGHT, this region was free of both FUNGAL DISEASES and phylloxera and European vines flourished here. Gradually plantings were made further north—in Los Angeles in the 1820s and NAPA and SONOMA in the 1850s (see CALIFORNIA, history).

Vines were introduced to AUSTRALIA by Captain Arthur Phillip in 1788 as part of the first British colony at Sydney. As this large country was invaded by the British, so the culture of the vine spread too. Viticulture was well established in all modern wine-producing states by the 1850s. Samuel Marsden, a missionary from Australia, is acknowledged as bringing the first vines to NEW ZEALAND in 1819.

Viticulture

New World viticulture is a phrase used to differentiate the viticultural practices in the New World from those of the Old World. It is difficult but not impossible to generalize about the viticultural practices of countries as diverse as the United States, Australia, New Zealand, South Africa, and the countries of South America as opposed to those more usual in Europe.

A common difference is in planting distances, or VINE DENSITY, with a particularly marked contrast between the 1 m by 1 m (3 ft by 3 ft) high-density planting of the MÉDOC and the 3.7 m by 2.5 m (12 ft by 8 ft) planting pattern that was long common in California and Australia. But no difference is absolute or constant. In some parts of the Old World, there is a trend towards wider spacings for reasons of economy, while some growers in the New World have been planting more densely, sometimes to an extreme extent, in a search for higher quality. POSTS characterize New World vineyards rather than the STAKES of the Old World.

The VINE VARIETIES planted in the New and Old Worlds are similar, as are the ROOTSTOCKS onto which they are GRAFTED, usually because the New World has concentrated on the INTERNATIONAL VARIETIES made famous in the Old World. New World regions are less likely to have a rich heritage of INDIGENOUS VARIETIES but some do have specialities, such as the PAIS and CARMENÈRE of Chile, and the PINOTAGE and almost extinct PONTAC of South Africa. Old World methods are more traditional, and many aspects of modern viticultural technology, especially MECHANIZATION and PRECISION VITICULTURE, have been developed and first used in the New World. MECHANICAL HARVESTING and MECHANICAL PRUNING, for example, were first developed in America, but by the early 1990s there was a high degree of acceptance, of the former at least, in Europe. Some vineyard sites in the Old World have been used for viticulture for hundreds of years, but there are still many potential new vineyard regions to be discovered in the New World (see VINEYARD SITE SELECTION).

Technological advance is by no means the sole prerogative of the New World, however. The development and application of new technology in Europe is the equal of anywhere in the world, as evidenced by work there on CLONAL SELECTION, VINE BREEDING, and CANOPY MANAGEMENT. R.E.S.

Wines and winemaking

If New World wines can be said to have a style of their own, it is that they are much more likely to be VARIETAL both in how they are described on the label and in how they taste, although a growing proportion of New World wines are now being made with the clear intention of expressing their geographical provenance (see REGIONALITY and TERROIR). FRUIT-DRIVEN is an essentially New World wine description, although it is not seen as such a desirable quality today as when the term was first coined in the 1980s.

New World winemaking, particularly in CALIFORNIA, has been subject to ever more rapid changes of direction and swings of FASHION than its Old World counterpart. This has been possible because both viticulturists and winemakers in the New World are much more willing, and much freer, to experiment. (Those in the Old World are more likely to be restrained by local regulations such as those enshrined in CONTROLLED APPELLATIONS.)

n

In the Old World, with its centuries of wine-making tradition, Nature is generally regarded as the determining, guiding force. In much of the New World, however, it was for long regarded with suspicion, as an enemy to be subdued, controlled, and mastered in all its detail, thanks to the insights provided by SCIENCE.

New World winemakers are still rather more likely to adopt PROTECTIVE WINEMAKING methods, attempting to shield grapes, juice, must, and wine from OXYGEN throughout the winemaking process, especially for white wines and light reds. This may involve BLANKETING and MUST CHILLING, using only fully enclosed PRESSES, and careful use of INERT GAS. However, as with so many New/Old World distinctions, this one is becoming more blurred as research into oxygen management in all corners of the wine world progresses, especially when it comes to BOTTLING and CLOSURES (see, for example, TOTAL PACKAGE OXYGEN and PREMATURE OXIDATION.)

Obsession with HYGIENE is generally more marked in the New World than the Old, with the consequence that WATER use is much higher. Rubber boots are much less de rigueur in the Old World.

In general, target TEMPERATURES throughout winemaking are lower in the New World than in the Old. This is especially true for FERMENTATION. Use of wild and/or ambient YEASTS is still relatively uncommon in the New World—although it has been becoming rarer in the Old World too. Again, more dialogue about contrasting practices and more careful analysis of yeast activity is leading to fruiful research and experimentation. (See also MICROBIAL TERROIR.)

The Old World red winemaking practice of following fermentation with an extended MACERATION in the fermentation vessel is increasingly replaced in the New World by RACKING some red wines into barrel before they have completed their first fermentation, in the belief that this, together with MALOLACTIC CONVERSION in barrel, results in a softer, fuller, earlier maturing wine. Although this is a tactic that has been adopted in the Old World, especially in Bordeaux by those seeking to make EN PRIMEUR samples flattering to taste.

ENZYMES, both for settling and for releasing flavours, are a more common winemaking addition in parts of the New World than in the Old.

New World wines tend to be immediately appealing on release, whereas some Old World wines may be positively off-putting to taste for their first year or two in bottle. In general, however, Old World wines are capable of more extended BOTTLE AGEING than their New World counterparts—although the proportion of exceptions to this rule is steadily increasing as New and Old Worlds move inexorably closer towards each other.

Some Old World observers identify three phases in the development of New World wine production. In the first, the technology phase, producers put all their faith in cellar techniques and technology. In the second, the viticulture phase, the importance of grape quality is acknowledged and techniques such as canopy management are introduced to the vineyard. In the third, terroir phase, producers introduce VINEYARD SITE SELECTION, cooler climates, reduced irrigation, and may eventually seek distinguished sites capable of producing distinctive single-vineyard wines.

See also NEW LATITUDE WINES.

New York, north eastern state of the UNITED STATES of America, between the Atlantic and the Great Lakes, historically an important source of wine but now third to CALIFORNIA and WASHINGTON as a US wine-producing state, as measured by acreage planted and annual tonnage (although its LABRUSCA-based products, including GRAPE JUICE, boost its wine volume total above that of Washington). Its inland wine regions share some characteristics with those of Ontario across the border in CANADA. The market for wine in the New York city metropolitan region is one of the world's most competitive and demanding, and its restaurants were slow to embrace the state's wines.

History

After unsuccessful trials with VINIFERA around Manhattan Island in the first days of settlement, nothing more is heard of viticulture in New York until the early 19th century. Vine-growing then developed in three regions across the state. The work with native grapes (see AMERICAN VINE SPECIES) of the Long island nurseryman William Robert Prince led to plantings along the Hudson river from which wine was produced in small quantities by the 1840s.

The second region was the Finger Lakes district of north central New York, where significant plantings of AMERICAN HYBRIDS began in the 1850s. From these a large industry developed, centred on the towns of Hammondsport, Penn Yan, and Naples, and specializing in white wines, both still and sparkling. By the end of the 19th century, there were 24,000 acres/9,700 ha of vines in the Finger Lakes region.

In western New York, along the Lake Erie shore, a 'grape belt' developed after the Civil War. A part of the region's grapes went into wine, but the vineyards were increasingly planted to CONCORD for GRAPE JUICE.

After PROHIBITION, vine-growing in New York was dominated by a few large wineries in the Finger Lakes, which continued the traditional trade in still and sparkling white wines from native grapes, but also used neutral blending wine from California. A special niche in New York is the production of sweet KOSHER wine

from the Concord grape, as well as dry kosher table wines from other grape varieties.

The new interest in wine that emerged in the 1970s had important results in New York. The Farm Winery Act of 1976 made it economically feasible for financially depressed grape growers to own and operate a small winery by allowing direct sales to consumers. First FRENCH HYBRIDS, then VINIFERA vines, began to be planted more and more widely; new wineries, mostly small, grew up; one entirely new region, the eastern end of Long island, was successfully developed; the large established wineries of the Finger Lakes passed through repeated changes of ownership, saw their traditional markets shrink under new competition, and fell into decline. By 2014, New York had 416 wineries, all but 140 of them established since the Farm Winery Act, and they produced about 36 million gal/1.4 million hl of wine a year.   T.P., H.G., & L.M.

Geography and climate

New York's grape and wine industry preserves from property developers about 37,000 acres/14,973 ha of vineyards, and is a significant part of the state's agricultural economy. The industry provides thousands of jobs, generates millions of dollars in sales, contributes millions of dollars in taxes, and attracts over 5.3 million TOURISTS each year. About a third of all grapes grown in the state are destined for wine production, while most are used for grape juice, jellies and jams, and TABLE GRAPES.

New York state has four distinct wine regions which represent nine American Viticultural Areas, or AVAS. The four regions are Finger Lakes (which is itself an AVA and includes Seneca Lake and Cayuga Lake AVAs) in the north central part of the state; Lake Erie at the western border; Hudson River, which begins about 40 miles/64 km north of New York City; Niagara Escarpment in the north west corner of the state; and Long Island (itself an AVA and including The Hamptons and North Fork AVAs), whose vineyards in the East End are at least 78 miles east of NYC. In spite of frequent low winter temperatures, the growing season typically has from 2,000 to 2,700 DEGREE DAYS. Its glacier-altered TOPOGRAPHY, strategic bodies of water, and deep, well-drained soils also encourage viticulture. The greatest viticultural hazard is WINTER FREEZE. A sustained period of record-low winter temperatures in early 2014, ranging from 7 to −18°F in 19 upstate counties contributed to crop losses as high as 85% in the Finger Lakes and 97% in Lake Erie.

Finger Lakes The picturesque Finger Lakes district is the oldest, and has been the centre of the New York wine industry, with grape-growing and wine production dating back to the 1820s. While Finger Lakes is the second

NEW YORK AND CANADA

largest wine-grape-growing area in the state, 90% of the state's wine is produced there in 119 bonded wineries in 2014. The narrow, deep lakes, so named because they look like the fingers of a hand, were carved by Ice Age glaciers, which deposited shallow topsoil on sloping shale beds above the lakes. This combination of steep slopes and deep lakes provides good AIR DRAINAGE and DRAINAGE of water, and fewer extremes of temperature in winter and summer. Since the lakes retain their summer warmth in winter, cold air sliding down the steep slopes is warmed by the lake and rises, permitting more cold air to drain from the hillside. Conversely, in spring, the now cold water of the lake retards budding until the

danger of FROST is past (see LAKE EFFECT). The lakes significant to the wine industry are Canandaigua, Keuka, Seneca, and Cayuga, which are big enough to moderate the climate. The official Finger Lakes AVA was established in 1982, with Cayuga Lake being granted its own AVA in 1988, since local wineries could demonstrate that its lower elevation and greater lake depth created a MESOCLIMATE suitable for the *V. vinifera* varieties most recently planted there. Cayuga now has 23 bonded wineries. Riesling does exceptionally well in this cool climate, and is attracting consumer attention. Recent plantings of Pinot Noir and Cabernet Franc have also made successful wines. Lake Seneca is emerging as an important wine-producing area with 40 wineries

spread around the lake's perimeter. Most of Finger Lakes' ESTATE WINE production is sold locally.

Lake Erie Lake Erie is one of the Great Lakes, and is the one that provides the most protection against extremes of weather to western New York, since it is lower in latitude and downwind from the Arctic air masses that prevail over lakes Superior and Huron. (Lake Michigan provides similar benefits to the states around its southern tip.)

Furthermore, besides the beneficial effects of the lake itself, the 3-mile wide Allegheny plateau, which runs parallel to lake Erie, extends the lake's moderating influence. The Lake Erie AVA was established in 1983, and includes three states spanning 40,000 acres/16,200 ha: New York around Chautauqua, Pennsylvania, and Ohio, with counties that border on the lake. About 19,000 acres/7,700 ha are planted, giving Lake Erie the largest acreage in NY, but it has only 17 wineries to date since most of the grapes planted in the region are for grape juice and table grapes—a result of pressure from Prohibitionists in the early 19th century.

Hudson River Wine has been made along the Hudson River continuously for the past 300 years, and it contains the oldest winery in the United States still in operation: Brotherhood Winery, established in 1839. Hudson River Region became an AVA in 1982. There are wineries on both sides of the Hudson River, but the moderating effects of the river on the local climate are seen as less important than the steep palisaded valley which acts as a conduit for maritime air and weather generated by the Atlantic ocean. Glaciers have deposited shale, slate, schist, and limestone throughout the region. Among the region's producers is Royal Kedem Winery/Royal Wine Corporation, one of the world's largest KOSHER wineries. SEYVAL BLANC is widely planted and some VINIFERA varieties, including Chardonnay, also do well. Just 235 acres/95 ha are planted in the AVA, yet there are a disproportionate number of wineries, 49, many of which buy in grapes from other regions.

Long Island The eastern Long Island region consists of three AVAs. Long Island, itself an AVA, had 2,400 acres/971 ha in 2014. Within the Long Island AVA are the North Fork of Long Island AVA (1986) and the Hamptons Long Island AVA (1985). Overall the East End has 66 producers, some of them using CUSTOM CRUSH FACILITY services. North Fork of Long Island is a peninsula surrounded by Long Island sound on the north, Peconic bay to the south, and the Atlantic ocean to the east. These bodies of water make the area temperate, sending breezes that moderate heat and cold, extending the periods when frost is not a threat, reducing daily temperature swings, and increasing winter precipitation. Local growers feel that the Atlantic's MARITIME influence is similar to its influence on BORDEAUX. Long Island's greatest viticultural hazard, however (apart from BIRDS), is the threat of ocean hurricanes, and some vineyards on the South Fork shore have been sprayed by salt water (see SALINITY). The growing season is at least three weeks longer than other wine regions in New York state, which means that dark-skinned V. vinifera varieties, especially Merlot and Cabernet Franc, predominate for they may be ripened fully almost every year. Lovely traditional method sparkling wines are also produced. The North Fork soils have less silt and loam than those on the South Fork, and require

IRRIGATION because of their reduced water-holding capacity. The first pioneers to buy potato fields and replant them with vines were Alex and Louisa Hargrave, who founded Hargrave Vineyard (now Castello di Borghese), the first commercial V. vinifera vineyard on Long Island in 1973. The Hamptons is also a peninsula, south of North Fork of Long Island. Thus, Peconic bay now forms the northern edge, and the Atlantic ocean washes the east and south. The Atlantic provides the same benefits to this area as it does to North Fork. Spring fogs keep the area cool and prevent premature BUDBREAK. The soils are deep and have a higher percentage of silt and loam, which makes for better water-holding capacity, requiring less irrigation. Eastern Long Island, with its desirability as a vacation area, enjoys increasingly strong sales of its wines to summer visitors.

Niagara Escarpment, relatively new AVA (2005) that borders Lake Ontario's southern shoreline. Grapes are grown on benchland under the LIMESTONE escarpment which runs some 700 miles from Rochester, New York, through southern Ontario, Canada, and into MICHIGAN. The ridge traps air warmed by Lake Ontario and protects vineyards from drastic temperature swings. With 883 acres of vines and 17 wineries in and near the AVA, Niagara Escarpment is a small cog in the New York wine machine, although a maker of outstanding, unctuous ICE WINES, the majority of which are made from VIDAL BLANC.

Vine varieties and wines

New York has more vinous diversity than any other major US wine state because it grows AMERICAN VINES, AMERICAN HYBRIDS, FRENCH HYBRIDS, and VINIFERA varieties (see VITIS).

American vines and hybrids The indigenous vines originally grown were *Vitis labrusca* and were valued for their resistance to PHYLLOXERA and their winter hardiness, although the early settlers found the grapes quite different in flavour from those of their European homelands. These native vines often hybridized by chance with other *labruscas* or even other American vine species, and produced a second generation of native grapes commonly grown today, of which the blue-black-skinned CONCORD is the most planted variety. These formed the backbone of the early New York wine industry, although they are often derided today for their FOXY flavour. (So pronounced is this flavour that such varieties were exempted when the US laws on VARIETAL labelling increased the minimum permitted percentage of the cited grape variety from 51 to 75%.)

The major red-pink native varieties are CATAWBA and DELAWARE, both of which are winter hardy and vigorous. Since Catawba has been

used in CHARMAT process sparkling wines, it is often subjected to THERMOVINIFICATION, or given limited SKIN CONTACT to yield pink juice. Delaware, on the other hand, is prized for use in fine sparkling wines, and it is fermented cold in stainless steel tanks without skin contact. It has higher sugars and lower acids than Catawba. Both grow in the Finger Lakes and Lake Erie regions.

The white native varieties currently grown include NIAGARA, DUTCHESS, Elvira, and Diamond (sometimes called Moore's Diamond), with Niagara showing the most promise as a TABLE GRAPE and for sparkling wine. Other varieties are declining due to susceptibility to disease, poorer tolerance to cold temperatures, limited use for table grapes, grape juice, and wine, and low grape prices, as well as the state's accelerating VINIFERA revolution. Most remaining acreage of these is in the Finger Lakes, Lake Erie, and Niagara Escarpment AVAs. The Niagara grape, however, is vigorous, winter hardy, and productive, and has a large following among those who enjoy its decidedly foxy flavour. It is grown mostly in Lake Erie and the Finger Lakes, but there is also a little in the Hudson valley. It is fermented cold, and finished with some RESIDUAL SUGAR to balance its intense aroma.

Of dark-skinned native varieties, Concord is widely planted, being grown in every area of New York except Long Island, and is highly productive. It has low sugars and high acids, and the wine is invariably sweetened, resulting in residual sugar ranging from 1% for table wines to more than 10% for DESSERT WINES. Thermovinification is used to extract colour for sweet red wines, or grapes may be pressed without skin contact when used in sparkling wines. Other red grapes include Fredonia, which was developed in the early 1900s at New York State Agricultural Experiment Station (NYSAES) in Geneva (see CORNELL). Fredonia is similar to Concord, but ripens a useful two weeks earlier. Today it is planted mostly in Lake Erie, and used as a table grape or for juice. Ives is used similarly to Concord, and is planted mostly in the Finger Lakes. ISABELLA, which used to be very popular, has been largely replaced by other varieties.

Traditional vine spacing for native varieties is 10 ft by 6 ft (3 m by 2 m) with vines trained to wires for maximum SUNLIGHT interception. William Kniffen developed the widely used umbrella, four cane, and double Kniffen vine-training systems in the 1850s. CHAPTALIZATION is permitted and is usually necessary here, while ACIDIFICATION is forbidden and usually unnecessary. DEACIDIFICATION is often practised, and MALOLACTIC CONVERSION is increasingly encouraged.

French hybrids French hybrids represent the majority of acreage devoted to dry table wines.

Most were developed by French hybridizers, working intensively from 1880 to 1950, to create new varieties that were hardy and disease and pest resistant. Newer hybrids (and some CROSSES) have been bred at NYSAES. The most important white hybrid is SEYVAL BLANC, which grows in every New York wine region except Long Island, and which, much to the confusion of some consumers, can be made clean and fruity in STAINLESS STEEL, or can be the much more complex result of BARREL FERMENTATION and malolactic conversion. VIDAL BLANC and, particularly, VIGNOLES both lend themselves to making late-harvest, dessert wines, Vignoles sometimes being beneficially affected by NOBLE ROT. AURORE, once the most widely planted white hybrid grape in New York, has given way to the prestige of Seyval Blanc. Two New York white hybrids, developed at NYSAES and released commercially in 1982, are Cayuga GW3 and Melody. Both of these are vigorous, resistant, and productive, and make fruity off-dry wines. Wine made from Melody is reminiscent of its Pinot Blanc parent. A third white, TRAMINETTE (1996), echoing Gewurztraminer, is finding favour with consumers. The red French hybrids are declining in acreage. The most famous are BACO Noir and CHAMBOURCIN, which are vinified in all styles from NOUVEAU to PORT-like; MARÉCHAL FOCH, which can also make a good nouveau using CARBONIC MACERATION; DE CHAUNAC; CHANCELLOR, which needs some OAK ageing to add complexity; and Chelois (Seibel 10878), which works well in blends, especially with Baco Noir.

Vinifera In the 1950s, Charles Fournier, winemaker at Gold Seal winery in the Finger Lakes and former winemaker at VEUVE CLICQUOT in Champagne, hired Dr Konstantin Frank, a *V. vinifera* expert from UKRAINE, to make experimental plantings of ROOTSTOCKS and *V. vinifera* varieties in a cold climate. By the early 1960s they had produced commercial *V. vinifera* wines. The most adaptable varieties were brought from Europe and, in descending order of total acreage in 2014, the state's white *V. vinifera* varieties were Riesling, Chardonnay, and Gewurztraminer. They are grown successfully in all of New York's regions, and while Sauvignon Blanc is not widely planted, it can make exceptional wines on Long Island, where the growing season is long enough to ripen it. Of the red *V. vinifera* varieties grown in New York—Merlot, Cabernet Franc, Pinot Noir, and Cabernet Sauvignon—Merlot and Cabernet Franc show particular promise. They both ripen earlier and give greater yields than Cabernet Sauvignon, are adaptable to different soil types, and can make fine varietal wines as well as blending well with other red Bordeaux varieties. Cabernet Sauvignon does best on Long Island, needing its long growing season to ripen, while the maritime climate of Long Island has proved too moist and warm for Pinot Noir, which performs better in the warmer areas of the Hudson Valley and Finger Lakes. *V. vinifera* plantings are increasing, as is VINE DENSITY, sometimes as close as 3 ft × 5 ft. In the warmer Long Island region, the open LYRE training system is gaining favour. In colder areas, especially the Finger Lakes, a multi-trunk FAN system is preferred to provide insurance against WINTER FREEZE of some canes.   H.L., H.G., & L.M.

Cass, B. (ed.), *Oxford Companion to the Wines of North America* (Oxford and New York, 2000).
Hedricks, U. P., *The Grapes of New York* (Albany, NY, 1908).
Robinson, J., and Murphy, L., *American Wine* (London and Berkeley, 2013).
www.newyorkwines.org

New Zealand, southern Pacific islands 1,000 miles/1,600 km away from the nearest land mass, AUSTRALIA, has an agricultural economy that is far more dependent on dairy products than it is on wine, the country's eighth-biggest export. Vines were first planted in 1819 but it took more than 150 years for New Zealanders to discover that their country's cool, MARITIME CLIMATE was suitable for high-quality wine production. Although production is small by world standards (one-tenth of Australia's relatively small wine output), vines are now grown on about 35,000 ha/86,450 acres (an increase of almost 60% between 2007 and 2013) in nine regions spanning 1,200 km/720 miles, almost the full length of the country's North and South Islands.

History

MISSIONARIES were responsible for New Zealand's first grapevines, planted by an Englishman, the Reverend Samuel Marsden, at Kerikeri on the far north east coast of the North Island in 1819. There is no record of Marsden making wine. That honour belongs to the first British resident, James BUSBY, who established a vineyard at nearby Waitangi in 1836 and subsequently sold his wine to the British troops.

New Zealand's early English working-class settlers preferred BEER to wine, their thirst founding and sustaining a substantial brewing industry. (The country's annual per capita consumption of beer still exceeds 70 l/18 gal per capita, while that of wine is just over 20 l.).

The wine industry has experienced a roller-coaster ride during its relatively brief history. Nature has played a part in its fortunes, thanks to pests such as PHYLLOXERA and diseases such as POWDERY MILDEW, but government policy has had by far the most significant impact. Economic peaks include the growth years 1890–1910, when New Zealand wine managed to capture 25% of the country's total wine consumption (imports, especially from Australia, have long dominated); the Second World War years when visiting American troops offered a new and affluent market; and the period ever since 1958 after the government raised the duty on beer, spirits, and imported wine, and restricted the importation of wine.

Significant developments in wine quality include the era of New Zealand's first government viticulturist, Romeo BRAGATO, who made improvements between 1895 and 1909 despite the ravages of phylloxera; the gradual replacement of AMERICAN HYBRIDS with European VINIFERA varieties from the late 1960s; the first vines planted in the Marlborough region in 1973; the founding of the official trade body the Wine Institute of New Zealand (now NZ Winegrowers) in 1975; the prohibition of wine dilution (as recently as 1983); and the Closer Economic Relations agreement with Australia, which, from 1990, forced New Zealand winemakers to compete against wines imported from Australia without the protection of tariffs.

Troughs in the economic fortunes of the wine industry are as common as peaks. Low points have included the damaging effect of the temperance movement between 1910 and 1919. New Zealand voted for national PROHIBITION by a narrow margin in 1919 but the votes of returning servicemen tipped the balance. The post-war economic depression had a predictably adverse effect on the wine industry. As one winemaker put it, 'We had to sell the grapes to get the money to buy the sugar to make the wine' (see CHAPTALIZATION). From 1945 to 1958 a flood of imports severely affected the viability of local winemaking and encouraged the industry to band together and lobby the government for relief, a move which ultimately resulted in significant protection. The rapid expansion of vineyards and a large harvest in 1983 led to a wine surplus, and heavy discounting in 1985 and 1986. The government intervened with a sponsored VINE PULL SCHEME in 1986, which meant that one-quarter of the country's vines were uprooted.

Troughs in national wine quality occurred after powdery mildew first appeared in 1876, and after the identification of phylloxera in 1895. In most of the rest of the world, vine-growers chose immunity from this voracious root louse by grafting European grape varieties onto American phylloxera-resistant ROOTSTOCKS. Their counterparts in New Zealand chose a second option: they simply planted phylloxera-resistant American hybrids. In 1960, the American ISABELLA vine, nicknamed Albany Surprise, was New Zealand's most widely planted grape variety.

Until 1881 wineries were not able to sell wine directly to the public but had to channel their produce through hotels, the country's only liquor outlets. Both hotels and wineries had to

daily average temperature above 10 °C/50 °F during the vine-growing season, New Zealand qualifies as Region I (along with BORDEAUX and BURGUNDY). This system ignores diurnal and seasonal TEMPERATURE VARIABILITY, however, and the largely MARITIME CLIMATE of New Zealand is very different from the CONTINENTAL climate of Burgundy. Bordeaux, with its proximity to the sea, is a closer match, in climate at least, to the North Island region of Hawke's Bay, which happens to produce New Zealand's finest Cabernet Sauvignon.

New Zealand is a green and pleasant land thanks to abundant RAINFALL throughout most of the country. Plentiful rain promotes good pastures but it can have a negative effect on wine quality, particularly during the critical RIPENING period. Excessive moisture, through poorly drained soils or heavy rainfall, encourages leaf and shoot growth. Dense vine CANOPIES tend to shade innermost leaves and grape bunches to produce green, HERBACEOUS flavours, to delay ripening, and to promote FUNGAL DISEASES. Excessive vine VIGOUR was one of New Zealand's major viticultural hindrances until Dr Richard Smart (this book's viticulture editor) preached the gospel of CANOPY MANAGEMENT during his tenure as government viticulturist between 1982 and 1990. As a result, many winemakers with vines that had produced excessively vegetal Cabernet Sauvignon reds and Sauvignon Blanc whites were able to make higher-quality wines within a single vintage of applying canopy management techniques. Some growers in the Marlborough region claimed that their HARVEST had been advanced by as much as seven days. Dr Smart's canopy management techniques made by far the greatest contribution to improved New Zealand wine quality during the 1980s.

Chief preoccupation of New Zealand vinegrowers in the 1990s was VINEYARD SITE SELECTION. New Zealand viticulture was for many years centred on the principal city of Auckland, an important market with one-third of the country's population. Between 1960 and 1983, wine production rose from 4.1 million l to 57.7 million l (15.2 million gal). New Zealand, it was claimed, had the fastest growing wine production in the world. In the late 1960s and early 1970s, the flat, fertile Gisborne River valley usurped Auckland's status as New Zealand's largest wine region. High yields of often relatively lowly grapes such as MÜLLER-THURGAU helped satisfy the nation's thirst for fresh, fruity, and slightly sweet table wine. Later, as PHYLLOXERA devastated Gisborne's grape crop and as demand for higher-quality wines increased, Hawke's Bay became the country's leading wine region. In 1990, Marlborough overtook Hawke's Bay and 23 years later had more than five times Hawke's Bay's productive vineyard area.

sell a minimum of 9 l/2.4 gal to every customer. From 1955, specialist wine shops were allowed to sell single bottles of New Zealand table wine, although the allocation of licences was carefully controlled. In 1960, restaurants were allowed to sell wine. A BYO licence was introduced in 1976 to allow diners to take their own wine to restaurants. Supermarkets were granted a licence to sell local and imported wine (but not beer or spirits) from 1990. Beer has been sold in supermarkets since 1999.

Geography and climate
New Zealand grows the world's most southerly grapes and, less significantly, the world's most easterly, thanks to an adjacent dateline. A parallel is sometimes made between the southern latitudes of New Zealand's wine regions and those of famous European regions. If New Zealand were in the northern hemisphere, the country would stretch from North Africa to Paris but the moderating influence of the Gulf Stream on European vineyards results in hotter growing conditions than in the vineyards of equivalent southern LATITUDES.

A broad climatic distinction can be made between the warmer North Island regions and those in the cooler South Island, although significant climatic differences exist within the five to six degree latitude span of each island. Under the imperfect HEAT SUMMATION measure of the

Viticulture

New Zealand's remote location has not, as it has done in CHILE, provided a barrier against the importation of vineyard pests and diseases. Phylloxera still threatens around one-tenth of the country's vines which are planted on their own, UNGRAFTED root while FANLEAF DEGENERATION and LEAFROLL VIRUSES have a detrimental effect on both the quality and quantity of the country's grape crop. Both are symptoms of an industry which has grown faster than the availability of grafted rootstock and virus indexed vines (see INDEXING). Strict QUARANTINE is of course enforced, and easily enforceable, on imported plant material.

As explained above, New Zealand has come to be regarded as a cradle of knowledge about canopy management techniques, and New Zealand VITICULTURISTS, like their winemaking colleagues, are able usefully to spend the New Zealand winter in northern hemisphere wine regions during their growing season. New Zealand's harvest generally takes place from February to May (and sometimes as late as June in parts of Central Otago).

New Zealand's vine-growers are free to IRRIGATE and there are no restrictions on PRUNING or YIELDS, which average about 70 hl/ha (3.6 tons/acre) nationally.

Much of the viticultural equipment has to be imported from Europe, but New Zealand technicians have even developed their own specialist equipment such as the Gallagher leaf-plucking machine (see LEAF REMOVAL) and MECHANIZED pruning equipment. As increasing attention is paid to the selection of vineyard sites (and land in New Zealand is relatively inexpensive), the wine industry may begin to reach its full potential. Flatlands viticulture is the norm in a country where land is plentiful, but wine PRICES now justify the additional expense and trouble involved in establishing HILLSIDE VINEYARDS.

Vine varieties

Sauvignon Blanc, the variety for which New Zealand established an international reputation, is the country's most planted variety (20,027 ha/49,488 acres in 2014) with Pinot Noir a distant second (5,569 ha/13,761 acres). A significant percentage of the Pinot Noir crop is destined for sparkling wine production. Chardonnay is in third place (3,211 ha), followed closely by rising star, Pinot Gris (2,412 ha). Merlot has declined in the last decade (1,256 ha). Plantings of Riesling (787 ha), the sixth most planted variety, continue to grow slowly (they have declined from 968 ha in 2010 and the growth now is barely perceptible, unchanged since 2013) as the often slightly sweet and frequently very good wine made from it battles to lose its unfashionable image in the local market place. Other varieties planted on a total of more than

100 ha/250 acres are, in declining order, Syrah, Gewürztraminer (often spelt without the umlaut), Cabernet Sauvignon, Malbec, and Cabernet Franc. All vine materials are screened for VIRUS DISEASES by an official government-run agency, and the number of CLONES available from the country's nurseries is considerably more limited than, for example, in Europe.

Winemaking

The youthful and dynamic New Zealand wine industry has been greatly influenced by Australia's ADELAIDE University, which provided training, and personnel, for many New Zealand winemakers. In recent years, however, local universities and technical institutes have begun to offer courses in viticulture and oenology. These include LINCOLN University, Blenheim Poly-Tech, Massey University, Hawke's Bay Poly-Tech, and Gisborne Poly-Tech. Auckland University now offers an MSc in Wine Science. Traditional winemaking techniques from benchmark European wine regions have also been adopted, however. The country's southern hemisphere location has had a positive effect on the development of wine styles and winemaking techniques. Many young New Zealand winemakers choose to work a second annual vintage in Europe and gain a wider perspective on the world of wine (see FLYING WINEMAKERS). A reverse migration of mostly young French winemakers has a similar effect.

The country's isolation does have disadvantages, however, such as adding to the cost of importing highly fashionable new oak BARRIQUES from France (or at the very least from the nearest cooperage in Australia). An efficient domestic STAINLESS STEEL industry, however, developed to serve New Zealand's dairy industry, has provided economy and ingenuity in winery tank design.

Winemakers in New Zealand operate relatively free from regulatory constraint, with ACIDIFICATION, DEACIDIFICATION, and ENRICHMENT all permitted. It is a remarkable tribute to the ambitions of the industry, especially abroad, that overall wine quality is as high as it is.

In 2001, a small number of winemakers adopted the SCREWCAP as a closure instead of traditional cork. They created an organization The Screwcap Initiative to assist members with any technical aspects of application and to promote the new seal to an often sceptical market locally and in export markets. Twelve years later, 99% of all New Zealand wine bottles were sealed with a screwcap.

New Zealanders for long tended to worship the winemaker rather than the vineyard, although interest in subregions, notably in Marlborough and Central Otago, is fast increasing. This NEW WORLD phenomenon is in direct contrast to the French view of the

primacy of TERROIR. A decade or two will no doubt reveal the ephemeral nature of winemakers and the permanence of geography, but until that time, New Zealand winemakers will continue to be revered by an adoring domestic public.

Industry organization

The industry is dominated by PERNOD RICARD NZ whose leading brand is BRANCOTT ESTATE; the Villa Maria/Vidals/Esk Valley group; the Nobilo Group, which is part of ACCOLADE; Matua, which is part of TREASURY WINE ESTATES; and Oyster Bay. The large wineries rely on fruit bought in from the country's grape-growers although many supplement their own grapes with grapes grown under contract.

As in other New World wine-producing countries such as ARGENTINA and AUSTRALIA, many wineries have traditionally been located far from vineyards, and the development of South Island wine regions, separated from many winery headquarters by the treacherous Cook Strait, has only exacerbated this phenomenon in New Zealand. Increasing attention to field CRUSHING facilities, and the construction of wineries, or at least PRESSING stations, closer to the vineyards, was a notable development during the 1990s.

Exports to Australia, where some of the biggest-selling white wine brands are from New Zealand, overtook those to the UK in 2013 with exports to the US catching up fast.

Wine regions

See map. They are listed below in declining importance by volume of wine grown.

Marlborough Marlborough is by far the biggest of New Zealand's wine regions. Industry giant Montana (see BRANCOTT ESTATE) planted the first vines in Marlborough when it established the South Island's first commercial vineyard in 1973. At the time it seemed an enormous gamble but after the vines reached full production Montana's investment returned a handsome dividend in terms of quality and profit. Other producers soon followed to establish wineries in the region or to secure a supply of grapes for the 18-hour journey north to Auckland or Gisborne. The single wine that put Marlborough Sauvignon Blanc on the international map was CLOUDY BAY, in 1985. Since 1989, winemakers based outside the region have been able to use the services of a growing number of CUSTOM CRUSH FACILITIES to process grapes into juice or wine which can then be transported in bulk with less risk of extracting astringent PHENOLICS from grape skins. The availability of contract winemaking facilities has encouraged an increasing number of vine-growers to process part or all of their crop into wine for sale under their own label.

Marlborough, at the north eastern tip of the South Island, consists of a large, flat, river valley with deep deposits of silt and gravel. A number of soil patterns are found throughout the valley and even within single vineyards, leading to significant variations in quality and style depending on the grape source. Shallow, stony soils, which aid DRAINAGE and limit fertility, are favoured for high-quality wine production although some of the region's best Pinot Noir is from heavier, clay-rich soils at the base of the Wither Hills. Irrigation is widely used throughout the valley to establish vines in the sometimes arid, free-draining soils and to relieve vine stress during the typically dry Marlborough summer. Many of Marlborough's best wines are made from irrigated grapes, which, it is claimed, would have suffered a loss in quality if the vines were forced to rely on a natural supply of ground water. Three subregions are now gaining increased recognition. The northern Wairau Valley's lighter, stonier soils tend to make riper and often more pungent wines. The Southern Valley's richer soils produce richer and more concentrated wines, while the cooler, lower-cropping Awatere Valley would be the country's second-largest if it were a region in its own right.

Sauvignon Blanc is Marlborough's best-known and most planted variety. These pungent, aromatic wines that blend tropical fruit flavours with gooseberry and capsicum herbaceousness are regarded as representative of New Zealand's national wine style. The scramble to meet growing world demand for Marlborough Sauvignon Blanc combined with an unexpectedly bloated 2008 crop resulted in a drop in grape, vineyard land, and export prices causing financial hardship for many producers. Sauvignon Blanc accounts for more than 80% of the country's exports while Marlborough has nearly 90% of the country's vines. In the early years of this century Marlborough Sauvignon Blanc enjoyed particular success in Australia where it captured 40% of the white wine market, to the annoyance of local wine producers. Marlborough Pinot Noir has overtaken Chardonnay to become the region's second most planted grape variety, and a small but growing proportion of the Marlborough Pinot and Chardonnay crop is used in traditional method SPARKLING WINE production. Pinot Gris, whose NZ wines tend to follow the richer Alsace style than the Italian Pinot Grigio model, has risen rapidly to follow closely in Chardonnay's wake, although growth appears to have tapered off. Riesling is another very successful Marlborough vine variety, reaching its apogee as a sweet, luscious, botrytis-affected dessert wine. BOTRYTIZED wines can be produced here most years although the results vary considerably with vintage conditions.

Hawke's Bay around the town of Napier is one of New Zealand's older wine regions and certainly one of the best. Complex soil patterns and MESOCLIMATES make it difficult to generalize about the wines of such a diverse region, particularly when they are made by such an eclectic group of winemakers. Situated on the east coast of the North Island, 215 km/130 miles south of Gisborne and 323 km/194 miles north of Wellington, Hawke's Bay frequently records the country's highest sunshine hours. The terrain varies from coastal ranges that rise to 1600 m/ 5,300 ft to wide, fertile plains consisting of alluvial and gravelly soils. A high water table and fertile soils can result in excessive vine vigour over much of the plains. In other parts of the region, deep, well-drained gravel soils encourage WATER STRESS and many vines require irrigation during long, dry periods. In pursuit of wine quality, vineyards were established on free-draining soils of lower fertility, at least from the mid 1980s. For ease of cultivation, vines have been almost exclusively planted on flat land, despite the allure of nearby limestone hills which may offer superior aspect and DRAINAGE. A collective of local grape growers and winemakers has identified an approximate 800 ha of deep shingle soils as an ideal area for the production of high-quality wines, particularly Syrah, Merlot, and Cabernet Sauvignon. The defined area has been named Gimblett Gravels, a district name that now appears on some of Hawke's Bay's better red wines.

Chardonnay and Merlot are the most planted Hawke's Bay varieties, with Sauvignon Blanc close behind. The best Hawke's Bay reds are a blend of Merlot and Cabernet Sauvignon, often with Cabernet Franc and/or Malbec playing a supporting role. They have intense berry and cassis flavours, often with a gently HERBACEOUS reminder of their moderately COOL CLIMATE origin and, sometimes, strong OAK influence from up to two years' maturation in new French BARRIQUES. The exalted status of BORDEAUX BLENDS is being tested by a small but rapidly expanding volume of Syrah, which at its best can perform with distinction. Hawke's Bay Chardonnay may lack the seductive charm of the Gisborne equivalent but the best have intense citrus flavours and a brooding elegance that are seldom matched by the wines of other regions. Hawke's Bay Sauvignon Blanc is a softer, fleshier wine than the better-known Marlborough Sauvignon Blanc. It often has a nectarine or stone fruit character, a useful indicator of regional identity.

Central Otago Central Otago grows New Zealand's, and the world's, most southerly grapevines, some of them cultivated south of the 45th parallel. It is New Zealand's only wine region with a CONTINENTAL climate, providing greater diurnal and seasonal TEMPERATURE VARIABILITY than any other. Most Central Otago vines are planted on HILLSIDE VINEYARDS to give better sun exposure and reduce frost risk. No other New Zealand wine region is as dependent on a single grape variety. Pinot Noir represents nearly 75% of the region's vines with Pinot Gris a distant second and Riesling in third place; this is one of New Zealand's very few Sauvignon Blanc-free zones. The growth in vineyard area, and development of new districts within the larger region, have been extraordinary. The now crowded valley at Gibbston was, with Wanaka, one of the orginal areas to be planted with vines as recently as the early 1980s. Bannockburn is widely regarded as the most successful district although subsequently planted vineyards in the Cromwell/Bendigo and Alexandra districts may challenge Bannockburn's crown. Central Otago's often voluptuous and intensely fruity Pinot Noir has helped put New Zealand red wine on the world map. The wines from this youthful and very experimental area have evolved rapidly in quality with potential for further gain.

Gisborne Total plantings in this east coast North Island region peaked in 2009, not least because of its dependence on once-popular Chardonnay when Pernod Ricard NZ decided that the future lay in Sauvignon Blanc. Gisborne Chardonnay is certainly the country's most distinctive regional example of the variety, with soft and charming fruit flavours that often resemble ripe peach, pineapple, and melon. Gewürztraminer is Gisborne's other claim to vinous fame. Pernod Ricard NZ sold off its large Gisborne winery and cancelled grape contracts there. Most Gisborne grapes are grown by farmers who sell them to wineries under long-term contract, or to the highest bidder. Several Auckland wineries buy Gisborne grapes and ship juice or wine to avoid extraction of unwanted PHENOLICS that might result from shipping grapes.

At the other end of the production scale are many small LIFESTYLE WINERIES that make only premium bottled table wine or TRADITIONAL METHOD sparkling wines. They include Millton Vineyards, New Zealand's first certified ORGANIC winery, which now produces grapes and wine according to the principles of BIODYNAMICS.

Canterbury/Waipara Canterbury, around Christchurch on the central east coast of the South Island, represents a collection of mostly small and very diverse subregions. Waipara, one hour's drive north of Christchurch, is by far the largest while each of Banks Peninsula to the east of the city, the plains west of Christchurch, the Cheviot Hills 40 minutes north of Waipara, and the limestone-rich Waikari Basin 15 minutes north west of Waipara have just a few producers each or, in the case of Cheviot Hills, a single winery. The region is cool and dry with a moderate risk of October and April FROSTS. Low rainfall and light soils of moderate fertility help control vine vigour and canopy here. Viticultural research at LINCOLN has had a considerable influence on selecting suitable vine varieties for the local growing conditions and in assisting local growers with viticultural techniques. Sauvignon Blanc and Pinot Noir are, yet again, the region's most planted varieties, with Pinot Gris in third place.

Nelson Nelson is the South Island's most northerly wine region, nearly two hours' drive across high ranges from Marlborough. The rolling hills of Nelson rise from a scenic coastline to form a beautiful setting for the region's 38 wineries. Sauvignon Blanc has overtaken Chardonnay to become the region's main grape variety, thanks to world demand for this varietal. Pinot Noir and Pinot Gris are second and third respectively with Chardonnay a distant fourth. The varied topography of Nelson makes it difficult to generalize about weather and soils, although records show that the region is slightly cooler and wetter than the Marlborough average.

Wairarapa/Martinborough Wairarapa, which includes the Martinborough region, is at the southern end of the North Island about one hour's drive from the nation's capital, Wellington. In 2012, Wairarapa had less than 3% of the country's vines but 9% of its winemakers. They are typically small-scale, LIFESTYLE producers with a quality-at-all-costs attitude to winemaking and a passionate faith in their region's potential. Pinot Noir occupies half the region's vineyard area and is undoubtedly the flagship wine. In their quest to make great wine, most producers crop their vines so that YIELDS are considerably below the national average, a significant factor in the region's success. In terms of topography, climate, and soils, Wairarapa might easily be considered a miniature Marlborough, were it not for the region's ability to make top-quality reds on a regular basis.

Auckland Auckland, the largest city, gives its name to the one New Zealand wine region where winery visitors can be assured of finding wines made from grapes grown as far south as Canterbury in the South Island, and are more likely to be offered wine from Marlborough and Hawke's Bay than the product of a local vineyard. Auckland viticulture declined during the rapid growth of Gisborne, Hawke's Bay, and Marlborough through the 1970s and 1980s but began to grow in the 1990s as grape-growers adopted canopy-thinning techniques to correct vine vigour. New subregions, including Clevedon, Matakana, and especially Waiheke Island, where some very fine BORDEAUX BLENDS are made, are now producing high-quality and highly fashionable reds which have

helped raise Auckland's profile and esteem as a wine region.

Northland Northland, at the very northern tip of the country, was the birthplace of New Zealand wine. The region's warm, wet, temperate climate has proved to be a barrier to good-quality wine production, particularly on the wetter west coast. Modern viticultural methods and careful site selection have allowed several producers to establish relatively rot-resistant varieties such as Cabernet Sauvignon and Syrah with promising results.

Waitaki on LIMESTONE in North Otago was rapidly being developed in the mid 2000s. That development has slowed although the quality of Waitaki's Pinot Noir and Pinot Gris may stimulate further growth.   R.F.C.

Cooper, M., *Wine Atlas of New Zealand* (Auckland, 2008).

Saker, J., *Pinot Noir: The New Zealand Story* (Auckland, 2010) .

Thomson, J., *The Wild Bunch* (Auckland 2012).

www.nzwine.com (NZ Winegrowers website).

www.nzwine.com

www.gisbornewine.co.nz

www.winehawkesbay.co.nz

www.winesfrommartinborough.com

www.canterburywine.co.nz

www.cowa.org.nz

www.centralotagopinot.co.nz

www.wine-marlborough.co.nz

www.winenelson.co.nz

Neyret, **Neret**, or **Neiret**, rare, dark-berried vine, strictly **Neret di Saint-Vincent**, still found in VALLE D'AOSTA and likely to be related to several transalpine varieties.

Niagara, American hybrid grown successfully in NEW YORK state. This VITIS *labrusca* variety is vigorous, productive, and withstands low temperatures well. Known as the white answer to CONCORD, one of its parents, it makes wines with a particularly FOXY flavour. It was created in Niagara, New York, in 1866 and is now planted widely in New York state, Canada, and Brazil. For details of Niagara, Canada, see ONTARIO.

Nieddera, promising Sardinian red wine grape.

Niederösterreich, or Lower AUSTRIA, is the state in which well over half of the country's vineyards are situated. In it are the wine regions CARNUNTUM, KAMPTAL, KREMSTAL, THERMENREGION, TRAISENTAL, WACHAU, WAGRAM, and WEINVIERTEL. Since the names Kamptal, Kremstal, Traisental, and Weinviertel between 2002 and 2008 became those of official DAC appellations of origin reserved for wines made from Grüner Veltliner or (in the first three of these) Riesling, wines made

from other varieties are labelled simply Niederösterreich, guaranteeing this name a prominence that it did not previously enjoy.   D.S.

Nielluccio, Corsica's name for SANGIOVESE, probably brought there by the GENOESE who ruled the island until the late 18th century. Often blended with SCIACARELLO (Mammolo), it constitutes an increasing proportion of the island's APPELLATION CONTRÔLÉE reds and, particularly, rosés, for which it is especially suitable. It is the principal ingredient in Patrimonio, on whose clay-limestone soils it thrives. It buds early and ripens late and is therefore susceptible to late frosts in spring and rot during the harvest.

nitrogen, mineral element and inert colourless, odourless, tasteless gas that is extremely useful in both grape-growing and winemaking. Nitrogen gas is an inert constituent of the atmosphere, making up 78% by volume. In its combined forms, nitrogen is an essential element in AMINO ACIDS, PROTEINS, and ENZYMES, without which life could not exist. In soil, it is an important constituent of ORGANIC MATTER, from which it is released during decomposition in the form of ammonium ions. Although these ions are taken up by plant roots, much of the ammonium is oxidized by specialist soil bacteria to nitrate ions, which are also absorbed by roots. Ammonium and nitrate compounds are important constituents of many FERTILIZERS.

Viticulture

Nitrogen has a major impact on vineyard VIGOUR, and potentially on wine quality. Nitrogen is essential for vine growth and is one of the three major elements, along with POTASSIUM and PHOSPHORUS, needed most for plant growth. It is an important component of proteins, and also of chlorophyll. The most common symptoms of nitrogen deficiency, which can be expected on sandy soils low in organic matter, are reduced vigour and uniformly pale green or yellow leaves. Soil and plant tests can be used as a guide to the use of nitrogen fertilizers.

Much more caution is needed with vines than with most other plants in applying nitrogen fertilizers, or large amounts of manure, or planting in soils naturally rich in nitrogen. The use of COVER CROPS containing clover and other legumes should also be monitored carefully as they might add excessive nitrogen to the vineyard soil.

Whatever the origin, too much nitrogen in a vineyard results in excessive vegetative vine growth, termed high vigour. Such vineyards typically show higher YIELDS than low-vigour vines and reduced quality owing to the SHADE effects. CANOPY MANAGEMENT procedures may be used to overcome some of these effects, but will not eliminate them completely. Vineyards with excessive nitrogen supplies are also prone to

n

poor FRUIT SET (COULURE, for example) and are more susceptible to BOTRYTIS BUNCH ROT. Excessive nitrogen is also considered to have a direct and negative effect on red wine quality, reducing SUGARS, COLOUR, and PHENOLICS, and increasing ACIDITY. High nitrogen levels in the soil also lead to increased wine levels of urea, ethyl CARBAMATES, and HISTAMINES. In some parts of Europe such as Germany, excessive nitrogen fertilization of vineyards has led to pollution of water supplies with nitrates, which may pose hazards to human health.

A feature of vineyards producing high fruit quality is that they have a restricted supply of nitrogen. Along with WATER STRESS, this is one of two important checks on vine growth which result in the vine BALANCE that is essential for premium wine quality. All grass or cereal cover crops can be grown to use up soil-rich supplies of nitrogen, and so make it less available to vines.

On the other hand, severe nitrogen deficiency is equally disadvantageous to quality, especially for white wines. Fruit from nitrogen-deficient vineyards can be lower in fermentable SUGARS and may also result in STUCK FERMENTATIONS, with the concomitant risk of forming undesirable SULFIDES. See also ATYPICAL AGEING.

R.E.S. & R.E.W.

Winemaking

In combination with phosphorus and potassium, nitrogen can serve as a critical factor in YEAST growth and therefore FERMENTATION, notably in HOME WINEMAKING of FRUIT WINES. Ammonium ions, primary amino acids, and small peptides, but not the secondary amino acids proline and hydroxyproline, are the principal forms of nitrogen present in grapes that can be used by yeast; these nitrogen components constitute what is often referred to as yeast assimilable nitrogen (YAN). Simple tests have only recently been developed for measuring YAN so that a deficiency of this essential yeast nutrient can now be easily determined. When a deficiency occurs, an ammonium salt, usually DIAMMONIUM PHOSPHATE (DAP), is often added. Nitrogen can also affect wine composition: in high concentrations it is associated with intensified AROMAS, while low concentrations favour the formation of HYDROGEN SULFIDE.

Obtained by fractional DISTILLATION of liquid air, nitrogen in both gaseous and liquid forms is a major commercial product used in a wide range of industrial activities. As ammonia, it is the starting material for most fertilizer mixtures. In liquid form, it has myriad uses in REFRIGERATION. In pure gas form, it is used to prevent a wide range of sensitive products from coming into contact with oxygen. Wine is just one of these.

Nitrogen as an inert gas is extremely useful to the winemaker in filling the head space in closed stainless steel tanks and bottles (see SPARGING and LEFTOVER WINE). Experiments have shown that if a bladder PRESS is enclosed in nitrogen, white wines are fresher and more fragrant and have higher levels of antioxidants (see wine and HEALTH). Nitrogen is more expensive but more effective than INERT GAS MIXTURE at preserving wine from potential harmful contact with oxygen.

A.D.W.

Bell, S.-J., and Henschke, P. A., 'Implications of nitrogen nutrition for grapes, fermentation and wine', *Australian Journal of Grape and Wine Research*, 11 (2005), 242–95.

Peyrot des Gachons, C., et al., 'The influence of water and nitrogen deficit on fruit ripening and aroma potential of *Vitis vinifera* L. cv Sauvignon blanc in field conditions', *Journal of the Science of Food and Agriculture*, 85/1 (2005), 73–85.

Rantz, J. M. (ed.), 'Nitrogen in grapes and wine', Proc. Int. Symposium, Seattle, June 1991, *American Society for Enology and Viti*culture (Davis, Calif., 1991).

Rantz, J. M. (ed.), *Proceedings of the International Symposium on Nitrogen in Grapes and Wine*, Seattle, June 1991, *American Society for Enology and Viticulture* (Davis, Calif., 1991).

White, R. E., *Understanding Vineyard Soils* (2nd edn, Oxford, 2015).

NMR. See NUCLEAR MAGNETIC RESONANCE.

Noah, seminal figure in the history of wine according to the BIBLE. See also ORIGINS OF VINICULTURE.

Noah is also the name of a relatively undistinguished AMERICAN HYBRID. It is particularly hardy and was once widely grown in France and eastern Europe. See HONDARRIBI.

noble rot, also known as *pourriture noble* in French, *Edelfäule* in German, *muffa* in Italian, and sometimes simply as botrytis, is the benevolent form of BOTRYTIS BUNCH ROT, in which the *Botrytis cinerea* fungus attacks ripe, undamaged white wine grapes and, given the right weather, can result in extremely sweet grapes which may look disgusting but have undergone such a complex transformation that they are capable of producing probably the world's finest, and certainly the longest-living, sweet wines. Indeed, the defining factor of a great VINTAGE for sweet white wine in areas specializing in its production is the incidence of noble rot. The malevolent form, which results if the grapes are damaged, unripe, or conditions are unfavourable, is known as GREY ROT.

Ideal conditions for the development of noble rot are a TEMPERATE CLIMATE in which the humidity associated with early morning mists that favour the development of the fungus is followed by warm, sunny autumn afternoons in which the grapes are dried and the progress of the fungus is restrained. In cloudy conditions in which the humidity is unchecked, the fungus may spread so rapidly that the grape skins split and the grapes succumb to grey rot. If, however, the weather is unremittingly hot and dry, then the fungus will not develop at all and the grapes will simply accumulate sugar rather than undergoing the chemical transformations associated with noble rot, so the result is less complex SWEET WINE.

In favourable conditions, the botrytis fungus *Botrytis cinerea* spreads unpredictably from grape to grape and bunch to bunch in different parts of the vineyard, penetrating the skins of whole, ripe grapes with filaments which leave minute brown spots on the skin but leave the skin impenetrable by other, harmful micro-organisms. The grapes turn golden, then pink or purple, and then, when they are in a severely dehydrated state, they turn brown, shrivel to a sort of moist raisin, and may seem to be covered with a fine grey powder that looks like ash (to which the word *cinerea* refers). It can take anywhere between five and 15 days to reach this stage, known in French as *pourri rôti*, literally 'roasted rot'. It is almost incredible that such unappetizing-looking grapes can produce such sublime wine, and there have been many instances in which nobly rotten grapes have been discarded, or at least unrecognized, in wine regions unfamiliar with the phenomenon.

These visible changes are an outward sign of the extraordinary changes that occur inside the grape. More than half of the grape's water content is lost due either directly to the action of the fungus or to loss by evaporation as the skins eventually deteriorate. Meanwhile, *Botrytis cinerea* consumes both the SUGAR IN GRAPES and, especially, ACIDS, so that the overall effect is to increase the sugar concentration, or MUST WEIGHT, considerably in an ever-decreasing quantity of juice. The fungus typically reduces a grape's sugar content by a third or more, but reduces the TOTAL ACIDITY by approximately 70%; TARTARIC ACID is generally degraded more than the usually less important MALIC ACID. In BOTRYTIZED wines, most of any balancing acidity is more often due to the concentration of acidity in the shrivelled but non-botrytized berries that are harvested, and then fermented, at the same time.

While it metabolizes these sugars and acids, the fungus forms a wide range of chemical compounds in the grape juice, including GLYCEROL (quite apart from that formed by alcoholic fermentation), ACETIC ACID, gluconic acid, various ENZYMES especially LACCASE and PECTINASE, as well as the yeast-inhibiting glycoprotein dubbed 'botryticine', which limits yeast growth and increases the production of acetic acid and glycerol during fermentation. The PHENOLICS in the grape skins are also broken down by the fungus so that the TANNIN content of the juice is significantly reduced. In sum, botrytized grape juice is very different from regular grape juice, and not just because of its intense levels of sugar. Masuda et al. identified SOTOLON as a contributor to the aroma of botrytized wines.

It is unusual for all grapes on a vine, or even on a single bunch, to be affected in exactly the same way, to exactly the same effect, and at exactly the same speed, which is why the HAR-VEST of a botrytis-affected vineyard can necessitate several passages, or TRIES, during which individual bunches, or parts of them, are picked at optimum infection level, and grapes affected by grey rot may have to be eliminated.

Weather conditions other than alternating early mists and warm afternoons can result in a satisfactory noble rot infection. In cold, wet weather, noble rot may form at a reasonable rate on fully ripe grapes, and grey rot be kept at bay. Wind can help to dehydrate the grapes and concentrate the sugars.

See SAUTERNES for details of common weather patterns there. See BOTRYTIZED WINES for details of where and how they are made, and their history.

Masuda, M., et al., 'Identification of 4,5-dimethyl-3-hydroxy-2(5H)-furanone (Sotolon) and ethyl 9-hydroxynonanoate in botrytised wine and evaluation of the roles of compounds characteristic of it', *Agricultural and Biological Chemistry*, 48/11 (1984), 2707–10.

Olney, R., *Yquem* (London, 1986).

Ribéreau-Gayon, P., et al., *Traité d'Œnologie 1: Microbiologie du vin: Vinifications* (Paris, 1998), translated by J. M. Branco, as *Handbook of Enology 1: The Microbiology of Wine and Vinifications* (Chichester, 2000), 255–66.

Nobling is a 1940 cross of Silvaner × Gutedel (Chasselas) that has declined in importance even in Baden, where all its 56 ha/138 acres grew in 2012. Wines are relatively neutral.

node, the part of a plant's stem at which a leaf is attached. In the grapevine, this zone is swollen and bears the leaf winter BUD and LATERAL SHOOT. TENDRILS or INFLORESCENCES are also borne at nodes on the side opposite to the bud.   B.G.C.

Noir, French for black and therefore a common suffix for dark-berried vine varieties.

Noirien is the most common eco-geogroup of related VINE VARIETIES, those found primarily in north eastern France that are related to or closely associated with Pinot Noir: notably Pinot Gris, Pinot Blanc, Auxerrois, Chardonnay, Melon, and Gamay Noir.

Robinson, J., Harding, J., and Vouillamoz, J., *Wine Grapes, a complete guide to 1,368 vine varieties, including their origins and flavours* (London, 2012).

non-alcoholic wine is a term sometimes used for wine with an ALCOHOLIC STRENGTH of less than 0.5%. For more details, see DEALCOHOL-IZED WINE.

non-vintage, often abbreviated to NV, a blended wine, particularly champagne or sparkling wine, which may contain the produce of several different VINTAGES, although in champagne-making practice it is usually substantially based on the most recent vintage, to which some additional ingredients from older years, often called 'reserve wines', may be added.

Some mass-market wines are sold without a vintage year and are in practice a blend made throughout the year so that the first blend of the winter season, typically, may contain a mixture of wine from both the new and last year's vintages.

normalized difference vegetation index (NDVI) is the most widely used indicator of plant biomass in agriculture. In viticulture, NDVI provides a relative measure of the size and density of the CANOPY and therefore correlates with VIGOUR. It is calculated from measures of reflected light at wavebands corresponding to red and infrared light. See also REMOTE SENSING and PLANT CELL DENSITY.   R.G.V.B.

Hall, A., et al., 'Optical remote sensing applications in viticulture—a review', *Australian Journal of Grape and Wine Research*, 8 (2002), 36–47.

North Coast, general CALIFORNIA umbrella region and AVA implying north of San Francisco although it also extends north east from San Francisco into a portion of Solano county. It includes all vineyards in LAKE, MARIN, MENDO-CINO, NAPA, and SONOMA counties and has rather more homogeneous growing conditions than many suspect. The name appears on some relatively prestigious wines assembled from, especially, Napa and Sonoma and also on some pretty ordinary blends.

North East Victoria Zone, wine zone in the Australian state of VICTORIA incorporating the wine regions of Alpine Valleys, Beechworth, Glenrowan, King Valley, and Rutherglen.

Northern Rivers Zone, on the north coast of NEW SOUTH WALES in Australia with one region, Hastings River.

Northern Slopes Zone, Australian wine zone parallel with NORTHERN RIVERS ZONE but on the western (inland) side of the Great Dividing range. The one region, New England, is developing rapidly, in part supplying its own wineries, and in part selling to QUEENSLAND wineries, particularly in the Granite Belt.

North West Victoria Zone comprises the high-yielding, irrigated vineyards of the Murray Darling and Swan Hill regions falling on the VICTORIA side of the Murray river in Australia.

Norton, arguably the only variety of AMERI-CAN VINE SPECIES origin making a premium quality wine. Little known and little grown outside the eastern and midwestern UNITED STATES, Norton is undoubtedly underrated because of entrenched bias against non-VINIFERA varieties. In Arkansas and MISSOURI, it was the mainstay of an extremely important wine industry. Leon D. Adams calls Norton 'the best of all native American red-wine grapes' and praises it for its wines' lack of FOXY character.

The origin of this dark-skinned variety is uncertain, but it takes its name from Dr D. Norton of Richmond, Virginia, a pioneer grape-grower. A recent DNA study has shown that it is a hybrid which has both *Vitis aestivalis* and *Vitis vinifera* (see VITIS) in its pedigree. It is also known as Cynthiana in Missouri, Arkansas, and Virginia.

Norton is tolerant of BUNCH ROTS, and other fungal diseases such as BLACK ROT, ANTHRACNOSE, DOWNY MILDEW, and POWDERY MILDEW, and its roots are tolerant of PHYLLOXERA. The vine is vigorous, and requires a long growing season. The grapes are acidic, but the wine is indistinguishable by taste from wine made from *V. vinifera* grapes. Grapes are very dark coloured and full flavoured, and Norton reliably produces healthy fruit in places with high summer rainfall even without SPRAYING. Chrysalis of Virginia is the Norton specialist.

Adams, L. D., *The Wines of America* (3rd edn, New York and London, 1985).

Norway has a vineyard on the southern coast in Kristiansand, although the Pinot Noir and Riesling vines have difficulty ripening a crop.

nose, the most sensitive form of TASTING equipment so far encountered, the sense of TASTE being so inextricably linked with the sense of smell. When the nose is blocked, whether by a cold or by mechanical means, the ability to taste either food or drink is seriously impaired—so much so that cold sufferers have to resort to decongestants if the need for their tasting skills is serious.

Nose is also used as a synonym for the smell, AROMA, or BOUQUET of a wine, as in wines having 'a nose of raspberries', 'a raspberry nose', or even 'raspberries on the nose'.

Nosiola, the only remaining white grape variety native to TRENTINO in northern Italy. It is grown principally on the hills around the village of Pressano, where it produces dry wines, and in the Valle dei Laghi to the west of Trento, where it is used to produce Vino Santo (see VIN SANTO). The 2010 vine census found only 79 ha/195 acres, but interest in the variety has been revived in recent years as several producers, notably Cesconi, have demonstrated that it can, when made with care, produce fragrant, zippy whites of real interest. DNA PROFILING at SAN MICHELE ALL'ADIGE revealed a surprising parent–offspring relationship with the Swiss RÈZE.

notch grafting, a method of GRAFTING vines that resembles CLEFT GRAFTING. It differs in that the cut trunk is not split across, but instead the scion pieces are cut to fit a V-shaped notch made on either side of the trunk to a length of about 3 cm/1 in. The scion pieces are often tacked into place. Notch grafts are not as secure as cleft grafts. A related method is the bark graft done later in spring when the bark lifts freely, but again the union is sometimes weak. B.G.C.

nouveau, French for new, and a specific style of wine designed to be drunk only weeks rather than months or years after the HARVEST. The most famous and successful nouveau is BEAUJO-LAIS Nouveau, which, at its peak, in 1988, accounted for more than 800,000 hl/21 million gal, or 60% of all Beaujolais produced. The Beaujolais producers themselves are keen to point out that their Nouveaux are not simply *un phénomène 'marketing'*, but that they owe their origins to the 19th century, when the year's wine would complete its fermentation in cask while en route to nearby Lyons, where the new wine provided a direct link with village life in the Beaujolais hills. The phenomenon originated in a group of villages just west of Ville-franche whose wines seemed to mature earliest. After the constraints of the Second World War, the Beaujolais producers were gradually allowed to release an increasing proportion of new wine. The original term was PRIMEUR, meaning 'young produce', and from 1951 the Beaujolais producers were allowed to release their primeurs from 15 December. These young, refreshing wines enjoyed great success in the bistros of Paris in the 1950s and 1960s, and by the end of the 1960s the phrase *Le Beaujolais Nouveau est arrivé* had been coined. In the 1970s, the phenomenon spread outside France, thanks to energetic work on the part of producers such as Georges Duboeuf and his agents around the world, and Alexis LICHINE in the United States. By the end of 1974, Beaujolais Nouveau had reached Great Britain to such an extent that the first Beaujolais Nouveau race (of bottles of purple ink to London) had been run. Eventually the Nouveau was flown, with inexplicable haste and brouhaha, to markets around the world: the craze reaching Australia in 1982 and Japan and Italy in 1985. Initially the release date was fixed at 15 November, but was eventually changed to the third Thursday in November, for the convenience of the wine trade and the media, who for much of the late 1970s and 1980s were apparently fascinated by this event.

The immense commercial success of Beaujo-lais Nouveau inevitably spawned other (much less successful) Nouveaux—infant wines from other regions of France, notably Gamays made in TOURAINE and the ARDÈCHE, a range of wines made in the LANGUEDOC and ROUSSILLON, MUSCADET

and many VINS DE PAYS, particularly Côtes de Gascogne.

Italy has produced a range of similar wines, described as **novello**, and Austria's HEURIGE could be said to be a version of the phenomenon. Many southern hemisphere producers have tried to sell their own early releases as 'Nouveau' because they carry the same year on the label and are available many months before the appearance of Beaujolais Nouveau (which has somewhat diluted the novelty that used to attach to bottles carrying the current vintage year).

Winemaking techniques have to be adapted to produce wines that are ready to drink so early. The majority of Nouveau wines are red and many of them are produced, like Beaujolais, by CARBONIC MACERATION or SEMI-CARBONIC MACERATION, which yields particularly fruity, soft, aromatic red wines suitable for drinking young and slightly cool, typically involving a fermentation of only about four days, and fairly brutal STABILIZATION. Those winemakers who do not or cannot practise any form of carbonic maceration may ferment the grapes traditional-ly but at lower temperatures than usual (in the low 20s °C (*c*.70 °F)) and allow only the briefest of MACERATIONS. White grapes, for which car-bonic maceration is not suitable, are generally fermented very cool, at 15 to 20 °C, and boiled candy aromas typically result.

The great attraction of Nouveau wines for producers is that they produce a financial re-turn so quickly. As one taster remarked, their characteristic aroma is the scent of cash flow. Their appeal for the wine drinker is that they are a refreshing and stimulating reminder of the passing of the seasons, a sort of liquid HARVEST TRADITION. Nouveau wines do not deteriorate in bottle substantially more rapidly than non-Nouveau wines, but their lifespan is inevitably shorter.

Nouvelle, vigorous, productive South Afri-can mid-20th-century cross of CROUCHEN and TREBBIANO Toscano which became popular from the mid 1990s for its ability to add obvious METHOXYPYRAZINE aromas to Cape Sauvignon Blanc. A few hundred hectares had been planted by 2005.

Nova Scotia. Midway between the equator and the North Pole, Nova Scotia in CANADA has a notably short growing season which restricts the number of varieties that can be ripened in the Annapolis Valley and Northumberland Strait. Plantings, which totalled 750 acres in 2014, include local speciality L'ACADIE, Char-donnay, and Pinot Noir (for sparkling wine), Riesling, Vidal, Seyval Blanc, and DeChaunac. The relatively new Tidal Bay appellation has particularly strict regulations. The region is known for classic sparkling, crisp aromatic

whites, late harvest and Icewines, and FRUIT WINES to which four of the 18 wineries are exclusively devoted. T.A.

Aspler, T., and Bergeron, J.-F., *Canadian Wineries* (Toronto, 2012).

www.winesofnovascotia.ca

novello, Italian for new, and therefore a name applied to Italy's deeply forgettable NOUVEAU wine.

nuclear magnetic resonance, NMR, or, more specifically, Site Specific Natural Iso-tope Fractionation by Nuclear Magnetic Reso-nance (SNIF-NMR), was in the mid 1990s the most powerful analytical tool for the AUTHENTI-CATION of alcoholic drinks. It is therefore an important weapon, and deterrent, against ADULTERATION AND FRAUD.

It was developed during the 1980s by Profes-sor Gérard Martin of Nantes University in north-west France and is officially approved as an analytical method both by the EU and, more internationally, by the OIV. This powerful re-search aid has been patented and marketed on a worldwide basis by the EU-funded Eurofins enterprise.

Its strength is that it can examine the precise structure of the ETHANOL molecule in such a way that it drastically reduces the potential for fraud. The principle is based on deuterium, the stable natural isotope of hydrogen, and its distribution in the ethanol molecule. There are three distinct sites of deuterium and NMR can differentiate between these sites, showing the abundance of deuterium in each of them.

The isotopic content of each site is linked to both the origin of the molecule and the condi-tions prior to the production of alcohol, i.e. FERMENTATION, showing the degree of CHAPTAL-IZATION (where the wine was enriched with sugar cane, sugar beet, or GRAPE CONCENTRATE, for example).

One obvious application is proving chaptal-ization in excess of legal limits. Another, much more far-reaching, long-term application has been the establishment of data-banks based on the analysis of representative sample wines from each wine area. This application, based on each region's unique deuterium ratios, can provide an absolute guarantee of geographical authenticity. While it may never be sufficiently detailed to distinguish a Ch LAFITE from a Ch LATOUR, it can distinguish between a BORDEAUX and a BERGERAC. G.T.

Nuits, Côte de, named after the principal town of Nuits-St-Georges, this is the northern half of the escarpment of the CÔTE D'OR, pro-ducing the greatest red wines of Burgundy, from the Pinot Noir grape, and very occasional white wines. The principal villages, from north to south, are GEVREY-CHAMBERTIN, MOREY-ST-DENIS, CHAMBOLLE-MUSIGNY, VOUGEOT, VOSNE-ROMANÉE,

Flagey-ÉCHEZEAUX, and NUITS-ST-GEORGES. See also MARSANNAY. The soils on the lower part of the slope tend to be much more fertile than the main parent rock because more immature soil has been incorporated.

Wines from FIXIN, Brochon, Prémeaux, Comblanchien, and Corgoloin may be sold as **Côte de Nuits-Villages**. These are usually but not exclusively red wines.

See also BEAUNE, CÔTE DE, and the map under BURGUNDY.   J.T.C.M.

Nuits-St-Georges, small market town in
Burgundy giving its name to the Côte de Nuits, the northern half of the Côte d'Or. Nuits-St-Georges has remained fully independent of BEAUNE to the south and Dijon to the north, with numerous NÉGOCIANTS making their headquarters here. The town also boasts its own charity auction, the Hospices de Nuits, held in March, when the wines can be better judged than those of the HOSPICES DE BEAUNE in November.

The appellation Nuits-St-Georges can be divided into three parts. North of Nuits, abutting Vosne, the wines combine elegance with a rich, heady quality. The heartiest wines, deepest in colour and most tannic, come from the heartland just south of the town, while furthest south, in the commune of Prémeaux, the wines are a little lighter, and should not be over-extracted.

Whereas the Intendant Bouchu noted in 1666 a preference for Nuits, 'where the wine is excellent', over Prémeaux, 'where the wine is of good quality', the king of Saxony specifically ordered in 1780 'the wine of Prémeaux, the colour of the stained glass windows of La Sainte Chapelle'.

Nuits boasts 27 PREMIER CRU vineyards but no GRANDS CRUS, perhaps because the town's leading vigneron, Henri Gouges, was too modest when the CLASSIFICATIONS were agreed in the 1930s. However, a dossier has been prepared to promote the eponymous Les St-Georges vineyard, first singled out as early as the 11th century, has always been cited as of the highest quality. Also particularly fine in the southern Nuits-St-Georges sector are Les Cailles and Les Vaucrains, both adjacent to Les St-Georges, while Les Murgers and Les Boudots on the Vosne-Romanée side and Clos St Marc, Clos des Forêts, and Clos de la Maréchale in Prémeaux have good reputations.

Some white wine is also made from the Chardonnay grape, as in the Clos l'Arlot, and from the Pinot Blanc grape in Domaine Gouges' premier cru Les Perrières.

Top producers include Henri Gouges, Robert Chevillon, Domaine de l'Arlot, Thibault Liger-Belair, Patrice Rion, and growers in neighbouring VOSNE-ROMANÉE such as Arnoux and Grivot.

See also CÔTE D'OR and BURGUNDY map.
J.T.C.M.

numbers and wine, a combination that has assumed increasing importance as WINE-MAKING has become more scientific, and as consumers, faced with a bewildering choice of wines, seek easily appreciated assessments of wine quality such as SCORES. As recently as the 1970s, winemakers had only the vaguest grasp of their wines' vital statistics; and the only numbers of significance to most wine drinkers were those of VINTAGE, PRICE, and, among more sophisticated connoisseurs of bordeaux, the numerical rankings associated with wine CLASSIFICATION.

Numbers are increasingly used for identification, however. Australian wine producers such as PENFOLDS have for decades exhibited a penchant for incorporating BIN numbers into the names of their wines. Individual CLONES of various VINE VARIETIES can be so numerous that they are usually identified by individual numbers, as are CASKS and individual BARRELS in some larger wineries. Some top German wines are identified by barrel (*Fass*) numbers and/or AP NUMBERS.

As the growing of grapes and the making of wine becomes more scientific, numbers as measurements play a key role, as they do in all scientific thinking (see in particular SCORING vineyards).

Consumers, as well as producers, have an interest in measurements taken at all stages of wine production, particularly RESIDUAL SUGAR, and the ALCOHOLIC STRENGTH which appears on most wine labels, even though they cannot be used on their own as a measure of how a wine will taste.   J.R.

The meaning of scores
Using a numerical score to denote a wine's quality offers the apparent appeal of brevity, objectivity, and precision. Scores provide an immensely convenient shorthand for the taster, being quick to record and simple to share. They transcend language barriers and are universally understood. With up to 100 values available (if one uses the standard 100-point scale, beginning at 50 but allowing the use of 'plus'), very fine discriminations can be recorded with absolute clarity

However, while the convenience of wine scoring is not in doubt, such objectivity and precision are somewhat illusory. This is because, despite appearances, scores do not measure an inherent property of wine against an independent scale. They are, rather, rankings of preference, which relate the perceived quality of several wines solely to one another. Although all scoring systems operate on a universal principle—that higher numbers denote higher quality—the choice of which specific numbers to ascribe to a given set of wines is completely arbitrary.

This is a quite separate issue to whether the five-, 20- or 100-point scale is preferable, as well as to the more fundamental debate concerning objectivity and subjectivity in assessing wine quality itself. Even if all the world's tasters were in complete agreement over the quality of every wine, and elected to use the same scale, their scores would in all likelihood significantly differ. Nothing other than whim governs where the qualitative boundary between two adjacent scores should lie.

It follows from this that we cannot assume different tasters mean the same thing by identical scores. They might choose a different score to represent an 'average' wine, and then distribute their marks either side according to a different method. The same is true for publications: 18 out of 20 in a specialist fine-wine journal does not necessarily refer to the same quality level as the same score in a more mainstream magazine.

An isolated score, therefore, carries no meaning. It can only be understood relative to the taster's overall mark distribution, possibly modulated by the context in which it is published. Furthermore, the averaged scores awarded by a tasting panel cannot be compared with scores awarded by a different panel, since the way each taster allocates points will vary.

The arbitrariness of point allocation undermines the precision as well as the objectivity of scoring. It is very tempting to start subdividing points, since rarely do two wines appear to be identical in quality, and so in the course of a large tasting, awarding quarter-points or plusses and minuses can feel like the honest thing to do. Although of some private value, the wider utility of this practice is doubtful. Tasters are not like machines that can be calibrated before each use; they cannot know for certain that what they mean today by 16 points is not what they meant by 15.5 points last month. The more finely subdivided the points become, the less sure it is that the boundaries between them are in the same place each time. The impression of precision is misleading, and beyond a certain point conveys no extra information to the reader.

Numbers fully deserve their place in the world of wine, but deserve also to be understood within the context of their fairly severe limitations. See also wine SCORING and WINE WRITING.   A. H.

Peynaud, E., *Le Goût du Vin* (Paris, 1983) trans. by M. Schuster as *The Taste of Wine* (London, 1987).
Schusterman, R., 'The logic of evaluation', *Philosophical Quarterly*, 30/121 (1980), 327–41.

Nuragus, ancient white Sardinian grape variety grown on 1,345 ha/3,324 acres according to the 2010 vine census, principally to produce the unremarkable varietal Nuragus di Cagliari on the island of SARDINIA.

nursery in viticultural terms is either a place set aside for nurturing young vines, or a name for a PROPAGATION and/or a GRAFTING establishment. Open-ground vine nurseries are where CUTTINGS are planted to develop roots and become ROOTLINGS. Cuttings are taken in winter, stored in a cold room, then CALLUSED by burying them in moist sand, often on heated beds, until young roots form at the base (after six to eight weeks). In spring they are planted in rows in the nursery, where the first-year shoots develop. Nursery soils need to be deep, friable, and well drained, free of pathogens and with a good water supply. In the following winter or spring, they are lifted, shoots and roots are trimmed, and the vines planted out in the vineyard. For grafted vines, the products of BENCH GRAFTING are callused in a humid room before planting in a nursery. B.G.C.

nursery budding and **nursery grafting**, methods for the PROPAGATION of grafted vines that complement BENCH GRAFTING, used in warm climates where the work can be done in the field. Great flexibility is possible in the type of SCION wood used and in the timing of grafting. Inserted scions are tied tightly with budding tape and, after the inserted bud has started to grow, the rootstock foliage is shortened back and later removed. B.G.C.

nutrients. All living things, including vines and yeasts, need NITROGEN, PHOSPHORUS, and POTASSIUM, along with CARBON, hydrogen, OXYGEN, and other MINERALS as nutrients. Lack of nutrients in MUST can lead to STUCK FERMENTATION. For more details of **nutrition** of the vine, see VINE NUTRITION.

NV. See NON-VINTAGE.

NYSAES, New York State Agricultural Experiment Station in Geneva. See CORNELL.

O

oak is hard and supple, and most oaks have watertight WOOD, which has the simple advantage over other WOOD TYPES used for COOPERAGE of displaying a natural affinity with wine, imparting qualities and flavours that today's consumers appreciate as enhancing or complementing those of many wines. Oak in general is one of the strongest of the common hardwoods of the temperate northern hemisphere. As well as being particularly good at holding liquids, oak is also physically easy to work; it encourages clarity and stability in red wines and adds new layers of complexity to many white wines.

There are hundreds of species of oak, all of which can be broadly separated into two categories, red and white. The red oaks are porous and cannot therefore be relied upon for watertight cooperage. For wine, three sorts of white oak are most important, one American and two European, all of them belonging to the botanical genus QUERCUS:

1. *Quercus alba*, also known as American white oak. This general name is also applied to the American oak species *Quercus bicolor*, swamp white oak; *Quercus lyrata*, overcup oak; *Quercus durandii*, Durand oak; *Quercus michauxii*, swamp chestnut oak; *Quercus macrocarpa*, bur oak; and *Quercus prinus*, chestnut oak. Some of these species can hybridize with each other.
2. *Quercus petraea*, once also known as *Quercus sessiliflora*, or *Quercus sessilis*, and as *chêne sessile* in France.
3. *Quercus robur*, once known as *Quercus pedunculata*, also called pedunculate or variously English, French, and Russian oak, *chêne pédonculé* in France.

In some forests, *Q. petraea* and *Q. robur* grow promiscuously together but are not systematically differentiated as far as timber quality is concerned, although the trees are fairly easy to tell apart (see under **European oaks**).

The anatomy of different oaks has implications for barrel making. A trunk can be thought of as a bundle of tubes or vessels and parenchyma cells running parallel to the trunk with groups of fibres called rays running radially from the outside towards the centre of the trunk. Oak is non-storeyed; the longitudinal tubes and fibres overlap so as to give strength. (In a soft wood such as pine, the tubes and fibres are stacked, making the wood much less resistant to pressure.) It is also ring-porous; there are distinct bands of large and small pores or tubes laid down at different times of the year (see GRAIN).

Oak is rich in tyloses, which are structures that plug the tubes. This is what makes it particularly good for holding liquids, as the path of the liquid through the wood is blocked by these tyloses. American white oaks, *Quercus alba*, are the richest in these tyloses, which is why American barrel STAVES can be sawn into shape without risk of leakage. With European oaks there are fewer tyloses so the wood is more porous and must be split to follow the tubes and then bent so that all the tubes are parallel to the stave, thus minimizing leakage.

American oak generally has a more obvious flavour, vanillin in character, and can be more astringent than the smoother, subtler oaks of Europe. Vital to barrel quality is not just the source of the oak, however, but its seasoning (see BARREL MAKING for more details).

World oak resources

All statistics regarding the amount of standing timber in a given country should be read with some caution, partly because it is hard to measure the contents of the forests and partly because, even when statistics are available, they are from different years and are not always directly comparable. The figures in the table below are the most recent available but sometimes they include species that are inappropriate for COOPERAGE. (See over for the various sources of information.)

The ages of the oak forests are often given and sometimes also the species. In Poland, for example, approximately 75% of the stands are less than 80 years old, as they are in Hungary. Cooperage quality oak should be at least 80 years old and preferably much older.

According to research done by Backman and Waggener of the University of Washington

Country (excluding ex-Soviet Union)	Growing stock (millions of cu m)
United States	1,019 (2012)
France	580 (2012)
Hungary	122 (2005)
Poland	120 (2005)
Bulgaria	87 (2005)
Croatia	86 (2005)
Turkey	75*
Germany	72*
Slovakia	64 (2007)
Portugal	52*
Sweden	36 (2005)
Great Britain	34*
Czech Republic	32 (2010)
Austria	26 (2000)
Georgia	24 (2005)
Greece	21*
Bosnia and Herzegovina	20 (2000)
Lithuania	14 (2005)
Slovenia	6 (2005)
Switzerland	5*
Netherlands	3*
Estonia	3 (2005)
Latvia	2 (2005)
Ireland	2*
Total	2,505

* = estimate

(US) in 1988, the former Soviet republics had approximately 9.7 million ha/24 million acres of oak, of which around 3.1 million are located in the far eastern region, close to the Pacific ocean. This is *Quercus mongolica*, not a species used for cooperage. About 1.7 million ha are in Ukraine and are said to add up to around 233 million cu m. Most of the balance, about 4.7 million ha with 763 million cu m/8,180 million cu ft of oak, is in European Russia, where the North Caucasus, the Urals, and Povolzhsk regions have the highest proportions of oak in their forests. If these estimates are correct, the former Soviet republics have the greatest oak resources in the world, even though they may have suffered from poor forestry management for many decades (see under **Eastern Europe**). These resources are not generally being exploited for wine barrels although there is one large cooperage in France that makes a small number of barrels with Russian oak.

FAO: www.fao.org/forestry/fra/67090/en

European Forest Institute: www.efi.int/portal/home

USDA Forest Service: www.fia.fs.fed.us

IGN Inventaire Forestier: inventaire-forestier.ign.fr/spip

American oaks

According to a report published by the US Forestry Service in 2014, there were 35,694 million cu ft/1,020 million cu m of commercially important selected white oaks in the eastern United States, although only a certain proportion of this would be suitable for cooperage, where the quality criteria are much higher than for pulp and veneer. The ratio of annual growth to annual harvest is around 1.5 to 1. *Quercus alba* covers most of the eastern United States, extending east from Minnesota, Iowa, Missouri, and Arkansas, north of Mexico, and south of Canada and Maine.

There is no general agreement as to which American regions provide the best oak for wine or whiskey barrels. Some people feel that oak from Minnesota and Wisconsin is best for wine barrels; others feel that it is too tannic. Wood from the more southerly parts of the US is condemned by some for being too sappy. Oregon white oak, *Quercus garryana*, which grows about 50 to 90 ft (15–27 m) tall, and around 24 to 40 in (60 cm–1 m) in diameter, has also been used experimentally for wine barrels, and began to be used on a limited scale for commercial production in the mid 1990s. There are approximately 6,000 million cu ft of various species of oak in California, Oregon, and Washington, but, other than Oregon oak, little is suitable for barrels. In the US alone, an estimated 150,000 to 200,000 American oak barrels are sold to producers each year but the success of BARREL ALTERNATIVES has affected sales of American oak barrels.

American oak is also used widely by the wine industries of Spain, North and South America, and Australia. Because American oak generally has a more powerful flavour than European oak, it was for long used mainly for relatively powerful red wines such as RIOJA and other Spanish reds, Australian SHIRAZ, and warm-climate CABERNET SAUVIGNON, but cooperage techniques improved so considerably in the 1990s that it is now routinely used on a much wider range of wine styles. See COOPERAGE, history.

European oaks

These oaks grow throughout Europe, as far east as the Urals, as far south as Sicily, as far west as Ireland, France, and Portugal, and as far north as southern Norway.

Quercus petraea can reach a height of 25 m/82 ft and can live over 300 years. Branches form high up the relatively straight trunk. Wood from this tree is usually tight grained (see GRAIN). This species grows well in sandy, silty soil with good drainage, but thrives in a variety of soils. In Europe it is found throughout the United Kingdom and from France east to Poland and the Baltic states and as far south as Italy and the former Yugoslavia. Austria and Hungary are increasingly prestigious sources of oak, mostly but not exclusively on home territory.

Quercus robur, thought of as English or French oak, also grows to over 25 m in height and can live over 300 years. Its branches spread out to provide more shade than *Quercus petraea* and it tends to produce wide-grained wood. It prefers fertile soils where there is plenty of water. As *Quercus robur* tolerates a wider range of growing conditions, it is more widespread in Europe than *Quercus petraea*. It extends further north into the Scandinavian countries, further south into Turkey, Georgia, and Portugal, and east as far as the Urals. Although wood from this species tends to have wider grains than *Quercus petraea*, the two species can be positively distinguished only by examination of leaves and acorns. The acorn of *Quercus robur* is attached via a long PEDUNCLE whereas that of *Quercus petraea* is attached directly to the twig. There is so much cross-fertilization that there are many hybrids of these two species, however.

Coopers do not usually distinguish the two species in their workshops. Like winemakers, they tend to pay more attention to geographical provenance and grain size than oak species. And, as winemakers increasingly understand, details of BARREL MAKING can have an even more significant effect on wine quality than exact forest location.

France Although Baltic and Slavonian oak were the most admired oaks in the 19th century, French oak has since become the standard by which all other oaks are judged. Thanks to

sound forestry management, French oak is available in viable commercial quantities and can add to wine flavours that appeal to modern consumers.

Almost a quarter of France, or nearly 14 million ha/34 million acres, is forest, constituting more than 40% of all forest in the EU. About one-third of this forest land is oak. There are around 4 million ha of *Quercus petraea* and *Quercus robur*, according to the French Office National des Forêts.

France is the world's major source of European oak, by quite a margin. According to Vivas, around 2 million cubic m of oak are harvested in France each year, whereas annual growth is around 10 million cubic m. At least 500,000 French oak barrels are made and sold every year, it is estimated, of which about one-third are to the US.

Since 1947, around 2 million ha/5 million acres of France have been naturally reforested. Unlike many other countries, France has done a good job of managing its forests since the Second World War. Supplies of French oak—barring unusual circumstances such as dramatic CLIMATE CHANGE—should remain abundant.

Concern about the condition of the French forests dates back to at least 1291, when scholars note the mention of 'maistre des fôrets' in the Royal Ordinances. The most famous of these Ordinances was written during the regime of Colbert in 1669. Colbert is commemorated in the Tronçais forest, where he ordered systematic replanting of oak trees for use in shipbuilding.

Sylviculture is actively practised in France so that trees in government-owned forests are not allowed to grow wild, but are carefully farmed to yield suitable wood, just like any other crop. Trees are encouraged to grow tall and straight, yielding grains appropriate for barrel making, for example, by a variety of physical techniques.

The following forests all over northern France provide oak for wine and brandy barrels:

Western Loire and Sarthe: woods from forests in the western LOIRE, from the *départements* of Indre, Cher, and Indre-et-Loire, and in the Sarthe near Le Mans, have tight grains and are highly prized.

Limousin: woods from the following regions in France: the eastern part of the *département* of Deux-Sèvres, Vienne, Haute-Vienne, the northern part of the Corrèze, the Creuse, the eastern part of the Charente and the southern part of the Indre, the northern part of the Dordogne. These oaks tend to have wide grains and are usually grouped together as Limousin. Soils here tend to clay-limestone or granite. These woods are more TANNIC than the tight-grained woods and are more popular with brandy makers than winemakers.

Nièvre and Allier: woods from these two central *départements* just south of SANCERRE go by many names. Sometimes this wood is sold under the name of the specific forest. Tronçais, for example, is a government-owned forest north of Moulins, while Bertranges is a forest near Nevers. This sort of oak may also be sold under the name of the region, such as Allier and Nevers. To many French winemakers, however, all of this wood is regarded simply as *bois du centre*, wood from the centre of France. However these forests are named, the wood is usually tight grained and is popular for both brandy and wine. Soil here tends to silica and clay. As stands are planted with close spacing, the trees tend to grow up, rather than out; hence the tighter grains.

Vosges: wood from the Vosges forests in ALSACE-Lorraine became popular with winemakers outside the region in the early 1980s. This wood is usually tight grained and resembles the oak from Nièvre and Allier. Oak experts say they can identify this wood by its 'clear' or 'white' colour. The character of Vosges woods varies according to the elevation of the stand.

Jura and Bourgogne: just to the east of BURGUNDY are forests which traditionally supplied Burgundy with oak. These forests are still important and supply wood mainly to Burgundian wine producers.

Argonne: located near CHAMPAGNE, this forest provides a small amount of oak for the cooperage business, principally for those few champagne producers who still ferment in barrel. Sometimes the wood is sold as Vosges.

According to L'Office Nationale des Forêts, the most important French *départements* for oak are, in declining order of importance, Haute-Saône, Nièvre, Yonne, Côte d'Or, Haute-Marne, Dordogne, Cher, Allier, Moselle, Saône-et-Loire, Loire-et-Cher, l'Orne, l'Eure, and la Sarthe.

There is no APPELLATION CONTRÔLÉE and much confusion of nomenclature in the world of oak. This means not only that winemakers are suspicious about proclaimed wood origins but that people use different definitions for the same name. Some would include wood from the western Loire in the category of 'bois du centre' while others would exclude anything but Nevers and Allier. Others will classify wood around Nevers with wood from the Yonne and CÔTE D'OR as 'Bourgogne'.

Eastern Europe Historically, the forests of Eastern Europe were extremely important sources of oak, mainly *Quercus robur* and *Quercus petraea*. In the 19th century, Baltic oaks were prized by the French and British, although it is not clear exactly how much oak suitable for cooperage is left in Lithuania, Latvia, and Estonia. Before the Second World War, Polish,

Russian, and Baltic oaks were important in both the beer and wine industries and in the 1990s coopers were scouting east keenly in search of good-quality wood that could be bought more cheaply than French oak. Political changes in Eastern Europe in the late 1980s immediately resulted in offers of Hungarian, Polish, Czech, Russian, and Moravian oak barrels to winemakers in the west. Some coopers have conducted successful trials of wines matured in eastern European oak and, although there is still much to be learnt about making barrels with these woods, sales have grown. Current estimates place annual sales at over 20,000 barrels. Hungary in particular has benefited from good forestry management for over two centuries. The ratio of annual growth of oak to annual harvest is around 2.5 to 1.

Slavonia (see CROATIA), BOSNIA AND HERZEGOVINA, and SERBIA have been a useful source of oak for the large casks and oval vats used by Italy's wine producers (who often called them simply Yugoslavian, or Slavonian). It is said these oaks are too tannic for French grape varieties but work well with Italy's NEBBIOLO and SANGIOVESE, but this could be a reflection of wood preparation or TERROIR. Much of this wood was sawn, rather than hand split (see BARREL MAKING) and the result was porous barrels that provided astringent flavours. These forests have been managed poorly, too many trees have been cut down, and access to these woods has been restricted for internal political reasons.

Portugal Oak grown in the far north of Portugal can, if well seasoned, be of use to Portugal's winemakers, being more subtle than the locally used chestnut and much cheaper than oak imported from France.

See also OAK FLAVOUR, WOOD INFLUENCE, BARREL, BARREL FERMENTATION, BARREL MAINTENANCE, BARREL MATURATION, BARREL RENEWAL, BARREL STORAGE, BARREL TYPES, BARREL INSERTS, INNER STAVES, OAK CHIPS, and OAK ESSENCES. M.K.

Burns, R. M., and Honkala, B. H. (eds.), *Silvics of North America*, ii: *Hardwoods* (Washington, DC, 1990).

Vivas, N., *Manuel de tonnellerie à l'usage des utilisateurs de futaille* (2nd edn, Bordeaux, 2002).

oak ageing, the process of AGEING a wine in contact with OAK. This typically involves BARREL MATURATION, ageing the wine in a relatively small oak container, although the phrase may also be used for CASK AGEING in a larger oak container, and can even be used for wines exposed to the influence of OAK CHIPS or INNER STAVES. Wines thus treated may be described as **oak aged**, **oak matured**, or **oaked**. (**Oaky** is a tasting term usually applied to wines too heavily influenced by OAK FLAVOUR, which smell and taste more of wood than fruit, and

may be aggressively tannic and dry.) See also BARREL ALTERNATIVES.

oak chips, useful if ersatz winemaking tool, an inexpensive alternative to top-quality BARREL MATURATION which imparts OAK FLAVOUR and aroma and may improve MOUTHFEEL and colour stability though the resultant wine may be less complex and have poorer ageing potential.

Oak chips vary considerably both in the provenance of the OAK (from subtle Cher to harsher American oak) and in the size of the chip (from pencil shaving to the more common cashew nut size). Oak chips, just like BARRELS, are also subjected to different degrees of TOAST. The quality of the oak, the method and duration of seasoning, and the degree and duration of toast are far more significant than the shape of the chip or shaving.

Oak chips are used either instead of barrel maturation or to supplement the oak flavour imparted by a used barrel. The average dose of chips is about 1 g/l, or 5 lb per 1,000 gal, typically added at the start of fermentation. Chips offer considerable savings over new cooperage: a sufficient quantity of American oak chips to impart some degree of oak flavour could cost less than a twentieth of the cost of a new American oak barrel (and an even smaller fraction of the cost of a new French barrel). They are most effective when added during FERMENTATION, when presumably a combination of heat and enzymatic activity combine to generate the most favourable flavour EXTRACTION. Such wines sometimes have such an overpoweringly oaky flavour that they must be blended with unoaked wine. In addition to cost savings, chips have other advantages over barrels: less oak is needed because of the greater surface area in contact with the wine, there is less oak wastage compared with producing barrel staves, the toast is more even, and they take up far less space in the winery.

Research by Wilkinson et al. has shown that the oak character imparted by the chips may intensify after the chips have been removed. This is because the formation of certain oak lactones (see OAK FLAVOURS) takes longer than the period during which the chips are in contact with the wine.

It is possible to buy oak chips impregnated with LACTIC ACID BACTERIA immobilized at the stage immediately prior to exponential growth so that they can be used to encourage MALOLACTIC CONVERSION but these are not widely used because of the additional costs involved.

Many wine producers are coy about admitting to using oak chips although, unlike OAK ESSENCE, oak chips may be used perfectly legally in many wine regions. A wine description which mentions 'oak maturation' or 'oak influence' without actually mentioning any form of COOPERAGE is a good clue.

The **oak shavings** which can result from BARREL RENEWAL may similarly be used, and larger **oak cubes** in a perforated bag are sometimes put into older barrels to impart oak flavour.

See also BARREL INSERTS and INNER STAVES.

G.T. & J.E.H.

Wilkinson, K. L., et al., 'Rates of formation of *cis*- and *trans*-oak lactone from 3-methyl-4-hydroxyoctanoic acid', *Journal of Agricultural and Food Chemistry*, 52 (2004), 4213–18.

oak essences, or **oak extract,** usually illegal winemaking additive (unlike OAK CHIPS) which can inexpensively substitute, at least in the short term, for some of the OAK FLAVOUR imparted by BARREL MATURATION in expensive new oak. Various powders and liquids are marketed based on extractions from different woods. In some cases, specific TANNINS are targeted and extracted so as to add structure as well as flavour to a wine (see OENOLOGICAL TANNINS).

Doses of powdered oak extracts can vary between 5 and 20 g/hl but powders are more difficult to use than liquids because of potential problems with CLARIFICATION. The usual dose of a liquid extract is about 0.01% and, since most liquids are based on ETHANOL or brandy, they can be extremely difficult to detect analytically. However, their ability to sustain a wine through BOTTLE AGEING is questionable.

G.T.

oak flavour. The wood in which a wine is fermented and/or aged has a profound and often complex effect on its characteristics and flavour (see WOOD INFLUENCE). Certain substances present in wood may also be directly extracted and absorbed into the wine, however. Those extractable substances identified in OAK, the most commonly used wood, are listed below. Pracotmtal et al. have shown that the flavours extracted change over time as the wine penetrates further into the STAVE beyond the depth that has been toasted (see TOAST).

Lactones These compounds, responsible for what is generally called the aroma of oak, or 'oakiness', are derived from lipids in the oak. There may be variances in lactone levels in different trees and even in different parts of the same tree. Lactones are more coconut-like at higher concentrations and can easily overpower a wine's inherent AROMA. Higher concentrations are found in American oak although studies by French cooper Taransaud have shown that during air drying of the STAVES prior to BARREL MAKING, some lactones increase while others decrease, and lactone levels decrease in American oak and increase in French. Toasting of the oak may increase the flavour. The specific compounds are the cis and trans isomers of ρ-methyl-g-octalactone. The former is more aromatic and imparts an earthy, herbaceous character; the latter imparts more spiciness and has a higher threshold value in wine. Seasoning affects the ratio of cis to trans isomers.

Phenolic aldehydes VANILLIN, a product of lignin degradation, is the best-known member of this group. Toasting increases the level of these (although they decrease at high toast levels), as does seasoning in the open air. BARREL FERMENTATION reduces their level because yeast metabolism reduces, for example, aromatic vanillin to odourless vanillic alcohol.

Volatile phenols These too are the product of lignin degradation and are not present in non-toasted wood. They impart a spice-like roasted character, ranging from clove to smokiness. These decrease with seasoning of the oak. The main volatile phenol associated with wood is eugenol (clove-like). Others include guaiacol and 4-methylguaiacol (smoky, charred aromas), which may increase at higher levels of toasting, and 4-vinylguaiacol (reminiscent of carnations).

Terpenes These essential oils important in fruit, tea, and perfume are found in American oak and to a lesser degree in some French oak. It is likely but as yet unproven that they have flavour effects.

Carbohydrate degradation products This is a large and complex group that includes furfurals, which are produced from toasting wood sugars. Maltol and cyclotene are also produced from the toasting process and have caramel-like flavours.

Tannins and other phenolics TANNINS and other PHENOLICS act as a reservoir to balance the oxidative/reductive reactions of the wine, protecting it from OXIDATION and lessening the chance of unpleasant REDUCTIVE aromas. Hydrolysable tannins derived from oak lignin are known as ellagitannins. Their concentration decreases with heavy toasting. It is worth noting that wine in the barrel is biologically active. The YEASTS that effect the FERMENTATION of sugars to alcohol also transform some of these directly extracted oak compounds into other compounds with flavours different from the original. The furfurals, for instance, are derived from hemicellulose, and are transformed by the yeasts into compounds which have a range of flavours from smoky to coffee. For example, during BARREL FERMENTATION of white wines, furfurylrthiol (FFT) is formed by yeast from the furfural released by toasted staves. Furfural levels increase with the duration of the toasting.

Those who cannot afford to extract their oak flavour from new BARRELS may use OAK CHIPS, BARREL INSERTS, INNER STAVES, or even OAK ESSENCE. Although the contribution made by oak barrels cannot be directly compared with that of BARREL ALTERNATIVES, some winemakers believe that the use of chips and inserts gives them better control over the type and amount of oak flavour extracted. Used carefully and in combination with MICRO-OXYGENATION, these products have allowed some wineries to achieve flavour effects in tank that are quite similar to those promoted by barrel ageing, and for a fraction of the cost.

L.B. & J.E.H.

Pracomtal, G. de, et al., 'Types of oak grain, wine élevage in barrel', *Practical Winery & Vineyard* (Jul 2014), 64–9.

oak influence. See WOOD INFLUENCE.

Oak Knoll. See NAPA.

oak root rot, vine disease. See ARMILLARIA ROOT ROT.

Oakville, important source of top quality NAPA Valley Cabernet.

Obaideh, hardy, vigorous, workmanlike indigenous grape of LEBANON, high in sugar, low in acidity, used extensively in the making of arak (local spirit), sacramental wines, and white Chateau Musar. The Obaideh was once believed to be a strain of Chardonnay, but without any DNA PROFILING of Lebanese CULTIVARS, it is difficult to determine its exact origins.

M.R.K.

Óbidos, DOP in LISBOA in western Portugal known particularly for SPARKLING WINES.

ochratoxin A (OTA) is a mycotoxin, i.e. a toxin produced in very small quantities by certain moulds, found in a range of food and beverages such as cereals, beer, coffee, cocoa, and wine. It has been shown to be carcinogenic and nephrotoxic (causing kidney damage) and has been reported in grapes and grape products since the mid 1990s. Studies have identified *Aspergillus ochraceus*, *A. carbonarius* and *Penicillium verrucosum* as the main synthesizers of OTA on grapes. (See also BUNCH ROTS and SOUR ROT.)

EU regulations were tightened in 2005 and the limit is currently 2 µg/l for wine and grape juice. Surveys conducted since 1999 have shown that warm climate wines, e.g. from the Mediterranean region, are more likely to be affected by OTA than wines from other regions. Healthy vineyards and good hygiene in the winery are the most important factors in limiting OTA.

Ochratoxin A is removed from wine at various stages of winemaking when solids are removed, particularly during FILTRATION, RACKING, CLARIFICATION, and FINING, but it is relatively stable and not destroyed by fermentation or maturation conditions.

Leong, S. L., 'Wine and fungi: implications of vineyard infections', in J. Dijksterhuis and A. Samson (eds.), *New Challenges in Food Mycology* (New York, 2005).

Oechsle, scale of measuring grape sugars, and therefore grape RIPENESS, based on the DENSITY of grape juice. Grape juice with a specific gravity of 1.075 is said to be 75 °Oechsle. This is the system used in Germany and it has its origins in a system of weighing grape must developed first by the Württemberg scientist J. J. Reuss, but much refined in the 1830s by the Pforzheim physicist Ferdinand Oechsle (see GERMAN HISTORY).

Like other scales used elsewhere (see BAUMÉ and BRIX), it can be measured with a suitably calibrated REFRACTOMETER or HYDROMETER. A similar scale, devised at KLOSTERNEUBURG, is used in Austria.

Each scale of sugar measurement relates to the others. For example, a grape juice of 14.7 °Brix has a specific gravity of 1.06 and an Oechsle value of $(1.06-1.0) \times 1000 = 60$. According to published scales, these relationships are not strict ones; see nomograms in Hamilton and Coombe.

For more details, see MUST WEIGHT.   B.G.C.

Hamilton, R. P., and Coombe, B. G., 'Harvesting of winegrapes', in B. G. Coombe and P. R. Dry (eds.), *Viticulture*, ii: *Practices* (Adelaide, 1992).

œil-de-perdrix, French for 'partridge's eye', used as a name and tasting term for pale pink wines made from Pinot Noir, especially in the Neuchâtel canton of SWITZERLAND.

Oeillade Noire, very old, now rare PROVENÇAL dark-skinned grape variety. **Oeillade Blanche** is a synonym for the unrelated PICARDAN.

oenocyanin, a TANNIN product extracted from the skins of black grapes, comprising a mixture of PIGMENTED TANNINS, some ANTHOCYANINS, and other PHENOLICS. Marketed as a food colourant, oenocyanin is a valuable source of natural pigments available from POMACE. Even though it is a tannin derived from grapes, and therefore of a composition more similar to the natural tannins of wine than many OENOLOGICAL TANNINS, regulations in most countries forbid the use of oenocyanin in RED WINEMAKING because it is classed as a colouring agent.   P.J.W.

oenological tannins, or commercial tannins, are products made by extraction of tannin from oak, chestnut, or birch woods and other suitable plant sources, including grape seeds. These have long been used (and are approved additives in many winemaking regulations) to improve the AGEING characteristics, TEXTURE, depth of colour, and colour stability of red wines and also to inhibit LACCASE activity from *Botrytis cinerea* on red grapes. Our understanding of the way in which oenological tannins achieve these often desirable outcomes is no less partial than our understanding of wine tannin chemistry in general, but many winemakers have discreetly built up considerable practical experience in using these materials.   P.J.W.

oenologist, or, in the United States and South Africa, **enologist**, one who practises OENOLOGY. A CONSULTANT oenologist is likely to concentrate on the activities traditionally considered WINEMAKING but increasingly concerns himself or herself with what happens in the vineyard as well as in the cellar. In general usage, an oenologist is either a scientifically qualified employee or a roving consultant, as opposed to a fully employed practitioner who may or may not have scientific training, the WINEMAKER. In California, certain winemakers are so adept and so modish that their input alone can be enough to double or treble PRICES and transform them into a CALIFORNIA CULT wine. Most famous of them is Helen Turley, and others include Heidi Peterson Barrett, Mia Klein, Philippe Melka, Andy Erickson, Thomas Rivers Brown, Celia Welch, and Martha McClellan. See also FLYING WINEMAKER.

oenology, or **enology**, the knowledge or study of wine, derived from the Greek *oinos* meaning 'wine'. The French and Italian terms are, respectively, *oenologie* and *enologia*.

Oenology has been used as a synonym for WINEMAKING, as distinct from VITICULTURE, which is concerned with vines. There is a general tendency towards including the study of viticulture as well as wine production in the term, however, as more people accept that wine is made to a great extent in the vineyard. See also OENOLOGIST.

Oenotria, name given to southern Italy when Greek colonists first arrived in the 8th century BC or soon after. The Greeks may have found the indigenous inhabitants already producing wine and using stakes to support the vines, and it is possible that they adopted a word meaning 'stake' (*oinotron*) as a name for the inhabitants. But this word is very rare; a different word (*kharax*) is used in most dialects of classical Greek; so it may be that Oenotria was the name already used by the local population and the similarity between it and the word meaning 'stake' is purely coincidental.   N.G.W. & H.M.W.

oïdium, much-used French name for POWDERY MILDEW, although Anglophones tend to omit the diaeresis.

OIV stands for **Organisation** (formerly **Office**) **Internationale de la Vigne et du Vin**, the Paris-based intergovernmental body which represents the interests of vine-growers, and the wine, DRYING GRAPE, and TABLE GRAPE industries of its members, 46 different countries (Armenia, the newest member, joined in 2014), including all the important wine producers. It was established in 1924, during PROHIBITION in the United States, charged with demonstrating the beneficial effects of wine consumption, as well as co-ordinating research and nomenclature and upholding high standards of production. It continued its work, with the benefit of diplomatic immunity, uninterrupted during the Second World War. Today it is more concerned with the wide spectrum of scientific, technical, economical, and social problems involving the vine and all its products. The OIV co-ordinates research, gathers statistics, and publishes books, papers, and journals, including the important *Bulletin de l'OIV*, not just on VITICULTURAL and OENOLOGICAL matters, but also on legal and economic aspects of wine production. The OIV also co-ordinates conferences to discuss the issues regarded as most pressing by the world's wine producers. In the late 1980s and early 1990s, topics included the possibility of increasing commercial controls as an indirect result of HEALTH concerns, and the increasing importance of ecological issues. More recent concerns have been various pests and diseases, CLIMATE CHANGE effects, BULK WINE, environmental impacts, and SUSTAINABILITY. Since 1986, the OIV's educational branch has offered an International Diploma in Management of Wine and the Vine, a master's degree taught in English and French while travelling around the world of wine.

OIV, *International Code of Oenological Practices* (2014), www.oiv.int/oiv/info/enplubication oiv.

Olasz Rizling, or **Olaszrizling**, is the most common name in HUNGARY for the white grape variety known in Austria as WELSCHRIESLING (under which more details appear). The variety is now Hungary's single most planted vine variety, although it was introduced less than a century ago. The Olaszrizling produced around lake Balaton, Somló, and Eger is particularly prized and, in general, the warmer climate imbues Hungarian versions of this variety with more weight than their counterparts in Austria. Plantings totalled 4,664 ha/11,520 acres in 2011, in virtually every wine region and a wide range of styles.

old vines are reputed to produce grapes which make better quality wine. See VINE AGE for a discussion of this common assertion. See also HISTORIC VINEYARD SOCIETY and VIEILLES VIGNES.

old wine. See AGEING and MATURITY.

Old World is Europe and the rest of the Mediterranean basin such as the Near East and North Africa. The term is used solely in contrast to the New World, the Old World having little sense of homogeneity. In very general terms, Old World techniques in vineyard and cellar have relied more on TRADITION and less on SCIENCE than in the New World but this is changing as more and more wine producers travel freely between Old and New Worlds, exchanging ideas and techniques. The notion of TERROIR is an important and well-established one in much of the Old World, especially France, Germany, and Italy. To typical Old World producers, geography is considerably more important than technology.

For more details of what characterizes the Old World, see NEW WORLD.

olfactory bulb, the most sensitive part of our personal TASTING equipment.

Olifants River, chiefly BULK grape-producing region in SOUTH AFRICA among mountains and along the Atlantic western seaboard. Most growers have supplied large local CO-OPERATIVES with wine for distillation but an increasing proportion is exported as wine. Vredendal, South Africa's biggest single winery and part of Namaqua, vinifies more than 110,000 tonnes of grapes annually. But there are pockets of vines with serious potential, particularly in Lutzville Valley district and the tiny Bamboes Bay ward.

oloroso, Spanish word with two related meanings in the sherry-making process, *oloroso* being the stronger, richer type of wine made in the bodega (as opposed to *fino*), Oloroso being one of the commercial styles of sherry. Pure Oloroso is a dry, dark, nutty wine that is basically bottled *oloroso*, and is often labelled Dry Oloroso. In some foreign markets, however, the term Oloroso is applied to any commercial sweet, dark blend of basic sherry plus colouring and sweetening wine that falls somewhere between AMONTILLADO and CREAM. Oloroso may have an alcoholic strength anywhere between about 18 and more than 20%. See SHERRY for more details.

Oltrepò Pavese, LOMBARDY's most sizeable viticultural area, administratively part of PIE-MONTE from 1741 to 1859, extends across the hills of a series of communes in the province of Pavia south of the Po river where the land begins to rise towards the Ligurian Apennines (the name means 'beyond the Po, in the Pavia region'). In 2012, vineyards totalled 11,657 ha/ 28,792 acres, of which 9,457 ha were registered for DOC wines. Oltrepò Pavese is also the name of an extensive, over-arching DOC, encompassing six DOCs and one DOCG, which lack true significance because production regulations and the permitted grape varieties are practically identical to those of the Oltrepò Pavese DOC. This is especially true of the DOC Pinot Grigio dell'Oltrepò Pavese and the DOC Pinot Nero dell'Oltrepò Pavese. Of real significance, however, is the DOCG Oltrepò Pavese Metodo Classico for TRADITIONAL METHOD sparkling

wines based on at least 70% Pinot Noir with Chardonnay, Pinot Grigio, and/or Pinot Bianco, and a minimum of 15 months on lees, 24 months for vintage-dated wines. Oltrepò Pavese has been producing base wines for SPARKLING WINEMAKERS since the 19th century and the large SPUMANTE houses of Piemonte have long relied on this neighbouring zone in Lombardy for varieties not cultivated in their own region. Significant amounts of BULK wine have always been sold in nearby Milan, encouraging abundant production at extremely low prices; the quality of Oltrepò wines has thus gained little from its proximity to Italy's largest and most affluent urban market. The small size of the properties (1.8 ha per grower) and the significant role played by CO-OPERATIVES have also tended to reward quantity over quality.

If the vast majority of the Oltrepò's production is not particularly interesting, there is no doubt that good, and occasionally very good, wine is made in this zone. One of the most interesting is the blended red Oltrepò Rosso, which is based on BARBERA grapes to which CROATINA (confusingly called Bonards, the name of a quite different, generally inferior grape variety here) adds spice and BODY and UVA RARA gives sweetness and aroma. Regrettably this blend accounts for only a small fraction of the total DOC production although there is a total of about 2,000 ha of each of Barbera and Croatina planted. Together with Uva Rara they form the blends for the DOCs Buttafuoco dell'Oltrepò Pavese and Sangue di Giuda dell'Oltrepò Pavese. The bland Riesling Italico (see WELSCHRIESLING) is the most significant white wine grape with a total of 1,172 ha planted. Many of these wines, both white and red, come in a lightly sparkling version, while Pinot Noir is principally used for SPUMANTE, most of whose production is controlled by the co-operatives and most of which is correct but hardly inspiring. An occasional good bottle of Oltrepò spumante and an occasional bottle of still Pinot Noir, given a Burgundian treatment and aged in OAK, indicate that the variety has real, if as yet unrealized, potential in the zone, although it currently lags far behind FRANCIA-CORTA.   W.S.

Omar Khayyám (d. AD 1132) was a Persian poet, made famous in the English-speaking world by Edward Fitzgerald's translation (and adaptation) of the *Rubáiyát* ('Quatrains') in 1859 (2nd edn, 1868). In his own life, he was known as a philosopher and a scientist, and was remembered for a long time, both in the Middle East and Europe, as one of the greatest mathematicians of medieval times. His quatrains would scarcely have been deemed original in his own society (see ARAB POETS). In a time of strict orthodoxy, this genre of occasional verse, which was popular in PERSIA in the 11th and

12th centuries, was the best medium for expressing dangerous personal doubts to a close circle of friends.

Khayyám's own quatrains are the outpourings of a non-conformist intellectual who was opposed to religious fanaticism; they range from a pious outlook to the extremes of scepticism. Wine is an important theme in this poetry. Given the ISLAMIC prohibition against wine, many of the *rubáiyát* may seem heretical; however, the defiant anti-Islamic stance of Bacchism in the 8th and 9th centuries had by the 12th century been transformed in significance by Sufism (Islamic mysticism). Some commentators have, therefore, viewed the *rubáiyát* as a mystical genre, with wine forming part of a sensitive allegory. More recently it has been accepted that wine merely serves to express religious scepticism and provides solace from existential anguish; Omar Khayyám sought to drown the world's sorrows in wine and thus rejected 'the hope of a diviner drink' offered by Islam. Khayyám's was a humanist protest that scorned sectarianism and intolerance: 'If I'm drunk on forbidden wine, so I am! | And if I'm a pagan or idolater, so I am! | Every sect has its own suspicions of me, | I myself am just what I am . . . To be free from belief and unbelief is my religion.'

Although Persian wine poetry was largely influenced by Arabic poetry, the range of Bacchic expression in the *rubáiyát* is far more limited than what we find in the detailed, sometimes exuberant, descriptions of wine amongst the earlier Arab poets.

See also PERSIA and ENGLISH LITERATURE, WINE IN.   P.K.

Avery, P., and Heath-Stubbs, J. (trans.), *The Ruba'iyat of Omar Khayyam* (London, 1979).

Ondarrabí. See HONDARRABI BELTZA.

Ondenc was once an important vine variety in GAILLAC and all over SOUTH WEST FRANCE but has fallen from favour because it yields poorly and is prone to rot. During the 19th century it must have been taken to Australia, where it was identified, called Irvine's White at Great Western in Victoria, by visiting French AMPELOGRA-PHER Paul Truel in 1976. Since then it has all but disappeared from Australian vineyards too.

Ontario produces the majority of CANADA's wine in three designated viticultural areas: the Niagara Peninsula, best known for the dramatic Niagara Falls, Lake Erie North Shore further to the south west, and Prince Edward County. Each of these areas is in the southern part of the province between the 41st and 44th latitudes and within sight and influence of two of the Great Lakes, Lake Ontario and Lake Erie, which temper the winter cold and the heat of summer (see LAKE EFFECT). In total, in 2013

Ontario grew 6,900 ha/17,000 acres of vines, of which 5,970 ha/14,746 acres were VINIFERA.

This cool climate growing region has a CONTINENTAL climate that is subject to extremes of very hot, often humid summers with occasional drought, to very cold winters where temperatures can fall below −20 °C. However, the median degree days (see CLIMATE CLASSIFICATION) during the growing season of 1500 °C are greater than Beaune, France (1315 °C), and Hawke's Bay, New Zealand (1200 °C). Long days and cool nights slow down fruit maturation while maximizing levels of acidity. The rich ethnic mix of grape-growers in Ontario is reflected in an unusually broad range of more than 50 different wine grape varieties, with a primary focus on Chardonnay, Riesling, Pinot Noir, and Cabernet Franc. Other varieties include Viognier, Gewurztraminer, Auxerrois, Syrah, and Zweigelt. Ontario, with more than 140 wineries, is also the home to the Cool Climate Oenology and Viticulture Institute at BROCK University in St Catharines.

The **Niagara Peninsula**, the largest wine region in Canada (13,000 acres of *V. vinifera*, 16,000 acres total) is dominated by the moderating effect of its position between Lakes Ontario and Erie. The proximity of the southern leg of the Niagara escarpment moderates air flow by acting as a passive barrier against continental winds. Climatically similar to Burgundy, the region regularly produces opulent Chardonnay, and Pinot Noir which has performed well enough to attract BOISSET of Burgundy to establish with CONSTELLATION's Canadian subsidiary a JOINT VENTURE winery dedicated to these varieties. Other Burgundian varieties such as Gamay Noir, Auxerrois, and Pinot Gris also thrive here. Because of the length of the growing season, Niagara can produce elegant Rieslings. Late-harvest wines, including ICEWINE, have gained international recognition. In warmer areas of the Peninsula, Cabernet Franc, Merlot, Malbec, and Cabernet Sauvignon can ripen fully, and recent years have seen successes with the northern Rhône varieties Viognier and Syrah. FRENCH HYBRIDS such as Maréchal Foch and Baco Noir, when taken seriously, have produced consistently successful reds, while Vidal is especially treasured for Icewine and other late-harvest wines.

Lake Erie North Shore in south western Ontario has Canada's longest growing season and the highest number of heat units but also the risk of WINTER FREEZE. It comprises a narrow band along the north shore over a large area but with only 142 ha/355 acres of mainly *V. vinifera* vines. Once a distinct appellation on its own, Pelee Island, 20 km offshore, is now part of the Lake Erie North Shore viticultural area totalling about 1,100 acres.

Prince Edward County, a 2½ hour drive east of Toronto, is Ontario's newest appellation and is on average 5° F cooler than Niagara. It was designated a viticultural area in 2007, had 800 acres of *V. vinifera* vines in 2013, and is the fastest-growing wine region in Canada. Exciting Chardonnay, Pinot Noir, and sparkling wines are being made here.

All three areas continue to hold promise when scrupulous attention is paid to site selection and cultivars planted. Wines carrying a viticultural designation must be made exclusively from *V. vinifera* grapes—except Icewine, which can also be made from Vidal. The fruit of VITIS LABRUSCA vines, still grown in Ontario, is used primarily for juice and some inexpensive non-VQA sparkling wine.   T.A.

Aspler, T., and Bergeron, J.-F., *Canadian Wineries* (Toronto, 2012).

www.vqaontario.com

www.wgao.ca

www.lcbo.ca

opening the bottle is an important and potentially difficult operation for bottles sealed with a cork. A wide range of CORKSCREWS is available for opening bottles of still wine. See CLOSURES for details of alternatives to CORK, most of which are much easier to remove and need no special equipment.

If the cork proves too recalcitrant for a corkscrew, the cork should simply be pushed in, if possible, and the wine poured out of the bottle, possibly into a jug, while the cork is held down with a long, thin instrument. See PORT TONGS for one way of opening bottles with very old corks.

But before the cork can be extracted any FOIL or wax seal has to be broached. A knife blade or FOIL CUTTER is the simplest way to cut a foil neatly, just below the lip of the bottle, which should be wiped of any residue from the foil, especially if it is an old one and contains LEAD. Wax seals are more difficult to penetrate and call for a sharp knife, or foil cutter, and tolerance of a certain amount of mess.

Opening a bottle of SPARKLING WINE is potentially extremely hazardous, as the pressure inside the bottle can expel a cork so fast that it can inflict grave injury. The bottle should be held at 45 degrees (to maximize the wine's surface area) with the cork pointing in the least dangerous direction (and certainly not at anyone, or at anything precious or fragile). The wire MUZZLE should be untwisted and discarded, while holding the cork in the bottle, usually with the top of the thumb. The bottle should then be very gently screwed off the cork with one hand while the cork is held in place with the other. The cork should be allowed to escape the bottle very slowly and the wine poured from the 45-degree angle, perhaps with a thumb in the punt (see BOTTLES). The racing driver technique of giving champagne a good shake and prising off the cork with two thumbs is about as dangerous as motor racing.

See SERVING WINE for the timing of opening a bottle.

Opimian wine is the wine of the consular year of Lucius Opimius, 121 BC. It owes its fame to the conjunction of an exceptionally hot summer and a momentous historical event, the assassination of C Gracchus, which temporarily ended the movement for social reform.

Writing in 46 BC, Cicero states that the Opimian vintage is already too old to drink (*Brutus* 287), and PLINY the Elder describes it as 'reduced to a kind of bitter honey' but still recognizably wine and exorbitantly expensive (*Natural History* 14. 55–7). Petronius (*Satyricon* 36) and MARTIAL (*Epigrams* 1. 26, 3. 82, 10. 49, etc.) treat Opimian as a literary commonplace rather than a real wine: drinking Opimian in large quantities is what the *nouveaux riches* do to flaunt their wealth, but this is satire, not fact.

To have lasted this long, the wines were almost certainly DRIED-GRAPE WINES.   H.M.W.

Oporto, Portugal's recently much-modernized second city and the commercial centre, known in Portuguese as Porto, which gave its name to PORT. Grapes grown in the harsh conditions up river of Oporto in the DOURO Valley would be crushed and vinified before being shipped to port shippers' LODGES across the Douro from Oporto in the suburb known as VILA NOVA DE GAIA. Oporto has long had a substantial population of British merchants, whose meeting place the FACTORY HOUSE survives to this day.

The PORTUGIESER red grape is sometimes known as Oporto in Romania.

optical sorting, relatively recent mechanical method of sorting grapes which may prove increasingly popular as LABOUR becomes more expensive. See TRIAGE.

Optima, also called **Optima 113**, is a 1970 GERMAN CROSS, of a Silvaner × Riesling with Müller-Thurgau. It ripens very early indeed, sometimes more than ten days before Müller-Thurgau, and can notch up impressive ripeness readings, even if the wines themselves are flabby and undistinguished. It will grow on some of the poorest of sites and has been regarded as a useful but ignoble blending ingredient. Its late budding makes it popular in the Mosel and it is also grown in Rheinhessen. Germany's plantings of Optima reached a peak of 420 ha/1,037 acres in 1990 but had declined, unlamented, to 45 ha by 2012.

options game, BLIND TASTING game which in practice allows novice tasters almost as great a chance of winning as professionals. Developed by Australian Len EVANS, it requires an informed quiz-master who presents players with a series of increasingly precise options for the identity of the wine. A typical series of options might be: 'Australia, California, or Bordeaux?', 'left or right bank?', 'St-Estèphe, Pauillac, St-Julien, or Margaux?', '20th or 21st century?', 'first or fifth growth?', 'Latour, Lafite, or Mouton?'. Players remain in the game only by choosing the correct successive options.

Orange, cool, high-ELEVATION, promising Australian wine region in one of the cooler parts of NEW SOUTH WALES.

Orange Muscat, white grape variety with MUSCAT characteristics that is a cross between CHASSELAS and MUSCAT BLANC À PETITS GRAINS. California plantings of 'Muscat Orange' had grown to about 300 acres by 2012 as well as a little in Oregon and Australia.

orange wine, distinctive dry and tannic white-grape wine style with links to the contemporary NATURAL WINE movement, but inspired by antiquity. As in RED WINEMAKING, orange wines are made by fermenting the juice of ripe white wine grapes on their skins and pips, usually for between a week and a year. The prolonged SKIN CONTACT results in wines darker than conventional whites, in the yellow/amber/gold/orange/pink spectrum depending on variety, ripeness, duration of maceration, extraction methods, and vessel type. Clay vessels such as AMPHORAE, QVEVRI, DOLIA, or TINAJAS are often but not necessarily employed, whether above ground or buried. TANNIN levels are also higher than conventional white wine, which can be useful in gastronomy and for natural wine adherents who bottle with low to no additions of SULFUR DIOXIDE. The genre was reintroduced west of the Caucasus for dry wine by Josko Gravner of FRIULI, who has bottled only orange and red wine since 1998, although he prefers the term amber to orange. However, traditional TOKAJI Aszu and Eszencia wines, foot-trodden white PORT, and many wines of GEORGIA were always macerated. The name was coined in 2004 by UK wine merchant David Harvey, then based in Italy and tasting such wines. There is no appellation: all are currently officially labelled as white wine.

See also CONDADO DE HUELVA.

M.W. & D.A.H.

order of wines to be served. This can affect how individual wines taste quite considerably. The general convention is a wise one for maximizing pleasure: dry before sweet, ordinary before fine, and, generally, young before old.

A sweet wine can make dry wines taste acidic and unpleasant if they are tasted afterwards, so it makes sense to serve wines in an increasingly sweet sequence (which matches the usual sequence of foods during a meal, although serving the sweet course before cheese can upset things).

Old wines are generally more complex than callow young ones and so it generally flatters all wines if the oldest in the sequence are served last. This is not infallible, however. Many young wines are so overwhelmingly robust in comparison to a delicate old wine that they overpower it, and increasing levels of average ALCOHOLIC STRENGTH with each vintage also provides an argument in favour of tasting from (weaker) old to (more powerful) young. For this reason, many tasters approach large tastings of PORT, especially vintage port, from the oldest to the youngest wine. Some wine producers, particularly but not exclusively in newer wine regions, also prefer to show their wines in chronological order of progress, and possibly prowess, from old to young. And those planning particularly generous meals may find that the nuances of the oldest, finest wine they serve last may be lost on some palates already soaked in too many younger wines.

Similar considerations apply to serving wines in an upward sequence of quality.

Oregon, one of the UNITED STATES known by wine lovers for its PINOTS and part of the PACIFIC NORTHWEST. Oregon lies between CALIFORNIA and WASHINGTON state but is markedly different from both. Its propensity for ripening grapes is the most marginal of the three, significant to those who hold that grapes which struggle to ripen achieve greater complexity, and fundamental therefore to the view that it may be from the Northwest—and Oregon in particular—that the best wines of the US will ultimately emerge. While Oregonian viticulture can be traced back for five generations, the growth of its wine industry has been a much more discreet affair than that of California and is only just maturing. Underfunded and somewhat shy by instinct, the Oregon wine industry was slow to find a native, high-profile spokesperson to project it on the wide international screen, although that may be changing. Oregon historically cultivated an image of rustic charm and natural simplicity as opposed to glamour or sophistication, although its producers are stubborn individualists rather than simple peasants. However, the lure of winemaking in the state has attracted increasingly moneyed producers (including DROUHIN and JADOT from Burgundy, JACKSON FAMILY WINES from California, and the relatively vast King Estate, as well as the LIFESTYLE seekers with their bags of gold).

History

VINIFERA vine varieties arrived in the late 19th century. A census of 1860 revealed Oregon's wine production was some 2,600 gal/98 hl. Twenty years later, Jackson county alone was producing 15,000 gal and a post-PROHIBITION boom saw 28 wineries making a million gal by 1938, even if much of that was FRUIT WINE. Little progress was made in the next 25 years as California dominated the market.

Oregon's modern era dates from 1961, when HillCrest Vineyard was established near Roseburg (well south of today's concentration of grape-growing) by Richard Sommer, a refugee from the University of California at DAVIS, where he had been firmly advised that *V. vinifera* grapes could not be grown in Oregon.

The Pinot Noir era dates from 1965. California refugee Charles Coury grew a wide range of Alsace varieties—including Pinot Noir—on the exact site in Washington county of an alleged 19th-century vineyard. But it is David Lett of the Eyrie Vineyard who is most frequently referred to as 'Papa Pinot', having first rooted Pinot Noir cuttings near Corvallis while researching a permanent vineyard site. In 1966, he replanted them in the north end of the Willamette Valley in the Dundee Hills—now the epicentre of Oregon's wine industry—convinced that Burgundian varieties could be grown better in Oregon than in California. He was followed by Dick Erath of Knudsen-Erath (now known as Erath Vineyards even though Dick Erath no longer owns it) among about six other true believers in those early years. The majority of the pioneers had done time in California before deciding that it was the wrong sort of place for their preferred style of wine.

Lett was to make the breakthrough that proved Davis wrong. It was his 1975 Eyrie Vineyard Pinot Noir that put Oregon under the spotlight with an eye-catching performance in a French-sponsored 1979 tasting comparing top French wines with their New World emulators: the Eyrie was placed second. Beaune merchant Robert DROUHIN staged a follow-up which served only to confirm the result. Drouhin eloquently endorsed it by purchasing land and building a state-of-the-art winery within a stone's throw of Lett's own vineyards in the Dundee Hills.

By 2013, the total area of vineyards had doubled in ten years to over 26,000 acres/10,522 ha with more than 400 wineries in production. In vineyard and volume terms, Oregon remains significantly smaller than WASHINGTON to its immediate north, but it has overall achieved a good deal more publicity—almost certainly because the state focused its attention on fashionable PINOT NOIR.

Geography and climate

While almost all Washington state vines are planted in the rain shadow and semi-desert east of the Cascade Mountains, most Oregon vines are directly exposed to the marine airflow of the Pacific ocean, giving milder winters but cooler and wetter summers than Washington. Oregon is notoriously wet, yet in most years the majority of the rain falls between October and

April, not during the crucial part of the growing season. In a late-ripening year, however, rain during HARVEST can cause ROT and dilution, while flocks of migrating BIRDS can ravage a vineyard within hours.

Weather patterns in the early years of the 21st century however have at least temporarily adjusted Oregon's cool climate image. Heat and drought from 2000 to 2005 resulted in stressed grapes and more alcoholic wines. Climatologists have predicted that these La Niña and El Niño weather patterns run in cycles, so a return to a more CONTINENTAL climate for Oregon was expected. What occurred from 2006 through 2012 was a mixed bag of cool and/or wet vintages (2007–2008 and 2010–2011) and warmer, drier years (2006, 2009, and 2012). There seems to be no such thing as normal in Oregon.

Promoters of Northwest wine are fond of pointing to the similarities in LATITUDE between this area and Bordeaux and Burgundy. Such a comparison can be misleading, however, since it takes no account of the influence of TOPOG-RAPHY. Where latitude does have an important influence is in the annual ration of SUNLIGHT, vital for PHOTOSYNTHESIS, but often overlooked by those preoccupied by temperature (see DEGREE DAYS).

In any marginal ripening climate, the choice of VINE VARIETY and selection of growing site take on added importance. Oregon's best-known wine district (and AVA) is the **Willamette Valley** (pronounced with the emphasis on the *am*), which stretches along the west bank of the Willamette River 150 miles/240 km from Portland in the north to Eugene in the south. Its vineyards lie on the foothills of the Coast Range that forms the western edge of this broad valley, specifically in the Red Hills of Dundee, so called for their ruddy-coloured clay-like Jory loam soils. Similar sites and soils, equally promising, can be found in the Eola Hills between Mc-Minnville and Salem, and the area just north of the Dundee Hills known as Ribbon Ridge with its prized Willakenzie soil mixture. (Dundee Hills, Red Hill Douglas County, and Ribbon Ridge are all AVAs.) It is reasonable to assume at least equal potential in many hitherto unexploited areas.

Contrary to common belief, Oregon vineyard soils owe little to volcanic origins and are not exceptionally fertile. Even as recently as the early 1990s, however, most vines were planted on their own roots, leaving them prey to PHYL-LOXERA (although its spread has been slowed, though not halted, by the scattered distribution of the state's vineyards). By the mid 1990s, though, the new Dijon CLONES (grafted onto phylloxera-resistant ROOTSTOCKS) had gained popularity both as replacement vines and new plantings. Vineyard elevations are commonly between 250 and 750 ft/110–330 m. Frost is rarely a problem. Summer temperatures show

little consistency, and harvest dates can vary from early September to late November. Wine characteristics differ accordingly. Pinot Noir ripened well in most of the 1980s vintages but, as in Burgundy, individual skill, or lack of it, has often been the greater influence on final wine quality. By the 1990s, winemaking skill had improved across the board, but a succession of rainy, difficult harvests from 1995 to 1997, and the heat-stressed 1994, 1998, and 2003 vintages, challenged even the most conscientious winemakers. As a result, recent years have seen great VINTAGE variation among the wines.

There are also significant wine districts south of the Willamette Valley: the **Umpqua Valley AVA** (which includes the **Red Hills Douglas County AVA** and **Elkton AVA**), the **Rogue Valley AVA**, the warmer and drier **Applegate Valley AVA**, and the **Illinois valley** just north of the California border and cooler and wetter by virtue of its proximity to the Pacific. The potential of south west Oregon is interesting and underdeveloped. Its main drawback may be commercial rather than climatic, for it lacks a major population centre. Its most extensive AVA is simply **Southern Oregon**, a blatant effort to distinguish itself from the cooler, more northerly Willamette Valley.

The wineries of the northern Willamette Valley (as well as the Columbia Gorge area) received an additional seven AVAs in the early 2000s in an effort to distinguish among and between the geographic differences, primarily for marketing purposes: **Ribbon Ridge**, **Chehalem Mountains**, **McMinnville**, **Eola-Amity Hills**, **Yamhill-Carlton District**, **Dundee Hills**, and the previously mentioned **Columbia Gorge**, which straddles both Oregon and Washington.

Grape varieties

Pinot Noir has passed the test with many wines of commendable depth and complexity. PINOT GRIS followed (again first planted by David Lett of Eyrie Vineyards), achieving growing popularity in a crisp, dry style of characterful white showing more flesh than Pinot Grigio and more acidity than Alsace versions. CHARDONNAY was initially widely but not wisely planted, but from the mid 1990s the produce of Dijon clones began a new chapter in the history of Chardonnay in Oregon. RIESLING is commercially useful and is increasingly fashionable, while GEWÜRZTRAMINER works but is hard to grow and even harder to sell. ICE WINES made from Riesling and Gewürztraminer have been more obviously successful.

Among red wine grapes other than Pinot Noir, GAMAY Noir has seen success, mostly vinified the same way as Pinot Noir to produce generally bigger wines than light, fruity Beaujolais. MERLOT is rare since FRUIT SET usually fails, while CABERNET SAUVIGNON finds most of Oregon

too cool, although fine examples have started to emerge from the south of the state. Syrah and Tempranillo are planted primarily in the south (with some limited plantings in the upper Willamette Valley, surprisingly) and have become very popular varieties.

Winemaking today

Oregon is a sympathetic home for any vine which does not like too much heat (although Pinot Noir grapes which ripen too fast may have to be picked before they reach full maturity in a particularly hot year). Increasingly mature vineyards and greater experience will reveal the extent to which the pioneers are justified in their hopes.

The economies of scale necessary for the production of cheap wine are not a feature of the Oregonian wine industry, which is therefore motivated by a need for quality rather than quantity. Crop YIELDS are small and the vines are mostly CANE pruned rather than CORDON pruned, thus demanding more time, care, and skill from the grower.

Some of Oregon's typically high prices softened in response to the American recession following September 11, 2001. Many wineries added a lower priced Pinot Noir to their line up, sometimes from their own vineyards, and occasionally produced from purchased wine. Independent négociants have also blossomed, with producers such as A to Z, Big Fire, and Union Wine Company cleverly buying oversupplied wines and blending them into well-priced bargains. The early 21st century's dramatic increase in plantings looks set to provide them with no shortage of BULK WINE.

The biggest issues of the 1990s were YIELD and CLONE choices. The lower yielding, earlier ripening Dijon clones promise potentially more complex Pinot Noir and Chardonnay. Many producers are deliberately reducing yields in an effort to produce superior, more concentrated wines. Oregon's wine producers are currently preoccupied by aspects of viticulture: the differing merits of ORGANIC, BIODYNAMIC, and merely SUSTAINABLE viticulture, this last best defined by the popular LIVE movement (a monitored Low Input Viticulture and Enology programme based on a Swiss model known as Vintura). It has been estimated that at least half of Oregon's vines are now at least effectively (if not necessarily certified) organic, and the number of converts to biodynamism was rising fast in the early years of the century.

A typical Oregon winery both owns vineyards and buys in fruit from specialist growers. Most wineries are relatively small, with an annual production of between 2,500 and 20,000 cases the norm. Most are proud to be run personally and relatively idiosyncratically. ACIDIFI-CATION is necessary only in the hottest vintages; and although CHAPTALIZATION may be practised, wines with a natural ALCOHOLIC STRENGTH of at least 12% are easily achieved. L.S.H. & L.M.

Cass, B. (ed.), *Oxford Companion to the Wines of North America* (Oxford and New York, 2000).

Robinson, J., and Murphy, L., *American Wine* (London and Berkeley, Calif. 2013).

www.oregonwine.org

www.oregonwinegrowers.org

organic matter,

the CARBON-containing matter formed in SOIL from the rotting of plant, animal, and microbial residues.

Normally most organic matter is in the top 10–20 cm/4–8 in of the soil, with some deeper as a result of deeply penetrating ROOTS and its distribution by EARTHWORMS and other burrowing animals. On undisturbed soils, much of the store of readily available plant nutrients is associated with the surface layer and its organic matter, having been extracted from the SUBSOIL over millennia and deposited at the surface in plant residues and the excreta of grazing animals. This applies especially to the less soluble nutrients such as PHOSPHORUS and the micronutrients (except BORON), which do not appreciably leach down the profile except in very sandy soils.

Fresh organic matter reflects the composition of the plant and animal materials from which it was formed but, as decomposition proceeds, the more soluble elements are progressively leached away, unless quickly taken up by microorganisms and plant roots. The end point of decomposition is a largely inert organic material called humus. Although humus has a carbon-to-nitrogen ratio of between 10:1 and 15:1, which is favourable for NITROGEN mineralization, the production of mineral nitrogen is slow because of the inert nature of humus. Humus helps to give the soil a desirable crumb structure and friability (see SOIL STRUCTURE). It also provides a framework for the retention and storage of water and CATION nutrients, in states of varying bondage and availability to plant roots.

The total result in undisturbed soils is a constant recycling of nutrients and their steady availability to plants. Importantly, it is at rates which broadly match the favourable conditions for plant growth, and plant nutrient requirements. Sound viticulture aims, if necessary, first to build up soil organic matter content and that of associated MINERAL nutrients, and then to maintain them at a level just high enough to ensure SOIL health and a steady supply of nutrients appropriate to the needs of the vines. On initially infertile soils, this may necessitate a substantial use of FERTILIZERS or, in the case of ORGANIC and BIODYNAMIC VITICULTURE, of imported plant materials or animal wastes to make good any mineral element deficiencies. Only then is it possible to ensure vigorous growth of the green manure and COVER CROPS needed to build up and maintain soil organic matter. At all stages, the increase or maintenance of soil organic matter demands that CULTIVATION, if any, be kept to a minimum.

Viticulture for high-quality winemaking nevertheless demands that soil organic matter content and fertility be just high enough to ensure a suitable BALANCE between fruiting and moderate vegetative growth. Fertile soils with high organic matter contents tend to be associated with excessive vegetative vigour and poor CANOPY MICROCLIMATES. Seguin discusses organic matter levels in relation to the top CRUS of Bordeaux. J.G. & R.E.W.

Seguin, G., ' "Terroirs" and pedology of wine growing', *Experientia*, 42 (1986), 861–72.

White, R. E., *Understanding Vineyard Soils* (2nd edn, Oxford, 2015).

organic viticulture,

a system of grape-growing broadly defined as shunning man-made (industrially synthesized) compounds such as FERTILIZERS, FUNGICIDES, HERBICIDES, and PESTICIDES, as well as anything that has been GENETICALLY MODIFIED. Organic viticulture is a prerequisite for the production of ORGANIC WINE. It contrasts with 'conventional', sometimes even called 'industrialized' or 'chemical' viticulture, in two main ways: by stressing management techniques such as CANOPY MANAGEMENT which seek to prevent rather than cure pests and diseases, and by using naturally occurring substances. The key organic management strategy for perennial crops such as vines, for which no crop rotation is possible, involves stimulating and maintaining healthy populations of a diverse range of soil microorganisms.

The primary route to achieving this in organic vineyards is through the application of organic fertilizer in the form of COMPOST. Unlike soluble fertilizer, this improves the structure and biological properties of the soil, rather than directly feeding the vine itself, and allows the slow release of MINERAL nutrients, by encouraging what in organic-speak is called a 'soil food web' of living organisms such as EARTHWORMS, beneficial bacteria, protozoa, and fungi (see SOIL BIOTA). Man-made soluble fertilizers provide nutrients but do not promote the intrinsic life in the soil. The principle of feeding the soil and not the plant also means that foliar feed fertilizers—those applied to the leaves of the vine—are prohibited under organic norms.

Growers who switch from conventional to organic soil and FERTILITY management claim that vine shoots need much less frequent TRIMMING as vine VIGOUR is reduced. This makes yields less erratic (organic growers claim to get lower annual YIELDS, but more regular yields overall compared with their conventional counterparts) and reduces the risk of attack by FUNGAL DISEASES. However, the second and especially third years of the three-year conversion period from conventional to organic (or biodynamic) management are critical. This period can produce uneconomically low yields and unsustainably high disease pressure, two not unrelated conditions arising because vines have been unable to begin accessing slow-release nutrients from the soil, its reserves of quick-release soluble fertilizers having been all but exhausted by then.

Therefore to make conversion to organics a success, would-be organic growers must adopt the prevention-rather-than-cure approach by putting in place the mechanisms first to create, and then to protect, both the soil humus and soil microbiology without which vines and soil nutrients will be unable to interact.

This usually means a combination of compost and COVER CROPS. Compost creates the preconditions for soil humification, being rich both in microbiology and in the basic building block of life, CARBON (organic wine-growers aim for finished compost with a carbon-nitrogen or C/N ratio of 15:1). Cover crops then protect this microbiologically rich resource from SOIL EROSION and nutrient leaching.

Humus-rich, cover-cropped soils are more likely to hold vital water and nutrients than impoverished ones, and to promote the growth of MYCORRHIZAL fungi on vine roots, organisms which allow vine roots to penetrate deeper into the soil and facilitate the uptake of micronutrients (see VINE NUTRITION), both of which are said by some to make wines taste more TERROIR-specific and thus more complex.

A small but increasing number of organic and biodynamic wine-growers (see BIODYNAMIC VITICULTURE) have moved to minimal or no till systems by which inter-rows are almost permanently covered by perennial sward, arguing that the tidiness of a vineyard's appearance has no direct bearing on wine quality. Such minimal cultivation preserves topsoil structure; it also means that the vineyard becomes a beneficial carbon-sink rather than the cause of the release of carbon and dust into the atmosphere, both of which may contribute to CLIMATE CHANGE and, in the case of dust, encourage certain vine MITES. Perennial swards can also provide MULCH to prevent weed growth directly under the vines if the inter-row vegetation is cut using the so-called mow and throw technique, leaving the mowings on the ground.

For disease prevention, organic growers are reliant on naturally occurring substances. For instance, elemental sulfur and the salt copper sulfate (see BORDEAUX MIXTURE) are used to control POWDERY MILDEW and DOWNY MILDEW respectively. Both these treatments and others commonly used in organic vineyards (e.g. soap, plant oils and teas, seaweed, and powders based on BENTONITE, silicates, milk, and wild herbs) are contact or barrier sprays which, unlike chemically produced systemic sprays, do not enter either the vine's sap or the grape pulp and so are less likely to produce RESIDUES in the wine. Organic growers, especially those in damp, humid climates, are often criticized for relying too heavily on copper-based treatments, leading to COPPER toxicity in the soil. Organic growers argue that copper residues are more easily mobilized where organic management fosters increased levels of soil microbiology, and that organic norms significantly restrict the amount of copper used compared with the amount allowed in conventional vineyards (to one-third in Europe, for example). Furthermore, these restrictions have either encouraged organic growers, especially those in marginal European climates, to switch from *V. vinifera* to DISEASE-RESISTANT interspecific CROSSES, or have inspired organic growers in both hemispheres to find genuinely SUSTAINABLE alternatives to copper and sulfur for mildew control. The most notable of these is aerated compost tea, a low-tech, low-cost, rain-fast way of colonizing vines with beneficial aerobic bacteria, fungi, and other microorganisms that inhibit, consume, or outcompete disease-bearing pathogens. Another increasingly relevant example of this type of approach is the application of strains of the *Trichoderma* fungus to either vine trunks or pruning wounds to protect vines from ESCA.

Other aspects of the organic prophylactic approach to farming in general, and to GREY ROT in particular, include employing canopy management techniques to open up the canopy and reduce the risk of rot. This can result in higher LABOUR costs compared with those of conventional farming. Organic growers who pass these costs on in the price of the wine argue that from a holistic standpoint, organic viticulture eliminates costs to the wider community such as cleaning up by local authorities of groundwater polluted by anti-rot sprays—an increasingly sensitive issue. Organic growers also argue that this predisposition towards manual labour provides employment opportunities in communities suffering rural depopulation due in part to increased MECHANIZATION; and may account for why organic vineyards in France are now more likely than their non-organic counterparts to be picked by hand rather than by machine and to be estate-bottled.

History

The origins of the organic agriculture movement are late-20th-century European. Like its predecessors the Enlightenment, the Romantic movement, and Darwinism, organics can be seen as attempting to redefine man's relationship to his natural surroundings. By the end of the 1920s, when the green movement was closely intertwined with reactionary cultural and political phenomena such as National Socialism in Germany and Guild Socialism in Britain, organics had declared itself as opposing the industrialization of agriculture for both social

and environmental reasons. Its main target was the mineral 'NPK' FERTILIZER devised in 1836 by Justus von Liebig and mass produced from 1913 using the Haber-Bosch process. These fertilizers transformed the agricultural landscape and economic and social structures. However, two World Wars, austerity, rural depopulation, rapidly rising metropolitan populations, and the ease with which NITROGEN production was switched post-1945 from making munitions to fertilizer meant the infant organic movement provided only a fringe argument against the inexorable industrialization of agriculture. And whereas industrial food conglomerates found GLOBALIZATION both necessary and desirable, organic activists struggled to form international bonds, and hence risked accusations of parochialism. The formation in 1972 of the International Federation of Organic Agriculture Movements (IFOAM) to oversee the setting of the majority of the world's organic standards and the certification bodies has helped change this perception.

Nevertheless, although the first organic vineyards were established after the Second World War, it took until the late 1980s for wines produced from organically grown grapes to begin to shake off a reputation for earnest amateurism, inconsistency, and poor value. Critics argue that organic wine's now steadily increasing market share, which began to grow in Europe in the early 1990s, was mainly due to EU subsidies, initially to help growers survive the three-year organic conversion process, but now provided to stimulate rural development and optimize the vineyard ECOSYSTEM. However, its advocates see the main selling point for organics in wine as reinforcing the key notion of TERROIR. This 'working with rather than against nature' handily chimed with increased public unease at the effects of industrialized farming on our food rather than in our wine, notably in the UK, where the food scandals of the mid-1990s and early 2000s involving BSE and foot-and-mouth disease provoked widespread public debate. Concern about the perceived threat that GENETIC MODIFICATION might have on food and wine also stimulated greater interest in the alternatives.

More particularly, though, growers themselves began adopting organics in greater numbers because they felt it would preserve and enhance their main equity, terroir, while giving the wines an organoleptic and marketing edge. More effective vineyard machinery for the control of weeds and disease, improved communication regarding which organic techniques work best, and consumer demand have also contributed to the steady growth in organic viticulture worldwide.

Conford, P., *The Origins of the Organic Movement* (Edinburgh, 2001).

Organic certification and terminology

To be described as 'organic', a vineyard and/or its wine (see ORGANIC WINE) must have third-party certification, usually from a non-governmental organization or 'certifier' accredited by a ministry of agriculture or its equivalent and to criteria which are ISO 17065 (formerly ISO65) compliant. This verifies that the certifier's standards conform to organic global baselines set by IFOAM (see above). Organic certification is granted after a three-year conversion period as wine grapes are a perennial crop (conversion takes two years for annuals such as cereals or carrots). Certification aims to protect both bona fide organic producers and consumers of organic products from anti-competitive activity or fraudulent claims. Certifiers can advise vineyard owners as to why their vineyard does not meet their standards, but cannot provide advice on which organic sprays might be best in any particular situation. Agreements in 2012 between the US, Canada, and the EU mean that organic production and labelling finally enjoy a strong degree of transnational if not yet global equivalence (previously an organic French vineyard exporting to the US needed both EU and American certification documents). Winegrowers who impose on themselves stricter standards than those of the organic baseline may join private organic associations such as France's Nature et Progrès or Germany's Ecovin. These bodies require, for example, wider buffer zones between conventional and organic plots, allow fewer FINING agents, and require lower levels of free and total SULFUR DIOXIDE than those permitted for organic wine.

See also ALTERNATIVE VITICULTURE, BIODYNAMIC VITICULTURE, and SUSTAINABLE VITICULTURE, and NATURAL WINE.

Organic viticulture worldwide

In 1999, 0.5–0.75% of the world vineyard was certified organic or biodynamic or in conversion, the majority of which comprised small, heritage organic estates prioritizing local rather than international markets. As more blue-chip estates in France, notably in the Loire, Alsace, and Burgundy, began converting to organics and biodynamics in the 1990s, conventional wine's potentially negative impact locally and on the wider environment started to be questioned. In California, organic/biodynamic pioneer Jimmy Fetzer's creation of a Mediterranean-style vine garden melding wine-growing with vegetables, olives, fruit, and both fluffy and feathered livestock, helped redefine organic wine as a colourfully positive lifestyle choice, finally providing the movement with sex appeal to go with its gravitas. By the end of the 2000s, Mediterranean France's Roussillon, Rhône, and Provence vineyards had become the global organic hotbeds, helped by a beneficial climate and a slew of second-careerists snapping up competitively-priced de facto organic old-vine vineyards, often from retiring or bankrupt co-operative growers. France's certified organic vineyard tripled in size between 2007 and 2011, and organic viticulture's share of the global vineyard went from under 2% to over 5% between 2007 and 2013, around two-thirds of which was in Europe. Austria's position as the world's wine-growing nation with the highest proportion of organic vineyards is due in large part to its pre-emptive investment in educating potential consumers about organics, thereby creating a ready market for organic food and wine.

Percentages of certified organic and biodynamic vines as part of the national/regional vineyard are as follows: France (7.4% in 2011; 2% in 2005; 0.5% in 1995), Italy (8% in 2011; 6.5% in 2010; 4.4% in 2000), Spain (5.2% in 2010; <1% in 1999), Portugal (c.1% in 2011); Germany (5.6% in 2011; 1.8% in 2003; 1.2% in 1994); Austria (9.2% in 2012; 6% in 2009; 1% in 1999; 0.3% in 1992); Greece (4% in 2010; 1% in 2000); Lebanon (4.5% in 2010); England and Wales (3.4% in 2010); California (c.4% in 2011; 1.1% in 1999; 0.17% in 1989); Oregon (12% in 2013; 8.6% in 2009; 1.4% in 1999); Washington state (2.5% in 2011; 0.6% in 1999); Canada (2.8% in 2011); New Zealand (7.6% in 2012; 2% in 2009; 0.7% in 1999); Australia (<4% in 2012; <1% in 1999); Chile (4.1% in 2011; 0.5% in 2001); Argentina (<2.5% in 2011); South Africa (<1.5% in 2012).

See also ORGANIC WINE, BIODYNAMIC VITICULTURE. M.W.

McGourty, G. T. (ed.), *Organic Winegrowing Manual* (Richmond, Calif., 2011).

organic wine, wine from grapes produced by ORGANIC VITICULTURE and processed (fermented) according to standards for organic winemaking, which, despite increasing harmonization, still vary from country to country, notably regarding the use of SULFUR DIOXIDE. From 1992 to 2011 wine produced or sold in the EU from organic grapes had to be labelled 'wine from organically grown grapes' rather than simply 'organic wine', even if the wines contained no added sulfur dioxide. However, from 2012 new EU rules created the term 'organic wine' for all its wines from organic grapes, whether they contained added sulfur dioxide or not, although maximum levels for the great majority that do are 25–35% lower than for conventional wines, depending on wine colour, sweetness, and style.

In the US and Canada, in contrast, the term 'organic wine' refers to wine made from organic grapes but with no added sulfites, while 'made *with* organic grapes' applies to similarly grown wines containing up to 100 mg/l of added sulfites. Therefore, paradoxically, all European wines from organic grapes sold in the US or Canada must be labelled 'made with organic grapes' rather than 'organic wine', even if they contain no added sulfites. This is because EU rules permit sulfite addition in both pre-2011 wines labelled 'from organic grapes' and those labelled as 'organic wine' from 2012 onwards.

Organic winemaking standards worldwide generally permit most other winemaking treatments, including, for example, adding DIAMMONIUM PHOSPHATE as a yeast nutrient and REVERSE OSMOSIS, because these have also been allowed for organic food, although their use in wine is under review in the EU. Although PVPP and potassium ferrocyanide (see BLUE FINING) are universally proscribed FINING agents for organic wine, most other fining agents are allowed, so that wines labelled in some way as organic may be unsuitable for vegetarians and vegans. (It is a common misconception that organic also equals vegetarian- or vegan-friendly.) Energy-intensive treatments (such as must CONCENTRATION, THERMOVINIFICATION, and PASTEURIZATION) are allowed by general organic standards, although members of organic wine producer groups such as Nature et Progrès in France voluntarily agree to shun them. Demeter-certified BIODYNAMIC winemakers cannot use processes that require large inputs of either energy or raw materials. Where possible, naturally derived additives, agents, and aids such as sugar for CHAPTALIZATION, yeast hulls to feed ferments, and egg whites for FINING should be from organic sources. Grape spirit used in organic fortified wines must have been distilled from certified organic grapes/marc/wine.

Organic wines made in the EU may carry the EU organic logo (stars in the shape of a leaf). M.W.

origins of viniculture. The beginning of viniculture, encompassing both VITICULTURE and WINEMAKING, cannot have begun where our species, *Homo sapiens sapiens*, originated in sub-Saharan Africa. While our ancestors might have exploited other high sugar fruits (e.g. fig and marula) for fermented beverages, the wild Eurasian grapevine (*Vitis vinifera sylvestris*; see WILD VINES) did not grow there. Only when humans came 'out of Africa', 60,000-100,000 years ago, did they encounter the grape. This occurrence, so auspicious for the future cultural and technological history of humanity, probably took place in the area of modern Lebanon, the southernmost point where wild vines grow in the Near East today and probably for the last 100,000 years.

No archaeological evidence of this initial encounter nor of the first wine exists for the Palaeolithic period. Containers, which can be chemically analysed, have not survived since they were made of perishable materials such as leather or wood. Yet, the centrality of FERMENTATION to life on Earth, as well as the physiological propensities (sensory, dietary, and mind-altering) of most animals for consuming alcohol, imply that humans would soon have discovered how to make wine from wild grapes.

Grapevines that festooned the forests of coastal and mountainous Lebanon would probably have captivated our ancestors and the colourful fruit, even if it were sour, would almost certainly have been gathered up for food and made into the 'first wine', whether accidentally or by applying traditional African traditions. We might imagine the following, according to the 'Palaeolithic Hypothesis' or 'Drunken Monkey Hypothesis': fruit was piled into a primitive container, juice was exuded from grapes near the bottom of the container under the weight of fruit above and, depending on its ripeness, fermentation of this liquid (the ideal, nutritious medium) would be initiated by YEAST on the skins of some of the grapes in a warm climate in several days. Reaching the bottom of the container, our ancestors would have been amazed by the aromatic and mildly intoxicating beverage that was produced. More intentional squeezings and tastings might well have ensued. You had to drink it quickly, since methods for preserving wine were likely poorly developed.

It is also possible that observation led to the discovery of LAYERING in which some vine woody parts, including STEMS and CANES, would have formed roots when growing along the ground. Once the new vine had sprung up, it might have been trained to grow up a nearby tree or even an artificial support.

A detailed knowledge of pruning and training would have come later, at least by c.3000 BC. By severing a rooted vine part from the parent plant, it could have been transplanted. Controlling the vine's height and shape would have enabled easier care and harvesting. Whoever did this was the world's first vine grower, and this would have been the world's first vineyard.

For larger-scale, more organized viniculture, we must cast a wider net than the Levant, to include the vast upland region of the eastern Taurus, Caucasus, and Zagros Mountains of north western Iran. These areas comprise a sort of world centre of the Eurasian grapevine, where its greatest genetic diversity is found and where a wine culture consolidated itself in the Neolithic period, c.9500–5000 BC.

Oldest grape wines

To date, the earliest chemically attested instance of grapes being used in a fermented beverage is at the Neolithic site of Jiahu in the Yellow River in the central plains of ancient China during the 7th millennium BC. Yet, the probable native wild grape was only one of several other fermentable ingredients in this mixed beverage. (With upwards of 30 native wild vine species, China accounts for more than half of the vine species in the world, some of which produce berries containing as much as 19% sugar by weight. No evidence, however, has yet been found to show that any of these species were ever domesticated until recent times.)

For an alcoholic beverage fermented solely from the Eurasian grape, the earliest chemical evidence for grape wine comes from the Neolithic village of Hajji Firuz Tepe, about 5400–5000 BC, in the northern Zagros Mountains of Iran. Six jars in a kitchen of an average household would originally have held some 55 l (15 gal) of wine, based on the presence of TARTARIC ACID which is found in large amounts in the Middle East only in grapes. The intended product was most likely wine and not vinegar or another grape product, because clay stoppers were used to stopper the narrow mouths of the jars and a tree resin, probably terebinth with anti-oxidant properties, was added to the wine as a preservative. Hajji Firuz was among the first year-round settlements based on newly domesticated plants and animals of the Neolithic period. The Eurasian VINIFERA grapevine might well have been one of those domesticates. The invention of pottery around 6000 BC gave impetus to the process, since special vessels for preparing, storing, and serving wine could now be made.

The large amount of wine for a single household implies that the Eurasian grape had already been domesticated at Hajji Firuz. In contrast to the wild dioecious plant (with separate male and female vines), the domesticated vine is hermaphroditic (with male stamen and female pistil on flowers of the same plant). It produces much more fruit, since it is not dependent on insects or wind for pollination.

For the vine to have been domesticated, either the sub-macroscopic sexual organs of a hermaphrodite need to be observed, which is quite unlikely since hermaphrodites comprise only about 6% of the wild population or, more probably, the would-be Neolithic viniculturalist noted that some vines yielded more fruit than others and proceeded to CLONE them by layering. Transplantation by CUTTINGS, roots, or buds was eventually discovered. Plants could also be selected for special characteristics (e.g. juicier and tastier fruit, different sizes and colour, fewer seeds, etc.) and moved to another place. Cloning could not have been done with the seeds of a desirable plant because they are genetically different to the parent plant. The magnitude of the accomplishment in domesticating *V. vinifera* vines can be appreciated by considering that of the many other grape species around the world, no evidence yet exists that any of them were domesticated by ancient humans. That distinction belongs solely to the Eurasian grapevine, which produces 99% of the world's wine today.

The Noah Hypothesis

But how early and where was the Eurasian grapevine domesticated? Was it at Hajji Firuz,

which lies within the modern distribution of the wild vine, or elsewhere in the Near East? Recent DNA PROFILING of modern wild grape and domesticated VINE VARIETIES in Europe and the Near East (including Turkey, Armenia, and Georgia but not yet Lebanon or Iran) points to a single Near Eastern domestication event (the so-called NOAH Hypothesis). Specifically, a very close relationship has been shown between wild and domesticated vines from eastern Turkey and Georgia and important western European cultivars, including Pinot Noir, Nebbiolo, Syrah, and Chasselas. Since the European *V. v. sylvestris* was far removed from these cultivars, it cannot fully account for their origin (see below).

As the domesticated grapevine was transplanted southwards to Egypt and SHIRAZ and westwards across the Mediterranean and the continent, there was introgression with wild vines in those areas such as Greece, Italy, France, and Spain to yield many more Middle Eastern and European varieties. At a later time, when the grapevine was better understood, independent domestication events may have taken place where the wild grapevine grew—in Spain, for example.

The Noah Hypothesis is plausible for other reasons. Exploitation of wild grapes had been going on since the Natufian period (*c*.11,000–10,000 BC) , as evidenced by the finding of pips at numerous sites along the middle Euphrates River in Syria. Several hundred kilometres upstream in the Taurus Mountains of Turkey, Çayönü, on the upper Tigris has yielded wild grape seeds dating back to around 9000 BC, and many other sites in the region have yielded similar evidence ranging in date as recently as the late Chalcolithic period, *c*.3500 BC.

The earliest domesticated Eurasian grape pips, which are generally longer and narrower than their wild counterparts (although Pinot is an exception), are reported from the Neolithic sites of Shulaveris-Gora in Georgia, Chokh in Dagestan, and Shomutepe in Azerbaijan. Once DNA PROFILING methods for extracting and testing ancient grapes have been developed, the wild/domesticated gene can be used to verify the equivocal botanical criteria.

Shulaveris-Gora and nearby Neolithic sites are also notable for having some of the earliest Near Eastern pottery which are decorated with motifs which may well be grape clusters and vines, and may have served as fermentation and drinking vessels. Chemical analyses were underway in early 2014. Since the later archaeology and history of Georgia was dominated by a wine culture intertwining almost every aspect of life—from everyday meals to special celebrations, religious rites, and the economy as a whole—it may be reasonably hypothesized that the newfound horticultural and technological advances of the Neolithic period laid the

basis for what followed, and which continues today.

Recent explorations in the eastern Taurus Mountains are revealing equally extraordinary developments in the Neolithic period there, going back to 9500 BC. At Göbekli Tepe and Nevali Çori, not far from Çayönü, 'sanctuaries' of three-dimensional monoliths with vivid, realistic portrayals of carved animals, humans, and symbolic motifs were constructed. Pottery had not yet made its appearance, but stone goblets and bowls were made of the highly absorbent clay mineral, chlorite, found at many other sites along the upper Tigris River extending into Syria. Celebratory scenes are again depicted, possibly fuelled by a fermented beverage. Wine again appears to be a distinct possibility, according to ongoing chemical analyses of copious amounts of ancient organic compounds extracted from the vessels using solvents. But wheat/barley beer cannot be ruled out, since einkorn wheat, one of the Neolithic founder plants, has been traced by DNA to the south eastern Taurus. A more complex fermented beverage of wine, beer, honey, and other botanicals, underlining the experimental prowess of our Neolithic ancestors, is also possible.

Another startling discovery was announced in 2011 from a cave at Areni in Armenia. In this mountainous area, humans constructed plaster floors for grape PRESSES designed to run the grape juice into underground jars, which constitute the earliest *karas* (in Armenian) or QVEVRI (in Georgian). Grape seeds in the vicinity suggested that the contents of the vessels were wine, and chemical analysis confirmed this. A contemporaneous cemetery within the cave suggests that the wine was used in burial services for the ancestors. This finding bridges the gap from winemaking during the Neolithic Period to the recent discovery of a probable wine cellar at Tel Kabri in the Galilee, *c*.1700 BC, and the enormous Urartian wine cellars of *c*.800–600 BC, some 2500 years later. The large-scale production at Areni points to a long gestation period after pottery was invented and large jars for fermentation were developed. But if Areni comes at the end of a long development, we are still left with the question, according to the Noah Hypothesis: where was *Vitis vinifera* first domesticated and wine first made?

Levantine influence spreads south and west

We do know that viniculture ultimately radiated out from the mountainous Near East to other areas on the western and eastern arms of the Fertile Crescent. It had reached CANAAN by *c*.3500 BC, to judge from grape seeds, wood, and even whole dried grapes (raisins) recovered from sites in the Jordan Valley. In MESOPOTAMIA transplantation of the vine and winemaking followed the spine of the Zagros Mountains and had arrived in Shiraz in south western Iran by at least 2500 BC.

The southern Levantine industry had matured to such a degree that by the time of Scorpion I (*c.*3150 BC), one of the first rulers of a united Egypt, his tomb at Abydos was stocked with 4,500 l of wine imported from southern Canaan. The wine was laced with terebinth tree resin, to which fresh fruit (grapes and figs) and various Levantine herbs such as thyme and savory had been added. The grapes might also have been added as raisins. It was essentially a medicinal powerhouse, and the well-documented Egyptian pharmacopeia of later times clearly drew inspiration, as well as the botanicals themselves, from the Canaanite world. Only the best beverage could serve to usher a pharaoh into the afterlife.

Once the kings and upper classes had been enticed by wine, the next logical step was to transfer viniculture to Egypt itself, so as to tailor the wines to individual tastes and exercise more control. Beginning around 3000 BC, the Egyptian pharaohs financed the establishment of a royal wine industry in the Nile Delta.

The new Egyptian industry was striking in its level of sophistication from the outset. Of course, the Canaanite specialists had many millennia of tradition behind them when they brought grapevines to the Nile Delta. Even the Egyptian hieroglyph meaning 'grape', 'vineyard' or 'wine' is a telling piece of evidence of viticultural expertise. As the earliest written character referring to the domesticated grapevine and wine from anywhere in the world, the hieroglyph graphically depicts a well-trained vine growing up on to a trellis of vertical poles, forked at their upper ends to hold the vine. The plant is rooted in a container, probably for ease of watering. In short, the best practices of modern vineyard management, including a drip irrigation system, were on display at the inception of the ancient Egyptian industry.

The Canaanite winemakers also had to be creative. Levantine vineyards, generally in hilly terrain with good drainage for winter rains, had a very different TERROIR than the flat, alluvial Nile delta where blistering summer heat and much less precipitation meant that crops, especially water-sensitive grapes, had to be irrigated. A trellising system minimized direct exposure of the grapes to intense sunlight. Fortunately the alluvial deposits of the delta, washed down from the upper Nile during the annual flooding, had produced well-drained and fertile soils.

Wine, which was specifically referred to by where it came from in the Delta—the ancient equivalent of today's vineyard-specific wines—had achieved canonical status as an essential funerary offering by Dynasty 6, around 2200 BC. In time, nearly every major religious festival, including the all-important *heb-sed* to guarantee the continued welfare of the pharaoh and the fruitfulness of the land, called for wine offerings and prolific drinking, often lasting for weeks.

With winemaking success in Egypt behind them, the Canaanites ventured further throughout the Mediterranean on their Byblos ships (telling Egyptian term for a sea-going vessel) made of Cedar of Lebanon. They applied a similar formula wherever they went: import wine and other luxury goods, entice the rulers with wine culture by presenting them with speciality wine sets, and then wait until they were asked to help establish native industries, including viniculture, by transplanting the domesticated Eurasian grapevine.

According to the biomolecular and archaeobotanical evidence, one of the first stops in the island-hopping jaunts of the Canaanites across the Mediterranean was CRETE. Nearly 1,000 kilometres from the port city-states of Lebanon and southern Syria, this large island lies on the threshold of the larger Greek world. Although modern scholars are understandably sceptical about the often-contradictory and fantastic tales of classical writers, a recurring theme in many accounts has the Greek wine god DIONYSUS voyaging from PHOENICIA to Crete as a daring seafarer. One beautifully painted drinking-cup (*kylix*) made by the master potter Exekias in the 6th century BC, shows the god single-handedly manning a small sailing boat, its mast festooned with a luxuriant grapevine. Apparently, Dionysus had been attacked by pirates, and fought back by miraculously growing the vine and dousing his attackers with wine; they were transformed into frolicking dolphins, who are seen circling around the boat. Could this tale be inspired by an actual voyage that carried the domesticated grapevine to Crete aboard a Byblos ship?

The earliest wine so far identified on Crete was from the late 3rd millennium BC farming community of Myrtos-Phournou Koryphe, along the southern coast. Numerous large jars (PITHOI) holding about 90 l were recovered from storerooms and kitchens of ordinary houses throughout the site. The pottery was locally produced, as was presumably the wine. Grape seeds, stems, and skins in some jars suggested fermentation on the lees, minimal filtration, and/or adding fresh grapes for flavor.

Numerous circular vats, often called 'bathtubs', were also found at Myrtos. Such finds, also well attested in ancient Egypt, are most often associated with industrial winemaking. The bathtubs, fitted with spouts for draining the grape juice into large jars, were ideal for FOOT TREADING. As one worker tired, the next would step into the vat and take over. Large-scale production was also marked by a massive funnel, the stock-in-trade of the Near Eastern winemaker, and impressions of grape leaves on the pottery pointed to vineyards in the vicinity.

Much like the royal winemaking industry in Egypt, the Myrtos enterprise appears to have sprung out of nowhere. Did the impetus to make wine at Myrtos come from elsewhere in Greece, or was it brought to this island by the Canaanites? The latter position is better supported. Myrtos lay at the terminus of a well-travelled maritime route for ships coming from Egypt and the Levant, and the distinctly Near Eastern character of its winemaking industry suggests influence from this quarter. The Canaanites were looking to spread their wine culture and they saw an opportunity in Greece to work with the local Cretan people to advance their interests.

Greek winemaking's debt to the Canaanites, as well as to their Egyptian trading partners, is also reflected in the later signs for 'grape', 'vineyard', and 'wine' in the earliest Greek scripts, including Cretan Hieroglyphic and Linear A. The characters are unquestionably derived from the Egyptian hieroglyph, which shows a well-trained vine growing on a horizontal trellis.

It is also possible that winemaking penetrated Greece from the north, especially from Macedonia where masses of grape skins and seeds, probably from pressings, have been recovered from late 5th millennium BC Dikili Tash, or perhaps came from western Anatolia via the Aegean islands where domesticated grape remains and leaf impressions on pottery have been found. A notable finding of domesticated grape pips inside a *pithos* was made at Aghios Kosmas in Attica. The large jar had a hole near its base, just like the Myrtos vessels. This is *prima facie* evidence that winemaking, perhaps along the same scale as that at Myrtos, was known on the mainland at about the same time.

The Canaanites, who became the Phoenicians of the Iron Age, did not stop at Crete. They sailed on to CARTHAGE in Tunisia and other parts of the western Mediterranean. The founders of Carthage, probably in the late 9th century BC, entered a territory only sparsely occupied by Berber pastoral nomads, who offered little resistance. Unlike more populous regions of the Mediterranean, it allowed the Phoenicians to play the role of true colonialists by foregoing trade agreements and building a settlement completely to their specifications. As Carthage grew in the following centuries, it became the capital of the Punic empire and the breadbasket of the Roman empire. Its ships plied the waters from Carthage through the Tyrrhenian Sea to the port of ROME at Ostia. Long lines of AMPHORAE spread out on the sea floor at a depth of as much as 1,000 m representing the cargo lost by foundering ships mark the approximately 600 km route, notably at Skerki Bank about 80 km north west of SICILY.

Wine was naturally the beverage of choice in ancient Carthage. One of the first AGRICULTURAL

TREATISES on viniculture and other forms of agriculture was composed by a 3rd-2nd century BC Carthaginian named Mago, who is quoted extensively in later Roman writings (VARRO, COLUMELLA, and PLINY THE ELDER). Presumably he drew on Phoenician traditions dating from the founding of the colony. To date, however, pips from the 4th century BC are the earliest excavated evidence for the domesticated grape at Carthage.

Although the wild vine grows in Tunisia, special precautions had to be taken to assure survival of the domesticated grapevine in such a hot climate. Mago advised on how to aerate the soil and plant vineyards (e.g. on north slopes to take advantage of rainfall coming from the Mediterranean) to compensate for the low rainfall. His recipe for raisin-wine involved picking the grapes at peak ripeness, rejecting damaged berries, drying the grapes on reed platforms in the sun for several days (taking care to cover them at night, so that they were not dampened by the dew), resaturating the raisins with fresh juice, and then treading the grapes. A second batch was prepared in the same way, and then the two lots were combined and fermented for about a month, finally being strained into vessels with leather covers. The end-result must have been a delicious, luscious elixir, also referred to in the earlier Anatolian texts of HOMER and HESIOD, much like a Tuscan VIN SANTO or Moscato di PANTELLERIA.

The huge Phoenician and Carthaginian shipments of wine, along with other luxury items, conveyed a new, wine-based way of life which gradually permeated the societies, religions, and economies of those they came in contact with. In the wake of the Phoenicians, native fermented beverages, including beers, and mixed fermented beverages of all kinds ('grogs'), were marginalized, modified, and displaced.

Wine culture invades Greece, then Italy, then France

Greece, which became a pre-eminent wine culture, was won over from its native 'Greek grog', made from Pramnian wine, honey, and barley, topped with cheese—the so-called *kykeon* of the Homeric epics. Even after the Greeks had become seafaring merchants in their own right and had begun vying with Phoenicia for control of the Mediterranean, their lasting debt to eastern Mediterranean wine culture was demonstrated by their adoption of the Phoenician alphabet which became the basis of our modern Western and Arabic scripts. The earliest archaic Greek inscription was incised on a wine jug (*oinochoe*) in the 8th century BC and reads: 'Whoever of all dancers performs most nimbly will win this *oinochoe* as prize.' Later in the same century, a Rhodian wine cup (*kotyle*) from the tomb of a young boy at Pithekoussai, an early Greek colony established on the island of ISCHIA in the Bay of Naples, states in elegant dactylic hexameter poetry, the language of the Homeric epics, that 'Nestor's cup was good to drink from, but anyone who drinks from this cup will soon be struck with desire for fair-crowned Aphrodite.' The Dionysiac interweaving of wine, women, and dance, inspired by Canaanite and Phoenician wine culture, is striking.

During the early first millennium BC, the Phoenicians ventured ever further into the western Mediterranean where they founded more bases and colonies along the north coast of Africa, on strategic islands (MALTA, CORSICA, Motya in western SICILY, LIPARI, IBIZA, etc.), and along the Spanish coast, even out into the Atlantic at Huelva, near Cádiz.

Greek traders followed suit, establishing colonies on many of the same islands (e.g. eastern Sicily and Corsica), southern Italy (OENOTRIA), northern Africa (e.g. Cyrene), and at Massalia (modern Marseille) in southern Mediterranean France.

Numerous Iron Age shipwrecks, loaded with amphorae and wine-related paraphernalia, have been located and excavated along the Italian and French coasts. The Phoenician and Greek impact throughout the Mediterranean was so pronounced that one can say that it was mediated by wine culture itself.

The 8th century BC saw the climax of Phoenician influence on the hearts, minds, and palates of native Mediterranean peoples. The ETRUSCANS of central Italy along the Tyrrhenian Sea illustrates the phenomenon and how it spread. They probably first came in contact with the Phoenicians before the Greeks arrived on their shores, as shown by their 'Orientalizing' industries, which closely reflected Phoenician style, technology, and iconography in metals, pottery, ivory, and glass. Their amphora was modelled after the Phoenician amphora, and where a similarity of form exists, it was likely because it served a similar function: primarily to hold grape wine, which soon began to be supplied by a nascent local industry.

As in other parts of Europe, the Etruscans already had a tradition of making a mixed fermented beverage before their culture was impacted by the Phoenicians. According to the available evidence, this 'grog' probably combined honey, barley, and wheat, even pomegranates, hazelnuts, herbs such as rosemary and thyme, tree resins, wild grapes, etc. The Phoenician traders lured them into a wine culture by presenting them with cauldrons, kraters (see CRATER), and other drinking vessels. The Etruscans probably first adapted the vessels to their native customs and mixed beverages, similarly to the CELT further north. After they had adopted the wine culture, they made their own wine vessels in pottery and precious metals, including gilded drinking-bowls of Phoenician-type.

In turn, the Etruscans became the principal conveyors of wine culture to coastal Mediterranean France by c.625–600 BC. It is not surprising that the Gauls or Celts there should have become equally entranced by the cultural and economic possibilities for wine and begun to substitute it for their native beverages.

The Gauls might have had a general knowledge of the Eurasian vine, which grew wild along the northern Mediterranean shore, but any successful exploitation of the domesticated vine to make wine would have required much more horticultural knowledge and technological proficiency, probably provided by the Etruscans. The domesticated grapevine needed to be transplanted and tended. Specialized equipment was needed to transform it into wine, which was preserved by a tree resin additive to stoppered vessels.

Plantings of the domesticated Eurasian grapevine in France were probably transported on Etruscan ships. A 4th century BC Punic shipwreck off the coast of Mallorca at El Sec illustrates how this might have been accomplished: grapevines on this ship were embedded in soil in the cool hull of the ship; this would have enabled them to travel safely enough to be replanted.

This supposition has now been corroborated by archaeological, chemical, and botanical findings at the heavily Etruscan-influenced site of Lattes (ancient Lattara), near Montpellier, where numerous Etruscan wine amphorae were imported in the 6th century BC and stored in harbour storehouses. As analyses have shown, the wine was resinated with pine and laced with botanicals (probably rosemary and/or thyme). A century later, local winemaking had begun at the site, as shown by the finding of masses of grape seeds, pedicels, and even fruit (grapeskins), commonly associated with treading activity, and what is so far the earliest wine press yet discovered in France.

The Etruscan role in the process was further revealed by a shipwreck (Grand Ribaud F), found just off Hyères east of Marseilles and dated c.515–475 BC. Its hold was filled with grapevines and some 700 to 800 amphorae. All the Etruscan amphorae on board this ship had been carefully stoppered with cork (among the earliest evidence for this technology, and also attested at Lattara) and stacked at least five layers deep in the hull. Significantly, they are of the same pottery type and are contemporaneous with the Etruscan amphoras at Lattara. The ship's final destination may have been Lattara.

The wine culture of Mediterranean France spread inland after the Roman conquest up the Rhône and Rhine rivers to the rest of Europe where, centuries later, monasteries such as the Cistercian Abbey of Vougeot in Burgundy, refined French viniculture so that it became a model for the world. It needs to be stressed, however, that France owes a debt of gratitude to earlier Levantine viniculture.

See also PALAEOETHNOBOTANY AND THE ARCHAEOLOGY OF WINE P.E.M.

Barnard, H., et al., 'Chemical evidence for wine production around 4000 BCE in the Late Chalcolithic Near Eastern Highlands', *Journal of Archaeological Science*, 38/5 (2011), 977–84.

Fleming, S. J., and Katz, S. H., *The Origins and Ancient History of Wine* (New York, 1995).

Mirzoian, A., and Hall, G. R., 'Ancient Egyptian herbal wines', *The Proceedings of the National Academy of Sciences USA*, 106/18 (2009), 7361–6.

McGovern, P. E., *Ancient Wine* (Princeton and Oxford, 2003).

McGovern, P. E., *Uncorking the Past: The Quest for Wine, Beer, and Other Alcoholic Beverages* (Berkeley, 2009).

McGovern, P. E., et al., 'Fermented beverages of Pre- and Proto-Historic China', *The Proceedings of the National Academy of Sciences USA*, 101/51 (2004), 17593–8.

McGovern, P. E., 'The beginning of viniculture in France', *The Proceedings of the National Academy of Sciences USA*, 110/25 (2013), 10147–52.

Robinson, J., Harding, J., and Vouillamoz, J., *Wine Grapes: A Complete Guide to 1,368 Vine Varieties, Including their Origins and Flavours* (London, 2012).

Orion, complex, recent OPTIMA x VILLARD Blanc hybrid, a DISEASE-RESISTANT VARIETY, which produces crisp, aromatic white wine not unlike SEYVAL BLANC, notably in Europe's northernmost wine regions.

Orléans, AOC created in 2006 for wines produced around the city of Orléans where the River Loire turns west. Burgundian influence is evident in the choice of grape varieties, principally Chardonnay and Pinot Meunier. At one time this was an important wine region but the development of the RAILWAYS changed all that and today fewer than 100 ha/250 acres of vineyards remain. They are too close to Paris to be of much practical interest to wine drinkers outside France, for the light, pale, fragrant wines have many devotees in the French capital. **Orléans-Cléry** is an even smaller AOC (just 32 ha in 2012) zone south west of the city on the left bank of the Loire for Cabernet-based reds.

See also LOIRE, including map.

Ormeasco, local name for DOLCETTO on the north-western coast of Italy. For more details, see LIGURIA.

Ornellaia, important BOLGHERI estate founded in 1981 by Lodovico ANTINORI, brother of Piero Antinori, following in the footsteps of nearby Tenuta San Guido's phenomenal success with SASSICAIA. The estate was created when Lodovico acquired 70 ha of land from his mother, sister-in-law of the owner of Tenuta San Guido. He hired André Tchelistcheff as his CONSULTANT. He planted Bordeaux grape varieties and the first commercial vintage, 1985, was an immediate success, eclipsed by the estate's release in 1986 of Masseto, a Pomerol-styled Merlot from a single vineyard. Michel ROLLAND succeeded Tchelistcheff. In 1999 Lodovico sold a share of Ornellaia to Robert MONDAVI who took complete control of the estate in 2003 with the Frescobaldi family (with whom Mondavi had already started a Tuscan JOINT VENTURE to produce the internationally styled SUPERTUSCAN Luce). In 2005 CONSTELLATION BRANDS, which had acquired Mondavi, sold the remaining 50% of Ornellaia to Frescobaldi. This recent somewhat stormy history has never compromised the wine's popularity nor its commercial value. Meanwhile, in 2001 Lodovico, together with Piero Antinori, founded a new estate in Bibbona north of Bolgheri, Tenuta di Biserno, where Rolland is involved in the production of Bordeaux-style wines. W.S.

Ortega was once popular as an OECHSLE booster in German wines, especially with the blenders of Rheinhessen. This CROSS of Müller-Thurgau and Siegerrebe produces extremely full-flavoured wines that often lack acidity but can reach high MUST WEIGHTS, if not quite as high as the equally early-ripening but less widely planted OPTIMA. Varietal wines are made, but a little goes a long way. The vine does not have good disease resistance, however, and its susceptibility to COULURE and ROT leaves Optima the more obvious choice for the Mosel. Germany's total plantings dropped from around 1,200 ha/2,960 acres in the the late 1980s to 561 ha in 2012. The variety is also quite popular in ENGLAND, for obvious reasons.

Ortrugo, white grape grown on about 600 ha/1,483 acres in the hills around Piacenza in EMILIA, often blended with Malvasia.

Orvieto, dry, medium dry, and sometimes—although increasingly rarely—sweet white wine produced near the medieval hill city of the same name, an important artistic centre during the late Middle Ages and Renaissance, is one of Italy's historically renowned white wines and by far the most important DOC in UMBRIA. Within the extensive DOC, partially shared with neighbouring LAZIO, is a historic CLASSICO zone. The vines are grown on TUFA and wines come in dry (secco), medium dry (abboccato), medium sweet (amabile), late harvest (vendemmia tardiva), and botrytized (muffa nobile) sweet versions. Due to the proximity of Lakes Corbara and Bolsano, and frequent autumn fogs, Orvieto is one of the very few places in Italy regularly affected by NOBLE ROT. The wine is a blend of PROCANICO, a local name for the bland TREBBIANO Toscano, and the much more characterful GRECHETTO, VERDELLO, MALVASIA BIANCA, and the tart DRUPEGGIO. Although Orvieto's reputation has been harmed by over-produced wines based on Procanico, recent changes to the production rules require a higher proportion of Grechetto at the expense of Procanico, while several producers have begun to bottle VARIETAL Grechetto, usefully demonstrating the grape's potential. While yields of up to 11 tonnes/ha are allowed, the actual average yield hovers around a much more reasonable 60 hl/ha, indicating a trend towards quality rather than quantity. Several producers have begun to produce a single-vineyard Orvieto.

Faced with declining sales and ever-lower prices for Orvieto at the beginning of this century, the local CONSORZIO created a red wine DOC Orvietano Rosso based on ALEATICO, CABERNET SAUVIGNON, and MERLOT, as well as MONTEPULCIANO and SANGIOVESE, blended or as single varieties. Such wines were in the past labelled IGT Umbria. Although considerable investments as early as the late 1970s were made in the region, notably by the likes of ANTINORI with their Castello della Sala estate, and a regular influx of consultant OENOLOGISTS, the focus tended to be on INTERNATIONAL VARIETIES and BARRIQUES. More distinctive expressions are expected as local varieties are re-evaluated. W.S.

www.consorziovinidiorvieto.it

Oseleta, revived red wine grape speciality of the VALPOLICELLA zone.

Osey, variously spelt **Oseye** and **Osaye**, fortified wine from PORTUGAL drunk in England in the 15th century, thought likely to have originated from vineyards near Lisbon, the name being an English corruption of the locality of Azóia northwest of Lisbon. See also CARCAVELOS and SETÚBAL. R.J.M.

Mayson, R., *The Wines and Vineyards of Portugal* (London, 2003).

osmosis. See CONCENTRATION and REVERSE OSMOSIS.

OTR. See OXYGEN TRANSMISSION RATE.

Ottavianello, Puglian name for the French red grape variety CINSAUT.

ouillage, French word meaning both ULLAGE and TOPPING UP. The term **ouillé** is used in the JURA to differentiate white wines made this way from those that are aged OXIDATIVELY or under FILM-FORMING YEASTS.

ovary, the ovule-containing part of the pistil of a FLOWER which, in the grapevine, develops into the grape berry. After FLOWERING, the ovary becomes a berry and the ovules become seeds (see GRAPE). B.G.C.

overcropping, a vine condition which delays grape RIPENING and therefore reduces wine quality. It is associated with low LEAF TO FRUIT RATIOS. Overcropping can be due to PRUNING to many buds with some fruitful varieties, or to a loss of leaf area as a result of INSECT PESTS or FUNGAL DISEASES. If climatic conditions are limiting for PHOTOSYNTHESIS, as with low temperatures or very limited sunlight, then vines may be considered overcropped. The grapes of overcropped vines are typically lower in sugar, colour, and flavour, and have an increased PH. Wines made from such fruit are typically termed thin.

Overcropping is a term which is also used emotively in arguments against high vineyard yields. Provided that the vine is in BALANCE and good health, even high yields can be properly ripened with good weather and good vineyard management. See also YIELD.   R.E.S.

overripeness. See SURMATURITÉ.

O.W.C. stands for 'original wooden case' and is frequently used as a description in the sale of FINE WINE. See CASE.

own-rooted vine. See UNGRAFTED VINE.

oxidation, the opposite of REDUCTION, is the chemical reaction in which a chemical compound loses electrons. Although controlled and moderate oxidation can be beneficial and is essential for some wine styles (see below), the term usually refers to a wine FAULT resulting from excessive exposure to OXYGEN (as opposed to AERATION, which is deliberate, controlled exposure to oxygen). Wines spoiled by oxidation are said to be **oxidized**. See also OXIDATIVE WINEMAKING.

Oxidation is a threat as soon as the grape is crushed, which is why high-quality grapes are transported to the winery as fast as possible in shallow containers, and why field pressing stations sited as close as possible to the vineyard are increasingly common. When the grape is crushed, unless special precautions are taken to exclude oxygen, it immediately starts to react with the liberated juice compounds. The most obvious change is the browning of the juice resulting from the oxidation of PHENOLICS catalysed by an ENZYME (polyphenol oxidase) present in grapes and thus referred to as enzymatic oxidation or enzymatic browning. The presence on the grapes of moulds associated with ROT introduces additional oxidative enzymes (LACCASES) which accelerate reactions with oxygen, especially those involved with browning. Small amounts of SULFUR DIOXIDE (5 g/hl) are therefore usually added to the must to inactivate enzymes and counter the oxidation of phenolics. See PROTECTIVE JUICE HANDLING for the techniques involved in minimizing the risk of oxidation.

Some winemakers, however, deliberately encourage a certain amount of prefermentation oxidation of grape varieties such as Chardonnay in order to develop a range of flavours other than those associated with primary fruit AROMA. Sometimes known as hyperoxidation, this also enhances enzymatic oxidation of phenolics and their conversion to insoluble polymers, which are then removed by CLARIFICATION treatments. As a result, the wine contains lower amounts of phenolic compounds that may generate brown pigments and haze through non-enzymatic oxidation reactions (see below) and is thus more stable. This technique is usually reserved for non-aromatic grape varieties. See WHITE WINE-MAKING for more details.

The last step of FERMENTATION, the REDUCTION of ACETALDEHYDE to ETHANOL, is coupled with the oxidation of the co-enzyme NADH, as shown in this equation:

$$CH_3CHO + NADH + H^+ \rightarrow CH_3CH_2OH + NAD^+$$

Note that no new oxygen is involved in this reaction, but that the essence of the reduction is the transfer of electrons from the co-enzyme to the acetaldehyde. Most oxidation–reduction reactions involved in growing grapes and making wine are of this type.

In wine itself, however, exposure to oxygen in the presence of an organism such as ACETOBACTER could result in a reversal of the above reaction, with alcohol being oxidized to acetaldehyde. The NADH produced by oxidizing alcohol is, in turn, oxidized by oxygen from the air. When this happens, the wine loses its fresh, fruity aroma and becomes vapid and flat smelling. Further exposure to oxygen converts the acetaldehyde to ACETIC ACID, the acidic component of wine VINEGAR, the winemaker's *bête noire*.

Oxygen reacts with the phenolics in both white and red wines through complex chemical oxidation processes that may also promote oxidation of ETHANOL to ACETALDEHYDE. In whites, the COLOUR changes from light yellow to amber and ultimately brown, and at this last stage the quality of a table wine is usually seriously impaired. In reds, with their greater complement of phenolics (ANTHOCYANINS, TANNINS, and PIGMENTED TANNINS), the colour change is much less apparent and a red wine can accommodate, and indeed benefit from, considerably greater exposure to oxygen than a white wine. While the natural formation of stable pigmented tannins in a red wine is a process requiring oxidation, other products of the reaction of the wine's phenolics with oxygen bring about highly desirable changes in the sensory properties of the wine. An appropriate level of oxygen exposure is usually accomplished through PUMPING OVER, DÉLESTAGE, RACKING, TOPPING UP, and the usual transfer operations imposed on a red wine.

Barrel maturation also involves regular exposure of the wine to small amounts of oxygen. This has inspired the development of technologies such as MICRO-OXYGENATION and the use of CLOSURES with controlled OXYGEN TRANSFER RATES to control oxygen exposure during ÉLEVAGE and BOTTLE AGEING.

To produce table wines attractive in aroma and colour, and certainly those designed to be drunk young, the winemaker generally restricts the exposure of must and wine to oxygen as much as is technically feasible (see PROTECTIVE WINEMAKING for more details).

Some wines, however, such as *oloroso* SHERRY, tawny PORT, MADEIRA, and some traditional white RIOJA, owe their character to deliberate exposure to oxygen. And those who make wines of all sorts are constantly experimenting with various aspects of controlled oxidation, often motivated by the role played by oxygen in AGEING. See WHITE WINEMAKING and RED WINEMAKING.

The term MADERIZATION is sometimes used interchangeably with oxidation, although it should theoretically also involve excessive exposure to heat.

See also OXYGEN.   A.D.W. & V.C.

oxidative winemaking contrasts with PROTECTIVE and REDUCTIVE WINEMAKING in that the winemaker deliberately exposes the wine to oxygen at various stages in the winemaking process in order to encourage certain reactions and achieve a particular style of wine—*oloroso* SHERRY being an extreme example. See also OXYGEN, AERATION, BARREL MATURATION, MICRO-OXYGENATION, and HYPEROXIDATION.

oxygen, colourless, odourless, tasteless gas that makes up nearly 21% of the atmosphere. It is essential to all animal life forms and for many other living systems. Unlike NITROGEN, which makes up a much higher proportion of air and is inert, oxygen is highly reactive, being essential for aerobic RESPIRATION in plants, animals, and soils. Oxygen interacts with grape juice, must, and wine in good ways (see AERATION) and bad ways (see OXIDATION).

Handling juice

A small amount of oxygen is required for the multiplication of the YEAST that will conduct the alcoholic FERMENTATION. Larger amounts may well be detrimental by oxidizing PHENOLICS. The aim of PROTECTIVE JUICE HANDLING is to minimize oxidation.

Making wine

During fermentation, the CARBON DIOXIDE given off by the nascent wine prevents exposure to oxygen, but, when fermentation ceases, the wine must be protected from access to oxygen if it is to remain wine. Early winemakers learned that, with very few exceptions, wines had to be kept in full containers at all times lest they change into VINEGAR.

Modern winemakers have equipment which allows most steps in making wine to exclude oxygen. One of the most effective has been the STAINLESS STEEL tank in which ULLAGE space can be filled with INERT GAS to exclude oxygen. Wooden vats, casks, and barrels are not sufficiently impervious for this blanketing technique. Some tanks have lids that can be raised or lowered depending on the volume of liquid in the tank. In older wineries, the oxidation of wine was minimized by frequent small additions of SULFUR DIOXIDE, which, although it is needed less frequently as an antioxidant in modern winemaking, is still used to inhibit microbial activity. ASCORBIC ACID has also been used to a certain extent as an antioxidant, but it must be employed in conjunction with sulfur dioxide (see ERYTHORBIC ACID too). REFRIGERATION of wine in storage slows all reactions, including oxidation, but it has the danger that oxygen solubility increases at low temperatures. The aim of PROTECTIVE WINEMAKING is to minimize oxidation, although see WHITE WINEMAKING for alternative approaches.

Oxygen plays a positive role during RED WINE-MAKING, when the small doses of oxygen which the wine receives during the inevitable operations of filling, RACKING, and TOPPING UP deepen and stabilize COLOUR, soften and intensify flavour, and assist natural STABILIZATION and CLAR-IFICATION by encouraging the precipitation of the less stable PHENOLICS.

Oxygen management throughout the winemaking process, especially at BOTTLING and in relation to wine bottle CLOSURES (see OXYGEN TRANSMISSION RATE and TOTAL PACKAGE OXYGEN), is currently the subject of increasingly sophisticated research in wine ACADEME around the world. SYNTHETIC CLOSURE producers Nomacorc,

in particular, have invested in an international research project that looks at all aspects of wine–oxygen interaction and how this highly significant aspect of winemaking may be controlled.

See also OXIDATION, AERATION, MICRO-OXYGEN-ATION, and SERVING WINE.   A.D.W. & P.J.W.

Goode, J., *Wine Science: The Application of Science in Winemaking* (2nd edn, London, 2014).

oxygen transmission rate (OTR) is a key property of wine bottle CLOSURES because the interaction between wine and OXYGEN is critical to the way a wine changes post bottling (see BOTTLE AGEING). It used to be widely thought that CORKS and alternatives such as SCREWCAPS and SYNTHETIC CLOSURES provided an airtight seal that allowed no oxygen into the bottle, except when the closure had failed. But with the advent of the first generation of synthetic corks, it quickly became clear that even though these were sealing bottles tightly so that they did not leak, they were allowing oxygen into the bottle, resulting in wines that showed signs of OXIDA-TION after a fairly short period of time. This is because the structure of plastic allows oxygen to diffuse through it. It also became clear that the screwcaps with a tin layer in the liner (almost all those used in Australia and New Zealand), were allowing virtually no oxygen transmission at all, and that natural corks were variable in their OTR but were mostly somewhere in between the OTR of synthetic closures and that of tin-lined screwcaps.

Subsequent research has focused on the effects of different OTRs on wine development, and closure manufacturers, in particular synthetic closure manufacturer Nomacorc, have developed products with engineered levels of OTR with a view to offering winemakers control over how their wine will develop post bottling. Screwcap manufacturer Alcan hase also

developed a range of liners offering winemakers alternatives to the almost-hermetic seal offered by the tin-lined screwcap. Technological cork manufactuer Diam Bouchage also offer products with different oxygen transmission rates. See also TOTAL PACKAGE OXYGEN.   J.A.G.

ozone is a form of OXYGEN having three instead of the usual two oxygen atoms per molecule. It is formed in the upper atmosphere by the action of ultraviolet light on normal oxygen; and, by being opaque to further incoming ultraviolet light, happily prevents most of the potentially very damaging ultraviolet wavelengths from reaching the earth's surface.

Some man-made molecules such as the chlorofluorocarbons, once widely used in REFRIGERATION, can, if released into the atmosphere, add to the effects of natural gases from volcanoes, etc. to destroy ozone. This occurs only at very low temperatures, such as occur over the poles in winter, but is nevertheless a matter of concern.

Some ozone is also released into the lower atmosphere as an industrial pollutant, and can cause a recognizable 'stippling' of vine leaves close to industrialized areas. Its significance to viticulture has been studied in California and New York state, but the economic effects remain uncertain.

In a winemaking context, ozone has been advocated as a sanitizing agent for the maintenance of HYGIENE in a winery and for use, for example, on stainless steel tanks, bottling equipment, and barrels, although it is not necessarily effective in killing off microflora (eg BRETTANOMYCES) in material such as oak. Ozone is sometimes used in cork manufacture as a preventive measure to retard microbial growth, though, again, its effectiveness is uncertain.   J.G. & P.J.W.

p

Paarl, important inland wine district in SOUTH AFRICA and home of an increasing number of well-known estates. It reaches north into TULBAGH and WELLINGTON and east towards FRANSCHHOEK, all separate areas of origin. The biggest cellars are KWV's and the most important branded wine producer is Nederburg, with a comprehensive range of 40 labels. Much of Paarl's fruit is blended with grapes from districts such as STELLENBOSCH and Wellington to be sold under the more generic regional origin COASTAL REGION.

Pacherenc du Vic-Bilh, defiantly GASCON name for tangy white wines made in the MADIRAN region mainly from a mixture of intensely local grape varieties COURBU, PETIT COURBU, GROS MANSENG, and PETIT MANSENG. The deep yellow wine can be either dry or more probably sweet, depending on the VINTAGE, and tastes like a slightly more alcoholic (thanks to Petit Courbu) version of JURANÇON, which is made further south. By 2012, 270 ha/667 acres were dedicated to this keenly priced wine, which may be picked as late as December. The sweet wines, made from PASSERILLÉ grapes, can last ten years or so in bottle. The Plaimont CO-OPERATIVE has access to some excellent fruit.

Perry, D. M., *Madiran and Pacherenc du Vic-Bilh* (Accrington, Lancs, 2014).

Pacific Northwest, self-conscious region in the far north west of the UNITED STATES. A beautiful and unspoilt landscape and some fine regional products, including food and wine, have brought a sense of pride to the states of WASHINGTON, OREGON, and IDAHO. Comparisons with CALIFORNIA, the state to the immediate south, are habitually made.

packaging of wine most often involves BOT-TLING, but alternative packages are proliferating.

BOTTLES are still by far the most popular form of wine packaging, not least because GLASS is inert and tasteless so, unlike other packaging materials, has no effect on the wine even over decades. It does have the disadvantages of being very fragile, relatively heavy, and uses up considerable natural resources during manufacture and TRANSPORT. See BOXES, CANS, CARTONS, KEGS, PLASTIC BOTTLES, and POUCHES, all of which are made from other materials.

Padthaway, a significant, moderately cool, primarily grape-growing (rather than wine-making) region in the LIMESTONE COAST zone in the south east of SOUTH AUSTRALIA. While all the mainstream varieties are grown, and while grape quality is, as elsewhere, sensitive to yield, Shiraz is a regional speciality, and can produce long-lived wine of high quality. It has just nine producers.

Pagadebit, occasionally **Pagadebito** or **Pagadebiti**, is used as a synonym for several different Italian varieties, most notably BOMBINO BIANCO in Puglia. The name refers to the vine's reliable yields which, in theory, should allow growers to pay their debts.

pago, Spanish term for a vineyard, used particularly in JEREZ and CASTILLA Y LEÓN. See also VINO DE PAGO.

Païen, Valais name for SAVAGNIN BLANC.

pairing food and wine. See FOOD AND WINE MATCHING.

País, Chilean name for the historic grape variety also known as CRIOLLA CHICA, MISSION, and Listán Prieto. It is most common in Maule and Bío-Bío in the south and is mainly grown in old, unirrigated plots by elderly farmers, often as FIELD BLENDS. Accurate statistics are elusive but

there are probably about 10,000 ha/25,000 acres in total. The variety used to be scorned but TORRES have made a thoroughly respectable sparkling pink from it and it is slowly appearing in more export quality bottlings.

Pakistan. According to OIV statistics, the total area of vines in this Asian ISLAMIC republic grew from 3,000 ha/7,400 acres in the late 1980s to 16,000 ha in 2011. They are dedicated to the production of TABLE GRAPES and DRYING GRAPES, but VINIFERA wine may occasionally be made from WILD VINES growing in the high valleys along the Silk Road, where one of the richest resources of ancient, genetically varied plant material may still be found.

palaeoethnobotany and the archaeology of wine. The study of the botanical remains of grapes and wine residues found in archaeological excavations is something of a detective story in which small pieces of evidence are put together to build up a picture of the development of mankind's use and, later, domestication of grapes.

The botanical evidence consists of the remains of vine LEAVES, BERRIES, STEMS, and SEEDS or pips; sometimes even the roots, or the hollows left by them, may subsist too. Their recovery is the result of painstaking examination of archaeological deposits. Usually the finds of grape remains form a very small proportion of the total botanical material recovered, the bulk of which is usually the seeds of annual crops such as cereals, pulses, and oilseeds.

The most common remains of grapes found are grape pips and they usually subsist because they have become charred at the time of deposition. Once converted to charcoal, they will subsist in recognizable form for many thousands of years buried in the ground. On other

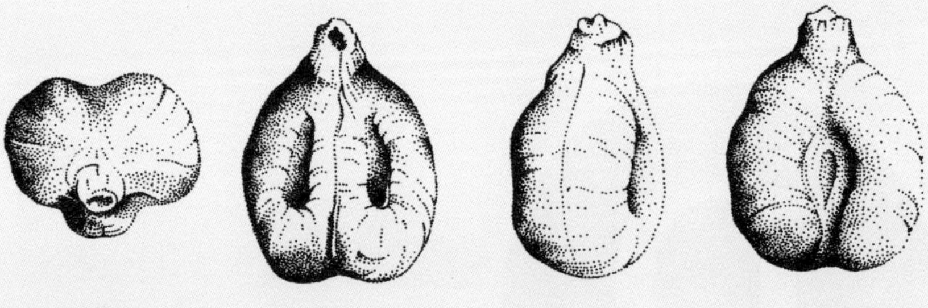

Fig 1. seed (pip) of wild vine *Vitis silvestris*

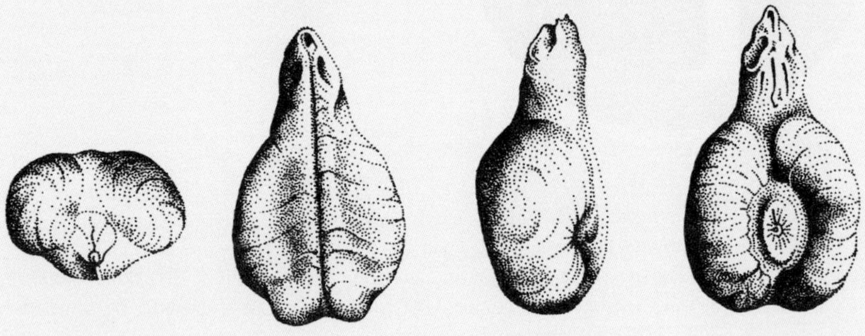

axial view   ventral (inner) view   lateral view   dorsal (outer) view

axial   ventral   lateral   dorsal

Fig 2. seed of cultivated vine *Vitis vinifera*

The exact shape of ancient grape pips helps **palaeoethnobotanists** determine whether the pips came from wild or cultivated vines.

Source: J. Renfrew, *Palaeoethnobotany*

archaeological sites they may be preserved in damp or wet soils in a waterlogged condition. Elsewhere, where there is a high concentration of calcium in the groundwater, they may become mineralized or semi-fossilized. Sometimes stray pips were incorporated in handmade clay pots and when the pots are fired, they burn out leaving a small hole the exact size and shape of the pip.

Occasionally, complete fruits survive in charred form, as when grapes were thrown on to a funeral pyre as part of the ritual, e.g. at Salamis and Athens. Exceptionally, finds of skins of fruits (possibly remains of pressings) survive, for example at early Minoan Myrtos, Crete (see Ancient GREECE).

Finds of burnt fruit stalks (PEDICELS) are exceptional but can be taken to indicate the presence of domesticated vines (the stems of bunches of WILD VINES are very strong and robust and do not come away with the fruit in the way that those of cultivated vines do). They have been recovered from the Greek prehistoric sites of Sitagroi and Myrtos.

The Greek prehistoric potters of the early Bronze Age developed the habit of standing their pots on upturned vine leaves to dry in the sun before firing. This resulted in the veins on the underside of these leaves being finely impressed and then baked on the bases of these pots. In some places—the Cyclades, for example—these are the only evidence that grapes were present on these islands at that time. Vine leaves were also used on clay sealings of Bronze Age pots, such as at Menelaion near Sparta. If vine leaves were being used in these ways by the Bronze Age Greeks, they may also have been used for cooking, as they are in Greece today.

The critical question in examining all this palaeoethnobotanical material is how can one tell whether it is derived from wild or cultivated sources. Apart from the fruit stalks, just discussed, it is the size and shape of the pips which give us the clue: the pips of wild grapes are spherical with a short stalk or beak and a small, round chalazal scar on one side, and two divergent grooves on the other side of the pip. The pips of cultivated grapes are usually larger and pear shaped. The stalk is usually longer, the chalazal scar larger and often oval in outline, and the grooves on the back of the pip parallel to each other. These features can be seen on the archaeological material, however it is preserved.

The domestication of grapes seems to have first taken place around 6000 BC in the region between the Black and Caspian seas. The domesticated grapevine provides fresh fruit, dried raisins, sultanas and currants (according to the VINE VARIETY), wine, vinegar, grape juice, and a light salad oil obtained by crushing the pips. The most significant product, however, was wine, which was greatly valued.

Finds of wild grape pips in archaeological contexts go back to the earliest palaeolithic sites in Europe, for example at Terra Amata in the south of France (*c.*350000 BC), where the fruits appear to have been eaten. There are a number of sites from the mesolithic period (12th–9th millenium BC) with finds of wild grape seeds: from Belma Abeurader, France, to Grotte del Uzzo in Sicily, the Frangthi Cave in southern Greece, Çayönü in Turkey, Tell Abu Heureya, Syria, and Jericho in Jordan. The earliest finds of pips from domesticated grapes come from the neolithic site of Shulaveris-Gora in Georgian Transcaucasia, dated *c.*6000 BC. From this site too comes a residue of resinated wine in a pot: the earliest find of wine to date. Another site which has yielded traces of neolithic wine is Hajji Firuz Tepe in northern Iran. Here a kitchen was excavated dating to 5400–5000 BC. In it were six jars set into the floor with their lids nearby. Chemical analysis has shown that they contained wine resinated with resin from the terebinth tree. It is not clear whether this wine was made from wild or cultivated grapes (wild grapes still grow close to the site today). If all these jars had contained wine they would have held around 50 litres, suggesting large-scale wine production at a very early date.

The excavations at the Areni 1 cave complex in ARMENIA have yielded remains of a wine-pressing structure dating to *c.*4000 BC. It consists of a shallow clay tub, a metre wide, with raised edges and a sloping base leading down to the mouth of a large jar. Desiccated grapes, pomace, grape seeds, and grape skins still attached to their pedicels have been found in close proximity to it. Biochemical analyses of the contents of associated pots revealed the presence of malvidin, the pigment responsible for red wine. It is thought that wine pressing here was not associated with regular consumption or feasting, but with rituals associated with the burial of the dead. Remains of both primary and secondary depositions of dismembered and complete human skeletons were found in the inner spaces in the caves.

It is not essential that vines were domesticated before WINEMAKING was invented. What appears to be necessary is having a suitable container in which to store the wine during and after the FERMENTATION process. All the ingredients—the sweet, juicy fruit, and airborne YEAST—are available for wild fruits. Thus, it is possible that the finds from palaeolithic sites (Old Stone Age) in the Mediterranean region of wild grape pips could indicate that winemaking had begun using leather bags even before the beginnings of agriculture.

The finds of grape remains such as pips, stalks, and skins in circumstances suggesting wine production are rare. The finds from House 1 at Dikili Tash in northern Greece of 2,460 grape pips, which have been directly dated to 4,460–4,000 BC, together with more than 300 empty, pressed grape skins, strongly suggest that they represent winemaking residues. The measurements of the pips suggest that they were morphologically grapes from WILD VINES or from plants in the process of domestication. Another exceptional find comes from Kurban Huyuk in eastern Turkey, where masses of grape pips, stem and vine fragments were found together with cakes of pressed fruits in a mid to late 3rd millennium BC pit. In prehistoric GREECE, they occur associated with spouted vessels on the early Bronze Age sites of Áyios Kosmas, Attica, and Myrtos in Crete. Remains of wine presses also occur occasionally as at Minoan Vathypetro in Crete, and there are a great number of drinking vessels made from exotic materials from Bronze Age sites suggesting that drinking wine was a special activity.

Analysis of residues found in the bottom of pottery containers has been undertaken by Patrick McGovern of MASCA in the University Museum, Philadelphia, using infrared, liquid chromatography and other chemical techniques to identify traces of tartaric acid, calcium tartrate and terebinth resin indicating the residues of wine. The actual residues in the bases of pithoi of wine have not been found very often (partly because the analysis of residues found in pottery vessels is still comparatively new in archaeology). Apart from identifying the earliest finds of wine residues, detailed above, these analyses have also given evidence of the earliest trade in wine. This dates back to 3500 BC at Godin Tepe, IRAN, where a reddish deposit turned out to be formed from TARTRATE crystals (similar to those which form on the bottom of wine corks today). Godin Tepe lies on a well documented trade route through the Zagros mountains to lowland Mesopotamia. Even stronger evidence of trade comes from the earliest finds of wine residues in Egypt from the royal tomb of Scorpion I at Abydos dating to 3100 BC. Here three rooms in the tomb formed a kind of wine cellar filled high with about 700 amphorae arranged in three or four layers one on top of another. They were stoppered with clay sealings bearing fine seal impressions. Deposits of crusty yellow residues inside the amphorae turned out to be of a resinated wine. In addition, 47 of them contained grape pips and several had raisins, stalks, skins, pips, and dried pulp intact. Eleven of the jars also contained the remains of sliced sycamore figs which had been strung together and suspended in the wine. Analysis of the clays from which the amphorae were made indicated that they probably came from various regions in the southern Levant. Viticulture was firmly established in the delta region of Egypt and in some of the western oases by the Sixth Dynasty (c.2323 BC). Processes of winemaking are shown in paintings and engravings on the walls of tombs from the Old Kingdom onwards, for example in the tomb chapels at Beni Hasan, especially nos. 15 and 17.

Recent finds in the CANAANITE PALACE at Tel Kabri in northern Israel, dating to 1700 BC, have revealed a wine cellar holding the remains of 40 jars that are 91 cm/3 ft tall. Chemical analysis of the residues of their contents, by Andrew Koh of Brandeis University, revealed traces of TARTARIC ACID, as well as flavourings of honey, mint, cinnamon bark, juniper berries, and resins used as preservatives. Of the 40 vessels, 38 contained wine residues all with the same constituents, the equivalent of 3,000 modern bottles of wine. The contents are consistent with winemaking recipes from the ancient texts found at the palace at Mari on the River Euphrates in modern SYRIA.

One of the most romantic finds of labelled wine jars must be that from Tutankhamun's tomb. They were sealed with clay and their contents were reduced to dried residues. The 26 wine jars have labels indicating the location of the vineyard, the year of the vintage (the majority belonging to the years 1345 BC, 1344 BC, and 1340 BC), the ownership of the vineyard and the name of the chief vintner. Most of them came from the western delta, one from the eastern delta, and one from the El Kharga oasis. Two of the vintners had Syrian names; four of the jars were labelled 'sweet wine'.

Analyses have also shown that sometimes wine was mixed with other alcoholic beverages. It appears that this was the case in Minoan Crete, where a number of residue analyses have shown that wine was mixed with barley beer and honey to form what McGovern has called 'Greek grog'. This was also the case in the finds from Midas` tomb at Gordion in Turkey (c.700 BC), where the funeral feast consisted of a tasty lamb and lentil stew washed down with an intoxicating beverage made from mixing wine, barley beer, and honey mead.

Other early residues of wine are known from 7th century BC CYPRUS, and from the contents of AMPHORAE in a Roman shipwreck off the southern coast of France, near Marseilles. There is a Roman glass BOTTLE containing what is claimed to be Roman wine in the museum in Speyer, Germany.

From apparently insignificant remains of grape pips, stalks, pulp, and leaves, and the analyses of dried up residues in the bottom of pots, found by chance to subsist in sediments on archaeological sites, and extracted with painstaking care, it is possible to begin to understand the ORIGINS OF VINICULTURE and its development. J.M.R.

Ancient biomolecules

In 2003, scientists at the Botanical Garden of Geneva, Switzerland, were able to analyse for the first time by DNA PROFILING a tiny amount of DNA from waterlogged and charred grape pips recovered from archaeological sites in France (Iron Age and Greek period, 5th century BC) and Hungary (Roman times, 2nd to 4th centuries AD). These remains could not be matched to any modern cultivar, but they could be assigned to their most likely geographic origin. DNA profiling of additional grape remains from archaeological sites as well as comparison between wild and cultivated grapes throughout the distribution of VINIFERA in the future might shed some new light on the place and time of the first domestication of grapes. J.V.

Areshian, G. E., et al., 'Wine and death: the 2010 excavation season at the Areni-1 Cave Complex, Armenia', Backdirt (2011), 65–70.

McGovern, P. E., Fleming, S. J., and Katz, S. H. (eds.), The Origins and Ancient History of Wine (New York, 1995).

McGovern, P. E., Fleming, S. J., and Katz, S. H. (eds.), Ancient Wine (Princeton and Oxford, 2003).

Renfrew, J., Palaeoethnobotany: The Prehistoric Food Plants of the Near East and Europe (London, 1973).

Sandler, M., and Pinder, R. (eds.), Wine, A Scientific Exploration (London and New York, 2003).

Valamoti, S. M., et al., 'Grape pressings from northern Greece: the earliest wine in the Aegean?', Antiquity, 81 (2007), 54–61.

palate, frequently mis-spelt term used when describing TASTING as a process and an ability. It is generally used to describe the combined human tasting faculties in the mouth and, sometimes, NOSE. The impact of a wine on the mouth may be divided chronologically, and somewhat loosely, into its impact on the front, middle, and back palate. The word may also be used more generally as in describing a good taster as 'having a fine palate'. A pallet of wine is dozens of CASES. Some may describe a BOUQUET as being composed of a palette of FLAVOURS.

Palatinate, originally territory under the jurisdiction of a local authority with sovereign powers, the term came to be used for that part of Germany which today includes both Rheinhessen and the PFALZ wine regions. It has been used as an alternative English name for the German wine region Pfalz. See also GERMAN HISTORY.

Palette, miniature appellation of just 43 ha/ 106 acres in 2005 in PROVENCE in the hills east of Aix-en-Provence. The appellation is a relatively old one, created in 1948 in recognition of a distinctive LIMESTONE outcrop on the north-facing bank of the River Arc. A single property, Ch Simone, produces most of the wine, and for many years was responsible for the most serious wine of the appellation. For seven generations, Ch Simone has been in the Rougier family, who continue to respect the traditional winemaking techniques, involving very old vines, prolonged fermentation, and BARREL MATURATION using very little new wood. FIELD BLENDS of southern vine varieties make extremely dense, long-lived reds, full-bodied rosés, and characterful white wines which belie modern white winemaking philosophy. The INDIGENOUS VARIETIES permitted are even more numerous than those allowed in CHÂTEAUNEUF-DU-PAPE.

palissage, French term for VINE TRAINING.

Palladius (4th century AD). Next to nothing is known about the life of this agrarian writer of Ancient ROME. He is the author of a treatise called, like Varro's earlier work, *De re rustica*, in 15 books. The first book is a general introduction to farming; the last two comprise a guide to veterinary medicine and an account of GRAFTING. The remaining 12 books deal with the tasks to be carried out throughout the agricultural year, one book for each month; Palladius has more to say about the vine than about any other crop. What he says, however, is sound but not original: he relies heavily on earlier authors, especially COLUMELLA (and, to a lesser extent, PLINY and VARRO). Unlike CATO, Varro, and Columella he was well known in the Middle Ages and in the early Renaissance: he is quoted by Albertus Magnus, Vincent of Beauvais, and PETRUS DE CRESCENTIIS, and an anonymous Middle English translation of his work, connected with Humphrey, duke of Gloucester, survives. There is no direct evidence for his influence on medieval English wine producers, however.

H.M.W.

Pallagrello Nero, red wine grape planted on about 170 ha/420 acres of Campania in 2010. Unrelated to the even rarer **Pallagrello Bianco**.

Palmela, DOP on the Setúbal peninsula in southern Portugal. See PENÍNSULA DE SETÚBAL.

Palo Cortado, a traditional and fully natural style of sherry based on a fluke of nature. This is a wine that was originally pre-selected to become a *fino* or, later, an Amontillado, i.e. a wine of greater finesse than those pre-selected to become *olorosos*, which are aged in OXIDATIVE fashion from the start. Yet some examples of these more delicate wines never develop the protective veil of FLOR yeast they need to become an Amontillado and end up ageing in *oloroso* fashion. As a result, such wines have an intermediate style—the elegance of the Amontillado with the power and body of the Oloroso. This is the rarest category of sherry, yet some of the greatest dry sherries are Palos Cortados. For more details, see SHERRY.

V. de la S.

Palombina, synonym for PIEDIROSSO.

Palomino Fino, white grape variety most closely associated with the making of SHERRY around JEREZ in southern Spain that is generally declining in importance there and elsewhere. It is almost certainly of Andalucian origin, supposedly named after one of King Alfonso X's knights and was introduced to the CANARY ISLANDS, where it is known as Listán Blanco.

The vine is relatively susceptible to DOWNY MILDEW and ANTHRACNOSE and responds best in warm, dry soils. Its loose, generous bunches of large grapes make it suitable for TABLE GRAPES as well as wine. Its yield is relatively high and regular, about 80 hl/ha (4.5 tons/acre) without irrigation, and the wine produced is, typically, low in both ACIDITY (as low as 3.5 g/l expressed in tartaric acid) and fermentable SUGARS. This suits sherry producers who pick Palomino grapes at about 19 °Brix (see MUST WEIGHT) and find Palomino must's tendency to oxidize no inconvenience, but for this very reason the variety tends to make rather flabby, vapid table wines, unless substantially assisted by ACIDIFICATION.

Spain's official 2011 vine variety statistics distinguished between the Canary Islands' 9,000 ha of Listán Blanco, 2,179 ha of Palomino Fino, and 13,689 ha of plain Palomino, but according to DNA PROFILING, they are all genetically identical. The only mainland Spanish regions with sizeable plantings of Palomino other than Andalucia are Galicia and Castilla y León, where productive Palomino was planted after PHYLLOXERA but is being systematically replaced by INDIGENOUS varieties. The great majority is in sherry country around Jerez but as sales of sherry have declined, so has the total area of Palomino planted.

Outside sherry country, in France, for example, it is often known as Listán, or Listán de Jerez, and sometimes just Jerez. In Portugal it is known as Malvasia Rei, planted on more than 3,000 ha/7,500 acres in 2012, mainly in the north of the country where it makes generally bland table wine. CYPRUS imported the Palomino vine because of its dependence on producing inexpensive copies of sherry but very little remains.

The country with the most Palomino planted outside Europe was at one stage South Africa, but the variety, known as Fransdruif in Afrikaans and White French in English, has been losing ground fast and is generally distilled or used for blending into basic table wines.

California's acreage of the variety, once wrongly identified as Golden Chasselas, has always been very limited, almost all in the SAN JOAQUIN VALLEY. In Australia, total plantings have shrivelled as dramatically as production of sherry-like wines. New Zealand once also grew a surprising amount of Palomino

considering its hardly ideal climate but the vines have been systematically replaced with more suitable varieties. Argentina has limited planting of the variety but PEDRO GIMÉNEZ predominates.

Pamid, BULGARIA's most widely planted and least interesting indigenous grape variety producing rather thin, early-maturing red wines with few distinguishing marks other than a certain sweetness. It does not play a major role in bottles bound for export. It is also planted quite extensively, on 2,852 ha in 2013 as Roşioară, in Romania.

Pampanuto, also known as **Pampanino**, minor Puglian white grape which is invariably blended with more acid wine.

Pannobile, a name derived from the Pannonian Plain, refers to a group of nine growers in AUSTRIA's NEUSIEDLERSEE region, all near the north eastern edge of the eponymous lake, and to a single prestige blended red each of them offers (from some combination of Zweigelt, Blaufränkisch, and St Laurent grapes) as well as, in some cases, a white (from some combination of Chardonnay, Pinot Gris, Pinot Blanc, and Neuburger).

D.S.

Pansa Blanca, synonym for the Catalan white grape variety XARELLO.

Pantelleria, VOLCANIC island at the extreme southern limit of Italy and closer in fact to Cape Bon in TUNISIA than to the southern coast of SICILY, to which it belongs administratively. Moscato di Pantelleria is one of Italy's finest dessert wines, made from the ZIBIBBO (MUSCAT OF ALEXANDRIA). The wine has enjoyed a certain reputation since the 1880s, when the MARSALA house of Rallo began to market it. The viticulture of the island is unusual: vines are GOBELET trained but buried in a hole (called a 'conca' by local growers) and vineyards surrounded by stone walls built from volcanic black rock to prevent dehydration by the hot scirocco winds that sweep across the island.

Moscato di Pantelleria comes in two different versions. The first is the regular Moscato, with at least 11% alcohol level and 68 g/l of RESIDUAL SUGAR, although many of the better producers raisin the grapes for 10 to 12 days to achieve a higher total alcohol level and a greater quantity of residual sugar (see DRIED-GRAPE WINES). The second version is lusher and richer and is true dessert style, which made the wine's reputation. This Passito di Pantelleria must have at least 14% alcohol and 100 g/l residual sugar, although a current trend is to seek a more decadently sweet style, raisining the grapes for up to 30 days and arriving at close to 140 g/l of residual sugar. This search for power can come at a cost: the Moscato perfumes tend to be destroyed by the very high level of VOLATILE

ACIDITY that may result from prolonged drying under the hot sun.

Both the Moscato and the Passito can come with the suffix 'liquoroso' indicating the addition of ethyl alcohol, which arrests the alcoholic fermentation while leaving a substantial amount of unfermented sugar in the wine. They may be additionally labelled Vino Dolce Naturale, the Italian equivalent of VIN DOUX NATUREL, but rarely achieve the complexity of the unfortified versions. And changes in the production rules in the early 2010s created a new category of dry white wines labelled as Pantelleria Bianco as well as sparkling wines.

After a period of neglect and decline, Moscato di Pantelleria continues to experience a period of revived popularity and recognition in Italy, with an undeniable increase in overall quality driven mainly by ambitious small-scale producers, notably Marco de Bartoli and biodynamic avantguardist Salvatore Ferrandes. French actress Carole Bouquet's Sangue D'Oro estate has also played a part in shining a spotlight on one of Italy's greatest sweet wines.   W.S.

Nesto, B., and Di Savino, F., *The World of Sicilian Wine* (Berkeley, 2013).

www.consorziopantelleria.it

Paraguay

Paraguay, in SOUTH AMERICA has more than 400 ha/1,000 acres of vines according to Goldstein, and one winery, Gerald Bühler of Vista Alegre, is a direct descendant of early-20th-century immigration from BADEN. TROPICAL conditions make Paraguayan wine more of a curiosity than a fine drink.

Goldstein, E., *Wines of South America* (Oakland Calif., 2014).

Pardillo

Pardillo, once known as Pardilla, is a vine variety planted on 2,500 ha/7,250 acres of LA MANCHA where it makes sturdy whites.

Pardina

Pardina, light-skinned grape producing rather ordinary wines in EXTREMADURA shown by DNA PROFILING in 2005 to be the same as CAYETANA Blanca.

Parellada

Parellada, highly regarded white grape variety originally Aragonese but now grown almost exclusively in Catalunya, especially around San Sadurn'I d'Anoia on just under 8,000 ha/20,000 acres in 2012 where it is widely used, with MACABEO and XAREL-LO, for the production of CAVA. It is the least planted of these three varieties in PENEDÈS, the region most closely associated with these Spanish sparkling wines. Parellada can produce aromatic, high-quality wine when grown in relatively poor soil and in cooler conditions. It has large, loose bunches, buds early, and ripens late. Occasionally made as a VARIETAL still wine.

Paris

Paris, capital of FRANCE, once the centre of a thriving wine region and still one of the few capital cities in which vineyards of any size may be found (although see also VIENNA). Rueil, Suresne, Nanterre, Coulombe, and Argenteüil were all renowned for their wine in the 17th century. Today there are still several suburban vineyards, of which only one, in the IGP Suresnes created in 2013, is commercial. There is even a small vineyard on the slopes of Montmartre, whose meagre produce, from 2,000 vines originally densely planted in 1933, is auctioned for charity. More IGPs are being sought for Île-de-France, or greater Paris.

History

Wine was grown around Paris in the 4th century, and its fame as a wine-growing area dates from long after the Roman empire. Clovis, king of the Franks 481–511, made Paris the capital of his kingdom and from the 8th century onwards Frisian, Saxon, and English merchants sailed up the river Seine to Paris to buy wine. Under the Merovingians and the Carolingians, Paris was an important centre of trade, and much of the wine sold there would have been produced locally.

A document from the beginning of the 9th century shows that viticulture was a major part of the local economy. The Roll of Irminon, named after the abbot of St-Germain-des-Prés who instigated this survey of his monastery's lands, is the only document of its kind dating back to the time of CHARLEMAGNE. Vineyards at Rambouillet, Dreux, Fontainebleau, Sceaux, and Versailles were cultivated not only by monks but also by laymen, and it is clear from the amounts produced that there must have been a surplus to sell on the open market. Documents from the Abbey of St-Denis, near Paris, show that St-Germain-des-Prés was not unique in this respect. In the 9th century, St-Denis had vineyards in the abbey precincts and possessed wine-growing estates in the Île-de-France, as the Paris basin was known; many smaller monasteries in the area also produced wine for sale (see MONKS AND MONASTERIES).

In the 10th century, Paris was well established as a centre of the wine trade. The main trade route was down the Seine to Rouen (today an important wine BOTTLING centre for northern European markets) and thence overseas. In the late 10th century, merchants from England, Ireland, Flanders, and Picardy visited Rouen, and later Henry II (king of England, including Normandy, 1154–89) gave Rouen the monopoly of transporting wine to England. The other, later (from the 13th century onwards), trade route from Paris was down the Seine or up the Oise as far as Compiègne, where the wine would be loaded on to carts and carried to Flanders by road. By then the merchants of Paris had managed to acquire for themselves privileges similar to those of their Gascon counterparts (see BORDEAUX). In an edict of 1190, Philip Augustus, king of France, declared that only the merchants of Paris, who were themselves usually wine producers as well (see CLIMATE CHANGE for details of the warmer MACROCLIMATE prevailing then), had the right to sell wine in Paris. They were able to prevent the sale of any wine they wished: thus they regulated the import of wines from outside the region and they controlled the quality of the wines sold as 'vins de France'. The wines of AUXERRE, CHABLIS, and Tonnerre had to pass through Paris before they were permitted to be transported further, and wines from other regions were not to be offered for sale before the 'vins de France' had all been sold. The wines of the LOIRE were also put on the market in Paris.

The 'vins de France' included not only the wines of Paris up to Vernon in Normandy but also those of CHAMPAGNE (Rheims, Épernay, Châlons-sur-Marne): this usage continued among wine producers until just after the French Revolution. The Capetian kings of France, who reigned from 987 to 1498, were particularly fond of the wines of Paris, but some of what they drank must have been from Champagne, since no distinction was made. In those days the region grew more than it could drink. Some of it was sold to the neighbouring areas of Normandy, Picardy, and Artois; the principal foreign export markets in the Middle Ages were England and Flanders. The 'vins de France' were highly esteemed both at home and abroad: in 1200 they fetched higher prices in London than the wines of ANJOU.   H.M.W.

Dion, R., *Histoire de la vigne et du vin en France* (Paris, 1959).

Lachiver, M., *Vins, vignes et vignerons* (Paris, 1988).

Parker, Robert M., Jr

Parker, Robert M., Jr (1947–), extremely influential American wine critic whose most obvious contribution to the LITERATURE OF WINE has been the concept of applying NUMBERS to wine. His scores, followed slavishly by some COLLECTORS and even more by INVESTORS, have a demonstrable effect on individual wine PRICES.

Robert Parker was born in farming country near Baltimore and both trained and worked as a lawyer there. He discovered wine at the age of 20 on his first trip to France. By the mid 1970s, at the height of active consumerism, Parker became frustrated by the lack of truly independent and reliable wine criticism, and began to think about launching his own consumer's guide to wine buying.

The first, complimentary, issue of his bimonthly newsletter the *Wine Advocate* appeared in 1978, and by 1984 he felt confident enough of its success to retire from the law and concentrate on the punishing schedule of tastings and travel on which it is based. By then he had made a name for himself with his enthusiastic, and unusually detailed, endorsement of the 1982 vintage in Bordeaux, and subscriptions grew rapidly with the American market for

P

wine FUTURES. By 1998, when a French language edition was launched, the *Wine Advocate* had more than 45,000 subscribers, mainly in the United States but in more than 35 other countries. There are no advertisements and little background, but hundreds of TASTING NOTES and assessments of individual, usually fine, wines. His judgements have had a significant effect on market demand, wine styles, and the commercial future of some producers.

Parker's was by no means the first American consumer wine newsletter, but it was the first to use scores, effectively between 80 and 100 for individual wines, quite so obviously. This system was easily and delightedly grasped by Americans familiar with high school grades, even though Parker himself urges caution, asking readers to use the numerical ratings 'only to enhance and complement the thorough tasting notes, which are my primary means of communicating my judgments to you'. Wine salesmen were less circumspect and used Parker's ratings mercilessly, while the notion of SCORING wine at all came under attack from some other wine authorities, notably Hugh JOHNSON, whose view is that wines themselves vary with time and conditions of tasting, and that wine tasting is an intrinsically subjective process. Parker's own view, stated on the cover of every issue of the *Advocate*, is that 'wine is no different from any consumer product. There are specific standards of quality that full-time wine professionals recognize.'

Parker's diligence in recording the impressions of his hard-worked palate provided the ingredients for several lengthy books, including *Wine Buyer's Guides*, essentially *Advocate* compendia. *Bordeaux* first appeared in 1985 and enjoyed considerable success in the United States, in Britain in 1987, and in France in 1989. The fourth edition appeared in 2003. *The Wines of the Rhône Valley and Provence*, which appeared in 1987 and was updated ten years later, reflected Parker's other great passion (he was instrumental in establishing the reputation and ambitious pricing policy of Côte Rôtie's GUIGAL). *Burgundy* (1990), with its complex mosaic of appellations, producers, and vintages, and its less predictable wines, succumbed less easily to being 'Parkerized'. Burgundian négociant François Faiveley's 1994 lawsuit was the first of several, subsequent ones involving past associates. By the late 1990s, Parker was no longer working alone and by 2012, when *The Wine Advocate* and erobertparker.com were sold to a Singapore ex-wine merchant for a reported $15 million, he had a substantial, fluctuating, team of fellow tasters. Bordeaux is likely to be the last region to be ceded to one of them.

Parker is recognized as a fervent, if critical, admirer of French wines. He was the first non-Frenchman to write a wine column for *L'Express* magazine, and was made a particularly

emotional Chevalier de l'Ordre du Mérite National in 1992. The Légion d'Honneur followed in 1999.

With a few notable and sometimes voluble exceptions, most agree that Parker is a gifted taster and diligent reporter. But his success won a degree of power over the wine market so great that at one stage it encouraged some producers, particularly red wine producers, to adapt the style of their wines to suit this one, compelling palate regardless of their own personal tastes. The sale and the emergence of a new, post-Parker generation of American wine enthusiasts, has resulted in a decline in Parker's power over wine in general, although not over Bordeaux's finest.

Langewiesche, W., 'The million-dollar nose', *The Atlantic Monthly*, 286/6 (2000) 42–62.

McCoy, E., *The Emperor of Wine* (New York, 2005).

Parraleta, interesting, fragrant red wine grape rescued from extinction in Spain's SOMONTANO region. It is also grown on Corsica and in Portugal under several aliases including Tinta Caiada.

partial rootzone drying, or **PRD**, Australian IRRIGATION technique designed to control vine VIGOUR and maintain wine quality with minimum interference to YIELD. PRD was developed by scientists Dry and Loveys from the University of ADELAIDE and CSIRO, after observation of basic vine physiology in response to WATER STRESS. Initially using vines with divided root systems, they discovered that when only a portion of a vine's root system was drying, TRANSPIRATION was reduced and shoot growth was slowed as a consequence of the production of the hormone ABSCISIC ACID by drying roots.

Field experiments with Cabernet Sauvignon showed that it was possible to control shoot vigour and reduce the amount of water needed while maintaining yield and quality. This was achieved with two DRIP IRRIGATION lines per row, used alternately for irrigation while the other part of the root system was drying. The results from these studies have been used to interpret some of the known beneficial effects of water stress, especially for red wine quality. Commercial adoption in vineyards has been limited thus far. However, research on grapevines and other crops has clearly shown that PRD can generate a unique physiological response that is distinct from what happens with conventional irrigation, including REGULATED DEFICIT IRRIGATION.

R.E.S. & P.R.D.

Iland, P., et al., *The Grapevine: From the Science to the Practice of Growing Vines for Wine* (Adelaide, 2011).

Pascal Blanc, almost extinct Provençal light-berried vine variety, very sensitive to POWDERY MILDEW and ROT.

Pascale di Cagliari, Sardinian dark grape speciality.

Paso Robles, very large California wine region and AVA on the inland side of the coastal mountains. See SAN LUIS OBISPO.

passerillage, French word for the process by which **passerillé** grapes are DRIED, shrivelled, or raisined on the vine, concentrating the SUGAR IN GRAPES—an alternative to wines whose sugars have been concentrated by BOTRYTIS.

Passerina, white variety from Italy's Adriatic coast making a wide range of wine styles on 894 ha/2,209 acres of vines in 2010.

Passetoutgrains. See BOURGOGNE PASSETOUTGRAINS.

passing the port. One of the wine trade's most cherished traditions is the rule that PORT, particularly a decanter of vintage port, must be passed round a table from the right hand of diners to the left. No single satisfactory explanation has ever been advanced, although so fiercely held is the custom that a miniature railway was constructed to transport decanters across an inconvenient fireplace in the Senior Common Room of New College Oxford.

Howkins, B., *Real Men drink Port . . . and Ladies do too!* (London, 2011).

passito, Italian term for DRIED-GRAPE WINE.

Pasteur, Louis (1822–95), a scientific genius and gifted scholar, has left a body of work which impinges on physics, chemistry, microbiology, agronomy, and medicine. On the centenary of his birth in 1922, the Institut Pasteur in Paris published a monograph on his principal discoveries listed under the following headings:

1847: Molecular dissymmetry
1857: Fermentations
1862: Supposedly spontaneous generations
1863: Study of wines
1865: Silkworm diseases
1871: Study of beers
1877: Virus diseases
1880: Viral vaccines
1885: Rabies protection

Pasteur's original work on what were supposedly spontaneous generations, or transformations, led him to interpret the process of alcoholic FERMENTATION and to demonstrate that this, far from being spontaneous, was the result of intervention by living cells, YEAST, using sugar for their own nutrition and transforming it into ALCOHOL and CARBON DIOXIDE. 'The chemical act of fermentation is essentially a phenomenon which correlates to a vital act . . . Now what for me constitutes this chemical division of sugar (into alcohol and carbonic gas), and what causes it? I admit that I have no idea' (*Œuvres de Pasteur*, ii. 77). With something approaching genius, Pasteur understood the phenomenon without being able to provide a precise explanation; contemporary biochemistry was able to explain in detail the different stages of the chemical fermentation mechanism only in the first half of the 20th century.

During his career as a scientist, Pasteur must have devoted only three or four years to the study of wine. Yet in this time he achieved as much as a good specialist researcher would have been delighted to achieve in an entire lifetime. Not only did he apply his theories to fermentation and ensure the mastery of the basics of vinification and conservation of wines, he also perfected the art of adding TARTARIC ACID, demonstrated the presence of SUCCINIC ACID and GLYCEROL, and made valuable suggestions about the role of OXYGEN in wine AGEING.

But it was above all in the field of microbiological diseases of wine that Pasteur's work has been most valued. One of the early problems assigned to Pasteur was to explain and prevent the vinegar spoilage of red wines shipped in barrel from Burgundy to England, as well as to try to explain some of the many FAULTS in French wine which had become apparent at the time. He identified the following transformations in various wine constituents:

mannitic acid: degradation of sugars
'tourne': degradation of tartaric acid
bitterness: degradation of glycerol
'graisse': production of a polysaccharide

From his discovery of the various micro-organisms which caused different wine maladies, such as the ACETOBACTER which turn wine into vinegar, came the whole science of bacteriology. He suggested that the application of heat (now called PASTEURIZATION) would destroy these micro-organisms and prevent microbial development, with beneficial effects on the quality of wine. The demonstration of the existence of these BACTERIAL DISEASES was extremely fruitful for the science of OENOLOGY; it resulted in the progressive reduction in VOLATILE ACIDS in wine which was an important factor in raising quality. Pasteur's research work on wine, and beer, also gave rise to his remarkable studies on the cause and prevention of infectious diseases in humans and animals.

From a drop of faulty wine, characterized by the presence of micro-organisms which could be seen with the aid of a microscope and by faults which could be tasted, Pasteur could contaminate a perfectly healthy wine. He expressed his thoughts thus: 'When one observes beer and wine experiencing fundamental changes because these liquids have given asylum to microscopic organisms which were introduced invisibly and fortuitously to them, where they since proliferated, how could one not be obsessed by the thought that similar things can and must sometimes happen to humans and animals?' (1866)

Whatever the undoubted merits of Pasteur's work, to which we owe the basis of wine microbiology, with all its practical consequences for vinification and wine conservation, it should be noted that he did not understand the positive role that LACTIC ACID BACTERIA could have in degrading MALIC ACID. Because of this it was particularly difficult to grasp the principles of MALOLACTIC CONVERSION, which, in 1930, Jean RIBÉREAU-GAYON elucidated as a bacterial transformation which could be of great benefit to a wide range of wines. It was not until the 1970s that the rest of the wine world was convinced. Not without reason, Émile PEYNAUD has written, 'the evolution of oenology would certainly have been very different if Pasteur, instead of leaving us the basis of a perfect method of adding tartaric acid, had taught us to add malic acid'.

For Pasteur 'yeast make wine, bacteria destroy it'. Pasteur truly created the science of winemaking; if today oenology is a discipline in so many universities throughout the world, it is to Pasteur that we owe this achievement.   P.R.-G.

pasteurization, process of heating foods, including wines, to a temperature high enough to kill all micro-organisms such as YEAST and BACTERIA. It is named after Louis PASTEUR, the French scientist who discovered that micro-organisms were alive and the cause of much wine spoilage.

Heat sterilization techniques have improved greatly since the early versions of pasteurization, which often resulted in burnt or cooked flavours in wines treated, particularly those that had not been subjected to complete CLARIFICATION. Wines are pasteurized by rapid heating to about 85 °C/185 °F for one minute, quick cooling, and return to storage tank or bottling line. Keeping the wine longer, for up to three days, at about 50 °C/122 °F is used to coagulate heat-unstable proteins and to speed ageing in low-quality red dessert wines. **Flash pasteurization** may also be effected by heating to temperatures as high as 95 °C for a few seconds, followed by rapid cooling. Some wine is **hot bottled** (at about 55 °C) and allowed to cool slowly or, for utmost effectiveness, closed bottles of wine are occasionally heated to about 55 °C and cooled to room temperature under a water spray. These techniques are relatively brutal, however, and are used only on ordinary wines which have no potential for improvement after BOTTLE AGEING. See also KOSHER wine.   A.D.W.

Patagonia. See ARGENTINA.

Patrimonio. See CORSICA.

Pauillac, small port and communal appellation in the MÉDOC district of BORDEAUX which has the unparalleled distinction of boasting three of the five first growths ranked in Bordeaux's most famous CLASSIFICATION within its boundaries—Chx LAFITE, LATOUR, and MOUTON ROTHSCHILD—as well as a bevy of other CLASSED GROWTHS rivalling them (and each other) with increasing insistence. For all the importance of its wines, Pauillac gives the impression of being the only settlement in the Haut-Médoc to have an existence independent of wine—an impression reinforced by its size and nearby industrial installations.

This, however, is Cabernet Sauvignon country *par excellence*, and while there is considerable variation between different properties' TERROIRS and winemaking policies and capabilities, certain expressions recur in Pauillac tasting notes: cassis (blackcurrant), cedar, and cigar box (the last two sometimes a reflection of the top-quality French oak cooperage which the selling prices of Pauillac permit). A high proportion of the Médoc's most concentrated wines are produced here.

About 1,200 ha/3,000 acres of vines produce this famous appellation in an almost continuous strip between Pauillac's boundary with ST-JULIEN to the south and ST-ESTÈPHE to the north, separated from the waters of the Gironde estuary by only a few hundred metres of *palus* too marshy for serious viticulture (although very suitable for grazing Pauillac's famous *agneaux présalés*, saltmarsh lamb). This strip of vines, 3 km/2 miles wide and more than 6 km long, dedicated to the production of the world's most famously long-lived red wine, is divided into two by the small river Gaët, whose banks are also unsuitable for vines. As elsewhere in the Médoc, the layers of GRAVEL here provide the key to wine quality, offering excellent DRAINAGE, aided by the almost imperceptibly undulating topography and a series of *jalles* or streams running water off the gravelly plateau and into the Gironde.

The stars of the northern sector of Pauillac are undoubtedly the two ROTHSCHILD properties Chx Lafite and MOUTON ROTHSCHILD, whose plots of vineyard are intermingled on the plateau of Le Pouyalet, reaching the considerable (for the Médoc) elevation of 30 m/100 ft at its highest point. Clustered around them are their satellite properties, whose wines benefit from the first-class winemaking ability of their owners. Ch Duhart-Milon is Lafite's fourth growth, made in the town of Pauillac. The fifth growths Ch Clerc-Milon and Ch d'Armailhac (the latter called Ch Mouton Baron Philippe and then Ch Mouton Baronne Philippe between 1956 and 1989) are made, to an often very high standard, close to Mouton itself. Other classed growths on this plateau just a stream away from St-Estèphe are the fifth growths Chx Pontet-Canet which has attracted considerable attention as a result of its unusual espousal of BIODYNAMIC VITICULTURE and the generally much less exciting Pédesclaux.

Throughout the 1970s, much was made of the inter-Rothschild rivalry in the northern half of Pauillac, resolved by the next generation. In the mid 1980s and early 1990s, the extreme south of the appellation around the village of St-Lambert was a battleground for wine supremacy, between first growth Ch Latour and, particularly, its near neighbours the two Pichons. All three of these have made considerable investments in their vineyards, *chais*, and more cosmetic aspects of their property, and the Pichons have demonstrated that, just like first growth Latour, they are capable of making sublime wine at the St-Julien end of Pauillac. The Pichon-Longueville estate was originally one, but had already been divided into a smaller 'Baron' portion and a larger Comtesse de Lalande portion by the time the 1855 classification ranked them in the bottom half of the second growths (a very much lower position than they merit today). Pichon-Baron has been lavishly renovated by AXA Millésimes while ROEDERER, new owners of Pichon Lalande, later did the same across the road.

In the hinterland of this southern extreme of Pauillac are neighbouring fifth growths Chx Batailley and Haut-Batailley, whose wines can challenge those of fifth growth Ch Grand-Puy-Lacoste to the immediate north, which is run impeccably by Xavier Borie and can offer some of Pauillac's best value. A dozen of the 18 fifth growths are in Pauillac, and none has been more successful than the Cazes family's flamboyantly styled Ch Lynch-Bages (the name betraying the original Irish connection), whose standing and fame suggest a considerably higher ranking. Chx Lynch-Moussas, Croizet-Bages, and Grand-Puy-Ducasse have rarely merited the limelight. Ch Haut-Bages-Libéral, between Chx Latour and Lynch-Bages, can be great value.

Two of Pauillac's most distinctive products do not feature in the 1855 classification. Les Forts de Latour, the SECOND WINE of Ch Latour, is regularly one of its most successful wines (and is priced as such), while the co-operative at Pauillac is a particularly important one, selling some of its considerable produce under the name La Rose Pauillac.

Brook, S., *The Complete Bordeaux* (rev. edn, London, 2012).

Penning-Rowsell, E., *The Wines of Bordeaux* (6th edn, London, 1989).

Paulée, La. Originally a HARVEST TRADITION, the term was appropriated for a huge BYOB extended lunch in MEURSAULT on the Monday after the annual HOSPICES DE BEAUNE sale and is now used for a series of bibulous events in the United States at which considerable predations are made in COLLECTORS' stocks of TROPHY WINES.

PCA, or **2,3,4,5,6-pentachloroanisole**. See TETRACHLOROANISOLE.

PCD. See PLANT CELL DENSITY.

PCR, abbreviation for **polymerase chain reaction**, a laboratory method based on DNA analysis used to detect vine pathogens. This technique has helped in determining strains of VIRUS, for example, and the INSECTS responsible for their spread.

Kumagai, L., and Fabritius, A.-L., 'Detection and differentiation of pathogenic *Agrobacterium vitis* and *A. tumefaciens* in grapevine using multiplex Bio-PCR', *Proceedings of the 2nd Annual National Viticulture Research Conference, July 2008* (Richmond. Calif). iv.ucdavis.edu/files/108864.pdf.

Weber, E., Golino, D., and Rowhani, A., 'Laboratory testing for grapevine diseases', *Practical Winery & Vineyard* (Jan/Feb 2002), 13–27.

PDO, abbreviation for **Protected Designation of Origin**, a superior EU wine category created as part of the 2008 wine reforms. It replaces the former Quality Wine Produced in Specified Regions category (France's Vin de Qualité Produit dans les Régions Délimitées or VQPRD) and encompasses the EU's CONTROLLED APPELLATION systems such as France's AOC, Spain's DO/DOCA, Italy's DOC/DOCG, and Portugal's DOC. Translations of PDO, such as AOP in France, DOP in Spain, Italy, and Portugal) are now also seen on wine labels. In 2012, PDO wines represented 44% of EU production, although the proportion of PDO wine produced—as well as the quality—can vary dramatically among member states. PDOs enjoy special privileges in the EU wine system, including protection against misuse as well as the right to use TRADITIONAL TERMS and the special EU PDO symbol on the label. Non-EU designations may be registered with the EU as PDOs as well, but only the US's NAPA Valley and BRAZIL's Vale dos Vinhedos had been registered by 2014.

The PDO category is regarded as a higher order of geographical designation than the PGI. The quality and characteristics of a PDO are required to be 'essentially or exclusively due to a particular geographical environment with its inherent natural and human factors'—a higher threshold than for the PGI category. The grapes must also be grown entirely in the delimited area and be sourced exclusively from VINIFERA grape varieties. PDOs generally have more stringent controls than PGIs, covering matters such as maximum yield, vineyard management techniques, permitted varieties, harvesting, and winemaking.   J.B.

pearls or **pearl glands**, small, spherical nodules that develop on the surface of vine stems, PETIOLES, and the underside of leaves along the large veins. They form under warm humid conditions, such as in a glasshouse, and when the vine's growth is exuberant. They are a multicellular outgrowth of the epidermis, even to the extent of an occasional STOMA, but collapse to a rusty colour and disappear when the humidity drops.   B.G.C.

Pécharmant, red wine appellation for BORDEAUX BLENDS within the BERGERAC district in SOUTH WEST FRANCE. A steady 400 ha/1,000 acres of vines were dedicated to the appellation in 2012, planted on gravelly, south-facing slopes just east of the town of Bergerac. The wines are some of Périgord's longest-lived reds but little of it escapes the region, however. Within the zone, some sweet white wine is made in the much smaller ROSETTE appellation.

Pecorino, vine speciality of the Marche and Abruzzo on Italy's east coast that has made a VARIETAL comeback because of its firm, dry, minerally white wine that compares well with the local Trebbiano. Total area planted grew from 87 ha in 2000 to over 1,110 ha/2,740 acres by 2010. Also a Calabrian synonym for GRECO BIANCO.

pectinase, an ENZYME used to break up grape PECTINS and thus speed up SETTLING. It is also used to promote juice and flavour extraction during SKIN CONTACT.

pectins, carbohydrate polymers made up of galacturonic acid units which have the important function of 'gumming' plant cells together. The group is diverse and includes pectic acid, hemicelluloses, and gums; the associated sugars are galactose, mannose, and arabinose. The pectin content of grapes increases steadily throughout ripening, reaching levels of about 1 g/l. Pectin is an important contributor to COLLOIDS. For the importance of pectin hydrolysing enzymes to winemaking, see ENZYMES.   B.G.C.

Pedernã, MINHO synonym for ARINTO.

pedicel, the stalk of an individual flower which, on a bunch of grapes, becomes the short stem bearing each berry. Its length varies with vine variety, from 5 to 15 mm (0.5 in), and its diameter varies with variety and BERRY SIZE. After FLOWERING, pedicels are liable to develop a separation layer at their base causing the flower to drop; the remainder adhere and can develop into berries (as in FRUIT SET). When berries of certain vine varieties ripen, the pedicels may develop a corky abscission at their top, at the junction with the berry. If this does not happen, then pulling off the berry tears the skin and leaves behind a chunk of pulp on the end of the pedicel that is called the BRUSH.   B.G.C.

Pedro Giménez, declining but still quite important white grape variety in ARGENTINA, where, along with the coarse and declining CRIOLLA GRANDE and CEREZA, it is one of the vines underpinning the country's substantial production of everyday wine for domestic consumption. Most of its approximately 12,000 ha/30,000 acres in 2013 were in Mendoza but is also found in Chile's pisco region. It is unrelated to PEDRO XIMÉNEZ.

Pedro Ximénez, white grape variety traditionally associated with ANDALUCÍA in southern Spain, found especially in MONTILLA-MORILES, where it accounts for about 70% of all plantings, but also in EXTREMADURA. Producers in JEREZ and MÁLAGA routinely import the dark, super-sticky wines made from Pedro Ximénez grown in Montilla-Moriles to sweeten blends. Many sherry producers now sell varietal PX under their own labels. The thin-skinned grapes are traditionally dried in the sun. They are generally lower in acid and alcohol than the sherry grape PALOMINO FINO, which is more productive and less disease-prone than Pedro Ximénez. By 2011 Pedro Ximénez was grown on a total of fewer than 8,500 ha/21,000 acres, virtually all in Montilla-Moriles. It is grown as Perrum on about 250 ha of Portugal's the ALENTEJO.

In Australia, Pedro Ximénez, often called breezily **Pedro**, was once quite widely grown but its total area has fallen to under 100 ha/247 acres. It has been known to shine, most particularly in BOTRYTIZED form to produce the rich, deep golden McWilliam's Pedro Sauterne (*sic*) made in irrigated vineyards near Griffith in NEW SOUTH WALES. Most of Chile's **Pedro Jiménez** (*sic*) is used for pisco production but a varietal dry white is made in Elqui Valley.

peduncle. See BUNCHSTEM.

Peel, warm coastal region just to the south of Perth in WESTERN AUSTRALIA with CHENIN BLANC and SHIRAZ its best wines.

Pelaverga, pale, rare, red grape of Piemonte making slightly fizzy, strawberry-flavoured wines. The even rarer and more admired **Pelaverga Piccolo** is a distinct variety.

Peloursin, obscure Isère red grape variety known mainly as a parent of PETITE SIRAH.

Penedès, sometimes spelt **Penedés** or **Panadés**, the largest and most important denominated wine zone in CATALUÑA in northeast Spain (see map under SPAIN), producing an innovative range of wines from 15,200 ha/36,500 acres of vineyard in 2013. With its proximity to Barcelona, Penedès has always had a ready outlet for its wines. In the 19th century, it

was one of the first regions in Spain to begin mass production and France, stricken by PHYLLOXERA, became an important market. The phylloxera louse reached Penedès in 1887, by which time José Raventós had laid the foundations of CODORNÍU and the CAVA industry. Vineyards that had once produced strong, semi-fortified reds were uprooted in favour of white grapes for sparkling wine. Cava has subsequently developed a separate nationally organized DO.

Penedès underwent a second radical transformation in the 1960s and 1970s largely because of Miguel Torres Carbó and his son Miguel A. TORRES, wine (and brandy) producers in the heart of the region at Vilafranca del Penedès. They were among the first in Spain to install TEMPERATURE CONTROL and STAINLESS STEEL tanks. Miguel Torres, Jr, who studied OENOLOGY in France, also imported and experimented with such revolutionary vine varieties as Cabernet Sauvignon, Chardonnay, Sauvignon Blanc, Merlot, Pinot Noir, Riesling, and Gewürztraminer, which were planted alongside and blended with native varieties. Other growers followed in the Torres family footsteps and Penedès was in the 1980s one of the most dynamic and varied wine regions in Spain. By the late 1990s, however, the region was failing to confirm the high hopes placed in its red wines, which were increasingly overshadowed by those of PRIORAT.

Penedès rises from the Mediterranean like a series of steps and divides into three distinct zones. Bajo, or Low, Penedès reaches elevations of 250 m/825 ft away from the tourist resorts of the Costa Daurada. This is the warmest part of the region which traditionally grew Malvasía and Moscatel de Alejandría (MUSCAT OF ALEXANDRIA) grapes for sweet FORTIFIED wines. With the expansion of the resort towns and declining sales of such wines, these vineyards have either been abandoned or replanted with GARNACHA, CARIÑENA, or MONASTRELL making sturdy reds. The second zone, Medio Penedès, is a broad valley 500 m/1,600 ft above sea level, separated from the coast by a ridge of hills, the Garraf chain, which has ambitions to be a separate subappellation. The Medio Penedès is the most productive part of the region providing much of the base wine for the sparkling wine industry at Sant Sadurní d'Anoia (see CAVA). MACABEO, XAREL-LO, and PARELLADA are grown for Cava, together with increasing quantities of Chardonnay and red varieties such as TEMPRANILLO (often called here by its Catalan name Ull de Llebre) and Cabernet Sauvignon. Penedès Superior, between 500 and 800 m above the coast, is the coolest part of the region where some of the best white grapes are grown. The native Parellada is the most important variety here, but Riesling, Muscat of Alexandria,

Gewürztraminer, and Chardonnay are also successful.   V. de la S.

Penfolds, makers of Australia's most famous fine wine **Penfolds Grange**, now owned by TREASURY WINE. Penfolds' first vineyard was founded in 1844 at Magill, South Australia, by Dr Christopher Rawson Penfold. For more than 100 years, Penfolds, in common with most Australian wineries, concentrated on producing FORTIFIED wines and brandy, much of which was exported to the UK. In 1950, Max Schubert, then chief winemaker, visited Europe, primarily to observe the making of sherry in Spain, but detoured on the way home to visit Bordeaux, where he was taken in hand by Christian CRUSE. This inspired him to adopt an entirely new approach to fermentation techniques and the use of new oak, the aim being simultaneously to protect the varietal flavour of Shiraz while adding a level of complexity previously unknown in Australia. Schubert's ambition was to create a red that would rival the finest wines of Bordeaux for both quality and the potential to improve with age for up to 50 years. This he achieved with Penfolds Grange (known as Penfolds Grange Hermitage until EU authorities objected to this misappropriation of a French place-name), now widely acknowledged to be Australia's greatest wine. The first vintage of Grange, named after Dr Penfold's cottage in Magill, was 1951; all early vintages were made from Shiraz grapes grown at Magill and Morphett Vale, Adelaide, and the wine was matured in new American oak for 12 months. So intense did the first vintages seem that they were rejected as maverick 'dry port'. In 1957, Schubert was ordered to cease production of Grange; instead he took the operation underground, emerging three years later when maturing vintages began to fulfil their promise. In fact, fine vintages of Grange improve for up to 30 years and beyond (the 1952 and 1953 vintages were still magnificent), and the wine became the first NEW WORLD wine to become an internationally acknowledged collectible. Fruit from Kalimna in the Barossa Valley was introduced in 1961, boosted by grapes from the Clare and Koonunga Hill vineyards. Small amounts of Cabernet Sauvignon are included in most vintages of Grange, and the wood-ageing period has been lengthened to between 18 and 20 months. The wine is not released until five years after the vintage.

A string of award-winning red wines from Penfolds followed, many identified by BIN numbers which originated in the winery stockkeeping system. Of particular note is Bin 707 Cabernet Sauvignon. In 1998 Penfolds released the first vintage of its super-premium Yattarna Chardonnay, now recognized as one of Australia's finest. A stream of 'Special Bin' luxury reds

p

followed in the early 2000s, not least the 2008 Bin 620 Cabernet/Shiraz, priced in line with first growth bordeaux, and 2010 Bin 170 Kalimna Shiraz that is even more expensive. If PRICES are a guide, Penfolds has truly arrived on the luxury catwalk. As of 2014 the brand was owned by TREASURY WINE ESTATES. See also RECORKING.   J.H. & H.H.

Hooke, H., *Max Schubert, Winemaker* (Sydney, 1994).

Caillaird, A., *The Rewards of Patience* (7th edn, Sydney, 2013).

Penicillium, one of a group of FUNGI commonly found on rotten grapes. See BUNCH ROTS.

Península de Setúbal, VINHO REGIONAL in southern PORTUGAL (called Terras do Sado until 2009) encompassing the SETÚBAL Peninsula between the Tagus and Sado estuaries and, to the south, the Troia Peninsula and a 60 km stretch of the Alentejo Litoral (see PORTUGAL map). The warm, MARITIME CLIMATE is particularly well suited to winemaking. In the 19th century, the north-facing slopes around the village of Azeitão were planted with a number of different Moscatel (MUSCAT) varieties for sweet, fortified Setúbal but, since this wine's decline in popularity, other varieties have largely taken their place.

Production is concentrated in the hands of one of Portugal's best CO-OPERATIVES, Cooperativa Agrícola de Santo Isidro de Pegões and two companies José Maria da Fonseca Successores in Azeitão and Bacalhôa Vinhos de Portugal (previously known as J. P. Vinhos) whose skilled OENOLOGISTS, trained respectively at DAVIS in California and ROSEWORTHY in Australia, helped to modernize the region's winemaking. Accordingly, the Península de Setúbal now produces a wide range of wines, from well-established brands such as Periquita to single-estate wines such as Quinta da Bacalhôa.

Within the region is the Palmela DOP, which has two distinct TERROIRS: the limestone hills of the Serra da Arrabida, and the sandy soils of the plain which extends eastwards from the fortress town of Palmela. Here, the widely planted, traditional CASTELÃO grape (which must represent at least two-thirds of any DOP red) performs at its best. Its distinctive, structured wines are capable of ageing well in bottle. Where the rules are more relaxed for VR Península de Setúbal, Castelão (here nicknamed Periquita) has become less important, especially where Cabernet Sauvignon, Merlot, and Syrah (and for whites, Chardonnay) have been grown so successfully on the limestone Arrabida Hills. Other grape varieties from the north of Portugal such as TOURIGA FRANCA, TOURIGA NACIONAL, and more recently ALVARINHO have taken hold here, too. To the south (on the Troia Peninsula and in the Alentejo litoral area) a number of

ambitious single estates were established in the early 21st century. The grapes of the ALENTEJO have been most popular, especially ALICANTE BOUSCHET, Aragones (TEMPRANILLO), and TRINCADEIRA—although one producer has made a name for itself with a Sangiovese. Wines here tend to be full-bodied.   S.A.

www.vinhosdapeninsuladesetubal.com

Peninsulas Zone, This Australian wine zone takes in the Southern Eyre Peninsula and the Yorke Peninsula on either side of SOUTH AUSTRALIA's Spencer Gulf.

Penning-Rowsell, Edmund (1913–2002), English wine writer with a scholarly interest in the history and wines of Bordeaux in particular. Educated at Marlborough College and a lifelong socialist, he was a journalist on the *Morning Post* from 1930 until 1935, when he began a career of almost 30 years as a book publisher. He was introduced to the pleasures of wine when his wife's employer at the BBC gave her as a leaving present (only unmarried females were then regarded as suitable employees) some non-vintage Moulin-à-Vent. Correspondence and eventual friendship with Bristol wine merchant Ronald AVERY was another formative influence.

The traditional but non-profit-making ethos of the co-operative buying group The WINE SOCIETY suited him perfectly and he joined the Society soon after his marriage in 1937. In 1959 he was elected to its Management Committee and served as its chairman from 1964 until 1987, a record length of time.

In 1949 he had reviewed wine books for the *Times Literary Supplement* and in 1954 wrote his first wine article for the magazine *Country Life*. After 1964, soon after his publishing career came to an end, he became wine correspondent of the *Financial Times*, scrupulously refusing to mention the Wine Society during his chairmanship. His wine primer *Red, White and Rosé* was published in 1967, and a second edition appeared in 1973, but his great gift to the LITERATURE OF WINE is *The Wines of Bordeaux*, which was first published in 1969 and whose sixth edition appeared 20 years later.

Until his sight failed him, he meticulously recorded the facts of his remarkable cellar in a series of cellar books and, typically, in his characteristic green ink. This unique archive included details of every purchase, every souvenir from his annual round of visits to the wine regions (continued into his ninth decade), and impressions of every bottle sampled.

A perennial figure in Bordeaux at vintage time and at the HOSPICES DE BEAUNE auction, Penning-Rowsell was made a Chevalier de l'Ordre du Mérite Agricole in 1971 and a Chevalier de l'Ordre du Mérite National in 1981.

Loftus, S., 'Purple prose: the wine writers', in *Anatomy of the Wine Trade* (London, 1985).

pepper, a tasting term for two very different aromas commonly found in red wines. **Bell peppers**, or **green peppers**, is used characteristically in the US of underripe CABERNET SAUVIGNON. A freshly sliced green pepper or capsicum liberates the chemical compound 2-methoxy-3-isobutyl-pyrazine (see METHOXYPYRAZINES), a vegetable-like or HERBACEOUS aroma to which many tasters have a very low threshold (see FLAVOUR COMPOUNDS).

Young wines made from the SYRAH grape, on the other hand, particularly if it does not reach full maturity, can smell of **black peppercorns** while GRÜNER VELTLINER sometimes smells of white peppercorns. See ROTUNDONE.

Per'e Palummo. See PIEDIROSSO.

pergola, a form of overhead VINE TRAINING. Where the canopy is horizontal, the pergola can alternatively be called TENDONE. Pergola trellises can be either one or two armed, depending on whether the vines are trained on one or both sides of the row. If the trellis is joined overhead, it is called a closed pergola.

The pergola is widely used in northern Italy, where the canopies vary but are often inclined rather than horizontal (in Trentino, for example, the slope is 20 to 30 degrees). In Emilia-Romagna the **pergoletta** system is used, while the **pergoletta Capucci** was developed by the eponymous Bologna professor. The **pergoletta a Valenzano** is very similar to the GENEVA DOUBLE CURTAIN. Where the vines have marked VIGOUR, the bunches which hang below the leafy canopy are in SHADE, with predictable negative effects on wine quality. This century there has been a resurgence of interest in pergola systems. It does intercept most if not all SUNLIGHT, and so has a high yield potential in marginal climates. The overhead leaf canopy may be an advantage as temperatures increase with CLIMATE CHANGE, and in AOSTA its value in protecting against HAIL has been noted.   R.E.S.

pericarp, the 'fruit wall' forming the bulk of a plant's ovary, consisting of sugary flesh and highly coloured skin attractive to animals, especially BIRDS, with the result that the SEEDS are spread. In the grape berry, the whole fruit except for the seeds (both the skin and the flesh) constitutes the pericarp. See GRAPE for more details.

Pérignon, Dom (1639–1715), Benedictine monk who has gone down in history as 'the man who invented champagne'. The title is the stuff of fairy-tales: the transition from still to sparkling wine was an evolutionary process rather than a dramatic discovery on the part of one man. The life of Dom Pérignon was in fact devoted to improving the still wines of

Champagne, and he deserves his place in the history books for that reason. Father Pierre Pérignon arrived at the Abbey of Hautvillers, north of Épernay, in 1668. His role was that of bursar, and in the 17th century that included being in charge of the cellars. He collected tithes from surrounding villages in the form of grapes and wine, fermenting and blending until he created wines that sold for twice as much as those of the abbey's rivals. Dom Pérignon introduced many practices that survive in the process of modern wine production, among them severe pruning, low yields, and careful harvesting. He also experimented to a great extent with the process, and was one of the first to BLEND the produce of many different vineyards. Dom Pérignon produced still white wines, favouring black grapes because a SECOND FERMENTATION was less likely. Ironically, he was often thwarted in his endeavours by the refermentation process, which produced the style of wine that was eventually to prove so popular. His fame as the 'inventor' of champagne probably spread after his death, embellished by Dom Grossard, the last bursar of the abbey, which closed at the time of the French Revolution. More modern champagne producers have jumped on the bandwagon, promoting the idea of a founder figure. Eugene Mercier registered the brand name Dom Pérignon before MOËT & CHANDON acquired it and used it to launch the first champagne marketed as a PRESTIGE CUVÉE, a 1921 vintage launched in 1936.

See also CHAMPAGNE. S.E.A.

Faith, N., *The Story of Champagne* (London, 1988).
Johnson, H., *The Story of Wine* (London, 1989).

Periquita, Portuguese word meaning 'parakeet' that is both a SETÚBAL name for CASTELÃO and a branded red wine from José Maria da FONSECA.

perlant, French term for a wine that is only slightly SPARKLING. **Perlwein** is the German equivalent. See FIZZINESS.

Perle, pink-berried, late-budding, rot-prone GERMAN CROSS of Gewürztraminer and Müller-Thurgau that can still be found in FRANKEN and, very occasionally England.

Pernand-Vergelesses, village in the Côte de Beaune district of Burgundy's Côte d'Or producing red and white wines. The former, made from Pinot Noir, are somewhat angular in style and do not always appear fully ripe as Pernand is set back from the main sweep of the Côte and many of its vineyards have a westerly, even north western exposition, which can retard RIPENING.

Pernand chose to suffix the name of its best red wine vineyard, east-facing Les Vergelesses, which it shares with neighbouring Savigny-lès-Beaune, although the most sought-after wines

are the whites on the Pernand side of the hill of Corton (see ALOXE-CORTON). Seventeen of the 72 ha/178 acres entitled to the GRAND CRU appellation Corton-Charlemagne lie within Pernand-Vergelesses. White Pernand wines have a hard but attractive flinty character which develops well during BOTTLE AGEING. As it ages, BOURGOGNE ALIGOTÉ from this area is said to resemble white Pernand-Vergelesses; and white Pernand to approach the quality of Corton-Charlemagne.

The most famous producer based in Pernand-Vergelesses is Bonneau du Martray, one of the top names in Corton-Charlemagne, while Domaines Dubreuil-Fontaine, Rapet, and Rollin also produce fine ranges of wine.

See also CÔTE D'OR, and map under BURGUNDY.
J.T.C.M.

Pernod Ricard, French spirits company whose wine portfolio is styled **Pernod Ricard Winemakers**. The company's first significant wine acquisition was in 1989, the Orlando Wyndham Group of Australia which included the BRAND JACOB'S CREEK. Etchart of Argentina, owner of Graffigna, followed in 1992, and then in 2005 Allied Domecq which included not just an array of spirits, but Montana (now BRANCOTT ESTATE), and Stoneleigh in New Zealand, Campo Viejo in Rioja, and Mumm and Perrier-Jouët champagnes. In 2013 the company invested in the Chinese wine brand Helan Mountain of Ningxia and in 2014 acquired Kenwood Vineyards of California. A project in GEORGIA begun in 1993 was abandoned. See GLOBALIZATION.

peronospora, European name for the very important VINE DISEASE more usually called DOWNY MILDEW.

Perricone, north west SICILIAN red grape variety whose total area had fallen to under 230 ha/560 acres by 2010; sometimes called by its synonym Pignatello.

Perricoota, large, sparsely populated, region bordering the Murray river in NEW SOUTH WALES to the east of Australia's Murray Darling region and south of the Riverina.

Perrum. See PEDRO XIMÉNEZ.

Persan, rare but promising SAVOIE red grape which can produce wines worth ageing. Interest in it is also increasing in neighbouring Isère.

Persia, Near Eastern country officially known as IRAN since 1935, which has known the consumption of wine since ancient times.

Ancient Persia

Much of this area was also known as MESOPOTAMIA in classical times. The earliest chemical evidence for grape wine comes from the Neolithic village of Hajji Firuz Tepe, about 5400–5000 BC, in the northern Zagros Mountains of

north western Iran. Six jars in a kitchen of an average household would originally have held some 55 l (15 gal) of wine, based on the presence of TARTARIC ACID which is found in large amounts only in grapes in the Middle East. The intended product was most likely wine and not vinegar or another grape product, because clay stoppers were used to stopper the narrow mouths of the jars and a tree resin, probably terebinth with antioxidant properties, was added to the wine as a preservative. Hajji Firuz was among the first year-round settlements based on newly domesticated plants and animals of the Neolithic period. The Eurasian VINIFERA grapevine might well have been one of those domesticates. The invention of pottery around 6000 BC, gave impetus to the process, since special vessels for preparing, storing, and serving wine could now be made. Similarly, two millennia later, pottery jars, one stored on its side, in rooms at the site of Godin Tepe, further south in the Zagros (dated to about 3500 BC) in central western Iran, were shown to contain a resinated wine.

More detailed evidence is available from the era of the Achaemenid Dynasty, which ruled Ancient Iran from c.559 to c.331 BC. Cyrus the Great and Darius extended Persia's power to cover all the lands from the Mediterranean in the west to the River Indus in the east, incorporating the old empires of BABYLONIA and Assyria, which were overwhelmed and extended. Dating from the period just before Persia and Greece became embroiled in the Persian Wars, an enormous archive of documents written on clay tablets in the Elamite language preserves detailed records of the administration of the Achaemenid royal capital Persepolis from 509 to 494 BC. Here there are records concerning distribution of large quantities of (grape) wine and *sawur*, another (probably weaker) sort of wine. Sometimes the wine was stored at, or issued from, the ancient city of SHIRAZ, whose name is now associated with so many wines. Wine was normally released in monthly amounts, although in certain cases the issue was daily. One *marrish* (a measure of 10 quarts) of wine was valued at one shekel.

Such 'rations' often amounted to far more than one person could consume: perhaps they would be better described as salaries. Some were given to important women with households of their own to support: these received 30 quarts per month. King Darius writes in one order that 100 sheep and 500 gal of wine should be issued for the royal princess Artystone, no doubt in order for her to give a lavish banquet at her own court. Persian royal ladies were very independent and maintained their own establishments and dependants.

Generally wine was not given to boy and girl workers (who did, however, receive other rations including sometimes beer), except according to one document where some boys received one-third of a quart daily for 156 days. Otherwise the general allowance was 10 or 20 quarts monthly for men and 10 for women. Some labourers received a good deal less.

Presumably in an effort to increase the proletarian population available for large-scale labour, special wine rations were provided under the Achaemenid dynasty as a reward for women labourers who had just given birth to children: women who bore sons received 10 quarts, and those who bore daughters 5 quarts. The issue was sometimes spread out over the entire subsequent year.

Important caravans of diplomatic visitors accompanied by élite guides travelled from as far afield as Kandahar, India, Sardis, and Egypt. Those due to arrive at the capital Persepolis during the cooler months of the year (November to May), when the king and his entourage were in residence, were issued with travel rations to ease their arduous journey at the various stations at which they put up on the Royal Road. The records indicate that these, naturally, included generous amounts of wine.

On occasions wine was issued, along with grain and beer, for the benefit of the royal horses, perhaps when they were used for long journeys. The amounts issued varied from half a pint to 10 pints per animal per month. *Sawur* wine was even made available to the king's camels as an occasional concession.

In the 5th century BC, HERODOTUS noted that the Achaemenids would make important decisions in a drunken state, then confirm these decisions when sober, and vice versa. The Persian empire was finally split up after the death of Alexander the Great in 323 BC.

See also ORIGINS OF VINICULTURE and PALAEO-ETHNOBOTANY AND THE ARCHAEOLOGY OF WINE.

J.A.B. & P.E.M.

Hallock, R. T., *Persepolis Fortification Tablets* (Chicago, 1969).

Shiraz as wine capital

The consumption of wine survived through the Sassanian Period, from the 3rd to the 7th centuries AD, influenced in part by Zoroastrian rite, and continued after the subsequent ISLAMIC conquest of the country.

Shiraz, a city rebuilt 50 km/30 miles from the site of Persepolis by the Arabs in the 8th century and the home town of Hāfiz, Persia's most famous mystic Bacchic poet (see ARAB POETS), had acquired a reputation by the 9th century for producing the finest wines in the Near East.

Thanks principally to the work of Edward Fitzgerald in the 19th century, the medieval polymath and poet OMAR KHAYYÁM has become famous in the west for poetry in which wine plays an important part.

From the diaries of 17th-century English and French travellers and especially the writings of C. J. Wills in the 19th century, we gain a picture

of the excellence of some Persian wines. Tavernier (17th century) wrote: 'the wine of Shiraz has by far the greatest foreign as well as native celebrity, being of the quality of an old sherry and constitutes an excellent beverage.' In the same century, Thomas Herbert commented: 'No part of the world has wine better than Shiraz.'

The wine most often described and praised was white, made from thick-skinned, pip-filled grapes grown on terraces round the village of Khoullar, four days' camel ride away from Shiraz (those grown in the immediate vicinity of the city produced watery wine, thanks to excessive IRRIGATION). C. J. Wills describes a 19th-century replication of the traditional Shiraz winemaking process in some detail. The wine, fermented on the skins with regular PUNCHING DOWN, was made either sweet and fruity for long keeping, the stems being removed immediately after fermentation in used jars, or dry and rich in PHENOLICS for drinking in its first year or so. A form of FILTRATION through coarse canvas bags was practised. Wills describes the wine as 'like a light BUCELLAS' when young, to be avoided on account of the headaches it induces. After five years, however, it attains a 'fine aroma and bouquet' and 'nutty flavour'.

See also DRIED-GRAPE WINES, for the Persians were certainly in the habit of drying their grapes.
P.K.

Hugh Johnson paints a fascinating and vivid picture of the export of wine from Shiraz to India by European merchants, in 1677 (already in BOTTLES 'wrapped in straw and packed in cases... swaying down to the Gulf Coast on mule back. There is scarcely any earlier instance of the regular use of bottles for shipping wine.' Tavernier notes that the 1666 vintage was so bountiful that the Persian king gave permission to export as much wine to the French, English, Dutch, and Portuguese trading companies as was retained by himself and his court. Wine was measured in 'mans', units of weight rather than volume.

For an outline of modern viticulture, see IRAN.

Johnson, H., *The Story of Wine* (London and New York, 1989).

Planhol, X., 'Une rencontre de l'Europe et de l'Iran: le vin de Shiraz', in D. Boidanovic and J. L. Bacque-Grammont (eds.), *Iran* (Paris, 1972).

Tavernier, J.-B., *Voyages en Perse* (Geneva, 1970).

Wills, C. J., *The Land of the Lion and the Sun* (London, 1891).

Wills, C. J., *Persia as it is* (London, 1886).

Perth Hills, picturesque, rapidly growing warm region just east of Perth in WESTERN AUSTRALIA. The region has moved from one of rustic, cottage craft to more polished winemaking with the arrival of Millbrook Winery and Western Range Wines.

Peru, the first country in SOUTH AMERICA to have encouraged systematic viticulture. Under orders from the famous conquistador Francisco Pizarro, the first Peruvian vineyard was planted in about 1547. Specific VINE VARIETIES were imported from Spain and by the 1560s Peru is thought to have had 40,000 ha/99,000 acres under vine, producing so much wine that it was exported to other South American countries and even, according to one document, as far as Spain. One of the several ways by which viticulture spread to Argentina was from Peru, with Nuñez de Prado, in 1550.

The arrival of the PHYLLOXERA louse in 1888 heralded the start of a serious decline in Peruvian viticulture, which was halted as recently as 1960. Only in the 1970s was progress made on establishing suitable planting material and there are now NURSERIES at Ica, Chincha, Moquegua, and Tacna, as well as a national wine research centre Centro de Innovación Tecnológica Vitivinícola (CITEVID).

According to OIV statistics, 23,000 ha/57,000 acres of Peru were planted with vines in 2011, yielding mainly TABLE GRAPES but also 630,000 hl of wine, more than twice as much as at the turn of the century. Almost all vines have traditionally been grown in Ica province south of Lima, close to the port of Pisco (which gives its name to the national drink, a grape brandy). Winter temperatures are so high (between 6 and 16 °C) that full vine DORMANCY cannot be relied on. Summer temperatures are also high, between 16 and 34 °C (60–93 °F) in the hottest month, and rainfall is low. Wells have traditionally supplied IRRIGATION water but levels are falling, as DRIP IRRIGATION is being introduced. Yields may reach 12 tons per ha (5 tons/acre) but attempts are being made to upgrade techniques and wine quality. New projects are being developed in areas such as Palpa (100 km south of Ica) where Syrah is promising, and also in the Sacred Valley near Cusco (although rain at harvest can be a problem at elevation). Peru's growing economy has been attracting investment from elsewhere in South America.

Vine varieties planted for wine include Cabernet Sauvignon, Malbec, Syrah, Tannat, Petit Verdot, Albilla, Moscatel, Chardonnay, Sauvignon Blanc, Torontel, and a little Chenin Blanc.

Tacama is the best-known producer but is not the only one with ambition.

Goldstein, E., *Wines of South America* (Oakland, 2014).

Pessac-Léognan, important BORDEAUX red and dry white wine appellation created in 1987 for the most celebrated part of the GRAVES district immediately south of the city (and often still referred to as Graves). It takes its somewhat cumbersome name from its two vinously most important communes, and includes all of the

WINEMAKING / WÜRZBURG / GERMANY Fashions in winemaking come and go. Wooden fermentation vessels were replaced by concrete, then stainless steel, then in some quarters by a return to wood, but by the second decade of the 21st century **concrete eggs** were increasingly used, as here at Weingut am Stein, Würzburg, Germany. The contact between lees and wine is considered optimal. © StockFood/Feig & Feig

properties named in the 1959 CLASSIFICATION of Graves, and many other fine châteaux too. This is Bordeaux's most urban wine area—indeed the vineyards of its most famous property Ch Haut-Brion and its neighbour and stablemate Ch La Mission-Haut-Brion are today surrounded by suburban development, including the campus of the University of BORDEAUX, on the boundary of the suburbs of Pessac and Talence. It is hardly surprising that Bordeaux's earliest wine estates were developed here, although the wines of Chx HAUT-BRION, LA MISSION-HAUT-BRION, and Pape-Clément justify the properties' existence on grounds far more solid than mere geographical convenience. Further from the city, vineyards are carved out of the pine forests which extend south west into the Landes. In all, about 1,435 ha/3,544 acres of vineyard within Pessac-Léognan produce red wine, and the total area devoted to white wine grapes was almost 270 ha by the early 2010s.

Soils here have particularly good DRAINAGE, being made up of gravel terraces of very different eras. The ENCÉPAGEMENT for red wines is very similar to that of the MÉDOC to the immediate north, being mainly Cabernet Sauvignon grapes with some Merlot and Cabernet Franc, but the wines can be quite different. It is not fanciful to imagine that the best wines of Pessac-Léognan have a distinct aroma that reminds some tasters of minerals, some of smoke, others even of warm bricks. Ch Haut-Brion is the most obvious exponent of this genre. Other current overachievers include Chx Pape-Clément, Smith Haut-Lafitte, and Haut-Bailly, while Chx de Fieuzal and La Louvière can provide some of Bordeaux's better value.

White wines made here can be some of the most characterful dry white wines in the world, made from Sauvignon Blanc, Sauvignon Gris, Sémillon, and Muscadelle grapes grown generally on the lighter, sandier parts of the vineyard, and often produced with considerable recourse to BARREL FERMENTATION and BARREL MATURATION. The most admired, Domaine de Chevalier and Chx Haut-Brion Blanc and La Mission-Haut-Brion Blanc, can develop in bottle over decades, and the dry white wines of Ch Malartic-Lagravière, for example, demand a decade in bottle at the very least. More recent, and more modern if still long-lasting, fine white wines are made at Ch Couhins-LURTON.

Brook, S., *The Complete Bordeaux* (rev. edn, London, 2012).

Penning-Rowsell, E., *The Wines of Bordeaux* (6th edn, London, 1989).

pesticides, substances or mixtures of substances applied to vineyards which are used to prevent, destroy, repel, or reduce the harmful effects of FUNGI, BACTERIA, INSECTS, NEMATODES, or other undesirable organisms regarded as VINE PESTS. Pesticides are made up of AGROCHEMICALS

and are usually classified according to their principal use as, for example, fungicides, bactericides, insecticides, nematicides, miticides, etc. Many pesticides have more than one mode of action and may be effective against more than one type of pest. For example, SULFUR is both a fungicide and a miticide in vineyards.

Most pesticides consist of an active chemical constituent in a concentrated form that is suitable for use after mixing with a diluent (water or oil). Less often, pesticides are formulated as dusts, granules, or fumigants and require DUSTING rather than SPRAYING. For reasons of worker safety, there is a move away from these latter formulations. Mixtures of active ingredients may be combined in one product for greater efficacy or versatility: two chemicals may be mixed, for example, to produce a DOWNY MILDEW fungicide with both protectant and eradicant properties. For convenience, two or more pesticides may be combined in a spray mixture. However, problems due to chemical incompatibility may arise when different pesticides are mixed.

Pesticides are, to varying degrees, toxic chemicals, and their potentially harmful effects on humans, other animals, and non-target organisms in the environment must be recognized. Since the 1990s, increasing attention has been paid to the safety of vineyard workers and the environment with chemicals classified according to toxicity and workers taught safe handling practices. Recycling spray machines are increasingly used to minimize drift onto the environment. See also RESIDUES.

The following factors should be taken into consideration when developing strategies for pesticide use in vineyards: use patterns, rates, the potential development of pesticide resistance, and potential effects on non-target organisms. Use patterns may involve routine application schedules or more flexible strategies that rely on pest warning services and/or the monitoring of pest activity, as in INTEGRATED PEST MANAGEMENT. Such flexible strategies are often adopted to minimize pesticide use.

The continuous use of some pesticides may result in a dramatic increase in the proportion of individuals in a pest population that are able to survive exposure to the pesticide. An example has been the development of resistance by the BOTRYTIS fungus to the fungicide Benomyl and also to the dicarboximide group of fungicides. A serious outcome of the development of pest resistance is the so-called 'treadmill effect': as resistance to a pesticide increases, the pesticide is used in increased dosages or, more frequently, until such time that pesticide treatment becomes ineffective or uneconomic. Even more serious is the development of resistance to a group of related (cross-resistance) or dissimilar (multiple-resistance) chemicals. Spray programmes that delay or prevent the development

of pest resistance are designed to avoid long-term exposure of the pest to a single pesticide or group of pesticides with similar mode of action.

See also FUNGICIDES and INSECTICIDES.

P.R.D. & M.E.

Emmett, R. W., et al., 'Grape diseases and vineyard protection', in B. G. Coombe and P. R. Dry (eds.), *Viticulture*, ii: *Practices* (Adelaide, 1992).

pests of vineyards. See VINE PESTS.

pétillant, French term for a lightly sparkling wine, somewhere between PERLANT and MOUSSEUX.

pétillant naturel, lightly sparkling wine that is relatively low in alcohol and usually contains some RESIDUAL SUGAR, made by the MÉTHODE ANCESTRALE. The style has been enthusiastically embraced by producers of NATURAL WINE who have coined the term PET-NAT for it. The first AOC created specifically for a style that has become increasingly FASHIONABLE in the 21st century was MONTLOUIS Pétillant Naturel but a wide range of very varied examples are now made all over the world of wine.

petiole, the stalk of a plant's leaf which supports the leaf blade or lamina. Petioles are stem tissue and branch from the main stem of the shoot having similar anatomical features. At both ends of the petiole are swellings that alter the position of the leaf blade according to such stimuli as water stress and low light. Samples of petioles taken at FLOWERING are used as a basis for assessing a vine's status in terms of VINE NUTRITION.

The characteristics of petioles vary with vine variety and growing conditions, being longer on vigorous vines. Between varieties, petiole length varies from 5 to 20 cm (2–8 in), petiole colour varies from green to red, and petioles may vary from smooth to hairy. These features help in the identification of varieties (see AMPELOGRAPHY).

B.G.C.

petit, 'small' in French and therefore often encountered in wine and grape names.

petit château. See PETITS CHÂTEAUX.

Petit Courbu, ancient, rescued white Basque grape variety capable of adding body, aroma, and quality to the wines of BÉARN, IROULÉGUY, JURANÇON, and PACHERENC DU VIC-BILH as well as those of Côtes de ST-MONT. Distinct from COURBU.

Petite Arvine. See ARVINE.

Petite Sirah, name common in both North and South America, and first mentioned in California wine literature in the early 1880s, for a related group of black grape varieties. DNA PROFILING techniques suggested in the late

1990s that the name had been applied in California vineyards to no fewer than four different vines: mainly DURIF, but also true SYRAH of the Rhône, PELOURSIN (an obscure French vine which turned out to be Durif's parent), and even PINOT NOIR.

Petite Sirah is relatively important in a wide range of warm wine regions, especially in both California and South America. In California, acreage declined until the mid 1990s but then began to climb again, reaching 4,400 acres/ 1,781 ha by 2003 and then almost doubling to more than 8,500 acres by 2012, mostly in the Italian-American enclaves of Sonoma, Paso Robles, Amador, Mendocino, and Napa. Accurate acreage assessment is difficult because so many of the old Italian vineyards were planted with a mixture of different varieties.

Although Petite Sirah has been valued as a relatively full-bodied, well-coloured blending partner for blowsier Zinfandels, it has been somewhat eclipsed by the fashionable true French Syrah. It has nevertheless carved out a place for itself in California, for it makes dark, well-balanced, sturdy red wine of agreeable if not highly distinctive flavour. As such, it has been essential as a backbone for some everyday red blends: useful when rain-weakened Cabernet Sauvignon needed shoring up, or Pinot Noir went too pale and soft in a sunny vintage. Sonoma and Mendocino counties seem to grow Petite Sirah best, especially the dry-farmed, elderly HILLSIDE VINEYARDS within the Russian river drainage from Redwood valley down through Healdsburg and out towards Guerneville. California producers started a new promotional push for the grape in 2004 called P.S. I Love You. L. A. Cetto champion it in Mexico.

Petit Manseng, top-quality white grape variety originally from SOUTH WEST FRANCE which is the superior form of MANSENG. Petit Manseng, which is much more suitable for sweet wines than its probable progeny GROS MANSENG, has particularly small, thick-skinned berries which yield very little juice (sometimes less than 15 hl/ha, although up to 40 hl/ha (2.3 tons/acre) is allowed for both JURANÇON and PACHERENC) but can withstand lingering on the vine until well into autumn, or even December, so that the sugar is concentrated by the shrivelling process known as PASSERILLAGE. The variety is however sensitive to both sorts of MILDEW. By 2011 France' total plantings had grown to 1,182 ha/2,919 acres, although those of Gros Manseng were more than 3,000 ha.

The variety, which makes firm, distinctively tangy, often slightly green-hued wines of all SWEETNESS LEVELS, has already been planted to a limited extent in the LANGUEDOC, Central Italy, Virginia, California, Australia, and New Zealand.

Petit Meslier, ancient and almost extinct white variety cultivated in Champagne. It used to produce fruity wines, but it has fallen out of favour because of its naturally low yields. DNA PROFILING at DAVIS showed in 2000 that Petit Meslier is a progeny of GOUAIS BLANC and SAVAGNIN. A tiny amount persists in Australia.

Petit Rouge, fine, ancient, dominant, indigenous red grape variety in the Valle d'AOSTA. making fruity, spicy wines. Plantings totalled 84 ha/207 acres in 2010.

petits châteaux, the French term meaning literally 'small castles' has a very specific meaning in the BORDEAUX wine region. These thousands of properties are modest in both their extent and in their reputation and price. A CLASSED GROWTH or equivalent is emphatically not a petit château, no matter how few hectares it encompasses, and nor is a CRU BOURGEOIS. The greatest concentration of petits châteaux, invariably family-owned and run, is in the BORDEAUX AOC and CÔTES DE BORDEAUX APPELLATIONS, although they are found throughout the region. Some of Bordeaux's best wine value is to be found at the most conscientious petits châteaux.

See also CHÂTEAU.

Petit Verdot is one of Bordeaux's classic black grape varieties, no longer planted in any great quantity but enjoying a small revival in some quality-conscious vineyards. The vine ripens even later than Cabernet Sauvignon and is equally resistant to rot. It shares Cabernet Sauvignon's thick skins and is also capable of yielding concentrated, tannic wines rich in colour. When it ripens fully, which in most Bordeaux properties happens only in riper vintages, its rich, age-worthy, sometimes rather spicy wines can make a valuable contribution to some of the best wines of the Médoc, but in a cool year it can add a distinctly raw, underripe note to a blend. Its inconveniently late ripening encouraged many producers to abandon it in the 1960s and 1970s so that total French plantings were just over 300 ha/740 acres in 1988, but by 2011 had increased to more than 1,000 ha, 673 ha of these in the Gironde.

Its qualities are increasingly recognized elsewhere. It is well suited to warm, dry parts of Spain such as Castilla-La Mancha where most of the 2012 total of 1,849 ha/4,567 acres are planted. The pioneer was Marqués de Griñon near Toleda. Italy's total plantings also increased dramatically in the first decade of the 21st century, to more than 650 ha by 2010, while even Portugal, not usually a great fan of INTERNATIONAL VARIETIES, grew 276 ha, mainly for blends in the Alentejo, by 2012. Outside Europe, it has performed exceptionally well in VARIETAL form in the irrigated inland regions of AUSTRALIA where by the mid 2000s plantings totalled more than 1,600 ha planted—although this had fallen to 1,200 ha by 2012 because of general viticultural difficulties there. California, where the state's total plantings were more than 2,000 acres/800 ha by 2012, mainly in Napa and Sonoma, it has so far been used mainly as an ingredient in MERITAGE blends. Washington state has much less and also tends to use it in BORDEAUX BLENDS, while a number of VIRGINIA producers make a speciality of varietal versions. It is also planted in Long Island and British Columbia, but it does need a warm summer. It is therefore well suited to both Argentina and Chile where several hundred hectares are grown and varietal versions of 'Verdot' (which may include the inferior Gros Verdot) abound, and to South Africa where total plantings reached 2,000 ha by 2012, concentrated in the prime regions of Paarl and Stellenbosch. Petit Verdot is welcomed as a seasoning for a Bordeaux blend.

pet-nat, name coined by the NATURAL WINE movement for an amorphous group of very varied lightly sparkling wines, usually with some RESIDUAL SUGAR and made by the MÉTHOD ANCESTRALE. See also PÉTILLANT NATUREL.

Petri disease, a decline affecting young vines and named after Italian plant pathologist Lionello Petri (1875–1946), who in 1912 first reported brown wood streaking and dark gummy sap (see BLACK GOO) in declining American rootstock mother vines. However, it was not until the mid 1990s that the fungi *Phaeomoniella (Pa.) chlamydospora* and *Phaeoacremonium* spp. were identified as the primary causal agents. Affected vines (generally younger than six years old) appear stunted and weak and show greatly reduced tolerance of stress. Internal symptoms are primarily found in the rootstock and are characterized by dark brown and/or black streaking of the wood. It has been well documented that infections can originate during PROPAGATION but the progress and spread of the disease have been shown to depend on the health of the vine. Clean propagation planting material and careful planting help to minimize disease levels. See also TRUNK DISEASES.

L.T.M. & J.R.U.-T.

Gubler, W. D., et al., 'Esca (Black Measles) and Petri disease', in L. J. Bettiga (ed.), *Grape Pest Management* (3rd edn, Oakland, Calif., 2013), 120–5.

Mostert, L., et al., 'A review of *Phaeoacremonium* species involved in Petri disease', *Phytopathologia Mediterranea*, 45 (2006), S12–29.

Petrus, the most famous wine of POMEROL and today the most expensive in BORDEAUX.

In the heart of the small Pomerol plateau, Petrus was partly bought in 1925, by Mme Loubat, wife of the owner of the Hotel Loubat in Libourne. By 1949, it consisted of 6.5 ha planted with 70% MERLOT vines and 30%

CABERNET FRANC. In 1969, 5 ha were purchased from the adjoining Ch Gazin. Although it won a gold medal at the 1878 Paris International Exhibition, and the London-based WINE SOCIETY listed the 1893, Petrus received little international attention until the remarkable, tiny crop of 1945, and the much more widely distributed 1947. Its exceptional concentration of colour, bouquet, and richness of flavour derives from a pocket of clay in the middle of the vineyard and the subsoil which affords exceptionally good DRAINAGE. Average production is 30,000 bottles.

However, its fame is largely due to M. Jean-Pierre MOUEIX of the Libourne merchants, who started his business before the Second World War. He took over the sole distribution of Petrus in 1945, and, after Mme Loubat died in 1961, he purchased from her nephew in 1964 50% of the shareholding, while Mme Loubat's niece Mme Lily Lacoste inherited the other 50%, which was acquired by Jean-Pierre's elder son Jean-François Moueix in 2001. Jean-François inherited his father's half in 2003. Olivier, son of the distinguished OENOLOGIST Jean-Claude Berrouet, now manages the property and is in charge of winemaking. The limited size of the property means that all the grapes can be harvested, at optimum ripeness, in a day and a half if necessary.

FERMENTATION VESSELS are neither wood nor stainless steel, but mundane cement.

There is no official CLASSIFICATION of Pomerol, but Petrus is unofficially recognized as a PREMIER CRU, and is distributed only through Moueix, with exclusive agents in the UK and restricted ones in the US. It tends to fetch a much higher price than any other red bordeaux (although see Le PIN), and at AUCTION achieves even higher prices relative to the rest. In 2005, a rather grander building superseded Petrus's modest farmhouse.
                        E.P.-R. & J.R.

Petrus de Crescentiis (1230–1310), Italian author whose writings on wine were much read in the Middle Ages (see LITERATURE OF WINE). Petrus de Crescentiis finished his *Liber ruralium commodorum* ('Book on agriculture') c.1304. Only part of his book, Book 4, is concerned with wine. He knows and quotes from the classical writers on agriculture (mainly PLINY, COLUMELLA, and VARRO) but he is no mere slavish follower of his authorities, for he has a great deal to say about medieval WINE-MAKING practice and his advice is reliable.

The ancients loved old wine, but Petrus knew that medieval wine was a different matter; if wine was kept in a wooden BARREL instead of an impermeable earthenware AMPHORA, it would not last long. Most medieval wine was drunk within a year of the vintage, but sweet or highly alcoholic wines, as some Mediterranean wines were, kept longer. Petrus divides wines into three categories: new (under a year); old (four years); and between new and old. New wine, he says, has no digestive or diuretic properties but inflates the belly. Old wine is bitter and can be off; unless it is mixed with water, it goes to the head. Two-year-old wine is best. Petrus also points out that TOPPING UP casks of wine is essential in order to stop the wine turning into vinegar; alternatively, a layer of olive oil can be floated on the surface of the wine. He also explains how to achieve the RACKING of a wine from one cask into another.

Given the soundness of his advice and the clarity of his prose style, it is not surprising that Petrus's book should have been popular. It survives in many manuscripts and early printed editions. By the end of the 15th century, it had been translated into German, French, and Italian.
                        H.M.W.

Marescalchi, A., and Dalmasso, G. (eds.), *Storia della vite e del vino in Italia*, 3 vols. (Milan, 1933).

Savastano, L. G., *Contribute allo studio critico degli scrittori agrari italici* (Acireale, 1922).

Peynaud, Émile (1912–2004), Bordeaux oenologist whose work had a profound and worldwide impact on winemaking and wine appreciation in the second half of the 20th century. After the Second World War, Peynaud worked with Jean RIBÉREAU-GAYON before joining him at BORDEAUX University's Institut d'Oenologie, while employed by the house of Calvet. It was here, in the late 1940s, that he began to advise numerous BORDEAUX châteaux on their winemaking. Because this CONSULTANCY work was the activity for which he later became best known, it is perhaps easy to forget his achievements as a taster, scientist, and teacher.

Peynaud wanted to understand the detail of the winemaking process, to eliminate its hitherto haphazard nature, and to produce consistently clean-tasting and healthy wines. Many of the practices that now seem unexceptional in winemaking were by no means axiomatic in the 1950s, and they are rooted in changes resulting from his wide-ranging scientific research. Among these were the complete control of MALOLACTIC CONVERSION, the understanding that quality starts in the vineyard with good-quality grapes, that red grapes should be fully ripe when picked, that dark grapes' skins (containing the PHENOLICS so crucial to red wine aromas and textures) should be treated more gently with softer CRUSHING, better-controlled fermentation temperatures, shorter MACERATION, and more moderate PRESSING of the skins for the PRESS WINE. Each technique aimed at improving the flavour and texture of the resulting finished wine.

Taste became the arbiter in winemaking decisions, and it underlay his other cardinal principle: selection. Select only healthy grapes when picking, vinify the produce of plots of vines of markedly different age or quality separately, choose only the best vats to be incorporated in the principal wine, and so on. Peynaud himself describes his method as 'monitoring the whole process of winemaking from grape to bottle' and this is the subject of his first book, *Connaissance et travail du vin*.

Peynaud considered the ability to taste accurately as essential to good winemaking as a thorough grasp of OENOLOGY. He says in his second book, *Le Goût du vin*, 'I am not sure whether I have contributed most by making tasting an introduction to oenology or oenology an introduction to tasting.' *Le Goût du vin* is as comprehensive and lucid on tasting wine as his first book was on making wine. It aimed to educate the palates not only of winemakers but of wine drinkers too. He was acutely aware of their symbiotic relationship.

As with his pupil Michel ROLLAND, critics used to complain that his winemaking methods so marked the wines that they were losing their individuality, but mature bottles tended to show genuine distinction and individuality.

Peynaud would have left his mark on the wine world had his gifts been limited to scientist, technician, and possessor of a refined palate; that his influence has been so widespread is due to his additional great gift as a teacher and communicator.
                        M.W.E.S.

Parnell, C., 'Émile Peynaud, Man of the Year', *Decanter* (Mar 1990), 36–40.

Peynaud, É., *Connaissance et travail du vin* (Paris, 1981).

Peynaud, É., *The Taste of Wine* (2nd edn, New York, 1996).

Pézenas, small, named CRU in the LANGUEDOC AOC producing red wines mainly from Syrah, Mourvèdre, and Grenache on lower land than some of the other crus between CABRIÈRES and the eponymous historic town.

Pfalz, until 1992 known as Rheinpfalz, is an important wine region in southern GERMANY in terms of both quantity and quality. The 23,567 ha/58,210 acres of vineyard follow the eastern edge of the Haardt range (a northern extension of Alsace's Vosges) for about 80 km/50 miles (see map under GERMANY) along the so-called Deutsche Weinstrasse, or German Wine Route, officially established in 1935 to link 40 villages. Viewed from a satellite, these vineyards would seem to reach in finger-like strips 8 km or so into the plain, which stretches a further 12 km to the Rhine. In some of the villages of the district in the southern half, the Südliche Weinstrasse, vines occupy nearly all the available land and viticulture has expanded greatly since the 1960s; only those parts of valleys at risk from cold air remain unplanted. Significant differences in character, especially with Riesling, emerge from varying elevations and striking

diversity of soils ranging from CALCAREOUS through SANDSTONE to the BASALT that characterizes the top vineyards of Forst, with many sedimentary, metamorphic, and volcanic variations in between. The relatively sunny, dry Pfalz, long a mecca for German TOURISTS and, like Rheinhessen, long associated with the cheap and cheerful, has since the 1980s acquired a national and international reputation as an innovative and exciting wine-growing region buoyed by demand for the red and dry white wines in which it excels and by the proximity of prosperous metropolitan Mannheim, Ludwigshafen, and Karlsruhe. Of the roughly 10,000 vinegrowers in the region, over half deliver their grapes to producers' associations, merchants' cellars, or one of 18 CO-OPERATIVES, of which a number boast not only high standards but also significant shares of top vineyards.

The vineyards to the north of Neustadt, collectively known as the Mittelhaardt, are the best known in the Pfalz, in large part thanks to wine estates with such historic reputations as Bassermann-Jordan, Bürklin-Wolf, von Buhl, and Dr Deinhard (von Winning). The top sites of the Mittelhaardt villages largely nestle between the western edge of the villages and the lower slopes of the Haardt, on sandstone and volcanic soils. The reputations of Riesling-dominated villages (from south to north, noting best vineyards) Ruppertsberg (Nussbien, Gaisböhl, Hoheburg, Reiterpfad), Deidesheim (Leinhöhle, Hohenmorgen, Kieselberg, Mäushöhle, Grainhübel, Kalkofen), Forst (Ungeheuer, Pechstein, Jesuitengarten, Kirchenstück), Wachenheim (Altenburg, Gerümpel, Goldbächel, Rechbächel), Bad Dürkheim (Michelsberg, Spielberg), Ungstein (Herrenberg, Weilberg), and Kallstadt (Saumagen) is secure. The resurgence of traditionally renowned growers, along with the maturation of vines in sites that were largely replanted in the FLURBEREINIGUNG (vineyard restructuring) of the 1980s, has resulted in increasingly impressive quality in recent years. Not to be underestimated is the continuing influence of Müller-Catoir excellarmaster Hans-Günter Schwarz, whose principles of 'minimalism in the cellar, activism in the vines' have been imparted to two generations of vineyard managers and winemakers who today fill dozens of the most important positions throughout the Pfalz.

Villages in the immediate vicinity of Neustadt and its suburbs, while a little less well-known for most of the 20th century, have more than demonstrated their excellence in recent years in the hands of several of the Pfalz's most meticulous growers. Outstanding villages and vineyards include Haardt (Bürgergarten, Herzog, and Mandelring), Mussbach (Eselshaut), Gimmeldingen (Biengarten, Mandelgarten) and Königsbacher (Idig, Ölberg). The low rolling calcareous and sandy hills east of the Weinstrasse—notably at Laumersheim

(Kirschgarten, Mandelberg), Grosskarlbach (Burgweg), and Freinsheim—have also demonstrated their ability to generate memorable wines, and here the energy of young vintners and small family wineries has been a driving force for quality.

South of Neustadt, the so-called Südliche Weinstrasse long endured a reputation for high yields of indifferent grape varieties. Nowadays though, thanks above all to the ambitions of local vintners and a boom in dry wines from red, Grauburgunder (see PINOT GRIS) and Weissburgunder (see PINOT BLANC) grapes, this area has become increasingly fashionable inside Germany. Its less common but often exceptional Rieslings—from such villages as Birkweiler (Kastanienbusch, Mandelberg), Burrweiler (Schäwer), Gleisweiler (Hölle), and Siebeldingen (Im Sonnenschein) have also stepped onto the international stage.

High yields, mechanical harvesting, and a reliance on such crosses as Müller-Thurgau, Kerner, and Morio-Muskat were long associated with the Pfalz. But Riesling, always dominant in the prestigious towns of the Mittelhaardt, has staged a comeback throughout the region and now accounts for one-quarter of vine surface. Red wine vines gained ground rapidly since the 1990s and now account for just over one-third of Pfalz production, while Kerner and the traditional Müller-Thurgau are the only white wine CROSSES that exceed 3% of the total vineyard. Pinot Noir, Weissburgunder, and Grauburgunder represented collectively 10% of Pfalz plantings by 2011. Scheurebe may be statistically relatively insignificant, but there are signs of a revival, as with Rieslaner. Traminer, traditionally associated with the Pfalz, has failed in recent decades to mirror its success in neighbouring Alsace, or even to maintain more than a residual toehold, but the best examples, dry and sweet, can still be excellent. Of all German regions Pfalz has the greatest area planted with such INTERNATIONAL VARIETIES as, in decreasing order of importance, Chardonnay, Sauvignon Blanc, Merlot, various Cabernets, and even Syrah.

Across the region, a majority of all wines are now dry (TROCKEN), at top estates overwhelmingly so, as befits both climate and demand. This explains why this region has been a leader in advocating the establishment of GROSSES GEWÄCHS full-bodied, dry wines (principally Riesling) from the best sites. The majority of non-dry Pfalz wine is nowadays destined for export. Pfalz red wines including Spätburgunder (Pinot Noir) today typically exceed 13% alcohol, and BARREL MATURATION is common, although there is still a local market for the traditional, light red as well as pink WEISSHERBST from PORTUGIESER (no more than 8% of total vineyard area now). DORNFELDER plantings increased five-fold between 1990 and 2010 so that

it is now Pfalz's second most-planted variety although stunning examples are few and far between. An increasing amount of Pfalz wine is made sparkling (see SEKT) according to demanding technical specifications, not least by the Sektkellerei Schloss Wachenheim that specializes in TRADITIONAL METHOD renderings of their own and other growers' generally high quality base wines, especially from Riesling, Weissburgunder, and Spätburgunder.   D.S.

Pigott, S., et al., *Wein Spricht Deutsch: Weine, Winzer, Weinlandschaften* (Frankfurt, 2007).

Reinhardt, S., *The Finest Wines of Germany* (London, 2012).

PGI, abbreviation for **Protected Geographical Indication**, a wine category created in 2008 as part of the EU wine reform. It encompasses what used to be known as TABLE WINES with a GEOGRAPHICAL INDICATION such as France's VIN DE PAYS, Italy's IGT, Spain's VINO DE LA TIERRA, and Germany's LANDWEIN. In 2012, PGI wines accounted for roughly 20% of total EU wine production. The equivalent abbreviation in many other countries, including France, Spain, Italy, and Portugal, is IGP, although the speed with which the reformed terminology has been adopted varies by country.

The qualifying criteria for a PGI are lower than those for the PDO, or Protected Designation of Origin category. A PGI need only 'possess a specific quality, reputation or other characteristics attributable to [its] geographical origin', in line with the international definition of a geographical indication. A minimum of 85% of the grapes must come from the delimited area and these may be either VITIS VINIFERA or a CROSS between *Vitis vinifera* and other VITIS species. PGIs enjoy special privileges in the EU wine system, including protection against misuse as well as the right to use TRADITIONAL TERMS and the special EU PGI symbol on the label.

Non-EU countries are, in theory, able to register their own geographical indications as PGIs in Europe, although by 2014 no third country PGIs had been registered—largely because many countries already have protection for their GIs within the EU by virtue of specific bilateral wine agreements.   J.B.

pH, a scale of measurement of the concentration of the effective, active ACIDITY in a solution and an important statistic, of relevance to how vines grow, how grapes ripen, and how wine tastes, looks, and lasts. (The technical definition is that pH is the negative logarithm of the all-important hydrogen ion activity or concentration.) Low values of pH indicate high concentrations of acidity and the tart or sour taste that occurs in lemon juice, for example. Values near 7 are effectively neutral; drinking waters have pH values near 7. Values between 7 and 14 are found in basic or alkaline solutions such as caustic or washing soda. Grape must and wine are acidic, with pHs generally between 3 and 4. The scale is logarithmic so a solution with a pH value of 3 has ten times as much hydrogen ion activity as one whose pH value is 4.

Soils

Soil pH measures the acidity or alkalinity of a soil. Acid soils have a pH less than 7 and alkaline soils a pH greater than 7. Soils formed on acidic parent materials (see SOIL), such as GRANITIC rocks or highly weathered SANDSTONES, generally have acid pH values, whereas those formed on basic parent materials, such as LIMESTONE, BASALT, or dolerite, generally have alkaline pH values. The optimum pH range for grapevines is from 5.5 to 8, although the grapevine is one of the domesticated plants most tolerant of soil pH outside this range. Soil pH is of some relevance to the resultant wine, although the effect is not direct. See also SOIL ACIDITY and SOIL ALKALINITY.   R.E.W.

White, R. E., *Understanding Vineyard Soils* (2nd edn, Oxford, 2015).

Grapes

The pH of grapes as well as wines can vary enormously since TEMPERATURE, RAINFALL, SOIL TYPE, viticultural practices, and VINE VARIETIES can all influence the different natural organic acids and minerals of mature grapes. In general, cool regions produce wines with low pH and hot regions produce wines with high pH. Part of the reason why white wines generally have a lower pH than red wines is that red wines have higher levels of POTASSIUM, which is extracted from the grape skin, where this ion is concentrated, during fermentation. See also GRAPE and ACIDITY.

The pH of grape juice is now well established as a factor affecting wine quality. In particular, high pH values are associated with high concentrations of potassium and low acidity, and red wine quality in particular is diminished (see below). Among factors known to affect the potassium concentration of grapes are potassium content of soils and SHADE within the canopy.

Wines

The pH range of most wines is between 2.9 and 4.2 (which incidentally, since the pH of the normal stomach is about 2, means that wines are 10 to 100 times less concentrated in the acid hydrogen ion than is the stomach interior). Wines with low pHs taste very tart while those with high pHs taste flat, or 'flabby'. White wines with a pH of 3–3.2 and reds with a pH of 3.4–3.7 not only tend to taste refreshingly rather than piercingly acid, they are also more resistant to harmful BACTERIA, age better, and have a clearer, brighter COLOUR (see below). Wines

with pH values higher than this tend to taste flat, look dull, and are more susceptible to bacterial attack. In the last twenty years, average pH levels have risen considerably as a result of longer HANG TIME and a FASHION for riper wines. While it is possible to manipulate pH values, with grapes and wines it is difficult because of the wine's high 'buffer capacity', which roughly correlates with TOTAL ACIDITY. The pH can be increased by decreasing the concentration of hydrogen ions, however, and vice versa. (See ACIDIFICATION and DEACIDIFICATION for discussion of the legal and practical aspects of these operations.)

The winemaker is interested in both the pH and the total acidity (the fixed and volatile acids) of both the grape juice and the resultant wine for several reasons. What one tastes in wines as the tart or sour sensation is influenced both by the total amount of acids present and by the concentration of hydrogen ions in the solution. Different YEASTS and bacteria have varying tolerances for hydrogen ion concentration and for the nature and concentration of the acid.

Finally, the resistance of the wine to changes of effective acidity (hydrogen ion concentration) during processing and STABILIZATION depends mainly on the total acid concentration. Keeping wine pH values low is of further importance because the hydrogen ion concentration of the wine controls the effectiveness of SULFUR DIOXIDE. Sulfur dioxide gas, when dissolved in wine, reacts with the water in the wine to form sulfurous acid, the form of the compound that is best at inhibiting bacteria and wild yeasts and countering OXIDATION. Sulfurous acid breaks down partially into hydrogen ions and bisulfite ions, a form having little effect on micro-organisms such as bacteria and wild yeasts. High hydrogen ion concentrations (low pH values) in the wine tend to combine with the bisulfite ions and thus keep more of the sulfur dioxide in the effective, anti-microbial form.

pH is also important in winemaking because the PIGMENTED TANNINS that colour red wines exist (like the monomeric ANTHOCYANINS from which they are formed) in several forms of different colours. At low pH values, the high concentration of hydrogen ions forces the pigment molecule into a form with a positive charge and a bright red colour. As pH increases (and hydrogen ion concentration decreases), the pigment molecules tend more and more to change through dull purple to blue, and ultimately greyish forms. The net result in the several pigments of red wine is a passage from bright to purplish red and finally to a dull brownish red as pH increases.

A.D.W., B.G.C., & P.J.W.

phenolic ripeness. See PHYSIOLOGICAL RIPENESS.

phenolics, very large group of highly reactive chemical compounds of which **phenol** (C_6H_5OH) is the basic building block. These include many natural colour pigments such as the ANTHOCYANINS of fruit and dark-skinned grapes, most natural vegetable TANNINS such as occur in grapes, and many FLAVOUR COMPOUNDS.

The terms **polyphenolics** or **polyphenols** are often used as synonyms of phenolics but should be restricted to plant secondary metabolites featuring more than one phenolic ring and derived from specific metabolic pathways, as Quideau et al. explain.

In grapes

These compounds occur in great profusion in grapes. They are particularly rich in stems, seeds, and skins but also occur in juice and pulp. The concentration of phenolics in grape skins increases if the berries are exposed to sunlight, in particular to ULTRAVIOLET RADIATION, because the phenolic compounds act as a natural sunscreen. Phenolic compounds strongly absorb ultraviolet light, a fact used in their laboratory analysis. Manipulating fruit exposure in the vineyard is therefore a way to affect the phenolic content of berries and wine made from them. See CANOPY MANAGEMENT.

Many hundreds of compounds belong to the phenolic category, and they can initially be classified as either non-flavonoid or FLAVONOID. The former include compounds derived from cinnamic and benzoic acids (one of the most abundant in grape juice is caftaric acid, the tartrate ESTER of caffeic acid) and stilbenes such as RESVERATROL. Flavonoids encompass CATECHINS and their polymers, called PROANTHOCYANIDINS or condensed TANNINS, which are an essential part of the taste and flavour of grapes and other fruits, and pigments, including FLAVONOLS and anthocyanins. With a few exceptions, such as the phenolic amino acid tyrosine that is a constituent of proteins, phenolics belong to the general group known as secondary metabolites, meaning that they are not involved in the primary metabolism of the plant. They are highly water-soluble and are secreted into the BERRY vacuole, many as GLYCOSIDES, and some are FLAVOUR PRECURSORS or precursors of off-flavours.

B.G.C., R.E.S., & V.C.

In wines

Phenolic acids (especially cinnamic acids) are the major phenolics in grape pulp and juice, and thus in white wines made without skin contact. Anthocyanins are localized only in the skins, except in red-fleshed *teinturiers*, so that red winemaking requires a MACERATION phase to extract them into the juice. Flavonols, which are constituents of skins, stems, and leaves, as well as catechins and tannins, which are also present in seeds, are simultaneously extracted. Alcohol, produced by FERMENTATION, greatly speeds up this extraction process. Additional phenolics (including gallotannins and ellagitannins as well as flavour compounds such as VANILLIN) may also be present in wine as a result of barrel ageing, the use of OAK CHIPS, or the addition of OENOLOGICAL TANNINS. Once extracted into the wine, the anthocyanins, catechins, and tannins are gradually converted to various types of derivatives, including PIGMENTED TANNINS. These reactions are responsible for the colour and taste changes observed during wine AGEING.

Catechins and proanthocyanidin oligomers taste bitter, while larger tannins are responsible for the mouth-puckering astringency in young wines. As the wine ages, tannins and their derivatives form larger and larger particles through aggregation and complexation with other molecules such as proteins and polysaccharides. This may result in the development of haze and sediments and other technological problems (e.g. clogging of filtration membranes, adsorption on tank surfaces).

A significant number of flavour precursors as well as FLAVOUR COMPOUNDS also have the phenol structure. Examples of these are VANILLIN, the key aroma compound of the vanilla bean, and raspberry ketone, the impact compound of raspberries. An ESTER, methyl salicylate, familiar as oil of wintergreen, is also a phenolic compound. These and many others are either grape constituents or are produced as trace components during alcoholic fermentation and by glycoside HYDROLYSIS during the subsequent processing and ageing phases. See also OAK FLAVOUR for details of the part played by the phenolics in new OAK.

A.D.W., P.J.W., & V.C.

As a tasting term
Phenolic is also sometimes used, imprecisely, as a pejorative tasting term, to describe (usually white) wines which display an excess of phenolics by tasting astringent or bitter.

As health benefit
It is in its high phenolics content that red wine is distinguished from white, and it is thought that it may well be the ANTIOXIDATIVE properties of phenolics which reduce the incidence of heart disease among those who consume moderate amounts of red wine. See HEALTH.

Frankel, E. N., et al., 'Inhibition of oxidation of human low-density lipoprotein by phenolic substances in red wine', *Lancet*, 341 (1993), 454–7.
Quideau, S., et al., 'Plant polyphenols: chemical properties, biological activities, and synthesis', *Angewandte Chemie International Edition*, 50/3 (2011), 586–621. doi: 10.1002/anie.201000044.
Somers, T. C., and Verette, E., 'Phenolic composition of natural wine types', in H. F. Linskens and J. F. Jackson (eds.), *Wine Analysis: Modern Methods of Plant Analysis*, NS 6 (Berlin, 1988).

phenology, the study of the sequence of plant development (see diagram). As applied to vines, it records the timing of specific stages such as BUDBREAK, FLOWERING, VERAISON, and LEAF FALL. Such studies indicate the suitability of VINE VARIETIES to certain climatic zones. See VINE GROWTH CYCLE.

pheromones are in a viticultural context synthetic products used in the biological control of vineyard INSECT PESTS. They work by causing sexual confusion (see INTEGRATED PEST MANAGEMENT).

philosophy and wine. Wine first played a part in the history of Western philosophy at the SYMPOSIUM of the early Greek philosophers where it enlivened and encouraged discussion. Later, during the Enlightenment, David Hume recommended drinking wine with friends as a cure for philosophical melancholy, and Immanuel Kant thought wine softened the harsher sides of men's characters and made their company more convivial. In recent times, philosophers have turned their philosophical attention to wine as an object of perception, assessment, and appreciation. Their enquiries have focused on the relationship between wine and our experience of it, including its intoxicating effect on us (see DRUNKENNESS), and the meaning and value it has for us in our lives (see Scruton 2009).

The issue of objectivity
To know the chemical WINE COMPOSITION and its method of VINIFICATION is not yet to know how it tastes. To know this, one must experience the wine itself by TASTING it. But in tasting a wine

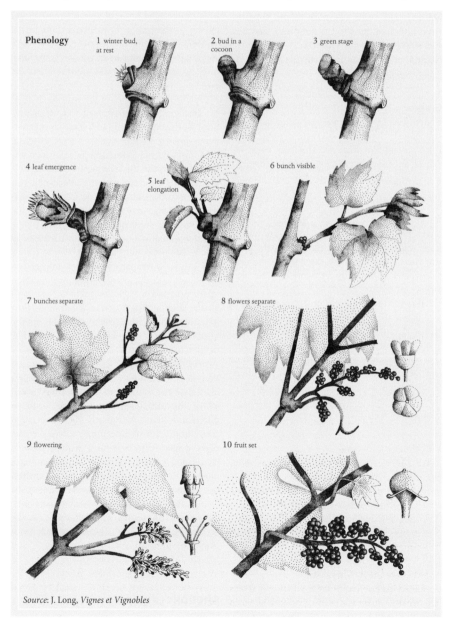

Phenology
1 winter bud, at rest
2 bud in a cocoon
3 green stage
4 leaf emergence
5 leaf elongation
6 bunch visible
7 bunches separate
8 flowers separate
9 flowering
10 fruit set

Source: J. Long, *Vignes et Vignobles*

are we discovering properties the wine has or just noting our SUBJECTIVE responses to it? And is every response as good any other? Here we have a key philosophical question: how subjective are tastes and tasting? On one view, the only objective knowledge we can have of wine is that provided by scientific analysis: the chemist describes the way the wine is, the wine critic describes the way it tastes. The former is objective, the latter is merely subjective. But are the two unconnected? Winemakers rely on scientific analysis to achieve the flavours they are aiming for, and experienced wine tasters rely on tasting to identify and describe compounds of flavours or aromas that arise from fermentation. For this to be so, wine tasters must draw objective conclusions about a wine from their subjective responses to it, and wine makers must create conditions they hope will produce a certain taste for us. A revised view would be that while tasting is a subjective experience of individual tasters, *what* we taste, the TANNINS, or ACIDITY in a wine, are objective properties or characteristics of the wine itself.

Nevertheless, many of the qualities we value in wine such as finesse, BALANCE, COMPLEXITY, HARMONY, and LENGTH can only be confirmed by tasting. And some philosophers would argue that these more complex properties depend on us and should be conceived as some kind of relation between the wines and our responses to them. The problem for this view is whether to treat all such responses as equally good. If we differ in opinion about whether a wine is round or balanced, does this mean there is no fact of the matter about who is right? Is it balanced for me but not for you? On such a subjectivist view, matters of taste are neither right or wrong: the conclusion is that *de gustibus non est disputandum*.

Tastes and tasting

Philosophers who reject this conclusion argue that taste properties, such as a wine's length or balance, *are* objective features of a wine and that under the right conditions, and with the right experience and training as tasters, they are revealed to us in experience. Tasting a wine involves the taster's subjectivity but verdicts based on those subjective experiences are not mere matters of opinion: so not subjective in that sense. Certain experiences will be more accurate than others, some people will be better tasters then others, and judgements of a wine can be right or wrong. On this objectivist view, *tastes* are in the wine, not in us, and by improving the skills of *tasting* we can come to know them more accurately (see Smith 2007).

What is meant by 'fine wine'?

A related issue concerns the evaluation of wines and whether there is a clear separation between describing a wine and assessing its QUALITY. Part of this issue is how we should characterize FINE WINE. From the absence of a definition we should not infer there is no category of fine wine any more than our inability to define 'chair' satisfactorily should lead us to conclude that there are no chairs. Criteria for being a fine wine can be given, as when we can say that a fine wine is one whose complex, individual character rewards the interest and attention paid to it, and affords the degree of discrimination we exercise in assessing its qualities and characteristics. But is a fine wine a wine that must be appreciated? Or can experienced wine tasters assess the qualities of a wine without enjoying it? The alternative view is that recognizing a wine's merits depends on the enjoyment, pleasure, or preferences of the individual taster. The dispute here concerns the ultimate nature of wine tasting and wine appreciation. Do we directly perceive the quality of a wine, or do we assess its quality on the basis of what we first perceive? Tasting seems to involve both perception and judgement. But does the perceptual experience of tasting—which relies on the sensations of touch, taste, and smell—already involve a judgement of a wine's quality? Is such judgement a matter of interpretation, and if so, does assessment require wine knowledge in order to arrive at a correct verdict?

Some philosophers would claim that one cannot assess a wine's quality on the basis of perceptual experience alone and that evaluation goes beyond what one finds in a description of its objective characteristics. According to these thinkers, something else is required to arrive at an assessment of a wine's merits. This may be the pleasure the taster derives from the wine, the valuing of certain characteristics, or the individual preferences of the taster. Is there room on such views for non-subjective judgements of wine quality?

To say that assessments of quality rest on interpretation is to say that one cannot recognize a wine's quality on the basis of perceptual experience alone. And yet according to some philosophers, a novice taster can recognize the merits of wine by taste without the expert knowledge of the wine critic. Moreover, expert knowledge may enable one to recognize a wine as an excellent example of its type but if that style of wine offers one no pleasure, could one, as a wine critic, still judge it to be or admire it as a great wine? Many philosophers would think not, but then on what basis does one judge something to be a great wine, and what could separate the experienced and the novice taster in evaluating wines? Is each taster's opinion equally good?

A standard of taste?

Here we address a question raised by Hume about whether there can be a standard of taste. Hume's solution was to rely on the excellence of JUDGES or critics who: showed delicacy of judgement; were free from prejudice; could draw on a wide range of experience for comparisons; paid due attention; and were unclouded by mood. These may be prerequisites for accurate tasting but on what basis does such an excellent critic appreciate a truly great wine? An answer to this question can be found in Kant's account of aesthetic judgement (which he did not himself extend to wine). To claim that a wine is great is not just to judge for oneself alone, but to judge for all. The judgement is made on the basis of pleasure but this is not a claim about what one finds personally pleasant or agreeable. It is a judgement about the pleasure the wine affords anyone suitably equipped to taste it. There is no such thing as a wine that is great *for me*. In claiming to recognize a great wine, I am claiming something about *the wine itself*, about how it will (and should) strike others. It is thus a universal claim about the delight all can take in it, and others would be mistaken were they not to judge it so. Kant's solution does not solve all problems of the objectivity of taste, however. Disagreements about a wine's qualities are still disagreements amongst ourselves, and not disagreements settled solely by the properties of the wine itself.

A further problem is created when two (or more) experienced, unprejudiced wine critics differ in their opinions regarding the excellence of a wine. Perhaps they agree in their descriptions of the wine's objective characteristics but diverge in evaluating its merits. If they merely point to divergent qualities, one can argue for pluralism about the qualities and flavours of a wine (see Todd 2010). However, if they genuinely conflict in judgement, but neither has overlooked any aspect of the wine's identifiable properties, and both agree in the terms they use to describe and classify wines, we may be tempted to conclude neither is right and neither is wrong. However, subjectivism about standards of taste can be resisted in this case by embracing relativism about matters of taste. According to relativist doctrine, both critics are right: both make true judgements about the wine in question. It is simply that the truth of each judgement is *relative* to a standard of assessment, or set of preferences, not shared by the other. Cultural differences could account for these divergences and there would still be a right answer according to one set of standards, or the other. In effect, this is to claim there can be more than one standard of taste, and each critic is right relative to a standard of assessment (see Burnham and Skilleas, 2012).

Finally, philosophers have stressed the meaning and value wine has in our lives as a celebration of our relationship with our natural surroundings. The place, culture, and history of a people that falls under the concept of TERROIR are celebrated and acknowledged in

p

drinking a wine that reflects that terroir and the efforts of people to uphold and maintain the traditions with which they transformed soil and vine into grape, and grape into wine. The final transformation, according to philosopher Roger Scruton (Smith, 2007), occurs when we take wine into ourselves and through its intoxicating effects it transforms us and opens us up to one another.   B.C.S.

Burnham, D., and Skilleas, O., *The Aesthetics of Wine* (Chichester, 2012).

Hume, D., 'Of the standard of taste', *Essays Moral, Political and Literary* (Oxford, 1965), 231–55.

Kant, I., *The Critique of Judgement*, Sections 1–7 (Oxford, 1952).

Scruton, R., *I drink therefore I am* (London, 2009).

Smith, B. C. (ed.), *A Question of Taste: Philosophy and Wine* (Oxford, 2007).

Todd, C., *The Philosophy of Wine: A Case of Truth, Beauty and Intoxication* (Durham, England, 2010).

phloem, the principal food-conducting tissue of the vine and other vascular plants. Phloem is composed of a mix of CELL types which lie alongside the XYLEM, the water-conducting tissue, and the combination makes up a system of veins or vascular bundles. Despite their proximity, phloem and xylem are entirely different: phloem has thin-walled tubes containing a strongly sugared sap under positive pressure which moves along from areas of strong to weak concentrations, while xylem consists of large, strong-walled tubes through which a dilute mineral solution moves under negative pressure (tension) by forces generated by TRANSPIRATION. During the thickening of woody parts, the CAMBIUM produces cells on the outside that become the new season's phloem; in later years these cells are added to the bark of the vine. Phloem of grapevine wood has the characteristic, unusual among deciduous trees, of reactivation after the next BUDBREAK and can remain functional for three to four years.

The vascular system permeates throughout the plant, but bundles of veins are particularly dense in the LEAF blade, as can be seen by holding it up to the light. This high density facilitates the loading of newly photosynthesized SUCROSE into the phloem tubes for its movement out of the leaf (see TRANSLOCATION).
                                                      B.G.C.

Phoenicia, ancient mercantile state of the Iron Age (*c.*1200–539 BC) and the Persian period until the capture of Tyre by Alexander the Great. The Phoenicians were the successors of the CANAANITES ethnically and culturally, and so inherited their aptitude for viniculture. Their territory at its widest extent included modern LEBANON and coastal southern Syria and northern Israel. Arwad, Byblos, Beirut, Sidon, and Tyre were among the famous city-states of Phoenicia. Vines and olives were grown along the coast and in fertile inland valleys, especially the Beqaá (Bekaa Valley). The Phoenicians were seafaring merchants and colonizers par excellence, spreading the Near Eastern 'wine culture' elsewhere in the Mediterranean. They applied a similar formula wherever they went: import wine and other luxury goods; entice the rulers with the wine culture by presenting them with speciality wine sets, and then wait until they were asked to help in establishing native industries, including viniculture, by transplanting the domesticated Eurasian grapevine. Their greatest colony, CARTHAGE in modern Tunisia, survived until destroyed by the Romans in 146 BC.

Evidently the Phoenician colonists found in North Africa a fertile region ideal for viticultural development. The Graeco-Roman historian Diodorus Siculus describes the Carthaginian countryside as being (in the 4th century BC) full of vines, olives, and cattle, especially in the Bagradas valley and in southern Tunisia. The Carthaginian author Mago left an extensive treatise on agriculture, including instructions on viticulture.

See also ORIGINS OF VINICULTURE and PALAEOETHNOBOTANY AND THE ARCHAEOLOGY OF WINE.   J.A.B. & P.E.M.

Harden, D., *The Phoenicians* (London, 1962).

McGovern, P. E., *Ancient Wine* (Princeton and Oxford, 2003).

McGovern, P. E., *Uncorking the Past: The Quest for Wine, Beer, and Other Alcoholic Beverages* (Berkeley, 2009).

Phoenix, a rot-prone DISEASE-RESISTANT VARIETY, a cross of BACCHUS and VILLARD Blanc which produces attractive, herbaceous, elderflower-scented wine in England with a minimum of SPRAYING. Despite its parentage, it produces remarkably VINIFERA-LIKE wine so has been registered as a *V. vinifera* variety. Consequently, it may be used in the production of UK QUALITY WINE. Very little is grown in Germany.

phomopsis, may refer to either **phomopsis cane and leaf spot** or **phomopsis dieback**. Both are caused by the fungus *Phomopsis viticola* but the symptoms are quite different.

Phomopsis cane and leaf spot, also known as *Diaporthe*, excoriose, and dead arm, occurs in most of the world's viticultural regions and is particularly severe in those characterized by a cool and wet spring followed by humid, temperate weather through the growing season. Under these conditions, the disease may cause crop losses of up to 30%. The fungus can infect all green parts of the grapevine, causing black lesions at the base of grape shoots, leaf petioles, and bunch stems; bleached patches on winter canes; the death of affected fruit buds; stunted shoots; small black spots with yellow halos on deformed leaves, and rot on infected berries.

Infected wood appears bleached during the dormant season and fruiting structures of the fungi (pycnidia) can be seen embedded in the bark. Although this disease poses the greatest threat in early spring, control measures to protect the fruit may continue into the summer in some regions. Because the fungus colonizes old wood, CANE PRUNING and hand harvesting reduce pressure from this disease. Wine grape varieties such as Cabernet Sauvignon, Chardonnay, Merlot, and Syrah are less susceptible than some TABLE GRAPES. However, GRENACHE is one of the most susceptible.

Phomopsis dieback is a TRUNK DISEASE that has received less attention than phomopsis cane and leaf spot. Field studies conducted in California in the mid 2000s found this fungus to be associated with other trunk diseases, especially BOTRYOSPHAERIA DIEBACK. *Phomopsis viticola* was isolated from perennial cankers in spurs and cordons from grapevines showing a lack of spring growth or reduced shoot growth. Later studies confirmed the presence and severity of *Phomopsis viticola* as a trunk disease pathogen in Arkansas, Missouri, and Texas.
                                          L.T.M., R.E.S., & J.R.U.-T.

Úrbez-Torres, J. R., et al., 'Phomopsis dieback: a grapevine trunk disease caused by *Phomopsis viticola* in California', *Plant Disease*, 97/12 (2013), 1571–9.

Vasquez, S. J., Leavitt, G. M., and Verdegaal, P. S., 'Phomopsis cane and leaf spot', in L. J. Bettiga (ed.), *Grape Pest Management* (3rd edn, Oakland, Calif., 2013), 126–30.

phosphorus, one of the most important MINERAL elements required for vine growth, yet the amounts required are sufficiently small that for most vineyards, the natural supply from the soil is enough. There is only about 0.6 kg of phosphorus in a tonne of grapes (1.3 lb per ton). Phosphorus in the vine is an essential component of compounds involved in PHOTOSYNTHESIS and sugar–starch transformations as well as the transfer of energy. Phosphorus deficiency in vines is uncommon, and found mostly on soils with a large content of iron and aluminium oxides, as in parts of the Yarra and King valleys in VICTORIA, Australia, and the WILLAMETTE VALLEY, Oregon, USA. Its symptoms are a gradual loss of VIGOUR and, sometimes, some red spots on the leaves.   R.E.S. & R.E.W.

photosynthesis, a biochemical reaction which combines water and atmospheric carbon dioxide using the energy of the sun to form SUGARS in plants, including vines. Important in this process are the green chlorophyll pigments in leaves which capture the sun's energy. Photosynthesis is the essential first step in the winemaking process, as the sugars formed in photosynthesis, along with other chemical products derived from sugar, are transported to grape berries (see SUGAR IN GRAPES), and eventually fermented into ETHANOL to produce wine. (According to the neat laws of nature, humans eventually metabolize wine's ethanol back to carbon dioxide and water; see CARBON DIOXIDE.)

Photosynthesis can be summarized by this chemical equation:

$$6CO_2 + 6H_2O + \text{light energy} = C_6H_{12}O_6 + 6O_2$$
(carbon dioxide + water + sunlight = sugar + oxygen)

The process of photosynthesis maintains atmospheric supplies of OXYGEN, essential for animal life on earth. Since these reactions take place inside the vine leaf, carbon dioxide must be able to diffuse in and oxygen out. This takes place through minute pores called STOMATA on the underside of vine leaves.

Photosynthesis is affected by environmental and plant factors, all of which have an effect on grape RIPENING and hence wine quality. SUNLIGHT, TEMPERATURE, and WATER STRESS are the three most important climatic controls. Photosynthesis is limited by low light levels, as, for example, under overcast conditions or, more commonly, for shaded leaves away from the canopy surface (see CANOPY MICROCLIMATE). Light levels of about 1% of full sunlight are too low for photosynthesis and can occur behind two leaf layers from the canopy surface. Leaves exposed to such light levels turn yellow and eventually fall off. Photosynthesis increases almost linearly with light up to about one-third full sunlight, and then is said to be light saturated, in that any further increase in sunlight intensity will not increase photosynthesis. So outside leaves on vine canopies are often light saturated in sunny conditions, and some sunlight is wasted.

Photosynthesis is highest with leaf temperatures from about 15 to 30 °C (59–86 °F), with a slight peak at about 25 °C. Photosynthesis is severely inhibited for temperatures below 15 °C and above 30 °C. During one day in hot DESERT regions, day–night TEMPERATURE VARIABILITY may be so great that vine leaf photosynthesis is inhibited by both low temperatures in the early morning and high temperatures in the afternoon. Low temperatures limit photosynthesis and hence grape ripening in cool climate wine regions such as those of northern Europe. High-quality vintages there are warm, sunny years when photosynthesis is highest.

Dry soil conditions will cause stomata to close, thus interfering with photosynthesis, but saving the vine from further desiccation. Such an effect of water stress on photosynthesis and grape ripening can be seen, especially towards HARVEST, in many of the world's wine regions, typically in MEDITERRANEAN CLIMATES. The vine can, however, tolerate mild water stress with no negative effect on wine quality. Indeed, if it occurs before VERAISON, and shoot growth is slowed, quality will probably be enhanced.

Wind can also cause stomata to close and interfere with grape ripening, as is common in MONTEREY in California, for example.

As a general rule, photosynthesis is enhanced by sunny conditions and mild temperatures. These conditions are known to give maximal sugar concentration in grapes and, conventionally, the best wine quality.   R.E.S.

Jackson, R., *Wine Science: Principles, Practice, Perception* (San Diego, 2000).

Keller, M., 'Photosynthesis and respiration', in *The Science of Grapevines: Anatomy and Physiology* (Elsevier, 2010).

Mullins, M. G., Bouquet, A., and Williams, L., *Biology of the Vine* (Cambridge, 1992).

phylloxera. This small yellow root-feeding aphid has probably had a more damaging impact on wine production than any other VINE PEST, or any VINE DISEASE. It attacks only grapevines, and kills vines by attacking their roots. For many years after it first invaded Europe there was no known cure.

The effects of phylloxera were first noted in France in 1863, just as the country was recovering from another great scourge of 19th-century European viticulture: oidium, or POWDERY MILDEW, which was first noted in 1847. Like powdery mildew, and the other FUNGAL DISEASES yet to arrive (DOWNY MILDEW in 1878 and BLACK ROT in 1885), the phylloxera louse was an unwelcome import from America which devastated European vineyards until appropriate control measures were found. In the history of agriculture it rivals the potato blight of Ireland as a plant disease with widespread social effects. In France, for example, almost 2.5 million ha/ 6.2 million acres of vineyards were destroyed, the aphid making no distinction between the vineyards of the most famous châteaux and those of humble peasants. For individual French vine-growers from the late 1860s, the sight of their vineyards dying literally before their eyes was particularly traumatic, although the epidemic soon spread elsewhere. Phylloxera invasion had a major social and economic impact, involving national governments and local committees, and requiring international scientific collaboration. For a while the very existence of the French wine industry was threatened. (See BURGUNDY, modern history, for example.)

Phylloxera has had several scientific names. Initially called *Phylloxera vastatrix* (the devastator) by the French scientist J.-E. Planchon, and also *Phylloxera vitifoliae* (A. Fitch), it is now more correctly known as *Dactylasphaera vitifoliae* (H. Shimer). See below for more detail.

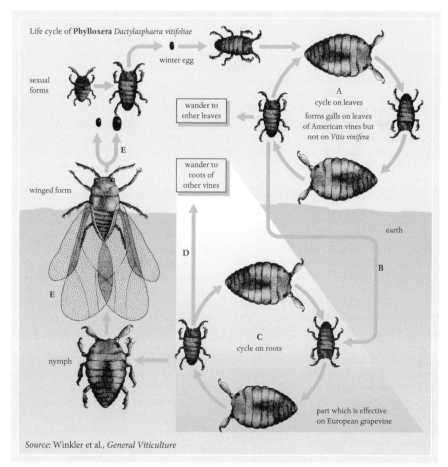

Life cycle of **Phylloxera** *Dactylasphaera vitifoliae*

sexual forms

winter egg

wander to other leaves

wander to roots of other vines

A
cycle on leaves
forms galls on leaves of American vines but not on *Vitis vinifera*

earth

B

C
cycle on roots

D

E

winged form

E

nymph

part which is effective on European grapevine

Source: Winkler et al., *General Viticulture*

Biology

The female phylloxera is yellow and about 1 mm/0.039 in long. Typically surrounded by masses of eggs, it is barely visible to the naked eye as it feeds on the roots. There are four to seven generations in the summer, each producing females capable of laying more eggs. As the eggs hatch, so-called 'crawlers' move to other roots of the vine, and some climb the trunk and can spread to other vines, or even vineyards, by the action of wind or machinery dislodging them from the foliage. Because of the movement of the crawlers through soil cracks, phylloxera tends to spread in a circle from the original infected vine. Wind-blown crawlers create secondary infections downwind.

It has a complex life cycle, existing in both root-living and leaf-living forms, and causes damage to vines by injecting saliva to produce galls, by feeding on the sap, and by causing root deformities.

In humid regions, there is also an associated life cycle whereby the root-hatched nymph produces a winged form which can travel longer distances, and which lays male and female eggs. The hatching female in turn lays a winter egg which develops into the stem mother or fundatrix, which lays eggs in a leaf gall (these galls typically being produced only on the leaves of AMERICAN VINES). Nymphs hatching from leaf galls can begin new infections as egg-laying females on roots.

The principal agent for the spread of phylloxera is humans. It is most commonly transported from one vineyard to another on the roots of ROOTLINGS (one-year-old dormant plants). However, phylloxera is easily moved in the soil that sticks to implements, and by irrigation water. Research by King and colleagues in New Zealand showed that crawlers present in vine foliage lead to secondary spread over considerable distances; they are moved by machines such as foliage trimmers and harvesters which brush against foliage, and also by wind.

Phylloxera is native to the east coast of the United States, and so native American vine species have generally evolved with resistance. Studies have shown that the basis of resistance is the development of cork layers beneath the wound made by phylloxera feeding on the root. This stops the invasion of other microbes (bacteria and fungi) which eventually rot the root and kill non-resistant vines.

Phylloxera kills vines which have not developed this resistance, such as the European VINIFERA vine species from which most wine is made, by destroying the root system. When first present, the phylloxera numbers build up quickly on roots, galls are formed, and there is little apparent root damage. Phylloxera can be diagnosed by the presence on the roots of the bright-yellow females, their eggs, and the characteristic gall symptoms. Studies in South Australia, whose phylloxera-free status is maintained by QUARANTINE, have developed a means of detection using DNA analysis of the soil. After a few years, the root rot affects the top growth, shoot growth is stunted, and leaves lose their healthy green colour. Normally a vine dies within several years of the first infection. Vines which are struggling for other reasons are more susceptible to phylloxera and succumb more quickly. Those growing on deep, fertile soil can continue to produce economic crops for many years after phylloxera attack. Phylloxera does not survive well in sandy soil, so vines planted in sand (such as on the Great Plain of HUNGARY, those planted by Listel on the French Mediterranean coast, or COLARES in Portugal) are immune from attack.

History

Attempts by early European colonists in North America to establish imported V. vinifera vines met with disaster, presumably substantially because of phylloxera, to which they had no resistance—although at this time phylloxera had yet to be identified, and other American vine diseases such as PIERCE'S DISEASE in Florida, downy and powdery mildew in all regions, and the very cold winters doubtless played a part. See UNITED STATES, history, for more details.

How did phylloxera come to Europe? In the mid 19th century there was considerable importation of living plants into Europe. This trade was supported by wealthy people who could afford elaborate gardens, greenhouses, and conservatories, and encouraged by the Victorians' keen interest in botany. Plants could be imported dormant, or kept alive and protected from salt spray by a glass container mounted on the ship's deck, like a modern terrarium. In 1865 alone, 460 tons of plants worth 230,000 francs were imported into France, and this trade had grown to 2,000 tons by the 1890s. In 1875, 50 tons were imported from the US and much of this was vines. Jules Planchon, Professor of Pharmacy at MONTPELLIER University, noted that rooted American vines were imported in particularly significant quantities between 1858 and 1862, and sent to parts of Europe as far apart as Bordeaux, England, Ireland, Alsace, Germany, and Portugal. No doubt phylloxera was an unsuspected passenger on vine roots at the same time.

Just like the fungal disease powdery mildew, the first reporting of phylloxera was in England, in 1863, when Professor J. O. Westwood, an entomologist at Oxford University, received insect samples from a greenhouse in the London suburb of Hammersmith. Since the insects were in a leaf gall, the vine species was probably American, and these plants may even have been a source of introduction of the pest to England. In 1863, an unknown vine disease in France was being talked about, with two vineyards in the southern Rhône affected. The first printed report in France was a letter written by a veterinarian in 1867 about a vineyard planted in 1863 at St-Martin-de-Crau (only about 30 km/20 miles north east of the site of the University of MONTPELLIER's 20th-century phylloxera-free vine collection on the Mediterranean coast, ironically), which developed unhealthy vines in summer 1866, failing to grow the following spring. It is likely that infection occurred several years beforehand. There were other reports from Narbonne in the Languedoc, and the Gard and Vaucluse *départements* in the southern Rhône in 1867, and from Bordeaux in 1869. (It was usually several years after the initial sighting that the louse's predations had a serious effect; the Médoc, for example, was not commercially compromised until the late 1870s.)

The first of many committees formed to resolve the phylloxera question was a Commission instigated by the Vaucluse Agricultural Society. On 15 July 1868 it began its investigation of affected vineyards in the southern Rhône. One member of the Commission was Jules Planchon, who had good training to work on phylloxera. He had spent a period at Kew Botanical Gardens in England, and subsequently became the brother-in-law of J. Lichtenstein, an amateur entomologist. Planchon noticed that dying vines had small yellow insects on their roots and noted the resemblance to an aphid *Phylloxera quercus* living on oak trees. He named the insect believed to be ravaging vineyards *Phylloxera vastatrix*. The form previously described by A. Fitch as living in the leaf galls of American vines was established by Planchon to be the same insect and therefore, according to the rules of priority, it became known as *Phylloxera vitifolii* (Fitch).

The Hérault Commission made its findings public in August 1868 but these caused little interest in any but the local newspapers. There was a marked reluctance to accept that this little yellow insect could be causing such devastation. Other explanations current at the time were over-production, winter cold and other bad weather, weakening of the vineyards as a result of continued vegetative reproduction, soil exhaustion, and also God's wrath at contemporary vices. Even eminent scientists of the time misdiagnosed the problem. The distinguished entomologist V. Signoret thought phylloxera was an effect not the cause, and Dr GUYOT thought its presence was due to over-severe pruning (the opposite of overcropping)! The debate was ended by the 1869 Commission of the Société des Agriculteurs de France headed by viticulturist L. Vialla, who gently but firmly debunked all false theories.

Total French wine production fell from a peak of 84.5 million hl/2,200 million gal in

1875 to a mere 23.4 million hl in 1889. But even by June 1873 the French government was sufficiently alarmed by the spread of phylloxera to offer a large prize (300,000 francs) for a remedy, which was to be verified by experimentation carried out by the School of Agriculture at Montpellier. Up to October 1876, 696 suggestions were forwarded to Professors Durand and Jeannenot at Montpellier and between 1872 and 1876 1,044 treatments were evaluated. Among the deluge of suggestions submitted were those verging on the ridiculous, which included burying a living toad under the vine to draw the poison, and irrigating the vines with white wine. Entries were received from other countries as different as Denmark and Singapore. All of this work, however, produced little benefit, as only two treatments based on the chemical application of various forms of SULFIDE appeared to show much advantage. Surprisingly, carbon bisulfide failed in the evaluation even though it was later used extensively.

Early attempts at commercial control of phylloxera included FLOODING, which was studied by the Commission in 1873. It was found that flooding in winter for weeks on end controlled the pest, but of course few vineyards were near enough to water supplies or sufficiently flat for this to be a widespread solution (although it is still used in parts of Argentina). Vineyards on sandy soils were noted to be immune, although this offered no control. The injection of the liquid carbon bisulfide was to become widespread, so that by 1888 some 68,000 ha/168,000 acres had been treated. The insecticidal properties of carbon bisulfide were found in 1854 on grain weevils, and Baron Paul Thénard evaluated it in Bordeaux in 1869. The first experiments used too high a dose, severely affecting the vines, but subsequently the practice of injecting it, mixed with water, into the soil, using about 30,000 holes per ha, became widespread.

By the time of the International Phylloxera Congress at Bordeaux in 1881, two distinct schools of thought on how the industry might be saved had emerged. The chemists considered salvation lay in carbon bisulfide or related chemicals, or in flooding. In opposition were the 'Americanists', who advocated grafting desired varieties on to American vine species used as ROOTSTOCKS. Gaston Bazille had suggested GRAFTING in 1869 and Leo Laliman of Bordeaux drew early attention to the resistance of these species to the phylloxera. Laliman had studied the resistance of American species to powdery mildew in a collection in his vineyards since 1840. (He subsequently tried to claim the prize for controlling phylloxera.)

Following successful demonstrations of the ability of American vines to withstand phylloxera, and the visit of Planchon to America in 1873, where his study was guided by the noted scientist C. V. Riley, state entomologist of Missouri, the use of grafted vines began, rising from 2,500 ha in 1880 to 45,000 ha in 1885. It was Riley who positively identified the unknown French insect as identical to the American one, a critical step in its eventual control; he was one of the first to suggest grafting European varieties to American rootstocks, and his authority and expertise on phylloxera gave weight to the suggestion. Initial American vine imports were from the north east, growing on acid soils. *Vitis labrusca* was found to lack resistance, but *V. aestivalis*, *V. rupestris*, and *V. riparia* were found to be most effective.

All was not plain sailing, however. Many American species could not tolerate the CALCAREOUS soils of France (see CHLOROSIS). A second visit to the US by Vialla led to the intervention of Texas nurseryman, breeder, and AMPELOGRAPHER T. V. MUNSON. The two met in 1878, and Munson guided Vialla to species resistant to calcareous soils, *V. berlandieri, V. cordifolia*, and *V. cinerea*. Munson was rewarded for his contribution to saving French viticulture by the medal of the French Legion of Honour, and a statue in Montpellier.

However, the transition to grafting was not simple. The amount of grafting to be done was almost overwhelming, and also there was a concern that the use of these foreign rootstocks (whose own wine is so often reviled for its FOXY flavour) might affect wine quality. The latter objection is voiced by the uneducated even today, and in Burgundy the importation of American vines was prohibited until 1887, although the clandestine activities of growers anxious to save their vineyards forced its repeal.

Eventually rootstock use became the established method for the control of phylloxera and this has had a dramatic effect on vine NURSERY operations worldwide, and subsequently on the spread of VIRUS and, more recently, TRUNK DISEASES. There was a period in the late 19th century, however, when it was thought that breeding HYBRIDS of European with American vine varieties might produce vines with sufficient phylloxera resistance not to need grafting, whose wines were not marked by the undesirable FOXY flavour of some American grapes. The class of varieties so created is loosely termed FRENCH HYBRIDS or DIRECT PRODUCERS. These efforts were generally unsuccessful, however, in that the vines had inadequate phylloxera tolerance and produced lower-quality wine, although they became popular with growers because of their high yields and their tolerance of FUNGAL DISEASES. While hybrids bred in this period were not destined to remain commercially viable, they did form a useful germplasm pool of disease tolerance for highly successful breeding projects in the latter part of the 19th century (see HYBRIDS). Nevertheless, many of the rootstocks used today (see ROOTSTOCKS for a detailed list) were bred in the late 19th and early 20th centuries—although hybrids with *V. vinifera* as one parent have been generally found to have insufficient tolerance to phylloxera (see below).

Geography

Phylloxera is now widespread around the world, having been found in California (1873), Portugal (1871), Turkey (1871), Austria (1872), Switzerland (1874), Italy (1875), Australia (1877), Spain (1878), Algeria (1885), South Africa (1885), New Zealand (1885), and Greece (1898). There are few parts of the world free from the pest, although these include parts of Australia (on which a strict QUARANTINE is imposed), parts of China, Chile, Argentina, India, Pakistan, and Afghanistan, and some Mediterranean islands such as Crete, Cyprus, and Rhodes.

There are also small sandy vineyards in otherwise affected wine regions (see BOLLINGER and COLARES) which have never been affected by phylloxera either because of isolation or because of the soil composition.

For much of the late 20th century, phylloxera has not been regarded as a serious problem, either because it was not known in a region, or because a wide range of rootstocks are available which are suited to different varieties, soil, and climate conditions along with tolerance to other pests such as NEMATODES. About 85% of all the world's vineyards were estimated in 1990 to be grafted onto rootstocks presumed to be resistant to phylloxera.

Late-20th-century outbreaks of phylloxera were noted on ungrafted vines in parts of Greece, England, New Zealand, Australia, Oregon, and, most dramatically, on vines grafted onto the AXR1 rootstock (see ROOTSTOCKS for details) in California where the so-called 'biotype B' strain of phylloxera was identified.

Phylloxera is known to occur naturally as a number of related strains or biotypes. King and Rilling exchanged phylloxera and vine cuttings between New Zealand and Germany, and confirmed evidence of the biotype differences between the two countries. Interestingly, the AXR1 rootstock was found not to be affected by phylloxera found in New Zealand, but it was affected by German phylloxera. New Zealand probably obtained phylloxera from California in 1885, which suggests that the biotype of phylloxera originally in California did not affect AXR1. With the introduction of other biotypes, probably on rooted vines imported from eastern American states at a time of nursery shortages in California, the demise of AXR1 began. It was found to offer insufficient phylloxera tolerance, and a significant proportion of grafted vineyards in Napa and Sonoma valleys succumbed to phylloxera and were replanted in the 1990s.

No doubt one of the most important effects of the phylloxera invasion of the world's vineyards was the inadvertent spread of VIRUS DISEASES. As grafting became widespread towards the end of the 19th century, virus diseases were also spread as a common result of grafting, because virus-infected cuttings were used in grafting. A virus originally present only in the rootstock would spread to the fruiting *V. vinifera* variety after grafting, and vice versa. Rootstocks do not show virus symptoms, and virology in viticulture was not well understood until the 1950s. With known effects on fruit ripening, perhaps it was virus diseases more than grafting which led to the debate as to the relative merits of 'PRE-PHYL-LOXERA' and 'post-phylloxera' wines.

Now, in the late 20th and early 21st centuries, grafting has been shown to spread TRUNK DISEASES, this time caused by fungi. These diseases can be minimized by protecting MOTHER VINES from infection, HOT WATER TREATMENT, and improved nursery sanitation.   R.E.S.

Campbell, C., *Phylloxera—How Wine was Saved for the World* (London, 2004).

Gale, G., *Dying on the Vine: How Phylloxera Transformed Wine* (Berkeley, Calif., 2011).

Herbert, K., et al., 'Developing and testing a diagnostic probe for grape phylloxera applicable to soil samples', *Journal of Economic Entomology*, 101 (2008), 1934–43.

King, P. D., and Rilling, G., 'Further evidence of phylloxera biotypes: variations in the tolerance of mature grapevine roots related to the geographical origin of the insect', *Vitis*, 30 (1991), 233–44.

phylogeny

phylogeny, or **phylogenesis**, is the chronological reconstruction of the evolutionary history of a given group of organisms. Formerly based on morphological comparisons (see VINE MORPHOLOGY), this field has been revolutionized in the last 20 years by phylogenetics, the DNA analyses of various molecular markers found in the nucleus (inherited from both parents), or in the organelles (e.g. the chloroplasts, maternally inherited in grapevines), and usually represented as a phylogenetic tree. See BOTANICAL CLASSIFICATION for the phylogeny of the GRAPEVINE.   J.V.

physiological ripeness

physiological ripeness, or sometimes **physiological maturity**, terms loosely used by some winemakers, especially in the New World, to contrast with RIPENESS measured by the normal analytical measures of MUST WEIGHT, ACIDITY, and PH. The terminology is imprecise because all grapes undergo physiological ripening irrespective of how it is assessed.

The concept of physiological ripening arose when winemakers realized that in many, particularly warmer, wine regions, these chemical measures were not sufficient to predict the optimum HARVEST date for wine quality. In its simplest form, the concept includes aspects of the berry's maturation which describe changes in a ripening grape berry important to eventual quality. These include skin colour, berry texture including skin and pulp texture, seed colour and ripening, flavour, and phenolic changes, often accompanied by LIGNIFICATION of the berry stem. It is increasingly common to measure ANTHOCYANINS and other PHENOLICS. The aim is to pick at as near optimum values of as many of these parameters as possible. Wine quality is thought to suffer if only a few parameters are at optimal value when the fruit is harvested; factors such as weather conditions, site, and viticultural technique, especially a shaded CANOPY MICROCLIMATE, can unbalance these relationships. A common example is the relatively faster rate of sugar increase in warm to hot climates compared with phenolic development, flavour increase, and acid decrease. The resulting wines tend to be high in alcohol without necessarily being accompanied by ripe fruit aromas and phenolics. On the other hand, VARIETAL flavour appears to increase more quickly relative to sugar in cooler climates.

Recent research into the effects of increased TEMPERATURE on grape composition by Sadras and colleagues in Australia has shown that, in Shiraz and Cabernet Franc, accumulation of anthocyanins is 'decoupled' from sugar accumulation during ripening. This was due to the delayed onset of anthocyanin accumulation at warmer temperatures.

A likely important aspect of physiological ripeness which is overlooked in conventional RIPENING considerations is that of the condition of the grape skin. There is empirical evidence that wine quality can be affected, even though other aspects of fruit condition seem similar.

In the late 20th century there was an increasing tendency to encourage growers to leave grapes longer and longer on the vine. The aim of this prolonged HANG TIME is riper tannins and phenolics but this is often achieved at the cost of excessively high sugar levels. As a consequence, winemakers may resort to adding WATER to the must, where local regulations allow, or the use of equipment such as the SPINNING CONE to reduce the ALCOHOLIC STRENGTH of the finished wine.

At the start of the 21st century, many wine producers were trying to find ways of encouraging physiological ripeness to coincide with optimal sugar accumulation. These included precisely timed IRRIGATION regimes, manipulating crop load, controlling fruit exposure, slowing sugar accumulation by careful reduction of the LEAF TO FRUIT RATIO, and research into YEASTS specifically designed to result in lower alcohol levels.

J.R., J.E.H., & R.E.S.

Sadras, V. O., and Moran, M. A., 'Elevated temperature decouples anthocyanins and sugars in berries of Shiraz and Cabernet Franc', *Australian Journal of Grape and Wine Research*, 18/2 (2012), 115–22. doi: 10.1111/j.1755-0238.2012.00180.x.

physiology of the vine

physiology of the vine. See VINE PHYSIOLOGY.

phytoalexins

phytoalexins, compounds produced by plants in response to bacterial or fungal attack. They are not normally present in significant quantities until a plant is invaded by disease. In grapevines, phytoalexins belong to a class of PHENOLICS called stilbenes (see RESVERATROL). When a fungus such as DOWNY MILDEW or BOTRYTIS invades the vine, resveratrol is synthesized and accumulates very rapidly near the infection point. At sufficient concentrations, resveratrol can slow or even stop the growth of the disease. Some grape varieties that are known to be resistant to fungi (Castor, for example) also have a high potential for stilbene production. Resveratrol was discovered in vines in 1976, and a related compound viniferin was discovered in 1977. This phytoalexin was studied with renewed interest when it was discovered also to be a constituent of the Asian medicinal herb *Polygonum cuspidatum*. The gene for resveratrol synthesis, stilbene synthase, has been cloned from VINIFERA vines and inserted into the ROOTSTOCK 41 B. The transgenic plants able to produce high concentrations of resveratrol were more resistant to BOTRYTIS infection, showing its value as a natural defence agent. However, botrytis and possibly other pathogenic fungi manufacture a LACCASE which can detoxify stilbenes and allow infection to proceed, but phenolics such as CATECHIN can inhibit this enzyme's activity, thus cancelling out the fungi's defence.   R.E.S. & G.L.C.

Goetz, G., et al., 'Resistance factors to grey mould in grape berries: identification of some phenolics inhibitors of *Botrytis cinerea* stilbene oxidase', *Phytochemistry*, 52 (1999), 759–67.

Langcake, P., 'Disease resistance of Vitis spp. and the production of the stress metabolites resveratrol, ε-viniferin, α-viniferin and pterostilbene', *Physiological Plant Pathology*, 18 (1981), 213–26.

Siemann, E. H., and Creasy, L. L., 'Concentration of the phytoalexin resveratrol in wine', *American Journal of Enology and Viticulture*, 43 (1992), 49–52.

phytoplasma

phytoplasma, once known as mycoplasma, small and sometimes microscopic organisms similar to BACTERIA associated with vine diseases of the PHLOEM, transmitted by insects and grafting. The most serious diseases caused, GRAPEVINE YELLOWS, may well have widespread implications for the world's wine industry in the 21st century. The relentless spread of various forms of phytoplasma continues in many European grape-growing regions, France, Germany, Slovenia, and Hungary among others. In recent years, CLIMATE CHANGE has been implicated, as the insect vectors spreading the disease migrate polewards. R.E.S.

Piacentini, Colli, diverse DOC zone centred on the hills of Piacenza in Emilia in north-central Italy. See EMILIA-ROMAGNA for more details.

Piave, mainly red wine DOC in the hinterland of Venice in north-east Italy. Like the neighbouring LISON-PRAMAGGIORE, the Piave DOC embraces vineyards in the plain of the Piave River, and is demarcated by the pre-alpine Conegliano and Montello hills to the north and the flatlands of the river's Adriatic delta to the south. The DOC is so large that it overlaps the DOCG Conegliano-Valdobbiadene, Colli Asolano, and the DOC Montello—so large that it accords little attention to terroir aspects. This is overwhelmingly MERLOT territory (some 4,323 ha/10.678 acres) with CABERNET (principally Franc) accounting for an additional 1,852 ha. VERDUZZO and TAI BIANCO account for the bulk of the white wine production. The wines, at their best, are fruity, fresh, and unpretentiously appealing; with permitted yields of up to 90 hl/ha for Merlot and over 80 hl/ha for Cabernet and Tai Bianco from the fertile soil, they seem destined to remain that way. The zone doubles as the DOCG **Piave Malanotte**, a potentially much more interesting red based on the local RABOSO grape of which between 15 and 30% of the grapes must be dried, arguably to counteract the grape's tannic, high-acid character. But in the right hands this variety can produce high quality, long lived, complex red wines. W.S.

Picapoll Blanco, vine variety making crisp white wine in the far north east of CATALUNYA which is genetically very similar to CLAIRETTE BLANCHE but is unrelated to PIQUEPOUL.

picardan, white wine, often sweet, developed from LANGUEDOC raw materials by the DUTCH WINE TRADE in the late 17th and 18th centuries. Picardan is also the name of one of the most neutral white grape varieties allowed in CHÂTEAUNEUF-DU-PAPE.

Piceno. See ROSSO PICENO.

picking grapes is apparently romantic but in practice often back-breaking work for humans. For more details, see HARVEST and LABOUR.

Pico, DOP on the island of the same name which is dominated by Portugal's highest mountain, Ponto do Pico, a volcano. Pico has more vines than other islands in the AZORES because its crust of black BASALT is an inhospitable environment for any other crop. Vines are planted in cracks filled with soil from the neighbouring island of Faial and protected from harsh winds and sea spray by volcanic rock walls (*currais*). This unique landscape has UNESCO World Heritage status. Traditionally

LICOROSO wine (some fortified, some late harvest) from VERDELHO was the mainstay but Arinto do Açores represents 95% of plantings today and table wines have become more common since the VINHO REGIONAL Açores was created. S.A.

Picolit, also written **Piccolit** and **Piccolito** in the past, fashionable and audaciously priced sweet white VARIETAL wine made in the FRIULI region of north east Italy, one of the more commercially successful of the DRIED-GRAPE WINES. The grape variety derives its name from the small, or *piccolo*, quantity of grapes it produces, thanks to its exceptionally poor pollination rate in the vineyard. The variety probably originates in Rosazzo in the COLLI ORIENTALI.

The wine was already famous in the 18th century but was almost extinct when the Perusini family of the Rocca Bernarda of Ipplis worked to identify and then reproduce hardier CLONES with a reduced failure rate.

Some better estates still make the wine much as it was in the past—Fabio Asquini left copious notes on his working methods—with the bunches, harvested late in mid October, left to dry and raisin on mats before pressing. Other producers have opted for a late-harvest style, with the grapes left even longer in the vineyard, picked with higher MUST WEIGHTS, but not raisined after picking. The use of small oak BARREL MATURATION is an innovation introduced in the mid 1980s. Although Picolit is generally considered a dessert wine, it is not luscious and is best considered a VINO DA MEDITAZIONE, a wine to be sipped alone in order to appreciate its delicate floral aromas and its light sweetness which suggests peaches and apricots.

The wine became the object of a cult enthusiasm in Italy in the late 1960s and 1970s, fetching extremely high prices that non-Italian connoisseurs find difficult to understand or justify; the Picolit boom has also resulted in frequent and illegal blending of the wine with the more neutral VERDUZZO, which has stretched the quantities available but has done no service to the wine's reputation. The Italian vine census of 2010 found only just over 125 ha/309 acres of the variety in total. A small amount is grown in western Slovenia.

Picpoul de Pinet, popular dry, aromatic LANGUEDOC white given its own AOC in 2013, when it appropriated the name Picpoul and decreed that PIQUEPOUL be used for the variety by all other appellations. The green-gold, full-bodied, lemon-flavoured white wine is grown on about 2,400 ha/5928 acres of fairly low-lying land between Pézenas and the Bassin de Thau lagoon exclusively from Picpoul Blanc grapes. This curious speciality, one of the country's few VARIETALLY named AOC wines, has in the post-modern age of vinification attracted new

interest. Millions of tourists each summer see the well-signposted CO-OPERATIVE at Pinet, the most important producer of this distinctive wine and clearly visible from the main *autoroute* along the Mediterranean coast. The co-operative at Pomerols and some individual domaines such as Félines Jourdan have made some good examples.

Pic-St-Loup, one of the most successful named CRUS within the LANGUEDOC AOC in southern France and the least dependent on CARIGNAN grapes or CO-OPERATIVES. The zone, with mixed but largely CALCAREOUS soils, includes 12 communes around the eponymous and dramatic 658 m peak north of Montpellier (including one called Claret—although the robust red wines made here much more closely resemble southern Rhône than any bordeaux). The mainly red with some rosé wines should be blends, with the Languedoc holy trinity of Syrah, Grenache, and Mourvèdre favoured, and Cinsaut allowed for rosés.

pièce, size and shape of barrel conventionally used in Burgundy. See BARREL TYPES for more details.

Piedirosso, one of CAMPANIA's relatively few red wine grapes, very much in second place after AGLIANICO, It is grown around Naples and on the islands of ISCHIA and Capri. Also known as Per'e Palummo and Palombina, it can make fresh, fruity reds but total plantings had declined to under 700 ha/1,730 acres by 2010.

Piedmont, Anglicized name for PIEMONTE.

pie franco, Spanish for UNGRAFTED VINE. There are at least 250,000 ha of ungrafted vineyards in CASTILLA-LA MANCHA alone, so this is hardly a rarity in Spain, but only a handful of producers such as Casa Castillo of JUMILLA use the term, or 'P.F.', on labels. Many of these vines are attacked by PHYLLOXERA. V. de la S.

Piemonte, qualitatively outstanding and highly distinctive wine region in north-west ITALY whose principal city is Turin (see map under ITALY). This subalpine part (its name means 'at the foot of the mountains') of the former kingdom of Savoy was the driving force behind Italian reunification in the 19th century and led the initial phases of Italy's industrial revolution. Its geographical position both isolated and protected it during the period of Habsburg, Bourbon, and papal domination which marked Italian life between 1550 and 1860, while its proximity, both geographical and cultural, to France (the kingdom's court and nobility were Francophone until well into the 19th century) gave it both an openness to the new ideas of the European enlightenment and relative prosperity—in stark contrast to the poverty of much of the rest of the peninsula.

P

In 2010, total annual wine production averaged over 3 million hl/79 million gal, with over 75% DOC or DOCG.

In Piemonte vines are planted at ELEVATIONS, which can vary from about 150 m to above 400 m (490–1,150 ft), with the best, south-facing sites typically devoted to NEBBIOLO, while the coolest positions are planted with DOLCETTO (or MOSCATO in the zones in which it is grown). BARBERA is widely planted in between. Average summer temperatures and rainfall are very similar to those in Bordeaux. Although there are 12 Nebbiolo-based DOCs or DOCGs, only the world-famous BAROLO and BARBARESCO supply significant amounts of wine. GATTINARA, for example, which is the largest of the Nebbiolo DOCs outside the LANGHE hills, encompasses hardly more than 100 ha/247 acres of vineyard. Very much more common is Barbera, planted virtually everywhere in the provinces of ALBA, ASTI, and Alessandria, often with scant attention to its viticultural needs, while the best sites are reserved for the more valuable Nebbiolo. It was therefore considered Piemonte's workhorse grape, resulting necessarily in modest wine, until the 1980s when high-quality and expensive oak-aged Barberas appeared on the market, showing its real potential and radically changing perceptions. DOLCETTO, almost as ubiquitous as Barbera and similarly considered modest rather than great, delivers most of Piemonte's fruity red wine for early drinking. It ripens even earlier than Barbera and is regularly vinified in less than a week to make sure the fermentation tanks are empty before Barbera and Nebbiolo are harvested.

White grapes, with the exception of the MOSCATO used extensively for various SPUMANTE and FRIZZANTE (most notably ASTI), used to be a virtual afterthought in Piemonte, but the region's production of white wine grew considerably in the late 20th and early 21st centuries. Part of this surge is due to the renewed popularity and commercial success of Asti and MOSCATO D'ASTI, but wines based on CORTESE such as GAVI and those from the Colli Tortonesi and Alto Monferrato have also become increasingly popular. Native Piemontese varieties such as ARNEIS and FAVORITA (Vermentino), mere curiosities in the early 1980s, were planted on 925 ha and 464 ha respectively in 2010. While the 1980s saw the arrival and a certain acceptance of INTERNATIONAL VARIETIES, they never established a real foothold here, no doubt due to Piemonte's many high-quality, unique INDIGENOUS VARIETIES. While the plantings of Chardonnay and Pinot Noir have helped trigger a budding and promising METODO CLASSICO production under the Alta Langa DOC, other white Piemontese varieties, such as ERBALUCE (dry as well as sweet), TIMORASSO, and NASCETTA, as yet produced in tiny quantities, are beginning to earn deserved recognition.

Piemonte is the only region in Italy that does not allow the production of IGT wine. Instead, an overarching DOC Piemonte, the size of the entire region, was created, encompassing more than 60 individual DOCs and DOCGs. The intention was to brand the region's entire production at the highest quality level in order to obtain greater prestige and success in the international market. But the system failed, because the Piemonte DOC's production rules had to be as flexible as those of an IGT to allow both INTERNATIONAL VARIETIES and higher YIELDS. This weakened the significance of the DOC system as well as the notion of origin in high-quality wines, while the expected added prestige for the region did not materialize. The only radical refinement of the Piemontese DOC system has been the creation of recognized smaller subzones or single-vineyard sites, called Menzioni Geografiche, of which especially Barolo and Barbaresco have taken advantage, but other DOCs and DOCGs are bound to follow, Barbera d'Asti being a case in point. See BAROLO for more detail.

For more details of individual wines, see ALBA, ARNEIS, ASTI, BARBARESCO, BARBERA, BAROLO, BRACHETTO, CAREMA, CORTESE, DOLCETTO, ERBALUCE, FAVORITA, FREISA, GATTINARA, GAVI, GRIGNOLINO, LANGHE, MOSCATO, NEBBIOLO, ROERO, RUCHÈ, SPANNA.   W.S.

Belfrage, N., *From Barolo to Valpolicella; The Wines of Northern Italy* (2nd edn, London, 2003).
www.ivinidelpiemonte.it

Pierce's disease, or **PD**, is one of the vine BACTERIAL DISEASES most feared around the world as it can quickly kill vines and there is no cure. The disease, along with FLAVESCENCE DORÉE, is a principal reason for QUARANTINE restrictions on the movement of grape cuttings and other plants between countries. In common with many other economically significant vine diseases, it originates on the American continent. The disease is a principal factor limiting grape-growing in the Gulf Coastal plains of the UNITED STATES (see TEXAS) and southern CALIFORNIA. The disease was first described in 1892 in southern California as Anaheim disease, but was later named after the Californian researcher Pierce. By 1906, the disease had destroyed almost all of the more than 16,000 ha/39,500 acres of vines, and there was another epidemic in the 1930s in the Los Angeles basin, which never recovered as a viticultural area. Pierce's disease has continued to cause chronic problems in coastal northern California (Napa and Sonoma) in isolated hot spots near riparian vegetation and in the Central Valley near insect vector breeding habitats such as pastures and hay fields. The disease is today found across the southern United States and throughout Mexico and Central America. It has also been reported in Venezuela.

Leaves develop marginal discoloration that advances to dead tissue. This progressively enlarges until only the PETIOLE remains attached. Vines die within one to five years after infection, depending on grape variety, vine age, and climate. Originally believed to be a virus, the disease is now known to be caused by a bacterium named *Xylella fastidiosa*. This bacterium lives in a wide range of host plants, and causes damage also to almonds and lucerne (alfalfa). Various strains of the bacterium differ from one another in their ability to multiply within, and cause disease to, certain plant species. For example, grape strains do not multiply in sweet orange, but orange strains (now in South America) cause disease in grape. The disease is spread by insects called sharpshooters (see LEAFHOPPERS), which transmit the bacterium from host plants to the vineyards during feeding. In coastal California, vectors originally fed and reproduced in natural vegetation along streams, and the largest numbers of infected vines were therefore typically within 100 m/330 ft of a vineyard edge. Only the spring infections of vines (April–May) establish chronic Pierce's disease; later infections do not survive until the following year.

However, the introduction of the GLASSY WINGED sharpshooter into southern California in the 1980s has led to far more widespread damage. This leafhopper also spreads the bacterium, and, significantly for vineyards, it can fly further and more frequently. Vineyards near Temecula, for example, were destroyed by an outbreak spread by this new insect vector. It has moved northwards in the Central Valley, and vigorous quarantine efforts are protecting vulnerable Napa and Sonoma counties for the moment. Since Pierce's disease exists in these counties, but the insect vector is limited, a new insect vector could have major implications.

There are no resistant VINIFERA varieties, and some varieties such as Chardonnay and Pinot Noir are especially susceptible. Varieties developed from MUSCADINE grapes or other wild grape species native to south eastern USA and Mexico have natural resistance or tolerance and are the only ones to be grown where the disease is endemic. In California, growers are advised to avoid planting near hot spots or use less susceptible varieties. There is no satisfactory chemical control of the bacterium.

However, the discovery of strong single-gene resistance to *Xylella fastidiosa* in forms of *Vitis arizonica* from Texas and northern Mexico led to the possibility of breeding high-quality PD-resistant wine grapes by classical BREEDING. Genetic mapping of this resistance gene enabled the marker-assisted selection of breeding populations, which when coupled with aggressive growing practices to force grapes into a two-year seed-to-seed cycle has allowed 97% *V. vinifera* PD-resistant selections to be created over about 12 years at the University of California, DAVIS.

Despite some scares in Europe, Pierce's disease has not become established there although it has been reported in Kosovo. Cold winters appear to limit where the disease occurs in North America and could do the same in northern Europe. In southern Europe, the failure of Pierce's disease to establish itself may be due to the lack of vectors that overwinter as infective adults since these are the only ones that could establish chronic infections in the spring. However, this situation could change if Europe were to be invaded by new vector species able to overwinter as adults. Climate studies indicate that both the bacterium and glassy winged sharpshooter if introduced might develop in European, South American, South African, and Australasian vineyard regions to a greater or lesser extent. FLAVESCENCE DORÉE is already quite widespread in Europe, however, and could perhaps pose a greater global threat to vineyards than Pierce's disease.

A.H.P. & R.E.S.

Goodwin, P., and Purcell, A. H., 'Pierce's disease', *Grape Pest Management* (2nd edn, California, 1992), 76–84.

Hoddle, M. S., 'The potential adventive geographic range of glassy-winged sharpshooter, *Homalodisca coagulata*, and the grape pathogen *Xylella fastidiosa*: implications for California and other grape growing regions of the world', *Crop Protection*, 23 (2004), 691–9.

Pearson, R. C., and Goheen, A. C. (eds.), *Compendium of Grape Diseases* (St Paul, Minn., 1988).

Tourney, J., 'PD resistant vines available in 2015?', www.winesandvines.com/template.cfm?section=news&content=125854.

Pierrevert, zone in the alpine foothills of northern PROVENCE, regarded by the INAO as an eastern satellite of the southern RHÔNE, promoted to AOC status in 1998. The appellation extends over a large area east of the LUBERON and includes some of the highest vineyards in France. The total vineyard area was 236 ha/ 583 acres in 2012. Wines of all three colours are produced with rosé the most important. Thanks to the relative harshness of the climate, they are usually marked more by acidity than body. Grenache and Syrah are the dominant grapes. Tourism in the Hautes Alpes de Provence is such that there has been little need to seek export markets.

Pigato, characterful white grape variety producing distinctively flavoured varietal wines in the north west Italian region of LIGURIA. DNA PROFILING showed that Pigato and VERMENTINO, both long-established in Liguria, and FAVORITA cultivated in Piemonte, are all genetically identical. The Italian vine census of 2010 distinguishes between them and found 264 ha/ 652 acres of Pigato Bianco.

pigeage, French term for PUNCHING DOWN.

pigmented tannins, also called **polymeric pigments**, are responsible for the colour of red wines, together with ANTHOCYANINS, which are the phenolic red PIGMENTS of dark-skinned grapes. Pigmented tannins comprise a great diversity of molecular species formed by the reactions of anthocyanins with non-pigmented CATECHINS, PROANTHOCYANIDINS (i.e. condensed tannins from grapes), and ellagitannins (i.e. hydrolysable tannins extracted from barrels or added as components of some OENOLOGICAL TANNINS), under the influence of acids and oxygen. Their formation begins in the course of MACERATION, and then progresses throughout the AGEING of a red wine, so that the grape anthocyanins as individual molecular species make only a transitory and ever-diminishing contribution to the colour of a red wine.

Although this process has been known for over thirty years, some of the structures postulated for pigmented tannins have only recently been shown to form in wine, owing to progress in the development of analytical techniques, whereas others have not yet been confirmed. Besides, several so far unsuspected reaction processes and products have been unravelled in the last few years. Formation of pigmented tannins occurs through both direct addition reactions between anthocyanins and tannins and reactions involving fermentation products such as ACETALDEHYDE and pyruvic acid. The nature and amounts of the resulting products depend on the nature and proportions of the phenolics present and the relative kinetics of the various reactions. Physico-chemical parameters such as pH and temperature and the presence of oxygen, of yeast metabolites, and of cofactors, such as metal ions, also affect the type and/or kinetics of the reactions.

Colour changes, from the purple nuance of young wines towards the red-brown tint of mature wine, are classically ascribed to the conversion of anthocyanins to pigmented tannins. However, pigmented tannins cover a wide range of colours, from orange to purple and blue. Besides, anthocyanin reactions also yield lower molecular weight orange pigments which are not pigmented tannins. Reactions of tannins under OXIDATIVE conditions also lead to brown-orange pigments that do not derive from anthocyanins. Most of these pigments show increased colour stability with respect to hydration and sulfite bleaching compared with anthocyanins but this property is neither characteristic of nor specific to pigmented tannins. Known pigments account for only a small proportion of wine colour, meaning that most pigmented tannins are of analytically intractable nature, due to their multiplicity and diversity of structure and the transient nature of individual molecular species as they equilibrate among each other.

There is also conjecture about interactions of pigmented tannins with PROTEINS and POLYSACCHARIDES and the influence of such putative interactions on the properties (particularly taste properties—see below) of the pigmented tannins.

Experience has also shown that the formation of pigmented tannins, as well as conferring stability on the colour of a red wine (for decades, in favourable circumstances) also modulates the ASTRINGENCY of the very high concentration of phenolics of the wine, improving its TEXTURE and other taste properties. The desirable effects of pigmented tannins on mouthfeel are well illustrated by a comparison of the taste properties of a red wine with those of a white wine made, like a red wine, with extensive maceration. Such highly tannic white wines (except for the few made deliberately in this way; see ORANGE WINE, QVEVRI, and SKIN-FERMENTED whites for examples) are not just unattractive, but crude and coarse on the palate; furthermore, they do not improve with age but remain tannic and undrinkable. In contrast, the pigmented tannins of the red wine make it palatable and soft with good ageing characteristics, and this despite the fact that their presence increases further the phenolic and tannin polymer content of the red wine relative to that of its macerated white wine counterpart.

Changes in astringency taking place during red wine ageing are usually attributed to an increase of tannin molecular weight as a result of the formation of co-polymers with anthocyanins since larger polyphenolic species have been claimed to be insoluble and thus non-astringent. However, recent studies have shown that tannin solubility does not decrease with molecular weight and that astringency in fact increases with the tannin size. Besides, tannin reactions in wine do not only yield larger polymers but also lead to lower molecular weight species. The latter reactions may contribute to the decrease of astringency observed during wine ageing. Nevertheless, the taste of pigmented tannins and the effect of incorporating anthocyanin units in a tannin structure on its astringency remain to be investigated.

P.J.W. & V.C.

Fulcrand, H., et al., 'The fate of anthocyanins in wine: are there determining factors?', in A. L. Waterhouse and J. A. Kennedy (eds.), *Red Wine Color: Revealing the Mysteries. ACS Symposium Series 886* (New York, 2004), 68–88.

pigments, inclusive name for the compounds which impart colour. Colour results from the presence in these compounds of structures or functional groups that absorb light of particular wavelengths. Young red wines get their colour from the ANTHOCYANINS and PIGMENTED TANNINS, with the former decreasing in concentration and the latter reciprocally increasing and making the dominant contribution to colour as the wine ages. In contrast to the broad understanding of the pigments (and their chromophores) responsible for red wine colour, the yellow to amber colours of white wines are less well understood. PHENOLICS present in the white grapes are evidently involved, and some limited OXIDATION of these is assumed to play a role in desirable white wine colour development. Brown polymers, resulting from excessive oxidation of white wine CATECHINS, are known to be responsible for the browning of oxidized wines. See AGEING and COLOUR.   P.J.W.

Pignatello, synonym for the Sicilian red grape variety PERRICONE.

Pignola Valtellinese, dark-berried vine almost certainly originating in VALTELLINA. The 2010 vine census found a total of 1,300 ha/3,350 acres in 2010. DNA PROFILING revealed a parent-offspring relationship with Rossolino Nero, also of Valtellina. It may be related to NEBBIOLO.

Pignoletto, lively, crisp white grape grown in Umbria and around Bologna in northern Italy on an area totalling about 500 ha/1,250 acres according to the 2010 vineyard census. This ancient variety is also known as Grechetto di Todi.

Pignolo, promising red grape variety native to the FRIULI region of north east Italy, probably first cultivated in the hills of Rosazzo in the COLLI ORIENTALI. Pignolo is a very shy bearer and it was generally ignored by local growers who preferred other, more productive grape varieties until, like SCHIOPPETTINO, it was given a new lease of life by a EU decree of 1978 authorizing its use in the province of Udine. Total plantings of Pignolo Nero were only 93 ha/230 acres according to the 2010 vine census.

Pin, Le. The original GARAGE WINE originally consisted of just one hectare of vines within sight of PETRUS, the traditional holder of the crown in POMEROL. This gentle, south-facing slope of gravel and sand, with about 10% clay, was bought for a million French francs in 1979 by three members of the Thienpont family, Belgian NÉGOCIANTS who also own nearby Vieux-Château-Certan in Pomerol and properties in the Côte de FRANCS. The vineyard had previously been farmed by a grower in Lalande-de-Pomerol *en* MÉTAYAGE, and its produce had for years been vinified there and sold as Le Pin, but not as a CHÂTEAU BOTTLED wine. When the Thienponts bought it, a third of the vines were only a year old. The first commercial vintage was 1979, and until the mid 1980s the wine was quite a hard sell. Jacques Thienpont, who

commuted between Belgium and Bordeaux, managed to buy out his two co-investors in 1988 and, by adding a further hectare and a half in three contiguous plots, now owns and manages the grand total of about six acres, all Merlot. The wine was always distinctive, deep, and luscious with an almost Burgundian richness, absolutely in tune with the FASHION for early-maturing, sensual wines. Le Pin was the first red bordeaux to have its MALOLACTIC CONVERSION completed in 100% new oak barrels (no great investment when the total production of the property averaged 600 cases). Demand for this rarity escalated towards the end of the 1980s and the price of the fashionable 1982 vintage reached a peak of £2,500 a bottle in 1997, just before the ASIAN boom began to falter. Le Pin's success inspired the rash of new, small, luxury RIGHT BANK estates (see GARAGISTES). In 2011 a new winery designed by Belgian architects Robbrecht en Daem was inaugurated. In 2010 Jacques Thienpont bought 8 ha of St-Émilion Grand Cru vineyard; the former Ch Haut Plantey, renamed L'If (the French word for a yew tree, another conifer). The cellars are located next door to Ch Troplong Mondot (incidentally also owned by the Thienpont family between 1921 and 1933).

Pineau, a word widely used in France as a synonym for the PINOT family of grape varieties. It seems to have been a portmanteau word for any better-quality vine in medieval France (probably a reference to the pine-cone shape of so many bunches of grapes) but is today a word associated primarily with the Loire. It is the first word of a wide range of vine synonyms, sometimes various forms of Pinot but often CHENIN, most notably as **Pineau de la Loire**.

Pineau d'Aunis, sometimes called Chenin Noir although unrelated to CHENIN BLANC, is a historic Touraine variety making light red wines once sought by the kings of both France and England according to Pierre GALET. France's total plantings, 442 ha/1,091 acres in 2011, has remained steady and is concentrated around Tours in the Loire Valley. The variety is one of the many sanctioned for the red and rosé appellations of Touraine and Anjou but is used only to a limited extent, mainly to bring peppery liveliness and fruit to rosés, although in ripe years it can yield a fine red, too, notably in Coteaux du LOIR. See also Coteaux du VENDÔMOIS.

Pineau des Charentes, or **Pineau Charentais**, is the VIN DE LIQUEUR of the Cognac region and has enjoyed some *réclame* in France as a strong, sweet aperitif more likely to be the product of an artisan than of big business. It is made by adding at least year-old cognac, which in practice usually means year-old cognac, straight from the cask to must that is just

about to ferment, thereby producing what is effectively a mixture of grape juice and brandy. The style most often encountered outside France is pale gold, decidedly sweet, and with young spirit much in evidence but there are many subtler examples, including soft, fruity rosé styles made from the same grapes as red BORDEAUX. See also FLOC DE GASCOGNE.

Pinenc, local name for the FER Servadou red wine grape variety in MADIRAN.

Pinot is the first word of many a French vine variety name and is thought to refer to the shape of Pinot grape bunches, in the form of a pine (*pin*) cone. Pinot is considered one of the most important and ancient grape varieties, possibly a selection from WILD VINES. The variety may well have existed for as long as two millennia. There is some evidence that Pinot existed in Burgundy in the 4th century AD. Although Morillon Noir was the common name for early Pinot, a vine called Pinot was already described in records of Burgundy in the 14th century and its fortunes were inextricably linked with those of the powerful medieval monasteries of eastern France and Germany (see BURGUNDY and GERMAN HISTORY). So long has Pinot existed an unusual number of CLONES have emerged, more than 1,000 according to Galet, of which PINOT BLANC, PINOT GRIS, PINOT MEUNIER, and PINOT NOIR are just some of the better known. CHARDONNAY is still occasionally called Pinot Chardonnay. The father of modern vine identification GALET maintained that Chardonnay was not a member of the Pinot family, but DNA PROFILING analysis in 1999 dropped the bombshell that at least 21 distinct varieties are the progenies of Pinot and the obscure and rather ordinary variety GOUAIS BLANC including ALIGOTÉ, AUBIN Vert, AUXERROIS, BACHET Noir, BEAUNOIR, CHARDONNAY, FRANC NOIR DE LA HAUTE-SAÔNE, GAMAY BLANC GLORIOD, GAMAY Noir, KNIPPERLÉ, MELON, Peurion, ROMORANTIN, ROUBLOT, and SACY. Furthermore, independent DNA analysis in Austria revealed a parent–offspring relationship between Pinot and SAVAGNIN. Other instances of DNA profiling have shown that Pinot is probably a grandparent of Terodego, Marzemino, Lagrein, and Dureza, parent of Syrah. A family tree in *Wine Grapes*, with Pinot, Gouais Blanc, and Savagnin at the top (and many blanks for unknown relatives) includes 156 Western European vine varieties, most of them well known. So much for Pinot's genetic importance. As for nomenclature, there are no fewer than 30 entries beginning 'Pinot' in the index of *Wine Grapes*, although they are by no means all distinct.

In German, members of the Pinot family frequently have the word Burgunder in their German names (SPÄTBURGUNDER, Weissburgunder, and GRAUBURGUNDER) in a reference to

Pinot's BURGUNDIAN homeland. There was a marked increase in the popularity of these grape varieties throughout the 1980s as tastes changed in favour of drier, fuller German wines. Throughout Eastern Europe, Pinots of various sorts have 'burgund' in their name.

Galet, P., *Dictionnaire encyclopédique des cépages* (Paris, 2000).

Robinson, J., Harding, J., and Vouillamoz, J., *Wine Grapes, a complete guide to 1,368 vine varieties, including their origins and flavours* (London, 2012).

Pinotage, a hardy and moderately vigorous red grape variety, is SOUTH AFRICA's most notable contribution to the history of the VINIFERA vine. In 1924 STELLENBOSCH University viticulturist A. I. Perold crossed Pinot Noir and Cinsaut, then commonly called Hermitage in South Africa, hence the contraction Pinotage. It took until 1961 for the name to appear on a label, that of a Lanzerac 1959. The grape has been controversial, particularly in earlier decades, when it frequently made reds with a flamboyantly sweetish paint-like pungency (from ISO-AMYL ACETATE) and, often, some degree of bitterness. Greater viticultural and winemaking understanding have made such problems increasingly rare, but local and international detractors remain. Many examples are indeed too powerful and jammy, with the excessiveness of a certain type of ambition taking its toll. Nonetheless, some unquestionably good VARIETAL and blended wines are produced, at all levels, from accessibly fruity rosés and lighter reds, to fine, deep-coloured, rich, seriously oaked examples, although examples made in the 1960s, long before the era of barrique vinification, reveal that Pinotage does not depend on the use of wood to acquire longevity and complexity. Most of the best of them come from mature BUSH VINE vineyards with restricted yields, and some have a perfume recalling the grape's parentage. Fairly simple CO-OPERATIVE winery examples from the 1960s and 1970s that have been drinking well (and rather elegantly) in the second decade of this century, as well as the complex maturation of older wines from the likes of Pinotage specialist Kanonkop in STELLENBOSCH, testify to Pinotage's longevity. So-called 'coffee Pinotage', with mocha notes deliberately derived from artful oaking, has become a notorious 21st-century success story in South Africa, and in some export markets. Pinotage works well in blends, and attempts continue to establish CAPE BLEND as a generic name for reds with a certain (but disputed) percentage of the grape. Since 1994, plantings of Pinotage, along with other major red varieties, have grown substantially and by 2012 the total area planted, 7,000 ha/17,500 acres, represented almost 7% of all South African vine plantings. Pinotage is also grown, to a much more limited extent, in Australia, New Zealand, Brazil, California, Oregon, Washington, Israel, Zimbabwe, and in most vine collections.

May, P. F., *Pinotage: Behind the Legends of South Africa's own Wine* (St Albans, 2009).

Pinot Beurot, ancient Burgundian synonym for PINOT GRIS.

Pinot Bianco, common Italian name for the white PINOT BLANC grape of French origin and much, much more widely grown than the French original in France. Introduced there as Weissburgunder well before the mid 19th century when the region was under Austrian rule, it was once very popular in north eastern Italy. By 2000, however, it had been decisively overtaken by Chardonnay and Pinot Grigio, and total plantings in 2010 were just 3,085 ha/7,620 acres.

It is grown particularly in TRENTINO-ALTO ADIGE, VENETO, FRIULI, and LOMBARDY although, as in Alsace but not in Germany or Austria, Pinot Grigio enjoys higher esteem here. Pinot Bianco is prized in Alto Adige, however, and has produced some of this region's finest white wines. It was first noted in Italy in Piemonte in the early 19th century and until the mid 1980s the name Pinot Bianco was used to describe Pinot Blanc, Chardonnay, or a blend of the two. Even today, there are vineyards in which both varieties grow side by side. Italians generally vinify Pinot Blanc as a high-acid, slightly SPRITZIG, non-aromatic white for early consumption, and often coax generous yields from the vine. In Lombardia, the high acid and low aroma are particularly prized by the SPUMANTE industry. Good Pinot Bianco from Alto Adige from low-yielding vineyards, fermented and aged in oak barrels, indicate that Pinot Bianco could give much better results in Italy if it were treated with more respect.

Pinot Blanc, French white vine variety, member of the PINOT family and particularly associated with ALSACE, where most of its French 1,245 ha/3,075 acres in 2011 were to be found. It was first observed in Burgundy at the end of the 19th century, a white mutation of PINOT GRIS, which is itself a lighter-berried version of PINOT NOIR. Although its base is Burgundian, today it is found all over central Europe.

For many years no distinction was made between Pinot Blanc and CHARDONNAY since the two varieties can look very similar. No Pinot Blanc is notable for its piercing aroma; its perfume arrives in a cloud. Most wines based on Pinot Blanc are also relatively full bodied, which has undoubtedly helped reinforce the confusion with Chardonnay, not only in Burgundy but also in north east Italy, where it is known as PINOT BIANCO. Although Chardonnay dominates white burgundy, Pinot Blanc is technically allowed into wines labelled BOURGOGNE Blanc and into some white MÂCON, but is no longer grown in any quantity in Burgundy.

Even in Alsace, Pinot Blanc's French stronghold, it is less important in terms of total area planted than Riesling, Silvaner, or even the white AUXERROIS with which it is customarily blended in Alsace, to be sold as 'Pinot Blanc'. In LUXEMBOURG, on the other hand, the higher acidity of Pinot Blanc makes it less highly regarded than Auxerrois.

While in Alsace it is regarded as something of a workhorse (and sometimes called Clevner or Klevner), it has been generally held in much higher esteem by the Germans, who have a much greater area planted, up to 4,449 ha/10,989 acres by 2012, than the French (although less in total than they have of the Pinot Gris they call Grauburgunder). Under the fashionable name Weissburgunder, it is now Germany's fifth most planted white wine CULTIVAR, with vinous personalities ranging from the full, rich, oaked examples of Baden and the Pfalz to relatively delicate, mineral-inflected variations along the Nahe and Mosel-Saar-Ruwer, and with quality aspirations ranging from a workaday norm to occasional brilliance. It is popular with growers seeking food-friendly wines that are softer than Riesling and can show local characters.

As PINOT BIANCO it is a popular dry white in Italy and is also grown in Switzerland but it is in Austria that, as Weissburgunder, the variety reaches some of its greatest must weights. Also the fifth most planted white wine grape on a total of nearly 2,000 ha/5,000 acres in 2012, it is grown in all regions. As a dry white varietal, Weissburgunder is associated with an almond-like scent, medium to high alcohol, and an ability to age, but it has achieved its greatest glory in Austria in ultra-rich, botrytized TROCKENBEERENAUSLESE form, often blended, typically with WELSCHRIESLING (acting out the respective parts of Sémillon and Sauvignon Blanc in Sauternes, according to top practitioner Alois Kracher of Burgenland).

Pinot Blanc is widely disseminated over eastern Europe. In Slovenia, Croatia, and Serbia, it is widely grown and may be called Beli (White) Pinot. It is also grown in the Czech Republic, Slovakia, and is widely used in Hungary to produce full-bodied, rather anodyne dry whites more suitable for export than INDIGENOUS VARIETIES.

Vinegrowers in the New World recognize that Pinot Blanc has lacked Chardonnay's glamour but there were still 444 acres/180 ha in 2012 of a variety called Pinot Blanc in California, mainly in Monterey, usually treated to barrel ageing and the full range of Chardonnay winemaking tricks, to creditable effect. Older vines bearing this name are almost certainly not Pinot Blanc but the Muscadet grape MELON (now proven to be another member of the extended Pinot family).

Viticulturally, if not necessarily commercially, Pinot Blanc seems particularly well adapted to the Okanagan Valley in Washington state. Elsewhere in the New World, Pinot Blanc is largely ignored in favour of the most famous white wine grape.

Pinot Blanco, common misnomer for CHENIN BLANC in Latin America.

Pinot Chardonnay is an old synonym for CHARDONNAY, the classic white grape of Burgundy. It was adopted at a time when Chardonnay was believed to be a white mutation of PINOT NOIR (correctly, as it turned out—see PINOT). **Pinot Chardonnay-Mâcon** has been an appellation recognized by INAO as virtually interchangeable with MÂCON Blanc but is not often seen.

Pinot Grigio, during the first decade of the 21st century, took over from Chardonnay as the name of the most popular white wine in the global mass market. It came to signify a vaguely aromatic, dryish, unoaked white. It is also the common Italian name for the French vine variety PINOT GRIS and, as such, is probably the name by which the variety is best known to many wine drinkers. Because of Pinot Grigio's popularity, many producers worldwide choose this name in preference to Pinot Gris. There were about 3,500 ha/8,600 acres of Pinot Grigio vineyard in Italy in 1990 (much less than the area planted with PINOT BIANCO, for example) but so great was demand for Pinot Grigio that its plantings had overtaken those of Pinot Bianco to reach 6,700 ha by 2000, and 17,280 ha/42,682 acres of Pinot Grigio by 2010, almost as much as Chardonnay's 19,709 ha.

The variety is said to have been introduced to Italy via Piemonte in the early 19th century but became a speciality of the north east. The best and richest wines are produced in Friuli, with the traditional version called Ramato, SKIN-FERMENTED, resulting in a copper-tinged ('ramato') wine, while those produced in Alto Adige can be particularly aromatic. But the bulk of Pinot Grigio produced today comes from Veneto, where large volumes are produced by growers for their local CO-OPERATIVES, and then sold to the large bottlers. These Veneto versions tend to be rather neutral and, at their best, inoffensive, the high yields diluting any true Pinot Grigio character. The variety is also grown widely in LOMBARDY although there is less fastidiousness here about distinguishing it from other hues of PINOT, especially when supplying grapes for the sparkling wine industry. Pinot Grigio is planted as far south as EMILIA-ROMAGNA and as far north as ALTO ADIGE.

Pinot Gris is the widely disseminated, fashionable VINE VARIETY (see PINOT GRIGIO) that can produce soft, gently perfumed wines with more substance and colour than most whites, which is what one might expect of a variety that is one of the best-known mutations of PINOT NOIR. If Pinot Noir berries are purplish blue and the berries of the related PINOT BLANC are greenish yellow, Pinot Gris grapes are anything between greyish blue and brownish pink—sometimes on the same bunch. In the vineyard, this vine can easily be taken for Pinot Noir for the leaves are identical and, especially late in a ripe year, the berries can look remarkably similar. At one time, Pinot Gris habitually grew in among the Pinot Noir of many Burgundian vineyards, adding softness and sometimes acidity to its red wine. Even today, as Pinot Beurot, it is sanctioned as an ingredient in most of Burgundy's red wine appellations and the occasional vine can still be found in some of the region's famous red wine vineyards. It was traditionally prized for its ability to soften Pinot Noir musts but older CLONES have a tendency to yield very irregularly.

But, within France, Alsace is where Pinot Gris (once known as Tokay, see GERMAN HISTORY) is most familiar and where by far the majority of the country's 2,792 ha/6,896 acres of the variety grew in 2011. Here it has been gaining ground and is revered as provider of super-rich, usually dry, wines that can be partnered with food without the distraction of too much aroma. For more on the wines, see ALSACE. There also remain small pockets of the variety in the Loire, where it is often known as Malvoisie (although even in such a small appellation as Coteaux d'ANCENIS both Malvoisie and Pinot Beurot are officially allowed as a suffix). It can produce perfumed, substantial wines in a wide range of different sweetness levels. It is also known as Malvoisie in SAVOIE and the Valais in SWITZERLAND, where its wines are also notably full bodied and richly aromatic—rather different from the neutral mouthwash that is typical commercial PINOT GRIGIO. The variety is also much admired for its weight and relatively low acidity in LUXEMBOURG.

As with Pinot Blanc, much more Pinot Gris is planted in both Germany (see GRAUBURGUNDER) and Italy (see PINOT GRIGIO).

The variety, like Pinot Blanc, is widely planted not just in Austria but throughout eastern Europe, particularly in HUNGARY, where it is widely planted on 1,623 ha and known as szürkebarát, although varietal versions may often be exported as the more familiar Pinot Gris, or even the more marketable Pinot Grigio. The area of Pinot Gris grown in MOLDOVA was also a substantial 2,000 ha in 2009. Many eastern European synonyms are inspired by the word RÜLÄNDER, the German name for sweeter styles of Pinot Gris, although the Slovenian name Sivi Pinot is more literal. (The variety can make fine wines in both eastern and western Slovenia.)

With the exception of OREGON where this mutation of its beloved Pinot Noir has long been the state's leading white wine grape and was planted on more than 2,500 acres/1,012 ha by 2011, Pinot Gris' impact on the New World has been more limited but has been increasing thanks to Pinot Grigio's commercial success. In the late 20th century there was a dramatic increase in plantings in California, mainly Monterey and Napa, and its 2012 total of 13,000 acres makes it the state's fourth most planted white wine grape after Chardonnay, French Colombard, and Sauvignon Blanc. In Washington state it is third most popular after Chardonnay and Riesling, and it is planted in much of the rest of North America. Pinot Gris has been a fixture in the Argentine vinescape since the LURTON brothers introduced it in the early 1990s but it is not common in Chile. T'Gallant of the Mornington Peninsula was Australia's Pinot Gris pioneer, using both French and Italian names, and the country's total area had reached 3,766 ha/9,302 acres by 2012. It was improved CLONAL SELECTION and increased interest in AROMATICS that precipitated a renewal of enthusiasm in New Zealand where Pinot Gris' total 2012 plantings of 2,400 ha were catching up fast with those of second most planted white wine grape Chardonnay.

Pinot Liébault, unusual and slightly more productive Burgundian selection of PINOT NOIR, first identified in GEVREY by A. Liébault in 1810, according to Galet.

Galet, P., *Dictionnaire encyclopédique des cépages* (Paris, 2000).

Pinot Meunier may be France's tenth most planted black grape variety but it is rarely encountered on a wine label. Pinot Meunier, sometimes called simply Meunier in the CHAMPAGNE region where almost all of its French total of more than 11,000 ha/27,170 acres is grown, is an early, particularly downy, MUTATION of PINOT NOIR. It earns its name (*meunier* is French for miller) because the underside of its downy leaves can look as though they have been dusted with flour. In Germany, it is known as Müllerrebe (miller's grape) as well, misleadingly, as Schwarzriesling.

The variety is treasured in Champagne, as it was in the once-extensive vineyards of northern France, because it buds later and ripens earlier than the inconveniently early budding Pinot Noir and is therefore much less prone to COULURE and more dependably productive. Acid levels are slightly higher although alcohol levels are by no means necessarily lower than those of Champagne's most-planted variety Pinot Noir. Pinot Meunier is therefore the popular choice for Champagne's growers, especially those in cooler north-facing vineyards, in the damp, frost-prone Vallée de la Marne, and in the cold valleys of the Aisne *département*. In fact, so commercially reliable is Meunier for Champagne's powerful vine-growers that until recently it was Champagne's most popular variety by far, but has now been overtaken by Pinot Noir. Common wisdom has it that, as an ingredient in the traditional three-variety champagne blend, Meunier contributes youthful fruitiness to complement Pinot Noir's weight and Chardonnay's finesse. Few producers boast of their Pinot Meunier, however (with the honourable exception of KRUG), although several Champagne growers make a VARIETAL Pinot Meunier, which is generally lower in pigments than Pinot Noir.

It has largely disappeared elsewhere in northern France although it is still technically allowed into the rosés and light reds of Côtes de TOUL, wines of MOSELLE, and, in the Loire, TOURAINE, and ORLÉANS.

As Müllerrebe or Schwarzriesling, a selection of Meunier is relatively popular in Germany, where the majority of its 2,162 ha/5,340 acres are in WÜRTTEMBERG where it is a local speciality. It is also grown in German-speaking SWITZERLAND, and to a much lesser extent in Austria. Elsewhere, Meunier tends to be grown by those slavishly following the champagne recipe (as in England and California, for example). But curiously, in Australia Pinot Meunier has a longer documented history as a still red varietal wine (at one time called Miller's Burgundy) than Pinot Noir, notably at Great Western (now called GRAMPIANS) in VICTORIA.

Pinot Nero is Italian for PINOT NOIR which is grown there chiefly for the SPUMANTE industry. There was a total of 5,046 ha/12,470 acres according to the 2010 vine census. The great majority is planted in the province of Pavia in LOMBARDY, but a few producers—Hofstatter, Haas, and Gottardi—are making a name for the variety in Alto Adige. Only 388 ha were grown in Brescia, the FRANCIACORTA zone, while plantings in TRENTINO-ALTO ADIGE totalled 595 ha, presumably reflecting the growing TRENTODOC spumante industry.

Pinot Noir is the most important and oldest form of PINOT. It is the grape variety wholly responsible for red BURGUNDY and one that suddenly became the height of FASHION, thanks to the 2004 film SIDEWAYS. It gives its name to the NOIRIEN family of grape varieties. Unlike Cabernet Sauvignon, which can be grown in all but the coolest conditions and can be economically viable as an inexpensive but recognizably Cabernet wine, Pinot Noir demands much of both vine-grower and winemaker (see CLIMATE AND WINE QUALITY, for example). It is a tribute to the unparalleled level of physical excitement generated by tasting one of Burgundy's better reds that such a high proportion of the world's most ambitious wine producers want to try their hand with this capricious and extremely variable vine. Although there is relatively little

consistency in its performance in its homeland, Pinot Noir has been transplanted to almost every one of the world's wine regions, except the very hottest, where it can so easily turn from essence to jam.

If Cabernet produces wines to appeal to the head, Pinot's charms are decidedly more sensual and more transparent. The Burgundians themselves refute the allegation that they produce Pinot Noir; they merely use Pinot Noir as the vehicle for communicating local geography, the characteristics of the individual site, the TERROIR on which it was planted. Perhaps the only characteristics that the Pinot Noirs of the world could be said to share would be a certain sweet fruitiness and, in general, lower levels of tannins and pigments than the other 'great' French red varieties Cabernet Sauvignon and Syrah. The wines are decidedly more charming in youth and evolve more rapidly, although the decline of the very best is slow.

Galet noted in 2000 that no fewer than 50 Pinot Noir clones (as opposed to 25 of the much more widely planted Cabernet Sauvignon) are officially recognized within France, with the most popular being one of first generation of virus-free Burgundy clones 115, followed by the productive Champagne clones 375 and 386. Marsh surveyed top Côte d'Or producers in the early 2000s and found second generation clone 677 marginally more admired for wine quality than the more widely planted 777 or 828. It is possible to choose a clone of Pinot Noir specially for the quality of its wine, its productivity, regularity of yield, resistance to rot, and/or for its likely ripeness (which can vary considerably). A major factor in the lighter colour and extract of so much red burgundy in the 1970s and 1980s was injudicious CLONAL SELECTION, resulting in higher yields but much less character and concentration in the final wine. The most reputable producers of all tend nowadays to have made MASS SELECTIONS from their own vine population. The clone called Pommard is well distributed in the New World, especially in North America, as has been one named after the WÄDENSWIL viticultural station in Switzerland. Often more sought-after now are Burgundian, 'Dijon', or in Australia 'Bernard' clones. In general the most productive clones, which have large-berried bunches, are described as Pinot Droit for the vines' upright growth, while Pinot Fin, Pinot Tordu, or Pinot Classique grows much less regularly but has smaller berries with thicker skin.

In as much as generalizations about a vine variety with so many different forms are possible, Pinot Noir tends to bud early, making it susceptible to spring FROST and COULURE. Damp, cool soils on low-lying land are therefore best avoided. Yields are theoretically low, although too many Burgundians disproved this with productive clones in the 1970s and early 1980s. The

vine is also more prone than most to both sorts of mildew, rot (grape skins tend to be thinner than most), and to viruses, particularly FANLEAF and LEAFROLL. Indeed it was the prevalence of disease in Burgundian vineyards that precipitated the widespread adoption of clonal selection there in the 1970s.

Pinot Noir generally produces the best-quality wine on CALCAREOUS soils and in relatively cool climates where this early-ripening vine will not rush towards maturity, losing aroma and acidity. In Burgundy, for example, where it is typically cultivated alongside the equally early-ripening Chardonnay, Pinot Noir may ripen after Chardonnay in some years, before it in others. There is general agreement, however, that Pinot Noir is very much more difficult to vinify than Chardonnay, needing constant monitoring and fine tuning of technique according to the demands of each particular vintage.

Pinot Noir is planted throughout eastern France and has been steadily gaining ground from less noble varieties so that by 2011 its total area of French vineyard was 31,323 ha/77,368 acres, up from 22,000 ha in 1988, and finally overtaking the area planted with Greater Burgundy's other red vine variety, the GAMAY of Beaujolais.

The extension of the CHAMPAGNE region from the 1980s saw Champagne's area planted with the variety, more than 13,000 ha in 2013, overtake that of Burgundy which grew just over 10,000 ha. Pinot Noir is also the principal red wine grape of ALSACE, JURA, SAVOIE, SANCERRE, MENETOU-SALON, and ST-POURÇAIN—and recent global demand for the variety has encouraged some planting in the Languedoc, even if few corners are as suitably cool as LIMOUX. Even in the Greater Burgundy region, Pinot Noir is rarely blended with any other variety, except occasionally with Gamay in a BOURGOGNE PASSE-TOUTGRAINS and, increasingly, to add class to a MÂCON. See under individual appellation names specified for the CÔTE D'OR and Côte CHALONNAISE for more detail on individual wines. Pinot Noir is the favoured black grape variety in northern Burgundy too where in 2011 there were 854 ha for such wines as IRANCY and particularly northern versions of BOURGOGNE. A tiny amount is cultivated even further north east for the light reds and VIN GRIS of Lorraine such as Côtes de TOUL and the wines of MOSELLE.

The greatest increase in Pinot plantings in Europe has been in Champagne, where it is used, as it is in the production of a wide range of sparkling wines made around the world in champagne's image, as a still, very pale pink ingredient in the base blend of still wines. The grapes are pressed very gently and any remaining pigments tend to agglomerate with the dead yeast cells during the champenization process.

In such a blend, Pinot Noir is prized for its body and longevity, as well it might be for that small proportion of champagne made exclusively from Pinot Noir is usually memorably substantial. In Champagne, only a tiny quantity of Pinot Noir is used for still red Coteaux CHAMPENOIS and ROSÉ DES RICEYS.

Pinot Noir has become increasingly well made, and desirable, in all areas where German is or was spoken. In Alsace, where it has been an important vine since the early 16th century (see GERMAN HISTORY), it is effectively the only black-berried vine variety planted, with a total area of more than 1,600 ha in 2011. Thanks to CLIMATE CHANGE, Alsace Pinot Noir has been getting darker and the wines much more substantial. The same phenomenon is even more marked in Germany where the variety, often but not always calls Spätburgunder, was the country's third most planted variety in 2012, only just behind the waning MÜLLER-THURGAU. See SPÄTBURGUNDER for more details.

So popular has the variety become in Switzerland that it is now the country's most planted, with more than 4,300 ha in 2012, even more than the area planted with Chasselas. Graubünden has a particularly strong reputation for its sturdy Pinots. In Austria, Pinot Noir is also sometimes called Blauburgunder but is not nearly as popular as BLAUFRÄNKISCH and ST-LAURENT.

Pinot Noir is spread widely, if not in great quantity, in the vineyards of eastern Europe, where its name is usually some variant on the local word for Burgundian (although Romania's Burgund Mare is Blaufränkisch). Moldova has most, more than 6,000 ha, but there are also several hundred hectares in each of Hungary, Romania, Ukraine, Russia, and Croatia. Elsewhere in Europe, the finicky nature of the Pinot Noir vine has set a natural limit on its spread. In Iberia, there has been some successful experimentation in SOMONTANO, and substantial plantings for CAVA in Spanish CATALUÑA where plantings surpassed 1,000 ha by 2012. Portugal grew just 300 ha in 2012, mainly in the north. There have been some noble experiments in some cooler Italian wine regions, notably LOMBARDY, where it is used for sparkling wine production. See more details under PINOT NERO.

It was wine producers in the New World, however, who turned the full heat of their ambitious attentions on Pinot Noir from the late 1980s and early 1990s. Some even relocated their wineries many hundreds of miles in order to be closer to sources of suitably cool climate Pinot Noir fruit. OREGON's wine reputation has so far rested almost entirely on its fine, fruity Pinot Noirs, although the state total had fallen to 12,560 acres/5,085 ha, well over 60% of the total vineyard area. Although for many years this Pacific Northwestern state, with its often miserably cool, wet climate, was popularly supposed to provide America's answer to red

burgundy, a number of fine Pinot Noirs has emerged from CALIFORNIA to redefine the more southerly state's reputation for Pinot, especially but not exclusively in regions such as the cooler reaches of the Sonoma Coast, Carneros, Chalone, the Gavilan mountains of San Benito, and, especially, Central Coast districts most affected by the Pacific. The state's total acreage remained steady into the 1990s but then took off after the SIDEWAYS effect so that by 2012 there were almost 40,000 acres/18,600 ha of Pinot Noir in the state (up from barely 24,000 acres when *Sideways* was made. The variety is also valued as an ingredient in champagne-like sparkling wines, one of Pinot Noir's most important uses in the New World.

(The variety once called **Pinot St George** in California, now in sharp decline, is NÉGRETTE.) There are pockets of Pinot Noir, generally accompanied by enthusiasm and ambition, all over the United States, but cool climates such as that of the FINGER LAKES are generally best. And over the Canadian border in ONTARIO with its more than 1,000 acres and BRITISH COLUMBIA with almost as much, there are some seriously successful Pinot Noirs. CLIMATE CHANGE has helped eastern Canada's Pinot producers considerably.

Much of South America is too hot for successful Pinot Noir production but newer, Pacific-cooled wine regions are being developed for the variety in CHILE where total planting had almost reached 4,000 ha by 2012. B'io B'io also shows promise. It can be more difficult to find suitably cool terrain in Argentina but plantings totalled 1,800 ha in 2012, mainly at the highest elevations of Tupungato.

Across the Atlantic in SOUTH AFRICA, on the other hand, at least one producer, Hamilton-Russell, managed to coax convincingly Burgundian flavours from Pinot Noir vines grown in the hinterland of WALKER BAY on the south coast many years ago and this continues to act as a spur to others, with increasingly encouraging results. Total plantings had reached 1,000 ha by 2012—a figure that would have been unthinkable at the turn of the century.

New Zealand, along with Oregon, is the New World wine producer that has been staking its red wine fortunes on Pinot Noir. By 2012 total plantings were more than 5,000 ha, making it this small country's second most popular variety by far, with the most impressive results coming from Martinborough, Canterbury, Marlborough, and rapidly growing Central Otago. See NEW ZEALAND for more details.

Fine Pinot Noir has been more elusive in Australia, and the total area planted was slightly less than New Zealand's in 2012, but increasingly interesting examples are being made in cooler spots such as Geelong, Gippsland, Macedon Ranges, Yarra Valley, and Mornington Peninsula, all relatively cool areas around

Melbourne in Victoria, as well as Tasmania. See AUSTRALIA for more details and more potential areas of exciting Pinot Noir production.

Wherever there is a wine producer with a palate, there will be experimentation with Pinot Noir.

Galet, P., *Dictionnaire encyclopédique des cépages* (Paris, 2000).

Marsh, S. A., 'The contribution of Pinot Noir clones to the vineyards of the Côte d'Or. An evaluation focusing on clones 114, 115, 667, 777' (MW dissertation, London, 2004).

Robinson, J., Harding, J., and Vouillamoz, J., *Wine Grapes, a complete guide to 1,368 vine varieties, including their origins and flavours* (London, 2012).

Pinot Noir Précoce, French name for FRÜHBURGUNDER.

Pinot St George, California red grape identified as NÉGRETTE and now difficult to find.

pipe, wine trade term, adapted from the Portuguese *pipa* meaning 'barrel', for a large cask with tapered ends, the traditional measure of PORT as well as of MADEIRA, other Portuguese wines, and MARSALA, although the volume can vary around the country. In the DOURO Valley, where port is produced, the yield of each vineyard is measured in pipes of 550 l/145 gal, while downstream in VILA NOVA DE GAIA, the suburb of Oporto where port is matured, a pipe may vary in size between 580 and 630 l, but is usually taken as 620 l. For shipping purposes, however, a pipe of port is 534.24 l, divided into 21 measures of 25.44 l called *almudes*, while pipes of madeira and Marsala are 418 and 423 l respectively. Gentlemen in Victorian England traditionally laid down a pipe of port for their sons and godsons, but inflation and changing consumption patterns have made this generosity exceptional.

Pipers Brook, unofficial but generally recognized wine region in TASMANIA.

pips. See grape SEEDS.

Piquepoul, ancient grape variety from the Vaucluse *département* of southern France that is encountered in Blanc, Noir, and very occasionally Gris versions, with the white being the most planted today, although they have frequently been mixed in the vineyard in their long history in the LANGUEDOC-ROUSSILLON. Piquepoul meaning 'lip-stinger', possibly signifying the high acidity of its must, was cited as a producer of good-quality wine as early as the beginning of the 17th century and, with CLAIRETTE, formed the basis of PICARDAN, exported northwards in vast quantities in the 17th and 18th centuries. Its susceptibility to FUNGAL DISEASES, however, together with its unremarkable yield, reduced its popularity considerably after PHYLLOXERA arrived. In the early

20th century, the variety's good tolerance of sand made it a popular choice for the coastal vineyards that serviced the then flourishing VERMOUTH industry. Today many of those vineyards are tourist campsites and vermouth is an Italian phenomenon but PICPOUL DE PINET has been a significant commercial success and France's total plantings of Piquepoul Blanc in 2011 were more than 1,500 ha/3,705 acres, virtually all in the Hérault. A small amount is also grown in California.

Piquepoul Noir produces alcoholic, richly scented, but very pale red that is best drunk young. Although it is allowed as a minor ingredient in CHÂTEAUNEUF-DU-PAPE and LANGUEDOC, it is rarely seen.

piquette, thin, vinous liquid made by adding water to the grape POMACE. Throughout history, from the time of classical GREECE and ROME to the mid 20th century, it has been given to slaves or low-paid workers. (See ancient PRESSES for details of *lorca*, the Roman version.) In the early 21st century, with its wine SURPLUS, LABOUR shortage, and concentration on quality, few employers would dare to offer even the most lowly worker such a drink.

Piros Szlanka. See PAMID.

Pirque, part of the MAIPO subregion of the Central Valley of CHILE.

pisco, aromatic brandy made in Peru and Chile, mainly from Moscatel (MUSCAT) grapes, rather like Bolivia's singani.

Pla de Bages, small but growing CATALAN wine region north west of Barcelona in Spain with just over 550 ha/1,300 acres under vine. Grape varieties are similar to those in neighbouring PENEDÈS, with INTERNATIONAL VARIETIES such as Merlot and Cabernet Sauvignon planted enthusiastically during the 1990s.   V. de la S.

Pla i Llevant, small (335 ha/800 acres) but thriving DO on the Spanish island of MALLORCA.

Planalto Mirandês, subregion of TRÁS-OS-MONTES in north-east Portugal.

plank, term used occasionally for STAVES when they are used to add OAK FLAVOUR to wine, hence plank in a tank.

Planta Fina or **Planta Fina de Pedralba**, grown in Valencia, south east Spain, to make fairly neutral whites. DNA PROFILING has shown that it is not, as has been suggested, identical to VERDEJO but is in fact the Damschino of Sicily and Alicante Branco of Portugal and Madeira.

Planta Nova, another undistinguished white Spanish grape variety planted on about 1,000 ha around Valencia.

plant cell density (PCD) is the most commonly used REMOTELY SENSED indicator of vine VIGOUR or canopy size in Australian viticulture. Like NDVI, it is calculated from measures of reflected light at wavebands corresponding to red and infrared light.
R.G.V.B.

Plantet, 5455 SEIBEL, once the Loire's most popular FRENCH HYBRID, has been more successfully eradicated from the French vinescape than some others (see BACO, COUDERC, VILLARD). France had 26,000 ha/63,000 acres planted in 1968 but under 1,000 ha by 2011. Its chief attributes are its productivity and its ability to crop regardless of the severity of the winter and spring frosts (although New York state winters have proved too harsh for it). Varietal versions are occasionally encountered and taste oddly of raspberries.

planting a vineyard ostensibly constitutes that vineyard's birth, but this viticultural operation can be undertaken only after a wide range of decisions have been taken. The potentially long process of VINEYARD SITE SELECTION is followed by SOIL PREPARATION and the choice of CLONES of both VINE VARIETY and ROOTSTOCK. Decisions must also be made about VINE DENSITY. Following delivery from the NURSERY, the young plants must be prevented from drying out before they are finally planted.

The planting operation is normally carried out in winter or spring. It consists of simply digging a small hole sufficient to take the normal dormant ROOTLING, or occasionally a CUTTING or, increasingly frequently, a growing plant. The hole can be dug by spade or post hole auger, but care must be taken, particularly in heavy clay soils, that holes dug by machine do not have such dense sides that roots cannot grow through them. In dry conditions, a high-pressure water jet can help to create a planting hole and at the same time provide moisture to assist early growth. For large estates, a planting machine adapted from forestry can be mounted behind a tractor to allow workers to put plants into a pre-formed furrow which is then filled in as the machine passes.

A cardinal rule of establishing grapevines, as for other plants, is to press the soil firmly in around the newly planted vine to avoid air pockets. Dry soil conditions around the roots of the young plant should be avoided.   R.E.S.

planting density. See VINE DENSITY.

planting rights became important when an EU scheme, in force since 1976, restricted the planting of new vineyards in member states. It was part of a group of control measures aimed at reducing the wine SURPLUS within the EU. The 2008 reform of the common market organization for wine (see EU) announced that the scheme would end in 2015 (or, exceptionally, with a transitional period until 2018), raising objections from the majority of wine-producing member states that this would lead to a free-for-all. This opposition led to the creation of a new system of 'authorizations to plant vines' which will be managed by national, sometimes regional, authorities and will regulate vineyard plantings not only for PDO and PGI wines but also, more controversially, for WINE WITHOUT GEOGRAPHICAL INDICATION. The annual maximum percentage growth in vineyard area is fixed at 1%.

plastic bottles, form of PACKAGING, usually from the material known to professionals as PET, an abbreviation for polyethylene terephthalate. They have the advantage of being generally much lighter, cheaper, and less breakable than glass BOTTLES, but the disadvantage that, depending on what they are lined with, they are not inert. Wine can start to taste of the package itself after only a few months.

plastic corks, a widely used but inaccurate term for SYNTHETIC CLOSURES.

plastic sheeting can be used in the vineyard to modify the climate. Studies in Canada and the UK have shown that transparent sheets suspended either side of the fruit zone will raise temperatures and protect the vine from wind, advancing vine development, which is helpful in cool climates. It has also been used experimentally on the ground in some vineyards to protect the vines from rain towards the end of the ripening period, thus allowing grapes to ripen fully but keeping vegetative growth to a minimum. However, when Michel ROLLAND first trialled this method in 1999 in Fronsac, the French regulatory body INAO judged it to be a modification of the soil and the wine had to be sold as a VIN DE TABLE. Plastic sheeting or patches can be used to keep weeds down and retain soil moisture around young plants (see MULCH). It can also be used on vines to protect grapes destined for EISWEIN from birds and rain.
R.E.S. & J.E.H.

Plavac Mali, grape variety with an interesting genetic history producing dense red wines all along the Dalmatian coast and on many of the Adriatic islands in CROATIA. Mali means 'small' and a white grape variety called simply **Plavac Žuti**, also **Plavec Žuti**, is also known, and results in tart, light wines. Both varieties thrive on sandy soil. Plavac Mali is Croatia's leading red wine grape and produces wines high in tannins, alcohol, colour, and ageability. Postup and Dingač are two of the better-known reds made from Plavac Mali. DNA PROFILING at DAVIS provided evidence that Plavac Mali, once suspected of being identical to ZINFANDEL, is a natural cross between it and Dobričić, an

P

obscure and ancient southern Croatian variety red wine grape.

Plavina, grape variety making light reds on the Dalmatian coast in CROATIA which may also be called Brajdica. DNA PROFILING has shown that it is a cross of VERDECA cultivated in Puglia and Croatia's ZINFANDEL.

Pliny (AD 23/4–79). Gaius Plinius Secundus is known in English as 'Pliny the Elder' to distinguish him from his nephew, also a man of letters and Pliny the Elder's adoptive son. Of Pliny the Elder's many works, the only one to survive is the *Natural History*, 37 books, dedicated to the Emperor Titus and published posthumously. Book 14 is devoted exclusively to wine, while Book 17 provides important information on the techniques of viticulture, and the beginning of Book 23 is devoted to the medicinal properties of wine (see MEDICINE). Although most of the *Natural History* is based on earlier authors rather than on scientific observation, and his information, invaluable as much of it is, must be used with discrimination, the fourteenth book, on wine, seems in large part to be the product of independent enquiry. It contains practical advice as well as literary and historical learning. Its most interesting part ranks Italian wines according to quality, and sweet wines seem to be favoured (although see also ATHENAEUS). The best wine used to be CAECUBAN, but in Pliny's day it is FALERNIAN, particularly Falernian of the Faustian CLOS. Setine is also a wine of the first rank. The next best wines are Alban, SURRENTINE, and MASSIC; Pliny awards third prize to Mamertine, of Messina in Sicily. An early proponent of TERROIR, he concludes that it is the country and the soil that determine quality, and not the vine variety; in any case, people's tastes differ. Pliny died during the eruption of Vesuvius when his extraordinary curiosity got the better of his common sense. In his much-quoted writings on wine, he drew on VARRO's *De re rustica*; PALLADIUS' treatise on husbandry is indebted to Pliny. H.M.W. & J.J.P.

André, J., *Pline l'Ancien: histoire naturelle, livre XIV* (Paris, 1958).

Beagon, M., *Roman Nature: The Thought of Pliny the Elder* (Oxford, 1992).

Pliny the Elder, *Natural History*, trans. by H. Rackham (London, 1945).

plonk, vague and derogatory English term for wine of undistinguished quality, is a term of Australian slang that has been naturalized in Britain. During the First World War, the French *vin blanc* with its un-English nasal vowels was adapted in various fantastic ways, from 'von Blink', which sounded like a German officer, to 'plinketty plonk', which suggested the twanging of a banjo. This was shortened to 'plonk', which coincidentally was also British soldiers' slang for 'mud'. By the Second World War this had given rise to 'A/C Plonk' for aircraftman 2nd class, the lowest of the low in the RAF and hence parallel to plonk in the glass.

Despite its etymology, plonk need not be white; and if the word suggests any kind of wine in particular it is cheap red served at a party. For this reason, colour-blind theories have sometimes been proposed, such as that it mimics the sound of a cork being withdrawn from a bottle. But it has no more to do with this sound than with the unceremonious plonking down of glass. L.H.-S.

ploughing. See CULTIVATION and LABOUR.

Ploussard. See POULSARD.

Plumpton in Sussex offers a variety of land-based courses and has been the leading centre of wine ACADEME in the UK since 1988, offering a wide range of WSET courses but also degree courses. Plumpton is the only European provider of undergraduate courses in wine production and wine business in English. With 8 ha/20 acres of its own commercial vineyards, Plumpton works closely with the ENGLISH WINE INDUSTRY. Its Rathfinny research centre, sponsored by a large local English wine producer, was opened in 2014, the same year that the UK's first MSc course in VITICULTURE and OENOLOGY was introduced.

www.plumpton.ac.uk

podere, Italian for a farm, usually smaller than a FATTORIA and usually a subdivision of a fattoria. The word stems from *potere*, meaning 'to be able to' and indicating that the size of the holding was sufficient for one sharecropping family.

points out of 100, common method of SCORING wine promoted notably by American writer Robert PARKER. See also NUMBERS.

Pokdum, Thai name for the dark-skinned Japanese hybrid Black Queen. It was propagated by grower Nong Pok in the Pak Chong area of Nakhon Ratchasima province in the early 1980s and now accounts for almost 10% of THAILAND's vines.

Poland. Although winemaking dates back to the introduction of CHRISTIANITY to Poland in 966 AD, it had all but died out by the end of the 15th century as beer and vodka became more popular and the climate became cooler. Vineyards persisted in Silesia (Śląsk), which was at that time German, and particularly, right up to the Second World War, around Zielona Góra (Grünberg). This was the region from which so many Silesians fled religious persecution and emigrated to BAROSSA in Australia. Nevertheless, modern Poland has hundreds of villages and cities whose names include some wine connection such as *winnica, winiary, winogrady* (vineyard), or even *moszcz* (most).

The modern Polish winemaking era started in the 1980s when the mountain climber Roman Myśliwiec planted his first vines by his home in Jasło (Podkarpacie), then importing cuttings from Ukraine, Hungary, the former Czechoslovakia, and Germany. He finally established his own vine nursery, in which he eventually developed his own white CROSS Jutrzenka (Sunrise or Morning Star), which is very popular now for sweet and FORTIFIED WINES. He became the first Polish wine CONSULTANT for many new growers. Anieszka Wyrobek-Rousseau was the first Polish FLYING WINEMAKER and worked in France, New Zealand, Australia, and even in Russia.

The most important grape varieties are RONDO and REGENT for reds, and SOLARIS, Hibernal, SEYVAL BLANC, Bianca, and Johanniter for whites, but Pinots, Chardonnay, and other VINIFERA varieties are also easy to find, as well as some other cold-hardy American crosses (LÉON MILLOT, MARQUETTE, FRONTENAC, and Prairie Star).

The five unofficial wine regions are Lubuskie (around Zielona Góra), Dolny Śląsk, Małopolska, Podkarpacie, and Małopolski Przełom Wisły but many prefer to use the official political names of districts or provinces. Poland's total vineyard area in 2014 was almost 1,000 ha/2,470 acres, but about half of these are small, hobby plantings since there are almost 1,000 producers. The total area of vines planted for official commercial purposes had not quite reached 150 ha, with official, legal production of around 65,000 bottles a year, expected to rise swiftly. The biggest producers are Jaworek (Dolny Śląsk, 22.8 ha), Srebrna Góra (Cracow, 12 ha), Dębogóra (Lubuskie, 8 ha), and Pałac Mierzęcin (Lubuskie, 6.7 ha). W.G.

politics and wine. While winemaking and TERROIR affect how wines taste in the glass, politics determines how and which wines make it to consumers. The relations that wine producers have with the state and with each other vary across winemaking and wine-consuming countries. This variation affects the quality, price, export profile, and availability of wine to consumers.

In France, where grapevines predated Roman times, wine and the state have had as cosy a relationship as the vines and the terroir. Indeed, the Church and aristocrats, key political allies of the monarchy, held many vineyards in feudal times and it was Emperor Napoleon III who commissioned the famous 1855 CLASSIFICATION of the wines of Bordeaux. Crisis struck in the late 19th century as the PHYLLOXERA louse devastated large swathes of vineyards, threatening the voluminous tax receipts from wine and the livelihood of a large number of citizens engaged in its production. The state came to the aid of the growers by organizing a major campaign to pool scientific knowledge and treatments and, eventually, tamed the pest.

With the resolution of the phylloxera blight, some regions developed an addiction to state aid that took decades to break, if it ever was broken. The wine boom that preceded phylloxera, the subsequent bust, and an early-20th-century boom so devastated producers of low-end TABLE WINES that they convinced the state to guarantee them a minimum price. But the market fluctuations led to other problems for better quality producers, notably ADULTERATION AND FRAUD. Underscoring the importance of wine in France, the strong French state delegated the power to set quality standards for superior producers through the formalization of the APPELLATION CONTRÔLÉE system in 1935. This system continues to this day with an ever-increasing number of qualifying regions. However, the tight historic relationship between French wine producers and the state appears to be weakening as opposition to wine has emerged under the aegis of public health with strict drink-driving and advertising restrictions. Domestic consumption has declined markedly (see Appendix 2C).

The politics of wine in the UNITED STATES could not be more different. Despite the best early personal and policy intentions of King James I during the colonial period and of Thomas JEFFERSON during the republic, the land proved inhospitable to vines suitable for winemaking until the mid 19th century in California. Even international recognition of some of California's best wines in the 1890s was not enough to propel the industry to success since wine fell victim to political shifts hostile to the industry.

The temperance movement was consolidating as a political force. So abhorrent was its view of any type of alcohol and so strong were its supporters that they succeeded in officially banning alcohol throughout the country for 13 years under PROHIBITION. Although no policy enshrined in the Constitution has ever been so quickly repealed, the damage to the wine industry was severe. During Prohibition, vineyard acreage paradoxically expanded through a loophole that permitted HOME WINEMAKING. Yet the quality of the vines plummeted to such an extent that it took the California wine industry three decades to recover.

An even longer lasting effect was that at Repeal in 1933, the states were left to regulate the distribution and sale of alcohol within their boundaries. This has left a patchwork of laws and a system that often prohibits wineries and retailers from selling directly to consumers (online for example) since most states mandate the intervention of a distributor, which can raise prices to consumers and limit choice (see THREE-TIER SYSTEM). Ironically, in a country that prides itself on free markets, the wine industry is arguably even more heavily regulated than that of France.

AUSTRALIA's industry growth and nearly three decades of surging exports (see AUSTRALIAN INFLUENCE) lay in part in overcoming a problem of collective action. With a small domestic market and tremendous productive potential, industry participants realized the importance of export markets. In the 1970s and accelerating in the 1980s, the industry participants and the state coordinated an upgrading of the country's international reputation through setting standards for export and initiating successful marketing campaigns. The relatively low number of producing, or at least exporting, firms made this coordination easier. The Australian example served as a model for other countries, although a reversal of fortunes for Australian wine from the late 2000s has demonstrated limits to this approach.

Changes in the national political regime can revolutionize the wine industry, as the example of SOUTH AFRICA vividly demonstrates. With the collapse of the apartheid regime in 1994, South Africa's international isolation ended as the numerous countries that had trade embargoes in place lifted them. Practically overnight, the number of outlets for South African wines expanded exponentially. Investment flowed in and increasingly high-quality wines flowed out to the rest of the world. A similar political opening has also made for a global market in the wines from Central and Eastern Europe, although their export potential has not yet reached the levels of South Africa.

A policy volte face can also lead to significant change: the HONG KONG government slashed import duties from 80% by value to zero in 2008, igniting the local wine trade, and propelling Hong Kong to the top spot in the global AUCTION market for wine.

Because wine is an important product in world trade, international politics play a role in structuring the wine. Certainly wine policy is most advanced at the international level within the EU, which now has the final say on many wine regulations and subsidies in the region and often negotiates the laws of the World Trade Organization for European producers. The EU has also been particularly vigilant in protecting its place names, or GEOGRAPHICAL INDICATIONS. And because of its highly symbolic value, wine, particularly French wine, has been the target of tariffs or, at the grassroots level, demonstrations, punitive tariffs, and boycotts.

Future political struggles in the wine world will almost certainly also provide support for the adage 'all politics is local'. The issues of environmental responsibility, SUSTAINABLE VITICULTURE, and land use have recently appeared on the agendas of wine-growing communities from Napa to Bordeaux and are likely to remain there for the foreseeable future.   T.C.

Colman, T., *Wine Politics* (Berkeley, 2008).

Pinney, T., *Wine in America*, vols 1 & 2 (Berkeley, 2007).

Yoon, S., and Lam, T.-H., 'The alcohol industry lobby and Hong Kong's Zero Wine and Beer Tax Policy', *BMC Public Health*, 12 (2012).

pollen, collective term for pollen grains which carry the male gametes in SEXUAL propagation for the vines as for other plants. Pollen develops within sacs of the ANTHER. Mature grains have a sculptured surface typical for each species. See FLOWERING. See also vineyard ECOSYSTEM.   B.G.C.

Pollera Nera, ancient dark-berried vine planted in 2010 on just over 50 ha/120 acres in Liguria and north-west Tuscany.

pollination, the transfer of pollen from the ANTHER to the receptive stigmatic surface. If pollination occurs with the pollen and pistil of the same flower, the process is called self-pollination and the progeny is known as a SELFLING or selfed vine; if it occurs between two different flowers (whether from the same vine or from different vines), the process is called cross-pollination. In cultivated grapevines, flowers are hermaphroditic and most are self-pollinated before the CALYPTRA has fallen (cleistogamy), but cross-pollination may also occur. Fertilization occurs two or three days after pollination depending on the ambient temperature (see FLOWERING). Wild grapes (*Vitis silvestris*) and some primitive cultivars are dioecious (male-only or female-only plants), therefore cross-pollination is essential.   B.G.C. & J.V.

See also POLLEN.

Vasconcelos, M. C., et al., 'The flowering process of *Vitis vinifera*: a review', *American Journal of Enology and Viticulture*, 60/4 (2009), 411–34.

pollution. Air pollution can damage grapevines in many parts of the world. Air pollutants arise from industrial gases and particles, exhaust gases including LEAD, AGROCHEMICALS, and fires. Principal pollutants are hydrogen fluoride, sulfur dioxide, OZONE, and SMOKE, and in restricted areas phenoxy herbicides such as 2,4-D (see AUXINS) applied to nearby crops. Hydrogen fluoride has reduced vineyard yields in many countries. While the leaves can accumulate high levels of fluoride, it is not translocated to the fruit. Mourvèdre is particularly sensitive to this type of pollution, while Carignan is tolerant. A reported EUCALYPTUS CHARACTER of wine is sometimes blamed on such trees near the vineyard.

Controls on wineries to reduce environmental pollution as a result of their operations are increasing. See WINERY WASTE.   R.E.S.

Pearson, R. C., and Goheen, A. C. (eds.), *Compendium of Grape Diseases* (St Paul, Minn., 1988).

Pol Roger, Champagne house founded in Épernay in 1849 and still in family hands. The founder's sons changed their surnames to Pol-Roger by deed poll, Pol being a champenois variant of Paul. The wines rank high among the top champagne houses for quality, although it is one of the smaller GRANDES MARQUES. Pol Roger owns 91 ha/224 acres of vineyards on prime sites in the Vallée d'Épernay and on the Côte des Blancs and latterly on the Montagne de Reims. Particularly deep cellars house nine million bottles, representing five years' supply. Sir Winston Churchill was a devotee of the house, even naming his racehorse Pol Roger. The compliment was repaid after his death, when all non-vintage labels exported to Britain were edged in black for 37 years. The Sir Winston Churchill Cuvée was launched in 1984 as Pol Roger's PRESTIGE CUVÉE. The great-grandsons of the original Pol Roger, Christian Pol-Roger and Christian de Billy were succeeded by the son of the latter, Hubert de Billy.   S.E.A.

polymeric pigments. See PIGMENTED TANNINS.

polymerization, the molecular process in which smaller molecules combine to form very large molecules. In all living material, the simple amino acids combine, or **polymerize**, in very large chains to create the PROTEINS, some of which function as ENZYMES. In AGEING wines, simpler PHENOLIC molecules combine to form larger TANNIN **polymers** and PIGMENTED TANNINS which eventually grow so large that they fall from the solution as SEDIMENT.   A.D.W.

polyphenols and **polyphenolics**. See PHENOLICS.

polysaccharides, a diverse group of carbohydrates found in all wines and distinguished by their high molecular weight. They can be grouped into three categories according to their origin: from YEAST (MANNOPROTEINS), grape (e.g. PECTINS), and fungi (notably glucans from *Botrytis cinerea*, see BOTRYTIZED wines). Their presence inhibits the formation of undesirable PROTEIN hazes and TARTRATE crystallization. Their ability to interact with wine TANNINS may also influence the perception of ASTRINGENCY and other aspects of MOUTHFEEL in both red and white wine.   R.G.

Le Bourellec, C., and Renard, C. M. G. C., 'Interactions between polyphenols and macromolecules: Quantification methods and mechanisms', *Critical Reviews in Food Science and Nutrition*, 52 (2012), 213–48.

polyvinylpolypyrrolidone. See PVPP.

pomace, a word used for centuries by English cider-makers (it comes from the Latin *pomum* meaning 'apple') meaning the debris of fruit processing. In WHITE WINEMAKING, the pomace is the sweet, pale brownish-green mass of grape skins, stems, seeds, and pulp left after PRESSING. In RED WINEMAKING, the pomace is a similar mass of grape debris coloured blackish red left after the FREE-RUN wine has been drained. Because red wine pomace is what is left after FERMENTATION rather than before, it also includes dead yeast cells and contains traces of alcohol rather than sugar.

In larger wineries, the significant amount of sugar which remains in white grape pomace may be washed out of the solid mixture and fermented to produce material for DISTILLATION into pomace brandy. Similarly, the smaller amounts of alcohol in red grape pomace may in large wineries be recovered by distillation. OENOCYANIN, a food colouring agent, is also recovered from red wine pomace, particularly in Italy. In some regions the solids from several wineries may be amalgamated for processing to recover TARTRATES and, occasionally, grapeseed oil.

The French call both pomace that has been drained dry and pomace brandy MARC. Some English speakers called this dry pomace the **press cake**.

In recent research by Goupil et al. in Clermont-Ferrand, France, powdered marc extract from dark-skinned grape varieties was shown to act like a vaccine and elicit natural plant defence mechanisms in tobacco plants. It is hoped that this could contribute to a reduction in PESTICIDE use and more SUSTAINABLE farming practices as well as offering a commercial use for a waste product.   A.D.W.

Goupil, P., et al., 'Grape marc extract acts as elicitor of plant defence responses', *Ecotoxicology*, 21 (2012), 1541–9. doi: 10.1007/s10646-012-0908-1.

Pomerol, small but distinctive wine region in Bordeaux producing opulent and glamorous red wines dominated by the Merlot grape. Although challenged by their counterparts in its much larger neighbour ST-ÉMILION, Pomerol's most successful wines are some of the world's most sought after, but the glamour attaches to the labels rather than the countryside.

Pomerol is produced from a steady 800 ha/ 2,000 acres of vineyard on a plateau immediately north east of LIBOURNE that is as geographically unremarkable as the MÉDOC, but without even any buildings or historical landmarks of note. A confusing network of narrow lanes connects about 150 smallholdings, most of which produce only a few thousand cases of wine a year in one of the world's most monocultural landscapes.

Vines were intermittently grown on this inhospitable, unfertile land from Roman times, but viticulture was abandoned during the HUNDRED YEARS WAR and the vineyards not re-established until the 15th and 16th centuries. For hundreds of years afterwards, Pomerol was regarded merely as a satellite district of neighbouring St-Émilion to the east, and it was not until the late 19th century that the wines began to be appreciated, and then only in France. In the early 20th century, they became known in northern Europe, notably in BELGIUM, whose wine merchants would import the wines in bulk; Belgian-bottled Pomerols of this period attract high prices at AUCTION. A succession of hard-working middlemen from the impoverished inland *département* of Corrèze made Libourne their base and developed markets for RIGHT BANK wines in such markets as Paris, Belgium, and Holland, leaving the traditional BORDEAUX TRADE to provide the British market with Médoc, Graves, and Sauternes. Such famous and well-educated British connoisseurs as George SAINTSBURY do not even mention Pomerol. It was not until the 1950s that British merchants Harry WAUGH and Ronald AVERY 'discovered' Pomerol, and its most famous property PETRUS.

The most successful of the Libourne merchants is Jean-Pierre MOUEIX, whose fortunes have been interlinked with those of Pomerol. After establishing a reputation for the appellation, the firm acquired a number of properties, as well as contracts to manage other properties, including Petrus, and still sells a significant proportion of the Pomerol made in each vintage.

The success of Petrus in particular, whose wines regularly fetch prices far above those of the Médoc FIRST GROWTHS, is mirrored by worldwide demand far in excess of supply for the wines of similarly minuscule properties such as Chx Lafleur, Le PIN, L'Église-Clinet, and La Fleur de Gay.

Pomerol's finest wines are in general made on the highest parts of the plateau, which is predominantly layers of gravel interleaved with clay, becoming sandier in the west, where rather lighter wines are made. The subsoil here is distinguished by a local iron-rich clay, the so-called *crasse de fer*, of which Petrus has a stratum particularly close to the surface.

Apparently as important in fashioning wines that are plump, voluptuous, and richly fruity enough to drink at less than five years old and yet which can last for as long as many a great Médoc are VINE AGE and low yields. (At Petrus, for example, the wine produced by vines less than 12 years old is usually excluded from the ASSEMBLAGE.) Yields here are often the lowest for red bordeaux and are zealously restricted at the best properties. The early flowering of the Merlot grape, and the fact that a single vine variety accounts for about 80% of plantings in the appellation, unusual in Bordeaux, means that in VINTAGES such as 1984 and 1991, the majority of the crop can be lost to, for example, poor weather at flowering or spring frosts.

Pomerol is also unusual in being the only one of Bordeaux's great wine districts to have no official CLASSIFICATION. The scores of properties are in general humble farmhouses with little to distinguish one from another, and only Ch de Sales has a building of any pretensions to grandeur, and an extent of more than 40 ha. The most sought-after wines, depending on the vintage, include Chx Petrus, Lafleur, Le Pin, La Conseillante, Trotanoy, Certan de May, La Fleur de Gay, L'Église-Clinet, Clinet, L'Évangile, Latour-à-Pomerol, and Vieux-Château-Certan.

See also LALANDE-DE-POMEROL.

Brook, S., *The Complete Bordeaux* (London, 2007).
Martin, N., *Pomerol* (Guildford, Surrey, 2012).

Pommard, prosperous village in Burgundy producing the most powerful red wines of the Côte de Beaune district of the Côte d'Or, from the usual Pinot Noir grapes. The pendulum of FASHION TENDS to swing between Pommard and Volnay, currently favouring the latter. However, a fine Pommard will be darker in colour than neighbouring VOLNAY, deeper in flavour, more tannic in structure, less charming when young but capable of developing into a rich, sturdy wine of great power after ten years in bottle. Claude Arnoux noted in 1728 that Pommard lasted longer than Volnay, only in those days he meant 18 months rather than 12.

Pommard stretches from the border of Beaune to the edge of Volnay. On the Beaune side, the finest vineyards are Les Pézerolles and Les Épenots, including the Clos des Épeneaux MONOPOLE of Comte Armand. Towards Volnay, the most impressive PREMIER CRU vineyards include Les Chanlins, Les Jarolières, Les Fremiers, and, in particular, Les Rugiens. The lower section of the latter, Les Rugiens Bas, has the potential to make the richest wines of all in Pommard, and is frequently mentioned as being worthy of elevation to GRAND CRU status. Clos de la Commaraine, Le Clos Blanc, and Les Arvelets have also been cited in the past as good sources for Pommard. Particularly high achievers are de Courcel, Comte Armand, and many of the best growers in Volnay such as de Montille and Pousse d'Or.

See also CÔTE D'OR, and map under BURGUNDY.
J.T.C.M.

Arnoux, C., *Dissertation sur la situation de Bourgogne* (Dijon, 1728).
Arnoux, C., *Histoire et chroniques du village de Pommard en Bourgogne* (Pommard, 1995).

Pompeii, ancient Roman settlement at the centre of an area of thriving viticulture which stretched round the southern bay of Naples from the slopes of Vesuvius to Sorrento and was at one time an important wine port. There was a Pompeian wine ('headache-inducing' according to PLINY (*Natural History* 14. 70)) and a local vine, the Holconia, which carried the name of one of the most prominent Pompeian families. The eruption of Vesuvius on 24 August AD 79 which destroyed Pompeii and its surrounding territory also preserved detailed evidence of all the processes involved in the production, sale, and consumption of wine. There are the farm-villas outside Pompeii, mainly excavated in the 19th century, which contained press rooms, and elaborate piping systems for running the must off into large DOLIA set in the ground in yards where fermentation took place. There is the more recent discovery of market vineyards within the walls of Pompeii. Then there are the incidental details: in the House of the Vettii one dining room has a painted frieze in which cherubs are engaged in what were doubtless the businesses of the owners, including working a wine press and the presentation of wine to be tasted by a prospective buyer. The local wine was widely exported in AMPHORAE. Finally there are the numerous inns, bars, and eating places, clustered significantly mainly around the gates of the town and in the busy public areas around the forum. Once again our imagination can be fuelled by lively scenes of inn-life painted on their walls. J.J.P.

Pontac, South African name for the distinctive red-fleshed TEINTURIER DU CHER grape variety probably imported from SOUTH WEST FRANCE in the late 17th century. Widely planted until PHYLLOXERA devastated the Cape's vineyards between 1866 and the 1880s, Pontac was superseded by higher-yielding and more fashionable varieties, although a vintage port-style wine was made from it as recently as 2008. While there are no longer any Pontac vineyards in South Africa, attempts are being made to produce virus-free material which, if successful, may herald its re-emergence. M.F.

port, a FORTIFIED WINE made by adding brandy to arrest fermenting grape must which results in a wine, red and sometimes white, that is both sweet and high in alcohol. Port derives its name from OPORTO (Porto), the second largest city in PORTUGAL, whence the wine has been shipped for over 300 years, notably by English merchants. Port production varies considerably from year to year, partly because of the conditions of each growing season but also reflecting the *benefício*, the amount of wine that may be fortified each year, officially calculated according to stocks and sales. The average annual production during the first decade of the 21st century was 157,000 pipes (86 million l). The production of unfortified DOURO wine averaged 56 million l between 2008 and 2011.

Fortified wines are made in the image of port in places as far apart as SOUTH AFRICA, AUSTRALIA, and CALIFORNIA but, within the EU, EU law restricts the use of the term port to wines from a closely defined area in the DOURO Valley of northern Portugal (one of the first examples of geographical DELIMITATION). See map under PORTUGAL.

History

Port originates from 17th-century trade wars between the English and the French. For a time, imports of French wines into England were prohibited, and then, in 1693, William III imposed punitive levels of TAXATION which drove English wine merchants to Portugal, a country with whom the English had always shared good relations. At first they settled on the northern coast but, finding the wines too thin and astringent (see VINHO VERDE), they travelled inland along the river Douro. Here merchants found wines that were the opposite of those they had left behind on the coast. Fast and furious FERMENTATION at high temperatures produced dark, astringent red wines that quickly earned them the name 'black-strap' in London. In a determined effort to make sure that these wines arrived in good condition, merchants would add a measure of brandy to stabilize them before shipment.

The English merchants are supposed to have discovered the winemaking technique which results in port in 1678 when a Liverpool wine merchant sent his sons to Portugal in search of wine. At Lamego, a town in the mountains high above the Douro, they found one of the important Cistercian vine-growing monasteries there where brandy was added to the wine during rather than after fermentation, killing off the active yeasts and so producing the sort of sweet, alcoholic red wine that port was to become.

British trade with France ceased altogether in the early 18th century with the outbreak of the War of the Spanish Succession. By this time, a number of port shippers were already well established and in 1703 England and Portugal signed the METHUEN TREATY, which laid down further tariff advantages for Portuguese wines. By the 1730s, however, the fledgling port industry was blighted by scandal. Sugar was being added and elderberry juice being used to give colour to poor, overstretched wines. Unprincipled over-production brought about a sharp fall in prices and a slump in trade. Prompted by complaints from British wine merchants, the port shippers contacted the Portuguese prime minister of the day, the marquis of Pombal. Partly to create a lucrative Portuguese monopoly on port production, in 1756 he instituted a series of measures to regulate sales of port. A boundary was drawn around the Douro restricting the production of port to those vineyards within it. Vineyards outside the official wine region, in BAIRRADA for instance, were summarily grubbed up by the authorities.

Geography and climate

Pombal's demarcation, modified a number of times since 1756 (see DOURO), corresponds closely to an area of pre-Cambrian SCHIST surrounded by granite. From the village of Barqueiros about 70 km/40 miles upstream from Oporto, the region fans out either side of the river stretching as far as the frontier with Spain. It is referred to by the port shippers as 'the Douro', or by those in charge of the UNESCO World Heritage sites as Alto Douro Wine Country. The vineyards are shielded from the influence of the Atlantic by the Serra do Marão, a range of mountains rising to an elevation of 1,400 m/4,600 ft. Inland, the climate becomes progressively more extreme. Annual rainfall, which averages 1,200 mm/47 in on the coast, rises to over 1,500 mm on the mountains and then diminishes sharply, falling to as little as 400 mm at Barca d'Alva on the Spanish border. Summer temperatures in the vineyards frequently exceed 35 °C/95 °F. It is hard to imagine a more inhospitable place to grow grapes. The topsoils in this mountainous region of Portugal are shallow, stony, and low in NUTRIENTS. Over a period of 300 years, however, the land has been worked to great advantage. The valley sides are very steep but TERRACES hacked from the schist, often with little more than a shovel and crowbar support, give vines a metre or two of soil in which to establish a root system. The bedrock fractures vertically, however, and, once established, vines root deeply in search of water and nutrients.

The Douro region divides into three officially recognized subzones. The Baixo (Lower) Corgo is the most westerly of the three and covers the portion of the region downstream from the river Corgo, which flows into the Douro just above the small city of Régua. This is the coolest and wettest of the three zones and tends to produce the lightest wines suitable for making inexpensive ruby and tawny ports (see Styles of port below). Upstream from the river Corgo, the Cima (Higher) Corgo is the heart of the demarcated region centred on the town of Pinhão. Rainfall is significantly lower here (700 mm as opposed to 900 mm or more west of Régua) and summer temperatures are, on average, a few degrees higher. All the well-known shippers own vineyards or QUINTAS here and this is where most of the high-quality tawny, Late Bottled Vintage, and vintage port is made. Much of the Douro Superior, the most easterly of the three subregions, is still pioneer country. Although it has long been a part of the demarcated zone, the country is remote and sparsely populated and in past centuries little headway was made in planting vineyards due to the impossibility of navigating upriver beyond the former rapids of Cachão da Valeira. The Douro Superior is also the most arid part of the region with average temperatures at least 3 °C higher than at Régua 50 km downstream. But rising LABOUR costs are forcing producers to consider planting the flatter land close to the Spanish border which is more suitable for MECHANIZATION and has considerable potential for high-quality port.

Viticulture

Viticulture in the Douro altered radically in the 1970s and 1980s, perhaps more than at any time since PHYLLOXERA swept through the region at the end of the 19th century, leaving many hillsides abandoned. The most noticeable change is the river itself, which was progressively dammed in the 1960s to form a string of narrow lakes.

Methods of cultivation have also changed the Douro landscape. Faced with an acute shortage of LABOUR at the end of the 1960s, along with escalating costs, growers began to look for alternatives to the tiny, step-like terraces built with high retaining walls in the 19th century. The first bulldozers arrived in the late 1970s to gouge out a new system of terraces called *patamares*. Inclined ramps bound together by seasonal vegetation replaced the costly retaining walls and, with wider spacing between the vines (resulting in a VINE DENSITY of 3,500 vines per ha (1,420 per acre) as opposed to 6,000 on some traditional terraces), small caterpillar tractors can circulate in the vineyards.

At much the same time, some growers pioneered a system of planting vines in vertical lines running up and down the natural slope. This 'up and down' planting has been a qualified success, although access and SOIL EROSION are problems where the gradient exceeds 30 degrees. In the 1980s, there was a flurry of new planting under a World Bank scheme which provided farmers with low-interest loans. The traditional, labour-intensive terraces, still impeccably maintained by some growers, now stand alongside the newer *patamares* and vine rows planted vertically up the hillside, both of which allow limited MECHANIZATION.

Most of the Douro's vineyards used to be pruned according to the French GUYOT system and were trained on wires supported by stakes hewn from local stone, but now all but the very old vines are spur pruned and VSP-trained on wires supported by wooden stakes. Most vines used to be GRAFTED *in situ* but now most are bench grafted. IRRIGATION is essential for young vines. July and August are generally dry and SPRAYING against FUNGAL DISEASES is necessary only in the early summer or in exceptionally wet years. Aside from the usual vineyard PESTS, most of which can be controlled by spraying, wild boar eat grapes and may occasionally damage new vineyards.

The Douro HARVEST usually starts in August in the Douro Superior and continues until early October. The steeply terraced vineyards, eerily quiet for most of the year, come alive as gangs of pickers descend from outlying villages for the duration of the harvest (see also HARVEST TRADITIONS). Yields in the Douro are among the lowest in any wine region in the world, with 500 to 750 g per vine from old vines the norm. From younger plantings, those up to 20 years old, 1.5 kg is the average production per vine in the best vineyards.

Vine varieties

More than 80 different grape varieties are authorized for the production of port but until the 1990s few growers had detailed knowledge of the identity of the vines growing in their vineyards. All old vineyards contain a mixture of grapes, often with as many as 20 or 30 different varieties intermingled in the same plot. But research conducted in the 1970s (mostly by Cockburn and Ramos Pinto), identified the best varieties and all new plantings since then have been more orderly. TOURIGA NACIONAL, TINTA BARROCA, TOURIGA FRANCA (often still referred to by its old name Touriga Francesa), Tinta Roriz (Spain's TEMPRANILLO), and TINTO CÃO are the favoured five black-skinned varieties, although varieties such as SOUSÃO, TINTA AMARELA, and MOURISCO find favour with certain growers. GOUVEIO, MALVASIA Fina, and VIOSINHO are generally considered among the best varieties for white port.

Port winemaking

Rapid EXTRACTION of COLOUR and TANNINS is the crux of the various vinification methods used to produce red port. Because FERMENTATION is curtailed by fortifying spirit after just two or three days, the grape juice or must spends a much shorter time in contact with the skins than in normal RED WINEMAKING. The MACERATION process should therefore be as vigorous as possible.

Until the early 1960s, all port was vinified in much the same way. Every farm had a winery equipped with LAGARES, low stone troughs, usually built from granite, in which the grapes were trodden and fermented. Some are still in use, mainly at the small, privately owned quintas, and some of the finest ports destined for vintage or aged tawny blends continue to be trodden in *lagares*. The human foot, for all its many unpleasant associations, is ideal for pressing grapes as it breaks up the fruit without crushing the pips that would otherwise release bitter-tasting PHENOLICS into the wine.

Lagares would be progressively filled over the course of a day, and trodden by the pickers themselves, thigh high in purple pulp, in the evening. Most *lagares* hold 10 to 15 PIPES (about 5,500 to 8,250 l (2,180 gal)) although a number of the larger quintas have *lagares* with a capacity of up to 30 pipes. As a rule of thumb, between one and two people per pipe are needed to tread a *lagar*. Fermentation begins as a result of the action of ambient YEASTS on the grapes' sugar. The alcohol produced, and the increasing TEMPERATURE of the mass of purple skins, juice, and stems, encourages the extraction of the phenolics vital for the character of port. After about two or three hours of hard, methodical treading, the CAP of skins and stalks starts to float to the surface. Regular PUNCHING DOWN of the cap was traditionally performed with long, spiked sticks from planks run across the top of the *lagares* which ideally need some form of cooling.

After 24 to 36 hours, the level of the grape sugar in the fermenting must declines from 12 or 13 °BAUMÉ to between 6 and 8 °Baumé. Depending on the intended sweetness of the wine, the wine would be run off the *lagar* into a vat, already about one-fifth full with grape spirit whose ALCOHOLIC STRENGTH is 77%. As the spirit is mixed with the wine, the yeasts are killed and the fermentation is arrested. At this stage the must becomes young, sweet, fiery port with an alcohol content of 19 or 20%.

In the 1960s and 1970s, treading grapes in *lagares* became much less widespread. The Douro valley and the remote TRÁS-OS-MONTES region which traditionally supplied labour at harvest time have suffered from marked emigration and the port shippers were forced to look for other, less labour-intensive, ways to make wine.

Most port producers abandoned *lagares* altogether. Many isolated properties were without electricity then and shippers set about building central wineries to which grapes from outlying farms could be delivered. Most of these were equipped with AUTOVINIFICATION tanks, which required no external power source and have proved to be a successful alternative to treading in *lagares*. The resulting wine is fortified just like foot-trodden young wines were.

In the late 1990s, however, a new generation of winemakers started to experiment with more novel ways of making port as the labour shortages in the region continued and production costs increased considerably. Two key types have emerged: cap plungers as introduced by the FLADGATE PARTNERSHIP and automated treading machines or 'robotic lagares' as designed by the SYMINGTON family. Both systems have become widely used for the making of premium quality ports, although they are too expensive to be used to make the large volumes of standard-quality ports.

All wineries are now equipped with PRESSES and the mass of grape skins and stems that remains after treading or crushing is forked into a press to extract the last of the juice. This deeply coloured, astringent wine is run off and fortified separately. It may be blended back at a later stage or used to bolster a lighter wine.

White port is made in much the same way (see Styles of port below).

The fortifying grape spirit for port used to be distilled from wine made in Portugal, mainly from the ESTREMADURA region north of Lisbon, although in recent years most of the spirit has been imported, and is distilled from the Europe's WINE LAKE. Until 1992, this spirit had to be purchased from the Casa do Douro (see Organization of the industry, below), which set a fixed price and controlled distribution. This monopoly was broken by the EU and producers have since been free to purchase any spirit they choose provided that it complies with the 77% norm of alcoholic strength and is approved by the Port and Douro Wine Institute (IVDP). Since 2000 there has been a marked improvement in the quality and purity of the fortifying spirit used for premium ports.

See VIN DOUX NATUREL for a comparison of port winemaking techniques with those in the production of French counterparts such as Banyuls.

Organization of the industry

By the mid 2010s, thanks to considerable new plantings in the Douro Superior, mostly EU-subsidized, the total number of grape growers in the Douro had grown to 34,000. They farmed a total of 45,000 ha/111,000 acres of vines in the Douro, mostly in the Baixo Corgo, nearly a third of which is under vine. In common with most of the north of Portugal, the region is fragmented into tiny holdings of which 142,000 were registered with the Casa do Douro, the official body set up in 1932 to represent the growers. Over 80% of these holdings are less than 0.5 ha/1.2 acres in size and a mere 0.01% have an area greater than 30 ha/74 acres. The development of the Douro Superior has caused a serious imbalance and brought a dramatic reduction in the price of grapes for Douro wine. Many growers, especially in the steeper Baixo Corgo region, have been producing grapes at below cost. Port grapes are better protected by the *benefício*, which some argue creates a false market.

Vineyards in the Douro are graded according to a complicated points system and classified into nine different categories rated A to I. Twelve different physical factors including site, aspect, exposure, and gradient are taken into consideration, each of which is allocated a numerical score. In theory, a vineyard could score a maximum of 2,031 points or a minimum of minus 400 points. A property with more than 1,200 points is awarded an A grade. On this basis, the annual *benefício* authorization (the total amount of port that may be made that year) is distributed to individual farmers. This is calculated annually by the port industry's regulating authority, the Instituto dos Vinhos do Douro e do Porto (Douro Port Wine Institute, or IVDP).

Permits are then distributed to farmers detailing the amount of grape must that they may fortify to make port. The amount varies according to the year but, typically, A and B grade properties may make 550 to 600 l of port per thousand vines, while properties with a grade of F or below are unlikely to be allowed to make port at all. The surplus is usually made into unfortified wine with its own denomination (see DOURO) but most of this sells for a much lower price than port.

This quality control system, instituted in 1947, served the port industry well for four decades, but pressure for its reform intensified when in 1990 the independence of the Casa do Douro was severely compromised by its purchase of shares in Royal Oporto, then one of the largest port shippers. After a period of instability, in the mid 1990s the Casa do Douro had most of its regulatory powers withdrawn and these were transferred to an independent interprofessional body representing both growers and shippers, the CIRDD, Commissão Interprofessional da Região Demarcada do Douro. This in turn was absorbed by the IVDP. The Casa do Douro continues to represent the farmers and to hold the register of vineyards.

After vinification, the bulk of the new wine traditionally stayed at the QUINTA or farm until the spring after the harvest when it was transported downstream to the shippers' LODGES in VILA NOVA DE GAIA across the river Douro from Oporto, where the shippers have traditionally been based. The cooler climate and markedly high humidity near the coast are thought to be beneficial for slow CASK AGEING but a number of shippers now have built temperature- and humidity-controlled lodges in the Douro which are being used successfully for ageing premium ports, especially aged tawnies. See DOURO BAKE for the traditonal effect on port of maturing it upstream in the Douro Valley.

Both growers and shippers have to submit to the authority of the IVDP. This government-run body employs inspectors to check the movement of stock. It ensures that shippers adhere to the so-called *lei do terço* (law of the third), which restricts shippers from selling more than a third of their stock in any one year. The IVDP is also empowered to analyse and taste a sample from each port shipment before issuing the guarantee seal which is stuck to the neck of every bottle of port leaving the region.

The market for port has altered dramatically since the Second World War. The so-called 'Englishman's wine' that used to be drunk everywhere from gentlemen's clubs to street corner pubs became the Frenchman's wine when France's imports of *le porto* (largely inexpensive wood ports; see Styles of port below) overtook those of the United Kingdom in the early 1960s. The British market is still highly coveted by port shippers, however, especially those of British descent, notably the SYMINGTONS who control shippers such as Cockburn, Dow, Graham, and Warre and the FLADGATE PARTNERSHIP (Croft, Fonseca, and Taylor). In the late 1990s, the United States became another important market for vintage port.

Styles of port

There are two broad categories of port, fortified wines whose style is shaped by either CASK AGEING or BOTTLE AGEING. Wood-matured ports, often called simply wood ports, are aged either in wooden casks or, sometimes, cement tanks, and are ready to drink straight after FINING, FILTRATION, and BOTTLING. Ports designed to mature in bottle, however, are aged for a short time in wood and are bottled without filtration. It may then take up to 20 or 30 years before such a wine is ready to drink. Within these two general categories there are many different styles of port. The official legislation governing the different categories of port was tightened up considerably in 2002 and the following are now permitted.

Ruby This is one of the simplest and least expensive styles of port. Aged in bulk for two or three years, it is bottled young while the wine retains a deep ruby colour and a strong, fiery personality. Young wines from more than one vintage are aged in all sorts of vessels (wood, cement, and occasionally stainless steel) before being blended, filtered, and bottled. PASTEURIZATION is sometimes applied to stabilize such wines and can result in 'stewed' flavours, but good ruby with its uncomplicated berry fruit aromas and flavours is often a good, warming drink. When the British FASHION for ruby port and lemonade faded in the 1960s, many shippers dropped the name ruby on the labels of such ports in favour of their own, self-styled brands.

Reserve/Reserva is the term now used to designate a premium ruby, a wine with more colour, character, and depth than a standard ruby. This category has supplanted 'vintage character', a misleading term which was largely used in English-speaking markets.

Tawny The word tawny is applied to a confusingly wide range of very different styles of port. In theory, tawny implies a wine which has been aged in wood for so much longer than a ruby that it loses colour and the wine takes on an amber-brown or tawny hue (see AGEING). In practice, however, much of the tawny port sold today is no older than the average ruby and may therefore be found at the same price. The difference between a commercial ruby and its counterpart labelled 'tawny' is that, whereas ruby is made from a blend of big, deep-coloured wines, tawny is often produced from lighter wines grown in the cooler Baixo Corgo vineyards where grapes rarely ripen to give much

depth or intensity of fruit. Vinification methods may also be adapted to produce paler coloured wines, and the colour of the final blend may be adjusted further by adding a proportion of white port so that the wine ends up with a pale pink hue rather than tawny brown. Many bulk tawnies are left upriver for longer than other wines for the heat to speed up the maturation (see DOURO BAKE). The resulting wines often display a slight brown tinge on the rim but tend to lack the freshness and primary fruit character normally associated with young port. The French typically drink inexpensive, light, tawny-style wines as an aperitif and supplying this market has become the major commercial activity for many of the larger port shippers.

Aged tawny Port that has been left to age in wooden casks for six or more years begins to take on a tawny colour and a soft, silky character as the PHENOLICS are POLYMERIZED (see AGEING). Most of these tawnies are bottled with an indication of age on the label, although a new category of *Tawny Reserve* or *Tawny Reserva* may be applied to wines that have spent at least seven years in wood. The terms 10, 20, 30, or Over 40 years old seen on labels are, however, approximations as tawny ports are blended from a number of years' production. Most aged tawnies are blended according to house style and must be tasted and approved by the IVDP as conforming to the character expected from the age claimed on the label. Aged tawnies are made from wines of the very highest quality: wines set aside in undeclared years that might have otherwise ended up as vintage port (see below). They mature in cask in the cool of the lodges at Gaia until the shipper considers that they are ready to blend and bottle. Labels on these wines must state that the wine has matured in wood and give the date of bottling, which is important since aged tawny port may deteriorate if it spends too long in bottle. Once the bottle has been opened, younger aged tawnies may be subject to quite rapid OXIDATION, losing their delicacy of fruit if left on ULLAGE for more than a few days. (Very old tawnies and colheita ports are usually more robust.) Port shippers themselves often drink a good aged tawny, chilled in summer, in preference to any other. The delicate, nutty character of a well-aged tawny suits the climate and temperament of the Douro better than the hefty, spicy character of vintage port, which is better adapted to cooler climes.

Colheita Meaning 'harvest' or 'crop' and therefore by extension 'vintage' in Portuguese, colheita ports are in fact very different from vintage ports (below). Colheitas are best understood as tawny ports from a single year, bottled with the date of the harvest on the label. The law states that colheita ports must be aged in wood for at least seven years, although most are aged for considerably longer. The wines take on

all the nuances of an aged tawny but should also express the characteristics of a single year. All colheita ports carry the date of bottling and most wines should be drunk within a year or so of that date. Colheita ports, once the speciality of the Portuguese-owned houses, have, in the 21st century, been taken up enthusiastically by the British shippers who sometimes use the word 'Harvest' on the label. (MADEIRA may also use the word 'colheita'.)

Vintage port The most expensive style of port is one of the world's simplest of wines to make. Vintage port accounts for hardly 1% of all port sold, yet it is the wine which receives the most attention. British shippers, in particular, have built vintage port into a flagship wine, 'declared' in an atmosphere of speculation when the quality of the wine, the quantity available, and the market are judged fit. Wines from a single year, or VINTAGE, are blended and bottled after spending between two and three years in wood. Thereafter, most of the wine is sold and the consumer takes over the nurturing for up to 30 or more years, although an increasing proportion is being drunk much earlier, especially in the US. Vintage port is distinguished from other ports by the quality of the grapes from which the wine is made. Only grapes grown in the best, usually Cima Corgo, vineyards, picked at optimum ripeness following an outstanding summer, are made into vintage port. Even then, nothing is certain until at least a year after the harvest when shippers have had time to reflect on the characteristics of the wine and the market. The vintage may be declared only after the IVDP has approved samples and proposed quantities in the second year after the harvest. With the steady improvement in vinification methods since the mid 1980s, some wine of vintage port potential is now made at the best quintas in most years. But a shipper will declare a vintage only if there is sufficient quantity and if it is felt that the market is ready to support another vintage (1931 being a classic example of a qualitatively superb vintage undeclared by most shippers for entirely commercial reasons). Vintage declarations may be very irregular but very roughly three vintages have been declared in each decade. Because they should be bottle aged for longer than almost any other style of wine, vintage port bottles are particularly thick, dark, and sturdy. The wines, extremely high in phenolics in their youth, throw a heavy DEPOSIT and need especial care when DECANTING and SERVING.

Single-quinta vintage Just as wine-producing CHÂTEAUX evolved in France in the 18th and 19th centuries, the cult of the single, winemaking QUINTA has developed in Portugal, and many of the better-known Douro quintas belong to a particular port shipper. Single-quinta ports are made in much the same way as vintage port, aged in wood for two or three years and bottled without filtration so that they throw a sediment (and should therefore be decanted before serving). Although some independent quintas produce a vintage port nearly every year, a number of significant differences distinguish single-quinta vintages from declared vintage ports. First of all, shippers' single-quinta ports tend to be made in good (but not outstanding) years which are not declared. In years which are declared for vintage port, many of these wines will be the lots that make up the backbone of the vintage blend and are not therefore available for release as wines in their own right. Secondly many single-quinta ports are kept back by shippers and sold only when the wine is considered to be ready to drink, perhaps eight or ten years after the harvest. Single quintas or individual vineyards in the Douro were given a fillip in 1986 when the law requiring all port to be exported via Vila Nova de Gaia was relaxed, opening the way for a number of small vineyard owners who, before, had been restricted to selling their wines to large firms.

LBV Late Bottled Vintage port is a wine from a single year, bottled between the fourth and sixth years after the harvest. Three different styles of LBV wines have evolved, however. First there are LBVs bottled without any filtration or treatment so that, like a vintage port, they need to be decanted before serving. These wines, once designated with the word 'traditional' tend to be made in good but undeclared years and are ready to drink earlier than vintage port, four to six years after bottling. Since the revision of the legislation in 2002, unfiltered LBV may also be sold as Envelhecido em Garrafa or 'bottle matured', provided the wine in question has been aged in bottle for a minimum of three years prior to release on the market. Many of the wines in this second style share much of the depth of a true vintage port.

A third style of LBV is the most common. These are wines which have been fined and sometimes filtered and cold stabilized before bottling to prevent the formation of sediment. These wines are made in large volumes and are popular with restaurateurs (obviating the need to decant) but do not have the intensity or depth of an unfiltered LBV.

Crusted port This port is so called because of the 'crust' or DEPOSIT that it throws in bottle. In spite of its rather crusty, establishment name, it is the fairly recent creation of British shippers, notably the SYMINGTON group. It is designed to appeal to vintage port enthusiasts, even though the coveted word 'vintage' does not appear on the label (because crusted ports are not wines from a single year or vintage but blends from a number of years bottled young with little or no filtration). Like vintage port, the wines continue to develop in the bottle, throwing a sediment or crust, so that the wine needs to be decanted

before it is served. Rather like traditional LBVs, many crusted or crusting ports offer an excellent alternative to vintage port, providing the port enthusiast with a dark, full-bodied wine at a much lower price. It may be exported from Oporto three years after bottling.

Garrafeira The word GARRAFEIRA, meaning 'private cellar' or 'reserve', is more commonly associated with Portuguese table wines than with port. Until 2002 it did not form part of the IVDP's officially authorized lexicon but was a style produced by a single shipper, Niepoort. Now a port may be designated as a garrafeira if it comes from a single year and is aged for a minimum of seven years in glass demi-john before bottling (like some MADEIRA). In practice the wines age in 5- or 10-l demi-johns for considerably longer than the minimum. After 20, 30, or even 40 years in glass, the wine is decanted off its sediment and rebottled in conventional 75-cl bottles. The wines combine depth of fruit with the delicate, silky texture associated with tawny port. Three dates appear on the label: date of harvest, date of bottling (i.e. when the wine was transferred to demi-john), and date of decanting (i.e. decanted from the sediment that has formed in the demi-john and transferred to a 75 cl bottle).

White port Ernest Cockburn remarked in the early 20th century that 'the first duty of port is to be red'. Nevertheless a significant proportion of white grapes grow in vineyards in the Douro and all shippers produce a small amount of white port, even if very few give it serious attention. White port is made in much the same way as red except that MACERATION during fermentation is much shorter, or non-existent. Most white ports have a certain amount of RESIDUAL SUGAR, even those labelled 'dry' or 'extra dry'. Intensely sweet wines, made mainly for the domestic market, are labelled *lagrima* (tears) because of their VISCOSITY (see also MÁLAGA). Another, drier style of white port, described as *leve seco* (light dry) is made by some shippers. These are wines with an alcoholic strength of around 16.5 or 17%, rather than the usual 19 to 20%. Most commercial white ports are aged for no more than 18 months, generally in tanks made of cement or stainless steel. Wood ageing lends character to white port, turning it gold in colour and giving the wine an incisive, dry, nutty tang. Superior white ports may also be bottled with a designation of age: 10, 20, 30, 40 Years Old. White port is sometimes used by shippers for blending cheaper tawnies.

Rosé This style was initiated by CROFT in 2008 and was initially classified by the IVDP as 'light ruby'. Made from red grapes with minimal SKIN CONTACT, it was subsequently introduced by many shippers, albeit with a huge variation in the style and colour of the wine, from pale salmon to light ruby. Not without controversy when it was launched, it is said by

some to have a new, younger group of port drinkers.

Moscatel One of over 30 different grape varieties used for making white port, Moscatel is occasionally used on its own to make a sweet fortified VARIETAL white wine with the grape aroma characteristic of MUSCAT. The village of Favaios on the north bank of the Douro makes a speciality of moscatel.

See also articles on individual port shippers COCKBURN, FERREIRA, FLADGATE PARTNERSHIP, QUINTA DO NOVAL, SANDEMAN, and SYMINGTONS.

R.J.M.

Bradford, S., *The Story of Port* (2nd edn, London, 1983).

Howkins, B., *Real Men Drink Port . . . And Ladies do Too!* (Shrewsbury, 2011).

Mayson, R., *The Wines and Vineyards of Portugal* (London, 2003).

Mayson, R., *Port and the Douro* (3rd edn, Oxford, 2013).

www.ivdp.pt

Portalegre, northernmost DOP subregion of the ALENTEJO in central-southern Portugal and the most distinctive. On the lower slopes of the predominantly GRANITE Serra de São Mamede, vineyards (up to around 800 m) are the Alentejo's highest and therefore coolest. This, combined with its unusual (for the Alentejo) mix of aged FIELD BLEND vineyards, has attracted talented newcomers whose wines are considerably more ambitious than those of its ailing CO-OPERATIVE. The best are excitingly individual, fresh, and well-structured compared with those from other the Alentejo regions.   S.A.

Portan, like CALADOC and CHASAN, is a CROSS made by French AMPELOGRAPHER Paul Truel at the INRA station at Domaine de Vassal. In this case he crossed Grenache Noir and Portugais Bleu (Blauer PORTUGIESER) to develop a Grenache-like variety that would ripen even in the Midi's cooler zones. By 2011, it was grown on just 200 ha of Languedoc vineyard.

Portimão, fishing port and DOP in Portugal's ALGARVE.

Porto, Portugal's second city (OPORTO in English) which has lent its name to PORT wine, Vinho do Porto.

Port Phillip Zone, Australian wine zone surrounding Melbourne, VICTORIA, and encompassing the Geelong, Macedon Ranges, Mornington Peninsula, Sunbury, and Yarra Valley regions.

port tongs, rare instrument for opening a bottle of vintage PORT so old that the cork is likely to crumble under the impact of a CORKSCREW. The specially shaped tongs are heated in a flame and applied to the neck of the bottle, which is then immediately cooled with a cold, damp cloth. The sudden temperature change should result in a clean break. Tongs can be used on other venerable bottles.

Portugais, or Portugais Bleu, French name for Blauer PORTUGIESER. Rare in France today.

Portugal.

Among European wine-producing nations, Portugal has been something of a paradox, arguably discussed in the greater world of wine more because of the CORK of which it is by far the dominant producer than for its wines. Sitting on the western flank of the Iberian peninsula, this seafaring nation which discovered so much of the NEW WORLD has long clung firmly to the Old—at least in terms of its tradition of myriad INDIGENOUS VARIETIES. Secluded both geographically and, for much of the 20th century until it joined the EU in 1986, politically as well, Portugal has developed in isolation from other countries, including neighbouring SPAIN. However, the sizeable wine industry that has grown up in this small country owes much to foreign trade. Total area under vine has declined from 385,000 ha/951,000 acres in the late 1980s to just under 234,000 ha producing about 7 million hl by the second decade of this century. Although the Portuguese rival the French and trump the Italians in terms of per capita wine consumption, the global financial crisis of 2007/08, which prompted the imposition of austerity measures in 2010, turned Portuguese wine producers' attention firmly to export markets.

History

The British have always enjoyed an amicable relationship with the Portuguese. As early as the 12th century, wines were being shipped to England from the MINHO in north west Portugal. In 1386, the Treaty of Windsor set the seal on a friendship that has persisted, virtually uninterrupted, to the present day. When England went to war with France in the 17th century, Portugal was therefore the natural alternative source for wine. PORT, often called 'the Englishman's wine', originated from this conflict. By the time England and Portugal signed the METHUEN TREATY in 1703, which laid down tariff advantages for Portuguese wines, a thriving community of English and German wine shippers was already well established in OPORTO. Out in the Atlantic, the island of MADEIRA, an important trading post for passing ships, began exporting wine to the newly colonized state and yet-to-be UNITED STATES of America. Renewed conflict between Britain and France over the French invasion of the Iberian peninsula in 1807 rekindled demand for Portuguese wines. BUCELAS, CARCAVELOS, and a red wine simply called 'Lisbon' were popular in Britain until the 1870s.

In the last 30 years of the 19th century, PHYLLOXERA devastated Portuguese vineyards as severely as those elsewhere in Europe. Some Portuguese wine regions never really recovered. Many growers resorted to planting high-yielding DIRECT PRODUCERS, which can still be found in the smallholdings of north and central Portugal. For much of the 20th century, Portugal turned her back on the outside world. Following 20 years of political and economic turmoil, the demure son of a DÃO smallholder, Antonio de Oliveira Salazar, became prime minister in 1932. His regime, which lasted for over 40 years, fostered a corporate, one-party state. Portugal's chaotic wine industry was thoroughly reorganized. The Junta Nacional do Vinho (JNV) founded in 1937 initiated a programme of co-operativization. Over 100 winery CO-OPERATIVES were built, mostly in northern Portugal, in less than 20 years. At the time they represented a significant advance but, all too often, the system imposed by central government was too inflexible and winemaking standards deteriorated.

It is paradoxical that, against this background of self-imposed seclusion, Portugal should give birth to one of the greatest international wine success stories of modern times: medium-sweet, lightly sparkling rosés called MATEUS and LANCERS.

In 1974, Portugal was once again thrown into turmoil by a military-led revolution. But after two years of upheaval the soldier politicians returned to barracks and subsequent democratically elected governments eventually returned Portugal to the European mainstream. Portugal's winemakers have benefited enormously from EU entry in 1986. Monopolistic legislation was overturned and, thanks to EU policies of supporting agricultural underdogs, money poured in to help update the wine industry, much of which had been hidebound by a lack of investment in modern technology.

During the 1980s and 1990s, the relaxation of state bureaucracy and the availability of grants and low-interest loans resulted in a country-wide wine revolution. It encouraged single estates, or QUINTAS, to cut their links with local co-operatives or PORT SHIPPERS and to make and market their own more distinctive wines. Private investors who had made millions in other industries injected a new entrepreneurial spirit into the business of winemaking, establishing estates from scratch (notably in the ALENTEJO, whose sprawling, flatter landscape offers relative economies of scale). The co-operatives were forced to adapt to survive and, while some struggled and others went under, some rose to the challenge. In 2011, there were 90 active co-operatives producing 43% of Portuguese wine. Vineyard transformation has inevitably been slower but the benefits of replanting vineyards in VARIETAL blocks rather than traditional FIELD BLENDS, experimentation with non-local and INTERNATIONAL VARIETIES, plus a considerable amount of research into Portugal's unique array of INDIGENOUS VARIETIES (see below) have become increasingly apparent, especially in the DOURO, DÃO, and the ALENTEJO, and more recently TEJO and LISBOA.

Geography and climate

For such a small country, Portugal produces a remarkable diversity of wines. Roughly rectangular in shape, it is under 600 km/360 miles long and no more than 200 km wide. The wines produced on the flat coastal littoral are strongly influenced by prevailing Atlantic westerly winds. Rainfall, which reaches 2,000 mm/78 in a year on the mountain ranges north of Oporto, diminishes sharply to less than 500 mm in some inland wine areas. The temperate MARITIME CLIMATE, with warm summers and cool, wet winters, becomes more extreme towards the south and east. An average annual temperature of around 10 °C/50 °F in the northern hills compares with more than 17.5 °C on the southern plains, where, in summer, temperatures frequently exceed 35 °C/95 °F.

Reflecting these contrasting climatic conditions, no two wines could be more dissimilar than VINHO VERDE and PORT, which are produced in adjoining regions. There are pockets of viticulture all over Portugal. Only the very highest mountain peaks of the central and northern mountain ranges are unable to support viticulture.

Vine varieties

Portugal's vineyards have evolved in isolation. Only a handful of varieties have crossed international frontiers, leaving Portugal like a viticultural island with a treasure trove of indigenous grape varieties, 248 of them according to a 2013 study produced by the Associação Portuguesa para a Diversidade da Videira (PORVID). Since Portugal joined the EU, the most promising have been identified and the overall quality and consistency of wines has commensurately improved. Among whites, whose quality has risen remarkably this century, LOUREIRO and ALVARINHO (in Vinho Verde), BICAL (in Bairrada), ENCRUZADO (in Dão), ARINTO (in Bucelas and throughout southern Portugal for blends), ANTÃO VAZ in the Alentejo and RABIGATO, CODEGA DO LARINHO, VIOSINHO, and GOUVEIO (in the Douro) have emerged as leading varieties. Red wine grapes account for around two-thirds of production. Some of the most celebrated so far are TOURIGA NACIONAL (originally from Dão and Douro but now prized country-wide), Spain's TEMPRANILLO (known as Tinta Roriz in the Douro and Aragonez in the Alentejo), BAGA (in Bairrada), TRINCADEIRA, and the French cross ALICANTE BOUSCHET (in the Alentejo). But as confidence and pride in native varieties has grown (and also a greater appreciation of the advantage of a point of difference in

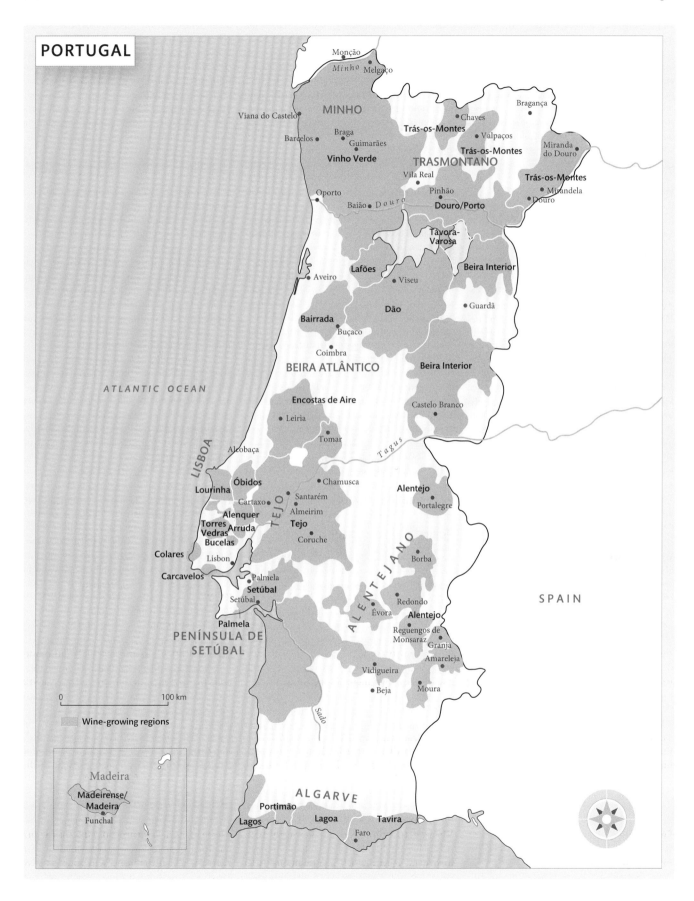

PORTUGAL

ATLANTIC OCEAN

Monção
Minho
Melgaço

MINHO

Viana do Castelo
Chaves
Bragança

Braga
Trás-os-Montes
Valpaços

Barcelos
Guimarães
Trás-os-Montes
Miranda
do Douro

Vinho Verde
TRASMONTANO

Vila Real
Trás-os-Montes

Oporto
Pinhão
Mirandela

Baião *Douro*
Douro/Porto
Douro

Tâvora-
Varosa

Lafões
Beira Interior

Aveiro
Viseu

Dão

Bairrada
Guardã

Buçaco

Coimbra

BEIRA ATLÂNTICO
Beira Interior

Encostas de Aire
Castelo Branco

Leiria

Tomar

Tagus

Alcobaça

LISBOA

Óbidos
Chamusca
Alentejo

Lourinha
Santarém
Portalegre

Cartaxo
Almeirim

Alenquer
Tejo

Torres
Arruda
Coruche

Vedras
Bucelas

Colares
Lisbon
Borba

Carcavelos
Palmela
Redondo

Setúbal
Évora
Alentejo

Setúbal
Reguengos de
Monsaraz

Palmela
Granja

PENÍNSULA DE
SETÚBAL
Amareleja

Vidigueira

Sado
Beja
Moura

ALENTEJANO

0   100 km

Wine-growing regions

ALGARVE

Madeira
Portimão

Madeirense/
Lagoa
Tavira

Madeira
Lagos

Funchal
Faro

SPAIN

an increasingly homogenized wine world), more indigenous varieties are being sought out and celebrated. INTERNATIONAL VARIETIES have made the most substantial inroads in LISBOA and TEJO, neither of which had a strong heritage of quality wines, unlike BAIRRADA where the relaxation of DOP rules about varieties has been controversial. Cabernet Sauvignon, Petit Verdot, and SYRAH are now not uncommon blend components of wines from the south of Portugal, especially the Alentejo.

Wine laws

Portugal's wine law predates that of most other European countries (although see also TOKAJ in Hungary). In 1756, the then prime minister, the Marquis of Pombal, drew a boundary around the vineyards of the Douro valley to protect the authenticity of port, one of the wine world's first examples of geographical DELIMITATION. Bucelas, Colares, Carcavelos, Dão, Madeira, Setúbal, and Vinho Verde were all awarded REGIÃO DEMARCADA (demarcated region) status between 1908 and 1929, followed by Bairrada, Algarve, and Douro (for table wine) in 1979 and 1980. Since Portugal joined the EU, the Regiões Demarcadas or RDs were initially redesignated Denominação de Origem Controlada (DOC), now Denominação de Origem Protegida (DOP). A second tier, Indicação de Proveniencia Regulamentada (IPR), has been replaced by generally larger regions known as VINHO REGIONAL. Underpinned by the WINE WITHOUT GEOGRAPHICAL INDICATION designation, labelled VINHO if Portuguese, this brings the country's wine laws roughly into line with that of other EU countries.

For details of Portugal's extremely varied viticultural techniques, winemaking practices and expertise, and individual regions, see also the ALENTEJO, ALGARVE, BAIRRADA, BUCELAS, COLARES, CARCAVELOS, DÃO, DOURO, LISBOA, MINHO, TEJO, PENÍNSULA DE SETÚBAL, TRÁS-OS-MONTES, VINHO VERDE, and, most importantly, PORT. The viticulturally important Atlantic islands of MADEIRA and the AZORES are autonomous regions of Portugal.   S.A.

Mayson, R. J., *The Wines and Vineyards of Portugal* (London, 2003).

Mayson, R. J., *Port and the Douro* (3rd edn, Oxford, 2013).

Metcalfe, C., and McWhirter, K., *The Wine and Food Lover's Guide to Portugal* (Haywards Heath, 2007).

www.winesofportugal.info

www.viniportugal.pt

www.ivv.min-agricultura.pt

Portugieser, or **Blauer Portugieser**, black grape variety common in both senses of that word in both Austria and Germany, its name suggesting completely unsubstantiated Portuguese origins. The vigorous, precocious vine is extremely prolific, easily producing 120 hl/ha (almost 7 tons/acre), thanks to its good resistance to COULURE, of pale, low-acid red that, thanks to robust ENRICHMENT, can taste disconcertingly inconsequential to non-natives.

Blauer Portugieser is synonymous with dull, thin red in lower AUSTRIA, where it is particularly popular with growers in Pulkautal, Retz, and the Thermenregion. It covers about 1,500 ha of vineyard and is the country's third most planted dark-berried vine variety after ZWEIGELT and BLAUFRÄNKISCH. Such wines are rarely exported, with good reason, and are only rarely worthy of detailed study.

Brought from Austria in the 19th century, Germany's everyday black grape variety Portugieser overtook even SPÄTBURGUNDER (Pinot Noir) in the 1970s in terms of total plantings, thanks to the prevailing German thirst for red wine regardless of its quality. By 2012 Portugieser's total area had fallen to 3,825 ha/9,448 acres, (Spätburgunder's was almost 12,000 ha), mainly in Rheinhessen and PFALZ, where a high proportion is encouraged to produce vast quantities of pink WEISSHERBST.

The variety is so easy to grow, however, that it has spread throughout central Europe and beyond (as PORTUGAIS Bleu it was once grown widely in south western France). It was ingeniously named Oportó or Kékoportó (*kék* meaning 'blue') in ROMANIA and HUNGARY, where its total area has fallen to below 600 ha but in the red wine region of Villány it can yield wines of real concentration in the right hands. It is also grown in northern Croatia as Portugizac Crni, or Portugaljka.

Pošip, impressive southern CROATIAN white wine grape probably originating on the island of Korčula.

post, substantial support for wires and vines which is common in NEW WORLD vineyards and usually made from wood, and driven into the ground at intervals down the row. Other materials used include concrete, steel, and plastic. Woods used for such posts are soft woods such as pine, treated to withstand insect and fungus attack, or naturally resistant hardwoods. A common spacing of about 6 m/20 ft between posts is close enough to stop the wire sagging. Smaller-diameter posts placed one beside each vine are called STAKES and these are more common for Old World vineyards but also found in California.   R.E.S.

potassium, one of the macronutrients required by the vine for healthy growth, along with NITROGEN and PHOSPHORUS. It constitutes about 1–3% of the vine's dry weight, and is an important component of grape juice. Potassium deficiencies show up first in older leaves as CHLOROSIS, which may become a marginal burn when severe. Potassium-deficient leaves are often shiny. Severe deficiencies can inhibit growth, yield, and sugar content. They can be confirmed easily by analysing for potassium levels in leaves or petioles, and 1 to 1.5% potassium is the optimal range. Potassium deficiency is more evident during DROUGHT or in cold soils in spring, both of which reduce the roots' uptake of potassium. However, soils containing a significant proportion of mica-type CLAY minerals can supply too much potassium, as occurs in parts of Sunraysia and the Riverland, Australia.

Potassium is widely regarded as the most important element directly affecting wine quality. This is because high potassium levels in grape juice cause high PH, which adversely affects wine quality. Juice potassium levels are influenced by soil potassium levels, although this is not always a straightforward relationship. (Delas and colleagues in Bordeaux have shown positive linear correlations between plant potassium levels and juice potassium, but this was for vines with potassium contents up to and exceeding three times the optimal value.)

ROOTSTOCKS also have an important effect on juice potassium, with lower-vigour rootstocks giving lower juice potassium. This effect has been shown both in France and Australia. Part of the explanation may be that more vigorous rootstocks tend to result in SHADE in the canopy, which is known to increase both juice potassium and pH. In hot climates with low humidity, must potassium and juice pH are high, which may be the result of the high TRANSPIRATION rate of vines growing in such an environment (see CLIMATE). It seems that distribution of potassium in the plant is important, and that shade causes accumulation in the leaves, which subsequently migrates to the fruit. CANOPY MANAGEMENT techniques which reduce shade can therefore be effective in reducing must potassium and pH. While skins are only about 10% of the berry weight, they contain 30 to 40% of grapes' potassium.   R.E.S. & R.E.W.

Delas, J., Molot, C., and Soyer, J. P., 'Fertilisation minérale de la vigne et teneur en potassium des baies, des moûts et des vins', in P. Ribéreau-Gayon and A. Lonvaud (eds.), *Actualités oenologiques 89: comptes rendus du 4e Symposium International d'Oenologie, Bordeaux, 15–17 juin, 1989* (Paris, 1989).

Smart, R. E., and Robinson, M., *Sunlight into Wine: A Handbook for Winegrape Canopy Management* (Adelaide, 1991).

White, R. E., *Soils for Fine Wines* (Oxford, 2003).

potential alcohol, measurement of a wine or must which equates to its total ALCOHOLIC STRENGTH if all the sugar were to be fermented out to alcohol. Thus, a Sauternes might have an alcoholic strength of 13%, but a potential alcohol of 20% if all the RESIDUAL SUGAR were fermented into alcohol.

pouches, relatively recent form of wine PACK-AGING made from polyethylene and aluminium. They have the advantage of being light (much lighter than a BOX, for example) and convenient, especially for smaller servings, but the disadvantage that wine stays fresh in a pouch for only a few months. Plastic taps ensure that wine in an opened pouch keeps reasonably fresh for three or four weeks. Relatively high SULFUR additions are needed, however.

Pouilly-Fuissé, important white wine appellation which commands the highest prices in the MÂCONNAIS district of Burgundy. The appellation, restricted to the Chardonnay grape, includes about 850 ha/2,100 acres in the communes of Fuissé, Solutré (which includes the hamlet of Pouilly), Vergisson, and Chaintré (see also MÂCON VILLAGES). The richest wines are said to come from Fuissé and Solutré-Pouilly, those of Vergisson being fresher and more mineral from vineyards at a higher elevation. a little lighter but elegant. Various single vineyards have traditionally been cited alongside the appellation and work is in progress to codify a CLASSIFICATION of PREMIER CRU vineyards.

As well as in the amphitheatre of Fuissé, grapes are grown in sun traps beneath the two impressive crags of Solutré and Vergisson which mark the end of the LIMESTONE plateau on which all burgundy save Beaujolais is grown. A popular myth is that the soil beneath the crags was enriched by the remains of animals driven from the top of the cliff by Stone Age hunters. The wines are full bodied and ripe but do not usually attain the elegance of the finer wines from the Côte de Beaune. Normally bottled after a year's BARREL MATURATION, they are capable of ageing well thereafter, particularly those of Domaine Ferret, the Ch de Fuissé and Guffens-Heynen (the family domaine associated with the NÉGOCIANT Verget). Prices can vary enormously depending on the demands of major export markets in a given year.

The small village of Pouilly also lends its name to two adjacent lesser appellations, POUILLY-VINZELLES and POUILLY-LOCHÉ. J.T.C.M.

Pouilly-Fumé, also known as **Pouilly Blanc Fumé** and **Blanc Fumé de Pouilly**, one of the Loire's most famous wines, perfumed dry whites that epitomize the SAUVIGNON BLANC grape (along with nearby MENETOU-SALON, QUINCY, REUILLY, and, most notably, SANCERRE). All Sauvignon here is Sauvignon Blanc (no Gris allowed) and was often called Blanc Fumé, because wines made from this variety when grown on the predominantly LIMESTONE soils, with some flint (*silex*), supposedly exhibit a 'smoky' flavour, or whiff of gunflint (*pierre à fusil*). The wines are certainly perfumed, sometimes almost acrid, and it takes extensive local knowledge reliably to distinguish Sancerres and

Pouilly-Fumés in a blind tasting of both. Pouilly-Fumé is arguably a more homogeneous appellation than Sancerre, which is not surprising since less than half as much Pouilly-Fumé is made as white Sancerre. Unlike that of Sancerre, the Pouilly-Fumé appellation applies only to white wines. The best Pouilly-Fumé (such as the range produced by Didier Dageneau) is perhaps a denser, more ambitiously long-lived liquid than Sancerre, for drinking at two to six years, for example, rather than one to four (although there are, as always with wine, exceptions). At the most historic estate, de Ladoucette's magnificently turreted Ch du Nozet, are bottles which prove that Pouilly-Fumé can last for decades, although whether it actually improves is a matter of taste. Some producers began experimenting with OAK for both fermentation and maturation in the mid 1980s and the wines of the region have become more complex. The appellation takes its name from the small town of Pouilly-sur-Loire on the right bank of the Loire in the Nièvre *département*. The name **Pouilly-sur-Loire** is given to the zone's less distinguished wine, a usually thin and short-lived liquid made in very much smaller quantities from the CHASSELAS grape, grown here in the 19th century for the tables of Paris. In the 1970s and 1980s, Pouilly-Fumé was much favoured by FASHION, and the total area planted with Sauvignon Blanc increased considerably. By 2012 it totalled 1,273 ha/3,144 acres. Some of the finest vineyards are on the slopes of St-Andelain north of Pouilly.

See also LOIRE, including map.

Friedrich, J., *Earthly Delights from the Garden of France, Wines of the Loire*, Vol 1: *The Kingdom of Sauvignon Blanc* (lulu.com, 2011).

Pouilly-Loché. See POUILLY-VINZELLES.

Pouilly-Vinzelles. Borrowing the prefix from its more famous neighbour in southern Burgundy POUILLY-FUISSÉ, the village of Vinzelles has its own small appellation of 51 ha/126 acres, most of which forms a steep, east-facing slope overlooking the valley of the Saône. The best vineyard is Les Quarts and the leading producer Domaine de la Soufrandière. Otherwise most production is in the hands of the local CO-OPERATIVE, as is the case also for **Pouilly-Loché**, an even smaller appellation of 29 ha which may be sold under the name of Pouilly-Vinzelles (but not vice versa).

Poulsard, sometimes called **Ploussard**, is a relatively rare speciality of the JURA, planted on a steady 300 ha/750 acres. Its long, thin-skinned, almost transluscent grapes make distinctive light tomato-red wines which may be left on the skins for as long as two weeks without tainting the wine too deeply, and are sometimes sold as rosé. It does particularly well on MARL in the northern vineyards of the Jura,

especially at Pupillin near Arbois, self-proclaimed capital of Ploussard. Its delicate pigment makes it much prized for adding colour to VIN DE PAILLE and it is also used for rosé CRÉMANT du Jura. Very prone to REDUCTION, Poulsard wines benefit from low or no SULFUR DIOXIDE additions, and in the 21st century they have often been made with semi-CARBONIC MACERATION. Poulsard may also be blended with TROUSSEAU and Pinot Noir. It is also grown to a very limited extent in BUGEY, mainly for the semi-sweet sparkling CRU Cerdon.

pourriture, French for ROT. *Pourriture noble* is NOBLE ROT. *Pourriture grise* is GREY ROT, or malevolent BOTRYTIS BUNCH ROT.

powdery mildew, also called oidium, *oïdium* in French, the first of the vine FUNGAL DISEASES to be scientifically described, in 1834 in the United States. It is native to North America, where it causes minor damage on native grapes. The fungus was given the name *Oidium tuckerii* after the gardener, a Mr Tucker, who first noted it in Europe, in Margate, England, in 1845 (Barron says 1831 or 1832). Today the fungus is more widely known as *Uncinula necator*. The disease was first noted in France in 1847, where it soon spread and caused widespread havoc to vineyards and wine quality. Today the disease is spread worldwide. There is a difference in susceptibility between different vine species, with many native AMERICAN VINES being very resistant.

Varieties of the European vine *Vitis* VINIFERA are generally very susceptible, although some variation is noted. For example, Aramon, Pinot Noir, Malbec, Merlot, and Riesling are noticeably more tolerant than Carignan, Colombard, Chardonnay, and Cabernet Sauvignon.

All green parts of the vine are attacked and the infection is very visible. A fine, translucent, cobweb-like growth spreads around the spot where the fungus first penetrates. After one to two weeks, grey-white ash-like spores are produced on short, upright stalks. The infection looks powdery, leading to the common name. Spores are spread by wind and, with favourable conditions, new infections rapidly occur. The fungus survives over winter inside buds or on the surface of the vine. If bunches are infected before flowering, then FRUIT SET and yield may be considerably reduced and berry RIPENING delayed. Yield can be further reduced if berries are infected before they reach full size. Surface cells are killed so that the berries never grow to full size. Fruit of coloured varieties also fails to colour properly.

Fruit infected with powdery mildew is universally avoided in winemaking, and until recently there has been surprisingly little research into the effects on wine quality. Studies in New York state and Australia agree on the following points: wine made from infected bunches loses its fruity aromas, to be replaced by mouldy, wet fur, and earthy characters; wines are described as 'oily' and 'viscous'. The greater the infection, the more obvious the effects.

The disease develops and spreads most rapidly in warm weather, 20 to 27 °C (68–80 °F). Unlike all other fungal diseases of vines, this one is little affected by humidity, making climate conditions which favour it different from those which favour many others. Powdery mildew is favoured by dense, shaded CANOPIES. In fact, bright sunlight, especially the ULTRAVIOLET part of the spectrum, inhibits the germination of spores. Fortunately the control of this disease was discovered soon after it appeared in Europe. Mr Tucker noted the similarity between this vine disease and that affecting peach trees, which could be controlled by a mixture of SULFUR, lime, and water. Dusting with sulfur was accepted after the disastrous French vintage of 1854, the smallest since 1788. This same technique is still used today.

In dry climates, sulfur dust is used; wettable powders are used in higher rainfall regions; and organic fungicides have been developed more recently. Cultural practices such as maintaining a non-shaded canopy (see CANOPY MICROCLIMATE) help prevent development of the disease. Recent developments in vine breeding have produced varieties with natural resistance and acceptable wine quality. These DISEASE-RESISTANT VARIETIES use the natural tolerance of native American species somewhere in their pedigree.

R.E.S.

Barron, A., *Vines and Vine Culture* (London, 1883).

Stumner, B. E., et al., 'Powdery mildew and grape and wine quality', *The Australian & New Zealand Grapegrower & Winemaker*, 464 (Sept 2002), 68–74.

University of California Agriculture & Natural Resources, 'Powdery mildew', www.ipm.ucdavis.edu/PMG/r302100311.html.

Prädikat

Germany

A Prädikat is a 'distinction', awarded to PDO wines on the basis of increasing grape MUST WEIGHT: either KABINETT, SPÄTLESE, AUSLESE, BEERENAUSLESE, TROCKENBEERENAUSLESE or EISWEIN. Long collectively known as Qualitätswein mit Prädikat (QmP), the wines are now officially known simply as **Prädikatsweine**. Depending on region and grape variety, the minimum must weights in OECHSLE (and equivalent potential alcohol) set by GERMAN WINE LAW for each Prädikat range as follows (with the low end applying in each case to the minimum for Riesling in the Mosel):

Kabinett 70–82 °Oe / 9.1–10.9%
Spätlese 76–90 °Oe / 10–12.2%

Auslese 83–100 °Oe / 11.1–13.8%
Beerenauslese and Eiswein 110–128 °Oe / 15.3–18.1%
Trockenbeerenauslese 150–154 °Oe / 21.5–21.9%

In practice, quality-conscious producers set their own estate-specific standards for what counts as Spätlese, Auslese, etc. These generally entail far higher must weights than the legal minima, which is unsurprising in this era of CLIMATE CHANGE. What counts as Kabinett, Spätlese, Auslese etc. is nowadays largely a matter of individual convention. One grower's Spätlese may be another's Auslese, and the choice of Prädikat is often made on the basis of intended style from among musts of nearly identical sugar content.

Germany's most prestigious growers' association, the VDP, may have 'Prädikatswein' in its name, but it took the lead in eliminating designations of Prädikat from the labels of dry wines, including those of their prestige class known as GROSSES GEWÄCHS. The idea is that a Prädikat designation should immediately indicate significant SWEETNESS, typically increasing with must weight. Dry German wines are more likely to be described as QUALITÄTSWEIN.

Austria

Prädikatswein officially excludes Kabinett wine in Austria but includes, in addition to the other Prädikats, Strohwein (or 'straw wine', see VIN DE PAILLE) and AUSBRUCH. As commonly used in Austria, Prädikatswein refers to overtly sweet wines of Auslese or higher must weight. The following minimum KMW must weights (with equivalent Oechsle and potential alcohols) are set for Prädikatswein:

Spätlese 19 °KMW / 94 °Oe / 12.8%
Auslese 21 °KMW / 105 °Oe / 14.5%
Beerenauslese 25 °KMW / 127 °Oe / 18%
Ausbruch 27 °KMW / 139 °Oe / 19.8%
Trockenbeerenauslese 30 °KMW / 156 °Oe / 21.8%
Eiswein 25 °KMW / 127 °Oe / 18%
Strohwein/Schilfwein 25 °KMW / 127 °Oe / 18%

Both German and Austrian laws stipulate certain characteristics that should be met by Prädikatswein over and above minimum must weights, such as that Spätlese or Auslese must be harvested from 'fully ripe' grapes; Beerenauslese from BOTRYTIZED grapes; and Trockenbeerenauslese from 'predominantly shriveled' grapes. But in practice, such unquantifiable criteria are virtually assured by the requisite must weight and are not enforced, except for two categories. Eiswein must be pressed from grapes that have frozen on the vine and not been allowed to thaw. And (in Austria) Strohwein/Schilfwein must be made from grapes suspended on racks or dried on straw or reed mats for at least three months without any use of heaters, fans, or dehumidifiers.

D.S.

Pramaggiore. See LISON-PRAMAGGIORE.

PRD. See PARTIAL ROOTZONE DRYING.

precipitates, solids which are deposited on the bottom of barrels, casks, tanks, or vats by wine stored in them.

Technically, precipitates are solids which deposit from solutions because of reactions or temperature changes, and differ from SEDIMENTS, which are suspensions of solids which settle from the mixture when agitation ceases. Technically, therefore, the stem, pulp, and skin fragments and the seeds and dead yeast cells which settle after fermentation as gross LEES are not precipitates, while subsequent deposits of TARTRATES and oxidized PHENOLICS are. Practical winemakers, however, tend to classify both groups as precipitates, along with COLLOIDS.

A.D.W.

precision viticulture is an approach to wine-grape production which recognizes that the productivity of individual vineyard blocks can show marked spatial variation in relation to variation in the land (SOIL, TOPOGRAPHY) underlying the vineyard. Thus, vineyard management is targeted rather than implemented uniformly over large areas. Research in Australia suggests that grape yield within a single vineyard under conventional uniform management will typically vary 10-fold (i.e. 2–20 tonnes/ha).

Critical to this approach to grape and wine production is the collection and use of large amounts of data relating to vine performance and the attributes of individual production areas (vineyards, blocks, sub-blocks, zones, etc.) at a high spatial resolution. This approach relies on a number of key enabling technologies including the GLOBAL POSITIONING SYSTEM (GPS), GEOGRAPHICAL INFORMATION SYSTEMS (GIS), REMOTE SENSING, PROXIMAL SENSING, and YIELD MONITORS, which, when used in conjunction with the GPS, enable geo-referenced records of yield to be collected 'on-the-go' during harvest. Such technologies, and the data derived from them, enable precision viticulture (PV) practitioners to manage vineyards by 'zones' rather than by blocks using targeted management to tailor production according to expectations of vineyard performance, and desired goals in terms of both YIELD and/or GRAPE COMPOSITION AND WINE QUALITY. This is feasible given recent research which has shown that patterns of spatial variation in vineyard performance tend to be constant from one vintage to another, which in turn lends itself to the adoption of ZONAL VITICULTURE and SELECTIVE HARVESTING, and the use of data collected in previous years to predict likely performance in subsequent years.

Targeted management may mean the timing and rate of application of water, fertilizer, ameliorants such as MULCH or sprays, or the use of machinery and labour for a range of vineyard operations such as pruning, shoot or crop thinning but selective harvesting is the most widely adopted form of targeted management. See ZONAL VITICULTURE.

Yield monitors and proximal fruit and canopy sensors are available as 'on-the-go' sensing technologies for attachment to existing vineyard machinery; methods to simultaneously predict yield and assess grapevine canopy conditions and GRAPE COMPOSITION are under development.   R.G.V.B.

> Bramley, R. G. V., 'Precision viticulture: managing vineyard variability for improved quality outcomes', in A. G. Reynolds (ed.), *Managing Wine Quality 1: Viticulture and Wine Quality* (Cambridge, 2010), 445–80.
>
> Proffitt, T., et al., *Precision Viticulture—A New Era in Vineyard Management and Wine Production* (Adelaide, 2006).

premature oxidation, known colloquially as premox, or even pox, is a phenomenon widely seen in white burgundy since the mid 1990s, but also evident in many other white wines and occasionally in reds. The first vintage to exhibit the problem was 1996, at about five years old, although it subsequently became clear that 1995 was also implicated.

A white wine which has oxidized naturally over a long period (see OXIDATION and BOTTLE AGEING) is likely to be deep yellow in colour, perhaps browning, with aromas of cooked fruit, sometimes quince, eventually dank, dead fruit, possibly sherrified and acetic (see ACETALDEHYDE). Typically these negative effects will be immediately apparent on opening and pouring.

A prematurely oxidized white wine will also show some advance in the colour, more in the dull yellow range, and this may happen after the bottle has been open for a minute or two. The first danger sign in terms of aroma is bruised apples or furniture polish, which can strengthen considerably with AERATION. A compound called SOTOLON, characterized by honey or beeswax, is also commonly identified in these wines. Aromas of stewed fruit and prunes are common in prematurely oxidized red wines.

Two specific reasons were identified early on: inadequate CORKS and low SULFUR DIOXIDE levels. This was the worst period for cork quality, with an increase in demand due to growing world wine production but prior to the widespread introduction of SCREWCAPS and alternative CLOSURES. Many producers had also reduced sulfur dioxide levels in the interests of elegance and purity.

These problems coincided with a period in which the oxidation potential of white wines has been higher than in the past thanks to CLIMATE CHANGE and the desire for riper styles of wine which may be enjoyed earlier in their life.

Some instances of premature oxidation seem to be temporary, similar to the AGEING trajectory of some white wines from the RHÔNE Valley. It is not clear if this is the apparent reversal of oxidation—a possibility if the oxidation process has not gone too far—or if the results of other complex processes are being blamed on premature oxidation.

Leading Bordeaux researchers Denis Dubourdieu and Valérie Lavigne believe that the production of the antioxidant GLUTATHIONE in vineyards is vital to the prevention of premox. Their overall preventive strategy comprises the following steps:

- ensuring adequate supply of NITROGEN to the vine for sufficient and appropriate VIGOUR
- limiting extraction of PHENOLIC compounds during pressing to preserve GLUTATHIONE
- protecting must and wine from oxidation (INERT GAS, sulfur dioxide)
- ensuring a rapid and complete alcoholic fermentation
- reducing the time lag between fermentation and MALOLACTIC CONVERSION (by LEES STIRRING and inoculation with LACTIC ACID BACTERIA)
- ageing the wines in REDUCTIVE conditions (sulfur dioxide, lees, moderate amounts of new oak)
- limiting the amount of dissolved oxygen when preparing the wine for BOTTLING (see TOTAL PACKAGE OXYGEN)
- choosing a closure that is suited to the wine.

See also RANDOM OXIDATION.   J.T.C.M.

> Goode, J., 'Beauty and the beast: premature oxidation', *World of Fine Wine*, 14 (2006), 86–92.
>
> Lavigne, V., Pons, A., and Dubourdieu, D., 'The premature oxidative ageing of wine', Faculty of Oenology, Bordeaux Institute of Vine and Wine Sciences (2010).
>
> Morris, J., 'White Burgundy out of the woods?', *World of Fine Wine*, 43 (2014), 100–9.
>
> www.oxidised-burgs.wikispaces.com.

premier cru, or **premier cru classé**, is a CRU judged of the first rank, usually according to some official CLASSIFICATION. The direct translation of the French term *premier cru*, much used in the context of BORDEAUX, is FIRST GROWTH. A **premier grand cru (classé)** or **premier cru supérieur** may, as in the case of ST-ÉMILION and Ch d'YQUEM, be a rung higher even than this. In Burgundy, scores of vineyards are designated premiers crus, capable of producing wine distinctly superior to VILLAGE WINE but not quite so great as the produce of the GRANDS CRUS. See BURGUNDY in general and each of the villages on the CÔTE D'OR in particular. See also ERSTES GEWÄCHS, ERSTE LAGE, and CHAUME.

Premières Côtes de Bordeaux, AOC created in 2011 specifically for sweet wine made in the narrow strip extending for 60 km/40 miles along the south-western edge of the ENTRE-DEUX-MERS appellation on the right bank of the GARONNE from Langon almost as far as the city of Bordeaux. It used to apply to the red wines produced in this strip too but from 2011 the reds have been known as CADILLAC CÔTES DE BORDEAUX. In 2013 just 123 ha/304 acres of vineyard were devoted to the production of these blends of Sémillon, Sauvignon Blanc, Sauvignon Gris, and Muscadelle that lack the intensity of great SAUTERNES. Dry whites are sold as AOC Bordeaux.

premium wine, debased and virtually meaningless term, not unlike RESERVE. See also ICON WINE.

Prensal. See MOLL.

pre-phylloxera, term used to differentiate European, and especially French, wines made from vines before the arrival of the devastating phylloxera louse towards the end of the 19th century from those made from the vines GRAFTED on to phylloxera-resistant American ROOTSTOCKS which replaced them. In the first half of the 20th century, there was much understandable discussion about the relative merits of pre- and post-phylloxera wines with, perhaps inevitably, overall agreement that the earlier generation of wines were distinctly superior. As pointed out at the end of PHYLLOXERA, however, it was probably not the grafting itself which resulted in an apparent drop in quality, but the effects of the VIRUS DISEASES imported into European vineyards along with all this phylloxera-resistant plant material from across the Atlantic.

pre-pruning. See MECHANICAL PRUNING.

press, in a wine context usually means **wine press**, a particularly ancient piece of winemaking equipment, used for the PRESSING operation of separating grape juice or wine from solids. Wine presses or their remains provide some of the longest-surviving evidence of the ORIGINS OF VINICULTURE. In ancient times, the design of presses was varied and ingenious. See Ancient EGYPT and GREECE for more details.

Ancient history

CATO (*De agricultura* 18–19) in the 2nd century BC provided the first detailed description of a press room. He describes a beam or lever press. This would be constructed on an elevated concrete platform with a raised curb, which formed a shallow basin, which sloped gently to a runoff point. On this was constructed the press, which consisted of a long, heavy horizontal beam, which slotted into an upright at the back and ran between two uprights at the front. The front end of the beam was attached by a rope to a windlass. The grape solids were put under the beam and pressure applied by winding down the end. As the pulp compacted, so wedges were hammered into the slot at the pivot end to lower it. Over time various refinements were introduced. Most notably, according to PLINY (*Natural History* 18. 317), a 'Greek-style' press was introduced in the late republic or early empire, in which the windlass was replaced with a vertical screw thread, sometimes with a heavy counterweight. There is ample archaeological evidence from Italy, and elsewhere, for the use of presses. All the Roman AGRICULTURAL TREATISES, apart from the writings of Palladius, assume the use of a press in their descriptions of winemaking. However, the press was an elaborate and comparatively expensive piece of equipment and its use was far from universal. Some farmsteads have large tanks for treading the grapes in, but no evidence of a press. It is not clear whether the must from the treading was always kept separate from that from the pressing. The grape pulp could be subject to a second pressing; but this was carefully kept separate. The pressed grape skins could even be soaked in water to produce *lorca*, a drink to be given to the farm hands (VARRO, *De re rustica* 1. 54), a forerunner of PIQUETTE.   J.J.P.

Rossiter, J. J., 'Wine and oil processing at Roman farms in Italy', *Phoenix*, 35 (1981), 345–61.

White, K. D., *Farm Equipment of the Roman World* (Cambridge, 1975), 112–15.

Presses today

Wine presses have evolved over the last thousand years or more into the relatively complicated machines used today. The **basket** presses used during the Middle Ages by religious orders were large devices built of wood in which grapes were squeezed by a horizontal wooden disc which just fitted into a cylindrical basket made of wooden staves bound into the cylinder shape by encircling wooden hoops. The juice from the crushed berries escapes through the spaces between the basket staves and flows into a tray below. Some of these traditional presses, usually depending on a giant lever for pressure, still exist and are occasionally used in Burgundy and parts of Italy. Similar, usually smaller versions of the basket press reliant on hand or hydraulic power can be found in many of the Old World's less mechanized wineries today and most producers of CHAMPAGNE and SAUTERNES still rely on variations on this vertical pressing theme, demanding though they are in terms of time and manpower. Modern basket presses, the wooden slats often replaced by stainless steel, are gaining in popularity among producers who wish to work with smaller batches and are willing to tolerate longer set-up and cleaning times in order to treat their fruit as gently as possible. If whole bunches are included, the stems improve drainage.

In modern **horizontal** presses, the basket press principle has been turned on its side. They can be divided into either batch or continuous presses, the latter almost never used for fine wines. Most batch presses depend upon squeezing a charge of crushed grapes or POMACE against a perforated screen. Pressure may be applied by a moving press head as in the old basket press or, more gently in theory, by using a pneumatic press, in which an airbag, or **bladder**, expands to squeeze the pomace against the inner wall of a perforated cylinder. A membrane may be used to perform a similar function. Horizontal batch presses that are fully enclosed are called **tank** presses. They reduce the exposure of the pomace and juice to air. The use of INERT GAS to flush the tank prior to pressing further reduces this exposure. (See also NITROGEN.)

Continuous presses, more common in the 1980s and 1990s, are much harsher and usually worked either by a screw or a belt. The screw press usually resembles a giant domestic food chopper. The decreasing pitch of an Archimedes screw subjects the pomace to increasing pressure as it is moved along within the perforated cylindrical housing. The juice obtained, especially near the exit end, is very cloudy and rich in PHENOLICS but the juice from the crushed grape or pomace entry point is much clearer. Belt presses are much rarer and function by pressing intact berries between two perforated moving belts arranged so that the clearance between them decreases. Juice from belt presses is much clearer and better quality than that from screw presses, but the screw press allows faster throughput and is therefore the cheapest form of press. Both screw and belt presses can also be enclosed. The belt press was really more of an alternative to the crusher since it was still necessary to drain the juice and press the skins further in some other form of press.

Many modern presses are controlled by a computer program designed to optimize the pressing cycle for each grape variety and wine type. The screw press is still found in some large commercial wineries but some form of tank press is increasingly common for fine wine production.   A.D.W.

Pressac, Bordeaux RIGHT BANK name for the red grape variety Cot or MALBEC.

pressing, winemaking operation whereby pressure is applied, using a press, to grapes, grape clusters, or grape POMACE in order to squeeze the liquid out of the solid parts, known as *pressurage* in French.

For most white wines, pressing takes place prior to FERMENTATION (for exceptions, see ORANGE WINES, QVEVRI, and SKIN-FERMENTED whites, for example). There are various options for extracting juice from grapes: immediate pressing of whole grapes without CRUSHING, immediate pressing of crushed and/or DESTEMMED grapes, or pressing after the crushed and destemmed grapes have undergone a period of SKIN CONTACT.

The most commonly used PRESSES today are pneumatic bladder presses. Using gentle pressure, this type of pressing makes it possible to extract juice containing little PULP. It also results in only a small increase in the level of PHENOLICS in the must. However, it is necessary to make sure that pressing lasts long enough for the grapes' aromatic qualities to be released into the must. In certain instances skin contact may take place in the press.

Red wines are usually pressed after fermentation (or just before the end) or following extended MACERATION, but see RED WINEMAKING for alternative approaches. The timing and the pressure influences the level of phenolic extraction.

See also PRESS, PRESS WINE, and FREE-RUN.
                                            V.L. & D.D.

pressure bomb, or **pressure chamber**, a device for measuring water potential in plants developed by the American plant scientist Scholander in the 1960s. Since then it has been used for studies in grapevine physiology, and more recently in California as a guide to the timing of vineyard IRRIGATION. The blade of the leaf is placed in an airtight chamber and pressure is increased until XYLEM fluid exudes from the cut PETIOLE end. However, water potential of the grapevine can vary from hour to hour, depending on sunshine, temperature, humidity and soil moisture content so it is difficult to interpret this dynamic value as an irrigation guide.   R.E.S.

Bogart, K., Measuring winegrape water status using a pressure chamber', www.extension.org/pages/33029/measuring-winegrape-water-status-using-a-pressure-chamber#.UyCqcOd_vbk.

Smart, R. E., 'Do not blow up your irrigation schedule with the pressure bomb!', *Practical Winery & Vineyard* (Nov/Dec 2001), 80–1.

press wine, dark red wine squeezed from POMACE (grape skins, stem fragments, pulp, dead yeast) in a wine PRESS. Press wine is generally inferior in quality to FREE-RUN wine, and certainly more astringent, although some presses are capable of exerting pressure in controlled stages so that the product of the first, gentle pressing is very close to free-run in quality. Continuous screw presses in particular often exert such pressure that the product is excessively bitter and astringent. A certain proportion of press wine may be usefully incorporated into the free-run wine, especially if it lacks TANNIN. Whether to include press wine in the blend, and how much to include, depends very much on the desired style of the wine and the vintage conditions. Otherwise it is used for a lesser bottling or, traditionally, given to workers at the establishment which produced it.

All white wine except for the free-run juice is effectively press wine, although its quality and characteristics are shaped considerably by how gently the white grapes were pressed. and whether there has been any SKIN CONTACT. See also the TAILLE produced in CHAMPAGNE.

A.D.W.

prestige cuvée, one of several names given to a CHAMPAGNE house's highest-quality wine. At one time the houses saw their NON-VINTAGE wine as their greatest expression. Vintage-dated champagne was added to the range and a premium usually charged for it. ROEDERER's Cristal bottling and MOËT & CHANDON's named after Dom PÉRIGNON scaled new heights, however, and today most of the major champagne firms offer one such product, available—at a price and, often, in a specially created bottle—in limited quantity at the top of their range. Also sometimes known as de luxe or luxury cuvées.

price is probably the single most important aspect of a wine to most consumers, just as the price of grapes is one of the most important variables of the viticultural year to most grape-growers. The price of vineyard land is not directly proportional to the price fetched by grapes grown on it, however. See below.

Grape prices

Wine grapes are an important item of commerce throughout the world, and the economic fortunes of many rural communities rise and fall with local wine grape prices. Although many wine consumers have the impression that most wine grapes are grown on estates which also process them into wine, nothing could be further from the truth. The majority of the world's wine grapes are sold in the form of fresh fruit, to be vinified quite independently of the grape-grower, whether by commercial wineries or CO-OPERATIVES.

The means to determine prices for wine grapes varies from region to region. Prices are normally fixed annually, taking into account supply and demand as well as individual VINTAGE characteristics. A buoyant wine market bolsters grape prices, whatever the size of the crop, with some wineries attracting fruit away from others by paying higher prices. When the market is depressed it is not unusual to see fruit left on the vine (as in Australia in the mid 2000s, for instance), since the cost of harvesting can be more than the potential income. In many areas, notably Europe and South Africa, surplus grapes are distilled into alcohol, which in turn often becomes SURPLUS to requirements.

Normally grapes are bought and sold according to VINE VARIETY and sugar content. The demand for different varieties is relatively stable, but prices can reflect longer-term changes as varieties move in and out of FASHION. In most

European regions, there is some sort of representative body which oversees grape prices. For example, in Bordeaux, the Conseil Interprofessionnel du Vin de Bordeaux (CIVB) has a board made up of wine producers and NÉGOCIANTS which seeks to organize the market for grapes and wine. As well as documenting wine sales, the CIVB may enter the market place in its own right and, for example, buy wine stocks for ageing in years of high supply. The regional organization in Champagne is the oldest of the French regional associations, and has powers and services which extend beyond grape price determination. The Comité Interprofessionnel du Vin de Champagne (CIVC) has in its time determined grape prices by means of a relatively complex series of calculations (see CHAMPAGNE).

For many European producers, grape prices are set by co-operatives, and although the formulae may not be so rigid as those traditionally employed in Champagne, they must take into account the same factors concerning supply, demand, and intrinsic quality. In much of the New World, the majority of grape-growers sell their produce to private wineries. In Australia, there are very few statutory bodies which are involved in setting minimum prices. In the United States of America, individual growers negotiate freely with individual wineries, even though they may voluntarily join an association which will set recommended prices. The US government does, however, report on prices paid after each vintage.

A basic problem in buying and selling wine grapes is that their true value is not known until they are made into wine, and indeed until that wine is sold. Region of origin, however, is well recognized as affecting wine style and quality, and in 2013 in Australia there existed more than six-fold variation in prices between regions, with fruit destined for bulk wine in hot inland areas being the lowest in value. Concentration of SUGAR IN GRAPES is the most common measure which can be related to grape quality. This is particularly important for grapes grown in cool climates, where better-quality wines are invariably made from grapes with higher MUST WEIGHTS. However, in warm to hot climates it is not difficult to reach the desired sugar level, and other aspects of GRAPE COMPOSITION are better related to quality. Increasingly, progressive wineries are implementing grape quality assessment schemes to reward growers for producing high-quality fruit. These schemes can be related to the vineyard site as well as to rootstock and clone, vineyard management methods, and also perhaps to a detailed chemical ANALYSIS of the fruit. Some wineries keep wine batches from different growers separate, and so are able to pay a bonus based on performance, but a lack of understanding of and agreement on vineyard factors which affect wine quality is likely to hamper widespread

application of wine grape quality bonus systems. Some enlightened wine producers pay growers per ha/acre and effectively manage grape quality themselves.   R.E.S. & J.R.

Vineyard land prices

Wine is acknowledged as a natural product, and there is a widespread acceptance that the region or even vineyard of origin has a major effect on wine quality (see CLIMATE AND WINE QUALITY, SOIL AND WINE QUALITY, and VITICULTURE). Needless to say, those vineyards with a reputation for high wine quality attract high land prices. Perhaps the clearest examples are to be found in the Bordeaux region, where, thanks partly to several important CLASSIFICATIONS of individual châteaux, land prices are also clearly stratified. In the mid 2000s, for example, the price of planted vineyard entitled to the basic Bordeaux appellation had fallen to very roughly 25,000 euros per ha (it was about 200,000 francs per ha in the late 1990s) while one of the most celebrated properties might cost the equivalent of 1.5 to 3 million euros per ha (very much less than Gérard Perse offered AXA-Millésimes in 2001 for Ch Petit Village in Pomerol, only to rescind the offer). According to the 2013 French government's valuation (for tax purposes) of vineyard land, the maximum value within the Gironde region was 2.35 million euros per ha in Pomerol, followed by 2.1 million euros in Pauillac.

Burgundy is a region in which geographical delimitation is even more precise, and prices vary considerably. GRAND CRU were valued at an eye-watering maximum of 9.5 million euros per ha while those qualifying only for AOC Bourgogne could be acquired for less than 30,000 euros per ha depending on their exact location. Champagne vineyard land was for long considered some of the world's most expensive but in 2014 the maximum price reported by SAFER, the French organization overseeing vineyard transactions, was 1.8 million euros per ha.

In 2013 Knight Frank published a global vineyard index comparing minimum and maximum prices of what they refer to as LIFESTYLE vineyards (vineyards greater than 5 ha/12 acres that are neither hobby purchases nor large commercial set-ups), in many regions around the world. Champagne was not mentioned but the highest values were for Bordeaux although they ranged widely there, from US$20,500 to $2,500,000 per ha. Next highest were Piemonte (bracketed with Lombardy), at a maximum of $1,200,000 per ha. Among NEW WORLD regions, land in the Napa Valley was the most expensive, with values from $135,000 to $588,000 per ha. Values for Chile's Colchagua Valley, Mendoza in Argentina, South Africa's Western Cape, and the Barossa Valley in Australia are lower, related to land availability, but for Hawke's Bay in New Zealand the values are surprisingly high (from $130,000 to $170,000).

p

Interestingly there are extensive tracts of land which have suitable soils and climate to grow quality grapes economically which are yet to be 'discovered' and planted to vineyards. As such, they have the value only of their existing land use. In many instances this might be low-value grazing. In HAWKE'S BAY, New Zealand, many of the vineyards are planted in soils which have alternative horticultural uses, which may explain why they are valued relatively highly. Regions with particular soil features, such as Gimblett Gravels in Hawke's Bay, have developed as well-regarded wine regions within a few decades. These ALLUVIAL gravel soils were rated poorly for grazing, and could be bought very cheaply by the initial vineyard investors but because the area is small and clearly defined, these vineyards are highly priced. Tasmania has Australia's coolest climate, similar to New Zealand, with ample cheap and suitable land, yet to date there has been limited outside investment, despite Australia's enthusiastic imports of COOL-CLIMATE wine styles from New Zealand.

R.E.S. & J.R.

http://my.knightfrank.co.uk/research-reports/global-vineyard-index.aspx

Wine prices

The price of a wine is a function of the price of the grapes, the price of LABOUR, the price of a winery or the debt outstanding on it, pricing policy on the part of the producer, pricing policy on the part of any merchants involved in selling it, the cost of TRANSPORT, BOTTLING, LABELLING, and marketing, quite apart from any DUTIES and TAXATION. The interest for the wine producer must be to maximize his or her return on capital, without acquiring a reputation for profiteering.

GLOBALIZATION continues to give bigger retailers increasing power to dictate prices and PRICE POINTS, which has had a generally deflationary effect on retail prices, if hardly an inflationary one on absolute value. See also ECONOMICS OF WINE.

The interesting question for the consumer, however, is the extent to which retail wine prices, which can vary more than a thousandfold, reflect wine quality. The answer is, of course, not very closely. All sorts of factors can depress the price of a wine to make it a bargain relative to the competition. Some national economies offer particularly low production costs (such as SOUTH AFRICA and some of SOUTH AMERICA) when translated into the currencies of many potential importers. Currency movements in general have far more (upward) impact on wine prices than most wine drinkers realize (merchants do not always pass on the benefit to consumers of downward movements). The enormous surge in demand for 1982 Bordeaux in the United States was partly the result of the strength of the American dollar relative to the French franc in 1983 when EN PRIMEUR purchases were made. Other political events can also affect wine prices. The fall of communism and the effect of GORBACHEV's anti-alcohol policies on eastern Europe left SURPLUS PRODUCTION in countries such as BULGARIA, HUNGARY, and ROMANIA, which used to ship enormous quantities to the Soviet Union, and these emerging economies' desire for hard, western currency led them to export goods such as wine at extremely keen prices, or as part of barter deals in the 1990s. Specific countries may also benefit from preferential import tariffs.

Pricing policy in general may be geared to gaining a foothold in a new market, as for example, South Africa needed to do after the lifting of sanctions in the early 1990s. Or it may have the result of bolstering prices in the belief that high prices automatically buy respect and prestige, a phenomenon associated with some aspirant CALIFORNIA CULT wines.

The above considerations relate to the prices of wine when it is first offered for sale. Serious wine COLLECTORS and those considering investing in wine are interested in what happens to the price of FINE WINE over time. As detailed in INVESTMENT and AUCTIONS, this depends on the precise wine, the era, and period of time, and also on the rarity value of a given wine, its PROVENANCE and condition, and the general state of the market.

Most ordinary wine drinkers took a certain comfort in the story of what happened to the world's most expensive bottle of wine sold, at Christie's for a record £105,000 in 1985: this particular bottle of Ch Lafite 1787, supposedly once the property of Thomas JEFFERSON, was stood upright on display under warm lights by its owner Malcolm Forbes so that, unnoticed, the cork dried out and dropped into the bottle, rendering the wine OXIDIZED and undrinkable.

Not least because of the ASIAN economic boom, the late 1990s saw the prices of the most sought-after fine wines, the so-called TROPHY WINES, draw away from those of other wines, a gap that widened as the CHINESE buyers poured into the market for top 2009 and 2010 bordeaux, making such wines seem even poorer value than ever. It is ironic perhaps that at a time when the difference in quality between wines at the top and bottom ends of the market has never been narrower, the price difference has never been greater. But presumably this reflects the hugely increased number of affluent wine consumers, the finite volumes of wine produced, and the significant position that wine now holds in a number of cultures round the world.

price points, the supposedly particularly significant retail prices that increasingly dominate wine selling, whether by producer to retailer or by retailer to consumer. Mass market wines are typically offered by the producer at a proposed retail price of x.99. Bigger retailers impose a carefully planned timetable of retail discounts and promotions on their main suppliers, thereby sometimes entailing artificially inflated base price points from which these 'reductions' can be made. In common usage 'price point' is often used instead of 'price'.

Prié, rare but genetically important AOSTA white wine grape that has close relatives in both Switzerland and Spain.

Prieto Picudo, unusual, musky, Spanish medium-red grape grown in 2012 on 4,465 ha/11,029 acres, mainly around the city of León in north central Spain. These red wines are light in colour but potent and distinctive. It is probably a sibling of Portugal's ALFROCHEIRO.

Primaticcio, occasional name used for both SANGIOVESE and PRIMITIVO.

primeur, French word for young produce which has been adapted to mean 'young wine'. French AOC rules allow all of the following to be released on the third Thursday of November following the harvest: Beaujolais, Côtes du Rhône, Grignan-les-Adhémar, Ventoux, Languedoc, Gamays from Touraine, Anjou, and Gaillac, Coteaux du Lyonnais, Côtes du Roussillon, Mâcon Blanc, Tavel Rosé, Rosé d'Anjou, Cabernet d'Anjou, Cabernet de Saumur, Bourgogne Blanc, Bourgogne Aligoté, Muscadet, and Gaillac Blanc. For more details of this style of wine, see NOUVEAU.

See also EN PRIMEUR for details of fine wines offered for sale as futures before they are bottled.

Primitivo, Italian name for the originally Croatian ZINFANDEL grape (see also TRIBIDRAG), grown principally in PUGLIA. Once highly prized for blending, in the 1990s it fell victim to the same EU VINE PULL SCHEME as NEGROAMARO. Plantings fell to under 8,000 ha by the turn of the century but the 1994 confirmation by DNA PROFILING that Primitivo was Zinfandel led to commercial success as a VARIETAL (rather than as a blending ingredient) and staunched the loss of vineyards in the 21st century. From 1999, Italian exporters have been allowed to label their Primitivo as Zinfandel and the Italian vine census of 2010 found a total vineyard area of 12,234 ha/30,231 acres, including non-DOC plantings. A move to limit the use of the name Primitivo solely to DOC wines was rejected by producers in 2005. Growers will be grateful, for the success of IGT Primitivo has meant that higher prices are now being paid for the grapes. This in turn has ensured that the variety is being replanted after years in which it was only grubbed up, as the backbreaking work involved in cultivating the BUSH VINES was not remunerative.

It was presumably brought across the Adriatic sea from Croatia to Puglia in the 18th century. Its name derives from the latter part of the 18th century, when a priest in Gioia del Colle selected vines from promiscuous old vineyards and noted that fruit from these vines matured earlier than those from other vines. As a result, he called the variety *primativo*, from the Latin *primativus*, or 'first to ripen'. In 1799, he planted these cuttings in a vineyard in Liponti, just outside Gioia del Colle.

Historically, it suffered from a poorly conceived DOC in Manduria: a minimum alcohol level of 14% for the regular production and higher alcohol for the *liquoroso* versions (both sweet and dry) which reach a leg-wobbling 18%. Puglians report it is highly prized as a high strength blending ingredient by many producers of AMARONE.

It is also DOC in its original homeland of Gioia del Colle. As an IGT Salento wine, it has enjoyed a boom since the late 1990s, where careful selection and modern vinification can result in wines of great appeal and value.

Priorat, one of Spain's most inspiring red wines made in an isolated zone in CATALUNYA inland from Tarragona (see map under SPAIN) that is one of the country's only two to qualify as a DOCA. (Its Spanish rather than native Catalan name is **Priorato**.) In the 1990s, a true revolution engulfed the region, where production methods for Priorat had barely altered since the 12th century when the Carthusian MONKS first established the priory after which the wine is named. Priorat is one of the world's few first-class wines to be made from Garnacha (GRENACHE) and Mazuelo/Cariñena (CARIGNAN) vines. The age of the vines and concomitantly extremely low yields, which average just 5 or 6 hl/ha (0.3 ton/acre), undoubtedly contribute to the intensity and strength of Priorat.

Poor, stony soils derived from the underlying SLATE and QUARTZ, called locally *llicorella*, support only the most meagre of crops. MECHANIZATION is almost impossible and many steeply terraced smallholdings had been abandoned as the rural population left to find work on the coast. The success of new-wave Priorat has been reviving viticulture, however.

The region was long dominated by CO-OPERATIVES but there is an increasing number of well-equipped estates, traditionally led by Scala Dei, while De Müller makes some good *generoso*. In the 1980s, René Barbier, the scion of the Franco-Spanish winemaking family (whose eponymous firm in Penedès belongs to FREIXENET), recognizing Priorat's potential for top-quality red wines, located some particularly promising vineyard sites, renaming them CLOS. Such French vine varieties as Cabernet Sauvignon, Merlot, Syrah, and some Pinot Noir were planted. A group of private growers took over. The wines of René Barbier (Clos Mogador), Costers del Siurana (Clos de l'Obac), Álvaro Palacios (Finca Dofí, L'Ermita), Mas Martinet (Clos Martinet), and Clos & Terrasses (Clos Erasmus) had won worldwide acclaim by the late 1990s with L'Ermita one of Spain's most expensive wines. Complex blends including small proportions of French varieties, careful winemaking, and ageing in new French oak barrels were the key innovations. Other small estates jumped on the bandwagon and by the mid 2000s there were more than 50 bodegas in Priorat, with a growing number now producing white wines too from Garnacha Blanca, Macabeo, Pedro Ximénez, and some Viognier.

V. de la S.

www.doqpriorat.org

proanthocyanidins, oligomers and polymers of FLAVONOLS. Proanthocyanidins are PHENOLICS belonging to the FLAVONOID group, also called condensed TANNINS. The term proanthocyanidin refers to the reactivity of these molecules that release red anthocyanidin pigments (i.e. anthocyanin aglycones) when heated in an acidic medium, still commonly used for their analysis.

Several classes can be distinguished by the differing nature of the anthocyanidin released. The most common proanthocyanidins are PROCYANIDINS, which are the only proanthocyanidins in grape seeds, whereas tannins of grape skins and stems consist of both procyanidins and PRODELPHINIDINS.

V.C.

Probus, Marcus Aurelius (AD 232–282), Roman emperor (276–282) who employed troops in the planting of vineyards in GAUL and along the Danube. (See GERMAN HISTORY.) This positive encouragement of viticulture was in marked contrast to the earlier Emperor DOMITIAN.

Procanico, Umbrian name for TREBBIANO Toscano.

processing aids, unlike ADDITIVES, are added to MUST or wine in order to react with and thus remove another component in the wine, so that only trace amounts will remain in the finished product. The purposes of such transient additions include CLARIFICATION, STABILIZATION, FINING, and the removal of off-flavours. However, in some countries, the use of certain processing aids, especially those based on animal products such as CASEIN, ISINGLASS, or GELATIN, must be stated on the label for the benefit of VEGETARIANS AND VEGANS or those with ALLERGIES AND INTOLERANCES.

procyanidin, a specific type of PROANTHO-CYANIDIN based on CATECHIN and epicatechin units which releases cyanidin when heated in acidic media. Found in the seed, skin, and stem TANNINS of grapes.

V.C.

procymidone, a systemic FUNGICIDE used to combat BOTRYTIS.

prodelphinidin, a specific type of PROANTHOCYANIDIN based on gallocatechin and epigallocatechin units which releases delphinidin when heated in acidic media. Found in the skin and stem TANNINS of grapes.

V.C.

production of a particular vineyard is normally measured as YIELD. The world's production of wine still totals between 260 and 290 million hl (6,800 million–7,650 million gal) annually, and is considerably in excess of CONSUMPTION, leading to continued surplus, but there is wide variation according to VINTAGE. See WORLD PRODUCTION and, for annual totals, SURPLUS PRODUCTION. The tables in Appendix 2 show the world's significant wine-producing countries and OIV figures for their total area of vineyard, annual wine production, and per capita consumption.

(See map under WORLD PRODUCTION for the location of different countries' wine regions.)

Prohibition in common parlance most often means a prohibition on the consumption of alcohol (which suggests the importance generally attached to the possibility of intoxication). Prohibition has officially been in force throughout the world of ISLAM for 12 centuries, and elsewhere there have been periods throughout history (usually just after a period of particularly heavy consumption) during which the arguments for Prohibition have seemed convincing. One of these periods was the early 20th century, when Prohibition was enforced in parts of Scandinavia, was put to a referendum in New Zealand, and was enforced most famously in the United States.

Prohibition in the US

'Prohibition' is generally considered the period in the United States, 17 January 1920–5 December 1933, during which, according to the language of the 18th Amendment to the Constitution, the 'manufacture, sale, or transportation of intoxicating liquors' was prohibited throughout the country. The passage of the 18th Amendment crowned a movement going back to the early 19th century.

Beginning with local, voluntary organizations concerned to foster temperance in a hard drinking country, the movement then undertook to pass restrictive legislation on a local or state basis (Maine went 'dry' in 1851). As the movement increased in vigour and confidence, total prohibition of alcohol consumption rather than temperance became the object. By the last quarter of the 19th century, the aim was to secure a complete national prohibition by means of a constitutional amendment. The work of propaganda to this end was in the hands of organized reformers, especially the Woman's Christian Temperance Union (1874) and the Anti-Saloon League (1895); they had the support of many Protestant churches, especially in the south and midwest. By the time the 18th Amendment was passed, 33 of the then 48 states were already dry.

The working out of the amendment was provided for by the National Prohibition Act (October 1919), usually called the Volstead Act: it defined 'intoxicating liquor' as anything containing 0.5% alcohol, so extinguishing the hope that wine and BEER might escape under a less stern definition. Some uses of wine were, however, allowed under the act: it could be used in religious ceremonies; it could be prescribed as medicine; and it could be used as a food flavouring or in other 'non-beverage' applications. All of these provisions could be and were greatly abused, and the act had to be amended and supplemented as experience showed the problems of enforcement.

The popular conception of Prohibition is that speakeasies abounded, gangsters and bootleggers of all sorts flourished, and every American gladly flouted the law. The reality is harder to determine, but there can be no question that the consequences for the American wine industry were disastrous. A number of American wineries, by obtaining licences to manufacture wine for the permitted uses, managed to continue a restricted operation (the apparent needs of communicants, for example, soared during this period). Effectively, however, the industry was wrecked. In 1919, the official production of wine in the US was 55 million gal/2 million hl; by 1925 it had sunk to just over 3.5 million gal. Winemakers received no compensation. Most wineries simply went out of business and their establishments were broken up.

The Volstead Act permitted the heads of households to manufacture up to 200 gal/7 hl of fruit juice annually and, by a benevolent inconsistency, this provision was construed to allow HOME WINEMAKING. In consequence, vineyard acreage in CALIFORNIA shot up to unprecedented size to meet the national demand for fresh grapes: the 300,000 acres/121,000 ha of vineyard in 1919 had nearly doubled by 1926. Most of the new planting was in very inferior grape varieties, however (THOMPSON SEEDLESS and ALICANTE BOUSCHET, for example), and the degradation of the California vineyards thus induced by the conditions of Prohibition had seriously damaging effects on California wine long after Repeal. Nor can the quality of the average home-made wine have done much to enhance national CONNOISSEURSHIP.

The first efforts of the opponents of Prohibition were to achieve 'modification' of the terms of the Volstead Act. They tried for example to alter the definition of 'intoxicating liquor', or to allow individual states to make regulations different from those of the act. These efforts got nowhere; in consequence, the 'Wets' concentrated on achieving Repeal by constitutional amendment. Aided by the economic collapse of 1929 (invalidating the argument that Prohibition was economically sound) and by the adoption of Repeal as a political question (the Democratic party made Repeal a plank in its platform for the 1932 elections), the repeal movement succeeded: in December 1933 the 21st amendment, repealing the 18th, was ratified. Unfortunately, the amendment left to the separate states the entire regulation of the 'liquor traffic' within their borders, with the result that US liquor laws—including local and state prohibition—remain a crazy quilt of inconsistent and arbitrary rules, another lastingly destructive effect of national prohibition.

The forces that achieved prohibition in the US remain potent, and protean. National prohibition in the simple terms of the 18th amendment is not likely to come again; but liquor—wine very much included—continues to be an object of punitive taxation, of moral disapproval in some quarters, and of obstructive legislation in the United States today. See UNITED STATES for more details.   T.P.

Asbury, H., *The Great Illusion* (New York, 1950).

Krout, J. A., *The Origins of Prohibition* (New York, 1925).

Sinclair, A., *Prohibition: The Era of Excess* (London, 1962).

Prokupac, old red grape variety grown all over SERBIA, where the strong wine it produces is often blended with more international vine varieties. It is also grown in KOSOVO and MACEDONIA. Within its native land, it is often made into a dark rosé. Its stronghold is just south of Belgrade.

proles, three categories of VINE VARIETIES of the VINIFERA species, grouped according to their geographical origin and, to some extent, their common end use (see BOTANICAL CLASSIFICATION). The classification is the work of Russian ampelographer Negrul in 1946. The differences between these groups may not only be a matter of response to environment, but also partly due to human selection for particular features related to end use, such as berry size for table grapes. Detailed observation of vine characteristics can reveal particularly close relationships which indicate that they are likely to have come from the same area. Thus are linked, for example, the CABERNET SAUVIGNON, CABERNET FRANC, MERLOT, PETIT VERDOT, and FER varieties.

Proles occidentalis: varieties native to western Europe, which were selected mostly for winemaking use. Most of the important wine grape varieties are in this group—RIESLING, CHARDONNAY, Cabernet Sauvignon, and so on—and they have common features of small bunches with small, juicy berries.

Proles pontica: the oldest varieties, and those native to the Aegean and Black Seas, which have shoot tips and leaf undersurfaces covered with dense, white hairs. Examples of varieties in this group are CLAIRETTE, FURMINT, HÁRSLEVELŰ, and Zante CURRANT.

Proles orientalis: varieties originating in the Middle East, Iran, and Afghanistan. These varieties were selected mainly for TABLE GRAPES, and so tend to have large, oval berries in loose, straggly bunches. The berries are often crisp, with less juice and sugar. This group of vines includes most varieties for DRYING GRAPES as well as most table grape varieties, such as SULTANA and MUSCAT OF ALEXANDRIA.   R.E.S. & J.V.

Negrul, A. M., 'Origin and classification of cultivated grape', in A. Baranov et al. (eds.), *The Ampelography of the USSR* (Moscow, 1946), 159–216.

propagation, the reproduction of a plant, whether by sexual or asexual means. Sexual propagation means reproduction by seed and involves the combination of two separate sets of chromosomes, one from the male (POLLEN) and the other from the female (the egg cell inside the ovule); their fusion during fertilization produces an individual with a set of genes different from its two parents. Asexual or vegetative propagation means reproduction without seed, by taking vegetative bits of the parent plant and getting them to form SHOOTS and ROOTS; the progeny are genetically identical to the parent unless MUTATIONS produce distinct CLONES.

For details of micropropagation, see TISSUE CULTURE. For more details of specific propagation methods, see SEXUAL PROPAGATION and VEGETATIVE PROPAGATION. See also LAYERING.
                                          B.G.C. & J.V.

Prosecco, extremely popular sparkling wine made in north-east Italy. Italy's largest DOC by far, the Prosecco zone now extends from the city of Vicenza to Trieste, and comprises more than 14,000 ha/34,580 acres. Extraordinarily high permitted yields of 18 tonnes/ha produced more than 300 million bottles of light sparkling white wine in 2013 made by the tank method (see SPARKLING WINEMAKING). As suggested by its extent, the DOC was once an IGT. To ensure that no one outside the region was able to jump on the lucrative Prosecco bandwagon, the eponymous grape variety on which the wine is based was renamed GLERA in 2009, and Prosecco was registered as a protected denomination of origin (DOC). This was enabled by enlarging the region many times to include the village of Prosecco in FRIULI, which triggered a frenzy of plantings, mostly on plains, while barring any other region or country from using the Prosecco name.

The classic production zone, with over 6,000 ha, was already considerable, situated in the hills between the towns of Conegliano and Valdobbiane, an area which has been elevated to the DOCG Conegliano-Valdobbiadene. Although most of these DOCG vineyards are on hills and terraces, between 50 and 500 m (164–1,640 ft), the high yields (some 13.5 tonnes/ha) can result in rather neutral wines whose apparent fruitiness owes much to the DOSAGE. Although BRUT versions exist, more common are Extra Dry (with RESIDUAL SUGAR of 12–17 g/l) and Dry (17–32 g/l). Allowed additions of up to 15% of international varieties such as Chardonnay, Pinot Bianco, and Pinot Grigio can help to increase alcohol and flavour. Superior wines are said to come from the Cru of Cartizze, a vineyard area of 107 ha on steep hills of San Pietro di Barbozza, Santo Stefano, and Saccol in the commune of Valdobbiadene whose grapes are generally much riper than most, although yields are not markedly lower here. Most Cartizze wines are Extra Dry.

Ambitiously, a system of crus has been introduced in Conegliano-Valdobbiadene DOCG, 43 communes or hamlets (called locally *Rive*) whose names may be mentioned on the label if yields are below 13 tonnes/ha, although little expression of origin has so far been evident.

Prosecco Col Fondo can offer more interest, on the other hand. Initially made by small-scale producers, often espousing ORGANIC techniques and, besides Glera, favouring other INDIGENOUS VARIETIES such as Verdiso, Bianchetta, and Pepera in the final blend, these wines are bottle-fermented and left undisgorged (see PÉTILLANT NATUREL). They are released with the original crowncap and with a sediment on the bottom of the bottle (*col fondo* means 'with sediment'). These wines are bone-dry, somehow mineral in character and, unlike most Prosecco, are worth ageing for a year or two. Conventional Prosecco producers have begun to experiment with this style, not least because it is so much more profitable than most Prosecco.

The DOCG **Colli Asolani Prosecco**, from a hilly outcrop on a plain southeast of Treviso, is similar to Conegliano-Valdobbiadene's vineyard area and structure, with the marked difference that its maximum permitted yields of 12 tonnes/ha are markedly lower.   W.S.

www.prosecco.it

Protected Designation of Origin
See PDO.

Protected Geographical Indication.
See PGI.

protected viticulture
, a form of vine-growing where the vines are protected from climatological excesses to avoid stress. In a conventional agricultural sense, this would involve protection from low temperatures using glass or plastic houses or cloches; such structures are rare in commercial wine grape vineyards because of the prohibitive costs although they can be seen in the cool climate of ENGLAND or very occasionally in cooler parts of California to protect some Chardonnay vines from poor FRUIT SET. Protected viticulture is more usual for TABLE GRAPES, as in northern Europe, Japan, and New Zealand.

Vines may also be protected from the wind by WINDBREAKS and from frost by various techniques (see FROST PROTECTION), and from drought by IRRIGATION.   R.E.S.

protective juice handling
, grape and must processing techniques with the aim of minimizing exposure to OXYGEN and therefore the risk of OXIDATION. This is regarded as especially important for white wines since, once grapes are crushed and juice liberated from the berry, the PHENOLICS react rapidly with oxygen to produce amber to dark-brown polymers (see POLYMERIZATION). Some ordinary wines are made encouraging this oxidation, the brown pigments being removed subsequently by FINING. Most better-quality white wines result from minimal oxygen exposure, saving the phenolics for later contribution to AROMA and BODY. (Some ambitious winemakers experimented with deliberate prefermentation oxidation of the must in the early 1980s but this is uncommon today.) The introduction of tank PRESSES has aided protective juice handling during the lengthy PRESSING operation enormously. See also NITROGEN. Grapes for red wines are far less vulnerable to damage from oxygen since they contain much greater concentrations of TANNINS and PIGMENTS.

See also SKIN CONTACT.   A.D.W.

protective winemaking
, winemaking philosophy founded on the need to minimize exposure to OXYGEN and concomitant risk of OXIDATION. It is less popular than it was at the end of the 20th century but still adhered to for many large-volume commercial white wines. It usually incorporates PROTECTIVE JUICE HANDLING. White wines are then fermented in closed-top tanks to exclude oxygen as much as possible while allowing for the escape of CARBON DIOXIDE from fermentation. All subsequent operations are then conducted as far as possible in closed equipment and small amounts of SULFUR DIOXIDE are added if exposure to oxygen occurs. Storage and processing at low temperatures favours the retention of some of the carbon dioxide, which has the effect of sweeping out any accidentally dissolved oxygen. Red wines, because of their greater PHENOLIC content, are much less sensitive to exposure to oxygen. Indeed, if they undergo BARREL MATURATION, some exposure to oxygen during TOPPING UP contributes to the wine's maturation.   A.D.W.

proteins
, very large polymers of the 20 natural AMINO ACIDS. Proteins are essential to all living beings.

In grapes
Proteins may function as ENZYMES, or as structural components of cells. While all functions are important, the enzymatic properties of proteins are the basis of all reactions within living systems.

In wines
Proteins from the grape remain in solution in all white wines but in some (notably those vinified from MUSCAT, GEWÜRZTRAMINER, SAUVIGNON BLANC, and SÉMILLON grapes), the concentration is often so high that the proteins coagulate to form an unsightly haze or cloud. Such haziness, which can be initiated when the wine is warmed, is irreversible. To avoid this happening after bottling, which renders the wine unstable, the heat-unstable proteins are removed by BENTONITE fining as part of normal winemaking STABILIZATION procedures. Research has shown that the troublesome, heat-unstable proteins of white wines belong to a particular group from the grape known as pathogenesis-related or PR proteins. The unique properties of PR proteins—their stability in acid conditions and resistance to degradation by proteolytic ENZYMES—means that fermentation and the other processes of winemaking selectively eliminate other proteins of the grape leaving the PR proteins as virtually the sole survivors.

The greater concentration of PHENOLICS in red wines means that much of the protein is removed in the LEES as an insoluble tannin–protein complex. See also PRECIPITATES and BOTTLE DEPOSIT.   V.L. & D.D.

Waters, E. J., et al., 'Preventing protein haze in bottled wine', *Australian Journal of Grape and Wine Research*, 11 (2005), 215–25.

provenance
, details of a wine's previous owner(s) and, ideally, STORAGE conditions, has become increasingly important in the FINE WINE market. Gone are the days when 'Property of an English Gentleman' would suffice as an AUCTION catalogue description, effectively implying that the source of the wine in question was beyond reproach. A number of factors have combined to bring provenance centre stage in the buyer's increasing need for a copper-bottomed guarantee of origin.

The growth of the ASIAN market has seen a new kind of collector, both more knowledgeable and more wary than many, and keen to ensure as impeccable a source of origin and storage for his or her wines as possible. At the same time, the huge increase in wine PRICES in recent years has generated a parasitic underbelly of COUNTER-FEITERS, fraudsters, forgers, and confidence tricksters keen to cash in on the bounty that a bottle of expensive fine wine (often bought, much less often opened) can bring. Budd tries to expose those he encounters from his UK base.

Most auction houses and BROKERS have responded to this growing demand for transparent provenance by sharpening up their inspection and AUTHENTICATION procedures, scrutinizing BOTTLES, CORKS, LABELS, and CAPSULES with greater care and rejecting wines of dubious origin or condition. Some, alas, have failed to see the warning signs or, unforgiveably, turned a blind eye.

The need for provenance and a history of optimum storage conditions and good-quality transportation goes beyond the auction room and back to the producer. Many now realize that taking measures to ensure traceability and authentication is a key part of protecting their BRAND. Despite this growing awareness, the relevant proofs are often neither required nor given.

One of the upshots of the demand for impeccable provenance has been the growing number of sales direct from the château or producer, or even from a famous owner such as the wine-loving football manager Sir Alex Ferguson. Christie's and Sotheby's, for instance, have held ex-château direct sales in which guaranteed provenance and condition have helped to set a premium over market price for many of the lots. Direct sales have included such notable names as Chx LATOUR, CHEVAL BLANC, and HAUT-BRION along with DROUHIN, Dujac, KRUG, MOËT & CHANDON, and VEGA SICILIA.   A.H.L.R.

Jim Budd, investdrinks-blog.blogspot.co.uk

Provence, region with considerable potential in the far south east of France (see map under FRANCE) whose associations with TOURISM and hedonism have perhaps focused too much attention on its relatively expensive rosés.

The precise period during which viticulture was introduced to the region is disputed. Certainly it appears unlikely that the Phocaeans, Greeks from Asia Minor, found vines when they founded Massilia (Marseilles) in about 600 BC. It is likely, however, that the Provincia of Ancient GAUL produced its own wines under the influence of classical ROME (although it is not certain that it preceded Narbo, or Narbonne, in the LANGUEDOC as a wine producer). See FRANCE for more details.

The region was much fought over, being under the influence in successive eras of the Saracens, Carolingians (see CHARLEMAGNE), the Holy Roman Empire, the counts of Toulouse, the Catalans, René of ANJOU, and the House of SAVOY. For much of the 19th century it belonged to SARDINIA. At the end of the 19th century, Provençal viticulture was nearly killed by the PHYLLOXERA louse, but was given a new lease of life by the arrival of a RAILWAY link with northern Europe.

As a result of its rich cultural heritage, Provence enjoys a particularly distinctive range of vine varieties, which show various historical influences from Italy, notably Sardinia. No fewer than 13 varieties are allowed in Côtes de Provence, for example, including particularly Cinsaut, Grenache Noir, Mourvèdre, Syrah, and TIBOUREN although the indigenous dark-berried Calitor (known in Provençal as Pécoui Touar) and Barbaroux are being phased out. Grenache is by far the most planted variety in Provence, followed by Cinsaut in the Var in the east (rosé country), and Syrah in Vaucluse and the Bouches-du-Rhône in the west where Provence meets the southern Rhône.

The climate here is France's most MEDITERRANEAN, with an average of 3,000 hours of sunshine a year, and less than 700 mm/27 in annual RAINFALL, which is concentrated in spring and autumn. Winters are mild, but usually allow full vine DORMANCY. The greatest climatological threat is WIND, in particular the famous *mistral*, a cold wind from the north. Proximity to the sea and careful vineyard siting on southern expositions can offer some protection. It has the advantage of minimizing the risk of FUNGAL DISEASES, and Provence is particularly suitable for ORGANIC VITICULTURE.

The magic attached to such names as the Côte d'Azur, St-Tropez, and Provence in general may have increased urban development, and pushed up land prices in habitable parts of the region, but it has also attracted outsiders prepared to make significant investments in vine-growing and winemaking, thereby raising standards overall.

Côtes de Provence

The 20,000 ha/50,000 acres of vineyard is by far the most significant appellation in Provence, although the sites vary enormously. The appellation applies to a large part of the Var *département* (other than the enclave entitled to the Coteaux Varois appellation) from the subalpine hills above Draguignan, cooled by the influence of the mountains to the north, to the coast at St-Tropez, the epitome of a Mediterranean wine zone. But it also includes pockets of hotter terrain between Cassis and Bandol, and land immediately south and east of the Palette appellation near Aix-en-Provence. The appellation even encompasses a tiny isolated area of vines at Villars-sur-Var high up in the mountains 40 km/25 miles north of Nice in the Alpes-Maritimes département.

About four-fifths of production is of pale pink dry rosé, which seems to find a growing local market almost regardless of quality. There is renewed interest in producing 'serious' rosé, however, with a distinctive new style combining flavour with a fashionably pale hue, and some producers even using a limited amount of OAK maturation. The best really do seem to have a special affinity with the garlic- and oil-based cuisine of Provence, particularly *aïoli*. Much of it is sold in a special 'skittle' bottle; almost all of it should be consumed as young and as cool as possible. Cinsaut and Grenache are typically used particularly for rosé, but Tibouren can add real interest to a blend.

The focus of attention for a new generation of serious wine producers in this appellation, however, is red wine, which accounts for just 15% of production. Great efforts have been made to replace the prolific Carignan vine with Grenache, Syrah, Cinsaut, Mourvèdre, and sometimes Tibouren.

An increasing number of producers, especially in the coastal sector, are paying as much attention to their white wines, which may be made from various permutations of Clairette, Sémillon, Ugni Blanc, and Vermentino, albeit in much smaller volumes.

Special named subappellations, for reds and rosés, include Fréjus, La Londe, Notre-Dame des Anges Pierrefeu, and Ste-Victoire.

See also the individual Provence appellations of coteaux d'AIX-EN-PROVENCE, BANDOL, les BAUX DE PROVENCE, BELLET, CASSIS, PALETTE, and Coteaux VAROIS en Provence.

www.provencewines.co.uk

proximal sensing is the measurement of attributes of the soil, vine CANOPY, or fruit using sensors mounted on vehicles or vineyard machinery operating in the vineyard, i.e. the sensor is operated close to the target of interest (cf. REMOTE SENSING). Hand-held sensors may also be used but are unlikely to be cost-effective if the intention is to collect sufficient data to produce a map. (See SOIL MAPPING.)

Proximal soil sensing is a common application in PRECISION VITICULTURE and provides key data input to ZONAL VITICULTURE. Electromagnetic induction (EMI) is the most common form of proximal soil sensing and is used to identify variation in soil properties which affect the electrical conductivity of the soil (SALINITY, SOIL TEXTURE, SOIL WATER status), or which are correlated with them. Research has shown that patterns of variation in vine performance often closely mimic patterns of variation in these soil attributes. A possible alternative to EMI sensing is to use electrical resistance tomography (ERT) to measure resistivity. Since resistivity is the inverse of conductivity, the information provided by these two types of sensors is essentially the same. However, the requirement for contact with the soil in the case of ERT, coupled with the much larger size of sensor, tends to make them a poor option in established vineyards or where the soil is stony; EMI instruments are generally smaller and do not require contact with the soil.

Proximal canopy sensing is being used increasingly to provide essentially the same PCD and NDVI information as is obtained by remote sensing, but has the advantage of timeliness, especially when canopy changes within the season are of interest.

New proximal sensors for the measurement of fruit attributes related to GRAPE COMPOSITION AND WINE QUALITY are being developed. The ability to use such sensors on the go during harvest is of key interest in precision viticulture, especially to support strategies such as SELECTIVE HARVESTING.   R.G.V.B.

Bramley, R. G. V., 'Precision viticulture: managing vineyard variability for improved quality outcomes', in A. G. Reynolds (ed.), *Managing Wine Quality 1: Viticulture and Wine Quality* (Cambridge, 2010), 445–80.

Bramley, R. G. V., et al., 'On-the-go sensing of grape berry anthocyanins during commercial harvest—development and prospects', *Australian Journal of Grape and Wine Research*, 17 (2011), 316–26.

Proffitt, T., et al., *Precision Viticulture—A New Era in Vineyard Management and Wine Production* (Adelaide, 2006).

Trought, M. C. T., and Bramley, R. G. V., 'Vineyard variability in Marlborough, New Zealand: characterising spatial and temporal changes in fruit composition and juice quality in the vineyard', *Australian Journal of Grape and Wine Research*, 17 (2011), 79–89.

Prugnolo Gentile, synonym for SANGIOVESE in VINO NOBILE DI MONTEPULCIANO.

pruners, devices used for winter PRUNING of grapevines. From ancient times until the 19th century, a pruning hook or knife was used. In modern times, pruning is normally carried out using hand-held SECATEURS. These were developed in the mid 19th century, and came into widespread use in the latter half of the century. Secateurs cut with a scissor action, and there are various forms available (including power-assisted versions). Sometimes pruning saws may be needed to remove old CORDONS or ARMS. Vineyard winter pruning is now being mechanized with tractor-mounted machines doing most of the cutting, as described in MECHANICAL PRUNING.   R.E.S.

pruning of vines involves cutting off unwanted vegetative parts in the form of canes in winter. For details of cutting off unwanted vegetative growth in the form of excess SHOOTS in early spring and shoot tips in summer, see SHOOT THINNING and TRIMMING respectively. **Summer pruning** is a misleading term for trimming.

Winter pruning is a vineyard practice developed primarily to produce fewer but larger bunches of riper grapes and is particularly important in cooler climates. More than 85% of each year's shoot growth may be removed.

There is an important relationship between vine pruning and VINE TRAINING, as the pruning method used depends on the training system employed.

Vines growing in their natural state, as in the WILD VINES of America and the Middle East, are of course not pruned. At the top of such vines, many of which grow up trees, and on other parts of the vine exposed to the sun, are many small bunches of grapes. While the vine may have had thousands of buds present in winter which could have produced shoots and fruit, only a small proportion will burst in spring. This reduced BUDBREAK is the principal means by which unpruned vines in their natural state avoid OVERCROPPING, which may weaken the vine and shorten its life. The wild vine is much branched, with many shoots growing apparently haphazardly.

History
It is not known when mankind began to prune vines but vine pruning was certainly known in Ancient EGYPT and was already a well-established practice by the beginning of the Roman era, described in detail by such writers as PLINY and VIRGIL. There are also numerous references to vine pruning in the BIBLE. For example, 'a Sabbath of rest unto the land, a Sabbath for the Lord: thou shalt neither sow thy field, nor prune thy vineyard' (Lev. 25. 4). Vine pruning also figures in the description of the Last Days (Mic. 4. 3): 'and they shall beat their swords into ploughshares, and their spears into pruning hooks'.

Aims of pruning
Among the early aims of vine pruning as practised by the Ancient Egyptians would have been to increase the size of individual berries and bunches, an important consideration even today in the production of TABLE GRAPES. A vine which is lightly pruned has many buds and will produce numerous bunches with small berries.

Another aim of vine pruning is to establish or maintain a shape of vine, which makes all other vineyard operations easier. For example, keeping vines pruned back to a more or less constant structure means they can easily be neatly trained in rows. Otherwise, vines would sprawl and quickly cover the space between rows.

But perhaps the most important aspect of pruning is that it regulates the next season's YIELD by controlling the number of buds which can burst and produce bunches of grapes. The number of buds retained after winter pruning may be influenced by TRADITION, local CONTROLLED APPELLATION regulations, the scientific principles behind BALANCED PRUNING, or greed.

Timing
Pruning is carried out in winter, normally once the first frost causes the leaves to fall, thereby exposing the woody CANES. Although the precise timing of winter pruning is not generally critical, it should be completed by the time of BUDBREAK in spring, as the PRUNERS can damage emerging shoots as they work. Some early-BUDDING varieties may be pruned very late in an effort to delay budbreak and minimize FROST DAMAGE. Vines lose water (see BLEEDING) from pruning wounds just prior to budbreak. In regions with warm winters, such as tropical and subtropical regions, the vines may not become completely dormant, and vines may have to be pruned when they are covered in leaves. See also TROPICAL VITICULTURE.

Two basic options
The basic principles of pruning have changed remarkably little since classical times, although the French viticulturist GUYOT in 1860 introduced firm suggestions as to the length and position of canes, formalizing some of the old ideas.

Along the canes, which were green, soft shoots during the previous growing season, are buds which are arranged on alternate sides of the cane about 8 cm/3 in or so apart. Basically there are two types of vine pruning: either to SPURS, or to CANES.

Spur pruning Spurs are cut to retain only two buds, while canes are longer, typically with five to 15 buds. In the spring, each bud on the two-bud spur normally produces one shoot. In autumn, these shoots become woody. During winter pruning the cane growing from the uppermost bud on the spur is removed, and the cane from the bottom bud is cut back to two buds, creating the new spur. The vine's physiology determines that, when a cane is cut, the last two buds will burst. This is the reason for

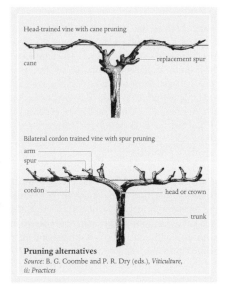

Pruning alternatives
Source: B. G. Coombe and P. R. Dry (eds.), *Viticulture, ii: Practices*

the common two-bud spur. If spurs were left with three buds, the bottom bud would often not produce a shoot, and so the spur position would move further and further from the cordon or head as the years passed.

Spur pruning is commonly used with free-standing vines, such as are widely seen in Mediterranean wine regions. The GOBELET-trained vines in the south of France are typical. The spurs arise from the trunk or from short arms on the trunk. This is of course a very simple form of vine training, requiring no supporting POSTS or WIRE; it is therefore among the oldest forms prevailing and was already known to the Roman writers COLUMELLA and PALLADIUS. This vine training is particularly common in the Old World. In Languedoc and Roussillon, for example, the great majority of vineyards are still pruned and trained in this basic way. It is common in the lower-rainfall areas of Spain, Italy, and Portugal, such vineyards being of lower VIGOUR, to which the system is best suited. Some of the older New World vineyards, for example in California, Australia, and South Africa, also have such vines, here often described as head trained.

Another spur-pruned form which is more common with higher-vigour vineyards is cordon training. Here the spurs arise from one or more horizontal arms or CORDONS. Known in France as CORDON DE ROYAT, this pruning method has been used for wine grapes since the end of the 19th century. The cordons are trained along a wire, and this method is particularly common in New World vineyards. Of all pruning methods, this one lends itself most readily to MECHANIZATION since all of the canes to be pruned are more or less in the one plane (see MECHANICAL PRUNING).

Cane pruning Cane pruning became common after the 1860 studies of the Frenchman Dr Guyot. In traditional French vineyards each vine is typically pruned to one cane with six to eight buds and one spur with two buds. During winter pruning the cane from the previous year is cut off and a new one laid down, using one of the canes arising from the spur. The number of buds on the cane depends on regional tradition and the small print of the APPELLATION CONTRÔLÉE laws. For example, eight buds may be left on Syrah canes in the Côtes du Rhône; eight on all major varieties in Burgundy; in Bordeaux seven buds is the maximum for Sémillon in Sauternes but six for Muscadelle. These small bud numbers per cane (and hence cane length) contrast greatly with those used for wine grapes in other regions where vine vigour is higher. For example, in vigorous irrigated vineyards in Australia it is not uncommon to see up to ten canes, each with up to 15 buds, left on a single vine after winter pruning. Of course, these vines are planted further apart than their Old World counterparts, as discussed in NEW WORLD.

A common observation with cane pruning is that buds in the middle of the cane often do not burst. There are often a few shoots growing near the head of the vine (at the base of the cane), and the last two shoots at the cut end of the cane will invariably grow. Where the cane was growing in shade the previous year the budburst is invariably poor, as outlined in CANOPY MICROCLIMATE.

In France, the colloquial name for canes varies regionally: *courgée* in Jura, for example, *aste* in Bordeaux, *baguette* in Burgundy, *archet* or *archelot* in Beaujolais, and, appropriately enough in view of the region's once notoriously high yields, *pisse-vin* in the Languedoc, although this last is used more generally to refer to high-yielding vines producing poor-quality wine.

Controlling yield

A fundamental question in relation to vine pruning is how many buds to leave on each vine at winter pruning. Does it matter? For many vignerons in the world this first question is never posed, as TRADITION or APPELLATION laws dictate how the vines are to be pruned. The winter pruning period can be a time when the mind is put into neutral, and the body is braced to survive long days spent outdoors, often in unpleasant and cold weather. Quite often, traditional pruning practices are followed, and vigorously defended against any suggestion of change.

When vines are pruned to just a few buds, most of them burst successfully, and the shoots will typically grow vigorously. They will be very long, with large leaves and many LATERAL SHOOTS. Early shoot growth is stimulated by the vine's food reserves in the trunk and roots being spread around only a few shoots. A low-vigour vine which has limited reserves of CARBOHYDRATES must therefore be pruned to few buds only compared with one of higher vigour which contains more reserves.

A vine that is very lightly pruned, to scores or even hundreds of buds, will produce many more shoots and bunches of grapes. Individual shoots will be shorter, and the number and size of berries will be reduced. However, the total yield of grapes will be greater, and the grapes will take longer to ripen. This may cause no problems in warm and sunny climates, but can be disastrous in cooler climates, where it can be a struggle to ripen the grapes anyway before autumn chill and frosts stop the ripening process.

There is therefore more concern about pruning levels in cooler climates than in warmer ones. In Germany, for example, the common rule is to leave about ten buds at winter pruning for each square metre of vineyard land surface. In New York state, Professor Nelson SHAULIS developed balanced pruning guidelines for

pruning which rely on the vine's growth as assessed by PRUNING WEIGHT (the weight of annual growth as canes removed at pruning); about 35 buds should be retained per kg of pruning weight. Having weighed a few vines, the grower can assess the pruning weight by eye as part of his or her pruning decision. For more vigorous vines with higher pruning weights, more buds are retained.

For high-vigour vineyards it may not be sufficient just to prune lightly, as this will lead to crowding of shoots in the vine CANOPY. Recognition of this problem has led to the development of CANOPY MANAGEMENT strategies to avoid dense canopies for vigorous vineyards. Similarly, yield cannot be limited by pruning high-vigour vineyards to just a few buds. The yield will still be considerable, as will BERRY SIZE (considered undesirable for wine quality). Bunches will be tight, increasing the risk of BUNCH ROT and there will be considerable shoot and leaf growth, which is likely to result in SHADE rather than vine BALANCE.

Mechanization

Winter pruning, along with hand harvesting, are the most labour intensive aspects of vine growing. During the 1960s and 1970s, increases in LABOUR costs and reductions in labour supply in Australia led to experimentation with and eventual development of MECHANICAL PRUNING. This in turn has led to the even more iconoclastic option of MINIMAL PRUNING, or not pruning at all, although the latter is now viewed with increasing disfavour.

By the 21st century, a full spectrum of vine-pruning practice was evident around the world, from the hand pruning of a lower-vigour vine in a traditional vineyard to less than 10 buds, to one essentially unpruned following the passage of a machine, with hundreds of buds remaining, to mechanical pruning using a tractor-mounted circular saw.

The time taken to prune a vineyard depends on how the vineyard is trained, the VINE DENSITY, and the pruning method. Pruning times can be up to 200 hours or more per ha for high-density cane-pruned vineyards. For wide-row, spur-pruned vineyards trained to cordons the figure may be as low as 50 hours per ha, and in combination with mechanical pre-pruning this may be reduced even further to less than 10 hours per ha.

Pruning and vine health

TRUNK DISEASES which invade pruning wounds are an increasing concern worldwide, and pruning systems such as cane pruning, which involve fewer wounds per vine than spur pruning and far fewer than mechanical pruning, are preferred. Marco Simonit of Italy has developed a modification to the Guyot system which encourages the maintenance of sap flow in the vine, thereby avoiding the potentially damaging effects of pruning wounds. This system is based on studies by Lafon in the Charentes, France, published in 1921. Care must be taken to treat pruning wounds, most commonly with a FUNGICIDE but also with a formulation that includes antagonistic fungi such as *Trichoderma*.   R.E.S.

Galet, P., *Précis de viticulture* (7th edn, Montpellier, 2000).

Simonit, M., *Manuale di Potatare della Vite Guyot* (Edizioni L'informatorore Agrario s.r.l., 2014).

pruning machines. See MECHANICAL PRUNING.

pruning weight, a measure of vine VIGOUR, or, more strictly, capacity, obtained by weighing the canes removed from a vine at winter PRUNING. This is the most useful and common measure of vine growth. The value may be used, for example, to assess how many buds might be left at winter pruning to achieve the best vine performance, using concepts of BALANCED PRUNING. Similarly, the ratio between the weight of prunings and the fruit produced is a good indication of BALANCE.   R.E.S.

Prynč, Czech synonym for TRAMINER.

Puente Alto, part of the MAIPO subregion of the Central Valley of CHILE.

Puerto de Santa María, one of the three towns making and maturing SHERRY. **Puerto Fino** is the name given to a FINO matured in Puerto de Santa María.

Puglia, Italian name for what is known by English speakers as Apulia, the long (350 km/ 210 mile) and fertile region on the 'heel' of Italy (see map under ITALY) which has long been of major importance for the production of wine and TABLE GRAPES. A MEDITERRANEAN CLIMATE and a predominance of soils well suited to grape-growing (a CALCAREOUS base from the Cretaceous era overlain by topsoils rich in iron oxide from the Tertiary and Quaternary eras) have created an ideal viticultural environment. Its name derives from the Roman *a-pluvia* or 'lack of rain'. Total vineyard area in 2012 was 107,000 ha/250,000 acres, of which a decreasing 60,000 ha is dedicated to basic table wine, and 24,000 ha to growing table grapes. Puglia rivals Sicily as Italy's second most productive wine region, well behind Veneto. Many growers have taken subsidies from the EU to grub up their vineyards but, unfortunately, many of these were of low-yielding BUSH VINES, while many remaining vines tend to be high-cropping inferior varieties planted on fertile soils.

While much of Puglia's viticulture is still focused on BULK WINE for blending, a reduction in compulsory DISTILLATION to drain the EU wine lake has forced producers to adopt a more market-oriented approach. Cue INTERNATIONAL VARIETIES, especially Chardonnay and Merlot, each of which were planted on about 1,000 ha by 2010. Although both varieties are allowed in several of Puglia's 32 DOCs and DOCGS, most are unremarkable and sold in bulk to large bottlers in the north to satisfy international supermarket demand. Sangiovese, with 12,500 ha, is Puglia's most planted variety, and together with the lacklustre but equally high-yielding TREBBIANO Toscano, constitutes much of the wine shipped in bulk, with hardly any plantings registered as DOC. More local varieties such as PRIMITIVO, NEGROAMARO, and NERO DI TROIA are slowly finding their way into DOC and IGT wines rather than the most basic table wine. While grape growers, as opposed to wine producers, are the norm here, with CO-OPERATIVES responsible for most winemaking, many have begun to bottle at least part of their production in order to compensate for plummeting bulk wine prices. Few of these first-timers have knowledge of or formal training in winemaking, which explains what is often very modest quality.

Puglia's propensity for bulk wine production combined with excessively high YIELDS even at DOC level, has tended to overshadow its unique wine styles based on indigenous varieties. In the north between Foggia and Bari Nero di Troia produces tannic, full-bodied reds under the Castel del Monte DOC. Confusingly, both Castel del Monte Nero di Troia Riserva and Castel del Monte Bombino Nero Rosato have been elevated to DOCG status, although the latter is of only marginal importance.

In the centre, between Bari and Matera, Primitivo is responsible for some of Puglia's most popular wines, dark, rich, and often marketed as IGT, although the best wines tend to be sold as DOC Gioia del Colle with its tangy acidity and DOC Primitivo di Manduria grown further south between Brindisi and Taranto and generally richer, although wines tend to be determined by winemaking rather than terroir.

The Salento peninsula, the heel of the boot, is home to Negroamaro. When grown on bush vines in the narrow Salento peninsula, where the proximity of both the Adriatic and the Ionian Seas brings a welcome night-time cooling, it can produce rich, spicy wines of considerable interest.

Puglia's biggest challenge is to reinvent itself as quality wine producer rather than bulk wine supplier. Unfortunately, because most of its production is either bulk or IGT, there are very few producer associations to help market the higher quality wines. Puglia's very few Consorzios, which may be formed only at DOC level, are practically defunct. What Puglia urgently needs is to ensure the survival of its centenarian bush vines and most interesting indigenous varieties, and, ideally, a viticultural and winemaking institute identical to SAN MICHELE ALL'ADIGE to help shape its future.
                                    W.S.

www.vinidipuglia.com

Puisseguin-St-Émilion, satellite appellation of ST-ÉMILION in Bordeaux on about 700 ha/ 1,750 acres of clay and limestone.

Puligny-Montrachet, village in the Côte de Beaune district of Burgundy's Côte d'Or producing very fine wines from CHARDONNAY and a tiny amount of less exalted red. Puligny added the name of its most famous vineyard, the GRAND CRU Le Montrachet, in 1879 and has benefited from the association ever since.

Puligny contains two grand cru vineyards in their entirety, Chevalier-Montrachet and Bienvenues-Bâtard-Montrachet, and two which are shared with neighbouring Chassagne: Le Montrachet itself and Bâtard-Montrachet. Below this exalted level, yet still among the finest of all white wines of Burgundy, are the PREMIER CRU vineyards. There are at least 13 of these, more if subdivisions are counted. At the same elevation as Bâtard-Montrachet lie Les Pucelles (made famous by the excellence of Domaine Leflaive's version), Le Clavoillon, Les Perrières (including the Clos de la Mouchère), Les Referts, and Les Combettes, which produces the plump wines to be expected of a vineyard adjacent to Meursault-Perrières.

A little higher up the slope, at the same elevation as Le Montrachet, lie Les Demoiselles, Le Cailleret, Les Folatières (including Clos de la Garenne), and Champ Canet. Part of Les Demoiselles is classified as grand cru Chevalier-Montrachet but a very small slice remains as premier cru, being regarded, along with Le Cailleret, as the finest example.

Further up the slope, where the terrain becomes rockier and the soil almost too sparse, are Le Champ Gain, Les Truffières, Les Chalumeaux, and the vineyards attached to the hamlet of BLAGNY, which are designated as Puligny-Montrachet premier cru for white wines, and Blagny premier cru for reds.

The VILLAGE WINES of Puligny-Montrachet are less impressive, perhaps because the water-table is nearer the surface here than in neighbouring MEURSAULT, for example. This phenomenon also means that the deep cellars ideal for AGEING wine are rare in Puligny, and few of the village's growers can prolong BARREL MATURATION for more than about a year. Although the Leflaive and Carillon families can both trace their origins as vignerons back to the 16th century, there are surprisingly few domaines in Puligny and a substantial proportion of its produce is contracted to the NÉGOCIANTS of Beaune. Sauzet is a third fine family producer.

p

In centuries past, Puligny, though less noted than Chassagne for its red wines, grew a significant amount of Pinot Noir grapes. Little is now grown.

See also MONTRACHET, CÔTE D'OR, and map under BURGUNDY. J.T.C.M.

Loftus, S., *Puligny-Montrachet* (London, 1992).

pulling out. See GRUBBING UP.

pulp, viticulturally, the soft tissue of grape berries inside the skin (also called the flesh or PERICARP) which is the source of the juice of the grape. The word may also be used by winemakers to refer to the solid matter that settles from the juice after must SETTLING. For more detail of grape pulp, see GRAPE. B.G.C.

pumping over. Winemaking operation involving the circulation of fermenting red wine through the CAP created by the grape skins and other solids. The French term is *remontage*. This can be carried out with or without AERATION, depending on the fermentation rate and the REDUCING CONDITIONS. It prevents drying out of the cap and encourages the EXTRACTION of the skins' valuable colouring matter and TANNINS into the wine. It may be done either in a closed or open-top vat, between one and three times a day depending on the temperature and rate of fermentation. The mechanical systems involved include some adaptation of the AUTOVINIFICA-TION system, ROTOFERMENTERS, and tanks which incorporate automatic PUNCHING DOWN. However, automation cannot replace the winemaker's decisions about the volume of fermenting wine that needs to be pumped over each day to get the right level of extraction. See also DÉLESTAGE, SUBMERGED CAP, and MACERATION.

pumps, mechanical devices for **pumping**, moving liquids such as wine and suspensions of solids such as grape juice from one location to another. Pumps are avoided by some of the most traditional—and some of the most modern (see WINERY DESIGN)—wineries that depend on gravity to move liquid from one level to another for different winemaking processes.

MUST from the CRUSHER-DESTEMMER is usually moved to the DRAINING tank or FERMENTATION VESSEL by means of a peristaltic or off-centre helical screw-type pump because this type performs particularly well with solid suspensions. Cloudy juice from the draining tank might well be moved by means of a rotor pump to the fermentation tank, and most of the semi-clear and clear wines being processed are also moved using these types of pump at any step of the winemaking process.

punching down, the winemaking operation of breaking up and submerging the CAP of skins and other solids during red wine fermentation to stop the cap from drying out, to encourage the EXTRACTION of colour and TANNINS, and to encourage useful AERATION in the making of a deeply coloured red wine. Keeping skins and liquid in contact is relatively simple with small batches of fermenting grapes. In tanks filled to a depth of 1–1.5 m/3–4 ft, a person can physically mix the floating solids into the fermenting grape juice using a wooden punch, stick or paddle, or even his or her feet. The cap may also be punched down by special metal devices, either by man or mechanically. It is usually done between one and three times a day depending on the fermentation rate. The French term is PIGEAGE. See also MACERATION, DÉLESTAGE, and SUBMERGED CAP.

punt, optional indentation in the bottom of wine BOTTLES, particularly common in bottles of sparkling wine.

pupitre, French name for a hand riddling rack, traditionally used for RIDDLING sparkling wines by hand. For more details, see SPARKLING WINEMAKING.

PVPP, **polyvinylpolypirrolidone**, a synthetic material used as a FINING agent. Its particular property is the removal of PHENOLIC components from white wine, especially those that are suffering from 'pinking' or 'browning' resulting from mild OXIDATION. D.B.

PX, common abbreviation for the Spanish grape variety PEDRO XIMÉNEZ, and particularly for the dark, sticky, ultra-sweet varietal FORTI-FIED WINE made from it that is so fashionable in Spain and increasingly so elsewhere. MONTILLA-MORILES is the usual source and top-quality wines can be almost as dark and viscous as molasses, though are generally lower in alcohol than the SHERRIES of nearby JEREZ.

pyrazines. See METHOXYPYRAZINES.

Pyrenees, hilly Australian wine region in the Western Victoria Zone sandwiched between the Grampians to the west and Bendigo to the east, named after the mountains separating France from Spain. It has nearly 50 producers.

pyruvic acid, three-carbon compound formed by YEAST at a midway stage in the complex FERMENTATION process. It is converted to ACETALDEHYDE and then to ETHANOL.

QbA, or **Qualitätswein bestimmter Anbaugebiete**, see QUALITÄTSWEIN.

QmP, or **Qualitätswein mit Prädikat**, German wine category now officially known as PRÄDIKATSWEIN.

Qualitätswein is what PDO wines are called in German. This is Germany's largest wine category and in practice includes all those wines once known as QBA (as opposed to QMP wines which have been renamed PRÄDIKATSWEIN). The grapes must originate in one of GERMANY's 13 official wine regions and reach minimum MUST WEIGHTS specified for each region, and which may vary by grape variety. In the cool Ahr, Mittelrhein, Mosel, and Saale-Unstrut, for example, Riesling need reach only 6% POTENTIAL ALCOHOL, in other regions 7%, while in Baden QbA must meet a minimum of 8% regardless of grape variety. Wines in this category may still be chaptalized but, thanks to CLIMATE CHANGE and improved viticultural techniques, chaptalization has become much rarer. Encouraged by VDP protocols, an increasing number of producers are selling all dry (TROCKEN and HALBTROCKEN) wines as Qualitätswein, reserving Prädikatswein designations for noticeably sweet wines.

Austria sets a national minimum for Qualitätswein equivalent to 9.7% potential alcohol.

quality assurance is a general concept covering the way in which a business is organized so that the quality of the product is assured at all stages. As applied to a wine business, good quality assurance will ensure that the original potential of the grapes and wine is not lost on the way to the bottle. Quality assurance is the totality of all the management actions and procedures that set out to achieve this high standard, and therefore incorporates QUALITY CONTROL.

An internationally recognized standard of quality management is ISO 9001:2008. This standard imposes a discipline that demands a uniformity of action throughout the business every time, all of the time.

Another useful though simple tool is Hazard Analysis and Critical Control Points (HACCP). The manufacturing process is divided into its basic stages, then each stage is examined to determine the problems that could occur at each one (hazard identification). Each hazard is then assessed for its potential danger to the process (the hazard analysis). Those that constitute the greatest danger are identified as the critical control points, to which the maximum attention is given. This procedure is now considered so important that it is mandatory throughout the EU for anyone involved in food and beverage handling, and is gaining worldwide recognition.   D.B.

Bird, D., *Understanding Wine Technology* (3rd edn, Newark, 2010).

quality control is a hands-on process of monitoring and controlling all parameters that verify a wine's palatability, STABILITY, compliance with regulations, TYPICALITY, and freedom from FAULTS and CONTAMINANTS. Most large wineries maintain laboratories capable of conducting all but the most difficult of the required ANALYSES, while smaller wine enterprises send samples to an independent commercial laboratory. For complete quality control, a chemical analytical laboratory, a microbiological laboratory, and a statistically controlled tasting panel are required. See also QUALITY ASSURANCE and SAMPLING.   A.D.W. & D.B.

quality in wine. The concept of quality is regularly used in connection with wine, both for marketing purposes and as a marker of personal evaluation. It is also widely used as an element in JUDGING in wine SHOWS. Nevertheless it is notoriously hard to pin down its precise nature. Even wine professionals comment at times that 'it is a matter of personal taste'. There are many—including Émile PEYNAUD—who argue that the denotation of quality is essentially the subjective enjoyment of pleasure, and others who claim that it exists only relative to other factors, such as PRICE or the circumstances of consumption. It is certainly true that our response to wine is in part idiosyncratic, dependent on varying physiological responses and the drinker's cultural background (see PHILOSOPHY AND WINE and TASTING) but that has not precluded a number of ways of trying to define quality. Whether wine quality has a SUBJECTIVE or objective nature is complex, as is the relationship of quality to preference. Arguably it is possible to assess a wine as high quality without actually liking it.

Some wine professionals believe that quality can be precisely measured. Certainly there are means such as INFRARED SPECTROSCOPY and GLYCOSYL-GLUCOSE ASSAY to evaluate grape quality, but Somers, formerly of the AUSTRALIAN WINE RESEARCH INSTITUTE, argues that, for red wines at least, it is possible to predict a wine's quality by using its ultra-violet absorbance to measure its PHENOLIC concentration. A more marketing-focused perspective is that a high-quality wine is one that is fit for its purpose, but given the complex motivations for drinking wine, this raises the question of precisely what the purpose is. The American oenologist Maynard AMERINE believed that wine is an aesthetic object and that its evaluation therefore calls for the use of aesthetic criteria.

Some commentators have suggested quality can be measured by such intrinsic indicators as a wine's BALANCE, LENGTH, intensity, harmony, varietal purity, and complexity. Such concepts are used in assessing wine throughout the world, although without any consistent application. Other means of grading quality, extrinsic to the drink itself, have also been used. These include the relationship of wine to the price it fetches, as in the best-known CLASSIFICATIONS. This does not however guarantee the actual organoleptic 'quality' of the drink as measured by critical or popular response.

Charters and Pettigrew suggest that drinkers consider that wine quality has a number of dimensions. Some of these are extrinsic to the wine, such as how it has been made; others are intrinsic, and include how the wine tastes (involving subdimensions such as concentration, balance, smoothness, drinkability, and interest), its capacity for AGEING, and its TYPICALITY. However, the most important quality dimension for consumers is the amount of pleasure afforded by the wine. Thus one can argue that for most drinkers quality has two components: a series of dimensions which catalyse quality and a sense of pleasure in the product which is the end result of those catalytic dimensions.

They also suggest a way out of the objective vs subjective quality conundrum. Employing a paradox which mirrors the sociological concept of intersubjectivity, it can be noted that wine drinkers often hold both perspectives simultaneously. Thus quality is partly objective, measured by external criteria which depend on a broad commonality in our response to the components of a wine (such as its balance and intensity) and subject to debate and agreement between drinkers. It is also partly personal, and related to the consumer's individual preference. S.J.C

Charters, S., and Pettigrew, S., '"I Like it But How do I Know if it's Any Good?": Quality and Preference in Wine Consumption', *Journal of Research for Consumers*, 5 (2003)

Charters, S., and Pettigrew, S., 'The dimensions of wine quality', *Food Quality and Preference*, 18(7) (2007), 997–1007.

Somers, C., *The Wine Spectrum: An Approach Towards Objective Definition of Wine Quality* (Adelaide, 1998).

quality wine is an expression widely and loosely used for any wine of good quality and was, until 2008, an official wine category throughout the EU, and therefore throughout most of Europe. It has been superseded by the PDO and PGI categories. Similarly, everything else, called 'table wine' in its strict pre-2008 EU sense, has been superseded by the cumbersome but clear WINE WITHOUT GEOGRAPHICAL INDICATION.

quarantine of imported plant material plays an important part in international viticulture, and can put a (necessary) brake on certain aspects of its development. Like any form of agricultural quarantine, it can annoy travellers but is designed to protect farmers from the ravages which may be caused by the introduction of pests and diseases from other countries or regions (see the history of DOWNY MILDEW, POWDERY MILDEW, and PHYLLOXERA). Most of the devastating pests and diseases of the vine species used commonly for wine production, VINIFERA, have in fact been spread from America, AMERICAN VINE SPECIES having developed a tolerance to these diseases which the European *V. vinifera* lacks.

Quarantine systems for viticulture are in place at national borders, and also sometimes at regional levels. Most wine-producing countries maintain strict quarantine on vine imports in an attempt to keep out the likes of PIERCE'S DISEASE, and FLAVESCENCE DORÉE, both of which could ravage a region's viticulture if they were to spread. Quarantine would appear less effective for flavescence dorée than for Pierce's disease, as the former is now found in most grape-growing countries and is continuing to spread. Quarantine also works to reduce the spread of other fungal, virus, and BACTERIAL DISEASES as well as insect and nematode PESTS which might not be lethal but may cause significant commercial damage. Licences issued for vine importation are typically restricted to a few cuttings of each lot which are subjected to disease testing. The quarantine delays can be up to two years, but diagnostic tests such as ELISA developed in the 1980s have reduced this period. Some countries, for example China and Canada, do allow imports of young GRAFTED vines but these are subject to guarantees about virus status. Nursery plants move freely around the EU with a plant passport to guarantee freedom from VIRUS DISEASE, but they are widely infected with TRUNK DISEASE fungi not covered by the passport. Smuggling of vines is not unknown, especially by impatient producers who believe that they are disadvantaged by not having access to better varieties or CLONES and are tempted to resort to what are sometimes referred to as 'suitcase clones'.

Sometimes there are quarantine areas within national boundaries, such as those that exist in South Australia in an attempt to avoid the further spread of phylloxera. Some countries and regions are free of major pests or diseases. CHILE, for example, has remained free of phylloxera, even though it is present in Argentina just over the Andes. Increasing international competition in the wine market makes the possibility of sabotage from another region or nation by introduction of a pest or disease less fanciful. The economic health of many of the world's viticultural regions depends on effective vine quarantine being maintained, and continuing vigilance and community support are essential. R.E.S.

Quarts de Chaume, extraordinary small enclave within the Coteaux du LAYON appellation producing, only in the best vintages and usually only as a result of NOBLE ROT infection, sweet white wines from BOTRYTIZED Chenin Blanc grapes or, increasingly, such grapes DRIED on the vine. Total annual production can often be as little as a few thousand cases, from just over 30 ha/74 acres of vineyard, supposedly the finest quarter, or *quart*, of the Chaume part near Rochefort-sur-Loire of Coteaux du Layon (see FRANCE, history, for details). The vineyards here have the advantage of a southerly exposition within a sort of amphitheatre. The brown SCHIST and carboniferous soils are distinctive and result in powerful wines, particularly since the average VINE AGE is high. The minimum grape sugar level in the must is 298 g/l, which is only rarely achieved, so few new investments are being made in this minuscule but potentially glorious appellation. The naturally high acidity of the Chenin Blanc grape endows these wines, similar to but rarer than those of nearby BONNEZEAUX, with impressive longevity. Domaine des Baumard has tried to secure permission for its continued use of CRYOEXTRACTION but in 2014 it was decreed that this freezing technique will be outlawed from 2019, and that Quarts de Chaume is officially the Loire's first GRAND CRU.

quartz, silicon dioxide (silica), a very common rock-forming mineral. It is seen as glassy, colourless grains in rocks such as GRANITE and SANDSTONE, producing sandy soils of low fertility. It also occurs as opaque white veins filling gashes in bedrock, which weathering loosens into fragments that become the milky white pebbles seen in many vineyard soils. See also GEOLOGY. A.J.M.

quartzite, a metamorphic rock that was originally a quartz-rich sandstone (see GEOLOGY). It is usually pale-coloured to white, with a 'sugary' appearance. It should not be confused with the mineral QUARTZ since it is a rock composed of myriad constituent grains. Once used for any tough quartz-rich rock, in modern usage quartzite refers to a compact, metamorphic fusion of the quartz grains and silica cement of the original sandstone, which makes it robust and resistant to SOIL EROSION.

Quartzite therefore tends to form relatively higher ground with thin, poorly fertile soils, generally not well suited to viticulture, although it does occur in Germany's NAHE and RHEINHESSEN regions, in Spain's CALATAYUD, and in the BAROSSA and CLARE VALLEYS, South Australia. Quartzite is much more commonly seen in vineyards as rock fragments in the soil, including the archetypal GALETS of CHÂTEAUNEUF-DU-PAPE. A.J.M.

Quatourze, one of the named CRUS within the LANGUEDOC AOC in southern France for reds based on Grenache, Syrah, and Mourvèdre. Production of appellation wine in this small wind-swept zone just west of Narbonne is small and dominated by Ch Notre-Dame du Quatourze.

Quebec is the least likely of all wine regions in CANADA. The centre of the province's small but enthusiastic winegrowing zone is the old town of Dunham. The wineries, for the most part strung out along the American border, have to battle the elements to produce wine for the tourist trade. The vines need time-consuming WINTER PROTECTION. Average sunshine hours during the growing season in Dunham are approximately 1,150 (in Burgundy they are 1,315; Niagara has 1,500, and the Okanagan Valley in British Columbia has 1,423). Despite relatively low temperatures, topographical features create highly localized warm spots that allow the hardiest vines to survive, if not flourish. The province had more than 115 cottage wineries by 2014, producing mainly white wines, mostly very fresh SEYVAL BLANC, Frontenac, Vandal-Cliché, Sainte-Croix, Vidal, Chardonnay, and Riesling, from a total of 647 ha/1,600 acres. There is no appellation system in Quebec, which makes some ICEWINE but its speciality is Ice Cider.   T.A.

Aspler, T., and Bergeron, J.-F., *Canadian Wineries* (Toronto, 2012).
www.quebecwines.com

Queensland. Australia's northern state appointed a Minister for Wine in 2004, although this move did not survive a change of government. The Queensland College of Wine Tourism remains a serious state asset, however. The industry has grown slowly since its early-20th-century growth spurt, with 148 wine producers at the end of 2013. The senior region, the **Granite Belt**, supports 50 producers. Humidity and summer rainfall are less of an issue than spring frost, for this is a high ELEVATION (700 m to 1,000 m) inland region with warm days and cold nights. Its principal white varieties are (in order of size) Chardonnay, Semillon, and Sauvignon Blanc (and 14 others), the red varieties Shiraz, Cabernet Sauvignon, and Merlot (likewise 14 others). The varietal pattern tells one that this is a normal region in climatic terms, with a two-thirds red, one-third white wine ratio. The Strange Bird marketing initiative encouraged planting of Spanish and Italian varieties (many producers are of Italian descent) and warm-climate ALTERNATIVE VARIETIES are expected to be increasingly important.

The state's largest winery, Sirromet, has its 200 ha/494 acres of vineyards here, although its high-tech 1,000-tonne winery is on the coast south of Brisbane. It and several smaller wineries (most under 100 tonnes) have made wines which have won gold medals at home and abroad and are taken increasingly seriously.

South Burnett was the first region to gain formal recognition as a GEOGRAPHICAL INDICATION. One large winery with 220 ha of plantings, Clovely Estate, and a crush capacity of 1,000 tonnes, makes wines of genuine quality.

Another 70 or so wineries are scattered along the Queensland coast and hillsides; although here the focus is fairly and squarely on the general LIFESTYLE tourist trade, there are more than a few wineries producing creditable wine as well as providing a host of scenic and other attractions. Two regions, the **Scenic Rim**, west of Ipswich, and **Somerset Valley**, north west of Brisbane, continue to expand with a range of varietally suited vineyards and growing CELLAR-DOOR trade. In the far western **Darling Downs**, Riversands Wines survived floods in both 2011 and 2012 but the floods drove Romavilla, the state's oldest wine property, which had traded continuously since 1863, out of business.
                                             J.H. & H.H.

www.queenslandwine.com.au
www.qwia.org.au

quercetin, also spelt **quercitin**, a yellow dyestuff with ANTIOXIDANT properties belonging to the FLAVONOL family, originally extracted from the bark of black oak (QUERCUS), hence the name.

Quercus is the botanical genus to which oak belongs and is therefore the most important family of plants to wine after the vine genus VITIS since it provides both CORK and wine's most classic storage material (OAK). It is subdivided into two subgenera, *Cyclobalanopsis*, and *Equercus*, to which all oaks used for wine containers and corks belong. The species most commonly used for BARRELS are the American white oak *Quercus alba*, and the European oaks *Quercus robur* and *Quercus petraea*. For more details, see OAK.

The species whose bark is stripped to provide cork is *Quercus suber*.

Quercy, Coteaux du, relatively recent AOC between Cahors and Gaillac in SOUTH WEST FRANCE for reds and some rosés made from Cabernet Franc with Cot (Malbec), Merlot, and Tannat. About 170 ha/420 acres of vineyard were in production in 2012.

Quincy, rapidly expanding, historic white wine appellation in the greater Loire region producing racy dry wines from Sauvignon Blanc (with up to 10% Sauvignon Gris) grapes from a total area of vines that had grown to 269 ha/664 acres by 2012 of sand and gravel on the left bank of the Cher tributary. Its long history (it was the second APPELLATION created, after CHÂTEAUNEUF-DU-PAPE) and early popularity owe much to its proximity to RIVER transport (especially in comparison with the much smaller nearby appellation REUILLY). The wines tend to be a little more rustic, less delicate, than those made in Menetou-Salon and Sancerre to the east.

See also LOIRE, including map.

quinta, Portuguese word meaning 'farm', which may also refer to a wine-producing estate or vineyard. Single-quinta ports are those made from a single year and from a single estate in the Douro Valley; see PORT.

Liddell, A., and Price, J., *Port Wine Quintas of the Douro* (London, 1992).
Mayson, R. J., *Port and the Douro* (3rd edn, Oxford, 2013).

Quinta do Noval. Founded in 1713, Noval is the name of both the estate and this historic, unusually vineyard-based, PORT shipper. Quinta do Noval was owned by the firm António José da Silva, who in 1973 changed their name to Quinta do Noval-Vinhos, because Noval represented their finest wine (and they also wanted to avoid confusion with all the other da Silva companies in OPORTO). The estate of Quinta do Noval, in the Pinhão valley, enjoyed a heyday in the mid 20th century when run by Luiz Vasconcellos Porto, before being inherited by the Van Zeller family. The firm's vineyards produce well over 60% of their needs, with the remainder being bought in from other properties in the DOURO valley. Noval's most prestigious wine is Nacional, produced from 2.5 ha/5 acres of vines which are not GRAFTED on to PHYLLOXERA-resistant American ROOTSTOCKS and are therefore 'national'. These vines yield particularly small quantities of fruit, so that a Nacional vintage port is made only in exceptional years. The wines these ungrafted vines produce are amongst the most concentrated of all vintage ports, however, with a deeper colour and much fuller texture than others. This results in these ports' commanding high prices on the market, with the Nacional 1931 VINTAGE (which Noval was virtually alone in declaring) enjoying almost legendary status. Quinta do Noval suffered a devastating fire at its lodges in Vila Nova de Gaia in 1981 and has continued to age its wines in air-conditioned lodges in the Douro Valley rather than in Gaia.

In 1993, the firm was acquired by the French insurance company AXA, and its winery, vineyards, and reputation have since been fully restored with more than three-quarters of the vineyard area having been replanted, mainly with Touriga Nacional, Touriga Franca, and Tinto Cão, innovatively retaining the original vineyard TERRACES while adapting them for modern cultivation wherever possible. A third vintage port Silval, sometimes produced in a generally declared vintage year alongside Quinta do Noval, sometimes on its own when Quinta do Noval is not declared, was introduced in 1995. Since 2004 Noval has produced a range of DOURO red wines under the labels Quinta do Noval and Cedro.

qvevri, uniquely GEORGIAN clay vessel used for FERMENTATION and AGEING of red and white wines for many centuries, especially, but by no means exclusively, in Kakheti in the east. The rounded, wide-mouthed earthenware jars vary enormously in size, from 50 l for a family's domestic production to 700–4,000 l for commercial use, the larger ones for ageing rather than fermentation. Unlike Roman AMPHORAE and Spanish TINAJAS, qvevri are buried underground, requiring no TEMPERATURE CONTROL and benefiting from natural SETTLING and CLARIFICATION. Procuring and then cleaning and maintaining these vessels are the main obstacles to their wider use.

The Kakhetian tradition for both red and white wines is to put the lightly crushed whole berries—including skins, pips, and stems, known as *chacha*—into the qvevri. Further west, where the jars are also known as *churi*, less *chacha* is used and maceration times are shorter. With red wines, the wine may be moved to a clean qvevri, or even to oak barrels, post fermentation. After fermentation and MALOLACTIC CONVERSION, the wide mouth of the qvevri is closed with a slate (occasionally wooden) lid and sealed with clay. Qvevri wines are quintessentially tannic, the best deeply satisfying and flavourful, but the whites are particularly distinctive thanks to their golden colour, tannic structure, and aromas of hay and chamomile, the winemaking sometimes obscuring the grape variety. Qvevri winemaking, recognized as a UNESCO 'intangible heritage' in 2013, is also practised by a few producers in Europe, most notably in FRIULI in north-east Italy and western Slovenia. Qvevri is both singular and plural.

r

Rabigato, grape that adds class and acidity to DOURO white blends and grown particularly in the Douro Superior. Total plantings were 2,172 ha/5,365 acres in 2012.

Rabo de Ovelha, white grape variety grown in Portugal, particularly the Alentejo, taking its name from the 'ewe's tail' shape of its bunches. Noted more for alcohol than subtlety and probably closely related to CAYETANA. Total plantings had fallen to 1,120 ha/2,766 acres by 2012.

Raboso, name of two closely related but distinct tough red grape varieties grown in the VENETO region of north east Italy. **Raboso Piave** is more common, on 730 ha/1,803 acres in 2010, as opposed to **Raboso Veronese** grown on less than 300 ha. Rabosa Piave is characteristic of the flat valley floor of PIAVE and most is grown in the province of Treviso. Raboso Veronese is sometimes interplanted with Raboso Piave but is also grown in Ferrara and Ravenna in Emilia-Romagna. The name is thought to derive from the Italian *rabbioso*, or angry, presumably a reference to consumer reaction to the uncompromisingly high ACIDITY and rough TANNINS which characterize the grape and its wine. This is a grape variety which has excellent resistance to disease and rot, but which makes CABERNET SAUVIGNON look rather mellow. Unfortunately Raboso is not notably high in ALCOHOL which might compensate for its astringency and can therefore taste extremely austere in youth. Stalwart defenders of the variety insist that with full ripeness and careful handling in the winery, wines produced can be truly distinguished, the Veneto's answer to the Nebbiolo of Piemonte or the Sangiovese of Tuscany. The reputation and price level of Raboso make it difficult to justify this kind of investment, and

vineyard plantings, which continue to decline, reflect this fact.

Raboso Veronese is also planted, to an extremely limited extent, in Argentina, presumably taken there by Italian immigrants.

rack, wine, common storage for wine bottles. See CELLAR.

rack and return. See DÉLESTAGE.

racking, the winemaking operation of removing clear wine from the settled SEDIMENT or LEES in the bottom of a container. The verb to **rack** has been used thus at least since the 14th century.

Racking is usually achieved by pumping or siphoning the wine away from the sediment into an empty container but special large **racking tanks** are used by some large wineries (and breweries). They are equipped with drain lines, the lower ends of which can be adjusted to just clear the sediment layer and permit more rapid and more complete wine removal from the solids.

Racking, or *soutirage* as it is known in French, forms an important part of the annual cycle of cellar work, or ÉLEVAGE, in the production of most fine wines matured in small BARRELS. Racking from barrel to barrel is very LABOUR-intensive and each racking inevitably involves a barrel that needs thorough cleaning to avoid any form of CONTAMINATION.

According to classical *élevage*, the first racking takes place soon after FERMENTATION and the ensuing MACERATION to separate the new wine from the gross LEES. In cooler regions, the second racking typically takes place just after the first frosts of winter have precipitated some of the TARTRATES, while in many cellars there is a third in spring and a fourth before the full heat of the summer. Wines may be racked once or

twice during a second year in barrel. New World winemakers have tended to rack less frequently.

Racking is not only part of the CLARIFICATION process, it also provides AERATION, which, in the case of red wines, is essential to the formation of PIGMENTED TANNINS and is beneficial to the sensory properties of the wine. Aeration also discourages REDUCTION of any excess SULFUR to malodorous HYDROGEN SULFIDE.

Raffiac, sometimes **Raffiat**, alternative names for ARRUFIAC.

railways. Until the arrival of a railway in their region, wine producers were almost totally dependent on water-borne means of transport. Without access to the sea or a navigable RIVER or canal, transport was too difficult and expensive for all but the finest and rarest wines. This gave an overwhelming advantage to regions such as BORDEAUX, which were served by a major port, or CHAMPAGNE, with access to the river system of northern France.

The construction of the railways enabled a number of wines previously unknown outside their region to be exported. In some cases—notably CHIANTI in central Italy and RIOJA in northern Spain—this enabled high-quality wines to achieve their deserved recognition for the first time. The construction of a railway line between the town of JEREZ and the coast in the mid 19th century greatly encouraged exports of SHERRY.

The railways also facilitated the transport of inferior wines. They allowed the late-19th-century development of the mass-production vineyards of the LANGUEDOC and ROUSSILLON in the south of France, whose rough wines were transported in vast quantities to northern France and Belgium, thus ruining such marginal northern

European vineyards as those around ORLÉANS and, to a lesser extent, those of the French MOSELLE. The railways in ARGENTINA were also crucial in establishing Mendoza as an important wine region so far from the capital Buenos Aires. During the 15 years of PROHIBITION in North America, efficient rail transport of fresh grapes from California to the suddenly numerous HOME WINEMAKERS in the eastern states played a part in maintaining a winemaking tradition in the United States.   N.F.

rainfall, a component of climate which affects grapevines in many and conflicting ways.

For vines depending directly on rainfall (see DRYLAND VITICULTURE), there needs to be enough rain, at the right times, to promote adequate growth and to avoid severe WATER STRESS during ripening. On the other hand, more than enough rainfall can lead to excessive vegetation growth and a poor CANOPY MICROCLIMATE, especially on soils high in NITROGEN. It can also cause waterlogging on soils prone to it (see DRAINAGE). Similarly, rainfall can promote fungal diseases such as DOWNY MILDEW and BOTRYTIS BUNCH ROT by wetting foliage and fruit.

The effects of irregular rainfall are moderated to the extent that the soil has sufficient depth and water-holding capacity, and is well enough drained for the vine roots to survive at depth (see SOIL WATER, SOIL DEPTH, TERROIR).

Alternatively, insufficient rainfall and/or insufficient soil water-holding capacity can be overcome by IRRIGATION. This is especially important in MEDITERRANEAN CLIMATES where the summer is dry. Under all these regimes the practical minimum annual rainfall for commercially adequate yields is somewhere around 500 mm/20 in in cool viticultural climates, rising to about 600–750 mm/24–30 in in warm to hot climates.

Hot regions with full irrigation typically have 300 mm/12 in of annual rainfall or less, and mostly depend on rivers, aquifers, or wells to provide water. The normal unreliability of rainfall means that full wetting of the SOIL PROFILE seldom occurs naturally, and frequent heavy watering is usually needed throughout the growing and ripening season.

No particular upper limit of rainfall is apparent for viticulture, provided that the soils are well drained, leached SOIL NUTRIENTS can be replaced, SUNLIGHT is enough, and HUMIDITY is not so high that FUNGAL DISEASES cannot be controlled. Some successful viticultural areas, such as the VINHO VERDE region in northern Portugal, and parts of southern SWITZERLAND, have annual rainfall totals exceeding 1,700 mm/67 in.

Heavy rain close to and at vintage is nevertheless nearly always detrimental to wine quality, especially if it follows water stress. The berries then swell suddenly and often split, resulting in fungal and bacterial infection of the bunches (see BUNCH ROT). At a minimum, the juice and its flavour are diluted. HAIL at this time is especially disastrous.   J.G. & R.E.S.

raisins, alternative generic name for DRYING GRAPES, from its direct French translation *raisins secs*, but also used specifically for relatively large, dark, dried grapes, particularly in California, where raisins are as important a viticultural crop as grapes for wine.

Grapes which have dried either on the vine or have been dried after picking, to produce either dried fruit or DRIED-GRAPE WINES, are often described as fully or partially **raisined**, one result of extended HANG TIME.

Rajinski Rizling and **Rajnai Rizling**, various eastern European names for the true RIESLING grape of Germany.

Ramandolo. See VERDUZZO.

Ramisco, red grape variety grown exclusively on just 17 ha by 2012 in the shrinking COLARES region of Portugal and therefore probably the only VINIFERA vine variety never to have been GRAFTED.

rancio, imprecise tasting term used in many languages for a distinctive style of wine, often FORTIFIED WINE or VIN DOUX NATUREL, achieved by deliberately MADERIZING the wine by exposing it to OXYGEN and/or heat. The wine may be stored in barrels in hot storehouses (as for some of Australia's TOPAQUE AND MUSCAT), or immediately under the rafters in a hot climate (as for some of ROUSSILLON's vins doux naturels), or in glass BONBONNES left out of doors and subjected to the changing temperatures of night and day (as in parts of Spain). The word rancio has the same root as 'rancid' and the wines which result have an additional and powerful smell reminiscent of overripe fruit, nuts, and melted, or even rancid, butter.

Key flavour compounds identified in aged vin doux naturel wines arise by MAILLARD REACTION of sugars with amino acids and by oxidation. These compounds are known to be present in, and responsible for, the characteristic flavour of other sweet food products. Thus, for example, furaneol, cyclotene, maltol, SOTOLON, which are known contributors to the flavour of honey and caramelized sugar products, have been found in these wines along with several lactones that are important to the flavour of dried fruits.

This richness emerges in a complex series of sensations on the nose and palate. 'Rankness, a special character of fullness and richness', was the unflattering description given by Charles Walter Berry, the wine merchant who was Britain's leading cognac connoisseur between the World Wars (rancio can often be found in oak-aged brandies). This richness, allied to a certain mild cheesiness in the nose, reminds some tasters of Roquefort cheese. But the richness, depth, and diversity of rancio can remind others of rich fruit cakes with their flavours of candied fruits, apricots, sultanas, almonds, and walnuts.   N.F., J.R., & P.J.W.

Cutzach, I., Chatonnet, P., and Dubourdieu, D., 'Study of the formation mechanisms of some volatile compounds during the aging of sweet fortified wines', *Journal of Agricultural and Food Chemistry*, 47 (1999), 2837–46.

random oxidation, also known as sporadic post-bottling oxidation, describes the premature browning that occurs in some white wines some months after BOTTLING. The problem is common enough for some industry figures to refer to it as the 'new CORK TAINT'. Wines are protected against oxidation through the addition of SULFUR DIOXIDE at bottling but if the level of free sulfur dioxide falls too low, the wine is unprotected, and browning can occur. The main explanation is oxygen transfer through the cork, which seems to be highly variable. However, some scientists suspect that random oxidation may be caused by as yet poorly understood chemical reactions independent of the CLOSURE. It has been suggested that the addition of the antioxidant ASCORBIC ACID just before bottling to keep white wines fresh may have the paradoxical effect of rendering the added sulfur dioxide less effective, and making some wines susceptible to oxidation. Worse still, when the level of free sulfur dioxide in the bottle becomes too low, ascorbic acid becomes a pro-oxidant, increasing the degree of oxidation. Another proposed cause is poor procedure or intermittent failure on the bottling line, allowing some wines to have much higher levels of dissolved oxygen from the outset (see TOTAL PACKAGE OXYGEN). Random oxidation is mainly a problem with white wines: while oxygen ingress through the closure will certainly damage red wines, they are more resistant to oxidation because of their high PHENOLIC content. Oxidation is also more likely to be spotted in white wines because of the dramatic colour change that accompanies it even though this change in colour is usually the last step in PREMATURE OXIDATION.

Ranina, Slovenian synonym for the BOUVIER grape.

Rapel, subregion of the Central Valley of CHILE, including most famously Cachapoal and Colchagua.

Rasteau, one of the more successful Côtes du Rhône villages in the southern RHÔNE making some wines to rival Châteauneuf-du-Pape from nearly 1,000 ha/2,470 acres of vineyard. Its heady, typically very concentrated red, white, and rosé table wines were sold as Côtes du Rhône-Villages, increasingly with the name

Rasteau as a suffix, but since 2010, the dry reds have had their own AOC. Grenache dominates with Mourvèdre and Syrah the main blending partners. Jérôme Bressy of Domaine Gourt de Mautens has fallen foul of the authorities because of his fondness for INDIGENOUS VARIETIES, some of them FIELD BLENDS, some outlawed by revised appellation regulations, others in too high a proportion.

Very much less common is the VIN DOUX NATUREL, sweet mixtures of just-fermenting grape juice and pure grape spirit in various shades of amber, brown, and red. They are essentially alcoholic Grenache juice (most of the grapes must be GRENACHE Noir, Gris, and/or Blanc) treated to a range of AGEING processes which may vary from the negligible through various forms of CASK AGEING. Although Rasteau is the chosen name for this variable drink, the grapes may be grown anywhere in the communes of three Côtes du Rhône villages: Rasteau, CAIRANNE, and Sablet.

ratafia is an old, usually domestically produced wine-based apéritif made in the French countryside by drying grapes to a raisin-like state and then moistening and fermenting them in the spring. Ratafia champenois is self-explanatory but nowadays there are more profitable things to do with Champagne grapes.

ratings, scores applied to individual wines. See NUMBERS AND WINE and SCORING.

Ratti, Renato (1934–88), industrious and dedicated winemaker based at La Morra in BAROLO in the north west Italian region of Piemonte. One of a group of so-called modernist Barolo producers seeking a more accessible Barolo (see BAROLO for more details), he was particularly keen to promulgate the notion of TERROIR. In 1979 he was one of the first to draw up a map of the best Barolo vineyards, or CRUS, which, with limitations, is still valid today.   W.S.

Räuschling, historic white grape variety today most commonly planted in German-speaking SWITZERLAND, where it can produce fine, crisp wines. In the Middle Ages, it was very widely cultivated in Germany, particularly Baden (see GERMAN HISTORY). DNA PROFILING has shown it is a natural GOUAIS BLANC x SAVAGNIN cross.

Ravat, French vine breeder who gave his name to a number of FRENCH HYBRIDS.

Ray, Cyril (1908–91), English war correspondent turned wine writer, famous more for his style and punctiliousness than for an obsession with wine itself.

In 1956, he edited the first of what were to be perhaps his most lasting contribution to the LITERATURE OF WINE, 16 volumes of *The Compleat Imbiber*, compilations of stories,

comments, and verses, although the 'pirate' edition, produced in later years without his seeing the proofs, provoked a special outburst of his famous rage against publishers. He also became wine correspondent of the *Observer* newspaper, *Punch* weekly magazine (where he was also a consultant to their purchases of wine), and the *Spectator*.

Cyril Ray founded the British organization the Circle of Wine Writers and was its first president. Among his books were strongly historical monographs on LAFITE-Rothschild, WARRE, BOLLINGER, MOUTON ROTHSCHILD, Langoa- and Léoville-BARTON, Ruffino Chianti, and, one of the last, Robert MONDAVI. His son Jonathan has followed him in to WINE WRITING.   P.V.P.

raya, Spanish word meaning 'stripe' or 'streak' and a term for the symbol used to classify SHERRY must. A *raya* is also a coarse style of OLOROSO used in blending medium-dry sherry.

RDI. See REGULATED DEFICIT IRRIGATION.

Rebe, German for vine. **Rebsorten** are vine varieties.

Rebula, Slovenian name for RIBOLLA Gialla.

Recioto, distinctive category of north-east Italian DRIED-GRAPE WINES, a historic speciality of VENETO. The word derives from the Italian for ear, *orecchio*, because the wine was originally produced only from the ripest grapes in the bunch, from the upper lobes, or ears, although selected whole bunches have long been substituted. The most common forms of Recioto are sweet red Recioto della VALPOLICELLA and the rare sweet white Recioto di SOAVE and Recioto di GAMBELLARA.

Recioto della Valpolicella, like its dry counterpart AMARONE, is produced from 45–95% CORVINA, the great native grape of Valpolicella up to half of which may be replaced by CORVINONE, and 5–30% RONDINELLA, with up to 25% of the INTERNATIONAL VARIETIES authorized in the province of Verona. As for Amarone, these grapes are raisined during the late autumn and winter months after the harvest in special drying rooms equipped with air conditioning and humidity control to avoid the development of BOTRYTIS which can lead to PREMATURE OXIDATION (although more traditional producers tend to embrace the complexity that botrytis under more natural drying conditions can add). Like Amarone it is produced in the Valpolicella DOC zone which has been divided into a CLASSICO subzone and a larger zone whose wines are simply called Recioto. As for Amarone, DOCG status was achieved for Recioto della Valpolicella in 2009. The wine is a decisively sweet one as the grapes need by law to be dried until at least 1 December following the harvest. The white Recioto di Soave must be made from at least 70% GARGANEGA and a maximum of 30%

TREBBIANO DI SOAVE, Pinot Bianco, and/or Chardonnay (although quality-oriented producers tend to eschew the last two which are generally included to compensate for lack of flavour and alcohol in grapes from high-yielding vineyards). Recioto di Gambellara must be 100% Garganega.

All three wines can represent some of Italy's finest sweet wines, but due to sluggish demand, and the mediocre quality associated with some dry Soave and Gambellara, the number of producers willing to sacrifice time and labour to produce these wines has been declining, while Valpolicella producers now definitively favour the much more lucrative Amarone.   W.S.

récolte, French for HARVEST. A **récoltant** is therefore a GROWER. In CHAMPAGNE, a **récoltant-manipulant** (identified by 'RM' on the label) is a grower who also makes his or her own champagne, of whom there are more than 3,000 in the region, as opposed to a **récoltant-coopérateur**, who sells champagne made by a CO-OPERATIVE, of whom there are slightly more.

recorking, a potentially hazardous exercise conducted by some top wine producers and some fine-wine traders. The aim is to prolong a wine's potential longevity after extended BOTTLE AGEING may have weakened the cork. At one stage Ch LAFITE would send its MAÎTRE DE CHAI on recorking tours which doubled as public relations exercises but, having encountered too many bottles of doubtful PROVENANCE and poor condition, they have abandoned this practice. Today PENFOLDS is the world's most determined recorker, holding 'clinics' for those who own Penfolds wines of more than 15 years old. In the 23 years to 2014, Penfolds had certified 120,000 bottles, typically topped them up with wine of a similar age and quality before recorking with advice on when to drink them. The FINE WINE market became suspicious of recorking in any circumstances other than the most public in the late 1980s, as it potentially offers too much possibility for ADULTERATION AND FRAUD.

rectified grape must, or RGM, is preserved GRAPE JUICE that has been rectified, processed to reduce the concentration of solids other than SUGARS. It is generally further treated by removing water to yield **rectified concentrated grape must**, or RCGM, which is a common commodity used principally in Europe for ENRICHMENT. The EU authorities were at one time keen to promote its use in place of sugar as a way of helping reduce the European WINE LAKE. Many winemakers who need to use it in northern Europe have a natural antipathy to introducing a product made from what they view as inferior grapes. There are several major producers of RGM in Europe who absorb SURPLUS grape production from areas such as the

LANGUEDOC, La MANCHA, SICILY, and PUGLIA. They submit it to such modern technological processes as ION EXCHANGE and REVERSE OSMOSIS together with super-efficient FILTRATION and evaporators to produce what is in effect a concentrated invert sugar (GLUCOSE and FRUCTOSE) solution from grape juice. See also CONCENTRATION.

red blotch virus, or **red blotch disease**, a new circular DNA geminivirus first described by scientists at CORNELL and UC DAVIS in 2012, is now being recognized as a serious problem in the US. At least two strains have so far been identified and more are likely. Much remains to be learned but this virus is known to seriously impair the RIPENING potential of the fruit in infected vines. Symptoms include red blotchy leaves in red wine varieties and yellow curled leaves in whites, although infected symptomless vines have also been seen. The origin of this 'new' disease is unknown but the primary source to growers now is infected plant material that was previously certified free of known viral pathogens. In addition, it is strongly suspected to be spread from sick to healthy vines via insect vectors, possibly LEAFHOPPERS. Virtually all NURSERIES in California, including the FOUNDATION PLANT SERVICE at UC Davis, are testing for and eliminating red blotch from their MOTHER VINES. They are planting new source blocks in virgin ground with the latest certified material that has also been tested for the new virus in the hope of eliminating it from the plant material stream. By the end of 2014, the presence of this virus had been recorded in nursery plants in California and it has spread in the US and perhaps in Canada. L.T.M.

Al Rwahnih, M., 'Association of a circular DNA virus in grapevines affected by red blotch disease in California', *Proceedings of the 17th Congress of ICVG* (Davis, Calif., 2012), 104–5. http://ucanr.edu/sites/ICVG/files/156711.pdf.

Morton, L., 'On the trail of Red Blotch virus: view from the East', *Wine Business Monthly* (Feb 2013), 132–9.

Redding, Cyrus (1785–1870), England's answer to the great wine explorer of France, André JULLIEN. Redding came from an old Cornish family and, after publishing several biographies and histories when working as a young journalist in London, was sent to Paris in 1814, where he was based for five years. It was during this time that he was introduced to wine regions and a wine-producing culture. Jullien's book was published two years after his arrival in Paris and Redding's most important work, *A History and Description of Modern Wines*, takes full account of both Jullien and CHAPTAL's previous publications, but Redding seems to have been independently inspired by the disparity between the wines then available in the British Isles and what he tasted in cellars all over Europe (see ADULTERATION). Like Jullien, he was an

intrepid traveller and his book includes observations not just on European wines but on those of Asia, Africa, and both North and South America. His emphasis on the word Modern owes much to his criticism of earlier writers such as Sir Edward Barry and Alexander HENDERSON (see LITERATURE OF WINE), whose reverence for CLASSICAL WINES he felt was misplaced. The first edition of *A History and Description of Modern Wines* was written when Redding had returned to England in 1833; modern facsimile editions have also appeared, so useful, fresh, and unpretentious are Redding's observations to this day.

Redondo, DOP subregion of the ALENTEJO in southern Portugal.

redox potential, or oxidation–reduction potential, is a measure of the summation of all of a wine's components' potentials to oxidize. Since wine is made up of components that are either oxidized or reduced (see OXIDATION and REDUCTION), it is a system composed of many joined redox pairs. Oxidation reactions are always coupled to reduction reactions. Electrons made available from an oxidation are taken up by the compound being reduced until an equilibrium is established. The reaction with the most positive value (in which electrons are most easily accepted) will occur at the expense of reactions with lower values. Thus an equilibrium is reached from all the redox pairs and a net redox potential can be determined.

Redox potentials are of only limited value to even the most scientific winemaker, however, since they do not express how rapidly the various reactions will occur. They reveal only the potential situation that will obtain given unlimited time. Redox potentials can also prove to be difficult to measure in practice. A determination of the concentration of dissolved OXYGEN in a given wine can often prove to be of more value in guiding the winemaker in his or her choice of cellar treatments. A.D.W.

Zoecklein, B., 'Understanding oxidation: redox potential', *Vineyard & Winery Management* (Nov–Dec 1989), 32–3.

reduced-alcohol wines are those with a lower than normal ALCOHOLIC STRENGTH, generally less than 5.5%. The easiest and cheapest way to produce these low-alcohol products is simply to dilute wine using water (to make a SPRITZER-type drink), natural or flavoured fruit juices, or even GRAPE JUICE to make an all-vinous product.

Another method is to arrest fermentation before it is complete by refrigeration, resulting in a sweet, low-alcohol, often lightly sparkling drink. This is a particularly common technique in Italy and is conducted at all sorts of quality levels, from the finest MOSCATO D'ASTI to partial fermentation of LAMBRUSCO must stored throughout the year at low temperatures and

transformed into relatively industrial 'Lambrusco Light' as required. See also DEALCOHOLIZED WINE.

reducing sugars are sugars that can act as very mild reducing agents (see REDOX and REDUCTION). In wine, GLUCOSE and FRUCTOSE are the primary reducing sugars. See also RESIDUAL SUGAR, which shares the same abbreviation but has a different meaning.

reduction, chemical reaction that is in effect the complement of OXIDATION and one in which an element or compound gains electrons. The essential feature of an oxidation is that electrons are transferred from the component being oxidized to the one being **reduced**. The reaction cannot be isolated; to have a reduction, something else must be oxidized. Common reduction reactions are those of iron ore to iron the metal, or the reduction of ACETALDEHYDE to ETHANOL as happens in the final stage of alcoholic FERMENTATION. Wine in a stoppered bottle or other airtight container is said to be in a **reductive** state.

Reducing conditions are desirable towards the end of fermentation so that alcohol is produced along with the carbon dioxide from the acetaldehyde. Reducing conditions are also generally preferable throughout ÉLEVAGE of wine in the cellar, especially for white wines, which can withstand oxidation much less well than reds with their higher content of PHENOLICS.

Wines, especially red wines held in the absence of oxygen, may suffer from excess reduction, resulting in the slow POLYMERIZATION of TANNINS and PIGMENTED TANNINS. **Reduction** is also used as a convenient, but rather inaccurate, term to describe the formation of sulfur compounds such as HYDROGEN SULFIDE and MERCAPTANS (thiols), which tend to form under reducing conditions. Typical descriptors for such compounds include rotten eggs, garlic, struck flint, cabbage, rubber, and burnt rubber. Such reduction is usually considered to be a wine FAULT, although sulfur compounds can add complexity at lower levels, depending on the wine style. In some cases, reduction faults can be cured by AERATION, perhaps careful RACKING, an operation which introduces some oxygen, an oxidizing agent strong enough to prevent the reduction of most sulfur compounds.

Reduction has become a much-debated topic in the wine trade since the more widespread adoption of tin-lined SCREWCAPS as closures. These make a near-impermeable seal and some commentators have suggested that the reductive conditions they create may discourage the loss of an aroma of struck flint, attributed to reduced sulfur compounds in some wines. The extent of this phenomenon is currently unclear because it is not unique to wines bottled with screwcaps and because the gas impermeability of a very good cork has been shown to be equivalent to that of a screwcap (see OXYGEN TRANSMISSION

RATE). What is clear is that reductive characters can appear in a wine regardless of the closure, unless these characters have been prevented or removed during the winemaking process. See also REDOX POTENTIAL.

A.D.W., P.J.W., & J.A.G.

Goode, J., *Wine Science: The Application of Science in Winemaking* (2nd edn, London, 2014).

reductive winemaking, increasingly fashionable approach, especially for high-end Chardonnay, that is in part a response to PREMATURE OXIDATION and aims at reducing the exposure of must and wine to oxygen in the winery by minimizing or eliminating practices such as RACKING, LEES STIRRING, and the use of new oak BARRELS. This is often done in combination with FERMENTATION using ambient YEASTS and tends to result in aromas and flavours of flint and struck match.

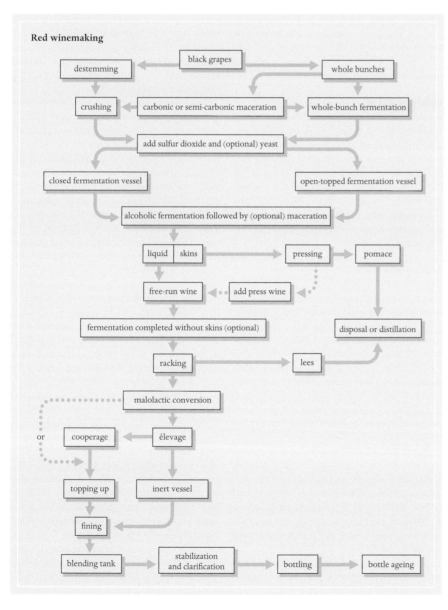

Red winemaking

red winemaking, the production of wines with reddish to purple colours. The great majority of today's red wines depend on CRUSHING and DESTEMMING of the grape clusters as a first step in their production (but see also WHOLE-BUNCH FERMENTATION and CARBONIC MACERATION).

The mixture of skins, seeds, and occasionally some stem fragments, along with the juice, then goes into a FERMENTATION VESSEL, where YEAST converts SUGARS into ALCOHOL. The natural ANTHOCYANIN pigments, which are contained in the skins of black grapes, along with FLAVOUR COMPOUNDS, FLAVOUR PRECURSORS, and large amounts of PHENOLICS (the latter originating from both the skins and the seeds) are extracted into the fermenting wine by the alcohol produced by yeast during FERMENTATION and MACERATION. Without some maceration of juice and skins, wine made from dark-skinned grapes is merely pink (as described in ROSÉ WINEMAKING). Duration of this EXTRACTION process can be anything from a fast two- or three-day fermentation for an everyday wine to a week-long fermentation followed by a further one, two, or even three weeks' maceration for a full-bodied red wine that is designed to age.

Red wine fermentations are almost always conducted at TEMPERATURES higher than those used for white wines. Red wines fermented at lower temperatures tend to be lighter in colour and body and to display the fruitier range of ESTERS. There is usually some producer somewhere in the world deliberately fashioning light reds in this style to be consumed chilled.

Red winemaking differs from white winemaking not only in terms of skin–juice contact and temperature but also because some exposure to OXYGEN is more generally desirable than with white wines, and BARREL MATURATION, or at least CASK AGEING, is also more common for red wines than white. The phenolic compounds extracted from skins, seeds, and stem fragments react more or less slowly with oxygen dissolved in the wine to form PIGMENTED TANNINS and these, together with the colourless TANNINS that were extracted directly or formed during the maceration, contribute to the TEXTURE of the wine. Another important difference between red and white winemaking is that most red wines undergo MALOLACTIC CONVERSION whereas with whites it is generally a deliberate choice on the part of the winemaker, related to factors such as grape variety, the level of ACIDITY in the grapes, and the intended wine style.

During barrel maturation, when the oxygen supply to the wine is restricted, both the substances produced in the earlier reactions between grape phenolics and oxygen and those derived from extraction of the wood phenolics interact and contribute an entirely new range of flavours (see OAK FLAVOUR).

Further reactions of the grape- and wood-derived phenolic constituents, and augmentation of the grape-derived flavour compounds, all progress during BOTTLE AGEING. The abundance and great diversity of compounds available in a red wine are the reasons that AGEING assumes particular importance for fine red wines. See also WINEMAKING.

A.D.W. & P.J.W.

red wines actually vary in COLOUR from dark pink to almost black, with an enormous variation in the amount of blue or yellow to be seen at the rim. Their colour depends on the grape varieties used, the vintage characteristics, the health of the grapes, the winemaking methods (in particular the extent of MACERATION and the method of EXTRACTION), the wine's PH, and the amount of time it has spent in tank, barrel, and bottle. A red wine that has suffered OXIDATION or is many decades old may be the same deep tawny colour as a very old white wine.

Red wines are produced in virtually all of the world's wine regions, although the proportion of red wines produced at the cool limit of wine production is low, since it can be difficult to develop sufficient pigmentation of most grapes' skins to produce a proper red wine (although see also TEINTURIERS).

French for red is *rouge*, Italian is *rosso*, Spanish and Portuguese more expressively *tinto*, Russian is *cherny*, and German is *rot*. Spain divides her red wines into those which really are *tinto* and lighter ones called CLARETE.

It has been only since the development of BOTTLES suitable for AGEING wine that red wines have been seen in any sense superior to white (see Ancient GREECE, ROME, medieval ITALY, and FASHION). In the late 20th century a general market preoccupation with white wines in the 1970s had been overtaken by what was called the **red wine boom** by the 1990s, encouraged by a belief in the emerging markets of ASIA that red wine is HEALTHIER (and visually more obviously wine) than white. In Mandarin only the word for red wine (not white) necessarily entails its being based on grapes.

reflection from soils and in some cases from water is considered by some to influence wine quality. Very white soils, such as the ALBARIZA soils of JEREZ, do indeed reflect high proportions of sunshine, and can add to the heating of vines growing on them. This is easy to demonstrate by calculation. More difficult to prove or measure is the theory that sunlight reflected from rivers may benefit nearby vineyards, as in the Mosel Valley. While the eye can behold the silvery sheen of water at low sun angles (specular reflection), it is unlikely that this can have any heating effect on adjacent vineyards.

R.E.S.

Refosco is a group of distinct red varieties cultivated in north east Italy, Slovenia, and Croatia producing very similar wines. The finest variety is known in Friuli as REFOSCO DAL PEDUNCOLO ROSSO but others include Refosco d'Istria (also called TERAN, Terrano, and Refošk).

Refosco dal Peduncolo Rosso, named after its red stem, is a member of the REFOSCO group of red grape varieties that makes usefully vigorous wine in the FRIULI region of north-east Italy. It has a long history in the area, apparently praised by PLINY the Elder and reputedly producing the favourite wine of Livia, the second wife of Augustus Caesar, cited in the *Annals of Friuli* of Francesco di Manzano in 1390. DNA PROFILING at SAN MICHELE ALL'ADIGE recently revealed a parent–offspring relationship with MARZEMINO, another ancient variety of Northern Italy.

This vine is cultivated both in HILLSIDE VINEYARDS and in flatter parts of Friuli and gives a deeply coloured wine with plummy flavours and a hint of almonds, a medium to full body, and a rather elevated ACIDITY which can be difficult to control or moderate, the variety being a notoriously late ripener. Refosco has the advantage of good resistance to autumn rains and rot.

There was a significant return of interest in Friuli's Refosco in the 1980s, and much greater care was taken in its cultivation and vinification in an effort to improve the wine's quality, although total plantings in 2010 were just over 1,000 ha/2,470 acres.

The most promising zone for Refosco is COLLI ORIENTALI and the Koper district in SLOVENIA. Others include GRAVE DEL FRIULI, LISON-PRAMAGGIORE (outside Friuli), Latisana, and Aquileia.

refractometer, an instrument for measuring a refractive index, which is related to the amount by which the angle of a light wave is changed when passing through the boundary between two media. The amount of refraction is a convenient way to measure solute concentration of a solution and is widely used in viticulture and winemaking to follow the ripeness of grapes (by measuring MUST WEIGHT) and changes during vinification. Refractometers may be precision laboratory instruments or pocket versions that can be used in the vineyard. In either case, TEMPERATURE correction or control is important for accuracy. B.G.C.

refrigeration, cooling process that has had a profound effect on how and where wine is made and how it tastes (see TEMPERATURE), enabling the winemaker to have a much greater degree of control than was possible before mechanical refrigeration became the norm for all but the least sophisticated wineries in the second half of the 20th century. More than any other factor, refrigeration has permitted warm and hot regions to produce wine of internationally acceptable quality.

Making wine

The essence of refrigeration is the transfer of heat from the body being refrigerated to some other place. The most obvious winery application of refrigeration is in the TEMPERATURE CONTROL of FERMENTATION—although refrigeration also allows winemakers to delay the processing of freshly picked grapes or must (see MUST CHILLING) until convenient, even in hot areas, where the use of chilled rooms to cool and store grapes prior to pressing has increased. The energy generated by the conversion of sugar to alcohol, carbon dioxide, and water is only partly used by the YEAST in building cells and by-products. The rest appears as heat, which, above a certain temperature, risks killing the yeast and therefore arresting the fermentation process. The amounts of heat generated by fermentation are large. Ten hl/260 gal of grape juice containing 20% sugar will generate about 3.6 million kilocalories, or enough to melt 45 tons of ice.

Not all the heat generated has to be removed by refrigeration, however. Because heat moves naturally by conduction from hotter bodies to cooler ones with which they are in contact, warm fermenting wine loses heat to the walls of the FERMENTATION VESSEL and from the outside of the wall to the atmosphere. Some of the fermentation heat will be removed by radiation from the outside of the fermenting vessel too, provided its temperature is higher than that of the objects in its vicinity. Heat may also be lost by radiation if open-topped fermentation vessels are used, or by volatilization of some of the water and alcohol in the wine.

All of these natural heat removal processes that function independently of refrigeration occur at the surfaces of the fermenting mass. Heat production, on the other hand, occurs throughout the entire volume of the mass. The amount of heat removed from a fermenting mass therefore depends on the surface to volume ratio of the fermentation vessel. A 225-l/59-gal BARRIQUE, for example, will probably lose enough generated heat for the temperature to remain within an acceptable range for fermentation. A typical large tank, on the other hand, which might contain several hundred hectolitres, will certainly need active heat removal to keep the temperature of the fermenting mass below danger point.

The development of mechanical refrigeration in the early 20th century at least made cooling a possibility in areas where insufficient naturally cold water was available. Early efforts to control temperature, used in France as recently as the 1970s, included the simple addition of blocks of ice to the fermenting wine (with concomitant dilution). More mechanical early systems of refrigeration cooled the wine by running cold water through metal tubes suspended in the tank. The development of more efficient PUMPS permitted systems which moved wine from the tank through coils immersed in cold water and then back into the tank.

In modern wineries, however, wines are seldom moved for cooling purposes. STAINLESS STEEL tanks with cooling devices, usually coils, inside the tank and cooling jackets incorporated in the external walls are now standard wine equipment. Temperature-sensing probes in tanks signal a computer system which controls the supply of refrigerant to the coils to a level predetermined for each tank by the winemaker.

Refrigeration has become increasingly important in other winemaking processes, however. Some producers, notably in Australia, store grape juice in refrigerated conditions for several months before fermentation. Others, notably in parts of North America, New Zealand, and SAUTERNES, may prior to fermentation apply heavy refrigeration to emulate the conditions necessary to produce EISWEIN (see freeze CONCENTRATION and CRYOEXTRACTION). Pre-fermentation cold MACERATION occasionally calls for refrigeration too. In warmer wine regions, some degree of refrigeration may be needed during wine maturation, and refrigerated tanks are routinely used for everyday wines to ensure that TARTRATES are not precipitated in bottle (see STABILIZATION).   A.D.W.

Serving wine

Refrigeration plays a part, and all too often a villainous part, in the SERVING of wine. Long before the advent of mechanical refrigeration, and its domestication, wine was deliberately chilled prior to serving (see Ancient GREECE, for example). It was fashionable to chill both red and white wines before serving at least from the 16th century. A wide range of wine coolers was used to achieve this until the 20th century, when mechanical refrigeration was domestically available. The modern successors of these large containers for both ice and bottles are the single-bottle wine coolers known as ice buckets and the gel-filled flexible sleeves kept frozen ready for use.

See also TEMPERATURE.

Regent, particularly successful dark-skinned DISEASE-RESISTANT VARIETY bred at GEILWEILERHOF in Germany and first registered in 1989. This complex hybrid of a SILVANER × MÜLLER-THURGAU cross with CHAMBOURCIN makes wine with good colour, moderate acidity, and it reaches full ripeness easily. It is already grown on a total of more than 2,000 ha/5,000 acres in Germany, particularly Rheinhessen and Pfalz, and is also planted in Switzerland, England, Belgium, and Scandinavia.

Reggiano, a DOC in EMILIA-ROMAGNA that used to be called Lambrusco Reggiano but its name was changed to allow the production of still and sparkling reds of up to 60% ANCELLOTTA. (It is notable that, according to the Italian agricultural census of 2010, total plantings of Ancellotta in Emilia-Romagna were 4,048 ha, almost as much as the 4,635 ha of the most-planted LAMBRUSCO, Salamino, which is presumably a reflection of producers' desire to add colour from the deep-tinted Ancellotta grape to their various Lambrusco grapes.) A wide range of Lambrusco varieties as well as Sangiovese, Cabernet Sauvignon, and Merlot are allowed in DOC Reggiano. Yields may be as high as 280 hl/ha.   W.S.

Região Demarcada, a demarcated region (RD) of PORTUGAL, although the expression is no longer seen on labels. See DOC for more details.

regionality, New World term for the concept, now fully accepted there, that the location of a vineyard plays an important part in shaping the character of the wine produced from it. It is less geographically precise and, importantly, less French, than the term TERROIR (although

as the century wears on, this last term is increasingly used by New World wine producers).

More and more wines in, for example, California and Australia, where the word was coined, are labelled and marketed on a geographical as well as VARIETAL basis, although many producers are wary of the restrictions that would ensue from CONTROLLED APPELLATIONS.

régisseur, French term used particularly of the director or manager of a Bordeaux estate.

Regner, declining, light-skinned 1929 German CROSS made in 1929 that still contributes the odd flabby white to German blends.

Régnié, the most recently created BEAUJOLAIS cru (in 1988), is a tribute to communal spirit, or at least the spirit abroad in the neighbouring communes of Régnié-Durette and Lantignié, whose vignerons lobbied for years to be allowed to join the other nine crus. The total area of vineyards had shrunk to 287 ha/709 acres by 2012, however. This is one of the highest and most westerly of the crus immediately east of Beaujeu and can taste more like a Beaujolais-Villages unless very well done.

Reguengos, subregion of the ALENTEJO in southern Portugal with a large and very successful co-operative winery.

regulated deficit irrigation (RDI), an IRRIGATION scheduling technique which uses mild WATER STRESS at key stages of fruit development to reduce vegetative growth and improve berry ripening and thus improve grape quality.

RDI was first applied on peach and pear orchards in Australia in the 1980s. Research showed that it restricted SHOOT growth without significantly affecting YIELD. It is now common practice in many vineyards around the world, especially in those planted to black grape varieties, due to the greater benefits to grape colour.

The main benefits of this strategically managed water stress are less competition between berry ripening and vegetative growth, better water conservation, and reduced BERRY SIZE. Successful application requires careful monitoring of EVAPOTRANSPIRATION and SOIL WATER content and typically results in slightly lower yields. It is most effectively applied through DRIP IRRIGATION, which allows the application of small amounts of water.

RDI is more stressful to the vine than PARTIAL ROOTZONE DRYING and its use in hot regions can cause problems if its application is followed by a spell of hot weather: vines with limited soil moisture can suffer extremes of water stress, which may, for example, lead to rapid loss of leaves. This situation can be alleviated by carefully monitoring weather forecasts and applying some irrigation.

Water deficit is generally applied between fruit set and a week or so after veraison but is generally avoided in the later stages of berry ripening.   J.E.H. & R.E.S.

Iland, P., et al., 'Water, soil and the vine', in *The Grapevine: From the Science to the Practice of Growing Vines for Wine* (Adelaide, 2011).

Kriedemann, P. E., and Goodwin, I., *Irrigation Insights 4: Regulated Deficit Irrigation and Partial Rootzone Drying* (Canberra, 2003).

McCarthy, M. G., et al., 'Regulated deficit irrigation and partial rootzone drying as irrigation management techniques for grapevines', in *Deficit Irrigation Practices*, FAO Water Reports 22 (Rome, 2002), www.fao.org/docrep/004/y3655e/y3655e11.htm#k.

Reichensteiner, white grape variety whose GEISENHEIM creator Heinrich Birk maintained it was the first EU cross, with French, Italian, and German antecedents. In 1939 he developed this cross of MÜLLER-THURGAU with a cross of the French table grape MADELEINE ANGEVINE and the Italian Early Calabrese. Its antecedents are hardly noble and both wine and vine most closely resemble its undistinguished German parent, but Reichensteiner with its looser bunches is less prone to rot and well-pruned plants stand a good chance of reaching PRÄDIKATSWEIN must weights in good years. Just 70 ha remained in Germany in 2012 but it has also been planted in England and to a limited extent in Switzerland, Japan, New Zealand, and British Columbia.

religion and wine. Wine is a wonderworking substance, and is therefore linked to metaphysics and to ritual. At the heart of the miraculous qualities of wine is the ALCOHOL it contains, and its capacity for quickly changing people's feelings, for better or worse.

Wine itself, however, has a quite specific history and geographical distribution (see ORIGINS OF VINICULTURE). It is associated with the peoples who live round the Mediterranean sea, in Europe, the Near East, and North Africa; and within this huge Circum-Mediterranean super-region the place of wine in the local values has been affected by the major revolution in the area whereby the old order, which was apparently partly monotheistic, partly polytheistic, and which presumably dated back into prehistory, was replaced by Christianity and ISLAM, rooted in the values of Judaic monotheism.

The different parts of the Circum-Mediterranean emerged from prehistory at different times, the western end of the Mediterranean basin far later than EGYPT and the Levant, for example, while northern and eastern Europe, outside the wine-producing area, acquired their first written records even later, and from Christian MISSIONARIES. A careful reading of the books of the Old Testament (see BIBLE) reveals the repeated emphasis on wine as a symbol of prosperity.

At a time when wine was so important to the prosperity of the human population, these people also saw it as a suitable offering to the superhuman authorities. Along with animal sacrifices, and offerings from other crops, LIBATIONS of wine were poured out to the gods by Italians and Greeks, and there were similar practices in the Levant. Although Israel, in the form of its remnant, the Jews, became, by reason of its monotheism, increasingly distinctive within the context of its neighbours, yet its rituals retained a mainstream familiarity. The offerings which were required in the temple in Jerusalem have been recorded, at least in part, in some of the books of the Old Testament, and they included cattle, sheep, and goats, which were ritually killed, together with cereal products, olive oil, and wine.

There was, however, another aspect to wine which probably had no Jewish counterpart, and this was obligatory, or almost obligatory, ritual DRUNKENNESS. In the Greek-speaking areas it was apparently normal to get drunk at the seasonal feasts of the god DIONYSUS, and his true devotees, presumably, felt bound to be drunk more often than that. In the same way, in Ancient ROME at the dark-of-the-winter festival of the Saturnalia, drunkenness was part of the general licence, and the reversal of normal sober (in every sense) behaviour. These examples emphasize the ambiguous nature of wine's effects. It can make you have a wonderful time, and it can make you dangerously irresponsible, as can the gods. (Indeed the gods themselves also get drunk—see, for example, SUMER.) Presumably, the Bacchanalia (see BACCHUS) and the Saturnalia were never fully respectable, but they were legal, because they emphasized the normality, and even value, of mundane daily life.

The period from prehistory to the revolution referred to above runs from c.3000 BC through to the opening centuries AD. The revolution itself began slowly and quietly. According to the prophetic critics of Israel, it is clear that Israel's abandonment of the various gods and spirits, most of them unrespectable (capricious, unpredictable, badly behaved), was a long, slow, bumpy, and incomplete process of conversion to the worship of God Almighty alone. However, by the time that some of them returned from the Exile in MESOPOTAMIA, in the 6th century BC, many were committed to devotional monotheism and to the sense of being the chosen people and the precious vine or vineyard of God's cultivation. This process initially made them peculiar, a minority among their neighbours, but it also led on later to the great crisis of the 1st century AD when the Jews split in two, and the Christian section set out on a world mission of evangelization.

The Christian achievement of banishing the multiplicity of gods from the Mediterranean area was reinforced by the Muslims, from the 7th century AD onward. There was a progressive impact on wine. Jews took wine for granted for secular use and for religious ritual, but rejected drunkenness as irresponsible. The early Christians accepted the Jews' position, apparently without debate, but rejected drunkenness at 'the Lord's table' as particularly disgraceful (see EUCHARIST). Muslims rejected wine absolutely, and they still do (see ISLAM). Their response to its ambiguity has been that it is too dangerous, not worth the cost. Much later, during the modern period, some Christian groups in the northern half of Europe have independently followed Muslims into total abstention, but they were stimulated into reaction not so much by wine as by distilled spirits. It was these various attitudes from northern as well as from southern Europe which were carried by colonists to the NEW WORLD, resulting in the most famous example of PROHIBITION, in the United States in the early 20th century.

See also MONKS AND MONASTERIES. J.D.K.

Fournier, D., and d'Onofrio, S. (eds.), *Le Ferment Divin* (Paris, 1992).

remontage, French word for various systems of PUMPING OVER.

The term may also be used in French for soil replacement after EROSION of vineyards.

remote sensing is the detection and/or measurement of features on the Earth's surface using sensors mounted on satellite or aircraft platforms. Its application in viticulture is almost entirely confined to the inference of VIGOUR and CANOPY condition. This is achieved by sensing the amount of sunlight that is reflected from a vineyard in the visible (blue, green, red) and near infrared parts of the electromagnetic spectrum and calculating ratios between them. Commonly used indices in viticulture are PLANT CELL DENSITY (PCD) and, to a lesser extent, NORMALIZED DIFFERENCE VEGETATION INDEX (NDVI). Research has shown VERAISON to be the optimal time to acquire remotely sensed imagery of vineyards, especially with respect to its use in PRECISION VITICULTURE or ZONAL VITICULTURE. Because patterns of variation in vine vigour and YIELD have been shown to be stable over time, many adopters of precision viticulture have tended to base their targeted management decisions on remotely sensed imagery rather than on maps derived from yield monitors.

A small number of producers, in Bordeaux and the US, for example, have carried out experiments using sensors mounted on unmanned aerial vehicles (otherwise known as drones), but this is expensive and unlikely to become cost-effective if the aim is to obtain imagery showing the same indices (e.g. PCD,

NDVI) as are obtained from airborne or satellite platforms. R.G.V.B.

Hall, A., et al., 'Optical remote sensing applications in viticulture—a review', *Australian Journal of Grape and Wine Research*, 8 (2002), 36–47.

Johnson, L. F., 'Temporal stability of and NDVI-LAI relationship in a Napa Valley vineyard', *Australian Journal of Grape and Wine Research*, 9 (2003), 96–101.

Lamb, D. W., Weedon, M. M., and Bramley, R. G. V., 'Using remote sensing to map grape phenolics and colour in a cabernet sauvignon vineyard—the impact of image resolution and vine phenology', *Australian Journal of Grape and Wine Research*, 10 (2004), 46–54.

remuage is French for the RIDDLING process. A person or machine that performs *remuage* is a **remueur**.

rendement, French for YIELD, usually expressed in hl/ha.

rendzina, a dark, interzonal type of soil found in grassy or formerly grassy areas of moderate rainfall, on limestones, especially in chalklands. It is characterized by a brown to black, friable surface and a light grey or yellow, soft underlying horizon. Such soils are associated with TERRA ROSSA soils of Coonawarra in SOUTH AUSTRALIA. See GEOLOGY.

research into grape-growing and wine production is officially and principally in the domain of academe, although some individual viticulturists and winemakers are more prone to experimentation and more subject to the rigour of SCIENCE than others. For a list of important wine research institutions, see ACADEME.

Reserva, term used in both Spain and Portugal to distinguish wines from a supposedly good vintage. In Portugal, a Reserva is a wine from a good vintage with an alcohol level at least half a per cent above the regional minimum. In Spain, a red wine labelled Reserva will have had at least three years' AGEING in cask and bottle, of which a year must be in oak cask (*barricas* are stipulated for Rioja). The wine may not be released until the fourth year after the harvest. Spanish white and rosé wines labelled Reserva must spend a total of at least two years in cask and bottle to qualify, with at least six months of this period in OAK.

See also GRAN RESERVA. R.J.M.

Reserve is a term liberally used by wine producers for various bottlings. It should be quite literally reserved itself, for superior wines, but, unlike RESERVA and RISERVA, the English term Reserve has few controls on its use. Some wineries release several bottlings, all of which may incorporate the word in their names (Proprietor's Reserve, Estate Reserve, Reserve Selection, Private Reserve, Vintner's Reserve, and the like). The French term is **Réserve** and there are moves to control the use of terms such as Cuvée de Réserve. In CHAMPAGNE, reserve wines are those held over from a given year for future blending, typically into the NON-VINTAGE cuvée.

residual sugar, occasionally **RS**, the total quantity of SUGARS remaining unfermented in the finished wine. This may include both fermentable sugars, mainly GLUCOSE and FRUCTOSE, which have for some reason remained unconverted to alcohol during FERMENTATION, and small amounts of those few sugars which are not readily fermented by typical wine YEAST. Some, but by no means all, residual sugar is tasted as SWEETNESS. REDUCING SUGARS, a term used by both the EU and the OIV, refers to all the sugars measured in a finished wine, including residual sugar and any sugars added post fermentation, for example, in the form of SÜSSRESERVE.

Residual sugar in wine is usually measured in grams of total sugars per litre of wine and can vary between about 1 g/l (0.1%) and 150 g/l (15%) or more. Wines with a residual sugar content of less than 2 g/l, such as the great majority of red wines and many white wines that do not taste at all sweet, are generally described as 'dry' (but see SWEETNESS for some more specific definitions). It is rare to find a wine with much less than 1 g/l residual sugar because some sugars are almost invariably impervious to the action of the yeasts. On the other hand, some wines with a residual sugar level even as high as 25 g/l may taste dry because the sweetness is offset by high ACIDITY. Some ordinary wines (usually white) that are naturally high in acids may have sugars (usually the particularly sweet fructose), sweet GRAPE JUICE, or sweet RECTIFIED GRAPE MUST added deliberately to increase their palatability or commercial appeal (see SWEET RESERVE).

Exceptionally sweet wines may be produced either in extraordinarily ripe years or by unusual winemaking techniques such as those involved in freeze CONCENTRATION, BOTRYTIZED, or DRIED-GRAPE WINES. The sweetest form of the unique Hungarian sweet wine TOKAJI, for example, must have a minimum residual sugar of 250 g/l—the 1947 vintage of Tokay Essencia managed 488 g/l.

Sugar levels in grapes are measured as MUST WEIGHT by various different scales, of which BAUMÉ, BRIX, and OECHSLE are the most common.

One German wine harvested at Nussdorf in the Pfalz in 1971 was picked at 326 °Oechsle, or about 870 g/l sugar, and had reached only 4.5% alcohol in a particularly slow fermentation 20 years later, producing a wine with about 480 g/l residual sugar.

In theory, 100 g of sugar should yield 51.1 g of alcohol, but numerous practical experiments show that only 47 to 48 g of alcohol are obtained. Between 16 and 17 g/l of sugar are required to produce 1% of alcohol in white wines (and about 18 g/l in reds).

There are many reasons why fermentable sugars may remain unfermented: yeasts vary enormously in their potency, especially their tolerance of higher sugar and higher alcohol concentrations; grape musts vary in their micronutrient and growth factor content; low TEMPERATURES and chemical additions can also arrest fermentation; and, probably the most influential factor, the expertise of the winemaker.

Residual sugar presents no great danger in a wine that is yet to be processed in bulk, but in a bottled wine the presence of such sugars may cause FERMENTATION IN BOTTLE. Small amounts of sugar are furthermore readily used by yeast or BACTERIA to produce unwanted ACETIC ACID, off-flavours, and, sometimes, CARBON DIOXIDE gas. The winemaker therefore must ensure either that a wine is effectively free of fermentable sugars or, in the case of most sweet and medium-dry wines, that the wine undergoes full STABILIZATION against the risk of further microbiological activity. This can be achieved by FILTRATION.   A.D.W.

residues. Residues of AGROCHEMICALS, the commercial preparations used in vineyards for the control of pests, diseases, or weeds, are that portion which is found on the grapes or in wine. Residues in viticulture and wine are typically different from those in other forms of agriculture and food processing. The time between application and harvest, known as the 'withholding period', commonly results in degradation of the agrochemical. Most of any remaining residue is likely to be eliminated with the skins after PRESSING, and more is removed or degraded during juice CLARIFICATION, FERMENTATION, and subsequent FILTRATION.

PESTICIDES may leave deposits or by-products that persist in plant or animal tissues or in soil, water, or air. Some pesticides are rapidly inactivated after application; others (or their by-products) may persist for years. Such residual contamination may affect human or livestock health, subsequent crop growth, and pollute the environment. Excessive or illegal pesticide residues in wine may lead to rejection on domestic and/or international markets, perhaps as a result of the use of inappropriate pesticides, incorrect application methods, or application too close to harvest. Residue effects on non-target organisms should also be considered. Useful insects such as bees or natural parasites and predators of insect pests may be affected by pesticide residues.

FUNGICIDE residues may inhibit fermentation by yeast, as discussed by Caboni and Cabras, but extensive trials have shown that the proper use of fungicides has no adverse effect on the taste or smell of wines, although residues of elemental SULFUR used to prevent fungal disease in the vineyard can be transformed, in REDUCING conditions, into foul-smelling HYDROGEN SULFIDE.

Maximum residue limits (MRLs) are established by governments for particular agrochemicals or their metabolites (breakdown products) in particular foodstuffs. MRLs are typically set at levels which are not likely to be exceeded if the chemicals are used in accordance with good agricultural practice and a dietary-exposure evaluation shows no undue hazard to human health. Trade in wine internationally can be hindered when markets differ in their MRLs. See also AGROCHEMICALS.

R.E.S., P.R.D., & M.E.

Caboni, P., and Cabras, P., 'Pesticides' influence on wine fermentation', *Advances in Food and Nutrition Research*, 59 (2010), 43–62.

resinated wines. Of the earthenware vessels in which the ancient Greeks and Romans kept their wines (see AMPHORAE) only the very best were airtight. Normally they were porous, and it is clear from the Roman writers on agriculture that the insides of jars were therefore coated with resin. It was therefore probably as a purely practical measure that resin was initially used. But soon people must have discovered that the wine would keep even better if they added resin to the wine itself. COLUMELLA deals at length with the different kinds of resin that can be employed in this way (*De re rustica* 13. 20–14), but he emphasizes that the best wines should not have resin put into them. Yet many people came to like the taste of resin and used it not only as a preservative but also as a flavouring agent. PLINY recommends that resin should be added to the fermenting must (*Natural History* 14. 124) and he discusses which kinds of resin are best: resin from mountainous regions has a more pleasant smell than resin from low-lying areas (16. 60).

The Romans abandoned amphorae in favour of wooden casks in the 3rd century AD because BARRELS were lighter and easier to handle. Wooden casks do not need an inside coating of resin, and this saved the winemaker time and money. Thus the Romans ceased to make resinated wines. Winemakers in Transalpine Gaul, most of whom did not have pine trees nearby, and those of Cisalpine Gaul, Illyria, and the alpine region, where the climate is cooler and wood does not crack so easily, had started using wooden casks in the 1st century AD. Unlike the west, however, Byzantium did not lose its taste for resin when it was no longer needed as a preservative. The pine forests of the eastern part of central Greece and of Euboea still provided the resin to enhance the flavour of some Greek wines after the 7th century.

This was very much not to the taste of one western visitor to Constantinople. In 968 Liudprand, bishop of Cremona, was sent there to arrange a marriage between the daughter of the late Emperor Romanos and the son of his own patron, Otto I, the Holy Roman Emperor. The mission was not a success. The Emperor Nicephorus treated Liudprand rudely and kept him a virtual prisoner. Liudprand's *De legatione Constantinopolitana* ('The mission to Constantinople') was his revenge. He has not a good word to say for the Byzantines in general and Nicephorus in particular. We are dealing with a masterpiece of invective, and since Liudprand's purpose is satirical, we should not believe his every word. But his observations on the food and wine he had are interesting. Horrified, he relates how he was given goat stuffed with onions, garlic, and leeks, swimming in fish sauce. Worst of all, and mentioned in his very first chapter, is the wine: undrinkable because it is mixed with resin, pitch, and gypsum. Like the fish sauce, not in the least remarkable to an Ancient Roman, but not a thing to serve a modern Lombard. Liudprand may have had perfectly decent, unresinated, wine at times during his enforced stay, but it would have spoilt his story to tell us about that.

For not all Greek wine was resinated in the Middle Ages. The strong, sweet wines that reached the markets of western Europe were not, but pilgrims travelling to the Holy Land say that some local wines were. The account of Pietro Casola, who sailed to Jerusalem in 1494, stopping off frequently on the way, is particularly valuable because he takes pains to describe the customs, the food, and the wines of every region. He often speaks of the excellent sweet wines in Greece, but in Modone, on the south-western tip of the Peloponnese (near Monemvasia which gave its name to MALVASIA), he is given a wine that has had resin added to it during fermentation in order, he explains, to preserve it. He objects to its strong unpleasant odour, but he goes on to describe the fine malmsey, muscatel, and rumney of Modone. Of Cyprus he says that he loves everything about it except the wine, which has resin in it. He must have been unlucky not to have tasted the famous sweet wines that Cyprus exported, but an earlier account by an anonymous French cleric, *Le Voyage de la Saincte Cyte de Hierusalem* of 1480, confirms what he observes about Cyprus and Modone.

See RETSINA for details of modern resinated wine. H.M.W.

Newett, M. M., *Canon Casola's Pilgrimage to Jerusalem in the Year 1494* (Manchester, 1907).
The Works of Liudprand of Cremona, trans. by F. A. Wright (London, 1930).

resins used in winemaking are natural or synthetic materials usually composed of long chains of simpler molecules that are capable of POLYMERIZING. Gum acacia is a natural resin used to stabilize the PIGMENTS in red wine.

Another natural resin is Aleppo pine resin, which is used in the preparation of RETSINA.

Synthetic resins, manufactured by polymerization processes, have several uses in winemaking. One of the commonest is epoxy resin, which can be used in the form of a two-part paint for coating the inside of CONCRETE vats, producing an inert and easily cleaned surface. Epoxy-resin compounds are also used for surfacing floors in wineries and bottling halls, being much more resistant than concrete to the acids in wine.

Silicone resins are used in the manufacture of BUNGS for wooden BARRELS; they have the flexibility of rubber but are taint-free and non-perishable.

ION EXCHANGE resins can be used in some countries for TARTRATE stabilization, for example. They are prepared in the form of small beads which are packed into a vertical cylindrical tank known as a column, through which the wine is passed. The particular property of these resins is their ability to exchange the ions which are loosely held on their surface with ions in the liquid phase. D.B.

Bird, D., *Understanding Wine Technology* (3rd edn, Newark, 2010).

respiration, biochemical process in animals and plants, including vines, which provides the chemical energy required for other reactions and for growth. Respiration may be considered the opposite of PHOTOSYNTHESIS in that OXYGEN is consumed and CARBON DIOXIDE and energy released, according to the following formula:

$$H_{12}O_6 \text{ sugar} + 6O_2 \rightarrow 6CO_2 + 6H_2O + \text{energy}$$

In addition to SUGARS, other compounds such as STARCH, fats, AMINO ACIDS, organic ACIDS, and other substances may be broken down to release energy.

In plants, temperature has a major effect on respiration rate. The rate of respiration approximately doubles for each 10 °C/18 °F increase in temperature. Of particular interest to wine drinkers is the respiration of MALIC ACID, which takes place in the grape during RIPENING. This reaction depends on temperature, an important reason why acidity levels are higher in wines from cooler climates.

(Respiration is also the name given to the metabolism of foodstuffs in humans; following ingestion of wine, the primary energy source, alcohol, is metabolized in the liver.) R.E.S.

resveratrol, PHENOLIC compound produced by grapevines (and other plants such as peanut and eucalyptus trees), particularly in response to microbial attack (see PHYTOALEXINS) or artificial agents such as ULTRAVIOLET RADIATION. It is one of a number of compounds (including CATECHIN and QUERCETIN) found in wine thought

to contribute to HEALTH aspects of its moderate consumption. Resveratrol is also found in other grape products such as juice and raisins. Resveratrol belongs to a class of compounds called stilbenes. In grapevines this also includes its derivatives, piceid, pterostilbene, and the viniferins. Woody parts of the vine normally contain large amounts of stilbenes, principally viniferins, which are thought to protect against wood decay. In the vineyard, leaves and berry skins produce resveratrol only in response to some action, such as fungal attack, where its subsequent accumulation may slow or stop the infection. There are numerous factors in the growing of grapes and vinification that can affect resveratrol concentration in the finished wine. Species, variety, clone, and rootstock influence potential stilbene production. For example, wines made from MUSCADINIA grapes or from PINOT NOIR tend to have high levels of resveratrol, whereas CABERNET SAUVIGNON has lower levels. Wines produced in cooler regions or areas with greater disease pressure such as Burgundy and New York often have more resveratrol, while wines from hot, dry climates such as Australia and California frequently have lower resveratrol concentrations.

Winemaking procedures have a great effect on resveratrol concentration in the final product. Red wines have a much higher resveratrol content, usually about ten times, than that found in whites. This is not necessarily because white grapes manufacture less resveratrol, but because stilbenes are manufactured in the grape skins and MACERATION, integral to the production of a red wine, encourages the extraction of these compounds. Much of the interest in resveratrol in the 1990s and early 2000s came from its suspected connection to wine's health benefits. It was known to play a part in herbal remedies for many years, but it was not until 1992 that New York researchers Siemann and Creasy made the link between it, wine, and its possible contribution to the FRENCH PARADOX. Resveratrol has been reported to reduce serum platelet aggregation, cholesterol levels, liver lipids, and act as a cancer chemopreventative agent. As part of the phenolic milieu in wine, its moderate consumption can contribute to good health. G.L.C.

Goldberg, D. M., et al., 'A global survey of *trans*-resveratrol concentrations in commercial wines', *American Journal of Enology and Viticulture*, 46 (1995), 159–65.
Siemann, E. H., and Creasy, L. L., 'Concentration of the phytoalexin resveratrol in wine', *American Journal of Enology and Viticulture*, 43 (1992), 49–52.

retsina, modern form of RESINATED WINE that is extremely common in GREECE, and a potent catalyst of taverna nostalgia outside it. Modern retsina is made like any other white (or rosé) wine, except that small pieces of resin from the *Pinus helepensis* pine are added to the must and left with the wine until the first RACKING separates the finished wine from all solids. Major producing areas are Attica, Euboea, and Boeotia, all in the southern part of central Greece close to Athens, but retsina is also made for local consumption all over the country. SAVATIANO is usually the principal grape, often enlivened with some RODITIS or occasionally ASSYRTIKO, but a wide range of local grape varieties are also used, and an interesting ATHIRI retsina is made on the island of Rhodes.

Poor-quality retsina was possibly the final nail in the coffin of Greek wine's image in the 1970s and thereafter. Low quality was the result of adding bad-quality resin to conceal bad-quality, often heavily oxidized, wine. Nevertheless, and perhaps surprisingly to many, a number of producers such as Kehris and Gaia decided to create top-quality retsinas, by using top-quality pine resin to elegantly flavour exceptional wine made from Assyrtiko or high-elevation Roditis. The final results prove that great retsina is no oxymoron.

Retsina is protected by the EU as a traditional APPELLATION. With one South Australian exception, it is rarely made outside Greece and southern Cyprus, where local palates are accustomed to its distinctively pungent flavour, and visitors expect it, even if in terms of shock to the palate, retsina can resemble a FINO sherry.   K.L.

Reuilly, small but expanding French appellation so far inside the bend of the Loire that it is often described as coming from central France. Its most useful manifestation is as a less expensive and sometimes purer version of the SANCERRE appellation to the east made from Sauvignon Blanc grapes in one of the riper vintages. Considerable amounts of red and rosé wine are also made, from Pinot Noir and Pinot Gris (the local Gamay is sold as IGP). Pale pink Reuilly has its devotees. Unlike nearby QUINCY, Reuilly is not just a sleepy viticultural centre, and the best wines yielded by its 215 ha/531 acres of vineyards scattered on the LIMESTONE base around the village of Reuilly can be impressive. This Loire AOC (which consisted of just 30 ha in the early 1990s) is not to be confused with that of RULLY in the Côte Chalonnaise.

See also LOIRE, including map.

Réunion. This French island in the Indian ocean, once mainly planted with ISABELLA, now produces small quantities of respectable red and white from French varieties at the CO-OPERATIVE Le Chai de Cilaos.

reverse osmosis is an increasingly popular though rather controversial winemaking intervention or MANIPULATION based on the principle of cross-flow or tangential membrane

filtration. In standard FILTRATION procedures, the liquid flows perpendicularly to the filter surface, making clogging a major problem. In cross-flow filtration, the liquid flows parallel to the filter membrane so that it helps scour the surface and prevent clogging. The liquid flows at pressure, and it is this pressure that causes water and some salts to pass through the membrane filter. Cross-flow filtration is highly promising for many winemaking applications but it is quite slow and expensive compared with traditional filtration techniques.

It is currently used chiefly for two distinct purposes: ALCOHOL REDUCTION and must CONCENTRATION. In the former, a possible alternative to HUMIDIFICATION, a portion of a high alcohol wine is passed through a reverse osmosis installation, which removes a colourless permeate that consists almost entirely of water and alcohol, and returns the retentate (the rest of the wine) to the tank. The alcohol may then be removed from the permeate by distillation and the water returned to the wine, to produce a wine of reduced alcohol content. This low alcohol wine can then be used as a blending component to produce a final wine of the desired alcohol level. An advantage of this technique is that only a portion of the wine need be subjected to this potentially intrusive manipulation, typically less than one-quarter.

In the case of must concentration, reverse osmosis is used to remove water from the unfermented grape must, achieving a similar result to vacuum evaporation. It has been widely adopted in Bordeaux, where many producers regard it as an insurance policy against the negative effects of a rainy harvest. Controversially, some have seen it as a way of producing more concentrated, denser wines of the sort that appeal to influential critics and the modern market place. In some countries, principally Australia, the main use of reverse osmosis is on finished wines, where the selective removal of water and alcohol concentrates all other components.

Another important use for reverse osmosis is the reduction of excessive levels of VOLATILE ACIDITY. Stuck fermentations are sometimes coupled with high levels of ACETIC ACID and some commentators have suggested that it is the volatile acidity that is arresting the fermentation.

More recently this technique has been proposed as a way of removing negative flavour compounds that result from BRETTANOMYCES spoilage in red wines.   J.A.G. & J.E.H.

Smith, C., 'The new filtrations', in *Postmodern Winemaking* (Berkeley, 2013), 202–18.

Wollan, D., 'Membrane and other techniques for the management of wine composition', in A. G. Reynolds (ed.), *Managing Wine Quality 2: Oenology and Wine Quality* (Cambridge, 2010), 133–63.

reviews, wine. See TASTING NOTES.

Rèze, very rare Swiss VALAIS white grape responsible for the sherry-like *vin des glaciers*. In 2005, DNA PROFILING at SAN MICHELE ALL'ADIGE revealed that Rèze has parent–offspring relationships with NOSIOLA and Groppello di Revò in Trentino and Cascarolo in Piemonte. Unexpectedly, DNA profiling in 2007 proved its presence in the Alpine Maurienne Valley and JURA. Coupled with additional genetic relationships, this makes Rèze one of the main founder varieties of the Alps. In Switzerland, the area of cultivation fell from 400 ha at the beginning of the 20th century to less than 3 ha at the beginning of the 21st century because Rèze and other Valais grapes were superseded by CHASSELAS to produce FENDANT.   J.V.

Vouillamoz, J., & Moriondo, G., *Origine des cépages valaisans et valdôtains* (Pontarlier, 2011).

Zufferey-Périsset, A.-D. (ed.), *Histoire de la vigne et du vin en Valais: des origines à nos jours* (Sierre, 2009).

Rhein, German name for the river RHINE.

Rheingau, for generations the most economically successful wine region in GERMANY and still one of its most famous abroad. The Church and nobility provided the discipline and organization necessary for a solid business in wine, which survived the unrest and secularization in the early 19th century (see GERMAN HISTORY). The region had 3,166 ha/7,820 acres of vines in 2013, over 90% of which lie on the right bank of the RHINE, between Wiesbaden and the MITTELRHEIN boundary at Lorchhausen (see map under GERMANY). The remainder of the Rheingau vineyards are near Hochheim (the origin of the word HOCK) on the banks of the Main, shortly before its confluence with the Rhine at Mainz.

The region has a favoured MESOCLIMATE. With its southern ASPECT, it is marginally warmer than much of Rheinhessen to the south, and its annual RAINFALL of a little over 600 m/23 in means that there is an adequate supply of water for the RIESLING vine to ripen its grapes long into the autumn. Critical to the differences among the Rheingau's diverse cast of Rieslings are soil type, proximity to the Rhine, and ELEVATION, with higher, cooler, breezier sites often performing better in recent warmer growing seasons than some of the traditionally most prestigious riverside vineyards, where potential alcohols and the risk of GREY ROT can be excessive.

At GEISENHEIM, the Rheingau has one of the world's leading viticultural institutes, but it has not been invaded by newer GERMAN CROSSES to the same extent as other German regions such as RHEINHESSEN and the Pfalz. Rather, the Rheingau has stuck by the grapes that brought it fame, Riesling representing 79% of surface area in 2011 and Pinot Noir 12% (scattered across the region but quite concentrated in Assmannshausen near the region's northern edge).

No German wines have ever achieved higher international standing (or prices) than did the Rieslings of the Rheingau in the late 19th century, and even in the mid 20th century prices were much higher than those of many of Bordeaux's CLASSED GROWTHS. The record of the late 20th century has been mixed. Under the stylistic inspiration of the late Bernard Breuer of Rüdesheim and the late proprietor of Schloss Vollrads, Graf Matuschka-Greiffenclau, this region led Germany in producing ever drier Rieslings, purporting to be closer to a late-19th-century model and inherently more adaptable to late-20th-century cuisine. The Rheingau CHARTA organization and the local VDP association were early activists in the promotion of low YIELDS, of a consistently TROCKEN (dry) style of Riesling, and of the CLASSIFICATION of top vineyards as ERSTES GEWÄCHS.

Proximity to the metropolitan markets of Mainz, Wiesbaden, and Frankfurt has further helped Rheingau wines re-establish high reputations and prices. But all of this has not been enough to secure the continued fortunes of many of the large, formerly noble, estates, several of which have in recent years been sold, closed, or continue to struggle economically. The Rheingau has also had stiff competition within Germany for both white and red wines from the increasingly fashionable and predominantly dry wines of the dynamic, warmer BADEN and PFALZ regions as well as from impressive Rieslings grown in formerly unfashionable sectors of RHEINHESSEN. And for those craving delicacy in Riesling or wines with a dynamic synergy of fruit acidity and residual sweetness, heightened awareness of the NAHE has brought the Rheingau further domestic competition. The Rheingau's best-known estates (and the state-owned KLOSTER EBERBACH) typically have holdings in multiple, far-flung villages, and many of today's family wineries follow a similar pattern, if on a smaller scale. When windows of opportunity become compressed, as has been the case with so many recent vintages, and as mustering crews of pickers becomes increasingly difficult despite the EU's open borders for LABOUR, having one's vineyards so scattered presents a huge challenge. It is not surprising that the new elite to have emerged among Rheingau growers since the 1990s consists largely of estates whose vineyards are in just one or two adjacent villages. The Rheingau was traditionally Germany's leader in selective and late-picking of botrytis-affected Riesling (see SCHLOSS JOHANNISBERG)—and continues to treasure its AUSLESEN, BEERENAUSLESEN, and TROCKENBEERENAUSLESEN even though dry wine today represents the overwhelming majority of wine produced. Almost 60% of Rheingau

wine today is bottled trocken, and a further 27% HALBTROCKEN. In fact, picking out BOTRY-TIZED Riesling berries has become essential to assuring healthy fruit and a suitable potential alcohol level in the dry Riesling made from the remaining grapes. The principle of picking selected bunches of grapes, AUSLESEN in German, was understood in the 18th century, but that of the widespread picking of grapes affected by NOBLE ROT dates, in the Rheingau, from about 1820.

In the Rheingau, seven CO-OPERATIVE cellars receive grapes from slightly less than 10% of the harvest. Their role is thus a relatively minor one compared with that of the private and state-owned estates. Many properties date from the 18th century and a few can trace their winemaking history to a much earlier period. Part-time growers own nearly one third of Rheingau vineyard area, and an encouraging late-20th-century trend has been the emergence of some top quality wines from some of them.

At Lorchausen and Lorch—the westernmost limit of the Rheingau, Riesling traditionally struggles to ripen, and Silvaner is far from uncommon. A couple of intrepid producers based outside these villages demonstrate the potential of such vineyards as Lorch's Kapellenberg, Krone, and Schlossberg. But the average vine holder in this sector does not vinify or bottle, and struggles to find a market. Immediately upstream at Assmannshausen, Pinot Noir dominates, above all in the south-facing Höllenberg. Rüdesheim is the westernmost limit of the Rhine's east–west orientation, exposing on the so-called Rüdesheimer Berg the first of the Rheingau's famous progression of south-facing slopes. The steep, stony SLATE, and QUARTZITE-dominated Berg Schlossberg, Berg Roseneck, and Berg Rottland sites, all directly overlooking the Rhine, can generate Rieslings of peachy richness, spiciness, and depth even in difficult vintages. The progression of small villages and top-class vineyards continues with Geisenheim (Kläuserweg, Rothenberg), Johannisberg (Goldatzel, Hölle, Klaus, Schloss Johannisberg), Winkel (Jesuitengarten, Schloss Vollrads), and Oestrich (Doosberg, Lenchen). All are capable of producing Riesling wines of a high order, but many would argue that they are surpassed by the best Rieslings from Hattenheim (Hassel, Pfaffenberg, Nussbrunnen, Schützenhaus, Wisselbrunnen), and Erbach (Marcobrunn, Siegelsberg, Schlossberg, Steinmorgen). Soils of LOESS, SAND, and MARL alternate in these central Rheingau villages, and sites further from the river are generally later-ripening and more ventilated due to their elevation. The wines of Hallgarten (Hendelberg, Jungfer, Steinberg, Schönhell), Kiedrich (Gräfenberg, Klosterberg, Wasseros, and Turmberg), and Rauenthal (Baiken, Gehrn, Nonnenberg, Rothenberg, Wülfen),

which lie on higher, stony, phyllite ground some distance from the Rhine, can yield long-lived, extraordinarily fine wines, featuring floral and mineral interaction. At lower elevations near the eastern edge of the Rheingau, the towns of Eltville (Langenstück, Sonnenberg) and Walluf (Walkenberg), while perhaps never quite rivalling the best Rieslings of the region, can produce wines that at their best are memorably complex and long-lived. On the other side of metropolitan Wiesbaden (whose own Neroberg is a serious source of Riesling) Hochheim boasts gentle slopes with CALCAREOUS underpinnings, stretching down to the River Main, often corpulent but minerally complex Rieslings quite distinct from those grown elsewhere in the Rheingau.   D.S.

Rheinhessen, huge, varied German wine region (see map under GERMANY) south and south west of Mainz with 26,582 ha/65,658–acres of vineyard in 2013. For some time it was best known as a source of inexpensive blending wine but all that has changed.

The part of the region traditionally most associated with quality is often referred to as the Rheinterrasse, where a third of the region's RIESLING vines grows. Its most famous vineyards are those in the so-called Roter Hang composed of *Rotliegenden* (Permian red soil) at Nierstein (with notable vineyards Hipping, Oelberg, Orbel, and Pettental) and neighbouring Nackenheim (Rothenberg). Aromas of peach, citrus, and a smoked meat pungency characterize wines grown on the red soils of the Rheinterrasse. A string of communes immediately south of Nierstein—Oppenheim, Dienheim, and Ludwigshöhe—also boast excellent eastern exposure on the edge of the Rhine. Most of the Rheinhessen is protected from winds and excessive rain by the hills on its western border, which rise to over 600 m (nearly 2,000 ft). But the temperature in the vineyards nearest the river RHINE is warmer throughout the year than that of the rolling country away from the river, and in severe winters they avoid the worst effects of FROST. LOESS, SAND, and CALCAREOUS soils in most of these villages can also yield Riesling such as in the underrated Brückchen and Paterberg on the south side of Nierstein, while Silvaner—a traditional Rheinhessen stalwart now reduced to 9% of surface area—is resurgent qualitatively in the hands of ambitious estate-bottlers.

But it is the south west, the so-called Wonnegau, whose wine villages feature predominantly calcareous vineyards, that have since the 1990s become the focus of international attention, rewarded with high prices for strikingly distinctive Rieslings as well as promising Pinot Noir and a revival of Silvaner. Dittelsheim (Geiersberg), Mölsheim (Frauenberg, Am Schwarzen Herrgott), and Hohen-Sülzen

(Kirchenstück), but most especially Flörsheim-Dalsheim (Bürgel, Hubacker), and Westhofen (Aulerde, Brünnenhäuschen, Kirchspiel, Moorstein) are now giants in the pantheon of German wine thanks to the efforts of a handful of ambitious vintners farming sites whose potential had been largely overlooked from the Middle Ages.

The north of Rheinhessen has its best-known vineyards at Ingelheim (traditionally associated with SPÄTBURGUNDER, or PINOT NOIR), at Bingen in the Scharlachberg site, and in the region's highest sector immediately south east of Bad Kreuznach, most notably the porphyric Heerkretz and Höllberg of Siefersheim.

Some INTERNATIONAL VARIETIES are grown in the region but much of Rheinhessen still produces uninspiring wines from GERMAN CROSSES, notably Müller-Thurgau (still nearly 17% of regional vine surface), Kerner (4%), and (red) Dornfelder (13%), wines that are largely traded in bulk for bottling by merchants at prices so low that smallholders and the CO-OPERATIVES struggle with a vicious cycle of high yields and low prices. Many quality-conscious growers still struggle to attract attention for their estate bottlings.

But the tide has turned in terms of this region's overall reputation, and the notion that it merely divides into Roter Hang and hinterlands has been definitively demolished. A significant number of Germany's pioneers in ORGANIC and BIODYNAMIC VITICULTURE have come from the ranks of Rheinhessen growers, further helping to attract attention to the region.   D.S.

Pigott, S., et al., *Wein Spricht Deutsch: Weine, Winzer, Weinlandschaften* (Frankfurt, 2007).

Reinhardt, S., *The Finest Wines of Germany* (London, 2012).

Rheinpfalz, German wine region. See PFALZ.

Rhein Riesling, or **Rheinriesling**, common synonym in German-speaking countries for the great white RIESLING grape variety of Germany.

Rheinterrasse, admired wine district in Germany. For more details, see RHEINHESSEN.

Rhenish, description of wines in common use in the Middle Ages which usually encompassed most of the wines then produced in what is GERMANY today and also those of ALSACE.

Rhine, English name for the river known in German as the **Rhein** and French as the **Rhin** (where it lends its name to the two ALSACE *départements* Haut-Rhin and Bas-Rhin). See also SWITZERLAND and LIECHTENSTEIN. 'Rhine' is frequently used as the name for German wines not from the MOSEL, and is used colloquially by Australians as an abbreviation for Rhine Riesling, their synonym for the RIESLING grape variety. The word Rhine has been incorporated into

a host of names associated in the English-speaking world with white, usually medium dry, but not necessarily at all Germanic, wines.

Rhine Riesling, synonym for the great white RIESLING grape variety of Germany, once common in Australia.

rhizopus, vine disease and one of a group of fungi commonly infecting grapes with rot. See BUNCH ROTS.

Rhoditis. See RODITIS.

Rhône, one of the most important wine RIVERS, linking a range of vineyards as dissimilar as those of CHÂTEAUNEUF-DU-PAPE in southern France, sparkling SEYSSEL, and Fendant du Valais in SWITZERLAND.

In wine circles, however, the term Rhône usually means the fashionable wines made in the Rhône Valley in south east France which themselves vary so much, north and south of an almost vine-free 50-km/30-mile stretch between approximately Valence and Montélimar, that they are divided into two very distinct zones (although the regional appellation Côtes du Rhône encompasses the less ambitious wines of the north as well as a large area of the south). The Rhône regularly produces more APPELLATION CONTRÔLÉE wine than any region other than Bordeaux, about 80% of the 2.5 million hl/66 million gal produced in 2013 being red and usually high in alcohol relative to other French wines.

The greater Rhône valley is divided into four wine districts, of which the **southern Rhône** (*Rhône méridionale* in French) is by far the most important in terms of quantity. The overwhelming majority of the approximately 2 million hl/53 million gal of wine that qualifies as **Côtes du Rhône** or **Côtes du Rhône-Villages** comes from the southern part of the Rhône valley.

The most important Rhône district in terms of the prestige of its wines is the **northern Rhône** (*Rhône septentrionale* in French), which includes the appellations of Hermitage and Côte Rôtie, representing serious rivals to the great names of Bordeaux and Burgundy in the quality and, especially, longevity of their best wines. The northern Rhône is quite different from the southern Rhône in terms of climate, soils, topography, and even vine varieties.

A third small but extremely ancient district about 64 km/40 miles east of Valence up the Drôme tributary comprises the Diois appellations, named after the town of Die, of CHÂTILLON-EN-DIOIS, CLAIRETTE DE DIE, CRÉMANT de Die, and Coteaux de DIE.

And finally there are the outlying appellations that are on the eastern borders of the southern Rhône and the northern borders of

PROVENCE. See GRIGNAN-LES-ADHÉMAR, LUBERON, PIERREVERT, VENTOUX, and Côtes du VIVARAIS.

It should be noted that COSTIÈRES DE NÎMES, for long considered part of the LANGUEDOC region, is effectively a western extension of the southern Rhône and now administratively considered part of the Rhône.

History

Finds of AMPHORAE show that the inhabitants of the Rhône valley drank wine from Baetica, the eastern province of Roman-occupied SPAIN, in the 1st century BC. In the 1st century AD, the Romanized élite of the Rhône valley drank FALERNIAN. From the 1st century BC onwards, wine was carried up the Rhône: Chalon-sur-Saône was a river port for the Gauls (see Côte CHALONNAISE). In his *Geography*, completed in AD 7, Strabo emphasized the importance of good RIVER connections for trade in Gaul. From the Mediterranean one can get to the Atlantic ocean and the Channel by river (*Geography* 4. 1. 2).

Strabo asserted categorically that viticulture was impossible beyond the Cévennes, which was north of the territory of the evergreen oak, *Quercus ilex*, and hence too cold for the vine, which he assumed needed a MEDITERRANEAN CLIMATE. He was proved wrong by the GAULS, who even in his day had probably discovered that the Côte Rôtie and the hill of Hermitage were superb sites for vineyards. They were certainly making wine by AD 71, when PLINY said that in Vienne the Allobroges were producing an excellent wine, still unknown in VIRGIL's day (*Natural History* 14. 18). There were three CRUS, Taburnum, Sotanum, and Helvicum. Pliny's observation that they tasted naturally of resin cannot be correct, for wine was stored and transported in earthenware vessels which were lined with resin to make them impermeable, so any wine, and particularly a wine that had come from afar or was old, would have tasted of resin (see RESINATED WINES).

Pliny calls the vine that the growers of Vienne used Allobrogica. It has black grapes and is resistant to cold (*Natural History* 14. 26–7). Given the latter, Allobrogica is unlikely to be SYRAH—unless Pliny, like Strabo, thought that the Rhône valley's climate was inclement and decided therefore that any vine variety growing there must be able to withstand the cold. The Allobroges are proud of their wines, which fetch a high price (*Natural History* 14. 57). Elsewhere, Pliny remarks that the Gauls have mastered the art of grafting and improved on CATO: the Romans in turn have learned from them (*Natural History* 17. 116). The Allobroges exported their wines not only to Rome but also to Britain.

The people living in the Rhône valley doubtless carried on making wine after the Romans left, but we have hardly any records at all until the late Middle Ages. Medieval wine merchants

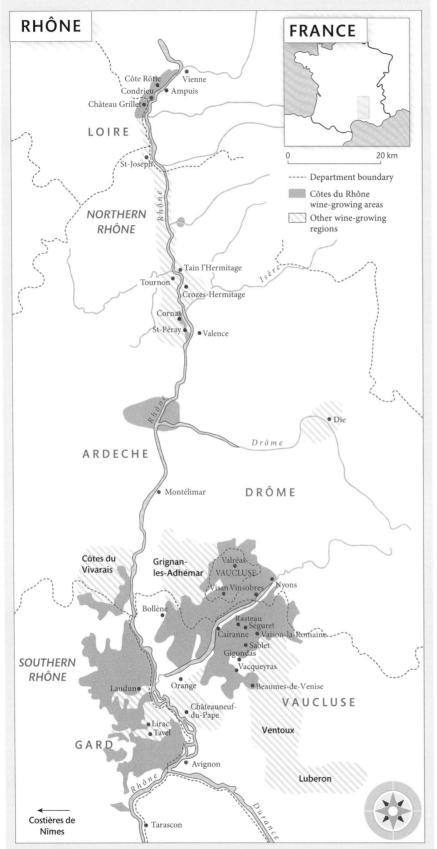

eagerly bought and sold the wine of Bordeaux, Gaillac, La Rochelle, the Île-de-France, and the Loire, but there was no trade in Rhône wines until the 14th century. This cannot have been because they were bad wines, for when Pope Clement V moved the papal court to Avignon in 1309 his entourage was quick to discover the local wines (see CHÂTEAUNEUF-DU-PAPE). Some three-quarters of the wines consumed at the papal court came from the Rhône valley, although the court was fond of Burgundy, too. When Urban V went back to Rome for three years from 1367 to 1370, he had a vine from the Côtes du Rhône planted there.

It was his hatred of political infighting, not his love of French wines, that drove Clement back to Avignon. After his successor Gregory XI returned to Rome for good in 1377, the pope and his Roman household continued to drink the wines of the Rhône.

Châteauneuf-du-Pape owes its name to a new castle built by John XXII, a summer residence in the hills 16 km/10 miles north of Avignon. It was destroyed by German bombers in the Second World War.

The name Hermitage La Chapelle has its origins in medieval legend. When the Crusader Gaspard de Stérimberg returned from the Holy Land, he gained the permission of Blanche of Castille, queen of France and regent during the minority of her son Louis IX (1226–70), to build a chapel and dedicate it to St Christopher; there he lived as a hermit for 30 years until he died. JABOULET's white Hermitage Chevalier de Stérimberg is named after this knightly recluse on the hill of Hermitage.

It was not only the Rhône which benefited from the extravagant habits of the papal court at Avignon: BURGUNDY, too, saw demand for its wines soar. As Burgundy became a major wine-producing region, it realized the dangers of competition from the south, especially because the wines of the Rhône were heavier than its own and hence more likely to survive transport unscathed. The duchy of Burgundy was in a powerful position, for in order to reach the markets of Paris and the north of France the wine of the Rhône had to be carried up the Saône through Burgundian territory. The solution was simple: Burgundy imposed severe restrictions on the entry and transit of all non-Burgundian wines. In 1446, the city of Dijon banned wines from Lyons, Vienne, and Tournon altogether, for the spurious reason that they were 'très petits et povres vins'. While these measures remained in force, from the 14th to the 16th centuries, they were successful. The wines of the Rhône valley were excluded from the trade with England and the Low Countries, and they were not available in Paris until the 17th century, when transport overland had become less expensive and merchants could afford to carry their wines to the lower reaches of the Loire by ox-drawn cart and then ship them down the Loire.   H.M.W.

Dion, R., *Histoire de la vigne et du vin en France* (Paris, 1959).

Livingstone-Learmonth, J., *The Wines of the Northern Rhône* (Berkeley, Calif., 2005).

Northern Rhône

The vineyards of the northern Rhône have probably been noticed by more tourists than any others, since so many millions of tourists are funnelled each year between northern and southern Europe down the narrow Rhône valley south of Lyons past Tain l'Hermitage. Here, high above the *autoroute du soleil*, TERRACES have been set to work as advertising hoardings for such producers as JABOULET and CHAPOUTIER. For a few seconds, the vineyards of the northern Rhône make an impression, but their produce is aimed in the main at the fine wine connoisseur rather than at the mass market. The total production of the northern Rhône is less than 5% of total Rhône valley wine, with Crozes-Hermitage alone representing well over half of all wine produced in the north.

At the southern limit of that part of Europe where CHAPTALIZATION is allowed, the northern Rhône is under the influence of a CONTINENTAL climate, with hard winters and summers whose effect on the grapes can be exaggerated by the steep slopes to which many of the better northern Rhône vineyards cling, although SOIL EROSION is a constant threat. The steep banks of this now heavily industrialized river naturally limited vine cultivation for many centuries, and the best wines are produced on inclines which are expensive to work and help to maximize the effect of the available SUNLIGHT (see TOPOGRAPHY). Since the 1980s, however, when the better wines of the Rhône were recognized as offering some of the best fine wine value (and winemaking recognized as a potentially noble way of earning a living), there has been considerable expansion, particularly in such appellations as St-Joseph and Crozes-Hermitage, but also in, and especially around, more restricted appellations such as Cornas and Condrieu. Most appellations are based on the right bank of the river, but the left bank vineyards of Crozes-Hermitage, and especially Hermitage, are particularly well exposed to afternoon sunshine.

This is the prime territory of the SYRAH grape, which is the only red wine grape permitted in northern Rhône red wines. Fashionable VIOGNIER is the defining grape variety of the white wines Condrieu and Château Grillet, while other white northern Rhône wines are made from the robust MARSANNE given nerve by the more delicate ROUSSANNE grape.

Most winemaking and all vine-growing is in the hands of individuals working a family holding. About half of all wines are bottled by merchants, of which Jaboulet, Chapoutier, Delas, and GUIGAL are some of the best known. Guigal's single-vineyard bottlings and distinctive, if controversial, use of new OAK did much to raise international awareness, and prices, of the northern Rhône in the 1980s. The district has benefited from an influx of winemaking perfectionists, whose hero is often Hermitage producer Chave. There are very few CO-OPERATIVES, although the one at Tain l'Hermitage is remarkably effective.

For more details, see the specific appellations CHÂTEAU GRILLET, CONDRIEU, CORNAS, CÔTE RÔTIE, CROZES-HERMITAGE, HERMITAGE, ST-JOSEPH, and ST-PÉRAY.

Livingstone-Learmonth, J., *The Wines of the Northern Rhône* (Berkeley, Calif., 2005).

Southern Rhône

The southern Rhône has only the river in common with the northern Rhône. The countryside here in the flatter, southern part of the valley is definitively southern, almost Provençal, with both houses and vegetation demonstrating the influence of a MEDITERRANEAN CLIMATE. Many other fruits are grown here, and one of the chief hazards is the sometimes cold WIND that can blow down the Rhône valley. Most vines are GOBELET trained, although Syrah vines are usually trained on wires in a single GUYOT system. If drought persists, some IRRIGATION is permitted.

Most wines are blends rather than made from a single vine variety. Although many growers have experimented with Syrah, much of the southern Rhône is too hot for it to ripen gracefully and two and a half times as much GRENACHE is grown. The dominant Grenache can in theory also be supplemented or seasoned by a wide range of other local varieties, but in practice only CARIGNAN, CINSAUT, and MOURVÈDRE are planted to any extent, with Mourvèdre becoming increasingly popular. Of white wine grapes, the most widely planted in the Vaucluse *départemente* where most southern Rhône wines are grown are Grenache Blanc, Ugni Blanc (Trebbiano), Clairette, Viognier, Vermentino, and Chardonnay (presumably for IGP wines).

CO-OPERATIVES are very important in the southern Rhône, responsible for about two-thirds of total production. The NÉGOCIANTS of the northern Rhône also have a long tradition of buying wine here for blending and bottling en route to the north. But there is also a swelling band of individual estates, especially in Châteauneuf-du-Pape, keen to etch their own stamp on a particularly accessible appellation. Winemaking techniques here are extremely varied, including everything from full-blown CARBONIC MACERATION to fly-blown ancient, open, wooden fermenting vats of uncertain age and certain lack of HYGIENE. New oak has been essayed and in many cases found less suitable that large old oak casks, or even concrete.

The southern Rhône is the only part of France other than the LANGUEDOC and ROUSSILLON to have a tradition of making sweet VIN DOUX NATUREL: a golden Muscat version in BEAUMES-DE-VENISE, and very varied colours and styles in RASTEAU.

For more details, see also CHÂTEAUNEUF-DU-PAPE, CLAIRETTE DE BELLEGARDE, COSTIÈRES DE NÎMES, Côtes du Vivarais, GIGONDAS, Grignan-les-Adhémar, LIRAC, LUBERON, Pierrevert, TAVEL, Ventoux, Vinsobres, and VACQUEYRAS.

Côtes du Rhône

This expression is sometimes used for the entire Rhône valley, but the specific appellation, granted in 1937, has almost become French for red wine. With BEAUJOLAIS and BORDEAUX AC, Côtes du Rhône has almost become a commodity, which must be discouraging for the increasing number of seriously quality-minded producers of it—even if this means that their wines are some of France's best value. The great majority of Côtes du Rhône comes from the flatter, arid, often windswept vineyards of the southern Rhône, typically a light fruity red wine made, using full or SEMI-CARBONIC MACERATION, by one of the many co-operatives in the region. But the extraordinary Domaine de Fonsalette, produced as an adjunct to Ch Rayas in Châteauneuf-du-Pape is a fine, ageworthy wines by any measure. A significant proportion of this wine is released as a PRIMEUR, in competition with Beaujolais Nouveau. Less than 4% of Côtes du Rhône is white, but rosé, specifically for summer drinking in the region, constitutes about 7% of the total.

The area of vineyard dedicated to the appellation has shrunk from about 42,000 ha/103,000 acres, in the mid-2000s to 33,510 ha by 2012. The area which qualifies for the appellation includes the fringes of smarter northern Rhône appellations as well as huge tracts of both the left and right banks of the southern Rhône. Most of the northern Rhône NÉGOCIANTS blend and bottle their own Côtes du Rhône, and that of Guigal can show the marked Syrah character of the northern Rhône.

The great majority of grapes used for Côtes du Rhône, however, are southern, which means officially those allowed in CHÂTEAUNEUF-DU-PAPE plus the scented white Viognier, and Carignan. Other than in the north, Grenache must constitute at least 40% of the blend, Syrah and/or Mourvèdre 15%.

Côtes du Rhône-Villages

This useful appellation represents a distinct step up in quality, and often value, from generic Côtes du Rhône. The basic maximum permitted YIELDS are considerably lower, 42 rather than 51hl/ha and the appellation has adopted the Châteauneuf-du-Pape's minimum alcoholic strength of 12.5% for red wines. The possibility for promotion to a specific appellation exists for each named village: first GIGONDAS then VACQUEYRAS, and in 2005, BEAUMES-DE-VENISE and VINSOBRES escaped the relative anonymity of the Villages appellation. RASTEAU followed. These particularly favoured communes may append their name to the appellation:

Rochegude, St-Maurice-sur-Eygues, Rousset-les-Vignes, and St-Pantaléon-les-Vignes in the Drôme *département*; Cairanne, Roaix, Séguret, Valréas, Visan, Sablet, Massif d'Uchaux, Plan de Dieu, and Puymeras in Vaucluse; and Chusclan, Laudun, St-Gervais, and Signargues on the right bank of the river Rhône in the Gard. Of these, Cairanne with such fine producers as Domaines Alary, Brusset, de L'Oratoire St-Martin, and Marcel Richaud has long been considered ripe for promotion. A further 80 or so communes, including some as far north as the ARDÈCHE, are allowed to submit wine for the appellation, although they may not append their village name. The total area of vineyard supplying wine for this appellation was 8,727 ha/21,556 acres in 2012, c, about a quarter of that producing generic Côtes du Rhône (it was one-eighth in the late 1990s). Some of the most energetic and thoughtful wine producers of France are based within this appellation.

See specifically BEAUMES-DE-VENISE, CHÂTEAUNEUF-DU-PAPE, CLAIRETTE DE BELLEGARDE, COSTIÈRES DE NÎMES, Côtes du VIVARAIS, DIE, DUCHÉ D'UZÈS, GIGONDAS, GRIGNAN-LES-ADHÉMAR, LIRAC, LUBERON, PIERREVERT, RASTEAU, TAVEL, VACQUEYRAS, VENTOUX, and VINSOBRES.

www.rhone-wines.com
www.drinkrhone.com

Rhône Rangers, loose affiliation of American wine producers who, led by Californians Bob Lindquist of Qupé winery and Randall Grahm of Bonny Doon, decided in the 1980s to produce wines in the image of the reds and, increasingly, whites of the RHÔNE valley in France. Such wines provided a useful outlet for the produce of old GRENACHE and Mataro (MOURVÈDRE) vines which had previously languished out of favour. It also resulted in a dramatic increase in plantings of such vine varieties as SYRAH (whose total California plantings grew from 2,000 acres/800 ha prior to 1995 to over 19,000 acres/7,700 ha in 2012) and VIOGNIER (500 acres/200 ha prior to 1995; 3,000 acres/1,214 ha in 2012). Joseph Phelps of NAPA was an early exponent, Bonny Doon of SANTA CRUZ a later but noisier one. The movement was regarded by some as providing welcome alternatives to the usual California diet of unblended Cabernet Sauvignon, Merlot, and Chardonnay, by others as an act of treachery against the state's own wine styles and vine varieties (PETITE SIRAH was only gradually accepted into the Rhône Rangers' blending vats).

Rías Baixas, the leading DO wine zone in GALICIA, north west Spain (see map under SPAIN), producing some of the country's most sought-after dry white wines. Between 1987 and 2012 the DO's vineyard area grew from 237 ha/570 acres to 4,050 ha/9,700 acres with the number of wineries rising from 14 to 177. Named after the flooded coastal valleys, or *rías*, that penetrate up to 30 km/19 miles inland, the zone's reputation is based on the white ALBARIÑO grape. Wines were exported to northern Europe in the 16th and 17th centuries but, after the ravages of PHYLLOXERA, many of the traditional vine varieties were abandoned, and by the 1900s the region's vineyards were largely planted with high-yielding HYBRIDS and by Jerez's PALOMINO, producing poor-quality wine. The revival began in the late 1970s, when growers were encouraged to replant native vine varieties and producers were given incentives to invest in modern winemaking equipment. The metamorphosis gathered pace with the application of EU funds following Spain's accession to the EU in 1986.

Rías Baixas has five separate subzones, all within the province of Pontevedra. Many of the purest Albariño wines come from Val do Salnés zone centred on the town of Cambados on the west coast. The two further subzones, O Rosal and Condado do Tea, are on the northern slopes of the river Miño facing the VINHO VERDE region in Portugal on the opposite bank. A fourth, small subzone, Soutomaior, was admitted in the late 1990s, to be joined later by Ribeira do Ulla in the far north. All five zones share the same GRANITE-based subsoils and relatively cool, damp, MARITIME CLIMATE. The Atlantic influence is strongest in Val do Salnés, where annual RAINFALL averages 1,300 mm/50 in. Vines were traditionally cultivated on pergolas (see TENDONE) to protect grapes from the constant threat of FUNGAL DISEASES, although modern vineyards are planted on a more practical local variant of the GENEVA DOUBLE CURTAIN vine-training system.

Twelve different vine varieties are officially permitted in Rías Baixas although Albariño accounts for 90% of the vineyard area. Other white grapes which may be blended with Albariño according to local regulations include CAIÑO BLANCO, as well as TREIXADURA, and Loureira (see LOUREIRO; locally known as Marqués), both of which are found in the Vinho Verde region. (TORRONTÉS and GODELLO are also permitted.) On its own, Albariño produces a fragrant, intensely fruity, dry white wine with a natural minimum alcohol often above 12%. Yields used to be low, which made the wines expensive, but abusive yield increases began to occur in the 1990s, sometimes aggravated by overreliance on selected, aroma-enhancing YEASTS. There have been experiments with OAK. The six permitted red grapes, including MENCÍA,

ESPADEIRO, and Caíño Tinto, were planted on a total area of just 190 ha/455 acres in 2012 but were beginning to make waves thanks to the work of some growers, particularly Eulogio Pomares (Zárate) and Gerardo Méndez (Forjas del Salnés). V. de la S.

Barquín, J., Guitiérrez, L., and de la Serna, V., *The Finest Wines of Rioja and Northwest Spain* (London, 2011).
www.riasbaixaswines.com

Ribatejo, former name of TEJO in Portugal.

Ribeira Sacra, growing Spanish DO, created in 1996. It is the only GALICIAN region specializing in red wines, from the MENCÍA grape, and some less well-known local varieties, together with some whites from Godello and Albariño. Since 2005 the region has won growing acclaim, particularly in the United States, where its top producers Algueira, Guímaro, Dominio do Bibei, Raúl Pérez, Ponte da Boga, and Envínate enjoy a certain cult status. V. de la S.

Ribeiro means 'river bank' or 'riverside' in the Galician language and is the name of a red and white wine DO zone in GALICIA, north west Spain (see map under SPAIN). Ribeiro spans the valleys of the river Miño and its tributaries and Arnoia downstream from Orense. In the 16th and 17th centuries wines from Ribeiro were exported as far afield as Italy and England but they disappeared from international markets until recently. PHYLLOXERA put paid to the region's prosperity at the end of the 19th century. As in RÍAS BAIXAS, for example, farmers, seeking a quick return to profit, replanted their holdings with the sherry grape PALOMINO. Over recent years, growers have been encouraged to uproot this productive but unsuitable variety in favour of TREIXADURA, TORRONTÉS, Lado, and other INDIGENOUS VARIETIES which perform well in the damp MARITIME CLIMATE of north west Iberia and can be made into aromatic, crisp white wines. But it is the red wine explosion that has been notable this century, with the recovery and discovery of local Brancellao (ALVARELHÃO), Caíño Redondo, Carabuñeira (Portugal's Touriga Nacional), and Ferrón varieties, and the rediscovery of the better vineyards planted to the long-reviled, post-phylloxeric Garnacha Tintorera (ALICANTE BOUSCHET). With help from EU funds, wineries have been updated and the traditional, labour-intensive pergolas (see TENDONE) are being replaced by lower VINE-TRAINING SYSTEMS. Emilio Rojo, Manuel Formigo, Luis Anxo Rodríguez, Antonio Cajide (Sameirás), Xosé Lois Sebio (Coto de Gomariz), and Casal de Armán are the new stars. V. de la S.

Ribera del Duero, important wine zone in CASTILLA Y LEÓN in north-central Spain that challenged RIOJA as the leading red wine-producing region in Iberia towards the end of the 20th century when it grew substantially. By 2012 it had a total of 21,500 ha/51,500 acres of vineyard, a third as much as Rioja. Ribera del Duero spans the upper valley of the River Duero (known as DOURO in Portugal), starting some 30 km/18 miles east of the city of Valladolid (see map under SPAIN). Although Bodegas VEGA SICILIA on the western margin of the denomination has been producing one of Spain's finest wines since the mid 19th century, the region was awarded DO status only in 1982. Since then more than 200 private estates have emerged.

At first sight, the Duero valley is not the most congenial place to grow grapes. At between 700 and 850 m/2,800 ft above sea level, the growing season is relatively short. FROST, commonplace in winter, continues to be a threat well into the spring. Temperatures, which can reach nearly 40 °C/104 °F in the middle of a July day, fall sharply at night—a phenomenon associated with wine quality elsewhere (see TEMPERATURE VARIABILITY).

The potential was recognized by Alejandro Fernández, who played a key role in the considerable development of the region in the 1980s. Pesquera, his wine vinified from grapes growing around the village of Pesquera del Duero a short distance upstream from Vega Sicilia, was released in the early 1980s to international acclaim. Other growers (many of whom had previously sold their grapes to the CO-OPERATIVES) were thereby encouraged to make and market their own wines, soon challenging Rioja's traditional hegemony inside Spain. In the 1990s, consumption of top-quality Ribera wines soared within Spain, causing deepening concern in Rioja. Several Ribera producers attained quality levels not much below those of Vega Sicilia and Pesquera. The leading challengers included Dominio de Pingus, Alión, Pérez Pascuas, Pago de los Capellanes, Emilio Moro, Aalto, Hermanos Sastre, Alonso del Yerro, Goyo García Viadero, Hacienda Monasterio, and Cillar de Silos. Several of these growers are in the east of the region, near Aranda de Duero, where a tradition of cheap rosés had previously inhibited production of top-quality reds.

The region's principal vine variety, the Tinto Fino (also called Tinta del Pais), is a local variant of Rioja's TEMPRANILLO. It seems to have adapted to the Duero's climatic extremes and produces deep-coloured, occasionally astringent, firm-flavoured red wines without the support of any other grape variety. White wine made from the ALBILLO, a white variety enjoyed as a table grape by the locals, is not entitled to the DO but may occasionally be blended into the intense red wine to lighten the load and add glycerine content. Cabernet Sauvignon, Merlot, and Malbec, introduced by Vega Sicilia 130 years ago, are now allowed throughout the

denomination. Garnacha is used in the production of rosé.   R.J.M. & V. de la S.

Peñín, J., *Guía Peñín* (Madrid, annually).
Radford, J., *The New Spain* (2nd edn, London, 2004).
www.riberadelduero.es

Ribera del Guadiana is the chosen name for a single denominated zone encompassing about 26,000 ha/64,000 acres of vineyards in Spain's EXTREMADURA region. The DO, awarded in 1998, includes such well-known areas as Tierra de Barros. The autonomous Extremadura government is actively encouraging the planting of INTERNATIONAL VARIETIES and improvements in wine quality but the results have been slow in coming.   V. de la S.

Ribera del Júcar, promising Spanish DO in the Cuenca province of CASTILLA-LA MANCHA whose first vintage was 2003.

Ribéreau-Gayon, dynasty of important OENOLOGISTS closely associated with the history of the Institut d'Oenologie at the University of BORDEAUX.

Ribolla, white grape variety also known as **Ribolla Gialla** to distinguish it from the less interesting **Ribolla Verde**, best known in FRIULI in north east Italy but also grown, as Rebula, in SLOVENIA. It is distinct from the ROBOLA of the island of Cephalonia in GREECE.

Ribolla's first historically documented appearance in Friuli was in 1296, as Rabola. The grape lost ground steadily in the 19th and 20th centuries, however, in the wake of the PHYLLOXERA epidemic and Friuli's subsequent enthusiasm for INTERNATIONAL (French) VARIETIES when vineyards were replanted. In the mid 1990s, Ribolla accounted for less than 1% of all the white DOC wines of Friuli, but by 2010, Italy's total plantings were 435 ha/1,075 acres, and there were champions of the variety on both sides of the Slovenian border. Rosazzo and Oslavia are generally considered Friuli's two classic areas for Ribolla Gialla but there is even more planted in western Slovenia, in both Brda and Vipava. Extended contact with the variety's particularly yellow skins is increasingly common and the wine produced can have firm structure and, neatly, yellow-fruit flavours.

Ribolla Nera is the SCHIOPPETTINO grape.

Ricasoli, one of the oldest and most powerful noble families of TUSCANY in central Italy, important landholders between Florence and Siena for over a thousand years. The vast size of their holdings led the medieval republic of Florence to bar them from holding public office lest the combination of territorial dominion and civic position create a threat to republican liberties. Bettino Ricasoli (1809–80), a dominant figure in the political life of his time and the second prime minister of the newly united

Italy in 1861, a dedicated agricultural experimenter and reformer, played a fundamental role in the revitalization of the viticulture of his time and invented what came to be the standard varietal formula for the production of CHIANTI. Like all Tuscan landowners of the time, he believed that the sharecroppers should grow the grapes and the large commercial houses—principally controlled by the Tuscan nobility such as ANTINORI and FRESCOBALDI—would age and distribute the finished wines.

He founded the Ricasoli NÉGOCIANT firm, which would assume a position of leadership in Tuscany for the better part of a century; André SIMON could still write after the Second World War that 'the most reliable brand of Chianti is that of Baron Ricasoli'.

The 1970s and 1980s were less kind to the fortunes of the house: a partnership with American distillers Seagram in the négociant part of the business in the 1960s, and others such as HARDYS of Australia, led to huge expansion of production and a general lowering of quality, and the marketing of Ricasoli wines in supermarkets and other mass distribution centres was extremely damaging to their image. In 1993, Francesco Ricasoli repurchased the family business and set about modernizing the estate. By the second decade of this century all the vineyards had been replanted, and Ricasoli had the largest number of hectares under vine of any producer in the Chianti Classico denomination. Very much in the model of a Bordeaux GRAND VIN, they produced a Castello di Brolio Chianti Classico for the first time in 1997. This wine became a GRAN SELEZIONE in the 2010 vintage.

The distinctive character of the neo-gothic *castello*, combined with the fame of both Brolio and the Ricasoli name, ensures visits from over 40,000 people a year to the Castle, the CELLAR DOOR tasting room, and the osteria which serves traditional local food.   D.C.G.

rich is a positive tasting term for, generally, a red wine that gives an appealing impression of power and sweetness even though it may have negligible RESIDUAL SUGAR. It may also be found as a label description on bottles of relatively sweet CHAMPAGNE (see DOSAGE).

Richebourg, great red GRAND CRU in Burgundy's CÔTE D'OR. For more details, see VOSNE-ROMANÉE.

riddling, an integral stage in the traditional method of making SPARKLING WINES, known as *remuage* in French. It involves dislodging the deposit left in a bottle after a second fermentation has taken place inside it and shaking it into the neck of the inverted bottle. It can be achieved either by hand or, more speedily, by machine (see GYROPALETTE). Modern alternative techniques may eventually render this cumbersome process superfluous, but they have not so far been commercially adopted. A **riddling rack** is English for a PUPITRE. For more details, see SPARKLING WINEMAKING.

Ridge Vineyards, the most internationally admired producer of American Cabernet Sauvignon, from the historic Monte Bello vineyard in the SANTA CRUZ MOUNTAINS. Ridge produces ageworthy, terroir-driven, single vineyard Cabernets and Zinfandels that demonstrate vineyard character and vintage variance over winemaking wizardry and homogeneity. Ridge's Sonoma outpost Ridge Lytton Springs, acquired in 1991 but a source of old-vine Zinfandel grapes for a quarter-century before that, is famous for its suave yet durable wines, as is their historic Geyserville vineyard.

Monte Bello was first planted in 1886 and the stone and redwood winery deep in a ravine at 2,600 feet above Silicon Valley produced its first wine in 1892. The vineyards were abandoned during PROHIBITION (1920–33), but were replanted to Cabernet Sauvignon in the 1940s. In 1959 Dave Bennion and two fellow Stanford Research Institute engineers purchased the winery and vineyard land as a weekend retreat and made a half barrel of such complex Cabernet that it inspired them to rebond the winery in time for the 1962 vintage. During the 1960s the group also made some exceptional Zinfandel from old vineyards both locally and in Sonoma. In 1969 Paul Draper, with winemaking experience from setting up a small winery in the coastal range of CHILE, joined the enterprise and is still in charge, having identified and secured long-term single vineyard sources of top-quality grapes. A small amount of Chardonnay has also been made since 1962. Draper, self-taught through tasting fine wines and studying 19th-century techniques, has been an outspoken critic of deliberately extended HANG TIME and of what he might call DAVIS dogma in winemaking.

Monte Bello 1971 performed particularly well in both JUDGMENT OF PARIS tastings. Ridge's export and pricing policies have been admirably and unusually consistent.

Ried, traditional term in AUSTRIA for a vineyard site—especially if considered one of particular value—that is sometimes seen on labels just before the site name. Not unlike BRICCO in PIEMONTE.

Rieslaner, increasingly rare, late-ripening Silvaner × Riesling cross that was grown on a total of 82 ha of Franken and Pfalz in southern Germany in 2012. Provided it can reach full ripeness, it can produce wines with race and currant fruit.

Riesling has for long been arguably the world's most undervalued, often mis-spelt, and certainly most often mispronounced grape. ('Reece-ling' is correct.) Riesling is the great vine variety of Germany and could claim to be the finest white grape variety in the world on the basis of the longevity of its wines and their ability to transmit the characteristics of a vineyard without losing Riesling's own inimitable style; in this sense it is very much more like Cabernet Sauvignon than Chardonnay (although DNA PROFILING in Austria in 1998 revealed a parent–offspring relationship with GOUAIS BLANC, a parent of Chardonnay, Pinot Noir et al.; see PINOT). Riesling has suffered, in an era when oak and heft have been considered the height of FASHION, because it is no friend of BARRIQUES, and its wines tend to be relatively low in alcohol. In the 1960s and 1970s, the name Riesling was debased by being applied to a wide range of white grape varieties of varied and often doubtful quality, the ultimate backhanded compliment. Rieslings were also associated with SWEETNESS (another black mark in the modern era) and lack the please-all blandness of, say, Pinot Grigio and Chardonnay.

In the late 19th and first half of the 20th centuries, on the other hand, German Riesling wines were prized, and priced, as highly as the great red wines of France. Connoisseurs knew that, thanks to their magical combination of ACIDITY and EXTRACT, these wines could develop for decades in bottle, regardless of ALCOHOLIC STRENGTH and RESIDUAL SUGAR. Riesling is made at all levels of sweetness, and in the second half of the 20th-century residual sugar, typically Süssreserve, was used by producers of basic German wine to compensate for a lack of full ripeness and uncomfortably high acidity. Today, thanks to CLIMATE CHANGE and more widespread determination to increase QUALITY IN WINE, fine dry Riesling is common in Germany. But while the average residual sugar of Riesling made everywhere has been declining fast, the variety is distinguished for its ability to produce great sweet wines, whether they be the cold weather speciality EISWEIN or ICE WINE, or the BOTRYTIZED, Beerenauslese and Trockenbeerenauslese and their counterparts outside Germany. Riesling's high natural level of TARTARIC ACID provides it with a much more dependable counterbalance to high residual sugar than, for example, the Sémillon grape of Sauternes.

Riesling wine, wherever produced, is also notable for its powerful, rapier-like aroma variously described as flowery, steely, honeyed, and whichever blend of quasi-mineral elements is conveyed by the individual vineyard site. This distinctive aroma, usually experienced in conjunction with Riesling's natural raciness and tartness, is particularly high in MONOTERPENES, 10 to 50 times higher, for instance, than WELSCHRIESLING, the quite unrelated white grape variety prevalent in central Europe which, much to German fury, borrowed the word Riesling for many of its aliases (RIESLING ITALICO, for example). An important contributor to the bottle-aged bouquet of Riesling wines is the norisoprenoid hydrocarbon 1,1,6-trimethyl-1,2-dihydronaphthalene (see TDN for more detail).

Viticulturally, true Riesling (sometimes called **Weisser**, **White**, **Rhein**, **Rhine**, or **Johannisberg Riesling**) is distinguished by the hardness of its wood, which helps make it a particularly cold-hardy vine, thus a possible choice for relatively cool wine regions, even if it needs the most favoured, sheltered site in order to ripen fully and yield economically. So resistant is it to FROST that winter pruning can begin earlier than with most other varieties. Its growth is vigorous and upright, and this is a top-quality variety which seems able to produce yields of 60 or 70 hl/ha (4 tons/acre), without any necessary diminution of quality. (Maximum yields allowed by the French INAO authorities are higher in Alsace, France's Riesling enclave, for example, than for any other comparable fine wine.) Its compact bunches of small grapes make it relatively prone to BOTRYTIS, and COULURE can be a problem, but its chief distinction in the vineyard is its late budding. Riesling ripens early relative to most INTERNATIONAL VARIETIES, but late relative to most other varieties planted in Germany such as the GERMAN CROSSES. In cool vineyards in the northern hemisphere, it is often not picked until mid October or early November (and sometimes even later). Riesling can ripen so early in warmer regions, however, that its wines can taste dull; a long, slow ripening period suits Riesling best and manages to extract maximum flavour and EXTRACT, while maintaining acidity. Thus, many of Germany's (and therefore most of the world's) most admired Rieslings are grown on particularly favoured sites in cooler regions such as the MOSEL, whose crackling, racy, feather-light style of Riesling is unique.

Germany

As outlined in GERMAN HISTORY, Riesling is by no means the oldest documented vine variety grown in Germany (including, as it did for so long, Alsace). ELBLING and SILVANER were widely grown throughout the Middle Ages, while RÄUSCHLING was the speciality of Baden in the south. An invoice dated 1435, from a castle in the extreme south east of the Rheingau on the river Main, mentions 'riesslingen in die wingarten', presumably Rieslings in the vineyard. Early spellings of words like Riesling have to be treated with care, since the similarly named Räuschling was so much more common then than today, but Riesling seems to have been recognized as a top-quality variety from the late Middle Ages and was planted throughout the Rhine and Mosel from the middle of the 16th century.

Riesling is first mentioned in connection with Alsace as one of its finer products in 1477 by Duke René of Lorraine, even if we have to wait until 1628 for the first documentary evidence of its actually being planted there.

In the 18th century, various prince-bishops and other ecclesiastical authorities did their utmost to encourage Riesling plantings at the expense of other lesser varieties, notably in the Mosel. But the habit of picking grapes earlier than is today customary did the late-ripening Riesling no favours and by 1930 the proportion of the Rheingau region, supposedly the classic Riesling heartland, planted with Riesling had fallen to 57% (as opposed to 80% by the turn of the century).

This provided a stimulus to Germany's burgeoning viticultural researchers (see GEISENHEIM) to select and develop top-quality CLONES of the variety. Today, partly thanks to the efforts of a special centre for the CLONAL SELECTION of Riesling at Trier, the German vine-grower can choose from more than 60, of which one of the more controversially perfumed is the N90 used by such innovative growers in the Pfalz region as Müller Catoir and Lingenfelder. (French-certified clones of Riesling still numbered precisely one, 49, in the mid 2000s, on the other hand.)

Much of the work of these viticultural institutes was also focused on developing the famous GERMAN CROSSES, designed to produce high yields of grapes with high MUST WEIGHTS but without the viticultural inconveniences of Riesling. In the second half of the 20th century, with their country awash in new money and an ocean of high sugar grape juice, many Germans gave up wine-growing, or at least the steep slope cultivation of the demanding Riesling vine, trends which sadly continue. In 1980, Riesling represented less than 20% of German vineyard area, and even amid signs of a Riesling renaissance among sophisticated wine drinkers, its share of area has barely increased since, although, after being overtaken by the lacklustre Müller-Thurgau, it has re-established itself as the most planted vine variety with a 2012 total of 22,837 ha/56,407 acres widely spread throughout the country.

Undeniably, though, the top vintners and sites not just of the Rheingau and Mosell, but also of the Nahe, Mittelrhein, Rheinhessen, and the Pfalz, are largely devoted to Riesling despite—in fact, precisely because of—its precarious, slow ripening in the face of climatic challenge. In these growing areas, Riesling is selected for the sunniest hillsides, steepest slopes, most sheltered rocky crenellations, and pockets of reflected heat. In such spots, Riesling shows dazzling diversity. It can be as delicate as a 7% Saar wine that is somehow satisfyingly complete—or it may be a refreshing, nervy, bone-dry GROSSES GEWÄCHS with 13.5% alcohol,

with many of the finest examples grown in Rheinhessen and Nahe. For more details see GERMANY.

Elsewhere

For some wine drinkers, Riesling is acceptable only in its French form, a wine from ALSACE, the only part of France where this German vine is officially allowed—a cause of some frustration with the strictures of INAO. Alsace's plantings of the variety wine producers there view as their most noble have slowly increased, passed the 3,000-ha mark in the late 1980s, and were almost 3,500 ha in 2011. What is needed to produce Alsace Riesling of real class is, as in Germany, a favoured site of real interest such as many of Alsace's famous grands crus vineyards.

The hallmark of Alsace has been dry wines from aromatic grapes such as Riesling and certainly the great majority of Alsace Rieslings follow the variety's alluring perfume with a taste that is generally full bodied and bone dry. The number of authorized clones of Riesling may be a tiny fraction of those available to German growers but the dry climate of Alsace minimizes the risk of rot and makes extended ripening a real possibility, however, often resulting in the prized late-harvest wines which qualify as VENDANGE TARDIVE or, even sweeter, SÉLECTION DE GRAINS NOBLES, the richest, most sumptuous ripeness category of Alsace wines. See ALSACE for more detail.

To the north, about 12% of the LUXEMBOURG vineyard is planted with Riesling, which tends to produce dry, relatively full-bodied wines (thanks to CHAPTALIZATION), closer in style to those of Alsace than to those of the Mosel just over the German border.

In AUSTRIA, Riesling (often called Weisser Riesling to distinguish it from the more widely planted WELSCHRIESLING) is quantitatively not nearly as important as Grüner Veltliner, planted on 2,036 ha/5,029 acres in 2012, but is regarded as one of the country's finest wines when made on a favoured site. The most hallowed Austrian Rieslings are dry, full-bodied, concentrated, and aromatic, and a high proportion of them come from the terraced vineyards of the Wachau in Lower Austria. Certain favoured sites in neighbouring Kamptal such as the Zöbinger Heiligenstein vineyard near Langenlois and those just over the border from the Wachau in Kremstal also enjoy a high reputation for their aristocratic, whistle-clean Rieslings. Riesling is a relatively important variety in the vineyards of Vienna, especially those of Nussberg and Bisamberg.

Not surprisingly, Riesling works well in the continental climate of the CZECH REPUBLIC and SLOVAKIA (where Egon Müller of the Saar valley in Germany makes fine Riesling) to the immediate north of Austria's vineyards, where

relatively light wines have real crackle and race. Most of SWITZERLAND is too cool to ripen Riesling properly, with the exception of some of the more schistous soils and warmest vineyards of the Valais around Sion.

Although practically unknown in Iberia (*pace* TORRES in Spain's high Penedès), Riesling has infiltrated the far north of Italy where plantings totalled just 446 ha/1,102 acres in 2010. It is grown with real enthusiasm in the high vineyards of ALTO ADIGE, where it produces delicate, aromatic wines quite unlike most Italian whites. It is also grown quite successfully in FRIULI, where it is known as **Riesling Renano**; and over the border in SLOVENIA, delicate **Renski Rizling** is produced in **Podravje.** Riesling, known as **Rizling Rajinski** and variants thereof, is also planted southwards in CROATIA.

It is planted throughout the rest of eastern Europe, with more than 1,000 ha in each of Hungary, Moldova, and Bulgaria, and apparently more than 2,000 ha of an unspecified Riesling in Ukraine, although in each of these countries summers can be too warm to coax real excitement from the variety and Welschriesling tends to reign supreme—as it does, for instance, in Romania.

In the New World, true Riesling was for a long time most widely grown in AUSTRALIA, where it was encouraged by the 19th-century influx of Silesians (see POLAND) and remained the most planted white wine grape variety of all until Chardonnay caught up with its nearly 4,000 ha/10,000 acres in 1990. But few new Riesling vines went into the ground and by 2012 total Australian plantings had fallen to 3,892 ha and become increasingly concentrated on proven hot spots of the Eden and Clare Valleys, Tasmania, and Great Southern, all producing dry Rieslings with a minerally raciness underlying the tangy, lime-accented fruit. A tiny quantity of botrytized sweet Riesling is also made. The wines are less phenolic than those of Alsace, and less alcoholic than Alsace or Austrian Riesling. They can also richly repay cellaring for up to, or even beyond, 20 years. In the early 21st century NEW ZEALAND began to produce convincing wines from its total plantings of just over 700 ha in 2012, mainly in Marlborough and Waipara, notably when some producers addressed themselves to making scintillating late-harvest sweet wines, but its production is dwarfed by that of Sauvignon Blanc, Chardonnay, and Pinot Gris.

Riesling (of some sort) is cultivated more widely in South America than one might think wise. Both Argentina and Chile have a few hundred hectares and some of Chile's is grown in the far south to good effect.

But the major change in Riesling's fortunes in the early 21st century was in North America, to the extent that by 2012 the US had the world's second biggest area of Riesling vineyard after Germany. The Riesling revolution began in WASHINGTON state, which claims a special affinity for Riesling, even organizing the world's first truly international conference on the subject (to be followed by similar events in Australia and the Rheingau). By 2011, Washington's total area devoted to Riesling had reached 6,320 acres/2,559 ha, almost as much as Chardonnay plantings. This growth was largely driven by a JOINT VENTURE between the dominant Washington wine producer Château Ste Michelle and Ernst Loosen of the Mosel, with the Eroica BRAND of Riesling a particular success. Washington Riesling is conveniently winter-hardy, and at their best the wines, with varying sweetness levels, benefit from the state's general brightness of fruit. In Oregon, too, Riesling's 700 acres are only just less than the Chardonnay acreage. California's total area of what is occasionally known as **White Riesling** remained at around 4,000 (1,600 ha) throughout the 1980s, and had declined to 1,850 acres by 2003, but had risen again to more than 4,000 acres by 2012, perhaps encouraged by Riesling's success in Washington. With the exception of Stony Hill's age-worthy wines and the Alsace-like offerings from Claiborne-Churchill, the variety is rarely made bone dry in California, and can command a decent price only if very sweet and described as Select Late Harvest (the equivalent of a German BEERENAUSLESE) or some such. Riesling is planted all over the state with one particularly faithful producer having been Navarro of Mendocino.

Because of its winter hardiness, Riesling tends to be treasured in the coolest wine regions of North America. In CANADA, Riesling is cultivated with particular success in Ontario, making fine, delicate ICEWINES just over the border from the Finger Lakes region of NEW YORK state, where it is increasingly recognized as the region's most successful variety. The sheer quality of Finger Lakes Riesling has contributed to a revived interest in the grape and wine and inspired the formation in 2007 of the International Riesling Foundation based there. One of its most obvious initiatives is the RIESLING TASTE PROFILE, a graphic for back labels designed to communicate SWEETNESS level. Riesling has also been emerging as a major VARIETAL in MICHIGAN, too.

Price, F., *Riesling Renaissance* (London, 2004).

Riesling Italico

Riesling Italico, or **Riesling Italianski**, white grape variety which Germans would like to see called RIZLING Italico to distinguish it from true RIESLING, known as Riesling Renano in Italy. In Austria, it is called WELSCHRIESLING (under which more details can be found); in much of what was YUGOSLAVIA, it is called LAŠKI RIZLING, in the CZECH REPUBLIC, it is called Ryzlink Vlašský, and in HUNGARY, it is called OLASZ RIZLING. In Romania it is known as Riesling Italico (*sic*). Within Italy, it is most common in the far north east, in FRIULI just over the border from SLOVENIA. Provided its tendency to overcrop is curbed, it can produce delicate, crisp, mildly flowery wines, most in COLLIO. It is grown to a limited extent in ALTO ADIGE and, more successfully, in LOMBARDY.

Riesling-Sylvaner

Riesling-Sylvaner is the flattering and misleading name for MÜLLER-THURGAU that is, curiously, preferred in SWITZERLAND, where the canton of Thurgau is to be found. It was also widely used in NEW ZEALAND when it was for some time the most planted variety.

Riesling Taste Profile

Riesling Taste Profile, a graphic for back LABELS designed by the New York-based International Riesling Foundation to indicate the SWEETNESS level of the Riesling in the bottle.

www.drinkriesling.com

right bank

right bank, an expression much used of that part of the BORDEAUX wine region that is on the right bank, or north, of the river DORDOGNE. It includes, travelling down river, CASTILLON Côtes de Bordeaux, FRANCS Côtes de Bordeaux, ST-ÉMILION and its satellite appellations, POMEROL and LALANDE-DE-POMEROL, FRONSAC and Canon-Fronsac, BOURG, and BLAYE. The most obvious characteristic shared by these appellations, and distinct from LEFT BANK appellations, is that the dominant red wine grapes are Merlot with Cabernet Franc rather than Cabernet Sauvignon. In recent years, much has been made of the rivalry between the established large estates of the left bank and the much smaller properties of the right bank (including many GARAGE WINES) with their more recent reputations.

ringing

ringing vines. See CINCTURING.

Rioja

Rioja. La Rioja is the oldest winemaking province in ARGENTINA but Rioja is probably best known in the wine world as the leading wine region of SPAIN, producing predominantly red wines in the north of the country. Named after the *río* (river) Oja, a tributary of the river Ebro, most of the Rioja wine region lies in the autonomous region of La Rioja in north east Spain, although parts of the zone extend into the neighbouring BASQUE country to the north west and NAVARRA to the north east. Centred on the regional capital Logroño, Rioja divides into three zones along the axis of the river Ebro. **Rioja Alta** occupies the part of the Ebro valley west of Logroño and includes the winemaking town of Haro. **Rioja Alavesa** is the name given to the section of the zone north of the river Ebro which falls in the Basque province of Alava. **Rioja Baja** extends from the suburbs of Logroño south and east to include the towns of Calahorra and Alfaro. In 2013, Rioja had 63,500 ha/152,400 acres of vines.

History

There is archaeological evidence that the Romans made wine in the upper Ebro valley (see SPAIN, history). Wine trade was tolerated rather than encouraged under the Moorish occupation of Iberia, but viticulture flourished once more in Rioja after the Christian reconquest at the end of the 15th century. The name Rioja was already in use in one of the statutes written to guarantee the rights of inhabitants of territory recaptured from the Moors. Rioja's wine industry grew around the numerous monasteries (see MONKS AND MONASTERIES) that were founded to serve pilgrims en route to Santiago de Compostela, and the region's first wine laws date from this period.

For centuries Rioja suffered from its physical isolation from major population centres, and the wines found a market outside the region only in the 1700s, when communications improved and Bilbao became an important trading centre. In 1850, Luciano de Murrieta (subsequently the Marqués de Murrieta) established Rioja's first commercial BODEGA in cellars belonging to the Duque de Vitoria and began exporting wines to the Spanish colonies. The Rioja region benefited unexpectedly, but substantially, from the all too obvious arrival of POWDERY MILDEW in French vineyards in the late 1840s. Bordeaux wine merchants crossed the Pyrenees in large numbers and in 1862 the Provincial Legislature in Alava employed a French adviser to help local vine-growers. Shunned by smallholders who were concerned only with the requirements of the local Basque market, Jean Pineau was finally employed by the Marqués de Riscal, who set about building a bodega at Elciego along French lines. It was finished in 1868, four years before Murrieta built its own similar installation at Ygay.

When the PHYLLOXERA louse began to devastate French vineyards in the late 1860s, yet more merchants came to Spain in search of wine. French duties were relaxed and Rioja enjoyed an unprecedented boom which lasted for nearly four decades. New bodegas were established, among them the Compañía Vinícola del Norte de España (CVNE), López de Heredia, La Rioja Alta, and Bodegas Franco-Españolas, all of which were heavily influenced by the French. During this period the 225-l/59-gal oak *barrica*, or BARRIQUE, was introduced from Bordeaux, and these influential maturation containers are still sometimes referred to as *barricas bordelesas* in Rioja (although American OAK was the popular choice). Helped by a new rail link (see RAILWAYS), Rioja sometimes exported 500,000 hl/13.2 million gal of wine a month to France in the late 19th century.

Phylloxera did not reach Rioja until 1901, by which time Bordeaux had returned to full production with vines grafted onto phylloxera-resistant ROOTSTOCKS. Spain also lost its lucrative colonial markets and Rioja's wine industry declined rapidly. A number of new bodegas were established in the period following the First World War and Spain's first Consejo Regulador was established in Rioja in 1926, but the Civil War (1936–9) and the Second World War which followed put paid to further expansion. Recovery came in the late 1960s and 1970s, when, encouraged by growing foreign markets and the construction of a motorway connecting Logroño and Bilbao, a number of new bodegas were built in the region, several with the support of multinational companies, which later sold back the wineries to Spanish firms.

Climate and geography

Rioja enjoys an enviable position among Spanish wine regions. Sheltered by the Sierra de Cantabria to the north and west, it is well protected from the rain-bearing Atlantic winds that drench the Basque coast immediately to the north. Yet Rioja's wine producers rarely experience the climatic extremes that burden growers in so much of central and southern Spain. It is difficult to make climatic generalizations, however, about a region that stretches about 120 km/75 miles from north west to south east. Indeed, Spanish critics argue that within this single DO there are several entirely different wine-producing regions.

The vineyards range in ELEVATION from 300 m/984 ft above sea level at Alfaro in the east to nearly 800 m on the slopes of the Sierra de Cantabria to the north west. Average annual RAINFALL increases correspondingly from less than 300 mm/12 in in parts of Rioja Baja to over 500 mm in the upper zones of Rioja Alta and Rioja Alavesa.

Rioja Alta and Rioja Alavesa share a similar climate and are distinct from each other for mainly administrative reasons, although there are soil differences between the two. Many of the best grapes are grown here on the cooler slopes to the north west around the towns and villages of Haro, Labastida, San Vicente, Laguardia, Elciego, Fuenmayor, Cenicero, and Briones. These zones share similar CLAY soils based on LIMESTONE. Downstream to the east, the climate becomes gradually warmer with rainfall decreasing to less than 400 mm at Logroño. Where the valley broadens, there is a higher incidence of fertile, ALLUVIAL soils composed chiefly of SILT. Around Calahorra and Alfaro in Rioja Baja the climate is more MEDITERRANEAN. In summer, DROUGHT is often a problem here, and temperatures frequently reach 30 to 35 °C/ 95 °F.

Viticulture and vine varieties

The number of permitted grape varieties was increased in 2009 to 14 (five red, nine white), and their distribution varies in different parts of the region. The most widely planted variety is the dark-skinned TEMPRANILLO, which ripens well on the clay and limestone slopes of Rioja Alta and Rioja Alavesa, where it forms the basis for the region's best wines and in 2012 was planted on 48,000 ha/115,000 ha, more than thee-quarters of the total vineyard surface.

Most Riojas are blends of more than one variety, however, and wines made from the GARNACHA vine, which after phylloxera superseded native varieties in the Rioja Baja, are often used to add BODY to Tempranillo, which can taste thin on its own in cooler VINTAGES. Two further red varieties, Mazuelo (Cariñena or CARIGNAN) and GRACIANO, are of relatively minor importance. Owing to its susceptibility to disease and its low productivity, Graciano fell from favour with Rioja's vine-growers before a strong revival in the 1990s, when the area devoted to this variety grew back to 200 ha/500 acres and VARIETAL versions are no longer oddities.

The CABERNET SAUVIGNON vines which arrived with the French in the 19th century are allowed as 'experimental' grapes and may be used, as MERLOT is too, in blends as minority components, but may not be mentioned on the label except as 'other varieties'.

The fifth red wine variety, authorized in 2009, was Maturana Tinta. But, in a chaotic turn of events, a different variety has actually been planted under that name which can be found on labels. When regional viticulturists began recovering old, minority grape varieties around the turn of the 21st century, several red ones showed good potential. Maturana was one. It was later identified through DNA PROFILING as Galicia's Merenzao, which, in turn, is the Jura's TROUSSEAU—present for centuries, under several names in Spain, Portugal, and the Canary Islands. Another red grape was named Maturana Tinta de Navarrete, as it was recovered and reproduced from a few vines in that Rioja village. Although the 'Trousseau' Maturana was the one registered with the Ministry of Agriculture, the deep-coloured, peppery one from Navarrete was preferred by growers and planted commercially. The Consejo Regulador looked the other way when it was identified as just 'Maturana Tinta' on labels. In 2011 it was shown to be Castets, an almost extinct member of the Bordeaux grape family.

Historically, until PHYLLOXERA arrived, Rioja's chief white grape variety was called MALVASÍA, a synonym for the lowly ALARIJE of west central Spain. On its own, it produced rich, alcoholic, dry white wines which responded well to ageing in oak. However, Viura (known elsewhere in Spain as MACABEO) took over as the most planted light-berried variety in the region and from the early 1970s, fresher-tasting, cool-fermented, early-bottled white wines were in FASHION all over Spain. By the 1990s, most white Riojas were made exclusively from Viura, and Malvasía vines were extremely difficult to find, although some of the traditional oak-aged whites and new barrel-fermented wines are blends of Malvasía and Viura.

A third traditional grape, Garnacha Blanca, was legal but rare. In 2009, Verdejo, Sauvignon Blanc, and Chardonnay were also permitted but may not be a majority component of blends. There has been very little interest in them. Also legalized then were three recovered white local varieties that have attracted considerably more attention: Tempranillo Blanco, a relatively recent mutation of Tempranillo; Maturana Blanca, which is not related to either one of the Maturana Tintas; and Turruntés, a local name for the ALBILLO Mayor which is more common further south, around the Duero/Douro River.

Vineyards in Rioja tend to be small, especially in Rioja Alta and Rioja Alavesa, where vines are often interspersed with other crops. Vines used to be free-standing BUSH VINES trained into low goblet shapes (see GOBELET), but of the thousands of hectares of new vineyard which have been planted since the 1970s, most are trained on WIRES. This resulted in a marked and alarming increase in YIELDS in the region in the 1990s, even before IRRIGATION was legalized in the late 1990s. Official DO limits are 63 hl/ha (3.5 tons/acre) for white wines and 45 hl/ha for reds.

Winemaking

Grapes are usually delivered to large, central wineries belonging either to one of the CO-OPERATIVES or to a merchant's bodega. Most wineries in Rioja are reasonably well equipped with a modern STAINLESS STEEL plant and facilities for TEMPERATURE CONTROL.

Rioja winemaking is characterized not by fermentation techniques but by BARREL MATURATION, however, and the shape and size of the 225-l *barrica bordelesa* introduced by the French in the mid 19th century is laid down by law. The regulations also specify the minimum ageing period for each officially recognized category of wine. In Rioja, red wines labelled CRIANZA and RESERVA must spend at least a year in oak, while a GRAN RESERVA must spend at least two years. In common with other Spanish wine regions, American OAK has been the favoured WOOD TYPE for wine maturation. New American oak barrels give the soft, vanilla flavour that has become accepted as typical of Rioja, but a similar effect can also be achieved by slow, OXIDATIVE maturation in older barrels. French oak is used increasingly, however. Over 40% of all Rioja falls into one of the three oak-aged categories above (the rest is either white, rosé, or sold as young, unoaked JOVEN red, much of it within Spain), and the larger bodegas therefore need tens of thousands of casks. Most bodegas renew their *barricas* on a regular basis; new oak use is on the increase and the

r

number of traditional producers who pride themselves on the age of their casks is dwindling. Some new producers are also spurning the tradional categories and bottling their oak-aged wine with a basic, generic Rioja back label. This enables them, among other things, to use different sized barrels or larger oak vats.

After the widespread adoption of cool fermentation techniques in the 1970s, the amount of oak-aged white Rioja progressively diminished. López de Heredia, Marqués de Murrieta, and only a few other bodegas upheld the traditional style by ageing their white wines in oak *barricas*. For whites labelled Crianza, Reserva, or Gran Reserva, the minimum wood-ageing period is just six months with a further year, two years, or four years respectively before the wines may be released for sale. By the mid 1990s, a large number of producers had switched to fashionable BARREL FERMENTATION, however, in effect reviving the region's traditional white wine vinification method.

Some reds as well as whites may occasionally need ACIDIFICATION.

Organization of trade

Rioja's vineyards are split among nearly 20,000 growers, most of whom tend their plots as a sideline and have no WINEMAKING facilities of their own, although in Rioja Alavesa they have been financially encouraged by the Basque regional government to acquire them. Many growers have an established contract with one of the merchant bodegas, whose numbers rocketed from about 100 in the mid 1990s to more than 500 a decade later. Others belong to one of the 30 CO-OPERATIVES that serve the region and receive around 45% of the grapes. Most co-operatives sell their produce, either as must or as newly made wine, to the merchant bodegas, who blend, bottle, and market the wine under their own labels.

In the 1980s, a number of bodegas bought up large tracts of land to plant their own vineyards, although few have sufficient to supply their entire needs. A number of single ESTATES, such as Contino and Remelluri, have also emerged, with the distinction, rare for the region, of growing, vinifying, and marketing their own wines.

Like other Spanish DOs, Rioja is controlled by a CONSEJO REGULADOR. Based in Logroño, the Consejo keeps a register of all vineyards and bodegas and monitors the movement of stocks from the vineyard to the bottle. The Consejo also maintains laboratories at Haro and Laguardia where tests are carried out on all wines before they are approved for export. After a long debate dating from the 1970s, Rioja was granted DOCA status in 1991. The qualifications have little to do with absolute quality, the single most important being that Rioja's grape prices are at least 200% above the national average.

The Consejo Regulador set itself the target of mandatory BOTTLING within the region, was defeated in the EU court in 1992, but finally won on appeal in 2000.   V. de la S.

Barquín, J., Guitiérrez, L., and de la Serna, V., *The Finest Wines of Rioja and Northwest Spain* (London, 2011).
uk.riojawine.com.
www.gruporioja.es

Ripaille, named CRU from a historic vineyard on the south eastern shore of Lake Geneva whose name may be added to the French appellation Vin de SAVOIE for wines from the Chasselas grape. Ch de Ripaille is the only producer.

riparia, species of the VITIS genus native to North America much used in developing suitably resistant ROOTSTOCKS and HYBRIDS.

ripasso, Italian term meaning literally 'repassed', for the technique of adding extra flavour, and alcohol, to VALPOLICELLA by refermenting the young wine on the unpressed skins of AMARONE wines after these DRIED-GRAPE WINES have finished their fermentation in the spring, and RACKED off. Regularly aged in new barriques to add a sweet note of vanilla and often with residual sweetness, Valpolicella Ripasso became a roaring success as a cheaper alternative to Amarone, with production rising from 7.5 million bottles in 2007 to more than 25 million bottles in 2013. By law the volume of ripasso obtained by this method may be double that of the Amarone that has been racked off before, while 15% of Amarone may also be added to improve its quality. This marked increase in the volume of Ripasso has been at the expense of straight Valpolicella, which decreased in the same period from 35.9 million bottles to under 20 million in 2013.   W.S.

ripeness, term used to describe that stage of the continuous process of grape RIPENING or development which is chosen by the winemaker and/or grape processor as that desired at HARVEST. What constitutes the ideal chemical and physical composition of grapes at this point is a subjective judgement dependent on wine style, the winemaker's current belief about optimal ripeness, FASHION, and many other factors, so ripeness is a relative term which can have many different meanings. Grapes considered at perfect ripeness by one winemaker for one purpose may be considered overripe or underripe by different winemakers for other uses.

Ripeness is often related to MUST WEIGHT or grape sugar concentration. Being directly related to POTENTIAL ALCOHOL, the concentration of SUGAR IN GRAPES has a major impact on wine type. The commercial table (non-fortified) wines of the world fall between two extremes.

One is represented by the very light whites, particularly from bigger brands in AUSTRALIA, for example, made from grapes harvested early, at night, and from cooler regions to give bottled wines that are refreshing, lower in calories, and low in ALCOHOLIC STRENGTH (9–11%). At the other extreme are the rich reds of the southern Rhône dominated by alcohol-rich GRENACHE or Cabernet from California's NAPA Valley that has been subjected to extended HANG TIME. These blockbusters may reach 16% alcohol or even more.

Sugar levels are not the only aspect of grape composition to affect what is considered ripeness. Especially in cool climates, ACIDITY levels can be closely monitored to determine the grapes' ripeness. The acidity in grapes declines with ripening, and must be below certain values (which differ for different wine styles) so that the resultant wine will not be too tart and unpalatable. In warm to hot regions it is more common that the acidity is too low and the PH is too high once sugars have reached the desired potential alcohol level.

Measures of sugar, acidity, and pH have been commonly used around the world to define grape ripeness and optimal harvest time, but growers and winemakers continue to search for better definitions of ripeness to improve wine quality. For red wine, measurements of grape PHENOLICS, including anthocyanins and tannins, are proving useful. For all grapes, a measure that indicates flavour is so eagerly sought that it may be said to be the grape researcher's holy grail (PHYSIOLOGICAL RIPENESS). This is a particularly difficult measurement because of the huge diversity of potential. See FLAVOUR COMPOUNDS, on the one hand, and their minute concentration on the other.

It is increasingly common for grapes to be tasted in the field, often by the winemakers, in an attempt to assess optimal harvest date. However, the ability to taste phenolic and other compounds in a sugar-rich substrate makes the practice subjective and of arguable merit. Flavour is also difficult to assess when it is partly present only as FLAVOUR PRECURSORS. The development of a measure of flavour precursors plus other GLYCOSIDES through analysis of the GLYCOSYL-GLUCOSE concentration of grapes and wines is another possible approach to this problem but INFRARED SPECTROSCOPY is proving to be more useful in the ANALYSIS of many different grape and wine components.

Individual grapes' physical condition, especially skin thickness and integrity, is also considered as an aspect of grape ripeness relevant to wine quality.

See also GRAPE COMPOSITION AND WINE QUALITY, and GRAPE JUICE COMPOSITION.   R.E.S. & B.G.C.

ripeness measurement. See MUST WEIGHT, RIPENESS, RIPENING, GRAPE.

ripening, grape. The important process of grape development which is a prelude to HARVEST. Ripening begins when the berries soften at the stage called VERAISON and is concluded normally by harvest, which can occur at different stages for different wine styles. Ripening can be affected by many plant, pest and disease, and environmental factors, and is in many ways the most important vine process affecting wine quality since it is so crucially related to the chemical and physical composition of the harvested fruit, and so to eventual wine quality.

Following FRUIT SET, grape berries grow in size but are hard, green, and very acidic (see GRAPE). When almost half their final size, veraison, or the inception of ripening, occurs. The timing of this will depend on variety and climate, but it is normally 40 to 60 days after fruit set, longer for cooler climates. The period from veraison to harvest will obviously depend on the harvest stage of ripeness required, but for grapes destined for dry table wine the period varies from about 30 days in hot regions to about 70 days in cooler regions. For early-ripening varieties such as Pinot Noir and Chardonnay, the ripening period is shorter than for a variety such as Cabernet Sauvignon, which ripens relatively late.

Not all bunches on a vine nor berries on a bunch are at the same stage of development; the first flowers to open set the first berries, which in turn go through veraison and ripen first. During the latter stages of ripening when the sugar content is above 20 °BRIX, the berry skin may lose some water. So for very ripe grapes the increase in concentration of sugar, for example, in the berry is due to a loss of water rather than more movement into the berry.

It is relevant to consider ripening in terms of the various chemical compounds of most interest to the winemaker. Sugar, or more precisely SUCROSE, is the most important. It is moved from the leaves to the berries by TRANSLOCATION, and is broken down to the constituent molecules GLUCOSE and FRUCTOSE by the enzyme INVERTASE. Sucrose may originate from current PHOTOSYNTHESIS or from stored CARBOHYDRATE reserves in the woody parts of the vine such as its trunk, arms, and roots. Heavy crop loads slow the increase in concentration of SUGAR IN GRAPES, as also do factors slowing photosynthesis such as low or high temperatures and cloudiness. There can also be competition for the products of photosynthesis; if shoot tips are growing actively, for example, then fruit ripening is slowed (see VIGOUR).

The second major indicator of grape ripening is ACIDITY. The concentration of TARTARIC ACID falls during ripening, due to dilution effects associated with berry growth. The concentration of MALIC ACID falls more quickly than tartaric during ripening, and this is because of temperature-dependent RESPIRATION in addition to dilution. Grapes ripening in cool climates therefore tend to have higher acidity as less malic acid is respired. Juice PH rises throughout ripening due to the decreases in free acids and increases in POTASSIUM. In hot regions, alarmingly high juice pH is a great concern for wine quality and ACIDIFICATION of the must may be necessary.

The skin colour of red grapes is due to ANTHOCYANINS; veraison is signalled as they replace the green colour of chlorophyll. Anthocyanin concentration rises during ripening and the value at harvest depends on both environmental and plant factors. Temperature and light have major effects; high temperatures and low light levels reduce skin coloration in many varieties. Grape TANNINS are distributed between the skins, seeds, and stems. They increase during ripening at a rate comparable to anthocyanins.

The most abundant minerals in the grape are POTASSIUM, CALCIUM, MAGNESIUM, and SODIUM, and they increase in concentration during ripening. Potassium is predominant and has a major effect on juice pH. Potassium is distributed between flesh and skins, and the potassium extracted from skins during fermentation is one reason why red wines have a higher pH than white wines.

Flavour compounds are all-important factors in wine quality, even if their measurement is many years away from becoming a universal practice (although see ANALYSIS). At the beginning of the 21st century, analytical techniques as well as knowledge about their role were still a developing science. See FLAVOUR PRECURSORS and FLAVOUR COMPOUNDS.

See also GRAPE JUICE COMPOSITION, GRAPE QUALITY ASSESSMENT, RIPENESS, and PHYSIOLOGICAL RIPENESS.   R.E.S. & B.G.C.

Coombe, B. G., 'Research on development and ripening of the grape berry', *American Journal of Enology and Viticulture*, 43 (1992), 101–10.
Hamilton, R. P., and Coombe, B. G., 'Harvesting of wine grapes', in B. G. Coombe and P. R. Dry (eds.), *Viticulture*, ii: *Practices* (Adelaide, 1992).
Tregoat, O., et al., 'Étude du régime hydrique et de la nutrition azotée de la vigne par des indicateurs physiologiques. Influence sur le comportement de la vigne et la maturation du raisin (*Vitis vinifera* L. cv Merlot, 2000, Bordeaux)', *Journal International des Sciences de la Vigne et du Vin*, 36/3 (2002), 133–42.

ripping is a viticultural operation conducted in many parts of the world before PLANTING a vineyard in order to to break up compact soils so that water can penetrate and roots can grow to a greater depth. Normally bulldozers or heavy tractors are used along row lines, which also makes it easier to insert vineyard posts.

Ripping also provides the opportunity to incorporate FERTILIZERS and soil amendments (see SOIL AMELIORATION) such as phosphates, forms of potassium or lime, as they will not readily leach through the soil.

Ripping is a procedure, like IRRIGATION, which can modify some important properties of the soil affecting wine quality; see TERROIR.   R.E.S.

Coombe, B. G., and Dry, P. R. (eds.), *Viticulture*, ii: *Practices* (Adelaide, 1992).

ripping out. See GRUBBING UP.

Riserva, nebulous Italian term usually denoting a wine given extended AGEING before release, and suggesting a higher quality than the normal version of the same wine. However, only few Riservas, notably COLLIO GORIZIANO Riserva and VINO NOBILE DI MONTEPULCIANO Riserva, have stricter production regulations, such as higher minimum ALCOHOLIC STRENGTH (therefore mirroring the SUPERIORE designation), and higher minimum EXTRACT. Chianti Classico Riserva, for example, questionably allows CHAPTALISATION to add up to 0.5% alcohol by volume. The ageing requirement for Riservas varies from DOC to DOC, but normally is a minimum of one year, up to 62 months for Barolo Riserva. In many cases this must include a period in CASK, as well as in bottle (with the notable exception of Chianti Classico Riserva, which does not require any wood ageing, however common it is in practice).

In most cases Riserva does not guarantee higher quality, because producers are not required to declare a Riserva before the harvest. They may decide to designate a wine Riserva on an ad hoc basis. This latitude has allowed some producers simply to reclassify their unsold inventory as Riserva in an effort to obtain a higher price, prompting calls for the abolition of the entire category. In some cases the prolonged oak ageing accelerates the wine's development, resulting in PREMATURE OXIDATION and stewed fruit flavours, even though the category is meant to denote wines with the inherent capacity for prolonged ageing. In some cases such as Barolo, it is not clear why a higher quality denomination is needed when there are so many single-vineyard, or CRU, bottlings.   W.S.

Rivairenc. See ASPIRAN.

Rivaner, another name for MÜLLER-THURGAU, used in LUXEMBOURG, where it is the most planted grape variety.

Riverina, major Australian wine region on the Murrumbidgee River in southern NEW SOUTH WALES. The base of McWilliam's, De Bortoli, and Casella, of YELLOW TAIL fame. Griffith is its main town. There may be only 20 producers, but the volumes are very substantial. Most wines made here are described coyly as coming from South Eastern Australia.

Riverland, the most productive wine region in AUSTRALIA, with 76 producers and a sprawl of vineyards irrigated by the River Murray mainly in the state of SOUTH AUSTRALIA. The same market forces as described in MURRAY DARLING are forcing grape growers to improve the quality, and also to ensure they have the right varietal mix in an ever-changing market place. Petit Verdot is an established speciality and hot-climate Italian varieties such as Vermentino, Fiano, Montepulciano, and Nero d'Avola are catching on. South Eastern Australia is the catch-all description usually found on labels.

rivers have played an important role throughout the history of wine, both as arteries of trade and also through their action in helping to shape valley slopes particularly well suited to the cultivation of the vine. More recently they have provided valuable IRRIGATION water.

A river is crucial to the earliest detailed account of the wine trade. HERODOTUS, writing in the 5th century BC, records how in MESOPOTAMIA wine in palm-wood casks was loaded onto boats in the upper reaches of the river Tigris, and then sailed down to Babylon, where the boats were broken up because of the impossibility of paddling them upstream against the current.

During the Roman era, rivers continued to play a vital role in the transport of bulky items such as wine. There were two main trade routes in GAUL: a western one from Narbonne to Toulouse and then along the river GARONNE to Bordeaux and the Atlantic; and a northern one up the RHÔNE to Lyons, and thence along the Saône, before cutting across country to the MOSEL and the RHINE, and eventually reaching the North sea. These routes witnessed the transport of thousands of AMPHORAE of wine, but they were also a highway along which the idea of vine cultivation and winemaking passed. By the 1st century AD, viticulture was thus well established along the Rhône and the Garonne, and gradually vineyards came to be cultivated along most of the other major river valleys of Gaul such as the LOIRE and the Seine (see PARIS).

By the year 1000, although vineyards were relatively widely established throughout southern Europe, in the north they were found most frequently in river valleys. The main reason for this was the high cost of overland transport, which gave those with easy access to the main fluvial transport routes a distinct competitive advantage. Environmental factors were also important, with the south-facing slopes of such valleys providing ideal sites because of the extra exposure to the sun that they afforded (see VINEYARD SITE SELECTION). This is particularly evident in the development of vineyards in the cool Mosel–Rhine area, where most of those established before 1050 were in close proximity to rivers.

Coastal transport became increasingly important during the later medieval period, but rivers also maintained their role as arteries of the wine trade, and, with the opening up of eastern Europe, rivers such as the Dnestr, the Vistula, and the Danube came to play as significant a role as did the Garonne, Loire, Seine, Rhône, and Rhine in the west.

In the 19th and 20th centuries, with the development of the RAILWAYS and, subsequently, efficient road transport, it is the environmental factors that have been most important in determining the location of vineyards along the slopes of river valleys. Above all, these locations provide additional sunshine, generally alleviate the problems associated with FROST and excess humidity (see HILLSIDE VINEYARDS), and frequently have soils well suited to vine cultivation (see TOPOGRAPHY). Moreover, in some special locations, as in SAUTERNES and along the Rhine, the proximity to water provides the ideal conditions for NOBLE ROT, which can result in some of the world's greatest sweet wines.

In the New World, certain rivers have been crucial to the development of several wine regions. The Murray river in Australia, for example, is responsible for the existence of that country's extensive RIVERLAND vineyards, California's CENTRAL VALLEY depends on riverwater, and most of the vineyards in WASHINGTON state depend on water from the Columbia river.

P.T.H.U.

Postan, M. M., and Miller, E. (eds.), *The Cambridge Economic History of Europe*, ii: *Trade and Industry in the Middle Ages* (2nd edn, Cambridge, 1987).

Pounds, N. J. G., *An Historical Geography of Europe 450 BC–AD 1330* (Cambridge, 1973).

Schenk, W., 'Viticulture in Franconia along the river Main: human and natural influences since AD 700', *Journal of Wine Research*, 3/3 (1992), 185–204.

Rivesaltes, town north of Perpignan in southern France that gives its name to two of the biggest appellations of ROUSSILLON, Rivesaltes and **Muscat de Rivesaltes**, both of them VINS DOUX NATURELS. Muscat de Rivesaltes, which represents about 70% of France's total Muscat production, can in fact be produced throughout most of Roussillon's recognized wine-producing area, together even with some sections of the Aude *département* to the north (including much of the FITOU appellation). The Rivesaltes production zone is similarly generous but specifically excludes those vineyards that produce BANYULS. In 2012 a total of 2,946 ha/7,277 acres were dedicated to the production of strong, sweet Rivesaltes in its many colours and styles.

The Muscats of 'Perpinyà' and 'Clayrà' (Claira is the next town to Rivesaltes) were already sought out by 14th-century wine buyers from as far away as Barcelona and Avignon. Their sweetness was originally concentrated by leaving the grapes on the vine to shrivel, as was still the custom in the 19th century (see DRIED-GRAPE WINES), and may even have been enhanced by adding honey, for which the region is still famous. Today Muscat de Rivesaltes is the only Muscat vin doux naturel which may be made from MUSCAT OF ALEXANDRIA as well as the finer MUSCAT BLANC À PETITS GRAINS, which was once unpopular for its degeneration and unreliable yields; but new clones are being replanted. Average yields of these low-trained vines, often on difficult-to-work dry terraces, can be as little as 17 hl/ha (1 ton/acre) (the official upper limit is 30 hl/ha). Since the 1980s, more skilled vinification has helped improve quality, despite the domination of Muscat of Alexandria. Techniques include SKIN CONTACT and MUTAGE *sur marc*, i.e. on the skins. Muscat de Rivesaltes is already on sale the spring after the harvest and should be drunk as young and cool as possible, either as an aperitif or with fruit or creamy desserts.

The even more common Rivesaltes, on the other hand, has the potential, not often realized, to be a more complex vin doux naturel, made in all conceivable colours and styles, generally depending on different producers' TERROIR. These sweet, heady, wines can be made from any permutation of Grenache Blanc, Noir, and Gris, Maccabéo, and to a much lesser extent Vermentino (here called Malvoisie du Roussillon), and the two Muscats allowed for Muscat de Rivesaltes. Varietal Rivesaltes are permitted, from a golden Maccabéo to a Grenache Noir that can be anything from crimson to deep chocolate brown, depending on its ÉLEVAGE. These tests for FOOD AND WINE MATCHING may be vinified 'en blanc', like white wines without any contact with the skins, or may be macerated for weeks in an effort to leach maximum colour, tannin, and flavour into the wine. They may be fermented in stainless steel and bottled young or fermented and aged in wooden casks of all ages and sizes, sometimes according to some sort of SOLERA. Some wines are made to taste deliberately RANCIO and, while some producers deliberately expose the maturing wine to the punishing heat and light of a Roussillon noon, others may include a period in glass BONBONNES in the ageing process. No Rivesaltes can be released until 16 months after the harvest. Rivesaltes may taste of raisins, coffee, chocolate, fruits, or nuts and the most concentrated can, like Banyuls, be some of the few wines that happily partner chocolate.

Riviera di Ponente, or **Riviera Ligure di Ponente,** extensive, overarching Ligurian DOC along the north-western coast of Italy producing wines made of VERMENTINO (called Pigato here) and ALICANTE (probably GRENACHE), and ROSSESE DI DOLCEAQUA. For more details, see LIGURIA.

Rizling, term for the white grape variety known variously in central Europe as

WELSCHRIESLING, OLASZ RIZLING, LAŠKI RIZLING, and RIESLING ITALICO. The Germans disapprove of any name for this inferior grape variety which suggests a relationship with their own noble RIESLING vine, but will accept Rizling as a suitably distinctive alternative.

Rkatsiteli, ancient, cold-hardy Georgian white grape variety which was so widely planted in what was the Soviet Union that in 1990 it was estimated to be the world's third most planted overall. Thanks to President GORBACHEV's vine pull scheme, by 2000 it had fallen to fourteenth place. It is still widely planted in the former Soviet republics, however, being grown in all of its wine-producing independent republics with the exception of TURKMENISTAN. It is, understandably, most important in GEORGIA, particularly in Kakheti. It is also the most planted variety in UKRAINE, second only to Muscat Ottonel in BULGARIA, is widely planted in MOLDOVA, and is commonplace in RUSSIA and ARMENIA. As Baiyu it reached China and has adapted well to the inland wine regions there with their cold winters. It was presumably its cold resistance that inspired Finger Lakes grower Konstantin Frank to plant it in New York state and it is now planted in Virginia and several other American states.

Much is demanded of this productive variety and it achieves much, providing a base for a wide range of wine styles, including fortified wines and brandy. The wine is distinguished by a keen level of ACIDITY, easily 9 g/l even when picked as late as October, and by good sugar levels too.

Roannaise, Côte, hand-crafted, lightish reds and some rosés made chiefly from locally adapted GAMAY grapes, called St-Romain à Jus Blanc here, using Beaujolais cellar techniques, usually SEMI-CARBONIC MACERATION. The south east-facing slopes of the upper Loire, on which vines are grown on a granitic base, are only one range of hills west of the BEAUJOLAIS region. Direct RIVER and canal links with Paris gave the region's wines relative fame and popularity in the 19th century so that annual production was almost 800,000 hl/21.1 million gal at the beginning of the 20th century. Production was down to 4,000 hl by 1994 when APPELLATION CONTRÔLÉE status was won and was 5,656 hl from 161 ha of vineyards in 2012. Wine quality is in the hands of individual winemakers (unlike Côtes du FOREZ to the south), egged on by the Troisgros family at their famous restaurant in the town of Roanne.

Robertson, important warm, dry, wine-producing district within the Breede River Valley region in SOUTH AFRICA. Home of many estates and CO-OPERATIVES, it produces some fine whites, including Chardonnays and Sauvignon Blancs, and an increasingly creditable array of reds, most notably Shiraz and Cabernet. Bonnievale is the best known of the district's wards. Most vineyards fringe the Breede River, which provides the essential IRRIGATION (rainfall is less than 400 mm/16 in annually) and ALLUVIAL soils although CALCIUM-rich outcrops are also found. Most of the INTERNATIONAL VARIETIES perform well here although Robertson has long enjoyed a reputation for lovely fortified MUSCADELS and off-dry Colombards. Robertson produces more than 15% of the national harvest. Average daily growing season temperatures are high.

Robola, wine and grape variety for which the Ionian island of Cephalonia in GREECE is most famous. The distinctively powerful, lemony dry white is made entirely from Robola grapes, which are cultivated almost exclusively on the island. The wine made from these early-ripening grapes is high in both acidity and extract and is much prized within Greece. DNA PROFILING established that Robola is quite distinct from REBULA (RIBOLLA Gialla). The few hundred hectares are mainly limited to the Ionian islands of GREECE.

robotic lagar, initial name for a computer-operated LAGAR pioneered by the SYMINGTONS for the production of PORT when LABOUR costs soared.

robots. See LABOUR and MECHANIZATION.

Rochelle, La. See LA ROCHELLE.

rock, a rigid, naturally bonded aggregate of geological MINERALS. A mass of sand or volcanic ash, or a molten lava, would not be be regarded as rock although this is the case in some historical texts; neither would concrete. The solid Earth is made chiefly of rock. Its outermost surface is known as bedrock (see GEOLOGY), which is generally overlain by a more or less disintegrated zone of SUBSOIL, and then possibly by agricultural SOIL, although in vineyards such divisions are unusually hazy.

A fragment of bedrock is commonly called a rock or a STONE, with more specific names used to indicate its size or smoothness (see GEOLOGY). The stones seen in many vineyard soils may or may not represent the local bedrock (see ALLUVIUM and COLLUVIUM). Vines cannot obtain nutrition directly from bedrock or from stones, except by the action of MYCORRHIZAL fungi.

A.J.M.

Rockpile, California AVA with vineyards but no winery. See SONOMA.

Roditis, or **Rhoditis**, slightly pink-skinned grape variety that is GREECE's second most common after SAVATIANO on a total of 9,127 ha/22,544 acres in 2013. Although its name is probably derived from the island of Rhodes, it was traditionally grown, often as a FIELD BLEND with other clones of Roditis, in the Peloponnese and was even more important in the pre-PHYLLOXERA era. The vine is particularly sensitive to POWDERY MILDEW. It ripens relatively late and keeps its acidity quite well even in such hot climates as that of Ankhíalos in Thessaly in central Greece, although it can also ripen well in high-elevation vineyards. It is often blended with the softer SAVATIANO, particularly for RETSINA.

Roditis Kokkinos, or **Rhoditis Kokkino**, meaning 'red of Rhodes', is a red-skinned Greek grape variety traditionally grown in the Peloponnese that has been shown by DNA PROFILING to be distinct from, even if often planted with, the more common pink-berried RODITIS. Also known as Tourkopoula.

Roederer, Louis, family-owned Champagne house known both for its early links with the Russian court and for its extensive vineyard ownership. The original company was founded by a M. Dubois around 1776; Louis Roederer joined in 1827, becoming owner in 1833. By the second half of the century, RUSSIA had become the major market for Champagne Louis Roederer: 666,386 bottles out of a total company production of 2.5 million were exported there in 1873. In 1876, Louis Roederer was commissioned by Tsar Alexander II to create a special personal cuvée in clear glass crystal bottles that was named Cristal. But in 1917 the Russian Revolution brought the immediate loss of the company's principal export market. Camille Orly-Roederer, widow of the great-nephew of Louis, rebuilt the company after this blow, in particular by strengthening Roederer's vineyard holdings at a time when other houses were selling, a move many later regretted. In 1924, responding to demand for the legendary Cristal, she reintroduced it, bottled in the original design of crystal glass with no PUNT, creating the first PRESTIGE CUVÉE champagne. By the mid 2010s the company's vineyards extended over 240 ha/593 acres, much of it in the Grands and Premiers Crus villages. Mainly thanks to these vineyard holdings, Roederer produces more vintages of Cristal than is usual for a prestige cuvée. The company, unusually for a substantial champagne house, remains independent. Jean-Claude Rouzaud, Camille's grandson, continued in expansionist vein, buying more vineyards and investing in other wine regions. Roederer Estate in ANDERSON VALLEY, first released in 1988, was one of California's finest sparkling wines. An investment in Jansz in TASMANIA was terminated. The company, now headed by Frédéric Rouzaud, seventh generation to lead the company, also owns Adriano Ramos Pinto in Portugal, Champagne Deutz, Delas Rhône wines, Domaines Ott in Provence, and in Bordeaux Chx de Pez and Haut-Beauséjour in

St-Estèphe and, since 2007, second growth Ch Pichon Longueville Comtesse de Lalande in Pauillac.

Roero, increasingly important vineyard area and DOCG on sandy hills on the left bank of the River Tanaro in the PIEMONTE region of north-west Italy which takes its name from the villages of Montaldo Roero, Monteu Roero, and Santo Stefano Roero to the north west of Alba. Geographically as well as administratively it is not part of the LANGHE, from which it is separated by the River Tanaro, but it shares its most important red grape variety, NEBBIOLO, although the wines tend to be softer and earlier-maturing than those from BARBARESCO and BAROLO. In spite of ongoing marketing efforts, Roero's expression of Nebbiolo deserves to be better known. This is perhaps why many Roero producers own vineyards in or buy grapes from the more famous Barbaresco. Significant quantities of red BARBERA and white ARNEIS are also grown in Roero.   W.S.

Arnulfo, C., *Langhe e Roero—From the Soil to the Glass* (Cuneo, 2012).

Rolland, Michel (1947–), the most famous CONSULTANT oenologist, responsible in several ways for the current FASHION for overtly ripe, deep-coloured, supple red bordeaux. He and his wife Dany have since 1973 run a laboratory in POMEROL on which many local growers depend for ANALYSIS. In 2013, after separating, they sold Michel's family properties Chx Le Bon Pasteur in Pomerol, Bertineau St-Vincent in Lalande de Pomerol, and Rolland-Maillet in St-Émilion to an Asian investor but continue to be responsible for their winemaking. They also farm Ch La Grande Clotte in Lussac-St-Émilion and Dany lives at Ch Fontenil in Fronsac, acquired in 1986. The Bordeaux RIGHT BANK enterprises to which he is consultant are too numerous to list (although they have included L'Angélus, Beau-Séjour Bécot, Clinet, Clos l'Église, La Dominique, La Gaffelière, Grand Mayne, Larmande, Pavie, Pavie-Decesse, and Troplong-Mondot). In the Médoc and Graves they have included many properties managed by négociants Dourthe and Chx Fieuzal, Kirwan, Léoville-Poyferré, Malescot St-Exupéry, Pape-Clément, Smith Haut Lafitte, and La Tour Martillac. He has also made wine for Skalli of the Languedoc, the arch-promulgator of varietal VIN DE PAYS. But it is his consultancies outside France that set him apart from all but a handful of his countrymen in the breadth of his experience: Simi, Newton, Merryvale, Cuvaison, St-Supéry, and Harlan in California; Marqués de Cáceres, Bodegas Palacio, Marqués de Griñon in Spain; ORNELLAIA in Italy (after TCHELISTCHEFF); Etchart and Trapiche in Argentina; Casa Lapostolle in Chile; Pajzos in Hungary; Grover in India; and many more, bringing

the total number of clients for him and his team of ten to more than 200 in 17 different countries. The Rollands and their two daughters also have holdings in Bonne Nouvelle in South Africa (with Remhoogte Estate), Campo Eliseo in Toro (with Francois LURTON), and Clos de los Siete, Val de Flores, and Mariflor in Argentina. He studied oenology at the University of BORDEAUX during the PEYNAUD era and has continued to declare his philosophy that wine should give maximum pleasure, although he has been criticized for a certain uniformity of style.

Rolle, officially accepted alternative southern French name for the increasingly popular VERMENTINO used traditionally in BELLET and parts of Languedoc-Roussillon. DNA PROFILING has shown it to be distinct from ROLLO.

Rollo, ancient Ligurian white wine grape with several names but distinct from ROLLE, planted on just 38 ha/94 acres according to the 2010 Italian vine census.

Romagna, eastern part of EMILIA-ROMAGNA.

Romagna Sangiovese, quantitatively important VARIETAL DOC made from the most widely cultivated red grape variety in ROMAGNA. In 2010 a total of 7,100 ha/17,537 acres of Sangiovese were planted, with some 3,000 ha registered for the production of DOC wine.

The reputation of the zone has been sullied by production rules geared towards high yields and quick turnover of wines, by the mediocre quality of much of the wine produced, especially by the CO-OPERATIVES that dominate here, and by the erroneous belief that the CLONES of SANGIOVESE in Romagna are inferior to those in Tuscany. Sangiovese di Romagna is part of the same Sangiovese Grosso group as, for example, BRUNELLO, but old bush vines around Predappio in Romagna appear to be of the Lamole variety, which has a higher phenolic content and produces smaller grapes resulting in higher extract in the final wines.

In the past the enormous size of the DOC made irrelevant any possible differences in clones as well as sites to all but the very few seriously ambitious Romagnan producers, but recent changes in the DOC's regulation have established the creation of 12 subzones, which can be broadly grouped in three different macro zones. Faentino, the vineyard area around Faenza (with the subzones of Serra, Brisighella, Modigliana, Marzeno, and Oriolo) whose vineyards are rich in iron and clay and planted at an elevation of up to 200 m, and with more calcareous soils over 200 m towards the Appenines. Forlivese around Forlì (with the subzones Castrocaro-Terra del Sole, Predappio, Bertinoro, and Medola), has predominantly clay soils, while soils towards the Appenines have a higher iron and sandstone content. Cesanese

around Cesena (with the sub zones of Cesena, San Vicinio, and Longiano) has hillside vineyards up to 200 m and, where due to the vicinity of the coast, a more moderate climate prevails and soils consisting of calcareous clay. Stylistic differences based on subzones are beginning to become a reality, but heavy-handed winemaking, and especially the overuse of new French oak, tends to obscure these for the moment, although a return to ageing the wines in large oak cask instead is noticeable. Producers willing to mention the subzone on their labels must include at least 95% Sangiovese in the wines and yields must not exceed 9 tonnes/ha (compared with 85% Sangiovese and 12 tonnes/ha for regular Romagna Sanviovese). In youth, Romagna Sangiovese tends to be a dense, muscular wine informed by the variety's hallmark acidity, but it can age well into a more complex, multi-layered whole.

A group of quality-oriented producers known as Convito di Romagna goes even further. A voluntarily imposed set of production regulations, including even lower yields and the production of at least one pure Sangiovese wine, often from a single vineyard, has been their main strategy in proving that the wines can be on a par with the best from Tuscany. Such determination and the creation of subzones represent the first steps on the road towards quality from the quantity that still determines the region's output.   W.S.

Masnaghetti, A., *Romagna Sangiovese* (Monza, 2013) including map.

www.consorziovinidiromagna.it

Romagna Trebbiano, DOC in EMILIA-ROMAGNA in central Italy for neutral dry whites from TREBBIANO Romagnolo grapes. Permitted yields of up to 14 tonnes/ha result in very ordinary wines.

Romanée, **Romanée-Conti**, **Romanée-St-Vivant**, great red GRANDS CRUS, for more details of which, see VOSNE-ROMANÉE. See also DOMAINE DE LA ROMANÉE-CONTI.

Romania, sometimes spelt **Roumania** or **Rumania**, is eastern Europe's quantitatively most important wine producer The quality of its wines has improved considerably in recent years. In 2012, there were 183,170 ha/452,623 acres of vineyard planted to wine grapes, of which just over 97,500 ha/240,928 acres were *Vitis* VINIFERA according to data from Romania's National Office for Vine and Wine Products. In 2013 the harvest reached 5.9 million hl/156 million gal, partly thanks to around 30,000 ha of productive new vineyards planted since 2007 coming onstream.

History

The beginnings of Romanian viticulture are claimed to date back at least 4,000 years. The

ROMANIA

UKRAINE

HUNGARY

REPUBLIC OF MOLDOVA

Prut

Diosig
Crișana
Silvania
Biharia

Cotnari

Iași
Bohotin
MOLDOVAN HILLS

Lechința

CRIȘANA and
MARAMURES

TRANSYLVANIA

Aiud

Huși
Iana

Miniș

Alba
Târnave
Sebeș-
Apold

Panciu
Nicorești

Odobești

Dealu
Bujorului

Cotești

Recaș

Mures

Olt

Cernatești

Sarica-
Niculițel
Babadag

BANAT

Pietroasa
Dealu Mare
Ștefănești

DOBROGEA

BLACK
SEA

Banat

Sâmburești
MUNTENIA

Danube
Terraces

Bucharest

Murfatlar

OLTENIA

Drăgășani

Oltina
DANUBE TERRACES

Mehedinți

SERBIA

Banu Mărăcine

Danube

0   150 km

Segarcea

Danube
Terraces

BULGARIA

r

Wine-growing regions

region known today as Dobrogea, on the Black Sea, was settled by the Ancient GREEKS in the 7th century BC and they may have introduced viticulture. It seems that Romania or Dacia had a well-established wine culture and a fine reputation for food and wine, but in an attempt to put an end to repeated invasions, the Dacian king Burebista (1st century BC), ordered the destruction of all vineyards. However, after the Roman Emperor Trajan had conquered Dacia (102 AD), coins were minted depicting a woman being offered grapes by two children, proof that not all the vineyards were uprooted.

The region was overrun by successive cultural influences, including Hungary, the Ottoman Turks (and, later, Russians and Austro-Hungarians), but vine-growing seems to have continued uninterrupted. Romania's existence as a united political unit comprising the old principalities of Wallachia and Moldavia dates only from 1861, and Transylvania and Banat did not join Romania until after the First World War.

The total vineyard area grew from 95,000 ha in the 1860s to 150,000 ha/370,500 acres by 1884, when the PHYLLOXERA louse began its devastation of Romanian vineyards. As a result, resistant HYBRIDS dominated wine production in 1930. In 1949 collectivism and state control of the wine industry were introduced two years after Romania became a Peoples' Republic under direct military occupation by the SOVIET UNION in the 1950s. In 1967 the notorious dictator Nicolae Ceaușescu came to power, imposing a brutal and repressive Stalinist regime, until his death by firing squad in 1989.

In the 1950s and 1960s, in an effort to increase productivity, the total vineyard area was expanded, reaching more than 340,000 ha by 1972. Vine material was also selected for quantity and FROST resistance rather than for quality. Immediately prior to the revolution of December 1989, this figure had decreased, largely as a result of uprooting hybrids, to about 275,000 ha. During the communist period, the state

gradually increased its direct share of vineyard holdings to about 30% of the total by the end of the 1980s. About 60% was owned by state-owned CO-OPERATIVES, leaving just 10% in private hands, and those of the state-funded viticultural institutes. Most wine was produced by state-owned Vinalcool wineries, but since the early 1990s wineries have been privatized.

Romania has a Latin culture with a Romance language and wine has a strong cultural role. Official per capita consumption was a robust 25.7 l/6.8 gal in 2012, and this does not include the significant black market in homemade wines. Such wines are sold by the roadside or through markets without any tax being paid and may account for 50% of all wine consumed in Romania. White wine accounts for approximately 58% of official production, reflecting changing tastes towards drier styles (from the traditional preference for semi-dry and semi-sweet styles) and increasing red wine consumption. Romania has become a net wine importer, with imports in 2012 reaching 546,500 hl/14.5 million gal and exports totalling just 110,200 hl. Five big wine producers dominate the domestic market, with a 68% share between them.

By 2013 most wineries had bought land and owned significant consolidated vineyard holdings, which represents a major structural change in the Romanian wine industry. Romania joined the EU in 2007 and since then a number of small private estates with high quality aspirations have emerged.

Geography and climate

Although there is a coastal plain on the Black Sea coast, the country is dominated by mountains, the north–south eastern Carpathians and the east–west Transylvanian Alps, whose average ELEVATION is *c.*1,000 m/3,280 ft. The Wallachian Plain stretches south to the River Danube and Bulgaria, while the Pannonian Plain lies between the hills and Hungary to the west. Romania's wine regions are widely dispersed throughout the country, in a wide range of different conditions.

Romania lies on much the same latitudinal span as France, although its climate is much more CONTINENTAL yet the Black Sea influence helps to moderate winter temperatures in Dobrogea by the coast. Temperatures are high but rarely excessive in the growing season, and rainfall during the harvest is unusual in most wine regions. Average July temperature is 23.5 °C/74 °F and average annual rainfall is 540 mm/21 in.

Viticulture

Vine-TRAINING SYSTEMS used here traditionally were mainly GOBELET or single, double, or multiple bows, as in the MOSEL. From the late 1950s, a state plan to raise foreign currency by export-funded research led to a predominance of neatly wired rows using concrete posts and mainly GUYOT and CORDON training. In older vineyards, VINE DENSITY is typically low, although new vineyards can have as many as 4,500 vines per ha. MECHANIZATION of all vineyard operations has become the norm, a change forced by difficulties in finding LABOUR. EU funds have poured in, to the benefit of Romanian vineyards. More than 30,000 ha/75,000 acres have been planted since EU accession in 2007, particularly in areas such as Dobrogea, Târnave, Banat, and Dealul Mare. High-quality CLONES have been planted, with VSP and much closer spacing (4,000–5,000 vines/ha). A further 250,000 to 300,000 tonnes of grapes were expected annually by 2015. Older plantings and lesser varieties such as MUSCAT OF HAMBURG and CHASSELAS are disappearing. By 2014 IRRIGATION has been installed on less than 5% of Romania's vineyards but this was expected to change, especially in new vineyards, in view of CLIMATE CHANGE concerns and severe DROUGHTS in 2011, 2012, and 2013.

Winters can be very harsh in parts of Romania, although many of the longest-established wine regions have MESOCLIMATES which offer some protection. Trees act as natural WINDBREAKS in new areas such as Ştefăneşti. Some particularly FROST-prone valley floor vineyards require WINTER PROTECTION. Other viticultural hazards include both POWDERY and DOWNY MILDEW, as well as GREY ROT, particularly in fragmented vineyards where vines may be left untreated due to the cost of SPRAYING. Another potential problem for grape growers is theft of fruit, young vine plants, and even metal posts and wires, requiring larger operations to employ full-time security guards and dogs. Concern about crop loss also discourages smaller growers from waiting for optimum ripeness.

Winemaking

Winemaking in Romania has widely been updated to modern international standards with STAINLESS STEEL equipment, TEMPERATURE control, pneumatic PRESSES, etc. Much of this has been subsidized by the EU through SAPARD, which gave 50% subsidies retrospectively. Some traditional CONCRETE tanks, ROTARY fermenters, and large old Carpathian oak casks still exist but are being replaced. Large old wood casks are still favoured by older winemakers. Such problems as a lack of winery HYGIENE, OXIDATION, lack of fruit, and excess VOLATILE ACIDITY have become much less prevalent. The use of OAK has become more sophisticated with premium wines often aged in BARRIQUES and sometimes fermented in oak. French oak is widespread but Hungarian, American, and some Romanian cooperages are now making high-quality barrels.

Vine varieties

Romania is notable for the number and scope of its grapevine collections, with 95 wine varieties recorded in 2013. It also has a significant proportion of HYBRIDS. These hybrids are largely American direct producers (89,620 ha in 2011) and were due to be uprooted by 2014 under the terms of EU accession agreements, but this target will not be met. Industry data for 2013 showed that the most planted varieties by far are two white FETEASCĂS, Fetească Albă (12,633 ha/31,217 acres) and Fetească Regală (12,933 ha/31,958 acres), both of which can produce fresh, perfumed, dry white wines, though may be vinified with varying degrees of perceptible sweetness for the domestic market. Fetească Regală has more body and can be successfully BARREL FERMENTED. The third most planted white wine variety is Riesling Italico, or WELSCHRIESLING, grown on 7,671 ha but usually marketed locally simply as 'Riesling'. Note that genuine RIESLING was only grown on 128 ha. Aligoté (6,325 ha), Sauvignon (5,459 ha) then Muscat Ottonel (4,330 ha) are next, with the latter two

showing significant increases in plantings in the five years to 2013. Other white varieties that have shown significant increases by area include Chardonnay, Pinot Gris (usually marketed as Pinot Grigio), and TĂMÂIOASĂ Românească (the 'frankincense grape', a local clone of MUSCAT BLANC À PETIT GRAINS). Merlot is the most planted red wine variety with 11,636 ha/28,741 acres, followed by CABERNET SAUVIGNON with much less vineyard, 5,308 ha. Local grapes Roşioară (Bulgaria's PAMID) planted on 2,852 ha and Băbească Neagră ('grandmother's grape') (2,73 6ha) are both losing ground and typically make light, ordinary reds. Of much greater interest is Fetească Neagră (the 'black maiden grape') planted on 2,508 ha whose area is increasing rapidly because of its potential as Romania's flagship red grape, although work still needs to be done on both viticulture, as it is prone to excessive yields, and winemaking to manage its combination of high acidity and high pH. Pinot Noir is viewed in certain export markets as Romania's signature grape variety, and the area planted has increased from an estimated 500 ha in 2005 to 1,796 ha in 2013. The variety was imported into Romania around 1900, particularly for sparkling wine production. The variety long known as Burgund Mare ('big Burgundian') is Kékfrankos, or BLAUFRÄNKISCH.

Other specifically Romanian varieties planted to a significant extent include the light-berried 'fat' GRASĂ planted on 567 ha and crisp Frâncuşă (375 ha), both grapes of COTNARI. Busuioaca (275 ha) is a violet-skinned Muscat making sweet wines of genuine character and quality, with typical aromas of peaches and honey, named after the Romanian word for basil, *busuioc*. It is best known around Bohotin in Moldova. The Galbenă vine of Odobeşti makes light, crisp whites—418 ha are officially registered—and the white Şarba (264 ha) is also found in this area. Other Romanian varieties planted to a limited extent include Majarca Albă, Mustoasă de Măderat, Iordana, Zghihară, and Plavaie grown in Odobeşti. There is also some interest in reviving old INDIGENOUS VARIETIES such as Crâmpoşie and relatively new local CROSSES such as Negru de Drăgăşani, which can produce long-lived reds, and the deeply coloured Novac. Other crosses enthusiastically developed by Romanian viticultural stations include Columna, a Pinot Gris x Grasă cross, and the red wine grape Codana.

Wine laws

Romanian wine law is fully compliant with EU regulations. PDO wines must be made from *Vitis VINIFERA* and in 2013 accounted for 653,186 hl (over 17 million gal) or 11% of the harvest.

DOC (Denumire de Origine Controlată) is the recognized traditional term for PDO wines, i.e. high-quality wines from a delimited area and produced within that area. It is supplemented by further classifications according to the grapes' maturity:

DOC-CMD wines harvested at full maturity bearing a designation of origin
DOC-CT late-harvest wines
DOC-CIB late-harvest/BOTRYTIZED sweet wines.

There are currently 32 PDO wines, though they are produced in only seven of the eight major regions.

PGI wines accounted for 534,424 hl in 2013 and are described as Vin cu Indicație Geografică. At least 85% of the grapes must be produced and vinified in the specified delimited area. By 2014, 13 PGIs were protected in law. Wines may be produced from *V. vinifera* or a cross with another VITIS species. Actual alcoholic strength must be a minimum of 9.5% or 10% depending on the wine-growing zone. Other protected traditional terms include Rezervă for wine matured for at least six months in oak and six months in bottle, and Vin de Vinotecă for wine matured at least one year in oak and four years in bottle.

Wine regions

The Romanian wine regions are divided into eight distinct zones (see map): the plateau of Transylvania in the middle of the country; the Pannonian Plain on the Hungarian border in the old province of Crișana and Maramures; the Moldovan hills on the eastern slopes of the Carpathians; the warm, central Muntenia and Oltenia region in the southern Carpathians; Banat towards the borders with Hungary and Serbia; the knolls of Dobrogea between the Danube and the Black Sea; and the flatter Danube Terraces and the clumsily named 'sands and other favourable lands in the south', the last two being relatively unimportant as producers of good-quality wine.

Transylvania is the high central region producing predominantly white wines. The total vineyard area in 2013 was 6,797 ha/16,795 acres. The most important and oldest Transylvanian delimited wine region is Târnave, with its subregions of Jidvei, Blaj, and Mediaș. Other DOC zones include Alba Iulia, Alba, Aiud, and Lechinta to the north with Sebeș-Apold in the south west. These are some of Romania's coolest vineyards at ELEVATIONS up to 500 m/1,800 ft. The mainly white wines typically have appealing fresh acidity and good aromatic expression when well made. Evidence of the medieval immigration of Saxon settlers from the MOSEL VALLEY is still common in the architecture and in the wine styles. Some of the most common varieties are Fetească Regală and Fetească Albă. Also grown are Muscat Ottonel, Traminer, Sauvignon Blanc, and recently some successful Pinot Noir, and even small amounts of Zweigelt

and Merlot. Apold's Iordană vine makes high-acid, low-alcohol wine used mainly for sparkling wines. Romania's largest vineyard owner is Jidvei with 2,460 ha although several smaller estates such as Liliac at Lechinta and Villa Vinea in Târnave have emerged, while UK specialist importers Halewood has a large, successful vineyard in Sebeș-Apold.

Crișana and Maramures is a region with two DOCs: Miniș in Arad county influenced by the lake and Crișana with the subdenominations of Diosig, Biharia, and Silvania. The total vineyard area is around 9,100 ha/22,487 acres. Permitted white wine varieties include Fetească Albă and Fetească Regală, Welschriesling, Muscat Ottonel, Traminer, Furmint, Pinot Gris, and Sauvignon Blanc. Miniș grows these, as well as a traditional white variety, in the Măderat region, Mustoasă which makes light, crisp wine. The MEDITERRANEAN climate here gives long warm autumns so red wine grapes such as Cabernet Sauvignon, Cadarca (KADARKA), Merlot, and Burgund Mare (BLAUFRÄNKISCH), while Pinot Noir and Oporto (PORTUGIESER) are also authorized. There has been some foreign investment in vineyard land and replanting here. Springs can be so mild on the south- and south west-facing slopes on the foothills of the Zarand Mountains that BUDBREAK is usually earlier than in the rest of Romania, although EROSION can be a problem on the steeper slopes. Annual rainfall is high, about 650 mm/23 in, and averages 365 mm during the growing season. Soils vary considerably and include VOLCANIC, SHALE, and LIMESTONE together with some GRAVEL, CLAY, and iron oxide.

Moldovan Hills in the eastern province of Romania known as Moldavia (the eastern part of the old Romanian province of Moldavia is now the republic of MOLDOVA) is home to possibly the country's oldest, and certainly most famous, wine region COTNARI, whose golden nectar was at one time almost as sought after as those of TOKAJ and CONSTANTIA. Romanian Moldavia lies north east of the Carpathians and is Romania's northernmost viticultural area at a latitude of 47°. It is also Romania's largest viticultural region encompassing some 69,134 ha/170,834 acres of vines in 2013, of which around 18,000 ha are for PDO or PGI wines. Vineyards are typically TERRACES on the slopes of south- and southwest-facing amphitheatres that protect the vines from the harsh north winds. Elevations vary from 200 m to almost 500 m. The region enjoys more than 2,000 hours of sunshine in an average year, and annual rainfall is only about 500 mm/20 in. Soil types include RENDZINA, chernozem, and podzols. GRASĂ is the variety responsible for most of the best sweet wines, supplemented by Tămâioasă, but Muscat Ottonel is also grown, together with Fetească Albă and Frâncusa, to produce dry and medium-dry lesser wines.

DOC regions include Bohotin, Cotești, Cotnari, Dealu Bujorului, Huși, Iași, Nicorești, Odobești, Panciu, Iana. On the surrounding hills, the traditional Moldavian Fetească Albă is grown, mainly for light, everyday wines, together with the more recently planted Fetească Regală, Frâncusa, Welschriesling, Aligoté, and Sauvignon Blanc. A range of red varieties, including Merlot, Cabernet Sauvignon, and Oporto (PORTUGIESER), is also cultivated around the capital Iași where Băbească shows perhaps its finest form. At Bohotin, sweet, scented, deep-coloured wine is made from Busuioaca (a dark-skinned aromatic grape, probably from the Muscat family). Another local variety is Zghihara, which is closely related to Galbena but ripens earlier and reaches higher sugar levels. Odobești is one of the largest and oldest viticultural centres in Romania and may well date from the Roman era. The gentle southwest-facing slopes are protected from the north by the Carpathians. Deep, fertile soils are mainly dedicated to everyday white table wine made from the local Galbena grape, but it is sensitive to both DROUGHT and GREY ROT. High-yield whites are made from Fetească Albă, Welschriesling, and Șarba, a CROSS between Welschriesling and Tămâioasă developed at the Odobești research station in 1972 which has a grapey aroma and good acidity. The local grape Plavaie is also grown here for light, high-acid, low-alcohol, everyday wines. In Panciu, to the immediate north of Odobești, winters are colder, winds stronger, and HAIL more frequent, but some good still white and sparkling wines are made. Cotești just south of Odobești, on the other hand, is distinctly warmer and can produce some deep-coloured reds. Nicoresti, east of Panciu, is another red wine region, particularly well known for its Băbească. This region has seen some new investments but is generally focused on supplying local market demands.

The large area of **Oltenia and Muntenia** in the Carpathian foothills north of the capital Bucharest grows 53,450 ha/132,078 acres of vines according to 2013 statistics. DOC areas include Dealu Mare, Drăgășani, Pietroasa, Stefănești, Sămburești, Banu Mărăcine, Mehedinți, and Segarcea. Most famous is the historic and extensive Dealu Mare, meaning 'big hill', best known for its reds and the source for some of Romania's most exciting wines, especially those of Davino and the French-owned SERVE. Promising newcomers include Lacerta, Rotenberg, Crama Basilescu, and Halewood's premium wines. Vineyards are at elevations of between 130 and 550 m/2,000 ft, protected from WINTER FREEZE by high hills and forests above the vineyards. Annual rainfall averages around 640 mm/25 in. This is principally a red wine district with Cabernet Sauvignon, Merlot, some Pinot Noir, recent plantings of Syrah, and considerable focus on Fetească Neagră, both as a varietal wine and blended. An outcrop of CALCAREOUS soil in the Pietroasa district is known for its lusciously sweet, golden, late-harvest wines, especially Tămâioasă from Pietroasele, which may be BOTRYTIZED. Archaeological finds suggest a long history of wine production in Ștefănești, an area noted for robust reds, possibly dating back to Alexander the Great. Towards the south west and River Olt basin lies the historic and extensive vineyards of Drăgășani, which are said to date from Roman times and stretch over 60 km/36 miles ranging from 200 m to 500 m in elevation. Average rainfall is nearly 700 mm/28 in and hail is a frequent hazard. This is a dynamic region of small estates which now has its own growers' association. Whites show crisp acidity and good aromas especially Feteasca Regală, Tămâioasă (sweet and dry styles), Sauvignon Blanc, and the local Crâmpoșie Selecționată. Local red specialities such as Negru de Drăgășani and Novac show promise and there are some good Merlot and Cabernet Sauvignon, too. Samburești is a much smaller wine region specializing in Cabernet Sauvignon. South west of the university town of Craiova lies the DOC of Banu Mărăcine, with a small vineyard area based around the viticultural research station. About 20 km south of Craiova is the DOC Segarcea, the site of a significant recent winery investment and much new planting. Mehedinți DOC covers the vineyard areas of Plaiurile Drânce and Severin county. This is the sunniest and warmest of the southern Carpathian wine regions and concentrates on red wine production. In the far south west, an outcrop of TERRA ROSSA around Oprisor produces some fine reds from Cabernet Sauvignon, Merlot, and Syrah. The climate here is temperate continental with a Mediterranean influence. Sunshine hours are typically 2,400 to 2,600 and rainfall can be up to 800 mm a year. Many vineyards here were grubbed up in the 1980s and have only recently been replanted.

In 2013, official statistics showed nearly 2,928 ha/7,235 acres of vines in **Banat** although in reality the area of vines in production is substantially smaller. Cramele Recaș is the most important producer in the region and is one of Romania's most successful wine exporters. Boutique estates such as Italian-owned Petro Vaselo are relatively recent. Historically, the region was part of the Transylvanian province of the Austro-Hungarian Empire and this influence is still clear in the varieties planted: Cadarca (KADARKA), Italian Riesling (WELSCHRIESLING), Furmint, Fetească Regală, Burgund (BLAUFRÄN-KISCH), and Muscat Ottonel. Today, substantial new vineyards have been planted with selected clones of INTERNATIONAL VARIETIES as well as Fetească Neagră. Banat has a moderate, MEDITERRANEAN climate, cooler than much of the rest of Romania, but warmer than most of Hungary. There are two DOC zones: Banat and Recaș.

The **Dobrogea** region on the Black Sea coast comprised 17,564 ha/43,400 acres of vines in 2013 and there are three DOCs, Murfatlar, Babadag, and Sarica Niculiţel. The region can have as many as 300 days of sunshine each year and rainfall between April and October averages only 150 mm to 200 mm. The climate is distinctly warm, although moderated by breezes from the Black Sea. Murfatlar, with its two sub-regions of Medgidia and Cernavodă, is the most important wine region here (and the name of Romania's top-selling winery). In the past the zone was best known for whites, including late-harvest wines, especially from Chardonnay. There are also substantial plantings of Pinot Gris, Welschriesling, Muscat Ottonel, and Sauvignon Blanc. Plantings of red grapes—especially Merlot, Cabernet Sauvignon, Fetească Neagră and Syrah—are increasing. The dry climate allows some producers to farm ORGANICALLY.

Danube Terraces Most vineyards here are devoted to TABLE GRAPES, and little wine of any quality is made. The only DOC is Oltina.

C.G.

www.wineromania.com
www.onvpv.ro (Romanian only)
www.oniv.ro
www.pnvv.ro

Roman Muscat, synonym for MUSCAT OF ALEXANDRIA.

Rome, classical. '*Vita vinum est*' ('Wine is life'), exclaimed Trimalchio to his dinner guests (Petronius, *Satyricon* 34).

Wine was deeply embedded in Roman culture at all levels; it was as much a staple for the poor as for the wealthy. So the evidence is particularly rich, detailed, and varied—as rich, indeed, as for any aspect of ancient society. There are the casual, but often illuminating, references in the poets, in letters, and even in the graffiti scratched on inn walls. All the AGRICULTURAL TREATISES, one of the largest bodies of technical literature to survive from antiquity, devote great space to detailed discussion of viticulture (see in particular CATO, *De agri cultura passim*, from the 2nd century BC, VARRO, *De re rustica*, Book 1, from the end of the 1st century BC, COLUMELLA, *De re rustica*, particularly Books 3–5, 12, and the separate work 'On trees' from the mid 1st century AD, and his contemporary PLINY, *Natural History*, Books 14, 17, and 23, and PALLADIUS from late antiquity). What these reveal is a lively debate, which has its modern counterpart, about CLIMATE, VINE VARIETIES, PLANTING and PRUNING techniques, technological developments, and the economics of viticulture. A more surprising source of information is Roman law; the sale of wine, particularly wholesale, raised considerable problems for the law of sale, when there was the question of what guarantee of quality the buyer might reasonably expect. The legal texts tell us much about the details of how wine was marketed. Equally interesting material comes from medical writers. Wine played an important role in medical treatment, and much of the information about the colour, quality, and effects of particular wines owes far less to the tasting books of Roman CONNOISSEURS than it does to the notes of the DOCTORS (see MEDICINE). Finally there is ARCHAEOLOGY, of which the most spectacular recent achievement, inspired by the underwater excavation of Roman wrecks, has been the identification of the types of AMPHORAE used to carry the wine and the recognition of the scale and pattern of the wine trade.

Both Pliny (*Natural History* 14. 21–39) and Columella (*De re rustica* 3. 2. 7–28) offer surveys of the main ANCIENT VINE VARIETIES. Columella's classification is the most revealing. His first class consists of the varieties used for the great Italian wines, most notably the types of Aminnean. His second class is high-yielding vines, which nevertheless can produce wines which can be aged successfully. The final group is those prolific vine types used largely to produce *vin ordinaire*. This reveals that wine producers were aware of the great diversity in the markets for their wines and chose their vines accordingly.

ROMAN ITALY

Rome
Alban
Setine
Caecuban
Falernian
Massic
Gauranum
Baiae
Naples
Surrentine
Aquileia
ETRURIA
SABINES
ADRIATIC SEA
Caeretanum
Nomentum
Mt Vesuvius
TYRRHENIAN SEA

0   50 km

'Classic wines can only be produced from vines grown on trees,' was Pliny's verdict (*Natural History* 17. 199). Although this was disputed by some agricultural writers, the most striking fact about Roman viticulture was that the great wines—CAECUBAN, FALERNIAN, etc.—nearly all came from vineyards in which the vines were trained up trees, usually elms or poplars. However, all the normal forms of VINE TRAINING were also known and described by agricultural writers, from the low, free-standing BUSH VINE to elaborate TRELLIS SYSTEMS. As in every age, the literature abounds with references to extraordinary YIELDS (for example, over 300 hl/ha (17 tons/acre), high but not unknown in modern terms); but Columella (*De re rustica* 3. 3) considers the economics of a vineyard on the basis of yields ranging from 21 to 63 hl/ha, which range may look familiar to modern vine-growers concerned with wine quality.

'Be the first to dig the ground . . . but the last to harvest the grapes' was the advice in VIRGIL's poem of the countryside (*Georgics* 2. 410). This is just one of many clues which suggest that the Romans sought to make their white wines—and nearly all the great wines were white—sweet.

The treading of the grapes was usually, but not invariably, followed by their PRESSING. The must obtained from the treading was sometimes kept separate, but more frequently added to that from the pressing. The grape pulp could be subject to a second pressing, or even, after being soaked for a day, a third, to produce a thin drink for slaves (see PIQUETTE). From the press room the must was run off to ferment in large DOLIA, which were frequently sunk in the ground. The wine could be racked off into amphorae at any stage from 30 days after being made, to various points through the winter and into the next spring. Many white wines of note were probably left SUR LIE, with the possible consequent enhancement of flavour and complexity. To those in the post-PASTEUR age of stainless steel vats, Roman winemaking must seem somewhat slapdash and uncertain. However, the accumulated wisdom and experience conveyed in all the agricultural treatises demonstrate a commitment to care (for example, in stressing the need for cleanliness at all stages) and sophisticated observation (as in the siting of the press room and *dolia* yard with regard to the ambient TEMPERATURE during fermentation).

'We consider the best wine is one that can be aged without any preservative; nothing must be mixed with it which might obscure its natural taste. For the most excellent wine is one which has given pleasure by its own natural qualities.' Columella's statement (*De re rustica* 12. 19) reflected current opinion. However, it is made at the beginning of a long discussion of additives for wine. Some of these are less objectionable to modern opinion than others. It was a normal practice to add boiled must to wine either during fermentation or soon after to act both as a sweetener and, so it was thought, a preservative. The addition of quantities of chalk or marble dust may be seen as attempts to modify the acidity of the wine (see DEACIDIFICATION). More surprising is the general advocacy of the addition of seawater or salt during fermentation. This was a distinctive Greek practice, taken over by the Romans. It was supposed both to 'enliven a wine's smoothness' (Pliny, *Natural History* 14. 120) (presumably increase acidity) and to prevent a mouldy taste (Columella, *De re rustica* 12. 23. 2). RESINATED WINE was common. So were FLAVOURED WINES with all kinds of herbal and plant additives, of which the primary effect was to disguise the inferior nature of the basic wine.

For Roman connoisseurs, the key to a good wine was AGEING. In Roman law the distinction between 'new' wine and 'old' was that the old had been aged for at least one year. Of course, vast quantities of wine were drunk within the first year. However, a higher price could be expected if the producer could hold back even for as short a period as the summer following the vintage. As for the great wines, both white and red, their key characteristic was their capacity to be aged for considerable periods. Falernian was considered drinkable after 10 years, but at its best between 15 and 20 years; SURRENTINE, another white wine, came into its own after 25 years. It may be that being sealed in an amphora which had an impermeable coating of resin meant that the ageing process was slowed. On the other hand, CATO recommends that air space should be left when amphorae are filled, which must have led to OXIDATION on a level which would be unacceptable now. The frequent mention of the darkening of the colour of the great whites suggests that MADERIZATION was normal and, indeed, desired. The final curiosity of Roman wines was the widespread practice of storing them in lofts over hearths, where they were exposed to smoke and heat. This was seen as a means of accelerating ageing, for which the nearest modern parallel may be the process of heating which MADEIRA is subjected to.

The heyday for Roman viticulture was the 1st century BC and the first two centuries AD. This was the time for the recognition and development of great wines in central ITALY which could compete successfully with those from the Greek world (see GREECE). It was a period of considerable experimentation and innovation, not least in western areas such as GAUL and SPAIN, which saw the creation of their own vineyards, often by Italian settlers after the areas had become part of Rome's empire. There was clearly a massive increase in the market for wine throughout the empire. Rome itself, with a fluctuating population of a million or more, sucked in imports from Italy and the provinces, while the process of the Romanization of the provinces included the stimulation of new markets for a commodity which was at the heart of Roman culture. The market for wine was a very diverse one, ranging from the élite's desire for great wine to the mass market for wines (for which the thousands of amphorae recovered from sites throughout the empire and beyond are ample testimony).   J.J.P.

Billiard, R., *La Vigne dans l'antiquité* (Lyons, 1913).

Negri, G., and Petrini, E., *Roma Caput Vini* (Milan 2011).

Purcell, N., 'Wine and wealth in Ancient Italy', *Journal of Roman Studies*, 75 (1985), 1–25.

Tchernia, A., *Le Vin de l'Italie romaine* (Rome, 1986).

Wilson, H., *Wine and Words in Classical Antiquity and the Middle Ages* (London, 2003).

Romorantin, a white, eastern Loire grape variety that is fast fading from the French *vignoble*. Cour CHEVERNY is an appellation especially created in 1993 for the rather tart Romorantin grown just west of Blois. DNA PROFILING has shown that this is yet another progeny of PINOT and GOUAIS BLANC.

Ronco, north-east Italian term derived from the verb *roncare* (to clear land, particularly land which is either wooded or overgrown with underbrush), which has been used for over a century in a wide swathe of northern Italy to indicate a HILLSIDE VINEYARD. The first appearance on a wine label dates from the early 1970s, when it was used by Mario Pasolini in the province of Brescia in LOMBARDY for his Ronco di Mompiano, a legendary VINO DA TAVOLA from MARZEMINO and MERLOT grapes grown within the city walls of Brescia. More or less contemporary examples can also be found from the OLTREPÒ PAVESE, frequently with the diminutive form **Ronchetto**. The widest current use is in FRIULI, often in plural as **Ronchi**, and where the dialect form is *ronc*. Examples can also be found in ALTO ADIGE and in ROMAGNA.

See also COLLI.

Rondinella, Italian red grape variety grown in VENETO, especially for Valpolicella. The vine yields profusely and is therefore extremely popular with growers but its produce is rarely sufficiently flavoursome to please consumers. Rondinella is not as widely planted nor as respected as its parent CORVINA VERONESE, with which it is usually blended.

Rondo, once known as GM6494–5, red-fleshed DISEASE-RESISTANT VARIETY grown to a limited extent in such northern European countries as DENMARK, ENGLAND, NETHERLANDS, SWEDEN, BELGIUM, and POLAND, where it is treasured for its combination of early ripening and depth of colour. It was bred using some VITIS *amurensis* genes to withstand cold winters, has small berries and makes light, fruity wines. It can occasionally suffer POWDERY MILDEW, however. Despite its parentage, it produces remarkably VINIFERA-like wine so has been registered as a *V. vinifera* variety. Consequently, it may used in the production of QUALITY WINE.

root, one of the three major organs of higher plants, the others being leaves and fruits/seeds. Roots' main functions are anchorage of the plant, storage of reserves of CARBOHYDRATES, absorption of WATER and MINERALS from the soil, and synthesis of specific compounds, such as reduced nitrogen compounds and such hormones as CYTOKININS and ABSCISIC ACID.

The roots of a commercial vineyard originate from the roots that develop at the base of CUTTINGS, which are more divided than the taproot style of a SEEDLING's root system. The position and number of the main framework roots, the 'spreaders' which extend out and down, are determined during the first three years. Although most vine roots occur in the top metre of soil (less if unfavourable soil horizons impede their penetration), there are many examples where roots have penetrated to 6 m/20 ft or more; often these examples are found in dry conditions such as the DOURO Valley. The root framework supports a large number of fibrous roots which, by their continuing growth, explore the soil for MINERALS and water. Root density is highest in friable soil with continuing supplies of minerals, water, and oxygen. MYCORRHIZAL fungi play an important role in increasing the surface area of the roots.

Vine roots are much less dense than those of many other crop plants. Different species of VITIS have different root distribution and habits, a difference that is deliberately used in the breeding of ROOTSTOCKS. B.G.C.

Smart, D. R., et al., 'Grapevine rooting patterns: a comprehensive analysis and a review', *American Journal of Enology and Viticulture*, 57/1 (2006), 89–104.

Van Zyl, J. L., 'The grapevine root and its environment', Republic of South Africa, Department of Agriculture and Water Supply, Technical Committee 215 (Stellenbosch, 1988).

root growth, that part of a vine's annual growth cycle which takes place below ground. In most fruit trees, the spring flush of root growth occurs at the same time as BUDBREAK, but for the vine it is delayed. There are two peaks of root growth during the year. The first takes place at FLOWERING of the shoots in early summer, and the second coincides with the normal HARVEST period in autumn. There is an important correlation between the size, health, and activity of the vine's root system and the growth of shoots and leaves above ground. This is because the roots act as storage sites for the vine's crucial reserves of CARBOHYDRATES and NITROGEN compounds, and also as the site for the production of HORMONES such as CYTOKININS GIBBERELLINS, and ABSCISIC ACID. Vines with restricted or unhealthy roots have low VIGOUR and this is the basis of the principles of BALANCED PRUNING. Root growth also varies according to VINE AGE. R.E.S. & R.E.W.

root knot nematode. See NEMATODES.

root lesion nematode. See NEMATODES.

rootling, a one-year-old vine grown in a NURSERY, the common material used for planting a vineyard. Typically, it is a GRAFTED rootling, with the fruiting variety, or SCION, grafted on to a ROOTSTOCK. Most species of the vine genus VITIS, especially VINIFERA varieties, form roots readily on their CUTTINGS, but some rootstocks such as *Vitis berlandieri* and *Vitis champini* form roots poorly. B.G.C.

rootstock, the plant forming the root system of a grapevine to which a fruiting variety, or SCION, is grafted. In most vineyards in the world, European wine-producing VINIFERA vines are grafted on rootstocks which are, with few exceptions, either varieties of one AMERICAN VINE SPECIES or more commonly HYBRIDS of several. See VITIS for details of the different species of this genus. Rootstocks are normally used to overcome soil pests or diseases, but may also be used for special soil conditions.

The use of rootstocks for grapevines became common around 1880 in France in order to

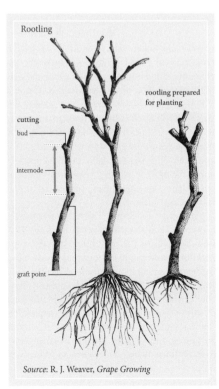

Rootling

rootling prepared for planting

cutting

bud

internode

graft point

Source: R. J. Weaver, *Grape Growing*

combat the devastating root louse PHYLLOXERA, which attacked the roots of the European grapevine *Vitis vinifera*, and the control of phylloxera remains a major, but by no means the only, reason rootstocks are used.

There are parts of the world where the choice of rootstock is more debated than the choice of the fruiting variety, since the latter might well be regulated by law or tradition. Even in the traditional viticultural regions of the Old World, the choice of rootstock tends to change with time, helped by long-term experiments and commercial experience. By contrast, in some parts of the New World, the use of rootstocks is relatively new, or prior use has been restricted to only a few locally available rootstock varieties.

While phylloxera has been present in California since 1873, for example, only a few rootstock varieties were used. The rootstock AXR1 (alternatively ARG1 or Ganzin 1) had been found so adaptable in California it was described by A. J. WINKLER as 'the nearest approach to an all-purpose rootstock', and was the majority rootstock, despite Winkler's qualifying phrase that 'resistance to phylloxera is not high'. In the 1980s, AXR1 succumbed to phylloxera, and now California uses a wide range of rootstocks, as is the case elsewhere in the world.

Choice of rootstock

Although at one time it was a common complaint that PRE-PHYLLOXERA wines are better than those since the invasion (perhaps partly because early rootstocks were not always ideally matched with soil types), more recent experiments have shown that little effect on wine quality can be attributed directly to rootstock. The effect of rootstock on wine quality is probably no greater than that of other factors such as soil, climate, fertilization, and irrigation. Certainly rootstocks can influence VIGOUR, and the high-vigour rootstocks such as Rupestris St George can produce canopies so dense that they affect wine quality (see CANOPY MANAGEMENT). Other studies indicate that the high-vigour rootstocks Harmony, Dog Ridge, Freedom, and Ramsey can result in high levels of POTASSIUM and PH in the resultant wine, but again this may be an indirect effect mediated through vigour and excessive canopy SHADE.

Any vigorous rootstock which stimulates vegetative growth late in the season will have a detrimental effect on fruit RIPENING and therefore on wine quality (see VINE PHYSIOLOGY). The use of rootstocks has also led to an increase in vine CHLOROSIS in those regions where limestone soils are common. Similarly, some rootstocks can induce MAGNESIUM deficiency, which, when severe, can inhibit PHOTOSYNTHESIS and ripening. Perhaps the most significant negative effect of all has been the impact of the universal adoption of GRAFTING on the spread of VIRUS DISEASES.

Rootstock vines do not always show virus symptoms, and it can easily be demonstrated that the spread of virus is increased by grafting. LEAFROLL VIRUS, in particular, delays ripening and can substantially reduce wine quality. Vine improvement has concentrated on avoiding the inadvertent spread of graft-transmitted virus diseases by sourcing virus-free plant material from certified MOTHER VINES of fruiting varieties and rootstocks. Since the early 1990s, a second major worldwide problem has been identified although not yet remedied: young, grafted vines are commonly infected by TRUNK DISEASES, typically in the rootstock, causing the plant to die early and/or grow irregularly.

Rootstocks can have a dramatic effect on YIELD. In the absence of a rootstock, a vine grown on its own roots may not grow at all and die because of root damage from phylloxera or NEMATODES. Grafting on to a rootstock with resistance to soil pests, and also suitable to LIME conditions or DROUGHT, can, on the other hand, increase yield dramatically.

Rootstock selection for any particular vineyard may be guided by known soil pests or diseases (especially nematodes and phylloxera), by suitability to the soil environment (especially lime content, fertility, drought incidence, and waterlogging), or by the effect on the performance of the scion variety that is desired, such as lower vigour or earlier ripening.

Rootstocks also differ in characteristics that are important to nurserymen. These include the ability of MOTHER VINES to produce plenty of wood, the ease with which cuttings root, and also the ease with which they can be grafted.

Rootstock characteristics

Phylloxera resistance The three most resistant AMERICAN VINE SPECIES are *V. riparia*, *V. rupestris*, and *V. berlandieri*, and the most susceptible species is the European VINIFERA (see VITIS). Interspecific HYBRIDS containing genes from any of the first three species will therefore have satisfactory resistance, and those hybrids including *V. vinifera* will have suspect resistance. Rootstocks of *V. vinifera* × *V. rupestris* (including AXR1, and Couderc rootstocks 1202 and 93–5) and *V. vinifera* × *V. riparia* parentage should be avoided as possessing insufficient phylloxera tolerance. Interestingly, *V. vinifera* × *V. berlandieri* rootstocks such as 41 B and 333 EM generally have sufficient resistance. A few examples of rootstocks with high phylloxera resistance are Riparia Gloire, 101–14 Mgt, SO 4, and 5 BB.

Nematode resistance Two principal types of NEMATODES are present in vineyard soils. VITIS species having the most resistance to root knot nematodes are *V. champini*, *V. longii*, and *V. cinerea*. Those having most resistance to the dagger nematode include *V. candicans*, *V. longii*, and *V. rufotomentosa*. Vines of the MUSCADINIA section of the *Vitis* genus are resistant to both types of nematodes, which explains the interest in this group of vines for rootstock breeding. As for phylloxera, *V. vinifera* is very susceptible to nematodes, so any one rootstock will not have resistance to all nematode species, nor indeed to all nematode races. Rootstocks commonly used for nematode tolerance include Ramsey, Dog Ridge, Harmony, 1613 C, 1616 C, SO 4, and Schwarzmann.

Lime tolerance Both *V. vinifera* and *V. berlandieri* contribute tolerance to the soils high in LIMESTONE common in Burgundy and Champagne. Rootstocks acknowledged to have the highest lime tolerance are 41 B, 333 EM, and the more recently bred Fercal.

Drought tolerance Berlandieri–rupestris hybrids are best able to tolerate drought, and these include 110 R and 140 Ru, followed by 1103 P and 99 R. *V. riparia* species and hybrids have low drought tolerance.

Salt tolerance The chloride component of salty soils can be toxic (see SALINITY). The *V. berlandieri* species is considered tolerant, but Australian research has found the *V. champini* rootstock Ramsey to be quite tolerant. *V. vinifera* is also tolerant.

Vigour The species *V. champini*, *V. berlandieri*, and *V. rupestris* and their hybrids give the most vigour, and *V riparia* the least. Among the most vigorous rootstocks are therefore Rupestris St George, 99 R, and 110 R, while Riparia Gloire and 101–14 are among the least vigorous. Vigorous vines tend to delay fruit maturity and can substantially reduce red wine colour.

Some internationally important rootstocks

AXR1, otherwise called **ARG1** in France, Australia, and New Zealand, is a *V. vinifera* × *V. rupestris* hybrid made by Ganzin in 1879. The rootstock was initially popular in France but at the turn of the century it was found there and in South Africa to have insufficient phylloxera resistance. It is popular with growers because the vines are vigorous and yield well, and is favoured by nurserymen because it is easy to graft. It was found satisfactory in California until the 1980s, when it succumbed to a supposed new biotype of phylloxera.

Dog Ridge is a seedling from the species *V. champini* which is suggested for use on light textured soils with high nematode contents. It is only moderately tolerant of phylloxera. This rootstock is extremely vigorous, so it should not be used in fertile soils, and vines need to be pruned lightly to achieve BALANCE. The rootstock is not suggested for high-quality vineyards.

Fercal was bred at INRA Bordeaux in 1959 and developed especially for high lime soils. It is a result of crossing Berlandieri-Colombard 2 (itself a *V. berlandieri* × Ugni Blanc hybrid) with 31 Richter. It is resistant to phylloxera, and grafts readily. Fercal is of moderate vigour, and more tolerant of chlorosis and drought than 41 B.

Harmony is a hybrid of open pollinated seedlings selected from *V. champini* and 1613 C. It was selected at Fresno, California, in 1966, and is quite tolerant of root knot and dagger nematodes. Phylloxera tolerance is, however, low, and vigour moderate to high.

Riparia Gloire de Montpellier is one of the oldest rootstocks used against phylloxera in France, bred in 1880. Of the several *V. riparia* crosses brought in at the time of the phylloxera crisis, this proved the best. It confers excellent phylloxera resistance and is of low vigour, providing for lower yields of improved-quality fruit and early ripening. It is widely used throughout Europe for the production of good-quality wine.

Rupestris St George is sometimes called **Rupestris du Lot** or **Rupestris-monticola**. Bred in 1879, it was another early introduction to France to fight phylloxera, and it is said to be a selection of *V. rupestris* Scheele. This is an extremely vigorous variety with a long growing season. It has excellent resistance to phylloxera, but vines grafted to it can easily overcrop or set poor crops because of extreme vigour. Because of high vigour, it is not used for high-quality vineyards.

Schwarzmann, a *V. riparia* × *V. rupestris* hybrid with high tolerance of phylloxera and nematodes but only moderate vigour. It is suited to deep, moist soils and is not as widely used as it might be.

SO 4, a *V. berlandieri* × *V. riparia* hybrid, is correctly known as **Selection Oppenheim de Teleki No. 4**, from the viticulture school at Oppenheim in Germany. This popular rootstock, used widely in France and Germany, shows excellent phylloxera resistance, and tends to favour fruit set and slightly advanced maturity. Vigour is moderate, as is tolerance to nematodes. SO 4 is not, however, suited to dry conditions, and is prone to magnesium deficiency.

5 BB Kober is sometimes called **5 BB Teleki**, and is a *V. berlandieri* × *V. riparia* hybrid. The seedling was raised by the Hungarian Sigmund Teleki from seeds produced by a French nurseryman. In 1904, some of the most interesting plants were sent to the Austrian Franz Kober, who selected 5 BB. This is quite a vigorous rootstock which is suited to more humid, clay soils. In many situations vigour is excessive. The rootstock 5 BB is widely used in Europe, especially in Germany and Switzerland.

5 C Teleki is a *V. berlandieri* × *V. riparia* hybrid selected in 1896 by Alexandre Teleki. and Heinrich Birk. The rootstock is similar to SO 4 in aptitude, and is mostly used in Germany.

41 B is an old rootstock obtained by Alexis Millardet and Charles de Grasset in 1882 at Bordeaux, and is a hybrid between Chasselas and *V. berlandieri*. This rootstock has the advantage of being highly tolerant of lime and so it is widely used in Cognac and Champagne. Its tolerance of phylloxera is sufficient but not absolute. This rootstock is moderately drought-tolerant.

99 Richter is a *V. berlandieri* × *V. rupestris* hybrid created by Franz Richter in 1902. This vigorous rootstock should not be used in cool regions because it can delay ripening. Phylloxera resistance is high and nematode resistance moderate.

101–14 Millardet et de Grasset is a lower-vigour and early-maturing rootstock used in some of the higher-quality vineyards in France. The vine is a *V. riparia* × *V. rupestris* hybrid made by Alexis Millardet and Charles de Grasset. It has high resistance to phylloxera but moderate nematode tolerance. The vine can tolerate only low lime content and has a shallow root system.

110 R, or **110 Richter**, is a relatively old *V. berlandieri* × *V. rupestris* hybrid made by Franz Richter in 1902. This rootstock is noted for its high vigour and thus tends to delay maturity, especially if planted in fertile soils. 110 R has high phylloxera tolerance but low nematode tolerance. It is moderately lime tolerant and quite drought tolerant, and so is widely used in MEDITERRANEAN CLIMATES. Initially it was not used extensively because of poor rooting in the nursery.

140 Ruggeri is a hybrid produced in 1894 in Sicily by Antonino Ruggeri using *V. berlandieri* and *V. rupestris*. This vigorous rootstock is well suited to dry soils high in lime, and Mediterranean climates. This rootstock should not be planted on fertile, moist soils because of possible excess vigour.

161–49 Couderc, *V. riparia* × *V. berlandieri* hybrid obtained in 1888 by Georges Couderc. This rootstock has high resistance to phylloxera but is susceptible to nematodes.

333 EM (École de Montpellier) is one of the few rootstocks used (with Fercal and 41 B) which has a *V. vinifera* parent. It was hybridized in 1883 by Gustave Foëx of MONTPELLIER by crossing Cabernet Sauvignon with *V. berlandieri*. Despite initial fears to the contrary, 333 EM has sufficient phylloxera tolerance. This rootstock is slightly more lime tolerant than 41 B, and is also drought tolerant.

420 A Millardet et de Grasset is one of the oldest rootstocks, obtained in 1887 by Alexis Millardet and his assistant Charles de Grasset. It is a *V. berlandieri* × *V. riparia* hybrid and is highly regarded for good-quality vineyards, being a lower-vigour rootstock which hastens

maturity. It is regarded as 'the *V. riparia* for chalky soils'. Phylloxera tolerance is high but nematode tolerance is low to moderate.

1103 Paulsen was bred in 1896 by Federico Paulsen, the director of an American vine nursery in Sicily, by crossing *V. berlandieri* with *V. rupestris*. It is regarded as a drought-tolerant rootstock with high phylloxera tolerance and moderate nematode resistance. Lime tolerance is intermediate, and vigour moderate to high. It is welcomed by nurserymen as being easy to graft and root.

1613 Couderc is a complex hybrid between Solonis (*V. riparia* × *V. rupestris* × *V. candicans*) and Othello (*V. labrusca* × *V. riparia* × *V. vinifera*) bred by Georges Couderc in 1881. Phylloxera resistance is low to moderate, but it finds favour because of moderate to high nematode resistance. It is well suited to fertile, sandy, loam soils, and is used mainly in California.

1616 Couderc is a *V. longii* × *V. riparia* cross bred in 1882 to produce a low-vigour rootstock with high nematode and phylloxera tolerance. It is best suited to more humid soils, and it advances maturity.

3309 Couderc is a *V. riparia* × *V. rupestris* cross made in 1881. Georges Couderc planted 18 seeds in a row of the nursery where he had added lime; of the five which did not show chlorosis, 3309 C became the most successful. Phylloxera tolerance is high and lime tolerance medium, and it is better suited to humid than drought-prone soils. Rooting and grafting are easy, and the use of this rootstock is widespread.

R.E.S.

Galet, P., *Précis de viticulture* (7th edn, Montpellier, 2000).

Institut Français de la Vigne et du Vin, *Catalogue des variétés et clones de vigne cultivés en France* (2nd edn, Montpellier, 2007).

Nicholas, P., 'Rootstock characteristics' (SARDI, 1999), www.sardi.sa.gov.au/viticulture/rootstocks/rootstock_characteristics.

van Leeuwen, C., and Roby, J.-P., 'Choix du porte-greffe', in *Un raisin de qualité: de la vigne à la cuve*, n° Hors Série du *Journal International des Sciences de la Vigne et du Vin* (2001), 61–6.

Roquebrun. See ST-CHINIAN.

Roriz. See TINTA RORIZ.

rosado is Spanish and Portuguese, and **rosato** is Italian, for ROSÉ. See also CLARETE.

Rosana, Spanish name for ROUSSANNE grape.

Rosé de Loire, general, and relatively important, appellation created in 1974 for ROSÉ WINE made from a blend of any dark-skinned grape you are likely to find in the Loire, including Cabernet Franc, Cabernet Sauvignon, Pineau d'Aunis, Pinot Noir, Gamay, and Grolleau Noir. The wine may be produced anywhere

within the ANJOU, SAUMUR, and TOURAINE zones and usually lies, in quality terms, somewhere between Rosé d'Anjou and Cabernet d'Anjou, with the distinction that it is always dry.

See also LOIRE.

Rosé des Riceys, rare, still, pink wine made in the commune of Riceys in the Aube *département*, the southern end of the CHAMPAGNE region. This dark, rose-coloured wine is made by careful SAIGNÉE of Pinot Noir grapes, by only a a handful of producers. It can be one of France's more serious rosés. Like Champagne's still red wine, Bouzy Rouge (see CHAMPENOIS, COTEAUX), part of its appeal may be its name.

Rosenmuskateller, German name for aromatic, pink-berried Moscato Rosa del Trentino, a minor but distinct grape variety particular to ALTO ADIGE, northern Italy.

Rosette, very limited sweet white wine appellation just north of Bergerac in SOUTH WEST FRANCE. It includes some of the PÉCHARMANT zone. Just 23 ha planted with the Bordeaux varieties were in production in 2012.

Rosette is also the name of an old FRENCH HYBRID, also known as Siebel 1000, which once produced pale red wines in New York state.

rosé winemaking, production of wines whose colour falls somewhere in the spectrum between red and white.

Historically, rosé wines have been made by a number of different processes, but today two methods are in general use: direct PRESSING or short MACERATION. The preferred technique is a short maceration of the juice with the skins (see SKIN CONTACT) of dark-coloured grapes just after CRUSHING, in the PRESS or in a tank, for a period long enough to extract the required amount of colour or ANTHOCYANINS. The juice is then separated from the skins by DRAINING or pressing, and FERMENTATION proceeds as in WHITE WINEMAKING. With the red-skinned GRENACHE grape, traditionally much used for rosés partly because of its relative lack of anthocyanins, a maceration of eight to 12 hours is usually sufficient. Highly pigmented grape varieties may need much less contact time, while very lightly coloured grapes may need a day or two's maceration. See also SAIGNÉE.

Some basic rosés are made by blending a small amount of finished red wine into a finished white wine. While a pinkish colour can be achieved by this process, the hue and flavour of such a wine are quite different from those of a wine made by short-term maceration. CHAMPAGNE is one of the few controlled appellations in which the blending method of rosé winemaking is sanctioned—and in practice rosé champagne is more often made by blending than by maceration.

Pink wines may also be made by using CHAR-COAL treatments to remove the colour from red wines which are for some reason not saleable as reds.

A VIN GRIS or BLUSH wine is made as above but with no maceration. Both tend to be even paler than most rosés. For a wine made pink by CO-FERMENTING red and white grapes, see SCHILLERWEIN.   A.D.W.

rosé wines, increasingly popular wines in any shade of pink, from hardly perceptible to pale red (see COLOUR). For some reason they are rarely known as pink wines, although the English word BLUSH has been adopted for particularly pale rosés. There was also a FASHION in California, from the late 1980s, when wine had to be white to be popular, to label pale pink wines made from dark-skinned grapes White, as in WHITE ZINFANDEL (which has spawned a host of supposedly White wines made from such darkly coloured grape varieties as Cabernet, Merlot, Grenache, and Barbera). Global production of rosé wines in 2011 was 24.1 million hl/637 million gal, up from 22.2 million hl in 2002.

In France, which is responsible for 27% of global production, rosés are particularly common in warmer, southern regions where there is local demand for a dry wine refreshing enough to be drunk on a hot summer's day but which still bears some relation to the red wine so revered by the French. PROVENCE is the region most famous for its rosé although, in the greater southern RHÔNE (especially TAVEL), the LANGUE-DOC, and ROUSSILLON, rosés are at least as common as white wines. Grenache and Cinsaut are two of the grapes commonly used for rosé in the south of France. The Loire Valley also produces a high proportion of rosé wine of extremely varied quality and sweetness levels, particularly around ANJOU, whether lowbrow Rosé d'Anjou or highbrow Cabernet d'Anjou. See also ROSÉ DE LOIRE. VIN GRIS and SAIGNÉE are French terms for particular types of rosé. See also ŒIL-DE-PERDRIX.

Spain also takes pink wines seriously—so seriously that it has at least two names for them, depending on the intensity of the colour. A *rosado* is light pink, while darker pink (light red) wines are labelled *clarete*. Portugal's best-known pink wines are exported, as in MATEUS and LANCERS. Pink wines are not especially popular in Italy, where the term used is usually *rosato* although *chiaretto*, meaning 'claret', is occasionally used for darker rosés. Official German terms for pink wines include WEISSHERBST, ROTLING, and, in WÜRTTEMBERG, SCHILLERWEIN.

The New World was for long rather bemused by the concept of rosé, although this changed fast in the early 21st century. Chile was innovative. Australia makes some swashbuckling deep pinks and South Africa (where red and white wines may be blended to produce a rosé) has a

growing market, with Blanc de Noir (*sic*) a legal category for those produced solely from red grapes.

Roseworthy, town north of Adelaide in the state of SOUTH AUSTRALIA, close to the Barossa Valley, known in the wine world for Australia's first agricultural college, established in 1883. It trained a high proportion of winemakers and viticulturists in Australia and New Zealand and contributed greatly to the technical standing of the Australian wine industry (see AUSTRALIAN INFLUENCE) until 1991 when it was relocated to the Waite campus of the University of Adelaide, where the AUSTRALIAN WINE RESEARCH INSTITUTE and CSIRO were already sited. For more details, see ADELAIDE.

Roșioară. See PAMID.

Rossese, name given to at least seven distinct north west Italian grape varieties, making both red and white wines in Italy where the 2010 vine census found only 7 ha/17 acres of 'Rossese Bianco' and 312 ha/770 acres of 'Rossese Nero'. **Rossese di Dolceaqua** is the best known. This esteemed red grape variety produces distinctively perfumed varietal wines in the north west Italian region of LIGURIA. The variety has a long history in the region and it has its own DOC in western Liguria. DNA PROFILING has shown it is the same as Provence's TIBOUREN.

Rossignola, optional, tart ingredient in VALPOLICELLA.

Rosso Conero, Italian red wine DOC based on MONTEPULCIANO grapes whose full potential is yet to be realized. See MARCHE.

Rosso di signifies a red wine from the Italian zone whose name it precedes, often a declassified version of a long-lived, more serious wine such as BRUNELLO DI MONTALCINO or VINO NOBILE DI MONTEPULCIANO.

Rosso Piceno, or Piceno, Italian red wine consisting of 35–85% MONTEPULCIANO and a maximum of 50% SANGIOVESE, while Conero Sangiovese is a wine containing at least 85% of the latter. See MARCHE.

rot, loose term for the decay, with microbial interference, of any part of the vine. Rot is most commonly used as a synonym for BOTRYTIS BUNCH ROT, which is the most important sort of rot for wine quality. Other fruit rots include BLACK ROT, SOUR ROT, WHITE ROT; rots of other vine parts include ARMILLARIA ROOT ROT and TEXAS ROOT ROT.

rotary drum vacuum filter (or RDV filter), specialized form of earth FILTRATION designed to cope with very 'dirty' liquids—those which contain a high concentration of

solids or particles that would rapidly block other filters. Such liquids arise during the wine-making process when hazy juice or wine is allowed to settle through the action of gravity; the resultant LEES, although still liquid, are frequently very thick and require mechanical sieving to separate the valuable liquid from the solid particles suspended in it.

RDV filtration relies on the constant regeneration of the filter medium, essential if these liquids with a high proportion of solid particles are to be clarified. This is achieved by shaving off a fine layer of the DIATOMACEOUS EARTH (DE) through which the liquid is passed.

The filter comprises a slowly rotating drum (or disk) covered in a fine stainless steel mesh and fitted with an internal vacuum pump, semi-immersed in a trough into which liquid is introduced. The filtration cycle begins when a significant quantity of DE is fed into the trough as a slurry in water; as the water is sucked through the mesh into the drum, the DE forms a 'cake', some centimetres thick, on the outer surface of the drum.

The water is largely removed from the trough and replaced with the turbid juice or wine, which is itself sucked through the earth by the vacuum and collected in a tank, while the solids are retained on the surface of the DE cake. As the quantity of solids retained quickly blocks the very fine holes in the cake, its surface is regenerated by the removal of the entrapped solids and a small quantity of DE (as little as possible) by a scraper knife, passed once every revolution of the drum or disk. When the entire cake of DE has been removed by the constant shaving off of a small amount, the filter is cleaned and prepared for another batch of juice or wine.

These filters are normally used to clarify the products of settled grape juice or wine, such as lees after crushing, pressing, and settling, and the residue of FININGS such as bentonite. If used carefully, they can recover good-quality wine that is otherwise impossible to separate from such solids and would therefore be either discarded or sent as POMACE for distillation.

Increasing concerns about the health risks of working with DE as well as its disposal have led many wineries to use alternative technologies such as cross-flow filtration or modern centrifuges (see FILTRATION), as well as other proprietary filtration media, such as self-cleaning ceramic filter discs, to recover juice and wine from heavy lees. Further technological developments will almost certainly make RDV filters much less commonly used in future.   P.L.

Rotbrenner, vine FUNGAL DISEASE found in most of Europe which can cause severe crop losses. Caused by the fungus *Pseudopeziicula tracheiphila*, the disease is encouraged by prolonged rainfall and attacks leaves and young bunches. It can be controlled by fungicides applied early in the growing season.   R.E.S.

Roter Traminer, German name for SAVAGNIN ROSE, non-aromatic relative of GEWÜRZTRAMINER.

Roter Veltliner, pink-skinned grape variety formerly widespread in Austria (once planted in California) for the production of table grapes and powerful white wine, in 2012 grown on 200 ha/500 acres of Lower Austria. In warm years, if yields are restricted, it can make intensely aromatic, concentrated wines with high extract, especially in the Wagram district of Donauland. DNA PROFILING in Austria revealed in 1998 that Roter Veltliner is a parent of ROTGIPFLER, NEUBURGER, and FRÜHROTER VELTLINER. A small amount is grown in SAVOIE, where the wines are labelled Malvoisie.

Rotgipfler, the marginally less noble of the two white wine grape varieties traditionally associated with the dramatically full-bodied, long-lived spicy white wine of Austria's Thermenregion. (The other is ZIERFANDLER.) Plantings have remained steady at about 120 ha/300 acres. It ripens late, but earlier than Zierfandler, and the wines are particularly high in EXTRACT, ALCOHOL, and BOUQUET. DNA PROFILING in Austria showed in 1998 that Rotgipfler is a natural cross of SAVAGNIN and ROTER VELTLINER.

Rothschilds and wine. The Rothschilds first entered the world of wine in 1853 when Baron Nathaniel (1812–70), grandson of Mayer Amschel and a member of the English branch of the family, bought Brane Mouton and renamed it Ch MOUTON ROTHSCHILD. This was common practice among more important CHÂTEAU owners. It was a buyer's market in Bordeaux vineyards then devastated by oidium, or POWDERY MILDEW, and the Rothschild purchase was viewed more as a property transaction than as the acquisition of a distinguished vineyard. When the important 1855 CLASSIFICATION placed Ch Mouton Rothschild top of the second growths, however, the Rothschilds were particularly exercised by what they regarded as its unfairly low placing.

Nathaniel was succeeded by his son Baron James (1844–81) and then Baron Henri (1872–1947), who was more interested in literature than wine, and James's widow was responsible for Mouton until the arrival of Henri's younger son Philippe (1902–88) in 1922.

Baron Philippe de Rothschild was to prove one of the most influential forces in the wine business of Bordeaux and beyond. Not only did he acquire two neighbouring Pauillac FIFTH GROWTH châteaux—Mouton d'Armailhacq (named at various stages Mouton-Baron-Philippe, Mouton-Baronne-Philippe, and, since the late 1980s, d'Armailhac) in 1933 and Clerc

Milon in 1970—he established the importance of château BOTTLING, established MOUTON CADET as one of the world's most successful wine BRANDS and an important NÉGOCIANT business in the Médoc, astutely developed the concept (and value) of ARTISTS' LABELS, established the finest collection of wine-related works of art in the world, and in 1979 initiated Opus One, the world's first high profile JOINT VENTURE with Robert MONDAVI of California. In 1996 a joint venture with Concha y Toro of CHILE was created to produce the ambitiously priced Cabernet blend Almaviva. Baron Philippe was succeeded at Mouton by his daughter Philippine (1933–2014). Under her leadership, Domaine de Baron'arques, a red LIMOUX AOC, was bought with her two sons in 1998. At the same time, Baron Philippe de Rothschild S.A. diversified into VARIETAL wines from LANGUEDOC.

Just next door to Mouton, Ch LAFITE was bought by Baron James of the French family in 1868 in the face of local competition. He died a few months later but is said to have visited the property briefly in the spring of that year. His son Edmond (1845–1934) was to sow, and indeed provide, the seeds for the establishment of the ISRAELI wine industry by making a vast donation in 1882. James's great-grandson Élie (1917–2007) was the family member who eventually took charge of Lafite, subsequently Lafite-Rothschild, until 1974 when his nephew Eric (1940–) became the château's head. In 1962, the fourth growth PAUILLAC Ch Duhart-Milon was acquired. In 1984, the leading SAUTERNES property Ch Rieussec was also purchased, L'Évangile in POMEROL being added in 1990. Since then joint ventures have been established in Los Vascos in CHILE in 1988, Ch d'Aussières in Corbières, Quinta do Carmo in Portugal (sold to their partners in 2007), Caro with Catena in Argentina, and, since 2008, a new estate in CHINA's Shandong region. The Lafite Rothschilds were on the point of expanding their California interests but sold Chalone to an acquisitive DIAGEO in 2004.

In 1973 Baron Edmond (1926–97), one of the family partners in Lafite but engaged in many other affairs, bought the semi-derelict Ch Clarke of LISTRAC and in 1977–8 built a very large new *cuvier* and *chai*. In 1979, he added Ch Malmaison in the adjoining commune of MOULIS, which was also treated to major renovation, as well as acquiring two more non-classified châteaux in the Médoc. Since 1998, this branch of the Rothschild family have had a JOINT VENTURE with Anton Rupert of South Africa, Rupert & Rothschild. In 2002, Baron Edmond's son Baron Benjamin created a joint venture with Laurent Dassault in Mendoza, Argentina. In 2003, he bought Ch des Laurets, straddling Puisseguin- and Montagne-St-Émilion. In 2013, two new ventures were

developed, one in Marlborough, New Zealand and a joint venture with VEGA SICILIA in Rioja, Spain.

In 1994, the English financier Lord (Jacob) Rothschild (1936–) opened a wine museum and cellar for the display and sale of Rothschild wines at Waddesdon Manor just north of London.   E.P.-R. & J.R.

Littlewood, J., *Milady Vine: The Autobiography of Philippe de Rothschild* (London, 1984).

Rotling, category of German wines made from a mix of red and white grapes or MUST, comprising SCHILLERWEIN from Württemberg, BADEN's Badisch Rotgold, and SACHSEN's Schielerwein.

rotofermenter, or **rotary fermenter**, a horizontal FERMENTATION VESSEL arranged so that the contents can be mixed mechanically either by rotating the vessel, or by rotating an inner shaft fitted with vanes in a stationary vessel. Designed to eliminate the need for PUNCHING DOWN or PUMPING OVER, this equipment speeds the MACERATION phase of RED WINE-MAKING. Some European wine producers, notably in Burgundy, have invested in them, as have a number of NEW WORLD winemakers. Like most mechanical systems that promote skin–juice contact, they are expensive and require extensive and robust framing structures to mount and hold the horizontal tank. Roto-fermenters are usually controlled by COMPUTERS, with cycles of rotation chosen by the winemaker.   P.J.W.

rotundone is a key aroma compound responsible for the distinctive 'spicy', 'peppery' aroma in some red wines, particularly SYRAH/Shiraz from cooler climates. It has also been found in Grüner Veltliner. In red wines, it has a very low aroma detection threshold of 16 ng/l but as many as one in five people cannot smell rotundone, even at very high concentrations. Rotundone is an oxygenated bicyclic sesquiterpenoid compound that was originally discovered in the tubers of *Cyperus rotundus*, a species of sedge. It is also present in black and white peppercorns and a number of herbs. In wine, rotundone originates mainly from the GRAPE SKINS of some varieties and is extracted during alcoholic fermentation. The concentrations of rotundone in Shiraz grapes have been shown to vary significantly between vineyards, between vintages for the same vineyard, and between grapevines within a vineyard, and its presence appears to be associated with variations in soil properties, TOPOGRAPHY, ambient TEMPERATURE, and vine water status (see SOIL WATER).

D.J. & M.H.

Wood, C., et al., 'From wine to pepper: rotundone, an obscure sesquiterpene, is a potent spicy aroma compound', *Journal of Agricultural and Food*

Chemistry, 56/10 (2008), 3738–44. doi: 10.1021/jf800183k.

Scarlett, N. J., Bramley, R. G. V., and Siebert, T. E., 'Within-vineyard variation in the "pepper" compound rotundone is spatially structured and related to variation in the land underlying the vineyard', *Australian Journal of Grape and Wine Research*, 20/2 (2014), 214–22. doi: 10.1111/ajgw.12075.

Rouchalin, sometimes **Rouchelin**, occasional name for CHENIN BLANC in south west France.

Rouchet, Italian red grape variety. See RUCHÈ.

Rouge du Pays, rare Swiss VALAIS red grape used to make deep-coloured red wines. Confusingly renamed Cornalin du Valais in 1972. The vine demands a fairly warm climate, and it took the research institute at CHANGINS to induce some sort of regularity of yield. DNA PROFILING at DAVIS showed that Rouge du Pays is the progeny of PETIT ROUGE and Mayolet, two varieties from the AOSTA Valley, and a parent of true CORNALIN, hence the confusion with the new name.   J.V.

Rougeon, Seibel 5898, FRENCH HYBRID red wine variety grown in the north eastern UNITED STATES. Very productive and winter hardy, it produces deep-coloured wines with few hybrid aromas, and sometimes has a meaty note, but needs considerable attention because of its susceptibility to both DOWNY MILDEW and POWDERY MILDEW.   D.F.

Roupeiro, the Alentejo name for the common Portuguese white grape variety SÍRIA.

rousing, alternative term for the winemaking operation of STIRRING.

Roussanne, sometimes **Rousanne**, fashionable white Rhône grape which doubtless owes its name to the russet or *roux* colour of its skin. With MARSANNE, with which it is often blended, it is one of only two vine varieties allowed into the white versions of the northern Rhône's red wine appellations HERMITAGE, CROZES-HERMITAGE, and ST-JOSEPH and into the exclusively white and often sparkling ST-PÉRAY. In each of these appellations, Marsanne is far more widely grown because the vine tends to be hardier and more productive. Roussanne's irregular yields, tendency to POWDERY MILDEW and rot, and poor wind resistance all but eradicated it from the northern Rhône until better clones were selected and even today it is preferred there by a minority of producers such as Paul JABOULET Aîné. Nevertheless, by 2011 French plantings had grown to 1,768 ha/4,367 acres, rather more than Marsanne with which a parent-offspring relationship has been strongly suggested by DNA PROFILING.

Roussanne's chief attribute is its haunting aroma, something akin to a particularly refreshing herb tea, but it can oxidize and age relatively easily. It does need to reach full maturity, however, in order to express itself elegantly. In the southern Rhône, Roussanne (but not Marsanne) is one of four grape varieties allowed into white CHÂTEAUNEUF-DU-PAPE, and Ch de Beaucastel here has demonstrated that their particular MASS SELECTION of Roussanne can respond well to oak ageing. The variety is also grown in Provence (although the more common pink-berried **Roussanne du Var** is a lesser, unrelated variety used for more basic wines) and, increasingly, in the Languedoc and Roussillon, where Roussanne's tendency to ripen late is less problematic than in the northern Rhône and where results can be impressive. Although it is usually classified with Marsanne and Vermentino in appellation regulations, it can make a fine blending partner with the fuller-bodied Chardonnay too. It can suffer in drought conditions, however.

The variety is also beguilingly fine and aromatic at Chignin in SAVOIE, where it is known as Bergeron, but should not be confused with ROUSSETTE. It is grown to a limited extent in Liguria and Tuscany, where it is a permitted ingredient in Italy's Montecarlo Bianco, and is grown for Clos d'Agon on the Catalan coast in Spain. Indeed, it has so much personality that many producers all around the wine world are experimenting with it on a small scale, both in aromatic, full-bodied white blends and as a VARIETAL. According to 2012 statistics there were more than 300 ha in Australia, even if Marsanne is much better established. Roussanne is decidedly more popular than Marsanne in California where there were more than 741 acres/300 ha by 2011, particularly in the Central Coast.

Roussette, former name for the ALTESSE grape of SAVOIE now used for a number of wines made in eastern France.

Roussette de Savoie is the Savoie appellation for whites made exclusively from Altesse. In good vintages, they age well and some producers now ferment and/or age in oak. Four CRUS' names may be suffixed to the appellation: Frangy, Monterminod, Monthoux, and most notably Marestel, a steep south-facing slope in the village of JONGIEUX that yields exceptionally ripe fruit.

Roussette de Seyssel is a SEYSSEL wine made from Altesse. In the nearby Ain *département*, **Roussette du Bugey** may be followed by the names of two crus, Virieu-le-Grand and the more notable Montaigneu.   W.L.

Roussillon, although first encountered by some outsiders as a suffix to LANGUEDOC, has a quite distinct identity, both cultural and geographical. Its inhabitants are Catalan rather than French or Occitan, with a history rich in Spanish influence, particularly between the 13th and 17th centuries, when it was ruled first from Mallorca and then from Aragón. They identify closely with the inhabitants of Spanish CATALUÑA just across the Pyrenees and many speak Catalan. Quite unlike the flat coastal plains of the Languedoc, Roussillon's TOPOGRAPHY can be guessed at by the fact that today it is effectively the *département* called Pyrénées-Orientales, the eastern section of the Pyrenees, a mountain range so high that much of it remains snow-covered throughout the summer. Vines and olives are two of the rare agricultural crops that can thrive in the tortured, arid valleys of the Agly, Têt, and Tech—although the lower, flatter land by the coast is today an important source of soft fruit. The climate is France's sunniest, with an average of 325 days' sunshine a year, frequent extremely strong winds accentuating the grape-drying process in summer. Wine styles and techniques as well as grape varieties have much in common with neighbouring Spain, as do the relatively low yields. Despite the prevailing temperatures, Roussillon's cellars were some of France's last to install efficient TEMPERATURE CONTROL, and new OAK arrived relatively recently, but the region has been making up for lost time and is now home to some of France's most exciting reds and whites.

Viticulture was probably introduced to the region via the Greek establishment of Marseilles in the 7th century BC and developed by the Romans. It seems highly likely that the MUSCAT vine was the first to be introduced, in an effort to ape the popular sweet wines of the AEGEAN ISLANDS. In the early 13th century, ARNALDUS DE VILLANOVA is credited with inventing MUTAGE, a process thought to have been applied particularly to the region's whites made from MUSCAT BLANC, Malvoisie (VERMENTINO), and MACABEU. The RIVESALTES region had certainly earned an important reputation for its Muscat by the 14th century, which probably pre-dated that of the Languedoc's FRONTIGNAN. Sweetness was often concentrated by leaving Muscat grapes to shrivel on the vine, a practice that continued at least until the late 19th century (see DRIED-GRAPE WINES) by which time a market for the wines had developed in northern France and red versions began to be made from GRENACHE NOIR. Roussillon became the world's foremost producer of VINS DOUX NATURELS, with BANYULS and to a lesser extent MAURY eventually overtaking Rivesaltes in *réclame* if not volume (see also GRAND ROUSSILLON). The wines proved particularly useful for the French army since, with their high sugar and alcohol, they were so much more stable than table wines. A good 70 million bottles of Rivesaltes were sold each year in the mid 20th century.

But this specialization was to be its downfall for much of the 20th century when strong, sweet wines were decidedly unfashionable (and relatively expensive to produce because of the ageing required). The region's table wines, rather Spanish in terms of their depth of colour and alcohol, were regarded as useful only for blending, particularly with the lighter wines of the Languedoc, which has about five times Roussillon's area under vine. Annual early-21st-century sales of Rivesaltes are just 3 million bottles.

Awarded APPELLATION CONTRÔLÉE status as recently as 1977, **Côtes du Roussillon** has been a name in search of an image outside the region in which it is, with the exception of COLLIOURE and the much more recent extension of the MAURY AOC, the sole appellation for table wines. **Côtes du Roussillon Les Aspres**, for wines made in the south of the département, gained its own appellation in 2004. Côtes du Roussillon, grown on 4,817 ha/11,898 acres of the *département*'s total vine plantings of about 27,200 ha in 2012, can be white and especially rosé as well as red, but the **Côtes du Roussillon-Villages** appellation (2,592 ha) that theoretically designates the region's finest wines is only for red wines made in the northern, hillier third of the region just south of CORBIÈRES and FITOU. The villages of CARAMANY, LATOUR-DE-FRANCE, LESQUERDE, and TAUTAVEL may append their names to the AOC Côtes de Roussillon. (See map under LANGUEDOC.)

The best reds, as geography suggests, tend to be like a Spanish rendering of Corbières. Côtes du Roussillon and Côtes du Roussillon-Villages reds must be made from at least three of Carignan, Grenache, Mourvèdre, and Syrah, with Carignan more strictly limited than the rest. Cinsaut and Grenache's relative Lledoner Pelut is also allowed. Grenache Gris takes the place of Cinsaut for the rosés. The most-planted varieties in Roussillon are, in descending order, Grenache Noir, Syrah, and Carignan. Next most planted are Muscat Blanc à Petits Grains and Muscat of Alexandria, grown traditionally for MUSCAT DE RIVESALTES but increasingly made as dry IGP wines. The principal grape varieties for the relatively rare dry white Côtes du Roussillon are Grenache Blanc, Macabeu, and Tourbat (TORBATO) known locally as Malvoisie du Roussillon. Roussillon dry whites, with their relatively low acidity, may be more difficult to make successfully, but they are also more distinctive and a much wider range of grape varieties than those embraced by the Côtes du Roussillon rules is grown. Like the most ambitious reds, many of Roussillon's finest whites come from the upper reaches of the three valleys and are sold as IGP Côtes Catalanes.

As for Languedoc reds, CARBONIC MACERATION has been much employed to counter Carignan's inherent astringency but more traditional vinification techniques are increasingly employed on the nobler varieties. The reds are robust, rarely subtle, but good value.

CO-OPERATIVES still dominate mass production but dozens of incomers from other French regions and other countries have invested in the potential of the schists, limestone, gneiss, and granite of these sunny valleys—no matter that they don't have a specific appellation to call their own.

A few producers, especially co-operatives on the coastal plain around Rivesaltes, have tried their luck with such INTERNATIONAL VARIETIES as Chardonnay and Merlot, although they ripen so early it can be difficult to preserve acidity in the first and fruit concentration in the second. These wines are also usually labelled IGP Côtes Catalanes, just to confuse things. IGP Côte Vermeille was created in the early 21st century for wines made close to the coast around Collioure and Banyuls.

The vine-growers of Roussillon have been some of France's least content with the details of their appellation regulations, which continue to evolve. There can be considerable scepticism about a system devised as far away as Paris and administered from Brussels, especially among those who identify so closely with the inhabitants of Barcelona.

See also BANYULS, COLLIOURE, MAURY, MUSCAT DE RIVESALTES, and RIVESALTES.

Ponsich, P., 'Histoire de la vigne et du vin en Roussillon', in Éditions Montalba, *Les Vins du Roussillon* (France, 1980).

row spacing, the space between rows of vines in the vineyard. See VINE DENSITY.

Royalty, also known as **Royalty 1390**, a complex CALIFORNIA hybrid vine variety with red flesh, a TEINTURIER. It was bred principally for its colour and was released in 1958 along with the similar but much more successful RUBIRED. There is little regal about this particular variety, which is difficult to grow, although a few hundred acres persist, almost exclusively in the hot SAN JOAQUIN VALLEY.

RS, common abbreviation for RESIDUAL SUGAR.

Rubin, distinctively BULGARIAN cross of Nebbiolo and Syrah developed around 1944. It ripens in mid September and has 50% more ANTHOCYANINS than Cabernet Sauvignon, although interest is waning since the wines seem to age too fast.   C.G.

Rubired, California winemaker's secret weapon, increasingly popular (in an age when depth of COLOUR is automatically associated with QUALITY in wine) red-fleshed HYBRID, released, along with the somewhat similar but much less successful ROYALTY, in 1958. Its productivity and depth of colour made the variety so popular with blenders of wine, juice, and some food products, that by 2003 there were more than 13,000 acres/5,200 ha in the state,

making it California's sixth most popular red grape. Total acreage was still 12,000 acres in 2012—almost as much as Sauvignon Blanc. It is grown, without any major viticultural problems, mainly in the hot SAN JOAQUIN VALLEY, and is never mentioned on a wine label.

ruby, style of fortified wine. See PORT.

Ruby Cabernet, red VINIFERA Carignan x Cabernet Sauvignon cross bred in and for CALIFORNIA in 1936 and released in 1948. Dr H. P. Olmo of the University of California at DAVIS (see also EMERALD RIESLING, CARNELIAN) was attempting to combine Cabernet characteristics with Carignan productivity and heat tolerance. The slightly rustic Ruby Cabernet enjoyed a heyday in California in the 1960s and even in 2012 was still grown on more than 6,000 acres/1,482 ha, mainly in the southern SAN JOAQUIN VALLEY (though is only half as popular as the red-fleshed hybrid RUBIRED). It is even more popular in South Africa where it was grown in 2012 on a total of 2,250 ha, mainly in hotter inland wine regions, and has also been grown quite extensively in Australia's inland regions; indeed Ruby Cabernet appeared increasingly on Australian wine labels during the country's red wine shortage of the late 1990s.

Ruchè, **Rouchet**, or occasionally **Roche**, very rare but distinctive red grape variety of the PIEMONTE region in north west Italy with its own varietal DOC around Castagnole Monferrato, occasionally labelled Rouchet. Like NEBBIOLO, the wine is headily scented and its TANNINS imbue it with an almost bitter aftertaste. The Italian vine census of 2010 found about about 100 ha/247 acres.

Rueda, historic Spanish white wine zone named after the unprepossessing town which straddles the main road from Madrid to León in CASTILLA Y LEÓN (see map under SPAIN). In the Middle Ages, vineyards flourished on this bleak Castilian plateau and cellars were hollowed out of the limestone under the town, but after PHYLLOXERA ravaged the zone, Rueda went into rapid decline. The high-yielding PALOMINO grape was used for replanting, a move that in this case was justified since the main local styles were FORTIFIED WINES in the image of SHERRY.

For much of the 20th century, the local VERDEJO grape was Rueda's sleeping beauty. It was awoken in the 1970s, when Bodegas Marqués de Riscal of RIOJA recognized the area's potential for dry white wine and sold a fresh Rueda white alongside its Rioja reds. Rueda was awarded DO status in 1980 and the local Consejo Regulador succeeded in relaunching the native variety of which there were nearly three times as much as of Palomino in the mid 2000s, a radical reversal of the previous situation. Fortified wines are hardly made today and modern Rueda is a light, fruity, dry white wine. It may be made from a blend of Viura (MACABEO) and Verdejo, the latter accounting for at least 50% of the blend, or it may be a SAUVIGNON BLANC varietal. Rueda Superior must contain at least 85% Verdejo and, as more farmers convert their vineyards, there are ever more VARIETAL wines. Sauvignon Blanc was introduced by Marqués de Riscal in the early 1980s. Some fine, elegant wines have resulted, including one from one of the LURTON family of Bordeaux.

TEMPRANILLO produces some typically firm red wine in the zone. In 2002, red wines were admitted in the Rueda DO but are rarely seen.

V. de la S.

Peñín, J., *Guía Peñín* (Madrid, annually).
www.dorueda.com

Rufete, late-ripening vine variety, previously known as Tinta Pinheira, capable of making fruity red wines and lightish port in the north of Portugal, where plantings had fallen to 3,342 ha/8,258 acres by 2012, and in Castilla-León where more than 700 ha grew in the same year. Grapes need to be fully ripe for the wine to succeed.

Ruffiac, Ruffiat. See ARRUFIAC.

rugose wood, a complex of four VIRUS DISEASES which comprises Rupestris stem pitting (RSP), Kober stem grooving (grapevine vitivirus A or GVA), CORKY BARK (grapevine vitivirus B or GVB), and LN33 stem grooving (LNSG). Additionally, grapevine vitiviruses C and D have been been identified but they have not yet been shown to cause disease in grapevines.

Although widespread, this complex of diseases is relatively unknown as all but corky bark are generally symptomless on *Vitis vinifera*. Rugose wood induces graft incompatibility and can kill the vines, especially in the first years after planting. Typical symptoms are pitting or grooving of the wood. All four diseases can be identified by INDEXING. The effect on wine quality of these diseases is still to be evaluated.

Constable, F., and Rodoni, B., 'Rugose wood–associated viruses', GWRDC factsheet (2011), www.gwrdc.com.au/wp-content/uploads/2012/09/2011-07-FS-Rugose-Wood-Disease.pdf.
Weber, E., Golino, D., and Rowhani, A., 'Laboratory testing for grapevine diseases', *Practical Winery & Vineyard* (Jan/Feb 2002), 13–27.

Ruländer is the more traditional German name for PINOT GRIS, which was propagated in the Rheinpfalz in the early years of the 18th century by wine merchant Johann Seger Ruland. Since the mid 1980s, the name has been reserved for sweeter—and increasingly unfashionable—styles of Pinot Gris, while the

increasingly common dry wines are labelled GRAUBURGUNDER.

The name Ruländer is also used in Austria and for some of the Pinot Gris that is widely planted in ROMANIA.

Rully, rambling village in Burgundy's CÔTE CHALONNAISE providing about 70% white wine. The wines are attractive early and rarely age well, being grown on light and sandy soil. Rully is also a good source of sparkling CRÉMANT de Bourgogne. Nineteen vineyards in the village, one-sixth of the total, are designated PREMIERS CRUS, with Grésigny, Rabourcé, and Les Cloux being the most frequently seen.

J.T.C.M.

Rumania. See ROMANIA.

rupestris, species of the *Vitis* genus native to North America much used in developing suitably resistant ROOTSTOCKS and HYBRIDS. For more details, see VITIS.

Russia. Only the most southern parts of the Russian Federation south of the Don River and the Caucasus are suitable for viticulture. The principal limiting factors are low temperatures (in both summer and winter) and a short vegetation period. After a turbulent post-Soviet and post-GORBACHEV period at the end of the 20th century, total vineyard area had dropped to 61,500 ha/153,750 acres by 2012, practically all in southern Russia: 24,100 ha in Krasnodar Krai; 21,100 ha in Dagestan; 6,800 ha in Stavropol Krai; 4,600 ha in Rostov Oblast; and 1,200 ha in Kabardino-Balkaria. In 2013, when the total yield was 404,500 tons of grapes, a system of viticultural macroregions (Kuban, Stavropol Krai, Don Valley, and Dagestan), was established while official recognition of their smaller viticultural zones and appellations was still pending.

In early 2014, the annexation of the CRIMEA, for long celebrated for its wines, added at least 25,000 ha to Russia's total area of vineyard, and later that year Prime Minister Medvedev announced plans to support the Russian wine industry by relaxing regulation and increasing total vineyard area to 140,000 ha by 2020.

History

South Dagestan is Russia's most important ancient viticultural area although WILD VINES growing around the Caspian, Black, and Azov seas and the greater Caucasus were selected and cultivated long ago. There is evidence of viticultural co-operation between the native tribes living on the Black and Azov seas and the Ancient Greeks who settled along the north east coast of the Black Sea from the 5th century BC.

The next important viticultural period was the time of the medieval Khazar Kaganate, who may have brought INDIGENOUS vines from

Dagestan to the banks of the Don and then—together with the Magyars—to Pannonia, modern HUNGARY.

After several centuries of viticultural oblivion, the first vineyards in the Novorossiysk zone of the Krasnodar region were established in 1870 and planted to Riesling and Portugieser. By 1914, the Russian vineyard area averaged 50,000 ha/123,500 acres, but this had halved by 1919, due mainly to the effects of the First World War and to PROHIBITION in the US. In 1940, vineyards occupied 42,000 ha of Russia. The great development of commercial vineyards came at the end of 1950, and throughout the Soviet era Russia had a highly efficient wine–production and, especially, processing and bottling system until President Gorbachev's anti-alcoholism campaign began in 1985. Just before then, in the mid 1970s PHYLLOXERA reached the Taman Peninsula just east of the Crimea (then part of UKRAINE). Vineyards were abandoned or GRUBBED UP, bottling plants converted to other uses, and then land privatization during the transition to a market economy further shrivelled the Russian wine industry. The Russian Federation's total vineyard area shrank to 72,000 ha by 2000, less than half the area cultivated in the late 1980s, while the total grape harvest shrank to less than a third of its previous level.

Climate and geography

Most commercial vineyards of pre-2014 Russia (see CRIMEA for separate details) are in the North Caucasus. The climate of most Russian viticultural zones is moderately CONTINENTAL and winters can be severe, so that all vines in the northern regions of Rostov Oblast and Stavropol Krai have to be buried for WINTER PROTECTION. The most favourable soil and climate conditions are in the Krasnodar region and Dagestan, with active annual temperature summations of 3,600 to 4,000 °C (see CLIMATE CLASSIFICATION) and, even more importantly, winters warm enough, thanks to the temperate influence of the Black Sea, to permit non-protected viticulture.

Krasnodar, the most important Russian wine region, is tentatively divided into five zones, of which the Anapa-and-Taman zone stretching along the ancient Kuban estuary is perhaps most promising for wine production, although its fertile soils can encourage excessive VIGOUR and call for disciplined PRUNING. No winter protection is required for vines here (apart from in the eastern zone where grapes are grown for brandy) and the active heat summation of 3,600 to 3,800 °C with 193 to 233 frost-free days is sufficient even for quite late ripening varieties. The Black Sea zone is much wetter but winters are not as severe and, thanks to the MARL and CALCAREOUS soils, still, sparkling, and dessert wines are produced here.

r

Dagestan with its extremely varied climate, some of it semi-desert, is Russia's second most important wine-producing region (and was its principal one in the late 1980s). The flat, southern zone along the Caspian Sea between the capital and AZERBAIJAN, with its strong tradition of viticulture, is one of the most propitious parts of the Russian Federation for wine and brandy production. Grape varieties grown include Pervenets Magaracha, Agadai, White Muscat, Asyl Kara, Red Tersky, Saperavi, Zálagyöngy, Premier, Codreanca, and Moldova.

About 13% of Russian wine is produced in the **Stavropol** region although the active annual temperature summation is only 3,200 to 3,400 °C and the frost-free period usually just 180–90 days. Winter protection is essential. The most common varieties are Levokumsky Ustoichivy (Stable), Sauvignon Blanc, Riesling, Rkatsiteli, and Aligoté.

Even less important as a wine producer is the **Rostov** region with its dry, hot summers, subzero winters that demand WINTER PROTECTION of vines, and low yields. **Kabardino- Balkaria** also produces considerable quantities of wine, while Chechnya now grows only TABLE GRAPES.

Industry organization

With large production centres in the cities, SPARKLING WINE is important to Russians and comprises an increasing proportion of wine consumption. In 2012, the Russians consumed 805 million l/213 million gal of still wine and 301 million l of sparkling wine, with official figures estimating that 65% of the market is domestically made wines and 35% is imported wines. The term 'domestically made' includes only 40 to 45% of wines made from Russian-grown grapes, the rest being based on imports of GRAPE CONCENTRATE and BULK WINE bottled in Russia. Another peculiarity of the Russian wine market is that medium-sweet wines, of all colours, represent up to 60% of sales, although this proportion is slowly declining.

Most Russian vineyards and wineries have now been privatized. Only in Dagestan, the nation's second largest wine-growing region, does the industry remain predominantly state-governed.

A recent trend in Russian wine production has been the development of the so-called GAR-AGISTE movement. Although its members were far from numerous, and had no legal status, in 2014 they had already started to play a role on the southern Russian gourmet and tourist scene.

Viticulture

Vine-TRAINING SYSTEMS changed enormously during the 20th century. Densely planted vineyards (5,000 to 10,000 vines per ha) with single vine supports have given way to TRELLIS SYSTEMS in wider-spaced rows. The many vineyards that need winter protection are either trained with long and medium canes left in one direction and covered with soil in winter by a vine-laying machine, or left to be covered with a high mound of soil. Row and vine spacing is generally 2.5 to 3.0 m and 1.25 to 2.0 m respectively. In warmer, non-protected viticultural zones, there may be IRRIGATION in areas with unsatisfactory rainfall.

In the Soviet era, the trunks of particularly vigorous vines are trained 1.2 m high, their canes being supported vertically, with free-hanging terminal shoots; such vines are planted in rows spaced between 3 and 4 m, the so-called broad-row training method. Vineyards on non-irrigated lands have medium- and high-TRUNKED forms with row and vine spacing at 2.5 to 3.0 m and 0.8 to 2.0 m respectively.

Vine varieties

The varietal assortment of Russia's vineyards is extremely diverse, with over 100 varieties allowed for commercial cultivation. Depending on the region, 70 to 85% of vineyards are planted to wine grapes, with TABLE GRAPES accounting for 15 to 30% of the total vineyard area. Among wine grapes cultivated in all viticultural regions of Russia, the most common, comprising almost half of all plantings, are Cabernet Sauvignon and the varieties most commonly grown for sparkling wines—the Pinots, Chardonnay, Sauvignon Blanc, and Riesling. Also planted are Aligoté, Traminer, Muscats, Saperavi, Merlot, the local red wine grape Tsimlyansky Cherny (Black), and the Soviet interspecific HYBRIDS Pervenets Magaracha, Moldova, and Augustin.

NEW VARIETIES with improved resistance to FUNGAL DISEASES and FROST have been developed by the All-Russia Potapenko Research Institute for Viticulture and Ecology. Most notable among the wine grape varieties are Saperavi Severny (Severny means northern) and CABERNET SEVERNY. They, and other new varieties such as Stepniak and Fioletovy Ranni occupy about 10,000 ha/25,000 acres on various Russian farms. Commercial cultivation of these new, specially bred varieties has allowed considerable expansion of non-protected viticulture.

In the early 1990s, there was a substantial expansion in the total area planted to new, high-yielding wine grape varieties such as Bianca, Pervenets Magaracha, Moldova, and 'all-purpose' varieties suitable for both wine and table grapes such as Muscat Derbentsky and Zálagyöngy, as well as to INDIGENOUS VARIETIES such as Sibirkovy, Tsimlyansky Cherny, Plechistik, Varyushkin, Narma, and Güliabi Dagestansky.   V.P.

Source: Centre for Research of Federal & Regional Alcohol Markets.

Russian River Valley, high-quality California wine region and AVA west of Healdsburg and centred in Sebastopol along that portion of the river that meanders through the hills of northern Sonoma county toward its mouth. See SONOMA.

Rust, important wine town on the western shore of the NEUSIEDLERSEE in the Burgenland region of AUSTRIA historically famous for the production of sweet white AUSBRUCH wines but now also for high-quality reds mainly from Blaufränkisch and Zweigelt and some excellent dry white wines. Rust is also the base of the Austrian Wine Academy, the largest wine education centre in mainland Europe.

Rutherford, important centre of wine production in California's NAPA Valley.

Rutherglen, historic wine region in NORTH EAST VICTORIA ZONE, famous for its FORTIFIED, extremely sweet TOPAQUE AND MUSCAT. There were 23 producers in 2014.

Ruwer, German river, just 40 km/25 miles long with viticultural significance well beyond its size, which rises in the Hunsrück Mountains and flows into the MOSEL, downstream from Trier. Ruwer wines are similar in structure to those of the SAAR, but have a touch of earthiness to add individuality. See MOSEL.

S

Saale-Unstrut, small wine region in eastern GERMANY of terraced and sometimes isolated vineyards, starting to recover from the forlorn condition in which they were left by the former East German regime (see map under GERMANY). The main producers in the 735 ha/1,816 acres under vine in 2013 are the cellars at Naumburg belonging to the state of Sachsen-Anhalt, and the co-operative cellar at Freyburg. As in nearby SACHSEN, white wine grapes dominate: Müller-Thurgau (with 17% of vineyard area), Weissburgunder (13%), Riesling (8%), and Silvaner (7%) although both Dornfelder and traditional Portugieser also hold significant shares. The decidedly CONTINENTAL climate entails frequent, dangerous FROSTS. The result is wines that are naturally light in alcohol but relatively rich in extract. The CALCAREOUS soils are thought to encourage BODY and balance in the overwhelmingly dry wines made here.   D.S.

Saar, river which rises in the Vosges Mountains and joins the Rivel Mosel at Konz, near Trier. Downstream from Serrig, Riesling vines grow on SLATE, resulting in wines of long-standing renown. The Saar's vineyards are today subsumed under the regional name MOSEL.

Saccharomyces. See YEAST.

Sachsen, Saxony in English, and one of GERMANY's smallest wine regions. Formerly in East Germany, it is also known colloquially as the Elbtal, and established the first German viticultural training institute (in Meissen) in 1811–12. The vineyard area, which had 499 ha/1,232 acres by 2013, follows the course of the river Elbe, from Pillnitz on the southern outskirts of Dresden, to Diesbar-Seusslitz north of Meissen. Sachsen and SAALE-UNSTRUT are the most northerly wine regions in Germany (see map under GERMANY) and have very similar climates. The granite and GNEISS-dominated soils are not unlike those of Austria's WACHAU, albeit with less dramatically steep slopes. Yields are low, usually under half the national average, and local demand for an extremely limited supply guarantees prices that should make reviving Saxony's neglected terraces and its reputation for fine wine attractive. It was in Meissen, known for its porcelain factory, that viticulture in Sachsen was first documented in 1161.

White wine grapes that collectively dominate this region's almost entirely dry wines are Müller-Thurgau (17% of vineyard area), Riesling (14%), Weissburgunder (12%), and Grauburgunder (Pinot Gris, 10%). A majority of the region's grapes are processed by the regional CO-OPERATIVE and state domaine (Schloss Wackerbarth), but two private estates account for over one-third of the region's production.   D.S.

sack, name for a white FORTIFIED WINE, imported from Spain or the Canary islands, which was much in vogue in England in the 16th and 17th centuries. Its most famous, fictional, consumer was Sir John Falstaff in Shakespeare's *2 Henry IV, Act IV, Scene ii* he delivers his classic speech in its praise. The etymology of sack is disputed. The *Oxford English Dictionary* derives the word from the French word *sec* meaning 'dry', but admits that it cannot produce a convincing explanation for the difference in vowels. Moreover, sack was probably sweet. It was matured in wood for up to two years so it would have been like a cheap OLOROSO. Hence Julian Jeffs proposes another derivation: Spanish *sacar*, to draw out, from which *sacas* became exports of wine. Often the place of production was put before the noun, as in Canary sack (see LA PALMA), Malaga sack, (see Málaga), Sherris (or Sherry) sack. Sherris is JEREZ, hence the modern word SHERRY. From the end of the 17th century, 'sherry' began to replace 'sack' as the generic term, but sack was still used in the 18th century.

Sack was popular in England, even more so when in 1587 Drake raided the Spanish fleet at Cádiz and captured 2,900 PIPES (not BUTTS at this stage) of sherry intended for the Armada and made drinking sack an act of patriotism. Undoubtedly the English colony did not welcome the second raid on Cádiz in 1595; yet sack continued to be exported to England. With the accession of James I in 1603, tension eased and the merchants flourished once more. Sack appears in the works of many of the major English writers of the 17th century, and, however much the Puritans disapproved of the theatre, they did drink sack: when Cromwell paid an official visit to Bristol he was presented with a pipe of sack.   H.M.W.

Jeffs, J., *Sherry* (4th edn, London, 1992).

sacramental wine, saviour of some CALIFORNIA wineries during PROHIBITION. For more details of the sacramental nature of wine, see EUCHARIST.

Sacramento Valley, northern part of the vast CENTRAL VALLEY of CALIFORNIA from Lodi northwards, including the vinously important University of California at DAVIS.

Sacy, white grape variety once widely grown in the Yonne *département*. Its productivity is its chief attribute, its acidity the wine's most noticeable characteristic. This has been used to reasonable effect by the producers of sparkling wines, and the variety, also called Tressallier, is still (just) grown as an ingredient in the white wines of ST-POURÇAIN. See also PINOT.

Sagrantino, lively, tannic red grape speciality of Montefalco in UMBRIA. **Sagrantino di Montefalco** was elevated to DOCG status in the mid 1990s. Sagrantino has been used as an ingredient in DRIED-GRAPE WINES but today shows promise as a carefully vinified dry red, sometimes blended with SANGIOVESE. Outstanding wines from the Arnaldo Caprai winery have created much interest in the variety, but the overall level of viticultural and oenological sophistication in the production zone is not high, as demonstrated by many wines. A total of 994 ha/2,456 were reported in the 2010 vine census.

saignée, French term meaning 'bled' for a winemaking technique which results in a ROSÉ WINE made by running off, or 'bleeding', a certain amount of FREE-RUN juice from just-crushed dark-skinned grapes after a short, prefermentation MACERATION. The aim of this may be primarily to produce a lightly pink wine, or to increase the proportion of PHENOLICS and FLAVOUR COMPOUNDS to juice, thereby effecting a form of CONCENTRATION of the red wine which results from fermentation of the rest of the juice with the skins. The second operation has often been undertaken by ambitious producers of both red bordeaux and red burgundy.

St-Amour, the most northerly of the BEAUJOLAIS crus and an area with some LIMESTONE in which a considerable amount of white Beaujolais Blanc (and ST-VÉRAN) is made. A steady 320 ha/790 acres of Gamay vines are planted for the production of relatively light but true red Beaujolais. The cru was added several years after most others. One theory is that its name, which indubitably adds to its appeal, comes from a Roman soldier who celebrated a narrow escape from death in Switzerland by converting to Christianity and establishing a mission. He was later canonized as St-Amour. There are other, earthier theories, as one would expect of Beaujolais, perhaps the earthiest of all wine regions.

St-Aubin, village in the Côte de Beaune district of Burgundy's Côte d'Or tucked out of the limelight between Meursault and Puligny-Montrachet. White wine production had increased to 80% of the total by 2013, an inversion of the situation a generation before. A high proportion, two-thirds, of the vineyard area is designated PREMIER CRU, notably Les Charmois, La Chatenière, En Remilly, and Les Murgers Dents de Chien, part of a swathe of mostly south west-facing vineyards lying between the borders of Chassagne-Montrachet and Puligny-Montrachet and the hamlet of Gamay, which is included in the St-Aubin appellation. The remaining vineyards have the ideal south and south easterly exposition but are less favourably situated further up the cooler valley.

White St-Aubin is a fresh, energetic wine, which has some of the character of Puligny-Montrachet, especially in the warmer vintages; the reds resemble a more supple version of red Chassagne-Montrachet. Hubert Lamy is one of several fine producers based in St-Aubin.

See also CÔTE D'OR, and BURGUNDY map.

J.T.C.M.

St-Bris was granted full appellation status from the 2001 vintage for its crisp, cool climate Sauvignon (Gris is now allowed as well as Blanc), having been a VDQS since 1974. Total vineyard area in the communes of St-Bris-le-Vineux, Chitry, IRANCY, Quenne, and parts of Vincelottes south of AUXERRE and west of CHABLIS had grown to 140 ha/349 acres by 2012. The wine is too obscure to be made with anything other than artisan passion, but it lacks the breed and concentration of great Loire Sauvignon Blanc made to the south west. Being technically Burgundian but made from a decidedly non-Burgundian grape, it is a curiosity.

St-Chinian, good-value, distinctive appellation in the LANGUEDOC in southern France which extends over spectacular, mountainous terrain in the foothills of the Cévennes between the MINERVOIS and FAUGÈRES appellations (see map under LANGUEDOC). Most wine is characterful red but some fresh, dry rosé and a small volume of increasingly interesting whites are also made. The small town of St-Chinian itself is in the middle of the zone, which extends upwards and northwards as far as Vieussan, including Berlou and its respected CO-OPERATIVE, whose wines are sometimes labelled Berloup. A steady total of about 2,800 ha/6,900 acres is dedicated to the production of appellation wine within the zone, which can be divided into two very different sections. In the northern zone around Berlou and Roquebrun, which earned their own appellations **St-Chinian Berlou** and **St-Chinian Roquebrun** for red wines in 2005, vines at around 200 m/656 ft elevation grow on arid schists and yield low quantities of extremely sharply etched wines with distinct minerality. In the southern zone closer to St-Chinian itself, the (sometimes purple) clays and limestone, typically at about 100 m, tend to result in fuller, softer wines. Carignan vines, limited to 30% of any red, are being gradually replaced by Syrah, Grenache, Lladoner Pelut, and Mourvèdre. Grenache Blanc, with Marsanne, Roussanne and some Vermentino are the main white grapes. Many producers here also grow other varieties with which to make some excellent IGP wines.

St-Christol, the easternmost named red wine CRU within the LANGUEDOC AOC in southern France, named after a village on the eastern boundary of the Hérault *département* with Gard. Production of appellation wine is relatively low here, and is chiefly in the hands of the village CO-OPERATIVE.

St-Drézéry, the smallest named red wine CRU within the LANGUEDOC AOC in southern France. Like neighbouring ST-CHRISTOL it is named after a village on the eastern boundary of the Hérault *département* with Gard and such appellation production as there is chiefly in the hands of the village CO-OPERATIVE although Ch Puech-Haut makes fine reds and whites.

Ste-Croix-du-Mont, most important of the sweet white wine appellations on the right bank of the GARONNE in the BORDEAUX region. At their best, these wines can be early-maturing answers to the wines made across the river in SAUTERNES and BARSAC, being high in alcohol, sugar, and concentration. But prices are considerably lower, so production techniques are generally slacker. The topography and soil structure of Ste-Croix-du-Mont's 380 ha/939 acres of vineyards are more promising than those of its right-bank neighbours LOUPIAC and CADILLAC, for some of the vineyards here are on gravel slopes well situated for the development of NOBLE ROT. An increasing number of producers are prepared to take the risks necessary to produce BOTRYTIZED wines, and BARREL FERMENTATION, such as introduced for the prestige cuvées of Chx des Arroucats, La Rame, and du Mont, is becoming increasingly common (see SAUTERNES for details). Some very ordinary, sugary MOELLEUX is also made, however.

Ste-Foy-Bordeaux, about 220 ha/543 acres of vineyards in the extreme east of the BORDEAUX region on the border with, and arguably more properly part of, BERGERAC. The appellation, technically part of the Côtes de BORDEAUX group, is named after its principal town, just 22 km/14 miles west of the town of Bergerac. Its red wines are very similar to red Bergerac and BORDEAUX AOC, while its much rarer white wines are often sweet and mostly undistinguished.

St-Émilion, important, fast-changing red wine district in Bordeaux producing more wine than any other RIGHT BANK appellation, and home of most of the extravagantly priced GARAGE WINES. It takes its name from the prettiest town in the Bordeaux region by far, and one of the few to attract tourists to whom wine is of no interest.

The town's historical importance is undisputed, and obvious to the most casual of visitors. In the 8th century it was a collection of caves hollowed out of the cliff on which a fortified medieval town was to be built. In the Middle Ages its port, Pierrefitte, played an important part in shipping wine down the DORDOGNE river, until it was overtaken by LIBOURNE a few miles downstream. It was on the pilgrim route to Santiago de Compostela, and even today its CONFRÉRIE the **Jurade de St-Émilion** prides itself on maintaining the district's reputation for hospitality. As outlined in BORDEAUX, history, St-Émilion was a wine region long before the Médoc on the left bank of the Gironde, even though for most of the 19th century it was less important commercially. In the early 20th century, the wines of St-Émilion were left to the merchants of Libourne to sell in northern France and northern Europe, while the BORDEAUX TRADE concentrated on selling LEFT BANK wines. The reputation of St-Émilion grew steadily throughout the second half of the 20th century, accelerating towards the end of the century, not least because of international interest in some of the garagistes. As a result, rivalry between the left and right banks intensified, with St-Émilion and the scores of wine shops lining its narrow cobbled streets being the focus of right-bank wine activity.

Whereas the Médoc is made up of large, grand estates, most of St-Émilion's 400 or so smallholders are essentially farmers, albeit dedicated to a single crop. That crop is dominated by the Merlot and Cabernet Franc (here called Bouchet) vine varieties, Merlot accounting for more than 60% of all vine plantings and imbuing the wines with their characteristic almost dried fruit sweetness. A little Cabernet Sauvignon is grown, but it can be relied upon to ripen profitably only in favoured spots in the generally cooler soils and MACROCLIMATE of the right bank, and then only if a suitable CLONE has been planted and is grown with care.

Grape varieties apart, variation is the hallmark of this extensive region. The quality of its wines can vary from light, fruity, serviceable clarets to the finest FIRST GROWTHS capable of ageing for a century or more. The diversity of soils in the district is such that Bordeaux's most diligent geologist, Henri Enjalbert, devoted his *tour de force* to the region.

Although conventionally the St-Émilion district has been divided into two general soil types—the *côtes* or hillsides below the town, and the clay-rich calcareous soil on the limestone plateau to the east and west of it—there are inevitably myriad soil types (see detailed map in Johnson and Robinson). At its north western limit is a distinctly gravelly district around Chx Cheval Blanc and Figeac. Much of the appellation zone lies on the plain between the town and plateau and the river Dordogne. Wines made on this lower land, a mixture of gravel, sand, and alluvial soils, tend to be lighter and less long lived than the wines produced on the plateau or the hillsides, and most, but not all, of them qualify for the most basic appellation, **St-Émilion**.

But the St-Émilion district also boasts a diversity of appellations and, uniquely in France, has a CLASSIFICATION of individual properties which is regularly revised, and depends on tasting. This classification was first drawn up in 1955 and is revised, often controversially, roughly every ten years, the most recent being that drawn up in 2012. Several hundred properties are accorded the misleadingly grand-seeming **St-Émilion Grand Cru** status. In 2013, for example, just 1,491 ha qualified for the simple St-Émilion appellation while 3,891 ha qualified as St-Émilion Grand Cru—far more than previously. But the classification's most significant task is to identify which properties rank as **St-Émilion Grand Cru Classé** and which few qualify as **St-Émilion Premier Grand Cru Classé**. See CLASSIFICATION for details of the 2012 classification, which rated 82 properties Grands Crus Classés, of which 18 are Premiers Grands Crus Classés and two, Chx Angélus and Pavie, were elevated to the same 'A' status as the historic Chx CHEVAL BLANC and AUSONE. Most of the district's most highly ranked properties are either on the steep, clay-limestone hillsides immediately below the town or on the gravelly section of the plateau 5 km/3 miles west of the town and immediately adjacent to the POMEROL appellation.

Of traditionally famous St-Émilion properties, Ch Figeac, which pre-dated and claims to rival Ch Cheval Blanc, is (unusually for the appellation) attached to Cabernet Sauvignon. Since most other St-Émilions lack this tannic ingredient, the district's wines in general mature much faster than their left bank counterparts.

This is particularly true of the new wave of small properties which emerged in the 1990s, some of whose wines have been offered (though did not necessarily sell) at prices in excess of the famous and established FIRST GROWTHS. See GARAGE WINES.

At the other extreme of value, the St-Émilion CO-OPERATIVE, l'Union des Producteurs de St-Émilion, is one of France's most ambitious, and bottles a quarter of St-Émilion's production. The whole region is characterized by a strong sense of local identity.

The satellite appellations
On the outskirts are the so-called St-Émilion satellites, LUSSAC-ST-ÉMILION, MONTAGNE-ST-ÉMILION, PUISSEGUIN-ST-ÉMILION, and ST-GEORGES-ST-ÉMILION, to the north east of St-Émilion. On this more rolling countryside north of the Barbanne (see LALANDE-DE-POMEROL), the vine is grown alongside other crops and viticulture now accounts for well over half of the total area, or 4,000 ha. Co-operatives are important here and Montagne- and Lussac-St-Émilion produce significantly more wine than either Puisseguin or, especially, St-Georges, which for many years sold as Montagne-St-Émilion. The grape varieties planted are similar to those in St-Émilion proper but the standard of winemaking is generally more rudimentary. There are, nevertheless, bargains to be sought out.

Brook, S., *The Complete Bordeaux* (rev. edn, London, 2012).

Johnson, H., and Robinson, J., *The World Atlas of Wine* (7th edn, London, 2013).

Penning-Rowsell, E., *The Wines of Bordeaux* (6th edn, London, 1989).

The vine variety
St-Émilion is also a synonym for the widely planted white grape variety called UGNI BLANC in France and TREBBIANO Toscano in Italy. The name is used particularly in Cognac in southwest France, where it is widely planted.

St-Estèphe, the northernmost of the four important communal appellations in the Haut-Médoc district of Bordeaux. St-Estèphe is separated from the vineyards of Pauillac's Ch LAFITE only by a stream—indeed Ch Lafite owns some land in the commune of St-Estèphe itself. To the immediate north of St-Estèphe, across a stretch of polder, lies the Bas-MÉDOC, the lower, lesser portion of this most famous region.

The soils of St-Estèphe contain their fair share of GRAVEL, but these layers of gravel are often to be found on a CLAY base. These more poorly drained soils are cooler and can delay ripening, leaving St-Estèphe grapes higher in acidity than their counterparts further south in the Médoc. In Bordeaux's low-rainfall vintages, such as 1990 and 2003, the water-retaining clays of St-Estèphe have an advantage.

A high proportion of grapes grown on St-Estèphe's area of just over 1,200 ha/2,960 acres of vines have found their way into the vats of the village's co-operative, which often uses the name Marquis de St-Estèphe. The village may boast fewer famous names and CLASSED GROWTHS than MARGAUX, PAUILLAC, and ST-JULIEN, but its wines have a distinctive style that is deep coloured, full of extract, perhaps a little austere in youth, but very long lived. This style was perceptibly softened during the 1980s as higher proportions of Merlot grapes blurred the edges of the Cabernet, and winemaking techniques, particularly CONCENTRATION, have been harnessed to make the wines seem softer and fuller.

The stars of St-Estèphe are its two second growths, Chx Montrose and Cos d'Estournel, whose fortunes and reputations have alternated throughout the village's relatively recent history as a fine wine producer. Cos (pronounced 'koss') d'Estournel has the Médoc's most eye-catching architecture, in a façade of pure oriental folly beside the main road through the Médoc's wine villages. Its wines are the commune's most ambitious, styled for many decades to come. Ch Montrose has traditionally produced much more traditionally structured, almost Ch LATOUR-like wines, but a new regime and reconstruction may change this.

S

St-Estèphe's other classed growths are the increasingly dramatic third growth Ch Calon-Ségur, the reliable fourth growth Ch Lafon-Rochet, well sited between Ch Lafite and Cos, and the distinctly modest fifth growth Ch Cos-Labory. Some of the village's most conscientiously made wines, however, are such CRUS BOURGEOIS as the exotic Chx Haut-Marbuzet, Meyney, de Pez, and Haut-Beauséjour (both owned by ROEDERER), Les-Ormes-de-Pez (the latter run in tandem with Pauillac's Ch Lynch-Bages), and Ch Beau-Site.

For more information, see MÉDOC and map of BORDEAUX.

Coates, C., *Grands Vins* (London, 1995).

Duijker, H., and Broadbent, M., *The Bordeaux Atlas* (London, 1997).

Ginestet, B., *St-Estèphe* (Paris, 1984).

Parker, R., *Bordeaux* (4th edn, New York, 2003).

Penning-Rowsell, E., *The Wines of Bordeaux* (6th edn, London, 1989).

Ste-Victoire, subappellation within Côtes de PROVENCE.

St-Georges d'Orques, named CRU within the LANGUEDOC AOC just west of Montpellier.

St-Georges-St-Émilion, very small satellite appellation of ST-ÉMILION in Bordeaux on fewer than 200 ha/500 acres of vines in 2013.

St-Jean-de-Minervois, small mountain village in the far north east of the MINERVOIS region that gives its name to the Languedoc's most individual VIN DOUX NATUREL appellation, Muscat de St-Jean-de-Minervois. It is made from MUSCAT BLANC À PETITS GRAINS, to which alcohol is added during fermentation to produce a wine with at least 15% alcohol and 125 g/l residual sugar. Unlike these other Muscats produced closer to the Mediterranean, however, St-Jean's vineyards are hacked out of the stony limestone and *garrigue* at 250 m/825 ft above sea level and the grapes ripen a good three weeks later. The elevation and less reliable weather can affect both quality and yields, which often have difficulty reaching the permitted maximum of 30 hl/ha, but the resulting wines are relatively delicate and refreshing.

St-Joseph, ambitiously expanding and improving northern RHÔNE right bank appellation producing mainly red wines from the SYRAH grape and less than 10% full-bodied dry whites from the MARSANNE and, occasionally, ROUSSANNE grapes. The vineyard area increased sixfold during the 1970s and 1980s although a more stringent development plan was put into place in the early 1990s as the better producers realized that the reputation of this relatively new appellation (1956) would hardly be enhanced by the produce of the new vineyards on the plateau. The appellation now extends from CONDRIEU in the north (where there is some overlap) to a small pocket of St-Joseph vineyards between ST-PÉRAY and the town of Valence. It totalled 875 ha/2,160 acres in 1996 and 1,211 ha by 2013. The heart of the region, however, is the stretch of old, terraced vineyards around the town of Tournon (including the communes of Vion, Lemps, St-Jean-de-Muzols, Tournon, Mauves, and Glun) just across the wide river Rhône from the hill of HERMITAGE. The wines are lighter and certainly faster maturing than the northern Rhône archetype across the river, not so much because the soils are very different—on the best sites granite predominates, supplemented by sand and gravel—but because St-Joseph's east-facing vineyards simply lose the sun up to two hours earlier in the crucial ripening season. For this reason, locals view St-Joseph as their answer to BEAUJOLAIS, a fruity wine for drinking in the first three years or so. Those less accustomed to the sheer weight of a good northern Rhône red may prefer to drink them at between two and six years old, depending on the character of the vintage, but the best wines of Bernard Gripa, CHAPOUTIER, and Chave can easily repay a decade's bottle age. Red St-Joseph can be a delightfully transparent expression of Syrah fruit, and is one of the most flattering northern Rhône reds to taste young but others can be too light and insubstantial to be worth the price premium that St-Joseph can, often inexplicably, command over the other basic northern Rhône appellation CROZES-HERMITAGE.

St-Julien, one of the most homogeneous, reliable, and underrated village appellations in the Haut-Médoc district of Bordeaux. St-Julien may suffer in popular esteem because, unlike PAUILLAC to its immediate north and MARGAUX a few miles to the south, there is no FIRST GROWTH property within its boundaries. Instead, however, it can boast five superb second growths, two excellent third growths, four well-maintained fourth growths, and, from the 1980s at least, an unrivalled consistency in winemaking skill. St-Julien has been the commune for wine connoisseurs who seek subtlety, balance, and TRADITION in their red bordeaux. The wines may lack the vivid, sometimes almost pastiche, concentration of a Pauillac, the austerity of a classic ST-ESTÈPHE, or the immediate charm of a stereotypical (if all too rare) Margaux, but they embody all the virtues of fine, long-lived blends of Cabernet and Merlot grapes, being deep coloured, dry, digestible, appetizing, persistent, intriguing, and rewarding.

The appellation, the smallest of the Médoc's most famous four, has for years encompassed about 900 ha/2,220 acres of vineyard within the communes of St-Julien and Beychevelle to its immediate south. Both gravelly soils and subsoils with clay-limestone and hardpan here are relatively homogeneous, broken only by a narrow strip of river bank on either side of the *jalle* that bisects the zone and flows into the Gironde north of the dramatically remodelled Ch Ducru-Beaucaillou. South of St-Julien is a considerable extent of land classified merely as Haut-Médoc, but to the north the appellation is contiguous with the southern border of Pauillac, and Ch LÉOVILLE-LAS-CASES in the extreme north of St-Julien shares many characteristics with some fine Pauillac wines, notably Ch LATOUR, which is well within sight.

The Léoville estate, as Penning-Rowsell points out, must have been the largest in the entire Médoc in the 18th century, before it was divided into the three second growths known today as Chx Léoville-Las-Cases, Léoville-Poyferré, and Léoville-Barton. Léoville-Poyferré, which includes the original château building, enjoyed a heyday in terms of its reputation in the 1920s, but also demonstrated something of a return to form in the 1980s. Best value, and perhaps most representative of the appellation, is Léoville-Barton, run from Ch Langoa-Barton, a fine third growth that is, unusually for the Médoc, the home of its owner Anthony BARTON. Chx Gruaud-Larose and Ducru-Beaucaillou are the other two St-Julien second growths, and produce two of the Médoc's finest wines in most vintages. The third growth Ch Lagrange was much improved in the 1980s by investment from SUNTORY of JAPAN, while fourth growths Chx St Pierre, Talbot, Branaire-Ducru, and Beychevelle are generally well run. St-Julien's classed growths account for about three-quarters of the appellation's total production, and even such unclassified properties as Chx Gloria, Hortevie, and Lalande-Borie do not believe in underpricing their admittedly admirable produce.

For more information, see MÉDOC and map of BORDEAUX.

Brook, S., *The Complete Bordeaux* (London, 2007).

Penning-Rowsell, E., *The Wines of Bordeaux* (6th edn, London, 1989).

St-Laurent, as well as being one of the few villages of any size in the MÉDOC, is the name of a black grape variety for long thought to be related to PINOT NOIR and today most commonly encountered in AUSTRIA where it is known as **Sankt Laurent**. In 2014 DNA PROFILING in New Zealand (where a little has been planted) apparently established that the variety is the progeny of PINOT and SAVAGNIN. It is capable of producing deep-coloured, velvety reds with sufficient concentration—provided yields are limited—to merit ageing in oak and then bottle. Thanks to the German red wine boom of the 1990s, total German plantings had reached 600 ha/1,500 acres by 2003 and were almost 700 ha by 2012, mainly in Pfalz and Rheinhessen. In

Austria its 761 ha in 2013 make it much more important than the viticulturally more demanding Blauburgunder (Pinot Noir). Certainly it has had several centuries to adapt itself to conditions in Thermenregion and Burgenland, where its viticultural disadvantages, dangerously early budding, tendency to drop its flowers and susceptibility to COULURE and rot, are less problematic than in Alsace, for example. St-Laurent wine can resemble a powerful Pinot Noir. It is even more important in the CZECH REPUBLIC and SLOVAKIA where it is once again known respectively as Svatovavřinecké and Svätovavřinecké, having been robbed of its sainthood during the communist regime when it was called simply Vavřinecké. Each country had more than 1,400 ha planted in 2009, making it one of their most planted red wine grapes.

St-Macaire, town in the BORDEAUX region just across the river GARONNE from Langon in the GRAVES district. It lends its name to **Côtes de Bordeaux-St-Macaire**, an appellation of just 42 ha/104 acres across the Garonne from Langon for mostly sweet white wines from the usual grapes.

St-Mont, previously Côtes de St-Mont, appellation in the Armagnac region dominated by the dynamic Plaimont CO-OPERATIVE which has worked so hard to identify and revive INDIGENOUS varieties. There is only a handful of other producers. The zone is effectively a northern extension of the MADIRAN area with much the same grape varieties are planted, although yields are generally higher. TANNAT must constitute at least 60% of some surprisingly juicy reds and rosés with FER Servadou and Cabernet Sauvignon the usual blending partners. For whites, GROS Manseng must make up at least 40% of the blend with ARRUFIAC and PETIT COURBU the preferred other ingredients, thereby differentiating this wine from PACHERENC DU VIC-BILH and JURANÇON to the south. Almost 950 ha/2,350 acres of vineyard are dedicated to this wine, just under 60% red and a quarter rosé. Quality is increasing with every vintage, as is the price differential between it and the local IGP Côtes de Gascogne.

St-Péray, white wine appellation of just 73 ha/180 acres for still and SPARKLING WINES made by the TRADITIONAL method that seem something of an anomaly in the northern RHÔNE, famous for the weight and longevity of its wines. Soils and MESOCLIMATE here are admittedly cooler than most of the rest of the Rhône, with some GRANITE in the area closest to CORNAS, and the Marsanne and Roussanne grapes grown here are now producing some wines of real finesse. A considerable proportion of sparkling wine production is given its first fermentation at the co-operative of Tain l'HERMITAGE before

being made sparkling in the St-Péray co-operative cellars.

St-Pourçain, sometimes called **St-Pourçain-sur-Sioule**, small appellation in the greater LOIRE region in cereal- and OAK-producing ALLIER *département* almost precisely in the centre of France. (Because of this St-Pourçain cannot be found on maps of French wine regions; only on detailed maps of the whole *hexagone*—see map under FRANCE.) It was an important site in Roman times, near RIVER transport and offering suitable HILLSIDE VINEYARDS. White St-Pourçain was one of the most respected wines in France in the Middle Ages (see LOIRE, history, and MEDIEVAL LITERATURE) but is today more of a cool climate curiosity. From about 550 ha/1,358 acres of vineyard on varied soils of limestone, granite, and gravel, a wide range of wine colours and flavours are made, being typically dry, light in body, and relatively high in acidity.

The traditional vine variety was SACY, but today the whites must be 50 to 80% Chardonnay with Sacy the minor blending partner. GAMAY is the most common grape used for pink and light red St-Pourçain, although some PINOT NOIR is also allowed in the reds. The increasingly effective CO-OPERATIVE in the town of St-Pourçain-sur-Sioule itself dominates production.

St-Romain, exquisitely pretty village perched on top of a cliff in the Côte de Beaune district of Burgundy producing red wines from Pinot Noir and white wines from Chardonnay. There are no PREMIERS CRUS in the appellation, which was granted only in 1947, and applies to just 98 ha/240 acres, of which two-thirds produce lively white wine.

The vineyards of St-Romain are situated behind those of Auxey-Duresses and at higher elevation, 300 to 400 m/985 to 1,310 ft above sea level, than is usual in the Côte d'Or. In lesser vintages, the grapes do not ripen as well as elsewhere but in warmer years the wines can be excellent value. St-Romain is also home to one of the region's best-known COOPERS, François Frères. Alain Gras makes particularly fine wines here.

See also CÔTE D'OR, and map under BURGUNDY.

J.T.C.M.

St-Sardos, small wine region on the left bank of the GARONNE near Montauban promoted to VDQS status in 2005 and AOC soon afterwards. Reds and rosés are mainly Syrah with some Tannat and a little Merlot and Cabernet Franc.

St-Saturnin, one of the more exciting of the named red wine CRUS within the LANGUEDOC AOC in southern France named after the eponymous village but including parts of St-

Guiraud, Jonquières, and Arboras. Just west of MONTPEYROUX, this zone is also in high, rugged country where little other than the vine will grow. The St-Saturnin CO-OPERATIVE is particularly dynamic, as are some individual producers.

Saintsbury, Professor George (1845–1933). Though a distinguished man of letters in his day, Saintsbury is now principally remembered for *Notes on a Cellar-Book*, a seminal work on wine which was an immediate success and has run to many editions.

He was born on 23 October 1845 in Southampton, where his father was superintendent of the docks. The family moved to London in 1850 and Saintsbury attended King's College School, where he acquired his deep love of literature. Aged 17 he won a Postmastership to Merton College, Oxford, but to his everlasting regret he failed to win a Fellowship. For ten years, from the age of 21, he was a schoolmaster but eventually settled in London with his wife and two sons, becoming a journalist, and for a time was assistant editor of the *Saturday Review*.

The actual cellar book was a simple exercise book in which Saintsbury listed the contents of just two cellars, the first in his London house in West Kensington, the second in Edinburgh, where from 1895 to 1915 he held the Regius Chair of Rhetoric and English Literature at Edinburgh University.

In June 1915 he retired from the Chair in Edinburgh, having some ten years previously developed gout, which prevented him from drinking red wine. He eventually retired to Bath, where he published 13 volumes, including *Notes on a Cellar-Book*, which first appeared in July 1920, as well as innumerable articles and pamphlets.

A London DINING club, the **Saintsbury Club**, was founded in his honour in 1931 but, although nominated as president, the Professor, due to ill health, never attended a meeting. The all-male membership, limited to 50, has always comprised men of letters, wine lovers, both professional and amateurs, with a good sprinkling of DOCTORS and lawyers. The Club meets in Vintners' Hall twice a year, as nearly as possible on his birthday 23 October and on his name day 23 April, St George's Day. He also inspired the name of a California winery, in CARNEROS. See also LITERATURE OF WINE. J.M.B.

Saintsbury, G., *Notes on a Cellar-Book* (16th edn, ed. T. Pinney, Berkeley, Calif., 2008).

St-Véran, appellation created in 1971 for white wines from the Chardonnay grape in southern Burgundy, between Mâconnais and Beaujolais, to include much of the wine that was once sold as Beaujolais Blanc. St-Véran encompasses seven communes: Davayé, Solutré-Pouilly, and Prissé on classic LIMESTONE soil adjacent to POUILLY-FUISSÉ and Chânes, Chasselas, Leynes, and St-Vérand, where the sandy red soil of Beaujolais is mixed with limestone. By 2011 703 ha/1,735 acres were declared under vine. The wines frequently have more body and ageing ability than a typical MÂCON-VILLAGES without rivalling the power and persistence of the wines of Pouilly-Fuissé, which forms an enclave within St-Véran. When the appellations were created, Davayé was offered the opportunity to be included in Pouilly-Fuissé but declined. J.T.C.M.

salary, wine as. The practice of paying workers in wine is an old one (and certainly older than the payments in salt from which the word 'salary' is derived). In Ancient PERSIA, for example, wine rations were strictly ordered and were often far in excess of any individual's possible personal consumption.

More recently, labourers, and in particular grape-pickers on the bigger BORDEAUX estates, would expect to receive some quantity of wine (rarely of great quality and often lowly PIQUETTE) in addition to wages.

The most notorious, and now outlawed, instance of paying workers with deliberately stupefying quantities of wine was the so-called *dop* system once prevalent in SOUTH AFRICA.

Salice Salento, DOC for robust red wine made mainly from NEGROAMARO grapes in south east Italy. The DOC Salice Salentino Bianco was created for Chardonnay-based whites, although the variety has no history nor much adaptability here. For more details, see PUGLIA.

salinity, the concentration of salt (sodium chloride) in soils or irrigation water. Among agricultural crops, grapevines are relatively sensitive to salt injury. Salt in the rootzone affects grapevines in two ways: firstly, it is harder for the vines to extract water from the soil, and they may suffer from drought. Secondly, salt can be toxic in high levels in the vines' tissues. When vines are irrigated by sprinklers with water containing excessive salt, or grown on excessively saline soils, leaves may be burnt, and in severe cases this leads to defoliation. Similar effects can occasionally be found in coastal vineyards affected by wind-borne salt. MERLOT vines are particularly susceptible. Saline soils are typically found in hot and dry climates where IRRIGATION has been introduced. For example, salinity is seen as a potential problem for the inland irrigated vineyards of Australia, along the Murray–Darling river systems. and also in PADTHAWAY. The problem is also found in southern France, where there are 10,000 ha/24,700 acres or more of vineyards planted on ancient marine deposits. Salinity can be overcome by applying more irrigation water than the vines use, so as to leach the salt. Some vine varieties such as

COLOMBARD are tolerant of salt, and there are ROOTSTOCKS such as Dog Ridge and Ramsey which show some salt tolerance. Grape juice and hence wine can contain elevated sodium and chloride levels. These appear unaffected by variety, and to result primarily from sprinkler irrigation (which wets the foliage) with saline water. Wine from vineyards with saline soils may contain elevated levels of salt. R.E.S.

Nicholas, P., *Soil, Irrigation and Nutrition* (Adelaide, 2004).

salt can affect vines. See SALINITY and ROOTSTOCKS. Some, although relatively few, wines may taste slightly salty (see TASTING).

Salvagnin, light red blend of Pinot Noir and Gamay (possibly with some GAMARET and GARANOIR), the first appellation created in SWITZERLAND in 1960. It accounts for about half of all wine produced in the canton of Vaud.

Salvagnin (Noir), sometimes just **Savagnin Noir**, is a Jura name for PINOT NOIR, disconcertingly similar to the name of one of the Jura's own vine varieties, SAVAGNIN BLANC.

Sämling 88, common AUSTRIAN synonym for the SCHEUREBE vine variety of which 373 ha/921 acres were planted in the southern Austrian wine regions of Burgenland and Styria in 2012.

Sámos. See GREECE.

sampling, important part of a continuum of wine quality control procedures which begin in the vineyard and may end when a consumer picks a bottle out of a CASE in his or her CELLAR.

A very small proportion of a vineyard's fruit may be sampled to assess its chemical composition to help predict the HARVEST date, as well as to indicate likely quality and, in some cases, eventual wine style. Grape sampling might simply consist of selecting some berries haphazardly from the vineyard and expressing juice into a REFRACTOMETER to measure sugar content (see MUST WEIGHT; see also RIPENESS). A more rigorous approach involves larger samples and winery laboratory analysis.

Vineyard sampling has become far more focused since the turn of the century, thanks to PRECISION VITICULTURE and to research into GRAPE COMPOSITION AND WINE QUALITY. Both approaches make it much easier to keep together batches of fruit that have similar quality potential, sometimes referred to as streaming when the fruit is fermented together in large vats. However, many vineyards are harvested without a fruit sample being taken, particularly in more traditional regions.

The person taking the sample must be careful to avoid any bias which might affect the sampling result. Either berries or bunches are taken, and a normal sample may weigh 300 g (10.5 oz) to several kilograms. Typically the sample is

crushed or pressed in the winery to obtain juice, which is then analysed for sugar and typically also ACIDITY and PH. Some modern laboratories use spectrophotometry or near infrared spectroscopy (NIRS) to analyse the concentration of extractable ANTHOCYANINS. Spectrophotometry can also determine the total PHENOLIC compounds in the grapes. The total extractable anthocyanin value has been shown to correlate well with the potential wine quality. See also PHYSIOLOGICAL RIPENESS.

A second sampling is frequently made when a load of grapes is delivered to the winery, particularly if the grapes have been bought by contract, since grape PRICES are often based on grape composition, typically on sugar levels.

During FERMENTATION samples are taken at least daily to verify the regular conversion of sugars to ALCOHOL. Later, during ÉLEVAGE, regular sampling provides the winemaker with valuable guidance. Finally, shortly before BOTTLING, samples are taken for detailed analysis to ensure that the wine meets all regulations and is free of FAULTS and CONTAMINANTS.

An important part of selling wine EN PRIMEUR is the release of **cask samples**, or *échantillons* in French, samples drawn from the containers in which the wine is still being matured, typically a BARREL, on which wine merchants and wine writers can base their assessments. Such raw wines, often roughly drawn off into small sample bottles, have not undergone STABILIZATION and can suffer OXIDATION and other faults after only a week or two. The best way to judge a young wine still in cask is sampling in the cellar or winery itself, tasting it straight from the barrel, but sampling the contents of a wide range of different barrels.

A.D.W., J.R., & R.E.S.

Samsó, confusing Catalan name used for both CARIGNAN and CINSAUT.

Samtrot. See MÜLLERREBE.

San Antonio, cool wine valley in CHILE, part of the Aconcagua region. Sometimes called Leyda.

San Benito, small CALIFORNIA county inland from MONTEREY county. The one exception to a prevailing mediocrity is a one-vineyard AVA named Mount Harlan (see map under CALIFORNIA) after the limestone-rich slopes on which Calera winery's several celebrated blocks of Pinot Noir grow. The county has other AVAs (Cienega Valley, Lime Kiln Valley, Paicines) from which little is seen. B.C.C.

Sancerre, dramatically situated hilltop town on the left bank of the upper Loire which lends its name to one of the Loire's most famous, and famously variable, wines: racy, pungent, dry white Sauvignon Blanc, which enjoyed enormous commercial success in the 1970s. The town's situation on such a navigable RIVER, and the favourable DRAINAGE and TOPOGRAPHY of the rolling countryside around it, assured Sancerre's long history as a wine producer; the suitability of the site for viticulture was obvious from Roman times. Until the mid 20th century, however, Sancerre produced red wines, and white wines from the Chasselas table grape. Sancerre's dramatically simple, piercing Sauvignon flavours of gooseberries and nettles were initially introduced into the bistros of Paris as a sort of white wine equivalent of Beaujolais, but, by the late 1970s and early 1980s, Sancerre was regarded as the quintessential white wine for restaurants around the world.

The average elevation of the Sancerre hills is between 200 m and 400 m/655–1,310 ft. The Sauvignon has adapted well to many of the varied TERROIRS around Sancerre, where, in 14 different communes, vines are cultivated, particularly on south-facing slopes. There are three distinct areas: the 'white' western vineyards are made up of clay and limestone soils with some Kimmeridgean marne, especially in the cru of Chavignol, that produce quite powerful wines; those between here and the town of Sancerre are high in gravel as well as limestone and produce particularly delicate wines; while those close to Sancerre itself are rich in flint (*silex*) and yield longer-living, particularly perfumed wines. Comparisons with POUILLY-FUMÉ, made just a few miles upstream on the opposite bank, are inevitable, although both are relatively large, heterogeneous appellations, Sancerre even more than Pouilly. The total area given over to the Sancerre appellation, which had declined to about 700 ha/1,730 acres in the 1960s, had reached almost 3,000 ha by 2012.

A wide range of agricultural activity takes place on this terrain, and in many of the outlying villages the vine plays a subordinate role, but viticulture is particularly important in Bué and in nearby Chavignol, where the meticulous grower Henri Bourgeois is based and which is famous for its goat's cheese.

The climate here is distinctly CONTINENTAL, and the vineyards are easily subject to spring FROSTS, but the river to the east and the forests to the west moderate low temperatures. Vines are generally CORDON or single GUYOT trained.

Sancerre's popularity has brought with it the inevitable increase in the proportion of mediocre wine produced, sometimes over-produced, within the zone. In particularly cool years, even the best producers have to work hard to avoid excessive VIGOUR, resulting in unpleasantly HERBACEOUS aromas and a lack of fruity substance but techniques such as grassing, de-budding, and leaf plucking result in healthier grapes and more concentrated wines. Most Sancerre is ready for drinking almost as soon as it is bottled, and rarely improves beyond two or three years, although the best certainly keep.

There have since been attempts to marry Sancerre fruit with OAK, with varying degrees of success. In years as ripe as 1989, some sweet VENDANGE TARDIVE wine was produced by the likes of Alphonse Mellot and Henri Bourgeois. Sancerre also exists in light, often beguiling, red and rosé versions, made from Pinot Noir grapes and representing approximately 10 and 6% of total production respectively. These wines enjoy a certain following, mainly in France, but need very high standards of winemaking and good weather to imbue them with a good core of fruit. CLIMATE CHANGE is helping.

See also LOIRE, including map.

Friedrich, J., *Earthly Delights from the Garden of France, Wines of the Loire*, Vol 1: *The Kingdom of Sauvignon Blanc* (lulu.com, 2011).

sand, description of sediment or soil which is made up of relatively large particles (bigger than SILT, and much bigger than CLAY). See SOIL TEXTURE and GEOLOGY for more details of this particular form of soil classification. Sandy soils can be difficult to cultivate because of their poor ability to store water and nutrients, but they are notable in viticulture for providing a good measure of protection from the PHYLLOXERA louse. Vineyards dominated by sand include those of COLARES in Portugal, the Camargue in the south of France, the Great Plain of HUNGARY, and Maipo Valley in CHILE.

Sandeman, port and sherry house with one of the most famous logos in the wine trade, the black-cloaked Sandeman Don created in 1928. It was founded in London by a Scotsman, George Sandeman, who in 1790 established his shipping business with a £300 loan from his father. He began by shipping sherry and moved swiftly on to port. After being taken over by the North American multinational corporation Seagram in 1980 for £17 million, Sandeman saw an increasing emphasis on quantity rather than quality. In 1990, George Sandeman (representing the seventh generation of the family to make port) moved to OPORTO to manage the company, becoming the first Sandeman to live in Portugal since 1868. In 2001, Sandeman's port and (less important) sherry interests were acquired by SOGRAPE. Sandeman sherries have been made by Garvey since 2004.

Halley, N., *Sandeman: Two Hundred Years of Port and Sherry* (London, 1990).

San Diego County. California's first wine grapes were planted in San Diego in 1769 by Franciscan MISSIONARIES. This modern CALIFORNIA appellation within the SOUTH COAST AVA includes the San Pasqual Valley and Ramona Valley AVAs. Orfila is a successful operation in San Pasqual Valley, specializing in Rhone-style wines, post-PIERCE'S DISEASE. Fallbrook Winery makes a good Sauvignon Blanc.   L.M.

sandstone, a sedimentary rock composed of SAND-size particles which are usually QUARTZ. The grains are commonly held together by natural cement formed by chemical precipitation in the pores. Typically this consists of silica, but may be another material such as calcium carbonate, forming a CALCAREOUS sandstone. These variations mean that sandstones vary greatly in fertility and drainage. Sandstones occur in the higher ALLUVIAL ground of the River Dordogne, just below the *Côtes* of ST-ÉMILION, and in similar settings elsewhere.   J.M.H. & A.J.M.

San Francisco Bay, commercially expedient, geographically extensive AVA that includes LIVERMORE VALLEY, SANTA CRUZ MOUNTAINS, and Contra Costa County where generally ancient red wine vines are still grown on more than 1,000 acres/405 ha of often sandy soils. The Bay Area is also home to many an URBAN WINERY, generally ageing wines grown well to the north.

Sangiovese, qualitatively variable red grape variety that is Italy's most planted wine vine and is particularly common in central Italy. In 1990, almost 10% of all Italian vineyards, or more than 100,000 ha/247,000 acres, were planted with some form of Sangiovese, although this had fallen to 71,558 ha/176,824 acres by 2010. In its various clonal variations and names (BRUNELLO, PRUGNOLO GENTILE, Morellino, NIELLUCCIO), Sangiovese is the principal vine variety for fine red wine in TUSCANY, the sole grape permitted for BRUNELLO DI MONTALCINO (in theory), and the base of the blend for CHIANTI, VINO NOBILE DI MONTEPULCIANO, and the vast majority of SUPERTUSCANS. It is, in addition, the workhorse red grape of all of central Italy, widely planted in UMBRIA (where it gives its best results in the DOCG wines Torgiano and Montefalco), in the MARCHE (where it is the base of Rosso Piceno and an important component of Rosso Conero), and in LAZIO. Sangiovese can be found as far afield as Lombardy and Valpolicella to the north and Campania to the south.

Sangiovese is widely thought to be of ancient origin, as the literal translation of its name ('blood of Jove') suggests, and it has been postulated that it was even known to the ETRUSCANS. Yet in 2004, researchers Vouillamoz and Grando at SAN MICHELE ALL'ADIGE identified the parents of Sangiovese: the Tuscan 'cherry grape' CILIEGIOLO and Calabrese Montenuovo, an obscure variety found in Campania though probably originating from Calabria. Other Italian researchers had established a direct link between Sangiovese and Ciliegiolo in 2002, but the parentage remained incomplete until Calabrese Montenuovo was DNA-typed by chance at San Michele all'Adige and identified as the other parent. Ciliegiolo was already cited in Tuscany in 1590 by Giovanvettorio

Soderini under the name Ciriegiulo. In his book, Soderini also mentioned the variety Sangiogheto. This is commonly accepted as the first historical mention of Sangiovese, but there is no evidence that Sangiogheto actually was Sangiovese. Indeed, when Soderini writes about the ways to make a very good wine, he says 'beware of the Sangiogheto, who thinks to make wine from it will make vinegar'. Moreover, Sangiovese was rare or almost unknown in Tuscany prior to 1700, whereas TREBBIANO and MALVASIA were the most widespread grapes. This is consistent with Sangiovese's probably being born some time before 1700 from a spontaneous cross between Ciliegiolo and Calabrese Montenuovo. Calabrese Montenuovo is not a registered variety, and its true identity is still not known, but researchers were prompt to make it clear that it is not NERO D'AVOLA from Sicily, a variety often called Calabrese. In fact, the name Calabrese is commonly used for several distinct CULTIVARS in Italy, even for Sangiovese.

Cosimo Trinci, in 1738, observed that wines made solely from Sangiovese were somewhat hard and acid, but excellent when blended with other varieties, a judgement echoed by Giovanni Cosimo Villifranchi in 1883. Bettino RICASOLI found a way to tame Sangiovese's asperity—a substantial addition of sweetening and softening CANAIOLO—which became the basis of all modern Chianti and of Vino Nobile di Montepulciano (although Ciliegiolo, MAMMOLO, and COLORINO as well as the white grapes Malvasia and, especially, Trebbiano were subsequently added to the authorised blend). The use of small oak barrels, begun in the 1970s, can be seen as a modern solution to the same problem of excessive asperity.

Conventional ampelographical descriptions of Sangiovese, based on the pioneering work of G. Molon in 1906, divide the variety into two families: the Sangiovese Grosso, to which Brunello, Prugnolo Gentile, and the Sangiovese di Lamole (of Greve in Chianti) belong, and the Sangiovese Piccolo of other zones of Tuscany, with the implicit identification of a superior quality in the former. Current thinking is that this classification is too simplistic, that there is a large number of CLONES populating the region's vineyards, and that no specific qualitative judgements can be based on the size of either the berries or the bunches. Significant efforts are at last being made to identify and propagate superior clones; MASS SELECTION in the past sought principally to identify high-yielding clones without any regard for wine quality. The variety adapts well to a wide variety of soils, although the presence of limestone seems to exalt the elegant and forceful aromas that are perhaps the most attractive quality of the grape.

Sangiovese's principal characteristic in the vineyard is its slow and late ripening—harvests traditionally began after 29 September and even today can easily be protracted until or even beyond mid October—which gives rich, alcoholic, and long-lived wine in hot years and creates problems of high ACIDITY and hard TANNINS in cool years. Over-production tends to accentuate the wine's acidity and lighten its colour, which can OXIDIZE and start to brown at a relatively young age. The grape's rather thin skin creates a certain susceptibility to ROT in cool and damp years, which is a serious disadvantage in a region where rain in October is a frequent occurrence. Too often Sangiovese has been planted with scant attention to exposure and ELEVATION in Tuscany, where the vine is often cultivated at up to or even above 500 m/ 1,640 ft. A good part of recent viticultural research in Tuscany—which has involved increased VINE DENSITY, lower YIELDS per vine, better clones, more appropriate ROOTSTOCKS, lower vine-TRAINING SYSTEMS, small oak BARRELS, more suitable supplementary varieties for blending, different temperatures and lengths of FERMENTATION—has been dedicated to resolving a single problem: how to put more meat on Sangiovese's bones, how to add flesh to its sizeable, but not always sensual, structure.

Throughout modern Tuscany, Sangiovese is now often blended with a certain proportion of the Bordeaux grape CABERNET SAUVIGNON, whether for Chianti (in which case the interloper should not exceed 15% of the total) or a highly priced VINO DA TAVOLA. Even in this commercially successful blend, sanctioned by the DOC authorities in CARMIGNANO, Cabernet can overwhelm the Sangiovese.

In UMBRIA, the variety dominates most of the region's best red wine, as in the Torgiano of the producer LUNGAROTTI. But in terms of quantity rather than quality, Sangiovese is most important in Romagna (see EMILIA-ROMAGNA), where SANGIOVESE DI ROMAGNA is as common as the LAMBRUSCO vine is in Emilia. Sangiovese di Romagna wine is typically light, red, ubiquitous, and destined, quite properly, for early consumption. The most widely planted Sangiovese vines planted in Romagna appear to have little in common with Tuscany's most revered selections, although there has been some careful CLONAL SELECTION in Romagna with promising results, and two of the best clones currently being used to repopulate Tuscan vineyards, R24 and T19, are in fact from Romagna. Some Sangiovese is grown in the south of Italy, where it is usually used for blending with local grapes, and the success of Supertuscans has inevitably led to a certain amount of experimentation with the variety to the north of Tuscany too.

DNA PROFILING has further suggested that Sangiovese is a parent of several significant southern Italian varieties including FRAPPATO, GAGLIOPPO, NERELLO MASCALESE, and PERRICONE.

Outside Italy

Like other Italian grape varieties, particularly red ones, Sangiovese was taken west, to both North and South America, by Italian emigrants. In South America it is best known in Argentina, where there were 2,000 ha/5,000 acres in 2012, mainly in Mendoza province, producing wine that few Tuscan tasters would recognize as Sangiovese.

In California, however, international recognition for the quality of Supertuscans brought a sudden increase in Sangiovese's popularity in the late 1980s and 1990s. By 2003, acreage had increased to nearly 3,000 but this had fallen to 1,800 acres by 2012, perhaps partly because California Sangiovese, typically more fruit-driven than the prototype, failed to establish a strong identity. ANTINORI, unsurprisingly, persists with the variety at their Antica winery on Atlas Peak above Napa Valley.

The grape also seems to be losing favour in Washington state where plantings had fallen to below 200 acres by 2011. In Australia, however, it has the allure of being classified an ALTERNATIVE VARIETY and total area exceeded 575 ha by 2012 even if renditions varied considerably in style and quality. It is a minor feature in South Africa and Chile.

Sangiovese di Romagna. See ROMAGNA SANGIOVESE.

sangría, a mixture of red wine, lemonade, and, sometimes, spirits and fresh fruit, served with particular gusto in Spain's tourist resorts. In 2014 the EU ruled that the name should be restricted to the produce of Spain and Portugal.

sanitation. See HYGIENE.

San Joaquin Valley, southern half of the vast Central Valley in CALIFORNIA, and that part of the state which produces the great bulk of its wine, and its TABLE GRAPES and DRYING GRAPES. It stretches almost 300 miles/480 km from Stockton down to Bakersfield, and approaches 60 miles in width at its widest. Its great expanses of vineyard included 151,000 acres/61,000 ha of wine grapes in 2013. It is California's Languedoc-Roussillon or Mezzogiorno, but so far only as a bottomless well of cheap, everyday wine. Except for the distinct AVAS of LODI and CLARKSBURG at its very northern end near the confluence of the San Joaquin and Sacramento rivers, it resists any internal dividing lines because its climate and soils are so relentlessly consistent.

Huge as it is, its wineries match. The immense E. & J. GALLO is unquestionably the most important name in it, although CONSTELLATION's huge Mission Bell winery, Bronco, and The WINE GROUP are major players too.

San Juan, wine-producing province in ARGENTINA whose Syrah is especially celebrated.

Sanlúcar de Barrameda, one of the three Spanish towns in which SHERRY is made and matured. MANZANILLA is a delicate, pale, dry sherry matured in Sanlúcar.

San Luis Obispo, wine-producing county in the CENTRAL COAST AVA of CALIFORNIA midway between Los Angeles and San Francisco. Many of California's coastal counties demonstrate why the American AVA system, its embryonic answer to France's APPELLATION CONTRÔLÉE, tries to avoid political boundaries in the shaping of vineyard districts. San Luis Obispo county does so more vigorously than most. A boiling summer sun beats down on the high, sheltered plain that is the Paso Robles AVA while fogs hang over a narrow, cool coastal shelf holding the Edna Valley AVA near San Luis Obispo city. The two AVAs are fewer than 20 miles/32 km apart, and well within the same county. A third AVA, Arroyo Grande, runs from the coast back up into the mountains, thus capturing examples of both extremes within its boundaries.

Arroyo Grande Valley AVA

A long range of hills sloping towards Pismo Beach at the southern edge of San Luis Obispo county, Arroyo Grande was viticulturally distinguished in the 1980s only by the painstaking decision to plant 350 ha/865 acres of it for Maison Deutz, the California arm of Champagne house Deutz. It was later sold, morphing into Laetitia winery. The location is one of the coolest in California. Hundred-year-old Zinfandel vines behind lake Lopez do magnificently well for Saucelito Canyon winery, while Chardonnay and Pinot Noir do well for Talley Vineyards in lower lying portions of the AVA.

Edna Valley AVA

Directly south of the coastal town of San Luis Obispo, Edna Valley won quick fame for its Chardonnays, beginning in the mid 1970s. Edna Valley Vineyards, now part of E. & J. GALLO, was the pioneer, and the principal wine company is Niven Family Wine Estates (the Nivens founded Edna Valley Vineyards), producer of Baileyana, Tangent, Zocker, and other labels. The AVA also claims Alban Vineyards, established by RHONE RANGER John Alban whose finest Syrahs, Grenaches, and Viogniers are sold strictly via mailing list. Gewürztraminer has also done well, but it is not widely planted. Pinot Noir has been variable. Low hills on three sides give the small valley a soup-turcen shape, allowing it to collect moisture-laden air from the Pacific, making FUNGAL DISEASES a frequent threat despite low rainfall. Cool, even temperatures and fog cover result in a very long growing season, often 50% longer than Burgundy.

Paso Robles AVA

An isolated inland plain, where the headwaters of the Salinas river congregate, Paso Robles earned an early reputation as a place where outlaws could hole up, no questions asked. Locals still cultivate the impression that this is a haven for the disconnected—James Dean ended his briefly rebellious life in a nearby automobile accident in the 1950s. From the 1880s onward, its role as a wine district was to produce the kind of sun-baked, high-alcohol, fiercely tannic Zinfandels that could pull an outlaw into a saloon on the bleak, wintry nights that are almost as common hereabouts as blistering summer days. Since its confirmation as an AVA, newcomers in an expanding roster of local wineries moved on to embrace Cabernet Sauvignon, Merlot, Syrah, Sauvignon Blanc, and Chardonnay in vineyards set on a restlessly rolling plain of former alfalfa fields east of Paso Robles town, and the cooler, CALCAREOUS viticultural areas west of the city. The Zinfandelists have stuck with their traditional haunts in high hills to the west of town, but now even they are joining up as growers of Cabernet and Rhône varieties. It surprises many that Cabernet, with 39% of acreage in 2013, is the most-planted wine grape in Paso Robles and that 'other reds' are second, at 16%. They include Petite Sirah, Cabernet Franc, Grenache, Mourvèdre, and Petit Verdot. Merlot follows at 14%, with Syrah and Zinfandel at 9% and 8% respectively. Chardonnay and Sauvignon Blanc have become rarities, replaced by 'other whites' including Grenache Blanc, Marsanne, and Roussanne. J. Lohr is the largest player, though not large by CENTRAL VALLEY standards, and its bottlings range from competent to exceptional across several price tiers. Justin, Wild Horse, Eberle, Adelaida, and Castoro are core producers, and the investment made by the Perrin family of Ch de Beaucastel in CHÂTEAUNEUF-DU-PAPE with their American importer Robert Haas has paid off handsomely in excellent Rhône varietal wines at Tablas Creek in the western sector of the appellation. Tablas Creek's vine NURSERY, established from cuttings taken from Beaucastel, has supplied US grape growers with top-quality plant material. Some of the beneficiaries are in Tablas Creek's own backyard, small Paso producers of blends made in the image of southern Rhône reds, more popular single-varietal examples.

The Paso Robles AVA is overwhelmingly extensive (666,000 acres/270,000 ha, of which 26,000 acres are planted with vines) and has no sub-AVAs, but there are moves afoot to change this. After an aborted attempt in 2007–2009 to create a Paso Robles Westside AVA (with state highway 101, and not geography and climate, dividing west from the east), wineries and growers ordered independent soil and climate studies and came up with 11 (pending in 2014) sub-AVAs within the current Paso Robles AVA.

York Mountain AVA

This tiny, single-winery AVA is not within the Paso Robles AVA boundaries, although it is contiguous on its western edge and within San Luis Obispo county.   B.C.C. & L.M.

www.pasowines.com
www.slowine.com

San Marino, tiny republic within Italy between the regions of EMILIA-ROMAGNA and the MARCHE. Its elusive wines, from 200 ha/500 acres of vineyards, are based on SANGIOVESE for its red, and PIGNOLETTO (here called, confusingly, Ribolla di San Marino), Biancame, and Cargarello for its whites.

San Michele all'Adige, Istituto Agrario di, or, strictly, since being renamed in 2008, the Edmund Mach Foundation, one of Italy's best-known viti-agricultural schools and centres of ACADEME. It was founded in 1874 in what was then the Austrian South Tyrol and is now the province of Trento in the far north of the country. Its aim is to promote cultural and socioeconomic growth in the agricultural sector and to develop SUSTAINABLE forestry and agriculture. Its first director Edmund Mach set up the institute to include an experimental station and a farm alongside the school. Today a wide range of agricultural and viticultural training and research is undertaken, including the genomics of INDIGENOUS VARIETIES in collaboration with international research institutes, and oenological concerns include the analysis of flavour and PHENOLICS, microbiology, and sensory analysis (see TASTING). The institute hosts the most important ampelographic collection in Italy, with varieties from Italy and all over the world, as well as producing a range of wines under the San Michele all'Adige label.

Santa Barbara, southern CALIFORNIA city and county which gives its name to the southernmost in a string of three heavily planted wine counties on California's CENTRAL COAST (see also MONTEREY and SAN LUIS OBISPO). Its southernmost vines grow hardly more than 100 miles/160 km from downtown Los Angeles. The city of Santa Barbara has one of the dreamiest climates one could hope to find, almost rain free, and so mild that semi-tropical plants grow in lush profusion. And yet Pinot Noir and Chardonnay are prized varieties in the county because many of its vineyards hug the Pacific shore north of Point Concepcion, where nearly eternal sea fogs create conditions cooler and cloudier than either CARNEROS or much of SONOMA county's Russian River. MISSIONARIES brought vines to the region in the 1770s (see CALIFORNIA, history), and a few commercial

S

wineries dotted the landscape during the later 19th century, but it was not until the wine boom of the 1970s that Santa Barbara began to assert any serious claims as a wine-producing area. Its potential seems particularly bright, in no small part because of its proximity to the trend-setting megalopolis of Los Angeles, and the 2004 movie SIDEWAYS set here that created an instantaneous American fascination with the district (and Pinot Noir). It has five AVAs, and they do not encompass all of its 17,000 acres/ 6,900 ha of vineyard, but its reliance on fog as a cooling agent gives it remarkably complex shadings. Ballard Canyon, Happy Canyon of Santa Barbara, Santa Maria Valley, Sta. Rita Hills, and Santa Ynez Valley are the current AVAs (see below); the Los Alamos, Los Olivos District, and the Santa Maria Bench may one day achieve AVA status.

Santa Maria Valley AVA

Located on the San Luis Obispo county border, this district is climatologically and geographically an extension of the coastal sections of its northern neighbour. A flock of distinctive Pinot Noirs brought this AVA swift identity during the 1980s. It also has proven well adapted to Chardonnay in a short career that began only with the 1970s. The floodplain of the Santa Maria river runs true east–west, and thus is wide open to the prevailing sea fogs of the region. Much more heavily planted than the Santa Ynez Valley to the south, it has only a dozen or so wineries. Byron, Qupé, and Au Bon Climat were its most prominent wineries at the outset of the 1990s, but more recently KENDALL-JACKSON's purchase of the Tepusquet Vineyard has made it an extremely important player (mainly under the Cambria label). Some small artisan wineries such as Foxen have also enjoyed acclaim, especially among day visitors from Los Angeles. Most of its grapes go to cellars outside the county. Much of the part that stays home goes to wineries in other parts of the county, and Rancho Sisquoc have also enjoyed acclaim, and the Miller family, owner of Bien Nacido Vineyard (whose grapes are prized by wineries throughout California) launched its own Bien Nacido label in 2010. Many of Santa Maria's grapes go to cellars outside the county, most notably the Ojai Vineyard in nearby Ventura county.

Santa Ynez Valley and Santa Rita Hills AVAs

Although far from being the only schizophrenic AVA in California, the Santa Ynez Valley comes close to being the extreme case. It starts as a narrow, fog-beset river course between steep east–west hills that run inland from the Pacific shore at Lompoc as far as the village of Solvang. There the main valley is joined by tributary canyons from the north, which are much warmer because they are sheltered from sea fogs by elevation and higher hills. The western end is best suited to Pinot Noir, Chardonnay, and, if anyone dares, Riesling. WIND is a serious consideration, and the best sites are in the lee of hills. In recognition of its climatological distinction, this section (west of the main coastal freeway, Highway 101) is the sub-AVA of Santa Ynez Valley now named Sta. Rita Hills. (It began life as the Santa Rita Hills AVA, but Chilean producer Viña Santa Rita objected.) Sanford, Sea Smoke, Babcock, Melville, Dierberg, Brewer-Clifton, Longoria, and Lafond are prominent producers in this western section.

Moving east from Sta. Rita Hills, Sauvignon Blanc, Cabernet Franc, Merlot, Syrah, and Cabernet Sauvignon come into play, in the warmer sub-AVAs Ballard Canyon and Happy Canyon of Santa Barbara. Firestone Vineyards was the pioneer, followed by Zaca Mesa. More recent entrants to have garnered acclaim include Fess Parker (known to Americans over 45 for his television roles as Daniel Boone and Davy Crockett) and Andrew Murray. Syrah is good at demonstrating the differences between western and eastern Santa Ynez Valley: in the Sta. Rita Hills AVA it tends to be lean and peppery while in the eastern Ballard and Happy Canyons it is fuller, more leathery, and berry-scented. Beckmen Vineyards in the heart of Santa Ynez Valley has a foot in both cool and warm zones, producing Syrah, Grenache, Sauvignon Blanc, and Cabernet Sauvignon. The same is true for Gainey Vineyard, which also makes Pinot Noir from Sta. Rita Hills.

The lower end seems best suited to Pinot Noir, Chardonnay, and, perhaps, Riesling. WIND is a serious consideration, and the best sites are in the lee of hills, not on top of them. In recognition of its climatological distinction, this lower section (west of the main coastal freeway, Highway 101) is now a sub-AVA of Santa Ynez Valley named Santa Rita Hills. Sanford, Babcock, Melville, and Lafond are prominent producers in this western section. The upper, eastern end appears to do better by Sauvignon Blanc and, mostly in blends, Cabernet Franc, Merlot, and Cabernet Sauvignon. Judgements on these varieties remain tentative, however; early plantings here came only after 1970, and acreage remains small. Firestone Vineyards was the pioneer, followed by Zaca Mesa.

B.C.C. & L.M.

www.sbcountywines.com

Santa Clara Valley, California wine region and AVA south of San Francisco. Its colloquial name, Silicon valley, explains its status in the computer high-tech industry. In spite of a long vinous history, factories, shopping malls, and homes began to supplant most of its vineyards in the 1950s. By the 1970s, the transformation was nearly complete and the final chapters were being written for once-important winery names such as Almadén and Paul Masson. Mirassou remains today but is now owned by E. & J. GALLO, the wines sourced from throughout California and its vineyards are now in the Salinas valley in MONTEREY. A few acres of Santa Clara vines persist to the west in the SANTA CRUZ MOUNTAINS and at its southern end in the Hecker Pass district, but the area's luxury homes for computer programmers make all these vineyards more of a toy than a viable agricultural investment. Twenty small wineries exist, largely for the benefit of TOURISTS. San Ysidro District AVA east of Gilroy is a single grower, owned by a New York winery.

B.C.C. & L.M.

Santa Cruz Mountains, diverse 350,000 acre/141,700 ha CALIFORNIA wine region and AVA immediately south of San Francisco. Its vineyards amount to a light dusting of freckles on a long, lopsided, bony body. In a stretch of coast ranges that begins as the ridgepole of the San Francisco peninsula and continues south as far as the city of Santa Cruz, climates and soils would be so diverse as to beggar description even if vineyards were not separated one from another by miles of redwood forest, meadows, and artist colonies populated by cyber-refugees earning a living through the optical fibre. The most useful points to make about it are: this is one of California's cooler growing regions; Pinot Noir has a rich history here, although Riesling and Zinfandel had their day in the last century; Cabernet Sauvignon has won the AVA its greatest fame albeit grown on the inland slopes of the ridgeline (see RIDGE Vineyards); and a prominent RHÔNE RANGER, Bonny Doon's Randall Grahm, started in the counterculture woods behind UC Santa Cruz. Jeffery and Ellie Patterson carry on Martin Ray's quest to produce pure, minerally Chardonnays and Pinot Noir at Mount Eden Vineyards, and stalwarts David Bruce and Thomas Fogarty wineries are also admirable. There is also much excitement for the wines being made by newer producers such as Rhys, Varner, and Big Basin. In the Corralitos area at the southern end of the AVA small producers such as Alfaro and Windy Oaks produce tiny quantities of precise, focused Pinot Noirs and Chardonnays that are relatively low in alcohol thanks to the cool growing conditions. Top wineries include Ridge, David Bruce, Mt Eden, Fogarty, and Storrs. At the southern end of the AVA, overlooking Monterey bay, the hamlet of Corralitos is the geographical centre of activity for many small-scale producers of Pinot Noir which have sprung up since the mid 1990s.

B.C.C. & L.M.

Santa Maddalena, known as **St Magdelener** by the many German speakers who make and drink it, was historically the most famous wine of ALTO ADIGE in north east Italy. (In an Italian government classification of 1941, it was for political purposes ranked after Barolo and Barbaresco as the country's most significant wine, a rating which would be unlikely to be repeated today.) An official subzone, and therefore suffix, of the enormous Alto Adige DOC, it takes its name from the hill of Santa Maddalena to the north of the city of Bolzano (Bozen), long considered a particularly suitable site for the cultivation of the SCHIAVA (Vernatsch) grape from which the wine is made. Since the late 20th century this light red wine has become so unfashionable that its total vineyard area has shrunk from 456 ha in 1978 to 220 ha in 2011 with an average yield of 76.2 hl/ha—much lower than the 12.5 tonnes per ha (close to 90 hl/ha) allowed by law. The production regulations decree a minimum 85% Schiava (no distinction being made between the three Schiavas). About 5% of the deep-coloured LAGREIN is routinely blended to give this pale speciality a deeper shade of red.

Like other Italian DOCs, when it sold well Santa Maddalena underwent a significant enlargement of its production zone from the original nucleus (now called Santa Maddalena CLASSICO) of the communes of Santa Maddalena, Retsch, Justina, Leitach, and St Peter. The zone with its well-known name now stretches all the way to Settequerce (Siebeneich) in the Val d'Adige to the west and to Cornedo (Karneid) in the Val d'Isarco to the east. These latter zones undoubtedly give a Schiava of good quality but with less personality than the Schiava of Santa Maddalena; fortunately over 85% of current production of Santa Maddalena is Santa Maddalena Classico. W.S.

Santa Maria Valley, California wine region and AVA. See SANTA BARBARA.

Santarém, capital of TEJO in central, southern Portugal.

Santa Rita Hills, promising California wine region and sub-AVA of Santa Ynez Valley. See SANTA BARBARA.

Santa Ynez Valley, California wine region and AVA. See SANTA BARBARA.

Santenay, somewhat forgotten village and spa in the Côte de Beaune district of Burgundy producing red wines from Pinot Noir and occasional whites. The soils in Santenay are a little richer in MARL than most of the Côte d'Or, producing red wines tending to the rustic more than the elegant. This is largely the fault of a poor selection of Pinot Noir vines whose vigour has often been tamed by the CORDON DE ROYAT training system in place of the usual GUYOT.

Most of the best vineyards, the PREMIERS CRUS La Comme, Clos de Tavannes, and Les Gravières, form an extension from Chassagne-Montrachet. Also reputed are La Maladière, situated behind the main village, and Clos Rousseau on the far border of Santenay, beyond the casino and thermal waters of the higher village.

See also CÔTE D'OR, and map under BURGUNDY.

J.T.C.M.

Santorini, one of the southern Cyclades islands that are part of GREECE, known in classical times as Thíra.

History

The island is a part of the core of an ancient volcano, which erupted c.1640–1620 BC (perhaps a century earlier), destroying the Minoan civilizations of Thíra and, it is thought, neighbouring Crete. A large part of Thíra became submerged, and has remained so to this day.

In antiquity, the island was not especially famous for its wine, but this was to change in the Middle Ages. It belonged to the Byzantine empire until the CRUSADERS sacked Constantinople in 1203–4 and Santorini was given to one of the Venetian conquerors, remaining in his family until 1336. It then became part of the duchy of Naxos but VENICE retained a strong influence; 1479–89 was another period of direct Venetian rule. It was Venetian enterprise that made Santorini an important wine producer. The wine it exported was made from a mixture of grapes, chiefly the white ATHIRI and red MANDILARIA, and it was prized for its sweetness and high alcohol which enabled it to withstand the six-month sea voyage, via Venice, to western Europe. Santorini was conquered by the Ottoman Turks in 1579, but the Turks did not discourage the production of the only cash crop that the island's volcanic soil could sustain.

Loanwords from Italian still in use in Santorini today testify to Venice's importance in its winemaking past. For example, the local dialect word for the vintage is *vendemma* from Italian *vendemmia*.

See GREECE. H.M.W.

Modern times have been equally kind to the wines of Santorini. Since at least 2005, Santorini has been the champion of modern Greek wine, at least in terms of visibility, media coverage, and prices commanded, with several producers enjoying superstar status, even in export markets. The fact that Santorini is one of the most beautiful islands in the Mediterranean, with millions of tourists every year, has helped.

Santorini is one of the most surreal terroirs for viticulture. The winds are extreme and, in most places, vines have to be trained in a low basket shape for protection. Everything that grows on the outside of the basket is pummelled by the wind, resulting in very low YIELDS. Recent trials with conventional TRELLIS SYSTEMS in sheltered areas have been successful, but highly controversial in the eyes of traditionalists. The island is very arid, with only mist rising from the caldera every morning to sustain any form of agriculture. The soils are VOLCANIC and not just free of PHYLLOXERA but immune to it. As a result, vines are UNGRAFTED, that portion below ground being up to 400 years old. Yields are seldom more than 15 hl/ha (0.8 tons/acre), which means that Santorini wine may eventually become a thing of the past.

The PDO Santorini allows for dry wines and sweet wines made from sun-dried grapes, based on Assyrtiko, with smaller amounts of Athiri and Aidani. The dry wines are, more often than not, pure Assyrtiko and generally present an outstanding combination of MINERALITY, high alcohol, and high acidity, often resulting in PHS below 3. Dry but late-harvest wines, harvested during the night, enjoy a short SKIN CONTACT and are then aged for at least three months in partly-filled old oak casks in order to initiate deliberate OXIDATION. These wines, called Nychteri, can reach 16% alcohol, are not for the faint-hearted but are clearly one of the most impressive and individual white wines in the world. Sweet wines are called Vinsanto, a term wrongly assumed to be a loanword from the Italian Vin Santo. However, it has been proved that Visanto, the Vino of Santorini, was exported, mainly for religious purposes, to Russia well before Italians initiated the style. Vinsanto is made from sun-dried grapes, mainly Assyrtiko, oak-aged for several years, if not decades. The best Vinsantos can age for ever but, given the yields in Santorini, they are necessarily extremely expensive. Mezzo is a less sweet, younger but delicious and cheaper alternative. The promising Mavrotragano variety can produce some exceptional reds, not (yet?) included in the appellation framework.

K.L.

Saperavi, ancient and distinctive south west GEORGIAN grape variety notable for the COLOUR and ACIDITY it can bring to a blend. It is Georgia's signature and most-planted red wine grape. As a VARIETAL wine, it is capable, not to say demanding, of long BOTTLE AGEING. The flesh of this dark-skinned grape is deep pink and it produces wines that command attention if not always devotion. It ripens late, is relatively productive, and is quite well adapted to cold winters, but not so well that the Russian Potapenko viticultural research institute has been discouraged from producing a **Saperavi Severny**, a hybrid of SEVERNY and Saperavi which was released in 1947 and incorporates not just Saperavi's VINIFERA genes, but also those of the cold-hardy VITIS *amurensis*.

Traditional Saperavi is planted throughout almost all of the wine regions of the former Soviet republics. It is an important variety in RUSSIA, UKRAINE, MOLDOVA, BULGARIA, ARMENIA, and AZERBAIJAN, as well as in its native GEORGIA although in cooler areas the acidity may be too marked for any purpose other than blending, despite its relatively high sugar levels. It was also used extensively for VINE BREEDING at MAGARACH, the Crimean wine research centre.

Sardinia, known as **Sardegna** in Italian (the Italian adjective is **Sardo**), Mediterranean island 200 km/125 miles off the coast of Italy at its nearest point, governed by CARTHAGE before conquest by Ancient ROME, and subsequently by Byzantines, Arabs, and Catalans. (See map under ITALY.) Sardinia became an integral part of Italy only in 1726, when it was ceded to the House of Savoy. Historically, linguistically, and culturally, as well as geographically, the island seems detached from the mainstream of Italian civilization, and it is no surprise that at least two of its significant grape varieties—CANNONAU (GARNACHA) and Carignano (CARIGNAN), also known as BOVALE Grande—are of Spanish origin.

Vines in any case play only a small part in a total agricultural economy in which much of the land is dedicated to the grazing of animals—sheep in particular—for milk and meat. Although the total area under vines and the total production of wine underwent a significant increase in the post-war period, due to the wholesale replacement of its low-yielding BUSH VINES with high-yielding TENDONE and wire-trained vineyards aided by lavish subsidies both from Rome and from the regional government, the result has not been a self-sustaining wine industry. As markets for Sardinian wines contracted and the flow of public funds to CO-OPERATIVE wineries dwindled to a trickle, the total vineyard surface decreased from a high of 70,000 to under 19,000 ha/47,000 acres in 2010. This dramatic contraction, however, has helped Sardinia's slow but certain transition from quantity to quality producer: of a total of 510,000 hl of wine produced in 2010, more than 330,000 hl qualified as DOC and over 80,000 hl of IGT, while basic BULK WINE represented a mere 15% of the total.

Little has been done within the DOCs to match individual vine varieties to proper soils and climates. The production zones of the most popular varieties—Vermentino and Cannonau—have been extended to include the entire surface of the island. Four smaller subzones have been created for Cannonau: Capo Ferrato, Jerzu (the smallest), Oliena, and Classico (comprising the provinces of Nuoro and Ogliastra and wines declared as such need to be at least 95% Cannonau compared to 85% in the other subzones), but they are still too large to represent a faithful expression of a specific terroir. With a maximum yield per ha of 11 tonnes (9 tonnes for the Classico zone) for Cannonau and an absurdly generous 16 tonnes for Vermentino, it is only logical that most quality-oriented producers turn their backs on the official DOCs, preferring the lowly IGT, which also has the benefit of less bureaucracy. The Arborea DOC, approved in 1987 and geared solely to producing enormous volumes of SANGIOVESE and TREBBIANO in a zone of commercial fruit cultivation, established 135 hl/ha as its official maximum permitted yield, and has not been a commercial success.

The existence of four different types of wine—dry, sweet, a *liquoroso*, or higher-alcohol, dry wine, and a *liquoroso* sweet wine—in many of the DOCs (Malvasia di Cagliari, Monica di Cagliari, Giro di Cagliari, Nasco di Cagliari, Cannonau di Sardegna) may seem confusing but at least reflects some of the island's traditional and highly original wine styles.

If the overall picture is far from encouraging, small quantities of good wines do exist and suggest that Sardinia's soil and climate have potential. Vernaccia di Oristano, although produced in dwindling quantities, can be a good approximation of a dry SHERRY with a clean and bitter finish, and the hard-to-find legendary Malvasia di Bosa justly enjoys a certain reputation as a dessert wine. Refreshing bottles of Vermentino di Gallura, produced in the island's north, do exist, though hardly in sufficient quantity to merit the wine's promotion to DOCG status in 1996, even though it was accompanied by the sensible lowering of yields to 10 tonnes/ha. An occasional good bottle of Nuragus di Cagliari only underlines the absurdity of allowing such high yields. Carignano del Sulcis has been responsible for some of the island's best wines, especially those from the co-operative in Santadi, Argiolas, and Barrua, a JOINT VENTURE between Santadi and the Incisa family of SASSICAIA set up by winemaker Giacomo Tachis. In the province of Alghero the giant Sella e Mosca has begun putting its energy into re-evaluating the local white TORBATO while also producing fine, long-lived Cabernet Sauvignon. But the real custodians of Sardinia's original wine styles and cultivation methods are several small producers who, following ORGANIC or BIODYNAMIC methods while tending old BUSH VINES, succeed in turning out wines that truly reflect their origin. Prime examples include Dettori in Sennori, Panevino in Nurri, Giovanni Battista Columbu in Bosa, and Contini in Oristano. These mavericks demonstrate the versatility and potential that Sardinia has in spades, but is frustratingly slow to develop.   W.S.

Belfrage, N., *Brunello to Zibibbo—The Wines of Tuscany, Central and South Italy* (2nd edn, London, 2003)

www.ctvsardegna.com

Sárga Muskotály, or **Sárgamuskotály**, occasional Hungarian name for the 'yellow Muscat' of TOKAJ (MUSCAT BLANC À PETITS GRAINS).

Sassicaia, trail-blazing Tuscan wine made, largely from CABERNET SAUVIGNON, originally by Mario Incisa della Rochetta at the Tenuta San Guido near BOLGHERI and one of the first Italian reds made in the image of fine red bordeaux. The first small commercial quantities were released in the mid 1970s. For more details, see VINO DA TAVOLA. In 1994 Sassicaia was granted its own DOC as an official subzone of Bolgheri (Bolgheri-Sassicaia DOC), the only wine from a single estate in Italy to enjoy this privilege.

Fini, M., *Sassicaia—The Original Super Tuscan* (Florence, 2000).

Saumur, town in the Loire just upriver from the ANJOU district giving its name to an extensive wine district and several appellations. Saumur is effectively a south western extension of TOURAINE, yet is more of a centre for the wine trade of Anjou–Saumur than is Angers. The grapes grown in these latter two neighbouring regions are very similar, except that Saumur does not have Anjou's range of potentially great sweet white wines.

Saumur's most important wine (and France's most important mousseux) is **Saumur Mousseux**, a well-priced white and rosé sparkling wine made from Chenin Blanc grapes, often with a mix of international and Loire varieties. These grapes can come from an even wider area than that permitted for still Saumur, and the quality of winemaking is high among the larger houses of the town of Saumur, such as Gratien & Meyer, Langlois Chateau, and Bouvet Ladubay, and also at the important CO-OPERATIVE at St-Cyr-en-Bourg, with its extensive underground cellars hewn out of the local TUFFEAU. This CALCAREOUS rock predominates around Saumur, and was much quarried, both locally and abroad (according to Duijker it was used for rebuilding after the Great Fire of London, and also extensively in the Dutch city of Maastricht). This left the Saumurois with ready-made wine cellars, perfect not just for mushrooms, one of their most important products, but also for the maturation of their acidic wines which, as in CHAMPAGNE, had a natural tendency to retain some carbon dioxide in spring. Ackerman-Laurance was the first producer of sparkling Saumur, in the early 19th century. The wines have enjoyed considerable commercial success, although an increasing proportion of the base material for Saumur Mousseux is expected to be fashioned into CRÉMANT de Loire, for which the criteria are rather more rigorous: yields of 50 rather than 60 hl/ha and 12 rather than nine months' TIRAGE.

Saumur Blanc can be remarkably difficult to distinguish from Anjou Blanc, being made from Chenin Blanc and being both high in acidity and potentially long lived. Only such conscientious growers as Chx du Hureau, de Targé, Villeneuve, and Domaine des Roches manage to coax much fruit out of them, however, by picking in TRIES and employing OAK for fermentation and maturation, resulting in a graceful, limestone alternative to the firmer dry white ANJOU made on schist.

Saumur Rouge is a much more successful wine, made on soils similar to those of CHINON and BOURGUEIL. It is made from at least 70% Cabernet Franc with Cabernet Sauvignon and/ or Pineau d'Aunis and can be a refreshing, relatively light, fruity wine. A little more Saumur Rouge is produced than Saumur Blanc, but the most significant still wine of the region is **Saumur-Champigny**, whose extraordinary expansion in the 1970s and 1980s was originally due to FASHION, and mainly Paris fashion at that, but has been sustained by growers' determination to maximize vineyard potential and reach full ripeness. The Saumur-Champigny zone, prettily named after the village of Champigny, is on a tuffeau plateau that lends itself well to viticulture, as in neighbouring Touraine. Its high LIMESTONE content made the Chenin Blanc vine traditionally grown here prone to CHLOROSIS in the post-PHYLLOXERA era, but by the mid 2000s more than 1,330 ha/3,200 acres of vines were producing Saumur-Champigny. It was the dominant St-Cyr-en-Bourg co-operative in particular that encouraged the planting of Cabernet Franc vines and developed the still red wine appellation with such success. Much Saumur-Champigny is too light to be worth ageing, although it is usefully, and quintessentially, fruity and flirtatious.

A small amount of light rosé **Cabernet de Saumur** is made, usually considerably drier and less ambitious than Cabernet d'Anjou, while **Coteaux de Saumur** is Saumur's medium-sweet white, made in very small quantities from Chenin Blanc grapes.

See also LOIRE, including map.

Friedrich, J., *A Wine and Food Guide to the Loire* (New York, 1996, and London, 1997).

Saussignac, very small (25 ha in 2012) sweet white wine appellation in SOUTH WEST FRANCE. It lies within the BERGERAC district to the west of Monbazillac and produces sweet white wines, from Sémillon, Sauvignon Blanc, Sauvignon Gris, and some particularly successful Muscadelle grapes. Since the mid 1990s, the appellation has become an enclave of great SWEET WINEMAKING, led by Clos d'Yvigne and Domaine de Richard. In 2004, appellation laws were strengthened to insist on manual picking and completely natural sweetness, generally due to BOTRYTIS.

Atkinson, P., *The Ripening Sun: One Woman and the Creation of a Vineyard* (London, 2004).

Sauterne, occasionally found on labels of GENERIC sweet white wine. Real SAUTERNES always ends in *s*.

Sauternes. The special distinction of this region of 1,767 ha/4,364 acres embedded within the Graves district south of BORDEAUX is that it is dedicated, in a way unmatched by any other wine region, to the production of unfortified, sweet, white wine. In Germany or Alsace, say, where superlative sweet wines are occasionally made, such wines are the exception rather than the rule, and emerge from vines that more usually produce much drier wines.

In Sauternes the situation is quite different. The appellation is reserved for wines from five communes that must adhere to regulations stipulating minimum levels of ALCOHOLIC STRENGTH (13%) and a tasting test that requires the wine to taste sweet. Sémillon, Sauvignon Blanc, Sauvignon Gris, and Muscadelle are responsible but Sémillon is the principal grape, because it is especially susceptible to noble rot, and it accounts for about 80% of a typical estate's ENCÉPAGEMENT. Sauvignon often attracts NOBLE ROT earlier than Sémillon, and its naturally high acidity can give the wine a freshness that balances the richer, broader flavours of Sémillon. Muscadelle's contribution is mostly aromatic, but its viticultural frailty leads many growers to find it more trouble than it is worth.

No one is exactly sure when sweet wine production became the norm here. The style was well entrenched by the late 18th century, when Thomas JEFFERSON and others were purchasing wines from the district's most famous property Ch d'YQUEM that were evidently sweet; and harvesting details from the 1660s suggest, but do not prove, that the wines made then were probably sweet.

Sauternes is the product of a specific MESOCLIMATE. The communes of Sauternes, Barsac, Preignac, Bommes, and Fargues are close to two rivers, the broad GARONNE and its small tributary, the Ciron. When, in autumn, the cool spring-fed Ciron waters flow into the warmer tidal Garonne, evening mists envelop the vineyards until late morning the following day, when the sun, if it shines, burns the mist away. This moist atmosphere encourages *Botrytis cinerea*, a fungus that attacks the grapes and causes them to shrivel and rot (see BOTRYTIS BUNCH ROT). Mist activates the botrytis spores in the vineyards, and the alternating sunshine completes the process of desiccation.

The onset of botrytis is crucial to the evolution of the grapes. Without it, they may indeed ripen sufficiently to ensure that a sweet wine can be made, if fermentation ceases before all the sugar has been converted into alcohol, but the result will lack complexity. As outlined in more detail in NOBLE ROT, the overall effect of a benevolent botrytis infection is to increase the concentrations of SUGAR IN GRAPES and, to a lesser extent, that of TARTARIC ACID; to stimulate the production of GLYCEROL; and to alter considerably the AROMA and flavour of the finished wine.

The essential difference between mediocre and great Sauternes hangs on the willingness of estate owners to risk waiting until botrytis arrives. There are years when botrytis either fails to develop at all or arrives very late in the year. Proprietors must then decide whether to delay or to begin the harvest. Delay is a risky strategy: the chances of frost or rain, both of which can wreck the harvest, clearly increase as the autumn months wear on, but by picking too early the estate can end up with insipid sweet white wine while its more scrupulous neighbours are in a position to market great BOTRYTIZED wine.

This introduces an economic issue unique to this region. Sauternes is exceptionally costly to make. There are a number of vintages each decade in which it is either impossible to make good sweet wine (and some grapes may be salvaged to make a dry white that qualifies only as a BORDEAUX AOC) or in which, as in 1991 for example, it can be produced only in minute quantities. Even in excellent VINTAGES, maximum YIELDS are restricted to 25 hl/ha (1.4 tons/acre), a quantity infrequently attained. At Yquem, the average yield is a trifling 9 hl/ha, and at most conscientious estates the yields probably fluctuate between 12 and 20 hl/ha—although total production of the appellation, perhaps tellingly, does not vary nearly as much. (In the red wine districts of MÉDOC or ST-ÉMILION, yields of more than 45 hl/ha are routine.)

In addition, the harvest is unusually protracted. Botrytis occasionally swoops over entire vineyards, as in 1990 and 2003, but this is rare. More commonly, it performs its unsightly activities patchily. A typical harvesting pattern might be as follows: an attack of botrytis on Sauvignon grapes allows half of them to be picked in late September; two weeks of drizzle follow, during which picking is suspended; finer weather resumes, grapes affected by undesirable GREY ROT are eliminated, and in late October another attack of botrytis allows the Sémillon and remaining Sauvignon grapes to be picked over a three-week period. The necessity for selective harvesting, or TRIAGE, essential for Sauternes, is expensive, as teams of pickers must be kept available for a very long period. More than any other wine, Sauternes is made in the vineyard. Once the grapes have been picked, they are difficult to manipulate. Their MUST WEIGHT (sugar content), their PHYSIOLOGICAL RIPENESS, and the degree of botrytis infection will all determine quality before the winemaker has got to work. None the less, Sauternes calls for careful vinification. Pressing should be as gentle as possible, and some leading estates still use old-fashioned hydraulic or basket PRESSES for this purpose. Fermentation takes place in tanks or, more usually since the mid 1980s, in BARRIQUES, of which 30 to 100% are likely to be new (see BARREL FERMENTATION). Fermentation either stops of its own accord when the wine has achieved a balance of about 14% alcohol and a RESIDUAL SUGAR level that is the equivalent of a further 4–7% alcohol, or it is arrested with the addition of SULFUR DIOXIDE. For more details, see BOTRYTIZED winemaking.

In weaker vintages, CHAPTALIZATION may be permitted, although better estates avoid the practice, which merely adds sweetness rather than complexity and is often used to disguise lazy harvesting. The wine is usually aged in oak barrels for between 18 and 36 months (see BARREL MATURATION). Less distinguished lots of wine are usually sold off to NÉGOCIANTS; in 1978, Yquem bottled only 15% of the crop under its own label, and in 1987, many estates marketed no wine at all. This is all the more remarkable because, despite having very much higher production costs, the Sauternais are not generally rewarded with much higher selling prices than the equivalent red bordeaux made in much greater quantity. Blame FASHION.

Although the prevalence of botrytis and overall geographical location are common to all Sauternes, specific MESOCLIMATES and SOIL STRUCTURES affect the styles of the different estates. BARSAC is the most distinctive commune, and is entitled to its own appellation, although it can also be sold as Sauternes. Its proximity to the Ciron and its ALLUVIAL soil give wines that are often lighter and more elegant than its neighbours. The communes of Bommes and Sauternes itself tend to give the fattest wines, although exceptions are numerous. There are also differences in maturation dates: the grapes at Ch Filhot, for instance, often ripen a week later than those of Barsac. The trend this century has increasingly been to seek HARMONY in the wines rather than maximum sweetness.

All these factors were taken into account when in 1855 the existing estates were classified. Successful candidates were ranked as either first or second growths, with Yquem rightfully given its own super-status (see CLASSIFICATION). In the 1960s especially, standards slumped. Producers were especially impoverished and there was a string of poor vintages. Only the richest estates could afford to maintain standards. Elsewhere, corners were cut, grapes were picked too early, and barriques were replaced with tanks. For two decades many classified growths produced wines that were mediocre at best, even in fine vintages. Only with the excellent 1983 vintage

did matters improve. Prices rose, and wise proprietors invested in long overdue improvements, which bore fruit in the superb 1986, 1988, 1989, and 1990 vintages and, more recently, the 1996, 1997, 2001, 2003, 2007, 2009, and 2011. The official 1855 classification is once again a reasonably reliable guide to quality, although a number of unclassified growths, such as Ch de Fargues (owned by Comte Alexandre de Lur-Saluces who used to manage Yquem), Gilette, and Raymond-Lafon, are often of first growth quality, and price.

After a bad patch, Sauternes is again showing the quality of which it is capable. It combines power, voluptuousness, and elegance, and good bottles can evolve and improve for up to 50 years (longer in the case of Yquem). Given the risks and costs involved in its production, it remains underpriced in relation to the enormous pleasure it brings to those growing numbers of wine lovers who find a fine Sauternes has an undeniable place on the dinner table.   S.B. & J.R.

Brook, S., *Sauternes, and Other Sweet Wines of Bordeaux* (London, 1995).

Olney, R., *Yquem* (London, 1986).

Sauvignonasse, old Bordeaux white grape hardly encountered there today but also known as Sauvignon Vert and, in Friuli, FRIULANO (once Tocai Friulano). It is quite distinct from the more famous SAUVIGNON BLANC but the two were long confused in Chile and the term 'Sauvignon' was once liberally applied. In general the wines produced from Sauvignonasse are much less crisp and aromatic than those of Sauvignon Blanc and this vine is much more sensitive to DOWNY MILDEW and ROT. According to official statistics Argentina may have more 'Sauvignon Vert' planted than Chile. In Slovenia the variety is now known as Zeleni Sauvignon. It can be found to a limited extent further east.

Sauvignon Blanc is the hugely popular vine variety solely responsible for some of the world's most distinctively aromatic dry white wines: Sancerre, Pouilly-Fumé, and a tidal wave of Sauvignon Blanc and Fumé Blanc from outside France, most notably New Zealand. The direct, obvious, easy-to-appreciate nature of varietal Sauvignon Blanc seems to answer a need in modern wine consumers who are perhaps more interested in immediate fruit than subtlety and ageing ability—which is not to deny that in many great white wines, both dry and sweet, it does also add nerve and zest to its most common blending partner SÉMILLON. It has always shared a certain aromatic similarity with the great red wine grape Cabernet Sauvignon (something approaching HERBACEOUSNESS) and in 1997 Sauvignon Blanc's standing in the world of wine rose when DNA PROFILING

established that, with Cabernet Franc, Sauvignon Blanc was a parent of Cabernet Sauvignon, the result of a spontaneous field crossing, probably in the 18th century, in Bordeaux. Further DNA studies have suggested that the variety's origins are probably in the Loire; that it has a parent-offspring relationship with the historic SAVAGNIN Blanc (and is therefore probably its progeny); that it is probably a sibling of the CHENIN BLANC of the Loire; and that it seems genetically close to Sémillon. It is certainly well-connected.

Sauvignon Blanc's most recognizable characteristic is its piercing, instantly recognizable aroma. Descriptions typically include 'grassy, herbaceous, musky, green fruits' (especially gooseberries), 'nettles', and even 'tomcats'. Research into FLAVOUR COMPOUNDS suggests that METHOXYPYRAZINES play an important role in Sauvignon's aroma. Over-productive Sauvignon vines planted on heavy soils can produce wines only vaguely suggestive of this but Sauvignon cautiously cultivated in the central vineyards of the Loire, unmasked by oak, can reach the dry white apogee of Sauvignon fruit with some of the purest, most refreshingly zesty wines in the world. The best Sancerres and Pouilly-Fumés served as a model for early exponents of New World Sauvignon Blanc, although by the 1980s it was the Loire vignerons, and winemakers all round the world, who were more likely to copy their counterparts in New Zealand (which achieved rapid fame with this variety) in experimenting with fermentation and maturation in oak, and picking the grapes at different levels of RIPENESS to add nuance and pungency to the aroma and weight to the palate.

Oak-aged examples usually need an additional year or two to show their best, but almost all dry, unblended Sauvignon is designed to be drunk young, although there are both Loire and Bordeaux examples that can demonstrate durability, if rarely evolution, with up to 15 years in bottle (see POUILLY-FUMÉ and Pavillon Blanc de Ch MARGAUX, for example). As an ingredient in the great sweet white wines of SAUTERNES, on the other hand, Sauvignon plays a minor but important part in one of the world's longest-living wines.

The vine is particularly vigorous, which has caused problems in parts of the Loire and New Zealand. If the vine's vegetation gets out of hand, the grapes fail to reach full maturity and the resulting wine can be aggressively herbaceous, almost intrusively rank. (And underripe Sémillon can exhibit very similar characteristics—just as underripe Cabernet Sauvignon can smell like Cabernet Franc. Recent discoveries of their relationships may help to explain this.) A low-vigour ROOTSTOCK and CANOPY MANAGEMENT can help combat this problem. Sauvignon buds after but flowers before Sémillon, with which it is typically blended in Bordeaux and, increasingly, elsewhere. Until suitable clones such as 297 and 316 were identified, and sprays to combat Sauvignon's susceptibility to POWDERY MILDEW and BLACK ROT were developed, yields were uneconomically irregular and the variety was not popular with growers. In 1968, for example, Sauvignon was France's 13th most planted white grape variety but within 20 years it had risen to fourth place and by 2011 its French total of nearly 30,000 ha/75,000 acres put it behind only Ugni Blanc and Chardonnay in France.

In Bordeaux it was not until the late 1980s that Sauvignon overtook Ugni Blanc, or TREBBIANO, as second most planted white grape variety after Sémillon, which in 2011 still outnumbered Sauvignon but not by that much—and the newer clones of Sauvignon are much more productive than the important but rapidly declining Sémillon. The Gironde's Sauvignon is concentrated in the Entre-Deux-Mers, Graves, and the sweet wine-producing districts in and around Sauternes. In each of these areas, it is dominated by and usually blended with Sémillon, particularly in Sauternes, where the typical blend incorporates 80% of the more rot-prone Sémillon together with a little Muscadelle. BORDEAUX BLANC owes much to Entre-Deux-Mers Sauvignon although low yields and, often, expensive oak ageing, as in the best dry white PESSAC-LÉOGNAN, GRAVES, and the handful of expensive Médoc whites (sold as BORDEAUX AOC), are prerequisites for a memorable performance from Sauvignon in Bordeaux. It is perhaps no coincidence that the average Loire Sauvignon has more Sauvignon character than the average all-Sauvignon Bordeaux Blanc when the official maximum yield for the first is 10 hl/ha (0.6 tons/acre) lower than the 65 hl/ha allowed in Bordeaux.

As with red wines, the satellite areas of SOUTH WEST FRANCE reflect Bordeaux's spread of vine varieties and Sauvignon is often an easily perceptible ingredient in the dry whites of such areas as BERGERAC, Côtes du MARMANDAIS, and Côtes de DURAS.

It is in the Loire that Sauvignon is encountered in its purest, most unadulterated form. In the often limestone vineyards of SANCERRE, POUILLY-FUMÉ, and their eastern satellites QUINCY, REUILLY, and MENETOU-SALON, it can demonstrate one of the most eloquent arguments for marrying variety with suitable TERROIR. The variety is often called Blanc Fumé here and has happily replaced most of the lesser varieties once common, notably much of the Chasselas in Pouilly-sur-Loire. The best examples need a few years in bottle to show their best. From this concentration of vineyards, Sauvignon's influence radiates outwards: north east towards Chablis in ST-BRIS, south to ST-POURÇAIN-sur-Sioule, and north and west to Coteaux du GIENNOIS and CHEVERNY, as well as to a substantial quantity of well-priced eastern Loire wines, typically labelled TOURAINE. Such Sauvignons tend to be light, racy, and, of course, aromatic. With Chardonnay, it has also been allowed into the vineyards of Anjou, where it is sometimes blended with the indigenous CHENIN BLANC.

Elsewhere in France, Sauvignon Blanc has been an obvious, though not invariably successful, choice for those seeking to make internationally saleable VARIETAL wine. In Languedoc-Roussillon its total plantings of 8,732 ha/21,568 acres in 2011 made it the region's second most planted white wine grape after Chardonnay, even if yields are often too high to extract quite enough varietal character. Small plantings of Sauvignon can also be found in some of the Provençal appellations.

Across the Alps, Sauvignon's most successful Italian region is the far north east in FRIULI, with some ALTO ADIGE and COLLIO examples exhibiting particularly fine fruit and purity of flavour. Many of the better bottles from the north east are made from the extremely pungent and recognizable R3 clone of the Rauscedo vine nursery. Attempts to transfer Sauvignon to central Italy have been notably less successful. In the 1980s, Italy's plantings of Sauvignon doubled to nearly 3,000 ha/7,410 acres but by 2010 growth had slowed, with just 3,744 ha/9,252 acres in total. Overall it's a relatively minor grape in Italy.

The Primorska region across the SLOVENIAN border from here is known as a source of delicate Sauvignon Blanc, with a particularly distinctive version coming from Meranovo in the Maribor district of Podravje. In Vipava and Brda districts both barrel-aged and unoaked styles are produced. The variety conspicuously thrives in Styria in AUSTRIA, stylishly combining fruit with aroma. Austria had more than 1,000 ha of Sauvignon Blanc in 2012, while Germany had about 700 ha in total, with almost half in the Pfalz. Parts of SERBIA, especially the Fruška Gora district, and some of the CZECH REPUBLIC, where it is widely planted, clearly have potential for racy Sauvignon. ROMANIA had even more Sauvignon Blanc planted than Cabernet Sauvignon: 5,548 ha, and neighbouring MOLDOVA also had sizeable plantings of the variety.

Sauvignon Blanc plantings in Spain have increased rapidly this century, reaching 4,482 ha in 2012, mainly in Castilla-La Mancha where varietals can lack definition. It has also been particularly popular with growers in RUEDA. Certainly Portugal and north western Spain have no shortage of indigenous varieties (see MINHO and GALICIA) capable of reproducing vaguely similar wine styles. There is a tendency for Sauvignon Blanc to taste oily when reared in too warm a climate, as it sometimes does in Israel and other Mediterranean vineyards where those with an eye to the export market put it through its paces.

This was clearly perceptible in many of Australia's earlier attempts with the variety, although by the early 1990s, there was even keener appreciation of the need to reserve it for the country's cooler sites (see AUSTRALIA for more on the wines produced) and since the second half of the 1990s plantings have soared, reaching nearly 7,000 ha by 2012. Chardonnay plantings outnumber those of Sauvignon Blanc by three to one in Australia but Sauvignon has been narrowing the gap, not least because of the extraordinary popularity of New Zealand examples of the varietal on the Australian market. Several of the best-selling whites in Australia were Marlborough Sauvignons by the start of the second decade of the 21st century—something that would have been unthinkable in the previous century.

New Zealand has built its wine industry and reputation on the particularly distinctive style of Marlborough Sauvignon Blanc. This is the variety that introduced New Zealand wine to the world and did it by developing its own pungent style: intensely perfumed, more obviously fruity than the Loire prototype, with just a hint of both gas and sweetness and, occasionally, gooseberries or asparagus. This style of Sauvignon can now be found in Chile, South Africa, the cooler areas of North America, and in virtually all parts of France where Sauvignon is grown. The area planted with Sauvignon Blanc had risen to almost 20,000 ha by 2012, representing three vines in every five in New Zealand and a far greater area of Sauvignon than anywhere else. The great majority, 88%, of the country's Sauvignon is grown in the rapidly expanded Marlborough region, although it is grown in all other regions, too. So popular has Kiwi Sauvignon become, that Chardonnay is relatively ignored in New Zealand.

Chardonnay overtook 'Sauvignon' in Chile only early this century although much of this, particularly older vines in the south, is almost certainly the widely planted SAUVIGNONASSE, for which Sauvignon Blanc is a legally accepted synonym in Chile. According to official statistics, total Chilean plantings of Sauvignon Blanc had risen rapidly to almost 14,000 ha by 2012, fuelled especially by the expansion of cooler, often coastal, wine regions from which some remarkably successful examples of true Sauvignon Blanc in which yields are limited, are emerging. High yields help depress the keynote aromas of Sauvignon Blanc in most other South American wines labelled Sauvignon although some of the higher elevation offerings from Argentina, where total plantings of 'Sauvignon' were 2,295 ha in 2012, are improving.

Thanks to Robert MONDAVI, who renamed it FUMÉ BLANC, Sauvignon Blanc enjoyed enormous success in California in the 1980s, and since the late 1990s a second great wave of popularity for California Sauvignon Blanc has boosted plantings to almost 16,000 acres/6,500 ha by 2012. See CALIFORNIA for more on the wines, which are very occasionally sweet and even botrytized, a sort of Semillon-free Sauternes. There has also been an increase, as elsewhere in the New World, in blending in some Semillon to dry white Sauvignon to add weight and fruit to Sauvignon's aroma and acidity. Like California, WASHINGTON state makes both Sauvignon Blanc and Fumé Blanc from its total area of 1,173 acres/475 ha in 2012, very much less important than Chardonnay and Riesling. Elsewhere in North America it is not especially notable, although fine white BORDEAUX blends have been made in British Columbia. But perhaps Sauvignon's real success in the New World, New Zealand excepted, has been in SOUTH AFRICA, where local wine drinkers fell upon the Cape's more successful early Sauvignons as a fashionable internationally recognized wine style. By 1990, there were 3,300 ha of Sauvignon Blanc to South Africa's barely 2,400 ha of Cabernet Sauvignon. By 2012 there were 9,471 ha/23,392 acres and the area was still growing. Cape Sauvignon Blanc, particularly from the cooler vineyards of Cape Point, Elgin, Darling, and Cape Agulhas, shows intense capsicum flavours and reasonable ageing potential.

Sauvignon Blanc is often simply called **Sauvignon**, especially on wine labels, but it has mutated into variants with darker-coloured berries, notably SAUVIGNON GRIS and Sauvignon Rouge, also grown to a limited extent in the Loire. SAUVIGNON VERT is genetically distinct.

Bowers, J. E., and Meredith, C. P., 'The parentage of a classic wine grape, Cabernet Sauvignon', *Nature Genetics*, 16/1 (1997), 84–7.

Sauvignon Gris, sometimes blended with SAUVIGNON BLANC, sometimes sold as a VARIETAL, is another name for Sauvignon Rose and has discernibly pink skins. It can produce more substantial wines than many a Sauvignon Blanc, and is increasingly specified as an authorized grape variety in AOC regulations, notably in Bordeaux and the Loire. It is also planted in Chile, Argentina, Uruguay, and New Zealand. See also FIÉ.

Sauvignon Vert, synonym for SAUVIGNONASSE, except in California where the variety called Sauvignon Vert is MUSCADELLE.

Savagnin is a very old, genetically important vine variety whose origins lie in north east France. Because it is so old, like PINOT, with which it has a parent-offspring relationship, it exists in many different mutations, including GEWÜRZTRAMINER, TRAMINER, and HEIDA (Païen), all with the same genetic fingerprint even if they display some clonal variation. DNA PROFILING has further shown that Savagnin is a parent of Chenin Blanc, Grüner Veltiner, Sauvignon Blanc, Silvaner, and Trousseau, may well be a parent of

Petit Manseng and, even more surprisingly, probably has a parent-offspring relationship with Verdelho.

Robinson, J., Harding, J., and Vouillamoz, J., *Wine Grapes, a complete guide to 1,368 vine varieties, including their origins and flavours* (London, 2012).

Savagnin Blanc is the white-berried, non-aromatic SAVAGNIN best known as the characteristic white wine grape of the JURA in eastern France. (Both this pale-skinned clone and a pink-skinned one may be called Traminer, the latter also Roter Traminer, while GEWÜRZTRAMINER is the aromatic, pink-skinned form.) Savagnin Blanc, often called simply Savagnin, is a fine but curious vine variety with a typically light crop of small, round, pale berries. In France, it is as much a viticultural curiosity as the wine it alone produces, VIN JAUNE, is a winemaking oddity. France's vineyard census of 2011 found a grand total of 510 ha/1,260 acres of this variety cultivated almost exclusively in Jura where it makes increasingly varied wines alongside—the sherry-like vin jaune. It may be included in any of the region's white wine appellations, although most start off as potential vin jaune. However, many barrels are withdrawn early, rejected for vin jaune, and used for OXIDATIVE dry white wines, sometimes blended with Chardonnay. Since the late 1990s, however, a new breed of fresh, unoxidized 'ouillé' Savagnin, in which exuberant floral aromas can bear witness to the variety's close relationship to TRAMINER et al., has emerged, and caused a stir amongst traditionalists. Whichever style of wine is produced, Savagnin is always a firm, long-lasting wine high in EXTRACT and, usually, acidity. The vine is well adapted to the ancient, west-facing MARL slopes of Jura but many believe it is at its finest in the steep vineyards of CHÂTEAU-CHALON, where it may sometimes be left to ripen as late as the end of October. The resulting distinctively nutty wine is the product of six years' ageing in cask, under a FLOR-like film, and it can continue to evolve for many years in bottle, the special 62 cl *clavelin*.

Official statistics showed that in 2012 Australia had almost 140 ha of Savagnin, virtually all planted in the early years of this century by growers supplied as ALBARIÑO by CSIRO, the result of a mis-labelling of cuttings imported from Spain via France. Producers have to decide whether to label the resulting wine as Savagnin or Traminer.

Savagnin Noir is a Jura name for PINOT NOIR.

Savagnin Rose, the pink-berried SAVAGNIN and non-aromatic version of GEWÜRZTRAMINER, also known in Germany as Clevner and Roter Traminer.

Savatiano, Greece's most common wine grape, widely planted on 11,306 ha/27,926 acres in 2012 throughout Attica and central GREECE. This light-berried vine, with its exceptionally good DROUGHT resistance, is the most common ingredient in RETSINA, although RODITIS and ASSYRTIKO are often added to compensate for Savatiano's naturally low acidity. On particularly suitable sites, Savatiano can produce well-balanced dry white wines.

Savennières, distinctive and much celebrated dry white wine appellation in the Anjou region of the Loire, immediately south west of the town of Angers on southeast–facing SCHIST and SANDSTONE slopes on the north bank of the Loire. Total production of the appellation has increased from the under 30,000 case norm at the turn of the century as these examples of dry CHENIN BLANC display such an unusual combination of nerve, concentration, and longevity that they attracted winemakers from outside the 6-km strip itself, notably from Coteaux du LAYON across the river. In its Napoleonic heyday, Savennières was a sweet wine, but today, although DEMI SEC, MOELLEUX, and DOUX versions have become more common in this era of CLIMATE CHANGE, most of it is dry or, if between 4 and 7 g/l RESIDUAL SUGAR, described unofficially as Sec Tendre. The best are unusually concentrated and can last for several decades, even if some are unappetizingly tart at less than seven years old. Within Savennières are the two subappellations **Savennières-Coulée de Serrant**, a single estate of just 7 ha/17 acres run by the Joly family on BIODYNAMIC lines, and the 33 ha of **Savennières-La Roche-aux-Moines**, in which several different producers struggle to make a living in this frost-prone corner of the Loire valley. More recently better vineyard management and selective picking techniques are achieving much higher ripeness levels which result in wines with both accessibility and complexity in youth, even if they may not last as long as more traditional Savennières. The appellation is bidding to become the Loire's second Grand Cru after QUARTS DE CHAUME.

See also LOIRE, including map.

Savigny-lès-Beaune, a small town in BURGUNDY near Beaune, as *lès* (Old French for near) implies, with its own appellation for red wine and a little white. The reds are agreeable, rivalling those of BEAUNE itself, but lack the depth and character of wines from villages such as Pommard or Volnay more prominently sited on the LIMESTONE escarpment.

The village is divided by the river Rhoin. Those vineyards on the southern side, including PREMIERS CRUS Les Peuillets, Les Narbantons, Les Rouvrettes, and Les Marconnets, are on sandy soil and produce wines similar to those of

Beaune, although lighter. Those on the other side of the village, towards Pernand-Vergelesses, including Les Lavières and Les Vergelesses, are on stonier soil.

An engraving dating from 1703 at the Château de Savigny describes the wines as nourishing, theological, and disease-defying—'nourrissants, théologiques et morbifuges'. A little white wine is produced from Chardonnay. Chandon de Briailles and Simon Bize have been the leading producers based here.

See also CÔTE D'OR, and map under BURGUNDY.

J.T.C.M.

Savoie, eastern French alpine region on the border with both Switzerland and Italy, sometimes Anglicized to **Savoy**, comprising the two *départements* Savoie and Haute-Savoie together with small parts of neighbouring Ain and Isère. The dramatic countryside is so popular with visitors for both winter sports and summer relaxation that the wines found a ready market and it was rare for them to leave the region. However, 21st-century interest in lighter wines and INDIGENOUS VARIETIES has encouraged exports.

Savoie became part of France only in 1860, and grows a highly distinctive group of vine varieties that seem to be unrelated even to those of nearby AOSTA. Most Savoie wine is sold under the much-ramified appellation **Vin de Savoie**, although there are individual appellations for ROUSSETTE de Savoie (for wines from ALTESSE) and for the area of SEYSSEL. Much of the terrain here is too mountainous for viticulture and the Savoie vineyards tend to be clustered on the more sheltered foothills. They are widely dispersed with varying climate and soil characteristics, justifying the separate appellations. Some vineyards are high above the banks of the River RHÔNE as it flows from Lake Geneva towards the wine region known as the Rhône Valley. Seyssel is here as well as the CHAUTAGNE district and the village of JONGIEUX, two of the 16 CRUS which can append their names to the appellation Vin de Savoie.

South of here, close to the town of CHAMBÉRY, once famous for its VERMOUTH, is a cluster of CRUS whose names may be more familiar to wine enthusiasts than the main appellation itself including ABYMES, APREMONT, ARBIN, CHIGNIN, and CRUET.

Further north, in Haute Savoie the Chasselas grape predominates in a cluster of vineyards on the southeastern shores of Lake Geneva and makes a range of light, dry, almost appley wines in the crus CRÉPY, MARIGNAN, Marin, and RIPAILLE. Towards Chamonix, the isolated cru of AYSE makes still and sparkling wine from the obscure GRINGET variety.

Total vineyard area for the Vin de Savoie appellation increased from about 1,650 ha/4,075 acres in 1990 to around 2,100 ha/5,190 in 2012. About two-thirds of production is white: crisp, delicate, lightly scented, and essentially alpine. The most widely planted variety is JACQUÈRE, popular with growers because of its productivity. The finest white varieties are Altesse, with its own appellation ROUSSETTE DE SAVOIE, and ROUSSANNE, or Bergeron, responsible for the cru CHIGNIN BERGERON. Chardonnay is declining.

Most of Savoie's wines are VARIETAL and, among reds, Gamay and Pinot Noir imported from Beaujolais and Burgundy respectively can be perfectly respectable, if relatively light. Most inspiring, however, is the late ripening MONDEUSE NOIRE with its deep colour, peppery flavour, and slight bitterness. Mondeuse grown at Arbin has a particular reputation for reds with notable structure and ageing ability at alcohol levels rarely above 12%. The rare PERSAN is enjoying a small revival too. A growing amount of Jacquère-based sparkling wine is expected to be sold as CRÉMANT DE SAVOIE, an appellation introduced in 2014.

W.L.

www.vindesavoie.net

scale, types of insects which attack grapevines, comprising at least 13 different species. Scale insects feed by sucking sap, and heavy infestations can weaken vine VIGOUR. Some scale insects excrete honeydew, which can spoil any bunches because a black, sooty mould usually grows on the honeydew. If many bunches are affected, this may taint the resultant wine.

R.E.S.

Scandinavia, part of northern Europe which includes NORWAY, SWEDEN, DENMARK, Finland, and Iceland (the first two of these being new recruits to vine-growing since the last edition of this book). Of these countries, only Denmark has a liberal attitude towards alcoholic drinks and their sale. Elsewhere wine has been sold by state MONOPOLIES, which has had the effect of restricting choice. High levels of TAXATION have made the lot of the Scandinavian wine drinker even harder, although Scandinavian cellars provide famously good, if slow, conditions for wine BOTTLE AGEING. The climate may make grape RIPENING difficult, but can be excellent for STORING WINE.

Scheurebe is the one early-20th-century GERMAN CROSS that deserves attention from any connoisseur, and the only one named after the prolific vine breeder Dr Georg Scheu, the original director of the viticultural institute at Alzey in Rheinhessen. Sometimes called simply **Scheu**, it was developed with specific, sandy, Rheinhessen soils around Dienheim in mind but has achieved its greatest popularity in the PFALZ. DNA PROFILING in 2012 showed that it is a cross of Riesling and Bukettrebe, a white-berried Silvaner x Schiava Grossa cross. It is much more than a riper, more productive replica of Riesling. Provided it reaches full maturity (like other such German crosses as BACCHUS and ORTEGA it is distinctly unappetizing if picked too early), Scheurebe wines have their own exuberant, racy flavours of blackcurrants or even rich grapefruit. It is one of the few varietal parvenus countenanced by quality-conscious German wine producers, not just because it can easily reach high PRÄDIKAT levels of ripeness, but because these are so delicately counterbalanced with the nerve of acidity—perhaps not quite so much as in an equivalent Riesling—but enough to preserve the wine for many years in bottle. Furthermore, for all its inherent aromatic exuberance, Scheurebe also follows its parent Riesling in reflecting soil and mesoclimate, generating some striking and site-typical variations not just in the Pfalz, but in Franken, and in rare instances along the Nahe, and around Boppart in the Mittelrhein.

Despite its distinct virtues and distinctive flavours, Scheurebe has been in steady decline in Germany over recent decades, slipping to 1,503 ha/3,712 acres by 2012, of which more than half were in Rheinhessen. This may be because it is associated with sweet wine, which is unfashionable in Germany but such prejudice seems unwarranted. Estates such as Müller-Catoir, Pfeffingen, and Lingenfelder in the Pfalz and Wirsching in Franken have for more than 20 years vinified impressive, full-bodied dry Scheurebe. (Dr Becker even makes a respectable sparkling version in Scheurebe's home base in Dienheim.)

The variety is also grown in southern Austria, where it is known as SÄMLING 88 and can make fine sweet wines such as those of Alois Kracher. It is also planted to a very limited extent elsewhere.

Schiava, Italian name for several distinct and generally undistinguished dark-skinned grape varieties known as Vernatsch by the German speakers of Alto Adige, or Südtirol as they would call it; and as TROLLINGER in the German region of Württemberg, where they are widely grown. The name Schiava, meaning 'slave', is thought by some to indicate Slavic origins.

The Schiava group is most planted in TRENTINO-ALTO ADIGE in northern Italy. The most common is **Schiava Grossa** (Grossvernatsch), which was used to breed many GERMAN CROSSES including KERNER and HELFENSTEINER, and has been shown to be a parent of MUSCAT OF HAMBURG. It is extremely productive but is not associated with wines of any real character or concentration. Schiava Grossa is also found in Japan and, as the table grape Black Hamburg, in one ancient vine at Hampton Court Palace in England. **Schiava Gentile** (Edelvernatsch) produces better quality, aromatic soft wines from smaller grapes. The most celebrated and least productive clone is Tschaggele. **Schiava Grigia** and **Schiava Lombarda** are even less important.

Light Schiava-based wines have become much less fashionable than in the late 20th century when they enjoyed much popularity in Switzerland, Austria, and southern Germany. Plantings are in decline as Schiava has been substantially replaced by INTERNATIONAL VARIETIES, although Schiava grapes are still found in most of the non-varietal light red wines of Trentino-Alto Adige. According to the 2010 Italian vine census total plantings of all Schiavas were 1,836 ha/4,537 acres. See TROLLINGER for details of the varieties in Germany.

Schiefer. See SLATE and SCHIST.

Schilcher, rosé wine found mainly in Western Styria in AUSTRIA that is light, acid, fruity and made from the ancient BLAUER WILDBACHER vine variety.

Schilfwein, literally 'reed wine', name used in Austria's NEUSIEDLERSEE for STRAW WINE, because in this area, grapes for such concentrated sweet wines are dried on reeds or mats made from the reeds that grow round the lake.

Schillerwein, pink wine speciality made by CO-FERMENTING red and white grapes or MUST in the WÜRTTEMBERG region in Germany. The term is also used in German SWITZERLAND but the grapes have to come from the same VINEYARD.

Schioppettino, perfumed red grape variety native to the FRIULI region of north east Italy, also known as Ribolla Nera but unrelated to RIBOLLA GIALLA. In spite of official attempts to encourage its replanting, Schioppettino was substantially neglected after the PHYLLOXERA epidemic of the late 19th century in favour of the new imports from France: Merlot, Cabernet Franc, and Cabernet Sauvignon. It seemed destined to disappear until an EU decree of 1978 authorized its cultivation in the province of Udine (see also PIGNOLO). The wine is deeply coloured, medium bodied, with an attractively aromatic richness hinting at violets combined with a certain peppery quality reminiscent of the RHÔNE. Although vine plantings and therefore wine production are still limited, and concentrated in the COLLI ORIENTALI, the potential seems notable. Prepotto close to Slovenia where, as Pokalca, it has virtually disappeared, is considered its elective home, but quite good quality has also come from the Buttrio-Manzano area. By 2010 total plantings had increased from 96 ha in 2000 to 154 ha/381 acres.

schist, a metamorphic rock with a distinct planar aspect due chiefly to the parallel alignment of some of its constituent MINERALS, best shown by mica and amphibole (see GEOLOGY). It has developed a coarser grain-size than SLATE, having been subjected to greater burial temperatures and pressures, and as a result splits less cleanly. The transition between slate and schist is therefore gradual, and the distinction rather subjective. The rocks of PRIORAT, for example, are described by some as slate and by others as schist. (To add to the confusion, the German word *Schiefer* is commonly used for both rocks, as is the French word *schiste*, which is also sometimes extended to include SHALE.)

The planes in schist can have any orientation but are commonly close to vertical—ideal for vine roots to penetrate and for rainwater to percolate through. This is probably why in the DOURO, vineyards sited on schist perform better than those on the region's massive, relatively impenetrable GRANITE. Schist is also important in parts of the Languedoc, such as BANYULS, FAUGÈRES, and parts of ST-CHINIAN, CORBIÈRES, and in NEW ZEALAND's Central Otago.   A.J.M.

Schloss Johannisberg, German wine estate in the RHEINGAU with a history closely interlinked with that of the entire region. First planted by Benedictine monks around 1100, it served in the 18th century under the prince-abbot of Fulda as a model for viticultural success with Riesling. Legend has it that Schloss Johannisberg played an important role in the discovery of BOTRYTIZED wines. Grapes affected by NOBLE ROT were allegedly first harvested at Johannisberg unwittingly, giving rise to the AUSLESE, BEERENAUSLESE, and TROCKENBEERENAUSLESE styles in which, among German growing regions, the Rheingau took the lead. In 1802, Johannisberg became secularized and the property of the prince of Orange. It was won four years later by Napoleon, who presented it to Marshal Kellerman, duke of Valmy, who owned it until 1813. From 1813 to 1815, the property was administered by the allies Russia, Prussia, and Austria; it was then given to the Habsburg Emperor Francis I of Austria at the Vienna Congress. In 1816, he presented it to his chancellor, prince of Metternich Winneburg, whose descendants sold their majority share in the property only in the 1970s. The property today belongs to the Oetker family whose vast network of businesses includes the sparkling wine producer Henkell as well as the G. H. von Mumm estate with which neighbouring Schloss Johannisberg has long had an interlocking relationship. The longstanding prestige of the estate has resulted in the name Johannisberg Riesling being a synonym for German RIESLING. See also GERMAN HISTORY.   D.S.

Schönburger, pink-berried 1979 GERMAN CROSS with Pinot Noir, Chasselas Rose, and Muscat of Hamburg among its antecedents which has been more useful to the wine industry of ENGLAND than to its native Germany, where it is hardly grown, although English plantings have been declining. Its wines are white, low in acid, and relatively full bodied.

Schoonmaker, Frank (1905–76), highly influential American wine writer and wine merchant. Born in South Dakota, he first became interested in wine when researching travel books in Europe in the late 1920s. Immediately after the Repeal of PROHIBITION, he wrote a series of wine articles for the *New Yorker* which were published as *The Complete Wine Book* in 1934. Soon afterwards he founded an eponymous wine import company and travelled extensively, becoming noted for his abilities as a judge of young wines, his espousal of DOMAINE BOTTLING in Burgundy, and his expertise in German wines. An early advocate of American wines, he was highly critical of the habitual GENERIC naming of them. In the 1940s, he was hired as consultant to the large California producer Almaden, for whom he created the best-selling VARIETAL Grenache Rosé, having been inspired by the French wine TAVEL. Schoonmaker employed Alexis LICHINE, who was to occupy a very similar, if not more public, post immediately before the Second World War and the two men were to publish the first editions of their respective wine encyclopedias in 1964 and 1967. He published five wine books and numerous shorter works on wine.

Bespaloff, A., *The New Frank Schoonmaker Encyclopedia of Wine* (New York, 1988).

Schwarzriesling, a German synonym for Pinot Meunier. See MÜLLERREBE.

Sciacarello (sometimes written **Sciaccarello** and **Sciaccarellu**) is a speciality of the French island of CORSICA where plantings had grown to 906 ha/2,238 acres by 2011. DNA PROFILING has established that both Sciacarello and the Corsican variety known as Malvasia Montanaccio are in fact the genetically important MAMMOLO of Tuscany. The grape variety is capable of producing red fruit-flavoured if not necessarily deep-coloured reds and fine rosés that can smell of the island's herby scrubland. The vine has good disease resistance and thrives particularly successfully on the granitic soils in the south west around Ajaccio and Sartène. It buds and ripens late and is less important than NIELLUCCIO.

science. For long it was maintained that WINEMAKING was an art, but the proportion of the world's wine made by individuals with little appreciation of science, even in the OLD WORLD, has shrunk substantially in the last century. Now most people practising OENOLOGY and VITICULTURE are scientifically trained, often to a tertiary level. Even by the late 1980s, it had become difficult to discuss wine with many of those who grow and make it without being conversant with a wide range of scientific terms and concepts, including a host of measurements such as PH, TA, RS, GA (GALLIC ACID), and IPT (*indice des polyphénols totaux*). The dramatically improved overall quality of wine since ACADEME took a role in teaching and researching wine-related subjects is eloquent testimony to the beneficial effect of the increasingly scientific approach of all those involved with wine. As in all fields, however, the best scientists are often those who seek to explain rather than dominate, and in Old World regions whose wines have been admired for centuries, the best results are often obtained by those who combine scientific knowledge with a respect for TRADITION. For specific applications of science, see, for example, DNA PROFILING, GLOBAL POSITIONING SYSTEMS, INFRARED SPECTROSCOPY, and PRECISION VITICULTURE.

scion, in viticulture, is the piece of the fruiting vine that is grafted on to the quite separate ROOTSTOCK. When grown, such a plant will have the leaves and desired fruit of one VINE VARIETY (Cabernet Sauvignon, for example), but the roots of the other, rootstock, variety (110 Richter, for example). GRAFTING is very widely used in viticulture since rootstocks are needed to combat soil-borne pests or diseases, such as PHYLLOXERA and NEMATODES.   B.G.C.

scoring individual wines, and many aspects of their production, became an increasingly popular pursuit with professionals and amateurs alike in the late 20th century.

Scoring vineyards

Vineyards may be scored to assess their suitability for producing good-quality wine grapes. The most famous system is that used in the DOURO valley of northern Portugal for PORT production. Vineyards are allocated points, from plus 1,680 for the most promising, to minus 3,340 for the least favoured, taking into account YIELD, SOIL TYPE, MESOCLIMATE, vineyard maintenance, GRAPE COMPOSITION, ENCÉPAGEMENT, and VINE AGE. Highly classified vineyards are entitled to produce as much wine as they are able each year, while the production from lower classifications can be restricted to meet demand. The CHAMPAGNE region of north east France has a similar, if considerably less precise, system whereby whole COMMUNES are given a percentage rating, between 80 and 100.

Vineyards may also be scored for their adherence to organic growing principles as part of their accreditation (see ORGANIC VITICULTURE).

For the growing practice of linking price to grape quality, see PRICE.

A newer system for assessing vineyards for potential wine quality was developed by this writer in New Zealand. This is based on the principles of CANOPY MANAGEMENT, but also allows for assessment of vine VIGOUR. This system, or variants of it, is being used as the basis of assessing both the potential quality and price of grapes in Australia and New Zealand.   R.E.S.

Smart, R. E., and Robinson, M., *Sunlight into Wine: A Handbook for Winegrape Canopy Management* (Adelaide, 1991).

Scoring wines

Wine drinkers are, happily, presented with more choice than ever before. Unhappily, we all seem to have less and less time to make decisions. A score which can be interpreted at a glance is one obvious way of solving those two problems and it was perhaps understandable that in the late 20th century many wine consumers and, particularly, retailers leaned heavily on scores as a means of buying and selling wine respectively. Some of the various scoring systems and their wider context are discussed in NUMBERS AND WINE. The prototype is that used by the American writer Robert PARKER, who did much to promote the controversial but highly influential practice of awarding points out of 100 between 50 and 100, modelled on the American high school system. Effectively, wines of interest to readers of his and the many other WINE WRITERS who adopted a similar scoring system are those which score more than 85. Serious COLLECTORS and INVESTORS tend to concentrate on those which score more than 90, or even 95, so-called TROPHY WINES. Other tasters use other scales, often in Europe points out of 20, but the 100-point scale is more popular with retailers.

These scores have had an extraordinary effect on the wine market. They enable potential INVESTORS, especially wine FUNDS, and even FINE WINE TRADERS, to take a position and affect the market, without necessarily knowing anything whatever about wine. They empower new wine drinkers to make decisions independently of wine traders. And because, unlike TASTING NOTES, they can be understood universally, they can guide potential wine buyers all over the world, thus opening up the wine market in general and the fine wine market in particular to countries without an established wine culture. Scores undoubtedly played a part in ASIA's dramatic and inflationary entry into the fine wine market in the mid 1990s, for example, just as they have since encouraged interest from new wine buyers not just in established markets but in expanding markets such as South America and Russia. The implications of extending the market so widely for a commodity as finite as fine wine are obvious, and the price gap between the trophy wines and the rest has continued to widen. Quite apart from price and demand, however, scoring affected the wines themselves. Because scores are invariably arrived at as a result of a comparative TASTING, of many different samples of the same sort of wine, it is inevitable that some of the more subtle wines are overlooked and, particularly with red wines, the deeper-coloured, stronger, more concentrated wines are likely to

make a more immediate, and often favourable, impression. Of course this varies with the taster(s), but it is undeniable that, overall, in the late 20th century wines became more alcoholic, more concentrated, smoother-textured, and less acid—all as an indirect result of comparative tasting in general, and possibly what has become known as Parkerization in particular.

There was another, more obviously beneficial, effect of the prevalence of scoring individual wines. New wine producers can make a name for themselves and their wines very much faster than has ever been the case. A sample judiciously sent to Robert Parker and the *Wine Spectator* can ensure immediate commercial success, and direct communication with potential consumers, within the vast American market, for example. The downside for wine drinkers, of course, is that prices will inevitably rise steeply.

Wine scores, as those who award them try vainly to point out, can never substitute for description however. Even if in the 1990s the market seemed much more interested in numbers than words, the 21st century has seen, perhaps as a reaction to over-reliance on scores in the US market and as a way for the army of new American recruits to wine drinking to distinguish themselves, an increased reliance on personal TASTE and on the stories behind wines rather than the numbers in front of them.

For more detail of the practicalities and weaknesses of wine scoring, see NUMBERS AND WINE.

Scotland, northern British country too cold for vine-growing but with some fine wine merchants and a long tradition of importing wine, notably from Bordeaux.

Kay, B., and Maclean, C., *Knee Deep in Claret* (Edinburgh, 1983).

Scott Henry, a vine-TRAINING SYSTEM whereby the CANOPY is divided vertically and the shoots are separated and trained in two curtains, upwards and downwards (see diagram overleaf). The canopy is about 2 m/6.5 ft tall, and the leaves are held in place by foliage wires. The system was developed by an Oregon vine-grower of the same name in the early 1980s when his vines were so vigorous that both yield and quality were reduced. The system was originally developed for CANE PRUNING; a later spur-pruned version has now generally been superseded by the SMART–DYSON system.

The Scott Henry system is suited to moderate-vigour vineyards with row spacing of about 2 m or more. It became widely used in many New World countries in the 1990s because of its suitability for MECHANICAL HARVESTING and potential for improving wine quality and yield. Adoption by Delegat in Hawke's Bay and

MARLBOROUGH, New Zealand, since 2005 has led to the world's largest vineyard area trained to this system, around 1,300 ha (3,212 acres), i.e. 90% of the company vineyards. R.E.S.

Smart, R. E. and Robinson, M., *Sunlight into Wine: A Handbook for Winegrape Canopy Management* (Adelaide, 1991).

screwcaps, sometimes known as ROTEs (roll-on, tamper-evident), and often by the brand name Stelvin®, have emerged as the leading competitor to cork in terms of performance if not yet in terms of usage. They are cheaper than top-quality corks, and no capsules are needed, but the cost of new bottling equipment and bottles can deter smaller producers.

Screwcaps as an alternative to cork for bottling wine were first used in 1959, when a French company introduced the Stelcap-vin, which had already proved successful for a range of spirits and liqueurs. The rights to manufacture this closure were acquired by Australian Consolidated Industries Ltd (ACI) in 1970 and it was renamed Stelvin® for the Australian market. ACI trials of four closures (three screwcaps with different wadding materials and a cork for comparison) on three red and three white wines, first reported in 1976, concluded that screwcaps were ideal for sealing wine bottles but only if they had the right wadding material and a satisfactory seal between bottle and cap. An industry push towards screwcaps at that time lost momentum, partly through lack of consumer acceptance, and partly because awareness of the shortcomings of cork were not as widespread then as now.

As dissatisfaction with cork gradually increased, there were sporadic attempts to introduce screwcaps to the market place. In 2000, winemakers in Australia's Clare Valley, famous for its Rieslings, banded together to take a stand on the issue. The Clare winemakers, many of whose wines are made in a style that shows up any cork-related faults particularly transparently, had to overcome a significant logistical obstacle: at the time, no Australian supplier could offer bottles and caps of the required style and quality. As a result, they had to gather together enough like-minded producers willing to adopt screwcaps to generate the threshold order of 250,000 bottles from Pechiney in France. Their effort made the headlines and the momentum increased so that by the 2004 vintage some 200 million wine bottles were sealed with screwcaps in Australia. This Clare initiative prompted New Zealand winemakers to form the New Zealand Screwcap Initiative in 2001. By 2004, an estimated 70% of New Zealand's wines were sealed under screwcap, up from just 1% three years earlier. Ten years later, in 2014, an estimated 95% of New Zealand wines and 80% of Australian wines are screwcap-sealed. Whether or not screwcaps establish such a presence in the Americas and the more traditional European wine-producing countries remains to be seen.

Screwcaps consist of two components: the aluminium alloy cap, which comes attached to the sleeve, and the liner, which is made of an expanded polyethylene wadding. The liner typically contains a tin-foil layer that acts as a barrier to gas exchange, overlain by a PVDC (Saranex®) film that provides an inert surface in contact with the wine. In production, the screwcap is not screwed on but is held down tight over the end of the bottle and a set of rollers moulds the sleeve of the cap over the ridges on the outside of the top portion of the neck. This holds the whole closure firmly in place. The cap itself is joined to the sleeve by a series of small metal bridges, which are broken when the cap is twisted. To obtain a tight seal it is especially important that the lip of the bottle be free of defects.

Although they are often considered as a single closure type, not all screwcaps are alike. The most significant difference is in the nature of the liner. In some caps this lacks the tin-foil layer; the closure therefore has higher oxygen transfer properties (see OXYGEN TRANSMISSION RATE) and is less suited to long AGEING of wines.

Trials have shown that screwcaps with tin/ Saranex® liners provide a more effective barrier to gas exchange than all but the very best corks. Screwcaps are inert and can last many years (and have kept white and red wine in good condition for more than 30 years). They also have the advantage of requiring no equipment to remove them. Screwcaps suitable for sealing sparkling wines at full pressure have been developed, but have yet to make much impact on the marketplace. Some industry commentators predict that they will eventually replace corks for almost all wine types. However, controversy remains over whether they are the best closure type for red wines destined for long ageing and for some styles of white wine. While some scientists argue that wine ageing is an anaerobic process most successful in the complete absence of extrinsic oxygen, others suspect that the tiny amounts of oxygen transmitted by the less than perfect seal of corks and diffused from within the cork cells—or the oxygen transmitted by screwcaps without a metal foil layer in the lining—are important for red wine ageing. Because the chemistry of wine ageing is incompletely understood, it is likely that only long-term trials with red wines sealed under different closures will settle this debate.

J.A.G. & T.M.S.

Goode, J., *Wine Science: The Application of Science in Winemaking* (2nd edn, London, 2014).

Stelzer, T., *Taming the Screw: A Manual for Winemaking with Screw Caps* (Brisbane, 2005).

Taber, G., *To Cork or Not to Cork* (New York, 2007).

Scuppernong, the best known of the vine varieties belonging to the *Vitis rotundifolia* species of the MUSCADINIA genus planted in the south east of the United States and in Mexico. Like other Muscadines, the grapes (in this case bronze-skinned) are very distinctively flavoured. Some well-structured, sweet, dark gold wines are made which taste markedly different from the much more widely known product of VINIFERA varieties. Scuppernong has been substantially replaced in the southern states by Muscadines specially bred for wine production.

sec is French for DRY while **secco** is Italian and **seco** is Spanish and Portuguese for dry. See SWEETNESS, and DOSAGE for official EU sugar levels.

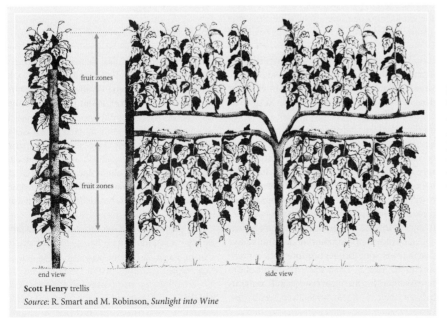

fruit zones

fruit zones

end view

side view

Scott Henry trellis

Source: R. Smart and M. Robinson, *Sunlight into Wine*

secateurs, hand-held scissors used for winter PRUNING of vines. Two-handled secateurs are used for cutting larger-diameter and older wood of the vine. Pruning can be faster, more effective, and less tiring with pneumatic or electric secateurs (see MECHANICAL PRUNING).   R.E.S.

secbutyl-methoxypyrazine (SBMP). See METHOXYPYRAZINES.

sécheresse, French for both DROUGHT and occasionally used to refer to WATER STRESS although the latter is more often referred to as *stress hydrique*. When the stress is mild, this is a recognized contributor to wine quality and then the term *déficit hydrique* is preferred.

second crop is one that may form after the main one on secondary LATERAL SHOOTS. The amount of lateral shoot growth is correlated with that of the whole shoot; on weak shoots, laterals can barely be seen, while on long, strong shoots and at NODES near the cut ends of trimmed shoots, laterals can grow so strongly as to resemble primary shoots. Second crop bunches are most abundant on strong laterals. In some varieties, a second crop is rare, but on others, such as PINOT NOIR and many MUSCAT varieties, this crop can be large. Usually the existence of a second crop is a negative factor for wine quality since its development runs six to eight weeks behind the main crop and it competes for nutrients, as well as complicating the development and control of VINE PESTS and VINE DISEASES. Worse, it adds a proportion of immature fruit to the HARVEST (especially where MECHANICAL HARVESTERS are used), which usually adversely affects the quality of the resulting wine.   B.G.C.

second fermentation, a fermentation that occurs after the completion of the normal alcoholic FERMENTATION. This may be a FERMENTATION IN BOTTLE, or the evolution of carbon dioxide that accompanies a MALOLACTIC CONVERSION, or simply a restarting in the winery of an alcoholic fermentation of a wine that still contains fermentable SUGARS. This can happen if, for example, there is a rise in TEMPERATURE or a more powerful YEAST is introduced. The GOVERNO winemaking process associated with TUSCANY in central Italy is another example of deliberate provocation of a second fermentation.

second growth. See the CLASSIFICATION of Bordeaux.

second wines are wines made from batches of wine or parcels of vines considered not good enough for the principal product, or *grand vin*, made at an estate. The phenomenon was born in BORDEAUX in the 18th century, and was revived in the early 20th century at Ch LAFITE but was hardly developed commercially until the 1980s, when increased competition forced ever

more rigorous selection at the ASSEMBLAGE stage. Some of the more famous second wines are Ch LATOUR's Les Forts de Latour, supplied by vineyards specifically designated for this purpose, and Ch MARGAUX's Pavillon Rouge. So important has the quality of second wines become that both these first growths also sell a third wine. The branded wine MOUTON CADET began life as the second wine of Ch MOUTON ROTHSCHILD, which much more recently created Le Petit Mouton as its modern second wine. Second wines are likely to contain the produce of young vines together with the least satisfactory lots. In particularly unsuccessful VINTAGES, some properties make no *grand vin* at all so that the second wine, or *second vin*, is the only wine produced that year. In general, a second wine from a poor vintage (when a *grand vin* was also bottled) is rarely an exciting drink, but a second wine from a quality-conscious producer in a good vintage can represent good value—so long as it is not consumed alongside the *grand vin*.

sediment, the solid material which settles to the bottom of any wine container, whether it be a bottle or a vat, tank, cask, or barrel. This sediment is a very heterogeneous mixture which in winemaking consists mainly of dead yeast cells (the gross LEES), the insoluble fragments of grape pulp and skin, and the seeds that settle out of new wine. At subsequent stages it consists of TARTRATES and, from red wines, PHENOLIC polymers, as well as any insoluble materials added to assist CLARIFICATION or to facilitate FILTRATION.

Sediments in bottled wines are relatively rare, and usually signal a fine wine that has already spent some years in bottle. So unaccustomed have modern wine consumers become to sediment that many (erroneously) view it as a fault. Many winemakers therefore take great pains to ensure, through clarification, STABILIZATION, and filtration, that the great majority of wines made today, and virtually all of those designed to be drunk within their first few years, will remain free of sediment for at least a few years. Wines designed for long periods of BOTTLE AGEING, on the other hand, frequently deposit crystals of tartrates, white in white wines and dyed red or black in red wines. Red wines, in addition, deposit some PIGMENTED TANNINS that are the result of phenolic polymerization. The heavy deposits in bottles of vintage port are a particularly dramatic example of this phenomenon. A bottle of wine containing sediment needs special care before SERVING.

Environmentally responsible disposal of sediment from wine production presents a problem: skins, stems, seeds, and pulp residues can be processed for the recovery of small amounts of sugar, tartaric acid, colouring agents (see OENOCYANIN), and grapeseed oil, but in most

wine regions the costs of recovery greatly exceed the market value of the recovered substances. The solid sediments are frequently returned to the vineyard and worked into the soil instead. See also WINERY WASTE.

See also the quite different phenomenon of BOTTLE DEPOSIT.   A.D.W.

seedling, the young plant that develops when a seed germinates. Grape seeds have tiny embryos which develop rapidly as the seed germinates, growing a freely branching tap-root and a shoot. The growth of seedlings is important in VINE BREEDING, but not otherwise in commercial viticulture, as vines are propagated from cuttings (see VEGETATIVE PROPAGATION).
   B.G.C.

seeds. For details of grape seeds, see GRAPE.

For details of the historical evidence provided by finds of ancient grape seeds (and other parts of the grape), see PALAEOETHNOBOTANY.

Ségalin, 1959 INRA cross of Jurançon Noir × PORTUGAIS Bleu which has good colour, structure, and flavour and is authorized in SOUTH WEST FRANCE. (See also CALADOC, CHASAN, PORTAN.)

Ségurs, important family in the history of the BORDEAUX wine region, originally from the village of PAUILLAC. In 1670, Jacques de Ségur, a notary who was a councillor of the legal Parlement of Bordeaux, became the second husband of Jeanne de Gasq, daughter of another Parlement councillor. As a dowry she brought with her the *seigneurie* of LAFITE, to add to others he had including Calon in ST-ESTÈPHE, and an estate of about 1,000 ha/2,470 acres to the north of Pauillac. Their son Alexandre de Ségur was born in 1674. His father died in 1691, but in 1695 he married Marie-Thérèse de Clausel, the heiress of LATOUR, which gave him all the southern part of Pauillac and another very large estate. Their son, the future Marquis Nicolas-Alexandre de Ségur, was born in Bordeaux in 1697, and when his father died in 1716 he took over the very large domaine, which then included the farm of MOUTON before it passed in the 1730s to the Marquis de Branne. The marquis, a vice-president of the Bordeaux Parlement, was said to have been called 'le prince de vignes' by Louis XV. He is reputed to have said, 'I make wine at Lafite and Latour, but my heart is at Calon,' and on the label of Ch Calon Ségur there is today a large heart. When he died in Paris in 1755 he left a substantial fortune. He had four daughters and their descendants owned Ch Latour until 1962.   E.P.-R.

Penning-Rowsell, E., *The Wines of Bordeaux* (6th edn, 1989).

Seibel, common name for many of the FRENCH HYBRID vine varieties bred by Albert

Seibel of the Ardèche in the late 19th and early 20th centuries, most of them identified by number and many of them given a more colloquially appealing name. Seibel 5455 is more often called PLANTET, for example, while Seibel 4986 is Rayon d'Or and Seibel 9549 is DE CHAUNAC. The variety once known simply as Seibel in France is Seibel 7053, which is known as CHANCELLOR in New York state. Small quantities of various Seibels such as VIGNOLES are planted in some cooler wine regions around the world.

Sekt, word used in German-speaking countries for SPARKLING WINE. Governed in Germany by manufacturing rather than wine law, most Sekt there is inexpensive and produced in bulk in tank from imported wine. The name Deutscher Sekt designates Sekt from German fruit, and a significant minority of German Sekt is BOTTLE FERMENTED wine made with ambition by family wineries, co-operatives, and houses specializing in the style from Riesling and Spätburgunder (Pinot Noir) grapes.

Austria's Sekt producers, some of which were already established during the era of the Austro-Hungarian empire, typically source their grapes from the WEINVIERTEL in Lower Austria. Some of the country's most quality-conscious estates also make sparkling wine.   D.S.

selection, increasingly important ingredient in maximizing wine quality whereby only the finest grapes or lots of wine are allowed in the final blend. See TRIAGE and ASSEMBLAGE. See also SELECTIVE HARVESTING.

Selection, was introduced into GERMAN WINE LAW in 2000 as a class of estate-bottled dry-tasting wine hand harvested at no less than 12.2% POTENTIAL ALCOHOL and subject inter alia to the unusual stipulation that the vineyard surface to be utilized had to be declared by 1 May before the harvest, ostensibly to permit greater administrative oversight. To say that this category failed to catch on appears to be an understatement.   D.S.

sélection clonale is French for CLONAL SELECTION, while **sélection massale** is French for MASS SELECTION.

Sélection de Grains Nobles, the richest, most sumptuous ripeness category of ALSACE wines.

selective harvesting is a key application of PRECISION VITICULTURE and the major management strategy employed in ZONAL VITICULTURE. It involves the split picking of fruit according to different yield/quality criteria in order to exploit the variation observed within a vineyard and to maximize the uniformity of individual fruit parcels delivered to the winery. These fruit parcels may then be selected for different wines—perhaps for different styles or at different price points. Typically, different parts of the same vineyard block are harvested into separate bins, either during a single operation or at different times. Early adoption of this strategy was predominantly by small-scale producers or by large companies with the equipment to process small lots. However, recent research has demonstrated that selective harvesting may be profitable even when production is geared to large fermentation volumes. For example, a block of Cabernet Sauvignon might be mechanically harvested into either of two bins, depending on location within the block, in order to maximize the volume produced of a high-value varietal wine by allocating fruit from areas producing lower-value material to a lower-value blended wine. Under conventional uniform management, only the latter would have been produced from the block.   R.G.V.B.

Bramley, R. G. V., Ouzman, J., and Thornton, C., 'Selective harvesting is a feasible and profitable strategy even when grape and wine production is geared towards large fermentation volumes', *Australian Journal of Grape and Wine Research*, 17 (2011), 298–305.

Bramley, R. G. V., et al., 'Generating benefits from Precision Viticulture through selective harvesting', in J. Stafford (ed.), *Proceedings of the 5th European Conference on Precision Agriculture* (Uppsala, 2005).

Trought, M. C. T., and Bramley, R. G.V., 'Vineyard variability in Marlborough, New Zealand: characterising spatial and temporal changes in fruit composition and juice quality in the vineyard', *Australian Journal of Grape and Wine Research* 17 (2011), 79–89.

Selektion, term without legal status or specific parameters but often used by growers in AUSTRIA to signify a wine with high quality pretensions or in some way unusual. The term is used, for example, by some growers in the WACHAU to designate wines that fail to qualify for the category SMARAGD because they have too high a level of residual sugar; and by certain growers in STYRIA to highlight single-vineyard bottlings as opposed to lighter KLASSIK bottlings. Not to be confused with SELECTION, a specific category of German wine.   D.S.

selfling, or **selfed vine**, a plant created by one VINE VARIETY crossed to itself. This is not a very successful breeding strategy, since most varieties carry deleterious recessive genes, and there is consequently a strong inbreeding depression. This is avoided by crossing unrelated vines, which is a feature of successful VINE BREEDING. See also NEW VARIETIES.   R.E.S.

semi-carbonic maceration, winemaking process which involves a short CARBONIC MACERATION phase followed by a normal alcoholic FERMENTATION. In such wines, winemakers rely upon an initial period of maceration of the grapes in an anaerobic (oxygen-free) atmosphere, followed by crushing, PRESSING, and then traditional fermentation of the resultant MUST. The great majority of Beaujolais NOUVEAU and most other PRIMEUR wines are made in this fashion. Such wines have a very distinct aroma reminiscent of bananas or kirsch, arising from the distinctive by-products of the intracellular fermentation occurring within the whole berries and without yeast, during the first phase.   A.D.W. & P.L.

Sémillon, often written plain **Semillon** in non-francophone countries, a golden grape variety from south west France, is one of the unsung heroes of white wine production. Blended with its traditional partner SAUVIGNON BLANC, to which it seems to be closely related (underripe Sémillon can taste remarkably like Sauvignon), this golden-, sometimes copper-, berried vine variety is the key ingredient in SAUTERNES, arguably the world's longest-living unfortified wine, as it is in most of the great dry whites of Graves (see PESSAC-LÉOGNAN). Unblended, in Australia's HUNTER VALLEY, it is responsible for one of the most idiosyncratic and historic wine types exclusive to the New World, but overall it is not fashionable and has been declining in importance.

Outside Sauternes, Sémillon seems destined to play a supplementary role. The wines it produces tend to fatness and, although capable of ageing, have little aroma in youth. Sauvignon Blanc, with its internationally recognized name, strong aroma, high acidity, but slight lack of substance, fills in all obvious gaps. In the early 1990s, in a world desperate for Chardonnay, Sémillon found itself the passive ingredient in commercially motivated blends sometimes, even, called SemChard—most notably but not exclusively in Australia. Sémillon's weight, and high yield, make it a useful base for commercial blends.

As a vine, Sémillon is easy to cultivate. It is almost as vigorous as Sauvignon Blanc with particularly deep green leaves, but flowers slightly later and is not particularly susceptible to COULURE. Nor is it a victim of disease, apart from rot, which, in favourable conditions, is the blessed NOBLE ROT rather than the destructive GREY ROT.

Its greatest concentration is still in Bordeaux, where, although Sauvignon Blanc has been catching up fast particularly for dry white BORDEAUX AOC wines in the Entre-Deux-Mers district, there were still more than 7,100 ha/17,537 acres in 2011. On the left bank of the Garonne, in the Graves, Sauternes, and its enclave BARSAC, Sémillon still outnumbers Sauvignon in almost exactly the traditional proportions of four to one. Sauvignon and Semillon fight for dominance in the great, long-lived dry whites of Graves and Pessac-Léognan. In Sauternes,

Sémillon's great attribute is its proneness to noble rot. This special mould, *Botrytis cinerea*, concentrates sugars and acids and shrinks yields so that the best of the resulting wines such as Ch d'YQUEM may continue to evolve for centuries. Again, oak ageing deepens Sémillon's already relatively deep gold (really ripe grapes may almost look pink). Similar, but usually less exciting, sweet whites, the most ordinary made simply by stopping fermentation or adding sweet grape must, are made in the nearby appellations of CADILLAC CÔTES DE BORDEAUX, CÉRONS, LOUPIAC, and STE-CROIX-DU-MONT.

Like Sauvignon Blanc, Sémillon is allowed in many other appellations for dry and sweet whites of SOUTH WEST FRANCE but is perhaps most notable in qualitative terms in MONBAZILLAC. Thanks to its (declining) importance throughout BERGERAC, Sémillon is the most planted white wine variety in the Dordogne by far, although its 3,678 ha in 2011 had been overtaken by Merlot. It is technically allowed in most appellations of PROVENCE, but has made little impact on the vineyards of the Midi, where acidity is at a premium.

Sémillon's other great sphere of influence has been South America in general and Chile in particular, although total plantings there had fallen below 1,000 ha by 2007 and Sauvignon is very much more common.

In North America, Sémillon is generally rather scorned, lacking the image of Sauvignon Blanc, although a significant number of producers use the former to add interest to the latter. Total area planted in California had fallen to below 900 ha/364 acres by 2012. A few producers have experimented with producing BOTRYTIZED wines in the image of Sauternes from it and it also adds weight to Sauvignon in white bordeaux MERITAGE blends. Historically LIVERMORE VALLEY has produced some of the best fruit. Sémillon was once nearly as important in Washington state as Sauvignon Blanc and the likes of L'Ecole 41 still make a fine dry varietal version, but plantings had fallen to just over 200 acres by 2012.

It is quite widespread, without being particularly important, throughout eastern Europe, but it is in both SOUTH AFRICA and AUSTRALIA where Sémillon had a particularly glorious past. In 1822, 93% of all South African vineyard was planted with this variety, imported from Bordeaux. So common was it then that it was simply called Wyndruif, or 'wine grape'. It was subsequently called Green Grape, a reference to its abnormally green foliage, but has been declining in importance so that today it was planted on less than 1,200 ha in 2013—although growth in Sauvignon Blanc plantings in South Africa has brought an increase in sophisticated white BORDEAUX BLENDS, often oak aged.

While all the Australian pale grape focus was on the growth of Chardonnay (and the decline of Riesling) since the early 1990s, Semillon's plantings stealthily grew from 2,713 ha/6,700 acres in 1990 to 6,200 ha/15,300 acres in 2004, although this had fallen slightly to 5,632 ha by 2013. Its role in the Hunter Valley is well known: to produce from early-picked grapes low alcohol (10.5 to 11%) wines with unmatched cellaring potential. It has also enjoyed success as a wooded style, blended with Sauvignon Blanc, in the Adelaide Hills, and in Margaret River where the blend is a popular speciality. See AUSTRALIA for more details.

In New Zealand it has been completely swamped by Sauvignon-mania and only 77 ha, mainly in Hawke's Bay, remained in 2012.

The variety was also exported to Israel to establish vineyards there at the end of the 19th century.

sensitivity, an important factor in TASTING. We all vary in our sensitivities to different compounds, sometimes a thousandfold or more in terms of tasting thresholds. Some of the most obvious examples are dramatic differences between tasters in sensitivities to the effects of BRETTANOMYCES, CORK TAINT, and ROTUNDONE.

sequence of wines to be served. See ORDER.

Serbia, officially the Republic of Serbia and independent since 2006, is a landlocked nation in the central Balkans and includes the autonomous province of VOJVODINA. Archaeological digs at Vinča near Belgrade found grape remains and AMPHORAE dating back to Neolithic times, but it was probably during the ROMAN era that grape growing became well established in this region. Sirmium, the present-day city of Sremski Mitrovica, was declared one of the four capitals of the Roman Empire in 294, and Emperor Probus is credited with ordering the first vines to be planted on the slopes of Fruška Gora. The Serbian state developed in the Middle Ages during the Nemanjić dynasty and the wine industry was encouraged by conversion to Christianity. It was during this period that the wine regions (more or less as they are today) were first identified. Ottoman rule brought destruction to much of the wine industry although some Serbians fled north to Srem and Banat taking vines with them. In 1699, the Karlovac Peace Agreement saw Srem and Banat join the Habsburg Empire, which encouraged wine production. As in the rest of the Balkan region, PHYLLOXERA was devastating and the early 20th century saw the development of growers' CO-OPERATIVES. Both world wars, collectivization when Serbia was part of YUGOSLAVIA, then the brutal wars of independence after the break-up of Yugoslavia, all seriously affected wine production, although the 21st century has seen considerable revival.

Serbia has been slow to develop a reliable vineyard register. The Serbian statistical office claimed 56,343 ha/138,379 acres of vineyard in 2011 although the Ministry of Agriculture believes that the true area of vineyards is closer to 27,000 ha/66,700 acres, with an average production of very roughly 1.65 million hl/43.6 million gallons of wine. There may be as many as 300 producers registered, though production is dominated by five large producers on one hand, and very small private family wineries making wine strictly for local consumption on the other. Of most interest is the development of small to mid-sized, quality-focused estates with vineyards and modern equipment, undoubtedly helped by significant government subsidies. A total of 45 wineries now produce PGI wines. Serbia has applied to join the EU although recognition of independence for KOSOVO remains a significant barrier to progress. Serbia, a net wine importer, has already put in place EU-compliant wine laws. PGI wines are described as Geografska Indikacija (GI), PDO wines are either Kontrolisano Poreklo i Kvalitet (KPK) or Kontrolisano i Garantovano Poreklo i Kvalitet (KGPK).

Vineyards and regions

The country's largely CONTINENTAL climate is moderated by mountains such as Fruška Gora and rivers, especially the Danube, Velika Morava, and Timok. Detailed grape variety statistics are not currently available but the most common white varieties are claimed to be Graševina (WELSCHRIESLING), Riesling, Chardonnay, SMEDEREVKA, ŽUPLJANKA, RKATSITELI, while reds are led by Cabernet Sauvignon, PROKUPAC, Merlot, VRANAC, and Pinot Noir with some Gamay and Frankovka (BLAÜFRANKISCH). Of INDIGENOUS VARIETIES Prokupac has the potential to become a local flagship—both vinified as a VARIETAL wine or in blends. White Smederevka is rather uninteresting, being neutral and lightweight. Temjanika is the local name for MUSCAT BLANC À PETITS GRAINS though it is widely regarded as a local variant, and certainly produces more expressive aromatic wines. Other local varieties include Neoplanta, Kreaca, Bagrina, Začinak, Bačka, Sila, and Sirmium but their potential is still under-researched.

The northern province of Vojvodina includes the regions of Srem, Subotica-Horgoš, and Banat. The Srem region is close to the Danube on the lower slopes of the Fruška Gora Mountains. The Danube influence moderates winter cold and aids earlier ripening in the summer, while an ELEVATION of around 200–300 m/660–980 ft helps keep freshness in the resulting wines. This is regarded as the heartland of Graševina while international white wine grapes including Chardonnay can thrive. Some Vranac and Portugieser (historically grown for vermouth-like Bermet) are present too.

S

The sandy soils of Subotica-Horgoš are of Pannonian origin so some overlap with Hungarian varieties such as Ezerjó, Kövedinka, and Kadarka are not surprising, although the area is best known for white wines from Graševina, Riesling, and Župljanka. The Banat region, and especially Vršac, lies on the western end of the Carpathians where the hills meet the plain and is dominated by wine producer Vršacki Vinogradi with 1,700 ha/4,200 acres of vineyards and a famous Y-shaped cellar. The rare Serbian white wine grape Kreaca is believed to originate here, and is also found over the border in Romania as Creață. In Central Serbia, the most important region is Šumadija-Velika Morava to the south of Belgrade. The subregion of Oplenac includes some of Serbia's best producers and has a long history of supplying wine to the royal cellars. Local red PROKUPAC is important here, along with some promising INTERNATIONAL VARIETIES such as Chardonnay, Sauvignon Blanc, Riesling, and even Pinot Noir. The town of Smederevo famously gave its name to Smederevka (DIMIAT). It lies between the Danube and Velika Morava Rivers on SAND and GRAVEL, so whites and light reds are typical but some of the country's top Cabernet Sauvignon can be found in this region too. The Timok region between the Danube and the river of the same name is very continental with a mixture of ALLUVIAL soils and some LIMESTONE. Negotin, once Serbia's biggest wine region, is the most famous subregion. Local grapes found here include Bagrina (making deep-coloured aromatic whites), Začinak (a red variety used for colour), and Prokupac. Zapadna Morava and especially the Župa area have long been famous for wine production. Vineyards lie across gentle hillsides of the western Morava River basin and are particularly noted for Temjanika and Prokupac.   C.G.

www.vinopedia.rs
www.serbia.travel/download/brosure/Serbian_wine_routes.pdf

Sercial, Portuguese white grape variety probably originally from BUCELAS where most is to be found today. It was once quite commonly planted on the island of Madeira but only about 20 ha grew there in 2010. The name came to be used to denote the lightest, most acid, latest-maturing style of MADEIRA rather than the grape variety from which it was made. On the Portuguese mainland it is also known as ESGANA CÃO and is notable for its late ripening and high acidity. It should not be confused with CERCEAL Branco.

service of wine. See SERVING WINE and SOMMELIER.

serving wine involves a number of fairly obvious steps, but mastering each of them can maximize the pleasure given by any individual wine. See OPENING THE BOTTLE, BREATHING, DECANTING, GLASSES, FOOD AND WINE MATCHING, ORDER OF WINES TO BE SERVED, and LEFTOVER WINE for details of these particular aspects of serving wine.

Perhaps the least obvious requirement of anyone serving wine is that they appear superficially mean, by filling glasses no more than two-thirds, and preferably less than half, full. This allows energetic agitation of the glass if necessary, and enables the all-important AROMA to collect in the upper part of the bowl (see TASTING).

The factor which probably has the single greatest effect on how a wine tastes, however, is temperature, and this is a factor which can be controlled by whoever is serving. Because of the well-known general rule that white (and rosé) wines should be chilled and red wines should be served at something called room temperature (see CHAMBRÉ), and because many refrigerators are set at relatively low temperatures, in practice many white wines are served too cool and many red wines dangerously warm. See TEMPERATURE for some guidance on specific recommended serving temperatures for certain styles of wine. Few wine drinkers have wine thermometers, however, so a certain amount of experimentation with ways of modifying serving temperatures is advisable.

Cooling wine in a refrigerator is much slower than cooling wine in a container holding water and ice (two hours rather than 30 minutes to cool an average bottle from 22 to 10 °C/50 °F). An ice box would do the job faster but has the serious disadvantage that the bottle will be cooled right down to icebox temperature if left there. This may well freeze the wine and push the cork out. Some main refrigerator cabinets are, furthermore, set at such low temperatures that wines may emerge simply too cool. (Note that a container full of ice cubes but no water is not a very effective cooler as it provides relatively little contact between the bottle and the cooling medium.)

It is a happy coincidence that the ideal cellar temperature, around 15 °C/59 °F, is also ideal for serving a wide range of wines such as complex dry white wines and light-bodied red wines, and is not so low that it takes long to warm tannic red wines to a suitable serving temperature.

In cool climates, wine drinkers may have difficulty in warming bottles of red wine to suitably high temperatures for serving. Direct heat should not be applied to a bottle, and even contact with a radiator can heat wine to such a dangerously high temperature that some of the more volatile FLAVOUR COMPOUNDS are lost and the ALCOHOL can dominate so that the wine tastes unbalanced.

One of the most effective ways of warming wine, whether intentionally or not, is to pour it out into glasses in a relatively warm environment or, even faster, to pour the wine into a decanter or glasses which previously held hot water. This effect is accentuated if the glasses are cupped in human hands. For this reason, it is usually wise to serve wines slightly cooler than the ideal temperature at which they are best appreciated. Warming wine in microwave ovens can be effective if the oven is big enough, and if great care is taken not to overheat the wine and to remove the FOIL if it is metallic.

Ambient temperature, or even the precise temperature of the taster, can affect how a wine tastes: crisp, light wines taste either delightfully refreshing or disappointingly meagre when the taster is hot or cold respectively. On the other hand, in tropical climates, where both temperature and HUMIDITY are high, it can be almost impossible to find suitable conditions in which to serve even the finest red wine as, without air conditioning, drinks heat up so rapidly that a red wine has either to be served well chilled or run the risk of being almost MULLED. Light red wines with marked ACIDITY such as BEAUJOLAIS and reds from cooler climates such as the LOIRE, NEW ZEALAND, TASMANIA, NEW YORK, and CANADA can taste more appetizing in hot climates than CLASSED GROWTH red bordeaux or fine burgundy.

One final aspect of serving wine, about which the Latin poet HORACE wrote extensively, is matching wine to guest and occasion. Part of what might generally be called CONNOISSEURSHIP, this is a pleasure associated with wine which can be almost as great as drinking it, but is too complex to prescribe or describe here.

See also TASTING for the special conditions of serving wine for this particular purpose, a very different one from actually drinking it.

set, the process by which vine flowers become berries. **Setting** is a stage in plant development after FLOWERING when the flowers either fall off or adhere to the plant and fruits start to grow. See FRUIT SET.

settling, the winemaking operation of holding MUST or wine in a vessel so that suspended solids fall to the bottom. The French term *débourbage* is sometimes used for the most common example of settling, to begin the CLARIFICATION of freshly drained and pressed white musts before FERMENTATION. Fermentation is delayed by adding SULFUR DIOXIDE and by cooling before pumping to the settling vessel.

Red wines, whose skins are included in the fermentation vessel, are settled after fermentation and MACERATION when the purpose is to remove not just grape debris but also dead yeast cells, or LEES.

Settling is governed by such factors as the size of the solid particles, the difference in their DENSITY from that of the liquid, and the extent to which the liquid moves within the settling vessel. Because must and cloudy grape juice are so much denser than wine, they are much more difficult to settle. Solids as large and dense as seeds and stem fragments settle rapidly. Finely divided pulp debris and dead yeast cells which are very small settle more slowly and are easily resuspended by currents within the settling vessel. COLLOIDS, which have dimensions of large molecular size, are very slow to settle because their movement is influenced by the smallest liquid movement within the vessel. The settling of colloids can be greatly assisted by the addition of clarifying or FINING agents such as BENTONITE, which adsorbs them and grows them into complexes large enough to settle. Settling of particularly viscous grape juice can also be encouraged by the addition of ENZYMES designed to break chains of PECTINS.

Settling, possibly followed by FILTRATION, may also be part of processing and finishing in winemaking. A.D.W.

Setúbal, port on the Sado estuary south of Lisbon, the capital of PORTUGAL, is also the name of a Portuguese FORTIFIED WINE with its own DOP region (see map under PORTUGAL). It is made predominantly from Moscatel (MUSCAT) grapes and the region was officially demarcated in 1907 for Moscatel de Setúbal. The finest examples grow on LIMESTONE soils on the cool, north-facing slopes of the Arrábida hills. Grapes are also grown on the plain around the town of Palmela. The principal type of Moscatel is MUSCAT OF ALEXANDRIA but a tiny amount (around 20 ha/ 49.5 acres) of pink-skinned, much earlier-ripening Moscatel Roxo is bottled separately and is generally slightly drier and more complex. Initially, Setúbal is made in much the same way as a VIN DOUX NATUREL. After vinification, however, pungent Muscat grape skins are left to macerate in the wine for five or six months, which imparts a taste of fresh grapes and gives Setúbal its intense aroma and flavour. Most Setúbal is bottled after four or five years in large oak vats (though one leading producer uses old whisky barrels), by which time the wine has an amber-orange colour and a spicy, raisiny character. Small quantities, however, are bottled after 20 years or more in cask, by which time the wine is deep brown and has a rich, grapey intensity. Leading producer José Maria da Fonseca Successores occasionally bottles and sells stocks dating back to the mid 19th century. Like historic MADEIRA, bottles labelled Moscatel Torna-Viagem crossed the equator twice by ship en route to and from the tropics and are considered the finest. For details of the unfortified wines made on the Setúbal peninsula, see PENÍNSULA DE SETÚBAL. R.J.M. & S.A.

Mayson, R., *The Wines and Vineyards of Portugal* (London, 2003).

Metcalfe, C., and McWhirter, K., *The Wine and Food Lover's Guide to Portugal* (Haywards Heath, 2007).

Severny, Russian vine variety developed at the All-Russia Potapenko Institute from a Précoce de Malingre seedling with a member of the famously cold-hardy VITIS *amurensis* vine species native to Mongolia. Severny means 'northern' and is a suffix of several crosses such as SAPERAVI Severny and CABERNET SEVERNY specifically bred for harsh winter climates.

sexual propagation, reproduction by seed involving the union of male and female sex cells (POLLEN and ovule respectively). The important feature of this type of propagation is that the parent plants are genetically different, so the seedling is in turn genetically different from either parent. Throughout the world of nature, this is how genetic diversity is continued, permitting selection of those progeny best suited to survive. In commercial viticulture, this process has been circumvented by propagating selected, desirable individuals and propagating them vegetatively (see VEGETATIVE PROPAGATION). Originally sexual seedlings, all grape varieties have been propagated asexually for many years, decades, or centuries with substantially the same genetic constitution. Sexual propagation is used for VINE BREEDING throughout the world to produce NEW VARIETIES. Success depends on selecting suitable parents, and many years of painstaking evaluation. B.G.C. & J.V.

Seyssel, the oldest appellation within the eastern French region of SAVOIE producing light, dry, and off-dry white still and sparkling wines from vineyards concentrated on the steep slopes of the upper Rhône valley about 40 km/ 25 miles downriver of Geneva. Historically, sparkling Seyssel was one of the few Savoie wines to escape the region itself, but since the BOISSET group closed the historic Varichon et Clerc winery, it has suffered a decline with less than 100 ha/247 acres of vines remaining in the appellation. ALTESSE (still often called Roussette) is the dominant grape variety here, although the local MOLETTE is also grown for sparkling wines, which must contain at least 10% Altesse, whose Savoyard roots are said to be here. The sparkling wines need to have a POTENTIAL ALCOHOL of just 8.5% at harvest and must be BOTTLE FERMENTED in the region. They are light, refreshing, and the best can develop in bottle, but most are drunk locally.

Seyssuel, village on which the dynamic IGP Comtés Rhodaniens is based.

Seyval Blanc, complex, light-skinned FRENCH HYBRID, the most widely planted SEYVE-VILLARD hybrid, number 5276, the result of crossing two SEIBEL hybrids. It is productive, ripens early and is well suited to relatively cool climates such as that of ENGLAND, where it was the single most planted vine variety in the late 20th century but has been superseded by the popularity of the Champagne grapes. It is also popular in CANADA and, to a lesser extent, in the eastern UNITED STATES, notably in NEW YORK state. Its crisp white wines have no hint of FOXY flavour and can even benefit from BARREL MATURATION. In the UK it is mainly used for blending and is particularly successful for sparkling wine production. As a sparkling wine, it can (somewhat unexpectedly in view of its hybrid origins) be labelled as Quality Sparkling Wine.

Seyve-Villard, series of about 100 FRENCH HYBRIDS developed by hybridizer Bertille Seyve and his partner and father-in-law Victor Villard, much planted in France in the mid 20th century. Perhaps the most famous, however, is SEYVAL BLANC.

Sforzato, or **Sfursat**, a dry red DRIED-GRAPE WINE made in the VALTELLINA zone in the far north of Italy from Nebbiolo, called Chiavennasca here.

SGN. See SÉLECTION DE GRAINS NOBLES.

shade, the absence of sunlight in a vine CANOPY. This is due to leaves blocking out sunlight, as the transmission of light through one leaf is less than 10% of full sunlight. In most vineyards, the blocking leaves are other vine leaves, but occasionally they may be the leaves of weeds or even adjacent trees, as occurs in the RÍAS BAIXAS region of north-west Spain. For most vineyards in the world, shade is due to vigorous vines being trained to restrictive vine-TRAINING SYSTEMS.

Sunlight levels in the centre of dense canopies with many leaf layers can be as little as 1% of the levels above the canopy. At this very low level of light, PHOTOSYNTHESIS is almost zero, and in time the leaves turn yellow and then fall off. Leaves deep in the canopy also experience filtered sunlight with altered spectral composition, in that red light is reduced and far red light relatively enriched. The ratio of red to far red light can act as a signal system for the vine and other plants, and may play a role in the vine's response to shade. Similarly, ULTRAVIOLET RADIATION (UV) is filtered in the canopy, which can have significant impact on PHENOLICS. Since the vine evolved in forests, it has mechanisms like tendrils for avoiding shade by climbing towards the sunlight.

Shade can reduce both vine YIELD and grape quality. Shade has been shown to reduce bud INITIATION, BUDBREAK, FRUIT SET, and hence berry number, as well as BERRY SIZE. So shade can reduce yield dramatically, and yields may increase up to threefold where shade has been removed by improving the training system and allowing the sunlight in.

Many studies around the world, for a range of vine varieties in a range of climates, have also demonstrated that shade alters grape chemical composition and reduces wine quality. Shade is known to decrease levels of SUGARS, ANTHOCYANINS, PHENOLICS, TARTARIC ACID, monoterpene FLAVOUR COMPOUNDS, and apparent varietal character. Other negative effects of shade on wine quality are increases in MALIC ACID, PH, POTASSIUM, and in the so-called HERBACEOUS characters. Shaded fruit is also more susceptible to BOTRYTIS BUNCH ROT and POWDERY MILDEW. CANOPY MANAGEMENT can reduce shade in the canopy and, in high-vigour vineyards, may improve yield and quality simultaneously. With CLIMATE CHANGE and warmer air temperatures, berry SUNBURN is more likely, and so a single leaf layer may be used to reduce the intensity of the suns's rays—although deep shade is not necessary,　　　　　　R.E.S.

Smart, R. E., and Robinson, M., *Sunlight into Wine: A Handbook for Winegrape Canopy Management* (Adelaide, 1991).

shale, a very fine-grained sedimentary rock, usually dark-coloured, which is weak and easily split because of the way the clayey sediment has settled, so that shale always breaks roughly parallel to the stratification of the sedimentary rock, unlike some metamorphic rocks (see SLATE and, especially, SCHIST). The splintered fragments are flaky and irrregular (unlike cleaved slate). Shale weathers easily, to give CLAY-rich soils. See also GEOLOGY.　　A.J.M.

shanking. See BUNCHSTEM NECROSIS.

sharpshooters, insects which feed on vine foliage and can carry important vine diseases. See LEAFHOPPERS.

shatter. See FRUIT SET.

Shaulis, Nelson (1913–2000). Born in Pennsylvania, Nelson Shaulis was destined to have a greater impact on world viticultural practice than most of his scientific contemporaries. His eastern US origin was appropriate, as this was the region of his greatest influence. He began his career at the Agricultural Experiment Station, Geneva (see CORNELL UNIVERSITY), in 1948, and retired as Professor of Viticulture in 1978.

Shaulis can be considered the father of CANOPY MANAGEMENT, although the term was not coined by him. In his early experiments with CONCORD grapevines, he realized that limits to YIELD and RIPENESS were a consequence of SHADE within the grapevine CANOPY. The solution was simple enough in hindsight, but revolutionary for the time. By dividing a dense canopy into two less dense canopies, shade could be reduced, and suddenly yield and ripeness could be dramatically increased. The new TRELLIS design, first published in the mid 1960s, was called the GENEVA DOUBLE CURTAIN. As an important further extension to this work, Shaulis and colleagues developed the world's first

MECHANICAL HARVESTER of grapes and subsequently undertook important primary research on MECHANICAL PRUNING.

The impact of Shaulis's research has been felt in every country of the world, but the NEW WORLD, free of yield limits, has benefited most. Shaulis influenced many younger researchers who made canopy management an accepted practice globally, including Carbonneau from Bordeaux (see LYRE), Intrieri and Cargnello from Italy, Kliewer from California, and Richard Smart, viticulture editor of this book.

　　　　　　R.E.S.

Shenandoah Valley is the name of two AVA wine regions. For details of the California region, see SIERRA FOOTHILLS. There is also a Shenandoah Valley in VIRGINIA.

sherry, seriously undervalued but slowly reawakening fortified wine from the region around the city of Jerez de la Frontera in ANDALUCÍA, south west Spain. 'Sherry' was used as a generic term for a wide range of FORTIFIED WINES made from white grapes, but in the mid 1990s the sherry trade successfully campaigned to have the name restricted—at least within the EU—to the produce of the Jerez DO. (For details of other once-prominent producers of similar wine styles, see CYPRUS, SOUTH AFRICA, and BRITISH MADE WINE.)

Despite renewed interest in high-quality sherry, overall production has dropped continuously for a quarter-century and was down to 450,000 hl/12 million gal a year by 2012. Apart from Spain, the two most important markets for sherry have been the Netherlands and Great Britain.

Sherry is the English corruption of the word Jerez, while Xérès is its French counterpart and is also the French name for sherry. The words Jerez-Xérès-Sherry appear on all bottles of sherry, on paper seals granted by the CONSEJO REGULADOR to guarantee the origin of the wine. Within the Jerez DO, there are three centres for sherry maturation: JEREZ DE LA FRONTERA, SANLÚCAR DE BARRAMEDA, and PUERTO DE SANTA MARÍA, each of which imparts subtle differences to the wines. Throughout this article, the types of wine made naturally in sherry BODEGAS are referred to in lower case italics, as in *oloroso*, while the sherry styles created for commercial use on the label are referred to with a capital letter, as in Oloroso.

Sherry is initially made to conform to two principal types: pale, dry *fino* (or, in Sanlúcar de Barrameda, *manzanilla*), which ages under the influence of the film-forming yeast FLOR, and dark, full, but dry *oloroso*. All sherry styles found on labels (Manzanilla, Fino, Amontillado, Oloroso, Pale Cream, Cream, etc., in generally ascending order of BODY) are derived from these two main types. The only exception is

Palo Cortado, which is a naturally resulting intermediate type and style between Amontillado and Oloroso. PEDRO XIMÉNEZ is an intensely sweet wine, usually for blending, made from the grape variety of the same name often grown outside the sherry region.

History

Jerez is one of the oldest wine-producing towns in Spain. It may well have been established by the PHOENICIANS who founded the nearby port of Cádiz in 1110 BC. The Phoenicians were followed by the CARTHAGINIANS, who were in turn succeeded by the ROMANS. Iberian viticulture advanced rapidly under Roman rule and Jerez has been identified as the Roman city of Ceritium. After the Romans were expelled around AD 400, southern Iberia was overrun by successive tribes of Vandals and Visigoths, who were in turn defeated by the Moors after the battle of Guadalete in 711 (see ISLAM). The Moors held sway over Andalucía for seven centuries and their influence is still evident, not least in the architecture of Seville, Cordoba, and Granada. Under Moorish domination, Jerez grew in size and stature. The town was named 'Seris' and this later evolved into Jerez de la Frontera, when it stood on the frontier of the two warring kingdoms during Christian reconquest in the 13th century.

Viticulture, which continued despite Moorish occupation, was revitalized by the Christians, although the region around Jerez continued to be plagued by war until the 15th century. Exports began and, in spite of periodic setbacks, trade with England and France was well established by the 1490s, when it was declared that wines shipped abroad would be free from local tax. In 1492, the Jews were expelled from Spain, their vineyards were confiscated, and foreigners, many of them English, took their place as merchants. Certain basic quality controls were established, including the capacity of the sherry cask or BUTT, which has not changed to this day.

At the end of the 15th century, after Christopher Columbus had discovered America from his base in Andalucía, the sherry town of Sanlúcar de Barrameda became an important port for the new transatlantic trade and in the 16th century large quantities of wine were shipped to the Americas from Jerez. In his book *Sherry*, Julian Jeffs speculates that Vino de Jerez (sherry) was almost certainly the first wine to enter North America.

Relations between England and Spain began to deteriorate in the 16th century and, although trade continued, the colony of English merchants trading from Sanlúcar began to suffer privations. In 1585, after a number of raids by Sir Francis Drake and his fleet, English merchants were arrested and their possessions seized. Exports ceased. Two years later, in an attack on Cádiz, Drake both 'singed the King of Spain's beard' and captured '2,900 pipes' of wine. This plunder helped to establish sherry as a popular drink in Elizabethan England.

After the death of Elizabeth I, trade became easier and 'sacke', or SACK, returned to royal circles. The English colony re-established itself and prospered, often by shipping poor-quality wines.

By the 17th century, 'sherris-sack' was well established in England and was drunk by Samuel Pepys, who in 1662 records that he mixed sherry and MÁLAGA. Pepys visited the English colony in Sanlúcar de Barrameda in 1683. At that time, until the construction of a railway in the mid 19th century, most of the sherry bodegas were located on the coast at Sanlúcar and Puerto de Santa María for easy export.

The sherry industry suffered many setbacks at the beginning of the 18th century, when England and Spain became embroiled in a series of conflicts beginning in 1702 with the War of the Spanish Succession. The METHUEN TREATY (1703) diverted trade to Portugal and a series of restrictive measures imposed by the Gremio or Wine Growers Guild of Jerez sent merchants to Málaga in search of wine. However, the latter half of the century was an era of increasing prosperity stimulated by the arrival of a number of French and British merchants. The firms of Osborne, Duff Gordon, and Garvey date from this period.

The Peninsular Wars (1808–14) devastated Jerez. Andalucía became a battleground, occupied for a time by the French, who pillaged the sherry bodegas and forced a number of families to flee to the relative safety of the Cádiz garrison. With the defeat of the French, merchants set about rebuilding their businesses with spectacular success. Pedro Domecq took over the firm of Juan Haurie in 1822 and Manuel María González Angel, founder of GONZÁLEZ BYASS, began trading in 1835. Sherry exports rose steadily from about 8,000 butts in the early years of the century to over 70,000 butts in 1873, a figure not exceeded again until the 1950s. In the 1850s, the sherry industry was greatly helped by the construction of a RAILWAY linking Jerez and Puerto de Santa María, and a number of merchants left their quayside bodegas. Many new producers took advantage of the sherry boom only to be wiped out by PHYLLOXERA and economic depression a few years later.

By the end of the 19th century, the sherry industry was on the brink of collapse. The boom gave rise to numerous spurious 'sherries' from South Africa, Australia, France—and from Germany, where a sherry-style potion was made from potato spirit. A spiral of price-cutting began and sherry was stretched with poor-quality wine imported from other parts of Spain. Demand fell as Victorian society refused sherry, alarmed by scare stories that the wine was detrimental to health. The predations of the phylloxera louse from 1894 helped to stabilize the market and the shippers who survived the depression held large stocks of unsold wine to tide them through the lean years when all the vineyards were replanted.

In 1910, the leading traders united to form the Sherry Shippers Association, which campaigned vigorously to restore the fortunes of the beleaguered industry. After the First World War exports returned to their late-19th-century levels. In 1933, a CONSEJO REGULADOR was formed to protect and control the sherry industry and in 1935, a year before the outbreak of the Spanish Civil War, Jerez established its own DO region. The Civil War (1936–9) had little effect on sherry exports, but trade collapsed during the Second World War.

The most dramatic episode in the recent history of sherry began in 1944 when Don Zoilo Ruiz-Mateos y Camacho, mayor of the town of Rota, bought out a small sherry stockholder whose business had suffered badly during the war. In the late 1950s, his son, the now legendary José María Ruiz-Mateos, secured a 99-year contract to supply the important BRAND owners HARVEYS OF BRISTOL with all their sherry requirements. With help from the banks, he began buying up other bodegas and in 1961 established the Rumasa empire. In the 1970s, Ruiz-Mateos acquired substantial wine interests outside Jerez (see RIOJA), as well as in banking, construction, retailing, tourism, chemicals, and textiles. The group is said to have bought three banks in a single day. Although Ruiz-Mateos contributed greatly to the modernization of the Spanish wine industry, Rumasa initiated a price-cutting spiral which continued to blight the long-term interests of sherry well into the 1990s. Ruiz Mateos's empire building came to an abrupt end in 1983 when, fearing imminent collapse, the government nationalized Rumasa, which at that point controlled about a third of the sherry industry. Rumasa's component parts were subsequently returned to the private sector.

Since the mid 1980s, the sherry industry has been facing decline. The total vineyard area has been reduced to 6,800 ha/16,300 acres; less than a third of what it was at the end of the 1970s. Plots of sunflowers and cereals are now commonplace among the vines. In the early 1990s, with a worldwide market estimated to be around 1.09 million hl/28.7 million gal, stocks were drastically reduced as the sherry industry attempted to bring supply and demand back into balance. By 2012 a new phenomenon surfaced as the supply of grapes from the dramatically smaller vineyard area dropped for the first time below demand. Ruiz Mateos briefly resurfaced in the early 21st century before his group again went under amid charges of assorted fiscal misdeeds. A few new names have appeared on the Jerez landscape, such as Tradición, Rey Fernando de Castilla, Dios Baco, and El Maestro Sierra. They have typically acquired older soleras from bodegas which either disappeared or were taken over by others.

Another leading actor has been the Estévez group, led by the idiosyncratic José Estévez (died 2005), the inventor of a controversial system to remove HISTAMINE from sherries. This group now includes Marqués del Real Tesoro, Tío Mateo, Hijos de Rainera Pérez Marín-La Guita, and Valdespino. Also showing signs of dynamism have been the Sanlúcar de Barrameda bodegas, from the giant Barbadillo to smaller ones such as Hidalgo-La Gitana and Pedro Romero. Equipo Navazos, formed by wine writer and criminologist Jesús Barquín and Estévez group winemaker Eduardo Ojeda has successfully contributed to the rebirth of interest in sherry worldwide by acquiring exceptional old butts from various bodegas and releasing small bottlings under the brand 'La Bota de . . .'.

Amid calls to rejuvenate the concept of sherry, including the promotion of a larger number of vintage-dated wines (a concept adopted by González Byass for some top-end Olorosos, Amontillados, and Palos Cortados), the Consejo Regulador responded in 2000 by creating two new categories of high quality sherry: VOS (Very Old Sherry or *Vinum Optimum Signatum*), for wines with an average age surpassing 20 years, and VORS (Very Old and Rare Sherry or *Vinum Optimum Rare Signatum*), for wines over 30, in four categories: Oloroso, Palo Cortado, Amontillado and Pedro Ximénez. Such methods as carbon dating were introduced to ascertain the age of the wines submitted by bodegas, and demanding blind tastings were instituted to accept or reject samples. This new category has stirred up fresh interest in sherry and qualified wines command high prices. But inevitably this is an elite category of minor presence on the market as most of the brands release just a few hundred bottles of their prized elixirs every year.

There is also increasing interest in the EN RAMA Fino and Manzanilla sherries that are perceived as more authentic and less manipulated than the regular versions.

See also SPAIN, history, and SACK.

Geography and climate

The climate of the Jerez region is strongly influenced by its proximity to the Atlantic. Sea breezes from the gulf of Cádiz alleviate extremes. The oceanic influence is strongest in the coastal towns of Sanlúcar de Barrameda and Puerto de Santa María, where temperatures in July and August may be 10 °C/18 °F lower than in Jerez, 20 km/12 miles inland. Winters are mild and damp with most of the region's annual average rainfall of 650 mm/25 in falling between late autumn and spring. There is almost no rainfall between June and October. Summer temperatures often reach 30 °C inland, occasionally rising to 40 °C with the *levante*, a piercing, dry, dusty wind from the south east.

The vines are sustained during the dry summer months by the porous, white ALBARIZA soils that are at the heart of the Jerez DO. The demarcated region is roughly triangular in shape and extends from the town of Chiclana de Frontera in the south east to the river Guadalquivir in the north west, tapering inland. However, the best albariza soils cover a stretch of rolling country north of the river Guadalete between Jerez and Sanlúcar de Barrameda. These outcrops of albariza are known collectively as Jerez Superior and the majority of these vineyards are within the municipality of Jerez de la Frontera, with secondary pockets around Sanlúcar de Barrameda, Puerto de Santa María, Chipiona, and Rota.

The albariza zone is divided into subdistricts. Those with the deepest, but not necessarily the most CALCAREOUS, albariza soils like the famous Balbaina, Macharnudo, Carrascal, and Añina districts produce the most delicate wines for the finest Finos and Manzanillas (see Winemaking below). The most calcareous soils, known as *tajón*, are generally unsatisfactory for viticulture because of potential CHLOROSIS. The finest albarizas include a proportion of sand and clay and tend to vary with depth, with a limestone content of 25% or more on the surface rising to 60% in the rooting zone 80 to 100 cm/39 in below the surface. In between the hills of albariza, barro soils have more clay and produce fuller, coarser wines and slightly higher yields. On the sandy soils known as arenas, yields are twice as great as on the albariza but the quality of the wine is poor. Arena soils were popular with growers at the end of the 19th century as the phylloxera louse found it difficult to survive in sand. However, with the recent rationalization of the sherry industry, viticulture is increasingly concentrated on the albariza soils and over 80% of the region's vineyards are situated in Jerez Superior.

Viticulture and vine varieties

In the 19th century, a variety of different vines were planted around Jerez but, after phylloxera wiped out most of the vineyards in the 1890s, many varieties were never replanted. Only three varieties are now authorized for new vineyards in Jerez: PALOMINO, PEDRO XIMÉNEZ, and MUSCAT OF ALEXANDRIA. Of these, Palomino is the most important and accounts for around 95% of the total vineyard area. There are in fact two types of Palomino: Palomino Basto (also known as the Palomino de Jerez) and Palomino Fino. Palomino Basto has largely been supplanted by Palomino Fino, which provides better YIELDS and is more resistant to disease. Palomino Fino has proved to be a particularly versatile grape and is used for most types of sherry.

Moscatel Gordo Blanco (Muscat of Alexandria) represents about 3% of the Jerez vineyard and is planted principally in the more sandy soils on the coast around Chipiona. It is mainly used for sweetening although some producers make and market their own VARIETAL Moscatel wines, including one of near-mythical proportions, Valdespino's Toneles.

Pedro Ximénez (known for short as PX) has given ground to Palomino and currently represents less than 100 ha/250 acres of vineyard since Palomino Fino is easier to cultivate. Most sweet wine is now made from Palomino although some smaller producers still maintain small PX SOLERAS which they bottle as a varietal wine. In recent years, special dispensation has been granted for the, now routine, importation of PX must from MONTILLA-MORILES to compensate for the lack of PX in Jerez.

Since phylloxera swept through Jerez, all vines have been grafted onto American ROOTSTOCKS which are selected according to the soil's LIME content. In the past vines were planted in a hexagonal pattern known as *tresbolillo* but, with increasing MECHANIZATION, vineyards are planted in orderly rows at a maximum VINE DENSITY of 4,100 vines per ha (1,660 per acre). Yields from the Palomino are high, although the maximum permitted yield for the entire DO has been set at 80 hl/ha (4.5 tons/acre).

With the onset of mechanization, modern vineyards are trained on WIRES, although the PRUNING method, called *vara y pulgar*, is unchanged, and similar to the GUYOT system. A *vara* (meaning stick or branch) with seven or eight buds produces the current year's crop. The *pulgar* (meaning thumb) is a short shoot with one bud which will produce the following year's *vara*.

Winemaking

The HARVEST begins when the Palomino has reached a MUST WEIGHT of at least 11 °BAUMÉ, traditionally on 8 September. It lasts for about a month.

Grapes are loaded into plastic crates and transported to large automated wineries, where they are destalked and pressed. Most bodegas use horizontal plate or pneumatic PRESSES to control the extraction rate, which may not legally exceed 72.5 l/19 gal of juice from 100 kg/220 lb of grapes (16% higher than the extraction rate permitted for CHAMPAGNE, for instance). Others, especially the CO-OPERATIVES, use continuous de-juicers which tend to produce coarser wines with more solids and PHENOLICS. Today acid levels are adjusted with the addition of TARTARIC ACID prior to fermentation, and cold STABILIZATION before bottling is usually essential.

After SETTLING or CENTRIFUGATION, fermentation generally takes place in temperature-controlled, stainless steel tanks, although a few shippers continue to ferment a small proportion of their wine in butt, mainly to impregnate and season new casks of American oak that are to be used for maturation. (New BARRELS are not valued in Jerez.)

The modernization of the sherry industry which began in the 1960s and continued through the 1970s and 1980s has removed much of the mysticism that once surrounded the production of sherry. The modern winemaker can predetermine which of the two initial sherry types—*fino* and *oloroso*—each lot of grapes becomes.

The first selection takes place in the vineyard. Wines for the best *finos* are sourced from older vines growing on the best albariza soils while *olorosos* are made from grapes grown on the heavier clays. Elegance is crucial to *finos*, also made from the best FREE-RUN juice, which has fewer impurities than the slightly coarser and more astringent juices from the press, which are set aside for *olorosos* or inferior *rayas*, particularly coarse *olorosos*. Wine destined for *fino* tends to be fermented at a lower temperature than that made for *oloroso*. Barrel-fermented wine is often too coarse and astringent for the production of *fino*.

The second selection takes place soon after the end of fermentation. Although many shippers producing table wine endeavour to persuade otherwise, Palomino-based wine is fairly flat and characterless with a natural alcohol content of 11 or 12%. Depending on the style of the wine, sherry is fortified with grape spirit to between 15 or 15.5 and 22%. The appearance of FLOR, the veil of yeast that forms on the surface of the wine and distinguishes *fino* from other styles of sherry, is determined by the degree of fortification. Growth is inhibited by an ALCOHOLIC STRENGTH much above 16%. Wines destined to develop into *finos* are therefore fortified to 15 or 15.5%. *Olorosos*, which mature without flor, are fortified to a higher strength of around 18%.

The sherry bodegas are teeming with the flor YEAST strains. This beneficial FILM-FORMING YEAST grows naturally on the surface of the wine, although some houses now choose to cultivate their own flor culture. Butts used for *fino* are only partially filled to around five-sixths of their 600- to 650-l (160–70-gal) capacity because flor, which both protects the wine from OXIDATION and changes its character, feeds off OXYGEN as well as alcohol.

Flor is also extremely sensitive to heat and in the warm summer months it tends to die. In Montilla, for example, flor is reduced to a scumlike film in July and August, while in the cooler Jerez region it grows all the year round. However, there are significant climatic differences

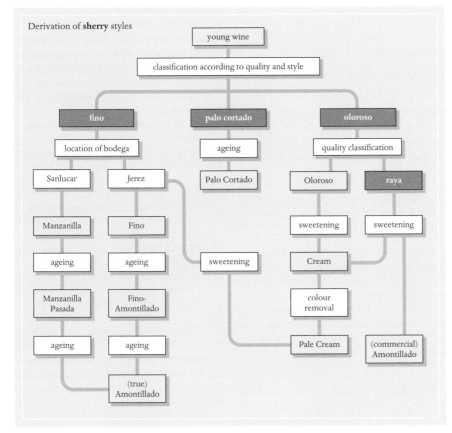

Derivation of **sherry** styles

within the Jerez region (see Geography above). Flor grows more thickly and evenly in the cooler, more humid coastal towns of Sanlúcar de Barrameda and Puerto de Santa María than it does in the bodegas situated in Jerez de la Frontera itself. This accounts for many of the subtle differences in style between Jerez Fino, Puerto Fino, and Manzanilla outlined below.

Left to its own devices, flor would feed on the nutrients in the wine and die before having a profound influence on the wine's character. However, flor is kept alive in casks of *fino* for six years or more by continually replenishing the butt with younger wine, and replenishing the yeast nutrients. This is the basis of the SOLERA system, a method of fractional blending which, apart from nurturing flor in *fino*, also maintains a consistent style for other sherry styles.

A sherry solera comprises a number of groups of butts, each of which is known as a criadera. Wine is withdrawn from the group containing the oldest wine, which is itself called the solera. This is replenished from the butts that form the first criadera, which is in turn replenished by wine from the second criadera, a process known as 'running the scales'. Simple soleras are fed by three or four criaderas while more complex systems run to as many as 14. The whole system is fed with new wine from the most recent harvest. Up to 33% of the wine in a solera may be withdrawn in any one year. *Fino* soleras need to be refreshed the most frequently, and by running the scales at regular intervals (usually two or three times a year) flor may be kept alive for eight to ten years.

Styles of sherry

The diagram above shows how commercial styles of sherry are made from the types of wine naturally formed.

Before bottling as Fino or Manzanilla styles of sherry, *finos* are filtered and fortified to a minimum of 15%. Some of the more commercial BRANDS are slightly sweetened.

Finos which lose their covering of flor become a sherry type known as *amontillados*, turning amber in colour and changing in character due to greater contact with the air. *Amontillados* evolve naturally if the flor has exhausted its supply of nutrients, or the style may be induced if the flor is killed off by fortification to 16% alcohol or above. A *fino* beginning to take on the characteristic of an *amontillado* may be bottled as a *fino-amontillado* or, in the case of a wine from Sanlúcar de Barrameda, a Manzanilla Pasada. True Amontillados are completely dry and the finest examples age for many years in their own soleras. Most so-called 'Amontillados' are no more than medium-dry

sherries blended from inferior quality *rayas* and sweet wines, however (see AMONTILLADO).

Having been fortified to 18%, *olorosos* on the other hand develop without recourse to flor. They age in greater contact with the air, turning dark brown and gaining in concentration with age. The alcoholic content increases with slow EVAPORATION such that the strength of an old *oloroso* may approach 24%. In their natural state, *olorosos* are dry, although old wines may taste full and concentrated. *Rayas* (inferior *olorosos* used in blending) may be aged in the open air. A certain proportion of Oloroso on the market is natural, dry OLOROSO; the majority is sweet wine of various quality levels.

Sweet sherries, most of them styled Cream, are made in a number of different ways. The finest sweet sherries such as Oloroso dulce (sweet oloroso) are produced by blending intensely sweet wines made from sun-dried Pedro Ximénez grapes. However, today Palomino grapes are frequently dried to raisins under plastic tunnels, pressed, and fortified before fermentation to make a MISTELA. This is never as sweet or as powerfully concentrated as PX, but the method is widely used for the production of more commercial sherries. Commercial Cream sherries may be very ordinary blends to which sweetening and colouring wines have been added.

The darkest sherries may be adjusted with ARROPE grape concentrate, or *vino de color*, a dark, sweet syrup that has been prepared by boiling down fresh grape must. Pale Cream sherry, typically a blend of *fino* and sweet wine, is normally adjusted with RECTIFIED CONCENTRATED GRAPE MUST and fresh Palomino must, vacuum CONCENTRATED, and the colour removed with activated CHARCOAL. A few bodegas sweeten their wines with fortified Moscatel but this tends to produce a rather obvious, aromatic, grapey style of sherry.

In the early 2000s, two new designations were introduced, with some success, for particularly old sherries: VOS, Very Old Sherry or *Vinum Optimum Signatum*, for blends at least 20 years old and VORS, *Vinum Optimum Rare Signatum* or Very Rare Old Sherry, for blends at least 30 years old. This provided some incentive for the release, or re-branding, of some bodegas' greatest treasures.

Organization of the trade

The majority of properties are small, averaging little over a hectare. Growers typically sell their grapes either directly to a shipper or to one of seven CO-OPERATIVES. Some co-ops maintain their own soleras but most sell the wine to one of the sherry bodegas.

Four classes of sherry bodega are recognized by the Consejo Regulador:

Bodegas de Producción: winemaking bodegas which are not permitted to mature wine.

Bodegas de Elaboración: winemaking bodegas which are allowed to hold stocks of wine for a short period of time before selling it on.

Bodegas de Crianza y Almacenado: firms which mature and keep stocks of wine or ALMACENISTAS. These bodegas are required to have a minimum of 1,000 hl/26,400 gal of which 60% must be from Jerez Superior.

Bodegas de Crianza y Expedición: firms which both mature and sell wine for consumption. These bodegas are required by law to maintain a minimum stock of 12,500 hl/330,000 gal of wine of which 60% must be from Jerez Superior. Exporters of sherry must hold a government licence.

See also individual articles on sherry shippers CROFT, GONZÁLEZ BYASS, HARVEY, and SANDEMAN; and see specific styles of sherry: FINO, MANZANILLA, AMONTILLADO, OLOROSO, CREAM, PALO CORTADO, and PEDRO XIMÉNEZ.

V. de la S.

Gonzalez Gordon, M., *Sherry: The Noble Wine* (London, 1990).

Jeffs, J., *Sherry* (5th edn, London, 2004).

Liem, P., and Barquín, J., *Sherry, Manzanilla & Montilla—A Guide to the Traditional Wines of Andalucía* (New York, 2012).

www.sherry.org

shipping. See TRANSPORT OF WINE.

Shiraz, the Australian name for the SYRAH grape, widely used elsewhere, and therefore a name better known by many consumers than its Rhône original. Because Australian Shiraz was so successful in European markets, the word Shiraz has been used on wine labels for Syrah grown all over the world, notably SOUTH AFRICA, although the word Syrah is also sometimes used to denote a lighter, fresher north RHÔNE style of wine rather than a typically concentrated, fruit-driven, potent Australian Shiraz. From the early years of the 19th century onwards, Shiraz (variously called Scyras, Syrah, or Hermitage) was the dominant red variety in Australia. When the concurrent red wine and export booms began in the second half of the 1980s, plantings in all regions, very cool to very warm, increased substantially. The result has been a range of styles from elegant, cool-grown Rhône styles (often with a dash of Viognier—see CO-FERMENTATION) through half a dozen important and regionally distinctive richer, riper styles, some traditional (Barossa Valley), some newer (Heathcote). Blends of Shiraz and Cabernet have been an Australian speciality for decades. For more detail, see AUSTRALIA.

The grape variety shares a name, but little else, with the medieval capital of PERSIA, although the (white) wine of Shiraz has been enthusiastically documented.

Shiroka Melnishka. See MELNIK.

Shoalhaven Coast, region on the NEW SOUTH WALES coast south of Sydney capable of producing surprisingly good Semillon. It also relies on CHAMBOURCIN.

shoestring root rot, vine disease. See ARMILLARIA ROOT ROT.

shoot, new growth in a plant that develops from a bud and consists of a stem with leaves and tendrils or INFLORESCENCES which become bunches of grapes. Collectively, the shoots and leaves of a vine form its CANOPY. The BUDS of a grapevine burst in spring to begin a new shoot (see BUDBREAK). Shoot growth gradually accelerates to a maximum rate before FLOWERING, then may slow to a stop at about VERAISON, common in unirrigated vineyards in a MEDITERRANEAN CLIMATE. When vines are well-supplied with water, shoots can continue to grow after veraison, which compromises fruit RIPENING; see WATER STRESS. See also WATER SHOOT.

VIGOUR, which effectively means shoot growth rate, varies hugely between and within vines. A vigorous shoot is evident by its long internodes, large leaves, strong LATERAL SHOOTS, and long tip tendrils well before flowering; weak shoots are the opposite. Despite these differences in growth rate and length at full bloom, shoots, whether weak or vigorous, have 17 to 20 visible internodes. Later in summer the stem of the shoot changes from green to brown (lignifies) and thus becomes a CANE (see CANE RIPENING). See also SHOOT TIP.

B.G.C. & R.E.S.

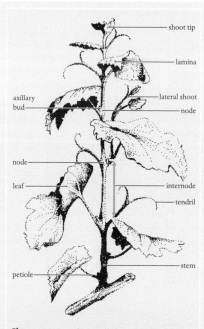

Shoot system: each spring buds burst and produce shoots as shown, which shoots in turn develop (axillary) buds at each node or leaf position along the shoot. If these buds are retained at winter pruning and burst in spring then a new sequence of shoot growth begins.
Source: J. Long, *Vignes et Vignobles*

shoot positioned, term used to describe vine-TRAINING SYSTEMS in a very general way. Shoot-positioned vines have shoots normally trained upwards and held between pairs of foliage or catch wires. Also the tips of the shoots are normally TRIMMED, because otherwise they can fall down the sides and cause SHADING. The typical vine-training system of Germany and many other countries is shoot positioned, as are all VERTICAL TRELLISES. Some important examples of non-shoot-positioned canopies are found in drier climates, such as the GOBELET-trained vines of the Mediterranean, and also the 'drooping' canopies of vigorous vines in California and Australia. See SHOOT POSITIONING.

R.E.S.

shoot positioning, spring and summertime viticultural practice of placing vine SHOOTS in the desired position to assist in TRIMMING, LEAF REMOVAL, and HARVEST operations, and to facilitate the control of VINE DISEASES and VINE PESTS.

The practice is by no means universal but is more common in wet and humid climates with high vineyard VIGOUR and a high risk of FUNGAL DISEASES, particularly in Germany, Alsace, and New Zealand. In the drier climates of southern France, Spain, Portugal, California, and Australia, the risk of fungal diseases is much lower and shoot positioning is not as common.

Typically the shoots are positioned upwards and are held between two pairs of so-called foliage wires, and sometimes the foliage wires themselves are moved to catch the shoots. Generally the operation is carried out manually, but a VINE FOLIAGE LIFTER may also be used. They are then trimmed to resemble a neat hedge. This then facilitates other vineyard operations such as SPRAYING and general cultivation, and enables mechanical operations such as leaf removal. For some training systems, such as GENEVA DOUBLE CURTAIN and SCOTT HENRY, shoots are positioned downwards.

R.E.S.

Smart, R. E., and Robinson, M., *Sunlight into Wine: A Handbook for Winegrape Canopy Management* (Adelaide, 1991).

shoot thinning, vineyard operation normally carried out by hand in the early spring which consists of breaking off unwanted shoots arising from the vine's HEAD or CORDON. Sometimes these shoots have no bunches and are called WATER SHOOTS. The shoot-thinning operation can be done most quickly when the shoots are 20–40 cm/8–15 in long and the bunches are quite visible, which allows discrimination between fruitful and non-fruitful shoots. The aim of shoot thinning is to reduce the density of the CANOPY and to avoid leaf congestion later in the season. This can help improve wine quality (see CANOPY MANAGEMENT) but is common only in regions with plentiful and relatively inexpensive LABOUR. Shoot thinning by machine is possible but not common. See also DESUCKERING.　　　　　　　R.E.S.

Morris, J. R., and Brady, P., *Vineyard Mechanization: Development and Status in the United States and Major Grape Producing Regions of the World* (ASHS, 2011).

shoot tip, the 1 cm/0.4 in of shoot furthest from the vine's original bud, also known as the shoot apex. This small piece of tissue competes very effectively with the grapes for food produced by the mature leaves, and so a vigorously growing vine may slow fruit RIPENING. These nutrients may be diverted to the grapes by TIPPING the shoots. The balance between shoot growth and fruit growth has important effects on grape RIPENING and wine quality (see BALANCE, LEAF TO FRUIT RATIO, and VINE PHYSIOLOGY). **Shoot tip growth** is being increasingly used to monitor vine growth as a guide to vine management. For example, irrigation should be regulated so that shoot growth stops by the time of VERAISON, and Californian, Australian, and French studies have related shoot tip appearance to measurements of vine WATER STRESS. Also, a vine which is in BALANCE and has been pruned appropriately will not have excessive numbers of shoot tips from the main and lateral shoots.　　B.G.C. & R.E.S.

Greenspan, M., 'Integrated irrigation of California winegrapes', *Practical Winery & Vineyard* (Mar/Apr, 2005), 21–34.

short, tasting term for a wine whose impact on the PALATE is not persistent; the opposite of LONG.

shot berry. A term once used for a small, immature, usually seedless berry resulting from insufficient pollination. See MILLERANDAGE.

shows, wine. Now a universal phenomenon, wine shows have occupied a particularly important place in Australia's wine culture, taking place in each AUSTRALIAN state's capital (originally offshoots of general agricultural shows), with some uniquely Australian features. Each class (established by variety and vintage(s)) is judged by a panel of three judges, one being panel chair, and three associate judges. If one or more of the judges has given gold medal points to a wine, it will automatically be retasted and discussed and the show chair may well be called in. The more experienced judges officiate at up to ten regional and capital city shows a year, know each other well, and have mutual respect for each other. While the discussion—in best Australian fashion—may be robust, it seldom, if ever, becomes ill-tempered. The most important part of the discussion usually turns on style issues.

The trophies and medals awarded to the more successful exhibitors are used extensively in marketing and promotion, and are accepted as reliable indicators of quality by retailers and consumers alike. But the greater long-term benefit has been for the winemaker judges, drawn from the leading wineries and schooled by chairs in the tradition of Len EVANS.　　J.H.

See also JUDGING WINE and COMPETITIONS, WINE.

shut down, vine. Some growers use this imprecise term for a cessation of the ripening process caused by WATER STRESS and/or temperatures over 35 °C/86 °F which cause STOMATA to close and PHOTOSYNTHESIS and TRANSPIRATION to stop.

Sichel, influential wine family now made up of two very distinct branches. The family originated in Germany and was involved with wine from the early 19th century. The direct descendants of the German founders established the wine and spirits distribution company H. Sichel Söhne at Mainz in Germany in 1857 and it grew to be an important commercial force (see JEWISH HERITAGE IN GERMAN WINE CULTURE). Its activities were severely curtailed during the First World War but a successful export business was developed in the 1930s, based increasingly on the branded wine BLUE NUN Liebfraumilch. Walter Sichel re-established a London office for Sichel in 1927 and had to work to overcome prejudice against all things German. In 1935, he became a naturalized British citizen, and the Sichels remaining in Germany were dispersed to Britain, France, and the United States. It was during the 1950s that Blue Nun began to establish itself as one of the world's most successful wines.

Peter M. F. Sichel directed the firm's fortunes from New York, widening the range of Blue Nun products in partnership with Sichel's American distributors Schieffelin Somerset, a subsidiary of LVMH, until his retirement when the Blue Nun trademark was sold (see BLUE NUN).

The Anglo-French-Scandinavian branch of the Sichel family is descended from a Dane who married a Sichel of Mainz, worked for the firm, and took his wife's name. He was sent to Bordeaux in 1883 to establish a Sichel & Company there. His son married another Dane, and extended the Bordeaux business into château ownership. His grandson Allan Sichel, who married a Swede, was an influential member of the British wine trade in the mid 20th century, introducing Harry WAUGH among others to the delightful, if hazardous, business of buying wine *sur place* in post-war France, and writing *The Penguin Book of Wines*, which was published in 1965.

Allan's son Peter A. Sichel continued his father's tradition of writing an annual report on Bordeaux, the vintage, and the market. He lived for many years in MARGAUX at the family's Ch Angludet running the Bordeaux NÉGOCIANT Maison Sichel, developing a number of French wine BRANDS. The Bordeaux Sichels are also substantial shareholders in Ch Palmer. Peter was a president of the Union des Grands Crus from 1988 to 1991, being one of the most articulate voices in defence of TRADITION and subtlety in the wines of Bordeaux. He took over the business of Pierre Coste of Langon in the GRAVES in 1992, and was an early investor in CORBIÈRES in the Languedoc, in Domaine du Trillol. The considerably expanded business is now run by his five sons, who have invested in Ch d'Argadens just across the Garonne from Langon.

Sicily (known as **Sicilia** in Italian), large, often hot, varied, and viticulturally important island off the toe of ITALY (see map under ITALY).

Ancient history

In startling contrast to the present day, Sicily was famed throughout classical antiquity for its agricultural produce, not least its wines. The settlement of colonies of Greeks around the island in the 8th century BC was an undoubted spur to the development of viticulture. Flourishing vineyards are testified for the 5th century at the later Greek settlement Akragas (Agrigento). Sicily may have played a key role in the development of viticulture on the Italian peninsula (see ITALY, ancient history). Vines from Morgantina and Tauromenium were transplanted to POMPEII around Vesuvius, the Colli ALBANI, and southern Etruria, where they were well established by the 2nd century BC (Pliny, *Natural History* 14. 25, 35, and 38). The most notable characteristic of Sicilian wines was their sweetness. The most famous were Mamertine, a sweet, light wine from the north east of the island around Messina, and a very similar wine from Tauromenium (Taormina); but there is evidence for wine production right down the east coast. Much of the rest of the island had its own wines. Inland there was the Murgentina vine from Morgantina (Serra Orlando). Inscriptions on AMPHORAE testify to a so-called 'Mesopotamian' wine from the south coast near Gela. Sicilian wines were certainly exported (references to Tauromenian, for example, appear on amphorae), but the scale of the trade is difficult to judge, since the identification of Sicilian amphora types remains a tantalizing problem.　　　　　　　J.J.P.

Wilson, R. J. A., *Sicilia under the Roman Empire* (Warminster, 1990).

Medieval history

Throughout the Middle Ages, Sicily's main export product was grain. It also produced olives, citrus fruits, and wine, but wheat has the advantage of being far less capital intensive: whereas olive trees, citrus fruit trees, and vines take years to come into full bearing, wheat can be harvested months after it has been sown. Medieval

Sicily owed its wealth to grain, and wine was not its most important commercial product.

Under the Normans, who governed Sicily from 1130 to 1194, smallholders owned most of the land, and they made their living mainly by growing wheat or, in the mountainous parts of the island, keeping livestock. They grew vines as well, but the wine made in these small vineyards was usually for domestic consumption. In the course of the 14th century, demand for high-quality wine rose, and vineyards spread through Sicily. Many of these vineyards, which produced wine for well-to-do Sicilians or for export, were owned by members of the feudal aristocracy or the local nobility. The principal winemaking towns were strung along the north eastern and eastern coasts: Cefalù, Patti, Aci, Catania, Augusta, and Syracuse. These not only produced large surpluses of wine, they were also able to ship their wine safely to Messina, from where it was taken to Africa and the Levant. From Patti, wine was carried to Constantinople, and Syracuse traded with nearby MALTA. Messina also imported wines from CALABRIA, which it then shipped to northern Italy; Messina and Palermo also carried Sicilian wines to the towns of northern Italy.

Palermo was Sicily's largest and most important city. In the early 14th century, it had 100,000 inhabitants, as did NAPLES; in the whole of Europe, only VENICE and Milan, with populations of 200,000, were larger. Because of its size, Palermo and its surrounding countryside could never make enough wine for the city's needs, and so it imported wine from Naples and Calabria, which was cheaper than transporting wine overland from eastern Sicily. This provoked the wrath of the citizens of Catania. Palermo exported wine as well.

From the late 14th century onwards, more and more vineyards around Palermo, Messina, and Catania came to be owned by members of the upper classes, and so, after 1400, did taverns. In the 15th century, most of the wine continued to be made in areas near ports: Aci, Catania, Messina, Taormina, and, in the west, Trapani. But further inland, Noto and Randazzo were also important. By far the biggest exporter was Messina, but Francavilla, Patti, Trapani, and Palermo handled a lot of the foreign trade in wine, too.

The wines that Sicily exported were, for the most part, the strong, sweet wines which were capable of surviving the sea voyage, such as VERNACCIA and Muscatello. Other names of wines mentioned in documents are Mantonico (also called Mantonicato), which could be red or white; a white wine named Cuctumini; and finally Mamertino, which shares its name with the classical Mamertinum, which PLINY tells us was grown in Messina (*Natural History* 14. 66).　　　　　　　　H.M.W.

Epstein, S. R., *An Island for Itself: Economic Development and Social Change in Medieval Sicily* (Cambridge, 1992).

Matthew, D., *The Norman Kingdom of Sicily* (Cambridge, 1992).

Modern wines and other vine products

With a total vineyard area of 114,290 ha/ 282,296 acres, Sicily produced 6 million hl of wine in 2013, making it Italy's second most important wine region after the Veneto. The 12,834 ha of DOC and IGT vineyards represent only 14% of the total, however, with 86% of the total still dedicated to the production of BULK WINE. The concentration on quantity over quality, systematically encouraged between 1960 and 1987 by the regional government's subsidies for the transformation of traditional BUSH VINES into more productive WIRE-trained or TENDONE systems led to a chronic cycle of over-production, with the EU's compulsory DISTILLATION regime encouraging CO-OPERATIVES to produce wine they knew would be distilled and GRAPE CONCENTRATE used for ENRICHMENT. However, the current increase in good wines produced is a strong indicator that Sicily is slowly beginning to turn the corner from a bulk wine to a quality producer, or at least that both can co-exist. The slow decline in the production of bulk wine is partly because of a decline in demand, and partly because compulsory distillation has largely been abandoned.

Sicily's bulk wine is still used, legally or not, to beef up weaker wines and vintages throughout Italy as well as in France and Germany. Nevertheless, Sicily produces much more white than red wine, notably from the island's 34,454 ha of the white wine grape Catarratto in 2010, more than twice as much as the second most planted variety Nero d'Avola with 16,342 ha. Although most Sicilian vineyard is planted with INDIGENOUS VARIETIES, there was 5,284 ha of Syrah, 4,865 ha of Chardonnay, 4,426 ha of Merlot, and 1,197 ha of Pinot Grigio, showing that Sicily was quick to adapt to demand for these varieties on the bulk market, while its diverse MESOCLIMATES, ELEVATIONS, and SOILS can supply even the ficklest of these with the right environment. Syrah shows particular potential in the province of Palermo, with Peter Vinding Diers' Montecarrubo near Modica probably the finest, if not exactly underpriced. From the 1980s these INTERNATIONAL VARIETIES not only satisfied international demand, they also spearheaded the production of quality wines, alerting the world to Sicily's potential, while blending them with indigenous varieties increased awareness of the likes of Grillo, Inzolia, Catarratto, and, especially, the widely planted Nero d'Avola.

In terms of climate and geology Sicily is often, rightfully, considered a continent itself, running counter to its perceived image as a hot, arid island. Climates range from distinctly alpine on Mount Etna, where vineyards up to 1,000 m/3,280 ft elevation are no exception, to the subtropical on the island of PANTELLERIA, which is closer to Tunisia than it is to the province of Trapani to which it administratively belongs. The island's centre can be hot and dry, although at higher elevations there can be favourable diurnal TEMPERATURE VARIABILITY, while many regions are close enough to the coast to benefit from such constant WINDS that FUNGAL DISEASES are a rarity except in the wettest of years.

The drive for quality began at the end of the 1980s when producers such as Planeta and Regeleali introduced smartly packaged international varietals that seemed to copy wines from the New World, especially Australia. This drew the attention of large producers from Italy's north, who, attracted by low land PRICES, and the virtual absence of a stringent DOC system, created large, fully mechanized estates, typically in the island's centre, which had traditionally been devoted to grain because of its arid climate. IRRIGATION and WIRE-trained international varieties were key ingredients in the recipe. It is partially owing to the influence of these large enterprises that the IGT Sicilia was promoted to DOC in 2012 without either stricter production rules or the requirement that the wines be bottled in the region of origin. Since by law IGTs may not take the same name as an existing DOC, the IGT Terre Siciliane was approved alongside the new DOC Sicilia.

All these recent developments tend to ignore Sicily's long history of producing wine from an abundance of INDIGENOUS VARIETIES. Several ancient wine regions have been rescued from the brink of extinction. From the island's eastern tip near Messina to Catania and the slopes of Etna, the distinct red Nerello Mascalese, in tandem with Nerello Cappuccio and Nocera, dominate the vineyards. The Faro DOC, which until 1994 existed only virtually since so many of the steep terraces had been abandoned, was resuscitated when the Palari estate began producing fine reds there. They have been followed by others, confirming Faro's exceptional TERROIR. Between Messina and Milazzo the DOC Mamertino, a wine region already appreciated by the Romans, declined fast after the introduction of international varieties and a controversial mandatory addition of Nero d'Avola to the elegant, local, crisp Nocera. Etna has seen an enormous rise in popularity resulting in huge investments and an influx of newcomers all keen to explore the cool VOLCANIC terraces and the UNGRAFTED and often centenarian Nerello Mascalese bush vines. The exposition of this sickle-shaped vineyard area situated around the volcano's snow-capped crest ranges from the south, where the white Carricante excels, to the north, where vineyards can be found up to 1,000 m and higher. The area is divided into *contrade* or hamlets, which have conveniently provided the first tentative steps towards a system of CRUS. Local consultant OENOLOGIST Salvo Foti educates newcomers in the ancient design of high-density vines trained on individual stakes and planted in a square, called *quinconce*, consisting of 13 vines each. He vinifies grapes from smallholdings in the ancient *palmenti*, large cellars which used to process the enormous production of grapes until PHYLLOXERA devastated what was then Europe's largest single wine-producing region. Such cellars are no longer allowed under EU law, which considers these edifices unhygienic.

Cerasuolo di Vittoria, situated near the town of the same name near Ragusa on the south eastern coast is Sicily's only DOCG so far. Several producers, notably COS, which ferments some of its wine in AMPHORAE, and Arianna Occhipinti, who espouses BIODYNAMICS, are producing high-quality examples of the classic Nero d'Avola–Frappato blend, while in the southeast the Eloro DOC with the subzone Pachino is Nero d'Avola's place of birth. The success of this accommodating variety is such that it has been planted in every corner of the island, regularly at the cost of other local varieties. The wines tend to be richly concentrated, and often oaked, which can disguise their origin.

Sicily's ancient sweet wine traditions can be found on the island of Lipari, where late-harvest or DRIED-GRAPE examples of MALVASIA are turned into Malvasia delle Lipari, while Passito di PANTELLERIA is the greatest expression of ZIBIBBO, or Muscat of Alexandria. Many ALBERELLO vineyards can be found in Sicily's extreme west between Erice and Trapani, but their future seems uncertain now that so many have been GRUBBED UP thanks to EU subsidies. Meanwhile, MARSALA, once western Sicily's raison d'être and one of the world's famous fortified wines, languishes on the margins, without any immediate prospect of being returned to its former glory.   W.S.

Belfrage, N., *From Brunello to Zibibbo: The Wines of Southern Italy* (2nd, edn, London, 2003).

Camuto, R., and Palmento. A., *Sicilian Wine Odyssey* (Lincoln, 2010).

Nesto, B., and Di Savino, F., *The World of Sicilian Wine* (Berkeley, 2013).

www.consorziodocsicilia.it

Sideritis, Greek light-berried vine variety found to a limited extent near Patra. It is mainly grown for TABLE GRAPES but can also make steely, peppery whites.

Sideways, a 2004 film by Alexander Payne of the eponymous book by Rex Pickett about a wine enthusiast's adventures in the CENTRAL COAST. One of its themes was the superiority of Pinot Noir over the then-popular Merlot. It had an immediate effect on demand for varietal Pinot Noir, particularly in the US—to such an extent that it resulted in a global shortage of BULK Pinot. One Languedoc supplier managed to sell GALLO vast quantities of a Grenache blend masquerading as varietal Pinot Noir until being found guilty of ADULTERATION AND FRAUD. An earlier edition of this volume figured prominently in the book but not the film. See also FILMS ABOUT WINE.

Siegerrebe, modern German vine cross grown principally, like certain giant vegetables, by exhibitionists, *Sieger* meaning 'champion'. In Germany it can break, indeed has broken, records for its ripeness levels, but the flabby white wine it produces is so rich and oppressively musky that it is usually a chore to drink. It was bred from SAVAGNIN ROSE and MADELEINE ANGEVINE and has been known to reach *double* the Oechsle reading required for a TROCKENBEERENAUSLESE. Total German plantings had blessedly dwindled by 2012 to under 100 ha/250 acres in Pfalz and Rheinhessen. The variety has also been used to bolster some blends in ENGLAND, Switzerland, Washington state, and British Columbia.

Sierra de Salamanca, DOP in the south of Salamanca province in western Spain. The Sierra de Francia mountain range has some 300 ha/750 acres of vineyards on acid, granite soils differing from the usual limestone of Spain's high plateaus. Five wineries led by the ambitious Viñedos del Cámbrico vinify the mainly Tempranillo and local RUFETE grapes.

V. de la S.

Sierra Foothills, wine region in GOLD RUSH country in CALIFORNIA and an AVA. This is basically the *piemonte* area on the western edge of the Sierra Nevada, the snowy mountains which separate California from the rest of the US (from reality in the minds of many). Thousands flocked here after 1849 and, miners being notoriously thirsty, the region's vineyards go back almost that far. The Sierra Foothills AVA blankets all of the vineyards in El Dorado, Amador, and Calaveras counties, takes in a few others in the flanking Nevada and Mariposa counties, and, in the process, points to most of the abandoned mines still there. California Shenandoah Valley and Fiddletown are AVAs within Amador county; El Dorado AVA and the subappellation Fair Play take in the vineyards in that county. North Yuba AVA is, not surprisingly, in Yuba county.

El Dorado county and Fair Play AVA
El Dorado county's vineyards are much higher than those of Amador county, starting close to 1,500 ft and ranging up above 3,600 ft/1,160 m. Predictably, conditions are cooler, and the choice of varieties leans toward Cabernet Sauvignon, Merlot, Chardonnay, and Riesling, with Syrah, Petite Sirah, and Zinfandel. Representative, established wineries include Sierra Vista, Boeger, Lava Cap, Holly's Hill, and Madroña. Cedarville Vineyards' Zinfandels and Grenaches can be superb. The subdistrict Fair Play AVA is south of the El Dorado vineyards, which cluster around Placerville (known as Hangtown during the Gold Rush), about halfway to Amador county, but not along the aptly named main road, Highway 49. Thus Fair Play is a mildly isolated destination. But the gaggle of small wineries in Fair Play has a justly deserved reputation for good times and for good value wines. So a steady stream of visitors regularly make the trek.

Amador county
The heart of the county's wine production is its two AVAs, Fiddletown and California Shenandoah Valley (see below), where pre-PROHIBITION Zinfandel vines thrive and old-school Barbera has found new life. Modernity also exists here, in Ann Kraemer's Shake Ridge Ranch, near the hamlet of Sutter Creek. Kraemer, an established Napa Valley viticulturist, has applied Napa vineyard expertise to a region unaccustomed to such precision. As a result, her Zinfandel, Syrah, Barbera, Tempranillo, and other varieties are highly sought after by boutique producers looking for authenticity over commercial appeal. Typical ELEVATIONS are 800 to 1,200 ft/ 240 to 360 m.

Fiddletown AVA
Amador county's Fiddletown AVA adjoins the upper, eastern end of California Shenandoah Valley, in the Sierra Nevada Mountain foothills east of the town of Plymouth. Amid rolling meadows and patchy pine forest, it grows some of the state's oldest plantings of ZINFANDEL in a region now most famous for that grape, and going back to gold rush days. There are few wineries in this AVA, but many elsewhere in Amador county purchase Fiddletown grapes.

California Shenandoah Valley AVA
California is tacked onto the front of Shenandoah Valley to distinguish this one from one, established earlier, in VIRGINIA. The California model is a mesa between two rivers east of the town of Plymouth. It became famous for hearty Zinfandels before the turn of the century and, after a long slumber, has regained some of its old momentum since the late 1970s, again with Zinfandel at the heart of the matter. More than a score of wineries share a modest acreage that also includes Sauvignon Blanc, Sangiovese, Syrah, and Petite Sirah. Monteviña initiated the resurgence after Sacramento retailer Darrell Corti encouraged Napa wineries to bottle some of the old-vine Amador Zinfandels. Leon Sobon's Shenandoah Vineyards and Bill Easton's Terre Rouge carry the region's banner

commercially, while Young's has become a cult destination selling mainly at the winery.

B.C.C. & L.M.

Sierras de Málaga, Spanish DO created in the early 21st century as effectively a subappellation of MÁLAGA to include a number of relatively new vineyards producing dry, unfortified wines, some in a subzone known as Serranía de Ronda around the inland town of Ronda, of which F. Schatz and Cortijo de los Aguilares are probably the best producers.

silica gel and **silica sol**, amorphous forms of silicon dioxide in which there is no crystalline structure, used in white winemaking and rosé winemaking as FINING agents. In white wines it is also used in conjunction with GELATIN, and it may be used after fining with BENTONITE to improve SETTLING. It has also been suggested that its use reduces the risk of overfining.

silt, description of particles of intermediate size between CLAY and SAND. See SOIL TEXTURE and GEOLOGY for more details of this particular form of soil classification. Grains of silt dominate LOESS and are often predominant in ALLUVIAL soils. Silt is a major component of many of the soils in California's Napa Valley.

Silvaner, called **Grüner Silvaner** in Germany, is an early-budding white grape variety grown mainly in Germany and central Europe (see SYLVANER for an account of it in France). Its very name suggests romantic woodland origins, and certainly it has a long history over much of eastern Europe, where it may indeed first have been identified growing wild. DNA PROFILING in Austria established that Silvaner is the progeny of SAVAGNIN (Traminer) and Österreichisch Weiss, a variety often mistaken for Silvaner and yet another progeny of GOUAIS BLANC. The cross probably took place in what is now Austria (although hardly any true Silvaner is grown there today) and it certainly came to Germany from the banks of the Danube. A vine known as Silvaner was widely grown throughout the extensive vineyards of medieval Germany. Its arrival from Austria at Castell in FRANKEN in 1659 is well documented and the variety is still the second most planted in Franken where distinctive clay-limestone soils seem to play a defining role in making full-bodied, firm, if aromatically discreet wines. Silvaner enjoyed its greatest popularity in the first half of the 20th century, when it overtook ELBLING to become Germany's most planted vine variety and established a dominant position in Rheinhessen. At 5,122 ha/12,651 acres in 2012, the variety is (just) a distant third among white wine grapes to the even more productive MÜLLER-THURGAU, which rapidly surpassed it in area after the Second World War. Grauburgunder (Pinot Gris) has been catching up rapidly, however.

This vigorous vine buds a few days before Germany's quintessential RIESLING, and can suffer spring frost damage. It is not notable for its disease resistance but it is productive. The chief characteristic of the wine produced is its high natural acid, generally lower than Riesling's in fact but emphasized by Silvaner's lack of body and frame. (It is significant that the German name for Sauvignon Blanc, a variety essentially notable for its aroma and high acid, is Muskat-Silvaner.) Provided yields are not too high, it can provide a suitable neutral canvas on which to display more geographically based flavour characteristics (see TERROIR). Most of Germany's finest Silvaners come from Franken, where Riesling is difficult to ripen and Silvaner has remained popular. Occasional and encouraging examples are made elsewhere, however—such as in certain calcareous, sandstone, or porphyry sites in Rheinhessen—where talented growers have achieved transparency of flavour and distinctively earthy character while avoiding the curse of a coarse, thick mid-palate. Silvaner is certainly more than capable of producing versatile, workhorse white wine, and the vintners of Rheinhessen, where more Silvaner is grown than anywhere else, have been at pains since the early 1990s to generate consumer awareness and a better image for this grape. It is particulary recommended with white asparagus.

Blauer Silvaner is a local, dark-berried mutation that is a speciality of Württemberg.

Outside Germany, Silvaner is relatively important, as Sylvánské Zelené, in the CZECH REPUBLIC, is still grown in SLOVENIA as Zeleni Silvanec, and is grown in Croatia, Ukraine, and Moldova. It is also planted in ALTO ADIGE, where there were more than 1,000 ha of Sylvaner Verde in 2010 making light, piercing wines for youthful consumption. In the Valais in SWITZERLAND, it is the fourth most-planted white wine grape. Also called Johannisberg, it can seem positively luscious in comparison with French Switzerland's ubiquitous CHASSELAS. Sylvaner is the second most planted white grape variety in the Valais, where it was once called Rhin, or Gros Rhin (as opposed to Petit Rhin, the local synonym for RIESLING). The variety ripens later than Chasselas and, in villages as warm as Chamoson, Leytron, and Saillon, can result in wines with more body, character, and race.

Despite its useful acidity levels, Silvaner is not widely grown in the New World, although California and New Zealand grow it to a strictly limited extent.

Simon, André Louis (1877–1970). Simon was the charismatic leader of the English wine trade for almost all of the first half of the 20th century, and the grand old man of literate CONNOISSEURSHIP for a further 20 years. In 66 years of authorship, he wrote 104 books. For 33 years he was one of London's leading champagne shippers; for another 33 years active president of the Wine & Food Society. Although he lived in England from the age of 25, he always remained a French citizen. He was both Officier de la Légion d'Honneur and holder of the Order of the British Empire.

Simon was born in St-Germain-des-Prés, between the Brasserie Lipp and the Deux Magots (the street has since been demolished), the second of five sons of a landscape painter who died (of sunstroke, in Egypt) while they were still youths.

From the first his ambition was to be a journalist. At 17 he was sent to Southampton to learn English and met Edith Symons, whose ambition was to live in France. They married in 1902 and remained happy together for 63 years in England. Simon was a man of judgement, single-mindedness, and devotion all his life.

He was also a man of powerful charm, the very model of his own description of the perfect champagne shipper, who 'must be a good mixer rather than a good salesman; neither a teetotaller nor a boozer, but able to drink champagne every day without letting it become a bore or a craving'.

He became a champagne shipper, the London agent of the leading house of Pommery, through his father's friendship with the Polignac family. It gave him a base in the centre of the City's wine trade, at 24 Mark Lane, for 30 years. From it he not only sold champagne; he soon made his voice heard as journalist, scholar, and teacher.

Within four years of his installation in London he was writing his first book, *The History of the Champagne Trade in England*, in instalments for the *Wine Trade Review*. A. S. Gardiner, its editor, can be credited with forming Simon's English prose style: unmistakably charming, stately, and faintly whimsical at once. He spoke English as he wrote it, with a fondness for imagery, even for little parables—but with an ineradicable French accent that was as much part of his persona as his burly frame and curly hair.

His first *History* was rapidly followed by a remarkable sequel: *The History of the Wine Trade in England from Roman Times to the End of the 17th Century*, in three volumes in 1906, 1907, and 1909—the best and most original of his total of over 100 books. None, let alone a young man working in a language not his own, had read, thought, and written so deeply on the subject before. It singled him out at once as a natural spokesman for wine, a role he pursued with maximum energy, combining with friends to found (in 1908) the Wine Trade Club, where for six years he organized tastings and gave technical lectures of a kind not seen before; the forerunner by 45 years of the Institute of MASTERS OF WINE. In 1919 he published *Bibliotheca vinaria*, a catalogue of the books he had collected for the Club. It ran to 340 pages.

The First World War ended this busy and congenial life, full of dinners, lectures, book-collecting, and amateur theatricals. Before war was declared Simon was in France as a volunteer, serving the full four years in the French Artillery, where as 'un homme de lettres' he was made regimental postman, before being moved on to liaison with the British in Flanders and on the Somme. It was in Flanders that the irrepressible scribbler wrote his best seller, *Laurie's Elementary Russian Grammar*, printed in huge numbers by the War Office in the pious hope of teaching Tommy, the British soldier, Russian.

In 1919, Simon bought the two homes he was to occupy for the rest of his life: 6 Evelyn Mansions, near Westminster Cathedral (where he attended mass daily), and Little Hedgecourt, a cottage with 28 acres beside a lake at Felbridge in Surrey. Gardening these acres, making a cricket pitch and an open-air theatre, and enlarging the cottage into a rambling country house for his family of five children were interspersed with travels all over Africa and South America to sell Pommery, until suddenly, in 1933, caught in the violent fluctuations of the franc–pound exchange rate when Britain came off the gold standard, he could no longer pay for his champagne stocks and Pommery, without compunction, ended their 33-year association.

Simon began a second life at 55: that of spokesman of wine and food in harmonious association. Already, with friends, he had founded the Saintsbury Club in memory of the crusty old author of *Notes on a Cellar-Book* (see SAINTSBURY, PROFESSOR GEORGE). With A. J. A. Symons he founded the Wine & Food Society (now INTERNATIONAL WINE & FOOD SOCIETY). Its first (Alsace) lunch at the Café Royal in London in the midst of the Depression (and for 10s. 6d.) caused a sensation. But its assured success came from the ending of PROHIBITION in America. Sponsored by the French government, Simon travelled repeatedly to the US, founding its first Wine & Food Society branch in Boston in December 1934 and its second in San Francisco in January 1935.

Meanwhile, while working briefly for the advertising agency Mather & Crowther, he conceived the idea of *A Concise Encyclopedia of Gastronomy* to be published in instalments. It sold an unprecedented 100,000 copies. Research, writing, and editing (and finding paper to print) the *Encyclopedia* and the Society's *Quarterly* occupied him throughout the Second World War. His daughter Jeanne and her family moved into Little Hedgecourt for the war and thereafter. His son André was a wine merchant. His two other daughters and a son all retired from the world into religious communities.

Simon was a better teacher than a businessman. He was repeatedly helped out of difficulties by adoring friends. Thus the National Magazine Company gave him an office in Grosvenor Gardens in 1941, to be followed by the publisher George Rainbird, still in central London at Marble Arch. In 1962, his friend Harry Yoxall suggested that at 85, daily responsibility for the Society and its magazine was too burdensome and bought the title from him for Condé Nast Publications. But in his 90s, Simon was still exceptional company at dinner and gave little picnics for friends beside his woodland lake.

His final book, *In the Twilight*, written in his last winter, 1969, recast the memoirs he had published as *By Request* in 1957. On what would have been his 100th birthday, 28 February 1977, 400 guests at the Savoy Hotel in London drank to his memory in CLARET he had left for the occasion: Ch LATOUR 1945.   H.J.

single-vineyard wines, wines made from the produce of one vineyard, and sometimes a single block within a vineyard, are becoming increasingly common throughout the world of wine. Arguably most of the better wines of GERMANY, AUSTRIA, and the Côte d'Or in BURGUNDY were the prototypes. (Many Bordeaux CHÂTEAUX are made up of several non-contiguous plots.) That the phenomenon is becoming so popular outside Europe suggests that the concept of TERROIR is widely embraced by producers in the NEW WORLD.

Sirah is the name by which some PETITE SIRAH is known in South America. It should not be confused with the true Syrah of the northern Rhône.

Síria, old, light-berried vine variety with many synonyms grown on 7,707 ha/19,036 acres all over Portugal where it is the second most planted white wine grape. Wines are aromatic but often age rapidly. It is known as Crato Branco in the Algarve, Roupeiro and Alva in Alentejo, and Códega in the Douro (distinct from CÓDEGA DE LARINHO). It was also known in Spain in the 16th century. Nearly 600 ha remained in 2011, mainly in Galicia. It is often known as Doña Blanca although it is known as Cigüente in Extremadura.

site climate, the climate of a specified site, for instance a vineyard or part of a vineyard. The scale of definition usually falls within that of MESOCLIMATE.

site selection. See VINEYARD SITE SELECTION.

Sizzano, tiny (3 ha/ 7 acre) DOC for seriously ageworthy reds in the Novara hills in the subalpine north of the PIEMONTE region of north west Italy. For more details, see SPANNA, the local name for Nebbiolo.

skin, grape. For details of grape skins, see GRAPE.

skin contact, *macération pelliculaire* in French, winemaking operation with the aim of extracting FLAVOUR COMPOUNDS, FLAVOUR PRECURSORS, and ANTHOCYANINS from grape skins into grape juice or wine. In its widest sense, it is identical to MACERATION, and some form of skin contact is usually essential to ROSÉ WINEMAKING, but the term is generally used exclusively for the maceration of white grapes for about four to 24 hours before PRESSING and FERMENTATION with the aim of increasing the extraction of constituents that contribute to the aroma of white wines. Destemmed and moderately crushed grapes are put into a vat and covered with INERT GAS and cooled down, if necessary, to a temperature of less than 15 °C/ 59 °F. A few hours later, the FREE-RUN juice is collected and the MARC is pressed. Skin contact can also take place directly in airtight pneumatic PRESSES. Skin contact tends to reduce must acidity and increase PH. It also increases the concentration of AMINO ACIDS, leading to a better rate of fermentation. Vine varieties frequently processed with skin contact are Sémillon, Sauvignon Blanc, Gros Manseng, Muscat, and Riesling. Grapes must be healthy, fully ripe, and have sufficient acidity and low tannin content. Denis DUBOURDIEU and his team have been responsible for its application to white bordeaux since the late 1980s. It is important to arrest skin contact before excessive amounts of bitter PHENOLICS (which may also darken colour) are extracted. In some vintages and in some regions, especially when the skin is rich in tannin due to a hot, dry climate, the technique simply does not work as too much undesirable material is extracted with the minimum amount of additional flavour compounds.

Ribéreau-Gayon, P., et al., *Traité d'Œnologie* 1: *Microbiologie du vin: Vinifications* (Paris, 1998), translated by J.M. Branco, as *Handbook of Enology* 1: *The Microbiology of Wine and Vinifications* (Chichester, 2000).

skin-fermented. All red wines are fermented in contact with the skins of the grapes (see RED WINEMAKING and MACERATION). Many wines are pink because the juice was briefly in contact with the skins of red wine grapes (see ROSÉ WINEMAKING). Most white wines are made by separating the juice from the grape skins before fermentation (see WHITE WINEMAKING). However, a small but increasing proportion of white wines are fermented in contact with grape skins, often described as **fermented on the skins**. Likely effects include increased COLOUR and TANNIN in the resultant wines. See, for example, ORANGE WINES and QVEVRI. Not to be confused with SKIN CONTACT.

slashing, vineyard operation of mowing or cutting a COVER CROP, or cutting vine shoots in summer (see TRIMMING).

slate, a moderately hard, very fine-grained metamorphic rock (see GEOLOGY), the result of the burial of pre-existing rocks such as mudstone, SHALE, and volcanic TUFF, with a marked propensity to cleave into thin sheets. With increased metamorphism, slate becomes SCHIST.

Slate is found, for example, in the Cederberg Mountains, SOUTH AFRICA, and the CLARE VALLEY, South Australia. It is particularly celebrated in Germany's MOSEL and RHINE regions, where it makes famously stony slopes and is thought to hold moisture and heat and radiate warmth at night.   A.J.M.

slip-skin. See AMERICAN VINE SPECIES.

slope, or incline, an important characteristic of any vineyard site that is not completely flat. For more details, see TOPOGRAPHY.

Slovakia. A relatively vibrant wine scene was one casualty when this eastern part of what was Czechoslovakia voted to split from the CZECH REPUBLIC in 1992, becoming officially independent in 1993. Total vineyard area fell from around 25,000 ha/62,000 acres to just 15,000 ha and yields are apparently extremely low. This shortfall may be explained by FROST, poor VITICULTURE, and small-scale, undeclared private production for barter or home consumption. Vineyards are much scattered but the most important wine-growing areas are the Malé Karpaty Hills (Small Carpathians) on the Czech border, where predominantly white wine is made from such grapes as Silvaner, Veltliner, Welschriesling, Riesling, Chardonnay, and various Muscats, and along the Hungarian border in the south where red wine production from the likes of Cabernet Sauvignon and Frankovka (Blaufränkisch) is more common. In the far east is what is effectively an extension of the Hungarian TOKAJ region. VINE BREEDERS have produced a host of new Slovak CROSSES such as Devín, Hetera, Hron, and Nitranka designed to reach high sugar levels rapidly in this decidedly CONTINENTAL climate. New wine laws combining the principles of both France and Germany came into force in 2009, and in the second decade of this century some interesting wine was beginning to emerge. But with notable exceptions such as the fine Rieslings of Kastiel Béla, a JOINT VENTURE involving renowned Mosel grower Egon Müller, Slovakia consumes virtually all the wine it produces except for that exported to the Czech Republic and some local Polish towns.   R.J.S.

Slovenia, small country in Central Europe with a long winemaking history. CELTS and Illyrian tribes were making wine here before the ROMANS. In the Middle Ages, wine production was undertaken by MONKS AND MONASTERIES. Slovenia was part of Austro-Hungarian Empire and since 1918 it was part of what was to become YUGOSLAVIA. After the Second World War, production was limited to CO-OPERATIVES, where quantity not quality ruled. However, some excellent and long-lived whites were produced in those times, especially in the Podravje region, and some are still available from cellar archives. Commercially important private-sector wine businesses started to emerge in the 1970s. In 1967, the PSVVS (Business Association for Viticulture and Wine Production), recently renamed Vinska družba, was founded and introduced a seal of approval for Slovenian wines. In 1991, Slovenia established its independence and in 2004 joined the EU. It was the first of the ex-Yugoslav countries to build a successful wine industry with fully implemented and well-policed wine laws and a thriving private sector incorporating many excellent estates. Slovenia has a total of 21,200 ha/52,300 acres of vines. Around 29,000 winegrowers and 2,000 bottlers are registered, resulting in highly fragmented vine-growing and winemaking. Annual production has fallen to between 0.7 and 0.9 million hl (18.5–23.8 million gal), 70% of it white. At about 40 l/10.5 gal a year, Slovene per capita wine consumption is one of the highest in the world, although by 2013 exports had reached about 10% of wine production, mainly to BOSNIA AND HERZEGOVINA, CROATIA, the UNITED STATES, AND THE CZECH REPUBLIC. Production is focused on quality PDO wines, with only about 30% PGI quality. TOURISM plays an important role in premium wine distribution.

Slovenia is divided into three wine regions: Podravje in the north east of the country; Primorska in the west, close to Italian border and the Adriatic; and Posavje in the south east. They are further divided to nine wine districts.

Geographically Slovenia is very diverse with many different MESOCLIMATES with vines growing on either gentle or steep slopes, many of them TERRACED. The climate is generally CONTINENTAL, with hot summers, and cold and wet winters. Annual rainfall averages 800 to 1,400 mm (31.5–55 in). The climate in Primorska is influenced by the MEDITERRANEAN, especially in the Slovenska Istra (Istrian Slovenia) district. Spring FROST, summer HAIL, and DROUGHT may be experienced in most wine districts.

Double or single GUYOT is the most common training system. The high-yield PERGOLA training system (*latnik*) and *casarsa* (similar to GDC), once common in Primorska, are being replaced with Guyot. As terrain is often steep, manual harvesting is the norm.

Wines were traditionally vinified in large old wooden casks either from Slovenian or Slavonian oak. Modern practice includes stainless steel and barrel maturation either in Slovenian or French oak of different sizes. MALOLACTIC CONVERSION for reds and whites is common in Primorska and for most reds in Podravje and Posavje. As in most ex-Austro-Hungarian Empire countries, the best wines have tended to be VARIETAL, while white and red blends are reserved for more basic wines and, more recently, for flagship wines in Primorska. The majority of wine is produced in large, often well-equipped wineries, either CO-OPERATIVES or privately owned. Small and mid-sized family estates are both important and in FASHION, often commanding higher prices.

By law all wines must be analysed, tasted, and scored to determine their quality level before going to market. Zaščitena Označba Porekla (ZOP) is the PDO equivalent, while Zaščitena Geografska Označba (ZGO) corresponds to PGI but is hardly used. Traditional designations still widely in use in the early years of the second decade of the 21st century were: *namizno vino* (table wine); *deželno vino PGO* ('Vins de Pays' coming from a single region); and *kakovostno vino ZGP* (quality wine) and *vrhunsko vino ZGP* (premium quality wine), both of which come from single district.

Priznano Tradicionalno Poimenovanje (PTP) is similar to Austria's DAC. According to the RESIDUAL SUGAR level, all wines in Slovenia are designated as either *suho* (dry), *polsuho* (medium-dry), *polsladko* (medium-sweet), or *sladko* (sweet).

Podravje With 8,900 ha/22,000 acres of vines, this is (just) the largest wine region in Slovenia and also an official PGI, divided into two districts (also PDOs). The extensive **Štajerska Slovenija** (Styrian Slovenia) district with its beautiful rolling hills is slowly regaining its former status, while the rather warmer **Prekmurje** district, a continuation of the Pannonian Plain in the far north east of the country, is of minor significance. In Maribor, the capital of Štajerska Slovenija, is the 400-year-old *Stara trta* ŽAMETOVKA vine, which locals claim is the oldest on the planet. In 1852, Slovenia's first sparkling wine (*penina*) produced by the TRADITIONAL METHOD was made in Gornja Radgona.

Laški Rizling (WELSCHRIESLING) is the dominant variety, usually ending up in BULK WINE or inexpensive blends. The increasingly popular Sauvignon Blanc (which thrives here as across the border in STYRIA) has enjoyed some export success, as has Šipon (Furmint), the traditional grape of the region. Renski Rizling (RIESLING), Chardonnay, Sivi Pinot (PINOT GRIS), Beli Pinot (PINOT BLANC), Dišeči Traminec (GEWÜRZTRAMINER), and Modri Pinot (Pinot Noir) are common for higher quality VARIETAL wines. Most of these varieties were introduced to the region by the Austrian Archduke Johann in 1823. Although most Podravje wines are white, reds represented 5% of production by 2014. Modri Pinot is the most planted dark-skinned variety with Modra Frankinja (BLAUFRÄNKISCH) being a recent development.

Many locals still prefer the traditional medium-dry whites but export markets prefer those that are dry, crisp, and medium bodied with distinctive and expressive varietal aromas.

Podravje and, to a lesser extent, Posavje (see below) is also where the country's best BOTRYTIZED wines are made, and labelled in German fashion according to sugar level: *pozna trgatev* (SPÄTLESE), *izbor* (AUSLESE), *jagodni izbor* (BEERENAUSLESE), *ledeno vino* (EISWEIN), and *suhi jagodni izbor* (TROCKENBEERENAUSLESE). The best sweet wines are made from Šipon, Laški Rizling, and Renski Rizling. Typically they are expensive and can be of world-class quality.

Other grape varieties planted in Podravje are the indigenous Ranina (BOUVIER) and Ranfol, Muškat Ottonel (MUSCAT OTTONEL), Zeleni Silvanec (SYLVANER), Rizvanec (MÜLLER-THURGAU), KERNER, Portugalka (PORTUGIESER), Kraljevina, Rdeča Žlahtnina and Beli Žlahtnina (red and white CHASSELAS), GAMAY, and ZWEIGELT.

Posavje With 4,300 ha/10,625 acres of vines, this is the smallest and least important wine region and PGI in Slovenia, producing slightly more reds than whites. Production is widely dispersed and bulk wine prevails. Posavje is divided into three wine districts or PDOs. **Bizeljsko Sremič** is known for sparkling wine Bizeljčan (white and red) and the highly acidic local white Rumeni Plavec. **Bela Krajina** can produce the best Rumeni Muškat (MUSCAT BLANC À PETITS GRAINS) in the country and some solid Modra Frankinja (BLAUFRÄNKISCH). It is home to the light red PDO blend Metliška Črnina and white PDO wine Belokranjec. **Dolenjska** is home to the highly popular Cviček, a light, pale ruby, highly acidic blend of red and white grapes, usually Žametovka and Kraljevina. Other grapes planted in this region are Sauvignon Blanc, Chardonnay, Beli Pinot, Sivi Pinot, Renski Rizling, Traminec, Šipon, Ranina, Neuburger, Modri Pinot, Šentlovrenka (ST-LAURENT), Gamay, Zweigelt, and Rdeča Žlahtnina (red Chasselas).

Primorska With a steady 8,000 ha of vines, this region has made great progress in quality since early 1990s and is today the most praised Slovenian wine region in certain quarters, having developed into an epicentre of NATURAL and ORANGE WINE production. It is also Slovenia's other PGI. Primorska is divided into four districts (PDOs). **Goriška Brda**, the continuation of Italy's COLLIO DOC and influenced by its Italian neighbours, boasts many good producers and is currently Slovenia's most esteemed wine district, having begun the quest for quality as early as the late 1980s. Many of the best wines are oak-aged white and red blends based on Rebula (RIBOLLA) and Merlot/

Cabernet Sauvignon respectively. The **Vipavska Dolina (Vipava** Valley) is proud of its native light, crisp Zelen and flashier Pinela. **Kras** (Carso), a plateau above Trieste, is the home of Teran, a distinctive, highly popular and highly acidic dark red made from Refošk (REFOSCO) grapes. **Slovenska Istra** on the Slovenian coast is the warmest district in the country. The most planted Slovenian red wine grape Refošk and the white Malvazija (MALVASIA ISTRIANA) prevail. In Primorska, some great sweet wines are made in PASSITO style. Other sweet wines are typically made from Rumeni Muškat. Sweet Verduc (VERDUZZZO) and Pikolit (PICOLIT) are specialities of Brda. Also grown in Primorska are Rumeni Muškat, Beli Pinot, Laški Rizling, Vitovska Grganja, Klarnica, Glera, Cabernet Franc, Barbera, Syrah, Cipro (possibly MAVRO), and Maločrn.

Slovenia makes very good, whites, especially from varieties such as Pinot Gris, Sauvignon Blanc, and Chardonnay. Reds, notably Pinot Noir, have improved considerably since the early 1990s. However, Slovenia is still trying to find its place on the international market with varieties such as Rebula, Šipon, Refošk, and local blends.   R.F.G.

Smaragd, the most valuable category of white wines made from the ripest grapes on the best sites of the Wachau in AUSTRIA. Alcohol levels in the unchaptalized Grüner Veltliners and Rieslings that qualify must be more than 12.5% and commonly range between 13 and 14.5%. The category is named after the green lizard that basks in the sun on the Wachau's steep stone terraces above the River Danube. See also STEINFEDER and FEDERSPIEL.

Smart–Dyson, vine TRAINING SYSTEM developed in the early 1980s in California and by the end of the 2000s adopted in new plantings in Spain and South Africa in particular. In South Africa, adoption has been encouraged by

companies such as DISTELL, where experience has shown an increase in both yield and quality following conversion from the often-shaded VERTICAL TRELLIS.

The system was devised by Richard Smart of Australia and John Dyson of New York, and initially trialled on Dyson's ranch in Gilroy, California, in 1992 with Merlot vines. It is a vertically divided training system like SCOTT HENRY, but the vine is CORDON trained and there are upwards- and downwards-pointing SPURS giving rise to the two canopies. It is compatible with MECHANICAL PRUNING, unlike the Scott Henry system, and it can be MECHANICALLY HARVESTED as readily.   R.E.S.

Smart, R., 'Introducing the Smart–Dyson trellis', *Practical Winery & Vineyard* (Nov/Dec 1993), 48–9.

Smederevka, white grape variety commonly planted in SERBIA and MACEDONIA, the name presumably being inspired by the town of Smederevo south of Belgrade. Often blended with other varieties, notably LAŠKI RIZLING, its wine is generally unremarkable. It is the same as Bulgaria's DIMYAT.

smell. The smell of a wine is probably its single most important attribute, and may be called its AROMA, BOUQUET, odour or off-odour if it is positively unattractive, or even FLAVOUR.

The sense of smell is the most acute human tasting instrument (blocked nose robs food and drink of any flavour) but since it is so closely related to what we call the sense of taste, it is considered in detail under TASTING. Those who lose their sense of smell, either temporarily or permanently, are said to be anosmic.

smoke taint in grapes and wine has become an increasing problem in the 21st century as the incidence of bushfires or wildfires escalates in many wine regions that are experiencing hotter and drier periods due to CLIMATE CHANGE.

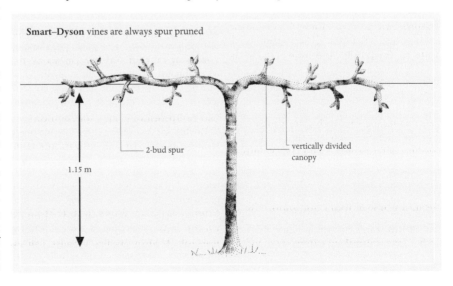

Smart–Dyson vines are always spur pruned

2-bud spur

1.15 m

vertically divided canopy

Grapevines become increasingly sensitive to any atmospheric smoke during the growing season, with the likely uptake most marked from VERAISON onwards. Depending on the stage of grapevine development and the level and duration of smoke exposure, smoke-tainted wines can display an array of different sensorial attributes, variously described as 'smoked meat', 'disinfectant', 'leather', 'burnt', 'smoky', 'salami', 'bacon', 'vinyl/plastic', 'medicinal/Bandaid', 'charry', and 'ashtray'.

Research since 2003 by the AUSTRALIAN WINE RESEARCH INSTITUTE (AWRI) related the exposure of grapevines to atmospheric smoke to the development of smoke-related flavour and aroma characteristics in the resultant wine. The compounds primarily responsible for the sensory perception of smoke taint characters include, but are not restricted to, a number of PHENOLS including guaiacols, cresols, and syringols. These phenols exist in grapes and wine as GLYCOSIDE FLAVOUR PRECURSORS which can be broken down during alcoholic FERMENTATION, MALOLACTIC CONVERSION, and through a chemical process as the wine ages. Perceived smoke taint character can become more obvious during maturation and after bottling.

Grape varieties tend to differ in the extent to which they are affected by smoke taint: Sangiovese appears to be particularly sensitive compared with, say, Chardonnay or Cabernet Sauvignon, having higher levels of volatile phenols in grapes and wine given a similar level of exposure to atmospheric smoke. The taint compounds appear to be concentrated under the berry skin so that vineyard and winery practices that reduce skin contact or damage help to mimimize the effects of the smoke. These include hand harvesting, WHOLE-BUNCH PRESSING, lower processing temperatures, less time on skins (before, during, and after fermentation), and separation of press fractions. REVERSE OSMOSIS has been used successfully to remove the free volatile phenol fraction but this method is currently not effective at removing the bound fraction.

These compounds can also occur naturally in grapes and wine which have not been exposed to smoke, especially in varieties such as Shiraz/Syrah, so comparing results to natural background levels is a key to assessing the potential risk prior to harvest if vines have been exposed to smoke. Risk assessment following smoke exposure includes conducting a mini-ferment and sensory assessment of the resultant wine. It may be necessary to submit grape or wine samples for laboratory analysis.   M.P.K. & C.A.S.

Hayasaka, Y., et al., 'Glycosylation of smoke-derived volatile phenols in grapes as a consequence of grapevine exposure to bushfire smoke', Journal of Agricultural and Food Chemistry, 58/20 (2010), 10989–98.

Kennison, K. R., et al., 'Effect of smoke application to field-grown Merlot grapevines at key phenological growth stages on wine sensory and chemical properties', Australian Journal of Grape and Wine Research, 17/2 (2011), 5–12.

Kennison, K. R., et al., 'Smoke derived taint in wine: the release of smoke-derived volatile phenols during fermentation of merlot juice following grapevine exposure to smoke', Journal of Agricultural and Food Chemistry, 56 (2008), 7379–83.

Ristic, R., et al., 'The effect of winemaking techniques on the intensity of smoke taint in wine', Australian Journal of Grape and Wine Research, 17/2 (2011), 29–40.

smudge pot, burner, usually fuelled with oil, lit in frost-prone parts of an orchard or vineyard on still nights when lethal frost seems imminent to create air convection currents which mix relatively warm upper air with the chilled air settled at ground level. They have lost favour because of the numbers of pots required, not to mention fuel, smoke, lost sleep, and the general inconvenience of operating them in the cold darkness of the early morning. Other approaches to FROST PROTECTION are available.   J.G. & R.E.S.

snails, vine pests of which at least two types can be of economic significance to wine production: the white Italian snail, *Theba pisana*, and the brown or English snail, *Helix aspersa*. They are mainly a problem in early spring, and can strip vines of young foliage if they are in large numbers, which happens particularly in wet conditions. They will contaminate fruit and wine if they are present at HARVEST time. Clean CULTIVATION is an important preventive measure, and sprays or baits used early can also control snails. Copper-based FUNGICIDES used on vines also affect snails by repelling and killing them. Ducks and geese feed on snails, and their presence in vineyards will keep numbers down.   M.J.E.

Soave, dry white wine from the VENETO region of north-east Italy. Like the neighbouring VALPOLICELLA zone, the Soave zone was expanded enormously with the creation of the Soave DOC in 1968. At the time, both regions were enjoying an export boom, so production flowed off the small hilly zone onto the alluvial plain of the Adige River. The CLASSICO zone of mostly HILLSIDE VINEYARDS first defined and delimited in 1927, is the source of superior Soave. The eastern part of the zone, in the commune of Monteforte d'Alpone, where the vineyards are planted on decomposed VOLCANIC rock, produces steelier wines than those from the western part in the commune of Soave, where the higher percentage of LIMESTONE in the soil and the warmer afternoon sun gives fuller, more forward wines.

By 2010 there were 3,319 ha/8,197 acres of vineyards on the plain, and these are responsible for the bulk of ordinary Soave. The quality-oriented producers from the hills have long struggled with the fact that their wines, no matter how good, are associated with these lower-priced wines. The real culprit responsible for insipid wines and Soave's tarnished reputation is excessive YIELDS, sometimes more than 15 tonnes/ha. It was hoped that the introduction of the DOCG in 2002 would deal with this situation, but instead of restricting the DOCG to the Classico hills, a general Superiore category was created, a half-baked compromise that included most of the produce of the omnipotent local CO-OPERATIVE. Maximum permitted yields for Soave Superiore DOCG are still high but are at least reduced to 10 tonnes/ha, and the minimum natural alcohol level is 12%. Confusingly, there are four official Soave denominations: Soave Classico DOC for the historical heartland; Soave Colli Scaligeri DOC, which includes all hillside vineyards outside the Classico zone; Soave DOC, which includes the plains, but is also an overarching DOC that producers can use for declassifying their wines; and Soave Superiore DOCG described above. All four can be seen on labels.

In an effort to elevate Soave's reputation, and align it with the current trend for single-vineyard wines, the whole region has been subdivided into 47 different subzones. Within each subzone, various single vineyards, or CRUS, have been identified, and most of them are located in the Classico zone. Their names may appear on labels. True Soave is medium bodied with fine acidity and a lively flowery aroma of white and yellow fruit, and garden herbs, taking on notes of chamomile and honey with age. Another potential improvement is that TREBBIANO Toscano has been excluded from both DOC and DOCG Soaves. This interloper was introduced to the area in the 1960s, when high yields were the driving force, and it soon displaced the local Trebbiano di Soave (which is, in fact, VERDICCHIO). Today, Soave must be at least 70% GARGANEGA and up to 30% Trebbiano di Soave, Chardonnay, Pinot Bianco, and/or the Sauvignon Blanc that has been used to add interest and body to wines from over-productive vines. When yields are controlled, Garganega can give wines of real class. A late-ripening variety, it has a thick skin that helps protect it against the autumn mists rising from the northern part of the Po Valley. Producers such as Pieropan, Gini, Pra, and Ca' Rugate have illustrated the potential not only of Garganega but also of the Soave zone.

Garganega is also the mainstay of the sweet RECIOTO di Soave DOCG, a PASSITO with a long local tradition made from raisined Garganega grapes.   W.S.

Lorenzoni, A., Zanichelli, M., and Ponchia, G., I Grandi Cru del Soave (Verona, 2008).

social media use mobile and web-based technologies for communicating and networking between individuals and organizations. Such networking shares, creates, discusses, and proliferates information in both textual and visual form. Social media have dramatically changed how information about wine is disseminated. Traditional media outlets still share information but have greatly decreased in number, leading to fewer permanent wine columns and paid WINE-WRITING positions. Increasingly, wine experts and consumers alike share wine information and opinion via social media channels such as Facebook, Twitter, Instagram, and wine blogs (see INFORMATION TECHNOLOGY).

Social media were initially differentiated from traditional media as being essentially consumer-generated, whereas traditional media were generated for consumers by experts selected to create such content, but the distinction is becoming increasingly blurred as wine producers and retailers are using social media to establish direct contact with consumers, often hiring wine professionals to create content for them. One of the effects of social media on wine criticism has been a general democratizing of authority, dispersing it broadly across online networks. Consumers increasingly turn to social media for information, thus relying less on expert authority, and more on crowd-sourced information. Prior to social media, influential information was concentrated around industrial media sources and established WINE WRITERS. But within social media, specific wine-focused communities have arisen via specialist websites, wine blogs, and mobile applications, most of which are designed to encourage sharing of consumer wine experiences, particularly impressions of specific wines (see CELLAR TRACKER, for example). Nielsen studies have shown that Internet users spend significantly more time on social media sites than on any other type of Internet site.

Social media have also led to a change in both wine publishing and wine marketing. Because of the dynamic nature of social media, the influence of any particular person or media source can change much more rapidly than in the past, and individuals who are charismatic but not necessarily expert can achieve prominence, even influence. Another consequence of social media is that traditional wine experts can now be in direct contact with their readers, who, along with wine bloggers (who include industry experts), can publish their reactions to them. Communication is very much a two-way process today.

However, what counts as a popular website or blog can also change quickly. Therefore, the impact of traditional marketing approaches such as ad campaigns simply seeking circulation numbers is less clear. Instead, many wineries have implemented social media marketing techniques. Such processes can integrate social media with information technology that tracks social media users' mentions of wine in general and specific wines, as well as their wine-based travel. Producers can thereby respond directly to consumers who mention their wines.

The proliferation of information online has also increased general discussion about even small-production and relatively obscure wines among consumers. Thus the democratization of wine information via social media has also encouraged consumers to experiment with a wider range of wines.   E.C.B.

sodium, element that is not a required nutrient for vine growth. Sodium chloride (common SALT) is, however, a major hazard for vine-growers, particularly in hot, irrigated areas where ground waters are saline, or where salty irrigation water is applied to the leaves. Sodium has an unfavourable effect on soil fertility because it reduces water infiltration due to its tendency to disperse clay particles. This can be overcome by addition of CALCIUM to the soil, normally as gypsum. See also SALINITY.   R.E.S.

Sogrape, Portugal's largest wine producer, owned by the Oporto-based Guedes family, whose success is founded on MATEUS Rosé. Since the 1980s, it has invested in new wine regions, acquiring Portuguese winemaking facilities and vineyards in the MINHO, DÃO, BAIRRADA, ALENTEJO, and DOURO (it owns port shippers FERREIRA, SANDEMAN, and Offley). Its Portuguese table wine brands include Douro icon FERREIRA's Barca Velha, Grão Vasco, Duque de Viseu, Gazela, Planalto, Quinta de Azevedo, Quinta dos Carvalhais, and Herdade do Peso. Global acquisitions include Finca Flichman (ARGENTINA), Framingham (NEW ZEALAND), Los Boldos (CHILE), and RIOJA-based Bodegas LAN.   S.A.

soil, mineral material at the Earth's surface formed by weathering of underlying bedrock (see GEOLOGY), or transported sediments, which form the parent material of a soil. The main distinction between soil and parent material is a soil's enrichment with plant and animal remains that undergo decomposition to form soil ORGANIC MATTER. Because soil formation is an ongoing process, determined by CLIMATE, vegetation, TOPOGRAPHY, and time, the boundary between a soil and its parent material is usually indistinct. Over very long periods, episodes of erosion and deposition followed by soil formation have led to layered soils, common in old weathered landscapes such as in Australia and southern Africa. However, where soils have formed on one parent material in situ, such as in north-west Europe and North America during the 11,000 years since the last Ice Age, distinctive zones called horizons can form in a vertical array, which is called a SOIL PROFILE. These horizons can be differentiated by their organic matter, colour, thickness, texture, structure, and stoniness. In addition to organic matter, soils are distinguished from rock materials by their structure (see SOIL STRUCTURE), which influences the rate of water infiltration (from RAINFALL or IRRIGATION), their resistance to SOIL EROSION, and ease of root penetration. The combined effect of SOIL TEXTURE and structure determines a soil's water-holding capacity, aeration, and DRAINAGE, and hence the soil's suitability for healthy ROOT GROWTH and vine performance.

In Australia, when there is a pronounced and relatively abrupt increase in soil CLAY content between a surface horizon (topsoil) and subsoil horizons, the soil is called duplex. This kind of profile is commonly found in soils referred to as podzolic in many vineyard regions around the world, notably in the US and South Africa. Duplex soils develop impermeable subsoils when the exchangeable sodium content (see CLAY) exceeds about 6% of the CATION EXCHANGE CAPACITY.

See GEOLOGY, STONES AND ROCKS, SUBSOIL, TERROIR, TOPOGRAPHY, and other entries prefaced by SOIL, most importantly, SOIL AND WINE QUALITY.   R.E.W.

van Leeuwen, C., and Chéry, P., 'Quelle méthode pour caractériser et étudier le terroir viticole: analyse de sol, cartographie pédologique ou étude écophysiologique?' in *Un raisin de qualité: de la vigne à la cuve*, n° Hors Série du *Journal International des Sciences de la Vigne et du Vin* (2001), 13–20.

White, R. E., *Understanding Vineyard Soils* (2nd edn, Oxford, 2015).

soil acidity, or low soil PH, occurs where hydrogen cations (H+) predominate relative to those of the alkaline elements CALCIUM, POTASSIUM, SODIUM, and MAGNESIUM adsorbed to the surfaces of CLAY and ORGANIC MATTER. Acidity is found mainly where the alkaline mineral elements have been leached out of the SOIL PROFILE under heavy rainfall over extended periods, and their place in the soil's CATION EXCHANGE CAPACITY has been taken by hydrogen ions.

In soils of less than pH 5, described as highly acid, exchangeable aluminium is released by slow decomposition of the clay and can inhibit grapevine root growth. Such soils are best avoided for viticulture; if this is not possible, then LIME should be applied. The soil acidity of the MÉDOC in Bordeaux, for example, promotes COPPER availability and consequent toxicity, wherever there has been a build-up of copper in the topsoil from spraying vines with BORDEAUX MIXTURE.

Acidity influences the speed at which organic matter is decomposed to release NITROGEN that predisposes to excess VIGOUR, whereas the release of nitrogen in soils of lower pH is limited. Problems of soil acidity are to be expected in most viticultural regions with high rainfall, and affect parts of Europe and some highly weathered soils in south-east Australia and South Africa.

Soil acidity should be contrasted with SOIL ALKALINITY, which is more common in arid areas. It does not follow that soil acidity bears any relation to wine ACIDITY.

R.E.S., C.v.L., & R.E.W.

soil alkalinity. A soil is said to be alkaline when the measured PH is above about 7. A pH above about 8.5 usually implies a content of free LIME or chalk (usually described as CALCAREOUS soil; see also LIMESTONE), or too high a content of soluble salts (including common salt, sodium chloride). In the latter case, such soils are described as SALINE. When these soils are leached, their pH can increase to 9 or more due to the hydrolysis of SODIUM ions (see CATION EXCHANGE) and the ORGANIC MATTER can disperse, forming a black alkali soil. Saline and black alkali soils should definitely be avoided for viticulture. However, some of the best vineyard soils in cool climates are associated with LIMESTONE or CHALK.

High lime and pH can induce deficiencies of IRON, ZINC, and MANGANESE or BORON in the vines. Lime-induced iron deficiency can cause CHLOROSIS. These deficiencies can usually be controlled by leaf sprays or the selection of particularly well-adapted varieties of ROOTSTOCK.

Soils high in free lime can sometimes create nutritional difficulties through the reduced availability of POTASSIUM.

J.G., C.v.L., & R.E.W.

soil amelioration, a viticultural practice for improving soils by the addition of so-called **soil amendments**. These can include FERTILIZERS to overcome mineral nutrient deficiencies (such as superphosphate to add phosphorus); LIME, which will overcome SOIL ACIDITY; gypsum and ORGANIC MATTER, which will improve SOIL STRUCTURE. These ameliorants are spread on the soil surface, and occasionally turned in by CULTIVATION. Where there is a need for deep placement, as in liming or the application of rock phosphate (see FERTILIZERS), then RIPPING implements drawn by powerful bulldozers are used before planting. When the lime and gypsum are finely ground, special applicators allow these normally insoluble products to be added through DRIP IRRIGATION systems but the drippers are easily blocked.

See also BIOCHAR.   R.E.S. & R.E.W.

Coombe, B. G., and Dry, P. R. (eds), *Viticulture*, ii: *Practices* (Adelaide, 1992).

soil and wine quality. The SOIL has many attributes that can influence the vine grown in it, and thence the quality and character of both grapes and wine. Quite how influential these attributes are remains a matter of debate, with a fairly marked but fast-decreasing divergence between the OLD WORLD and NEW WORLD, if not of opinion, then of interpretation.

Old World versus New World

Old World opinion, especially in France, strongly emphasizes soil effects on vines, grapes, and wines at a vineyard level, particularly in relation to vine water status. These are fundamental to the concept of TERROIR which underlies the official French APPELLATION CONTRÔLÉE system, although the influence of soil is generally regarded as less significant than that of climate. In Germany, large local differences in climate associated with TOPOGRAPHY are often considered to override soil effects (see MESOCLIMATE and CLIMATE AND WINE QUALITY), although soils are still regarded as an important factor governing wine quality.

Until a few decades ago, New World opinion had tended to minimize the role of soil, and instead to stress major differences in regional climate, or MACROCLIMATE. Amerine and Winkler's 1944 CLIMATE CLASSIFICATION of California into five temperature regions epitomizes this view. Much of the divergence in approach can be ascribed to differences in historical, geographical, and commercial background. Traditional European vineyards were small, and the identities of their wines often uniquely established over many generations. It was observed that certain sites consistently produced different and/or better wines than others, apparently regardless of VINE MANAGEMENT and WINEMAKING practices, and sometimes in the absence of discernible differences in mesoclimate. One general observation, especially marked in Bordeaux, was that the best sites stood out most clearly in poor VINTAGE YEARS. These sites maintained a relative consistency of high quality, whereas others, superficially similar and often very close, suffered greatly diminished quality. The only possible reason seemed to lie in unalterable (and perhaps invisible) properties of the soil.

New World viticulture has generally lacked this experience. Individual vineyards were often much larger, and until recently grapes from individual plots were rarely fermented separately. Moreover, the dominant commercial organizations tended to employ extensive BLENDING of wines from different soils and regions, so that any individualities are often masked or lost.

Differences in agricultural history have also influenced the choice of soils for planting vines. In Europe, all the fertile land was needed for cereal production or grazing to provide sufficient food for the people. Since vines would grow almost anywhere, they were planted on the poorest soils to optimize land use. In the New World, there was generally no shortage of land so that viticulture developed on a wide range of soils, from infertile to fertile, with irrigation a common, and in many cases necessary, practice.

Nevertheless, the absolute need for quality (and, in particular, wine individuality) in a now highly competitive world market means that winegrowers in the New World have increasingly emphasized the importance of soil as contributing to a site's terroir. This has become especially evident with recent advances in SOIL MAPPING as part of VINEYARD DESIGN and in PRECISION VITICULTURE, notably in North America and Australia. This approach enables different plots to be identified by soil type and to be managed and harvested separately, even in extensive vineyard developments. The results obtained support Old World experience, as reported by Smart. It is important to note, however, that the effect of soil on wine quality is reduced in warmer climates, which is why the influence of terroir is so much more marked in marginal climates such as that of Burgundy.

The Old World meanwhile is busy trying to identify more closely the reasons why some soils can give better wines than others. Preeminent in this field has been the work of the Bordeaux researcher Dr Gérard Seguin, which forms a background to the discussion that immediately follows. In this account we distinguish between chemical and physical soil attributes.

Physical soil attributes

Scientific opinion now almost universally agrees with Seguin's conclusion that soil physical characteristics predominate as the main influence over grape and wine quality other than CLIMATE; and further, that, among the physical characteristics, the most important are those which govern water supply to the vine. These and their relationship to individual soil types are discussed in some detail under TERROIR. See also SOIL WATER, SOIL TEXTURE, DRAINAGE, and VINE PHYSIOLOGY.

Here we may note briefly that the best wines come from soils that are very well drained, and furnish a steady, but only moderate, water supply to the vines. When combined with appropriate restrictive mineral VINE NUTRITION, this ensures that growth is restrained. The leaf area, especially the secondary leaf area on the LATERAL SHOOTS, remains relatively small, and nearly all leaves and bunches are well exposed to SUNLIGHT. Smaller berries are also usually less liable to congestion and compression within the bunch, and are therefore less likely to split or suffer spoilage as a result of FUNGAL DISEASES or BACTERIA. WATER STRESS needs to be just enough to attain these ends, and not enough to reduce photosynthesis too much.

Some other physical properties of soils almost certainly influence wine quality and characteristics in subtle ways.

SOIL COLOUR affects soil temperature and that of the air immediately above. Dark-coloured soils absorb and convert much of the sunlight falling on them into heat, and so are warmer than light-coloured soils, and, at night and during daytime cloud cover, radiate more warmth back to the vines and bunches. This can be critical in some cold marginal viticultural climates, allowing fuller RIPENING and thus better wine quality (as in the very dark soils of the Neckar Valley in WÜRTTEMBERG or the Meuse Valley of southern BELGIUM, for example).

The presence of STONES AND ROCKS in the soil or on its surface influences both water and temperature relations. A high proportion of stones or GRAVEL throughout the SOIL PROFILE is commonly associated with very good DRAINAGE, but at the same time reduces water-holding capacity and encourages desirably extensive ROOT GROWTH to assure a vine's water supply. In Bordeaux, where the main risk is excessive water supply to the vines, the most important positive effect on wine quality of stones in the soil is the limitation on water-holding capacity, leading to the level of water stress that promotes red wine quality. A cover, or mulch, of stones or rocks also protects against surface EVAPORATION, leading to a greater consistency of water supply. The steep, rubbly slate surfaces of many of the MOSEL vineyards in Germany are a good example. Stony soils, whether sloping or not, usually have the further advantage for wine quality that they are at most only moderately fertile, as discussed below.

Soils containing a large proportion of rocks or stones have the additional advantage that they most readily absorb heat and transmit it to depth, because rocks are a comparatively good conductor of heat: much better than dry or loose soil. Stony soils are warm mainly because they hold less water. Water has a high specific calorific capacity and needs a lot of energy to warm it. Wet soils are therefore cold soils. Moderately damp soil beneath surface stones is both a reasonable heat conductor and a good heat storer, because of the high heat storage capacity of its water content. It is also protected from evaporative cooling. Such soils are efficient at absorbing and storing warmth, and retransmitting it to the above-ground vine parts during cloud cover and in the evening. See TEMPERATURE VARIABILITY and CLIMATE AND WINE QUALITY.

Whatever the mechanisms, there can be little doubt that stony and rocky soils produce many of the world's great wines; and that, within given areas, the stoniest or rockiest usually produce the best. Typical are the coarse gravels that characterize the most eminent châteaux of the MÉDOC in Bordeaux, the large stones (GALETS)

that completely cover some of the best sites of CHÂTEAUNEUF-DU-PAPE in the southern Rhône, the coarsely stony gravels that give wines of outstanding quality in the Marlborough region of NEW ZEALAND's South Island, and more recently in the Gimblett Gravels region of Hawke's Bay in the North Island.

Chemical attributes

The relationship between soil chemistry and wine quality and individuality is in the main poorly understood. In some quarters there is the belief that soil influences wine character because the vine takes up flavour compounds direct from the soil but this viewpoint is totally unsubstantiated (see, for example, MINERALS and MINERALITY).

Soil NITROGEN is in part an exception to this lack of knowledge. It is clear from Seguin's work, and that of other European researchers, that the optimum nitrogen supply to the vine is at most only moderate. The optimum supply for red wine production is lower than for white wine because nitrogen deficiency increases berry skin PHENOLICS but also limits the build up of FLAVOUR PRECURSORS in white grapes (see Peyrot des Gachons et al. and Choné et al.). Vines receiving much nitrogen, unless severely constrained by other factors, have vigorous and leafy growth. This leads readily to excessive SHADE within the canopy, and thence to poor fruit quality (see CANOPY MICROCLIMATE). The effects of nitrogen, water supply, and various other nutritional and environmental factors can to varying degrees reinforce or counteract each other in this regard. The best combination among them is that giving optimum vine BALANCE. Excessive nitrogen fertilization, leading to excessive vigour, can sometimes be problematic in both Old World and New World vineyards. However, this tendency is countered by the more widespread use of grass or cereal COVER CROPS, which can compete with the vine for nitrogen or even cause a deficiency.

A further complication has arisen from research showing that low nitrogen contents in the berries can be a cause of difficulties in winemaking, leading to STUCK FERMENTATIONS and the presence of HYDROGEN SULFIDE and its malodorous MERCAPTAN derivatives in the wine. This is especially common with grapes grown in warm, sunny climates. While it is now known that at least much of the problem can be overcome by adding nitrogen-based YEAST nutrients during fermentation, the problem of combining suitable nitrogen nutrition for vine balance with optimum concentrations of natural nitrogen compounds in the berries remains largely unsolved.

POTASSIUM availability is another soil factor with mixed relationships to wine quality. Deficiencies are common in cool and humid climates, where the efficiency of water use for growth and yield (see HUMIDITY and CLIMATE

AND WINE QUALITY) means that potassium and some other elements are diluted in the plant. Potassium-deficient vines are more than usually susceptible to DROUGHT and VINE DISEASES, and the fruit lacks sugar (see SUGAR IN GRAPES) as well as COLOUR and flavour.

Conversely, vines in hot, atmospherically arid climates can accumulate excess potassium in the leaves, stems, and fruit, especially if the soil contains reserves of mica-type clay minerals that release potassium. High potassium levels in grapes can lead to high wine PH, with all its attendant quality defects. Excessive leaf shading in a poor canopy microclimate contributes importantly in many cases, and improved CANOPY MANAGEMENT can help greatly in assuring more appropriate fruit potassium levels. However, the effect of potassium on grape quality is far less significant than that of nitrogen.

The rule for other nutrient elements appears to be that adequate supplies are needed equally for vine health and for fruit and wine quality though there is very little evidence concerning the possible role of elements such as magnesium, phosphorus, or iron.

Possible specific roles for the micronutrients (COPPER, ZINC, MANGANESE, IRON, BORON, and MOLYBDENUM) remain obscure but potentially interesting. Their contents in the soil and availability to the plant vary enormously from soil to soil, and, in often disparate ways, with SOIL MANAGEMENT. Champagnol cites some cases where differences in wine quality or character from different soils could conceivably be associated with the amounts or balances of micronutrients in the soil, vines, or grapes. At the moment, however, no micronutrient constituent has been shown to be a decisive factor, either in wine quality or in any particular wine characteristic, and opinions about the effect of micronutrients on grape quality are highly speculative and sometimes exaggerated in non-scientific literature.

SOIL ACIDITY and SOIL ALKALINITY are further possible influences; but again, little firm evidence exists at present. Extremes in either direction, sufficient to upset vine nutrition and health seriously, seem unlikely to improve wine quality. On the other hand, vines can tolerate a fairly wide soil pH range without evident harm, while the potential micronutrient deficiencies that are often encountered at high pH levels can in most cases be readily overcome by foliar sprays or judicious choice of ROOTSTOCKS. Robinson gives a comprehensive account of this and other aspects of VINE NUTRITION.

Although little studied by the Bordeaux school, properties related to the SOIL BIOTA can also affect vine growth and fruit quality. In particular, the ORGANIC MATTER in soils for viticulture needs careful evaluation. On the one hand, soils naturally high in organic matter tend to be too fertile, and to supply too much nitrogen, for good wine quality (as explained above). Soils naturally low in organic matter have a reduced nitrogen supply (unless fertilizers are added), which is good for red winemaking. On the other hand, many respected TERROIRS that have otherwise favourable characteristics for wine quality are naturally too low in organic matter, or have become so, so that both their physical and biological condition would benefit from its build-up and maintenance (see ORGANIC VITICULTURE). Very sandy soils need organic matter to give them sufficient capacity to store water and nutrients. All soils, and especially clayey soils, benefit from having an adequate organic matter, content (1.5–3%), to give them friability (see SOIL STRUCTURE), and to encourage the activity of EARTHWORMS, which help to keep them well aerated and freely draining.

The nature and geological origin of the ROCKS or sediments from which soils are formed (see SOIL and GEOLOGY) are further factors sometimes held to influence wine quality and character. Soils formed from CHALK and LIMESTONE, for example, are highly valued in some cool climates, although not generally in warm regions such as the south of France (see, for instance, Champagnol) or inland Australia. Most researchers consider the advantages of chalk and limestone to be related to their free DRAINAGE and the ability of the SUBSOIL to store water. Certain grape varieties, particularly Pinot Noir and Chardonnay, are also regarded by some as having a special requirement for chalk or limestone soils to produce their best wines; but again, this seems to be a largely northern French viewpoint. Experience elsewhere, especially in the New World, lends it little support. One universally positive role of chalk and limestone (or deliberately adding LIME) is that the resulting high level of calcium absorption to the soil clay particles helps to maintain a friable and stable SOIL STRUCTURE, thus encouraging aeration and drainage, even at high clay contents.

On the general role of geology, we can conclude that any influence is mostly indirect, via the shaping of TOPOGRAPHY determined by the underlying GEOLOGY, and through effects which are more properly those of the derived soil rather than of the rock or sediment. There can be some direct effects on water supply, however, where vine roots penetrate into the geological stratum underlying the soil. Chalk in Champagne (see above), the limestone of St-Émilion, and the Médoc gravel beds of Bordeaux (see SOIL WATER) have been cited in this regard.

Other factors

The great variation of soils over even short distances means that generalizations of any kind are dangerous. In some vineyards, especially those on ALLUVIAL soils, the soil type may change dramatically over a few metres, despite an apparent uniformity at the surface. For the same reason, SOIL MANAGEMENT procedures are seldom equally appropriate across an entire vineyard, let alone between different vineyards.

A second point is that, despite this, management technologies are increasingly becoming available which obviate many of the effects of this variability. This is especially so in the New World. Among the more important is adoption of DRIP IRRIGATION, which in climates with a dry summer can go far towards giving the vines a controlled water regime that is little influenced by soil type. Similarly, techniques of soil and (especially) leaf or PETIOLE analysis are making possible a more controlled vine nutritional regime, so that differences in nutrient supply by the soil are moderated, or even, potentially, eliminated.

A third point is that most vineyards throughout the world are now grafted to PHYLLOXERA-tolerant ROOTSTOCKS. The various rootstocks differ in their ability to take up mineral elements and water, in their capacity to root to depth, and in their effects on the VIGOUR of the vines grafted onto them. It is therefore possible to compensate for and adapt to particular soils as a means of approaching an optimal combination of vigour, nutrition, and canopy management for vine balance. Rootstocks are particularly effective in modulating water supply to the vines, and drought-resistant rootstocks such as 110R should be used in soils with low water-holding capacity in dry climates. Any consideration of soils now has to acknowledge the role of rootstocks.

At the same time it is salutary to remember that no single rootstock variety can be identified in France which distinguishes the GRAND CRU vineyards from their less celebrated neighbours; nor have vineyard reputations changed much, whereas rootstock usage has. These facts support the conclusion that the main effects of both soil and rootstock on wine quality are mediated by observable effects on the vine that can be subsequently manipulated by management, and are not due to any direct influence of the soil or rootstock itself.

The growing awareness of soil effects on wine quality and character in the New World has several repercussions. One is to plant vineyards on the less fertile hillside soils, as is evident in California and Chile, for example. Another is to perform detailed SOIL MAPPING before planting as a prerequisite to VINEYARD DESIGN. More recently, ZONAL VITICULTURE, employing GLOBAL POSITIONING SYSTEM and GEOGRAPHICAL INFORMATION SYSTEM technologies, allows differential management, including harvesting separate zones of a vineyard block to maximize quality. These effects, identified by REMOTE SENSING or PROXIMAL SENSING, are by and large due to soil differences and can be managed by means of PRECISION VITICULTURE techniques.

Conclusions

There can be no doubt that soil characteristics do influence grape quality, yield, and wine individuality, as has been shown by Renouf et al. in grand cru vineyards in Bordeaux. However, in most situations the effects of soil are subsidiary to those of CLIMATE, VINE VARIETY, and VINE MANAGEMENT (see van Leeuwen et al.). Of the influential soil characteristics, the most important are those governing the supply of water to the vine, probably followed by those influencing temperatures in and above the soil. Provided that vine growth is healthy, soil chemistry and vine nutrition do not play any particular role, other than the effect of nitrogen in vegetative vigour and berry nitrogen content, and in some situations that of excess potassium on the pH of must and wine.

Identifying the 'best' soil for wine growing depends on the objectives of the winegrower and whether the vines are dry-grown or irrigated. If the objective is to produce large yields of grapes for blending and producing lower-priced wines, then deep well-drained soils that are fertile and either naturally well-watered or irrigated are best. However, if the objective is to produce low to moderate yields of high quality grapes that can be used for higher-priced wines, and wines that reflect the particular TERROIR of a site, then infertile soils in which the vines suffer a certain amount of stress perform best. It appears that this stress should be primarily through the water supply to the vine (see WATER STRESS), which can be achieved naturally, under DRYLAND conditions, in deep well-drained soils that have a significant proportion of sand and gravel. In the case of irrigated vines, where usually the soil water content of only the top 40–60 cm is controlled, this stress can be applied through REGULATED DEFICIT IRRIGATION or PARTIAL ROOTZONE DRYING. In all cases, free drainage is very important. This is usually achieved in sandy gravelly soils, and in heavier textured soils that are well-structured, generally due to a predominance of calcium on the CLAY particles. An organic matter content of 1.5–3% is also important to support a good soil structure, especially of the topsoil, and to sustain an active and diverse SOIL BIOTA.

R.E.S., C.v.L., & R.E.W.

Champagnol, F., *Éléments de physiologie de la vigne et de viticulture générale* (St-Gely-du-Fesc, 1984).

Choné, X., et al., 'Terroir influence on water status and nitrogen status of non-irrigated Cabernet Sauvignon (*Vitis vinifera*): vegetative development, must and wine composition', *South African Journal of Enology and Viticulture*, 22/1 (2001), 8–15.

Peyrot des Gachons, C., et al., 'The influence of water and nitrogen deficit on fruit ripening and aroma potential of *Vitis vinifera* L. cv Sauvignon blanc in field conditions', *Journal of the Science of Food and Agriculture*, 85/1 (2005), 73–85.

S

Renouf, V., et al., 'Soils, rootstocks and grapevine varieties in prestigious Bordeaux vineyards and their impact on yield and quality', *Journal International des Sciences de la Vigne et du Vin*, 44/3 (2010), 127–34.

Robinson, J. B., 'Grapevine nutrition', in B. G. Coombe and P. R. Dry (eds.), *Viticulture, ii: Practices* (Adelaide, 1992).

Seguin, G., ' "Terroirs" and pedology of wine growing', *Experientia*, 42 (1986), 861–72.

Smart, R., 'Terroir unmasked', *Wine Business Monthly* (June 2004), 34–8.

Tregoat, O., et al., 'Étude du régime hydrique et de la nutrition azotée de la vigne par des indicateurs physiologiques. Influence sur le comportement de la vigne et la maturation du raisin (*Vitis vinifera* L. cv Merlot, 2000, Bordeaux)', *Journal International al des Sciences de la Vigne et du Vin*, 36/3 (2002), 133–42.

van Leeuwen, C., et al., 'Influence of climate, soil, and cultivar on terroir', *American Journal of Enology and Viticulture*, 55/3 (2004), 207–17.

White, R. E., *Understanding Vineyard Soils* (2nd edn, Oxford, 2015).

soil biota is the generic term used to describe the population of organisms living in soil. Broadly speaking, these organisms can be divided into the 'reducers', such as EARTHWORMS, slugs and SNAILS, beetles and their larvae, mites and springtails, Protozoa, and NEMATODES, which feed on leaf litter and animal excreta to break it down into smaller fragments (without achieving much chemical decomposition), and the 'decomposers', which are much smaller organisms that colonize these organic fragments and gradually convert them into humus (see CARBON and ORGANIC MATTER). The decomposers, comprising Archaea, bacteria, actinomycetes, and fungi, are commonly called microorganisms and the microbial biomass is measured by their collective weight. An active and diverse microbial biomass, interacting with the reducers, is important for ORGANIC MATTER decomposition and NUTRIENT turnover in soil, which is a prerequisite for good SOIL HEALTH. This applies equally well to conventional viticulture as to ORGANIC and BIODYNAMIC VITICULTURE. See also MYCORRHIZA, MICROBIAL TERROIR, and BIOCHAR. R.E.W.

soil colour, a term normally referring to the surface colour of a soil although it may also be applied to various layers or horizons in a SOIL PROFILE. Some viticultural folklore associates red wine with red soils, and white wines with white or grey soils. However, topsoil colour is very heterogeneous, as is the spatial distribution of SOIL TYPES within vineyards potentially planted to a single variety. So any support for such a relationship is at best circumstantial.

Colour can affect soil temperature, and that of the air immediately above it. Dark-coloured soils or rocks absorb much of the incoming SUNLIGHT energy and convert it to heat. Therefore, whereas they reflect less light than light-coloured soils, they radiate more heat at night and when the sun is shaded. This may be especially beneficial in cool climates. Other examples of the exploitation of these thermal characteristics include the vineyards of Deidesheim in the PFALZ region of Germany, where black BASALT rock is mined and spread on the vineyards to help produce wines of unusual sweetness. Fragmented dark grey SLATE helps Riesling to ripen in the otherwise very cool MOSEL. Dark-coloured SCHIST soils are reportedly the only ones on which grapes can be ripened at the extreme northern limit of viticulture in BELGIUM. At the other extreme, the exceedingly reflective white ALBARIZA soils of JEREZ in southern Spain produce the best (white) grapes for sherry in a very hot climate, which would seem counter-intuitive.

The relationships of soil colour to temperature suitability for vine-growing are far from straightforward, however. Many reddish and brown soils are used for viticulture in hot areas such as the Mediterranean wine regions and also in much of Australia and California. However, such soils predominate in these regions, and are not known to offer any advantage to viticulture because of their colour: see CLIMATE AND WINE QUALITY. Differences in soil colour have little effect on sunlight reflected back into the CANOPY which might affect PHOTOSYNTHESIS. Recent French experiments have shown an improvement in grape (and apple) colour from using reflective foil on the soil surface. See further discussion under SUNLIGHT.

Soil colour is in any case a useful indicator of some of a soil's other properties, which probably have more effect on VINE PHYSIOLOGY, and therefore on wine quality. For example, black soils may indicate a high content of ORGANIC MATTER. Red or brown are due to the presence of oxidized IRON compounds, and normally indicate good DRAINAGE. A pale grey soil surface, or soil layer, shows that most of the original iron compounds have been reduced as a result of bad drainage and waterlogging, and eventually leached downwards, often to be deposited in a heavier-textured SUBSOIL.

The colour of the subsoil is a particularly important indicator of soil suitability for viticulture. Except where it consists largely of decomposing chalk or LIMESTONE, a blue-grey, or mottled subsoil shows drainage that is usually too poor for viticulture; or at least, a need for artificial drainage. J.G., R.E.S., & R.E.W.

soil compaction in vineyards is due to the passage of machinery, especially if it is heavy and the soil is wet and CLAY-textured. Vineyards are particularly prone to compaction because tractor wheel tracks are confined to narrow strips, often in close proximity to the vine row. The soil is compressed so that the surface absorbs less water and soil pores are destroyed, and the supply of air and water to vine roots is diminished (see SOIL STRUCTURE). Further, soil strength is increased, providing a physical barrier to root growth and EARTHWORM activity. Soil compaction can reduce vine VIGOUR and thus YIELD, and, in some instances, wine quality. Soil compaction, which may be the most serious environmental damage done in many vineyards, can be reduced by avoiding the use of heavy machinery on wet soils, and by using tracked rather than wheeled vehicles. Horse-drawn equipment is both a more traditional—and modern—alternative. R.E.S.

Lagacherie, P., et al., 'Spatial variability of soil compaction over a vineyard region in relation with soils and cultivation operations', *Geoderma*, 134/1–2 (2006), 207–16. doi:10.1016/j.geoderma.2005.10.006.

soil depth, a loose term for the depth to the boundary between the SOIL and its parent material; or, alternatively, the depth to which plant ROOT GROWTH is possible before reaching some impermeable barrier. Examples of the latter include the tight and/or poorly drained subsoils of many duplex soils (see SOIL), which occur in south-eastern Australia, South Africa, and the Piedmont region of the eastern US; cemented ironstone, or 'coffee rock', which forms at the base of some iron-rich podzolic soils that have been subject to leaching; or subsoils with poor structure due to exchangeable SODIUM, or excessively high concentrations of salt or acidity, or some other toxic factor which effectively prevents further root penetration.

Soil fertility is a combination of fertility per soil volume unit and the rooting depth, which determines the amount of soil available for each vine. Seguin's work shows that if soil is fertile or moderately fertile per soil volume unit, deep rooting leads to excessive soil fertility (due to the availability of water and nutrients) and thus excessive VIGOUR. As a result, in most cases, shallow rooting is a quality factor, because it reduces vigour and yield. Only in soils with very poor fertility per soil volume unit, such as the gravelly soils of the MÉDOC or MARLBOROUGH, New Zealand, is deep rooting an advantage. These soils have such a low water-holding capacity per soil volume unit that, unless the vines are irrigated, deep rooting is necessary to provide a regular supply of water to the vine. Seguin has also shown that deep rooting in these soils where water drains very rapidly prevents the rapid absorption by the root system of rain shortly before harvest, thus helping to prevent rot.

There is a great deal of evidence that in many other situations, great wines are produced on soils where vine rooting is shallow. For example, most great ST-ÉMILIONS are produced on the limestone plateau, where vine rooting rarely exceeds 60 cm/23 in and can be as little as 30 cm (as in parts of the vineyard of Ch AUSONE). The roots do not penetrate the rock, although Duteau et al. have shown that water can move from the bedrock to the roots by capillarity. On the heavy clay soils in PETRUS and Ch CHEVAL BLANC, vine rooting does not exceed 130 cm/50 in because of the clay's physical resistance to root penetration. In the Languedoc, the best wines are produced on shallow soils on the hillsides and simple wines are produced on the plains, where rooting is much deeper.

Shallow soils are therefore of major importance in cool, wet climates, while somewhat deeper soils might be an advantage in very dry climates, especially when irrigation is not allowed or not possible.   J.G., C.v.L., & R.E.W.

> Duteau, J., 'Contribution des réserves hydriques profondes du calcaire à Astéries compact à l'alimentation en eau de la vigne dans le Bordelais', *Agronomie*, 7/10 (1987), 589–865.
>
> Seguin, G., 'Influence des terroirs viticoles', *Bulletin de l'OIV*, 56 (1983), 3–18.
>
> Seguin, G., '"Terroirs" and pedology of wine growing', *Experientia*, 42 (1986), 861–72.

soil disinfection. See FUMIGATION.

soil erosion, shifting or removal of soil by wind or running water. Wind erosion is fairly uncommon in established vineyards, because the vines themselves constitute an effective WINDBREAK at ground level, although it can be a problem in young vineyards. Driving sand, in particular, can seriously injure young vines, and there can in addition be irreparable loss of the most valuable topsoil. The danger can be minimized by growing COVER CROPS such as rye, which act as windbreaks as well as directly binding the soil. More recently, VINE GUARDS have been used to protect young vines from sand blasting.

Erosion by water, on the other hand, is always a potential problem on the sloping sites that normally afford the best MESOCLIMATES for wine quality (see HILLSIDE VINEYARDS). Some steeply sloping sites, such as in the MOSEL region of Germany and the northern RHÔNE, necessitate a constant and laborious replacement of soil from the bottom of the slope to the top. Even in more moderately sloping sites in the Côte d'Or, clean CULTIVATION of the mid rows may lead to soil erosion during summer storms.

Planting vines across a slope, rather than up and down the slope, provides some measure of erosion control, especially if the vine rows are hilled. Constructing TERRACES is an effective means of erosion control on steeper slopes (between 7 and 15%), as practised in the NAPA Valley, California, and the FRIULI region of

north-east Italy. However, vineyard cultural operations are usually easier with rows oriented up and down a slope, in which case other methods must be used to control erosion, such as avoiding unnecessary cultivation, spreading MULCHES (including vine prunings) to protect bare soil surfaces, and planting mid-row COVER CROPS. Permanent grass cover crops offer the best protection but are feasible only in those situations where water and NITROGEN supplies are sufficient for both grass and vines. Planting on convex hill slopes helps too, to the extent that there are no external sources of flowing water. Where occasional water flowing onto or across a site cannot be avoided, it can often be made harmless by diversionary banks, directing the flow into drains or permanently grassed waterways which follow the natural flow line.

Other measures to control erosion include maintaining the soil's ORGANIC MATTER content and stable SOIL STRUCTURE (see also SOIL MANAGEMENT). These conditions enable rain to be absorbed readily where it falls. Row orientation and such cultivation as is unavoidable should ideally be directed just a little off the contour, so that any water flow along furrows will be gentle and harmless, and able to spill out onto permanently grassed natural waterways. Cultivation straight up and down slopes lends itself to general erosion but the practicalities of vineyard design often limit control over the direction and slopes of cultivation.   J.G. & R.E.W.

> White, R. E., *Soils for Fine Wines* (Oxford, 2003).

soil fertility, the physical, chemical, and biological characteristics of a soil determining its ability to support vigorous plant growth. A fertile soil is generally understood to be one with a high content of available plant nutrients, moderate to high ORGANIC MATTER content, supporting an active and diverse SOIL BIOTA, good SOIL STRUCTURE and DRAINAGE, and typically a LOAMY SOIL TEXTURE that can store large amounts of water. Neither SOIL ACIDITY nor SOIL ALKALINITY will be excessive, so that the nutrient elements will all be in a favourable balance of availability for plant growth. Recent research in Australia by Oliver et al. and Riches et al. have identified a minimum set of important biophysical and chemical properties and their optimum ranges for healthy vine growth and yields of quality fruit.

Highly fertile soils, especially those rich in NITROGEN, are undesirable for wine grapes because they encourage excessive vegetation and a congested CANOPY MICROCLIMATE. This in turn can reduce both YIELD and, especially, the composition and suitability of the grapes for winemaking. Although vineyard management cannot greatly improve this state of affairs, vigour may be reduced by planting permanent grass COVER CROPS, using low-vigour ROOTSTOCKS, avoiding the use of fertilizers except to

correct nutrient deficiencies, and by not over-irrigating the vines. On the other hand, the notion that only infertile soils can make good wines is undoubtedly mistaken. CANOPY MANAGEMENT techniques can allow vigorous vines on moderately fertile soils to mimic the canopy microclimates of traditional vineyards on less fertile soils, with resultant improvements in quality. Carbonneau and Casteran have elucidated these principles, which have been successfully applied in many situations, in the Bordeaux environment.

See also SOIL AND WINE QUALITY, CLIMATE AND WINE QUALITY, and BALANCE.

J.G., R.E.S., & R.E.W.

> Carbonneau, A. P., and Casteran, P., 'Interactions "training system × soil × rootstock" with regard to vine ecophysiology, vigour, yield and red wine quality in the Bordeaux area', *Acta Horticulturae*, 206 (1987), 119–40.
>
> Oliver, D. P., et al., 'Review: soil physical and chemical properties as indicators of soil quality in Australian viticulture', *Australian Journal of Grape and Wine Research*, 19 (2013), 129–39.
>
> Riches, D., et al., 'Review: soil biological properties as indicators of soil quality in Australian viticulture', *Australian Journal of Grape and Wine Research*, 19 (2013), 311–23.
>
> Smart, R. E., and Robinson, M., *Sunlight into Wine: A Handbook for Winegrape Canopy Management* (Adelaide, 1991).

soil health, is, for a soil scientist, synonymous with soil quality, but the term emphasizes the living nature of soil, dependent on the healthy function of SOIL BIOTA. Soil quality may be defined holistically as 'the capacity of a soil to function within ECOSYSTEM boundaries to sustain biological productivity, maintain environmental quality, and promote plant and animal health'. A soil's condition and capability depend on the interaction of many chemical, physical, and biological processes and determine its suitability for the specific aims of a viticulturist or winegrower in a particular location. See also VINEYARD SITE SELECTION.   R.E.W.

> Doran, J. W., and Parkin, T. B., 'Defining and assessing soil quality', in J. W. Doran, et al. (eds.), *Defining Soil Quality for a Sustainable Environment* (Madison, 1994).

soil management, the practices of CULTIVATION, or non-cultivation, of soils in vineyards, including the use of COVER CROPS, COMPOST, and MULCHES, and other measures to improve the soil's physical, chemical, and biological condition (see SOIL FERTILITY.). In the broadest sense this term can also embrace IRRIGATION, the use of HERBICIDES, and the addition of FERTILIZER.

In the past, soil management has consisted primarily of clean cultivation to control WEEDS. The advantages of this approach include the avoidance of herbicides and forcing roots to go deeper. The disadvantages of this approach are increasingly recognized, however. Over time, clean cultivation leads to a deterioration in SOIL STRUCTURE and also to a decline in SOIL BIOTA, particularly EARTHWORMS. Modern soil management seeks to conserve and, if necessary, increase the ORGANIC MATTER content; to conserve and improve soil structure and porosity, and thereby improve aeration and free absorption and DRAINAGE of SOIL WATER and resistance to SOIL EROSION; and to maintain a reserve of nutrients in organic and slowly available inorganic forms to provide a steady and balanced supply of SOIL NUTRIENTS matched to the plants' needs.

Aspects of soil management include growing COVER CROPS, with minimal cultivation for their establishment; using inorganic fertilizers (as needed) mainly to grow these crops, and thence to supply the vines as far as possible from organic sources; summer mulching with the residues of the cover crop grown *in situ*, or with imported vegetable materials or manures, preferably composted; and, when essential, the use of environment-friendly herbicides to control cover crops and weeds. These practices force the roots to go down deep, improve machine access to the vineyard after rain, help to control vigour, and reduce the use of herbicides. However, it may also lead to too much competition for NITROGEN in low-fertility soils, especially in the case of white grapes (see ATYPICAL AGEING).

Measures by which undesirable SOIL COMPACTION can be reduced include the use of lighter equipment in the vineyard, and avoidance of all traffic when the soil is wet. In large vineyards it is feasible to apply some sprays from the air (see HELICOPTERS). The use of LIME or gypsum may be required for some soils. All these measures serve to improve soil physical conditions for vine ROOT GROWTH, thereby improving vine health, YIELD, and in some instances wine quality.

J.G., R.E.S., & R.E.W.

McCarthy, M. G., et al., 'Soil and management and frost control', in B. G. Coombe and P. R. Dry (eds.), *Viticulture*, ii: *Practices* (Adelaide, 1992).

White, R. E., *Understanding Vineyard Soils* (Oxford 2nd edn, 2015).

soil mapping, procedure used before vineyard planting to assist in decisions about irrigation layout, location of varieties and rootstocks, application of FERTILIZERS and soil amendments such as LIME and GYPSUM, and choice of TRAINING SYSTEM. Soil mapping is becoming more common in vineyard developments in the New World, and represents acceptance of the Old World notion that local conditions, especially the soil, have important effects on fruit quality. It is also used after a vineyard has been planted, often much later, to help understand vineyard variability.

Ideally, an electromagnetic survey should be carried out (see PROXIMAL SENSING) to identify soil variations within a vineyard block. Accurately located by GPS, these data are fed into a GIS so that high-resolution maps of the soil's variability can be prepared. Based on this knowledge, soil pits are dug, usually by a backhoe, at sites covering the full range of variation so that SOIL PROFILES can be described in detail. Where such a preliminary survey is not carried out, pits may be dug on a grid so that the soil can be sampled and described by a soil specialist, although this is less effective at capturing variability. Single- or multi-property soil maps can be used in vineyard design, one of the most useful of which is that of 'readily available water' or RAW. See TERROIR for a full discussion of the relevant issues, also SOIL, SOIL AND WINE QUALITY, and PRECISION VITICULTURE.

R.E.S. & R.E.W.

Proffitt, T., et al., *Precision Viticulture: A New Era in Vineyard Management and Wine Production* (Adelaide, 2006).

soil nutrients, elements (see MINERALS) and ions occurring in the soil which are taken up by plant root systems. Soils which are rich in nutrients are often termed fertile, but such soils do not usually produce good-quality wine (see SOIL FERTILITY). The amounts of nutrients that are available to the vine depend on the soil's mineralogy, the amount and nature of ORGANIC MATTER, and also the soil PH. Soils with a long history of COVER CROPS have high levels of surface organic matter and are often rich in NITROGEN. However, grass and cereal cover crops compete with vines for nitrogen, so nitrogen is not as available to the vine as when the cover crop contains legume species. Soils in old vineyards, especially if clean CULTIVATED, are often relatively impoverished of organic matter and may have high levels of available COPPER as a result of repeated FUNGICIDE application. Many nutrients including nitrogen and PHOSPHORUS, for example, are less available in acid soils (see SOIL ACIDITY). Others such as IRON, MANGANESE, COPPER, and ZINC are less available in alkaline soils. Nutrient deficiencies are diagnosed by symptoms on the vines, or by plant and soil tests, and can be remedied by applying FERTILIZERS and MANURES.

R.E.S. & R.E.W.

Robinson, J. B., 'Grapevine nutrition', in B. G. Coombe and P. R. Dry (eds.), *Viticulture*, ii: *Practices* (Adelaide, 1992).

soil potential, a viticultural term coined in South Africa to describe the ability of a soil to support vigorous vine growth, sometimes referred to as **site potential**. A soil of high potential will be well supplied with water (by rainfall or irrigation), nutrients, and air, and will be free-draining, promoting a large and healthy root system. Such a soil will create vines of high VIGOUR, which in turn may require special management.

R.E.S.

soil preparation, the treatment of SOIL before PLANTING a vineyard, can be an important viticultural operation. Proper attention at this stage can determine the long-term success or otherwise of a vineyard.

Having selected the best possible site (see VINEYARD SITE SELECTION, TOPOGRAPHY, and TERROIR) and vineyard layout, and assured suitable DRAINAGE, the potential vine-grower should in most soils, especially in duplex soils (see SOIL) and shallow soils over LIMESTONE and SHALE, undertake deep RIPPING along the paths of the future vine rows. This should be done when the soil is dry enough for compacted layers (see SOIL COMPACTION) and any hard pans (cemented layers) to be shattered by the ripper. Such treatment opens up the SUBSOIL and facilitates penetration by the vine roots.

If a vineyard is replanted, particular care must be taken to remove the roots of the old vines since these can harbour VIRUS DISEASES or FUNGAL DISEASES. Where populations of pathogenic NEMATODES are large, FUMIGATION may be necessary.

If the SOIL ACIDITY is high, with a pH at a depth of 3 cm/1.2 in of less than, say, 5.5, adding LIME will be beneficial. SOIL TESTING should be used to establish the suitable application of lime and other FERTILIZERS, and whether GYPSUM should be applied to improve SOIL STRUCTURE, especially in clayey soils.

Finally, WEEDS need to be controlled. In most climates it is usual to grow an autumn–winter green manure crop to add ORGANIC MATTER prior to vine planting in spring.   J.G. & R.E.W.

Boehm, E. W., and Coombe, B. G., 'Vineyard establishment', in B. G. Coombe and P. R. Dry (eds.), *Viticulture*, ii: *Practices* (Adelaide, 1992).

soil profile, the vertical face of a SOIL, exposed by digging, that generally consists of visually and texturally distinct layers (known as horizons) which are more or less parallel to the earth's surface. These are typically labelled from top to bottom of the profile. During SOIL MAPPING, the soil surveyor describes the properties of each layer (sometimes also sublayers) especially those that will have an impact on vine root growth. See also GEOLOGY and TERROIR.

R.E.S.

soil structure, the physical structure of soils, is an important vineyard characteristic, as governed by bonding of the mineral particles (as described in SOIL TEXTURE) into larger aggregates. The size, shape, and stability of these aggregates help to determine the friability of the surface soil and its ability to accept rainwater and resist erosion (see SOIL EROSION). A soil's structure also determines its porosity for air movement, water DRAINAGE, and ROOT penetration, and its capacity to withstand the effects of CULTIVATION and compaction (see SOIL COMPACTION) by vineyard machinery.

To a varying degree in different soil types, soil structure depends on the following factors:

1. The amount and chemical nature of the CLAY. To have stable structure, a soil must have a moderate clay content. Montmorillonite clays swell and shrink with wetting and drying, leading to a desirable 'self-mulching' of the soil surface, provided the content of exchangeable SODIUM is not too high (see SOIL). On the other hand, soils with predominantly kaolinitic clays form stable structures at pH less than 6, especially in the presence of iron and aluminium oxides. Illitic clays are intermediate in behaviour.

2. The relative contents of exchangeable CALCIUM and SODIUM (see CATION EXCHANGE). Calcium helps to build up good soil structure, whereas sodium causes clay dispersion and breakdown of the aggregates. In CALCAREOUS soils, calcium carbonate can be an effective bonding agent for aggregation.

3. Organic matter content. Organic matter in the form of humus (see CARBON and CLAY) bonds to clay particles and iron and aluminium oxides, and so lays the foundation for good structure. Additionally, gums and mucilages secreted by roots and soil micro-organisms play an important part in forming and preserving soil aggregates, and fine roots can form a mesh holding larger aggregates together.

4. Soil disturbance by CULTIVATION. All cultivation can be destructive of soil structure, especially in clayey soils when wet. Repeated cultivation exposes organic matter to faster decomposition, which weakens soil structure. Cultivation is sometimes done to improve the 'tilth' of the surface soil, but this is a temporary effect and does not improve soil structure in the longer term.

Good SOIL MANAGEMENT aims principally to preserve and strengthen soil structure.

J.G. & R.E.W.

White, R. E., *Understanding Vineyard Soils*, (2nd edn, Oxford, 2015).

soil testing involves measurements made in the field or laboratory of soil properties that indicate the physical, chemical, and biological condition of the soil (see SOIL FERTILITY). Soil testing is a necessary adjunct to SOIL MAPPING to determine soil PH (see SOIL ACIDITY, SOIL ALKALINITY), the amounts of available vine nutrition, and any adverse conditions such as SALINITY or too much SODIUM (see CATION EXCHANGE), a lack of healthy biological activity (see SOIL BIOTA), or high populations of pathogenic organisms (see SOIL PREPARATION). Soil tests can give useful preliminary information as to which macronutrients are needed. When the tests are carried out before planting, the results allow the application of any necessary nutrients such as PHOSPHORUS, POTASSIUM, CALCIUM, MAGNESIUM, and BORON under the vines, at

depths where they will remain readily, and more or less permanently, available to the roots. However, because the grapevine is a perennial plant, tissue analysis of leaf blades or PETIOLES, rather than soil testing, usually gives a better guide to any ongoing FERTILIZER requirements.

Field inspection to determine SOIL TEXTURE and its natural DRAINAGE to as great a depth as possible is an essential preliminary to any vine planting. See also SOIL AND WINE QUALITY, TERROIR, and VINEYARD SITE SELECTION.

J.G., R.E.S., & R.E.W.

Proffitt, T., 'Assessing soil quality and interpreting soil tests' (GWRDC/Wines of Western Australia, 2014), www.winewa.asn.au/images/Technical%20Papers/ Assessing_soil_quality_Wine_grape.pdf.

soil texture, describes the size distribution of soil particles (those less than 2 mm diameter), simplified to indicate the proportions of clay, silt, fine, and coarse sand (STONES AND ROCKS and ORGANIC MATTER are excluded). The individual constituents are defined below. Soils predominantly of clay are described as heavy textured. Loams are medium-textured soils, normally containing a fairly even balance of clay, silt, and sand. Sands are light-textured soils, often loose and gritty, with a low clay content. Certain mineral elements, most notably CALCIUM, complement textural differences in helping to determine soil friability (see SOIL STRUCTURE).

Clay is the finest of the size fractions, with particles less than 0.002 mm diameter. When mixed with water, clay particles may remain in colloidal suspension for some time, especially if the proportion of exchangeable SODIUM is greater than 6% of the CATION EXCHANGE CAPACITY. Because their surface areas are so large relative to their volumes, they have by far the greatest capacity for combining with, adsorbing, and holding plant nutrient elements and water. Fertile soils normally have at least a moderate proportion of clay.

Silt is an intermediate fraction, comprising particles between 0.002 and 0.02–0.05 mm diameter (the upper limit for silt varies according to the particle size classification used). Silt particles are small enough to be carried large distances by wind and are also carried in suspension by turbulent rivers. Both clay and silt particles are prominent in ALLUVIAL soils deposited by river floods.

Sand particles are divided into fine sand (0.02 to 0.2 mm) and coarse sand (0.2 to 2 mm diameter); again this size division varies according to the particle size classification used. Unless mixed with a proportion of clay, sand remains loose under most conditions. In contrast to clay, the surface area of a sand particle is small relative to its volume, so it has little capacity for surface binding and storing of plant nutrients or water.

Soil texture can be measured by a rigorous particle size analysis in a laboratory or by a soil specialist in the field, who determines texture by feel. ORGANIC MATTER is destroyed before reaching a laboratory, but in the field it can make sandy soils feel more silty and clay soils feel less sticky.

Stones and rocks appear to have particular significance for viticulture, through their effects on limiting soil water-holding capacity and, additionally, on TEMPERATURE both within and immediately above the soil. Stony soils are also usually well drained and have a low water-holding capacity, while a surface layer of stones greatly enhances resistance to SOIL EROSION and reduces surface water loss by evaporation.

Commercial viticulture is carried out across a very wide range of soil textures. Clay and clay loam soils can be suitable provided that they contain ample calcium (as in most LIMESTONE- or CHALK-derived soils) and organic matter to improve their structure. The strongest growth of vines, as with most other plants, is usually on loams and clay loam soils. Whether or not this is desirable depends on various other management and environmental factors, as described for example under SOIL FERTILITY and VIGOUR. Soils of clay loam to sandy clay loam texture can store in the vicinity of 15 mm/0.6 in of available SOIL WATER per 10 cm/4 in of soil depth, in forms that the vine roots can extract.

Soils consisting mostly of sand can pose problems for viticulture because of their lack of storage capacity for both water and nutrients. Typically they will hold 10 mm or less of plant-available water per 10 cm of soil depth. The great depth of some sandy soils can be an off-setting factor, however, as in parts of the Bordeaux region, because vine roots penetrate many metres if the SUBSOIL texture and DRAINAGE permit, and can thus exploit a large enough volume to compensate for the low water-holding capacity per soil volume unit. In soils of low water-holding capacity, the problems of water availability can be overcome by supplying IRRIGATION.

An ideal soil for wine quality, depending on CLIMATE and the rate of EVAPORATION, together with the potential for irrigation, will balance texture against root-available depth to give an adequate storage capacity for water and nutrients, and to provide the vine with a steady moderate supply of both for BALANCED growth and fruiting. No single soil texture has a monopoly of these characteristics. Seguin notes that in the Bordeaux region the soils giving the best water regimes and producing the best wines range from the dominant deep, stony sands of the MÉDOC, because of their low water-holding capacity, to heavy (but well-structured) clays in POMEROL, because the water is present but not easily available to the vines. Thus in Bordeaux, extreme textures are generally better than intermediate textures such as clay loam soils, which can hold significant supplies of water readily available to the vine.

See also GEOLOGY, SOIL, CLAY, and SOIL WATER.

J.G., C.v.L., & R.E.W.

Seguin, G., 'Influence des terroirs viticoles' ('Influence of viticultural terroirs'), *Bulletin de l'OIV*, 56 (1983), 3–18.

White, R. E., *Understanding Vineyard Soils* (2nd edn, Oxford, 2015).

soil types. For types of SOIL and ROCK, see individual entries on ALBARIZA, ALLUVIUM, BASALT, CALCAREOUS, CHALK, CLAY, COLLUVIUM, GALET, GNEISS, GRANITE, GRAVEL, GREYWACKE, LIMESTONE, LOAM, LOESS, MARL, MUSCHELKALK, QUARTZ, QUARTZITE, RENDZINA, SAND, SANDSTONE, SCHIST, SHALE, SILT, SLATE, TERRA ROSSA, TUFF, TUFFEAU, and VOLCANIC. See also SOIL AND WINE QUALITY and GEOLOGY, however, for evidence of soil's relatively indirect role in shaping wine and wine quality.

soil water, that water held in the pore spaces of the soil within the potential rooting zone for vines. When all the pore space is filled with water, the soil is said to be saturated (this defines its water-holding capacity). Unless the soil is a very heavy clay (see SOIL TEXTURE), it will normally drain within 48 hours to a state called its field capacity (FC), which corresponds to a soil water suction of about 10 kiloPascals (kPa) (see WATER STRESS). Ideally, 10–15% of the pore space should be filled with air at the FC. With soil EVAPORATION and, most importantly, extraction of water by the vines, the soil water content decreases until a point is reached when the vine can no longer extract water fast enough to prevent its wilting during the day, and non-recovery at night. This condition is called the permanent wilting point (PWP). The amount of water held between FC and PWP, per metre depth of soil, defines the available water capacity (AWC). The amount of plant available water (PAW) in a SOIL PROFILE is the product of the AWC and SOIL DEPTH. Soils that do not drain to an FC remain waterlogged, in which case a lack of OXYGEN quickly kills the vine roots.

Water supply to the vines is the key factor in grape quality. Vines are Mediterranean plants that need very little water: they can easily grow in climates with only 400 mm/15 in of rainfall a year, providing that the soil has at least an average PAW and EVAPOTRANSPIRATION rates are not too extreme. Water deficits resulting in a certain level of WATER STRESS are essential to grow good quality grapes, particularly for red winemaking.

Water supply to the vine depends on climatic parameters (RAINFALL, potential evapotranspiration), soil parameters (AWC and soil depth), and plant-related factors (rooting depth, leaf area, crop load). Studies on TERROIR by Morlat

and van Leeuwen et al., for example, show that terroir that produces high-quality red wine supplies only moderate amounts of water to the vines, thus inducing water deficit stress. The gravelly soils of the Médoc were the first in the world to be seriously studied by Gérard Seguin, who used a neutron moisture probe to investigate vine–water relations in these soils as early as 1966. However, the fact that these soils are deep is rather an exception than a general rule, and can be explained only by their high gravel content and their low clay content (see SOIL DEPTH). These soils can be subject to temporary waterlogging until flowering, but generally the water table is not within reach of the roots during ripening. If it is, wine quality suffers, as explained in van Leeuwen et al. (1994).

Regular or permanent waterlogging, even if only of the subsoil or the zone immediately overlying it, is a clear counter-indicator for vines, particularly if it occurs during the vine growing season. The optimum soil water regime is thus usually found where there is an adequate depth of well-drained soil, with at least moderate contents of CLAY, SILT, and ORGANIC MATTER so that water can be supplied steadily from soil reserves over a long period. The less clay and organic matter, the deeper the soil needs to be to achieve that end. Note, however, that too much available soil water can be counter-productive in viticulture if it promotes too much vegetative VIGOUR, or helps to prolong vegetative growth into the fruit-ripening period. (See also CLIMATE AND WINE QUALITY, SOIL AND WINE QUALITY.)

Ideally there should be ample available soil water during FLOWERING and FRUIT SET, diminishing so as to create just enough mild WATER STRESS before VERAISON to inhibit further vegetative growth. Opinions vary as to the optimum water supply between veraison and RIPENING, but most agree at least that there should be no severe stress through this period; nor should there be so much water available, especially after preceding stress, as to encourage a sudden uptake into the berries or renewed vegetative growth.

The binding capacity of the soil for the water that remains after draining to its FC has its own significance for vine–water relations. Some is so tightly bound to the CLAY that roots cannot extract it at all, and some can only be extracted slowly. This explains why heavy clay soils, such as those of PETRUS in Pomerol which induce early water deficits, can produce very fine red wines (see van Leeuwen et al. (1994)). The small amount of available water in sandy soils, on the other hand, is readily extracted and therefore easily exhausted. However, in sandy soils, vine rooting is often very deep and the PAW can be too large to grow high quality fruit. See van Leeuwen et al. (1994, 2004).

Even in Mediterranean climates with very low summer rainfall, the best soils are not those on the plains with a large PAW, but the more shallow, stony soils of the slopes, which have a much lower PAW. However, when the PAW is very small (shallow and very stony soils on hard limestone bedrock, as in La Clape, near Narbonne), water stress might be so severe as to reduce wine quality. In such climates, relatively shallow soils, or sandy/stony soils with limited PAW, combined with supplementary irrigation when needed (and permitted), can have advantages in allowing the best control over water availability to the vines. In hot inland regions, such as the CENTRAL VALLEY, California, and the MURRAY DARLING region in Australia, evapotranspiration rates are so high in summer that, irrespective of soil type, irrigation is essential to grow healthy vines and produce reasonable yields.

R.E.S., C.v.L., & R.E.W.

Morlat, R., 'Characterization of viticultural terroirs using a simple field model based on soil depth. I–Validation of the water supply regime, phenology and vine vigour, in the Anjou vineyard (France)', *Plant and Soil*, 281 (2006), 37–54.

van Leeuwen, C., and Seguin, G., 'Incidences de l'alimentation en eau de la vigne, appréciée par l'état hydrique du feuillage, sur le développement de l'appareil végétatif et la maturation du raisin (Vitis vinifera variété Cabernet franc, Saint-Emilion, 1990), *Journal International des Sciences de la Vigne et du Vin*, 28/2 (1994), 81–110.

van Leeuwen, C., et al., 'Influence of climate, soil, and cultivar on terroir', *American Journal of Enology and Viticulture*, 55/3 (2004), 207–17.

van Leeuwen, C., et al., 'Vine water status is a key factor in grape ripening and vintage quality for red Bordeaux wine. How can it be assessed for management purposes?' *Journal International des Sciences de la Vigne et du Vin*, 43/3 (2009), 121–34.

White, R. E., *Understanding Vineyard Soils* (2nd edn, Oxford, 2015).

solera, system of fractional blending used most commonly in JEREZ for maintaining the consistency of a style of SHERRY which takes its name from those barrels closest to the *suelo*, or floor, from which the final blend was customarily drawn. The system was created for commercial reasons in the second half of the 19th century. Previously, sherry was vintage-dated just like claret.

The system is designed to smooth out the differences between vintage years and is effectively a more subtle, and very much more labour-intensive, version of the BLENDING of inexpensive table wines between one vintage and another, although the solera system concerns barrel-aged liquids and is made up of several different scales. Depending on market demand, a fraction of wine is removed from the oldest scale of the solera, the so-called solera barrels themselves, and replaced (although the barrels are never filled completely) with wine from the next scale of barrels containing wine of the same type but one year younger, the so-called first criadera. They in turn are replenished from the scale two years younger (the second criadera) and so on, the youngest scale being replenished with new wine. This system is particularly useful for FLOR wines because it refreshes each barrel with younger wine and provides micronutrients to sustain the flor yeast for several years. It takes several years' operation for a solera to reach an equilibrium average age. Many soleras in Jerez were started decades ago and, since no barrel is ever emptied, there is always some of the oldest wine in the final blend. Fewer scales are needed to produce a consistent AMONTILLADO or OLOROSO sherry than a FINO or MANZANILLA sherry because these fuller, richer wines vary less from year to year.

Even using modern pumps, a solera system is extremely labour-intensive and it is only in regions where LABOUR costs are relatively moderate that a large solera is feasible.

The solera system is also used for blending Brandy de Jerez, and for many other fortified wines such as MÁLAGA, MONTILLA, MADEIRA, TOPAQUE AND MUSCAT in Australia, as well as in the production of top-quality VINEGAR. If a product is labelled 'Solera 1880', for example, it should come from a solera established in 1880.

For mathematical calculations of the average age of a solera, and the time required to reach equilibrium average age, see Baker et al.

Baker, G. A., Amerine, M. A., and Roessler, E. B., 'Theory and application of fractional blending programs', *Hilgardia*, 21 (1952), 383–409.

soluble solids, also called total soluble solids (TSS) and total dissolved solids (TDS), refers to the collective concentration in unfermented grape juice of all solutes (dissolved molecules and ions). The predominant solutes, accounting for about 90% of the total, in the juice of ripe grapes are the reducing sugars GLUCOSE and FRUCTOSE; others are acids (MALIC and TARTARIC), ions (organic and inorganic), and literally hundreds of inorganic and organic molecules that together contribute to the characteristics that make grapes such an adaptable and useful product. Collective concentrations of TSS range from 5 to over 25% and may be expressed in many ways, most usually either as degrees BRIX, BAUMÉ, or OECHSLE. See also MUST WEIGHT. B.G.C.

sommelier, widely used French term for a specialist wine waiter or wine steward, sometimes abbreviated to 'somm' in the US where an eponymous 2013 FILM was devoted to four sommeliers' efforts to pass the Master Sommelier exam. The sommelier's job is to ensure that any wine ordered is served correctly and, ideally, to advise on the individual characteristics of every wine on the establishment's wine list and on FOOD AND WINE MATCHING. In some establishments, the sommelier may also be responsible for compiling the list, buying and storing the wine, and restocking whatever passes for a CELLAR. (All too few restaurants today have their own serious collection of wines, although there are notable exceptions such as, in Paris, the Tour d'Argent whose cellar is but a few feet from the River Seine, and Taillevent, whose cellar is so important that it has spawned a retail wine business.)

A sommelier should present the wine or wines ordered to the host before they are opened to ensure that there has been no misunderstanding (and so that the host can especially check that the vintage corresponds to expectations). This is a good time for the host to check that the bottle feels at the right SERVING temperature. The bottle should be opened in view of the host, and, if a wine is to be DECANTED (and that is an option that any decent sommelier should be able to offer), that operation should be performed in public too.

Some sommeliers offer the cork to the host to smell, which is well meaning but is no certain guide to whether or not the wine is FAULTY. Some sublime wines come from under some rather unpleasant-smelling corks, and vice versa.

A surer guide to whether a particular bottle happens to be one of the relatively few to exhibit a FAULT (CORKINESS is the most common) is to examine the small tasting sample usually offered by the sommelier to the host for this very purpose. A glance will confirm that it is not cloudy, dull, or fizzing when it should not. A swift inhalation should confirm that it smells 'clean'. Few people can then resist actually tasting a mouthful, but it is generally unnecessary as the most common faults are apparent to the eye or nose. Besides, tasting a wine should clearly reveal its all-important TEMPERATURE. This is the moment to ask for an ice bucket (for red wines if necessary) or for a bottle of white wine to be taken out of an ice bucket.

In many countries there are official associations of sommeliers, often with a series of examinations, qualifications, or at least competitions. The Court of Master Sommeliers (www.courtofmastersommeliers.org) holds exams and awards the initials MS not unlike the Institute of MASTERS OF WINE, although there is less context and rather more rote. French, and other, sommeliers compete in these events all over the world and, such is the average French person's reverence for the wine knowledge of a sommelier, to win the title Meilleur Sommelier du Monde (Best Sommelier in the World) is henceforth to inhabit another world.

Somontano, wine zone in the foothills of the central Pyrenees, in ARAGÓN in north-east Spain (see map under SPAIN). Somontano (meaning 'under the mountain') is one of Spain's newer wine regions. There are currently some 4,750 ha/11,400 acres under vines. In stark contrast to much of inland Spain, Somontano looks like winemaking country. The heavy winter rains are supplemented by a network of rivers and streams flowing off the mountains. Even in summer, when temperatures can easily reach 35 °C/95 °F, the fields remain green and productive.

Bodega Pirineos, once the region's CO-OPERATIVE, together with the ultra-modern, recently created wineries Viñas del Vero (vintage 1986) and Enate (1991), make most of Somontano's wine. The main early selling point of Somontano in the early 1990s was its dedication to INTERNATIONAL VARIETIES but by 2010 this had become its main problem as competing on a varietal basis with Cabernets and Syrahs made all over the world proved an arduous task. The native MORISTEL and Parraleta varieties represent only 3.5% of the vineyard surface. Tempranillo, with 15%, is the only significant Spanish variety. The native Garnacha was on the wane, and mainly used for rosés, until Viñas del Vero discovered and relaunched the impressive old vineyards at Secastilla with a very distinctive single-estate Garnacha red. Some 160 ha of Garnacha remain. For whites, the traditional Macabeo and almost extinct Alcañón have been joined by Chardonnay and Gewürztraminer, which together represent 81% of the 870 ha/2,090 acres planted to white wine varieties. V. de la S.

www.dosomontano.com

Sonoma, northern CALIFORNIA town, valley, and one of the state's most important wine counties. **Sonoma county** is one of the larger of northern California's coastal counties, and one of its most historic. **Sonoma Valley** is a very small portion of Sonoma county but it rivals and occasionally beats nearby NAPA Valley for *réclame*. Vineyards are everywhere in the county, and have been since the last third of the 19th century. Sprawling, geologically and climatically diverse, it is the most resolutely amoebic of all the fine wine regions, having divided and redivided itself into AVAs and sub-AVAs until they run three layers deep in several places, four in a few, and eight in one. Growing conditions are a little more homogeneous than the welter of names suggests, but Sonoma still gives would-be gurus some of their most engaging opportunities to define subtle boundaries by taste and taste alone. The full roster follows.

Alexander Valley and Pine Mountain-Cloverdale Peak AVAs

The largest and most fully planted of Sonoma county's many vineyard valleys, Alexander

Valley takes in the Russian River watershed upstream of Healdsburg north all the way to the Sonoma–Mendocino county line north of Cloverdale. In 2011, the Pine Mountain-Cloverdale Peak AVA was created within Alexander Valley at its northernmost edge and spilling into MENDOCINO county. If the general history of the area is long, with vines dating back to the 1850s, the particular history of superior varieties is—a few rare plantings excepted—as short here as almost everywhere else in California. Before PROHIBITION, hops and prunes blanketed the Alexander Valley and remained the major crops, along with some plantings of mixed black grapes for bulk red, into the late 1960s and early 1970s. Simi winery started the renaissance in 1970, when a new owner breathed life into a moribund cellar. Chateau Souverain picked up the traces in 1973 and then Jordan Vineyards added a stamp of elegance in 1976. Growth has been steady since then and by 2013 there were more than 50 wineries and 15,000 acres/6,070 ha of vines. KENDALL-JACKSON's 1996 purchase of the mountain vineyards on Gauer Ranch, renamed Alexander Mountain Estate, represented another step forward for Sonoma, while GALLO's acquisition of nearly 1,500 acres/600 ha since 1988 in Alexander Valley alone signalled a new era for both Gallo and Alexander Valley, and encouraged others to follow suit.

Alexander Valley is noteworthy among other Sonoma county appellations for the fleshy voluptuousness of its wines. A wide range of grape varieties is grown at least passably well, which has distracted from the question of what the district does best. Accessibility is much more likely to be a general descriptor than longevity, however. Cabernet Sauvignon and Merlot have gained a certain currency, with a signature note of chocolate warmth and agreeable MOUTHFEEL. Chardonnays also tend to bold statement and ample girth, although some grown close to the Russian River can have an unexpectedly stony character. These varieties, market driven, dominate plantings. Sauvignon Blanc and Zinfandel succeed often enough to make one wonder if they are not suited best to these particular suns and soils. Most of its substantial plantings are on a broad and nearly flat valley floor very nearly bisected by the river, but some significant ones creep into the east hills. Kendall-Jackson's Alexander Mountain Estate plantings reach as high as 2,400 ft, and other daring growers seeking more complexity and structure in their wines are moving to mountain-grown grapes. Jordan boldly moved away from its valley floor plantings to HILLSIDE VINEYARDS for Cabernet and the Russian River Valley for Chardonnay, with excellent results. Other wineries that have drawn attention to Alexander Valley include Geyser Peak, Clos du Bois, and Stuhlmuller—and RIDGE and Seghesio for Zinfandel. Wineries outside the area whose significant reputations have been based primarily on grapes grown in Alexander Valley include Rodney Strong, Silver Oak, and Chateau St Jean.

Bennett Valley AVA

With just four wineries and 650 acres of wine grapes, Bennett Valley is not especially important but it does contribute significantly to the quality of Sonoma county Merlot. Its volcanic-laced, clay soils and moderately cool climate encourages the extended HANG TIME ideal for the variety. The long growing season helps maximize flavours and increase concentration, while the cooler temperatures preserve the grape's natural acidity. Matanzas Creek, sold to Jackson Family Wines (see KENDALL-JACKSON) in 2000, is the pioneer here. Sauvignon Blanc, Grenache, and Syrah also show promise, although spring FROST is a perennial concern.

Chalk Hill AVA

Small sub-AVA within the Russian River Valley AVA in the foothills on the far eastern boundary of the district near the town of Windsor. Some objected to its inclusion in the Russian River Valley AVA, arguing that its location on the western slope of the Mayacamas range and its volcanic soils mean that it has little in common with the gravel and sandy loams more common in the valley below. Yet studies of the daily Pacific fog incursions that define Russian River showed that they reached into Chalk Hill, and it remains in the larger AVA. Chalk Hill Estate is the dominant winery, and growers have had success with Chardonnay, Sauvignon Blanc, and Cabernet Sauvignon

Dry Creek Valley and Rockpile AVAs

For years a sparsely settled tributary of the Russian River drainage, Dry Creek Valley has emerged as one of Sonoma county's most intriguing appellations. Among white varieties, Sauvignon Blanc stands head and shoulders above Chardonnay, although smatterings of Viognier and Italian white varieties, including Arneis and Fiano, are grown. Among reds, the race is more even between Zinfandel and Cabernet Sauvignon. The sad thing, from the point of view of Zinfandel fanciers, is that nowhere else is that grape nearly so voluptuous, while Cabernet does at least as well and perhaps better in several other zones in California. Still, until the mid 1990s, economic considerations favoured Cabernet to a degree that no farmer could ignore, and plantings shifted accordingly. Since 1995, however, (red) Zinfandel has been resurgent and an undersupply has made these highly regarded vineyards tantalizing to second careerist refugees from San Francisco as well as local farmers wanting to diversify their crops and to cash in on the wine bonanza. Vines aged 35 to 100-plus years, on phylloxera-resistant St George ROOTSTOCK, produce Dry Creek's most acclaimed Zinfandels, with Petite Sirah and sometimes Carignane joining the blend.

The valley heads north and west from Healdsburg, where Dry Creek trickles into the Russian River. For many years plantings stopped at Warm Springs dam which created Lake Sonoma. The reservoir drowned some good patches of Zinfandel; but now the area north west of the lake has been planted and christened Rockpile AVA, parts of which are within the Dry Creek Valley AVA. Although there are no wineries in the rugged Rockpile district, vines contribute Zinfandel grapes to the likes of Carol Shelton, J. C. Cellars, Mauritson, Rosenblum, and Seghesio. Italian immigrants planted the early vineyards, and their names remain common among vineyard and winery owners, including A. Rafanelli and Pedroncelli. But they are far from having a monopoly in the modern era. Dry Creek's most prominent wineries in 2014 included Bella, Dry Creek Vineyard (a Sauvignon Blanc trailblazer), Ferrari-Carano, Lambert Bridge, Nalle, and RIDGE VINEYARDS' Zinfandel outpost at Lytton Springs.

Fort Ross-Seaview AVA

From the confounding mass that is the Sonoma Coast AVA the admirably focused Fort Ross sub-AVA emerged in 2012. Vineyards are sited on rounded ridges with summits exceeding 1,800 ft, above the fog line yet within the path of Pacific winds that ensure a COOL CLIMATE. Yet these summits receive longer periods of sunlight and are warmer than the land below, allowing for the maturation of Chardonnay, Pinot Noir, and Syrah grapes with high acidity and lean, angular character—a style gaining increasing acceptance. Hirsch, Flowers, Wild Hog, Fort Ross, and Peay are among the well-known producer-growers; Marcassin, Pahlmeyer, and Peter Michael have vineyards here, too.

Green Valley of Russian River Valley AVA

A sub-AVA of California's Russian River Valley AVA described above, this cool corner began life in 1983 as Sonoma County-Green Valley AVA, but later changed to its present name. It lies at the south western edge of the larger region, bordered by the towns of Sebastopol, Forestville, and Occidental, and is the coldest, foggiest wedge of Russian River Valley, prized for its Goldridge soils. Its best-known estate is Iron Horse, yet recent years have seen Littorai, Dutton-Goldfield, Marimar Estate, and Hartford Family Winery emerge as stars, their wines focused and crisp.

Knights Valley AVA

A small, handsome, upland valley in Sonoma county separates the upper end of the Napa Valley from the lower end of the Alexander

Valley. It was originally developed by Beringer Vineyards, and has since been joined by several growers and a prominent winery owned by British businessman Sir Peter Michael. The most impressive grape variety to date has been Cabernet Sauvignon, which embraces the heat that is trapped in the valley during the day, with the vines being cooled by refreshing breezes overnight.

Moon Mountain District Sonoma County AVA

This was approved in 2013 on the western slopes of the Mayacamas and encompasses some 17,000 acres, with just 1,500 planted to grapevines. It has yet to establish its viticultural significance.

Northern Sonoma AVA

This oddity of an AVA encompasses all of Sonoma that drains into the Pacific, which is to say all but Sonoma Valley and some of the Petaluma river watershed; it was proposed and is mainly used by E. & J. GALLO, but has proven useful to a few others with scattered vineyards.

Russian River Valley

Most of the Russian River's course is through other AVAs in MENDOCINO and Sonoma counties. Only when the river escapes from Alexander Valley through a narrow gorge in the mountains at Healdsburg, then flows on, first south, then west, in its journey to the Pacific do the watercourse and the Russian River Valley AVA become one and the same.

Cool, often foggy, the AVA blossomed as a wine-producing region in the 1970s when new winery owners in the area began bottling locally grown grapes under Sonoma county labels. It took the district fewer than 20 years to prove itself eminently well adapted to Chardonnay and Pinot Noir. In a few HILLSIDE locations such as Martinelli's Jackass Vineyard, Zinfandel does amazingly well. Joe Swan was an early pioneer. Dehlinger, Sonoma-Cutrer, Rochioli, Gary Farrell, Merry Edwards, Kosta Browne, Paul Hobbs, and Williams & Selyem are among the region's best-known producers, and dozens more emerged in rapid fire in the early 2000s—some without vineyards of their own, some without production facilities, and a few with neither, creating brands first, and finding the grapes as LABOUR as they went along. The boom was ignited by interest in the region's Pinot Noir that surged from the late 1990s, with total vineyard acreage ballooning from around 4,000 acres then to over 18,000 acres/7,287 ha in 2013. Chardonnay remains the most-planted variety, but Pinot Noir is not far behind; this one—two Burgundian punch countering Napa's mastery of Bordeaux varieties. Such is the cachet of Russian River Valley that various interested parties have twice successfully petitioned to have the AVA expanded, in 2003 and 2011, thereby blurring the lines of authenticity, and contributing to the rapid increase in vine acreage totals since 2003. Russian River Valley is widely thought of as being chilly during the growing season, yet some vineyard sites on the eastern side of the AVA can be as warm as ALEXANDER VALLEY.

Sonoma Coast AVA

This misleadingly named AVA stands out as a purely artificial construction. Its sponsors (including Sonoma-Cutrer) drew boundaries to include widely scattered vineyards so they could continue to describe their wines as ESTATE BOTTLED after tightened federal regulations began requiring that both winery and vineyard be within the same AVA to qualify. The AVA stretches all the way from San Pablo Bay to the border with Mendocino county, encompassing vast inland tracts including parts of the Carneros, Russian River Valley, and Sonoma Valley AVAs.

The fringe vineyards along Sonoma county's shore that hug the Pacific have emerged as statement makers for what is regarded by many to be the 'real' Sonoma Coast, where the ocean is actually in sight. The marine soils, temperatures, and breezes yield wines that are very much less ripe, more structured, and higher-acid wines than could ever be produced in the much warmer CARNEROS. Much-needed fragmentation of the Sonoma Coast AVA began in 2011 with the establishment of the Fort Ross-Seaview sub-AVA (see above). More segmentation is expected in the future as winemakers seek more specificity within the broader appellation. One prime area is the so-called Petaluma Gap, a break in the coastal mountains near Petaluma through which ocean fog and wind intrudes on a daily basis, making optimum conditions for fine-boned Chardonnay, Pinot Noir, and cool-climate Syrah.

Sonoma Mountain AVA

A sub-AVA of Sonoma Valley (see below) best known for Cabernet Sauvignon, it occupies the east-facing slopes of the 2,400-ft/730-m mountain from which it draws its name and which separates Sonoma Valley from the Petaluma River watershed to the west. The AVA sits above the towns of Glen Ellen and Kenwood. Its most prestigious winery is Laurel Glen, its most characteristic Benziger Family. The Richard Dinner Vineyard is an outstanding Chardonnay source for Paul Hobbs.

Sonoma Valley AVA

For history, especially romantic history, no other AVA in California compares with Sonoma Valley. In addition to being the site of the ragtag 1846 Bear Flag revolt, which eventually secured Alta California for the US rather than Mexico, it had the last of the Franciscan MISSIONARY vineyards, one of the earliest commercial vineyards north of San Francisco (General Mariano Vallejo appropriated the Franciscan plantings), and, courtesy of public relations master Agoston HARASZTHY, the first great winery name of northern California, Buena Vista (now owned by BOISSET). In more modern times, its Hanzell Vineyard started the rush to using French oak BARRELS to age California wines and thereby revolutionized their style, most especially Chardonnay's. The valley runs parallel to the Napa Valley to the east, its southern extremity doubling as the Sonoma portion of CARNEROS. A long, thin comma of a trough in the coast ranges, it warms markedly from south to north because San Francisco Bay's influence dwindles mile by mile. Steep mountains on each side make it geologically as well as climatically complex. Some of its memorable wines portray that diversity: Zinfandel, Gewurztraminer, Pinot Noir, Chardonnay, and Cabernet Sauvignon. Sonoma Mountain (see above) is a sub-AVA. The Monte Rosso Vineyard, planted in 1838 by Louis M. Martini, looms large over the valley, with views of San Francisco on clear days, and produces Cabernet Sauvignon and Zinfandel fruit for several producers, including GALLO's Louis M. Martini Winery in Napa.

Above all else, Sonoma Valley is known for its ancient Zinfandel vines, many well over 100 years old (see HISTORIC VINEYARD SOCIETY) and continuing to pump out small yields of intensely flavoured, spicy grapes. Many old vineyards were planted to FIELD BLENDS of Zinfandel, Petite Sirah, Carignane, and other 'mixed blacks', and there is a growing appreciation in the valley for such vineyard-specific blends.

Sebastiani and Gundlach-Bundschu are the old-timers of the valley. Others of note include Chateau St Jean, Arrowood, Kenwood, Cline, St Francis, Kunde, and Ravenswood which specializes in old-vine Zinfandel and is now part of CONSTELLATION. L.M.

Sopron, wine region and PDO in the extreme north west of HUNGARY which is geographically part of the NEUSIEDLERSEE wine regions of Austria. Its climate is much more temperate than that of most of the rest of Hungary, with cooler, wetter summers and milder winters. From the 14th century, when Hungary was recognized as a useful source of fuller, richer wines than those of northern Europe, Sopron was an important centre of the wine trade, dispatching not just its own wines but those of the rest of Hungary to Austria, Poland, and Silesia. Today Sopron produces mainly red wines, more tannic than the Hungarian norm, from grape varieties such as KÉKFRANKOS, Cabernet, and Merlot.

sorbic acid (2,4-hexadienoic acid), winemaking additive and preservative discovered in 1940 to inhibit the growth of YEAST and other FUNGI. Sorbic acid, or its salt potassium **sorbate**, is used widely in food and drink production to inhibit the growth of yeast and mould, notably on cheese and meat. It is classified as one of the safest food preservatives. Sorbic acid use has permitted the wide range of everyday commercial wines currently available which contain some RESIDUAL SUGAR but whose ALCOHOLIC STRENGTH alone is not sufficient to inhibit yeast metabolism.

There is a drawback, however. While most people detect about 135 mg/l, a small proportion of humans are sufficiently sensitive to sorbic acid to find about 50 mg/l in wines. It has a particular taste and a rancid odour to some palates, even at levels that are hardly high enough to inhibit yeast. The EU and OIV limit in finished wines is 200 mg/l.

Sorbic acid inhibits the growth of some BACTERIA but not, unfortunately for winemakers, the large group of LACTIC ACID BACTERIA. SULFUR DIOXIDE must be used together with sorbic acid in sweet wines that are low in alcohol in order to prevent the growth of lactic acid bacteria. Some of these lactics metabolize sorbates to produce compounds such as 2-ethoxyhexa-3,5-diene, which has a perception threshold of around 10 ng/l and smells of crushed GERANIUM leaves—definitely a wine FAULT.   A.D.W.

sorbitol, one of the sugar ALCOHOLS present in trace amounts in grapes and wines, and closely related to GLUCOSE. It has a mildly sweet taste, is very soluble in water and, when present in high concentrations, confers a sense of BODY on a liquid.

Since sorbitol can be made easily and cheaply from many agricultural raw materials, this property has been harnessed by a few unscrupulous wine bottlers to increase consumer acceptance of thin, acid, ordinary wines. Sorbitol is not harmful to humans but its use is prohibited by most wine regulations.   A.D.W.

sorì is a PIEMONTESE dialect term used for vineyard sites of the highest quality, particularly for those with an exceptional favourable southern exposure. More subtle variations also exist: a 'morning' sorì (*sorì di mattino*) with a south-eastern exposure or an 'evening' sorì (*sorì di sera*) with a south-western exposure. The term was first used on a wine label by Angelo GAJA for his Sorì San Lorenzo Barbaresco 1967 and was widely imitated in the subsequent quarter-century.

sorting of grapes. See TRIAGE.

sotolon, compound (3-hydroxy-4,5-dimethyl-2(5H)-furanone) formed from ACETALDEHYDE that is an important component of the spice fenugreek and is found in a wide range of products from BOTRYTIZED wines to roasted tobacco.

It is responsible for the hazelnut and particularly spicy 'curry' aromas found notably in VIN JAUNE from the Jura but also in TOKAJI and some fortified wines including VIN DOUX NATUREL and PORT, especially those that are RANCIO. It forms partially during the ageing process, particularly if this is oxidative, but in vins jaunes it is known to increase after bottling. It is also commonly identified by a honey or beeswax aroma in wines suffering from PREMATURE OXIDATION. Discovered by Japanese scientists in the late 1970s as a flavour compound in raw cane sugar, sotolon has a very low flavour threshold (7 µg/l) and is formed in carbohydrate-rich media.

W.L. & P.J.W.

Kobayashi, A., 'Sotolon identification, formation and effect on flavor', in American Chemical Society, *Flavor Chemistry Trends and Developments* (Washington, DC, 1989).

Lavigne, V., Pons, A., and Dubourdieu, D., 'The premature oxidative ageing of wine', Faculty of Oenology, Bordeaux Institute of Vine and Wine Sciences (2010).

sour rot, known as *pourriture acide* in French, is a breakdown of mature grapes caused by a mixture of fungi, bacteria, and yeast which invades damaged berries. The fruit takes on the smell of vinegar, and juice from rotting berries can spread the infection, as can FRUIT FLY. Common entry points for the mixture of microbes are bird pecks as well as splits in berry skin caused by rain. Some organisms involved are the fungi *Aspergillus, Botryosphaeria, Cladosporium, Monilia, Penicillium*, and *Sclerotinia* and the yeast *Saccharomyces*. The rot is encouraged by rain and high humidity, and control relies on avoiding fruit damage as well as encouraging fruit aeration.   R.E.S.

Pearson, R. C., and Goheen, A. C. (eds.), *Compendium of Grape Diseases* (St Paul, Minn., 1988).

Sousão, is a dark-skinned grape variety widely planted in northern Portugal, where the wine is notably high in acidity as well as colour and is therefore increasingly valued in PORT blends. It is an ingredient in QUINTA DO NOVAL Nacional, and in the nearby Minho it is known as Vinhão, its official Portuguese name, and makes particularly tart red VINHO VERDE. Portuguese plantings totalled almost 4,000 ha/10,000 acres in 2012 and a few hundred hectares in Galicia where most goes into tart blends. Spelt variously **Sousão, Souzao**, and all stations in between, it has also been planted by aspirant makers of port-style wines in California, South Africa, and Australia, with a certain degree of success.

South Africa, prolific southern hemisphere wine producer with a lustrous past and now in the midst of a significant renaissance. The famous Muscat-based dessert wines of CONSTANTIA seduced 18th and 19th-century Europe at a time

when names such as LAFITE and Romanée-Conti (see DOMAINE DE LA ROMANÉE-CONTI) were still in the making. The two centuries which followed were, by comparison, a disappointment, with the ordinary being too plentiful and the individual too rare. Only since the early 1990s has the Cape begun to shake off its political notoriety and vinous obscurity.

The Cape (most South African vineyards are in the hinterland of the Cape of Good Hope) functioned as a vast distillery for much of the 20th century, draining a partly subsidized annual wine lake and guaranteeing a certain quality of life to a politically powerful farming lobby. The growers' body founded in 1918, the KWV (Co-operative Wine Growers' Association), was until 1998 legally empowered to determine production quotas, fix minimum prices, and predetermine production areas and limits—a system which tended to handicap the private wine producer and favour the bulk grape-grower. Under pressure, the KWV began to relinquish most of these powers in 1992, and set the stage for a much freer, livelier production scene.

By the late 1990s, the requirements of the country's considerable brandy industry were more or less separately met, with plantings of high-yielding varieties increasingly developed expressly for this purpose. This forced growers of poorer vine varieties in lower-yielding regions to reconsider their commercial strategies. At the same time, increased demand for superior wines and the enthusiasm of a new generation of winemakers led to new vine-growing ventures in completely new viticultural areas and to the rediscovery of certain regions whose potential had long been overlooked.

Until recently, the Cape's wine industry could be divided between the quantity-producing majority and the quality-conscious minority. However, the export-led boom which followed democratic elections in 1994 transformed an industry in which as recently as 1990 less than 30% of the harvest reached the market as wine. By 2012, 75% of the grape crop was used to produce wine, with the remainder supplying the domestic brandy industry and the fruitjuice sector.

With 1.7% of the world's vineyards, South Africa ranks about 11th in area under vines, but its annual output, at just 10 million hl/264 million gal, makes it definitively one of the world's top ten wine producers. Total area of vineyard for wine grapes has stabilized at around 100,000 ha/247,000 acres. By 2014, there were almost 600 cellars which crush grapes, a small proportion of the 3,440 registered grape growers.

The risks and discipline of cooler environments suited to classic, low-yielding varieties have been braved by those who represent the innovative side of the South African wine

SOUTH AFRICA

0 _____ 100 km

▨ Wine-growing regions

Upington
Central Orange River
Douglas
Orange
0 _____ 100 km

Lutzville Valley
• Vredendal

OLIFANTS RIVER
Citrusdal   **Citrusdal Valley**
Mountain
• Citrusdal
• Piketberg
Olifants

Swartland   **Tulbagh**
Malmesbury   • Tulbagh
Groenekloof
Darling • **Wellington**
COASTAL **Breedekloof**
REGION Paarl • Worcester
Tygerberg **Paarl** **Worcester**
Durbanville • **Franschhoek** **Robertson** • Bonnievale
Cape Town • Stellenbosch **BREEDE RIVER VALLEY**
Constantia • **Stellenbosch**
Cape Peninsula **Elgin** **Overberg**
• Caledon
Hermanus • **Walker Bay**
Cape Agulhas

Touws
Montagu
• Robertson
• Swellendam
Swellendam **CAPE SOUTH COAST**
Breede

Calitzdorp
Calitzdorp
• Oudtshoorn
KLEIN KAROO
Langeberg-Garcia

• Mossel Bay

Johannesburg
• Durban
Cape Town

Cape Agulhas
INDIAN OCEAN

industry. Together with a few wholesale merchant-producers (notably DISTELL and Douglas Green Bellingham), such wine-growers began to revolutionize the Cape wine scene in the 1980s, preparing the way for the significant transformation—in both plantings and in quality—which characterized the first post-apartheid decade.

An ever-strengthening export market which is slowly recognizing the nuances possible in the higher-priced brackets has been helped by a buoyant domestic demand for good quality wine.

As in Europe and America, people are drinking less, but better, with average per capita consumption around 8 l per year. Meanwhile,

to an increasing extent, wine is the beverage of choice of middle-class families in many of the urbanized areas. This shift away from a beer-and-spirit-only consumption pattern has seen the growth of a more sophisticated domestic market. Coupled with a virtual twenty-fold increase in exports between 1992 and 2012, there is now a significant incentive to vine-growers to pursue quality rather than quantity.

This scramble for excellence has confirmed the benefits both of cooler sites and matching locality to grape varieties. The historic Constantia area has been rediscovered and replanted. Climatic conditions here and in recently

pioneered areas such as ELGIN, WALKER BAY, and CAPE AGULHAS on the eastern seaboard and alongside the cold Benguela current along the west coast differ dramatically from those in the hot hinterland. This century many of the country's more adventurous winemakers have been exploiting the fit between locality and variety, and the warmer SWARTLAND district and Olifants River region have come to yield some of the country's most exciting new-generation wines.

Chenin Blanc remains the farmers' favourite vine variety, making almost any and every style of white wine and comprising just over 17% of all plantings. In the late 1990s, less than 18% of

Cape vineyards produced red grapes. By 2012 this proportion was more than 45%. As a result, the traditional red blends featuring Cabernet Sauvignon, Shiraz, Cinsaut, Tinta Barroca, and the Cape's own cross PINOTAGE have been joined by newer styles. Growth in plantings of the premium red varieties has seen Cabernet Sauvignon move from 4.9% of total plantings in 1996 to 11.8% in 2012. In the same period, Shiraz vineyards increased ninefold, Merlot trebled, and Cabernet Franc more than doubled. Small OAK AGEING was introduced in the late 1970s and became widely used for commercial wines in the second half of the 1980s. Now most of the country's smaller cellars, and all of the producing wholesalers, use French oak for both reds and whites. Controlled MALOLACTIC CONVERSION is widely practised while reduced dependence on flavour-stripping FILTRATION and STABILIZATION processes has also helped improve the quality of the better wines. New CANOPY MANAGEMENT strategies and increasing VINE DENSITIES also played a role.

However, poor grape quality—often due to VIRUS-infected planting material—has hindered even greater progress. LEAFROLL, FANLEAF, and CORKY BARK viruses affect tens of thousands of hectares of vineyards.

While counterparts elsewhere in the New World streaked ahead, South Africa's progress was slowed in the 1980s by the application of unnecessarily arduous plant importation regulations and the steadfast refusal by members of the industry's own vine improvement body to recognize the extent of the problem. Initially, poor handling techniques in disseminating this material as well as virus-infected ROOTSTOCKS ensured that many of the newer vineyards would succumb to viruses, although more rigorous protocols now appear to be playing a role in raising the average age of virus-free plantings on the better-managed properties.

A few fundamental natural handicaps exist. Apart from isolated CALCAREOUS outcrops, Cape soils tend to be excessively acid, requiring heavy LIME amendments, tartaric acid adjustments to musts and wines, and severe TARTRATE removal procedures before bottling (see SOIL ACIDITY).

History

The father of the South African wine industry was a 33-year-old Dutch surgeon sent to establish a market garden to reduce the risks of scurvy on the long sea passage between Europe and the Indies. Jan van Riebeeck, the Cape's first European settler, was a reluctant pioneer, and no viticulturist. But his brief was to set up a supply station for DUTCH EAST INDIA COMPANY sailors on the spice routes; and the Cape's MEDITERRANEAN CLIMATE suggested vines might well flourish.

Seven years after sailing into Table Bay on 6 April 1652, at the head of a ragtag mercenary band, he recorded: 'Today, praise be to God, wine was pressed for the first time from Cape grapes.' The cuttings came from 'somewhere in western France' according to viticulturist Professor C. Orffer. Conditions and quality improved when a new governor, Simon van der Stel, established the legendary 750-ha/1,850-acre CONSTANTIA wine estate outside Cape Town in 1685.

Constantia again became the focal point of the wine industry in 1778, when a portion of the now-divided estate was bought by a talented and ambitious grower, Hendrik Cloete. His Constantia dessert wines soon became the toast of European aristocracy. Cape wine exports flourished under British rule, even if mainly of cheap wines. When in 1861 the Gladstone government removed empire-preferential tariffs, French wines had only the Channel to cross to capture the British market and far-flung Cape colony products became uncompetitive.

PHYLLOXERA struck in 1886, adding a 20-year recuperation period to the trade's already unhealthy fortunes. Making up for lost time, growers rebuilt the industry, planting some 80 million high-yielding vines such as Cinsaut by the early 1900s. A manageable flow swelled into a deluge; unsaleable wine was poured, literally, into local rivers.

This fuelled the formation in 1918 of the Co-operative Wine Growers' Association (KWV), which, over time, was granted statutory authority to enforce production quota limits to prevent unmanageable surpluses. It also fixed annual minimum wine PRICES. Its powers—weighted in favour of producers rather than consumers and often oblivious to market forces—were criticized by free-marketeers and some producers who, even if non-members, were subject by law to KWV regulations. The KWV argued it spared government the embarrassment of direct grower subsidies. Grower benefits, however, were indirect. Wine CO-OPERATIVES and farmers enjoyed Land Bank credit terms well below commercial interest rates, opportunities that were not available to non-whites until the end of the apartheid era. Such was KWV's political influence in pre-democratic South Africa that wine, alone among alcoholic drinks in South Africa, was exempt from excise duty for many years.

In the late 1990s, the newly structured KWV was relieved of all the statutory functions previously performed by the 4,600-strong growers' co-operative. Its conversion from co-operative to company was not without controversy. The process was challenged by the Minister of Agriculture, who cited the statutory void which would result from the process and a concern about the real ownership of some of the organization's assets as grounds for his intervention. Resolution was reached through an out-of-court settlement in which the KWV undertook

to pay a sum of 369 million rand (equal at the time to $77 million) into the South African Wine Industry Trust to redress inequalities of the past and to assist in the management and promotion of the industry. Financial mismanagement, together with a controversial decision to allow the residue to be used to fund the purchase of 25% of KWV's shares by a black consortium, led to its being wound up after less than 10 years.

The export boom which followed South Africa's first democratic elections in 1994 saw an end to wine SURPLUSES for the first time since the 1950s. By 1996, South Africa was importing GRAPE CONCENTRATE, BULK table wine, and wine for DISTILLATION. While large-scale producers and co-operatives crush a significant percentage of the 1.4 million-ton (2012) crop, most top-quality South African table wine, however, comes from private cellars and a few wholesaler-producers. The biggest wholesaler, DISTELL, still dominates the market in South Africa's vine-related alcohol products, as it has since 1979.

The organizations which are now independent but which were formerly part of KWV still fulfil functions such as research, vine PROPAGATION, advisory services, and administration of the WINE OF ORIGIN system. These include Vinpro, the service organization for the country's primary producers, SAWIS, which collects, processes, and disseminates industry information, and Winetech, which coordinates research, training, and technology transfer.

Burman, J., *Wine of Constantia* (Cape Town, 1979).

Fridjhon, M., and Murray, A., *Conspiracy of Giants* (Johannesburg, 1986).

James, T., *Wines of the New South Africa: Tradition and Revolution* (Berkeley, Calif., 2013).

Leipoldt, C. L., *Three Hundred Years of Cape Wines* (Cape Town, 1952).

Climate and geography

It has been suggested that if South Africa jutted another 200 km/124 miles south into the Atlantic, the cooler climate would slow grape ripening in line with European expectations. That said, the Benguela current from Antarctica makes the Cape cooler than its LATITUDE may suggest and many new vineyard areas south towards Agulhas as well as on the Cape west coast offer the prospect of a long, slow ripening season.

Warm summers from November to April are moderated by cold, wet, blustery winters, frequently with snowfalls on the higher mountains. Late frosts are rare; so are unseasonally heavy summer rains.

The winelands are widely dispersed throughout the Western and Northern Cape, some 700 km/420 miles from north to south and 500 km across, strung between the Atlantic and Indian oceans.

Climates and soils vary as dramatically as landscapes: mountains rear out of the sea,

S

unfolding into lush valleys, sere drylands, and a series of inland mountain chains. In the Stellenbosch district alone, just outside Cape Town, there are more than 50 soil types. On the hillsides, decomposing GRANITE prevails. Soils tend to be low in PH (4.5), with a predominance of clay (25% and more), but are well drained and moisture retentive. That portion of the harvest reserved mainly for brandy and fruit juice comes from hot, irrigated river valleys such as the Orange, Olifants, and Breede, where vineyards yield prodigiously. Around inland Robertson there are some CALCAREOUS lime-rich outcrops akin to the calcareous soil of Burgundy's CÔTE D'OR. But in the cooler coastal areas, the ancient soils depend on substantial LIME additions.

Annual rainfall rises from 250 mm/9.7 in in the near-desert Klein Karoo to 1,500 mm in the lee of the Worcester Mountains, about 100 km inland from Cape Town. Growers, particularly in the semi-desert areas who depend on IRRIGATION, argue they merely make up the shortfall to reach the 900 mm annual rainfall of a vineyard in the Bordeaux region of France.

Average summer daily temperatures often exceed 23 °C/ 73 °F during the February and March harvest months, and maximum summer temperatures can rise to nearly 40 °C. However, an increasing proportion of new, cooler vineyard sites are making this caricature of the Cape as a hot-climate viticultural region as questionable a generalization as the old belief that Cape vintage variations are insignificant.

A unique but mixed blessing is the frequent gale-force summer south easter, the 'Cape Doctor' WIND, that reduces humidity, mildew, and other FUNGAL DISEASES, but also sometimes batters vines.

Most wine regions would, according to the WINKLER scale, be classified Region III sites (as in Oakville, Napa Valley), IV (like Sydney and Florence), and some in V (Perth). But a number of areas experience cooler European (or Winkler II) conditions, especially in high-elevation or sea-cooled vineyards. New appellations such as Walker Bay (on sandy SHALE), Constantia (granite and SANDSTONE), Elgin (shale), and Cape Agulhas have stretched horizons and broadened the Cape's climatological repertoire.

Burger, J., and Deist, J., *Viticulture in South Africa* (Cape Town, 1981).

Winegrowing areas

South African wine country is divided into geographical units in which are regions, then districts, and then wards as in this table. For more explanation of their significance, see Wine of Origin below.

See separate articles on some of the most frequently encountered geographical names—COASTAL REGION, CONSTANTIA, ELGIN, ELIM, FRANSCHHOEK, GROENEKLOOF, KLEIN KAROO, OLIFANTS RIVER, PAARL, ROBERTSON, STELLENBOSCH, SWARTLAND,

Production Areas Defined in Terms of the Wine of Origin Scheme

Geographical Unit	Region	District	Ward
Western Cape	Breede River Valley	Breedekloof	Goudini
			Slanghoek
		Robertson	Agterkliphoogte
			Bonnievale
			Boesmansrivier
			Eilandia
			Hoopsrivier
			Klaasvoogds
			Le Chasseur
			McGregor
			Vinkrivier
		Worcester	Hex River Valley
			Nuy
			Scherpenheuvel
	Cape South Coast	Cape Agulhas	Elim
		Elgin	No ward
		Overberg	Elandskloof
			Greyton
			Klein River
			Theewater
		Plettenberg Bay	No ward
		Swellendam	Buffeljags
			Malgas
			Stormsvlei
		Walker Bay	Bot River
			Hemel-en-Aarde Ridge
			Hemel-en-Aarde Valley
			Sunday's Glen
			Upper Hemel-en-Aarde Valley
			Stanford Foothills
		No district	Herbertsdale
			Napier
			Stilbaai East
	Coastal Region	Cape Peninsula	Constantia
			Hout Bay
		Darling	Groenekloof
		Franschhoek/ Franschhoek Valley	No ward
		Paarl	Simonsberg-Paarl
			Voor Paardeberg
		Stellenbosch	Banghoek
			Bottelary
			Devon Valley
			Jonkershoek Valley
			Papegaaiberg
			Polkadraai Hills
			Simonsberg-Stellenbosch
		Swartland	Malmesbury
			Riebeekberg
			St Helena Bay
		Tulbagh	No ward
		Tygerberg	Durbanville
			Philadelphia
		Wellington	No ward
	Klein Karoo	Calitzdorp	No ward
		Langeberg-Garcia	No ward
		No district	Montagu
			Outeniqua

			Tradouw
			Tradouw Highlands
			Upper Langkloof
	Olifants River	Citrusdal Mountain	Piekenierskloof
		Citrusdal Valley	No ward
		Lutzville Valley	Koekenaap
		No district	Bamboes Bay
		No district	Spruitdrift
			Vredendal
	No region	Ceres Plateau	Ceres
		No district	Cederberg
			Lamberts Bay
			Prince Albert Valley
			Swartberg
Northern Cape	No region	Douglas	No ward
		Sutherland-Karoo	No ward
		No district	Central Orange River
			Hartswater
			Rietrivier FS
Eastern Cape	No region	No district	St Francis Bay
Kwazulu-Natal	No region	No district	No ward
Limpopo	No region	No district	No ward
	Boberg (region)—for use in respect of fortified wines from Paarl, Franschhoek, Wellington and Tulbagh		

Source: SAWIS (20/01/2014)

TULBAGH, WALKER BAY, WELLINGTON, WESTERN CAPE, and WORCESTER—although new areas are emerging all the time.

Viticulture

The stark contrast between the traditional and the progressive in South African viticulture, often visible on adjoining farms, reflects the disparate objectives of growers. The bulk grape-farmer delivering to one of the less progressive co-operatives strives for quantity; the grower bottling his own crop knows quantity can be the enemy of quality. From the second half of the 20th century, TRELLISING, low VINE DENSITY, and chemical pest and weed control became common features of the South African viticultural landscape. However, in this century closer planting, more restrained ORGANIC and biological pest controls, careful CLONAL SELECTION, painstaking SOIL PREPARATION that can involve additions of over 20 tons of LIME per hectare to achieve higher PH, and PRUNING for lower yields have become the norm on many properties.

Average planting densities are around 3,300 vines per ha (1,300 per acre). Yields in cooler, coastal climates are appreciably lower than the national average: about 49 or 56 hl/ha (2.8 or 3.2 tons/acre) for Cabernet Sauvignon and Chardonnay are considered consistent with quality in Cape conditions. Yields from a still significant number of virus-infected vineyards can drop to below 28 hl/ha (1.6 tons/acre).

Most vineyards are IRRIGATED in summer, with DRIP IRRIGATION having replaced overhead sprays or fixed sprinkler systems on the better estates.

The most common TRELLISING SYSTEM is a simple vertical 'hedge row' developed from a split vine cordon, supported by a wire raised about 750 mm/2.4 ft for ease of pruning. The summer foliage is trained upright in a canopy held by one or more wires above the cordon. Short-SPUR PRUNING is commonly practised (eight to ten spurs, four to five on each cordon, pruned back to two or three buds each).

Most vine diseases and pests found their way from the northern hemisphere long ago. Chemical pesticides are widely used, especially in the higher-yielding vineyards, although farmers are now encouraged by way of the INTEGRATED PRODUCTION OF WINE (IPW) programme to minimize the use of insecticides and to use a more ORGANIC approach. Baboons are also a pest in several areas.

POWDERY MILDEW, locally called 'white rust', is the most serious common disease. DOWNY MILDEW poses a seasonal threat. Both are containable by systemic fungicides. BOTRYTIS is not a serious problem most years, and is welcomed by growers specializing in dessert wines.

Cape vineyards were decimated by PHYLLOXERA from 1886 and virtually all vines are grafted onto resistant American ROOTSTOCKS, the most common being Richter 99, 110, and 101–14.

Virus-infected vines are widespread, shortening the productive lifespans of vineyards. Affected vines succumb to LEAFROLL, CORKY BARK, and FANLEAF, inhibiting PHOTOSYNTHESIS and ripening, diminishing yields but not improving grape quality.

From the mid 1980s, HEAT-TREATED, virustested plant material was more freely available, along with a greater selection of imported CLONES

of classic varieties. Healthier, earlier-ripening vineyards are the result. However, developing a significant pattern of regional/varietal characteristics is Cape viticulture's current challenge.

Burger, J., and Deist, J., *Viticulture in South Africa* (Cape Town, 1981).

Winemaking

Winemaking in South Africa remains in a state of flux and experimentation, with younger winemakers who travel extensively, many working vintages in the northern hemisphere, challenging the orthodoxies of earlier generations and transforming the face and taste of the Cape's best wines. While many of the more commercial wines reflect an environment where irrigation, higher yields, a warm climate, and low pH soils are the dominant factors, an increasing number of the better producers are offering wines which reflect considered viticultural practices, thoughtful vinifications, and ÉLEVAGE which does not depend on new OAK to achieve results.

Vine varieties

In South Africa, a vine variety is usually known as a cultivar, and South Africa is a cultivar-conscious wine country. Regional wine characteristics are still not sufficiently defined to challenge grape variety as the determining factor for quality, style, and even labelling and marketing of a wine, although increased VINE AGE and a greater focus on site are beginning to change this. While white varieties used to dominate South African vineyards, the post-1994 transformation of the wine industry has seen premium red varieties reach virtual parity. Chenin Blanc was for long the most planted variety in South Africa, and still comprises 18% of the national vineyard. From the 1980s, Sauvignon Blanc and Chardonnay were energetically planted and by 2012 comprised 9.5% and 7.9% of all plantings respectively. Other major white wine grapes include, in decreasing quantity: Colombar(d), Muscat of Alexandria, Sémillon, and Viognier.

Cabernet Sauvignon is South Africa's most planted red INTERNATIONAL VARIETY, comprising just under 12% of the nation's vineyard. Syrah (often called Shiraz in South Africa) has come to rival Cabernet Sauvignon, and in 2012 accounted for more than 10% of all plantings. Merlot, often blended but popular enough in its own right, occupies roughly half the area dedicated to Cabernet. Pinot Noir has improved dramatically as new CLONES have been planted and cooler regions established. PINOTAGE, the Cape's own cross of Pinot Noir and Cinsaut, remains relatively stable at just less than 7%. For most of the first half of the last century, high-yielding Cinsaut was the most widely planted red wine grape, but it has declined dramatically in importance and now represents less than 2% of all vineyards. There are yet smaller plantings of Grenache, Mourvèdre, Carignan, Zinfandel, Ruby Cabernet, Cabernet Franc, and some port varieties—most commonly TINTA BARROCA, often made

S

into a dry red. Italian varieties, notably Nebbiolo and Sangiovese, are beginning to attract attention.

Orffer, C. J., *Wine Grape Cultivars in South Africa* (Cape Town, 1979).

Wine of Origin and labelling

Wine of Origin (WO) legislation introduced in 1973, and variously updated since then, ended decades of a labelling free-for-all in which confused South African wine nomenclature and unverified vintage and grape variety claims baffled the consumer. The following types of wine production zones are now classified: geographical unit (e.g. Western Cape), region (e.g. Coastal), which may represent a merging of several districts, district (e.g. Stellenbosch), and ward (e.g. Bottelary). While the larger units are broadly geographical and/or political, a ward is based on shared soils, climate, etc. (i.e. aspects of TERROIR). 'Estates' are no longer official places of origin, but registered 'estate wines' must be grown, made, and bottled on a single property. Single vineyards may be indicated as such on labels provided they are not larger than 6 ha/15 acres, are planted to a single variety, and are registered in accordance with the legal provisions.

A wine may also be 'certified' for vintage provided at least 85% comes from one harvest. For a wine to be labelled as a single VARIETAL, it must contain at least 85% of the variety stated. Varieties in a blend may be indicated on the label providing they are stated in descending percentages and only if they are vinified separately.

A certified wine is identified by a seal which contains a tracking number enabling the authorities to trace every component batch or variety (in the case of a blend) back to the vineyard and the date of harvest. Vineyards are subject to inspection and wines may be monitored in the cellars. Certification follows an official analysis, tasting, and final label approval. Participation is voluntary and around 60% of the country's wine production is now certified. The process is under the supervision of the government-appointed Wine & Spirit Board. Non-certified wine is liable to spot-check analysis for health requirements.

South Africa meets requirements on prohibition of ADDITIVES, and for LABELLING, which must state the ALCOHOLIC STRENGTH (from 1992) to within half a per cent. TRADITIONAL METHOD Cape sparkling wine is labelled Méthode Cap Classique even locally. FLOR-yeast FORTIFIED WINES matured in a SOLERA system are in decline, and may no longer be sold as sherry. But wines made in the image of PORT, generally using very similar varieties and the same techniques as in port country, have been very successful.

Although the WO regulations borrow from France and Germany, there are no rulings on crop YIELDS, FERTILIZER quantities, or IRRIGATION levels. CHAPTALIZATION and all other forms of ENRICHMENT are banned, although grape juice concentrate may be added as a sweetener to most wines (see SWEET RESERVE). ACIDIFICATION is permitted. Wines sold as 'dry' on the domestic market may not have a RESIDUAL SUGAR content exceeding 5 g/l (see www.sawis.co.za).

J.P. & M.F.

James, T., *Wines of the New South Africa: Tradition and Revolution* (Berkeley, Calif., 2013).

Platter, J., *Platter's South African Wine Guide* (Stellenbosch, annually).

www.wosa.co.za

South America, the world's second most important wine-producing continent, after Europe, with ARGENTINA and CHILE now rivalling each other as most productive, followed by BRAZIL. Other, relatively minor, wine producers are, in descending order of importance, URUGUAY, PERU, BOLIVIA, and PARAGUAY, although see also COLOMBIA, ECUADOR, and VENEZUELA. The North American wine producer MEXICO produces much more wine than Uruguay, for example. Spain and, in some parts, Portugal were important influences in the 16th and 17th centuries, although more recently France, Italy, and the United States have helped to shape South America's wine industries. Wine quality has improved extremely rapidly in those countries—Chile, Argentina, and to a lesser extent Brazil and Uruguay—which have (relatively recently) turned their attention to exporting.

History

The late-15th-century European voyages of discovery, notably to the Americas, were followed by migrations of European settlers there, associated with substantial movement of animals and plants between the two continents. Although indigenous varieties of vine grew in Central America (see VITIS), there is no evidence that the Aztecs made wine from them, and it was thus with the arrival of the Spanish conquistadores in the 16th century that vine cultivation and winemaking were first introduced to the region. Mexico was the first part of the continent to witness the introduction of European VINIFERA vines, and as early as 1522 Cortés is recorded as having sent for vine cuttings from Spain. Moreover, by 1524 the planting of vines was a condition of *repartimiento* grants, through which the Spaniards were granted land and labour on the foundation of Mexico City. From Mexico, the spread of viticulture followed swiftly on the heels of Spanish conquests.

Vines were planted in Peru soon after Pizarro's defeat of the Incas between 1531 and 1534, and within 20 years Spanish commentators described vineyards producing a substantial quantity of grapes. Some of the earliest Peruvian vines appear to have been introduced from the CANARY ISLANDS, whereas others seem to have been derived from the seeds of dried grapes brought from Spain. From Peru, viticulture and winemaking then spread south to Chile and Argentina, where vines were cultivated as early as the mid 1550s, although there were even earlier experimental plantings on Argentina's coast. See also MONKS AND MONASTERIES.

The traditional explanation for the rapidity of this spread was that the Spanish conquerors required a ready supply of wine for the EUCHARIST, and that monks therefore played a central role in establishing vineyards. There is, however, little evidence to support this view, and many of the early vineyards and attempts to produce wine were on secular estates. Economic factors, such as the cost of importing wine and the difficulties of transporting it overland, meant that the early Spanish conquerors had a very real interest in establishing vineyards if they wished to continue to consume the main alcoholic beverage that they had known in Iberia. In particular, the long sea voyage across the Atlantic, followed by an overland haul across Panama, and then a further voyage down the Pacific coast, meant that most wine reaching Peru and Chile from the Iberian peninsula was likely to have been of poor quality.

By the end of the 16th century, Spanish restrictions on wine production in 'New Spain', designed to protect the metropolitan wine producers and merchants in Iberia, served to limit further secular development of viticulture in Mexico, but they also appear to have provided an incentive to Peruvian producers, who rapidly became the dominant wine suppliers to the region as a whole. Subsequently, in the 17th century, Jesuit MISSIONS along the coastal valleys of Peru became the most important centres of viticulture in the region.   P.T.H.U.

Blij, H. de, *Wine Regions of the Southern Hemisphere* (Totowa, NJ, 1985).

Dickenson, J., and Unwin, T., *Viticulture in Colonial Latin America: Essays on Alcohol, the Vine and Wine in Spanish America and Brazil* (Liverpool, 1992).

Hyams, E., *Dionysus: A Social History of the Wine Vine* (London, 1965).

South Australia, *the* wine state in AUSTRALIA, responsible for 45 to 50% of the annual CRUSH. This share may have fallen from the 75% of the 1940s and 1950s, but the state still dominates the country's wine output. Vine-growing and winemaking are major contributors to South Australia's gross domestic production, yet they occupy only a small percentage of the state's vast land mass. Vine-growing is concentrated in the south eastern corner, much of it within an hour's drive of the capital Adelaide. The two outposts are the Riverland sprawling along the Murray river (the Lower Murray Zone); and Coonawarra and nearby Padthaway 325 km/200 miles south east of Adelaide, not far from the border with VICTORIA (the Limestone Coast Zone).

The BAROSSA VALLEY, an hour north of Adelaide, is Australia's best-known wine region with 140 producers. To this day, the Germanic influence of its 19th-century Silesian immigrants is everywhere to be seen—in the town names, the Lutheran churches, the stone buildings, and in the names of the leading families. The once-dominant Riesling has bowed to the inevitable as Chardonnay (and also Semillon) has swept past it, although part of the change has come about as a consequence of Riesling's move to the Eden Valley, Clare Valley, and (less importantly in absolute terms), the Adelaide Hills.

This shift reflects two things: first, the warm climate of the valley floor, more suited to red wine production; second, a fundamental reappraisal of the function of the Barossa Valley proper. For decades vine plantings shrank while production soared, not because of increased yields, but because the Barossa Valley wineries process a major part of the grapes grown in the Riverland, Coonawarra, Padthaway, McLaren Vale, and Langhorne Creek.

Most of Australia's largest companies are based here. The presence of PENFOLDS, and the creation of its masterwork Grange, embody the glory of the Barossa Valley: substantial plantings of Shiraz dating as far back as 1860, dry farmed (no IRRIGATION) and BUSH trained, often yielding as little as 16 hl/ha (1 tonne/acre) of inky, dark purple essence.

CLARE VALLEY, just to the north west of the Barossa Valley, but joined with the Adelaide Hills in the Mount Lofty Ranges Zone, is one of the unspoilt jewels of South Australia. The narrow, twisting folds of the hills provide an attractive intimacy. Like the Barossa Valley, it is steeped in history, with splendid stone buildings and wineries. Its strongly CONTINENTAL climate, with warm days but cool to cold nights in summer, produces outstanding Riesling, a fragrant yet steely wine which ages superbly, taking on the aroma of lightly browned toast with a twist of lime as it ages. Most of the 43 wineries are small; almost all produce Riesling, Shiraz, and Cabernet Sauvignon, the red wines being intensely coloured, deeply flavoured, and long lived, often with a patina of EUCALYPT mint. MALBEC also flourishes here, used as a blend component with Cabernet Sauvignon (sometimes with a dash of Shiraz thrown in for good measure).

EDEN VALLEY, in spite of its name, is a range of hills adjacent to the Barossa Valley proper, approximately 200 m/656 ft higher than the Barossa floor at 400–450 m and commensurately cooler. The soils are also different: poor, quartz-based podsols. The history is as old as the Barossa floor, as Joseph Gilbert planted the original Pewsey Vale in 1947. The cooler climate has led to a focus on white varieties, especially lime-juicy and long-lived Riesling, which

is outstanding here, but reds can also excel—witness Henschke Hill of Grace and Mount Edelstone Shirazes. Shiraz is more spicy and elegant than on the Barossa floor with finer tannins and generally lower alcohol.

ADELAIDE HILLS has rapidly become one of South Australia's most important fine-wine regions. Grapes have been grown there as long as anywhere in the state but plantings took off in the 1980s when Petaluma and others made major commitments, sniffing the wind, and realizing that lighter table and sparkling wines were the future. Plantings were further encouraged in the 1990s by its proximity to Adelaide (30 minutes by car) and by the second decade of this century there was an oversupply of grapes which depressed prices and profitability. Major players include Henschke, The Lane, Nepenthe, and Shaw + Smith. Contrary to the pioneers' plans, Sauvignon Blanc and Shiraz are the most notable varieties, together with the more-predictably successful Chardonnay.

MCLAREN VALE, 45 minutes due south of Adelaide, is often called the home of the small winery. These wineries represent a mixture of the old and the new, thus reflecting the dynamics which have operated here no less than in the Barossa Valley. At the northern end, urban sprawl has swallowed up many once-substantial vineyards, and encircles the few remaining plantings at Reynella. However, with one important qualification, the southern end of the fashionably cool and increasingly important Adelaide Hills to the east, the open plains of McLaren Vale, and the hills of the Fleurieu Peninsula offer abundant suitable land for future plantings. The qualification is the availability of increasingly scarce WATER, and ever-more stringent controls on the use of surface water (by dams), artesian water (by bores), and river water.

MCLAREN VALE is a strongly maritime-influenced region, with considerable variation in MESOCLIMATE. Once famous for its supposedly iron-rich red wines exported to England under the Emu and Glenloth labels and prescribed by (surely enlightened) physicians around the turn of the century as tonics, the emphasis in the 1970s and 1980s turned to its melon-and tropical fruit-tinged Chardonnay, pungent gooseberry Sauvignon Blanc, and full-flavoured Semillon. But with the resurgence of the red wine market, attention has once again focused on its generous, gutsy red wines. Here the long-forgotten virtues of its DRYLAND Grenache have been rediscovered; whether used to make a single varietal red wine, or blended with Shiraz, many consider it Australia's best example of Rhône-style red. The high quality of the grapes, and hence the wines, is better understood by the industry than by the public, and (even more with neighbour LANGHORNE CREEK) much of the

production ends up in multi-regional blended wines, the labels of which may or may not show the composition of that blend. Langhorne Creek is the principal source of Jacob's Creek and these two regions between them account for 20% of the state's output.

The LIMESTONE COAST ZONE in the far south east of the state includes the regions of growing importance: Mount Benson, Robe, Wrattonbully, Coonawarra, and Padthaway. COONAWARRA was traditionally recognized as producing Australia's finest Cabernet Sauvignon while PADTHAWAY grows very serviceable, mid-priced Chardonnay, Sauvignon Blanc, and Shiraz. Both are cool regions (Coonawarra is the cooler of the two) with considerable LIMESTONE (TERRA ROSSA in Coonawarra), and an extensive underground watertable. While vines were first planted in Coonawarra in 1890 (by John Riddoch), for all practical purposes both regions date from the early 1960s. This explains why both areas are exclusively planted to premium grape varieties, and why the major wine companies are the dominant landholders (there are six wineries in Padthaway, more than 40 in Coonawarra). After two decades of darkness in the 1980s and 1990s, when the focus was on the cost of growing grapes and not on maximizing their quality, there has been a major turnaround in the approach of the major companies. Cabernet Sauvignon, the flagbearer, accounts for 60% of the 5,700 ha under vine; white grapes just 10%.

WRATTONBULLY had a face lift in 2004 with the formation of the Tapanappa joint venture between Brian Croser, Jean-Michel Cazes (of Ch Lynch Bages in Pauillac), and the parent company of Champagne Bollinger (now an all-Australian enterprise). It purchased the original Koppamurra Vineyard, from which it produces estate-based wines, setting a formula for future ventures elsewhere.

MOUNT BENSON is cooler, with sand and limestone interspersed, and seems destined to produce wines of greater elegance but less weight and structure.

The FLEURIEU ZONE, as well as being home to McLaren Vale and Langhorne Creek, takes in the exotic KANGAROO ISLAND, plus CURRENCY CREEK, and SOUTHERN FLEURIEU. All are highly MARITIME, and hence cooler than McLaren Vale. Kangaroo Island is one of the (largely) undiscovered nature paradises of Australia, viticulture as yet of small compass. Southern Fleurieu is also largely unspoilt and of considerable beauty.

Finally, there is the RIVERLAND, the South Australian portion stretching along the mighty Murray River from Waikerie to Renmark, producing 59% of South Australia's total crush and 27% of the nation's. The continuing increase in premium grape plantings, and the decline in lesser or multipurpose varieties, is nowhere more evident than in the fact that Chardonnay,

Shiraz, Cabernet Sauvignon, and Merlot accounted for 71% of total Riverland plantings by 2012, the once-dominant Muscat Gordo Blanco and Sultana for well under 10%.

J.H. & H.H.

www.winesa.asn.au

South Burnett, young, relatively hilly Australian wine region in south east Queensland. It has a subtropical climate, with summer rainfall a real problem; coupled with generally fertile red soils. Ripening tannins can be challenging, but in the right vintages there have been impressive results with Semillon, Chardonnay, Shiraz, and Cabernet Sauvignon. It is also a very pretty region, well worth the two and a half hours' drive from Brisbane.

South Coast, extensive AVA defining vineyards close to the CALIFORNIA coast from south of Los Angeles to the Mexican border. TEMECULA in Riverside county within it has the only substantial vineyards within the region and is resurgent. San Diego county's San Pasqual and Ramona Valleys also fall within it.   L.M.

South Coast Zone of NEW SOUTH WALES stretches more than 400 km from north of Sydney, Australia, to the Victorian border in the south, but extends inland to take in Sydney itself, the Blue mountains, and the Southern Highlands and Shoalhaven Coast regions.

South Eastern Australia, official 'super zone' which takes in all relevant wine regions in QUEENSLAND, NEW SOUTH WALES, VICTORIA, and SOUTH AUSTRALIA, used for multi-region, inexpensive blended wines constituting a significant proportion of all wine exported from Australia.

Southern Fleurieu, strongly maritime wine region in SOUTH AUSTRALIA, one of the most westerly regions in the state. ELEVATION is the key moderator of climate.

Southern Flinders Ranges, newest and most northerly wine region of SOUTH AUSTRALIA.

Southern Highlands, Australian wine region high on the Great Dividing range south west of Sydney. A somewhat schizophrenic climate, cold in winter and humid in late summer with rainfall then a problem. A popular weekend retreat for wealthy Sydney residents is a partial explanation for its development. It is growing gradually, with 18 producers, mostly between 500 and 700 m (1,640–2,300 ft) elevation.

Southern Wine & Spirits is the biggest wine company you've never heard of. The behemoth American distributor stands between wineries and retailers, serving as a licensed wholesaler in 35 US states. *Forbes* estimated the company was the 29th largest private

company in the US with revenues of $10.5 billion in 2013.

The company was founded in 1968 when Walter Jahn, a drinks executive from New York, bought out a local wine and spirits distributor in Miami. The original financing came from a bank with ties to organized crime, which competitors but not Southern frequently mention. The company grew first in Florida and then nationally, with its sales force championing the emergent interest in wine.

While they have some enormous facilities, such as a streamlined 40,000 sq m (425,000 sq ft) warehouse in Nevada, the company has also been known to use sharp elbows in its rise to become the country's largest wine and spirits wholesaler. As with other large distributors, it is a donor to politicians of all stripes and at all levels of politics. The policy goals include maintaining the legally mandated middle-tier in the controversial THREE-TIER SYSTEM or otherwise tilting the playing field in their direction.   T.C.

Emshwiller, J., and Freedman, A., 'Early relationships help shape Southern Wine & Spirits', *Wall Street Journal*, 4 October 1999.

http://online.wsj.com/news/articles/SB938998156171122649

Blain, G., 'Booze plan may cost ya', *New York Daily News*, 4 February 2014.

South West Australia Zone comprises the Blackwood Valley, Geographe, Great Southern, and Margaret River wine regions, not to be confused with the South East Australia Super Zone.

South West France, recognized region within FRANCE which incorporates all of the wine districts in the south western quarter of the country with the exception of BORDEAUX and Cognac. This means in effect all of the upriver wines once regarded as serious commercial rivals by the Bordelais (most notably Bergerac, Monbazillac, Côtes de Duras, Cahors, Buzet, Fronton, and Gaillac travelling away from and roughly clockwise round Bordeaux), together with those made in GASCONY and BASQUE country (St-Mont, Madiran, Pacherenc du Vic-Bilh, Jurançon, Béarn, and Irouléguy). Few generalizations can be made about such an extensive area, except that the climate is heavily influenced by the Atlantic.

The vine was cultivated in most of these districts in the Roman era (see FRANCE and GAUL) but winemaking was developed only under the medieval influence of MONKS AND MONASTERIES. During the Crusades some of these areas came under direct English protection.

The history of the first group of wines described above has been heavily influenced, nay hampered, by the commercial muscle of protectionist Bordeaux. The fact that these wines were

made up river of but outside Bordeaux in the 'high country', or HAUT PAYS, meant that they were penalized at their exit port, and the HUNDRED YEARS WAR was to have an everlasting effect on their trading history, opening the door for the DUTCH WINE TRADE to take the place of once-powerful ENGLAND. The commercial progress of wines from the second group was long hindered by the difficulty of navigating the Adour river down to the port of Bayonne, and by competition with other crops.

The grape varieties grown in the first group of wine districts is generally very similar to the ENCÉPAGEMENT of Bordeaux, while the southern districts can boast one of the most exciting collections of INDIGENOUS VARIETIES in Europe, including the likes of ABOURIOU, ARRUFIAC, BAROQUE, COURBU, DURAS, FER (Servadou), GROS MANSENG, LEN DE L'EL, MAUZAC, NÉGRETTE, PETIT COURBU, PETIT MANSENG, and TANNAT. Culturally, Gascony is one of the proudest and greediest regions of France; the region needs wines to drink with *foie gras*, duck, and goose.

For more details, see the individual entries for all the AOC wines BÉARN, BERGERAC, BRULHOIS, BUZET, CAHORS, Côtes de MILLAU, Côtes de DURAS, Côtes du MARMANDAIS, Coteaux du QUERCY, ENTRAYGUES-LE FEL, ESTAING, FRONTON, GAILLAC, IROULÉGUY, JURANÇON, MADIRAN, MARCILLAC, MONBAZILLAC, MONTRAVEL, PACHERENC DU VIC-BILH, PÉCHARMANT, ROSETTE, ST-SARDOS, ST-MONT, SAUSSIGNAC, and TURSAN.

www.southwestfrancewines.com

soutirage, French term for RACKING, or moving clear wine off its sediment and into a clean container. It can also be used for the wine serving process of DECANTING.

Soviet sparkling wine is a specific term which, in tune with EU law, replaced the term Soviet champagne, or *champanskoe*, in the early 1990s. Although BOTTLE-fermented sparkling wines have been made in what has variously been called Russia, the Soviet Union, the CIS, and the ex-Soviet republics since the 18th century, consumer demand for sparkling wine was most notably demonstrated at the end of the 19th-century, when the imperial court of Tsar Nicholas II regularly imported 800,000 bottles of, usually sweet, CHAMPAGNE a year. (The late-19th-century Champenois defined champagne sweetened to satisfy the *goût russe* as one with 273 to 330 g/l of RESIDUAL SUGAR, as opposed to the *goût anglais* of 22 to 66 g/l for the English.)

High import taxes led to the development of a domestic industry initially constructed on base wines imported from France in barrel, made sparkling according to champagne production techniques. This led to the development of vigorous sparkling wine industries based on grapes grown in the CRIMEA and around Odessa in UKRAINE, where Henri ROEDERER of Rheims established a Franco-Russian sparkling winery in 1896. Inexpensive sparkling wine is still very popular in RUSSIA.

Soviet Union, the Union of Soviet Socialist Republics, which, following the fall of communism, fragmented into its constituent republics. See, in very approximate declining order of wine production (not the same as order by vineyard area), RUSSIA (thanks to considerable BULK imports), MOLDOVA, UKRAINE, CRIMEA, GEORGIA, UZBEKISTAN, KAZAKHSTAN, TURKMENISTAN, AZERBAIJAN, ARMENIA, KYRGYZSTAN, and TAJIKISTAN. See also BALTIC STATES.

spacing of vines. See VINE DENSITY.

Spain, country in the grip of vinous revolution with the most land under vine in the world (954,000 ha/2,289,600 acres in 2012, after extensive EU-subsidized GRUBBING UP), of which 34% was (mainly drip) irrigated and yet most years only the world's third most important producer of wine. The dramatic 21st-century increase in irrigated surface and a more controversial insistence on high-yielding CLONES have abundantly offset a 30% reduction in vineyard surface over the past quarter-century, with current yields averaging about 43 hl/ha (3.0 tons/acre)—up from 30 hl/ha in 2005. The introduction of IRRIGATION increased Spain's annual average wine production from 35 million hl/924 million gal in the early 1990s to an average of more than 40 million hl after 2010.

Spain occupies most of the Iberian peninsula and is the third largest country in Europe, extending from the Pyrenees that form the frontier with France in the north to the strait of Gibraltar just 15 km/9 miles from Africa to the south. Spain is a diverse country with distinct regional and cultural differences. The principal language spoken throughout Spain is Castilian, although Galician is dominant in GALICIA, Catalan and Spanish are roughly tied in CATALUÑA, and Basque remains a minority language in the BASQUE region.

The country's regional diversity is reflected in her wines, which range from light, dry whites in the cool Atlantic region of Galicia to heavy, alcoholic reds in the Levante and the Mediterranean south. ANDALUCÍA in the south west is known for the production of fortified and dessert wines, the most famous of which is SHERRY.

Spain is a significant beneficiary of recent improvements in winemaking TECHNOLOGY. Modern production methods were slow to reach Spain but, when they did, typically in the early 1990s, they did so with a vengeance, with modernization sweeping one region after the other, including some (but not all) of the less glamorous ones. A programme of investment which began a decade earlier was further helped by Spain's accession to

the EU in 1986. In 1996, vineyard IRRIGATION was legalized throughout the country, radically changing prospects for the drought-stricken central and south-eastern areas.

History to Columbus

Although the wine-growing PHOENICIANS founded Cádiz c.1100 BC on the coast of southern Spain, they did not introduce viticulture to the Iberian peninsula, for the vine had been cultivated in Spain since between 4000 and 3000 BC. Grapes, found in Spain from the close of the Tertiary era onwards, pre-date *Homo sapiens* by millions of years.

Cádiz, gateway to the Atlantic, was an important Phoenician trading post. After the Phoenicians came the Carthaginians, themselves inhabitants of a city—CARTHAGE—founded by Phoenicians. The Carthaginians grew wine in Spain; more importantly, they were a threat to the emerging republic of Ancient ROME.

The 2nd century BC was a time of much unrest under Roman rule in Spain, and no systematic colonization was attempted until Rome finally 'pacified' the whole of the peninsula under Augustus. Political stability furthered trade: as the evidence from AMPHORAE shows, a great deal of wine from Baetica (which approximated to ANDALUCÍA) and Tarraconensis (TARRAGONA) was sold in Rome, and Spanish exports far exceeded exports of Italian wine to Aquitaine and south eastern GAUL via Bordeaux. Spanish wine reached the Loire valley, Brittany, Normandy, and England, and it was given to the troops guarding the Roman frontier with Germany. Literary evidence confirms the discoveries of archaeology. Strabo says in his *Geography* (completed AD 9) that, since the fall of Carthage, Baetica has been famous for the beauty of its many vineyards. COLUMELLA, a native of Cádiz in Baetica, sees the wine imports from Baetica and Gaul as symptomatic of the decline of Roman agriculture (1, *Praefatio*. 20).

Most of the Spanish wines, and particularly that of Saguntum, sold in Rome appear to have been PLONK: perfect for getting the porter of one's mistress drunk on, is Ovid's advice (*Ars amatoria* 3. 645–6). Some wines earn praise, however: PLINY says that Tarraconensis is good (*Natural History* 14. 71) and so repeatedly does MARTIAL, himself a native of Spain.

Spain was no mere outpost of empire. It was the birthplace of other Roman authors besides Martial and Columella: Seneca, Lucan, and Quintilian. The emperors Hadrian and Marcus Aurelius came from Spanish families. When the Roman empire disintegrated, Spain was invaded by barbarians, first by the Suevi and then by the Visigoths. We do not know what happened to viticulture and the wine trade: presumably it continued.

The overthrow of the Visigoths by the Moors in 711 did not mean the end of viticulture, for

the ISLAMIC conquerors were enlightened rulers, who did not impose their own way of life on their subjects. Better still, many of them liked wine themselves. The Moorish position with regard to wine was ambiguous. Although the Prophet forbade the use of wine, the emirs and caliphs of Spain grew wine; although its sale was illegal, it was subject to excise (see TAXATION). By the time ENGLAND was importing considerable quantities of wine from Spain, the mid 13th century, the Christians had largely succeeded in their reconquest.

Around 1250, wine was regularly shipped from Bilbao to the English ports of Bristol, Southampton, and London. The quality of the wines varied. The best wines were very good indeed: when Edward III fixed maximum prices for wines in 1364, a cask of the best Spanish wine was to cost as much as a cask of the best GASCON, which fetched more than wine from LA ROCHELLE. Spanish wines were popular because being from a hot climate they were high in alcohol and therefore kept better than French or German wines. But some of these wines were just high in alcohol, and that was their only merit. Hence they were often used to ADULTERATE more expensive and weaker wines. Laws forbidding this practice were widely disregarded.

See also SACK, and ARNALDUS DE VILLANOVA and EIXIMENIS, two important medieval commentators on aspects of wine who were Catalan by birth.   H.M.W.

Blazquez, J. M., 'La economía de la Hispania Romana', in A. Montenegro et al. (eds), *Historia de España: España romana* (Madrid, 1982).

Curchin, L. A., *Roman Spain* (London, 1991).

Jeffs, J., *Sherry* (4th edn, London, 1992).

Keay, S. J., *Roman Spain* (London, 1988).

Tchernia, A., *Les Vins de l'Italie romaine* (Paris, 1986).

History from Columbus

Spain emerged as a united, Christian country under a single crown in January 1492 following the final defeat of the Moors at Granada. Christopher Columbus discovered the West Indies in October of the same year, opening up a whole NEW WORLD to Spanish trade.

The wine regions around Cádiz and MÁLAGA, both important Spanish ports, were the first to attract the attention of foreign traders, and SHERRY, often called SACK, became a popular drink at the English court. Foreign traders in the sherry town of SANLÚCAR DE BARRAMEDA were granted special privileges by the duke of Medina Sidonia in 1517 and an English church was built to encourage more merchants. But relations between England and Spain began to deteriorate in the 1520s and after Henry VIII's divorce from Catherine of Aragón in 1533 brought English merchants into direct conflict with the Spanish. In the latter part of the century, war erupted between the two countries. English

S

settlers fled fearing the Spanish Inquisition and trade between the two nations diminished.

The English defeat of the Armada in 1588 destroyed Spain as a seafaring power and, on the death of Philip II ten years later, the country was left with a crippling debt despite its immense colonial wealth. Trade in wine soon resumed and, after the death of Elizabeth I, sack became a favoured drink in the court of James I. But 17th-century trade was sporadic and trade in Spanish wines was blighted by excessive English import duties. Not surprisingly, the Spanish fostered markets elsewhere in Europe and the New World.

Spanish wine has historically depended on exports to a larger extent than the wines from other traditional producing nations in Europe (and this continues to be the case today). During the 17th and 18th centuries, exports to Spain's American colonies surpassed in volume and value those to Britain and northern Europe. Vines had been planted all over the

Americas since the very first days of Spanish colonization, and wine was made in MEXICO from the early days of the 16th century. But successive monarchs, particularly Philip III, tried to stop the development of a local industry, to protect the flourishing export trade from the mainland. Between 1605 and 1620 he wrote edicts curtailing the spread of American vineyards. These were followed very unevenly—the local administration practically ignored them in Chile, but in Argentina they served to virtually quell all attempts at developing a national wine industry until independence came in the early 19th century. For more details, see SOUTH AMERICA.

See SHERRY for details of 18th- and 19th-century trade in that important SPANISH WINE.

At the same time, Málaga also enjoyed a spectacular increase in popularity, producing an estimated 35,000 BUTTS of wine in 1829, equivalent to 175,000 hl. 'Mountain', as the wine was popularly known in its 19th-century

heyday, sat alongside PORT, MADEIRA, and sherry as one of the world's great FORTIFIED WINES.

By all accounts there was little wine of exportable quality from the rest of Spain. Even RIOJA, already Spain's leading table wine at the turn of the 19th century, found few markets other than neighbouring Basque country and South America. The chronicler Richard Ford writing in 1846 notes that Spanish 'wine continues to be made in an unscientific and careless manner'. Cyrus REDDING writing in the 1851 edition of the *History and Description of Modern Wines* observes 'the rude treatment of the grape' in Spain. It seems that outside Jerez and Málaga little had changed since Roman times. In central and southern Spain, wines continued to be made in crude earthenware TINAJAS, while to the north wooden casks were used. Wine was frequently stored in *cueros*, pigskins lined with pitch or resin which tainted the wine. Winemaking progressed slowly in Spain.

From the middle of the 19th century, wholesale change was forced on the Spanish wine industry, first by POWDERY MILDEW, which was found in Cataluña in the 1850s, and then much later by PHYLLOXERA. This devastating aphid was to arrive in Málaga in 1878, where it destroyed the livelihoods of thousands of vine-growers, many of whom left to establish a new life in South America, and Málaga's wine industry never fully recovered. But phylloxera spread relatively late and slowly through Spain, partly because of the long distances between the various Spanish wine regions, and in the 1860s the French, who had also suffered powdery mildew (oidium) for ten years, had crossed the Pyrenees to compensate for the shortfall in French wine. Rioja and NAVARRA, the closest wine regions to BORDEAUX, benefited most from France's misfortune, and the resulting influx of French influence and expertise.

The BARRICA (225-l/59-gal oak cask) which is now used throughout Spain was introduced from Bordeaux and winemaking was refined along the Bordelais lines (although American OAK continued to be preferred thanks to Spain's flourishing transatlantic trade in the late 18th century, to the hardness of American oak—much appreciated in Jerez—and to its relatively low cost). Rioja BODEGAS belonging to Marqués de Murrieta, Marqués de Riscal, López de Heredia, and CVNE date back to this period when up to 500,000 hl of wine a month were shipped across the Pyrenees to France.

Phylloxera took hold in Jerez in 1894 and reached Rioja in 1901, by which time the epidemic had been controlled by grafting European vines on to resistant American ROOTSTOCKS. Vineyards were replanted throughout the country but many traditional, INDIGENOUS VARIETIES in such regions as Galicia and Cataluña were rendered virtually extinct. In Cataluña, the post-phylloxera period coincided with the development of the sparkling wine industry which is today one of the largest in the world. Following a visit to the Champagne region, José Raventós introduced the TRADITIONAL METHOD for the production of sparkling wine to the family firm of Codorníu in 1872. The wine, originally christened *champaña*, was a success, and vineyards around the town of San Sadurni de Noya were replanted with the trio of white grapes that now produce over a million hl of CAVA annually.

The first half of the 20th century was a turbulent era for Spain. Political infighting led to the abdication of Alfonso XIII in 1931 and the proclamation of a republic. However, one of the lasting measures introduced by the monarchist dictator General Primo de Rivera was the DO system of controlled appellations administered by a CONSEJO REGULADOR, which was first established in Rioja in 1926. Jerez and Málaga followed suit respectively in 1933 and 1937.

In July 1936, following the election victory of the Popular Front, Spain erupted into civil war. For three years sentiment ran high and Spain tore itself apart, often along regional, separatist lines. Some parts of the country, notably Cataluña and VALENCIA, were affected more than others but throughout the country vineyards were neglected and wineries were destroyed. The Nationalist victory in 1939 brought political stability to Spain under General Franco but economic recovery was hampered by the Second World War, which effectively closed European markets to Spanish exports.

In the 1950s, the wine industry began to revive, helped by the nationwide construction of large CO-OPERATIVE wineries which had begun some years earlier. This turned Spain, with its vast area of vineyard, into a natural source for inexpensive bulk wine either sold under proprietary BRAND names, or labelled with spurious GENERIC names such as Spanish Chablis or Spanish Sauternes, subsequently outlawed by EU authorities.

The post-war history of the Spanish wine industry was for some time marked by the Rumasa saga, outlined under SHERRY. But Rumasa's horizons ran far beyond Jerez and by the late 1970s José María Ruiz-Mateos seemed to control Spain. Ruiz-Mateos contributed greatly to the much-needed modernization of the Spanish wine industry but by the early 1980s there were signs that the empire was in trouble—see SHERRY.

The 1960s sherry boom was followed by the international 'discovery' of Rioja, which had reached the top in the domestic market early this century. In the 1970s and 1980s, the family firm of TORRES wrought a single-handed transformation of the wines of PENEDÈS. The death of General Franco in 1975 and the restoration of the monarchy set the foundations for a modern, multi-party democracy in Spain. Greater economic freedom has led to the growth of an urban middle class which has in turn stimulated a new interest in high-quality wine. Economically deprived rural regions such as La Mancha and Galicia have further benefited from EU finance, which is helping to change the face of the Spanish wine industry. In the 1990s, a fast-paced chain of events brought about more changes than during possibly the previous 90 years. International FLYING WINEMAKERS flocked to Spain; private estates overtook CO-OPERATIVES in most regions; INTERNATIONAL VARIETIES became commonplace in vineyards from La Mancha to Navarra; irrigation and WIRE-trained vineyards sprouted up everywhere; and wine styles changed radically to the fruitier type favoured on international markets.

Spanish wine law

Since joining the EU, Spain has brought her wine law into line with that of other European countries. There is now a four-tier system administered by INDO, acronym for the Madrid-based Instituto Nacional de Denominaciones de Origen. Every autonomous region, however, controls its own appellations, following the lead of Cataluña through INCAVI, the Institut Català de la Vinya i del Vi, and Castilla-La Mancha through IVICAM, the Instituto de la Viña y el Vino de Castilla-La Mancha. Only the appellations encompassing more than one autonomous region (Rioja, Jumilla, and Cava) are controlled by the Ministry of Agriculture through INDO.

Recent EU changes in wine DENOMINATIONS have been mirrored in Spain by the disappearance of Vino de Mesa, replaced simply by 'Vino', and a progressive shift from Vino de la Tierra to terms such as Vino de Calidad and Denominación de Origen Protegida (DOP). But older appellations have kept their old denominations.

DO regions are the mainstay of the system, each with its own Consejo Regulador which regulates the growing, making, and marketing of wines, ensuring that they comply with specified regional standards. In 2005, there were 64 DO regions covering two-thirds of the total vineyard area of Spain. In the 1990s, INDO introduced a new category: Denominación de Origen Calificada (DOC, previously known as DOCa), which equates with Italy's DOCG. Rioja was the first region to be awarded DOC status, in 1991, and was followed in 2003 by Priorat, which calls itself DOQ, Denominaciò d'Origen Qualificada in Catalan.

Geography and climate

Around much of Spain, the land rises steeply from the coast reaching a maximum elevation of 3,482 m/11,420 ft at Mulhacén in the Sierra Nevada just 50 km/30 miles from the Mediterranean. Iberia's dominant feature is the vast plateau that takes up much of central Spain. Known as the *meseta*, this undulating table land ranges in elevation from 600 to 1,000 m, tilting slightly towards the west. Four of Iberia's five major rivers (the Duero, Tajo, Guadiana, and Guadalquivir) drain westwards into the Atlantic, with the Ebro flowing south east to the Mediterranean. Other rivers are seasonal, many drying up completely in the summer months.

Great mountain ranges known as *cordilleras* divide Spain into distinct natural regions. The north coast, from Galicia to the Pyrenees, is relatively cool and humid with few extremes. Annual RAINFALL in this part of Spain ranges from 1,000 mm/39 in on the coast to over 2,000 mm on the mountain peaks inland. Galicia, Asturias, and the BASQUE country are intensively cultivated and densely populated.

The Cantabrian cordillera, a westerly spur of the Pyrenees which rises to over 2,600 m in the Picos de Europa, protects the main body of

Spain from cool, rain-bearing north westerlies. Rioja in the upper Ebro valley is therefore shielded from the bay of Biscay so that, although annual rainfall reaches around 1,500 mm on the Basque coast, it declines sharply to the east and is just 450 mm at Haro, the wine-making capital of Rioja, only 100 km inland.

The Spanish climate becomes more extreme towards the centre of the central plateau. Winters are long and cold with temperatures falling well below freezing point (the lowest recorded temperature is −22 °C/−7.6 °F in Albacete). Summers here can be blisteringly hot with day-time temperatures sometimes rising above 40 °C. Little rain falls in the summer months and DROUGHT is a constant problem. Agriculture has adapted to the lack of rainfall, which struggles to reach 300 mm in places. Much of this comes in sudden downpours in spring and autumn which sometimes cause devastating flash floods.

South and east from the central plateau the climate is increasingly influenced by proximity to the Mediterranean. The climate on the narrow coastal littoral is equable with long, warm summers giving way to mild winters. These are Spain's holiday Costas, but there are lush market gardens producing rice and citrus fruit around Valencia, and, on the mountain slopes inland, olives, almonds, and TABLE GRAPES are important crops. The hottest part of Spain is the broad Guadalquivir valley in Andalucía, north of the Sierra Nevada, where summer temperatures rise to 45 °C. The south west corner of Andalucía has a climate of its own, strongly influenced by the gulf of Cádiz and the Atlantic (see SHERRY).

Viticulture

The drip irrigation that became prevalent in the early years of this century markedly changed the vinous landscape of inland Spain. In most of central and southern Spain, the old BUSH VINES are widely spaced to survive the summer drought with VINE DENSITIES ranging from 900 to 1,600 vines per ha (375–650 per acre) according to the amount of water available (less than one-eighth of the vine density in some MÉDOC or CÔTE D'OR vineyards, for example). Growers have adopted a system of planting known as the *marco real* with 2.5 m between each vine in all directions. Yields from the shrinking proportion of old vines are frequently less than 20 hl/ha (1.1 tons/acre). However, one considerable advantage that accompanies a dry climate is the lack of FUNGAL DISEASES. POWDERY MILDEW, DOWNY MILDEW, and BOTRYTIS BUNCH ROT are virtually unknown in central Spain.

IRRIGATION was one of the most important new developments of the 1990s. The practice had begun to spread unofficially—particularly during the DROUGHTS in south-east Spain of 1994 and 1995—and was formally legalized in 1996. Drip irrigation, pioneered on the Marqués de Griñón Valdepusa estate in Toledo province under the supervision of Australian viticulturist Richard Smart, is the favourite of many growers. Subsurface drip irrigation, which minimizes the losses due to EVAPORATION, became increasingly popular in the early 21st century. Irrigation has been followed by considerably increased yields throughout the country. This, together with a rapid increase in new plantings and productive clones, has triggered concerns about wine quality.

Viticultural practices vary sharply from one part of Spain to another. In areas such as Rioja and Penedès, where more systematic replanting is taking place, vines are more densely planted (up to 5,000 vines per ha) and are increasingly trained on wires. With irrigation, yields may reach 70 or 80 hl/ha, far above official limits. In Galicia, vines were traditionally trained on pergolas (see TENDONE), both to make maximum use of the limited space in this densely populated part of Spain and to lessen the risk of fungal diseases in this humid climate. Newer vineyards are planted on lower vine-TRAINING SYSTEMS to ease cultivation but have to be regularly sprayed to combat disease. Yields are frequently high, sometimes surpassing 100 hl/ha in RÍAS BAIXAS.

Traditionally, most grapes were harvested by hand and grapes frequently arrived at co-operative wineries already starting to ferment, having been squashed when loaded into large trailers. Quality-conscious bodegas increasingly provide growers with stackable plastic containers to keep the grapes whole during transportation (see HARVEST). Some firms also set out a harvest regime refusing grapes delivered after midday when they have been heated by the sun. Some estates are now harvesting at night. The number of MECHANICAL HARVESTERS is increasing as fast as the acreage of vineyards supported on wires.

Vine varieties

The Spanish claim to have up to 600 different grape varieties, although 80% of the country's vineyards are planted with just over 20 of them. Since the arrival of phylloxera at the end of the 19th century, farmers tended to favour varieties well adapted to local climatic conditions, but irrigation has changed this tendency considerably. The drought-resistant white AIRÉN is planted throughout central Spain, although by 2013 it had been overtaken as Spain's most planted grape by TEMPRANILLO whose total of 210,000 ha represents an increase of more than 70% on the area planted with Tempranillo ten years earlier. It travels under such aliases as Cencibel, Ull de Llebre, and Tinto Fino in different parts of the country. BOBAL is the second most planted red wine grape with 75,000 ha/180,000 acres and the traditional GARNACHA is third with 65,000 ha/156,000 acres. Monastrell

(the MOURVÈDRE of France) is fourth with 55,000 ha/132,000 acres. Other white varieties which are also important in Spain are the sherry grapes PALOMINO (planted in Jerez, RUEDA, and parts of Galicia) and PEDRO XIMÉNEZ (Montilla-Moriles and Málaga). The white MACABEO (also called Viura) is widely planted in Rioja and Cataluña, especially Penedès, where, along with Parellada and Xarel-lo, it is grown for Cava sparkling wine. High-quality white varieties which are gaining ground include ALBARIÑO (Galicia) and VERDEJO (Rueda), while other promising grapes which are making a more limited comeback include the white LOUREIRA, TREIXADURA, and GODELLO (all three in Galicia) and the red GRACIANO (Rioja) and MENCÍA (Galicia and Castilla y León).

INTERNATIONAL VARIETIES have made significant inroads in some parts of Spain. CABERNET SAUVIGNON, SYRAH, MERLOT, PETIT VERDOT, SAUVIGNON BLANC, and CHARDONNAY have become increasingly important in Cataluña, Somontano, Navarra, Castilla y León and Castilla-La Mancha. Cabernet Sauvignon, with a total of 23,000 ha/55,000 acres of vineyards, is the most important of these.

Winemaking

Spanish winemaking has changed radically since the 1960s. Stainless steel, once a rarity, is now commonplace and virtually all bodegas have the means of TEMPERATURE CONTROL for fermentation. These improvements transformed Spanish wines, especially in La Mancha and the Levante, where temperature control is essential to preserve the primary fruit character in both red and white wine. The epoxy-lined concrete tanks still to be found in some co-operative wineries are regaining favour with top producers for red wines, as are oak vats, in a return to traditional fermentation vessels which ensure less temperature variation than stainless steel tanks.

A vogue for crisp, technically perfect, simple young whites was followed in the 1990s by a resurgence of barrel-fermented whites.

Spain continues to foster the long-established tradition of ageing red wines in OAK. The use of wooden BARRELS as vessels for fermentation and storage dates back many centuries but in the second half of the 19th century the French introduced the 225-l BARRIQUE (*barrica*) to Rioja, and its use has subsequently spread throughout the country. Unlike the French, however, most Spanish winemakers use American oak, which is not only considerably cheaper than French oak, it can also impart a stronger flavour to the wine. The Tempranillo grape in particular seems to produce wine that responds to maturation in new oak. However, French oak has made significant inroads since the early 1990s. Spanish oak-aged reds are usually denoted by the words CRIANZA, RESERVA, or GRAN RESERVA, which are enshrined in local legislation. From the 1970s to the 1990s, the wines often showed a pungent, vanilla character but this was superseded by more FRUIT-DRIVEN aromas and flavours, partly in response to FASHION. After 2000, a return to some TRADITIONS, sometimes including the use of TINAJAS, was apparent among a newer generation of producers keenly attuned to the worldwide trend towards using less technology in high quality wines.

Most Spanish DOs also stipulate minimum BOTTLE AGE and traditionally very few Spanish wines were released before they were were ready to drink. But some growers, led by the PRIORAT newcomers, started a new habit of renouncing both Crianza and Reserva back labels, selling oak-aged wine as vino JOVEN, often with little bottle age.

For specific wine regions, see ANDALUCÍA, ARAGÓN, BASQUE, CASTILLA-LA MANCHA, CASTILLA Y LEÓN, CATALUÑA, GALICIA, NAVARRA, and RIOJA.

See also SHERRY. V. de la S.

Peñín. J., *Peñín Guide to Spanish Wine* (Madrid, annually).

Radford, J., *The New Spain* (2nd edn, London, 2004).

www.winesfromspain.com

www.fev.es

www.oemv.es

Spanna, local name for the NEBBIOLO grape grown in the north of PIEMONTE in north-west Italy, particularly in a historic wine zone in the hills of Vercelli and Novara provinces.

Five DOC wines and two DOCGS, Gattinara and Ghemme, are made either wholly or in part from Spanna: three in the Vercelli hills (BRAMATERRA, GATTINARA, LESSONA) and four in the province of Novara (BOCA, FARA, GHEMME, and SIZZANO). Only Gattinara and Ghemme, responsible for some of the longest-lived Spanna wines, are made in any quantity today but in the 19th century this area had greater plantings, and was more famous for its wines, than the LANGHE. Spanna wines had an excellent reputation before the Second World War and were quite popular in the major market of nearby Milan, but the post-war period saw a loss of ground to the richer and more professionally made Nebbiolo wines of the Langhe, particularly BAROLO and BARBARESCO. The extreme fragmentation of vineyard property and a workforce that moved to the textile factories of nearby Biella accelerated the decline of winemaking in this area, but this group of wine zones is attracting attention once more, not least because of the finesse of its best wines. W.S.

sparging a wine means stripping it of OXYGEN or CARBON DIOXIDE by purging it with fine bubbles of an INERT GAS, usually NITROGEN. The technique is not widely used because it removes not only oxygen but also significant amounts of volatile FLAVOUR COMPOUNDS. A tank or bottle may also be sparged with an inert gas. Sparging can also refer to the injection of carbon dioxide into the wine, with or without nitrogen, to increase the concentration of carbon dioxide in the wine. A.D.W.

sparkling wine, wine which bubbles when poured into a glass, an important and growing category of wine. The bubbles form because a certain amount of CARBON DIOXIDE has been held under pressure dissolved in the wine until the bottle is unstopped (see FIZZINESS).

Sparkling wine may vary in as many respects as still wine: it can be any wine COLOUR (it is usually white or pink but sparkling reds such as Australian sparkling Shiraz enjoy a certain following); it can be any degree of SWEETNESS (although a high proportion tastes bone dry and may be labelled BRUT, while Italians specialize in medium-sweet SPUMANTE and a wave of sweetish fizzy MOSCATO washed the US in the early 2010s); it can vary in ALCOHOLIC STRENGTH (although in practice most dry sparkling wines are about 12%, while the sweeter, lighter Spumante are between 5.5 and 8%); and it can come from anywhere in the world where wine is produced.

According to EU regulations, the sweetness level of EU wines and those marketed in the EU must be shown on the label. For official EU definitions, see DOSAGE.

Sparkling wines also vary in FIZZINESS, not just in the actual pressure under which the gas is dissolved in the wine, but also apparently in the character of the foam. Some sparkling wines froth aggressively in the mouth while others bubble subtly. The average size, consistency, and persistence of the bubbles also vary considerably. Study of foam and foaminess, along with research into YEASTS, are two of the few areas which unite the (sparkling) wine industry with the BEER industry.

To the winemaker, however, the most obvious way in which sparkling wines differ is in how the gas came to be trapped in solution in the wine: traditional method, transversage, transfer, Charmat, or carbonation, in declining order of cost, complication, and likely quality of sparkling wine, together with the rarer *méthode ancestrale* and *méthode dioise ancestrale*. (See SPARKLING WINEMAKING for details of each method.)

The most famous sparkling wine of all is CHAMPAGNE, the archetypal sparkling wine made in north-eastern France, which represents about 13% of global sparkling wine production. A significant proportion of all sparkling wine is made using the same basic method as is used in Champagne (now called the traditional, rather than the champagne, method), much of it from the same grape varieties Pinot Noir, Chardonnay, and, to a lesser extent outside Champagne, Pinot Meunier, even though different wine regions often stamp their own style on the resulting sparkling wine. Examples of such wines were made with ever-increasing frequency from the 1980s onwards in CALIFORNIA, AUSTRALIA, and ITALY particularly.

A host of fine, very individual sparkling wines is made using the traditional method but with non-champagne grapes, however. The most prodigious example of this is the popular Spanish CAVA. The LOIRE region of France also produces traditional method sparkling wine in great quantity, notably in SAUMUR. All of France's CRÉMANTS also use the traditional method. In almost every wine region in the world with aspirations to quality, some traditional method wine has been made. Wines made by this, the most meticulous method, may be described on the label within Europe as *méthode traditionnelle, méthode classique,* or *méthode traditionnelle classique.* Other descriptions include bottle fermented (although strictly speaking wines made by the transfer method, described below, may be labelled 'bottle fermented', while only those made by the traditional method can be labelled 'Fermented in *This* Bottle').

Similarly, in almost every wine region in the world, Charmat process sparkling wine is made in considerable quantity, often for specific local BRANDS, especially for SEKT in Germany and a host of wines such as PROSECCO, LAMBRUSCO, and ASTI in Italy. RUSSIA has been an enthusiastic market for sparkling wines ever since the imperial court imported such vast quantities of champagne (and base wine to make sparkling) at the end of the 19th century. Today SOVIET SPARKLING WINE is still made in enormous quantity in both Russia and UKRAINE. Asti and a number of other low-alcohol, sweet Italian, or Italianate, sparkling wines are made using a variation of the Charmat process.

The transfer method is used for some better-quality branded wines, particularly in Germany and the United States (giving rise to the defiant description on some American sparkling wine labels 'Fermented in *This* Bottle' for products made by the traditional method).

Some characterful sparkling wines are made eschewing DISGORGEMENT and selling the part-fermented, still-sweet wine together with the LEES of its second fermentation in bottle. These include some GAILLAC, LIMOUX, and CLAIRETTE DE DIE made by specific but similar local methods sometimes called *méthode ancestrale.*

See also OPENING THE BOTTLE, LABELLING INFORMATION, and DOSAGE.

sparkling winemaking, making SPARKLING WINES, most obviously involves the accumulation of gas under pressure in what was initially a still 'base wine' or, ideally, blend of base wines. The most common methods of achieving this are discussed below but these are matters of technique rather than substance. Almost all of them depend on initiating a second FERMENTATION, which inevitably produces CARBON DIOXIDE, and most of them incorporate some way of keeping that gas dissolved under pressure in the wine (see FIZZINESS), while separating it from the inconvenient by-product of fermentation, the LEES. What matters most to the quality of a sparkling wine, however, is the quality and character of the blended base wines.

Making and blending the base wine

Wines that are good raw material for the sparkling winemaking process are not usually much fun to drink in their still state. They are typically high in acidity and unobtrusively flavoured. There is a school of thought that the austerity of the still wine of the CHAMPAGNE region, Coteaux CHAMPENOIS, is the most eloquent argument of all in favour of champagne's carbon dioxide content.

It is not just in Champagne, however, that sparkling winemakers argue that BALANCE is the key to assembling a base wine to make sparkling, and that the best sparkling wines are therefore essentially blended wines. Some fine VARIETAL sparkling wines exist (some of the best BLANC DE BLANCS champagnes, for example), but a great sparkling wine never tastes just like the still wine version plus gas; the very nature of sparkling winemaking is to try to make a sum that is greater than the parts (although this may not be achieved, or even attempted, for cheaper wines). Those who aspire to make good sparkling wine are acutely aware that any minor fault in a base wine may be amplified by the sparkling winemaking process.

Accordingly, for better sparkling wines, grapes had invariably been hand picked up to the early 1990s since WHOLE-BUNCH PRESSING was the norm, and such MECHANICAL HARVESTERS as had been tested by then risked splitting berries and extracting harsh PHENOLICS into the grape juice, which could cause astringent, coarse characteristics which would be magnified by the pressure of bubbles. It is possible that gentler mechanical harvesters will change this, although it is essential to press grapes as soon as possible after picking. Press houses in the vineyards have long been *de rigueur* in Champagne and are increasingly common for other top-quality sparkling wines.

Grapes destined for sparkling wines are usually picked at lower MUST WEIGHTS than the same varieties would be if they were to be sold as a still wine. In very general terms, average YIELDS can be higher for sparkling wines than for still wines (see below), partly because there is no imperative to achieve high sugar levels. In California, for example, HARVEST begins in mid, or sometimes early, August for Pinot Noir and Chardonnay destined for sparkling wines. In Australia, the aim is to pick such varieties just as HERBACEOUS characters have been lost when ripe fruit FLAVOUR COMPOUNDS are beginning to develop (in practice at about 17 to 20 °BRIX in Australia's cooler areas).

PRESSING is an important stage in sparkling winemaking, particularly in Champagne, where black grapes are used, as it is essential that the concentration of phenolics, both ASTRINGENCY and COLOUR, is kept to a minimum. There has been much experimentation with horizontal PRESSES of various types, and modern pneumatic or tank presses can certainly offer a reliably high standard of HYGIENE, but modern technology has found it difficult to improve upon the traditional vertical presses of Champagne, although they are LABOUR intensive. So-called 'thin layer' presses which minimize pressure, and therefore the extraction of phenolics, by pressing a layer of grapes no more than 70 cm/27 in thick, are used increasingly.

The winemaker can then make the usual still white wine choices concerning OXIDATIVE versus PROTECTIVE methods of JUICE HANDLING; juice CLARIFICATION; choice of YEAST strain and FERMENTATION rate; protein STABILIZATION; and MALOLACTIC CONVERSION.

Then comes the crucial blending stage, the true art of making sparkling wine, and one in which experience is as important as SCIENCE. A large champagne house such as MOËT & CHANDON may be able to use several hundred base wines in order to achieve the house style in its basic expression, that year's NON-VINTAGE blend.

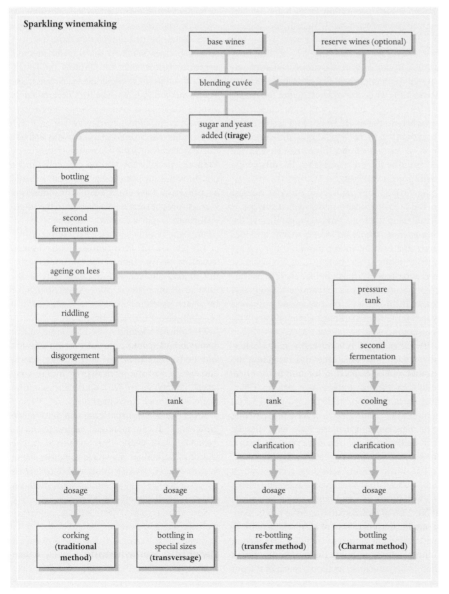

Sparkling winemaking

base wines → reserve wines (optional)

→ blending cuvée ←

→ sugar and yeast added (**tirage**)

→ bottling → second fermentation → ageing on lees → riddling → disgorgement

pressure tank → second fermentation → cooling

tank | tank | clarification → cooling → clarification

→ dosage → corking (**traditional method**)

→ dosage → bottling in special sizes (**transversage**)

→ dosage → re-bottling (**transfer method**)

→ dosage → bottling (**Charmat method**)

A small, independent concern, especially outside Champagne, may have access to only a very limited range of base wines—a disadvantage in a poor vintage, although not necessarily in a good one. And a producer of the most basic Charmat process wine may simply blend the cheapest vaguely suitable ingredients available in the market place.

Traditional method

This method, once known as the champagne method and now known variously as traditional method, classical method, classical traditional method, *méthode traditionnelle*, and *méthode classique*, is the most meticulous way of making wine sparkle; the raw ingredients vary considerably but the basic techniques do not.

Pressing and yield Pressing is the first operation defined in detail by the traditional method, which understandably differentiates rigorously between the fractions of juice from each press load, for the first juice to emerge from the press is highest in sugar and acidity and lowest in phenolics, including pigments. A maximum extraction rate is usually defined in any regulations concerning sparkling wine production (such as those for France's CRÉMANTS). Those who produce traditional method sparkling wine acknowledge that the first juice to emerge from the press is generally the best, even if there is a certain amount of VINTAGE variation. From 1992, the permitted extraction rate for champagne was reduced so that 160 kg (350 lb) of grapes rather than 150 kg of grapes were required to produce 102 l (27 gal) of wine, about the same extraction rate as that used by producers of top-quality sparkling wine anywhere in the world. (This compares with an approximate average extraction rate of 100 l of wine from about 130 kg of grapes for still red wines; see YIELD.)

Base wines After the making of the base wines (described above), which usually takes place over the winter following the harvest, the final blend is made after extensive tasting, assessment, and ASSEMBLAGE. There is extreme flexibility in blending a non-dated wine and a high proportion of 'reserve wine' made in previous years may be used. Some champagne houses include up to 45% of reserve wines in their NON-VINTAGE blend. (KRUG indulge in the luxury of using base wines from up to ten different vintages being held in reserve.) The ingredients in a vintage-dated sparkling wine are more limited (often by necessity for those new to sparkling winemaking, and by law in Champagne). Many of the base wines made from dark-berried grapes, however lightly pressed, may have a light pink tinge at this stage, although the PIGMENTS are precipitated during *tirage*, the crucial next stage during which the blended wine rests on the lees of a second fermentation in bottle. As soon as the new blend has been made in bulk blending tanks, it usually undergoes cold STABILIZATION in order to prevent subsequent formation of TARTRATES in bottle.

Second fermentation This new blend then has a mixture of sugar and yeast added to it before bottling in particularly strong, dark BOTTLES, usually STOPPERED with a CROWN CAP, so that a second fermentation will occur in bottle, creating the all-important fizz. Conventionally, an addition or *tirage* of about 24 g/l of sugar is made. This creates an additional 1.2 to 1.3% ALCOHOLIC STRENGTH and sufficient carbon dioxide to create a pressure inside the bottle of 5–6 atmospheres after disgorgement (see below), which is roughly the FIZZINESS expected of a sparkling wine, and one which can safely be contained by a wired champagne cork. During this second fermentation, known as *prise de mousse* in French, the bottles are normally stored horizontally at about 12 °C/54 °F until the fermentation has produced the required pressure and bubbles, usually for four to eight weeks.

Special types of YEAST culture which help sparkling winemakers have been developed (and are much used for still wines too). Such yeasts are particularly good at flocculating, and produce a granular deposit that is easy to riddle, or shake, to the neck of the bottle for extraction.

At this stage, RIDDLING agents are increasingly added with the yeast and sugar. Made of some combination of TANNINS, BENTONITES, gelatines, or alginates, they help to produce a uniform skin-like yeast deposit that does not stick to the glass but slips easily down it during the riddling process. The development of smoother glass bottles has also helped.

Ageing on lees Timing of the riddling process after the second fermentation is a key element in quality and style of a traditional method sparkling wine, the second most important factor affecting quality after blending the base wine. The longer a wine rests on the lees of the second fermentation in bottle, the more chance it has of picking up flavour from the dead yeast cells, a process known as yeast AUTOLYSIS.

Most regulations for traditional method sparkling wines specify at least nine months' ageing on lees, and the minimum period for non-vintage champagne was increased to 15 months in the early 1990s (vintage champagnes are usually aged for several years). During the bottle ageing process, the yeast cells autolyse, releasing increasingly complex flavour compounds. The chemistry of autolysis is not fully understood, but it seems that autolysis has significant effects only after about 18 months on the lees, and that the most obvious changes occur after five to ten years of lees contact, which inevitably increases production costs considerably. It may be that compulsory periods of lees contact in bottle of only a few months have less effect on quality than has been imagined.

Riddling The riddling process, known as *remuage* (or shaking) in French, is one of the most cumbersome (and most publicized) parts of the traditional method, but it is undertaken for cosmetic rather than oenological reasons: to remove the deposit that would otherwise make the wine cloudy (as it does in the *méthode ancestrale* described below).

Traditionally, bottles were gradually moved from the horizontal to an inverted vertical by hand, by human *remueurs* or riddlers who would shake them and the deposit every time they moved them towards the inverted vertical position in special *pupitres* or riddling racks. This was a slow and extremely labour-intensive way of moving the deposit from the belly of the bottle to its neck. The CAVA industry based in Cataluña developed an automatic alternative in the 1970s, the *girasol* or GYROPALETTE, which has since been widely adopted for traditional method sparkling winemaking the world over. The bottles are stacked, 504 at a time, in large metal crates, and their orientation changed at regular intervals (including night time, unlike the manual method), with accompanying shake, from the horizontal to inverted vertical by remote control. Using riddling agents, well-adapted yeasts, and gyropalettes, bottles may now be riddled in as little as three days, as opposed to the six weeks or more needed for hand *remuage* without riddling agents.

Disgorgement and dosage The final stage in a complicated production process—though it may be shorter than, say, that of a fine oak-aged red—is to remove the deposit now in the neck of an inverted bottle. The conventional way of achieving this is to freeze the bottle neck and deposit by plunging the necks of the inverted bottles into a tray of freezing solution. The bottles are then upended, the crown cap flipped off, and the 2 cm deposit flies out as a solid pellet of ice. Bottles are then topped up with a mixture of wine and sugar syrup, the so-called DOSAGE, stoppered with a proper champagne CORK held on with a wire MUZZLE, and prepared for labelling. Many of the bigger producers employ a technique known as jetting, long familiar to brewers, to protect the wine from OXIDATION: just before the cork is inserted, a small dose of wine, or bisulfite diluted in water, is injected into the neck of the bottle at high pressure; this creates bubbles that rise just to the lip of the bottle, pushing out any oxygen in the head space. Most dry sparkling wine is sweetened so that it contains between 5 and 12 g/l RESIDUAL SUGAR, the higher the natural ACIDITY of the wine, the more dosage is generally required to counterbalance it, although the longer a wine is aged on lees, the less dosage it needs. One of the apparent effects of CLIMATE CHANGE seems to be a noticeable trend to reduce the amount of sugar added as grapes are picked riper, with lower acidity.

Alternative methods Riddling and disgorgement are unwieldy processes which contribute nothing to the innate quality of the sparkling wine. It is not surprising therefore that, in the 1980s, as LABOUR costs spiralled, there was considerable research into alternative methods of expelling the sediment.

One of the most successful has been the development of encapsulated yeast. Yeast can be trapped in a 'bead' made of calcium alginate. Such beads are about a few millimetres in diameter and are able to hold the yeast trapped in their interior while having big enough pores to admit sugar and nutrients into the bead so that a full second fermentation can proceed as normal. The great advantage is that the riddling stage takes seconds as the beads simply drop into the neck of the inverted bottle. The only brake on the adoption of encapsulated yeasts has been the development of reliable machinery which will dispense beads into bottles without shearing them. Although MOËT & CHANDON successfully trialled the use of such beads, the company decided it was more practical and economical to continue to use gyropalettes to move the sediment to the neck of the bottle.

Another possible method is to insert a membrane cartridge into the neck of the bottle. Yeast is dispensed into it and it is then plugged before the bottle is stopped with the usual crown cap. Like the beads, the cartridge allows ingress of sugar and nutrients for fermentation to take place there, as well as allowing the carbon dioxide gas out. In this case there is no need at all for riddling, and disgorgement simply entails taking off the crown cap and allowing the pressure inside the bottle to expel the cartridge.

Neither of these alternatives has been commercially adopted so far, partly because of cost, although the membrane method could be useful to small wineries for whom the investment in riddling and disgorgement equipment has been prohibitive, but perhaps also out of concern that the use of such technology might be seen to undermine the 'traditional method' image so cherished by the big champagne houses.

Transversage

Transversage is an occasional twist on the traditional method whereby, immediately after disgorgement, the contents of bottles of sparkling wine made by the traditional method are transferred into a pressure tank to which the dosage is added before the wine is bottled, typically in another (often small) size of bottle, under pressure. This is how many half-bottles, all airline 'splits' or quarter-bottles, and virtually all BOTTLE SIZES above a jeroboam of champagne are filled.

Transfer method

The transfer method, known as *méthode transfert* in French and Carstens in the United States, also depends on inducing a second fermentation by adding sugar and yeast to a blend of base wines and then bottling the result. It differs from the traditional method, however, in that riddling and disgorgement are dispensed with and, after a period of lees contact, the bottles are chilled, and their contents transferred to a bulk pressure tank where the sediment is removed by clarification, usually FILTRATION. A suitable dosage is then added and the result is once again bottled, using a counter pressure filler, before being corked and wired. The transfer method is likely to be abandoned in the long term because it has all the disadvantages of the traditional method but does not produce all its qualities in the wine.

Continuous method

This process was developed in the USSR for SOVIET SPARKLING WINE and is now used in Germany and Portugal. but only for large-volume inexpensive fizz. The method involves a series of usually five reticulated tanks under five atmospheres of pressure, the same FIZZINESS as in most sparkling wines. At one end, base wine together with sugar and yeast (usually rehydrated dried yeast) is pumped in and the second fermentation crucial to virtually all methods of sparkling winemaking begins. This creates CARBON DIOXIDE, which increases the pressure in the tank, but the yeast cannot grow under this pressure and so further yeast has to be added continuously. The second and third tanks are partly filled with some material such as wood shavings, which offer a substantial total surface area on which the dead yeast cells accumulate and a certain amount of AUTOLYSIS, or at least reaction between the dead yeast cells and the wine, takes place. In the fourth and fifth tanks there are no yeast cells and the wine eventually emerges relatively clear, having spent an average of perhaps three or four weeks in the system. See also LANCERS.

Charmat process or tank method

This very common method, also called *cuve close* (French for sealed tank), tank, or bulk method, *granvas* in Spanish, *autoclave* in Italian, was developed by Eugene Charmat in the early years of the 20th century in Bordeaux. Its advantages are that it is very much cheaper, faster, and less labour intensive than the above processes, and is better suited to base wines which lack much capacity for AGEING. A second fermentation is provoked by yeast and sugar added to base wine held in bulk in a pressure tank and, after a rapid fermentation, the fermentation is typically arrested by cooling the wine to −5 °C when a pressure of about 5 atmospheres has been reached. The result is clarified, a dosage is added and the resulting sparkling wine is bottled using a counter pressure filler. This style of sparkling wine is the most likely to taste like still wine with bubbles in it, rather than to have any of the additional attributes which can result from fermentation in bottle.

Carbonation

Also known as the injection, or simply the 'bicycle pump', method, carbonation of wine is achieved in much the same way as carbonation of fizzy soft drinks: carbon dioxide gas is pumped from cylinders into a tank of wine which is then bottled under pressure, or very occasionally it is pumped into bottles. The result is a wine which has many, and large, bubbles when the bottle is first opened, but whose mousse rapidly fades. It must have a pressure of at least 3 atmospheres and in EU parlance is referred to as aerated sparkling wine. This is the cheapest, least critical, and least durable way of making wine sparkle and is used for perhaps the cheapest 10% of all sparkling wines.

Méthode ancestrale or méthode rurale

This method (given new life by the PÉTILLANT NATUREL vogue) results in a lightly sparkling wine, often with some sweetness and sediment, and most closely parallels how wines were originally made sparkling. It involves bottling young wines before all the RESIDUAL SUGAR has been fermented into alcohol. Fermentation continues in bottle and gives off carbon dioxide. Today it is becoming increasingly common in parts of France such as the Loire and the Jura, and is spreading throughout the wine world, but variants on this theme are still made in GAILLAC, LIMOUX, and for CLAIRETTE DE DIE Tradition (see below).

The resulting wine, generally stoppered by a CROWN CAP, is sweeter and less fizzy than a traditional method sparkling wine and no dosage is allowed. The wine may in some cases be decanted off the deposit and rebottled under pressure in a form of transfer method.

Méthode dioise ancestrale

This is an unusual variation on the *méthode ancestrale* above and the transfer method, producing wines similar to ASTI. It is used for the sweet wine CLAIRETTE DE DIE Tradition, most of which is made by the local CO-OPERATIVE. The base wines are fermented in stainless steel tanks at very low temperatures over several months. The wine is then filtered to remove most but not all of the yeast, bottled, and fermentation continues in bottle until an alcoholic strength of between 7 and 8.5% has been reached. The wine is disgorged six to 12 months after bottling (the minimum time on lees is four months) before being filtered again and immediately transferred to new bottles. The use of liqueur de tirage and liqueur d'éxpedition is both prohibited and unnecessary.

Spätburgunder is the chief German synonym for PINOT NOIR and the grape variety that experienced the most dramatic rise in popularity in Germany in the 1990s. Such is German enthusiasm for red wine that Germany's total plantings increased from 3,400 ha/8,400 acres in 1980 to more than 11,000 ha by 2003 at which level it has remained. There is considerable dispute over the vine's importance in Germany during the Middle Ages but in modern times, until the late 1980s, it was cultivated largely in parts of the RHEINGAU (notably Assmannshausen) where it owes its toehold to the same 13th-century Cistercian MONKS responsible for its rise to fame in the Côte d'Or, and along the steep slate slopes of the AHR. Then the typical Spätburgunder was pale, sweetish (and all too often tinged with rot-related odours). Today it is at least as deep coloured, dry alcoholic, and well structured as a red burgundy, thanks to much lower yields, longer MACERATION, BARREL MATURATION, and CLIMATE CHANGE. For many years demand in Germany was so strong that very little Spätburgunder was exported but the best bottles of the Ahr, Baden, and Pfalz, in particular, are increasingly appreciated abroad too.

Spätlese, means literally 'late harvest' but, as a so-called PRÄDIKAT, is officially defined by grape sugar at harvest. In Germany, specific minimum MUST WEIGHTS are laid down for each combination of vine variety and region and range from 76 to 90 °OECHSLE. In Austria, where the designation is no longer used for dry wines and seldom for sweet, the minimum across the board is 19 °KMW (approximately 94 Oechsle). Since the mid 20th century, many German growers have considered a Spätlese the ideal vehicle for conveying the complexity of ripe Riesling and its influence by site. It is thus not surprising that during the 1980s revival and subsequent domination of dry wines in domestic markets, the conjunction Spätlese trocken would be treated as a mark of excellence. When the term GROSSES GEWÄCHS was introduced by the VDP growers' association as its prestige dry wine category, such wines were usually also labelled as Spätlese trocken, but from vintage 2011 that option was discontinued.

D.S.

Spätrot, synonym for ZIERFANDLER.

special late harvested, term which should according to EU labelling law be applied to wines made in Australia from 'fresh ripe grapes of which a significant proportion have been desiccated under natural conditions in a manner favouring the concentration of sugars in the berries'. In South Africa, the term refers to a lighter style of dessert wine harvested at a minimum of 22 °Balling and with at least 11% alcohol. If the RESIDUAL SUGAR is less than 20 g/l, the label must indicate whether the wine is extra dry, dry, semi-sweet, or sweet.

www.wosa.co.za/sa/varieties_styles.php

specific gravity. See DENSITY.

Spergola, grape variety from the Emilia region of Italy making tart whites.

spiced wines. See FLAVOURED WINES and MULLED WINE.

spinning cone column, gas-liquid counter-current device for making DEALCOHOLIZED WINE or GRAPE CONCENTRATE and for removing SULFUR DIOXIDE from juice, and reducing some wines' ALCOHOLIC STRENGTH, particularly in California. Spinning cone technology is an advance on the processes operating in a one- or two-stage vacuum evaporator. The device consists of a vertical stainless steel column containing two internal and alternating series of inverted cones; one series is fixed and attached to the column wall, the second series is parallel to the first and attached to a central rotating shaft. Liquid flows down the upper surfaces of the stationary cones under gravity, and moves up the upper surfaces of the rotating cones in a thin film due to the centrifugal force from the spinning action. Vapour that is evaporated from the thin film of liquid (under vacuum at low temperature, and with the aid of an inert stripping gas) flows up the column in the spaces between the successive fixed and rotating cones. Through a process of repeated evaporation and condensation on the cones, the volatiles are enriched in the up-flowing vapour stream. The volatiles, after passing through a condenser, are finally captured in liquid form at the top of the column while the stripped liquid is pumped out the bottom of the column. Spinning cone technology offers extremely high separation efficiency, with a low pressure drop across the column and low liquid hold up, hence the juice or wine has a short residence time in the column. Accordingly, alcohol and aroma removal are achieved with much less of the product evaporated than in a traditional evaporator. Also, the aroma fraction is recovered separately from the alcohol and can be back added to the wine to restore the flavour profile at a lower alcohol concentration. One application of the spinning cone column is reducing the alcoholic strength of excessively alcoholic wines by between one and 3% without loss of FLAVOUR COMPOUNDS to produce a wine with the flavour intensity afforded by fully ripe fruit but without an unacceptable alcohol content. About 10% of the wine is passed through the spinning cone column and, after having the volatile flavour compounds restored, is then added back to the remainder.

Advocates of the spinning cone column claim it can be used to selectively remove unwanted flavours from a finished wine such as those from HYDROGEN SULFIDE, MERCAPTANS, and even excess HERBACEOUS notes. Because of the cost of equipment, this is mainly a service industry since very few producers can afford to buy a spinning cone themselves. An alternative and equally popular technique for reducing alcohol levels in wines is REVERSE OSMOSIS.

P.J.W.

spitting is an essential practice at professional TASTINGS where several dozen, often more than 100, wines are regularly offered at the same time. Members of the wine TRADE, and WINE WRITERS, rapidly lose any inhibitions about spitting in public. Since there are no taste receptors in the throat, spitting allows the taster to form a full impression of each wine, while minimizing the blunting effects of ALCOHOL. It does not, unfortunately, leave the taster completely unaffected by alcohol. Some ethanol is vaporized and absorbed in the nose and mouth and, no matter how assiduous the taster, it can also be extremely difficult to prevent any liquid from dribbling down the throat. According to the estimates of this writer, tasting 30 wines can involve ingesting almost a glass of wine, depending on the personal mechanics of TASTING.

Whatever tasters spit into is a **spittoon**. These can vary from specially designed giant funnels on a stand, through wooden CASES filled with sawdust, to ice buckets, jugs, or, particularly convenient at a seated tasting, personal plastic or cardboard beakers. Most professional tasting rooms are equipped with channels, or sinks with running water designed to drain away expectorated wine.

spontaneous fermentation refers to alcoholic FERMENTATION that occurs due to AMBIENT rather than inoculated, cultured yeast. Some producers and marketers prefer the term 'wild ferment'. See YEAST for the terminology used in this book.

spraying, a vineyard practice of applying liquids and powders to control pests, diseases, and weeds. Late last century, vineyard sprayers were often drawn by draught animals and operated with manual pumps; nowadays they are usually mounted on TRACTORS or drawn by them, and sometimes mounted on MECHANICAL HARVESTERS in order to spray several rows at once.

The aim of economically and environmentally sound spraying is to achieve maximum coverage of the 'target' (leaves, bunches, or weeds) by applying minimum amounts of the

S

appropriate AGROCHEMICAL (or other products). There should be ideally no spray material lost to the surrounding environment as 'spray drift'. Good coverage depends on having very small droplets, although these are more readily blown off target by WIND than large drops. A welcome development is the so-called tunnel sprayer, which prevents spray escaping into the environment. The vine canopy beside the tractor is enclosed by a cover or tunnel, usually made of fibreglass, with the spray jets mounted inside the tunnel. Any spray droplets not caught by the vine are caught by the opposite side of the tunnel and can therefore be retrieved and returned to the spray cart. Such units save a lot of spray material, especially early in the growing season when the 'target' is small.

Vineyards can be sprayed from the air as well as from the ground, using fixed-wing aircraft or HELICOPTERS. Costs can be lower, but coverage is typically not as good as for ground spraying and low wind conditions are required. Aerial spraying can be used when ground conditions are unsuited for tractors, such as following heavy rain. However, spray drift may endanger the ORGANIC or BIODYNAMIC status of a neighbouring vineyard.

Relatively few vineyards are now sprayed from containers strapped on workers' backs, although this is still done in Portugal's DOURO valley and on one-man properties. The costs of such spraying operations are of course very high, and generally not sustainable for most commercial vineyards. Agrochemicals in dry powder form are applied by a process known as DUSTING.

See also RESIDUES.   R.E.S.

Coombe, B. G., and Dry, P. R. (eds.), *Viticulture*, ii: *Practices* (Adelaide, 1992).

sprinklers are used for IRRIGATION, and in some vineyards to control FROST (the water freezes to form a protective coating of ice round the young vine buds). Sprinkler irrigation has largely been replaced by DRIP IRRIGATION, which uses much less water, and does not leave wet leaves vulnerable to FUNGAL DISEASES and possible SALINITY damage. It is important to avoid waterlogging, which can readily cause injury to the newly growing roots. It has also been used in hot regions of Australia for vineyard cooling, by operating the system intermittently during the hottest part of the day, but this is not economical and wastes WATER.   J.G. & R.E.S.

spritzer, common name for a mixture of white wine and sparkling water that is usually drunk as an APERITIF.

spritzig, German term for wines with a slight, attractive prickle of CARBON DIOXIDE. **Spritz** has become an international tasting term, perhaps for onomatopoeic reasons.

spumante, Italian word for sparkling wine from the verb *spumare*, to foam or froth, which can appear on labels as *Vino Spumante*, *Vino Spumante di Qualità*, or *Vino Spumante di Qualità* followed by a denomination of origin. It is allowed only for wines made sparkling by a second fermentation, either in bottle (METODO CLASSICO) or by the tank method (see SPARKLING WINEMAKING). The most important example in terms of volume is PROSECCO, of which 300 million bottles were produced in 2013. Second best-selling is ASTI made from the MOSCATO Bianco grape cultivated in the provinces of Asti, Cuneo, and Alessandria, of which over 80 million bottles may be made in an average year.

Significant quantities of sparkling wines from CHARDONNAY and PINOT NOIR, the classic grapes of CHAMPAGNE, are also produced in Italy, principally from three areas: the TRENTINO-ALTO ADIGE, the OLTREPÒ PAVESE, and FRANCIACORTA. The Italians, unlike the Champagne houses, regularly employ PINOT BLANC and PINOT GRIS in their blends. Some of these wines are produced using the tank method, but the majority are fermented in bottle like champagne and are labelled 'metodo classico'. TrentoDOC is the name adopted for TRADITIONAL METHOD sparkling wines made in TRENTINO and the only other Italian fizz to have eliminated the word spumante from labels, is FRANCIACORTA whose DOCG applies only to sparkling wine, thus emulating CHAMPAGNE with which it is often compared.

A vast number of other types of sparkling wine are made in Italy from a wide range of grape varieties, in a dazzling array of colours, ALCOHOLIC STRENGTHS, and RESIDUAL SUGAR levels. Inspired by the extraordinary commercial success of Prosecco, almost every DOC now has a provision for the production of sparkling wine. Some of the more significant white spumantes are from Bianco di CUSTOZA, Colli Albani, Colli Euganei, Colli PIACENTINI, COLLI Tortonesi, CORTESE dell'Alto Monferrato, FRASCATI, GAVI, GRECO DI TUFO, Locorotondo, Marino, Roero ARNEIS, TREBBIANO di Romagna, Velletri, and VERDICCHIO dei Castelli di Jesi. Red sparkling wines are permitted within the AGLIANICO, BRACHETTO, Cesanese di Olevano Romano, Elba Rosso, FREISA, and LISON-PRAMAGGIORE (from MERLOT, CABERNET, or REFOSCO) DOCs. Several famous sweet wines, such as the three major RECIOTOS, may be produced in sparkling versions, too. In addition to these there are myriad more basic sparkling wines. One can conclude that Italians simply like CARBON DIOXIDE in their wine and do not, unlike the French perhaps, require that it resembles a single paradigm.

See also FRIZZANTE.   W.S.

spur, a viticultural term for a shortened grapevine cane. A spur is a stub formed by pruning the CANE to between one and four NODES, usually two. Spurs are used to provide the next season's

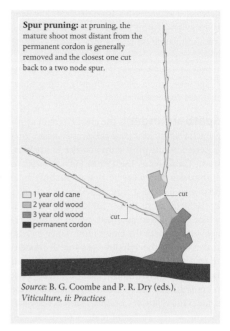

Spur pruning: at pruning, the mature shoot most distant from the permanent cordon is generally removed and the closest one cut back to a two node spur.

☐ 1 year old cane
☐ 2 year old wood
▨ 3 year old wood
■ permanent cordon

Source: B. G. Coombe and P. R. Dry (eds.), *Viticulture*, ii: *Practices*

fruiting SHOOTS. Of all PRUNING systems, SPUR PRUNING is the most severe since over 90% of the previous year's cane growth is removed. Spurs are also left on cane-pruned vines to augment replacement canes at next pruning.   B.G.C.

spur pruning, a form of winter vine PRUNING whereby the canes are cut back to two-bud SPURS (see diagram). Normally the spurs are spaced along a CORDON top and point upwards (although see SMART–DYSON). There are several advantages to spur pruning, in that it takes less time to prune by hand and the operation can also be mechanized easily (see MECHANICAL PRUNING). Also, setting the spur spacing results in the correct shoot spacing in the canopy, which in turn leads to well-exposed leaves and fruit (see CANOPY MICRO-CLIMATE). Spur pruning is not particularly well suited to very vigorous vineyards, however, as excessive SHADE can lead to the loss of both yield (due to low bud fruitfulness) and quality. The other main form of vine pruning is CANE PRUNING. See also CORDON TRAINING.   R.E.S.

Sri Lanka (formerly Ceylon), tropical Indian Ocean island nation where two fledgling, very small-scale ventures have tried to make wine from established plantings of Cardinal, Black Muscat, and a variety called Israel Blue vines originally grown for TABLE GRAPES. In 2014, two companies were licensed to make wine from imported MUST and GRAPE CONCENTRATE as well as local fruit, including grapes. One is a collaborative venture with an Italian company.   D.G.

stabilization, group of wine-processing operations undertaken to ensure that the wine, once bottled, will not form hazes, clouds, or unwanted deposits; become gassy; or undergo rapid deterioration of flavour after BOTTLING.

A quick recovery from BOTTLE SICKNESS and subtle changes in flavour that occur with lengthy AGEING are considered normal in a **stable** wine. BARREL MATURATION has the effect of stabilizing a wine naturally, if more slowly.

Stabilization includes two sorts of operations: one to counter physical and chemical changes and another to counter microbiological changes.

Physical and chemical stability

Young wines are supersaturated in TARTRATES; REFRIGERATION and cold FILTRATION will reduce the concentration of tartrates below the level that would subsequently form crystals in the bottle.

Young white wines often contain high concentrations of rapidly browning PHENOLICS which, if left in the wine, will cause undue darkening of the wine after bottling. Selective FINING, with CASEIN, for example, can remove the offending type of phenolic and ensure longer light colour in young white wines. Young red wines may also contain excessive amounts of TANNINS which taste bitter and astringent. If they are designed to be drunk young, they can be fined to remove some of these tannins.

White wines contain large amounts of heat-unstable PROTEINS which can coagulate and appear as a haze in the bottle unless it is kept at a constant, low temperature. These proteins can be removed by fining with BENTONITE.

Microbiological stability

Measures to ensure microbiological stability have to counter the growth of either YEAST or BACTERIA. The simplest way to avoid yeast growth, which could result in a SECOND FERMENTATION, is to ensure that the wine is free of fermentable sugar, and that its RESIDUAL SUGAR is negligible. If some residual sugar is necessary to balance, say, high ACIDITY in the wine, then sterile filtration and STERILE BOTTLING are the surest way of guaranteeing stability. Failing the necessary equipment and trained personnel, additions of SULFUR DIOXIDE and SORBIC ACID will sufficiently inhibit most yeast growth, at some marginal depreciation of wine quality.

Stabilization of wine against bacterial attack is not so much of a problem in clean, modern wineries where the level of HYGIENE is high. The most harmful bacteria, those which turn wine into vinegar, ACETOBACTER, can operate only in the presence of OXYGEN and so stability can be assured by protecting the wine from air. Furthermore, sulfur dioxide, which is invariably used by winemakers, helps by suppressing the growth of acetobacter, and that of LACTIC ACID BACTERIA. Lactic acid bacteria can also be inhibited by removing all fermentable sugars and all of the MALIC ACID (by MALOLACTIC CONVERSION), two substrates for growth of some lactics.

No cellar treatments are needed against micro-organisms harmful to humans since wine's high levels of acidity and alcohol naturally inhibit their growth.   A.D.W.

Stags Leap District, California wine region and AVA. See NAPA.

stainless steel, sometimes referred to as inox (from the French *acier inoxydable*), is widely used for holding wine, both for AGEING and, especially, for FERMENTATION. For wines made PROTECTIVELY it has the great advantage over wood that it is easy to clean and OXYGEN can be completely excluded from it, by the use of INERT GAS to fill the HEAD SPACE if necessary. It has the advantage over CONCRETE that TEMPERATURE CONTROL is even easier, especially with REFRIGERATED jacketing and cooling/warming coils, and any TARTRATES can be hosed out rather than having to be chipped off the concrete walls. For some wines, the exclusion of oxygen can be a disadvantage, however, and there is a risk of REDUCTION.

Nor is there any possibility of the gradual, natural CLARIFICATION and STABILIZATION process that is possible in wooden containers.

stake. The simplest form of vine support is a stake driven into the ground beside the vine. A stake supports an individual vine, whereas POSTS, which are usually thicker than stakes, support several vines from suspended wires. Stakes are a very traditional form of vine support, having been used for centuries. Vines trained to stakes are most common in the OLD WORLD, although the vineyards of California are a significant exception. Since vines are climbing plants, they are unable to support themselves unless specially trained with a short trunk which thickens with age, as for GOBELET vines.

Materials used for stakes vary enormously between different wine regions, reflecting local availability. Most common is WOOD, which has been used for centuries, although it is only recently that timber has been treated chemically, preventing softwoods from rotting in the ground. However, such treated wood requires special handling for disposal as it is toxic when burnt. Sometimes stakes are made from round timber, as in much of Europe, or from sawn timber, as in California. They can also be made from stone (slaty schist), as in the Douro Valley of Portugal, or from concrete, as in parts of Italy and China. Stakes made from steel, plastic, or fibreglass have become more common in recent times and can be installed already notched and punched for wires.

See also POST.   R.E.S.

stalk. For information about the stalk of an individual grape or berry, see PEDICEL. For information about the stalk of a bunch of grapes, see BUNCHSTEM. See also STEM.

stamen, pollen-bearing part of a flower that consists generally of an ANTHER borne on a filament. A grapevine flower is small and has five erect stamens that become evident after the CALYPTRA or cap has fallen off at FLOWERING.   B.G.C.

standard drinks, unit of measurement used by governments to quantify a normal or regular pour of alcoholic drink by the amount of pure ALCOHOL it contains; also known as a unit of alcohol. Once this has been agreed upon, the theory goes, it is easier for authorities to set safe limits for consumption. There are many stumbling blocks, however, including wide variance among countries with regard to how much alcohol a 'standard drink' contains: 14 g in the US, 13.6 g in Canada, 12 g in France, 10 g in Australia and 8 g in the UK. In addition, both standard servings and the average ALCOHOLIC STRENGTH of wine are greater than when the standards were first set (see HEALTH, Sensible drinking). In some countries such as Australia, it is compulsory to state on wine labels the number of standard drinks each bottle contains.   B.B. & C.S.S.

starch, vine, an insoluble carbohydrate polymer composed of GLUCOSE residues. It is non-osmotic and is the principal storage substance in plants, forming as starch grains. Starch grains occur in the leaf and in cells of storage tissue in stems and roots of the vine. During daylight hours, when SUCROSE levels rise in leaves due to PHOTOSYNTHESIS, starch grains build up. At night they are metabolized to provide the sugar needed for RESPIRATION (this is also their fate in the human gut). Starch, natural storage reserves, are remobilized when buds burst and shoots begin to grow. Unlike many fruits, grape berries do not contain much starch, which is one reason why grapes do not ripen after picking (apart from changes associated with dehydration). Starch is the principal CARBOHYDRATE reserve of vines.   B.G.C.

state winemaking though less common than it once was, has been important, not just in eastern Europe during the communist era when all activity took place under the auspices of the state, but also in TURKEY, Germany, where the state has owned a number of important vineyards and cellars, including KLOSTER EBERBACH, and at certain points in their history in North African countries such as ALGERIA, EGYPT, and MOROCCO.

staves are the shaped wooden planks that are cut and formed into BARRELS. See BARREL MAKING for more details.

Shorter lengths designed to impart OAK FLAVOUR to wines stored in used barrels or in tanks may be called **inner staves** (see BARREL INSERTS and INNER STAVES, respectively).

S

Steen, name by which CHENIN BLANC used to be known in South Africa.

Steiermark, wine region in AUSTRIA known in English as Styria, comprising the southeast corner of the country and incorporating the official wine regions of SÜD-OSTSTEIERMARK, SÜDSTEIERMARK, and WESTSTEIERMARK. In the age of Imperial Austria, adjacent wingrowing tracts of what is now SLOVENIA were also considered part of Steiermark, making a total viticultural area more than twice the size of that remaining in Austria today. In 2006 Slovenia officially renamed a large share of the Podravje region 'Stajerska Slovenija', about which some Austrian neighbours had misgivings initially. The traditional centre for Styrian viticulture was in fact Maribor in Slovenia (Marburg in German), where in the early 19th century Archduke John of Austria directed expansion and improvements in winegrowing, including the introduction of most grape varieties found there today, for which he is still revered by both Austrian and Slovenian vintners.   D.S.

Steinfeder, the lightest in terms of MUST WEIGHT and alcohol among the trio of dry white wine categories in AUSTRIA's WACHAU region—specifically for unchaptalized grapes of 73 to 83 °OECHSLE (15 to 17 °KMW) which result in wines with no more than 11% alcohol. Consumers have been willing to pay much higher prices for the fuller-bodied wines of the other categories FEDERSPIEL and SMARAGD, and it can be difficult to achieve attractive flavours in Wachau grapes at such low levels of POTENTIAL ALCOHOL. So Steinfeder wines today, however charming and refreshing, tend to be made only from a few comparatively cool sites or ones considered otherwise expendable, from Grüner Veltliner, and solely for local consumption. The name comes from a feathery grass species indigenous to the local vineyard terraces.   D.S.

Stellenbosch, important wine district in SOUTH AFRICA, named after the charming university town at its heart 45 km/28 miles east of Cape Town with its Cape Dutch, Cape Georgian, and Victorian buildings shaded by long-established oaks.

Stellenbosch is the Cape's most famous wine district, traditionally associated with the country's most celebrated reds. It has been producing wine since 1679. As well as Stellenbosch University, it is also home to the Wine & Spirit Board and the biggest wine wholesaler DISTELL with its 10,000-barrel maturation cellars. Stellenbosch is surrounded by valleys of vines and the soaring blue-grey mountains of Stellenbosch, Simonsberg, and Helderberg. The district's wards—Banghoek, Bottelary, Devon Valley, Jonkershoek Valley, Papegaaiberg, Polkadraai Hills, and Simonsberg-Stellenbosch in

2014—all yield wines capable of displaying distinctive differences. Vineyards on the Helderberg (which runs from Stellenbosch to False Bay at Somerset West) enjoy a considerable reputation. Soils and climate vary, from sandy ALLUVIAL loam along the valley floors and river courses to deep, moisture-retaining decomposed GRANITE on the hillsides. The climate is tempered by the Atlantic sweeping into False Bay, a 15-minute drive from the town. Average daily summer temperatures range from 20 °C/68 °F.

Stellenbosch returns low average YIELDS; it makes less than 9% of the country's wine despite having 17% of the country's vines and the greatest concentration of leading estates, an extensive wine route network, and scores of restaurants.

Stellenbosch University is the only one in South Africa offering professional degrees in both VITICULTURE and OENOLOGY. Informal teaching in these two subjects started in 1889 but the Department of Viticulture and Oenology was formally opened only in 1917, with Professor A. I. Perold as chair. The university has been an important influence on the Cape wine industry over the decades, and continues to produce most of the Cape's leading viticulturists and winemakers. The town is also home to the Agricultural Research Council's ARC Infruitec-Nietvoorbij Institute for Horticulture, Viticulture, and Oenology; and the College for Agriculture and Oenology at nearby Elsenburg. Stellenbosch University is also home to the Institute of Wine Biotechnology.

As elsewhere (see the University of BORDEAUX, DAVIS, GEISENHEIM, for example), the PHYLLOXERA crisis was a powerful motivation for viticultural research, and from 1890 until about 1920 most of Stellenbosch's work was concentrated on re-establishing the phylloxera-devastated vineyards of the Cape.

During the 1920s, considerable effort was expended on improving the quality of fruit-bearing vine SCIONS, a range that was naturally restricted by strict QUARANTINE regulations. This involved VINE BREEDING which led to NEW VARIETIES, of which PINOTAGE has been the most widely acclaimed. Under the guidance of Stellenbosch oenologists, South Africa was one of the first wine-producing countries to apply widespread TEMPERATURE CONTROL to fermentations. Other globally admired advances have been in plant material quality, ROOTSTOCKS, root systems, PRUNING, CANOPY MANAGEMENT, vine spacing, vine row orientation, grape and wine flavour profiles, and optimal ripeness for different wine styles.

Stelvin. See SCREWCAPS.

stem. The terms stem and stalk tend to be used somewhat carelessly by winemakers, if not by viticulturists. For information about

the stem of an individual grape or berry, see PEDICEL. For information about the stem of a bunch of grapes, see BUNCHSTEM. See also DESTEMMING.

stemming, paradoxically alternative term for DESTEMMING grapes.

stem pitting, vine virus disease. See RUGOSE WOOD.

stemware. See GLASSES.

sterile bottling, or, more correctly, **aseptic bottling**, is the technique of getting wine into a closed bottle without incorporating any micro-organisms (notably YEAST and harmful BACTERIA). Borrowed from the pharmaceutical packaging industry, this technique does the job of PASTEURIZATION without the use of heat. Aseptic techniques have become the norm for wine bottling because the use of membrane filters (see FILTRATION) has made the task very simple. Many everyday modern wines have small amounts of RESIDUAL SUGAR and therefore require bottling in an aseptic manner, but the degree of care needed depends upon the levels of residual sugar and alcohol.

An aseptic bottling line involves the creation of a clean room, modifying the usual equipment so that it may be sterilized easily. The room is kept under a slight positive pressure of filtered air and entry is restricted to the few specially trained and clothed personnel required. Microorganisms are removed from the wine by sterile FILTRATION using membranes, and the corks or other CLOSURES are sterilized by gaseous SULFUR DIOXIDE or other chemical sterilizing agents such as peracetic acid. The bottling and corking machines are usually sterilized by steam, or by chemical sterilants. Frequent sample bottles are removed at random for microbiological analysis, and each bottling run is held in storage until it is certain that no organisms are growing.   D.B.

Bird, D., *Understanding Wine Technology* (3rd edn, Newark, 2010).

steward, wine. See SOMMELIER.

stickie, Australian term for sweet, usually fortified, wines. Typical examples are the TOPAQUES AND MUSCATS of RUTHERGLEN and Glenrowan in North East VICTORIA.

stigma. See FLOWERS, VINE.

stilbene. See RESVERATROL.

stirring, winemaking term which may be used as a synonym for LEES STIRRING or may refer to the important operation of stirring, usually in much larger containers, when blending disparate components in a blend. This is particularly necessary when grape spirit is added to wine, as during FORTIFICATION, since

TERRACES / DOURO / PORTUGAL The monocultural Douro Valley in northern Portugal, upriver of the city of Oporto, is one of the world's most haunting wine regions. It is exclusively responsible for port and Douro table wine. Many of the vineyards are so steep that **terraces** are often essential. © Alan Copson/Getty Images

the spirit, with its lower DENSITY, tends to float on top of the wine. Stirring, or dynamizing, also plays an important role in the production of some BIODYNAMIC preparations.

stomata (plural of **stoma**), minute openings on the surface of leaves bordered by two guard cells which open and close, thus regulating the exchange of gases between the atmosphere and the air chambers inside the leaf, especially of water out and carbon dioxide in (see TRANSPIRATION and PHOTOSYNTHESIS). The stomata of the grapevine occur only on the underside of each leaf blade, and there are also some on berries.   B.G.C.

stones and rocks are fragments of bedrock and, in the context of SOIL, the two words are synonymous (see also GEOLOGY). As visible constituents of the soil or its surface they loom large in the folklore of wine quality. They figure prominently in the older French concepts of TERROIR. Nineteenth-century French writers such as Rendu and Petit-Lafitte laid particular emphasis on the proportions of stone or gravel in the soils of the best vineyards. The stonier the soil, they said, the better in general is the wine quality.

Present thinking broadly supports the old ideas. Rocky and stony soils are usually well drained, but at the same time not too fertile. A high proportion of stones also reduces water-holding capacity (see SOIL WATER, which is especially critical to red wine quality in Bordeaux, for example). Both factors are significant in climates and management systems where excessive vine VIGOUR, leading to unsatisfactory CANOPY MICROCLIMATES, is a threat. Forcing the vine to develop a sparse, but extensive, ROOT system also helps to buffer it against sudden changes in nutrition or water supply. Beyond that, a rocky or stony soil is thought to help by efficiently absorbing heat during sunshine and reradiating it during the evening and cloudy periods—thereby perhaps affording the ripening fruit a better temperature regime for flavour RIPENING (see CLIMATE AND WINE QUALITY). Stones and rocks also form an efficient mulch against surface evaporation, and offer protection against SOIL EROSION.

See also SOIL AND WINE QUALITY.
                                                    J.G. & A.J.M.

Fanet, J., 'Geology and soil: effects on wine quality', VIII International Terroir Congress (2010), terroir2010.entecra.it/atti/pdf/session4.pdf

Lanyon, D. M., Cass, A., and Hansen, D., 'The effect of soil properties on vine performance', *CSIRO Land and Water Technical Report* 34/04 (2004), www.clw.csiro.au/publications/technical2004/tr34-04.pdf

Morlat, R., and Jacquet, A., 'The soil effects on the grapevine root system in several vineyards of the Loire Valley (France)', *Vitis*, 32 (1993), 35–42.

stoppers, wine bottle. See CLOSURES.

storing wine is an important aspect of wine consumption, since wine is relatively sensitive to storage conditions and is one of the very few consumer products that can improve with age (although see AGEING for details of how few, and which, wines this applies to). Until the era of inflation, wine producers and merchants regarded storing and ageing wine as part of their business, but since the 1960s they have steadily relinquished this role. The development of the EN PRIMEUR market and the increase in the number of wine COLLECTORS leaves many more ordinary wine drinkers with the problem of how to store wine over long periods, often a decade or two.

There are two basic choices: to consign the bottles to professional storage and/or to establish some form of domestic cellar. If wine is put in storage, it is vital that a specialist in wine storage is found, since wine is a much more fragile commodity than most things kept in warehouses, and needs specialist treatment and conditions. It is important that the wine storage specialist is in sound financial health itself, it understands the detail of storage conditions needed, and that it provides some facility for marking individual CASES with some identification of their owner. In the case of business failure, this can make the difference between establishing possession and not.

For more details of how to identify and, if necessary, convert part of a home into a suitable place to store wine, see CELLAR.

Ideal storage conditions

Even in Ancient GREECE there was some appreciation of the importance of storage conditions on the evolution and health of wine. The key factors are TEMPERATURE, light, HUMIDITY, and security.

If wine is kept too hot, or exposed to strong sunlight, it rapidly deteriorates. If it is kept too cold, it can freeze, expand, and push out the stopper of whatever container it is held in.

For bottles stored for a few weeks, the primary concern is to keep them from strong direct light (white wines in colourless glass are most at risk) and to ensure that they do not reach temperatures more than about 25 °C/77 °F (although there is some latitude here, depending on the fragility of the wine), at which point the wine may be spoilt and forever afterwards taste cooked.

A fairly wide range of temperatures is suitable for wine storage, although, in general, the lower the storage temperature, the slower the reactions involved in wine maturation and, the theory goes, the more complex the wine eventually. Dramatic temperature swings should be avoided and an average temperature somewhere in the range 10–15 °C (50–9 °F) is

considered suitable (see TEMPERATURE for more details).

Some degree of humidity is beneficial, to ensure that the exposed end of corks don't dry out and allow in oxygen. A level of 75% relative humidity is usually cited, although this, like so many aspects of wine consumption rather than production, suffers from a lack of scientific research. The disadvantage of very damp cellars is that damp labels eventually deteriorate and make identification difficult (and some COLLECTORS prefer pristine labels so any resale price is not prejudiced).

Bottles to be stored for more than a few weeks, however, should be stored so that any cork is kept damp and there is no possibility of its drying out and allowing in the enemy, OXYGEN. This usually entails storing the bottles horizontally, ideally in a wine rack so that individual bottles can easily be extracted, or in a BIN full of wines of the same sort. Many wine producers deliberately mark their CASES in an effort to keep bottles upside down, and corks damp, during shipment. The increased use of alternative CLOSURES however, particularly SCREWCAPS, suggests that horizontal storage may no longer be strictly necessary, although the stopper is much less likely to be damaged than if bottles are stored vertically.

The wine itself in an inverted bottle comes to no harm. Research in the late 1990s suggested that an ideal storage position for wine bottles stoppered with a natural cork is at a slight angle from the horizontal so that the cork is kept damp but the air bubble of ULLAGE just touches the cork rather than lying on top of the middle of the bottle. It has also been suggested by some that champagne ages most gracefully when stored in bottles that are kept upright rather than horizontal but this has not been proven.

If a maturing wine is agitated, it may disturb the sediment and therefore the AGEING process (although this is an unproven hypothesis). Some cellars are specifically designed with rubber racks for bottles in order to minimize any likely vibration. The need for a secure storage space is obvious, especially since bottles of alcoholic drink seem to be widely regarded as common currency rather than private property.

It is also important that there are no strong, persistent smells in a long-term wine storage area.

See also BULK STORAGE.

Straccia Cambiale, synonym for the white grape BOMBINO BIANCO.

Strathbogie Ranges, hilly, elevated Australian wine region in central VICTORIA. Elevation, aspect, and soil differences provide a multiplicity of opportunity for the 14 producers here.

straw wines, sweet wines made from grapes dried on straw. See VIN DE PAILLE, ALSACE, AUSTRIA, CZECH REPUBLIC, VIN SANTO, and DRIED-GRAPE WINES.

Strevi, independent DOC for a sweet white wine made from late-harvested or dried MOSCATO Bianco grapes made in the hills around Strevi in the east of the ASTI zone. As it is usually riper in flavour than most MOSCATO D'ASTI thanks to Strevi's warmer MESOCLIMATE and steep vineyards, it has also been granted subzone status within the Moscato d'Asti DOCG zone.   W.S.

structure, TASTING term that refers not to any FLAVOUR but to the TANNINS, particularly their intensity. It may sometimes incorporate ACIDITY.

Stück, German term for a large wooden BARREL, typically one with a capacity of 1,200 l/317 gal used in the RHINE regions of GERMANY. (In the MOSEL region the FUDER is more common.) A **Halbstück** contains 600 l, and was commonly used for transporting wine in the pre-tanker era, while a **Doppelstück** contains 2,400 l.

stuck fermentation, winemaker's nightmare involving an alcoholic FERMENTATION which ceases before completion. Such fermentations are notoriously difficult to restart and the wine is at risk of spoilage from OXIDATION and BACTERIAL DISEASE. Before cooling equipment was commonplace, fermentation TEMPERATURES could reach a dangerously high level, often in excess of 35 °C/95 °F. In extreme cases, with temperatures nearing the range at which YEASTS are killed, over 40 °C, the yeast cells release compounds which inhibit future yeast growth, thereby making it difficult or impossible to restart such fermentations, even after cooling.

Stuck fermentation has many documented causes, and because there can be several concurrent causes, diagnosis is often difficult. However, one clear cause is the tendency over recent decades to harvest grapes at higher maturity levels (see PHYSIOLOGICAL RIPENESS) which has resulted in grapes with higher sugar levels and wines with a higher alcohol content. Unless fermentation conditions are optimal, various stresses culminate in reduced or, in some cases, complete cessation of fermentation activity before the target sugar content has been reached. One common stress is deficiency of the essential nutrient NITROGEN. Grapes which come from vineyards deficient in nitrogen have a low level of available nitrogen, or yeast-assimilable nitrogen (YAN). This limits the development of yeast cells, and fermentation activity is not sustained after they have become starved of nitrogen. This problem is exacerbated in the fermentation of highly clarified musts (see CLARIFICATION), with which the winemaker is aiming

to produce wine low in phenolics. The very low content of suspended grape solids in such musts means that the level of LIPIDS, the compounds that allow yeast to build strong membranes needed to limit the toxic effects of alcohol, is also low. Fermentation at low temperatures (below 15 °C/60 °F) with strict protection from air (oxygen), which prevents yeast from making lipids, greatly increases the risk of stuck fermentation.

There are several ways to reduce the risk of stuck fermentation: adding nitrogen to the juice, either in the form of an ammonium salt (most commonly DIAMMONIUM PHOSPHATE) or a proprietary yeast food which contains significant nitrogen; adding back the 'fluffy' or light fraction of must settlings to increase the level of grape solids (lipids); using a yeast starter culture of a high-alcohol-tolerant strain that has been propagated with excess air; or adding nitrogen and exposing the fermentation to a small amount of air once the yeast is active. These options are usually effective, especially when several are used in combination. The last treatment is most simply achieved by stirring, SPARGING with air or OXYGEN, or PUMPING OVER. Failure of the yeast inoculum to dominate the ambient yeasts that are invariably present in grape must can result in a stuck fermentation if the ambient yeasts have a lower tolerance to alcohol. Ambient yeasts which produce 'killer toxin' (called zymocidal yeasts; yeast toxin has no effect on human cells) can be especially aggressive by actively eliminating the killer-sensitive wine yeast. Certain LACTIC ACID BACTERIA, which can grow rapidly during the early stages of fermentation when sulfites have not been added to the must prior to fermentation, can interrupt fermentation. Inhibition of fermentation by ambient yeasts and bacteria can be diminished considerably by using a highly active yeast starter culture, choosing a yeast that is resistant to killer toxin (broad spectrum resistant strains are not yet available commercially), and by any method that reduces the number of wild micro-organisms present in the must. Should a ferment become stuck despite the use of these procedures, increasing concentrations of the problem stuck wine should be added to a new rescue-yeast starter culture, in the presence of adequate nutrients, including oxygen.   P.A.H.

Alexandre, H., and Charpentier, C., 'Biochemical aspects of stuck and sluggish fermentation in grape must', *Journal of Industrial Microbiology and Biotechnology*, 20 (1998), 20–7.

Bisson, L. F., and Butzke, C. E., 'Diagnosis and rectification of stuck and sluggish fermentations', *American Journal of Enology and Viticulture*, 51 (2000), 168–77.

Henschke, P. A., 'Stuck fermentation: causes, prevention and cure', in M. Allen, P. Leske, and G. Baldwin (eds.), *Proceedings of the Australian*

Society of Viticulture and Oenology: Advances in Juice Clarification and Yeast Inoculation (Adelaide, 1997), 30–8, 41.

Styria, small but fashionable wine area in the far south east of AUSTRIA known as STEIERMARK in German and most famous for aromatic, lively dry whites.

subjectivity plays an unavoidable part in wine TASTING. Personal preferences inevitably play some role in wine assessment. For more discussion of this, see PHILOSOPHY AND WINE and QUALITY IN WINE.

submerged cap is a way of keeping the CAP wet and mixed with the fermenting wine to facilitate EXTRACTION. A perforated screen is positioned just under the surface of the liquid to keep the cap submerged but the pressure of the rising CARBON DIOXIDE tends to force the cap against the screen, making extraction less efficient. A pipe to allow the gas to escape can help to resolve this. It is still quite common to see head boards performing the same function in traditional CONCRETE tanks in the BAROSSA VALLEY. See also PUNCHING DOWN, PUMPING OVER, and MACERATION.

subsoil, the usually heavier-textured layer of a SOIL PROFILE which underlies the main zone containing ROOTS and ORGANIC MATTER. It overlies the bedrock (see ROCK) or sediments from which the soil is formed. The contrast in texture between surface soil and subsoil is greatest in ancient soils and in forest (especially pine forest) regions, due to the progressive downward leaching of the heavier minerals and fine CLAY particles. Such subsoils are, however, typically depleted of many of the important nutrient elements, because roots have continuously extracted them from depth and deposited them at the surface in leaf litter and derived organic matter.

A fairly heavy-textured subsoil, provided that it drains freely enough, can have advantages for viticulture because it provides a good store of moisture that is well protected against direct EVAPORATION and exploitation by shallow-rooted WEEDS. The usual relative sparseness of vine roots in the subsoil, together with the strength with which clay particles hold water (see SOIL WATER and SOIL TEXTURE), ensures that the stored water can be used only at a limited rate. Seguin cites the clay soils of POMEROL as an example of this. It helps to provide the vine with the consistent regime of water supply that Seguin believes to be important for wine quality. See also TERROIR and SOIL AND WINE QUALITY.

On the other hand, many heavy subsoils impede DRAINAGE, particularly those formed from acid rock materials. These can be detrimental to viticulture, unless carefully drained and, possibly, LIMED to overcome SOIL ACIDITY and improve the SOIL STRUCTURE. J.G.

Seguin, G., 'Influence des terroirs viticoles', *Bulletin de l'OIV*, 56 (1983), 3–18.

Seguin, G., '"Terroirs" and pedology of wine growing', *Experientia*, 42 (1986), 861–72.

White, R. E., *Understanding Vineyard Soils* (2nd edn, Oxford, 2015).

subsoiling. See RIPPING.

succinic acid, an acid found to a limited extent in both grapes and wine. Present in low concentrations in ripe grapes, it is a contributor to the fresh or tart taste of the fruit, albeit to a much lesser extent than TARTARIC ACID or MALIC ACID. Like these two principal grape acids, pure succinic acid is a white crystalline solid that is very soluble in water and alcoholic water solutions such as wine.

Succinic acid concentrations tend to be higher in wine than in grapes because the acid is a by-product of the complex nitrogen metabolic processes involved in YEAST growth during FERMENTATION. Concentrations are generally higher in red wines than in whites. In some wines, a considerable proportion of the succinic acid reacts with one molecule of ETHANOL to form an ESTER, mono-ethyl succinate, which has a very mild, fruity aroma. A.D.W. & G.T.

Coulter, A. D., Godden, P. W., and Pretorius, I. S., 'Succinic acid: how is it formed, what is its effect on titratable acidity, and what factors influence its concentration in wine?', *Australian and New Zealand Wine Industry Journal*, 19/6 (Nov/Dec 2004), 16–25.

suckering. See DESUCKERING.

sucrose, cane sugar, the most common of the SUGARS, is ubiquitous in plants because it is the preferred compound for PHLOEM translocation of energy and carbon around the plant. Sucrose consists of a GLUCOSE molecule joined to a FRUCTOSE molecule. Breakdown (HYDROLYSIS) of sucrose is achieved readily by the enzyme INVERTASE, which 'inverts' it to these hexoses.

Invertase in the vine occurs in CELL wall spaces but not in those of the leaf, which is why sucrose is confined in vines mainly to leaves and phloem tubes. Invertase is abundant in grape berries both in the cell walls and in the vacuoles; hence the sugars that accumulate in berries are mainly glucose and fructose. B.G.C.

Südburgenland, stretches along AUSTRIA's south-east border with Hungary as far south as SLOVENIA but the region's 500 ha/1,200 acres of vines represent just 1% of the country's total. While fascinating white wines of Grüner Veltliner, Welschriesling, and Weissburgunder (Pinot Blanc) are emerging, the region is best known for its profoundly complex and ageworthy Blaufränkisch, particularly that grown in Deutsch-Schützen and neighbouring EISENBERG. Pioneers in the 1990s were the Krutzler family of Weingut Perwolf and Uwe Schiefer, who did much to define Südburgenland's official appellation of origin, Eisenberg DAC. (A curious regional relic of PHYLLOXERA's aftermath is UHUDLER.) D.S.

Süd-Oststeiermark, wine region of AUSTRIA that covers a vast area, yet harbours only around 1,300 ha/3,200 acres of vineyard, little more than half that planted by its much smaller but densely planted neighbour SÜDSTEIERMARK. Süd-Oststeiermark's top growers, however, stake claims for the distinctiveness of their individual sectors and villages, of which the best-known are Kapfenstein, Straden, Klöch, and Bad Radkersburg. Important varieties include Chardonnay, MUSKATELLER, Pinot Blanc (Weissburgunder), Pinot Gris, Sauvignon Blanc, Welschriesling, and Traminer, which has a long association with several south-east Styrian communities. D.S.

Südsteiermark, a dramatically hilly AUSTRIAN wine region fanning south from Graz, the capital of STEIERMARK, and hugging some 40 km/25 miles of frontier with SLOVENIA. Its reputation and densely planted 1,950 ha/4,816 acres (yielding around 7% of national production) are disproportionate to its deceptively small outline on a viticultural map. Südsteiermark gained national prominence in the wake of Austria's 1985 wine scandal, when wine lovers sought out small wine estates which had little truck with NÉGOCIANTS and whose vineyards were within walking distance of the point-of-sale. That said, one's shoes and heart need to be stout to tackle the steep terrain of a region whose cool, well-watered growing season and complex mingling of VOLCANIC and sedimentary soils support success with a wide range of white wine grapes, most importantly Sauvignon Blanc, Chardonnay (here generally labelled Morillon), Muskateller, and Welschriesling, but also Pinot Blanc, Pinot Gris, and Traminer. The few reds are made primarily from Austria's ubiquitous Zweigelt, although there is some fine Pinot Noir and Blaufränkisch. Varietal diversity was already a feature of greater Steiermark in the early 19th century, but the choice of principal grapes today—and especially the pre-eminent Sauvignon Blanc—stem from regional pioneers in the 1980s, in particular Manfred Tement.

South Styrian wines are generally marketed in two categories. Steierische KLASSIK refers to tank-aged, early bottled, bracing, dry varietals with 11.5–12.5% alcohol and no MALOLACTIC CONVERSION. Vineyard-designated wines—usually varietals but occasionally blends—tend to be fuller-bodied and more ambitiously vinified and matured, often featuring SKIN CONTACT, malolactic conversion, and LEES CONTACT during BARREL AGEING. Both size and age of casks have been increasing in recent years after a period during the 1990s and early 21st century when new BARRIQUES were FASHIONABLE. There are signs of these two stylistic categories blurring at some important addresses, and a small but strong cadre of contrarian growers espousing NATURAL winemaking techniques has also emerged.

South Styria features many locations so minuscule that they have to borrow other localities' postal addresses. Frequently encountered wine-growing addresses, all within the southern half of Südsteiermark, include Eckberg, Ehrenhausen, Gamlitz, Glanz, Grassnitzberg, Leutschach, Nussberg, Ottenberg, Ratsch, Spielfeld, Steinbach, Sulztal, and Welitsch. Given this region's penchant for single-site bottlings, not to mention the scenic beauty of those sites, it is hardly surprising that the names of certain vineyards, particularly the tight cluster of Obegg, Hochgrassnitzberg, and Zieregg, which straddles the border with Slovenia, are well known. Styrian growers such as Gross and Tement have established sister wineries over the border in Slovenia, or been involved in collaborations with Slovenian vintners. Ten of the region's most prominent growers, under the name Steierische Terroir & Klassik, have classified their best vineyards as premier or grand cru using the abbreviations '1-STK' and 'G-STK' on price lists and labels. D.S.

Südtirol, or South Tyrol. See ALTO ADIGE.

sugar addition, winemaking practice more usually called CHAPTALIZATION or, in EU parlance, ENRICHMENT.

sugar concentration in grapes. See MUST WEIGHT.

sugar in grapes, the *raison d'être* of VITICULTURE. The central role of sugar in the utility of grapes for wine, TABLE GRAPES, DRYING GRAPES, and other viticultural products cannot be overemphasized. SUGARS produce SWEETNESS and ferment to produce ETHANOL, both of which are valued by humans. However, of all sugary plant produce, none yields a commodity as highly valued or widely produced as grape wine.

The free sugar that accumulates in grapes, GLUCOSE and FRUCTOSE, is the result of translocation of SUCROSE photosynthesized in leaves and moved via PHLOEM tubes into grape berries during RIPENING, where it is inverted (hydrolysed) by the enzyme INVERTASE. The astonishing feature of grapes is that this accumulation occurs at the same time as water is accumulating in the berry, yet concentration is also increasing; in other words, sugar is increasing proportionately more than water. Other phloem-provided sucrose moves throughout the vine dispensing energy and the carbon skeletons for all organic molecules throughout the vine. Additionally, sugar is used for carbon storage, as STARCH in wood, and for the formation of GLYCOSIDES in the storage of secondary metabolites in vacuoles of cells (see FLAVOUR PRECURSORS and FLAVOUR COMPOUNDS).

While total sugar content (see MUST WEIGHT) is a key factor in determining optimum RIPENESS of grapes for wine, sugar–acid balance is equally important; hence the use of sugar–acid ratio as a guide to the date of harvest. See also PHYSIOLOGICAL RIPENESS and GRAPE QUALITY ASSESSMENT. B.G.C.

Keller, M., *The Science of Grapevines: Anatomy and Physiology* (Elsevier, 2010).

sugars, simpler members of the large group of natural organic chemical compounds called CARBOHYDRATES. The sugar of common parlance, SUCROSE, comes from either sugar cane or sugar beet plants and is a major international commodity. To scientists, sucrose is a molecule made up of one unit of each of GLUCOSE and FRUCTOSE linked together with the elimination of a molecule of water.

Plants produce sucrose by PHOTOSYNTHESIS, many of them accumulating sucrose within their cells but others, such as the common wine vine VINIFERA, breaking this sucrose down into its two simpler constituent parts, glucose and fructose, which are stored in the berries. AMERICAN VINES store small amounts of sucrose in the fruit along with the two simpler forms. Over the millennia during which people have selected grape vines, they have chosen those capable of photosynthesizing an excess of sugars and storing them in berries. For more detail, see SUGAR IN GRAPES.

Although the amounts of sugars other than glucose and fructose detected in grape must are very small, the process of photosynthesis involves sugars with three, four, five, and seven carbon atoms as well as the six-carbon glucose and fructose.

Sucrose, usually in the form of sugar beet concentrate or some form of GRAPE CONCENTRATE, may be added to some grape musts during fermentation in order to increase the ALCOHOLIC STRENGTH of the resultant wine (see CHAPTALIZATION).

The total amount of sugars left in a finished wine is called its RESIDUAL SUGAR.

Some of the sucrose resulting from photosynthesis, stored in the berries as glucose and fructose before grape harvest, is converted into STARCH and stored in the vine's trunk and larger arms and roots during winter DORMANCY until spring temperatures begin the annual cycle of leaf and fruit production once more, and the starch is remobilized to soluble sugars, mainly glucose.

See also MUST WEIGHT. A.D.W.

sulfide and **disulfide** are the compounds of SULFUR with hydrogen or metallic elements in which the sulfur atom exists in its most reduced state, that is having gained two electrons from the other element or elements in the compound (see REDUCTION).

Sulfides occur naturally during FERMENTATION. Elemental sulfur residues on the grapes from fungicides can be reduced to HYDROGEN SULFIDE. The winemaker can detect this problem easily because hydrogen sulfide has an intense smell of bad eggs. Fortunately, the compound is very volatile and can usually be removed by simple AERATION.

In a winemaking context, any reference to 'sulfide' or 'sulfides' is invariably a criticism and usually means hydrogen sulfide. Sulfides should not be confused with SULFITE, however. A.D.W.

sulfite and **bisulfite**, the negatively charged ions liberated when sulfurous acid dissociates, as shown below:

$$H_2SO_3 \quad \rightleftharpoons \quad H^+ \quad + \quad HSO_3^-$$
sulfurous acid   hydrogen ion   bisulfite ion

$$HSO_3^- \quad \rightarrow \quad H^+ \quad + \quad SO_3^{--}$$
bisulfite ion   hydrogen ion   sulfite ion

The analytical method usually used for the measurement of sulfite determines all of the various forms which are active in terms of smell, effect on YEAST and BACTERIA, and potential danger to asthmatics (see SULFUR DIOXIDE). The term sulfites, or sulphites, is therefore used on wine labels (as in 'Contains sulfites/sulphites') as an inclusive term for free sulfur dioxide, sulfurous acid (hydrated sulfur dioxide), bisulfite ion, sulfite ion, and some forms of complexed sulfite. See LABELLING INFORMATION and ALLERGIES AND INTOLERANCES. A.D.W.

sulfur, an element that constitutes about 0.5% of the weight of the Earth's crust and one of the more important elements for mankind. It is extremely important in wine production because of the wide-ranging uses of SULFUR DIOXIDE. A pale yellow, brittle, solid substance at room temperature, it was already known to the speakers of Ancient Sanskrit as *sulvere*. The book of Genesis in the Bible refers to sulfur as brimstone. In its combined form as sulfuric acid, sulfur is used in so many manufacturing processes that the tonnage consumed by a nation can be taken as an indication of the health of its economy.

History

Sulfur has been used as a cleansing agent and wine preservative since antiquity. Among the various substances, such as pitch and resin, used by the Romans to prepare vessels in which wine was stored and to assist in the preservation of wines, authors such as CATO and PLINY also mention the use of sulfur. It seems probable that the pungent smells given off when ores containing sulfur were burned led to their association with a cleansing action, and experimentation would then have revealed the most efficacious methods of use. In the late 15th century, a German decree specifically refers to the use of sulfur, with wood shavings, powdered sulfur, herbs, and incense being burned in barrels before they were filled. By the 18th century, sulfur wicks were being regularly used to sterilize barrels in the best châteaux of Bordeaux (having been introduced by the DUTCH), and advances in chemistry had also led to the synthesis of derivatives of elemental sulfur, thus enabling inorganic salts containing sulfur to become widely used in winemaking. Sulfur dioxide is today used in the production of virtually all wines, albeit kept to a minimum in high-quality winemaking. and in many NATURAL WINES. In the vineyard, sulfur products are widely used to protect vines against POWDERY MILDEW. P.T.H.U.

Johnson, H., *The Story of Wine* (London, 1989).

Viticulture

Sulfur is essential for vine nutrition, although sulfur deficiency in vineyards is very rare. Vines usually obtain sufficient quantities from soil supplies, or from FUNGICIDES. Continued application of sulfur to vineyards to control powdery mildew for over a century has led to excess SOIL ACIDITY in many European vineyards. Sometimes periodic LIMING may be needed to counter soil acidification. See also SULFIDE. R.E.S.

Winemaking

Sulfur is most familiar to winemakers as sulfur dioxide. It may be reduced by YEAST during fermentation to produce foul-smelling HYDROGEN SULFIDE.

See also SULFITE. A.D.W.

sulfur dioxide, or SO_2, formed when elemental SULFUR is burned in air, is a colourless, pungent, choking gas and is the chemical compound most widely used by the winemaker, principally as a preservative and a disinfectant. Sulfur dioxide, as fumes from burning sulfur, has been used since antiquity to preserve and disinfect during the production and storage of foods (see SULFUR for more historical detail).

Sulfur dioxide is said to react with OXYGEN and so prevent wine or juice OXIDATION. This is an oversimplification because the chemical reaction between sulfur dioxide and oxygen is not rapid so it is not totally effective in preventing chemical oxidation. However, sulfur dioxide reduces oxidation in other ways.

The addition of sulfur dioxide during CRUSHING and PRESSING deactivates ENZYMES that catalyse oxidation, which leads to juice browning and modification of aromas and flavours, which is why it is often added to freshly picked grapes in the salt form of metabisulfite. (The compound is widely, often more liberally, used in the preparation of other foods and drinks, particularly fruit juices and dried fruits.) Sulfur dioxide is also an effective antimicrobial agent, so that maintaining sufficient free sulfur dioxide (see below) in juice or wine reduces the occurrence of oxidation due to microbial activity, for example acetification by ACETOBACTER. Sulfur dioxide is also used in combination with the antioxidant ASCORBIC ACID.

The antimicrobial properties of sulfur dioxide also help minimize undesirable aromas and flavours that may be produced by spoilage yeasts such as BRETTANOMYCES and by BACTERIA, although the activity of such organisms is largely controlled by harvesting sound grapes and by practising good winery HYGIENE. However, when non-inoculated FERMENTATION is effected by ambient YEASTS, care has to be taken if sulfur dioxide is added to the must as this may reduce the population of the desirable wild yeast strains.

Sulfur dioxide's efficacy is influenced by the wine's PH. Less is needed at lower pH because the pH level determines how much of the free sulfur dioxide is molecular (see below), the form in which it is effective as an anti-microbial agent.

Sulfur dioxide exists in wine and juice in free and bound forms. Total sulfur dioxide equals free sulfur dioxide plus bound sulfur dioxide. Bound sulfur dioxide is sulfur dioxide which has reacted or combined with up to 50 other wine constituents, including ACETALDEHYDE and PYRUVIC ACID. The free sulfur dioxide in wine or juice is an equilibrium between molecular sulfur dioxide (as a dissolved gas), bisulfite ion (HSO_3^-), and sulfite ion (SO_3^{2-}). This equilibrium depends on pH, with lower pH shifting the equilibrium towards molecular (gaseous) sulfur dioxide. It is only the free fraction that is effective as an antioxidant and microbicide and it is only free sulfur dioxide that affects aroma. Excess free sulfur dioxide may be perceived as an unpleasantly pungent odour that tickles the throat. In white wines, depending on pH, levels of free sulfur dioxide as low as 30 mg/l may produce molecular sulfur dioxide levels that are evident in the aroma and taste of the wine.

In the late 20th century, concerns about the allergenic properties of sulfur dioxide led to a widespread reduction in the permitted levels of total sulfur dioxide in wines. Permitted levels of up to 500 parts per million (ppm) in 1910 had fallen to well under half this limit for dry wines by the early 1990s. By the early 2000s most countries had made it mandatory to declare on the label 'contains sulfites' (or variations on that theme) if the overall content in the wine was greater than 10 mg/l. (For more details, see LABELLING INFORMATION and ALLERGIES AND INTOLERANCES.)

Within the EU, maximum permitted levels of total sulfur dioxide are 150 mg/l in dry red wines, 200 mg/l in dry white, dry rosé, and sweet red wines, 235 g/l in sparkling wines, and 250 mg/l in sweet white and rosé wines. Certain very sweet wines may contain up to 400 mg/l, however, including all sweet white bordeaux, JURANÇON, a number of sweet white Loire wines, BEERENAUSLESE, TROCKENBEERENAUSLESE, and AUSBRUCH wines. Maximum levels in the EU regulations for ORGANIC WINE agreed in 2012 are lower still: 100 mg/l for dry reds and 150mg/l for white and rosé. For sweet wines, the maximum is 30 mg/l lower than for non-organic wine. The maximum level permitted in Australia was reduced to 250 mg/l in the 1990s, except for wines with 35 g/l or more RESIDUAL SUGAR, for which up to 300 mg/l sulfur dioxide is permitted. The limit in the US is 350 mg/l in all types of wine. In South Africa, the limit is 150 mg/l for dry reds, 160 mg/l for dry white, rosé, and sparkling, and between 200 and 300 mg/l for sweet wines depending on style and level of sweetness. Argentina: 130 mg/l for dry reds, 180 mg/l for dry white and rosé wines and sweet reds, 210 mg/l for sweet white and rosé. Chile: 300 mg/l for all dry wines and 400 mg/l for sweet wines.

Most producers use far lower levels than those officially permitted and there is an increasing tendency to reduce the amount of sulfur dioxide used and to think more strategically about the timing of additions. Attempts to produce wines without any addition of sulfur dioxide (see, for example, NATURAL WINES) have met with varying degrees of success since such wines are particularly prone to oxidation and the off-flavours generated by wild yeast and bacteria. They need careful handling and storage, and possibly even PASTEURIZATION, although this is an unlikely solution for most winemakers who prefer so-called minimum intervention. It would be impossible to produce an entirely sulfur-free wine since a small amount of sulfur dioxide is one of the by-products of the metabolic action of yeast during fermentation when the material being fermented contains sulfate salts. Since sulfate salts are natural components of such fermentable materials as dough and fruit juices, it is normal to encounter small amounts of sulfur dioxide in such fermented products as bread and wine.   J.A.G. & T.J.

Bird, D., *Understanding Wine Technology* (3rd edn, Newark, 2010).

Goode, J., *Wine Science: The Application of Science in Winemaking* (2nd edn, London, 2014).

Robinson, E. M. C., and Godden, P. E., 'Revisiting sulphur dioxide use', *Australian Wine Research Institute Technical Review*, 145 (2003).

Sulfur dioxide and grapes

Recent research by Considine and Foyer has revealed unexpected effects of sulfur dioxide on the chemical composition of grapes, including PHENOLICS, FLAVONOIDS, and ANTHOCYANINS. Just as plant leaves can assimilate atmospheric sulfur (sulfur dioxide, hydrogen sulfide), so, too, can grape berries. As little as 2–3 mg/l sulfur dioxide (applied to the berries after harvest) caused massive changes to gene expression and synthesis of phenolic acids and other plant metabolites. This has implications for sulfur-containing compounds including GLUTATHIONE, other thiols (see MERCAPTANS), and AMINO ACIDS, and conjugated FLAVOUR PRECURSORS, as well as secondary effects on REDOX-sensitive wine qualities, through effects on primary fermentation. Possibilities include increased levels of glutathione and an altered balance of glutathione and conjugated precursors.   M.J.C.

Giraud, E., et al., 'Sulphur dioxide evokes a large scale reprogramming of the grape berry transcriptome associated with oxidative signalling and biotic defence responses', *Plant, Cell & Environment*, 35/2 (2012), 405–17.

Considine, M. J., and Foyer, C. H., 'Metabolic responses to sulfur dioxide in grape, wine and non-photosynthetic tissues', *Frontiers in Plant Science* (in press). doi: 10.3389/fpls.2015.00060.

sulphate, **sulphide**, **sulphite**, and **sulphur**, the British and non-technical spellings of SULFATE, SULFIDE, SULFITE, and SULFUR respectively. This volume follows the International Union of Pure and Applied Chemistry (IUPAC) nomenclature recommendations and uses sulfate, sulfide, sulfite, and sulfur throughout since the terms are generally used in a technical context.

Sultana, also known as **Sultaniye**, **Sultanina**, and **Sultanine**. Its origins are thought to be eastern Mediterranean. Even further east it is known by variants on Kismis and in Egypt as Banati. It is the most important white grape variety used to produce the pale brown DRYING GRAPES sometimes called sultanas and has in its time been the single most-planted vine variety in the world covering an estimated 344,000 ha/ 850,000 acres of vineyard, much of it in the Middle East. The fruit of the Sultana vine, called THOMPSON SEEDLESS in California, is remarkable for its versatility. As well as being dried, it can be vinified into a neutral white wine and, especially after treatment with GIBBERELLIN growth regulators to increase BERRY SIZE, is a much sought-after crisp, green, seedless TABLE GRAPE. In widely varying locations, it has provided base material for some, usually undistinguished, wines. In some viticultural regions, such as Australia's RIVERLAND and California's CENTRAL VALLEY, the Sultana harvest has occasionally been diverted to whatever happens to be the most profitable end use, including wine in times of wine grape shortage.

Sumer. In Ancient Sumer (3500–1900 BC), the earliest literate civilization of southern

MESOPOTAMIA, wine and BEER were both widely consumed, and are often mentioned as being drunk on the same occasion. 'Wine' almost certainly refers to grape wine in most contexts, although date wine was also prepared by the Sumerians.

At the sacred city of Nippur, just downstream from Babylon, which stood on an important branch of the river Euphrates, the principal quay of the temple was known as the 'Quay of the Vine', although it is not clear if this refers to an original commercial activity, irrigation, or is simply an ornate epithet of the sort beloved of Sumerian poets. In praise poetry addressed to King Shulgi, who was deified in his own lifetime (c.22nd century BC), the king's martial prowess with the double-edged axe is eulogized with the image of him 'spilling his enemies' blood on the mountain-side like the contents of a smashed wine jug'.

DRUNKENNESS seems to have carried no stigma of disapprobation. In a number of Sumerian literary works, the gods get drunk on wine and beer in circumstances which are not merely amusing but are dramatically important.

See also ORIGINS OF VINICULTURE and PALAEOETH-NOBOTANY AND THE ARCHAEOLOGY OF WINE.

J.A.B.

Bottéro, J., 'Getränke', Reallexikon der Assyriologie und vorderasiatischen Archäologie (the standard reference work) (Berlin, 1928–).

Kinner Wilson, J. V., The Nimrud Wine Lists (London, 1972).

Powell, M. A., 'Wine and the vine in Ancient Mesopotamia', in Fleming, S. J., and Katz, S. H. (eds.), The Origins and Ancient History of Wine (New York, 1995).

summer pruning. See TRIMMING.

Sumoll, minor CATALAN red wine grape usually blended, known as Vijariego Negra on the Canary Islands.

sunburn can damage grapes and is a viticultural term used loosely for a range of conditions. Classical sunburn produces a round halo of burnt skin on the side of the berry facing the sun's position in the western sky, as damage normally occurs in the afternoon. Such sunburn is due to a combination of bright sunshine, high air temperatures, and low winds, and the so-called 'hot spot' can be up to 12 °C/54 °F above air temperature. Berries which were previously shaded from the sun are most sensitive, as their skins have not been conditioned by exposure to sunlight. Sunburn sensitivity is higher for vineyards suffering WATER STRESS.

The condition in which grapes develop pigmentation in response to the ULTRAVIOLET component of sun exposure is also loosely called sunburn. This is particularly obvious with some white varieties, and the skin can develop deep yellow or even brown colours. Whether such exposure is harmful to the berry is arguable, and exposure to sun encourages the production of a range of PHENOLIC compounds, including QUERCETIN (see FLAVONOLS), which are generally associated with wine quality, especially for red varieties. R.E.S.

Smart, R. E., and Sinclair, T. R., 'Solar heating of grape berries and other spherical fruits', Agricultural and Forest Meteorolgy, 17 (1976), 241–59.

Sunbury, historic Australian cool-climate wine region in VICTORIA close to Melbourne's northern suburbs, and even closer to its domestic and international air terminal. Of the 14 wine producers, Craiglee and Goona Warra are steeped in history, Craiglee a top-flight producer of spicy, elegant SHIRAZ.

sunlight, the ultimate energy source of all life, and of wine itself. Through a process known as PHOTOSYNTHESIS, part of its energy is used by grapevines to combine CARBON DIOXIDE from the air with WATER taken up from the soil, to form SUGAR IN GRAPES. This is the building block for other plant products, as well as being the immediate source of energy for all of a plant's biochemical processes, via its RESPIRATION back to carbon dioxide and water.

In climatology, the traditional measurement of sunlight was as hours of bright sunlight but it is now generally measured in terms of total energy using electronic sensors. This is more pertinent in viticulture since PHOTOSYNTHESIS of grapevine leaves is 'light-saturated' at around one-third full sunlight, although a CANOPY of leaves will photosynthesize at higher rates with increased sunlight. Photosynthesis is reduced at very low light levels in a shaded canopy. It is also reduced by high (> 35 °C) or low (< 15 °C) temperatures, and by WATER STRESS.

Another important role of sunlight in viticulture is that of heating the vines and the soil. Grape berries for example may be heated up to 15 °C above air temperature for black berries exposed to bright sunlight in low wind conditions. Leaves are heated less when exposed to sunlight, as they are evaporatively cooled by the process of TRANSPIRATION. Berry temperatures are of considerable importance in affecting the chemical make-up of the grapes. Similarly, leaf temperatures have important effects on photosynthesis and respiration and this also directly affects GRAPE COMPOSITION AND WINE QUALITY. Soil temperature depends on the reflectivity to sunlight of the soil surface; thus dark soils absorb more sunlight and are warmer than white or light-coloured soils (see SOIL COLOUR). The total amount of sunlight energy over all of the spectrum is important in heating vines and soils.

The intensity of sunlight is not its only characteristic of importance to grapevines. Another is spectral quality or the proportion of sunlight at different wavelengths. This does not vary greatly from region to region, or under full sunlight versus cloud; but it does vary enormously within the vine canopy.

The total spectrum of solar radiation comprises ULTRAVIOLET RADIATIONS, visible light, and infrared (heat) radiations, in order of increasing electromagnetic wavelengths. Visible light is in the wavelength range 400 to 760 nanometres (nm) (1 nm is a millionth of a millimetre). Within that range, in order of increasing wavelength, are the component colours of the visible light spectrum: violet, indigo, blue, green, yellow, orange, and red.

Most of the wavelengths between 400 and 700 nm are absorbed by leaves, and are used to varying degrees for photosynthesis. Those absorbed and used most efficiently are in the blue and (especially) red parts of the spectrum, centred around 440 and 660 nm respectively. It is the partial reflection of the intermediate wavelengths, by the photosynthetically active pigment chlorophyll, that gives plant leaves their characteristic green colour. Thus shade light, as well as being much less intense than full sunlight, is still more impoverished of its photosynthetically useful wavelengths. If overall light intensity is reduced eight- or tenfold, that of red light around 660 nm can be reduced a hundredfold in deep canopy shade.

Also important physiologically are the barely visible 'far red' wavelengths, between 700 and 760 nm. These and the adjacent infrared wavelengths are hardly absorbed at all, being either reflected or transmitted through the leaves. Canopy shade light is therefore relatively rich in them. The ratio of normal red to far red wavelengths (measured as 10-nm-width bands centred around 660 and 730 nm, and known as the R : FR ratio) is between 1.0 and 1.2 in the open, whereas in deep canopy shade it can be 0.1 or less.

It is the R : FR ratio, rather than light intensity as such, that appears to govern many plant reactions to shading within the canopy, probably through the action of a wavelength-sensitive pigment known as phytochrome. A low R : FR ratio, characteristic of deep canopy shade, promotes rapid spindly stem growth (trying to reach the light); sparse leaves and light green colour; sparse lateral branching; and poor bud FRUITFULNESS. Conversely, a high R : FR ratio, as in normal external light, promotes stocky growth, with strong lateral branching; deep green leaf colour; and good bud fruitfulness. Direct exposure of the bunches to such light also promotes the formation of ANTHOCYANIN pigments in the berry skins of red wine grape varieties, and appears to be associated with superior flavour and potential wine quality. The practice of LEAF REMOVAL around the bunches is in part a response to this.

The fact that such wavelength discrimination can still occur at quite low light intensities raises further interesting questions on which, at present, there is little direct information for grapevines. They include the effects of height, orientation, and distance between rows on the quality of the light reaching the lower canopy and bunches; also those of different soil colours, MULCHES, or COVER CROPS on the intensity and spectral quality of light reflected back to the lower canopy and bunches.

Smart reviews general aspects of light-quality effects on grapevine growth and fruit composition. He also deals comprehensively with sunlight relations in the context of vine canopy microclimate, canopy management, and wine quality.

See also VINE PHYSIOLOGY.   J.G. & R.E.S.

Smart, R. E., 'Principles of grapevine canopy microclimate manipulation with implications for yield and quality', *American Journal of Enology and Viticulture*, 35 (1985), 230–9.

Smart, R. E., 'Canopy management', in B. G. Coombe and P. R. Dry (eds.), *Viticulture*, ii: *Practices* (Adelaide, 1992).

Suntory, traditional Japanese food and alcoholic drinks company that has discreetly become a significant player in the world's wine business. Founded in 1899, the company was selling a sweet red wine in 1907, and by 1936 was developing its vineyards in the Tomi no Oka region of Yamanashi prefecture. It has since invested considerably in developing viticultural and oenological prowess in JAPAN and is one of the country's most important wine producers.

Its first foreign acquisition was Ch Lagrange in ST-JULIEN in 1983 when Suntory became the first non-Western company to own a Bordeaux CLASSED GROWTH. Five years later they acquired Weingut Robert Weil, one of the best-run estates in the RHEINGAU, still run by Wilhelm Weil. Both properties have benefited from considerable investment. In 2010, when the Chinese wine market was booming, they acquired ASC, one of China's most successful importers, together with its Hong Kong and Macau operations. In Bordeaux, Suntory first participated with CASTEL in Grands Millésimes de France in 1989 and the company now operates both Châteaux Beychevelle and Beaumont as well as the négociant Barrière Frères.

'A yen for quality' (June 2013) www.jancisrobinson.com/articles/a201306051.html.

Supérieur, **Supérieure**, or **Supérieures** may be found suffixed to the name of an AOC wine. See BORDEAUX AOC and GRAVES.

Superiore, Italian term applied to DOC wines which are deemed superior because of their higher minimum ALCOHOLIC STRENGTH, usually by a half or one per cent, a longer period of AGEING before commercial release, or a lower maximum permitted YIELD, or all three. Among the more significant wines which fall into this category are the three BARBERA DOCs or DOCGs of PIEMONTE (Alba, Asti, Monferrato), BARDOLINO, CALDARO, GRAVE DEL FRIULI, SOAVE, VALPOLICELLA, and VALTELLINA (where the Superiore-designated area includes the crus of Grumello, Inferno, Maroggia, Sassella, and Valgella). Triggered by the EU reforms of 2008, the Superiore versions of several DOCs such as FRASCATI have been elevated to DOCG status while, confusingly, the normal DOC continues to co-exist. These promotions, notably that of Agliancio del Vulture Superiore and, earlier, Soave Superiore, are often petty compromises, born out of resistance to elevating the often much smaller historic CLASSICO heartland of a zone to DOCG status.   W.S.

super second, a specialist term in the FINE WINE market for CLASSED GROWTH wines from BORDEAUX to denote the best-performing wines that are not actually FIRST GROWTHS. There is no absolute agreement about which properties qualify as super seconds, and reputations are constantly changing, but in the Médoc and Graves Chx Pichon-Lalande, Pichon-Baron, Pontet Canet, Lynch Bages, and Les Forts de LATOUR in PAUILLAC, Cos and Montrose in ST-ESTÈPHE, all three LÉOVILLES and Ducru-Beaucaillou in ST-JULIEN, Ch Palmer in MARGAUX, and Ch La MISSION-HAUT-BRION in PESSAC-LÉOGNAN have all been nominated at one time or another.

Supertuscan, term sometimes used by English speakers to describe the innovative wines labelled as VINO DA TAVOLA made in the central Italian region of Tuscany which emerged in the 1970s. Prototype Supertuscans were TIGNANELLO and SASSICAIA, both initially marketed by ANTINORI. The Vino da Tavola denomination was replaced by IGT in 1994, but the term Supertuscan remains. For more details, see TUSCANY.

sur lie, French term meaning 'on the lees', customarily applied to white wines whose principal deviation from everyday WHITE WINEMAKING techniques was some form of LEES CONTACT. The term has been used most commonly for the French dry white MUSCADET to differentiate those wines which remained on their lees after fermentation, usually in tank, in an effort to increase flavour and texture. The practice, and term, has since spread south to the LANGUEDOC and even outside France and has proved a useful way of adding flavour and value to the produce of relatively neutral grape varieties.

surmaturité, French expression sometimes used by Anglophones for overripeness, a usually undesirable stage in grape maturity whereby grapes start to shrivel and acid levels fall to a dangerously low level. Some Australians refer to this stage as exhibiting 'dead fruit' flavours. It may well be the result of the continuing fashion, in parts of CALIFORNIA in particular, for extended HANG TIME.

surplus production was for years the single greatest problem facing the world's wine industry, aggravated by improved efficiency in the vineyard and falling consumption in Europe's important wine markets. The most palatable effect of this surplus for wine consumers has been its dampening impact on PRICES at the bottom end of the wine market.

Even in the late 1950s, relatively soon after the shortages of the Second World War, the world produced almost 15% more wine than it consumed, but wine consumption was rising rapidly, and it was assumed that it would catch up. By the late 1970s, average YIELDS began to increase substantially. This was largely the result of increased viticultural proficiency, but also reflected the availability of particularly productive CLONES of established vine varieties, as well as the more widespread use of AGROCHEMICALS to combat VINE DISEASES, and FERTILIZERS. Just at this point, consumption began to decline, especially markedly in the principal wine-producing countries (which had been the principal wine markets): France, Italy, USSR, Spain, and Argentina.

The exceptionally large European harvests of 1979 and 1980 plunged what is now the EU into crisis and forced measures which included compulsory DISTILLATION of about a fifth of total production (only of the lowest-quality wine), a VINE PULL SCHEME, and a somewhat fruitless attempt to control yields, which continued to rise by an average of about 0.5% a year. By the late 1980s, the world was producing 19% more than it could consume (see table), with particularly marked surpluses in France, Italy, and Spain, and a marked surplus of industrial alcohol as a result of compulsory distillation.

The breakup of the Soviet Union, for long a net wine importer, and the introduction of free market economies within the former Soviet Republics in the early 1990s deprived many eastern European wine producers of their traditional, and none too fastidious market, creating fresh pressure on the world's wine suppliers.

Surpluses on a smaller scale, sometimes simply of the wrong type of wine, have resulted in national vine pull schemes such as those enacted in NEW ZEALAND and ARGENTINA in the late 1980s and early 1990s respectively.

By the early and mid 1990s, there was overproduction in all continents except the Americas, but most especially in Europe and particularly of poor quality TABLE WINE. This did nothing to alleviate severe shortages in the

World totals in million hl of wine

	Production	Consumption	Surplus	% Surplus
1976–80	326.0	285.7	40.3	12
1981–85	333.6	280.7	52.8	16
1986–90	292.8	237.0	55.8	19
1991–95	261.3	222.7	38.6	15
1996	272.5	223.2	49.3	18
1997	264.4	223.5	40.9	15
1998	262.1	227.8	34.4	13
1999	281.2	225.1	56.1	20
2000	280.0	226.6	53.4	19
2001	266.6	226.9	39.7	15
2002	257.8	228.6	29.2	11
2003	266.7	234.7	32.0	12
2004	296.4	237.6	58.8	20
2005	278.0	236.9	41.1	15
2006	282.6	244.7	37.9	13
2007	267.8	252.4	15.4	6
2008	268.7	248.7	20.0	7
2009	272.2	240.9	31.3	11
2010	264.3	240.3	24.0	9
2011	267.4	241.2	26.2	10
2012	254.7	241.2	13.5	5
2013	278.6	238.7	39.9	14

Note: These figures are based on OIV official statistics.

mid to late 1990s of red wines suitable for export in many countries, however, most notably in South Africa and Australia, where there was a shortage of commercially desirable wine grapes of both colours. Substantial plantings of Chardonnay vines in the mid 1990s in Australia and California resulted in a surplus of that grape variety.

In the late 2000s the EU, concerned about the size of its WINE LAKE, embarked on a rigorous programme of draining it with a vine pull scheme and limitations on new plantings. The result was a dramatic decrease in total EU vineyard area, and total vineyard area shrank throughout the ex-Soviet republics, but this was partly outweighed by extraordinary vineyard expansion in China.

The total annual volume of wine produced varies considerably according to the weather. As the table above shows, the overall surplus is declining overall but is still uncomfortably high.

Surrentine wine from vineyards on the slopes of the Sorrento peninsula in southern Italy achieved prominence from the latter half of the reign of Augustus in the first decade of the 1st century AD. It ranked high in Classical ROME, but behind CAECUBAN and FALERNIAN, in PLINY's assessment. It was produced from the vine known as the Aminnea Gemina Minor, which, unusually for one of the classic wines, was trellised rather than grown up trees. The wine itself was a rather thin white wine, which nevertheless could be described as 'strong'. It may well have had a high acidity. There are recommendations to age it for 20 to 25 years. It never won universal approval—'a high class

vinegar' was the opinion of both the emperors Tiberius and Caligula, and there are some signs that its MEDICINAL properties were among its most important selling points. J.J.P.

Pliny the Elder, *Natural History*, trans. by H. Rackham (London, 1945), Book 14.

sur souches, French expression meaning 'on the stumps' or, in the context of a purchase of a future vintage of wine, 'on the vine'. The BORDEAUX TRADE has, at times of particularly buoyant sales, occasionally bought futures in a crop even before it was harvested.

Süss, literally 'sweet' in German. Used on labels in AUSTRIA to designate wines whose RESIDUAL SUGAR is more than 45 g/l.

Süssreserve, German term for SWEET RESERVE, the unfermented or part-fermented MUST much used in the 1970s and 1980s to sweeten all but the finest or driest German wines. Its use has declined considerably because GERMANY is making an increasing proportion of dry wines (see TROCKEN and HALBTROCKEN) and because better producers of sweeter wines prefer to stop the fermentation while there is still some RESIDUAL SUGAR in the wine rather than add unfermented juice.

sustainability has become an increasing concern for wine producers, shippers, merchants, and consumers. In an era of CLIMATE CHANGE, environmental concerns have been uppermost, but considerations of economic and social sustainability are becoming increasingly common, too.

For producers, and certainly vine growers, SUSTAINABLE VITICULTURE is the most obvious first step, but an increasing number are considering their entire carbon footprint, including thorough consideration of all vehicles, equipment, and products used in the vineyard, winery, cellar, packaging, and even shipping. Some producers market themselves on their sustainable credentials, planting trees to act as carbon sinks, insulating their buildings, recycling with a vengeance, and switching to low-input vehicles and alternative energy sources. Many of these decisions result in increased costs, however, demanding a reconciliation of environmentally sound choices with economically feasible ones—and all of these decisions have to be made with potential wine QUALITY in mind. For example, TEMPERATURE-CONTROLLED shipping containers can increase carbon use, but many producers and retailers of fine wine would argue that they are necessary to avoid heat damage. On the other hand, a producer of more basic wine may well decide that shipping to export markets in BULK is more sustainable than BOTTLING at source. Others may decide to reduce the amount of energy needed for packaging and shipping by choosing ALTERNATIVE PACKAGING for their wine.

Within the winery, some of the most important considerations are water and energy usage and what happens to the wide range of WINERY WASTE. Winery waste-water recycling is becoming more widespread worldwide, often through legislative pressure, with waste water typically recycled for non-potable purposes such as IRRIGATION and cooling systems. But temperature control can use enormous amounts of energy. Sustainability-aware producers are increasingly locating or relocating temperature-sensitive operations (i.e. most of them) in hillsides or underground where temperatures are naturally low. Sustainability concerns are becoming increasingly important in WINERY DESIGN. Outside pressure, including generous tariffs for adopters (notably in Germany and California), is also encouraging the use of renewable energy, often helped by dramatic reductions in the price of alternative energy sources such as solar-powered cells.

The final stage of production, BOTTLING, is the heaviest consumer of energy via glass BOTTLE production. Wineries may select lighter glass, and recycled glass bottles to reduce energy consumption.

Around the globe, many regions have developed sustainability schemes to encourage producers to improve their practices. Oregon, California (especially Napa Valley), New Zealand, and South Africa were quicker off the mark than most. The social and economic elements of long-term sustainability depend fundamentally on the overall health of the LABOUR force, a business's compliance with local laws, the financial stability of the business, and the local ECONOMY.

For many consumers, recycling wine bottles is one of their most obvious contributions to sustainability of any sort. In some parts of the world it is possible to recycle other aspects of wine packaging, including CLOSURES. There has also been a discernible increase in selling wine in bulk to environmentally aware consumers with their own recycled bottles, a throwback to traditional practice in some of Europe's wine producing areas.

Sachs, J., 'Free exchange: the next frontier', *The Economist* (21 Sep 2013).

www.wineinstitute.org/resources/pressroom/04022014

sustainable viticulture, a form of viticultural practice informed by the United Nations' seminal definition of sustainability: 'the principle that we must meet the needs of the present without compromising the ability of future generations to meet their own needs'.

In reality, the term is applied quite liberally and almost invariably falls short of environmentalist ideals of being completely self-sustaining. The Sustainable Winegrowing New Zealand (SWNZ) initiative, for example, was established in 1995 to provide a 'best practice' environmental model for both vineyard and winery. SWNZ is independently audited but stops short of prohibiting man-made inputs such as PESTICIDES. However, such programmes can, via grower education, significantly reduce the number and strength of chemical SPRAYINGS, which is of both environmental and economic benefit. A related approach is INTEGRATED PEST MANAGEMENT, as are LISA or LEISA, acronyms which stand for Low (External) Input Sustainable Agriculture, terms often used for programmes in North America and Australia.

Even in biodynamic wine-growing, in which external inputs are to be minimized to create self-sustaining farms, growers are invariably reliant on copper sulfate (as BORDEAUX MIXTURE) and SULFUR, both of which are finite resources and, in the case of COPPER, decompose in the soil only with great difficulty. However, a small but steadily growing number of the world's ORGANIC

and BIODYNAMIC vineyards have replaced copper- and sulfur-based sprays with aerated compost teas rich in beneficial micro-organisms, or with drenches, fresh teas, and essential oils made from seaweed, whey, or wild herbs, and often sprayed by hand or HORSE rather than by machine.

See also LUTTE RAISONNÉE and SUSTAINABILITY.

M.W.

'Report of the World Commission on Environment and Development', *United Nations General Assembly Resolution 42/187* (11 Dec 1987).

Susumaniello, lively, deep-coloured PUGLIAN red wine grape. One of GARGANEGA's many offspring.

Svatovavřinecké, Czech name for ST-LAURENT.

Swan District, the hot, traditional, once-dominant wine region of WESTERN AUSTRALIA. **Swan Valley** is now a subregion fighting back from the brink of oblivion, and very dependent on TOURISM, although in 2014 there were still more than 40 producers.

Swan Hill, Australian wine region on the Murray River, partly in VICTORIA and partly in NEW SOUTH WALES.

sward. See COVER CROP.

Swartland. Fashionable wine-producing district in SOUTH AFRICA which, since the late 1990s, has attracted some of the country's most adventurous and least interventionist winemakers. This focus is partly explained by the relatively high percentage of older vineyards planted with varieties well suited to predominantly DRYLAND VITICULTURE. For red wines these are mainly Rhône varieties, while the whites are typically blends based on low-yielding old Chenin Blanc vineyards. There is a strong community spirit here and an annual wine festival known as the Swartland Revolution.

Sweden has an extremely marginal climate for wine growing, well outside the natural area for VINIFERA. The current trend for wine production started in the 1990s and is centred around the southernmost municipality Skåne (Scania). Other winegrowing areas include the Baltic

islands Gotland and Öland, Halland on the west coast, and Blaxta outside Stockholm. By 2013 it was estimated that Sweden already had 100 ha/250 acres under vine. That winemaking is nascent, though rapidly improving, is particularly evident in cooler vintages. Key challenges include RIPENESS and ROT, and early-ripening varieties such as Solaris and RONDO are favoured. Léon Millot, ORTEGA, and REGENT are also grown, as is Vidal for ICEWINES. Sweden does not have to apply for EU planting rights and does not currently have any CONTROLLED APPELLATIONS.

Barely a tenth of Sweden's 350 wine growers operate commercially. Because of the Swedish MONOPOLY, cellardoor sales are illegal, which presents a major financial challenge for wineries which have to rely simply on wine TOURISM. E.L.

www.svenskavinodlare.se

sweetness, one of the primary tastes involved in TASTING and a fundamental component of wine. It varies considerably and is sensed by taste buds principally on the tongue. Wines taste sweet mainly because of the amount of RESIDUAL SUGAR they contain (although the impact of this on the palate is greatly influenced by factors such as the levels of ACIDITY, TANNINS, and CARBON DIOXIDE in the wine as well as by the serving TEMPERATURE). ETHANOL, or alcohol, can also taste sweet, as can GLYCEROL and a high level of PECTINS. Any wine with less than 2 g/l residual sugar is considered bone dry, but a dry wine with residual sugar of less than 2 g/l that is relatively high in alcohol, such as many a Chardonnay for example, can taste quite sweet. A sweet VOUVRAY, on the other hand, made in a cool region from the naturally acidic grape variety CHENIN BLANC, may contain well over 30 g/l residual sugar, but in youth can taste dry.

A wide variety of different terms in different languages are used to describe sweetness, although they invariably relate strictly to the residual sugar rather than to the taste impression. The table below gives the official EU classification of sweetness levels. Producers are not obliged to put this information on the label of a still wine, though it is mandatory for sparkling wines. See DOSAGE for specific terminology.

Some wine drinkers have been conditioned to be suspicious of any sweetness in a wine,

RS g/l	English	French	German	Italian	Spanish
up to 4 (or not exceeding 9 provided that the total acidity expressed as grams of tartaric acid per litre is not more than 2 grams below the RS content)	dry	sec	trocken	secco or asciutto	seco
more than 4 and not exceeding 12 (or not exceeding 18 provided that the total acidity expressed as grams of tartaric acid per litre is not more than 10 grams below the RS content)	medium dry	demi-sec	halbtrocken	abboccato	semiseco
more than 12 and not exceeding 45	medium (or medium sweet)	moelleux	lieblich	amabile	semidulce
at least 45	sweet	doux	süss	dolce	dulce

perhaps because neophytes generally prefer some residual sugar (which is why so many wine BRANDS contain some, up to 20 g/l in even red wines in some cases) and sweetness is therefore associated with a lack of sophistication. Some of the greatest wines of the world are sweet, however. So long as there is sufficient ACIDITY to balance the sweetness, a sweet wine is by no means cloying. Indeed, a comparative tasting of great young sweet wines is more likely to leave the taster with the impression of excess acidity than excess sugar.

See SWEET WINES and SWEET WINEMAKING for more details of sweeter wines.

sweetness codes

are becoming more common on back labels and in sales literature. This is particularly true of RIESLINGS and ALSACE whites because they can vary so widely in how sweet they taste. They may take the form of a scale of numerical rating. See, for example, the RIESLING TASTE PROFILE.

sweet reserve

, preserved GRAPE JUICE held for BLENDING purposes, usually to sweeten, or at least soften, wines high in ACIDITY. The unfermented grape SUGARS counterbalance the sometimes tart flavours of wines produced from grapes grown in cool regions such as parts of GERMANY (where such juice is known as *Süssreserve*) or grapes naturally high in acidity such as RIESLING, UGNI BLANC, and COLOMBARD.

Historically grape juice was preserved simply by adding offensively high doses of SULFUR DIOXIDE.

Modern REFRIGERATION and near-sterile FILTRATION enable the production of sweet reserve that does not reek of sulfur dioxide. The sweet juice usually undergoes CLARIFICATION and refrigeration so as to precipitate any TARTRATES and can be stored at very low temperatures for up to 12 months.

In many wine regions, sweet reserve is being replaced by GRAPE CONCENTRATE or RECTIFIED GRAPE MUST. Grape concentrate is cheaper to store because it is much richer in sugar, which also prevents the growth of micro-organisms so that it can be stored without recourse to expensive refrigeration. Rectified grape must is preferred simply because it more closely resembles a solution of sugar and water than does preserved juice.   A.D.W.

sweet winemaking

, the production of wines with noticeable amounts of RESIDUAL SUGAR which may vary considerably in ALCOHOLIC STRENGTH and production techniques. Local regulations differ significantly but, with a few exceptions, non-grape sugar may be added only (and rarely) for the purposes of CHAPTALIZATION, to increase the final alcoholic strength, and not to add sweetness after fermentation. The most common method of sweetening basic wine is the addition of some form of sweet grape juice, followed by STABILIZATION (for any wine containing sugar is theoretically susceptible to a SECOND FERMENTATION).

The finest sweet wines are made by concentrating the SUGAR IN GRAPES, however, and the combined effect of the alcohol produced and the residual sugar tends to inhibit further YEAST activity. The four common ways of doing this are by the benevolent NOBLE ROT effect of the botrytis fungus on the vine as it nears maturity in perfect conditions (see BOTRYTIZED WINES); by processing frozen grape clusters (see EISWEIN and CRYOEXTRACTION); or by drying mature grapes either on the vine or after picking (see DRIED-GRAPE WINES). Many sweet wines are made by simply leaving the grapes on the vine for as long as possible in order to concentrate the grape sugars. (see LATE HARVEST). If BOTRYTIS BUNCH ROT fails to materialize, the grapes simply start to raisin or shrivel, a condition known in French as *passerillage*. Such wines, sweet JURANÇON, for example, described as *moelleux* in French, can be extremely rich and satisfying, but are typically less complex and less long-lived wines than those made from grapes transformed by the action of noble rot.

Some everyday sweet wines are made simply by fermenting the wine out to dryness and subsequently adding SWEET RESERVE, GRAPE CONCENTRATE, or RECTIFIED GRAPE MUST just before a sterilizing membrane FILTRATION and sterile BOTTLING. These wines owe their stability not to their composition but to the fact that all micro-organisms have been filtered out. They are best drunk within a year of bottling and within a day or two of opening the bottle. LIEBFRAUMILCH is an example of this type of wine, and the sweetening agent is called SÜSSRESERVE in German.

Another technique, commonly employed for inexpensive sweet white French wines, is to ferment a must relatively high in sugars, between 200 and 250 g/l, until the alcohol level has reached about 11 or 12%, and then add a substantial dose of SULFUR DIOXIDE.

One quite different way of transforming grapes into a liquid that is both sweet and stable is to add spirit to grape juice either before fermentation (see MISTELA) or during it (see VIN DOUX NATUREL). Such liquids are usually more than 15% alcohol, much stronger than most table wines.

Many FORTIFIED WINES are sweet. See also LATE HARVEST, BOTRYTIZED WINES, DRIED-GRAPE WINES, and EISWEIN for details of how these particularly fine sweet wines are made.

sweet wines

are widely under-appreciated, especially in view of how difficult some of them are to make (see SWEET WINEMAKING). Sweet wines have been popular for various periods since ancient times; indeed most of the most admired wines of classical ROME were sweet and white, many of them DRIED-GRAPE WINES made by deliberate raisining to concentrate the sugars. In the Middle Ages the great city states of Italy such as VENICE and GENOA profited from the popularity of wines made so much sweeter than northern European wines by the effects of

the MEDITERRANEAN CLIMATE. By the late 17th century. the DUTCH WINE TRADE was energetically profiting from the sweet wines of western France. And subsequently the sweet wines of CONSTANTIA and TOKAJ in particular were considered the height of FASHION.

For specific modern sweet wines see AUSLESE, BANYULS, BARSAC, BEERENAUSLESE, BONNEZEAUX, BOTRYTIZED WINES, CÉRONS, CLAIRETTE DE DIE, EISWEIN, JURANÇON, LAYON, LOUPIAC, MAURY, MOELLEUX, MONBAZILLAC, MONTLOUIS, various MOSCATELS, MOSCATO, MUSCAT, PICOLIT, PREMIÈRES CÔTES DE BORDEAUX, QUARTS DE CHAUME, RASTEAU, RECIOTO, RIVESALTES, SÉLECTION DE GRAINS NOBLES, STE-CROIX-DU-MONT, SAUTERNES, SPECIAL LATE HARVESTED, TROCKENBEERENAUSLESE, VENDANGE TARDIVE, VIN DE PAILLE, VIN SANTO, and VOUVRAY.

See SWEETNESS for details of sweet wine descriptions in various languages and what they entail.

Switzerland

, small, alpine country in central Europe beginning to look outwards into the greater world of wine. Annual wine production is steady at more than a million hl/26.4 million gal from about 15,000 ha/37,050 acres of often spectacular vineyards. The majority of these are in the western, French-speaking part of the country, Suisse romande. There are also extensive vineyards all over eastern, German-speaking Switzerland (or Ostschweiz), and many vineyards in Ticino, the Italian-speaking south of Switzerland (or Svizzera italiana). The country is divided into 26 cantons, of which all produce some wine (see map). For many years, Swiss wine labelling lacked the discipline applied to the north in Germany or the controls imposed to the west in France, but from the early 1990s a CONTROLLED APPELLATIONS system was applied with increasing rigour, initially in French-speaking Switzerland. Since controls on wine imports were relaxed in the mid 1990s (and disappeared altogether in 2006), the Swiss wine industry has been forced to up its game, replacing much of the light, white, and relatively neutral wine that was once the norm with serious offerings of both colours. CHASSELAS is the principal white grape variety and, when well vinified, it can express well the country's diversity of soils and climates. The Valais has a clutch of interesting INDIGENOUS VARIETIES and some increasingly sophisticated red wines are made in all Swiss wine regions, particularly Ticino and Graubünden. Switzerland is able to supply only 40% of domestic consumption; 60%, mainly red wine, has to be imported.

History

Seeds from WILD VINES of the Neolithic age, between 3000 and 1800 BC, have been found at St-Blaise in Neuchâtel, and recent findings of a significant amount of VITIS pollen in deposits below a lake near Sion in the Valais, as well as grape pips and pedicels at the Iron Age archaeological site of Gamsen near Brig in the Haut-

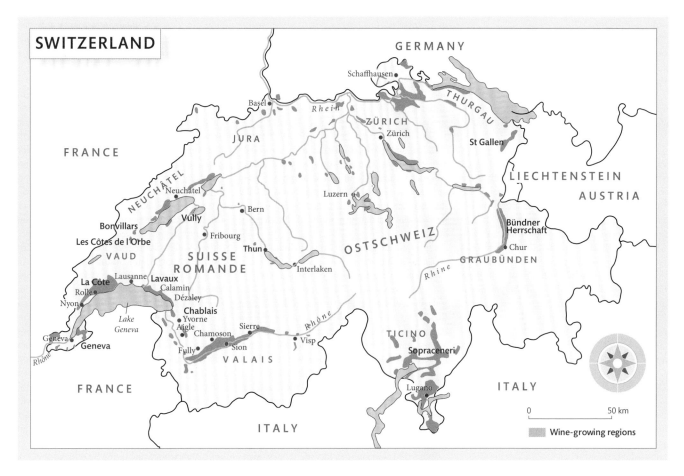

Valais, suggest that winemaking already existed *c.*800–600 BC, before the ROMAN era. In the Middle Ages, vine-growing spread under monastic influence, notably that of the Cistercians (see MONKS AND MONASTERIES), who planted the original Dézaley vines in Vaud. As elsewhere, medieval wines were thin, acid, and often helped by the addition of honey and other flavourings. In the 17th century, Swiss vignerons were already feeling the effects of wine imports from hotter climes, notably from further down the RHÔNE Valley.

Switzerland was far more seriously affected by the viticultural catastrophes of the late 19th century (DOWNY MILDEW, PHYLLOXERA, POWDERY MILDEW) than most other wine-producing countries. Between 1877 and 1957 the total Swiss vineyard declined by 60% from 33,000 to 12,500 ha/30,890 acres, a decrease encouraged by competition from cheaper imported wines, increasing industrialization, and development of the all-important lakesides. In the mid 20th century, CLONAL SELECTION and FERTILIZERS were harnessed with particular enthusiasm in attempts to increase productivity from Switzerland's relatively inconvenient, expensive-to-work vineyards. More recent developments in both vineyard and cellar are concerned with quality.

Climate

Although Switzerland is on a particularly suitable latitude for wine production, between 45 and 47 degrees, a high proportion of the country is simply too high. However, the country's lakes and the föhn, a local wind which warms up sizeable portions of the south of the country, particularly Graubünden in the upper Rhine Valley, enable full grape ripening to take place in many valleys and on lakesides. And in the Valais in the south west, the upper Rhône Valley, sunshine is so dependable (an average of more than 2,000 hours a year, rising sometimes to more than 2,500 hours) that vineyards can be as high as 750 m/2,460 ft, and some, such as Vispterminen, reach 1,150 m above sea level. The Valais is sheltered by the alps and, like south east Switzerland, benefits particularly from the föhn, but it can be dry and IRRIGATION with mountain water is sometimes necessary. Most Swiss wine regions have an annual rainfall of between 500 and 1,800 mm/19.5–70 in a year, the wettest region being Ticino, which suffers violent but short (HAIL) storms and is also the hottest with average July temperatures of more than 21 °C/70 °F. Elsewhere, average July temperatures are between 17.5 and 20 °C, there is good day–night TEMPERATURE VARIABILITY, and winter temperatures in the vineyards rarely

fall below danger level for vines. The Valais is most at risk.

Viticulture

The slope, as steep as 90% in places, and, in some regions, rainfall make SOIL EROSION many Swiss vine-growers' prime concern. TERRACES are common in Switzerland's steep vineyards, and COVER CROPS are increasingly common. Sophisticated MECHANIZATION is possible only on some of the flatter vineyards on the plain, or on some of the terraces of eastern Switzerland. A wide variety of training methods are used, including CORDON, GOBELET, GUYOT, TENDONE (in Ticino), and the Swiss German speciality *taille à l'onglet* designed to protect the vines against spring FROST danger there. Elaborate monorail systems, and sometimes even helicopters may be used to transport equipment and, at harvest, grapes.

Many vine-growers sell their grapes direct to NÉGOCIANTS or CO-OPERATIVES. YIELDS are nationally restricted, according to Switzerland's somewhat microscopic unit of measurement, to 1.4 kg/sq m for Chasselas grapes and 1.2 kg/sq m for red and superior white grapes, quite generous allowances although some cantons, such as those of eastern Switzerland and Geneva, Neuchâtel, and the Valais, apply their own stricter limits, and national average yields are about the same as in France.

The most common viticultural problems are downy mildew, powdery mildew, BOTRYTIS BUNCH ROT, soil erosion, and occasional spring frost in the east of the country.

Switzerland's most famous viticultural research stations are at WÄDENSWIL in German-speaking Switzerland and CHANGINS at Nyon in Suisse romande.

Winemaking

The essential stylistic difference between Swiss wine and that of neighbouring Germany and Austria is that ACIDITY is seen as an evil rather than a virtue and MALOLACTIC CONVERSION is routinely practised. The resulting softness in Swiss wine is emphasized by the additional alcohol provided by CHAPTALIZATION. This prefermentation sugar addition has been almost *de rigueur* for many Swiss wines, although the practice is unnecessary in much of the Valais and the Rhine Valley, and is declining elsewhere. Ordinary wines may have their alcohol content increased by up to 3%, although Swiss consumers are increasingly favouring lighter, drier wines.

Swiss PRESSES, made by Bucher and Sutter, are known throughout the winemaking world, and are put to particularly effective work in their native land, where the aim is to extract as much juice as possible from the country's precious grapes with only the gentlest of pressure from an inflatable membrane.

DESTEMMING is the norm and some form of CARBONIC MACERATION is often employed for German-speaking eastern Switzerland's red wines. As elsewhere, BARREL MATURATION has become increasingly popular for Swiss reds in general.

Switzerland has several pink wine specialities: white wines made from Pinot Noir and/or Gamay grapes such as the Valais's DÔLE Blanche. Œil de Perdrix, 'partridge eye', is made only from Pinot Noir, originally in Neuchâtel, while Gamay provides rosé. Federweisser (sometimes Federweiss) or WEISSHERBST are respectively white or rosé wine made from dark-skinned grapes in German Switzerland, where SCHILLERWEIN is a local rosé made from both red and white grapes.

BLENDING once played a much more important part in the Swiss wine industry than it does now. Before the practice was banned in 2005, Swiss wine merchants depended on imported wines, particularly deeply coloured red ones, to add bulk to many of their less expensive blends, and although Switzerland remains outside the EU, its CONTROLLED APPELLATIONS are in some instances stricter than those of the EU.

Vine varieties

Switzerland's most planted grape variety is now Pinot Noir, or Blauburgunder as it is known by German speakers, planted on 29% of the country's vineyard land. CHASSELAS, or Gutedel in German, is the most planted white variety with 27%. In the Valais it is called Fendant, a name used until the late 19th century in Vaud where wines have since then been sold under their geographical appellations. Dorin in Vaud and Perlan in Geneva are brand names introduced in the late 20th century with mitigated success.

The conveniently early-ripening MÜLLER-THURGAU, in Dr Müller's native land erroneously still known as Riesling–Silvaner or Riesling-Sylvaner, is the most common white grape variety in German Switzerland, having substantially replaced the historic RÄUSCHLING vine, particularly around Zurich just south of the German border.

Other white grape varieties include, in decreasing order of importance, CHARDONNAY, which can be elegant in the cantons of Neuchâtel and Geneva, and richer in Vaud and the Valais; SILVANER, whose wines, fuller bodied than Chasselas, are sold as Johannisberg in the Valais; PINOT GRIS, called Malvoisie in the Valais, and PINOT BLANC; Arvine, the Valais' most revered indigenous variety (see below); SAUVIGNON BLANC, notably in Geneva canton; and SAVAGNIN BLANC, known in the Valais as Heida, especially high up at Visperterminen, and its pink and aromatic variant Gewurztraminer; and Marsanne, also known as Ermitage, exclusive to the Valais.

Other red wine grapes include GAMAY, Switzerland's second most widely planted dark-skinned variety, which is widely planted in Vaud, the Valais, and Geneva; MERLOT, reigning in Ticino to such an extent that it accounts for 80% of production; and SYRAH, which can produce respectably ripe wine in sheltered parts of the Valais. The northern Ticino speciality Bondola has largely been replaced by Merlot. A number of quite popular CROSSES have been developed since 1965 at CHANGINS as suitable for Switzerland's very particular growing conditions: Charmont and Doral (both Chasselas × Chardonnay); GAMARET and GARANOIR (both Gamay × REICHENSTEINER); and, a Valais speciality, Diolinoir (Robin Noir × Pinot Noir). Garanoir is today the country's fourth most planted red wine grape.

But of most interest to students of AMPELOGRAPHY is the Valais' rich collection of a dozen ancient INDIGENOUS VARIETIES, each with substantial body, ageing potential, and its own whiff of history: the dry or sweet AMIGNE, mainly in Vétroz; the powerfully scented and complex ARVINE; the elegant HUMAGNE BLANCHE; the almost extinct RÈZE; the local rarities of the Haut-Valais Lafnetscha and Himbertscha; and, among dark-skinned varieties, the noble and historical Rouge du Pays, today more usually known as CORNALIN, and the powerful HUMAGNE ROUGE, both initially originating from the neighbouring AOSTA VALLEY in Italy; Rouge de Fully (or Durize) and Eyholzer Rote are even rarer; COMPLETER is Graubünden's indigenous white wine grape.

The wine regions

Swiss wine country is divided into six main regions, in decreasing order of importance: Valais, Vaud, German-speaking Switzerland, Geneva, Ticino, and Trois-Lacs (Neuchâtel). The country's emerging Appellation Contrôlée system is applied by each canton individually.

Valais The 5,000 ha/12,500 acres of productive vineyards of this south western canton produce 40% of every Swiss vintage. Concentrated on the south-facing slopes of the sunny upper Rhône Valley, the region is known as 'the California of Switzerland'. Many of these beautiful vineyards are terraced with historic dry-stone walls into so-called *tablars*, horizontal slices of vineyard cut into the mountainside, farmed as a part-time activity by 20,000 smallholders. Typical of what they produce is the ubiquitous FENDANT (made from the Chasselas grapes which cover one-quarter of the *vignoble*), and medium-weight reds labelled either Pinot Noir or DÔLE, a blend in which Pinot Noir must dominate the Gamay element, and up to 15% of other varieties may be included. (Dôle Blanche is a pale rosé made from a blend of Pinot Noir and Gamay grapes, with the permitted inclusion of up to 10% white wine in the final blend.)

Some of the most concentrated Silvaners, sold here as JOHANNISBERG, come from particularly well-favoured sites at Chamoson. ARVINE of Fully is accorded the greatest respect, however, for its exotic intensity; while Cornalin (or Rouge du Pays) and Humagne Rouge (confusingly known as Cornalin in Aosta) make some of Switzerland's most characterful reds. Fine, sweet, late-harvest wines, made from Amigne, Ermitage (Marsanne), Malvoisie (Pinot Gris), and Arvine picked in November and December, can easily reach 20% POTENTIAL ALCOHOL. They may be described as FLÉTRI, or withered, a reference to partial raisining on the vine. In 1996 a few dozen of the best producers, introduced a strict quality charter Grain Noble ConfidenCiel. Wines made from such indigenous varieties as Rouge de Fully (Durize), Lafnetscha, Himbertscha, or Rèze are curiosities, the last featuring historically in the VIN DES GLACIERS from the Val d'Anniviers above Sierre. Superior Valais producers include Marie Thérèse Chappaz, Jean-René Germanier, Domaine des Muses, and Didier Joris.

Vaud Switzerland's second most important wine canton is also in French Switzerland, round the northern shore of Lake Geneva, or Lac Léman (almost everything has at least two names in Switzerland). The canton's six wine regions are La Côte, Lavaux, and Chablais on the north shore of Lake Geneva, Les Côtes de l'Orbe on the plain between lakes Geneva and Neuchâtel, Bonvillars on Lake Neuchâtel, and Vully on Lake Morat. The canton's eight appellations encompass the six regions as well as two GRANDS CRUS: Dézaley in the commune of Puidoux and Calamin in the commune of Epesses. Chasselas accounts for 70% of the production from about 3,800 ha/9.390 acres, although, under the influence of the Vaud's varied soils, its character can vary from almost insultingly innocuous to an almost POUILLY-FUMÉ-like steeliness. In La Côte, the aromatic floral notes of the variety itself tend to dominate the wines. In Yvorne, Aigle, Bonvillars, and Calamin the mineral character of individual soils can easily dominate the fruit, while Dézaley and St-Saphorin often manage to demonstrate both fruit and minerals.

A little Chardonnay and Pinot Gris are also grown here. Red wines, especially Gamay, are a speciality of La Côte. Salvagnin, a designation accorded by a special tasting panel, approximates to a Vaud version of the Valais' Dôle, although it can be made from Pinot Noir or Gamay or both. Similarly, Terravin is a Chasselas whose quality has a local seal of approval. Many of Switzerland's largest NÉGOCIANTS are based here.

In 2002 some of the best producers including Domaine La Colombe, Pierre-Luc Leyvraz, and Blaise Duboux created the quality-oriented association Arte Vitis to promote Vaud's TERROIRS.

Geneva The 1,400 ha/3,460 acres of vineyards around the city at the south western end of the lake are much flatter than those of the Valais and Vaud and benefit from good sunlight, those next to the lake often escaping spring frost danger. Chasselas dominates white wine production, Riesling–Sylvaner (Müller-Thurgau) is on the wane, while all manner of newcomers, including Chardonnay, Aligoté, Sauvignon, Sémillon, and Kerner, have become popular. In reds, Gamay clearly dominates and is particularly successful here, whether as a well-structured red, a PRIMEUR, or a rosé. Pinot comes second, closely followed by GAMARET, planted extensively in recent years (120 ha by 2012). GARANOIR, Merlot, and even Cabernet Sauvignon are increasingly popular with growers and consumers alike. This was the birthplace of Switzerland's burgeoning controlled appellations. Reliable producers include Jean-Michel Novelle of Le Grand Clos, Domaine Grand Cour, and Domaine Les Hutins.

Neuchâtel Only 600 ha/1,480 acres of the ancient CALCAREOUS soils, on the well-situated south-facing slopes above Lake Neuchâtel, grow vines, but with characterful results. Pinot Noir and Chasselas as usual. The pale pink Pinot Œil de Perdrix is a Neuchâtel invention, as is the Chasselas *non filtré* (unfiltered) released on the third Wednesday in January following the harvest. This was the first canton to restrict yields.

Eastern cantons In the 17 German-speaking cantons of Switzerland are 2,600 ha/6,425 acres of vines, ranging from 0.2 ha in Nidwald to more than 600 ha in the canton of Zürich. Schaffhausen, effectively an outcrop into south BADEN in Germany, has nearly 500 ha of vines. Here in eastern Switzerland nearly 80% of production is red wine, particularly the rot-resistant Mariafeld and 2–45 clones of Blauburgunder (Pinot Noir) and, to a lesser extent, the crosses Gamaret and Garanoir developed locally at the CHANGINS viticultural research station. Räuschling is once again gaining ground in Limmatal and on the shores of the lake south of Zürich, where Blauburgunder is often labelled Clevner. Riesling–Sylvaner (Müller-Thurgau) is the dominant white grape variety of eastern Switzerland, while Completer is a local speciality of Bündner Herrschaft near the border with Austria and Liechtenstein in Graubünden, where a small quantity of sweet Freisamer and serious red wine, mainly Blauburgunder, is also produced. Donatsch, Fromm, Gantenbein, and Schlossgut Bachtobel are some of the most effective producers.

Italian-speaking Switzerland There are just over 1,000 ha/2,470 acres of vineyard in the southern canton of Ticino, and barely 30 ha over the border with Graubünden in the Italian-speaking Mesolcina Valley. This makes Ticino Switzerland's fourth most important wine canton, and 80% of its production is of the Bordeaux red variety Merlot, imported in 1906. Here, vineyards lower than 450 m/1,475 ft are sunny enough to ripen this variety, although higher vineyards may have to concentrate on Pinot Noir. Merlot del Ticino can be relatively light or, from well-sited vineyards and carefully vinified, often using new oak, can be a serious challenge for fine red bordeaux. The pale yellow Merlot Bianco, made from gently pressed black-berried Merlot, has become quite popular. Sopraceneri, north of Monte Ceneri, is an important wine region of which the local red grape variety Bondola is a speciality. It tends to be included in the rustic local version of 'house wine' called Nostrano, or 'ours', as opposed to Americano, which may include the HYBRIDS and AMERICAN VINES still representing 7% of total production here. Some of the most interesting producers are Castello Luigi, Guido Brivio, Daniel Huber, Kopp von der Crone Visini, Werner Stucky, and Christian Zündel.

Other cantons The German-speaking but central canton of Bern has more than 200 ha/495 acres of vines, mainly on the north shore of Lake Bienne, although there are some vines on the Thunersee west of Interlaken. On the southern shores of Lake Neuchâtel are 100 ha of mainly Chasselas and Pinot Noir in the canton of Fribourg, most of them on the north shore of Lake Morat. The Swiss canton of Jura also has a few hectares of vines.   J. R. & J. V.

Pigott, S., et al., *Wein Spricht Deutsch: Weine, Winzer, Weinlandschaften* (Frankfurt, 2007).
Wallace, E., *Vineglorious! Switzerland's Wondrous World of Wines* (ebook, 2014).
Swiss Wine Guide (Zofingen, 2010).
www.swisswine.ch

Sylvaner is the French name for the eastern European variety known in German as SILVANER (under which name details of all non-French plantings appear). In France, it is practically unknown outside ALSACE, where it was the most planted vine in the lower, flatter, more fertile vineyards of the Bas-Rhin until Riesling overtook it in the 1990s. Total plantings had fallen to 1,237 ha/3,055 acres by 2011.

Sylvaner may be an old vine and, at one time, an extremely important one in Germany at least, but in Alsace many of the wines are dull, even if quite full bodied with good acidity (unlike many Pinot Blancs). Only specific TERROIRS such as the Grand Cru Zotzenberg and old vines manage to imbue Alsace Sylvaner with as exciting a character as the best FRANKEN Silvaners.

Sylvoz, a vine-TRAINING SYSTEM developed by the Italian grower Carlo Sylvoz in which canes of up to, say, ten buds in length are tied to a wire below a high CORDON. The vines can be trained with a high cordon, about 2 m/6.5 ft, or a mid height cordon at about 1 m. Depending on the number of buds retained, the system can be very high yielding. A variation of the Sylvoz is the Casarsa system common in northern Italy, where the canes are not tied below the cordon, but fall downward as a result of their own weight when bearing leaves and fruit. The Sylvoz system is suited to vines of high vigour, where high yields are acceptable, and where it is necessary to minimize pruning labour (see over).

R.E.S.

Eynard, I., and Dalmasso, G., *Viticoltura moderna: manuale pratico* (Milan, 1990).

Symingtons, dominant family of port wine shippers for five generations whose group of port companies includes W. & J. Graham, Warre, Dow, Quinta do Vesúvio, Smith Woodhouse and COCKBURN. They also own Quinta de Roriz. Founder of the family firm was Andrew James Symington, who arrived in Oporto from Glasgow in 1882 at the age of 19 and afterwards married the Anglo-Portuguese Beatriz Leitão de

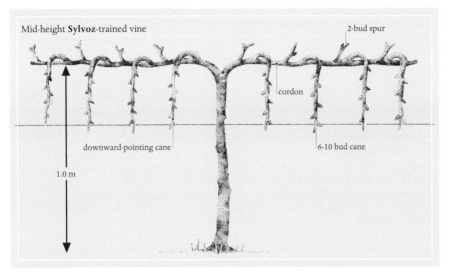

Mid-height **Sylvoz**-trained vine

2-bud spur

cordon

downward-pointing cane

6-10 bud cane

1.0 m

Carvalhosa Atkinson whose ancestors had been in port since the 17th century. Originally he joined the firm of Warre & Co., rising to become a partner. At the time George Warre was senior partner in Dow's, and in 1912 a swap took place whereby Symington took a share in Dow's while Warre regained a part of the firm that his family had founded. The Symingtons ran production and the vineyards for the two firms while the Warre family ran sales and marketing in London. The Warre family sold their remaining shareholding to the Symingtons in 1961. W. & J. Graham & Co. was purchased from the Graham family in 1970 along with the smaller sister company of Smith Woodhouse. The family owns Quinta do Bomfim near Pinhão, which provides much of the fruit for Dow's (along with Quinta da Senhorada Ribeira, acquired in 1998, having originally been sold by the family in 1954 when the fortunes of port were at a particularly low ebb). It also owns Warre's Quinta da Cavadinha in the Pinhão valley and Graham's Quinta dos Malvedos at Tua. The group was instrumental in reviving interest in single-quinta ports in the late 1980s (see PORT, styles). In 1989 the Symingtons acquired Quinta do Vesúvio, a 400-ha/990-acre estate widely regarded as one of the finest vineyards in the Douro, but in need of restoration (see FERREIRA). The vineyards have been extended and improved and, from 1991, Quinta do Vesúvio has been marketed as a brand in its own right. The family own substantial additional vineyards whose fruit is sold to their various different port companies. In 1988, the extensive Quinta do Marco plant in VILA NOVA DE GAIA was opened and it bottles more than 1.5 million cases of port annually. In 1996, a new winery, Quinta do Sol near Regua, was opened with an annual winemaking capacity of 3.2 million litres of port. The Symingtons operate another six small wineries

on individual vineyards throughout the Douro, some of them equipped with the ROBOTIC LAGARES that the family pioneered in 1998. In 2006, Symingtons bought the COCKBURN vineyards, cellars, and stock, and in 2010 acquired the brands. Despite this integration, each company within the group has its own separate stocks and the group maintains a full range of vintage and wood ports for each company.

In 1988, the BLANDY family approached the Symingtons and offered a partnership in their MADEIRA business, hoping to reverse a general decline in sales of madeira. The Symingtons acquired a controlling interest in the Madeira Wine Company and ran it until 2011 when the Blandy family regained control. The Symingtons have established their own distribution companies in Portugal, Britain, and the US.

The Symingtons have become firm believers in DOURO table wines. Their flagship wine Chryseia is made jointly with Bruno Prats, past owner of Ch Cos d'Estournel of ST-ESTÈPHE. The two families acquired Quinta de Roriz in 2009 and Chryseia is now made at this estate, with its related wines. The Douro table wines Quinta do Vesúvio and the Altano range are made from the family's Douro vineyards.

Mayson, R., *The Story of Dow's Port (1798–1998)* (London, 1998).

Symphony, white-berried vine cross of red-skinned Grenache and Muscat of Alexandria developed in CALIFORNIA at DAVIS by Dr H. P. Olmo. It has lived the tenuous existence of all crosses, especially ones that make powerfully aromatic wines, although in the early 1990s it enjoyed a small vogue as an off-dry table wine something like a MALVASIA Bianca, and a flurry of new plantings in 2010 brought the state total to 1,600 acres/648 ha in 2012.

symposium (meaning 'drinking together') was one of the most important social forms in the world of Ancient Greece, and was a considerably less cerebral affair than its 20th-century counterpart. From Greece it spread to Etruria and the rest of Italy and flourished until the end of antiquity. Symposia were usually intimate gatherings: the room normally held seven or 11 couches, on each of which two men reclined on their left side, a custom adopted from oriental feasting; respectable women did not take part, and the servants and entertainers were mostly handsome slaves, both male and female. As part of the lifestyle of the leisured class, symposia were lavish affairs: in the richest households, the vessels for the mixing and drinking of wine would have been of gold or silver, although most will have been content with fine painted pottery. Both the shapes and the decoration of Greek pottery bear witness to the strong influence of the symposium.

The drinking of wine at the symposium followed the meal and was distinct from it, although a dessert of nuts, fruit, cakes, and the like often accompanied the wine. The end of the meal proper was marked by the drinking of a small amount of neat wine in honour of the 'Good Daemon' as a 'demonstration of the power of the good god', after which the tables were removed and the guests washed their hands and were offered garlands and perfumes. The wine was then mixed with water in a *krater* (mixing bowl; see CRATER) according to one of the numerous possible ratios (as detailed under Ancient GREECE). From each bowl, a LIBATION was first offered together with a prayer (the god or gods invoked seem to have varied), and the Paean, a hymn of praise to Apollo, was also sung at the beginning of the proceedings by the whole company. A standard *krater* had a capacity of 14 l/3.7 gal, and various ancient writers indicate that three *kraters* would be emptied at a temperate symposium, so, although the alcoholic strength of the mixture was not high, the amount consumed must have been considerable (42 l for 14 or 22 people, apparently). The ratio for the dilution of the wine was determined by a *symposiarch* or master of ceremonies, chosen from the company, who also regulated the progress of the drinking: he could propose toasts, and order any member of the company to drink more, the aim being to maintain a level of pleasurable but controlled intoxication. However, since the drinking involved an element of competition, and since the proceedings might last all night, the outcome was often outright DRUNKENNESS, as VASE PAINTINGS and literary evidence make clear.

The most basic forms of entertainment arose out of the drinking itself: there were various drinking challenges with forfeits, and the heeltaps of wine were used to play the game of *kottabos*, in which each drinker would shoot the last drops of wine from his cup with a flick of the wrist at the target, which was usually a light bronze disc, balanced on top of a stand or tripod; when hit, it would fall into the basin beneath with a satisfying clatter.

Music and poetry played an important part in the entertainment: most, if not all, of the LYRIC POETRY of archaic Greece is now thought to have had its origins in the symposium, with its preoccupations of warfare and politics, wine and feasting, and love. Some extemporized poetry was no doubt sung at classical symposia, but it was more normal to perform existing poems, which often celebrated the great men and deeds of the past: the collection of Athenian songs of this type (*skolia*) preserved in ATHENAEUS' *Deipnosophistae* (694–96 BC) offers a sample of the traditional songs of one city.

Like the drinking, the singing was both communal and competitive: a branch of myrtle was passed round, and each man as he received it had to sing, sometimes picking up the song from the last singer, although good singers might be called on for a 'party piece'. Singers often accompanied themselves on the lyre, but slave girls were also hired to play the flute to entertain the company, to accompany singers, and to provide music for dancing, and professional dancers, acrobats, and mimes might also perform. Flute players would also be expected to provide sexual services at the end of the evening if required (hence the assumption that any women present at a symposium were not respectable).

Urbane and cultured conversation was also an essential feature; at times this might be structured, and given a competitive aspect, by the posing of riddles or the exchange of witty (and often abusive) comparisons applied to fellow guests. This too might be stimulated by professional help: the career of the parasite who pays for his dinner with his jokes and clowning can be traced back to HOMER. The genre of the literary symposium, a gathering of learned figures conversing on literary or philosophical issues, as in Plato's *Symposium* (whence the modern use of 'symposium'), may give a misleadingly high-minded impression of the average Greek symposium, but such discussion clearly had its place, albeit at a less rarefied level.

Finally, those revellers still awake might go out into the street as a *komos*, a mobile party with wine and music, calling on other symposia or making rowdy attempts to rouse those now asleep. R.B.

Bibliographical note: the most recent general study is Hobden, F., *The Symposion in Ancient Greek Society and Thought* (Cambridge 2013). O. Murray (ed.), *Sympotica* (Oxford, 1990) and O. Murray and M. Tecuşan, *In vino veritas* (Rome 1995) chs. 6–10 are collections of essays on particular aspects, with very full bibliographies, while

J. Davidson, *Courtesans and Fishcakes* (London 1997), ch. 2, analyses Athenian attitudes to drinking.

Athenaeus' *Deipnosophistae* collects many stories of symposia, while XENOPHON's *Symposium* gives the flavour of a classical symposium better than the more famous one of Plato; both are accessible in translation in the Loeb Classical Library.

synthetic closures, also known rather imprecisely as 'plastic corks'. See CLOSURES.

Syrah, one of the noblest and most fashionable red wine grapes, if nobility is bestowed by an ability to produce serious red wines capable of ageing majestically for decades and if fashionability is measured by the extent to which new cuttings have been going into the ground all over the world, despite the depredations of SYRAH decline. So valued was the durability of France's HERMITAGE, arguably Syrah's finest manifestation, that many red bordeaux were in the 18th and 19th centuries *hermitagé* (see ADULTERATION AND FRAUD). And so popular is the variety that in 2010 it was the world's sixth most planted wine grape of either colour, with a global total of 185,568 ha/458,353 acres.

Syrah's origins have been the subject of much debate and hypothesis, involving Syracuse in SICILY, Ancient PERSIA (SHIRAZ being its most common synonym, especially in Australia), the vine family VITIS *allobrogica* recognized as producing fine wine in the Rhône since Roman times (see RHÔNE, history). DNA PROFILING at DAVIS and MONTPELLIER in 1998 however established that, unexpectedly, Syrah is in fact the progeny of two vines from southeast France, MONDEUSE BLANCHE and DUREZA. DNA probability analysis strongly suggests that PINOT is a great-grandparent of Syrah, and both Viognier and Mondeuse Noire seem to be closely related to Syrah, too.

The vine is relatively productive and disease resistant, sensitive to COULURE but conveniently late budding and not too late ripening. Care has to be taken with rootstocks because it is sensitive to CHLOROSIS. Its distinctively savoury qualities are much reduced once the yield is allowed to rise and it has a tendency to lose aroma and acidity rapidly if left too long on the vine.

Many vignerons in the northern Rhône, Syrah's homeland, distinguish between a small-berried, superior version of Syrah, which they call Petite Syrah (not to be mistaken for the variety known in North and South America as PETITE SIRAH), and the larger-berried Grosse Syrah, which produces wines with a lower concentration of PHENOLICS. AMPELOGRAPHERS reject this distinction; Grosse Syrah is a synonym of Mondeuse Noire. The total ANTHOCYANINS in Syrah can be up to 40% higher than those in the tough, dark Carignan, which makes it, typically, a wine for the long term that responds

well to OAK maturation, even new oak when the grapes are really ripe.

The most famous prototype French Syrahs—Hermitage and CÔTE RÔTIE—are distinguished by their longevity or, in the case of newer producers, ambition. Only ST-JOSEPH and that paler shadow CROZES-HERMITAGE can sensibly be broached within their first five years. Syrah that has not reached full maturation can be simply mean and astringent, with more than a whiff of black pepper or burnt rubber. When planted on the fringes of the Rhône such as in the ARDÈCHE, Syrah may avoid this fate only in the ripest vintages.

Until the 1970s, French Syrah plantings were almost exclusively in and around the very limited vineyards of the northern Rhône valley and were dwarfed in area by total Syrah plantings in the vine's other major colony, Australia, where it is known as Shiraz and has been that country's major black grape variety for decades (see AUSTRALIA).

Since then, however, Syrah has enjoyed an extraordinary surge in popularity throughout southern France so that total French plantings rose from 2,700 ha/6,670 acres in 1968 to exactly ten times that 20 years later and had reached 66,859 ha by 2011, making it the country's third most planted red wine. The increases were noticeable throughout the southern Rhône, particularly in Châteauneuf-du-Pape country, where there was a vogue for planting Syrah (although Mourvèdre is increasingly regarded as a more suitable blending partner for Grenache this far south). And in Languedoc-Roussillon Syrah has been so enthusiastically adopted as an officially approved 'improving variety' that has added structure and savour to blends as well as yielding exciting VARIETAL wines that its 41,000 ha in 2011 made it the region's most planted variety. Yields very much in excess of the low yields that characterize the arid hill of Hermitage have tended to dilute its northern Rhône characteristics in many cases, producing a much more supple, more obviously fruity, if still savoury, style of Syrah, often characterized by a particularly polished TEXTURE. In the northern Rhône it is rarely blended, except perhaps with a little Viognier (the original CO-FERMENTATION recipe), while in the south it is typically blended with Grenache, Mourvèdre, Carignan, and/or Cinsaut. In Provence, the very Australian blend of Syrah and Cabernet Sauvignon is relatively common, and Syrah is one of the most successful noble vine imports to Corsica, where there are several hundred hectares in production.

Shiraz, then known as Scyras, was probably taken to Australia, possibly from Montpellier, in 1832 by James BUSBY. It flourished so obviously that it was rapidly adopted by New South Wales and spread therefrom. For more details, see SHIRAZ.

Another unexpectedly successful site for mature, concentrated Syrah is the Valais in Switzerland, particularly around the suntrap village of Chamoson on the upper reaches of the Rhône valley. Here classic northern Rhône techniques are employed, sometimes to great effect. Although keener on Bordeaux grapes, Italians have been planting Syrah, whose total area was 6,738 ha/16,650 acres according to the 2010 vine census, most successfully so far around Cortona in southern Tuscany. The variety was initially introduced from MONTPELLIER, in 1899 in Piemonte. Spanish growers have embraced the variety with even more enthusiasm with 2012 plantings exceeding 20,000 ha, two-thirds of them in Castilla-La Mancha. Spanish Syrah tends to be plumper than most but pioneer Marqués de Griñon has made convincingly fine examples. In Portugal on the other hand, it is relatively rare although is certainly known in the Alentejo. Syrah is planted to a limited extent in most warmer wine regions of Europe and the eastern Mediterranean but only Turkey has more than a few hundred hectares planted. To ripen fully, Syrah demands a warm climate, but if temperatures are too high, its telltale fragrance is lost. This has acted as a brake on American Syrah's success in the US. Perhaps partly thanks to the RHÔNE RANGERS, California growers rushed to plant the variety in the late 20th century; there were still barely 400 acres of it in the state in 1992 but by 2003 there were 17,000 acres/6,800 ha. But many of these plantings were opportunistic, Syrah the wine had no clear identity, the SIDEWAYS effect suggested Pinot Noir was more fashionable, and the variety may have been damaged by the low quality image of cheap Australian SHIRAZ (see YELLOW TAIL, for instance). In 2012 total plantings were 19,000 acres, with a much more significant proportion of them in suitable areas and vinified by a sensitive hand. For more details, see CALIFORNIA.

Promising results from such vineyards as Red Willow, Cayuse, and various Red Mountain vineyards suggest that WASHINGTON state may have considerable potential for fine, bright Syrah wines. In 1999, only a handful of Washington Syrahs were produced but by 2011 total plantings exceeded 3,000 acres, surpassed only by Cabernet and Merlot. Syrah has become markedly FASHIONABLE in Washington, with many producers releasing fine examples. It is

much less important in Oregon but is planted to a limited extent in many other US states warm enough to ripen the variety. Syrah, generally but not always labelled Shiraz, has been hugely popular in South Africa, so that its 2012 total plantings of more than 10,000 ha make it the country's second most planted red wine grape after Cabernet Sauvignon. It is planted in all but the very coolest spots and makes wines in a wide range of styles. The introduction of virus-free clones has improved wine quality, but the variety is so susceptible to South Africa's own, fatal vine virus that can be transmitted via grafts that it is known as Shiraz disease.

Much of New Zealand is too cool for Syrah but plantings have increased to over 350 ha, chiefly Hawke's Bay. (See SHIRAZ for informaion about Australia.)

The variety has been hugely successful in CHILE, on the other hand, where total plantings grew from under 700 ha in 1998 to nearly well over 7,000 ha by 2012. The wines are generally relatively rich and dense although the range of styles has been widening as cooler areas are developed, and most wines recognizable as Syrah. Argentina, for whom Malbec rather than Syrah is an obvious alternative to the Bordeaux grapes, nevertheless has even more land planted with Syrah, nearly 13,000 ha by 2011, making it the country's sixth most planted variety of any colour. San Juan province seems particularly well suited to the variety which is also grown in Bolivia, Peru, and Uruguay. It is not far-fetched to suggest that Syrah/Shiraz may soon be as popularly familiar a name as Cabernet.

'La Syrah', supplement to *Le Vigneron des Côtes du Rhône et du Sud-Est* (1992), 341.

Syrah decline, mysterious fatal phenomenon affecting SYRAH exclusively, known as *dépérissement* in French, whereby a part of the trunk swells and becomes bulbous, generally around the graft, forming splits in the wood. The vine may continue to function normally for a few years but eventually the leaves redden prematurely during summer, VIGOUR rapidly declines and, within a year or two, the vine is dead. It was first noticed in the Languedoc in the 1990s and has affected Syrah virtually wherever it is grown apart from Australia. This led researchers to investigate clonal material selected after the original Syrah cuttings arrived in

Australia. As a result the seven most susceptible French clones (73, 99, 301, 381, 382, 383, and 585) were withdrawn from sale, while the three least susceptible (470, 524, and 747) were strongly recommended for new plantings. New high-quality, low-susceptibility clones have since been promulgated.

Syria, country in the Middle East with, almost incredibly considering its recent history (see WAR, EFFECTS ON WINE), at least one first-class wine producer. Domaine Bargylus was founded in 2005 by the Saade family (also owners of Château Marsyas in LEBANON) in the mountains above the port city of Latakia. A fine red and very respectable white have been made from INTERNATIONAL VARIETIES on a site with a Roman connection.

Syria has a particularly long history of wine production (see ORIGINS OF VINICULTURE and MESOPOTAMIA).

Szekszárd, wine region and PDO in southern HUNGARY with a special LOESS soil as deep as 10 to 15 m (35–50 ft) in places. The landscape is very varied, which allows different MESOCLIMATES to shape the wines. The Szekszárd Hill is 100–120 m/330–395 ft high on average. The steep slopes are dissected by erosional valleys and ravines with the eastern and southern slopes generally providing the best wines. The KADARKA grape, once the chief component of BIKAVÉR, made Szekszárd's viticulture famous in the 18th and 19th centuries and its attractively scented, relatively soft wine can once again be found fairly easily, either as a varietal Kadarka, Kékfrankos, Bikavér (a blend now based on Kékfrankos), or a BORDEAUX blend.   G.R. & G.M.

Szepsy, István, The most respected winemaker in HUNGARY. Records of his winemaking forebears date from at least the 16th century. He currently owns about 79 ha/179 acres of the best vineyard land in the Tokaj villages of Mád, Bodrogkeresztúr, Tarcal, Tállya, Mezőzombor, and Rátka, of which 51.5 ha/126 acres are planted. He created the new style of Tokaj dry wines and has a special interest in the selection of old Furmint and Hárslevelű CLONES.

G.R. & G.M.

Szürkebarát, HUNGARIAN name for PINOT GRIS.

table grapes, the common term for those grapes specially grown to be eaten as fresh fruit. Of the grapes grown worldwide, table grapes represent the third most frequent use, following wine and dried grapes. About 21 million tonnes are grown each year and the trend is upwards. The most important producing country is China, followed at quite some distance by Turkey, India, Iran, Italy, and Egypt. The fruit is consumed primarily within the producing country because it is relatively low in value and perishable. However, with refrigeration the opportunities for export are increasing and Chile, for example, has developed a substantial export trade in table grapes over the last four decades. Table grapes are used widely by the emerging wine industries of ASIA.

The varieties of grapes for fresh consumption are usually specialized and different from those for wine and drying. They should taste good, have a reasonably consistent BERRY SIZE, bright colour, firm flesh texture, not too many seeds, and skins tough enough to withstand storage and transport. Recently developed seedless varieties are increasingly popular. Some important table grape varieties are Barlinka, Calmeria, CARDINAL, CHASSELAS, Dattier, Emperor, Flame Seedless, Gros Vert, Italia, MUSCAT OF ALEXANDRIA, MUSCAT OF HAMBURG, Perlette, Ruby Seedless, Alphonse Lavallée (Ribier), and SULTANA (or Thompson Seedless).

Table grapes are typically grown in warm to hot regions to encourage early maturity and freedom from any ROT brought on by rain. Low night temperatures assist the colour development of some varieties, while both very high and very low day temperatures may inhibit colour development. Many of the table grape regions of the world are inland DESERT areas.

There are some important differences between table grape and wine grape vineyard management. For table grapes, the aim is generally to produce maximum berry size, and so IRRIGATION and FERTILIZERS are used more liberally than for wine grapes. Sloping and overhead trellis systems such as the pergola and TENDONE are common, where the shoots and leaves form a canopy over the fruit, avoiding excessive and direct sun exposure (see SUNBURN).

Because they are worth more than most wine grapes (although see Ch d'YQUEM, MONTRACHET, and DOMAINE DE LA ROMANÉE-CONTI), table grapes typically require more manual vineyard work. This can include SHOOT THINNING, CROP THINNING, and sometimes berry thinning. These practices lead to larger berries which ripen early. GROWTH REGULATORS are also commonly used to thin flowers, but more particularly to increase berry size of seedless varieties such as Sultana. CINCTURING or girdling can also be used to hasten ripening.

Table grapes are harvested earlier than wine grapes as a lower sugar level and higher acidity make them taste more refreshing, in the range of 15 to 18 °BRIX (whereas wine grapes would preferably be harvested for dry wines at about 22 °Brix).

Some table grape varieties can be kept in cool stores for up to 20 weeks, although eight to 12 weeks is more common. Long storage life is promoted by low temperatures such as −1 °C (at which the sugar content stops them freezing), a relative humidity of about 96%, and SULFUR DIOXIDE fumigation for mould control.   R.E.S.

table wine, term used internationally to distinguish wines of average ALCOHOLIC STRENGTH from FORTIFIED WINES, which have been strengthened by the addition of alcohol. In this context, 'table wines' rely solely on FERMENTATION for their alcoholic strength, which tends to be between 9 and 15%.

Within the EU, the term 'table wine' had until the reforms of 2008/2009 a specific meaning and was applied to the vast but declining quantity of wine produced within it that did not qualify as superior so-called QUALITY WINE. Within Italy, the situation was rather different, as explained in VINO DA TAVOLA.

In the US, the term table wine denotes wine with less than 14% alcohol while wines with between 14 and 24% alcohol are officially 'dessert wines' whether fortified or not, and attract a higher tax rate.

Tâche, La, great red GRAND CRU in Burgundy's CÔTE D'OR. For more details, see VOSNE-ROMANÉE and DOMAINE DE LA ROMANÉE-CONTI.

Tacoronte-Acentejo, DO wine region of 1,730 ha/4,270 acres of vines on the west-facing slopes up to 800m in the north east of the volcanic island of Tenerife in the CANARY ISLANDS. Tacoronte-Acentejo produces red wines made predominantly from the dark-berried LISTÁN Negro and Negramoll grapes. The fertile volcanic soil imparts a peculiar character to these improving wines.   V. de la S.

Tahiti in French Polynesia has a planting of Carignan and some TABLE GRAPES on the Tuamutus archipelago which supplies Domaine Dominique Auroy with two harvests a year using TROPICAL VITICULTURE techniques.

Tai Bianco, north-east Italian synonym for SAUVIGNONASSE that has replaced Tocai Bianco, to which Hungarians objected.

taille, French term for PRUNING. The name is also used in CHAMPAGNE and sometimes elsewhere for the coarser, later juice which flows from the press in the traditional method of SPARKLING WINEMAKING.

taint is the term used to refer to the effect of an external CONTAMINANT once its presence can be tasted in a wine. See, for example, CORK TAINT, LADYBUG TAINT, SMOKE TAINT. An off-flavour, on the other hand, is generally the result of a chemical or microbial action within the must or wine.

Tai Rosso, north-east Italian synonym for GRENACHE.

Taiwan, otherwise known as the Republic of China, island off, and independent of, CHINA with about 3,000 ha/7,500 acres of vines in 2011 according to the OIV. Prior to the dismantling of the government alcohol MONOPOLY following Taiwan's accession to the World Trade Organization in 2002, grape growers were not permitted to make wine. They were instead encouraged to sell their grapes to the government agency. Since then, under a government-backed industry development project, wine production has become increasingly popular. Among the many new ventures producing a diverse range of FRUIT WINES are a growing number now producing grape wine—primarily from Black Queen for red wines and Golden Muscat for whites. An indication of progress was the awarding of a gold medal to a Taiwanese wine, a Golden Muscat ICE WINE produced by Domaine Shu-Sheng winery, at Vinalies Internationales in 2014.   D.G.

Tajikistan, mountainous, former Soviet, central Asian republic between UZBEKISTAN and CHINA producing only about 10,000 hl/264,170 gal of wine from 40,000 ha/100,000 acres of vineyards in 2011 according to the OIV.

Viticulture and winemaking were developed in Tajikistan even before the military campaigns of Alexander the Great in the 4th century BC. Ancient documents testify to the cultivation of numerous VINE VARIETIES in the country, which were made into wine, vinegar, and *bekmes* (CONCENTRATED GRAPE MUST), as well as being traded as TABLE GRAPES and RAISINS. Viticulture was highly developed in Osrushan in Ura-Tyube, Fergana, and in the Zeravshan River valley.

The adoption of ISLAM in the north prohibited the consumption of wine and changed the country's range of grape varieties. Wine varieties were grubbed up and table and raisin varieties were planted in their place. Central, south, and south-eastern parts of the country were also affected by this trend but to a lesser extent. In the 1920s, small private vineyards were amalgamated to form large farms, and the total vineyard area continued to increase in order to meet the needs of commercial wine production in the Soviet era.

Tajikistan can be divided into three viticultural zones: the Leninabad region in the north, the Ghissar Valley in the centre, and the Vakhsh Valley together with the Kuliab regions in the south. Most vineyards need WINTER PROTECTION and IRRIGATION.

In the 1990s, 25 grape varieties were in commercial cultivation, with ten wine varieties such as RKATSITELI, SAPERAVI, CABERNET SAUVIGNON, RIESLING, Tagobi, Bayanshira, and Muscat Rosé. Tajikistan's wine is mainly strong and sweet.
                                                                V.R.

Kirillov, I. F., et al., *Viticulture of Tajikistan* (Russian) (Dushanbe, 1969).

Kiselev, N. A., *Viticultural Regions and Wines of Tajikistan* (Russian) (Moscow, 1967).

Savchenko, A. D., 'The Soviet Socialist Republic of Tajikistan' (Russian), in A. I. Timush (ed.), *Encyclopaedia of Viticulture* (Kishinëv, 1986).

Tália, occasionally written **Thalia**, Portuguese name for the ubiquitous white grape variety known in France as UGNI BLANC and in Italy as TREBBIANO Toscano.

Tămâioasă, name for MUSCAT grape or wine in ROMANIA. Thus **Tămâioasă Alba** is Romanian for MUSCAT BLANC À PETITS GRAINS, **Tămâioasă Hamburg** or **Tămâioasă Neagră** is MUSCAT OF HAMBURG, **Tămâioasă Ottonel** is MUSCAT OTTONEL. **Tămâioasă Românească** is another Romanian synonym for Muscat Blanc à Petits Grains, and there were more than 1,450 ha planted in Romania in 2013.

Tamarez, old but relatively uninspiring white grape grown in the Alentejo.

Tamar River, wine region in TASMANIA.

Taminga, grape variety bred specifically for hot AUSTRALIAN conditions (see also TARRANGO) by A. J. Antcliff from TRAMINER. Taminga is not widely planted but is capable of ripening and producing white wine of fair quality in a wide variety of different sites with an average yield of 90 hl/ha (5 tons/acre).

Tamyanka, Bulgarian, Russian, and Serbian name for MUSCAT BLANC À PETITS GRAINS.

tank method, alternative name for a bulk SPARKLING WINEMAKING process which involves provoking a second fermentation in wine stored in a pressure tank. Other names include Charmat process and *cuve close*.

tanks. See CONTAINERS.

Tannat, distinctive, tough, deep black-berried vine variety most famous as principal ingredient in MADIRAN, where its inherent astringence is mitigated by blending with Cabernet Franc, some Cabernet Sauvignon, and FER, and wood ageing for at least 20 months. If Madiran is Tannat's noblest manifestation, slightly more approachable, if more rustic, wines are made to much the same recipe for Côtes de ST-MONT, as well as for the distinctively hard reds and rosés of IROULÉGUY and the rare reds and pinks labelled TURSAN and BÉARN.

Overall plantings in France have remained fairly static and were 2,849 ha/7,037 acres in 2011. Although it may owe its French name to its high tannin content, the vine may well be Basque in origin and, like MANSENG, was taken to URUGUAY by Basque settlers in the 19th century, where it is by far the most important vine variety and, rather like MALBEC in ARGENTINA, seems to thrive better in the warmer climate of its new home in South America than SOUTH WEST FRANCE. In Uruguay, where it has been called Harriague after its original promulgator, there were more than 1,800 ha in 2013. Strategies for softening the grapes' tannins include blending with such grapes as Pinot Noir and Merlot as well as all the usual winemaking techniques (see MACERATION, and MICRO-OXYGENATION which was developed for Tannat in Madiran in particular). Port and Beaujolais styles have also been made from it. From Uruguay it spread to other wine-producing countries in South America, and there are several hundred acres in California. The variety is seen as a minor but intriguing challenge by winemakers all over the world.

tannins, diverse and complex group of chemical compounds that occur in the bark of many trees and in fruits, including the grape. Strictly speaking, a tannin is a compound that is capable of interacting with PROTEINS and precipitating them; this is the basis of the process of tanning animal hides (hence the name tannin) and is also a process that is believed to be responsible for the sensation of ASTRINGENCY. Tannins in wine come predominantly from the grapes and, to a much lesser extent, from the WOOD in which the wine is aged. See also OAK FLAVOURS.

The natural tannins of grapes, or condensed tannins, also called PROANTHOCYANIDINS since they release red anthocyanidin pigments when heated in acidic media, are FLAVONOIDS consisting of oligomers and polymers of CATECHINS. Formation of proanthocyanidins occurs under the control of ENZYMES as part of the metabolism of the grape but they may rearrange to longer or shorter molecules in the acidic wine medium. Other catechin polymers can be formed in wine as a result of enzymatic or chemical oxidation reactions. These polymeric flavonoids that can range from colourless through light yellow to amber, as well as PIGMENTED TANNINS resulting from reactions of anthocyanins with catechins and tannins, may also be regarded as tannins. Wine may also contain hydrolysable tannins, deriving from gallic acid and ellagic acid, extracted from oak cooperage in the course of barrel ageing, from OAK CHIPS, or added as OENOLOGICAL TANNINS.

Tannins play an important role in the AGEING of wine, particularly red wines, where pigmented tannins are crucial to the colour and sensory properties. Handling tannins during RED WINEMAKING is one of the most critical steps in optimizing the quality and character of a red wine, yet the process is based almost totally on experience and intuition because our understanding of the principles involved is still incomplete.

The tannins in grapes are predominantly in the SKINS and SEEDS of each berry and also the STEMS, the amount of tannins in grape pulp being much lower. Thus, the more skins, seeds, and stems are involved in the winemaking process, the higher the possible resultant level of tannins. Tannin levels in white and rosé wines, which are made largely by excluding or minimizing these grape components, are therefore lower than in reds. Although white wines contain structures similar to the pigmented tannins of a red wine, the absence of ANTHOCYANINS condensed into the tannins of white wines accounts for how different they look.

Tannins are most often encountered by the human palate in over-steeped tea, and by wine drinkers in young reds designed for a long life in bottle and in whites made with prolonged or excessive SKIN CONTACT. They produce the taste sensation of bitterness and the physical tactile 'drying' sensation of astringency. Catechins and small tannins are said to be responsible for bitterness, while larger ones elicit the astringency sensation, presumably by interaction with the proteins of the mouth but also by the adherence of the tannins to the oral mucous membranes (see below).

Traditional methods for measuring tannins report them as if they were all gallic acid, and such analyses, including the widely used Folin Ciocalteu method, are popular because of their analytical convenience. Alternative methods for measuring the phenolic compounds of grape tannins more directly and as other than gallic acid are time consuming and require considerable analytical expertise. Gallic acid or GA equivalent concentration averages about 300 mg/l in white wines, but 1,800 mg/l in reds. The tannin types and their extraction rates vary considerably with VINE VARIETY and WINEMAKING methods. Varieties notably high in tannins include CABERNET SAUVIGNON, NEBBIOLO, SYRAH, and TANNAT.

Since the late 1980s, much research into red winemaking has been aimed at minimizing the bitter and astringent impression made by tannins on the palate while enhancing the TEXTURE and ageing properties which they confer on a wine. These studies have involved, among other variations, ever more refinement of MACERATION techniques and deliberately controlled exposure to OXYGEN at various points during the winemaking process (see MICROOXYGENATION, for example). It is also widely recognized that the influence of such

viticultural factors as grape RIPENESS and grape composition on the properties of tannins is not yet understood.

Different WOOD TYPES contain different sorts of tannins, but these have most effect on wine when the COOPERAGE is new. The tannins of the various species and varieties of OAK, the most common wood used in winemaking, vary among themselves, and according to how the oak was seasoned (see BARREL MAKING). Oak tannins differ in significant ways from grape tannins, although the consequences of such differences on the stability of wine colour and on the sensory properties (including mouthfeel) of barrel-matured red wines in particular are yet to be scientifically rationalized. For more details, see OAK FLAVOUR. Wine consumers may experience a certain amount of wood oak flavour in a wide range of wines, including some relatively immature wines, both red and white, whether the result of genuine BARREL MATURATION or the use of OAK CHIPS. They are therefore often exposed to the effects of tannin on the palate, which can be considerably mitigated by the right choice of accompanying FOOD.

Winemakers can adjust excessively high tannin levels by FINING with casein, gelatin, or albumin, which selectively precipitate large-sized astringent tannins. Formation of soluble complexes with macromolecules such as proteins may also prevent tannins from interacting with salivary proteins and eliciting astringency. Given sufficient time, tannins are removed naturally, however, during wine ageing. The tannins polymerize and form aggregates that eventually precipitate as SEDIMENT so that they no longer have any bitter or astringent effect on the palate. Depending on the wine composition and PH, reactions of tannins can also yield smaller tannins and pigmented tannins, thus resulting in lower astringency.

See also OENOLOGICAL TANNINS, which may be deliberately added in the course of winemaking to increase a wine's tannin level.

A.D.W., P.J.W., & V.C.

Cheynier, V., 'Flavonoids in wine', in O. M. Andersen and K. R. Markham (eds.), *Flavonoids: Chemistry, Biochemistry and Applications* (Boca Raton, Fla., 2006).

Tasting tannins

Tannins cannot be smelt or tasted; they cause tactile sensations. A significant development of the 1990s was a keener appreciation of the different sorts of sensory impact of tannins on the palate (see TEXTURE). In Australia, this led in particular to the development of a MOUTHFEEL wheel rather like the AROMA WHEEL. Tannins may be variously described as hard, bitter (if accompanied by BITTERNESS), green, ripe (if perceptible but only after the impact of fruit that has reached PHYSIOLOGICAL RIPENESS has been felt on the palate), coarse, grainy, wood (if

obviously the effect of CASK AGEING), long chain (an American expression for POLYMERIZED), short chain, and polymerized. Research in the US by Revelette et al. has shown that it is not just the quantity of tannins in a wine that determines its astringency but also the quality of those tannins, specifically their tendency to 'stick' to another surface such as the mucous membranes.

Cheynier, V., et al., 'The structure of tannins in grapes and wines and their interactions with proteins', in T. Watkins (ed.), *Wine: Nutritional and Therapeutic Benefits* (Washington, DC, 1997).

Noble, A. C., 'Astringency and bitterness of flavonoid phenols', in P. Given and D. Paredes (eds.), *Chemistry of Taste: Mechanisms, Behaviors, and Mimics* (Washington, 2002), 192–201.

Revelette, M., et al. 'High-performance liquid chromatography determination of red wine tannin stickiness', *Journal of Agricultural and Food Chemistry*, 62/28 (2014), 6626–31. doi: 10.1021/jf501666z.

Vidal, S., et al., 'Taste and mouth-feel properties of different types of tannin-like polyphenolic compounds and anthocyanins in wine', *Analytica Chimica Acta*, 513/1 (2004), 57–65.

Tanzania. Although less than eight degrees south of the equator, Tanzania produces wine from two vintages a year (see TROPICAL VITICULTURE). INTERNATIONAL VARIETIES are planted, notably around the city of Dodoma. German settlers planted vines just south of Mount Kilimanjaro in the 1930s and an ambitious vine nursery was established by another German in the 1980s.

Platter, J. & E., *Africa Uncorked* (London, 2002).

Tarragona, Mediterranean port in Spanish CATALUÑA which has played an important part in a flourishing wine industry since Roman times (see SPAIN, history, and map). Until the 1960s, wines called Tarragona were predominantly sweet, red, fortified, and drunk as a cheap alternative to PORT. Awarded DO status in 1976, Tarragona continues to ship communion wine all over the Christian world (see EUCHARIST). Over 70% of Tarragona's wine production today is white, however, a large proportion of which is sold to the CAVA houses in PENEDÈS. The MONTSANT DO created in 2001 was carved out of the original Tarragona zone.

V. de la S. & J.R.

Tarrango, red wine grape variety developed at Merbein in AUSTRALIA in 1965. The aim of this TOURIGA × SULTANA cross was to provide a slow-ripening variety suitable for the production of light-bodied wines with low TANNINS and relatively high ACIDITY. As a result, some Australian wines have been fashioned in the image of BEAUJOLAIS but the variety will ripen satisfactorily only in the hot irrigated wine regions of

Australia such as the RIVERLAND. Brown Brothers of Milawa have been particularly persistent with this variety, planted on almost 200 ha in Australia in the mid 2000s.

tartaric acid, the most important of the ACIDS found in grapes and wine. Of all the natural organic acids found in plants, this is one of the rarer. The grape is the only fruit of significance that is a tartrate accumulator, and yet it is of critical importance to the winemaker because of the major part it plays in the taste of the wine. Furthermore, because tartaric acid exists in wine partially as the intact acid and partially as the acid tartrate, or bitartrate ion, it is the principal component of the mixture of acids and salts that constitutes wine's all-important buffer system (see BUFFERING CAPACITY) and maintains the stability of its ACIDITY and COLOUR.

Tartaric acid is of further interest because its potassium acid salt, potassium tartrate or cream of tartar, while being moderately soluble in grape juice, is only partially soluble in alcoholic solutions such as wine. Most winemakers therefore try to ensure that no excess tartrates remain in the wine when it is bottled lest these crystals frighten less sophisticated consumers by their resemblance to glass shards. See TARTRATES for more on this important by-product of the wine-making process.

Grapes and the resultant wines vary considerably in their concentrations of tartaric acid. Among the thousands of cultivated VINE VARIETIES, some are noted for their high concentrations of tartaric acid, while others are remarkably bland. In general, wine grapes have higher concentrations of acids than table grapes. Among wine grape varieties, however, there is considerable variation in concentrations of the two principal acids: tartaric acid and MALIC ACID. Palomino, the sherry grape, for example, is particularly high in tartaric acid, while the Pinot Noir of Burgundy and Malbec, or Côt, are relatively low in tartaric.

The relative amounts of these two acids that are present in grapes, which varies with VINTAGE, do not necessarily govern the relative amounts in wines, however. Precipitation of potassium acid tartrate, as outlined above, limits total tartaric acid concentration, while malic acid is frequently decomposed by MALOLACTIC CONVERSION. Wines that have not undergone this conversion generally have slightly more tartaric acid than malic acid, while those which have undergone this 'softening' process usually have many more times tartaric than malic acid; they are also more stable.

Weather and soil, as well as grape variety, affect the amounts of different acids in the grape and wine. Cooler climates in general favour higher concentrations of acids and lower levels of POTASSIUM in the grape skins. Malic acid

is much more effectively decomposed by excessive heat during the grape ripening period than is tartaric acid. Soils deficient in potassium, or potash, may result in grapes of high acid concentration and low PH because low potassium levels allow greater concentrations of acid tartrate ion to stay in solution. Another curious difference is that tartrate levels are very high in grape flowers. Tartaric acid is not respired during ripening, meaning that its amount per berry stays relatively constant during berry RIPENING. More than half of the tartrate in ripe berries can be present as a salt. The proportion of free to salt form varies with variety and the concentration of metal cations in the juice; potassium is by far the most abundant.   A.D.W. & B.G.C.

tartrates, the general term used by winemakers to describe the harmless crystalline deposits that separate from wines during FERMENTATION and AGEING. In English the substances are also called argols, in French *tartres* and in German *Weinsteine* (literally, 'wine stones'). The principal component of this deposit is potassium acid tartrate, the potassium salt of TARTARIC ACID, which has therefore given rise to the name. Small amounts of pulp debris, dead yeast cells, precipitated phenolic materials such as TANNINS and PIGMENTED TANNINS, and traces of other materials make up the impurities contaminating the potassium acid tartrate (see SEDIMENT).

The LEES, the thick layer of dead yeast and grape skins, seeds, and pulp fragments that sinks to the bottom of the FERMENTATION VESSEL during the later stages of fermentation as deposit, contains lower concentrations of tartrates than do the crystalline deposits that form on the walls of the vessel. Lees are a commercial source of tartrates, but extraction and purification of potassium acid tartrate from lees is much more expensive and time consuming than from the crystalline deposits on walls, the preferred source for commercial tartrates.

The main forms of tartrates used commercially are pure crystalline tartaric acid used as an acidulant in non-alcoholic drinks and foods, cream of tartar (pure potassium acid tartrate) used in baking, and Rochelle salt (potassium sodium tartrate) used mainly in electroplating solutions. The wine industry is the only source of tartrates available to commerce and the crystalline encrustations left inside fermentation vessels are therefore regularly scraped off and purified for eventual commercial use.

Tartrates separate from new wines because potassium acid tartrate is less soluble in solutions of alcohol and water such as wine than it is in plain water, or grape juice. The exact figures for wines vary slightly according to grape variety and region, but experience shows that about a half of the tartrate soluble in grape juice is insoluble in wine. The problem is that the

tartrate may remain in a supersaturated state in the complex wine mixture only to crystallize at some unpredictable later time.

Only the most informed consumers appreciate the harmlessness of tartrate crystals in bottle. Although tartrates precipitated in red wines usually take on some red or brown colouring from adsorbed wine pigments and are commonly regarded as mere sediment, in white wines they can look alarmingly like shards of glass to the uninitiated. The modern wine industry has in the main decided that tartrate STABILIZATION is preferable to consumer education.

Tartrate instability was recognized as a problem only in the 19th century when, with greater wine production and standardization of BOTTLE production, bottle-aged wines first became common. Previously wines were not expected to be perfectly clear and many would routinely be strained, but producers of most modern wines, and all inexpensive white wines, believe that their customers expect a brilliantly clear liquid to emerge from the bottle, no matter how long it has been there.

With the efficient degrees of FILTRATION possible today, it is relatively easy to ensure perfect clarity immediately prior to BOTTLING. The problem is to ensure that the wine will remain clear. Historically, wines were stabilized against tartrate precipitation by letting the cellar cool to temperatures near or below freezing during the winter. Low temperatures for three to four months would usually remove so much potassium acid tartrate that further precipitation was unlikely. The modern equivalent is to use REFRIGERATION to chill the wine before bottling to between −5 and −10 °C/24 to 14 °F for two to three weeks. Precipitated tartrate crystals are then filtered from the cold wine before it is warmed back to cellar temperature. Sometimes small amounts of finely divided CHARCOAL or BENTONITE clay are mixed into the wine to be chilled to act as nucleation centres for the supersaturated potassium acid tartrate and therefore induce crystal formation. A more recent and faster technique involves the stirring up of finely ground potassium acid tartrate in the wine, which is then cooled to a low temperature and the cold wine and crystal mixture immediately filtered. This method depends on the rapid crystallization of tartrates from the wine on the millions of fine crystals added that act as nucleation centres. This method saves both time and power. Yeast MANNOPROTEINS may be added to wine to inhibit tartrate precipitation. Carboxymethyl cellulose (CMC) is also used. See also ELECTRODIALYSIS.

Metatartaric acid, produced by heating tartaric acid, is used widely in the UK and occasionally in Germany at a maximum level of 100 mg/l. Its use is permitted in Australia and elsewhere but it is not very popular because it is effective only for a matter of months. Metatartaric acid dissolves in wine and inhibits the formation of tartrate crystals. However, it is unstable and reverts to tartaric acid within 3–18 months (depending on temperature), with the risk of yet more tartrate crystals.

Some everyday wines produced in large quantities contain enough calcium to cause precipitation of calcium tartrate during bottle ageing, although this was most common in the era of the concrete tank. When the concrete tanks were new, or had had their protective coating of tartrates removed, wine dissolved enough calcium carbonate from the concrete surface to cause subsequent calcium tartrate instability. Stainless steel tanks, or lined concrete ones, have largely overcome the problem of calcium tartrate instability.

Tartrates are most commonly encountered in bottles of German wine because, coming from a relatively cool region, they have the greatest concentration of tartaric acid. In white wines, colourless, perfectly shaped crystals of potassium acid tartrate are found. In red wines, there are usually sufficient adsorbed TANNINS and PIGMENTED TANNINS to colour the crystals reddish brown and to ensure that they are small and irregular in shape.   A.D.W.

Ribéreau-Gayon, P., et al., *Traité d'Œnologie 2: Chimie du vin: Stabilisation et traitements* (Paris, 1998), translated by Aquitrad Traduction as *Handbook of Enology 2: The Chemistry of Wine Stabilization and Treatments* (Chichester, 2000).

Tasmania, small island state to the cool south of AUSTRALIA, with most of its vineyards clustered round Launceston in the north or Hobart in the south of the island and on the east coast around Bicheno. So far there has been no move to seek registration of any regions, or even zones, notwithstanding the diversity of climate noted below. The creation of two zones, one north and one south, would be a logical first step, the boundary easy to draw. Regions could then follow once they gained the sufficient critical mass of 500 tonnes.

In volume terms, the Tasmanian wine industry is as tiny as its potential is large. The island state has 1,320 ha/3,260 acres of planted vineyards, which is less than 1% of Australia's total, but Tasmania has for several years been the one Australian wine region where demand for grapes outstrips supply. It crushed a total of 7,388 tonnes of grapes in 2010, a figure virtually unchanged since 2004.

Outside observers not only habitually exaggerate the extent of Tasmania's viticulture, but are oblivious to the diversity of TERROIR and climate in the island's extremely complex geography. There are sites which are both warmer and very much drier than southern Victoria (for example the **Coal River/Richmond** region in the east of Hobart, and, in terms of warmth, the **Tamar Valley** north of Launceston) and

there are sites cooler and wetter (for example **Pipers River**, east of Launceston). The one clear pattern is that Pinot Noir finds itself at home in all parts of the state, with the qualified exception of parts of the Tamar River.

Zinfandel was once grown successfully at the Coal River; the colour and extract of the Tamar River red wines is extraordinary, hinting misleadingly at a warm to very warm climate. The island's major producers have hitched their future to such cool-climate varieties as Riesling, Pinot Gris, Chardonnay, and Pinot Noir (the latter two for both table and sparkling wine use). However, the apparent effect of climate change—or at least, some warm vintages—has led to some impressive MERLOT, CABERNET SAUVIGNON, and SHIRAZ coming from the warmer sites of the Tamar River and from the Coal River, where Domaine A struts its stuff.

Tasmania has seen many changes in recent years. After selling Tamar Ridge to Gunns Limited, Joe Chromy bought another vineyard and created his third wine company, Josef Chromy Wines, at Relbia in 2004. Heemskerk was relaunched as TREASURY WINE ESTATES' key Tasmanian brand. Belgian-owned Kreglinger took control of Pipers Brook in 2001, the same year that Hardys developed the Bay of Fires BRAND. Andrew Pirie, who abruptly left Pipers Brook in 2003, launched his new Apogee brand in 2013. Andrew Hood sold Wellington Wines to the principals of organic producer Frogmore Creek in 2003. Art collector and professional gambler David Walsh, who bought Moorilla Estate in 1995, has reinvented it with a new winery, excellent brewery, restaurant, and the internationally celebrated MONA art museum. The Hill Smith family of Yalumba bought Dalrymple in 2007, having bought Jansz some years earlier. Brown Brothers bought Tamar Ridge from Gunns in 2010 and immediately became the biggest single player in the state. Shaw + Smith bought Tolpuddle Vineyard in 2011.

Over this period, Tasmania has emerged as a serious producer of the country's finest sparkling wines as well as high-level Pinot Noir, Chardonnay, and Riesling table wines. While some larger vineyards have been established, most of the 112 producers remain tiny. Pinot Noir has improved out of all recognition and is being made in larger volumes; the distinctively elegant Riesling and Chardonnay, with high natural acidity, are increasingly admired. Hardys, Australia's pre-eminent sparkling winemaker (Arras, Sir James, etc.), now sources all of its ultra-premium base wine from the island.

The quality of Tasmanian wine has never been in dispute, and will presumably only improve as VINE AGE increases, and the terroir/variety dating game becomes even more sophisticated.   J.H. & H.H.

www.winetasmania.com.au

taste. What we call the sense of taste is to a very great extent the sense of SMELL. See TASTING for more details. As for our own personal taste in wine, it is overall SUBJECTIVE, even if subject to our own personal SENSITIVITIES. There are no rights and wrongs in wine preferences. See also QUALITY IN WINE.

tastevins, or wine tasters, as they are known by collectors of wine antiques, are shallow, often dimpled, saucers used for TASTING by professionals (and occasional self-conscious amateurs). Because they were usually used in a cellar, or on purchasing journeys where robust construction was essential, they were almost invariably made of silver. The earliest English references to tasters date from the 14th century but only a single extant example pre-dates 1600. British tasters mostly copy the BORDEAUX model, being 65–110 mm (2.5–4.5 in) in diameter with sloping sides, a domed base, and lacking a handle. Extremely rare tasters were made of glass or porcelain, usually Worcester.

Tastevins are far more plentiful in France than elsewhere. Most have a single handle and a slightly domed base. Many are decorated with a different pattern on either side of the handle. Late-19th- and 20th-century examples are often plated.   R.N.H.B.

Some BURGUNDY producers still use tastevins in their own cellars, where they can be useful to demonstrate hue and clarity even in a dim light. For actual tasting, GLASSES are more efficacious, even if more fragile and less easily portable. Contemporary manufacture of tastevins is sustained by many CONFRÉRIES, most obviously the Burgundian Chevaliers du Tastevin.

Butler, R., *Great British Wine Accessories 1550-1900* (Sudbury, Suffolk, 2009).

Mazenot, R., *Le Tastevin à travers les siècles* (Grenoble, 1973).

tasting, the act of consciously assessing a wine's quality, character, or identity (see BLIND TASTING). It is certainly not synonymous with, nor necessarily contemporaneous with nor accompanied by, the act of drinking it. The ideal conditions for the act of tasting, and the organization and classification of formal wine tastings, is outlined under TASTINGS. This article is concerned with the activities and mechanisms involved in consciously receiving the sensory impressions a wine can stimulate.

Ancient Greek tasters

The existence of an organized trade in wine in Ancient GREECE must have created a class of specialized MERCHANTS. Both for them and for discerning members of the public, skill in tasting was necessary, and the Greeks had a word for the wine tasters and their art: *oinogeustes/-geustikē*. The first attestation of this activity is through the cognate verb meaning 'to taste wine', found as early as the 4th century BC.

References to the professionals are extremely rare; one is found in a document of the 3rd century AD from Roman Egypt (*Oxyrhynchus Papyrus* 3517), where it is said, 'The wine taster has declared the Euboean wine to be unsuitable.'

The most enlightening ancient text is by Florentinus, a writer of the early 3rd century AD, who gives the following advice (preserved in the *Geoponica* 7. 7):

When and how to taste wine. From Florentinus. Some people taste wines when the wind is in the north, because then the wines remain unchanged and undisturbed. Experienced drinkers prefer to taste when the wind is from the south, because this has the most effect on the wine and reveals its nature. One should not taste when hungry, because the sense of taste is blunted, nor after heavy drinking or a large meal. The person tasting should not do so after consumption of food with a sharp or very salty taste, or anything which affects the sense of taste strongly, but should have eaten as lightly as possible and be free from indigestion.

See MERCHANTS for a continuation of this advice, as applied to the art of selling wine.

N.G.W.

How we taste

Most of what is commonly called the sense of taste is in fact the sense of SMELL, whether applied to wine, or any food or drink, since by chewing we transform our food into liquid which gives off smellable vapour. To verify this it is enough to eat or drink something with the nose pinched shut, or to consider the extent to which we 'lose our appetite' when we have a head cold which blocks the nose. The human brain senses what we call flavours and aromas in the olfactory bulb, which, as Buck and Axel so elegantly demonstrated in their Nobel prize-winning work, is reached via a thousand different olfactory receptor cells, each expressing a single odorant receptor gene, these genes representing about 3% of an individual's genetic make-up. Unexpectedly, each olfactory receptor cell is sensitive to a very small group of related aromas. From the olfactory bulb these messages are sent to other parts of the brain and processed, combining them and forming a pattern. Most aromas are made up of many different molecules, each of which activates several of these olfactory receptors, making odorant patterns, so that humans are able to recognize and, particularly, memorize up to 10,000 different aromas. The olfactory bulb is reached mainly by the nostrils, and to a lesser extent by a channel at the back of the mouth called the retronasal passage (which is why most healthy people can still perceive some flavour even if they do not consciously smell

what they consume). The human olfactory sense is extremely acute and possibly as acute as that of most mammals. Concentrations of some compounds of one part per trillion (see Bushdid et al.) can be sensed, recognized, and remembered by the average person. A single whiff can transport us immediately to something experienced many years before.

The tasting capacity of the mouth is much more limited. In the mouth, our tactile sense can register FIZZINESS, TEMPERATURE, VISCOSITY, EXTRACT, the apparent heat generated on the palate by excessive ALCOHOL, and the sensation induced by TANNINS of drying out the insides of the cheeks.

The tongue also has certain taste receptors we call taste buds, which can sense the five 'primary tastes' of SWEETNESS, ACIDITY, BITTERNESS, SALTINESS, and the more recently recognized UMAMI. There is considerable genetic variation in how many taste buds we have, with roughly a quarter of the population considered extremely sensitive 'supertasters'. To supertasters the substance PROP (6-n-propylthiouracil) tastes extremely bitter and taste sensations in general are intensified and exaggerated. To so-called 'non-tasters', PROP is virtually tasteless, while about half of us are 'medium tasters', find PROP mildly bitter, and experience taste sensations without distorting extremes. It was long thought that different parts of the tongue were particularly sensitive to one of these primary tastes but Bartohuk et al. showed that in fact we have taste receptors for all the primary tastes in each taste bud.

With the exception of some wines matured near the sea such as MANZANILLA or some produced from vineyards with a serious SALINITY problem, very few wines taste salty, and in even fewer can umami be detected. Sweetness and acidity, on the other hand, are two of the most important measurements of a wine, although it is important to recognize that the apparent sweetness of a wine is not necessarily the same as its RESIDUAL SUGAR. High acidity can easily make a wine taste much drier than it actually is, for example.

It is clear that the mouth's tasting ability, apart from being usefully linked to the olfactory bulb by the retronasal passage, is in *measuring* the wine, assessing its dimensions of sweetness, acidity, bitterness, fizziness, viscosity, potency, and ASTRINGENCY. The mouth is capable of making an overall assessment of a wine's TEXTURE and STRUCTURE, while the nose senses what we call its flavour. Just as what is commonly called the sense of taste is really the sense of smell, so what is commonly called flavour is really AROMA or, in older wines, BOUQUET. (See FLAVOUR, however, for a proposal that the word be used to

incorporate all the measurements sensed by the mouth.)

The essential character and most complex distinguishing marks of any wine are in its smell, which is made up of hundreds, probably thousands, of different FLAVOUR COMPOUNDS, present in widely varying permutations and concentrations in different wines.

What is commonly called tasting therefore involves persuading as many of these flavour compounds as possible to reach the olfactory bulb, while ensuring that contact is made between the wine and all of the inside of the mouth for the purposes of assessing a wine's dimensions and texture.

How to taste

The operation of tasting is generally divided into three stages involving sequentially the eye, the nose, and the mouth (although, as outlined above, this is not the same as the simple sequential application of the senses of sight, smell, and taste).

Eye The job of the eye in wine tasting is mainly to assess clarity and colour, as well as to monitor the presence of CARBON DIOXIDE and ALCOHOL (the former indicated by bubbles, the latter possibly by any TEARS of the wine that may form on the inside of the glass when it is rotated).

The clarity of a wine is an indication, hardly surprisingly, of the extent to which CLARIFICATION has been carried out, but also of the wine's condition. Many wine FAULTS result in a haze of some sort. In the late 1990s, anti-FILTRATION sentiment was so strong in California that some highly priced Chardonnays looked positively cloudy, a common characteristic in many NATURAL WINES. A wine with particles floating in it, however, may simply be an innocent casualty of poor SERVING technique in which a wine has not been properly separated from its entirely harmless SEDIMENT. Experienced tasters can sometimes discern quality simply by looking at a wine's luminescent clarity and subtle range of hues.

The colour of a wine, both its intensity and its hue, is one of the potentially most valuable clues to any BLIND TASTER. Intensity of colour is best judged by looking straight through a glass of wine from directly above (preferably against a plain white background). Different grape varieties tend to make deeper or lighter coloured wines (Cabernet Sauvignon, Syrah, Tannat, and Malbec make particularly deep red wines; Gewürztraminer and Pinot Gris are examples of varieties which make particularly deep white wines, because the grape skins are deep pink). A deep colour also indicates youth, long MACERATION (possibly over-EXTRACTION), and thick-skinned grapes in a red wine; sometimes age, SKIN-FERMENTATION, some OXIDATION, BARREL

MATURATION, although not if preceded by BARREL FERMENTATION, in white wines.

The actual hue can also provide clues, and can be best assessed by tilting the glass away at an angle so that the different shadings of colour at the rim can be seen, again preferably against a plain white background. A bluish tinge in a red wine indicates youth, while orange/yellow indicates AGE (or OXIDATION). Very pale green in a white wine may indicate Riesling, while a pink tinge suggests that the wine was made from pink-skinned grapes such as Gewürztraminer and Pinot Gris. For more information, see COLOUR.

This stage in tasting for any purpose other than identification is usually very short and, if tasters are SCORING various aspects of a wine, many wines gain maximum points for appearance.

Nose As demonstrated above, this is the single most important stage in wine tasting. The trick is to persuade as many flavour compounds as possible to vaporize and come into contact with the olfactory bulb (although what we smell is in fact an AZEOTROPIC mixture of many, rather than isolated, individual, flavour compounds). It is then necessary, of course, to be in a suitable frame of mind to interpret the messages received by the olfactory bulb, which is why the act of tasting requires concentration.

The simplest way to maximize the evaporation of a wine's volatile elements is by the judicious use of TEMPERATURE and agitation. Higher temperatures encourage any sort of evaporation, so ideal tasting temperatures tend to be slightly higher than ideal SERVING temperatures. It is unwise to taste wines so hot that the alcohol starts to evaporate at such a rate that it dominates the flavour, however, so an ideal tasting temperature for wines, red or white, is somewhere between 15 and 20 °C/59–68 °F. At these relatively elevated temperatures, faults as well as attributes should be perfectly apparent. What is lost is the refreshment factor, but then the point of tasting rather than drinking is analysis rather than pleasure. Sparkling wines tend to be tasted slightly cooler to retain the carbon dioxide.

Many professional tasters first smell, or 'nose' a wine without agitating it to see how powerful its aroma is without this encouragement before deliberately increasing the number of molecules liberated by a wine by agitating the wine and increasing its surface area, preferably rotating it in a bowl-shaped glass with a stem (see GLASSES) so that no wine is lost.

As soon as the wine has been agitated, the aroma collects in the bowl of the partly filled glass above the wine and can be transmitted to the olfactory bulb up the nostrils with one thoughtful inhalation.

The taster monitors first whether the wine smells fresh and clean, or whether any off-odours indicate the presence of a wine FAULT.

The next basic measurement might well be of the intensity of the aroma (if it is an attractive smell, then intensity is preferable). And then comes the complex part of the operation which is much more difficult to describe: the sensation and attempt at description of the individual components that make up the aroma, or 'bouquet' as it is called if it has taken on the complexities associated with AGEING. For a discussion of this, see TASTING TERMS.

Quite apart from those components which result from the grapes themselves, the aroma can provide certain overall hints about viticulture and winemaking techniques. LEAF ALDEHYDES suggest that the grapes were less than fully ripe. Oak ageing may be betrayed by a certain amount of OAK FLAVOUR; scents of spices and toast can be the result of the degree of TOAST which the barrels received. Tropical fruit aromas suggest that the fermentation was particularly long and cool. DIACETYL, which can smell like butter and other dairy products, is a particularly obvious sign of MALOLACTIC CONVERSION. The subject is too complex for more than the most cursory treatment here, but the books cited below provide more detail.

As a wine undergoes gentle AERATION in the glass, it may well begin to give off other compounds with time. World-famous taster Michael BROADBENT, for example, keeps a series of records of how a single glass of wine tastes, marked according to how long after pouring each note was made. Most good wines seem to get better with time and then to start to deteriorate. In blind tasting, however, a taster's first impressions are usually the most accurate, and insights are rarely provided by constant repetition of the 'nosing' process.

Mouth In terms of aroma, 'flavour' in its narrow sense, the mouth, or palate as it is sometimes called, usually merely confirms the impressions already apparent to the nose when some vapour escapes the mouth and reaches the olfactory bulb via the retronasal passage. Many tasters take in a certain amount of air over their mouthful of wine to encourage this process (and are often mocked for the accompanying noise).

The main function of the mouth in the tasting process is to assess the texture and measure the dimensions rather than the character of a wine by assessing sweetness, acidity, bitterness, saltiness, and umami if any, viscosity, and tannin level. Monitoring the combination of sweetness, viscosity, and any sensation of 'heat' gives a good indication of the likely alcohol content of any individual wine, ETHANOL tending to leave a burning sensation in the mouth. The insides of the mouth may also register the TEXTURE, analysing the impact of the TANNINS. For this reason, it is a good idea to rinse the mouth thoroughly with wine so that all possible

taste receptors may come into contact with it—another reason why wine tasting looks both ridiculous and disgusting to outsiders.

After rinsing a wine around their mouths, and noting the impressions given by the vapour rising up the retronasal passage, most professional tasters then demonstrate their devotion to duty rather than alcohol by SPITTING. There are no taste receptors in the throat. The taster then notes how LONG the impressions given by the wine seem to persist after spitting, or swallowing.

Conclusions Perhaps the most important stage, however, is a fourth stage of analysis, in which all previous impressions are evaluated. This includes most particularly considering whether the measurements taken by the mouth suggest that the wine is in BALANCE, and monitoring the LENGTH of the aftertaste, these last two factors being important indicators of quality. A fine wine should continue to make favourable sensory impressions throughout the entire tasting process.

Experience is necessary to judge balance. A significant, if decreasing, proportion of young red wines designed for long-term evolution, for example, are not by any objective criterion in balance. Their tannins may still be very marked and make the wine an unpleasantly astringent drink, even if they suggest that the wine will keep well. (Making red wines with less obvious tannins so that they can be both aged and drunk in their youth has been one of the prime recent preoccupations of winemakers.) Similarly, the acidity in a young German wine may be aggressively dominant, but experience shows that it is essential to preserve a top-quality Riesling, for example, for the ten or 20 years' bottle ageing it may deserve. (Some would also argue that a perceptible level of SULFUR DIOXIDE was also acceptable in such a wine.)

Professional tasting usually involves making TASTING NOTES, typically under the four headings noted above. It may also involve SCORING by allotting NUMBERS to different elements according to a carefully predetermined scale, especially if wine JUDGING is involved. Tasting notes can be set out in many different ways and experienced tasters tend to devise their own abbreviations and symbols.

Tasting for pleasure, which is what most wine drinkers do every time they open a bottle, requires nothing more complicated than a moment's concentration and an open mind.

Factors affecting taste

We cannot know what other tasters experience for the tasting mechanism is far from public. Furthermore, individuals vary in their SENSITIVITY to different compounds and dimensions of wine. But even as individuals, the way our brain processes information sent from sensory receptors changes all the time so that the same wine will have a different effect on us depending on the state of our PALATE. The most obvious example of this is how different something tastes before and just after we have had a mouthful of red hot chili, or brushed our teeth with a mint toothpaste. But even something as apparently innocuous as a particularly hot drink or salty solution can affect the way we taste. An acid wine will seem less acid if tasted immediately after a very acid one, which is why the ORDER of serving and tasting is crucial, but extremely difficult to get right until every wine has been tasted. See also FOOD AND WINE MATCHING.

Our overall physical well-being affects how we taste. If we are run down, we tend to produce less saliva and, because saliva contains compounds which have a buffering effect on many aspects of taste, both foods and drinks can taste quite different (this is quite apart from the fact that good HEALTH is needed to tackle a succession of alcoholic liquids).

How we taste can be quite markedly affected by our mood, and of course by the physical environment in which we taste (see TASTINGS below). Tasting in a very humid atmosphere is markedly more difficult than when the atmospheric pressure is high, flavour compounds are readily volatilized, and taste impressions seem crystal clear.   J.R. & Hg.H.

Bartoshuk, L. M., et al., 'The biological basis of food perception and acceptance', *Food Quality and Preference*, 4 (1993), 21–32.

Broadbent, M., *Wine Tasting* (9th edn, London, 2003).

Buck, L., and Axel, R., *Cell*, 65 (1991), 175–87.

Bushid, C., et al., 'Humans can discriminate more than 1 trillion olfactory stimuli', *Science*, 343 (2014), 1370–2.

Duffy, V. B., Miller, I. J., and Bartoshuk, L. M., '6-n-propylthiouracil (PROP) supertasters and women have greater number of fungiform papillae taste buds', *Chemical Senses*, 19 (1994), 465.

Peynaud, É., *The Taste of Wine* (2nd edn, New York, 1996).

Robinson, J., How to Taste (Wine), (rev. edn, London, 2008).

Schuster, M., *Essential Winetasting* (London, 2000).

tasting notes are the usual record of professional or serious wine TASTINGS. They are conventionally divided into notes (sometimes together with SCORES or NUMBERS) for what is sensed by the eye, the nose, and the mouth, together with overall conclusions (see TASTING). The thoughtful organizer of a tasting prepares a **tasting sheet** which provides as a minimum a list of complete names of all the wines served, in the relevant ORDER of serving, with sufficient space to write full tasting notes. Sometimes these are carefully divided into sections—Appearance, Aroma/Bouquet, Taste, and Conclusions, for example—but this is an optional extra as tasters vary according to how much

they want to write on each aspect. Most experienced tasters develop their own shorthand, and good and bad habits. The number of words in a personal average tasting note can vary between one and 100 or, in the case of a particularly complex wine which evolves in the glass, more. Tasting notes, especially of wines worth AGEING, are all the more valuable if they are dated. Most tasting notes remain of personal use only, but Michael BROADBENT has produced two important books based entirely on his, and the majority of Robert PARKER's output has been made up of his. Comparison of the two authors provides a reasonable guide to the different styles of British and American tasting notes respectively. The advent of sophisticated INFORMATION TECHNOLOGY has introduced the possibility of entering tasting notes directly into a computer database, and many wine websites are made up principally of tasting notes, although any nearby liquid poses a threat to a keyboard (which can become unpleasantly sticky during a tasting of sweet wines). This method of record-keeping should, in theory at least, lessen the usual problem of declining legibility of tasting notes towards the end of a tasting.

tasting notes language. The language we use to write or speak about wine may vary according to our intended audience—is the aim to sell to a potential customer, to inform an enthusiast, or to display academic rigour in an exam or a BLIND-TASTING competition? The language of wine can be descriptive (what is this wine like?) or evaluative (how good a wine is this?).

Using language to convey sense impressions, as we do when we describe a wine's properties, is inherently problematic. The brain receives so many data through the senses of smell, taste, vision, and touch that it has to select in order to prevent it from being overwhelmed. Thus the brain does not measure the world around us but models it by constant filtering (known as higher-order processing), and there is no one-to-one correspondence between sense data and conscious perception. Hence a TASTING NOTE cannot be an exact representation of a wine: it conveys the taster's interaction with the wine.

A further problem is that an individual's experience shapes their later perceptions, giving people not only different prototypes of sense impressions (i.e. different notions of what a typical X should be) but also different grids with which to make sense of the raw data received by the brain: a taster who has never encountered a gooseberry cannot detect the smell of gooseberries in a wine. In other words, what is selected in the brain's higher-order processing is determined by a taster's personal history and culture and, if he or she is part of a tasting-group, for example, other tasters' comments.

Finally, due to physiological and genetic factors, individuals vary in their perceptual acuity,

especially in their sensitivity to the thousands of possible AROMAS. It follows that no two people will describe a wine in identical terms. Anne Noble's AROMA WHEEL is an excellent teaching aid in that it can be used to broaden tasters' vocabularies and sharpen their perceptions, but its range of aromas can be neither exhaustive nor definitive.

This is not to say that everything we say about a wine is subjective: some components of wine, such as ACIDITY, RESIDUAL SUGAR, and ALCOHOLIC STRENGTH, are measurable, so it is possible for a taster to be right or wrong about these. However, human tasters are not calibrated scientific instruments, and perception of one component may influence that of another: high acidity can make residual sugar less noticeable, and, conversely, low acidity can make a sweet wine appear cloying. Hence a good tasting note will not just list observations about appearance, NOSE, PALATE, and finish, but must attempt a holistic description by considering how a wine's components balance each other. BALANCE and LENGTH being criteria for quality assessment, a holistic tasting note must inevitably be evaluative as well as descriptive.

Although tasters who resort to florid use of metaphor and simile are often mocked as pretentious, we cannot analyse a wine without using figurative language. Some descriptive terms are literal—adjectives denoting colour, for instance—but to describe the TEXTURE of a wine, a taster will need figurative language such as 'silky', 'grainy', or 'chewy'. Some descriptions of the nose will be literal because they are grounded in fact, others are analogies. Yet a taster who describes a Gewürztraminer as smelling of roses without knowing that one of the variety's constituents is damascenone (rose oil) would regard his choice of language as figurative. Dullness is not a virtue: a dry list of the component parts of a wine may fail to communicate the beauty and complexity of a high-grade wine; on the other hand, excessive inventiveness is liable to be counterproductive. A tasting note should not only be precise but also comprehensible, and this means that competent tasters must draw, to a greater or lesser extent, on a shared vocabulary which needs to be taught.

An agreed vocabulary, such as the systematic approach that is mandatory for the WSET diploma, represents a learnt culture of wine. The discipline of putting sense impressions into words is indispensable if the taster is to analyse and remember a wine and later to recognize and identify examples of the same wine style. Competence develops with experience, and this means not only knowing what to look for but also how to describe it.

See also LANGUAGE OF WINE and PHILOSOPHY AND WINE.   H.M.W.

Allhoff, F. (ed.), *Wine and Philosophy: A Symposium on Thinking and Drinking* (Malden, Mass. and Oxford, 2008).

Lehrer, A., *Wine and Conversation*, (2nd edn, Oxford, 2009).

Smith, B. C. (ed.), *Questions of Taste: The Philosophy of Wine* (Oxford, 2007).

Todd, C., *The Philosophy of Wine: A Case of Truth, Beauty and Intoxication* (Durham, 2010).

tastings, events at which wines are tasted. Informal tastings take place every time a bottle of wine is opened by a wine enthusiast. More formal ones take place when wine producers show their wines to potential buyers or commentators. The most common sort of formal tasting is one held for the purposes of wine assessment, typically by wine MERCHANTS keen to sell their wares, sometimes by a generic body keen to promote wines of a particular style or provenance. Formal tastings are also held by wine clubs and societies for less commercial purposes: EDUCATION or simple pleasure perhaps.

A **horizontal tasting** is one in which a number of different wines of the same VINTAGE are compared, while a **vertical tasting** is a comparison of different vintages of the same wine, most commonly the same Bordeaux CHÂTEAU. George SAINTSBURY is credited with the first recorded use of these expressions.

A BLIND TASTING is one whose purpose is that the taster assesses and possibly identifies unknown wines as closely as possible.

A **comparative tasting** is one in which various different examples of the same sort or style of wine—CLASSED GROWTHS of the same vintage, or wines from the same APPELLATION, or a single VARIETAL, for example—are tasted and compared. Such tastings form the basis of much modern WINE WRITING and should be conducted blind for a true, unprejudiced assessment.

Equipment

The only essential equipment for a wine tasting, apart from the wine, is suitable GLASSES and, if bottles are stoppered with a cork, a CORKSCREW, but it is almost impossible to hold a tasting without a substantial area of flat surface on which to put bottles and glasses safely, usually in the form of a table to which there is good access. Next most useful objects are undoubtedly spittoons (see SPITTING), and something in which to pour away LEFTOVER WINE from a tasting sample (bottles plus funnels are customary although spittoons can also be used for this purpose). The thoughtful organizer ensures that there is some plain white surface against which to hold a glassful of wine (see TASTING). This typically involves lining up bottles on a table with a white surface (to see a wine's colour and clarity most easily) or a covering such as a tablecloth or sheet. A truly assiduous host provides tasters with a tasting sheet on which is a full and accurate list of wines to be tasted, in the correct order, with appropriate space for tasting notes. Water for rinsing of glasses and palates and some neutral-tasting food for 'cleaning the palate' can be helpful too. Cheese is usually too strong (see FOOD AND WINE MATCHING); bread or dry, savoury crackers are generally preferred by professionals.

Conditions

Ideal conditions include a strong natural light, ambient temperature between 15 and 18 °C/ 59–64 °F, and an absence of any extraneous smells. (It is clear therefore that tasting in most cellars, even those of the finest winemakers, is far from ideal.) In practice, a tasting that involves many people inevitably generates its own heat and smell, so it is wise to begin at a lower ambient temperature and not to be too exercised about a whiff of aftershave or polish, which is soon absorbed into the ambient atmosphere.

Organization

One glass per taster usually suffices, and between a fifteenth and a twentieth of a bottle is enough for a decent tasting sample. Ensuring that tasters are served rather than serving themselves can limit wine consumption.

The suitable number of different wines to be shown at a single tasting is controversial. Some tasters claim to be able to assess up to 200 wines in a day at JUDGING sessions such as the Australian wine SHOWS, while the most experienced professionals in CHAMPAGNE deliberately limit themselves to fewer than a dozen wines at a time. A novice taster should probably start with no more than four wines while a professional might feel a tasting which offered only 15 was hardly worth the detour.

What is clear is that it is difficult to *enjoy* more than a dozen wines at a time, and that the ORDER in which any selection is served is vital to the impression they give.

tasting terms, the myriad and oft-mocked words used by tasters in an often vain attempt to describe sensory impressions received during TASTING.

The difference between a taster and a social drinker is this need to describe, to attempt the difficult task of applying words to individual, invisible sensations, particularly the aromas sensed by the olfactory bulb.

The sense of smell is an exceptionally private one, for which there is no common public domain which can be codified. The best we can do is describe aromas by other aromas of which they remind us. Hence 'blackcurrant' or CASSIS, frequently for Cabernet Sauvignon; 'strawberry' or 'raspberry' perhaps for Pinot Noir; 'vanilla' for OAK, and so on. Science is starting to correlate the FLAVOUR COMPOUNDS found in different GRAPE VARIETIES (if not yet different TERROIRS) with those found in the objects used as taste descriptors.

There is as yet no official wine-tasting LANGUAGE, or even TASTING NOTES LANGUAGE, although there have been many valiant attempts at establishing one and, particularly as research on flavour compounds and FLAVOUR PRECURSORS continues apace, this is becoming an increasingly attainable goal. The Scottish doctor Alexander HENDERSON was one of the first to attempt it in the English language in *The History of Ancient and Modern Wines* in 1824, CHAPTAL having applied about 60 French terms in his *L'Art de faire le vin* in 1807. These early tasting vocabularies tended to concentrate on the dimensions of a wine rather than its flavour or aroma, and applied words such as 'acidic, sweet, bitter, light'.

Terms used for mouth sensations

The most straightforward of these 'dimensional terms', which describe what is sensed in the mouth (and the even more public and obvious visual impressions), are still in use today and, since for the most part they describe what is measurable, are useful, indisputable, and not affected by SUBJECTIVITY or SENSITIVITY. Inevitably, some jargon has evolved, of which the following are the most obvious examples.

Body—a noun; see BODY.
Big—high in alcohol.
Concentrated—having intense (though possibly) subtle flavours.
Crisp—attractively high in ACIDITY.
Fat—full bodied and viscous.
Flabby—lacking in ACIDITY.
Finish—a noun for aftertaste.
Full—of BODY.
Green—too acid, made of unripe fruit; see GREEN.
Hard—too much TANNIN and too little fruit.
Heavy—too alcoholic; too much EXTRACT.
Hot—too alcoholic.
Light—agreeably light in BODY.
Long—impressively persistent aftertaste; see LONG.
Short—opposite of LONG.
Smooth—imprecise term for pleasing TEXTURE.
Soft—low in tannins.
Well balanced—having good BALANCE.

Terms used for aroma

It is in their attempts to find 'character terms' to apply to these more subtle, more private olfactory sensations that wine tasters can seem so foolish.

Some 'idioterms' are just plain fanciful, descriptions obviously applied in sheer desperation at the apparent impossibility of the task. In this category come the 'fading but well-mannered old lady', and who can forget James Thurber's 'naive domestic burgundy but I think you'll be amused by its presumption'? A more recent example is 'sexy', an increasingly common, but delightfully imprecise, tasting term.

Other sorts of terms, 'simile terms', are applied in a serious attempt to recall palpable objects which give rise to similar aromas: the fruits, flowers, vegetable, and mineral descriptors, for example.

Particularly common terms used to describe aroma, or flavour, include:

Buttery—see DIACETYL.
Fruity—intense impact of fruit flavours, sometimes a euphemism for 'slightly sweet',
Grapey—mixture of intensely aromatic and the aromas associated with MUSCAT grapes.
Oaky—pejorative term for a wine excessively marked by OAK.
Toasty—see TOAST.

There are also 'derivative terms', which must once have been coined by an authority and continue to be widely used even though they are literally inaccurate. So many wine tasters have been taught to describe the powerful and characteristic smell of GEWÜRZTRAMINER as 'spicy', for example (perhaps because *Gewürz* is German for 'spiced'), that this is the most common tasting term for the aroma, even though it does not smell like any particular spice at all (much more like lychees or rose petals, in fact).

It will be of the 'simile terms' that a common tasting vocabulary is finally composed— although there is the obstacle of many different languages and national conventions to be overcome first. Max Leglise, a researcher in Burgundy, has attempted to concoct essences of each of his approved terms so that there is an objective standard for them. (Unfortunately, synthetic flavourings deteriorate.) Professor Ann C. Noble at DAVIS, clearly frustrated by the looseness with which tasting terms are applied, has done sterling work with her AROMA WHEEL. This corresponds sufficiently closely with the tasting terms suggested by Professor Émile PEYNAUD, Bordeaux's tasting guru, to give us all hope that an international tasting language that is no more ambiguous than any other will one day be available to the world's wine tasters.

Brochet and DUBOURDIEU established in 2001 that each expert taster has his or her own set of tasting terms which typically correspond to a personal set of prototypes, 'ideal' wines, rather than detailed analytical description. In a separate study involving white wines coloured red, they also demonstrated that many tasting terms are colour-specific and that if tasters see red wine, they will assign tasting terms associated with objects of that colour.

See also AROMA WHEEL and LANGUAGE OF WINE.

Broadbent, M., *Wine Tasting* (9th edn, London, 2003).

Brochet, F., and Dubourdieu, D., 'Wine descriptive language supports cognitive specificity of chemical senses', *Brain and Language*, 77 (2001), 187–96.

Brochet, F., and Dubourdieu, D., 'The color of odors', *Brain and Language*, 79 (2001), 309–20.

Peynaud, É., *The Taste of Wine* (2nd edn, New York, 1996).

Taurasi, full-bodied red from CAMPANIA produced from the distinctive AGLIANICO grape grown on 1,000 ha/2,470 acres of vineyards in a zone north east of the city of Avellino. The wine has such high levels of acidity and tannins that it demands BOTTLE AGEING, which is why it is regularly referred to as 'the Barolo of the south'. Taurasi demonstrates the heights which Aglianico can reach in the VOLCANIC soil which it favours (see also AGLIANICO DEL VULTURE, produced in BASILICATA to the east). A total of 17 villages on both sides of the River Calore in the province of Irpinia form the Taurasi DOCG. This hilly terrain has a multitude of different soil types, elevations, and exposures. The left bank of the river with full southern exposition is the warmest part of the zone while the west-facing slopes have a more CONTINENTAL climate. In the central valley on the right bank, on CALCAREOUS soils with rock fragments, a cooler macroclimate prevails. On the southern slopes vines are planted as high 700 m (2,300 ft), harvest can be as late as November, and the wines are marked by higher acidity. DOCG regulations require three years of ageing, one of which must be in wood, and RISERVA bottlings must be aged for four years.

By 2013 there were 50 producers of Taurasi (up from a mere ten in the 1980s) and more than 227 grape growers tending an extremely parcellated vineyard area. MASTROBERARDINO was until the early 1990s the only label on the market. Taurasi has been a hotbed of activity this century with several new estates striving for the highest quality, experimenting with ORGANIC VITICULTURE, AMBIENT YEAST fermentations, and ageing in large casks rather than French BARRIQUES, resulting in muscular, concentrated, and complex wines which need age to develop notes of red berries, cherry, tobacco, and, often, hints of tamarind and iron.

Although its two largest producers, Mastroberardino and Feudi di San Gregorio, give Taurasi some visibility, the wine arguably needs a CONSORZIO to promote it. W.S.

www.campaniastories.com

Tautavel, subappellation of Côtes du ROUSSILLON-Villages which applies to the relatively low clay-limestone vineyards of communes Tautavel (famous for its ancient man) and Vingrau. The opulent reds are not unlike FITOU.

Tavel, one of France's few all-rosé appellations on the right bank in the southern RHÔNE.

Its historic reputation is still sufficient to justify a sometimes unwarranted price premium over other rosés, although Tavel at its best manages to combine refreshment with interest and concentration of flavour. Tavel was already favoured by Louis XIV in the 18th century, and writers Balzac and Mistral continued to promulgate its superiority.

The wine is always bone dry, but the Grenache and Cinsaut grapes give the blend a certain apparent sweetness. Chilling is essential, and the wine should be drunk young, as an alternative to red wine in hot weather. Grenache in all three hues is the dominant grape variety, as throughout the southern Rhône, and should constitute between 30 and 60% of the blend.

Such was demand for the wine in the 1950s that the area was considerably extended, by clearing garrigue. A steady 900 ha/2,220 acres of sand and clay is shared mainly by members of the Tavel CO-OPERATIVE, although there are some quality-minded estates. Ch d'Acqueria was for long the best-known estate but some of the best wine is made by Domaine de la Mordorée in nearby LIRAC, a more dynamic and often more remarkable appellation.

Tavira, fishing port and DOP in ALGARVE in southern Portugal.

Távora-Varosa, DOP immediately south of the DOURO in central northern Portugal. Much of the region's production is dry, white base wine for the local sparkling wine industry, not entitled to the denomination.

tawny, style of FORTIFIED WINES usually associated with extended CASK AGEING. See PORT, for example.

taxation. Wine has attracted the attention of the taxman since ancient times. Its production, sale, and distribution have been so closely regulated by the authorities for one simple reason: revenue, whatever their attitude to alcohol. The civilizations of the ancient Middle East (see Ancient EGYPT and MESOPOTAMIA) were the first to recognize this useful attribute. It was carefully regulated in parts of Ancient GREECE, but it was the Romans who, in this as in many other aspects of wine history, helped realize its potential.

In Ancient ROME tax was paid from the moment the grape appeared on the vine (Roman vine-growers paid a vineyard tax calculated on the quality of the land) to when it was consumed. It was paid either in kind or in cash and represented a huge proportion of state income. Some areas in the empire, CALABRIA, then the heel of Italy, for example, paid their entire tax to Rome in wine, which was then sold or distributed free to the urban masses.

Medieval kings found wine taxation fabulously lucrative. During England's occupation of western France, for example, the crown benefited doubly by receiving DUTIES paid on wine exported from BORDEAUX, and then again on the same wine as customs when it entered London. During the early part of the 14th century, when this trade was at its peak, wine duties collected in Bordeaux surpassed the king's total tax revenue in England.

Not surprisingly, taxes on wine have been perceived as a fast, easy way of raising cash and the state has shown no scruples in doubling or tripling them at times of emergency—often to pay for wars such as the HUNDRED YEARS WAR, the English Civil War, and the Napoleonic Wars.

Although they may complain, in certain circumstances wine merchants have been happy to pay tax because it legitimizes their business. Wine merchants within the Islamic empire of the caliphs (usually Jewish or Christians) viewed their payments as a kind of insurance policy; the state would not outlaw their activities, despite the Koranic ban on alcohol, because the income was so useful (see ISLAM).

Wine taxation has uses beyond mere revenue. Different levels can be used to reward or punish trading partners. For example, throughout the 18th century, French wines attracted twice as much DUTY as Portuguese wines (see METHUEN TREATY). Not surprisingly, trade in French wines suffered and port became the staple English wine (see WAR).

Differential taxation has also been used to manipulate consumer tastes for reasons of health or morality. Gladstone's Act of 1860 reduced the duty on light, less alcoholic wines in an attempt to switch the British palate away from the heavy, fortified wines and spirits that earlier taxation had favoured.

Taxation has at times had indirect consequences. During the 18th century, when duties were high and complicated (French wines were subject to 15 separate duties), ADULTERATION AND FRAUD and smuggling increased in England. Grievances against excessive taxation of wines entering Paris have been recognized as one of the sparks that lit the fire of revolution in 1789.

It was inevitable that, as soon as wine was taxed, certain parties should be exempt. Traditionally these have included the crown, the Church, and sections of the nobility; such exemptions go back at least as far as Ancient EGYPT. This privilege has been extended in modern times (so far as customs duties go) to travellers via the system of duty-free allowances.

H.B.

Briggs, A., *Wine for Sale: Victoria Wine and the Liquor Trade 1860-1984* (London, 1985).

Francis, A. D., *The Wine Trade* (London, 1972).

Hyams, E., *Dionysus: A Social History of the Vine* (2nd edn, London, 1987).

Taylor's, important independent PORT shipper and a key part of the FLADGATE PARTNERSHIP. The original firm of port shippers was established in 1692 by Job Bearsley, and his son Bartholomew bought Casa dos Alambiques at Salgueiral near Régua, the first known British port shipper's property in the DOURO Valley. Between then and 1844 there were no fewer than 21 name changes. However, with the arrival of Joseph Taylor in 1816, John (later Baron) Fladgate in 1837, and Morgan Yeatman in 1844, the company assumed the name **Taylor**, **Fladgate**, & **Yeatman**, Taylor's for short. See The FLADGATE PARTNERSHIP for more details.

Foulkes., C. (ed.), *A Celebration of Taylor's Port* (London, 1992).

Tazzelenghe, relatively obscure 'tongue-cutting' red grape of Italy's Colli Orientali in FRIULI.

TBA, understandably common abbreviation for TROCKENBEERENAUSLESE. And also for **2,4,6-tribromoanisole**; see TRIBROMOANISOLE.

T-budding, a BUDDING method used extensively in woody horticultural plants, including the grapevine, normally for field GRAFTING onto a ROOTSTOCK. The method entails making a T-shaped cut in the bark of the rootstock, when the bark is slipping, then lifting back the flaps to permit insertion of a shield-shaped piece cut from the scion with a bud on it. After insertion, the bud is wrapped tightly with budding tape to ensure close contact of the tissues and high humidity around the cuts. T-budding can be done when the bark of the stock lifts freely, during two to three months over midsummer. Scion buds may be taken from stored winter cuttings or green current shoots. As with CHIP BUDDING, T-budding may be used for TOP GRAFTING.

B.G.C.

TCA, or **2,4,6-trichloroanisole**, is a potent TAINT compound associated with musty odours and flavours in a range of food and beverages. It is the unpleasant-smelling compound most commonly considered responsible for CORK TAINT. The formation of TCA begins when chlorine reacts with organic phenols to form chlorophenols such as trichlorophenol (TCP). These in turn react with mould in the presence of moisture to form TCA. The ENZYME methylase acts as a catalyst. Such phenols are present in all organic matter and are highly prevalent in the winery—in CORKS, BARRELS, wooden pallets, and in wood used in the structure of the building such as beams. TCA is extremely potent, with an aroma threshold in wine of 2–5 ng/l in red and white wines, reduced to 1–1.5 ng/l in

sparkling wine because the CARBON DIOXIDE volatilizes taint compounds. A recent study by Chatonnet found evidence of TCA in new BARRELS, a finding fiercely contested by French COOPERS.

J.A.G. & J.E.H.

Chatonnet, P., Fleury, A., Boutou, S., 'Identification of a new source of contamination of *Quercus sp.* oak wood by 2,4,6-trichloroanisole and its impact on the contamination of barrel-aged wines', *Journal of Agricultural and Food Chemistry*, 58/19 (2010), 10528–38.

Tchelistcheff, André (1901–94), consultant OENOLOGIST and founding father of the modern California wine industry. Tchelistcheff was born in Moscow, the sickly son of a Russian professor of law. After a brush with death in the army, he trained as an engineer-agronomist in Czechoslovakia, then at the age of 36 decided to study VITICULTURE and OENOLOGY in more detail, in Paris. While working on a farm near Versailles, he became a graduate assistant to the director of the department of viticulture at the National Institute of Agronomy as well as taking a course in wine microbiology at the Institut PASTEUR. An obviously talented student, who combined intellectual rigour with a philosophical bent, he worked briefly at MOËT & CHANDON and had already been offered jobs in Chile and China before being introduced to his future employer. Georges de Latour was a Frenchman who had established himself as a highly successful businessman and owner of Beaulieu Vineyard in the Napa Valley but was anxious to import a French-trained winemaker for the post-PROHIBITION era.

During his 35-year career at Beaulieu, Tchelistcheff introduced the principles of winery HYGIENE as well as pioneering TEMPERATURE-CONTROLLED fermentation, mastery of MALOLACTIC CONVERSION, and FROST DAMAGE prevention techniques such as the orchard heaters and WIND MACHINES which dominated Napa Valley for so long. He also made considerable progress in the prevention of various VINE DISEASES and established a reputation as both wine and vineyard CONSULTANT.

From his first years in California, Tchelistcheff established an identity independent of Beaulieu, with his own small laboratory in St Helena advising other Napa and Sonoma wineries and training a younger generation of winemakers such as the young MONDAVI brothers. He was a consultant to Buena Vista winery, for example (see HARASZTHY), from 1948, and in 1967 began a long association with Ch Ste Michelle in WASHINGTON state. He was also one of the first to recognize the viticultural potential of the CARNEROS district of northern California. Although he retired from Beaulieu in 1973, four years after it was sold to the Heublein corporation, he continued to be an active consultant to a host of California wineries as well as to ORNELLAIA of BOLGHERI in Italy (where his son Dimitri subsequently advised). In 1991, however, he was wooed back to Beaulieu by the multinational corporation which by then owned it.

Tchelistcheff was a charter member of the American Society of Enologists and was made a Chevalier de l'Ordre du Mérite Agricole by the French government in 1954, being promoted to Officier in 1979. Tchelistcheff was unique in the wine world for the geographical breadth and historical depth of his singularly acute views on the contemporary wine scene.

TCP. See TRICHLOROANISOLE.

TDN, the FLAVOUR COMPOUND norisoprenoid hydrocarbon 1,1,6-trimethyl-1,2-dihydronaphthalene found particularly in RIESLING. TDN formation responds to fruit MICROCLIMATE and is increased by high temperatures and solar radiation. Low-PH wines seem to be more prone to TDN formation, and yeast strain also affects it. At or just above the detection threshold, it adds to the complexity of a bottle-aged wine but at relatively high concentrations, particularly in wines that have been in bottle for two or more years, and in excess, TDN can impart an undesirably pronounced kerosene-like flavour.   H.S.

Black, C., et al., 'Aged Riesling and the development of TDN', *Wine & Viticulture Journal* (Sept/Oct 2012), 20–6.

tears (to rhyme with 'ears'), term used to describe the behaviour of the liquid climbing and falling in a glass of relatively strong wine. The wine wets the inside of a clean glass and climbs up a few millimetres. or even centimetres. At the upper edge of the thin layer on the inside wall patches of the film thicken, become more drop-like, and eventually roll back down the inside wall to the liquid surface. These traces of what look like particularly viscous droplets are also sometimes called 'legs', and may give some indication of a wine's ALCOHOLIC STRENGTH. (But note that some of the finest German wines may have only 7 or 8% alcohol but still form very obvious tears.)

James Thomson, a British physicist and engineer, observed in 1855 what he called 'tears of strong wine' and related the phenomenon to surface tension. Unfortunately, his work was overlooked and this relation to surface tension is usually credited to Italian physicist Carlo Marangoni, who published it in 1871. However, the exact physical explanation of the phenomenon was not obtained until 2009.

A few physical relationships are involved in producing tears. The attractive forces between molecules in the liquid–air interface give rise to surface tension forces. A similar type of force also acts between a liquid molecule and the molecules of a solid surface, and yet another intermolecular force acts between the solid and the air molecules. These are called interfacial tensions.

If the interfacial tension between the solid glass and the air is higher than the interfacial tension between the solid and the liquid, then molecules of liquid will adhere to the glass and wet areas higher and higher above the liquid surface. A point is reached at which the weight of the liquid clinging to the wall just balances the force trying to lift more liquid up the wall surface.

Wine is mainly a solution of alcohol and water. While the thin film of wine climbs up the inner wall of the glass, another physical action occurs: the alcohol evaporates faster than the water from the film surface. This changes the composition of the film, increasing its concentration of water and thereby increasing both its air–liquid and solid–liquid surface tensions. This increase in surface tensions, and especially in the solid–liquid surface tension, causes perpetual tears: the tears keep going down and the wine keeps going up. Eventually the drop becomes so heavy that interfacial tension can no longer hold it to the glass surface. It then runs down the wall, forming a tear or leg.

Dubious readers can convince themselves of this somewhat complicated explanation of an apparently simple phenomenon by observing the lack of tears in glasses of pure water. That evaporation is necessary can be demonstrated by simply covering a glass that previously demonstrated **tearing**. Tearing ceases, and will resume upon removal of the cover.

It is often thought that tears are the result of GLYCEROL but in fact entirely unrelated phenomena are responsible. Tears are *not* a measure of viscosity.

Tears occur in many multicomponent liquid mixtures but not in all. For example, it is most obvious in wines above about 12% alcoholic strength, but at lower concentrations the effect is either small or completely non-existent because the surface tension of the air–solid is no longer higher than that of the liquid–solid.

Tadmor, R., 'Marangoni flow revisited', *Journal of Colloid and Interface Science*, 332 (2009), 451–4.

TeCA, or **2,3,4,6-tetrachloroanisole**. See TETRACHLOROANISOLE.

teinturier literally means 'dyer' in French, which is the function for which these vines with their red-fleshed grapes were initially grown, notably in the Midi, to add at least apparent depth to the pale wines of the dominant ARAMON in the early years of the 20th century.

The original variety called **Teinturier**, or sometimes **Teinturier du Cher**, was probably extremely ancient, and was first noted around Orléans in the 17th and 18th centuries, where it imbued the pale pink wines of the region with valuable colour. DNA PROFILING strongly suggests a parent-offspring relationship with SAVAGNIN.

As long ago as 1824, the Frenchman Louis BOUSCHET decided to try to breed vines with coloured flesh, and the 1828 cross of Aramon × Teinturier du Cher resulted in the popular Petit Bouschet. Henri Bouschet, Louis's son, crossed Petit Bouschet with Grenache to produce the very popular ALICANTE BOUSCHET, a deeply coloured *teinturier*, known as Garnacha Tintorera in Spain, *tintorera* being Spanish for *teinturier*. Other red-fleshed varieties bred by the Bouschet family and used for their 'dyeing' properties at one time include Morrastel Bouschet, Carignan Bouschet, and GRAND NOIR DE LA CALMETTE.

Red-fleshed versions of the lightly coloured GAMAY grape have been widely grown, not just in the Loire but outside France. The Gamay *teinturiers* include Gamay Fréaux, Gamay de Bouze, and Gamay de Chaudenay. Gamay Fréaux and Gamay de Chaudenay are said to be mutants of Gamay de Bouze. Colobel (Seibel 8357) is a *teinturier* FRENCH HYBRID which was the only such variety to be authorized in France.

Germany's useful red-fleshed varieties include Carmina, Deckrot, DUNKELFELDER, Kolor, and Sulmer. ROYALTY 1390, Salvador, and the increasingly popular RUBIRED are all California creations, while the important Georgian *teinturier* is SAPERAVI, which is, if not red fleshed, then certainly deep pink fleshed.

Galet, P., *Dictionnaire encyclopédique des cépages* (Paris, 2000).

Robinson, J., Harding, J., and Vouillamoz, J., *Wine Grapes: A Complete Guide to 1,368 Vine Varieties, Including their Origins and Flavours* (London, 2012).

Tejo, DOP and VINHO REGIONAL (called Ribatejo until 2009) in central-southern Portugal. It corresponds to the province of the same name on both sides of the River Tagus (Tejo) inland from the capital Lisbon (see map under PORTUGAL). Its new name reflects a desire to distance it from its historic reputation for vast quantities of indifferent wine produced by its CO-OPERATIVES from ultra-high yielding vines grown on the river's fertile floodplains. Of its six DOP subregions (Almeirim, Cartaxo, Chamusca, Coruche, Santarém, and Tomar), Almeirim and Cartaxo (each, quantitatively at least, still dominated by a large co-operative) have been the most important. However, since the late 20th century, soils not subregions have come to define the region's best wines. Large, family-owned agricultural estates, which started to make wine themselves in the 1990s rather than selling to the co-operatives, led the migration to poorer soils, grubbing up vineyards along the river, and concentrating production on less fertile, well-drained sandy soils, calcareous clay, and sandstone. New plantings favoured better-quality vine varieties such as CASTELÃO and TRINCADEIRA for reds and FERNÃO

PIRES for whites, but also introduced TOURIGA NACIONAL from northern Portugal and such INTERNATIONAL VARIETIES as Syrah, Cabernet Sauvignon, Sauvigon Blanc, Chardonnay, and Viognier. Around the same time the region also benefited from major investment by two export-focused enterprises, Falua and Fiuza, whose brands helped raise the region's profile with bargain-hunters abroad. Regrettably, the region's most ambitious newcomer Vale D'Algares swiftly became a casualty of the global credit crunch. However, the promising white wines which it produced, together with the improved quality of DOP and Vinho Regional wines, attest to Tejo's potential.   S.A.

www.cvrtejo.com

Temecula, CALIFORNIA high DESERT wine region and AVA inland of the coastal mountain range 35 miles north of San Diego. Temecula is the viticultural aspect of a mixed-use residential and industrial development called Rancho California. Beginning in the late 1960s, insurance company developers used vineyards as part of their sales pitch to urban-weary escapees from Los Angeles and San Diego. Rainbow Gap, a narrow opening in the coastal ridge, funnels cool marine air across a 5-mile swathe of sanded desert allowing grapes to be grown in what would otherwise be a deeply inhospitable home for vines. IRRIGATION water is imported by pipeline. As the vineyards began to weave an image of moderate, salubrious weather, housing developments came swiftly to the undulating mesas all the way from Riverside south to San Diego. Within 20 years, grape-growers in the band of cool afternoon breezes at Temecula began to find themselves squeezed between rows of residences. Then viticultural disaster struck in the mid-1990s in the form of PIERCE's DISEASE infestation, forcing the removal of some 850 acres/344 ha of diseased vines by 2002. The region's largest winery and grapegrower at the time, Callaway, had to resort to buying in grapes from elsewhere. Yet many took the opportunity to replant with varieties better suited to the conditions, among them heat-loving Grenache, Petite Sirah, Syrah, and Tempranillo. South Coast Winery is Temecula's largest producer and grand experimenter with myriad varieties. Callaway rebounded under new owners, although on a much smaller scale and with mostly local grapes.   B.C.C. & L.M.

temperate, a broad class of climates, usually taken to include those with an annual average temperature of less than 20 °C/68 °F, but a warmest month average temperature greater than 10 °C/50 °F, the latter being the approximate poleward limit of tree growth.

Just as wine is considered a beverage of temperate people, so the grapevine is a plant of temperate climates. It is specially so when the grapes are to be used for WINEMAKING, and still more so for table wines. Excessive heat during ripening leads to a loss of the more delicate fruit aromas and flavours from the grapes, and therefore from the wines. Insufficient warmth leads to incomplete RIPENING in which FLAVOUR COMPOUNDS, which become manifest only late in the ripening process, are lacking. (The gross geographical limits for commercial viticulture resulting from temperature constraints are noted under LATITUDE.)

See TEMPERATURE VARIABILITY and CLIMATE AND WINE QUALITY.   J.G.

temperature is critically important to VITICULTURE, WINEMAKING, wine MATURATION, and wine SERVICE, each in very different ways.

Climate, viticulture, and temperature

Temperature is widely considered the most important climatological factor affecting grapevines, although others such as SUNLIGHT, RAINFALL, HUMIDITY, and WIND are also important. Gladstones comprehensively reviews the role of temperature in viticulture. Temperature records are available from climate recording stations, and modern statistical procedures allow the calculation of temperatures between station locations that may be more representative of actual vineyard sites (see TOPOGRAPHY, MESOCLIMATE, CLIMATE CHANGE).

Vines in cool climates start growing in the spring at about the time when the mean air temperature reaches 10 °C/50 °F. The rate of vine growth and development then increases to a maximum at a mean temperature of about 22 to 25 °C (72–7 °F). Temperature is often discussed in viticulture as mean temperature, that is maximum plus minimum temperatures divided by two. These facts underlie the traditional methods for viticultural CLIMATE CLASSIFICATION, which are based on excesses of monthly average mean temperatures over 10 °C. Such classifications can at best be only approximate, however, if only because mean temperatures seldom truly reflect the real average temperatures as they might be measured continuously throughout the 24 hours, and as experienced by the vine.

Average mean temperatures for the full growing season and temperature of the warmest month can also be a reasonable basis for broad comparisons (see CLIMATE CLASSIFICATION, COOL-CLIMATE).

The risk of killing dormant vines in winter is a second basis for defining climatic suitability for viticulture, being the main limiting factor in cool climates with marked CONTINENTALITY. Most fully dormant VINIFERA vines with well-matured canes can withstand air temperatures down to about −15 °C/5 °F. Native AMERICAN VINE SPECIES are in general hardier, and AMERICAN HYBRIDS, their hybrids with European varieties, intermediate. However, there is considerable variation among VINE VARIETIES within each group.

The winter hardiness of RIESLING, for instance, is almost certainly one of the reasons for its historical success in Germany. See also WINTER FREEZE.

The chance of winter killing of vines in Europe increases from south west to north east (see RUSSIA, for example). Extensive commercial viticulture without WINTER PROTECTION reaches its limit where the average mean temperature of the coldest month falls below about −1 °C/30 °F.

Air temperature is not the only kind governing vine growth and fruiting, however. Vines and soils are warmed by sunlight, which has major effects on grape berry temperature, leaf temperature, grape composition, and hence wine quality (see VINE PHYSIOLOGY). Some evidence now confirms the old belief that soil temperature is also important. This control appears to be mediated by the root-produced hormone CYTOKININ, although soil temperature can also affect vine temperature, especially at night. The composition of the soil, its colour, drainage, and duration and angle of exposure to the sun are all important factors in this respect. See SOIL COLOUR, STONES AND ROCKS, TOPOGRAPHY, MESOCLIMATE.

Soil and air temperatures at particular stages of vine growth or during ripening can have specific effects. Winter and early spring temperatures govern BUDBREAK in spring. Air TEMPERATURE VARIABILITY largely determines the risk of FROST DAMAGE after budbreak. Temperatures around FLOWERING contribute to differences in FRUIT SET (by influencing COULURE, most notably) and to the FRUITFULNESS of the developing new buds which form shoots and bunches the following year. Both fruit set and bud fruitfulness are favoured by moderately high temperatures. Finally, both average temperature and temperature variability during ripening can have a direct influence on fruit and wine qualities, as discussed under CLIMATE AND WINE QUALITY.   J.G.

Gladstones, J., *Viticulture and Environment* (Adelaide, 1992).

Winemaking and temperature

Temperature and TEMPERATURE CONTROL are of critical importance in making good-quality wine (although great wine may have been made fortuitously, long before the theory of temperature control was understood and temperature was deliberately manipulated). Temperature has direct effects on the rates of the biochemical reactions involved in FERMENTATION, and on the slower reactions involved in CLARIFICATION and STABILIZATION of wine. Years of experiment and calculation have demonstrated that most chemical reactions happen about twice as fast if the temperature is raised by 10 °C/18 °F—and it is for this reason that

REFRIGERATION slows down the reactions of harmful BACTERIA, as well as the reactions involved in AGEING.

In warm regions, therefore, care should be taken to ensure that grapes arrive at the winery in a cool, and relatively undamaged, condition. The harmful effects of ACETOBACTER and wild YEAST are encouraged by high temperatures. Low temperatures are vital if there is any interval between HARVEST and CRUSHING; the potential quality of white wines in particular can be lost through carelessness at this early phase of winemaking. During DESTEMMING and crushing, when the PHENOLICS in grape juice are in direct contact with oxygen, OXIDATION begins at a rate proportional to the temperature. To slow browning of white grape juice, therefore, care is usually taken to keep temperatures as low as possible (see MUST CHILLING). SULFUR DIOXIDE may also be added. Oxidation of red grape juice is less of a problem because its higher phenolic content, including the red colour compounds, can conceal small amounts of amber or brown, although lower temperatures during prefermentation processes are in general desirable whatever the colour of the grape skins.

If temperature control is desirable prior to fermentation, it is critical during it. At temperatures below 10 °C/50 °F most yeasts will act prohibitively slowly or not at all, while at temperatures above 45 °C/113 °F they are damaged and finally killed. Secondly, higher fermentation temperatures speed up some reactions so that undesirable flavour compounds become apparent. Thirdly, at higher temperatures, some of the desirable FLAVOUR COMPOUNDS are volatilized in the rapidly evolving stream of carbon dioxide, literally 'boiled off'. The result of this is a wine low in fruit and marked by 'hot' fermentation characteristics. In the extreme case of temperatures nearing the range at which yeasts are killed, the yeast cells secrete compounds which inhibit future yeast growth, thereby making it difficult or impossible to restart this STUCK FERMENTATION even after cooling.

There are yeast strains which grow and ferment very slowly at very low temperatures, only just above freezing. Such strains are particularly useful in cool wine regions such as Switzerland and parts of Germany but fermentation rates are so slow that a single FERMENTATION VESSEL can be used only once after each harvest, which therefore affects the capital cost of production, as it does at the most ambitious wineries elsewhere where there has been investment in fermentation capacity for any year's total production.

White wines are in general fermented at lower temperatures than red, partly in order to conserve the primary grape AROMAS, partly because there is no MACERATION for which heat may be useful in encouraging the extraction of phenolics and other flavour compounds from the grape skins. White wine temperatures between 12 and 17 °C (50–54 °F) are common for fermentation in the New World to yield fruity, well-balanced, light coloured wines quickly enough that the fermentation vessel can be used two or three times in a season (although see also BARREL FERMENTATION). Grape varieties such as Sauvignon Blanc, Riesling, and Muscat tend to be fermented at the lower end of this temperature range, whereas more neutral varieties, with a less complex blend of grape flavours to be conserved, may be fermented at the upper end and rely on the accumulation of secondary fermentation aromas. Old World white wine fermentation temperatures are likely to be 18 to 20 °C (64–68 °F) or cooler. The techniques of barrel fermentation and LEES CONTACT, such as are often applied to Chardonnay grapes, often involve slightly higher fermentation temperatures too, although the small size of the barrel (in comparison with the normal stainless steel tank) helps to control temperature.

Temperature control is also extremely important during RED WINEMAKING. The main concern here is the extraction of sufficient TANNINS, ANTHOCYANINS, and flavour compounds from the grape skins. Temperature is one of the factors governing this extraction, agitation and time being the others. Fermentation temperatures between 25 and 30 °C (generally produce the best flavour and extraction in red wines, provided other conditions (and grape variety, agitation, and time all play a part interlinked to temperature in the maceration process) are optimal. Temperatures higher than this threaten the yeast activity, while temperatures below it inhibit extraction.

Temperature continues to be an important factor in wine production long after the fermentation phase. Oxidation and loss of fruitiness in white wines can be discouraged by low temperatures, while the bacterial activity that stimulates MALOLACTIC CONVERSION can be positively encouraged by storing the newly fermented wine between 25 and 30 °C (77–86 °F) until this conversion is completed.

Fermentation temperatures govern the types of ESTERS that are formed and accumulate in the wine. Lower temperatures (10 to 15 °C/50–59 °F) favour both the production and retention of the fruity esters, which have lower molecular weights. Among these are nearly all of those possible by reactions between ACETIC, propionic, isobutyric, and isovaleric acids with ETHANOL, propyl, isobutyl, and FUSEL OILS. These are the esters which give tropical fruits their characteristic flavours (ISOAMYL ACETATE, for example, is the flavour material of ripe bananas), which is why cool-fermented wines so often taste of tropical fruits. The aroma compounds of each grape variety are also better retained at these lower temperatures.

Higher fermentation temperatures (20 to 25 °C/68–77 °F) favour heady, heavier esters and, at the same time, destroy more of the VARIETAL character of the grape. Temperatures of 30 °C and higher result in the loss of much of the fruity ester complex through hydrolysis and volatilization and its replacement by substances which smell 'cooked'. A.D.W.

Storage temperature

In the same way that it affects the reactions involved in winemaking, temperature becomes the governing factor in the much slower reactions in bottle that constitute wine AGEING. Interactions among the thousands of natural organic chemicals in the wine during this important phase of its maturation are directly affected by temperature. Applying the general scientific formula for temperature's effect on chemical reactions, a CELLAR temperature of 30 °C/86 °F should in theory mature a wine twice as fast as storage at 20 °C/68 °F—except that at such a high temperature compounds with a cooked or jammy note are formed and may well dominate the more desirable compounds. A cellar temperature of 10 °C/50 °F should in theory age wine at half the speed of a 20 °C cellar, which is to say very slowly, although not quite so slowly as a cellar kept at 0 °C/32 °F, which would also result in extremely high deposits of TARTRATES and PHENOLICS. In practice, a reasonable cellar temperature for ageing wines to be drunk within one's own lifetime is somewhere between 10 and 15 °C (50–59 °F). (The cellars of the Swedish state MONOPOLY were so cold that any fine, old wine bought in Sweden would taste markedly different from the same wine aged in the more temperate climate of France, for example.)

Even lower down the temperature scale, wine freezes at a temperature below 0 °C, that is roughly half its ALCOHOLIC STRENGTH, so usually somewhere between −5 and −8 °C (23 and 18 °F). For this reason, in cool climates, care should be taken to insulate wine stored in places such as garden sheds or garages where winter temperatures are not maintained at a level acceptable to humans.

Serving temperature

The temperature at which a wine is served has a profound effect on how it smells and tastes. Different styles of wine deserve to be served at different temperatures to enhance their good points and try to mask any faults. The following are some general observations, with suggested guidelines in italics.

The higher the temperature, the more easily the volatile FLAVOUR COMPOUNDS evaporate from the surface of wine in a glass. So, to maximize the impact of a wine's AROMA or BOUQUET, it is sensible to serve it relatively warm, say between 16 and 18 °C (61–4 °F) (at temperatures over

20 °C/68 °F the ALCOHOL can begin to evaporate so markedly that it unbalances the wine). *Serve complex and mature wines relatively warm.*

Conversely, the lower the temperature, the fewer volatiles will evaporate and, at a serving temperature of about 8 °C/46 °F, all but the most aromatic wines appear to have no smell whatsoever. *The gustatory faults of a low-quality wine can be masked by serving it very cool.*

The higher the temperature, the more sensitive is the PALATE to sweetness, so it makes sense to serve sweet wines which may not have quite enough ACIDITY to counterbalance the sweetness quite cool, say at about 12 °C/54 °F. For the same reason, medium-dry wines served with savoury food will probably taste dry if served well chilled. *In general, chill sweet wines.*

The lower the temperature, the more sensitive the palate to TANNINS and BITTERNESS. Peynaud points out that the same red wine will taste 'hot and thin at 22 °C/72 °F, supple and fluid at 18 °C/64 °F, full and astringent at 10 °C/50 °F'. *Tannic or bitter wines such as many Italian red wines and any young red designed for ageing should be served relatively warm.*

The effect of temperature on apparent acidity is more widely disputed by scientists, but it is generally observable that flabby wines can seem more refreshing if they are served cold, say at 10 °C/50 °F. (This may be related to the effect of temperature on sweetness described above.) *To increase the refreshment factor of a wine, serve it cool.*

Temperature also has an observable effect on wines containing CARBON DIOXIDE. The higher the temperature, the more gas is released, which means that fizzy wines can be unpleasantly frothy at about 18 °C/64 °F. *Sparkling and lightly sparkling wines are generally best served well chilled.* Since very few wines with a complex bouquet ever have any perceptible gas, this is no great limitation (those who make Australia's extraordinary sparkling Shiraz claim it is best served at room temperature, but these sparkling wines are not particularly fizzy).

General rules are therefore:

Serve tannic red wines relatively warm, 15–18 °C (59–64 °F).

Serve complex dry white wines relatively warm, 12–16 °C (54–61 °F).

Serve soft, lighter red wines for refreshment at 10–12 °C (50–5 °F).

Cool sweet, sparkling, flabby white, and rosé wines, and those with any off-odour, at 6–10 °C (43–50 °F).

Of course wine tends to warm up to match the ambient temperature, so initial serving temperatures at the bottom end of these brackets are no bad thing, especially in warmer environments. For more details of how to cool and warm bottles, see SERVING WINE.

See also TASTING (as opposed to drinking) for its different requirements of wine temperature.

Peynaud, E., *The Taste of Wine* (2nd edn, New York, 1996).

temperature control during WINEMAKING is crucially important, as outlined in TEMPERATURE. Although it has been widely and systematically practised only since the 1960s and 1970s, its efficacy was appreciated as long ago as Roman times (see DIE). See REFRIGERATION for details of how wine may be cooled at various points in its life. In cool wine regions or particularly cool years, a FERMENTATION VESSEL may need to be heated to encourage alcoholic FERMENTATION, most easily by circulating warm water in equipment also designed to carry cooling cold water or, in smaller cellars, simply by closing doors and installing a heater or two. Some form of heating may also be required to encourage MALOLACTIC CONVERSION.

temperature variability, a characteristic of climates referring to the short-term variability of temperature between night and day (diurnal temperature variation or thermal amplitude), and from day to day. It is unrelated to annual temperature range, as described under CONTINENTALITY, and clearly distinct in its viticultural and oenological implications (see TEMPERATURE). Temperature variability plays an important role in determining the risks of FROST DAMAGE to dormant vines in spring and autumn, and of HEAT STRESS and direct heat damage to the vines and fruit in summer. Gladstones speculates that restricted temperature variability is important for improved wine quality in cool regions since it may influence the formation of PIGMENT, AROMA, and FLAVOUR in the vines and ripening berries: these processes being favoured, relative to the mere accumulation of SUGAR IN GRAPES, by a narrow daily temperature range and minimal temperature fluctuations from day to day. However, in warm to hot regions, a greater temperature variability may be an advantage for wine quality as it implies cooling effects at night (see CLIMATE AND WINE QUALITY).

Commercial experience around the world does not always support Gladstones' view. Indeed, much is made in certain regions (e.g. WACHAU in Austria, the Uco Valley in ARGENTINA, much of CHILE, NAPA Valley and the SANTA CRUZ MOUNTAINS in California) of the beneficial effects of a wide diurnal temperature variation (night temperatures must be lower than 15 °C)—often due to ELEVATION—but it is not clear whether this is simply because the ripening period is thereby extended, allowing grapes to reach PHENOLIC RIPENESS without losing the desired sugar/acid balance, or whether the variation has some more complicated, as yet unidentified,

influence on the ripening process and the accumulation of phenolics.   J.G. & J.E.H.

Gladstones, J., *Viticulture and Environment* (Adelaide, 1992).

Tempranillo has been planted so enthusiastically in Spain that it was the world's fourth most popular wine grape variety in 2010. In some ways it is Spain's answer to Cabernet Sauvignon, the vine variety that puts the spine into a high proportion of Spain's most respected red wines, and is increasingly planted elsewhere. Its grapes are thick skinned and capable of making deep-coloured, long-lasting wines that are not, unusually for Spain, notably high in alcohol. Often replacing GARNACHA, BOBAL, or MONASTRELL, it became the most popular red wine grape in Spain in the early 21st century and by 2011 was planted on a total of more than 206,000 ha/508,800 acres in virtually all regions except for those in the far south and north west, and challenged AIREN as the country's most-planted variety of either colour.

Temprano means early in Spanish and Tempranillo probably earns its name from its propensity to ripen early, certainly up to two weeks before the Garnacha (GRENACHE) with which it is still regularly blended to make RIOJA. This relatively short growing cycle enables it to thrive in the often harsh climate of Rioja's higher, more Atlantic-influenced zones Rioja Alta and Rioja Alavesa, where it constitutes by far the majority of all vines planted with a total of 34,383 ha in 2011. Tempranillo has traditionally been grown in widely spaced bushes here, but this relatively vigorous, upright vine has also responded well to training on WIRES.

Wine made from Tempranillo grown in relatively cool conditions, where its tendency to produce musts slightly low in acidity is a positive advantage, can last well but the variety does not have a particularly strong flavour identity. Some find strawberries, others spice, leather, and tobacco leaves, but yields and winemaking skill are critical in determining its style.

In Rioja, it is traditionally blended with Garnacha, plus a bit of Mazuelo (Carignan), Graciano, and Viura. In Penedès, where it is known as Ull de Llebre, Tempranillo softens the local Monastrell. In Valdepeñas, it is known as Cencibel. The variety is ideally suited to the cool conditions of Ribera del Duero, where, as Tinto Fino, it is by far the principal grape variety, but the seasoning of varieties imported from Bordeaux is an ingredient of some importance in that high plateau's most famous wine VEGA SICILIA. Indeed, throughout Spain, blends of Tempranillo with Cabernet Sauvignon and/or Merlot are common, notably in Navarra and Castilla-La Mancha.

Its Spanish synonyms also include Tinta Madrid, Tinta del Pais, and Tinta de Toro, where its particularly concentrated form has played a major part in the newfound popularity of TORO wines.

Tempranillo is one of relatively few Spanish varieties to have been adopted to a great extent in Portugal, where it is known both as Aragonez and (Tinta) Roriz and, after a dramatic increase in popularity, was the country's single most planted variety. For more, see TINTA RORIZ.

As Tempranillo or **Tempranilla** and making rather light, possibly over-irrigated reds, it has been important in Argentina's wine industry but lost ground to more marketable varieties in the late 1980s. Plantings increased slighty this century, to over 6,000 ha by 2012, mainly in Mendoza, although the Spanish-owned O. Fournier makes a particularly interesting example.

There were 578 ha in southern France in 2011, most notably in the Aude and used for blending. Thanks to mildly increased interest in the variety and all things Spanish, in 2012 California grew just under 1,000 acres/400 ha of Tempranillo, once known there as Valdepeñas. Abacela pioneered fine Tempranillo in southern Oregon where there were just under 200 acres in 2012, and there has been small-scale enthusiasm for the variety in Washington state.

As vine-growers the world over search for new, recognizably high-quality ALTERNATIVE VARIETIES, Tempranillo is spreading around the world, notably in Australia, where plantings had reached 711 ha by 2012.

Italy grows a tiny amount of vines called Tempranillo, but DNA PROFILING unexpectedly showed that some Tempranillo has been grown in Tuscany and Basilicata under the widely applied name Malvasia Nera. It has also revealed as a likely parent-offspring relationship with the old Spanish white wine grape ALBILLO Mayor.

Tempranillo Blanco, a pale-berried MUTATION, has been identified in Rioja where varietal versions have been made.

tendone, the Italian name for the overhead vine-TRAINING SYSTEM widely used in southern Italy, especially in ABRUZZO. It is also common in South America, where it is used for both TABLE GRAPES and wine grapes, and is called *parral* (Argentina) or *parron* (Chile). English terms used include both arbour and pergola, although the system is little used in English-speaking countries.

The vines are normally trained with trunks about 2 m/6.5 ft high and a system of wooden frames and cross wires supports the foliage and fruit. Typically in Abruzzo the vines are planted in a 2.5 x 2.5 m square (up to 3 x 3 m for TREBBIANO) and from each staked vine four shoots are trained in different directions along the wires.

Arbours are normally high enough from the ground to allow tractors and implements to pass underneath, but not so high as to make

hand work difficult. The vines are pruned to either canes or spurs (see PRUNING). Because all of the sunlight is captured, the system can be very productive: 30 to 70 tonnes of grapes per hectare (12–28 tons/acre) when water supply is plentiful.

Such training systems are limited in use because of the expense of their construction and the high cost of LABOUR required to manage them. Worker productivity is lower because of fatigue, and, where the vines are vigorous, the leaves form a very dense CANOPY on top and so the fruit and lower leaves are heavily SHADED. This reduces both yield and quality, and increases the risk of POWDERY MILDEW.

Furthermore, the ventilation under such canopies is very restricted and the build-up of humidity favours BOTRYTIS BUNCH ROT. The arbour system is used for table grapes in many parts of the world, and has the advantage that the fruit hangs freely and makes access easy. Inclined overhead trellis systems which do not completely cover the ground are often used for table grapes, as in South Africa (where it may be called the verandah system), and occasionally for wine grapes around the borders of fields in the VINHO VERDE region of Portugal.   R.E.S.

tendril, coiling, clasping organ that enables the stems of plants to climb (see WILD VINES). In many plants, these organs are modifications of stems, leaves, or leaflets, but in the grapevine they are modified INFLORESCENCES, developing at two of every three consecutive NODES. Tendrils are sensitive to touch (thigmotropic); when sufficiently elongated, they react to pressure on their surface by coiling around the touched object, be it a wire, a part of the vine, or any other adjacent material. Once coiled, the tendrils become lignified, very tough, and difficult to remove.   B.G.C.

tent, medieval term for strong red wine from Iberia, mainly Spain (notably deeper in colour that the CLAIRET then still associated with Bordeaux). It is an Anglicized version of the word TINTO, Spanish and Portuguese for red.

tenuta, Italian word for an agricultural holding, estate, or farm, usually larger than, for example, a PODERE.

Téoulier Noir, old Provençal red wine grape variety.

Teran, **Terrano**, names for Refosco d'Istria, a subvariety of the REFOSCO group, used, respectively, in CROATIA and the Kras district of SLOVENIA and the CARSO DOC in the extreme east of Friuli. The Slovenians registered Kras Teran as a geographical entity with the EU and object to the Croatian use of the word on labels. Often confused with the distinct REFOSCO DAL PEDUNCOLO ROSSO.

Terlano, or **Terlaner** in German, long-lived white wines from around the town of Terlano in ALTO ADIGE. It is also the name of a large subzone of the Alto Adige DOC many times the size of the original area.

Termeno Aromatico. See GEWÜRZTRAMINER.

termites can be pests in older vineyards, where they tunnel into old wood and can weaken it so much that the vine may partially collapse. Very occasionally newly planted cuttings are attacked where growing conditions are poor.   M.J.E.

Teroldego, old, well-connected grape variety which makes deep-coloured, seriously lively, fruity wines named Teroldego Rotaliano because they are made almost exclusively in the Rotaliano plain in TRENTINO, north-east Italy, with suitable tannins for relatively early drinking. Wine made from this variety is rather prone to REDUCTION. Teroldego was traditionally trained on PERGOLAS, but from 1985 Elisabetta Foradori initiated a qualitative revolution by introducing MASS SELECTION and GUYOT vine training in Trentino. Foradori's Granato became the benchmark for classic, age-worthy Teroldego. The variety was known in the Rotaliano plain as early as the 15th century, and DNA PROFILING at SAN MICHELE ALL'ADIGE has shown a parent-offspring relationship with LAGREIN from Alto Adige and that the variety is quite closely related, through DUREZA, to Syrah. Total plantings in Italy in 2010 were 796 ha/1,967 acres. See also MARZEMINO.   J.V.

Robinson, J., Harding, J., and Vouillamoz, J., *Wine Grapes, a complete guide to 1,368 vine varieties, including their origins and flavours* (London, 2012).

terpenes, distinctive FLAVOUR COMPOUNDS associated with the floral and citrus aromas found in wines made from such varieties as Muscat, Gewürztraminer, and Riesling. They are also found in oak, particularly American oak (see OAK FLAVOUR).

terpenoids, an important group of plant chemicals including many essential oils, CAROTENOIDS, plant HORMONES, sterols, and rubber. They contribute much to the unique qualities of the vine. Chemically, they are multiples of branched, five-carbon (isoprene) units yielding a variety of compounds with diverse properties: the C10 monoterpenes make an important contribution to floral aromas (see FLAVOUR COMPOUNDS); the C15 sesquiterpenoids include the hormone ABSCISIC ACID, and the C20 diterpenes include the GIBBERELLIN hormones. Carotenoids, with 40 carbon atoms, contribute to the skin colour of so-called white grapes and are metabolized to norisoprenoid flavour compounds

that contribute to non-floral aroma of grapes. See also terpenes in OAK FLAVOUR.

B.G.C. & P.J.W.

Terra Alta, Spanish for 'high land', is the highest of the DO wine zones in Spanish CATALUÑA (see map under SPAIN). Its recent development parallels that of TARRAGONA, which adjoins Terra Alta to the east. As in Tarragona, growers are following the lead of PRIORAT, notably recovering and relaunching their formerly despised GARNACHA BLANCA grapes and making some impressive red blends. R.J.M. & V. de la S.

terraces make work in vineyards planted across sloping land considerably easier, and can also help combat SOIL EROSION. Terraces more or less follow the contours of the land, and so row spacing may be irregular. Terraces are created when the hillside is re-formed into a series of horizontal steps between the rows. The world's most famous vineyard terraces are those of the PORT wine region of the DOURO Valley in northern Portugal, where there has been considerable experimentation with different designs, although they are common in much of SWITZERLAND, the northern RHÔNE, and elsewhere.

In centuries past, such terraces were laboriously constructed by hand and supported by stone walls. For modern vineyards, the cost of laying stones by hand can be prohibitive and skilled craftsmen hard to find, so most modern terraces are formed by bulldozers. Terraces are expensive to create, and are therefore justified only for expensive wines. There is a modern tendency to avoid planting vineyards on such slopes.

An alternative to creating terraces is to plant vines up and down the hillsides, as in Germany and other parts of northern Europe. This practice avoids the expense of forming terraces but can lead to soil erosion and worker fatigue, and some slopes are too steep for tractors. See also HILLSIDE VINEYARDS. R.E.S.

Terrano. See TERAN.

Terrantez, Portuguese white wine grape that is practically extinct on the island of MADEIRA but can occasionally be encountered in historic bottles. It is not, as some have suggested, a synonym for FOLGASÃO.

terra rossa, red-brown LOAM or CLAY directly over well-drained LIMESTONE found typically in regions with a MEDITERRANEAN CLIMATE. Such soils are found in southern Europe (in Spain's La MANCHA, for example), North Africa, and parts of Australia. The quality of many wines made from Cabernet Sauvignon and Shiraz grapes grown at Coonawarra in SOUTH AUSTRALIA is said to owe much to the terra rossa soils there. However, similar soils are found in Australia's inland irrigated districts, associated with much lower quality wines. M.J.E.

Terras do Sado, former name of PENÍNSULA DE SETÚBAL.

Terras Madeirenses, IGP (Indicação Geográfica Protegida) for the unfortified wines of the island of MADEIRA that are mostly unchallenging liquids for local consumption. Although VERDELHO shows great promise, plantings are limited and the competition for grapes for the island's famous fortified wines is fierce. Attempts at producing Cabernet Sauvignon, Merlot, and Syrah seem misconceived. S.A.

Terrasses du Larzac. The highest named TERROIR in the LANGUEDOC was promoted to full AOC status for its distinctive reds in 2014. The elevation of these foothills of the Cévennes entails dramatic TEMPERATURE VARIATION, sometimes as much as 20 °C/36 °F between day and night. The decidedly infertile soils include clay, limestone, pebbles, and shingle. The required blend of Languedoc grape varieties is dominated by Grenache Noir, Syrah, and Mourvèdre with, possibly, some Cinsaut and Carignan.

Terret is one of the Languedoc's oldest vine varieties and, like PINOT, has had plenty of time to mutate into different shades of grape, which may even be found on the same plant. **Terret Gris** was once by far the most planted white wine variety in the Languedoc, even if it was concentrated in the Hérault *département*. Both Terret Gris and **Terret Blanc**, both in decline, can be made into a relatively full-bodied but naturally crisp varietal white. The French vineyard survey of 2011 notes 1,281 ha/3,164 acres of Terret Blanc, less of Terret Gris. Some VARIETAL versions are made and both are allowed into the white wines of Minervois, Corbières, and Languedoc.

Terret Noir is the even rarer dark-berried version, one of the permitted varieties in red CHÂTEAUNEUF-DU-PAPE, to which it can add useful structure and interest. All Terrets bud usefully late and keep their acidity well.

terroir, much-discussed term for the total natural environment of any viticultural site. No precise English equivalent exists for this quintessentially French term and concept. Laville describes it fully, and how it underlies and defines the French APPELLATION CONTRÔLÉE system. A definition is given in van Leeuwen et al. (2004). Discussion of terroir is central to philosophical and commercial differences between OLD WORLD and NEW WORLD approaches to wine, although these viewpoints have been converging.

Major components of terroir are SOIL (as the word suggests, *terra* being Latin for 'earth' or 'land') and local TOPOGRAPHY, together with their interactions with each other and with MACROCLIMATE, which in turn affects

MESOCLIMATE and vine MICROCLIMATE. The holistic combination of all these is held to give each site its own unique terroir, which is reflected in its wines more or less consistently from year to year, to some degree regardless of variations in methods of VITICULTURE and WINEMAKING. Thus every small plot, and in generic terms every larger area, and ultimately region, may have distinctive wine-style characteristics which cannot be precisely replicated elsewhere. The extent to which terroir effects are unique is, however, debatable, and of course commercially important, which makes the subject controversial.

Opinions have differed greatly on the reality and, if real, the importance of terroir in determining wine qualities. Major regional classifications of European vineyards have been largely founded on the concepts of terroir, although these may be based on climate rather than soil. New World viticulturists and researchers, on the other hand, tended to dismiss terroir as a product of mysticism and established commercial interest. Dickenson canvasses the issues in detail, and is likewise mostly sceptical. But against these views it might also be justly charged that 'newer' viticulture has notoriously attempted to imitate the products of the great vineyards without regard to terroir, and therefore has a commercial reason for belittling its potential contribution.

It can certainly be argued that modern improvements in vineyard and winery technology, by raising and unifying standards of wine quality, have to some extent obscured differences in both style and quality of wines that in the past were (sometimes wrongly) attributed to terroir in its true sense. But paradoxically, the same improvements can serve to unmask genuine differences due to terroir. By eliminating extraneous odours and tastes derived from faulty winemaking, they allow the fuller expression of intrinsic grape qualities, which can be related to site. The wines of Burgundy are most often cited as evidence of the reality of the terroir effect. Many growers have different plots which they cultivate in the same way. They then vinify the grapes from these plots in a similar way, yet the wines produced differ significantly in quality and style. GUIGAL's single-vineyard bottlings in Côte Rôtie are one famous example of this approach to terroir, which is increasingly being followed by producers in the New World who espouse REGIONALITY.

Laville lists the following factors (components) as determining terroir:

- Climate, as measured by TEMPERATURE and RAINFALL.
- Sunlight energy, or insolation, received per unit of land surface area (see SUNLIGHT).
- Relief (or TOPOGRAPHY, or geomorphology), comprising elevation, slope, and aspect.

- Geology and pedology, determining the soil's basic physical and chemical characteristics (see GEOLOGY).
- Hydrology, or SOIL–WATER relations.

An essential notion of terroir is that all its components are natural, and that they cannot be significantly influenced by management, although Moran argues that terroir also includes human input in the vineyard and winery.

The main emphasis in nearly all recent French writings is on the soil, and especially its role and interactions with other elements of the environment in governing water supply to the vine. The most important evidence for this comes from the studies of Dr Gérard Seguin, of the University of BORDEAUX. He found that, while many of the acknowledged best Bordeaux vineyards are on the Quaternary (recently laid down) gravelly sands, by no means all are. Neither geological origin nor SOIL TEXTURE could explain the region's best terroirs, as judged by the wines they produce. The best in fact covered extremely diverse soil textures, ranging from heavy CLAYS, as in Pomerol, through CALCAREOUS brown soils, to sandy LOAMS and SANDS over clay (podzols), to the deep, gravelly sands most typical of the Médoc. An analysis of the soils' chemical properties showed them also to be extremely variable.

Two unifying themes did, however, emerge among the top CRUS. First, none of their soils was very fertile, but then none of the vines showed mineral element deficiencies either (see VINE NUTRITION). Secondly, their soils regulated water supply to the vines in such a way that it was nearly always just moderately sufficient, without extremes in either direction. DRAINAGE was always excellent, so that both water-logging and sudden increases in water supply to the vines were avoided no matter how much the rainfall. In the case of clay soils, this depended on their having fairly high ORGANIC MATTER and/or CALCIUM contents, so that they maintained friability and an open pore structure through which water could move readily (see SOIL STRUCTURE).

At the same time, the capacity to store soil water within a SOIL DEPTH accessible to the vine ROOTS was great enough to ensure supply through prolonged rainfall deficits. This might be achieved either by great soil depth and a deep, sparse root system, in the case of sandy soils with little water storage capacity per unit volume; or a lesser depth in heavier soils, combined with a capacity of the clay and organic matter to hold some of the water tightly enough that it is only slowly available to the roots. The deep, gravelly sands of the MÉDOC exemplified the former situation, the heavy clays of POMEROL, the latter. This explained why the best terroirs maintain their wine quality notably better in poor seasons than the rest, a

consistency which has always been one of the most striking features of the Bordeaux CLASSED GROWTHS. Renouf et al. showed that the wine quality produced on each individual block in Bordeaux grands crus classés was related to the soil type of the block.

van Leeuwen et al. found that the effect of soil is secondary to that of climate. However, both the climate and the soil effects are mediated through their influence on water supply to the vine.

Studies of terroir in Burgundy, cited and illustrated by Johnson, and by Halliday and Johnson, have led to similar conclusions. There the best wines are from stony clay loam soils, formed on the middle slopes from MARL (a clay and soft limestone mixture) mixed with SILT and rubble from outcropping hard LIMESTONE further up. These soils combine good drainage with just the right capacity to store and supply water to the vines.

Extensive studies by Carbonneau and colleagues in the Bordeaux region, and by Smart and colleagues in Australia and New Zealand, have revealed a further common feature of vineyards producing the best wines. All have a high degree of leaf and bunch exposure to direct sunlight, with little complete shading of internal and lower leaves (see further discussion under SUNLIGHT, CANOPY MICROCLIMATE, and CANOPY MANAGEMENT). Variation in this respect is explained by differences in vegetative VIGOUR and vine BALANCE. Best quality is associated with only moderate vigour, which typically results from a somewhat restricted water supply, limited NITROGEN, and (in some cases) appropriate TRAINING SYSTEMS. These studies suggest that soil effects on wine quality are indirect; i.e. soil conditions regulating water and nitrogen supply to the vine affect vine vigour, which in turn affects fruit and leaf exposure to sunlight, which in turn affects wine quality. While exposure to sunlight is amenable to management control on soils that are not too fertile, vine supply of water, in the absence of IRRIGATION, is very largely not. It is therefore a prime contributor, together with local TOPOGRAPHY, to the immutable influence of terroir.

An implication is that GEOLOGY, often cited as a basis of terroir, has in general no more than an indirect role. To varying degrees, parent ROCK materials do contribute to the natures of the soils derived from them; they also shape local topography and therefore MESOCLIMATE. Occasionally the parent materials contribute directly because vine roots can penetrate fissures in them, as in the cases of CHALK subsoils and the SCHISTS of the Douro Valley. In the broad sense, however, it remains the soil itself, and its water relations, that play the decisive role.

The effect of terroir on wine quality is now quite well understood: it is mainly mediated through vine water supply by the soil and the

climate, although mineral supply (and especially nitrogen supply) can also play a role. This effect of terroir can partly be obtained by good canopy and irrigation management in dry climates. However, the effect of terroir on wine style is still poorly understood. The high quality of Ch AUSONE (limestone), Ch CHEVAL BLANC (gravel and clay), and PETRUS (heavy clay) can be explained by the water regime. But why do they taste different and why do they each have their own style, despite very similar viticultural and oenological practices? This aspect of terroir is extremely interesting, because top wines are not only very good, but also unique, with their own style.

Another aspect of terroir is that its greatest expression occurs when grape ripening is relatively slow and therefore late in the season. This occurs in cool climates, or in warmer climates when varieties are sufficiently late ripening. In all quality wine regions in Europe, growers have chosen varieties that just achieve ripeness under the local climatic conditions. When grapes ripen in August in the northern hemisphere, or in February in the southern hemisphere, it is very difficult to produce refined wines with sought-after aromatic expression. Terroir can only be understood when soil, climate, and vine are taken into account simultaneously. A poor understanding of terroir in New World countries has in some instances led producers to plant varieties regardless of the local climatic conditions. When early-ripening varieties are planted in warm climates, wines are heavy, lacking freshness and aromatic expression (except for aromas produced by winemaking practices). This is the case with warm-climate Chardonnay, for instance. A much better expression is obtained in cool climates (Chardonnay in Chablis, Sauvignon Blanc in New Zealand). Growers in the New World are becoming more aware of this and seeking out cooler regions—Carneros instead of the Napa Valley, for example, New Zealand, Tasmania, or high-ELEVATION vineyards in Argentina.

An international concept?

The question remains as to how far the French concept of terroir, with its primary emphasis on soil, is relevant to other regions and viticultural systems. An overriding influence of soil and its water relations can be easily enough understood in the Bordeaux environment, with its relatively flat topography and, as a consequence, few really major differences in mesoclimate. The situation is clearly different in areas such as Germany's MOSEL region at the cold limit of commercial viticulture. The topographic differences between individual sites decide whether grapes, particularly the high-quality varieties such as RIESLING, will ripen fully at all. Topography and mesoclimate are inescapably major components of terroir (or its German equivalent).

Moreover, it has been argued that mesoclimatic differences may not merely govern the degree of ripeness attained. Some believe that they could also affect more subtle grape and wine qualities of the kinds commonly attributed to terroir; see CLIMATE AND WINE QUALITY and TEMPERATURE VARIABILITY. Soil might similarly influence grape and wine qualities through its effect on MICROCLIMATE; see STONES AND ROCKS, SOIL COLOUR, and SOIL AND WINE QUALITY.

The New World approach to vineyard design is now much more likely to take soil differences into account. New World vineyards were once most likely to have been subdivided according to existing boundaries, shape, topography, or whim, and to have been much larger and newly planted. Today it is increasingly common to allow a soil survey and SOIL MAPPING to determine choice of variety, rootstock, even trellis system—a concession to the wisdom of Old World experience. The growing number of single-vineyard wines is further evidence of this trend.

All these effects serve, of course, to underline terroir as a real concept, and not something expressed merely through the relationships between vine vigour, balance, and the vine canopy. The distinction is critical because, to the extent that the latter is true, other approaches are often available to achieve the same end. Two stand out in importance.

1. The use of larger or more complex vine TRAINING SYSTEMS, such as Carbonneau's LYRE trellis, making it possible to maintain good leaf and fruit exposure on larger and more productive vines. This in turn allows the exploitation of moister, and possibly more fertile, soils, giving higher yields without any necessary loss of fruit and wine quality.

2. In regions with dry summers, the use of controlled IRRIGATION, especially that made possible by DRIP IRRIGATION. This allows vegetative vigour to be held at appropriate levels for vine balance, but water to be supplied during ripening as needed. It is an important advance in regions of MEDITERRANEAN CLIMATE, enabling them to duplicate many of the terroir characteristics of the long-established best table wine areas, but with fewer climatic risks.

It seems inconceivable, however, that these developments will ever totally eliminate the regional and local differences in wine qualities that have been traditionally ascribed to terroir. Differences in MACROCLIMATE, MESOCLIMATE, and soil MICROCLIMATE remain, while there are many conceivable avenues by which differences in soil chemistry—for instance, in trace element balances—might have small effects on wine flavours and aromas which are nevertheless detectable by the sense of TASTE. To the extent that terroirs remain unique, and poorly understood, one can therefore hope that they will continue to help mould the infinite variety and individuality of the best wines, giving the special nuances of character that make wine such a fascinating study for winemaker and consumer alike. *Vivent les différences!*

See also MICROBIAL TERROIR.

J.G., R.E.S., & C.v.L.

Bohmrich, R., 'Terroir', *Journal of Wine Research*, 7/1 (1996-7), 33-46.

Dickenson, J., 'Viticultural geography: an introduction to the literature in English', *Journal of Wine Research*, 1 (1990), 5-24.

Halliday, J., and Johnson, H., *The Art and Science of Wine* (London, 1992).

Johnson, H., and Robinson, J., *The World Atlas of Wine* (7th edn, London and New York, 2013).

Laville, P., 'Le Terroir, un concept indispensable à l'élaboration et à la protection des appellations d'origine comme à la gestion des vignobles: le cas de la France', *Bulletin de l'OIV*, 709-10 (1990), 217-41.

Moran, W., 'Terroir—the human factor', *Australia and New Zealand Wine Industry Journal*, 16/2 (2001), 32-51.

Renouf, V., et al., 'Soils, rootstocks and grapevine varieties in prestigious Bordeaux vineyards and their impact on yield and quality', *Journal International des Sciences de la Vigne et du Vin*, 44/3 (2010), 127-34.

Riou, C., Morlat, R., and Asselin, C., 'Une approche intégrée des terroirs viticoles. Discussion sur les critères de caractérisation accessibles', *Bulletin de l'OIV*, 68/767-8 (1995), 93-106.

Seguin, G., ' "Terroirs" and pedology of wine growing', *Experientia*, 42 (1986), 861-73.

Smart, R. E., 'Vineyard design to improve wine quality the Orlando way', *Australian and New Zealand Wine Industry Journal*, 11 (1996), 335-6.

van Leeuwen, C., and Chéry, P., 'Quelle méthode pour caractériser et étudier le terroir viticole: analyse de sol, cartographie pédologique ou étude écophysiologique?', in *Un raisin de qualité: de la vigne à la cuve*, n° Hors Série du *Journal International des Sciences de la Vigne et du Vin* (2001), 13-20.

van Leeuwen, C., Friant, P., Choné, X., Tregoat, O., Koundouras, S., and Dubourdieu, D., 'Influence of climate, soil, and cultivar on terroir', *American Journal of Enology and Viticulture*, 55/3 (2004), 207-17.

van Leeuwen, C., Roby, J. P., Pernet, D., and Bois, B., 'Methodology of soil based zoning for viticultural terroirs', *Bulletin de l'OIV*, 83/947-948-949 (2010), 13-29.

van Leeuwen, C., and Seguin, G., 'The concept of terroir in viticulture', *Journal of Wine Research*, 17/1 (2006), 1-10.

tête de cuvée, term occasionally used for selected top bottlings.

tetrachloroanisole, more properly **2,3,4,6-tetrachloroanisole**, or **TeCA**, is a musty- or dusty-smelling compound that can taint wine if the concentration is above the perception threshold of around 20 ng/l in red or white wine and 4 ng/l in water. It is caused by the microbial degradation by fungi in the winery of pentachlorophenol (PCP) used in wood-treatment products. PCA or 2,3,4,5,6-pentachloroanisole has a much higher perception threshold, at around 5000 ng/l, but is nearly always present with TeCA.

Texas, south-western state in the UNITED STATES, currently the country's fifth largest wine-producing state after California, New York, Washington, and Oregon with about 4,400 acres/1,619 ha planted mainly with VINIFERA vines. The first vineyard was planted by the Spanish at the Ysleta Mission near what is now El Paso in the early 1660s. The production built to more than 200,000 gal/7,570 hl by 1853. In the 1880s, the famous VITIS taxonomist T. V. MUNSON, from Denison, Texas, shipped native Texas vine species to France and saved the European wine community from devastation by PHYLLOXERA. In the early 20th century, the Texas wine industry was almost eliminated by PROHIBITION. Dr Clint McPherson and Robert Reed of Texas Tech University revived the modern wine industry in 1976 with the creation of Llano Estacado Winery in Lubbock, experimenting with multiple grape varieties and spurring others to do the same. The industry has grown steadily ever since, to the point that there were 275 bonded wineries in Texas in 2014.

Wine is grown in all parts of the state and conditions vary greatly. Texas is divided into three main regions. The **North-Central Region** runs across the northern third of the state from the Panhandle border with New Mexico east towards Dallas, but excludes north east Texas. One of the best quality wine regions, the Texas High Plains AVA, and the largest concentration of grape growers are both in the western part of the North-Central Region. To the east around Dallas, Fort Worth, and Grapevine, which has fashioned itself as a major wine destination, the humidity makes it difficult to grow VINIFERA vines though a few hardy souls persevere.

The eastern third of Texas, the **South-Eastern Region** around the cities of Austin, San Antonio, and Houston, suffers from PIERCE'S DISEASE, the biggest problem for the Texas grape-growing industry over the long term, although DROUGHT has become an equal adversary. In the far north east portion of the South-Eastern Region are warm, humid pine forests suitable for MUSCADINE grapes. Pierce's disease-resistant Lenoir (Black Spanish), Cynthiana (NORTON), and Blanc du Bois varieties are grown in this north east area. In the centre of the South-Eastern Region, however, including the Texas Hill Country AVA, Bell Mountain AVA, and Fredericksburg in the Texas Hill Country AVA, fine VINIFERA wines are produced. In the south of the South-Eastern Region, on the Mexican border, is DESERT and the oldest winery in Texas, Val Verde, which has operated continuously for over a century and is known mainly for sweet, FORTIFIED WINES.

The central-western third of the state is the **Trans-Pecos Region** whose high-elevation vineyards amidst arid mesas produce about 40% of the grapes in Texas, about the same production as that of the Texas High Plains vineyards.

Mesa Vineyards, which owns 1,000 acres/400 ha of vineyards first planted by the University of Texas near Fort Stockton, grows a substantial amount of grapes for Texas wineries, including its own Ste. Genevieve Winery, the state's largest wine producer of mostly grocery-store bottlings, with a higher-end Peregrine brand.

Like many modern US vintners, Texans first planted and vinified the traditional French varieties Cabernet Sauvignon, Merlot, and Chardonnay, often with disappointing results. In recent years, many have come to accept that Mediterranean grape varieties that thrive in hot growing conditions are the state's ticket to winemaking success. Syrah, Tempranillo, Sangiovese, Viogniers, and Vermentino seem much more at home, notably in the Texas High Plains AVA in the north western Panhandle of Texas, particularly from growers such as Bingham, Newsom, and Reddy. Vineyards are planted at elevations of 3,000–4,000 ft (915–1,220 m), affording plenty of daytime sunshine for ripening and relatively cool night temperatures for acid retention. Even pioneering Texas Hill Country wineries are adding High Plains grapes to their repertoires.

Texas vines have to combat not just Pierce's disease and drought but also WINTER FREEZE, HAIL, WIND, BLACK ROT, TEXAS ROOT ROT, black berry moth, and CROWN GALL. It is hardly surprising perhaps that grapes are routinely imported from California, New Mexico, and Washington state to augment Texas production. In 2014 there was a move afoot to require Texas wines to contain at least 75% Texas-grown grapes.

Texas has eight AVAs, listed below in chronological order.

The Mesilla Valley (1985) extends from New Mexico into Texas, but is generally considered a New Mexico AVA.

Bell Mountain (1986), won on behalf of the quality and concentration of Cabernet Sauvignon grown in this small area in northeast Gillespie county 15 miles north of Fredericksburg.

Fredericksburg (1989), within Texas Hill Country is known for good-quality Cabernet Sauvignon and Chardonnay, and burgeoning TOURISM that has spawned a plethora of tasting rooms.

Texas Hill Country (1991), the largest AVA in the US, includes 15,000 square miles but fewer than 800 planted acres of vineyard. It produces mainly pleasant whites and relatively soft reds with some producers here importing grapes from the Texas High Plains AVA to boost quality and complexity.

Escondido Valley (1992), an area of about 50 square miles in Pecos county in the Trans-Pecos Region near Fort Stockton is home to Mesa Vineyards' St Genevieve, the state's biggest winery.

Texas High Plains (1993), the state's most consistent AVA so far, initially for Cabernet Sauvignon and Chardonnay, and more recently for Tempranillo, Syrah, Sangiovese, Vermentino, and Roussanne. A high elevation with fertile red soils, hot days, cool nights, and frigid winters that allow full vine DORMANCY.

Texas Davis Mountains, (1998) produces good Cabernet Sauvignon and a small quantity of Sauvignon Blanc.

Texoma (2006) includes parts of both Texas and Oklahoma. L.M.

English, S. J., *The Wines of Texas* (4th edn, Austin, Tex., 2002).

Robinson, J., and Murphy, L., *American Wine* (Berkeley, Calif., 2013).

Texas root rot, caused by the fungus *Phymatotrichum omnivorum,* which lives in the soil. This vine FUNGAL DISEASE can prevent grape-growing in parts of the south western United States. A circular patch of vines can suddenly die in summer. The disease is avoided by planting disease-free material in non-infested soil. The vigorous ROOTSTOCK Dog Ridge can be planted where the fungus is suspected. R.E.S.

texture, the dimension of TASTING that draws together attributes such as smoothness and ASTRINGENCY that produce tactile rather than flavour sensations on the surface of the mouth. These sensations are often referred to collectively as MOUTHFEEL, especially in relation to red wines. In practice, the sensory perception of texture, experienced through the sense of touch and arising from the trigeminal nerve, is closely intertwined with the senses of taste and smell. ASTRINGENCY, BODY, VISCOSITY, BITTERNESS, and ACIDITY are among the interrelated factors influencing texture. Because of the complexity of the interactions among the many wine constituents that may be involved, formal sensory studies relating wine composition to texture are limited. Nevertheless, a start has been made on this daunting task and evidence to date indicates that wine TANNINS, PIGMENTED TANNINS, and ETHANOL are all involved with this sensation. Research in 2004 showed that wine POLYSACCHARIDES also probably play an important role in the textural properties of wine. Current work at DAVIS, ADELAIDE, and INRA MONTPELLIER is aimed at discriminating among the ways astringency manifests itself, and relating these to the texture and tannin composition of the wine. TASTING NOTES sometimes try to describe the texture of a wine by comparing it to a type of material such as silk or velvet, or by likening it to the texture of a foodstuff, e.g. grainy or chewy. A mouthfeel wheel was developed in Adelaide in Australia in answer to Davis's AROMA WHEEL (illustrated under MOUTHFEEL). Its purpose is to establish a vocabulary for describing the sensations of texture in red wines.

P.J.W. & J.E.H.

Gawel, R., Oberholster, A., and Francis, I. L., 'A "mouth-feel wheel": terminology for communicating the mouth-feel characteristics of red wine', *Australian Journal of Grape and Wine Research*, 6 (2000), 203–7.

Vidal, S., et al., 'The mouth-feel properties of polysaccharides and anthocyanins in a wine like medium', *Food Chemistry*, 85 (2004), 519–25.

Thailand, South East Asian country where viticulture began in the 1960s on the low plain around the capital Bangkok and has flourished, despite the challenges involved in TROPICAL VITICULTURE. Although the early vineyards were developed to produce TABLE GRAPES, the main varieties planted were VINIFERA, including MALAGA BLANC, MUSCAT OF HAMBURG, Perlette, CARDINAL, and POKDUM. A total of around 5,000 ha/12,350 acres of vines had been planted by 2013.

In the mid 1980s, grapes from these vineyards became the raw material for a popular wine cooler (called Spy) produced by the Siam Winery, a venture established by the man who devised the energy drink Red Bull. A more conventional winemaking operation, Château de Loei, based on mainstream wine grape varieties (principally Chenin Blanc and Syrah) began in 1991 in the cooler Phurua Highland district in north-east Thailand (at 600–800 m/1,970–2,635 ft) along the Loei River, close to the border with Laos. A third frontier was forged in the mid 1990s by an offshoot of the giant Boon Rawd Corporation, brewer of Singha beer, with trial plantings of 50 wine grape varieties in the highlands around the Khao Yai National Park north of Bangkok. Chenin Blanc and Syrah also performed well here, forming the backbone of the premium wines released by the founding winery, PB Valley, and by Chateau des Brumes, GranMonte Estate, and Alcidini that have followed PB Valley. Other varieties for which expectations are high in this region include Viognier, Cabernet Sauvignon, Pinot Noir, Tempranillo, and Dornfelder.

Meanwhile, Siam Winery has strengthened its position as the largest producer of wine in Thailand, with a capacity of more than half a million cases a year. It has progressed through a variety of labels with wines based on Malaga Blanc and Pokdum from the so-called 'floating vineyards' in the Chao Phraya delta to a more upmarket range, appropriately named Monsoon Valley. This label is supplied with INTERNATIONAL VARIETIES grown in Siam Winery's vineyards at Khao Yai and, more recently, at Hua Hin, south west of Bangkok. Silverlake is a modern winery in the tourist resort region of Pattaya with a substantial area of vines.   D.G.

Theophrastus (370–288 BC), philosopher and botanist from Lesbos who discusses viticulture in his 'plant researches'.

thermal amplitude. See TEMPERATURE VARIABILITY.

Thermenregion, AUSTRIAN wine-growing region named for its thermal springs, also unofficially known as the Südbahn for the railway south from VIENNA that forms its backbone, encompassing 2,500 ha/6,100 acres of vines. The region grows two indigenous white wine varieties seldom encountered anywhere else that, amounting to little more than 7% of Thermenregion's vines, are often taken to define the region. ROTGIPFLER produces wines with a striking combination of body and brightness, while ZIERFANDLER (sometimes called Spätrot) recalls CHENIN BLANC in its juxtaposition of opulence with brightness with spiced quince and citrus notes. Weingut Stadlmann's Zierfandler from the Mandel-Höh vineyard demonstrates how profound, seductive, and long-lived this varietal can be. NEUBURGER, PINOT BLANC (Weissburgunder), GRÜNER VELTLINER, RIESLING, PINOT NOIR (Blauburgunder), and ST LAURENT have all selectively demonstrated promise in this region that once had a major presence in foreign as well as domestic markets. Two reds, ZWEIGELT and Blauer PORTUGIESER, evenly split a 25% share of the region's vineyards, but without similar successes to show for it. Chardonnay, MUSKATELLER, and TRAMINER wines have recently found their way abroad, although these varieties are not widely planted in Thermenregion.   D.S.

thermotherapy, a technique to eliminate VIRUS DISEASES from grapevines by growing infected plants at high temperatures (about 38 °C or 100 °F), and then propagating from SHOOT TIPS. These shoot tips can produce plants free of virus diseases, but diseases such as FANLEAF DEGENERATION virus are eliminated much more easily than others—LEAFROLL, for example. Each tip produced must be checked to see whether it is virus-free, and can become registered as a new CLONE. New techniques of TISSUE CULTURE have generally been found more effective at virus elimination. Thermotherapy should not be confused with HOT-WATER TREATMENT.   R.E.S.

thermovinification, process sometimes used in RED WINEMAKING, particularly in cool climates such as those of upper NEW YORK state or after particularly cool growing seasons, whereby heat, about 70 °C/158 °F, is applied to grape clusters or MUST before FERMENTATION to liberate ANTHOCYANINS, or colour, from the skins (see TEMPERATURE). The heat treatment is immediately followed by cooling then PRESSING to liberate coloured juice, which is then fermented much as in traditional WHITE WINEMAKING. Thermovinification is particularly valuable in making everyday wines from grape varieties low in anthocyanins, or from better-coloured grape varieties that are not fully ripe or are affected by moulds such as BOTRYTIS rot, which destroys colour in dark-skinned grapes. In the latter case, the heat inactivates the colour-destroying enzymes secreted by the mould. The heat also destroys pectoclytic ENZYMES, making CLARIFICATION more difficult, and oxidases such as LACCASE, reducing the risk of OXIDATION, especially useful for botrytis-affected grapes. Heat treatment also volatilizes ISOBUTYL-METHOXYPYRAZINE, thereby reducing GREEN aromas. Thermovinification is rarely used in making fine wines, however, which almost invariably rely on extended MACERATION to extract colour and flavour from the grape skins. However, at Ch de Beaucastel in the Rhône, the Perrins have for many years heated the grapes very briefly to 80 °C/176 °F immediately after DESTEMMING. The grapes are then cooled to cellar temperature prior to fermentation. This is said to increase the extraction of colour and flavour and avoid the addition of sulfur to the must. See also FLASH DÉTENTE.

A.D.W. & J.E.H.

thiamine. See VITAMINS.

Thiniatiko, red grape occasionally found on the Greek island of Cephalonia making rich wines. It may be related to MAVRODAPHNE.

thinning vines. See CROP THINNING and SHOOT THINNING.

thiols. See MERCAPTANS.

third growth. See the CLASSIFICATION of Bordeaux.

Thompson Seedless is the common CALIFORNIA name for the seedless white grape variety SULTANA. It acquired this name from an early grower of the variety, near Yuba City, one William Thompson. Thompson Seedless is California's most planted grape variety by far. Almost all of California's Thompson Seedless is planted in the hot, dry SAN JOAQUIN VALLEY, with nearly two-thirds in Fresno county, the powerhouse of California raisin production. In 1960, almost 70% of all grapes crushed for white wine were Thompson Seedless, clearly indicating what made up the 49% of 'other grapes' then allowed in wines labelled as VARIETALS. In the 1970s, Thompson Seedless was particularly useful to the California wine industry in helping to bulk out inexpensive white JUG WINE blends at a time when demand far outstripped supply of premium white wine grape varieties. Today, however, it is used mainly either for DRYING GRAPES, as material for DISTILLATION, or for GRAPE CONCENTRATE to sweeten bottled waters or cold tea drinks.

Thrapsathiri, Greek island vine variety making richy fruity reds. Probably identical to the Cyclades' Begleri.

three-tier system. With the repeal of PROHIBITION, most US states promulgated regulations that made vertical integration of the industry illegal, mandating that it be separated in to three 'tiers': producer (or supplier in the case of imports), wholesaler, and retailer (or restaurant). As a result of the legal protection of the middle tier and the rapid consolidation of wholesalers, notably SOUTHERN WINE AND SPIRITS, many producers, retailers, and consumers chafe at the lack of a full liberalization of the US wine market. For more, see UNITED STATES, regulation and DIRECT SHIPPING.   T.C.

thrips, tiny (1–2 mm long), winged insects which readily feed on grapevine flowers and developing bunches, causing scarring and disfigurement of grapes by feeding on the small berries. While thrips are sometimes thought to be the cause of poor FRUIT SET, there is little evidence to support this.   M.J.E. & R.E.S.

Tibouren could almost be said to be *the* Provençal grape variety but DNA PROFILING has shown it to be identcal to ROSSESE di Dolceacqua. It has a long history in south east France and the ability to produce such quintessentially Provençal wines as earthy rosés with a genuine scent of the garrigue (its wine is not naturally deep in colour). In 2011 total French plantings were still about 450 ha/1,110 acres, almost all in the Var. Tibouren is cultivated by a number of the more quality- and history-conscious producers of Provence and some of them bottle it as a varietal rosé. Particularly early-budding, it is sensitive to COULURE and therefore yields irregularly. Its original sphere of influence was around St-Tropez, where it is thought by some to have been imported as recently as the end of the 18th century by a naval captain Antiboul, after whom it was named.

Tierra de Barros, Spanish wine zone. See EXTREMADURA.

Tierra de León, promising DOP created in 2008, encompassing some 1,465 ha/3,515 acres of vineyards south of the BIERZO appellation in north west SPAIN on well-drained, limestone-based alluvial terraces. This is the birthplace of the red PRIETO PICUDO grape and shares with Asturias the white Albarín, so that its wines are quite different from those of its neighbours that are dominated by Tempranillo and Mencía. V. de la S.

Tierra del Vino de Zamora, DOP just west of TORO with 800 ha/2,000 acres and just eight wineries. Tempranillo dominates terrain similar to its better-known neighbour.

tight spacing, American colloquial expression for closely planted vineyards; see VINE DENSITY.

Tignanello, seminal central Italian wine first produced by the house of ANTINORI as a single-vineyard Chianti Classico in the 1970 vintage and then as a ground-breaking VINO DA TAVOLA in the 1971 vintage. For more details, see VINO DA TAVOLA and SUPERTUSCANS.

time and wine. See AGEING.

Timorasso, relatively rare Piemontese vine variety enjoying a renaissance for its aromatic, durable white VARIETALS. The 2010 vine census found only 129 ha in total.

tinaja, large, earthenware vessel, probably developed from the Roman AMPHORAE, occasionally still used to ferment and store wine in central and southern SPAIN and southern CHILE. *Tinajas* are used by some producers in La MANCHA, VALDEPEÑAS, and MONTILLA-MORILES, although modern versions are mostly made from reinforced concrete. They are relatively cheap, but have the disadvantages that they are not very efficient in terms of space, are difficult to clean, especially if the neck is narrow, and offer relatively poor TEMPERATURE CONTROL unless they are buried underground like QVEVRI. Increased interest in amphorae in winemaking has led to a certain reprise, however.

tinta, the Spanish and Portuguese feminine adjective for red, is therefore the first word of many, unrelated Spanish and Portuguese names and synonyms for dark-skinned vine varieties. For Tinta Roriz, see RORIZ, for example.

Tinta Amarela, productive dark-skinned Portuguese grape variety grown in the DOURO for PORT. It can yield fine, attractively scented wines but suffers the singular disadvantage of being particularly sensitive to ROT. Nonetheless it accounts for around 20% of vines in the Baixo Corgo, the coolest and wettest of the Douro's three subregions. As TRINCADEIRA, its official name, it is a highly regarded variety in the more arid regions of the Alentejo and southern Portugal, where it produces rich, powerful dry reds.

Tinta Barroca, common, relatively thick-skinned port grape variety which is the third most planted in Portugal's DOURO Valley, mainy for port, and grown on a total of 5,444 ha/ 13,447 acres of Portuguese vineyard in 2012. It is favoured by growers for yielding large quantities of grapes with exceptionally high levels of sugar and is widely planted on higher or north-facing slopes. However, Barroca is prone to both mildews and is easily damaged by extreme heat and the berries have a tendency to shrivel on the vine. By no means as highly prized as the other leading port grapes, Touriga Franca and Tinta Roriz (Tempranilloa), Barroca produces reasonably well-structured but slightly jammy, rustic wines which can be useful in a blend. In Portugal, Tinta Barroca is rarely used as a varietal but it has been one of the most popular varieties for fortified port-like wines in South Africa's vineyards, and full-throttle, unfortified VARIETAL Tinta Barroca dry(ish) red (sometimes misspelt and referred to as **Tinta Barocca** or **Tinta das Baroccas**) is a speciality in South Africa where there were 215 ha in 2012.

Tinta Caiada, Portuguese red grape variety also known as Tinta Lameira in the Douro. It is the same as Spain' s PARRALETA.

Tinta de Toro. See TEMPRANILLO and TORO.

Tinta Francisca (not to be confused with TOURIGA FRANCA), lesser red grape variety used in the production of port in Portugal's DOURO Valley. The wine produced can be notably sweet but is not particularly concentrated. Some see similarities with Pinot Noir. It has been planted in South Africa.

Tinta Miúda, 'small red one', Portuguese red wine grape grown traditionally around LISBON but now found in ESTREMADURA. The vine is low-yielding but can produce seductive and powerful wines. Identical to the GRACIANO of Rioja and MORRASTEL of the Languedoc, it ripens late and is susceptible to rot but is valued by winemakers for the colour and acidity it contributes to a blend. There were 290 ha/716 acres in Portugal in 2012.

Tinta Negra, previously **Tinta Negra Mole**, name for NEGRAMOLL on the island of MADEIRA.

Tinta Pinheira, former name for the Portuguese grape variety RUFETE.

Tinta Roriz, official name for the Spanish vine variety TEMPRANILLO in northern Portugal. (ARAGONEZ is more common in the south.) Thanks to recent popularity, it has become Portugal's most planted variety by quite a margin with total plantings of 21,150 ha/52,240 acres by 2012. It is particularly important in the Douro Valley, where it vies with TOURIGA FRANCA as the most planted variety, particularly in the Cima Corgo and Douro Superior. It is relatively easy to grow in the Douro but has a tendency to over-produce and performs best in those years when yields are inherently low. Varietal wines are also made in Dão, and in the Alentejo where it is known as Aragonez. Here it is sometimes bottled as a VARIETAL but is often blended with the local TRINCADEIRA. It has also gained ground in the Dão region (where it is also known as Tinta Roriz), and in other parts of Portugal.

Tintilla de Rota, Andalucian name for a variety shown by DNA PROFILING to be GRACIANO. Here it can make rather charming sweet fortified reds.

tinto, Spanish and Portuguese for red, so that *vino* (*vinho* in Portuguese) *tinto* is red wine (as opposed to the lighter red CLARETE produced in Spain). This is the origin of name of the red wine once known in England as TENT.

Like TINTA, Tinto is also the first word of many Spanish and Portuguese names and synonyms for black grape varieties. TEMPRANILLO, for example, is known as Tinto Fino in Ribero del Duero.

Tinto Cão, meaning 'red dog', top-quality black grape variety for the production of PORT. Having almost disappeared from the vineyards of the DOURO Valley in northern Portugal (despite its long history there), it is being planted with greater enthusiasm since it was identified as one of the five finest port varieties, although it is not one of the deepest coloured nor especially productive. It is also grown for varied table wines in the Dão region and has also been planted experimentally at DAVIS in California, and in Australia were it has been known as Tinta Cao.

Tinto del Pais, synonym for TEMPRANILLO, as is **Tinto Fino**, in RIBERA DEL DUERO.

tipping, the viticultural practice of cutting off SHOOT TIPS at flowering. Normally about 10 to 20 cm (8 in) of shoot tip are removed. This can help reduce the problem of COULURE, or poor FRUIT SET, for some susceptible varieties.

tirage, French for that part of the SPARKLING WINEMAKING process during which sugar and yeast are added to the blended base wines in order to provoke a second fermentation, thereby creating CARBON DIOXIDE gas. It is sometimes used to refer to the entire period during which the sparkling wine matures on the LEES of this second fermentation.

tissue culture, the culturing of excised cells, tissues, and organs using artificial media of salts and nutrients, used especially in PROPAGATION and GENETIC MODIFICATION. The techniques can be used to develop vines with particularly useful properties much faster than by conventional PROPAGATION. Usually a CALLUS develops first, then roots and buds develop within the callus, leading to a new vine that can flower and set seed. The formation of roots or buds is achieved by subtle changes in the ingredients of the culture solution,

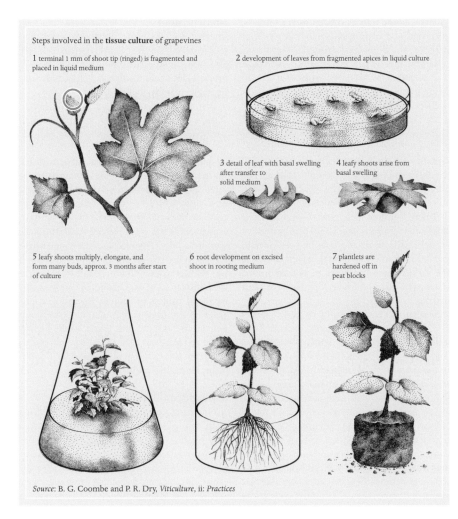

Steps involved in the **tissue culture** of grapevines

1 terminal 1 mm of shoot tip (ringed) is fragmented and placed in liquid medium

2 development of leaves from fragmented apices in liquid culture

3 detail of leaf with basal swelling after transfer to solid medium

4 leafy shoots arise from basal swelling

5 leafy shoots multiply, elongate, and form many buds, approx. 3 months after start of culture

6 root development on excised shoot in rooting medium

7 plantlets are hardened off in peat blocks

Source: B. G. Coombe and P. R. Dry, *Viticulture*, ii: *Practices*

especially in the relative amounts of the hormones AUXIN and CYTOKININ. Aseptic conditions are essential. Meristem culture, or the culture of the terminal 1 mm of vine shoot, especially after its fragmentation, has permitted the production of large numbers of plantlets in tubes that are free of some VIRUSES and CROWN GALL disease. Large numbers of vine plantlets can be 'micropropagated' by these methods, which can rapidly build up populations of scarce VINE VARIETIES. See diagram above. B.G.C.

titratable acidity. See TOTAL ACIDITY.

toast (*chauffe* in French), given to a barrel towards the end of the process of forming it over a heat source, is one of the processes in BARREL MAKING that most obviously affect eventual wine flavour. The heat source also inevitably toasts the inside of the barrel to a degree that varies according to the heat of the fire and the length of time the barrel is held over it. This heating process dramatically alters the wood's physical and chemical composition. The toasted wood provides a buffer between the ALCOHOL in wine and the TANNINS in wood.

In general, the less a barrel is toasted, the more tannins and other wood characteristics will be leached into the wine by the alcohol. Wine matured in lightly toasted barrels therefore tends to taste 'oaky', 'woody', or even 'vegetal', while wine matured in heavily toasted barrels is more likely to taste 'toasty' or 'spicy'. See also OAK FLAVOUR.

Burgundy barrels are in general more heavily toasted than Bordeaux barriques, perhaps partly because the STAVES are thicker, and partly because a heavy toast is better suited to the flavours of Pinot Noir and Chardonnay grapes than to those of Cabernet Sauvignon, Merlot, Sauvignon Blanc, and Sémillon. The following terms are used, although they are imprecise and cannot really be compared between coopers.

Light toast: there is little colour change in the wood, which has probably been toasted over the fire, after the shaping has been completed, for about five minutes at a surface temperature of 120–180 °C/248–356 °F. Wines aged in these barrels are usually quite fruity but can be somewhat tannic.

Medium toast: the wood is browner, probably having been toasted for approximately 10 minutes at 200 °C/392 °F. Wines aged in such barrels are said to have smells of vanilla and coffee. Wines aged in these barrels will normally be less tannic than those aged in light toast barrels. They are often described as rounder, smoother, and more persistent.

Heavy toast: the wood is very dark, having been toasted for around 15 minutes at 225 °C/ 440 °F. Wines aged in these barrels are usually marked by aromas of roasted coffee beans, toasted bread, ginger, nutmeg, cloves, and smoked meats. The above flavour descriptions apply to wine aged in French oak barrels.

The word 'char' is usually associated with American whiskey barrels, which are made over steam or natural gas but then set on fire. Traditionally American oak wine barrels were simply un-charred bourbon barrels but American cooperages now toast to the customer's specifications.

The higher the toast, the greater the risk of blisters inside the staves. Coopers have recently developed new toast levels using different combinations of temperature and duration.

In addition to the origin of the wood and the way it was seasoned, toast is a crucial factor when ordering a barrel. M.K.

Tocai, or **Tocai Friulano**, old Friulan name for SAUVIGNONASSE, now replaced by FRIULANO.

California grows a few hundred acres of the variety they still call Tocai Friulano which is also produced by Millbrook in the Hudson Valley, NEW YORK.

Tocai Rosso is used as a synonym for GRENACHE NOIR in the VENETO.

Tokaj, town, PDO (*Oltalom alatt álló eredet megjelöléssel* or OEM in the local language), and the most famous wine region in HUNGARY, whose sweet wine was once revered throughout Europe. Mount Tokaj is the prominent VOLCANIC cone at the southernmost tip of the region, which includes the foothills of the entire Zemplén Mountains (which, in turn, form the southern range of the Tokaj-Eperjes Mountains). Hungarians often use the name Tokaj to mean the whole region, but the people living in the area refer to themselves as being from the Hegyalja, to emphasize their separateness from the residents of the town of Tokaj itself. However, even they prefer to call their wine **Tokaji** (the –i ending is a suffix indicating place of origin, as the –er in New Yorker) regardless of any more precise location within the region.

History

The first known occurrence of the name, in the form 'Tokay', is in a 13th-century genealogy and history entitled *Gesta Hungarorum*. The *Gesta*, and many sources after it, refer to the emblematic hill of the region not as Tokaj but as Tarcal, today the name of a village at the

t

western foot of the hill. Remarkably, Tarcal was also the name of the hill in Syrmia far to the south, today known as Fruska Gora in SERBIA, which yielded the most famous wine of medieval Hungary. Records enumerating the administrative units have existed since 1641, but these early sources are rife with gaps and contradictions. Hungarian wine legislation of the time lists 27 communities with a right to label their wines as Tokaj. The vineyards around most of these communities were first CLASSIFIED in the 18th century, in a manner that was rigorous at the time but is not entirely useful today. By the 18th century, this extraordinary wine had been introduced to the French court (see HUNGARY, history), and was subsequently introduced to the Russian imperial court by the Habsburgs. Only CONSTANTIA from the Cape of Good Hope, and to a lesser extent Moldavian COTNARI, rivalled the reputation of this wine, generally known outside Hungary as 'the wine of kings and king of wines' during this period of sweet-wine worship, with Tokaji Esszencia regarded as an all-purpose restorative.

During most of the 20th century, Tokaj languished however. Its recovery from PHYLLOXERA was slow, and was far from complete even at the outset of the Second World War. Its reputation suffered with the dissolution of the Austro-Hungarian Empire in 1918. Under Soviet domination, quantity rather than quality was encouraged, although a surprising number of individual growers and winemakers continued to uphold traditions and some exceptional wines were made. As the birthplace of a world-famous wine, Tokaj has a better-documented history than most Hungarian wine regions. It potentially encompasses 11,149 ha/27,549 acres but only 5,946 ha/14,692 acres are planted today. It seems unlikely that all of the 9,829 hectares/24.287 acres rated Class I will ever be fully planted.

Geography

Located in north-eastern Hungary, the Zemplén Mountains have a cool climate, as does the entire Tokaj-Eperjes range within the Carpathian volcanic chain. The mean temperature in the foothills is 9–10 °C/48–50 °F annually, 21 °C in July, and −3 °C in January. The favourable south-south-eastern aspect of the foothills contributes to the excellent MESOCLIMATES found on the slopes. High levels of humidity, due to the location of the vineyards above the confluence of the Bodrog and Tisza rivers, encourage special fungoid flora, including the all-important BOTRYTIS.

The best vineyard sites occupy the southern slopes, where they are sheltered from northern and north-westerly winds by relatively high, forested peaks. Of these, the top sites are open to the east or west to promote air circulation and to discourage FROSTS.

The volcanic activity which began 15 million years ago and dominated geological processes here for 6 million years created a great TOPOGRAPHICAL diversity in the Tokaj-Eperjes range. The spectrum of VOLCANIC rocks that can be found in the area includes rhyolite, rhyodacite, dacite, andesite, and even BASALT, which is much more typical of the volcanic hills of western Hungary. These various rock types occur as lavas and differ mainly in terms of silica content. In addition, pyroclastic rocks, most significantly TUFFS, are also found. During and after the principal eruptions, a variety of post-volcanic alterations left their stamp on the rocks of Tokaj. Volcanic rocks tend to weather faster than other igneous types and the process is accelerated here by the flow of post-volcanic groundwater and hot springs, which deliver to the surface large quantities of potassium and trace elements, which enrich the volcanic detritus.

The major centres of post-volcanic changes are in the area of Mád (sites such as Szent Tamás, Úrágya, Betsek, Urbán), Erdőbénye, Tolcsva, and Sárospatak. The southern fringes of the range were overlain by LOESS at a much later stage, during the Quaternary period when the region's main soils were developed. On the steeper slopes, the thin soils are typically mixed with weathered andesite, and are quite hard to till. In the low valleys, loess soils of the slope, clay, and glacial deposits evolved. Easily weathered volcanic glass still mingles with the soils today, enriching them in NUTRIENTS that are available to the vines. The most widespread soil type is the clayey nyirok, a red soil created by weathering volcanic rocks, particularly stony andesite. When too wet, nyirok is so sticky that it adheres to the spade; if it dries out, it will yield to nothing short of a pick-axe. It does not absorb water very well, and has low permeability. Its red colour, from ferrous hydroxide, turns darker as its HUMUS content increases. Slightly less common is the soil type known as yellow earth, which forms from loess and clayey loess, as well as sandy loess on the Kopaszhegy near Tokaj and the hills north of Olaszliszka. Loess has good drainage, and here has a low LIME content. Szarvas near Tarcal is a famous example of a vineyard with loess soil. Loess is not found in the interior of the Tokaj-Eperjes chain nor in the valleys, but on the south eastern slope of Mount Tokaj it can be found at ELEVATIONS as high as 405 m/1,330 ft.

A further soil type is the rock flour that forms from the mechanical weathering of white rhyolite, pumice, and perlite. It is crumbly, does not retain water, and has a low heat capacity, so vines planted in it may easily dry out during a DROUGHT, or freeze in extreme cold. Rock flour is the soil type of the Pereshegy at Erdőbénye, the Tolcsvaihegy, and the Oremus vineyard at Sátoraljaújhely.

Nomenclature

The two leading grape varieties, FURMINT and HÁRSLEVELŰ, have their genetic origin in Tokaj and seem to be related. Both varieties tend to produce dry wines worth ageing based on acidity, tension, body, and BALANCE.

For centuries, the two main categories of Tokaj were szűrt bor (filtered wine) and csinált bor (made wine). The former were wines made much the same way as most wine is made today, by simply pressing the grapes and fermenting the must. The latter were wines produced by the more complicated Aszú process. Clearly distinct from this noble sweet category was the typically dry ordinarium. Even in the old days, a distinction was made between free-run juice and press juice, although they were not necessarily handled separately. Főbor (principal wine) was the old name of Szamorodni-style wine, at least insofar as it was made by pressing the harvested fruit as is, without separating BOTRYTIZED berries from grapes unaffected by NOBLE ROT. From 1707 onward, Eszencia, the highest grade of Tokaj, was also increasingly referred to as legfőbb bor, meaning 'supreme wine' (legfőbb is the superlative of the adjective fő).

Dry and semi-dry wines

An increasing proportion of dry wine is made from Tokaj grapes. These are wines matured only briefly. They are typically fermented dry but may contain some RESIDUAL SUGAR (even if at a level well below semi-sweet wines). With a few exceptions, they are fermented in stainless steel and will last three to five years, depending on the vintage.

Matured dry wines. These are invariably matured in wood, with a small proportion also fermented in wooden casks, and have a very long cellaring potential. As botrytis is undesirable in these wines, the grapes must come from high-elevation vineyards (about 250 m/820 ft) designed specifically for this purpose. These are mostly single-vineyard wines and expensive wines.

Szamorodni. The grape ripeness level is comparable to that of BEERENAUSLESE, but they are fermented dry (száraz) and subjected to subtle maturation under a FILM-FORMING YEAST. These wines, which contain botrytized berries, are very like the Jura's VIN JAUNE.

Főbor. This category was known and used for centuries, but has become extremely rare. Closest to Szamorodni in style without being matured under OXIDATIVE conditions, Főbor can be either dry or sweet, depending on the natural proportion of over-ripe fruit and shrivelled, possibly botrytized, berries.

Sweet wines

Szamorodni. Typically made in the sweet style (édes), when the sugar content of the grapes is so high that the must will not ferment fully dry.

Style	Residual sugar (g/l)	Dry extract (g/l)
Aszú	120	35
Eszencia	450	50

Average residual sugar is 80–120 g/l although the minimum is 45 g/l. This barrel-aged, selected botrytized wine is matured for two or three years partly in oak. It is lightly oxidized.

Late Harvest/Cuvée. These are mostly RE-DUCTIVE sweet wines ready for release 12–16 months after harvest. This new style emerged in the early 21st century as a consequence of the substantial time and capital investment required to mature Aszú wines for a longer period in compliance with regulations. Often marked by a MINERAL character, they may contain 50–180 g/l residual sugar and (optionally) a proportion of botrytized berries similar to that for Aszú wines. Cuvée wines are generally made from botrytized grapes but barrel ageing is not mandatory. These two categories are made in the same way as other natural sweet wines in other regions, by a single fermentation of selected bunches.

Aszú and Aszúeszencia

This is the classic sweet Tokaj and usually the sweetest wine of any producer. The table above shows minimum RESIDUAL SUGAR and EXTRACT required for these designations.

Tokaj Aszú always has a high concentration of residual sugar and is made from hand-selected shrivelled, botrytized grapes. Before pressing, the harvested botrytized grapes are soaked for a period of 16 to 36 hours in fresh must, *murci* (fermenting wine), or new wine that has completed fermentation. The wine is then matured under oxidative conditions without any FORTIFICATION, including at least two years in barrel. The unique second fermentation gives a special, deeper character to the wines. The classification of sweetness by the number of *puttonyos* is no longer part of Hungarian wine law.

The following categories of sweet Tokaji are relatively rare:

Eszencia. The free-run juice of hand-picked botrytized berries. Residual sugar should be at least 450 g/l but levels of 800 g/l or more are not unheard of. Eszencia takes years to achieve a modest alcohol level of 4–5%. It is rarely sold commercially, and smaller wineries will not handle it separately. It is typically used for blending to improve the concentration of Aszú wines.

Fordítás. Made by refermenting wine or must poured on Tokaj Aszú 'paste' (marc) left after pressing sweet wines, typically with more than 60 g/l sugar (minimum 45 g/l).

Máslás. Rarity made by refermenting new wine or must poured on Tokaj Aszú lees.

Sweet wines, typically with 50–90 g/l sugar. No longer an official category.

The Mádi Kör, the local wine authority, has drawn up a rather Burgundian vineyard classification which means in practice that the member wineries are obliged to follow stricter regulations in vine-growing and winemaking than are required by general Hungarian rules.

The most highly regarded producers include István Szepsy, Tokaj Hétszőlő (owned by the Michel Reybier of Ch Cos d'Estournel), Hold-völgy, Tokaj Oremus (owned by VEGA SICILIA), Disznókő (owned by AXA), Királyudvar, István Balassa, Zoltán Demeter, Judit Bott, Barta Pince, DemeterVin, and the Royal Tokaji Wine Company. Wine writer Hugh JOHNSON and other private investors set up the Royal Tokaji Wine Company in 1989 and the early 1990s saw an unusually cosmopolitan range of investors dedicated to restoring the image of this noble wine.   G.R & G.M.

Alkonyi, L., *Tokaj* (Budapest, 2000).

Alkonyi, L., *Tokaj—the Myth of Terroir* (Budapest, 2004).

Balassa, I., *Tokaj-Hegyalja Szőleje és Bora* (Tokaj, 1991). Tokaj-Hegyalja Vineyard and Wine, English summary.

Rohály, G., Mészáros, G., and Nagymarosy, A., *Terra Benedicta—Tokaj and Beyond* (Budapest, 2003).

Tokaj-Hegyaljai Album (1867).

Tokay was the name under which TOKAJ used to travel. It was also the original name of the Australian STICKIE made from raisined Muscadelle grapes that, because the Hungarians objected, has been renamed TOPAQUE.

Tokay d'Alsace, or simply **Tokay**, was also for long the Alsace name for PINOT GRIS but was officially outlawed from 2007.

Tomar, DOP subregion of TEJO in central, southern Portugal.

tonneau, traditional Bordeaux measure of wine volume, once a large wooden cask holding 900 l, or 252 imperial wine gallons, the equivalent of four BARRIQUES. A PARIS tonneau was 800 l, but, because of the prominence of GASCON merchants in London and English merchants in Bordeaux, the Bordeaux measure became the standard. By the end of the 18th century, tonneaux had been replaced by the easier to transport smaller barrique, yet the tonneau, the exact equivalent of 100 CASES of wine, is still the measure in which the Bordeaux wine trade deals.

Such was the importance of wine to medieval trade in general (see BORDEAUX and DUTCH WINE TRADE), that a tonneau, or ton in English, evolved from being the space occupied by a tun of wine, to become the unit of measurement

for the carrying capacity of any ship, whatever its load.

Topaque and Muscat, extremely sweet FORTIFIED WINES that used to be called Liqueur Tokay and Liqueur Muscat. They taste something like a cross between MADEIRA and traditional dark MÁLAGA, and are two of AUSTRALIA's great gifts to the world made from, respectively, MUSCADELLE, traditionally known as Tokay in Australia, and a very dark-skinned strain of MUSCAT BLANC À PETITS GRAINS, called here Brown Muscat. The centre of production is a hot north eastern corner of the state of Victoria around the towns of Rutherglen and Glenrowan. Grapes are semi-raisined on the vine, partially fermented, and then fortified with grape spirit before being subjected to an unusual wood-ageing programme that resembles a cross between a sherry SOLERA and, under many a hot tin roof, a Madeira ESTUFAGEM. The results can be uncannily fine quality, are bottled when they are ready to drink, and do not change with BOTTLE AGE. These wines are quite sweet enough to serve with virtually any dessert. In the late 1990s, the winemakers of Rutherglen joined forces to create a four-tier nomenclature for Muscat (and, by extension, Topaque). At the bottom is Rutherglen Muscat, next is Classic, then Grand, and finally Rare. It is a voluntary, self-regulated system, but is a very real guarantee of style, which becomes progressively richer and more complex with each tier. Rare is released in tiny quantities each year, limited by the maintenance of a very old Solera base.

top grafting, or **top working**, the viticultural operation of changing the fruiting VINE VARIETY of a mature vineyard by inserting a bud of the selected variety in each vine, but retaining the established root system. An array of approaches is available: CLEFT GRAFTING, NOTCH GRAFTING, CHIP BUDDING, or T-BUDDING, usually applied high on the original trunk just below the HEAD. If the operation is done well, only one season's crop is lost. The main risk is that of systemic disease spread from the original planting, especially VIRUS DISEASES to which different varieties and rootstocks have different tolerances.   B.G.C.

topoclimate, a local climate as determined by TOPOGRAPHY, for instance that of a particular hill, valley, or slope. It is commonly subsumed under the broader term MESOCLIMATE.

topography, a term describing the land surface features of any area, which can have considerable implications for local climate (see MESOCLIMATE) and therefore for viticulture. The classic reference work by Geiger gives the most comprehensive general account of topographic effects on local climate. Topographic elements having the most influence on the climate are

Topography: Surface-chilled air drifts down the hillsides and side valleys and away down the main valley floor, bypassing a projecting hill (A) and an isolated hill (B). Because the projecting and isolated hills have no external sources of chilled air, they remain more or less entirely in the stable or circulating warm upper air.

local ELEVATION; slope; the relative isolation of hills; aspect; and proximity to water masses such as oceans, lakes, and rivers.

Local elevation Other things being equal, temperature falls by about 0.6 °C/1.1 °F per 100 m/330 ft greater elevation. This is known as the lapse rate.

Slope At night, air is chilled by direct contact with a land surface which is rapidly losing heat by radiation. The chilled air, being denser, flows down slopes to the flat land or valleys below, and is replaced by warmer air from above the land surface. The turbulent surface air over slopes at moderate elevations is therefore usually warmer at night, and in the early morning, than that settled over the adjacent flats and valley floors. This band on a hill slope is known as its 'thermal zone', and especially in cool climates is valued for viticulture because of its enhanced ripening potential and length of frost-free period. The steeper the slope, the more pronounced is its thermal zone. See also HILLSIDE VINEYARDS.

Relative isolation of hills Thermal zones are strongest on isolated and projecting hills or mountains, because these have little or no external source of surface-chilled air. Cooled air from their own surfaces that slips away can be replaced only by totally unchilled air from above. The implications of this are discussed under CLIMATE AND WINE QUALITY; see also TERROIR. Examples of viticulturally famous isolated hills include the hill of Corton at ALOXE-CORTON in Burgundy; the Kaiserstuhl in BADEN; and, on a

larger scale, the Montagne de Reims in CHAMPAGNE.

Aspect Slopes which face the sun through much of the day (southerly aspects in the northern hemisphere, and northerly aspects in the southern hemisphere) are the warmest, and those facing away from the sun are the coolest. The influence of aspect is modified by other climate parameters. For example, the degree of daytime warming is increased by more sunshine and by protection from wind. Differences in soil temperature are important not only for nutrition of the vine, but also for growth and fruiting through export of the growth substance CYTOKININ to the vine tops.

The climatic contrasts among aspects are greatest at high latitudes and in cooler vineyard regions, and also early and late in the vine-growing season. The steeper the slope, the more aspect will affect its climate.

Easterly aspects of slopes facing the equator have the advantage that they are warmed earliest in the day, when soil and air temperatures are lowest. Notable examples of this are found in the CÔTE D'OR of Burgundy, and in the RHINE Valley of Germany and Alsace. West-facing slopes can, however, induce higher daytime air temperatures because absorption of sunlight and warmer air temperatures are complementary. This is important in very cool climates.

Proximity to oceans, lakes, and rivers Water absorbs and stores large quantities of heat, with relatively little change in temperature because of the depth to which the heat penetrates, together with the high specific heat of water

compared with rocks or dry soil. Its resulting temperature inertia greatly modifies the temperature regimes of adjacent land. Cool air from over the water is drawn to replace heated air rising over the land in the afternoons, while at night a reverse convection results from chilled air descending from the cold land surface and rising over the now relatively warm water. In some vineyard areas, these breezes may, in fact, be very strong winds if they are funnelled by mountains, as in the Salinas Valley in MONTEREY, California. This daily alternating pattern of air circulation makes the climate adjacent to water bodies significantly more constant than it would otherwise be, in terms of both temperature and humidity. Both factors are important in CLIMATE AND WINE QUALITY. There is also a reduced incidence of spring FROSTS and WINTER FREEZE injury in regions liable to these. Examples of this LAKE EFFECT are found in NEW YORK state, in the vineyards of Ontario in CANADA, and around RUSSIA's Black Sea coast.

The effects of rivers and lakes are normally confined to their immediate valleys, but MARITIME influences can extend considerable distances inland from coasts in the form of land and sea breezes. Notable examples of the latter occur in the BORDEAUX region of France; the NAPA Valley and SONOMA and other near-coastal regions of California; and the HUNTER VALLEY and SWAN VALLEY of Australia's east and west coasts respectively.   J.G. & R.E.S.

Geiger, R., *Das Klima der bodennahen Luftschicht* (4th edn, Brunswick, 1961), trans. as *The Climate near the Ground* (Cambridge, Mass., 1966).

topping. See TRIMMING.

topping up, *ouillage* in French, the operation of refilling any sort of wooden container to replace wine lost through EVAPORATION. The container should be kept full or nearly full lest the ubiquitous ACETOBACTER use OXYGEN from the head space to start the process of transforming wine into VINEGAR. The well-run winery will have a strict regime of topping up all wooden containers on a regular basis.

A BARREL closed with a sound, new, inert plastic BUNG loses liquid by diffusion through the barrel's staves. The HEAD SPACE created by this liquid loss is filled with water and alcohol vapours, together with traces of CARBON DIOXIDE. Since no oxygen can enter the head space, there is no danger of acetification and topping up is not necessary.

Winemakers differ in what they view as the ideal topping-up regime for various different wines, but modern practice is to top up at least monthly, using wine of the same provenance and, often, filling the barrel so that some wine is ejected when the BUNG is driven into the bung-hole.

Depending on the amount of evaporation, which is affected by fluctuations in temperature and humidity in the cellar, and the spare time available to the winery staff, topping up is done anything from twice a week to once every six weeks. The cellar temperature should be about 50–55 °F (10–13 ºC): not so cold as to hinder development but not so warm as to encourage bacterial growth. New barrels may also need more frequent topping up since the new oak absorbs up to 5 l of wine. In Bordeaux the bung is often left at the top of the barrel so as to maximize AERATION of the young wine for the first six months, after which the barrel may be rolled to one side so that the bung is in the so-called bung-over position. Thus the bung and bung-hole region are kept moist and aeration is reduced. Many New World wineries have adopted this practice, even for Burgundian varieties, as it is much less labour intensive than constant topping up.

See also ULLAGE.   M.K., V.L., & D.D.

Torbato, mid to late ripening vine variety today most obviously associated with SARDINIA, where varietal dry whites are produced from a grand total of under 20 ha in 2010, with particular success around Alghero.

It was once quite widely cultivated in ROUSSILLON, where it is known as TOURBAT, or Malvoisie du Roussillon, but was almost abandoned before new and healthier plant material was imported from Sardinia in the 1980s. As with GRENACHE NOIR, known as Cannonau in Sardinia, it is believed to have been brought to the island from Spain when Sardinia was part of the Aragón kingdom, but this is unproved.

Torgiano, small hillside DOC zone between Perugia and Assisi in the central Italian region of UMBRIA. It was considered Umbria's finest red wine in the 1960s and 1970s when the production of bottled wine was almost entirely in the hands of the Lungarotti family, who demonstrated that the SANGIOVESE vine could yield excellent wine outside TUSCANY. Production rules have regrettably been changed to allow VARIETALS based on INTERNATIONAL VARIETIES with no history in the zone such as Torgiano Pinot Grigio and Torgiano Pinot Noir. Up to 50% Merlot and/or Cabernet Sauvignon are now allowed in Rosso di Torgiano, originally a Sangiovese-based wine. At least 70% Sangiovese is required in DOCG Torgiano Rosso Riserva, but overall the current spirit of Torgiano appears to be marketing-oriented.

torna viagem, literally means 'round trip' in Portuguese and is occasionally found on labels of ancient SETÚBAL which have been subjected to lengthy sea voyages for ageing purposes. This is the equivalent of the *vinho da roda* of MADEIRA.

Toro, revolutionized Spanish red wine zone in CASTILLA Y LEÓN (see map under SPAIN) whose wines were famous within Spain in medieval times. This wild and remote zone spans the Duero valley east of Zamora. It was accorded DO status in 1987. At an ELEVATION of between 600 and 750 m/2,000–2,800 ft, growing conditions are severe. The dry, stony soils can support cereals or vines. The region's principal grape variety, Tinta de Toro, is a local variant of Rioja's TEMPRANILLO which has adapted to the climatic extremes of this part of Spain. The grapes need careful handling. Left to their own devices, they will easily ripen to a POTENTIAL ALCOHOL level of 16%. Local regulations permit a maximum ALCOHOLIC STRENGTH of 15% but the best wines usually have a strength of around 13.5. A small number of producers have fostered a move away from the heavy, bulk reds of recent times, a move which gained notable momentum when some of the greatest names in Ribera del Duero, Rioja, and even Bordeaux were awakened to the region's potential and launched their own estates, particularly Vega Sicilia's Pintia, Mauro's San Román, Sierra Cantabria's Numanthia-Termes (subsequently acquired by LVMH), Michel Rolland's Campo Elíseo, Telmo Rodríguez's Pago La Jara, Jacques Lurton's El Albar, in addition to the home-grown Bienvenida Sitio del Palo, Paydos, and Quinta Quietud. By 2010, Toro's 5,700 ha/ 14,000 acres of vineyard supplied nearly 50 bodegas.   V. de la S.

www.dotoro.com

Torontel, Chilean white wine grape that is probably identical to the aromatic TORRONTÉS Riojano of Argentina. There were still 585 ha/ 1,445 acres in 2013, mainly BUSH VINES in MAULE.

Torres SA, Miguel, Spain's largest family-owned producer of premium wine and Spanish brandy, based in PENEDÈS in north-east Spain. The present company was founded in 1870 by Miguel and Jaime Torres with the fruits of a chance investment by Jaime in a Cuban oil company. A winery was established at Vilafranca del Penedès near Barcelona and its produce was shipped to Cuba in a fleet also belonging to Torres. Miguel's son Juan expanded the business within Spain and left a thriving family business to his son, another Miguel, in 1932. After confiscation, disruption, and even winery destruction during the Spanish Civil War, Miguel rebuilt the business and as early as the 1940s decided to concentrate on selling wine in bottle rather than in bulk.

Perhaps the most significant development in the history of Torres came in 1959 when Miguel's son Miguel A. Torres went to study in DIJON. This resulted in experimental plantings of vine varieties imported from France and Germany such as Cabernet Sauvignon, Chardonnay, Riesling, Gewürztraminer, and Sauvignon Blanc. Torres also introduced vine TRELLIS SYSTEMS. A modern laboratory was established, temperature-controlled stainless steel fermentation vessels were installed, and red wines were bottled after just 18 months' BARREL MATURATION in cool cellars hewn out of the hillside. All of these techniques, and a host of other innovations, were then quite unknown elsewhere in Spain.

Vindication of Miguel A. Torres's achievements came in 1979, when, in the well-publicized 'wine olympics' organized by the French gastronomic magazine *Gault-Millau*, Torres Gran Coronas Black Label 1970 was voted winner of the top Cabernet class. In 1982/3 he spent a sabbatical year at MONTPELLIER, and has since introduced higher VINE DENSITIES, increasingly ORGANIC methods, MECHANICAL PRUNING, and a programme to recuperate Catalan INDIGENOUS VARIETIES. About 75% of all Spanish wine produced by Torres is exported.

On the death of his father in 1991, Miguel A. Torres became president of the company with particular responsibilities for winemaking. He has also been one of Spain's most prolific wine writers, and was one of the first wine producers in the world to take SUSTAINABILITY issues seriously. In 2004, the company invested in Ribera del Duero, Jumilla, and Toro and by the mid 2010s, Torres owned about 2,000 ha of vineyard in Penedès, Priorat, and other areas of Spain, 400 ha in Chile, part of which belong to the estate near Curicó in CHILE which he established in 1978, and 32 ha in California. His sister Marimar is a food writer based in San Francisco and manages Marimar Estate in SONOMA county's Russian River Valley. In 1997, a decade earlier than most of its peers, the Spanish company embarked on a JOINT VENTURE in China involving a bottling plant and viticulture experiments. In 1999 Torres founded its own distribution company in Shanghai which today employs 300 people and has become the second largest wine distributor in China. Since September 2012 Miguel A.'s son, another Miguel, has been general manager of Torres group while his daughter Mireia directs the Jean Leon winery which Torres acquired in 1994 and the winery in Priorat that was built in 1996.

Torres Vedras, DOP subregion of LISBOA in western Portugal.

Torrontés, name of many distinct white grape varieties grown in Argentina and Spain, not always named with precision.

Argentina grows at least three different varieties with Torrontés in their name. The most common, planted on 7,683 ha/18,977 acres in 2011, is **Torrontés Riojano**, a natural cross of MUSCAT OF ALEXANDRIA and CRIOLLA CHICA (California's MISSION grape), as shown by DNA

PROFILING in 2003. It is the most planted white wine grape after the undistinguished Pedro Giménez and is regarded as Argentina's most distinctive white wine grape. See also TORONTEL. **Torrontés Sanjuanino**, a distinct speciality of San Juan province and another natural cross of Muscat of Alexandria and Criolla Chica, was planted on just 2,048 ha (and, as Moscatel de Austria, 53 ha of Chile), while plantings of **Torrontés Mendocino** were under 700 ha. This third variety is also the result of a natural cross of Muscat of Alexandria, but the other parent is so far unknown.

The fragrant **Torrontés Riojana** is often seen as the Argentine white wine variety with the greatest potential although some wines can be over-alcoholic and bitter. Carefully grown and vinified, **Torrontés Riojana** can produce wines that are high in acidity, and intriguingly aromatic in a way reminiscent of but not identical to MUSCAT, although much is also used for blending. Grown all over the country, and to a limited extent in Uruguay, the variety seems particularly well adapted to the arid growing conditions of Argentina, particularly the high, sandy vineyards of Cafayate where at ELEVATIONS of over 1,600 m/5,250 ft its high natural acidity and assertive flavour are particularly distinguished.

Torrontés Sanjuanino is less aromatic, and has bigger berries and more compact clusters. Despite its name, Torrontés Mendocino is most common in Río Negro province in the south, and lacks Muscat aroma.

DNA PROFILING has shown that the name Torrontés is applied to at least four distinct varieties in Spain: in Montilla-Moriles, Navarra, Ribeiro in Galicia (which may be identical to either FERNÃO PIRES or BICAL), and in Extramadura where it is a synonym of ALARIJE. Torrontes is also a common synonym for several different varieties in Portugal. Altogether, Torrontes represents an identification minefield on the Iberian Peninsular. The situation is much clearer in Argentina, even if the varieties' parents are not the most noble.

Toscana, important central Italian region known in English as TUSCANY.

total acidity (TA), measure of the total ACIDITY, both FIXED ACIDS and VOLATILE ACIDS, present in grape juice or wine. With ALCOHOLIC STRENGTH and RESIDUAL SUGAR, total acidity is one of the most common wine measurements involved in any wine ANALYSIS.

It is obtained by a laboratory process called titration (which is why it is also referred to as titratable acidity, although technically they are not exactly the same, according to Boulton), in which very small additions of an alkali of known strength are made to a measured quantity of the grape juice or wine until the amount of added alkali just equals the amount of acids in the sample. The value of these total acids can be calculated and expressed as grams of any number of different acids per litre of juice or wine. By tradition, different wine regions have chosen to express total acidity variously as TARTARIC ACID or sulfuric acid, or milliequivalents.

France and a few other European countries tend to express total acidity as sulfuric, even though the amount of this compound in grapes and wine is minuscule. However, the growth of international trade has demanded consistent terminology so that most major producers and exporters report acidity as tartaric. A further complication arises with what is termed the end point of the titration, with some countries using pH 7.0 and others pH 8.2. For many years both the OIV and EU methods of analysis have specified a pH 7.0 end point, but some countries are slow to change.

The total acidity of wines expressed as tartaric acid normally varies between about 4 g/l and 9 g/l, and primarily depends on the grape variety and the climate. Warmer-climate wines generally have lower acid levels; some of the highest levels can be found in bottle-fermented SPARKLING WINES and in cool-climate late-harvest wines. The total acidity of ripe grape juice or must should ideally be in the general range of 7 to 10 g/l expressed as tartaric acid, although it may in practice be between 3 and 16 g/l. (Some acid is usually lost during winemaking, as a result of MALOLACTIC CONVERSION and cold STABILIZATION, so one may need to start with a higher acidity than the final one desired.)   G.T.

Boulton, R., 'The relationship between total acidity, titratable acidity and pH in wine', *American Journal of Enology and Viticulture*, 31/1 (1980), 76–80.

total dry extract, or TDE. See EXTRACT.

total package oxygen (TPO) is the awkward but efficient neologism used to refer to the total amount of OXYGEN that can influence the development, quality, and longevity of a wine once it has been bottled. It includes any oxygen that passes through the CLOSURE (see OXYGEN TRANSMISSION RATE), oxygen that diffuses out of the closure itself, oxygen in the HEAD SPACE, and dissolved oxygen in the wine. New non-destructive methods based on luminescence, as well as other destructive methods based on the use of dyes, have enabled the accurate measurement of TPO. It is clear that unless the pick up of oxygen throughout the winemaking and BOTTLING processes is controlled, there is little point in stoppering the bottle with closures that are highly engineered to control oxygen ingress.

Ugliano, M., et al., 'Controlling oxygen at bottling to optimize post-bottling development of wine', *Practical Winery & Vineyard* (Winter 2013), 1–4.

Toul, Côtes de, small AOC in the far north east of France which remains, with the even more northerly French wine region on the MOSELLE, as a reminder of what was once a flourishing Lorraine wine industry. It was subsequently marginalized by industrialization, injudicious replanting after PHYLLOXERA, the First World War, and the delimitation of the nearby CHAMPAGNE region which had once drawn wine from here. Gamay with some Pinot Noir is responsible for the local pale pink speciality VIN GRIS. Pinot Noir is the only ingredient in Toul's relatively light reds. AUXERROIS is the most successful variety for dry whites.

Touraine, the most important Loire region centred on the town of Tours (see map under LOIRE). This is 'the garden of France', and Loire château country *par excellence*, a series of playgrounds for France's pre-revolutionary aristocrats, and now the Parisian weekender's rural paradise. The local TUFFEAU was quarried extensively to build these and more distant châteaux, leaving caves ideal for winemaking and wine maturation.

Touraine's most famous wines are the still red wines from the individual appellations of BOURGUEIL, CHINON, and St-Nicolas-de-Bourgueil and its still and sparkling, dry to sweet whites from VOUVRAY and MONTLOUIS.

Wines called simply Touraine AOC come from a much larger zone, incorporating about 3,683 ha/9,097 acres of vineyard (much less than in the 1990s) in total extending from SAUMUR in the west as far as the city of Blois in the east, encompassing very varied soils which may include clay, sand, tuffeau, and gravel. Viticulture is concentrated on the steep banks of the Loire and its tributary the Cher east of Tours. Cereals predominate on the cooler soils of the plateaux between river valleys. The climate of the region also shows considerable variation, with that of the most eastern vineyards being distinctly CONTINENTAL and affected by seriously cold winters, while vineyards at the western extreme are tempered by the influence of the Atlantic.

If soil and climate vary considerably throughout Touraine, there is an enormous range of grape varieties too. White Touraine, the most important colour, must be made substantially from Sauvignon Blanc with only Sauvignon Gris, up to 20%, allowed as a blending partner. The best of these can provide a less expensive alternative to SANCERRE and POUILLY-FUMÉ.

Touraine Rouge should be based on Cot (Malbec) and Cabernet Franc, with the latter favoured in the Atlantic-influenced sector west of Tours, although varietal Gamay is also allowed within the Touraine appellation, especially for PRIMEUR wines. Rosés have to be blends from the wide range of dark-skinned grapes grown in the region.

About 600 ha of vines are dedicated to the production of the **Touraine Mousseux** that is so much less important than SAUMUR Mousseux.

Five communes may attach their name to Touraine. From its 187 ha/462 acres of vines on both banks of the Loire close to the famous château of Amboise, **Touraine-Amboise** produces mainly rosé wines from Gamay, Cabernet Franc, Cabernet Sauvignon, and Cot. The appellation's white wines, dry to medium dry (or even moelleux—notably produced by Amboise's excellent viticultural college Domaine de la Gabillière) depending on the year, are made exclusively from the long-lived Chenin Blanc.

By 2013 **Touraine-Azay-le-Rideau** comprised just 36 ha of vineyard on both banks of the Indre, south of the Loire between Tours and Chinon on soil that is superior to that of the general Touraine appellation. It produces roughly equal quantities of crisp whites from Chenin Blanc and light rosés mainly from Grolleau, rather sprightlier than Rosé d'ANJOU. **Touraine-Mesland** in 2013 comprised about 110 ha of vineyard on a sand and gravel plateau immediately above the right bank of the Loire between Amboise and Blois. Chenin and Gamay are responsible for wines of all three colours. **Touraine–Chenonceaux** and **Touraine–Oisly** in Sauvignon Blanc country were authorized in 2011, the latter for whites only. The Chenonceaux reds depend on Cabernet Franc and Cot.

Touraine-Noble Joué is an unusual appellation of barely 30 ha just south of Tours for pink wines made from at least 40% Pinot Meunier with Pinot Gris and Pinot Noir.

Tourbat is the ROUSSILLON name for Sardinia's white grape variety TORBATO. It is alternatively known as Malvoisie du Roussillon and is one of the many varieties allowed into the several VINS DOUX NATURELS of the region and Côtes du Roussillon whites.

Touriga is used as a synonym for TOURIGA NACIONAL, particularly in Australia.

Touriga Franca (formerly known as **Touriga Francesa**) is the most widely planted grape variety in the DOURO Valley, accounting for around one-fifth of all vines, and is the more common of Portugal's two Tourigas with a total of 14,357 ha/35,462 acres in 2012. Despite the name, it has no connection with France and has been shown by DNA PROFILING to be the relatively recent progeny of the Douro varieties TOURIGA NACIONAL and MARUFO. On warmer south-facing slopes it is valued for both port and Douro wines. It is classified as one of the best port varieties, although the wine it produces is not as concentrated as that of Touriga Nacional and is more susecptible to ROT. Favoured by growers for its consistent yields, it is respected by winemakers for its wines' perfume and persistent fruit. It is also widely planted in TRÁS-OS-MONTES and is spreading to other Portuguese regions such as Lisboa, Tejo, and the Alentejo.

Touriga Nacional, the most famous vine variety for port and, increasingly, for fine dry reds, and not just in PORTUGAL. It produces small quantities of very small berries in the DOURO Valley and the Portuguese DÃO region (where it probably originated) which result in deep-coloured, very tannic, concentrated wines, often with a floral aroma in youth. The vine is vigorous and robust but is prone to COULURE and may produce just 300 g/10 oz of fruit per vine, making it unpopular with growers. This almost led to its extinction in the mid 20th century but considerable work has been done on CLONAL SELECTION of the variety so that newer cuttings are slightly more productive and average sugar levels even higher. Touriga Nacional is proportionately more important in its native Dão than the Douro and can make fine VARIETAL reds here, although the variety is regarded by many as better in a blend. Touriga Nacional plantings have been increasing considerably, not least because it has migrated south into most other Portuguese wine regions. Its total area had reached 10,531 ha/26,012 acres by 2012. Touriga Nacional has also been travelling extensively outside Portugal—notably to Australia in its capacity as an ALTERNATIVE VARIETY, California, and South Africa—although each of them had only about 100 ha by 2014. Its distinctive name, proliferation of varietal versions from Portugal, and its nominal hint at the glories of QUINTA DO NOVAL Nacional are expected to continue its worldwide spread.

tourism. Wine-related tourism continues to be increasingly important to both producers and consumers. For many centuries, not even wine merchants travelled, but today many members of the general public deliberately make forays to explore a wine region or regions. This is partly a reflection of the increased interest in both wine and foreign travel generally, but also because most wine regions and many producers' premises are attractive places. VINEYARDS tend to be aesthetically pleasing in any case, and the sort of climate in which wine is generally produced is agreeable at least during the growing season and very possibly for most of the year. Getting to grips with this specialist form of agriculture combines urban dwellers' need to commune with nature with acquiring privileged, and generally admired, specialist knowledge. And then there is the possibility of TASTING, and buying wines direct from the source, which may involve keen prices and/or acquiring rarities. (CELLAR DOOR sales can be particularly attractive to wine drinkers living in countries with high DUTY levels on alcohol.)

Wine tourism is certainly not new to Germany. The RHINE has long welcomed tourists, who are encouraged to travel by steamer and stop at wine villages en route, and the MOSEL Valley is surely one of the most photographed in the world. German tourists, on the other hand, have long plundered the Weinstuben of ALSACE and represent an important market for the region's wines.

In France, wine tourism was often accidental. Northern Europeans heading for the sun for decades travelled straight through BURGUNDY and the northern RHÔNE and could hardly fail to notice vineyards and the odd invitation 'Dégustation–Vente' (tasting–sale). (And it is true that a tasting almost invariably leads to a sale.) Wine producers in the LOIRE have long profited from their location in the midst of châteaux country, and within an easy Friday night's drive of Paris.

BORDEAUX was one of the last important French wine regions to realize its potential for wine tourism, although the city itself is determinedly making up for lost time. The village of ST-ÉMILION has had scores of wine shops and restaurants for decades but it was not until the late 1980s that the MÉDOC, the most famous cluster of wine properties in the world, had a hotel and more than one restaurant suitable for international visitors. Alexis LICHINE was mocked for being virtually the only CLASSED GROWTH proprietor openly to welcome visitors but there are now others, albeit fewer than one would expect.

Much of southern Europe is simply too hot, and too far from suitable resorts, to make wine tourism comfortable and feasible, but AGRITUR-ISMO has played an extremely important part in the viticultural economy of Italy.

In various NEW WORLD wine regions, tourism has also become an important aspect of business. Prominent examples here include NAPA Valley, now almost part and parcel of the San Francisco tourist experience; SOUTH AFRICAN vineyards within easy reach of Cape Town; NEW ZEALAND, the most southerly wine areas of which are just as breathtakingly beautiful as those of the Cape; HUNTER VALLEY for visitors to and residents of Sydney; upper NEW YORK state; and even the vineyards of ENGLAND, whose owners depend heavily on income from 'farmgate' sales.

Some tour operators and travel agents specialize in wine tourism, and the number of wine regions without their own special wine route or winery trail is decreasing rapidly. The first annual wine tourism conference was held in 2011.

www.greatwinecapitals.com

tourne, wine fault caused by BACTERIA which turn the wine brown and cloudy.

tractor, the most common vineyard machine. Tractor dimensions have had a significant impact on vineyard design. In many parts of Europe where tractors replaced horses, tractor designers obliged by creating either narrow, or row-straddling, tractors (known in France as *tracteurs-enjambeurs*). The narrowest vineyard tractors are not much wider than their drivers, about 80 cm/31 in. In the New World, however, vineyards were changed to accommodate the tractors, which included row spacings of 3 to 4 m (10–13 ft) to allow early and wide tractor models between the rows. Modern New World tractors are much narrower and can fit down rows less than 2 m apart.

The introduction of tractors and other forms of MECHANIZATION to viticulture has had profound economic and sociological effects. Less LABOUR was required, encouraging the population drift to the cities. However, a very few growers concerned about SOIL COMPACTION or constrained by steeply sloping vineyards have returned to HORSE-drawn ploughs, especially popular among those practising BIODYNAMIC VITICULTURE. R.E.S.

trade, wine. The world of wine is better known for its sociability than its profitability. What is needed to make a small fortune in the wine business is said to be a large fortune. The wine trade is considerably more amusing, however, than many others. It routinely involves immersion in an often delicious product, travel to some of the more beautiful corners of the world (TOURISM), typically with a MEDITERRANEAN CLIMATE, and provides widely admired expertise.

One of the attractions of the wine trade is the people. It has for long attracted a wide range of individualists who, if they were not interesting and amusing before they or their visitors have tasted their wares, seem so afterwards. Producers and merchants alike tend to be generous, and to appreciate the fact that it is difficult to sell or buy wine without tasting and sharing it.

Apprenticeship is probably the easiest route into the wine trade, although some form of specialist EDUCATIONAL qualification can help too. The general areas in which full-time employment may be found include vineyard management, winemaking and quality control, sales and marketing, wholesaling, retailing, and, the job with potentially the most power and perks, buying. There are also the overcrowded fields of WINE WRITING, consulting (in some form), and INVESTMENT. See also wine MERCHANTS.

tradition, defined by oenologist Émile PEYNAUD as an experiment that has worked, is an extremely important ingredient in viticulture and winemaking in many Old World regions and is increasingly emulated outside Europe. A significant proportion of older small-scale producers in regions such as Burgundy and the Rhône, for example, do things in the vineyard and cellar precisely because their fathers did, even if their own children are likely to have been exposed to SCIENCE through some sort of formal training. These graduates of ACADEME may understand the reasons for some of these supposedly traditional methods better than their parents, but they do not necessarily change them.

Some peasant wine-growers, for example, will perform operations such as RACKING or BOTTLING only when the moon is in a certain phase (see BIODYNAMIC VITICULTURE), or when the wind is, or is not, blowing from a certain direction. Superstition plays a very small part in making wine, and these traditions are likely to have evolved for a reason, often one that is eventually explained by science. Some French wine producers, such as those in CHÂTEAUNEUF-DU-PAPE, informally call their regular bottlings Tradition.

traditional method, official EU term for the most painstaking way of making wine sparkle, once known as the champagne method. As explained by Tom Stevenson in the website article cited below, the English have a strong claim to have invented the method or *méthode champenoise*. See SPARKLING WINEMAKING for how it works.

www.wine-pages.com/guests/tom/no-merret-in-digby.htm

traditional terms are words or phrases used on wine labels that enjoy special protection within the EU. They can be phrases such as Appellation d'Origine Contrôlée or Vin de Pays which are alternatives to PDO or PGI. They can also be 'the description of a product characteristic' referring to production method (e.g. RANCIO, PASSITO, EISWEIN), ageing method (e.g. SUR LIE, RISERVA, GARRAFEIRA), colour (e.g. *chiaretto*), place of production (e.g. *château*), or, rather more obscurely, 'a particular event linked to the history of a PDO or PGI wine' (e.g. Liebfraumilch). Terms such as *château, sur lie*, vintage, CLASSIC, etc. have been the source of some controversy as non-EU producers have protested that the EU should not limit the rights of all producers to use words that are purely descriptive or in the public domain. J.B.

ec.europa.eu/agriculture/markets/wine/e-bac chus/index.cfm?event=searchPTradTerms&lan guage=EN.

Traditionsweingüter Österreich, promotional organization of 17 growers in NIEDERÖSTERREICH in AUSTRIA that has developed a CLASSIFICATION of selected and ostensibly superior vineyard sites under the rubric ERSTE LAGE, pledging not to market wines dedicated to those sites prior to September following their harvest, a restraint rare in the context of Austria's general fixation on young wine. The name simply means traditional wineries of Austria. In attempting to set an example of model vineyard classification, the Traditionsweingüter invites growers from outside its group to participate so that in theory all of the best sites will receive their due. Growers propose candidates both for Erste Lage status as well as for a much larger cast of merely *Klassifizierte Lagen* (classified sites), with promotion or demotion to be determined ultimately on the basis of blind tastings among the participants. Because their VINEA WACHAU association pre-dates and is structured entirely differently from the Traditionsweingüter, growers in the WACHAU are not participants, initially anyway. D.S.

training in a wine context usually means VINE TRAINING. See below.

training systems, methods of VINE TRAINING, which vary considerably around the world. They are known in French as *systèmes de*

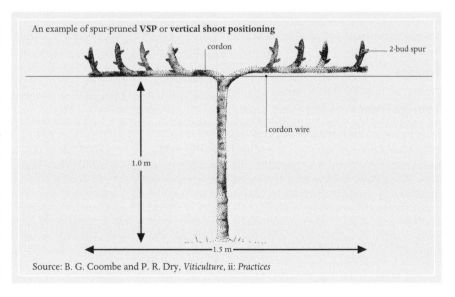

An example of spur-pruned **VSP** or **vertical shoot positioning**

cordon
2-bud spur
cordon wire
1.0 m
1.5 m

Source: B. G. Coombe and P. R. Dry, *Viticulture*, ii: *Practices*

conduite. Since the grapevine is a true VINE, and is not self-supporting like a tree, innumerable training systems for vines have been devised over the millennia of cultivation (see OENOTRIA for example). Confusion between the terms training systems, TRELLIS SYSTEMS, and PRUNING is widespread. In fact they are three distinct, if closely related, entities. A trellis is a man-made physical structure, consisting normally of POSTS, generally made of wood, and WIRES. The word training describes the actions of pruning in winter and summer, and SHOOT and CANE placement, so that the vine's TRUNK, ARMS, and CORDONS and BUDS are appropriately located on the trellis system. Those training systems which involve trellises are often named after the trellis.

The viticulturist's choice of training system will be affected by the cost of the system, the availability of any materials required, the availability of the skilled LABOUR required to install and manage it, CLIMATE, TOPOGRAPHY, vine VIGOUR, VINE VARIETY, MECHANIZATION requirements, and, in many instances, knowledge of alternative systems. In many places in the world, especially the OLD WORLD, little thought is given to using any but the region's traditional system. In the New World, more consideration is given to the choice of training system, because of recent research into CANOPY MANAGEMENT which has shown substantial benefits in terms of YIELD, wine quality, and disease reduction by adopting new designs. Training systems may be dictated by requirements for MECHANICAL HARVESTING and MECHANICAL PRUNING.

A basic difference in training systems about which the casual observer may wonder is why some vineyards have trellis systems with wires, and others not. While self-supporting GOBELET vines are common in southern Europe, in many countries such vineyards are considered old-fashioned, and WIRES to suspend foliage are used instead. A particular disadvantage of gobelet training is that the yield has to be limited when the vines are young while the trunk and arms grow sufficient girth and strength to be self-supporting. The control of vine VIGOUR and VINE DISEASES are the principal reasons for adopting more elaborate systems. If vines were planted to the gobelet system in an area of summer rainfall such as northern France, the vines could be more prone to FUNGAL DISEASES because the leaves and fruit would be in a shaded, humid environment; no SHOOT POSITIONING is used with gobelet systems. It would also be difficult to gain access to the vineyard, as the shoots would cover the ground. Lifting the foliage up and containing it between wires allows TRIMMING of the ends and LEAF REMOVAL for better fruit exposure. Both tractor access to the vineyard and airflow within it are also improved by shoot positioning.

The vine is pruned in winter as a means of training the framework and buds into an appropriate position to be supported by the trellis system.

A vine-training system should aim to maximize yield and quality, and to facilitate cultural operations such as spraying, cultivation, harvesting, and pruning. As the degree of mechanization increases, so does the need for the vineyard to be uniform and orderly. For example, mechanical leaf removal and harvesting are made easier by locating the bunches of grapes in a single zone. Similarly, mechanization of summer and winter pruning is made easier if the vine shoots and canes all point in the same direction, vertically upwards, for example. The vine framework should ideally be at a convenient height for any hand operations, neither too high nor too low. Some would argue that the fruit should be near the ground to absorb reflected heat, although this can involve back-breaking labour at HARVEST and pruning, and is more difficult to mechanize.

Until the 1960s, it was extremely rare for any training system other than that traditionally used in a given region to be considered. In many parts of the world, little has changed, although the recently developed vineyards of some NEW WORLD regions have evaluated the various systems and adopted those best suited to their requirements.

There is an almost infinite variety of vine-training systems; there are few plants whose cultivation can vary as much as between the densely planted (10,000 vines per ha or 4,000 per acre), neatly trimmed vertical hedges of the vineyards of the Médoc and the vineyards of a few hundred vines per hectare trained up trees around agricultural fields in the Vinho Verde region of Portugal.

Vine-training systems can be classified in a number of ways. In France, it is common to classify vines as low-trained (*vignes basses*) or high-trained (*vignes hautes*). For low vines, the trunk is up to 50 cm/20 in high, but usually shorter. Such training systems are suited to lower-vigour vineyards. Grape RIPENING may benefit from the fruit being closer to the ground, but both HARVEST and PRUNING are much less comfortable manual operations, and vines may also be more disease prone. The many examples of low-trained vines in France include the extensive southern areas of GOBELET, the CORDON DE ROYAT vines of Burgundy and Champagne, and the double GUYOT of Bordeaux.

High vines are less common in modern France but were certainly known by Roman authors (see AGRICULTURAL TREATISES). Interest in high vines was more recently rekindled by the 1950 publication of the Austrian viticulturist LENZ MOSER. He recommended low-density vineyards with wide rows of trunks about 1.25 m/4 ft high. Higher training does reduce FROST risk, but requires thicker and more expensive supports, although vineyard work is made easier. 'High-culture' vines can be trained either cordon or Guyot. Vineyards of the New World have typically used high vine-training systems. Overhead trellises such as Italy's TENDONE are special examples of high vines.

There are other possible ways of classifying vine-training systems, however. The cordons may be classed as short, as in the 0.5 m in a closely spaced cordon de Royat, or many metres in length as for the Portuguese cruzeta (see below). An alternative classification takes account of whether the foliage is free, as for example in the gobelet vines of the Midi, or SHOOT POSITIONED or constrained into a plane, such as the vertical systems common in Alsace and Germany in which the foliage is held in place by WIRES and maintained by TRIMMING.

The vine canopies can also be classified by their plane: arbours or tendone-trained vines have horizontal canopies about 2 m above the ground, and most shoot-positioned canopies are vertical. Some canopies have shoots all growing upwards, as in the lyre trellis, while the GENEVA DOUBLE CURTAIN (GDC) has shoots which are trained downwards, and the SCOTT HENRY and SMART–DYSON systems have shoots trained both upwards and downwards. Vines may have a DIVIDED CANOPY in either the horizontal plane such as the GDC or LYRE trellis, or vertically as in the Scott Henry or Smart-Dyson. Training systems can be simple, like the free-standing gobelet vines of the Rioja, or elaborate, like the Ruakura twin two tier (RT2T) developed in New Zealand, which is both horizontally and vertically divided, and requires 20 wires per row to support fruit and foliage.

The following list gives brief details of some of the training systems in use around the world, including traditional and some new ones being used for deliberate CANOPY MANAGEMENT.

alberate, an old form of vine-training system used in parts of Italy where the vines are trained on or between trees. There are local variations, such as those in Bologna, Tuscany, Veneto, and Romagna, with the common feature being that trees are used for support.

alberello, see GOBELET.

arbour, see TENDONE.

arched cane, a variation on many different forms of training systems where canes are arched rather than being tied horizontally, see GUYOT. Alternative names include bow trained, *arcure* in French, Capovolto or Guyot *ad archetto* in Italy. This practice is claimed to lead to better BUDBREAK in the centre of the canes, where buds do not normally burst well (see APICAL DOMINANCE). It can be considered a variation of Guyot training.

ballerina, a form of Smart–Dyson developed in King Valley, VICTORIA, Australia. One vertical and two transverse curtains are created from one or two cordons trained to spurs pointing upwards. Many bilateral cordon training systems can easily be converted to ballerina.

barra, used for monoculture in Vinho Verde whereby vines are trained in one direction along a single wire at shoulder height.

basket training, often used for free-standing vines where canes are wound one around the other for mutual support. Common for some BUSH VINE systems which are pruned. Typically they are of low vigour.

bush vines, see BUSH VINES and GOBELET.

Casarsa, or Casarsa Friuli, an Italian training system like the SYLVOZ, except the canes are not tied down after pruning.

cassone padavano, a horizontally divided Italian system, pruned like the Sylvoz.

Cazenave, an Italian vine-training system which uses a modified form of Guyot pruning where short arms containing spurs and canes (five to six buds) are arranged along a horizontal CORDON. The canes are tied about vertically to a wire above. Because the pruner is able to leave so many buds per vine, this system is suited to fertile soils.

Château Thierry, a form of GUYOT training where the cane is tied in an arch to a stake beside the free-standing vine.

cordon de Cazenave, an Italian and French system used for fertile soils, with one or more canes left on a CORDON DE ROYAT.

cordon de Royat, see CORDON DE ROYAT.

cordon trained, term to distinguish a training system using cordons as opposed to a vine head and canes. These are typically horizontal and bilateral but they may also be unilateral. They are used in warm to hot regions.

cordon vertical, a vertical cordon with alternating spurs to either side. Not used very commonly as growth tends to be mainly from the top buds.

cruzeta, a system used in the VINHO VERDE area of Portugal where vines are trained to a wide cross arm about 2 m off the ground. More sophisticated than *latada* but less so than *barra*.

double header, a system developed by Terry Bennett, a grower in Tasmania, to allow CANE pruned vines in his COOL-CLIMATE vineyard to achieve BALANCE by pruning to more buds, but avoiding shoot crowding. This was achieved by removing each second vine in the row.

duplex, a system developed in California in the 1960s with flexible cross arms to allow for machine harvesting. While the fruiting wires are horizontally divided by 1 m/3 ft, the foliage was not shoot positioned to create two separate curtains as for the GENEVA DOUBLE CURTAIN. As a consequence, it is not nearly as beneficial in terms of yield, quality, and disease avoidance and is now little used.

espalier, see ESPALIER.

éventail (meaning 'fan'), a French system with multiple arms, each giving rise to a spur or short cane. Originally the form used in Chablis, with the arms lying on the ground, this has been modified to the taille de Semur system, where each arm is tied to a lower wire in the one plane.

factory roof system, commonly used for TABLE GRAPES, in South Africa and Israel, for example, where the CANOPY is trained up at an angle to meet in a gable near the row centre. This may also be called a closed, one-arm PERGOLA, and provides excellent access to the fruit for any hand work required.

fan shaped, a training system distantly related to *éventail* that is used in central Europe, particularly Russia, where the vine trunks are spread out in the shape of a fan, which makes it easier to bury vines for WINTER PROTECTION. The Italian version is called *ventagli*.

Flachbogen, the German name for a training system like the Guyot whereby one cane is laid horizontally either side of the head, and shoots trained vertically between foliage wires. The shoots are trimmed at the top. See VERTICAL TRELLIS.

Geneva double curtain (GDC), see GENEVA DOUBLE CURTAIN.

gobelet, see GOBELET.

Guyot, see GUYOT.

Halbbogen, a German training system whereby the vine is pruned to one cane of about 15 buds' length, and is arched in the middle over a wire about 25 cm/10 in above the base and end of the cane. Shoots are trained each year vertically between foliage wires, and are trimmed at the top. See APICAL DOMINANCE.

head trained, common term for a vine trained so that spurs and canes arise in one zone, called the head. Such vines are normally cane pruned.

Hudson River umbrella, a system used in the eastern US, where canes are arched downwards from a high head.

Isère, a training system much like Château Thierry (see above).

latada, traditional 3-m-high trellis used on Madeira for vines grown around fields of other crops, equivalent to VINHO VERDE's *ramada*.

Lenz Moser, see LENZ MOSER.

Lincoln canopy, a horizontal canopy developed at LINCOLN University in New Zealand but rarely used commercially. It is like the arbour, but is at waist height and allows tractor access between rows.

lyre, see LYRE.

MPCT, or minimal pruned cordon trained, which describes the system developed and extensively used in Australia, mainly for BULK WINE production. Young vines are trained to a form of CORDON at about 1.5 m height and, apart from wrapping early cane growth on the wire, receive minimal hand work, including pruning. See MINIMAL PRUNING.

palmette, an Italian training system, with one vine trained to four horizontal canes, one pair above the other.

parral, see TENDONE.

parron, see TENDONE.

Pendelbogen, the German name for the arched cane training system described above. There is a 50-cm height difference between the end of the cane and the highest point, which is thought to improve budbreak in the middle of the cane. Most of the shoots are trained vertically upright between foliage wires, and normally require trimming at the top. Pendelbogen means 'pendulum bow', and there are related training forms called not just Halbbogen ('half bow'), but also Rundbogen ('round bow') and Doppelbogen ('double bow'). The name has also been applied to a mid-height Sylvoz system in New Zealand.

pergola, see PERGOLA.

Perold, a South African term for vertical trellis, named after A. I. Perold, the breeder of PINOTAGE.

pyramid, an Italian training system where vine shoots are trained over a group of stakes tied together at the top, forming a pyramid.

ramada, VINHO VERDE name for *latada* above.

raggi Belussi, an Italian overhead training system suspended from above and with two vines planted together and trained in four directions. Pruned like the Sylvoz.

raggiera or **raggi,** an Italian training system where vines are trained overhead on wires like the spokes of a wheel. Either one vine may be trained up a central stake or tree and divided into cordons, or several vines may be at the one position with each trained along a different radius.

Ruakura twin two-tier (RT2T) trellis, a system developed at the Ruakura Research Centre in New Zealand with the canopy divided into four curtains, two above two. Related to the SMART–DYSON, this is an experimental system that has not been used commercially.

Scott Henry, see SCOTT HENRY.

shelf, or *tana*, local name for overhead trellis in Japan.

slanting trellis. The canopy is trained along an inclined support. This trellis can be used for both table- and wine-grape production.

Smart–Dyson trellis, see SMART–DYSON.

Sylvoz, see SYLVOZ.

Te Kauwhata two tier (TK2T). Developed at the Te Kauwhata Research Station in New Zealand, this system is vertically divided, with shoots trained vertically upwards. Limited commercial use in California and New Zealand.

tendone, see TENDONE.

three-wire trellis, another California trellis system with a pair of fixed foliage wires above the cordon. Shoots are not positioned, and fall across these wires under their own weight.

traverse trellis, European name for the T trellis.

T trellis, common in Australia, where the vine is trained to two horizontal cordons about 0.5 m apart. It takes its name from the appearance of the vine trunk and cordons. Shoots are not positioned, and so the canopy is not divided. Can be machine pruned and harvested, and is widely used in bulk wine-producing areas.

tunnel, an alternative name for a form of overhead vine training where the vines are planted in two rows and trained overhead.

two-wire vertical trellis, common terminology in California, where one wire is occupied by the cordon and the second is a fixed foliage wire. Shoots grow up and over this wire and fall under their own weight to form a bell-shaped canopy. When the vines are vigorous, the canopy is very shaded.

U, an alternative name for the LYRE trellis.

umbrella kniffin, a system used in eastern America, where canes from a mid-height head are trained over a top wire and tied below.

V, a vine-training system in the shape of the letter where shoots are trained upwards into two curtains. This form does not work as well as the LYRE or U system, where the cordons are separated at the base.

vase, another name for the GOBELET training system.

vertical cordon, a rare training system as top buds tend to burst first, making it difficult to manage.

vertical trellis, see VERTICAL TRELLIS.

VSP, or vertical shoot positioning, which describes a system used throughout the world where annual shoot growth is trained vertically upwards and held in place by foliage wires. See VERTICAL TRELLIS.

Y, a vine-training system in the shape of the letter and equivalent to the V system except that the trunk of the vine forms the vertical part of the letter.

The above cannot pretend to be a comprehensive list of the multitude of training systems used worldwide, nor of all their local names, and how patterns of usage are changing, especially in the New World, but it does give some indication of the extraordinary variation in vine-training systems. The greatest complexity of training systems in the world is to be found in Italy, while those used in France tend to be determinedly regional.   R.E.S.

Eynard, I., and Dalmasso, G., *Viticoltura moderna: manuale pratico* (Milan, 1990).

Galet, P., *Précis de viticulture* (7th edn, Montpellier, 2000).

Smart, R. E., and Robinson, M., *Sunlight into Wine: A Handbook for Winegrape Canopy Management* (Adelaide, 1991).

Traisental, wine region in AUSTRIA astride a roughly 12 km/7 mile stretch of the Traisen River just before it empties into the right bank of the Danube below KREMS. This relatively small region of 700 ha/1,730 acres of vineyard, inaugurated in 1995, benefits from diurnal temperature variation (see TEMPERATURE VARIABILITY) similar to that of the WACHAU and distinctive and unusual conglomerate soils (see GEOLOGY), especially on the left bank of the Traisen. These are rich in active LIME, and whose efficacy grower Ludwig Neumayer of Inzersdorf, has demonstrated with Grüner Veltliner and Riesling, and also with Pinot Blanc (Weissburgunder), Sauvignon Blanc, and wine based on an old GEMISCHTER SATZ. The enthusiastic young vintners emerging here may render the Traisental more important.

Traisental DAC is an official Austrian appellation of origin for varietal Grüner Veltliner and Riesling free of BOTRYTIS and WOOD notes. Wines referred to as KLASSIK must be at least 12% alcohol and can be sold as early as 1 January following their harvest. Wines from this DAC labelled Reserve must be at least 13% alcohol and are not sold before 15 March. Since the DAC's 2006 inception, wines that do not qualify for the Traisental DAC must be labelled NIEDERÖSTERREICH for their state of origin. This applies in particular to wines produced from the 40% of grape varieties that are neither Grüner Veltliner nor Riesling.   D.S.

Trajadura, white grape variety used to add body and a certain citrus character to Portugal's VINHO VERDE if it is picked sufficiently early. It was planted on 1,662 ha of Portugal in 2012, more than the area devoted to TREIXADURA as it is known across the Spanish border in Galicia. It is often blended with LOUREIRO and sometimes with ALVARINHO.

Traminer, name applied both to white-berried and pink-berried non-aromatic clones of the more famous, distinctly aromatic, pink-skinned grape variety GEWÜRZTRAMINER or Traminer Aromatico (see also SAVAGNIN). All are known in various parts of the world, particularly in central and eastern Europe, by names which are derivations of the word Traminer.

Traminette, relatively recent, complex AMERICAN HYBRID showing promise in cooler American states. Its heady whites hint strongly at its GEWÜRZTRAMINER genes.

transfer method, SPARKLING WINEMAKING process, now less common than it was, involving provoking a second fermentation in bottle and then transferring its contents into a tank, where the wine is separated from the deposit.

translocation, plant physiological process whereby soluble materials such as dissolved salts, organic materials, and growth substances are moved around the vine in the PHLOEM. (The phloem tissue is in the outer part of the trunk or stems, and so can be disrupted by CINCTURING.) Sucrose is the principal form in which CARBOHYDRATES are moved, and the phloem sap also contains amino acids and organic acids, inorganic nutrients, plant hormones, and alkaloids. Examples of translocation are the movement of inorganic nutrients absorbed by roots from the soil to other parts of the vine, for example POTASSIUM going into the fruit, which may prejudice wine quality. Translocation also includes the important movement of SUCROSE formed by PHOTOSYNTHESIS away from the leaves to the fruit which will eventually become ALCOHOL in wine. From the point of view of wine, the translocation of sucrose, MALIC ACID, TARTARIC ACID, elements, and compounds containing NITROGEN during RIPENING are crucial to the chemical composition of grapes, and thus to eventual wine quality.

Movement of foodstuffs is invariably towards points of need, such as growing shoot tips for the early part of the season, flowers, then developing berries, and also towards the permanent vine parts such as trunks and roots for the accumulation of reserves later in the season. HORMONES such as auxins, cytokinins, and gibberellins play an important role in regulating translocation. The vine is capable of translocating products over long distances and so, even though the shoot supporting a bunch may be shaded, the grapes will still ripen depending on materials imported from other parts of the vine.
                                                                    R.E.S.

Champagnol, F., *Éléments de physiologie de la vigne et de viticulture générale* (St-Gely-du-Fesc, 1984).

Transmontano, large, mountainous VINHO REGIONAL in north-east Portugal with the same borders as TRÁS-OS-MONTES. Vinho Regional wines labelled Transmontano feature a broader range of grape varieties; Valle Pradinhos makes an exceptional blend of Riesling and Gewürztraminer with local variety Malvasia Fina.

transpiration, physiological process whereby water taken up from a vine's roots is evaporated through the leaves, important in preventing the vine from overheating in sunny weather. Water and dissolved elements move in the so-called transpiration stream through the woody part of the vine called the XYLEM. The xylem fluid also contains relatively large amounts of amino acids, especially glutamine, organic acids, especially malic, and small amounts of sugars. Total water loss from a vineyard is called EVAPOTRANSPIRATION, and this includes transpiration from the vines and also any weeds or cover crop present, plus EVAPORATION from the soil surface.

Transpiration is an energy-driven process due to leaves absorbing SUNLIGHT. Water vapour passes from the leaf to the atmosphere via small pores on the underside called STOMATA. Energy is required to provide the latent heat of evaporation for the phase change from liquid (water) to gas (water vapour), which takes place in the cavity below the stomata. The cell walls of the substomatal cavity are wet owing to a long column of water extending from the roots. Provided the vine is well supplied with water, leaves facing the sun will be only 2–3 °C (36–7 °F) warmer than the air, while if water supply is limited then this figure can exceed 10 °C (18 °F) and the vine will suffer both HEAT STRESS and WATER STRESS.

Transpiration is controlled by both atmospheric and plant factors. High transpiration rates are due to low humidity, high sunshine, temperature, and wind speed. Typically, during the day as temperature rises, humidity falls, and so transpiration is fastest in the early afternoon. As soils dry, the risk of water stress increases and so, by partially closing stomata, the vine is able to regulate its water status to some extent. However, as stomata close then PHOTOSYNTHESIS stops, as carbon dioxide entry into the leaf is inhibited.

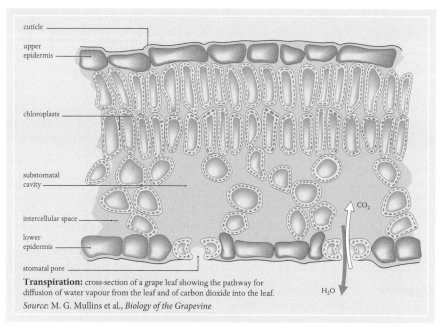

Transpiration: cross-section of a grape leaf showing the pathway for diffusion of water vapour from the leaf and of carbon dioxide into the leaf.
Source: M. G. Mullins et al., *Biology of the Grapevine*

Labels on figure: cuticle; upper epidermis; chloroplasts; substomatal cavity; intercellular space; lower epidermis; stomatal pore; CO_2; H_2O

Rates of transpiration vary with the weather and growth stage of the vineyard. For a vineyard in full leaf in the middle of the season, daily evapotranspiration rates may be as high as 40,000 l/ha for a hot, dry, and sunny climate. For a vineyard planted with 2,000 vines per ha, this rate is equivalent to 20 l (4.4 gal) per vine per day. The amount of water transpired is very high relative to both the vine's growth overall and the fruit produced. For example, measurements cited by Smart and Coombe show 5,000 g and 80 g of water respectively for each gram of plant dry weight and gram of fruit produced.

Recent research has shown that, contrary to earlier assumptions, vines transpire at night as well as during the day. This transpiration is driven by a vapour pressure gradient of water, from wet cell walls in the sub-stomatal cavity to the drier atmosphere outside. A study by Rogiers et al. investigated the fact that SÉMILLON is more prone to water stress than many other varieties because its stomata are more open, both day and night, and are slow to shut under water stress.   R.E.S.

Rogiers, S. Y., et al., 'Does night-time transpiration contribute to anisohydric behaviour in a *Vitis vinifera* cultivar?', *Journal of Experimental Botany*, 60/13 (2009), 3751–63.

Smart, R. E., and Coombe, B. G., 'Water relations of vines', in T. T. Kozlowski (ed.), *Water Deficits and Plant Growth*, vii (New York, 1983).

transport of wine has changed considerably over the ages but a wide variety of different methods, from tanker to a bottle sent by mail, are still used.

Ancient history
Wine was transported in bulk in antiquity in a variety of ways: in huge wineskins loaded on the backs of two- or four-wheeled carts or in BARRELS on carts, but water-borne transport had a great advantage because of the inefficiency of the harnesses used on animals. For most of the Mediterranean area, wine was carried in large AMPHORAE, which were loaded in the holds of ships. The pottery jars required considerable packing (heather, straw, etc.) to cushion them against breakages. They could be transferred to smaller vessels for transport up inland waterways. A recent discovery has been of wrecks carrying DOLIA, as a kind of tanker for the bulk transport of wine. Barrels were widely used in northern Europe (see CELTS) and later in the Mediterranean, although the amphora tradition died out completely only in the medieval period.   J.J.P.

Moulin, M. M., 'Le Transport du raisin ou du vin par la route à l'époque romaine en Gaule et dans les provinces voisines', in R. Chevallier et al., *Archéologie de la vigne et du vin* (Paris, 1990).

Peacock, D. P. S., and Williams, D. F., *Amphorae and the Roman Economy* (London, 1986).

Modern transport
In the Middle Ages, RIVERS played an important role in transporting wine, and only those wine regions with access to good water transport (by sea and/or river) were likely to develop much trade. In the 19th and early 20th centuries, the advent of a RAILWAY system transformed wine regions as dissimilar as the LANGUEDOC, ROUSSILLON, Mendoza in ARGENTINA, RIOJA, and CHIANTI. Today wine is generally transported by road and sea (although, at the height of Beaujolais NOUVEAU's popularity in the early 1980s, planes, parachutes, and vintage cars were just some of the means used to race that particular wine to the consumer).

For centuries, the transport of wine meant BULK TRANSPORT, and the most common container used for transporting wine was the barrel. SHERRY, for example, was still shipped to British bottlers in its special casks, or BUTTS, until well into the 20th century (when the empty butts were used for Scotch whisky maturation). In the latter half of the 20th century, however, container shipment in bulk tankers became the norm, although, as an increasing proportion of wine is bottled not just in its country or region of origin but actually at the winery (see BOTTLING), the most common container for transport today is probably the BOTTLE, although for both financial and SUSTAINABILITY reasons, the proportion of wine shipped in bulk rose dramatically in the seven years to 2012 to reach 40% (see BULK TRANSPORT). Unlike wine in bulk, bottles are breakable, and can easily be pilfered. Wine transport across national frontiers or state lines can involve the additional problems associated with any product subject to TAXATION.

From the consumer's point of view, the most important aspect of the transport of wine is TEMPERATURE. If wine is exposed to high temperatures, it may well deteriorate considerably, even if it has been subject to effective STABILIZATION. Spikes of temperature can also lead to spoilage due to OXIDATION. Conscientious producers try to avoid shipping wine in high summer, while scrupulous wholesalers insist that insulated containers sometimes called reefers are used for shipments in hot weather and/or through the TROPICS, although they are more expensive. Stowing the wine below sea level minimizes the temperature variation. Some shippers of fine wines include temperature sensors in the shipment.

Exposure to light can also be a problem: research indicates that exposure to UV light at any point in the distribution chain may convert amino acids into MERCAPTANS, thus damaging wine quality (see LIGHTSTRIKE). The risk is reduced by the use of brown rather than clear bottles.

In the late 1990s, the transport of wine, and DIRECT SHIPMENT in particular, became even more legally restricted in the UNITED STATES, although a Supreme Court ruling in 2005 suggested some relaxation of controls.

transversage. See SPARKLING WINEMAKING.

Trás-os-Montes, large DOP in north-east Portugal. Meaning 'behind the mountains', Trás-os-Montes is bounded by high mountains on one side and the Spanish frontier on the other (see map of PORTUGAL). The mountains which isolate Trás-os-Montes from the rest of Portugal cast a rain shadow over the region, although it becomes progressively more arid towards Spain. With varied microclimates and soil types (mostly SCHIST, but the region also has GRANITE and CALCAREOUS soils) Trás-os-Montes has three DOP subregions, from west to east: Chaves, Valpaços, and Planalto Mirandês. Climatic extremes and poor soils make cultivation difficult, although farmers have been helped considerably by funds from the EU and the World Bank. Wine is an important commodity in Trás-os-Montes and there are more vineyards here than in any other part of Portugal: 69,000 ha/170,000 acres. However, as yields are low, both LISBOA and TEJO produce more wine. The high vineyards here, north of the DOURO Valley, also supply wine for MATEUS Rosé and a number of imitative brands. See also TRANSMONTANO.

S.A.

Trbljan, relatively important light-berried vine variety grown particularly on the coast of CROATIA just north of Zadar. Several hundred hectares are planted. The grape is also sometimes called Kuč.

Treasury Wine Estates, Australia's biggest wine group in terms of revenue, and second-biggest (after ACCOLADE) in terms of wine production and grape crush. Treasury is a public listed company created in 2011 when Foster's separated its wine interests from its brewing business. Its brands include some of Australia's most prestigious, including PENFOLDS, Wolf Blass, Wynns Coonawarra Estate, Seppelt, Coldstream Hills, Devil's Lair, St Huberts, Heemskerk, and Saltram. Others include Annie's Lane, Ingoldby, Jamiesons Run, Leo Buring, Lindemans, Rosemount Estate, T'Gallant, Tollana, and Yellowglen. It also owns Matua in New Zealand and many California brands of which the best known is Beringer, acquired in 2001 when Foster's set up Beringer Blass, the first Australo-American wine group. In 2013 the company wrote off US$35 million worth of wine in response to sluggish sales in the US. Bottling facilities in Australia and the UK are shared with rivals ACCOLADE.

Trebbiano. At least six distinct varieties grown in Italy are known principally as Trebbiano, including **Trebbiano Toscano**, whose national total of 22,702 ha/56,098 acres in 2010 made it one of the most planted white wine grapes in Italy. Next most planted, largely in Emilia-Romagna, on 15,893 ha was the remarkably similar **Trebbiano Romagnolo**. **Trebbiano Giallo** is found on 10,663 ha, particularly in Lazio, and **Trebbiano Spoletino** is an Umbrian speciality grown on 200 ha. **Trebbiano Modenese** is grown on 363 ha and is associated with production of the local vinegar while **Trebbiano d'Abruzzo** is quite unrelated to any other Trebbiano (see ABRUZZO). Meanwhile, many an Italian synonym incorporates the word Trebbiano, most notably Trebbiano di Soave, Trebbiano di Lugana, and Trebbiano Valtenesi, which are all the Marche grape VERDICCHIO. There are almost as many possible histories of Trebbiano as there are different

varieties called Trebbiano (the index of *Wine Grapes* has no fewer than 28 entries for grape names beginning with Trebbiano). The Bolognese agronomist PETRUS DE CRESCENTIIS certainly described a vine called Tribiano as early as 1303, but which? Today, Trebbiano is planted all over Italy (with the exception of the cool far north), to the extent that it is likely that the great majority of basic *vino bianco* will contain at least some of the variety, if only to add acidity and volume.

The stronghold of Trebbiano Toscano, shown by DNA PROFILING to have a parent-offspring relationship with the GARGANEGA of Soave, is central Italy. It is known as UGNI BLANC and St-Émilion in France, Tália in Portugal, and is widely planted around the world. Any grape called simply Trebbiano is likely to be Trebbiano Toscano.

See under its most common French name UGNI BLANC for details of Trebbiano in France.

This gold-, even amber-berried grape variety is so productive, and so much planted in both France and Italy, the world's two major wine-producing countries, that it may well still produce more wine than any other vine variety in the world—even though the total area it was planted on appears to have slipped from fifth to ninth place between 1990 and 2010. It is cited in more DOC regulations than any other single variety (about 80) and may well account for more than a third of Italy's entire DOC white wine production. Trebbiano Toscano the wine is typically light, crisp, and wet.

Some idea of Trebbiano Toscano's ubiquity is given by listing just some of the wines in which it is an ingredient: VERDICCHIO, ORVIETO, FRASCATI, together with SOAVE (Trebbiano Toscano was planted in place of Trebbiano di Soave in the 1960s and 1970s when yield was a more important consideration than quality but has now been outlawed). The variety has after all had many centuries to adapt itself to local conditions. Between Tuscany and Rome, in UMBRIA, the variety can be known as Procanico, which some agronomists believe is a superior, smaller-berried Trebbiano. Only the fiercely varietal-conscious north eastern corner of Italy is virtually free of this bland ballast.

Trebbiano's malign influence was most noticeable in central TUSCANY in much of the 20th century, however, where Trebbiano was so well entrenched that CHIANTI and therefore VINO NOBILE DI MONTEPULCIANO laws sanctioned its inclusion in this red wine, thereby diluting its quality as well as its colour and damaging its reputation. Trebbiano is now very much an optional ingredient, however, increasingly spurned by quality-conscious producers. Once Trebbiano fell out of favour with Chianti producers, an attempt was made to transform it into innocuous dry whites such as GALESTRO. Fortunately, the market for these wines has dwindled,

and in the 2000s much Trebbiano in Tuscany was grubbed up, or used in VIN SANTO.

Trebbiano Toscano has also managed to infiltrate Portugal's fiercely nationalistic vineyards, as Tália or Thalia, and is widely planted in BULGARIA and in parts of Croatia, and GREECE. As well as being used for MEXICO's important brandy production, Trebbiano is well entrenched in the southern hemisphere, where its high yields and high acidity are valued. There were still nearly 2,000 ha of 'Ugni Blanc' in Argentina in 2012 as well as plantings in Brazil and Uruguay.

South Africa also calls its relatively limited plantings Ugni Blanc but relies more on COLOMBARD for brandy production and cheap, tart blending material, as does California, whose 200 remaining acres of the vine called 'St-Emilion' there are exclusively in the Central Valley, although interesting VARIETAL versions called Trebbiano are not entirely unknown. Australia, where Colombard is also more important, has about 200 ha of Trebbiano, planted mainly in the irrigated areas, where it provides a usefully tart ingredient in basic blended whites and is also sometimes used by distillers.

The influence of Trebbiano/Ugni Blanc will surely continue to decline as wine drinkers seek flavour with increasing determination.

Trebbiano Romagnolo, and its almost amber-berried clone Trebbiano della Fiamma, dominates white wine production in EMILIA-ROMAGNA and results in generally remarkably undistinguished dry whites. The variety is cultivated across a wide swathe of ROMAGNA in the provinces of Bologna, Forlì, and Ravenna, and only about a fifth is registered for the production of DOC wines. It is permitted on its own or as a blending component in no fewer than 12 of Emilia-Romagna's total of 21 denominations. Permitted yields of almost 100 hl/ha (5.7 tons/acre) do little to assist a grape not known for its striking personality, and most Trebbiano di Romagna is, at best, suitable for a picnic.

Perhaps Italy's most exciting Trebbiano, **Trebbiano d'Abruzzo** (see ABRUZZO) is thought to be not a Trebbiano at all but probably the BOMBINO BIANCO of Puglia but this has yet to be proved by DNA PROFILING, which has suggested the variety is related to Trebbiano Spoletino. Trebbiano Spoletino was rescued from extinction by Cantina Novelli in Umbria at the beginning of this century and has clearly gained ground at an extraordinary rate if the 2010 vine census is accurate. Trebbiano Giallo and Trebbiano Modenese are, perhaps appropriately, closely associated with vinegar production.

Robinson, J., Harding, J., and Vouillamoz, J., *Wine Grapes, a complete guide to 1,368 vine varieties, including their origins and flavours* (London, 2012).

Treixadura, Galician name for Portugal's scented, delicate white TRAJADURA and treated in much the same way. This is the main grape of Ribeiro and may be blended with Galician Torrontés and Lado. It is also grown in the Rías Baixas region, where it is often blended with ALBARIÑO, LOUREIRA, and/or GODELLO. Total Spanish plantings had grown to almost 1,000 ha/2,500 acres by 2011.

trellis systems, support structures for the vine framework required for a given TRAINING SYSTEM. Normally these are man made, although vines are still occasionally trained to trees. The trellis system in its simplest form consists of a STAKE driven beside a vine to which the vine trunk or shoots are tied. Nowadays WIRES are used to support vines and foliage, as posts are installed at intervals along the row.

There are several designs of end assemblies but they are all firmly anchored in the ground so as to support the strain in the wire due to the weight of the crop, the vines, and any wind stresses. At intervals along the row are intermediate posts, which also help carry the vine weight. In a well-constructed trellis system, the wires should be strained so tight that the wire does not sag, and this in turn facilitates MECHANIZATION. Details of some common trellis systems and end assemblies are given by Smart and Robinson. Vineyard POSTS are made from wood, concrete, plastic, steel, stone, or even cane. If made from softwood, vineyard posts must be chemically treated to stop wood-rotting fungi.

The majority of the world's vineyards, however, have very simple trellis systems. For many, the vines are free standing (see GOBELET), or have loose wires running from vine to vine supported by occasional stakes. The major support for the weight of the vine and crop is from the vine trunk.

For more information on the wide range of trellis systems used in various regions, see TRAINING SYSTEMS.   R.E.S.

Freeman, B. M., Tassie, E., and Rebbechi, M. D., 'Training and trellising', in B. G. Coombe and P. R. Dry (eds.), *Viticulture*, ii: *Practices* (Adelaide, 1992).
Smart, R. E., and Robinson, M., *Sunlight into Wine: A Handbook for Winegrape Canopy Management* (Adelaide, 1991).

Trentino, the southern and principally Italian-speaking half of Italy's central alpine region of TRENTINO-ALTO ADIGE. Trento is the regional capital. Viticulture is centred on the valley of the Adige and the hills immediately to the east and west of the river, with an occasional excursion to side valleys such as the Valle dei Laghi and the Val di Cembra. The terrain further east and west into the Dolomites and the Gruppo di Brenta mountains is too rugged and mountainous for viticulture. Although the region is far to Italy's north, and Trento is on the 46th degree of LATITUDE, the climate is not necessarily cool, as heat rapidly builds up at lower elevations during the summer months (see TOPOGRAPHY).

Viticulture is therefore by no means confined to early-ripening vine varieties.

Of Trentino's 10,000 ha/24,700 acres, all of 9,500 ha are registered for the production of DOC and IGT wines. In 2010 more than a million hl of wine were produced. Although these figures seem to indicate a region focused on quality, the reality is very different and geared towards large volumes of international varietals. Chardonnay and Pinot Grigio, planted on respective totals of 2,835 ha and 2,353 ha, are followed by Müller-Thurgau on 894 ha and Merlot on 694 ha of vineyards. A good 90% of the region's total output is controlled by 15 CO-OPERATIVES and 14 NÉGOCIANTS who have the power to set the region's agenda. This commercial model has led to overproduction of Chardonnay and Pinot Grigio, while INDIGENOUS VARIETIES and local wine specialities have been neglected.

The region's DOC system has been designed with large-scale production of international varieties in mind, with scant interest in the notion of TERROIR. The overarching Trentino DOC permitting yields up to 15 tonnes/ha as well as innumerable grape varieties extends to the entire region. It is, however, subdivided into four historic subzones with some local focus: Trentino Isera and Trentino Ziresi for MARZEMINO grapes, Trentino Castelbenes for MOSCATO, and Trentino Sorni for NOSIOLA and SCHIAVA. The DOC Valdadige, covering the same area and varieties as the Trentino DOC, seems void of sense.

The confusingly named Trento DOC (for marketing reasons written as TrentoDoc) designates the entire region for the production of METODO CLASSICO sparkling wine based on Chardonnay and Pinot Noir. The base wine requires high levels of acidity, guaranteed in grapes coming from elevations of 400 to 700 m (1,310–2,300 ft). An extended minimum period of 18 months on the LEES has proven to be an efficient way of ensuring truly high quality wines. Ferrari is the leader, ageing the non-vintage wine for 24 months and longer, but the many small producers tend to turn out equally good wine. Trento DOC is surely set to become Trentino's flagbearer. The other candidate is Teroldego Rotaliano, one of the few DOCs that have been sensibly demarcated, in this case limited to the gravelly Rotaliano Plain, with only a handful of producers, notably the pioneering Elisabetta Foradori who has so successfully proved that with low yields TEROLDEGO can produce serious wines. Most quality-conscious producers refuse to bottle the wines as DOC Teroldego Rotaliano, preferring the more anonymous but less tarnished IGT Vigneti delle Dolomiti. Two other independent DOCs, Casteller and Lago di Caldaro (the latter shared with ALTO ADIGE to the north), are devoted almost exclusively to light, pale, Schiava-based reds, but its 340 ha in Trentino is dwarfed by Alto Adige's more than 1,000 ha.

Although Trentino's greatest handicap is the market-driven spirit of mass-market wine production, there are significant traditions of matching individual varieties and subzones: Müller-Thurgau in the Val di Cembra; Cabernet in the Vallagarina and between Pressano and Lavis; LAGREIN in the Campo Rotaliano; NOSIOLA in the Valle dei Laghi and Pressano; Pinot Noir in Civezzano and in the hills to the north of Trento; Marzemino in the Vallagarina. The local centre of ACADEME is SAN MICHELE ALL'ADIGE, which is instrumental in researching the detail of the region. This undertaking has so far been largely in the hands of a tiny group of small-scale growers who have set up I Dolomitici association. They have received official CONSORZIO status and are virtually the only ones carrying the quality banner, which would otherwise be sorely lacking in Trentino.   W.S.

www.vinideltrentino.com

Trentino-Alto Adige, autonomous, alpine northern Italian region through which flows the Adige River (called Etsch by the region's many German speakers). It is made up of ALTO ADIGE, or the South Tyrol, in the north and TRENTINO in the south (see map under ITALY).

TrentoDOC, TRADITIONAL METHOD sparkling wines from TRENTINO, thus written for marketing reasons.

Trepat, increasingly fashionable indigenous red-skinned wine grape of north-east Spain, particularly in Conca de Barberá and Costers del Segre. Total plantings were just over 1,000 ha/2,500 acres in 2011, producing mainly light rosés, both still and sparkling, but it has shown some intriguing potential for light reds.

Tressallier, ST-POURÇAIN synonym for SACY.

Tressot, ancient red grape variety of Burgundy, already described in the 14th century along with PINOT NOIR. Tressot is exclusively cultivated in the Yonne (CHABLIS country) where it has now almost disappeared. DNA PROFILING at DAVIS suggested, unexpectedly, that Tressot is a natural cross between DURAS and PETIT VERDOT. Confusingly, it is also a Burgundian name for the Jura's (unrelated) TROUSSEAU vine.   J.V.

tri, French for a sorting process, notably postal but, in a winemaking context, it means the selection of suitable grapes. This usually takes the form of a TRIAGE on reception of the grapes at the winery or cellar, using a sorting table or *table de tri*. However, in the production of BOTRYTIZED wines a *trie* (note the feminine form), or several *tries*, is made in the vineyard whereby the pickers proceed along the rows selecting only those clusters, and occasionally only those berries, that have been successfully attacked by NOBLE ROT.

tri, table de, French for 'sorting table'. See TRIAGE.

triage is the French and common winemaking term for the sorting of grapes according to quality prior to winemaking. Most commonly, freshly picked bunches of grapes are spread on a *table de tri*, a sorting table or slowly moving and sometimes vibrating belt, so that substandard examples can be manually plucked off and thrown away (along with any leaves and stems, or MOG, that have crept in). For most wines, clusters that are unevenly ripe, or underripe, or have suffered DISEASE or VINE PEST damage are rejected. In some wineries, the grape berries are sorted after the bunches have been through the destemmer, and may even be sorted twice, both before and after DESTEMMING. Such sorting is a labour-intensive process that requires training. However, an automated sorter which works on the basis of grape density and is used after destemming has been developed in France. Ripe grapes sink in the floating tank; unripe grapes remain on the surface. The cost of sorting can be justified only for relatively fine wines but the practice increased considerably in the early 2000s with the emergence on the market of highly sophisticated mechanical and optical sorting systems. See also GRAPE COMPOSITION AND WINE QUALITY.

A.D.W. & J.E.H.

Tribidrag, earliest known name for ZINFANDEL in its CROATIAN birthplace.

tribromoanisole, more properly **2,4,6-tribromoanisole**, or **TBA**, is a musty- or dusty-smelling compound which may affect wine produced in a contaminated winery. The cause so far identified is the microbial degradation by fungi in the winery of tribromophenol (TBP) used in wood preservatives or as a flame retardant in paints and plastics. It is therefore only indirectly related to cork, which can act as a 'carrier' of the taint. The perception threshold in red and white wines is approximately 3–4 ng/l, down to 2 ng/l in sparkling wine. Further research is needed to assess the frequency of this FAULT. It has not so far been possible to distinguish TBA from TCA by TASTING.

Tricastin, Coteaux du, old name for GRIGNAN-LES-ADHÉMAR.

trichloroanisole, more properly **2,4,6-trichloroanisole**, the unpleasant-smelling compound associated with CORKED wine. See TCA.

Trimbach, family-run wine producer based at Ribeauvillé in ALSACE. The company was established in 1626. Its wines are characterized by very fine fruit and high acidity. Riesling constitutes half of production and even its most basic offering can stand many years' BOTTLE AGEING. Two of its most famous bottlings are

Rieslings: the very fine, rare, and long-lived Clos Ste-Hune (in fact from the Alsace Grand Cru Rosacker) and Cuvée Frédéric Émile, named after the 19th century Trimbach who expanded the business to become an important merchant house as well as vine-grower. The family owns 45 ha of vineyards in eight different villages around Ribeauvillé, famous for the diversity of its soils. Recent additions have included 2 ha in the Grand Cru Schlossberg and holdings in Geisberg and Kirchberg rented from the local convent.

trimming, the vineyard operation of removing unwanted SHOOT growth which can cause SHADING and hinder SPRAYING. Although it is usually done with a trimming machine mounted on a tractor, it may also be carried out with a hand-held machete or similar device. The operation normally removes the SHOOT TIP and a few leaves below it, or about 30 cm/12 in of growth, thus leaving the shoots trimmed to about 15–25 NODES, or 70–150 cm/31–58 in. Trimming is essential in vineyards with high VINE DENSITY to stop shoots from adjacent rows from growing together. Regrowth may be such as to demand up to six trimmings a year, particularly in vineyards well supplied with water (by rainfall or irrigation) and NITROGEN. If shoots are trimmed too short then there may be insufficient leaf area to ripen the crop properly (see LEAF TO FRUIT RATIO). Resulting wines will be lower in alcohol and of lighter body and colour. Sometimes vineyards are trimmed so neatly on the top and sides that vine rows can look like a recently trimmed hedge, hence the alternative term hedging.

R.E.S.

Trincadeira, sometimes called **Trincadeira Preta**, or black Trincadeira, is a red grape highly valued by winemakers in southern PORTUGAL and grown on a total of 11,674 ha/28,835 acres of vineyard all over the country. Known in the DOURO as TINTA AMARELA, it is very susceptible to rot and therefore only performs well in the driest of climates. Trincadeira is therefore ideally suited to the ALENTEJO, where it can produce deep-coloured, spicy wines in the right conditions but tends to herbaceousness if not picked at the right time.

R.J.M.

Trincadeira das Pratas, traditional minor Portuguese white grape grown on just over 100 ha, mainly in Tejo. It can, but does not always, produce delicate, perfumed dry whites.

Triomphe (d'Alsace), HYBRID bred by Kuhlmann in Alsace from KNIPPERLÉ and a *riparia-rupestris* AMERICAN VINE. It has good resistance to mildew but the wine produced, however deep coloured, tastes FOXY. The vine is responsible for some English reds.

trocken, German for dry, a legally defined term when applied to the wines of GERMANY.

Wines so-labelled first appeared in the 1970s and in the decade following became the overwhelming preference of German consumers. By the late 1980s, German vintners of all regions were selling largely trocken or HALBTROCKEN wines in their domestic market although there has been a gradual return of consumer interest within Germany in sweeter styles of Riesling. It took the produce of riper vintages to win over foreign lovers of German wine to trocken styles.

The term can be applied in German-speaking countries within the EU to a still wine with a maximum of 4 g/l RESIDUAL SUGAR, or up to 9 g/l if the TOTAL ACIDITY is less than the residual sugar by no more than 2 g/l (9 g/l residual sugar and total acidity not less than 7 g/l). The proportion of German still wine that is described as trocken (as opposed to halbtrocken) varies considerably between regions (with a higher proportion in southern regions) but averages about 28% (from just 16% in the mid 1990s). This legal definition of dryness should not be confused with an organoleptic impression that most tasters would describe as dry. A Riesling HALBTROCKEN would commonly be described as tasting dry; whereas, for example, a low-acid, high-alcohol Baden Grauburgunder (Pinot Gris) that has undergone MALOLACTIC CONVERSION and harbours 4 g/l of residual sugar would probably be described as slightly sweet, just as would an analytically comparable white burgundy or California Chardonnay.

Because CARBON DIOXIDE reduces the impression of sweetness, a sparkling wine containing between 17 and 35 g/l residual sugar may be described as trocken. Many of the big-volume sparkling wines produced in Germany (see SEKT) are trocken, while top-quality versions are usually drier and labelled BRUT or extra brut. See also DOSAGE.

See also HALBTROCKEN, FEINHERB, and SWEETNESS.

J.R. & D.S.

Trockenbeerenauslese, sometimes known as **TBA**, the highest MUST WEIGHT PRÄDIKAT defined by Austrian and GERMAN WINE LAW. *Trockenbeeren* refers to grapes (*Beeren*) shrivelled on the vine, typically under the influence of NOBLE ROT. Many VINTAGES have yielded no Trockenbeerenauslese wine at all in Germany (it is more frequent in Austria's Neusiedlersee region), but warmer weather and scrupulous standards of selection have dramatically increased the frequency of TBA bottlings by many top German estates since 1988. An even higher minimum POTENTIAL ALCOHOL is required than for SAUTERNES, generally produced in a much warmer climate. It is inevitable therefore that these rarities command exceptionally high PRICES, which go some way to compensating the producer for the many passages (see TRI) through the vineyard, the risk of losing all the grapes to GREY ROT or rain, and the difficulty of vinifying such viscous juice. High must weight

TBA (and musts in the upper 200s of OECHSLE are no longer freakishly uncommon) can sometimes take a year or more to ferment to the 5.5% alcohol requisite for wine—all the while risking the acquisition of excessive VOLATILE ACIDITY—and a significant share of any TBA is lost to the filter pads in the process of bottling it in stable condition.   J.R. & D.S.

Trois Glorieuses, annual weekend devoted to wine, and food, in and around Beaune. See HOSPICES DE BEAUNE and PAULÉE for more details.

Trollinger, or **Blauer Trollinger**, is the most common German name for the distinctly ordinary black grape variety known as SCHIAVA in Italy, VERNATSCH in the Tyrol, and Black Hamburg by many who grow and buy table grapes. It almost certainly originated in what is now the Italian Tyrol (see ALTO ADIGE) and its German name is a corruption of Tirolinger. In Germany, it is associated exclusively with WÜRTTEMBERG, where it has been cultivated since the 14th century (see GERMAN HISTORY). This southern region's 2,350 ha/5,804 acres sufficed as of 2003 to sustain the variety's position as Germany's fourth most planted red wine vine, a rather astonishing statistic when one considers that virtually all of the resultant pale red is drunk by thirsty Württembergers.

Tronçais is a sort of French OAK named after a forest near NEVERS.

trophy wines, small group of wines more expensive than any others and becoming more so under sustained attack from the world's best-heeled COLLECTORS, INVESTORS, and drinkers. A Bordeaux FIRST GROWTH, PETRUS or Le PIN from a fine VINTAGE is a trophy wine. Most wines from DOMAINE DE LA ROMANÉE-CONTI and Domaine LEROY count, as do the single-vineyard bottlings of GUIGAL, most PRESTIGE CUVÉES from Champagne, TROCKENBEERENAUSLESEN from top German growers and Austrians such as Kracher, VEGA SICILIA, L'Ermita of PRIORAT, Dominio de Pingus, and the most lauded SUPERTUSCANS and GAJA bottlings. New World trophy wines include PENFOLDS Grange and all the CALIFORNIA CULT wines. The key to identifying trophy wines is their international fame (often determined by a particularly high SCORE, notably from the American wine critic Robert PARKER) and, especially, PRICE. Their prices rose markedly in the late 1990s because of the dramatic increase, particularly in ASIA, in the number of potential buyers of these 'limited edition' wines prepared to acquire them at any price.

tropical viticulture. Although the grapevine is regarded by many as a strictly temperate plant, it is now increasingly grown in the tropics, defined approximately as the region bordered by the tropics of Cancer and Capricorn. Countries in which some grapes, generally

TABLE GRAPES, are cultivated in tropical conditions include AUSTRALIA, CAMBODIA, Colombia, BOLIVIA, BRAZIL, ECUADOR, INDIA, INDONESIA, KENYA, Laos, MEXICO, MYANMAR, NAMIBIA, Nigeria, the Philippines, SRI LANKA, TANZANIA, THAILAND, VENEZUELA, and VIETNAM.

Within the tropics there are many different climates, modified by differences in ELEVATION and RAINFALL. Lowland tropical areas can be divided into those regions which are almost continuously wet, those with pronounced wet and dry seasons, and those which are virtually arid. In the lowland wet tropics, grapevines adopt an evergreen growth habit and can be manipulated into cropping more than once per year, mainly by PRUNING twice, immediately after harvest, and by the application of chemicals which induce dormant buds to burst. Other chemicals are used, particularly for TABLE GRAPES, which retard growth and induce flower buds to form (see GROWTH REGULATORS).

In areas with pronounced wet and dry seasons, pruning and removing all vegetation can induce a form of DORMANCY, which leads to BUDBREAK and a second VINE GROWTH CYCLE. In some tropical countries, grapes can be ripening as temperatures are rising, contrary to most TEMPERATE areas, where ripening proceeds as temperatures fall.

In arid tropical areas, IRRIGATION is essential to permit vine growth. Here budburst is initiated by pruning and withholding irrigation water. Highland tropical areas with elevations in excess of 1,000 m/3,280 ft can have climates that are almost temperate with temperatures that are sufficiently low (less than 15 °C/59 °F) to induce normal dormancy and allow grapevines to follow a climate-controlled growth cycle, as for non-tropical areas.

The majority of tropical grapes are consumed as TABLE GRAPES. However, increasing amounts are used as DRYING GRAPES, especially in India, or fermented into wine. Grapevines can be very productive in the tropics, giving YIELDS of fresh fruit of 140 to 280 hl/ha, or 8 to 16 tons/acre, more than once a year—so tropical viticulture can yield relatively inexpensive wine, as in the far north of Brazil, for example, although in Thailand producers are increasingly encouraging vines to produce a single higher quality crop every 12 months.

Depending on the climate, tropical grapes can be programmed to reach maturity at times of the year when other fresh fruit is not available, or when international prices are very high.
                                    J.V.P., H.-P.H., & R.E.S.

Trousseau, well-connected and well-travelled red wine grape indigenous to the JURA, where it makes distinctively perfumed, powerful wines that age well and are much more deeply coloured than POULSARD provided yields are controlled. Since early-21st-century

research pinpointed the best (warmer) vineyard sites for the variety, plantings had increased: 177 ha/437 acres by 2011. It buds early and may be affected by spring frosts, and it is an irregular yielder. In the mid 19th century, the early French AMPELOGRAPHER Comte A. Odart maintained that Trousseau is the same as Portugal's BASTARDO, as DNA PROFILING has confirmed. Under the names Bastardo, Maturana Tinta, Merenzao, and Verdejo Negro, it has been grown in Iberia for at least two centuries, although its journey from eastern France remains a mystery. DNA parentage analysis strongly suggests that the variety is a sibling of both CHENIN BLANC and SAUVIGNON BLANC, and probably has a parent-offspring relationship with that other Jura variety SAVAGNIN. Grapes called Bastardo are grown in Oregon, Crimea, and Moldova.

Trousseau Gris is a colour mutation that was once known as Gray Riesling in California and is enjoying a small renaissance there.

trunk, the main stem of a tree, from the ground to the first branches or, in the case of a grapevine, to the CORDONS or HEAD. Newly formed vine trunks are pliable and need support (see VINE TRAINING). The height of the trunk of a grapevine is variable, from 10 cm/4 in (in BUSH VINES) to more than 10 m/30 ft (in vines growing up trees), and is determined by the specifications set for each TRAINING SYSTEM and TRELLIS. The trunk height determines the position of the CANOPY relative to the ground. Vine trunks are woody and form part of the bulk needed for storage reserves, especially of CARBOHYDRATES and NITROGEN compounds. In climates with freezing winters, multiple trunks are used to facilitate replacement after winter killing, and in extremely cold climates trunks are buried during the winter (see WINTER PROTECTION).

The trunk of any plant (including the OAK tree, used for COOPERAGE and CORKS) contains a sleeve of conducting tissue with the CAMBIUM in its centre, bark (with PHLOEM) on the outside, and wood (with XYLEM) on the inside. Through these tissues, xylem sap moves upward, carrying water, minerals, and compounds from the roots to the leaves, and phloem sap moves multidirectionally carrying sugars and elaborated molecules from the leaves to the rest of the vine. The downward passage of phloem sap in vines can be interrupted by trunk CINCTURING or girdling. See also TRUNK DISEASES.   B.G.C.

trunk diseases, group of FUNGAL DISEASES that infect the wood of the vine and other perennial crops primarily through PRUNING wounds. They are caused by *Ascomycete* and, to a lesser extent, *Basidiomycetes* fungi. Grapevine trunk diseases affect both young and mature vineyards and occur wherever grapes are grown.

In young vineyards, BLACK FOOT and PETRI DISEASE are the most prevalent and devastating of these diseases, constituting what is currently known as the young vine decline complex, which can be observed as early as a few months after planting. Though spread of these diseases can occur in the vineyard, one of the main sources of infection is compromised plant material since it has been well demonstrated that fungi responsible for causing young vine decline can be introduced to the grapevine propagation process in nurseries from infected MOTHER VINES.

Trunk diseases affecting mature vineyards include ESCA and the canker diseases BOTRYO-SPHAERIA DIEBACK, EUTYPA DIEBACK, and PHOMOP-SIS dieback. Symptoms are characterized by dieback and death of spurs, canes, cordons, trunks, and eventual vine death due to canker formation in the vascular tissue. Grapevine canker diseases are currently recognized as one of the primary factors limiting vineyard longevity and productivity, causing significant economic losses to the grapevine industry worldwide due to YIELD reduction and increased production costs, including both prevention and the removal of diseased wood. Since establishing and maintaining a vineyard is very costly, a long lifespan for vines is essential for economic success, as well as for the widely reported relationship between VINE AGE and wine quality. The decline and death of young and mature vines can cause substantial economic loss to grape-growers. Management strategies satisfactorily to control and/or eradicate the different fungi infecting and colonizing the wood of the grapevine are not currently available.

The International Council of Grapevine Trunk Diseases, formed in 1998, meets biannually to co-ordinate research into tackling these increasing threats. J.R.U.-T.

Carter, M. V., *The Status of Eutypa lata as a Pathogen*, monograph, Phytopathological Paper 32, Commonwealth Agricultural Bureau, International Mycological Institute (UK, 1991).

Gramaje, D., and Armengol, J., 'Fungal trunk pathogens in the grapevine propagation process: potential inoculum sources, detection, identification, and management strategies, *Plant Disease*, 95 (2011), 1040–55.

Mostert, L., et al., 'A review of Phaeoacremonium species involved in Petri disease and esca of grapevines', *Phytopathologia Mediterranea*, 45 (2006), S12–S29.

Smart, R., 'Grapevine trunk diseases—a larger problem than ever posed by phylloxera?', *Practical Winery & Vineyard* (Jan 2014), 9–13.

Úrbez-Torres, J. R., 'The status of Botryosphaeriaceae spp. infecting grapevines', *Phytopathologia Mediterranea*, 50 (2011), S5–S45.

Úrbez-Torres, J. R., et al., 'Phomopsis dieback: a grapevine trunk disease caused by Phomopsis viticola in California', *Plant Disease*, 97/12 (2013), 1,571–9.

trunked, a common form of VINE TRAINING where the vine has a trunk of variable height which ends in a HEAD or CORDONS. The term trunked is particularly used in eastern Europe and the former Soviet Republics, where such vines are considered high or low trunked, in contrast with trunkless vines, which are easier to bury for WINTER PROTECTION.

Tsaoussi, white grape speciality of the Greek island of Cephalonia, where it may be blended with the more distinctive ROBOLA.

Tsimlyansky Cherny, vine speciality of Rostov in RUSSIA making tannic, characterful reds.

Tsolikouri, relatively important white wine grape of GEORGIA, although only about a tenth as widely planted there as the popular RKATSITELI. It makes semi-sweet and dry wines.

TTB, acronym for the Alcohol and Tobacco Tax and Trade Bureau, the US regulatory body responsible for AVA approvals, federal taxation, and label approvals and winemaking protocols (although states are permitted to enact more stringent rules than those applied nationally). TTB is an offshoot of the Bureau of Alcohol, Tobacco, and Firearms, which previously was the overseer of alcohol beverage regulation.

tufa, a rock formed by the localized precipitation of calcium carbonate, typically in association with springs, caves, river beds, and lake edges. It should not be confused with the marine LIMESTONE of the Loire region known in French as TUFFEAU, nor with the widespread non-calcareous volcanic deposit called TUFF that is much more relevant to viticulture. A.J.M.

tuff is a fine-grained VOLCANIC rock created when fine, ashy material ejected during a volcanic eruption settles, accumulates, and through time becomes progressively hardened. Tuffs vary in composition and colour, depending on the chemistry of the parent volcano but all comprise several silicate minerals (see GEOLOGY) and so have plenty of potential nutrients for the vine. Geologically, young tuffs can still be relatively soft and easily weathered. **Tuffaceous** soils, such as those found in parts of southern Italy and SICILY, can therefore be deep and fertile. The relative softness of young tuff is exploited in places such as TOKAJ, EGER, and Bükk in Hungary for excavating extensive wine cellars. Confusingly, some wine literature refers to tuff as TUFA, which is geologically quite different. In Italy, *tufo* is sometimes used rather inexactly to refer to certain limestone soils as well as to those of volcanic origin. A.J.M.

tuffeau, a common rock type in the central LOIRE. *Tuffeau blanc* is CALCAREOUS but provides much better DRAINAGE than most LIMESTONES. This is the rock used to build many of the châteaux of the Loire and remaining hollows in the rock have been adapted for winemaking and storage. The overlying *tuffeau jaune* is more sandy, and is particularly suitable for the Cabernet Franc vine, underlying some of the best vineyards in CHINON and SAUMUR-CHAMPIGNY. It is distinct from both TUFA and TUFF. A.J.M.

Tulbagh, inland wine district in SOUTH AFRICA just east of SWARTLAND that is best-known for its whites but produces some fine reds too.

Tumbarumba, relatively new high-ELEVATION, cool Australian wine region especially suited to Sauvignon Blanc, Chardonnay, and Pinot Noir, the last two both for table and sparkling wine production. Spring frost is the major threat. See NEW SOUTH WALES.

Tunisia, North African country which was once an important wine producer. Viticulture was probably introduced when the Phoenicians established the city of CARTHAGE on the coast and was certainly developed during the Roman occupation. The Phoenician agronomist MAGO recorded contemporary vine-growing and winemaking practices in his *Treatise of Agronomy*.

French occupation until 1956 led to vineyard development on a vast scale, but independence was followed by a decline in local expertise. The total vineyard area devoted to wine production fell from 17,500 ha/43,240 acres in 2000 to 9,000 ha in 2013 when 238,000 hl/6.3 million gal of wine were made in the country's 16 wineries, about 60% of it rosé and only 30% red. About 40% of all wine is classed as AOC. Italians, Swiss, Germans, and Austrians have all invested in the Tunisian wine industry since the late 20th century, bringing with them winemaking and viticultural expertise, and an overall improvement in wine quality.

Annual rainfall is between 250 mm/10 in and 500 mm/20 in, with the great majority of precipitation in mid autumn. The average annual temperature is 20 °C/68 °F. The most important varieties traditionally planted included Carignan, Mourvèdre, Cinsaut, Alicante Bouschet, Grenache, Syrah, and Merlot for reds and Muscat of Alexandria, Chardonnay, and Pedro Ximenez for whites. More recently Petit Verdot, Touriga Nacional, and Marselan have been planted for reds and rosés with the likes of Viognier, Verdejo, Sauvignon Blanc, and Grenache Blanc for whites. The vast majority of wine production is centred in and around the Cape Bon region in the north east of the country. Most Tunisian wine is drunk by tourists.

Platter, J. & E., *Africa Uncorked* (London, 2002).

Turkey, eastern Mediterranean country with the fifth largest vineyard area in the world

(517,000 ha/1,277,500 acres in 2012) where only 3% of the produce is destined for wine. Most grapes are eaten fresh, used for DRYING, molasses, and the popular aniseed-flavoured spirit rakı, produced in nearly equal volumes to wine. Of the 552,000 hl/14.6 million gal of wine produced, less than 5% was exported in 2012. Despite the crackdown on alcohol consumption by the long-serving, Islamist-leaning government, the early 21st century saw a marked increase in wine quality and interest in Turkey's rich heritage of INDIGENOUS VARIETIES.

History

Turks settled in ANATOLIA in the late 11th century as fresh converts to ISLAM. Alcohol consumption was forbidden, which conflicted with the Turks' old customs of drinking, and promulgated turbulent encounters with alcohol over the next thousand years. The non-Muslim community was allowed to produce and control strong drink and its consumption by all was tolerated for economic reasons. There were PROHIBITIONS time and again, a dilemma that has continued throughout the short history of the modern republic, resulting today in burdensome regulations and a punitive tax regime. Nonetheless, a deep-rooted wine culture in Anatolia can be observed even today.

Most importantly, south eastern Turkey is one of the most likely locations of the ORIGINS OF VINICULTURE, a thesis supported by linguistic evidence.

The ancient civilizations that inhabited the land, from Hittites and Assyrians to Thracians and Lydians, had all been involved in growing grapes and making wine with their relevant customs, ceremonies, and festivities, continuing through Greek, Roman, and Byzantine periods. Alongside its religious attributes, wine was a commodity traded in volume along major river routes and through ports. Between 1650 and 1200 BC, when the Hittites ruled most of Anatolia, there were enhanced laws safeguarding viticultural practices and trade routes, identifying the different types of wine consumed. Hittites used the word *wiyana* for wine, influencing the words used in many modern languages.

Thracians, the residents of Thrace in what is now north-western Turkey, were in ancient times famous for their wines and drinking habits, and in their Mysteries described DIONYSUS, 'the god of the grape harvest, winemaking, and wine' as Thracian. Western Anatolia is home to the ruins of the largest temple dedicated to Dionysus, located in Teos near İzmir. Numerous artefacts depicting grapes and wine-related rituals are displayed in the award-winning Museum of Anatolian Civilizations in Ankara. See also ANATOLIA.

Modern history

Boosted by the construction of a RAILWAY network, vineyards in the Aegean and Thrace were the source of vast quantities of wine exported to Europe during the 19th-century PHYLLOXERA devastation.

In the aftermath of the First World War, the forced migration of Armenian and Greek settlers, who had been responsible for most of the production of and trade in wine, abandoned Turkish viniculture, with the exception of few Alavi and Syriac villages that persevered in making wine for their own consumption.

In the early years of the modern republic, foreign CONSULTANTS were hired to aid reconstruction. Most wineries were acquisitions from Greeks but Kemal Atatürk, the founder of the republic, established Atatürk Orman Çiftliği Wine Factory in 1925 to revive Turkish wine production. Doluca in southern Thrace and Kavaklıdere in Ankara, still important wineries today, were in the vanguard during the 1920s. Competition from the state monopoly Tekel and some regional growers encouraged both companies to focus on marketing and sales rather than wine quality and diversity well into the last decade of the 20th century.

A new chapter began in the mid 1990s when Sarafin and Gülor, early BOUTIQUE wineries in southern Thrace, planted their own vineyards with INTERNATIONAL VARIETIES and produced VARIETAL wines. Their success spurred many similar new producers in the early 21st century. The concurrent interest in imported wine, despite protective tax policies, helped create a wine culture in Turkey and an overall increase in Turkish wine quality, aided by thoroughly modern technology and foreign consultants hired to improve viticultural and winemaking practices.

Domestic wine consumption of a mere one litre per head per year forced producers to search for new markets. Attempts to introduce and promote Turkish wine in western markets through tastings and competitions swiftly demonstrated that Turkey needs to focus on its own grape varieties and winemaking styles to find a place in export markets already sated with international varietals from elsewhere.

Wines of Turkey, the generic organization founded in 2008 by leading wineries to promote Turkish wine, has been expanding its scope. The focus of Turkey's Tobacco and Alcohol Market Regulatory Authority is to prevent illegal sales rather than organizing viticulture and winemaking. In effect, the wine scene in Turkey is based on the practice of individual producers rather than on regulations and an accumulation of customs.

In 2013 the government imposed largely unpopular curbs on the sale and promotion of wine.

Geography, climate, and grape varieties

Owing to prolonged administrative neglect, the wine-growing regions of Turkey are not officially designated. Geographically, the country is divided into seven regions with a wide variety of climatic conditions.

The relatively wet coastal **Black Sea** region grows three-quarters of the world's hazelnuts and good quality tea rather than grapevines. In the central Black Sea province of Tokat there is a tradition of grape growing based around the white variety Narince, well adapted to the cold winters and cool summers. Most vineyards lie at 400 m/1,300 ft ELEVATION, around the course of Kelkit River, the longest tributary of the Yeşilırmak River. It makes rich, opulent wines, often oak aged. Diren, established in 1958, is the only winery based in the region.

The southern shores of the **Mediterranean** region with dry, hot summers and mild, wet winters do not provide the best conditions for viticulture. Such vineyards and wineries as are there are at high elevations only.

The vast **Aegean** region, responsible for more than half of Turkey's wine production, consists of the coastline and the mountainous interior. The climate is typically MEDITERRANEAN on the coast and inland around Manisa, Turkey's leading province for grape production. Kavaklıdere's Pendore vineyards here focus mainly on black varieties under the consultancy of Stéphane DERENONCOURT.

The area further inland, around Güney in Denizli, has a semi-arid CONTINENTAL climate with hot, dry summers and cold, snowy winters, at elevations of up to 800 m/2,600 ft. The local Çalkarası grape is used mainly for rosé wines. Pamukkale and Küp are the leading producers here with, unusually, experience of more than 50 vintages.

The Aegean is known for two local white grape varieties. The seedless Sultaniye (SULTANA), Turkey's most widely planted grape, is basically used for DRYING but has more recently been the source of some fresh, aromatic wines. Bornova Misketi, associated with the Bornova area of Izmir, is related to MUSCAT BLANC À PETITS GRAINS and is used for dry and semi-sweet wines as well as for DRIED-GRAPE WINES, a style gaining in popularity. Dark-skinned local varieties Foça Karası and Urla Karası are relatively recent (re?) discoveries by local producers. Cabernet Sauvignon, Syrah, Merlot, and Petit Verdot produce richly structured wines while the fruit of generally older Alicante Bouschet and Carignan vines is used mostly for blending. Chardonnay and Sauvignon Blanc can make fine wines when grown at high elevations, as proven by Sevilen, founded in 1942.

A good 40% of all registered producers are based in the **Marmara** region that includes eastern Thrace. Surrounded by three seas, the peninsula has a unique TERROIR with two low mountain ranges, Ganos to the south and Strandja to the north. The most valuable vineyard areas are located in their foothills.

Influenced by the Sea of Marmara, the climate is typically Mediterranean in southern Thrace, where local black Karalahna grapes give deeply coloured, tannic wines. Adakarası, an aromatic variety grown on the island of Avşa in the Sea of Marmara, is often used for rosé. The success of recently revived white varieties Yapıncak and Kolorko has triggered a spate of new plantings. Doluca has for long been the leading winery of the region. Kayra, since taking over the former state monopoly Tekel in 2005, has won instant recognition for creativity and dynamism despite the staid image of its predecessor.

The province of Kırklareli in the foothills of Strandja Mountains is close to the Black Sea that influences the mild continental climate here. Soils are particularly varied and include decomposed GRANITE, LIMESTONE, TERRA ROSSA clay, and QUARTZ gravels. The region's late-ripening Papaskarası yields smooth, fruity reds with bright acidity. Some of Turkey's most energetic newcomers are based in this relatively cool climate.

The windy island of Bozcaada is home to some of the oldest wineries and vineyards in Turkey and grows mainly local varieties such as the dark Kuntra and pale Çavuş and Vasilaki, mostly as BUSH VINES. Despite this traditional wine culture, the island was put on the wine map thanks to the efforts of the visionary winery Corvus.

The vineyards in **Central Anatolia** follow the course of Turkey's longest river, the Kızılırmak. North east of the capital Ankara lies the town of Kalecik, home to the native black grape Kalecik Karası, saved from extinction during the 1970s. Its soft, fresh reds enjoyed cult status in the early 1990s. The vineyards are planted at an elevation of 650 m/2,130 ft, in LIME-rich LOAM and GRAVEL. The river and the surrounding mountains moderate what is otherwise a severe continental climate.

Upriver in the south east, Cappadocia has an elevation of over 1000 m/3,280 ft, with sandy, VOLCANIC soils. The climate is continental and arid with low rainfall. Winters are very cold and mostly snowy while summers are hot and dry. Winter and spring FROSTS can pose problems. The most promising grape variety in Cappadocia for dry and sparkling wines is the white Emir. Other white wine grapes Narince, Sauvignon Blanc, and Chardonnay have also performed well. Kavaklıdere, based in Ankara, has vineyards in Cappadocia focusing on white varieties branded Côtes d'Avanos. Established in 1943, Turasan is the oldest and the leading producer in Cappadocia with two main vineyard areas. Their winery is carved out of one of Cappadocia's spectacular rock formations in the town of Ürgüp, a well-known tourist destination.

In **eastern Anatolia** vineyards are on the course of the Euphrates River in the provinces of Malatya and Elazığ, at elevations of 1000 to 1100 m or more with a markedly CONTINENTAL climate. Annual rainfall can be under 400 mm and diurnal TEMPERATURE variation is wide. The principal variety planted is Öküzgözü along with some Boğazkere. Most vineyards here are well managed and free of PHYLLOXERA.

The vineyards of **south-eastern Anatolia** are less well cared for than those of Elazığ, and phylloxera infestations are common. Although only 130 km from Elazığ, the area around the city of Diyarbakır, the principal city of south east Turkey where Kurdish influence is strong, is very different. Much lower elevation, in the basin of the Tigris River, this area is extremely hot in summer. The best grapes come from higher land in the Çüngüş and Çermik areas northwest of Diyarbakır which is closer to the Euphrates than the Tigris but more influenced by the conditions of Diyarbakır. South-eastern Anatolia's harvest is the latest in Turkey, extending into late October.

Gigantic dams have been built on both the Euphrates and Tigris which have had the effect of making the climate milder.

Of the two main varieties this part of Turkey is known for, Öküzgözü is Turkey's most widely planted red wine grape, giving medium-bodied, fruity wines. Boğazkere, a thick-skinned grape from the area around Diyarbakır, makes tannic wines with ageing potential. They are traditionally blended for well-balanced, structured wines which go well with the meat-based cuisine of the region. Although both varieties are also planted in other areas of Turkey, many producers choose to source their grapes from Elazığ and Diyarbakır. The former Tekel facility in Elazığ, run by Kayra for the famous Buzbağ label, is one of very few wineries in the region.

U.C.

Atilla, A. N., *Batı Anadolu Şarap Kültürü* (İstanbul, 2011) [Wine culture in Western Anatolia].

Aydınoğlu, Ü. and Şenol, A. K. (eds.), *Olive Oil and Wine Production in Anatolia during Antiquity*, International Symposium Proceedings (Mersin, 2008).

Yankı, M., *Periler Diyarında Şarap Yolculuğu* (Ankara, 2012) [Wine's journey in fairy land—about wine culture and the history of Cappadocia].

www.winesofturkey.org

Turkmenistan, central Asian republic and former state of the Soviet Union that sprawls between the Caspian Sea, UZBEKISTAN, AFGHANISTAN, and IRAN. Its approximately 29,000 ha/71,630 acres of vineyards specialize in TABLE GRAPES and RAISINS but according to OIV figures, 170,000 hl/4.5 million gal of strong, mainly sweet wine were produced in 2011. The vast Karakumy Desert occupies a large part of this hot, dry country.

There are large daily and annual temperature fluctuations (see TEMPERATURE VARIABILITY). The average January temperature is −4 °C/25 °F; that of July is 28 °C. The annual rainfall is 80 mm/3 in in the north east and 300 mm in the mountains, the largest amount of rainfall being recorded in spring and winter. Evidence of vine-growing in the country dates back to the 3rd century BC. Greek and Roman writers report that grapes were cultivated in Marghian (the Murghab Valley) and in Aria (the Tejen Valley). The Kopetdag ravines still have a great diversity of WILD VINES that have served as a basis for many INDIGENOUS VARIETIES. Different wine vessels depicting grape bunches found during excavations of the village of Baghir near the capital Ashkhabad testify to the fact that Turkmenistan has a long history of winemaking.

For many years the nomadic way of life of Turkmenistan's population did not favour the development of agriculture, viticulture included, which had to wait until the country was annexed to RUSSIA at the end of the 19th century and the Ashkhabad RAILWAY was built. In 1898, the total vineyard area was just 308 ha/760 acres. Thereafter it increased and reached 2,500 ha in 1928, 4,000 ha in 1940, 11,000 ha in 1975, and 27,000 ha in 1990. Almost all vineyards need IRRIGATION, but only the north part of the Tashauz region needs WINTER PROTECTION. The Karakumy canal provided the chance to increase vineyard areas and their production. Vineyards are mainly in the Ashkhabad region with some in Mary and Chardzhou regions.

Turkmenistan is a unique region suitable for early-, mid-, and late-maturing table and raisin grapes but only a limited selection of wine grapes are grown including Terbash, Tara Uzüm Ashkhabadski, RIESLING, SAPERAVI, Kizil Sapak, and Bayanshira.   V.R.

Tursan, 320 ha/790 acre AOC in the Landes in SOUTH WEST FRANCE producing wine in all three colours, mainly rosé made from Cabernet Franc and TANNAT grapes with Fer, Cabernet Sauvignon, and Merlot, mostly from the Geaune CO-OPERATIVE and sold locally. The white version is of more interest and is virtually a one-producer wine, but what a producer: three-star chef Michel Guérard of Eugénie-lès-Bains who sells his oaked version of the local white grape variety BAROQUE under the name Baron de Bachen.

Tuscany, the most important region in central ITALY (see map under ITALY), where it is known as Toscana. Today Tuscany is at the centre neither of Italy's economic life nor of its political life, but it is the region which formed Italy's language, its literature, and its art, and has thus assumed a central place in the country's culture and self-image. The landscape, immortalized in the work of artists from Giotto to Michelangelo and part of every European's cultural baggage, has remained largely unchanged to this day: a succession of hills and valleys covered with cypresses, umbrella pines, olive groves—and vineyards.

Ancient history

In the ancient world, Tuscany, and at certain points of its history a much larger area, was known as Etruria. See ETRUSCANS for the ancient history of Tuscany.

Medieval history

If we know more about the wines of medieval Tuscany than we do about the wines of other regions of medieval Italy, it is not because they were better or there were more of them: the reason is the region's, and particularly Florence's, economic and political importance.

Viticulture flourished despite the frequent, small-scale civil wars. The region produced more or less equal amounts of oil and wine, but by far the largest crop was wheat. Smallholders were rare in this part of Italy, since the land was mostly owned by monasteries, the local aristocracy, and, increasingly, by merchants in the cities. The system of agriculture was often that known as *mezzadria*, sharecropping whereby the landowner would provide the working capital and the land in return for half (*mezzo*, hence the name) the crop. In 1132, for instance, the Badia (Abbey) di Passignano (whose wine is now made and sold by the merchants ANTINORI) leased some of its land to a wealthy cobbler for half his crop of olive oil and wine.

The regional centre for selling wine was the Mercato Vecchio in Florence. The earliest reference to wine retailers in the city dates from 1079, and in 1282 the wine sellers formed a guild, the Arte dei Vinattieri. Giovanni di Piero Antinori joined it in 1385, a member of the noble family that continues to make and sell wine in Tuscany today. In order to uphold the profession's reputation, the guild imposed a strict code of practice. The statutes insisted on cleanliness and exact measures; the shop was not to be situated within 100 yards of a church and it was not to serve children under 15. No cooked food could be sold, and shops were not to shelter ruffians, thieves, or prostitutes. The wine trade was vital to the Florentine economy. Tax records show that more than 300,000 hl/7.9 million gal of wine entered the city every year in the 14th century. The Florentine historian Villani, writing in 1338, estimated that weekly consumption of wine was a gallon a head. Given that Florence had approximately 90,000 inhabitants, this meant that well over 90% was sold elsewhere, to the surrounding country or other Tuscan cities, some overseas via the port of Pisa, mainly to Flanders, PARIS, and Marseilles.

By no means all of this wine would have been Tuscan: a lot of it had come from CRETE (Candia), CORSICA, or NAPLES. Tuscany itself produced red wine, which was usually called simply *vino vermihlio*, but occasionally names appear. The reds of MONTEPULCIANO and Cortona were heavy, those of Casentino lighter. In the late 14th century, we find Montalcino referred to as BRUNELLO. The most important of Tuscany's white wines were called 'Vernaccia' and 'Trebbiano', probably named after their respective grape varieties VERNACCIA and TREBBIANO, but neither was an exclusively Tuscan wine. Of the two, Vernaccia was the more highly reputed. In its sweet form it was associated primarily with LIGURIA, and particularly with Cinqueterre and Corniglia, although sweet Vernaccia was also made in Tuscany. The dry style of Vernaccia, made in San Gimignano (but also elsewhere), which is not found before the 14th century, was not exported overseas, because only the sweet version was capable of surviving the long sea voyage to France, Flanders, or England. Trebbiano, too, could be dry or sweet. The first recorded mention of CHIANTI is in the correspondence of the Tuscan merchant Francesco di Marco Datini in 1398, and it is a *white* wine. Datini was fond of it: in 1404 Amadeo Gherardini of Vignamaggio, which is still a well-known estate, wrote to Datini sending him half a barrel of his personal stock. Another of Datini's favourites was (red) CARMIGNANO.

Datini's letters give us an idea of what a rich merchant bought for his own consumption. He had MALMSEY sent to him from Venice and Genoa, and, more exotically, the equally strong, sweet wine of Tyre from Venice. These foreign wines were luxury items. Another expensive wine from outside Tuscany that Datini loved was Greco. It was grown in PUGLIA and so highly prized was it that in the 14th century the commune of San Gimignano abandoned its tradition of giving distinguished visitors a few ounces of saffron and instead made them a present of the precious Greco.

Dante and Boccaccio both mention Vernaccia, a byword for luxury. No Tuscan author wrote exclusively about the wines of the region until Francesco Redi. His *Bacco in Toscana* ('Bacchus in Toscana'), published in 1685, is subtitled *ditirambo*, the Greek dithyramb being a choral lyric in praise of DIONYSUS. Redi's poem, however, has little to do with the classical genre and is no more than an excuse for showing off his learning to fellow members of the Accademia della Crusca: he provides 228 pages of unhelpful and pretentious notes to deluge 980 lines of verse. Neither the poem nor the notes contains anything interesting or new about Tuscan wine and viticulture, and the notes Leigh Hunt wrote to his translation (1825) of *Bacco in Toscana* are a good deal more amusing (although of more use to the historian of language than to the historian of wine). The only wines Redi mentions, and praises, are VERNACCIA, CHIANTI, CARMIGNANO, and, finally, MONTEPULCIANO, which he regards as the king of all wines. H.M.W.

Flower, R., *Chianti: The Land, the People and the Wine* (London, 1979).

Melis, F., 'Produzione e commercio dei vini italiani nei secoli XIII–XVIII', *Annales cisalpines d'histoire sociale*, 1/3 (1972), 107-33.

Modern history

Tuscan viticulture was dominated historically by large estates owned by wealthy local families, the majority of them of noble origin, and tilled by a workforce of sharecroppers. The demise of this system in the 1950s and 1960s led to a hiatus in investment or even ordinary maintenance, deterioration of the vineyards and cellars, plummeting wine quality, and eventual sale of the properties to new owners with the requisite capital and energy to carry on the viticultural traditions of the past. Tuscan ownership of Tuscan viticulture is no longer the norm but the new wave of vintners from Milan, Rome, and Genoa—joined in the 1980s by a sizeable contingent of foreigners—has shown both a commendable commitment to quality and an equally commendable openness to new and more cosmopolitan ideas. See also ANTINORI, FRESCOBALDI, and RICASOLI, local noble families with considerable wine interests.

Geography and vine varieties

Tuscany produces wines in a wide variety of ELEVATIONS, EXPOSITIONS, and SOILS. Vineyards spread from the plains of the MAREMMA on the Tuscan coast and steep HILLSIDES as high as 550 m/1,800 ft above sea level in Gaiole-in-Chianti and Lamole in Greve-in-Chianti. A full 68% of the region is officially classified as hilly (a mere 8% of the land is flat) and HILLSIDE VINEYARDS, at elevations of between 150 and 500 m (500–1,600 ft) supply the vast majority of the better-quality wines. The SANGIOVESE vine, the backbone of the region's production, seems to require the concentration of SUNLIGHT that slopes can provide to ripen well in these latitudes, as well as the less fertile soils on the hills. Growers also value the significant day-night TEMPERATURE VARIABILITY as an important factor in developing its aromatic qualities.

Sangiovese, with more than 38,000 ha/93,860 acres planted in 2010 is by far Tuscany's most planted grape variety. The second most planted, the insipid white TREBBIANO Toscano was planted on just 3,095 ha and continues to decline now that it has lost its classic role as ingredient in the many Sangiovese-based wines made in the region. In the past enormous yields were demanded from both varieties and the generously demarcated DOCs that were set up in the 1960s encouraged large-scale plantings of high yielding CLONES with scant attention to the suitability of the site, giving

Sangiovese an undeserved reputation as a mediocre grape variety. As the DOC laws did nothing to encourage the production of good quality wines, many producers enthusiastically embraced INTERNATIONAL VARIETIES, especially Merlot and Cabernet Sauvignon, which they aged in French BARRIQUES and sold at high prices. The popularity of these SUPERTUSCANS is only now slowly subsiding. Several iconic producers persevered with Sangiovese, devoting their best sites to it and drastically lowering YIELDS. As they refused to blend the then-obligatory Trebbiano Toscano into the wine, they also had to resort to the lowly VINO DA TAVOLA category. The situation has been redressed, especially in CHIANTI CLASSICO where intensive research in clonal material and site specifics led to a noticeable increase in quality, while the creation of the IGT Toscana brought the Supertuscan rebels back into the fold of a slightly higher denomination. Although many producers in Chianti Classico still use Merlot as a blending partner (up to 20% varieties other than Sangiovese is allowed), the unstoppable trend is for varietal Sangiovese wines, and regularly from single vineyards. Many ferment with AMBIENT YEAST with wines aged in traditional large oak casks rather than small French barrels.

BRUNELLO DI MONTALCINO, a 100% Sangiovese wine by law, and in spite of the recent lapse in credibility caused by a blending scandal, has long shown that Sangiovese can produce world-class, long-lived wines. Its neighbour VINO NOBILE DI MONTEPULCIANO has been more reluctant to embrace Sangiovese fully; the production rules were changed in 2010 to allow for a 30% inclusion of INTERNATIONAL VARIETIES, although quality producers tend to concentrate on Sangiovese and its ability to transmit a transparent expression of the Monepulciano terroir.

BOLGHERI has been Tuscany's Cabernet Sauvignon, Cabernet Franc, and Merlot hotspot (see SASSICAIA for more details) although many of the wines contain a portion of Sangiovese to add acidity to Cabernet and Merlot which can be too ripe and flabby when grown on the hot Maremma plains. Further inland and higher up in the hills where a cooler climate prevails, the previously unremarkable DOC Montecucco has attracted newcomers who regularly produce wines on a par with the best from Chianti Classico even if their number is still small. DOC Monteregio di Massa Marittima seems equally promising for fine wine, especially when vineyards are planted on elevations above 300 m, but it may take some time (as well as more producers) to convincingly show its potential.

Not all of the myriad of DOCs and DOCGs in Tuscany (48 in total in 2014) are either significant or particularly different from the supposedly lower IGT category. Producers

therefore often prefer to label their wines with the more widely recognized IGT Toscana. More than half of Tuscany's 60,000 ha are registered for the production of DOC and IGT wine with their stricter production rules than for basic table wine. While the Chianti DOCG continues to supply the mass market with distinctly modest wines, the majority of Tuscany's wine regions are now focused on high quality. While the trend for indigenous varieties seems unstoppable, the international varieties, which are still widely planted, excel in several areas (notably in CARMIGNANO, Bolgheri, Suvereto, and, for Syrah, Cortona). While the whites from international varieties fared less well, there was still almost as much Chardonnay (585 ha/1446 acres) as Vermentino (652 ha/ 1611 acres) but most of Tuscany seems too warm to produce truly great whites. Vermentino, a relative newcomer in central Tuscany arriving from nearby LIGURIA, seems to be the most credible indigenous answer, while the minerally and elegant VERNACCIA di San Gimignano deserves a comback after it became a victim of its own success which led to the overproduction of rather technical wines.

For more details of specific Tuscan wines, see BOLGHERI, BRUNELLO DI MONTALCINO, CARMIGNANO, CHIANTI, CHIANTI CLASSICO, CHIANTI RUFINA, ELBA, GALESTRO, VERNACCIA, VINO DA TAVOLA, VINO NOBILE DI MONTEPULCIANO, VIN SANTO.   W.S.

Belfrage, N., *Brunello to Zibibbo—The Wines of Tuscany, Central and Southern Italy* (2nd edn, London, 2003).

Txakoli

Txakoli, usually white wine made in Spain's BASQUE country, known as **Chacolí** in Castilian. Like VINHO VERDE it is strongly Atlantic influenced and is usually sold young, very slightly sparkling, and low in alcohol. A century ago over 1,000 ha of vines stretched from Bayonne to Bilbao, but after PHYLLOXERA ravaged the region, few vineyards were replanted. With cool summers, and an annual RAINFALL of 1,500 mm/ 58 in, this is hardly ideal grape-growing country. The high trained Hondarribi Zuri white grape variety, which accounts for 85% of Txakoli, traditionally produced thin wines, but quality noticeably improved during the 1990s. Hondarrabi Beltza makes light reds for local consumption.

Getariako Txakolina is the principal appellation yet is still one of Spain's smallest DO regions and a matter of considerable pride to those few BASQUE farmers who stubbornly refuse to give in to the elements and have even increased their vineyards to reach 84 ha/201 acres on the rocky Biscay coast west of San Sebastian (see map under SPAIN). **Bizkaiko Txakolina** is an even smaller DO region with just 60 ha/ 144 acres of vineyards scattered in Vizcaya province around the main city of Bilbao. The

predominance of FOLLE BLANCHE grapes makes for more acidic and herbaceous wines than in Getariako. **Arabako Txakolina** is the newest DO for Txakoli and comprises just 50 ha of vineyards in the Ayala valley near Vizcaya. Hondarribi Zuri and Hondarrabi Beltza are the main grape varieties, while Petit Manseng, Petit Courbu, and Gros Manseng are also permitted.   V. de la S.

Barquín, J., Guitiérrez, L., and de la Serna, V., *The Finest Wines of Rioja and Northwest Spain* (London, 2011)

typicality

typicality, the original English word for **typicity**, a wine tasting term adapted from the French *typicité* or Italian *tipicità* for a wine's quality of being typical of its type, geographical provenance, and even its VINTAGE year—a wine characteristic much discussed by professionals. And it is perhaps because typicality is a SUBJECTIVE notion, rather than a physical attribute that can be measured by ANALYSIS, that it is so much discussed. Individual tasters are likely to differ as to what they consider typical of a particular wine description, just as they are likely to differ in their impressions of the wine under consideration.

Typicality need not and may not concern the average wine drinker, who is right to demand merely that the wine tastes good, but it becomes important in wine JUDGING if the wine has been entered into a particular class. It is also important to professional wine buyers, particularly when choosing wines to represent a GENERIC style.

Each wine type demands a different set of characteristics. For example, a deep white wine of modest ACIDITY and relatively high ALCOHOLIC STRENGTH, smelling strongly of ALDEHYDES, would be extremely atypical of Chablis, but would display the typicality of a FINO style of SHERRY. Similarly, a very young red wine smelling strongly of CARBONIC MACERATION would be typical of many a young BEAUJOLAIS, but very unlike a young BORDEAUX.

It should be added, however, that as winemakers increasingly travel between wine regions, absorbing and applying different techniques, some distinctions between what were regarded as wine archetypes are being eroded, and there is more disagreement than ever as to what constitutes typicality. See also REGIONALITY.

typicity

typicity. See TYPICALITY.

Tyrian

Tyrian, Australian NEW VARIETY, a cross of SUMOLL and CABERNET SAUVIGNON. See CIENNA.

Tyrol

Tyrol. Hardly any wine is made in this western part of Austria, but considerable quantities are made in that part of the Tyrol ceded to Italy after the First World War, now known as the South Tyrol, Südtirol in German, or ALTO ADIGE in Italian.

Uclés, promising Spanish DO in the Cuenca province of CASTILLA-LA MANCHA.

Ugni Blanc (which is in fact Italy's ubiquitous TREBBIANO TOSCANO) is France's most planted white grape variety by far, with almost twice as much French vineyard devoted to it than Chardonnay, and yet it is rarely seen on a wine label. Just as AIRÉN, Spain's most planted white variety, supplies that country's voracious brandy stills, so the copious, thin, acid wine of Ugni Blanc washes through armagnac and, especially, cognac stills. In Charentes it is often known as St-Émilion.

But despite EU encouragement to pull up poorer-quality vines, and a distinctly sluggish market for brandy, France's total plantings of Ugni Blanc fell by well under 20% between the late 1980s and 2011 to 83,230 ha/205,578 acres.

Ugni Blanc supplanted the FOLLE BLANCHE that was pre-PHYLLOXERA the main ingredient in French brandy production because of its good resistance to POWDERY MILDEW, and grey rot. It was probably imported from Italy during the 14th century when the papal court was established at Avignon. Other Italian varieties were presumably similarly transported but Trebbiano Toscano's extraordinarily high yields and high acidity may have helped establish it in southern France, where it is still grown widely today. It is still the most planted white wine grape in Provence and is grown in the southern Rhône and in and around Bordeaux, but the great majority of plantings are in the Charentes. It is, like most copiously produced wines, low in extract and character, relatively low in alcohol, but usefully high in acidity. This exceptionally vigorous vine buds late, thereby avoiding most spring frost damage which makes it popular with growers. Yields can easily reach 150 hl/ha (8.5 tons/acre). Because it

ripens relatively late, there is a natural geographical limit on its cultivation, but in areas such as Charentes it is simply picked before it is fully ripe.

For more details of this variety, see TREBBIANO Toscano (although it is usually known throughout South America, where it is widely planted, as Ugni Blanc).

Uhudler, wine speciality of SÜDBURGENLAND in AUSTRIA—usually pink, sometimes white—made from the several AMERICAN HYBRIDS introduced post-PHYLLOXERA to this region (as to so many others in Europe, though very seldom with such lasting influence). D.S.

Ukraine, former Soviet Union state on the Black Sea. Ukraine's total vineyard area was declining even before the annexation of the vine-growing CRIMEA by RUSSIA in early 2014, after which it fell to about 50,000 ha/125,000 acres.

As so often, MONKS AND MONASTERIES were responsible for introducing viticulture to northern Ukraine in the 11th to 12th centuries. Viticulture and wine production waxed and waned since this part of the world suffered numerous raids of nomadic tribes and witnessed long periods of war. The development of capitalism in Ukraine necessitated new profitable branches of agriculture, vine-growing and winemaking included. In 1913, the total vineyard area of Ukraine was 54,000 ha/133,000 acres but due to the effects of the First World War and PHYLLOXERA, it had shrunk to 13,000 ha/3,212 acres by 1919.

Thereafter viticulture was steadily restored so that by 1940 the total vineyard area was 103,000 ha. However, the Second World War also caused great damage to the industry. The total vineyard area decreased once more, to 68,000 ha. Vineyards were completely neglected, with

the proportion of missing vines reaching 40 to 50%. In the post-war Soviet period, state farms specializing in viticulture were established and were subsequently amalgamated into specialized trusts and large companies. Nurseries were also established to meet the need for propagation material.

When the CRIMEA was ceded to Ukraine by Russia in 1954, the national total vineyard area was boosted to an estimated 400,000 ha, but since then there has since been a steady and significant decline.

Ukraine is mostly flat and sometimes hilly, with the Ukrainian Carpathian Mountains in the south west. The climate is mild, mostly CONTINENTAL. The difference between summer and winter temperatures increases in the south, which is drier and has a longer season free of snow. The frost-free period is 230 days in the north and 290 days in the south. The active temperature summation (see CLIMATE CLASSIFICATION) is 2,900–3,700 °C. The annual rainfall is 350–400 mm (13–15 in) in the south east and 1,200–1,500 mm in the Carpathian Mountains.

Commercial viticulture is concentrated in the Odessa region (31,600 ha), but also in the Kherson region (6,400 ha), the Nikolayev region (6,500 ha), the Transcarpathian region (4,100 ha), and in the Zaporozh'ye region (400 ha).

Some but not all wine regions need WINTER PROTECTION. Since most vineyards are located in drier zones, IRRIGATION has played a major part in increasing yields, with DRIP IRRIGATION employed for some higher-quality wines.

Vineyards are planted mostly to VINIFERA varieties grafted on phylloxera-resistant ROOTSTOCKS. The most planted grape variety was for long Rkatsiteli, which has accounted for as much as 40% of all plantings in some regions, but other varieties have been taking over. These are notably Chardonnay, Aligoté, Sauvignon

Blanc, Pinot Noir, Pinot Gris, Gewurztraminer, Riesling (the German sort), Podarok Magaracha, Pervenets Magaracha, Muscat white, Muscat rose, Cabernet Sauvignon, Merlot, Saperavi, Saperavi Severny, Bastardo Magarachsky—as well as the indigenous Cevat Kara, Kefessyia and Telti Kuruk (mostly in Shabo south west of Odessa)—Kokur Bely, which is thought to have Balkan roots, Sary Pandas, believed to have Greek origins, and Odessa Black, a selection of the Tairov Institute (see below).

Wine grapes account for 80% of the total vineyard area but TABLE GRAPES are gaining ground.

In 2003, Ukraine produced 1.9 million hl/50 million gal of wine, a steep decline from the 5.8 million hl average of the early 1980s before GORBACHEV's anti-alcohol campaign, although according to OIV statistics, total production had risen to 3.2 million hl by 2009. For much of the 20th century viticultural and oenological research in Ukraine was carried out by the famous centre of wine ACADEME in the former Soviet Union, the Institute for Vine and Wine MAGARACH, founded in 1828 in Yalta in the Crimea. The Tairov Institute for Viticulture and Oenology was founded in Odessa in 1905.

Of all former Soviet states, Ukraine has made most notable progress towards establishing its own wine law. Sixty viticultural regions have been specified for Ukraine.   I.N.

www.ukrvinprom.ua (Ukrainian only)

ullage, which derives from the French *ouillage*, has had a variety of meanings and uses in the English-speaking wine trade. It can mean the process of EVAPORATION of wine held in wooden containers such as a BARREL. The HEAD SPACE left in the container is also called the ullage, or 'ullage space', and the wine in that state is said to be 'on ullage'. The word ullage is also used for any space in a stoppered wine bottle not occupied by wine (see FILL LEVEL). And ullage is also used as a verb so that a bottle or barrel not entirely full is said to be 'ullaged'.

The ullage space in a barrel is not empty but contains water and alcohol vapours together with some CARBON DIOXIDE previously dissolved in the wine. If the container is not completely gas tight, some air will seep in around the tank head or the BUNG. New barrels tend to allow greater oxygen ingress than old because the pores in the wood have not been obstructed by previous fillings. When wine is matured in any form of container, it is particularly important that the ullage space is minimized by regular TOPPING UP to protect the wine from unwanted OXIDATION.   A.D.W.

Ull de Llebre, meaning 'hare's eye', is the CATALAN name for TEMPRANILLO.

ultrafiltration, a form of cross-flow FILTRATION which can be used for ALCOHOL REDUCTION and, more controversially, for TANNIN removal or CONCENTRATION. It is looser than REVERSE OSMOSIS but tighter than sterile FILTRATION. It can also be used to separate COLLOIDS from their solution. It is used as an alternative to FINING. Proponents suggest it is useful for removal of browning and for reducing tannins in press wines but it is subject to strict regulation and is not permitted in the EU.

Smith, C., 'The new filtrations', in *Postmodern Winemaking* (Berkeley, Calif., 2013), 202-18.
Wollan, D., 'Membrane and other techniques for the management of wine composition', in A. G. Reynolds (ed.), *Managing Wine Quality 2: Oenology and Wine Quality* (Cambridge, 2010), 133-63.

ultraviolet radiation, or **UV radiation**, radiation of shorter wavelength (< 400 nm) than so-called visible SUNLIGHT, and which is very damaging to all life because of its mutation-inducing properties. PHENOLIC compounds absorb ultraviolet radiation, and levels of QUERCETIN in grape berries are related to ultraviolet exposure. It is proven that ultraviolet exposure increases levels of phenolics and therefore COLOUR in red wines, which can be an advantage of vineyards at high ELEVATION, and those closer to the 'ozone hole' over the Antarctic. This raised the intriguing possibility that the more southerly regions of the southern hemisphere have a wine quality advantage over northern hemisphere wine regions due to higher UV levels.   R.E.S.

Jug, T., and Rusjan, D., 'Advantages and disadvantages of UV-B radiations on grapevine (*Vitis* sp.)', *Emirates Journal of Food and Agriculture*, 24/6 (2012), 576-85. doi: 10.9755/ejfa.v24i6.14676.

umami, Japanese term derived from two words meaning 'delicious' and 'essence' and used to refer to what some consider to be the fifth primary taste (see TASTING). More a quality than a specific flavour, it is variously described as 'savoury' or 'meaty' and is found in high levels in foods such as soy sauce, Parmesan, fresh tomato juice, tuna and seaweed. Umami levels in other foods are increased by the addition of monosodium glutamate.

Eastern thinking has for many centuries recognized five primary tastes but it was not until 1907 that Professor Ikeda of Tokyo Imperial University identified and isolated the AMINO ACID glutamate, or glutamic acid, as the source of the flavour he named 'umami'. He subsequently developed the seasoning monosodium glutamate so that umami levels in other foods might be increased. Recent research identifying the receptors on the tongue that detect amino acids gives further credibility to the existence of this fifth taste.

The level of amino acids in wine is thought to be affected by the ripeness of the grapes and the process of fermentation. However, it is extremely difficult to isolate the taste of umami in wine because of the way it interacts with the other four primary tastes.

Proponents of umami suggest that its presence brings a 'completeness' to the flavour of a wine but warn that it may increase the BITTERNESS and ASTRINGENCY of some tannic reds.

Umbria, fourth smallest of ITALY's 20 regions in terms of both physical size and population (see map under ITALY), and one of the country's very few landlocked regions. It shares many geological and climatic similarities with Tuscany to the north, which produces five times as much wine. Umbria's DOCs seem repetitive at best, obstructive of the distinction of different TERROIRS at worst. Most of its 15 DOCs are similar in terms of GRAPE VARIETIES, YIELDS, and minimum ALCOHOLIC STRENGTH, with a strong bias towards INTERNATIONAL VARIETIES. Sangiovese, with a total of 2,460 ha/6,080 acres planted in 2010, is Umbria's most important red wine grape, followed by Merlot with 1,297 ha, the indigenous SAGRANTINO with 905 ha, and Cabernet Sauvignon with 567 ha. Of white wine grapes, the lacklustre Tuscan import TREBBIANO Toscano (also called Procanico in Umbria) comes first with 1,452 ha followed by the superior GRECHETTO (1,357 ha), and Chardonnay (344 ha). All of these varieties are an obligatory component in every DOC's production regulations, regardless of their suitability for the different local conditions.

Regrettably, Trebbiano Toscano is the dominant component in Umbria's most important white DOC, ORVIETO. The blend must include at least 60% of a mix of Trebbiano and Grechetto. Orvieto's terroir is very suitable for the production of high quality whites, and in the 1980s the region attracted the attention of Tuscan wine producers and CONSULTANTS keen to broaden their portfolio with a white from a nearby location. But instead of working with local varieties, they planted Chardonnay and Sauvignon Blanc, which may have promised a higher return, but it has done little to increase Orvieto's reputation. Although Orvieto's quality has undoubtedly improved, currently almost none of it is made without the inclusion of one or more international white varieties. Spoleto, Umbria's other all-white DOC, requires at least 50% Trebbiano Spoletino, which, at least in theory, is considered more characterful than Trebbiano Toscano.

SANGIOVESE gives pleasant, if not memorable, wines in the Colli Altotiberini, Colli Amerini, Colli Martani, Colli Perugini, and Colli del Trasimeno DOCs, more often than not blended with Merlot and Cabernet Sauvignon. The best Umbrian Sangioveses have been produced by Lungarotti (see TORGIANO). Some good Rosso di Montefalco is also made in the HILLSIDE VINEYARDS of the small Montefalco DOC zone between Assisi and Terni. It is blended with a small percentage of the local SAGRANTINO, a grape that comes into its own in the DOCG Montefalco Sagrantino. This ancient variety was already documented in the 16th century, but was almost extinct in the 1960s; however, total plantings grew from 122 ha in 2000 to 906 ha in 2010 thanks to a flowering of interest in it in the 1980s and 1990s. This tannic grape, used traditionally for PASSITO sweet wines, now makes full-bodied, oak-aged, concentrated dry reds which, by law, must be aged for at least 37 months. Regularly compared with BRUNELLO in its aromatics and with BAROLO in tannic grip, Montefalco Sagrantino's density and high alcohol quenched international thirst for high-octane wines at the time, although some are simply too oaky and alcoholic. Research into sites that can provide an extended ripening season and into the best clones should help.

W.S.

Belfrage, N., *Brunello to Zibibbo—The Wines of Tuscany, Central and Southern Italy* (2nd edn, London, 2003).

ungrafted vine, also known as an own-rooted or self-rooted vine, is a vine which has not been grafted to a ROOTSTOCK (see GRAFTING). Ungrafted vines grow perfectly well, although some varieties, e.g. SÉMILLON, are known to produce weak root systems, while SYRAH, for example, produces strong ones. The terms *pie franco, pe franco*, and *franc de pied* are occasionally used on labels in Spain, Portugal, and France respectively. See also PHYLLOXERA. R.E.S.

United Kingdom. See Great BRITAIN for general matters, and ENGLAND and WALES for wine produced there.

United States of America, now an important wine importer and producer of wine and DRYING GRAPES. In the 2010s it became the world's most significant importer of wine, thanks to a growing interest in wine among important, often youthful, segments of its 319 million population. The US is the globe's fourth largest producer of wine, behind Spain, France, and Italy, with CALIFORNIA contributing 90% of the country's 750 million gal/28 million hl output in 2013. California is by far the most important wine-producing state in both volume and prestige, followed by WASHINGTON, OREGON, and NEW YORK. Total US vineyard area was over 1,005,000 acres/407,000 ha in 2011 according to OIV statistics.

More than 375 million nine-litre cases of wine were sold in the US in 2013, 3% more than in 2012. This represents 21 consecutive years of volume growth as Americans, previously unaccustomed to enjoying wine with meals, have steadily been embracing the activity (while it declines in Europe).

History

European settlement in what is now the US goes back to the late 16th century (see also VÍNLAND), but it was two centuries later that wine was first successfully produced there. The long delay was not for lack of trying. The abundant native AMERICAN VINE SPECIES immediately drew the attention of the first settlers; winemaking was an official aim of the VIRGINIA and Carolina colonies, and it was encouraged and repeatedly tried in all of the American colonies.

The first trials quickly showed that wine acceptable to European palates could not be made from the unameliorated native grape varieties. The next step was to import cuttings of European VINIFERA vines, beginning in Virginia around 1619. The experiment was frequently repeated over the whole length of the Atlantic seaboard with vines from every great European wine region, but the result was uniform failure. The vines were destroyed by extremes of climate, by native PESTS, and by previously unknown VINE DISEASES. The facts were not clearly understood for more than two centuries, since the trials were isolated and uncoordinated, and no adequate knowledge of plant pathology existed. The cycle of hopeful experiment followed by complete failure went on in profitless repetition (see Thomas JEFFERSON for example).

All Europe took part in the effort. French VIGNERONS were imported along with French vines by the Virginia Company in 1619, and French expertise continued to be sought thereafter: Huguenot exiles were employed in Carolina in 1680, in Virginia in 1700, in Pennsylvania in 1683. Germans attempted wine-growing at Germantown in Pennsylvania; in Florida a colony of Greeks, Italians, Frenchmen, and Spaniards tried vine-growing in 1767. All of these, and innumerable other efforts, were based on VINIFERA varieties and were accordingly doomed to rapid and entire failure (see PHYLLOXERA and FUNGAL DISEASES).

A new direction was taken through the discovery of a chance HYBRID—the combination of a native *Vitis labrusca* and an unknown *V. vinifera*—called the Alexander grape, in Pennsylvania, not far from where William Penn had planted *V. vinifera* in 1683. Its hybrid character was unrecognized for many years, but it in fact showed the way in which vine-growing in the eastern United States would be developed. The first successful commercial wine production in the US, based on the Alexander, began in Indiana around 1806. Thereafter, many new AMERICAN HYBRIDS of American vine species either with each other or with a European *V. vinifera* variety, formed almost invariably by chance, were introduced and contributed to the possibilities of winemaking in the US.

The most important were the CATAWBA, DELAWARE, ISABELLA, and NORTON, all introduced in the first half of the 19th century. With the exception of Norton, most were better adapted to white wine production than to red, and most had more or less of the so-called FOXY aroma. Whatever their defects, they would at least survive under American conditions, and they made wine production possible.

Permanent and extensive wine production was first established around Cincinnati, Ohio, in the 1830s by Nicholas Longworth; when the Cincinnati *vignoble* was devastated by BLACK ROT, the Ohio wine industry moved north to the shores of Lake Erie. The other main winemaking centres were around Hermann, MISSOURI, a German colony on the Missouri River, and around the Finger Lakes of upstate New York (see NEW YORK for more historical detail of the state's wine industry).

In the south before the Civil War, some winemaking, based both on the native hybrids and on the native MUSCADINE vines of the American south, grew up in the Carolinas and Georgia. Scattered vineyards, all growing American native or hybrid vines, and small wineries could be found throughout the settled regions, and extended to the frontiers of TEXAS and Kansas. The federal government supported vine-growing through plant exploration, the distribution of plants, and experimental work in the analysis of grapes and wines. In the decade before the Civil War, interest in vine-growing burgeoned and many new hybrid varieties were introduced, some of them now the outcome of controlled rather than accidental hybridizing.

The most important single result of this activity was the CONCORD, a vine with good resistance to pests and diseases, well adapted to the extreme growing conditions of the area that then constituted the United States, but whose extremely FOXY grapes were particularly unsuitable for wine (or at least wine as most wine drinkers know it). The ubiquity of the Concord has had a large part in establishing a taste for grape juice rather than for wine among Americans.

Meanwhile, although the fact was quite unknown in the US, *V. vinifera* grapes were successfully grown and wine made in the Spanish settlements on the Rio Grande in New Mexico and Texas (beginning around 1626) and in the Franciscan missions of California (beginning around 1779). The Mexican-American War of 1846–8, followed by the GOLD RUSH of 1849, brought the *V. vinifera*-growing regions of the south west into the US; since then, California has dominated American wine production. At the time of the US conquest of Mexico, the vine was already grown on a small but commercial scale in Los Angeles. Plantings thereafter spread over the state and production grew rapidly, from a few hundred thousand gallons in 1860 to more than 30 million gal/1.1 million hl by the end of the century.

The first *V. vinifera* variety grown in New Mexico and California was the MISSION. Importations and trials of many superior *V. vinifera* varieties quickly began, and although the Mission grape long dominated California, plantings of other, better varieties increased steadily. Among the most interesting is ZINFANDEL, for long associated specifically with California, which is still widely grown.

The economic growth of the California industry was unstable: a cyclical pattern of boom and bust persisted until 1894 (see CALIFORNIA, history), when the California Wine Association, a union of the largest producers and dealers in the state, was formed. The CWA was not a MONOPOLY, but it controlled so large a share of the state's wine wine production that it could stabilize costs and prices, and did so until Prohibition. The CWA distributed its wines throughout the US (where wine drinking continued to be almost wholly confined to the cities) and developed export markets, particularly Great BRITAIN.

Outside California, vine-growing continued to develop slowly, in much the same way. New Jersey, Virginia, and Arkansas were added to the states where viticulture was already established: New York (where the production of sparkling wine had become a speciality), Ohio, and Missouri. By 1919, the last year before national PROHIBITION was enforced, the US produced 55 million gal of wine. During the Prohibition years, from 1920 to 1933, some commercial wine production was allowed, for SACRAMENTAL and 'medicinal' purposes, and HOME WINEMAKING became more popular than ever before or since, resulting in an increase in total vine acreage thanks to demand for GRAPE CONCENTRATE, but the industry was destroyed.

Upon Repeal (from 1934), the US industry had to reconstitute itself. Some of the old firms reappeared; many new firms mushroomed. But it took time to put things right: the market was ignorant, or perverted by the intemperate habits encouraged by Prohibition; the producers were uninstructed or, sometimes, unscrupulous. The country was in the lowest depths of economic depression, and wine was an unfamiliar luxury. High-alcohol sweet wines became the mainstay of the trade, and remained so for the next generation. The federal government failed to re-establish its research programmes for wine, but important OENOLOGICAL and VITICULTURAL research was carried out by the state universities of California at DAVIS and New York. Promotional work was largely in the hands of the Wine Institute of California, founded in 1934.

The Second World War, by cutting off European supplies, brought new prosperity to US industry but brought new instability as well. Large distilling companies bought up established wineries in order to have a product to sell. A seller's market prevailed until, after the war, the artificially stimulated demand collapsed. The distillers departed from the wine trade, which fell into somnolence. Little effort was made to develop new markets; wineries typically sold their wines in BULK to wholesalers for bottling under their own brands; American wines, after the bad old example set in the 19th century, continued to use GENERIC names such as Burgundy, Chablis, Sherry, and Champagne, and most wineries produced an entire 'line' of such types from a severely limited range of grape varieties.

In the east, especially, the decline was marked; in Ohio, for example, the 149 wineries of 1940 had dwindled to 47 by 1960. One valuable new development was the introduction, by Philip WAGNER, of hybrid grape varieties developed in France (see FRENCH HYBRIDS) such as SEYVAL, SEIBEL, and BACO into the eastern vineyards; these gave larger yields and made more attractive and interesting wines than the old American hybrids could produce. Another innovation was the effective introduction of VARIETAL labelling by the American merchant Frank SCHOONMAKER, a practice that was to become standard.

Beginning around 1970, wine production in the US suddenly took on a new energy and a new glamour, a development not entirely explained but doubtless the result of many different, slowly gathering social forces. New wineries, large and small, were started in California where there were 240 wineries in 1970, 770 in 1989, almost 1,700 in 2004, and 3,800 by 2014. New vineyards were planted, and wine-growers made unprecedented efforts to find the best matches between grape variety and location. They increasingly concentrated on relatively few grape varieties and wine types instead of producing the old comprehensive ranges, aspiring to new levels of quality and complexity. Innovation in technology was eagerly sought, at the same time as traditional European methods were introduced and adapted. Large-scale foreign investment from Japanese, British, French, Spanish, Swiss, and German companies was attracted to the American wine industry, notably a number of French CHAMPAGNE firms who invested, some of them briefly, in California sparkling wine production in the 1980s.

The explosion of new activity in the industry was matched by consumer developments: wine classes, internet sales and websites, wine societies, wine publications proliferated to exploit the interest and anxieties of a public long ignorant and indifferent but now eager to learn. Consumption of wine—now dominated by table wine—rose from 267 million gal/10 million hl in 1970 to 856 gal in 2013, about 4 gal (18 l) per adult (18 year-olds are classified adults by America's census-takers but have to wait three years before being allowed to drink legally in most states). As wineries proliferated, they offered a variety of choices such as Americans had never before seen. One firm, GALLO of Modesto, California, succeeded in becoming the largest winery in the world, surpassed only temporarily in 2004 through the legerdemain of mergers and acquisitions by CONSTELLATION.

Outside California the boom in wine was, proportionately, even greater. The old regions—New York and Ohio especially—began to sprout new enterprises after a long quiescence. The vineyards were transformed by the introduction not only of hybrids developed in France such as Seyval and Seibel, but by *V. vinifera* varieties, now, thanks to modern understanding of plant pathology and the availability of PESTICIDES and FUNGICIDES, at last grown successfully in the eastern US after more than three centuries of failure. States such as New Jersey, Pennsylvania, and Virginia which had once supported viticulture on only a modest scale now saw the growth of a renewed and expanded industry. Texas and New Mexico, sites of very old but very small-scale *V. vinifera* winemaking, now boasted large viticultural developments. The Yakima Valley in WASHINGTON and the Willamette Valley in OREGON undertook large plantings of *V. vinifera* and began to develop a reputation for particular types of wine. Although, thanks largely to the *labrusca*-based products of Constellation Brands' Canandaigua Wine Company, New York has continued to produce a greater volume of wine than any state other than California. Michigan embraced Riesling and other AROMATIC varieties suited to its cold winters, and Minnesota, Wisconsin, and the Midwest embraced cold-climate HYBRIDS such as Brianna, La Crescent, and Marquette developed by the University of Minnesota. The number of commercial wineries in the entire country reached 8,400 in 2014.

Many obstacles to the production and sale of wine still exist, however, some of them natural, such as climate, some of them man made, such as the complex web of taxes and restrictions imposed by the different states. The spirit of Prohibition is still vigorous in some states, whether it takes the old form of moral disapproval or the protectionism of alcohol beverage MONOPOLIES. Since 1989, the federal government has required warning labels on all bottles of wine sold in the US. And in the late 1990s further, sometimes severe, restrictions were placed on the shipment of wine between states, making it even more difficult for consumers to buy wine direct from wineries (although see Regulations below).

But, on any view, the US wine industry in the latter half of the 20th century underwent a remarkable development from the ruins left after Prohibition, renewing old activities, spreading into new regions, expanding production, developing new methods in viticulture and winemaking, and reaching new levels of quality.

T.P., J.R., & L.M.

Adams, L., *The Wines of America* (4th edn, New York, 1990).

Lapsley, J. T., *Bottled Poetry: Napa Winemaking from Prohibition to the Modern Era* (Berkeley, Calif., 1996).

Pinney, T., *A History of Wine in America—From the Beginnings to Prohibition* (Berkeley, Calif., 1989).

Pinney, T., *A History of Wine in America—From Prohibition to the Present* (Berkeley, Calif., 2005).

Robinson, J., and Murphy, L., *American Wine* (Berkeley, 2013).

Sullivan, C., *Napa Wine: A History from Mission Days to the Present* (San Francisco, 1994).

Regulations

Following repeal of Prohibition in 1933, each of the 48 (now 50) states was allowed to set its own regulations governing the sale and distribution of alcoholic beverages. As a result an arcane, confusing regulatory environment involving in effect 50 separate countries has evolved. The prevailing THREE-TIER SYSTEM is, however, under increasing economic and legal pressures. The consistent theme throughout the rules is that no enterprise can act as supplier, wholesaler (distributor), and retailer. A chief exception to this rule is California, where wineries can circumvent this structure. In many states, boutique (farm) wineries can sell their wines directly to consumers, but most sell them to wholesalers, which then sell to retailers and restaurateurs. After a series of aggressive acquisitions, the number of different wholesalers was dramatically shrunk between 1985 and 2005, each enjoying what is effectively a state-sanctioned monopoly on alcohol sales and profits. An actual state MONOPOLY operates in Pennsylvania and New Hampshire.

A potentially revolutionary 2005 US Supreme Court ruling gave all states a choice: either allow inside-the-state and into-the-state shipping by wineries, or prohibit both; such shipments would enable consumers interested in DIRECT SHIPPING to bypass the three-tier system. But that system has not disintegrated, because all but the smallest producers need wholesalers to display and to distribute their wares across the immense continent. Seeking to protect their privileges, wholesalers have amassed clout in state legislatures nationwide by giving sizeable contributions to office-holders' fund-raising campaigns.

Label approval, AVAS, and federal taxation, are overseen by the TTB.   D.F. & H.G.

Modern wine production

Wine is made in each of the 50 states comprising the US. Some of it is humble, created only for the TOURIST traffic that provides the majority of sales for most small wineries. While small wineries on the West Coast have garnered boutique and even cult status, only now are critics and the wine trade recognizing the quality of wines produced in Michigan, New York, Virginia, and the rest of the US.

The American wine industry comprises an odd collection of monied hobbyists, enthusiastic HOME WINEMAKERS, retired professionals in search of a glamorous lifestyle, and a diminishing number of increasingly powerful international wine and spirits conglomerates (see GLOBALIZATION).

A gradual easing of regulatory constraints has kept pace with these developments, and many states can now boast of official wine trails and state grapes, wine festivals, concerts, and events, even if the majority of states still limit or prohibit altogether the shipping of wines within or across their borders.

Despite these successes, the national retail chains and the behemoth wholesalers have rarely been interested in the pioneering work required to promote wines from little-known US wine regions. The dramatic growth of these wineries has come despite the wineries' inability to ship wines in most states and the lack of support from the powerful retail companies.

Most of the wineries in the lesser-known areas are reliant on the tourist trade in order to provide consistent revenue. Few wineries in these regions have a well-established distributor network nearly as effective as their sales at the winery. And those that use HYBRID grapes have the challenge of educating customers accustomed to drinking Chardonnay and Merlot, yet might not have heard of Vignoles, Norton, or Marechal Foch.

The developing wine industries in NEW YORK, VINIFERA, MARYLAND, TEXAS, and in the southwest may increasingly use VINIFERA varieties but much of the rest of the US is dependent upon hybrids or native AMERICAN VINE varieties such as Delaware, Catawba, Niagara, or Norton. *V. vinifera* has consistently struggled in these areas, due to pressures from PHYLLOXERA, PIERCE'S DISEASE, and the numerous other challenges associated with hot, humid summers and/or fiercely cold winters. In many of eastern America's vineyards, winter hardiness has been the overriding selection criterion.

Red hybrid grapes such as BACO NOIR, CHANCELLOR, CHAMBOURCIN, MARECHAL FOCH, MARQUETTE, and ROUGEON are increasingly common as new vineyards and wineries spring up in America's viticultural hinterlands. White hybrid plantings are dominated by AURORE, Brianna, CAYUGA, La Crescent, SEYVAL BLANC, VIGNOLES, and VIDAL BLANC.

Some wineries eschew these hybrids as inappropriate for dry table wines, but many of America's best dessert wines have so far been based on such hybrids as Vidal Blanc and Vignoles. As the significant wine-producing states of Texas, Virginia, and New York are abandoning hybrids (except for dessert wines), it will increasingly be left to other, less important wine-producing states to explain and market these grapes and wines to buyers.

However, regional pride, local media, and plain old curiosity offer small wineries opportunities that are unavailable to large-scale wine areas.

Other US states

While CALIFORNIA, IDAHO, MICHIGAN, MISSOURI, NEW YORK, OREGON, TEXAS, VIRGINIA, and WASHINGTON have their own entries in this book, much of the wine made in every other US state is surprisingly good. Greater understanding of the viticultural and winemaking challenges associated with these areas, and the hybrid and native American varieties upon which they often rely, has given rise to a burgeoning wine industry far from the famous coastal wine regions.

The states of **Hawaii** and **Alaska** can be said to have derived a marketing advantage from their tourist industries. Many other states, **North Dakota** and **Maine** being extreme examples, suffer from the considerable limitation of having such a short growing season that they have no commercial vineyards and therefore have to import grapes, must, or grape concentrate and/or produce FRUIT WINES. But wineries exist in these states in response to perceived interest in local agricultural products, as well as an increasing curiosity about, and acceptance of, wine in American society. While Maine and the other New England states (excluding New York) support about 300 wineries, many are dependent upon grapes purchased from New York or Pennsylvania. This is a common phenomenon in new US wine regions where many wineries function as BRANDS built upon grapes imported from more famous wine-producing states, particularly California, Washington, and New York.

The creation of new AVAS in New England, as in so many of the new regions, reflects wishful thinking, and marketing more than viticultural reality. Only the minority of these AVAs host legitimate commercial wine production from locally grown grapes and many are so large as to make a mockery of the concept supposedly enshrined in the AVA definition. The Ohio River Valley AVA, for instance, is a delimited region of over 16 million acres/6.5 million ha. Southeastern New England AVA is hardly better defined. At just under 2 million acres/750,000 ha, it sprawls across three states' coasts, but at least it has coastal proximity as its common thread. But with so few successful vineyards to draw on, the two dozen or so wineries in the three states of **Massachusetts**, **Rhode Island**, and **Connecticut** have found it necessary to create such a flexible AVA. Sakonnet, Rhode Island's best known winery, utilizes grapes grown throughout the AVA for its well-made sparkling wines. The Western Connecticut Highlands AVA abuts the New York state border and New York's famously picturesque Hudson valley. The short growing seasons and cool nights throughout the northeastern US necessitate a reliance on white varieties if *V. vinifera* grapes are grown—and Riesling, Gewurztraminer, and Muscat are more successful than the ubiquitous Chardonnay grown in response to the perceived market demands.

The newfound fame and financial rewards reaped by New York's Finger Lakes' producers of Riesling and other aromatic wines is being emulated elsewhere in the north east. **New Jersey**'s Warren Hills AVA, the Central Delaware Valley AVA (shared by New Jersey and **Pennsylvania**), and Pennsylvania's Lancaster Valley AVA and the Cumberland Valley AVA, have all produced some well-balanced examples of white *V. vinifera*-based wine, but have had more success with hybrids of both colours. Pennsylvania's more than 150 wineries, including the ubiquitous Chaddsford, are almost wholly dependent upon hybrids. Yet in New Jersey's Outer Coastal Plains AVA, Amalthea, Heritage, Tomasello, and Unionville wineries have enjoyed success with red Bordeaux varieties.

The Lake Erie AVA is shared by New York, Pennsylvania, and Ohio and its 20,000 acres of vineyard produce vast quantities of grapes, less than a quarter of which is converted to wine. Most is CONCORD for jelly and juice.

Although wine production has been sporadically attempted along the eastern seaboard since the founding of the Jamestown colony in the 16th century, it has only recently become a product worthy of national and international trade. Philip Wagner of **Maryland**'s Boordy Vineyard played an important role in the story in the improvement of eastern US wines through its adoption of hybrid vines in the late 20th century. Black Ankle Vineyards, also in Maryland, has become a superstar with its fine *V. vinifera* wines, including Albarino and blended reds. See also VIRGINIA.

North Carolina boasts over 100 wineries as well as one of the area's chief tourist destinations, the Biltmore Estate. This sprawling mansion sees more than a million visitors annually, many of whom taste the estate's well-made wines. Surprisingly, many of the grapes used are from the state of **Georgia**, which has more acres under vine than any southeastern state apart from Virginia; estate-grown and California grapes supplement the production. **South Carolina** and Georgia's vineyards hug the Atlantic coast, many perched upon hills close to the sea. Although the mainstay has always been hybrid and the well-known if little-respected MUSCADINE vines, *V. vinifera* plantings have

increased considerably, and Georgia's Blackstock Vineyards, while producing no wine itself, is the source of many estimable *V. vinifera* wines from this part of America. Frogtown Cellars in Lumpkin county, Georgia, has had the courage to enter its wines in California competitions with remarkable success.

Florida's hot and humid weather is ideal for citrus crops but offers only a suffocating hothouse environment for *V. vinifera* and even hybrid grapevines. Gulf Coast states Alabama, Mississippi, and Louisiana fare little better and generally import grapes.

But there has been progress for the grapevine in the interior states of **Arkansas**, **Illinois**, **Indiana**, and, to a much lesser degree, in **Tennessee**, **Kentucky**, and **West Virginia**. In Arkansas, the Altus and Arkansas Mountain AVAs are finding their feet with hybrid plantings. In these states, WINTER FREEZE may be only a marginal issue, but the hot, humid summers have so far proved to be discouraging to efforts with *V. vinifera* vines.

The two largest producing states in this part of America are **Ohio** and MISSOURI. Ohio features prominently in the story of American wine (see above), but its $500 million wine TOURISM industry suffered a setback when a 2014 spring freeze wiped out most of the crop. Ferrante Winery, Valley Vineyards, and Chalet Debonné are the old hands among the 150 wineries in Ohio. The small AVAs of Grand River Valley and Loramie Creek are home to small wineries producing both *V. vinifera* and hybrid wines. Although Ohio's grapevine production is more *V. vinifera* than hybrid, much of the *V. vinifera* wine has so far been lacklustre. The most reliable wines have been dessert wines created from hybrid grapes, but Troutman and Tarula wineries suggest that *V. vinifera* quality is rising. One of the more unusual American AVAs is the Isle St George AVA encompassing four islands in the middle of Lake Erie, a ferry boat ride away from Cleveland.

Indiana, the state to the immediate west of Ohio, hosts a smaller wine industry but one with equal promise and Oliver Winery, Huber Winery, and Turtle Run have all produced reliable wines including Huber's Heritage, a blend of hybrid and *V. vinifera* grapes. Throughout the Midwest, FUNGAL DISEASES are a constant concern and fuel the continued interest in hybrids.

Until recently, **Illinois** lagged behind but its vineyard acreage has overtaken Indiana's and some exciting hybrid wines are being produced in the southwest of the state not far from Missouri's Augusta AVA. Alto Vineyards, Galena Cellars, and Illinois Sparkling Wine Co are notable producers among the state's 100-plus wineries and, since climatic conditions are similar to MISSOURI, many of the same hybrids such as Seyval Blanc, Vidal Blanc, and Chambourcin are likely to succeed.

The states to the north are mostly afflicted by the severity of the winters. MICHIGAN may be protected by its Great Lakes but **Wisconsin**, **Iowa**, **Minnesota**, **Nebraska**, and the **Dakotas** have very little wine production and as yet relatively few vineyards, but their small successes have been based upon some of the grapes and styles proven in MISSOURI, as well as varieties created by the late Elmer Swenson. An amateur viticulturist for most of nine decades of life, Swenson created dozens of winter-hardy hybrids for the University of Minnesota, and his cuttings continue to see experimentation and commercialization in these High Plains states as well as Canada. So, in addition to the usual hybrids, Plains vineyards are planted with Brianna, Diamond, Fredonia, FRONTENAC, La Crescent, LaCrosse, St Croix, and St Pepin. Notable wineries include Alexis Bailly and WineHaven (Minnesota), Tabor Home (Iowa), Cuthills Vineyards and James Arthur Vineyards (Nebraska), HolyField Winery (Kansas), and Stone Bluff Cellars (Oklahoma). But most are still working to match hybrid varieties and site.

Only Wisconsin's eastern portion and the Lake Wisconsin AVA seem to offer the hope of *V. vinifera* production. Wisconsin's most prolific wineries, Cedar Creek and Wollersheim, make very good wine but principally use grapes purchased from less viticulturally challenging states.

The Mountain states are relatively unimportant wine producers but **Colorado**'s increasing vineyard area (1,200 acres) and growing number of wineries (100) are beginning to make decent wine. The dry conditions allow healthy *V. vinifera* production from Riesling, Chardonnay, Gewurztraminer, Merlot (the most widely planted), Cabernet, Syrah and, perhaps surprisingly, LEMBERGER. Wineries such as Alfred Eames, Bookcliff, Boulder Creek, Canyon Wind, Carlson, Garfield, Plum Creek, and Stone Cottage are all notable.

The rest of the Southwest, including TEXAS, **New Mexico**, and **Arizona**, also has warm, dry growing conditions resulting in short seasons and grapes that can lack flavour and PHENOLIC RIPENESS. But, as with Colorado's best vineyards, ELEVATION seems to be the solution for both New Mexico and Arizona's best vineyards. Arizona's sole AVA, Sonoita, includes vineyards at 4,000 to 5,000 feet /1,200 to 1,500 m, and many of the best of the 50 or so wineries in the state use fruit from these lofty vineyards. Syrah and Zinfandel can be almost shockingly good here and Dos Cabezas, Sonoita, and Callaghan have also made impressive white wines. In the Verde Valley region to the north, Arizona Stronghold, Caduceus, and Page Springs produce wines every bit as good as those from Sonoita. New Mexico has 30 wineries and the best of their vines are grown at more than 4,000 feet. Good reds have been produced by wineries such as

Milagro Vineyards but Gruet Vineyards is one of the few US wineries outside the major wine-producing states to have genuinely national distribution. This is no mere stroke of luck but reflects the high quality sparkling wines produced in high-ELEVATION vineyards, vineyards which might be as warm as 90 °F/32 °C during the day but will usually cool to less than 60 °F/15 °C during the night.

See also AVA and specific entries on CALIFORNIA, WASHINGTON, OREGON, IDAHO, TEXAS, VIRGINIA, MICHIGAN, MISSOURI, and NEW YORK.

D.F. & L.M.

Adams, L., *The Wines of America* (4th edn, New York, 1990).

Cass, B. (ed.), *Oxford Companion to the Wines of North America* (Oxford and New York, 2000).

Lukacs, P., *American Vintage: The Rise of American Wine* (New York, 2000).

Morton, L. T., *Winegrowing in Eastern America* (Ithaca, 1985).

Robinson, J., and Murphy, L., *American Wine* (Berkeley, Calif., 2013).

www.wineamerica.org

www.wineinstitute.org

Upper Goulburn, high-ELEVATION, cool Australian wine region in VICTORIA with the snowfields of mount Buller on one extremity, Strathbogie Ranges on the other.

urban wineries, a 21st-century phenomenon that has introduced city-dwellers from London to HONG KONG to winemaking. Wine was long made in unglamorous warehouses on the outskirts of American cities and much of the wine produced in the Soviet era was finished in urban processing plants close to centres of consumption. But the first of this new era of self-consciously artisanal urban wineries was probably Edmunds St John, established in the San Francisco Bay Area in 1985, vinifying grapes grown in nearby California wine country. The Bay Area still has one of the greatest concentrations of the several hundred urban wineries located in North American cities, including New York. One of these, Crushpad, established in San Francisco in 2004, was the model for a new type of DIY urban winery, in which amateur 'members' could make their own wine—at a price. Crushpad, a sort of micro CUSTOM CRUSH FACILITY for the well-heeled, subsequently opened a branch in Bordeaux, and relocated to Sonoma. Both operations have been restructured and renamed.

http://eater.com/archives/2011/03/01/americas-urban-winery-revival-what-does-it-mean.php

Uruguay is South America's fourth most important wine-producing country with an area under vines of more than 9,000 ha/ 22,200 acres, of which more than 95% is for wine production. Total wine production in 2011 was of 900,000 hl/19.5 million gallons.

The history of winemaking in the country is comparatively recent, starting as late as 1870, with vineyards planted by immigrants, mainly Basques and Italians. This tradition of 'peasant' smallholdings continues, with the average vineyard size being no more than 5 ha/12 acres. In all there are over 1,750 growers but fewer than 300 wineries, and only about 15% of those focus on higher quality and export. Wine was initially produced for local consumption and, with half the population of the country living in the capital Montevideo, four-fifths of the vineyards are in the immediately neighbouring *departmentos*, especially in Canelones. Most other vineyards are in the west, close to the Río de la Plata (River Plate), which forms the border with Argentina. Domestic wine consumption is high, and stable, currently standing at 22.5 l/ 6 gal per person per year.

With the formation of Mercosur, announced at the end of the 1980s, the Uruguayans realized that they would have to protect their wine industry from Chilean and Argentine wine, with their lower production costs. In order to achieve this, the Uruguayan National Institute for Vitiviniculture (INAVI) embarked on a three-pronged campaign. Firstly, encouragement was given to growers to plant VINIFERA varieties, rather than the AMERICAN VINES and HYBRIDS that then dominated. Secondly, the Uruguayans were urged to be proud of their own wines, with stress being laid on their purity and 'naturalness'. (In an American report published at the 2004 World Economic Forum, Uruguay was ranked third most environmentally SUSTAINABLE country in the world after Finland and Norway.) Finally efforts were made to conquer export markets despite limited promotional resources. BRAZIL, because of a shortage of domestic red wine, is by far the most important export market, accounting for 60% of the total, followed at a considerable distance by the UNITED STATES and RUSSIA.

Wines are divided into two classes, VCP (*Vino de calidad preferente*) and VC (*Vino Común*). VCP wines, which account for about 12% of total production, must be made from *V. vinifera* grapes and be sold in 75 cl, or smaller, bottles. VC wine, which is sold widely in demi-johns and tetrapacks, is predominantly rosé based on MUSCAT OF HAMBURG grapes, although this variety is in sharp decline thanks to increasing demand for *V. vinifera* wines even in this market sector.

For better quality wines the dominant grape variety is TANNAT, introduced to Uruguay by Basque settlers and made with increasing enthusiasm and expertise. In 2013 it accounted for 24% of all plantings of wine grapes. Other red wine grapes are Merlot (11%), Cabernet Sauvignon (8%), and Cabernet Franc (4%), while white wines (around a quarter of total production) tend to be made from Sauvignon Blanc and Chardonnay.

Most of the vineyards lie on deep CLAY soils on gently rolling hills to the north of Montevideo, but there are vines in 16 out of the 19 *departmentos*. More recent plantings in the Cerro Chapeu region on the Brazilian border and in El Carmen and Carpinteria in the centre of the country are on poorer soils where there is a bigger diurnal temperature variation (see TEMPERATURE VARIABILITY).

The climate in Uruguay is influenced by the Atlantic, and often compared with that of Bordeaux, although the average rainfall (particularly in the south) and the average annual temperature are higher than in Bordeaux. Humidity can be excessive even though the climate seems to be getting warmer and drier, so the ESPALIER training system is popular, gradually replacing the once-widespread LYRE. High soil fertility has to be controlled by producers aiming high. The newest vineyard area to be developed is around Garzón in Maldonado. Here GRANITE soils, higher elevations (up to 300 m/ 1,000 ft), and constant cooling breezes from the Atlantic promise less humid conditions for crisp whites, refined reds, and expanding olive plantations.

International interest in Uruguayan wines has been shown by several recent investments, including Argentinian pesos at Garzón and Narbona, Brazilian Real at Filgueira, and California dollars at Artesana. International consultants are few in number (e.g. Alberto Antonini, Paul Hobbs, and Michel ROLLAND) but more and more young winemakers such as Gabriel Pisano, scion of the family that more than any other has spread the word about Uruguayan quality wine, are gaining overseas experience to reinvest in Uruguay.

C.C.F. & J.E.H.

Dominé, A., and Herrera, M., *The Unique Wines of Uruguay* (Montevideo, 2013).

Goldstein, E., *South American Wines* (Berkeley, Calif., 2014).

www.winesofuruguay.com

US. See UNITED STATES of America.

USSR. See SOVIET UNION.

Utiel-Requena, large, workmanlike Spanish wine region producing some sturdy reds, and mostly rosés, in the hills inland from VALENCIA in south-east Spain (see map under SPAIN). Utiel-Requena is the coolest of the five wine regions of the LEVANTE and was once famous for its heavy DOBLE PASTA reds. Consequently the region is dominated by the sweet, dark BOBAL grape variety although the TEMPRANILLO vine has become important this century, followed by Syrah, Merlot, and Cabernet Sauvignon. Utiel-Requena produces large amounts of GRAPE CONCENTRATE.

V. de la S. & J.R.

Uva Abruzzese, occasional name for the red MONTEPULCIANO grape.

Uva di Troia, old name for NERO DI TROIA.

Uva Rara, red wine grape variety too widely grown in north west Italy to justify its Italian name, whose literal translation is 'rare grape'. In the Novara hills it is often used to soften the SPANNA grapes grown here in a range of scented red wines.

Uzbekistan, independent central Asian republic with Tashkent as its capital. The most prolific grower of grapes of the former Soviet republics, it is a major supplier of TABLE GRAPES. Wine production has been declining fast but it still produced 210,000 hl/5.5 million gal—mainly strong and sweet—from its substantial vineyard total of 117,000 ha/289,000 acres in 2011, according to OIV figures.

History

The grapes and wines of Uzbekistan have long been famous beyond its own frontiers. Between the 6th and 2nd centuries BC, people in the Fergana Valley grew wheat, barley, and grapes using artificial IRRIGATION and Fergana grapes were prized in CHINA to the east.

It is thought that some central Asian VINE VARIETIES originated as the wild subspecies VITIS silvestris Gmel as a result of long-term selection. Some varieties were brought to Uzbekistan from IRAN between the 6th and 4th centuries BC and other varieties were brought by Greeks and Arabs in the 7th and 8th centuries AD.

Archaeological excavation has revealed grape seeds dating back to the 5th century BC during excavations of Tali Barzu near Samarkand.

Viticulture and winemaking flourished in Uzbekistan until the end of the 7th century, when, as a result of the Arab conquest of central Asia, wine grape varieties gave way to table, RAISIN, and seedless raisin varieties (see ISLAM).

After central Asia was annexed to RUSSIA in the second half of the 19th century, demand for table grape varieties with good shipping qualities developed rapidly. European wine varieties from MOLDOVA, CRIMEA, and other regions were also imported into Uzbekistan. In 1917, Uzbekistan had 37,000 ha/91,000 acres of vineyards, mainly owned by individual smallholders. The first specialized Soviet state farms were established in the 1920s.

Modern viticulture

Uzbekistan is in the very heart of central Asia, on the same latitude as Italy. The country's relief varies considerably, with the Tian-Shan and the Pamir and Alai spines in the east, and mountains accounting for about 30% of the total area of the country. The climate of Uzbekistan is very CONTINENTAL. The average January temperature is 3 to -3 °C/37–22 °F and that of July is 26 to 32 °C/79–89 °F. Late spring and early autumn FROSTS are commonplace. The active temperature summation (see CLIMATE CLASSIFICATION) is 4,000 to 4,500 °C. The annual rainfall is 100 mm (4 in) in the lowlands to 1,000 mm in the mountains.

The leading viticultural zones, accounting for about 75% of vines, are the Samarkand, Surkandaria, Namandan, Tashkent, Bukhara, and Kashkadaria regions. About 90% of vines need WINTER PROTECTION. Only vineyards in the mountains, at an ELEVATION of 800–1,500 m (2,600–5,000 ft), where the annual rainfall is at least 450 mm, do not require IRRIGATION.

The country's assortment of vines, all UNGRAFTED, still has features typical of the viticulture of central Asia. Table grape varieties predominate and the grape conveyor system is employed whereby early-, mid-, and late-maturing grapes are harvested continuously for about 120 days. Wine grape varieties include ALEATICO, RIESLING, Kuljinkski, Hungarian Muscat, MUSCAT Rosé, Soiaki, Bayanshira, SAPERAVI, RKATSITELI, MORRASTEL, and Khindogni.

Uzbekistan's wine industry was still run substantially by the state in the early 2000s and was more dynamic than that of many other central Asian republics. Wines tend to be sweet, often strong, and many are sparkling.

The Shreder Research Institute for Horticulture, Viticulture, and Oenology is Uzbekistan's centre of wine ACADEME and sole vine NURSERY.

V.R.

Akhramov, I. K., 'The history of viticulture and enology in the Fergana valley' (Russian), *Vinodelie i vinogradarstvo SSSR*, 7 (1966), 43.

Julia, F., and Beillon, D., *Uzbekistan–Rehabilitation of the Vine and Wine Sector* (Bordeaux, 2001).

Mirzayev, M. M., 'The Soviet Socialist Republic of Uzbekistan' (Russian), in A. I. Timush (ed.), *Encyclopaedia of Viticulture* (Kishinëv, 1986).

u

Vaccarèse, rare, relatively light red grape variety permitted in CHÂTEAUNEUF-DU-PAPE producing wines similar to CINSAUT. Also known as Brun Argenté and Camarèse.

Vacqueyras, after GIGONDAS, the second of the Côtes du Rhône villages to be awarded its own appellation, in 1990. Vacqueyras may be red, white, or rosé, although only a minuscule proportion of a dramatically expanded vineyard total that had reached 1,406 ha/3,473 acres by 2013 (more than neighbouring Gigondas, for example) is planted with white grape varieties. Most of the wine is like a super-concentrated Côtes du Rhône-Villages, made in the communes of Vacqueyras and Sarrians between Gigondas and BEAUMES-DE-VENISE (see map under RHÔNE). The appellation rules are very similar to those of Gigondas, and thus to those of Châteauneuf-du-Pape, although only half the grapes in a red Vacqueyras have to be Grenache. The rest are usually Syrah, Mourvèdre, and Cinsaut. Vacqueyras tends to be slightly more rustic than good Gigondas, but producers such as Ch des Tours, now operated in conjunction with Ch Rayas of CHÂTEAUNEUF-DU-PAPE, at least back up that rusticity with power and concentration.

vacuole, the central compartment of plant CELLS, separated from cytoplasm by a membrane. In grape berries, vacuoles within flesh cells contain the solution that forms grape juice.   B.G.C.

vacuum evaporation. See CONCENTRATION.

Valdadige, or Etschtaler in German, basic appellation of the Adige (Etsch) Valley that, unusually, extends across three regions, though is used principally by producers in TRENTINO and also by some in north-western VENETO. Vineyards in ALTO ADIGE theoretically qualify but the Alto Adige appellation is usually used instead.

Valdeorras, easternmost wine zone in GALICIA in north-west Spain (see map under SPAIN). Steeply terraced vineyards are planted predominantly with inappropriate but productive vine varieties such as Garnacha Tintorera (ALICANTE BOUSCHET) and the white PALOMINO. The indigenous white GODELLO, which had all but disappeared from Galicia in the wake of PHYLLOXERA, is being aggressively replanted. This moderately productive variety is susceptible to disease, but Valdeorras is protected from the Atlantic by mountains immediately to the west. If carefully vinified, it can produce an aromatic wine with an ALCOHOLIC STRENGTH of 12 to 13%. In the late 1990s, some of Spain's most acclaimed BARREL-FERMENTED whites were Godello wines from Valdeorras made by the Guitián family, who pioneered this style, now artfully practised by the likes of Rafael Palacios and Valdesil. The MENCÍA grape, which makes fruity reds, is similarly respected by a new wave of producers in Valdeorras.

Valdepeñas, wine region in CASTILLA-LA MANCHA in south central Spain producing soft, ripe red wines. The sea of rolling vineyards that is Valdepeñas is really an extension of LA MANCHA (see map under SPAIN), but Valdepeñas has developed a reputation for quality over and above its larger neighbour and has consequently earned a separate denomination, or DO. Physical conditions in Valdepeñas are similar to those in La Mancha. The Sierra Morena dividing CASTILE from ANDALUCÍA immediately to the south is a barrier to the moderating influence of the Mediterranean. At an elevation of 700 m/ 2,300 ft above sea level, Valdepeñas shares the arid, CONTINENTAL conditions that prevail through much of central Spain.

As in La Mancha, the white, DROUGHT-resistant AIRÉN is the dominant grape variety but the red Cencibel, as the TEMPRANILLO of Rioja is known here, has been gaining ground in Valdepeñas' 28,000 ha/67,000 acres of vineyard. Much of the 'red' wine made in the region is a blend of red and white grapes somewhat lacking in colour and BODY. The best red wines, however, are made exclusively from Cencibel, which has the capacity to age well in OAK and increasingly they include Cabernet Sauvignon, Merlot, Syrah, and even Petit Verdot. The best wines have the soft, smooth, vanilla character, although not the price tag nor the complexity, of a well-aged RIOJA.   V. de la S.

Val di Cornia. See MAREMMA.

Valdiguié, sometimes called Gros Auxerrois, enjoyed its finest hour in the late 19th century when, as a dark-berried grape variety from the Lot, it was valued for its productivity and its resistance to POWDERY MILDEW. In the early 20th century, it was known as 'the ARAMON of the south west' for its emphasis on quantity at the expense of quality. It has now been all but eradicated from France, where a few hectares remain, mainly in the Tarn *département*.

In 1980, French ampelographer Galet visited the US and identified the variety then sold rather successfully as Napa Gamay as none other than this undistinguished vine from south-west France, of which there were then 4,000 acres/1,600 ha planted in California. By the 1990s, it had disappeared from official statistics but occasionally turned up on the label of a fruity VARIETAL wine.

Galet, P., 'La Culture de la vigne aux États-Unis et au Canada', *France viticole* (Sept–Oct 1980 and Jan–Feb 1981).

Valdobbiadene. See CONEGLIANO-VALDOBBIADENE.

Valençay, small AOC region on the south bank of the Cher tributary of the Loire in northern France with about 180 ha/444 acres in production by 2013. Limestone, flint, and silt are planted with a wide range of LOIRE grape varieties. Whites must be at least 70% Sauvignon Blanc (Valençay is only about 20 miles/30 km from QUINCY and REUILLY) but crisp reds and some rosés are made from a mix of grapes dominated by Gamay.

Valencia, Spain's biggest port and third largest city, also lends its name to an autonomous region and one of five wine denominations (see DO) in the Comunidad Valenciana region (see map under SPAIN). The vineyards are well away from the city, inland from the fertile market gardens and paddy fields bordering the Mediterranean. Production of white wine exceeds red. Neutral dry whites are made from the MERSEGUERA grape, although the local Moscatel Romano (MUSCAT OF ALEXANDRIA) produces some good, pungent dessert MISTELAS. MONASTRELL and the dark-fleshed Garnacha Tintorera (ALICANTE BOUSCHET) together produce rather coarse red wines, although the latter can produce some fresh, dry rosé. Five large producers dominate Valencia and the surrounding DOs.

Valle d'Aosta. See AOSTA.

Valle de Güimar, denominated wine region of just under 1,000 ha/2,470 acres at up to 1,400 m/4,593 ft occupying a valley in the dry south-eastern part of Tenerife in the Spanish CANARY ISLANDS. A few tiny wineries, technically improved with EU subsidies, make surprisingly distinguished wines from the white LISTÁN Blanco grape, but in such small quantities that they are hardly known even on the island.

V. de la S.

Valle de la Orotava, denominated wine region with just under 1,000 ha/2,470 acres of vines on the lush northern flanks of Mount Teide on Tenerife in the Spanish CANARY ISLANDS. Much improved reds, whites, and rosés are made from INDIGENOUS VARIETIES and exported by the likes of Suertes del Marqués.

V. de la S.

Valle Isarco, or Eisacktaler in German, source of pure, dry white wines from the upper reaches of ALTO ADIGE.

Valpaços, subregion of TRÁS-OS-MONTES in north-east Portugal.

Valpolicella, lively red wine from the VENETO region in north-east Italy. Vines are grown in a series of adjacent valleys descending from the pre-alpine Lissini Mountains north of Verona down to the plains in the south. The Fumane, Marano, and Negrare valleys, with vineyards on hillsides rising up to 400 m/1,312 ft, form the historic nucleus and have their own DOC Valpolicella Classico with 3,325 ha/8,213 acres of vines. Between the Classico zone and the plains to the east lie the 433 ha of Valpantena vineyards on both hillsides and plains. The total area of vineyard given over to regular DOC Valpolicella is 3,587 ha. Valpolicella, like a number of other historic areas of Italy, saw its production zone greatly enlarged when it achieved DOC status in 1968. It was extended eastward as far as the boundary of the SOAVE white wine zone, and south onto the fertile plains on the northern edge of the Po Valley. Although the total Valpolicella zone is large and varied, in general soils are more CALCAREOUS and temperatures lower in the north and on the hillsides, in the Classico area, while soils on the plains are distinctly heavier and deeper and temperatures higher. The majority of quality-conscious producers' vineyards are to be found on HILLSIDES only.

The name Valpolicella is derived from a mixture of Latin and Greek, as in 'the valley of many cellars'. CORVINA has historically been regarded as the best grape of Valpolicella, being used to produce a wide range of styles, all from the same hills. The youthful wines resemble a good Beaujolais in that they can be enjoyed chilled and have, at their best, a delicious sour-cherry character. The fuller wines come from better sites on the hills, as do the RECIOTO and AMARONE wines made from dried grapes.

By the late 1960s, when the DOC regulations were drawn up, any pretence of quality wine production seemed to have been abandoned. Lesser grape varieties MOLINARA and RONDINELLA were allowed as part of the blend, and excessive yields were permitted. As a result, quality fell almost as quickly as the prices paid to growers for their grapes. By the late 1980s, many of the vineyards on the hills in the Classico zone were abandoned, as viticulture there became less and less profitable. Only those growers on the plains, where yields were several times higher than those from the hills, were able to make money. Consequently, the grapes from these prolific vineyards made most Valpolicella, and these were the wines that shaped—one might say tarnished—the image of the wine.

Hillside viticulture was salvaged by Amarone, a wine with virtually no tradition and once considered a 'faulty' RECIOTO that had fermented to complete dryness, and only commercially produced since the 1960s. As described in the AMARONE entry, there has been an explosion in total production this century. As the price paid for Amarone grapes is about three times that paid for regular Valpolicella grapes, the total area of vines for Amarone has increased enormously and there are plans to extend the region further. Efforts to prevent overproduction of Amarone by restricting the total amount of grapes coming from a single estate that may be dried from 70 to 60% have been shelved, not least due to pressure from the many CO-OPERATIVES. The commercial success of Amarone has reduced average annual production of regular Valpolicella from 41 to 19 million bottles between 2005 and 2013. Meanwhile the production of Valpolicella RIPASSO, a normal Valpolicella run over Amarone skins, adding alcohol and extract to the wine, has soared from 7 million bottles in 2007 to more than 25 million bottles in 2013. Ripasso's rapid growth is a direct result of Amarone's popularity, as the volume of Ripasso obtained by this method may be double the volume of the Amarone that has been racked off before, while 15% of Amarone may also be added to improve its quality. With falling prices for both Amarone and the Ripasso marketed as a cheaper alternative, this policy may prove toxic in the long run.

This concentration on only two styles has also led to the slow demise of RECIOTO della Valpolicella. This truly historic wine is produced in ever-shrinking quantities because it is not seen as nearly as profitable by producers, and sweet wines can be a hard sell on the international market, while Amarone is rapidly turning into BRAND rather than a wine that reflects its origin.

Some authentic Valpolicella can still be found, however, from the highly concentrated, almost elixir-like Amarone from Romano Dal Forno wines to the traditional long-lived Amarones from Quintarelli and the historic house of Bertani, as well as a handful of mavericks continuing to pursue TERROIR rather than volume, such as Ca' La Bionda, Corte Sant'Alda, Meroni, and Monte Dall'Ora.

W.S.

Belfrage, N., *Barolo to Valpolicella: The Wines of Northern Italy* (London, 1999).

Masnaghetti, A., *Valpolicella, Amarone: The Vineyards* (Monza, 2013) (map).

www.consorziovalpolicella.it

Valtellina, Italy's northernmost wine zone in the alpine far north of LOMBARDY where the NEBBIOLO grape (here called Chiavennasca) is cultivated, is a narrow valley formed by the River Adda as it flows from east to west before emptying its waters into Lake Como. Despite its 46-degree latitude, the valley—protected to the north by the Alpi Retiche and to the south by the Alpi Orbie—has a relatively privileged climate (not unlike the warmer wine regions across the border in SWITZERLAND) with a high percentage of sunny days and moderate and evenly spread rains throughout the year. The steep, terraced vineyards optimize solar radiation for grape RIPENING. A certain amount of daytime heat is also stored and released during the cooler hours of the evening and night by the dry stone walls of the terraces and the very rocky soils of the vineyards. All of this helps compensate for lower median temperatures than in Nebbiolo's classic areas in PIEMONTE to the south west. Nonetheless, the wines themselves, while unmistakably Nebbiolo, do tend to be rather lighter, with more perceptible TANNINS and ACIDITY than the wines of the LANGHE or those made from SPANNA in the Novara-Vercelli hills.

Although Nebbiolo seems well adapted to Valtellina, it arrived relatively recently: the detailed works of Francesco Saverio Quadrio in the 17th century make no mention of the grape and the beginning of its cultivation in Valtellina appears to date from the early 19th century, when more than 6,000 ha/15,000 acres of vineyards were registered here, more than a third planted with Nebbiolo. In the early 2010s the region had just 850 ha of vineyards planted on a thin 45 km strip of terraces on the right bank of the Adda. This isolated zone has been sensibly demarcated, with the whole region classified as DOC Valtellina Rosso, whose maximum yield of 10 tonnes/ha is unlikely to be achieved in practice. A step up is Valtellina Superiore (215 ha) from separate demarcated areas where yields are restricted to 8 tonnes/ha and the wine must be aged for at least 24 months, of which 12 in oak cask (36 for Riserva). At the pinnacle of quality are five subzones which lie within the Superiore area, each with a distinctly different style of Nebbiolo: delicate Maroggio (25 ha), elegant and mineral Sassella (114 ha), harmoniously precocious Grumello (78 ha), earthy and powerful Inferno (55 ha), and fresh and fruit-driven Valgella (137 ha). All these DOCs must contain at least 90% of Nebbiolo. The handful of INTERNATIONAL VARIETIES planted here, among them Pinot Noir and Sauvignon Blanc, may be sold as IGT Terrazze Retiche di Sondrio. The zone's only DOCG is reserved for the SFORZATO di Valtellina (or Sfurzat in local dialect), a full-bodied, dry red made from Nebbiolo grapes that have been dried for three months, and which must be aged for at least 20 months.

The vineyard area has declined significantly because of the increasing cost of working the narrow TERRACES which are impossible to mechanize. The region's vineyards are extremely fragmented with many small smallholders whose produce was traditionally bought and bottled by NÉGOCIANTS who, together with the four local CO-OPERATIVES, were long the dominant economic force in the zone. However the dynamics in the region are changing, with négociants now playing a much more active role in grape growing, and more and more producers bottling their own wines, often from single vineyards. Ar.Pe.Pe, founded in 1984, has achieved virtual cult status while other notable producers include Rainoldi, Fay, the négociant Nino Negri, the stalwart of Valtellina, Rainoldi and Mamete Prevostini, and it is becoming difficult to find a mediocre bottle of wine from Valtellina.   W.S.

Masnaghetti, A., *I Cru di Enogea: Valtellina* (Monza 2012) (map).

www.vinidivaltellina.it

vandalism has long affected wine production but as wine prices have risen, so has the cost of wine vandalism, which can now be publicized so easily. Disgruntled ex-employees, commercial rivals, and pranksters are the usual culprits. Perhaps the most famous instance was the loss of six vintages of BRUNELLO DI MONTALCINO in the cellars of its most famous producer, Gianfranco Soldera of Case Basse in 2012. A former employee went to jail for opening the taps on every cask. The year before the cellars of lauded PRIORAT producer Terroir Al Limit were broken into and tank taps opened with bleach added to contaminate various casks. Foreign ownership may have been a factor here, as at Domaine Jones in FITOU, where wine was destroyed in early 2013. Moana Park in Hawke's Bay, NEW ZEALAND, was the next victim.

Vineyards are generally more public but much more accessible. In 2010 someone threatened to poison the venerable vines of DOMAINE DE LA ROMANÉE-CONTI unless a substantial ransom was paid. In the same year, anti GENETIC MODIFICATION protesters vandalized a trial planting of GM vines in Alsace.

vanillin, a phenolic ALDEHYDE that is a component of the lignin structure of OAK wood; responsible for the vanilla note in wines. It is especially extracted from barrel wood. If new oak casks are used for wine maturation, this vanillin adds complexity to the flavour (see OAK FLAVOUR). Vanillin levels tend to be higher in American than in French oak.

varietal, adjective and descriptive term for a wine named after the dominant grape variety from which it is made. The word is increasingly misused as a noun in place of VINE VARIETY. A varietal wine is distinct from a wine named after its own geographical provenance (as the great majority of European wines are), and a GENERIC wine, one named after a supposed style, often haphazardly borrowed from European geography, such as 'Chablis' and 'Burgundy'. Varietal wines are most closely associated with the NEW WORLD, where they constitute the great majority of wines produced. The concept was nurtured by Maynard AMERINE at the University of California at DAVIS in the wake of PROHIBITION as a means of encouraging growers to plant worthy vine varieties. It was advocated with particular enthusiasm by Frank SCHOONMAKER in the 1950s and 1960s, and was embraced during the CALIFORNIA wine boom of the 1970s to distinguish the more ambitious wines, often made from Cabernet Sauvignon and, increasingly, Chardonnay, from the lack-lustre generics of old. Varietal labelling was also adopted, for a similar purpose, in AUSTRALIA, SOUTH AFRICA, NEW ZEALAND, and elsewhere.

Originally, when the United States' acreage of classic vine varieties was relatively limited, a varietal needed only 51% of that variety in the blend to be so labelled. In 1973, this requirement was increased to 75% (although some particularly strongly flavoured NEW YORK state vine varieties were exempted from this increased requirement; see FOXY). Despite the emergence of the MERITAGE category of superior blends, varietal wines continue to be viewed by many as California's premier statement of quality. See also LABELLING INFORMATION.

The French INAO authorities are hostile towards varietal labelling, understanding that they have nothing to gain and much to lose by entering into this commonwealth of nomenclature. Within France, varietal wines (typically IGP) are called *vins de cépage*, and are widely regarded as of lower rank than AOC wines.

In their 1990s attempts to reformulate the DOC system and wine-quality categories, the Italian authorities were equally keen to emphasize their uniqueness, place, over grape variety whenever possible. Such attitudes are understandable and, in the long term, may pay dividends, but there is little doubt that an important factor in the success of many New World wines has been the ease with which consumers can grasp the concept of varietal labelling. In the 1980s, Chardonnay and Cabernet Sauvignon became the most recognizable names in the world of wine.

Most varietal wines are based on a single vine variety but examples made up of a blend of two or even three different varieties have become increasingly common, especially when there is a shortage of certain popular varieties. Common varietal blends are Sémillon/Chardonnay (possibly stretched with some Colombard or Chenin Blanc) and Sauvignon/Sémillon among white wines and Cabernet/Merlot, Cabernet/Shiraz, Syrah/Merlot, and Grenache/Shiraz/Mourvèdre (GSM) among reds. It is usual to list the varieties on the label in declining order of importance in the blend.

Changes introduced by the EU reforms of 2008 that allow variety and vintage to be indicated on the labels of WINES WITHOUT GEOGRAPHICAL INDICATION are intended to help such European wines compete with varietal wines from the New World.

For more details, see VINE VARIETIES.

variety of vine or grape. See VINE VARIETIES.

Varois, Coteaux, enclave within the Côtes de PROVENCE appellation which takes its name from the Var *département*. Of wines produced from the 2,505 ha/6,187 acres in production by 2013, 90% were rosé. The wooded hills around Brignoles are based on LIMESTONE and are so buffered from warming MARITIME influence by the hills of Ste-Baume that vines will not ripen at all reliably at elevations of more than about 350 m/1,100 ft.

Reds and rosés may incorporate a wide array of grapes: the rosé varieties Grenache and Cinsaut but also Syrah and Mourvèdre (which will ripen only in the warmest sites) are the principal dark-skinned grapes but Cabernet Sauvignon, Carignan, and the Provençal speciality TIBOUREN are allowed a minor role. This gives the better producers an exciting palette from which to work; some of them produce several different blends which vary in style by virtue of both varietal mix and ÉLEVAGE. For white wines, Grenache Blanc is added to those varieties permitted for Côtes de Provence Blanc (see PROVENCE), although Vermentino is increasingly appreciated.

Varro, Marcus Terentius, (116–27 BC) was a prolific Roman writer who wrote on subjects as diverse as grammar, geography, history, law, science, philosophy, and education; the rhetorician Quintilian called him 'the most learned man among the Romans' (*Institutio oratoria* 10. 1. 95). Yet the only one of his works to survive in its entirety is his manual of agriculture, *De re rustica*. Varro started it in his 80th year and addressed it to his wife, who had bought a farm. Varro was a man of letters, and, unlike CATO's treatise, from which he borrows occasionally, his own is a literary exercise, written in a highly wrought style. *De re rustica* is full of antiquarian learning as well as practical advice, and Varro often looks back to the time when the inhabitants of Italy were all hardworking honest farmers and there was none of the decadence that prevails among the city dwellers of his day. The treatise is divided into three books, each of which is a dialogue; most of the material on wine comes in the first book. He defines old wine as at least a year old; some wine goes off before that, but some, like FALERNIAN, becomes the more valuable the longer it is kept. Varro's work was used by later writers such as VIRGIL, PLINY, COLUMELLA, and PALLADIUS. Varro's own chief authority, by his own admission, is Mago of CARTHAGE, about whom nothing is known and of whose work nothing survives. Among the many Greek authors he mentions as his sources are Aristotle, Xenophon, and Theophrastus.   H.M.W.

Skydsgaard, J. E., *Varro the Scholar* (Copenhagen, 1968).

vase painting. Vases in Ancient GREECE from 600 to 300 BC are an important source of information about the SYMPOSIUM, the VINTAGE, and VITICULTURE generally.

vat, large CONTAINER for STORING wine and/or AGEING or maturation. A vat may also be used as a FERMENTATION VESSEL. In English-speaking countries they may also be known as tanks; in France they are called CUVES.

For many centuries, WOOD was the most common material but in the mid to late 20th century inert materials such as CONCRETE, enamel, epoxy resin, and STAINLESS STEEL replaced wood except in particularly traditional or traditionalist areas. At the start of the 21st century, wooden fermentation vats were once again becoming more fashionable though they are very expensive.

For details of wine maturation in wooden vats, see CASK AGEING; for more on fermentation and maturation in smaller clay vessels, see AMPHORAE, QVEVRI, and TINAJAS.

vat size varies enormously. FERMENTATION VESSELS in large commercial wineries contain, typically, between 50 and 300 hl, (1,320–8,000 gal), although smaller enterprises may use much smaller wooden or CONCRETE vats. The ratio of height to width has implications for red winemaking in determining the area of the CAP. Blending tanks in large commercial wineries usually hold around 3,500 hl (92,000 gal) and may contain up to 10,000 hl. Grupo Peñaflor, Argentina's largest wine company, boasts the largest wine vat in the world, with a capacity of about 53,000 hl—large enough to hold a dinner party for several hundred inside, though it is no longer used in winemaking.

Vavřinecke, former Czech name for the red ST-LAURENT grape.

VDN is sometimes used as an abbreviation for VIN DOUX NATUREL.

VDP, or the Verband Deutscher Prädikatsweingüter, the most influential and prestigious German growers' association, incorporating 202 (in 2014) of the finest wine estates in GERMANY. In 1910, just two years after consolidating the top MOSEL estates into the GROSSER RING, the mayor of Trier persuaded like-minded organizations in the RHEINGAU and PFALZ to band together to form a national association for the purpose of selling its members' wines at AUCTION. Over the years, other regional groups joined the VDP and by the late 1990s its membership included estates in all 13 wine-growing regions. Although its collective holdings account for a mere 3.5% of Germany's total vineyard area, this group produces a remarkable proportion of its finest wines.

In their effort to preserve German wine culture, the national and regional branches of the VDP still maintain their tradition of wine auctions, although auction prices today, prestige notwithstanding, have little bearing on market prices. The VDP's contribution to the image of fine and rare German wines is based on its members' uncompromising dedication to high quality, starting with stringent, self-imposed regulations. These stipulate that members must have holdings in the top vineyard sites; produce lower YIELDS and higher MUST WEIGHTS than required by the GERMAN WINE LAW; plant at least 80% of their vineyards with varieties traditionally associated with their regions; practise environmentally sound methods; be established as full-time growers of sound reputation; and submit to regular (at least every five years) VDP compliance inspections. Members' labels and capsules carry the VDP name and logo, an eagle and grape cluster. The VDP's efforts at vineyard classification and QUALITY CONTROL as well as its LABELLING practices are influential beyond its membership, transcending the categories and minimal qualitative stipulations of the German Wine Law, even if the organization has been unable to effect significant changes in the law itself.

See also GROSSES GEWÄCHS.

VDQS, or Vin Délimité de Qualité Supérieure, was France's minuscule interim wine quality designation between VIN DE PAYS and APPELLATION CONTRÔLÉE, which accounted for less than 1% of the nation's wine production. The VDQS category was scrapped after the 2010 vintage and most have been promoted to AOC.

Vega Sicilia, concentrated and long-lived red wine that is Spain's undisputed equivalent of a FIRST GROWTH, made on a single property now incorporated into the RIBERA DEL DUERO denomination. The wine was being made long before the present DO region took shape in the 1980s. This 1,000-ha/2,500-acre farm either side of the main road east of Valladolid has been making wine in its present form since 1864 when Eloy Lacanda y Chaves planted vines from Bordeaux alongside Tinto Fino, also known as Tinta del País (a local strain of TEMPRANILLO). The current style was defined around 1910, when the winery was leased by Cosme Palacio, a Rioja grower. A succession of different owners has since managed to maintain the quality and reputation of Vega Sicilia as Spain's finest red wine. However, Vega Sicilia fell on lean times at several junctures, and was able to make a substantial leap in quality and, more importantly, in consistency after being bought by the Alvarez family in 1982.

The more than 200 ha/500 acres of vineyard on LIMESTONE soils overlooking the River Duero (DOURO in Portugal) are planted mainly with

Tinto Fino but CABERNET SAUVIGNON, MERLOT, and a little MALBEC together make up about 20% of the total production. A tiny quantity of old-vine white ALBILLO remains.

Bodegas Vega Sicilia produces three wines, all red. Valbuena is a five-year old VINTAGE-dated wine aged in American oak. Vega Sicilia Unico, which is restricted to the best VINTAGES and is often released after spending about ten years in a combination of wooden tanks, small, new BARRIQUES, large, old barrels and bottles, attracts the most attention. The best vintages of Vega Sicilia Unico and the third wine produced here, the rare multi-vintage Reserva Especial, last for decades.

In 1991, Bodegas Vega Sicilia acquired the nearby Liceo winery and created the immediately acclaimed Bodegas Alión, which makes much more modern reds from 100% Tempranillo grapes, aged in new French oak. In 2001, Pintia, Vega Sicilia's bodega in the TORO region, produced its first vintage. Then, in a JOINT VENTURE with Benjamin de ROTHSCHILD, Vega Sicilia created the Macán estate in Rioja. As the bodega celebrated its 150th anniversary in 2014, tensions between different members of the Álvarez family who acquired it in 1982 were widely publicized.   V. de la S.

Peñín, J., *Vega Sicilia—Journey to the Heart of a Legend* (Madrid, 2002).

vegetarian and vegan wines

are increasingly requested by consumers. The main area of concern is the use of animal-based products for FINING and STABILIZING wine. Of the most common agents, only BENTONITE is suitable for vegans as well as vegetarians; CASEIN and albumin (see EGG WHITES) are acceptable to most vegetarians; ISINGLASS and GELATIN would be unacceptable to most vegetarians and vegans. Although such materials are PROCESSING AIDS rather than ADDITIVES, it is impossible to guarantee that there is absolutely no residue in the wine and some wine drinkers may object to the use of an animal-derived product. Some winemakers and retailers have started to make this information available on the bottle or at the point of sale. See also LABELLING INFORMATION and INGREDIENT LABELLING.

vegetative propagation

reproduction of a plant by asexual means. In viticulture, CUTTINGS on which both roots and shoots will grow are used. In those limited locations where PHYLLOXERA and other root pests are not present and ROOTSTOCKS are not used, LAYERING can be used to replace missing vines. Micropropagation (see TISSUE CULTURE) is a modern application in which small amounts of a MOTHER VINE may be propagated in large numbers rapidly. Unlike SEXUAL PROPAGATION, the progeny of vegetative propagation is genetically identical, unless MUTATION intervenes.   B.G.C.

vein banding, vine disease. See FANLEAF DEGENERATION.

Veltliner, Valtlin Zelene, Veltlinske Zelené, Veltini, common Eastern European names for the four distinct Austrian grape varieties supposedly originating from VALTELLINA in Lombardy (northern Italy): GRÜNER VELTLINER, ROTER VELTLINER, FRÜHROTER VELTLINER, and occasionally Brauner Veltliner.   J.V.

vendange, French word for HARVEST. A *vendangeur* is a grape-picker, and a temporary lodging for grape-pickers may be called a *vendangeoir*.

Vendange Tardive, means literally 'late harvest' and in France is restricted to ALSACE, where strict regulations cover its production, even if too many producers are meeting only the bare minima. Although all Alsace Vendange Tardive wines are made from ripe grapes, and without the aid of CHAPTALIZATION, the wines themselves vary considerably in how sweet they are, with some of them tasting rich but almost bone dry. Labels give no clue as to how sweet these wines taste, making FOOD AND WINE MATCHING particularly difficult. SÉLECTION DE GRAINS NOBLES is Alsace's even riper category. See also AUSLESE and BEERENAUSLESE, their counterparts in Germany, and LUXEMBOURG.

vendange verte. See CROP THINNING.

vendemmia, Italian for VINTAGE YEAR or HARVEST. **Vendimia** is Spanish for harvest.

Vendômois, Coteaux du, AOC producing a wide range of light wines between the Coteaux du LOIR and the city of Vendôme in the greater LOIRE Valley. The wines are necessarily crisp, this far from the equator, but a pale pink VIN GRIS from the PINEAU D'AUNIS grape can be an attractive local speciality. Pineau d'Aunis must also constitute at least half of any blend for the slightly more solid reds, while Chenin Blanc is the principal white wine grape, often aided and abetted by Chardonnay, for some particularly tart white wines which represent about one bottle in six.

See also LOIRE, including map.

Veneto, Italy's most productive wine region in the north east (see map under ITALY). It stretches westward to Lake Garda and northward to the Alps and the Austrian border from the terra firma behind the lagoons and city of VENICE, an important power in the wine trade of the Middle Ages whose legacy has shaped some wines in Veneto and even elsewhere. In the mid 1990s the volume of wine produced in Veneto overtook that of PUGLIA and SICILY, and in 2012 was more than 8.2 million hl/205 million gal. Much of this growth has been due to the runaway success of PINOT GRIGIO, followed by that of PROSECCO, although the entrepreneurial spirit of the producers, CO-OPERATIVES, and large bottlers has also played a pivotal role.

In theory, a significant proportion of Veneto wine is of good quality, with DOC wine representing well over half the total. The reality is somewhat different. This proportion has been artificially inflated both by drastic enlargements of the DOC zones (to plains which were cereal-growing areas prior to the Second World War in the case of Valpolicella and Soave) and/or by sanctioning extremely generous YIELDS which, even for DOCs and DOCGs, in 2012 averaged an exceptionally high 95 hl/ha. The resulting wines, although nominally of DOC level, are too frequently characterless. Good bottles of Bardolino, Valpolicella, and Soave are not difficult to find, however, and the CORVINA vine variety which forms the basis of Valpolicella, and GARGANEGA, the basis of Soave, are capable of making seriously interesting wines if grown in the right place: the hills on the 45 degrees 30 minutes of LATITUDE which run eastward from Lake Garda, to the north of the fertile Adige river plain. Other HILLSIDE zones of real potential are scattered around the region and include the Colli Berici to the south; Breganze to the north of Vicenza, especially for Tai Rosso (GRENACHE); the Colli Euganei to the south west of Padua; and the hillside part of the Piave DOC zone. Native varieties such as Friulano, Garganega, and Verduzzo are cultivated in these zones, as are imports such as Merlot and Cabernet, mainly Franc (brought to the area in the wake of the Napoleonic invasion in the early part of the 19th century). The Garganega-based Bianco di Custoza and Gambellara, two country cousins of Soave, the lightly sparkling Prosecco of Conegliano, and the Fior d'Arancio of the Colli Euganei (a fuller-bodied answer to MOSCATO D'ASTI) round out the regional picture, a picture characterized by large quantities of pleasant, easy-drinking wines which seem to suffer from a lack of ambition and the devaluation of many of the DOCs, resulting in dumping and further erosion of quality. Individual producers throughout the region provide exceptions, especially those who show an interest in TERROIR rather than volume. The small Lessini DOC, producing TRADITIONAL METHOD sparkling wine from the Durella grape, was one bright spot in the mid 2010s.

Veneto's centre of ACADEME is the experimental viticultural institute at CONEGLIANO.

For details of notable specific wines, see AMARONE, BARDOLINO, BREGANZE, CUSTOZA, GAMBELLARA, LISON-PRAMAGGIORE, PIAVE, PROSECCO, RABOSO, RECIOTO, SOAVE, and VALPOLICELLA.   W.S.

Belfrage, N., *Barolo to Valpolicella—The Wines of Northern Italy* (2nd edn, London, 2003).
www.uvive.it
www.winesofveneto.com

Venezuela is a very minor South American wine producer, and consumer, but TROPICAL VITICULTURE has been practised, mainly for TABLE GRAPES, since the arrival of European immigrants at the end of the 19th century—although there is evidence that Jesuit MISSIONARIES first planted vines at Cumana in the 16th century, and vine-growers emigrated here from Baden in the early 19th century; see GERMAN HISTORY. According to OIV estimates, there were only about 1,000 ha/2,500 acres of vines in the early 21st century and a thriving DRIED-GRAPE industry. Producers have tended to use GRAPE CONCENTRATE or bulk wine imports as their raw material for products that range from LAMBRUSCO-like blends to base wines for SANGRÍA. Average temperatures are about 27 °C/81 °F, vine DORMANCY is impossible, and the two harvests per year are dictated by the rainy seasons. High ELEVATIONS are necessary for the tropical viticulture practised. Bodegas Pomar is the only producer of note.

Goldstein, E., *Wines of South America* (Oakland, Calif., 2014).

Venice, overarching DOC created in the early 2010s stretching from the hills of CONEGLIANO-VALDOBBIADENE to the Venetian lagoon in an attempt to capitalize on the name of this world-famous Venice city which was the cultural and, once, commercial centre of north east Italy.

In its time Venice has exerted considerable and sometimes lasting influence on the wines of the world. Medieval Venice had no agriculture or viticulture and obtained its wine and grain from LOMBARDY to the west; Venice's importance was in its trade. In 840 a treaty, known as the Pactum Lotharii, between CHARLEMAGNE's grandson Lothair and the doge of Venice, protected Venice's neutrality and guaranteed its security from the mainland. This treaty made Venice independent from the west and from Byzantium. Thus Venice became the most important of the Italo-Byzantine ports, and its position was strengthened when the Byzantines discovered that Venice's rivals Amalfi, NAPLES, and Gaeta had been collaborating with the Saracens. Initially Venice owed its wealth to its trade, acquiring possession of Crete, Modon, and Coron in the Aegean and being granted exemptions from the TAXATION in Constantinople that was to ruin the Byzantine economy (see GREECE, medieval history). The Crusades only strengthened Venice's position at the frontier between northern Europe and the eastern Mediterranean.

With its eastern expansion came the trade in sweet wines, so much more esteemed by northern Europeans than their own thinner FERMENTS. Most of these were from Crete, known then as Candia. Many of them carried the name of the Greek port from which they were shipped, Monemvasia (hence MALVASIA di Candia, and MALMSEY). Some of these wines were sold in Constantinople, others were taken to Venice for redistribution, either overland to Florence (via Ferrara), or by sea to Paris, England, and Flanders. In addition to buying and selling Aegean wines, Venice also dealt in Italian wines, from Trevi, the northern Adriatic, and the MARCHE, and in the even richer wines of Tyre (in modern LEBANON), which was owned by the Venetians for most of the 13th century.

However, in trade with Syria and Palestine, Venice came second to GENOA, and the rivalry extended to the trade with northern Europe: Genoa led the way there, and Venice, which was less well placed, did not start shipping wine to northern Europe until the early 14th century. By that time Genoa had already won the battle: at the end of the 13th century, Venice had ceased to be the richest and most important port in Italy, but not before having imported the Greek techniques of increasing sugar and alcohol content by deliberately making DRIED-GRAPE WINES. Johnson suggests a direct link between such practices, employed on the islands along the Dalmatian coast, and those subsequently, indeed currently, used by some in the VENETO hinterland of Venice to make RECIOTO versions of Valpolicella and Soave.

Venice was also to become the centre of GLASS production, and therefore played an important, if indirect, role in the history of wine.

See also ITALY.   H.M.W.

Johnson, H., *The Story of Wine* (London, 1989).
Lopez, R. S., 'The trade of mediaeval Europe: the south', in *The Cambridge Economic History of Europe*, 7 vols., ii: *Trade and Industry in the Middle Ages* (Cambridge, 1987).
Melis, F., 'Produzione e commercio dei vini italiani nei secoli XIII–XVIII', *Annales cisalpines d'histoire sociale*, 1/3 (1972), 107–33.
Nicol, D. M., *Byzantium and Venice* (Cambridge, 1988).

Ventoux, large and growing appellation on the south-eastern fringes of the southern RHÔNE between GRIGNAN-LES-ADHÉMAR and the LUBERON. The nearly 6,000 ha/15,000 acre appellation takes its name from Mont Ventoux, the 2,000-m/6,500-ft high peak which dominates the region. The communes entitled to the appellation are on the western and southern flanks of this land mass, which has a significant cooling effect on the southern Rhône's generally MEDITERRANEAN CLIMATE. Historically this has been an area for producing TABLE GRAPES (along with other tree fruits such as cherries) but vines thrive up to 450 m elevation, and Syrah can be much more successful here than in hotter, lower vineyards to the south.

The almost exclusively red and rosé wines are blends from a wide variety of southern Rhône grapes. Ventoux is even more dominated by the CO-OPERATIVES than Grignan, and the less ambitious wines can taste even lighter than those of Grignan, but since the 1990s, a number of ambitious, distinctly superior producers have emerged, notably Domaine de Fondrèche and Chx Pesquié and Valcombe. Clairette, Bourboulenc, and Grenache Blanc are the principal varieties for the little white produced.

veraison, word used in viticulture for that intermediate stage of grape berry development which marks the beginning of RIPENING. It is derived from the French term *véraison*. At the beginning of veraison, the berries are hard and green, and about half their final size. During veraison, the berries change skin colour and soften, SUGARS and volume increase, and ACIDITY decreases. The colour of the grape before veraison is due to green chlorophyll, and at veraison berry skin changes colour to red-black (see ANTHOCYANINS) or yellow-green (see CAROTENOIDS), depending on the variety.

The inception of veraison is rapid and dramatic, but not all berries on a vine, nor indeed in a bunch, show veraison simultaneously. After about six days the berries soften and begin to accumulate GLUCOSE and FRUCTOSE, and begin to grow. The first to soften are those which are exposed and in warmer MICROCLIMATES (on the west-facing part of exposed bunches, or near a POST, for example); the last berries to undergo veraison are those in the CANOPY shade and on short shoots. It is difficult therefore to be precise about the single date of veraison; more commonly a date is recorded when, say, 50% of the berries on a vine show veraison. At about the same time as veraison occurs, CANE RIPENING begins.

The onset of veraison (and cane ripening) is controlled by both plant and environmental factors. Exposed grapes on vines which have a high LEAF TO FRUIT RATIO and which are experiencing mild WATER STRESS (and hence no active shoot growth) undergo veraison first. By contrast, veraison is delayed in vines with large crops, with many actively growing shoot tips and shaded fruit. Veraison is observably early in vineyards producing high-quality fruit, with both veraison and cane ripening developing quickly. Environmental factors associated with the early onset of veraison are warm, sunny, and dry weather.   B.G.C. & R.E.S.

Keller, M., 'Phenology and growth cycle', in *The Science of Grapevines: Anatomy and Physiology* (Elsevier, 2010).

Verdea, ancient Tuscan light-berried vine now a speciality of the Colli Piacentini in north central Italy.

Verdeca, Puglia's most popular light-berried vine producing neutral wine suitable for the VERMOUTH industry and declining in popularity.

According to the 2010 Italian vine census, 795 ha/1,965 acres remained. DNA PROFILING has shown that it is a parent, with TRIBIDRAG (Zinfandel) of the widespread Dalmatian variety PLAVINA, interestingly indicating an ancient viticultural bridge across the Adriatic Sea. More recently, Verdeca has been shown to be identical to the much more highly regarded Greek variety LAGORTHI.   J.V.

Verdejo, characterful grape so FASHIONABLE in Spain that its total plantings increased threefold between 2004 and 2011 to just over 18,000 ha/44,460 acres. Its distinctive blue-green bloom, which presumably inspired its name, is RUEDA's pride and joy (and helped stave off a challenge for primacy from imported SAUVIGNON BLANC, with which it is often blended). The variety ripens relatively early but is very susceptible to POWDERY MILDEW. DNA parentage analysis suggests Verdejo and GODELLO may be siblings. Wines produced are aromatic, herbaceous (somewhat reminiscent of laurel), but with great substance and extract, capable of ageing well into an almost nutty character.

Verdelho, name once given to several Portuguese white grape varieties, and most closely associated with the island of MADEIRA, where the Verdelho vine became increasingly rare in the post-PHYLLOXERA era but the name was for long used to denote a medium-dry style of wine somewhere between SERCIAL and BUAL levels of richness. Of the original four VINIFERA varieties that were traditionally grown on Madeira, Verdelho is the most planted today, with 47 ha/116 acres in 2010. Musts have moderate levels of sugar and notably high acidity. The Verdelho found on Madeira is the same as that found growing in the Azores and this Verdelho, cuttings of which were presumably picked up on one of these Atlantic islands en route to the antipodes, was extremely important in 19th-century Australia. Planted on 1,338 ha/3,305 acres in 2012, it has had notable success in vibrant, tangy, full-bodied table wines in more recent times, particularly in the Hunter valley of New South Wales, Victoria, and some of the hotter regions of Western Australia. See AUSTRALIA for more details. Verdelho has been planted to a very limited extent in SAVENNIÈRES in the Loire for just as long and makes some interesting varietal wine there. It is also grown in New Zealand, California, and Argentina.

A quite distinct variety once called Verdelho or Verdelho do Dão but now officially renamed Gouveio and identified as Spain's GODELLO, is planted on the Portuguese mainland, particularly in the Alentejo, Dão, and Douro.

Verdelho Roxo is a red-berried colour mutation of Verdelho (while the now virtually extinct Verdelho Tinto of the MINHO is unrelated).

Verdello, white Umbrian grape variety once prized for its ACIDITY. Just 287 ha/709 acres remained in 2010.

Verdesse, revived white grape of SAVOIE in eastern France whose wine can be powerful and highly aromatic.

Verdicchio, one of central Italy's classic white wines, is produced from the Verdicchio grape in two DOC zones of its home territory (since at least the 14th century) of the MARCHE: Verdicchio dei Castelli di Jesi, to the west of Ancona and a mere 30 km/20 miles from the Adriatic Sea, and the much smaller Verdicchio di Matelica zone, considerably further inland and at higher elevations, close to the regional border with UMBRIA. The best wines are cool with minerally mandarin fruit, lifted lemony acidity, and a slight chew on the finish. The finest can age ten or more years. Verdicchio di Matelica, with marginally lower yields and better exposed HILLSIDE VINEYARDS, was for long supposed to produce fuller, more characterful wine but this is no longer a given, since average yields in Castelli di Jesi have decreased to a sensible 65 hl/ha. Matelica's 300 ha/750 acres are dwarfed by the 2,762 ha/6,822 acres of the Castelli di Jesi, Marche's largest DOC and one which makes no distinction between vineyards on plains and the hills, with the exception of the much smaller historic Classico zone in the hills near the town of Cupano. Here several small producers produce complex wines, often from single vineyards. Under their initiative a start was made in the early 2010s to identify subzones based on exposition, elevation, and soil composition.

Close to 60% of the production of the Castelli di Jesi DOC is controlled by CO-OPERATIVES, and NÉGOCIANT houses control most of the remaining 40%. The wine's fame was largely due to the efforts of Fazi-Battaglia, a large négociant firm with extensive vineyard holdings. It was Fazi-Battaglia which introduced the amphora-shaped bottle and scroll-shaped label, initially a positive factor in gaining recognition for the wine but later responsible for the image of kitsch and frivolity with which Verdicchio has been saddled.

Like many central Italian white wines, Verdicchio was once fermented on its skins, giving it a certain fullness and authority but most Verdicchio is now made in a modern style, without SKIN CONTACT and with temperature-controlled fermentations, although some are returning to traditional methods.

Perhaps partly because of its high natural acidity, Verdicchio can also produce fine PASSITO wines while it was one of the first Italian SPUMANTES, with a tradition which can be traced back to the middle of the 19th century. Pleasant bottles of bubbly

Verdicchio remain an integral part of the DOC production.

Two DOCGs were created in 2011: Castelli di Jesi Verdicchio Riserva and Verdicchio di Matelica Riserva, for wines aged for at least 18 months before release. Bucci, La Distesa, La Moncesca, Pievalta, San Lorenzo, as well as the Colonnara CO-OPERATIVE all provide ample evidence of Verdicchio's capacity for ageing.

Verdicchio, the grape

The Verdicchio grape has been in the Marche for centuries but it has recently been established as identical to TREBBIANO di Soave, Trebbiano di Lugana, and Trebbiano Veltenesi. In SOAVE it can add perfume to the steely GARGANEGA while further west, on its own in a warmer zone, it gives full-bodied LUGANA of real interest.

The 2010 Italian vine census found a total of 2,838 ha/7,000 acres of Verdicchio in Italy, of which more than 2,300 ha/5,681 acres were in the Marche. A further 2,226 ha of Trebbiano di Soave is also recorded.   W.S.

Robinson, J., Harding, J., and Vouillamoz, J., *Wine Grapes, a complete guide to 1,368 vine varieties, including their origins and flavours* (London, 2012).

Verdiso, revived grape speciality of the Colli Euganei in north-east Italy making lively, varied whites.

Verdoncho, undistinguished La Mancha white grape grown on 1,718 ha/4,243 acres in 2011 and used almost exclusively for blending.

Verdot. See PETIT VERDOT for details of both this and Gros Verdot.

Verduzzo, wine made from VERDUZZO FRIULANO and/or VERDUZZO TREVIGIANO, principally in FRIULI and in the PIAVE DOC in the bordering province of Treviso in Veneto in seven different DOC zones: AQUILEIA, COLLI ORIENTALI, GRAVE, ISONZO, Latisana, FRIULI Annia, and LISON-PRAMAGGIORE. Only the Grave and the Colli Orientali produce significant quantities and the latter is qualitatively far superior, the grape showing a decided preference for HILLSIDE VINEYARDS. The wine exists in a dry, occasionally sparkling, and regularly sweet version, although the latter, obtained either by late harvesting or by raising the grapes (see DRIED-GRAPE WINES), can frequently be more medium dry than lusciously sweet. Sweet Verduzzo, less common than dry Verduzzo, is the more interesting wine, golden in colour, and often with a delightful density and honeyed aromas, even if it lacks the complexity of an outstanding dessert wine. Dry Verduzzo is less characterful, and the grapes' TANNINS often impart an odd astringency which is more noticeable when it has been fermented dry.

Ramandolo, to the north of Udine, is considered the classic zone for fine sweet Verduzzo, but the Colli Orientali di Friuli DOC, when first established, permitted the use of the name Ramandolo for any sweet Verduzzo in the production zone, converting, as it were, a place-name into a generic name. This anomaly has been corrected with the establishment of a separate Ramandolo DOCG for generally sweet wines, with maximum yields of 8 tonnes/ha (as opposed to the 11 tonnes/ha permitted for Colli Orentali Verduzzo) from anywhere in the Colli Orientali di Friuli zone.

Verduzzo Friulano, also known as **Verduzzo di Ramandolo**, white grape variety recorded as early as 1409 in north-east Italy.

According to Italy's 2010 vineyard survey, total plantings had fallen to 548 ha/1,354 acres.

Verduzzo Trevigiano makes much duller wine than the distinct VERDUZZO FRIULANO and was planted on almost 4,000 ha/10,000 acres in 2010—mainly in the provinces of Treviso and Venezia. Its origins are so far unknown.

verjus, or **verjuice**, the tart, apple-flavoured juice of unripe grapes, has many variations and many culinary uses, especially in dressings and sauces. It adds ACIDITY to a dish but unlike vinegar does not clash with wine. Traditional in many countries of the world, it is made from underripe grapes cut during CROP THINNING or from second crop berries that are unripe at harvest. One method is to press the grapes then preserve the partially fermented but highly VOLATILE juice with salt. Alternatively, the grapes may be boiled before pressing to kill the yeast and prevent fermentation but must then be used immediately or frozen. Most commercial producers gently press the grapes, cold settle and filter the juice before packaging, in which case STERILE BOTTLING is essential to prevent the verjus from fermenting.

Vermentino, attractive, aromatic white grape variety widely grown in north western Italy, Sardinia, to a limited extent in Corsica, and in southern France, where it is a recently permitted variety in many appellations. DNA PROFILING showed it is identical to the Ligurian PIGATO, the Piedmont variety FAVORITA and has long been considered identical to the ROLLE of Provence (although this has yet to be confirmed by DNA profiling).

France has the world's greatest area planted with Vermentino/Rolle: 4,721 ha/11,660 acres by 2011, considerably boosted by recent plantings in the Languedoc, fuelled by varietal FASHION. The Var département grows about 1,500 ha, about the same as the entire Languedoc-Roussillon, and it is both the southern Rhône's and Corsica's most planted white grape variety dominating the island's white APPELLATION

CONTRÔLÉE wines. The wines vary from floral to citrus but are almost always refreshing.

The Italian vine census of 2010 records 4,562 ha/11,273 acres of Vermentino Bianco, 220 ha of Favorita (the traditional pale-skinned grape of ROERO), and 264 ha of Pigato. (Ligurians long distinguished between their Pigato and Vermentino, and they may well be different clones of the same variety.) In Sardinia, Vermentino is the most planted white wine grape and is often picked deliberately early to retain acid levels but still manages to produce lively wines of character, although attempts at a richer, fuller style have also emerged, notably from Capichera in the **Vermentino di Gallura** DOCG. The interest in indigenous white grape varieties has been a boon for those growers along the Tuscan coast who had either the foresight or good fortune to plant Vermentino, for prices have been firm, with demand far outstripping supply.

Some Vermentino is also grown on Malta, in Lebanon, in California, Virginia, Texas, and North Carolina but of the non-European wine producers, the land of ALTERNATIVE VARIETIES, Australia, has been quickest to embrace this popular variety with plantings in many different regions.

Vermentino Nero is a minor, unrelated Tuscan red wine grape once almost extinct.

vermouth, herb-flavoured FORTIFIED WINE available in many different styles and qualities but usually a much more industrial product than wine. The Romans certainly made herb-flavoured wines, and the Greeks before them used a wide range of additives (see Ancient GREECE), often using wormwood or *artemesia absinthum*, which was thought to have curative powers for gastric ills. Such FLAVOURED WINES were strictly of local minority interest until the 16th century when a Piemontese, d'Alessio, began to market a medicinal wine similar to those he had noted in Bavaria flavoured with wormwood, there called *Wermuth*. The medicine, which enjoyed a certain success in French royal circles, subsequently became known as *vermutwein* and, in Anglicized form, vermouth. The diarist Samuel Pepys noted 'a glass of wormwood wine' without the comment it would have elicited had it been anything other than commonplace in late-17th-century London. Modern large-scale vermouth production dates from 18th-century PIEMONTE, close to the Alps which could supply the necessary herbs. Brands such as Cinzano, Martini, and the French Noilly Prat threw off any pretence at curative powers during the cocktail age and were particularly popular in the early and mid 20th century.

So many herbs and spices are now used to flavour fortified wines that the definition of vermouth is necessarily elastic. The more classic version is the almost dry, bitter drink with the

strong aroma of wormwood and other bitter herbs. The Italian Punt e Mes is one of the better-known examples. But the more popular version by far is sweeter, about 17% alcohol, and more vaguely herbal. Such vermouths are traditionally known as Italian if red and sweet and French if gold and drier, although most styles are made wherever vermouth is produced. France's most delicately alpine vermouth is CHAMBÉRY, while the vermouth most closely linked to fine wine is Lillet of Bordeaux, for long owned by the Borie family of the ST-JULIEN property Ch Ducru-Beaucaillou.

With the exception of Barolo Chinato, based on the bark of the cinchona tree macerated in BAROLO wine, the modern vermouth industry has never sought fine wine as its base and has been a useful outlet for some of the European WINE LAKE, absorbing millions of litres of basic table wine from the south of Italy and France. The alcohol used for FORTIFICATION came from much the same source until the EU abandoned its policy of compulsory DISTILLATION. Traditionally vermouths were flavoured by infusion of 'botanicals', herbs, peels, and spices gathered from the wild. Modern vermouth is more likely to be flavoured by the addition of a concentrate designed for consistency to match an imagined ideal blend of botanicals. After sweetening, usually with MISTELA, and fortification, most modern vermouth is chilled for tartrate STABILIZATION and subjected to PASTEURIZATION and FILTRATION.

Vernaccia, name used for several, unrelated Italian grape varieties, mainly white but sometimes red, *vernaculus* meaning 'native' or 'indigenous' in Latin. These vary from the extreme north of the peninsula (VERNATSCH being merely a Germanic version of Vernaccia) to the fizzy red **Vernaccia di Serrapetrona** of the MARCHE made from the vine variety known locally and in Umbria as **Vernaccia Nera** which is actually GRENACHE, Vernaccia di Pergola which is a southern Italian synonym for ALEATICO, and VERNACCIA DI ORISTANO, which is an almost SHERRY-like Sardinian varietal. The most highly regarded form is the dry white Tuscan varietal VERNACCIA DI SAN GIMIGNANO. Wines called Vernaccia, or sometimes **vernage**, are often cited in the records of London wine merchants in the Middle Ages, but the term could have been used for virtually any sort of wine, Latin being the common language then. Vernaccia was a particularly common product of LIGURIA in north-west Italy and Tuscany. For more details of medieval trade in Vernaccia, see GENOA, ITALY, and TUSCANY.

Vernaccia di Oristano, distinct variety (see VERNACCIA) grown almost exclusively on 272 ha/672 acres (in 2010) of western SARDINIA and making a wide range of white wines with varying SWEETNESS levels and sometimes fortified and oxidatively.

Vernaccia di San Gimignano, potentially distinctive dry white wine made from the historic local vine variety of the same name, probably unrelated to any other Vernaccia, cultivated in the sandstone-based soils around the famous towers of San Gimignano in the province of Siena in TUSCANY in central Italy. There are references to Vernaccia in the archives of San Gimignano as early as 1276. The wine was the first ever awarded DOC status, in 1966, and was elevated to DOCG status in 1993 in recognition of its unquestioned superiority over the standard bland Tuscan white blend of Trebbiano Toscano and Malvasia.

In the late 20th century Vernaccia di San Gimignano enjoyed some export success and producers were encouraged to make crisp, refreshing wines. Demand for them has since declined, despite attempts to provide complexity via small BARREL MATURATION. Since the beginning of this century the Consorzio has promoted SUSTAINABLE VITICULTURE, and some producers have adopted ORGANIC VITICULTURE—even going so far as to ferment Vernaccia grapes on their skins in AMPHORAE. The best examples have a 'minerally', salty impact on the palate and gain both complexity and notes of ripe yellow fruit and beeswax with age.

Total plantings of Vernaccia have declined, to 500 ha/1,236 acres by 2010, perhaps because of sales success with serious red wines based on SANGIOVESE grapes (which have always been grown around San Gimignano), and because it was usurped by an influx of INTERNATIONAL VARIETIES. W.S.

www.vernaccia.it

Vernatsch, German name for the undistinguished light red grape variety SCHIAVA.

Veronelli, Luigi (1926–2004), Italy's most influential food and wine critic from 1956, when he founded the magazine Il Gastronomo and began to collaborate with Italy's major daily newspapers, news weeklies, and the national television network RAI-TV, until his death. Born into an affluent cosmopolitan Milanese family, Veronelli was an unabashed Francophile and a frank admirer of the French APPELLATION CONTRÔLÉE system, in particular of its designated CRUS, a CLASSIFICATION which he attempted to apply to Italian vineyards and their products in his many books on his country's wines. Polemical in character and a romantic anarchist in his political convictions, Veronelli long championed the cause of the small peasant proprietor and was a particularly bitter opponent of Italy's DOC systems, which he considered rigged in favour of the country's large commercial wineries. His campaigns against the DOC system earned him a period of banishment from Italian

television in the 1970s and 1980s. A trip to California in the early 1980s turned him into a promulgator of the BARRIQUE, then almost unknown in Italy, and his writing was extremely influential in spreading the use of small oak barrels in Italy.

For many years Veronelli represented the only possible means of obtaining commercial recognition and visibility for Italy's small producers and he can be credited with the discovery and identification of many of the country's better producers, a role which won him a group of devoted friends and an equally large group of sworn enemies.

Belfrage, N., *Life beyond Lambrusco* (London, 1984).

vers de la grappe, insect pest and an important cause of BOTRYTIS BUNCH ROT. The term is generally used to refer to the European grapevine moth and the vine moth (see MOTHS).

vertical trellis, a vine-TRAINING SYSTEM widely used throughout the world, in which the shoots are trained vertically upwards in summer. The system is commonly called **vertical shoot positioning**, or **VSP**, in the New World. The shoots are held in place by foliage wires which, in turn, are attached to vineyard posts. In many vineyards there are two pairs of foliage wires, and commonly the vines are subjected to TRIMMING at the top and sides to maintain a neat, hedge-like appearance. Both SPUR PRUNING and CANE PRUNING are possible. This trellis system is widely used in Alsace, Germany, eastern Europe, the United States, Australia, and New Zealand, with high vines (trunks of about 1 m/3 ft) and relatively low-density plantings. The vineyards of Bordeaux, Burgundy, and Champagne are also vertically shoot positioned, although the vines are planted closer together and the trunks are much shorter. R.E.S.

verticillium wilt, FUNGAL DISEASE which causes apparently healthy vines to collapse suddenly. The fungus *Verticillium dahliae* lives in the soil, and attacks new vineyards. Young vines are usually affected, and often the vine recovers. There is no control apart from avoiding planting on sites where the fungus exists. R.E.S.

Vespaiola, white wine grape speciality of Vicenza in the VENETO region of north-east Italy, said to take its name from the wasps (*vespe*) attracted by the sugar levels of its ripe grapes. Its most famous product is the Torcolato sweet wine of BREGANZE, although in this Vespaiola is blended with Tocai and Garganega, and the DRIED-GRAPE winemaking technique may well be the most important ingredient. As a dry white wine, Vespaiolo is acidic and neutral. Total plantings were just 94 ha/232 acres in 2010.

Vespolina, low-yielding red grape variety known almost exclusively in, and probably native to, the area around GATTINARA in the PIEMONTE region of north-west Italy. Commonly blended with its close relative NEBBIOLO, it was planted on just 134 ha/331 acres in 2010, occasionally in the OLTREPÒ PAVESE zone across the border in LOMBARDY, where it is known as Ughetta.

Veuve Clicquot Ponsardin, Champagne house as famous for its eponymous founder, the first great champagne widow (*veuve* in French), as for its wines. Nicole Barbe Ponsardin (1777–1866) married François Clicquot, the son of the house's founder, in 1798. After the premature death of her husband in 1805, the 27 year-old widow took over the reins of the company, which she renamed Veuve Clicquot Ponsardin. Despite her youth, she steered the house carefully through the turbulent years of the First and Second Empires, defying Napoleon's blockades to ship the wine to Russia, and finding an export market in virtually every European court. 'La grande dame de la Champagne' is credited with inventing the riddling process called REMUAGE, and adapting a piece of her own furniture into the first riddling table for that purpose. In 1818, she was first to elaborate a rosé champagne by addition of red wine from Bouzy. On her death, the company passed to her former chief partner, another shrewd operator, Édouard Werlé who introduced the famous yellow label, still used for the non-vintage wine, and the house remained in the hands of the Werlé family until in 1987 it became part of the Moët Hennessy-Louis Vuitton group (see LVMH). The house style is based on Pinot Noir grapes and, in particular, those grown at Bouzy, where the house has large holdings. La Grande Dame is Clicquot's PRESTIGE CUVÉE, named, of course, after the widow. In 1990, the Champagne house purchased a majority stake in the WESTERN AUSTRALIAN winery Cape Mentelle and its New Zealand subsidiary CLOUDY BAY, completing the purchase in 2000.

Crestin-Billet, F., *Veuve Clicquot, la grande dame de la Champagne* (Grenoble, 1992).

Vézelay, commune near AUXERRE whose white wines from local Chardonnay grapes have their own appellation Bourgogne Vézelay, given a fillip by the village's well-known restaurant.

Victoria, third most important wine state in AUSTRALIA in terms of volume of wine produced. From its nadir in the mid 1950s, when there were fewer than 30 wineries in operation, Victoria has recovered to the point where its viticultural map once again resembles that of the 19th century, populated by almost 800 wine producers, more than any other state.

Hubert de Castella came to Victoria in 1854 from his native Switzerland, and was a leading figure in the golden age of Victorian viticulture up to 1890 (when it produced half the wine made in Australia). He wrote several books, the most famous entitled *John Bull's Vineyard*, a eulogy suggesting Victoria could supply England with all the wine it might ever need. Instead, a combination of PHYLLOXERA, changing land use, changing consumption patterns, the removal of inter-state duties, and the First World War saw the end of the hundreds of vineyards and wineries spread across the very cool southern half of the state.

What is now the North East Victoria Zone, with **Rutherglen** as its epicentre, became the focus of winemaking, producing a range of FORTIFIED and red TABLE WINES, some of the latter almost indistinguishable from some of the former. Foremost among the former are the supersweet TOPAQUES AND MUSCATS, fortified wines of unique style and extraordinary concentration of flavour. Rutherglen and **Glenrowan** also produce massively rich, full-bodied dry reds (from mainly Shiraz and Durif), and a range of other, less convincing, table wines, but with their very warm summer and autumn days (and cold nights) they are best suited to fortified wines.

The North East Victoria Zone is currently divided into five regions: Rutherglen, Glenrowan, King Valley, Alpine Valleys, and Beechworth, although there was a move in the mid 2000s to excise parts of the King Valley and create a new region called Whitlands High Plateau. **Alpine Valleys** and **Beechworth** provide a total contrast to Rutherglen and Glenrowan. Their elevation creates a significantly cooler climate eminently suited to table wines, albeit with a wide spectrum of varieties. **King Valley** is an incubator for varietal wines of every hue and shape: Prosecco (GLERA), ARNEIS, VERDUZZO, GRACIANO, MARZEMINO, MONDEUSE, PETIT MANSENG, SAGRANTINO, SAPERAVI, and TANNAT.

The Port Phillip Zone has five regions clustered around Melbourne: **Yarra Valley, Mornington Peninsula, Geelong, Sunbury**, and **Macedon Ranges**. Over 310 wineries here enjoy a range of climatic conditions all cooler than those of Bordeaux, variously cooled by ELEVATION or MARITIME influences. Pinot Noir and Chardonnay are the dominant varieties, capable of producing wines of world class, with the Yarra Valley, Mornington Peninsula, Geelong and the southern part of Gippsland leading the way.

Shiraz is sometimes seen as a newcomer in Victoria, but Craiglee (at Sunbury) made superb Shiraz evidenced by a cache of 1872 discovered almost 100 years later buried in the then defunct winery. Yeringberg removed its Shiraz in 1981 because it didn't sell as well as its other wines (and has since replanted it), while Yarra Yering has been producing its No. 2 Dry red for over 40 years, quietly using

a little VIOGNIER. Shiraz–Viognier is the new star, with Geelong, and the Yarra Valley (Yering Station) seen as leaders. With appropriate VINEYARD SITE SELECTION, and warmer rather than cooler vintages, both Cabernet Sauvignon and Merlot can be superb. Pinot Gris has become extremely significant in many Victorian wine regions.

Heathcote is the darling of the Central Victoria Zone, with its ancient (500 million-year-old Cambrian) soils, decompressed igneous greenstone which has become a vivid red-brown with age. The temperate climate and soil combination is producing some of Australia's most striking Shiraz, deeply coloured and velvety rich, albeit with the high alcohol (14% to 15.5%) levels necessary for full sensory ripeness. **Bendigo**, which once included Heathcote, is likewise red wine country, with Cabernet Sauvignon also excellent.

The **Goulburn Valley** is the oldest Victorian region with a continuous history of viticulture thanks to Tahbilk (formerly Chateau Tahbilk), which still makes an icon Shiraz exclusively from vines planted in 1860. Marsanne grows alongside Shiraz, Cabernet Sauvignon, and, of course, the ever-present Chardonnay. The newcomers are Roussanne and Viognier.

The **Upper Goulburn** and **Strathbogie Ranges** are paired in much the same way as the Alpine Valleys and Beechworth. Here elevation provides a cooler climatic background, but not cool enough in the Strathbogie Ranges to prevent generous flavours and MOUTHFEEL in the red wines. Riesling, Gewurztraminer, Pinot Gris, Chardonnay, and Viognier are the dominant white varieties.

The **Pyrenees** (quaintly named, for the slopes are gentle and far from dramatic) on the eastern side, abutting the **Grampians** (with Great Western registered as a subregion in 2007) continue the red wine dominance, this time in the Western Victoria Zone. The Pyrenees on the eastern side can provide Shiraz and Cabernet Sauvignon every bit as sumptuous as that of Heathcote or Bendigo, but as you move west into the Grampians, the subtly cooler climate yields wines with more elegance and finesse, pepper, spice, and EUCALYPT mint along with the vibrant red fruit flavours.

The sparsely populated **Henty** in the far south west is dramatically cooler; indeed on some criteria it is the coolest region on the Australian mainland. Ultra-fine and intense Riesling, Semillon, Sauvignon Blanc, and steely, elegant Chardonnays are the mainstays, but micro-quantities of magnificent Pinot Noir have emerged on occasion.

North West Victoria Zone takes in the **Murray Darling** and **Swan Hill** regions on the Murray River as it meanders for 500 km/305 miles marking the border between New South Wales and Victoria before moving through

South Australia's Riverland. The story is no different: modified hydroponics in desert sand with historically unlimited WATER provide sky-high yields of at times surprisingly good quality grapes. But recent DROUGHTS have encouraged both more effective water usage and an increase in Mediterranean vine varieties suitable for dry climates. The focal point is Lindemans' Karadoc winery, the eastern states' winemaking, bottling, and packaging centre for TREASURY WINE ESTATES.

J.H. & H.H.

www.winevictoria.org.au

Vidal, white grape variety and a FRENCH HYBRID more properly known as **Vidal Blanc** or **Vidal 256** and widely grown in CANADA, where it is particularly valued for its winter hardiness. Grown to a limited extent in the Midwest and eastern UNITED STATES, particularly NEW YORK state, it is a hybrid of UGNI BLANC and one of the Seibel parents of SEYVAL BLANC. The wine produced, like Seyval's, has no obviously FOXY character and can smell attractively of currant bushes or leaves. Its slow, steady ripening and thick skins make it particularly suitable for sweet, late-harvest (non-botrytized) wines and ICEWINE, for which it, with RIESLING, is famous in Canada. Vidal-based wines do not have the longevity of fine Rieslings, however.

Vidigueira, DOP subregion of the ALENTEJO in southern Portugal which marks the dividing point of the upper (Alto) and typically lower, hotter (Baixo) parts of the region. Vidigueira's relative proximity to the coast and cold air descending from the Serra de Portel escarpment tempers the heat, hence the region's tradition of making white wine from ANTÃO VAZ, upheld by the large CO-OPERATIVE. However, attracted by the scope for producing balanced reds, most other producers are now focused on red wine.

S.A.

vieilles vignes is French for 'old vines'. The term is used widely on wine labels—as is *vinhas velhas* (Portugal), *alte Reben* (Germany)—in the hope that potential buyers are aware that wine quality is often associated with senior VINE AGE. BOLLINGER was one of the first producers to use the term, for the produce of UNGRAFTED VINES in one walled vineyard. Italian *vecchie vigne* and Spanish *viñas viejas* are less commonly flaunted and generally only on back labels.

There are few effective controls on the use of the term, however, and little agreement about exactly how many years it is before a vine can be deemed old, although over 50 years seems like a good starting point. In the early 21st century, there have been concerted efforts to preserve and protect these viticultural treasures by California's HISTORIC VINEYARD SOCIETY. Other examples include the Barossa Old Vine Charter and JancisRobinson.com's online Old Vines Register.

www.barossa.com/wine/wine-chapters/the-barossa-old-vines.

www.jancisrobinson.com/files/pdfs/Old_Vines_Register.pdf.

Vien de Nus, special red grape variety grown on 13 ha/32 acres in 2010, and mainly blended, around the town of Nus in Italy's Valle d'AOSTA.

Vienna, capital city of AUSTRIA and, unusually, a wine region and wine area in its own right. See WIEN.

Vietnam, small, South East Asian country with a history of viticulture dating from French colonial times. Recent attempts to revive viticultural traditions and make wine have had mixed results. The most suitable locations for conventional viticulture in this hot and wet country are in the highlands—on the slopes of Ba Vi Mountain west of Hanoi, for example, where VINIFERA vines were grown by French colonists about a century ago, or on the upper slopes of the central highlands. Contrarily, however, Vietnam's first commercial grape winemaking venture, the Thien Thai Winery, was established on the steamy southern coastal plain at Phan Rang, in Ninh Thuan province, 350 km/210 miles north east of Ho Chi Minh City (formerly Saigon). The attraction was the existence of established vineyards producing substantial quantities of TABLE GRAPES a year, mostly from red-berried CARDINAL vines grown on PERGOLAS. The first wines, both still and sparkling, were released in 1995 but the winery was mothballed in 2002. Subsequently, though, two of the biggest FRUIT WINE producers began drawing on grapes grown in Ninh Thuan for still and sparkling grape wines. Hanoi-based Thang Long Liquor uses primarily Cardinal and more recently planted Shiraz and Sauvignon Blanc for its grape wines. Lam Dong Foodstuffs, through its beverage subsidiary Vang Dalat (Dalat Wine), is now Vietnam's largest grape wine producer and has also drawn on these grapes as well as a large vineyard it has developed close to the Central Highlands city of Dalat. Many domestic wine labels also rely, sometimes exclusively, on imported BULK WINE bottled locally.

Under natural conditions, the southern vines bear almost continuously (see TROPICAL VITICULTURE). Systematic PRUNING has been adopted in some wine grape vineyards, however, to induce three output peaks ('vintages') in order to facilitate a manageable crushing schedule. INTERNATIONAL VARIETIES have been trialled under Australian technical supervision—on land which was, until 1995, a minefield left over from the Vietnam war. CHAMBOURCIN produces prolifically and copes best with the humidity. In the trials, a number of varieties progressed from CUTTINGS to fruit in a single year. D.G.

vigna is Italian for VINEYARD, while a **vignaiolo** is a vine-grower.

vigne is French for a VINE, and sometimes VINEYARD. **Vigneron** is French for a vine-grower, or for someone who is both grower and winemaker, whereas a VITICULTEUR merely grows vines. The term *vigneron* is now used widely outside France for a wide range of people engaged in wine production.

A **vignoble** is French for a VINEYARD, although the term *vignoble* can be used more broadly as in 'the entire French *vignoble*'.

Vignoles, also known as Ravat 51, late-budding, early-ripening FRENCH HYBRID popular in cooler wine regions in the Midwest and eastern UNITED STATES. It can make fresh, delicate white wine and is particularly well suited to sweet wine production.

vigour in a viticultural sense is the amount of vegetative growth, an important aspect of any vine. This may seem of unlikely interest to wine drinkers but it is a vital factor in wine quality. Very low-vigour vines do not always have sufficient leaf area to ripen grapes properly, while high-vigour vines typically produce thin, pale, acidic wines often wrongly thought to result from OVERCROPPING. Vigour changes through a vine's lifetime, as discussed in VINE AGE.

Vines of high vigour show a lack of BALANCE between shoot and fruit growth. Vigorous vineyards show rapid shoot growth in the spring, and shoots continue to grow late into the growing season, even past VERAISON, the beginning of fruit ripening. Shoots on vigorous vines have long INTERNODES, thick stems, large leaves, and many, usually long, LATERAL SHOOTS. Vigorous vineyards are generally, but not necessarily, associated with high YIELDS. Rank vegetative growth may produce so much SHADE that FRUITFULNESS declines, leading to even more vegetative growth and a loss of varietal character, colour, body, and general wine quality.

Vine vigour is easy to quantify using PRUNING WEIGHTS and other vine measurements as outlined by Smart and Robinson, and these approaches, along with SCORING, can be used as a form of quality control. For an alternative but related approach to the assessment of vine vigour using REMOTE SENSING, see NORMALIZED DIFFERENCE VEGETATION INDEX.

The vigour of a vineyard is essentially dependent on two features: the size and health of the root system, and the pruning level. First, what grows above ground is some sort of mirror of what grows below. A vine with a large and healthy root system will have the reserves of CARBOHYDRATES and balance of HORMONES to support considerable vigorous shoot growth. On the other hand, a vine with a small and/or unhealthy root system, be it due to shallow soil,

drought, root pests such as PHYLLOXERA, or diseases such as TRUNK DISEASE or ARMILLARIA ROOT ROT, will support only low-vigour growth.

Vines should be pruned to bud numbers relative to the amount of early shoot growth they can support. This is the concept of BALANCED PRUNING, and one criterion used is to retain at winter PRUNING about 25–30 buds per kg of pruning weight. Use of this sort of rule means that the subsequent shoot growth will be in balance with the vine's carbohydrate reserves, ensuring balance between shoot and fruit growth, and moderate vigour.

High vigour is a common problem of modern vineyards, for many and varied reasons. The vines may be planted in a region with a benign climate on too deep a soil, which is well supplied with water (from rainfall and/or irrigation) and nutrients, especially NITROGEN (from natural fertility or fertilizers or added compost). Such soils are said to have high SOIL POTENTIAL in that they promote excessive vine vigour. Modern control methods can also keep vines free of stress associated with weeds, pests, and diseases. CANOPY MANAGEMENT techniques are used to maintain yield and wine quality in such situations.

An alternative approach is to devigorate the vines, most commonly by controlling the water supply, which is of course easier to do when irrigating in an arid climate than when vineyards are supplied by rainfall alone. COVER CROPS that compete for the available water are another useful tool. Other techniques include nutrient stressing, increasing crop load by leaving more buds at winter PRUNING, or by growing shoots downwards as in the GENEVA DOUBLE CURTAIN training system. R.E.S.

Smart, R. E., and Robinson, M., *Sunlight into Wine: A Handbook for Winegrape Canopy Management* (Adelaide, 1991).

Vijariego (also known as **Bujariego** and **Vijiriega**), white grape variety from the CANARY ISLANDS which produces distinctive dry wines there on vineyards totalling 452 ha/1,116 acres, with varietal versions made by Bodegas Viñátigo. A little is also planted in Andalucia.

Vilana, white grape variety that is native to and the most widely grown on the island of CRETE. It is solely responsible for the delicate spicy dry white Peza PDO, and is blended with THRAPSATHIRI for Sitia PDO.

Vila Nova de Gaia, or Gaia New Town, cramped, cobbled suburb on the opposite side of the DOURO estuary from the Portuguese city of OPORTO where PORT is traditionally aged. From the waterfront, long, single-storey buildings called LODGES rise in steps up the hillside. Under the clay-tiled roofs, shippers mature their stocks of port, as well as TASTING, BLENDING, BOTTLING, and selling it. Until 1986, the law required that all port destined for export had to be shipped from within the strictly defined area of the Gaia entrepôt. Port may now be shipped from anywhere within the demarcated Douro region so that export markets are open to small firms, quintas, and co-operatives without premises in Vila Nova de Gaia. R.J.M.

Villages, common suffix of an APPELLATION CONTRÔLÉE name for a French wine. Generally speaking, an X-Villages wine must be made from one or several of a selection of communes whose produce is known to be superior to that of the rest of the X zone. See, for example, BEAUJOLAIS, MÂCON, and Côtes du RHÔNE.

village wine is a term used particularly in BURGUNDY for a wine which qualifies for an APPELLATION that coincides with the name of the village or commune in which the wine is made. It contrasts with a lesser GENERIC wine, which takes the name of a region, and wines from PREMIER CRU and GRAND CRU vineyards.

Villány, wine region and PDO in HUNGARY on the terraced southern and eastern slopes of the Villány Mountains, which protect the vineyards from cold northern influences resulting in a special sub-MEDITERRANEAN MESOCLIMATE. (See map under HUNGARY.) The Villány Mountains consist of CALCAREOUS rocks deposited in the marine basins of the Mesozoic. Dolomite, MARL, and LIMESTONE are covered direct with sandy LOESS. This layer is sometimes mixed with limestone debris, having a higher concentration of calcium. This is the cropland of more acidic wines, while the purely loess soil produces softer wines. Villány is mostly known for its red BORDEAUX BLENDS, sometimes rather heavy and tannic but with good ageing potential. Cabernet Franc grows well here and Cabernet Sauvignon also produces exciting wines. The everyday drinking wine is the softer PORTUGIESER, and KÉKFRANKOS is often used in blends. In the last decade, Pinot Noir and Syrah have been planted, producing wines that can be heavy and lacking elegance. The whites are mostly grown around Siklós. As in SZEKSZÁRD, wines are often low in acid, high in alcohol, and do not suit long ageing. Olaszrizling, Chardonnay, and Hárslevelű are widely planted. The region is well suited to TOURISM.

Villard is the common French name for a great French viticultural secret, their most commonly planted HYBRIDS. Most are members of the vast SEYVE VILLARD group. G.M.

In France, **Villard Noir** is Seyve-Villard 18.315 while **Villard Blanc** is Seyve-Villard 12.375. Villard Noir was planted all over France, from the northern Rhône to Bordeaux, and was treasured for its resistance to DOWNY MILDEW and ROT. Villard Blanc made slightly more palatable wine (though the must can be difficult to process). Both varieties yield prodigiously and for that attribute were so beloved by growers that in 1968 there were 30,000 ha/74,000 acres of Villard Noir and 21,000 ha of Villard Blanc in France (making them fifth and third most planted black and white grape varieties respectively).

To the great credit of the authorities, and thanks to not inconsiderable bribes for grubbing up, by the turn of the century these respective totals had been shaved to 600 ha and 740 ha, mainly in Tarn and Ardèche. According to the 2011 vine survey, Villard Noir plantings had grown again, to 1,283 ha, while Villard Blanc, now planted in many American states, is grown on only 238 ha of France.

vin, French for wine and therefore a much-used term (see below). **Vin blanc** is white wine, **vin rosé** is pink, **vin rouge** is red wine, **vin mousseux** is sparkling wine, and so on. For **vin ordinaire**, see VIN DE FRANCE. For **vin biologique** (more correctly, **vin issu de raisins biologiques** or **vin issu d'agriculture biologique**), see ORGANIC WINE. For **vin blanc cassis**, see KIR.

viña, viñedo, Spanish word for VINEYARD.

Vin de France, category for the most basic French wine, that which used to be called vin de table, the French version of wine known in the EU as WINE WITHOUT GEOGRAPHICAL INDICATION, known in French as VSIG. Unlike the old vin de table, a vin de France may be labelled with a vintage and/or vine variety, although by 2013 only about half of the wine sold as vin de France has taken advantage of this relatively recent development, designed to make it more competitive with inexpensive VARIETAL wine produced outside Europe. This category is much less tightly regulated than the AOC/AOP and IGP categories. On average during the period 2010–12 this lowly category accounted for less than 8% of all French wine, but it includes an increasing number of superior quality wines made outside the strictures of AOC/AOP and IGP regulations. See also FRANCE.

vin de liqueur, strong, sweet drink made by adding neutral grape spirit or eau de vie to grape must, so-called MUTAGE, either before or during fermentation. The resulting liquids have an alcoholic strength of 16–22% but no secondary products of fermentation such as GLYCEROL or SUCCINIC ACID. Confusingly, the term is also used by the EU to refer to all FORTIFIED WINES. See LIQUEUR WINE.

The principal members of this special category of French specialities, known as *mistelles* (see MISTELA) if the fortification takes place before fermentation has started, are the PINEAU DES CHARENTES of Cognac country, its Armagnac counterpart FLOC DE GASCOGNE, MACVIN DU JURA, made from local MARC added to grape juice and tasting strongly of the former, and CLAIRETTE DU LANGUEDOC. Most vins de liqueur are pale gold, but soft, fruity rosé versions of both Pineau and Floc can be found in the regions of production. Vin de liqueur differs from VIN DOUX NATUREL in that the alcohol is generally added earlier and the resulting drinks therefore tend to be, and taste, more spirit dominated. Some Muscat de FRONTIGNAN may also qualify. Many wine regions have their own versions of this easy-to-make strong, sweet aperitif: Champagne has its Ratafia, while the Languedoc has Cartagène. Where there are no regulations governing their production, they are sometimes made further along the scale towards vins doux naturels. Like vins doux naturels, these sweet wines can be enhanced by serving them cool, and the wine in an opened bottle should retain its appeal for well over a week.

vin de paille is French for 'straw wine' (*Strohwein* in German), a small group of necessarily expensive but often quite delicious, long-lived, sweet white wines. These are essentially a subgroup of DRIED-GRAPE WINES made from grapes dried on straw mats. Cyrus REDDING's catalogue of wines produced in the early 19th century makes it clear that vins de paille were much more common then and, although he was most enthusiastic about 'Ermitage-paille' (from HERMITAGE vines), he found vins de paille in JURA, ALSACE, and Corrèze. At about the same time some producers in Rust in AUSTRIA were also using the technique.

For much of the 20th century no vin de paille was made in Hermitage, but Gérard Chave revived the practice with healthy, not late-picked, Marsanne grapes in 1974, dried on straw in the attic, and has since been followed by CHAPOUTIER and others.

Average yields are minuscule once the grapes have been raisined, but the results are luscious in the extreme, and are invariably sold in half-bottles.

Around 1% of Jura's wine production is of Vin de Paille from ARBOIS, L'ÉTOILE, and Côtes du JURA made from SAVAGNIN, POULSARD, or Chardonnay grapes picked relatively early and dried for at least six weeks, but today rarely on straw. The minimum POTENTIAL ALCOHOL allowed is 19% (as opposed to 14% in Hermitage). The grapes are generally pressed in January, and 100 kg/220 lbs of grapes may yield fewer than 20 l/5 gal of juice. Jura producers must age their vins de paille in cask for at least 18 months and the wines must have a natural alcoholic strength of at least 14%. They are capable of long BOTTLE AGEING. Many Jura producers flout these appellation rules to make a lower alcohol version under a table wine designation. Such is the importance of the wine in the Jura that in 2014 the region won a court case preventing Corrèze producers from using the term vin paillé for their version.

There is renewed, if limited, experimentation with making vin de paille in Alsace and, unlike BOTRYTIZED wine, this is one wine style with which any curious and dedicated winemaker can experiment. See also LUXEMBOURG.

Livingstone-Learmonth, J., *The Wines of the Northern Rhône* (Berkeley, Calif., 2005).

Vin de Pays

Vin de Pays, French expression meaning 'country wine' which was adopted for an intermediate category of wines created in FRANCE in 1973, and formalized in 1979, to recognize and encourage the production of wines between VIN DE TABLE, and APPELLATION CONTRÔLÉE in quality. This category has been superseded by IGP wines.

vin de presse, French for PRESS WINE.

Vin de Savoie. See SAVOIE.

Vin des Glaciers, also known as **Vin du Glacier**, or **Gletscherwein** in German, 'glacier wine', is a local speciality in the Val d'Anniviers near Sierre in the Valais in SWITZERLAND. The white wine, traditionally made of the now obscure Rèze vine, comes from communally cultivated vines and is stored at high ELEVATIONS in casks refilled just once a year on a SOLERA system. The resultant product is deliberately MADERIZED and valued for its rarity.

vin de table, the old name for France's most basic level of wine, which, having been a copious embarrassment, has dwindled to a relative trickle. It has been replaced by VIN DE FRANCE.

vin doux naturel translates directly from French as a wine that is naturally sweet but is a term used to describe a French wine speciality that might well be considered *un*naturally sweet. Nature's sweetest wines contain so much grape sugar that the yeasts eventually give up the fermentation process of converting sugar into alcohol, leaving a residue of natural sugars in a stable wine of normal alcoholic strength (see SWEET WINEMAKING). Vins doux naturels, on the other hand, are made by MUTAGE, by artificially arresting the conversion of grape sugar to alcohol by adding spirit before fermentation is complete, thereby incapacitating yeasts with alcohol and making a particularly strong, sweet half-wine in which grape flavours dominate wine flavours. They are normally made of the grape varieties MUSCAT and GRENACHE, and should have an alcoholic strength of between 15 and 18% and a POTENTIAL ALCOHOL of at least 21.5%. The minimum RESIDUAL SUGAR level varies from 45 g/l for Rasteau and Banyils, to 100 g/l for the various Muscat de Somethings.

The Greeks, happily ignorant of DISTILLATION, already knew how to make a sweet wine by adding concentrated must. Almost as soon as the techniques of distillation were introduced into western Europe, it was discovered that distilled wine, or alcoholic spirit, had the power to stop fermentation, thereby reliably retaining the sweetness so prized by our forebears. The Catalan alchemist ARNALDUS DE VILLANOVA (Arnaud de Villeneuve) of Montpellier University's then flourishing medical school perfected the process and in 1299 was granted a patent from the king of Majorca, then ruler of ROUSSILLON, which was to become the world's centre of vin doux naturel production.

This is essentially how PORT as we know it, created nearly 400 years later, is made strong and sweet, and the technique is also used in the production of MADEIRA and MÁLAGA. In each case, spirit is added when the fermenting MUST has reached about 6% alcohol, except that whereas the added spirit constitutes between 5 and 10% of the final volume of a vin doux naturel, typically resulting in an alcoholic strength of just over 15%, the added spirit usually represents 20% of the final volume of port, whose alcoholic strength is closer to 20%. The spirit added to vins doux naturels is considerably stronger than that added to port, however: about 95% alcohol as opposed to the traditional 77% used in port FORTIFICATION. Nowadays, however, the spirit may well come from exactly the same source, one of France's larger distilleries.

A young vin doux naturel therefore, like young port, tastes relatively simply of grapes, sugar, and alcohol (although, since some fermentation has usually taken place, it may contain a more interesting array of fermentation products than most VINS DE LIQUEUR, which are made by adding spirit before fermentation or just as fermentation is starting). Naturally aromatic MUSCAT BLANC À PETITS GRAINS grapes are therefore particularly well suited to the production of vins doux naturels designed to be drunk young (and, usually, chilled to offset the sugar and alcohol). The best known of these golden sweet liquids that are made exclusively from this, the finest MUSCAT vine variety, was historically Muscat de FRONTIGNAN. The Languedoc has three other Appellation Contrôlée vins doux naturels, however: Muscats de LUNEL, MIREVAL, and, an exception far from the coast, ST-JEAN-DE-MINERVOIS, whose vineyards are even higher than most of those for the red, pink, and dry white wines of MINERVOIS. A similar Muscat is made in the Côtes du Rhône village of BEAUMES-DE-VENISE and is probably easier for non-locals to appreciate than the southern Rhône's other vin doux naturel appellation of RASTEAU, whose Grenache-based heady red and tawny sweet wines, some of them deliberately made RANCIO, have more in common with the vins doux naturels of Roussillon. The best of these, like the best ports, owe their complex flavours necessarily to ageing, whether in cask, BONBONNE, or, occasionally, bottle. The greatest name is BANYULS, which has benefited from some impeccable winemakers and, most important in this context, wine-éleveurs (see ÉLEVAGE). MAURY is a smaller appellation in the mountains with enormous and, occasionally, realized potential (although most wine made there now is dry table wine), while the extensive coastal RIVESALTES and Muscat de Rivesaltes appellations are much more varied and sometimes traduced. Grand Roussillon is a largely theoretical vin doux naturel appellation designed as a lesser Rivesaltes.

Non-vintage-dated vins doux naturels are common, particularly among the Languedoc Muscats into which a little of the previous year's output may be blended so as to smooth out vintage differences. It is common in Roussillon, however, to find indications of age and vintage dates, although most vins doux naturels are ready to drink as soon as they are sold. Many, particularly the Muscats, benefit from being served young and chilled, but the alcohol preserves the freshness of wine in an opened bottle for at least a week.

Vin du Bugey. See BUGEY.

vine, the plant, often known as the grapevine, whose fruit is transformed into WINE.

A vine in its broadest sense is any plant with a weak stem which supports itself by climbing on neighbouring plants, walls, or other supports. Of this group of plants the grapevine is the most famous, and the most commercially important. (In this work the word vine is used to mean the grapevine.) There are various forms of climbing vines which rely on different mechanisms for attachment. The so-called ramblers rest on each other's plants and some, as for roses, have spines to help adhesion. The grapevine is one of the so-called tendril climbers with TENDRILS on the stem; the garden pea has leaf tendrils.

Because the vine is unable to support itself, it is generally grown on TRELLIS SYSTEMS. Some TRAINING SYSTEMS still use trees for support, as for the *alberate* of Italy. However, most vineyards of the world are trained to some combination of POSTS, commonly made of wood, and wire. Vines can be trained so that they are free standing but this requires special pruning and training to keep the trunk short, otherwise the vine will fall over. The GOBELET of the Mediterranean region is the most widespread of the free-standing forms.

Most of the world's wine is made from the VINIFERA species of the VITIS genus (see BOTANICAL CLASSIFICATION for a more detailed explanation of where the vine fits into the world of plants).

Grapevines are the world's most important fruit crop, with about 7.4 million ha/18.4 million acres of vineyards producing more than 258 million hl/6,822 millon gal in 2012.

Grapes are used for winemaking in all of its forms, for brandy, for consumption as TABLE GRAPES and DRYING GRAPES, for fresh GRAPE JUICE, for GRAPE CONCENTRATE, RECTIFIED GRAPE MUST, and for limited industrial products. However, wine production is the major use and accounts for 70% of all vineyard output.

The grapevine is grown on all continents except Antarctica, but most of the world's vineyards are in Europe. Spain had more than 1 million ha/2.5 million acres of vineyards in 2011, France and Italy around 0.8 million ha, and between them these three countries produced almost half of the world's wine in 2011, Italy nearly 16%, and Spain 12.5%.

Vitis vinifera cannot tolerate extreme winter cold. Requiring warm summers for fruit maturation, the vine is grown approximately between the 10 and 20 °C isotherm in both hemispheres, or about between latitudes 30 degrees north and 50 degrees north, and 30 degrees south and 40 degrees south, although CLIMATE CHANGE has seen the vine planted ever closer to the poles (see map of WORLD PRODUCTION). Principally in order to minimize the damage associated with FUNGAL DISEASES, the grapevine has traditionally been grown in MEDITERRANEAN CLIMATES with warm, dry summers and mild, wet winters. The ready availability of AGROCHEMICALS, and to a lesser extent disease-tolerant varieties, has allowed this range to be extended, especially since the Second World War. Winter DORMANCY is essential for vine longevity, and the hot and humid climates nearer the equator are not conducive to either grape production or wine quality (although see TROPICAL VITICULTURE).

Most of the world's vineyards are planted with traditional VINE VARIETIES, which have been perpetuated for centuries by vegetative propagation. Different CLONES of these varieties may also be distinguished.

Many viticultural practices are very traditional, especially in Europe, where in many cases they are prescribed by law. Cultural operations and the reasoning behind them are introduced under VITICULTURE, VINE PHYSIOLOGY, VINE DISEASES, and VINE PESTS. The effects of climate and soils are also discussed in, respectively, CLIMATE AND WINE QUALITY and SOIL AND WINE QUALITY.

See VINE MORPHOLOGY for discussion of the parts of the vine, and VINE PHYSIOLOGY for details of how the vine functions. See also VINE GROWTH CYCLE and, for a historical perspective, ORIGINS OF VINICULTURE.   R.E.S.

Mullins, M. G., Bouquet, A., and Williams, L., *Biology of the Grapevine* (Cambridge, 1992).

Winkler, A. J., et al., *General Viticulture* (2nd edn, Berkeley, Calif., 1974).

vine age, easily observable by the girth of the vine's trunk (unless it is multi-trunked, as many very old vines are), is widely considered a factor affecting wine quality. Many believe that, in general, older vines make better wine. Although there is no agreement and certainly no legislation as to what constitutes 'old', vines more than 50 years old could justifiably be described as such. APPELLATION CONTRÔLÉE legislation in many cases specifically excludes the produce of vines less than two or three years old, although this probably represents a bias against the fruit of very young vines rather than an affirmation of the qualities of older ones, and it is unusual for vines to crop before their third year. Some French producers deliberately exclude wine from vines under a certain age from their top bottlings, and put it into SECOND WINES. The concept that older vines make better wine is much used in marketing wine in the Old World (see VIEILLES VIGNES) and has more recently been adopted in the New World, notably by some California and Barossa and Eden Valley producers whose UNGRAFTED VINES remain alive and producing after more than a century. Conversely, some winemakers observe that young vineyards produce their highest-quality wine in the first year or two of production. For example, in the world-famous blind tasting in Paris in 1976 which first pitted California Cabernets and Chardonnays against top-quality red bordeaux and white burgundies, Stag's Leap Wine Cellars S.L.V. Cabernet Sauvignon 1973 came out on top, scoring more highly than Ch MOUTON ROTHSCHILD 1970 and Ch HAUT-BRION 1970, even though this was the first vintage of this Napa Valley red and the vines were only three years old. Both of these apparently opposed viewpoints may be correct, as will be discussed below.

Conventional VINE TRAINING takes two to three years to form the vine framework, and if any bunches are formed they may be discarded before they ripen, although this is a conservative and perhaps unnecessary precaution. Once a vine produces one to three or so normal crops and is about three to six years of age, it usually fills its allotted growing space above ground, and so the YIELD and annual shoot growth normally stabilize, and will change only with a major alteration to management or growing conditions. Vineyards which are protected from stresses, pests, and diseases, and from too much or too little water and mineral nutrients, can be long lived. An outstanding example is the famous vine at Hampton Court Palace near London, which is still producing large crops of grapes (under glass) despite having been planted in 1769. Vineyards free from stresses are, however, rare.

The vigour and yield of many commercial vineyards begin to decline after 20–30 years, and by 50 years many vineyards are yielding at such a low level as to be normally considered uneconomic, sooner if the vines are diseased (see TRUNK DISEASES).

Below ground, however, the picture can be different. Champagnol defines three stages of ROOT GROWTH. During the first stage the root system colonizes available space, and this takes until the seventh to tenth year, taking longer in poor soils and with low VINE DENSITY. In the so-called adult stage there is little change in the volume of soil exploited, but the final, senescent stage sees a reduction in root activity. This can be through the accumulation of cultivation wounds, or from the effects of drought, or from SOIL COMPACTION by machinery, or lack of oxygen at depth. It has also been noted that root pests and diseases may weaken the root system, and the continued application of some fertilizers and spray materials can worsen SOIL ACIDITY and so reduce root health.

The parts of the vine above ground also weaken with age, and senescence is more obvious. Winter PRUNING weakens the vine, the increasing number of pruning wounds allowing the invasion of wood-rotting fungi (see TRUNK DISEASES). While some fungal species and especially virulent strains can kill a vine within a few years, others called epiphytes can live in the vine with little impact on vine health. In addition to this there are the continued effects of cultivation, which can prune shallow roots, and the possible exhaustion of the soil's mineral reserves. Since very old vines contain a lot of dead wood due to fungal invasion, TERMITES can often weaken the trunk.

The normal course of events, then, is for very young vines to show reduced VIGOUR for the first crop or so, and then to remain vigorous and out of balance for several decades. As they age, after perhaps 50 years, vigour may decline. This is particularly evident for vines planted on sites with low SOIL POTENTIAL. The conventional explanation for improved quality with vine age is because of reduction in yield, and indeed for many celebrated vineyards the two go hand in hand. However, since older vines are lower in vigour, exposure of the leaves and fruit to sunlight is better, which may offer an indirect but equally plausible explanation for the effect of vine age on wine quality (see MICROCLIMATE).

This BALANCE between leaves and fruit can also explain the apparent paradox that some vineyards seem to produce their best quality when very young, often with the first few crops. Such vines have very open CANOPIES and so in the first fruiting year there is very good exposure of both to sunlight. Commonly the vine is more vigorous in subsequent years, the shoots grow longer and quality is reduced because of increasing SHADE. So such vineyards can produce premium quality for the first few crops and then quality may decline until the vine is old and vigour is low again. However, appropriate CANOPY MANAGEMENT can improve wine quality in these in-between years of higher vigour.   R.E.S. & J.E.H.

Champagnol, F., *Éléments de physiologie de la vigne et de viticulture générale* (St-Gely-du-Fesc, 1984).

Smart, R. E., and Robinson, M., *Sunlight into Wine: A Handbook for Winegrape Canopy Management* (Adelaide, 1991).

vine architecture, *architecture de la vigne* in French, encompasses VINE DENSITY, TRELLIS and TRAINING SYSTEMS, and PRUNING.

Vinea Wachau (full title Vinea Wachau Nobilis Districtus), is an organization representing most wine estates (nearly 200) in Austria's WACHAU region. Called into existence in 1983 by a quartet including the late Josef Jamek, who helped define the styles of dry, unchaptalized wine that came to characterize this region and eventually the wines of NIEDERÖSTERREICH as a whole. The Vinea Wachau established three stylistic tiers—STEINFEDER, FEDERSPIEL, and SMARAGD—imposing them on the region in the aftermath of Austria's 1985 wine scandal. By the late 1990s, the Vinea Wachau executive board that featured Toni Bodenstein of Prager, Franz Hirtzberger, Emmerich Knoll, and F. X. Pichler had, together with BURGENLAND sweet-wine pioneer Alois Kracher and KAMPTAL vintner Willi Bründlmayer, come to represent increasingly prestigious Austrian wine on export markets. These founding members of the Vinea Wachau declared their independence from KREMS—traditionally thought of as the Wachau's unofficial capital. Thus did the much-restricted viticultural sector upstream from that city come to define Wachau for a new generation of Austrians. The far more numerous vineyards around Krems and points immediately east had to create their own new identities, KREMSTAL and Kamptal. In 2006, the Vinea Wachau strengthened its founding principles by publishing a Wachau Codex, unusual for the number of cellar procedures—including any form of must CONCENTRATION or separation (such as DEALCOHOLIZATION)—that it proscribes, as well as for its explicit rejection of any new WOOD flavours. The Vinea Wachau has successfully deflected recent challenges to their members' exclusive use of the terms Steinfeder, Federspiel, or Smaragd, and the few important Wachau growers who are not members—either by choice or because their degree of viticultural involvement in neighbouring regions disqualifies them—have to market their wines without those designations. D.S.

vine breeding, the crossing of one vine variety or species with another to produce a new variety. Grapevines are highly heterozygous outcrossers and do not breed true from seed, which is the reason for their universal vegetative PROPAGATION. If both parent varieties belong to the same species (in practice, usually the European VINIFERA) of the VITIS genus, then the result is commonly called a CROSS (occasionally crossing), while the results of crossing varieties from more than one species (typically, a *V. vinifera* variety and a member of an AMERICAN VINE SPECIES) are commonly called HYBRIDS.

These NEW VARIETIES are traditionally created by dusting POLLEN from the male parent on to the receptive stigma of the female parent (see VINE flower), and then germinating the seed from the berry which subsequently grows (although see GENETIC MODIFICATION for more recent techniques). There is a very low probability that any one seedling will be a useful variety, and extensive testing, probably over more than ten years, for viticultural and winemaking suitability is required before any new variety is released.

The convention is to express the female parent first, thus KERNER is a Schiava Grossa × Riesling cross, while BACO 22A is a Folle Blanche × Noah hybrid (Noah itself being an AMERICAN HYBRID).

Vine breeding was particularly important in the early 20th century, notably in France, Germany, and Romania, as a European response to the spread of the PHYLLOXERA pest (see HYBRIDS and FRENCH HYBRIDS). Breeding of new varieties which combined high yields with high MUST WEIGHTS, and subsequently those which combined high wine quality with good resistance to pests and diseases, has been an important activity in such German centres as GEILWEILERHOF and GEISENHEIM.

The prospects for the breeding of new varieties are outlined by Alleweldt and Possingham. They emphasize the availability of germplasm among *Vitis* species which contains resistance to the major pests, diseases, and environmental stresses of *vinifera*. *V. amurensis* and *V. riparia*, for example, contain genes for winter hardiness, and *V. vinifera* and *V. berlandieri* for lime soil tolerance (see CHLOROSIS). Among various *Vitis* species can be found genetic resistance to the fungal diseases DOWNY MILDEW, POWDERY MILDEW, BOTRYTIS BUNCH ROT; the bacterial diseases of CROWN GALL and PIERCE'S DISEASE; and the soil pests of PHYLLOXERA and NEMATODES. A desire to minimize the use of AGROCHEMICALS has encouraged breeding DISEASE-RESISTANT VARIETIES to combine these natural resistances, notably in Germany and the United States.

Because of increasing emphasis on a few familiar VINE VARIETIES, and also the lingering suspicion of hybrids caused by the poor wine performance of the early French hybrids, some consumers view the results of breeding programmes with suspicion. Yet such programmes can offer the opportunity of an improved range of flavours and styles produced from vineyards which do not require any other means of pest and disease protection.

See also NEW VARIETIES. R.E.S.

Adam-Blondon, A.-F., Martinez-Zapater, J.-M., and Kole, C. (eds.), *Genetics, Genomics and Breeding* (CRC Press, 2011).

Alleweldt, G., and Possingham, J. V., 'Progress in grape breeding', *Theoretical and Applied Genetics*, 75 (1988), 669–73.

Burger, P., Bouquet, A., and Striem, M. J., 'Grape breeding', in S. M. Jain and P. M. Priyadarshan (eds.), *Breeding Planation Tree Crops: Tropical Species* (Springer, 2014).

Huglin, P., *Biologie et écologie de la vigne* (Paris, 1986).

vine density is a measure of how closely spaced vines are in the vineyard, both within the row and between rows. The choice of vine spacing is one of the most fundamental decisions in PLANTING a vineyard, and between, even within, the world's wine regions there is enormous variation in spacing. The traditional vineyards of France's Bordeaux, Burgundy, and Champagne regions have about 10,000 plants per ha (4,050 per acre) (and sometimes more), with vines spaced typically 1 m apart both within and between the rows. In many NEW WORLD vineyards, on the other hand, a spacing of 2.5 m/8 ft between vines along the row and 3.7 m/ 12 ft between rows, or 1,080 vines per ha, is quite common. Probably the most widely spaced vineyards of the world are those of the Vinho Verde region in Portugal, La Mancha in Spain, and some parts of Chile, Japan, and Italy (see TENDONE), with spacings as wide as 4 m by 4 m, or just 625 vines per ha.

Some argue that high vine densities lead to improved wine quality. It is true that many of the world's most famous vineyards, almost invariably in the Old World, have very narrow spacings, and so high densities, but it is difficult to argue that this is a prerequisite for quality production. Narrow spacings are indeed appropriate to vineyards of moderate VIGOUR, which is a feature of the low SOIL POTENTIAL of these vineyards (see TERROIR and SOIL AND WINE QUALITY). Some New World vignerons have been encouraged to plant high-density vineyards on fertile vineyard soils in expectation of matching the quality of famous Old World vineyards. The theory is that such dense planting will cause root competition and substantial devigoration, but this has infrequently, if ever, been demonstrated, and the result is often a vineyard of high vigour which is very difficult to manage. The quality of fruit is affected by excessive SHADE, and this reduces quantity. The belief that 'tight spacing' encourages wine quality was widely promulgated in the 1980s and 1990s in California. Despite many commercial experiments, it remains to be demonstrated that wine quality is automatically increased, while the costs of establishing and running such a high-density vineyard certainly are. Research and commercial experience in Europe indicate that close row and vine spacings are suited only to vineyards of low SOIL FERTILITY, or more correctly of low soil potential. In high-vigour situations, some New World vine-growers have responded by removing one vine in two down the row, and sometimes two in three. This has been found to restore vine BALANCE, and yield and quality have subsequently improved.

High-density vineyards are the traditional form of viticulture in many parts of the world, as spacing need only be sufficient to allow the workers unhindered access. Some vineyards are not even planted in rows but were haphazardly arranged, like a field of wheat. Before PHYLLOXERA invaded Europe, unhealthy plants could be replaced by LAYERING a cane from an adjacent vine. These considerations, and the fact that vines then were generally less vigorous, encouraged high-density vineyards and densities were as high as 40,000 plants per ha, or just a quarter of a square metre per plant. Once GRAFTING to ROOTSTOCKS developed as a response to phylloxera, however, then the additional cost of each plant encouraged lower vine densities. The introduction of first animals and then TRACTORS led to the planting of vineyards in rows with a further reduction in vine density. The final factor leading to wider spacing between vines has been the need to provide sufficient space for modern, more vigorous vines. This follows from effective control of vine pests and diseases and weeds using AGROCHEMICALS, as well as the use of plants both VIRUS free and subject to CLONAL SELECTION.

Many New World vineyards were planted after the introduction of tractors, necessitating row spacings of about 3 m/10 ft or more. By contrast, most European vine-growers have chosen to persist with narrow rows and to develop either narrow tractors, or over-row tractors, known in France as *tracteurs enjambeurs*.

Vineyard density is a major consideration affecting the vineyard's yield, quality, cost of establishment and maintenance, and therefore profitability. Planting costs are proportional to the number of plants used; costs for TRELLIS SYSTEMS and DRIP IRRIGATION are higher with narrower row spacings. The time taken to plough and spray is also greater when rows are closer together.

Under most circumstances, the YIELD of densely planted vineyards is higher, especially in the first years of the vineyard's life and with vines planted on low soil potential.   R.E.S.

Champagnol, F., *Éléments de physiologie de la vigne et de viticulture générale* (St-Gely-du-Fesc, 1984).
Galet, P., *Précis de viticulture* (7th edn, Montpellier, 2000).

vine diseases.
Diseases caused by microbes can limit the distribution of vines and affect both yield and quality. See BACTERIAL DISEASES, FUNGAL DISEASES, TRUNK DISEASES, VIRUS DISEASES, PHYTOPLASMA diseases, and the names of individual diseases. See also CLIMATE EFFECTS ON VINE DISEASES.

vine foliage lifter,
machine which lifts vine foliage in the growing season. Once the foliage is vertical it can be secured by WIRES and is then well placed for TRIMMING to maintain a constant CANOPY outline. This is a particular aid to CANOPY MANAGEMENT. See also SHOOT POSITIONING.

vinegar,
sour liquid condiment that depends etymologically, and often materially, on wine. The French word for it, composed of *vin* (wine) and *aigre* (sour), is a direct descendant of its Latin equivalent. Not just wine but any solution containing a low concentration (less than 15%) of ETHANOL will turn to vinegar if exposed to OXYGEN. The ethanol is oxidized first into an ALDEHYDE and then to ACETIC ACID by the oxygen in the atmosphere. Winemakers over the centuries have learned to shelter wine from the action of atmospheric oxygen, and nowadays will do all they can to prevent their wines turning to vinegar, and 'vinegary' is a tasting term of great disapprobation (while 'winey' is quite a compliment when applied to a vinegar). Once the VOLATILE ACIDS in a wine have reached a certain point, however, it can have a potable future only as wine vinegar.

The OXIDATION of any dilute aqueous alcohol solution is greatly hastened by the action of a group of bacteria known as ACETOBACTER from the environment. These bacteria also hasten the reaction of some of the alcohol with some of the newly produced acetic acid to form the ESTER known as ETHYL ACETATE. This compound, when added to the tart taste of acetic acid, gives the complex character to a good wine vinegar.

The everyday vinegar of the market place varies geographically. In southern Europe wine vinegar is the norm, for example, while in northern Europe malt, cider, and distilled vinegars predominate, and in the Far East rice vinegar is most usual.

Today a wide range of vinegars are produced, many flavoured with herbs and fruits, some, such as Italian balsamic vinegar, given BARREL MATURATION according to rules as strict as those governing APPELLATION CONTRÔLÉE wine production. The most powerful vinegars are so strong in ethyl acetate that their flavour can overpower that of a subtle wine. In foods served with subtle wines, wine itself can be used as a condiment, contributing the same sort of ACIDITY as a vinegar would have done. See also VERJUS.

A domestic vinegar SOLERA is one solution for LEFTOVER WINE.   A.D.W.

vinegar fly.
See DROSOPHILA.

vine growth cycle,
the annual march of the vine's development, which begins at budbreak in the spring, and concludes at leaf fall in the autumn. There are distinct developmental stages along the way (see PHENOLOGY), the principal ones being BUDBREAK, FLOWERING, FRUIT SET, VERAISON, HARVEST, when the grapes are mature, and LEAF FALL. The pace of development between these phenological stages varies greatly with vine variety. Very early varieties, such as MADELEINE ANGEVINE, go through the stages up to ripeness in a short time, and can therefore ripen in regions with a short growing season and relatively cool temperatures. In late varieties, such as MOURVÈDRE, CARIGNAN, and CLAIRETTE, all stages are prolonged and much more heat and time are needed to bring them to maturity. The length of the growth cycle also depends on climate, especially temperature. In hot regions, the period from budbreak to harvest may be as short as 130 days for early varieties, but in cooler regions this period can be over 200 days.

The vine often begins to grow later in the spring than most other deciduous plants, when the average air temperature is normally about 10 °C/50 °F in cool climates. The first sign of impending growth is vines BLEEDING as the soil warms, then the buds swell, and eventually the first tinges of green are seen in the vineyards as the shoot tips burst from the buds. The young shoots grow very slowly at first, producing small leaves on each side of the shoot. This early shoot growth depends on the reserves of CARBOHYDRATES stored in the vine, but soon the leaves are old enough for PHOTOSYNTHESIS and produce the carbohydrates which become the tissue of further shoot growth.

After about four weeks in warm climates, the principal period of most rapid shoot growth begins. Shoots may grow more than 3 cm/1 in a day, and differences in shoot length can be observed from day to day. Shoot growth slackens at flowering or bloom, 40 to 80 days after budbreak depending on TEMPERATURE, but can continue to the end of the season under conditions of mild temperatures and over-generous supplies of water and NITROGEN. More commonly, especially for DRYLAND VITICULTURE, WATER STRESS reduces shoot growth between flowering and veraison (or the beginning of grape RIPENING), and it may cease altogether later in the season. The shoot tips are sometimes TRIMMED, but will often grow again from lateral buds.

Small flower clusters are apparent on the young shoots as buttons, and in the few weeks before flowering the BUNCHSTEMS and the individual flowers are obvious. Flowering takes place when the average daily temperatures are about 15 to 20 °C (59–68 °F), and is followed by the so-called fruit set process.

The next significant stage is that of veraison, when grapes change colour and begin to ripen about 40 to 50 days after fruit set. Between set

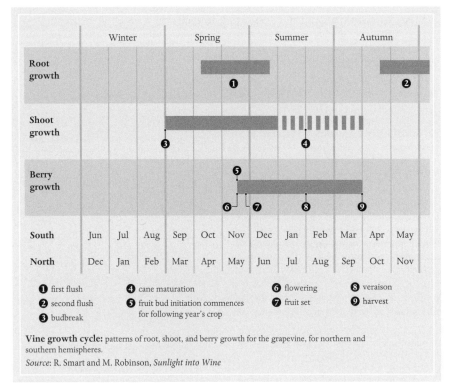

	Winter			Spring			Summer			Autumn		

Root growth ❶ ❷

Shoot growth ❸ ❹

Berry growth ❺ ❻ ❼ ❽ ❾

South	Jun	Jul	Aug	Sep	Oct	Nov	Dec	Jan	Feb	Mar	Apr	May
North	Dec	Jan	Feb	Mar	Apr	May	Jun	Jul	Aug	Sep	Oct	Nov

❶ first flush ❹ cane maturation ❻ flowering ❽ veraison
❷ second flush ❺ fruit bud initiation commences ❼ fruit set ❾ harvest
❸ budbreak   for following year's crop

Vine growth cycle: patterns of root, shoot, and berry growth for the grapevine, for northern and southern hemispheres.
Source: R. Smart and M. Robinson, *Sunlight into Wine*

and veraison, the berries grow to about half their final size, but remain green and hard. They contain low concentrations of SUGARS, but are high in organic ACIDS. Veraison is an easily observable stage when the berries change colour to either red-black or yellow-green, depending on the variety. The berries also soften, and they begin rapidly to build up sugar. During this stage, the vines also rapidly accumulate carbohydrate reserves in the roots, trunk, and arms.

The most appropriate date of harvest depends on the desired stage of RIPENESS for WINE-MAKING. It is earliest for sparkling wines, intermediate for table wines, and delayed for dessert and fortified wines. Harvest date may also be influenced by weather conditions and by disease levels (see BUNCH ROTS). Fruit ripening normally proceeds quickly in hot areas, with rapid increases in sugars and PH and a decline in ACIDITY, especially MALIC ACID. In cooler regions the rate of ripening is slower, and the fruit typically has lower sugars and higher acidity. Rainfall near harvest can cause problems due to berry splitting, BOTRYTIS, and other bunch rotting fungi (see ROT). After rain, there is normally a rush to harvest grapes while they are still sound.

Leaf fall marks the end of the season, and of all the developmental stages it is the least precisely marked. Some leaves may fall off during the growing season, especially if the vine comes under stress, for example by drought, disease, or shade. A significant proportion of the leaves may also be removed by MECHANICAL

HARVESTING. With continued warm and sunny weather following harvest, the leaves remain healthy and are photosynthetically active in replacing carbohydrate reserves in the vine trunk and roots. Once these levels are built up, the vines often lose their green chlorophyll colour and turn yellow. The first frost or the low temperatures of the winter season usually cause leaf fall, and the vines are then in a dormant state. After PRUNING in winter, the vines are ready for the growth cycle to begin again.

See also VINEYARD ANNUAL CYCLE. R.E.S.

Coombe, B. G., 'Grape phenology', in B. G. Coombe and P. R. Dry (eds.), *Viticulture, i: Resources* (2nd edn, Adelaide, 2004).

Keller, M., 'Phenology and growth cycle', in *The Science of Grapevines: Anatomy and Physiology* (Elsevier, 2010).

vine guards, plastic tubes which became popular internationally in the 1980s and 1990s to protect young vines. As well as protecting vines from WIND, they also protect from HERBICIDES and vineyard PESTS, especially rabbits, and reduce vine-training costs, although in warmer wine regions they can create an excessively hot MICROCLIMATE around the young plant. The guards are normally in place for one year, sometimes two. Wine tourists now witness coloured vine guards as the most obvious feature of new plantings. R.E.S.

vine identification. See AMPELOGRAPHY and DNA PROFILING for details of these two very different methods of identifying different VINE VARIETIES.

vine improvement, a group of practices designed to improve vine planting material for the benefit of vineyard YIELD and the quality of the fruit and wine produced. This is currently focused on eliminating harmful VIRUS DISEASES and also on genetic improvement. Some virus diseases such as LEAFROLL cause delayed RIPENING and can therefore have dramatic effects on wine quality. CLONAL SELECTION is a technique which, by selecting high-performance vines, can achieve both ends. Other techniques of virus elimination include THERMOTHERAPY and TISSUE CULTURE. Genetic improvement can also be achieved through beneficial MUTATION and selection, by GENETIC MODIFICATION, and by VINE BREEDING.

Although virus diseases had affected European vines since the end of the 19th century, it took some time for preventive action to be taken on a national scale. The first attempt at controlling the quality of planting material in France was made in 1944, when the Section de Contrôle des Bois et Plantes de Vigne was formed (its functions now subsumed within FranceAgriMer, the intermediary body between the French ministry of agriculture and the grape and wine sectors), charged with avoiding the spread of virus diseases, and also with ensuring that all rootstocks used had sufficient resistance to phylloxera. Previously, nurserymen had been free to propagate whichever vines they chose, with sometimes disastrous effects for their clients. Nurserymen were encouraged to take healthy CUTTINGS from specially planted and disease-free MOTHER VINES.

In Germany there has been a high regard for the health of buds and rootstock for grafting, and rigorous clonal selection programmes and registration of CLONES has ensured high-quality planting material. Similar schemes operate in other European countries.

In non-European countries there has also been an awareness of the importance of quality control of propagation material. After the Second World War, the California wine industry created a model system for improving the quality of planting material. Research at the University of California at DAVIS had demonstrated the importance of virus diseases, and had shown how they might be detected. A so-called 'clean rootstock program' was developed which aimed to distribute only virus-free cuttings to nurseries, using thermotherapy and INDEXING in particular to produce virus-free plants. This has subsequently become known as FOUNDATION PLANT SERVICES (FPS), and has distributed high-health vines all around the world. In Australia and New Zealand, government officials worked with industry personnel to create at regional or state level a Vine Improvement Organization which became self-funding by the sales of improved planting material.

Recently all such programmes around the world have been challenged by the discovery of fungi associated with TRUNK DISEASES in mother vines, meaning that once again nurseries the world over are distributing diseased plants. This situation is yet to be resolved.   R.E.S.

McCarthy, M. G., 'Grape planting material', in B. G. Coombe and P. R. Dry (eds.), *Viticulture*, i: *Resources* (2nd edn, Adelaide, 2004).

vine management

vine management, a term embracing all management practices in the vineyard, including especially SOIL PREPARATION and DRAINAGE; PRUNING and CANOPY MANAGEMENT; use of FERTILIZERS, MULCHES, and COVER CROPS; CULTIVATION and WEED CONTROL; use of FUNGICIDES and PESTICIDES; IRRIGATION; vine TRIMMING and LEAF REMOVAL; CROP THINNING to control YIELD; and HARVEST methods.

vine morphology

vine morphology is the study of the form and structure of the vine plant, as distinct from VINE PHYSIOLOGY, which is the study of its function. See ANTHER, ARM, BEARER, BERRY, BRUSH, BUD, BUNCH, BUNCHSTEM, CALYPTRA, CAMBIUM, CANE, CELL, CORDON, FLOWERS, GRAPE, HEAD, INFLORESCENCE, INTERNODE, LATERAL SHOOT, LEAF, NODE, OVARY, PEDICEL, PERICARP, PETIOLE, PHLOEM, POLLEN, PULP, ROOT, SEEDS, SHOOT, SPUR, STAMEN, STEM, STOMATA, TENDRIL, TRUNK, VINE, WATER SHOOT, and XYLEM.   B.G.C.

vine nutrition

vine nutrition, the supply of inorganic nutrients (sometimes called mineral nutrients or nutrient elements) to the vine. Vines, like other plants, require the essential macronutrients NITROGEN, PHOSPHORUS, POTASSIUM, SULFUR, CALCIUM, MAGNESIUM, and chlorine (at concentrations greater than 1,000 ppm in their tissues), and the micronutrients MANGANESE, IRON, ZINC, COPPER, MOLYBDENUM, and BORON (at concentrations less than 1,000 ppm in their tissues). See MINERALS.

Among horticultural plants, the vine is regarded as having low nutrition requirements. A common recommendation for vineyards,

depending on the soil and the grower's objectives for the wine to be made, would be 0–50 kg/ha nitrogen, 0–25 kg/ha phosphorus, and 0 to 100 kg/ha potassium. These low requirements reflect the low levels of nutrients that are removed from the vineyard each year by the grape HARVEST. Fertilizers supplying the macronutrients (see SOIL NUTRIENTS) nitrogen, phosphorus, and potassium are normally applied in amounts giving up to 50, 25, and 100 kg/ha per year of nitrogen, phosphorus, and potassium, respectively.

Measurements have been made in many countries of the amounts of elements contained in the grapes picked, and also in the leaf litter and winter prunings. These values vary with region, variety, and yield but are in the range of 12–24 kg/ha of nitrogen, 3–6 kg/ha of phosphorus, and 25–40 kg/ha of potassium for a 10 t/ha crop. A general recommendation therefore would be to apply this amount of fertilizer if there was any doubt that the vineyard soil would be able to supply it. In general, SOIL TESTING before PLANTING can indicate any likely deficiencies. In mature vineyards, the standard procedure is to test either the leaves or the leaf stalks (PETIOLES) for their nutrient content, and apply fertilizers only as the need is indicated. For many crops, an annual addition of fertilizer will do little harm if it is not needed. For vines, however, such an addition is likely to be unnecessary and even wasteful since their needs are low, and there is always the danger of over-fertilization, especially with nitrogen, which can directly and indirectly reduce wine quality. Furthermore, repeated applications of nitrogen as ammonium-based or urea fertilizers leads to acidification of the soil over time. Similarly, high levels of potassium in soils can reduce wine quality because of increased wine PH.

Continued use of the same parcel of land for viticulture over extended periods of time reduces the levels of nutrients. Studies of old vineyard soils in Bordeaux have shown that fertility can be restored by heavy applications of ORGANIC MATTER, LIME, phosphorus, and potassium. Organic matter such as MULCHES, COMPOST, and animal MANURES can be used to fertilize vineyards, but they are typically lower in nutrient content and may be more expensive. They often, however, improve SOIL STRUCTURE by their organic matter content. Such forms of fertilizer are favoured for ORGANIC VITICULTURE.

Although research shows little connection between nutrition of the vine and a wine's quality or specific character, other than through influences on vine VIGOUR, there is a perception that soil directly affects wine character by giving wines a special chemical signature that is unique to the site. Recent studies in Canada and elsewhere have shown that the vineyard origin may be determined by analysis of a wine's trace elements, but there is not

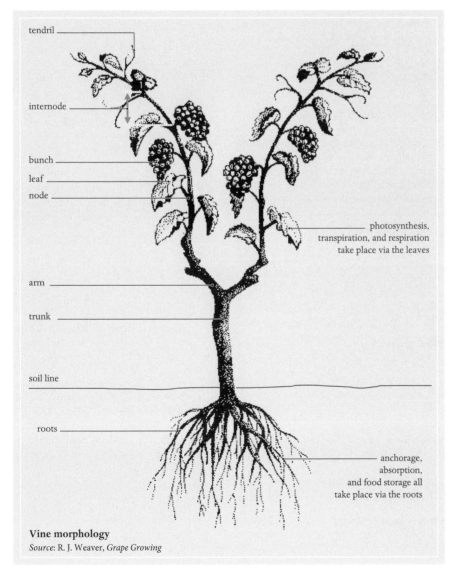

Vine morphology
Source: R. J. Weaver, *Grape Growing*

tendril

internode

bunch

leaf

node

photosynthesis, transpiration, and respiration take place via the leaves

arm

trunk

soil line

roots

anchorage, absorption, and food storage all take place via the roots

necessarily any relationship to wine character. See MINERALS for more explanation, and also SOIL AND WINE QUALITY and TERROIR.

R.E.S. & R.E.W.

Danzer, K., et al., 'Classification of wine samples according to origin and grape varieties on the basis of inorganic and organic trace analyses', *American Laboratory* (Oct 1999), 26–34.

White, R. E., *Understanding Vineyard Soils* (2nd edn, Oxford, 2015).

vine pests can make viticulture uneconomic and can have drastic effects on wine quality unless controlled. They include ANIMALS, INSECTS, and NEMATODES (while VINE DISEASES include the microbes bacteria, fungi, phytoplasma, viroids, and virus).

The principal commercial wine grape VITIS VINIFERA is indigenous to Eurasia, while the majority of severe vine pests and diseases come principally from east and south east North America. Their accidental introduction to Europe from the 1850s onwards had dramatic consequences for local viticulture. The fungal disease POWDERY MILDEW was bad enough but fortunately a control was soon at hand. The insect pest PHYLLOXERA was not so easy to control, and for a period following its introduction in 1863 the entire French wine industry was threatened. Fortunately it was solved by grafting *V. vinifera* vines on to ROOTSTOCKS derived from AMERICAN VINE SPECIES which have natural resistance to phylloxera. This practice is now used worldwide.

In general, vine pests are easier to control than diseases, although the AGROCHEMICALS used to control insects (PESTICIDES) are among the most potent used in viticulture. The modern tendency is to depend less on pesticides and to develop strategies such as INTEGRATED PEST MANAGEMENT. Phylloxera is a threat to only a small proportion of the world's vineyards as over 85% are grafted to rootstocks considered resistant. However, at present there is only limited chemical control of the insect pest MARGARODES, which is currently confined to a few vineyard regions of the southern hemisphere.

Vine pests can have dramatic effects on wine quality. One end of the spectrum is the pest causing the vine severe stress, as for example with root damage due to NEMATODES or phylloxera. Indeed this effect is frequently transient as it is a prelude to death and/or vine removal (see GRUBBING UP).

The following are some examples of how some pests can affect vines and reduce wine quality. Leaf area removal by beetles, deer, kangaroos, LOCUSTS, MOTHS, rabbits, and SNAILS can jeopardize PHOTOSYNTHESIS and grape RIPENING. Leaves can also be damaged and photosynthesis reduced by LEAFHOPPERS and MITES. Vine growth and yield are reduced by attacks on roots from gophers, badgers, phylloxera, margarodes,

nematodes, and squirrels, and by destruction of the trunk and arms by BORERS and TERMITES. Monkeys can cause significant damage to shoots, leaves, and fruit in JAPAN. Damage to the grapes themselves by insects and birds can lead to BUNCH ROTS, which can be spread by fruit fly. Some pests can taint grapes, as for example the LADYBUG, or the honeydew of MEALY BUGS and SCALE. Last but not least is the very important role of pests in carrying (vectoring) diseases. The dreaded and lethal bacterial PIERCE'S DISEASE is spread by leafhoppers, as is the phytoplasma disease FLAVESCENCE DORÉE. Important VIRUS DISEASES which can substantially reduce wine quality and yield are spread by nematodes and mealy bug.

For more detail, see major entries under ANIMALS, BEETLES, BIRDS, FRUIT FLY, INSECT PESTS, MITES, NEMATODES, PHYLLOXERA; other entries are to be found under the pests' common name.

R.E.S.

vine physiological status, term often used to describe the condition of the vine. How the vine is responding to its environment is a most important consideration for the production of premium wine quality, especially during the fruit RIPENING period, but its status during the preceding year may also affect YIELD.

R.E.S.

vine physiology, the science of the function of the VINE, including the growth and development of the vine shoot and root systems, its fruiting, and the major physiological processes such as PHOTOSYNTHESIS, TRANSLOCATION, and TRANSPIRATION. Physiology is also concerned with controls on plant growth and development, including both environmental and internal control by HORMONES. Both VINE NUTRITION and degree of WATER STRESS are affected by the vineyard soil, and TEMPERATURE and SUNLIGHT are the most important climate influences.

The vine's physiology can be manipulated by vineyard management techniques to alter growth, yield, and quality. For example, decisions on TRAINING SYSTEMS and PRUNING levels will alter the light incident on leaves, thus affecting photosynthesis and sugar supply to the grapes during RIPENING. Irrigation is another important form of manipulation. The term VINE PHYSIOLOGICAL STATUS is often used to describe the condition of the vine, as for example the degree of water stress it is experiencing. Manipulating such conditions is the aim of the vineyard manager intent on maximizing wine quality.

R.E.S.

Keller, M., 'Phenology and growth cycle', in *The Science of Grapevines: Anatomy and Physiology* (Elsevier, 2010).

vine products, the range of products produced from the vine. The GRAPEVINE is the world's most important fruit crop, and WINE

and its brandy distillates are by far the most important of its products. Other products include DRYING GRAPES, TABLE GRAPES, GRAPE JUICE, GRAPE CONCENTRATE, VINEGAR, VERJUS, grapeseed oil, and RECTIFIED GRAPE MUST. There are other minor products: grapevine cuttings (*sarments* in French) can be used for propagation or for barbecue firewood (although the latter is indeed a minor use); vine leaves are used in Middle Eastern and Greek cuisine and for wrapping certain cheeses; a range of cosmetics based on grapevine products exists; and pharmaceutical companies have even started selling grape-derived RESVERATROL tablets with supposed HEALTH benefits.

R.E.S. & J.E.H.

vine pull schemes have been instituted in various parts of the world at different times, generally in response to a perceived wine SURPLUS.

In the late 1980s and early 1990s, smallholders in the south of France and Italy in particular took advantage of substantial financial inducements to abandon viticulture on all or part of their land in an effort to drain the European WINE LAKE. About 300,000 ha/741,000 acres of French vineyard and about 400,000 ha of Italian vineyard were ripped out between the late 1970s and 1991. France's total vineyard was reduced by a further 80,000 ha and Italy's by about 150,000 ha between 1991 and 1996, while a further 284,000 ha were ripped out in Spain and 126,000 ha in Portugal. In the following decade, the uptake was greatly reduced, with just 30,000 ha grubbed up, mainly in France.

As a result of the EU reforms of 2008, there were further financial incentives to grub up vines in much of Europe but this time farmers were able to apply directly to the EU. As a result, 161,164 ha (398,244 acres) of vines were grubbed up between 2008 and 2011, equivalent to 10% of the European vineyard area. During the same period, 111,364 ha (275,186 acres) were grubbed up without the inducement of a subsidy. However, this has not necessarily resulted in a reduction in wine production. In SPAIN, for example, vineyard restructuring has increased yields despite the ripping out of 150,000 ha of vines.

Such schemes are not exclusive to the EU. An even more comprehensive vine pull scheme was enacted within a single country, the Soviet Union, as part of GORBACHEV's attempts to curb alcohol consumption. Between 1985 and 1990, the total area under vine in the old USSR fell from more than 1.3 million ha to 880,000 ha/2.2 million acres.

Other national vine pull schemes may be directed at particular types of vine in an effort to reduce production of certain wine types—usually in recent history wine of the most basic sort. Such schemes were applied in both

ARGENTINA and NEW ZEALAND in the late 1980s, for example.

For details of the mechanics of pulling out vines, and why a grower might do so, see GRUBBING UP.

vine removal. See GRUBBING UP.

vine spacing. See VINE DENSITY.

vine training, the process of establishing a vine framework in the required shape. It may begin in summer by tying down and trimming growing shoots, followed by suitable winter PRUNING. Normally vines are trained to a supporting structure which may be as simple as a stake in the ground, or may be a more complex trellis system made from wire and wood, metal, or concrete posts. Training is normally complete within the first two or three years of a vine's life and is well established before grape production begins. It will, however, take longer where vines are planted at wide distances apart and with complex trellis systems such as the TENDONE. Training normally consists of forming the TRUNK, the CORDONS or HEAD, and any arms required.

See under TRAINING SYSTEMS for more details of individual forms, and see also TRELLIS SYSTEMS for more details of their supports.   R.E.S.

vine-training systems. See TRAINING SYSTEMS.

vine varieties, distinct types of vine within one species of the vine genus VITIS (see also BOTANICAL CLASSIFICATION). Different vine varieties produce different varieties of grape, so that the terms vine variety and grape variety are used almost interchangeably. Each variety of vine, or grape, may produce distinct and identifiable styles and flavours of wine. Vine variety is *cépage* in French, *cepa* in Spanish, *Rebsorte* in German, *vitigno* in Italian., and *casta* in Portuguese. Professional botanists favour the term grapevine CULTIVARS.

All of the vine varieties we know today initially originated from WILD VINES. Domestication was made possible by propagating the best vines (see ORIGINS OF VINICULTURE) either by CUTTINGS or LAYERING (see PROPAGATION), thus producing genetically identical new plants. Afterwards, new vine varieties could originate from natural crosses between the vine varieties that had been selected, or between vine varieties and wild vines, or by selecting other wild vines.

Most important vine varieties used to produce wine are of the European vine species *Vitis* VINIFERA. A number of varieties of AMERICAN VINE SPECIES and their AMERICAN HYBRIDS have also been used to make wine, however, although many suffer a bad reputation because of the resultant wines' FOXY character (the dark-skinned NORTON is a notable exception). American species are also used as ROOTSTOCKS. Wine has also been made from a range of Asian vine varieties and from the FRENCH HYBRIDS.

It is clear that specific vine varieties were recognized in Ancient GREECE and ROME, since some are already described in CLASSICAL TEXTS such as those of Pliny and Columella (see ANCIENT VINE VARIETIES). The extent to which the vine varieties of Europe originate from wild vines or were introduced is not known. Also, with the fall of the Roman empire, cultivated vineyards were abandoned, and such varieties as were deliberately cultivated presumably interbred with local wild vines and native *Vitis vinifera*. The result of this intermixing over time is that many European regions have developed their own INDIGENOUS VARIETIES.

There are between 5,000 and 10,000 known varieties of *V. vinifera*. Ampelographers Pierre Viala and Victor Vermorel listed about 5,000 different varieties in their great seven-volume AMPELOGRAPHY published between 1901 and 1910 (see MONTPELLIER). Many of these were synonyms, and Robinson, Harding, and Vouillamoz proposed a total of 1,368 varieties cultivated around the world for commercial wine production in 2012. Italy had the richest heritage of cultivated vine varieties (377), followed by France (204), Spain (84), Portugal (77), and Greece (77). Thousands of other varieties exist in grape germplasm collections but they are not cultivated for commercial bottling and sale. VINE IDENTIFICATION and the study of individual varieties' characteristics and aptitudes is a scientific activity known as ampelography, recently supplemented by DNA PROFILING.

Vine varieties are often named for the colour of their berries, with many French varieties, for example, coming in *noir* (black), *rouge* (red), *violet, rose* (pink), *gris* (grey-pink), *jaune* (yellow), *vert* (green), and *blanc* (white) hues. This book uses the convention of adopting a capital letter for each word in a vine variety's name, without quotation marks, even though 'Pinot Noir' would be botanically more correct for a cultivar name. Examples of MUTATIONS are Pinot Blanc and Pinot Gris, while Sauvignon Vert is a quite different variety from Sauvignon Blanc. See individual variety names for more details.

Varieties were classified and grouped into families by Levadoux, but DNA profiling is now shedding light on the true origin for many varieties, and is now being harnessed to yield the pedigrees of both traditional and modern vine varieties. Varieties can be broadly grouped into three major botanical categories called PROLES, which are related to their geographical origins, and to some extent their end use. Varieties can also be classified in more detail by their country or region of origin, although as some varieties have been planted widely throughout the world (see INTERNATIONAL VARIETIES) this distinction is becoming unclear.

Another classification is by end-product use, and so vine varieties may be described as being for wine, TABLE GRAPES, DRYING GRAPES, GRAPE JUICE, or for ROOTSTOCKS (although some varieties, such as SULTANA, are in practice used for several of these). Among wine vine varieties, some varieties are particularly well suited to different styles of wine: sparkling, fortified, sweet, or dry still wine, for example. Within each group there are varieties more likely to make notable, ageworthy wines and those suitable only for lower-value products.

Most widely planted varieties

Of all vine varieties, remarkably few have achieved an international reputation, and most of these are French. Obvious examples of these international varieties include Cabernet Sauvignon, Pinot Noir, Syrah/Shiraz, Merlot, Chardonnay, Sauvignon Blanc, and Riesling. As an increasing proportion of all wine is labelled VARIETALLY, there has been an increasing correlation between these most famous varieties and those which cover the greatest total area of vineyard land (see TABLE GRAPES). Nevertheless most estimates agree that more of the Earth's surface is devoted to Sultana/Thompson Seedless than it is to any well-known wine grape.

The table overleaf lists the 20 most planted wine grape varieties in the world, based on Kym Anderson's 2013 research.

Choice of variety

Vine-growers are rarely free to choose which vine variety to plant in a given vineyard. They may have acquired a planted vineyard in full production and cannot afford the crop loss involved in changing variety either by GRUBBING UP established vines or by FIELD GRAFTING a new variety onto the trunk and root system of the old one. Different varieties need different conditions of soil and climate. Cabernet Sauvignon simply will not ripen regularly in cool regions, for example.

In France, and much of the EU, the varieties permitted may be regulated. Some of these restrictions can be traced back to the Middle Ages (see PINOT NOIR), but formalization took place from 1935 with the APPELLATION CONTRÔLÉE (AOC) laws which authorize only specified varieties for each appellation, distinguishing between principal and secondary varieties (see Appendix 1 for full details). Similarly, some varieties were completely banned (although it required more than 30 years for this law to have its effect). For the production of more basic VIN DE TABLE, l'Institut des Vins de Consommation Courante (IVCC, the precursor of ONIVIT) decreed in 1953 for each viticultural region three classifications of varieties: recommended, authorized, and tolerated until eventual removal. These laws have subsequently been overtaken by EU laws with the similar intent

Prime variety	Global area 1990			Global area 2000			Global area 2010		
	ha	acres	rank	ha	acres	rank	ha	acres	rank
Cabernet Sauvignon R	127,678	315,500	8	220,890	545,831	2	290,126	716,916	1
Merlot R	154,752	382,400	7	211,967	523,783	4	267,638	661,349	2
Airen W	476,396	1,177,201	1	387,978	958,714	1	252,364	623,605	3
Tempranillo R	47,429	117,200	24	92,985	229,770	10	232,561	574,670	4
Chardonnay W	69,282	171,200	13	145,344	359,152	5	198,841	491,346	5
Syrah R	35,086	86,700	35	101,516	250,853	8	185,568	458,548	6
Grenache R (Garnacha, Cannonau)	282,997	699,301	2	213,987	528,774	3	184,735	456,490	7
Trebbiano Toscano W	207,442	512,600	5	136,572	337,476	6	111,222	274,836	8
Sauvignon Blanc W	44,677	110,400	25	64,889	160,345	15	110,194	272,295	9
Pinot Noir R	41,539	102,644	30	60,099	148,509	16	98,395	243,140	10
Carignan R (Mazuelo, Carignane)	202,869	501,300	6	126,650	312,960	7	80,178	198,124	11
Bobal R	106,149	262,300	10	100,128	247,422	9	80,120	197,981	12
Sangiovese R	98,946	244,500	11	68,877	170,200	13	77,709	192,024	13
Monastrell R	108,213	267,400	9	76,304	188,551	12	69,850	172,604	14
Graševina W	19,384	47,900	48	92,306	228,093	11	61,200	151,227	15
Rkatsiteli W	280,569	693,301	3	67,354	166,435	14	58,641	144,904	16
Cabernet Franc R	39,619	97,900	32	48,551	119,971	19	53,615	132,486	17
Riesling W	52,164	128,900	21	43,166	106,665	23	49,974	123,488	18
Pinot Gris W				18,879	46,651	44	43,630	107,812	19
Macabeo W	43,504	107,500	26	48,125	118,919	21	41,046	101,428	20

Source: Kym Anderson, *Which Winegrape Varieties are Grown Where? A Global Empirical Picture*, Wine Economics Research Centre, University of Adelaide (2013)

of allowing only specified varieties. For discussion of these restrictions, see VINE VARIETIES, EFFECT ON WINE.

In the New World, the choice of vine variety or varieties is often in practice determined by the style of wine that is eventually desired, many of them involving just one vine variety (typically sold as a VARIETAL wine). Examples of mono-varietal AOC wines within France are Beaujolais (Gamay), Muscadet, (Melon), and Sancerre (Sauvignon Blanc). Blends of two varieties often include those which are complementary, such as the productive and full-bodied Marsanne mixed with the lighter, rarer Roussanne for the white Hermitage. Celebrated blends of three varieties include Sémillon, Sauvignon Blanc, and Muscadelle in Sauternes, and Pinot Noir, Chardonnay, and Pinot Meunier in champagne. Even more complex blends of varieties are common in red bordeaux and in Châteauneuf-du-Pape, both styles which are emulated in the New World. The mix of vine varieties that go into a single wine is called an *assemblage* in French and *uvaggio* in Italian, and the mix of vine varieties that are planted on a single property, appellation or region, is called *encépagement* in French. Varieties themselves are often subdivided into various CLONES. While particular clones of many varieties have been selected through performance evaluation by CLONAL SELECTION, in many cases they cannot be separated by appearance.

See also NEW VARIETIES. J.R., J.E.H., & J.V.

Anderson, K., *Which Wine grape Varieties are Grown Where?* www.adelaide.edu.au/wine-econ/databases/winegrapes-front-1213.pdf

Galet, P., *Dictionnaire encyclopédique des cépages* (Paris, 2000).

Mullins, M. G., Bouquet, A., and Williams, L., *Biology of the Grapevine* (Cambridge, 1992).

Robinson, J., Harding, J., and Vouillamoz, J., *A Complete Guide to 1,368 Vine Varieties, including their Origins and Flavours* (London & New York, 2012).

van Leeuwen, C., 'Choix du cépage en fonction du terroir dans le Bordelais', in *Un raisin de qualité: de la vigne à la cuve*, n° Hors Série du *Journal International des Sciences de la Vigne et du Vin* (2001), 97–102.

vine varieties, effect on wine. Of all the factors such as SOIL, CLIMATE, VITICULTURE, and detailed WINEMAKING techniques which have an effect on wine quality, vine variety is probably the easiest to detect in a BLIND TASTING. The colour of the grapes' skin determines what COLOUR of wine can be produced: red wine can be produced only from dark-skinned grapes. Only grape varieties which ripen readily and/or are prone to NOBLE ROT are likely to produce good SWEET WINES, while only those with high levels of natural acidity are likely to produce good brandy or SPARKLING WINES. But, even more important in identification, individual grape varieties tend to produce wines with identifiably different flavours. Indeed, in very general terms, it is a mark of quality in a vine variety that it is capable of producing wines with distinguished and distinctive flavours, even if those flavours are heavily influenced by weather, TERROIR and, vineyard practice. Lesser vine varieties tend to produce wines that are neutral and undistinguished, however promising the vineyard site.

When more than one vine variety is used to produce a single wine, it is important that the wines produced by those varieties are complementary. Cabernet Sauvignon tends to blend well with wines that have more obvious fruit such as Merlot or warm-climate Syrah/Shiraz, for example, while the weight of Sémillon is a good foil for the aroma and acidity of Sauvignon Blanc. Another French example widely copied elsewhere is Grenache with Syrah and, possibly, Mourvèdre.

Wine quality is maximized if the vine variety or vine varieties are well suited to the site, in terms of climate, soil structure, ROOTSTOCK, VINE DENSITY, TRAINING SYSTEM, PRUNING regime, and other viticultural methods. Although to an increasing extent varieties are selected for new vineyards on the basis of climatic similarity with a classic wine region (see HOMOCLIMES), matching vine variety to site is considered in its infancy in most of the NEW WORLD (even if certain combinations such as Coonawarra for Cabernet Sauvignon vines, or the Central Coast and Oregon for Pinot Noir, established themselves earlier than most). In parts of the Old World, on the other hand, the matching of vine variety to site, or even whole regions, is so entrenched (see VINE VARIETIES above) that some would argue it amounts to restriction. The varieties Cabernet Sauvignon and Merlot undoubtedly perform extremely well in Bordeaux, but it is perhaps an unnecessary constraint to forbid Bordeaux vinegrowers from planting, say, the Syrah grape of Hermitage.

Varieties vary in the range of environments they can tolerate. Chardonnay, for example, is extremely versatile and can produce good wine in climates which vary from the coolness of Chablis to the hot interior valleys of California. Varieties such as Pinot Noir and Nebbiolo, on the other hand, appear to be extremely fastidious. See also CLIMATE AND WINE QUALITY.

The French APPELLATION CONTRÔLÉE system, which generally disapproves of citing vine varieties on the label, even as interpretation of a geographical appellation, is predicated on the belief that for every appellation there is an ideal vine variety or ENCÉPAGEMENT, or that the character of the appellation is stronger than that of any vine variety. While this is an attractive proposition (and it is certainly true that, for example, the appellation of a red bordeaux or a white Alsace wine is often more strongly identifiable than any single vine variety), it seems questionable for most wine regions, even within France. Regulations in other EU wine-producing countries tend to emulate those of France.

R.E.S. & J.R.

Galet, P., *Précis de viticulture* (7th edn, Montpellier, 2000).

Moran, W., 'The wine appellation: environmental description or economic device', *Auckland Cool Climate Symposium* (1988), 356–60.

Robinson, J., Harding, J., and Vouillamoz, J., *Wine Grapes: A Complete Guide to 1,368 Vine Varieties, including their Origins and Flavours* (London & New York, 2012).

vineyard, name given to the agricultural field where grapevines are grown.

The contrast in connotations between the very words vineyard and field illustrates something of the special nature of vines as a crop. This may be partly connected with the symbolism of and pleasures associated with wine, but is also a function of the aesthetic appeal of vineyards in all seasons, whether the increasingly luxuriant green canopy of spring and summer, the flame-coloured leaves of autumn (even if these indicate the presence of VIRUS DISEASE), or the rows of poignant black stumps in winter. The beauty of vineyards and vines plays an important part in wine TOURISM; it is difficult to imagine substantial numbers of people making a pilgrimage to a region famous for any other agricultural crop.

In most parts of the world, the vineyard is a well-defined entity, generally well demarcated by the borders of the straight rows. *Vignoble* is a common French term for a vineyard at all quality levels. In Bordeaux, and elsewhere, CRU may be used synonymously with a top-quality vineyard, while in Burgundy the terms CLIMAT or, in the case of a walled vineyard, CLOS are more common. In Italy the terms cru, VIGNA, SORÌ, and RONCO are all used. Recognition of single vineyards is less developed in Spain although VINO DE PAGO is a classification for single-estate wines.

In an agricultural sense, vineyards are typically monocultures with vines the only plants growing, apart from COVER CROPS and WEEDS. Less frequently, however, vineyards are grown intermingled with other crops, the so-called *coltura promiscua* that was once the norm in much of central Italy. In the VINHO VERDE region of northern Portugal, vines are still sometimes grown as borders around other fields which may contain field crops or orchards. Originally trained to wires attached to bordering trees, the vines of Vinho Verde are nowadays more commonly trained on wooden or metal supports, known as *ramada*, although they may still surround fields in which other crops are grown.

Any one vineyard may be made up of smaller units, parcels, or fields, which may contain different vine varieties, clones, rootstocks, or vines of different ages. Sometimes fields are separated, as for example by headlands, hedges, or drainage ditches, and otherwise may be contiguous one with another.

Even relatively small vineyards are rarely homogeneous in terms of SOIL, TOPOGRAPHY, and MESOCLIMATE. Soils in particular may vary considerably within one single vineyard (see VOUGEOT or MONTRACHET, for example). Sometimes, when the soil, topography, and climate are uniform over an area much larger than a single vineyard, as in COONAWARRA in South Australia (although the soils are much, much more varied than the climate or topography), then the region as a whole may earn a reputation for good quality rather than certain vineyards within it.

Vineyards vary in size, depending on many factors. Owing to fragmentation of vineyards by inheritance, some vineyard owners in BURGUNDY may lay claim to only a few rows often indistinguishable to outsiders from the adjacent vines. At the other end of the scale in the New World, there are often large corporate vineyards. One of the world's largest vineyards is the 2,800-ha/6,920-acre San Bernabe ranch in the Salinas valley of MONTEREY in California.

Some vineyards are particularly famous for their wine because of their specific combination of VINE VARIETY, CLONE, ROOTSTOCK, and climate conditions, which can be distinguished at the various levels of MACROCLIMATE, MESOCLIMATE, and MICROCLIMATE. Of particular importance are the soil conditions, which, together with TOPOGRAPHY, mesoclimate, and CANOPY MICROCLIMATE, constitute what the French (and others) call TERROIR. See under each of these entries for a discussion of their relative contribution. For example, a feature of the famous Bordeaux PREMIERS CRUS is that as well as producing great wine in good years they are also able to do well in acknowledged low-quality years. This is a function not just of appropriate vineyard management, but also of the terroir which allows the vine to ripen the fruit adequately when other, less exalted vineyards cannot.

See also HILLSIDE VINEYARDS, PLANTING, VINEYARD ANNUAL CYCLE, VINEYARD SITE SELECTION.

R.E.S. & J.R.

vineyard annual cycle. The march of the seasons through the year dictates the work to be done in vineyards (see VINE GROWTH CYCLE). Spring is the time of budbreak, and early ploughing and spraying must be done. Early spring is also the common time for PLANTING vineyards, once the danger of FROST is past. As the temperatures rise, the vine shoots grow more rapidly, and FLOWERING takes place in early summer. This can be a busy period as often fungicide SPRAYS are to be applied, and the first SHOOT POSITIONING is carried out. Soon after FRUIT SET is the time for the second shoot positioning. In those vineyards of the world where IRRIGATION is practised, the first applications of water are often made around this time, and may continue up to the time of harvest. About this period the nurseryman is doing BENCH GRAFTING, and it is also the time for FIELD BUDDING AND GRAFTING. As the summer progresses, TRIMMING is carried out, typically before VERAISON. Many vine-growers are involved with further spraying of AGROCHEMICALS and often continued CULTIVATION. Depending on the vine variety and region, the HARVEST may be in early, mid, or late summer, and sometimes in the autumn. Whenever it occurs, it is one of the busiest periods in the vineyard, often involving SAMPLING to test grape RIPENESS before the harvest itself. Depending on the spread of varieties, the harvest may be brief or protracted, but few other jobs are attended to in the vineyard at this time. The period immediately following harvest is busy in the wineries but not so in the vineyards, and vineyard workers and viticulturists often take their annual leave then. This is also the common time for soil RIPPING and maintenance of machinery and TRELLIS SYSTEMS. Once the leaves fall, the serious business of PRUNING begins, and, depending on the scale of operations, this may continue right up until budbreak. This is also the time when CUTTINGS are taken for PROPAGATION.

R.E.S.

vineyard design, important component of vineyard planning before vineyard planting (except in traditional OLD WORLD areas where spacings, variety, and rootstock may well be prescribed). In a new vineyard, normally the first step is a topographic survey, followed by a soil survey and SOIL MAPPING, today in some instances using GLOBAL POSITIONING SYSTEM technology. Based on this important information, block layout and irrigation design proceeds, and finally on a block by block basis decisions are made about variety, clone, rootstock, row and vine spacing, and training system. In this way, the vineyard will optimize use of local resources and the potential of the site.

R.E.S.

vineyard site selection can be the single most important aspect of grape production in the NEW WORLD, even if it is not always appreciated as such. If, for example, the new vineyard is in a cool region, then the TOPOGRAPHY of the site may be a critical factor in avoiding FROST DAMAGE and the ASPECT chosen may be vital to ensure adequate warmth for ripening (see HILLSIDE VINEYARDS). On the relatively rare occasions when a vineyard site may be selected in the Old World, it is, of course, just as crucial. (Most Old World vineyards have been in existence for centuries, and when a new vineyard is created, or recreated, another important consideration may be whether or not it qualifies for a certain APPELLATION.)

Vineyard site selection embraces more than just choosing the vineyard location, as the decision will affect the vineyard's YIELD, quality of the wine produced, and therefore the vineyard's long-term profitability. The site's regional climate, or MACROCLIMATE, for example, determines by virtue of temperature and sunshine hours which VINE VARIETIES should be grown, and the resulting likely wine style and quality. For example, lower temperatures produce more delicately flavoured wines, and hot climates produce wines relatively high in alcohol. Such effects are discussed under CLIMATE AND WINE QUALITY. Vineyards are often planted at higher ELEVATIONS to take advantage of lower temperatures. The site selection process might include evaluating climatic data from distinguished wine regions in an attempt to locate similar climates, or HOMOCLIMES, as has been done with considerable success in Australia. With its enormous range of LATITUDE and ELEVATION, Chile has a greater opportunity than most countries to match climates.

Modern science is creating new methods of vineyard site selection, especially based on GEOGRAPHICAL INFORMATION SYSTEMS (GIS) and digitized databases. Researchers at VIRGINIA TECH in the US, for example, have identified sites with the greatest potential by overlaying maps of the same area according to different selection criteria such as elevation and land use, slope and aspect, and winter freeze risk. Such approaches provide a useful alternative to the trial and error more usually employed.

Similarly, rainfall and humidity affect the likelihood of many VINE DISEASES, especially important fungal diseases such as POWDERY MILDEW, DOWNY MILDEW, and BOTRYTIS BUNCH ROT. The likelihood of these diseases can be estimated by reference to climate records. In addition, the threat of NEMATODES may be evaluated by knowledge of indigenous types, or of the previous crops grown on the site. It may even be possible to avoid the introduction of PHYLLOXERA and other pests and diseases by creating a local QUARANTINE. If phylloxera and nematodes are considered a likely problem, the appropriate ROOTSTOCKS can be used.

The site climate, or MESOCLIMATE, affects, for example, the extent to which cold air drains away, and the likelihood of spring and autumn FROST. A site's proximity to bodies of water such as lakes (see LAKE EFFECT) can be important in providing protection from injury due to particularly low temperatures, as in NEW YORK state and SWITZERLAND. These attributes depend on local TOPOGRAPHY.

The balance between rainfall and evaporation indicates the likelihood of DROUGHT, and for some regions at least whether IRRIGATION is desirable, and the amount of water required. In many parts of the world availability of high-quality water for irrigation is an essential factor in site selection. This may involve locating vineyards near streams or rivers, or with access to underground (artesian) water, or opportunities to build dams or reservoirs.

SOIL conditions present at the site will determine vineyard VIGOUR, with deep, fertile soils, for example, leading to vigorous growth and the possibility of high yields, but the concomitant need to manage the problems this creates (see CANOPY MANAGEMENT). Premium-quality vineyards are typically found on soils with low water-holding capacity, and low SOIL FERTILITY. Site selection normally involves a process of SOIL MAPPING and physical and chemical analysis of soil samples. This allows potential problems such as poor DRAINAGE or SOIL ACIDITY to be treated appropriately before the vineyard is planted. Knowledge of soil depth indicates likely vine vigour.

Vegetation growing at the site, and the productivity and quality of other agricultural crops grown in the region, can be used as an indicator of the vineyard performance. The types of trees present give guidance as to the soil properties, and their size for their age indicates soil fertility and water supply.

Not all important features of potential vineyard sites are natural ones. Frontage to busy roads is essential if retail sales are expected from the vineyard site. Good communications with markets and proximity to a supply of LABOUR can also be significant. The performance and reputation of other vineyards in the area can also be commercially important.   R.E.S.

Virginia Cooperative Extension, 'Vineyard site selection', http://pubs.ext.vt.edu/463/463-020/463-020.html.

vineyard weather stations contain a number of electronic instruments to measure the climate within a vineyard. Normally they comprise sensors for sunshine, air and soil temperatures, wind speed and direction, humidity, rainfall, leaf wetness, and occasionally evaporation. Data are stored in a data logger which may be downloaded to a portable computer, or remotely interrogated by a computer over a wireless or cable telephone connection or may be available via the Internet. Such weather stations are used primarily for disease prediction, especially for fungal diseases such as DOWNY MILDEW and POWDERY MILDEW, and also for predicting vine PHENOLOGY.   R.E.S.

vin gris is not, happily, a grey wine but a pink wine that is usually decidedly paler than most ROSÉ, made exactly as a white wine from dark-skinned grapes, and therefore without any MACERATION. No rules govern the term *vin gris*, but a wine labelled **gris de gris** must be made from lightly tinted grape varieties described as *gris* such as GRENACHE GRIS. or Grolleau Gris.

In France, where it is a speciality of the Côtes de TOUL in north-east France and in certain parts of the LOIRE, *vin gris* is usually made from PRESSING, but not macerating, dark-skinned grapes, often Gamay, which rarely ripen sufficiently to produce a deeply coloured red. It is also made in the Midi, notably beside the saltpans of the Camargue by Listel, where care is needed to tint rather than dye the resultant wine. The term is also occasionally encountered in the New World—although BLUSH wines are extremely similar to, if almost invariably sweeter than, *gris* wines. See also SCHILLERWEIN and other German light pinks.

The style is particularly popular in Morocco, which produces gris with an orangey-pink hue, mainly from traditional varieties such as Cinsaut and Grenache Gris, but also from Merlot and Cabernet Sauvignon. Moroccan Gris de Boulaouane is one of CASTEL's French supermarket staples.

Vinhão, official Portuguese and local MINHO name of the dark-skinned grape SOUSÃO.

vinho, Portuguese for wine, **vinho** is how Portugal's WINE WITHOUT GEOGRAPHICAL INDICATION is described on the label.

Vinho Regional, second tier of designated wine regions in Portugal. Although new terms Indicação Geográfica Protegida (IGP), sometimes shortened to Indicação Geográfica (IG), meaning Protected Geographical Indication (PGI), have been introduced since the EU wine market reforms of 2008, most Portuguese regions have chosen to keep the old denomination Vinho Regional (VR).

These large regions covering entire provinces—MINHO, TRÁS-OS-MONTES, DURIENSE for wines from the Douro, BEIRA ATLÂNTICO, TERRAS DO DÃO, TERRAS DA BEIRA, TEJO, LISBOA, Alentejano for the ALENTEJO, PENÍNSULA DE SETÚBAL, ALGARVE, and Terras Madeirenses for MADEIRA—allow greater flexibility in terms of permitted grape varieties and ageing requirements. The Vinho Regional denomination is therefore popular with innovative winemakers wishing to bottle relatively young wines or blend Portuguese and INTERNATIONAL VARIETIES. In the centre and south of the country (Lisboa, Tejo, Península de

Setúbal, and the Alentejo), producers are largely ignoring the DOCS in favour of Vinho Regional.

S.A.

Vinho Verde, dramatically improving DOP in north-west PORTUGAL known for its distinctively light, fresh wines. Vinho Verde originated as a rough and ready local wine on a domestic scale. Following fermentation in open stone LAGARES, the wine would be run off into cask where the secondary MALOLACTIC CONVERSION produced carbon dioxide. This was retained in the wine, giving it a slight sparkle. The better-known BRANDS are typically slightly sweet, sparkling, non-vintage white wines made for early consumption (*vinho verde* means 'green wine', a reference to the youthful state in which wines were customarily sold). However, since the 1980s a shift towards better viticultural practices and more PROTECTIVE WINEMAKING has challenged the old stereotype, resulting in a growing middle and upper tier of higher-quality wines from individual estates (the latter typically sub-regional VARIETAL wines). The region's verdant coastal strip (known as the Costa Verde or Green Coast) extends from Vale da Cambra south of the River DOURO to the River Minho that forms the frontier with Spain over 130 km/ 80 miles to the north (see PORTUGAL map), and the big brands (these days better made), represent most of production where rain-bearing westerly winds from the Atlantic support intensive cultivation on its granitic soils. Moreover, these fertile soils extend inland, along the rivers which criss-cross the region (and act as conduits for tempering ocean winds).

In 2011, over 129,000 vineyards totalled around 21,000 ha/51,892 acres, many little bigger than a suburban back garden. In order to make the best use of these small plots, vines were traditionally grown high above the ground on PERGOLAS, stout granite posts up to 4 m/13 ft high, leaving space for other crops underneath. Similarly, farmers trained vines on pergolas around the perimeters of fields planted to corn (once the region's biggest crop). These high-trained vines also helped to reduce the risk of GREY ROT, which is endemic during the warm, damp growing season where average annual RAINFALL is as high as 1,500 mm. However, this culture of polyculture, which remained embedded well into the last century, was neither conducive to MECHANIZATION nor quality, both of which factors had become critical to making economically viable wine once the Portuguese wine industry entered a new, more entrepreneurial (and competitive) phase following the country's EU accession. New vineyards planted (or restructured) since the 1990s are on lower TRAINING SYSTEMS, the new norm and dominant form, resulting in riper, healthier grapes. Increased professionalism in the vineyard has been mirrored in winemaking. Since the

1980s, the average ALCOHOLIC STRENGTH has increased from 9–10% to 11–12% without sacrificing the region's signature freshness.

The Vinho Verde DOP is officially divided into nine subregions, distinguished by climatic differences and the white grape varieties grown there. The subregion of MONÇÃO E MELGAÇO on the Spanish border produces one of the best but least typical Vinhos Verdes from the ALVARINHO grape, which can be up to 13% and is relatively expensive. Further south along the River Lima around the towns of Braga, Barcelos, and Guimarães, the dominant grape varieties are LOUREIRO (which thrives in the subregion of LIMA), TRAJADURA, and Pedernã (see ARINTO). Inland towards the River Douro around the town of Baião, AVESSO is the most important variety, producing a slightly fuller style of wine in a warmer, drier climate. Basic Vinhos Verdes must be between 8 and 11.5% cent alcohol so more potent basic wines are sold as VINHO REGIONAL MINHO. Vinho Verde labelled with a single variety, subregion, or quality level (Escolha, Grande Escolha, Superior, Colheita Selecionada) have different (generally higher) minimum alcohol levels and are subject only to a maximum POTENTIAL ALCOHOL of 14%. Since 1999, the DOP extends to sparkling wines (labelled espumante) made by the TRADITIONAL METHOD, which must be bottled-aged for at least nine months.

Until the 1980s, Vinho Verde was predominantly red, made in a naturally fizzy, acidic, bone-dry style from red grapes such as Azal, Vinhão, and Espadeiro. Examples of deep-coloured, rasping reds still exist and are prized locally, but little leaves the north of Portugal. Some of the new breed of single estates now make deeper-fruited, still reds, sometimes even oaked.

See also MINHO.   S.A.

de Castro, R., 'The viticulture of Vinho Verde—the early days and from the turn of the century to the present', in Fundação Francisco Girão, *Francisco Girão: An Innovator in Viticulture in the North of Portugal* (Volume II, 2011, Porto).

www.cvrtejo.com

viniculture. While some use this term interchangeably with VITICULTURE, we use it to denote both vine-growing and a culture of wine drinking.

vinifera, more correctly *Vitis vinifera* or *V. vinifera*, the European species of VITIS that is the vine most used for wine production, to which all the most familiar VINE VARIETIES belong. *Vinifera* is not a classical Latin word, but one made up by Linnaeus (see BOTANICAL CLASSIFICATION) to denote 'wine-grape bearing'.

The species is thought to originate in south-eastern Anatolia or in Transcaucasia (see ORIGINS OF VINICULTURE), and has been spread through the Mediterranean and Europe by the

Phoenicians and Greeks and later by the Romans. *Vinifera* was spread through the New World, initially by Cortés in SOUTH AMERICA, and subsequently into western North America. The Dutch took *vinifera* grapevines to the Cape of Good Hope in 1616 (see SOUTH AFRICA), and the English to Australia, then New Zealand, beginning in 1788.

Vinifera is one of about 60 species of the *Vitis* genus, the majority of which originate in the Americas or Asia. *Vinifera* grapes are used principally for winemaking, table grapes, and drying grapes. See VINE for more details. There are some 5,000 to 10,000 *vinifera* VINE VARIETIES, grouped into three PROLES.

Vitis vinifera is distinguished from other *Vitis* species by a range of general botanical features, including vigorous shoots mostly free of hair, prominent NODES and BUDS, regularly intermittent TENDRILS, leaves generally orbicular, more or less deeply lobed, PETIOLAR sinus often in a U or lyre shape, and conspicuous dentation (so-called teeth) around the edge of the leaf. *Vinifera* flowers are typically hermaphroditic (both male and female), and there are differences in seeds too (see GRAPE). Because *vinifera* vines are selected for their fruit characters, the seeds typically represent a small proportion of the berry weight, 10% compared with 80% for *Vitis berlandieri*.

Further details about *vinifera* can be found under the following entries, which describe more fully aspects of the commercial culture of this species, emphasizing its use in winemaking. Especially important are the effects of CLIMATE and SOIL. See also VINE VARIETIES, VINE GROWTH CYCLE, VINE BREEDING, VINE DISEASES, VINE MORPHOLOGY, VINE PESTS, VINE PHYSIOLOGY, VINE PRODUCTS, VINE TRAINING, and VITICULTURE.

R.E.S. & J.V.

Robinson, J., Harding, J., and Vouillamoz, J., *Wine Grapes: A Complete Guide to 1,368 Vine Varieties, including their Origins and Flavours* (London & New York, 2012).

vinification, the practical art of transforming grapes into wine. In its widest sense, it is synonymous with WINEMAKING, but strictly encompasses only those processes which take place in the winery up to the point at which the ÉLEVAGE of the new wine begins. See also OENOLOGY.

vin jaune, meaning literally 'yellow wine' in French, extraordinary style of wine made in France, mainly in the JURA region, using a technique similar to that used for making SHERRY but without FORTIFICATION.

In the Jura, where the most famous *vin jaune* appellation is CHÂTEAU-CHALON, the wine must be made from the signature local white grape variety the SAVAGNIN, grown ideally on MARL. The grapes are picked well ripened, often not until late October, ideally at about 13 to 13.5% POTENTIAL ALCOHOL, to allow for an increase during the ageing process, and fermented as normal. The wine is then put into old 228-l/ 60-gal casks usually not quite filled so that the local benevolent FILM-FORMING YEAST, called here the *voile* or veil, can develop on the surface. It is similar to the FLOR which is responsible for FINO sherries but can develop at a lower alcoholic strength and a much thinner layer, coloured grey, is considered the best. The ageing 'cellars' (which may be above or below ground) are ventilated deliberately to allow temperature fluctuations during which the activity of the *voile* will change. The presence of the veil prevents severe OXIDATION, but the important factor in making *vin jaune* is that for at least five years the wine is left in cask, untouched other than to allow regular sampling to check the amount of ETHANAL formed (a crucial compound for the taste of *vin jaune*) and for a dangerous rise in VOLATILE ACIDS. It may not be bottled for a full six years and three months after the harvest. Inoculation or seeding of yeasts to form the *voile* for Savagnin and even Chardonnay wines was introduced in the 1970s, and today this is used by some producers, but is disapproved of by purists who believe that natural methods produce a better wine and are reliable if 'cellar' conditions are right and barrels have previously held wine aged under the *voile*.

The finest *vin jaune* from the best vintages will last for 50 or more years in its distinctive 62-cl *clavelin* bottle (the amount of wine left after keeping a litre in a cask for six years, supposedly). Research in the 1990s showed that the compound SOTOLON develops in bottle, providing the distinct spicy or light 'curry' flavours in *vin jaune*. The wine should be served at cellar temperature or warmer and the bottle should be opened well in advance. The wine may be drunk with all sorts of savoury dishes, particularly of course chicken cooked in the wine itself, a classic dish, and the local Comté cheese.

A similar wine, called *vin de voile*, is made by at least one producer in GAILLAC. Other isolated French producers are also experimenting, as are some Australian producers growing Savagnin.

W.L.

Vínland. Driven westward by overpopulation in the second half of the 9th century, the Scandinavians colonized Iceland, then Greenland, and finally, a century later, as some sources tell us, Vínland, 'Wine Land', which must have been on the east coast of America.

Two sagas, Grenlinga Saga, the 'Saga of the Greenlanders', composed in the late 12th century, and Eirik's Saga, dated mid 13th century, give accounts of the discovery of Vínland,

where wild vines, wheat, grassland and game are found.

Scholars do not agree on the precise location of Vínland. The sagas do not give clues, and, although archaeologists have found what appear to be traces of Norse settlements on the east coast of America, the evidence is not conclusive. Besides, the climate was warmer around AD 1000 than now (hence the colonization of Greenland; see CLIMATE CHANGE) so that vines could survive further north.

Even though the stories told in the sagas differ in some respects, they are not fantasy. An earlier and unrelated source supports the existence of Vínland. Around 1075 Adam of Bremen wrote a history of the archbishopric of Bremen and Hamburg, which until 1104 included the Scandinavian countries. Adam travelled to the royal court of Denmark, where King Svein Ulfsson, nephew of King Canute, tells him that Vínland has wild vines, which make excellent wine, and also wild wheat. So were the first winemakers in America Norse colonists? But if they were, the wine must have been made not from the European *Vitis* VINIFERA, but from native AMERICAN VINE SPECIES, almost certainly VITIS *labrusca*, which grows wild on the eastern coast of the United States.   H.M.W.

Jones, G., *The Norse Atlantic Saga Being the Norse Voyages of Discovery and Settlement to Iceland, Greenland, America* (Oxford, 1964).

Magnusson, M., and Pálsson, H., *The Vínland Sagas* (Harmondsworth, 1965).

vin muté, wine that has undergone MUTAGE.

vino, Italian and Spanish for wine and, colloquially and unfairly, English for basic quaffing wine, or PLONK. In Italy and Spain, the term has replaced VINO DA TAVOLA and VINO DE MESA respectively as the most basic level of wine, WINE WITHOUT GEOGRAPHICAL INDICATION.

vino da meditazione, unofficial Italian category of wines considered too complex but often simply too alcoholic and/or sweet to drink with food. Such wines, many of them extra strong and/or sweet because they are DRIED-GRAPE WINES, are probably best sipped meditatively after a meal.

Although they do not employ the same terminology, and produce wines much lighter in alcohol, some Germans effectively treat fine wine as a *vino da meditazione* to be drunk once the table has been cleared of food and, often, beer.

vino da tavola, Italian for TABLE WINE, was the official EU category denoting the lowest of the vinous low until 2009 when it was replaced with VINO. It also played a key role in the transformation of Italian wines in the late 20th century. Historically the great majority of each Italian wine harvest qualified as basic Vino da

Tavola, but the designation was for a period worn as a badge of honour by some of the finest, and most expensive, wines produced in Italy but that did not conform to the DOC laws of the time.

These new **vini da tavola** were born in 1974 with the commercial debut of TIGNANELLO and SASSICAIA, both marketed by the Florentine house of ANTINORI. Although the wines were produced in different geographical zones (CHIANTI CLASSICO and BOLGHERI respectively) and from different grape varieties (a predominance of Sangiovese and Cabernet Sauvignon respectively), they shared four significant characteristics that were to mark the evolution of this category of wines. They both represented an attempt to give more body, intensity, and longevity to Tuscan red wines, which had become lean and attenuated. Unlike the prevailing Tuscan red wine norm, these blends excluded white grapes. Non-traditional, non-Italian varieties were used in both blends (from 1975 when Tignanello substituted Cabernet Sauvignon for the native CANAIOLO). And, in a move that was to delight French COOPERS, small oak barrels, principally of French origin, were used for the BARREL MATURATION of both wines. This latter innovation was a radical break with the traditional practice of using large casks of Slavonian oak, and marked a general movement towards an international style. The move was not welcomed by all in the domestic market and forced Antinori to seek a wider international public for the wines.

The vini da tavola were born out of frustration with the DOC laws that came into practice in the late 1960s. These laws enshrined the practices of low quality and high quantity that prevailed in Italy in the post-war years, so producers trying to pursue a quality route found their way blocked by absurd laws. In Chianti, for instance, producers were compelled by DOC laws to add at least 10% white grapes to their blend. Any producer wishing to produce a superior red wine had to ignore this stipulation. Rather than do battle, they stepped outside the legal framework at the urging of Italian wine journalist Luigi VERONELLI, a vehement opponent of the mediocrity of the DOC laws.

INTERNATIONAL VARIETIES were enthusiastically planted and other Cabernet Sauvignon-based wines began to appear in the image of Sassicaia, particularly after the mid-1980s. The native Sangiovese grape was hardly neglected, however, and a substantial number of BARRIQUE-aged, 100% Sangiovese wines were also launched, as vini da tavola, in the 1980s, following in the path of Montevertine's Le Pergole Torte whose first vintage was 1977.

Experiments with earlier maturing varieties SYRAH and, with notable success, MERLOT became increasingly common in the late 1980s, both for blending with Sangiovese and for VARIETAL wines. Some non-traditional white varieties were also planted, notably CHARDONNAY and SAUVIGNON BLANC, and various OAK treatments essayed with variable success.

Sassicaia was a pioneering wine, not only in its use of Cabernet but also in its revaluation of a zone never known for producing fine or even commercial wine. When first offered commercially, Sassicaia had to be sold as a Vino da Tavola, not because, as with Tignanello, it eschewed the legal constraints of the area, but because there was no DOC for BOLGHERI reds at the time. Its example was rapidly followed by other peripheral areas of Tuscany. At the time, these could not qualify as DOC wines, just as non-traditional varietal wines in an area such as Chianti Classico cannot be given DOC status. Such wines, with their ambitious price tags, came to be known as SUPERTUSCANS.

Inspired by these highly-priced Tuscan 'outlaws', ambitious producers in other regions, saddled with poorly conceived DOCs and/or a poor image for the wines of their zone, were quick to launch their own vini da tavola, in some instances even when they could have qualified as DOC wines. Some of these wines returned to the DOC fold in the 1990s, partly as a result of the greater prestige and credibility now accorded to the wines of their zones and regions, but many important wines were still deliberately sold as vini da tavola in the mid 2000s. In 1992, the Italian government finally bowed to EU pressure and introduced the Goria law, named after the then Minister of Agriculture. This led to the introduction with the 1994 vintage of the IGT designation, which eventually resulted in the phasing out of such vini da tavola.

See also SUPERTUSCAN.

Vino de Calidad (con indicación geográfica), transitory Spanish denomination between VINO DE LA TIERRA/IGP and DOP/DO, of which there were seven in 2014. It identified wines 'produced and vinified in a specific area or place, with grapes of the same origin' with some degree of recognition and quality. Eventually this denomination is to be merged, with DO, into DOP. V. de la S.

Vino de la Tierra, wines from legally designated zones in SPAIN which have not qualified for DOP status. With changes to EU denominations (see PGI), this category is now known as IGP or Indicación Geográfica Protegida, a term which can also be found on Spanish labels and which may eventually replace it.

Vino de Mesa, the old Spanish term for TABLE WINE, the most basic category of wine now known as WINE WITHOUT GEOGRAPHICAL INDICATION.

Vino de Pago, special Spanish category of supposedly exceptionally high-quality, single-estate wines, granted their own appellation. By

2014 there were 15, arguably too many. See also PAGO.

Vino Nobile di Montepulciano, potentially majestic and certainly noble red wine based on SANGIOVESE, called Prugnolo Gentile here, made exclusively in the township of Montepulciano 120 km/75 miles south east of Florence in the hills of TUSCANY in central Italy. Vino Nobile has an illustrious history, having been lauded as a 'perfect wine' by the cellarmaster of Pope Paul III in 1549, by Francesco Redi in his 'Bacchus in Toscana' of 1685 (he called it 'the king of wines'), while the first record of the official name dates from 1787 when it was listed in the expense accounts of Giovan Filippo Neri for a trip to Siena. After the introduction of the DOC in 1966, from 1970 and 2011, the total vineyard rose from less than 150 ha/370 acres in 1970 to 1,300 ha in 2011, while the number of producers bottling their own wine increased from seven or eight to 230.

Vino Nobile di Montepulciano was one of the first four DOCGs conferred in 1980. Traditionally, producers would have blended in Canaiolo, Mammolo, Trebbiano, and even Gamay, but since the mid 1980s Sangiovese has come to the fore as the principal variety of Montepulciano. Following a change to the DOCG regulations in 1999, the wine must contain between 70 and 100% Sangiovese, while in 2009 the production regulations were changed to allow up to 30% of varieties such as Cabernet Sauvignon, Merlot, and Syrah into the blend, reflecting what was already common practice. This amendment was criticized widely as the 'internationalization' of a historic Tuscan wine.

The region is generally higher in sand than either Montalcino or Chianti Classico, and consists of two distinct zones: the hills around the township of Montepulciano and, about 10 km to the west and separated by the Val di Chiana plain, the hills around the township of Valiano, the latter dominated by extensive holdings. It is further divided into 20 subzones whose names may appear on labels, although further research into their individual characteristics is needed. Vines are planted on east- to southeast-facing slopes at elevations of 250 m to 600 m/2,000 ft, while vineyards on the plain do not qualify as Vino Nobile.

Stylistically Vino Nobile sits between CHIANTI CLASSICO and BRUNELLO DI MONTALCINO, combining the elegance of the first with the firm structure of the latter. It is notably deep in colour, due to the heavy, cool clay and sand soils which result in austere, muscular Sangiovese that demands BOTTLE AGE. Many producers blend in Merlot to accelerate the wine's evolution but it can blur TERROIR expression. The DOC Rosso di Montepulciano, which allows the wines to be released in March following the vintage (Vino Nobile must be aged for two years), was created

for earlier-maturing wines but, because it is much less profitable than Vino Nobile, it is not widely used.

Two contrasting philosophies determine the style of Vino Nobile produced today: a traditional approach using Sangiovese either on its own or blended with CANAIOLO and aged in large casks of Slavonian oak and generally requiring prolonged ageing; and a more modern approach in which Sangiovese is blended with INTERNATIONAL VARIETIES, notably Merlot and Syrah, and aged in new French oak. This modern style, although still dominant, has been losing ground because it results in wines that are less recognizably Vino Nobile. The traditional approach has been criticized as outdated, but a few practitioners such as Contucci and Boscarelli have shown that it can yield wines on a par with Brunello and Chianti Classico. W.S.

www.consorziovinonobile.it

Vino Santo. See VIN SANTO.

Vin Santo, 'holy wine', TUSCANY's classic amber-coloured dessert wine, is produced throughout this central Italian region. It is made traditionally from the local white grapes TREBBIANO Toscano and MALVASIA (although the red SANGIOVESE is also used to produce a wine called Occhio di Pernice, or eye of the partridge) which have been dried on straw mats under the rafters, in the hottest and best-ventilated part of the peasant home (see DRIED-GRAPE WINES). The grapes were normally crushed between the end of November and the end of March, depending on the desired RESIDUAL SUGAR level in the wine (the longer the drying process, the greater the evaporation and the sweeter the must), and then aged in small barrels holding between 50 l and 300 l/79 gal. These barrels, often bought second hand from the south of Italy, were frequently made of chestnut, but the 1980s saw a decisive turn towards OAK. The barrels themselves are sealed and never topped up, resulting inevitably in ULLAGE and OXIDATION which gives the wine a RANCIO-like aroma and its characteristic amber colour. Some producers believe in using a madre, or starter culture, comprised of yeast cells from previous batches of Vin Santo in order to help the fermentation and to add complexity to the blend. Others, in true Tuscan fashion, view the madre as a throwback to the time when all Vin Santo was marred by faults and refuse to countenance its use.

The wine comes in a bewildering range of styles from the ultra-sweet to a bone-dry version which more closely resembles a dry FINO sherry than a dessert wine. The habit of keeping the barrels under the roof in a space called the vinsantaia encouraged refermentation each year when warm weather arrived and tended to exhaust the unfermented sugars that had remained in the wine. Today, most producers keep their Vin Santo in a cellar with a more constant temperature so as to retain a degree of freshness in the finished wines.

Until recently, most Vin Santo was sold as a VINO DA TAVOLA, simply because the authorities had struggled to codify the bewildering array of styles contained within the many localized traditions. The DOCs under which Vin Santo is now produced include Chianti Classico, Chianti Rufina, Chianti, Montepulciano, Colli dell'-Etruria Centrale, and Val d'Arbia. Trebbiano and Malvasia remain the mainstay of many of these DOCs, as a number of producers argue that the production technique is far more important in determining the style of the eventual wine than the grape varieties used.

The quality of the wine itself varies wildly, not only as a result of variation in grape composition, RESIDUAL SUGAR, and winemaking competence, but because the land is divided between so many smallholders, all of whom seem to feel obliged to produce Vin Santo as an obeisance to the tradition of offering this wine to guests as a gesture of esteem. Although some delicious Vin Santo is made, there is also a considerable proportion with serious wine FAULTS, particularly an excess of VOLATILITY, usually a direct consequence of lengthy BARREL MATURATION. DOC rules insist the wine is matured for at least three years, and the better producers rarely release their Vin Santo before five years. Cask maturation, without RACKING, may last for up to ten years for the most traditionally made wines.

Producers who manage to produce traditional yet fault-free Vin Santo include Avignonesi, Capezzana, Fontodi, Isole e Olena, Felsina Berardenga, Poliziano, Rocca di Montegrossi, San Giusto a Rentennano, and Selvapiana. The advent of DOC for Vin Santo sounded the death knell for **Vin Santo Liquoroso**, which was made by adding grape spirit to sweet must, and produced in four months rather than four years. An official decree stated that the name Vin Santo could only be used on wines of orgin (DOCs), so Vin Santo Liquoroso was thankfully eased off the shelves.

Trentino also produces its own version of Vin Santo called **Vino Santo**, made from the NOSIOLA grape and a decisively sweet DRIED-GRAPE WINE. These wines are quite different from Tuscan Vin Santo since they are aged in barrels subject to regular TOPPING UP, although they too are decidedly artisanal and very variable in quality.

D.C.G.

Vinsanto is the official term for the sweet wines of SANTORINI.

Tachis, G., *Il libro del Vin Santo* (Florence, 1988).

Vins de Moselle. See MOSELLE.

Vinsobres, one of the better Côtes du Rhône villages, awarded its own red wine appellation in 2006. The relatively high, cool vineyards, which suit Syrah better than most in the southern Rhône, totalled 441 ha/1,089 acres in 2013. The wine must include at least 80% Grenache with the rest of the blend made up of the usual southern RHÔNE varieties.

vintage can either mean the physical process of grape-picking and winemaking, for which see HARVEST, or it can mean the year or growing season which produced a particular wine, for which see VINTAGE YEAR. A vintage wine is one made from the produce of a single year.

vintage assessment is important enough to have an immediate effect on PRICE but is also notoriously difficult because quality and character can vary so much between producers and properties. A vintage is often assessed at the most difficult stage in its life, its infancy, for reasons of commerce and curiosity. Wine MERCHANTS and WINE WRITERS habitually taste wines from the most recent vintage in a wine region important for INVESTMENT when they are just a few months old and are still in cask (see EN PRIMEUR). Quite apart from the fact that the wines are at this stage still being made (see ÉLEVAGE), samples may give a misleading impression because they have been specially chosen and groomed to show particularly well at this early stage, or too long has elapsed since they were drawn from cask (OXIDATION is a common problem), or, if they are tasted directly from cask, because they are undergoing a distorting treatment such as FINING. Furthermore, this sort of vintage assessment may be before the ASSEMBLAGE process and provides only a snapshot of embryonic wine from a small proportion of the total number of barrels produced.

This sort of comparative tasting can usually give some indication as to which are the most and least successful wines of a given vintage, but it can be difficult to stand back from the individual samples, accurately remember exactly how the same wines from previous vintages tasted at the same stage, and make any reliable assessment of the likely characteristics and potential of the young vintage as a whole. Vintages of which the collective assessment at this young stage was subsequently agreed to have been too enthusiastic include 1975 in Bordeaux and 1983 and 1996 in Burgundy, but other examples abound. (Wine merchants have proved themselves much less likely to err on the side of caution, although 2001 Bordeaux is generally agreed to have been underestimated.)

The assessment of a mature vintage is a much less hazardous process that is usually undertaken in the form of a horizontal TASTING, although of course SUBJECTIVITY plays its part as it does in all tasting.

Broadbent, M., *Great Vintage Wine Book II* (London, 1991).
Broadbent, M., *Wine Vintages* (London, 1998).

vintage charts are both useful and notoriously fallible, partly because young VINTAGE ASSESSMENT is so fraught with difficulty. Most vintage charts take the form of a grid mapping ratings for each combination of wine region and year. The least sophisticated vintage charts content themselves with a NUMBER for each major wine region: Bordeaux 2010 was given '9' (out of 10), for instance. More sophisticated charts (such as that regularly updated in Robert PARKER's newsletter) divide Bordeaux into its main districts, and add a letter indicating maturity: Margaux 2003 '91T' (91 out of 100, T for Still Tannic) in 2013, for instance. The fact that this same vintage chart suggests that Pomerol 2003 is '84E' (E for Early maturing) already demonstrates how difficult it is to generalize about a district in which there may be hundreds of different producers, each with a different winemaking policy and style of wine.

The most useful vintage charts are the most detailed, but also those that are regularly updated on the basis of continuous and relevant tasting. The INTERNATIONAL WINE & FOOD SOCIETY was one of the first to issue a vintage chart, in 1935. The Society has since then issued an annual vintage chart, updated by a committee expressly charged with this task.

vintage port, in France often called *le vintage*. See PORT.

vintage year, the year in which a wine was produced and the characteristics of that year. Most, but not all, of its characteristics result from particular WEATHER conditions experienced. In the southern hemisphere, a **vintage-dated** wine invariably carries the year in which the grapes were picked, even though much of the VINE GROWTH CYCLE was actually in the previous year. In the northern hemisphere, vintage-dated wines carry the year in which both the vine growth occurred and the grapes were picked (with the exception of those rare examples of EISWEIN picked in early January, which are dated with the year whose vine growth produced the wine). The expression 'vintage year' is also sometimes used of a year producing particularly high-quality wines.

In a literal sense, all newly fermented wine is vintage wine, being from a single year. Only at the BLENDING stage may wine of a recent year, or vintage, be mixed with older wines into an undated blend. Many everyday wines—such as the JUG WINES of the US and CASK WINE in Australia—are not vintage dated. Some top-quality CHAMPAGNE, most SHERRY is, and many other FORTIFIED WINES are NON-VINTAGE too. In most other circumstances, however, a non-vintage wine is inferior to a vintage-dated one. For wines designated within the EU as WINE WITHOUT GEOGRAPHICAL INDICATION, the vintage date is now optional.

The vintage year printed on a wine label can help the consumer decide when to open a particular bottle, being particularly relevant to wine meant for AGEING (others, the great majority of wines, should simply be drunk as young as possible). Since the capacity of a wine to improve with age is one obvious test of its quality, a vintage's status is only fully established in retrospect (whatever those charged with selling it may say; see VINTAGE ASSESSMENT).

The concept of vintage year has a long history. OPIMIAN wine, made in the consular year of Lucius Opimius, 121 BC, was celebrated for decades afterwards as a particularly fine vintage. The celebrated RHINE Steinwein of AD 1540, last drunk in 1961, was made in a freak year so hot and dry that the Rhine dried up, and people could walk across its bed.

Vintage years did not become a normal commercial consideration until the end of the 17th century, when BOTTLES and CORKS replaced BARRELS for long-term wine storage. Vintages became particularly important towards the end of the 18th century, when the modern bottle shape evolved, allowing bottles to be stored on their sides. The better red wines of Bordeaux came to be 'laid down' for many years, and it was then that what is now regarded as the traditional Bordeaux style of winemaking for prolonged BOTTLE AGEING became established.

Broadbent gives details of some of the more famous Bordeaux vintages. The celebrated 1784 clarets, sought out and imported by America's wine-loving President Thomas JEFFERSON, were from one of the many fine vintages spanning the late 18th century and first years of the 19th century, culminating in the reputedly outstanding 'comet' year of 1811. Other runs of predominantly good Bordeaux vintages followed in the 1840s and again in the 1860s and the first half of the 1870s: a period long remembered as the crowning glory of the PRE-PHYLLOXERA era. The limited climatic records available suggest that these were predominantly warm periods.

Vintage years in contemporary Bordeaux, and throughout central and western Europe, tend still to be those of ample sunshine (especially in spring, and again in late July and August), and average or higher TEMPERATURES leading to a normal or early HARVEST date. Bad vintage years have almost invariably been cool and/or wet, with below-average sunshine.

In hot and reliably sunny viticultural climates, on the other hand, the best years for table wines are usually average or cooler than average. This generalization does not apply to sweet FORTIFIED WINES, which need more or less unlimited warmth and sunshine. Nor does it necessarily apply to all table wines, or all hot areas. For instance, wet, cloudy, and relatively cool summers in the very warm Hunter Valley of NEW SOUTH WALES are usually inferior for red table wines, although they may still produce good-quality white table wines.

The reactions of vines and grapes to seasonal conditions or weather events can also differ widely according to SOIL TYPE within an area. As demonstrated by the extensive studies of Seguin in Bordeaux, vines on well-drained, deep soils may be little affected by variations in RAINFALL, whereas those on shallow and poorly drained soils will alternate between drought stress and waterlogging under the same rainfall. For this reason the best vineyards, with favourable TERROIR, are the least subject to vintage variation and can maintain consistently high quality.

In addition, VINE VARIETIES can react quite differently to the weather conditions depending on their individual timings of BUDBREAK, FLOWERING, and RIPENESS, and the relative sensitivities of their berries to rain, diseases, or damaging heat. PINOT NOIR, like most other early-maturing red grape varieties, is very sensitive to heat or direct exposure of the berries to SUNLIGHT, readily suffering *coups de soleil*, or SUNBURN. ZINFANDEL, with its tightly packed bunches, is notoriously sensitive to any rain towards harvest time. The least rain and water uptake causes berry splitting and subsequent total BUNCH ROT. This is probably the main reason its extensive use is confined to California and Puglia, where the ripening season is free of rain. CHENIN BLANC is similarly susceptible, at least in climates such as those of California and South Africa, where the preceding weather is mostly hot and dry. By contrast the CABERNET SAUVIGNON of Bordeaux is relatively tolerant of both heat and rain, and is therefore generally less affected by vintage differences, so long as the weather has been warm enough to ripen it.

A final point is that critical weather events, particularly heavy rainfall and HAIL, are not necessarily uniform within a given district and year. Even if they were, management decisions can lead to quite different results—depending, for instance, on the extent to which SPRAYING has been practised, or whether grapes are picked before, during, or after rains at harvest time.

Nor is weather the only possible external influence on the characteristics of a particular vintage year. Market conditions may dictate how or whether certain viticultural practices such as PRUNING and CROP THINNING are carried out so as to influence crop quality or yield. Social history may also dictate some characteristics of a vintage year, as in some of the vintages ripened in European vineyards during the Second World War. There have also been rare instances of CONTAMINANTS from a new pesticide, for example, which have affected particular vintages of certain wines, sometimes on a less than localized scale, as in the use of Orthene in Germany in 1983.

For all these reasons, vintages are seldom uniformly good, medium, or bad, even within a small area (see VINTAGE ASSESSMENT). A

generally recognized 'vintage' year can have its failures, often for reasons totally beyond the competence of vignerons and winemakers. Equally, 'poor' vintages can usually still produce good wines from particular locations and grape varieties, either because of the characteristics of the TERROIR or thanks to more precise vineyard management, or both.

See AUCTIONS and INVESTMENT IN WINE. See also LABELLING INFORMATION.   J.G. & R.E.S.

Seguin, G., ' "Terroirs" and pedology of wine growing', *Experientia*, 42 (1986), 861–72.

Broadbent, M., *Vintage Wine* (London, 2002).

www.jancisrobinson.com/categories/vintages. html.

vintner, late Middle English word for wine MERCHANT which superseded **vinter**. Mainly because of England's links with BORDEAUX, vintners were some of the most important people in the City of London in the 14th and early 15th centuries (four mayors of London were vintners in Edward II's reign). The **Vintners' Company** evolved from the 'Mistery of Vintners', a group of London and Gascon merchants who enjoyed a practical monopoly on London's important wine trade with Gascony from at least 1364. It was formally incorporated in 1437, and was recognized by Henry VIII as one of the '12 great' livery companies. It is still based at **Vintners' Hall** by the Thames in London, in a section of the City known as Vintry ward, where for centuries wine would be unloaded from ship for sale throughout southern England. Independently of UK licensing restrictions, the Vintners' Company may grant Free Vintner status to members, allowing them to sell wine under certain conditions. Both the WSET and the Institute of MASTERS OF WINE are the result of initiatives of the Vintners' Company.

The word has also come to be used for a wine producer as well as a wine merchant, particularly in North America. KENDALL-JACKSON's Vintners Reserve Chardonnay is one of the most successful BRANDS in the US.

Simon, A., *History of the Wine Trade in England*, ii (London, 1964).

vin viné is a traditional term for a wine made strong and sweet by the addition of alcohol to grape must at some point before fermentation is complete. A VIN DOUX NATUREL and a VIN DE LIQUEUR are both therefore *vins vinés*. See also MUTAGE.

Viognier became one of the world's most fashionable white grape varieties in the early 1990s, mainly because its most famous wine CONDRIEU is distinctive, was associated with the modish RHÔNE, and was then relatively scarce. By the mid 2000s, it was planted all over the Languedoc and had spread to the great majority of the world's wine regions, and in Australia had become a common blending partner with various red grapes, especially SYRAH, for CO-FERMENTATION, copying traditional practice in CÔTE RÔTIE. CHÂTEAU GRILLET is the only other all-Viognier French appellation. DNA PROFILING has shown a parent–offspring relationship with MONDEUSE BLANCHE, and therefore, not unexpectedly, a close one with SYRAH. It also suggests a close genetic relationship with FREISA from Piedmont, a likely progeny of NEBBIOLO, making Viognier a cousin of Nebbiolo—something of a surprise.

The vines need a relatively warm climate and can withstand drought well but are prone to POWDERY MILDEW. The grapes are a deep yellow and the resulting wine is high in colour, alcohol, and a very particular perfume redolent of apricots, peaches, and blossom sometimes with a deeply savoury undertow. Condrieu is one of the few highly priced white wines that should probably be drunk young, while this perfume is at its most heady and before the wine's slightly low acidity fades.

The vine was at one time a common crop on the farmland south of Lyons and has been grown on the infertile terraces of the northern Rhône for centuries but its extremely low productivity, often due to COULURE, saw it decline to an official total of just 14 ha/35 acres in the French agricultural census of 1968—mostly in the three northern Rhône appellations in which it is allowed, Condrieu, the only other all-Viognier French appellation CHÂTEAU GRILLET, and, to an even lesser extent, CÔTE RÔTIE, in which it may be included as a stabilizing agent up to 20% but usually closer to 5% of the Syrah-dominated total.

French nurserymen saw an increase in demand for Viognier cuttings from the mid 1980s, however (when the red wines of the Rhône enjoyed a renaissance of popularity), and by 1988 were selling half a million a year. By 1997, more than 100 ha/250 acres of Viognier qualified for the Condrieu appellation and by the turn of the century, Viognier plantings throughout the LANGUEDOC-ROUSSILLON had reached 1,540 ha (from 139 ha in 1993). By 2011, this total was almost 4,000 ha. Considerable further plantings in the northern and southern Rhône, many of them outside appellation boundaries, took the total French area of Viognier up to 5,874 ha by 2011—quite a contrast to 50 years earlier. French Viognier is often sold as a relatively inexpensive VARIETAL although here and elsewhere the variety has shown itself a willing and able blending partner, not just with other Rhône varieties such as ROUSSANNE, MARSANNE, GRENACHE BLANC, and VERMENTINO/ROLLE, but also, usefully, with Chardonnay. This latter blend has had some success in Italy, where total plantings had grown to more than 1,000 ha by 2010. Graf Hardegg makes some fine varietal Viognier in Austria

and it has its champions, such as Gerovassiliou of Greece, in many European wine regions but is rarely planted to any great extent.

California has the world's second biggest area of Viognier planted: just over 3,000 acres/1,215 ha in 2012, much of it in the Central Coast. Many examples are notably high in alcohol when ripened under the reliable California sun, but Viognier has to be fully ripe before it reveals its trademark heady aromas. So seductive is it that there has been considerable experimentation with it all over North America, particularly in VIRGINIA which has adopted it as its signature white wine and also in Washington, Oregon, Texas, and British Columbia. By 2011, Argentina had more than 800 ha and Chile had almost 300 ha, both of them having made some convincing examples of this popular variety which is also planted in Brazil and, with particular success, in Uruguay. Australian producers, led by Yalumba, have welcomed it with particular enthusiasm, using it both as a varietal white wine and as a 5–10% blend with Shiraz. Total plantings had reached 1,194 ha by 2012. In New Zealand it is generally slightly less expressive but was planted on 160 ha by 2012. South Africa has been catching up fast and had 884 ha widely spread around the country by 2012. Today the consumer can choose from a range of recognizably perfumed, if slightly light, southern French varietal Viogniers, some of them produced from vines FIELD GRAFTED over to Viognier from less fashionable varieties, some of them perhaps perfumed by other aromas including a dollop of Muscat. The California way with Viognier is a notably alcoholic one, but when it works these monsters can be magnificent.

Viosinho, distinctive white variety producing some fine, aromatic white wines, especially at higher elevations, in the DOURO and Trás-os-Montes. Traditionally a constituent of white PORT, Viosinho is now also used to make unfortified wines and, partly because of its low yields and tendency to oxidize, it is generally blended with RABIGATO and GOUVEIO (Godello). Total plantings were 783 ha/1,934 acres in 2012.

Viré-Clessé, white wine appellation created in 1998 by separating out two of the top Mâcon-Villages, noted not just for their quality but for the rich style of their wines. Bizarrely, the appellation initially banned wines with residual sugar such as those made by Jean Thévenet of Domaine de la Bon Gran, but common sense subsequently prevailed. Although most wines are vinified dry, Viré-Clessé tends to produce heady, full-bodied whites of a sunny disposition. J.T.C.M.

Virgil (Publius Vergilius Maro) (70–19 BC), Latin poet and good, if unoriginal, source of information on viticulture in Ancient ROME.

Like HORACE, Virgil benefited from the patronage of the Emperor Augustus, and much of his poetry was written in praise of Roman and Italian virtues. The rural virtues are expounded in the *Georgics*, a didactic poem about agriculture, published in 37 BC. The second of the four books is devoted mainly to vine-growing. Although it is of little use as a practical manual, it does give a lively and colourful picture of the life and problems of the vine-grower. Like HESIOD, Virgil's purpose was moral, and his main concern is to describe the farmer's virtues of austerity, integrity, and hard work, which made Rome great. Although Virgil is from a literary point of view a more interesting writer than his chief source VARRO, he is not an independent authority, and it is to his predecessors CATO and Varro, and to the later COLUMELLA and PLINY, that we must turn for first-hand information about Roman viticulture. H.M.W. & H.H.A.

Griffin, J., *Latin Literature and Roman Life* (London, 1985).

Johnston, P. A., *Virgil's Agricultural Golden Age: A Study of the Georgics* (Leiden, 1980).

Virginia, mid-Atlantic state in the eastern UNITED STATES in which wine production has increased substantially since 1980. Grapes have been planted there since the early settlers came to Jamestown in 1607, making the first wine in the New World from indigenous grapes. It is to Thomas JEFFERSON, however, that credit is given for importing fine French wines to his estate at Monticello (now an AVA in central Virginia), and for attempting, unsuccessfully, to grow and vinify VINIFERA varieties. *Vinifera* grapes now outnumber HYBRIDS and native grapes by almost 4 : 1. Chardonnay and the red Bordeaux varieties do exceptionally well, and interesting wines are also made from Norton, Touriga Nacional, Tannat, Petit Verdot, Viognier and Petit Manseng. The growing season is warm and humid so growers have to guard against FUNGAL DISEASES by careful selection of site and variety, CANOPY MANAGEMENT, and SPRAYING regimes. The total number of wineries increased from 6 in 1979 to more than 200 by 2014. Six other AVAs are Virginia's Eastern Shore, influenced by the Chesapeake bay; Northern Neck George Washington Birthplace in northern Virginia close to the ready market of Washington, DC; Shenandoah Valley (not to be confused with the California AVA) bounded by the Allegheny mountains to the west, the Blue Ridge mountains to the east, the James river to the south, and the Potomac river to the north; North Fork of Roanoke; Rocky Knob in southwest Virginia, and the newest, Middleburg, 50 miles west of Washington, DC.

Encouraged by an unusually engaged state government mindful of the TOURISM potential, Virginia winemakers have lifted their game and diversified in recent years. Thibaut-Janisson produces beautiful sparkling wine made by the TRADITIONAL METHOD. Jim Law at Linden is known for his pure Chardonnays and Bordeaux reds, and for mentoring many a Virginia winemaker. RdV is a relative newcomer producing high-end Bordeaux-style reds with style. Ankida Ridgehas found the sweet spot with Chardonnay and is trying hard with Pinot Noir. Jenni McCloud of Chrysalis is a passionate disciple of Norton and Petit Manseng. Italian-owned Barboursville is arguably Virginia's most versatile producer, with exceptional bottlings including Vermentino, Nebbiolo, and their Octagon BORDEAUX BLEND.

B.W.Z., T.K.W., & L.M.

www.virginiawine.org

Virginia Tech (VT) in Blacksburg, VIRGINIA, is home to the Enology–Grape Chemistry Group, established by B. W. Zoecklein in 1986 within the Department of Food Science and Technology. Oenology research at VT aims to improve wine AROMA and flavour through increasing precursor concentration in grapes and applying targeted FERMENTATION management practices. Oenology extension supports the growing Virginia wine industry through workshops and analytical services. Oenology, brewing, and fermentation courses are offered at undergraduate and graduate level.

Virginia Tech's viticulture research and extension programmes are conducted through the Agricultural Research and Extension Center (www.arec.vaes.vt.edu/alson-h-smith/index.html) at Winchester in the northern Shenandoah Valley. Grape research has focused on aspects of cold stress physiology, vine and vineyard management to optimize YIELD; evaluation of wine QUALITY, VINE VARIETIES, and CLONES; and PEST management. Technical information is disseminated through industry meetings, web-based resources, and a Wine Grape Production Guide (palspublishing.cals.cornell.edu/nra_winegrapecontent.html).

B.W.Z., T.K.W., & A.C.S.

www.vtwines.info

viroids, particles smaller than VIRUSES which are thought capable of producing virus-like disease effects in the grapevine. Viroids can be found in nominally virus-free vines following THERMOTHERAPY, and are known to cause significant diseases for other crops. They are transmitted by vegetative PROPAGATION as for viruses, but viroid-free grapevines can be produced by TISSUE CULTURE. No viroids have so far been identified with commercially important grapevine diseases. The viroid Yellow Speckle is widespread in Australia but is not known to harm the vines.

R.E.S.

Mullins, M. G., Bouquet, A., and Williams, L., *Biology of the Grapevine* (Cambridge, 1992).

virus diseases, group of VINE DISEASES caused by very small and simple organisms, consisting of ribonucleic acid (RNA) wrapped in a protein sheath. Some virus diseases can seriously affect grapevine yield and wine quality, and since they are mainly spread by PROPAGATION in CUTTINGS, there has been an emphasis on VINE IMPROVEMENT and CLONAL SELECTION to prevent their spread. Virus diseases began to affect European vines from about 1890, when ROOTSTOCKS were used in France to control PHYLLOXERA. GRAFTING doubles the risk of virus spread and, unlike many fruiting varieties, rootstocks do not always show virus symptoms.

Virus diseases are mostly spread by taking cuttings from infected plants, although some are spread by NEMATODES and insects. They are mostly detected by inoculating sensitive plants (see INDEXING), and more recently by serological techniques based on immunological reactions (see ELISA) and RNA analysis. Often viruses do not kill the vine but each year they reduce both growth and yield. For example, rootstocks infected with LEAFROLL VIRUS show no symptoms but the virus can greatly reduce wine quality as it delays fruit ripening. It is probably the most important vine virus disease in many parts of the world. Considerable viticultural effort has been expended in vine improvement and in developing virus-free vines. However, the increased use of NURSERY-propagated cuttings taken from virus-free MOTHER VINES, especially rootstocks, has inadvertently led to the spread of TRUNK DISEASES, causing greater harm than the virus diseases they were meant to control.

Common virus diseases are CORKY BARK, FANLEAF DEGENERATION, LEAFROLL VIRUS, RUGOSE WOOD, NEPOVIRUSES. See also BACTERIAL DISEASES, FUNGAL DISEASES, PHYTOPLASMA diseases. R.E.S.

Bovey, R., et al., *Virus and Virus-Like Diseases of Vines: Colour Atlas of Symptoms* (Lausanne, 1980).

Pearson, R. C., and Goheen, A. C. (eds.), *Compendium of Grape Diseases* (St Paul, Minn., 1988).

Weber, E., Golino, D., and Rowhani, A., 'Laboratory testing for grapevine diseases', *Practical Winery & Vineyard* (Jan/Feb 2002), 13–27.

Visan, one of the Côtes du Rhône villages. See RHÔNE.

viscosity, the quality of being **viscous**, the extent to which a solution resists flow or movement. Honey is more viscous than sugar syrup, for example, which is considerably more viscous than water. Viscosity, which approximates to what wine tasters call BODY, can be sensed by the human palate in the form of resistance as the solution is rinsed around the mouth.

A very sweet wine is more viscous than a dry one, even if they have the same ALCOHOLIC STRENGTH. Alcohol itself is more viscous than water, and higher-strength wines are therefore more viscous than lower-strength wines. An

increase of 1% in alcoholic strength increases viscosity relative to water by about 0.04 units, while an increase of 10 g/l in RESIDUAL SUGAR increases viscosity by about 0.03 units. The most viscous wines of all, therefore, are those that are both sweet and strong.

It has been thought that the viscosity and the (quite unrelated) GLYCEROL content of a wine were the main factors in the formation of 'tears' on the inside of a wine glass. While they may be minor factors, the explanation is very different. See TEARS. A.D.W.

Vitaceae, the family in the plant kingdom which includes the genus VITIS containing the grapevine. There are 14 genera altogether with about 900 species, which are spread through tropical and temperate zones around the world. The plants in the family are characteristically climbers with leaves opposite tendrils. See also BOTANICAL CLASSIFICATION.

R.E.S. & J.V.

Vital, low-acid white grape grown in central Portugal, known as MALVASIA Corada in the Douro. Total Portuguese plantings of this vigorous productive vine were 1,251 ha/3,090 acres in 2012 and Casa Figueira has shown that the variety can make fine wine if planted in cool enough terrain.

Vitales, the order in the plant kingdom which includes the family Vitaceae, including the genus VITIS, the grapevine. See BOTANICAL CLASSIFICATION.

vitamins, a group of organic compounds that are essential dietary components, deficiencies causing a variety of well-known disorders in humans. The levels of vitamins in grapes increase during ripening but the final values are relatively low compared with those of many other fruits. The most abundant is ASCORBIC ACID (vitamin C), the levels of which vary considerably—from 15 to 150 mg/l, which is only 10% of that in oranges (although ascorbic acid is often added during winemaking). Average values for the concentrations of other vitamins are about 1 to 10 parts per million (ppm) for niacin, pyridoxine, and pantothenic acid; 0.1 to 1 ppm for thiamine and riboflavin; and 0.001 to 0.01 ppm for biotin and folic acid. These levels in grapes are too low to be considered as a serious dietary source and are further reduced in wine by the use of SULFUR DIOXIDE and YEAST growth (although AUTOLYSIS can add others). Wine also contains low concentrations of vitamin B_{12} (cobalamine).

The 'bioflavonoids', or vitamin P, a complex that includes D-catechin and many other FLAVONOIDS, occur in grape juice in large amounts, especially in dark-skinned berries., and may play a part in warding off heart disease (see HEALTH). B.G.C. & A.D.W.

viticulteur, French term for a vine-grower.

viticulture, the science and practice of grape culture. Viticulture is practised consciously by VITICULTURISTS, often instinctively by grape-growers or vine-growers. Practices vary enormously around the world; some of these differences are highlighted under NEW WORLD.

Grapes can be grown, over a wide range of LATITUDES, in CLIMATES ranging from very hot (southern California, inland Australia) to very cool (England, Luxembourg, Denmark). Viticulture is practised in very wet climates (parts of England and New Zealand) to very dry ones (Atacama in Chile, Central Valley in California). The TOPOGRAPHY can be very steep, as in the Mosel valley of Germany or the Douro of Portugal, or very flat plains, as in many regions of Australia and Argentina. VINE DENSITY can vary enormously: from vineyards planted with large numbers of very small vines, as is common in Champagne and Bordeaux (10,000 vines per ha (4,050 per acre)), to few, large vines as in the Vinho Verde vineyards of Portugal (600 vines per ha). Some vineyards may be tended entirely by manual LABOUR, while others are MECHANIZED. Vineyards may rely on IRRIGATION for their survival where they are grown in deserts, while in others, such as parts of France, irrigation is severely restricted.

The following entries follow the sequence of vineyard development from initial planning through to picking: VINEYARD SITE SELECTION; choice of ROOTSTOCK, VINE VARIETY, and CLONE; SOIL TESTING and SOIL PREPARATION; choice of VINE DENSITY and TRELLIS SYSTEM; vine PLANTING, VINE TRAINING, and PRUNING; control of VINE PESTS, VINE DISEASES, and WEEDS; fruit SAMPLING and HARVEST. See also VINEYARD ANNUAL CYCLE.

Effects on wine quality

For still wines, the VITICULTURIST may well have a greater impact on wine quality than the WINEMAKER since so many of the factors affecting quality are determined in the vineyard. The belief that 'wine is made in the vineyard not the cellar' became increasingly widespread during the 1990s and is now probably more widely quoted than ever.

Quite apart from the decisions involved in vineyard site selection, there are obvious ways in which viticulture can influence wine quality—selection of vine variety, rootstock, clone—and some where the effects are more difficult to identify.

Usually premium-quality wines come from vineyards planted to soils with good DRAINAGE and of low SOIL FERTILITY (see also TERROIR). However, inappropriate vineyard management can destroy the potential for wine quality. For example, over-enthusiastic applications of nitrogen FERTILIZERS will result in excess vineyard VIGOUR which may delay RIPENING and encourage FUNGAL DISEASES. The SPRAYING regime adopted by the vine-grower can determine whether the grapes are affected by BUNCH ROT or not.

The choice of vine-TRAINING SYSTEM and associated trellis system can have fundamental effects on wine quality. Limits on YIELD are also imposed by appellation laws in some regions. Where vines are pruned lightly to many buds and carry too low a LEAF TO FRUIT RATIO then the fruit will not ripen properly and wine quality will be reduced.

Vineyards may require judicious IRRIGATION to prevent excessive WATER STRESS (although the practice is banned or restricted in many European regions), but excessive irrigation (like excessive rainfall) can cause delayed ripening and a loss of wine quality. Vineyards should be subject to grape sampling programmes so that harvest takes place when the fruit has reached the level of maturity appropriate for the wine style. More broadly, lack of concern for the vineyard SOILS and ECOSYSTEM will not make the most of the vineyard site, nor promote its SUSTAINABILITY. R.E.S.

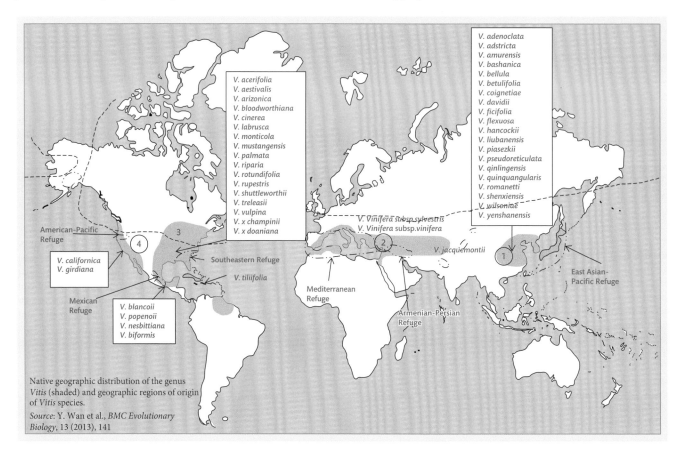

Native geographic distribution of the genus *Vitis* (shaded) and geographic regions of origin of *Vitis* species.

Source: Y. Wan et al., *BMC Evolutionary Biology*, 13 (2013), 141

Coombe, B. G., and Dry, P. R., *Viticulture*, i: *Resources* (2nd edn, Adelaide, 2004).

Coombe, B. G., and Dry, P. R., *Viticulture*, ii: *Practices* (Adelaide, 1992).

Galet, P., *Précis de viticulture* (7th edn, Montpellier, 2000).

viticulturist, someone who practises VITICULTURE. In many countries the grape-grower is termed simply 'grower' rather than 'viticulturist', which word is more often used for professionals who typically have some formal tertiary training in viticulture. Grape-growers or vine-growers may also be termed winegrowers.   R.E.S.

Vitis, the genus of the plant kingdom which includes the VINE (see BOTANICAL CLASSIFICATION). *Vitis* is one of 14 genera in the family Vitaceae and contains in turn about 60 species. Centres of *Vitis* diversity are equally divided between the east and south east of North America and Asia, mainly in the temperate zones of the northern hemisphere, with a few in the tropics. The most important species for wine production is the single European species (strictly, Eurasian) *Vitis vinifera*, often written *V. vinifera*, described in detail in VINIFERA.

As shown on the map (opposite) there are many different AMERICAN VINE SPECIES. They became the subject of attention by early European settlers as *V. vinifera* failed to cope with indigenous diseases in the early colonies on the east coast. However, they proved generally unsatisfactory for wine because of their strongly flavoured berries (see FOXY). These native American species have since been crossed with *V. vinifera* to form new varieties (see AMERICAN HYBRIDS), and among themselves to produce the ROOTSTOCKS used in modern viticulture.

Among Asian species, *V. amurensis* is the world's most northerly vine species, and has been used to introduce cold hardiness into VINE BREEDING programmes (see AMURENSIS). Varieties of *V. amurensis* and *V. cognetiae* are grown in JAPAN.

Note: The systematic botanical classification of species within the *Vitis* genus has been a subject of confusion for more than a century. Hedrick documents this early confusion, especially that concerning *V. vulpina*, which has often been wrongly confused with *V. riparia*, the great taxonomist Linnaeus being the origin of the confusion. GALET clarified the taxonomy in 1967, but there is still some doubt about the taxonomy of Asian species. The French taxonomist Planchon proposed that *Vitis* species be divided into two so-called sections. The first, *Vitis* (but originally called *Euvitis*), contains the great majority of species including the 'European' wine grape species *V. vinifera*, and the second MUSCADINIA contains only two species indigenous to the Americas. These two sections differ in chromosome number and many morphological features. The species of the section *Vitis* have proven to be closely enough related to interbreed easily when this has been attempted, but crosses between members of the two sections typically produces sterile hybrids. *Muscadinia* is sometimes considered a separate genus but recent DNA PHYLOGENIES do not support this distinction.

For *Vitis sylvestris* see WILD VINES. See also VINE, VINIFERA, AMERICAN VINE SPECIES, VINE VARIETIES, PROLES, CLONE, HYBRIDS, CROSS.

     R.E.S. & J.V.

Antcliff, A. J., 'Taxonomy: the grapevine as a member of the plant kingdom', in B. G. Coombe and P. R. Dry (eds.), *Viticulture*, i: *Resources* (2nd edn, Adelaide, 2004).

Galet, P., *Précis de viticulture* (7th edn, Montpellier, 2000).

Hedrick, U., *The Grapes of New York* (Albany, NY, 1908).

Soejima, A., and Wen, J., 'Phylogenetic analysis of the grape family (Vitaceae) based on three chloroplast markers', *American Journal of Botany*, 93/2 (2006), 278–87.

Wan, Y., et al., 'A phylogenetic analysis of the grape genus (*Vitis* L.) reveals broad reticulation and concurrent diversification during neogene and quaternary climate change', *BMC Evolutionary Biology*, 13 (2013), 141. doi:10.1186/1471-2148-13-141.

Vitis vinifera, the species of vine from which most of the world's wine is made. The relationship of *vinifera* to other species of the *Vitis* genus is described above under VITIS, and details about the species and wine grapes in general are given under VINIFERA. There are many thousands of *vinifera* VINE VARIETIES, which in turn are classified into three PROLES. The relationship of *Vitis vinifera* to other members of the plant kingdom is discussed under BOTANICAL CLASSIFICATION. The commercial culture of *Vitis vinifera* is introduced within the VITICULTURE article.

Viura is the RIOJA synonym for the MACABEO grape.

Vivarais, Côtes du, wine region promoted to AOC status in 1999 on the right bank of the RHÔNE immediately opposite GRIGNAN-LES-ADHÉMAR in the wild and beguiling Ardèche. Widely dispersed vineyards on mainly LIMESTONE soils in a much cooler and wetter climate than the rest of the southern Rhône had fallen to 321 ha/793 acres by 2013. Most of the wine is light reds and rosés from Grenache and Syrah. A small amount of white is made, mainly from, Grenache Blanc. Production is dominated by CO-OPERATIVES, whose more profitable business may be producing varietal IGP Ardèche from INTERNATIONAL VARIETIES.

Vizetelly, Henry (1820–94), prolific English wine writer whose detailed accounts of the history of port and champagne are particularly celebrated. Vizetelly came from a family of printers, and so it is particularly appropriate that today his influence is perhaps most marked in the continued, and increasingly imprecise, reproduction of the engravings which distinguished his many and various books about wine. He was introduced to wine in 1869 when he was sent to Paris to report on the French vintage for the *Pall Mall Gazette*, narrowly escaping execution during the Franco-Prussian War the next year. He spent much of the 1870s visiting the vineyards of France and Germany and in 1877 visited Portugal, Madeira, and the Canary Islands. Whereas JULLIEN and REDDING provided global wine surveys for the specialist reader, Vizetelly managed both to delve more deeply into specific wine regions, and to produce books which appealed to a wider market. When based in France he was one of the first acknowledged wine 'experts' who was invited to serve as a judge of wines at the Vienna and Paris Exhibitions. On his eventual return to England, he became a publisher and as Zola's English publisher, he was imprisoned and financially ruined.

Gabler, J. M., *Wine into Words: A History and Bibliography of Wine Books in the English Language* (Baltimore, 1985).

vocabulary, tasting. See LANGUAGE OF WINE, TASTING NOTES LANGUAGE, and TASTING TERMS.

Vojvodina, autonomous region within SERBIA.

volatile. All wines are volatile in that they contain volatile FLAVOUR COMPOUNDS and some level of VOLATILE ACIDS, but volatile is used as a pejorative tasting term for a wine in which the level of ACETIC ACID has risen unacceptably high.

volatile acidity of a wine is its total concentration of **volatile acids**, those naturally occurring organic ACIDS of wines that are separable by DISTILLATION. Wine's most common volatile acid by far is ACETIC ACID (more than 96%), which is why it is used as the routine measure of volatile acidity (VA). A few other acids such as formic, propionic, SUCCINIC, and LACTIC, normally present in trace amounts in wines, are also volatile. The EU limit for VA (expressed as acetic) is 1.2 g/l for red wine and 1.08 g/l for white and rosé.

Acetic acid, in small amounts, is a by-product of the normal action of YEAST in grape juice. However, the major source is the action of a group of BACTERIA known as ACETOBACTER which require OXYGEN for their growth and survival, and cause a reaction between the

V

alcohol of the wine and the oxygen to produce acetic acid. Very low concentrations of acetic acid, below 0.2 g/l, do not affect the taste adversely. Increasing concentrations change the taste of the wine, however, from added complexity and fruitiness to a frankly vinegary flavour at levels much above 1.5 g/l. Most everyday wines are very low in acetic acid but some red wines may be excessively acetic. A few fine wines, usually mature reds in bottle, are rich enough in BODY, TANNINS, and ALCOHOL to bear low concentrations of acetic acid that are sometimes said to LIFT the flavour, although they would probably be even better without the VA.

It is not the acetic acid itself that causes changes in the aroma but the ESTER known as ETHYL ACETATE, the reaction product of acetic acid and ETHANOL.

Exposure of wines to air in the presence of acetobacter starts the process of VINEGAR production, although if exposure to air is limited the wine will probably not be spoiled.

It was the research work of Louis PASTEUR, trying to find a reason for the spoilage of so much burgundy shipped to England, that resulted in the discovery of acetobacter. It also resulted in the discovery that yeast is responsible for the conversion of grape sugars to wine.

A.D.W.

volatility, property of having excessive VOLATILE ACIDS.

volcanic describes the processes and products of volcanic eruptions. The solid volcanic products include recently deposited ash and rocks such as BASALT and TUFF, together with the soils derived from them. Such materials are very variable in composition, but all involve several silicate minerals (see GEOLOGY) and are therefore rich in potential SOIL NUTRIENTS. Volcanic rocks are often relatively easily weathered so soils formed from them tend to be particularly fertile (unusually so for vineyards) and most are well drained. The various silicate minerals and the nutrients they yield are identical to those in non-volcanic rocks but anecdote and marketing often claim that vines grown on volcanic soils give something extra to wine.

Mediteranean islands such as SICILY and SANTORINI are composed of volcanic rocks, as are parts of mainland Italy such as CAMPANIA, SOAVE in the Veneto, and Monte Vulture in BASILICATA. The TOKAJI of Hungary is produced from grapes grown on volcanic rocks, mainly andesite. Numerous vineyards in the states of IDAHO, WASHINGTON, and OREGON are underlain by volcanic materials, as are parts of the NAPA and SONOMA valleys, California. In the Kaiserstuhl-Tuniberg region of BADEN in Germany,

vines are grown in clays derived from volcanic rocks, while the Pfalz to the north is underlain by BASALT, and there are numerous other examples around the world.

A.J.M.

Volnay, attractive small village in the Côte de Beaune district of Burgundy's Côte d'Or producing elegant red wines from Pinot Noir. The wines of Volnay were celebrated under the *ancien régime* for their delicacy: Claude Arnoux describes them as partridge-eye pink in colour, and the finest of all the wines of the Côte de Beaune, although they had to be drunk very young. Since then they have alternated in fame with those of neighbouring Pommard depending on whether FASHION dictated wines of breeding or of power.

More than half Volnay's vineyards are of PREMIER CRU status, stretching in a broad swathe from Pommard to Meursault, continuing into the latter village. Because Meursault is renowned for its white wines, its single really fine red wine vineyard of Les Santenots is sold as **Volnay Santenots**, which has its own appellation. The best part of this vineyard is Les Santenots-du-Milieu, although it is not as typical of Volnay as Le Cailleret, which it abuts, or Champans. These two vineyards express the astonishing, velvety finesse of Volnay. Clos des Chênes, just above Le Cailleret, is also very fine but a little lighter as the soil is even thinner.

Excellent vineyards close to the village include Taillepieds, the Clos de la Bousse d'Or, MONOPOLE of Domaine de la Pousse d'Or, which also owns an excellent enclave within Le Cailleret known as the Clos des 60 Ouvrées, and the Clos des Ducs of the Marquis d'Angerville, whose father pioneered DOMAINE BOTTLING in the 1930s. Volnay's finest producers include Michel Lafarge, Pousse d'Or, de Montille, d'Angerville, and most of the best producers in MEURSAULT who also have vineyards in Volnay.

See also CÔTE D'OR, and map under BURGUNDY.

J.T.C.M.

Arnoux, C., *Dissertation sur la situation de Bourgogne* (Dijon, 1728).

VORS and VOS, classifications for age-dated SHERRY.

Vosges OAK comes from the mountains to the immediate west of ALSACE.

Vosne-Romanée, village in the Côte de Nuits district of Burgundy's CÔTE D'OR producing arguably the finest red wines made anywhere from Pinot Noir grapes (see map under BURGUNDY). As well as excellent wines at VILLAGE and PREMIER CRU level, there are six GRAND CRU vineyards, three of which share the name Romanée, the suffix to which Vosne was hyphenated in 1866.

The grands crus are Romanée-Conti, La Romanée, La Tâche, Richebourg, Romanée-St-Vivant, and La Grande Rue. Between them they produce, with Musigny and Chambertin, the greatest wines of the Côte de Nuits. They have more finesse than any other but to this is allied as much power and stuffing as their nearest rivals.

A vineyard formerly known as Le Cloux was rechristened La Romanée in 1651, presumably on account of Roman remains being discovered nearby. In 1760, the property was bought by the Prince de Conti, subsequently becoming known as Romanée-Conti. Just above this sublime vineyard, whose wines can be the most expensive in the world, is La Romanée. Romanée-Conti has brown, CALCAREOUS soil about 60 cm/23 in deep with 45 to 49% CLAY and liable to serious erosion in the upper, steeper part. La Romanée also has a notably steep slope with less clay and more RENDZINA in the make-up of the soil. The former is the monopoly of the DOMAINE DE LA ROMANÉE-CONTI (DRC), the latter of Comte Liger-Belair. About 300 cases are made each year from the tiny 0.84 ha/2 acres of La Romanée, double that is produced from the 1.80 ha of Romanée-Conti.

Another monopoly of the Domaine de la Romanée-Conti, and regarded as nearly as fine as the vineyard from which it takes its name, is La Tâche, whose 6 ha (including the vineyard of Les Gaudichots, which used to be separate but is regarded as being of the same quality) produce a wine which is explosively seductive even when young, whereas Romanée-Conti takes longer to show its astonishing completeness. La Tâche seems to thrive even in lesser years, being judged the only wine worthy of bottling by the Domaine de la Romanée-Conti in 1950 and 1951.

The next most sought-after Vosne-Romanée wine is Richebourg, whose 8 ha are shared between ten growers, notably Domaine de la Romanée-Conti, Domaine LEROY Grivot, branches of the Gros family, and Domaine Méo-Camuzet. As the name suggests, this is one of the most voluptuous wines of Burgundy and can equal La Tâche in some years.

Romanée-St-Vivant, taking its name from the monastery of St-Vivant founded at Vergy *c.*900 and subsequent owner of the vineyard, can also make very fine wine but it is usually lighter and less powerful than its neighbours, being further down the slope and having deeper soil. There are half a dozen owners, of which the largest is Domaine de la Romanée-Conti (5.3 ha out of 9.43). Domaine Leroy and Louis LATOUR's Domaine de Corton Grancey are the next largest owners.

Between La Tâche to the south and La Romanée-Conti to the north lie the 1.4 ha of La Grande Rue, originally classified as PREMIER

CRU but promoted, as its location suggests is only right, to grand cru. The vineyard is a monopoly of Domaine Lamarche. Among the best of Vosne-Romanée's premier cru vineyards are Les Malconsorts on the Nuits-St-Georges side, Cros Parantoux made famous by Henry Jayer, above the grands crus, and Les Beauxmonts and Les Suchots abutting Flagey-Échézeaux. Part of Les Beauxmonts is actually in the latter commune, although it is sold as Vosne-Romanée, as is the village wine of Flagey.

While the renown of the Domaine de la Romanée-Conti dominates Vosne-Romanée, it should not overshadow other significant influences: Henri Jayer, for his unparalleled winemaking skills; René Engel for his patriarchal influence and local historical research and publications; Lalou Bize-LEROY, who has bought and transformed the former Domaine Nöellat. Other particularly fine domaines are those owned by the various members of the Gros family, Domaine Jean Grivot, and Sylvain Cathiard.   J.T.C.M.

Meadows, A., *The Pearl of the Côte* (Winnetka, Calif., 2010).

Norman, R., *Grand Cru* (London 2010).

Olney, R., *Romanée-Conti* (Paris, 1991).

Rigaux, J., *Ode aux grands vins de Bourgogne* (Précy-sous-Thil, 1997).

Vougeot, small village in the Côte de Nuits district of Burgundy producing red wines from the Pinot Noir grape. The name is derived from the diminutive of Vouge, a small stream flowing through the village. There are only 4.8 ha/11.8 acres of vineyards producing VILLAGE WINE and 11.7 ha designated PREMIER CRU; the village's fame rests squarely with the 50.6 ha GRAND CRU, Clos de Vougeot.

The fame of Clos de Vougeot is historical since it was the flagship vineyard of the Cistercians, who planted and enclosed what is significantly the largest grand cru vineyard of the Côte d'Or. Geologically, this is not a homogeneous site: the top, abutting Musigny and Grands Échézeaux, has a light CALCAREOUS and gravelly soil on oolitic limestone which drains beautifully and gives the wines of greatest distinction; the middle section is on softer limestone with clay and some gravel, with moderate drainage on a very gentle slope. The bottom section, almost flat, stretching down to the main D974 road, consists of poorly drained alluvial clay.

When the wines could be blended by the MONKS to produce a complete wine from differing constituent parts, Clos de Vougeot doubtless deserved its reputation. Now that the vineyard is fragmented between 80 or more owners, too many of the wines are below standard through the inadequacies of some of the raw material and many of the production techniques of the less conscientious producers.

Classic Clos de Vougeot is likely to be dense and ungiving when young, robust rather than elegant. However, after a decade it opens out into one of the most complete wines of the Côte d'Or with deep, rich flavours reminiscent of truffles and undergrowth.

Of the premier cru vineyards, Le Clos Blanc, the monopoly of Domaine de la Vougeraie in succession to Héritiers Guyot, has produced white wine since first planted by the monks in 1110. The other premier crus are les Cras, les Petits Vougeots, and Clos de la Perrière, monopoly of Domaine Bertagna.

Reliable producers of Clos de Vougeot include Château de la Tour (the largest owners), Méo-Camuzet, Anne Gros, and Domaine d'Eugénie.

See also CLOS DE VOUGEOT, CÔTE D'OR, and map under BURGUNDY.   J.T.C.M.

Vouvray, the most important individual white wine appellation in the TOURAINE district of the Loire. The wines of Vouvray vary enormously in quality, thereby offering a true representation of the grape variety from which Vouvray is exclusively made. Vouvray is CHENIN BLANC and, to a certain extent, Chenin Blanc is Vouvray (although up to 5% MENU PINEAU grapes are theoretically allowed into Vouvray too). No other wine made only from this long-lived middle Loire grape, often called Pineau de la Loire, is made in such quantity, from more than 2,000 ha/5,000 acres of vineyard. (The proportion of sparkling wine produced increased during the 1990s.) Only Coteaux du LAYON can begin to rival Vouvray for the total area of Chenin Blanc planted.

Vouvray itself is a particularly pretty small town on the northern bank of the Loire just east of Tours, whose wines owe much to the MONKS AND MONASTERIES who refined local viticulture from the Middle Ages. It was not until the creation of the Vouvray appellation in 1936 that Vouvray established an identity of its own; before then most of it was shipped out for blending by the energetic DUTCH WINE TRADE, and much of the wine sold as Vouvray came from anywhere in Touraine.

Houses, and wine cellars, have habitually been created out of the TUFFEAU on this right bank of the wide river, with vines planted in the clay and gravel topsoil over the tuffeau on the plateau above, dissected by small rivers and streams so that many vineyards have an ideal sheltered southerly aspect. The locals claim that this is where the Atlantic climate meets the CONTINENTAL climate.

Making top-quality Vouvray MOELLEUX is as hazardous as making any top-quality sweet white wine which owes its sweetness to NOBLE ROT or extreme RIPENESS. The vine-grower is entirely at the mercy of the weather, and the harvest in Vouvray is one of France's last, usually lasting until well into November, often involving a number of TRIES through the vineyard. An increasing number of producers have mastered the art of making top-quality dry Vouvray in less ripe vintages however.

Winemaking here is distinguished by the need to bottle pure fruit and its naturally high acidity as early and as unadorned as possible. Thus, this is one of the few wine regions of the world of little commercial interest to the COOPERAGE business. Neutral fermentation vessels such as large old oak casks or stainless steel tanks are used, MALOLACTIC CONVERSION is generally avoided, and the AGEING process is expected to occur, extremely slowly, in bottle.

In the least generous VINTAGES, only dry and possibly sparkling wines are made. The best years yield very sweet, golden nectars that are naturally MOELLEUX, or even LIQUOREUX, but are so high in acidity that most are almost unpleasant to drink in their middle age between about three years old and two to three decades. Some of the finest Vouvrays can still taste lively, and richly fruity, at nearly a century old. A relatively high proportion of demi-sec (medium dry) is also produced in many years, and it too has demanded a considerable amount of BOTTLE AGEING before the acidity has muted and the wine can be served as a fine accompaniment to many savoury, richly sauced dishes. Better vineyard management, however, is resulting Vouvrays of all sweetness levels that are more broachable in youth. The leading producer, Huet, changed hands in 2003 and has been accused of changing direction towards a higher proportion of dry wines.

Commercial Vouvray also exists, on the other hand, as simply a medium-sweet, reasonably acid, white wine that has little capacity for development.

Vouvray Mousseux can often offer more interest than other Loire sparkling wines, to those who appreciate the honeyed aromas of Chenin Blanc, at least. The wines have weight and flavour, and are suitable for drinking with as well as before meals.

See also LOIRE, including map.

VQA, Vintners Quality Alliance, was initially formed as a voluntary organization to identify wines made entirely from grapes grown in CANADA, as opposed to the many on sale that are merely blended or bottled there. Today Ontario and British Columbia's VQA APPELLATION systems are legally enforceable.   T.A.

www.vqaontario.ca/Home

Vranac, very promising indigenous Balkan red grape variety grown in southern CROATIA,

Herzegovina (see BOSNIA), KOSOVO, MONTENEGRO, the republic of MACEDONIA (where it is known as **Vranec**), and SERBIA. The wines produced are deeply coloured and can be rich in EXTRACT, responding unusually well to oak AGEING. There is an element of refreshing bitterness on the finish of these wines. DNA PROFILING at Zagreb in 2001 suggested a parent–offspring relationship with TRIBIDRAG, better known in California as ZINFANDEL.

VSIG stands for Vin Sans Indication Géographique, the French equivalent of a WINE WITHOUT GEOGRAPHICAL INDICATION, and official EU category for wines sold as VIN DE FRANCE.

VSP, **vertical shoot positioning.** See TRAINING SYSTEMS.

VT. See VENDANGE TARDIVE.

Wachau, important wine region in AUSTRIA comprising roughly 1,400 ha/3,500 acres of spectacular, typically south-facing vineyards upstream of KREMS on the Danube. The term was long used to refer collectively to the vast array of vineyards within a radius of roughly 15 km/9 miles of Krems, then regarded as its capital. But in the aftermath of Austria's 1985 wine scandal, the recently formed growers' association VINEA WACHAU lobbied successfully for a more restricted delimitation. Today the Wachau constitutes only about 3% of Austria's vine surface and, owing to relatively low yields, represents an even smaller proportion of total wine production; but it is arguably the most prestigious, certainly since the 1990s, due in part to initiatives by the Vinea Wachau.

The region and its growers' association are best known for the stylistic division of their dry, unchaptalized wines into the weight classes STEINFEDER, FEDERSPIEL, and SMARAGD, each defined by a distinct range of MUST WEIGHT and finished alcohol. The designation Wachau is much more inclusive than contemporary Austria's DAC of that name. Wines that fall outside the parameters of the region's three characteristic categories, including any that fail (or were not intended by their makers) to ferment to complete dryness, may still be labelled Wachau. Wines made from any of the many grape varieties grown here—Grüner Veltliner and Riesling most prominently, but also Chardonnay, Pinot Blanc (Weissburgunder), Pinot Gris, Sauvignon Blanc, Neuburger (of local origin), Muskateller, Roter Veltliner or Zweigelt—may be labelled Wachau. This contrasts with the DAC regulations elsewhere.

Much of the Wachau is dramatically terraced and defined by ancient rocks of VOLCANIC origin—along with their metamorphic and decomposed variants. Gravel and alluvium characterize some

level stretches near the Danube, and LOESS—the ancient glacial dust that dominates many vineyards east of Krems—has settled among rocky slopes in certain places. The role of fast-draining, nutrient-poor soils based on rocks of crystalline structure is far from understood, but local growers as well as many consumers with a penchant for Wachau wine are confident of their ability to distinguish this region's wines according to their vineyards or at least their basic soil types, often regardless of grape variety. Wachau soils, and in particular its towering terraces, accumulate heat and drain moisture so quickly that they can cause vines to SHUT DOWN in years characterized by heat or DROUGHT. So, paradoxically, such vintages historically produced wines as high in unripe acidity and marginal in must weight as cool, rainy vintages, so that only vintages that experienced neither hot and sunny nor cool and rainy conditions were entirely successful. To meet this difficulty, in the Vinea Wachau era IRRIGATION lines were constructed, an initiative not without controversy, but one that seems to have resulted in more than two decades of Wachau wines with consistently higher must weights, more harmonious acidity, and greater prestige than at any time during the past century. A further effect of selective irrigation—which nowadays also characterizes top sites in the neighbouring KREMSTAL and KAMPTAL—when combined with other viticultural refinements, is to extend the Wachau's already late harvests into November and sometimes December, thus resulting in record HANG TIME for any wine region anywhere. The Wachau also experiences some of the wine world's most extreme diurnal temperature variation (see TEMPERATURE VARIABILITY), thanks to a dependable daily pattern by which warm air is sucked upstream along the Danube from the Pannonian-Hungarian Plain, then displaced by

cold moving in the opposite direction from the pre-Alps and forests that dominate the west and north of the region.

In recent decades, Wachau growers have placed increasing emphasis on vineyard-designated offerings, which today make up virtually the entire production for most growers, beyond a few reasonably priced generic bottlings. The best-known villages, travelling upstream from east to west, with some of their most famous vineyards, are:

Unterloiben (Kreutles, Steinertal)
Oberloiben (Loibenberg, Schütt)
Dürnstein (Hollerin, Kellerberg)
Weissenkirchen (Achleiten, Kaiserberg, Klaus, Steinriegel, Weitenberg)
Joching (Kollmitz)
Wösendorf (Hochrain, Kollmütz)
Spitz (Axpoint, Hochrain, Setzberg, Singerriedel, Tausendeimerberg a.k.a. Burgberg)

The Spitzerbach, with its associated village of Viessling and its vineyards Brück and Schön, extends west into high hills from Spitz and away from the Danube, offering favourable conditions in an era of CLIMATE CHANGE. And while the Wachau's right-bank vineyards generally generate little excitement, those of former Roman garrison Mautern—immediately opposite the Danube from Stein, which is part of the official KREMSTAL—are of contemporary as well as historical importance, thanks primarily to the Nikolaihof estate, where St Severin is thought to have initiated Wachau viticulture in the 5th century. Average holdings in the Wachau have largely resisted the national trend towards consolidation, thanks to the continuing success of the Domäne Wachau (formerly Freie Weingärtner Wachau) co-operative, whose more than 200 members collectively own nearly one-third of the Wachau's vineyard area. D.S.

Wädenswil, site of a viticultural research station on Lake Zurich in German-speaking SWITZERLAND. It was founded in 1890 in response to the viticultural catastrophes of FUNGAL DISEASES and PHYLLOXERA. SUSTAINABLE VITICULTURE, in which pests and diseases are controlled by biological or biotechnological methods, has developed in this environment.

Today Wädenswil is concerned with research, development, testing, control, and extension services in viticulture and wine microbiology. The station has developed a number of YEAST strains for the repair of STUCK FERMENTATIONS and some grapevine CLONES, notably of PINOT NOIR, which have been planted as far away as Oregon, California, New Zealand, and South Africa. A number of plant protection methods have been developed, such as the introduction of predators and PHEROMONES for trapping and confusing INSECTS.

Wädenswil and the research station at CHANGINS in western Switzerland combined under the administration of Agroscope (ACW) in early 2006.

Wagga, abbreviation for the School of Agricultural and Wine Sciences, Wagga Wagga, now part of CHARLES STURT UNIVERSITY.

Wagner, Philip (1904–96), Baltimore newspaper editor, VITICULTURIST, WINEMAKER, and author of books on vines and wine. Beginning as a HOME WINEMAKER during PROHIBITION, Wagner published *American Wines and How to Make Them* (1933). Interested in improving the basis of eastern American winemaking, Wagner began to import and test FRENCH HYBRID vines in 1939 and to distribute them from the nursery and vineyard he founded, Boordy Vineyard, in Maryland. His *A Wine-Grower's Guide* (1945) was the first work to publicize French hybrids in the US; in the same year he opened a winery at Boordy Vineyard and produced the first French hybrid wine on record in the US. Wagner's success with his wines, his activity in supplying French hybrids from his nursery, and the persuasiveness of his writing in favour of a better selection of VINE VARIETIES entitle him to be regarded as the man who changed the course of winemaking in the eastern US. The clarity, grace, and authority of his books gave him an influence far beyond the sphere of Boordy Vineyard.   T.P.

Wagram is a 2,800-ha/6,900-acre wine region of AUSTRIA comprising just over 5% of the nation's vineyards on the left bank of the Danube between KREMSTAL and VIENNA. Known officially, if misleadingly, until 2007 as Donauland, and incorporating under that description today's TRAISENTAL as well as the right-bank vineyards of KLOSTERNEUBURG, the Wagram derives its name from the wall-like embankment of LOESS that dominates this sector of the Danube

and its viticulture. Grüner Veltliner accounts for roughly half of all vines and Bernard Ott—the one Wagram grower to have achieved Austrian star status—devotes his attention almost entirely to it. Yet, Roter Veltliner and GEMISCHTER SATZ vineyards, which make up just 3% and 5% respectively of Wagram vineyards, were dominant in large parts of Wagram until the late 20th century. Some strikingly successful wines, both white and red, have been made from them, as well as from other varieties, including Pinot Blanc and Riesling.   D.S.

waiter, wine. See SOMMELIER.

Wales has around 21 vineyards totalling 30 ha/75 acres, mainly in the southern part of the principality. Wales has the same appellation system as ENGLAND, allowing producers to make Welsh Quality Wine and Welsh Regional Wine in both still and sparkling (see ENGLAND).

Walker Bay, southerly, relatively cool MARITIME wine district in SOUTH AFRICA. Its most important wards are Hemel-en-Aarde Valley, Upper Hemel-en-Aarde Valley, and Hemel-en-Aarde Ridge. Walker Bay's vineyards produce many of South Africa's most promising wines made from Chardonnay and Pinot Noir.

Wälschriesling. See WELSCHRIESLING.

war, effects on wine. Wine is a way of life literally rooted in the soil. It is also capital and labour intensive and reliant on a complex distribution network, which make it highly vulnerable during time of war.

The most visible effect of war is the destruction of vineyards. Just as it was customary for warring ancient Greeks to cut down or burn the vines of their enemies, so the barbarian invaders of Roman Europe signalled victory in the same way.

Planting on newly captured territory likewise symbolized success. When the Christians drove the Moors from medieval SPAIN, they planted vines behind them, as did the Crusaders who briefly held parts of the Holy Land. It is difficult to imagine a clearer expression of a battle won and determination to stay than the planting of such a long-term crop as vines.

Certain regions have suffered ruin disproportionately because of their strategic geographical position. The location of the CHAMPAGNE region at the crossroads of northern Europe has ensured the destruction of its vineyards dozens of times, most famously when they were bisected by the trenches of the First World War.

The short-term effects of war have sometimes had permanent consequences. The Thirty Years War (1618–48) which ravaged 17th-century Europe was so destructive that many northern German vineyard areas were never replanted (see GERMAN HISTORY). Recovery was hampered by the sheer scale of the devastation,

by lack of manpower through depopulation, and by destruction of capital equipment.

Plundering of existing wine stocks is another common feature of European war, with Champagne, once again, an obvious example. When Russian soldiers occupied the region in 1814 they were not slow to help themselves. In this case the Champagne houses did at least have the subsequent consolation that the Russians became their wines' most loyal peacetime consumers until 1917. In general, however, terrible hardship was the result of forced requisitioning and outright plunder. Civil conflicts, such as the French Wars of Religion in the 16th century, were at least as destructive.

The sale and distribution of wine is a complex operation which is inevitably dislocated by war. TRANSPORT becomes hazardous. During the HUNDRED YEARS WAR (1337–1453) ships carrying wine between Bordeaux and England were attacked so often that convoys were arranged for safety.

Wars also frequently led to a ban on trade with the enemy. When Britain and France were at war in the early 18th century, French wine imports into Britain were prohibited. Smuggling was one answer to the problem, switching to wine produced by the ally Portugal was another. Thus war altered trading and consumption patterns, and PORT became the staple wine of Georgian England.

Wars do not bring uniform misfortune. The demand for wine to provision troops in some cases provided a stimulus to wine regions not directly involved in the fighting. The Roman army needed huge supplies to send it into battle. Records show that, when Edward I embarked on his Scottish campaign in 1300, he first bought in vast quantities of wine from Bordeaux.

It is also probable that the influx of American forces into Second World War Europe and its aftermath was an important factor in building the wine market in the UNITED STATES.

Historically the effects of war on wine, as on so many other commercial activities, have been mixed and in some cases one grower's suffering made another's fortune.

From 2012, wine production in SYRIA was affected by the civil war there, as that in neighbouring LEBANON had been three decades earlier.   H.B.

Bonal, F., *Le Livre d'or de Champagne* (Lausanne, 1984).

Johnson, H., *The Story of Wine* (London and New York, 1989).

Kladstrup, D. and P., *Wine and War: The French, the Nazis, and the Battle for France's Greatest Treasure* (New York, 2001).

Warre, important port shipper. See SYMINGTONS.

Washington, dynamic fruit-growing state in the PACIFIC NORTHWEST of the United States which occupies second position behind California as an American VINIFERA wine producer. Producing just 5% of the national wine total, Washington state's 50,000 acres/20,234 ha of vines are still considerable.

History
In the 1930s, the Washington wine industry was based on the native American grape variety CONCORD, which grows well in the Columbia Valley (see below). It is still planted there although its acreage is rapidly shrinking, and today its fruit is almost exclusively limited to the making of juice, jellies, and other non-wine confections. In 1969, when California's wine boom was well under way, there were just two wineries in Washington. By 2014 there were well over 800 and small-scale producers are continuing to emerge. California producers such as GALLO, Cakebread, and Duckhorn have invested in the state's wine industry too.

Geography and climate
Washington is the USA's leading apple and hop state, both crops being good viticultural markers, but there is a sharp difference between the climates of western and the viticulturally much more important eastern Washington.

Western Washington is mild and damp the year round because of the proximity of the Pacific Ocean and the inland sea called the Puget Sound, overlooked by Seattle. Population, limited space, and marginal growing conditions combine to limit *vinifera* plantings in western Washington to less than 1% of the state's total. The **Puget Sound** appellation covers the islands and land adjoining the waters of the Puget Sound, into the Cascade foothills.

Eastern Washington, a vast DESERT with patches of irrigated farmland screened from marine air by the towering barrier of the Cascade mountains (which extend south into OREGON and help shape the viticultural landscape there), has hot, dry summers and cold to arctic winters. The dependable summers east of the Cascades have encouraged vine plantings, with the Columbia River providing most of the much-needed IRRIGATION in summer and early autumn. Painful experience has led growers to plant vines in areas less susceptible to WINTER FREEZE. In January and February, temperatures occasionally plummet to −15 °F/−26 °C. Such freeze-susceptible varieties as Merlot are particularly vulnerable in the winter freeze years such as 1996, and that of 2004. The severity of Washington winters has encouraged growers to explore higher sites where AIR DRAINAGE helps protect the vines, not only from the coldest winter nights, but also the more common early spring/late autumn FROSTS.

Except for the Columbia Gorge, which straddles Washington and Oregon, and Lake Chelan AVAs, virtually all the vineyards in eastern Washington fall within the 11 million-acre/4.4 million-ha embrace of the Columbia Valley AVA. Inside the Columbia Valley are the important Yakima Valley appellation (which includes Snipes Mountain, the Rattlesnake Hills, and Red Mountain as sub-AVAs), the Walla Walla Valley AVA, Horse Heaven Hills AVA; Wahluke Slope AVA, and recently added Ancient Lakes and Naches Heights AVAs. Many of these smaller AVAs such as Snipes Mountain, Lake Chelan, Naches Heights, and Ancient Lakes are relatively new, suggesting that Washington is only now identifying its myriad growing conditions.

Eastern Washington soils tend to be sandy loam, a generally inhospitable environment for PHYLLOXERA, so most vines are planted UNGRAFTED, which helps recovery from winter freeze, widely spaced, and trained in bilateral CORDONS. With no exposed graft unions, these vines are better preserved in the cold winters. About 80% of grapes are MECHANICALLY HARVESTED. Clonal diversity used to be limited, but by the early 21st century, more diverse plant material became available. Washington also claims an average of two hours more sunlight each day during the growing season than California, due to its more northerly, yet still sunny, position. Cool nights help maintain a fresh acidity in the grapes despite the heat of the days.

Vine varieties and wine styles
Virtually all wines are *vinifera*, and are generally distinguished from those of California by bright fruit and relatively crisp acidity. Although the state was initially celebrated for its Merlot, later followed by Cabernet Sauvignon and Syrah, there were just as many white wine grapes as red according to the 2013 vine census. Riesling (6,320 acres/2,558 ha) is a variety that the state grows particularly well, for both drier wines and sweeter late-harvest ones, some of the latter being BOTRYTIZED. The Eroica JOINT VENTURE (see below) together with Allen Shoup and Armin Diel's joint venture Poet's Leap have raised Washington's Riesling game and, as a result, many fine examples have emerged. Washington has been closely associated with Riesling since the dominant company Ste Michelle claims to be the world's biggest producer of it and hosts international Riesling events. Nevertheless, Chardonnay dominated vineyard and cellar alike in Washington throughout the 1990s and continues to be so widely planted that total acreage was 7,654 acres/3,097 ha in 2013. Washington Chardonnays range from merely good to very good, with a handful of committed winemakers intent on achieving complexity and TERROIR expression. White wine varieties with good track records from more limited plantings are Sauvignon Blanc, Pinot Gris, Sémillon, and Viognier.

Chenin Blanc and Gewurztraminer, once workaday in quality, have steadily declined in acreage yet can achieve great heights in the state. Müller-Thurgau can succeed in the scattering of vineyards in the cool Puget Sound basin.

For red wines, Merlot enjoyed great popularity in the 1990s while Cabernet Sauvignon and Syrah are current favourites for those planting new vineyards, so that by 2011 Cabernet Sauvignon was king with 10,300 acres/4,168 ha, followed by Merlot (8,235 acres/3,333 ha), and the more recent incomer Syrah was planted on 3,103 acres/1,256 ha. In warm years such as 2009 and 2012 Washington reds lean towards ripe flavours and noticeable alcohol levels. BORDEAUX BLENDS, with or without the state's fourth most-planted red wine grape Cabernet Franc with 972 acres/393 ha, are increasingly common and show promise. Malbec and GSM blends have been successful, and Tempranillo, Barbera, and even Zinfandel can thrive in the right spot.

The producers
The dominant force in Washington wine is Ste Michelle Wine Estates (formerly Stimson Lane), a subsidiary of tobacco company, the Altria Group, and the owner of a range of labels which includes Chateau Ste Michelle, Michelle, Columbia Crest, and Northstar, with important high-quality joint ventures with Ernst Loosen of Germany (for Eroica Riesling) and Piero ANTINORI of Italy (for Col Solare). The company collectively controls more than one-third of all vineyard land in Washington, and produces a wide range of wines, including a number of superior single-vineyard bottlings. Some of the state's most sought-after wines are made in Walla Walla by Cayuse, Gramercy Cellars, Leonetti, Pepper Bridge, and Woodward Canyon and in western Washington (with fruit grown in some of Columbia Valley's top vineyards) by Andrew Will, Betz Family, Cadence, and Quilceda Creek. Other widely distributed labels by volume and reputation include the Seattle-based Columbia Winery, now owned by GALLO, and Yakima Valley-based Hogue Cellars, a consistent producer of well-priced wines.   L.M. & P.G.

Gregutt, P., *Washington Wines and Wineries: The Essential Guide* (2nd edn, Seattle, 2011).

Robinson, J., and Murphy, L., *American Wine* (Berkeley, Calif., 2013).

www.washingtonwine.org

www.wawgg.org

water is the most important constituent of wine (see WINE COMPOSITION) and access to reliable supplies of good-quality water, particularly for IRRIGATION, is becoming a pressing problem for an increasing number of wine producers, particularly in inland Australia and much of California—not least because of CLIMATE CHANGE, DROUGHT, and problems associated with SALINITY.

SOIL WATER, the product of RAINFALL and/or irrigation, is a prerequisite for vine growth and survival. PHOTOSYNTHESIS, without which grapes would never ripen, depends on water being available (which is why RIPENING stops if WATER STRESS is too severe). Water in the form of well-timed rain can also be useful in dusting off grapes immediately prior to HARVEST.

Water is also vital in the winery: HYGIENE's best friend is the hosepipe, and many systems of TEMPERATURE CONTROL depend on copious supplies of water. In warmer regions, the operation known euphemistically as HUMIDIFICATION is sometimes undertaken for ALCOHOL REDUCTION.

And then there is water as a drink. For centuries wine was always diluted with water, indeed drinking undiluted wine was the mark of a barbarian in Ancient GREECE and Ancient ROME. Wine was a safer drink than most available water until the 17th century in major cities, and much later than that elsewhere. In the late 1960s, this writer was offered unlimited wine as part of her board when working in a smart Italian hotel, but had to pay for bottled water, the only reliable drinking water.

The modern wine drinker rarely chooses to dilute his or her wine (other than to make the occasional SPRITZER) but for HEALTH reasons he or she is well advised to drink at least as much water alongside every glass of wine. Despite its incontrovertible appeal, wine is a poor quencher of thirst.

water addition. See HUMIDIFICATION.

water berry, an alternative name, current in California, for BUNCHSTEM NECROSIS, the physiological disorder of grape berry stems, drying and shrivelling grapes as they approach RIPENESS.

water deficit. See WATER STRESS.

water shoot, a shoot that arises from the wood of the vine, not from buds left at pruning. In fact they mostly arise from BASAL BUDS embedded in the wood and are generally not FRUITFUL. Suckers are a type of water shoot which arise at the base of the TRUNK at or below soil level. B.G.C.

water stress is the physiological state of plants, including vines, suffering from a shortage of water. Water stress during the later stages of the viticultural growing season is common, since a considerable proportion of the world's vines are grown in MEDITERRANEAN CLIMATES, where rain falls principally in the winter months and irrigation is restricted or not used. By the time of ripening, the amount of SOIL WATER may well be low. It is commonly held that mild water stress, often referred to as water deficit, is desirable for optimum wine quality, especially for red wines, but there is little agreement about exactly how much. There is,

however, almost universal agreement that water deficit should be sufficient before VERAISON to stop SHOOT TIPS actively growing. Otherwise the shoot tips attract assimilates, the products of PHOTOSYNTHESIS, away from the ripening fruit, to the detriment of wine quality.

Water deficit is essential for growing good-quality dark-skinned grapes. It not only reduces shoot growth but also limits berry size and increases the PHENOLICS in the skins. However, these beneficial effects require a CANOPY free from SHADE and, generally, low yields. A combination of high yields and water stress leads to poor ripening due to insufficient photosynthesis. This explains why great wines may be produced in very dry climatic conditions in southern France or Spain, for example, but only when yields are kept to 30 hl/ha or less. Peyrot des Gachons et al. have shown that water stress is not generally favourable for the quality of white wines, causing them to be less aromatic.

IRRIGATION can be used to overcome water stress, although it is outlawed or severely restricted in some European countries. Water stress results in restriction of growth and loss of yield. Unirrigated DRYLAND vineyards in hot climates may yield only 2 to 5 tonnes/ha, for instance. PARTIAL ROOTZONE DRYING is an irrigation method which aims to stimulate the vines' perception of water stress while minimizing any drop in YIELD. Another irrigation strategy designed to induce water stress is REGULATED DEFICIT IRRIGATION. However, this technique is more likely to reduce yield and can induce excessive water stress in hot weather if not applied judiciously. Both techniques are used in California and Australia to control water stress in vines at critical times to achieve better fruit and wine quality.

Water stress depends on two components: the available water content in the root zone of the vine (see SOIL WATER), and the evaporative demand of the atmosphere. The latter depends on factors affecting the rate of EVAPORATION, which is high on sunny, hot, windy days with low humidity. On days with extremely high evaporation, even well-watered vines can show temporary wilting. On the other hand, vines growing in dry soils but in overcast, cool, and humid climates do not show as much water stress. The combination of climate, soil, and VINE ARCHITECTURE which results in maximum vine stress is high evaporation, low soil water content, and large leaf area; minimum stress results from low evaporation, wet soils, and small leaf area.

Water stress is measured by vine physiologists as water potential in the plant, but is more easily understood in terms of the effect on the vine. One of the first signs of impending water stress is the drooping, or wilting, of tendrils near the shoot tip, followed by wilting of the young, then the mature, leaves. With severe

stress, the leaves exhibit yellowing, then NECROSIS, and may eventually fall off. Berries start to shrivel. As water stress develops in the vine, the plant responds by endeavouring to reduce water loss. In NEW WORLD countries in particular, where irrigation is more common, water stress is sometimes indicated by measurements of SOIL WATER content or suction, with irrigation decisions based on this information.

The direct measurement of water stress as experienced by the vine (through so-called 'physiological indicators') has been made possible by the commercial availability in the last decade of the 20th century of equipment such as PRESSURE BOMBS, which measure leaf or stem water potential. Although time-consuming, this measurement can indicate day-to-day fluctuations in vine water status and is widely used in the Central Valley, California. It can be used either to monitor the response of dry-farmed vines to the site, or to fine-tune irrigation, although such data are not always easy to interpret.

A very promising technique to measure the water deficit experienced by vines is to analyse carbon isotope discrimination by measuring the ratio of ^{13}C to ^{12}C in the sugar content of fully ripe grapes. In the process of photosynthesis, plants incorporate preferentially ^{12}C and thus 'discriminate' against ^{13}C but in water stress conditions, isotope discrimination is less effective so that the ^{13}C/^{12}C ratio is lower. This ratio can therefore be used as a measurement of average water uptake conditions from veraison through to ripeness, as described in van Leeuwen et al. (2009). The measurement can be outsourced to specialized laboratories and requires no other field work than grape sampling. Possible applications are the assessment of vine water status in terroir studies and validation of irrigation strategies at the end of the season.

A well-watered vine opens the pores called STOMATA on the underside of the leaf in response to the first light of dawn, and they remain open all day, allowing the free exchange of water vapour (the air humidity) and CARBON DIOXIDE between the leaf interior and the atmosphere. Water stress causes the vine leaf partially to close stomata during the day, and the hormone ABSCISIC ACID regulates this response. Initially, this may be in the middle of the day, but subsequently, as the stress worsens, they are shut for most of the day. While this action is sufficient to reduce further water loss, photosynthesis is reduced because of the lack of carbon dioxide. Recent studies have shown that stomata may stay open during the night, so that night-time water stress may occur.

Water stress also affects a range of other vine functions. It can substitute for winter cold in promoting DORMANCY in TROPICAL VITICULTURE. During the growing season, drought causes shoot growth to slow and then stop as the leaf tip loses activity. Leaves are smaller and paler in colour, and the growth of LATERAL SHOOTS is also inhibited. Severe stress early in the season can reduce FRUIT SET, and later stress reduces BERRY SIZE.

The effect of water stress on wine quality is not straightforward. There is no doubt that severe water stress interrupts grape RIPENING and reduces wine quality (especially when yields are high), as for example may be observed in Algeria. It is not clear whether water stress leads to higher SUGARS and better wine in dry viticultural areas such as the LANGUEDOC and ROUSSILLON in southern France. In humid maritime climates, such as that of BORDEAUX, however, there has been ample demonstration that mild water stress during ripening is favourable to wine quality. For example, the Bordeaux growing seasons of 1989, 1990, 1995, 1998, 2000, 2005, 2009, and 2010, all superior VINTAGES, were all relatively dry. Van Leuwen et al. (2009) show that all the driest vintages produced good quality and all the wettest vintages were relatively poor.   R.E.S., C.v.L., & R.E.W.

Peyrot des Gachons, C., et al., 'The influence of water and nitrogen deficit on fruit ripening and aroma potential of Vitis vinifera L. cv Sauvignon blanc in field conditions', Journal of the Science of Food and Agriculture, 85/1 (2005), 73–85.

Tregoat, O., et al., 'Étude du régime hydrique et de la nutrition azotée de la vigne par des indicateurs physiologiques. Influence sur le comportement de la vigne et la maturation du raisin (Vitis vinifera L. cv Merlot, 2000, Bordeaux)', Journal International des Sciences de la Vigne et du Vin, 36/3 (2002), 133–42.

Smart, R. E., 'Aspects of the water relations of the grapevine (Vitis vinifera)', American Journal of Enology and Viticulture, 25 (1974), 84–91.

van Leeuwen, C., et al., 'Vine water status is a key factor in grape ripening and vintage quality for red Bordeaux wine. How can it be assessed for vineyard management purposes?', Journal International al des Sciences de la Vigne et du Vin, 43/3 (2009), 121–34.

White, R. E., Understanding Vineyard Soils (2nd edn, Oxford, 2015).

Waugh, Harry (1904–2001), English wine merchant famous for his longevity, courtesy, and open mind. He did not enter the wine trade until he was 30, joining as a clerk in a long-established City of London business associated with the fashionable West End company of Block, Grey & Block, where he went to work and first displayed his ability in selecting and selling fine wines. At that time, few British wine merchants visited the sources of their wines, but relied on agents or their principals, who paid regular visits to Britain. In this way, Waugh met such well-known Bordeaux merchants as Christian Cruse, Jean Calvet, and Ronald BARTON. He also spent an annual holiday in the leading French wine areas with the late Allan SICHEL, wine importer and part-owner of Ch Palmer (see MARGAUX).

During the Second World War, Waugh served in the Welsh Guards, and then at the beginning of 1946 joined the London office of HARVEYS OF BRISTOL. With wine in very short supply after six years of war, there was great demand for red bordeaux, the favoured table wine among regular wine drinkers. Waugh took a further holiday in Bordeaux, where he was introduced by Édouard Cruse to the wines of POMEROL, then almost unknown in Britain. In 1950, he acquired and imported in cask the distinguished 1949 vintage of the then obscure PETRUS; as by coincidence did that other Bristol wine merchant Ronald AVERY. He also visited for Harveys other French wine regions, including Beaujolais, then imported as a somewhat anonymous quaffing blend. He bought individual CRU Beaujolais and was invited to form a London chapter of the still flourishing Compagnons de Beaujolais CONFRÉRIE.

After the devastating FROSTS of February 1956, Waugh, by then a director of Harveys, went with a colleague to Bordeaux and, through broker Jean-Paul Gardère, bought large quantities of the fine 1955 vintage, thereby bypassing the BORDEAUX TRADE, for which he was long remembered. He was a regular visitor for his firm to Oxford and Cambridge colleges, and in 1953 instituted an annual Oxbridge undergraduate wine-tasting competition, sponsored until 1990 by Harveys (and subsequently by POL ROGER champagne).

In 1962 the families who owned Ch LATOUR decided to sell, and offered this famous Bordeaux first growth to Harveys. Although Waugh and his chairman were in favour, so that the majority of the board was against, so that Pearson, publishers of the Financial Times, acquired a 51% stake, while Harveys were allotted only 25%. Waugh became one of two Harvey representatives on the board, on which he remained during two changes of ownership. He introduced as joint managers Jean-Paul Gardère and his friend Henri Martin, proprietor of Ch Gloria (see ST-JULIEN). In 1966 when Harveys was bought by Showerings, producers of Babycham, a popular perry, Waugh, then 62, retired. (Seven years later his first children, twins, were born, both of them going on to work in the UK wine trade.)

Then began Waugh's close association with wine amateurs in the United States. For many years he made regular lecture tours, and achieved a reputation in the US unequalled by any other British wine professional. Several volumes of Harry Waugh's Wine Diary were published as a record of his punishing itineraries. He did much to publicize Ch Latour, as well as other Bordeaux châteaux's wines. He also introduced California wines to British (and east coast American) wine connoisseurs in the early 1970s when they were little known. For his services to French wines, he received the French Mérite Agricole in 1984 and in 1988 he was made a Chevalier de l'Ordre du Mérite National. In 1989, he was made an honorary member of the Institute of MASTERS OF WINE. He will always be remembered for his reply to someone who asked whether he had ever mistaken claret for burgundy: 'not since lunch.'   E.P.-R.

Waugh, H., Harry Waugh's Wine Diaries vols. i–ix (vols. i–v were individually entitled) (London, 1966–81).

weather, probably the single most exasperatingly unpredictable variable in the viticultural equation, as in most other farming activities. For details of overall weather patterns, see CLIMATE, MACROCLIMATE, and CLIMATE CLASSIFICATION. For accounts of specific climatological phenomena with implications for wine production, see DEW, DROUGHT, FLOODING, FROST, HAIL, RAINFALL, SUNLIGHT, TEMPERATURE, and WIND. The weather in a specific growing season is the most important influence on the characteristics of a particular VINTAGE YEAR.

websites, increasingly important way of selling and communicating about wine. See INFORMATION TECHNOLOGY.

weed control, a range of viticultural practices to avoid WEEDS competing with vines—particularly young vines—for water and NUTRIENTS. The practices vary from region to region and with VINE AGE, with the common options being CULTIVATION (ploughing) or HERBICIDES.

Mechanical control of weeds involves cultivating down the row alley using discs or tines. Cultivation directly under the row is more difficult, as the weeding device needs to avoid the trunks. A number of appropriate cultivators have been developed, with the swing back action achieved manually in early models but now controlled automatically by touch sensing the trunk. Even so, such cultivation disturbs the ground under the vine row where the majority of roots are, and many machines can cause some vine damage. Hand hoeing of weeds is still found in some vineyards, although often this is restricted to the control of particularly difficult weeds in young vineyards. The alternative is to use herbicides, and spraying an undervine strip is common.

Mowing between the rows is common in summer rainfall areas, or where there is plentiful irrigation, otherwise the weeds growing there cause excessive WATER STRESS and sometimes NITROGEN deficiency, leading to incomplete fermentations. Other methods of weed control include mulching, using cereal straw, for example, placed as a mat under the rows. This has the added advantage of increasing ORGANIC MATTER, EARTHWORM populations, and water infiltration. During the vines' early years, weeds may also be controlled by planting through a strip of plastic. R.E.S.

University of California Agriculture & Natural Resources, 'Integrated weed management', www.ipm.ucdavis.edu/PMG/r302700111.html.

weeder, implement used in vineyards for removing WEEDS, typically from the vine row. These machines, usually mounted on a tractor, have fallen from favour owing to the death of some vines, and the introduction of some diseases because of vine injury. In many parts of the world, the use of undervine weeders has been replaced by HERBICIDES. R.E.S.

weeds. A weed is defined as a plant out of place. Although vine-growers have traditionally regarded a weedy vineyard as a sign of poor management, attitudes changed in the late 20th century and the sight of a 'weedy' vineyard is now commonplace. Weeds, now referred to as volunteer COVER CROPS, are considered environmentally desirable as part of the vineyard ECOSYSTEM. Alternatively, some vineyards are frequently ploughed to keep them free of weeds, to the detriment of SOIL STRUCTURE. HERBICIDES are used, perhaps in combination with less frequent CULTIVATION.

There is no doubt that weed growth can inhibit the growth of vines, especially when they are young. When the vine root system is small and shallow, weeds compete for water and nutrients, especially NITROGEN, but with older vines the competition can be less as the vine root system is larger and deeper. Some plant species seem to have a further effect in inhibiting others, a phenomenon known as allelopathy. In very weedy vineyards, the weeds may also compete with the vines for light.

Weeds can cause inconvenience and discomfort to vineyard workers and can also harbour vine PESTS and DISEASES, although they can also usefully shelter predators of insect vine pests. Weeds play an important part in the spread of the disease FLAVESCENCE DORÉE. In some vineyards, other plants may be deliberately encouraged to grow between the rows as a COVER CROP.

Weeds which occur in vineyards obviously vary from region to region, and are representative of the local flora. Those present depend on prior land use, soil preparation, seed reserves in the soil, and the extent to which seeds arrive in the vineyard, by wind or on implements, for example. Weeds which are difficult to control and can be found in many vineyards worldwide include field bindweed (*Convolvulus arvensis*), Johnson grass (*Holcus halepensis*), and Bermuda or couch grass (*Cynadon dactylon*). R.E.S.

Bettiga, L. J. (ed.), *Grape Pest Management* (3rd edn, Oakland, Calif., 2013).

weevils. See BEETLES.

weighing of grapes is an important operation at any centre where grapes are received from a number of different growers who are paid by weight. This applies to most wine CO-OPERATIVES and many individual wineries, even if the more progressive take other factors such as grape quality and health into account before determining PRICE. Weighing is normally done with large platform scales on which the lorry is weighed full and empty.

It is also important to weigh grapes before PRESSING in order to measure the volume of juice extracted in relation to the fruit weight. See, for example, CHAMPAGNE for the regulations concerning pressing and yield.

Wein (pronounced 'vine') means 'wine' in GERMAN and is therefore how a WINE WITHOUT GEOGRAPHICAL INDICATION would be described in Germany and Austria. It is also the first syllable of a host of important German wine names such as **Weinbau** (vine-growing), **Weinbrand** (basic brandy), and **Weingut** (wine estate) as distinct from a **Weinkellerei**, which buys in grapes, must, or wine but probably owns vineyards only if it describes itself as the all-purpose **Weingut-Weinkellerei**. A **Weinprobe** is a wine tasting, **Weinsäure** is TARTARIC ACID, some of which may eventually be precipitated as crystal TARTRATES, or **Weinsteine**. A wine made by blending ingredients from more than one EU country is a **Wein aus der europäischen Gemeinschaft**.

Weinviertel, a vast arc of viticulture in AUSTRIA north of the Danube, extending along the borders of the CZECH REPUBLIC, then east and south along the River March and Austria's frontier with SLOVAKIA, its western edge abutting KAMPTAL and WAGRAM, and its southern fringes abutting the urban vineyards of VIENNA. With 16,650 ha/41,000 acres of vines, the Weinviertel is Austria's largest official wine region, and produces more than a third of Austrian wine. Volume has gone hand in hand with modest prices and relative lack of cachet when compared with other wine regions, but it has also made the Weinviertel an indispensable feature of Austria's passionate wine-drinking culture, and an increasing number of quality-conscious growers are carving a niche for themselves and this region among their country's many wine sophisticates.

Half of the Weinviertel's vineyard area is planted with GRÜNER VELTLINER, but that dominance came about only after the middle of the last century. In a region, this large and diverse geologically, climatically, and culturally, it is not surprising that growers have scored striking successes with many grape varieties: Pinot Blanc (Weissburgunder), Riesling, and Zweigelt as well as Austrian specialities BLAUBURGER, Blauer PORTUGIESER, MUSKATELLER, and WELSCHRIESLING,

and mixed plantings of GEMISCHTER SATZ. Among the more important wine communities of the Weinviertel are Retz and Röschitz in the west of the region; Falkenstein, Poysdorf, and Wolkersdorf in the north-east (prominent for SEKT base wine but capable of far greater distinction). Also included are a cluster of tiny villages on the edge of the Bisamberg and Vienna's 21st District, of which the best known is Stetten, because it is home to the Weinviertel's most prominent pioneer of ambitious quality, Roman Pfaffl.

Weinviertel DAC was the first Austrian DAC appellation for wines from the region made from Grüner Veltliner. Those referred to as KLASSIK must be of at least 12% alcohol and be free of BOTRYTIS and wood notes. They may be commercialized as early as 1 January following harvest. Wines from this DAC labelled Reserve must be at least 13% alcohol; are permitted to evince 'subtle' botrytis or wood tones, and are not approved for sale before 15 March. Other than slight differences in the adjectives used to characterize their styles, the above sets of criteria are not materially different from those governing the KAMPTAL DAC, KREMSTAL DAC, and TRAISENTAL DAC, in all of which, however, they apply to Riesling as well. Since its inception in 2002, wines that do not qualify for the Weinviertel DAC or are not successfully submitted by their growers for inclusion may not be labelled Weinviertel but must instead be labelled NIEDERÖSTERREICH for their state of origin. This applies most importantly to wines produced from grape varieties other than Grüner Veltliner, which represent around half of the Weinviertel's vineyard area. D.S.

weisser, meaning 'white', is a common prefix in German for pale-skinned grape varieties, e.g. **Weissburgunder** or **Weisser Burgunder** is PINOT BLANC in German-speaking wine lands.

Weisser Riesling, common synonym for the great white RIESLING grape variety of Germany.

Weissherbst is by German law a rosé wine at least 95% of which is made by direct pressing of a single red wine grape variety named on the label (SPÄTBURGUNDER and PORTUGIESER are especially common). In practice, the 5% red wine permitted to achieve a desired colour is rarely added since consumers expect Weissherbst to be very pale. The term is also used in German-speaking SWITZERLAND for very much the same style of wine. See also SCHILLERWEIN.

Wellington, warm inland wine district in SOUTH AFRICA just north of PAARL, which produces full-bodied wines, mainly reds.

Welschriesling, or **Wälschriesling**, important white grape variety which, as Germans are keen to point out, is completely unrelated to the great RIESLING grape of Germany. Indeed it rankles with many Germans that the noble word is even allowed as a suffix in the name of this inferior variety; they would prefer that the word Rizling were used, as in **Welsch Rizling** or **Welschrizling**, which it is in many of its many synonyms. Welsch simply means 'foreign' in Germanic languages, which provides few clues but suggests that the variety may well have originated in a non-German-speaking country. It is widely planted in much of central and eastern Europe.

Welschriesling may be the variety's most common name in AUSTRIA, but Welschrizling is obediently used in BULGARIA, its most common name in HUNGARY is OLASZ RIZLING (under which more details of its importance in Hungary are to be found), in SLOVENIA and SERBIA it is LAŠKI RIZLING, and in the CZECH REPUBLIC and SLOVAKIA it is the very similar Rizling Vlassky. Only in CROATIA, where it is also the single most planted vine variety, does it acquire a name of any distinction, Graševina. The Italians call it RIESLING ITALICO (as opposed to Riesling Renano, which is the Riesling of Germany) and variants of this are used all over Eastern Europe. In ROMANIA most of the 6,346 ha/15,680 acres of 'Riesling' noted in 2013 are this variety, although new plantings are increasingly of the German Riesling. Welschriesling is one of the few common white wine grapes in ALBANIA, as it is in what was for long its close political ally CHINA.

It does best in dry climates and warmer soils, and has a tendency to produce excessively acid wines in cool climates. Like German Riesling, it is a relatively late-ripening vine whose grapes keep their acidity well and produce light-bodied, relatively aromatic wines. Welschriesling can easily be persuaded to yield even more productively than Riesling, however, and indeed this and its useful acidity probably explain why it is so widely planted throughout eastern Europe and, partly, why so much of the wine it produces is undistinguished (although poor-quality viticulture and winemaking equipment may also have played a part).

As a wine, Welschriesling reaches its apogee in AUSTRIA, specifically in some particularly finely balanced, rich late-harvest wines made on the shores of the Neusiedlersee in Burgenland, where nearly half of Austria's total 3,436 ha/8,487 acres of the variety is planted. Welschriesling is Austria's most planted white wine grape after Grüner Veltliner. In particularly favoured vintages, the NOBLE ROT forms to ripen grapes up to TROCKENBEERENAUSLESE level, while retaining the acidity that is Welschriesling's hallmark. Welschriesling may not have the aromatic character of Germany's Riesling, but since aroma plays only a small part in the

appreciation of really sweet wines, this leaves Welschriesling at less of a disadvantage than Riesling addicts might imagine, although Austrian TBAS, sometimes a blend of Chardonnay with Welschriesling, rarely have the longevity of their German counterparts. The bulk of Austria's Welschriesling, however, goes into light dryish wines for early drinking, notably in Weinviertel, Burgenland, and Styria. It is also used for production of Austrian SEKT.

Croatia grows almost three times as much of the variety as Austria, all over the country with the finest wines produced in Slavonia in the east. It is second only to Grüner Veltliner in the CZECH REPUBLIC with more than 3,000 ha/7,413 acres planted and its 1,200 ha/2,965 acres in SLOVAKIA make it almost as important as German Riesling. According to Anderson at the University of Adelaide's calculations this was the world's 15th most planted wine grape variety in 2010.

Western Australia, or WA. AUSTRALIA's biggest state has the country's most isolated wine regions in its south-west corner.

Nowhere have the winds of change blown harder since 1970 than in Western Australia. In that year, more than 90% of the state's wine was made from grapes grown in the then Swan Valley (now a subregion of the **Swan District** in the Greater Perth Zone); by 1980 the figure was 59%; and by 2003 it was less than 11%. The other side of the coin has been the emergence of the Margaret River and Great Southern regions spanning the far south western corner of the state.

In a manner reminiscent of the Barossa Valley in South Australia, the Swan Valley, with the dubious distinction of being the hottest region in Australia, with harvest typically beginning in January, remains the production centre of much of Western Australia's wine, largely through a single company, Houghton (part of HARDYS). As well as producing Houghton White Burgundy (or HWB, as it is called in Europe) from Verdelho, Chenin Blanc, and Chardonnay grown in the Swan Valley and at Gingin (just to the north), Houghton has large vineyards at Frankland in the Great Southern, and is a major purchaser of grapes throughout that region and the Margaret River. Houghton's ultra-premium Jack Mann and Gladstones red wines from these regions are among Australia's very best full-bodied wines based on Cabernet Sauvignon and Shiraz.

The **Margaret River** has grown considerably in both size and reputation since the mid 1990s. It is now recognized as the source of some of Australia's finest Cabernet Sauvignon as well as of pungently grassy and intense Semillon and Sauvignon Blanc, more often than not blended with each other. Chardonnay is the other grape

of importance, making wine which is invariably complex and often long lived. Leeuwin Estate is regarded by many as Australia's best, Giaconda of Beechworth being the other obvious contender. Such wines, together with Margaret River's year-round TEMPERATE CLIMATE, physical beauty, and diverse attractions from surf to woodworks make it a prime centre for wine TOURISM, while, 240 km/146 miles to the south of Perth, it is still at a latitude of 34 degrees south, and therefore completely reliant upon the cooling influence of the Indian Ocean.

With one or two exceptions such as Leeuwin Estate's, Riesling has never succeeded in the Margaret River, but comes emphatically into its own in the far-flung, cooler, and usually more CONTINENTAL subregions of the Great Southern region: **Porongurup**, **Mount Barker**, and **Frankland River**. Here it produces crisp, tightly structured wines which evolve slowly but with grace, mirroring the slow development of the equally taut yet fragrant Cabernet Sauvignon. This is a huge and diverse region. Chardonnay and Shiraz also do well, balancing cool-climate elegance and intensity of flavour. The coastal subregions of **Albany** and **Denmark** are far more suited to Sauvignon Blanc, Chardonnay, and (intermittently) Pinot Noir.

The other regions within the South West Australia Zone are of lesser importance in terms of production, and will remain so. The adjacent regions of **Pemberton** (north east) and **Manjimup** (south west) failed to agree on the name of a region which should probably have been called Pemberton/Manjimup, which has resulted in two separate, adjacent ones. This somewhat schizophrenic attitude is also reflected in the varietal wines of the regions. The distinctly cool, moderately high rainfall, and varied soils (some very fertile) caused the Pemberton pioneers to see their region as a Burgundy equivalent. In fact Merlot and Shiraz have performed as well, if not better than, Pinot Noir while Verdelho challenges Chardonnay. That challenge intensifies in Manjimup, but will likely remain undecided for a while yet.

The **Blackwood Valley** lies immediately to the north of Manjimup, taking its name from the Blackwood river. The first plantings were in 1978, and there are just as many questions about the future direction here as there are in Manjimup and Pemberton.

The last region in the South West Australia Zone is **Geographe**, altogether more important and with a clearer focus, albeit with varied climate as one moves inland from the coast. The coastal town of Bunbury is the centre (on the north/south axis), while Capel Vale is the dominant winery. The most important of four rivers are the Collie and Ferguson, creating valleys as they flow to the coast, and a cross-hatch with the Darling range running north–south. Varied terroir is the order of the day, but Chardonnay, Verdelho, Semillon, and Sauvignon Blanc lead the white wines and Shiraz, Cabernet Sauvignon, Merlot, and Tempranillo the reds, all with flavour and attitude. J.H. & H.H.

www.winewa.asn.au

Western Cape, the most important of the five geographical units making up SOUTH AFRICA's production areas defined by the country's WINE OF ORIGIN scheme and accounting for well over 90% of the nation's vineyards and wineries. (Even the extensive COASTAL REGION is a region within it.) On wine labels it generally indicates a multiregional BLEND.

western grapeleaf skeletonizer, a vine pest and native insect of Mexico and the states of Arizona, New Mexico, and Texas, first found in California in 1941 in San Diego county. The young larvae feed on the soft leaf tissue, leaving a skeleton framework. Chemical control is effective, but timing is critical. Left unchecked this insect will completely defoliate a vine, seriously affecting RIPENING. M.J.E.

Western Victoria Zone comprises Grampians, Henty, and Pyrenees regions in Australia.

Weststeiermark, the least known of the three subdivisions of STEIERMARK (Styria)—indeed, the least known of any official AUSTRIAN wine region. Its significant total expanse harbours a mere 450 ha/1,100 acres of vines, dominated by the local speciality, SCHILCHER, made from Blauer Wildbacher grapes and most often as rosé.

whip graft, the form used in GRAFTING which simply involves an angled slice across the SCION stem and a similarly angled cut of the stock, with the two cuts then matched and the graft tied tightly with grafting tape. **Whip-and-tongue** is the same except that another cut is made to raise 'tongues' of stem tissue that dovetail with each other and improve the strength of the graft. B.G.C.

white has a special meaning when applied both to grapes and wine. Any light-skinned grape may be called a white grape, even though the grape skin is not white but anything from pale green through gold to pink. In a similar fashion, white wines are not white, but vary in colour from almost colourless to deep gold. See COLOUR.

White Riesling, common synonym for the great white RIESLING grape variety of Germany.

white rot, FUNGAL DISEASE affecting vines that occurs in those parts of Europe most prone to hailstorms, also known as hail disease. Crop losses can be as high as 80%. The fruit is attacked after a hailstorm and, because the berry skin is lifted from the flesh, the berries appear white, hence the name. High summer rainfall, high humidity, and high temperatures also favour the disease. The fungus responsible is *Coniella diplodiella*, which is controlled by a range of chemical sprays. R.E.S.

white winemaking, the production of wines with almost imperceptible to golden COLOUR. If the juice is separated from the grape skins gently and soon enough (as in the production of CHAMPAGNE), white wines can be made from black-skinned grapes, but the great majority of white wines are made from grapes with yellow or green skins. White wines can be made from grapes of all hues, so long as there is no SKIN CONTACT or MACERATION with dark-skinned grapes. The only exception to this is the red-fleshed TEINTURIERS. White wines are distinguished from their red counterparts by their absence of ANTHOCYANINS and PIGMENTED TANNINS. As with any WINEMAKING operation, the production of white wines generally entails CRUSHING and DESTEMMING the grape clusters on arrival at the winery, although occasionally white grapes may be crushed beforehand at a field pressing station (and see also WHOLE-BUNCH PRESSING). After crushing and destemming, the sweet POMACE requires draining and PRESSING to separate the liquid from the solids. The timing of the separation of juice from solids constitutes the major difference between red and white winemaking: before FERMENTATION for whites and afterwards for reds.

Prolonged contact between juice and grape skins (see SKIN CONTACT and MACERATION) encourages the transfer of soluble materials, including PHENOLICS, FLAVOUR COMPOUNDS, and FLAVOUR PRECURSORS, from the skins to the juice. The extracted phenolics, which are

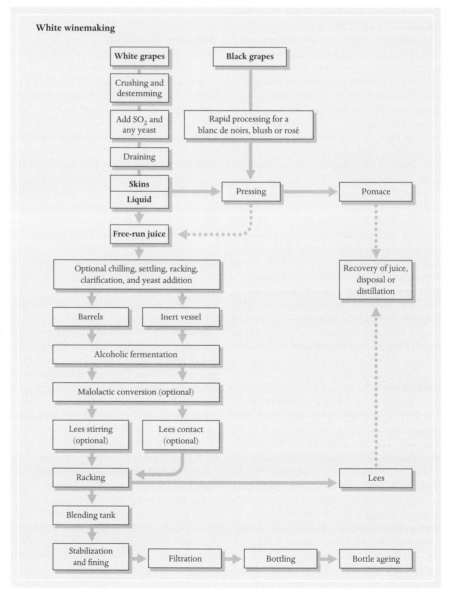

White winemaking

essential to a red wine, providing both colour and TANNIN, are generally undesirable in a white wine, for they promote OXIDATION and can lead to ASTRINGENCY. The skin phenolics also lead to the development of amber to brown colours deemed inappropriate for most white wines (but see ORANGE WINES and other SKIN-FERMENTED whites). The challenge for the white winemaker is therefore to find the balance, through appropriate juice handling techniques, between appropriate transfer of the flavour compounds and minimal phenolic extraction. Because of their light colour and delicate flavours, white wines show the unappetizing effects of oxidation much faster than red wines and so white winemaking is in general a more delicate operation than RED WINEMAKING. Small amounts of ACETALDEHYDE are produced by the reaction of oxygen with alcohol, and this compound can easily spoil the AROMA of a fresh, fruity young wine. There are two possible solutions to this inconvenience. Exposure to oxygen may be minimized during extraction, winemaking, AGEING, and right up to and including BOTTLING (see PROTECTIVE WINEMAKING, for example). Alternatively, a policy of unprotected handling is adopted whereby the MUST is deliberately, and sometimes in the case of everyday wines violently, aerated so that its susceptible phenolics oxidize, these brown compounds being removed during must clarification. This technique is sometimes referred to as hyperoxidation. The disadvantage of this preferment oxidation is that it removes some of the compounds that would have contributed to AROMA.

White wines are usually fermented at cooler TEMPERATURES than reds, now much easier to control than in the past thanks to REFRIGERATION. However, BARREL FERMENTATION followed by BARREL MATURATION is a common phenomenon for more ambitious white wines, particularly for wines made from the CHARDONNAY grape. Among these barrel-fermented white wines, LEES STIRRING is also popular (though less so than in the past), as is MALOLACTIC CONVERSION.
A.D.W. & P.J.W.

white wines, made with much less SKIN CONTACT, are much lower in PHENOLICS than red wines (see WHITE WINEMAKING). This does not necessarily mean, however, that they are inherently less interesting, or shorter lived (see AGEING). They vary enormously in colour from virtually colourless to deep gold or ORANGE, and even, in extreme age, deep tawny (not unlike the colour of some very old red wines). They are made in virtually all wine regions, although in hot regions ACIDIFICATION and some form of REFRIGERATION are usually needed to produce white wines suitable for modern tastes.

French for white is *blanc*, Italian is *bianco*, Spanish is *blanco*, Portuguese is *branco*,

German is *weiss*, while in most eastern European languages, including Russian, the word for white is some variant of *byeli*.

White Zinfandel, undeterred by the fact that it is neither white nor crucially Zinfandel, was California's great commercial success story of the 1980s. Although he was not the first to vinify California's heritage ZINFANDEL grapes as a white, and therefore BLUSH, wine, Bob Trinchero of Sutter Home launched 'White' Zinfandel down the commercial slipway in 1972 and was to see his own sales rocket from 25,000 cases in 1980 to 1.5 million cases six years later. Other producers quickly jumped on board and experienced similar success. The wine evolved as a way of making California's vast acreage of Zinfandel acceptable to the predominantly white wine-drinking American public, and it also saved many old-vine Zin vineyards from being converted to Merlot and Cabernet Sauvignon. The wine is usually pale pink, decidedly sweet, often scented with more than a dash of other, more obviously aromatic, grape varieties such as Muscat or Riesling. So successful was the wine that it begat styles such as **White Grenache** and **White Merlot**. White Zinfandel sales remain strong, although US consumers are increasingly gravitating to drier rosés.

whole-bunch fermentation, ultra-traditional method of red wine FERMENTATION in which grape berries are not subjected to DESTEMMING. This was the default position before the introduction of the CRUSHER-DESTEMMER. Aside from the influence of the stems themselves, the process generally involves an element of CARBONIC MACERATION at the start of the ferment. The possible disadvantages are that, unless the STEMS are very ripe, i.e. well LIGNIFIED, and the MUST is handled very gently, the stems may impart harsh TANNINS to the wine. The technique also involves a greater total capacity of FERMENTATION VESSELS, which are often open-topped to allow PUNCHING DOWN of the CAP. The practical advantages are that the stems can ease the drainage of the juice through the cap, aerate the ferment so that it is slightly cooler, and encourage healthy oxygenation by increasing the cap's interface with the atmosphere during MACERATION. The level of potassium in the juice is also increased slightly, resulting in lower ACIDITY in the wine.

Whole-bunch fermentation is most common in BURGUNDY and now more generally with Pinot Noir. Cabernet Sauvignon seems to be particularly unsuited to this technique, partly because of the risk of increasing GREEN flavours, which may already be a problem in cooler regions, and partly because there is no lack of tannin in Cabernet skins. An increasing number of winemakers in both hemispheres are experimenting with the inclusion of stems,

varying the percentage of whole bunches according to the vintage conditions, the overall character of the fruit, the ripeness of the stems, and the desired wine style. Proponents suggest that whole-bunch fermentation imparts organoleptic benefits such as firmer tannins and increased aroma, freshness, elegance, and complexity. Opponents—most famously the late Henri Jayer of Burgundy—point to the potential loss of colour (absorbed by the stems), tougher tannins, and increased herbal or green characters in the wine.

Goode, J., 'Stemming the tide', *World of Fine Wine*, 37 (2012), 90–7.

whole-bunch pressing, WHITE WINEMAKING technique whereby the grapes are not subjected to DESTEMMING and bunches of ripe grapes are pressed whole, with the stems used as conduits for what can often be particularly viscous juice. This works best for very ripe grapes and would not be suitable if a period of SKIN CONTACT precedes PRESSING since excess TANNINS could be leached into the must from the STEMS. This technique is almost universal in the production of top-quality SPARKLING WINES and most other white wines from dark-skinned grapes and in the direct pressing of BOTRYTIS-affected clusters of super-ripe grapes as in SAUTERNES. It is also increasingly popular with some quality-conscious producers of white wines in some wine regions since the juice that results tends to be low in PHENOLICS and high in quality.

whole-cluster fermentation. See WHOLE-BUNCH FERMENTATION.

whole-grape fermentation. Alternative name for CARBONIC MACERATION.

Wien is how the natives of Vienna refer to the AUSTRIAN capital and the official wine-growing region it comprises. Vienna serves as an axis between Danubian growing regions, nowadays dominated by Grüner Veltliner but also starring Riesling, and those regions more strongly influenced by the warmth of the Pannonian-Hungarian Plain and significantly planted with red wine grapes. Just under a quarter of the metropolis's roughly 700 ha/1,700 acres of vines are dark-skinned. Red wine production dominates the two important viticultural neighbourhoods on Vienna's southern fringe, Oberlaa and Mauer (abutting the THERMENREGION), which feature Zweigelt, Pinot Noir (Blauburgunder), and smaller contingents of diverse other red wine grapes. The reputation of Vienna as an important wine-growing region, however, rests on Grüner Veltliner, Riesling, less prominently Chardonnay and Pinot Blanc (Weissburgunder), along with white-grape-dominated GEMISCHTER SATZ. Although these old FIELD BLENDS have shrunk to a mere 11–12% of the city's vineyard area, they represent a distinctive contribution to its wine-growing and drinking culture, and provide the basis for the relatively recent Wiener Gemischter Satz DAC (see below). Nearly all of these field blends are dominated by or consist exclusively of white wine grapes, with older vineyards generally incorporating significant shares of Grüner Veltliner as well as vaguely Burgundian varieties such as Chardonnay, Pinot Blanc, Pinot Gris, and Neuburger. Riesling, Rotgipfler, Silvaner, Traminer, Welschriesling, Zierfandler, and unidentified vines are also frequently found.

Predominantly white wine grapes, they grow mainly on either side of the Danube in the city's north west. The Kahlenberg and Nussberg vineyards, along with sites in the nearby suburbs of Grinzing, Sievering, and Neustift—all in Vienna's 19th District—offer a stunning panorama of the city thanks to the ELEVATION and sunny exposure that, along with attendant breezes and soils typically rich in fossils and LIMESTONE, commend them as high-quality sites. Musts seldom dip below 12.5% POTENTIAL ALCOHOL. On the Danube's left bank, important vineyards extend north and west from the suburbs of Stammersdorf and Strebersdorf to the edges of the Bisamberg and the WEINVIERTEL, a vast growing region many of whose locally important growers also have holdings in Vienna. Each wine district has managed to keep the look of a wine village, even within the borders of a large city. Their often-bucolic wine taverns are a refuge for thirsty urbanites and an emblematic part of Austria's HEURIGER culture of grower-dispensed new wine. No account, however brief, of modern Viennese wine history would be complete without mention of the role played by Fritz Wieninger as a model vintner and international ambassador for his vine-rich native city.

Weiner Gemischter Satz DAC is the official Austrian appellation of origin designed to showcase Vienna's mixed vine plantings. As officially defined from the 2013 vintage, these wines must include at least three white grape varieties, though these may be planted in dedicated blocks as opposed to truly intermingled, provided those blocks are contiguous. No single variety may constitute more than half of a wine's volume and if it consists of just three varieties, then none may constitute less than 10% of the total volume. Wines from grapes grown in Vienna but vinified and bottled in another region—and there are many producers just outside the city limits in the neighbouring WEINVIERTEL or THERMENREGION as well as in KLOSTERNEUBURG—may apply for a dispensation to allow their Viennese wines that meet all other DAC requirements to be bottled as Wiener Gemischter Satz DAC. Wines of this DAC that are bottled without vineyard designation may not (with the usual half percentage

labelling tolerance) exceed 12.5% alcohol, whereas those labelled for single sites must reach a minimum 12.5%, which nowadays happens as a matter of course. It seems possible that the creation of this DAC will encourage Viennese growers to plant more vineyards with GEMISCHTER SATZ. Since Wien is the name of an Austrian state, as well as of an official wine region, Viennese wines that do not qualify for the Wiener Gemischter Satz DAC may be labelled Wien (see other DAC regulations). D.S.

WIETA, or Wine and Agricultural Ethical Trade Association, is an organization dedicated to improving social and employment conditions in the wine industry of SOUTH AFRICA. Members include grape-growers, wine producers, trades unions, retailers, agents, importers, and exporters of South African wine. Its code of conduct includes a prohibition on child and enforced labour and obliges members to provide a safe and healthy working environment with freedom of association, the right to collective bargaining, a living wage, reasonable working hours, regular employment, security of tenure, and protection against unfair discrimination. Members are subject to regular audits, and, when compliant, are accredited by WIETA. In 2014 certification arrangements were being extended with a view to ensuring that over time WIETA compliance will be incorporated in a single seal, issued by the Wine & Spirit Board and covering not merely compliance in terms of the WINE OF ORIGIN scheme but also environmental SUSTAINABILITY (see INTEGRATED PRODUCTION OF WINE) and ethical responsibility. M.F.

Wildbacher. See BLAUER WILDBACHER.

wild vines, plants of the genus VITIS growing in their natural state without any cultivation by humans. Such vines are lianas and are often found climbing trees but may also grow as shrubs. They are widespread in the Americas, especially in the east and south east, in Asia, and up until the late 1800s in Europe. Indigenous wild grapevines can sometimes be confused with feral or naturalized vines derived from plants once cultivated. Examples of feral vines are the wild vines of the Pays BASQUE and the AMERICAN VINE SPECIES *Vitis riparia* and *Vitis rupestris* along the Rhône and Garonne rivers after importation as ROOTSTOCKS. Wild vines are typically spread by BIRDS eating the berries and passing the seeds. Where wild vines of different species grow together, it is common for natural HYBRIDS to develop, as for example in the east of America (see AMERICAN HYBRIDS). Such hybrids can also develop from natural pollen interchange with cultivated grapes.

Perhaps the most famous of all wild vines are those described in the legend about the

discovery of VÍNLAND. The early settlers and explorers in the Americas and the Caribbean found profuse growth of wild vines in the woods. Such vines had tolerance to the harsh winter climate and indigenous pests such as PHYLLOXERA, and FUNGAL DISEASES such as DOWNY MILDEW and POWDERY MILDEW, and to PIERCE'S DISEASE, and so could grow without check, while the *Vitis* VINIFERA vines imported from Europe perished in cultivation.

Wild vines of the wine-producing V. vinifera species were once widespread in Europe and western Asia, although they have disappeared from large areas of Europe since the introduction of the American pests and diseases noted above. Sometimes such wild vines are called *Vitis vinifera* subsp. *silvestris*, while cultivated vines are called *Vitis vinifera* subsp. *vinifera* (sometimes *sativa*). The main difference between the two forms lies in the sexes of the flowers: the subspecies *silvestris* is dioecious, with flowers that are either male-only or female-only on the same plant, while the subspecies *vinifera* is hermaphroditic, with flowers containing functional male and female parts. This feature of subspecies *vinifera* results in better FRUIT SET, and has been the basis of selection from the wild by humans.

Wild vines are important to modern viticulture as they are the source of many resistance genes that can used in breeding NEW VARIETIES. The genetic diversity of wild *Vitis* varieties has not yet been extensively explored, and the possibilities for improving modern varieties' resistance to pathogens and environmental stresses such as DROUGHT are endless. See also GENETIC MODIFICATION. R.E.S. & J.V.

Arrigo, N., and Arnold, C., 'Naturalised *Vitis* rootstocks in Europe and consequences to native wild grapevine', PLOS ONE, 2/6 (2007), e521. doi: 10.1371/journal.pone.0000521.

Grassi, F., et al., 'Phylogeographical structure and conservation genetics of wild grapevine', *Conservation Genetics*, 7/6 (2006), 837–45. doi: 10.1007/s10592-006-9118-9.

Myles, S., et al., 'Genetic structure and domestication history of the grape', *Proceedings of the National Academy of Sciences of the United States of America*, 108/9 (2011), 3530-5. doi: 10.1073/pnas.1009363108.

wild yeast. See YEAST.

wind, or strong air movement, is a problem on many coastal and otherwise exposed viticultural sites. Major valleys can also be windy, because they can act as funnels, and have their own distinctive systems of wind force and directions. The mistral of the southern Rhône is one of the more notorious examples of this, as is the Salinas Valley in MONTEREY. The detrimental effects of wind on vines are described under

WIND STRESS; installing WINDBREAKS can provide a solution.

Hot, dry winds in summer are a particular hazard of viticultural regions bordering deserts. The sirocco of North Africa afflicts the vineyards of southern Europe, occasionally reaching France, for example. The hot, very dry, strong *zonda* winds of ARGENTINA can cause major problems for vineyards.

The effects of wind are by no means all detrimental, however. The normally regular afternoon sea breezes of coastal regions with otherwise summer-dry climates, such as those of Portugal, California, and much of southern Australia, have a useful moderating effect on viticultural climate, and are thought to contribute significantly to the quality of their wines (see CLIMATE AND WINE QUALITY). In all environments some air movement is needed to prevent excessive build-up of HUMIDITY within the vineyard, and to encourage drying of wet foliage and bunches, thereby reducing the risk of FUNGAL DISEASES. Night winds (or WIND MACHINES) largely prevent radiation FROSTS, while during sunlight hours the moderate movement of leaves encourages a more uniform spread of intermittent sunlight exposure among them, thus promoting a more efficient use of SUNLIGHT. Some degree of windiness is also often an unavoidable concomitant of the TOPOGRAPHIES that are viticulturally the best in other respects, for example in Waipara in NEW ZEALAND.

In summary, winds cannot be entirely avoided; nor are they wholly undesirable. The selection of sheltered sites, where possible, is important in windy regions. Beyond that, the answers to wind problems lie mainly in suitable vineyard strategies of TRELLISING and where necessary in the use of WINDBREAKS.   J.G.

windbreak, a barrier of vegetation or other materials to break the force of WINDS and avoid WIND STRESS. The benefits of windbreaks go beyond reducing physical vine damage. A combination of reduced wind force and (in dry atmospheres) the maintenance of higher HUMIDITIES among the vines reduces closure of the leaf pores (STOMATA), and therefore enhances potential PHOTOSYNTHESIS. Quite substantial yield increases are commonly recorded in the lee of effective windbreaks, amply exceeding any losses that might be incurred through any reduced area of vineyard or SHADING by the windbreaks.

The best natural windbreaks are fast-growing trees or tall shrubs whose roots do not extend too far laterally. Tall winter COVER CROPS such as cereal rye, planted between the vine rows, can also afford useful protection to young vineyards in early spring. VINE GUARDS can also protect young vines from wind.   J.G. & R.E.S.

Neel, D., 'Windbreaks mitigate climate', *Practical Winery & Vineyard* (May/June 2000).

wind machine, a strong fan for stirring up and mixing cold, dense air settled on the land surface with warmer air from above, thereby preventing FROSTS on still spring nights when there is no WIND to do the job. Such machines, introducing an aeronautical look to vineyards, have been used on valley floors that are prone to radiation frosts, such as in the NAPA Valley of California. HELICOPTERS can be used to the same effect.   J.G.

wind stress can reduce vine YIELD and RIPENING in some exposed vineyards. Severe gusts of wind can have dramatic effects on vineyards, breaking shoots and removing leaves. However, even lower velocity wind can also cause vine problems which are apparent only to the trained eye. Wind cools plants by removing the warming effects of the sun's rays, as well as other more substantial effects on physiology. For some plants, including vines, wind can have a major effect on growth. Shoot length, leaf area, and fruit growth can all be substantially reduced. The problem is particularly acute for young vines, as in older vineyards the CANOPY can usually offer some degree of self-protection.

Some vines respond negatively to movement of shoots and leaves, probably a response involving plant HORMONES. A major effect of wind is that of closing STOMATA. Freeman and colleagues of the University of California showed that wind speeds of 3 m/10 ft per second in the Salinas Valley caused stomata to close partially, which has the effect of reducing both PHOTOSYNTHESIS and TRANSPIRATION. Vines ripening in windy places will show reduced ripening and higher PH.

Simon studied the effects of WINDBREAKS on vines in the San Rafael region of Argentina. Malbec vines adjacent to the 10-m/33-ft tall poplar windbreak showed earlier FLOWERING, FRUIT SET, and VERAISON and longer shoots with more grapes near the windbreak. The windbreak was also effective against occasional very strong winds in reducing mechanical damage.   R.E.S.

Freeman, B. M., Kliewer, W. M., and Stern, P., 'Influence of windbreaks and climatic region on diurnal fluctuation of leaf water potential, stomatal conductance, and leaf temperature of grapevines', *American Journal of Enology and Viticulture*, 33 (1982), 233–6.

Simon, J. C., 'Étude des influences agronomiques des brise-vents dans les périmètres irrigués du Centre-Ouest de l'Argentine. 1: Effets des brise-vents sur la croissance et le développement d'une culture type: la vigne', *Annales agronomie*, 28 (1977), 75–93.

wine, alcoholic drink made by fermenting the juice of fruits or berries (see FRUIT WINES). By extension, this most general definition can also include products of the FERMENTATION of sugar solutions flavoured with flowers or herbs, but it normally excludes those of hydrolysed barley starches involved in brewing, and the products of the fermentation of sugar-containing liquids destined for DISTILLATION. There are also certain drinks, such as mead, cider, and perry, which depend on sugar fermentations for their alcohol content but for historical reasons merit their own names.

The narrower definition, relevant to this book and accepted throughout Europe, is that wine is 'the alcoholic beverage obtained from the fermentation of the juice of freshly gathered grapes, the fermentation taking place in the district of origin according to local tradition and practice'. This is to distinguish 'proper' wine from alcoholic drinks made from imported grape concentrate, which are known in Europe as MADE WINE. These include BRITISH MADE WINE and a significant proportion of the liquid produced by HOME WINEMAKING. New World definitions of wine are very similar except that the last phrase is omitted and wine may be made from a mixture of grapes grown many hundreds of miles apart.

Etymology

The modern English *wine* comes from Old English *wīn*, pronounced like modern 'wean': that indeed was how Chaucer pronounced his *wyn*, but Shakespeare's pronunciation was closer to our own. The Old English form was in turn descended from the Latin *vīnum*, or as the Romans wrote it *vinvm*, by way of a loanword represented in all Germanic languages (e.g. German *Wein*, Icelandic *vín*); a similar loan into Celtic has yielded Welsh *gwin* and Irish *fíon*. The explanation is that the Germans and CELTS, whose native beverage was BEER, learnt to drink wine from the Romans; with it came the Latin word, borrowed while Latin *v* was still pronounced [w]. From Germanic territory drink and name passed in turn to the Slavs (e.g. Russian *vinó*) and Balts (Lithuanian *vỹnas*, Latvian *vīns*).

Within Latin itself, from *vīnum* comes the noun *vīnea* 'vineyard'; this word, reinterpreted of a single vine (classically *vītis*, whence 'viticulture'), yielded French *vigne*, which was naturally brought over to England by the Normans. However, once the native English began to learn their masters' language, they adjusted it to suit their own speech habits; since English then as now lacked the palatal sound of French *gn*, it was simplified to *n*, so that *vigne* became *vine*. This was adopted into English and subjected to the normal sound-changes of the late medieval and early modern period: the final *-e* ceased to be pronounced and the long *i* became a diphthong. The French word was also substituted in the term for the place where vines were grown, originally *wīngeard*, now 'vineyard', with the vowel shortened as often in compounds (e.g. 'shepherd' vs. 'sheep').

Whereas *vitis* can be related to an Indo-European verb-root meaning to 'wind' or 'twine', as in English *withy*, the ultimate origins of *vinum* and *vinea* are less clear: similar words are found in many Mediterranean languages, even those belonging to different language-families, but few interrelations can be established. For instance, although Latin *ī* often comes from *ei*, since the change did not take place till the late 2nd century BC it cannot have occurred in *vinum*, for which forms with *vin-* are found in the kindred languages of ancient Italy. This rules out a direct link with the term current in Ancient GREECE, according to dialect *woinos* (ϝοῖνος) or *oînos* (οἶνος), as in OENOLOGY, akin to the **woiniyo-* (*denotes a reconstructed form) underlying Armenian *gini* and sometimes associated with Sanskrit *veṇi* or *veṇī* 'braid'. The form *wiyana* and *wayana* are quoted from the ancient Anatolian languages (see ASIA MINOR) Hittite and Luvian: outside Indo-European, a Semitic noun **wayn*, 'grape, vine, wine', which yields Hebrew *yayin* and Ethiopic *wäyn* besides an Arabic *wayn* 'black grape' found in an ancient lexicon, has sometimes been considered the source of the Greek word and sometimes a derivative. Even Georgian ɣ*vino* (see GEORGIA) has been proposed: no theory is convincing, except after a few glasses.   L.H.-S.

Editorial note:
See WINE COMPOSITION, WINEMAKING, WINE TYPES and the other entries which immediately follow. The word 'wine' appears in only these titles. Otherwise, for instance, for wine press see PRESS, for wine and religion see RELIGION AND WINE, for wine trade see TRADE, etc. For details of specific wines, see under their names or their provenance.

Wine & Spirit Education Trust. See WSET.

wine composition differs quite considerably from GRAPE COMPOSITION, partly because parts of the grape are discarded during WINEMAKING, and partly because the processes involved effect a complicated series of transformations. Alcoholic FERMENTATION, for example, transforms sugars into alcohol, while MALOLACTIC CONVERSION reduces the level of malic acid in favour of lactic acid. The precise composition of a wine varies with WINE TYPE, HARVEST conditions and date, VINTAGE characteristics, and the age of the wine (see AGEING for details of how wine composition may change with age). Nevertheless, the table gives some guidance as to the likely range of concentrations of the essential constituents of the approximately 1,000 so far identified.

Navarre, C., and Langlade, F., *L'Oenologie* (Paris, 7th edn, 2010).

wine grape, a term used to describe grapes used for winemaking, as opposed to TABLE GRAPES for eating and DRYING GRAPES for use by the dried fruit industry. For discussion about the plant which bears wine grapes, see VINE, and for more detail of the fruit itself, see GRAPE.

Wine Group, The, Based in Livermore, California, The Wine Group (TWG) is the second-largest wine producer by volume in the world, behind E. & J. GALLO and just ahead of CONSTELLATION. Privately owned and relatively secretive about its financial affairs, it boasts among its brands Concannon, established in 1883 in LIVERMORE by Irish immigrant James Concannon and the first to bottle Petite Sirah as a stand-alone varietal in the US. TWG's considerable market clout, however, comes from the JUG and BOXED California wine juggernauts Franzia and Almaden; the moderately priced Cupcake bottled line; and Big House, which it purchased from Randall Grahm of Bonny Doon in 2006.

wine-growing, expression used for the process of growing vines with a view to making wine.

wine lake, term coined for Europe's wine SURPLUS. With the introduction of compulsory DISTILLATION in 1982, it was rapidly transformed into an ALCOHOL lake. See EU for the various reforms that have been introduced to try to balance supply and demand.

winemaker, one who makes WINE. In its broadest sense, the term includes those who engage in HOME WINEMAKING as a hobby, although in a professional sense a winemaker is someone employed (sometimes by themselves) to produce wine. An increasing proportion of such people recognize that wine production includes every aspect of vineyard management, and there are wine producers all over the world whose production is so small that they personally conduct, or at least oversee, every stage from planting to marketing.

A wine production unit of any size, however, will employ both a VITICULTURIST, or vineyard manager, and a winemaker whose active responsibilities begin with receiving grapes from the vineyard and continue with their SAMPLING, CRUSHING, PRESSING, FERMENTATION, ÉLEVAGE, BOTTLING, and storage—all those operations outlined in WINEMAKING. Larger wine producers may even employ a team of winemakers, each with different responsibilities.

Curiously, there is no obvious synonym for the word winemaker in any of the major European languages, perhaps because historically

Wine composition		
Component	**Proportions per l**	**Comments**
Dissolved gases		
CARBON DIOXIDE	0–50 cc	
SULFUR DIOXIDE		
Total	80–200 g	More in some sweet wines
Free	10–50 mg	More in some unstable wines
Volatile substances		
WATER	700–900 g	
ETHANOL (alcohol)	8.5–15% by vol	More in fortified, less in low-alcohol wines
HIGHER ALCOHOLS	0.15–0.5 g	
ACETALDEHYDE	0.005–0.5 g	Higher amounts in sherry and similar wines
ESTERS	0.1–0.3 g	
ACETIC ACID	0.35–0.6 g	
Fixed substances		
RESIDUAL SUGAR	0.8–180 g ⎫	According to type of wine; more in sweet and
GLYCEROL	5–12 g ⎬	botrytized wines
PHENOLICS	0.2–0.5 g; 1.5–4.0 g	Lower range for white wines, higher range for reds
Organic acids		
TARTARIC ACID	3–10 g	Depending on grape origin
MALIC ACID	0–4 g ⎫	According to climate and extent of malolactic
LACTIC ACID	0–1 g ⎬	conversion
SUCCINIC ACID	0.2–1.5 g	
CITRIC ACID	0–1 g	Found in wines where additions have been made
Mineral salts		
Sulfates	0.1–0.4 g ⎫	
Chlorides	0.25–0.85 g ⎬	Expressed as potassium salts
Phosphates	0.08–0.5 g ⎭	
Mineral elements		
POTASSIUM	0.7–1.5 g	
CALCIUM	0.06–0.9 g	
IRON	0.002–0.006 g	

Based on Navarre, C., *L'Oenologie* (7th edn, Paris, 2010)

wine was thought to make itself. The most common candidates have very different literal translations into English: *maître de chai* in Bordeaux; *Kellermeister* in Germany; *enologo* in Italy; *œnologue* in some French wineries. While most (though not all) modern winemakers have studied OENOLOGY, and will certainly consider themselves oenologists, the term OENOLOGIST is more usually applied to an outside CONSULTANT rather than to a full-time employee in Europe. The most temporary winemakers of all are the breed known colloquially as FLYING WINEMAKERS or, if lower down the pecking order, CELLAR RATS.

During the early 1980s, some winemakers enjoyed a brief period of near cult status, most notably in the New World, until VITICULTURISTS re-established their status, to become the wine gurus of the 1990s and early 2000s. Today there are ever closer links between those responsible for vineyard and cellar and in an increasing number of cases they are the same person.

Most successful winemakers understand that making fine wine depends not only on a respectful understanding of the complicated biochemistry involved but also, perhaps more importantly, on an appreciation of the greatest potential within each lot of grapes and then the skill and patience to reveal that potential in the finished wine.

winemaking

winemaking, the practical art of producing WINE. In its most general sense, it encompasses all operations in both vineyard and cellar but for the purposes of this article, winemaking excludes vine-growing, or VITICULTURE.

Winemaking, while a sophisticated practical art for several millennia, became an applied SCIENCE only towards the end of the 19th century after Louis PASTEUR's discovery of the existence and activities of BACTERIA and YEAST. Since then, knowledge of the detailed chemical and biochemical reactions involved in their metabolic processes has steadily increased, as has the sophistication of the containers and equipment used in the professional cellar.

Winemaking in brief is a series of simple operations, the first of which is CRUSHING or smashing the fruit to liberate the SUGAR in the juice for FERMENTATION, which is the second step and occurs naturally when YEAST cells come into contact with sugar solutions. The new wine must then be subjected to various treatments to ensure CLARIFICATION and STABILIZATION and various other cellar operations which are collectively called *élevage* before the final step, BOTTLING.

Details in this sequence of operations vary considerably with WINE TYPE and its origin. General (as opposed to local) differences of technique dictated by different sorts of wine are outlined in WHITE WINEMAKING, RED WINEMAKING, ROSÉ WINEMAKING, SWEET WINEMAKING, SPARKLING WINEMAKING, and under the names of various FORTIFIED WINES.

Halliday, J., and Johnson, H., *The Art and Science of Wine* (London, 1992).

Rankine, B., *Making Good Wine: A Manual of Winemaking Practice for Australia and New Zealand* (1989, rev. edn, Sydney, 2004).

Wine of Origin, area of origin designation scheme described in detail in SOUTH AFRICA. Established in 1973, it is the oldest and arguably the most extensive and rigorous in the NEW WORLD.

wine press. See PRESS for details of the equipment used during PRESSING. For the interface between wine and the press, see WINE WRITERS.

winery, modern, essentially NEW WORLD term for the premises on which wine is made; its first recorded use was in the United States in 1882. It may mean either the entire enterprise, or it may mean specifically the building or buildings used for WINEMAKING. The nearest French equivalent is CAVE (but see also CHAI and CUVE). WINERY DESIGN is a specialist art most dramatically practised in RIOJA and northern CALIFORNIA, where, neatly, the FASHION is for caves: winemaking facilities burrowed into hillsides, the cost of maintaining suitable temperatures and humidity in such subterranean tunnels being minimal. However, there are spectacular examples all over the wine world today, with increasing emphasis on SUSTAINABILITY.

winery design is a specialist branch of building design. Although WINEMAKING can take place almost anywhere, modern wineries are much more than mere processing facilities. Nowadays wineries should be efficient in energy and resource consumption, suit the individual styles of wine and winemaking and, of equal importance, support the BRAND image, often through architectural appearance, public display of winemaking processes, specialized hospitality and cellar door facilities, and other amenities designed to engage the TOURIST and customer.

To ensure functionality and efficient workflow, a winery layout is based on a thorough understanding of the logistics of the specific winemaking practices and processes from grape receipt through production, bottling, storage, and shipping. Other issues include winery offices, laboratory, tasting bench, equipment sizes and types, and finish materials. The impacts of site conditions, environmental concerns, health and safety matters, and maintenance are also considered. Finally architectural requirements in terms of style and functionality of the winery and associated facilities, including CELLAR DOOR sales, amenities, access, and infrastructure are incorporated.

Building a winery to make an architectural statement is not new; the 19th-century CHÂTEAUX of Bordeaux, like the imposing Ch MARGAUX or

the whimsical Ch Cos d'Estournel in ST-ESTÈPHE, or Andrea Palladio's 16th-century Villa di Maser in the VENETO make that clear. There are also 21st-century icons created by the world's greatest architects. Ysios by Santiago Calatrava and Marques de Riscal by Frank Gehry are two examples, both in RIOJA, in the Old World; Clos Pegase of NAPA Valley by Michael Graves, Craggy Range in NEW ZEALAND by John Blair, and Graham Beck Coastal Cellar in SOUTH AFRICA by Johan Wessels are three examples in the New World.

Other wineries find beauty in their simplicity and clarity. Many top producers aim for quick, cool, and gentle processing, which means GRAVITY flow instead of PUMPS wherever possible, as at Ridge in the SANTA CRUZ MOUNTAINS. If the site permits, as many as seven different levels may be achieved, where grapes are received at the highest level and shipping takes place from the lowest, as at Calera in MONTEREY. If the winery can be part-buried into a hillside, it aids natural TEMPERATURE and HUMIDITY control. Otherwise, creating cellars deeply dug from ancient limestone deposits is a possibility, as in Champagne or on the South Downs in England. Perhaps the most ambitious winery project thus far has been realized in the Loisium Wine Centre in Langenlois, Austria, by Stephen Holl with clients Karl and Brigitte Steininger. The entire medieval wine-village with its subterranean cellars has been transformed to include hotel, spa, and restaurant set amid the vineyards.

A well-planned winery development can conserve resources, manage waste and noise pollution, and be easy to maintain. If located in a vineyard, a winery offers the potential of a high level of SUSTAINABILITY.   P.K.C.S.

Eue, R., and Seiler, C., *Wine Architecture: The Winery Boom* (Ostfildern, 2008).

Dethler, J. (ed.), *Chateaux Bordeaux* (London, 1989).

Richards, P., *Wineries with Style* (London, 2004).

Stanwick, S., and Fowlow, L., *Wine by Design* (New York, 2010).

Zoecklin, B. (ed.), *Winery Planning and Design* (16th edn, Blacksburg, 2010).

winery waste comprises the liquid and solid waste that results from the process of turning fruit into wine. Globally the wine industry has been working to establish SUSTAINABLE systems to deal with both these waste streams so as to maintain the beautiful rural environments in which wine is typically made. In many wine regions, there are now stringent local and sometimes national guidelines, policies, and legislation covering this area.

Water is a by-product of the HYGIENE or sanitation required to make wine, for example washing tanks, fermenters, and barrels. Roughly 1.5 volumes (litres/gallons) of water is used in

W

the production of 1 volume of wine, though the exact amount depends on winemaking processes, winery equipment, and winery practices. Over a year, about 70% of the total volume of waste water generated is during the VINTAGE period, so sustainable waste-water systems need to be designed to handle these loads at this time.

Liquid winery waste tends to have a high oxygen requirement or BOD (organic acids, sugars, alcohol, etc.), low levels of nitrogen and phosphorus relative to carbon, and high solids content; it is generally acidic (low PH) due to organic acids, moderately saline (from sodium-based cleaning chemicals); and there may be imbalances in sodium, calcium, and magnesium.

This kind of waste water stored for a period of time releases malodours and degrades any land/vegetation that it continually comes into contact with. There are winery waste-water treatment systems all over the world that are now able to turn this liquid waste stream into a reusable resource via solids removal, pH adjustment, anaerobic digestion and/or aeration, clarification, and final polishing. Treated water is often then reused to irrigate golf courses, vineyards, winery gardens, or used back in the winery.

What are collectively known as cleaner production procedures can help minimize water use in the winemaking process and thereby reduce treatment costs and reliance on potable water. These procedures include waste stream segregation, for example keeping stormwater out of the waste system, diverting heavily polluted waste water (from crushing or fermentation areas, for example) away from less polluted; improved operating practices, for example screening solids from the waste system, high-pressure hoses, sweeping floors rather than hosing them down with water; personnel practices, including management initiatives, employee training and incentives; procedural measures, including documentation, material handling and storage, material tracking, and inventory control.

Winery solid wastes include stalks, MARC, LEES (tartrates, grape solids, and dead yeast cells), spent DIATOMACEOUS EARTH used in FILTRATION, and sludge, which is a by-product of wastewater treatment.

Stalks and marc are produced only during the vintage period. Approximately 1 unit of marc is generated for every 10 units of grapes processed. Marc can be distilled to recover alcohol, colour extract, and tannin extract. Lees can also be collected and sent to the still for alcohol recovery. Stalks can be used to improve the organic levels of soils if they are thinly spread and worked into the soil. Many garden COMPOSTS use grape stalks and sludge as an ingredient.

Spent diatomaceous earth can be processed by third parties to produce TARTARIC ACID, which may be used as a wine additive in various parts of the world. Spent earth also has agronomic benefits and can be worked into most soil types to improve the SOIL STRUCTURE. However, many filtration processes now use cross-flow membrane technology instead of diatomaceous earth, thereby reducing waste.

When the correct resources, management initiatives, and support are allocated to ensuring winery waste is treated in an environmentally sustainable manner, wineries will continue to exist in harmony with their surroundings (see ECOSYSTEM, VINEYARD). S.J.G.

CSIRO, 'Winery wastewater management', www. clw.csiro.au/publications/projects/ WineryWastewaterManagement2006.pdf.
GWRDC, 'Winery wastewater online resource kit', www.gwrdc.com.au/tools-resources/winery-wastewater-management-recycling.

Wine Society, The, seminal British member-owned wine club-cum-wine merchant. The International Exhibition Co-operative Wine Society (IECWS), generally known as The Wine Society, was founded in 1874 by an architect, an eye surgeon, and a prominent Customs and Excise official following a food and wine exhibition in London's Albert Hall that year. The objects and rules included a membership holding of one share only, no dividends to be paid on these until extinction on the member's death, and the introduction of unfamiliar wines as well as those in general use—all to be bought 'for ready money only' at the lowest possible price. The Society remained small for many years, and attained its 5,000th member only in 1922, but grew substantially between the two World Wars. The number of shares exceeded 390,000 by 2014.

Prospective members are sponsored by existing members and elected by the Committee. Edmund PENNING-ROWSELL was the Society's longest-serving chairman, from 1964 until 1987.

The Society's cellars were under the London Palladium theatre and London Bridge railway station (where the London AUCTIONEERS subsequently stored their wine) until the Society moved out of London to purpose-built and regularly extended premises in Stevenage in 1965. The Wine Society is one of the two biggest independent retail wine merchants in Britain (the other being its mail order direct rival Laithwaites) with a turnover exceeding £90 million. The policy of cash-with-order is retained. The Society is distinguished by its fair prices, distinguished buying, the efficiency of its bureaucracy, and the quality of wine STORAGE offered to members.

Australia has a similar, but independent, operation.

wine tasters. The animate sort are humans, often of widely varying abilities, experiences, preferences, and prejudices, engaged in the pursuit of wine TASTING. The inanimate sort are shallow, usually silver, saucers for tasting young wines, known in French, and often in English, as TASTEVINS.

wine types may be classified in several ways, the most usual being by alcohol level. Those whose ALCOHOLIC STRENGTH is entirely due to FERMENTATION, and usually in the range of 9 to 15%, are what we tend to call simply 'wine' or sometimes 'table wine' (although TABLE WINE used to have a specific meaning within the EU). Such wines may be further classified by COLOUR into RED WINES, WHITE WINES, and ROSÉ WINES. Or they may be classified according to their concentration of dissolved carbon dioxide as SPARKLING WINES, still wines, and a host of terms in between such as PERLANT and FRIZZANTE. Wines may also be classified according to SWEETNESS.

Wines with higher concentrations of alcohol, between 15 and just over 20%, are called FORTIFIED WINES in this book since (with the exception of some DRIED-GRAPE WINES) they owe some of their alcoholic strength to the process of FORTIFICATION, i.e. the addition of spirit. PORT and SHERRY are the best known of these wines, officially called *vins de liqueur* in EU terminology. This higher-strength category also includes sweet alcoholic drinks made by adding grape spirit to grape juice or partly fermented grape juice at various points, for details of which see VIN DOUX NATUREL and VIN DE LIQUEUR as well as MISTELA.

Wines which have been deliberately manipulated so that their alcohol levels are particularly low, say below 5.5%, are sometimes called LOW-ALCOHOL wines. (Some regular wines, such as MOSCATO D'ASTI and lighter SAAR wines, may have a natural alcoholic strength of between 5 and 9%.)

Wine types may also be loosely, and somewhat subjectively, classified according to when they are drunk into APERITIF wines (sometimes called 'appetizer wines'), 'food wines' or 'dinner wines', and SWEET WINES. See also VINO DA MEDITAZIONE.

Although geographical classifications are of wines not wine types, once-popular GENERIC wines represent an attempt at a geographical classification of wine types.

wine without geographical indication is the EU term adopted since 2008 to designate those wines, previously categorized as TABLE WINES, that have neither a PROTECTED DESIGNATION OF ORIGIN (PDO) nor a PROTECTED GEOGRAPHICAL INDICATION (PGI). Such wines must be labelled with the word 'wine', in the appropriate language(s), and the country of origin must also appear somewhere on the label. Examples include **Vin de France** in France, **Vino** in Italy and Spain, **Vinho** in Portugal, and **Deutscher Wein** in Germany. They are also permitted to specify on the label VINTAGE YEAR and/or grape variety (varieties).

wine writers, imprecise term to include all those who communicate via today's burgeoning media on the subject of wine. Some of them style themselves wine critics (notably the consumerist Robert PARKER) while such literary stylists as Hugh JOHNSON and Gerald Asher are undoubtedly wine writers. One sort of commentator hardly ever writes at all but occupies regular slots on radio or television, often reaching a much wider audience than most authors could hope to. And INFORMATION TECHNOLOGY, through myriad wine WEBSITES and blogs, has provided some wine writers with an international reputation far quicker than is usually possible with the printed word.

Such was the increase in wine writing opportunities in the late 20th century that by the early 1980s, for probably the first time ever, it was possible, with luck and hard work, to make a living as a wine writer with no other source of income. But it would be unreasonable to expect an activity as pleasurable as wine writing to be lavishly rewarded financially and many wine writers also rely either on a private income or on income from dangerously closely related activities such as trading in wine or undertaking specific commissions for wine companies. Wine writer ethics became a hot topic after several well-publicized cases of unseemly activity. As detailed in the LITERATURE OF WINE, Britain had a long tradition of wine merchants who wrote, who sometimes became wine writers who used to trade. Kermit Lynch is an American example of this phenomenon, Michael Fridjhon a South African one while John Platter and James Halliday are wine producers turned wine writers in South Africa and Australia respectively.

Wine writers in continental Europe such as France's Michel Bettane and Thierry Desseauve, Spain's Jose Peñín, and Italy's phalanx of specialists, tend to concentrate on the wines of their own countries.

Britain may have the greatest concentration of full-time wine writers in the world, perhaps partly because it is a centre of wine book publishing—and possibly because the British wine market is so diverse that British consumers need more advice than most. It certainly has the highest proportion of women among the country's wine writers, whereas in the United States and most European countries, wine writing is still dominated by men even if this is at last changing.

Changes in wine writing have wrought changes in wine writers. Given the 1990s preponderance of buyer's guides, TASTING NOTES, and SCORING in place of writing, there was a time when it would have been quite possible

to be a highly successful wine writer without ever visiting a vineyard or cellar. A sound palate and a good database (see INFORMATION TECHNOLOGY) would in theory be quite sufficient, if a poor substitute for the excitement of exploring the world of wine.

See also WINE WRITING.

wine writing, a parasitical activity undertaken by WINE WRITERS enabled by vine-growing and winemaking but more usually associated with wine TASTING, and even wine drinking, than with either of the former. For an analysis of wine books through the ages, see LITERATURE OF WINE and for a discussion of words used to describe wine, see LANGUAGE OF WINE.

Wine writing can now be found not just between hard covers in specialist books but on WEBSITES and blogs, in specialist magazines and newsletters, in academic journals, and in general interest magazines and newspapers of even the most populist sort. It is now quite usual for an upmarket and not unusual for a mass-market newspaper to have a regular wine column, although the lack of associated advertising revenue has tended to shrink the total space devoted to wine in print media in the 21st century.

Newsletters are a mainly American phenomenon with Robert PARKER's *Wine Advocate* being particularly influential in the late 20th century.

Virtually all countries of any interest to wine exporters have at least one specialist wine consumer magazine (and major wine-producing and wine-trading countries tend to have specialist trade publications too). The world's best-selling wine magazine is the glossy, New York-based *Wine Spectator*. Its distant American consumer rival is the *Wine Enthusiast* but there are several lively wine trade publications including *Wine Business*. Britain fields *Decanter* (of which there is also a Chinese edition) and *The World of Fine Wine*. Europe's three major wine-producing countries can offer much less consumer wine coverage than might be imagined: France, for example, has exactly the same number of specialist wine magazines as Singapore. Few print publications are without an online version and associated app(s).

In the world of books, food outweighs wine very substantially; indeed many bookstores locate such wine titles as they do stock in an obscure corner of their cookery section. New wine titles continue to appear, perhaps sometimes the result of publishers' famous fondness for the fruits of the vine, but only a handful of authors can generate the sort of sales the increasingly agglomerated book trade now seeks worldwide.

Buyer's guides, typically annual, proliferate and for a while more and more of the words written about wine resembled shopping lists with SCORES rather than literature. But specialist wine books have been striking back.

Winkler, Albert Julius (1894–1989), scientist at the University of California at DAVIS whose name (and that of Maynard AMERINE) is commonly associated with a particular method of CLIMATE CLASSIFICATION involving heat summation whereby California was divided into five viticultural regions, Regions I (the coolest) to V (the warmest). He edited *General Viticulture*, published in 1962 and revised in 1974, which was for long considered the most comprehensive book on VITICULTURE in the English language.

winter freeze, a climatic stress which can be lethal to parts or all of the vine. In areas of high LATITUDE and high ELEVATION the risk of very cold winter weather is substantial, particularly in CONTINENTAL climates away from the moderating effects of oceans (although even in MARITIME climates winter freeze can kill thousands of vines in exceptionally cold winters such as that of 1956 in St-Émilion and Pomerol). Such continental climates typically show colder temperatures, but also greater TEMPERATURE VARIABILITY.

Cold-hardy varieties, such as the American vine CONCORD, can be grown in the midwestern United States in sites with annual minimum temperatures of −29 °C/−20 °F occurring once in three years. European VINIFERA varieties sensitive to cold require relatively warmer sites, however, where annual minimum temperatures of −20 °C/−4 °F are recorded no more than once in a decade. CROWN GALL disease commonly develops on vines injured by winter freeze.

An essential first step towards avoiding winter freeze injury is wise VINEYARD SITE SELECTION. Sites which export cold air, such as those offering AIR DRAINAGE on free-standing hills, can avoid winter injury by being up to 5 °C/9 °F warmer than sites which import cold air, such as those on valley floors. Vineyard sites within a few kilometres of large bodies of water (such as the Médoc, which suffered far less from the great winter freeze of 1956 than the inland vineyards of St-Émilion and Pomerol, for example) are also preferred because of the moderating effects on temperature (and see LAKE EFFECT in North America).

Selecting varieties with noted winter hardiness is also important. Varieties such as CABERNET FRANC and RIESLING are more winter-hardy than Pinot Noir, Chasselas, and Cabernet Sauvignon. In turn, *Vitis vinifera* is less hardy than some interspecific HYBRIDS such as SEYVAL, which in turn are less winter-hardy than such American varieties as DELAWARE and CONCORD. VINE BREEDERS have used *V. amurensis* as a parent to produce winter-hardy varieties such as CABERNET SEVERNY. Choice of ROOTSTOCKS which avoid stress is also critical for vine survival.

The vine's reserves of CARBOHYDRATES act like a biological antifreeze. The aim of vine management to avoid winter stress is to achieve maximum carbohydrate reserves at the end of the growing season. This entails choice of suitable TRAINING SYSTEM, appropriately severe PRUNING level, and THINNING so as to restrict YIELD, which, when excessive, can act to reduce levels of vine carbohydrates.

An alternative strategy to avoid winter kill is to bury the vines in autumn (see WINTER PROTECTION).
R.E.S.

Covert, C., 'Cold climate grape varieties from eastern U.S. breeding programs', *FPS Grape Program Newsletter* (Oct 2008). http://iv.ucdavis.edu/files/24502.pdf.

Howell, S. A., 'Cultural manipulation of vine cold hardiness', in R. E. Smart et al. (eds.), *Proceedings of the Second International Symposium for Cool Climate Viticulture and Oenology: 11–15 January 1988, Auckland, New Zealand* (Auckland, 1988).

winter protection, cumbersome viticultural technique aimed at protecting vines in cold, CONTINENTAL climates against the effects of WINTER FREEZE. Vines are buried in autumn to benefit from the fact that winter temperatures below the soil surface are never more than a few °C below freezing point, whereas the air temperature can be more than 20 °C/36 °F colder. Burying vines is, however, LABOUR-intensive and expensive. This was traditionally practised in central Europe and North America, but is uncommon now because of the cost. Only in the vineyards of RUSSIA, parts of UKRAINE, some of the central Asian republics, and CHINA is it still considered an acceptable price to pay for viticulture, although some severe winters in upper NEW YORK state in the early 21st century have engendered some reconsideration. The procedure has been modified so that just those few canes to be used for fruiting the following year are buried. Vines are also trained so that they have several trunks, so that those killed in winter can easily be replaced. See fan-shaped TRAINING SYSTEMS.   R.E.S. & J.R.

Winzer, which is the German equivalent of the French VIGNERON, is a common prefix in Germany for a CO-OPERATIVE wine cellar, as in **Winzergenossenschaft**, **Winzerverein**, and **Winzervereinigung**.

wire, used to form vine TRELLIS SYSTEMS, along with POSTS. Wine consumers might never credit

W

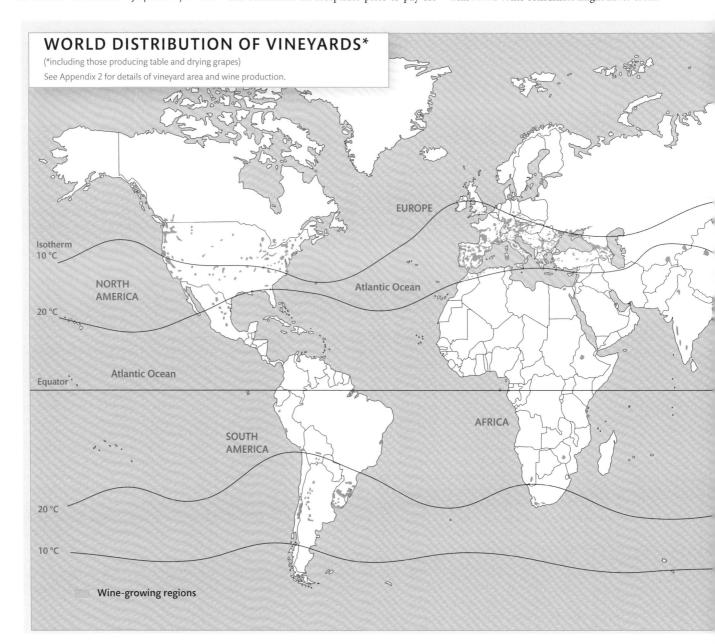

WORLD DISTRIBUTION OF VINEYARDS*
(*including those producing table and drying grapes)
See Appendix 2 for details of vineyard area and wine production.

Isotherm 10 °C

EUROPE

NORTH AMERICA

Atlantic Ocean

20 °C

Atlantic Ocean

Equator

AFRICA

SOUTH AMERICA

20 °C

10 °C

Wine-growing regions

something as mundane as wire in vineyards with their enjoyment, yet it is difficult to conceive of how wine could be so widely produced without it. The widespread use of wire has revolutionized trellising of vines, since it is now possible to train vines to forms which maximize their production and MECHANIZATION. High-tensile wire can support very heavy loads without breaking. Normally, thicker wire is used to support the weight of grapes in a trellis, and thinner wires to support foliage. See TRELLIS SYSTEMS and TRAINING SYSTEMS.   R.E.S.

WO. See WINE OF ORIGIN.

wood has been the most popular material for wine CONTAINERS both for transport and storage for centuries and even today trees are almost as

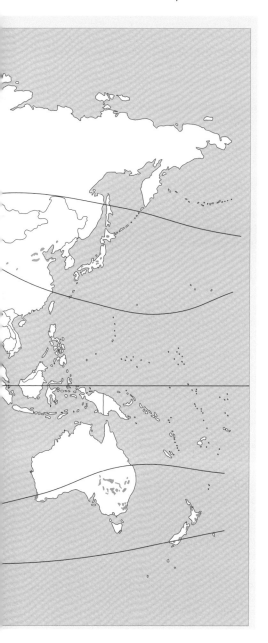

important to some wines as vines. Merchants in Ancient ARMENIA shipped wine down the Tigris in palm-wood casks seven centuries BC, according to HERODOTUS. Wooden BARRELS eventually succeeded AMPHORAE as containers for both shipping and storage in the 3rd century AD.

It was not until the mid 20th century, however, that wood was irrevocably replaced by the bottle and tanker for TRANSPORT and widely replaced by inert materials such as CONCRETE and STAINLESS STEEL for STORAGE and FERMENTATION.

For fine wines, wood is still valued as the prime material for maturing (see BARREL MATURATION and CASK AGEING) and for fermenting certain types of white wine and for some handmade red wines (see BARREL FERMENTATION) as well as for some larger fermentation vats.

The chemistry of wine's maturation in wood is still not fully understood but experience shows that wood (unlike sealed tanks made of inert materials) exposes the wine to a certain amount of OXYGEN, and actively aids CLARIFICATION and STABILIZATION of the wine matured in it—quite apart from the wide range of flavours and characteristics which may be added and transformed as a result of exposure to that particular wood, either directly as OAK FLAVOUR or indirectly as WOOD INFLUENCE.

See also WOOD TYPES.

Wood also plays a part in viticulture, not just because the vine's own wood is important (see CANE and TRUNK), but also because wood is a common material for POSTS and STAKES in the vineyard.

For more detail of wood structure, see CAMBIUM and XYLEM.

Guimberteau, G. (ed.), *Le Bois et la qualité des vins et eaux-de-vie* (Martillac, 1992).

wood alcohol. Alternative name for harmful METHANOL.

wood influence. If a wine is fermented or matured in a wooden container, many different aspects of that container may shape its character and flavour, quite apart from those compounds that may be directly extracted from the oak wood and absorbed into the wine as wood flavour (see OAK FLAVOUR). The most obvious advantage of holding a wine in wood (see BARREL MATURATION and CASK AGEING) rather than in an inert material is that wood encourages natural CLARIFICATION and STABILIZATION. The precise influence of a wooden container on any wine held in it is a function of the way that wine was made as well as of the following aspects.

Wood type
Barrels and tanks have been made from a variety of different woods although OAK is generally preferred. The exact choice of wood, or even oak, type can have a powerful effect on flavour and structure. See WOOD TYPES for more.

Manufacturing techniques
Several aspects of barrel making can have a marked impact on wine flavour. One particularly controversial issue is whether barrels made from hand-split staves are perceptibly superior to their counterparts made from sawn staves; carefully controlled research in this area is rare.

The method of drying the wood can also affect wine character. Wines, particularly those naturally low in tannins themselves, can taste aggressively tannic after being matured in barrels made from kiln-dried, as opposed to air-dried, wood. Finally, the degree to which the staves are heated while being bent, or the level of barrel TOAST, also has an obvious and profound effect on flavour (see BARREL MAKING).

Size of container
The larger the container, the lower the ratio of surface area to volume will be. Barrels holding less than 190 l/50 gal can overwhelm wine with OAK FLAVOURS. Containers holding more than 570 l/150 gal will provide little wood oak flavour, particularly after their first use. (See BARREL TYPES for detail of barrel sizes most commonly used.)

The use of large wooden VATS or tanks as FERMENTATION VESSELS fell out of favour after the advent of STAINLESS STEEL and other inert materials, because the latter are much easier to clean than wood and because TEMPERATURE is harder to control in large-volume wooden containers, but there is currently a resurgence of interest in them (and in CONCRETE).

Many of Italy's and some of the southern Rhône's, Germany's, and Alsace's most revered wines are the product of CASK AGEING in large, old wooden casks. Proponents of such wooden vats note that some of the greatest wines in the world are made in them and suggest that ageing in large wooden tanks provides a gentle oxygenation of the wine and, hence, a desirable form of pre-bottling maturation. Taransaud compared oak-matured wines that had been fermented in oak with those that had been fermented in stainless steel and found that the former had more ellagitannins and colour stability.

Age of container
Barrels may be valued simply because they are containers made from a material that clarifies and stabilizes the wine naturally, offers the wine some mild but useful oxygenation, or also because they can actually add OAK FLAVOUR to the wine. The newer the barrel, the more wood flavour it is capable of imparting and in most wine regions new barrels command a premium, with one-year-old barrels selling for approximately 70%, two-year-old barrels selling for less than 50%, and five-year-old barrels selling for just 10% of the cost of a new barrel.

New barrels may be the most expensive but they are not necessarily valued most highly by all winemakers because their strongly oaky flavour can overwhelm subtle wines, and some winemakers deliberately minimize this effect by using only a small proportion of new barrels or by 'breaking in' new barrels on lesser wines. Within a given type and style of wine, the richest wines will absorb the most oak with positive effects.

Although there is a trend towards increasing the average age of barrels used, when new barrels are used, they tend to be reserved for the best wines. In Burgundy, GRAND CRU wines, both red and white, might be aged in over 50% and sometimes 100% new barrels; PREMIER CRU, one-third to two-thirds new. In Bordeaux, FIRST GROWTHS and GARAGISTES usually employ 100% new oak nearly every year, although it may vary according to the VINTAGE. New barrels are also used for a high proportion of better quality wines made by ambitious and well-funded winemakers in newer wine regions., although here too there has been a trend to greater restraint over the last decade or so.

Older barrels are important for wines where the winemaker seeks slow oxygenation of the wine but no perceptible oak flavour, such as in making PORT, SHERRY, and, in many cases, RIOJA.

Some producers, most famously such as Dominique Laurent, NÉGOCIANT in Nuits-St-Georges, boast of using '200% new oak', meaning that wines are first put into one new barrel and then into another. Very few wines can withstand such an onslaught.

Time
Time remains the winemaker's greatest tool. A wine's character is also influenced by how long it remains in wood, which can vary from about two months for relatively light white wines to two years or even three for certain red wines and top-quality SAUTERNES. More traditionally minded producers in Spain, Italy, and Portugal may keep wines in old wooden cooperage for even longer. Some BRUNELLO DI MONTALCINO is given four years' CASK AGEING and VEGA SICILIA, for example, has sometimes been matured for ten years in barrel.

Vintage
The character of individual VINTAGE YEARS also affects how they react to wood and therefore the influence of any wood on a wine's flavour. Wines, especially red wines, vary so much from vintage to vintage that it is impossible to specify the perfect barrel for a given wine. For this reason, many winemakers order a range of different WOOD TYPES and with variation of TOAST in anticipation of each harvest.

Wine-making techniques
Up to this point our concerns have been with direct flavour effects from the wood, but equally important are the indirect or secondary flavour effects that are more the result of the wooden tank's or barrel's environment. For more details, see CASK AGEING and BARREL MATURATION respectively. White wines fermented in barrel may be changed enormously in character. For more details, see BARREL FERMENTATION.

Storage conditions
Exact temperature and humidity, even draughts, can affect the character of a wine held in a wooden container. For more details, see BARREL STORAGE.   L.B. & M.K.

Naudin, R., L'Élevage des vins de Bourgogne en fûts neufs (Beaune, 1989).

Singleton, V. L., 'Some aspects of the wooden container as a factor in wine maturation', in American Chemical Society, Chemistry of Winemaking (Washington, DC, 1974).

Spillman, P. J., Sefton, M. A., Gawel, R., 'The effect of oak wood source and location of seasoning on the chemical composition of oak matured wines', Australian Journal of Grape and Wine Research, 10 (2004), 216–26.

wood types. Over the years, many different kinds of wood have been used to make small BARRELS and larger VATS and casks. Acacia, cypress, chestnut, ash, redwood, pine, eucalyptus, and poplar are just a few of the woods that have been used.

Chestnut has long been popular for large oval casks in the Rhône, Beaujolais, and in parts of Italy and Portugal, but as this wood offers strong TANNINS and is also relatively porous, chestnut barrels and tanks are often coated with paraffin or silicone to neutralize the wood. Wines made in unlined new chestnut barrels can be so tannic as to be undrinkable.

In other countries, pine and eucalyptus have been used for casks, but these woods produce wines with flavours that strike many consumers as odd unless the wood is very well seasoned (see BARREL MAKING) or coated on the inside. Acacia is used successfully, notably in Austria and Istria, although some coopers say it is very porous. In Chile, the local evergreen beech, or rauli, wood was once common. Redwood was used for large upright tanks in America for many years, although very few have been built since the early 1970s. Redwood is rarely made into barrels because the wood is difficult to bend and the flavours are aggressive. Since the advent of neutral STAINLESS STEEL and enamel-lined tanks, wooden COOPERAGE must offer something extra to the wine to be worth the premium.

By far the most popular wood type in use in winemaking today is OAK, which has none of the disadvantages outlined above and whose particular aspects of WOOD INFLUENCE and OAK FLAVOUR have come to be appreciated by both winemakers and wine drinkers.   M.K.

Worcester, warm inland wine district within the Breede River Valley region in SOUTH AFRICA. This extensive, fertile district beyond the Du Toitskloof Mountains and within the Breede River Valley region produces about 12% of the national wine crop. Generally warm and dependent on IRRIGATION, the region used to be heavily dependent on Colombard and Chenin Blanc but Chardonnay, Sauvignon Blanc, Viognier, and Shiraz have all become relatively important too.

world production of wine is concentrated in two bands of generally TEMPERATE to MEDITERRANEAN CLIMATE in each hemisphere, as shown on the map on p. 822. TROPICAL VITICULTURE is becoming increasingly common but so far on a small scale relative to the established wine-producing countries.

Total production of wine is affected by each year's weather (particularly by FROST, poor FRUIT SET, or HAIL, particularly but not exclusively within Europe), by the effects of VINE PULL SCHEMES, offset by those of new plantings. The underlying trend is downwards, largely because of determined efforts by the EU to reduce its wine SURPLUS.

See also PRODUCTION, CONSUMPTION, and, for precise figures, SURPLUS of wine as well as Appendices 2A, 2B, and 2C.

Wrattonbully, now substantial wine region just north of Coonawarra in SOUTH AUSTRALIA with a strongly LIMESTONE-based soil. Significant players among the 22 producers are Tapanappa, Yalumba/Smith & Hooper, Hollick, Patrick, Pepper Tree, and Terre à Terre.   J.H. & H.H.

WSET. The Wine & Spirit Education Trust is the world's leading provider of wine EDUCATION, based in London, offering courses and qualifications for both wine trade and consumer at several different levels. A WSET Diploma is the usual pre-requisite for studying to become a MASTER OF WINE. In the academic year ended 2014 there were more than 56,000 WSET students in 62 countries, of which those in the UK, China including HONG KONG, the US, and Canada were most numerous.

Württemberg, wine region in southern GERMANY with 11,373 ha/28,091 acres of vineyard which loosely follow the River Neckar and its tributaries (see map under GERMANY). Much of the region lies between Stuttgart (including several suburbs) and Heilbronn with vineyards to the north contiguous with those of BADEN's Kraichgau. In these sectors, steep, DROUGHT-sensitive and demanding terraced slopes look down on the Neckar. The climate varies from south to north, but is at its most CONTINENTAL along the Kocher, Jagst, and Tauber, three tributaries at the north-eastern edge of the region, where winters can be severe. Some 18% of the region's vineyards are planted in RIESLING, while other white wine varieties are in decline and collectively amount to little more than 10% of the vineyard surface. Dark-skinned grapes dominate Württemberg's vineyards, notably Trollinger with 21%, Lemberger (Blaufränkisch) with 15%, Schwarzriesling/Müllerrebe (Pinot Meunier) with 14%, and Spätburgunder (Pinot Noir) with 11%.

Württemberg's Swabian populace is known for its thirst and the local wines for being drunk before leaving the region, but an increasing number of growers who believe their reds are world-class are showing their bottlings abroad. They represent sites spread across the region, some of which also excel with Riesling. And while Swabians are also notorious for thrift, their wines sell for prices well above German averages and comparable to those prevailing in Baden and Franken. Also in common with those two regions, the majority of Württemberg's production represents smallholders who sell to CO-OPERATIVES which process their fruit at a single huge central cellar (see ZENTRALKEL-LEREI).   D.S.

Würzer is a Gewürztraminer × Müller-Thurgau CROSS made at the German viticultural station of Alzey in 1932 and only planted in any significant quantity in the 1980s, peaking in 1995 at 121 ha/300 acres, mainly in Rheinhessen. Planted on only 61 ha/150 acres in 2012, it is overpoweringly heady, yields well, but a little goes a very long way indeed.

Xarello, or **Xarel-lo**, fine white grape variety planted on a fairly static total of 8,662 ha/21,395 acres of CATALUNYA in 2011, producing powerful, ageworthy still and sparkling wines. It is particularly important in ALELLA, where it is known as Pansa Blanca. It is most commonly found in PENEDÈS, however, where, with Parellada and Macabeo, it makes up most CAVA blends. It needs careful pruning and the wine it produces can be very strongly flavoured. It is the rather vegetal smell of Xarel-lo that often distinguishes so many Cavas from other TRADITIONAL METHOD sparkling wines.

Xenophon, writer in Ancient GREECE in the late 5th century BC famous for his *Anabasis*. In the *Economics*, a dialogue between a farmer, Ischomachos, and the famous philosopher Socrates, the planting and care of vines is discussed: vines should be planted in well-dug earth, at an angle, and the earth should be trodden down around the vine. H.H.A.

Xérès, French name for both JEREZ and SHERRY.

Xinomavro, black grape variety grown in 2013 on 2,239 ha/5,530 acres all over northern GREECE as far south as the foothills of Mount Olympus, where Rapsani is produced, but most famous as the grape of Naoussa. Its name means 'acid black' and the wines can indeed seem harsh in youth but they age well. One of the few Greek vine varieties which may not reach full ripeness in some years, it is blended with a small proportion of the local Negoska to produce Goumenissa and is also used as a base for sparkling wine on the exceptionally cool, high vineyards of Amyndeo. The wines tend to be relatively soft but to have good acid, attractive bite, and age well. It has also been planted in Gansu in CHINA at a JOINT VENTURE project by Mihalis Boutaris of Kir-Yianni in Naoussa.

xylem, the principal water-conducting tissue in vascular plants. In woody stem tissues, the secondary xylem forms the wood. The CAMBIUM differentiates xylem tissue on its inside. A single ring of xylem is produced each year with the first-formed vessels (in spring) being larger than those of late wood. This is how the annual rings which help to assess the age of a plant are formed (see OAK). In the grapevine, the vessels are large and porous so that its wood is very water conductive, a feature of vines generally. In autumn, however, vessels may become blocked by structures which plug the tubes, called tyloses, formed by the 'ballooning' of adjacent cell material into the vessel through pits in the walls; some vessels remain functional for up to seven years, but most become blocked by tyloses in their second or third year. The secondary xylem of QUERCUS forms the wood from which oak barrels are made. (See also PHLOEM.)
B.G.C.

Xynisteri, the most common white grape variety grown on Cyprus, more than 2,200 ha/5,500 acres in 2010, almost a quarter of the island's vineyard. It is preferred to the dark-skinned MAVRO for the rich fortified wine COMMANDARIA, the island's most distinctive wine and also makes dry whites of varying quality.

Yarra Valley, historic Australian wine region just north east of Melbourne, VICTORIA, that is cool in both senses of the word. Its 120 producers make internationally recognized Chardonnay and Pinot Noir and, increasingly, Shiraz as well as iconic Cabernet blends including Mount Mary Quintet, Yarra Yering Dry Red No 1, and Yeringberg. Ever-changing vistas from hillsides of valley floor make it a thriving centre for wine TOURISM. Melbourne is but one hour away.   H.H.

Ycoden-Daute-Isora, complicated name from the Guanche pre-Hispanic times, for the most ancient, but recently denominated, wine region in the Spanish CANARY ISLANDS. It is centred on the town of Icod de los Vinos, where wine has been made since the Spanish conquest in the 15th century. It now produces some of the best dry whites in the islands, from LISTÁN Blanco (PALOMINO) and, increasingly, from the much more distinctive VIJARIEGO and MARMAJUELO grapes. The region has 1,350 ha/ 3,300 acres under vines. In the 1990s, coastal vineyards were consistently uprooted and replaced by inland vineyards at much higher ELEVATIONS on the verdant VOLCANIC slopes.
                                    V. de la S.

yeast, microscopic, single-celled fungi, having round to oval cells which reproduce by forming buds, are vital to the alcoholic FERMENTATION process, which, starved of oxygen, transforms grape juice to wine. SUGARS are used as an energy source by yeast, with ETHANOL and CARBON DIOXIDE as major by-products of the reactions.

The word yeast (which may be singular or plural unless it encompasses yeasts from more than one species) is an old one whose meaning has changed significantly with the flowering of

microbiological science. It originally derived from an ancient word meaning 'to boil', 'to seethe', or 'to be troubled'. In 16th-century English, it referred to the froth on the top of a brewing tank and to the semi-solid material that could be collected both from that froth and from the bottom of the tank. From the mid 17th century, the meaning of the word yeast changed to that of a single-celled plant, a *thallophyte* and one of the lowest members of the plant kingdom along with algae, lichens, and fungi.

In common with other fungi, yeasts are differentiated from plant cells by absence of chloroplasts, which contain the plant cell's chlorophyll. The modern fermentative yeasts have evolved from an ancestral yeast by a process of genome duplication, rearrangements and deletions, estimated to have occurred over the past 100 million years, most likely in response to the high availability of sugar as flowering plants evolved. The genetic, and hence phenotypic, diversity of the pre-eminent fermentation yeast, *Saccharomyces cerevisiae*, is now immense.

Nomenclature

The nomenclature of various yeasts is far from straightforward and is in the process of being revised. Taxonomists—scientists who classify and name plants and animals—have traditionally had difficulty with the various microorganisms because early microscopes revealed little detail, and because the appearance of an organism depended on the conditions of its growth, isolation, and preparation for observation. The result has been that names have changed over time as laboratory equipment improved and as new techniques were perfected. In particular, the development of methods to study the genetic information contained in chromosomal DNA has provided

more reliable ways to characterize and classify yeasts. Indeed, a *Saccharomyces cerevisiae* yeast was the first higher organism to have its whole genome sequenced, by 1996. Genome analysis has revealed that some yeasts which were thought to be closely related were in fact only distantly related, and vice versa. Furthermore, some characteristics of yeasts that were used to differentiate species, such as the pattern of sugars that can be fermented, were found to represent natural variation within that species, and consequently did not represent different species. For this reason, many yeast names in common usage several decades ago are no longer accepted.

Saccharomyces cerevisiae is the name now most frequently used for the yeast involved in making wine and beer and in leavening bread. *Saccharomyces*, the genus name, means 'sugar fungus', and *cerevisiae* derives from the same root as 'cereals'. Older literature frequently called this yeast *Saccharomyces ellipsoideus* because the cells associated with fruit juices appeared more elliptical than the often-circular bakers' yeast. Within this yeast species are several hundred different strains or selections, each with real or fancied minor differences. Some strain differences relate to fermentation vigour, lack of off-flavour formation, ESTER production, and enhancement of a wine's VARIETAL character, such as fruity notes in Sauvignon Blanc. Many strains are being DNA-sequenced to reveal the genetic basis of their important winemaking characteristics, which will ultimately facilitate the breeding of strains with enhanced fermentation characteristics (see GENETIC MODIFICATION). Another species within the same genus, *Saccharomyces uvarum*, is often used in the distilling and brewing industries. It can grow at lower temperatures than *S. cerevisiae* and is often the dominant yeast fermenting musts located in cool-climate viticultural regions of countries including New Zealand, France, and Italy. It and other closely related species, *Saccharomyces bayanus* and *Saccharomyces paradoxus*, and their hybrids made by breeding with *Saccharomyces cerevisiae*, are showing potential for increasing the diversity of wine aromas and flavours. Several of the non-*Saccharomyces* yeast species which are commonly associated with grapes and fermentation (see below), such as *Candida zemplinina* (previously called *stellata*), *Lachancea* (previously *Kluyveromyces*) *thermotolerans*, and *Torulaspora delbrueckii*, are now being used in combination with *Saccharomyces cerevisiae* to introduce new and diverse flavour profiles in wine.

Editorial note:

In this article and throughout the book we use the term **ambient yeasts** to refer to yeasts of any genus that are present in the vineyard or winery, i.e. the opposite of inoculated yeasts; some writers refer to non-inoculated yeasts as 'native' or 'indigenous' yeasts. We use **wild yeasts** to refer to non-*Saccharomyces* yeasts, although 'wild yeasts' is used by many writers to refer to non-inoculated yeasts of any genus.

Cultured versus ambient yeasts

Ecology studies have shown that intact grape berries harbour a number of other yeast genera in significant populations. Spread around wineries and vineyards by insects, particularly fruit flies (DROSOPHILA), and possibly air currents, the most common genera are *Klöckera/Hanseniaspora* and *Candida*, with *Pichia*, *Lachancea* (formerly *Kluyveromyces*), *Metschnikowia*, *Zygosaccharomyces*, and *Torulaspora* usually representing a low proportion. *Saccharomyces* species are rarely isolated from grape berries unless they are damaged by, for example, disease, birds, insects, or hail. More sensitive to SULFUR DIOXIDE, and intolerant of an ALCOHOLIC STRENGTH much above 5%, these wild yeasts are generally active during the early stages of non-inoculated or 'spontaneous' fermentations, those occurring when insufficient or no sulfur dioxide is added to the grape juice or must. Fortunately, there are usually enough *Saccharomyces cerevisiae* cells present on the surfaces of harvesting, transportation, and winery processing equipment that enter the grape juice or must, so that these latter yeasts continue the fermentation above the unstable alcoholic strength of 5%, depleting the supply of sugar and producing a stable wine. Inoculation with *Saccharomyces* yeast does not suppress wild yeasts which are naturally present in juices and musts during the early stages of fermentation. Therefore, wine is commonly the result of a mixed microflora, although the impact of wild yeasts on the wine is usually restricted by the inoculated yeast. These populations are believed to stabilize with a particular mixture of yeasts

suitable for wine fermentation, so that ambient yeast, generally a mixture of yeast genera and species, have in the past been much more commonly used than cultured yeast in the traditional wine regions of Europe. The concept of 'château' or resident/indigenous populations of ambient yeast which promote the particular character of an estate wine is controversial among wine scientists. See also MICROBIAL TERROIR.

Increasing numbers of Old World producers, the majority of New World winemakers, and certainly all of those worried about minimizing risk, use **cultured yeast**, however, sometimes called **pure culture**, **selected (natural or native) yeast**, or **inoculated yeast**. The advantage of cultured yeast, of which only one strain is usually added, is that it has been specially selected (from ambient yeasts) so that its behaviour is predictable and the fermentation will proceed smoothly and, of greatest importance, to completion without the risk of a STUCK FERMENTATION or formation of off-odours. Individual winemakers often favour certain strains of cultured yeast for practical WINEMAKING reasons. Depending on the strain of yeast, the flavour differences in the wines produced, particularly as the wine ages, is likely to be too small to be detected by the average consumer. Strains have been selected and exploited by oenologists and winemakers for characteristics such as fermentation vigour, high alcohol and sulfur dioxide tolerance, tolerance to temperature extremes, ability to referment wine to make sparkling wine, freedom from acetic (VOLATILE ACIDITY) and sulfidic off-flavours, film or FLOR formation needed for SHERRY production, enhancement of wine varietal character, fruity ester profile and intensity, low-foaming, sedimentation (flocculant) property, yeasticidal properties, improved red wine colour, better tolerance to nutrient deficiencies, lower potential to form sulfur dioxide, and compatibility with LACTIC ACID BACTERIA. Because the selection and characterization of new yeast isolates is a laborious and time-consuming process, a variety of conventional breeding techniques are increasingly being used. These include selecting natural variants from a population or using mutagenesis, such as ultraviolet light, to increase genetic variability, or culturing yeast under specific stressful conditions (often referred to as adaptive or directed evolution) and by hybridization or rare-mating, which exploits the sexual cycle in yeast. See also GENETIC MODIFICATION.

The advantage of a well-adapted population of ambient yeast is that there are many different strains and, because of their different abilities and aptitudes, they may be capable of producing a wine with a better balanced, wider range of flavours and characteristics. In an attempt to verify such a view, current research is working systematically with mixed-culture fermentations in combination with chemical analysis of flavour

compounds (referred to as 'metabolic footprinting') and sensory evaluation of wines to compare inoculated with the somewhat riskier so-called wild ferments. Given the unpredictable nature of wild yeast fermentations, it is likely that even more sophisticated blended yeast cultures, which better simulate the apparent characteristics of wild ferments, will be developed in the future.

Cultured yeast characteristics

Yeast are cultured in large sterile tanks with vigorous aeration under conditions which encourage biomass but discourage alcohol formation. They are then filtered, washed, dried, and packed in sterile containers, often under vacuum, for transfer to the winery (or brewery or bakery). Well over one hundred different strains are now produced worldwide as active dried wine yeast preparations. Active dried yeast is quickly and simply reactivated with warm water or diluted grape juice at 40 °C/ 104 °F for 15 minutes. Some wineries culture their favoured yeast in grape juice with or without vigorous aeration and add about 2–4% by volume to the juice or must to initiate fermentation. Following use in winemaking, the yeast and grape debris are freed of as much wine as possible and usually discarded. A minor proportion may be processed to recover alcohol, TARTRATES, and occasionally grapeseed oil.

Among the many genera of yeasts, there are astounding variations in terms of the production and tolerance of alcohol, aroma and flavour, rate of fermentation, temperature tolerance, flocculation characteristics, sulfur dioxide tolerance, REDUCING potential, and micronutrient requirements. Although some wild yeasts cannot tolerate alcohol concentrations above 5%, a tolerance of up to 13 or 15% is the norm for yeasts used in the production of dry wine, and hence strains of *Saccharomyces cerevisiae* are preferred. Some strains can tolerate concentrations of more than 20% during the special conditions of sake fermentation. Yeast with a high alcohol production and tolerance may be chosen for FORTIFIED WINES or dry red wine made from over-ripe grapes with very high sugar content in some New World wine regions; yeast which flocculate particularly well, such as that called Épernay, may be used for SPARKLING WINEMAKING; FILM-FORMING YEAST are used to make sherry; while a yeast with good tolerance of sulfur dioxide may be useful in certain examples of SWEET WINEMAKING. Strains with well-defined flavour characteristics are becoming popular, and can offer better colour and tannin structure, improved fruity/estery notes, or greater enhancement of varietal flavour; strains which emphasize, for example, the tropical/passion fruit aroma in Sauvignon Blanc are now widely available. Some cultured yeast strains are known internationally while others may be used merely locally.   A.D.W. & P.A.H.

How yeast works

Yeast, like most living organisms, need a good supply of carbon and NITROGEN, a source of SULFUR, PHOSPHORUS, and OXYGEN, various MINERALS and micronutrients (e.g. trace elements, and several VITAMINS) for growth and reproduction. The usual carbon sources are the six-carbon sugars, GLUCOSE and FRUCTOSE. Wine yeast can also use SUCROSE, which may be added to the juice of underripe grapes (CHAPTALIZATION) and is used in SPARKLING WINEMAKING to induce the second fermentation. Grape amino acids and ammonium compounds most often supply the nitrogen, and most fruit juices, including grape juice, provide the other components necessary for growth. Nutrients, based on nitrogen or vitamins, may be specially added to encourage yeast activity at the beginning of fermentation. This is especially important in the case of underripe grapes, ROT, grapes from low SOIL POTENTIAL vineyards, or grape- and must-processing conditions that deliberately or unwittingly lead to nutrient depletion, such as harvesting and transport under hot conditions that permit extensive microbial growth, or excessive CLARIFICATION. Grape solids provide a source of LIPIDS, which, in the absence of oxygen, are used to build stronger cell membranes that confer better tolerance to fermentation stresses, such as extremes of alcohol and temperature. Oxygen is an especially important nutrient, which is supplied in large quantity during production of the yeast starter culture. Small amounts of oxygen may also be supplied during the early or middle stage of fermentation to improve yeast survival and fermentation activity later in fermentation, especially in anaerobic, high-sugar, highly clarified musts at low temperatures (see STUCK FERMENTATION).

All cells require energy to exist, to grow, and to reproduce. Yeast can release a small amount of the energy stored in glucose and fructose of grape juice by a series of complex biochemical reactions known as glycolysis. This nearly universal process among living organisms is so complex and involves so many steps that it has taken scientists years of research to understand it. Using internal ENZYMES, the yeast cell, through a series of reactions, splits the six-carbon sugar molecule into two molecules of three-carbon PYRUVATE. The final two steps, known collectively as fermentation, convert pyruvate to ETHYL ALCOHOL and carbon dioxide. In this fermentative decomposition of pyruvate, the first step is removal of the terminal carbon dioxide from the pyruvate, leaving the two-carbon fragment ACETALDEHYDE. Acetaldehyde is then converted to ethyl alcohol and carbon dioxide. A small amount of acetaldehyde is also converted to ACETIC ACID, which is required for cell processes, e.g. biosynthesis of lipids, needed to make cell membranes; some acetic acid escapes from the cell and contributes to wine VOLATILE ACIDITY.

When all of the sugar is fermented to alcohol and carbon dioxide, and a small amount of oxygen is present, yeast can reconvert some of the ethyl alcohol back to acetaldehyde. Further oxidative decomposition occurs, by a complex series of reactions, to carbon dioxide and water. This process, which takes place in the mitochondria within the cell and which releases most of the energy originally stored in sugar, is known as RESPIRATION. The exposure of wine to oxygen is, however, rigorously prevented except in some circumstances, such as in the making of FLOR wines such as FINO sherry. Normally wine is protected from air during fermentation by the blanket of carbon dioxide produced.

During fermentation of grape juice, yeast produce small amounts of other compounds from sugar glycolysis, and the metabolism of amino acids and other nutrients. Some of these compounds are volatile and contribute fermentation-derived characteristics to a wine's AROMA. The most important compounds are esters, aldehydes and ketones, fatty acids, higher alcohols, and volatile sulfur compounds (HYDROGEN SULFIDE and MERCAPTANS). Recent research has shown that some of these volatile compounds play a much greater role in the distinctive aroma profile of certain grape varieties than previously believed. Furthermore, advances in the understanding of how yeast control the formation of these aroma compounds is leading to the development of new yeast strains which can alter the emphasis of various aroma notes in wine. GLYCEROL, ACETIC ACID, and SUCCINIC ACID, which contribute to the taste of wine, are the most important non-volatile compounds produced by yeast.

So far this century research has focused on and revealed the complex metabolic/enzymatic interactions that yeast have with various grape-derived compounds, many of which contribute to the characteristic aroma and flavour of specific grape varieties. For example, certain hydrolytic enzymes, glycosidases, are released by the cell which can hydrolyse various FLAVOUR PRECURSORS, notably sugar conjugates of MONOTERPENES, norisoprenoids, aliphatics, PHENOLS, and benzene derivatives. Monoterpenes are important to the aroma of wines made from floral grape varieties such as MUSCAT, RIESLING, and TRAMINER. β-damascenone, responsible for stewed apple, rose, and honey aromas in young wine is an example of a norisoprenoid. See FLAVOUR COMPOUNDS.

Another class of grape-derived flavour precursors are the cysteine- or glutathione-linked compounds, which, when hydrolysed by enzymes present in some strains of yeast, generate polyfunctional volatile thiols (see MERCAPTANS) with fruity aromas. These compounds, which contribute box tree, passionfruit, grapefruit, guava, and gooseberry aromas, are important

in Sauvignon Blanc wines, and have also been identified in wines made from Colombard, Riesling, Sémillon, Merlot, and Cabernet Sauvignon.

Some yeasts also have the ability to degrade phenolic acids to volatile vinyl phenols (e.g. 4-vinylphenol and 4-vinylgaiacol), which contribute a phenolic off-flavour. BRETTANOMYCES yeasts are able to convert these unstable vinylphenols to the stable ethylphenols (e.g. 4-ethylphenol and 4-ethylgaiacol), responsible for phenolic, medicinal, and barnyard aromas in wine. Yeast also produce carbonyl compounds, which, under some circumstances, can enhance red wine colour. For example, acetaldehyde and pyruvic acid can react with anthocyanins to form more stable pigmented pyroanthocyanins that can contribute to the stable colour of aged red wines. On the other hand, most aldehydes are ultimately converted to the corresponding alcohol (just as acetaldehyde becomes ethyl alcohol), such that the oak-derived aldehyde vanillin is reduced to vanillic alcohol, thereby lowering flavour intensity.

After the yeast have converted all of the sugar, they slowly die, flocculate, and fall to the bottom of the vessel, forming a sediment known as gross LEES. In bottle-fermented sparkling wines, the interaction between this sediment and the wine in the bottle is an important element in sparkling winemaking (see AUTOLYSIS). The traditional STIRRING of wine on yeast lees in barrel and in tank is now becoming widely practised as a means to improve palate weight and texture.   P.A.H.

Boulton, R. B., et al., *Principles and Practices of Winemaking* (Gaithersburg, 1998).

König, H., Unden, G., and Fröhlich, J. (eds.), *Biology of Microorganisms on Grapes, in Musts and in Wine* (Springer, 2009).

Swiegers, J. H., et al., 'Yeast and bacterial modulation of wine aroma and flavour', *Australian Journal of Grape and Wine Research*, 11 (2005), 139–73.

Ugliano, M., and Henschke, P. A., 'Yeasts and wine flavour', in M. V. Moreno-Arribas and C. Polo (eds.), *Wine Chemistry and Biochemistry* (Springer, 2009), 313–92.

Varela, C., et al., 'Discovering a chemical basis for differentiating wines made by fermentation with "wild" indigenous and inoculated yeasts: role of yeast volatile compounds', *Australian Journal of Grape and Wine Research*, 15/3 (2009), 238–48.

Yecla, denominated wine zone in the LEVANTE, south east Spain. Sandwiched between JUMILLA, ALICANTE, and ALMANSA (see map under SPAIN), Yecla is dominated by La Purísima, the single largest CO-OPERATIVE in Spain. The red MONASTRELL represents 85% of all grapes grown in the region. The private Bodegas Castaño is pioneering more ambitious wines by adding Cabernet Sauvignon, Tempranillo, and Merlot to Monastrell.   V. de la S.

yellow mosaic, vine disease. See FANLEAF DEGENERATION.

yellows. See GRAPEVINE YELLOWS.

Yellow Tail, Australian wine BRAND whose early-21st-century growth in the US, from a standing start, set records in the history of branding and gave birth to the infamous 'critters' (small animals on labels) wine category. The Casella family had just 16 ha/40 acres of vines in RIVERINA and supplied BULK WINE until John Casella with an aggressive, export-orientated manager planned an assault on the embryonic US market for Australian wines in the late 1990s. A first attempt failed but new branding involving a yellow kangaroo image and the irritating but eye-catching logo [yellow tail] (*sic*), together with particularly fruity, not to say sweet, wines and a bold profit-sharing scheme with their US importer W. J. Deutsch & Sons. Annual US sales rose from 200,000 cases in the launch year of 2001 to 7.5 million in 2004, by which time Yellow Tail was the top imported wine brand in the US. By 2014 the Casellas were exporting 12.5 million cases to more than 50 countries.

yema bud, alternative name for CHIP BUDDING.

yield, how much a vineyard produces is an important statistic in wine production and has been a subject of intense interest from at least the time of classical ROME, not least because of alleged effects on wine quality.

Factors affecting yield

Vineyard yield depends on many factors, which will be briefly described here. For a more complete discussion, see the individual factors listed.

Yield may be measured as either a weight of grapes or a volume of wine (see below), and is usually considered per unit area of vineyard, since this is what matters in agricultural terms. Those who believe that increasing VINE DENSITY is associated with improved wine quality argue that yield per vine is a more important consideration. Disciples of CANOPY MANAGEMENT, on the other hand, argue that the amount of sunlit leaf area per unit of land is more important than yield per vine. or per hectare

Yield per vine depends on the number of bunches per vine, and the average bunch weight. The number of bunches per vine depends on the winter PRUNING policy, the BUDBREAK, and the number of bunches per shoot, or FRUITFULNESS. Bunch weight depends on the number of FLOWERS per bunch, and the success of FRUIT SET in forming berries, then on the weight of individual berries.

Yield per vine also depends on VINE AGE (very old vines often produce very little), the way the vines have been managed, and on the WEATHER over at least the last two years, together with other factors such as VINE PESTS and VINE DISEASES.

After VIGOUR and pruning, the weather is one of the most important factors affecting vineyard yield. Cold winters may promote budbreak, but FROSTS in spring can kill young shoots and bunches. Warm, sunny weather promotes FLOWERING and POLLINATION, but cold, wet, and windy weather can cause poor FRUIT SET. Some varieties are more prone than others to poor set. DROUGHT conditions commonly reduce berry size—to less than half that of vines well supplied with water in extreme cases. Rain will generally increase yield as it causes berries to swell, but too much rain near harvest causes BOTRYTIS BUNCH ROT and potentially a considerable loss in yield.

Perhaps surprisingly, the weather the preceding season can also have an effect on yield. It has been shown that warm, sunny weather during flowering encourages bunch INITIATION in the buds that are forming to produce shoots and bunches for the next growing season. So this weather pattern can prepare the vine for a high potential yield the following year.

How yield is measured

Conventional units of yield are the weight of fresh grapes per unit land area, such as tonnes/ha, or tons/acre. (One ton/acre is about 2.5 tonnes/ha.) This is the standard measurement in most NEW WORLD wine regions.

Although many Italians and Swiss measure yield in weight of grapes, in most European countries production is measured in volumes of wine per unit area, normally expressed as hectolitres per hectare, or hl/ha. In many cases, this measurement is an extremely important one, often limited to a maximum (depending on the VINTAGE) specified by local regulation (see APPELLATION CONTRÔLÉE, DOC, etc. and the note below).

The two measurements interrelate, although the volume of wine produced by a given weight of grapes can vary considerably according to vine variety, individual vintage conditions, winery equipment, winemaking policy, and, most importantly, wine type. To make 100 litres of red wine, which is fermented in the presence of grape skins that can be pressed rather harder than white grape skins, about 130 kg (0.13 tonnes) of grapes are needed. To make 100 litres of white wine, about 150 kg are needed (more like 160 kg for top-quality SPARKLING WINEMAKING). Assuming an average of 140 kg of grapes per 100 litres of wine, one tonne/ha is about 7 hl/ha, while one ton/acre is about 17.5 hl/ha (typically slightly less for whites, slightly more for reds).

Despite its importance in measuring yield, there is no uniform approach in determining the area of a vineyard. Excluding the essential and normally cultivated areas along the ends (called headlands) and at the sides, which are indubitably part of the productive unit, effectively reduces the size of many vineyards by 10% or so, and the figure may be higher for small vineyards.

Yields and wine quality

A necessary connection between low yields and high-quality wine has been assumed at least since Roman times when *Bacchus amat colles* encapsulated the prevailing belief that low-yielding HILLSIDE VINEYARDS produced the best wine. Wine law in many European countries is predicated on the same belief and the much-imitated APPELLATION CONTRÔLÉE laws of France specify maximum permitted yields for each appellation (even if an additional allowance is often permitted; see below).

There is little doubt that heavily cropped vines with a low LEAF TO FRUIT RATIO ripen more slowly, so that in cooler climates the fruit may not reach full RIPENESS and wine quality suffers. It is less widely understood that undercropping can also adversely affect wine quality. A high leaf to fruit ratio will certainly ripen grapes, but the shaded CANOPY MICROCLIMATE will produce grapes high in POTASSIUM and PH and low in PHENOLICS and flavour.

It should also be noted that, within a given wine region (Bordeaux is a notable example), there is no correlation between size of the crop and quality of the wine. Some of the finest red bordeaux VINTAGE YEARS of the 1980s, for example, were also those in which yields were relatively high; while the lowest crop levels of the decade were recorded in lesser vintages such as 1984 and 1980.

There are countless commercial examples of high vineyard yields associated with low quality, however. Very high yields are common to vineyards of high vigour, which in turn is typically due to planting on very fertile soil, well supplied with water and nutrients, but the negative effects are more likely to be the result of excessive shoot and leaf growth and canopy SHADE. High-yielding vineyards are also often in hot climates, where the climate reduces the potential for wine quality anyway.

Very low yields may be the deliberate result of careful pruning, SHOOT THINNING, or even CROP THINNING, but they may also be associated with excessive vine stress. This can be due, for example, to weeds, pests, or disease, or to very shallow soils and WATER STRESS (as in many traditionally dry-grown vineyards of Mediterranean Europe), and a vine that is too severely stressed will not function properly and will not produce premium wine.

The yield which a vineyard can ripen properly will depend on the VINE VARIETY, the region, vine management practices (particularly pruning and vine-TRAINING SYSTEMS), and climate as well as weather. For example, a yield of 8 tonnes/ha, or 56 hl/ha, might be considered excessive in a very cool climate, but a yield five times this figure might be easily ripened to a similar or higher sugar level in a warmer climate. Some varieties seem more prone than others to crop-level effects on wine quality, and in general red wine varieties are more affected than white. PINOT NOIR is an outstanding example, as the inverse relationship between yield and quality in red burgundy demonstrates. Both Pinot Noir and MERLOT show less colour in the skins and wine whereas yield effects are much less evident in deeply pigmented varieties such as Syrah.

Some specific examples

Vineyard yields vary enormously around the world and, in some regions with less dependable climates, from year to year. Among the highest reported yields are about 100 tonnes/ha for TABLE GRAPES grown on complex trellises in Israel (if their juice were made into wine, this would convert into about 1,750 hl/ha!). The Argentine vine-breeder Angel Gargiulo was in the 1970s and 1980s encouraged to breed new wine grape varieties specifically designed for the Argentine environment which can yield up to 500 hl/ha (but were commercially planted only to a very limited extent). Commercial, well-managed vineyards in irrigated DESERT regions in California, Australia, and Argentina can routinely produce 15 tons/acre, almost 38 tonnes/ha (260 hl/ha). At the other end of the spectrum, pests, disease, drought, or bunch rot can all reduce yields to less than 1 tonne/ha, or 7 hl/ha. See Ch d'YQUEM as well as Domaine LEROY and CHAPOUTIER for some examples of particularly low yields, encouraged for the sake of wine quality.

Some attempt at calculating national average yields may be made using OIV statistics, although these are more reliable for some countries than for others. and they include vineyards dedicated to table or drying grapes as well as to wine grapes. According to figures for 2011, the US has one of the highest national average yields, at 6.5 tons/acre (115 hl/ha). See EU for a discussion of yields in Europe.

Certain wine types, most red wines, for example, are apparently more sensitive to yield, perhaps because wines from higher yielding vineyards are often lighter in colour but this is more likely the result of a vine vigour producing a shaded canopy, which is known to depress PHENOLIC synthesis. Vineyards dedicated to sparkling wines, or base wines for brandy, are in general allowed to yield rather more than those dedicated to still wine production. In Champagne, for example, permitted yields of 12 tonnes/ha (5 tons/acre) or over 80 hl/ha are common.

From a financial point of view, high yields are attractive to vine-growers, who have traditionally been paid on the simple basis of weight (although quality factors such as MUST WEIGHT are also taken into account; see PRICE OF grapes). Vine-growers whose aim is to produce good-quality wine may, however, deliberately restrict yields by such measures as pruning, crop thinning, and shoot thinning, although the evidence for a direct yield–quality equation is lacking. One of the most important economic issues facing modern viticulture is whether high-vigour and high-yielding vineyards can produce high-quality wine using vineyard management techniques such as CANOPY MANAGEMENT.

The fact that yields are officially limited by regulation in the two most important wine-producing countries of France and Italy has undoubtedly encouraged worldwide respect for low yields, and perhaps some inertia in researching ways of increasing both quality and quantity. Alternatively, such restrictions could be seen as a device to avoid production surplus. It should be noted, however, that the official maxima cited in wine regulations were almost routinely increased in France by a device called the *plafond limite de classement*, or PLC, which allowed a certain increase (often 20%) on the base yield according to the conditions of the year. Average yields for the top appellations of the MÉDOC in 1989, 1990, and 1996, for example, were between 55 and 60 hl/ha when the theoretical maximum yield is 45 hl/ha.

Although the PLC has been abolished and the wording has changed, the practice has not. Leeway still exists thanks to the so-called *rendement butoir*, which is higher than the basic maximum. Derogations are also made when yields are severely reduced by severe weather such as HAIL.

See also PRUNING.   R.E.S. & J.R.

Coombe, B. G., and Dry, P. R., *Viticulture, i: Resources* (2nd edn, Adelaide, 2004).

Gargiulo, A. A., 'Quality and quantity: are they compatible?', *Journal of Wine Research*, 2/3 (1991), 161–81.

Ross, J., 'Balancing yield and quality, parts I–IV', *Practical Winery & Vineyard* (Mar/Apr 1999, May/June 1999, Nov/Dec 1999, May/June 2000).

yield monitors, sensors fitted to mechanical grape harvesters which assess and record the amount of fruit being harvested in real time. When used in conjunction with a differential GLOBAL POSITIONING SYSTEM, they allow maps of yield to be produced. Such maps are a tool in the implementation of PRECISION VITICULTURE and ZONAL VITICULTURE. See also REMOTE SENSING.

R.G.V.B.

York Mountain, California wine region and AVA. See SAN LUIS OBISPO.

Yquem, Château d', the greatest wine of SAUTERNES and, according to the famous 1855 CLASSIFICATION, of the entire BORDEAUX region. It is sweet, golden, and apparently almost immortal.

The origin of the name is obscure, although the Germanic *aig-helm* (meaning 'to have a helmet') is claimed. Probably the first vineyard-owning family were the Sauvages, who, from being tenants, bought the estate in 1711. It was acquired by the Lur Saluces family in 1785, when the last Sauvage d'Yquem married Comte Louis-Amadée de Lur Saluces. By then the wine was very well known, for in 1787 Thomas JEFFERSON wrote to 'M. d'Yquem', asking to buy some, stating, 'I know that yours is one of the best growths of Sauterne [*sic*]'. It is not known when Yquem was first made with BOTRYTIZED grapes, those affected by NOBLE ROT, but this painstaking technique probably originated early in the 19th century, although very sweet bottles dating from the latter part of the 18th century have been found. In the second half of the 19th century, Yquem had a worldwide reputation, not least in tsarist RUSSIA. From before the First World War until 1968, the estate was run by the Marquis Bernard de Lur Saluces who was succeeded in 1968 by Comte Alexandre, who also owns Ch de Fargues in Sauternes (although in 1999 LVMH acquired majority ownership after a bitter family struggle). Pierre LURTON, also manager of Ch CHEVAL BLANC, was subsequently installed by LVMH.

The château, dating back to the 15th century and the Renaissance, stands on the crest of a small hill, with small towers at each corner and a large inner courtyard. The vineyard on all sides extends to 99 ha/245 acres in production out of a total of 125 ha. The vines planted are 80% SÉMILLON and 20% of the usually more productive SAUVIGNON BLANC. Production averages 8,000 cases, a fraction of the typical output of a top red wine property in the MÉDOC. The secret of Yquem's renown is its susceptibility to noble rot, and its ability to run risks and sacrifice quantity for painstakingly upheld quality. An average of five passages, or TRIES, are made through the vineyard each year so that only the BOTRYTIS-affected grapes are picked. The maximum yield is 9 hl/ha (0.5 tons/acre), compared with the normal 25 in Sauternes. The juice is pressed three times, and then treated to three years' BARREL MATURATION in new OAK casks. The cost of the whole operation makes Yquem a very expensive wine. CRYOEXTRACTION, or freeze concentration, was controversially used on the 1987 vintage and, experimentally, in the early 1990s.

Since 1959 a dry white wine, Y, or Ygrec, has been produced but intermittently. Notably alcoholic, it has more than a hint of a Sauternes. In 2004, Pierre Lurton began experimenting with a fresher style of dry white bordeaux from grapes unaffected by botrytis.

E.P.-R. & J.R.

Olney, R., *Yquem* (Paris, 1985; London, 1986).

WESTERN BALKANS

Wine-growing regions

0   100 km

Yugoslavia, eastern European union of peoples that existed for barely 60 years before breaking up amid bloodshed, privation, and extreme ethnic tension at the beginning of the post-communist era in the early 1990s.

Viticulture in this region dates back at least to Roman times and almost certainly earlier, to the Illyrians in the 4th and 5th centuries BC. In the communist era, production of volume at low prices was the priority in large state-controlled CO-OPERATIVES, and winemaking standards were often poor. At its peak in the 1970s, former Yugoslavia was one of the world's top ten wine producers, making around 6 million hl/158 million gal a year, and was famous for wines such as Lutomer Laski Rizling, once the UK's best-selling white wine. Marshal Tito's regime was less hardline than other Eastern Bloc countries and some degree of private land ownership, and even private wine production, was permitted. Some family producers were able to start bottling their wine as early as the 1970s. The first private producer, industry hero Stanko Čurin, and, Tito's favourite, Movia of SLOVENIA kept producing throughout this era. This meant that some connection between land and vine growing was retained and provided a strong foundation for the emergence of today's private wine producers. Yugoslavia has since been split into (roughly from north to south) SLOVENIA, CROATIA, SERBIA, KOSOVO, MONTENEGRO, BOSNIA AND HERZEGOVINA, and MACEDONIA.   C.G.

Zalagyöngye, Muscat-like TABLE GRAPE cross of an EGER grape variety and Pearl of Csaba that is planted on more than 1,700 ha/ 4,200 acres in Hungary, where some undistinguished wine is also made from it, mainly in Kunság. It is also grown in Italy, Croatia, Romania, and Israel for table grapes and is usually called by a local translation of the expression 'Queen of the Vineyards'.

Zalema, Spanish white grape variety still making light, neutral whites from 4,113 ha/ 10,159 acres of Andalucia in 2011, particularly in the southern CONDADO DE HUELVA zone, where its musts and wine can oxidize easily. It is being replaced by higher-quality varieties such as PALOMINO.

Žametovka, SLOVENIAN dark-skinned grape variety most famous for a single plant. Wine made from this speciality of the Dolenjska wine region in Posavje in the south of the country has usually been an ingredient in the pale, tart, local Čvicek but in Maribor is a vast, productive 400-year-old vine that is one of the world's oldest.

Zefir, early-ripening 1951 Hungarian CROSS of LEÁNYKA and HÁRSLEVELŰ producing soft, spicy white wine.

Zelen, old, south-west SLOVENIAN vine variety making crisp, dry whites in Vipavska Dolina.

Zenit, 1951 Hungarian CROSS of EZERJÓ and BOUVIER which ripens usefully early on just under 560 ha/1,384 acres in 2011 to produce crisp, fruity but not particularly aromatic white wines.

Zentralkellerei, a vast central co-operative wine cellar peculiar to GERMANY. See CO-OPERATIVES.

Zéta, Hungarian vine CROSS of FURMINT and BOUVIER, formerly known as Orémus, which, with Furmint, Hárslevelű, and Sárga Muskotály, is permitted in TOKAJ where there were 120 ha/ 296 acres in 2011. The Bouvier character can dominate unless it is very ripe.

Zibibbo, Sicilian name for the MUSCAT OF ALEXANDRIA white grape variety, sometimes made into wine, notably Moscato di PANTELLERIA, although more usually sold as TABLE GRAPES. It is very much less common in Italy than Moscato Bianco (MUSCAT BLANC À PETITS GRAINS) and in 2010 there were 1,521 ha/3,758 acres. The rich, dark Moscato di Pantelleria is geographically closer to Tunisia than to Sicily, which administers it. In fact this is the only wine with even a modicum of international renown that is made remotely near the city after which the variety is named.

Zierfandler, the finer of the two white wine grape varieties traditionally associated with Gumpoldskirchen, the dramatically full-bodied, long-lived spicy white wine of the THERMENREGION district of AUSTRIA. (The other is ROTGIPFLER.) Plantings had fallen to just 85 ha/210 acres by 2013. It ripens late, as its synonym Spätrot suggests, but keeps its acidity better than Rotgipfler. Unblended, Zierfandler has sufficient nerve to make late-harvest wines with the ability to evolve over years in bottle, but many Zierfandler grapes are blended, and sometimes vinified, with Rotgipfler. The variety, as Cirfandli, is also known in Hungary. DNA parentage analysis suggests it may be a natural cross of ROTER VELTLINER and a relative of SAVAGNIN.

Žilavka, the most famous grape variety in Herzegovina (see BOSNIA AND HERZEGOVINA). This characterful variety makes distinctive whites that manage to combine high alcohol with high acidity and a certain nuttiness of flavour. The Žilavka made around the inland town of Mostar is particularly prized. It is not, however, necessarily made exclusively from Žilavka grapes. Žilavka is also found in CROATIA, the Republic of MACEDONIA, and SERBIA.

Zimbabwe, southern AFRICAN country with small-scale commercial wine industry. After a slow start in the 1960s and 1970s, investment and foreign CONSULTANTS led to an improvement in wine quality from the late 1980s to the mid 1990s. However, President Mugabe's land-acquisition policies and a deeply unstable economy have had a devastating impact on both quantity and quality, drastically reducing the area of vineyard, financial potential, and access to knowledge and equipment.

Production is mostly in East Mashonaland and Manicaland, on the same latitude as much of BOLIVIA and southern BRAZIL. The TEMPERATE climate averages eight hours of daily sunshine and mean annual TEMPERATURES are just under 19 °C/66 °F. Summer rain falls from November to April, but DROUGHT is a constant threat. Uneven budding and ROT are annual hazards in the long, hot, humid summers, and the grapes can be affected by dilution and HAIL. The better vineyard areas lie at an ELEVATION of about 1,500 m/4,920 ft. Shortcomings in the vineyard are frequently addressed by ACIDIFICATION and sometimes ENRICHMENT (Zimbabwe has no official labelling or wine-production regulations). Chenin Blanc, Colombard, Sauvignon Blanc, Chardonnay, and Crouchen vines produce dry and off-dry whites, with Pinotage, Merlot, Shiraz, and Cabernet Sauvignon planted for reds.

The most promising vineyards are east of the capital Harare towards Marondera. The Cairns Group (which produces wines under the

Mukuyu label) and African Distillers own the biggest wineries, but each lost significant farms in the land grab, and the quality of their production provides evidence of the general decline. Some attempt has been made to create boutique wineries, of which Bushman's Rock has proved the most tenacious. T.D.C.

zinc, essential element for healthy vine growth. A deficiency of zinc affects the plant's ability to synthesize the hormones AUXINS, deficiency in which results in a failure of the shoots to grow normally. The principal symptoms are CHLOROSIS between the veins of young and old leaves, their small size, and a widened leaf sinus where the PETIOLE attaches. FRUIT SET can also be poor. Zinc deficiency commonly occurs in vineyards on sandy soils and on some high-PH soils, and is treated by daubing pruning wounds with pastes containing zinc, or applying a zinc spray to the leaves in summer. R.E.S. & R.E.W.

Zinfandel is the best-known California name of the black grape variety known in its native CROATIA as both TRIBIDRAG and CRLJENAK KAŠTELANSKI and in Puglia as PRIMITIVO. California grows far more of the variety than anywhere else: nearly 48,000 acres/19,433 ha in 2012. The wines produced there have tended to mirror the giddily changing fashions of the American wine business.

For much of the 20th century, the viticultural 'pioneer' Agoston HARASZTHY was credited with introducing this important variety to California from his native Hungary, but a more worthy Zinfandel hero is the California historian Charles L. Sullivan, who unearthed the truth, or at least part of it, about Zinfandel's route to California. It was he who pointed out that there was no mention of Zinfandel in Haraszthy's copious promotional literature in the early 1860s, and that, long before Haraszthy arrived in California in 1849, the variety was well known on the American East Coast.

The vine was imported, possibly unnamed, to the US from the Austrian imperial nursery in Vienna by George Gibbs of Long Island, probably in 1829. He took it to Boston and by the early 1830s it had acquired such names as 'Zenfendel' and 'Zinfindal' among New England growers, many of whom added it to the range of VINIFERA vines they grew under glass as a TABLE GRAPE.

Many of those who participated in the California GOLD RUSH of 1849 turned to agriculture, often dependent on shipments of plant material from the East Coast. 'Zinfindal' was included in a particularly important consignment which arrived in 1852 and by 1859 the variety was grown in both Napa and Sonoma. In 1862, the secretary of the Sonoma Horticultural Society gave some wine made from these grapes to a French winemaker working in California who reported that it tasted like 'a good French claret'.

Because Zinfandel has no French connection, it had escaped the detailed scrutiny of the world's ampelographic centre in MONTPELLIER and its European origins rested on local hypothesis rather than internationally accredited fact until the application of DNA PROFILING to vines in the early 1990s. Only then was it irrefutably demonstrated what had been suspected, that Zinfandel is one and the same as the variety known as Primitivo in Puglia. Subsequent DNA profiling at DAVIS established that the Croatian variety PLAVAC MALI is in fact a cross between Zinfandel and Dobričić, an obscure and ancient Croatian variety found on the island of Šolta near Split. This suggested a probable Dalmatian origin for Zinfandel too, and Croatian researchers Pejic and Maletic collaborating with Carole Meredith at Davis intensively searched the coastal vineyards for Zinfandel until in 2001 they discovered an ancient and almost extinct variety on the island of Kaštela near Split called Crljenak Kaštelanski (literally 'red grape of Kaštela') that was established as Zinfandel by DNA. Analysis of this variety's DNA showed an exact match with that of a 90-year-old herbarium specimen of an ancient Croatian vine known locally as Tribidrag.

Zinfandel took firm hold on the California wine business in the 1880s, when its ability to produce in quantity was prized above all else. Many was the miner, and other beneficiary of California's gold rush, whose customary drink was Zinfandel. By the turn of the century, Zinfandel was regarded as California's own claret and occupied some of the choicest North Coast vineyard. During PROHIBITION, it was the choice of many a HOME WINEMAKER but since then its viticultural popularity has become its undoing.

In 20th-century California, Zinfandel occupied much the same place as SHIRAZ (Syrah) did in Australia and for many decades suffered the same lack of respect simply because it was the most common black grape variety, often planted in unsuitably hot sites and expected to yield more than was good for it. Zinfandel may not be quite such a potentially high quality grape variety as Syrah but it is certainly capable of producing fine wine if yields are restricted and the weather cool enough to allow a reasonably long growing season, as Ridge Vineyards and others have proved. And the fact that so many of California's oldest vines are Zinfandel means that the best wines labelled with the varietal, sometimes FIELD BLENDS, are exceptionally complex (see VINE AGE).

Zinfandel's viticultural disadvantages are uneven ripening and thin-skinned berries in compact clusters. Bunches often ripen unevenly with harsh, green berries on the same cluster as those that have reached full maturity, and that once grapes reach full ripeness, in direct contrast to its great California rival Cabernet Sauvignon for example, they will soon turn to raisins if not picked quite rapidly. Zinfandel performs best in warm but not hot conditions and prefers well-drained HILLSIDES since it is subject to BUNCH ROT if caught by autumn rains.

Although Zinfandel has been required over the years to transform itself into virtually every style and colour of wine that exists, it is best suited to dry, sturdy, vigorous reds that mature rather earlier than a comparable Cabernet Sauvignon. Dry Creek Valley in SONOMA has demonstrated a particular aptitude for this underestimated variety. See CALIFORNIA for more details of Zinfandel the wine, both red and white.

In the late 1980s, thanks to the enormous popularity of WHITE ZINFANDEL, Zinfandel plantings, which had been declining, increased by up to 3,000 acres/1,215 ha a year, mostly in the Central Valley, so that they totalled 34,000 acres/13,760 ha in 1992, just ahead of California's total acreage of Cabernet Sauvignon at the time. The resurgence of Zinfandel continued in the late 1990s as red Zinfandel began to enjoy mildly cult-like status (with many examples commanding prices over $30), driving total plantings to 50,000 acres/20,000 ha in 2003, only slightly less than Merlot and two-thirds as much as California's most important black variety Cabernet Sauvignon.

Zinfandel is also grown to a much more limited extent in warmer sites in other western states in the US, and Mexico. Because of its prominence in California, where it is still definitively the second most planted red wine grape, Zinfandel is grown in many of the world's wine regions, albeit to a very limited extent—quite apart from Puglia where it is known as Primitivo and in MONTENEGRO on the other side of the Adriatic where it is known as Kratošija. There is some 'Zinfandel' in the Languedoc, South Africa, and Australia where there were more than 100 ha/247 acres in 2012 and Cape Mentelle in Western Australia has been particularly successful with it.

Darlington, D., *Zin: The History and Mystery of Zinfandel* (Cambridge, Mass., 2001).

zonal viticulture, form of PRECISION VITICULTURE in which vineyards are divided into zones of characteristic performance in terms of YIELD and/or grape composition. These are then managed as separate units with respect to SELECTIVE HARVESTING and/or particular inputs. Typically, zones are identified either on the basis of visual inspection of yield maps, imagery acquired by REMOTE SENSING, or PROXIMAL SENSING and/or maps of other vineyard attributes, simple classification of such data, or through the use of statistically based clustering algorithms.

This approach has been adopted in several locations in Australia, Chile, Spain, and the US. R.G.V.B.

Zweigelt, or **Blauer Zweigelt** (formerly Rotburger), is Austria's most popular dark-berried grape variety planted on 6,539 ha/16,151 acres in 2013, even though this cross was bred only relatively recently, by a Dr Zweigelt at the KLOSTERNEUBURG research station in 1922. It is a BLAUFRÄNKISCH × ST-LAURENT cross that at its best combines some of the bite of the first with the elegance of the second, although it is sometimes encouraged to produce too much dilute wine. It is popular with growers because it ripens earlier than Blaufränkisch but buds rather later than St-Laurent, thereby tending to yield generously. It is widely grown throughout all Austrian wine regions and can increasingly make a serious, age-worthy, exuberantly fruity wine, even though most examples are best drunk young. So successful has it been in Austria that the variety is also popular over the border in the Czech Republic and Slovakia as well as in western Hungary. It has also been planted in British Columbia and, surprisingly widely, on Hokkaido in JAPAN. The export fortunes of the variety may, oddly enough, be hampered by its originator's uncompromisingly Germanic surname. If only he had been called Dr Pinot Noir.

zymase, group of ENZYMES which encourage the conversion of GLUCOSE and FRUCTOSE into ETHYL ALCOHOL during fermentation.

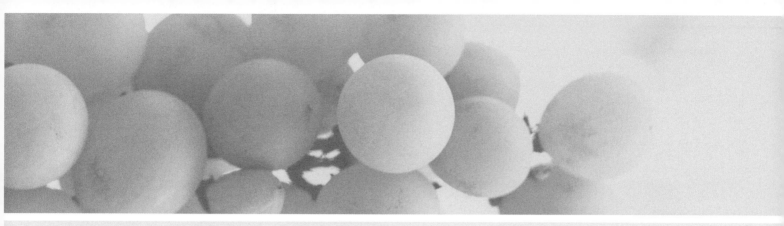

Appendix 1

CONTROLLED APPELLATIONS AND THEIR PERMITTED GRAPE VARIETIES

It is still impossible to tell from the labels of most geographically named wines which grape varieties were used to make them. The following is a unique guide to the varieties officially allowed into the world's CONTROLLED APPELLATIONS (therefore by no means all known wine names), listed by local name alphabetically by country, grouped where appropriate into alphabetically listed regions within that country. Italics denote minor grapes and the varieties are listed alphabetically, not in order of importance. R, W, P, and S denote red, white, pink, and sparkling wines respectively.

VARIETAL appellations and appellations that permit a very wide range of varieties are not included in this list because they are so numerous and because the region of origin and the grape variety are, in most cases, clearly stated on the label.

AUSTRIA

Eisenberg (R) Blaufränkisch
Kamptal (W) Grüner Veltliner, Riesling
Kremstal (W) Grüner Veltliner, Riesling
Leithaberg (W) Chardonnay, Grüner Veltliner, Neuburger, Pinot Blanc (R) Blaufränkisch, *Pinot Noir, St Laurent, Zweigelt*
Mittelburgenland (R) Blaufränkisch
Neusiedlersee (R) Zweigelt, *other local red varieties*
Traisental (W) Grüner Veltliner, Riesling
Weinviertel (W) Grüner Veltliner
Wiener Gemischter Satz (W) at least three quality white varieties that have grown together in one vineyard

CROATIA

Dingač (R) Plavac Mali

CYPRUS

Commandaria (R, W) Mavro, Xynisteri

FRANCE

For more detail on subappellations such as Grés de Montpellier or St-Christol (within the Languedoc AOC), see www.inao.gouv.fr or www.vitis.org.

Alsace and North East
Crémant d'Alsace (S) Auxerrois, Chardonnay, Pinot Blanc, Pinot Gris, Pinot Noir, Riesling
Vin d'Alsace Edelzwicker (W) Auxerrois, Chasselas, Gewürztraminer, Muscat Blanc à Petits Grains, Muscat Ottonel, Pinot Blanc, Pinot Gris, Pinot Noir, Riesling, Savagnin Rose, Sylvaner
Other Alsace wines are varietally labelled.
Côtes de Toul (R) Pinot Noir (P) Gamay, Pinot Noir, *Aubin, Auxerrois, Pinot Meunier* (W) Aubin, Auxerrois
Moselle (R) Pinot Noir (P) Pinot Noir, *Gamay* (W) Auxerrois, Müller-Thurgau, Pinot Gris, *Gewürztraminer, Pinot Blanc, Riesling*

Bordeaux
Blaye (R) Cabernet Franc, Cabernet Sauvignon, Merlot, *Carmenère, Côt, Petit Verdot*
Bordeaux, Bordeaux Clairet, Bordeaux Rosé, (R, P) Cabernet Franc, Cabernet Sauvignon, Carmenère, Malbec, Petit Verdot
Bordeaux Supérieur (R) Cabernet Franc, Cabernet Sauvignon, Carmenère, Côt, Petit Verdot (W) Muscadelle, Sauvignon Blanc, Sauvignon Gris, Sémillon, *Colombard, Merlot Blanc, Ugni Blanc*
Bordeaux Sec (W) Muscadelle, Sauvignon Blanc, Sauvignon Gris, Sémillon, *Colombard, Merlot Blanc, Ugni Blanc*

Bordeaux Haut-Benauge (W) Muscadelle, Sauvignon Blanc, Sauvignon Gris, Sémillon

Bourg, Côtes de Bourg, Bourgeais (R) Cabernet Franc, Cabernet Sauvignon, Côt, Merlot (W) Colombard, Muscadelle, Sauvignon Blanc, Sauvignon Gris, Sémillon

Côtes de Blaye (W) Colombard, Ugni Blanc, *Muscadelle, Sauvignon Blanc, Sauvignon Gris, Sémillon*

Blaye Côtes de Bordeaux, Francs Côtes de Bordeaux (R) Cabernet Franc, Cabernet Sauvignon, Malbec, Merlot, *Carmenère, Petit Verdot* (W) Muscadelle, Sauvignon Blanc, Sauvignon Gris, Sémillon, *Colombard, Ugni Blanc*

Côtes de Bordeaux, Cadillac Côtes de Bordeaux, Castillon Côtes de Bordeaux (R) Cabernet Franc, Cabernet Sauvignon, Malbec, Merlot, *Carmenère, Petit Verdot*

Crémant de Bordeaux (WS) Cabernet Franc, Cabernet Sauvignon, Carmenère, Malbec, Merlot, Muscadelle, Petit Verdot, Sauvignon Blanc, Sauvignon Gris, Sémillon, *Colombard, Merlot Blanc, Ugni Blanc* (PS) Cabernet Franc, Cabernet Sauvignon, Carmenère, Malbec, Merlot, Petit Verdot

Entre-Deux-Mers, Entre-Deux-Mers Haut-Benauge (W) Muscadelle, Sauvignon Blanc, Sauvignon Gris, Sémillon, *Colombard, Mauzac, Merlot Blanc, Ugni Blanc*

Fronsac, Canon Fronsac (R) Cabernet Franc, Cabernet Sauvignon, Merlot, *Carmenère, Malbec, Petit Verdot*

Graves, Graves Supérieures (R) Cabernet Franc, Cabernet Sauvignon, Carmenère, Malbec, Merlot, Petit Verdot (W) Muscadelle, Sauvignon Blanc, Sauvignon Gris, Sémillon

Graves de Vayres (R) Cabernet Franc, Cabernet Sauvignon, Carmenère, Malbec, Merlot, Petit Verdot (W) Muscadelle, Sauvignon Blanc, Sauvignon Gris, Sémillon, *Merlot Blanc*

Haut-Médoc, Listrac-Médoc, Margaux, Médoc, Moulis, Pauillac, St-Estèphe, St-Julien (R) Cabernet Franc, Cabernet Sauvignon, Carmenère, Malbec, Merlot, Petit Verdot

Lalande-de-Pomerol, Lussac-St-Émilion, Montagne-St-Émilion, Puisseguin-St-Émilion, St-Georges-St-Émilion (R) Cabernet Franc, Cabernet Sauvignon, Malbec, Merlot, *Carmenère, Petit Verdot*

St-Émilion (R) Cabernet Franc, Cabernet Sauvignon, Carmenère, Malbec, Merlot, *Petit Verdot*

Ste-Foy-Bordeaux (R) Cabernet Franc, Cabernet Sauvignon, Malbec, Merlot, *Carmenère, Petit Verdot* (W) Muscadelle, Sauvignon Blanc, Sauvignon Gris, Sémillon, *Colombard, Ugni Blanc*

Sauternes, Barsac, Ste-Croix-du-Mont, Loupiac, Cadillac, Cérons, Premières Côtes de Bordeaux, Pessac-Léognan, Côtes de Bordeaux St-Macaire (W) Muscadelle, Sauvignon Blanc, Sauvignon Gris, Sémillon

Pomerol (R) Cabernet Franc, Cabernet Sauvignon, Malbec, Merlot, Petit Verdot

Burgundy
Regional appellations

Bourgogne Passetoutgrains (R, P) Gamay, Pinot Noir, *Chardonnay, Pinot Blanc, Pinot Gris*

Bourgogne Mousseux (S) César (Yonne only), Gamay, Pinot Noir, *Aligoté, Chardonnay, Gamay Teinturier de Bouze, Gamay Teinturier de Chaudenay, Melon, Pinot Blanc, Pinot Gris*

Bourgogne, Bourgogne La Chapelle Notre-Dame, Bourgogne La Chapitre, Bourgogne Chitry, Bourgogne Côtes d'Auxerre, Bourgogne Côte Chalonnaise, Bourgogne Côte St-Jacques, Bourgogne Coulanges-la-Vineuse, Bourgogne Hautes Côtes de Beaune, Bourgogne Hautes Côtes de Nuits, Bourgogne Montrecul or Montre-Cul or En Montre-Cul (R) Pinot Noir, *Chardonnay César, Pinot Blanc,*

Pinot Gris, (P) Pinot Noir, Pinot Gris, *Chardonnay, Pinot Blanc, César* (Yonne only) (W) Chardonnay, Pinot Blanc, *Pinot Gris*

Bourgogne Clairet (P) Pinot Gris, Pinot Noir, *Chardonnay, Pinot Blanc, César* (Yonne only)

Bourgogne Côtes du Couchois (R) Pinot Noir, *Chardonnay, Pinot Blanc, Pinot Gris*

Bourgogne Epineuil (R) Pinot Noir, *Chardonnay, Pinot Blanc, Pinot Gris* (P) Pinot Gris, Pinot Noir, *Chardonnay, Pinot Blanc*

Bourgogne Tonnerre (W) Chardonnay, Pinot Blanc, *Pinot Gris*

Bourgogne Vézelay (W) Chardonnay

Bourgogne Aligoté, Bourgogne Bouzeron (W) Aligoté

Crémant de Bourgogne (S) Aligoté, Chardonnay, Gamay, Melon, Pinot Blanc, Pinot Gris, Pinot Noir, Sacy

Coteaux Bourguignons (R) Gamay, Pinot Noir, *César* (Yonne only), *Aligoté, Chardonnay, Gamay de Bouze, Melon, Pinot Blanc, Pinot Gris* (P) Gamay, Pinot Gris, Pinot Noir, César (Yonne only), *Aligoté, Chardonnay, Melon, Pinot Blanc* (W) Aligoté, Chardonnay, Melon, Pinot Blanc, Pinot Gris

Beaujolais

Beaujolais, Beaujolais Supérieur, Beaujolais-Villages (R, P) Gamay, *Aligoté, Chardonnay, Gamay de Bouze, Gamay de Chaudenay, Pinot Gris, Pinot Noir, Melon,* (W) Chardonnay

Brouilly, Chénas, Chiroubles, Côte de Brouilly Fleurie, Juliénas, Morgon, Moulin-à-Vent, Régnié, St-Amour (R) Gamay, *Aligoté, Chardonnay, Melon*

Chablis region

Bourgogne-Vézelay (W) Chardonnay, Pinot Blanc

Irancy (R) Pinot Noir, *César, Pinot Gris*

Petit Chablis, Chablis, Chablis Premier Cru, Chablis Grand Cru (W) Chardonnay

St-Bris (W) Sauvignon Blanc, Sauvignon Gris

Côte Chalonnaise

Note: The communes indicated with an asterisk contain premier cru vineyards.

Givry (R) Pinot Noir, *Chardonnay, Pinot Gris* (W) Chardonnay, *Pinot Blanc, Pinot Gris*

Mercurey*, Rully* (R) Pinot Noir, *Chardonnay, Pinot Gris* (W) Chardonnay, *Pinot Gris*

Montagny* (W) Chardonnay

Côte d'Or

Note: The communes indicated with an asterisk contain premier cru vineyards.

Côte de Beaune, Beaune*, Nuits-St-Georges* (R) Pinot Noir, *Chardonnay, Pinot Blanc, Pinot Gris* (W) Chardonnay, Pinot Blanc, *Pinot Gris* (the last allowed in Beaune and Côte de Beaune only)

Aloxe-Corton*, (R) Pinot Noir, *Chardonnay, Pinot Blanc, Pinot Gris* (W) Chardonnay, *Pinot Blanc*

Côte de Beaune-Villages (R) Pinot Noir, *Chardonnay, Pinot Blanc, Pinot Gris*

Auxey-Duresses*, Blagny, Chassagne-Montrachet*, Chorey-lès-Beaune, Côte de-Nuits Villages, Fixin*, Meursault*, Monthelie, Morey-St-Denis*, Pernand-Vergelesses*, Puligny-Montrachet*, St-Aubin*, St-Romain, Santenay*, Savigny-lès-Beaune* (R) Pinot Noir, *Chardonnay, Pinot Blanc, Pinot Gris* (W) Chardonnay, Pinot Blanc

Ladoix (R) Pinot Noir, *Chardonnay, Pinot Blanc, Pinot Gris* (W) Chardonnay, Pinot Blanc, *Pinot Gris*

Chambolle-Musigny*, Gevrey-Chambertin*, Marsannay Rosé, Pommard*, Volnay*, Volnay Santenots*, Vosne-Romanée* (R) Pinot Noir, *Chardonnay, Pinot Blanc, Pinot Gris*

Maranges (R) Pinot Noir, *Chardonnay, Pinot Blanc, Pinot Gris* (W) Chardonnay

Marsannay (R) Pinot Noir, *Chardonnay, Pinot Blanc, Pinot Gris* (P) Pinot Gris, Pinot Noir, *Chardonnay, Pinot Blanc* (W) Chardonnay, Pinot Blanc, *Pinot Gris*

Vougeot* (R) Pinot Noir (W) Chardonnay, Pinot Blanc

Côte d'Or—Grands Crus

Bonnes-Mares, Chambertin, Chambertin-Clos de Bèze, Chapelle-Chambertin, Charmes-Chambertin, Griotte-Chambertin, Latricières-Chambertin, Mazis-Chambertin, Mazoyères-Chambertin, Ruchottes-Chambertin, Clos des Lambrays, Clos de la Roche, Clos St-Denis, Clos de Tart, Clos de Vougeot, Échezeaux, La Grande Rue, Grands Échezeaux, Richebourg, Romanée-Conti, Romanée-St-Vivant, La Romanée, La Tâche (R) Pinot Noir, *Chardonnay, Pinot Blanc, Pinot Gris,*

Charlemagne (W) Chardonnay, *Pinot Blanc*

Corton (R) Pinot Noir, *Chardonnay, Pinot Blanc, Pinot Gris* (W) Chardonnay, *Pinot Blanc*

Corton-Charlemagne (W) Chardonnay, *Pinot Blanc*

Montrachet, Bâtard-Montrachet, Bienvenues-Bâtard-Montrachet, Chevalier-Montrachet, Criots-Bâtard-Montrachet (W) Chardonnay

Musigny (R) Pinot Noir, *Chardonnay, Pinot Blanc, Pinot Gris* (W) Chardonnay

Mâconnais

Mâcon-Villages (W) Chardonnay

Mâcon (R, P) Gamay, Pinot Noir (W) Chardonnay

Mâcon followed by a commune name (R, P) Gamay (W) Chardonnay

Pouilly-Fuissé, Pouilly-Vinzelles, Pouilly-Loché, St-Véran (W) Chardonnay

Viré-Clessé (W) Chardonnay

Champagne

Champagne, (S) Chardonnay, Pinot Meunier, Pinot Noir, *Arbane, Petit Meslier, Pinot Blanc, Pinot Gris*

Coteaux Champenois (R, P, W) Chardonnay, Pinot Meunier, Pinot Noir, *Arbane, Petit Meslier* (W)

Rosé de Riceys (P) Pinot Noir

Corsica. See Provence and Corsica.

Jura

Arbois, Arbois Mousseux, Arbois Pupillin (R, P) Pinot Noir, Poulsard Noir, Trousseau, *Chardonnay, Savagnin* (W) Chardonnay, Savagnin Blanc, *Pinot Noir, Poulsard, Trousseau* (S) Chardonnay, Pinot Noir, Poulsard Noir, Savagnin Blanc, Trousseau, *Pinot Blanc*

Note: Pinot Noir and Pinot Blanc are not permitted for the production of *Vin de Paille*

Arbois Vin Jaune (W) Savagnin Blanc

Château-Chalon Vin Jaune (W) Savagnin Blanc

Côtes du Jura (R, P) Pinot Noir, Poulsard, Trousseau, *Chardonnay, Savagnin Blanc* (W) Chardonnay, Savagnin Blanc, *Pinot Noir, Poulsard, Trousseau*

Côtes du Jura Vin Jaune (W) Savagnin Blanc

Crémant du Jura (S) Chardonnay, Pinot Gris, Pinot Noir, Poulsard, Savagnin, Trousseau

L'Étoile (W) Chardonnay, Savagnin Blanc, *Poulsard*

L'Étoile Vin Jaune (W) Savagnin Blanc

Languedoc and Roussillon

Cabardès (R, P) Cabernet Franc, Cabernet Sauvignon, Grenache, Merlot, Syrah, *Cinsaut, Côt, Fer*

Collioure (R) Carignan, Grenache, Mourvèdre, Syrah, *Cinsaut, Counoise* (P) Carignan, Grenache, Grenache Gris, Mourvèdre, Syrah, *Cinsaut, Counoise* (W) Grenache Blanc, Grenache Gris, Maccabeu, Marsanne, Roussanne, Tourbat, Vermentino, *Carignan Blanc, Muscat Blanc à Petits Grains, Muscat d'Alexandrie*

Corbières (R) Carignan, Grenache, Lladoner Pelut, Mourvèdre, Syrah, *Cinsaut, Grenache Gris, Piquepoul Noir, Terret Noir* (P) Carignan, Cinsaut, Grenache, Lladoner Pelut, Mourvèdre, Piquepoul Noir, Syrah, *Bourboulenc, Clairette, Grenache Blanc, Grenache Gris, Maccabeu, Marsanne, Muscat Blanc à Petits Grains, Piquepoul, Roussanne, Terret Blanc, Terret Noir, Vermentino* (W) Bourboulenc, Grenache Blanc, Maccabeu, Marsanne, Roussanne, Vermentino, *Clairette, Muscat Blanc à Petits Grains, Piquepoul, Terret Blanc*

Corbières-Boutenac (R) Carignan, Grenache, Mourvèdre, *Syrah*

Costières de Nîmes (R, P) Grenache, Mourvèdre, Syrah, *Carignan, Cinsaut, Marselan* (W) Grenache Blanc, Marsanne, Roussanne, *Bourboulenc, Clairette, Maccabeu, Vermentino, Viognier*

Côtes de Millau (R) Gamay, Syrah, *Cabernet Sauvignon, Duras, Fer* (P) Gamay, *Cabernet Sauvignon, Duras, Fer, Syrah* (W) Chenin Blanc, *Mauzac*

Côtes du Roussillon (R) Carignan, Grenache, Mourvèdre, Syrah, *Cinsaut, Lladoner Pelut* (P) Carignan, Grenache, Mourvèdre, Syrah, *Cinsaut, Grenache Gris, Lladoner Pelut, Maccabeu* (W) Grenache Blanc, Maccabeu, Tourbat, *Grenache Gris, Marsanne, Roussanne, Vermentino*

Côtes du Roussillon-Villages (R) Carignan, Grenache, Mourvèdre, Syrah, *Lladoner Pelut*

Faugères (R, P) Grenache, Lladoner Pelut, Mourvèdre, Syrah, *Carignan, Cinsaut* (W) Grenache Blanc, Marsanne, Roussanne, Vermentino, *Clairette, Viognier*

Fitou (R) Carignan, Grenache, *Mourvèdre, Syrah*

Grand Roussillon (R, P, W) Grenache, Grenache Blanc, Grenache Gris, Macabeu, Tourbat, *Muscat Blanc à Petits Grains, Muscat d'Alexandrie*

Languedoc (R) Grenache, Lladoner Pelut, Mourvèdre, Syrah, *Carignan, Cinsaut, Counoise, Grenache Gris, Morastel, Piquepoul Noir, Rivairenc, Terret Noir* (P) Grenache, Lladoner Pelut, Mourvèdre, Syrah, *Bourboulenc, Carignan Blanc, Carignan, Cinsaut, Clairette, Counoise, Grenache Blanc, Grenache Gris, Maccabeu, Marsanne, Morrastel, Piquepoul Blanc, Piquepoul Noir, Rivairenc, Roussanne, Terret Blanc, Terret Noir, Tourbat, Vermentino, Viognier* (W) Bourboulenc, Grenache Blanc, Marsanne, Piquepoul Blanc, Roussanne, Tourbat, Vermentino, *Carignan Blanc, Macabeu, Terret Blanc, Viognier*

Malepère (R) Merlot, *Cabernet Franc, Côt* (P) Cabernet Franc, *Cabernet Sauvignon, Cinsaut, Côt, Grenache, Merlot*

Minervois (R) Grenache, Lladoner Pelut, Mourvèdre, Syrah, *Carignan, Cinsaut, Piquepoul Noir, Rivairenc, Terret Noir* (R) Grenache, Lladoner Pelut, Mourvèdre, Syrah, *Bourboulenc, Carignan, Cinsaut, Clairette, Grenache Blanc, Maccabeu, Marsanne, Piquepoul Blanc, Piquepoul Noir, Rivairenc, Roussanne, Terret Blanc, Terret Noir, Vermentino* (W) Bourboulenc, Grenache Blanc, Maccabeu, Marsanne, Roussanne, Vermentino, *Clairette, Muscat Blanc à Petits Grains, Piquepoul Blanc, Terret Blanc*

Minervois-La Livinière (R) Grenache, *Lladoner Pelut,* Mourvèdre, Syrah *Carignan, Cinsaut, Piquepoul Noir, Rivairenc, Terret Noir*

St-Chinian (R, P) Grenache, Lladoner Pelut, Mourvèdre, Syrah, *Carignan, Cinsaut* (W) Grenache Blanc, Marsanne, Roussanne, Vermentino, *Carignan Blanc, Clairette, Viognier*

Loire and Central France

Anjou, (R) Cabernet Franc, Cabernet Sauvignon, *Grolleau, Pineau d'Aunis* (W) Chenin Blanc, *Chardonnay, Sauvignon Blanc*

Anjou Coteaux de la Loire (W) Chenin Blanc

Anjou Mousseux (W, S) Chenin Blanc, *Cabernet Franc, Cabernet Sauvignon, Chardonnay, Gamay, Grolleau, Grolleau Gris, Pineau d'Aunis* (P, S) Cabernet Franc, Cabernet Sauvignon, Gamay, Grolleau, Grolleau Gris, Pineau d'Aunis

Anjou-Villages, Anjou-Villages-Brissac (R) Cabernet Franc, Cabernet Sauvignon

Bourgueil, St-Nicolas-de-Bourgueil (R) Cabernet Franc, *Cabernet Sauvignon*

Bonnezeaux (W) Chenin Blanc

Cabernet d'Anjou, Cabernet de Saumur (P) Cabernet Franc, Cabernet Sauvignon,

Châteaumeillant (R, W, P) Gamay, *Pinot Gris, Pinot Noir*

Cheverny (R, P) Pinot Noir, *Cabernet Franc, Cabernet Sauvignon, Côt, Gamay* (W) Sauvignon Blanc, Sauvignon Gris, *Chardonnay, Chenin Blanc, Orbois*

Chinon (W) Chenin Blanc (R, P) Cabernet Franc, *Cabernet Sauvignon*

Coteaux d'Ancenis (W) Pinot Gris (R, P) Gamay

Coteaux de l'Aubance (W) Chenin Blanc

Coteaux du Giennois (R, P) Gamay, Pinot Noir (W) Sauvignon Blanc

Coteaux du Layon, Coteaux du Layon Chaume (W) Chenin Blanc

Coteaux du Loir (W) Chenin Blanc (Pineau de la Loire) (R) Pineau d'Aunis, *Cabernet Franc, Côt, Gamay* (P) Pineau d'Aunis, *Côt, Gamay, Groslleau*

Coteaux de Saumur (W) Chenin Blanc

Coteaux du Vendômois (W) Chenin Blanc, *Chardonnay* (R) Pineau d'Aunis, *Cabernet Franc, Gamay, Pinot Noir* (P) Pineau d'Aunis

Côtes d'Auvergne (R, P) Gamay, *Pinot Noir* (W) Chardonnay

Cour-Cheverny (W) Romorantin

Crémant de Loire (WS, PS) Cabernet Franc, Cabernet Sauvignon, Chardonnay, Chenin Blanc, Grolleau Gris, Grolleau Noir, Menu Pineau, Pineau d'Aunis, Orbois, Pinot Noir

Fiefs Vendéens (R) Cabernet Franc, Négrette, Pinot Noir, *Cabernet Sauvignon, Gamay* (R) Gamay, Pinot Noir, *Cabernet Franc, Cabernet Sauvignon, Grolleau Gris, Négrette* (W) Chenin Blanc, *Chardonnay, Sauvignon Blanc*

Gros Plant du Pays Nantais (W) Folle Blanche, *Colombard, Montils*

Haut-Poitou (W) Sauvignon Blanc, Sauvignon Gris (R) Cabernet Franc, *Gamay, Gamay de Bouze, Gamay de Chaudenay, Merlot, Pinot Noir* (P) Cabernet Franc, Gamay, Pinot Noir

Jasnières (W) Chenin Blanc

Menetou-Salon (W) Sauvignon Blanc (R, P) Pinot Noir

Montlouis-sur-Loire (W) Chenin Blanc

Muscadet, Musacadet-Côtes de Grandlieu, Muscadet-Coteaux de la Loire, Muscadet-Sèvre et Maine (W) Melon

Orléans (R) Pinot Meunier, *Pinot Noir* (W) Chardonnay, *Pinot Gris* (P) Pinot Meunier, *Pinot Gris, Pinot Noir*

Orléans-Cléry (R) Cabernet Franc

Pouilly-Fumé, Blanc Fumé de Pouilly (W) Sauvignon Blanc

Pouilly-sur-Loire (W) Chasselas

Quarts de Chaume (W) Chenin Blanc

Quincy (W) Sauvignon Blanc, *Sauvignon Gris*

Reuilly (W) Sauvignon Blanc (R) Pinot Noir (P) Pinot Gris, Pinot Noir

Rosé d'Anjou (P) Cabernet Franc, Cabernet Sauvignon, Côt, Gamay, Grolleau, Grolleau Gris, Pineau d'Aunis

Rosé de Loire (P) Cabernet Franc, Cabernet Sauvignon, Gamay, Grolleau, Grolleau Gris, Pineau d'Aunis, Pinot Noir

St-Pourçain (R) Gamay, Pinot Noir (P) Gamay (W) Chardonnay, *Sacy, Sauvignon Blanc*

Sancerre (W) Sauvignon Blanc (R, P) Pinot Noir

Saumur (R) Cabernet Franc, *Cabernet Sauvignon, Pineau d'Aunis* (W) Chenin Blanc (S) Chenin Blanc, Chardonnay, Sauvignon Blanc, Cabernet Franc, Cabernet Sauvignon, Gamay, Grolleau, Grolleau Gris, Pineau d'Aunis, Pinot Noir

Saumur-Champigny (R) Cabernet Franc, *Cabernet Sauvignon, Pineau d'Aunis*

Savennières, Savennières Coulée de Serrant, Savennières Roche aux Moines (W) Chenin Blanc

Touraine (R) Cabernet Franc, Côt, *Cabernet Sauvignon, Gamay, Pinot Noir* (P) Cabernet Franc, Cabernet Sauvignon, Côt, Gamay, Grolleau, Grolleau Gris, Meunier, Pineau d'Aunis, Pinot Gris, Pinot Noir (W) Sauvignon Blanc, *Sauvignon Gris* (S) Chardonnay, Chenin Blanc, Cabernet Franc. Grolleau, Grolleau Gris, Orbois, Pineau d'Aunis, Pinot Noir

Touraine Amboise (R, P) Cabernet Franc, Cabernet Sauvignon, Côt, Gamay (W) Chenin Blanc

Touraine Azay-le-Rideau (P) Grolleau, *Cabernet Franc, Cabernet Sauvignon, Côt, Gamay* (W) Chenin Blanc

Touraine Chenonceaux (R) Cabernet Franc, Côt, *Gamay* (W) Sauvignon Blanc

Touraine Mesland (R) Gamay, *Cabernet Franc, Côt* (P) Gamay, *Cabernet Franc, Côt* (W) Chenin Blanc, Chardonnay, Sauvignon Blanc

Touraine Noble Joué (P) Pinot Meunier, *Pinot Gris, Pinot Noir*

Touraine Oisly (W) Sauvignon Blanc

Valençay (R) Côt, Gamay, Pinot Noir, *Cabernet Franc* (P) Côt, Gamay, Pinot Noir, *Cabernet Franc, Pineau d'Aunis* (W) Sauvignon Blanc, *Chardonnay, Orbois, Sauvignon Gris*

Vouvray (W) Chenin Blanc, *Orbois*

Loire fringes

Côte Roannaise (R, P) Gamay

Côtes du Forez (R, P) Gamay

Provence and Corsica

Ajaccio (P, R) Barbarossa, Nielluccio, Sciacarello, Vermentino Blanc, *Aleatico, Carcajolo Blanc, Carignan, Cinsaut, Grenache, Morrastel* (W) Vermentino Blanc, *Biancu Gentile, Codivarta, Genovese, Ugni Blanc*

Bandol (R) Cinsaut, Grenache, Mourvèdre, *Carignan, Syrah* (P) Cinsaut, Grenache, Mourvèdre, *Bourboulenc, Carignan, Clairette, Syrah, Ugni Blanc* (W) Bourboulenc, Clairette, Ugni Blanc, *Marsanne, Sauvignon Blanc, Sémillon, Vermentino*

Bellet, Vin de Bellet (R) Braquet, Fuella Nera, *Cinsaut, Grenache* (P) Braquet, Cinsaut, Fuella Nera, *Grenache, Rolle, Roussanne, Spagnol (Mayorquin), Clairette, Bourboulenc, Pignerol* (W) Rolle, Roussanne, Spagnol (Mayorquin), *Clairette, Bourboulenc, Chardonnay, Pignerol, Muscat Blanc à Petit Grains*

Cassis (R) Cinsaut, Grenache, Mourvèdre, *Barbaroux, Carignan, Terret Noir* (P) Cinsaut, Grenache, Mourvèdre, *Barbaroux, Doucillon, Carignan, Clairette, Marsanne, Pascal Blanc, Sauvignon Blanc, Terret Noir, Ugni Blanc* (W) Clairette, Marsanne, *Doucillon, Pascal Blanc, Sauvignon Blanc, Ugni Blanc*

Coteaux d'Aix-en-Provence (R, P) Cinsaut, Counoise, Grenache, Mourvèdre, Syrah, *Cabernet Sauvignon, Carignan* (W) Clairette, Grenache Blanc, Sauvignon Blanc, Ugni Blanc, Vermentino *Bourboulenc, Sémillon*

Coteaux Varois en Provence (R, P) Cinsaut, Grenache, Mourvèdre Syrah, *Cabernet Sauvignon, Carignan, Tibouren* (W) Clairette, Grenache Blanc, Sémillon, Ugni Blanc, Vermentino

Côtes de Provence (R, P) Cinsaut, Grenache, Mourvèdre, Syrah, Tibouren, *Barbaroux, Cabernet Sauvignon, Carignan, Clairette, Sémillon, Ugni Blanc, Vermentino* (W) Clairette, Sémillon, Ugni Blanc, Vermentino

Côtes de Provence Fréjus (R) Grenache, Mourvèdre, Syrah (P) Grenache, Mourvèdre, Syrah, Tibouren, *Cinsaut*

Côtes de Provence La Londe (R) Grenache, Mourvèdre, Syrah, *Cabernet Sauvignon, Carignan* (P) Cinsaut, Grenache, *Carignan, Clairette, Mourvèdre, Sémillon, Syrah, Tibouren, Ugni Blanc, Vermentino.*

Côtes de Provence Ste-Victoire (R, P) Cinsaut, Grenache, Syrah, *Cabernet Sauvignon, Carignan, Clairette, Mourvèdre, Sémillon, Ugni Blanc, Vermentino*

Les Baux-de-Provence (R) Grenache, Mourvèdre, Syrah, *Cabernet Sauvignon, Carignan, Cinsaut, Counoise* (P) Cinsaut, Grenache, Syrah, *Cabernet Sauvignon, Carignan, Counoise, Mourvèdre* (W) Clairette, Grenache Blanc, Vermentino, *Bourboulenc, Marsanne, Roussanne, Ugni Blanc*

Palette (R, P) Cinsaut, Grenache, Mourvèdre, *Brun Fourca, Cabernet Sauvignon, Carignan, Castets, Durif, Muscat Blanc à Petits Grains, Muscat de Hamburg, Petit Brun, Syrah, Téoulier, Terret Gris, Tibouren* (W) Bourboulenc, Clairette, Clairette Rose, *Araignan, Colombard, Furmint, Grenache Blanc, Muscat Blanc à Petits Grains, Panse Muscade, Pascal, Piquepoul Blanc, Terret Gris, Ugni Blanc, Ugni Rosé*

Patrimonio (R, P) Nielluccio, *Grenache, Sciacarello, Vermentino* (W) Vermentino Blanc

Pierrevert (R, P) Grenache, Syrah, *Carignan, Cinsaut, Grenache Blanc, Marsanne, Mourvèdre, Piquepoul Blanc, Roussanne, Téoulier, Ugni Blanc, Vermentino, Viognier* (W) Clairette, Grenache Blanc, Marsanne, Piquepoul, Roussanne, Ugni Blanc, Vermentino, Viognier

Vin de Corse (R, P) Grenache, Nielluccio, Sciacarello, *Cinsaut, Mourvèdre, Barbarossa, Syrah, Carignan, Vermentino (Malvoisie de Corse)* (W) Vermentino (Malvoisie de Corse), *Biancu Gentile, Codivarta, Genovèse, Ugni Blanc (Rossola)*

Rhône

Beaumes de Venise (R) Grenache, Syrah, *Bourboulenc, Brun Argenté, Carignan, Cinsaut, Clairette, Clairette Rose, Counoise, Grenache Blanc, Grenache Gris, Marsanne, Mourvèdre, Muscardin, Piquepoul Blanc, Piquepoul Noir, Roussanne, Terret Noir, Ugni Blanc, Viognier*

Châteauneuf-du-Pape (R,W) Bourboulenc, Cinsaut, Clairette, Clairette Rose, Counoise, Grenache Blanc, Grenache Gris, Grenache Noir, Mourvèdre, Muscardin, Picardan, Piquepoul Blanc, Gris, and Noir, Roussanne, Syrah, Terret Noir, Vaccarèse

Châtillon-en-Diois (R, P) Gamay, *Pinot Noir, Syrah,* (W) Aligoté, Chardonnay

Condrieu, Château Grillet (W) Viognier

Cornas (R) Syrah

Coteaux de Die (W) Clairette

Côte Rôtie (R) Syrah, *Viognier*

Côtes du Rhône (R, P) Grenache Noir, Mourvèdre, Syrah, *Carignan, Cinsaut, Clairette Rose, Counoise, Grenache Gris, Marselan, Muscardin, Vaccarèse/Camarèse, Piquepoul Noir, Terret Noir* (both red and rosé may include a small percentage of the white grapes allowed in the appellation, as follows) (W) Bourboulenc, Clairette Blanc, Grenache Blanc, Marsanne, Roussanne, Viognier, *Piquepoul, Ugni Blanc*

Côtes du Rhône-Villages (R) Grenache Noir, Mourvèdre, Syrah, *Carignan, Cinsaut, Counoise, Muscardin, Vaccarèse/Camarèse, Piquepoul Noir, Terret Noir* (R) Grenache, Mourvèdre, Syrah, *all the red and white varieties plus Clairette Rose, Grenache Gris* (W) Bourboulenc, Clairette,

Grenache Blanc, Marsanne, Roussanne, Viognier, *Piquepoul, Ugni Blanc*

Côtes du Vivarais (R, P) Grenache Noir, Syrah, *Cinsaut, Marselan* (W) Clairette, Grenache Blanc, Marsanne, *Roussanne, Viognier*

Crémant de Die (S) Clairette, *Aligoté, Muscat Blanc à Petits Grains*

Duché d'Uzès (R, P) Grenache, Syrah, *Carignan, Cinsaut, Mourvèdre* (W) Grenache Blanc, Viognier, *Clairette, Marsanne, Roussanne, Ugni Blanc, Vermentino*

Gigondas (R, P) Grenache Noir, *Syrah, Mourvèdre* (with the exclusion of Carignan, all the other grapes that go into Côtes du Rhône are also allowed)

Grignan-les-Adhémar (R, P) Grenache, Syrah, *Bourboulenc, Carignan, Cinsaut, Clairette, Grenache Blanc, Marsanne, Marselan, Mourvèdre, Roussanne, Viognier* (W) Bourboulenc, Clairette, Grenache Blanc, Marsanne, Roussanne, Viognier

Hermitage, Crozes-Hermitage, St-Joseph (R) Syrah, *Marsanne, Roussanne* (W) Marsanne, Roussanne

Lirac (R, P) Cinsaut, Grenache Noir, Mourvèdre, Syrah, *Carignan, Clairette Rose, Counoise, Grenache Gris, Marsanne, Piquepoul Blanc, Piquepoul Noir, Roussanne, Ugni Blanc, Viognier* (W) Bourboulenc, Clairette, Grenache Blanc, Roussanne, *Marsanne, Piquepoul Blanc, Ugni Blanc, Viognier*

Luberon (R, P) Grenache, Mourvèdre, Syrah, *Bourboulenc, Carignan, Cinsaut, Clairette, Grenache Blanc, Marsanne, Marselan, Roussanne, Ugni Blanc, Vermentino, Viognier* (W) Bourboulenc, Clairette, Grenache Blanc, Marsanne, Roussanne, Vermentino, *Ugni Blanc, Viognier*

Rasteau (R) Grenache, Mourvèdre, Syrah, *Bourboulenc, Brun Argenté, Carignan, Cinsaut, Clairette, Clairette Rose, Counoise, Grenache Blanc, Grenache Gris, Marsanne, Muscardin, Piquepoul Blanc, Piquepoul Noir, Roussanne, Terret Noir, Ugni Blanc, Viognier*

St-Péray (W, S) Marsanne, Roussanne

Tavel (P) Bourboulenc, Cinsaut, Clairette, Clairette Rose, Grenache Blanc, Grenache Gris, Grenache Noir, Mourvèdre, Piquepoul, Piquepoul Gris, Piquepoul Noir, Syrah, *Calitor, Carignan Blanc, Carignan*

Vacqueyras (R) Grenache, Mourvèdre, Syrah, *Bourboulenc, Brun Argenté, Carignan, Cinsaut, Clairette Rose, Counoise, Grenache Blanc, Grenache Gris, Marsanne, Muscardin, Piquepoul, Roussanne, Terret Noir, Viognier* (P) Cinsaut, Grenache Noir, Mourvèdre, Syrah, (W) Bourboulenc, Clairette, Grenache Blanc, *Marsanne, Roussanne, Viognier*

Ventoux (R, P) Carignan, Cinsaut, Grenache, Mourvèdre, Syrah, *Bourboulenc, Clairette, Counoise, Grenache Blanc, Marsanne, Marselan, Piquepoul Noir, Roussanne, Vermentino, Viognier* (W) Bourboulenc, Clairette, Grenache Blanc, Roussanne, *Marsanne, Vermentino, Viognier*

Vinsobres (R) Grenache, Mourvèdre, Syrah, *Bourboulenc, Brun Argenté (Camarèse/Vaccarèse), Carignan, Cinsaut, Clairette Rose, Counoise, Grenache Blanc, Grenache Gris, Marsanne, Muscardin, Piquepoul Blanc, Piquepoul Noir, Roussanne, Terret Noir, Ugni Blanc, Viognier*

Rhône fringes

Coteaux du Lyonnais (R, P) Gamay, *Gamay de Bouze, Gamay de Chaudenay* (W) Aligoté, Chardonnay, *Pinot Blanc*

Savoie and Bugey

Bugey, Bugey followed by a commune name (R) Gamay, Mondeuse Noire, Pinot Noir (P) Gamay, Pinot Noir, *Mondeuse, Pinot Gris, Poulsard* (W) Chardonnay, *Aligoté, Altesse, Jacquère, Mondeuse Blanche, Pinot Gris*

Bugey Manicle (R) Pinot Noir (W) Chardonnay

Bugey Montagnieu (R) Mondeuse Noire (S) Altesse, Chardonnay, Mondeuse, *Gamay, Jacquère, Molette, Pinot Noir*

Bugey Mousseux, Bugey Pétillant (S) Chardonnay, Jacquère, Molette, *Aligoté, Altesse, Gamay, Mondeuse Blanche, Pinot Gris, Pinot Noir, Poulsard*

Bugey Cerdon (S) Gamay, Poulsard

Note: Varietal labelling is used for all the Bugey appellations where a wine is made exclusively from one variety.

Crémant de Savoie (S) Aligoté, Altesse, Chardonnay, Jacquère, Mondeuse. For the *département* Haute-Savoie: Chasselas, Molette

Roussette de Bugey, Roussette de Bugey followed by a commune name (W) Altesse

Roussette de Savoie, Roussette de Savoie followed by a cru name (W) Roussette

Seyssel (W) Altesse (S) Altesse, Chasselas, Molette

Seyssel Molette (W) Molette

Vin de Savoie (P, R) Gamay, Mondeuse, Pinot Noir, *Cabernet Franc, Cabernet Sauvignon, Etraire de l'Aduï, Joubertin, Persan, Servanin* (W) Aligoté, Altesse, Chardonnay, Jacquère, Mondeuse, Velteliner Rouge Précoce, *Chasselas, Gringet, Marsanne, Roussette d'Ayze, Verdesse*

Note: Marsanne, and Verdesse are permitted only in the *département* of Isère. Gringet, Roussette d'Ayze, Molette and Chasselas are permitted only in the *département* of Haute-Savoie.

Vin de Savoie followed by cru names: Abymes, Apremont, Cruet, Montmélian, St-Jeoire-Prieuré (W) Jacquère, *Aligoté, Altesse, Chardonnay, Marsanne, Mondeuse, Velteliner Rouge Précoce, Verdesse*; **Arbin** (R) Mondeuse; **Ayze** (W, S) Gringet, *Altesse, Roussette d'Ayze*; **Chautagne, Chignin, Jongieux** (R) Gamay, Mondeuse, Pinot Noir, *Cabernet Franc, Cabernet Sauvignon, Persan* (W) Jacquère, *Aligoté, Altesse, Chardonnay, Marsanne, Mondeuse, Velteliner Rouge Précoce, Verdesse*; **Chignin-Bergeron, Bergeron** (W) Roussanne; **Crépy, Marignan, Marin, Ripaille** (W) Chasselas, *Aligoté, Altesse, Chardonnay, Gringet, Mondeuse, Roussette d'Ayze, Velteliner Rouge Précoce*

Vin de Savoie Pétillant, Vin de Savoie Mousseux (W, P) Aligoté, Altesse, Chardonnay, Gamay, Jacquère, Mondeuse, Mondeuse Blanche, Pinot Noir, Velteliner Rouge Précoce. For the *département* of Haute-Savoie: Chasselas, Gringet, Molette, Roussette d'Ayze. For the *département* of l'Isère: Marsanne, Verdesse

South West France

Béarn (R, P) Cabernet Franc, Cabernet Sauvignon, Tannat, *Fer, Manseng, Courbu Noir* (W) Gros Manseng, Petit Manseng, Raffiat de Moncade, *Camaralet de Lasseube, Courbu, Lauzet, Petit Courbu, Sauvignon Blanc*

Bergerac, Bergerac Sec (W) Muscadelle, Sauvignon Blanc, Sauvignon Gris, Sémillon, *Chenin Blanc, Ondenc, Ugni Blanc*

Bergerac (R, P) Cabernet Franc, Cabernet Sauvignon, Côt, Merlot, *Fer Servadou, Mérille*

Blanquette de Limoux, (S) Mauzac, *Chardonnay, Chenin Blanc*

Blanquette Méthode Ancestrale Mousseux (S) Mauzac

Brulhois (R, P) Cabernet Franc, Merlot, Tannat, *Abouriou, Cabernet Sauvignon, Côt, Fer Servadou*

Buzet (R, P) Cabernet Franc, Cabernet Sauvignon, Côt, Merlot, *Abouriou, Petit Verdot* (W) Muscadelle, Sauvignon Blanc, Sauvignon Gris, Sémillon, *Colombard, Gros Manseng, Petit Manseng*

Cahors (R) Malbec, *Merlot, Tannat*

Coteaux du Quercy (R, P) Cabernet Franc, Côt, Merlot, Tannat, *Gamay*

Côtes de Bergerac (R) Cabernet Franc, Cabernet Sauvignon, Côt, Merlot (W) Muscadelle, Sauvignon Blanc, Sauvignon Gris, Sémillon, *Ugni Blanc, Chenin Blanc, Ondenc*

Côtes de Duras (W) Chenin Blanc, Mauzac, Muscadelle, Sauvignon Blanc, Sauvignon Gris, Sémillon, Ondenc, *Colombard, Ugni Blanc* (R, P) Cabernet Franc, Cabernet Sauvignon, Malbec, Merlot

Côtes du Marmandais (R, P) Cabernet Franc, Cabernet Sauvignon, Merlot, *Abouriou, Malbec (Côt), Fer, Gamay, Syrah* (W) Sauvignon Blanc, Sauvignon Gris, *Muscadelle, Sémillon*

Côtes de Montravel, Haut-Montravel (W) Muscadelle, Sauvignon Blanc, Sauvignon Gris, Sémillon, *Ondenc*

Crémant de Limoux (W) Chardonnay, *Chenin Blanc, Mauzac, Pinot Noir*

Entraygues–Le Fel (R, P) Cabernet Franc, Cabernet Sauvignon, Fer, Mouyssaguès, Négrette (W) Chenin Blanc, *Mauzac, St-Côme*

Estaing (R, P) Fer, Gamay, *Abouriou, Cabernet Franc, Cabernet Sauvignon, Castets, Duras, Merlot, Mouyssaguès, Négret de Banhars, Pinot Noir* (W) Chenin Blanc, Mauzac, St-Côme (Roussellou)

Fronton (R, P) Négrette, *Cabernet Franc, Cabernet Sauvignon, Cinsaut, Côt, Fer, Gamay, Mérille, Syrah*

Gaillac (R, P) Duras, Fer, Syrah, *Cabernet Franc, Cabernet Sauvignon, Gamay, Merlot, Prunelard* (W, S) Len de L'el, Mauzac, Mauzac Rosé, Muscadelle, *Ondenc, Sauvignon Blanc*

Gaillac Premières Côtes (W) Len de L'el, Mauzac, Mauzac Rosé, Muscadelle, *Ondenc, Sauvignon Blanc*

Gaillac Mousseux (doux) (S) Mauzac, Mauzac Rosé

Irouléguy (R) Cabernet Franc, Tannat, *Cabernet Sauvignon* (P) Cabernet Franc, Cabernet Sauvignon, Tannat, *Courbu, Gros Manseng, Petit Courbu, Petit Manseng* (W) Courbu, Gros Manseng, Petit Courbu, Petit Manseng

Jurançon, Jurançon Sec (W) Gros Manseng, Petit Manseng, *Camaralet de Lasseube, Courbu, Lauzet, Petit Courbu*

Limoux (R) Merlot, *Cabernet Franc, Cabernet Sauvignon, Côt, Grenache, Syrah* (W) Chardonnay, Chenin Blanc, Mauzac (S) Mauzac, *Chardonnay, Chenin Blanc*

Madiran (R) Tannat, *Cabernet Franc, Cabernet Sauvignon, Fer*

Marcillac (R, P) Fer, *Cabernet Sauvignon, Merlot, Prunelard*

Monbazillac (W) Muscadelle, Sauvignon Blanc, Sauvignon Gris, Sémillon, *Chenin Blanc, Ondenc, Ugni Blanc*

Montravel (R) Merlot, *Cabernet Franc, Cabernet Sauvignon, Côt* (W) Muscadelle, Sauvignon Blanc, Sauvignon Gris, Sémillon, *Ondenc*

Pacherenc du Vic Bilh (W) Courbu, Gros Manseng, Petit Courbu, Petit Manseng, *Arrufiac, Sauvignon Blanc*

Pécharmant (R) Cabernet Franc, Cabernet Sauvignon, Malbec, Merlot

Rosette (W) Muscadelle, Sauvignon Blanc, Sauvignon Gris, Sémillon

Saussignac (W) Muscadelle, Sauvignon Blanc, Sauvignon Gris. Sémillon, *Chenin Blanc, Ondenc, Ugni Blanc*

St-Mont (R, P) Tannat, *Cabernet Franc, Cabernet Sauvignon, Fer, Merlot* (W) Gros Manseng, *Arrufiac, Courbu, Petit Courbu,Petit Manseng*

St-Sardos (R, P) Syrah, Tannat, *Cabernet Franc, Merlot*

Tursan (R, P) Cabernet Franc, Tannat, *Cabernet Sauvignon, Fer, Merlot* (W) Baroque, Gros Manseng, *Chenin Blanc, Claverie, Petit Manseng, Raffiat de Moncade, Sauvignon Blanc, Sauvignon Gris*

GREECE

Amyndeo (R, P, S) Xinomavro

Ankhíalos (W) Roditis, *Savatiano*

Archanes (R) Kotsifali, Mandilaria

Dafnés (R) Liatiko

Goumenissa (R) Xinomavro, *Negoska*

Lemnos (W) Muscat of Alexandria

Mantinia (W) Moschofilero

Messenikola (R) Messenikola, *Carignan, Syrah*

Monemvasia-Malvasia (W) Monemvasia, Assyrtiko, Asproudes, Kydonitsa

Náoussa (R) Xinomavro

Neméa (R) Agiorgitiko

Paros (R) Mandilaria, Monemvassia (W) Monemvassia

Pátras (W) Roditis

Peza (R) Kotsifali, Mandilaria (W) Vilana

Rapsani (R) Krassato, Stavroto, Xinomavro

Rhodes (R) Mandilaria (W) Athiri

Sámos (W) Muscat Blanc à Petits Grains

Santorini, Santorini Vissanto (W) Assyrtiko, *Aidani, Athiri*

Sitia (R) Liatiko, *Mandilaria* (W) Vilana, *Thrapsathiri*

Slopes of Meliton (R) Cabernet Franc, Cabernet Sauvignon, Limnio, (W) Assyrtiko, Athiri, Roditis

Zitsa (W, S) Debina

HUNGARY

Egri Bikavér (Bulls Blood of Eger) (R) Blauburger, Cabernet Franc, Cabernet Sauvignon, Kadarka, Kékfrankos, Kékmedoc, Merlot, Pinot Noir, Portugieser, Zweigelt

Tokaji (W) Furmint, Hárslevelű, Kövérszőlő, Muscat Blanc à Petits Grains (Sárga Muskotály), Zéta

ITALY

Abruzzo

Cerasuolo d'Abruzzo (R) Montepulciano, *other non-aromatic red grapes authorized for Abruzzo*

Controguerra (W) Trebbiano Abruzzese, Trebbiano Toscano, *Malvasia, Passerina* (R, P) Montepulciano

Ortona (W) Trebbiano, *other local white varieties* (R) Montepulciano

Terre Tollesi or Tullum (W) Trebbiano Abruzzese, Trebbiano Toscano, *other local white varieties* (R) Montepulciano, *other local red varieties*

Villamagna (R) Montepulciano

All other DOC and DOCG wines are varietal.

Basilicata

Grottino di Roccanova (R, P) Sangiovese, *Cabernet Sauvignon, Malvasia Nera di Basilicata, Montepulciano* (W) Malvasia Bianca di Basilicata

Matera (R) Sangiovese, Primitivo (P) Primitivo (W) Malvasia Bianca di Basilicata, *other local white varieties*

Terre dell'Alta Val d'Agri (R) Cabernet Sauvignon, Merlot, *other local red varieties* (P) Cabernet Sauvignon, Malvasia di Basilicata, Merlot, *other local varieties*

Other DOCs are varietal.

Calabria

Bivongi (R, P) Gaglioppo, Greco Nero, *Castiglione, Nero d'Avola,* Nocera (W) Greco Bianco, Guardavalle, Montonico Bianca, *Ansonica, Malvasia Bianca*

Cirò (R, P) Gaglioppo (W) Greco Bianco

Donnici (P, R) Gaglioppo (Montonico Nero), *Greco Bianco, Greco Nero, Malvasia Bianco, Pecorello* (W) Greco Bianco, Malvasia Blanca, Montonico Bianco, Pecorello

Lamezia (W) Greco Bianco, *other local white varieties* (P, R) Gaglioppo, Greco Nero, Magliocco, Marsigliana

Melissa (W) Greco Bianco, *Malvasia Bianca, Trebbiano Toscano* (R) Gaglioppo, *Greco Bianco, Greco Nero, Malvasia Bianca, Trebbiano Toscano*

Pollino (R) Gaglioppo, Greco Nero, Guarnaccia Bianca, Malvasia Bianca, Montonico Bianco

Sant'Anna di Isola Capo Rizzuto (R, P) Gaglioppo, Greco, Nerello Cappuccio, Nerello Mascalese, Nocera, Malvasia Bianca, Malvasia Nera

San Vito di Luzzi (W) Greco Bianco, Malvasia Bianca, Trebbiano Toscano (R, P) Gaglioppo, *Greco Nero, Malvasia, Sangiovese*

Savuto (W) Chardonnay, Greco Bianco, Montonico, *Malvasia Bianca, other local white varieties* (R, P) Aglianico, Gaglioppo, *Greco Nero, Nerello Cappuccio, other local red varieties*

Scavigna (W) Chardonnay, Traminer, *Pinot Bianco, Riesling Italico, other local white varieties* (P, R) Aglianico, Magliocco, Marsigliana, *other local red varieties*

Terre di Cosenza (W) Greco, Guarnaccia, Montonico Bianco, Pecorello (R, P) Magliocco Canino, *Aglianico, Cabernet Sauvignon, Gaglioppo, Greco Nero, Merlot, Nero d'Avola, Pecorello, Sangiovese*

Verbicaro (R, P) Gaglioppo (Guarnaccia Nera), Greco Bianco, Greco Nero, Guarnaccia Bianca, Malvasia Bianca (W) Greco Bianco, Guarnaccia, Bianca, Malvasia Bianca

Campania

Aversa (W, S) Asprinio

Campi Flegrei (W) Falanghina, *other local white varieties* (R) Aglianico, Piedirosso, *other local red varieties*

Capri (W) Falanghina, Greco, *Biancolella* (R) Piedirosso, *other local red varieties*

Castel San Lorenzo (R, P) Barbera, Sangiovese (W) Malvasia Bianca, Trebbiano Toscano

Cilento (R) Aglianico, Piedirosso, Primitivo, *other local red varieties* (P) Sangiovese, *Aglianico, Piedirosso, Primitivo, other local red varieties* (W) Fiano, Trebbiano Toscano, *Greco Bianco, Malvasia Bianca, other local white varieties*

Costa d'Amalfi (R, P) Aglianico, Piedirosso, Sciascinoso (W, S) Biancolella, Falanghina

Falerno del Massico (W) Falanghina (R) Aglianico, Piedirosso

Galluccio (W) Falanghina, *other local white varieties* (R, P) Aglianico, *other local red varieties*

Guardia Sanframondi or **Guardiolo** (W) Falanghina, Malvasia di Candia (R, P) Sangiovese (S) Falanghina

Irpinia (W) Fiano, Greco, *other local white varieties* (P, R) Aglianico, *other local red varieties*

Ischia (W) Biancolella, Forastera (R) Guarnaccia, Piedirosso (Per'e Palumno)

Penisola Sorrentina (W) Biancolella, Falanghina, Greco, *other local white varieties* (R) Aglianico, Piedirosso, Sciascinoso, *other local red varieties*

Sannio (R, P) Sangiovese, other local red varieties (W, S) Malvasia Bianca di Candia, Trebbiano Toscano, *other local white varieties*

Sant'Agata dei Goti (R, P) Aglianico, Piedirosso (W) Falanghina, Greco

Solopaca (W) Coda di Volpe, Falanghina, Malvasia di Candia, Malvasia Toscana, (R, P) Aglianico, Piedirosso, Sangiovese, Sciascinoso (S) Falanghina

Taburno Falanghina, (W) Trebbiano Toscano (R) Aglianico, Sangiovese (S) Coda di Volpe, Falanghina

Taurasi, DOCG (R) Aglianico

Vesuvio (W) Coda di Volpe Verdeca, *Falanghina, Greco* (R, P) Piedirosso, Sciascinoso, *Aglianico*

Emilia-Romagna

Bosco Eliceo (W) Trebbiano Romagnolo, *Malvasia di Candia, Sauvignon Blanc*

Cagnina di Romagna (R) Refosco (Terrano)

Colli Bolognesi (W) Albana, Trebbiano Romagnolo

Colli Romagna Centrale (W) Bombino, Chardonnay, Pinot Bianco, Sauvignon Blanc, Trebbiano (R) Barbera, Cabernet Sauvignon, Merlot, Montepulciano, Sangiovese

Colli di Faenza (W) Chardonnay, Pignoletto, Pinot Bianco, Sauvignon Blanc, Trebbiano Romagnolo (R) Ancellotta, Cabernet Sauvignon, Ciliegiolo, Merlot, Sangiovese

Colli di Parma (R) Barbera, Bonarda Piemontese, Croatina (S) Chardonnay, Pinot Bianco, Pinot Nero

Colli di Rimini (W) Trebbiano Romagnolo, *Biancame, Mostosa* (R) Sangiovese, *Ancellotta, Barbera, Cabernet Sauvignon, Ciliegiolo, Merlot, Montepulciano, Terrano*

Colli di Scandiano e Canossa (W, S) Spergola, *Malvasia di Candia, Pinot Bianco, Pinot Grigio, Trebbiano Romagnolo* (R) Marzemino, *Cabernet Sauvignon, Malbo Gentile*

Colli d'Imola (W) one or more non-aromatic local white varieties (R) one or more non-aromatic local red varieties

Colli Piacentini Monterosso Val d'Arda (W) Malvasia di Candia Aromatica, Moscato Bianco, Ortrugo, Trebbiano Romagnolo, *Beverdino, Sauvignon Blanc*

Colli Piacentini Trebbianino Val Trebbia (W) Malvasia di Candia Aromatica, Moscato Bianco, Ortrugo, Sauvignon Blanc, Trebbiano Romagnolo

Colli Piacentini Valnure (W) Malvasia di Candia, Ortrugo, Trebbiano Romagnolo

Gutturnio (R) Barbera, Croatina

Modena (W, S) Montù, Pignoletto, Trebbiano (R, P, S) Lambrusco, *Ancellotta, Fortana, Malbo Gentile*

Pagadebit di Romagna (W) Bombino Bianco

Reggiano (S) Lambrusco (R) Ancellotta, *Cabernet Sauvignon, Fogarina, Lambrusco, Malbo Gentile, Marzemino, Merlot*

Reno (W, S) Albana, Trebbiano Romagnolo, *other local white varieties*

Friuli-Venezia Giulia

Carso (R) Terrano, *Merlot, Refosco dal Peduncolo Rosso*

Collio Goriziano or **Collio** (W) Chardonnay, Friulano, Malvasia, Picolit, Pinot Bianco, Pinot Grigio, Ribolla Gialla, Riesling, Riesling Italico, Sauvignon Blanc, *Gewürztraminer, Müller-Thurgau* (R) one or more local red varieties

Friuli-Annia (W) Chardonnay, Friulano, Gewürztraminer, Malvasia, Pinot Bianco, Pinot Grigio, Sauvignon Blanc, Verduzzo Friulano (R, P) Cabernet Franc, Cabernet Sauvignon, Merlot, Refosco dal Peduncolo Rosso

Friuli Aquileia (P) any local red varieties (R) Refosco dal Peduncolo Rosso, *other local red varieties* (W) Friulano, *other local white varieties*

Friuli Colli Orientali (W) Chardonnay, Friulano, Malvasia Istriana, Picolit, Pinot Bianco, Pinot Grigio, Ribolla Gialla, Riesling, Sauvignon Blanc, Verduzzo Friulano (R, P) Cabernet Franc, Cabernet Sauvignon, Merlot, Pignolo, Pinot Nero, Refosco dal Peduncolo Rosso, Refosco Nostrano, Schioppettino, Tazzelenghe

Friuli Grave (W) Chardonnay, Friulano, Pinot Bianco, Pinot Grigio, Riesling, Sauvignon Blanc, Verduzzo Friulano (R, P) Cabernet Franc, Cabernet Sauvignon, Carmenère, Merlot, Pinot Nero, Refosco dal Peduncolo Rosso

Friuli Isonzo (W) Chardonnay, Friulano, Gewürztraminer, Malvasia, Pinot Bianco, Pinot Grigio, Riesling, Riesling Italico, Sauvignon Blanc, Verduzzo Friulano (R, P) Cabernet Franc, Cabernet Sauvignon, Franconia, Merlot, Pignolo, Pinot Nero, Refosco dal Peduncolo Rosso, Schioppettino

Friuli Latisana (R, P) Merlot, *Cabernet Franc, Cabernet Sauvignon, Carmenère* (W, S) Friulano, *Chardonnay, Pinot Bianco*

Ramandolo, DOCG (W) Verduzzo Friulano

Rosazzo, DOCG (W) Chardonnay, Friulano, Pinot Bianco, Sauvignon Blanc, *Ribolla Gialla*

Lazio

Aprilia (R, P) Cabernet Sauvignon, Merlot, Sangiovese (W) Trebbiano Toscano, *Chardonnay*

Atina (R) Cabernet Sauvignon, *Cabernet Franc, Merlot, Syrah*

Bianco Capena (W) Malvasia del Lazio e Toscana, Malvasia di Candia, Trebbiano, *Bellone, Bombino (Uva di Spagna)*

Cannellino di Frascati, DOCG (W) Malvasia Bianca di Candia, Malvasia del Lazio, *Bellone, Bombino Bianco, Greco, Trebbiano*

Castelli Romani (R) Cesanese, Merlot, Montepulciano, Nero Buono, Sangiovese (P) one or more local red and white varieties (W) Malvasia, Trebbiano

Cerveteri (W) Malvasia di Candia, Trebbiano Toscano, *up to 15% other white varieties authorised for Lazio* (R, P) Merlot, Montepulciano, Sangiovese, *other red varieties authorised for Lazio*

Circeo (W, S) Malvasia del Lazio, Trebbiano Toscano (R, P, S) Cabernet Sauvignon, Merlot, Sangiovese

Colli Albani (W, S) Malvasia del Lazio, Malvasia di Candia, Trebbiano di Soave, Trebbiano Giallo, Trebbiano Toscano

Colli della Sabina (W) Malvasia del Lazio, Trebbiano Toscano (R, P) Montepulciano, Sangiovese,

Colli Etruschi Viterbesi or **Tuscia** (W, S) Malvasia del Lazio, Malvasia Toscana, Trebbiano Toscano (R) Montepulciano, Sangiovese

Colli Lanuvini (W, S) Malvasia Candia, Trebbiano Toscano, Trebbiano Giallo, Trebbiano Verde (R) Merlot, Montepulciano, Sangiovese

Cori (W) Bellone, Greco, Malvasia del Lazio (R) Cesanese, Montepulciano, Nero Buono

Est! Est!! Est!!! di Montefiascone (W, S) Malvasia Bianca Lunga, Malvasia del Lazio, Trebbiano Giallo, Trebbiano Toscano

Frascati (W, S) Malvasia Bianca di Candia, Malvasia del Lazio, *Bellone, Bombino Bianco, Greco, Trebbiano Giallo, Trebbiano Toscano*

Frascati Superiore, DOCG (W) Malvasia Bianca di Candia, Malvasia del Lazio, *Bellone, Bombino Bianco, Greco, Trebbiano*

Genazzano (W) Malvasia di Candia, *other local white varieties* (R) Ciliegiolo, *other local red varieties*

Marino (W, S) Malvasia Bianca di Candia, *other local white varieties*

Montecompatri-Colonna (W) Malvasia Bianca di Candia, Trebbiano, *Bellone, Bonvino*

Nettuno (W) Bellone, Trebbiano Toscano, *other local white varieties* (R) Merlot, Sangiovese, *other local red varieties* (P) Sangiovese, Trebbiano Toscano, *other local varieties*

Roma (W, S) Malvasia, *Bellone, Bombino Bianco, Greco, Trebbiano Giallo, Trebbiano Verde* (R, P) Montepulciano, *Cabernet Franc, Cabernet Sauvignon, Cesanese Comune, Cesanese di Affile, Sangiovese, Syrah*

Tarquinia (W) Trebbiano Giallo, Trebbiano Toscano, *Malvasia del Lazio, Malvasia di Candia, other local white varieties* (R, P) Montepulciano, Sangiovese, *Cesanese Comune, other local red varieties*

Velletri (W) Malvasia, Trebbiano Giallo, Trebbiano Toscano, Trebbiano Verde, *other local white varieties* (R) Montepulciano, Sangiovese, *Cesanese, other local red varieties*

Vignanello (W) Trebbiano Giallo, Trebbiano Toscano, *Malvasia Bianca di Candia, Malvasia del Chianti, other local white varieties* (R, P) Ciliegiolo, Sangiovese

Zagarolo (W) Malvasia, *Bellone, Bonvino, Trebbiano*

Liguria

Cinque Terre (and subzones) (W) Albarola, Bosco, Vermentino, *up to 20% other white varieties approved for cultivation in Spezia*

Colli di Luni (R) Sangiovese (W) Trebbiano Toscano Vermentino

Colline di Levanto (W) Vermentino, *Albarola, Bosco* (R) Ciliegiolo, Sangiovese, other local red varieties

Golfo del Tigullio-Portofino (W, S) Bianchetta Genovese, Vermentino, *other local non-aromatic white varieties* (R, P) Ciliegiolo, Dolcetto, *other local non-aromatic red varieties*

Pornassio or **Ormeasco di Pornassio** (R, P) Dolcetto

Val Polcèvera (W, S) Albarola, Bianchetta Genovese, Vermentino, *other local white varieties* (R, P) Ciliegiolo, Dolcetto, Sangiovese, *other local red varieties*

Lombardy

Botticino (R) Barbera, Marzemino, *Sangiovese, Schiava Gentile*

Buttafuoco dell'Oltrepò Pavese (R) Barbera, Croatina, Ughetta, Uva Rara

Capriano del Colle (R) Marzemino, Merlot, Sangiovese, *up to 10% other red grapes authorised in Lombardia* (W) Trebbiano di Soave, Trebbiano Toscano, *up to 40% other white grapes authorised in Lombardy*

Casteggio (R) Barbera, *Croatina, Pinot Nero, Ughetta, Uva Rara*

Cellatica (R) Barbera, Incrocio Terzi No. 1, Marzemino, Schiava Gentile

Curtefranca (R) Cabernet Franc, Cabernet Sauvignon, Carmenere, Merlot (W) Chardonnay, Pinot Bianco

Garda (W) Riesling, Riesling Italico (R, P) Groppello, *Barbera, Marzemino, Sangiovese*

Garda Colli Mantovani (R, P) Cabernet, Merlot, Rondinella, *Molinara, Negrara, Sangiovese* (W) Chardonnay, Garganega, Riesling, Riesling Italico, Sauvignon Blanc, Trebbiano Toscano

Franciacorta, DOCG (WS) Chardonnay, Pinot Bianco, Pinot Nero (P, S) Pinot Nero, *Chardonnay, Pinot Bianco*

Lugana (W) Trebbiano di Soave

Oltrepò Pavese (R, P, S) Barbera, Croatina, Pinot Nero, Ughetta (Vespolina), Uva Rara (W) Riesling, Riesling Italico, *other local white varieties*

Oltrepò Pavese metodo classico, DOCG (S) Pinot Nero, *Chardonnay, Pinot Blanco, Pinot Grigio*

Riviera del Garda Bresciano or **Garda Bresciano** (W) Riesling Italico, Riesling Renano (R, P) Barbera, *Groppello di Mocasina, Groppello Gentile, Marzemino, Sangiovese*

San Colombano al Lambro (R) Barbera, Croatina, Uva Rara (W) Chardonnay, Pinot Nero

San Martino della Battaglia (W) Friulano, *other local white varieties*

Sangue i Giuda dell'Oltrepò Pavese or **Sangue di Giuda** (S) Barbera, Croatina, Pinot Nero, Uva Rara, Vespolina

Scanzo, DOCG (R) Moscato di Scanzo

Sforzato di Valtellina, DOCG (R) Nebbiolo

Valcalepio (R) Cabernet Sauvignon, Merlot, (W) Chardonnay, Pinot Bianco, Pinot Grigio

Valtellina Rosso (R) Nebbiolo

Valtellina Superiore, DOCG (R) Nebbiolo

Valtènesi (P, R) Groppello Gentile, Groppello Mocasina, *other local red varieties*

Marche

Colli Maceratesi (W, S) Maceratino, *Chardonnay, Grechetto, Incrocio Bruni 54, Malvasia Toscana, Pecorino, Sauvignon Blanc, Trebbiano Toscano, Verdicchio* (R) Sangiovese, *Cabernet Franc, Cabernet Sauvignon, Ciliegiolo, Lacrima, Merlot, Montepulciano, Vernaccia Nera*

Colli Pesaresi (R, P) Sangiovese (W) Biancame, Chardonnay, Pinot Bianco, Pinot Grigio, Pinot Nero, Riesling Italico, Sauvignon Blanc, Trebbiano, Verdicchio (S) Biancame, Chardonnay, Pinot Bianco, Pinot Grigio, Pinot Nero, Riesling Italico, Sauvignon Blanc, Trebbiano Toscano, Verdicchio

Conero, DOCG (R) Montepulciano, Sangiovese

Esino (R) Montepulciano, Sangiovese (W) Verdicchio, *other local white varieties*

Falerio (W) Trebbiano, *Passerina, Pecorino, Verdicchio, Malvasia Toscana*

Focara Rosso (R) Cabernet Franc, Cabernet Sauvignon, Merlot, Pinot Nero, Sangiovese

Offida, DOCG (R) Montepulciano, *other local red varieties*

Pergola (R, P, S) Aleatico, *other local varieties*

Roncaglia Bianco (W) Pinot Nero, Trebbiano

Rosso Conero (R) Montepulciano, *other local red varieties*

Rosso Piceno (R) Montepulciano, Sangiovese

San Ginesio (R) Sangiovese, *Cabernet Franc, Cabernet Sauvignon, Ciliegiolo, Merlot, Vernaccia Nera* (S) Vernaccia Nera

Serrapetrona (R) Vernaccia Nera, *other local red varieties*

Terre di Offida (S) Passerina, *other local white varieties*

Terreni di Sanseverino (R) Vernaccia Nera, *other local red varieties*

Molise

Biferno (R, P) Montepulciano, *Aglianico* (W) Trebbiano Toscano, *Bombino Bianco, Malvasia*

Molise (R, P) Montepulciano, *other local red varieties* (S) Chardonnay, Falanghina, Fiano, Malvasia, Montepulciano, Moscato, Pinot Bianco, Pinot Grigio, *other local white varieties*

Pentro di Isernia or **Pentro** (W) Falanghina, *Trebbiano Bianco* (R, P) Montepulciano, *Tintilia*

Piemonte

Albugnano (R) Nebbiolo, *Freisa, Barbera, Bonarda*

Alta Langa, DOCG (S) Chardonnay, Pinot Nero

Asti, DOCG (S) Moscato

Barbaresco, DOCG (R) Nebbiolo

Barbera d'Asti, DOCG, Barbera del Monferrato, DOCG (R) Barbera, *Dolcetto, Freisa, Grignolino*

Barolo, DOCG (R) Nebbiolo

Boca (R) Nebbiolo, *Bonarda Novarese, Vespolina*

Brachetto d'Acqui or **Acqui, DOCG** (R, S) Brachetto

Bramaterra (R) Nebbiolo, *Bonarda, Croatina, Vespolina*

Calosso (R) Gamba Rossa

Canavese (R, P, S) Barbera, Bonarda, Freisa, Neretto, Uva Rara (W) Erbaluce

Carema (R) Nebbiolo

Cisterna d'Asti (R, S) Croatina

Colli Tortonesi (R, S) Aleatico, Barbera, Bonarda Piemontese, Cabernet Franc, Cabernet Sauvignon, Croatina, Dolcetto, Freisa, Grignolino, Lambrusca di Alessandria, Merlot, Nebbiolo, Pinot Nero, Sangiovese (W, S) Barbera Bianca, Chardonnay, Cortese, Favorita, Müller-Thurgau, Pinot Bianco, Pinot Grigio, Riesling Italico, Riesling Renano, Sauvignon Blanc, Sylvaner Verde, Timorasso

Collina Torinese (R) Barbera, Freisa

Colline Novaresi (R, P) Nebbiolo, *other local red varieties* (W) Erbaluce

Colline Saluzzesi (R) Barbera, Chatus, Nebbiolo, Pelaverga

Coste della Sesia (R, P) Nebbiolo, *Barbera, Bonarda, Croatina, Vespolina* (W) Erbaluce

Dogliani, DOCG (R) Dolcetto

Fara (R) Nebbiolo, *Uva Rara, Vespolina*

Gabiano (R) Barbera, *Freisa, Grignolino*

Gattinara, DOCG (R) Nebbiolo, *Uva Rara, Vespolina*

Gavi or **Cortese di Gavi, DOCG** (W) Cortese

Ghemme, DOCG (R) Nebbiolo, *Uva Rara, Vespolina*

Langhe (W) any proportions of authorized non-aromatic white grapes, (P) Barbera, Dolcetto, Nebbiolo (R) any proportions of authorized non-aromatic red grapes

Lessona (R) Nebbiolo, *Bonarda, Vespolina*

Loazzolo (W) Moscato

Monferrato (R) any local red varieties (W) any local white varieties (P) Barbera, Bonarda, Cabernet Franc, Cabernet Sauvignon, Dolcetto, Freisa, Grignolino, Nebbiolo, Pinot Nero

Piemonte (W) Chardonnay, Cortese, Erbaluce, Favorita, *other local white varieties* (R, P) Barbera, Croatina, Dolcetto, Freisa, Nebbiolo, *other local red varieties* (S) Chardonnay, Pinot Bianco, Pinot Grigio, Pinot Nero

Pinerolese (R, P) Barbera, Bonarda, Nebbiolo, Neretto, *other local red varieties*

Roero, DOCG (R) Nebbiolo, *Arneis* (W) Arneis

Rubino di Cantavenna (R) Barbera, *Freisa, Grignolino*

Ruchè di Castagnole Monferrato, DOCG (R) Ruchè, *Barbera, Brachetto*

Sizzano (R) Nebbiolo, *Uva Rara, Vespolina*

Valli Ossolane (W) Chardonnay, *other local white varieties* (R) Croatina, Merlot, Nebbiolo

Valsusa (R) Avanà, Barbera, Dolcetto, Neretta Cuneese, *other local red varieties*

Verduno (R) Pelaverga Piccolo

Puglia

Alezio (R, P) Negroamaro, *Malvasia Nera, Montepulciano, Sangiovese*

Barletta (R, P) Uva di Troia, *Malbec, Montepulciano, Sangiovese* (W) Malvasia Bianca

Brindisi (R, P) Negroamaro, *Malvasia Nera, Montepulciano, Sangiovese, Susumaniello*

Cacc'e Mmitte di Lucera (R) Uva di Troia, *Bombino Bianco, Malvasia Bianca Lunga, Malvasia Nera di Brindisi, Montepulciano, Sangiovese, Trebbiano Toscano*

Castel del Monte (W, S) Bombino Bianco, Chardonnay, Pampanuto (R) Aglianico, Montepulciano, Nero di Troia (P, S) Aglianico, Bombino Nero, Uva di Troia

Colline Joniche Tarantine (W, S) Chardonnay, *other local white varieties* (R, P) Cabernet Sauvignon, *other local red varieties*

Copertino (R, P) Negroamaro, *Malvasia Nera di Brindisi, Malvasia Nera di Lecce, Montepulciano, Sangiovese*

Galatina (R, P) Negroamaro (W) Chardonnay, *other local white varieties*

Gioia del Colle (R, P) Primitivo, *Malvasia Nera, Montepulciano, Negroamaro, Sangiovese* (W) Trebbiano Toscano, *other local white varieties*

Gravina (W) Greco, Malvasia Bianca Lunga, *Bianco d'Alessano, Chardonnay, Fiano, Verdeca* (P, R) Montepulciano, Primitivo, *Aglianico, Cabernet Sauvignon, Merlot, Uva di Troia*

Leverano (P, R) Malvasia Nera di Lecce, Montepulciano, Negroamaro, Sangiovese (W) Malvasia Bianca, Vermentino

Lizzano (P, R) Bombino Nero, Montepulciano, Negroamaro, Pinot Nero, Sangiovese (W) Chardonnay, Pinot Bianco, *Bianco d'Alessano, Malvasia Bianca Lunga, Sauvignon Blanc*

Locorotondo (W) Bianco d'Alessano, Verdeca, *other local white varieties*

Martina or **Martina Franca** (W, S) Bianco d'Alessano, Verdeca, *Bombino, Fiano, Malvasia Toscano*

Matino (P) Negroamaro, *Malvasia Nera, Sangiovese*

Nardò (P, R) Negroamaro, *Malvasia Nera di Brindisi, Malvasia Nera di Lecce, Montepulciano*

Orta Nova (P, R) Sangiovese, *Lambrusco Maestri, Montepulciano, Trebbiano Toscano, Uva di Troia,*

Ostuni (W) Francavilla, Impigno, *Bianco d'Alessano, Verdeca*

Rosso Canosa (R) Uva di Troia, *Montepulciano, Sangiovese*

Rosso di Cerignola (R) Negroamaro, Uva di Troia, *Barbera, Malbec, Montepulciano, Sangiovese, Trebbiano Toscano*

Salice Salentino (P, R) Negroamaro, *other local red varieties* (W) Chardonnay, *other local white varieties*

San Severo (W) Bombino Bianco, Trebbiano Toscano, *other local white varieties* (P, R) Montepulciano, Sangiovese, *other local red varieties*

Squinzano (P, R) Negroamaro, *Malvasia Nera di Brindisi, Malvasia Nera di Lecce, Sangiovese* (W) Chardonnay, Malvasia Bianca, *other local white varieties*

Tavoliere delle Puglie or **Tavoliere** (R, P) Uva di Troia, *other local red varieties*

Terra d'Otranto (W, S) Chardonnay, *other local white varieties* (R, P) Malvasia Nera, Negroamaro, Primitivo, *other local red varieties*

Sardinia

Alghero (R, P, S) one or more local non-aromatic red varieties (W) one or more local non-aromatic white varieties

Campidano di Terralba or **Terralba** (R) Bovale di Spagna, Bovale Sardo, *up to 15% other approved red varieties for the region of Sardinia*

Mandrolisai (P, R) Bovale Sardo, Cannonau, Monica

Sicily

Alcamo (W) Catarratto Bianco, *Chardonnay, Grecanico, Grillo, Inzolia, Müller-Thurgau, Sauvignon Blanc* (R) Calabrese, *Cabernet Sauvignon, Frappato, Merlot, Nero d'Avola, Perricone, Sangiovese, Syrah* (P, S) Cabernet Sauvignon, Calabrese, Frappato, Merlot, Nerello Mascalese, Nero d'Avola, Perricone, Sangiovese, Syrah

Cerasuolo di Vittoria, DOCG (R) Frappato, Nero d'Avola

Contea di Sclafani (W) Catarratto, Grecanico, Inzolia (R) Nero d'Avola, Perricone (P) Nerello Mascalese

Contessa Entellina (W) Inzolia, *Catarratto Bianco Lucido, Grecanico Dorato, Grillo, Müller-Thurgau, Pinot Bianco, Sauvignon Blanc* (R, P) Calabrese, Syrah

Delia Nivolelli (W) Grecanico, Grillo, Inzolia (R) Cabernet Sauvignon, Merlot, Nero d'Avola, Perricone, Pignatello, Sangiovese, Syrah (S) Chardonnay, Damaschino, Grecanico, Grillo, Inzolia

Eloro (P, R) Frappato, Nero d'Avola, Pignatello

Erice (W) Catarratto Bianco (R) Calabrese, Nero d'Avola, *other local varieties*

Etna (W) Carricante, *Catarratto Bianco Comune, Catarratto Bianco Lucido, Minnella Bianca, Trebbiano* (P, R, S) Nerello Mascalese, *Nerello Mantellato, (Nerello Cappuccio)*

Faro (R) Nerello Mascalese, *Calabrese, Gaglioppo, Nerello Cappuccio, Nocera, Sangiovese*

Mamertino di Milazzo (W) Catarratto, Grillo, Inzolia (R) Calabrese, Nero d'Avola, *other local red varieties*

Marsala (Oro, Ambra) Catarratto, Damaschino, Grillo, Inzolia (Rubino) Calabrese, Nerello Mascalese, Perricone

Menfi (W) Catarratto Bianco Lucido, Chardonnay, Grecanico, Inzolia, *other local white varieties* (R) Cabernet Sauvignon, Merlot, Nero d'Avola, Sangiovese, Syrah, *other local red varieties*

Monreale (W) Catarratto, Inzolia, *other local white varieties*
(R) Calabrese, Nero d'Avola, Perricone, *other local red varieties* (P)
Nerello Mascalese, Perricone, Sangiovese, *other local red varieties*

Noto (R) Nero d'Avola, *other local red varieties*

Pantelleria (W, S) Zibibbo

Riesi (W) Chardonnay, Inzolia (R) Cabernet Sauvignon, Calabrese
(P) Cabernet Sauvignon, Calabrese, Nerello Mascalese

Salaparuta (W) Catarratto, *other local white varieties* (R) Nero d'Avola,
other local red varieties

Sambuca di Sicilia (W) Inzolia, *other local white varieties* (R, P) Nero
d'Avola, *other local red varieties*

Santa Margherita di Belice (W) Catarratto Bianco Lucido, Grecanico,
Inzolia (R) Cabernet Sauvignon, Nero d'Avola, Sangiovese

Sciacca (W) Catarratto Bianco Lucido, Chardonnay, Grecanico Dorato,
Inzolia (R) Cabernet Sauvignon, Merlot, Nero d'Avola, Sangiovese
(P) Ansonica, Cabernet Sauvignon, Catarratto, Chardonnay, Grecanico
Dorato, Merlot, Nero d'Avola, Sangiovese

Sicilia (W) Catarratto, Grecanico, Grillo, Inzolia, *other local white varieties* (R, P) Frappato, Nerello Mascalese, Nero d'Avola, Perricone, *other
local red varieties* (WS) Carricante, Catarratto, Chardonnay, Grecanico,
Grillo, Inzolia, Moscato Bianco, Pinot Nero, Zibibbo, *other local white
varieties* (PS) Frappato, Nerello Mascalese, Nero d'Avola, Pinot Nero,
other local red varieties

Siracusa (W) Moscato Bianco, *other local white varieties* (R) Nero
d'Avola, *other local red varieties*

Vittoria (R) Nero d'Avola, Frappato

Tuscany

Bianco dell'Empolese (W) Trebbiano Toscano

Bianco di Pitigliano (W) Grechetto, Trebbiano Toscano, *Chardonnay,
Greco, Malvasia Toscana, Pinot Bianco, Riesling Italico, Sauvignon
Blanc, Verdello*

San Torpè (W) Trebbiano Toscano, *other local white varieties* (P) Sangiovese, *other local red varieties*

Bolgheri (W) Vermentino, *Sauvignon Blanc, Trebbiano Toscano* (R, P)
Cabernet Franc, Cabernet Sauvignon, Merlot, *Sangiovese, Syrah*

Bolgheri Sassicaia (R) Cabernet Sauvignon, *other local red varieties*

Brunello di Montalcino, DOCG (R) Sangiovese

Candia dei Colli Apuani (R, P) Sangiovese, *Merlot, up to 20% other red
grapes authorized in the region of Tuscany* (W, S) Vermentino, *up to
30% other white grapes authorised for the region of Tuscany*

Capalbio (R, P) Sangiovese, *Cabernet Sauvignon, up to 50% other red
grapes authorized in the region of Tuscany with the exception of Aleatico*
(W) Trebbiano Toscano, Vermentino, *up to 50% other white grapes
authorized in the region of Tuscany with the exception of Moscato Bianco*

Carmignano, DOCG (R) Sangiovese, *Cabernet Franc, Cabernet Sauvignon, Canaiolo Bianco, Canaiolo Nero, Malvasia del Chianti, Trebbiano Toscano*

Barco Reale di Carmignano (R, P) Canaiolo Nero, Sangiovese, *Cabernet
Franc, Cabernet Sauvignon, Canaiolo Bianco, Malvasia, Trebbiano Toscano*

Chianti, DOCG (R) Sangiovese, *Cabernet Franc, Cabernet Sauvignon,
Canaiolo Nero, Trebbiano, Malvasia del Chianti*

Chianti Classico (R) Sangiovese, *other authorized red varieties*

Colli dell'Etruria Centrale (R, P) Sangiovese, *Cabernet Franc, Cabernet
Sauvignon, Canaiolo Nero, Malvasia, Merlot, Trebbiano Toscano*
(W) Trebbiano Toscano, *Chardonnay, Malvasia del Chianti, Pinot
Bianco, Pinot Grigio, Sauvignon Blanc*

Colline Lucchesi (R) Canaiolo, Ciliegiolo, Merlot, Sangiovese, Syrah
(W) Chardonnay, Grechetto, Greco, Malvasia, Sauvignon Blanc,
Trebbiano Toscano, Vermentino Bianco

Cortona (R) Syrah, *Merlot*

Elba (W, S) Inzolia, Trebbiano, Vermentino (R, P) Sangiovese, *other local
red varieties*

Grance Senesi (R) Sangiovese, *other local red varieties* (W) Malvasia
Bianca Lunga, Trebbiano, *other local white varieties*

Maremma Toscana (W) Trebbiano Toscano, Vermentino, *other local
white varieties* (R) Sangiovese, *other local red varieties*

Montecarlo (W) Trebbiano Toscano, *Pinot Grigio, Pinot Bianco, Roussanne, Sauvignon Blanc, Sémillon, Vermentino* (R) Sangiovese, *Cabernet Franc, Cabernet Sauvignon, Canaiolo Nero, Ciliegiolo, Colorino,
Malvasia Nera, Merlot, Syrah*

Montecucco (R) Sangiovese, *other local red varieties* (P) Cilieglio, Sangiovese, *other local red varieties* (W) Trebbiano Toscano, Vermentino,
other local white varieties

Monteregio di Massa Marittima (R) Sangiovese, *other local red varieties*
(W) Trebbiano Toscano, Vermentino, *other local red varieties*

Montescudaio (W) Trebbiano Toscano, *other local white varieties*
(R) Sangiovese, *other local red varieties*

Morellino di Scansano, DOCG (R) Sangiovese, *other local red varieties*

Orcia (R, P) Sangiovese, *other local red varieties* (W) Trebbiano Toscano,
other local white varieties

Parrina (R, P) Sangiovese, *other local red varieties* (W) Ansonica, Chardonnay, Trebbiano Toscano, Vermentino

Pomino (R) Merlot, Pinot Nero, Sangiovese, *other local red varieties*
(W) Chardonnay, Pinot Bianco, Pinot Grigio, *other local white
varieties*

Rosso della Val di Cornia, DOCG (R) Cabernet Sauvignon, Merlot,
Sangiovese

Rosso di Montalcino (R) Sangiovese

Rosso di Montepulciano (R) Sangiovese, *other local red varieties*

San Gimignano (R, P) Sangiovese, *Cabernet Sauvignon, Merlot, Pinot
Nero, Syrah*

Sant'Antimo (W) Chardonnay, Malvasia, Pinot Grigio, Sauvignon
Blanc, Trebbiano (R) Cabernet Sauvignon, Malvasia Nera, Merlot,
Pinot Nero, Sangiovese

Sassicaia (R) Cabernet Sauvignon

Sovana (R, P) Sangiovese, *other local red varieties*

Suvereto, DOCG (R) Cabernet Sauvignon, Merlot, Sangiovese

Terratico di Bibbona (W) Vermentino, *other local white varieties*
(R, P) Merlot, Sangiovese, *other local red varieties*

Terre di Casole (W) Chardonnay, *other local white varieties* (R) Sangiovese, *other local red varieties*

Terre di Pisa (R) Cabernet Sauvignon, Merlot, Sangiovese, Syrah, *other
local red varieties*

Val d'Arbia (W) Trebbiano Toscano, Malvasia Bianca Lunga, *other local
white varieties* (P) Sangiovese, *other local red varieties*

Val d'Arno di Sopra or **Valdarno di Sopra** (W) Chardonnay, Malvasia
Bianca Lunga, Trebbiano Toscano, *other local white varieties*
(R, P) Merlot, *Cabernet Sauvignon, Syrah, other local red varieties*

Val di Cornia (W) Ansonica, Malvasia Bianca Lunga, Trebbiano, Vermentino, Viognier (P) Cabernet Sauvignon, Merlot, Sangiovese, *other
local red varieties*

Valdichiana (W) Chardonnay, Grechetto, Pinot Bianco, Pinot Grigio,
Trebbiano Toscano (R, P) Cabernet Franc, Cabernet Sauvignon, Merlot, Sangiovese, Syrah

Valdinievole (W) Trebbiano Toscano, *other local white varieties*
(R) Canaiolo Nero, Sangiovese, *other local red varieties*

Vino Nobile di Montepulciano, DOCG (R) Sangiovese, *other local red
varieties*

Vino Santo Occhio di Pernice (P) Merlot, Sangiovese

Trentino-Alto Adige

Caldaro or **Lago di Caldaro** (R) Schiava

Casteller (R) Lagrein, Lambrusco, Merlot, Schiava Gentile, Schiava Grossa, Teroldego

Trentino (W) Chardonnay, Pinot Bianco, *Manzoni Bianco, Müller-Thurgau, Sauvignon Blanc* (R) Cabernet Franc, Cabernet Sauvignon, Carmenère, Merlot (P) Lagrein, Lambrusco a Foglia Frastagliata, Schiava, Teroldego

Trento (SW, SP) Chardonnay, Pinot Bianco, Pinot Meunier, Pinot Nero

Valdadige or **Etschtaler** (W) Chardonnay, Garganega, Müller-Thurgau, Nosiola, Pinot Bianco, Pinot Grigio, Riesling Italico, Sauvignon Blanc, Trebbiano Toscano, (R, P) Lambrusco a Foglia Frastagliata, Schiava, *Cabernet Franc, Cabernet Sauvignon, Lagrein, Merlot, Pinot Nero, Teroldego*

Umbria

Amelia (W) Grechetto, Malvasia Toscano, Trebbiano Toscano (R) Ciliegiolo, Merlot, Sangiovese

Assisi (W) Grechetto, Trebbiano (R, P) Merlot, Sangiovese

Colli Altotiberini (W) Trebbiano Toscano (S) Chardonnay, Grechetto, Pinot Bianco, Pinot Grigio, Pinot Nero (R, P) Sangiovese

Colli del Trasimeno (R, P) Cabernet Sauvignon, Ciliegiolo, Gamay, Merlot, Sangiovese (W, S) Chardonnay, Grechetto, Pinot Bianco, Pinot Grigio, Trebbiano

Colli Martani (W) Trebbiano Toscano (R) Sangiovese

Colli Perugini (R, P) Sangiovese (W) Trebbiano Toscano (S) Chardonnay, Grechetto, Pinot Bianco, Pinot Grigio, Pinot Nero

Lago di Corbara (R) Cabernet Sauvignon, Merlot, Pinot Nero, Sangiovese, *other local red grape varieties* (W) Grechetto, Sauvignon Blanc

Montefalco (W) Grechetto, *Trebbiano Toscano, other local white varieties* (R) Sangiovese, *Sagrantino, other local red varieties*

Orvieto (W) Grechetto, Trebbiano Toscano (Procanico), *other local white varieties*

Rosso Orvietano (R) Aleatico, Cabernet Franc, Cabernet Sauvignon, Canaiolo, Ciliegiolo, Merlot, Montepulciano, Pinot Nero, Sangiovese, *other local red varieties*

Spoleto (W, S) Trebbiano Spoletino, *other local white varieties*

Todi (W) Grechetto, *other local white varieties* (R) Sangiovese, *Merlot, other local red varieties*

Torgiano (W) Trebbiano Toscano, *other local white varieties* (R, P) Sangiovese, *other local red varieties* (S) Chardonnay, Pinot Nero

Torgiano Riserva, DOCG (R) Sangiovese, *other local red varieties*

Valle d'Aosta

Arnad-Montjovet (R) Nebbiolo, *Dolcetto, Freisa, Neyret, Pinot Nero*

Chambave (R) Petit Rouge, *Dolcetto, Gamay, Pinot Nero* (W) Moscato

Donnaz (R) Freisa, Nebbiolo (Picutener), Neyret

Enfer d'Arvier (R) Dolcetto, Gamay, Neyret, Petit Rouge, Pinot Nero, Vien de Nus

Nus (R) Petit Rouge, Pinot Nero, Vien de Nus (W) Malvoisie

Torrette (R) *Dolcetto, Fumin, Gamay, Mayolet, Petit Rouge, Pinot Nero, Premetta, Vien de Nus*

Valle d'Aosta (W) any local white varieties (R, P) any local red varieties

Veneto

Amarone della Valpolicella, DOCG (R) Corvina Veronese, *Rondinella*

Arcole (R, P) Merlot, *Cabernet Franc, Cabernet Sauvignon, Carmenère* (W, S) Chardonnay, Garganega, Pinot Bianco, Pinot Grigio

Bagnoli Friularo, DOCG (R) Raboso Piave

Bagnoli di Sopra/Bagnoli (R) Cabernet Franc, Cabernet Sauvignon, Carmenère, Merlot, *Raboso Piave, Raboso Veronese* (P) Merlot, Raboso Piave, Raboso Veronese, *Cabernet Franc, Cabernet Sauvignon, Carmenère* (W) Chardonnay, Sauvignon Blanc, Tocai Friulano, *Raboso Piave, Raboso Veronese, Sauvignon Blanc* (S) Raboso Piave, Raboso Veronese, Cabernet Franc, Cabernet Sauvignon, Carmenère, Merlot

Bardolino (R) Corvina, Molinara, Rondinella, *Barbera, Garganega, Negrara, Rossignola, Sangiovese*

Bardolini Superiore, DOCG (R) Corvina Veronese, Rondinella, *Barbera, Cabernet Sauvignon, Marzemino, Merlot, Molinara, Rossignola, Sangiovese*

Bianco di Custoza (W) Garganega, Trebbiano Toscano, *Chardonnay, Cortese, Malvasia, Manzoni Bianco, Pinot Bianco, Riesling Italico, Tocai Friulano,*

Breganze (W) Tocai Friulano, *Chardonnay, Pinot Bianco, Pinot Grigio, Sauvignon Blanc, Vespaiolo* (R) Merlot, *Cabernet Franc, Cabernet Sauvignon, Marzemino, Pinot Nero*

Colli Asolani Prosecco, Asolo Prosecco DOCG (W) Glera, *Bianchetta Trevigiana, Perera, Verdiso* (S) Glera, *Bianchetta Trevigiana, Chardonnay, Perera, Pinot Bianco, Pinot Grigio, Pinot Nero, Verdiso*

Colli Berici (W) Garganega, *Chardonnay, Manzoni Bianco, Pinot Bianco, Pinot Grigio, Sauvignon Blanc* (S) Chardonnay, Pinot Bianco, Pinot Nero (R) Merlot

Colli di Conegliano, DOCG (W) Chardonnay, Incrocio Manzoni 6.0.13., Pinot Bianco, *Riesling Renano, Sauvignon Blanc* (R) Cabernet Franc, Cabernet Sauvignon, Marzemino, Merlot, *Incrocio Manzoni 2.15*

Colli Euganei (W) Garganega, Sauvignon Blanc, Tai, *Moscato Bianco, Moscato Giallo* (R) Cabernet Franc, Cabernet Sauvignon, Carmenère, Merlot, *Raboso Piave, Raboso Veronese*

Colli Euganei Fior d'Arancio, DOCG (W, S) Moscato

Conegliano Valdobbiadene Prosecco, DOCG (W) Glera, *Bianchetta Trevigiana, Perera, Verdiso* (S) Glera, *Bianchetta Trevigiana, Chardonnay, Perera, Pinot Bianco, Pinot Grigio, Pinot Nero, Verdiso*

Corti Benedettine del Padovana (W) Chardonnay, Friulano, Pinot Bianco, Pinot Grigio, Sauvignon Blanc (R) Merlot, Raboso Piave, Veronese

Gambellara (W, S) Garganega, *Chardonnay, Pinot Bianco, Trebbiano di Soave*

Garda (W) Riesling, Riesling Italico (R, P) Barbera, Groppello, Marzemino, Sangiovese (S) Chardonnay, Garganega

Lessini Durello/Durello Lessini (S) Durella, *Chardonnay, Garganega, Pinot Bianco, Pinot Nero*

Lison, DOCG (W) Friulano, *other local white varieties*

Lison-Pramaggiore (R) Merlot, *Cabernet Franc, Cabernet Sauvignon, Carmenère, Malbec, Refosco* (W) Friulano, *Chardonnay, Pinot Grigio, Sauvignon Blanc, Verduzzo Friulano*

Merlara (R) Merlot, *Cabernet Franc, Cabernet Sauvignon, Carmenère, Marzemino, Raboso, Refosco dal Peduncolo Rosso* (W) Friulano, *Chardonnay, Malvasia, Pinot Bianco, Pinot Grigio, Riesling, Riesling Italico*

Montello, DOCG (R) Cabernet Franc, Cabernet Sauvignon, Carmenère, Merlot

Montello-Colli Asolani (R) Cabernet Franc, Cabernet Sauvignon, Carmenère, Merlot (W) Bianchetta, Chardonnay, Glera, Manzoni Bianco, Pinot Bianco

Monti Lessini (W) Chardonnay, *Durella, Garganega, Pinot Bianco, Pinot Grigio, Pinot Nero, Sauvignon Blanc*

Piave (R) Merlot, *other local red varieties*

Piave Malanotte, DOCG (R) Raboso Piave, *Raboso Veronese*

Prosecco (W, S) Bianchetta Trevigiana, Chardonnay, Glera, Perera, Pinot Bianco, Pinot Grigio, Pinot Nero

Recioto della Valpolicella, DOCG (R) Corvina Veronese, Rondinella

Recioto di Gambellara, DOCG (W) Garganega

Recioto di Soave, DOCG (W) Garganega, Trebbiano di Soave

Riviera del Brenta (W) Friulano, *other local white varieties* (R) Merlot, *other local red varieties* (S) Chardonnay, *other local white varieties*

Soave, Soave Superiore, DOCG (W) Garganega, *Chardonnay, Trebbiano*

Valpolicella (R) Corvina Veronese, Rondinella, *other local red varieties*

Valpolicella Ripasso (R) Corvina, Corvinone, *Rondinella, other local red varieties*

Venezia (W) Glera, Verduzzo Friulano, Verduzzo Trevigian (R) Merlot, *other local red varieties* (P) Raboso, *other local red varieties*

Vicenza (R, P) Merlot, *other local red varieties* (W) Garganega, *other local white varieties*

PORTUGAL

Alenquer (R) Aragonez, Castelão, Tinta Miúda, Touriga Nacional, Trincadeira, *Alicante Bouschet, Amostrinha, Baga, Cabernet Sauvignon, Caladoc, Camarate, Jaen, Preto Martinho, Syrah, Tinta Barroca, Touriga Franca* (W) Arinto, Fernão Pires, Rabo de Ovelha, Seara Nova, Vital, *Alicante Branco, Alvarinho, Chardonnay, Jampal, Malvasia Rei, Ratinho, Sauvignon Blanc, Viosinho*

Alentejo (including the subregions of Portalegre, Borba, Redondo, Evora, Reguengos, Moura, Granja-Amareleja and Vidigueira) (R) Alfrocheiro, Alicante Bouschet, Aragonez, Cabernet Sauvignon, Castelão, Touriga Nacional, Trincadeira, (W) Antão Vaz, Arinto, Fernão Pires, Manteúdo, Perrum, Rabo de Ovelha, Roupeiro, Síria, Tamarez, Trincadeira das Pratas

Arruda (R) Aragonez, Castelão, Tinta Miúda, Touriga Nacional, Trincadeira, *Alicante Bouschet, Cabernet Sauvignon, Camarate, Jaen, Syrah, Tinta Barroca, Touriga Franca* (W) Arinto, Fernão Pires, Rabo de Ovelha, Seara Nova, Vital, *Alicante Branco, Chardonnay, Jampal, Malvasia Rei, Sauvignon Blanc, Viosinho*

Bairrada (R, P) Alfrocheiro, Baga, Camarate, Castelão, Jaen, Touriga Nacional, *Aragonez, Bastardo, Cabernet Sauvignon, Merlot, Pinot Noir, Rufete, Syrah, Tinta Barroca, Tinto Cão, Touriga Franca* (W) Arinto, Bical, Cercial, Chardonnay, Fernão Pires, Pinot Blanc, Rabo de Ovelha, Sauvignon Blanc, Sercealinho, Verdelho

Beira Interior (R) Baga, Bastardo, Jaen, Marufo, Rufete, Tinta Roriz, Touriga Nacional, *Alfrocheiro, Alicante Bouschet, Aragonez, Cabernet Sauvignon, Caladoc, Camarate, Merlot, Mourisco, Petit Bouschet, Petit Verdot, Pinot Noir, Rabo de Ovelha, Syrah, Tinto Cão, Tinta Barroca, Tinta Carvalha, Touriga Franca, Trincadeira* (W) Arinto, Bical, Chardonnay, Fernão Pires, Folgasão, Folha de Figueira, Fonte Cal, Malvasia Fina, Malvasia Rei, Sauvignon Blanc, Rabo de Ovelha, Riesling, Síria, Tamarez

Biscoitos (W) Arinto, Terrantez, Verdelho

Bucelas (W) Arinto, Rabo de Ovelha, Sercial

Carcavelos (R) Castelão, Preto Martinho (W) Arinto, Galego Dourado, Ratinho

Colares (R) Ramisco (W) Malvasia

Dão (R) Alfrocheiro, Alvarelhão, Aragonez, Bastardo, Jaen, Rufete, Tinto Cão, Touriga Nacional, Trincadeira (W) Barcelo, Bical, Cerceal, Encruzado, Malvasia Fina, Rabo de Ovelha, Terrantez, Uva Cão, Verdelho

Douro (R) Alicante Bouschet, Alvarelhão, Alvarelhão Ceitão, Aragonez, Aramon, Baga, Barca, Barreto, Bastardo, Bragão, Camarate, Carignan, Carrega Tinto, Casculho, Castelã, Castelão, Cidadelhe, Concieira, Cornifesto, Corropio, Donzelinho Tinto, Engomada, Espadeiro, Gonçalo Pires, Grand Noir, Grangeal, Jaen, Lourela, Malandra, Malvasia Preta, Marufo, Melra, Mondet, Mourisco de Semente, Nevoeira, Patorra, Petit Bouschet, Pinot Noir, Português Azul, Preto Martinho, Ricoca, Roseira, Rufete, Santareno, São Saúl, Sevilhão, Sousão, Tinta Aguiar, Tinta Barroca, Tinta Carvalha, Tinta Fontes, Tinta Francisca, Tinta Lameira, Tinta Martins, Tinta Mesquita, Tinta Penajóia, Tinta Pereira, Tinta Pomar, Tinta Tabuaço, Tinto Cão, Tinto Sem Nome, Touriga Fêmea, Touriga Franca, Touriga Nacional, Trincadeira, Valdosa, Varejoa (W) Alicante Branco, Alvarelhão Branco, Arinto, Avesso, Batoca, Bical, Branco Especial, Branco Guimarães, Caramela, Carrega Branco, Cercial, Chasselas, Côdega de Larinho, Diagalves, Dona Branca, Donzelinho Branco, Estreito Macio, Fernão Pires, Folgasão, Gouveio, Gouveio Estimado, Gouveio Real, Jampal, Malvasia Fina, Malvasia Parda, Malvasia Rei, Moscadet, Moscatel Galego Branco, Mourisco Branco, Pé Comprido, Pinheira Branca, Praça, Rabigato, Rabigato Franco, Rabigato Moreno, Rabo de Ovelha, Ratinho, Samarrinho, Sarigo, Sémillon, Sercial, Síria, Tália, Tamarez, Terrantez, Touriga Branca, Trigueira, Valente, Verdial Branco, Viosinho, Vital

Encostas d'Aire (R) Aragonez, Baga, Castelão, Tinta Miúda, Touriga Nacional, Trincadeira, *Alfrocheiro, Alicante Bouchet, Amostrinha, Bastardo, Cabernet Sauvignon, Caladoc, Grand Noir, Syrah, Rufete, Touriga Franca* (W) Arinto, Fernão Pires, Ratinho, Seara Nova, Tamarez, Vital, *Alicante Branco, Bical, Boal Branco, Cercial, Chardonnay, Diagalves, Jampal, Malvasia Fina, Rabo de Ovelha, Trincadeira Branca*

Graciosa (W) Arinto, Fernão Pires, Malvasia Fina, Terrantez, Verdelho

Lafões (R) Amaral, *Jaen, Pilong* (W) Arinto, Cercial, *Dona Branca, Rabo de Ovelha, Sercial*

Lagoa (R) Negra Mole, Trincadeira, *Alicante Bouschet, Aragonez, Cabernet Sauvignon, Castelão, Monvedro, Moreto, Syrah, Touriga Franca, Touriga Nacional* (W) Arinto, Síria, *Manteúdo, Moscatel Graúdo, Perrum, Rabo de Ovelha, Sauvignon Blanc*

Lagos (R) Castelão, Negra Mole, Trincadeira, *Alicante Bouschet, Aragonez, Bastardo, Cabernet Sauvignon, Monvedro, Touriga Nacional* (W) Arinto, Malvasia Fina, Manteúdo, Moscatel Graúdo, Perrum, *Síria*

Lourinha (R) Cabinda (W) Alicante Branco, Alvadurão, Boal Espinho, Malvasia Rei, Marquinhas, Tália

Madeira (R) Bastardo, Malvasia Roxa, Tinta de Madeira, Tinta Negra, Verdelho Tinto, *Complexa, Deliciosa, Tiunfo* (W) Boal, Malvasia Candida, Sercial, Terrantez, Verdelho, *Babosa, Caracol, Carão de Moça, Listrão, Malvasia Babosa, Moscatel, Rio Grande, Valveirinho*

Madeirense (R, P) Bastardo, Cabernet Sauvignon, Complexa, Deliciosa, Malvasia Cândida Roxa, Maria Feld, Merlot, Tinta Barroca, Tinta Negra, Touriga Franca, Touriga Nacional (W) Arnsburger, Carão de Moça, Chardonnay, Chenin Blanc, Lilás, Malvasia Bianca, Malvasia Branca de São Jorge, Malvasia Cândida, Malvasia Fina (Boal), Rio Grande, Sauvignon Blanc, Sercial, Tália, Terrantez, Verdelho

Óbidos (R) Alicante Bouschet, Amostrinha, Aragonez, Baga, Cabernet Sauvignon, Caladoc, Camarate, Carignan, Castelão, Jaen, Merlot, Pinot Noir, Preto Martinho, Syrah, Tinta Barroca, Tinta Miúda, Touriga Franca, Touriga Nacional, Trincadeira (W) Alicante Branco, Alvarinho, Antão Vaz, Arinto, Chardonnay, Encruzado, Fernão Pires, Jampal, Loureiro, Malvasia Rei, Moscatel Graúdo, Rabo de Ovelha, Ratinho, Riesling, Sauvignon Blanc, Seara Nova, Verdelho, Viognier, Viosinho, Vital

Palmela (R, P) Alicante Bouschet, Aragonez, Bastardo, Cabernet Sauvignon, Castelão, Merlot, Moscatel Galego Roxo, Petit Verdot, Syrah, Tannat, Tinta Miúda, Tinto Cão, Touriga Franca, Touriga Nacional, Trincadeira (W) Alvarinho, Antão Vaz, Arinto, Chardonnay, Fernão Pires, Loureiro, Malvasia Fina, Moscatel Galego Branco, Pinot Blanc, Rabo de Ovelha, Roupeiro, Sauvignon Blanc, Sémillon, Tamarez, Verdelho, Viosinho

Pico (W) Arinto, Terrantez, Verdelho

Portimão (R) Castelão, Negra Mole, Trincadeira, *Alicante Bouschet, Aragonez, Cabernet Sauvignon, Monvedro, Syrah, Touriga Nacional* (W) Arinto, Síria, *Manteúdo, Moscatel Graúdo, Perrum, Rabo de Ovelha*

Port (R) Bastardo, Cornifesto, Donzelinho Tinto, Malvasia Preta, Marufo, Mourisco, Rufete, Tinto Cão, Touriga Franca, Touriga Nacional, Tinta Roriz, Tinta Amarela, Tinta Barroca (W) Arinto, Donzelinho Branco, Folgazão, Gouveio, Malvasia Fina, Moscatel Galego Branco, Rabigato, Samarrinho, Sémillon, Sercial, Síria, Verdelho, Viosinho, Vital

Setúbal (W) Antão Vaz, Arinto, Fernão-Pires, Malvasia Fina, Moscatel Galego Branco, Moscatel Graúdo (R, P) Aragonez, Bastardo, Castelão, Moscatel Galego Roxo, Touriga Franca, Touriga Nacional, Trincadeira

Tavira (R) Castelão, Negra Mole, Trincadeira, *Alicante Bouschet, Aragonez, Cabernet Sauvignon, Syrah, Touriga Nacional* (W) Arinto, Síria, *Diagalves, Manteúdo, Moscatel Graúdo, Tamarez*

Távora-Varosa (R) Alvarelhão, Bastardo, Castelão, Mourisco, Pinot Noir, Rufete, Tinta Barroca, Tinta Roriz, Touriga Nacional, Touriga Franca, Vinhão (W) Bical, Chardonnay, Fernão Pires, Gouveio, Malvasia Fina, Malvasia Rei, Síria, Viosinho

Tejo (subregions Almeirim, Cartaxo, Chamusca, Coruche, Santarém, Tomar) (R, P) Alfrocheiro, Alicante Bouschet, Amostrinha, Aragonez, Baga, Bastardo, Bonverdo, Cabernet Franc, Cabernet Sauvignon, Cabinda, Caladoc, Camarate, Carignan, Castelão, Cinsaut, Grand Noir, Grenache, Grossa, Jaen, Merlot, Molar, Monvedro, Moreto, Negra Mole, Parreira Matias, Petit Verdot, Pinot Noir, Preto Cardana, Preto Martinho, Ramisco, Rufete, Sousão, Syrah, Tannat, Tinta Barroca, Tinta Caiada, Tinta Carvalha, Tinta Miúda, Tinta Pomar, Tintinha, Tinto Cão, Touriga Franca, Touriga Nacional, Trincadeira, Valbom (P only) Fernão Pires Rosado, Gewürztraminer, Pinot Gris (W) Alicante Branco, Almafra, Alvadurão, Alvarinho, Antão Vaz, Arinto, Bical, Boal Branco, Boal Espinho, Cerceal Branco, Cercial, Chardonnay, Chenin, Côdega de Larinho, Diagalves, Encruzado, Fernão Pires, Galego Dourado, Gouveio, Jampal, Loureiro, Malvasia, Malvasia Fina, Malvasia Rei, Marquinhas, Moscatel Galego Branco, Moscatel Graúdo, Pinot Blanc, Rabo de Ovelha, Ratinho, Riesling, Sauvignon Blanc, Seara Nova, Sémillon, Sercial, Síria, Roupeiro, Tália, Tamarez, Trincadeira Branca, Trincadeira das Pratas, Verdelho, Viognier, Viosinho, Vital

Torres Vedras (R) Aragonez, Castelão, Tinta Miúda, Touriga Nacional, *Alicante Bouschet, Cabernet Sauvignon, Caladoc, Camarate, Jaen, Syrah, Tinta Barroca, Touriga Franca, Trincadeira* (W) Arinto, Fernão Pires, Rabo de Ovelha, Seara Nova, Vital, *Alicante Branco, Alvarinho, Chardonnay, Jampal, Malvasia Rei, Ratinho, Sauvignon Blanc, Viosinho*

Trás-os-Montes – Chaves (R) Alicante Bouschet, Aragonez, Baga, Bastardo, Castelão, Cornifesto, Malvasia Preta, Marufo, Moscatel Galego Roxo, Tinta Barroca, Tinta Carvalha, Tinto Cão, Touriga Franca, Touriga Nacional, Trincadeira (W) Alvarinho, Arinto, Bical, Boal Branco, Côdega de Larinho, Fernão Pires, Gouveio, Malvasia Fina, Moscatel Galego Branco, Rabigato, Síria, Viosinho

Trás-os-Montes – Valpaços (R) Aragonez, Bastardo, Cornifesto, Marufo, Tinta Barroca, Tinta Carvalha, Tinto Cão, Touriga Franca, Touriga Nacional, Trincadeira (W) Arinto, Bical, Boal Branco, Côdega de Larinho, Donzelinho Branco, Fernão Pires, Gouveio, Malvasia Fina, Moscatel Galego Branco, Rabigato, Síria, Viosinho

Trás-os-Montes – Planalto Mirandês (R) Alicante Bouschet, Aragonez, Bastardo, Castelão, Cornifesto, Gorda, Marufo, Rufete, Tinta Barroca, Touriga Franca, Touriga Nacional, Trincadeira (W) Bical, Boal Branco, Carrega Branco, Côdega de Larinho, Donzelinho Branco, Fernão Pires, Gouveio, Malvasia Fina, Moscatel Galego Branco, Rabigato, Samarinho, Síria, Viosinho.

Vinho Verde (R) Alvarelhão, Amaral, Borraçal, Espadeiro, Padeiro, Pedral, Rabo-de-Anho, Vinhão (W) Alvarinho, Arinto, Avesso, Azal, Batoca, Loureiro, Trajadura

SPAIN

Note: Single-estate DOs such as Dominio de Valdepusa or Pago Guijoso are not listed below.

Abona (W) Bastardo, Forastera, Listán Blanco, Pedro Ximénez, *Bermejuela, Gual, Moscatel Verdello* (R) Bastardo, Malvasía Rosada, Tintilla, Vijariego, *Moscatel Negro, Negramoll*

Alella (W) Chardonnay, Xarello, *Chenin Blanc, Garnacha Blanca, Macabeo, Malvasía, Pansá Rosado, Parellada, Picapoll Blanco* (R) Garnacha Tinta, Merlot, Tempranillo, *Cabernet Sauvignon, Garnacha Peluda*

Alicante (R) Monastrell, *Bobal, Cabernet Sauvignon, Garnacha Tinta, Garnacha Tintorera, Merlot, Petit Verdot, Pinot Noir, Syrah, Tempranillo* (W) Moscatel de Alejandría, *Airén, Chardonnay, Macabeo, Merseguera, Planta Fina, Sauvignon Blanc, Subirat, Verdil*

Almansa (R) Cabernet Sauvignon, Garnacha Tintorera, Merlot, Monastrell, Syrah, Tempranillo (W) Chardonnay, Sauvignon Blanc, Verdejo, *Garnacha Blanca, Moscatel de Grano Menudo, Petit Verdot*

Arabako Txakolina/Chacolí de/Txakoli de Álava (W) Hondarribi Zuri, *Gros Manseng, Petit Courbu, Petit Manseng*

Arlanza (R) Cabernet Sauvignon, Garnacha, Mencía, Merlot, Petit Verdot, Tintilla del País (W) Albillo, Viura

Bierzo (R) Mencía, *Garnacha Tintorera* (W) Doña Branca, Godello, *Malvasía, Palomino*

Binissalem Mallorca (R) Manto Negro, *Cabernet Sauvignon, Callet, Merlot, Monastrell, Syrah, Tempranillo* (W) Chardonnay, Macabeo, Moscatel, Parellada, Prensal Blanc

Bizkaiko Txakolina/Chacolí de Vizcaya/Txakoli de Bizkaia (W) Folle Blanche (Gros Plant), Hondarribi Zuri (R) Hondarribi Beltza

Bullas (R) Monastrell, *Cabernet Sauvignon, Garnacha, Merlot, Petit Verdot, Syrah, Tempranillo* (W) Macabeo, *Airén, Chardonnay, Malvasía, Moscatel, Moscatel de Grano Menudo, Sauvignon Blanc*

Calatayud (R) Cabernet Sauvignon, Garnacha Tinta, Mazuela, Merlot, Tempranillo, Syrah, *Bobal, Monastrell* (W) Chardonnay, Macabeo, Malvasía, *Garnacha Blanca, Gewürztraminer, Moscatel, Sauvignon Blanc*

Campo de Borja (R) Cabernet Sauvignon, Garnacha, Mazuelo, Merlot, Syrah, Tempranillo (W) Chardonnay, Macabeo, Moscatel

Cariñena (R) Cariñena, Garnacha, Tempranillo, *Cabernet Sauvignon. Juan Ibáñez, Merlot, Monastrell, Syrah, Vidadillo* (W) Viura, *Chardonnay, Garnacha Blanca, Moscatel Romano, Parellada*

Cava (S) Garnacha, Macabeo, Monastrell, Parellada, Subirat, Xarello, *Chardonnay, Pinot Noir, Trepat*

Cigales (R) Garnacha, Tempranillo, *Cabernet Sauvignon, Merlot, Syrah* (W) Verdejo, *Albillo, Sauvignon Blanc, Viura* (P) the principal red varieties and any of the authorized white varieties

Conca de Barbera (W) Macabeo, Parellada, *Chardonnay, Chenin Blanc, Garnacha Blanca, Moscatel, Sauvignon Blanc* (R) Tempranillo, Trepat, *Cabernet Franc, Cabernet Sauvignon, Garnacha, Mazuelo, Merlot, Pinot Noir, Syrah*

Condado de Huelva (W) Cabernet Franc, Cabernet Sauvignon, Chardonnay, Colombard, Garrido Fino, Merlot, Moscatel de Alejandría, Palomino Fino, Pedro Ximénez, Sauvignon Blanc, Syrah, Tempranillo, Zalema

Costers del Segre (W) Albariño, Chardonnay, Garnacha Blanca, Macabeo, Parellada, Riesling, Sauvignon Blanc, Xarello, *Gewürztraminer, Malvasía, Moscatel de Alejandría* (R) Cabernet Sauvignon, Garnacha Tinta, Merlot, Monastrell, Pinot Noir, Samsó, Syrah, Tempranillo, Trepat

El Hierro (W) Baboso Blanco, Bremajuelo, Gual, Vijariego Blanco, *Listán Blanco, Malvasía, Pedro Ximénez, Verdello* (R) Baboso Negro, Listán Negro, Verijadiego Negro, *Negramoll*

Empordà (W) Garnacha Blanca, Macabeo, Moscatel de Alejandría, *Chardonnay, Malvasía, Moscatel, Picapoll Blanco, Sauvignon Blanc, Xarello* (R) Cariñena, Garnacha, *Cabernet Franc, Cabernet Sauvignon, Garnacha Peluda, Merlot, Monastrell, Syrah, Tempranillo*

Getariako Txakoli/Chacolí de Guetaria/Txakoli de Getaria (W) Hondarribi Zuri (R) Hondarribi Beltza

Gran Canaria (W) Listán Blanco, *Albillo, Breval, Gual, Marmajuelo, Moscatel, Pedro Ximénez, Vijariego* (R) Listán Negro, *Negramoll, Tintilla*

Jerez-Xérès-Sherry (W) Moscatel, Palomino Fino, Pedro Ximénez

Jumilla (R) Cabernet Sauvignon, Garnacha Tinta, Garnacha Tintorera, Merlot, Monastrell, Syrah, Tempranillo (W) Airén, Macabeo, Malvasía, Pedro Ximénez, *Chardonnay, Moscatel de Grano Menudo, Sauvignon Blanc*

Lanzarote (W) Breval, Burrablanca, Diego, Listán Blanco, Malvasía, Moscatel, Pedro Ximénez (R) Listán Negro, Negramoll

Málaga (W) Moscatel de Alejandría, Moscatel Morisco, Pedro Ximénez, *Doradilla, Lairén* (R) Cabernet Sauvignon, Merlot, Romé, Syrah, Tempranillo, *Cabernet Franc, Garnacha, Petit Verdot, Pinot Noir*

Manchuela (W) Albillo, Chardonnay, Macabeo, Sauvignon Blanc, Verdejo (R) Bobal, Cabernet Sauvignon, Garnacha, Merlot, Monastrell, Moravia Dulce, Syrah, Tempranillo

Manzanilla-Sanlúcar de Barrameda (W) Moscatel, Palomino Fino, Pedro Ximénez

Monte Lentiscal (R, P) Listán Negro, *Malvasía Rosada, Negramoll, Tintilla* (W) Listán Blanco, *Albillo, Bermejuela, Breval, Gual, Malvasía, Moscatel, Pedro Ximénez, Vijariego*

La Mancha (R) Tempranillo, *Cabernet Sauvignon, Garnacha, Moravia, Merlot, Syrah* (W) Airén, *Chardonnay, Macabeo, Sauvignon Blanc*

Méntrida (R) Cabernet Sauvignon, Merlot, Syrah, Tempranillo, *Garnacha* (W) Albillo, Chardonnay, Macabeo, Sauvignon Blanc

Mondéjar (W) Macabeo, Malvar, Torrontés (R) Cabernet Sauvignon, Tempranillo

Monterrei (W) Doña Blanca, Godello, Treixadura, *Albariño, Branca de Monterrei, Caíño Branco, Loureira* (R) Bastardo, Mencía, *Caíño Tinto, Sousón, Tempranillo*

Montilla-Moriles (W) Pedro Ximénez, *Airén, Baladí, Moscatel, Torrontés, Verdejo*

Montsant (W) Chardonnay, Garnacha Blanca, Macabeo, Moscatel, Parellada, Xarello (R) Cabernet Sauvignon, Garnacha Peluda, Garnacha Tinta, Mazuela, Merlot, Monastrell, Picapoll Negro, Syrah, Tempranillo

Navarra (R) Cabernet Sauvignon, Graciano, Tempranillo, *Garnacha Tinta, Mazuelo, Merlot, Pinot Noir, Syrah* (W) Chardonnay, Viura, *Sauvignon Blanc*

La Palma (W) Albillo, Bastardo Blanco, Bermejuela, Bujariego, Burrablanca, Forastera, Gual, Listán Blanco, Malvasía, Moscatel, Pedro Ximénez, Sabro, Torrontés, Verdello (R) Almuñeco, Bastardo Negro, Castellana, Malvasía Rosada, Moscatel Negro, Negramoll, Tintilla

Penedès (R) Cabernet Sauvignon, Cariñena, Garnacha Tinta, Merlot, Monastrell, Samsó, Tempranillo, *Cabernet Franc, Pinot Noir, Syrah* (W) Chardonnay, Macabeo, Parellada, Subirat Parent, Xarello

Pla i Llevant (W) Chardonnay, Macabeo, Moscatel, Parellada, Prensal Blanc (R) Cabernet Sauvignon, Callet, Fogoneu, Manto Negro, Merlot, Monastrell, Tempranillo, Syrah

Pla de Bages (W) Chardonnay, Gewürztraminer, Macabeo, Parellada, Picapoll Blanco, *Sauvignon Blanc* (R) Cabernet Franc, Cabernet Sauvignon, Garnacha, Merlot, Tempranillo, Sumoll, Syrah

Priorato (R) Garnacha Tinta, Samsó, *Cabernet Franc, Cabernet Sauvignon, Garnacha Peluda, Merlot, Picapoll Negro, Pinot Noir, Syrah, Tempranillo* (W) Chenin Blanc, Garnacha Blanca, Macabeo, Moscatel de Alejandría, Moscatel de Grano Menudot, *Pedro Ximénez, Picapoll Blanco, Xarello*

Rias Baixas (W) Albariño, Caíño Blanco, Loureira, Treixadura, *Godello, Torrontés* (R) Caíño Tinto, Espadeiro, Loureira Tinta, Sousón, *Brancellao, Mencía, Pedral*

Ribeira Sacra (W) Albariño, Doña Blanca, Godello, Loureira, Torrontés, Treixadura (R) Brancellao, Mencía, Merenzao, *Caíño Tinto, Mouraton, Sousón, Tempranillo*

Ribeiro (W) Albariño, Godello, Loureira, Torrontés, Treixadura, *Albillo, Jerez, Macabeo* (R) Brancellao, Caíño, Ferrón, Mencía, Sousón, *Garnacha, Tempranillo*

Ribera del Duero (R) Tempranillo, *Cabernet Sauvignon, Garnacha Tinta, Malbec, Merlot* (W) Albillo

Ribera del Guadiana (W) Alarije, Borba, Cayetana Blanca, Chardonnay, Chelva, Cigüente, Malvar, Moscatel de Alejandría, Moscatel de Gran Menudo, Pardina, Parellada, Pedro Ximénez, Perruno, Sauvignon Blanc, Verdejo, Viura (R) Bobal, Cabernet Sauvignon, Garnacha Tinta, Garnacha Tintorera, Graciano, Jaén Tinto, Mazuela, Merlot, Monastrell, Pinot Noir, Syrah, Tempranillo

Ribera del Júcar (R) Bobal, Tempranillo, *Cabernet Franc* (W) Moscatel de Grano Menudo, *Sauvignon Blanc*

Rioja (R) Garnacha, Graciano, Maturana Tinta, Mazuelo, Tempranillo (W) Chardonnay, Garnacha Blanca, Malvasía Riojana, Maturana Blanca, Sauvignon Blanc, Tempranillo Blanco, Torrontés, Verdejo, Viura

Rueda (W) Verdejo, Viura, *Palomino Fino, Sauvignon Blanc* (R) Cabernet Sauvignon, Garnacha, Merlot, Tempranillo

Sierras de Málaga (W), Chardonnay, Macabeo, Moscatel, Pedro Ximénez, Sauvignon Blanc, *Colombard, Doradilla, Lairén* (R) Cabernet Sauvignon, Merlot, Romé, Syrah, Tempranillo, *Cabernet Franc, Garnacha, Petit Verdot, Pinot Noir*

Somontano (R) Cabernet Sauvignon, Garnacha Tinta, Merlot, Moristel, Pinot Noir, Syrah, Tempranillo (W) Alcañón, Chardonnay, Garnacha Blanca, Gewürztraminer, Macabeo, Riesling, Sauvignon Blanc

Tacoronte-Acentejo (R) Listán Negro, Negramoll, *Bastardo Negro, Cabernet Sauvignon, Castellana Negra, Listán Prieto, Malvasía Rosado, Merlot, Moscatel Negro, Ruby Cabernet, Syrah, Tintilla, Vijariego Negro* (W) Gual, Listán Blanco, Malvasía, Marmajuelo, *Albillo, Bastardo Blanco, Breval, Burrablanca, Forastera, Moscatel, Pedro Ximénez, Sabro, Torrontés, Verdello, Vijariego*

Tarragona (R) Cabernet Sauvignon, Cariñena, Garnacha Tinta, Merlot, Syrah, Tempranillo (W) Chardonnay, Garnacha Blanca, Macabeo, Moscatel, Parellada, Xarello

Terra Alta (W) Garnacha Blanca, Macabeo, Parellada, *Chardonnay, Chenin Blanc, Moscatel de Alejandría, Moscatel de Grano Menudo, Pedro Ximénez, Viognier* (R) Garnacha Peluda, Garnacha Tinta, Samsó, *Cabernet Franc, Cabernet Sauvignon, Garnacha Tintorera, Merlot, Morenillo, Syrah, Tempranillo*

Tierra de León (R) Mencía, Prieto Picudo, *Garnacha, Tempranillo* (W) Albarín, Godello, Verdejo, *Malvasía, Palomino*

Tierra del Vino de Zamora (R) Tempranillo, *Cabernet Sauvignon, Garnacha* (W) Malvasía, Moscatel, Verdejo, *Albillo, Godello, Palomino*

Toro (R) Tempranillo, *Garnacha Tinta* (W) Malvasía, Verdejo

Uclés (R) Cabernet Sauvignon, Garnacha Tinta, Merlot, Syrah, Tempranillo (W) Chardonnay, Macabeo, Moscatel, Sauvignon Blanc, Verdejo

Utiel-Requena (R) Bobal, Cabernet Sauvignon, Garnacha Tinta, Merlot, Syrah, Tempranillo (W) Chardonnay, Macabeo, Merseguera, Planta Nova, Sauvignon Blanc

Valdeorras (R) Albarello, Mencía, Merenzao, Sousón, Garnacha, Gran Negro, Tempranillo (W) Dona Branca, Godello, *Palomino*

Valdepeñas (R) Cabernet Sauvignon, Garnacha, Merlot, Petit Verdot, Syrah, Tempranillo (W) Airén, Chardonnay, Macabeo, Moscatel de Grano Menudo, Sauvignon Blanc, Verdejo

Valencia (W) Gewürztraminer, Malvasía, Merseguera, Moscatel de Alejandría, Planta Fina, Pedro Ximénez, Sauvignon Blanc, Tortosí, Verdejo, Verdil (R) Bobal, Bonicaire, Cabernet Sauvignon, Garnacha Tinta, Garnacha Tintorera, Mando, Merlot, Monastrell, Petit Verdot, Pinot Noir, Syrah, Tempranillo

Valle de Güímar (W) Gual, Listán Blanco, Malvasía, Moscatel, *Verdello, Vijariego* (R) Cabernet Sauvignon, Listán Negro, Malvasía Tinta, Merlot, Moscatel Negro, Negramoll, Pinot Noir, Ruby Cabernet, Syrah, Tintilla, Vijariego Negro

Valle de la Orotava (W) Gual, Malvasía, Verdello, Vijariego, *Bastardo Blanco, Forastera, Torrontés, Listán Blanco, Marmajuelo, Moscatel, Pedro Ximénez* (R) Listán Negro, Malvasía Rosada, Negramoll, *Bastardo Negro, Moscatel Negra, Tintilla, Vijariego Negro*

Vinos de Madrid (R) Garnacha, Tinto Fino, *Cabernet Sauvignon, Merlot, Syrah* (W) Airén, Albillo, Malvar, *Moscatel de Grano Menudo, Parellada, Torrontés, Viura*

Ycoden-Daute-Isora (W) Albillo, Bermejuela, Gual, Malvasía, Moscatel, Pedro Ximénez, Sabró, Torrontés, Verdello, Vijariego, *Bastardo Blanco, Forastera, Listán Blanco* (R) Baboso Negro, Castellana, Listán Negro, Malvasía Rosada, Negramoll, Tintilla, *Bastardo Negro, Moscatel Negra, Vijariego Negro*

Yecla (R) Cabernet Sauvignon, Garnacha Tinta, Garnacha Tintorera, Merlot, Monastrell, Syrah, Tempranillo, *Petit Verdot* (W) Airén, Chardonnay, Macabeo, Malvasía, Merseguera, *Petit Verdot*

SWITZERLAND

Dôle (R) Gamay, Pinot Noir, *Ancellotta, Carminoir, Diolinoir, Gamaret, Garanoir, Merlot, Syrah*

Dôle Blanche (P) Pinot Noir, *Gamay* (optionally blended with up to 10% Valais AOC white wine)

Dorin (W) Chasselas

Ermitage du Valais/Hermitage du Valais (W) Marsanne

Goron (R) Gamay, Pinot Noir, *Ancellotta, Carminoir, Diolinoir, Gamaret, Garanoir, Merlot, Syrah*

Johannisberg du Valais (W) Silvaner

Malvoisie du Valais (W) Pinot Gris

L'Œil-de-Perdrix (Valais) (P) Pinot Noir, *Pinot Blanc, Pinot Gris*

L'Œil-de-Perdrix de Neuchâtel (P) Pinot Noir, *Pinot Gris*

Appendix 2A

TOTAL VINEYARD AREA BY COUNTRY

These 2000 and 2012 OIV figures include vineyards dedicated to TABLE GRAPES and DRYING GRAPES. OIV figures are given in hectares so the equivalent figures in acres are approximate. For accuracy, totals are taken directly from the OIV figures, and therefore may not equal the sum of the individual numbers because these are all rounded.

	2000 (000 ha)	2000 (000 acres)	2012 (000 ha)	2012 (000 acres)
Spain	1,229	3,037	1,018	2,516
France	907	2,241	792	1,957
Italy	908	2,244	704	1,740
China	300	741	660	1,631
Turkey	575	1,421	497	1,228
United States	412	1,017	407	1,006
Portugal	246	607	233	576
Iran	292	722	226	558
Argentina	201	497	222	549
Chile	174	431	206	509
Romania	248	613	192	474
Australia	140	346	162	400
Moldova	147	363	142	351
South Africa	124	307	132	326
Uzbekistan	104	257	121	299
India	43	106	120	297
Greece	131	323	110	272
Germany	104	257	102	252
Brazil	63	156	91	225
Ukraine	110	272	78	193
Algeria	55	136	74	183
Egypt	64	159	71	175
Bulgaria	115	284	67	166
Hungary	113	279	64	158
Russia	72	178	62	153

continued

	2000 (000 ha)	2000 (000 acres)	2012 (000 ha)	2012 (000 acres)
Afghanistan	52	128	62	153
Georgia	66	163	48	119
Syria	74	184	48	119
Marocco	50	123	48	119
Serbia	–	–	44	109
Austria	51	125	44	109
Tajikistan	36	90	44	109
New Zealand	14	34	38	94
Croatia	63	157	29	72
Mexico	42	104	29	72
Turkmenistan	29	72	29	72
Peru	10	25	26	64
Macedonia (Republic of)	28	70	23	57
Other Asian countries	28	69	22	54
Tunisia	29	71	21	52
Japan	22	54	19	47
Slovakia	18	44	19	47
South Korea	31	78	18	44
Czech Republic	14	34	17	42
Armenia	15	37	17	42
Pakistan	12	31	17	42
Slovenia	17	41	16	40
Azerbaijan	14	35	16	40
Switzerland	15	37	15	37
Lebanon	15	37	14	35
Yemen	24	60	14	35
Kazakhstan	12	31	13	32
Canada	8	21	12	30
Irak	14	34	12	30
Albania	6	15	10	25
Montenegro	–	–	9	22
Libya	9	21	9	22
Other African countries	3	7	9	22
Uruguay	10	24	9	22
Cyprus	19	48	9	22
Israel	8	19	8	20
Other American countries	4	10	8	20
Bosnia and Herzegovina	4	10	6	15
Kyrgyzstan	8	19	6	15
Bolivia	4	9	5	12
Thailand	4	10	5	12
Tanzania	3	6	4	10
Jordan	4	10	4	10
Madagascar	2	5	3	7
China and Taiwan	3	8	3	7
Malta	0	1	2	5
Venezuela	1	2	1	2
Luxembourg	1	3	1	2

	2000 (000 ha)	2000 (000 acres)	2012 (000 ha)	2012 (000 acres)
UK	1	2	1	2
Yugoslavia (incl Serbia and Montenegro)	72	178	–	–
WORLD TOTAL	7,847	19390	7,440	18,385

www.oiv.int/oiv/info/enpublicationsstatistiques

Appendix 2B

WINE PRODUCTION BY COUNTRY

These 2000 and 2012 OIV figures include vineyards dedicated to TABLE GRAPES and DRYING GRAPES. OIV figures are given in hectares so the equivalent figures in acres are approximate. For accuracy, totals are taken directly from the OIV figures, and therefore may not equal the sum of the individual numbers because these are all rounded.

	2000 (000 hl)	2000 (000 gal)	2012 (000 hl)	2012 (000 gal)
France	57,541	1,520,072	41,548	1,097,582
Italy	51,620	1,363,656	45,616	1,205,047
Spain	41,692	1,101,386	31,123	822,183
United States	21,500	567,970	21,740	574,310
Argentina	12,537	331,192	11,778	311,142
China	10,500	277,381	13,810	364,822
Australia	8,064	213,021	12,260	323,875
Chile	6,674	176,308	12,554	331,634
South Africa	6,949	183,578	10,550	278,702
Germany	9,852	260,254	9,012	238,072
Russia	3,050	80,572	6,250	165,108
Portugal	6,710	177,259	6,308	166,640
Romania	5,456	144,124	3,311	87,457
Brazil	3,638	96,106	3,115	82,290
Ukraine	1,290	34,078	2,400	63,401
Austria	2,338	61,774	2,125	56,123
Greece	3,558	93,992	3,115	82,290
Hungary	4,299	113,568	1,818	48,026
New Zealand	601	15,877	1,940	51,249
Serbia	–	–	2,175	57,457
Croatia	1,891	49,955	1,293	34,157
Moldova	2,500	66,043	1,214	32,070
Bulgaria	3,305	87,309	1,442	38,094
Switzerland	1,276	33,701	1,004	26,523

	2000 (000 hl)	2000 (000 gal)	2012 (000 hl)	2012 (000 gal)
Georgia	1,138	30,063	1,127	29,772
Uruguay	904	23,881	990	26,156
Japan	974	25,730	800	21,134
Macedonia (Republic of)	1,238	32,695	781	20,632
Czech Republic	525	13,869	470	12,416
Peru	270	7,133	650	17,171
Algeria	424	11,191	490	12,944
Turkey	248	6,551	546	14,424
Canada	428	11,304	570	15,058
Slovenia	412	10,897	507	13,394
Mexico	1,041	27,507	389	10,276
Slovakia	463	12,231	384	10,144
Israel	75	1,981	270	7,133
Morocco	299	7,899	345	9,114
Belarus	97	2,562	272	7,185
Tunisia	411	10,857	240	6,340
Uzbekistan	410	10,831	215	5,680
Kazakhstan	273	7,212	200	5,283
Albania	74	1,958	190	5,019
Turkmenistan	360	9,510	180	4,755
Montenegro	–	–	160	4,227
Luxembourg	132	3,485	85	2,245
Other American countries	19	502	125	3,302
Cyprus	570	15,058	107	2,827
Bolivia	20	541	76	2,008
Madagascar	89	2,351	85	2,245
Lebanon	170	4,491	90	2,378
Azerbaijan	77	2,034	79	2,087
Armenia	42	1,110	57	1,506
Lithuania	40	1,065	65	1,717
Other African countries	40	1,057	43	1,136
Egypt	30	779	40	1,057
UK	14	372	8	211
Bosnia and Herzegovina	48	1,260	34	898
Paraguay	56	1,479	29	766
Latvia	0	0	23	608
Malta	50	1,321	22	581
Kyrgystan	22	593	13	347
Tajikistan	39	1,038	10	264
Belgium	2	53	3	79
Other Asian countries	3	79	1	26
Estonia	33	861	0	0
Yugoslavia (incl Serbia and Montenegro)	1,973	52,113	–	–
WORLD TOTAL	280,373	7,406,683	258,238	6,821,926

www.oiv.int/oiv/info/enpublicationsstatistiques

Appendix 2C

PER CAPITA CONSUMPTION BY COUNTRY

These 2000 and 2012 figures are based on official OIV statistics. Those for 2000 are unrealistically low because the OIV at that time used the UN's Food and Agriculture Organization population database. The 2012 figures are based on the UN's population database of those aged 15+ and are therefore more realistic. OIV figures are given in litres so the equivalent figures in gallons are approximate. All figures are rounded.

	2000 (litres)	2000 (gal)	2012 (litres)	2012 (gal)
Luxembourg	62.1	16.4	60.7	16.0
France	58.4	15.4	57.9	15.3
Portugal	44.5	11.7	55.4	14.6
Italy	54.0	14.3	43.3	11.4
Denmark	33.7	8.9	39.7	10.5
Switzerland	43.1	11.4	39.1	10.3
Croatia	40.2	10.6	38.9	10.3
Slovenia	34.4	9.1	38.0	10.0
Austria	30.9	8.2	35.8	9.5
Greece	26.0	6.9	32.5	8.6
Argentina	33.8	8.9	32.3	8.5
Belgium	24.4	6.5	31.0	8.2
Serbia	–	–	29.4	7.8
Georgia	10.1	2.7	29.3	7.7
Australia	20.3	5.4	28.8	7.6
Germany	24.5	6.5	28.7	7.6
Netherlands	19.5	5.2	26.3	6.9
New Zealand	1.1	0.3	26.1	6.9
Sweden	13.3	3.5	26.0	6.9
Spain	34.9	9.2	24.8	6.6
UK	16.4	4.3	24.6	6.5
Uruguay	28.5	7.5	24.2	6.4
Montenegro	–	–	24.0	6.3
Hungary	30.9	8.1	23.3	6.2
Chile	14.7	3.9	22.9	6.0
Ireland	11.0	2.9	22.7	6.0